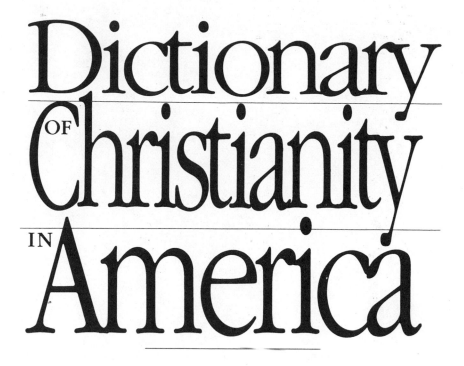

Dictionary of Christianity in America

Coordinating Editor
Daniel G. Reid

Consulting Editors
Robert D. Linder
Bruce L. Shelley
Harry S. Stout

INTERVARSITY PRESS
DOWNERS GROVE, ILLINOIS 60515

InterVarsity Press is the book-publishing division of InterVarsity Christian Fellowship, a student movement active on campus at hundreds of universities, colleges and schools of nursing. For information about local and regional activities, write Public Relations Dept., InterVarsity Christian Fellowship, 6400 Schroeder Rd., P.O. Box 7895, Madison, WI 53707-7895. Distributed in Canada through InterVarsity Press, 860 Denison St., Unit 3, Markham, Ontario L3R 4H1, Canada.

ISBN 0-8308-1776-X

Printed in the United States of America

Library of Congress Cataloging-in-Publication Data

Dictionary of Christianity in America/coordinating editor, Daniel G.
  Reid: consulting editors, Robert D. Linder, Bruce L. Shelley, Harry
S. Stout.
      p.   cm.
    Includes bibliographical references.
    ISBN 0-8308-1776-X
    1. Christianity—United States—Dictionaries.   2. United States—
Church history—Dictionaries.   I. Reid, Daniel G., 1949-   .
II. Linder, Robert Dean.   III. Shelley, Bruce L. (Bruce Leon), 1927-
IV. Stout, Harry S.
BR515.D53   1990
277.3'003—dc20   89-29953
                                                    CIP

16	15	14	13	12	11	10	9	8	7	6	5	4	3	2	1
99	98	97	96	95	94	93	92	91	90						

EDITORIAL STAFF

Managing Editor
Andrew T. Le Peau

Reference Book Editor
Daniel G. Reid

Editorial Support Staff Supervisor
James Hoover

Editorial Assistants
Kathleen Carlson, Cindy Bunch, Melissa Ramer, Dorothy Bowman

Manuscript Editor
Lorraine M. Davis

Principal Proofreader
Robin Sheffield

Proofreaders
Jeron Frame, Nancy Hines, Randy Hines, Susan Holton,
Melissa Ramer, Susan Young

Bibliographic Research Assistant
David Rogers

PRODUCTION STAFF

Production Manager
Nancy Fox

Production Coordinators
Deborah Keiser, Shirley Peska

Design
Kathy Lay Burrows

Design Assistant
Amy Craft

Typesetters
Marjorie Sire, Gail Munroe

Programming Consultant
Richard E. Ecker

CONTENTS

PREFACE

The idea for the *Dictionary of Christianity in America* was born when a managing editor reached for a volume that would give ready information on the individual men and women, denominations and organizations, events and movements, ideas and practices that have contributed to the history of Christianity in America. But such a book did not exist.

Until now the available resources on reference shelves have been narrative histories of American religion, reference books covering North American religious bodies, denominational encyclopedias, biographical dictionaries and multivolume reference books on religion or worldwide church history in general. All of these books serve their purposes, but the need has remained for a one-volume reference book providing easy access to the full range of topics related to the past and present of Christianity in America. One of our chief editorial goals has been to produce such a volume.

As the word *dictionary* indicates, this book arranges its topics alphabetically. It awaits to serve a natural human impulse—the need to know. And because knowledge begets further questions, each article has been amply cross-referenced to other topics covered in the *Dictionary,* while most articles have bibliographies directing readers to further resources. These features make the *Dictionary of Christianity in America* a valuable resource for users at every level. For those who are new to the field of American religion, the *Dictionary* is designed to provide the foundations for understanding the breadth and diversity of the Christian tradition. More serious students should find the *Dictionary* a helpful traveling companion through yet unexplored corridors in the labyrinthine maze of Christianity in America. The *Dictionary's* breadth of coverage and bibliographic resources will also prove of value to scholars of religion.

As a dictionary of Christianity, this book covers its topic in the broadest sense of the term. The *Dictionary* seeks to cover the numerous religious bodies, movements, individuals and institutions that have laid claim to the Christian tradition. It does not attempt to arbitrate in matters of religious conviction, but to report fairly, accurately and objectively the beliefs and practices of the respective groups. It seeks to be descriptive rather than prescriptive. Many of the articles have been contributed by experts with religious commitments to the traditions on which they write. If any emphasis may be detected in the *Dictionary,* it would be an attempt to give comprehensive attention to the evangelical tradition in America. But given the prominent role the evangelical tradition has played in America's religious history, it is doubtful that this emphasis upsets the balance of coverage.

Inevitably, there are topics that have not been included. This may be attributable to several factors. Since the *Dictionary* has no direct forebear, the task of establishing a list of entries was made doubly troublesome. An initial list of topics was compiled by consulting the indexes of the standard histories of religion in America as well as a variety of specialized resources. It was thought that any topic mentioned in a standard text on American religious history, inasmuch as it related to the Christian tradition, was a candidate for inclusion in the dictionary. With the help of the consulting editors this list was refined and expanded, and in time it was fortified through the suggestions of numerous experts in particular fields of American religion, most of whom contributed to the *Dictionary*. But in the end, a number of worthy topics were regretfully left behind either because of a lack of space (the capacity of one volume is stretched as it is) or shortness of time (production schedules could not wait for further assignments).

If *Christianity* has been given broad definition, *America* embraces far less than its widest possible reference. The *Dictionary* is primarily focused on the United States, and even more so on the forty-eight contiguous states. It does not include Latin America; however, a substantial amount of space has been devoted to Canada. This coverage reflects the continued religious interaction between the United States and Canada and the sharing of a prevailing linguistic and cultural background. But, out of respect for the differences between the two nations, it should be emphasized that the *Dictionary* does not pretend to provide comprehensive coverage of Christianity in Canada.

One point the title may not make clear—the *Dictionary of Christianity in America* is predominantly historical in perspective. Although the reader will find a great deal of information on contemporary movements, denominations and even some prominent living religious figures, by and large the book deals with the past. More than anything else it is a historical reference work, though it inevitably reaches into the present. Editorially, a far safer policy would have been to include only those individuals who had passed away. But with religious history being made before their eyes, the editors succumbed to the temptation to include a few popular and well-known contemporary religious figures and a handful of contemporary theologians whose contributions were judged significant and/or mature enough to be treated in separate entries. The list could have been extended, and in the end we must beg the forbearance of those who would have liked to have seen it so.

By any reckoning the Christian tradition in America is baffling in its diversity. And yet in its history lie clues to the meaning of America's cultural and spiritual heritage. The editorial goal of this dictionary has been to provide reliable and accessible information on as many aspects of that story as can reasonably be treated in one volume. If the *Dictionary* helps unlock the richness of that story, it will have succeeded in its mission. Beyond that, perhaps it can help promote mutual understanding and good will between men and women of faith—and aid those outside the faith in understanding the ever-changing expressions of the Christian faith within an increasingly pluralistic society.

Daniel G. Reid
Coordinating Editor

How to Use This Dictionary

Abbreviations

A list of abbreviations used in this dictionary will be found on pages xv-xviii.

Authorship of Articles

The authors of articles are indicated by their initials and last name at the foot of each article. A full list of contributors will be found on pages xix-xxix, in alphabetical order of their last name.

Bibliographies

A bibliography has been appended to nearly every article. In the case of biographical articles, bibliographies usually list secondary sources, while important primary sources are listed in the body of the article. Many biographical articles also contain references to articles in important biographical dictionaries, which are noted by their standard abbreviations. All bibliographical items are listed in alphabetical order by the author's last name or, in the case of standard reference works, by the abbreviation of that work.

Cross-references

Subjects will frequently be found covered in both lengthy, comprehensive articles and brief, focused treatments. Thus information on the Evangelical Lutheran Church in America will be found under that heading as well as in a comprehensive article entitled "Lutheran Churches in America." A system of cross-references has been utilized as an aid to finding subjects:

1. One-line entries direct the reader to the title of the article where the topic is treated:

   Episcopal Church. *See* PROTESTANT EPISCOPAL CHURCH IN THE U.S.A.

2. An asterisk after a word or phrase indicates that further relevant information will be found in an article approximating that title. Readers should note:

   a. The *form* of the word asterisked will not always be precisely the same as that of the title of the article to which the asterisk refers. For example, "Methodism*" directs the reader to the article on **Methodist Churches** and "ordained*" to **Ordination**.

   b. The asterisk sometimes applies to two or three words rather than to the word immediately preceding the asterisk. Thus "Civil War*" refers to **Civil War and the Churches** and "Social Gospel*" to **Social Gospel Movement.**

3. References such as (*See* Restoration Movement) have been used within the body of articles.

4. Cross-references have been appended to the end of many articles:

    See also HOLINESS MOVEMENT; PERFECTIONISM.

Introductory Essay

This dictionary includes a lengthy introductory essay entitled "Division and Unity: The Paradox of Christianity in America." It is intended to provide readers a synoptic overview and interpretive perspective on a subject the *Dictionary* has otherwise parsed into alphabetical segments. Since the essay also utilizes asterisks as cross-references, it can serve as a launching point for those who wish to use the *Dictionary* as something more than a quick reference. It may even make the volume a candidate for classroom use.

ABBREVIATIONS

Books and Journals

AAP	*Annals of the American Pulpit,* ed. W. B. Sprague, 9 vols.
ABQ	*American Baptist Quarterly*
ABR	*American Benedictine Review*
ACR	*American Church Review*
AGR	*American German Review*
AHC	*Annuarium Historiae Conciliorum*
AHP	*Archivum Historiae Pontificae*
AHR	*American Historical Review*
AP	*American Presbyterians*
APTR	*American Presbyterian and Theological Review*
AQ	*American Quarterly*
AS	*American Studies*
ASR	*American Sociological Review*
ATR	*Anglican Theological Review*
AUSS	*Andrews University Seminary Studies*
BASOR	*Bulletin of the American Schools of Oriental Research*
BHH	*Baptist History and Heritage*
BE	*The Brethren Encyclopedia,* ed. D. F. Durnbaugh, 3 vols.
CathDi	*Catholic Digest*
CBQ	*Catholic Biblical Quarterly*
CCen	*The Christian Century*
CCri	*Christianity and Crisis*
CDCWM	*Concise Dictionary of the Christian World Mission,* ed. S. Neill et al.
CH	*Church History*
CHR	*Catholic Historical Review*
Con	*Concilium*
CongQ	*Congregational Quarterly*
CQR	*Church Quarterly Review*
CSR	*Christian Scholars Review*
CT	*Christianity Today*
CTJ	*Calvin Theological Journal*
CTM	*Concordia Theological Monthly*
CTQ	*Concordia Theological Quarterly*
CW	*The Catholic World*
DAB	*Dictionary of American Biography,* ed. A. Johnson, D. Malone et al. (vols. I-X, 1892-1974; 1-7, 1944-1988)
DACB	*Dictionary of American Catholic Biography,* J. J. Delaney
DARB	*Dictionary of American Religious Biography,* H. W. Bowden
DCB	*Dictionary of Canadian Biography,* ed. G. W. Brown et al., 11 vols.
DNB	*Dictionary of National Biography,* ed. L. Stephen et al.

DPCM	*Dictionary of Pentecostal and Charismatic Movements,* ed. S. M. Burgess and G. B. McGee
DTC	*Dictionnaire de theologie catholique,* ed. A. Vacant, et al.
EAL	*Early American Literature*
EAR	*The Encyclopedia of American Religion,* J. G. Melton
EARE	*Encyclopedia of the American Religious Experience,* ed. C. H. Lippy and P. W. Williams, 3 vols.
EDT	*Evangelical Dictionary of Theology,* ed. W. Elwell
ELC	*Encyclopedia of the Lutheran Church,* ed. J. Bodensieck
EncyR	*The Encyclopedia of Religion,* ed. M. Eliade
ER	*An Encyclopedia of Religion,* ed. V. Ferm
ERS	*Encyclopedia of Religion in the South,* ed. S. S. Hill
ESB	*Encyclopedia of Southern Baptists,* ed. C. J. Allen et al., 4 vols.
Eter	*Eternity*
Ethn	*Ethnicity*
FH	*Fides et Historia*
Foun	*Foundations: A Baptist Journal of History and Theology*
GOTR	*Greek Orthodox Theological Review*
HDSB	*Harvard Divinity [School] Bulletin*
HERE	*Encyclopaedia of Religion and Ethics,* ed. J. Hastings
HMPEC	*Historical Magazine of the Protestant Episcopal Church*
HTR	*Harvard Theological Review*
IBMR	*International Bulletin of Missionary Research*
IRM	*International Review of Mission*
JAAR	*Journal of the American Academy of Religion*
JASA	*Journal of the American Scientific Affiliation*
JCCHS	*Journal of the Canadian Church Historical Society*
JCMHS	*The Journal of the Calvinistic Methodist Historical Society*
JCS	*Journal of Church and State*
JEH	*Journal of Ecclesiastical History*
JER	*Journal of the Early Republic*
JETS	*Journal of the Evangelical Theological Society*
JHBS	*Journal of the History of Behavioral Sciences*
JHI	*Journal of the History of Ideas*
JNH	*Journal of Negro History*
JPH	*Journal of Presbyterian History*
JPHS	*Journal of the Presbyterian Historical Society*
JPT	*Journal of Psychology and Theology*
JR	*The Journal of Religion*
JSH	*Journal of Southern History*
JSocH	*Journal of Social History*
JTS	*The Journal of Theological Studies*
JUHS	*Journal of the Universalist Historical Society*
LCQ	*Lutheran Church Quarterly*
MarS	*Marian Studies*
McCQ	*McCormick Quarterly*
ME	*Mennonite Encyclopedia,* ed. H. S. Bender et al., 4 vols.

MH	*Methodist History*
MHR	*Maryland Historical Magazine*
MissRev	*Missiology: An International Review*
MQR	*The Mennonite Quarterly Review*
NAW	*Notable American Women: 1607-1950,* 3 vols. (1971)
NAWMP	*Notable American Women: The Modern Period,* 1 vol. (1980)
NCAB	*National Cyclopedia of American Biography,* 55 vols. (1892-1974); Current Series, A-L (1930-1972).
NCE	*New Catholic Encyclopedia,* ed. W. J. McDonald, 18 vols.
NEQ	*The New England Quarterly*
NIDCC	*The New International Dictionary of the Christian Church,* ed. J. D. Douglas
NYHSQ	*New York Historical Society Quarterly*
OBMR	*Occasional Bulletin of Missionary Research*
ODCC	*The Oxford Dictionary of the Christian Church,* ed. F. L. Cross
PAPS	*Proceedings of the American Philosophical Society*
PC	*The Presbyterian Communique*
PI	*The Public Interest*
PP	*Pastoral Psychology*
PPR	*Philosophy and Phenomenological Research*
Presb	*Presbyterian*
PRR	*The Presbyterian and Reformed Review*
PR	*Philosophical Review*
PSB	*Princeton Seminary Bulletin*
PTR	*The Princeton Theological Review*
QR	*Quarterly Review*
RACHAP	*Records of the American Catholic Historical Association of Philadelphia*
Rat	*Ratio*
RE	*Review and Expositor*
RelEd	*Religious Education*
RelS	*Religious Studies*
RR	*Reformed Review*
RRR	*Review of Religious Research*
RTR	*The Reformed Theological Review*
RQ	*Restoration Quarterly*
RSR	*Religious Studies Review*
RUL	*Revue de l'université Laval*
RUS	*Rice University Studies*
SHERK	*The New Schaff-Herzog Encyclopedia of Religious Knowledge,* ed. S. M. Jackson
SJT	*Scottish Journal of Theology*
SSR	*Social Service Review*
SVTQ	*St. Vladimir's Theological Quarterly*
SwJT	*Southwestern Journal of Theology*
Theol	*Theology*
TheolEd	*Theological Education*
Tht	*Thought*

Abbreviations

TS	*Theological Studies*
TT	*Theology Today*
USQR	*Union Seminary Quarterly Review*
USCH	*U. S. Catholic Historian*
VC	*Vigilae Christianae*
VoxT	*Vox Theologica*
WDCH	*The Westminster Dictionary of Church History,* ed. J. Brauer
WTJ	*Wesleyan Theological Journal*
WMQ	*William and Mary Quarterly*
WmTJ	*Westminster Theological Journal*

General Abbreviations

b.	Born
c.	*Circa,* about, approximately
d.	Died
ET	English Translation
fl.	*Floruit,* flourished
vol(s).	Volume(s)
?	Date uncertain
*	Indicates subject included in the *Dictionary of Christianity in America*

LIST OF CONTRIBUTORS

Adeney, Bernard T., Ph.D., Graduate Theological Union—Berkeley. Associate Professor of Social Ethics and Cross-Cultural Studies, New College, Berkeley, California.

Adeney, Frances S., Ph.D., Graduate Theological Union. Assistant Professor of Religion and Society, New College for Advanced Christian Studies, Berkeley, California.

Airhart, Phyllis D., Ph.D., University of Chicago. Assistant Professor of Church History, Emmanuel College, University of Toronto, Toronto, Ontario.

Aivazian, Arshen A., M.Div., St. Vladimir's Orthodox Seminary. Parish Priest, St. Leon's Armenian Church, Fair Lawn, New Jersey.

Albin, Thomas R., M.A., Fuller Theological Seminary. Ph.D. candidate, Cambridge University. Instructor of Christian Formation and Faith Education, University of Dubuque Theological Seminary, Dubuque, Iowa.

Anderson, Clifford V., Ed.D., Teacher's College, Columbia University in conjunction with Union Theological Seminary. Professor of Education and Associate Dean and Director of Bethel Theological Seminary, West Campus, San Diego, California.

Angell, Stephen W., Ph.D., Vanderbilt University. Assistant Professor of Philosophy and Religion, South Dakota State University, Brookings, South Dakota.

Appleby, R. Scott, Ph.D., University of Chicago. Associate Project Director, The Fundamentalism Project, The American Academy of Arts and Sciences, Chicago, Illinois.

Armentrout, Donald S., Ph.D., Vanderbilt University. Professor of Church History, Associate Dean for Academic Affairs, Director of the Advanced Degrees Programs, School of Theology, University of the South, Sewanee, Tennessee.

Ashcraft, William M., M.Div., Southern Baptist Theological Seminary, Ph.D. candidate, University of Virginia, Charlottesville, Virginia.

Auge, Thomas E., Ph.D., Iowa University. Director of Loras College Historical Research Center, Dubuque, Iowa.

Avella, Steven M., Ph.D., University of Notre Dame. Assistant Professor of Historical Studies, St. Francis Seminary, Milwaukee, Wisconsin.

Bachman, E. Theodore, Ph.D., University of Chicago. Archivist, New Jersey Synod, Evangelical Lutheran Church in America, Princeton Junction, New Jersey.

Baker, Vaughn W., D.Min., Perkins School of Theology, Southern Methodist University. Pastor, St. Andrew's United Methodist Church, Arlington, Texas.

Balmer, Randall H., Ph.D., Princeton University. Assistant Professor of Religion, Columbia University, New York, New York.

Barbour, Hugh S., Ph.D., Yale University. Professor of Religion and Church History, Earlham School of Religion, Richmond, Indiana.

Barcus, James E., Jr., D.Phil., University of Pennsylvania. Professor of English and Chair, Department of English, Baylor University, Waco, Texas.

Barker, William S., II, Ph.D., Vanderbilt University. Professor of Church History, Westminster Theological Seminary, Philadelphia, Pennsylvania.

Barron, Bruce, B.A., Michigan State University. Ph.D. candidate, University of Pittsburgh.

Bays, Daniel H., Ph.D., University of Michigan—Ann Arbor. Professor of History and Chair, Department of History, University of Kansas, Lawrence, Kansas.

Bechtel, Paul M., Ph.D., Northwestern University. Professor Emeritus of English, Wheaton College, Wheaton, Illinois.

Bekker, Gary J., Ph.D., Michigan State University. Assistant Professor of Missions, Gordon-Conwell Theological Seminary, South Hamilton, Massachusetts.

Bell, Marty G., Ph.D. candidate, Vanderbilt University. Assistant Professor of Religion, Belmont College, Nashville, Tennessee.

Bendroth, Margaret L., Ph.D., Johns Hopkins University. Adjunct Professor, Northeastern University, Cambridge, Massachusetts.

Berk, Stephen E., Ph.D., University of Iowa. Professor of History, California State University, Long Beach, California.

Birkel, Michael L., Ph.D., Harvard University. Assistant Professor of Religion, Earlham College, Richmond, Indiana.

Blantz, Thomas E., C.S.C. Ph.D., Columbia University. Associate Professor of History, University of Notre Dame, Notre Dame, Indiana.

Bloesch, Donald G., Ph.D., University of Chicago. Professor of Theology, University of Dubuque Theological Seminary, Dubuque, Iowa.

Blumhofer, Edith L., Ph.D., Harvard University. Project Director, Institute for the Study of American Evangelicals; Associate Professor of History, Wheaton College, Wheaton, Illinois.

Bolt, Robert, Ph.D., Michigan State University. Professor of History, Calvin College, Grand Rapids, Michigan.

Bowen, John W., S.S., M.A., Catholic University of America; S.T.L., St. Mary's Seminary and University. Archivist, Sulpician Archives, Baltimore, Maryland.

Boylan, Anne M., Ph.D., University of Wisconsin. Associate Professor of History, University of Delaware, Newark, Delaware.

Bracken, W. Jerome, C.P., Ph.D., Fordham University. Associate Professor, St. Charles Borromeo Seminary, Philadelphia, Pennsylvania.

Brackney, William H., Ph.D., Temple University. Principal and Professor of Historical Theology, McMaster Divinity College, Hamilton, Ontario.

Bratt, James D., Ph.D., Yale University. Professor of History, Calvin College, Grand Rapids, Michigan.

Brown, Beth E., Ed.D., University of Northern Colorado. Assistant Professor of Christian Education, Denver Seminary, Denver, Colorado.

Brown, Joanne C., Ph.D., Boston University. Professor of Church History and Ecumenics, St. Andrew's

College, Saskatoon, Saskatchewan.

Browning, W. Neal, D.Min., Vanderbilt University Divinity School. Associate Professor of Japanese Studies, William Carey International University, Pasadena, California.

Bruce, Marcus C., M.Div., Yale University Divinity School. Instructor, Philosophy/Religion Department, Bates College, Lewiston, Maine.

Bruins, Elton J., Ph.D., New York University. Evert J. and Hattie E. Blekkink Professor of Religion, Hope College, Holland, Michigan.

Buckley, Thomas E., S.J., Ph.D., University of California—Santa Barbara. Professor of History, Loyola Marymount University, Los Angeles, California.

Bundy, David D., Licentiate, Universite Catholique de Louvain. Associate Professor of Christian Origins and Collection Development Librarian, Asbury Theological Seminary, Wilmore, Kentucky.

Buss, Dietrich G., Ph.D., Claremont Graduate School. Professor of History and Chairman of the Department of History, Biola University School of Arts and Sciences, La Mirada, California.

Butin, Philip W., M.Div., Fuller Theological Seminary. Co-Pastor, Oxford Presbyterian Church (PCUSA), Oxford, North Carolina.

Byrne, Patricia, C.S.J., Ph.D., Boston College. Assistant Professor, Department of Religion, Trinity College, Hartford, Connecticut.

Cairns, Earle E., Ph.D., University of Nebraska. Professor Emeritus of History, Wheaton College, Wheaton, Illinois.

Campbell, Debra, Ph.D., Boston University. Dana Faculty Fellow and Assistant Professor of Religion, Colby College, Waterville, Maine.

Carden, Allen, Ph.D., University of California—Irvine. Vice President for Academic Affairs and Professor of History, Spring Arbor College, Spring Arbor, Michigan.

Carey, Patrick W., Ph.D., Fordham University. Associate Professor of American Religious History, Marquette University, Milwaukee, Wisconsin.

Carlson, Douglas W., Ph.D., University of Illinois—Urbana/Champaign. Associate Professor of History, The King's College, Briarcliff Manor, New York.

Carlson, Gordon William, Ph.D., University of Minnesota. Associate Professor of History and Political Science, Bethel College, St. Paul, Minnesota.

Carmody, John T., Ph.D., Stanford University. Senior Research Fellow, University of Tulsa, Tulsa, Oklahoma.

Carpenter, Joel A., Ph.D., The Johns Hopkins University. Director of Religion Program, The Pew Charitable Trusts, Philadelphia, Pennsylvania.

Carper, James C., Ph.D., Kansas State University. Associate Professor of Foundations of Education, The University of South Carolina, Columbia, South Carolina.

Cassidy, Keith M., Ph.D., University of Toronto. Associate Professor, University of Guelph, Ontario.

Cathey, Robert A., Ph.D., Duke University. Assistant Professor, Department of Philosophy and Religious Studies; College Chaplain, Monmouth College, Monmouth, Illinois.

Cheseborough, David B., D.A., Illinois State University. Assistant Chair and Academic Advisor, Department of History, Illinois State University, Normal, Illinois.

Chilton, Roger H., M.Div., Regent College. Ph.D. candidate, Oxford University, Oxford, England.

Cizik, Richard C., M.Div., The Conservative Baptist Theological Seminary. Research Director, National Association of Evangelicals, Office of Public Affairs, Washington, D.C.

Clapp, Rodney R., M.A., Wheaton Graduate School. General Books Editor, InterVarsity Press, Downers Grove, Illinois.

Clifford, Anne M., C.S.J., Ph.D., The Catholic University of America. Assistant Professor of Theology, Duquesne University, Pittsburgh, Pennsylvania.

Clouse, Robert G., Ph.D., University of Iowa. Professor of History, Indiana State University, Terre Haute, Indiana.

Clutter, Ronald T., Th.D., Dallas Theological Seminary. Professor of Church History and Theology, Grace Theological Seminary, Winona Lake, Indiana.

Coalter, Milton J., Jr., Ph.D., Princeton University. Library Director and Associate Professor of Bibliography and Research, White Library, Louisville Presbyterian Theological Seminary, Louisville, Kentucky.

Coggins, Wade T., M.A., University of Maryland. Executive Director, Evangelical Foreign Missions Association, Washington, D.C.

Conforti, Joseph A., Ph.D., Brown University. Director of New England Studies, University of Southern Maine, Portland, Maine.

Conn, Harvie M., Th.M., Westminster Theological Seminary. Professor of Missions and Chairman of the Practical Theology Department, Westminster Theological Seminary, Philadelphia, Pennsylvania.

Connelly, James T., Ph.D., University of Chicago. Archivist, Congregation of Holy Cross, Indiana Province, Notre Dame, Indiana.

Cooper, James F., Jr., Ph.D., University of Connecticut. Assistant Professor of History, Oklahoma State University, Stillwater, Oklahoma.

Cooper, Wilmer A., Ph.D., Vanderbilt University. Dean Emeritus and Professor of Quaker Studies, Earlham School of Religion, Richmond, Indiana.

Corduan, Winfried, Ph.D., Rice University. Professor of Philosophy and Religion, Taylor University, Upland, Indiana.

Cort, John C., B.A., Harvard University. Freelance writer, Contributing Editor, *New Oxford Review*.

Corwin, Gary R., M.Div., Trinity Evangelical Divinity School; D.Miss. candidate, Trinity Evangelical Divinity School. International Research and Education Coordinator for SIM International, Charlotte, North Carolina.

Craig, John M., Ph.D., College of William and Mary. Assistant Professor, Department of History, Slippery Rock University, Slippery Rock, Pennsylvania.

Crews, Clyde F., Ph.D., Fordham University. Chairperson, Department of Theology, Bellarmine College, Louisville, Kentucky.

Crocco, Stephen D., Ph.D., Princeton University. Librarian and Assistant Professor, Pittsburgh Theological Seminary, Pittsburgh, Pennsylvania.

Crocker, Richard R., Ph.D., Vanderbilt University. College Chaplain and Lecturer in Religion, Bates College, Lewiston, Maine.

Crow, Paul A., Jr., Ph.D., Hartford Seminary Foundation. President of Council on Christian Unity, Disciples of Christ, Indianapolis, Indiana.

Cruz, Virgil A., Ph.D., Free University, Amsterdam. Senior Professor of New

Testament, Louisville Presbyterian Theological Seminary, Louisville, Kentucky.

Cunningham, Lawrence S., S.T.L., Gregorian University, Rome, Ph.D., Florida State University. Professor of Theology, University of Notre Dame, Notre Dame, Indiana.

Currey, Cecil B., Ph.D., Kansas University. Professor of Military History, University of South Florida, Tampa, Florida.

Davis, Lorraine Mulligan, B.A., Houghton College. Manuscript Editor, InterVarsity Press, Downers Grove, Illinois.

Dawson, Cole P., Ph.D., Miami University. Professor and Chair of the Division of Arts and Sciences, Warner Pacific College, Portland, Oregon.

De Chant, Dell, M.A., University of South Florida. Adjunct Professor, University of South Florida, Tampa, Florida.

De Marco, Donald T., Ph.D., St. John's University—Jamaica, New York. Professor of Philosophy, The University of St. Jerome's College, Waterloo, Ontario.

Detzler, Wayne A., Ph.D., University of Manchester. Senior Pastor, Calvary Baptist Church, Meriden, Connecticut. Adjunct Professor of Church History, Temple Baptist Seminary.

DeVries, George., Jr., M.A., University of Iowa. Professor Emeritus of History, Northwestern College, Orange City, Iowa.

Diefenthaler, Jon T., Ph.D., University of Iowa. Pastor, Bethany Lutheran Church, Waynesboro, Virginia.

Dieter, Melvin E., Ph.D., Temple University. Professor of Church History and Director of Wesleyan/Holiness Studies, Asbury Theological Seminary, Wilmore, Kentucky.

Dolan, Jay P., Ph.D., University of Chicago. Professor of History, University of Notre Dame, Notre Dame, Indiana.

Donnelly, John P., S.J., Ph.D., University of Wisconsin—Madison. Professor of History, Marquette University, Milwaukee, Wisconsin.

Dorn, Jacob H., Ph.D., University of Oregon. Professor of History, Wright State University, Dayton, Ohio.

Dorsett, Lyle W., Ph.D., University of Missouri. Director of the Wade Center and Professor of History, Wheaton College, Wheaton, Illinois.

Durnbaugh, Donald F., Ph.D., University of Pennsylvania. Carl W. Ziegler

Professor of Religion and History, Elizabethtown College, Elizabethtown, Pennsylvania.

Dyck, Cornelius J., Ph.D., University of Chicago. Professor of Anabaptist and Sixteenth Century Studies, Associated Mennonite Biblical Seminaries, Elkhart, Indiana.

Dyrness, William A., D.Theol., Strasbourg University. Professor of Theology, New College Berkeley, Berkeley, California.

Edelman, Hendrik, M.L.S., George Peabody College—Nashville. Professor, School of Communication, Information and Library Studies, Rutgers University, New Brunswick, New Jersey.

Edwards, John H., M.A., San Francisco State University. Associate Editor, Works of Jonathan Edwards, New Haven, Connecticut.

Edwards, Lillie J., Ph.D., University of Chicago. Associate Professor of History, DePaul University, Chicago, Illinois.

Eller, David B., Ph.D., Miami University. Senior Editor, Social Studies, Glencoe/Macmillan Publishing Company, Schaumburg, Illinois.

Elliott, C. Mark, M.Div., Holy Cross Greek Orthodox School of Theology. Adjunct Instructor of American History, Hellenic College, Brookline, Massachusetts.

Ellis, Walter E., Ph.D., University of Pittsburgh. Senior Minister, Fairview Baptist Church, Vancouver, Canada.

Ellis, William E., Ph.D., University of Kentucky. Director, Oral History Center, Professor of History, Eastern Kentucky University, Richmond, Kentucky.

Enns-Rempel, Kevin M., M.A., University of California—Riverside. Archivist, Center for Mennonite Brethren Studies, Fresno, California.

Enroth, Ronald M., Ph.D., University of Kentucky. Professor of Sociology, Westmont College, Santa Barbara, California.

Erickson, Millard J., Ph.D., Northwestern University. Executive Vice President and Dean, Professor of Theology, Bethel Theological Seminary, St. Paul, Minnesota.

Erickson, Nancy L., Ph.D., University of North Carolina—Chapel Hill. Professor of History, Erskine College, Due West, South Carolina.

Ernst, Eldon G., Ph.D., Yale University. Associate Dean and Professor of American Religious History,

Graduate Theological Union, Berkeley, California.

Estep, William R., Th.D., Southwestern Baptist Theological Seminary. Distinguished Professor of Church History, Chairman of the Historical Division, School of Theology, Southwestern Baptist Theological Seminary, Fort Worth, Texas.

Evans, George P., S.T.D., The Catholic University of America. Spiritual Advisor, St. John's Seminary, Boston, Massachusetts.

Evans, John W., Ph.D., University of Minnesota. Associate Professor, College of St. Scholastica, Duluth, Minnesota.

Evans, William B., Th.M., Westminster Theological Seminary. Ph.D. candidate, Vanderbilt University, Nashville, Tennessee.

Ewert, David, Ph.D., McGill University, Montreal. Professor Emeritus, Mennonite Brethren Bible College, Winnipeg, Manitoba.

Farina, John, Ph.D., Yale University. Editor, Paulist Press/Paulist Office of History, Mahwah, New Jersey.

Feldmeth, Nathan P., Ph.D., University of Edinburgh. Adjunct Assistant Professor, Fuller Theological Seminary, Pasadena, California.

Fields, Kathleen R., Ph.D., University of Notre Dame.

Fischer, Robert H., Ph.D., Yale University. Emeritus Professor of Church History, Lutheran School of Theology, Chicago, Illinois.

Fitzgerald, Thomas, Th.D., University of Thessaloniki. Associate Professor of Religious Studies and History, Hellenic College, Holy Cross Greek Orthodox School of Theology, Brookline, Massachusetts

Fitzmier, John R., Ph.D., Princeton University. Assistant Professor of American Religious History, Vanderbilt Divinity School, Nashville, Tennessee.

Fletcher, David B., Ph.D., University of Illinois—Urbana. Associate Professor of Philosophy, Wheaton College, Wheaton, Illinois.

Floding, Matthew D., M.A., Wheaton College. Chaplain of the College, Northwestern College, Orange City, Iowa.

Flowers, Ronald B., Ph.D., School of Religion, University of Iowa. Professor of Religion-Studies, Texas Christian University, Fort Worth, Texas.

Frank, Albert H., D.Min., Drew University Theological School. Pastor, First Moravian Church of Dover, Ohio.

Franklin, Stephen T., Ph.D., University of Chicago. Pastor, Hope Evangelical Covenant Church, East Grand Forks, Minnesota.

Fraser, M. Robert, Ph.D., Vanderbilt University. Associate Professor of Theology and Church History, Asia-Pacific Nazarene Theological Seminary, Makati, Metro Manila, Philippines.

Freundt, Albert H., Jr., D.Min., McCormick Theological Seminary. Professor of Church History and Polity, Reformed Theological Seminary, Jackson, Mississippi.

Fry, C. George, Ph.D., Ohio State University. Protestant Chaplain, St. Francis College, Fort Wayne, Indiana.

Gaffin, Richard B., Jr., Th.D., Westminster Theological Seminary. Professor of Systematic Theology, Westminster Theological Seminary, Philadelphia, Pennsylvania.

Garrett, James L., Jr., Ph.D., Harvard University; Th.D., Southwestern Baptist Theological Seminary. Professor of Theology, Southwestern Baptist Theological Seminary.

Garrett, Paul D., M.Div., St. Vladimir's Orthodox Theological Seminary. Director of Information Services, Antiochian Village Heritage and Learning Center, Latrobe, Pennsylvania.

Geisler, Norman L., Ph.D., Loyola University—Chicago. Dean, Liberty Center for Research and Scholarship, Lynchburg, Virginia.

George, Timothy, Th.D., Harvard University. Dean, Beeson Divinity School, Samford University, Birmingham, Alabama.

Getz, Gene A., Ph.D., New York University. Director, Center for Church Renewal, Plano, Texas. Senior Pastor, Fellowship Bible Church North. Adjunct Professor, Dallas Theological Seminary, Dallas, Texas.

Glass, James M., M.Div., Southwestern Baptist Theological Seminary. Pastor, Chapel Hill Baptist Church, Millry, Alabama.

Glenn, Alfred A., Ph.D., Northwestern University. Professor of Theology, Bethel Theological Seminary—West, San Diego, California.

Goen, Clarence C., Ph.D., Yale University. Professor Emeritus, Wesley Theological Seminary, Washington, D.C.

Goodpasture, H. McKennie, Ph.D., University of Edinburgh. Professor of Christian Mission, Union Theological Seminary, Richmond, Virginia.

Goodwin, Grover F., Ph.D., Princeton University. Associate Professor, Department of History, Carleton University, Ottawa, Canada.

Graham, Stephen R., Ph.D., The Divinity School, University of Chicago. Assistant Professor of American Church History, North Park Theological Seminary, Chicago, Illinois.

Grant, John W., D.Phil., Oxford University. Professor Emeritus, Victoria University, Toronto, Ontario.

Grasso, Christopher D., M.Phil., Yale University. Graduate student, Yale University, New Haven, Connecticut.

Gration, John A., Ph.D., New York University. Professor of Missions/Chair, Missions/Intercultural Studies Department, Wheaton Graduate School, Wheaton, Illinois.

Gravely, William B., Ph.D., Duke University. Professor of Religious Studies, University of Denver, Denver, Colorado.

Green, Roger J., Ph.D., Boston College. Professor of Biblical and Theological Studies, Gordon College, Wenham, Massachusetts.

Grenz, Stanley J., D.Theol., University of Munich. Professor of Systematic Theology and Christian Ethics, North American Baptist Seminary, Sioux Falls, South Dakota.

Groothuis, Douglas R., M.A., University of Wisconsin—Madison. Freelance Writer and Lecturer, Eugene, Oregon.

Gross, Leonard, D.Phil., Universität Basel, Switzerland. Executive Secretary, Historical Committee of the Mennonite Church. Director, Archives of the Mennonite Church, Goshen College, Goshen, Indiana.

Guelzo, Allen C., Ph.D., University of Pennsylvania. Academic Dean, Theological Seminary of the Reformed Episcopal Church, Philadelphia, Pennsylvania.

Guenther, Karen E., M.A., Pennsylvania State University. Instructor of History, San Jacinto College District, Houston, Texas.

Gunter, W. Stephen, D.Theol., University of Leiden, The Netherlands. Professor of Historical and Systematic Theology and Dean, Bethany College of Ministry and the

Humanities, Southern Nazarene University, Bethany, Oklahoma.

Hähnlen, Lee W., M.A., Western Kentucky University; D.Theol. candidate, University of South Africa. Assistant Professor of Church History/Theology, Liberty University, Lynchburg, Virginia.

Hall, Cline E., Ph.D., University of Tennessee. Department Chair and Associate Professor, History Department, Liberty University, Lynchburg, Virginia.

Hall, Joseph H., Th.D., Concordia Seminary, St. Lewis. Knox Theological Seminary, Ft. Lauderdale, Florida.

Hambrick-Stowe, Charles E., Ph.D., Boston University Graduate School. Pastor, Church of the Apostles, United Church of Christ, Lancaster, Pennsylvania.

Handy, Robert T., Ph.D., University of Chicago. Henry Sloane Coffin Professor Emeritus of Church History, Union Theological Seminary, New York, New York. Visiting Professor, Drew University, Madison, New Jersey.

Hannah, John D., Th.D., Dallas Seminary; Ph.D., University of Texas, Dallas. Department Chairman, Professor of Historical Theology, Dallas Theological Seminary, Dallas, Texas.

Hanson, Calvin B., M.A., University of Minnesota. Director of Internship, Trinity Evangelical Divinity School, Deerfield, Illinois.

Harakas, Stanley S., Th.D., Boston University. Archbishop Iakovos Professor of Orthodox Theology, Holy Cross Greek Orthodox School of Theology, Brookline, Massachusetts.

Hardesty, Nancy A., Ph.D., University of Chicago. Independent Scholar, Writer, and Book Copyeditor. Visiting Assistant Professor of Philosophy and Religion, Clemson University, Clemson, South Carolina.

Harper, George W., M.Div., Gordon-Conwell Theological Seminary; Ph.D. candidate, Boston University. Adjunct Lecturer in Church History, Gordon-Conwell Theological Seminary, South Hamilton, Massachusetts.

Harrell, David E., Jr., Ph.D., Vanderbilt University. University Scholar in History, University of Alabama, Birmingham, Alabama.

Hart, D. G., Ph.D., Johns Hopkins University. Director of the Institute for the Study of American Evangelicals, Wheaton, Illinois.

Hassey, Janette R., Ph.D., The Divinity School, University of Chicago. Adjunct Professor, Asian Theological Seminary, Manila, Philippines.

Healey, Robert M., Ph.D., Yale University. Professor of Church History, University of Dubuque Theological Seminary, Dubuque, Iowa.

Henery, Charles R., S.T.M.; Th.D. candidate, The General Theological Seminary. Instructor in Church History, Nashotah House Seminary, Nashotah, Wisconsin.

Hennesey, James, Ph.D., Catholic University of America. Professor of the History of Christianity, Canisius College, Buffalo, New York.

Hesselgrave, David J., Ph.D., University of Minnesota. Professor of Mission, Trinity Evangelical Divinity School—School of World Mission And Evangelism, Deerfield, Illinois.

Hesselgrave, Ronald P., Ph.D., Drew University. Assistant Professor of Sociology, Trinity College, Deerfield, Illinois.

Hexham, Irving, Ph.D., Bristol University. Associate Professor, Department of Religious Studies, University of Calgary, Calgary, Alberta.

Hill, Samuel S., Ph.D., Duke University. Professor of Religion, University of Florida, Gainesville, Florida.

Hillis, Bryan V., Ph.D., University of Chicago. Assistant Professor, Luther College, University of Regina, Regina, Saskatchewan.

Hitchcock, James F., Ph.D., Princeton University. Professor of Law in History, St. Louis University, St. Louis, Missouri.

Hoffecker, W. Andrew, Ph.D., Brown University. Professor of Religion, Grove City College, Grove City, Pennsylvania.

Holifield, E. Brooks, Ph.D., Yale University. Charles Howard Candler Professor of American Church History, Candler School of Theology, Emory University, Atlanta, Georgia.

Hollinger, Dennis P., Ph.D., Drew University. Associate Professor of Preaching and Church and Society, Associated Mennonite Biblical Seminaries, Elkhart, Indiana.

Holmes, David L., Ph.D., Princeton University. Professor of Religion, College of William and Mary, Williamsburg, Virginia.

Horn, Henry E., S.T.M., Lutheran

Theological Seminary—Philadelphia. Pastor Emeritus, University Lutheran Church, Cambridge, Massachusetts.

Howe, Claude L., Jr., Th.D., New Orleans Baptist Theological Seminary. Chairman, Theological and Historical Studies Division, New Orleans Baptist Theological Seminary, New Orleans, Louisiana.

Howes, John F., Ph.D., Columbia University. Professor Emeritus, University of British Columbia; Professor, Obirin University, Tokyo, Japan.

Hummel, Charles E., M.S., Massachusetts Institute of Technology. M.A., Wheaton College. Faculty Specialist, InterVarsity Christian Fellowship.

Hummel, Horace D., Ph.D., Johns Hopkins. Professor of Exegetical Theology, Chairman of Department of Exegetical Theology, Concordia Seminary, St. Louis, Missouri.

Hunt, Everett N., Jr., Ph.D., The Divinity School, University of Chicago. Lecturer at Large, OMS International, Greenwood, Indiana; Adjunct Professor of Missions, E. Stanley Jones School of World Mission and Evangelism, Asbury Theological Seminary, Wilmore, Kentucky.

Hunt, Thomas C., Ph.D., University of Wisconsin. Professor and Chair, Division of Curriculum and Instruction, Virginia Polytechnic Institute and State University, Blacksburg, Virginia.

Hunter, Harold D., Ph.D., Fuller Theological Seminary. Executive Director, Sunday School Department, Church of God of Prophecy, Cleveland, Tennessee.

Hussey, M. Edmund, Ph.D., Fordham University. Pastor, St. Paul Church, Yellow Springs, Ohio; Adjunct Professor of Historical Theology, Mt. St. Mary Seminary, Cincinnati, Ohio.

Ingersol, Robert S., Ph.D., Duke University. Denominational Archivist, Church of the Nazarene International Headquarters, Kansas City, Missouri.

Japinga, Lynn W., M.Phil., Union Theological Seminary, New York. Adjunct Professor, Western Theological Seminary, Holland, Michigan.

Johnson, James E., Ph.D., Syracuse University. Professor of History and Department Chair, Bethel College, St. Paul, Minnesota.

Johnson, John F., Th.D., Concordia

Seminary; Ph.D., St. Louis University. President and Professor of Religion, Concordia College, St. Paul, Minnesota.

Jones, Charles E., Ph.D., University of Wisconsin. Historian and Bibliographer, Oklahoma City, Oklahoma.

Joy, Mark S., M.A.; Ph.D. candidate, Kansas State University. Instructor, Department of History, Kansas State University, Manhattan, Kansas.

Juhnke, James C., Ph.D., Indiana University. Professor of History, Bethel College, North Newton, Kansas.

Kane, Paula M., Ph.D., Yale University. Assistant Professor of History, Texas A&M University, College Station, Texas.

Kane, Stephen M., M.A., Boston College. Teaching Assistant, Brown University, Providence, Rhode Island.

Kantowicz, Edward R., Ph.D., University of Chicago. Freelance Historian, Chicago, Illinois.

Keiss, Issabelle, R.S.M., Ph.D., University of Notre Dame. President, Gwynedd-Mercy College, Gwynedd Valley, Pennsylvania.

Kennedy, Earl W., Th.D., Princeton Theological Seminary. Professor of Religion, Northwestern College, Orange City, Iowa.

Kern, Richard, Ph.D., University of Chicago. Professor of History, University of Findlay, Findlay, Ohio.

Kidd, Karen, M.A., Fuller Theological Seminary; Ph.D. candidate, Claremont Graduate School, Claremont, California.

Klejment, Anne, Ph.D., State University of New York at Binghamton. Associate Professor, Department of History, College of St. Thomas, St. Paul, Minnesota.

Kolb, Robert A., Ph.D., University of Wisconsin, Madison. Professor of History and of Religion, Concordia College, St. Paul, Minnesota.

Kreeft, Peter J., Ph.D., Fordham University. Professor of Philosophy, Boston College, Chestnut Hill, Massachusetts.

Kress, Robert L., S.T.D., University of St. Thomas (Angelicum), Rome. Professor, Department Chair, Theological and Religious Studies, University of San Diego, San Diego, California.

Lagerquist, L. DeAne, Ph.D., University of Chicago. Assistant Professor, St. Olaf College, Northfield, Minnesota.

Land, Gary G., Ph.D., University of California, Santa Barbara. Professor, Chairman, Department of History, Andrews University, Berrien Springs, Michigan.

Lawrence, William G., Ph.D., Drew University. Senior Pastor, Owego United Methodist Church, Owego, New York.

Leahy, William P., S.J., Ph.D., Stanford University. Assistant Professor, Department of History, Marquette University, Milwaukee, Wisconsin.

Leliaert, Richard M., Ph.D., Graduate Theological Union—Berkeley, California. Staff Chaplain, St. Joseph Mercy Hospital, Pontiac, Michigan.

Leonard, Bill J., Ph.D., Boston University. Professor of Church History, The Southern Baptist Theological Seminary, Louisville, Kentucky.

Lewis, Donald M., D.Phil., Oxford University. Associate Professor of Church History, Regent College, Vancouver, British Columbia.

Linder, Robert D., Ph.D., University of Iowa. Professor of History, Kansas State University, Manhattan, Kansas.

Lippy, Charles H., Ph.D., Princeton University. Professor of Religion, Clemson University, Clemson, South Carolina.

Logan, Samuel T., Jr., Ph.D., Emory University. Academic Dean and Professor of Church History, Westminster Theological Seminary, Philadelphia, Pennsylvania.

Longfield, Bradley J., Ph.D., Duke University. Instructor in American Christianity, Duke Divinity School, Durham, North Carolina.

Loux, Gordon D., M.Div., Northern Baptist Theological Seminary; L.H.D., Sioux Falls College. President, International Students, Inc., Colorado Springs, Colorado.

Lundeen, Joel W., L.H.D., Bethany College, Lindsborg, Kansas. Retired, Associate Archivist, Lutheran Church in America.

Lundquist, Carl H., Th.D., Northern Baptist Theological Seminary. President, Christian College Consortium, St. Paul, Minnesota.

Lynch, John E., Ph.D., University of Toronto. Professor of the History of Canon Law and of Medieval History, The Catholic University of America, Washington, D.C.

Maas, David E., Ph.D., University of Wisconsin, Madison. Professor of History, Wheaton College, Wheaton, Illinois.

McBeth, Harry L., Th.D., Southwestern Baptist Theological Seminary. Professor of Church History, Southwestern Baptist Theological Seminary, Fort Worth, Texas.

McGreal, Mary N., O.P., Ph.D., Catholic University of America. Director of Research, Dominican History Project: OPUS, Chicago, Illinois.

MacHaffie, Barbara J., Ph.D., University of Edinburgh, Scotland. Assistant Professor of History and Religion, Marietta College, Marietta, Ohio.

McIntire, C. T., Ph.D., University of Pennsylvania. Professor of History, Trinity College, University of Toronto, Toronto, Canada.

McKenzie, Brian A., Ph.D., University of St. Michael's College—Toronto School of Theology. Pastor, Nobles Memorial Baptist Church, Windsor, Ontario.

McKim, Donald K., Ph.D., University of Pittsburgh. Interim Pastor, Trinity Presbyterian Church, Berwyn, Pennsylvania.

McKinley, Edward H., Ph.D., University of Wisconsin, Madison. Professor of History, Chairperson, Division of Social Sciences, Asbury College, Wilmore, Kentucky.

Macleod, Donald, Ph.D., University of Toronto. Francis L. Patton Professor of Preaching and Worship, Princeton Theological Seminary, Princeton, New Jersey.

McNally, Michael J., Ph.D., University of Notre Dame. Professor of Church History, St. Vincent de Paul Regional Seminary, Boynton Beach, Florida.

McNamara, Robert F., M.A., Harvard University. S.T.L., Gregorian University, Rome. Professor Emeritus of Church History, St. Bernard's Seminary. Archivist, Roman Catholic Diocese of Rochester, Rochester, New York.

McNeal, Patricia, Ph.D., Temple University. Associate Professor, History, Indiana University, South Bend, Indiana.

McShane, Joseph M., S.J., Ph.D., University of Chicago. Associate Professor of Religious Studies, LeMoyne College, Syracuse, New York.

Maffly-Kipp, Laurie F., M.Phil., Yale University. Assistant Professor of American Religious History, University of North Carolina, Chapel Hill, North Carolina.

Magnuson, Norris A., Ph.D., University of Minnesota. Professor of Church History and Resource Center Director, Bethel Theological Seminary, St. Paul, Minnesota.

Marsden, George M., Ph.D., Yale. Professor of the History of Christianity in America, The Divinity School, Duke University, Durham, North Carolina.

Marty, Martin E., Ph.D., University of Chicago. Fairfax M. Cone Distinguished Service Professor of the History of Modern Christianity, University of Chicago, Chicago, Illinois.

Massa, Mark S., S.J., Th.D., Harvard University. Assistant Professor, Theology Department, Fordham University, Bronx, New York.

Mathisen, Robert R., D.A., Illinois State University. Professor of History and Political Science, Grace College, Winona Lake, Indiana.

Means, James E., Ph.D., University of Denver. Associate Professor of Pastoral Ministries and Homiletics, Denver Seminary, Denver, Colorado.

Meier, Samuel A., Ph.D., Harvard University. Assistant Professor of Hebrew, The Ohio State University, Columbus, Ohio.

Mennell, James E., Ph.D., University of Iowa. Associate Professor of History, Slippery Rock University, Slippery Rock, Pennsylvania.

Meno, Chorepiscopus John P., M.A., American University of Beirut, M.S.T. Union Theological Seminary, New York, New York. General Secretary of the Archdiocese of the Syrian Orthodox Church in the United States and Canada. Dean of St. Mark's Syrian Orthodox Cathedral, Hackensack, New Jersey.

Menzies, William W., Ph.D., University of Iowa—Iowa City. President, Far East Advanced School of Theology, Baguio City, Philippines.

Mercadante, Linda A., Ph.D., Princeton Theological Seminary. Assistant Professor of Theology, Methodist Theological School, Delaware, Ohio.

Michell, David J., D.Miss., Trinity Evangelical Divinity School. Director of Overseas Missionary Fellowship, Toronto, Ontario.

Mickey, Paul A., Ph.D., Princeton Theological Seminary. Associate Professor of Pastoral Theology at Duke University Divinity School, Durham, North Carolina.

Miethe, Terry L., Ph.D., St. Louis University. Ph.D., University of Southern California. Dean and Professor of Philosophy and Theology for the Oxford Study Centre, Oxford,

England, and Lynchburg, Virginia.

Miller, Randall M., Ph.D., Ohio State University. Professor of History and Director of American Studies, St. Joseph's University, Philadelphia, Pennsylvania.

Miller, Robert M., Ph.D., Northwestern University. Professor of History, University of North Carolina, Chapel Hill, North Carolina.

Minkema, Kenneth P., Ph.D., University of Connecticut. Executive Editor, *Works of Jonathan Edwards,* Yale University.

Miranda, Jesse, D.Min., Fuller Theological Seminary. Superintendent of the Pacific Latin American District Council of the Assemblies of God, La Puente, California.

Moberg, David O., Ph.D., University of Minnesota. Professor of Sociology, Marquette University, Milwaukee, Wisconsin.

Monti, Dominic V., O.F.M., Ph.D., University of Chicago. Assistant Professor, Church History, Washington Theological Union, Silver Spring, Maryland.

Moody, Barry M., Ph.D., Queen's University, Kingston, Ontario. Associate Professor of History, Acadia University, Wolfville, Nova Scotia.

Moran, Bob, C.S.P., Ph.D., University of California at Santa Barbara. Director, McGill Newman Center, McGill University, Montreal, Quebec.

Moran, Gerald F., Ph.D., Rutgers University. Professor of History, University of Michigan—Dearborn, Dearborn, Michigan.

Mott, Stephen C., Ph.D., Harvard University. Professor of Christian Social Ethics, Gordon-Conwell Theological Seminary, South Hamilton, Massachusetts.

Mouw, Richard J., Ph.D., University of Chicago. Professor of Christian Philosophy and Ethics, Fuller Theological Seminary, Pasadena, California.

Mullin, Robert B., Ph.D., Yale University. Assistant Professor of Religion, North Carolina State University, Raleigh, North Carolina.

Nelson, F. Burton, Ph.D., Northwestern University—Garrett Evangelical Theological Seminary. Professor of Theology and Ethics, North Park Theological Seminary, Chicago, Illinois.

Nemer, Lawrence J., Ph.D., Cambridge University. Professor of Church History and Director of the World Mission Program, Catholic Theological Union, Chicago, Illinois.

Newell, Mark Bishop, Ph.D. candidate, University of Notre Dame. Assistant Professor of History and Bible, Northeastern Bible College, Essex Falls, New Jersey.

Noll, Mark A., Ph.D., Vanderbilt University. Professor of History, Wheaton College, Wheaton, Illinois.

Nord, David P., Ph.D., University of Wisconsin—Madison. Associate Professor of Journalism and American Studies, Indiana University, Bloomington, Indiana.

Nordbeck, Elizabeth C., Ph.D., Harvard University. Professor of American Church History, Lancaster Theological Seminary, Lancaster, Pennsylvania.

North, James B., Ph.D., University of Illinois—Urbana. Professor of Church History and Chairman of the Department of General Studies, Cincinnati Bible College and Seminary, Cincinnati, Ohio.

Numbers, Ronald L., Ph.D., University of California—Berkeley. Professor of the History of Medicine and the History of Science, University of Wisconsin, Madison, Wisconsin.

Olbricht, Thomas H., Ph.D., University of Iowa; S.T.B., Harvard Divinity School. Chair, Religion Division, Pepperdine University, Malibu, California.

Oliver, John W., M.A., University of Pittsburgh. Associate Professor of History, Malone College, Canton, Ohio.

O'Malley, John S., Ph.D., Drew University. Professor of Church History and Historical Theology, Asbury Theological Seminary, Wilmore, Kentucky.

Ostwalt, Conrad E., Jr., Ph.D., Duke University. Assistant Professor, Appalachian State University, Boone, North Carolina.

Patterson, James A., Ph.D., Princeton Theological Seminary. Associate Professor of Church History, Mid-America Baptist Theological Seminary, Memphis, Tennessee.

Patterson, W. Morgan, Th.D., New Orleans Baptist Theological Seminary. President and Professor of Religion, Georgetown College, Georgetown, Kentucky.

Payne, Rodger M., Ph.D., University of Virginia. Instructor in Religious Studies, University of Virginia, Charlottesville, Virginia.

Peake, Thomas R., Ph.D., University of North Carolina—Chapel Hill. Professor of History, Chairman of Social Science Division, King College, Bristol, Tennessee.

Perko, Francis Michael, S.J., Ph.D., Stanford University. Associate Professor of Education and History, Loyola University of Chicago.

Petersen, Rodney L., Ph.D., Princeton Theological Seminary. Adjunct Professor, Departments of Human Resource Development, Management, and International Affairs, Webster University, Geneva, Switzerland.

Pierard, Richard V., Ph.D., University of Iowa. Professor of History, Indiana State University, Terre Haute, Indiana.

Pierson, Paul E., Ph.D., Princeton Theological Seminary. Dean, Professor of History of Mission and Latin American Studies. School of World Missions, Fuller Theological Seminary, Pasadena, California.

Pitts, Bill L., Ph.D., Vanderbilt University. Professor of Religion, Baylor University, Waco, Texas.

Pitzer, Donald E., Ph.D., Ohio State University. Professor of History and Director of Center for Communal Studies, University of Southern Indiana, Evansville, Indiana.

Pointer, Richard W., Ph.D., The Johns Hopkins University. Associate Professor of History, Trinity College, Deerfield, Illinois.

Pointer, Steven R., Ph.D., Duke University. Associate Professor of History, Trinity College, Deerfield, Illinois.

Portier, William L., Ph.D., University of St. Michael's College. Associate Professor of Theology, Mount Saint Mary's College, Emmitsburg, Maryland.

Prichard, Robert W., Ph.D., Emory University. Associate Professor of Church History, Protestant Episcopal Theological Seminary, Alexandria, Virginia.

Raser, Harold E., Ph.D., Pennsylvania State University. Associate Professor of the History of Christianity, Nazarene Theological Seminary, Kansas City, Missouri.

Reed, Gerard A., Ph.D., University of Oklahoma. Professor of History, Philosophy, and Religion, Point Loma Nazarene College, San Diego, California.

Reher, Margaret M., Ph.D., Fordham University. Professor, Chair,

Department of Religion, Cabrini College, Radnor, Pennsylvania.

Reid, Daniel G., Ph.D., Fuller Theological Seminary. Reference Book Editor, InterVarsity Press, Downers Grove, Illinois.

Rennie, Ian S., Ph.D., University of Toronto. Vice President and Academic Dean, Ontario Theological Seminary, Willowdale, Ontario.

Riforgiato, Leonard R., Ph.D., Pennsylvania State University. Associate Professor of History, Pennsylvania State University, Shenango Campus, Sharon, Pennsylvania.

Ringenberg, William C., Ph.D., Michigan State. Professor and Chair of the Department of History and Director of the Honors Program, Taylor University, Upland, Indiana.

Rippinger, Joel A., O.S.B., S.T.L., Pontifical Academy of Saint Anselm, Rome. Professor, Marion Abbey/Academy, Aurora, Illinois.

Roark, Dallas M., Ph.D., University of Iowa. Professor of Philosophy, Chairman, Division of Social Sciences, Emporia State University, Emporia, Kansas.

Robert, Dana L., Ph.D., Yale University. Assistant Professor of International Mission, Boston University School of Theology, Boston, Massachusetts.

Robins, Roger G., M.Div., Harvard Divinity School. Ph.D. student, Duke University Divinity School, Durham, North Carolina.

Robinson, David M., Ph.D., University of Wisconsin—Madison. Professor of English and Director of American Studies, Oregon State University, Corvallis, Oregon.

Rommen, Edward, D.Theol., University of Munich, West Germany. Associate Professor of Mission, Trinity Evangelical Divinity School, Deerfield, Illinois.

Ronan, Charles E., S.J., Ph.D., University of Texas—Austin. Professor Emeritus, History Department, Loyola University, Chicago, Illinois.

Rose, Anne C., Ph.D., Yale University. State College, Pennsylvania.

Rosell, Garth M., Ph.D., University of Minnesota. Professor of Church History and Director of the Ockenga Institute, Gordon-Conwell Theological Seminary, South Hamilton, Massachusetts.

Rudnick, Milton L., Th.D., Concordia Seminary—St. Louis. President, Concordia Lutheran Seminary, Edmonton, Alberta.

Ruegsegger, Ronald E., Ph.D., University of Toronto. Head, Department of Philosophy, Nyack College, Nyack, New York.

Russell, C. Allyn, Ph.D., Boston University. Professor Emeritus of Religion, Boston University, College of Liberal Arts, Concord, Massachusetts.

Ryan, John B., S.T.D., Institut Catholique, Paris, France. Professor, Manhattan College, Bronx, New York.

Sable, Thomas F., Ph.D., Graduate Theological Union. Assistant Professor of Theology/Religious Studies, University of Scranton, Scranton, Pennsylvania.

Salvaterra, David L., Ph.D., University of Notre Dame. Associate Professor and Chairman, History Department, Loras College, Dubuque, Iowa.

Sawyer, Kenneth S., Ph.D. candidate, University of Chicago Divinity School. Adjunct Instructor in Church History, McCormick Theological Seminary, Chicago, Illinois.

Sawyer, Mary R., Ph.D., Duke University. Assistant Professor of Religious Studies, Iowa State University, Ames, Iowa.

Scalberg, Daniel A., Ph.D., University of Oregon. Professor of History, Multnomah School of the Bible, Portland, Oregon.

Schaaf, James L., D.Theol., Ruprecht-Karl Universität—Heidelberg. Professor of Church History, Trinity Lutheran Seminary, Columbus, Ohio.

Schlereth, Thomas J., Ph.D., University of Iowa. Director of Graduate Studies in American Studies, University of Notre Dame, Notre Dame, Indiana.

Schneider, Lenore, Ph.D., Carnegie-Mellon University. Teacher, New Canaan High School, New Canaan, Connecticut. Visiting Professor, King's College, Briarcliffe Manor, New York.

Schneider, Mary L., Ph.D., Marquette University. Professor, Department of Religious Studies, Michigan State University, East Lansing, Michigan.

Schoepflin, Rennie B., M.A., University of Wisconsin—Madison. Assistant Professor of History, Loma Linda University, Riverside, California.

Schrag, Martin H., Ph.D., Temple University. Professor Emeritus of History of Christianity, Messiah College, Grantham, Pennsylvania.

Schreck, Alan E., Ph.D., University of St. Michael's College—Toronto. Professor of Theology and Chairman, Department of Theology/Philosophy, Franciscan University of Steubenville, Steubenville, Ohio.

Schultze, Quentin J., Ph.D., University of Illinois. Professor of Communication Arts and Sciences, Calvin College, Grand Rapids, Michigan.

Scott, Stephen E., Writer-Researcher, People's Place, Columbia, Pennsylvania.

Seamands, John T., Th.D., Serampore University, India. Professor Emeritus, Asbury Theological Seminary, Wilmore, Kentucky.

Seamands, Stephen A., Ph.D., Drew University. Professor of Christian Doctrine, Asbury Theological Seminary, Wilmore, Kentucky.

Selleck, Ronald E., Ph.D., University of Chicago. Pastor, West Richmond Friends Meeting, Richmond, Indiana.

Seymour, Jack L., Ph.D., Peabody College of Vanderbilt University. Professor of Religious Education, Garrett-Evangelical Theological Seminary, Evanston, Illinois.

Shanaberger, Manuel S., M.A., University of Virginia. Pastor of Purcellville Baptist Church, Purcellville, Virginia.

Shelley, Bruce L., Ph.D., University of Iowa. Professor of Church History, Denver Seminary, Denver, Colorado.

Shelly, Harold P., Ph.D., Temple University. Professor of Church History, Alliance Theological Seminary, South Nyack, New York.

Shenk, Wilbert R., Ph.D., University of Aberdeen. Vice President for Overseas Ministries, Mennonite Board of Missions.

Showalter, Nathan D., Th.D. candidate, Harvard Divinity School. Director, Partnership Services, World Vision International, Monrovia, California.

Sider, E. Morris, Ph.D., State University of New York—Buffalo. Professor of History and English Literature; Archivist for the Brethren in Christ Church, Messiah College, Grantham, Pennsylvania.

Silk, Mark, Ph.D., Harvard University. Member, Editorial Board, Atlanta Constitution, Decatur, Georgia.

Silva, William A., Ph.D., Yale University. Assistant Professor of American Studies, Trinity College, Hartford, Connecticut.

Sittser, Gerald L., Ph.D., University of Chicago. Assistant Professor of Religion, Whitworth College, Spokane, Washington.

Smith, Gary S., Ph.D., Johns Hopkins University. Associate Professor of Sociology, Grove City College, Grove City, Pennsylvania.

Smylie, James H., Ph.D., Princeton Theological Seminary. E. T. Thompson Professor of Church History, Union Theological Seminary, Richmond, Virginia.

Sobolewski, Gregory L., Ph.D., Marquette University. Assistant Professor of Religious Studies, College of St. Francis, Joliet, Illinois.

Spivey, James T., Jr., D.Phil., The University of Oxford, England. Assistant Professor of Church History, Southwestern Baptist Theological Seminary, Fort Worth, Texas.

Sprunger, Keith L., Ph.D., University of Illinois. Professor of History, Bethel College, North Newton, Kansas.

Stackhouse, John G., Jr., Ph.D., University of Chicago. Assistant Professor of History, Northwestern College, Orange City, Iowa.

Staggers, Kermit L., Ph.D., Claremont Graduate School. Associate Professor of History and Political Science, Sioux Falls College, Sioux Falls, South Dakota.

Stamoolis, James J., Th.D., University of Stellenbosch. Dean of the Graduate School, Wheaton College, Wheaton, Illinois.

Stanislaw, Richard J., Ph.D., University of Illinois. Vice President for Academic Affairs, Taylor University, Upland, Indiana.

Stanley, John E., Ph.D., Iliff School of Theology—University of Denver. Associate Professor of Religion, Warner Pacific College, Portland, Oregon.

Stanley, Susie C., Ph.D., Iliff School of Theology—University of Denver. Professor of Church History and Women's Studies, Western Evangelical Seminary, Portland, Oregon.

Steeves, Paul D., Ph.D., University of Kansas. Professor of History, Stetson University, DeLand, Florida.

Stockwell, Clinton E., Th.D., New Orleans Baptist Theological Seminary; D.Min., Chicago Theological Seminary. Director, Chicago Center for Public Ministry, Chicago, Illinois.

Stoeffler, F. E., S.T.D., Temple University. Professor of Religion, Emeritus, Temple University, Philadelphia, Pennsylvania.

Stout, Harry S., Ph.D., Kent State University. Professor of American Religious History, Yale University, New Haven, Connecticut.

Stowe, David M., Th.D., Pacific School of Religion. Executive Vice President Emeritus, United Church Board for World Ministries, New York, New York.

Strege, Merle D., Th.D., Graduate Theological Union. Associate Professor of Historical Theology, School of Theology, Anderson University, Anderson, Indiana.

Strong, Douglas M., Ph.D., Princeton Theological Seminary. Assistant Professor of the History of Modern Christianity, Wesley Theological Seminary, Washington, D.C.

Stylianopoulos, Theodore G., Th.D., Harvard Divinity School. Professor of New Testament, Holy Cross Greek Orthodox School of Theology, Brookline, Massachusetts.

Sullivan, Larry B., M.A., Fort Hays State University; Ph.D. student, Kansas State University. Associate Professor of History, Manhattan Christian College, Manhattan, Kansas.

Sunquist, Scott, Ph.D., Princeton Theological Seminary. Lecturer in Church History, Trinity Theological College, Singapore.

Sutherland, John D., M.A., University of California—Irvine. Senior Pastor, St. Andrew Lutheran Church, Whittier, California.

Swierenga, Robert P., Ph.D., University of Iowa. Professor of History, Kent State University, Kent, Ohio.

Talley, Thomas J., Th.D., The General Theological Seminary. Professor of Liturgics, The General Theological Seminary, New York, New York.

Taylor, Thomas T., Ph.D., University of Illinois—Urbana-Champaign. Assistant Professor of History, Department of History, Wittenberg University, Springfield, Ohio.

Teague, Fred A., Ed.D., University of Oklahoma. Dean of Graduate Studies, Southwest Baptist University, Bolivar, Missouri.

Thielman, Samuel B., M.D., Ph.D., Duke University. Assistant Professor, Head, Geriatric Psychiatry Section, Medical College of Georgia, Augusta, Georgia.

Thigpen, Thomas P., B.A., Yale University; Ph.D. candidate, Emory University. Editorial Director for Magazines, Strang Communications Company, Altamonte Springs,

Florida.

Tinder, Donald G., Ph.D., Yale University. Christian Missions in Many Lands, Belgium.

Tipson, L. Baird, Jr., Ph.D., Yale University. Professor of Religion and Provost, Gettysburg College, Gettysburg, Pennsylvania.

Touchstone, D. Blake, Ph.D., Tulane University. Instructor, History Department, Tulane University, New Orleans, Louisiana.

Toulouse, Mark G., Ph.D., University of Chicago Divinity School. Associate Professor of Church History, Brite Divinity School, Texas Christian University, Fort Worth, Texas.

Towns, Elmer L., D.Min., Fuller Theological Seminary. Dean, School of Religion and Vice President, Liberty University, Lynchburg, Virginia.

Travis, William G., Ph.D., New York University. Professor of Church History, Bethel Theological Seminary, St. Paul, Minnesota.

Trollinger, William V., Jr., Ph.D., University of Wisconsin—Madison. Assistant Professor of History, The School of the Ozarks, Point Lookout, Missouri.

Troutman, Richard L., Ph.D., University of Kentucky. Head, Department of History, Western Kentucky University, Bowling Green, Kentucky.

Tucker, Ruth A., Ph.D., Northern Illinois University. Visiting Professor, Trinity Evangelical Divinity School, Deerfield, Illinois.

Turley, Briane K., M.A.; Ph.D. candidate, University of Virginia.

Turner, William C., Jr., Ph.D., Duke University. Assistant Professor of Theology and Director of Black Church Affairs, Duke University, Durham, North Carolina.

Tuttle, Robert G., Jr., Ph.D., University of Bristol, England. E. Stanley Jones Professor of Evangelism, Garrett-Evangelical Theological Seminary, Evanston, Illinois.

Tyson, John R., Ph.D., The Graduate School, Drew University. Associate Professor, Theology, Houghton College, Houghton, New York.

Van Allen, Rodger, Ph.D., Temple University. Professor of Religious Studies, Villanova University, Villanova, Pennsylvania.

Van Ness, Daniel W., J.D., DePaul University College of Law. President, Justice Fellowship, Washington, D.C.

Van Til, L. John, Ph.D., Michigan State

University—East Lansing. Professor of History, Geneva College, Grove City, Pennsylvania.

Vande Kemp, Hendrika, Ph.D., University of Massachusetts—Amherst. Associate Professor of Psychology, Fuller Theological Seminary, Pasadena, California.

Vaudry, Richard W., Ph.D., McGill University. Assistant Professor of History, Camrose Lutheran College, Camrose, Alberta.

Vos, Howard F., Ph.D., Northwestern University; Th.D., Dallas Theological Seminary. Professor of History and Archaeology, The King's College, Briarcliff Manor, New York.

Wacker, Grant, Ph.D., Harvard University. Associate Professor of Religious Studies, University of North Carolina, Chapel Hill, North Carolina.

Waddell, Chrysogonus, O.C.S.O., Abbey of Gethsemani, Trappist, Kentucky.

Wade, William J., Ph.D., University of North Carolina. Professor of History, Director of Institutional Research, King College, Bristol, Tennessee.

Wainwright, Geoffrey, D.D., University of Cambridge; D.Theol., University of Geneva. Professor of Systematic Theology, Duke University, Durham, North Carolina.

Wakelyn, Jon L., Ph.D., Rice University. Professor and Chairman, Department of History, The Catholic University of America, Washington, D.C.

Walsh, Brian J., Ph.D., McGill University. Senior Member in Worldview Studies, Institute for Christian Studies, Toronto, Canada.

Wangler, Thomas E., Ph.D., Marquette University. Associate Professor, Department of Theology, Boston College, Chestnut Hill, Massachusetts.

Warner, Wayne E., Dipl., Eugene Bible College. Director, Assemblies of God Archives, Springfield, Missouri.

Warnock, James H., Ph.D., University of Washington. Instructor in History, Eastern Oregon State College, La Grande, Oregon.

Weaver, C. Douglas, Ph.D., Southern Baptist Theological Seminary. Assistant Professor of Christianity, Brewton-Parker College, Mount Vernon, Georgia.

Weaver, J. Denny, Ph.D., Duke University. Professor of Religion, Bluffton College, Bluffton, Ohio.

Webber, Robert E., Th.D., Concordia Theological Seminary. Professor of Historical Theology, Wheaton College, Wheaton, Illinois.

Weber, Timothy P., Ph.D., University of Chicago. Professor of Church History, Denver Seminary, Denver, Colorado.

Weeks, Louis B., Ph.D., Duke University. Paul T. Jones Professor of Church History, and Dean of the Seminary, Louisville Presbyterian Seminary, Louisville, Kentucky.

Weir, David A., Ph.D., University of St. Andrews. Assistant Professor of History, Centenary College, Hackettstown, New Jersey.

Wenger, J. C., D.Theol., Universität Zürich, Zürich, Switzerland. Professor Emeritus of Historical Theology, Goshen Biblical Seminary, Elkhart, Indiana.

Wenig, Scott A., Ph.D. candidate, University of Colorado. Adjunct Faculty, Denver Seminary, Denver, Colorado.

Wentz, Frederick K., Ph.D., Yale University. Visiting Instructor, Lutheran Theological Seminary, Gettysburg, Pennsylvania.

Westermeyer, Paul, Ph.D., University of Chicago. Professor of Music, Elmhurst College, Elmhurst, Illinois.

White, Charles E., Ph.D., Boston University. Associate Professor of Christian Thought and History, Spring Arbor College, Spring Arbor, Michigan.

White, James F., Ph.D., Duke University. Professor of Liturgy, University of Notre Dame, Notre Dame, Indiana.

White, Joseph M., Ph.D., University of Notre Dame. Freelance Writer, Indianapolis, Indiana.

White, Susan J., Ph.D., University of Notre Dame. Visiting Assistant Professor of Liturgics, School of Theology, University of the South, Sewanee, Tennessee.

Whiteman, Curtis W., Ph.D., St. Louis University. Associate Professor of Historical Theology, Westmont College, Santa Barbara, California.

Whitlock, David B., Ph.D., The Southern Baptist Theological Seminary. Pastor, Livingston First Baptist Church, Livingston, Alabama.

Whitney, Evans J., Ph.D., University of Minnesota. Associate Professor, History and Religious Studies, College of Saint Scholastica, Duluth, Minnesota.

Wiers, John R., M.Div., Trinity Evangelical Divinity School. Ph.D.

candidate, University of Iowa, Iowa City, Iowa.

Williams, David R., Ph.D., Brown University. Visiting Assistant Professor of English and American Studies, George Mason University, Fairfax, Virginia.

Williams, Peter W., Ph.D., Yale University. Professor of Religion, Miami University, Oxford, Ohio.

Wills, David W., Ph.D., Harvard University. Professor of Religion, Amherst College, Amherst, Massachusetts.

Wilshire, Leland E., Ph.D., University of Southern California. Professor of History, Biola University, La Mirada, California.

Wilson, J. Christy, Jr., Ph.D., The University of Edinburgh, Scotland. Professor of World Evangelization, Gordon-Conwell Theological Seminary, South Hamilton, Massachusetts.

Wilson, Everett A., Ph.D., Stanford University. Academic Dean, Professor of History, Bethany Bible College, Scotts Valley, California.

Wilson, John R. M., Ph.D., Northwestern University. Professor of History, Southern California College, Costa Mesa, California.

Wilson, Marvin R., Ph.D., Brandeis University. Ockenga Professor of Biblical and Theological Studies, Gordon College, Wenham, Massachusetts.

Wilson, Robert S., Ph.D., University of Guelph. Academic Dean and Professor of History, Atlantic Baptist College, New Brunswick, Canada.

Wilt, Paul C., Ph.D., American University. Professor of History, Westmont College, Santa Barbara, California.

Wimmer, John R., M.Div., Duke Divinity School. Ph.D. candidate, The Divinity School, University of Chicago.

Wood, James E., Jr., Ph.D., Southern Baptist Theological Seminary. Director, J. M. Dawson Institute of Church-State Studies; Simon and Ethel Bunn Professor of Church-State Studies, Baylor University, Waco, Texas.

Woodbridge, John D., Doctorat de Troisiéme Cycle. Université de Toulouse, Toulouse, France. Professor of Church History, Trinity Evangelical Divinity School, Deerfield, Illinois. Visiting Professor of History, Northwestern University, Chicago, Illinois.

Wright, Conrad E., Ph.D., Brown University. Editor of Publications,

Massachusetts Historical Society, Boston, Massachusetts.

Wright, J., Robert, D.Phil., Oxford University. St. Mark's Professor of Ecclesiastical History, General Theological Seminary, New York, New York.

Yocum Mize, Sandra A., Ph.D., Marquette University. Assistant Professor, Saint Mary's College, Notre Dame, Indiana.

Yoo, David K., M.Div., Princeton Seminary. Ph.D. student, Yale University, New Haven, Connecticut.

Zeman, Jarold K., D.Theol., University of Zurich. Professor of Church History, Acadia Divinity College, Acadia University, Wolfville, Nova Scotia.

Zwier, Robert, Ph.D., University of Wisconsin—Madison. Vice President for Academic Affairs, Northwestern College, Orange City, Iowa.

Introduction

Division and Unity:
The Paradox of Christianity in America

W*e are a religious people whose institutions presuppose a Supreme Being." So wrote liberal* U.S. Supreme Court Justice William O. Douglas for the majority of the Court in the 1952 "released time" religious education case of *Zorach* v. *Clauson*. So Americans have been, and so they continue to be. In the 1980s more than ninety per cent of all Americans still identified with some religious faith, and on any given Sunday morning more than forty per cent could be found in a place of worship.* By most measurable indices the U.S. is a more religious nation than any European country, except perhaps for Ireland and Poland.

Religion, especially the Christian religion, played an important part in motivating colonists to come to the New World, and religion was a major factor in the movement which led to the American Revolution* and the formation of the United States of America. Religion was so important to the nation's founders that they specifically guaranteed its "free expression" in the First Amendment* to the Constitution in 1791. Moreover, throughout American history Christian teachings have undergirded the national search for order, freedom and social justice. On the one hand, in its support of the orderly growth of civilized society and its ability to provide the nation with a foundational consensus of evangelical* values, the Christian faith has fostered societal unity. On the other hand, its advocacy of freedom and social justice has often led to widespread unrest, agitation for political and social reform and societal division. This paradoxical impact of Christianity on the course of American history in terms of division and unity has remained to the present day.

This essay undertakes in brief compass to highlight the developmental motifs of religious faith in America from the entrance of sixteenth-century Europeans into what is now the U.S. to the religious ferment which characterizes American life in the late twentieth century. It is a story of spiritual vitality and decay, revival and reform, divisive controversy and interdenominational cooperation, the search for a place simply to be left alone, the rise and fall of utopian dreams, as well as the influences of the Christian faith and American culture on each other.

Christian Beginnings, 1492-1700.† Christianity was transplanted in North America during one of the most tumultuous periods of Christian history, as new expressions of the faith took shape in what

---

†The dates of the subdivisions in this essay are based on the historical judgment of the author and sometimes overlap. They are usually, but not always, set off by the date of a significant historical event and are meant to provide general guidelines for the periodization of American religious history.

were to become Lutheran,* Reformed,* Anglican* and Anabaptist* forms. This historical context—the time of the Renaissance and Reformation—would determine not only the original configuration of Christianity in America but also the continuing religious ethos of the U.S. to the present day.

Shortly after the discovery of the New World by Christopher Columbus,* the rulers of Spain appealed to Pope Alexander VI to settle the dispute between Spain and Portugal over their claims to the new lands. In the protocols of 1493 and 1494, Spain was granted control of an area that was still only vaguely comprehended. From Cuba and then Mexico, the Spanish began a program of conquest and settlement which included North America. The government's drive to develop the Spanish Empire and the Church's desire to convert and Christianize the native populations often came into conflict. While the Church won a number of smaller victories in its attempts to ensure humane treatment of the native peoples, in the end the government usually dominated the situation.

Interestingly enough, however, the first Christian "thanksgiving day" on what is now U.S. soil was celebrated by French Huguenots.* Admiral Gaspard de Coligny, one of the prominent leaders of the French Protestants, dreamed of an American haven for his persecuted co-religionists. Thus, in 1564 a contingent of French Calvinists* under his sponsorship settled a Florida site near the mouth of the St. Johns River and named it Ft. Caroline. Saved by Coligny's re-enforcements from what seemed like certain failure, the Huguenot settlers held the first thanksgiving festival on the continent on June 30 of that year.

It was in response to this perceived threat to their claimed but not yet settled Florida territory that the Spanish acted. They established the oldest permanent European settlement in North America at St. Augustine on August 28, 1565, and from there attacked and massacred the fledgling Protestant* colony. It was also from St. Augustine that Spanish priests* established missions* that at one point reached as far north as the Carolinas and briefly into the Chesapeake Bay area. Despite numerous ups and downs, the missions in Florida were generally successful through several generations. Other important early Spanish Catholic missionary activity in this period took place in the U.S. Southwest, from today's Texas to California.

While Spanish missionaries worked to spread the faith in Florida and the Southwest, the French moved from their original settlements in the St. Lawrence River Valley of Canada to claim territory along the Atlantic coast, in the Great Lakes region, down the Mississippi Valley and along the Gulf Coast west of Florida. In the early seventeenth century, the efforts of French Catholic missionaries* to reach the Native Americans were spearheaded by the Jesuits* operating out of Quebec and Sulpicians* based in Montreal. French missionaries also were active in the same period in what is now Maine and along the strategic Champlain-Lake George-Hudson-Mohawk waterways. These Spanish and French missionaries were noted for their zeal and heroism, but not for the numbers of their converts.

The first permanent English settlment in what would become the U.S. was at Jamestown in 1607. Like most European colonists in the sixteenth and seventeenth centuries, the English at Jamestown were motivated by "God, gold and glory," although probably not in that order. Nevertheless, there was a strong sense of religious purpose in the Jamestown settlement from the beginning. One of the first acts of the newly landed English settlers at Jamestown in May, 1607, was to join the Anglican* divine* Rev. Robert Hunt in a Eucharist* of thanksgiving and praise. Shortly before their departure for the New World on April 25, 1609, the Rev. William Symonds, minister of St. Savior's Church, Southwark, had preached to Jamestown-bound re-enforcements from Genesis 12:1-3, saying that as did Abraham of old, they were to go to a new land that the Lord had shown them and become a great nation, blessed of God.

From the beginning, the Church of England was established by law as the official religion of the Virginia colony. When the English Civil War broke out in 1642, Virginia sided with the Royalist-High Church* cause against the Parliamentarian-Puritan* side. However, this did not mean that the Virginia Anglicans lacked a Puritan element nor that they were entirely in sympathy with the episcopal* establishment of the Church of England. Their worship was biblically oriented and their concerns were spiritual as well as political.

The settlements which followed in New England would be different. Both the Pilgrim* Separatists who landed at Plymouth in 1620 and the Congregational* Puritans who settled Massachusetts Bay Colony in 1630, arrived in America alienated from their Anglican roots. The Pilgrims were radical Protestants who had completely given up any hope of purifying the Church of England and reforming it according to their strict biblical norms. The Massachusetts Puritans represented the left wing of their movement, that segment which had growing doubts similar to the Separatists but would not break off fellowship with the Mother Church.

Both Separatists and Puritans came to America espousing Calvinist theology* and a congregationalist church government,* the latter considered unusually radical for its time. They also both came with a profound conviction that they were fulfilling the will of God and playing a part in his cosmic plan. This was illustrated by the Pilgrims' Mayflower Compact,* which acknowledged God as the basis of all civil and religious authority, and by the Puritans' dream of establishing a new kind of state in the American wilderness, a veritable "city upon a hill" which would be a model Christian community and a light to the nations.

In 1662 two other Puritan colonies, New Haven and Connecticut, merged, followed by Plymouth and Massachusetts Bay in 1691. With the principal exception of Rhode Island, which was founded by Roger Williams* in 1636, most of New England in the seventeenth century remained under Puritan domination. Exiled from the Bay Colony because of his controversial views on church and state and advocacy of religious liberty,* Williams first established Providence and then helped obtain a royal charter for the Rhode Island and Providence Plantations in 1663. Because from the beginning it allowed complete religious liberty to all, Rhode Island soon became a stronghold of Baptists,* Quakers* and other religious nonconformists who joined Williams in promoting this concept. By embracing religious freedom and by encouraging nonconformity and individualism,* Rhode Island in a real sense adumbrated the future American nation.

As Anglicanism took root in Virginia and Congregational Puritanism spread over New England, other colonies were being formed with different denominational bases. The Dutch founded the colony of New Netherlands in 1624 and two years later established New Amsterdam on Manhattan Island. Although officially tolerant of most religious groups in the homeland, the Dutch both at home and abroad maintained an established Reformed* Church and, in America at least, attempted to discourage competing worship centers. One significant exception were the Jews, whom the Dutch welcomed as refugees in 1654 from former Dutch colonies in Brazil and who organized the first Jewish congregation in America soon thereafter. Otherwise, the officially sanctioned Reformed Church spread quickly over Long Island and up the Hudson River Valley, and included the foundation of the Marble Collegiate Church in New Amsterdam in 1628, the oldest continuously existing Protestant church in North America. In 1664 the English captured New Netherlands, changed the name to New York, built an Anglican church and adopted a policy of toleration concerning non-Anglican groups in the colony. However, a generation later the government imposed an Anglican establishment on New York, while allowing the Dutch and others to continue their distinctive worship.

The Swedes founded Ft. Christiana in present-day Delaware in 1638, and the following year a Lutheran* minister,* the Rev. Reorus Torkillus, arrived to establish a Lutheran church. Lutheranism flourished among the Swedish and Finnish settlers in the area until 1655, when the Dutch took over the colony. They permitted one Lutheran pastor to remain and Lutheran worship to continue.

Nearby, in what became known as Maryland, a small band of English Roman Catholics and Protestants, accompanied by two Jesuits, arrived in 1634 to establish what was intended to be a primarily Catholic colony. Struggling with an increasingly religiously mixed settlement as well as with the continuing unpopularity of Catholics in England, the Maryland Assembly passed a Toleration Act* in 1649, granting freedom of worship to all Christians. That law remained in effect until 1692, when the Church of England was officially established. However, the passage of the Act of Toleration in England in 1689 and the presence of large numbers of non-Anglicans kept the establishment weak and allowed a strong Catholic presence to remain unmolested.

But the most important Middle Colony in terms of the history of Christianity in America was Pennsylvania, established by William Penn* in 1682 as a haven for Quakers and other religious minorities. Convinced that government was a gift from God and a part of religion itself and, therefore, that it could be good, Penn exuded optimism and good will. Building on these theological presuppositions and a munificent land grant, Penn established a "Holy Experiment" which guaranteed religious toleration for all who believed in God. He recruited colonists not only from among England's Quakers but also from Germany's persecuted religious minorities and soon large numbers of Mennonites,* Amish* and Brethren* descended on Pennsylvania. They were followed by an influx of other Germans, mostly Lutheran and Reformed.

As the various Southern Colonies developed, they embraced an Anglican establishment and in the seventeenth century were populated overwhelmingly by immigrants from the British Isles. However, since the Anglican establishment in the areas south of Virginia was little more than nominal, Presbyterians* and Baptists began to multiply rapidly in the South toward the end of the century.

Therefore, in the period of original European settlement, generally speaking, the New Englanders bequeathed to the future American republic the vision of a redeemer nation, the Middle Colonies handed down the notions of freedom and pluralism,* and the Southern Colonies passed on an emphasis on materialism and a success ethic where church was subordinate to plantation. In common, they shared a Reformation background and embraced a world view which included reverence for the Bible,* emphasis on a personal relationship with God through Jesus Christ, biblical norms for social ethics and a special stress on work as a calling. Historians disagree over just how similar they were beyond these few Protestant commonalities. However, nearly all scholars affirm that they injected an energetic religious dimension into the settlement of the New World and that the Puritans constituted the most dynamic Christian force of all in the colonies in the period before 1700.

Religious Decay, 1700-1725. Second-generation New England Puritans confronted a problem faced by Christians throughout the centuries: how to sustain religious fervor from generation to generation. This became complicated in Puritan New England, where conversion* was so closely tied to church membership* and church membership was so closely tied to civil participation in the community. Moreover, the Puritans desired to have a state church with a regenerate membership, but their frustration grew as it became apparent that a number of those of the second generation could not testify to a conversion experience. A synod* of the Massachusetts churches tried to solve the problem in 1662 when it declared that adults who had been baptized as infants and who now professed faith and lived uprightly but who had not had a conversion experience might be accepted as church members. Further, the synod asserted that children of such church members could now be baptized as "half-way members," even though they could not receive the Lord's Supper* or participate in church elections. Thus, the so-called Half-Way Covenant* opened the door to receive the unconverted into church membership. Many Puritan leaders of the day saw this sort of development as decay. Increase Mather's* lamentation *The Glory Departing from New England* (1702) is but one example of this opinion.

Even though the Half-Way Covenant had been an accommodation to the spiritual facts of life, it obviously had taken its toll. In addition, the Act of Toleration of 1689 (applicable throughout the colonies) had made it more difficult to maintain doctrinal purity in New England. More important, when the Bay Colony was rechartered in 1691, the franchise was based on property rather than church membership, thus diluting the ability of the churches to maintain their communal emphasis and the friendly integration of church and state. The ubiquitous frontier aided and abetted the presence of spiritually lax and lukewarm elements in society, not to mention dissenters and heretics, and made spiritual oversight difficult. Further, Britain's involvement in a series of continental wars which spread to North America affected the New England churches adversely as they attempted to minister in a climate of bloodshed and hatred.

The other colonies experienced similar problems. There was growing spiritual indifference as many colonists lost their memory of the reasons for the exodus from Europe, became preoccupied with economic activities, moved out to inaccessible places on the frontier, or simply lost interest in religion. There were complaints about the increasingly poor quality of clergy who came to America to serve the churches and some indication that the new rationalism in the universities was beginning to affect the educated leadership. In short, it became increasingly apparent in the years around the turn of the eighteenth century that Christianity in the New World was having trouble maintaining its spiritual vitality.

The First Great Awakening,* 1725-1775. Beginning in 1725 and lasting until around 1775, a series of revivals* swept the American colonies. The earliest stirrings occurred among the Reformed churches of the Raritan Valley of New Jersey, mostly due to the fervent preaching* of T. J. Frelinghuysen.* A religious tinder box, the colonies provided abundant spiritual fuel for the revivalistic firestorm which quickly spread to the Presbyterian churches in the Middle Colonies, then up to New England and finally down through the American South. The individual who more than any other made these regional awakenings a colony-wide movement was the itinerant English evangelist* George Whitefield.* A close associate of John Wesley,* Whitefield, beginning in 1740, traveled up and down the Atlantic seaboard, preaching such basic gospel themes as repentance and faith in Christ and giving the Awakening an ideological unity which a short time later would help create a new nation.

In New England, beginning in 1734-1735, the Awakening came under the scholarly and spiritual dominance of Jonathan Edwards,* a Congregational minister-theologian and America's first native-born intellectual genius. When the revivalists met criticism and resistance, Edwards became their vigorous defender. In his works *Some Thoughts Concerning the Present Revival of Religion in New-England* (1742) and *A Treatise Concerning Religious Affections* (1746), Edwards discriminated between the natural and the supernatural effects of the revival. On the one hand, he acknowledged that persons could be saved without the apparent outbursts of enthusiasm and bodily tics which marked some phases of the Awakening and that some aberrant manifestations might be demonic. On the other hand, he defended the revival as authentic religious experience on the basis of the Holy Spirit's work in changing thousands of individuals' lives for good and bringing high standards of Christian morality to hundreds of communities.

Nevertheless, the Awakening split denominations and congregations in many places. In New England, Congregationalists who opposed Edwards and the other revivalists were called Old Lights* and, conversely, those who favored the revivals were known as New Lights.* Presbyterians split into the pro-revivalist New Sides* and the anti-revivalist Old Sides.* The issue was not orthodox* theology but a new form of preaching and spirituality.*

Despite its divisive tendencies, the Awakening united more than it separated—with the revivalists eventually prevailing. In general, Christianity in the colonies was renewed, with the Congregationalists in New England, the various Presbyterian and Reformed churches in the Middle Colonies, and the Baptists, Presbyterians and Wesleyans* in the South making heavy gains. Reverence for the Bible and biblical values were restored throughout the colonies, and the American outlook was given an "evangelical" cast that increasingly moved away from a reliance on Old World hierarchies to a more individualistic and experimental faith. This rejuvenated faith was new in form if not in doctrine, introducing a heightened emotionalism, lay exhorting, itinerant* preaching and a more dramatic style of pulpit delivery. In addition, vigorous, optimistic postmillenialism,* which emphasized the bringing in of God's kingdom* on earth, was firmly established as the eschatology* of the Protestant churches. Thus, a religious revolution preceded, and helped prepare the way for, the political revolution in America.

The American Revolution* and Religious Decline, 1775-1800. Some historians have argued that the Revolutionary epoch constituted a watershed in the history of American Christianity. During that period, Enlightenment* ideas and evangelical* Christian values combined to produce what sociologist Seymour Martin Lipset has called "the first new nation." Not only was the U.S. the first major colony in modern history successfully to revolt against colonial rule, but it also was unique in the extent to which republican and biblical beliefs flowed together and influenced each other. The birth of the republic served to re-enforce this interlocking relationship. It was also in this period that Thomas Jefferson* and James Madison, with the support of their Baptist, Quaker, Mennonite and Presbyterian allies, hammered out the First Amendment of the Constitution. This guaranteed religious liberty and established the principle of separation of church and state* in the new land.

During the Revolutionary period many of the emphases of the First Great Awakening were subtly secularized and appropriated by the new nation—such as the transfer of millennial expectations from the province of the churches to that of the new country. This was not the view of evangelicals such as Edwards and most other leaders of the First Great Awakening, nor of Roman Catholic Americans, who well into the twentieth century continued to define America as "a mission field" rather than "a promised land." However, for the vast majority of Protestant ministers, the revolutionary experience deepened the conviction that God had chosen America for a special purpose. The revolutionary settlement rewarded those churches which reflected the ethos of the common people and engaged in persuasion and competition. Moreover, those churches (such as the Baptists and Methodists) which best reflected the new republican environment flourished best in the new nation.

However, the Revolutionary War itself helped to bring on a period of decline in the churches. Whereas many clergymen had hoped the Revolution would serve to strengthen and purify the churches, in reality the war had the opposite effect. The issue of the Revolution itself had badly divided Americans, both inside and outside the churches. Opinion ranged from enthusiastic endorsement of the Revolution by most Congregationalists, Presbyterians and Baptists to non-participation on moral grounds by the Quakers, Mennonites and other Christian pacifists.* Further, the unleashed animosities of war left their mark. Many ministers who had joined the Continental army were wounded or crippled, serving as visible reminders of the pain and division of war. The conflict blunted the religious conscience of a generation of Americans and encouraged many to become apathetic toward Christianity.

The war also accelerated the acceptance of Enlightenment values in America, often at the expense of Christianity. In the last quarter of the century, rational religion made inroads in the colleges where ministers were trained. For instance, the College of William and Mary* had reportedly become a hotbed of French skepticism, and when Timothy Dwight* became president of Yale* in 1795, he claimed that he could find only two young men in the entire student body of 110 who would admit that they even believed in God. In the schools and among American intellectuals, deism*—the religious expression of the Enlightenment which ridiculed the idea of a personal God and supernaturalism—became popular. Revolutionary leaders such as Ethan Allen* and Thomas Paine* preached deism and launched attacks on revealed religion. The first three presidents of the U.S. (George Washington,* John Adams, Thomas Jefferson*), although nominal church members, were in reality Unitarians* or deists who rejected Christian orthodoxy, advocated rational belief in a "Supreme Being" and embraced a generalized civil religion.*

Finally, a great westward movement during this period presented a new challenge to the colonial denominations. By the war's end in 1783, a westward-bound human torrent was pouring into Appalachia, the Northwest Territory and the southern hinterland. It was difficult for colonial denominations like the Congregationalists, Episcopalians* and Presbyterians to keep up with this development and to supply the frontier people with trained ministers. Also, the unsettled conditions of the wilderness made evangelism* difficult and religious indifference easy. One survey in 1790 found only five per cent of the American people claimed formal affiliation with any denomination. These factors, taken as a whole, illustrate that the churches reached a lower ebb of vitality during the last twenty-five years of the eighteenth century than at any other time in the country's previous religious history.

The Second Great Awakening and the Evangelical Golden Age, 1800-1861. As historian Edwin S. Gaustad has pointed out, the task of the churches at the turn of the nineteenth century was not only the "conquest of the West," but also the "reconquest of the East." Both of these conquests were closely interrelated and can be understood only as part of a single surge of new religious life and activity now known as the Second Great Awakening.* The Protestant experience in the earlier Great Awakening led many to embrace a re-emphasis on "plain gospel truths" as the remedy to the current spiritual malaise. This revivalistic preaching produced a great wave of spiritual awakenings that swept back and forth across the country for two generations after 1800.

[7]

The exact beginning of this Second Great Awakening is difficult to pinpoint for it appeared in many localities, especially in the East, almost simultaneously. In 1801, just as it began to diminish in the New England towns, revival came to Yale College under the earnest preaching of President Timothy Dwight. Many other colleges had similar experiences during the period, as the revival proceeded in a calm and orderly fashion to engulf the entire northeastern seaboard.

Such would not be the case in the West where conditions were much more unsettled and church attendance much less respectable. With little formal education and an atmosphere of political and economic insecurity, frontier revivals tended to be direct and expressive in their zeal and religious emotions. The half-tamed nature of the American West called for a different approach from that of the frock-coated preachers of the East. That approach was embodied in the camp meeting,* a distinctive feature of frontier* religious life and a massively successful institution of Western evangelism.

As in the East, the Western phase of the Second Great Awakening had no obvious and precise beginning. The first memorable actor was Presbyterian minister James McGready,* an aggressive, strong-willed Scots-Irishman who pastored three churches in rough-and-tumble Logan County, Kentucky. Revival began under his leadership, culminating in a great week-long outdoor meeting for preaching and observance of Communion at the Gasper River Church held in July 1800. There, McGready and his associates gave decisive impetus to the Western tradition of evangelism through camp meetings, great outdoor religious services of several days' duration held for a gathering of people who had to take shelter on the spot because they were a distance from their permanent homes. Shortly thereafter, Barton W. Stone,* converted under McGready's preaching, carried the revival to Cane Ridge, Kentucky, where, in August 1801, a much larger interdenominational camp meeting was held for six days and nights with between ten and twenty-five thousand people in attendance.

The camp-meeting technique was so compelling that it was soon widely used with great success by Methodists, Baptists and Presbyterians alike. They were the means by which tens of thousands were converted to Christ and swept into the churches, often to the accompaniment of great emotion and excitement, which aroused misgivings in the minds of many church leaders in the more staid East. As the focus of the awakening shifted from region to region, the popularity of the camp meetings waned. Eventually domesticated into permanent camp grounds, by mid-century they had been transformed into Bible conference* centers or summer religious resorts.

Meanwhile, the revivals burned on in other parts of the nation, particularly in central and western New York State where they came under the influence of Charles G. Finney,* the most prominent national evangelist of the era. Finney, himself dramatically converted at age twenty-nine, left his law practice to become a full-time evangelist in 1821. As such, he shifted the focal point of revival preaching from settled ministers who confined their efforts to an area in and around their home parishes to professional evangelists who traveled full time across large sections of the country holding increasingly well-organized, long-term, city-wide, interdenominational evangelistic campaigns. Finney's controversial "new measures,"* including the participation of women in the conduct of his revival services, added dynamic new dimensions to the awakening and established new patterns of church life. Most important, Finney virtually institutionalized revivalism and adapted it to an urban environment. His well-organized, community-wide revival campaigns of several weeks' duration foreshadowed the urban evangelism of Dwight L. Moody,* Billy Graham* and many others who followed.

The end of this great era of revivalism occurred in the 1850s when lay leaders, especially big-city businessmen, sponsored simple prayer meetings,* frequently held at noon, which resulted in thousands of reconsecrations and fresh conversions. By 1858 twenty such noon prayer meetings were being held daily in New York City, and more than two thousand people jammed Chicago's Metropolitan Theatre for a daily service. The noted Methodist lay* evangelist Phoebe Palmer* and the newly formed Young Men's Christian Association* (YMCA) also played prominent roles in the Prayer Meeting Revival* of 1857-1858 and its subsequent extension to the Old World.

By the time of the outbreak of the Civil War* in 1861, the Second Great Awakening, it seemed, had run its course. But it had established evangelical Christianity as the mainstream of American religion and had inaugurated an evangelical golden age. Biblical Christianity and democratic* idealism became the twin hallmarks of America and Americans as the revivalists preached their decreasingly Calvinistic and increasingly Arminian* gospel of "all have sinned" and "salvation for all."

Perry Miller and others have argued that the Second Great Awakening transformed Puritan covenant theology* into the current of nationalism and created an ethos of evangelical democracy in America. Further, just as the revivals altered the nature of American religion and politics, so they also helped give decisive form to the first American civil religion—the public faith that would dominate the scene for nearly a century. Earlier deistic elements now combined with a virile evangelical faith to produce for the fledgling republic a civil religion which emphasized America's godly connections, unique history and millennial mission to convert the world to Christianity and democracy.

The Second Great Awakening also saw the religious initiative shift from the East and New England to the West and the frontier. This occurred largely as a result of, and in conjunction with, the emergence of the Methodists and Baptists as the dominant Protestant denominations and the decline of the Congregationalists and Episcopalians. Presbyterians in general held their own, with the newly formed Cumberland Presbyterian Church* adapting well to the frontier. However, the Methodists and Baptists in particular seemed perfectly suited to the new land. They were extremely mobile. Since their ministers were willing and able to preach anywhere, anyplace, anytime and were unencumbered by any requirements for a formal education, they could deploy new circuit riders* and bivocational pastors with great speed. Moreover, they gave evangelistic activity their highest priority and endured great hardships to carry the gospel to the furthest corners of the frontier.

As in any time of great religious enthusiasm and expectation, not only were older denominations revived and transformed, but new religious enterprises were born and flourished. Among the most important of the new Christian groups which came into existence during the Second Great Awakening was the Disciples of Christ* (also sometimes called the Churches of Christ* but more properly the Restoration Movement,* which its founders claimed was not a denomination) under the leadership of Barton W. Stone and Alexander Campbell.* There were many others, some rejuvenated and some newborn, some on the radical fringes and some just outside the periphery of Christianity: the Church of Jesus Christ of Latter-day Saints (popularly known as the Mormons,* which eventually became the largest of these new religious undertakings), various Adventist* groups, the Unitarians, the Universalists,* the Transcendentalists,* the Shakers,* the Oneida Community* and the Spiritualists—to name the most interesting and most important. In addition, it was a period of Christian renewal and growth among African-Americans, as large numbers of African-American slaves were converted to Christ in Baptist and Methodist revival meetings.

The period was also a time of significant increase for the Roman Catholic Church in America as millions of Irish Catholics immigrated* to America in the wake of the deadly potato famine of the 1840s. Many German Catholics came to the U.S. in this period as well, and the purchase of the Louisiana Territory in 1803 brought thousands of French Catholics into American religious life. Catholic evangelism, inspired by the Finney revivals and led by gospel-preaching priests like Walter Eliot,* Clarence Walworth,* Francis X. Weninger* and Joseph Wissel, using the technique of parish missions,* also pumped new spiritual life into the American Catholic Church while at the same time adding many fresh converts to Church rolls. By 1860 Roman Catholicism had become the largest single denomination in America, with 3.5 million members, rivaling combined Methodist-Baptist strength.

Perhaps most important from the overall historical perspective were the political and social fruits of the Second Great Awakening. The revivals stimulated and intensified the abolitionist movement,* especially that branch which called for "immediate emancipation." The Awakening also led to the establishment of scores of voluntary organizations dedicated to evangelism, education,* Bible and tract* publication and distribution, and missions* to Native Americans and to foreign lands. Crusades were launched not only against slavery, but also against Sabbath*-breaking, alcohol* abuse, gambling and the exploitation of labor, and for women's rights. More than 150 colleges* were established by evangelicals in the Transappalachian West between 1820 and 1860 in order to provide for an educated ministry and to promote Christian culture. Shelters and homes were built for orphans, unwed mothers, the mentally impaired, the handicapped and the poor. Thousands of sermons were preached and meetings held to condemn slave-owning, political corruption and the abuse of women.

In the course of the nineteenth century, scores of Christian believers came into national prominence as reformers: Charles G. Finney, Arthur and Lewis Tappan,* Orange Scott,* Jonathan Blanchard,* Theodore Weld,* Angelina and Sarah Grimké,* Harriet Beecher Stowe,* William Lloyd Garrison,* Phoebe Palmer,* Catharine Beecher, Frances Willard,* Charles Crittendon* and William Jennings Bryan,* to name a few. Home mission societies established Sunday schools* to educate unchurched children and distribute clothing, food and money to the needy. All of these enterprises represented a tremendous outburst of evangelical reforming energy generated by the revivalism of the Second Great Awakening.

Civil War and Religious Decline, 1861-1877. Ironically, the revivalism of the Second Great Awakening contributed to the coming of the Civil War (1861-1865) and in so doing to its own demise. An increasingly strident abolitionism, fueled in great part by evangelical zeal, sharply divided the nation and brought it to the brink of civil conflict. Once the slavery issue came to a head, the bonds of religion could no longer hold the various sections of the country together, and brothers, in more than one sense of the term, took up arms against one another. The war was a watershed between the old and the new America. Following the conflict, the American people became much more heterogeneous in background in almost every respect, including religion. The advent of modern science* drastically altered the intellectual climate, making it more hostile to Christianity than at any previous time in history. And the quickening pace of urbanization and industrialization created new centers of power in national life.

The war cost billions of dollars and more casualties than any other in U.S. history, ruined and impoverished many Southern states and left a lasting legacy of sectional and racial hatred. Despite a significant revival in the Confederate army during the war, Christianity in general did not fare well in the conflict. Besides killing and wounding tens of thousands of faithful church members, four years of carnage blunted the American moral and religious conscience. Both during and immediately after the war, church membership and attendance declined.

President Abraham Lincoln* and a number of American church leaders—such as Horace Bushnell* and Philip Schaff*—saw the war as an act of divine judgment on the nation because of slavery. They interpreted the conflict as the humiliation of an arrogant and boastful people, a supreme hour of trial designed to help the nation fulfill rather than forfeit its destiny. They concluded that the war represented not only divine judgment because of the sin of slavery but also presented the possibility of national redemption and renewal. Unfortunately, Lincoln's tragic assassination in 1865 made this possibility much more difficult to achieve than any of these men had dreamed.

The generation following the Civil War—dubbed "the Gilded Age" by Mark Twain in 1873—proved disastrous in terms of the advancement of Christianity and Christian ideals in America. It was an era marked by the assassination of one president (Lincoln), the impeachment of another (Andrew Johnson) and rampant corruption in the adminstration of a third (U. S. Grant), as well as far-reaching exploitation and greed in the nation's business community. The period of Reconstruction (1865-1877) following the war was a failure, largely because the removal of Lincoln's strong hand left the nation with weak leadership as the federal government could not decide what to make of its victory. Efforts at Reconstruction were confused and halfhearted, and the increasing disposition of a war-weary North was to leave the South to its own devices and to get on with the business of reaping the profits of a booming post-war economy. The issues which had stood at the center of the recent conflict were subordinated to partisan politics, and the task of restoring the Union by protecting the fundamental rights of all its people was neglected. Methodists, Baptists and Presbyterians, who represented the majority of church members in the defeated South, had split on a national basis before the war over the issue of slavery. They remained divided after the war and consequently were unable to contribute much to the healing process.

Even though a veneer of evangelical piety covered almost everything in the culture, the rhetoric of idealism and virtue no longer seemed to touch the core of the materialism of the political and commercial interests. It was in this period that Darwinism* made its appearance in America, first as a biological theory of the origin of human life and shortly thereafter as a social doctrine with widespread political implications. Darwinian aphorisms like "natural selection" and "the survival of the fittest" increasingly became bywords within the American business community. Episcopalian clergyman and sociologist William Graham Sumner embraced Social Darwinism, resigned his ministry and in 1872 became professor of political and social science at Yale, where he preached the virtues of the evolutionary process and unrestrained private enterprise for more than thirty-eight years. Sumner's popularity reflected the spirit of the times and made difficult the task of those Christian intellectuals who disagreed, especially those who viewed the increasing brutalization of life brought about by the new age of materialism as un-Christian and unacceptable.

The New Urban Revivalism in Victorian America, 1877-1890. Hard times had fallen on America's "evangelical empire." Although there was little doubt that evangelical religious norms and values still prevailed in rural America, the burgeoning cities were a different matter. More and more evangelical leaders acknowledged a growing decline in religious vigor and expressed uneasiness concerning the increasing breach between lip service and reality. The traditional evangelical cure for such a spiritual malady was revivalism—and Victorian America was no exception.

Dwight L. Moody* became the most prominent evangelist of the period. Unusual in that he was a lay preacher with a business background, Mr. Moody (as he was called) both challenged and reflected the age. Captivating his audiences with a homey and sentimental style of storytelling, he declared a message that was simple and direct: God loves sinners, and sinners can be saved through faith in Jesus Christ!

The one constant factor which dominated both Moody's personal faith and public proclamation was biblical authority. In this respect he stood in the preaching tradition of Edwards and Finney. However, he was also a product of Victorian America, especially its extravagant sentimentalism. Moody and his great songleader, Ira D. Sankey,* and hundreds of other lesser evangelists of the period, wove this sentimentality into the warp and woof of American Protestantism through sermon and song. In the process the strong prophetic element in evangelical Christianity was transformed into a sentimental moralism. Perhaps in these subtle nuances and emphases lies the chief import of the new revivalism.

It was in this period and under these conditions that the old informal evangelical consensus began to give way to the emergence of a Protestant Establishment. This Protestant Establishment was more self-conscious of the paramount place of Protestantism in society, more concerned with respectability and more keenly aware of its self-interests. This mentality stemmed from the assurance that the cultural dominance of the Protestant faith rested on a strong base of the wealthiest and the oldest American families and institutions. Protestants had been the first to settle almost everywhere in the American colonies and had provided the ideology and ethic for the development of a dynamic new nation; therefore, their descendants held most of the positions of power and influence in America. These families and institutions controlled most of the national wealth. During this period they became mutually supportive, their interests increasingly interlocking.

The Era of the Protestant Establishment and the Age of the New Immigrants, 1890-1918.
Protestants were clearly in control of American political, economic and social life in the era between the disappearance of the old frontier, around 1890, and the end of World War 1* in 1918. The mainline* Protestant denominations, with the possible exception of the Baptists, had become respectable, and the Roman Catholics were making giant strides in that direction. However, there were signs of increasing hostility toward Christianity among intellectuals—based on the new science in the universities and on growing theological liberalism in the seminaries—although confidence in orthodoxy still prevailed in most of the educational institutions of the land. Protestant hopes for a "Christian America" still burned bright and American civilization, although never "Christian" in a biblical sense, clearly cohered in the main because of a shared set of values resting on an evangelical understanding of the Scriptures.*

With the possible exception of Cardinal* James Gibbons,* all of the best-known religious figures of the period were members of mainline Protestant denominations and had national reputations: Dwight L. Moody, Henry Ward Beecher,* Lyman Abbot,* Phillips Brooks* and Josiah Strong,* to name a few of the most prominent. Moreover, the presidential election of 1896 reflected the age: the voters of America had a choice between William McKinley,* a born-again,* testifying Methodist on the Republican ticket and William Jennings Bryan, a born-again, testifying Presbyterian on the Democrat ticket.

The Puritan Dream was now transmogrified into the American Dream, meaning primarily that every individual supposedly had a chance to be whatever he or she wanted to be and to achieve whatever he or she wanted to achieve in America. In this period, however, the Dream became inextricably tied to making money—so much so that even the nation's religious leaders praised the accumulation of wealth and endorsed its pursuit as the will of God. Chief spokesman for this new "Gospel of Wealth"* was Massachusetts-lawyer-turned-Philadelphia-minister Russell H. Conwell,* whose energetic life illustrated his mission to bring all Americans into the Protestant middle class. He founded Temple University (1888), preached to one of the largest congregations in America, and made his Baptist church into a neighborhood social-service institution—all the time declaring that Jesus had provided the opportunity for salvation* and America the opportunity for success. He set forth his gospel-of-wealth ideology in his famous lecture "Acres of Diamonds," which he delivered an incredible 6,000 times.

Other Protestant leaders saw the American economic system in a different light—not as one primarily of opportunity but of exploitation. They pointed out that by 1900, ten per cent of American families had cornered ninety per cent of the nation's wealth. It appeared to many Christians with a sensitive social conscience that something had gone wrong and that unregulated capitalism was controlled by unregulated greed.

Although it had evangelical roots in institutions such as the rescue mission movement* and The Salvation Army* (established in 1878), the Social Gospel* itself became a bona fide, powerful, trans-denominational movement in the 1890s. Sometimes called "social Christianity" or even "Christian socialism," it stressed the need to remember the social dimension of the gospel of Christ and to apply Christian social principles to the present economic order. A combination of factors—such as inhumane conditions in the factories, bloody labor management disputes, wretched tenement life in the increasingly crowded cities, and a growing awareness that middle-class Protestantism was out of touch with the urban working class—led to a plethora of sermons, newspaper articles, books and interdenominational organizations calling for the Christianization of the American social order. Many of the country's best-known Christian leaders became Social Gospel activists: Washington Gladden,* often called "the father of the movement," Josiah Strong, Francis Greenwood Peabody,* Richard T. Ely,* Albion W. Small* and most of all Walter Rauschenbusch,* who typified the movement's passion and soul. These advocates and their allies believed that through concerted moral effort the political and economic institutions of American society could be shaped to biblical standards of ethics* and morality.

In many ways a continuation of the reforming zeal generated by the Second Great Awakening, the Social Gospel Movement was also in large part a direct response to the growing social ills caused by the rapid industrialization and urbanization characteristic of America in the last decades of the nineteenth century. It combined the residual of the old evangelical consensus with the new social concern to produce a great wave of progressive-populist reform around the turn of the twentieth century. As many foreign visitors of the time noted, America was a land of mind-boggling paradoxes: ruthless robber barons and exploitative slum landlords on the one hand and crusading political reformers and religious social critics on the other. Whatever the case, America was, indeed, the home of passionate crusaders—represented by such diverse causes as the Sunday-school movement, the Student Volunteer Movement* for Foreign Missions, educational reform, the temperance movement,* the drive for women's rights (especially female suffrage*), world peace associations and the Men and Religion Forward Movement.* In many ways the Protestant Establishment exhausted and to some extent discredited itself in its last great moral crusades: namely, World War 1* (1914-1918) and the passage of the Prohibition* Amendment to the U.S. Constitution in 1920.

While the Protestants of the nation struggled with their social consciences, U.S. Catholics struggled to become genuine Americans. Although long present in one form or another, the Americanism* crisis of American Catholicism became particularly intense during this period. The central question was: Given the central teachings of the Roman Catholic Church in the nineteenth century, could Catholics in the U.S. ever hope to become "real Americans"—that is, genuine adherents of Americanism?

Although Americanism was never a clearly defined concept, then or now, in the nineteenth century it generally meant accepting the established Protestant-American traditions of liberalism, republicanism, democracy, free enterprise, reverence for biblical authority, denominationalism,* hostility toward Old World hierarchies, and, most of all, religious liberty and separation of church and state. Since these had been periodically condemned by nineteenth-century popes such as Pius IX,* it was often difficult for American Catholics to convince their non-Catholic fellow Americans that they were good citizens of the republic. This problem was compounded by the fact that as the century wore on this "immigrant church," for a variety of reasons, adopted what has been described as a "ghetto culture," which fostered personal and group identities independent of, and separate from, the mainstream Protestant culture. These difficulties gradually were overcome mostly thanks to the hard work of certain Americanists within the hierarchy of the American Catholic Church—mainly Cardinal Gibbons and his chief supporters: Archbishop* John Ireland* of St. Paul, Minnesota; John J. Keane,* rector* of the Catholic University of America*; and Denis J. O'Connell,* rector of the North American College,* Rome.

Although the full fruit of their efforts was not realized until much later (symbolized first by the nomination of Alfred E. Smith* for president in 1928 and second by the election of John F. Kennedy* to that office in 1960), these men and others made their greatest impact in this period as a result of the growing numbers of Catholic immigrants from southern and southeastern Europe. The Protestant Establishment may not have particularly liked Catholics, but it had to pay more attention to their growing numbers and wealth. In fact, the dramatic increase in immigration, resulting largely from the insatiable demands of the big industrialists for cheap labor, dramatically changed the religious landscape of America in the period from 1880 until the stringent immigration law of 1924.

This spurt of immigration markedly increased the variety of religious expression in America and challenged the assimilative powers of the Protestant Establishment. Greeks, Romanians, Bulgarians and Serbians brought all the variations of Eastern Orthodoxy.* Russian and Polish Jews eventually outnumbered and recreated the small German Jewish community. The Japanese added their expressions of Buddhism to the Chinese forms, and Indians brought Sikhism and Hinduism. Most of all, large numbers of Roman Catholics came from southern and eastern Europe. As northern European immigration tapered off, it became increasingly apparent that the piety of Italian, Polish and Portuguese Catholics differed significantly from that of the Irish and German Catholics who had preceeded them. This factor would create new problems of assimilation.

Rapid change in the social order also provoked insecurity among many mainstream Protestants and resulted in a revival of nativism.* Arising first during the massive influx of immigrants in the period 1830-1860, fueled by tribal Protestantism and typically aimed at European Catholics, it issued in the burning of an Ursuline* convent in Charlestown, Massachusetts (1834), and riots in Philadelphia (1844) and Louisville (1855). A second wave emerged during the decade of 1886-1896, when the rural Midwestern American Protective Association (APA)* revived anti-Catholic sentiments. Hard times were blamed on Irish Catholic labor leaders and one APA official even claimed to have uncovered a plot for a Catholic rebellion and the massacre of American Protestants. Urban Catholic political power and new immigrants were again the focus of sporadic Protestant animosity during the years 1900-1930.

Related to the religious changes brought by the new immigrants and the new patterns of thinking required by this pluralism were other factors, such as accelerated urbanization, bigger big business, bellicose nationalism and the entry of the U.S. into world-power status with its first major venture in imperialism with the coming of the Spanish-American War* of 1898. All of these placed additional pressure on the Protestant Establishment to provide leadership to solve the massive new problems created in the wake of these developments and to assimilate the newcomers into the American way of life.

The increasing loss of nerve in this respect on the part of the mainline Protestant churches was complicated by the impact of Darwinism and the inroads of theological liberalism which tended to split the Protestant intellectual community and divide denominations. These were not like the divisions of the past—which had been more about means than substance—but divisions based on fundamental differences in theology. More and more of the energy of the Protestant churches, internally at least, came to be spent on defending orthodoxy and deflecting heresy.* For what would prove to be the last time, Protestants joined hands in significant numbers to support America's efforts in World War 1; but even as this happened many leaders knew that a major theological confrontation between the forces of the older theologically conservative America, represented by the evangelicals, and the forces of the newer theologically liberal America, represented by the modernists, was in the offing.

The Fundamentalist-Modernist Controversy and the Dominance of the Liberal Establishment, 1918-1965. As historian Sydney Ahlstrom* has pointed out, "The decade of the twenties is the most sharply defined decade in American history." It was "sharply defined" not only chronologically (from the end of World War 1 to the beginning of the Great Depression*) but ideologically. Moreover, especially in terms of the religious history of the nation, it has proved to be the most momentous decade of the twentieth century. The wild fulminations, furious debates and bloated ballyhoo of the Jazz Age, the development of the movies, the radio and the automobile—all of which deeply affected church life in America—and the future-shaping struggle for the soul of the nation by the fundamentalists* and modernists all helped to make it so.

In the course of events the fundamentalists, representing the militantly conservative wing of American evangelical Christianity, emerged as the champions of the old Protestant orthodoxy, while the modernists, representing the militantly liberal wing of the new theology, emerged as the champions of the new Protestant naturalism. During the 1920s the public began to perceive the fundamentalists as the voice of the evangelical movement and of the old America, on the one hand, and that of the modernists as the voice of the liberal movement and the new America on the other. As it turned out, this was a great public relations coup for the modernists because the media, with a certain amount of justification, saw the fundamentalists as fighting a rearguard action on behalf of a former way of life as much as attempting to defend historic Christianity against the inroads of German rationalism, scientific naturalism and the new historicism. Ironically, even though the modernists won in the short run, they did not prevail over the long run.

The story of the fundamentalist-modernist controversy* constitutes a complex chapter in American religious history. Despite the protestations of some historians to the contrary, it was a time of crisis for both the Protestant Establishment and the historic evangelical Christianity which undergirded it. The cultural face of the nation was changed forever by the events of the period. By 1930 the old evangelical consensus had been replaced by a new pluralism, the old Protestant establishment had been replaced by the new Liberal Establishment, and the older Christianity-in-general civil religion had been replaced by the newer Judeo-Christian-tradition* brand of civic faith. The years that followed saw evangelicals in general and fundamentalists in particular become a despised subculture as the Liberal Establishment held sway in the media and in the universities, theological schools and denominational hierarchies of the land.

The Methodists, Episcopalians, Congregationalists and Disciples were most heavily influenced by the new theological liberalism, with Presbyterians and Northern Baptists badly divided over the issue. Harry Emerson Fosdick's* down-home pulpit liberalism came to dominate the church pews of the country, while John Dewey's liberal civil-religion educational philosophy took the colleges of education of the land by storm. Most important, the institutions of higher education of the leading Protestant denominations (with the possible exception of the National Baptist* Convention of the U.S.A., Inc., the National Baptist Convention of America, the Southern Baptist Convention,* the various Pentecostal* and Holiness* groups and certain Lutheran and Reformed bodies) became the focal points of liberal dominance of the American Protestant churches in the period.

The hold of the Liberal Establishment on the hearts and minds of American Christianity, however, was weakened shortly after its triumph over fundamentalism in the 1920s, first by the Great Depression (1929-1933), then by the impact of neo-orthodoxy* and finally by the excesses of World War 2* (1939-1945). The Depression and the Second World War were blows to liberal optimism and represented a setback for its peace initiatives and Social Gospel agenda. Moreover, the economic depression was accompanied by a time of religious depression in the churches. This not only led to spiritual stagnation but also to what historian Robert T. Handy has described as a turning by American Protestantism from its historic "quest for a Christian America" to grappling with religious pluralism and new social forces.

More serious than the Depression in terms of the erosion of confidence in theological liberalism was the emergence of neo-orthodoxy on the American scene in the late 1920s and early 1930s. This movement was initiated in Europe by Karl Barth* and Emil Brunner,* and championed on the American side of the Atlantic by the brothers Reinhold* and H. Richard* Niebuhr. The term *neo-orthodoxy* loosely designates certain forms of twentieth-century Protestant theology which sought to recover the distinctive insights and themes of the Reformation while at the same time integrating certain aspects of modern scientific methodology into biblical scholarship. Beginning in the 1930s, many of those who had previously embraced theological liberalism turned to neo-orthodoxy for religious meaning.

As liberal ideas and assumptions concerning human nature and social progress collapsed before the onslaught of the increasing pessimism concerning human nature produced by World War 1, the Great Depression, the Stalinist Era in the Soviet Union, World War 2, the Holocaust* and the Vietnam War,* a new general religiosity developed in America, based partly on a longing for religious certainties from the nation's past and partly from a general impression that modern science could not provide all of the answers once expected from it, especially concerning the nonmaterial aspects of life. This new religiosity became especially strong during the presidency of Dwight D.

Eisenhower* (1953-1961). During that period Billy Graham became an established figure on the national religious scene and a confidant of presidents. It was also a time of renewal for civil religion as the public faith was expanded from the Judeo-Christian* tradition to theism*-in-general under a civically pious President Eisenhower who declared: "Our form of government has no sense unless it is grounded in a deeply felt religious faith, and I don't care what it is."

It was also during the Eisenhower years that the modern Civil Rights Movement* (1954-1968) began. This drive for basic civil rights for minorities, especially African-Americans, rested largely on the substructure of African-American church life, which provided the leadership, ideology and energy to launch and sustain the movement, and the residual of the Social Gospel which had sensitized Anglo-Americans to the plight of the nation's minorities. Building on earlier organizational activities among free black Christians prior to 1865 and the evangelistic successes of the Second Great Awakening in the South, several important African-American religious fellowships emerged in the post-Civil War era which were as large and vital as their Anglo-American counterparts. For example, the African Methodist Episcopal Church* was founded by Richard Allen,* the first ordained* African-American Methodist minister, in 1816. Then in 1822 the African Methodist Episcopal Church Zion* was formed with James Varick* as its first bishop. The National Baptist* Convention (now the National Baptist Convention of the U.S.A., Inc.) was officially constituted in 1895, and from it several other African-American Baptist conventions of churches have been formed as a result of splits, the most important being the National Baptist Convention of America, 1917, and the Progressive National Baptist Convention, 1961.

In the twentieth century, the number of African-Americans who identify as Baptists has remained at about seventy per cent and as Methodists at about twenty per cent, with most of the remainder affiliated with Pentecostal and Holiness churches. Beginning in the 1930s, the proportion of African-Americans who are church members has been higher than that of the white population. Until recently, "the Black Church" has not only served as a needed refuge from a hostile world but also as the social and economic center of the African-American community. And the leader of this community, set apart by God and humans through ordination and education, has been the minister. Martin Luther King, Jr.*—Baptist preacher, civil rights leader, Nobel Peace Prize recipient—was the heir of this tradition. His courageous leadership in the struggle for social justice made a significant impact on American society. Following the teachings of Jesus with a proximity seldom witnessed among American Christians, King headed a nonviolent movement which raised the public consciousness regarding racism, discrimination and the exploitation of African-Americans and achieved many of its legislative goals. Its successes rested in a large measure on his inspirational leadership and on the vitality of the African-American churches.

The social upheaval of the 1960s led to the rejection of the liberal consensus which had prevailed in American society since the early 1930s. The new young radicals not only turned their collective backs on Franklin Roosevelt's New Deal politics, but also on liberal mainline Protestantism's brand of Christianity. The collapse of the liberal consensus brought with it a new crisis in American cultural values. The new pluralism made it increasingly difficult to formulate a new cultural consensus and led to what theologian Richard John Neuhaus has called a "naked public square" in American civic life. The moral crisis of the 1960s directly and deeply affected the course of Christian history in America from that time forward to the end of the century.

Religious Ferment and the Evangelical Resurgence, 1965-the Present. The evangelical resurgence which began to take shape in the 1960s took many observers of the religious scene by surprise. However, a closer examination reveals that the evangelicals had been quietly rebuilding their strength and increasing their numbers since the debacle of the 1920s. The foundation for this resurgence was provided by unpublicized-but-effective programs of personal evangelism; the continuation of the revival tradition in many parts of the country; the replacement of lost seminaries with new theological schools and Bible colleges;* the stirrings of a powerful transdenominational neo-Pentecostal/charismatic* movement; and the unheralded, continuing presence of large numbers of evangelicals in nearly all of the major Protestant denominations. In addition, widespread disillusionment with the leadership in the liberal denominations and with the liberal political establishment also provided fertile fields for evangelism. The historic certitudes of the Bible-based message of the evangelicals resonated in the hearts and minds of a generation of Americans brought up on liberal uncertainties, capped in the mid-1960s by the announcement of God's death.*

The evangelical resurgence coalesced around Billy Graham and his evangelistic ministry. Graham, representing a new mainstream evangelicalism, grew in national stature over the years and became the main spokesperson for progressive evangelical Christianity in the 1980s. The founding of the theological journal *Christianity Today** in 1956, with distinguished evangelical theologian Carl F. H. Henry* as its first editor, provided the intellectual underpinnings for the resurgence and gave direction to the movement. Norman Vincent Peale* recovered his biblical faith in the 1960s and joined Graham as a leading evangelical advocate. During the 1970s and 1980s, a whole galaxy of TV evangelists joined pioneer religious telecommunicators Billy Graham and Bishop Fulton Sheen* and became religious celebrities in their own right as they drew the attention of the American viewing public to evangelical themes and concerns. Best known among them were Kathryn Kuhlmann,* Oral Roberts,* Robert Schuller,* Marion G. "Pat" Robertson,* Jerry Falwell,* Jim and Tammy Bakker,* and Jimmy Swaggart.*

These TV evangelists came from a variety of backgrounds, but most commonly fundamentalism and/or the charismatic movement. By this means and through burgeoning evangelistic, missionary and quasi-political organizations, the fundamentalist movement, beginning in the 1960s, enjoyed a renaissance within the larger framework of evangelicalism. Moreover, many of these new fundamentalists became political activists during the 1970s.

By 1980 there was a direct correlation between the level of Christian commitment on the part of fundamentalists and the desire to be politically active. The result was that moral questions once again came to the forefront of political discussion in American life. The catalyst for this change was the Supreme Court's *Roe* v. *Wade* decision on abortion* in 1973, which overrode the laws of all fifty states by permitting abortion on demand. Evangelicals in general and fundamentalists in particular soon joined hands with American Catholics to oppose this ruling, which they felt violated church teaching and the Christian principle of the sacredness of human life. It was out of this kind of concern that fundamentalists, Catholics, Mormons and other religious conservatives soon organized in large numbers for political action. The Moral Majority* (founded in 1979 and disbanded in 1989 by TV evangelist Falwell) was the largest of several of these groups which combined conservative theology with conservative politics. Other evangelicals, such as those who founded Evangelicals for Social Action in 1974, took a different point of view and linked conservative theology to basically liberal politics. In either case, it was clear that evangelical spiritual vitality once again was translating into a drive for political and social reform.*

Perhaps even more important for evangelical renewal and for the impact which Christianity made on American culture in the period after 1965 was the emergence of the charismatic movement. This movement is an international interfaith revival which takes its name from the fact that its adherents believe that they have recovered one or more of the gifts (Greek *charismata*) described in 1 Corinthians 12—14 in the New Testament, especially the gifts of speaking in tongues,* spiritual healing* and exorcism. It began in the 1960s and quickly spread to nearly every major Protestant denomination as well as to Roman Catholic and Eastern Orthodox churches. By this means, charismatic and evangelical themes were introduced into a variety of new ecclesiastical settings and thus helped to spread the evangelical revival. Moreover, in the 1980s large numbers of independent charismatic fellowships, often female-led, came into existence as the movement continued to spread and sometimes fragment.

For their part, American Catholics have experienced spiritual uncertainty and spiritual renewal in about equal amounts since the conclusion of Vatican Council II* (1962-1965). The Second Vatican Council opened the Catholic Church in America to new possibilities in terms of relationships with Protestants (as in the charismatic movement) and new opportunities for Protestants to fraternize and make common cause with Catholics (as in the pro-life, anti-abortion movement). However, it also has caused a certain amount of confusion in American Catholicism concerning identity and goals. In the main, the American Catholic Church has experienced a loss of active communicants since 1965 but an increase in activism among those Catholics who regularly attend Mass.*

The period since 1965 also has been one of religious ferment in general. Numerous new non-Christian and quasi-Christian groups have appeared on the scene to challenge Christian orthodoxy. Chief among these new groups are Islam, occultism and the New Age Movement,* all of which have made their appearance as important forces in American religious life since the mid-1960s.

Another aspect of the general religious renewal of the period has been the intermingling of evangelical Christianity with national politics. This has been particularly true in the presidencies of Richard Nixon* (1969-1974), Gerald Ford* (1974-1977), Jimmy Carter* (1977-1981), Ronald Reagan* (1981-1989) and George Bush (1989-present). All of these chief executives claimed to have been converted to Christ, all openly professed reverence for the Bible and biblical values, and all claimed a special relationship with Billy Graham or other evangelical leaders. Moreover, a new, more virile brand of civil religion developed alongside of, and sometimes in conjunction with, these "religious presidencies." In particular, under the guiding hand of President Reagan, civil religion took on a more decidedly priestly cast and was expanded to religion-in-general to accommodate the growing religious pluralism of the American public during the 1980s.

Paradoxically, as evangelical Christianity in particular and religion in general enjoyed a resurgence during this period, an increasingly secular component in American society also flexed its cultural muscles and made its presence felt. This was especially true of the media, which grew markedly more secular in the era. In addition, the American nation continued to become more pluralistic in every respect, including religion and irreligion, and the new pluralism became different in quantity and kind from that of early America. For example, with the rescission of the Asian Exclusion Act by Congress in 1965, a fundamental adjustment in the religious map of the American nation took place. This action has allowed the flow of immigrants from those countries which had been excluded in 1917 and 1924. Other subsequent changes in the immigration laws have allowed a great ingress of new peoples from non-European countries. Many of the recent immigrants have been Roman Catholics and consequently have found a home in that denomination, while many others have joined the burgeoning Asian-American* and Hispanic-American* evangelical churches that now

[19]

dot the land. Millions of others have come from non-Christian cultures and have resisted assimilation. As a result, by 1990 America contained, in addition to its legions of Christian denominations, more than three million Muslims, as well as more than 100 different Hindu subgroups and more than seventy-five forms of Buddhism. The appointment of the first Buddhist chaplain* in the armed forces in 1987 signaled a new era of religious pluralism in U.S. history.

In the meantime, as religiosity abounds, theological confusion likewise also abounds. Polls indicate that Americans continue to be an overwhelmingly religious people with a firm belief in God. However, beyond this there seems to be little theological consensus concerning what is believed about God. These same Americans want their political leaders to have strong religious beliefs. Evangelicals, the single largest and presumably most theologically cohesive group, are badly divided over politics, economics and social issues. Neuhaus's public square continues to be largely unclothed and value free. The scandals of the Reagan administration, noted for its close identification with fundamentalist concerns, left doubts in the minds of many Americans concerning the ability of evangelicals to lead. And the secular media of the era continued to remind religious Americans of their shortcomings. The spiritual ferment appears destined to continue into the foreseeable future, and so does the moral drift and indecision.

Finally, in terms of the future of Christianity in America and perhaps the future of America itself, there is the paradox of American Christian history. Christianity in its evangelical expression historically has been the dominant faith of the nation. As such, it has fostered both division and unity. Through its sponsorship of religious liberty, it has generated the very pluralism which increasingly threatens national cohesion. At the same time, until recently, it has provided America with a set of common values by means of an evangelical consensus. Revivalism historically has transmitted both division and unity—by making sharp distinctions between the saved and the unsaved in any community, on the one hand, and by converting large segments of the population to evangelical faith and values, on the other. This paradox has not been resolved and may never be.

Whatever the case, the certitude of the Christian message, with its concomitant emphasis on evangelism, continues to divide as it unites. As in the past, that message of certitude has supplied an organizing principle for millions of individuals and groups while at the same time stressing gospel freedom and prophetic social justice. Historically speaking, this has been the main ingredient responsible for producing an ordered society in which both freedom and justice have expanded. Perhaps that has been the supreme paradox in the story of Christianity in America. The potential for order, freedom and social justice inherent in the Christian faith provides both hope and a challenge for the future.

In the meantime, Americans continue to be both "a religious people whose institutions presuppose a Supreme Being" and a religiously divided people. The U.S. is currently the home of more than 1,500 different churches, denominations, sects,* religious societies or cults,* each seeking the primary religious loyalty of its adherents. The majority of these organizations are Christian denominations or churches, and the overwhelming majority of Americans who engage in any outward religious activity are members of one of the more than 900 different Christian groups which are now resident in the U.S. These facts alone illustrate the continuing themes of division and unity generated by the presence of Christianity in America.

BIBLIOGRAPHY

S. E. Ahlstrom, *A Religious History of the American People* (1972); C. L. Albanese, "Religion and the American Experience: A Century Later," *Church History* 57 (September 1988):337-351; L. Baritz, *City on a Hill: A History of Ideas and Myths in America* (1964); R. N. Bellah, *The Broken Covenant: American Civil Religion in Time of Trial* (1975); D. J. Boorstin, *The Americans,* 3 vols. (1958-1973); H. W. Bowden, *American Indians and Christian Missions* (1981); P. A. Carter, *The Spiritual Crisis of the Gilded Age* (1972); C. Cherry, *God's New Israel: Religious Interpretations of American Destiny* (1971); W. R. Cross, *The Burned Over District* (1950); D. W. Dayton, *Discovering an Evangelical Heritage* (1976); J. P. Dolan, *The American Catholic Experience: A History from Colonial Times to the Present* (1987); J. P. Dolan, *Catholic Revivalism: The American Experience, 1830-1900* (1978); R. H. Gabriel, *The Course of American Democratic Thought,* 2nd ed. (1956); E. S. Gaustad, *Faith of Our Fathers: Religion and the New Nation* (1987); E. S. Gaustad, *Historical Atlas of Religion in America,* rev. ed. (1976); R. T. Handy, "The American Religious Depression, 1925-1935," *CH* 29 (March 1960):3-16; R. T. Handy, *A Christian America: Protestant Hopes and Historical Realities,* rev. ed. (1984); R. T. Handy, *A History of the Churches in the United States and Canada* (1979); N. A. Hardesty, *Women Called to Witness: Evangelical Feminism in the Nineteenth Century* (1984); N. O. Hatch, *The Sacred Cause of Liberty: Millennial Thought in Revolutionary New England* (1977); N. O. Hatch and M. A. Noll, eds., *The Bible in America: Essays in Cultural History* (1982); N. O. Hatch and H. S. Stout, eds., *Jonathan Edwards and the American Experience* (1988); A. E. Heimert, *Religion and the American Mind from the Great Awakening to the Revolution* (1966); J. Hennesey, *American Catholics: A History of the Roman Catholic Community in the United States* (1981); W. Herberg, *Protestant—Catholic—Jew,* rev. ed. (1960); C. H. Hopkins, *The Rise of the Social Gospel in American Protestantism, 1865-1915* (1940); W. S. Hudson, *Religion in America,* 4th ed. (1987); R. T. Hughes, ed., *The American Quest for the Primitive Church* (1988); W. R. Hutchison, *The Modernist Impulse in American Protestantism* (1976); J. W. James, ed., *Women in American Religion* (1980); C. A. Johnson, *The Frontier Camp Meeting* (1955); S. M. Lipset, *The First New Nation,* rev. ed. (1979); R. W. Lovin, ed., *Religion and American Public Life* (1986); W. G. McLoughlin, ed., *The American Evangelicals, 1800-1900* (1968); W. G. McLoughlin, *Revivals, Awakenings, and Reform* (1978); N. A. Magnuson, *Salvation in the Slums: Evangelical Social Work, 1865-1920* (1977); G. M. Marsden, ed., *Evangelicalism and Modern America* (1984); G. M. Marsden, *Fundamentalism and American Culture* (1980); M. E. Marty, "Ethnicity: The Skeleton of Religion in America," *CH* 41 (March 1972):9-14; M. E. Marty, *The Kingdom of God in America,* rev. ed. (1988); M. E. Marty, *Modern American Religion, vol. I: The Irony of It All, 1893-1919* (1986); M. E. Marty, *A Nation of Behavers* (1976); M. E. Marty, *Pilgrims in Their Own Land: 500 Years of Religion in America* (1984); M. E. Marty, *Protestantism in the United States: Righteous Empire,* 2nd ed. (1986); M. E. Marty, *Religion and Republic: the American Circumstance* (1987); D. G. Mathews, *Religion in the Old South* (1977); H. F. May, *The Enlightenment in America* (1976); H. F. May, *Protestant Churches and Industrial America* (1949); S. E. Mead, *The Lively Experiment: The Shaping of American Christianity* (1963); S. E. Mead, *The Nation with the Soul of a Church* (1975); J. G. Melton, *The Encyclopedia of American Religions,* 3rd ed. (1989); P. Miller, *Errand into the Wilderness* (1956); P. Miller, *The Life of the Mind in America: From the Revolution to the Civil War* (1965); E. S. Morgan, *Visible Saints: The History of a Puritan Idea* (1963); H. M. Nelson et al., *The Black Church in America* (1971); R. J. Neuhaus, *The Naked Public Square: Religion and Democracy in America* (1984); M. A. Noll, *Christians in the American Revolution* (1977); M. A. Noll et al., eds., *Eerdmans' Handbook to Christianity in America* (1983); M. A. Noll et al., *The Search for a Christian America* (1983); R. V. Pierard and R. D. Linder, *Civil Religion and the Presidency* (1988); R. Quebedeaux, *The New Charismatics: The Origins, Development, and Significance of Neo-Pentecostalism* (1976); A. J. Raboteau, *Slave Religion* (1978); W. C. Roof and W. McKinney, *American Mainline Religion: Its Changing Shape and Future* (1987); B. L. Shelley, *Evangelicalism in America* (1967); A. Simpson, *Puritanism in Old and New England* (1955); J. W. Smith and A. L. Jamison, eds., *The Shaping of American Religion* (1961); T. L. Smith, *Revivalism and Social Reform in Mid-Nineteenth Century America,* rev. ed. (1980); J. B. Stewart, *Holy Warriors: The Abolitionists and American Slavery* (1976); A. P. Stokes, *Church and State in the United States,* 3 vols. (1950); H. S. Stout, *The New England Soul: Preaching and Religious Culture in Colonial New England* (1986); V. Synan, *The Holiness-Pentecostal Movement in the United States* (1972); L. I. Sweet, ed., *The Evangelical Tradition in America* (1984); V. Synan, *The Twentieth-Century Pentecostal Explosion* (1987); R. Tucker and W. Liefeld, *Daughters of the Church: Women and Ministry from New Testament Times to the*

Present (1987); E. L. Tuveson, *Redeemer Nation: The Idea of America's Millennial Role* (1968); T. L. Weber, *Living in the Shadow of the Second Coming* (1981); D. L. Weddle, *The Law as Gospel: Revival and Reform in the Theology of Charles G. Finney* (1985); D. F. Wells and J. D. Woodbridge, eds., *The Evangelicals: What They Believe, Who They Are, How They Are Changing*, rev. ed. (1977); R. A. Wells, ed., *The Wars of America: Christian Views* (1981); Williamsburg Charter Foundation, *The Williamsburg Charter Survey on Religion and Public Life* (1988); G. S. Wilmore, *Black Religion and Black Radicalism*, rev. ed. (1983); J. F. Wilson and D. L. Drakeman, eds., *Church and State in American History*, 2nd ed. (1987); J. D. Woodbridge et al., *The Gospel in America* (1979).

R. D. Linder

A

Abbott, Lyman (1835-1922). Congregationalist* minister* and editor. A graduate of New York University (1853), Lyman Abbott had a brief career as a lawyer before being ordained* as a Congregationalist minister in 1860. After serving a church in Indiana during the Civil War,* Abbott moved to New York City where he both pastored a church and helped direct the educational efforts of the American Freedmen's Union Commission in the South (1865-1869). Later Abbott was Henry Ward Beecher's* successor as minister of the Plymouth Church in Brooklyn, New York (1888-1899).

Abbott's widest influence came through his editorial labors. He edited the *Illustrated Christian Weekly* for six years before assuming the editorship of the *Christian Union* in 1876. For the next forty-six years that journal (renamed *Outlook* in 1893) functioned as a religious weekly paper of liberal opinion.

Unlike Beecher in his socio-economic views, Abbott was always interested in social reform and championed Theodore Roosevelt's Progressivism for nearly two decades. Like Beecher, though, Abbott's earlier evangelical* convictions gave way to a decidedly liberal* theology. Neither an accomplished theologian nor scientist, Abbott did, nonetheless, popularize the "assured results" of a skeptical biblical criticism* and in works such as *The Evolution of Christianity* (1892) and *The Theology of an Evolutionist* (1897) applied the principle of evolution to his elaboration of religious faith. Not content with being labeled a Darwinist,* Abbott was an optimistic evolutionist who believed that "what Jesus was, humanity is becoming."

See also BEECHER, HENRY WARD

BIBLIOGRAPHY. L. Abbott, *Reminiscences* (1915); I. V. Brown, *Lyman Abbott: Christian Evolutionist* (1953); *DAB* I; *DARB;* W. W. Sweet, *Makers of Christianity: From John Cotton to Lyman Abbott* (1937). S. R. Pointer

Aberhart, William ("Bible Bill") (1878-1943). Radio pioneer and premier of Alberta. Born in Ontario and trained as a schoolteacher, Aberhart first emerged into prominence as a Baptist* Bible* teacher in Calgary, Alberta. His weekly classes on dispensationalism* filled the downtown Grand Theater and were broadcast to a radio audience that was estimated at 350,000. When the Depression came, Aberhart shifted his attention to the economic and political needs of the province and founded the Social Credit Party on the ideas of Englishman C. H. Douglas. With Aberhart devoting much time in his weekly broadcasts to politics, the party won two provincial elections (1935 and 1940). Aberhart died in office, having introduced reforms particularly in the areas of education and farm relief. His increasingly unorthodox theology,* egocentricity, sectarianism and especially his involvement in politics, eventually alienated him from large numbers of evangelicals.* But the Social Credit Party remained in power in Alberta until 1971.

BIBLIOGRAPHY. W. Aberhart, *The Douglas System of Economics* (1933); J. A. Boudreau, *Alberta, Aberhart, and Social Credit* (1975); D. R. Elliott and I. Miller, *Bible Bill: A Biography of William Aberhart* (1987). J. G. Stackhouse

Abolition and the Churches. At the time of the Revolutionary War,* none of the denominations* had a tradition of opposition to slavery. However, the growing emphasis on natural rights in the post-Revolutionary era led the Methodists,* many Baptist* associations and the Scotch-Irish Presbyterians* either to adopt pro-emancipation statements or specifically to condemn slavery. Accommodation to the Southern institution had become the rule again by the 1820s as these groups, along with the more regional denominations (e.g., Congregationalists,* Unitarians,* Universalists* and Disciples of Christ*), refused to condemn slaveholders as sinners or to take disciplinary measures against slaveholding members.

Many did support the American Colonization Society* (organized 1817), which sought to emancipate slaves gradually with remuneration to their masters and to send free African-Americans to Africa. Before 1830 only the Quakers* (as early as 1776), the Freewill Baptists* and the small Scottish* Presbyterian groups had actually debarred slaveholding members. With few exceptions, the more liturgical* Lutheran,* Episcopal* and Roman Catholic* churches remained aloof from the issue and defended the status quo. It was the movement for "immediate emancipation," developing primarily from the Second Great Awakening,* that began to challenge the equivocal stance of the traditionally evangelical* churches.

The surge of revivalism* in the 1820s and 1830s stressed immediate and complete repentance from sin and encouraged* disinterested benevolence and perfectionism.* Many Northern evangelicals soon related these ideas to the issue of slavery and became advocates of immediate abolition. Most prominent among them was Theodore D. Weld,* a convert of the great revivalist Charles G. Finney.* Early in 1833 Weld began to denounce the colonization movement for diverting criticism from slavery and to proclaim slaveholding and the condoning of it as sinful. He called on Christians of both North and South to repent immediately and to work to end the institution of slavery. Later that year Northern Christian abolitionists, including William L. Garrison,* formed the American Antislavery Society to work for emancipation and to win the churches to moral condemnation of slaveholding.

As this agitation for abolition continued within the denominations, several schisms resulted. Of major proportions were the North-South divisions among the Methodists (1844) over the acceptance of a slaveholding bishop* and among the Baptists (1845) over the appointment of slaveholding missionaries. In both cases the Southern constituencies forced the issues and by their intransigency made division inevitable. The Northern factions were motivated in their opposition to these issues both by growing antislavery sentiment and concerns about loss of members to come-outer groups such as the Wesleyan* Methodist Connection and the American Baptist Free Mission Society, which had left the denominations in protest over lack of abolition action. (Similar groups split off from the Presbyterians, Lutherans and Friends.*) Nevertheless, Baptists and Methodists in the North continued to compete for members in the border states with no prohibition against slaveholding.

Thus, while abolitionist agitation succeeded in moving most of the major Northern denominations away from neutrality on the slavery issue, it did not move them to unqualified moral condemnation. It also hardened Southern churches in their arguments that slavery was scriptural and indeed a positive good. Consequently, America abolished slavery not through moral or religious persuasion but through political and military means.

See also Civil War and the Churches; Emancipation Proclamation.

Bibliography. G. H. Barnes, *The Antislavery Impulse, 1830-1844* (1933); J. R. McKivigan, *The War Against Proslavery Religion: Abolitionism and the Northern Churches, 1830-1865* (1984).

M. S. Shanaberger

Abortion. Much of the impetus, organization and financing of the antiabortion movement in contemporary American society owes to the leadership of conservative Christian bodies. The presence of American Christians at the forefront of the antiabortion, or "pro-life," movement is so pronounced that a casual observer might be led to think that there has always been a single position on the nature of unborn human life and a single position on the morality of abortion in American Christianity and its European predecessors. Such observations, while understandable in light of the vigor and absoluteness with which the antiabortion position is held by many Christians, would not be entirely accurate. While Christianity in all its forms has never rested easy with abortion, European and American Christians historically have held a variety of opinions on the nature of the fetus and on whether its protection must be absolute. Even today they represent a wide range of convictions and viewpoints.

Roman Catholic* Christianity, in the U.S. as elsewhere, has held to the view that the fetus receives its soul very early in its development, although the Catholic position has never actually specified the exact point when this happens prior to birth. As ensouled, it was innocent humanity, to be protected against nearly every action that would destroy it. By 1869 it was ruled that all who were involved in performing abortions would be excommunicated.* Although Catholic teaching on abortion has been strict, its impact on American policy has been limited in the late nineteenth and the twentieth centuries by American Catholicism's relative newcomer status as an alien and immigrant faith.

For theological reasons Protestantism historically had been even more forcefully opposed to abortion than had Catholicism. The Protestant Reformers had taught that the fetus inherited its sin* nature at conception and thus was fully human at that time. They were led by the logic of this theological point to reject the option of abortion, even at the earliest stages of pregnancy. American Protestants of the eighteenth and nineteenth centuries were less concerned about the status of the fetus, since to those in the Calvinist* tradition the issue of predestination* to salvation* or damnation was the crucial concern, and this was settled even before conception. At the same time, those in the revivalist* tradition were more interested in adult conversion* than in the nature of the fetus. In American Protestantism, opposition to abortion was more likely to be grounded on the fact that it enabled people to evade the consequences of their sinful sexual behaviors, a reason which also would underlie their continued opposition to artificial birth control* well into the twentieth century. Abortion was also opposed as an option for nineteenth-century American Protestants because they believed themselves to have a divine responsibility to reproduce offspring who would have a role in shaping a (Protestant) Christian America.

In this century American Protestant theologians have tended to maintain an antiabortion position, based not on church tradition but on Scripture.* Notable European Protestant theologians who upheld the sanctity of fetal life included Dietrich Bonhoeffer,* Helmut Theilicke and Karl Barth,* while in this country Presbyterian* theologian Paul Ramsey led the antiabortion camp.

Biblical themes that tended to maintain an antiabortion stance include the value of each life as a divine creation, a stress on the woman's body as her responsibility for stewardship rather than as her possession, and an emphasis on the communal rather than individualistic nature of Christian believing. The dignity of the fetus and newborn was implied by the tradition of infant baptism,* since as David H. Smith has affirmed that "it would be hard to hold . . . that a being who might be baptized was lacking in human dignity." In all of these affirmations, Christians have found themselves increasingly at odds with an egoistic, individualistic, reductionistic and pluralistic society.

On the other side of the issue, the Protestant tradition has resources that would lead at least to a grudging support for abortion in some circumstances, and for retaining this decision as a matter for individual conscience.* Views more permissive on abortion appeared first in the Protestant laity* and then in the theological leadership, generating a Protestant minority that has maintained that women's rights to self-determination and other social concerns would justify not only the right of women to choose for themselves but also the decision for abortion itself. Joseph Fletcher, in his earlier years, was among the most visible supporters of this view.

Nineteenth-century Protestant optimism about social progress and its strong social conscience would contribute to a developing liberalized view on abortion, particularly as abortion could be seen as a way to alleviate social ills as well as to express support for the dignity of women. Other Protestant values that would compete with the dominant antiabortion view include the stress on the liberty of individual conscience, the unavoidability of complex and ambiguous choices, and the availability of grace and forgiveness. It has been argued that the Protestant emphasis on individual liberty, now secularized, has become the secular American ethic of self-determination, autonomy and resistance to legislated morality.

A review of positions taken on abortion by American Christian denominations* shows substantial variation. A strong opposition to abortion under any circumstance except to save the mother's life is maintained by the various Orthodox churches.* At the other extreme, the United Church of Christ* "calls for repeal of all legal prohibitions of physician-performed abortions, thus making voluntary and medically safe abortions available to all women." Others aligned with the strong antiabortion position include the Church of the Brethren,* the Reformed Church of America* and many smaller evangelical* bodies. Churches supporting individual choice in abortion decisions, include the Lutheran Church in America* and the American Lutheran Church* (now united as the Evangelical Lutheran Church of America*), the Episcopal Church* and the Presbyterian Church (U.S.A.).

Opposition to government intrusion in the decision whether to abort is strong in many Protestant bodies, including the conservative Southern Baptists.* This opposition must not, however, be taken to imply an unqualified acceptance of abortion; most of the denominations speak forcefully against abortion "for convenience" as a method of birth control and as a means of population control, and call for the clergy and the church as a whole to provide care and counseling. In the late 1980s, however, there is a noticeable movement in the assemblies of the major Protestant denominations to introduce more conservative statements on abortion and to relax their opposition to governmental restrictions on the availability of abortion. It seems likely that this trend will continue.

In the years following the 1973 Supreme Court decision, evangelicals have entered into the abortion debate. It is noteworthy that Carl F. H. Henry's* *Christian Personal Ethics* (1957) does not contain an entry on the topic. As abortions become more widespread in this country, evangelicals have become increasingly aware of the problem of abortion. Evangelical thinking has followed the work of Francis Schaeffer,* Harold O. J. Brown, James Dobson and others in repudiating abortion and in seeking legislation to make it unavailable. An evangelical minority has attempted to offer alternatives to the dominant evangelical position, expressing a desire to maintain greater freedom for women in making these decisions, based on concern for women's self-determination and social welfare. Others, such as philosopher Robert Wennberg and scientist D. Gareth Jones, have argued for the limited permissibility of abortion in special cases, such as serious fetal defects. Despite these efforts, a strong antiabortion position has taken its place among doctrinal assertions to become virtually an item of faith for many evangelicals, as they have united with secular antiabortion groups to lobby for the repeal of permissive legislation. *See also* BIRTH CONTROL; RIGHT TO LIFE.

BIBLIOGRAPHY. "Church Policy Statements," in *Biomedical-Ethical Issues: A Digest of Law and Policy Development* (1983); J. R. Connery, "Abortion: Roman Catholic Perspectives," and J. B. Nelson, "Abortion: Protestant Perspectives," in W. T. Reich, ed., *The Encyclopedia of Bioethics* (1978); J. Hoffmeier, ed., *Abortion: A Christian Understanding and Response* (1987); M. E. Marty, *Health and Medicine in the Lutheran Tradition* (1983); J. T. Noonan, Jr., ed., *The Morality of Abortion: Legal and Historical Perspectives* (1970); D. H. Smith, *Health and Medicine in the Anglican Tradition* (1986); K. L. Vaux, *Health and Medicine in the Reformed Tradition* (1984).

D. B. Fletcher

Absolution. Declaration of forgiveness of sins. Absolution may be viewed as the human side of the sinner's finding forgiveness. Biblical teaching shows that only God forgives sin. It also shows that a person's subjective experience of forgiveness may be aided by other believers (Jn 20:23; 2 Cor 2:6-8; Gal 6:1).

In some churches, notably Catholic* and some Episcopal,* absolution is performed by the priest,* who announces forgiveness in the form "I absolve thee" to the penitent making confession. This is called "positive" or "indicative" absolution. Most American Protestant* churches reject this sacramental* view of absolution. They consider a more biblical pattern to be proclamation of assurance

that God forgives sins through Christ, such as "In Jesus Christ we are forgiven." This public affirmation often follows a prayer of confession, which might be private, pastoral or congregational. This is called "declaratory" or "precatory" absolution, although often Protestants do not actually use these words.

BIBLIOGRAPHY. J. R. W. Stott, *Confess Your Sins* (1964). P. D. Steeves

Abstinence. In its most technical sense, *abstinence* denotes a restricted form of fasting* that limits the type of food but not the quantity. For example, the Catholic* church distinguishes between abstinence from flesh-meat on Fridays and fasting, which allows only one meal in twenty-four hours. A wider application of the term advocates refraining from other actions such as alcohol* consumption, marriage and participation in larger society. Abstinence took an important place in the early church, especially among monastic communities. Friday abstinence by Christians in commemoration of the Passion is mentioned by Clement of Alexandria (c.155-c.220) and Tertullian (c.160-c.215) as an established custom. Benedict required all but the sick of the monks of his order to "abstain from the flesh of four-footed beasts." The sixteenth-century Protestant* reformers attacked the medieval Catholic views of abstinence, while the nineteenth-century evangelical* revivals stimulated societies in the U.S. to espouse total abstinence from alcohol (*See* Prohibition Movement; Temperance Movement). D. A. Scalberg

Acadian Expulsion. The expelling of the French Catholic population of Nova Scotia in 1755-1763. The Acadians, or Neutral French, were the descendants of fur traders, fishermen and laborers who had settled in the French colony of Acadie (now Nova Scotia) in the early 1600s. Largely neglected by the French government, these settlers evolved a successful lifestyle based on farming of the marshlands (which they dyked), fishing and trading with the native peoples and the nearby merchants of Boston.

Acadie was formally ceded to England by the Treaty of Utrecht in 1713. The treaty guaranteed the Acadians freedom of religion if they remained in the colony, an unusual concession to Roman Catholics in this period. However, their Catholicism and suspected French sympathies brought distrust from their new government and that of nearby Massachusetts. Fearing the loss of the colony to the French, the Nova Scotia government finally decided on expulsion. Between 1755 and

1763 approximately 10,000 Acadians were deprived of their farms and homes and sent into exile in the thirteen colonies, England and France. In the U.S., Canada and France, the Acadians have remained a distinct entity down to the present day. A large number of Catholics in today's southern Louisiana and southeast Texas owe their heritage to the Acadians, and a distinctive Cajun culture still exists in southern Louisiana (the word *Cajun* being an alteration of *Acadian*).

BIBLIOGRAPHY. A. G. Doughty, *The Acadian Exiles* (1916); N. Griffiths, *The Acadians: Creation of a People* (1973).   B. M. Moody

Adams, Hannah (1755-1831). Religious writer and historian. Born at Medfield, Massachusetts, and self-educated, Adams attempted to turn her academic interests into a profession. Her first book, *An Alphabetical Compendium of the Various Sects* (1784), was a survey of the Calvinist-Arminian debate in America, describing the various denominations present at the time. The work appeared, in her words, at a time "when a book from a female hand was almost without precedent," and appeared in four editions. Another major compendium of information, *A Summary History of New-England* (1799), brought her the patronage of Boston's leading intellectuals and a public controversy with the Reverend Jedidiah Morse,* who charged that it was a deliberate infringement on a volume he was about to publish. Two other books, *The Truth and Excellence of the Christian Religion Exhibited* (1804) and *A History of the Jews* (1812) helped establish her reputation as a woman of learning and literary skill, and reflected her Unitarian* beliefs. She was the first self-supporting female author in America—though she consistently characterized herself as timid and socially awkward.

BIBLIOGRAPHY. H. Adams, *A Memoir of Miss Hannah Adams, Written by Herself* (1832); *DAB* I; *NAW* 1.   M. L. Bendroth

Adams, Theodore Floyd (1898-1980). Baptist* pastor,* educator and leader in the Baptist World Alliance.* Born in Palmyra, New York, the son of a Baptist minister, Adams graduated from Denison University (B.A., 1921) and Colgate Rochester Divinity School (B.D., 1924). Ordained* in 1924, he served as pastor of the Cleveland Heights Baptist Church in Cleveland, Ohio (1924-1927), and the Ashland Avenue Baptist Church in Toledo, Ohio (1927-1936), before accepting the pastorate of the historic First Baptist Church of Richmond, Virginia, where he remained as pastor (1936-1968)

and pastor emeritus (1968-1980) until his death. For a decade (1968-1978) he taught preaching* at Southeastern Seminary.

His balanced ministry at Richmond stressed missions,* pastoral care and social concern. He conducted a daily radio program for twenty-six years and became involved in television locally and nationally. An active trustee of Virginia Union University (from 1941) and the University of Richmond (from 1942) for almost four decades, he encouraged the founding of Richmond Memorial Hospital (1957) and chaired its board. Adams received ten honorary doctorates and many awards. He served the Baptist World Alliance on its executive committee (1934-1980), as vice president (1947-1950) and president (1955-1960). He published four books, including *Baptists around the World* (1967).

BIBLIOGRAPHY. John W. Carlton, *The World in His Heart: The Life and Legacy of Theodore F. Adams* (1985).   C. L. Howe

Addams, Jane (1860-1935). Settlement house* founder, social reformer, suffragist and peace activist. Born in Cedarville, Illinois, Addams was educated at Rockford Female Seminary in Rockford, Illinois (B.A., 1882), where she steadfastly resisted the institution's attempt to shape her into a Christian missionary.* Addams studied medicine at Women's Medical College of Pennsylvania for one year (1881-1882) but decided against the medical profession. Addams spent several years in Europe (1883-1885, 1887-1889) and did some graduate study in England. There she also observed firsthand the miseries of urban poverty. Upon returning to her hometown in 1885, she joined the Presbyterian Church,* though she had been raised a Quaker.*

Addams is best known for her work with Ellen Gates Starr* in founding Hull House (1889). Located in Chicago's impoverished Nineteenth Ward, Hull House provided clubs, classes and activities to meet the needs of the primarily immigrant neighborhood. Politically, Addams advocated progressive reforms and was influenced more by the pragmatism of William James* and John Dewey than she was by religious considerations.

Addams held office in several national organizations. In 1909 she became the first woman president of the National Conference of Charities and Correction. She served as a vice president of the National American Woman's Suffrage Association from 1911 to 1914. Her belief in free expression led her to help found the American Civil Liberties

Union in 1920. She was the first president of the Women's International League of Peace and Freedom, serving from 1919 until her death. In 1931 she received the Nobel Peace Prize.

BIBLIOGRAPHY. J. W. Linn, *Jane Addams* (1935); *NAW* 1. S. C. Stanley

Adger, John Bailey (1810-1899). Presbyterian* minister* and missionary.* Born in Charleston, South Carolina, Adger attended Union College and Princeton Theological Seminary.* From 1834 to 1847 he served with the American Board of Commissioners for Foreign Missions* as a missionary among the Armenian people in Constantinople and Smyrna.

Adger moved back to Charleston in 1847, where he organized the Anson Street Chapel, later known as Zion Presbyterian Church, and operated a plantation. Called in 1857 to the faculty of Columbia Theological Seminary, Adger taught church history and church polity there until he retired in 1874. In a Southern Presbyterian dispute over the teaching of evolution, Adger sided with James Woodrow,* a faculty colleague who favored the reconciliation of science and theology. Active as a writer and leader in the Presbyterian Church in the U.S. (PCUS),* Adger served as an editor of the *Southern Presbyterian Review* from 1857 until 1885 and helped draft the PCUS *Book of Church Order* (1879).

BIBLIOGRAPHY. J. B. Adger, *My Life and Times, 1810-1899* (1899). L. B. Weeks

Adopting Act (1729). An action of the Synod* of Philadelphia whereby the Westminster Confession of Faith* and Catechisms* were adopted as the doctrinal position of the Presbyterian Church* in colonial America. Subscription to these standards was required of all ministers and ministerial candidates. The Synod, created in 1717 out of the Presbytery of Philadelphia, was the highest Presbyterian governing body *(see* Church Government: Presbyterian*) in America.

Until 1729 American Presbyterianism* operated without an official doctrinal standard and without requiring creedal subscription of its ministers. The Adopting Act was the result of a compromise between the dominant Scotch and Scotch-Irish party, which desired strict subscription, and those of English and New England background, led by Jonathan Dickinson,* who did not want to see fallible, human documents imposed as tests of orthodoxy* and ordination.* The Act required all ministers and licentiates to subscribe to these doctrinal standards "as being, in all the essential and necessary articles, good forms of sound words and systems of Christian doctrine; and . . . as the confession of our faith." The Act provided that one who had scruples regarding one or more of the articles in these standards could still be approved, if one's synod or presbytery* judged that these differences were over nonessentials. In fact, all members of the synod did take exception to the Confession's statements on the role and responsibility of the civil magistrate in religious matters.

See also SCOTTISH PRESBYTERIANISM; SUBSCRIPTION CONTROVERSY.

BIBLIOGRAPHY. L. J. Trinterud, *The Forming of an American Tradition: A Reexamination of Colonial Presbyterianism* (1949); G. S. Klett, ed., *Minutes of the Presbyterian Church in America, 1706-1788* (1976). A. H. Freundt

Advent. A season of preparation for Christmas,* more characteristic of Western liturgical* churches. The advent theme, focused on the coming of Christ at the consummation of history, is found in the fifth century at Rome in sermons of Leo I for the winter seasonal fast, a fast lasting for only three days in one week. The extension of the fast to several weeks appeared first in Gaul in the sixth century. Canon 17 of the Synod of Tours (567) assigned three times of intensified fasting for monks: Lent,* a period following Pentecost* and the month of December up to Christmas. A fast before Christmas was enjoined for all the church by a council at Mâcon in 581, beginning from the Feast of St. Martin of Tours (November 11), from which it came to be called "St. Martin's Lent." The forty days of the season could be marked with either six or five Sundays of Advent, but most now observe only four.

While Advent has always been characterized by a heightened soberness, it has not been strictly penitential as has Lent, a time for public penitential exercises. The contrast is shown by the decision of a council at Toledo in 656 to observe the feast of the Annunciation a week before Christmas rather than on the previously accepted date of March 25, because that March date inappropriately fell during Lent. In recent lectionary reforms, Annunciation accounts have been assigned to the fourth Sunday of Advent. The four Sundays are popularly marked in homes by lighting, in order, four candles mounted on an evergreen "Advent wreath."

BIBLIOGRAPHY. A. A. McArthur, *The Evolution of the Christian Year* (1953); T. J. Talley, *The Origins of the Liturgical Year* (1986).

T. J. Talley

Africa Inland Mission. Interdenominational and international mission agency. Founded in 1895 by Peter Cameron Scott,* AIM was first promoted by the Philadelphia Missionary Council. Almost concurrently the Philadelphia Bible Institute was established, and one of its leaders, Charles Hurlbert, became the Mission's first general director following Scott's death in 1896.

During Hurlbert's twenty-five years of leadership, the Mission advanced into new areas and tribes. He was assisted by the pioneering triumvirate of Lee Downing, Albert Barnett and John Stauffacher. Ministries of social concern began early and have continued as an integral part of the Mission's primary commitment to evangelization, church planting and nurturing.

The Mission is a member of the Interdenominational Foreign Mission Association* which it helped to found in 1917. Because of a financial policy of nonsolicitation, this group became known as a faith mission.* As with other missions of this genre, AIM's financial approach has seen significant modification, especially in recent years.

The Mission has approximately eight-hundred active members from fifteen countries, over one hundred of which are on short-term assignments. A growing number come from Asia and Latin America. Its missionaries serve in fourteen fields in East, Central and Southern Africa, the Indian Ocean and three urban centers in the U.S. The churches related to the Mission, all fully autonomous, have an estimated membership of two million, with many thousands of adherents.

The Mission's international headquarters is located in Bristol, England, and serves a coordinating role in AIM's infrastructure and as a liaison with external agencies.

See also MISSIONS, EVANGELICAL FOREIGN.

BIBLIOGRAPHY.   C. S. Miller, *Peter Cameron Scott: The Unlocked Door* (1955); G. Stauffacher, *Faster Beats the Drum* (1977); J. H. Westervelt, *On Safari for God: The Life and Labors of John Stauffacher* (1950).   J. Gration

African Methodist Episcopal Church. The largest African-American Methodist* denomination.* The African Methodist Episcopal Church (AMEC) was founded by Richard Allen* and his followers, who refused to accept their second-class status in St. George's Methodist Episcopal Church in Philadelphia. At Sunday services in November 1787, the trustees of St. George's tried to remove the African-American members from their places of prayer at the altar.* Allen and Absalom Jones led the African-American members of the congregation

out of the church in protest. With his own money, Allen purchased a blacksmith shop and began holding services there. Most of the African-American members of St. George's were also members of the Free African Society,* a nonreligious benevolent society organized by Allen. The Free African Society was the foundation upon which Allen built his blacksmith-shop congregation, later named Bethel.

Bishop Francis Asbury* of the Methodist Episcopal Church dedicated Bethel Church in Philadelphia in 1793 and ordained Allen a deacon* in 1799. Although St. George's tried to keep the rebel African-American congregation and its property under its jurisdiction, Allen sued to maintain the autonomy of the Bethel congregation.

African-American members of two white churches in Baltimore also declared their independence and established the Colored Methodist Society. In 1801 Daniel Coker* became the leader of the Baltimore group, which also named their church Bethel. In April 1816 representatives from the Bethel churches in Philadelphia and Baltimore, and African-American Methodists from other communities, met at Bethel Church in Philadelphia to establish the AMEC. Bishop Francis Asbury* consecrated Allen as the first bishop of the church. The AMEC Discipline, Twenty-Five Articles of Religion, General Rules and the episcopal* structure remained close in doctrine and practice to the Methodist Episcopal Church. Allen had a fundamental belief in the spiritual and moral teachings and doctrines of the founder of Methodism, John Wesley.* Yet, he wanted to insure that the rituals of the church responded to the conditions of the African-American community. In place of the emphasis on rituals and dogma,* Allen wanted African-American Methodists to focus on a pious, moral life.

The church began the AME Book Concern, the first publishing house owned and operated by African-Americans. In 1847, the church began publishing a weekly magazine, which became *The Christian Recorder,* the oldest African-American newspaper in the world. The first AME college, Wilberforce University, was founded in 1856. In 1883 they began the *AME Church Review,* the oldest African-American magazine published by African-Americans.

After Reconstruction the AMEC expanded from 20,000 members in 1856 to over 200,000 members by 1876. The church established foreign missions* to the Caribbean, South America and Africa. Before the Civil War,* the church had fulfilled a strongly felt obligation to Africa with missionaries like

Daniel Coker, who went to Liberia in 1820 under the auspices of the American Colonization Society,* and Scipio Bean, who went to Haiti in 1827. After the Civil War, Bishop Henry McNeal Turner* and Martin Delaney continued to advocate a religious pan-Africanism and black nationalism.

The denomination has thirteen districts with thirteen bishops. The last statistics provided in 1981 showed that there were 6,200 churches with a membership of 2,210,000 in the U.S. There are nine AMEC congregations in Canada.

BIBLIOGRAPHY. R. Allen, *The Life, Experience and Gospel Labors of the Rt. Rev. Richard Allen* (1793); C. V. R. George, *Segregated Sabbaths: Richard Allen and the Rise of Independent Black Churches, 1760-1840* (1973); R. C. Ransom, *Preface to the History of the A.M.E. Church* (1950); G. S. Wilmore, *Black Religion and Black Radicalism: An Interpretation of the Religious History of Afro-American People* (1983).

L. J. Edwards

African Methodist Episcopal Zion Church.
Second-largest African-American Methodist* denomination.* In 1796 Peter Williams, James Varick,* George Collins and Christopher Rush led disaffected African-American members out of John's Street Methodist Episcopal Zion Church in New York. The African-American members refused to accept the discrimination and segregation imposed by the John's Street Church where they were not allowed to preach* or to be official voting members of the conference. James Varick and other African-American leaders petitioned Bishop Francis Asbury* to let them hold their own meetings apart from the John's Street Church. Bishop Asbury approved the request and separate meetings began in 1796 and the first church, called Zion, was built in 1800. A year later, the church received its charter under the name *African Methodist Episcopal Church of the City of New York.*

In 1813 a group of members left the Zion Church to form Asbury Church. Until he left the Methodist Episcopal Church in 1820, a white member of the John's Street Church, William Stillwell, served as minister for both congregations. In spite of this loose affiliation, the members of Zion Church refused to be reabsorbed into the John's Street Church. Nor did they want to join another independent African-American church, the African Methodist Episcopal Church,* which had been incorporated in 1816 in Philadelphia.

When the church members could find no one in the Episcopal or the Methodist churches to ordain

or consecrate* their elders, they consecrated them independently. At the first annual conference held on June 21, 1821, nineteen preachers representing six African-American Methodist churches in New York, New Haven, Newark and Philadelphia organized the African Methodist Episcopal Zion Church (AMEZC) with Varick as the first bishop. The AMEZC adopted the rituals and doctrines of the Methodist Episcopal Church as found in the Twenty-five Articles of Religion, the Discipline, the General Rules and the episcopal* structure. The denomination's episcopal polity divides the church into twelve districts with twelve bishops. The name *African Methodist Episcopal Zion Church* was adopted in 1848.

After the Civil War,* the AMEZ churches spread throughout the South. Home missions were established in Louisiana, Mississippi and Oklahoma. By 1880 the church not only had fifteen annual conferences in the South, but in that same year it established Livingstone College at Salisbury, North Carolina, the church's largest educational institution. Eventually the church founded five secondary schools and two colleges, including Hood Theological Seminary. The church has foreign missions* in the Caribbean, Africa and South America. In 1892 the church started the departments of missions, education and publications and currently publishes four major publications: *Star of Zion,* published weekly; *Quarterly Review,* published quarterly; *Missionary Seer,* published monthly; and *Church School Herald,* published quarterly.

In 1906, the denomination had 184,542 members in 2,197 churches in the U.S. In the 1980s the AMEZ Church was the second-largest African-American Methodist denomination, with 1,202,229 members in 6,057 churches reported in 1984.

BIBLIOGRAPHY. D. H. Bradley, *A History of the A.M.E. Zion Church* (1956); G. S. Wilmore, *Black Religion and Black Radicalism: An Interpretation of the Religious History of Afro-American People* (1983). L. J. Edwards

Agassiz, Jean Louis Rodolphe (1807-1873).
Naturalist, Harvard* professor. Born at Motier-en-Vuly, Switzerland, Agassiz earned his Ph.D. at Erlangen (1829) and his M.D. from Munich (1830). He soon distinguished himself in the fields of natural history, zoology and geology and in 1846 immigrated to America. Through his lectures and accomplishments he soon emerged as the country's leading figure in natural sciences. In 1849 he began teaching at Harvard College, where he remained until his death in 1873. There he founded the Harvard Museum of Comparative

Zoology and was instrumental in founding the National Academy of Sciences. Agassiz published widely and was admired by his students. Yet, his involvement in the evolution controversy,* beginning in 1855 and heightened by Darwin's publication of the *Origin of Species* in 1859, would diminish his stature and illustrate a transition in the intellectual climate of the nation.

Though Agassiz seldom expressed interest in organized religion and was certainly not a biblical literalist, he resisted evolutionary theory on both religious and scientific grounds. Influenced by German idealism and theistic* ideas, Agassiz argued for a "special creation," including the view that every race of humans had been specially created for its particular geographical zone. Living organisms, he maintained, represented different examples of "a thought of God" and that the "study of nature is an intercourse with the highest mind." These ideas were wedded to a good deal of empirical research, and eventually shaped an influential school of thought combining precise observation with speculative theory. But Agassiz found himself swimming against the tide of Darwinism. One of his most notable opponents was his colleague at Harvard, Asa Gray,* who was a devout Christian, a theistic evolutionist and an eminent naturalist.

Public lectures and publications promoting his views increasingly alienated Agassiz from the mainstream of the scientific community, but won for him wide public acclaim. Agassiz is remembered for articulating the differences between creationism* and evolution and is sometimes appealed to as a notable scientist who opposed evolutionary theory in the nineteenth century.

BIBLIOGRAPHY. *DAB* 1; D. N. Livingstone, *Darwin's Forgotten Defenders* (1987); B. J. Lowenberg, "The Reaction of American Scientists to Darwinism," *AHR* 38 (1932-1933):687-701; E. Lurie, *Louis Agassiz: A Life in Science* (1960).

C. P. Dawson

Aggiornamento. An Italian term broadly defined as modernization or adaptation. The term was popularized for Catholics* by Pope John XXIII,* who explained its meaning as "the renewal of traditions by interpreting them in harmony with the new conditions and needs of the time." It represented the effort by the Catholic Church "to understand the diverse circumstances of life so that she can adapt, correct, improve and be filled with fervor." As the goal of the Second Vatican Council,* *aggiornamento* was to be "a leap forward in doctrinal insight and the education of consciences in ever greater fidelity to authentic teaching as this authentic doctrine is studied and expounded in the light of research methods and the language of modern thought." The results of *aggiornamento* stemming from Vatican II may be seen in the reform and renewal represented in the use of modern languages in the Catholic liturgy* and the increased role of the laity* in ministry.
See also VATICAN II.

BIBLIOGRAPHY. P. Hebblethwaite, *Pope John XXIII: Shepherd of the Modern World* (1985).

J. W. Evans

Agnosticism. The belief that humans cannot know the answers to the ultimate questions of the existence of God or the nature and destiny of the human soul. For the agnostic such questions must be left open and unanswered. The term should not be confused with atheism,* which denies the reality of God.

The word *agnostic* was coined by Thomas Huxley (1825-1895) in 1869 as an antithesis to the claim of early gnostic sects that secret knowledge of the universe was available to certain individuals. For Huxley, agnosticism was more a method than a formal belief system. He argued that one must follow reason as far as it would go, but then a point is reached beyond which it is impossible to know. Huxley questioned the truthfulness of any belief that could not be supported by factual, verifiable evidence.

This concept is rooted in the British skepticism of David Hume (1711-1776), who, in questioning the idea of causality, rejected the historical veracity of the New Testament miracles. It also owes much to German philosopher Immanuel Kant's (1724-1804) arguments that human knowledge is limited by the categories of time and space. In the nineteenth century the Scottish philosopher William Hamilton (1788-1856), who held that knowledge was relative to human mental faculties, believed that the superiority of human intellect could be partially seen in its willingness to accept ignorance when it comes to the ultimate questions. A popular thinker among America's learned churchmen, Hamilton helped introduce them to elements of German philosophical skepticism. The British evolutionary thinker Herbert Spencer (1820-1903), writing in 1862, made the point even sharper in saying that neither science nor religion can answer all questions. For the American philosopher William James (1842-1910), however, belief must sometimes be embraced not on the basis of its metaphysical claims but because of its consequences for human behavior and conduct.

By the mid-twentieth century the term had come to be used loosely to describe all forms of skepticism. An influential modern American exponent of agnosticism is scientist Carl Sagan.

BIBLIOGRAPHY. R. A. Armstrong, *Agnosticism and Theism in the Nineteenth Century* (1905); T. H. Huxley, "Agnosticism" and "Agnosticism and Christianity," in *Collected Essays,* vol. V (1902); R. W. Hepburn, *Christianity and Paradox* (1958).

N. P. Feldmeth

Ahlstrom, Sydney Eckman (1919-1984). Historian of modern religion and American history. Born in Cokato, Minnesota, Ahlstrom studied at Gustavus Adolphus College (B.A., 1941), the University of Minnesota (M.A., 1946) and Harvard University* (Ph.D., 1952). He enlisted in the U. S. Army in 1942 and left the service as a captain in 1946.

Ahlstrom served as a teaching fellow in the Harvard history department in 1948. He studied at Strasbourg, France, from 1951 to 1952, where he was instructor in history and general education. Joining the Yale* history faculty in 1954, he was promoted to assistant professor in 1960 and full professor in 1964; he was named the first incumbent of the Samuel Knight Chair in 1979. His numerous honors included an invitation to serve as lecturer for the Lutheran World Federation* throughout Europe in 1957 and as chairman of the Consulting Committee on the Bicentenary of the Lutheran Church in America.* He delivered the Rauschenbusch* Lectures at Colgate Rochester Divinity School in 1967, the Stone Lectures at Princeton Seminary* in 1974, and the Lyman Beecher* Lectures at Yale Divinity School in 1981.

Ahlstrom retired from teaching in 1983, having spent thirty years teaching students from the Yale Divinity School and the departments of American studies, religious studies and history. His encyclopedic study, *A Religious History of the American People* (1972), received the National Book Award in Philosophy and Religion in 1973 and was honored in a *TIME* magazine poll of book reviewers as the outstanding book on religion published in the 1970s. His other publications include *The Harvard Divinity School* (joint author, 1954), *The American Protestant Encounter with World Religions* (1962), *Theology in America: the Major Protestant Voices from Puritanism to Neo-Orthodoxy* (1967), *American Religious Values and the Futures of America* (1978, edited by R. Van Allen) and numerous articles. Two works have been published posthumously: *An American Reformation: A Documentary History of Unitarian Christi-*

anity (1985, edited with J. S. Carey); *The Scientific Theist: A Life of Francis Ellingwood Abbott* (1987, with R. B. Mullin). In his teaching and writing, he distinguished himself as one of the nation's foremost scholars in the field of American religious and intellectual history.

BIBLIOGRAPHY. Obituary, *New York Times* (July 4, 1984). P. M. Kane

Albright, Jacob (1759-1808). Itinerant preacher,* first bishop* of the Evangelical Association. Albright was born into a family of pietistically* inclined German Lutherans* near Pottstown, Pennsylvania. His grandfather, Johannes Albrecht, had emigrated from Coburg, in the Palatinate, and arrived in Philadelphia in 1732.

In 1785 Jacob married Catharine Cope and moved to Lancaster County, where he became a prosperous farmer and tile manufacturer. There his skill in his trade and fairness in business dealings earned him the sobriquet "The Honest Tiler." Around 1790 three of the Albrights's children died. This crisis brought Jacob into spiritual turmoil, and he sought advice from three men: Anthony Houtz, the German Reformed* minister who conducted the Albright children's funerals; Isaac Davies, a neighboring farmer and Methodist* lay preacher; and Adam Riegel, a United Brethren in Christ lay preacher. In 1791, through Riegel's influence, Albright experienced a conversion and subsequently joined the class meeting in Davies' home. Granted a Methodist exhorter's license in 1796, he began preaching throughout eastern Pennsylvania and Maryland.

Albright's abiding concern was the spiritual welfare of German-speaking people. When Methodist leaders failed to organize special meetings for Germans, Albright began contemplating the necessity of a separate group to meet the needs of his flock. In 1800 he organized his converts into three classes, after the Methodist fashion. By 1803 the number of classes had increased to five, and in that same year a conference of class leaders organized themselves and ordained Albright as elder preacher. Albright was named bishop in 1807 but died in May 1808, probably of tuberculosis, while on a preaching mission not far from his home. Known to outsiders as Albright People or Albright Brethren, from 1816 they called themselves the Evangelical Association.

See also GERMAN-AMERICAN REVIVALISM, UNITED METHODIST CHURCH.

BIBLIOGRAPHY. R. W. Albright, *A History of the Evangelical Church* (1942); J. B. Behney and P. H. Eller, *The History of the Evangelical United*

Brethren Church (1979); *DAB* I; *DARB*.

M. D. Strege

Albright, William Foxwell (1891-1971). Biblical archaeologist. Born in Coquimbo, Chile, the son of missionaries, Albright showed an early interest in ancient history. He graduated from Upper Iowa University (1912) and then pursued graduate studies at Johns Hopkins University's Oriental Seminary (Ph.D., 1916). After a year in the army (1918), Albright studied in Jerusalem at the American Schools of Oriental Research (ASOR), becoming acting director in 1920 and director from 1921 to 1929. In 1929 he became the W. W. Spence Professor of Semitic Languages at Johns Hopkins, a position he held until his retirement in 1958. His commitment to ASOR was reflected in his directorship again in 1933-1936 and his thirty-eight years as editor of the *Bulletin of the American Schools of Oriental Research*. ASOR has renamed its Jerusalem school, Albright Institute.

Albright's career was characterized by extensive field work (with excavations at Gibeah, Bethel, Petra and Tell Beit Mirsim), an ability to assimilate a wide range of historical and archaeological data and a remarkable scholarly output and erudition. He wrote over a dozen books, including *Archaeology of Palestine and the Bible* (1932), *From the Stone Age to Christianity* (1940) and *Archaeology and the Religion of Israel* (1942). His extensive studies, articles and collaborated volumes comprise a bibliography of over 1,000 entries. For his many achievements he received thirty honorary doctorates.

Albright's archaeological and historical studies led him to increasingly conservative conclusions regarding the historicity of the Bible, and he was influential in attracting many scholars in his field to similar conclusions. During his thirty years at Johns Hopkins, he trained a whole generation of biblical scholars, many of whom are leaders in the field today.

BIBLIOGRAPHY. F. M. Cross, "William Foxwell Albright: Orientalist," *Bulletin of the American Schools of Oriental Research* 200 (1970):7-11; L. G. Running and D. N. Freedman, *William Foxwell Albright* (1975).

H. F. Vos

Alcohol, Drinking of. The Scriptures illustrate the consumption of alcohol in several ways. On the one hand, alcohol is recognized as potentially evil (Prov 20:1; Is 5:11, 22), and intemperate use of wine is said to lead to poverty (Prov 21:17). The apostle Paul commands Christians not to get drunk on wine (Eph 5:18) and teaches that Christian leaders must limit their wine consumption (1 Tim 3:3, 8). On the other hand, the use of alcohol is not normally prohibited in Scripture. Christ illustrates spiritual truth through the use of wine as a teaching tool (Jn 2:1-11; Mk 2:22; Mt 26:27-29), and wine is described as having medical value and the ability to refresh, gladden and rejuvenate (1 Tim 5:23; Ps 104:15; Prov 31:6). Moreover, Isaiah uses wine as a symbol of spiritual blessing (Is 55:1-2). References to wine in the Scriptures make it clear that it was a part of the regular diet (Gen 14:18; 1 Sam 16:20). No evidence exists to support the idea that the wine mentioned in the Bible was unfermented grape juice. In fact, when juice is referred to it is not called wine (Gen 40:11).

Christians have generally been in agreement that moderation is the clear Scriptural injunction on the use of alcohol. While the Bible does not require complete abstinence on the part of Christians, Christians have concurred that drunkenness plays no legitimate role in the life of the Christian, and so drunkenness has generally been proscribed by the church. Attitudes toward alcohol have varied throughout the history of the American church. New England Puritans,* for example, viewed alcoholic drinks as an enjoyable creation of God to be consumed along with other produce of the soil. Rum was an essential part of the New England economy, and alcohol was an accepted part of momentous occasions and private hospitality. However, as early as 1784 Dr. Benjamin Rush of Philadelphia warned that distilled liquor could injure health. Nineteenth-century American evangelicals,* influenced by revivalism,* perfectionism* and the accompanying movements for social reform, began to call not only for temperance* but for total abstinence.* Protestant churches after 1840 commonly required members to pledge their abstinence from all drinking of alcohol, and communion wine was often replaced with grape juice. Many twentieth-century evangelicals continue to practice abstinence from alcohol, and evangelical churches generally encourage abstinence. Nineteenth-century Catholics for the most part did not share the evangelical campaign against "demon rum," nor did many Protestants more closely identified with European confessional traditions. In these traditions the use of alcohol has remained a matter of personal choice, regulated more by medical and social opinion than by theological rationale.

See also ABSTINENCE; PROHIBITION MOVEMENT; TEMPERANCE MOVEMENT. D. A. Scalberg

Alemany, Joseph Sadoc (1814-1888). Domini-

[33]

can* missionary* and archbishop* of San Francisco.* A native of Vich, Spain, Alemany entered the Dominican order in 1829 and was ordained* eight years later. Between 1840 and 1847 he worked as a missionary* in Ohio, Tennessee and Kentucky, becoming an American citizen in 1845. In 1848, his superiors appointed him provincial of Dominicans in the U.S.; and in 1850 Pope* Pius IX* named Alemany bishop* of Monterey, California, placing him in charge of Church affairs in not only California but also northwestern Mexico and parts of Utah, Nevada and Arizona. In 1853 Alemany became the first archbishop of San Francisco. He attended the First Vatican Council* in 1870 and strongly supported the definition of papal infallibility.* Church authorities in Rome granted his request for a coadjutor in 1883, and he retired to Spain in 1884. During his years in California, Alemany achieved a settlement of church land claims and obtained a share of the "Pious Fund," an endowment established in the seventeenth century for the support of Spanish missions* in California and seized by the Mexican government in 1842.

BIBLIOGRAPHY. J. B. McGloin, *California's First Archbishop: The Life of Joseph Sadoc Alemany, O.P.* (1965).   W. P. Leahy

Alexander, Archibald (1772-1851). First professor at Princeton Theological Seminary and founder of the Princeton Theology.* Born in Rockbridge County, Virginia, Alexander grew up in a frontier environment and was converted at the age of seventeen. Having little formal education, he studied theology* with William Graham at Liberty Hall Academy (Washington and Lee University). Prior to assuming his duties at Princeton in 1812, Alexander pastored churches, led revivals and served as president of Hampden-Sydney College (1796-1807) in his native Virginia and ministered in the Pine Street Presbyterian Church in Philadelphia (1807-1812).

Recognizing the need for institutions providing formal training for Presbyterian ministers, Alexander issued a call for schools in 1808, and in 1812 Princeton Theological Seminary emerged as the first Presbyterian seminary in America, with Alexander as its first professor. By his academic diligence Alexander established Princeton's main themes and set a standard of excellence that his successors at Princeton, Charles* and Archibald Alexander Hodge* and Benjamin B. Warfield,* vigorously maintained. Alexander implemented the General Assembly's* plan that Presbyterian pastors not only experience a call to the ministry*

but also receive rigorous intellectual training. They should obtain a thorough knowledge of the Bible* (including the original languages of Scripture) and be skilled defenders of its content and authority.

To accomplish these ends Alexander taught Scottish Common Sense philosophy,* which he had learned from William Graham. Under this school of thought the defense of Christianity begins with reason judging external evidences for the truthfulness of Scripture: the credibility of its witnesses, fulfilled prophecy and cultural benefits attending the spread of the gospel. But more effective in establishing biblical truth are internal evidences: the self-authenticating purity and sublimity of its content as attested by the Holy Spirit. To this philosophical base Alexander added seventeenth-century Reformed theology*—the Westminster Confession* and the work of Swiss theologian François Turretin (1623-1687).

Undergirding his teaching, preaching* and writing was a fervent piety* and vital interest in religious experience* which had its roots in his revival* preaching and continued to be a characteristic feature of the Princeton Theology.

BIBLIOGRAPHY. *AAP* 3; J. W. Alexander, *The Life of Archibald Alexander* (1854); *DAB* I; *DARB;* A. W. Hoffecker, *Piety and the Princeton Theologians: Archibald Alexander, Charles Hodge and Benjamin Warfield* (1981); *NCAB* 2; M. A. Noll, ed., *The Princeton Theology, 1812-1921.*

W. A. Hoffecker

Alexander, Charles M. (1867-1920). Singing evangelist* with R. A. Torrey* and J. Wilbur Chapman.* Born at Meadow, Tennessee, and educated at Maryville Academy and College, Alexander studied music at Washington College and prepared for his work as an evangelist at the Bible Institute of Chicago (later called Moody Bible Institute*).

In 1893 Alexander worked with Dwight L. Moody's* revival* meetings held during the Chicago World's Fair and then spent several years (1894-1901) with Milan B. Williams in evangelistic campaigns in the Midwest. The most notable phase of his ministry was his work with R. A. Torrey, with whom he traversed the globe (1902-1906). In Australia alone they covered fifty engagements in one month (1902), advertising their meetings with small white cards inscribed in bold red letters, "Get Right With God." Wherever they went, "Charlie" would "warm up the crowd" and sing songs such as the "Glory Song" and "Where Is My Wandering Boy Tonight?"

In 1904 Alexander married Helen Cadbury of Birmingham, England, whom he had met as she did personal evangelism in the "after-meetings" of an evangelistic campaign. At their wedding feast in Liverpool, 2,100 poor were fed, a brass band played and a 2,500-voice choir sang. Their honeymoon consisted of a series of evangelistic services in the U.S. From 1906 until the end of his life, Alexander, now living in Birmingham, traveled internationally with evangelist J. Wilbur Chapman and supported the work of Pocket Testament League,* which was founded by his wife, Helen.

George Stebbins, Alexander's voice teacher at Moody Bible Institute, wrote in 1924 that Alexander had not aspired to be a composer nor a singer, but he was "one of the most magnetic and successful leaders of Gospel song in the history of modern evangelism."

BIBLIOGRAPHY. C. M. Alexander, *Soul Winning Around the World* (1907); G. T. B. Davis, *Torrey and Alexander: The Story of a Worldwide Revival* (1905); H. C. A. Dixon, *Charles M. Alexander* (1920); T. S. Fitchett, *The Chapman-Alexander Campaigns, 1909-1913* (1913), R. Harkness, *With the Torrey and Alexander Missions Round the World* (1904); P. I. Roberts, *"Charlie" Alexander: A Study in Personality* (1920).

R. J. Stanislaw

Alexander, Joseph Addison (1809-1860). Old School* Presbyterian* biblical scholar. The son of Archibald Alexander,* Joseph was born in Philadelphia, and graduated from the College of New Jersey* at Princeton. A prodigiously gifted linguist, he was instructor of ancient languages and literature at Princeton (1830-1833), studied a year in Europe, and taught Old and New Testament (1834-1860) and (after 1851) church history at Princeton Theological Seminary.* He published many articles in the *Biblical Repertory and Princeton Review,* which he helped edit, as well as commentaries on the Psalms, Isaiah, Matthew, Mark and Acts. Although Alexander supported Princeton's rational orthodoxy* and often echoed German biblical scholar E. W. Hengstenberg's attacks on radical biblical criticism, he was more open than other Old Princeton theologians to a historical and critical approach to the Bible and cautiously introduced German biblical scholarship into his writings.

BIBLIOGRAPHY. H. C. Alexander, *The Life of Joseph Addison Alexander . . . ,* 2 vols. (1870); *DAB* I; J. H. Moorhead, "Joseph Addison Alexander: Common Sense, Romanticism and Biblical Criticism at Princeton," *JPH* 53 (1975):51-65.

E. W. Kennedy

Alien Immersion. A term still used by many Baptists* in the South to refer to baptism* by immersion administered by non-Baptists. Although the term was used before the rise of the Landmark Movement* in the mid-nineteenth century, it came to prominence through the exclusivistic ecclesiastical theories of J. R. Graves,* J. M. Pendleton* and A. C. Dayton.

Landmarkers stressed baptism more than any other issue in their ecclesiology. Graves and others insisted that since only Baptist churches and ministers* are valid, only baptism administered in the context of a local Baptist church is valid. Landmark leaders were particularly troubled because some Baptist churches were accepting members who had only been immersed by Paedo-baptists *(see* Baptism*)* or Campbellites *(see* Restoration Movement*).*

A similar concept of baptismal exclusivism arose among some in the Restoration Movement, with leaders of the Churches of Christ* refusing to accept the validity of immersion outside their fellowship. However, the term "alien immersion" did not become popular with them.

BIBLIOGRAPHY. *BIIH,* 10.1 (1975); J. E. Barnhart, "Alien Immersion," *ERS* (1984); J. R. Graves, *Old Landmarkism: What Is It?* (1880). M. G. Bell

Alison, Francis (1705-1779). Presbyterian* educator and political theorist. Born in Leck, County Donegal, Ireland, Alison studied at the Royal Academy of Raphoe and Edinburgh University, and with the moral philosopher Francis Hutcheson. He arrived in America in 1735 and soon pastored a Presbyterian church in New London, Chester County, Pennsylvania (1737-1752). Concerned by the lack of educational opportunities in the Middle Colonies, Alison established New London Academy in 1743 (later relocated to Newark, Delaware, a predecessor of the University of Delaware). In 1752, at Benjamin Franklin's behest, Alison left New London to become rector* of the Philadelphia Academy and, later, vice provost and professor at the College of Philadelphia (now the University of Pennsylvania*). Concurrently, he co-pastored the First Presbyterian Church of Philadelphia and became a major spokesperson for Old Side* Presbyterianism.

In his teaching, Alison trained a whole generation of students in the inductive empiricism of Scottish Common Sense Realism,* demonstrating the relevance of Scottish academic philosophy to pressing American problems, particularly in political theory. Alison's students, many of whom became prominent political leaders in the Revolutionary* era, learned from their mentor concepts such as the right of resistance to tyranny, government by contract and consent, and the necessity for balanced forms of government. Alison also actively opposed British encroachments upon American prerogatives, both ecclesiastically and politically.

BIBLIOGRAPHY. J. L. McAllister, Jr., "Francis Alison and John Witherspoon: Political Philosophers and Revolutionaries," *JPH* 54 (1976):33-60.

D. M. Strong

All Saints Day. A feast celebrated in the Western Church on the first of November to commemorate Christian martyrs and all those who have led conspicuously holy lives. In the Eastern Church it is observed on the first Sunday after Pentecost. It is also known as All Hallows, and so the popular celebration of Halloween (traditionally spelled Hallowe'en) began as a celebration of All Hallows Eve.

Both Catholics* and Protestants* consider all the saved in heaven* as saints, but the term *saint* is customarily used specifically for those persons of conspicuous holiness whom the church officially recognizes. From at least the end of the second century the Christian church paid official honors to the saints in its liturgy.* By the end of the fourth century the sources speak of a celebration of all the martyrs of the church without specifying a date. The idea of celebrating the first day of November as the day of all the saints can be traced back to the eighth century in the West. It has been argued that the date was chosen because it was on that day, in the reign of Pope Gregory IV (d. 741), that a chapel to all the saints was dedicated in Saint Peter's Basilica in the Vatican.

All Saints Day is in particular a recognition of those who have not been assigned a special day in the church year. On the day after the feast, All Souls Day, the Catholic Church prays for all departed souls, but particularly those undergoing purgation. In some Anglican* churches the day is observed in honor of all the saved in Christ, whether or not they were distinguished by their life or death.

The feast of All Saints has historically been a major feast of the Roman Catholic Church. One indication of its importance is that in the British Isles over a thousand churches bear that name, a title only surpassed by the Virgin Mary.* In the Reformed* tradition All Saints Day has been maintained among many communions as a day to remember and thank God for the faithful departed while the observance of All Souls Day, except within Anglicanism, has been abandoned since the Reformation.

See also CHRISTIAN YEAR; SAINTS, CULT OF THE; PIETY, POPULAR CATHOLIC.

BIBLIOGRAPHY. "All Saints," *The Oxford Dictionary of Saints,* ed. D. H. Farmer (1978); P. Brown, *The Cult of the Saints* (1982); L. Cunningham, *The Meaning of Saints* (1980).   L. S. Cunningham

All Souls Day. *See* ALL SAINTS DAY.

Allen, Alexander (V)iets (G)riswold (1841-1908). Episcopal educator. Allen was a leading figure in the late nineteenth-century liberal* or broad church* movement within Anglicanism.* Son of a low church* Episcopal* priest,* Allen was nurtured in an evangelical* household. After graduating from Kenyon College (1862), he studied at Bexley Hall. There he lost his early evangelical faith while discovering the writings of Samuel Taylor Coleridge (1772-1834) and F. D. Maurice (1805-1872). Transferring to Andover Seminary* (1864-1866), he graduated in 1866 and a year later began teaching ecclesiastical history at the Episcopal Theological School (now Episcopal Divinity School) in Cambridge, Massachusetts. Allen emphasized—particularly in his most famous book *The Continuity of Christian Thought* (1884)—the inadequacy of the Latin, or Augustinian,* theological emphasis upon human sinfulness* and the separation of God from creation. Instead he urged a revival of Greek theology with its emphasis upon divine immanence, and the connectedness between God, man and nature. Allen also wrote notable biographies of Jonathan Edwards* (1889) and Phillips Brooks* (1900).

BIBLIOGRAPHY. *DAB* I; C. L. Slattery, *Alexander Viets Griswold Allen, 1841-1908* (1911).

R. B. Mullin

Allen, (A)sa (A)lonzo (1911-1970). Healing revivalist.* Born in Sulphur Rock, Arkansas, Allen's childhood was characterized by abject poverty and alcoholic parents. In 1934 he was converted in a "tongues speaking" Methodist* church. Licensed* as a minister* of the Assemblies of God* (c. 1936), Allen began his career in a small Colorado congregation and gradually built a reputation as a preacher. During World War 2* he worked as a full-time revival preacher, but his early years of Pentecostal* ministry were difficult. By 1947 he had found a more stable ministry in a church in Corpus Christi, Texas, but he resigned in 1949 and returned to an itinerant revival ministry.

Inspired by the success of Oral Roberts,* Allen began his own healing ministry and by 1951, claiming hundreds of healings in his meetings, he had launched a tent ministry. By 1953 the *Allen Revival Hour* was being broadcast over eighteen American stations and seventeen in Latin America. His ministry was characterized by an appeal to the poor, an emphasis on eccentric healings and miracles, and an old-time Pentecostal message. During this period Allen published *The Price of God's Miracle Working Power* (1950) and *How to Have Freedom From Fear, Worry, and Nerves* (1954).

In 1955, having been arrested for drunken driving in Knoxville, Tennessee, Allen lost the support of his fellow revivalists and his ordination with the Assemblies of God. Telling of "unprecedented persecution," Allen retained a faithful following and launched an independent ministry featuring several irregular "miracles" and victories over numerous demons. In 1954 Allen began *Miracle Magazine* and in 1956, the Miracle Revival Fellowship. In 1958 he established Miracle Valley near Bisbee, Arizona. From these new headquarters he developed a variety of ministries. An early forerunner of the faith movement,* Allen stressed financial as well as spiritual healing.

Allen's meteoric career ended in tragedy. In 1967 he divorced his wife of over thirty years, and in 1970 he died alone in a San Francisco motel while his team was conducting a campaign in West Virginia. The ministry was continued by Allen's associate, Don Stewart.

BIBLIOGRAPHY. D. E. Harrell, *All Things Are Possible* (1975). H. D. Hunter

Allen, Cary (1767-1795). Presbyterian* revivalist* and home missionary.* Raised in a large family in Cumberland County, Virginia, Allen attended Hampden-Sydney College and in 1787, while home on vacation from college, attended a Methodist* meeting and experienced a dramatic evangelical* conversion.* Returning to Hampden-Sydney, he helped precipitate a revival among the students. This revival is now viewed by historians as one of the first outbreakings of the Second Great Awakening.* Allen and many others from the school entered the Presbyterian ministry,* spreading this heightened religious interest throughout the South and trans-Appalachian Southwest. Allen spent three years as an evangelist* for his synod,* and was a home missionary to various parts of Virginia and Kentucky, eventually settling in Kentucky in 1794. His message had a socially levelling influence; he even invited African-American slaves to join their white masters on the equal ground of evangelical experience. Blessed with a remarkable speaking ability and an unusually good sense of

humor, Allen was a very popular preacher. He died unexpectedly at age twenty-eight and was buried near Danville, Kentucky.

BIBLIOGRAPHY. W. H. Foote, *Sketches of Virginia, Historical and Biographical,* Second Series (1852). D. M. Strong

Allen, Ethan (1738-1789). Revolutionary War* figure and controversial religious freethinker. Born in Litchfield, Connecticut, Allen was largely self-educated but throughout his life concerned with the weighty religious and theological issues of his day. His victory at Fort Ticonderoga in 1775 for the Continental Army and his ongoing efforts on behalf of a "free" Vermont earned him the enduring reputation of a boisterous frontier hero. But his religious views, moving from an anti-Calvinist* to an outspoken anti-Christian position, earned him enmity among the orthodox.* In his one published work, *Reason the Only Oracle of Man* (1785), Allen argued against reliance on biblical revelation that he perceived to be full of contradictions and errors, and against the "superstitions" of traditional Christian belief, including miracles, prayer* and the divinity of Christ. Allen wielded little practical influence for change, either theologically or among the clerical elite whom he militantly opposed. Yet he was an early representative of the anti-authoritarian, democratizing currents of thought that after the turn of the century effectively undercut New England's Congregational* establishment.

BIBLIOGRAPHY. *DAB* I; *DARB;* C. A. Jellison, *Ethan Allen: Frontier Rebel* (1969); *NCAB* 1; J. Pell, *Ethan Allen* (1929). E. C. Nordbeck

Allen, Richard (1760-1831). Black clergyman and founding bishop* of the African Methodist Episcopal Church* (A.M.E.). Born into slavery in Philadelphia on February 14, 1760, Allen grew up on the Stokeley farm near Dover, Delaware. In 1777 he was converted and began preaching on the plantation and in local Methodist* churches. Among his early converts was his owner who was impressed by young Allen and allowed him to purchase his freedom. From 1781 to 1786, just after the Revolutionary War,* Allen traveled the Methodist preaching circuits* in Delaware and surrounding states and worked at odd jobs to help support himself. Prominent Methodist leaders, including Bishop Francis Asbury,* took him under their care and arranged preaching engagements.

In 1786 Allen returned as a free man to his native Philadelphia and joined the predominantly white St. George's Methodist Church. His series of prayer-study services attracted dozens of blacks into the church, and with that came increased racial tension and formal segregation of seating and the altar. In April 1787 Allen, his associate Absalom Jones (also a former slave) and a contingent of blacks from St. George's left the church to worship as the Free African Society.* The Society provided both alternative religious services that reflected Quaker* influences and a means of mutual economic support. Absalom Jones secured ordination from the Protestant Episcopal Church* and his followers soon formed the African Church of St. Thomas, while Allen led his congregation toward separatist Methodism.*

Convinced that African-Americans needed a distinct religious identity, Allen formally established the Bethel African Methodist Episcopal Church in 1794, with Bishop Asbury leading the dedication. For twenty-two years Allen sought its legal independence and throughout his life combined his experiential religion grounded in Methodism with widespread efforts to uplift African-Americans economically and socially. Allen was ordained a bishop* in 1799, and after a court victory the A.M.E. Church was officially recognized in April 1816. Its membership climbed to some seventy-five hundred by the 1820s. Allen died on March 26, 1831.

See also BLACK RELIGION; FREE AFRICAN SOCIETY.

BIBLIOGRAPHY. R. Allen, *The Life, Experience, and Gospel Labors of the Rt. Rev. Richard Allen* (1793); *DAB* I; *DARB;* C. V. R. George, *Segregated Sabbaths; Richard Allen and the Emergence of Independent Black Churches, 1760-1840* (1973); C. S. Smith, *History of the African Methodist Episcopal Church, 1856-1922* (1922); C. H. Wesley, *Richard Allen, Apostle of Freedom* (1935); C. G. Woodson, *The History of the Negro Church* (1921). T. R. Peake

Alline, Henry (1748-1784). Leader of the Great Awakening in Nova Scotia. Born in Rhode Island, Alline moved with his family to present-day Nova Scotia in 1760. He underwent a profoundly emotional conversion* experience in 1775, and shortly thereafter went out preaching* the "new birth."* Although he reached much of the Maritime Provinces, his most enthusiastic audiences were his fellow Yankees in rural Nova Scotia. Their experience of economic hardship and psychological rootlessness, exacerbated by their decision to remain neutral during the American Revolution,* made them particularly receptive to Alline's message.

Alline's peculiar anti-Calvinistic mysticism*

influenced the Free Will Baptist* movement in the United States, but most of the Canadian "New Light"* churches he founded either collapsed or became Calvinistic Baptists.* Many of his more than five hundred hymns* and songs, however, were popular in Alline's own day, and several were printed in standard hymnals of the nineteenth century. His views on the relationship between the physical and spiritual worlds were published in *Two Mites on Some of the Most Important and much disputed Points of Divinity . . .* (1781). Alline returned to New England to begin a preaching tour in 1783 but died soon afterward of tuberculosis.

See also NEW LIGHTS, CANADIAN; BAPTIST CHURCHES IN CANADA.

BIBLIOGRAPHY. J. M. Bumsted, *Henry Alline: 1748-1784* (1971); *DAB* I. J. G. Stackhouse

Allis, Oswald (T)hompson (1880-1973). Presbyterian* clergyman, Old Testament scholar and educator. The son of a Philadelphia medical doctor, Allis was reared in a Presbyterian home. Before taking a Ph.D. in archaeology and Assyriology from the University of Berlin in 1913, he studied at the University of Pennsylvania (A.B.) and Princeton Theological Seminary* (B.D.). Beginning in 1910, Allis served as a member of Princeton Seminary's faculty for nineteen years, where in addition to teaching Old Testament, he served as an editor of the *Princeton Theological Review.*

In 1929 he left Princeton to teach at the newly founded Westminster Theological Seminary in Philadelphia, where he served for six years. Allis resigned in 1935 after Westminster Seminary was implicated in a controversy within the Presbyterian Church in the U.S.A. Freed from the constraints of the teaching schedule and independently wealthy, Allis devoted the rest of his life to writing and editing. In addition to compiling extended studies of English translations of the Bible, Allis focused on the Pentateuch and Old Testament prophecy. In *Prophecy and the Church* (1945) Allis registered significant objections to dispensational* premillennialism* and his *God Spake by Moses* (1951) became a standard defense of the traditional conservative understanding of pentateuchal authorship. Meanwhile, he served as a contributing editor for *Christianity Today* (Philadelphia) and as an associate editor for the *Evangelical Quarterly* (Edinburgh).

BIBLIOGRAPHY. M. A. Noll, *Between Faith and Criticism* (1986). D. G. Hart

Altar. A place of sacrifice, either of animal offerings

or of incense, in the Old Testament. In the New Testament the term is found in several places, but not applied to Christian liturgical furnishings. In Christian use it refers to the table upon which the Eucharist* is celebrated and from which Holy Communion is distributed. The use of such terms as the Latin *ara* or the Greek *thusiasterion* (classic terms for *altar*) for this table derives from the understanding of the Eucharist as memorial of Christ's sacrifice on Calvary and thus as closely related to that unique event. Modern altars usually stand in a free space so that the presiding minister can stand behind the altar and face the congregation.

BIBLIOGRAPHY. C. E. Pocknee, *The Christian Altar* (1963). T. J. Talley

Altar Call. In the revivalistic* tradition the altar* call is a period following the sermon* in which the hearers are challenged to publicly respond by coming to a designated place, usually in the front of the congregation. Today it is frequently referred to as the invitation.

Although it is difficult to trace precisely the origin of the practice, no instances of the practice are recorded prior to the nineteenth century. The practice became popular during the first half of the nineteenth century, growing out of the camp meetings* and protracted meetings on the Southern frontier and in the "burned-over district"* of western New York. The practice of seekers "repairing to the woods" was accompanied by reports of immorality, and revival leaders constructed "pens" for those in spiritual struggle.

The tension between Calvinism *(see* Reformed Tradition*) and Arminianism* in revivalism* played a part in the development of the altar call. At first the altar call was not identified with a conversion* experience but was an occasion for inquiry and prayer as reflected by the various names employed—"mourner's bench,"* "anxious bench," "praying pen" and others. However, increasingly throughout the nineteenth century, the altar call became institutionalized and tantamount to a conversion* experience. Many churches today that stand within the revivalistic tradition maintain the altar call as a frequent, if not weekly, practice.

See also CAMP MEETINGS; REVIVALISM; MOURNER'S BENCH.

BIBLIOGRAPHY. D. D. Bruce, *And They All Sang Hallelujah* (1974); W. R. Cross, *The Burned-over District* (1950); C. A. Johnson, *The Frontier Camp Meeting* (1955); T. H. Olbricht, "The Invitation: An Historical Survey," *RQ* 5:1 (1961):6-16.

M. G. Bell

Altar Fellowship. The practice of Christians receiving Communion* at the same altar.* The restrictions to this fellowship vary among the denominations but may be depicted by the following general categories: (1) open Communion, in which a church allows members of other churches to receive Communion with its members; (2) close Communion, in which fellowship is limited to those who either belong to the same denomination or are in doctrinal agreement with each other; and (3) closed Communion, in which fellowship is restricted to those who are members of the same local church. The issue of intercommunion was a major element in the heightening of denominational* sensitivity in the nineteenth century.

BIBLIOGRAPHY. D. Baillie and J. Marsh, eds., *Intercommunion* (1952). J. M. Glass

Altar Societies. The general name for a variety of groups formed in local Roman Catholic* parishes or congregations with the aim of assisting the clergy* and serving God through care of the church appointments, especially the altar.* These societies are usually composed of women who take responsibility for the cleaning and decoration of the altar, the sanctuary area, the sacristy, church vestments, candles and flowers.

While these societies serve a practical and religious purpose, they also promote friendship among members and seek to develop spiritual growth. Typically called "the altar and rosary society," they combine two central Catholic themes, the centrality of the altar and the rosary.*

Regular meetings for prayer and religious instruction are held, presided over by leaders chosen by the members. The society's programs are coordinated to fit the needs of the particular congregation and the religious celebrations of the liturgical calendar. Annual plans typically include guest speakers and a day of prayer for members. In many congregations women are encouraged to join the altar society and men urged to join either the Knights of Columbus,* a fraternal order, or the St. Vincent de Paul Society, famous for its help to the poor.

Since the Second Vatican Council* these typically Catholic societies have lessened in their vigor. This is partly due to the development of other groups which have arisen. Some of the altar and rosary society tasks have been given to sacristans or worship committees.

BIBLIOGRAPHY. S. A. Heeney, "Altar Societies," *Encyclopedic Dictionary of Religion* (1979).

B. Moran

Altham, John (1589-1640). Jesuit* missionary* in Maryland. Born in Warwickshire, England, Altham entered the Society of Jesus in 1623. After his ordination* to the priesthood,* Altham worked at missions in Devon and London districts. Due to the penal laws against Catholic priests in England, he sometimes used the alias John Gravener.

In 1634, along with Father* Andrew White,* and Brother* Thomas Gervase, he accompanied the first settlers who came to Maryland aboard the *Ark* and the *Dove.* From their residence at St. Mary's City, the Jesuits began to evangelize* the Native Americans. For the first five years Governor Leonard Calvert* would not permit the priests to live outside the English settlement because the Native Americans were considered hostile, but in 1639 Altham* was assigned to Kent's Island on the Eastern Shore. Though not possessed of great intellectual gifts, he was esteemed by his Jesuit companions for his missionary zeal. Altham died on Nov. 4, 1640, at St. Mary's City.

BIBLIOGRAPHY. E. W. Beitzell, *The Jesuit Missions of St. Mary's County, Maryland* (1976); *DAB* I; T. Hughes, *The History of the Jesuits in North America: Colonial and Federal,* 4 vols. (1907-1917). T. E. Buckley

Amana Church Society. Pietist* sect previously known as the Community of True Inspiration. Formed in Hesse in 1714 by Johann Friedrich Rock and Eberhardt Ludwig Gruber, these "new prophets" taught that the age of true and direct divine inspiration (with authority equal to Scripture*) had not ended. The inspired community lived simply, practiced nonresistance and held love feasts much like other radical Pietists. Although they expanded in areas of toleration, a period of quietism and spiritual decline set in after the death of Rock in 1749.

The movement was renewed during the early nineteenth century through two new inspired leaders, Barbara Heinmann (later Landmann) and Christian Metz. Inhospitable conditions, however, led to their immigration* to New York in 1842. There they established the village of Ebenezer, near Buffalo, and were reorganized into a communal* society. Between 1855 and 1864 the Inspirationists moved from corrupting urban influences to a large tract near Iowa City, Iowa. Seven prosperous villages, collectively known as the Amana colonies (Amana means "remain faithful") were eventually established. Membership in the society reached its peak of 1,813 in 1880.

In 1932, however, internal dissension and external pressures led to a dissolution of communal ties and the creation of an independent church society. The assets of the community were divided and a joint stock company created in which the members received shares. Worship* is conducted in seven congregations by the society's elders* and includes reading testimonies from previous inspired prophets, the last of whom died in 1883.

BIBLIOGRAPHY. M. Goebel, "Geschichte der wahren Inspirationsgemeinde von 1688-1850" *ZHT* 19 (1854):267-322, 377-438; 20 (1855):94-160, 327-425; 22 (1857):131-151; R. S. Fogerty, *Communal and Utopian History* (1980); B. Richling, "The Amana Society: A History of Change," *The Palimpsest* 58 (1977):34-47; B. M. Shambaugh, *Amana That Was and Amana That Is* (1932).

D. B. Eller

American Baptist Association. A Landmark* Baptist* organization. The formation of the American Baptist Association in Arkansas in 1905 was the culmination of the struggle of Landmarkism in the Southern Baptist Convention* (SBC). In the 1850s Landmarkism, under the leadership of J. R. Graves,* advocated an ecclesiology which emphasized the local church. Tenets included: Baptist churches are the only true churches; the true church is a local visible institution; the churches and the kingdom of God are coterminous; valid ordination* derives from a Baptist church; only valid ministers can administer the Lord's Supper* and baptism;* Baptist churches have an unbroken historical succession back to the New Testament; and missionary work is to be done by local churches rather than convention boards.

In 1899 Landmarkers formed their first state organization, the East Texas Baptist Convention, later known by the name the *Baptist Missionary Association* (BMA). With Samuel A. Hayden as its most prominent leader, the BMA was outspoken against the SBC and its method of carrying out missionary work through a convention rather than through local churches.

In 1902 Arkansas's "anticonvention" forces rallied against the state convention and formed the General Association of Arkansas Baptists in 1902. Under the dynamic leadership of Ben M. Bogard, an attempt was made in 1905 to convert the SBC to Landmark views regarding mission methods. Although the attempt failed, Bogard's movement absorbed smaller Landmark bodies, including the BMA of Texas, and was renamed the *American Baptist Association* in 1924. With headquarters in Texarkana, Arkansas, the ABA operates several schools, a seminary in Little Rock and a publishing house. In the late 1980s there were over 1700 affiliated churches and an inclusive membership of approximately 250,000.

BIBLIOGRAPHY. E. G. Hinson, *A History of Baptists in Arkansas* (1979); H. L. McBeth, *The Baptist Heritage: Four Centuries of Baptist Witness* (1987).

C. D. Weaver

American Baptist Board of International Ministries.

Foreign mission* agency of the American Baptist Churches in the U.S.A.* In 1812, Adoniram Judson* and Luther Rice* sailed for India under the American Board of Commissioners for Foreign Missions,* converted en route to the Baptist* view of baptism* by immersion, and soon resigned their appointments with the ABCFM. The Judsons started a Baptist mission in Burma and Rice returned to the U.S. to raise support. Baptists in America responded by organizing the General Missionary Convention and the Baptist Board for Foreign Missions in 1814.

Baptist missions functioned through the Baptist Board and a Triennial Convention* until 1845, when a conflict primarily over slavery led to the formation of the Southern Baptist Convention.* Baptists in the North restructured their program as the American Baptist Missionary Union. During the nineteenth century, new fields were opened in Europe, Asia, Africa and Central America.

In 1910, the ABMU was renamed the American Baptist Foreign Mission Society and nine years later became more fully integrated into the Northern Baptist Convention (organized in 1907). Meanwhile, new ministries commenced overseas, particularly in Central America and the Philippines. However, the Board suffered setbacks with fundamentalist* defections to Baptist Mid-Missions* (1920), the Association of Baptists for World Evangelism* (1927) and the Conservative Baptist* Foreign Mission Society (1943). In 1973 the ABFMS was renamed the American Baptist Board of International Ministries, which currently employs almost 200 missionaries and reports an annual income of over $10 million.

BIBLIOGRAPHY. R. G. Torbet, *Venture of Faith* (1955); H. C. Vedder, *A Short History of Baptist Missions* (1927). J. A. Patterson

American Baptist Churches in the U.S.A.

A major Baptist denomination,* formerly known as the American Baptist Convention (1950-1972) and the Northern Baptist Convention (1907-1950). On May 17, 1907, delegates from local churches, Baptist state conventions and city mission societies of the Northern U.S., leaders of the American Baptist Foreign and Home Mission Societies plus the American Baptist Publication Society, met at Calvary Baptist Church in Washington, D.C., to organize formally the Northern Baptist Convention. Charles Evans Hughes, governor of New York, was elected the first president of a loosely federated body of churches and benevolent organizations dedicated to "better and more coherent action as a purely advisory body."

From the establishment of the first Baptist congregation in America at Providence, Rhode Island, around 1638, Baptists cherished the local governance of their churches. Even with the creation of the first regional association of churches in New England in 1670 (General* Six Principle* Baptists) and Philadelphia in 1707 (Philadelphia Baptist Association), each local congregation was said to have complete power and authority from Jesus Christ. Gradually, in the second half of the eighteenth century, Baptists grew in numbers and sought to cooperate in evangelism,* missions* and educational enterprises. Permanent organizations beyond local churches evolved slowly. In general, associations gathered as confessional bodies of fellowship* and mutual support, and to review and debate matters of concern.

Beginning in 1802 and modeled on English Baptist and American Congregationalist* bodies, Baptists in New England organized a series of benevolent societies to advance the denominational interests. Until 1845, when the Southern Baptist Convention* was formed, these societies represented congregations in the South and West as well. An organizational principle of voluntary* individual membership* with independent charters, dominated Baptist life in the Northern states throughout the nineteenth century. This was in marked contrast to the more centralized convention model which Baptists in the Southern states created in 1845.

The driving impulse of Baptists in the North from 1814 was foreign missions. The first national body was organized that year as the General Baptist Missionary Convention, which soon grew to include a college, a seminary* and domestic mission endeavors. In 1824 the Baptist General Tract Society was organized (later the American Baptist Publication and Sunday School Society), and in 1832 the American Baptist Home Mission Society started in New York City. Women's missionary societies* were chartered in the 1870s, and separate conferences for ethnically and racially diverse peoples emerged, beginning in 1851, for German, Swedish, Danish-Norwegian, Italian and Hispanic Americans. Sometimes overlapping in programs, often competing in stewardship drives, the Baptist society model in the North was focused sharply on the local churches which jealously guarded their autonomy. When financial exigency threatened around 1900, interagency agreements and planning meetings eventually led to the creation of a unified Northern Baptist Convention (NBC) in 1905.

After organization, the leaders of the NBC took some bold steps in ecumenism and centralization. In 1911 the Convention became a charter member of the Federal Council of Churches of Christ* and the International Faith and Order Movement. The same year a merger was effected with the Free Baptist General Conference, the organization of the Freewill* Baptists in America. Structurally, Northern Baptists created boards for ministerial pensions and education and several commissions for stewardship, missions and social service. Controversy ensued over these rapid advances, and the Convention delegates found themselves embroiled in self-destructive debates by 1920 between the modernists* and fundamentalists.* Clusters of churches in the Northeast, Ohio Valley and Oregon bolted the Convention and organized new theologically conservative associations which prevented binding legislative action beyond the local congregations. The main body of Northern Baptists in 1922 assumed a mediating position, affirming the New Testament as the "all sufficient ground of faith and practice."

In the era of World War 2,* Northern Baptists looked for a new theme and a revival of denominational life. Following a review commission report, delegates to the 1950 annual meeting of the convention voted to change the name to American Baptist Convention (ABC) and to create an office of the general secretary. An open invitation was given to other Baptist bodies to unite with the ABC and achieve a national Baptist body. While many congregations in the African-American Baptist traditions achieved a dual-alignment status and the Convention negotiated an associated relationship with the Church of the Brethren,* no organic union took place. Instead, American Baptists have participated in more collegial efforts such as the Baptist World Alliance* and the Baptist Jubilee Advance in 1964.

In 1972 a second major revision of American Baptist denominational structures was adopted and a new, more connectional polity resulted in the American Baptist Churches in the U.S.A. (ABC-USA). A greater share of authority was given to the regional bodies and local churches, with policy matters being ratified by a more democratic general board, composed of clergy* and laity.* The older national societies became program boards of the Convention with interlocking directorates and common annual meetings. A series of "covenants of relationships" unites the interests, tasks and resources of sixty distinct regional, national and general organizations.

As of 1988, the ABC-USA claimed 5,805 churches and 1,568,778 members in all fifty states. About 800 congregations were dually aligned with one or more of the African-American Baptist or mainline* Protestant* groups. Of the 7,678 ordained clergy which the ABC recognized, 434 were women in ministry. Theologically, American Baptists are broadly evangelical,* with churches and pastors* representing conservative, neo-orthodox* and liberal* traditions.

Denominational interests are coordinated at the national offices in Valley Forge, Pennsylvania, and at thirty-seven regional, state and city locations across the U.S. Churches in a region or state generally meet annually in conventions, while elected convention delegates, representatives to the General Board and program administrators hold a Biennial Meeting in various cities throughout the U.S. and Puerto Rico. There are fifteen colleges or universities, six theological schools and 122 homes, children's centers and hospitals affiliated with the denomination. The official periodical, *The American Baptist,* is said to be the oldest Christian magazine continuously in print in North America.

See also BAPTIST CHURCHES.

BIBLIOGRAPHY. W. C. Bitting, ed., *A Manual of the Northern Baptist Convention* (1918); W. H. Brackney, ed., *Baptist Life and Thought, 1600-1980* (1983); W. H. Brackney, *The Baptists* (1988); R. G. Torbet, *History of the Baptists* (1963); *Yearbook of the American Baptist Convention* (later the American Baptist Churches in the U.S.A.), 1920-1987.

W. H. Brackney

American Baptist Convention. *See* AMERICAN BAPTIST CHURCHES IN THE USA.

American Baptist Foreign Mission Society. *See* AMERICAN BAPTIST BOARD OF INTERNATIONAL MINISTRIES.

American Baptist Missionary Union. *See* AMERICAN BAPTIST BOARD OF INTERNATIONAL MINISTRIES.

American Bible Society. A nondenominational organization dedicated to distributing the Bible* throughout the world. The American Bible Society (ABS) was founded in New York City in 1816 for the purpose of distributing the Scriptures throughout the world. At the time of its formation some 130 Bible societies had sprung up in twenty-four states or territories. Their purpose was chiefly to supply Americans, especially the many immigrants,* with Bibles in their own languages. Although some Bibles were published in America prior to 1816, the American societies received most of their Bibles from the British and Foreign Bible Society.

As the number of societies in America increased, there was a call for a national association that would function as an umbrella for the many regional societies. At first this move was strongly opposed by some local societies, particularly by the Philadelphia Bible Society. However, in May 1816, delegates from the many regional societies met in New York and formed the American Bible Society. The British and Foreign Bible Society served as a kind of model for this new organization. Elias Boudinot* was chosen as first chairman of the board, which was comprised mainly of Christian laymen.*

The purpose of the ABS was to offer help to the existing societies and not to replace them. Regional societies were encouraged to join the "parent" society (ABS) as auxiliaries. Within a year forty-one societies had become auxiliaries of ABS. The ABS was designed to supply the regional agencies with Bibles and money. The "daughter" societies acted as agents for the ABS, not only in the distribution of the Scriptures but also in the collecting of monies. Eventually, however, most of these auxiliaries disappeared. As time went on the ABS began to see its mission in other lands more clearly. Working in close cooperation with missionaries of various denominations, the ABS has now printed Bibles in more than a thousand tongues. In 1986 the ABS distributed 289,486,970 Bibles and portions of Scripture. The ABS headquarters is in New York. On the initiative of the ABS, the United Bible Society, which serves as an umbrella organization over the national societies, was formed in 1946.

BIBLIOGRAPHY. C. Lacy, *The Word Carrying Giant* (1977). D. Ewert

American Bible Union. A nineteenth-century Baptist* Bible* society. The American Bible Union grew out of a controversy over the translation of the Greek verb *baptizein,* which the King James Version translates as *baptize* and Baptists wished to translate as *immerse.* The controversy split the American Bible Society* (ABS) and dragged on for more than a decade. The occasion for the controversy was the work in Calcutta of British Baptists, who asked the American Bible Society for help in publishing a second edition of the Bengali New Testament, after the British and Foreign Bible Society had turned them down because of its policy not to print sectarian versions.

In 1835 the ABS appointed a commission to look into the matter. But the issue created a schism in the ABS board, to the embarrassment of all sides, for the battle was fully reported in the secular press. However, the ABS held firm to its policy not to publish sectarian versions, and that the Greek verb *baptizein* was simply to be transliterated in English.

The Baptists then formed the American and Foreign Bible Society in 1836. This name offended the ABS, and there was acrimonious debate when both societies applied for a government charter in 1841. Among Baptists, too, there was sharp disagreement on the name of the Baptist society, and on the new society's publication policies. Out of this controversy the American Bible Union was born, on June 10, 1850, with the financial backing of William Colgate* and with Spencer Cone, former secretary of ABS, as president.

The policy of the American Bible Union was to circulate "only such versions as are conformed as nearly as possible to the original text." Its avowed object was "to procure and circulate the most faithful versions of the Sacred Scriptures in all languages throughout the world." The rift between Baptists and the ABS was eventually healed, and Baptists in various conventions resumed their earlier place among the most loyal supporters of the ABS.

BIBLIOGRAPHY. J. Edmunds, *Discussion on Revision of the Holy Oracles* (1856); C. Lacy, *The Word Carrying Giant* (1977); W. H. Wyckoff, *Documentary History of the American Bible Union,* 4 vols. (1857-1867). D. Ewert

American Board of Catholic Missions. A standing Committee of the National Conference of Catholic Bishops* to distribute funds to the home missions. The Board had its origin in a meeting of seventeen directors of Catholic home and foreign missionary societies at Notre Dame University,* Indiana, in 1919. Their plan for cooperation in fund raising was accepted by the U.S. bishops* who that same year appointed a committee to coordinate and stimulate the missionary* endeavors all over the U.S. It was called the American Board of Catholic Missions (ABCM).

The ABCM was restructured in 1924 in connection with the Society for the Propagation of the Faith, and in 1925 George Cardinal Mundelein* of Chicago became the first president of the new board. Since the SPF would be responsible for all fund raising and for supporting the foreign missions, the ABCM, receiving forty per cent of the funds raised through the society's annual collections and memberships, would distribute these funds to the missions at home—an arrangement that still exists.

Grants are distributed annually, especially in support of black and Hispanic parishes. Since 1970 the ABCM also has given grants to inter-diocesan organizations and religious institutes connected with special ministries, such as black, Hispanic, Asian and handicapped. The amount of funds distributed has gone from $55,715 in 1926 to $6,343,780 in 1985.   L. Nemer

American Board of Commissioners for Foreign Missions. The first American foreign missions society. The presence of Native Americans* had facilitated crosscultural missions since the earliest days of European settlement in North America, but the challenge of planting new churches on the frontiers and reviving the older ones delayed overseas mission outreach. In 1806 some concerned students from Williams College in Massachusetts were caught in a rainstorm; there they held their now-famous "haystack prayer meeting,"* committing themselves to service overseas as God led. Many of them attended Andover Seminary* where in 1810 they successfully petitioned the Congregationalists of Massachusetts to organize the American Board of Commissioners for Foreign Missions (ABCFM), the first American foreign mission society. (However, Native American work was also initially a major focus.)

Various other Reformed denominations used the board as their agency also, but by 1870 it had become basically Congregational in sponsorship. Nevertheless, both before and since that time about half the missionaries have come from other denominations. The first five missionaries included two from the original haystack meeting; they sailed for India in 1812. However, Luther Rice* and Adoniram Judson* changed their views on baptism en route to India, and subsequently founded the American Baptist Foreign Mission Society.* By 1877 there were 375 missionaries, with the peak of 724 reached in 1920. In 1961 ABCFM merged to form the United Church [of Christ]* Board for World Ministries. At that time it had some 300 missionaries, but the institutions

they served had more than 14,000 indigenous teachers, preachers and healers (compared to about 1,000 in 1870).

Probably the most successful field in terms of church-planting was Hawaii. Other large concentrations of missionaries were in China, India, Sri Lanka, Japan and southern Africa (where the churches that were planted are now generally part of United Churches), plus Turkey and Syria (where Greeks and Armenians responded). Fewer numbers served in several European countries and Micronesia. Bible translation, schools and hospitals were always among the emphases, with evangelism gradually receding as a priority.

BIBLIOGRAPHY. F. F. Goodsell, *You Shall Be My Witnesses* (1959); W. E. Strong, *The Story of the American Board* (1910).   D. G. Tinder

American Board of Missions to the Jews. An independent mission agency engaged in evangelism* to Jews. The American Board of Missions to the Jews (ABMJ) was founded as the Williamsburg Mission in 1894 by Leopold Cohn. A Jewish immigrant from Hungary, Cohn came to the U.S. in 1892 and converted* to Christianity. After studying theology* for a year in Scotland, he returned to Brooklyn, New York, as a missionary.*

An initial monthly stipend from the American Baptist Home Mission Society enabled Cohn to concentrate on evangelism. He began preaching* in rented halls in the Jewish neighborhoods of Brownsville and Williamsburg. Working out of these buildings, he organized sewing schools and English classes and occasionally operated a dispensary where immigrants received free medical treatment. His magazine *The Chosen People* served to interest Christians in Jewish evangelism and to spread news of the Mission's evangelistic successes. In the 1920s, the Mission expanded into several North American and European cities, a fact reflected in its change of name in 1924 to the American Board of Missions to the Jews.

When Cohn died in 1937, his son Joseph succeeded him as director. Educated at Moody Bible Institute,* he became a familiar figure at prophecy conferences* and greatly broadened the ABMJ's base of support. During the Jesus Movement* of the 1970s, the ABMJ's San Francisco branch, under the leadership of career missionary Moishe Rosen, became the focal point of the Jews for Jesus* movement. A separate evangelistic agency was organized under that name in 1973.

See also JEWS, CHRISTIAN MISSIONS TO; JEWISH CHRISTIANS; JEWS FOR JESUS.

BIBLIOGRAPHY. J. H. Cohn, *I Have Fought a Good*

Fight: The Story of Jewish Mission Pioneering in America (1953); L. Cohn, *A Modern Missionary to an Ancient People* (1908); M. Rosen with B. Proctor, *Jews for Jesus* (1974).

J. H. Warnock

American Christian Commission. The first post-Civil War* Protestant* response to the challenge of urban ministry.* By the end of the Civil War, Protestant leaders were becoming aware of the physical, moral and spiritual poverty in America's burgeoning cities. In 1865, James Yeatman* of St. Louis published a *Circular of Inquiry* outlining the church's ignorance of conditions and lack of organization for urban ministry. In response, the American Christian Commission (ACC) was formed in Cleveland in September by clergy* and laymen* who had been active in the wartime United States Christian Commission.*

A year later the ACC presented a lengthy report, based on observations from thirty-five cities, describing urban needs and mission* efforts. One scholar called the report "the first truly significant picture of Protestant prospects in urban America." For two decades the ACC held local, state and national conventions. The ACC's monthly paper, *The Christian at Work,* encouraged churches to adopt programs of neighborhood visitation, humanitarian endeavors, street preaching and rescue work.

BIBLIOGRAPHY. A. I. Abell, *The Urban Impact on American Protestantism, 1865-1900* (1962).

D. W. Carlson

American Colonization Society. An early-nineteenth-century organization for the resettlement of freed African-American slaves in Africa. The American Colonization Society was founded in 1817 with Henry Clay and John Randolph among its prominent members. The purpose of the organization was to raise funds to remunerate slave owners and establish a colony in Africa for the repatriation of American blacks. In 1820 the organization sent the first African-American Methodist* missionary,* Daniel Coker,* to Sierra Leone, West Africa. By 1830 the society had resettled 1,420 former slaves, most of them in Liberia, West Africa.

The African-American colony of Liberia was founded in 1822, and as many as twelve thousand blacks immigrated to West Africa under the auspices of the American Colonization Society. But the organization failed in its ultimate purpose. Christian supporters of colonization hoped that African-Americans would help to Christianize Africa. While some white Northerners believed that colonization would help bring an end to slavery, others, like Thomas Jefferson,* wanted the nation to be rid of the African-American population which was regarded as a blight upon the new republic. Many Southerners who supported colonization did so in order to protect the institution of slavery from the anomaly of the free African-American in their midst.

Free African-Americans were insulted by these racial motives for colonization, and most of them preferred to immigrate to Canada. Prominent free African-Americans in the North, like Richard Allen,* and white abolitionists, like William Lloyd Garrison* rejected colonization, demanding that African-Americans deserved a full share in the nation they had helped build. The Society itself was plagued by insufficient funding, planning, transportation, housing, medical care and military defense. In Africa, colonists died from disease and suffered from mismanagement and lack of support from the Colonization Society. By 1834 factionalism had weakened the parent organization, which survived only until the 1850s.

BIBLIOGRAPHY. J. H. Franklin and A. A. Moss, Jr., *From Slavery to Freedom: A History of Negro Americans* (1980); G. S. Wilmore, *Black Religion and Black Radicalism* (1983).

L. J. Edwards

American Council of Christian Churches. An agency representing separatist* fundamentalists.* The American Council of Christian Churches (ACCC) was founded on September 17, 1941, in New York City in a meeting of the Bible Protestant Church and the Bible Presbyterian Church. In the years that followed, several other denominations* joined the ACCC.

The initial impetus for organizing the group was to witness to Protestant* orthodoxy* in the face of the modernism* represented by the Federal* Council of Churches (FCC)—now known as the National Council of Churches* (NCC)—and to provide a united organization of separatist churches. Carl McIntire,* a militant defender of orthodoxy, was the first president of the ACCC.

McIntire challenged the right of the FCC to speak for American Protestantism, protesting that the ecumenical movement* had compromised the truth of the gospel, was attempting to build a "one-world church" and advocated pacifism and peaceful coexistence with Communism. Two early victories for the ACCC were the gaining of free radio time and the granting of a quota of chaplains* in the U.S. armed forces, both in addition to what had already been apportioned to the FCC.

The ACCC remains firmly committed to the doctrine of the plenary, verbal inspiration of Scripture* as the basis for Protestant orthodoxy and adheres to a separatist doctrine of the church that calls for true believers to depart from what it judges to be apostate denominations. McIntire's strong views regarding separatism and authoritarian leadership inevitably led to clashes within the organization during the 1950s. In 1968 his leadership was rejected by the ACCC, a decision he attempted—but failed—to reverse in 1970.

In the late 1980s the ACCC reported a total membership of 1.5 million, including denominations, independent churches, associations and individuals. Membership consists of constituent members, who have severed all ties with the NCC, and auxiliary members, who still maintain some ties with the NCC (such as in the case of individuals in denominations that are members of the NCC). The ACCC publishes the *Christian Beacon* and maintains headquarters in Valley Forge, Pennsylvania. It is a member of the International Council of Christian Churches.*

BIBLIOGRAPHY. L. Gasper, *The Fundamentalist Movement, 1930-1956* (1963).

The Editors

American Friends Service Committee. Independent Quaker* peace and service organization. Founded in 1917 to provide conscientious objectors with an opportunity to aid civilian victims during World War 1,* today the American Friends Service Committee (AFSC) carries on projects of service, development, justice and peace.

AFSC workers in Central and Latin America, Indochina, Africa and the Middle East conduct projects of social and technical assistance designed to strengthen self-sufficiency and community. In the U.S., AFSC provides support for the rights of undocumented workers, small farmers, farmworkers and refugees, advocating for people who are hungry, poorly housed, homeless or unemployed.

In its programs for disarmament and peace, and for non-military solutions to conflict, AFSC reflects the Quaker conviction that all life is sacred. AFSC staff work to build informed public resistance to war, militarism and the nuclear arms race, and for peaceful U.S. policies. In 1947 the AFSC and its British counterpart were jointly awarded the Nobel Peace Prize. The AFSC's international headquarters are in Philadelphia, with nine regional and more than forty program offices located across the U.S.

W. A. Cooper

American Home Missionary Society. A cooperative and then Congregational* home mission agency. Since the 1801 Plan of Union* between Presbyterians* and Connecticut Congregationalists, there had been formal cooperation between these branches of Reformed* Protestantism, particularly in planting new churches. But the competition and confusion resulting from independent actions of numerous locally based societies led in 1826 to the formation of the American Home Missionary Society (AHMS). As a coordinating body it had some 400 local auxiliaries within a few years, but the intentions to become multidenominational were never realized. Most Presbyterians cooperated until their 1839 split into New* and Old School* factions; then, the New School alone cooperated and only until 1861. Thereafter AHMS was only what the name change of 1893 acknowledged, the Congregational Home Missionary Society. In 1937 it became part of the United Church of Christ.*

The AHMS purposed to help new congregations that were unable to support a minister until they could do so. The congregation's share of ministerial support was expected to increase gradually. It thereby promoted resident ministry rather than the itinerancy which had prevailed. From the initial 170 missionaries (in fifteen states), there was rapid growth to more than 500 by 1832 and nearly 1,100 by 1853. Final Presbyterian withdrawal did not hurt the AHMS because after the Civil War* Congregationalists were proportionately the largest donors for organized home missions of any major group. By 1892 there were more than 2,000 missionaries, a tenth of them in the South. Meanwhile, the society began responding to the massive increases in immigration so that by 1903 some 230 of the 1,907 missionaries then employed were ministering in foreign languages. By the turn of the century, more than four-fifths of the 5,650 Congregational churches then in America were planted by AHMS/ CHMS. In the twentieth century comparable growth has not been sustained, doubtless owing to changes in the parent constituency.

BIBLIOGRAPHY. C. B. Goodykoontz, *Home Missions on the American Frontier, with Particular Reference to the American Home Missionary Society.*

D. G. Tinder

American Lutheran Church. A large Lutheran* denomination* that merged to form the Evangelical Lutheran Church in America (ELCA).* The American Lutheran Church (ALC) for the most part arose out of nineteenth-century Lutheran immigrants* to America who tended to stress a blend of confessionalism* and pietism.* In time these

Lutherans formed various bodies, including four Germanic groups: the Evangelical Joint Synod of Ohio and Other States (1818); the Buffalo Synod (1845); and the Iowa Synod (1854), which had been established under the influence of Wilhelm Loehe.* In 1930 these three bodies formed the original American Lutheran Church.

They were joined in 1960 by a group with Norwegian origins, the Evangelical Lutheran Church. This body had been formed in 1917 out of Hauge's Synod (1846), the Norwegian Synod (1853) and the United Norwegian Lutheran Church of America (1890). At its founding it included over 1,000 congregations and approximately 500,000 members. It brought nearly 2,700 congregations and 1.5 million members to the merger of 1960.

The third member of the union of 1960 was United Evangelical Lutheran Church, which was of Danish lineage. Founded in 1896 with 127 congregations and nearly 14,000 members, it brought 181 congregations and 70,000 members to the union of 1960.

A later addition to the ALC was the Lutheran Free Church, which did not join until 1963. It was formed in 1897 by a splinter group from the United Norwegian Lutheran Church of America. Numbering 6,250 members and 125 congregations at their founding, they added 88,500 members and 288 congregations to the ALC.

The ALC confessed the canonical Scripture* as inspired and inerrant* and adhered to the ancient ecumenical* creeds, the unaltered Augsburg Confession and Luther's Small Catechism. The ALC was strongest in the Upper Midwest and was a member of the Lutheran World Federation* and the World Council of Churches.* When the ALC merged to form ELCA in 1987, it consisted of 2.3 million members.

BIBLIOGRAPHY. E. C. Nelson, ed., *The Lutherans in North America* (1975); A. C. Piepkorn, *Profiles in Belief,* vol. 2 (1978); R. C. Wiederaenders and W. G. Tillmanns, *The Synods of American Lutheranism* (1968). The Editors

American Missionary Association. A congregational* mission* agency with a nineteenth-century focus on ministry to African-Americans. Believing that the mission* societies serving the Congregational churches were not taking a staunch antislavery position, the American Missionary Association (AMA) was formed in 1846, building on four earlier groups. Soon it was sponsoring some eighty missionaries in Africa and Asia, Jamaica and Hawaii, as well as among African-Americans in Canada and American states. Nearly half of the missionaries worked with non-Congregational churches. With the coming of the Civil War* the society focused on educating newly freed slaves, becoming the most significant of many such agencies. What is now Hampton University became, in 1861, the first of hundreds of schools founded and staffed for many years by the AMA. Most did not evolve into universities, but those that did include Atlanta, Dillard, Fisk and Howard universities. Some 500 African-American secondary schools begun by the AMA were eventually transferred to local governments. After the Civil War the AMA returned its foreign work to the older American Board of Commissioners for Foreign Missions* and resumed its work among Native Americans. Efforts to plant Congregationalism among African-Americans and Appalachian whites were not very successful. In this century, AMA became part of the Congregational home missions department, moving with it as that denomination merged to form the United Church of Christ.*

BIBLIOGRAPHY. J. M. Richardson, *Christian Reconstruction: The American Missionary Association and Southern Blacks, 1861-1890* (1986); A. F. Beard, *A Crusade of Brotherhood: A History of the American Missionary Association* (1909).
D. G. Tinder

American Missionary Fellowship. Nondenominational home mission* agency. The American Missionary Fellowship's earliest forerunner was Philadelphia's First Day Society, organized in 1790 by Bishop William White* of the Episcopal Church.* Impressed with the British Sunday-school movement, he offered non-sectarian religious training to many of the unchurched lower classes. In 1817 several Philadelphians established the Sunday and Adult School Union, which became the American Sunday School Union* in 1824.

The Union aimed to support Sunday schools, provide Christian literature, distribute Bibles,* attack vice and uphold the Lord's Day. Later Union ventures included a Reconstruction ministry and renewed literature efforts to counteract Darwinism* after the Civil War,* and new programs in camping* and daily vacation Bible schools in the early twentieth century. In response to changing patterns in American church life after World War 2,* the Union reassessed its mission and phased out its publication and literature ministry in 1968. In 1973 the society moved to suburban Philadelphia and in 1974, changed its name to American Missionary Fellowship. The current AMF general director is E. Eugene Williams, who supervises about 125 missionary families and a total annual income of almost $3.5 million.

See also AMERICAN SUNDAY SCHOOL UNION.

BIBLIOGRAPHY. W. Rice, *The Sunday School Movement, 1780-1917 and the American Sunday School Union, 1780-1917* (1917); R. Mattocks, *On the Move: A Pictorial History of American Missionary Fellowship, 1790-1980* (1980).

J. A. Patterson

American Peace Society. The first nonsectarian national peace organization in the U.S. Peace societies appeared in New York and Massachusetts in 1815, spurred by the writings of David Low Dodge and Noah Worcester,* who argued the incompatibility of Christianity and war. In 1828 William Ladd formed the American Peace Society (APS) as a national organization, though New England remained its focal point. Considering war unchristian, the society aimed to discuss "the evils of war and the best means for effecting its abolition." The APS was one of the most idealistic antebellum expressions of evangelical* Protestant* millennialism* and perfectionism.* By the 1840s, the society had split into factions, but nevertheless it developed and disseminated thoughtful arguments against war.

Slavery posed a dilemma to the APS, since most members were abolitionists.* When the Civil War* began the society endorsed the Union cause, labelling it a "rebellion" not a war. The society revived after the War, mainly as an advocate of international arbitration. Nationalism prevailed in World War 1,* however, and the society endorsed American participation.

BIBLIOGRAPHY. P. Brock, *Pacifism in the United States, From the Colonial Era to the First World War* (1968); M. E. Curti, *The American Peace Crusade, 1815-1860* (1965).

D. W. Carlson

American Protective Association. A nativistic* anti-Catholic society. Organized in 1887 by H. F. Bowers and a group of businessmen in Clinton, Iowa, the American Protective Association (APA) developed its strongest foothold in the Midwest. Chief among the concerns of the APA was what many American nativists perceived as an ongoing Roman Catholic* plot to undermine American democratic institutions. With the establishment in 1894 of an Apostolic Delegation* to the American Catholic hierarchy, the APA experienced an accelerated rate of growth. It is difficult, if not impossible, to determine how large the membership of the APA actually became. Typical of secret societies that flourished at the time, the organization failed to keep reliable records of dues-paying members. William Traynor, president of the APA in 1896, claimed a membership approaching two-and-a-half million, but it is doubtful whether the APA ever attracted more than a fraction of that figure. Hailing nearly every major Republican Party triumph as an APA victory, the organizational leadership made a career of inflating its importance in American political affairs. Actually, the organization was incapable of marshaling the votes necessary to influence elections at the national level. Established upon a quixotic vision of salvaging the fleeting myth of a unified Protestant* social order, the APA collapsed almost as rapidly as it had risen. Holding its final national convention in 1898, the APA remained little more than a token movement until its dissolution in 1911.

BIBLIOGRAPHY. H. J. Desmond, *The A.P.A. Movement* (1912); D. L. Kinzer, *An Episode in Anti-Catholicism: The American Protective Association* (1964).

B. K. Turley

American Revolution, Christianity and the. In 1776 religion and political sentiments merged in an unforgettable moment in history. The mingling of these two forces altered both the nature of the American Revolution and religion. But what exactly was the relationship between religion and politics in the American Revolution? How did Christians, known more for Bible* than gun toting, justify armed revolt? The answer unfolds in three separate scenes: religion shaping ideology, religion in wartime actions and the consequences of the war on religion.

Christianity and Other Ideological Causes of the Revolution. Ministers* from such diverse religious perspectives as libertarians, liberals* and evangelicals,* all planted the seeds of rebellion. Along with the usual Sunday* message of repentance, ministers gave numerous weekday occasional sermons,* such as fast day,* militia, thanksgiving and election sermons, as well as Thursday-evening lectures. On these occasions ministers catechized* more on politics than on religion.

Lacking a coherent all-encompassing world view from which to work, the ministers tried to sort out a number of competing ideologies about the nature of society and government. Some of these ideologies were Christian, others were secular. Even within the same ideological school, systematic ideas were often mixed with biases.

One major ideology came from Puritanism.* Ever since the founding of Massachusetts in 1620, Puritanism had stressed covenant theology*—both for the individual and the nation. In the past the special covenant people of God had been Israel, but now New England stood at the center of God's work in history. In return for obedience and acknowledgement of his sole sovereignty, God promised to defend and protect America. Furthermore, God gave Americans a unique mission to serve as a redemptive agent. Puritans must redeem their children from sin.* If successful, New England would provide a model of a godly community. A model which, if replicated by other nations, could redeem the whole world and prepare the way for the establishment of the millennial* kingdom.*

Drawing on the covenant concept, preachers in 1765 began to develop a rationale for armed revolt. They warned further allegiance to England might result in God's displeasure and loss of America's special covenant relationship. In a message to the Connecticut legislature from the text "Let every soul be subject unto the higher powers," Reverend Samuel Lockwood interpreted the Bible typologically, directly equating America with Old Testament Israel. God punished sin in Israel by temporarily allowing rule by evil men such as King Jeroboam of Israel or Haman, prime minister of Persia. Originally, God had intended rulers to serve the people. Instead, some rulers act as the "tyrant" and "indulge sloth, luxury, and avarice . . . oppress the subjects with unconstitutional decrees and unrighteous measures." Other pastors argued that both nations, contrary to God's perfect will, foolishly asked for a king. Some advocates of the national covenant argued America could never agree with England's insistence on "unlimited" control over the colonies, as expressed in the Declaratory Act of 1766. Such a demand was a religious heresy,* an affront against God's word, which demands "no other gods." Further, it would end America's covenant relationship, as God would immediately cast away any people putting loyalty to country ahead of loyalty to God.

Many upper-class individuals and their pastors held a rival world view: the commonwealth or Whig ideology. This theory of government and society had its roots in sixteenth-century Italian Renaissance writers such as Niccolo Machiavelli (1469-1527). Whig ideology further developed under the libertarian thoughts of English commonwealth (1680-1740) writers James Harrington, John Trenchard, Thomas Gordon and James Burgh. Whiggism warned that uncontrolled political power always degenerated into corruption. The best governments balanced power between three separate branches (monarchy, aristocracy and democracy*) to prevent any faction from gaining

too much power. Whigs stressed that history was a struggle between power and liberty. Since humans were basically evil, freedom was perpetually in danger from the temptations of wealth, luxury and bribery. Great nations in the past fell not from the force of invading armies, but internally from lack of character and spirit in their citizens. When a leader had too much unchecked power, that leader could always maintain power by corrupting followers with bribes of jobs and money. Finally, Whigs developed a compact theory of government. Americans need only obey the king if he secured the rights of the people.

Influenced by radical Whig writers, many Americans interpreted British actions as evidence of corrupt, unchecked power. Since Americans had no voice in Parliament, there was no constitutional balance; no check against arbitrary British rule. The new tax laws, beginning with the Stamp Act of 1765, called for collection by appointed revenue agents. History showed one way a balanced constitution had been corrupted was by appointed officials who obeyed ruling powers. Next came a standing army to support appointed officials. Money collected from the new taxes might bribe key Americans and pay judges' salaries.

After reciting this list of abuses, ministers applied the contractual notion to argue that King George III had broken his compact with the people, and the people had a right to revolt. Further, they suggested the best antidote to corruption and self-interest was moral character in a nation's citizens. Like Puritanism, the American Whigs stressed frugality, industry, simplicity and sacrifice of individualism for the collective good. Whigs taught that governments existed to strengthen public virtue and to encourage the individual to set aside self-interest for the sake of the community.

After 1765 ministers increasingly strengthened their arguments for revolution by intertwining Whig ideology with Puritan covenant theology. They translated and elevated political arguments to the sacred plane of religious and moral language. The evils of British tyranny became magnified as ministers used biblical imagery—Israel captive in Babylon, an oppressive Pharaoh or an evil advisor like Haman—to explain the Christian's duty to disobey evil rulers. Finally, a symbiosis of Puritanism and Whiggism was possible since both ideologies held many similar beliefs: humans were basically sinful; governments must serve the common good; history was a struggle between good and evil; there were God-given "unalienable" rights. This double-stranded ideology became a defense for liberty and a doctrine justifying revolution.

Christians cannot take exclusive credit or blame for promoting revolution. There were other ideologies which stimulated armed revolt. For example, middle-class tradespeople preferred the ideas of economic liberalism as expressed by Adam Smith. In his *The Wealth of Nations* (1776), Smith argued that God had established a natural law of competition and self-interest. Smith enthroned self-interest and materialism as virtues. Since the best government was the one ruling least, England had no right to tax or pass trade laws for the colonies. Another competing intellectual framework was the radical, popular ideology which appealed to many lower-class townspeople. This ideology championed the levelling of society by advocating maximum power for the people. A final intellectual stimulus came from the concepts of European Enlightenment* theorists (1680-1789) who argued that rational thinking would bring liberal progress to civilization.

Since the War took place within this pluralistic context of competing world views, it is difficult to disentangle Christian influences and ideologies from secular thinking. An American revolutionist in a pamphlet or a pastor in a political sermon could without any sense of incongruity cite a seventeenth-century Puritan, a Radical Whig like John Trenchard, the economist Adam Smith or an Enlightenment thinker like Jean Jacques Rousseau—all on the same page.

Ministerial Support for the War. Many ministers did not restrict their activities to preaching an ideology of revolution. They lent their names and spiritual support first in local town committees, then county conventions, later at state conventions and finally in national politics. They also participated directly in political action, serving on their town's committee of correspondence, recruiting men for the army, serving as chaplains* and even as common soldiers, and drafting new state constitutions.

This key role of the clergy* in the Revolution is easy to document. There are numerous specific examples of such clerical political action. For example, when citizens in Talbot County, Maryland, set up the Committee of Observation to stop importation of British merchandise, they selected Reverend John Gordon as its chairman. When Virginia in March 1775 held an extra-legal patriotic convention, Reverend Charles Thruston from Frederick County served as a delegate, and the convention selected another minister, named Selden, to read daily prayers.* And in May 1775, seven out of ninety-eight towns elected their local

minister to a state convention which New Hampshire set up in the process of transferring power from royal to state authority. One of these ministers, Samuel Webster, also served on the state's Committee of Safety, the committee running the government when the legislature was not in session. In May 1775, the Committee of Correspondence of Albany, New York, asked Samuel Kirkland,* missionary to the Oneida Indians, to use his influence to keep the Native Americans neutral.

Ministers seemed most active in politics in Massachusetts. For example, in 1775 Massachusetts appointed Reverend Murray as president *pro tempore* of the Provincial Congress. This same congress then allowed Reverend William Gordon to interrogate all prisoners and gave Gordon custody of Governor Thomas Hutchinson's abandoned letters. Gordon promptly printed excerpts from Hutchinson's letters to prove Hutchinson's sinister actions as former governor.

Many ministers also served as fighting soldiers or praying chaplains.* As colonies formed local armies to resist England, regiments needed chaplains. Thus when Connecticut formed a state army of six regiments, it appointed six chaplains. Probably the most conspicuous examples of revolutionary fervor were ministers who served as privates and officers in the army. In 1776 John Peter Gabriel Muhlenberg,* the Lutheran* minister in Woodstock, Virginia, preached from Ecclesiastes, "A time to be born, and a time to die . . . a time to fight." Immediately afterwards, he took off his clerical robe, revealed a colonel's uniform, marched to the door of his church and recruited 300 soldiers. Similarly, when news of Lexington and Concord reached the Reverend David Avery of Windsor, Vermont, he finished his sermon, went outside the church, called his parishioners to arms and marched off with twenty men. Avery served not as chaplain, but as the captain of Windsor's minutemen.

Although clergymen played a vital role promoting, nourishing and serving in the American Revolution, their most significant function was establishing a Christian milieu for the American revolutionary generation. Even if a majority of nonclerical members on local committees, or delegates to state conventions, or the "Founding Fathers" at the Continental Congress cannot be classified as godly men, all placed a high value on religion for the good of society. Even Deists* acknowledged that all religions shared a common morality which supplied inner strength in wartime. Many states legislated religious laws. For example, among New Hampshire's first legislative acts were laws encouraging citizens to faithfully attend religious services on the Sabbath,* a requirement that all New Hampshire regiments have chaplains and a request that all citizens spend a day in fasting and prayer for the colony.

The Religious Consequences of the War. Wars inevitably herald change. After the eight-year-long war, Abigail Adams, wife of the second president of the U.S., commented that she had lived to see the colonial world "turned up side down." Ministers lent fervent support to the war effort, but at what cost to religion? Religion and politics entered the war locked arm in arm, but the partnership would prove to be short-lived.

Unfortunately, the revolutionary fervor resulted in some negative religious trends. The almost-total marriage of Whig and Puritan ideology during the Revolution produced an American civil religion*— America was God's chosen people. For nineteenth-century Americans this meant that they had a spiritual responsibility to reform society and bring on the millennial kingdom. Even today many still believe that America is the New Israel, a nation singularly blessed by God and responsible for worldwide reform.

Furthermore, the clergy's unreserved support for revolution meant forgoing criticism of revolutionary policies. Ministers ever since colonial days had played the role of Old Testament prophets like Jeremiah, warning the people of sin or serving as critics of government policy. Yet, once evangelical pastors enthusiastically embraced the Revolution, it was difficult for them to maintain an objectivity about patriot policies. Nowhere was this more apparent than in their treatment of War dissenters—both pacifists* and Loyalists. Evangelical pastors, like most Whig politicians, were intolerant of the significant minority of Americans who found military conflict incompatible with their religious or political convictions.

Another negative outcome was that ministers often became the dupes of politicians, who promoted secular political goals in the guise of religion. For example, politicians in Virginia's House of Burgesses, hoping for grounds for revolt, cleverly arranged a religious confrontation with the royal governor. Although it was the governor's prerogative to establish days of thanksgiving and fasting, in 1774 the legislature called for a day of fasting and prayer to mourn England's closing of Boston's harbor. Unable to ignore this challenge to his authority, Governor Dunmore immediately dissolved the Virginia legislature.

Later that same year at the Continental Congress, the nation's first national assembly, the first divisive issue arose over a proposal, by Massachusetts delegate John Adams, to appoint a permanent chaplain. The major motivation for proposing a chaplain and then suggesting that he be an Anglican* was political. Massachusetts delegates desired to remove prejudices against New England Congregationalists,* who were rumored to be emotional extremists. For Adams and his cohorts, supporting a chaplain was a satisfactory mixture of pious religion and beneficial politics. Gradually, as politicians adopted the rhetorical style of preachers, politicians displaced ministers as the intellectual leaders in America. As one historian has observed, "political ideology had assumed religion's role as the fashioner of the most creative ideas in America."

Not all of the consequences, however, were negative. The Revolution did bring greater religious freedom. Prior to the Revolution, many colonial Americans suffered under severe religious intolerance because every colony, except Rhode Island and Pennsylvania, had an official "church of the standing order." All citizens were required to pay church taxes, and those not belonging to an established church* were discriminated against. Thus in Massachusetts no adult male could vote in civil elections unless he was a member of a local Congregational church. Every citizen was required to attend a church on at least one Sunday a month or pay a fine. Religion was defined so narrowly that Massachusetts nonconformists suffered banishment (Roger Williams* and Anne Hutchinson*) or death (the Quaker* Mary Dyer*).

But the War meant an end to such religious intolerance. American independence could only be obtained with the support of the majority. Therefore, in a society so diverse—religiously, ethnically and ideologically—once the War began, most colonies attempted to build as broad a political and religious consensus as possible. This resulted in greater religious toleration and freedom after the War. For example, Virginia's 1776 constitution became the first state constitution to mandate religious freedom.* The Virginia model was followed in the First Amendment* of the nation's federal constitution. The Revolution had thus precipitated the movement which ultimately resulted in the liberation of the churches from state control.

Conclusion. In 1776 religion and political sentiments merged as ministers promoted political ideology and eventually catechized the people on their sacred duty to resist British tyranny. Drawing on both Puritan covenant theology and Whig ideology, ministers rationalized revolution. Ministers also participated directly in political action, serving on their town's committee of correspondence, recruiting men for the army, serving as chaplains and even as common soldiers, and drafting new state policies. Religion and politics entered the war locked arm in arm, but the marriage produced both negative (America's civil religion, decline in ministers' influence, false religious cant) and positive results (greater religious tolerance and freedom).

BIBLIOGRAPHY. J. Appleby, "The Social Origins of the American Revolutionary Ideology," *JAH* 64 (1978):935-958; A. Baldwin, *The New England Clergy and the American Revolution* (1965); P. Force, ed., *American Archives*, 6 vols. (1837-1846); E. S. Gaustad, *Faith of Our Fathers: Religion and the New Nation* (1987); N. O. Hatch, *The Sacred Cause of Liberty: Republican Thought and the Millenium in Revolutionary New England* (1977); J. S. Herbert, ed., *America, Christian or Secular? Readings in American Christian History and Civil Religion* (1984); R. Isaac, *The Transformation of Virginia, 1740-1790* (1982); M. Noll, *One Nation Under God? Christian Faith and Political Action in America* (1988); M. A. Noll, N. O. Hatch and G. M. Marsden, *The Search for Christian America* (1983); H. S. Stout, *The New England Soul: Preaching and Religious Culture in Colonial New England* (1986); G. S. Wood, *The Creation of the American Republic, 1776-1787* (1969).

D. E. Maas

American Society of Missiology. Ecumenical* society to promote mission studies in the U.S. The idea for such a society was proposed to the Association of Professors of Missions at their annual meeting, June 9-10, 1972, on the campus of Scarritt College, Nashville, Tennessee. It received support, and a continuation committee of Gerald Anderson, Ralph D. Winter and Donald M. Wodarz, SSC, was established. The constituent assembly was held at Concordia Seminary in St. Louis, Missouri, June 8-10, 1973. More than ninety attended and membership surpassed 450. Since then the Society has had annual meetings, and membership has remained at approximately 500.

The society is ecumenical in membership and representation, and includes Roman Catholics and both evangelical and mainline Protestants. It seeks to stimulate mission studies through its annual meetings, its journal *Missiology: An International Review* (since 1973) and its series of monographs, published through Orbis Press since 1980.
See also MISSIOLOGY, PROTESTANT.

BIBLIOGRAPHY. W. R. Shenk, *The American So-ciety of Missiology, 1972-1987* (1987).

L. Nemer

American Sunday School Union. Primary agency for the early development of the Sunday school.* Founded in 1824, the American Sunday School Union (ASSU) was as an outgrowth of the Sunday and Adult School Union in Philadelphia. The ASSU leaders, primarily laity,* saw the Sunday school as a means to provide society with education in Christian and democratic* values. The ASSU had three purposes: organizing Sunday-school leaders, publishing moral and religious books and developing Sunday schools "wherever there is a population." To avoid theological conflict, the ASSU was founded on the "union principle," emphasizing a general evangelical* Protestant* Christianity; however, the lack of theological clarity stimulated some denominations* to form competing Sunday-school organizations.

Prior to the Civil War,* the ASSU was responsible for the calling of the first national Sunday-school conventions in 1832 and 1833. In publishing, it provided a significant quantity of material, including the first widely used Sunday-school curriculum ("Selected Lessons" and "Union Questions") and a 100-volume library for children. As a missionary society, it initiated in 1830 the Mississippi Valley Enterprise that founded over 3,000 schools. Similar less successful projects were later initiated in the South and for foreign missions. After the Civil War, when leadership for the Sunday school shifted to the convention system and to denominations, the ASSU continued in a more limited manner to form and support Sunday schools, primarily in rural areas. In 1970 the name was changed to the American Missionary Society* to reflect its task of assisting multi-cultural and ethnic groups to form new churches in rural and inner-city areas.
See also AMERICAN MISSIONARY FELLOWSHIP; SUNDAY SCHOOL MOVEMENT.

BIBLIOGRAPHY. A. M. Boylan, *Sunday School: The Formation of an American Institution, 1790-1880* (1989); E. W. Rice, *The Sunday School Movement, 1780-1917 and the American Sunday School Union, 1817-1917* (1917). J. L. Seymour

American Tract Society. A religious publisher. The American Tract Society (ATS) was the chief innovator of mass publication of religious material in early nineteenth-century America. Born of the merger of tract societies in New York and Massachusetts in 1825, the ATS quickly became a leader in the development of printing technology, including stereotyping, steampowered printing, and woodcut and lithographic illustration. By the late 1820s the ATS was annually printing and distributing more than five million tracts (plus books and magazines)—at least five pages of material for every person in America. In addition to its publication work, the ATS was an innovator in the use of traveling agents known as Colporteurs.*

From its founding, the ATS was nondenominational. All publications were approved by a committee representing mainstream Calvinist* churches. Early tracts were usually brief homilies on common vices (especially intemperance) or narratives on salvation* and damnation (often anti-Catholic). Two of the most popular were "The Swearer's Prayer" and "The Dairyman's Daughter," both imported from England. The society prospered through the 1850s, despite increasing sectarian disagreements and the temporary secession of the Boston society in 1858 over the unwillingness of the ATS to oppose slavery. After the Civil War,* the ATS was widely heralded for its evangelical* work among freed slaves. But after 1870 the ATS's financial support and publishing activities declined steadily as it turned its attention more to foreign-language and book publication. In 1947 the society returned to its original mission: the publication of small, English-language, gospel tracts. By 1975—its sesquicentennial—the ATS was regularly publishing some thirty million tracts per year.

See also PUBLISHING, RELIGIOUS.

BIBLIOGRAPHY. D. P. Nord, "The Evangelical Origins of Mass Media in America, 1815-1835," *Journalism Monographs,* no. 88 (1984); L. Thompson, "The Printing and Publishing Activities of the American Tract Society from 1825 to 1850," *Papers of the Bibliographical Society of America* 35 (1941):81-114; E. Twadell, "The American Tract Society, 1814-1860," *CH* 15 (1946):116-132.
D. P. Nord

American Unitarian Association. Unitarian*

denomination.* The American Unitarian Association (AUA) was established in Boston in 1825 "to diffuse the knowledge and promote the interests of pure Christianity." The organizers of the AUA belonged to the liberal wing of New England Congregationalism,* the church of the Puritan* founders. The "pure Christianity" which Unitarians wished to promote, however, rejected certain Calvinist* doctrines* in favor of the Arian belief that Christ, although not merely human, was not divine, and the Arminian* belief that sinners were not predestined* but could make themselves deserving of salvation* through their own efforts.

Until the mid-1860s Unitarians used the AUA primarily for missionary* purposes, including issuing liberal religious publications and gathering new churches outside their stronghold in eastern Massachusetts. Following the Civil War,* the AUA began to take on more of the trappings of a formal denomination, including a professional bureaucracy and an assembly of delegates from each congregation convened periodically to set church policy. In 1961 the AUA merged with the Universalist Church of America to form the Unitarian Universalist Association.*

See also UNITARIAN CONTROVERSY.

BIBLIOGRAPHY. D. Robinson, *The Unitarians and the Universalists* (1985); C. C. Wright, ed., *A Stream of Light* (1975).
C. E. Wright

Americanism. A nineteenth-century term for patriotism which entered the lexicon of Catholic theology in 1899 when Pope Leo XIII* used it in his apostolic letter *Testem Benevolentiae.** In the Catholic context, the term has five dimensions: (1) the ideas censured in the letter; (2) a series of controversies between 1884 and 1899 dividing the U.S. Catholic community over the desired extent of accommodation to American culture; (3) ideas of American Catholic messianism held by the progressive or Americanist Party; (4) the international Catholic reform movement (1887-1899) through which Americanists sought to implement their ideas; (5) a French controversy occasioned by the 1897 French version of Walter Elliott's* *The Life of Father Hecker* (1891).

Presuming a rigid neo-scholastic nature-grace distinction, *Testem Benevolentiae* condemned the notion that the Church should adapt to the age in essentials, and, more specifically, that the Church should imitate contemporary states by introducing greater individual liberty. While noting the legitimacy of political Americanism, Leo rejected the term as applied to the censured opinions.

On Being American and Catholic: The Conflict, 1884-1899. How could the Catholic Church in the U.S. provide the large numbers of Catholic immigrants* with the kind of pastoral care needed to sustain their faith in a new environment? This concern preoccupied the Third Plenary Council of Baltimore* in 1884. Among its strategies were a proposed system of parochial schools* and a cautious attitude toward Catholic membership in organizations known in Europe as "secret societies" (e.g., Freemasons, Odd Fellows, etc.). Subsequent divisions grew out of diverging interpretations of these strategies and ultimately from conflicting estimates of "the age." Was the culture of the late nineteenth-century U.S. benign or hostile to the Catholic faith? Two views emerged.

The Americanists, led by John Ireland,* archbishop* of St. Paul, Minnesota, advocated mainstreaming immigrant Catholics into American society and adapting Catholicism, wherever doctrine allowed, to the genius of the American character. "There is no conflict," Ireland proclaimed in a sermon at the third council of Baltimore, "between the Catholic Church and America." The Conservative Party, led by Michael A. Corrigan,* archbishop of New York, thought Ireland and his friends minimized the hostility of the American environment to Catholicism and accused them of "a spirit of false liberalism." Where the Americanists were confident about Catholic prospects in America, the conservatives saw reason to be more cautious and protective of the Catholic people. "Our love for the country must not in any way blind us to errors which are serious," warned Corrigan's vicar general, Thomas Preston.*

These two approaches clashed for the first time over the "social question" raised by Catholic immigrant participation in the incipient American labor movement. The bishops could not agree on whether the Knights of Labor,* condemned by the Church in their Canadian form in 1884, ought to be treated as a suspect secret society or supported for the sake of the workers' social betterment. A "memorial," submitted by Baltimore's Cardinal* James Gibbons* during the winter of 1887, won Vatican toleration for the Knights as well as the enmity of Corrigan who correctly perceived that the Americanists had conspired at Rome against his position. They also lent their support to Edward McGlynn,* a New York priest and social activist, whom Corrigan had excommunicated for insubordination. The Knights of Labor dispute, with its McGlynn subplot, solidified the reflex opposition of the two parties.

Subsequent conflicts included a tangle of related issues: the school question, involving Ireland's controversial plan to have Catholic schools in two Minnesota districts financed by the state; the German question, which pitted Frederick Katzer, archbishop of Milwaukee, and the German-Americans who wished to retain their language and culture against the Irish-American bishops of the Americanist party; the Catholic University of America* at Washington, D.C., opened in 1889 with Ireland's ally, Bishop John J. Keane,* as rector, viewed by the liberals as a symbol of intellectual rapprochement with the age and opposed by the conservatives as a needless duplication of re-

sources; the issue of interreligious cooperation, raised by the participation of Keane and Gibbons in the 1893 Parliament of Religions* at Chicago; and, finally, the advocacy of temperance* by Keane and Ireland.

The bishops' disagreement on these issues led to appeals to the Vatican. These, added to the conflicting reports on American church affairs from both parties and their Roman agents, prompted Pope Leo XIII in 1893 to send Archbishop Francesco Satolli* to the U.S. as apostolic delegate.* Although Satolli seemed initially favorable to the Americanists, he was eventually won over to the conservative side and returned to Rome to become one of the putative authors of *Testem*. The first sign of the shift in momentum in favor of the conservatives was Leo's January 1895 encyclical,* *Longinqua Oceani*,* warning against universalizing the American arrangement of separation of church and state.* The following spring, Denis O'Connell,* Roman agent for the Americanists, was dismissed as rector of the North American College.* In September of 1896, Keane was removed from his post at Catholic University. Despite these setbacks O'Connell remained at Rome as vicar of Gibbons's titular church, soon to be joined by Keane for their final efforts to export Americanist ideas to Europe.

American Catholic Messianism. These ideas had come together nearly a decade before during the winter of 1886-1887, when the Americanist inner circle of Ireland, Keane and O'Connell was formed at Rome. Having come to the Vatican for different purposes, the three, along with Gibbons, worked together on the Knights of Labor issue. During the months they spent together at Rome, they became convinced of the need to grasp the present historical moment and committed themselves to a common body of ideas which would serve as a basis for church reform.

Their subsequent writing and speeches reveal a characteristic ideology of near-mythic proportions. The world had entered upon a new democratic* age. The U.S., with its institution of separation of church and state, embodied the spirit of the new age. As Denis O'Connell would argue in his 1897 address before the International Catholic Scientific Congress at Fribourg, the Church must adapt, always in nonessentials, to the new age. To American Catholicism fell the messianic mission of leading the Catholic Church into the new age.

With the adoption of this world view, the Americanists had bought uncritically into the ambivalent Puritan* idea of American election.* This theme of America's "Manifest Destiny"* had entered the American Catholic conversation with the conversions* of Orestes Brownson* and Isaac Hecker* in 1844. While they stand in the remote background of Americanism as a body of ideas, its intellectual roots have been traced to other sources as well. A sense of the providential ripeness of the historical moment and a fascination with the prospect of contributing to history's movement, account for the confident tone of apocalyptic* urgency which characterizes Americanist thought and distinguishes it from that of other Catholic thinkers who shared the concern to adapt Catholicism to the American situation.

Americanism and the International Catholic Reform Movement. Historians who dismiss Americanism as a "phantom heresy" tend to ignore the extent to which the Americanists considered themselves part of an international reform movement. The 1897 appearance of *La Vie du Père Hecker* in Europe was part of a wider attempt to export Americanist ideas to Europe. This effort had begun in 1887 when the Americanists first discovered that they could form public opinion in their favor by manipulating the flow of information in the European Catholic press. As the U.S. moved closer to the mood of the Spanish-American War* in the years after the Americanist setbacks of 1895 and 1896, these efforts intensified.

Transposing American nationalist expansionism to the sphere of church affairs, O'Connell and Keane formed alliances and networks of communication with liberal Catholics in Germany and Italy. Ireland was already well known in France where his discourses had been translated as *L'Église et le siècle* (1894). Here the main contact was Abbé Félix Klein, a professor at the Institut Catholique, whose exaggerated preface had given instant notoriety to the French version of Hecker's *Life*. In Germany Franz Kraus's "Spectator" letters, appearing in Munich's *Allegemeine Zeitung* in 1897 and 1898, publicized the Americanist point of view and tried to overcome their anti-German image. In Italy, where the Italian question still exercised the Vatican, Countess Sabina Parravicino di Revel translated the discourses of Ireland and John Lancaster Spalding* as well as Satolli's American speeches. She also provided Americanists access to the columns of Milan's *Rassegna nazionale.*

In addition to its general openness to the age, liberal Catholicism in the nineteenth century was primarily political and implied sympathy for popular government. In their appeals to Leo XIII as a liberal and "Pontiff of the Age," the Americanists and their allies underestimated his intransigence on the Italian question and failed to interpret *ralliement* in France in the context of his commitment to restore the papal states.

Isaac Hecker: Symbol of Americanism. Charles Maignen's *Études sur l'Américanisme: Le Père Hecker, est-il un saint?* (1898) represents the response of French monarchists and Vatican intransigents to the issue of Americanist expansionism. It is a vehement attack on the persons and ideas of Keane, Ireland and Gibbons. All three protested to the Vatican, which had granted Maignen the *imprimatur* denied him at Paris. Maignen was definitely concerned to cut Klein's model priest of the future down to size, but his real targets were the Americanists. Isaac Hecker and his thought function here, as they had for the Americanists in the 1897 *Vie*, largely at the symbolic level. By October of 1898, amid rumors that Elliott's *Life of Hecker* would be placed on the Index of Forbidden Books,* the pope reserved the question of Americanism to himself. No record of the commission he reputedly appointed to study the matter has yet been found. *Testem* followed at the beginning of 1899.

Whether the aging pope thought any Americans actually held the opinions reproved in the letter may never be known with certainty. Scholars have debated the question of whether Hecker or any of the Americanists held them. Given a classical understanding of theology as a body of truths above history, it is relatively easy to understand the Americanists' distinction between political and religious Americanism, and consign whatever theological content Americanism might have had to the mind of Maignen. In the recent past theologians have given increasing attention to the religious ideas of Hecker and the Americanists, but it is now more difficult to separate religious and political Americanism and to deny the theological content of Americanist thought.

In addition to theological considerations, however, the victory of the U.S. over Spain* and Leo's position on the Italian question are political factors which cannot be ignored in interpreting *Testem.* Its diplomatic ambiguity was calculated to warn the Americanists off while leaving them, in the distinction between political and religious Americanism, a face-saving escape route. They took it. But the end of their reflections delayed for decades the potential Catholic contribution to the public discussion of the religious significance of the American reality.

See also IMMIGRATION AND ETHNICITY, CATHOLIC; LONGINQUA OCEANI; TESTEM BENEVOLENTIAE.

BIBLIOGRAPHY. A. Houtin, *L'Americanisme* (1904); T. T. McAvoy, *The Great Crisis in American Catholic History, 1895-1900* (1957); R. D. Cross,

The Emergence of Liberal Catholicism (1958); G. P. Fogarty, *The Vatican and the Americanist Crisis: Denis J. O'Connell, American Agent in Rome, 1885-1903* (1974); G. P. Fogarty, *The Vatican and the American Hierarchy from 1870 to 1965* (1985); T. E. Wangler, "The Birth of Americanism: 'Westward the Apocalyptic Candlestick,' " *HTR* 65 (1972):415-436; "American Catholic Expansionism: 1886-1894," *HTR* 75 (1982):369-393; M. M. Reher, "Pope Leo XIII and 'Americanism,' " *TS* 34 (1973):679-689; R. C. Ayers, "The Americanist Attack on Europe in 1897 and 1898," in *Rising from History,* ed. R. J. Daly (1987).

W. L. Portier

Americans United for Separation of Church and State. An organization promoting a policy of strict separation of church and state.* Americans United for Separation of Church and State (AUSCS) (also called Protestants and Other Americans United for Separation of Church and State) began as a coalition of liberals* and conservatives, under the leadership of Joseph Dawson,* which opposed the Supreme Court's decision in *Everson* v. *Board of Education* (1947) to allow federal assistance in transporting children to parochial schools. In that year the group issued a manifesto which clearly stated its rejection of any use of public funds for religious purposes, its opposition to any efforts to breach the "wall" of separation between church and state and its belief that the greatest threat to religious liberty lay in "clericalism" or the manipulation of political power by churches for their own personal ends. Not surprisingly, this view of church-state relations brought the AUSCS into frequent conflict with the Catholic Church.* This conflict came to a head during John F. Kennedy's* 1960 presidential campaign, when AUSCS issued its "questions for a Catholic candidate" which called for the candidate to clarify his stance on the relationship of church and state.

AUSCS experienced rapid growth under Glen Archer, who served as executive director from 1948 to 1975. It now claims a membership of 50,000, with headquarters in Washington, D.C., and 115 local chapters. In addition, it maintains an archive of some 30,000 volumes on church-state issues and seeks to educate the public on the importance of church-state separation for religious freedom. These include a monthly magazine, *Church and State,* books and pamphlets, films, speakers and a yearly national conference. It has also been involved in lobbying efforts in Washington and in various court cases involving alleged violations of separation of church and state.

BIBLIOGRAPHY. L. P. Creedon and W. D. Falcon, *United for Separation: An Analysis of POAU Assaults on Catholicism* (1959); C. S. Lowell, *Embattled Wall; Americans United: An Idea and a Man* (1966). R. P. Hesselgrave

Ames, Edward Scribner (1870-1958). Philosopher, theologian* and Disciples of Christ* minister. Born in Eau Claire, Wisconsin, Ames attended Drake University (B.A., 1889; M.A., 1891), Yale* Divinity School (B.D., 1892) and the University of Chicago (Ph.D., 1895). After graduating from Chicago, Ames taught at Disciples Divinity House, Chicago (1895-1897), and Butler College (1897-1900), and then returned to teach at the University of Chicago (1900-1935). He was pastor of Hyde Park (later University) Church of the Disciples (1900-1940), editor of *The Scroll* (1903-1951) and dean of Disciples Divinity House (1927-1945).

Ames's long and prominent career showed him to be among the most radical of the theological modernists* of the Chicago School,* boldly revising traditional theology* according to the insights of psychology.* Among his writings are *The Psychology of Religious Experience* (1910) and *The New Orthodoxy* (1918). Indebted to William James,* John Dewey (1859-1952) and Henri Bergson (1859-1941), his functionalism examined the search for human values in a universe characterized by process and social existence in which traditional dogma* had no positive meaning. Ames's sympathetic reading of the function of religion in human experience led him to reinterpret religious terms according to functionalist, modernist meanings, so that religion could exemplify the highest of human ideals. For Ames, terms such as *Uncle Sam* or *alma mater* (Latin for "nourishing mother") are examples of the use of analogies to express the ideals of human experience. While Ames repudiated any understanding of God as an ontological reality, a person in space and time, the term *God* was given to that set of attributes which, as an ideal, characterize the fulfillment of human value in the advancement of intelligence, order, personality and love.

BIBLIOGRAPHY. V. M. Ames, ed., *Beyond Theology: The Autobiography of Edward Scribner Ames* (1959); *DARB.* K. S. Sawyer

Ames, Jessie Daniel (1883-1972). Suffragist* and anti-lynching reformer. Born in Palestine, Texas, Jessie attended Southwestern University, a Methodist school in Georgetown, Texas, where her family had moved when she was ten years old. Though her father disliked religion, Jessie became a member of the Methodist* Church. In 1905 she married Roger Post Ames, an Army doctor thirteen years her senior. Most of their married life he helped Walter Reed fight yellow fever in Central America, where he died in 1914. A widow at 31, with three children to support, she lived with her mother, helped run the family business, and became involved in Methodist women's groups, which led her into the women's suffrage movement. In 1916 she organized a local suffrage association and helped Texas become the first Southern state to ratify the Nineteenth Amendment. Ames was founding president in 1919 of the Texas League of Women Voters and a delegate to the Democratic National Conventions of 1920, 1924 and 1928. Her involvement in interracial meetings of church women's groups led in 1924 to her becoming director of the Texas council of the Atlanta-based Commission on Interracial Cooperation. Five years later she moved to Georgia to head its women's division. In 1930 she founded the Association of Southern Women for the Prevention of Lynching. The organization disbanded in 1942, but Ames continued to promote interracial harmony until her death in 1972.

BIBLIOGRAPHY. J. D. Hall, *Revolt Against Chivalry: Jessie Daniel Ames and the Women's Campaign against Lynching* (1979).

N. A. Hardesty

Ames, William (1576-1633). British Puritan* theologian* important to separating and non-separating Congregationalists.* Born in Ipswich, Suffolk, England, Ames was educated at Christ's College, Cambridge, where he studied under William Perkins, one of the fathers of experimental Puritan theology. He was suspended, but not expelled, from Christ's College for his Puritan tendencies. After trying to settle in Colchester, England, he moved to Leyden, Holland. There he became involved in the Arminian* controversy at the Synod of Dordt (1618-1619), serving as an observer for the Calvinistic* side. He became professor of theology at the University of Franeker in Friesland, Holland, and served from 1622 to 1632. He was elected rector of the University in 1626. At Franeker his international reputation attracted students from all over Europe. Ames moved to Rotterdam, Holland, in 1632 and died there in 1633. His family settled in New England, bringing his library with them; it formed the nucleus of the original library for Harvard College,* though most of the books were later destroyed by fire.

Ames was highly revered by the leaders of both Plymouth Colony and the Massachusetts Bay Colony. His *Marrow of Theology* (*Medulla Theologiae,* 1623) provided a good summary of Calvinistic theology, while his theological methodology (*Technometry*) affected generations of New England divinity* students. Some of his thinking laid the groundwork for non-separating Congregationalism in New England, a movement which held that the members of the Congregational churches of the Massachusetts Bay Colony and its offshoots had not separated from the Church of England* but were providing an example for its reformation.

BIBLIOGRAPHY. W. Ames, *The Workes* (1643); *DAB* I; P. Miller, *The New England Mind: The Seventeenth Century* (1939); P. Miller, *Orthodoxy in Massachusetts, 1630-1650* (1933); K. L. Sprunger, *The Learned Doctor William Ames* (1972).

D. A. Weir

Amillennialism. The view that the 1,000 years of Revelation 20:1-10 is not a literal millennial rule of Christ on earth but is a symbolic reference to the period between the ministry of Christ and his Second Coming. Amillennialism teaches that there will be a continuous development of good and evil in the world until the return of Christ, when the dead shall be raised and the last judgment conducted. This interpretation emphasizes the present reality of the kingdom of God as Christ rules his church through the Word and the Spirit. There will not be a future perfect and glorious age until the establishment of the new heaven and the new earth. Thus, Revelation 20 refers to the souls of the believers reigning with Christ in heaven.

Amillennialism was given its most influential expression in the writings of the church father Augustine. The eschatology* of the early church was dominated by premillennialism,* but with the excesses of the Montanists, the allegorical interpretation popularized by Origen, and the legalization of Christianity by Constantine, the countercultural emphasis of primitive Christianity began to die out. Augustine's interpretation of the book of Revelation as referring to the church in its struggle with evil became the dominant view of Roman Catholic Christianity. The major Protestant* traditions, including the Lutheran,* Reformed* and Anglican,* also accepted amillennialism, and such statements as the Augsburg Confession, the Thirty-Nine Articles* and the Westminster Confession* condemn premillennialism. Most of the leading churches of the twentieth century follow amillennial eschatology.

See also ESCHATOLOGY.

BIBLIOGRAPHY. R. G. Clouse, ed., *The Meaning*

of the Millennium: Four Views (1977); A. A. Hoekema, *The Bible and the Future* (1979).

R. G. Clouse

Amish, Old Order. One of several North American groups whose roots go back to the sixteenth-century Swiss Anabaptists.* During the years 1693-1697 the Swiss Brethren (today called Mennonites*) experienced a schism. The one faction, led by Jakob Ammann, decided to reject the new spirit of Pietism* that was influencing many Swiss Mennonites, and introduced some Dutch Mennonite elements, as found in the Dutch Dordrecht Confession of 1632. These included the ordinance of foot washing* and a strict approach to the *Meidung* (shunning, or the avoidance of excommunicated persons). Ammann believed men should wear untrimmed beards and promoted a modest attire.

Various Swiss Mennonite congregations decided in favor of Jakob Ammann's views; some residing in Switzerland, and several in Alsace and the Palatinate, where Swiss Mennonites had relocated for economic and political reasons. Sometime after 1710 Amish families began immigrating* to North America, so that by 1787 some seventy congregations were established in Pennsylvania. Soon thereafter the Amish joined in the general westward movement into Ohio, Indiana and elsewhere.

From 1862 to 1878 the Amish entered into formal conference discussions (called *Dienerversammlungen,* or *ministerial meetings*) which led to a schism. One group decided for the "Old Order"; the other accepted more progressive ideas. Most congregations in the latter group, called Amish-Mennonites, eventually merged with the Mennonite Church. Today the Old Order Amish live in several states and the Province of Ontario, with their largest concentrations in Ohio (Holmes County), Pennsylvania (Lancaster County) and northern Indiana. In the late 1980s adult membership in the U.S. numbered about 35,000, with about 700 in Canada.

BIBLIOGRAPHY. H. Bender, C. Krahn et al., eds., *Mennonite Encyclopedia* (1955-1960); J. F. Beiler, "Old Order Amish," *Mennonite World Handbook* (1978); J. A. Hostetler, *Amish Society* (1980).

L. Gross

Anabaptist Tradition and Vision. *Anabaptist* is derived from the Greek word *anabaptizein,* meaning "to rebaptize," and given to the movement by its opponents in the sixteenth century. A sixteenth-century reform movement, Anabaptists were neither Catholic* nor Protestant,* but stressed pacifism, the separation of church and state,* church membership* consisting of adult believers only, and the conviction that ethics* are a part of the good news of Jesus Christ. Anabaptists wanted to restore the New Testament church in both essence and form. Mennonites,* Amish* and Hutterites* are the lineal and doctrinal descendants of that earlier movement.

The cradle of Anabaptism was Zurich in 1525 with the followers of the Swiss reformer Huldreich Zwingli (1484-1531), but the movement's roots drew on the work of many others. These included the writings of Martin Luther (1483-1546), the theological and pastoral emphases of Andreas Karlstadt (1480-1541), late medieval asceticism and mysticism,* and peasant unrest brought about by economic and social injustice. Monastic reform movements also played a part, as did sacramentarianism, anticlericalism and humanism.

The Anabaptists did not announce a program for changing the social order, but their doctrine of a believers' church, their simple egalitarianism, as well as their missionary* zeal so threatened both church and state in central Europe that persecution and martyrdom swiftly descended upon them. An abortive and atypical attempt by some Dutch Anabaptists in 1534-1535 to establish by force of arms an Old Testament theocracy* in the city of Munster gave a useful alibi for officials to ruthlessly suppress the movement. *The Martyrs Mirror* (1660) is a summary of earlier martyrologies.

Geographical dispersion increased the variety of influences on early Anabaptism. Consequently, some scholars believe that no normative theological core can be identified for them. There was, however, significant doctrinal uniformity among Anabaptists. The September 1524 letter of Conrad Grebel (c.1498-1526) and his circle to Luther, Karlstadt and Thomas Muntzer (c.1490-1525) outlined this core as follows: (1) Scripture* as the primary authority; (2) the Lord's Supper* as a memorial and sign of love among believers; (3) Matthew 18:15-18 as the pattern for church discipline*; (4) the belief that baptism* must follow personal faith and that it is a sign rather than a sacrament*; (5) that children are saved by the redemptive work of Christ; (6) that weapons of violence have no place among Christians; and (7) that the church is called to be a suffering church. The Anabaptists who drafted the *Brotherly Union* at Schleitheim in 1527 would have agreed with most of these points. They added three others: the rejection of the oath, belief in a radical church-world dualism and the importance of church order.

Mennonites came to North America for many reasons, but the longing for freedom of religion* was primary. This included the freedom to exercise their pacifism, congregational autonomy, the right not to swear oaths and control over their own educational programs. Mennonites are non-creedal and affirm the Bible* as their primary authority* for faith and life. Still, the *Dordrecht Confession* of 1632 was reaffirmed and signed by the early group in Germantown in 1725, and the 1527 *Brotherly Union* of Schleitheim was also indirectly influential in the New World. Except during the colonial era, Mennonites preferred cultural and geographic isolation, in part a legacy of earlier persecutions. Thus tradition controlled most of their lives almost to the late nineteenth century.

All this has changed for most Mennonites. The dynamic sixteenth-century missionary zeal has been recovered. Mennonite theologians* and historians have called their tradition to the recovery of the Anabaptist vision of community, nonconformity, discipleship and nonresistance. In so doing they have forged a viable Anabaptist alternative to the prevailing American Protestant options. Instead of continued withdrawal from society, many Mennonites seek involvement and have become voices for social justice. Some, especially in Canada, hold elective political office even at the national level. On any given day approximately 1,000 volunteers serve at home and abroad under the Mennonite Central Committee,* alleviating human need. Education is given high priority among most groups. Dialog with other theological traditions is encouraged. The Swiss-Dutch-German ethnic ethos (*See* Immigration and Ethnicity, Protestant) of the early immigrants is being enriched by new members of African-American,* Hispanic,* Chinese and other cultural traditions. Rapid urbanization has led to full involvement in the professional and business worlds of North American society.

The Amish and Hutterite wings of the Anabaptist tradition reflect the values of their tradition in the most visibly distinctive ways. Their separation from the world is evident in their avoidance of agricultural mechanization, their legendary frugality and their ecologically efficient farming. They forbid the use of electricity and maintain their own elementary schools, maintaining that education beyond the eighth grade is superfluous. Amish regard humility as a primary virtue and rely on each other for help in times of health emergencies or other crises. In basic doctrines they affirm traditional Mennonite beliefs, but Old Order Amish only worship in homes.

As with the Amish, the Hutterites affirm basic Anabaptist and Mennonite doctrines, but yieldedness and community of goods are also practiced. Education to the eighth grade, in their own schools, is considered sufficient for faithful living. In contrast to Old Order Amish, Hutterite farms are fully mechanized with modern equipment but cars, radios and television are not permitted. There is a diligent effort to simplify life and to pattern their communal experience after the church of New Testament times.

BIBLIOGRAPHY. H. S. Bender and C. H. Smith, eds., *Mennonite Encyclopedia,* 5 vols. (1955-1969); H. S. Bender, *The Anabaptist Vision* (1943); C. J. Dyck, ed., *An Introduction to Mennonite History* (1981); J. R. Hostetler, *Amish Society,* 3rd ed. (1980); J. R. Hostetler, *Hutterite Society* (1974); J. H. Kauffman and L. Harder, *Anabaptists Four Centuries Later* (1975); W. Klaassen, ed., *Anabaptism in Outline* (1981); G. H. Williams, *The Radical Reformation* (1962).   C. J. Dyck

Anaphora. The Greek term means "oblation," but in discussing liturgical* forms it refers to the eucharistic prayer,* what medieval and Reformation writers spoke of as "the prayer of consecration." Twentieth-century liturgical studies have given a great deal of attention to this prayer, especially since the discovery of the earliest indisputable example in *The Apostolic Tradition,* a church order most commonly ascribed to Hippolytus of Rome in the early third century. There, a thanksgiving for the redemptive work of Christ culminates in the narrative account of the Last Supper and the paragraph known technically as the *anamnesis,* a carefully balanced formula that associates remembrance of Christ's death and resurrection with the offering of bread and wine in thanksgiving. From that memorial oblation the prayer turns to supplication, specifically to a petition to God to "send your holy Spirit on the offering of your holy Church." This thanksgiving/supplication pattern subsequently developed differently in different areas, but it has remained the core of eucharistic prayer. The earlier supposition that there could be but one eucharistic prayer has given way to the writing of multiple forms in many traditions: Roman Catholic,* Episcopal,* Lutheran,* Methodist,* Presbyterian* and Reformed.* One prayer found in several North American traditions is "A Common Eucharistic Prayer," prepared by an ecumenical committee and based on the Alexandrian version of an anaphora attributed to Basil of Caesarea (d. 379). Such liturgical developments promise to contribute significantly to ecumenical convergence in eucharistic understanding.

See also EUCHARISTIC DEVOTIONS.

BIBLIOGRAPHY. R. C. D. Jasper and G. J. Cuming, *Prayers of the Eucharist: Early and Reformed* (1980); F. C. Senn, ed., *New Eucharistic Prayers: An Ecumenical Study of Their Development and Structure* (1987). T. J. Tally

Anderson, Isaac (1780-1857). Presbyterian* minister* and educator. Born in Rockbridge County, Virginia, Anderson attended Liberty Hall Academy, but when the family moved to Tennessee in 1801, he continued his theological studies under Samuel Carrick* and Gideon Blackburn.* Ordained* to the Presbyterian ministry in 1802, he was pastor* of churches near Knoxville and in 1812 assumed the pastorate of New Providence Church at Maryville, whose congregation came to number seven hundred. Anderson was also a schoolteacher and numbered Texas leader Samuel Houston as one of his students.

Disappointed at the reluctance of Princeton* graduates to serve on the frontier, Anderson played a leading role at the Synod* of Tennessee in 1819 in the formation of the Southern and Western Theological Seminary. During its first six years, he was its only teacher, and classes were held in his Maryville home. As most applicants lacked adequate background, it became necessary to establish a collegiate program in conjunction with theological studies, and a college farm kept costs low. Anderson trained about one hundred fifty ministers in his lifetime and so contributed toward a broad base of New School* sentiment and support in Tennessee. But declining numbers of theological students caused the seminary program to falter after 1840, and in time the school became Maryville College.

An indefatigable worker, Anderson averaged two hundred sermons a year, organized nine churches in his lifetime, served as moderator of Union Presbytery on forty occasions, was its treasurer for thirty-one years, its stated clerk for eleven and moderator of the Synod of Tennessee seven times.

BIBLIOGRAPHY. J. J. Robinson, *Memoir of Rev. Isaac Anderson, D. D.* (1860). W. J. Wade

Anderson, Rufus (1796-1880). Missionary* statesman and theorist. Born in Yarmouth, Maine, Anderson was educated at Bowdoin College (1818) and Andover Seminary* (1822). At Andover he acquired a compelling interest in missions. In 1826 he was named assistant secretary to the American Board of Commissioners for Foreign Missions* (ABCFM), the agency chartered in Massachusetts and responsible for the overseas projects of the Congregational,* Presbyterian* and Reformed* Churches until the 1850s. From 1826 to his retirement in 1866, he was the Board's foreign secretary.

Anderson's missionary principles developed gradually in a succession of tracts published throughout his career, gaining definition, however, after his voyage to India in 1855. Observing the restrictive influence of the foreign-directed work, Anderson became a strong advocate of decentralization that would encourage local initiative and make better use of overseas resources. He supported the ordination of national pastors and affirmed that all missionary institutions should be directed at strengthening the nascent church. The guidelines adopted for missions by the ABCFM in 1856 incorporated these principles. In effect, Anderson propounded the doctrine of self-government, self-support and self-propagation that has been affirmed by most subsequent American foreign missions agencies in advocating the indigenous church. Active in his promotion of missions, he conducted a monthly missions meeting at Park Street Church, Boston, for many years. His collected works demonstrate the development of modern missionary thought from the motives of compassion and a desire to subdue the whole world for the kingdom of Christ, to a comprehensive program of individual salvation, church formation and social regeneration.

BIBLIOGRAPHY. R. P. Beaver, *To Advance the Gospel: Selections from the Writings of Rufus Anderson* (1967); R. P. Beaver, ed., *Pioneers in Mission; The Early Missionary Ordination Sermons, Charges, and Instructions* (1966). E. A. Wilson

Anderson, William Madison, Jr. (1889-1935). Presbyterian* pastor* and educator. A third generation Presbyterian minister, Anderson was born in Rock Hill, South Carolina. He received training at Vanderbilt University (1907-1910), Austin College (A.S., 1911) and Austin Theological Seminary (B.D., 1914). Ordained* to the ministry of the Presbyterian Church in the U.S. (1914), he pastored the East Dallas Church (1914) before becoming secretary of schools and colleges of the Presbyterian Church in Texas (1915). He served as assistant pastor under his father at First Church, Dallas (1916-1924), becoming pastor in 1925, a position held until his death.

Concern for children resulted in Anderson establishing the Freeman Memorial Clinic at the church in 1921. His influence on Lewis Sperry

Chafer* resulted in the locating of the proposed Evangelical Theological College (later Dallas Theological Seminary*) in Dallas. Anderson served that institution as vice president and professor of homiletics.* A pioneer radio preacher in Dallas, he conducted a weekly Bible class which enrolled about 30,000 members.   R. T. Clutter

Andover Controversy. The debate over the doctrine of "future probation," involving the faculty of Andover Theological Seminary* from 1886 until 1893. The seminary had been established by New England Congregationalists* in 1808 to counter the Unitarian* tendencies of Harvard,* especially the appointment of Henry Ware* in 1805 as Hollis Professor of Divinity. Attempting to guarantee Andover's orthodoxy,* the founders required faculty subscription to the Andover Creed, summarizing Edwardsean theology as it had been restated by Samuel Hopkins.* Each year faculty members were required to subscribe to the theological statement.

After the Civil War,* however, faculty members joined other New England progressives in restating their faith along the lines of the liberal emphasis upon the immanence of God, emerging biblical criticism and the doctrine of progress. Future probation, the center of the controversy, developed when the Andover men applied the "new theology" to missions.* In a series of articles in the *Andover Review,* E. C. Smyth and his colleagues argued that heathen who die without knowledge of the gospel will have an opportunity in the future life either to accept or to reject the gospel before facing final judgment. This aroused opposition of conservative Congregationalists. In 1887 they succeeded in removing Smyth from his teaching position at the seminary,* but in 1892 his dismissal was voided by the Supreme Court of Massachusetts.

See also ANDOVER THEOLOGICAL SEMINARY.

BIBLIOGRAPHY. F. H. Foster, *The Modern Movement in American Theology* (1969); W. R. Hutchison, ed., *American Protestant Thought: The Liberal Era* (1968); D. D. Williams, *The Andover Liberals: A Study in American Theology* (1941).

    B. L. Shelley

Andover Theological Seminary. Congregational* seminary.* In 1805 Unitarians gained control of Harvard.* Old Calvinists* and New Divinity* Men responded by planning to create their own seminaries. As an alternative, Timothy Dwight,* Jedidiah Morse* and Leonard Woods* were among those who proposed one orthodox* institution. After complicated negotiations, Andover Seminary was founded in 1808 on the campus of Andover Academy in northeast Massachusetts. Although a compromise seminary, Andover favored the New Divinity theology* because Nathaniel Emmons and Woods were indebted to the work of Samuel Hopkins. Woods was the head of the faculty and a bulwark of Andover's orthodoxy until his retirement in 1846.

True to its mission, Andover Seminary produced zealous ministers eager to resist growing Unitarian and Arminian* tendencies in Massachusetts and beyond. In later decades, Romanticism* and German rationalism eroded the orthodoxy of the Andover faculty. Shortly after Edwards Amasa Park's retirement as Abbot Professor of Christian Theology in 1881, the faculty openly embraced liberal theological methods. The Andover controversy* of the 1880s led to a drop in enrollment, and by 1900 the school's future was in doubt. The pull of urban life and university ties prompted the Andover trustees to move to Cambridge and affiliate with Harvard* Divinity School in 1908. In 1922 plans were made to merge the two institutions, but fearing a loss of control, the board of visitors thwarted the plan by evoking a legal requirement for Andover faculty to subscribe to an orthodox creed*—something that had not been required for years. The faculty resigned in protest, and the Seminary's operations were suspended until 1931 when the trustees became affiliated with a local Baptist seminary, Newton Theological Institute, to form Andover-Newton Theological School—an institution that continues to train ministers today.

BIBLIOGRAPHY. R. D. Pierce, "The Legal Aspects of the Andover Creed" *CH* 15 (1946):28-47; H. K. Rowe, *History of Andover Theological Seminary* (1933); L. Woods, *History of the Andover Theological Seminary* (1885).   S. D. Crocco

Andrew, James Osgood (1794-1871). Methodist* bishop.* Born in Wilkes County, Georgia, James early on demonstrated a gift for ministry* and soon followed his father, John Andrew, Georgia's first native-born Methodist itinerant, into the ministry. He received a license* to preach at age eighteen and served various congregations in South Carolina and Georgia in the early decades of the 1800s. In 1832 the Methodist Episcopal Church made Andrew one of two bishops. Andrew disliked slavery and advocated religious education* for African-Americans, although he did not advocate separate African-American churches. When he acquired slaves through his second marriage, he renounced all legal claims to them, but Georgia law would not allow him to free them. A majority of Northern delegates to the General Conference of 1844 asked for his suspension, and Andrew offered to resign. Southern delegates insisted that his resignation would undermine the Church's ability to minister to slaves and slave owners. Despairing of resolving this and other issues, they instead proposed an amicable separation—though one that Andrew himself did not favor. The Plan of Separation was adopted, and in 1845 Southern Methodists created the Methodist Episcopal Church, South, with Andrew as a bishop, in which capacity he served until 1866. His most important published works were *Family Government* (1847) and *Miscellanies* (1855).

BIBLIOGRAPHY. *DAB* I; A. C. Loveland, *Southern Evangelicals and the Social Order, 1800-1860* (1980); D. G. Mathews, *Slavery and Methodism: A Chapter in American Morality, 1780-1845* (1965).
T. T. Taylor

Angelus. A popular devotion* in honor of the Virgin Mary* which developed in the Middle Ages. The word *angelus* derives from the first word of the versicle which precedes the recitation of the Aves, "The angel *(angelus)* of the Lord announced unto Mary, and she conceived of the Holy Spirit." From the twelfth century it became customary to say the *Ave Maria* at the sound of the evening curfew bell. Monks said the same prayers at the morning bell calling them to the first hour of prayer. Sometime in the fourteenth century there arose the custom of saying the prayers at noon, and by the sixteenth century it was a standard custom to say the prayers when the Angelus bell tolled at the appropriate hour, morning, noon and night. This pious custom was recommended to Catholics* as late as 1974 in Pope Paul VI's* exhortation *Marialis Cultus,* but the custom has never been as common in North America as it was in Europe.

BIBLIOGRAPHY. "Angelus," *Theotokos: A Theological Encyclopedia of the Blessed Virgin Mary,* ed., M. O'Carroll (1982).
L. S. Cunningham

Anglican Church of Canada. Although the first Anglican* worship* service on Canadian soil was conducted by Robert Wolfall at Frobisher Bay, Baffin Island, on September 2, 1578, it was over two years before the first bishop* was appointed. In the meantime, the young British colonies in eastern Canada were ministered to by naval or military chaplains* or by missionaries* sent from England by the Society for the Propagation of the Gospel in Foreign Parts* (SPG).

The Irish-born Loyalist, Dr. Charles Inglis,* be-
came the first Anglican bishop in Canada, then British North America (BNA) in 1787. Based in Halifax, he had episcopal oversight of all BNA colonies. Inglis, who, like his successors in 1851, was appointed by the Crown, strongly believed in the establishment of the Church of England in Nova Scotia. Since this was never legislated in the colonies, attempts by Inglis and his son Charles, who succeeded him as bishop, to prevent other denominations* from exercising religious functions recognized by the Crown often brought them into conflict with Loyalist Dissenters.

In the Canadas, Bishop Jacob Mountain* of Montreal (appointed in 1793) and Archdeacon John Strachan* of York, faced similar hostility to the establishment principle, owing to the ambiguous wording of the *Constitution Act* of 1791, which provided for the reservation of one-seventh of all Crown land as an endowment for "Protestant Clergy." Originally understood to mean Anglicans, the principle was challenged first by Presbyterians* and later by other denominations, culminating in the *Clergy Reserves* Act* of 1840, which recognized religious pluralism* and rejected the principle of an Anglican establishment in Canada.

As bishop of Toronto, Strachan convened the first diocesan synod* in the history of the Church of England in 1856 and, in the following year, Benjamin Cronyn* of Huron became the first bishop to be elected to office by a synod. In 1860 Bishop Francis Fulford* was elected as the first Metropolitan* of the self-governing Ecclesiastical Province of Canada. Apart from British Columbia, the other dioceses* in Western Canada formed themselves into the Province of Rupert's Land in 1875. Its first Metropolitan, Archbishop Robert Machray,* was elected Primate of All Canada at the inaugural General Synod of the Church of England in Canada in September 1893. There are now thirty dioceses grouped into four Ecclesiastical Provinces. In 1985, the Anglican Church of Canada (as it was called after 1955) claimed approximately 856,000 members (3.4 per cent of the Canadian population), of whom almost half live in Ontario.

Troubled over liberal trends in the Anglican Church, the Provincial Synod of Canada petitioned the archbishop of Canterbury in 1865 to convene an international synod of the Anglican Communion.* The archbishop responded by calling a meeting of all bishops at Lambeth Palace in 1867, the first of the famous Lambeth Conferences.*

In this century, the Anglican Church of Canada has inaugurated many liberalizing policies involving significant changes in structure, theology* and outlook, which have given rise to the ordination of women* to the priesthood, liturgical revision (including the recent publication of the *Book of Alternative Services*), the peace* movement, the use of inclusive language,* homosexual* rights and support for native land claims. However, since each diocese is autonomous in its government, there are differences across the country in the extent to which such policies have been adopted.

BIBLIOGRAPHY. R. W. Bibby, *Fragmented Gods: The Poverty and Potential of Religion in Canada* (1987); T. C. B. Boon, *The Anglican Church from the Bay to the Rockies* (1962); S. Ervin, *The Political and Ecclesiastical History of the Anglican Church of Canada* (1967); J. W. Grant, *The Church in the Canadian Era* (1972).   R. H. Chilton

Anglican Churches in America. Historically Anglicanism* has put far greater emphasis on church unity than have other Reformation churches. Because of this there are comparatively few ecclesiastical divisions within American Anglicanism. Two communions, The Episcopal Church* of the U.S. and the Anglican Church of Canada,* make up almost ninety-nine per cent of the Anglican population of English-speaking North America. Since the organization of American Methodism* in 1784, there has been only one significant schism from these churches, though the second half of the twentieth century has witnessed the formation of a number of splinter groups. Some question whether any of these latter groups are technically Anglican at all, since they are neither recognized by the archbishop of Canterbury nor do they participate in the decennial Lambeth Conferences;* but they are all heirs of different facets of the Anglican heritage.

The Episcopal Church (or the Protestant Episcopal Church in the U.S.A.—since 1967 both names are in use, though the former is more widely used) was organized between 1784 and 1789. At the General Convention of 1789 its canons and constitution were drawn up. Its organization consists of a house of bishops* (who have been elected by clergy* and laity*) and a house of deputies* consisting of lay and clerical representatives. It is headed by a presiding bishop.* Before the twentieth century this office had little authority and was simply held by the most senior bishop, but since 1919 it has become an elected office with major administrative responsibility. Also in 1789 a revised American prayer book, combining elements from both the English and Scottish Episcopal liturgies, was given final shape. The Episcopal Book of Common Prayer* underwent further revision in 1893, 1928 and 1979.

The Anglican Church of Canada* was gradually organized over the course of the second half of the nineteenth century. Earlier it had been viewed as an extension of the Church of England and had received state support, largely through the resources of the 675,000-acre Clergy Reserve.* With the selling of the reserve in 1854 and the separation of church and state,* there was an increased move toward ecclesiastical autonomy. In 1861 the provincial synod* of the Canadas became self-governing. Organizationally, Canadian Anglicanism has differed from American Episcopalianism because of the importance it has placed on ecclesiastical provinces or groups of territorially contiguous dioceses.* Each province in the Canadian Church is governed by a synod* and headed by a metropolitan archbishop. In 1893 the churches in western Canada (the Province of Rupert's Land) became autonomous from England, and the different provincial synods were united in one general synod. The head of this united church is known as the Primate of All Canada.

The most significant schism in the history of the Episcopal Church occurred in 1873. Throughout the late 1860s and early 1870s there arose increasing evangelical* or low church* dissatisfaction, both over the willingness of the church to tolerate the new theology* and practices of the high church* party and over Episcopal unwillingness to extend full fellowship with non-Episcopal Protestants. The breaking point came in October of 1873 when George D. Cummins,* assistant bishop of Kentucky, was criticized for participating in an interdenominational service of holy communion* at the meeting of the Evangelical Alliance.* In December 1873 he and others organized the Reformed Episcopal Church.* A second bishop, Charles E. Cheney,* was also consecrated. Both in liturgy* and doctrine, this church was pointedly Protestant and more open to fellowship with other Protestant communions. A small Reformed Episcopal movement also broke away from the Anglican Church of Canada in 1874 over the Tractarian* sympathies of the bishop of British Columbia (George Hills).

A second, smaller movement that can qualify as a schism was the African Orthodox Church,* organized in 1921 under George A. McGuire,* an Episcopal priest who later received Episcopal consecration by the hands of a "wandering bishop." The African Orthodox Church combines a concern for African-American autonomy (McGuire having been inspired by the African-American nationalist Marcus Garvey*) and a profession of Eastern Orthodox* doctrines such as rejection of the *filioque* clause.

During the 1950s and 1960s a number of small splinter movements broke away from the Episcopal Church, such as the Southern Episcopal Church (1953), the Anglican Orthodox Church (1963) and the American Episcopal Church (1968). In general these groups protested the heterodox theology, liberal politics and sacerdotal ecclesiology of the national church.

A final wave of splinter groups can be traced to the early 1970s over prayer book revision and the ordination of women.* The decision in favor of both by the General Convention of 1976 led a number of conservative high church Episcopalians to believe that the Episcopal Church had fallen into apostasy,* and that churches for "continuing Anglicanism" needed to be established. The largest of these groups are the Anglican Catholic Church, the Anglican Rite Jurisdiction of America and the Diocese of Christ the King. All told, these groups include fifteen thousand members.

See also ANGLICAN CHURCH OF CANADA; ANGLICAN COMMUNION; ANGLICANISM; CHURCH GOVERNMENT: EPISCOPAL; PROTESTANT EPISCOPAL CHURCH IN THE U.S.A.; REFORMED EPISCOPAL CHURCH; TRACTARIANISM.

BIBLIOGRAPHY. D. Armentrout, *Episcopal Splinter Groups* (1985); S. Ervin, *The Political and Ecclesiastical History of the Anglican Church of Canada* (1967); R. T. Handy, *A History of the Churches in the United States and Canada* (1976); J. G. Melton, *The Encyclopedia of American Religions* (1986); A. D. Price, *A History of the Formation and Growth of the Reformed Episcopal Church, 1873-1902* (1902).

R. B. Mullin

Anglican Communion. A term for those worldwide churches who are the heirs of the Anglican Reformation and who stand in full communion with the archbishop of Canterbury. As of 1987 the Anglican Communion contained over sixty million members found in twenty-seven self-governing churches and distributed through approximately one hundred sixty-four countries. In the centuries following the British Reformation, Anglicanism began extending itself throughout the world, both in conjunction with British colonialism and emigration (such as to North America and Australia) and through the nineteenth-century foreign missionary endeavor. Yet as late as the middle of the nineteenth century, the relationship between these national churches was undefined.

The concept of an Anglican communion was an effort to emphasize the common tradition and fellowship shared by these churches. It was given institutional shape by the calling in 1867 of the first Lambeth Conference,* in which bishops from the different churches met together at Lambeth Palace in London. This conference has continued to be held (except when postponed by war) every ten years and has played an important part in giving shape to the Anglican communion. Lambeth resolutions, however, are not binding since each national church or province is autonomous. A second unifying institution, the Anglican Consultative Council, has met since 1971 and includes representatives of bishops,* clergy* and laity* of the different constitutive churches. It was established to aid in the communication between parts of the Anglican communion, as well as to coordinate ecumenical endeavors.

See also ANGLICAN CHURCH OF CANADA; ANGLICAN CHURCHES IN AMERICA; CHICAGO-LAMBETH QUADRILATERAL; EPISCOPAL CHURCH; LAMBETH CONFERENCES.

BIBLIOGRAPHY. S. Neill, *Today's Church and Today's World* (1977). R. B. Mullin

Anglicanism. An ecclesiastical tradition arising from the British Reformation of the sixteenth century. Anglicanism has often proven something of a puzzle for outsiders since it views itself as both a Reformation and a pre-Reformation church, and as both Catholic* and Protestant.* This paradoxical nature, which has shaped in turn both American and Canadian Anglicanism, stems from sixteenth- and seventeenth-century developments.

The first phase of the Anglican Reformation (1531-1547) arose from England's King Henry VIII's failure to receive papal support for annulling his marriage to Catherine of Aragon. In response both king and parliament repudiated papal primacy and asserted the supremacy of the crown over the church. However, they introduced little if any change in doctrine or practice. The cooperation of the church hierarchy in these changes became an important part of the later Anglican claim that their Reformation only cleansed the older church and did not create a new one. Edward VI (1537-1553) attempted to place the English Church more firmly into the Protestant camp in both theology* and practice.

With Edward's death his half-sister Mary became monarch and attempted (by force at times) to bring the English church back to the Roman primacy. She ultimately failed and instead left a popular mistrust for Roman Catholicism that has lasted in branches of Anglicanism for centuries. During her reign many English Protestants found refuge in the Rhineland and Switzerland and became convinced that the English church should become modeled after the continental Protestant churches.

With the accession of Elizabeth (1558)—and largely through her influence—Anglicanism began to take on its present form. Although firmly a Protestant church, it kept much of the organization of the pre-Reformation English church by maintaining offices such as those of archbishop,* dean, canon and archdeacon. Second, it strove to be theologically flexible by allowing for various theological understandings. Finally, it placed strong emphasis on practical uniformity, both by emphasizing its Book of Common Prayer* as the center of worship and by insisting on the continuation of certain pre-Reformation customs and rules for clerical dress.

This Elizabethan Settlement (1559) provoked increasing opposition among more radical Protestants (later known as Puritans*) who wanted the English church more fully reformed. Thus, by the end of the sixteenth century, proponents of the Church of England found it necessary to defend the peculiarities of their Reformation settlement against both Roman Catholics and Puritans.* What resulted was the unique Anglican understanding of itself as a *via media,* a middle way between the excesses of both Geneva and Rome, theologically reflected by the balancing of Scripture,* tradition and reason.

This was the religious heritage brought to the New World by the English explorers. Although Anglican chaplains* undoubtedly performed services on earlier exploratory expeditions, continuous services began with the founding of English colonies: Virginia in 1607 for America and Nova Scotia in 1713 for Canada. As the extension of the Church of England in the British colonies, it was legally established in Virginia, Maryland, North Carolina, South Carolina, Georgia and certain counties of New York, though numerically it always remained strongest in Virginia and Maryland. Its growth increased markedly after 1701 and the establishment of the Society for the Propagation of the Gospel* (SPG), which began sending missionaries to the colonies. SPG missionaries focused their efforts on those colonies where Anglicanism was not established or where it was weak, and their labors in the New England Puritan colonies resulted in a number of notable conversions, in particular that of Samuel Johnson* and faculty members of the newly founded Yale College.* This proselytizing* created tension between Anglicans and non-Anglicans.

The defeat of the French in 1763 placed Canada under British control and with it extended the influence of Anglicanism in Canada. But it also ushered in a period of conflict between Britain and her American colonies. During this period the campaign by a number of northern Anglican clergy for an American episcopate provoked both political and religious fears among other religious groups. The Revolutionary* era was a period of crisis for American Anglicans. Generally speaking, Anglican clergy north of Philadelphia were overwhelmingly Loyalist in their sympathies, while those in the South were largely patriotic. (Tory spirit, it should be noted, was everywhere less strong among the laity.)

As a result of the Revolution, Anglicanism in the colonies was greatly weakened: in large areas of the North controlled by patriots, clergy closed their churches rather than remove from the liturgy prayers for the monarch. Other clergy returned to England, and thousands of Loyalists (among them many Anglicans) fled to Canada and other British provinces after the War. This factor in turn proved beneficial to Canadian Anglicanism, and it was an expatriated Loyalist, Charles Inglis,* who in 1787 became its first bishop.* Finally, as a result of the War, the Anglican church was legally disestablished in every colony—an event which had its greatest consequences in Virginia and Maryland.

After the Revolution American Anglicans faced the challenge of securing bishops and organizing themselves into an independent denomination.* In New England generally, and particularly in Connecticut, bishops were seen as paramount, and hence the Connecticut clergy in 1783 voted to send Samuel Seabury* to Britain to secure episcopal consecration. He received this from the hands of Scottish nonjuring bishops in 1784. In contrast William White* and others argued that the church must be organized before bishops could be secured. Furthermore, they advocated a greater role for the laity* in governing the church.

In 1785 church representatives from a number of states met in convention, and the Protestant Episcopal* Church in America began organizing itself. White and Samuel Provoost* of New York received episcopal consecration* from the hands of English bishops in 1787. After a number of compromises, Connecticut Episcopalians in 1789 joined the convention, and the two movements came together. One of the compromises resulted in the unique organizational feature of the American Episcopal Church: a house of deputies* composed of both clergy* and laity, and an independent house of bishops. In Canada, at approximately the same time, the English church began receiving increased support both from the SPG and the legislature of Nova Scotia, as well as the British crown.

The early nineteenth century witnessed an increase in party tension in both America and Canada. Many Anglicans were inspired by the great English evangelical revival of the eighteenth century associated with George Whitefield* and John Newton (1725-1807). Although loyal to traditional polity and order, they emphasized a conversion*-centered piety,* strict evangelical* morality and a willingness to cooperate with other Protestant communities. In Canada this movement was given great impetus through the labors of the Church Missionary Society.* Others, characterized as "high church,"* emphasized a piety based on baptism* and the liturgy,* the importance of apostolic succession,* and the need for independence from the rest of Protestantism.

This high church/evangelical tension shaped much of Anglican religious life in the nineteenth century, giving rise to competing educational institutions (for example, General Theological Seminary vs. Virginia Theological Seminary in America and Trinity College vs. Wycliffe College in Canada) as well as missionary endeavors. The tension reached a peak during the 1840s and 1850s with the growing influence of the Oxford Movement (see Tractarianism*) and its more positive appreciation of Catholicism and medievalism. The immediate result in America was a flurry of trials of bishops and a number of secessions to Roman Catholicism, including one American bishop, Levi S. Ives.* The long-term effects of the movement, along with the revival of Gothic architecture* and advanced ceremonialism, can be seen in vast areas of later Anglicanism.

After the middle of the nineteenth century a third voice began to be heard among American Anglicans, a "broad church"* movement, inspired by English writers such as F. D. Maurice (1805-1872), which called for the church to be open to the intellectual and social trends of the age. Associated with this movement was the "Memorial" (see Memorial Movement*) of William A. Muhlenberg* that advocated a more flexible and aesthetically richer worship to lighten the drabness of urban* life, and a recognition of the ecumenical* mission for the Episcopal Church. The ecumenical* role of the Episcopal Church as a bridge church was most clearly set forth in the Chicago/Lambeth Quadrilateral* (1886/1888) that called for the reunion of Christianity on the foundation of Scripture, creed,* sacrament* and Episcopal ministry.

The middle of the nineteenth century also witnessed significant changes within Canadian Anglicanism. From 1839 to 1854 Anglicans progressively lost all governmental aid, and beginning at that point there was an increasing movement toward church self-government. Anglican synods were granted legal status, and the Province of Canada was founded in 1861 and that of Rupert's Land in 1875. A general synod* was organized in 1893. In the early 1860s Anglicans adopted the name the Church of England in Canada, which in 1955 was changed to the Anglican Church of Canada.* During these years much effort was spent in extending the church into the western provinces.

In the twentieth century American Episcopalians have developed an elaborate central administration headed by a presiding bishop (an elected office since 1919). Like many other mainline* denominations,* its membership increased sharply through the mid-1960s, declined markedly after this, finally stabilizing in the 1980s. During these years it has taken the lead in both ecumenical* issues and in directing the focus of Christians toward social questions. High church/evangelical party strife has declined in the twentieth century, though this has been at least in part replaced by a conservative/liberal* split on questions such as prayer book reform, social outreach and the ordination of women* (the latter accepted by American Anglicans in 1976, by Canadians in 1975). Recent years have also witnessed a strong charismatic movement* in the Episcopal Church.

See also ANGLICAN CHURCH OF CANADA; ANGLICAN CHURCHES IN AMERICA; ANGLICAN COMMUNION; ANGLO-CATHOLICISM; CHURCH GOVERNMENT: EPISCOPAL; EPISCOPAL CHURCH; REFORMED EPISCOPAL CHURCH; TRACTARIANISM.

BIBLIOGRAPHY. R. W. Albright, History of the Protestant Episcopal Church (1964); P. Carrington, The Anglican Church in Canada (1963); E. C. Chorley, Men and Movements in the American Episcopal Church (1946); G. E. De Mille, Episcopal Church Since 1900 (1955); R. B. Mullin, Episcopal Vision/American Reality (1986); J. F. Woolverton, Colonial Anglicanism in North America (1984).

R. B. Mullin

Anglo-Catholicism. The common name for the most extreme wing of the high church* party within Anglicanism.* As a concept it arose out of the Oxford Movement's (see Tractarianism) emphasis upon the historic continuity of the Church of England with the pre-Reformation English church.

Anglo-Catholics generally believe that the term

catholic is only rightly attributed to those churches historically connected with and exhibiting the polity,* theology* and sacramentality of the church of the first four centuries. This catholicity is found in three streams: Greek (Greek and Russian Orthodoxy*), Latin (Roman Catholicism*) and English (Anglo-Catholicism). The Reformation was a severe blow to the true church of England but did not destroy its fundamentally Catholic nature. Anglo-Catholics have seen their task as reviving the spirit and forms of Catholicism within Anglicanism, particularly through emulating the theology and practice of the Middle Ages, Eastern Orthodoxy and post-Reformation Roman Catholicism. Three important areas of concern have been sacramentalism,* the revival of religious communities and an emphasis upon a richer and more aesthetic ceremony in Christian worship.

In the nineteenth century Anglo-Catholicism was extremely controversial, but it gradually gained grudging acceptance, particularly as a result of its extensive inner-city ministry. This experience in the slums of industrial Britain led many individual Anglo-Catholics to become early advocates of Christian Socialism. Anglo-Catholicism has never been as strong in America as England (and it has been even weaker still in Canada), but it has played an important part in shaping Episcopal Church* life in large urban communities and the upper Midwest and, more generally, in advocating a Catholic understanding of Anglicanism. In recent decades it has lost some of its vigor partially because of a broader acceptance of its eucharistic concerns, but largely as a result of changes in Roman Catholic theology and practice in the aftermath of Vatican II.*

See also TRACTARIANISM.

BIBLIOGRAPHY. N. P. Williams, ed., *Northern Catholicism* (1933); G. E. DeMille, *The Catholic Movement in the American Episcopal Church* (1941).   R. B. Mullin

Annual Conference. A geographical and organizational body within a Methodist* church, the annual conference is the heartbeat of Methodism, "the basic body of the Church." The general church is a loose confederation of annual conferences. In the early history of Methodism only clergy* were members of the annual conference, including those of probationary, associate, local-pastor and full-connection status. By 1910 lay* delegates, elected by their charge conferences on an annual basis, became members of the annual conference.

The Methodist *Discipline* requires an equal number of clergy and laity as conference members. Meeting in annual sessions lasting from three to five days, the conference sets the budget, adopts programs, debates issues of the day, receives the reports of the conference program agencies and the episcopal address and every four years, based upon population, elects an equal number of clergy and lay delegates to the general conference.

Only the general conference, which in the United Methodist Church* ordinarily meets quadrennially, can change the official policies of the Church. All general-conference action must be done in conformity with the Restrictive Rules of the Church established by John Wesley.*

P. A. Mickey

Anointing. To apply oil or ointment as a sign of consecration* and invocation of the Holy Spirit. The term comes from the biblical practice of anointing persons or objects consecrated to holy service. Priests, prophets and kings were separated for service and anointed with oil, signifying their appointment and the outpouring of God's Spirit upon them to enable them to fulfill their role (Ex 28:41; 1 Sam 16:12). In the New Testament, *anointing* describes the presence of the Holy Spirit with Jesus (Acts 10:38) and his disciples (1 Jn 2:20). In the Epistle of James anointing, prayer and forgiveness of sins are associated with healing (Jas 5:14-15). In the ancient Catholic Church, the oil of anointing was termed *Chrism** and was used as a sign of invoking the Holy Spirit in baptism,* confirmation* and ordination.*

Protestant* commentators understand the efficacy of anointing the sick to arise from the "prayer of faith," while Roman Catholics* associate it with the Markan account of Jesus commissioning his disciples (Mk 6:7-11) and so speak of a sacrament* of anointing the sick. Until recently, this sacrament was termed *extreme unction.** Post-Vatican II* Catholicism significantly modified the rite: it is now described as "anointing of the sick," a means of strengthening and healing the elderly or infirm in body or soul. Anointing is still considered a sacrament and hence, a holy obligation. Protestants, beginning with Luther's *Babylonian Captivity* (1520), have rejected the sacramental understanding of anointing. The Episcopal Church* maintains a provisional rite for anointing but does not consider it a sacrament or Christian obligation.

American Protestants generally do not practice anointing, though some groups—such as the Christian and Missionary Alliance,* Church of the Foursquare Gospel* and Fire-Baptized Holiness Church*—anoint with oil as they pray for healing.

Anointed is sometimes used in a metaphorical sense, as in Pentecostal* churches, to describe persons who are spiritually gifted in preaching* or other forms of Christian service.

See also BAPTISM; CHRISM; UNCTION.

BIBLIOGRAPHY. A. C. Piepkorn, *Profiles in Belief,* 4 vols. (1977-1979). J. R. Tyson

Anointing of the Sick, Sacrament of the. *See* EXTREME UNCTION, SACRAMENT OF.

Anthony, Susan Brownell (1820-1906). Quaker social reformer. Born in South Adams, Massachusetts, into a family of independent-minded Quakers,* Anthony took on the moral zeal of her father, an early abolitionist,* and followed in the footsteps of outspoken women in her Quaker family tree. Her whole career reflected her devotion to reform. A schoolteacher during the 1840s, she actively advocated equal pay for women teachers. A temperance reformer in the early 1850s, she was denied the floor at a Sons of Temperance meeting and responded by organizing the Woman's State Temperance Society of New York. A radical abolitionist herself, she served as an agent of the American Anti-Slavery Society from 1856 to 1861 and then pushed hard to include women in the constitutional amendments designed for male African-Americans after freedom was won. The theme of women's rights ran through all of these efforts, and following the Civil War* she devoted her life to endless lecture tours and state campaigns to win women the right to vote.

The suffrage crusade linked her with Elizabeth Cady Stanton* in one of the most productive intellectual partnerships in American history. The two women worked hard and enjoyed themselves immensely. Together they published *The Revolution,* a weekly newspaper, from 1868 to 1870. In 1869 they organized the National Woman Suffrage Association (*See* Woman's Suffrage Movement) and then merged it with its rival to form the National American Woman Suffrage Association in 1890. From 1892 to 1900 Anthony served as president. She also helped organize the International Council of Women in 1888 and the International Woman Suffrage Alliance in 1904. Along with other activists she authored the four-volume *The History of Woman Suffrage* (1881-1902), providing a firsthand account of their struggle.

As a young woman Anthony was straight-laced, prudish, highly moral and very serious minded. Despite admirers, there is no evidence that she ever had any romantic interest. Instead, she gave her heart to reform and used her strength and indomitable spirit to reshape the role of women in America and the world.

BIBLIOGRAPHY. K. Anthony, *Susan B. Anthony: Her Personal History and Her Era* (1954); *DAB* I; E. C. DuBois, ed., *Elizabeth Cady Stanton/Susan B. Anthony: Correspondence, Writings, Speeches* (1981); *NAW* 1. J. R. M. Wilson

Anticlericalism. Opposition to perceived undue influence of clergy* in church and society. Although a tradition of some individual scorn for ministers* exists, without a hierarchical state church, anticlericalism as a movement, as in revolutionary France or Mexico, never took root in the U.S. Even in the original colonies, with their established churches, congregations were almost uniformly governed by popular coalitions of clergy and laity.* In the American Revolution* ministers were leading spokespersons, solidifying their place at the center of society. In 1835 Alexis de Tocqueville* observed of Protestant* and Catholic* clergy alike, "Public opinion is therefore never hostile to them but rather supports and protects them" (*Democracy in America*).

Criticism of particular ministers and priests,* reflecting religious freedom and the power of the laity, still is a familiar mark of American religious life. Classic examples include Anne Hutchinson's* charge that Massachusetts ministers preached a covenant* of works rather than grace (1636) and Gilbert Tennent's* warning against "The Danger of an Unconverted Ministry" (1740).

Groups such as the Quakers,* Christians,* Disciples* and Mormons* displayed mild anticlericalism in asserting the priesthood of believers.* Disdain for "hireling ministers" was part of a general frontier antipathy toward parasitic professionals such as lawyers. Outright anticlericalism existed rarely, as among German secular rationalists in the Midwest with Old World notions of an oppressive clerical caste. Protestant fear of Catholic priestly power cannot be separated from anti-Romanism and nativism.* In the nineteenth century such hatred expressed itself in violence but usually took the form of rumors and smirks regarding priests and nuns.*

Since the mid twentieth century an anger displayed toward the national leadership of some denominations* has reflected a gap between clergy and laity. In the late 1980s, while polls showed ministers among the most admired people in America, a certain anticlericalism was perceptible in the secular media's treatment of news stories regarding popular religious figures.

BIBLIOGRAPHY. J. M. Sanchez, *Anticlericalism: A Brief History* (1972). C. E. Hambrick-Stowe

Antimission Movement. A nineteenth-century Calvinistic Baptist* response to denominational* innovations and the growth of voluntary* societies. During the 1820s and 1830s, the development of state conventions as well as missionary,* benevolence and educational societies evoked a hostile reaction among some Baptists living in the underdeveloped areas of the Ohio and lower Mississippi River Valleys. Mistrusting the leadership of such efforts, they suspected their motivation and questioned the theological validity of their innovations.

Recent scholarship has tended to emphasize social and cultural factors that brought about the movement rather than the theological issues that were reportedly at stake. Accordingly, those who opposed the new denominational structures and societies did so out of an acute sense of local community and stood in opposition to the structures and cosmopolitan vision of the Eastern ecclesiastical establishment. From a theological standpoint, the Antimission Movement was fueled by hyper-Calvinism* (an extreme form of predestinarianism*) and the perceived threat to the autonomy of local congregations.

Daniel Parker,* John Taylor and Alexander Campbell* played important leadership roles in the Antimission Movement. From their strongholds in Kentucky and Tennessee these leaders spread their views throughout the rural South. Taylor and Campbell later reversed their position on voluntary mission societies and left the movement. Parker became the leader of the Two-Seed-in-the-Spirit doctrine, a hyper-Calvinistic group teaching that every person was born of the seed leading either to election* or to reprobation.

The Antimission Movement divided Baptists in the South into missionary* and primitive* wings. Because of their aggressive evangelism, in subsequent years the missionary wing was to far outstrip the primitive Baptists in growth. In many areas of the South today congregations are identified as Missionary or Primitive Baptist.

See also BAPTISTS; MISSIONARY BAPTISTS; PARKER, DANIEL; PRIMITIVE BAPTISTS.

BIBLIOGRAPHY. W. B. Posey, *The Baptist Church in the Lower Mississippi Valley, 1776-1845* (1957); R. G. Torbet, *A History of the Baptists* (1963); B. Wyatt-Brown, "The Antimission Movement in the Jacksonian South: A Study in Regional Folk Culture," *JSH* 36 (1970):501-529. M. G. Bell

Antinomian Controversy. Meaning literally "against law," *antinomianism* describes a theological position in which the role of objective, external elements of Christianity (such as obedience to the moral law) are underemphasized and subjective, while internal elements of Christianity (such as the work of the Holy Spirit) are overemphasized.

In America this position is first associated with the teachings of Anne Hutchinson* of Boston. Hutchinson immigrated with her husband to Boston in May 1634, and shortly after her arrival she began holding small meetings in her home on Sunday* afternoons to discuss that morning's sermon with interested individuals. In the course of those discussions, Hutchinson disclosed her belief that many of the Massachusetts Puritan* ministers* were emphasizing external morality to such a degree that she believed them guilty of preaching* a "covenant of works." Only John Cotton, teaching elder* at the Boston church and a minister whom she had come to admire back in England, was, according to Hutchinson, faithfully proclaiming the "covenant of grace."

Hutchinson's ideas attracted supporters in Boston and the ensuing controversy nearly destroyed the colony. At the heart of the debates was the question of the nature of the believer's union with the Holy Spirit. Hutchinson was understood to be teaching that the believer is so united to the Holy Spirit that no human categories (such as the requirements of the moral law) can any longer be applied to the believer. Though neither Hutchinson nor her followers were ever charged with immorality, their position was regarded as being so dangerous to the church that she was brought to trial. During her trial, her belief in her total union with the Holy Spirit led her to claim direct revelation from the Spirit rather than Scripture* alone as the source of her authority. As a result, she was banished from the colony; she left for Rhode Island on March 28, 1638. She and her family later moved to New York where, in August of 1643, she and most of those with her were killed in a Native American raid on their settlement.

BIBLIOGRAPHY. D. D. Hall, *The Antinomian Controversy, 1636-1638: A Documentary History* (1968); I. Murray, "Antinomianism: New England's First Controversy," *The Banner of Truth* 179-180 (1978):7-75. S. T. Logan

Anti-Saloon League of America. A national prohibition organization. In December 1895, delegates gathered in Washington, D.C., representing nearly fifty temperance* and religious organizations, to found a national organization under the name American Anti-Saloon League. Its professed goal was the destruction of the saloon—that is, the businesses which manufactured, distributed and sold alcoholic beverages—but its ultimate goal was a "dry" society. The League was dominated by the leaders of such evangelical* Protestant* denominations* as the Presbyterians,* Methodists* and Baptists,* who made it into a politico-ecclesiastical machine, or as they called it, "The Church in Action Against the Saloon." The League reflected nineteenth-century evangelical antipathy toward the use of alcohol* and the demand that Christian standards govern the private behavior even of nonbelievers. Drawing only limited support from Catholics* and Jews, the League did, however, have considerable appeal to the urban and rural middle class, which was concerned about the effects of alcohol consumption and feared the economic and social corruption of the saloon.

Under the able leadership of its first general superintendent, Howard Hyde Russell, a Congregational* minister,* the League quickly gained ascendancy in the anti-liquor crusade, using evangelical congregations as League units focusing on the single issue of prohibition. League leaders shrewdly sought to attain national prohibition on a step-by-step basis, calling first for local option laws to remove the saloon from specific areas, next state prohibition and then congressional regulation of interstate liquor shipments. Victory came in January 1919, with the ratification of the Eighteenth Amendment, which prohibited the manufacture, sale or transportation of intoxicating beverages, beginning in January 1920. To League supporters, the Amendment was the greatest achievement of evangelical Protestantism in the U.S.

Throughout the 1920s, the League was an influential pressure group, but growing public disenchantment with national prohibition, financial problems, discredited leadership and strategic errors led to the repeal of the Eighteenth Amendment in 1933 and an almost complete erosion of the League's power and influence. In 1964 the League became part of the National Council on Alcohol Problems.

See also PROHIBITION MOVEMENT; TEMPERANCE MOVEMENT.

BIBLIOGRAPHY. K. A. Kerr, *Organized for Prohibition: A New History of the Anti-Saloon League* (1985); P. H. Odegard, *Pressure Politics: The Story of the Anti-Saloon League* (1928); N. H. Clark, *Deliver Us from Evil* (1976).

G. F. Goodwin

Anxious Bench. *See* MOURNER'S BENCH.

Apocalypticism. From the Greek root *apokalyptein* ("to uncover" or "unveil"), a term denoting the expectation of imminent, cataclysmic events related to the Second Coming of Jesus Christ or the end of the age. Although similar to millenarianism,* it has broader applications and is not tied to any one millennial position. The apocalyptic tradition has deep roots in Jewish and Christian history, but particularly relevant for early American Christianity was the apocalyptic strand in seventeenth-century English Puritanism,* shaped by the Reformation view of the pope* as Antichrist and forged in the revolutionary traumas of the 1640s.

In colonial America, Puritan divines such as John Cotton,* the Mathers* and Jonathan Edwards* retained the image of the Papal Beast and often supported it with allegorical interpretations of the Book of Revelation. Their confident postmillennialism,* however, tempered the speculative elements in their thought, and they did not regard the Roman Church as an immediate threat to Protestant* America. During the Revolutionary War,* the image of Rome as Antichrist faded, displaced by a far more foreboding enemy, the British Empire. Several sermons of the period pictured America as the messianic "Woman in the Wilderness" and Great Britain as the Beast of Revelation 12 and 13. The pulpit rhetoric of the Revolution thus invested the war effort with an acute sense of prophetic significance, a key characteristic of apocalyptic thought.

Following the Revolution, a new apocalyptic model emerged as many Americans expressed horror at the excesses of the French Revolution. In 1797, Scottish professor John Robison warned of an "illuminati conspiracy" based on Enlightenment* rationalism and anticlericalism.* Soon New England preachers like Timothy Dwight* and Jedidiah Morse* incorporated the Illuminati plot into their own millennial visions, suggesting a theme that still lingers in the American apocalyptic imagination.

The proliferation of apocalyptic cult movements in the nineteenth century—such as the Shakers,* the Mormons* and the Jehovah's Witnesses*—convinced many evangelical* Protestants that Satan was deceiving even the elect. On a broader scale, the protracted, emotionally charged struggle between abolitionists* and defenders of slavery produced new Antichrist images that magnified the apocalyptic proportions of the Civil War.* But the most enduring nineteenth-century symbol for Satanic evil was the Roman Catholic Church.* Samuel Morse and Lyman Beecher* warned fellow Protestants of a Catholic plot to undermine American freedoms and subjugate the West. Such apocalyptic alarms intensified the feelings of hatred toward Catholics, the residues of which continue to exist today (*See* Nativism).

In the twentieth century, dispensationalist* interpretations of Ezekiel 38 and 39 have provided a convenient framework for viewing the Soviet Union in apocalyptic terms. In addition, two world wars* have generated Antichrist candidates, including Kaiser Wilhelm II, Adolf Hitler and Benito Mussolini. In more recent years, Hal Lindsey, Mary Stewart Relfe and Constance Cumbey have respectively understood the European Common Market, universal product codes and the New Age movement* as dangers of apocalyptic proportions. Common to most apocalypticists are the inclinations to relate contemporary events directly to biblical prophecy and to equate America's enemies with God's enemies.

See also ESCHATOLOGY; MILLENARIANISM.

BIBLIOGRAPHY. G. Alexander, "The Final Threat: Apocalypse, Conspiracy, and Biblical Faith," *SCP Newsletter* 10 (January-February 1984):1, 6-8, 11-12; D. B. Davis, ed., *The Fear of Conspiracy* (1972); J. H. Moorhead, "Between Progress and Apocalypse," *JAH* 71 (1984):524-542; J. A. Patterson, "Changing Images of the Beast: Apocalyptic Conspiracy Theories in American History," *JETS* 31 (1988): 443-452; T. P. Weber, *Living in the Shadow of the Second Coming, American Premillennialism, 1875-1982* (1987).   J. A. Patterson

Apologetics. Christian apologetics, broadly conceived, is argumentation on behalf of the Christian faith. Its substance is derived from revelation, while its packaging reflects the culture it addresses. Presumably, apologetics is directed toward those outside the Christian community, but in reality the audience is usually those within the Christian community.

Apologetics was imported to America ready-made from Great Britain. At the close of the eighteenth century, English and French deism* penetrated most facets of American life. College presidents such as Timothy Dwight* at Yale* and Mark Hopkins* at Williams spoke out against deism, and courses in Christian evidences soon appeared at Transylvania (1789), Harvard* (1807), Princeton* (1821), Amherst (1822), Dartmouth* (1822), Williams (1822) and Yale (1822). Christian evidences were required in the newly founded state universities of Michigan, Ohio, Indiana, South Carolina, Wisconsin and Mississippi. Evidences were taught at Mississippi in the regular curriculum from 1850 to 1930. The British anti-deistic

apologetic became the standard, particularly that of Joseph Butler (1692-1752) and William Paley (1743-1805). Many schools required both Butler and Paley as texts, but almost always, Paley.

A consensus on apologetics was possible among Protestants because of a commonly accepted epistemology, agreed upon by deists and traditionalists alike. This was the epistemology of the British philosopher John Locke (1632-1704), which was mediated through Scottish Common Sense Realism* and later flew under the flag of *Baconianism.* Locke held that all ideas are derived from experience, either sensation or reflection. The mind can synthesize these raw data and engage in rational demonstration with profit, especially in matters pertaining to God. Scientific knowledge came from empirical data, and religious knowledge from Scripture* and experience. Despite differing nuances, all eighteenth- and nineteenth-century American apologists agreed epistemologically. At stake was the deist rejection of miracles, as well as the necessity of revelation. The burden of apologetics, therefore, consisted in marshaling historical evidence for the miracles, and the necessity and authenticity of the Scriptures.

Butler argued in *Analogy of Religion* (1736) that neither miracles nor Scripture can be proven with final certainty, but then neither can scientific propositions. Conclusions in either case are probable. For Paley (*View of the Evidences of Christianity,* 1794), the miracles, fulfilled prophecies and the triumph of Christianity establish the veracity of the Christian faith. The miracles are attested by at least twelve credible witnesses. Americans who drew upon these British predecessors were Alexander Campbell* in his debate with Robert Owen* on *Evidences of Christianity* (1829) and Mark Hopkins's *Lectures on the Evidences of Christianity* (1858).

The influence of deism had waned by the 1850s, but new challenges appeared on the horizon—first evolution* and then the new form of biblical interpretation,* higher criticism. Discussions of evolution only became incorporated into apologetics proper after the turn of the century. Higher criticism, however, was another matter. The traditionalists defended the veracity of the Scripture and set out to prove that the documents were written by Moses, the prophets and the apostles, and therefore were a credible witness to the revelation from God. Such was the thrust of books by George P. Fisher* (1889), Harvey W. Everest (1884) and J. W. McGarvey* (1886).

After 1900 apologetics became more and more problematic. The American epistemological consensus gradually eroded. The first challenge was Hegelianism in its various forms. But it was the rigorous empiricism of neo-Kantianism, with its severe reservations about the possibility of divine action, which destroyed the possibility of a pan-apologetic. Liberals* and fundamentalists* could no longer talk with each other because the fundamentalists retained the older Lockian epistemology while the liberals followed first Hegel and then Kant or the pragmatists.

A revival followed World War 2* with the apologetic theology of Paul Tillich* and the conservative apologetics of Gordon H. Clark,* Edward J. Carnell* and Bernard Ramm. Tillich argued that culture provided the questions, specifically the alienation of modern man, and biblical faith the answers. His views drew considerable attention in a decade intrigued with depth psychology. Clark championed fundamentalistic Calvinism* by showing that all other positions violated the law of noncontradiction. His defense was therefore philosophical rather than historical. Carnell and Ramm hoped to command the attention of the wider Christian community—Carnell through the law of noncontradiction and history, and Ramm by characterizing the varieties of apologetics—but they primarily captivated fellow conservatives. They did, however, enter the international arena by discussing the classical apologists as well as neo-orthodox* theologians.*

By the late 1960s the neo-orthodox theologians were passing from the scene, and American intellectuals were increasingly fractured epistemologically, affirming logical positivism, language analysis, phenomenology, existentialism,* neo-Kantianism, process,* personalism, pragmatism and neo-Thomism* (with its attendant Roman Catholic* and Anglican* apologetics). The conservatives, in contrast, embraced either Cartesian rationalism, Lockian empiricism or both, and turned their attention to experiential and relational* theology, which retained an empirical foundation but without the prosaic Lockian confines.

BIBLIOGRAPHY. B. Willey, *Christianity Past and Present* (1952); E. Flower and M. G. Murphey, *A History of Philosophy in America* (1977); R. C. Sproul, J. Gerstner, A. Lindsley, *Classical Apologetics* (1984); J. O. Filbeck, *The Christian Evidence Movement* (1946).   T H. Olbricht

Apologist. *See* APOLOGETICS.

Apostasy. The abandonment of true Christian faith. In contrast to heresy,* which would constitute an aberration of doctrine,* apostasy refers to

the total renunciation of Christianity through either word or deed. Apostasy may take the form of outright renunciation or the abandonment of a recognizably Christian life style. The concept presupposes that the person who commits apostasy appeared to be a genuine believer at one time.

The issues surrounding apostasy concern its theological interpretation and pastoral treatment. The fact that apostasy occurs is hardly put into question. Among Christians in America several theological explanations have gained widespread support. Some groups would claim that those who commit apostasy have lost their salvation.* Others maintain that since salvation is an act of God, external acts by human beings cannot undo it. Still others argue that apostasy is evidence that those who commit it were never truly saved. In traditional Roman Catholic* thought, apostasy can be brought about through mortal sin.* The pastoral response to apostasy corresponds to the theological interpretation.

See also ASSURANCE OF SALVATION; ETERNAL SECURITY.

BIBLIOGRAPHY. J. F. Strombeck, *Shall Ever Perish* (1966); G. C. Berkouwer, *Faith and Perseverance* (1958).   W. Corduan

Apostolate. In general, *apostle* refers to both the mission and the representational authority* of someone sent on a mission by a superior. In Christianity, *apostle* refers to the authoritative mission conferred by Christ on his disciples, with special emphasis on the Twelve and other specific people, to continue his mission on earth after his resurrection-ascension. Later, *apostolic* would refer to any and everything connected in any way with the mission or apostolate of the Catholic Church, viewed as the successor of the apostolic church. The apostolic church came to be viewed as the successor to the first apostle, Jesus Christ (Heb 3:1). In the mid-nineteenth century, the term *lay apostolate* or *apostolate of the laity* came into very frequent usage to describe the role or mission of the laity* in contrast to but also in communion with the apostolate of the hierarchy. *Apostolate* was a very important term in Catholic Action,* especially as this existed in the U.S. in such forms as the Christian Family Movement,* Young Christian Students and Young Christian Workers from 1940 to 1960.

BIBLIOGRAPHY. Y. M. Congar, *Lay People in the Church* (1957).   R. L. Kress

Apostolic Delegate. A papal diplomat. As official papal representative to the local (i.e., regional or national) church, this ecclesial diplomat promotes the unity of the Roman Catholic Church* by fostering relations between the Vatican and the local church, as well as relations within that territorial church. In practice, one of the delegate's most notable duties is mediation between the local church and the Vatican in the selection of bishops.* Unlike the papal nuncio,* or pro-nuncio, the delegate is not also accredited to the territorial government. The apostolic delegation to the U.S. was founded in 1893, and Francesco Satolli* was appointed the first apostolic delegate. The delegation became an apostolic nunciature in 1984.

See also VATICAN-U.S. CATHOLIC CHURCH RELATIONS.

BIBLIOGRAPHY. R. A. Graham, *Vatican Diplomacy: A Study of the Church and State on the International Plane* (1959); M. Oliver, *The Representatives: The Real Nature and Function of Papal Legates* (1982). G. L. Sobolewski

Apostolic Succession. Like *apostle* and *apostolate,* *apostolic succession* has a wide range of usages. In general, the whole church in any age may be viewed as the successor or follower of the apostolic church. All members of the church are successors of the first disciples and apostles of Jesus. In Catholic usage, *apostolic succession* is a technical term designating the college of bishops,* in which the bishop of Rome, the pope,* plays a special role. This college of bishops succeeds the college of apostles, especially the Twelve, in the administration and governance of the church, so that it will be an orderly and peaceful society and community of believers as befits the communion of saints.*

Included in the contemporary Catholic understanding of *apostolic succession* is the historical continuity of any contemporary church with the apostolic church. This historical continuity is not sustained solely by or on the basis of a literary document, not even the Bible,* which even as God's Word must be read and interpreted. *Apostolic succession* in this sense describes the mutual relationship and dialog between the authoritative written Word from the past and the authoritative preservation, preaching and interpretation of the present. The concept of apostolic succession does not place the college of bishops above the gospel or even the Bible, but describes their role in the handing on of the gospel in its written form. Apostolic succession thus understood presupposes both the succession of the whole church in the faith of the first disciples and the promised presence of the Holy Spirit with the church until the end of time (Mt 28:18-20).

Historically, most Protestant* churches have rejected any notion of apostolic succession validating Christian ministry. However, nineteenth-century Anglo-Catholics* (*See* Tractarian Movement) claimed validity for Anglican ministerial orders by appealing to an unbroken succession through the pre-Reformation church in England. This claim was rejected in 1896 by Pope Leo XIII's* *Apostolicae Curae.* Contemporary ecumenical* dialog has often focused on the issue of apostolic succession and ministry, with a more biblical understanding of ministry emerging on both sides. *See also* LAY MOVEMENT, CATHOLIC.

BIBLIOGRAPHY. *Baptism, Eucharist and Ministry,* Faith and Order Paper No. 111 (1982); H. Küng, *The Church* (1967); K. Rahner and J. Ratzinger, *The Episcopate and the Primacy* (1962); K. Rahner and J. Ratzinger, *Revelation and Tradition* (1965). R. L. Kress

Apthorp, East (1733-1816). Episcopal* minister* and founder of Christ Church, Cambridge, Massachusetts. Born in Boston, Apthorp graduated from Jesus College, Cambridge University (B.A., 1755; M.A., 1758). Appointed in 1759 as a missionary by the Society for the Propagation of the Gospel in Foreign Parts* (SPG), an organization devoted to the spread of Anglicanism,* Apthorp returned to Massachusetts and founded the first Episcopal church in Cambridge. The Congregational* establishment, becoming concerned about the number of Anglican churches being formed in New England, made verbal attacks upon the spread of episcopacy,* and Apthorp wrote a tract defending the SPG, *Considerations on the Institution and Conduct of the Society for the Propagation of the Gospel in Foreign Parts.* . . . Jonathan Mayhew* of Boston responded, and a pamphlet warfare erupted, to which Thomas Secker, the archbishop* of Canterbury, contributed. Mayhew contended that the constitution of the SPG prohibited it from going to established colonies, while the supporters of the SPG maintained that the constitution directed such activity. Apthorp immigrated to England in 1765 and never returned to New England.

BIBLIOGRAPHY. *AAP* 5; G. M. Day, *The Biography of a Church: A Brief History of Christ Church, Cambridge, Massachusetts* (1951); C. F. Pascoe, *Two Hundred Years of the S.P.G., 1701-1900,* 2 vols. (1901). D. A. Weir

Archbishop. An episcopal office higher than that of bishop.* The term usually designates those bishops whose jurisdiction extends over an ecclesiastical province, rather than over a single diocese.* Bishops of dioceses within the province are called suffragan bishops. This means that every metropolitan* is an archbishop. Not every archbishop, however, is a metropolitan. Some gain the title because of the unusual status of the area governed (perhaps including an important church or city), an area which yet has no suffragan dioceses and so is not a metropolitan center. Others receive it as a personal honor, not to be transferred to the diocese or to their successors, and still others receive it because of their special functions as members of the Roman curia or of the papal diplomatic corps.　　　J. G. Stackhouse

Archdiocese. A preeminent diocese* presided over by an archbishop.* In a practice dating back to at least the fourth century, several neighboring dioceses are grouped into provinces. The most significant of these dioceses is then designated the metropolitan see, or archdiocese; the others are called *suffragan dioceses* (from *suffrage,* insofar as their bishops have a vote in synod*). (For Episcopalians,* however, a *suffragan* is an auxiliary, or subordinate, bishop under the bishop of the diocese.) The Eastern, or Byzantine, churches prefer the terminology of *eparchy* and *archeparchy.* By way of exception there can be an archdiocese without a province or suffragan dioceses and an archbishop who does not govern an archdiocese. In the U.S. and Canada only the Roman Catholic Church* makes extensive use of the archdiocesan structure. Though the Episcopal Church organizes dioceses into provinces, it does not recognize any archdioceses (as does, e.g., the Anglican Church* in England). The Greek Orthodox Church in North and South America consists of one archdiocese and a dozen dioceses. In the Orthodox Church in America, one of the diocesan bishops has by election the title "Metropolitan of All-America and Canada."

The first Roman Catholic bishop in the U.S. was John Carroll,* named bishop of Baltimore in 1789 and archbishop in 1808, when Baltimore became a metropolitan see. By 1988 there were thirty-four archdioceses (including the military and two Eastern rites*). Quebec, the mother church of Catholicism in Canada and its primatial see, became a bishopric in 1674, an archdiocese in 1819 and a metropolitan see in 1844. There are now about twenty Roman Catholic archdioceses in Canada.　　　J. E. Lynch

Architecture, Church. During the colonial period, three major types of churches were introduced into what would become the United States—Spanish-style churches from Roman Catholic* missionaries* in the Southwest, meeting-house churches from the Puritans* in New England, and "auditory churches" from Anglican* influence throughout the colonies.

First, Catholic missionaries in the Southwest *(see* Missions to North America, Spanish), primarily Franciscans* such as Junipero Serra,* brought with them memories of the Renaissance and Baroque styles that were popular in Spain. With the help of native labor they erected mission churches and compounds from Texas to California that combined Iberian style (itself influenced by centuries of Islamic contact) with local materials such as adobe bricks and Native American workmanship. The eighteenth-century California missions stretching from San Francisco to San Diego are the best known of those that remain, although many in Texas and New Mexico are more striking in their design.

Another type of colonial building was that of the Puritans, who began to settle southern New England in the early 1600s. Building on their Reformed* Protestant heritage that had arisen in Zurich and Geneva and filtered through the Netherlands and Old England, these Puritans rejected the notion of a church as a building and created a new architectural mode called the meetinghouse. Where the church building of Medieval Catholicism* had been regarded specifically as a sacred space—a *domus dei* or "house of God"—the meetinghouse was a purely functional structure for the preaching* of the Word and the occasional performance of the two sacraments.*

New England meetinghouses were therefore built in the "plain style," with no pictorial representations of religious themes. A massive pulpit dominated the interior, and the congregation was seated in box pews arranged to reflect social rank. (Galleries or balconies were also provided for those not qualified for the pews.) Communion* was administered from a movable table or a hinged board attached to a wall. Since the building itself was not sacred, the meetinghouse could also be used for other public functions, such as town meetings, schooling or even defense. The meetinghouse was frequently sited at the center of town on the green, thus providing a visual orientation for the entire community. The only meetinghouse from the seventeenth century that still survives is the Old Ship Church (1681) in Hingham, Massachusetts, which is still used for worship by a Unitarian* congregation.

The third important architectural model for a house of worship* did not emerge until later in the colonial era. These were the "auditory churches" developed after the style introduced by England's Christopher Wren in his master plan for rebuilding the Anglican* churches destroyed in the Great Fire of London in 1666. Wren's churches were designed to fulfill the goals of both the audible preaching and sacramental worship that characterized the Anglican "middle way." Externally these Anglican churches resembled their Gothic and Romanesque predecessors in their general shape: rectangular, with the main entrance located at one of the short ends (traditionally the north); and a tower, steeple or spire built near the entrance. The general style, however, was in the Neo-Classical tradition of the Renaissance.

The earliest Anglican church that has survived from colonial times to the present is St. Luke's in Isle of Wight County, Virginia (1632?). The church is basically Gothic in style, with pointed-arch windows, but elements of Neo-Classical design point toward the influence of the Renaissance. Later churches in colonial Virginia, such as Bruton Parish (1711-1715) in the colonial capital of Williamsburg, were usually built of brick and exhibit more clearly the Wren style in its Georgian form (the term used to describe most Neo-Classical buildings of the eighteenth century).

Christ ("Old North") Church in Boston (1723) was one of the first Anglican churches in that Puritan city, and its Congregationalist* neighbors were quick to imitate its Wren-style features in the nearby Old South Meetinghouse (1729). From then on the meetinghouse model began to fade as even Baptists* adapted their houses of worship to the new fashion (e.g., the First Baptist Meetinghouse in Providence, 1774-1775). The influence of the English architect James Gibbs, who introduced a trend toward more complex steeples and massive columned porches, spread throughout the colonies during the eighteenth century (e.g., St. Michael's, Charleston, 1752-1761), but the basic Wren style remained fundamental to these embellishments. The Quakers (Friends*), together with the Shakers* in their nineteenth-century heyday, were the only significant Christian groups to resist this abandonment of the Puritan ideal.

Independence brought with it visions of a new republic modeled on the ancient democracies of Greece and Rome, and religious as well as secular architecture was deeply influenced by the styles of those eras. When offered a choice between Gothic and Roman Revival styles for the first American Catholic cathedral* (1804-1818), Bishop John Carroll* of Baltimore directed his architect, Benjamin Latrobe, to utilize the domed style of the Romans that President Jefferson was favoring in his own designs. Similarly, St. Peter-in-Chains Catholic Cathedral in Cincinnati was erected in 1845 on the plan of a Greek temple. During the antebellum period, as a sign of their identification with the American democratic experiment, many denominations built dozens of smaller churches in these styles.

As the popularity of first the Roman and then the Greek Revival flourished, a new model of "what a church should look like" was being introduced—again by the Anglicans. This was the Gothic Revival which began to flourish first in England and then in the U.S. Its success was in considerable measure the result of the militant campaign of the Cambridge Camden Society, or "Ecclesiologists," who argued strenuously that Gothic was "the only proper style" for Christian worship. This Cambridge Movement gained an American branch in the New York Ecclesiological Society, founded in 1848, and a brilliant practitioner in the English emigrant and architect Richard Upjohn.

Upjohn's Trinity Church in Manhattan (1839-1846) was a major force in popularizing among a receptive public the picturesque appeal of pointed-arch windows, crockets, crenelations and the other ornamental characteristics of Gothic style. Although he designed a number of churches (mostly Episcopal) in stone and along traditional lines, his greatest contribution was his adaptation of the medieval style to a distinctively American idiom expressed in board-and-batten construction (vertical planks with their joints bridged and sealed by thinner wooden strips). These "Carpenter Gothic" churches rapidly became a common feature of the American and Canadian religious landscape, and were used widely by the whole denominational spectrum.

Another medieval style that became popular later in the nineteenth century was the Romanesque, characterized by rounded arches and vaults. Trinity (Episcopal) Church in Boston (1872-1877), designed by the great H. H. Richardson for Phillips Brooks,* the "Prince of the Pulpit," introduced "Richardsonian Romanesque" into the American idiom, and became widely used in secular public buildings and by Baptists, Methodists* and other denominations with no direct links to the medieval tradition. The same was true of the Gothic Revival in its later phases, although its foremost advocate at the turn of the century, Ralph Adams Cram, was as militant an Anglican as had been his predecessor, Upjohn. Cram employed Gothic in a wide variety of contexts, including collegiate, monastic and "prep" school chapels, but his greatest monument remains the Cathedral Church of St. John the Divine in New York City, which was not begun until 1892 and still awaits completion.

Revival styles of various sorts remained popular until the Depression,* a period in which church construction lagged, not to gain momentum again until the religious revival of the 1950s and the burgeoning of the suburbs. Although much of the new building was still in traditional modes—Presbyterians* and Baptists,* especially in the South, continued to favor the Georgian—the Liturgical Movement* in the Catholic Church, fostered by Vatican II* and nurtured in other denominations as well, began to question the suitability of medieval and Renaissance forms for biblically based worship.

As a result, semicircular designs and other shapes thought to promote interaction between the minister or celebrant and the congregation frequently displaced the traditional rectangle. The doctrine that "form follows function," originating with Horatio Greenough and Louis Sullivan in the previous century, now found expression in Frank Lloyd Wright's Unity Temple (Unitarian; 1904-1906) in Oak Park, Illinois. This building combined textured concrete, horizontal lines and minimal ornament to produce a radically new physical context for worship. Post-war experiments with this new geometrical austerity, often carried out in America by such European architects as Marcel Breuer and Pietro Belluschi, continued to provide alternatives to the Georgian and Gothic standbys. Outstanding examples are Breuer's Benedictine Abbey Church in Collegeville, Minnesota, and Belluschi's St. Mary's Cathedral in San Francisco.

An emphasis on functionality also characterized the architecture generated by the burgeoning evangelical* and Pentecostal* churches of the 1970s and 1980s. Black* churches in these traditions had often adapted storefronts or abandoned white churches, while rural white churches were frequently humble frame or brick structures of no distinct style. The new interstate temples of more recent times, however, have often been daring in their shapes and massive in size, reflecting their congregations' wealth and freedom from traditional constraints. Many of these structures continue the theatrical model that was popular in many nineteenth-century Protestant churches (even those with Gothic or Romanesque exteriors), which were fundamentally auditoria with platforms at the front for speakers and choirs, and rows of linked individual "opera seats" rather than pews. Although rivaled for a time during the late nineteenth century by the "Akron Plan," which permitted the conversion of auditorium space into Sunday-school* classrooms and vice versa, the auditorium remains today a dominant model within denominations where worship focuses on preaching, testimonials and song, rather than on elaborate fixed liturgy.

See also CATHEDRAL; CHAPEL.

BIBLIOGRAPHY. J. De Visser and H. Kalman, *Pioneer Churches* (1976); R. G. Kennedy, *American Churches* (1982); W. H. Pierson, Jr., *American Buildings and Their Architects,* 4 vols. (1976); P. B. Stanton, *The Gothic Revival and American Church Architecture* (1968); H. W. Turner, *From Temple to Meeting House* (1979); J. F. White and S. J. White, *Church Architecture* (1988); P. W. Williams, "Religious Architecture and Landscape," *Encyclopedia of the American Religious Experience,* eds. C. H. Lippy and P. W. Williams (1987). P. W. Williams

Argue, Andrew Harvey (1869-1959). Pentecostal* pioneer in Canada. Born and raised in a Methodist* home in the Ottawa Valley, Argue was converted as a young man. He only had a sixth-grade education, but after moving to Winnipeg, Manitoba, he became a successful real estate salesman and ministered as a lay* preacher* with the Holiness Movement* Church. Argue went to Chicago in 1907 on hearing of William Durham's* mission there and received the Pentecostal experience. Returning to Winnipeg he became the leading figure among Pentecostals, emphasizing divine healing,* Spirit baptism* and the premillennial* return of Christ. There he founded Calvary Temple, an Assemblies of God* congregation that for many years was one of Canada's largest Pentecostal churches.

Argue was a key figure in the emergence of the Pentecostal Assemblies of Canada in the late 1910s. He published several magazines promoting his views, notably *The Apostolic Messenger.* Perhaps even more important is the fact that his children and their spouses became leaders in Canadian Pentecostalism.

See also PENTECOSTAL CHURCHES; PENTECOSTAL MOVEMENT.

BIBLIOGRAPHY. G. F. Atter, *The Third Force* (1962). D. M. Lewis

Armenian Church. A non-Chalcedonian Orthodox* church. Christianity in Armenia dates at least from the third century, though the official conversion of Armenia into the Christian faith came after the extensive evangelization of St. Gregory the Illuminator, who, in the year 301 baptized the king of Armenia, Tiritades III (298-330), and the entire royal family. Christianity was proclaimed the official state religion in the same year, making Armenia the first Christian nation. Gregory received episcopal* consecration* in 305 from Metropolitan Leontius of Caesarea (Cappadocia), thus becoming the first *catholicos* (chief bishop) of Armenia.

The Armenian Church belongs to the family of Eastern Orthodox churches commonly referred to as Oriental, or Non-Chalcedonian, Orthodox churches because of their opposition to the Council of Chalcedon (451) and advocacy of the Christological doctrine of St. Cyril of Alexandria. The Oriental Orthodox churches adhere to the doctrinal decrees of the Councils of Nicaea (325), Constantinople (381) and Ephesus (431).

The first Armenian to ever set foot in the New World is believed to have been a tobacco trader who settled in Virginia in the early seventeenth century and was known as "Martin the Armenian." Very few Armenians arrived on the shores of the U.S. until the first half of the nineteenth century, when a number of young men arrived to pursue higher education at Princeton,* New York and Yale* universities and at Andover Theological Seminary.* Larger numbers of Armenian immigrants from the Ottoman Empire came to the U.S. during the last quarter of the nineteenth century, many planning to make their fortunes and return to their homeland. But political instability in Armenia kept them in America. By 1888 there were approximately twelve hundred Armenians in the U.S., concentrated mostly around New York City; Providence, Rhode Island; Boston and Worcester, Massachusetts; and Fresno, California.

To minister to the spiritual needs of the growing community, the Rev. Hovsep Sarajian arrived in the U.S. from Constantinople in 1889 and celebrated the first Divine Liturgy in Worcester, Massachusetts, on July 28 of that same year. As he traveled throughout the Northeast, the presence of an Armenian priest* created a new enthusiasm in the Armenian communities. The first Armenian church was consecrated in Worcester on January 18, 1891. As the flow of immigrants continued and as the community grew, so did the number of parishes. New churches were consecrated in Fresno, California (1900); West Hoboken, New Jersey (1907); and Fowler, California (1910).

Catholicos Mugurditch I (1892-1907) gave permanence to the presence of the Armenian Church in America when his encyclical* of 1898 formally established the Diocese of the Armenian Church of America. The Rev. Hovsep Sarajian, now a bishop,* was its first primate. At the turn of the century the Armenian community in the U.S. numbered over 15,000, with four established churches and six priests. The community grew further during the first two decades of the twentieth century, especially after 1915, with the arrival of many Armenians who had survived the massacres perpetrated by the Ottoman government against its Armenian population. Toward the end of the 1920s, there were nineteen churches in the U.S. and over thirty-five parishes, in various stages of formation, served by more than thirty priests.

The 1930s were turbulent years, with an internal conflict within the community in 1933 leading to the establishment of a rival diocesan jurisdiction. The schism remains unresolved to this day. The next decades brought further growth to the Church. In the early 1960s the St. Nersess Theological Seminary was established.

Beginning in the early 1970s, a major and ongoing wave of new immigrants from various Middle Eastern countries has brought the number of Armenians in the U.S. to an estimated population of over 750,000, making it the largest Armenian population in any country outside Armenia. In 1984 the Diocese of Canada was established, which was part of the Eastern Diocese of the U.S. Presently there are over one hundred churches and mission parishes in the U.S., divided into two jurisdictions: the Eastern Diocese with its headquarters in New York City, and the Western Diocese centered in Los Angeles. Since 1959 the Armenian Church has been a member of the National Council of Churches.*

BIBLIOGRAPHY. M. Ormanian, *The Church of Armenia* (1955); P. Gulesserian, *The Armenian Church* (1939); C. Long, ed., *Armenians in America* (1987).   A. A. Aivazian

Arminianism. A theological reform movement within the Dutch Reformed Church in the early seventeenth century, Arminianism had considerable influence in Anglo-American theological developments, particularly as it came to be championed by Methodists.* The movement is traced to the work of Jacob Arminius (1560-1690). A convinced Calvinist* who was educated at the University of Leyden and at Geneva, he eventually departed from the teachings of Calvin on several points of doctrine. Although the movement associated with Arminius came to be synonymous with "anti-Calvinism," it was actually a reaction against an orthodox* expression of Calvinism that was placing particular emphasis on predestination* and a cluster of doctrines* associated with it.

[77]

Arminius was requested by the authorities of the Dutch church to examine and refute what was regarded as the humanist views of Dirck Koornbert, a leader of an anti-Calvinist party in Holland, who objected in particular to the "high" Calvinist doctrine of predestination. In the course of this investigation, Arminius became convinced of the truth of significant aspects of Koornbert's position. With this altered doctrinal perspective, Arminius began to clash with Franciscus Gomarus (1563-1641), his strict Calvinist colleague on the theological faculty at the University of Leyden. Gomarus's view on predestination, known as *supralapsarianism,* maintained that God's double decree for the election* of some and the reprobation of others was made sovereignly by God before the Fall of Adam and Eve, rather than as a response to their Fall. Hence, God permitted the Fall as the event through which he would make effective his eternal decrees. As corollaries of this position, Gomarus held that human nature is totally depraved and that the atoning death of Christ is limited to the elect.

After the death of Arminius in 1609, his theological position was maintained by his successor at Leyden, Simon Bisshop (1583-1643), and consequently Gomarus and his allies began to call for the expulsion of all Arminian teachers from their teaching positions. In response, forty-six pastors signed a document called the *Remonstrance* in 1610, that rejected the supralapsarian doctrine of predestination as well as the alternative infralapsarian view, which held that God's decrees were not eternal but were made after and in light of the Fall. They also rejected the doctrine of limited atonement* that affirmed Christ died only for the elect, and the doctrine of irresistible grace.

The positions stated in the *Remonstrance* were essentially those that had been held by Arminius. In Arminius's view, God's decrees were based on his foreknowledge of the future faith of the elect and not foreordained so as to permit no room for a free human response to God's offer of saving grace. Moreover, this human response was not simply the exercise of free will, which would be to repeat the ancient Pelagian heresy. Arminius maintained that since the human will is enslaved to sin, it is necessary for God to assist people in responding to the invitation to salvation.* He does this by providing prevenient grace, so enabling the will to respond freely to God. In his view, God also foreknows who will persevere in their Christian faith after conversion, although once again God's foreknowledge does not mean that he foreordains that they cannot fall from grace if they choose to do so.

A major reason for the Calvinist's opposition to Arminius' position was their desire to uphold at all costs the sovereignty of God, whereby all credit for human salvation rests with God. This view is also called *monergism,* which indicates that God is the sole party operative to effect human salvation. Arminius's view may be described as *synergism,* which indicates that God's grace initiates the act of salvation but, to become effective, grace cooperates with the human act of response to grace. For Arminius this meant that "the grace sufficient for salvation is conferred on the Elect, and on the non-Elect; that, if they will, they may believe or not believe, may be saved or not be saved."

The publication of the *Remonstrance* led to a heightening of the controversy, as it now became embroiled in a web of social and political issues. The Arminian position appealed to the growing middle class, especially in the maritime provinces of Holland. However, under the leadership of Maurice of Nassau, the anti-Remonstrant party, also known as the *Gomarists,* consolidated their position and, at the Synod of Dort in 1618, they secured the condemnation of the Remonstrant tenets. The five principal tenets of the Synod are represented in the acronym TULIP—total depravity, unconditional election, limited atonement, irresistible grace and the perseverance of the believer in salvation.

Undoubtedly, Arminius and the Remonstrants would have been still perceived as Calvinists by Lutherans* and Catholics* of their day, particularly given their Calvinist views of the church and sacraments.* However, in the course of the succeeding two centuries, their views came to be regarded as distinctly anti-Calvinist, particularly in the Anglo-American context. While the distinguishing mark of Calvinism came to be its focus on God's irresistible grace, for Arminianism the distinguishing feature had come to be a conditional view of grace. Further, while the Arminians of the early seventeenth century tended to place a greater emphasis on God's role in the divine-human synergism, the emphasis on irresistible grace led to a growing ethical emphasis that would merge into a Pelagianism that emphasized human moral effort on the basis of free will. Later Arminianism also tended to merge into deism or natural religion, where the moral emphasis wholly replaces the theological.

By the eighteenth century Arminianism had become a generic label for a wide variety of moral thinkers who objected to strict Calvinism. The leading representatives of such liberal Arminianism in America were such eighteenth-century

Boston churchmen as Charles Chauncy* at Boston's First Congregational Church and Jonathan Mayhew* of Boston's West Church. They were products of a broad, latitudinarian culture that was fostered at Harvard,* beginning with the presidency of John Leverett* in 1707. This anti-clerical* spirit had merged with a critical attitude toward the Calvinistic tenets of New England Puritanism.* These ministers became locked in theological controversy with Jonathan Edwards,* whose leadership in the Great Awakening* served to renew the older Calvinist tradition. Yet, they were slow to break from the older Calvinists, due to longstanding social and intellectual ties with that heritage. Their successors were to pass over into the ranks of New England Unitarianism* amid theological controversy that disrupted the Massachusetts churches between 1805 and 1820.

The original tenets of Arminius enjoyed a restoration in the eighteenth century, emerging with evangelical* warmth in the Wesleyan* revival. There was probably more affinity between this revived Arminianism and Edwards's defense of Calvinist orthodoxy than there was between the early Methodists and the Arminianism of Chauncy or Mayhew. Wesley overtly identified with the Arminian label during a dispute that erupted in 1770 between himself and his disciples, on one hand, and the Calvinist chaplains of the Countess of Huntingdon on the other. In their attack on the minutes of the Methodist conference of 1770, these Calvinists labeled the Methodists as *Arminians,* although there is little indication that Arminius had heretofore been a major source in Wesley's theological reading. Wesley, accepting this label, named his new Methodist theological journal, *The Arminian Magazine,* that began publication in 1778. There he advocated the case for "conditional salvation" in terms of "universal redemption" in Christ, in opposition to the Calvinist doctrines of predestination and the irresistibility of grace. Wesley also wrote major treaties against the Calvinists, entitled "Predestination Calmly Considered" and "Thoughts Upon Necessity."

Methodism became the largest Protestant* denomination within nineteenth-century America, and with it the Arminian ascendancy prevailed in the Second Great Awakening,* as well as in numerous other denominations that were divided over the issues of the Awakening (including Presbyterians,* Congregationalists,* Baptists* and, to some extent, the Lutherans,* German Reformed and Mennonites*) and still others that were indigenous products of the Awakening (including the United Brethren in Christ, the Evangelical Association, the Restoration Movement* or Christian Churches* and the Churches of Christ*). The Arminian outlook that informed this Methodist age of American Protestantism fit well with the emphasis upon voluntarism* and purposiveness that came to characterize American evangelical Protestantism.

BIBLIOGRAPHY. J. Arminius, *Works,* 3 vols. (1825, 1828, 1875); C. Bangs, *Arminius* (1985); A. W. Harrison, *Arminianism* (1937); J. Miley, *The Atonement in Christ* (1879); A. Outler, ed., *John Wesley* (1964); C. Pinnock, ed., *Grace Unlimited* (1975); P. Ramsey, ed., *The Works of Jonathan Edwards; Freedom of the Will* (1957); H. O. Wiley, *Christian Theology,* 3 vols. (1941). J. S. O'Malley

Armitage, Thomas (1819-1896). Baptist* historian and pastor.* Born in England, Armitage began his pastoral career in the Methodist Church of England in 1815 at age sixteen. Immigrating to the U.S. in 1838, he served as a Methodist Episcopal* pastor in New York until 1848. He then joined the Baptist Church after becoming convinced of the Baptist doctrine* of believer's baptism* by immersion. Subsequently, he was pastor of Washington Avenue Baptist Church, Albany, New York (1839-1848), and served nearly forty years as pastor of the Fifth Avenue Baptist Church of New York City (1848-1896). A contemporary Baptist, William Cathcart, suggested that Armitage was "regarded by many as the foremost man in the American pulpit."

In 1850 Armitage led in the formation of the American Bible Union* and served as its second president. This organization advocated rendering the Greek word *baptizein* as *immersion* rather than *baptism* in translations of the Bible. Armitage is best known, however, for his publication of *A History of the Baptists* (1887). While not claiming an unbroken succession of organized Baptist churches all the way back to Christ (as did the "Landmarkers"*), Armitage attempted to trace the continuation of Baptist teachings (i.e., certain biblical truths) from the New Testament to the present.

BIBLIOGRAPHY. J. F. Eller, *Thomas Armitage, D.D., the Man, the Preacher, the Leader* (1896). H. L. McBeth

Armstrong, Annie Walker (1850-1938). Leader of the Southern Baptist* Woman's Missionary Union. Born into a prosperous and traditional Baltimore family, she joined a local Baptist* church around the age of twenty. She and her sister Alice, both of whom never married, became involved in the woman's missionary movement* which was sweeping the country during the 1870s and 1880s.

At Richmond in 1888, Annie led the way in forming the Women's Missionary Union. From her election as corresponding secretary in 1888 until she left that postion in 1906, Armstrong continued to exert her influence in shaping the Union, both in its publications and missionary offerings. She was instrumental in instituting the famous Lottie Moon* Christmas Offering among Southern Baptists.

Perhaps more than any other person in the Convention's history, Armstrong helped advance the cause of Southern Baptist home and foreign missions. Talented, but at times struggling with her leadership role, she is representative of many late-nineteenth-century women who felt torn between the opportunities for leadership in church and society and the traditional roles of women. Today her name is honored among Southern Baptists by the Annie Armstrong Offering for Home Missions. *See also* MISSIONARY MOVEMENT, WOMEN'S.

BIBLIOGRAPHY. A. Hunt, *History of Woman's Missionary Union* (1976); B. Sorrill, *Annie Armstrong: Dreamer in Action* (1984).   M. G. Bell

Armstrong, George Dod (1813-1899). Southern Presbyterian* pastor* and scientist. Born in Morris County, New Jersey, Armstrong graduated from Princeton* College (1832) and Union Theological Seminary, Virginia (1837). He then taught chemistry and geology at Washington College (now Washington and Lee University) from 1838 to 1851. For the next forty-eight years he pastored the First Presbyterian Church of Norfolk, Virginia (1851-1899).

As both a prominent pastor and as his denomination's* leading spokesman on the relationship between religion and science,* Armstrong significantly influenced Southern Presbyterian opinion in the second half of the nineteenth century. His published works covered many topics. He defended slavery as a positive good (*The Christian Doctrine of Slavery,* 1857), vividly described a yellow fever epidemic in Norfolk and explained basic Christian doctrines* such as the sacraments* (*Doctrine of Baptism,* 1857) and religious experience.* Especially important was his persistent attack upon Darwinism* as unsubstantiated by the facts of nature and contradictory to scriptural teaching (*The Two Books of Nature and Revelation Collated,* 1886). He played a major role at the 1886 Southern Presbyterian General Assembly* which affirmed static creationism* and rejected the theistic evolutionary* position of James Woodrow* of Columbia Theological Seminary.

BIBLIOGRAPHY. *DAB* I; E. T. Thompson, *Presbyterians in the South,* vol. 2 (1963).   G. S. Smith

Armstrong, Laura Dell Malotte (1886-1945). Southern Baptist* missions* leader. Armstrong served on the executive board of the Missouri Baptist General Association from 1919 to 1936 and on the executive committee of the Southern Baptist Convention from 1927 to 1945. For the last ten years she was the board's only female member. She also served as a member of the executive committee of the Baptist World Alliance.* Armstrong is best known for her leadership in the Woman's Missionary Union. She headed the statewide organization at the Baptist World Congress in Berlin in 1934, and in Atlanta, Georgia, in 1939. As Woman's Missionary Union president and chairman of the Board of Trustees of its Training School, she guided the erection of a new facility outside Louisville and proposed a $10,000 fund-raising drive to benefit black Southern Baptist colleges and churches.

BIBLIOGRAPHY. K. Mallory, "Mrs. Frank W. Armstrong," *Royal Service* 40 (July 1945):3-4.
M. L. Bendroth

Armstrong, William Park (1874-1944). Presbyterian* New Testament scholar. Born in Selma, Alabama, Armstrong graduated from Princeton University* (B.A., 1894; M.A., 1896). He attended Princeton Theological Seminary* in 1897, and then studied in Germany (Marburg, 1897; Berlin, 1897-1898; Erlangen, 1898), where above a thousand Americans were engaged in theological studies at the time. Upon completing his studies at Princeton Seminary (B.D., 1899), he was appointed instructor in New Testament at Princeton and then to the chair of New Testament literature and exegesis in 1903.

Armstrong was on the board of *The Princeton Review* through all its years (1903-1929), did most of the editorial work during the years 1909-1917 and prepared the final index. Armstrong, who was better known for his classroom skills than his written scholarship, published seven articles in *The Review* and several book reviews, mostly on the Gospels and especially on the resurrection accounts. His response to German biblical criticism was knowledgeable and fair, though he clearly argued for the historicity of the resurrection. A contemporary of J. Gresham Machen,* he chose to remain at Princeton Seminary in 1929 when Machen and other conservatives left to form Westminster Theological Seminary.

BIBLIOGRAPHY. *PSB* 37 (1944):64-66.
T. H. Olbricht

Arndt, William Frederick (1880-1957). Lutheran New Testament scholar. A member of the Lutheran Church—Missouri Synod,* Arndt graduated from Concordia College in Milwaukee, Wisconsin, and Concordia Seminary in St. Louis, Missouri, and earned graduate degrees at the University of Chicago* (M.A., 1923) and Washington University in St. Louis, Missouri (Ph.D., 1933). After pastoring from 1902 to 1912, Arndt taught at St. Paul's College (1912-1921) and then served as professor of New Testament exegesis and literature at Concordia Seminary, St. Louis (1921-1951). There he served on the editorial staff of *Concordia Theological Monthly* from 1930 to 1949.

Arndt is best known for his work (1949-1955) with F. Wilbur Gingrich of Albright College in producing an English translation and adaptation of Walter Bauer's magisterial Greek-German lexicon of the New Testament and early Christian writings. Published in 1957 as *A Greek-English Lexicon of the New Testament and other Early Christian Literature,* the volume became known among students of the New Testament as "Arndt and Gingrich." The lexicon was largely funded by the Centennial Thank-Offering of the Lutheran Church—Missouri Synod.

BIBLIOGRAPHY. P. M. Bretscher, "William Frederick Arndt," *CTM* 28 (1957):401-408.

J. E. Stanley

Art, Christianity and. As art itself has not been valued in American culture, so Christian art has not developed a characteristic American tradition. Except for within the Catholic* tradition and academic circles, the influence of European religious art has not been great. Within their own domestic setting, Christian artists in America have sought either to encourage Christian morality or to stimulate religious feelings through their portrayal of nature—or in the case of twentieth-century artists, through their use of light and composition.

The Puritan Heritage. The Puritans* inherited from the reformers the fundamental shift of imagination away from the allegorical and visual toward the verbal and literal. As a result, their religious life centered around the preaching* of the Word and the moral life, which was equated with simplicity. Though they insisted that faith must inform all of life, since clarity of language was valued over visual impact, the text supplanted the image. Not until the turn of the nineteenth century did Americans produce paintings with religious subject matter.

The congregational* character of church life in America has in general made any direct patronage of art difficult. So expressions of faith became the personal choice either of the artist or the patron. This individualism of religious expression was further encouraged by the great revivals* that swept New England in the 1740s and the East Coast and West in the early 1800s. While Jonathan Edwards's* "consent of being to being" encouraged an aesthetic that limited drama and the visual arts, painting of religious themes was permissible when it served moral purposes.

In many ways the highest symbolic expression of these values (perhaps even the central symbol of American culture) was the Constitution. There the ideals of freedom and justice were enshrined. The art of that period, even when explicitly Christian, served these ideals: it was meant to provide refined knowledge and exhibit true piety.* Portraiture, for example, was to portray the moral fiber and character of the person. Ezra Stiles* believed that in his portrait "emblems are more descriptive of my Mind than the effigies (painting) of my face."

The Nineteenth Century: Art and Nature. From the beginning, a dominant influence on American culture in general and on art in particular was the vast American landscape. As European painters went to the Louvre, Americans went to the wilderness. Washington Allston (1779-1843) introduced to American art the romantic* conception that art is a great mediator between spirit and matter, freeing the sensuous from earthly bonds. Though he was an Episcopalian* who attempted many biblical subjects, his importance lay in developing art not as an expression of faith, but as a means to a more universal religious experience.*

Meanwhile, people of faith continued to distrust imagery. Edward Hicks's portrayals of "The Peaceable Kingdom" (ca. 1820-1830) may be the most famous image of Quaker* spirituality, but he was never confident of their ultimate worth: "If the Christian world was in the real spirit of Christ, I do not believe there would be such a thing as a fine painter in Christendom." But insofar as American artists did create religious imagery of power, it was often by using the dynamics of their natural environment.

Thomas Cole (1801-1848), for example, imbued his landscapes both with the terror of nature (usually associated with biblical events) and with a paradise lost or regained. Always beginning his work with prayer, he sought to stimulate his viewers to lives of moral discipline, freed from any sensuous distractions. Interestingly, as Cole became more religious, he found it more difficult to express himself in his art.

Raised as a strict Methodist,* Albert Pinkham

Ryder (1847-1917) painted works steeped in devotion. Often the life of Christ inspired him to paint tender and moving scenes, but in almost every case the human figures are embedded in nature, and derive much of their power from that setting.

Christian subjects in American art often make a moral or personal appeal, as we have noted, and the sufferings and death of Christ have ordinarily not been featured. An interesting exception is the famous crucifixion depicted by the agnostic Thomas Eakins (1844-1916). This portrayal of a stark naked man, face darkened and looking downward, is a powerful yet strangely disinterested image which anticipated the way modern artists would make use of Christian themes.

Catholic religious art stands in contrast to the dominant tradition of Protestant religious art in America. In one sense Catholic art was the first Christian art in America, for it was present in the Spanish missions of the Southwest from an early period. Unlike the Protestants, Catholics brought with them a rich tradition of visual arts which played a central role in worship.* Indeed for Catholic worship, images were more real than words. In Mexican culture as well, sight was a central mode of expression. As a result, Catholic art flourished in the Southwest, reaching its highest expression from 1820 to 1840, though often in ways that showed little Renaissance, or Counter-Reformation influence. In the Eastern U.S., Catholic art during the nineteenth century was heavily influenced by European sources.

The Twentieth Century: Secular Art with Sacred Theme. The development of art in our century has displayed little Christian influence. This is largely due to the mutual estrangement that has characterized until very recently the relationship between Christianity and the arts. This is not to say that modern art is purely secular and irreligious. Scholars have recently begun to recognize the influence of spiritualist writers, especially on the various schools of abstract art. For example, Emanuel Swedenborg (1688-1772), with his emphasis on correspondences between the physical and spiritual world, exercised a large influence in nineteenth-century American art. This was especially true of the luminism movement, a tradition that may have played a role in the development of modern art.

But where modern artists have used Christian themes, it is usually for more generally religious purposes. Two significant examples are Mark Rothko's chapel in Houston and Barnett Newman's stations of the cross (1965). Rothko states his purpose in this way: "I'm interested only in expressing basic human emotions." Newman, a faithful Jew, seeks to capture the horror of Jesus' question: "Why have you forsaken me?" This query, Newman believes, has been fundamental to humanity since the beginning of time, and he wants these "stations" to describe this question which has no answer.

The visual arts in America, John Dillenberger notes, are epiphenomenal to culture. Therefore, Christian art has had to overcome the bias that images are illustrative, rather than constitutive of our imaginative experience in the world. As Christianity has stressed moral development, so its art has tended to encourage moral excellence; as it has focused on cognitive propositions, so its art has tended to be literal and unimaginative. Art has had to do with taste and refinement, rather than with an essential element of the human spirit. Reformed* writers and thinkers since World War 2,* such as Hans Rookmaaker of the Netherlands and Calvin Seerveld of Canada, have begun to stress the importance of the visual dimensions of Christian discipleship* and have had some influence on evangelicals in particular.

See also ART, LITURGICAL.

BIBLIOGRAPHY. J. Dillenberger, *The Visual Arts and Christianity in America: From the Colonial Period to the Present* (1988); *The Hand and the Spirit: Religious Art in America, 1700-1900,* eds. J. Dillenberger and J. Taylor (1972); G. Gunn, ed., *The Bible and American Arts and Letters* (1983).

W. A. Dyrness

Art, Liturgical. *See* LITURGICAL ART.

Articles of Religion (1784). Articles of doctrine prepared by John Wesley* for American Methodists.* When Methodists in America separated from the Anglican Church,* Wesley sent over, as standards of worship* and doctrine, a Sunday Service and the Articles of Religion, which the founding conference of the Methodist Episcopal Church* adopted in 1784. He sent twenty-four of the original Anglican articles, and the Americans added one more by inserting a statement affirming the new national government. When the denomination's* General Conference became a delegated body in 1808, it protected those twenty-five articles by passing the first "Restrictive Rule," which made it almost impossible for any future conference to alter them.

Wesley maintained most of the doctrines in the Anglican original. His articles affirmed the Trinity, the Christology* of the ancient ecumenical councils, the unique authority* of Scripture,* the doctrine of original sin,* the redemptive work of Christ, justification* by grace through faith, the expectation that the faithful would do good works and the sacraments* of baptism* and the Lord's Supper.* He excised, however, the articles on predestination* and election,* as well as the assertion that sin invariably remained within the regenerate—positions Wesley associated with Calvinism.* He also eliminated, as unsuited for Americans, the articles on church governance and the supremacy of the King.

Along with Wesley's *Sermons* and his *Explanatory Notes upon the New Testament,* the Articles of Religion have served as doctrinal standards for Methodists in America.

BIBLIOGRAPHY. H. M. DuBose, *The Symbol of Methodism* (1907); H. M. DuBose, "Articles of Religion," *Encyclopedia of American Methodism,* ed. N. B. Harmon, 2 vols. (1974); T. C. Oden, *Doctrinal Standards in the Wesleyan Tradition* (1988).   E. B. Holifield

Asbury, Francis (1745-1816). First Methodist* general superintendent, or bishop,* in America. Asbury was born near Birmingham, England, to Anglican* parents who were also members of a Methodist society. He received little formal education and was apprenticed to a blacksmith at age sixteen. He was converted* at about the same time and became a Methodist local preacher, eventually joining the Wesleyan Conference in 1767 as a circuit preacher. In 1771, in response to a plea from John Wesley* for preachers to go to America to aid the fledgling Methodist work there, Asbury volunteered. He arrived in Philadelphia in late October, together with another volunteer, Richard Wright.

Aggressively evangelistic, Asbury was distressed to find many Methodist preachers in America "settled" in one location, principally in cities. He set out immediately to prod them into "circulation," the better to reach persons with the Methodist message of free grace and Christian perfection.* Asbury was highly successful in this, giving rise to the Methodist circuit rider,* the seemingly ubiquitous preacher on horseback who followed the advancing frontier and sought out potential converts in the most remote settlements. Asbury set the example for these Methodist itinerants. He traveled almost incessantly for forty-five years, covering an estimated three hundred thousand miles and preaching over 16,000 sermons. He literally had no home, finding shelter as he could, and once telling a correspondent in England to address letters to him simply "in America."

Asbury exercised tremendous influence over American Methodism in part because he was the only one of the original Methodist missionaries* sent by Wesley before the Revolutionary War* who remained in America for the duration of the conflict. Wesley's opposition to the war made Methodists suspect, but instead of fleeing, Asbury remained—sometimes in hiding—and maintained contact with the scattered Methodist societies. By war's end he was the acknowledged leader of American Methodists. His status was recognized and endorsed by John Wesley when he appointed Asbury general superintendent of the Methodists, along with Thomas Coke,* who was dispatched from England in 1784 to ordain* Asbury and so provide a ministry* qualified to administer sacraments* for Methodists in America. Asbury, however, refused to accept simple appointment and held out instead for action by a conference of Methodist preachers. Such a conference convened in Baltimore on December 24, 1784, and continued until January 3, 1785. Dubbed the "Christmas Conference,"* this body brought into being the Methodist Episcopal Church and elected Asbury and Coke as general superintendents (Asbury would later use the term *bishop* against Welsey's advice).

Asbury used his office and influence to spur Methodism into a tremendous period of growth which continued well beyond his death in 1816. He was an early advocate of camp meetings* and did much to make these a central Methodist institution. Crossing the Appalachians more than sixty times, he presided over 224 annual conferences and ordained more than 4,000 preachers. He encouraged Sunday schools* among Methodists, was the first to raise money for Methodist education in America, and promoted the "Book Concern" which developed into the Methodist Publishing House. Active to the very end of his life, only a week before his death he delivered his last sermon from a table supported by pillows. His remains lie in Mount Olivet Cemetery in Baltimore among those of other Methodist notables.

BIBLIOGRAPHY. E. T. Clark, ed., *The Journal and Letters of Francis Asbury* (1958); W. L. Duren, *Francis Asbury; Founder of American Methodism* (1928); L. C. Rudolph, *Francis Asbury* (1966); E. S. Tipple, *Francis Asbury: The Prophet of the Long Road* (1916).   H. E. Raser

Ash Wednesday. The first day of Lent* in Western churches, so designated from the custom of sprinkling ashes on the heads of the people as a sign of mortality, accompanied by the words "Remember that you are dust, and to dust you shall return" (Gen 3:19). This ceremony is first mentioned in ninth-century Germany in connection with the dramatic expulsion of penitents from the church as Adam and Eve were driven from Eden. This was the beginning of their public penance, to be terminated by solemn reconciliation on Thursday in Holy Week. There was no such sprinkling of ashes at the expulsion of penitents in Rome, but in the eleventh century this ceremony was enjoined for all the faithful of the Western church, the rites of public penance having fallen into desuetude. In its later medieval form the imposition of ashes preceded the Eucharist* and is allowed in that position in Lutheran* churches in this country today, while the ceremony now follows the sermon of the eucharistic liturgy in Roman Catholic* and Episcopal* churches.

BIBLIOGRAPHY. H. Thurston, "Ash Wednesday," *NCE* 1.   T. J. Talley

Asian-American Protestants. Protestantism has played a significant role among a variety of groups who are of Asian ancestry. But though connections to the Asian continent are important for understanding these groups, their experiences as immigrants and as American-born generations who have played an integral part in American history should not be overlooked. Moreover, although Chinese-, Japanese- and Korean-American communities are more generally recognized, they only partially represent those referred to by the collective term *Asian-American.*

Chinese-Americans. The early period of Chinese immigration spans the years 1850 to 1882, when approximately 322,000 Chinese arrived in the U.S. Many Chinese, mostly male and predominantly from the Southeastern province of Kwangtung, came in search of work as they faced overpopulation and a strained agricultural economy at home. With its newly discovered gold and with railroad and agricultural industries in need of cheap labor, California became the primary base of most Chinese immigrants.

Protestant efforts among the Chinese became firmly rooted toward the end of the 1860s. By 1892 eleven denominations* were involved in home mission* efforts with Presbyterians,* Baptists,* Methodists* and Congregationalists* in the forefront. Chinese-American Christians and missionaries worked together to found churches, to offer instruction—whether it be Sunday school or English/Chinese language skills—and to serve other needs of the community.

The Chinese in America represented a vital link in the Protestant vision to evangelize China. Since many immigrants planned to return to China, missionaries felt that conversion* of the Chinese could greatly aid Protestant work in China. While some immigrants (including Christians) did return, many also stayed in the U.S., despite intense anti-Chinese agitation.

Nativist* sentiments culminated in the Chinese Exclusion Act of 1882, which effectively barred further Chinese immigration well into the twentieth century. The Chinese-American churches provided one of the few lines of defense against anti-Chinese activity, and also remained an important dimension of the Chinese-American experience as they served constituencies throughout the country.

Protestantism, however, would not claim the allegiance of more than a small portion of the total Chinese-American population. In 1955 a National Council of Churches* study of Chinese-American churches reported that there were sixty-five Protestant congregations in the U.S., with a combined membership of 7,500-7,700 members. That figure had grown to an estimated 360 churches by 1986, but total membership still only accounted for about six per cent of the Chinese-American population. According to the 1980 census, Chinese-Americans were the single-largest Asian-American group, with approximately 820,000 persons.

The Chinese-American community today is comprised not only of American-born Chinese, but also of more recent (post-1943) immigrants from Taiwan, Hong Kong and the People's Republic of China. It remains to be seen whether more Chinese-Americans will embrace Christianity in the years to come, as the Chinese-American community continues to undergo changes brought on by the co-existence of these various segments.

Japanese-Americans. Japanese immigration to the U.S., which began around 1860, was a sign of changing times for Japan. In the early years of the Meiji period, Japan was brought into contact with the West. The peak period of immigration to America occurred at the turn of the century. At that time an estimated 130,000 Japanese filled the need for labor in the agricultural-, mining- and fishing-related industries of the West Coast, as well as providing much of the labor for the sugar-cane industry in Hawaii.

The beginnings of Protestantism among the Japanese can be traced to San Francisco in 1877 when the Gospel Society was formed by several Japanese immigrants. Home mission efforts also were sponsored by many Protestant denominations (as well as the YMCA* and The Salvation

Army*). Like the Chinese, the Japanese suffered from the nativism and hysteria of those who claimed that the Japanese posed a threat not only to industry but to their perception of the American way of life. The Gentleman's Agreement of 1907 between Japan and the U.S. prohibited further Japanese immigration to America.

In the decades that followed, work progressed and the churches provided leadership, spiritual guidance and services for Japanese-Americans. The ministry of the churches continued through World War 2 and the tragedy of February 19, 1942. On that date Executive Order 9066 placed over 110,000 persons of Japanese ancestry (over two-thirds of whom were American-born citizens) into ten "relocation centers." Morning prayer meetings,* Bible studies* and worship* services were held within the armed, barbed-wire surroundings. After the people were released, many neighborhood churches served in coordinating the resettlement processes of Japanese-Americans.

Despite their presence within the community, the churches did not reach a large number of Japanese-Americans. In 1977, the year marking the centennial of Japanese mission work in North America, it was estimated that there were about 150 churches and 200 pastors in the U.S. Current estimates (1988) show a slight growth to about 170 congregations, numbering close to 30,000 members. This represents about three per cent of the current Japanese-American population. The 1980 census reported that there were approximately 720,000 Americans of Japanese ancestry.

Some are confident that an emerging third generation *(Sansei)* of leadership will expand the work of the churches to include more of the Japanese-American population. While international students from Japan continue to come to the U.S., overall immigration from Japan has been very minimal for the last few decades. This trend seems likely to continue as Japan enjoys continued economic growth and prosperity.

Korean-Americans. Between the years 1903 and 1905, a small group of Koreans left for the shores of Hawaii, and from there they would travel to the West Coast of the U.S. Some left their country due to the unwelcome presence of Japanese, who would annex Korea from 1910 to 1945. Others sought relief from the difficult socioeconomic situations in northern Korea.

In contrast to the immigration patterns of the Chinese and Japanese, Protestant Christianity has had a major influence within the Korean-American community from the outset. In fact, groups of Korean Christians organized services and sought to reach out to other passengers en route to their destinations. Establishment of a church was often among the first collective actions taken by Koreans after their arrival.

Protestantism undoubtedly took root in Korean-American communities because some immigrants were adherents of Christianity prior to their arrival. These Koreans provided a base for the churches, and many others joined after they arrived because of the ethnic identification and affirmation that the churches offered. In particular, the churches were places where the community could gather to support the Korean independence movement—the desire to see Korea free of Japanese rule sparked the community for many years.

The overall Korean-American population did not grow much during the years 1910-1945 because it too suffered from the nativism and anti-Asian legislation that was imposed on other Asian-American groups. As contact increased between the U.S. and Korea after World War 2* and throughout the Korean Conflict, international students and military wives were added to the number of Koreans in America. It was not until 1965, however, when the Immigration and Nationality Act eased long-standing restrictionary policy, that large numbers of Koreans began to arrive in the U.S.

The Korean-American community has grown tremendously in the past twenty years and, as throughout the entire history of the Korean-American community, the Protestant church has been a central institution. It is estimated that there are 1,000 Korean-American churches, accounting for approximately sixty-five per cent of the population. Census projections estimate that there will be about 850,000 Korean-Americans by 1990.

In terms of the future, it is questionable whether the church will continue to grow as quickly as it has, since its current strength is heavily concentrated within its immigrant generation. The church must begin investing in the next generation so that new leadership will be able to make the transition with the community as it expands to include a rapidly emerging American-born generation.

Conclusion. The summaries which have been presented of Protestantism within the Chinese-, Japanese- and Korean-American communities really represent three separate journeys within American Christianity. Nevertheless, within these stories there is a common thread in the suffering and challenge that each group has had to face as a racial-ethnic minority. In many ways, the issue of identity remains a crucial one for Asian-Americans, who live in a country where their fellow Americans often fail to distinguish between them or to recognize the richness that each group has contributed to the collective history of the U.S.

Protestant faith has been and will continue to be important for many Asian-Americans. The call of the churches is to a new identity in Christ. The hope is that in Christ, Asian-Americans will find meaning which both transcends and affirms their particularity.

BIBLIOGRAPHY. Hyung-chan Kim, ed., *Dictionary of Asian-American History* (1986); W. S. Woo, "Protestant Work Among the Chinese in the San Francisco Bay Area, 1850-1920" (unpublished Ph.D. dissertation, Graduate Theological Union, Berkeley, California, 1983); *Chinese Around the World,* a monthly publication of the Chinese Coordination Centre of World Evangelism (CCCOWE), Hong Kong; S. Koga, ed., *A Centennial Legacy: History of the Japanese Christian Missions in North America, 1877-1977,* vol. 1 (1977); *JEMS Journal,* a bimonthly publication of the Japanese Evangelical Missionary Society, Los Angeles; S. S. Shim, *Korean Immigrant Churches Today in Southern California* (1977); E.-Y. Yu et al., eds., *Koreans in Los Angeles: Prospects and Promises* (1982). D. K. Yoo

Assemblies of God. Pentecostal* denomination.* Formed in April 1914 in Hot Springs, Arkansas, the Assemblies of God (AG), with well over 15 million adherents, is today the largest Pentecostal denomination in the world. The denomination began inauspiciously when some 300 believers responded to a call to a convention at Hot Springs. Approximately 120 of them were delegates from scattered Pentecostal ministries who shared concerns about their movement's future. While they nurtured an intense dislike for established denominations, they concluded that limited cooperation would be in their best interests and created the General Council of the Assemblies of God. Refusing to adopt a statement of faith, they did agree to encourage support for foreign missions* and Bible institute* education and to issue credentials to would-be workers who met certain qualifications. They also stated their intention to disapprove theological and practical "error."

The people who formed the AG often shared backgrounds in one or another of the settings that had proved receptive to Pentecostal teaching—the Christian and Missionary Alliance*; John A. Dowie's* Zion City; Charles Parham's* Apostolic Faith Movement in Texas; Elizabeth Baker's* Rochester Bible Training Institute; one or another local holiness* association. Their sense of participation in a broader religious awakening was nurtured through such networks by a wide variety of Pentecostal periodicals, and frequent camp meetings* and conventions. Otherwise, they worked independently, with a strong stress on the restoration of New Testament Christianity, evangelism,* healing* and the imminence of the Second Coming. They reveled in intense religious experiences*; for them Pentecostalism was a way of life, a way of perceiving reality.

Their reluctance to adopt a creed was challenged by the emergence of unorthodox Trinitarian views within the constituency. In 1916 the fledgling denomination adopted a Statement of Fundamental Truths, which addressed the Trinitarian question and defined a Pentecostal distinctive but omitted such doctrines as the virgin birth. In 1962, as the denomination became more thoroughly evangelical* and asserted its evangelical identity more formally, statements on the verbal inspiration of Scripture,* the virgin birth and other doctrines affirmed in the National Association of Evangelicals'* statement of faith were added to the Statement of Fundamental Truths.

Those who formed the AG had already rejected the necessity of a crisis sanctification* experience. They anticipated that believers should experience one work of grace, not two (as their Holiness counterparts urged) and a crisis enduement with power, which they called the baptism with the Holy Spirit.* Their ideas on sanctification had been influenced by William Durham,* an independent Pentecostal with centers of influence in Chicago and Los Angeles. Durham emphasized the "finished work of Calvary," and urged spiritual discipline and growth as the means to progressive sanctification. For the first decade of its history, the AG embraced some who differed with Durham. Over the years, however, views on progressive sanctification or the Trinity have most clearly defined the differences between the Assemblies of God and several other predominantly white Pentecostal groups. In 1918 the denomination excluded some who questioned its view of evidential tongues.* The trend toward conformity was reinforced. In four years it had become evident that, rhetoric aside, the Assemblies of God was a denomination rather than the loosely structured fellowship* it claimed to be. When it adopted a constitution in 1927, the formal process was complete.

From the outset the denomination supported a growing missions program. By the mid-1980s the Assemblies of God annually devoted some $135 million (nearly seventy-five per cent of its total expenditures) to its various world ministries, in which some 1,500 missionaries served in 118 countries. More than 250 Bible institutes abroad train nationals; the denomination's radio program, "Revivaltime," is aired in over 100 countries. Home missions efforts started more slowly, but since 1937 they have targeted various ethnic and handicapped constituencies in North America.

When the AG denomination was formed, numerous small, nondenominational Pentecostal Bible schools operated around the country. In 1922 the denomination opened Central Bible Institute (now Central Bible College) in Springfield, Missouri, primarily conceived to offer practical training for Pentecostal pastors,* evangelists* and missionaries. Other schools were sponsored by local districts. In the mid-1980s, the denomination's fifty-seven districts sponsored thirteen colleges and several nonaccredited institutes. In 1955 the Assemblies of God opened Evangel College, a four-year liberal arts institution in Springfield, Missouri. In 1973 the AG opened a theological seminary at the denomination's headquarters in Springfield. A denomination that had once disavowed formal training except at the institute level (with a practical, rather than a reflective, emphasis) had discovered a commitment to Christian education* that now extends to local-church-sponsored elementary and high schools as well (*See* Schools, Protestant Day).

Since the mid-1970s the AG has been cited in several years as the fastest-growing American denomination. Although congregations average about 115 members, the denomination has numerous congregations with membership in the thousands. Its visibility had been enhanced by the ministries of various televangelists.* Scandals involving two AG televangelists, James Bakker* and Jimmy Swaggart,* have made apparent some of the recent trends in the denomination. Both ministers were defrocked and the denomination has sought to rediscover a more moderate stance than either personality projected. The trends they symbolize remain as the denomination struggles to define its relationship to American culture.

The AG, despite strong centralizing tendencies, continues to assert the primacy of the local congregation. Congregations are organized into districts, and districts ordain* and discipline* ministers. Each district is governed by a district council, which has its own superintendent and presbytery. All fifty-seven district superintendents, plus two elected representatives from each district, compose the denomination's general presbytery,* which meets annually. Every two years all ordained and licensed* ministers meet in General Council sessions. The General Council governs the denomination through thirteen elected executives.

Early in the 1940s AG leaders affiliated with the National Association of Evangelicals* (NAE). General Superintendent Thomas F. Zimmerman (1959-1985) was the first AG member to serve as an NAE president. Evangelicalism as represented in the NAE has had far more influence on the AG than the Assemblies of God has had on it. Since World War 2,* AG adherents have been solidly conservative and often Republican. Their vision for America was largely shaped by the men who formed the NAE. They shared several basic predispositions: anti-Communism,* anti-Catholicism and the hope for a Christian America.

The denomination's record on women is more impressive on paper than in reality. Although the AG has offered women ordination* since 1935, no woman has ever served on the denomination's governing boards, and, in a denomination with over 13,000 congregations, fewer than 280 women have held pastorates in their own right at any given time.

The denomination's first headquarters was in Findlay, Ohio, where T. K. Leonard, an independent Pentecostal who operated a small Bible institute, publishing house and mission, offered the use of his facilities. Early in 1915, the denomination's leaders decided to move the headquarters to St. Louis, Missouri. In 1918 they moved the headquarters to Springfield, Missouri, where it is housed today in a multimillion-dollar complex. The Gospel Publishing House produces over 23 tons of literature every day. *The Pentecostal Evangel,* the denomination's weekly publication, has a circulation of some 278,000, the largest weekly circulation of any American religious weekly magazine.

Doctrinally, the AG has become more precise since 1914. Efforts to discourage dissent have resulted in strong affirmations of both premillennialism* and the denomination's distinctive doctrine of tongues as uniform initial evidence of Spirit baptism. Growth and problems have stimulated centralization and organization. Upward mobility and higher education have challenged assumptions of an earlier era when Pentecostalism was less an intellectual persuasion and more a way of experiencing and interpreting reality.

Its size and affluence have helped assure the AG a leadership role in white classical Pentecostalism. It is misleading, however, to base generalizations about American Pentecostalism on the AG. A large and growing denomination, the Assemblies of God perceives itself as an evangelical denomination with a difference. But the difference is increasingly obscured by religious and cultural change.

BIBLIOGRAPHY. E. L. Blumhofer, *The Assemblies of God: A Chapter in the Story of American Pentecostalism* (1989); W. Menzies, *Anointed to Serve* (1971).   E. L. Blumhofer

Assistant/Associate Pastor. An ordained* minister who works with the senior pastor of a larger congregation. The role of assistant pastor developed in response to the need for younger pastors to gain on-the-job expertise in the ministry, with the example, support and supervision of a more experienced senior minister. Assistants often share in preaching* and visitation, or specialize in Christian education* or youth ministry.*

The role of associate pastor has become increasingly significant as the knowledge and skills required for effective ministry have become more specialized. Associates with particular gifts or training are frequently called to mid-sized and large churches in order to concentrate their energies more specifically on education, pastoral care,* counseling, youth, evangelism,* missions,* congregational life or visitation. An associate generally works in partnership with the senior pastor, taking full responsibility for assigned areas and coordinating this work with the ministry of the larger church.

BIBLIOGRAPHY. H. R. Niebuhr and D. D. Williams, eds., *The Ministry in Historical Perspectives* (1981).   P. W. Butin

Associate Reformed Presbyterian Church. *See* GENERAL SYNOD OF THE ASSOCIATE REFORMED PRESBYTERIAN CHURCH.

Associated Gospel Churches. A Canadian evangelical* denomination.* One of the few Christian bodies indigenous to Canada, the roots of the Associated Gospel Churches (AGC) lay in the intense evangelistic/revivalistic* and missionary* movement of the late nineteenth century. Its founders, fearing the rise of non-evangelical views of theology* and the Christian life, found meaning in premillennialism,* with its pessimistic understanding of the future of the church and society in this age. Moving in the orbit of fundamentalism,* with its generally Calvinistic* orientation, it laid great stress on the eternal security of the believer.

The key figure in the formation of the AGC was Peter W. Philpott.* A handsome young blacksmith from Dresden in southwestern Ontario, Philpott, who became a member of The Salvation Army,* was soon promoted to the rank of Brigadier. Growing restive with the institutionalism of the

Army, he eventually departed. Drawn toward the Christian and Missionary Alliance* for a time, he found he could not espouse their emphasis on healing.* From 1896 to 1922 he ministered in Hamilton, Ontario, where he established the downtown Gospel Tabernacle. Drawing heavily on the migrant Scottish steelworkers, the Tabernacle soon was filled with 1,600 people, frequently spilling over into a nearby theatre. Satellite congregations were also founded.

In order to provide mutual encouragement, a few of these congregations came together in 1921 to form the AGC. In 1922 Philpott left for the pastorate of the Moody Church, Chicago, and later the Church of the Open Door, Los Angeles. With its leader gone, and the group facing a somewhat different era, the new denomination developed slowly but nonetheless steadily. It has now grown to a membership of some 10,000 in 115 congregations across Canada, more than half of which are in southern Ontario. A group of young pastors, largely from the U.S., are giving the AGC renewed presence, with the outstanding example being the new $5 million edifice of the Park Avenue Bible Church on the hillside above Burlington, across the bay from Hamilton.

BIBLIOGRAPHY. S. D. Clark, *Church and Sect in Canada: Encyclopedia Canadiana* (1948).
                                    I. S. Rennie

Association of Baptists for Evangelism in the Orient. *See* ASSOCIATION OF BAPTISTS FOR WORLD EVANGELISM.

Association of Baptists for World Evangelism. Independent Baptist* foreign mission* society. The fundamentalist-modernist controversy* in the Northern Baptist Convention contributed to the formation of the Association of Baptists for Evangelism in the Orient (ABEO) in 1927. The founder, Raphael C. Thomas, a veteran medical missionary* in the Philippines under the American Baptist Foreign Mission Society (ABFMS),* launched the new faith mission following disagreements with ABFMS policies on doctrine and evangelism.* In 1928 Thomas and other former ABFMS missionaries returned to the Philippines to begin their new work. At home, ABEO opened a headquarters in Philadelphia and chose Lucy M. Peabody* as its first president.

For over a decade, ABEO concentrated on its Philippine field. In 1939 it extended its operations into Peru and changed its name to the Association of Baptists for World Evangelism (ABWE) to reflect a new scope of ministry. During and after World

War 2,* ABWE developed additional stations in South America and the Orient. In more recent years the mission has initiated new efforts in Africa, Australia and Europe. In 1971 ABWE moved its home office to Cherry Hill, New Jersey. Today it primarily engages in church planting, theological education, medicine and Bible translation. ABWE employs over 450 full-time missionaries in over twenty countries, handles a total annual income of $10.5 million, and is affiliated with the Fellowship of Missions, a fundamentalist* agency based in Cleveland, Ohio.

BIBLIOGRAPHY. H. T. Commons, *Heritage and Harvest* (1981); W. W. Kempton, "The Faithfulness of God," *The Message* 45 (Spring 1987):2-5.

J. A. Patterson

Association of Evangelical Lutheran Churches.

A Lutheran* denomination* now part of the Evangelical Lutheran Church in America (ELCA).* The Association of Evangelical Lutheran Churches (AELC) was made up of a group of Lutherans who left the Lutheran Church—Missouri Synod* after a conservative element took over leadership of the Missouri Synod in 1969. Beset by conservatives who had set out to bring the moderates into line or purge them, the moderates formed "Seminex," a "Concordia Seminary in Exile," representing the large majority of faculty and students of Missouri Synod's Concordia Seminary in St. Louis. The AELC understood itself as a provisional association awaiting merger with the American Lutheran Church* or the Lutheran Church in America.* Ultimately, in 1987 its 110,000 members and 272 congregations merged with both bodies to form the Evangelical Lutheran Church in America. The Editors

Assumption of Mary.

The Roman Catholic* doctrine that Mary, at the completion of her earthly life, was taken up to heaven, body and soul. Attested to by the proliferation of New Testament apocrypha surviving in Greek, Latin, Syriac, Coptic, Ethiopic and Arabic sources from the late fourth century onwards, the belief also found expression in feasts celebrating the death of Mary, perhaps as early as the fourth century at Antioch. The precise object of such feasts, however, was often unclear (the mere death of Mary? her purely spiritual assumption into heaven? her anticipated resurrection and glorification, body and soul?).

Patristic discussion from the sixth century on, continued and refined by later theological reflection, was based chiefly on deductive theology concerning the special union of Mary with her Son

in his redemptive incarnation. This prepared the way for the apostolic constitution, *Munificentissimus Deus* (Nov. 1, 1950), in which Pius XII* defined as dogma that "Mary, having completed the course of her earthly life, was assumed body and soul into heavenly glory."

BIBLIOGRAPHY. V. Bennet and R. Bench, *The Assumption of Our Lady and Catholic Theology* (1950). C. Waddell

Assurance of Salvation.

The certainty or confidence which Christians have with respect to their own salvation.* The New Testament indicates that through the intercession of Christ one may draw near to God with a true heart in "full assurance of faith" (Heb 10:22) and that the word of the gospel and the power of the Holy Spirit produce in believers a "full conviction" (1 Thess 1:5). There are two salient features that make up the doctrine of assurance: The first aspect is its objective basis, which Christians identify as being the death and resurrection of Christ. The second aspect, a subjective basis, entails the Christian's sense of acceptance before God.

While almost all Christian traditions affirm both the objective and subjective bases of assurance, they vary in the emphasis and shape given to those affirmations. Roman Catholics,* for example, look to the sacramental* ministry of the Church (especially penance* and the Eucharist*) as the means whereby assurance is communicated. But the Council of Trent rejected the teaching that believers may achieve certainty of their salvation apart from special revelation.

Reformed* Christians, following the *Westminster Confession of Faith,* affirm "an infallible assurance of faith, founded upon the divine truth of the promises of salvation, the inward evidence of those graces upon which these promises are made, the testimony of the spirit of adoption witnessing with our spirit that we are children of God, which spirit is the earnest of our inheritance, whereby we are sealed to the day of redemption" (Article 18). Methodists like William B. Pope* also embrace the "objective and external ground of assurance provided in [Christ's] work of redemption and the means of grace," but their more characteristic emphasis has been upon "individual assurance of faith and hope of understanding based upon or flowing from the former [objective grounds] through the operation of the Holy Spirit" (*Compendium of Christian Theology,* 1875-1876).

In a similar fashion, Christians differ over the constancy of the certainty they have about their salvation. For those, like Calvinists, who embrace doctrines of election and eternal security,* present assurance is directly connected to their future life with God. For others, including Roman Catholics and Wesleyan*-Arminians,* a present sense of assurance does not necessarily imply inclusion in a future state of blessedness, since salvation can be lost through faithlessness.

The doctrine of assurance has often been a point of controversy in American Christianity. The Puritans* came to emphasize external signs of election ("the covenant of works") over the more subjective "internal marks of assurance." Cotton Mather's* *Menachem* (1716) listed four marks which might indicate one's inclusion among the elect: turning from idols, a zeal for Christ's work, a fear of God and a willingness to take up the cross. As the Great Awakening* brought revival* to the colonies, Puritans like Jonathan Edwards* sought to reconcile revivalism's interest in personal experience with the traditional Puritan perspective that located assurance more directly in God's "covenantal promises" of election.

Revivalism profoundly shaped American Protestantism as many Presbyterians,* Baptists* and Methodists* gradually lost some of their traditional differences and came to share a common interest in personal religious experience* as a basis of assurance. Revivalism also produced theological hybrids, like Charles G. Finney,* who merged his Presbyterian roots with a Wesleyan conception of sanctification* to produce a theology that emphasized a personal sense of assurance found in conversion* and a final salvation that looked toward "entire sanctification."

The results of revivalism were manifold; traditional Presbyterians, like Charles Hodge,* sought to return to more objective bases for Christian assurance. In his *Systematic Theology* (1872-1873) he argued that "to make assurance of personal salvation essential to faith, is contrary to Scripture and to the experience of God's people." Hodge did not believe a believer's assurance of salvation should be dependent on introspection; hence, he listed five appropriate grounds which located assurance in the nature and promises of God, the work of Christ and the witness of the Spirit.

Methodist theologians of the same period followed Wesley in emphasizing "the witness of the Spirit" (Rom 8:16) as the focal point of their doctrine of assurance. For William Pope, the witness of the Spirit formed a bridge between objective and subjective bases of assurance. John Miley* demonstrated the impact of revivalism and emerging rationalism as he tried to analyze and categorize the direct and immediate witnesses of God through his Spirit.

Others took the results of revivalism in new directions. Horace Bushnell* eschewed the revivalist emphasis on conversion experiences and looked to Christian nurture* as a process for forming Christian attitudes and dispositions; assurance could be cultivated and shaped within a person. Walter Rauschenbush* found faith and assurance shaped by the social crises of an urban, industrialized society. In *A Theology of the Social Gospel* (1917), he argued, "It is faith to see God at work in the world and to claim a share in his job," thus linking inner assurance to outer involvement with God's work in the world.

As modern thinkers found life increasingly less certain and heaven above less appealing, existentialist theologians, such as Paul Tillich,* transformed questions of Christian assurance into *The Courage to Be* (1952) in the face of uncertainty and human finitude. In such a theological climate theologies of hope, oriented toward the transforming potential of the future, used *hope* to replace *assurance.* For theologies of liberation,* assurance is found in one's willingness to identify with the cause of the oppressed or disadvantaged and be involved in their liberation.

See also ETERNAL SECURITY.

BIBLIOGRAPHY. D. Ferm, *Contemporary American Theologies* (1981); C. Hodge, *Systematic Theology* (1872-1873); W. Pope, *Compendium of Theology* (1875-1876). J. R. Tyson

Atheism. The word *atheism* is a transliteration of a Greek word which means "without God." The term has come to mean a disbelief in the existence of God, but historically its use was more ambiguous, as in the ancient world where it was used to describe someone who held a personal belief in God yet who denied the official pantheon of Greece, as did Socrates, or the gods of Rome, as did the early Christians.

There are many kinds of atheists, the types determined by their reasons for rejecting theism.* Charles Darwin is an example of those who reject the existence of God on the grounds that there is an inherent cruelty in nature, as seen in the struggle for existence among animal species. Karl Marx represents the view which sees religion and God as manmade institutions invented to ease emotional pain and explain life and death. For Marx faith in God was an aberrant belief arising out of the pressures of the class struggle. Marx went on to call religion the "opiate of the masses," in that it deadened the desire for social change in the present with a hope of heaven. For Sigmund Freud, the founder of psychoanalysis, God was an illusion, a childish projection which grew out of the insecurity of knowing that parents will die someday and the subsequent wish for a "father" who was perfect and would not die.

Some reject God on purely philosophical grounds. An example of this type of atheism is seen in the logical positivists who argue that since it is impossible to define God in intelligible terms (i.e., one cannot verify statements about God empirically), any statement about God's existence is meaningless.

For centuries one of the standard proofs of God's existence was the teleological argument which begins with the fact of life and the harmony of nature and argues that there had to be a grand and purposeful designer, God. The classic biblical reference for this line of reasoning is found in Romans 1:19-20. In the twentieth century such a view has been countered by scientific humanism,* which sees no evidence for God in the design of nature since everything that exists, they argue, can be explained by scientific laws or human decisions.

One of the most visible atheists in twentieth-century America has been the activist Madalyn Murray O'Hair (b.1919), whose efforts contributed to the 1963 Supreme Court* ruling that declared unconstitutional the devotional reading of the Bible and the recitation of the Lord's Prayer in public schools.*

BIBLIOGRAPHY. *Encyclopedia of Unbelief,* 2 vols. (1985); S. Freud, *The Future of an Illusion* (1975); J. Hick, ed., *The Existence of God* (1964); H. Küng, *Does God Exist?* (1980).   N. P. Feldmeth

Athenagoras I (Aristoclis Spyrou) (1886-1972). Greek Orthodox* archbishop* of North and South America and patriarch of Constantinople. Born in what is now northern Greece, he entered the Patriarchal Theological School of Halki in Constantinople in 1903 and was ordained* deacon in 1910. In 1918 he became archdeacon to Metropolitan Meletios Metaxakis* of Athens. Elected bishop of Corfu in 1922, Athenagoras held the post with distinction for almost a decade, giving leadership to refugee, youth, philanthropic, ethnic and ecumenical* activities.

Elected archbishop of the Greek Orthodox Church in the Western Hemisphere in 1931, he inherited a politically divided church membership. Fostering a strong central administration headquartered in New York City, he succeeded in uniting the parishes under a new constitution and bylaws. Athenagoras recognized the importance of the laity,* and established biennial clergy-laity congresses as the supreme administrative body for nondoctrinal affairs. Among the organizational steps taken were the establishment of local chapters of a national philanthropic women's organization, *"Philoptohos"* ("Friends of the Poor"); a teacher training college; and a seminary,* Holy Cross Greek Orthodox School of Theology, in Brookline, Massachusetts.

Elected patriarch in 1948, Athenagoras cultivated cooperation among the various Orthodox churches through a series of Pan-Orthodox Conferences, the first of which was held in Rhodes in 1961. He also developed a wide-ranging ecumenical ministry, meeting in Jerusalem in 1964 with Pope Paul VI.* A year later, the anathemas which marked the beginning of the division between the two churches in 1054 were revoked, allowing for further developments in the relations between Eastern and Western Christianity.

BIBLIOGRAPHY. G. Papaioannou, *From Mars Hill to Manhattan: The Greek Orthodox in America Under Patriarch Athenagoras I* (1976); D. Tsakonas, *A Man Sent By God: The Life of Patriarch Athenagoras of Constantinople* (1977).

S. S. Harakas

Atonement, Theories of. Early New England theology* was basically Calvinistic,* emphasizing the holiness and righteousness of God and, consequently, the seriousness of humanity's sinful state. This meant that God could not lightly forgive or overlook sin* on the one hand and that humans were unable to atone for their own sin on the other. Thus, the view of the atonement advocated by Jonathan Edwards* and other early American theologians* saw the death of Christ as primarily affecting God. This view, often referred to as the substitutionary-penal view, emphasized that by his death Christ paid the penalty for sin to which humans were liable.

As this strict Calvinism began to diminish in its influence, the substitutionary-penal view was gradually replaced by what is often referred to as the governmental view of the atonement. In this understanding the death of Christ primarily affects humanity and only secondarily affects God. Its primary purpose was to demonstrate the seriousness of sin by showing the extremity of God's action in putting his Son to death. The aim of this demonstration was both to serve as a deterrent to sin and to induce the sinner to repentance so that God could forgive him. Theologians such as Joseph Bellamy,* Samuel Hopkins,* Jonathan Edwards, Jr.* and Edwards Park* espoused this view.

Another category of views of the atonement are those that are primarily subjective in orientation. That is, they view the atonement as fundamentally acting upon humans and moving them to some particular action or response. A notable form of this is the moral-influence theory, of which the leading American exponent was Horace Bushnell.* Bushnell's view was not a perfect example of this theory since he also provided for a secondary effect of Christ's death upon God, but it does set forth clearly the subjective dimension. Bushnell emphasized that moral renovation of humanity requires more than mere good example and instruction. There must be some supernatural influence, and this was accomplished by Christ's work. Christ identified with humanity through his suffering, and his demonstration of divine love powerfully moves us to turn from our selfishness and respond in love and gratitude toward God. We are attracted to Christ. Bushnell wrote, "We like the Friend before we love the Saviour." Beyond that, however, when we recognize that Christ's suffering and death were innocent and on our account, we are moved to a conviction of sin. Thus, both repentance and faith are evoked by Christ's death.

While in Bushnell's view the effect of Christ's death is primarily on human beings, there is also, said Bushnell, a secondary influence or impact on God. It helps remove God's resentment toward humanity and facilitate his forgiveness. This effect upon God is likened to when we do something for someone who has done evil to us—we are consequently moved to forgive that injury when forgiveness is sought.

Perhaps the most subjective view of the consequence of Christ's death is the so-called Socinian or example theory of the atonement. Originally propounded in the sixteenth century by Laelius and Faustus Socinus of Poland, it became the view commonly held by Unitarians* in America. Since human nature has not been radically corrupted by sin, humanity does not need a moral and spiritual transformation or regeneration, but a living example of virtue and righteousness. The death of Jesus Christ accomplishes this. We find in it the most complete example of total dedication to doing the will of the Father.

These theories, which emphasize the influence of Christ's death upon the human person, became popular within Protestant liberalism* of the late nineteenth and early twentieth centuries. In part, this was because liberal theology did not see human beings as too seriously disabled by sin. Human nature is basically intact and, therefore, humans are capable of doing right. To a consider-

able extent sin was seen as an ethical concept, the doing of wrong actions, rather than a religious concept, a rebellion against God.

While Protestant* orthodoxy* had generally emphasized an objective or sacrificial view of Christ's death, the fundamentalist-modernist controversy* of the late nineteenth and early twentieth centuries forced a clear restatement of the conservative, orthodox view of the atonement. Figures such as Charles Hodge,* A. A. Hodge* and B. B. Warfield,* shapers and guardians of the Princeton Theology,* clearly stood in this tradition. Accordingly, human sin was seen as a violation of God's law and intention for the human race. Sinners are liable to punishment, and since sin is ultimately an offense against the infinite God, the ultimate punishment is executed: eternal death, or everlasting separation from God. There is nothing else that man can offer on his own behalf to God other than this eternal death. Christ, however, as the perfect God-man, offered his life in the place of sinful humanity and thus paid the penalty for them.

This insistence upon the substitutionary-penal view of atonement came to be expressed in *The Fundamentals** (1910-1915), a twelve-volume restatement and defense of essential Protestant orthodox belief against the claims of modern criticism. Strongly objective in its orientation, this view emphasized Christ's atonement as primarily directed toward God, enabling him to forgive and justify humans and accept them back into his fellowship.

A variation of this view was the ethical theory of the atonement espoused by Augustus H. Strong.* Strong argued that because of Christ's union with humanity, he was so identified with the human predicament that he was not only capable of suffering on their behalf but was actually obligated to do so. Strong wrote, "Being one with the race, Christ had a share in the responsibility of the race to the law and the justice of God." Christ assumed no personal guilt, but he did inherit the guilt of Adam's sin. Strong's view brought him under criticism by conservatives who felt that he had conceded too much to the more liberal kenotic view of the incarnation and thus had compromised the integrity of Christ's deity. On the other hand, Strong's view appeared to jeopardize the integrity of Christ's humanity.

An issue that has concerned conservative theologians is the extent of the atonement. Did Christ die for the sins of the entire human race, or did he simply die for the elect,* that group of persons whom God has chosen and designated to be the recipients of salvation? Proponents of each view can appeal to Scriptures that appear to support their position. In general, Arminians* have held to the former view, known as unlimited atonement or general redemption, while Calvinists* have espoused the latter view, known as limited atonement or particular redemption. The Arminian view has been a potent theological rationale behind American Protestant revivalism,* with its broad invitation to the masses to "accept Christ" and "be saved by his blood."

Some Protestants have asked whether Christ died for humanity's sin and guilt alone. Did not Jesus in his death assume more than merely the sins of human beings? Some, such as A. B. Simpson,* have insisted that Christ bore not only the guilt of sin, but also human sickness. Basing their argument upon Matthew's citation (Mt 8:17) of Isaiah, they would argue that physical healing is also included in Christ's atonement. Thus, physical healing is a right which believers can claim. This view of the atonement has influenced some within the Pentecostal* and charismatic* movements and has shown its more extreme fruit in some of the teachings and practices of the Faith Movement.*

An issue that has traditionally divided Protestants and Catholics* concerns the control and application of the benefits of Christ's atonement. This raises the question of who the recipients of the benefits of Christ's death are. Generally, conservative Protestants have held that the benefits of the atonement are available to all who believe. Some, called Universalists,* have held that all persons, even those who may not espouse faith in Christ, are saved by Christ's death. Some have even held that there is no need for atonement, either in terms of God accepting persons or of humans turning to God.

The traditional Roman Catholic position, on the other hand, has been that the church controls the "treasury of merit.'"* Only those who are linked to its sacramental* system receive the benefits of Christ's death. Vatican II,* however, greatly extended this concept, so that while only Catholics are fully incorporated into the body of Christ, communicants of other Christian denominations are "linked" to the church, and non-Christians are "related" to it.

See also ARMINIANISM; FUNDAMENTALS; NEW ENGLAND THEOLOGY; NEW HAVEN THEOLOGY; PRINCETON THEOLOGY; REFORMED TRADITION.

BIBLIOGRAPHY. L. J. Averill, *American Theology in the Liberal Tradition* (1967); H. Bushnell, *The Vicarious Sacrifice* (1866); D. W. Ferm, *Contemporary American Theologies: A Critical Survey*

(1981); H. D. McDonald, *The Atonement of the Death of Christ* (1985); G. O'Collins, *The Cross Today: An Evaluation of Current Theological Reflections on the Cross of Christ* (1978); D. P. Rudissill, *The Doctrine of the Atonement in Jonathan Edwards and His Successors* (1971).

M. J. Erickson

Atwater, Lyman Hotchkiss (1813-1883). Princeton* College professor and apologist.* After graduating from Yale* in 1831 and studying for the ministry at Yale Divinity School, Atwater pastored the First Presbyterian Church of Fairfield, Connecticut, from 1835 to 1854. For the remainder of his life he taught at Princeton College and was a bulwark of conservative Presbyterianism.*

First as a professor of the relationship between Christianity and philosophy (1854-1869) and then as professor of logic, moral and political science (1869-1883), Atwater wrote extensively on a wide range of topics: theology,* apologetics,* biography, history, education, philosophy, ethics, economics and finance. More than one hundred of his articles were published in the *Princeton Review,* which he helped to edit for many years. Along with Charles Hodge,* he defended Old School* Calvinism against the mediating theologies of Nathaniel Taylor* and Horace Bushnell.*

During the mid nineteenth century Atwater was probably the greatest champion of conservative Calvinist political, social and economic views. He defended private ownership of property, promoted "benevolent" capitalism,* worked for civil service reforms, criticized socialism and objected to many labor union practices.

BIBLIOGRAPHY. *DAB* I; G. S. Smith, *The Seeds of Secularization* (1985). G. S. Smith

Auburn Affirmation (1924). A document, entitled "An Affirmation," designed to safeguard the unity and liberty of the Presbyterian Church in the U.S.A.,* issued during the Fundamentalist* controversy by a group of ministers meeting in Auburn, New York. It was intended as a liberal* protest against the Five Point Deliverance* of the 1910 General Assembly* of the Presbyterian Church in the U.S.A. (reaffirmed in 1916 and 1923), that affirmed biblical doctrines* that were "essential and necessary."

The Affirmation was published January 1924 with the signatures of one hundred fifty ministers* and was reissued in May 1924 with 1,274 signatures. Without denying the particular doctrines, the Auburn Affirmation opposed attempts to make the five points a test for ordination* or orthodoxy.* They were regarded as theories about facts or doctrines, concerning which other explanations or theories, deduced from Scripture* and Presbyterian standards, might be acceptable. The 1926 General Assembly opened the way to greater theological pluralism by declaring that Presbyterianism admits diversity of views, the limits of which the church, rather than the individual, must ultimately decide. *See also* FIVE POINT DELIVERANCE; FUNDAMENTALS; PORTLAND DELIVERANCE.

BIBLIOGRAPHY. L. A. Loetscher, *The Broadening Church: A Study of Theological Issues in the Presbyterian Church since 1869* (1954); G. M. Marsden, *Fundamentalism and Modern Culture* (1980); E. H. Rian, *The Presbyterian Conflict* (1940). A. H. Freundt

Auburn Declaration (1837). A theological statement issued by New School* Presbyterians* in August 1837, intended to confirm their Presbyterian orthodoxy.* The Declaration defended the New School against accusations of heresy* made by the Old School* majority at the 1837 General Assembly* of the Presbyterian Church in the U.S.A.* At that Assembly, the Old School forced out three New School synods* in New York and one in Ohio.

The accusation of the Old School was that the New School party held to a modified Calvinism* or "Taylorism"* that compromised the Westminster Confession of Faith.* Secondary issues were the New School's support of the 1801 Plan of Union,* a cooperative agreement between Presbyterians and Congregationalists* by which they would combine their efforts in evangelizing the West and in New School antislavery activity.

The Declaration affirmed a moderate but generally orthodox Calvinism, which its signers believed reflected Presbyterian doctrinal standards. It also denied sixteen accusations alleged against them by the Old School. The 1838 General Assembly refused to reconsider its decision, and for a time Presbyterians continued to exist in separate New School and Old School denominations, both claiming the title, "The Presbyterian Church in the U.S.A." Finally, in 1868, the Old School General Assembly admitted that the Auburn Declaration contained "all the fundamentals of the Calvinistic creed," and in 1870 the Old School/New School schism among northern Presbyterians was healed. Among Presbyterians in the South, the Civil War* facilitated reunion of the two groups in 1864.

BIBLIOGRAPHY. "The Auburn Declaration," in *The Presbyterian Enterprise*, ed. M. W. Armstrong et al. (1956); G. M. Marsden, *The Evangelical Mind*

and the New School Presbyterian Experience (1970). A. H. Freundt

Augustinianism. A tradition of theological and philosophical thought based on the work of St. Augustine of Hippo (A.D. 354-430). Augustine's major writings include *The Confessions* (400) and *The City of God* (413-426). His writings exemplify Christian theology* within the context of a neo-Platonic heritage. Although there are many variations among representatives of this tradition, in general it is characterized by five emphases:

(1) The primacy of the will over the intellect. In relation to God, this notion manifests itself in the need to love God before attempting to know him with the mind. Thus, faith must precede reason: *credo ut intelligam* (I believe so that I may understand).

(2) Knowledge as illumination from God. God is seen as the original repository of all true knowledge (divine exemplars), and thus what we know does not come to us by way of the senses or through reason, but through an immediate disclosure by God to the soul.

(3) The soul as the human being. In Augustinianism the soul is thought of as complete in itself. It does not require the body to be truly human. But the body should not be understood as evil in a dualistic sense.

(4) The pervasive effects of the fall into sin.* Augustine carried on a significant controversy with the monk Pelagius, who denied original sin. In Augustinian thought, original sin is usually thought of as propagated by concupiscence, which must be understood as a misdirection of the human will.

(5) God's grace as manifested in divine election.* Augustine himself, in the controversy with Pelagius, who minimized the need for divine grace, argued that grace is seen in God's predestination* and in the efficacy of the sacraments* apart from a particular human disposition (*ex opere operato*). Many of Augustine's followers have diverged from him on either or both of these two points.

Augustinianism has been present in America in both Roman Catholic* and Protestant circles. The Catholic Augustinian* monastic order has been present here since 1794. In 1843 Villanova University was founded under its auspices. Presently the order has parish* and educational work throughout the U.S.

The advancement of Augustine's thought by Catholic scholars continues on many fronts but has received particular impetus by the work done at the Pontifical Institute of Medieval Studies in

Toronto, Canada. Even though contemporary Catholic theology as a whole does not always lean explicitly on Augustine's categories, he can still be seen wherever there is emphasis on action (the will) before abstract theology (the intellect), knowledge through self-knowledge or the centrality of the sacraments. As diverse as American Catholicism is, these themes recur frequently, and with them Augustinianism as a conceptual heritage.

Among Protestants, Augustinianism can be seen particularly in the various Calvinistic* or predestinarian theological traditions. Thus the thought of Jonathan Edwards* is an interesting combination of Augustinian commitments with the philosophy of John Locke. Twentieth-century evangelicals,* such as Gordon Clark* and Cornelius Van Til,* have upheld the Augustinian tradition with their emphasis on unconditional election and knowledge on the basis of faith presuppositions.

BIBLIOGRAPHY. E. Gilson, *The Christian Philosophy of Saint Augustine* (1960); H. de Lubac, *Augustinianism and Modern Theology* (1969); R. H. Nash, *The Light of the Mind: St. Augustine's Theory of Knowledge* (1969). W. Corduan

Auricular Confession. *See* PENANCE, SACRAMENT OF.

Austin, Anne (d. 1665). Quaker* missionary.* Little is known of Austin's early life. She was a mother of five and "well stricken in years" when she volunteered to accompany Mary Fisher* to New England. After stopping in Barbados, they arrived in Massachusetts Bay Colony in July 1656. They were immediately imprisoned. Their books, about one hundred in number, were seized and burned, and they were strip-searched for marks of witchcraft. The windows of their cell were boarded up so no one could talk with them or bring food. A fine was imposed on anyone who would try to help—though one man paid the fine and brought food. The ship captain who brought them was forced to post bond and take them back to Barbados. In England, Austin became housekeeper for a leading Quaker. In 1659 she was again imprisoned for speaking at a Quaker meeting in London. She died in the Great Plague and is buried in Bunhill Fields.

N. A. Hardesty

Authority. The term *authority,* derived from the Latin *auctoritas,* originated in the social world of western Europe. It means the power to author, command or sanction certain forms of life or ways of being, both corporate and personal, and to proscribe others. Within the traditions of Christian faith, all Protestants* and Roman Catholics,* and some Eastern Orthodox,* agree that the God of Jesus Christ is the ultimate source of both true authority and freedom. God's authority is the persuasive power of divine truth to create, sustain and perfect an historical community of royal, priestly and prophetic persons as the living image of divine freedom in the world.

The theological meaning of authority is an enduring issue in the West due to the breakdown of obedience to traditional sources and institutions of authority during the Reformation and the Enlightenment.* The division of Christians into Catholics and Protestants, and then into the various Protestant movements and churches became the occasion for intense religious and political conflict leading to persecution, revolution and war. In response to the religious division of Europe, both Christians and post-Christians of the Enlightenment created and employed new secular forms of discourse in the spheres of philosophy, politics, science and history.

Authority was redefined in terms of individual consent to probable reason, and internal evidence was judged without invoking external theological authorities or doctrines. Autonomy (the rational individual's free self-rule, supposedly without final dependence on authoritative traditions or communities) radically redefined or replaced traditional modes of authority. Christians in North America inherited this orientation and continue to struggle with it, as evidenced by ongoing debates over biblical authority and papal infallibility.*

Christians have always disagreed over how God's authority is mediated in the world over time. In North America the many authorities by which Christian communities or individuals have claimed to live, act and speak in God's name include: the gospel or revelation as the living word of God, canonical Scripture,* apostolic tradition and succession,* the church and sacraments* as divinely instituted, Christian doctrine* (whether as dogma,* creeds* and confessions*), church tradition (embodied in liturgies,* sermons,* letters and personal narratives), church structures and offices (such as the papacy,* bishops,* church councils,* elders,* deacons, priests* or ministers*), *consensus fidelium* ("the consent of the faithful"), charismatic, prophetic or holy individuals (whether canonized saints* or mass evangelists*), Christian experience, human reason and theology.*

In the context of Protestant communities, North American religious history has witnessed a critical tension between institutional and charismatic forms of authority. Institutional forms of authority include *sola Scriptura,* the authority of an educated clergy and secular reason embodied in the scientific disciplines. Charismatic forms of authority include Jonathan Edwards's* "sense of the heart," the "New Light"* churches of the Great Awakening,* and the rise of fundamentalist* and Pentecostal* Protestants as a kind of third teaching office over against the teaching authority of established,* or mainline,* church officials and theologians.* The conflicts and conversations between institutional and charismatic authorities have encouraged a broader recognition among Protestants that their own churches and communities, like Catholics and Eastern Orthodox, also employ extra-biblical sources of authority in the interpretation and use of Scripture.

It is hard to underestimate the impact of Vatican II* on how authority is conceived and exercised among Catholics today. In the post-conciliar document *Mysterium ecclesiae* (June 24, 1973), both the transcendent nature of God's revealed mysteries and the historically relative condition of all human expressions of revelation are recognized. An example is Catholic theologian Avery Dulles (1918-), who has developed a model of the Church as a "community of disciples" following Christ, with popes and bishops as successors of the apostles but also disciples under the authority of Christ. He thus proposes a theory of "moderate infallibilism" for the teaching authority of the pope and Church councils that accentuates a concern shared by all Christians: God's preservation of his community of (fallible) disciples in the truth of the gospel.

In the context of Eastern Orthodoxy, the issue of authority takes a different turn. The Orthodox theologian Alexander Schmemann has argued for "the Orthodox Principle" as "the rejection of freedom understood and defined in terms of authority." "The Church is *not* authority, and therefore there is no freedom *in* the Church, but the Church herself *is* freedom, and only the Church is freedom." Schmemann's Orthodox Principle is based on the belief that "The Church is the presence and action of the Holy Spirit" and the Holy Spirit is "Freedom itself." The Eastern Orthodox critique of Protestant and Catholic concepts of authority has contributed to greater ecumenical understanding among some Christians.

BIBLIOGRAPHY. D. M. Campbell, *Authority and the Renewal of American Theology* (1976); A. R. Dulles, S. J., *A Church to Believe In: Discipleship and the Dynamics of Freedom* (1982); A. Flannery,

ed., *Vatican Council II: The Conciliar and Post Conciliar Documents* (1975); A. Flannery, ed., *Vatican Collection,* vol. 2: *Vatican Council II: More Post Conciliar Documents* (1982); A. Schmemann, "Freedom in the Church," in *The Word in History: The St. Xavier Symposium,* ed. T. Patrick Burke (1966); J. Stout, *The Flight from Authority: Religion, Morality and the Quest for Autonomy* (1981).

R. A. Cathey

Autocephalous Orthodox Church. The status of a self-governing local Orthodox* church having the right to elect its own primate. The Patriarchate of Moscow granted autocephaly to the jurisdiction in America known as the Metropolia on April 10, 1970. Since then, it has used the title The Orthodox Church in America. After the Greek Orthodox Archdiocese (Ecumenical Patriarchate),* it is the second-largest Orthodox jurisdiction in America, claiming about three hundred fifty parishes serving over five hundred thousand communicants.

The Metropolia, known formally as the Russian Orthodox Greek Catholic Church, claimed to be the direct continuation of the Alaskan Mission* established by the Church of Russia in 1794. The Metropolia broke relations with the Church of Russia in 1924 and was viewed as being schismatic by the latter from the year 1933. Between the years 1937 and 1946, the Metropolia became associated with the Russian Orthodox Church Outside of Russia. By the year 1970 the Metropolia was one of at least twelve Orthodox jurisdictions in America, each of which had a direct or indirect link to an autocephalous mother church in Europe. Viewing the Metropolia as its daughter jurisdiction, the Church of Russia claimed to have the right to grant it an autocephalous status in 1970.

The autocephaly of the Metropolia was subsequently recognized by the autocephalous Churches of Bulgaria, Georgia and Poland. However, the autocephaly has not been recognized by the autocephalous Churches of Constantinople, Alexandria, Antioch, Jerusalem, Serbia, Romania, Cyprus and Greece. These latter churches have not broken communion with the Metropolia but simply refuse to recognize its autocephalous status.

As the first see of Orthodoxy, the Patriarchate of Constantinople has been quite outspoken in its opposition to the grant of autocephaly to the Metropolia. First and foremost, Constantinople claims to have ultimate authority over the Orthodox living in lands beyond the boundaries of other autocephalous churches. This position is based on the twenty-eighth canon of the Council of Chalcedon (451) and subsequent ecclesiastical practices. Constantinople also claims that the Church of Russia does not have the authority to grant autocephaly. It has affirmed that only the Patriarchate of Constantinople can grant autocephaly apart from the context of an ecumenical council—and even then it must be confirmed by a subsequent council. Furthermore, Constantinople has also noted that the situation of American Orthodoxy is such a unique and complex one that a pan-Orthodox resolution must be found.

BIBLIOGRAPHY. M. Efthimiou, ed., *A History of the Greek Orthodox Church* (1984); T. E. FitzGerald, "Orthodoxy in the United States," in *A Companion to the Greek Orthodox Church,* ed. F. Litsas (1984); C. J. Tarasar and J. H. Erickson, ed., *Orthodox America, 1794-1976* (1975).

T. E. FitzGerald

Awakenings, College. Religious revivals* on university campuses. Perhaps the earliest religious awakening among students occurred at the University of Paris in the seventeenth century. As a result of that revival, three students from Germany went to Africa as missionaries,* and Peter Heiling went to Egypt (1632) and Abyssinia (1634). Count Nicholas von Zinzendorf* participated in a revival movement when he was a student at August Herman Francke's *Paedagogium* in Halle (1710-1716). At that time von Zinzendorf established a student club called the Order of the Grain of Mustard Seed. Later he founded the Moravians* as a major missionary* movement.

In 1726 John Wesley* gathered the Holy Club at Oxford. From this small group issued the Wesleyan revival, the Methodist Church,* and a missionary movement among Native Americans in the Southern colonies of America. Later, Charles Simeon (1759-1836), a Fellow of King's College, Cambridge, and vicar* of Holy Trinity Church, brought many students to evangelical faith. On the continent of Europe there was also a series of campus revivals. The Scottish evangelist Robert Haldane (1764-1842) led Bible studies among theological students at Geneva (1816-1819). In Berlin, Baron Hans Ernst von Kottwitz won many students for the evangelical cause. One of von Kottwitz's proteges was August Tholuck (1799-1877), who had a similar revival ministry at Halle after 1826. In 1877 the Cambridge Inter-Collegiate Christian Union was founded as the forerunner of the InterVarsity Christian Fellowship.* The movement at Cambridge was fanned into revival by the visit of Dwight L. Moody* (1882). Three years later the "Cambridge Seven" sailed for China to serve with

James Hudson Taylor. From this group came C. T. Studd, the missionary statesman.

Meanwhile, in America revival had also touched university campuses. The "Haystack Prayer Meeting" (1806) led by Samuel J. Mills, Jr.,* issued in the birth of the American foreign missionary movement.* The Second Great Awakening had touched Yale College* (1802) under the leadership of President Timothy Dwight.* Afterwards it spread to Princeton,* Dartmouth,* Amherst, Williams, and Washington and Lee. Later in the nineteenth century, the focus of revival shifted to Oberlin College,* where the revivalist Charles G. Finney* served as president (1851-1866). In 1888 the Student Volunteer Movement* (SVM) was organized as the result of Dwight L. Moody's student conference at Mount Hermon, Massachusetts. Leadership of the SVM was taken by Robert P. Wilder* and John R. Mott.* It is estimated that by 1945 more than 20,000 had volunteered for missionary service as a result of the Student Volunteer Movement.

After World War 2* returning servicemen brought a renewed zeal for foreign missions to college campuses in Britain and America. This was enhanced by revival movements at Wheaton College* (Illinois) and Asbury College (Kentucky). Additionally, the death of the Auca missionary martyrs (1956) contributed to the awakening of missionary interest among students. This interest has been fostered by the triennial Urbana Student Missions Convention* sponsored by InterVarsity Christian Fellowship.*

BIBLIOGRAPHY. C. E. Hummel, *Campus Christian Witness* (1958); R. P. Wilder, *The Student Volunteer Movement* (1935); J. C. Pollock, *A Cambridge Movement* (1953); D. Howard, *Moving Out: The Story of Student Initiative in World Missions* (1984). W. A. Detzler

Ayer, William Ward (1892-1985). Fundamentalist* Baptist* pastor,* evangelist,* radio voice and Bible conference* speaker. Born in Shediac, New Brunswick, Canada, Ayer ran away from home some time after the death of his mother in 1897. Converted* at a 1916 Billy Sunday* revival meeting in Boston, Ayer later attended Moody Bible Institute,* graduating in 1919. He went on to serve Baptist churches in Mason City (c. 1919-1920) and Atlanta, Illinois (1920-1922); Valpariso (1922-1927) and Gary, Indiana (1927-1932); and the nondenominational Philpott Tabernacle in Hamilton, Ontario (1932-1936).

He is best remembered as minister of Calvary Baptist Church, New York City (1936-1949). Under

Ayer's leadership the church grew from 400 to 1,600 members, with some 5,000 people professing conversion and as many as a quarter-million persons listening to him each week over radio station WHN (later WMGM). In 1947 a radio poll to discover "New York's Number One Citizen" placed Ayer third, behind Francis J. Spellman* and Eleanor Roosevelt but ahead of Harry Emerson Fosdick.* He served as trustee of Bob Jones University (which awarded him a D.D. in 1937) and Eastern Baptist Seminary and was elected the first president of the National Religious Broadcasters.*

Among his more controversial views were his belief that America should take an unequivocal stand against Russian atheism, his assertion that the success of Fulton J. Sheen* had been overestimated and overpublicized, and his conviction that the Roman Catholic Church* was the enemy of religious freedom.* Ayer wrote ten books, among them *Questions Jesus Answered* (1941) and *God's Answer to Man's Doubts* (1943).

Ayer resigned as minister of Calvary Baptist Church in 1949, desiring to give greater time to evangelism and Bible conference* work. But he continued his radio ministry independently of the church. During his active ministry, Ayer traveled widely, making evangelistic trips to England and to Central and South America. Ayer was a well-known spokesperson for fundamentalism, although he chose to work within the framework of the Northern Baptist Convention.

BIBLIOGRAPHY. M. G. Larson, *God's Man in Manhattan: A Biography of William Ward Ayer* (1950).   C. A. Russell

Azusa Street Mission. The site of early Pentecostalism's* legendary Azusa Street revival, which began in April 1906 under the leadership of an African-American Holiness* preacher,* William J. Seymour,* and continued for approximately three years. Although it was not Pentecostalism's point of origin, the Azusa Street Mission quickly emerged as its epicenter, providing the greatest impetus for its early growth and expansion.

William Seymour arrived in Los Angeles in February 1906 after a brief apprenticeship under Pentecostal progenitor Charles F. Parham* in Houston. Dismissed from his first Los Angeles pastorate over the "tongues"* doctrines, he began holding cottage meetings with a small band of African-American saints. On April 9, in a home on North Bonnie Brae Street, the group experienced its first outbreak of glossolalia. Crowds burgeoned and within a week the now racially integrated company sought larger facilities in a depressed industrial section of downtown Los Angeles. The dilapidated building they acquired, located at 312 Azusa Street, would become the premier landmark in Pentecostal-charismatic* history.

Over the next three years, thousands of people from around the world made pilgrimages to Azusa Street to hear the Pentecostal message. Workers from the mission, such as Florence Crawford* and Frank Bartleman,* spread the revival through their articles and evangelistic* travels. Countless others, like Gaston B. Cashwell* and Charles H. Mason,* journeyed to Azusa, found their "Pentecost" and returned home as emissaries of the movement.

Services were held three times daily at the peak of the revivals and were characterized by spontaneity, informality and ecstatic charismatic worship.* Reports of miraculous healings* abounded. Another trademark of the mission was its remarkable racial diversity, a scandal to some but a sign of divine endorsement to the Azusa faithful. Azusa was also noted for its fivefold doctrine of salvation,* sanctification,* tongues as evidence of Spirit-baptism,* divine healing and the imminent Second Coming of Christ (*See* Eschatology).

By 1909 the revival tides had begun to ebb, although meetings continued at the Azusa Street Mission until the city of Los Angeles condemned and razed it in 1929. The influence of the mission had all but evaporated by that time, but the revival it had once harbored remained for most Pentecostals the formative and definitive event of early Pentecostalism.

BIBLIOGRAPHY. F. Bartleman, *How Pentecost Came to Los Angeles* (1925, reprinted as *Azusa Street* [1980]); D. J. Nelson, *For Such a Time as This: The Story of William J. Seymour and the Azusa Street Revival* (unpublished Ph.D. dissertation, University of Birmingham, England, 1981); R. M. Anderson, *Vision of the Disinherited: The Making of American Pentecostalism* (1979).
R. G. Robins

B

Babcock, Rufus (1798-1875). Baptist minister in the North. Born in Colebrook, Connecticut, Babcock graduated from Brown University* (B.A., 1821) and studied theology* under William Stoughton in Washington, D.C., while serving as a tutor at Columbian College (1821-1823). Babcock was active in a variety of leadership roles in American Baptist life of the first half of the nineteenth century. He served as pastor in Baptist churches at Poughkeepsie, New York (1823-1826), and Salem, Massachusetts (1826-1833), before becoming the second president of Waterville College of Maine (now Colby College) from 1833 to 1836. He later served as pastor of Spruce Street Baptist Church, Philadelphia (1836-1840), followed by pastorates in Poughkeepsie, New York; New Bedford, Massachusetts; and Paterson, New Jersey (1840-1875).

Babcock served as president of the American Baptist Publication Society, the corresponding secretary of the American Bible Society* and the American Sunday School Union.* A prolific writer, he founded and edited from 1841 to 1845 *The Baptist Memorial,* a monthly journal that encouraged an awareness of denominational heritage through biographical sketches and current religious news. Other works included *Memoirs of Andrew Fuller* (1830) and *Forty Years of Pioneer Life: Memoir of John Mason Peck* (1864). His major contribution to his denomination* was in advocating interdenominational cooperation in areas of common mission, an emphasis that helped Northern Baptists overcome their sectarian tendencies.

BIBLIOGRAPHY. H. S. Burrage, *History of Baptists in Maine* (1904); *DARB; NCAB* 8.

C. D. Weaver

Bachman, John (1790-1874). Lutheran* minister,* naturalist. Born in Rhinebeck, New York, Bachman won fame as a "Patriarch of Southern Lutheranism" and an American naturalist. After attending Williams College, Bachman taught school in Ellwood and Philadelphia, Pennsylvania,

and was licensed by the New York Ministerium (1813) to serve three churches near Rhinebeck ("the Gilead Pastorate"). Ordained* in December 1814, Bachman pastored the St. John's Lutheran Church, Charleston, South Carolina (1815-1868). He was an organizer of the South Carolina Synod (1824), the General Synod (president, 1835, 1837), Lutheran Southern Seminary (1831), Newberry College (1858), Evangelical Lutheran General Synod Confederate States (1863) and the United Synod of the South (1866).

Admitting that "from my earliest childhood I had an irrepressible desire for the study of Natural History," Bachman founded the South Carolina Horticultural Society (1833), taught biology at the College of Charleston and collaborated with John James Audubon on *Birds of America* (1827) and *Viviparous Quadrupeds of North America* (1845-1849, 3 vols.). His books, such as *The Unity of the Human Race* (1850), attempted to reconcile Scripture* and science.* 240461

See also SCIENCE AND CHRISTIANITY.

BIBLIOGRAPHY. C. C. Bachman, *John Bachman* (1888); R. M. Bost, "The Reverend John Bachman and the Development of Southern Lutheranism" (unpublished Ph.D. dissertation, Yale, 1963); *DAB* I.

C. G. Fry

Backus, Isaac (1724-1806). Baptist* minister* and champion of religious liberty* during the Revolutionary* era. Born in Norwich, Connecticut, into the ruling elite of Puritan* Connecticut, as a New England farm boy Isaac imbibed the principles of Calvinism* and learned that religious training and the laws of the state maintained the good order of society. The crumbling of these social foundations came in the 1740s with the turbulent Great Awakening.* Seventeen-year-old Isaac was "born again"* without unusual emotion, but he confessed that he was "enabled by divine light" to see "the riches of God's grace."

Backus soon plunged into itinerant* evangelism.* Near Middleborough, Massachusetts, he found a gathering of converts who were anxious to have a revivalistic* pastor, so he was ordained* to serve the church. Slowly he came to Baptist beliefs. After agonizing prayer* and intense Bible study,* he, along with six fellow church members, was immersed on profession of faith in Christ. For five years the Titicut church tried to live in peace as a mixed fellowship. But finally Backus followed his conscience and, with his wife and four others, formed a Baptist church, the First Baptist Church in Middleborough.

Freed of his indecision, Backus plunged into evangelistic tours, pastoral responsibilities and, most importantly, the cause of religious freedom. As spokesman for the Warren Association of Baptists, Backus wrote tracts,* drew up dozens of petitions, and carried on a constant warfare of words in the newspapers, public disputes and private letters. In 1773 his most important tract, *An Appeal to the Public for Religious Liberty Against the Oppression of the Present Day,* appeared— the best exposition of the eighteenth-century evangelical* concept of separation of church and state.* Backus lived to see the birth of the U.S. and found comfort in the nation's adoption of the First Amendment,* guaranteeing religious freedom. It is estimated that Backus traveled over 67,000 miles and preached close to 10,000 sermons in the course of his nearly sixty years of ministry.

BIBLIOGRAPHY.   *DAB* I; *DARB;* W. G. McLoughlin, *Isaac Backus and the American Pietistic Tradition* (1967); W. G. McLoughlin, *New England Dissent 1630-1833: The Baptists and the Separation of Church and State,* 2 vols. (1971); W. G. McLoughlin, ed., *The Diary of Isaac Backus,* 3 vols. (1979).
B. L. Shelley

Bacon, Leonard Woolsey, Jr. (1830-1907).
Congregational* minister* and controversialist. Born in New Haven, Connecticut, the son of well-known Congregationalist minister Leonard Bacon, Leonard, Jr., followed in his father's footsteps by graduating from Yale (B.A., 1850) and Andover Theological Seminary (B.D., 1852). After studying medicine at Yale and becoming a doctor, he was ordained* a Congregational minister at Litchfield, Connecticut. During the succeeding thirty-five years Bacon pastored nine churches in regions as diverse as Geneva, Switzerland, and Savannah, Georgia. Leaving the ministry for ten years (1892-1902), he devoted himself to polemical writing, resuming pastoral work again in 1902 at Assonet, Massachusetts.

A forceful speaker and a vigorous, combative writer, Bacon found his niche in polemics. Not noted for charitability, he was an intense thinker—both brilliant and erratic—with a taste for historical investigation. His essays on "Two Sides of a Saint," [St. Francis de Sales] and "William Lloyd Garrison" in *Irenics and Polemics* (1895) reveal his delight in discrediting romanticized renderings of de Sales and in further discrediting the agnostic* Garrison.* Interest in the Old Catholic movement led him to translate a number of volumes of Pére Hyacinthe and to write *An Inside View of the Vatican Council* in 1872. Bacon wrote the capstone volume to the noted American Church History Series, *History of American Christianity* (1897). There he expressed his optimistic vision of American Protestantism progressing by divine providence to a wonderful but undisclosed future.

BIBLIOGRAPHY.   *DAB* I.
J. E. Mennell

Bacon, Leonard, Sr. (1802-1881).
Congregational* minister* and reformer. Born in Detroit, Michigan, the son of missionaries* in the Old Northwest Territory, Bacon was educated at Yale* (B.A., 1820) and Andover Theological Seminary* (B.D., 1823). After post-graduate study at Andover (1823-1824), he intended to go as a missionary to the Western frontier, but he received an unexpected invitation to supply the pulpit at New Haven's First Congregational Church. There he was installed in March 1825, succeeding Nathaniel W. Taylor* who had left the pulpit in 1822. Bacon spent his entire ministerial career at First Church (1824-1866; emeritus, 1866-1881). In his later years he was acting professor of revealed theology* (1866-1871) and then lecturer in church polity and American church history at Yale Divinity School (1871-1881). Over the course of his career, Bacon edited *The New Englander* for approximately twenty years, the *Christian Spectator* (1826-1838) and the antislavery publication *The Independent* (1846-1881).

Bacon became a widely respected Congregational churchman and a formidable polemicist, particularly on issues of social reform. Much of his writing and debate in the public arena was focused on the institution of slavery, which he opposed. Bacon was not an abolitionist* but argued for a gradual emancipation and supported the efforts of the Colonization Society to settle freed African-American slaves in Liberia. His volume *Slavery Discussed in Occasional Essays* (1846) is known to have had an influence on Abraham Lincoln's* thinking about slavery. As a churchman he was known as a charitable diplomacist who supported cooperative ventures between churches as long as congregational autonomy was not at stake. For this reason he championed the Congregational withdrawal from cooperation with the Presbyterians* in the Plan of Union.* Among historians of American religion, Bacon is remembered for his work *The Genesis of the New England Churches* (1874), which related the story of New England Congregationalism. Bacon's son and namesake was also a well-known Congregational polemicist and author.

BIBLIOGRAPHY. T. D. Bacon, *Leonard Bacon: A Statesman in the Church* (1931); *DAB* I; *DARB*; *NCAB* 1; W. Walker, *Ten New England Leaders* (1901).   D. G. Reid

Badin, Stephen Theodore (1768-1853). Catholic* frontier missionary.* Badin entered the Sulpician* seminary* in his native city of Orléans, France, in 1789. But along with other seminarians, he withdrew from the school two years later when his bishop* took the constitutional oath supporting the revolutionary government. In 1792 Badin went to the U.S. with Benedict Flaget* and enrolled at the newly established St. Mary's Seminary in Baltimore, Maryland. The next year he became the first Catholic priest* ordained* in the U.S. Assigned after ordination by his bishop, John Carroll,* to work as a frontier missionary, Badin played a key role in the establishment of Roman Catholicism in Kentucky, Indiana and Tennessee in the late eighteenth and early nineteenth centuries. He returned to France in 1812, mainly because of disagreements with Bishop Benedict Flaget concerning ownership of church land, but also because he needed a rest. After pastoring a parish in the vicinity of Orléans, Badin came back to America in 1828, ministered to Native Americans in Michigan and Indiana for five years and then focused his pastoral efforts on spreading Catholicism in Indiana and Ohio. Badin donated property on which the University of Notre Dame was later built, and he is buried on the campus.

BIBLIOGRAPHY. *DAB* I; J. H. Schauinger, *Stephen T. Badin: Priest in the Wilderness* (1956).
W. P. Leahy

Bainton, Roland (1894-1984). Church historian. Born in Darbyshire, England, the son of a minister,* Bainton moved with his family to Vancouver, British Columbia, when he was eight years old. Later the family moved to Colfax, Washington, where Bainton spent most of his childhood. After graduating from Whitman College in Walla Walla (B.A., 1914), Bainton went to Yale* Divinity School (B.D., 1917) and then earned a Ph.D. in Semitics and Hellenistic Greek at Yale University in 1921. In 1920 he joined the Yale Divinity School faculty as an instructor in church

history and New Testament. In 1927 he was ordained* a minister* of the Congregational Church,* though he also maintained an associate membership in the Society of Friends.* In 1936 Bainton became Titus Street Professor of Ecclesiastical History at Yale, a post he held until his retirement in 1962.

Bainton wrote over thirty-two books, but he is best known for his book *Here I Stand: A Life of Martin Luther,* which was published in 1950 and went on to sell over 1.2 million copies. Both historically accurate and entertaining, the book was an instantaneous hit with readers, both lay* and clerical, and remains today the most readable biography of its kind on Luther. In addition, *The Church of Our Fathers* (1971), a history of the church, has become almost a classic. *Behold The Christ* (1974) is a life of Christ as represented in works of Western and Eastern art, showing how and why cultural expression gradually changed the interpretation of who and what Christ was. Bainton's sound scholarship combined with his readable clarity made him one of the most influential historians of the church in his time.

J. E. Mennell

Baird, Robert (1798-1863). Presbyterian* minister,* ecumenical* pioneer and leader of voluntary societies.* Born of Scotch-Irish descent in Western Pennsylvania, Baird was educated at Washington (1816-1817) and Jefferson (B.A.,1818) colleges and Princeton Theological Seminary* (B.D., 1822). He was ordained* to the Presbyterian ministry in 1822 and directed the Princeton Academy for the next five years (1822-1828), during which he strongly advocated and influenced public education in New Jersey. He was thus launched on a career of advocacy not only for public education, but also for religious education as an agent of the American Sunday School Union* (1829-1834). Prior to that he was agent for the New Jersey Missionary Society (1828-1829). His concern for temperance* took him to many foreign capitals (crossing the Atlantic eighteen times). Baird also had an interest in missions* and ecumenism.* He was a supporter of the Evangelical Alliance* and formed his own society, which came to be known as the American and Foreign Christian Union. Baird's pioneering work as a leader and shaper of voluntary societies found him drawing support from several denominations* while frequently placing them under broad interdenominational governance. His influence on voluntary movements was both seminal and enduring.

A prolific author, Baird charted the movements

[101]

of voluntary societies, evangelicalism* and the American church scene in his classic *Religion in America* (1843; rev. ed. 1856). While he nowhere strictly defined the nature of the church, the work was deeply sympathetic toward broad American evangelicalism. Moreover, though Baird was a Presbyterian, he was charged by at least one conservative Princeton Seminary faculty member with identifying Presbyterian theology too closely with aberrant New England Theology.*

BIBLIOGRAPHY. J. W. Alexander, "Religion in America . . . by Robert Baird," in *The Biblical Repertory and Princeton Review* 17 (January 1895); H. M. Baird, *Life of the Rev. Robert Baird, D.D.* (1866); *DAB* I; *DARB*; *NCAB* 8. J. H. Hall

Baker, Elizabeth V. (1849-1915). Faith healer* and educator. The daughter of a Methodist* minister,* James Duncan, Baker's first marriage to W. A. Dawson, a seminary* administrator, ended in divorce. She then married C. W. Baker, a physician. Meanwhile, she became interested in the higher life, divine healing and missionary* movements. After an experience of healing in 1881, she began devoting her life to Christian service, first with the Women's Christian Temperance Union* and then independently. In 1895 she and her four sisters opened the Faith Mission in Rochester, New York. By the time of her death, their efforts had grown to include the Elim Faith Home, Elim Publishing House, Elim Bible Training School, Elim Tabernacle and a monthly publication, *Trust,* edited by Elizabeth Baker. All of these were operated on a freewill-offering basis, the sisters believing that funds came in answer to prayer. They identified their work with the fledgling Pentecostal Movement in 1907. In 1924 the surviving sisters discontinued the ministry.

BIBLIOGRAPHY. E. V. Baker et. al., *Chronicles of a Faith Life* (1918); G. B. McGee, "Three Notable Women in Pentecostal Ministry," *AG Heritage* 1 (1986):3-5, 12, 16. E. L. Blumhofer

Bakker, James (Jim) Orson (1940-). Televangelist* and founder of PTL and Heritage Village. Born in Muskegon Heights, Michigan, Bakker grew up in a conservative, Pentecostal* family. In 1961, while attending the Assemblies of God's* North Central Bible College in Minneapolis, Minnesota, Bakker married Tamara (Tammy) Faye LaValley. The marriage resulted in their expulsion from North Central and the end of Bakker's formal education. The two embarked on an itinerant preaching* ministry* in the small towns of North Carolina. But Bakker's early obscurity was not to last. Ordained* by the Assemblies of God in 1964, in 1965 he and Tammy started "The Jim and Tammy Show," a puppet show for children that was part of Pat Robertson's* Christian Broadcasting Network (CBN). Jim later became a cohost with Robertson on CBN's "700 Club." It was there that Bakker realized the power of the electronic medium and developed his own mastery of televangelism. From there he and Tammy helped start the Trinity Broadcasting Network in Southern California and eventually moved to Charlotte, North Carolina, where in 1974 they developed their television ministry, the PTL Club.

The magnetic Jim and the effervescent Tammy built a Christian empire out of PTL (standing for "Praise the Lord" and "People that Love"), mingling their charismatic theology with themes of health and wealth—the proof of which was exhibited in the Bakkers's own extravagant lifestyle. The Bakkers and PTL prospered through the seventies and eighties, and by 1987 the Bakkers were drawing lavish salaries. Their organization included a cable-TV program reaching 13 million homes and a 2,300-acre Christian theme park and resort, Heritage USA.

Nevertheless, the prosperity that marked the Bakkers's accomplishments eventually led to the downfall of their empire. Critics attacked Jim and Tammy's extravagant lifestyle, which was paid for by contributors' money; the IRS began investigating the ministry as early as 1981 and, finally, on March 19, 1987, Jim Bakker resigned from his ministry amidst revelations of Jim's 1980 sexual affair with a church secretary, Jessica Hahn, and subsequent hush money paid her by the ministry. Bakker turned the ministry over to Baptist televangelist Jerry Falwell* who guided the ministry through a turbulent period in which fellow Assemblies of God televangelist Jimmy Swaggert* brought further accusations against the Bakkers, and Jim Bakker accused Falwell of stealing his ministry. Investigations revealed that PTL had paid the Bakkers at least $1.6 million in salaries and bonuses for the 1986-1987 fiscal year before PTL, $71 million in debt, filed for bankruptcy in 1987. On December 5, 1988, following a sixteen-month investigation, Jim Bakker and his former aide Richard Dortch were charged in a twenty-four-count federal grand jury indictment with alleged mail fraud, wire fraud and conspiring to defraud the public through the sale of thousands of lifetime memberships to Heritage USA. On October 5, 1989, he was convicted on all twenty-four counts and on October 24, 1989, he was fined $500,000 and sentenced to forty-five years in prison.

BIBLIOGRAPHY. J. Bakker, *Move That Mountain!* (1976); J. E. Barnhart, *Jim and Tammy* (1988); "Fresh Out of Miracles," *Newsweek* (May 11, 1987):70-72; "Heaven Can Wait," *Newsweek* (June 8, 1987):58-65; "The Rise and Fall of 'Holy Joe'," *Time* (August 3, 1987): 54-55.

C. E. Ostwalt

Balch, Hezekiah (1741-1810). Presbyterian* minister* in East Tennessee. Born in 1741 in Maryland, Balch was reared in Mecklenburg County, North Carolina. He graduated from the College of New Jersey* and was ordained* by Hanover Presbytery, March 8, 1770. For some years he was an evangelist* in North Carolina and western Pennsylvania, but by 1782/83 he had moved to Greeneville in northeastern Tennessee, where his Mount Bethel congregation became the largest church in the Holston-Tennessee River Valley.

In 1794 Balch organized Greeneville College and in the following year journeyed to New England in search of funds and library books. At Newport, Rhode Island, he met Samuel Hopkins,* and was attracted to his "New Divinity"* theology.* Introducing these views into East Tennessee, Balch stirred up a fratricidal controversy among Presbyterians, marked by acerbic denunciations in the local press and endless judicial hearings in church courts. In the next few years Balch was attacked by the conservatives, led by Samuel Doak,* and brought sixteen times before presbytery,* four times before synod* and once before the General Assembly* on heresy* charges. Despairing of permanent peace, the church courts sought to separate the dissenting brethren by organizing Union (1797) and Greeneville (1800) presbyteries. Balch's introduction of Hopkinsian theology was significant because it led to the growth of liberal currents which spurred large defections of Tennessee Presbyterians into the New School* following the schism of 1837/38. Balch remained in Greeneville until his death in April 1810.

See also DOAK, SAMUEL; HOPKINS, SAMUEL; NEW ENGLAND THEOLOGY.

BIBLIOGRAPHY. *AAP* 3.

W. J. Wade

Baldwin, Harmon Allen (1869-1936). Pentecost Band leader, Free Methodist* minister* and theologian.* After several terms as a rural Ohio schoolteacher, Baldwin began to prepare for ministry in the Methodist Episcopal Church* at Mt. Union College, but joined Vivian Dake's* Pentecost Band and the Free Methodist Church* (1890). In 1896, forced to choose between Band and Church, he was ordained* deacon* (1896) and began forty years of pastoral ministry in western Pennsylvania, Ohio, West Virginia and Georgia. He married Clara Etta Baldwin (1896), a Pentecost Band member who was ordained and who co-pastored with him. A careful scholar of Christian theology* and history, and a prolific author, he argued against the trends of absolutist perfectionism,* premillennialism* and the Keswick* understanding of sanctification.* He called for a return to an eighteenth-century Wesleyan* understanding of Christian perfection, congruence with the patristic theological tradition, and for Christian social responsibility.

BIBLIOGRAPHY. H. A. Baldwin, *Lessons for Seekers of Holiness* (1918); D. D. Bundy, *Keswick: A Bibliographical Introduction to the Higher Life Movements* (1975).

D. D. Bundy

Ballou, Hosea (1771-1852). Leader of New England Universalism.* The son of a Baptist minister of Richmond, New Hampshire, Hosea was the youngest of eleven children. He studied at Quaker* academies in Richmond and Chesterfield, New Hampshire. By 1791 he and his brother David had embraced Universalism.

Ballou taught school for a number of years in Rhode Island and preached* as an itinerant* on Sundays. In 1803 he moved from a pastorate at Dana, Massachusetts, to Barnard, Vermont, where he wrote *A Treatise on Atonement* (1805). The work reflects the rationalist influences of his day, and in particular the writings of Ethan Allan,* Ferdinand Olivier Petitpierre and Charles Chauncy.* Here Ballou set forth a Unitarian* view of God that relegated Christ to the role of divine agent. Ballou also rejected the orthodox* view of Christ's atonement* as vicarious and substitutionary. The *Treatise,* as is true for Ballou's theology generally, made God's love the central tenet, and concluded that God through Christ's redeeming love will reconcile all men to himself, irrespective of their creeds or deeds in this life. In *An Examination of the Doctrine of Future Retribution* (1834) he developed more fully his view that there is no divine punishment beyond the grave.

Ballou started the *Universalist Magazine* in 1819, the same year that William Channing* articulated the tenets of New England Unitarianism.* The two denominations* shared many beliefs but remained socially distanced, with Universalists attracting the lower classes. Ballou served as pastor at Portsmouth, New Hampshire, and Salem, Massachusetts, and for thirty-five years he was pastor of the Second Universalist Society in

Boston. In 1830 he founded the *Universalist Expositor*. As the most respected Universalist preacher, he was chosen many times to serve as the moderator of the annual Universalist General Convention. In his lifetime, he saw Universalism grow from a handful of New England societies to a denomination of over 800,000 adherents nationwide.

See also UNITARIANISM: UNIVERSALISM.

BIBLIOGRAPHY. J. C. Adams, *Hosea Ballou and the Gospel Renaissance of the Nineteenth Century* (1903); E. Cassara, *Hosea Ballou: The Challenge to Orthodoxy* (1961); *DAB* I; *DARB;* R. E. Miller, *The Larger Hope,* 2 vols. (1986); *NCAB* 5; T. Whittemore, *Life of Rev. Hosea Ballou,* 4 vols. (1854-1855). D. G. Buss

Baltimore, Councils of. Meetings of the U.S. Roman Catholic* bishops* in the nineteenth century to consider church concerns and to legislate uniform Church discipline.* When Bishop John Carroll* called a synod* for his clergy* in 1791, his diocese* included all of the new U.S. It was the only such meeting held during his twenty-five years as bishop and later archbishop* of Baltimore, though after the creation of additional dioceses, Carroll met with his suffragan bishops in 1810. Urged by Bishop John England* of Charleston, South Carolina, Archbishop James Whitfield* convoked the first provincial council of Baltimore in 1829. Over the next twenty years seven provincial councils promulgated decrees concerning such matters as liturgy* and sacraments,* the clergy,* trusteeism,* education* and seminaries.* Most important, these meetings promoted a sense of unity for a rapidly growing Church in America.

In the late 1840s the Church in America was divided into several provinces; and the first plenary council was held in 1852, with six archbishops and twenty-eight bishops in attendance. Its concerns ranged from parochial schools* to the administration of Church property. After the Civil War* a second plenary council in 1866 codified Church legislation. The Church's rapid growth required a third plenary council in 1884. Seventy-two archbishops and bishops dealt with issues such as ecclesiastical jurisdiction, procedures for naming new bishops, the relationship of the U.S. Church to the Vatican Congregation for the Propagation of the Faith, and, especially, the development of the parochial school system. This council's decrees directed Church development for the following decades, and no further meetings of the entire hierarchy were held until the formation of the

National Catholic War Conference* in 1917.

See also CONCILIAR TRADITION, AMERICAN.

BIBLIOGRAPHY. P. Guilday, *A History of the Councils of Baltimore, 1791-1884* (1932). T. E. Buckley

Bangs, Nathan (1778-1862). Methodist* minister* and editor. Born in Stratford, Connecticut, Bangs moved to Canada shortly before being licensed* as a Methodist itinerant* preacher* in 1801. Essentially self-educated, he was ordained* in 1804 and proceeded to minister on circuits from Niagara to Quebec where, until 1812, he worked to effectively establish Methodism in the lower St. Lawrence Valley. Returning to the U.S., he ministered in New York for several years, becoming head of New York's Methodist Book Concern in 1820. Always committed to evangelism,* Bangs founded the Methodist Missionary Society, serving as its first secretary (1836-1841) and drawing up its constitution. Bangs worked to ensure the salaries of Methodist missionaries working in frontier settings among Native Americans, African-Americans and poor whites, as well as raising the educational requirements of Methodist ministers. For a short period he served as president of Wesleyan University (1841-1842), followed by a decade of ministry in several churches in New York (1842-1852).

In addition to editing several denominational periodicals, including the New York *Christian Advocate and Journal* (1828-1832), he wrote a number of historical and doctrinal works, including his four-volume *The History of the Methodist Episcopal Church* (1838-1840), *The Errors of Hopkinsianism Detected and Refuted* (1815) and *The Reformer Reformed* (1816). His writings frequently reflected his antipathy toward the Calvinist* doctrine of election* and predestination,* which he regarded as contrary to Scripture, reason and experience. Though he retired in 1852 he continued to be actively involved in the ministry until his death in 1862.

BIBLIOGRAPHY. *DAB* I; *DARB; NCAB* 9; A. Stevens, *The Life and Times of Nathan Bangs* (1863); A. H. Tuttle, *Nathan Bangs* (1909). P. D. Airhart

Bapst, John (1815-1887). Jesuit* missionary* and educator. Born in LaRoche, Switzerland, Bapst attended St. Michael's College at Fribourg, entered the Society of Jesus in 1834 and after further education and spiritual training was ordained* in 1846. He was exiled to New York in 1848, and from then until 1859, served in Maine on a missionary circuit of thirty-three towns. There Bapst became noted for his converts to Catholicism* and his founding of several temperance* societies.

In 1853 at Ellsworth, Maine, he was tarred and feathered by members of the nativistic* Know Nothing Party, barely escaping with his life. Upon being transferred to Bangor, Bapst received a public welcome and honors from its Protestant* citizens. In 1860 Bapst became rector of the Jesuit Seminary in Boston, in 1864 served as first president of Boston College and from 1869 to 1873 was superior of the New York and Canadian Missions. Mental deterioration, blamed upon the Ellsworth trauma, plagued him during the final years of his life. He finally died in Mt. Hope, Maryland.

BIBLIOGRAPHY. *DAB* I; R. H. Lord, J. E Sexton and E. T. Harrington, *History of the Archdiocese of Boston in the Various Stages of Its Development, 1604 to 1943,* 3 vols. (1944).   J. W. Evans

Baptism. The initiation rite practiced by most Christian churches, in which water is applied to the participant. The rite is related to certain spiritual truths bound up with one's new status, including death and new life, cleansing from sin* and the presence of the Spirit.

New Testament Background and History. The term "baptism" is a transliteration from the Greek words referring to the action of washing with, or plunging into (literally, "surrounding with") water. While some scholars have tried to trace the early Christian practice to various sources, including Jewish and pagan rituals, the church has claimed the New Testament precedent of Jesus' baptism by John the Baptist (Mt 3:13) and Jesus' command to baptize disciples (Mt 28:19) as the origin and authority* for the Christian rite.

The practice of both John the Baptist and the early church seems to have included the dipping of the participant in the baptismal water (as in Acts 8:38-39), although it is possible that the practice of pouring water over the participant had already been introduced. In the early church the name of "the Lord Jesus" (Acts 19:5) or the trinitarian formula (Mt 28:19) was invoked at baptism, for by this rite the participant was symbolically placed "into the Lord."

The New Testament employs several models from the Old Testament to indicate the meaning of baptism, including the exodus (1 Cor 10:1-2), circumcision (Col 2:11-12) and the flood (1 Pet 3:19-20). But of greater importance than these Old Testament events for Christian baptism are the paradigm of Jesus' death and resurrection (Rom 6:3-5). The rite of baptism indicates a person's

union with Christ and the spiritual realities of forgiveness of sins (Acts 2:38; 1 Pet 3:21) and the reception of the Spirit (1 Cor 12:13).

By extension this union with Christ also includes union with the body of Christ, the church (1 Cor 12:13). And it symbolizes the confirming of a covenant with God, for the rite is an outward pledge of a person to God made possible by the salvation which comes through the resurrection of Jesus (1 Pet 3:21). This baptismal confession is subsequently reaffirmed through participation in the Lord's Supper* (1 Cor 10:14-21).

In each of these senses, baptism is a visual word of proclamation, declaring the death and resurrection of Christ on behalf of sinners and the baptized person's participation in Christ. At the same time, the practice of the rite issues a call for response. The baptizing community is called to nurture its own and to complete the mandate to baptize all nations (Mt 28:19-20). Onlookers are called to make the same confession being declared by the rite. And the participant is called to walk in newness of life, reaffirming in daily living the baptismal vow (Rom 6:3-8).

In linking the participant with Christ's death and resurrection, baptism carries an eschatological orientation. It points beyond initiation into the Christian life to the process of sanctification* and the continual renewal of the believer by the Spirit (2 Cor 3:18; Rom 8:10). This process will one day result in a final, total transformation at the Lord's return (Rom 8:11; 1 Cor 15:51-57).

Specific instructions for baptism were developed in the patristic era. The *Didache,* for example, stipulated the type of water to be employed (preferably a running stream of cold water). And later writings reveal the growth of an involved initiation process, as the church sought to incorporate a large number of converts from pagan backgrounds. Sometime after the second century, the baptism of infants and the mode of sprinkling were introduced. However, believer's baptism (the rite as a profession of the personal faith of the participant) and immersion (placing the participant fully under water) continued in general use up to the Middle Ages. Eventually the sprinkling of infants gained ascendancy throughout the church, a practice which the Protestant* Reformers affirmed against the so-called Anabaptists* in the sixteenth century. Nevertheless, believer's baptism and immersion have been seen as valid options by nearly all Christian traditions and are the sole practice of several Protestant groups.

Baptism in Church Traditions. Christian churches have understood the meaning of baptism in various ways. While all declare baptism to be both a divine and a human act, pedobaptist groups (those who practice infant baptism) have tended to emphasize the side of the divine action, whereas believer baptists stress the human response. The divine agency involved in baptism is variously interpreted. According to one view, baptismal regeneration, the rite works regeneration, as God produces through the act what baptism signifies. The Roman Catholic* and Eastern Orthodox Churches* tie the Spirit's regenerative action closely to the act itself *(ex opere operato).* Some Episcopalians* *(See* Anglicanism) and confessional* Lutherans* understand the regenerative nature of baptism more in covenantal terms, as the rite places one within the church covenant (Episcopal) or as it constitutes God's covenantal promise of life (Lutheran). An understanding akin to baptismal regeneration is also maintained in a believer-baptist context by certain followers of the nineteenth-century American churchman Alexander Campbell.*

Traditional Roman Catholic theology* speaks of the efficacy of baptism in remitting original sin* and the actual guilt brought by sin. At the same time, the virtues of faith, hope and love are poured into the participant. The Orthodox Church, in contrast, speaks of the regeneration worked in baptism in terms of divinization. The participant partakes of the divine nature and from that point on carries the very life of God.

Many Protestants deny any direct correlation between baptism and the regeneration of the participant. For some, including many Lutherans, the rite is rather the sign of God's claim on an individual prior to personal response. Churches in the Reformed tradition,* while accepting this emphasis, tend to see the significance of baptism in terms of covenant theology.* Baptism is the sign and seal of the covenant God makes with God's people or which God's people make with their Lord. Some (like low church* Episcopalians and many Methodists*) emphasize the conditional nature of this covenant, requiring future repentance and faith. Other Reformed bodies highlight the permanent nature of the covenant in the case of God's elect.

The concept of baptism as covenant is present among some believer baptists as well. However, they tend to emphasize the human response to the covenant sealed by the rite. Two alternative but interrelated outlooks on baptism have developed out of this understanding. Some believer's baptists describe baptism as a significant, divinely given means of responding personally to the gospel.

Others view it as a public testimony to an inner spiritual transformation. In either case, baptism is linked to discipleship.* It is a public affirmation of one's conscious decision to place oneself under the lordship of Jesus. For this the baptism of Jesus serves as a model, and the disciple is often said to be "following the Lord in baptism."

Related to this discussion of the theology of baptism is the question of terminology. The normal word for a sacred rite in the Orthodox church is *mystery,* emphasizing the mystery of God's love and grace proclaimed by the church. Most churches in the Western tradition refer to the rite as *sacrament.* Although there are differences concerning the definition of the term, it is generally meant to suggest a close connection between the sign and the reality it signifies.

Many believer baptists reject *sacrament* in favor of another term, *ordinance.* *Sacrament,* they claim, carries the "magical" understanding of medieval Catholic theology, in which the rites of the church were supposed to infuse divine grace into the recipient. *Ordinance* avoids this danger. The term is derived from *ordain,* suggesting that these rites are ordained or commanded by Jesus. Participation in them, therefore, symbolizes the obedience of the disciple to the Lord and corresponds to the personal and voluntary character of the sacred practices emphasized by believer's baptists.

Some Christian groups focus more on the underlying spiritual reality symbolized by baptism than on the rite itself. In the Holiness* and Pentecostal* movements the baptism of the Spirit tends to be separated from water baptism entirely and linked with a "second work of grace" experienced subsequent to conversion* and initiation. This experience of Spirit baptism* is viewed as more significant than human rites, such as water baptism. For the Evangelical Free Church of America,* baptism is optional and not required for local church membership. The Salvation Army* and the Society of Friends* do not practice water baptism at all; the spiritual reality (Spirit baptism) has eliminated the need of its symbol.

Baptism and the American Churches. Baptism has been controversial through much of Christian history. Controversy has been especially acute in America, where Christian groups with widely divergent views have flourished, coexisted and competed. The debate over the role of baptism in the life of American churches goes back to colonial New England.

In the first half of the seventeenth century the Puritan* settlers of Massachusetts developed a distinctive form of church life known as the "New England Way."* Full communicant status in the congregations required not only the older requisites (acceptance of the doctrines of the church and baptism) but also verbal evidence of a religious experience* which had made the candidate aware of his or her elect status. In this way the Puritans attempted to produce and maintain churches composed of the elect only (regenerate church membership*). At the same time the Puritans sought to develop a Christian commonwealth ordered according to divine law, in which civil government acknowledged and protected true religion.

As the seventeenth century unfolded, the New England Way faced dissension and challenge. The first leading dissenter was Roger Williams.* Soon after his arrival in Massachusetts, Williams concluded that the principle of regenerate church membership required believer's baptism. Although he was banished from Massachusetts, his thinking made inroads throughout New England.

The New England Way faced other challenges as church membership declined. The Puritans had simply assumed that most of the children born to the elect, if brought under the covenant through infant baptism, would later experience a confirmation of their own elect status and thereby be eligible for church membership. When the numbers of nominal Christians* swelled, however, the problem of the status of the seed of the elect became acute. In response, the Half-Way Covenant* was adopted in 1657, whereby those baptized in infancy but who could not give evidence of election could bring their children for baptism, but could not receive communion or vote in congregational meetings.

The face of American religion was radically changed by the Great Awakening* of the 1740s and the resultant rise of evangelical* fervor. The Awakening led to division in the colonial churches and to the formation of separate congregations by many who were converted during the revival. The renewed commitment to regenerate church membership that characterized the Separates,* or revivalists, led to a reopening of the question of baptism. Many adopted believer's baptism and eventually joined the Baptists.

The nineteenth century was characterized by lively debates between believer's baptists and pedobaptists and by the birth of new developments that affected the older denominations. One such development, the Restoration Movement,* arose in western Virginia, Tennessee and Kentucky. At the turn of the century Thomas Camp-

bell* was instrumental in forming the Christian Association of Washington with the watchword "Where the Scriptures speak, we speak; where they are silent, we are silent." He and his son, Alexander, broke with Presbyterianism* and became convinced that believer's baptism by immersion was the only scriptural initiation rite. After joining the Baptists* in 1813 Alexander became a controversial leader in the region. He and his followers saw themselves as "Reformers," desiring "the restoration of the ancient order of things." Baptist leaders, however, accused Campbell of teaching baptismal regeneration. Certain churches and associations withdrew fellowship from the Campbellites and separate Campbellite churches were organized, generally known as the Disciples of Christ* or the Christian Church.*

A second development, the Landmark movement,* nearly divided the Southern Baptist Convention.* In an essay James M. Pendleton* raised the issue of the status of non-Baptist clergy.* The Big Hatchie Association, meeting at Cotton Grove, Tennessee, in 1851, declared all non-Baptist churches to be religious societies, whose clergy should not be recognized and whose members should not be addressed as "brethren." The term "Landmarkism" was derived from the republication of Pendleton's essay by James R. Graves* in 1854 under the title *An Old Landmark Reset*. The movement focused on five major doctrines: an unbroken succession of true churches from the Jerusalem Church to the Baptists, no church apart from local churches, the rejection of alien immersion* (baptism administered in any church except a Baptist congregation), closed Communion (only the faithful members of the celebrating local congregation are admitted to the Lord's Supper) and a rejection of cooperative mission programs.

Although the tide in the Southern Baptist Convention had turned against the Landmarkers by 1862, the controversy simmered for many years until a separate Landmark denomination was formed early in the twentieth century. Landmarkers continue to maintain that the divine pattern for baptism includes a proper candidate (a believer), mode (immersion), design (a picture showing forth the gospel) and administrator (one whose authority is derived from a scriptural church).

As the nineteenth century drew to a close, the debates of the earlier era began to subside. The rise of Protestant theological liberalism* led to a de-emphasis on traditional doctrine and a reduction of the role of the sacraments. In liberal theology baptism lost its stature as a regenerative rite or as a sign of the covenant. Instead it was viewed as a formality for church membership or, in the case of infant baptism, a dedicatory rite for parents. Likewise the nondenominationalism of liberalism called into question the importance of church divisions based on theology or polity.

Although many of the older questions persist into the twentieth century, the outlook toward baptismal controversies has been reshaped by a new interest in ecumenism.* The establishment of the Faith and Order Commission in 1927 is a striking example of this shift in outlook. The work of the Commission came to a climax in a widely disseminated document, *Baptism, Eucharist and Ministry*, which seeks to articulate a basic agreement among the churches on these three topics. The understanding of baptism reflected in the document is inclusive. The act is seen as both a divine gift and a human response. Churches are invited to see believer's baptism and infant baptism as "equivalent alternatives." At the same time, faith is declared to be necessary for the reception of the salvation set forth in baptism. In the case of infants, this personal response, which is integral to baptism, is to be offered later in the person's life.

Baptism, Eucharist and Ministry holds forth the hope that the divisions produced or enhanced by divergent understandings of baptism can be overcome. The current cooperative mood, whether among churches committed to future organizational union or among those loosely allied in evangelical organizations, calls on all traditions to learn from each other, while offering one's own tradition as a contribution to the whole church.

See also ALIEN IMMERSION; BAPTISM IN THE SPIRIT; BAPTISMAL FONT; BAPTISTERY; LANDMARK MOVEMENT; SACRAMENTS AND ORDINANCES.

BIBLIOGRAPHY. *Baptism, Eucharist and Ministry* (Faith and Order Paper No. 111) (1982); G. R. Beasley-Murray, *Baptism in the New Testament* (1981); C. E. Braaten and R. W. Jenson, eds., *Christian Dogmatics,* 2 vols. (1984); D. Bridge and D. Phypers, *The Water that Divides* (1977); G. W. Bromiley, *Children of Promise* (1979); A. M. Coniaris, *Introducing the Orthodox Church: Its Faith and Life* (1982); M. J. Erickson, *Christian Theology,* vol. 3 (1985); J. D. C. Fisher, et. al., "Baptism," *The New Westminster Dictionary of Liturgy and Worship,* ed. J. G. Davies (1986); S. J. Grenz, *Isaac Backus—Puritan and Baptist* (1983); J. A. Hardon, *The Catholic Catechism* (1966); P. K. Jewett, *Infant Baptism and the Covenant of Grace* (1978); D. Moody, *Baptism: Foundation for Christian Unity* (1967); W. M. Nevins, *Alien Baptism and the Baptists* (1951); L. H. Stookey, *Baptism: Christ's Act in the Church* (1982). S. J. Grenz

Baptism in the Spirit. A term referring to the bestowal of the Holy Spirit on believers. It is not used in the New Testament and was rarely used before the rise of the Pentecostal Movement* in the late nineteenth and early twentieth centuries. For classic Pentecostals it is a distinct experience in which believers are consciously immersed in the power of the Holy Spirit and are imparted the gift of speaking in tongues.

Spirit baptism is based on the announcement by John the Baptist that the Coming One would baptize "with the Holy Spirit" (Mk 1:8) and the bestowal of the Spirit on the early Christians as it is described in Acts 2, 9, 10 and 19. Christians disagree regarding the nature of the baptism of the Spirit and when it can be expected to take place. At least five interpretations can be distinguished.

(1) The classic Reformed* Protestant* view is that the baptism of the Spirit occurred at the birth of the church as a singular historical event in which the believers who had come to faith prior to the giving of the Spirit received the Spirit on a subsequent occasion in order to make their Christian experience complete. Proponents of this view would argue that believers today receive the gift of the Spirit at conversion*—the beginning of the Spirit's work of transformation, assurance and enablement—and though some may wish to refer to it as "baptism in the Spirit," it is not accompanied by speaking in tongues or any other signs. Some evangelicals within this tradition would refer to successive "fillings" of the Spirit, enabling the believer to live a life of holiness and powerful service to God. But these particular impartings of the Spirit have not traditionally been called "baptism in the Spirit."

(2) The nineteenth-century Holiness Movement* adopted the Wesleyan* idea of a second work of grace—an enhanced sanctifying work of the Spirit that lifts a believer to a new level of holiness and Christian experience. W. E. Boardman* called this the "higher Christian life."* Charles Finney* spoke of an experience subsequent to conversion which he called "the Baptism of the Holy Ghost." Many who were Wesleyan in their orientation spoke of this as a "second blessing"* in which a believer achieved sinless perfection or near perfection.* Others, particularly those within the Keswick Movement,* were more Reformed* in their orientation and spoke of the gradual, lifelong work of sanctification* in a believer, aided by successive "fillings" of the Spirit.

(3) These two strains of Holiness thought reappear in the classical Pentecostal churches. The so-called Keswick (e.g., Assemblies of God,*

International Church of the Foursquare Gospel*) and "Oneness"* groups are most alike in their view of Spirit baptism. Like traditional Reformed Protestants, they speak of sanctification beginning in the initial experience of salvation and progressing throughout a believer's lifetime. The so-called Holiness Pentecostals, on the other hand, maintain that entire sanctification—a second work of grace whereby the adamic nature is eradicated—precedes the baptism in the Spirit.

But while Pentecostals differ regarding the relationship between the saving and sanctifying works of grace, both groups understand Spirit baptism as a logically and temporally independent event in Christian experience. For Keswick Pentecostals, Spirit baptism takes place somewhere in the process of sanctification and may be referred to as the true "second work of grace." For Holiness Pentecostals the Baptism of the Spirit is a third event in Christian experience, in addition to regeneration and the "second blessing" of entire sanctification. In either case, the baptism is not for purification but empowerment. Though Pentecostals will also refer to the gift of the Spirit at conversion, they speak of it with qualification—the Spirit is received "in a sense." But when classical Pentecostals refer to having "received the Holy Spirit," they are referring to Spirit baptism. Pentecostals have recognized the priority of faith in receiving the Holy Spirit, but have also spoken of prayer,* obedience and yielding as conditions for the experience.

Pentecostals have traditionally been united in arguing that Spirit baptism is evidenced in the tangible sign of speaking in tongues.* But this stance has been mitigated by the fact that some present-day Pentecostal leaders and scholars do not support this claim and, experientially, all Pentecostals who profess to have been baptized in the Spirit cannot claim to have spoken in tongues.

(4) Protestant charismatics,* or neo-Pentecostals, were until recently found largely within Protestant mainline* denominations. Their leaders have, with a few exceptions, agreed that Spirit-baptism can be distinguished from the Spirit's regenerating work, but opinions have varied regarding its relationship to sanctification. Charismatics within the Episcopal,* Lutheran* and Presbyterian* churches generally do not believe that sanctification is an intervening stage between regeneration and Spirit baptism. Charismatics as a whole are less inclined to identify speaking in tongues as the initial evidence of Spirit baptism, regarding it as one of several possible gifts accompanying the baptism.

(5) Roman Catholic* charismatics, tracing their recent history back to the 1967 charismatic revival at Pittsburgh's Duquesne University, usually agree that Spirit baptism is at least logically and objectively associated with Christian initiation—even though chronologically there may be little connection between the two. Initiation is usually defined sacramentally* as water baptism* or confirmation.* Spirit baptism is the conscious experience of the Spirit who has already been bestowed. Speaking in tongues is not regarded as an exclusive or necessary sign of Spirit baptism.

BIBLIOGRAPHY. F. D. Bruner, *A Theology of the Holy Spirit: The Pentecostal Experience and the New Testament Witness* (1970); J. D. G. Dunn, *Baptism in the Holy Spirit* (1970); H. D. Hunter, *Spirit Baptism: A Pentecostal Alternative* (1983); W. Menzies, *Anointed to Serve* (1971); E. D. O'Connor, *The Pentecostal Movement in the Catholic Church* (1974); R. Quebedeaux, *The New Charismatics II* (1983); K. McDonnell, *The Holy Spirit and Power: The Catholic Charismatic Renewal* (1975); V. Synan, *The Holiness-Pentecostal Movement* (1971).   H. D. Hunter

Baptismal Font. A vessel containing water used for baptism.* The term is derived from the Latin *fons,* meaning "a spring of water." The shape and meaning of the baptismal font have changed considerably through the centuries of church history. In the early church the font was large enough for an adult to step down into it for immersion or affusion. The advent of infant baptism introduced the font as an elevated basin in which a child could conveniently be immersed. Later still the change from immersion to affusion as a mode of baptism introduced a font shaped like a small basin or a cup. The prominence of the font in church furnishings varies widely. In some traditions it is a rather ornate vessel mounted on a pedestal, while in others it is a simple, small cup viewed only during baptism.

See also BAPTISM; BAPTISTERY.

BIBLIOGRAPHY. F. Bond, *Fonts and Font Covers* (1908); J. G. Davies, *The Architectural Setting of Baptism* (1962).   M. G. Bell

Baptist Bible Union An alliance of fundamentalist* Baptists during the years 1923-1932. The First Annual Conference of the Baptist Bible Union (BBU) was held in Kansas City, Missouri, May 10-15, 1923. Support for the BBU came from three sources: fundamentalists in the Northern Baptist Convention (NBC), led by William B. Riley*; Southern fundamentalists, led by J. Frank Norris*;

and Canadian fundamentalists, led by Thomas T. Shields.* The primary purpose of the BBU was expressed by Shields—who was elected president—as "declaring and waging relentless and uncompromising war on Modernism." The two most significant fronts on which the BBU did battle were missions* and education.

At the 1925 meeting of the NBC the BBU supported the Hinson resolution, intended to put an end to the "inclusive policy" in missions, only to be defeated. The BBU then created the Missionary Society of the Baptist Bible Union of North America. However, the program never materialized. Turning to education, the BBU purchased Des Moines University in 1927 for the purpose of creating a bastion of fundamentalism. Problems immediately arose concerning the moderate stance of some faculty toward fundamentalism and the question of who should control the institution—the university president or Shields. Following a student riot, the university closed in 1929. Riley subsequently withdrew his support from the BBU, and Norris had already dissociated from the BBU due to a shooting incident in his church. Shields shortly returned to Canada. The final meeting of the BBU was held in 1932, and a new organization was begun, the General Association of Regular Baptist Churches.*

BIBLIOGRAPHY. R. Delnay, "A History of the Baptist Bible Union" (unpublished Th.D. dissertation, Dallas Theological Seminary, 1963); G. W. Dollar, *A History of Fundamentalism in America* (1973). C. W. Whiteman

Baptist Board for Foreign Missions. *See* AMERICAN BAPTIST BOARD OF INTERNATIONAL MINISTRIES.

Baptist Churches in U.S.A. Members of a Christian denomination* that originated within seventeenth-century English Puritanism.* Puritans believed that the established* Church of England* demonstrated far too few signs of the true church of Christ. As a territorial church the Church of England welcomed sinners in a neighborhood to worship* just as readily as it welcomed saints. Puritans believed that the church should be congregations of the saints, men and women who could testify to the grace of God in their lives.

Baptists, at first a handful of radicals on the fringe of the Puritan movement, agreed with the Puritan majority in their criticism of the Anglican Church, but they disagreed with most Puritans at two important points: (1) they said that church membership* should be limited, not only to those families who could testify of the grace of God, but

that even children of believers must be denied baptism* and church membership until they too can personally confess their faith in Christ; (2) they argued that God had instituted the state as well as the church, and that the two were designed by God to serve two distinct purposes. While the state was intended to bear the sword of justice, the church was designed to worship, preach* and grow by voluntary means alone, freed of the state's power.

The name *Baptist* came from the group's insistence that baptism be limited to those old enough to confess personally faith in Jesus Christ. But perhaps more significant was the view of the church as a community of Christian believers gathered by the witness of the Spirit, not by the state.

In the U.S., by 1984, scholars could identify fifty-two distinct Baptist groups, with a total membership of just over 30 million, the largest Protestant denominational family in North America. The largest Baptist convention is the mammoth Southern Baptist Convention,* numbering almost 14 million. It is followed by two predominantly African-American Baptist conventions; the National Baptist Convention, U.S.A., Inc., with an estimated six million members, and the National Baptist Convention of America with an estimated 3.5 million members *(See* National Baptists).

The multiplicity of Baptist groups in America is traceable to four primary developments in Baptist life: (1) Baptists started with two distinct theological groups, Calvinists* (or Regular Baptists*) and Arminians (or General Baptists*); (2) Baptists have separated over the use of "means" in church activity, thus producing missionary* and primitive* (or anti-missionary*) bodies; (3) Baptists have divided between those with Northern cultural roots and those with Southern cultural roots, thereby creating Northern-oriented and Southern-oriented bodies; (4) in the twentieth century Baptists have separated over the issues of centralized denominational structures and theological inclusivism (or liberalism*).

Colonial Period. While some Baptists immigrated to the New World from England and Wales, many more adopted Baptist views after their arrival in the American colonies. Henry Dunster,* the first president of Harvard College,* and Roger Williams,* the founder of Rhode Island Colony, are representatives of the latter group.

Roger Williams, shortly after his banishment from the Massachusetts Bay Colony for preaching "new and dangerous opinions," led in the establishment of the first Baptist church in America. The location was Providence, Rhode Island; the year was 1639. Less than a year later Williams came to the conclusion that all existing churches lacked proper foundations, and that the true church could only be re-established by a new dispensation of apostolic authority.*

Williams's defection left the Providence church without adequate leadership, but a short distance away, at Newport, Rhode Island, between 1641 and 1648 John Clarke* established another congregation with Baptist convictions. Due to Puritan opposition, however, the Baptist witness in New England remained weak throughout the seventeenth century.

Baptists found a more favorable atmosphere in the Middle Colonies. In 1707 five churches in New Jersey, Delaware and Pennsylvania united to form the Philadelphia Baptist Association. This first association in America enabled Baptists to launch a vigorous missionary effort. By 1760 the Philadelphia Association extended from Connecticut in the North to Virginia in the South. In 1751 Baptists in the South formed the Charleston Association, and others soon followed.

Most of this growth is traceable to the colonial revival* called the Great Awakening* during the decades immediately preceding the American Revolution.* In addition to strengthening the existing "regular" Baptist churches, the revival drew to Baptist churches in New England large numbers of awakened believers from established Puritan Congregationalism.* These revivalistic believers were called Separate Baptists.* Through the ministry of Shubal Stearns,* the revivalistic spirit spread to the South and marked the region for generations to come. Stearns was a New England Separate Baptist who moved to Sandy Creek, North Carolina, in 1755 and initiated a widespread revival that eventually penetrated the entire Piedmont area.

At the same time Baptist work began in Canada. Ebenezer Moulton, a Baptist emigrant* from Massachusetts, organized a church in Nova Scotia in 1763. The earliest churches in Ontario were planted by United Empire Loyalists who crossed the border following the American Revolution. Still other churches were started by immigrant Baptists from Scotland and by missionaries from Vermont and New York.

The Nineteenth Century. Scholars have estimated that, at the outbreak of the American Revolution, Baptist congregations numbered 494. Twenty years later in 1795, Isaac Backus,* a leader of Baptists in New England, estimated that Baptists could claim 1,152 churches. Thus, on the threshold of the nineteenth century, Baptists were poised to make a major contribution to American life.

Their first need, however, was some unifying cause. This came in the form of the missionary* challenge. Early in the century the newly formed Congregational mission board sent Adoniram Judson* and Luther Rice* to India as their first missionaries. En route to India, however, both men came to the Baptist conviction that only believers should be baptized. Upon their arrival in Calcutta they agreed that Judson should go on to Burma and that Rice should return to America to enlist support for missions among American Baptists. As a result, in 1814 Rice succeeded in rallying Baptists in the formation of a General Convention of the Baptist Denomination. Since it met every three years, most Baptists called it the Triennial Convention.*

Initially the convention tried to support home missions, education and publications, as well as foreign missions. In 1826, however, the convention decided to limit its role to foreign missions. Other independent societies were formed to meet the needs of home missions, publications and education.

Many Baptists, however, especially on the Southern frontier, objected to these new agencies on the grounds that they were without biblical precedent. The sovereign God of the Bible,* they said, had no need of these modern "means" to reach the lost. This resistance to voluntary societies* gave birth to the Primitive, or anti-missionary, Baptists. Their strict Calvinism gave rise to their "hard shell" label.

The Primitive Baptist protest was a regional crisis. The greatest challenge to the newly found Baptist unity was the slavery controversy that enveloped the whole country by mid-century. During the decade prior to 1845, Baptists considered various compromises for the proslavery and antislavery parties in their ranks, but all proposals proved unacceptable. As a result in 1845 Southern churchmen organized the Southern Baptist Convention in Augusta, Georgia *(See* Civil War and the Churches). The division between North and South was consolidated in 1907, when eight once-independent agencies joined in the formation of the Northern Baptist Convention (later renamed American Baptists).

As early as the eighteenth century, African-American Baptists organized independent local congregations. The first African-American Baptist church was organized around 1773 at Silver Bluff across the Savannah River from Augusta, Georgia. Others soon followed in Virginia, Kentucky and other states. The great influx of African-Americans

Baptist Churches

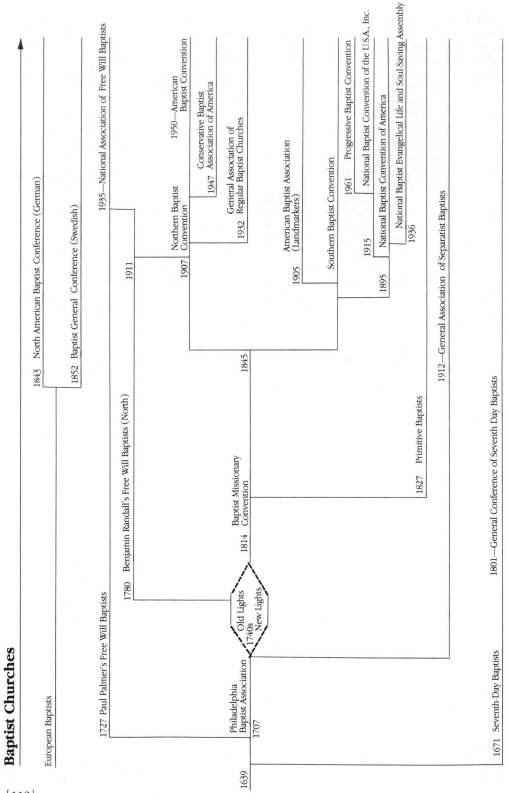

European Baptists

1727 Paul Palmer's Free Will Baptists

1843 North American Baptist Conference (German)

1852 Baptist General Conference (Swedish)

1780 Benjamin Randall's Free Will Baptists (North)

1935—National Association of Free Will Baptists

1911

1907 Northern Baptist Convention

1950—American Baptist Convention

1947 Conservative Baptist Association of America

1932 General Association of Regular Baptist Churches

1814 Baptist Missionary Convention

1845

1905 American Baptist Association (Landmarkers)

Southern Baptist Convention

1895

1915 National Baptist Convention of America

1961 Progressive Baptist Convention

National Baptist Convention of the U.S.A., Inc.

1936 National Baptist Evangelical Life and Soul-Saving Assembly

1827 Primitive Baptists

1912—General Association of Separatist Baptists

Old Lights
1740s
New Lights

Philadelphia Baptist Association
1707

1639

1671 Seventh-Day Baptists

1801—General Conference of Seventh Day Baptists

into Baptist churches, however, awaited the Emancipation Proclamation.*

The lack of formality in Baptist churches, together with their absence of ritual and the democratic* spirit in their congregations, appealed to African-American believers more than the formal and priestly denominations. Within fifteen years after the Civil War* nearly one million African-American Baptists worshiped in their own churches.

In 1866 African-American leaders organized a state convention in North Carolina, and in 1880 the first national organization was formed at Montgomery, Alabama: the Foreign Mission Baptist Convention. The National Baptist Convention was created at Atlanta, Georgia, in 1895. Early in the twentieth century (1915), however, a dispute over the adoption of a charter and control of a publishing house led to the two largest conventions of African-American Baptists today.

The Twentieth Century. After 1900 Baptists in the South as well as the North were divided by theological controversy and the growth of denominational bureaucracies. In 1905 churches located primarily in Texas, Oklahoma and Arkansas—called Landmarkers*—protested the "conventionism" of the Southern Baptist Convention. The result was the American Baptist Association,* which by 1980 numbered about 200,000. Later, in the 1950s, another conservative group arose from Southern fundamentalism*: the Baptist Bible Fellowship.* By 1980 membership within the Fellowship was an estimated 750,000.

In Northern Baptist circles, theological differences centering in the fundamentalist-modernist* debate generated two conservative bodies: the General Association of Regular Baptist Churches* in 1932 (240,000 in size by 1980) and the Conservative Baptists* in the 1940s (210,000 by 1980). A third conservative body in the North, the Baptist General Conference,* traces its roots to nineteenth-century Swedish immigrants in the Midwest. General Conference churches, counting about 120,000 members in 1980, were scattered across the North and the West.

Twentieth-century theological controversy was also evident among the 220,000 Baptists in Canada.* In 1944 three regional conventions—Atlantic Provinces, Ontario and Quebec, and Western Canada—formed the Baptist Federation of Canada.* Conservatives, however, objected to the presence of theological liberalism in the older conventions and created several separate bodies.

In 1953 the Fellowship of Evangelical Baptist Churches in Canada united most of the conservatives in eastern Canada; then in the 1960s two conservative bodies in western Canada joined the Fellowship. In 1980 these shifts and mergers resulted in 127,000 members within the Baptist Federation and 47,000 within the Fellowship of Evangelical Baptists, the second-largest group in Canada.

See also BAPTIST CHURCHES IN CANADA.

BIBLIOGRAPHY. C. Allen and L. May, eds., *Encyclopedia of Southern Baptists,* 4 vols. (1958-1982); W. H. Brackney, *The Baptists* (1988); W. L. Lumpkin, ed., *Baptist Confessions of Faith* (1963); H. L. McBeth, *The Baptist Heritage: Four Centuries of Baptist Witness* (1986); R. G. Torbet, *A History of the Baptists* (1950); A. W. Wardin, Jr., *Baptist Atlas* (1980); J. K. Zeman, ed., *Baptists in Canada* (1980). B. L. Shelley

Baptist General Conference. A Baptist* denomination.* The Baptist General Conference originated in the great evangelical revival of the nineteenth century. Its specific roots were Swedish Pietism.* Simple biblical faith, dedicated evangelism,* rejection of formalism and a demand for a regenerate clergy were the trademarks of the Baptists in the Scandinavian homeland.

The first Swedish Baptist congregation in America was founded in 1852 at Rock Island, Illinois, by Anders Wiberg and Gustaf Palmquist. Known for their energetic witness to newly arrived Scandinavian immigrants, by 1871 the Swedish Baptists had grown to 1,500 members, in congregations dispersed over seven states. The church grew with the influx of Swedish immigrants in the late nineteenth century, and by 1902 there were 22,000 members in 324 churches. A Canadian branch was established at Winnipeg in 1894.

The national body became known as the Swedish Baptist General Conference in 1879. Prior to World War 2* the Conference maintained its ethnic* identity, though English gradually replaced Swedish in worship* services. In 1940 the denomination's official organ, *Nya Wecko-Posten,* was renamed *The Standard.* In 1945 the Conference, by then numbering 40,000 adherents and more comfortable with its American identity, dropped *Swedish* from its title.

The Conference operates Bethel Seminary and Bethel College in St. Paul, Minnesota, originally founded in Chicago during the late nineteenth century by pastor John Alexis Edgren. The college, established as a four-year liberal arts college in 1947, began as a Bible and missionary school in 1922. The Conference operates a foreign missions program reaching Asia, Africa and Latin America. In 1980 there were 135,000 members in 779 churches.

BIBLIOGRAPHY. N. Magnuson, *How We Grew: Highlights of the First Hundred Years of Conference History* (1988); A. Olson, *Seventy-Five Years: A History of Bethel Theological Seminary* (1946).

J. E. Johnson

Baptist Mid-Missions. An independent Baptist* foreign missionary* agency. The founder of Baptist Mid-Missions, William C. Haas, first sailed to Africa in late 1911 under the Africa Inland Mission,* with the primary goal of reaching the Zande tribe in the Belgian Congo. Following some exceptional achievements in reducing tribal languages to writing, Haas joined Ralph Buxton and C. T. Studd, English missionaries who were establishing the Heart of Africa Mission (later the Worldwide Evangelization Crusade). After several years of linguistic and evangelistic ministry, Haas returned to the U.S. to build support for a new mission to French Equatorial Africa. On October 15, 1920, the General Council of Cooperating Baptist Missions of North America was organized at Elyria, Ohio. The new missions sent six missionaries to Africa on a project known as the Mid-Africa Mission. Haas died in 1924 and was buried in Africa.

In addition to an expanding work in Africa, the agency eventually opened new stations in Central and South America, the Caribbean, Europe, Asia, Australia and the Pacific islands. The name Baptist Mid-Missions replaced its unwieldy predecessor in 1953. The mission emphasizes evangelism, church planting, theological education, medicine and Bible translation. Since 1983 C. Raymond Buck has served as mission president and supervises over 600 full-time missionaries in over thirty countries and a total annual income of almost $17 million. The home office is in Cleveland, Ohio, and the mission is affiliated with the Fellowship of Missions, a group of eleven mission societies in the fundamentalist*/separatist* tradition, also based in Cleveland.

J. A. Patterson

Baptist World Alliance. An international fellowship* of Baptist* organizations. The Alliance, the first international Baptist organization of its type, was formed in 1905 at a meeting in Exeter Hall, London. The primary purposes of the Alliance include: safeguarding and maintaining religious liberty* everywhere; propagating Baptist principles and tenets of faith; arranging and conducting preaching* missions throughout the world; gathering and disseminating Baptist news; and coordinating relief efforts as occasions arise. Between 1905 and 1985 the Baptist World Alliance has held fifteen world congresses, usually at five-year intervals.

At present the Baptist World Alliance consists of 136 bodies in 94 nations and dependencies. This includes about 126,000 churches with a total membership of over 32 million. Recently the Alliance has been engaged in projects such as providing Bibles and commentaries in translation to the Soviet Union, providing relief and development assistance to Nicaragua, Argentina, Bangladesh, Lebanon and Zaire, and conducting friendship tours to the Soviet Union and China. Dr. Gerhard Class was the general secretary of the Baptist World Alliance until his death in March 1988.

Two historic Baptist commitments have received the attention of the Baptist World Alliance: religious liberty and congregational autonomy. The preamble of their Constitution stated that the Alliance may "in no way interfere with the independence of the churches or assume the administrative functions of existing organizations."

The major periodical of the Alliance is *The Baptist World,* and its headquarters are in McLean, Virginia. Until 1941 it was located at the Baptist Church House in London, when for safety reasons it was moved to Washington, D.C.

BIBLIOGRAPHY. F. T. Lord, *Baptist World Fellowship* (1955); J. Nordenhaug et al., *Baptists of the World, 1950-1970* (1970); W. B. Shurden, ed., *The Life of Baptists in the Life of the World* (1985).

G. W. Carlson

Baptistery (also Baptistry). A term referring to the place of baptism.* The changing practices concerning baptism in church history have been reflected in the various architectural* settings for the rite. The term carries at least three distinct meanings: (1) a round or polygonal building used for baptismal services in the early and medieval church; (2) an area in a church building containing a font for use in baptism; and (3) a large tank, often below floor level, utilized by churches practicing immersion as the mode of baptism. In churches within the Baptist tradition,* the baptistery is located behind the chancel and may be entered by steps descending into the water on either side. Catholic* churches have generally placed the baptistery in a location apart from the main sanctuary, and other denominations* have adopted a variety of locations, each seeking to enhance the meaning of the rite by its architectural setting.

See also BAPTISM, BAPTISMAL FONT.

BIBLIOGRAPHY. K. F. Brown, *Baptism through the Centuries* (1965); J. G. Davies, *The Architectural Setting of Baptism* (1962).

M. G. Bell

Baptistry. *See* Baptistery.

Baptists in Canada. There are about 2,000 Baptist* congregations in Canada, with a total membership of around 230,000. The 1981 Census of Canada reported 696,850 persons as Baptist, including children and adherents.

In contrast to the U.S., Baptists in Canada, with the exception of the provinces of Nova Scotia and New Brunswick, are a small minority (2.9 per cent of the population), and yet the largest evangelical* denomination* in Canada. They share their distinctive beliefs and practices with Baptists in the U.S.,* but congregations and denominational bodies differ among themselves in interpreting particular doctrines and in their attitudes to such issues as ecumenical* cooperation and moral standards. Regional loyalties, conflicting American and British influences, diverse ethnic origins and the fundamentalist-modernist controversy* of the 1920s have contributed to dividing Canadian Baptists into two larger and several smaller bodies.

Canadian Baptist Federation. This is the largest body (1,125 churches, 135,000 members) and represents the mainstream Baptist tradition. Organized in 1944 as the Baptist Federation of Canada (BFC) and renamed CBF in 1983, it coordinates programs in national, international and interdenominational spheres but also provides opportunities for consultation and cooperation in other areas of work. Regionalism has prevented the CBF from functioning as a national denomination. Most programs are administered by each of the four constituent bodies: The United Baptist Convention of the Atlantic Provinces (UBCAP; organized 1906; 550 churches; 67,000 members); Baptist Convention of Ontario and Quebec (BCOQ; organized 1888; 390 churches; 47,000 members); Baptist Union of Western Canada (BUWC; organized 1909; 160 churches; 21,000 members) and Union of French Baptist Churches (UFBC; organized 1969; 25 churches; 1,000 members).

The Baptist movement in the Maritimes began in the 1760s under the influence of New Light* and Baptist preachers* from New England. Repeated revivals* produced church growth unmatched elsewhere in Canada. In Ontario and English-speaking Quebec, Baptists suffered from conflicting influences brought by ministers* and immigrants from the U. S. (predominantly Regular Baptists* practicing closed Communion), England (open Communion), Scotland (revivalist tradition) and later by immigrants from elsewhere. The earlier tensions were overcome when the Baptist Convention of Ontario and Quebec was formed in 1888, only to reappear during the fundamentalist-modernist controversy in the 1920s (*see* Shields). Black Baptists, many of whom originally were slaves who escaped from the U.S., have maintained a distinct piety* and separate organizations in the Maritimes (African Association) and Ontario (Amherstburg Association).

Baptists have pioneered in Protestant mission to French Canadians in Quebec since the 1830s (Grande Ligne Society, 1855), but persecution and lack of resources hindered growth until the "quiet revolution" in French Canada during the 1970s. Baptist missionaries* arrived late in the prairies (Winnipeg, 1875) and in British Columbia (Victoria, 1876). Denominational growth was further impeded by schism in the 1920s and economic factors during the depression* of the 1930s.

Fellowship of Evangelical Baptist Churches in Canada. The second-largest group (an estimated 475 churches and 56,000 members), was formed in 1953 through the merger of two groups which appeared in Central and Western Canada (*see* T. T. Shields) after the fundamentalist-modernist controversy: The Union of Regular Baptist Churches of Ontario and Quebec (1927) and Fellowship of Independent Baptist Churches of Canada (1933). In the 1960s, Regular Baptist churches in Western Canada joined the FEBC. In recent years, a few churches have been planted in the Atlantic provinces. About ten churches in Ontario, led by Jarvis Street Baptist Church in Toronto, continue a separate Association of Regular Baptist Churches (Canada).

Ethnic Baptist Churches. The multiracial and multicultural mosaic of Canadian society has been mirrored in a variety of ethnic Baptist churches for more than a century. German-speaking and Swedish-speaking congregations appeared in Central and Western Canada in the 1850s and 1880s respectively. Originally, they maintained dual affiliation with one of the Canadian conventions and with ethnic conferences in the U.S. Several factors led to severance of links with the Baptist Convention of Ontario and Quebec and the Baptist Union of Western Canada in the 1930s. Churches in both ethnic groups are now English-speaking, and the two conferences have formalized their independent status in Canada: Baptist General Conference of Canada* (BGC; originally Swedish; 75 churches; 6,000 members) and North American Baptist Conference in Canada* (NABC; originally German; 120 churches; 18,000 members). Many other ethnic churches appear and disappear, reflecting the changing patterns of Canadian immigration. Through the years, churches related

[115]

to the Canadian Baptist Federation have assisted work among immigrants in more than thirty languages. Of all Baptist churches in Canada, the Chinese are now the fastest growing. Oddly enough, Baptists have largely ignored native Indians and Eskimos.

Other Baptist Bodies. Other Baptist groups include the Canadian Convention of Southern Baptists (CCSB; 80 churches; 5,000 members) which was organized in 1985 after three decades of slow invasion of Western and Central Canada by missionaries sent by churches affiliated with the Southern Baptist Convention* in the U.S. Other Baptist bodies in the United States, such as Bible Baptists and Seventh-Day Baptists,* have also expanded their work into Canada in recent years. In the Maritimes the Alliance of Reformed Baptist Churches, founded in 1888 as part of the Holiness Movement,* united with the Wesleyan Methodist Church in 1966 and then became part of the Wesleyan Church* in a subsequent merger with the Pilgrim Holiness Church in 1968. The Primitive* Baptist Conference of New Brunswick emerged in the 1870s and recently linked up with the Association of Free Will Baptists* in the U.S.

Canadian Baptists remain divided over relations with cooperative Baptist and ecumenical organizations. Only the Canadian Baptist Federation and North American Baptist Conference belong to the Baptist World Alliance.* The conventions and unions which form the Canadian Baptist Federation were among the founding bodies of the Canadian Council of Churches* in 1944. Since 1980 only the Baptist Convention of Ontario and Quebec retains membership in the Canadian Council of Churches while the Baptist Union of Western Canada and the Baptist General Conference joined the Evangelical Fellowship of Canada.* No Canadian Baptist body has ever held membership in the World Council of Churches.*

In the nineteenth century, Canadian Baptists made major contributions to the clarification of church-state relations *(See* Clergy Reserves) and to higher education.* Even though they relinquished control of three universities (Acadia, McMaster and Brandon), the various conventions and conferences now operate two colleges, eleven seminaries* and several Bible schools* and lay training centers.

With contrasting political convictions, several Baptists have given leadership in federal and provincial governments: prime ministers Alexander MacKenzie (1822-1892), Charles Tupper (1821-1915) and John George Diefenbaker*; premiers of Alberta, William Aberhart* and Ernest Charles Manning*, and of Saskatchewan, Thomas Clement Douglas.*

See also BAPTIST CHURCHES IN THE U.S.A.

BIBLIOGRAPHY. P. G. A. Griffin-Allwood, G. A. Rawlyk and J. K. Zeman, *Baptists in Canada 1760-1990: A Bibliography of Selected Printed Resources in English* (1989); H. A. Renfree, *Heritage and Horizon: The Baptist Story in Canada* (1988).

J. K. Zeman

Barber, Virgil Horace (1782-1847). Roman Catholic* convert, missionary* and educator. Born in Simsbury, Connecticut, Barber was educated at the nearby Episcopal* academy in Cheshire and at Dartmouth College.* After teaching briefly at the Cheshire academy, he took holy orders* in the Episcopal Church and was rector* of St. John's Church, Waterbury, Connecticut, from 1807 to 1814. He then moved to Fairfield, New York, where he became rector* of Trinity Church and principal of the Episcopal academy. There Barber began to have doubts about the claims of the Episcopal Church, and eventually he and his family decided to enter the Catholic Church; they were received into the Church in 1816. Several other relatives also converted afterwards, among them his father, who was the Episcopal rector in Claremont, New Hampshire.

In 1817, on receiving permission to enter the religious life, he joined the Jesuits* at Georgetown and his wife entered the Visitandine convent there. In 1822 he was ordained* priest* and sent as a missionary to Claremont, New Hampshire, where he founded the first Roman Catholic parish and school in that region. After mission* work among the Native Americans in Maine, he was recalled to the Georgetown area in 1830. There he spent the rest of his life chiefly in educational pursuits, acting for a time as professor of Scripture* at Georgetown college. He lived to see all five of his children prominent members of religious societies.

BIBLIOGRAPHY. L. Gibson, *Some Anglo-American Converts to Catholicism Prior to 1829* (1943); H. Mitchell, "Virgil Horace Barber," *Woodstock Letters* 79 (1950):297-334.   C. R. Henery

Barclay, Robert (1648-1690). Quaker* theologian* and colonial governor. Heir of an adventurous Scottish family, Robert Barclay inherited the family estate of Ury, studied Catholicism* under an uncle in Paris and Presbyterian* doctrine at Aberdeen University. At Aberdeen he became a friend of George Keith.* In 1667, following his father's example, he became a Quaker. From a series of systematic summaries and *A Catechism* (1673) of Quaker beliefs, he evolved *An Apology for the True Christian Divinity* in Latin (1675) and English (1678), accepted as the authoritative statement of Quaker doctrines. His own experience is laid out in his central sections on "Worship" and "Ministry": these must begin from God's own Spirit or Light working within each worshiper, stilling human self-will and increasingly giving truth and power. Barclay defended the universal and saving nature of this Light and the possibility of perfect obedience to it. It is "the real presence of Christ" making outward sacraments* unnecessary. In 1677 Barclay traveled with George Fox*, William Penn* and George Keith* in Germany. Through Penn he became organizer and absentee governor of the Scottish committee that bought and settled East New Jersey as a colony, but few Quakers settled there.

BIBLIOGRAPHY. E. E. Trueblood, *Robert Barclay* (1968). H. S. Barbour

Barnes, Albert (1798-1870). New School* Presbyterian* minister.* Born in Rome, New York, Barnes graduated from Hamilton College, Clinton, New York, (1820) and Princeton Seminary* (1824) and was ordained* as a Presbyterian minister at Morristown, New Jersey (1825). During his early years in the ministry Barnes shaped a theology* compatible with his revivalist* preaching* in the New School tradition. In a famous sermon entitled "The Way of Salvation" (1829), Barnes contradicted several Old Calvinist doctrines, particularly the doctrine of original sin,* and drew the fire of conservative Presbyterians who questioned his doctrinal soundness. When the First Presbyterian Church, Philadelphia, called Barnes as pastor in 1830, charges were brought against him in the Philadelphia Presbytery,* but they were ultimately adjudicated by the General Assembly* of 1831, which merely censured him for "unguarded and objectionable passages."

In 1835 it was alleged in Second Philadelphia Presbytery that his *Notes on Romans* departed from the traditional interpretation of the Westminster Confession of Faith* on essential doctrines such as original sin,* justification* by faith, the imputation of the guilt of Adam and the righteousness of Christ. This case, too, was appealed to the Assembly, which acquitted Barnes and restored him to his pastorate. Again the Old School* party, which upheld the traditional interpretation of the disputed doctrines, asserted itself and eventually brought about a division of the Presbyterian Church into Old School and New School denominations* (1837).

Barnes supported revivalism and social reform, including the campaign against slavery, and wrote popular biblical commentaries, including the eleven-volume *Notes, Explanatory and Practical on the New Testament* and his commentaries on four Old Testament books. His other publications included his own autobiography and significant books on revivals, the anti-slavery issue, the atonement,* Christian evidences and St. Paul's life. He provided leadership to New School Presbyterianism, while he continued to serve his Philadelphia congregation until his retirement (1868). He lived to see the reunion of the two denominations in the North (1869-1870).

BIBLIOGRAPHY. S. J. Baird, *History of the New School* (1868); A. Barnes, *Life at Three-Score and Ten* (1871); *DAB* I; *DARB;* G. Junkin, *The Vindication, Containing a History of the Trial of the Rev. Albert Barnes* (1836): G. M. Marsden, *The Evangelical Mind and the New School Presbyterian Experience* (1970); *NCAB* 7. A. H. Freundt

Barnhouse, Donald Grey (1895-1960). Presbyterian* fundamentalist* pastor,* Bible* expositor* and journalist. Born in Watsonville, California, to devout Methodist* parents, Barnhouse enrolled at age seventeen in the Bible Institute of Los Angeles (BIOLA), where he learned dispensational* theology* under Reuben A. Torrey.* After a brief sojourn at the University of Chicago,* Barnhouse entered Princeton Theological Seminary* in 1915, but left in 1917 to join the Army Signal Corps. Spending six years in Europe after the war, Barnhouse served the Belgian Gospel Mission in Brussels (1919-1921) and then pastored two Reformed* churches in the French Alps. He married missionary Ruth Tiffany in 1922. Barnhouse returned to the U.S. in 1925 and settled in Philadelphia, where he took graduate courses at the University of Pennsylvania and pastored the Grace Presbyterian Church.

Barnhouse became the pastor of Tenth Presbyterian Church in 1927 and served there until his death. From that base he began a network radio program in 1928; a monthly magazine, *Revelation,* in 1931 (renamed *Eternity* in 1950); and a circuit of weekly Bible classes. Eventually his tours took him all over the world. Barnhouse published a dozen volumes during his life and produced other material that was posthumously made into books and audiotapes.

In doctrine* and temperament, Barnhouse was a fundamentalist, but he never fully conformed to the party line. He did not leave the Presbyterian Church when many of his allies did, and he criticized them as freely as he did the liberals.* His

[117]

famous resolution in 1953 to be more loving indicated some mellowing, but it was consistent with his earlier independent-mindedness. Accused of treason by fundamentalists, distrusted by liberals and personally distant from other conservatives, Barnhouse was still, in his own way, a leader of the new evangelical* movement.

BIBLIOGRAPHY. C. A. Russell, "Donald Grey Barnhouse: Fundamentalist Who Changed," *JPH* 59 (1981):33-57; M. N. Barnhouse, *That Man Barnhouse* (1983).   J. A. Carpenter

Barth, Karl (1886-1968). Swiss Reformed* theologian.* The son of a Reformed minister* and professor, Barth attended Berne, Berlin, Tübingen and Marburg universities, studying under Adolf Harnack (1851-1930), Wilhelm Herrmann (1846-1922) and other leading European theologians of his day. In his earlier years, while serving as a village pastor in Safenwil, Switzerland (1911-1921), Barth became convinced of the poverty of his own liberal* theology* and so began a gradual reorientation that would finally lead him to a renewed theological quest in dialog with Scripture* and Protestant* orthodoxy.* From the pastorate Barth's career was to take him through a series of academic posts at Göttingen (1921-1925), Munster (1925-1930) and Bonn 1930-1935), Germany, and finally to Basel, Switzerland (1935-1962). Throughout these years he would set forth the so-called "Barthian theology" *(See* Neo-orthodoxy) that would have such an impact on Western theology of the mid-twentieth century.

Barth's commentary *The Epistle to the Romans* (1919; rev. ed. 1922) was said to have fallen "like a bomb on the playground of the theologians." Yet it was not translated into English until 1935. The first English translation of Barth's writings was *The Word of God and The Word of Man* in 1928. This volume was widely read and reviewed, but it was not until 1933 that further Barth volumes were translated into English.

American liberal theologians decisively rejected the early Barth. They saw his emphasis on the "infinite qualitative distinction" between God and humanity as making God completely inaccessible and communication about God impossible. On the other hand, American conservative theologians feared Barth was producing a "new modernism"* since he was building his theology on something other than rational foundations.

By the later 1930s, however, American theologians such as Reinhold Niebuhr* (who later disagreed with Barth), Edwin Lewis* and Elmer Homrighausen* began to show the influence of

Barth in the theologies they produced. This led to the ascendency of Barth's thought in the 1940s and 1950s. But it was not until 1956 that translations of his developing multi-volumed *Church Dogmatics* (1932-1968; ET 1936-1969) began to appear regularly in English. Later, English editions would appear soon after the German editions, giving English readers more immediate access to Barth's theology. By contrast, the writings of Emil Brunner,* Barth's early theological companion, appeared in English earlier and more frequently than Barth's.

Karl Barth's influence in America has extended in a number of directions. His impact on American Protestantism has been strongest in the major Presbyterian* traditions. Other denominations* have been affected to lesser degrees. But as American ministers read the translated works of Europeans such as Paul Tournier or Jacques Ellul, they would meet some of Barth's views filtered through these writers.

Barth has also had an ongoing impact in American evangelicalism.* This is seen in the works of Donald Bloesch and Bernard Ramm and marks a significant change from earlier appraisals of Barth by writers such as Cornelius Van Til* and Charles Ryrie, who from different perspectives rejected Barth's theology as a deviation from orthodoxy. The Dutch theologian G. C. Berkouwer, whose writings have been influential among Reformed evangelical theologians in America, while critical of aspects of Barth's thought, has long been in dialog with it.

Though many professional theologians have turned away from Barth, his influence lives in America through those who have continued to do theology in ways similar to what Barth advocated. These include Europeans such as Hendrikus Berkhof, Thomas Torrance and Otto Weber, as well as those who work in America such as Arthur Cochrane and Paul Lehmann. Others such as Robert McAfee Brown, Harvey Cox and Langdon Gilkey* also recognize the impact of Barth on their thinking.

A steady stream of literature on Barth's thought is produced in America, as well as English translations of European studies of Barth. The Karl Barth Society of North America continues to hold both national and regional meetings. While Barth's theology as a whole may not enjoy a full-scale revival in America, his influence continues in indirect, diffuse and distilled forms.

BIBLIOGRAPHY. G. C. Bolich, *Karl Barth and Evangelicalism* (1980); E. Busch, *Karl Barth* (1976); D. K. McKim, ed., *How Karl Barth Changed*

My Mind (1986); B. Ramm, *After Fundamentalism* (1984); D. N. Voskuil, "America Encounters Karl Barth, 1919-1939," *FH* 12 (1980):61-74.

D. K. McKim

Bartleman, Frank (1871-1936). Pentecostal* evangelist* and author. Born near Carversville, Pennsylvania, Bartleman's father was a Roman Catholic* and his mother a Quaker.* Leaving home at the age of seventeen, Bartleman worked in Philadelphia, where he attended Russell H. Conwell's* Grace Baptist Church, was converted* on October 15, 1893, and baptized* by Conwell. Feeling called to the ministry during the summer of 1894, he attended Conwell's Temple College and later Moody Bible Institute.*

Over the next several years, he ministered in Holiness* settings, including The Salvation Army,* Wesleyan Methodists* and the Pillar of Fire. Bartleman married Anna Ladd in 1900, and the family moved in 1903 to Los Angeles where they suffered the loss of their first child. Deeply affected by this event, Bartleman recommitted himself to ministry, and by 1906 he was in contact with William J. Seymour,* who would soon be leading the Azusa Street Revival.* Bartleman became convinced of the Pentecostal message and soon opened his own mission in Los Angeles. But he was soon launched on what would be a lifelong career of itinerant ministry that would take him many times around the country and once around the world (1910-1911).

A prolific author, he is said to have written over 500 articles, 100 tracts* and six books—several of which described his own experiences and ministry. A voice for unity among Pentecostals and a critic of sectarianism, he was also a pacifist and a strong advocate for the separation of church and state.* His book *How Pentecost Came to Los Angeles* (1925) is an important historical resource for understanding the Azusa Street Revival.

BIBLIOGRAPHY. C. M. Robeck, Jr., "The Writings and Thought of Frank Bartleman," in *Witness to Pentecost: The Life of Frank Bartleman* (1985); V. Synan, "Frank Bartleman and Azusa Street," in F. Bartleman, *Azusa Street* (1980).

D. G. Reid

Barton, Bruce Fairfield (1886-1967). Journalist, advertising executive and popular religious author. Barton was born into a Congregationalist* minister's home and grew up near Chicago. At Amherst College he was a successful leader and student. From 1910 to 1920 he worked for such journals as *Home Herald, The Continent, Collier's*

Weekly and *Every Week.* He also began to publish articles and editorials in such popular magazines as *Red Book* and *American Magazine.* Crisp, anecdotal and inspirational, these articles were later reprinted in a series of books, among them *More Power to You* (1917) and *Better Days* (1924). Barton believed that through hard work, creativity, independence and humility one could become successful, like the many businessmen he knew and esteemed. He also believed that faith and success were not enemies but allies. To prove his point he ventured into the world of theology.*

There he discovered that the typical portrait of Jesus was hopelessly outdated and irrelevant to modern life. He attempted to alter that portrait in his *The Man Nobody Knows,* a best seller about Jesus (1925), *The Book Nobody Knows* (1926) and *He Upset the World,* a biography of the apostle Paul (1931). Ignoring the fundamentalist-modernist controversy,* Barton put the accent on a human Christ whose boundless energy, personal magnetism, physical strength and simple teachings revealed who God was and showed how people could live. Barton's religion was practical and positive.

In 1918 Barton helped to start the advertising firm of BBDO. Barton himself was a master at writing copy. One of his phrases—"A man may be down but he's never out"—eventually became the slogan for The Salvation Army.* In 1937 he won a seat in Congress, representing a district in New York City. He ran for the U.S. Senate in 1940 on a Republican ticket but lost. He returned to advertising, where he remained until he suffered a stroke in 1957.

BIBLIOGRAPHY. *DAB* 8; L. P. Ribuffo, "Jesus Christ as Business Statesman: Bruce Barton and the Selling of Corporate Capitalism," *AQ* 33 (1981): 206-231; W. Susman, "Piety, Profits and Play: The 1920's," in *Men, Women and Issues in American History* (1980).

G. L. Sittser

Barton, Clarissa ("Clara") Harlowe (1821-1912). Founder of the American Red Cross. Born in North Oxford, Massachusetts, Barton was raised in a universalist* environment and devoted her life to public service. Nevertheless, her career seems to have arisen from humanitarian concern rather than her religious faith. She began her career as a schoolteacher in Massachusetts and in New Jersey, but it was her service as a nurse during the Civil War* that led to her enduring fame. Her relief efforts started when she solicited supplies for some soldiers whose train had been mobbed en route to Washington. Gradually, she began to consider direct aid to soldiers on the battle lines, and her timely assistance during the Second Battle of Bull Run led to an army official calling her an "Angel of the Battlefield." Barton fed the wounded, provided surgeons with medical supplies and coordinated the dispensation of provisions to the forces. After the War, she assisted in locating and identifying missing soldiers.

Barton traveled to Europe in 1869 in order to recover from physical ailments, and while touring the Continent she met Dr. Louis Appia, a member of the International Committee of the Red Cross. During the Franco-Prussian War, Barton saw her first service under the Red Cross badge and recognized its usefulness. By 1878 she had begun to promote the ratification of the Treaty of Geneva that had created this agency. Recognizing that the American public did not expect to be engaged in another war, Barton emphasized the peacetime uses of the organization. In 1881, she formed the American Association of the Red Cross, and the agency first provided disaster relief in that year. Barton continued to supervise aid for victims of floods, fires, hurricanes, epidemics and the Spanish-American War* until her retirement in 1905.

BIBLIOGRAPHY. *DAB* I; *DARB*; *NAW* 1; *NCAB* 15; I. Ross, *Angel of the Battlefield: The Life of Clara Barton* (1956).   K. E. Guenther

Bashford, James Whitford (1849-1919). Methodist* pastor,* educator, bishop* in China. Born in Fayette, Wisconsin, Bashford graduated from Boston University School of Theology in 1875 and served pastorates in Massachusetts, Maine and New York. In 1889 he was called to be president of Ohio Wesleyan University, and in 1904 he was elected bishop of the Methodist Episcopal Church* and assigned to China. He was greatly interested in united Christian work and helped establish Yenching University at Peking and the China Medical Board which sponsored Peking Union Medical College. In 1912 he urged President Taft to recognize the new Chinese Republic, and in 1915 appealed to the U.S. Government to protect China's territorial integrity. He was author of 200 pamphlets and articles, two books on China (1908 and 1916), *Wesley and Goethe* (1902) and *The Oregon Mission* (1918).

BIBLIOGRAPHY. *DAB* I; G. R. Grose, *James W. Bashford, Pastor, Educator, Bishop* (1922).

D. M. Stowe

Bashir, Antony (1898-1966). Antiochian Orthodox* archbishop* of New York. The Lebanese-born Bashir had achieved renown as a writer and translator of Arabic literature before coming to America in 1922 as his patriarch's representative to the General Convention of the Episcopal Church. Following ordination* to the priesthood* that year, he served a variety of parishes* and as a roving missionary* across the Midwest while continuing to acquaint the Arab world with Western thought, and vice versa, through translations.

In 1936 Bashir was consecrated* bishop* in New York by one faction of Russian hierarchs the same day as a rival candidate, Samuel David, was elevated in Toledo. Thus conceived in conflict, Bashir's episcopacy saw the final separation of the Syrians from the Russian jurisdiction. Though supported by his patriarch, Bashir had to overcome tragic ethnic division, doing so chiefly through energy and administrative prowess. He created a youth-oriented Society of Orthodox Youth Organizations (SOYO); shifted the archdiocesan magazine, the *Word,* to an English format; and instituted a Western Rite to accommodate converts.

Bashir had a keen vision of what American Orthodoxy as a whole ought to be and pushed to achieve it. He was an early advocate in his tradition of the use of English and of comprehensive religious-education programs and was the inspirational force behind the formation in 1938 of the Federation of Primary Jurisdictions of the Orthodox Greek Catholic Churches in America, precursor to the Standing Conference of Orthodox Bishops in the Americas,* which latter body he served as vice president from its formation in 1960 until his death.   P. D. Garrett

Bauman, Louis Sylvester (1875-1950). Brethren pastor, evangelist, conference speaker. Born in Nora Springs, Iowa, into a German Baptist* (Dunker) family, Bauman was influenced by his father who was a leader of the Progressive Brethren Movement in the 1880s. He was ordained* without college or seminary education and pastored at Morrill, Kansas (1894-1895); Auburn and Cornell, Illinois (1895-1897); Mexico and Roann, Indiana (1897-1900); Philadelphia, Pennsylvania (1900-1908); Long Beach, California (1913-1948); and Washington, D.C. (1948-1950).

At Philadelphia he became devoted to the cause of world missions,* serving as secretary of the Brethren Foreign Missionary Society (1906-1945) and as field representative (1908-1912). His evangelistic services in Long Beach, California, gave birth to a new church which called him as pastor and grew to be the largest in the denomination. His desire for a Brethren seminary saw fruit as Ashland College (Ohio), but when his close friend Alva J. McClain* was dismissed as dean, Bauman supported the establishment of Grace Theological Seminary (1937). An emphasis on eschatological preaching* and writing led to articles in *The Sunday School Times, The King's Business* and two books: *Light on Bible Prophecy* (1940) and *Russian Events in the Light of Bible Prophecy* (1942).

BIBLIOGRAPHY. *The Brethren Missionary Herald* 13:1 (January 6, 1951); *BE* I.   R. T. Clutter

Bäumler, Joseph Michael. *See* BIMELER, JOSEPH MICHAEL.

Bay Psalm Book. First American psalter. *The Whole Booke of Psalmes* was produced by the Massachusetts Bay clergy in 1636-1640 (the principal editors being Richard Mather,* Thomas Welde and John Eliot*), and was published by Stephen Daye at Cambridge, Massachusetts, in 1640. It was the first book printed in English in North America. Though several Reformed* psalters were available to the New English settlers, including metered versions of the Psalms by Stenhold and Hopkins (1562) and Henry Ainsworth (1612), these were deemed by the Massachusetts Bay ministry to be either too closely associated with separatism* (as was the Ainsworth version, which continued in use in the Plymouth church until 1692), or too shallowly rooted in the new Hebrew scholarship.

The new psalter incorporated the advances in scriptural scholarship included in the Bible* of 1611, and was quickly adopted by nearly every church in Massachusetts Bay, hence the sobriquet Bay Psalm Book. In 1651 it was revised and enlarged as *The Psalms Hymns and Spiritual Songs of the Old and New Testament,* and in this form reached twenty-seven editions, the last printed at Boston in 1762. The original and revised psalters were also popular in England and ran through twenty editions, the last dated 1754. Beginning with the 1750s the *Bay Psalm Book* gradually gave way to the newer versions of Tate and Brady, and of Isaac Watts.

BIBLIOGRAPHY. *The Bay Psalm Book,* intro. W. Eames (1973); Z. Haraszti, *The Enigma of the Bay Psalm Book* (1956).   G. F. Moran

Bayley, James Roosevelt (1814-1877). Catholic* Archbishop* of Baltimore. Born at Rye, New York, the son of Guy Carleton and Grace Roosevelt Bayley and a nephew of Elizabeth Ann Bayley Seton,* Bayley first contemplated a naval career and was educated at Amherst College in Massachusetts. But later he decided to study for priesthood*

in the Episcopal Church* and pursued studies at Trinity College in Hartford, Connecticut. He was ordained* in 1840 and was appointed the head of St. James Church in Harlem.

After reading an early biography of his aunt, Elizabeth Ann Seton, he became interested in Catholicism. He moved to Rome in 1841 and was received into the Church in 1842. He pursued theological studies at St. Sulpice in Paris and was ordained a Roman Catholic priest on March 2, 1844, by Bishop John Hughes* of New York. Appointed to the faculty of St. John's College in Fordham, he subsequently served as vice president and president. He also served Bishop Hughes as secretary, chancellor and personal theologian.* On October 30, 1853, he was consecrated* bishop* of the newly created diocese* of Newark, New Jersey, by Archbishop Gaetano Bedini. In Newark he established Seton Hall College and Immaculate Conception Seminary and recruited priests and religious to serve in the rapidly growing diocese. He attended the Second Plenary Council of Baltimore* and the First Vatican Council.* A man of cultural and literary interests, Bayley was an amateur historian, writing short treatises on the history of Catholicism in New York and on the life of Simon Gabriel Bruté de Remur.*

In 1872 he was chosen to succeed Martin John Spalding* as archbishop of Baltimore. As leader of the premier see of the American Church, Bayley attempted to exercise some influence over Native American affairs and spoke often on the matter of temperance.* He also was instrumental in the establishment of the American College* at Rome. But his poor health consistently sapped his efforts to do much more. In 1877 he requested the services of a coadjutor bishop. Even before the brief arrived appointing Bishop James Gibbons* of Richmond to this post, Bayley had left the country for Vichy, France, to find relief from his illness. He soon returned to the U.S., but died in Newark on October 3, 1877.

BIBLIOGRAPHY. *DAB* I; *DARB; NCAB* 1; *NCE* 2; M. H. Yeager, *The Life of James Roosevelt Bayley: First Bishop of Newark and Eighth Archbishop of Baltimore, 1814-1877* (1947).   S. M. Avella

Beatific Vision. A Roman Catholic* technical term for the vision of God. In Catholic theology it is used to refer to the experience of the saved in heaven,* who will experience a direct vision of God, which is the great joy of heaven. The vision comes not from human effort but as a free gift of a saving God who grants what the theologians call the *lumen gloriae*—the light of glory. In the words of the fifteenth-century Council of Florence, they will clearly see "God, one and three, as God is, though some more perfectly than others, according to the diversity of merits."

The notion of the beatific vision flows out of a long tradition of Catholic reflection on the gospel promise that the pure of heart will see God (Mt 5:8) and on Paul's statements about seeing God "face to face" without any mediation (1 Cor 13:12; 2 Cor 3:12-18). The most powerful meditation on this direct vision of God is to be found in the final canto of Dante's *Paradise,* where the poet gains a momentary glimpse of the majesty of God as a foretaste of his own salvation.*

See also HEAVEN AND HELL.

BIBLIOGRAPHY. R. McBrien, *Catholicism* (1981).

L. S. Cunningham

Beatification. A step toward the canonization of a saint,* by which the pope* permits religious honor to be paid to the deceased, or commands such veneration, but not with regard to the whole Church. In the Roman Catholic Church,* canonization is the final declaration of the pope by which he publicly and solemnly places on the catalog of saints a person who has already been beatified (declared "blessed") and commends him or her to the perpetual veneration and invocation of Christians throughout the universal Church. A canonized saint is one about whom the Church has declared that he or she is irreversibly united with Jesus Christ. The saint's life serves as a model of challenge and hope for the Christian community.

The process of beatification and canonization developed in various stages throughout the Middle Ages. Since then it has been adapted slightly, most recently in reforms following the Second Vatican Council.* It begins with an investigation of a would-be saint initiated by a local bishop, the results of which are then investigated by the Congregation for the Causes of Saints. The process does not usually begin until fifty years after the death of the candidate. In 1988, for example, one North American was canonized (Rose Philippine Duchesne, July 3) and two were beatified (Junipero Serra,* September 25; Mother Katherine Drexel,* November 20).

BIBLIOGRAPHY. L. S. Cunningham, *The Meaning of Saints* (1981).

G. P. Evans

Becker, Peter (1687-1758). First Brethren* minister* in America. A native of Duedelsheim, Germany, Becker and his wife were converts to the Brethren movement in 1714. Along with co-religionists, in 1715 they found asylum among Mennonites* in Krefeld, where Becker worked as a weaver. In 1719 he led a group of Brethren families to Pennsylvania, where Becker settled in Germantown. He helped organize the first Brethren congregation in America in late 1723 and was chosen its leader. Although not a strong preacher, he was admired for his piety, his ardent prayers and his warm pastoral care. When Alexander Mack* (the leading Brethren minister) arrived in Germantown in 1729, Becker deferred to Mack but again led the congregation after 1735, upon Mack's death. For a time Becker employed Johann Konrad Beissel* as an apprentice. Despite Beissel's later defection from the Brethren, he long retained his respect for the Germantown weaver. The only known literary creation by Becker was a lengthy hymn advocating patience.

BIBLIOGRAPHY. D. F. Durnbaugh, ed., *Brethren in Colonial America* (1967); M. G. Brumbaugh, *History of the German Baptist Brethren in Europe and America* (1899).

D. F. Durnbaugh

Beecher, Edward (1803-1895). Congregational* minister,* educator and abolitionist.* Born in East Hampton, Long Island, the son of the famous Congregational preacher Lyman Beecher,* several of Edward's siblings were to make their mark: Catharine Beecher as a champion of female higher education, Henry Ward Beecher* as a popular Brooklyn pulpiteer and Harriet Beecher Stowe* as the author of the influential *Uncle Tom's Cabin* (1852). Edward graduated from Yale* (B.A., 1822), studied divinity* for a time at Andover Seminary* (1822-1824) and tutored for a year at Yale (1825-1826). In 1826 he became pastor of the prominent Park Street Church on Boston Common. Four years later he left the church to become president of Illinois College, a small frontier school in Jacksonville, Illinois. There, with a vision of an expanding Protestant* republic, Beecher was faced with the challenges of building up an institution always in need of outside funding. This responsibility frequently took him to the East Coast, and though he enjoyed some success, the task ill fit his natural inclinations toward preaching and scholarship.

With the slavery controversy gaining momentum, Beecher eventually felt compelled to take a stand against slavery. In 1837, when abolitionist minster Elijah P. Lovejoy's press was threatened at Alton, Beecher helped him stand guard the night before Lovejoy was murdered. Beecher's *Narrative of Riots at Alton* (1838) and his subsequent articles on the nature of "organic sin" helped galvanize the evangelical abolitionist cause. Beecher was active in establishing the state's first anti-slavery society, and the college and its students became the focus of controversy and threats from local residents, many of whom were from the South.

Returning to Boston in 1844, he pastored the Salem Street Church and edited the *Congregationalist* (1849-1853), only to return to Illinois several years later to minister at the Galesburg First Congregational Church (1855-1871). In his later years he returned to Brooklyn, where, with his brother Henry, he was assistant editor of the *Christian Union* (1871-1873) and continued to preach and write.

BIBLIOGRAPHY. *DAB* I; *DARB;* R. Merideth, *The Politics of the Universe: Edward Beecher, Abolition, and Orthodoxy* (1963); *NCAB* 3.

D. G. Reid

Beecher, Henry Ward (1813-1887). Congregational* minister* and religious editor. Born in Litchfield, Connecticut, son of Lyman Beecher,* one of the great church leaders of the pre-Civil War years, Henry became one of the premier preachers in the late nineteenth century. He graduated from Lane Seminary in 1837 and, after some years as an itinerant* preacher in Indiana, accepted a call to become pastor of the newly formed Plymouth Church on Brooklyn Heights, overlooking lower New York City. Under his preaching (1847-1887), Plymouth Church became one of the first large middle-class suburban churches in America. As editor of two well-read journals, the *Independent* (1861-1863) and the *Christian Union* (1870-1881), Beecher's influence reached well beyond the confines of his own church's membership. Yale University* invited him to deliver the prestigious Lyman Beecher Lectures for three years straight (1872-1874).

A proponent of "evangelical liberalism,"* also known as the "new theology," Beecher's preaching demonstrated his belief that theology* should be adapted to meet the needs of contemporary culture. He interpreted the humanity of Jesus as an indicator of what human beings could achieve. Though a social conservative with a tendency to associate poverty with sin,* Beecher preached openly about social issues, including women's rights, civil corruption and slavery. In an effort to guarantee that Kansas would become a free state, he used the pulpit to raise funds to buy rifles ("Beecher's Bibles") for Northern settlers willing to make the move into the territory.

None of these activities raised the level of controversy associated with his later years. During the 1870s, he endured a public scandal after charges of adultery were brought against him. In the early 1880s, his lectures publicizing his adoption of evolution,* denial of eternal punishment and rejection of Calvinism* led to his resignation from the Congregational Association of New York.

BIBLIOGRAPHY. L. Abbott, *Henry Ward Beecher* (1887); *DAB* I; *DARB;* J. A. Elsmere, *Henry Ward Beecher: The Indiana Years, 1837-1847* (1973); W. G. McLoughlin, *The Meaning of Henry Ward Beecher: An Essay on the Shifting Values of Mid-Victorian America* (1970); *NCAB* 3.

M. G. Toulouse

Beecher, Lyman (1775-1863). Congregational* and Presbyterian* clergyman.* A native of Connecticut, Beecher entered Yale College* in 1793. During his sophomore year, Yale President Timothy Dwight* launched a preaching campaign against religious skepticism among Yale undergraduates. As Beecher later recalled in his *Autobiography* (1865), Dwight led a class disputation on the question "Is the Bible* the Word of God?" and soon "all infidelity skulked and hid its head." Beecher himself was "awakened" the following year, during which he began a friendship with Dwight that lasted until the latter's death in 1817.

Although Beecher was licensed a Congregational clergyman in 1798, his first pastoral charge was the East Hampton Presbyterian Church on Long Island. Initially indifferent to his attempts to begin a revival,* his congregation was finally stirred by Beecher's "The Remedy for Duelling," a lament delivered in 1806 after Aaron Burr, Jr., fatally wounded Alexander Hamilton in a duel. A subsequent salary dispute led Beecher to accept an offer of the Congregational Church in Litchfield, Connecticut, in 1810.

During the Litchfield years, Beecher's reputation as a revivalist, social reformer and political observer grew. As a respected member of the Connecticut "Standing Order"—a group of conservative clergymen who jealously defended the privileged position of the Congregational Church against the more democratic* notions of Jeffersonian Baptists*—Beecher fought against the disestablishment of Congregationalism in the state. When Connecticut Congregationalism was finally disestablished in 1817, Beecher lamented the loss, believing that the "injury done to the cause of Christ . . . was irreparable." Soon thereafter, however, Beecher realized that disestablishment was, ironically, a positive development. "It cut the churches loose from dependence on state support. It threw them wholly on their own resources and on God." Beecher left Litchfield in 1826 to assume pastoral duties at the Hanover Street Church in

Boston. From there he launched his strenuous campaign against New England Unitarianism.*

In 1832 Beecher began concurrent terms as president of Lane Seminary and pastor of the Second Presbyterian Church, both in Cincinnati, Ohio. Over the following decade, Beecher developed a keen sense of the power of voluntaryism.* He discovered that the voluntary efforts of Christian groups organized to resist social ills were extremely useful tools for social reform and revivalism. Perhaps more important, this discovery led Beecher to reshape his understanding of the doctrine of sin.* Having been greatly influenced by Charles G. Finney* and Nathaniel W. Taylor,* Beecher adjusted the Calvinism* of the Puritans* and Jonathan Edwards,* a move that stirred resistance among Beecher's ministerial colleagues. In 1835 he was tried for heresy* on the grounds that he had departed from the Westminster Confession of Faith.* Efforts to censure Beecher eventually failed, and he was cleared of the charges.

Beecher retired from his pastoral duties in 1843, and from the presidency of Lane Seminary in 1850. The final years of his life were spent lecturing and writing. He died in 1863, and was survived by ten of his eleven children, several of whom—notably Harriet Beecher Stowe* and Henry Ward Beecher*—played important roles in the continuing development of Christianity in New England.

BIBLIOGRAPHY. L. Beecher, *The Autobiography of Lyman Beecher,* ed. B. M. Cross, 2 vols. (1961); M. Caskey, *Chariot of Fire: Religion and the Beecher Family* (1978); *DAB* I; *DARB;* S. C. Henry, *Unvanquished Puritan: A Portrait of Lyman Beecher* (1973); S. E. Mead, *Nathaniel W. Taylor, 1786-1858: A Connecticut Liberal* (1942); *NCAB* 3.

J. R. Fitzmier

Beecher, Willis Judson (1838-1912). Presbyterian* Old Testament scholar. After attending Auburn Theological Seminary in New York during the Civil War* and being ordained* as a Presbyterian minister* in 1864, Beecher pastored a church in Ovid, New York, until 1865. He then taught at Knox College, Illinois (1865-1869), and pastored a church in Illinois (1869-1871), before returning to Auburn Seminary where he remained until retirement as professor of Hebrew language and literature (1871-1908). Beecher served the wider Christian public as a contributor to the *Sunday School Times.* He delivered the 1902 Stone Lectures at Princeton Theological Seminary* and served as president of the Society of Biblical Literature* in 1904.

As biblical scholar at a time when European higher critical theories were beginning to be influential in America, Beecher perceived his task as primarily apologetic* in nature; not simply defending orthodox* views of the Bible* but articulating them to appeal persuasively to his readers. Concentrating his work on the prophets and prophecy, as well as the reliability of the Bible, in *Reasonable Biblical Criticism* (1911) he acknowledged that "my conclusions are simply the old orthodoxy." In this effort he sided with Benjamin B. Warfield* by defending an evangelical* view of biblical criticism in the pages of the *Presbyterian Review.*

BIBLIOGRAPHY. M. A. Noll, *Between Faith and Criticism* (1986). S. Meier

Beissel, Johann Konrad (1691-1768). Communitarian* leader. A gifted but imperious man in later life, Beissel was orphaned as a child in his native Eberbach/Neckar in the Rhenish Palatinate. As a journeyman baker in Heidelberg, he joined pietist* circles and was persecuted. For a time in Germany he was associated with the Community of True Inspiration, members of which later founded the Amana* Colonies in Iowa. Beissel journeyed to Pennsylvania in 1720, expecting to join the mystic community of the Woman in the Wilderness near Philadelphia. He was disappointed in his aim, for the community had disbanded before his arrival. He then apprenticed himself to the weaver Peter Becker,* a Brethren* minister,* and was later chosen as the leader of a Brethren group in what is now Lancaster County. In 1728 he broke with the Brethren and in 1732 founded the Ephrata Community,* a monastic colony with three sections: sisters, brothers and "householders"—families living in the vicinity who worshiped* at Ephrata.

Under Beissel's direction the Ephrata Community ("Cloister") was noted for its choral singing, illumination of manuscripts (*Fraktur*), economic achievements and philanthropic* outreach. The community's printing press, which began operating in 1745, produced the largest book issued in the American colonies, a German-language martyrology for the Mennonites* (*Martyrer Spiegel,* 1748). At its height Ephrata numbered more than 300 members who were noted for their piety, asceticism, discipline and erudition. The community's celibate orders ceased in 1814, though a small, non-monastic group known as the German Seventh-Day Baptist Church has survived.

Beissel was both revered and reviled for his highhanded leadership and undoubted brilliance during his lifetime, and his character is disputed among historians to the present day. Thomas Mann featured him in his novel *Doktor Faustus* (1947), emphasizing his unusual musical creativity.

See also EPHRATA SOCIETY.

BIBLIOGRAPHY. E. G. Alderfer, *The Ephrata Commune: An Early American Counterculture* (1985); *DAB* I; *DARB;* W. C. Klein, *Johann Conrad Beissel: Mystic and Martinet* (1942); J. E. Ernst, *Ephrata: A History* (1963). D. F. Durnbaugh

Believers' Church. A term referring to those within the Free Church* tradition that regard the church* as the gathering of regenerate, committed disciples, living in the fellowship of mutual correction, support and abiding hope. Membership* is based on a voluntary* and uncoerced confession of Jesus Christ as Lord. Such a confession eliminates citizenship in a certain territory or infant baptism* as rites of entrance into the church. To allow this uncoerced confession, there must be no entanglement between church and state* which would give jurisdiction to one over the other. As committed disciples, members of believers' churches are to manifest a new quality of life brought about by the work of the Holy Spirit and accept the necessity of being reproved or corrected by those within the fellowship. The model of this life is the life of Jesus Christ. Every believer participates in the full ministry of Christ according to the priesthood of the believer,* and is given the task of sharing the gospel with the world while remaining unstained by it. The Word of God is the final authority in all matters of faith and practice.

The term seems to have been first coined by Max Weber in order to make a clearer distinction between groups within the Free Church* tradition. Several study conferences have been held to delineate the marks of the believers' church: the General Conference of the Mennonite Church (August 23-25, 1955), the Louisville Conference (convened by the faculty of the Southern Baptist Theological Seminary, June 26-30, 1967) and the Study Conference of the Believers' Church in Canada (May 15-18, 1978).

BIBLIOGRAPHY. D. F. Durnbaugh, *The Believers' Church* (1968); J. L. Garrett, *The Concept of the Believers' Church* (1969); J. K. Zeman and W. Klaassen, eds, *The Believers' Church in Canada* (1979). J. M. Glass

Bell, Eudorus N. (1866-1923). Assemblies of God* founder. Eudorus and his twin brother, Endorus, were born in Lake Butler, Florida. Determined to become a Baptist* pastor,* Bell worked his way through Stetson University in DeLand,

Florida, and then attended Southern Baptist Theological Seminary in Louisville, Kentucky. Following graduation he spent three years studying at the University of Chicago. After some seventeen years as a Southern Baptist* pastor, primarily in Texas, Bell accepted Pentecostal* teaching. He became editor of a paper, *The Apostolic Faith* (later called *Word and Witness),* and a prominent participant in camp meetings* and conventions throughout Texas, Arkansas and Missouri. In 1913 he signed the original call for the General Council at Hot Springs, Arkansas, which convened in April 1914 and created the Assemblies of God. Bell was twice voted to the denomination's highest executive office, serving as chairman from April through November 1914, and again from 1920 until 1923. He also served as general secretary (1919-1920), as editor (1914-1916) and as an Assemblies of God pastor (1917-1918).

BIBLIOGRAPHY. C. Brumback, *Suddenly . . . from Heaven* (1961); *DARB.* E. L. Blumhofer

Bell, (L)emuel Nelson (1894-1973). Medical missionary* and cofounder of *Christianity Today.** Born in Longsdale, Virginia, Bell was converted at age eleven during an evangelistic* service held at his church. Educated at Washington and Lee College (B.A., 1912) and Medical College of Virginia (M.D., 1916), Bell spent twenty-five years as a Southern Presbyterian medical missionary in Tsing kiang pu (now Huaiyin), China (1916-1941). Forced out of China by the Japanese occupation, he took up a medical practice in Asheville, North Carolina (1941-1956).

A conservative evangelical* and devoted churchman, Bell urged other conservatives within the Presbyterian Church in the U.S. (PCUS) not to withdraw from the denomination.* In 1942 he founded the *Southern Presbyterian Journal* (renamed *The Presbyterian Journal* in 1959) in order to promote evangelical and Reformed* orthodoxy* within the denomination. Bell successfully led the 1950 struggle against the proposed merger of the PCUS with the Northern body, the Presbyterian Church in the U.S.A.,* a move he believed would dilute the more conservative nature of Southern Presbyterians. Bell served on the board of the PCUS Board of World Missions (1948-1966). In 1972 he was elected moderator of the 112th General Assembly* of the Presbyterian Church in the U.S.

In 1956, along with his son-in-law Billy Graham,* Bell founded *Christianity Today.** A member of the journal's board of directors, he managed the production of the periodical, wrote occasional articles on missions in the Far East and wrote a regular column entitled "A Layman and his Faith." Because of its popularity, selected articles were reprinted in the journal for many years after his death. As a missionary, churchman and national leader, Bell made a significant contribution to twentieth-century evangelicalism.

BIBLIOGRAPHY. J. C. Pollock, *A Foreign Devil in China* (1971). L. E. Wilshire

Bellamy, Joseph (1719-1790). Congregational* minister and a leader of the New Divinity Movement.* Born in Cheshire, Connecticut, Bellamy attended Yale College* from which he graduated in 1735, at the age of sixteen. Interested in the reports of revival* emanating from the parsonage in Northampton, Massachusetts, Bellamy went there for theological tutoring by Jonathan Edwards.* Enthused by Edwardsean theology,* Bellamy emerged as one of the most fervent of the New Light* ministers, as supporters of the Great Awakening* came to be known. In the aftermath of the Awakening, Bellamy, like Edwards, began training young men for the ministry of his own parsonage at Bethlehem, Connecticut, where he ministered for over fifty years (1738-1790).

In 1750 Bellamy published *True Religion Delineated,* and in 1758 he published his most famous work, *The Wisdom of God in the Permission of Sin.* Scholars differ sharply on the nature and impact of Bellamy's theology. While there is no doubt that Bellamy sought to be faithful to the experiential Calvinism* of Edwards, there is significant doubt regarding his success, and this doubt applies equally to Samuel Hopkins,* Nathaniel Emmons* and Jonathan Edwards, Jr.,* who, with Bellamy, comprised the New Divinity Movement of the 1760s and 1770s. Among the accusations levelled at the group and specifically at Bellamy is the charge that, in attempting to defend orthodoxy* against the challenge of deistic* humanism, these men adopted the presuppositions of their opponents and thereby hastened the downfall of Calvinistic orthodoxy in New England.

See also NEW ENGLAND THEOLOGY.

BIBLIOGRAPHY. *AAP* 1; G. P. Anderson, *Joseph Bellamy: The Man and His Work* (unpublished Ph.D. dissertation, Boston University, 1971); J. Conforti, *Samuel Hopkins and the New Divinity Movement* (1981); *DAB* I; *DARB;* J. Haroutunian, *Piety Versus Moralism: The Passing of the New England Theology* (1932); B. Kuklick, *Joseph Bellamy: Works,* 2 vols. (1987); *NCAB* 7.

S. T. Logan

Bellavin, Tikhon Basil (1865-1925). Russian

Orthodox* archbishop* in America and later patriarch of Moscow. Born near Pskov, Russia, he studied at the seminary there and at the theological academy of St. Petersburg. He subsequently taught at the seminaries in Pskov, Kholm and Kazan before being consecrated* bishop* of Lublin and auxiliary to the archbishop of Kholm and Warsaw in 1897. He was elected as the bishop of the Aleutians and Alaska* in 1898, making him responsible for the Russian Orthodox mission in North America begun in 1794. With the permission of the Holy Synod of the Church of Russia, he guided the transfer of the diocesan center from San Francisco to New York in 1905. This placed him closer to the parishes* in the East recently established by immigrants from Carpatho-Russia, the Ukraine, the Balkans and the Middle East. After 1904 he was assisted by two auxiliary bishops, Innocent Pustynsky and Raphael Hawaweeny.* Given the title *archbishop* in 1905, Tikhon was an early proponent of Orthodox unity in America and the use of English in liturgical services.

Tikhon was transferred to the See of Iaroslav in 1907 and to Vilno in 1914. He was elected metropolitan of Moscow in 1917, following the abdication of Tzar Nicholas II. The historic church council of 1917-1918 in Moscow restored the office of patriarch, suppressed by Peter the Great in 1700, and by lot elected Tikhon from three candidates on November 5, 1917.

In the face of the Bolshevik revolution and the Russian Civil War, Tikhon excommunciated those whom he termed the "enemies of Christ, open or disguised" on November 1, 1918, although he maintained political neutrality and advised the Russian clergy to do the same. He opposed the "Living Church" movement within Russia and did not sanction the Russian emigres who advocated the restoration of the monarchy. Tikhon was imprisoned from May 1922 to June 1923. He died on April 7, 1925, under mysterious circumstances. While not formally canonized as a saint,* Tikhon is widely venerated as a confessor of the faith.

BIBLIOGRAPHY. C. J. Tarasar and J. H. Erickson, eds., *Orthodox America, 1794-1976* (1975); D. Pospielovsky, *The Russian Church under the Soviet Regime, 1917-1982* (1984).

T. E. FitzGerald

Beman, Nathan S. S. (1785-1871). Presbyterian* minister* and educator. Born at New Lebanon, New York, of German and Scottish ancestry, Beman graduated from Middlebury College, Vermont, in 1807, after which he taught in Lincoln Academy in New Castle, Maine. Ordained* to the Presbyterian ministry in 1810, his subsequent vocational experience was concurrently that of a pastor and teacher. In 1845 he was appointed president of Rensselaer Polytechnical Institute.

Beman's eloquent preaching, his teaching of philosophy and his college administration were all superseded by his influence as national leader of the New School* Presbyterian movement of 1837. His New School evangelistic* and abolition* fervor, as well as his advocacy of the voluntary movement, all placed Beman at the front of the New School. Later he became a signatory of the Auburn Declaration,* a document intending to affirm the New School's genuine Presbyterian heritage.

While Beman's chief contribution was as a New School Presbyterian leader, he gained some prominence by attacking prelacy in the Episcopal Church,* and even primarily in the Roman Catholic Church.*

BIBLIOGRAPHY. *DAB* I; H. B. Nason, *Biographical Records of the Officers and Graduates of the Rensselaer Polytechnical Institute* (1887); *Proceedings of the Centennial Anniversary of the First Presbyterian Church, Troy* (1891).

J. H. Hall

Bender, Harold Stauffer (1897-1962). Mennonite* historian, educator and churchman. Born in Elkhart, Indiana, Bender studied at Goshen College (B.A., 1918), Garrett Biblical Institute (D.D., 1922), Princeton University* and Princeton Theological Seminary* (M.A. and Th.M., 1923), the University of Tübingen (1923-1924) and the University of Heidelberg (Th.D., 1935). He taught Bible and church history at Goshen College, beginning in 1924, becoming dean of the college in 1933 and dean of the seminary in 1944. In 1926 he began the *Goshen College Review Supplement,* which became the *Mennonite Quarterly Review* in 1927, and served as its editor through 1962. Bender was a leader on the Historical Committee of the Mennonite General Conference, the Mennonite Central Committee* and the Mennonite World Conference. His most important works were *The Anabaptist Vision* (1943) and *The Mennonite Encyclopedia,* for which he was general editor (1955-1959). His research and teaching contributed significantly to the recovery of the history and significance of sixteenth-century Anabaptism.*

BIBLIOGRAPHY. J. C. Wenger et al., *Harold S. Bender* (1964); G. F. Herschberger, ed., *Recovery of the Anabaptist Vision* (1957).

J. M. Glass

Benedictines. The Benedictine Order refers to a federation of independent monasteries living under the Rule of St. Benedict (of Nursia, c.480-c.547). Benedictines date back to the lifetime of St. Benedict, who first established a hermitage at Subiaco, Italy, and later at Monte Cassino. Benedictines established monasteries throughout Europe and Britain, and in their coming to the U.S. they served as a transmitter of an ancient European Christian tradition.

The immediate impulse for the journey of Benedictine men and women to North America was the tide of immigration* in the Catholic Church of the U.S. during the nineteenth century. More particularly, it was the desire to provide pastoral and educational care for German-speaking immigrants that attracted Benedictines from the Abbey of Metten in Germany, under the leadership of Boniface Wimmer,* to establish the first stable community of Benedictine monks at St. Vincent, Pennsylvania, in 1846. Within the next decade they were followed by Benedictine sisters from Bavaria and Benedictine monks from Switzerland. By the close of the nineteenth century, the Order's presence in North America had undergone considerable numerical and geographical expansion.

The Benedictine monks were organized according to two major congregations: the American Cassinese Congregation, emanating from the Abbey of St. Vincent, Pennsylvania, and the Swiss-American Congregation, emanating from the Abbeys of St. Meinrad, Indiana, and Conception, Missouri. At least four different strains of Benedictine women added to the diversity. In addition to their interior life of prayer* and work, the principal external activity of the Benedictine houses in this founding era was that of education and evangelism.*

The twentieth century witnessed a widening of the ministry of the Benedictine Order and a continued geographical expansion across the entire map of North America. Monks of the Benedictine Confederation in the United States numbered approximately 2500 approaching the final decade of the twentieth century and Benedictine women numbered between 4,000 and 5,000. The influence of individual Benedictines and their communities during the last century in the area of liturgical* reform, ecumenical* relations and spirituality* has reached beyond Catholic monastic circles and touched a widening number of American Christians.

BIBLIOGRAPHY. C. Barry, *Worship and Work* (1980); J. Rippinger, "Some Historical Determinants of American Benedictine Monasticism, 1846-1900," *ABR* 27:1 (1976):63-84.

J. A. Rippinger

Benevolent Fraternity of Unitarian Churches. Voluntary* association of Boston-area Unitarian* churches for support of local ministries to the urban* poor. This early expression of American Unitarianism's characteristic social impulse was founded in 1834 as the Benevolent Fraternity of Churches, at the urging of Ezra Stiles Gannett,* who was elected the first secretary of the Fraternity's Central Board. The Fraternity's first action was to take over from the American Unitarian Association support of Joseph Tuckerman's ground-breaking "ministry-at-large" in Boston's slums. In subsequent years, the Fraternity underwrote a number of chapels* in working-class neighborhoods, incidentally using its patronage to enforce these parishes' conformity to mainstream Unitarian theological and social perspectives. John T. Sargent, pastor of one such chapel, was disciplined by the Fraternity in 1844 for practicing pulpit exchange with the "radical" Unitarian minister Theodore Parker.* With a change of name in 1915, the Benevolent Fraternity of Unitarian Churches continues active today in a wide range of local social ministries, supported by churches of the Unitarian Universalist Association throughout the metropolitan Boston area.

BIBLIOGRAPHY. C. R. Eliot, *The Story of the Benevolent Fraternity of Unitarian Churches* (1930).

G. W. Harper

Benezet, Anthony (1713-1784). Quaker* educator and social reformer.* Born in San Quentin, in Picardy, France, of Huguenot* parents, his family fled their homeland in the wake of persecution that followed the revocation of the Edict of Nantes. The family dwelt briefly in Rotterdam, then lived in London for sixteen years, finally settling in Philadelphia. His parents were active in both Quaker and Moravian* circles, joining the latter while their son chose membership in the former. The peaceful ways of both groups and their concerns for the non-whites left their mark on Anthony. He was trained in both mercantile business and coopering, but he eventually found his calling in teaching, first at the Friends' English Public School, now known as the William Penn Charter School. He successfully urged Friends to establish adequate schooling for girls (1755) and African-American children (1770).

In 1756 he effectively mobilized Quaker support for the Acadian* population who made their way to Philadelphia after expulsion from Nova Scotia. By then he had already begun to labor on behalf of slaves. His most influential writings on slavery are *A Caution and Warning to Great Britain and Her Colonies on the Calamitous State of the Enslaved Negroes* (1766) and *Some Historical Account of Guinea with an Inquiry into the Rise and Progress of the Slave-Trade, its Nature and Lamentable Effects* (1771). It seems most likely that the latter won John Wesley* to the anti-slavery* cause, and Benezet and Wesley corresponded for a decade. Benezet's correspondence was perhaps as influential as his published works, and his associates in the anti-slavery movement included John Woolman,* Granville Sharp, Benjamin Rush, Thomas Clarkson, William Wilberforce, as well as British Friends John and Henry Gurney and David Barclay. Benezet likewise devoted his pen and energies to seeking better treatment of Native Americans, not an enviable task during the French and Indian War of the 1750s. His other writings concern themselves with international peace, with teaching and with the interior religious life.

BIBLIOGRAPHY. R. Vaux, *Memoirs of the Life of Anthony Benezet* (1817); G. S. Brookes, *Friend Anthony Benezet* (1937).

M. L. Birkel

Bennett, Belle Harris (1852-1922). Southern Methodist* missions* leader and social reformer.* Born at Whitehall, near Richmond, Kentucky, the younger daughter of eight children of Samuel and Elizabeth (Chenault) Bennett. At twenty-three, after a largely social life, she joined the Methodist Church her family attended. She received a "baptism of the spirit" in 1884, which propelled her into her lifelong work of organizing in the church. Much of her work centered on home missions. She conceived the idea, urged the establishment of and raised the funds for Scarritt Bible and Training School (dedicated September 11, 1892). She was president of the Home Mission Society (1896) and after 1898 of its new governing body, the Woman's Board of Home Missions (*See* Missionary Movement, Women's).

Her major concern was the condition and needs of the cities. After a trip to London in 1901, she established more than forty settlement houses* throughout the South. These were named Wesley Community Houses and Bethlehem Houses for blacks. Bennett was responsible for the development of the deaconess* movement in the South as well. She was active in working for rights for African-Americans, taking personal initiative and urging the church to do the same. She was an early member of the National Child Labor Committee, and she worked for women's suffrage.* In 1906 she was named president of the newly created Woman's Missionary Council, a union of the home and foreign boards. She worked diligently for lay rights for women in the Southern church, a goal she achieved in 1918. She was then elected as the first woman delegate to the General Conference in 1922. She could not attend because of illness and died of cancer that July.

Bennett was a woman of spirit as well as talent, a speaker and an organizer, traveling throughout the Methodist connection, exhorting, encouraging and helping institute programs which put the church firmly in the center of social reform for the betterment of all people, wherever and whoever they were.

BIBLIOGRAPHY. S. E. Haskin, *Women and Missions in the MEC, South* (1920); R. W. MacDonnell, *Belle Harris Bennett, Her Life Work* (1928); *NAW* I; C. L. Stapleton, "Belle Harris Bennett: Model of Holistic Christianity," *MH* 21 (April 1983):131-142.

J. C. Brown

Bennett, John Coleman (1902-). Protestant theologian,* ethicist* and ecumenical* leader. Born in Kingston, Ontario, the son of a Presbyterian minister, Bennett grew up in Morristown, New Jersey. He was educated at Williams College; Mansfield College, Oxford; and Union Theological Seminary in New York.* Bennett held teaching posts at Auburn Seminary in New York (1931-1938) and Pacific School of Religion at Berkeley, California (1938-1943), before returning to Union Seminary, where from 1943 to 1970 he served as professor of Christian theology and ethics, as Reinhold Niebuhr Professor of Social Ethics, and as president. Bennett was a delegate to the first assembly of the World Council of Churches,* in 1948, and served as secretary of the section on the Church and the Disorder of Society. He has been an active participant in the work of the World Council of Churches' Department on Church and Society. Bennett's theological and ethical reflection has focused on problems of society and politics. His numerous books and articles have addressed such specific topics as nuclear weapons, Communism, U.S. foreign policy and the relationship between the Christian and the state. Bennett is senior contributing editor of *Christianity and Crisis,* of which he was a founding sponsor.

BIBLIOGRAPHY. R. Lee, *The Promise of Bennett* (1969); E. L. Long, Jr., and R. T. Handy, eds., *Theology and Church in Times of Change: Essays in Honor of John Coleman Bennett* (1970); D. H.

Smith, *The Achievement of John C. Bennett* (1970).

W. A. Silva

Bennett, Mary Katharine Jones (1864-1950). Presbyterian home missions leader. Born in Englewood, New Jersey, Bennett graduated from Elmira College (B.A., 1885) and taught school in Englewood for several years. In 1898 she married Fred Bennett, a prosperous New York manufacturer. A woman with wide interests and leadership abilities, Bennett served as president of the Woman's Board of Home Missions for her denomination,* the Presbyterian Church in the U.S.A.* from 1909 until its merger with the Presbyterian Board of National Missions in 1923. She was an influential voice for women during this difficult period of change. In 1916 she was the first woman to make a board report to the General Assembly,* and in 1923 she became vice president of the newly created National Board of Home Missions. With Margaret Hodge,* vice president of the Board of Foreign Missions, she compiled a blunt report on the "Causes of Unrest among Women of the Church" (1927). One of the leading churchwomen of her day, she also represented the denomination in ecumenical* causes, including the Council of Women for Home Missions (president from 1916 to 1923). She served with the Federal Council of Churches* and the National Committee on the Cause and Cure of War, alongside Carrie Chapman Catt and Jane Addams.*

BIBLIOGRAPHY. L. A. Boyd and R. D. Breckenridge, *Presbyterian Women in America* (1983); *NAW* 1.

M. L. Bendroth

Berkenmeyer, Wilhelm Christoph (1686-1751). Lutheran* minister* in New York. A native of Bodenteich in the Duchy of Luneburg, Berkenmeyer was ordained* to the Lutheran ministry by the conservative Amsterdam Consistory on May 24, 1725 for service in America. His ministry encompassed New York and eastern New Jersey, which he divided into five parishes.* Berkenmeyer was pastor of the Lower Hudson parish, centered around Loonenburg in upstate New York and attracted like-minded European Lutheran missionaries to staff the other four parishes.

In 1735 Berkenmeyer wrote a constitution known as the General Church Order that detailed rules for the liturgy* and parish governance. A synod* of sorts was provided for, but it was an ad hoc body called only to resolve congregational disputes whose decisions could be appealed to European superiors. His failure to cut himself off from European ties hampered his ministry and led

[129]

to a loss of authority. A dispute between the Raritan, New Jersey, congregation and its pastor, Johann C. Wolf, whom Berkenmeyer supported, caused the congregation to seek a new pastor from Henry Melchior Muhlenberg's* pietistic* Pennsylvania Ministerium.* In 1751 another lay*-clergy* dispute in the New York City parish prompted the congregation to appoint Muhlenberg as its pastor. Isolated in his own parish, Berkenmeyer died in late August 1751.

BIBLIOGRAPHY. *DAB* I; L. R. Riforgiato, *Missionary of Moderation: Henry Melchior Muhlenberg and the Lutheran Church in English America* (1980). L. R. Riforgiato

Berkhof, Louis (1873-1957). Reformed* theologian. Born in the Dutch province of Drenthe, Berkhof's parents belonged to the pietist* orthodox* Seceder (1834) branch of the Reformed church. (Herman Bavinck, whose work Berkhof's theology relies on most, shared this regional and religious cast.) The family emigrated to the U. S. in 1882, settling in Grand Rapids, Michigan, where Louis spent virtually all the rest of his life. In 1900 he graduated from the Christian Reformed Church's* Theological School in Grand Rapids and, between two Christian Reformed pastorates, did two years (1902-1904) of graduate work in theology at Princeton.* In 1906 he was appointed to the Grand Rapids (later Calvin) Seminary, where he served the rest of his career as professor of biblical theology (1906-1914), New Testament (1914-1926) and, finally, systematic* theology (1926-1944). From 1931 to 1944 he served as president of that institution.

Around 1920, Berkhof helped purge the Christian Reformed Church of the perceived influx of dispensational* fundamentalism* and higher-critical modernism.* The latter struck him as the far-graver error. Consequently, the second half of his career, devoted to articulating a Reformed theological consensus, was marked by a consistent anti-Modernist agenda. Berkhof produced his monumental works in the early 1930s: *Reformed Dogmatics* (1932; in later editions, *Systematic Theology)* and its popular distillation, *Manual of Reformed Doctrine* (1933). These bear the influence of Berkhof's Princeton mentor, Gerhardus Vos,* and of Herman Bavinck, whose *Gereformeerde Dogmatiek* (1906-1911) Berkhof followed in format, substance and much detail. Throughout, the works show his tradition's taut theocentricity. All initiative, virtue and certainty reside with God; all the opposite, with man. Accordingly, the crucial task of life is obedience to divine authority, which

is presented for human appropriation in Scripture.* For theology in particular, Berkhof insisted that Scripture is the only source and norm. Human reason, experience or church tradition should neither supplement it nor affect its reading. On these bulwarks Berkhof erected his systematics, hewing to a moderate line on the classic issues of Calvinist controversy and reproving Modernist proposals throughout.

Berkhof rejected rationalistic* strictures on the Bible and orthodoxy, yet showed a rationalistic frame of mind himself. Faith alone could appropriate the saving truth of revelation, but reason's job of arraying these truths in systematic unity was vital. Ideas dictated action, and true Christian experience had to follow doctrinal formulations. Thus, after 1920 Berkhof largely gave up his earlier talent for social-cultural commentary and concentrated instead on creating a theological fortress for a beleaguered group facing troubled times. The scope and rigor of his work, as well as its appeal beyond its original audience (particularly among evangelicals* of a generally Reformed persuasion), show the strength of his tradition and the talent with which he defended it.

BIBLIOGRAPHY. J. D. Bratt, *Dutch Calvinism in Modern America* (1984); H. Zwaanstra, "Louis Berkhof," in *Reformed Theology in America,* ed. D. F. Wells (1985). J. D. Bratt

Berlin Congress on World Evangelism. *See* WORLD CONGRESS ON EVANGELISM.

Berry, Martha McChesney (1866-1942). Southern educator. Born on a cotton plantation near Rome, Georgia, Berry began her career teaching informal Sunday-school classes for the rural mountain children near her home. A devout Episcopalian,* she decided to use her sizable inheritance to establish a nondenominational school for mountain boys. In 1902 she established the Mount Berry School for Boys and in 1909 opened the Martha Berry School for Girls. Both schools stressed vocational as well as academic instruction; students' tuition was paid by two days a week of manual labor. In 1926 she founded Berry College. By 1960 the Berry schools had graduated over 16,000 students and offered education from nursery school to selected master's degrees. Widely known in philanthropic circles as a consummate fund raiser, she was aided by Theodore Roosevelt, Andrew Carnegie (who donated her first $50,000) and Henry Ford ($4 million). Berry was the first woman elected to the University of Georgia's Board of Regents and the first person named a "Distinguished Citizen of the State of Georgia."

BIBLIOGRAPHY. T. Byers, *The Sunday Lady of Possum Trot* (1932); *DAB* 3; H. Kane and I. Henry, *Miracle in the Mountains* (1956); *NAW* 1.

M. L. Bendroth

Bessette, Alfred ("Brother Andre") (1845-1937). Canadian Roman Catholic* saint.* Born in Quebec and orphaned at the age of five, Bessette, who was functionally illiterate for half his life, worked at various manual labor jobs before joining the Congregation of Holy Cross* as a lay* brother.* Although just a porter in a church-run boys' school for the next four decades, Brother Andre became the most popular religious figure in French Canada. A million visitors from Canada and the U.S. viewed his body as it lay in state after his death. Despite poor personal health and his opinion that accepting suffering was better than healing, since the former makes Christ's suffering more real, Brother Andre was credited with tens of thousands of miraculous healings. Since he attributed the miracles to "the good St. Joseph," his followers erected St. Joseph's Oratory in 1924-1925, a basilica* which still is one of Montreal's most impressive landmarks. Pope John Paul II beatified* Bessette in 1982.

BIBLIOGRAPHY. H.-P. Bergeron, *Brother Andre, C.S.C.: Apostle of Saint Joseph* (1938).

B. A. McKenzie

Bethune, Joanna Graham (1770-1860). Founder of charitable societies. Born in Canada and raised in Scotland, Joanna Graham came to New York City in 1789 with her widowed mother, the noted Presbyterian* laywoman Isabella Graham. After her marriage to Scottish-born merchant Divie Bethune in 1795, Bethune devoted much of her life to educational and philanthropic causes, often in concert with her mother and husband (she also bore six children, three of whom survived to adulthood). Among the groups she founded or co-founded were: the Society for the Relief of Poor Widows with Small Children (1797), an early Sunday school* (1803), the Orphan Asylum Society (1806), a House of Industry (1814), the Female Union Society for the Promotion of Sabbath Schools (1816), and an Infant School Society (1827). During the latter portion of her life, she devoted herself especially to the orphan asylum and to the infant school cause. Before paid careers became available to women, Joanna Bethune forged a successful, if voluntary, career in the field of benevolence.

BIBLIOGRAPHY. *NAW* 1; G. W. Bethune, *Memoirs of Mrs. Joanna Bethune* (1863).

A. M. Boylan

Bethune, Mary McLeod (1875-1955). African-American educator and advocate for African-American women. Born to former slaves and raised on her parents' thirty-five-acre farm in Mayesville, South Carolina, Mary was chosen from among her seventeen siblings to attend the local Presbyterian school. She continued her education at Scotia Seminary in Concord, North Carolina, and graduated from Moody Bible Institute* in Chicago (1895). Twice rejected for missionary* service in Africa, she turned her attention to educating African-Americans in America. After teaching school in Georgia and Florida for several years, she opened her own Daytona Normal and Industrial School for Girls in Daytona Beach, Florida, on October 3, 1904. From five students in a four-room cottage she rented for $1.50 in 1904, the institution emerged as a fully-accredited liberal arts college for African-Americans—Bethune-Cookman College. She remained president of the college until 1942.

As early as 1909 the National Association for Colored Women (NACW) raised funds for Bethune College. In 1927, Mary Bethune became president of the NACW. Under her leadership, the organization became an advocate for school desegregation, anti-lynching legislation, help for rural women, women's training programs and prison reform. She joined with white women to address racial problems and in doing so developed a close friendship with Sara Roosevelt and her daughter-in-law Eleanor.

In 1935, Bethune founded the National Council of Negro Women, a national coalition of women's organizations, to present a comprehensive agenda to the federal government. During the Depression* Bethune joined Franklin Roosevelt's "Black Cabinet," as director of the Division of Negro Affairs from 1935 to 1943. Bethune continued to build alliances and coalitions between African-American women's organizations, between African-American and white women and between the African-American community and the federal government until her death in 1955.

BIBLIOGRAPHY. *DAB* III; *DARB;* R. Holt, *Mary McLeod Bethune: A Biography* (1964); *NAWMP;* NCAB 49; C. O. Peare, *Mary McLeod Bethune* (1951); B. J. Ross, "Mary McLeod Bethune and the National Youth Administration: A Case Study of Power Relationships in the Black Cabinet of Franklin D. Roosevelt," in *Black Leaders of the Twentieth Century,* ed. J. H. Franklin and A. Meier (1982).

L. J. Edwards

Bible and American Culture. From the very first explorations by the French, Spanish and English, the Bible has been a part of the American landscape. The Bible's place in North America is so instinctive and so vast, however, that only recently have scholars singled out the subject for special study. For most of American history, the general situation for both testaments was that which Perry Miller,* America's greatest twentieth-century historian, once described for an earlier period: "The Old Testament is truly so omnipresent in the American culture of 1800 or 1820 that historians have as much difficulty taking cognizance of it as of the air people breathed." If the many dimensions of this subject defy comprehensive summary, it is still possible to recognize the importance of the Bible in America, most simply by seeing its publication as a noteworthy phenomenon, but also by realizing its powerful and multifaceted role in American social and cultural history.

The Bible in Print. The publishing history of the Bible in America is a long and fascinating story, extending from the earliest Spanish explorers in what would become the U.S. to the present, where the sale of Bibles approaches $200 million in annual business. Most impressive about this aspect of the Bible's history is its sheer immensity.

Throughout their history, Americans have sustained an incredible rate of Bible publication and an even more stupendous appetite for literature about the Bible. Over 2,500 different English-language editions of the Bible were published in the U.S. between 1777 and 1957. More recently, modern translations* have joined the Authorized, or King James, Version (KJV) in racking up breathtaking sales. Over fifty million copies of the Revised Standard Version (RSV) were distributed in the first thirty years after its publication in 1952. The Living Bible, a paraphrase by Kenneth Taylor, had over thirty million copies in print from just the 1970s and 1980s. Other versions, arising like the RSV and the Living Bible from largely Protestant* efforts, have also been overnight million sellers in recent years. Of these, a joint effort by conservative Protestants, the New International Version (published in 1978), has been the most successful, with annual sales by the end of the 1980s beginning to reach those of the KJV. Catholics* and Jews have also been active Bible publishers as well. The RSV has been adopted for use by Catholics, and the Catholic Church in America has also sponsored the New American Bible, among several other authorized projects. And the Jewish Publication Society completed in the early 1980s its new version of the translation of the Hebrew Scriptures into English.

Publication of the Bible has been a lucrative business in America, but not without peril. Before the Revolutionary War,* the publication of English-language Bibles was prohibited in America, since the King's printers in England enjoyed an exclusive copyright to printing the KJV. This meant that the first Bibles and biblical portions printed in America were in languages other than English. In 1743, Christopher Sauer* published an edition of Luther's Bible on type carried from Frankfurt and in so doing established his family as America's leading publisher of Bibles for speakers of German. Even earlier, the Bible had made its appearance in native tongues. Spanish Franciscans* were translating biblical liturgies and other Catholic literature for the Rimucuan Indians of Florida in the sixteenth and very early seventeenth centuries, before permanent English colonies existed in New England. Decades later the Massachusetts Puritan* minister* John Eliot* translated the Bible into Algonquin (New Testament, 1661; entire Bible, 1663). Eliot fully expected this Indian-language Bible to provide the foundation for the Christianization of Native Americans. In spite of failure on that score, other laborers since Eliot have translated at least parts of the Bible into a whole series of Native American languages, including Apache, Cherokee, Cheyenne, Choctaw, Dakota, Hopi, Inupiat, Kuskokwim, Muskogee, Navajo and Ojibwa.

Once American printers began producing their own editions of the KJV, business boomed. Mason Weems,* who fabricated the story of Washington and the cherry tree, made his living in the early years of the new nation selling Bibles in Virginia. From there he reported to his publisher: "I tell you this is the very season and age of the Bible. Bible Dictionaries, Bible tales, Bible stories—Bibles plain or paraphrased, Carey's Bibles, Collins Bibles, Clarke's Bibles, Kimptor's Bibles, no matter what or whose, all, all, will go down—so wide is the crater of public appetite at this time." As successful as Bible publishing was in general, however, that success did not extend to efforts at producing new translations. Until well into the twentieth century, the Authorized Version for Protestants and the Douay-Rheims version for Catholics reigned supreme as America's Bibles of choice. Nineteenth-century publishers who underwrote efforts to produce a Bible specifically for their countrymen found great market resistance to any version that departed from the KJV. Noah Webster, father of the American dictionary, in 1833 finished his translation of a Bible shorn of British spellings and archaic usages. His contemporary

Andrew Comstock devised a phonetic "purfekt alfabet" for his "Filadelphia" New Testament of 1848. But these and similar efforts met with little success. Only with the production of the American Standard Version in 1901 did publishers begin to enjoy the market for newer versions that has burgeoned since the early 1950s.

One of the ways Scripture was circulated in the early history of the U.S. was through Bible societies.* Although Britain had the first formal Bible society, American groups would be even more active. The American Bible Society,* the largest of the societies, has distributed nearly four billion complete Bibles, testaments, scriptural portions and selections since its founding in 1816. Bible societies received the support of many who held traditional Christian views on the Bible's supernatural character, like the first president of the U.S. Congress, Elias Boudinot* of New Jersey, who also became first president of the American Bible Society. But they also were patronized by others with unconventional religious ideas, like Thomas Jefferson,* who twice prepared editions of the Gospels with the supernatural parts removed.

Modern organizations that specialize in Bible translation and distribution are the descendants of America's early Bible societies. Of these, the Wycliffe Bible Translators*/Summer Institute of Linguistics has been the most visible. Since its founding in the 1930s, workers with Wycliffe have translated at least a portion of the Scriptures into over one thousand of the world's languages.

As great as the quantity of Bibles printed in America has been, even greater has been the quantity of literature about the Bible. Statistics can suggest the merest outlines of a literary mountain: four large volumes (with 63,000 entries in 700 languages) in the Library of Congress's catalog of books held by American libraries before 1956; sixty pages of Bible materials in the closely packed type of the 1985-1986 edition of *Books in Print;* ninety-four columns of academic citations to the Bible in the 1983-1984 *Religious Index One: Periodicals;* seven thousand members of the Society of Biblical Literature,* only the largest of many academic societies organized around study of Scripture and many pages in annual surveys by learned journals and popular magazines.

Society and Culture. The vast stretches of literature on the Bible, as well as the booming business of Bible-selling, testify to the prominence that Scripture has enjoyed in American religious life. Discussions concerning the doctrines of revelation and of Scripture itself, suggestions for applying the Bible's message to daily life and study

of the Bible in its linguistic and historical settings account for the vast bulk of publications about the Bible. The 1963 Supreme Court ruling that prohibited the Bible's use as a religious text in public schools* but that encouraged its study for cultural purposes has also fueled a publishing surge on the Bible as literature. This flood of Bibles and literature on the Bible, however, also points to the immense signficance of Scripture more generally in American life.

The Bible has clearly influenced the way Americans write, talk, think and think of themselves. From William Bradford,* whose *Of Plymouth Plantation* recorded the efforts of the Massachusetts Pilgrims to live up to biblical conceptions of a faithful Christian community, to Senator Sam Ervin, who entertained a national television audience during the Watergate hearings with biblical quotations—leaders in the public eye have freely employed material from the Bible. Many of the nation's presidents have been lifelong readers of the Bible, from John Adams and Thomas Jefferson at the start of the nation's history, through Abraham Lincoln,* James Garfield,* Grover Cleveland, William McKinley* and Woodrow Wilson,* to Jimmy Carter* in the very recent past. In 1864 a group of grateful African-Americans from Baltimore presented President Lincoln with a pulpit Bible—bound in violet-tinged velvet, finished in gold, with a raised design depicting the emancipation of the slaves—as a token of their respect for his efforts on their behalf. In response, Lincoln called the Bible "God's best gift to man." Some years before, the skeptical John Adams wrote to his even more skeptical friend, Thomas Jefferson, that the Bible "contains more of my little philosophy than all the libraries I have seen." Woodrow Wilson, in a speech shortly before he became president, called the Bible "the 'Magna Charta' of the Human Soul."

America's common people have also reflected a pervasive respect for Scripture. The use of biblical names for children continues into the late twentieth century and extends a much longer pattern of employing biblical nomenclature. As Americans in the nineteenth century settled new towns and named new features of the terrain, it was instinctive to turn to the Bible for names like Zoar (from Gen 13:10) in Ohio and Mount Tirzah (Josh 12:24) in North Carolina, or the forty-seven variations on Bethel to be found across the country, sixty-one on Eden and ninety-five on Salem. Bibles were often listed in the estate inventories of common people in the colonial period, and Bible societies in the nineteenth century, no less than the Gideons* in the twentieth century, often aspired to put a copy of the Scriptures in the hands of every person in a given locality. Public polling suggests that the hold of the Bible on ordinary people remains strong, even in an America that is more secular than it once was. A Gallup Poll from 1979 showed, for example, that forty-two per cent of the population believed that "the Bible is the word of God and is not mistaken in its statements and teachings" and that thirty per cent of the population read the Bible at least once a week.

Many of the country's great writers have also reflected the impact of the Bible. From titles (like Ernest Hemingway's *The Sun Also Rises,* from Ecclesiastes; William Faulkner's *Absalom, Absalom!* and *Go Down, Moses;* or "Lazarus" from both Eugene O'Neill and Sylvia Plath) and characters (Ishmael, Ahab and Leviathan in Melville's *Moby Dick;* Adam from Nathaniel Hawthorne* and Walt Whitman) to ethos and moral structure (Harriet Beecher Stowe,* Flannery O'Connor,* Walker Percy), American authors have found the Scriptures an inexhuastible resource.

In American social history the Bible has acted as both a conservative and a radical force. It has provided a vocabulary for traditional deference, but also innovative egalitarianism. It has fueled both stability in the face of anarchy and freedom in the face of tyranny. Scripture penetrated to such a deep level nationally that it became a major prop for both sides in the conflict leading to the Civil War.* Thus, to many Southerners the Bible was the sure foundation for their way of life. The Reverend Frederick Ross of Huntsville, Alabama, for one, insisted that Southern slavery amounted to a direct parallel of the Bible and was a biblical pattern: "Every Southern planter is not more truly a slaveholder than Abraham. And the Southern master, by divine authority, may today, consider his slaves part of his social and religious family, just as Abraham did." From the North it was a much different story, but based on the same foundation. As the Presbyterian* Albert Barnes* from Philadelphia put it, "The principles laid down by the Saviour and his Apostles are such as are opposed to Slavery, and if carried out would secure its universal abolition." Only occasionally did an observer pause to reflect on the tragedy of two Scripture-quoting societies moving implacably toward war. In his Second Inaugural Address, Abraham Lincoln pointed out that "both [sides] read the same Bible" before concluding that God's purposes might be higher and different than the purposes of Bible-readers in either the North or South.

The Bible has been a charter of social liberty for many who have felt constrained by traditional boundaries or dominating cultural fashions. "The Bible only" was the liberating cry of the energetic men and women who formed many of the new denominations* established between the Revolution and the Civil War. On the other side of the picture, the Bible has also played a part in reinforcing social conformity. When the Roman Catholic bishop* of Philadelphia, Francis Patrick Kenrick,* petitioned city officials in 1842 to allow school children of his faith to hear readings from the Douay Version instead of the King James Version, strong Protestant protests followed. Evangelical* ministers formed national anti-Catholic organizations and Protestant laymen* vented their anger by rioting against Philadelphia's Catholic churches.

The most important instance of the Bible's social liberation in America belongs to the history of African-Americans. Slaves made a sharp distinction between the Bible that their owners preached to them, with its emphasis on not stealing and obeying masters, and the Bible they discovered for themselves, with its message of liberation for the captive and redemption for the oppressed. Under slavery stringent regulations often existed against unsupervised preaching* or sometimes even against owning Bibles. But with permission or not, slaves went to great lengths to possess Scripture for themselves. Many made a special effort to hear African-American preachers* expound the Scriptures in circumstances unsupervised by masters. One slave left a striking testimony of the difference: "A yellow [light-complexioned] man preached to us. She [the slave owner] had him preach how we ought to obey our master and missy if we want to go to heaven, but when she wasn't there, he came out with straight preachin' from the Bible." African-Americans sang and preached about Adam and Eve and the Fall, about "wrestlin' Jacob" who "would not let God go," about Moses and the exodus from Egypt, about Joshua possessing the Promised Land, about Daniel in the lion's den and Daniel's three friends in the fiery furnace, about Jonah in the whale, about the birth of Jesus and his death and future return. The narratives of the Old Testament in particular lent slave use of the Bible its special social dimension. For slaves, the figure of Moses assumed a special importance as the one whom God had raised up to free his people. To the hope of liberation in this world, the slaves added a concentration on the figure of Jesus, who suffered innocently and who ministered particularly to the oppressed, as the source of hope for the future.

The slave's profound embrace of Scripture created the climate for the ongoing importance of Bible reading and biblical preaching among African-Americans since the Civil War.

If the Bible deserves special attention for its place in American society, it deserves no less for its place in American intellectual history. The celebrated debate over evolution between William Jennings Bryan* and Clarence Darrow at Dayton, Tennessee, in 1925, represented only the most visible instance of the ongoing effort to integrate the Bible and the various fields of human learning. During its first three centuries, most American intellectuals assumed that scientific knowledge proceeded within a framework provided by Scripture. In the twentieth century there has been more controversy. From the side of science and the side of the Bible have come extravagant claims about "warfare" between Scripture and science, and these claims have been the source of endless public attention. More generally, if also less visibly, American Bible-believers have followed many paths to reconcile faith and science.

The Bible has also played an important role in efforts to define the character of the country. Borrowing liberally from Old Testament precedents, many early Americans and not a few in more recent days have regarded the U.S. as God's New Israel, a nation established in this new-world Canaan as a land flowing with wealth and freedom. Puritan preachers, with a firm covenant theology,* often spoke as if God had made special promises to, and was extracting special duties from, his children in New England. More recently, leaders in efforts for national moral reform have used the prophetic language of the Old Testament to call "my people" (2 Chron 7:14) back to God. Although Canadians have never indulged such notions to the extent of their fellows in the U.S., Canada too has seen notions of a special divine covenant. In both the nineteenth and twentieth centuries, at least a few Canadian leaders have spoken of "his dominion" with the understanding that God had bestowed special blessings on that northern land.

To balance the picture of the Bible and American culture, however, we must also note a different perspective, because African-American slaves before the Civil War and not a few Christian radicals in the late twentieth century have reversed the typology: America was Egypt, and *escape* from American institutions and influence was the exodus. Particularly at moments of crisis, however, the themes of Scripture have easily slid over into the terms of national identity, whether apocalypse*

during the Revolutionary and Civil Wars, redemption during the Civil War by the one whom some called "Father Abraham," or judgment during national disasters. Late into the twentieth century the messages of American politics still sometimes echo the words and themes of the Bible.

There is not time enough to write of the many other ways in which the Bible has played a part in American culture, often shaping that culture by the power of its own message, but also often shaped itself by the social, economic and artistic patterns of life in America. The Bible has informed the spirituals* of African-Americans and Shakers* and the more formal hymnody* of the churches; it has provided material for paintings both refined and primitive; it has been a primary textbook itself in many American schools and a decisive influence on the curriculum in many more; it has been a factor in legal decisions and jurisprudential reasoning; it has provided the raw material for historical novels, plays, mass art, country music, humor, broadcasting, children's literature and much, much more. In sum, the Bible has been an ever-present force in American life. Americans have perhaps been more prone than people elsewhere to bend, twist and abuse the Bible for their own sometimes very un-Christian purposes. But from its pages they have also drawn insight, strength and wisdom for life more in keeping with Scripture's central themes. For good and for ill, it remains true that the person who would understand the history of America must understand the history of the Bible in America.

See also BIBLE SOCIETIES; BIBLE, AMERICAN VERSIONS; BIBLICAL INTERPRETATION.

BIBLIOGRAPHY. W. D. Adams, ed., *Jefferson's Extracts from the Gospels* (1983); C. Baker, "The Place of the Bible in American Fiction," in *Religious Perspectives in American Culture,* ed. J. W. Smith and A. L. Jamison (1961); D. Barr and N. Piediscalzi, ed., *The Bible in American Education* (1982); E. S. Gaustad and W. Harrelson, ed., "The Bible in American Culture," including E. S. Frerichs, ed., *The Bible and Bibles in America* (1988); E. D. Genovese, *Roll, Jordan, Roll: The World the Slaves Made* (1972); G. Gunn, ed., *The Bible and American Arts and Letters* (1983); C. V. Hamilton, *The Black Preacher in America* (1972); N. O. Hatch and M. A. Noll, ed., *The Bible in America: Essays in Cultural History* (1982); M. T. Hills, *The English Bible in America: A Bibliography of Editions of the Bible and New Testament Published in America, 1777-1957* (1961); J. T. Johnson, ed., *The Bible in American Law, Politics, and Political Rhetoric* (1985); J. Leighly, "Biblical Place-Names in the

United States," *Names* 27 (1979):53-56; M. Marty, *Religion and Republic* (1987); M. A. Noll, "Review Essay: The Bible in America," *JBL* 106 (1987):493-509; A. S. Phy, ed., *The Bible and Popular Culture in America* (1985); E. R. Sandeen, ed., *The Bible and Social Reform* (1982).   M. A. Noll

Bible and Prophetic Conference Movement.

A series of conferences that helped to shape early fundamentalism,* the movement played an important role in forming coalitions of conservative evangelicals,* serving to train new leaders and introducing dispensational* premillennialism* into the churches.

Borrowing from an English practice already underway, in 1869 a group of American evangelicals associated with the millenarian journal *Waymarks in the Wilderness* began scheduling summer conferences for intense Bible* study* and fellowship.* The most important of these conferences was founded in 1875 and permanently located at Niagara-on-the-Lake, Ontario, in 1883. Originally called the Believers' Meeting for Bible Study, the Niagara Conference* became a prototype for scores of others which were held in the following decades.

The conference met for one week during the summer, beginning with a Wednesday-evening prayer meeting. Then for the next week the daily schedule included two morning study sessions, two in the afternoon and one in the evening. On Sunday, conferees attended a worship* service, observed the Lord's Supper* and met to consider foreign missions.* Participants came from many evangelical denominations*; and speakers maintained a broad evangelical theology.* The special emphasis on the Scriptures led them to develop a new kind of exposition called the "Bible Reading." To keep human distortions to a minimum, speakers used a concordance to select various passages on a given doctrine* or theme and then read them with few expository* comments.

The Niagara Conference served as an important gathering place for those who wanted the old evangelical doctrines affirmed and defended against their liberal* detractors. Yet Niagara emphasized premillennialism, which was not accepted by many evangelicals at the time. From its inception the conference was under the control of millenarian teachers and pastors. Nathaniel West,* Henry M. Parsons,* A. J. Gordon,* William J. Erdman,* A. T. Pierson,* George Needham,* Robert Cameron* and, most significantly, James H. Brookes* guaranteed that premillennialism in one form or another had an honored place in the

proceedings. Such advocates challenged the prevailing postmillennial* view and worked hard to prove that the world was getting worse and could not be won to Christ before his Second Coming.

When such views caused controversy, in 1878 James Brookes issued a fourteen-point "Niagara Creed," which affirmed the verbal inerrancy* of the Bible; a Calvinist* view of human depravity; salvation by faith in the blood of Christ; the personality and continuing work of the Holy Spirit in believers' lives; the need for personal holiness*; and the premillennial Second Coming of Christ. Millenarians insisted that their distinctive doctrine was not only compatible with more standard evangelical fare, but was actually necessary in the increasingly fierce battle with liberalism. Ironically, belief in premillennial doctrine proved to be the undoing of the conference. As J. N. Darby's* dispensationalism became more popular among speakers and conferees, serious disputes over details of interpretation arose. Finally, arguments over the any-moment, pretribulation rapture* of the church drove a wedge between the millenarians in charge, and the conference was cancelled in 1901.

The Niagara Conference served as a model for many others. Evangelicals in different parts of the country, many of whom had Niagara connections, established annual Bible conferences at permanent sites, where attenders could combine solid Bible teaching and wholesome recreation. Other more ad hoc conferences were organized around specific doctrines. There was a Bible Inspiration Conference (Philadelphia, 1887) and a Bible Conference on the Holy Spirit (Baltimore, 1890). Of more long-term significance, however, were those organized to promote biblical prophecy. In 1878, Niagara Conference leaders who wanted to give their full attention to Christ's return organized the First American Bible and Prophetic Conference in New York. Others were held in Chicago, 1886; Allegheny, Pennsylvania, 1895; Boston, 1901; Chicago, 1914; and Philadelphia and New York, 1918. Speakers analyzed current events in light of biblical prophecy, speculated about the signs of the times and the any-moment coming of Christ, and defended premillennialism against its evangelical and non-evangelical opponents. These meetings gave premillennialism an unprecedented platform and increased the popularity of dispensationalism within millenarian circles to such an extent that by World War 1* nondispensationalist premillenarians found it difficult to get a hearing at the prophecy conferences.

These conferences helped to give rise to fundamentalism by forming a self-conscious coalition with recognized leaders and a distinctive perspective which increasingly became militant and separatistic. By the early twentieth century, most of the promoters of the Niagara Conference had been replaced by new millenarian leaders, most of whom played an important role in the developing fundamentalist movement. Arno C. Gaebelein,* William B. Riley,* C. I. Scofield,* James M. Gray* and R. A. Torrey,* to name a few, used their connections in the Bible and Prophetic Conferences to forge new fundamentalist clienteles and mobilize them for a new crusade. For the most part the new leaders were more militant than their predecessors and more willing to draw sharp distinctions between other believers and themselves. With the growing religious and cultural crisis following World War 1, such millenarians were able to convince more and more evangelicals that apostasy was on the rise, that the end of the age was fast approaching, and that true believers should withdraw from liberal denominations. Such views helped to make the fundamentalist movement possible and account for much of fundamentalism's distinctive spirit.

See also ESCHATOLOGY; FUNDAMENTALISM.

BIBLIOGRAPHY. E. R. Sandeen, *The Roots of Fundamentalism* (1970); G. Marsden, *Fundamentalism and American Culture* (1980); T. P. Weber, *Living in the Shadow of the Second Coming* (1987).

T. P. Weber

Bible Belt. A term coined by H. L. Mencken to describe the fundamentalist* South, *Bible Belt* usually has a pejorative intent. Obviously it points to the formidable strength of the Scriptures* of the Old and New Testaments as the basis of Southerners' faith. Indeed, the great majority honor no other religious authority,* whether creed,* person or institution, and they have their suspicions about Christian groups that locate authority anywhere else.

Beyond that, it refers to the literalistic, uncritical reading of the biblical text concerning scientific and historical facticity no less than religious truthfulness. Thus the Bible often is more than authoritative, being authoritarian as well. Such a view easily becomes argumentative, and may result in absolutist and triumphalist claims. While most Southern biblicists are resolute without being contentious, some have pled their case with such fervor, ridiculing any and all others, that the entire region is associated with their extreme position and harsh spirit.

Bible Belt, when used to describe rather than to evaluate, highlights the comprehensively Protestant,* and even evangelical* Protestant, character of Southern society.

S. S. Hill

Bible Chairs. A program of religious education* and nurture intended to supplement learning at state universities. In the late nineteenth century members of the Christian Church (Disciples of Christ)* became increasingly concerned over the growing number of Disciples students attending tax-supported, state universities. Such students were thought to be deprived of the nurture and opportunity for spiritual growth available at the Disciples colleges.

In 1882 Leonard Bacon proposed a program of religious studies adjacent to the University of Michigan in Ann Arbor. Eleven years later his proposal was realized in the creation of the first Disciples' Bible Chair, created through the joint cooperation of the Michigan Christian Missionary Association and the Christian Women's Board of Mission. Other chairs soon followed at the universities of Kansas (1900), Texas (1900) and Virginia (1906). A building, usually a house located near the university campus, served as a place to instruct and nurture the church's young people, offering guidance for their moral and spiritual lives. However, since the more general development of religion departments at state universities, Bible Chairs have tended to take on the form of ministry to students.*

BIBLIOGRAPHY. R. B. Flowers, *The Bible Chair Movement in Disciples of Christ Tradition: Attempts to Teach Religion in State Universities* (unpublished Ph.D. dissertation, University of Iowa, 1967); W. E. Tucker and L. G. McAllister, *Journey in Faith: A History of the Christian Church (Disciples of Christ)* (1975).

M. D. Strege

Bible Church Movement. The name generally applied to the hundreds of denominationally* unaffiliated churches which developed primarily in the U.S. during the twentieth century. Although some Bible churches have no affiliation with any group, many are in fellowship with organizations such as the Independent Fundamental Churches of America,* the American Council of Christian Churches* and the National Association of Evangelicals.*

The movement has its roots in the teaching of John Nelson Darby* (1800-1882) and his followers who rejected the concept of a state church and urged believers to deny the legitimacy of all denominations.* Darby's view of the church emphasized the apostate nature of Christendom and argued for total separation from existing denominational structures. Darby viewed the true church as temporary, established by God to cover the dispensation of grace from the cross to the Second Coming. He believed that denominationalism is wrong because it appeals to the outward profession, whereas the true church consists of the inward "unity of the Spirit." The movement received further support from the revivalistic* efforts of D. L. Moody* and his successors, who resisted denominationalism and led cooperative, interchurch campaigns, appealing for support to all evangelical denominations. Moody's Chicago Avenue Church was one of the earliest nondenominational ministries in the U.S.

Darby made six trips to the U.S. and Canada between 1859 and 1874. He visited most of the major cities and spoke in many pulpits of prominent American churchmen, particularly those who embraced premillennialism.* Darby's eschatological views were widely accepted by American pastors and teachers, but his ecclesiology was not endorsed by most American churchmen during his lifetime. When the modernist-fundamentalist* conflicts arose in the denominations during the late nineteenth and early twentieth centuries, many then accepted Darby's views on apostasy* and separated from their denominations, although most did not join the Plymouth Brethren* movement, which he had helped found.

Bible churches emphasize biblical preaching.* This often means expository* preaching. The attempt is made to compare Scripture* with Scripture in an effort to determine all that the Bible has to say about a particular subject or theme. Communicants typically follow closely the preaching and teaching which is centered on the text. A strictly maintained doctrinal position, including in most cases dispensationalism* as taught in the *Scofield Reference Bible,* is characteristic of these churches. Bible churches are fully autonomous. Church officials rule over the local church only.

Bible churches receive their support entirely from the freewill offerings of the communicants. They refuse to solicit funds through bake sales, rummage sales, games of chance or other so-called "secular" fundraising activities. They emphasize tithing by the members, and some refuse to pass an offering plate because that might entice a nonbeliever to contribute to the work of the church. These churches normally shun any emphasis which might suggest a social gospel.* They are typically apolitical, emphasize individual conversion,* interpret the Scriptures in a literal manner and advocate a strict separation* from the world in

personal conduct. They stress evangelism,* although they often have a strong disposition against collaboration with city-wide campaigns that include ecumenical* representations. They contribute generously to the support of interdenominational home and foreign missions,* particularly the faith missions.*

See also FUNDAMENTALISM.

BIBLIOGRAPHY. J. G. Melton, ed., *Encyclopedia of American Religions* (1986); J. O. Henry, *For Such a Time as This, A History of the I.F.C.A.* (1983).

P. C. Wilt

Bible College. *See* BIBLE INSTITUTES AND COLLEGES.

Bible Commonwealth. The Puritan* application of scriptural teachings to political and ecclesiastical organization. As a product of the Calvinist* wing of the Protestant* Reformation, the Puritans were committed to following the revealed Word of God. This commitment was reflected in the tenet of *sola scriptura,* which stated that the Bible* was the ultimate source of truth and the guide for all spheres of life.

The Puritans took their literal interpretation of Scripture* to New England, where they attempted to construct a Bible Commonwealth, a society that adhered in every particular to the Word of God and emulated the simplicity of the early New Testament churches. The most important aspect of this plan was the idea to build a society controlled by visible saints, those who, according to behavior and profession, were savingly converted* and therefore members of God's elect.* To insure the perpetuation of the Bible Commonwealth, the saints were responsible for granting access to both temporal and spiritual ordinances. Those adult males who could not be judged as saints were barred from voting and from partaking in communion.*

See also HALF-WAY COVENANT; NEW ENGLAND WAY.

BIBLIOGRAPHY. N. O. Hatch and M. A. Noll, eds., *The Bible in America* (1982); E. S. Morgan, *Visible Saints: The History of a Puritan Idea* (1963).

K. P. Minkema

Bible, English Translations and Versions in North America. The Bible has been a significant feature of American culture since the first European settling of North America (*See* Bible and American Culture). The early British settlers brought their Bibles* with them, and for nearly two hundred years most Bibles would be imported from England. While the Plymouth Pilgrims* brought with them their treasured *Geneva Bible,* produced in 1560 by English Protestant exiles in Geneva, the standard Bible for English-speaking Americans soon became the King James, or Authorized Version (AV) of 1611. Because the AV could only be printed by those authorized by the Crown, it was not until the Revolutionary War* that English Bible publishing became an American concern. Thus, apart from significant efforts to translate the Bible into Native American languages, such as John Eliot's* complete Algonquin translation of the Bible, published in 1663, the story of Bible translation in America begins with the birth of the Republic.

In 1777 Robert Aitken printed the first American edition of the AV, a New Testament. Bibles were again imported from England following the war, a notable example being the London "Polyglot Bible" (1824), which in its most popular form was the English portion of an eight-language edition of the Bible. Generally speaking, in nineteenth-century America if a new version of the English Bible was produced, it was an attempt to improve on the AV. Such was the intent of Noah Webster's versions of 1833 and 1841, in which he updated the archaic usages and Americanized the British spellings found in the AV. Some English versions were eccentric (such as Julia Smith's in 1876); others were sectarian (such as the Baptist* "immersion" version produced by the American Bible Union* in 1850). But such was the appetite for Bibles in new and familiar forms, that between 1777 and 1957 over 2500 different English-language editions of the Bible were published in the U.S. Space allows only an overview of the more significant versions and translations that have been produced in America over the past century.

In 1870 British scholars of various denominations began a major revision of the AV and asked for American cooperation. The church historian Philip Schaff* chaired the American committee. American scholars made numerous suggestions on how to improve the AV, but many of them were rejected. The English Revised Version was completed in 1885 and the American committee, remaining intact after 1885, produced the American Standard Version (ASV) in 1901. The ASV became very popular in America, especially among students.

The arrival of the twentieth century marked the beginning of modern speech versions. The archaeological discovery of secular Greek papyri in the sands of Egypt convinced biblical scholars that the Bible was originally written in the language of its day, and this in turn encouraged scholars to translate Scripture into contemporary English.

James Moffatt (1870-1944), a Scotsman, published a modern speech version in 1928, after moving to America. Called "A New Translation of the Bible," the final version appeared in 1935. Between the two world wars, Moffatt's Bible was the most popular modern-speech version in America. About the same time Edgar J. Goodspeed* of the University of Chicago published his Twentieth Century New Testament (1923). His colleague J. M. P. Smith, together with several other scholars, undertook the translation of the Old Testament into current American English. In 1931 Goodspeed's New Testament and Smith's Old Testament were combined to form The Bible—An American Translation. Goodspeed then translated the Apocrypha as well, and in 1939 The Complete Bible—An American Translation was published. In 1937 Charles B. Williams published The New Testament in the Language of the People. Following similar principles of translation was The Expanded Translation of the New Testament by Kenneth Wuest (1956-1959).

In 1937 the International Council of Religious Education accepted a recommendation to revise the ASV. Under the chairmanship of Luther Weigle, some thirty-two scholars began the task of preparing the Revised Standard Version on behalf of some forty major denominations* in the USA and Canada. The New Testament was published in 1946, and in 1952 the entire Bible was available. A second edition, incorporating numerous improvements, was published in 1962. Sales of the RSV were phenomenal, with over fifty million copies sold in the first thirty years since its appearance. In 1966, after only a few changes, it was published in Britain as an officially acceptable version for English-speaking Roman Catholics.* With the inclusion of the Apocrypha, the RSV Common Bible was published in 1973.

In 1945 Gerrit Verkuyl had published the Berkeley Version of the New Testament. Zondervan Publishing Company then invited him to undertake the translation of the Old Testament into modern English as well. With the help of Old Testament scholars, the complete Bible was published in 1959. The revised version of the Berkeley Bible, under the title The Modern Language Bible, appeared in 1969.

English-speaking Roman Catholics used the Douay-Rheims Bible as their "authorized version" up to 1937. That had not prevented several Catholic scholars from translating the New Testament from time to time. Between 1849 and 1860 appeared the Kenrick New Testament. In 1901 the Spencer Version of the Four Gospels was pub-

[139]

Notable American Bible Translations, Versions and Editions

John Eliot's Algonquin Bible	1663
C. Sauer's printing of Luther's German Bible	1743
R. Aitken's first American printing of AV (King James Bible)	1777
G. R. Noyes	1827-1869
N. Webster (Americanizing of AV)	1833-1841
American Bible Union "Immersion" Version of AV	1859
F. B. Kenrick	1849-1862
F. W. Grant (Revision of AV)	1891-1931
American Standard Version	1901
Scofield Reference Bible	1909
American Bible Union	1912
Spencer Version of the New Testament	1913
Moffatt Bible	1926
J. M. P. Smith and E. J. Goodspeed, The Bible—An American Translation	1931
C. B. Williams, The New Testament in the Language of the People	1937
Confraternity New Testament	1941
Revised Standard Version	1946-1952
Catholic Edition	1966
Berkeley Version	1945-1959
Kleist-Lilly New Testament	1952
K. Wuest, The Expanded Translation of the New Testament	1956-1959
New World/Watchtower Society	1950-1960
Phillips New Testament	1957-1972
New American Standard Bible	1963-1971
Amplified Version	1965
American Bible Society (Revision of AV)	1966
Today's English Version/ Good News Bible	1966-1976
New American Bible	1970
New Scofield Reference Bible	1970
Living Bible	1971
RSV Common Bible	1973
New American Standard Bible	1971
New International Version	1973-1978
New King James Version (Revision of AV)	1982
Reader's Digest Bible	1982

lished, and in 1913 the entire New Testament appeared in this version. The Kleist-Lilly version of the New Testament was published in 1952. In contrast to earlier versions, which were based on the Latin Vulgate, this translation was made from the Greek text.

An official version of the New Testament, based on the Latin Vulgate, was published for American Catholics in 1941, known as the Confraternity New Testament. With a change in the Vatican's policy in 1943 (*See* Divino Afflante Spiritu), members of the Catholic Biblical Association subsequently translated the Scriptures from the original languages, and in 1970 The New American Bible was published.

The New American Standard Version (NASV), sponsored by the Lockman Foundation of California, was published in 1971. The forerunner for this was The Amplified Bible, published between 1958 and 1965. The New American Standard Version itself was a revision and modernization of the ASV

of 1901. Although it is a reliable translation of the original languages, it lacks felicity in its English.

The Living Bible, a paraphrase developed by Kenneth N. Taylor, was the outcome of sixteen years of work which began in 1954. It was published in installments to begin with, but in 1971 Tyndale House in Wheaton, Illinois, published the complete Bible. While not very dependable in its representation of the text in the original languages, its colloquial American English has attracted millions of readers.

Even more phenomenal have been the sales of The Good News Bible (Today's English Version). In 1966 the American Bible Society* published a modern-speech version of the New Testament. Its popularity was so great that four editions were published—the fourth, together with the completed Old Testament, appearing in 1976 as The Good News Bible. The work was spearheaded by Robert Bratscher and was geared to readers whose first language might not be English.

The New International Version arose out of a dissatisfaction among American evangelicals* with existing English versions. In 1965 a Committee on Bible Translations, representing various denominations, made plans for a new translation. Over 100 scholars were involved in the actual translation work, under the leadership of Edwin Palmer. The New York Bible Society agreed to sponsor and finance the project, with printing being done by the Zondervan Publishing House. In 1973 the New Testament was published, and in 1978 the completed Bible came off the press. The translation has been widely accepted by evangelicals, who have appreciated its accuracy and readability.

Despite the variety of translations and versions available, many twentieth-century Americans still prefer the Authorized Version of 1611. To meet this continued demand, in 1961 Jay Green published the King James II, though it was hardly an improvement over the 1611 version. In 1982 Thomas Nelson and Sons published The New King James Bible—a moderate revision of the 1611 version by a group of 119 scholars from various American denominations. With the numerous revisions the AV has undergone, one wonders how many times it can be revised and still retain its original name.

The year 1982 also saw the publication of the Reader's Digest Bible. A condensed version of the Revised Standard Version, the publishers hoped that by putting together selections from the Bible, non-Bible readers would be encouraged to begin reading the Scriptures. This was not the first time the Bible had been abridged for the sake of America's consumers, but the renewed attempt caused some to question whether Holy Scripture should be presented in anything less than full strength.

BIBLIOGRAPHY. F. F. Bruce, *History of the Bible in English,* 2nd ed. (1970); D. Ewert, *From Ancient Tablets to Modern Translations* (1983); M. T. Hills, *The English Bible in America* (1961); J. P. Lewis, *The English Bible/From KJV to NIV* (1982); L. A. Weigle, "Bible IV: United States" *NCE* 2.

D. Ewert

Bible Institutes and Colleges. The Bible college or institute (also popularly called "Bible school") is primarily a North American evangelical* Protestant* innovation and development. As an educational institution, a Bible college occupies an intermediary position between a Bible institute and a Christian liberal arts college. Like a Bible institute its students all earn a major in religion and participate in a formal program of practical Chris-

tian service. Like the Christian liberal arts college, however, the Bible college enrolls all of its students in a series of general-education courses. Generally the Bible college curriculum is four years in length and results in a B.A. degree, whereas the Bible institute program is shorter—frequently three years—and results in a diploma.

Origins of a Movement. While the founders of the earliest American Bible schools found inspiration in the precedents set by London pastors Charles Spurgeon and H. G. Guinness, nowhere has the movement blossomed as in America. Where it has appeared elsewhere throughout the world, it has usually been introduced by American missionaries.* While most of the North American Bible colleges are located in the U.S., the Bible schools have played a larger role in the development of evangelicalism* in Canada than in the U.S.

The American Bible-institute movement arose in the late nineteenth and early twentieth centuries as a response to the widespread revivalism* of Dwight L. Moody* and others, as a reaction to the growth of liberal* thought in American Protestantism in general and its colleges and seminaries* in particular and as a reflection of the American movement toward popular education. The first two Bible schools, Nyack in New York City and Moody* in Chicago, sought to provide quick, practical training for the sharply increasing number of young people who wished to become so-called full-time Christian workers, even though they were in reality lay* persons. In this period before the development of universal secondary education, many of them were unprepared for admittance to a college or seminary and preferred not to commit many years to formal study. They received encouragement from Moody and from Nyack's founder, A. B. Simpson,* both of whom deeply believed that if the Christian message was to reach all classes in all countries, the efforts of the regularly trained clergy* must be supplemented with those of the less well-trained but often more zealous Christian lay workers. The earliest Bible institutes, then, came into existence to serve as an auxiliary means of securing Christian workers.

Although neither Nyack nor Moody was founded primarily to counter the growth of liberal theology, the Bible schools which followed them were increasingly motivated by this purpose. Indeed, in many ways the early Bible institutes served the interdenominational fundamentalist* movement like the headquarters of a denomination.* As the major denominations and their colleges became less orthodox,* the individual churches which separated from them, as well as the small denominations which had never operated any educational institution, increasingly looked to Moody and the other early Bible schools as a model to follow when establishing a school for their own young people. For many students the choice was a Bible-school education or none at all. By 1960 most of the Bible colleges with denominational affiliation represented groups which directly or indirectly had withdrawn from a mainline* denomination in reaction to growing liberal tendencies. In 1960 the Christian Churches and Churches of Christ ("Centrist"),* formerly known as the North American Christian Convention, as well as several Baptist* groups and the combined Holiness* and Pentecostal* denominations each had between thirty and thirty-five Bible colleges. In addition, the Mennonites* sponsored a significant number of Bible colleges, especially in Canada.

Essentially, pioneers Simpson and Moody sought to develop schools to provide minimal training for the type of Christian workers who in earlier eras had pursued their spiritual endeavors with no training at all. These so-called "gap men" streaming forth from Nyack, Moody and the other early Bible schools were the turn-of-the-century counterparts of the earlier Wesleyan* Sunday-school* teachers in England and the Methodist* circuit riders* and Baptist farmer-preachers on the American frontier.

The personal fame of Moody as the best-known evangelist of his time, the solid financial and academic base established by early administrators Henry Crowell and R. A. Torrey,* and the institute's central location in Chicago, one of the most rapidly growing cities in the world, combined to bring Moody Bible Institute to a position of leadership in the Bible-school movement. If Yale,* Princeton* and Oberlin* each gained reputations in the nineteenth century as the mother of many of the liberal arts colleges that began in that period, Moody Bible Institute became known as the mother of numerous Bible institutes and colleges, including Toronto Bible College (later Ontario Bible College), the first permanent Canadian school.

The early Bible schools offered a very limited curriculum. The typical school usually listed some courses in the liberal arts and a large amount of work in biblical studies, theology* and practical Christian training. Every Bible college from the beginning of the movement to the present has made the English Bible* the heart of its curriculum. Almost invariably, each Bible-college student has majored in biblical studies even when pursuing a second major. Also, even though not listing it as a formal part of the curriculum, the schools have given major attention to developing a pietistic* lifestyle in their students.

Bible Colleges and the Evangelical Missions Movement. It is difficult to exaggerate the extent to which the early Bible schools emphasized foreign missionary activity. For example, forty per cent of the 2500 students attending Nyack between 1882 and 1902 eventually entered foreign missionary service in forty countries. The intense missionary emphasis of the early Bible-school movement joined other forces, including the efforts of the Student Volunteer Movement* in the liberal arts colleges and universities, to allow the U.S. by the early twentieth century to surpass England as the supplier of the majority of both personnel and funds for Protestant foreign missions.*

So great was the early and continuing missionary emphasis at the Bible colleges that by the mid-twentieth century they were probably producing the majority, and by the 1980s the large majority, of the Protestant missionary recruits in this country. Indeed this large number of missionary trainees has been one of the unique features of the Bible-college movement. Perhaps no other type of American educational institution can be said to have had a more noteworthy record abroad than in its home country.

While not all Bible college alumni could become missionaries, studies show that historically a high percentage—perhaps even a majority—have entered full-time Christian service, while probably an even higher percentage originally planned for such a career. Today the progressive Bible colleges actively encourage their students to consider a broad variety of Christian callings that include but are not limited to professional ministry.

Practical training—now known as Christian service—has been a part of the curriculum of most schools since their beginning years. Accordingly Bible colleges have usually been located in cities where they could exert a wider influence and find more opportunities for Christian witness than would be possible in rural areas.

Development, Organization and Growth. The most significant recent development in the academic organization of the Bible-college movement has been the tendency for institutions to evolve from Bible institutes to Bible colleges and even, in a few cases, from Bible colleges to Christian liberal-arts colleges. By 1960 approximately half of these schools in North America identified themselves as Bible colleges rather than Bible institutes.

While efforts to create an organization that would establish standards for the total program of the Bible colleges began as early as 1918, they finally succeeded only in the late 1940s under the leadership of President Howard Ferrin of Providence Barrington, President Safara Witmer of Fort Wayne and Dean Samuel Sutherland of Biola. These men led in the organization of the Accrediting Association of Bible Institutes and Bible Colleges (AABIBC). In the late 1950s the organization shortened its name to the Accrediting Association of Bible Colleges (AABC) and hired Witmer as its first full-time executive secretary.

The number of North American institutions accepted as fully accredited members increased to thirty-six in 1960, forty-seven in 1969 and seventy-seven in 1980. In each case the accredited and candidate members represented approximately twenty per cent of the Bible institutes and colleges. In recent years, the AABC manual lists the following standards for its member schools: (1) a desirable student-faculty ratio of 15:1 with the maximum allowable being 25:1; (2) a minimal academic training for faculty members of the first graduate or professional degree beyond the baccalaureate; and (3) a high-school graduation requirement for admission.

The Canadian schools have participated in the AABC, but they have also organized the Association of Canadian Bible Colleges (incorporated in 1968). While eighty-five per cent of the Canadian schools are denominational in affiliation, the most widely recognized ones are independent. These include the aforementioned Ontario, Prairie (Alberta) and Briarcrest (Saskatchewan). Also noteworthy is the number of Bible colleges in Canada's western provinces, the region in which seventy per cent of Canada's Bible colleges have been founded. In part, this may be due to the influence of the spirit of prairie populism.

Like American higher education in general, the Bible-college movement has witnessed significant growth during the twentieth century. While many of the leading Bible colleges began before 1920, the great majority of the approximately 400 contemporary institutions came into existence after 1940. The recent Bible-college enrollment pattern compares favorably with the enrollment figures of the graduate theological schools. The average enrollment in the accredited schools is approximately 425 (accredited seminaries, by comparison, average about 300 students). Most schools, however, are much smaller.

See also HIGHER EDUCATION, PROTESTANT; HIGHER EDUCATION, CATHOLIC; EDUCATION, PROTESTANT THEOLOGICAL; SEMINARIES, CATHOLIC DIOCESAN.

BIBLIOGRAPHY. V. L. Brereton, "Education and Evangelism: Protestant Fundamentalist Bible Schools." (Ph.D. dissertation, Columbia University, 1981); H. W. Boon, "The Development of the Bible College and Institute in the United States and Canada Since 1880." (Ph.D. dissertation, New York University, 1950); G. A. Getz, *MBI: The Story of Moody Bible Institute* (1969); R. G. Sawatsky, "Bible Schools," *Canadian Encyclopedia,* vol 1 (1985); S. A. Witmer, *The Bible College Story: Education with Dimension* (1962).

W. C. Ringenberg

Bible Presbyterian Church. A small Presbyterian* denomination* born out of the modernist-fundamentalist controversy.* In 1936 The Presbyterian Church of America (later Orthodox Presbyterian Church*) was founded by a small group of pastors and elders who left the Presbyterian Church-U.S.A. The immediate cause for this exodus was the suspension of J. Gresham Machen* and J. Oliver Buswell, Jr.,* from the Presbyterian ministry due to their support of an independent mission board that sought to insure biblical teaching on Presbyterian mission fields. The newly formed denomination was soon drawn into internal conflict. Genuine differences in doctrine,* ethics* and church government,* coupled with suspicions and disagreements, led Buswell, Carl McIntire,* Allan MacRae and others to separate and form the Bible Presbyterian Church (BPC) in 1937.

At its first synod the BPC amended the Westminster* standards to teach premillennialism.* A piety* which included alcoholic* abstinence was enjoined, and a church government allowing greater freedom to the local church and both independent and church-controlled agencies was established. The chief characteristic was a self-conscious denominational "testimony" for the Bible* and Jesus Christ, which issued in separatist* stance calling for separation from apostasy* as well as from those having fellowship with apostates. This ultimately isolated the BPC and hindered evangelistic efforts.

The BPC was originally supportive of the American and International Councils of Christian Churches* (ACCC; ICCC) presided over by Carl McIntire. Disagreement during the 1950s over the denomination's association with the ACCC and ICCC and the autonomy of BPC agencies led to the withdrawal of McIntire and others at the 1956 General Assembly to form the Bible Presbyterian Church, Collingswood Synod. The majority continued as the Bible Presbyterian Church, Columbus Synod, until 1961, when the denomination changed its name to the Evangelical Presbyterian

Church (EPC). In 1965 the EPC then merged with the Reformed Presbyterian Church in North America, General Synod, to form the Reformed Presbyterian Church, Evangelical Synod.*

BIBLIOGRAPHY.   G. P. Hutchinson, *The History Behind the Reformed Presbyterian Church, Evangelical Synod* (1974); *The Constitution of the Bible Presbyterian Church* (1946).

J. H. Hall

Bible Societies. Organizations founded for the purpose of distributing Bibles* and portions of Scripture. The Bible society movement began with the spiritual awakening in Germany known as Pietism.* The Van Canstein Bible Society grew out of this movement in 1710 and is considered to be the oldest Bible society in the world. The modern Bible society movement began in 1804, with the founding of the British and Foreign Bible Society in London. Prior to that the Society for the Propagation of Christian Knowledge* (SPCK), founded in 1698, attempted to provide English readers, both in Britain and in her colonies, with Bibles. The Society for the Propagation of the Gospel* (SPG), founded in 1701, did something similar. From England the Bible society movement spread to Europe and the British colonies.

In America, prior to the American Revolution,* most books, religious and secular, were imported from Europe. Publication of English-language Bibles was the prerogative of the Oxford and Cambridge University presses. The War of Independence cut off shipments of English Bibles to America, but with the end of hostilities the flow of Bibles was resumed. That, however, did not prevent American publishers from printing the Bible. In 1782 Congress recommended to the people of the new republic an edition of the Bible printed by Robert Aitken of Philadelphia. At the time only the King James, or Authorized, Version was considered acceptable for English readers.

In 1808 the Philadelphia Bible Society was founded. At first the plan was to form a society that would embrace every state in the Union. However, this could not be achieved at the time and so a smaller society was formed with the purpose of supplying Bibles in English, Welsh, German and French for all denominations.* Such Bibles were to be offered to readers "without money or price."

In 1809, at least seven new Bible societies in New York, Connecticut, Massachusetts, Maine and New Jersey, came into being. All were funded by voluntary donations. Independent as well as interlocking Bible societies continued to be formed, some regionally, others along other lines

(e.g., "Young Men's," "Women's," etc.). In New York a group of Episcopalians,* fearful that readers would have only the plain words of Scripture, established the New York Bible and Common Prayer Society. They objected to the policy of the British and Foreign Bible Society not to publish the Book of Common Prayer.* When the American Bible Society* was founded in 1812, and adopted the policy of the British Society—to publish the Scriptures "without note or comment"—the Episcopal group refused to participate in the founding of this new society.

By 1816 some 130 Bible societies had sprung up in twenty-four states or territories, including fifteen "women's" societies. The British and Foreign Bible Society (BFBS) contributed generously to many of these, both in Bibles and finances. Some of these American societies dispensed fewer than 500 Bibles a year, others went far beyond their regional boundaries. Some of the larger societies took it upon themselves to supply the smaller societies with copies of the Scriptures or portions thereof. All of them depended on freewill offerings to finance their activities. Many of these local societies took a great interest in distributing the Bible to Native Americans, soldiers, prisoners and immigrants who spoke many different languages. Some American societies sent Bibles to other lands.

As the number of societies increased, there was a growing need for a national organization that would somehow keep the movement from becoming chaotic. A pioneer in this regard was Samuel J. Mills,* who was also instrumental in the formation of the American Board of Commissioners for Foreign Missions* in 1812. Mills traveled extensively in the West, distributing Bibles and frequently reporting on the deplorable lack of Bibles among Americans on the frontier. He made a strong case for the formation of a national Bible society but met considerable resistance to the idea. Some regional societies felt their independence threatened, and some Episcopalians hesitated to cooperate with Nonconformists, desiring the Book of Common Prayer to be included among the publications of such a society. The chief argument in favor of a national society was the model established by the BFBS, in which the parent society supplied the auxiliaries with Bibles and these regional societies in turn served as its agents, not only in the distribution of the Scriptures, but also in collecting monies for the parent society. Surely, it was believed, a national society could function more effectively than 108 (in 1814) independent regional societies.

In 1816, fifty-six delegates of various local societies met in New York to form what came to be known as the American Bible Society* (ABS). Like the BFBS, its goal was to distribute the Scriptures "without note or comment." It was designed to help the existing regional societies, not to replace them. By 1817, forty-one established societies had joined the ABS as auxiliaries. Other societies were reluctant to join and, in fact, new Bible societies continued to emerge. The ABS did what it could to help these many societies. Sometimes they even loaned them the printing plates of an edition of the Bible and allowed the regional society to print as many copies as it wished. Often such publications lacked in quality because of lack of proper supervision. By 1818 the ABS began to appoint "stationary agents" all over the country, to receive and solicit donations and subscriptions. Traveling agents who could assist regional societies were also appointed.

Although the name did not suggest it, the charter of the ABS made it clear that it was there to serve not only Americans but also people living in other lands. The original name of the ABS was to have been the American and Foreign Bible Society, but this was not accepted. In order not to compete with the BFBS, arrangements and agreements were made to lessen the potential for conflict and for overlap. The ABS decided to work with missionaries from various denominations in the country where these were active, with missionaries often carrying out the translation and the Society printing the Bibles.

During the Civil War* the ABS remained neutral and sought to serve both the North and the South without discrimination. This helped bring about a reconciliation eventually with the many Southern Baptists* who had formed their own Bible society (American Bible Union*) when the ABS refused to produce English Bibles that plainly rendered the Greek word *baptizein,* commonly translated as *baptize,* as *immerse.*

As the ABS broadened its scope of mission, it also relaxed its policy of printing Bibles without the Apocrypha or other helps. Eventually it became a leader in printing translations based on modern linguistic theories.

The rapid growth of the ABS resulted in the establishment of similar societies in other countries. Plans for closer international cooperation were made prior to World War 2* but were delayed until hostilities ceased. In 1946 the major Bible societies of Europe joined the ABS in forming the United Bible Society (UBS). As a result of the formation of the national Bible society in America

(ABS), with its international connections (UBS), most of the regional Bible societies in the U.S. have disappeared.

See also BIBLE, ENGLISH TRANSLATIONS AND VERSIONS IN NORTH AMERICA; BIBLE AND AMERICAN CULTURE.

BIBLIOGRAPHY. L. A. Bushinski, "Biblical Societies," *NCE* 2; E. W. Frerichs, ed., *The Bible and Bibles in America* (1988); N. O. Hatch and M. A. Noll, *The Bible in America: Essays in Cultural History* (1982); C. Lacy, *The Word Carrying Giant* (1977); W. P. Strickland, *History of the American Bible Society* (1856); R. T. Taylor, *Wings for the Word* (1978). D. Ewert

Bible Study. Throughout American history the systematic study of the Bible* has been a dominant force in the spiritual and intellectual development of the populace. A central feature of colonial religious life was the exposition of Scripture* through sermons.* This was supplemented by personal Bible reading, normally guided by the use of a devotional manual. In addition the Bible was used as a means of teaching reading. This commitment wrought an educational system that made eighteenth-century Americans one of the most literate peoples in the world.

In the nineteenth century the widespread popularity of William McGuffey's* *Eclectic Readers,* which overtly reflected the contents of Scripture, reinforced the influence of the Bible on American education and society. In the early part of the twentieth century, the Protestant emphasis on Bible study was reflected in the Bible conference movement,* the establishment of Bible schools* and the publication of the Scofield Reference Bible* (1909). Although these developments weakened after 1920, the Bible was still studied on an immense scale within the realm of fundamentalism.* Fundamentalists regarded the Bible as the primary vehicle of saving truth for themselves and others. It was studied in order to mold character and ward off temptation, but its most important use was evangelistic.*

Following in this tradition, twentieth-century evangelicals* have used the Bible as their primary authority* for both faith and practice. The post-War religious revival in America brought about an upsurge in the publishing and use of the Bible. This coincided with the publication of the complete text of the Revised Standard Version in 1952. The continuing emphasis of evangelicalism on reading and understanding the written Word of God has also been reflected in the development of nondenominational ministries like Bible Study Fellowship and Neighborhood Bible Studies, Inc.

While the principle of *Sola Scriptura** and the consequent study of Scripture has always been a cornerstone of Protestantism,* a significant move toward systematic Bible study occurred among Catholics in the late 1950s. This was reinforced by Vatican II,* which encouraged the reading and study of the divine Word and its use in liturgy.* As a result, articles, periodicals and classes on Bible study abounded. The most significant of these was *The Bible Today* (1962), a periodical devoted to promoting the appreciation of the Bible among Catholics.

The Bible has also had a profound effect on the African-American community. Prior to the Civil War,* slaves were often punished for reading the Bible, but its study became a central tenet of African-American religious culture. While there were occasional moralistic overtones in their approach to Scripture, African-American Christians have used the Bible as a symbol of hope as well as a tool by which to critique white American society.

The Bible has functioned as an influential element in the development of Christian faith and practice for major segments of American society. At present the study of Scripture is gaining momentum among many of the charismatic* renewal groups. While these groups have normally emphasized the importance of Scripture in evangelism, they are now using it as a basis for prayer,* meditation and teaching. In addition, the current popularity of Bible study programs such as The Bethel Series and Walk Thru the Bible, as well as the spread of small-group Bible studies, reveals the underlying influence which the Scriptures continue to have on American religious life and thought in the last decade of the twentieth century.

BIBLIOGRAPHY. D. L. Barr and N. Peidiscalzi, eds., *The Bible in American Education* (1982); O. Beguin, *Roman Catholicism and the Bible* (1963); N. O. Hatch, *The Bible in America: Essays in Cultural History* (1982); G. Martin, *Scripture and the Charismatic Renewal* (1979).

S. A. Wenig

Biblical Interpretation. Biblical interpretation in America has always had a formal and an informal side. Formally, it is the history of learned men (and since the mid-nineteenth century, women) who have employed technical skills in language, archaeology, history and hermeneutics, often in structured settings of church* and school, for studying the biblical text. Informally, it is the history of how general social and cultural values have influenced the way all Bible readers, whether lay* or cleric, relatively uneducated or professionally certified, have understood the Scriptures.* Formal and informal interpretations of the Bible have proceeded side-by-side and have often affected each other profoundly. The informal story includes the democratic* tendency in America that has led to great creativity and great individualism* in the interpretation of the Bible. But the democratic approach to Scripture has also been balanced by a history of deference—to ecclesiastical authority,* especially among American Catholics*; to academic authorities, especially among more liberal* denominations* over the last century; and to populist leaders of sectarian movements, especially among evangelicals* and fundamentalists.* Informal factors in the interpretation of Scripture have been just as important as the formal, but students of the subject have yet to explore informal patterns of interpretation with the attention they have devoted to the formal.

Before the Critical Era. Academic study of Scripture was one of the trademarks of Puritan* ministers* who took part in the early settlement of New England. Many of these ministers were graduates of Cambridge University, where they participated in the growing European interest in formal biblical study. New concern for Hebrew grammar, a well-established emphasis on the Greek of the New Testament and interest in the derivation of biblical words—all accompanied Puritan ministers to the New World. Harvard College,* founded in 1636, was named in honor of a young minister, John Harvard, who at his death bequeathed his library to the new Massachusetts college. That library of 329 titles was more than half taken up with biblical commentaries, texts and grammars. Puritan preachers* not only brought over a scholarly concern for Scripture from England, but they also tried to promote study of Scripture themselves. The most dedicated example of that promotion was Cotton Mather's* *Biblia Americana,* a manual of 6,000 manuscript pages incorporating textual commentary, Jewish antiquities, harmonization of contradictions and discussions of fulfilled prophecy—all worked up with full attention to the most recent productions of European scholars. Mather died in 1727 without having found a publisher, and the book still awaits printing at the end of the twentieth century.

The Puritans studied the Scriptures so intently because, as Reformed* Protestants,* they felt that the Bible held the key to personal salvation,* social harmony and national well-being. As children of the Reformation, they continued the learned study of Scripture that had characterized the lives of

Martin Luther, John Calvin and leaders of England's Reformation. Technical study was not an end in itself, but a means to better understanding the covenant* that God had established with the church and of better following the divine will to be discovered in the words of Scripture. A certain relaxation in formal biblical study probably did set in during the course of the eighteenth century, but desire to understand the Scriptures still drove the New England descendants of the Puritans and a growing number of learned persons in the Middle and Southern colonies to serious technical study of the Bible.

Immediately after the American Revolution,* the views of free-thinking *philosophes* found a hearing in America and caused a flurry of concern about the Bible. Under the influence of exteme Enlightenment* views, the notion was spread by popular heroes of the Revolution, such as Ethan Allen* and Thomas Paine* (especially in his book, *The Age of Reason*), that the Bible was merely an unusual human book. A little later, some transcendentalists* like Theodore Parker* came to accept the radical conclusions about the human origin of Scripture that had become popular in Europe by the beginning of the nineteenth century. The decades before the Civil War* did see an increasing flow of Americans crossing the Atlantic for study in England, France and especially Germany, as preparation for teaching in American colleges and seminaries. But most of the scholars who pursued a European education did so to buttress traditional views of the Bible. Thus, the Harvard Unitarian* Andrews Norton* studied European biblical scholarship, but used it to support the Bible's divine character and its record of supernatural events. Moses Stuart* of Andover Seminary* was the leading Bible scholar of the period, but he too pursued his studies with the hope of better understanding Scripture as a revelation from God.

As late as the 1870s most American students of Scripture would have shared the belief that Scripture recorded the infallible words of God. It was assumed that the Bible was true, and (with the possible exception of the early chapters of Genesis) true in a commensensical way: events described as historical were historical, statements about matters of fact were matters of fact. Over the first two-thirds of the nineteenth century, the leaders of the American denominations, both those coming from Europe and those started in the New World, disagreed heartily among themselves on what the Bible taught concerning such matters as baptism,* the role of the individual in conversion,* the nature of the church,* the legitimacy of slavery* and other matters. But almost all, Catholic as well as Protestant, would have agreed on the divine character of the Bible and its essential truthfulness.

The Critical Age. The consensus on the divine character of Scripture began to change during the last third of the nineteenth century. Biblical scholarship on the continent, and to some extent in Great Britain, was beginning to look more modern. Conclusions from both "textual criticism" (comparative study of the manuscript evidence for the original words of the New and Old Testaments) and "higher criticism" (the application of modern philosophical notions to the Bible) were calling settled opinions into question. Some of these adjustments concerned simpler matters of translation, like the growing conviction that the King James Version was based on inferior Greek and Hebrew manuscripts. Others, however, dealt with larger questions and seemed to point to a new understanding of Scripture.

The discoveries of inscriptions and other documents dating from the biblical era, along with advances in philology, archaeology and the study of non-Christian religions, led to the conclusion that the Old Testament Hebrews and the New Testament Christians shared more with their surrounding cultures than had previously been thought. Some Americans began to feel that European scholars had demonstrated the relativity of all facts to their historical contexts, that is, that minds were always a function of the cultures in which they existed. This meant, among other troubling conclusions, that the experience of divinity rose as much or more from human conditions and circumstances as from a divine revelation. Historical consciousness of this sort had revolutionary implications when applied to the Bible. Scripture might retain its status as a revered document, but only because of the way it provided a unique focus for the religious experience of Jews and Christians.

The entrance of these views into the American scene corresponded with a surge of professionalization in the country's universities. In 1880 a new academic organization, the Society of Biblical Literature,* was founded as a way of focusing the energies of Bible scholars. In the 1870s and 1880s, graduate study on the European model began to be offered at older universities like Harvard and newer ones like Johns Hopkins. At such centers science was exalted as the royal road to truth, and the new professional academics reacted scornfully to what was perceived as parochial, uninformed and outmoded scholarship. All fields, including the study of the Bible, were to be unfettered for free inquiry.

The result was growing curiosity about the newer critical views of Scripture. Did Moses really write the first five books of the Old Testament, or was Julius Wellhausen correct that the Pentateuch was written by many hands long after the events it purported to describe? Did the prophetic books represent messages to Israel and Judah largely from the eighth through sixth centuries B.C., or were they written later, in fact, after the events they supposedly "foretold"? Did the Gospel writers report the facts about Jesus or the idealized thoughts of the early Christian community? Did Paul really write the pastoral epistles and Peter the letters that bear his name, or were they composed later by individuals who exploited the reputations of the apostles for communicating their own ideas? In general, the newer scholarship relied heavily upon evolutionary notions; histories, stories and writings all evolved over time, as did religious consciousness itself. They also tended to be skeptical about the miraculous and to reflect the view that the religious experience* of the Jews and Christians was not essentially different from that of other peoples in the world.

Very few Americans accepted such views without reservation in the decades before World War 1.* The earliest difference of opinion came rather over the question of whether it was possible to incorporate some elements of the new scholarship into older, more traditional views. An internal debate among Presbyterians* in the years 1881 through 1883 highlighted these questions. Writing in the *Presbyterian Review,* three authors, led by Charles A. Briggs* of Union Seminary* in New York, argued for a cautious acceptance of the new criticism. To them, the results of responsible criticism did not overthrow historical faith in Scripture. Where scholars did not rule out the miraculous in advance, the newer work was helpful since, as Briggs put it, "theories of text and author, date, style, and integrity of writings" cannot establish or undercut the more general confidence in the Bible. Five other Presbyterians, led by Benjamin B. Warfield* (who later taught at Princeton Seminary*), disagreed. They held that the newer views compromised the very notion of a divinely inspired Bible. The Scripture's own account of itself, which was also the traditional understanding of the church, could still be shown to be true if only scholars would abandon the prejudices of modern scholarship.

For the next two decades a noisy series of clashes between conservatives and moderates engaged many American denominations. Professors resigned or were ousted for teaching the more liberal views at Southern Baptist Seminary in Louisville (1879), the Baptist Newton Theological Institution (1882), Congregationalist Andover (1885), Methodist Boston University (1905) and at other institutions. Three prominent Presbyterians, including Charles Briggs, left the denomination during the same period for holding the newer views. The academic tide, however, was swinging in the direction of critical scholarship. After about 1900, most of the recognized universities and seminaries* swung over to the new views, and exponents of more radical notions in which little remained of traditional conceptions of Scripture grew in number and importance.

The result by about 1930 was a fragmented field of Bible scholarship in the U.S. The division was not between scholars and non-scholars, but between advocates of traditional, more mechanical notions of study and critical, more evolutionary ideas. Both sides thought of themselves as truly scientific, while each thought the other had sacrificed science to ideology. The burgeoning academic literature from university presses and scholarly journals came, with a few exceptions, to be the preserve of modern critical views. Arguments upholding traditional notions of Scripture opinions found expression in *The Fundamentals** (1910-1915) and in the works of leading fundamentalists during the 1920s. In general, those who upheld the new criticism thought that when conservatives stubbornly failed to recognize the recent gains in scholarship and philosophical perspective and when they clung to outmoded conceptions of the supernatural, they forfeited their right to existence in the modern academy. The conservatives held that the evolutionary speculations and the anti-supernatural bias of the new critics disqualified them as scholars altogether.

Conservative attitudes toward biblical interpretation moved further away from opinions in the academy, as powerful renewal movements, with little place for modern learning, strengthened their various constituencies. Among Southern Baptists,* the leading theological positions of the period stressed the importance of Christ-centered faith and the renewal of the heart, and so were not preoccupied with academic questions. The new and growing Pentecostal movement* relied faithfully on the Bible, but mostly as a source for mediating the direct witness and activity of the Holy Spirit. The growth of dispensationalism,* with its insistence that the Bible be interpreted literally wherever possible and with its abiding concern for the fulfilling of prophecy, pushed conservative constituencies further away from modern academic standards. Southern Baptists, Pentecostals and dispensationalists could all be painstaking students of the Bible, but their standards of interpretation grew out of a traditional confidence in the Bible as a divinely revealed book, rather than from the modern academy's understanding of Scripture as a human record of ancient religious experience.

By 1930, only a few places remained in America where older notions of the Bible's divine character coexisted alongside involvement with modern academic research. Such places included institutions like Princeton Seminary which, after a reorganization in 1929, stood on the conservative end of the academic mainstream; Westminster Seminary, founded by Presbyterian conservatives as a protest against the Princeton reorganization; institutions sustained by European-based denominations, where academic work was often carried on in Dutch, German or a Scandinavian language; the colleges* and seminaries* of the Roman Catholic Church, where views on Scripture continued to be very conservative until after World War 2*; and some denominational seminaries in the South (a region always more immune to the newer criticism), where intensive work on the biblical languages was combined with traditional opinions.

In Canada roughly the same divisions prevailed, except that lines of demarcation were never drawn as sharply as in the U.S. Scholars at major centers of research largely accepted the newer critical conclusions, while conservative evangelicals and some groups of immigrant Pietists* followed traditional approaches to Scripture. Because of the influence of Britain, where biblical scholarship, especially in the New Testament, never became as radical as in the U.S. or on the Continent, there was still some room for moderate or conservative views. The Canadian practice of incorporating denominational colleges into university systems also meant that where churches maintained conservative practices of biblical interpretation, they remained in closer dialog with critical views than was the case in the U.S. Beginning in the 1930s, moreover, the growth of InterVarsity Christian Fellowship* presaged a new interest by conservatives in university-level academic work. On the model of recent biblical scholarship in the United Kingdom, and somewhat more rapidly than in the U.S., Canadian evangelicals who pursued Bible scholarship were able to win at least a modest hearing in the academy.

The Post-War Period. Since World War 2,*

critical scholarship in the U.S. has been nudged back in a more traditional direction, especially by the influence of neo-orthodox* theology and by the realization that some of the supposedly scientific discoveries of the nineteenth century were more a product of their times than of genuine breakthroughs. A biblical theology movement,* strong in the 1950s and 1960s, was an effort to season standard critical views with the increased respect for Scripture as divine revelation that characterized neo-orthodoxy. More recently, proposals to treat the canon of Scripture as the central focus of biblical research (as opposed to the historical process thought to lie behind the canonical documents) has led some scholars in mainstream academic institutions partway back to more traditional views of biblical understanding. Still, however, the "academic orthodoxy" remains predominately under the influence of non-traditional opinions. In addition to advocates of higher criticism in the nineteenth-century model, contemporary scholars who promote radical versions of form and redaction criticism usually discount the idea that the Bible is a unique revelation from God. For such ones, similarities between the religion of the Bible and the religion of other peoples still loom larger than differences, and the bias against the supernatural is as pronounced as ever. Developments of the 1970s and 1980s—in the application of post-modernist literary theory and the deployment of self-conscious ideologies—reinforced the trend away from traditional opinions.

On the opposite side, study of Scripture that has no use for modern criticism has grown rapidly in almost all parts of North America and among many groupings of Christians. The more general conservative turn in religion has been accompanied by a plethora of books, articles and organizations serving the needs of those who reject the academic conventions of the modern secular university. The creation of universities by leading television evangelists, the growth in public promotion of "creation science"* and "flood geology," and an immense flow of literature on the Bible from anti-modernist publishers testify to the capacity of theological conservatives to maintain their own standards of biblical interpretation in direct opposition to the conventions of the academy.

Between the two extremes recent decades have also witnessed a growing contingent of scholars who could be called "believing critics." Such ones may be self-styled evangelicals; they may come from Catholic, Reformed, Lutheran,* Methodist* or other older denominations; or they may be at home in the newer denominations of the Churches of Christ,* Pentecostals or Seventh-Day Adventists.* Such scholars concur with conservatives who reject the modern academy and believe in the divine character of Scripture, but they also share with modern critics the conviction that modern discoveries and theoretical proposals can sometimes provide a clearer grasp of the Bible. Representatives of such convictions began returning to university graduate schools in the 1930s. Soon they were establishing their own academic institutions, publishing their commentary series and other scholarly efforts and also organizing new translations. A major boost to their work has come from Great Britain, where academics relatively conservative on issues of Bible scholarship have gained positions in the universities, sponsored graduate students (many from the U.S.) and paved the way for more fruitful interaction with scholars who did not share traditional views.

At the end of the twentieth century, the history of formal biblical interpretation in America remains divided. Despite the growing number of "believing critics," the divisions over criticism dating from the late nineteenth century remain deep. The religious and social circumstances that nurtured a common view of Scripture in the years before the American Civil War are gone. It remains to be seen how successful the efforts of "believing critics" will be to bridge the gap between traditions of the church and the practices of the modern academy.

See also DIVINO AFFLANTE SPIRITU; SCRIPTURE.

BIBLIOGRAPHY. J. W. Brown, *The Rise of Biblical Criticism in America, 1800-1870* (1969); G. P. Fogarty, *American Catholic Biblical Scholarship: A History from the Early Republic to Vatican II* (1989); N. O. Hatch and M. A. Noll, ed., *The Bible in America: Essays in Cultural History* (1982); R. Lundin, "Our Hermeneutical Inheritance," *The Responsibility of Hermeneutics,* ed. Lundin, C. Walhout, and A. C. Thiselton (1985); N. H. Maring, "Baptists and Changing Views of the Bible, 1865-1918," *Foun* 1 (July 1958):52-75, and (Oct. 1958):30-61; G. M. Marsden, *Fundamentalism and American Culture: The Shaping of Twentieth-Century Evangelicalism, 1870-1925* (1980); M. A. Noll, *Between Faith and Criticism: Evangelicals, Scholarship, and the Bible in America* (1986); T. Olbricht, "Biblical Primitivism in American Biblical Scholarship, 1630-1870," *The Restoration Tradition in America,* ed. R. Hughes (1988); J. B. Rogers and D. K. McKim, *The Authority and Interpretation of the Bible: An Historical Approach* (1979); J. Stackhouse, "Proclaiming the Word: Canadian Evangel-

icalism Since World War I" (unpublished Ph.D. dissertation, University of Chicago, 1987); J. Woodbridge, *Biblical Authority: A Critique of the Rogers-McKim Proposal* (1982).   M. A. Noll

Biblical Theology Movement. The biblical theology movement in America is generally believed to have begun in the 1940s and to have lasted until the early 1960s—roughly parallel to the flourishing of neo-orthodoxy* in America. The movement's inception is marked by the appearance of studies related to biblical theology, such as Millar Burrows' *Outlines in Biblical Theology* (1946) and G. Ernest Wright's *God Who Acts: Biblical Theology as Recital* (1952). The demise of the movement, as charted in Brevard Child's *Biblical Theology in Crisis* (1970), could be seen in Langdon B. Gilkey's article "Cosmology, Ontology, and the Travail of Biblical Language" (1961) and James Barr's inaugural address at Princeton Theological Seminary, "Revelation through History in the Old Testament and Modern Thought" (1962). Contrary to Childs, James D. Smart has argued that there never was a distinct movement, that biblical theology has been a long-term interest in international biblical scholarship and that the interest was still alive in the late 1970s.

Biblical theology as a self-conscious discipline has roots at least as far back as 1787 in Johann Philipp Gabler's (1753-1826) distinction between biblical and systematic theology: "Biblical theology is historical in character and sets forth what the sacred writers thought about divine matters," while dogmatic theology is "didactic in character, and teaches what a particular theologian philosophically and rationally decides about divine matters, in accordance with his character, time, age, place, sect or school, and other similar influences." Nineteenth-century European scholarship produced numerous examples of biblical theology in this vein, but by century's end the philosophical influence of G. W. F. Hegel (1770-1831) and the literary and historical criticism of Julius Wellhausen (1844-1918) in the Old Testament and the work of Ferdinand Christian Bauer (1792-1860) and Wilhelm Wrede (1859-1906) in the New Testament, had turned the attention of the mainstream of biblical scholarship away from biblical theology. Emphasis was placed on the development of religious ideas and theologies within Israel and primitive Christianity, with little or no regard for the issue of revealed truth or its unity.

The influence of this European movement on English-speaking scholarship could be seen in British scholar H. Wheeler Robinson's *The Relig-

ious Ideas of the Old Testament (1913) and American theologian Albert C. Knudsen's* *The Religious Teaching of the Old Testament* (1918). Conservative Continental scholars such as Ernst W. Hengstenberg (1802-1869), Johann von Hofmann (1810-1877) and Georg H. A. Ewald (1803-1875) did resist this movement, each with their own distinctive approach to the issue of the unity and authority of the biblical message. Nevertheless, by the 1920s biblical scholarship had contributed to the spiritual poverty of liberalism,* which was left with a Bible that could be viewed with little more than skepticism and far less than an authoritative canon for Christian truth. The appearance of Karl Barth's* 1918 commentary on the Epistle to the Romans is often cited as the beginning of liberalism's rediscovery of the Bible as the Word of God and consequently, a return to biblical theology.

In Europe the Old Testament theology of Walter Eichrodt (1933-1938) marked a revival of interest in biblical theology. This was followed by the work of Wilhelm Vischer (1934), Theodorus C. Vriezen (1949) and, somewhat later, the magisterial work of Gerhard von Rad (1957-1960). In New Testament theology there were contributions by Adolf Schlatter (1909-1918), Ethelbert Stouffer (1941) and later that of Rudolf Bultmann (1948-1953). All of these works had their gradual effect in shaping American biblical theology. Just as liberalism and biblical criticism had been slower to take root in North America than in Europe, so the reaction to the old liberalism and the parallel return to biblical theology had a delayed entrance onto the American theological scene. This was as much due to the lingering cultural optimism in America as it was to the geographical and linguistic barriers.

Though the movement was characterized by a diversity of methods, confessional orientations and results, James Barr has identified eight characteristics that were widely shared: (1) a contrast drawn between biblical and philosophical categories of thought; (2) a preference for the organic nature of biblical theology rather than the systematizing tendency of dogmatic theology; (3) an argument that the Bible was pervaded by Hebrew thought patterns in contrast to the Greek thought of later Christian theology; (4) a confidence in the unity of biblical theology and an optimism that a unifying theme could be found; (5) an emphasis on word studies as a legitimate approach to the meaning of biblical language; (6) a contrast drawn between the Bible over against its cultural and religious environment; (7) a stress on revelation in history; and (8) a conviction that theological concern should pervade biblical study, bearing fruit in preaching and the life of the church.

All of these features can be seen as a reaction against the sterility of the purely analytic biblical criticism that had prevailed for over half a century in America. The movement gave fresh impetus to scholars and publishers, who sought to bridge the gap between biblical exegesis and pulpit exposition. One journal that still remains, *Interpretation: A Journal of Bible and Theology,* was founded in 1947 at Union Theological Seminary, Richmond, Virginia, to encourage biblical theology and convey its fruit to the pulpit. Biblical theology, if no longer a movement, remains today as a theological discipline that seeks to disclose the theological meaning of the Bible.

BIBLIOGRAPHY. J. Barr, "Biblical Theology" in *The Interpreter's Dictionary of the Bible* Supplementary Volume (1976):104-111; B. Childs, *Biblical Theology in Crisis* (1970); W. J. Harrington, *The Path of Biblical Theology* (1973); J. D. Smart, *The Past, Present and Future of Biblical Theology* (1979). D. G. Reid

Biederwolf, William Edward (1867-1939).

Popular Presbyterian* evangelist.* Born at Monticello, Indiana, Biederwolf was converted* as a teen-ager under the evangelistic* ministry of Frank N. Palmer, pastor of the Presbyterian* Church of Monticello. Biederwolf attended Wabash College, Indiana (1889-1890), and Princeton University,* where he received his B.A. and M.A. (1890-1894). Graduating from Princeton Theological Seminary* in 1895, he spent two years under a Princeton Fellowship at the Universities of Berlin and Erlangen in Germany, and the Sorbonne in Paris. After pastoring a Presbyterian church in Logansport, Indiana (1897-1900), he became an assistant to revivalist* J. Wilbur Chapman.* In 1906 he launched out on his own, spending much of the next three decades in evangelistic campaigns, primarily in small towns and medium-sized cities in the U.S. Biederwolf combined soul-winning* with advocacy of civic reform, prohibition* and Americanism. In his later years premillennialism* was a favorite theme. He wrote several books on the topic, including *The Millenium Bible* (1924). Biederwolf was also active in efforts to reduce corruption among revivalists.

In 1922 Biederwolf became director of the Winona Lake Bible Conference, rescuing it from near-bankruptcy. In 1923 he became director of the Winona Lake Bible School of Theology, a position he held until he became its president in 1933. Later he organized and owned The Winona Publishing Company of Chicago. In his final decade (1929-1939), he also pastored the Royal Poinciana Chapel in Palm Beach, Florida, called by some the "richest congregation in the world."

BIBLIOGRAPHY. R. E. Garrett, *William Edward Biederwolf: A Biography* (1948); W. G. McLoughlin, Jr., *Modern Revivalism: Charles Grandison Finney to Billy Graham* (1959).

W. V. Trollinger

Bill of Rights. *See* FIRST AMENDMENT TO THE CONSTITUTION.

Billings, William (1746-1800). Composer and singing master. An untutored tanner by trade, Billings became the first important American composer and a major force in the development of New England musical practices. Despite his unusual appearance and habits (he had a short leg, withered arm and blind eye; and he dipped large amounts of snuff), he was able to give up his tannery to teach singing and train choirs in Boston, including those of the Brattle Street and Old South churches. Billings introduced the use of the pitchpipe and cello to New England's previously unaccompanied choirs. Alone among his American peers, he wrote or sought out original texts for his tunes, and he advocated the pleasure, as well as the spiritual benefits, to be derived from music. In composition, he utilized meter changes and "fuguing" to dramatically interpret his texts. His several publications included *The New England Psalm-Singer* (1770), *The Singing Master's Assistant* (1778) and *The Psalm Singer's Amusement* (1781). His reputation sagged in the 1800s, but his works are often sung today.

BIBLIOGRAPHY. R. Crawford, "Watts for Singing: Metrical Poetry in American Sacred Tunebooks, 1761-1783," *Early American Literature* 11 (1976): 139-146; *DAB* I; M. G. DeJong, " 'Both Pleasure and Profit': William Billings and the Uses of Music," *WMQ* 42 (1985):104-116; D. P. McKay and R. Crawford, *William Billings of Boston: Eighteenth-Century Composer* (1975).

T. T. Taylor

Billington, Dallas Franklin (1903-1972). Baptist* preacher. Born in a log house in western Kentucky and raised in a devout Christian home, Billington did not respond to the gospel until, at the age of twenty-one, he was converted* at a tent meeting* in Paducah, Kentucky, where he had been invited by his fiancée, Nell Stokes. In 1927, after moving to Akron, Ohio, to gain employment and during a serious illness of his infant son, Billington answered God's call to preach. In June

1934, he was invited to organize a group of people into a Baptist church. Beginning with thirteen people meeting in an elementary school and an offering of $1.18, the Akron Baptist Temple was born. Under his ministry over the next thirty-eight years, the church grew to sixteen thousand members and physical assets of several million dollars. The church was among the first to have its own television studio. Its radio, television and missionary outreach made its ministry worldwide. In 1968 the church was recognized by *Christian Life* magazine as having the world's largest Sunday schools. Having had heart trouble since 1941, Billington died of a heart attack August 26, 1972, at age sixty-nine. His only son, Charles, who had served as associate pastor for twenty-four years, succeeded him as pastor of the Akron Baptist Temple.

E. L. Towns

Billy Graham Center. An agency of Wheaton College* devoted to research, strategy and training for evangelism* and missions.* The idea for a Billy Graham Center began in 1970 when the Billy Graham Evangelistic Association* formed a committee to gather materials that documented its history and the ministry* of Billy Graham.* Also in 1970, the Association established a separate entity, the World Evangelism and Christian Education Fund, which would finance the project.

Early on the idea arose of establishing a center that would contain an archives, library and museum, each of which would document the Graham ministry and collect resources on the history of evangelism and missions. Such a center, it was thought, might also sponsor programs to advance the cause of world evangelization. Several sites were considered, but Wheaton College, Graham's alma mater, was chosen in 1974. Groundbreaking took place in 1977, and the building was dedicated in 1980. It housed the Billy Graham Center, which included an archives, a library, a museum and eventually a cluster of programs; and it was the site of the Wheaton College Graduate School.

The substantive shape and thrust of the Graham Center's ministry developed slowly at first, but by 1988 it included a variety of activities and agencies, notably a missionary-scholar-in-residence program, professional workshops and conferences, and strategic institutes in the areas of Chinese studies, prison ministries and evangelism. Adjunct agencies also located at the Center included the Extension Studies Department and research institutes on American evangelicals, Christianity and Marxism and Muslim studies.

BIBLIOGRAPHY. J. Maust, "Graham Center Provides Evangelism Focal Point," *CT* (October 10, 1980):74-75; R. Shuster, "Library and Archival Resources of the Billy Graham Center," *IBMR* 5 (1981):124-126; C. H. Malik, *The Two Tasks* (1980).   J. A. Carpenter

Billy Graham Evangelistic Association. The nonprofit religious corporation which conducts the ministries* of Billy Graham,* his associate evangelists and affiliated agencies. The Billy Graham Evangelistic Association (BGEA) was the vehicle that brought evangelist Billy Graham's gospel message to scores of millions around the globe and made him one of the best-known persons in the twentieth century. The BGEA was founded in 1950 in order to dispel criticism over Graham's finances as his crusade ministry grew, and to provide organization for his expansion into other endeavors. By the late 1980s, the BGEA, which maintained its headquarters in Minneapolis, Minnesota, had become a large and varied international religious agency, with offices serving every major continent and a North American budget in excess of $70 million.

Among the activities and subsidiaries of the BGEA by the 1980s were Graham's crusades and those of his seven associate evangelists; telecasts of Graham's crusades; the "Hour of Decision" radio program, broadcast in six languages; World Wide Pictures, which produced documentary and dramatic evangelistic films; *Decision* magazine, which was published in six languages and had a monthly circulation of 4 million; a counseling department, which handled nearly a quarter of a million letters and 6,000 calls a year; Grason/World Wide Publications, which published and distributed Graham's writings and a selection of other evangelical books and pamphlets; radio stations in North Carolina and Hawaii; a World Emergency Fund, which distributed about $400,000-500,000 a year in relief activity; and the Schools of Evangelism, sixty of which were conducted between 1967 and 1987.

Over the years, the BGEA's activity has reflected Graham's importance as an evangelical* leader. Among the events and agencies which owe their existence to the BGEA's influence and support are *Christianity Today** magazine, which Graham helped to found in 1956; the World Congress on Evangelism, held in Berlin in 1966; the International Congress on World Evangelism, held in Lausanne in 1974, and the continuing Lausanne Committee on World Evangelization; the Evangelical Council for Financial Accountability (ECFA), founded in 1978; the Billy Graham Center* of Wheaton College,* dedicated in 1980 as an agency

for research, strategy and training in world evangelization; the International Conferences for Intinerant Evangelists in Amsterdam in 1983 and 1986; and The Cove, near Asheville, North Carolina, projected in 1987 as a lay retreat center for training in Bible and evangelism.

These ventures distributed the influence of Graham and the BGEA in a variety of directions. *Christianity Today* has given evangelicals a forum for intelligent and thought-provoking religious discourse. The international conferences and the ongoing Lausanne Committee have been landmarks of evangelicals' deepening understanding of the church's worldwide mission* and the relationship between gospel and culture. The founding of the ECFA showed evangelicals' growing concern over the conduct and reputation of their parachurch* agencies. The Billy Graham Center reflected both the spirit of Lausanne and a desire to restore advanced scholarship to the status of kingdom work. And The Cove embodied an abiding evangelical goal: to help ordinary people know God's Word and spread the gospel.

In sum, Billy Graham and the executives of the BGEA have been remarkably single-minded in their commitment to evangelism, but they have used their influence and resources to stimulate evangelical advances in other strategic fields.

BIBLIOGRAPHY. W. Martin, "Billy Graham," in *Varieties of Southern Evangelicalism,* ed. D. F. Harrell, Jr. (1981); Billy Graham Evangelistic Association and Affiliated Organizations, *Annual Report* (1987); *Guide to Collection 74,* Graham, William Franklin, Jr., Ephemera, Archives of the Billy Graham Center, Wheaton, Illinois; J. C. Pollack, *Billy Graham: The Authorized Biography* (1966).   J. A. Carpenter

Bimeler (Bäumler), Joseph Michael (1778-1853). Communitarian leader. Born in Wurttemberg, Germany, Bimeler was a weaver and schoolteacher. He joined, and later led, a company of peasants who broke away from the Lutheran Church,* refused to send their children to German schools and would not allow their young men to serve in the military. Harassed because of their nonconformity, Bimeler's group immigrated* to the U.S. In 1817 they settled in Ohio. Calling themselves the Society of the Separatists of Zoar, or the Zoarites, they founded the community of Zoar. Bimeler served as Zoar's agent general until his death. In this capacity he acted as the intermediary between the community and the outside world. He was also their physician and spiritual leader. Zoarites adhered to a strict personal piety, and though they were initially celibate, they later permitted marriage within the community. In 1819 they adopted communistic practices. Zoar survived Bimeler's death in 1853, finally disbanding in 1898.

BIBLIOGRAPHY. *DAB* I; M. Holloway, *Heavens on Earth* (1966); *NCAB* 13.　　　W. M. Ashcraft

Bingham, Hiram, Jr. (1831-1908). Missionary* to the Gilbert Islands. Born in Honolulu, the son of missionary Hiram Bingham, Sr., he graduated from Yale College* and attended Andover Theological Seminary.* Bingham was appointed a missionary of the American Board of Commissioners for Foreign Missions* in 1856 and sailed on the missionary ship *Morning Star,* arriving at Apiaiang in the Gilbert Islands where he started a mission station. He returned to the U.S. in 1865, and in 1866 he was made commander of the second *Morning Star,* sailing from Boston and making a circuit of missions in the Marquesas and Micronesia. After making another unsuccessful attempt (1873-1875) to adjust to health conditions on Apaiang, he lived from 1875 in Honolulu.

Bingham reduced the Gilbertese language to writing and provided the beginnings of a Christian literature in that language: the Bible* (1890), a hymn* and tune book (1880), a *Gilbert Islands Bible Dictionary* (1895) and a commentary on the Gospels and Acts. For these achievements Yale granted him the D.D. in 1895. He was for a time corresponding secretary of the Hawaiian Board of Missions and held a government appointment as protector for the colony of Gilbert Islanders.

BIBLIOGRAPHY. *DAB* I.

D. M. Stowe

Bingham, Hiram, Sr. (1789-1869). Pioneer missionary* to Hawaii. Born in Bennington, Vermont, Bingham graduated from Middlebury College and Andover Theological Seminary.* In 1819 he was ordained* a missionary of the American Board of Commissioners for Foreign Missions* and sailed with the first company of Protestant* missionaries to the Sandwich Islands.

Courageous and strong-willed, yet good-natured, cheerful and calmly persistent, Bingham was the natural leader of the mission. He was stationed at Honolulu, the seat of government and the principal port of call, where he represented the mission before the Hawaiian king and chiefs as well as foreign residents and visitors. Bingham's force of personality and high moral principles won the general allegiance of the Hawaiians but brought him into conflict with foreigners who resented missionary interference with their com-

mercial, political or sexual interests.

Bingham was the first pastor of Kawaiahao Church and helped create a written Hawaiian language, translated several books of the Bible* and published numerous books, including *First Book for Children* (1831) and *Scripture Catechism* (1831). His wife's ill health forced a withdrawal in 1841. Following her death in 1848, changes in Hawaii made it difficult for him to return. For a few years he was pastor of an African-American church in New Haven, Connecticut, and was later supported by an annuity given by friends. He died just before a planned return to the Islands for the semicentenary celebration in 1870. Bingham privately published *A Residence of Twenty-one Years in the Sandwich Islands* (1847), recounting the early history of the mission.

BIBLIOGRAPHY. R. Anderson, *History of the Sandwich Islands Mission* (1870); *DAB* I; O. Gulick, *Pilgrims of Hawaii* (1918); A. Loomis, *Grapes of Canaan: Hawaii, 1820* (1951).

D. M. Stowe

Bingham, Roland Victor (1872-1942). Evangelical* publisher and missionary.* Bingham was born in East Grinstead, Sussex, England, and moved to Canada as a young man, shortly after his conversion* under the Salvation Army.* While in Toronto Bingham became convinced that God was calling him as a missionary to the Sudan. In 1893 he arrived in Lagos in the company of Walter Gowans and Tom Kent, both of whom were to lose their lives as they attempted to penetrate the Sudan. Bingham, however, having contracted malaria, was forced to return to Canada. In 1898, after brief medical training, followed by studies at Simpson's Bible College in New York, he founded the Sudan Interior Mission.* In 1901 the first mission station was established in Patagi, West Africa; and by the time of his death, he had built it into the largest Protestant presence in Africa, with nearly a thousand missionaries engaged in medicine, education, printing and Bible* translation.

Bingham's influence was not limited to Africa. In Canada he edited the only transdenominational evangelical magazine (the *Evangelical Christian and Missionary Witness*), founded Evangelical Publishers (1912) and established a summer resort and spiritual retreat, the Canadian Keswick Conference (1924). Bingham used his magazine, summer conference and personal prestige to promote British, American and domestic missions and organizations (Shantyman's, InterVarsity,* Scripture Gift, etc.), which sought an introduction to the Canadian evangelical community. Although critical of the tactics of T. T. Shields* and the eschatological* stance of other fundamentalists,* Bingham, an ordained* Baptist,* strenuously opposed the spread of evolutionary* theory and higher criticism in his denomination and in the larger Christian community.

See also SIM INTERNATIONAL

BIBLIOGRAPHY. J. Hunter, *A Flame of Fire* (1961).

B. A. McKenzie

Bioethics. Bioethics is the intellectual discipline that attempts to resolve specific ethical problems brought about by innovations in biology. Until recently, religious and medical values, with the notable exception of induced abortion* to save the mother's life, were largely in fundamental agreement. The four ends of medicine—preventative, diagnostic, curative and alleviatory—were not in conflict with religion's mandate to love oneself and one's neighbor.

Recent biological advances, however, especially in the areas of genetics, reproductive physiology and life-prolonging techniques, have given medicine new powers that go beyond their four traditional ends. The gap between medical technology—what medicine *can* do—and traditional religious ethics* has prompted religious leaders and religious institutions to re-evaluate their positions on medical ethics and, in some instances, provide carefully reasoned statements to serve as guidelines for their adherents.

Speaking in behalf of an Orthodox Jewish tradition, Rabbi Immanuel Jakobovits reiterates Judaism's attribution of *infinite* value to human life. Because infinity is indivisible, any fraction of life, however limited its expectancy or health, remains equally infinite in value. Reformed Jews, in general, take a more permissive approach to bioethical issues.

Paul Ramsey speaks for the Protestant* tradition on the matter of the integrity of the marital act when he states that "an ethic that in principle sunders the unitive from the procreative good of sexual intercourse pays disrespect to the nature of human parenthood." Likewise, Helmut Thielicke asserts that the totality of the marriage is threatened when the couple conceives a child through the biotechnological means of artificial insemination by an anonymous donor (AID), an act which he regards as the ruin of the one-flesh unity of husband and wife.

On the other hand, some Protestant ethicists and theologians* deviate from their Christian tradition. Joseph Fletcher, for example, an Episcopalian* minister, accepts a utilitarian argument in defending the use of a wide variety of new bio-technologies, including *in vitro* fertilization and the bio-engineering of "para-humans." Fletcher believes that a proportionately good end can justify the introduction of actions that are in themselves disvalues and evils. Some Protestant as well as Catholic* moral theologians depart from a traditional ethic of the sanctity of life and argue for an ethic centered on the quality of life.

The most definitive and comprehensive ecclesiastical declaration on the matter of bioethics is that released by the Vatican on March 10, 1987, entitled "Instruction on Respect for Human Life in Its Origin and on the Dignity of Procreation." The "Instruction" is based on two principles: the integrity of the marital act and the fundamental good of all forms of human life. The "Instruction" finds that such techniques as artificial insemination, freezing and experimenting with human embryos and fetuses, *in vitro* fertilization and surrogate motherhood are essentially incompatible with these two principles. At the same time, the "Instruction" encourages scientists to develop techniques that are aimed at *assisting* insemination and restoring fertility. These aims are consistent with a Catholic tradition that affirms medical intervention that is truly therapeutic and is concerned about restoring the patient to health or wholeness.

See also ABORTION; BIRTH CONTROL; ETHICS, CATHOLIC PERSONAL; ETHICS, PROTESTANT PERSONAL

BIBLIOGRAPHY. I. Jakobovits, "Some Recent Jewish Views on Death and Euthanasia," *Death, Dying, and Euthanasia,* ed. D.J. Horan and D. Mall (1977); D. G. Jones, *Brave New People* (1984); W. May, *Sex and the Sanctity of Human Life* (1984); H. Thielicke, *The Ethics of Sex* (1964).

D. T. DeMarco

Birth Control. A term made popular in the U.S. by Margaret Sanger (1883-1966), it could in principle refer to any voluntary control of the reproductive effect of sexual intercourse, but it is popularly used to refer to the various mechanical or chemical means used before, during or after coitus to prevent conception. In the latter sense it is often called contraception.

U.S. Catholic* and Protestant* views on birth control developed in the context of Christian thinking on marriage and its purposes, particularly in response to modern Western social conditions. Until about 1930, a broad consensus existed. Both Catholics and Protestants, regardless of how or on what basis they perceived the purposes of marriage, viewed voluntary prevention of conception by means other than abstinence as offensive to God's purposes for creation. This consensus found its way into U.S. law as Protestant social reformers, beginning in the 1870s, campaigned against the birth-control movement and won highly restrictive federal and state legislation against contraception. Catholic moral theologians* such as Francis P. Kenrick* in the nineteenth century and John A. Ryan* in the twentieth also gave voice to this consensus.

By the 1930s societal support for such legislation had eroded. For many, birth control had become a medical question. U.S. Protestants, with the freedom afforded them by the Reformation's scriptural principle, had begun to respond to new social conditions by rethinking the purposes of marriage in terms of a biblically based appreciation for the interpersonal dimensions of married love. During the years between England's 1930 Lambeth Conference* of Anglican* bishops* and the 1958 Conference, U.S. Protestant thought moved gradually away from the traditional consensus to a new one which recognized contraception as a means to responsible Christian parenthood in a global perspective. From an early emphasis at Lambeth 1930 on a presumption in favor of procreation in the family setting, with a cautious approval of contraception and a hierarchy of means, discussion moved to a later emphasis at Lambeth 1958, and in statements from U.S. mainline* denominations in the 1950s, on the responsibility to limit family size in a world population context. By 1956 a United Lutheran* Church in the U.S.A. statement could view "irresponsible" reproduction to be as detrimental as "selfish limitation."

Criticisms from U.S. black Christians and others have tempered initial enthusiasm for the ambivalent overpopulation rhetoric about "bombs" and "explosions." With less emphasis on the population question, the 1968 evangelical* statement, "An Affirmation on the Control of Human Reproduction," presented a comparatively conservative Protestant view. While it appreciated the potentially positive role birth control might play in Christian marriage, the Affirmation also insisted that the reasons for it must be "in harmony with the total revelation of God for marriage." Once a couple has made the decision, recognized as a morally serious one, to limit conception, questions of means become primarily medical rather than moral. Voluntary sterilization is not excluded.

Until the 1960s U.S. Catholic views on birth control were shaped largely by papal reaffirmations of the traditional consensus in terms of what was "natural," that is, in keeping with God's purposes for creation. Pope Pius XI's* 1930 encyc-

lical *Casti connubii* repeated, partly in response to Lambeth 1930, the traditional ban on contraception. In 1951 Pope Pius XII* approved the use of rhythm (birth regulation by abstinence during the wife's fertile period). During the next decade many factors spurred discussion of the issue and led to widespread expectation of a development in papal teaching: (1) marketing of the anovulant pill, often called "the pill," and the involvement of Catholic physician John Rock; (2) publication by Catholic laity of reflections on their past decade of experience with rhythm; (3) theologians' recognition of intercourse as an expression of married love; (4) Pope Paul VI's* establishment in 1964 of a commission of experts to study birth control; (5) the second Vatican Council's* emphasis on "conjugal love" in marriage (procreation was no longer referred to as the primary end); and (6) the 1967 leak to the press of the papal Commission's Report recommending a change.

When *Humanae Vitae** appeared in July 1968, a sizable majority of U.S. Catholics rejected its teaching on birth control. Among these dissenters were many theologians, the most prominent of whom is C. E. Curran who holds that spouses may decide that contraception is sometimes "permissible and indeed necessary" to safeguard Christian marriage. As a symbol of dissent, birth control dramatizes the issue of church authority. U.S. Catholic bishops have publicly supported *Humanae Vitae*. Empirical research indicates that U.S. Catholics use artificial contraception in the same proportion as the general population. Three out of four believe that one can practice birth control and still be a good Catholic. Since the early 1970s, many U.S. Catholics have advocated Natural Family Planning or the Billings Method. NFP teaches women to recognize the bodily indicators for ovulation and provides an effective alternative or accompaniment to calendar and temperature rhythm.

In general Catholics and Protestants agree that, in the biblical view, procreation and mutual love are purposes of marriage. They also agree on the necessity of responsible parenthood. The official Catholic position excludes artificial contraception as a means to that end. U.S. Protestants in general would not oppose the use of contraception, including voluntary sterilization, in responsible family planning. Deeper differences on the relative importance of the purposes of marriage, however, may divide conservative Protestants and Catholics from their more liberal counterparts.

See also ABORTION; BIOETHICS; BODY, THEOLOGY OF THE; HUMANAE VITAE.

BIBLIOGRAPHY. J. T. Noonan, *Contraception: A History of its Treatment by the Catholic Theologians and Canonists* (1965); R. M. Fagley, *The Population Explosion and Christian Responsibility* (1960); W. O. Spitzer and C. L. Saylor, eds., *Birth Control and the Christian* (1969); C. E. Curran, *Faithful Dissent* (1986); G. Gallup and J. Castelli, *The American Catholic People* (1987).

W. L. Portier

Bishop. The chief pastor* or overseer in a church. The term comes from the Greek *episkopos* by way of the vulgar Latin *biscopus* and Old English *biscop.* In the Roman Catholic,* Eastern Orthodox* and Anglican* communions, the bishop stands in the ecclesiastical hierarchy above the priest* and below the archbishop.* The office derives its authority* from the apostles who, according to church teaching, designated the bishops as their successors.

Normally the bishop presides over a diocese* as its chief pastor, responsible for the full range of pastoral duties (especially the administration of Communion* and the preaching of the Word) and in particular for two duties reserved to the episcopal office: administration of the sacrament* of confirmation* and the ordaining* of clergy.* In large dioceses or in the case of a bishop hampered by age or disease, some or all of these duties may be exercised by suffragan, auxiliary or coadjutor bishops.

Bishops were recognized as distinct from presbyters or elders* from at least the third century until the Reformation. Since then, most Protestant* churches have done away with the office. Some maintain the title, but among these most deny the doctrine of apostolic succession,* seeing the bishop instead as a supervisory pastor. Scandinavian Lutheran,* Methodist* (in America, including the African Methodist) and Moravian* churches are among those which retain some version of the office.

BIBLIOGRAPHY. W. Telfer, *The Office of a Bishop* (1962).

J. G. Stackhouse

Bishop's Pastoral Letters. There are two types of pastoral letters, the individual pastoral written by a bishop* to his own diocese,* and the group pastoral written by several bishops to all their dioceses. The latter are usually national pastoral letters and addressed to the faithful of an entire country and should be distinguished from statements issued by national episcopal* conferences, which are not pastoral letters as such.

A bishop has governing power over his diocese, similar to that which the pope exercises over the entire church. He addresses letters to his diocese in the same manner as the pope* issues encyclicals.* These episcopal letters are the most common expression of the ordinary magisterium* of the bishops throughout the world. In the U.S. the national letters are usually the result of a general meeting of the hierarchy of the church. The letters can be doctrinal, devotional or disciplinary in purpose.

For example, one of the first pastoral letters issued in the U.S. was by Bishop Carroll* of Baltimore in 1792. Written after the First National Synod held in Baltimore in 1791, it addressed the question of the Christian education of youth, but was also concerned with the founding of a new seminary* in Baltimore, maintenance of the clergy,* financial support of the churches, attendance at Sunday Mass,* prayers for the dead* and devotion to Mary.* The first truly national pastoral letter was written in 1829 after the first Provincial Council of Baltimore which met to discuss the disorganized affairs of some of the dioceses, episcopal authority,* foreign interference in the nomination to vacant dioceses in the U.S. as well as the necessity of founding a national Catholic parochial school* system. The resulting pastoral letter addressed all of these issues.

Another example is that of 1919, which addressed the problems caused by World War 1* and the church's duties in reconstruction. It also concerned itself with the sanctity of marriage,* the evils of divorce, industrial relations, the rights of labor and education in general. A more modern pastoral letter issued in 1983, The Challenge of Peace: God's Promise and Our Response, is the result of the deliberations of the National Conference of Catholic Bishops.* It addresses various aspects of the nuclear age, from testing and the threat of nuclear war to the philosophy of deterrence, and it assesses their morality. In recent years national bishops' pastoral statements on issues of justice and peace have had an influence in America far beyond the Catholic Church.

BIBLIOGRAPHY. P. Guilday, ed., *The National Pastorals of the American Hierarchy* (1923); National Conference of Catholic Bishops, *Summary of the Challenge of Peace: God's Promise and Our Response* (1983).

C. E. Ronan

Bishops' Program of Social Reconstruction (1919). Social platform adopted by the American Catholic* hierarchy after World War 1.* After the First World War the American Catholic bishops,* like many other social and religious groups, proposed a comprehensive program of social reform, "The Bishops' Program of Social Reconstruction." Written by Father John A. Ryan,* who was known for his books *A Living Wage* (1906) and *Distributive Justice* (1916), "The Bishops' Program" was adopted by the Administrative Committee of the National Catholic War Council* on February 12, 1919. It focused on three defects in the American system: "enormous inefficiency and waste in the production and distribution of commodities; insufficient incomes for the great majority of wage-earners, and unnecessarily large incomes for a small minority of privileged capitalists" ("Bishops' Program").

The Program proposed practical ways of addressing these defects, including: government agencies to find jobs and housing for returning veterans; vocational training programs; minimum wage legislation; comprehensive state insurance programs for the sick, unemployed and elderly; and the elimination of child labor. Those women who during the war had entered occupations dangerous to their health or morals were to be replaced by returning veterans. However, women "engaged in the same tasks as men should receive equal pay for equal amounts and qualities of work." Labeled socialistic by its critics in the 1920s, much of the Program was implemented during the New Deal years. John A. Ryan earned the nickname "Right Reverend New Dealer."

BIBLIOGRAPHY. "The Bishops' Program," in J. T. Ellis, *Documents of American Catholic History*, Vol. II: 1866-1966 (1987); F. L. Broderick, *The Right Reverend New Dealer: John A. Ryan* (1963); J. A. Ryan, *Social Doctrine in Action* (1941).

D. Campbell

Bjerring, Nicholas (1831-c.1883). Founder of first Orthodox* parish* in the Eastern U.S. Born and educated in Denmark, Bjerring became a naturalized U.S. citizen following his appointment as professor of philosophy and history at St. Mary's Roman Catholic Seminary in Baltimore in 1868. After the promulgation of the dogma* of papal infallibility* in 1870, he left the Roman Catholic Church* and joined the Orthodox Church. During a visit to Russia, he was ordained* a priest in St. Petersburg in the same year and returned to New York with a mandate from the Russian Holy Synod to establish an Orthodox parish there. During the next decade, he was also engaged in translating Orthodox liturgical* texts and doctrinal essays into English. His best-known publication was the quarterly *Oriental Church Magazine* (1879-1881). His ministry, lectures and publications encouraged many American Protestants to seriously examine Orthodoxy.

BIBLIOGRAPHY. C. J. Tarasar and J. H. Erickson, ed., *Orthodox America, 1974-1976* (1975).

T. E. FitzGerald

Black Catholics. The earliest Black Catholics were slaves located primarily in Maryland and Louisiana. The 1865 population of 100,000 remained constant until the Church created in 1884 the Commission for Catholic Missions among the Colored People and the Indians. The best-known Black Catholic of the century was Patrick Healy, who served as president of Georgetown University from 1873 to 1882. The number of black Catholics increased from 200,000 in 1929 to 600,000 in 1959; 900,000 in 1975 and 1.3 million in 1984. Approximately two per cent of all Catholics in the U.S. are black; approximately four per cent of all blacks are Catholic.

During the migrations of the World Wars,* many Southern black Catholics moved to the North and West. Patterns of segregation in schools and churches established in the late 1800s remained intact as blacks moved into inner-city parishes* abandoned by white Catholics. Growth in black Catholics is attributable to efforts of some inner-city priests* to convert new black residents; the presence of parochial schools* in urban parishes and increased activism of the Church in the 1950s and 1960s in social justice issues. The civil rights* and black power movements of the 1960s resulted in increased recognition by the Church of black cultural forms in worship services, and in the formation of organizations such as the Black Catholic Clergy Caucus, National Black Sisters Conference, Black Catholic Lay Caucus and the National Office of Black Catholics. Approximately 700 women are members of four predominately black religious communities, and 100 men are members of three such male communities. Seminaries* began accepting blacks as candidates for the priesthood in the 1950s. As of 1983, there were 300 black priests. Between 1966 and 1984, ten black bishops* were ordained.*

See also BLACK RELIGION.

BIBLIOGRAPHY. L. N. Jones, "The Organized Church: Its Historic Significance," in *Negotiating the Mainstream*, ed. H. Johnson (1978); J. P. Dolan, *The American Catholic Experience* (1985); J. P. Dolan, "The Black Catholic Experience," *USCH* 5 (1986).

M. R. Sawyer

Black Colleges. Of the 116 black colleges and universities currently in operation, over fifty were founded by religious and voluntary associations.* Aided by white philanthropists* George Peabody, John F. Slater, Anna T. Jeanes and others, denominational and religious organizations such as the American Missionary Association,* the American Baptist Home Missionary Association, the African Methodist Episcopal Church* and the Freedman's Aid Society played crucial roles in the nineteenth-century movement to fund and build colleges for both African-American freedmen and newly freed slaves. This movement was so successful and influential that a majority of black colleges and universities (ninety-six), including those with no formal religious affiliation, were established before the turn of the century.

Two organizations led the way in the move to educate African-Americans, sending not only funds but teachers to staff the new institutions. The African Methodist Episcopal Church* (1816), one of the first African-American denominations, founded over nine colleges between 1854 and 1890. Among these were Wilberforce University (1856) in Ohio; Edwards Waters College (1866) in Florida; St. Augustine's College (1867) in North Carolina; Paul Quinn College (1872) in Texas; Livingstone College (1879) in North Carolina; and Morris Brown College (1880) in Georgia. The American Missionary Association, an evangelical* and abolitionist* organization formed in 1846, founded seven colleges: Fisk University (1866) in Tennessee; Hampton Institute (1868) in Virginia; Tougaloo University (1869) in Mississippi; and Atlanta University (1869), a consortium of colleges that included Morehouse College, Spelman College, Clark University and Morris Brown College in Atlanta, Georgia.

The majority of these religious associations and black colleges viewed education as a way to Christianize newly freed slaves and prepare them for citizenship. There was also the hope that black schools would eventually train a sufficient number of African-Americans teachers to continue the work of educating African-Americans. To achieve these ends, many colleges and associations advocated a form of industrial education popular during the nineteenth century. Seeking to cultivate order, industry, economy and self-reliance in their students, these institutions offered practical training in blacksmithing, wagon-making, carpentry, printing, bricklaying, masoning, forge work, shoemaking and animal husbandry.

One notable exception to this early form of education was Fisk University, where students were offered liberal arts instruction in Latin, Greek, higher mathematics, natural science, world history,

Bible* study and music. By the twentieth century, most black colleges and universities had abandoned various forms of industrial education in favor of a liberal arts curriculum.

BIBLIOGRAPHY. H. M. Bond, *The Education of the Negro in the American Social Order* (1934); A. Meier, *Negro Thought in America* (1966); J. M. Richardson, *A History of Fisk University, 1865-1945* (1980); W. L. Rose, *Rehearsal For Reconstruction: The Port Royal Experiment* (1964).

M. C. Bruce

Black Religion. Black religion in America is not exclusively Christian, but even where it is, it bears a distinct character from the Christianity of predominantly white churches. Black religion, in its Christian manifestation, has its origins in a synthesis of African traditional religions brought to the Americas by enslaved Africans and the evangelical* Christianity of North American Anglo-Saxons, shaped as it was by the revivalism* of the First and Second Great Awakenings.* As with all religions, the particular form of the synthesis was influenced by the social circumstances of the believers. In the case of African-Americans this was the oppression they experienced from the time of their arrival in America and for over 300 years thereafter.

The religion of slaves as it developed during the antebellum period is referred to as the "invisible institution." The phrase denotes the fact that severe restrictions in numbers, hours and locations were often imposed on African-Americans wishing to congregate for worship.* Consequently, most services took place clandestinely, or under the watchful eye of the slavemaster. The apprehension on the part of slave owners that Christianity might fuel rebellion was confirmed as slave revolts led by religious personalities increased in numbers after 1800. Among the more famous revolts were those led by Gabriel Prosser, Denmark Vesey* and Nat Turner.* More commonly, however, religious conviction gave impetus to subtle protest in the form of sabotage or deception.

Black Denominations. Several independent African-American Baptist congregations were organized in the South in the 1700s and in the North around 1900. However, the independent church movement among free African-Americans in the North, which began in the latter part of the eighteenth century, was primarily Methodist.* From its beginnings in the colonies, the membership of Methodism included African-Americans. As their numbers grew, restrictions in seating, communion* services, ordination* policies and property ownership caused many African-Americans to seek autonomy in their own congregations and, ultimately, separate denominations.*

In 1787 Richard Allen,* Absalom Jones and others withdrew from St. George's Methodist Episcopal Church in Philadelphia. Two African-American congregations resulted: St. Thomas African Episcopal Church and Bethel Church. In 1816 Bethel Church joined with four other congregations to organize the African Methodist Episcopal Church.* In a similar development, African-American congregants of John Street Church in New York City withdrew in 1796. Under the leadership of James Varick,* the resulting church joined with four other congregations in 1821 to form another denomination, which became known as the African Methodist Episcopal Zion Church.* The doctrines* and polity* of the two African-American denominations differed little from white Methodism; their separation was overwhelmingly a function of racial discrimination.

African-American ministers in these denominations—as well as in the predominantly white denominations—demonstrated their social and political consciousness in their organizing of the Negro Convention Movement of the 1830s and 1840s and in their abolitionist* activity. Ministers or lay* church leaders, such as Martin Delany, Henry Highland Garnet* and Henry M. Turner,* were among the nationalist leaders of that century, some of whom became emigrationists, advocating a return to Africa. Following the Civil War,* the memberships of the African Methodist churches grew dramatically as their missions extended to newly emancipated Southern African-Americans. In 1870, these two denominations were joined by a third when African-Americans withdrew from the Methodist Episcopal Church, South. Originally called the Colored Methodist Episcopal Church, the name was changed in 1954 to Christian Methodist Episcopal* (CME).

In the post-Civil War period, African-Americans who had been part of the "invisible" church organized separate Baptist* congregations, associations and conventions. In 1895 three such conventions merged to form the National Baptist Convention.* This Convention suffered a schism in 1915, resulting in the National Baptist Convention, U.S.A., Inc., and the National Baptist Convention of America. A second schism in the incorporated body in 1961 produced the Progressive National Baptist Convention, Inc.

The Holiness Movement* of the second half of the nineteenth century and the Pentecostal Movement* in the first decade of the twentieth—led by African-American Holiness preacher William Seymour*—resulted in dozens of African-American Holiness-Pentecostal bodies, the largest of which is the Church of God* in Christ, founded by Charles Mason.*

Character and Significance. Resisting the dichotomizing of the sacred and the secular, black religion has always held in tandem the emphases of spirituality* and social consciousness. Consequently, black religion has served two critical functions: survival under circumstances of the most extreme oppression and struggle through liberation movements aimed at moderating the oppression. African-American worship often is characterized by expressiveness and spontaneity, with sermon and song assuming particular importance. As the one institution fully controlled by the African-American community, the church historically functioned as the center of African-American political, economic and social life. The church has served as a critical source of identity for its members; its clergy have assumed the leadership roles in the community, often serving as the primary contacts with the larger white world. From the time of emancipation, African-American churches were preoccupied with responding to the needs of a largely illiterate population through the provision of benevolent and educational services. Schools were founded, insurance companies organized, and training in homemaking skills provided.

Beginning in the 1890s and continuing through World War 2,* many African-Americans migrated from the rural South to the cities and to the North and West, seeking economic opportunities. Often the ministers migrated with them, starting new congregations in urban areas. One result was the proliferation of "storefront" churches. Other migrants were introduced to parochial schools* and parish priests* in the emerging urban ghettos and became converts to Catholicism.* Still seeking to meet the needs of their congregants, a number of the largest churches—Abyssian Baptist in New York City being an example—developed comprehensive community-service programs oriented to the peculiar stresses of urban life.

Today the larger African-American churches are involved in such projects as housing, credit unions and health-care programs. The church continues to be important in both protest and electoral politics. Beginning in 1934 most of the African-American religious groups participated at least nominally in the first African-American ecumenical* organization, the Fraternal Council of Negro Churches, which in its objectives for social change anticipated in important respects the civil rights movement* of the 1950s and 1960s. The African-American churches figured largely in the Civil Rights Movement, providing a large proportion of the movement's leadership, meeting facilities, communications network and source of funding. Organizationally, the church was most evident in the Southern Christian Leadership Conference* (SCLC).

During the Black Power phase of the movement, SCLC and the more conservative National Black Evangelical Association* were joined by the National Conference of Black Churchmen,* which played a central role in the development of African-American liberation theology.* The 1970s produced yet other ecumenical organizations in the form of Partners in Ecumenism, the Black Theology Project and the Congress of National Black Churches.* The larger Methodist and Baptist communions also participate in the National Council of Churches of Christ* and the World Council of Churches.*

Current Organization. Not all black religion is Christian. In recent years, numerous neo-African religions have developed in urban settings. Other African-Americans, if relatively few in number, identify themselves as black Jews or black Hebrews. More significant are Black Muslims. While an unknown number of slaves brought to America's shores were Muslim, none were able to sustain the tradition in any systematic or enduring fashion. Most African-Americans who are practicing Muslims today trace their roots to an indigenous movement known as the Moorish Science Temple, begun by Noble Drew Ali in 1913. More directly, present-day Muslims are a product of the Nation of Islam organized and led by Elijah Muhammad from the 1930s until his death in 1975. This movement became visible to the larger public in the 1960s, largely as a result of the ministry of Malcolm X. Following the death of Elijah Muhammad, the movement experienced a schism. The larger segment, under the leadership of Warith Deen Muhammad, took the name American Muslim Mission and moved toward a position of orthodoxy. The smaller segment, led by Louis Farrakhan, continues to promulgate the more extremist teachings of Elijah Muhammad.

The majority of African-Americans who claim a religious identity, however, are Christian. Collectively they make up what is referred to as the *black church.* Structurally, the black church contains numerous components. The overwhelming majority of church members—nearly 18 million—belong to one of the seven largest denominations: African Methodist Episcopal (1.7m); African Meth-

odist Episcopal Zion (1.1m); Christian Methodist Episcopal (850,000); Church of God in Christ (3.5m); National Baptist Convention of America (2.2m); National Baptist Convention, U.S.A., Inc. (7.1m) and Progressive National Baptist (1.0m). A minimum of 1.2 million African-Americans belong to the eighty or so smaller African-American denominations and sects,* most of which are Holiness-Pentecostal bodies. Approximately 1.3 million African-Americans are Roman Catholic, while an additional 1.1 million hold membership in a range of predominantly white Protestant denominations. Among these, United Methodists* claim some 360,000 African-American members. American Baptist* churches also have significant numbers of African-American members, although African-Americans often hold dual affiliation in this convention and in one of the African-American conventions. Other Protestant bodies with sizable numbers of African-American members (from 70,000 to 150,000) are the Episcopal Church,* Southern Baptist Convention,* Presbyterian Church (U.S.A.) and United Church of Christ.* African-Americans are also well represented in Jehovah's Witnesses* and Seventh-day Adventist* churches.

See also BLACK AMERICANS AND MISSIONS; BLACK CATHOLICS; BLACK COLLEGES; BLACK THEOLOGY.

BIBLIOGRAPHY. E. F. Frazier, *The Negro Church in America* (1974); C. E. Lincoln, *The Black Church Since Frazier* (1974); H. V. Richardson, *Dark Salvation: The Story of Methodism as It Developed in Blacks in America* (1976); M. C. Sernett, *Afro-American Religious History: A Documentary Witness* (1985); J. M. Washington, *Frustrated Fellowship: The Black Baptist Quest for Social Power* (1986); G. S. Wilmore, *Black Religion and Black Radicalism: An Interpretation of the Religious History of Afro-American People,* 2nd ed. (1983). M. R. Sawyer

Black Theology. Derived from both traditional African-American religion and the historical process of liberation, Black Theology focuses on God in Christ as deliverer of oppressed people, and blackness as the key to understanding that deliverance.

"It is my contention," wrote James H. Cone* in *A Black Theology of Liberation* (1970), "that Christianity is essentially a religion of liberation." In a society where people "are oppressed because they are black," he adds, "Christian theology must become Black Theology, a theology that is unreservedly identified with the goals of the oppressed community and seeking to interpret the divine character of their struggle for liberation."

A similar note was sounded by Albert B. Cleage, Jr., author of *The Black Messiah* (1968). Like Cone, Cleage perceived an essential connection between the African-American experience of oppression and the liberating themes of Christianity. Both argued that this had been ignored or distorted by traditional white European and American theologians.* To Cleage and Cone it appeared that any religion that did not meet the needs of a people was flawed in its theological understanding. As the two leading advocates of Black Theology in the late twentieth century, they have called for reorientation of Christian theology in both its theory and applications. Blackness, defined more symbolically than physically, appears in their theology as the cornerstone of authentic Christian thinking. Jesus Christ, in this view, is "black" and embodies God's liberation of black (i.e., oppressed) people.

Black Theology as a distinct movement within Christianity is relatively young. The Civil Rights Movement* of the 1950s and 1960s not only quickened African-American political consciousness but also engendered widespread interest in African-American culture, identity and religious experience.* Dr. Martin Luther King, Jr.,* a Baptist* minister* and president of the Southern Christian Leadership Conference* (SCLC), constantly proclaimed a message of divine deliverance of African-American people. Throughout the organizational structure of SCLC and the broader Civil Rights Movement, religious faith linked to a deliverance theology was the major energizing force.

At the same time, the unyielding problems of ghetto life produced frustration and violence in the 1960s, underscoring the plight of millions of people to whom the Civil Rights Act of 1964 and the Voting Rights Act of 1965 appeared remote and irrelevant. Integration of public facilities, and even the right to vote, did not mean that their most pressing problems were solved. The wave of urban violence that began in Watts in Los Angeles in 1965, continued throughout the decade and reached such serious proportions in 1967 that a special commission was appointed by the Johnson administration to study its causes and possible solutions. This same period witnessed a dramatic affirmation of black power by Stokely Carmichael and others in the wake of the shotgun attack on James Meredith in Mississippi in the summer of 1966. Their message—less mindful of love and the refusal to resist evil with violence—affirmed the uniqueness and beauty of black identity and the need to combine political and social potential to effect basic change, together with the possession

of land and other economic resources by African-American people.

African-American Christian leaders were varied in their responses to the plight of African-American people in the U.S., but there was general agreement that their problems could neither be understood nor resolved by piecemeal civil rights reforms. From several religious groups came endorsements of black power understood in both historical and theological perspectives. Robert A. Paxton, executive of the Commission on Religion and Race of the National Council of Churches* (NCC), issued an influential statement in behalf of the NCC in July 1966, calling on Americans who had reacted negatively to black power to consider the historical condition of African-American people. He argued that African-American men had "long ago been forced out of the white church" and had to create and use "black power" long before the contemporary black-power movement. Several other Christian organizations joined the chorus of affirmation of black-power in the light of Christian theology. The influential National Committee of Black Churchmen (originally the National Committee of Negro Churchmen) not only endorsed in principle the black-power concept but also appointed a commission to formulate a theology that would incorporate the historical experience of African-Americans and their quest for liberation.

If the shift of thought in 1966 and 1967 marked the beginning of a major transformation of African-American religious philosophy, the assassination of Dr. Martin Luther King, Jr., in 1968 added to the momentum. To some, his death indicated that nonviolence had failed. King's successor as president of the Southern Christian Leadership Conference, the Rev. Ralph David Abernathy, appealed to African-Americans who engaged in rioting following the assassination not to discredit King's memory by using the violent means he had long opposed.

That same year Cleage's *The Black Messiah* was published. In it Cleage averred that Christ was *black* and did *not* preach universal love. And Vincent Harding's widely discussed article "The Religion of Black Power" appeared in *The Religious Situation: 1968*. The early 1970s brought a host of additional articles and books on African-American religion by Calvin B. Marshall, Preston N. Williams, C. D. Coleman, C. Eric Lincoln and others. The most influential was James H. Cone's *Black Theology and Black Power* (1969), published during the period when a dramatic statement delivered by Student Non-Violent Coordinating Committee

(SNCC) leader James Forman was stirring widespread debate. Interrupting the morning services at the prestigious Riverside Church in New York on May 4, 1969, Forman had asked American churches and synagogues for some $500 million in reparations to help African-Americans advance economically. Cone's book thus appeared at a circumstantially favorable time when interest was high and a commission of the National Conference of Black Churchmen was searching for a theology that would synthesize the basic content of traditional theology with the African-American experience.

Historical Precedents. Although the intensity and scope of such works were unprecedented, the convergence of religion and social experience was not new for African-Americans. Pulled away from their African heritage by slave traders in the seventeenth and eighteenth centuries, African-Americans had to adjust to the new and hostile environment of slavery. From the beginning African-American people were sensitive to the tension within white churches between their religion of love and salvation and the hard realities of slavery and segregation. We now know that African-American accommodation to American Christianity was only partial. Vestiges of African religious experience persisted and later intermingled with Christian aspects. God as deliverer and source of strength was indigenous to African faith, and that theme was reinforced by the historical burden of slavery. During the days of slavery, African-Americans gathered in the backwoods for their own variety of religious services. There is sufficient historical evidence to conclude that themes later developed by Black Theology were present in at least a nascent form.

There is no single definitive thread of African-American religious experience or African-American theology. By the late eighteenth century separate African-American churches emerged, the first sizable one being the African Methodist Episcopal* (AME) Church developed by Richard Allen* and his associates, who seceded from the predominantly white Methodist Episcopal* Church in Philadelphia in 1787. Many others followed throughout the next century, providing an environment in which the African-American cultural heritage could be preserved while giving African-American preaching its distinctive tone. But separate African-American churches were only one of several strands of the complex African-American religious ethos. Antislavery activity, including uprisings like the Southampton Insurrection of Nat Turner* in 1831, was often motivated by religious convictions. In addition, a significant number of African-Americans, in association at times with white-sponsored efforts like the American Colonization Society* (ACS), sought to help African-Americans immigrate to nonslave countries and to carry Christianity back to Africa.

As time passed the original antislavery/anti-segregationist zeal of African-American religious leaders waned. The segregationist patterns that followed the Reconstruction period contributed, as did the risks involved in overt clerical resistance at a time when the churches lacked adequate resources or motivation to resist social and legal restrictions. Also, it can be argued, an otherworldliness permeated the atmosphere of African-American religion* by the turn of the twentieth century, adding to the slackening of African-American churches' involvement in resistance activities. Nonetheless, the African-American churches remained basic to the continuance of liberation thinking and would eventually provide the matrix for the nonviolent movement of SCLC, SNCC and other organizations during the heyday of the Civil Rights Movement. Early twentieth-century African-American scholars like W. E. B. DuBois, even if not personally very religious, emphasized the vital importance of religion to African-American identity and hope for a better life.

Although he cannot be classified as an advocate of Black Theology as it is usually understood, Martin Luther King, Jr., drew heavily on the tradition of liberation in African-American religion. Combining an unusually strong educational background, the experience of growing up under the influence of the Ebenezer Baptist Church in Atlanta where his father was pastor, and his own synthesis of Gandhian nonviolence and Christian theology, King contributed powerfully to the setting that produced Black Theology. This was recognized by Cone and Cleage, even as they disagreed with some of King's emphases, notably the principle of love as the energizing force of the nonviolent cement.

Diversity continued to characterize both African-American religion and the theology of African-American churches. There are wide differences among African-American ministers and teachers, as well as traditional laity, on such matters as the role of African culture, the relative weight of love and social pressure, and a host of other specifics. The theological approach that is defined formally as Black Theology thus exists within a shifting and complex matrix. What differentiates Black Theology from other forms is its persistent emphasis on the African-American experience as the pivotal reality of theology. "Blackness" is seen as both the quintessential human experience of suffering injustice, and the focus of divine revelation. The action of God in history is directed toward its resolution.

Black Theology seeks to do more than meet African-American people's material and spiritual needs; it envisages what Cone calls the destruction "of the oppressor's definition of blackness." The major objective of Black Theology is not simply to dismantle segregation and correct false images about African-American people, but to expose the inherent evil of making blackness ugly and symbolic of oppression. Blackness, in this view, characterizes more than one race. It also refers to Native Americans, Hispanic* Americans and others who have been denied full freedom and access to the benefits of society. At a deeper level, Black Theology argues that traditional eschatology has failed to note the connection between the end of history and the present order. Affirming that the future is God's future and pessimistic expectations are thus inappropriate, Black Theologians have nonetheless attempted to shift the focus to the present, in the light of God's redemptive activity in the past and in view of the present conditions that remain oppressive to many people.

If there is obvious kinship with other varieties of Liberation Theology,* Black Theology is also different in some respects, particularly in its stress on existential blackness as the key to divine providence. It is also less directly related to social philosophies that emanated from European social history. It is grounded in the slave experience, the interaction of African and American Christian history, and the Civil Rights Movement. Adjustments and refinements in Black Theology, as well as dialog with traditional European-American theologians has continued well beyond the period of civil-rights activism.

BIBLIOGRAPHY. H. A. Baer, *The Black Spiritual Movement: A Religious Response to Racism* (1984); J. B. Childs, *The Political Black Minister: A Study in Afro-American Politics and Religion* (1980); A. B. Cleage, Jr., *The Black Messiah* (1968); J. H. Cone, *Black Theology and Black Power* (1969); J. H. Cone, *A Black Theology of Liberation* (1970); C. E. Ellis, Jr., *Beyond Liberation: The Gospel in the Black American Experience* (1983); J. H. Evans, Jr., "Keepers of the Dream: The Black Church and Martin Luther King, Jr.," *ABQ* 5 (March 1986):75-84; M. L. King, Jr., *Strength to Love* (1963); C. E. Lincoln, *The Black Experience in Religion* (1974); J. R. Washington, Jr., ed., *Black Religion and Public Policy* (1978); G. S. Wilmore, *Black Religion and Black Radicalism,* 2nd ed., (1984).

T. R. Peake

Blackburn, Gideon (1772-1838). Presbyterian* minister,* educator and missionary* to Indians.* Blackburn was born in Augusta County, Virginia, August 27, 1772, but during his boyhood the family moved to Greene County, Tennessee. Attending Samuel Doak's* Martin Academy, he studied theology* privately, was licensed as a Presbyterian minister in 1792, and became pastor* of New Providence and Eusebia churches near Knoxville.

Increasingly concerned for missions among the Indians, Blackburn urged the matter in a paper he presented to the 1803 General Assembly.* Appointed missionary by the Assembly, he opened a school for Cherokee youth near Charleston, Tennessee, in 1804, adding a second in Hamilton County in 1805. His curriculum stressed religious instruction, agricultural and mechanical arts, as well as self-government. Personal exhaustion, as well as unproven charges of illegal whiskey trade with the Indians, led in 1810 to his withdrawal from the work, which passed into the hands of the American Board of Commissioners for Foreign Missions.*

Blackburn moved to central Tennessee and settled at Franklin, where he opened Harpeth Academy. He also founded Presbyterian churches in Franklin and Nashville and converted Rachel Jackson (wife of Andrew Jackson), who referred to him as her "father in the Gospel." In 1821 Blackburn became pastor of the Presbyterian church in Louisville, Kentucky, and in 1829 was made president of Danville (now Centre) College. His outspoken antislavery* and New School* views forced his resignation in 1830, and he moved to Carlinville, Illinois, where he founded a Presbyterian church and became active in the formation of the Illinois Anti-Slavery Society in cooperation with David Nelson, Elijah Lovejoy* and Edward Beecher.* Blackburn was also active in efforts to establish a college in Carlinville, an institution that now bears his name (Blackburn College).

BIBLIOGRAPHY. *AAP* 4; *DAB* I; *DARB; NCAB* 13.

W. J. Wade

Blackstone, William Eugene (1841-1935). Author and Christian Zionist.* Born into a Methodist* family in Adams, New York, William Blackstone converted to Christianity* at age eleven. A successful business career in building and property investments helped finance his religious interests. Blackstone was a zealous dispensationalist* who authored *Jesus Is Coming* (1908). This popular and widely translated book explained how the signs of the times pointed to the imminent return of Christ. Blackstone's millennial* concerns also led him to aid in the founding of the Chicago Hebrew Mission, which he superintended from 1887 to 1891. He is best remembered for a "Memorial" sent to President Benjamin Harrison in 1891. Signed by 413 prominent Americans, the document advocated the settlement of persecuted Russian Jews in Palestine and antedated the first Zionist Congress by six years. A second memorial in 1916 may have influenced President Woodrow Wilson* to favor the Balfour Declaration.

See also JEWS, CHRISTIAN MISSIONS TO; MILLENNIALISM; ZIONISM.

BIBLIOGRAPHY. B. M. Lindberg, *A God-Filled Life: The Story of William E. Blackstone* (1985); T. P. Weber, *Living in the Shadow of the Second Coming: American Premillennialism, 1875-1925* (1979).

J. H. Warnock

Blackwell, Antoinette Louisa Brown (1825-1921). First regularly ordained* woman in America. Born in Henrietta, New York, to Joseph and Abby Morse Brown, the seventh child of ten, Antoinette graduated from Oberlin College's* literary course in 1847 and completed requirements for the theology* degree in 1850, but she was denied the degree. On September 15, 1853, she was ordained* a Congregational* minister* in South Butler, New York. She resigned that post on July 20, 1854, and eventually became a Unitarian,* pastoring All Souls' Unitarian Church, Elizabeth, New Jersey, from 1908 until her death in 1921. On January 24, 1856, she married Samuel Charles Blackwell; they had seven children, with five daughters surviving to adulthood. Brown's books include *Shadows of Our Social System* (1856), *Sexes Throughout Nature* (1875), *The Physical Basis of Immortality* (1876) and *The Philosophy of Individuality* (1893). Throughout her life she was an ardent feminist* and suffragist.*

BIBLIOGRAPHY. *DAB* I; E. Cazden, *Antoinette Brown Blackwell* (1983); E. R. Hayes, *Those Extraordinary Blackwells: The Letters of Antoinette Brown and Lucy Stone* (1967); C. F. Hitchings, "Universalist and Unitarian Women Ministers," *JUHS* 10 (1975):155-156; L. Kerr, *Lady in the Pulpit* (1951); *NAW* 1.

N. A. Hardesty

Blackwood, Andrew Watterson (1882-1966). Presbyterian* minister* and professor of homiletics.* Born in Clay City, Kansas, Blackwood was educated at Muskingum and Harvard* and then at Princeton* and Xenia Theological Seminaries. He served Presbyterian churches in Pittsburgh, Pennsylvania; Columbia, South Carolina; and Columbus, Ohio. In 1925 he became professor of English

Bible at the Presbyterian Theological Seminary in Louisville, Kentucky, until 1930 when he became professor of homiletics at Princeton Theological Seminary. From 1950 to 1958 he was professor of preaching at Temple University.

Blackwood published twenty-two books, including *The Fine Art of Preaching* (1937), *Preaching from the Bible* (1941) and *The Preparation of Sermons* (1948). He was the most prominent homiletician among American Protestants in his era. For resources Blackwood drew upon his own training and experience, and quasi-scholarly religious works. His observations were largely practical, and therefore especially helpful to beginners. Little influence is obvious from medieval or Scottish homileticians, studies in rhetoric and modern communication, hermeneutics or the scholarly exegetes.*

BIBLIOGRAPHY. *NCAB* 53.

T. H. Olbricht

Blair, James (1656-1743). Anglican* commissary, and founder and president of the College of William and Mary.* Born in Alvah, Scotland, the son of a Scottish clergyman,* James Blair graduated from the University of Edinburgh (M.A., 1673), entered the ordained* ministry* (1679), and became the vicar of Cranston parish (1679) in Scotland. His tenure was cut short, however, by his refusal to sign the Stuart test oath, acknowledging a Roman Catholic* James II as the heir to the British throne. Thereafter Blair made his way to London (1682), and on Bishop of London Henry Compton's suggestion, he immigrated to Virginia (1684). Blair made the colony his home, marrying Sarah Harrison (1687) and persuading his brother Archibald to join him in Virginia (1690).

In 1689 Bishop Compton designated Blair as his first colonial commissary. Compton hoped that commissaries—clergymen who represented bishops* in remote portions of their dioceses*—could provide discipline* and direction for the colonial church. As the first such officeholder in the colonies, Blair had no clear model to follow. He quickly learned that his effectiveness rested more on his abilities of persuasion than on any acknowledgment of his authority.* While he failed in his campaigns to establish ecclesiastical courts and to stabilize clergy salaries, he was able to summon regular clergy conferences, secure the dismissal of two unfriendly colonial governors, and found the College of William and Mary* (1693).

In addition to serving as commissary, Blair was the president of William and Mary, a member of the Governor's Council (1694-1743) and the rector* of Henrico (1684-1694), Jamestown (1694-

1710) and Bruton (1710-1743) parishes. His major published work was *Our Saviour's Divine Sermon on the Mount* (1722). Near the end of life, he was one of the few colonial commissaries warmly to welcome evangelist* George Whitefield.*

BIBLIOGRAPHY. *AAP* 5; *DAB* I; *DARB; NCAB* 3; P. Rouse, Jr., *James Blair of Virginia* (1971).

R. W. Prichard

Blair, John (fl. c.1700). Early Anglican* missionary* in North Carolina. In 1701, soon after his ordination* to the Anglican priesthood,* John Blair visited the colony of North Carolina on a missionary tour that was financed by Thomas, Lord Viscount Weymouth. Blair baptized* approximately one hundred persons, preached* twice each Sunday, called for the formation of vestries* in the places he visited and provided the three lay readers* whom he met with books. Neither the colonial assembly nor any individual vestry agreed, however, to contribute to his support, and he soon expended the funds with which he had come. After a return trip to England, which was interrupted by capture by the French, Blair wrote an account of the religious situation in North Carolina for the Society for the Propagation of the Gospel.* The letter is the chief source of information about his ministry.

BIBLIOGRAPHY. J. F. Woolverton, *Colonial Anglicanism in North America* (1984).

R. W. Prichard

Blake, Eugene Carson (1906-1985). Presbyterian* minister,* ecumenist* and civil rights* leader. Born in Missouri, Blake attended Princeton University,* New College of Edinburgh and Princeton Theological Seminary.* Ordained* in the Presbyterian Church in the U.S.A., he served churches in New York and California before being elected stated clerk of the denomination* in 1951. Serving in that capacity until 1966, Blake oversaw the merger of his denomination with the United Presbyterian Church of North America in 1958 to form the United Presbyterian Church in the U.S.A.*

From 1966 until 1972 Blake was the general secretary of the World Council of Churches,* based in Geneva, Switzerland. In that work he enabled the 1968 Assembly in Uppsala to take place, a benchmark gathering for its leadership by churches from emerging nations. As an ardent advocate of ecumenical relationships, Blake helped start the Consultation on Church Union.* Equally fervent in behalf of racial justice, he led many white Protestants in the 1963 March on Washington, where he proclaimed, "We are late,

but we are here."

See also BLAKE-PIKE UNITY PROPOSAL; ECUMENICAL MOVEMENT.

BIBLIOGRAPHY. R. D. Brackenridge, *Eugene Carson Blake, Prophet with Portfolio* (1978).

L. B. Weeks

Blake-Pike Unity Proposal. A suggestion for the union of major Protestant* churches in the U.S. At the request of Bishop James A. Pike* of the Protestant Episcopal Church,* Eugene Carson Blake,* stated clerk of the United Presbyterian Church,* delivered a sermon in 1960 at Grace Cathedral in San Francisco. Blake invited the Methodist* Church, the United Church of Christ* and other interested denominations* to join the Episcopalians and the United Presbyterians in drafting a plan of union that would be truly "catholic and reformed." With these key words, Blake wanted to bridge the "chasm of the Reformation" by joining what the universal (catholic) church had preserved with the contributions of the churches of the Reformation. In calling for the proposal's immediate implementation, Blake and Pike suggested that the new denomination be named the "Reformed and Catholic Church in the U.S.A." Though no new denomination was formed, their proposal did result in the organization of the Consultation on Church Union* which met early in 1962.

BIBLIOGRAPHY. R. T. Handy, *A History of the Churches in the United States and Canada* (1976); "Four Major Denominations Nominated for Amalgamation," *CT* 5 (December 19, 1960):25, 29.

B. V. Hillis

Blanchard, Charles Albert (1848-1925). Congregational* minister* and president of Wheaton College (Illinois).* Born in Galesburg, Illinois, when his father, Jonathan, was president of Knox College, Blanchard graduated from Wheaton College (B.A., 1870) when his father was president of that institution. His career as an educator began when he became principal of the preparatory school at Wheaton College (1872-1874). He then became professor of English language and literature at Wheaton (1874-1878), vice president of the college (1878-1882) and finally succeeded his father as president (1882-1925). Paralleling his career as educator were some years as a clergyman. He held brief pastorates in Presbyterian* churches in Paxton and Streator, Illinois. In 1878 he was ordained* to the Congregational ministry and was pastor of the College Church of Christ in Wheaton (1878-1883) and the Chicago Avenue Church in

Chicago (1883-1885), known today as Moody Memorial Church.

Under his presidency, Wheaton College made great advances as a center of conservative Christian influence and as an academic institution. Blanchard was a leader in the fundamentalist* movement and served as first vice president of the National Fundamentalist Association. As did his father before him, he engaged in an aggressive campaign against secret societies. Some of his publications included *Modern Secret Societies (1903), Light on the Last Days* (1913) and *Getting Things from God* (1915).

BIBLIOGRAPHY. F. C. Blanchard, *The Life of Charles Albert Blanchard* (1932).

D. B. Chesebrough

Blanchard, Jonathan (1811-1892). Presbyterian* minister,* abolitionist* and president of Wheaton College.* Born in Rockingham, Vermont, Blanchard graduated from Middlebury College (B.A., 1832) and went on to study at Andover Seminary* and Lane Theological Seminary in Cincinnati. In 1838 he was ordained* as pastor of the Sixth Presbyterian Church in Cincinnati. During this pastorate he founded and edited a church paper, the *Herald and Presbyter.*

In 1834 Blanchard became an ardent abolitionist. He attended the World's Anti-Slavery Convention in London (1843) and was elected American vice president of the body. Though often met by strong opposition, Blanchard was unyielding in his attacks upon slavery. On one occasion he debated the slavery issue with Stephen A. Douglas. Blanchard was equally passionate in his dislike of, and attacks upon, secret societies, especially the Masonic order.

From 1845 to 1857 Blanchard served as president of Knox College in Galesburg, Illinois. During his tenure the college's indebtedness was liquidated and student enrollment doubled. His outspokenness brought about great controversy during the latter years of his administration. At Galesburg he began publication of a religious periodical, *The Christian Era.* In 1860 Congregationalists* called him to be the first president of Wheaton College. At Wheaton he founded and edited the *Christian Cynosure,* a publication devoted to the denunciation of secret societies. He became president emeritus in 1882, a position he held until his death. His son, Charles Albert Blanchard,* succeeded him as president of Wheaton College in 1882.

BIBLIOGRAPHY. *DAB* I; C. S. Kilby, *Minority of One* (1959); R. S. Taylor, "Religion and Higher Education in Gilded America: The Case of Wheaton College," *AS* 22 (Spring 1981):57-70.

D. B. Chesebrough

Blanchet, François Norbert (1795-1883). Catholic* missionary* to the Pacific Northwest and first archbishop* of Oregon City. Born near St. Pierre, Quebec, Blanchet studied at the Sulpician* seminary in Quebec and was ordained in 1819. For seven years he served the Acadians and Micmac Indians in New Brunswick and then for a decade served St. Joseph de Soulages Church in Montreal (1827-1837). But he longed for missionary service and accepted the challenge to establish the church in the Oregon Territory, where he arrived November 24, 1838.

In 1843 Blanchet became vicar apostolic and titular bishop of Oregon and was consecrated* July 25, 1845. In 1846 he was elevated to the newly created archbishopric of Oregon City. Blanchet recruited missionaries,* raised money and planted Catholicism in the Pacific Northwest. In 1862 he moved his see to Portland, where he built a cathedral,* college and hospital. His writings include *Historical Sketches of the Catholic Church in Oregon* (1878) and *Historical Notes and Reminiscences* (1883). Blanchet attended the first (1852) and second (1866) Plenary Councils of Baltimore, as well as Vatican I* (1869-1870), where he supported the doctrine of papal infallibility.* For his nearly four-and-a-half decades of planting the Catholic Church in the Northwest, he has been remembered as the "apostle of Oregon."

BIBLIOGRAPHY. C. B. Bagley, *Early Catholic Missions in Old Oregon,* 2 vols. (1932); *DAB* I; L. M. Lyons, *Francis Norbert Blanchet and the Founding of the Oregon Missions, 1838-1848* (1940).

G. A. Reed

Bland, Salem Goldworth (1859-1950). Canadian Methodist* reformer. Born in Quebec and ordained* in 1884, Bland ministered in several churches in Ontario and Quebec before accepting a professorship in New Testament and church history at the Wesley College in Winnipeg in 1903. After controversy culminated in his dismissal in 1917, Bland wrote for the prairie *Grain Grower's Guide* until securing a pulpit in Toronto in 1919. Bland continued to use the printed page both as columnist in the *Toronto Star* daily and as author of *The New Christianity* (1920), to promote reform and socialism in general and the Social Gospel* in particular. Bland supported the labor movement, Sunday* observance, prohibition of alcohol,* the Cooperative Commonwealth Federation (a political party in Ontario), as well as doctrinal liberalization. Bland was also an advocate of the 1925 merger of the Methodist, Congregationalist* and much of the Presbyterian* church to produce the United Church of Canada.*

BIBLIOGRAPHY. R. Allen, *The Social Passion: Religion and Social Reform in Canada, 1914-1928* (1971).   B. A. McKenzie

Bliss, Daniel (1823-1916). Missionary* educator in the Near East. Born in Georgia, Vermont, Bliss graduated from Amherst College (1852) and Andover Seminary* (1855) and was sent by the American Board of Commissioners for Foreign Missions* to Syria in December 1855. After serving at Abeih and Suk Al Ghurb, he prepared a proposal for a Syrian Protestant* Collegiate Institute at Beirut and in 1864 became its first president, resigning from the Board to facilitate access to the Muslim community. His vision was to "originate, in the bosom of the native Protestant* community of Syria, all the educational institutions necessary for its permanent existence, growth and prosperity." In 1920 the Syrian Protestant College became the American University of Beirut, a premier educational institution in the Arab world. His son, Howard, succeeded him as president of the institution. A major thoroughfare in Beirut was named Rue Bliss.

BIBLIOGRAPHY. D. Bliss, *The Reminiscences of Daniel Bliss*, ed. and supplemented by F. J. Bliss (1920); *DAB* I.   D. M. Stowe

Bliss, Phillip Paul (1838-1876). Writer of hymns* and hymn tunes. Born in a log cabin in Clearfield, Pennsylvania, Bliss joined the Elk Run Baptist* Church at the age of twelve. He studied music with J. G. Towner (father of the hymnodist Daniel B. Towner), with hymnodist William B. Bradbury* and with several summer musicians at the Normal Academy of Music in Geneseo, New York. By the winter of 1860 he was an itinerant teacher in singing schools, traveling about on "Old Fanny" and carrying a twenty-dollar melodeon.

In 1864 Bliss sold his first song, and by 1865 he had moved to Chicago and was being published by music publishers Root and Cady, sometimes writing in collaboration with George F. Root or Ira Sankey.* Through Sankey he met Dwight L. Moody* and Major D. W. Whittle,* the latter whom he joined for twenty-five revival* meetings. Representative of his hymn texts and tunes are "Almost Persuaded," "Free from the Law," "I Am So Glad That My Father in Heaven," "Man of Sorrows," "Sing Them Over Again to Me," "The Whole World Was Lost in the Darkness of Sin" and the text of "I Will Sing of My Redeemer."

Bliss died December 29, 1876, in a fiery train wreck near Ashtabula, Ohio, while on his way to Moody's tabernacle. Bliss brought authentic personality to his music ministry, folksy humor to his newspaper column and spiritual dedication to every aspect of his short life.

BIBLIOGRAPHY. D. W. Whittle, ed., *Memoirs of Philip P. Bliss* (1877).   R. J. Stanislaw

Bliss, (W)illiam (D)wight (P)orter (1856-1926). Episcopal* priest,* Christian socialist* and advocate for the Social Gospel.* Born in Turkey, the son of Congregationalist* missionaries,* Bliss received his education at Amherst College (B.A., 1878) and Hartford Theological Seminary (B.D., 1882). He began his career as a Congregational* minister* in Denver, Colorado, and South Natick, Massachusetts (1882-1885). Attracted to the catholicity of the Protestant Episcopal Church,* he became an Episcopal rector in Lee, Massachusetts (1885-1857), and was ordained* by the Episcopal Church in 1887. He then became rector of Grace Episcopal Church in Boston (1887-1890).

While in Boston, Bliss came under the influence of Anglican* Christian Socialists Frederick D. Maurice (1805-1872) and Charles Kingsley (1819-1875) and the writings of Henry George (1839-1897). In 1887 Bliss joined a socialist labor union, the Knights of Labor,* and ran unsuccessfully as a candidate for lieutenant governor of the state of Massachusetts on the Labor Party ticket. In 1889 he organized the Society of Christian Socialists, the first organization of its kind in America. In 1890 Bliss founded the Christian Socialist Church of the Carpenter and attempted to apply the New Testament to both his inner-city experience and prevailing social problems. He lectured widely in Canada, the U.S. and England, and in 1899 became the president of the National Reform Union. In that same year he cofounded the Church Association for the Advancement of the Interests of Labor.

From 1909 to 1914, Bliss and Josiah Strong* established the American Institute of Social Services. The purpose of the Institute was to gather data on "everything that tends to the social betterment of humanity." From 1917 to 1919, he served as a special investigator for the Department of Labor in charge of educational work among French and Belgian soldiers in Switzerland during World War 1.* In 1921 Bliss returned to parish ministry as rector of the St. Martha's Episcopal Church in New York City (1921-1925).

Not known as a scholar, Bliss nevertheless

turned his energies toward publications supporting his goals. From 1889 to 1896 Bliss was the editor of *The Dawn,* the organ of the Christian Socialist Society. Among his edited works were *The Communism of John Ruskin* (1891), a collection of his own essays entitled *Handbook of Socialism* (1895) and *Encyclopedia of Social Reform* (1897).

As a liberal evangelical* and a supporter of the left wing of the Social Gospel Movement, Bliss generally distinguished between the kingdom of God* and the secular vision of a socialist utopia. He believed that the solution to social ills lay not in an improved environment, but in repentance, faith, baptism* and the sacraments.* Christocentric in theology,* his Christian socialism* was rooted in the cross and resurrection of Jesus Christ. He attacked social evils of all sorts, particularly unjust labor practices. Committed to urban issues, Bliss nevertheless carefully distinguished between the goals of Christian regeneration and secular utopianism.

BIBLIOGRAPHY. *DAB* I; *DARB;* R. B. Dressner, "William Dwight Porter Bliss' Christian Socialism," *CH* 47 (1978):66-82; C. H. Hopkins, *The Rise of the Social Gospel in American Protestantism, 1865-1915* (1940); *NCAB* 20:91-92; C. L. Webber, "William Dwight Porter Bliss (1856-1926): Priest and Socialist," *HMPEC* 28 (1959):9-39.

C. E. Stockwell

Blue Laws. Civil legislation regulating Sunday* activities, including works, commerce, travel and public entertainment. Some colonial laws required attendance at Sunday church services. The name *Blue Laws* originated from laws printed on blue paper in England for New Haven, Connecticut, in 1781. All of the American colonies enacted and enforced such ordinances, which generally favored the Christian faith and penalized those of other religious orientations.

Sunday legislation dates back to Constantine the Great, who decreed in 321 that Sunday was to be a day of rest and worship, although the law was not exclusively Christian, since it pleased sun-god pagans as well. English laws governing Sunday first appeared in the thirteenth century and were greatly enlarged throughout the sixteenth and seventeenth centuries, eventually spreading to the American colonies.

Blue Laws in the U.S. have constantly been a source of controversy and continuing legal action. Opponents have argued that Sabbath* regulations violate the First Amendment*: "Congress shall make no law respecting an establishment of religion, or prohibiting the free exercise thereof. . . ." Many of the original laws lapsed or simply were not enforced after the Revolutionary War.* Others, including compulsory church attendance, were struck down by the courts during the nineteenth century. In more modern times, laws regulating Sunday activities have been upheld by the Supreme Court* on the basis of secular considerations (*McGowan* v. *Maryland,* 1961), although original religious orientation was admitted. In 1963 the Court modified its position (*Sherbert* v. *Verner*) to soften the impact of Sunday closing laws where hardship was demonstrated. Current Sunday laws are largely oriented toward public health, safety, recreation, welfare and cultural activities, but are gradually being eroded or are not enforced.

J. E. Means

Boardman, George Dana (1801-1831). Pioneer Baptist missionary* to Burma. Born at Livermore, Maine, Boardman graduated from the Maine Literary and Theological Institute (now Colby College) and taught there 1822-1823. Feeling an imperative call to foreign missionary service, he attended Andover Theological Seminary* and then was sent by the Baptist* Missionary Board to Burma in 1825. He served in Calcutta until 1827 and then founded the station at Moulmein, Burma. In 1828 he founded a station at Tavoy, where he inaugurated extensive educational work. Boardman baptized Kyo Tha Byu, the first convert among the Karen people, who became the first of many effective evangelists* among a people whose own religious legends had prepared them in an extraordinary way to receive the gospel. Boardman died at Tavoy at the end of a jungle tour among the Karens. His wife, Sarah Boardman (Judson),* stayed on to continue work in Burma and in 1834 married Adoniram Judson,* founder of the Burma mission.

BIBLIOGRAPHY. *AAP* 6; J. C. Robbins, *Boardman of Burma* (1940). D. M. Stowe

Boardman, William Edwin (1810-1886). Presbyterian* minister* and advocate of the higher Christian life.* Born in Smithfield, New York, Boardman pursued a number of unsuccessful business ventures and led a restless life until he had a religious experience* while working in the small mining town of Potosi, Wisconsin. There he assumed leadership of the small "Plan of Union"* church, and by 1843 he had enrolled in Lane Theological Seminary in Cincinnati, where he remained for three years. Ordained* a Presbyterian minister, by 1852 he was serving in a New School* Presbyterian church in Detroit, Michigan, where he later served as a missionary* of the American Sunday School Union,* eventually moving to their central office in Philadelphia in 1855. After a brief sojourn in California (1859-1862) for the sake of his wife's health, Boardman worked for the United States Christian Commission* during the Civil War* (c.1862-c.1865), serving as its executive secretary. In 1870, after several years in business, Boardman became publicly associated with holiness* teachings.

A biography of James Brainerd Taylor had provided Boardman his first acquaintance with the "higher life" concept, and an itinerant Methodist* minister had pointed him to the writings of Charles G. Finney* and Asa Mahan.* Boardman had read them eagerly, but his Reformed* background naturally inclined him to resist Wesleyan* terminology in describing the believer's spiritual pilgrimage. Boardman's frequent attendance at Phoebe Palmer's* "Tuesday Meetings for the Promotion of Holiness" and his brief term as leader of the Union Holiness Convention reveal how closely he sympathized with the Holiness emphasis. His description of his own "second conversion" reflects the language of second blessing* Holiness revivalists.* The Wesleyan and Oberlin* Perfectionist* teaching and expression that flow through his book *The Higher Christian Life* (1858) combined to produce a statement of the nature and reality of the holy life which was more widely received than the expositions in the more classic traditions.

Boardman later participated with Robert Pearsall Smith* in the English Holiness conferences at Brighton and Oxford in 1874 and 1875. After a brief trip to America in June 1875, he returned to England in December 1875 to make his permanent home there. The last years of his life were spent in a healing* ministry, reflected in his book *The Lord that Healeth Thee* (1881).

Boardman's ministry and writings were instrumental in opening the doors of non-Methodist churches to the teachings of the Holiness revival. Drawing on his own spiritual pilgrimage and denying any personal theological sophistication, Boardman described in simple language a religious experience characterized by victory over sin.

BIBLIOGRAPHY. Mrs. W. E. Boardman, *Life and Labors of the Rev. W. E. Boardman* (1887); M. E. Dieter, *The Holiness Revival of the Nineteenth Century* (1980); B. B. Warfield, *Perfectionism* (1931). W. S. Gunter

Body, Theology of the. Between September 5, 1979, and November 28, 1984, Pope John Paul II*

developed what he calls a "Theology of the Body." He delivered this "Theology of the Body" (which is alternately referred to as a "Theology of Marriage" and a "Theology of Masculinity and Femininity") to large and enthusiastic throngs in St. Peter's Square. Dealing with a continuous theme, as one would chapters in a book, for the first time in public catechesis the pope made use of the higher criticism of the Old Testament and freely cited a number of Protestant* theologians.*

The pope's 133 presentations have been collected and published in four separate volumes. These four works, entitled *Original Unity of Man and Woman, Blessed Are the Pure of Heart, Theology of Marriage and Celibacy* and *Reflections on Humanae Vitae,* have become the substance for university and college courses offered at various Catholic educational institutions throughout North America and have had a considerable influence on Christian writers and thinkers.

BIBLIOGRAPHY. G. H. Williams, *The Mind of John Paul II: Origins of His Thought and Action* (1981); K. Wojtyla, *Love and Responsibility* (1981). D. T. DeMarco

Boehm, John Philip (1683-1749). German Reformed* pioneer in Pennsylvania. Born the son of a Reformed pastor in Hochstadt, a small town in the German principality of Hesse-Cassel, Boehm served as schoolmaster to Reformed congregations in Worms and Lambsheim. Because of conflict with town authorities in Lambsheim, Boehm immigrated to southeastern Pennsylvania, arriving with his family in 1720. Settling in the Perkiomen Valley with other German Reformed people, Boehm was soon asked to lead worship* services. In 1725 the Reformed settlers persuaded Boehm to assume the pastoral office, and the sacrament* of the Lord's Supper was first celebrated late that year, a point marking the inception of regular German Reformed worship in Pennsylvania.

The legitimacy of Boehm's ministry* was challenged by Georg Michael Weiss, a Heidelberg-educated Reformed minister who arrived in 1727. In response, the congregations served by Boehm requested that the classis of Amsterdam of the Dutch Reformed Church ordain* him. The classis agreed to do so, and Boehm was ordained November 23, 1729. The German Reformed group continued under the oversight of the Dutch Church until 1791.

After Weiss's departure in 1730, Boehm faced challenges from John Peter Mueller, a mystical individualist who opposed the developing relationship with the Dutch Reformed Church, and from John Henry Goetschy (Goetschius*), the son of a Swiss minister who interfered in Boehm's congregations from 1735 to 1739. The arrival of the Moravian* leader Count Zinzendorf,* whose aim it was to unite all the German sects, represented a more serious threat to the young church's existence. Through much effort Boehm prevented his congregations from joining the Moravians.

Realizing the need for permanent ecclesiastical structure, Boehm worked with Michael Schlatter* to establish a German Reformed coetus (Convention) in 1747, which adopted the Heidelberg Catechism* and the Canons of Dordt as its confessional* standards. Boehm died on April 29, 1749, after twenty-four years of ministry and the founding of twelve congregations.

BIBLIOGRAPHY. *DAB* I; *DARB;* W. J. Hinke, *Life and Letters of the Reverend John Philip Boehm* (1916); W. J. Hinke, *Ministers of the German Reformed Congregations in Pennsylvania and Other Colonies in the Eighteenth Century* (1951).
W. B. Evans

Boehm, Martin (1725-1812). Co-founder of the United Brethren in Christ. Of Mennonite* upbringing, Boehm came to the spiritual crisis of his life when, upon being chosen by lot to be a Mennonite minister,* he found he had no message to deliver. Disturbed by this discovery, Boehm came to believe he was lost, but after a time of spiritual struggle he experienced a pietistic* crisis conversion* (c. 1758) and felt the joy of regeneration. Now assured of his salvation,* he proceeded to preach* and within a few years his influence had moved beyond the Mennonite fold as he spoke in homes, churches and mass meetings. At one of these mass meetings (c. 1767), the German Reformed* pastor* Philip W. Otterbein* heard Boehm and recognized the spiritual kinship between them. This began a partnership that was to last for many years.

Under the leadership of Otterbein and Boehm, a revival* spread throughout the German communities of Pennsylvania, Maryland and Virginia, with Boehm working primarily in Pennsylvania. The focus of his message was the necessity of the crisis conversion experience and the possibility of a subsequent life of personal piety. Some Mennonites were drawn into the movement, but the Mennonite Church as a body excommunicated Boehm (c. 1775) because of his association with Christians who were "walking on the broad way." As the revival continued many converts met in informal groups for edification and enrichment. From these groups leaders emerged, usually

Reformed or Mennonite in background, and in turn these pastors-evangelists* periodically met together. In 1800 the movement organized itself as the United Brethren in Christ with Otterbein and Boehm as the first superintendents of the movement. In his later years Boehm also associated with a local Methodist* class meeting.*
See also GERMAN-AMERICAN REVIVALISM.

BIBLIOGRAPHY. *DAB* I; A. W. Drury, *History of the Church of the United Brethren in Christ* (1924); H. G. Spayth, *History of the Church of the United Brethren in Christ,* 2 vols. (1851).
M. H. Schrag

Bogardus, Everardus (1607-1647). Dutch Reformed* minister* in New Netherland. Everardus Bogardus, ordained* by the Classis* of Amsterdam in 1632, arrived in New Amsterdam the following year to become minister *(dominie)* of the Dutch Reformed church there. In 1642, during a besotted wedding feast, Bogardus secured subscriptions for a new church building, including some rather lavish commitments which he refused later to forgive.

During his career in New Netherland, Bogardus ran afoul of two of the West India Company's directors-general. The dominie criticized Wouter Van Twiller for incompetence, a charge no one was likely to refute. When Bogardus condemned Willem Kieft's slaughter of neighboring Indians in 1643, however, he touched off a bitter feud with the director-general, who boycotted Dutch services, instigated others to disrupt them and pressed charges against the dominie. In 1647 both Kieft and Bogardus sailed for the Netherlands to resume their quarrel before officials there. Their boat, however, was shipwrecked off the coast of Wales, and both men perished.

BIBLIOGRAPHY. *DAB* I; Q. Breen, "Dominie Everardus Bogardus," *CH* 2 (1933):78-90; E. T. Corwin, *A Manual of the Reformed Church in America* (1879).
R. H. Balmer

Bomberger, John Henry Augustus (1817-1890). German Reformed* minister.* Born in Lancaster, Pennsylvania, Bomberger graduated from Marshall College (1837) and Mercersburg Theological Seminary (1838). He served as pastor of various German Reformed churches in Pennsylvania until 1870 when he accepted the position of president of Ursinus College at Collegeville, Pennsylvania. His most prestigious pastorate was of the Race Street Church in Philadelphia. Some of Bomberger's best-known writings were penned in opposition to the Mercersburg Theology* of John

W. Nevin* and Philip Schaff.*

From 1868 to 1877 he edited *The Reformed Church Monthly,* which served as the primary organ for his anti-Mercersburg views. A main area of contention was the proposed revision of the liturgy* of the German Reformed Church. Nevin was appointed chairman of the revision committee in 1849, and a year later Schaff took over as chairman. Bomberger served on the committee, and work was completed in 1857. In 1861 the committee was again at work considering suggested revisions, but by that time a rift had developed between factions led by Nevin and Bomberger. From that point on, Bomberger, who had defended Nevin and Schaff against charges of heresy* in 1845, was a vigorous opponent of Nevin and the entire Mercersburg system. In 1867 he published *The Revised Liturgy, a history and criticism of the ritualistic movement in the German Reformed Church* and *Reformed, not Ritualistic: a reply to Dr. Nevin's "Vindication."* Other notable publications by Bomberger were two volumes of a condensed translation of Johann Jakob Herzog's *Realencyklopadie* (1856-60); a revised translation of Johann Heinrich Kurtz's *Text-book of Church History* (1860); *Infant Salvation in Its Relation to Infant Depravity, Infant Regeneration, and Infant Baptism* (1859); and *Five Years at the Race Street Church* (1860).

BIBLIOGRAPHY. *DAB* I.　　　　　S. R. Graham

Bompas, William Carpenter (1834-1906). Anglican* missionary* and bishop* in Canada. Born in England, but accepted for missionary service in Canada by the Church Missionary Society* (CMS), Bompas arrived at Fort Simpson on Christmas Day 1865. For the next forty-one years he exercised a roving evangelistic* and pastoral ministry* to the Native American and Inuit peoples of western Canada. Named by the CMS as first bishop of Athabasca in 1873, he was consecrated* in England, and he married his cousin, Charlotte Selina Cox. In 1884, he became bishop of Mackenzie River and subsequently bishop of Selkirk (now Yukon) in 1891. He died at the Carcross Mission, Yukon Territory, in June 1906.

A conservative evangelical,* staunchly opposed to ritualism and resistant to any concession to Roman Catholic* missions, Bompas maintained tight control of missionary appointments to his dioceses* to preserve their evangelical purity. He deprecated episcopal titles and dignity, seeing his function primarily as a CMS missionary to the native people. Although he preferred the isolation of the North, Bompas kept abreast of current theological debates, studied Syriac and published many articles on Native American languages as well as a book on the Mackenzie River Diocese.

BIBLIOGRAPHY. H. A. Cody, *An Apostle of the North: Memoirs of Bishop W. C. Bompas* (1908); T. C. B. Boon, *The Anglican Church from the Bay to the Rockies* (1962).　　　　　R. H. Chilton

Bonhoeffer, Dietrich (1906-1945). German Lutheran* pastor* and theologian* esteemed for his theological writings and life sealed by martyrdom. Bonhoeffer earned his doctor's degree in theology* at Berlin University at the age of twenty-one with a dissertation entitled *The Communion of Saints* (1963). He did postgraduate work at Union Seminary* in New York and then became a lecturer at Berlin University while ministering as a Lutheran chaplain.* When Hitler came to power in 1933, Bonhoeffer was a leader in the resistance of the breakaway Confessing Church which issued the famous Barmen Declaration in 1934. The need for a distanced perspective on the German situation led Bonhoeffer to a two-year pastorate in London. He then returned to Germany to establish a clandestine seminary* for the Confessing Church at Finkenwalde. Two books emerged from this period, both of which have been enormously influential: *The Cost of Discipleship* (1948) and *Life Together* (1954).

When the seminary was closed by the Nazis, Bonhoeffer was brought under the aegis of German military intelligence—not the Gestapo—ostensibly as a courier, to secretly collaborate in the overthrow of the Third Reich. This identity enabled Bonhoeffer to both continue his church ministry and participate in the plot to assassinate Hitler. Though constantly on the move, he resided for a short period in a monastery at Ettal, writing his incomplete yet profound volume *Ethics* (1955). The last two years of his life were spent in prison as a result of the abortive plot against Hitler. While in prison the pastor became a mystic and the theologian became a prophet, evinced in his widely read *Letters and Papers from Prison* (1953). He was put to death by hanging at the Flossenberg concentration camp on April 9, 1945, ironically, just as the Allied armies approached a few miles away.

Bonhoeffer's influence in North America has risen in three successive waves. The first came with the English translations of *The Cost of Discipleship* and *Life Together.* Post-World War 2* Americans were especially receptive to the concepts of "costly grace"—a meaningful discipleship beyond first-step conversion,* with a corresponding church life that would nurture growth in grace.

Next, radical thinkers—including the ephemeral "death of God"* theologians—picked up on Bonhoeffer's nascent thoughts about "religionless Christianity" in *Letters and Papers from Prison.* The phrase is based on a distinction between "religion" and biblical faith found especially in the writings of Karl Barth,* who strongly influenced Bonhoeffer. It is doubtful that the more secularized interpretations accurately reflect what Bonhoeffer intended, though he never lived to sufficiently develop what he meant by "religionless Christianity." It is probable that he became disenchanted with the state church in both its capitulation to Hitler and the creation of religion as a specialized department of culture isolated from the rest of life. Bonhoeffer was advocating a Christianity that would depend more on the inward resources of faith and less on the outward institutional aspects of organized religion—a "Christian Christianity" without provincial religious wrappings.

The third and most recent wave of Bonhoeffer's influence stems from detailed studies in the entire Bonhoeffer corpus, with special attention to church-state* relations, which so occupied Bonhoeffer. He is the inspiration for Christians today, both in North America and the Third World, who are either opposed to or suffering under oppressive political regimes. Ultimately it is Bonhoeffer's life that has so pervasively challenged Christians. He did what he said; he was a person of intense Christological piety* who died as a martyr for his Lord.

BIBLIOGRAPHY. E. Bethge, *Dietrich Bonhoeffer* (1977); A. Dumas, *Dietrich Bonhoeffer, Theologian of Reality* (1971). A. A. Glenn

Book of Common Prayer. The primary liturgical book of Anglican churches. The short title refers more narrowly to the forms for daily morning and evening prayer, the longer title including *and Administration of the Sacraments and Other Rites and Ceremonies of the Church.* The first *Book of Common Prayer* (BCP), primarily the work of Thomas Cranmer (1489-1556), archbishop of Canterbury, was issued in 1549. That first BCP compressed the traditional eight hours of prayer into two. The eucharistic* rite had a conservative shape but already reflected the reformers' theological agenda.

The second BCP, issued in 1552, gave full expression to Cranmer's reformed sacramental* theology. Upon the accession of Elizabeth I, in 1559 a new book was issued that sought to strike a mean between those of 1549 and 1552. With but little change (in 1604), the Elizabethan Prayer Book continued in use until the Puritan* suppression of the BCP in 1645. At the accession of Charles II, the Savoy conferences were held to address Puritan grievances. When these failed to produce significant results, convocation proceeded to revise the Prayer Book, producing the BCP of 1662. That continues in legal force as the Book of Common Prayer of the Church of England. One of the sources employed in that revision was the abortive BCP for Scotland issued in 1637 and discontinued immediately. It continued to influence later Scottish Episcopalian worship, and a revision of its eucharistic liturgy* found a lasting place in that church's liturgy from 1764. That in turn influenced the Episcopal Church in the U.S. in its first BCP of 1789 (revised in 1892 and 1928). The present American BCP, the result of a much more extensive revision and enrichment, was authorized in 1979.

See also LITURGICAL BOOKS.

BIBLIOGRAPHY. F. E. Brightman, *The English Rite,* 2 vols. (1915); G. J. Cuming, *A History of Anglican Liturgy* (1969); M. Hatchett, *Commentary on the American Prayer Book* (1979). T. J. Talley

Boone, William Jones (1811-1864). First American Episcopal* missionary* bishop* to China. Born in Walterborough, South Carolina, Boone was ordained* a priest* in the Protestant Episcopal Church in 1837. Appointed a missionary to China in 1835, Boone finished medical studies and went to Batavia in 1837, working among the Chinese there. From 1840 to 1843 he was in Macao and Hong Kong. In 1844, after the death of his first wife, he was consecrated* missionary bishop to China. His station from 1845 until his death in 1864 was Shanghai.

Boone was a significant participant in the committee of delegates who gathered in the late 1840s to make a new Chinese translation of the Bible.* Controversies arose over the proper Chinese term to use for *God,* and Boone, with some other missionaries, commenced their own translation in 1851. Boone presided over the initial expansion of the American Episcopal China operation and ordained the first Chinese Episcopal priests. His son, also named William Jones Boone, was later missionary bishop of Shanghai.

BIBLIOGRAPHY. *An Historical Sketch of the China Mission* (1885); M. Boone, *The Seed of the Church in China* (1973). D. H. Bays

Booth, Ballington (1857-1940). Salvation

[173]

Army* leader and founder of the Volunteers of America.* Born on July 28, 1857, the second child of William and Catherine Booth,* founders of The Salvation Army, Ballington was to devote much of his life to the Army. After several appointments he was placed in command of Army operations in the U.S. in 1887.

Ballington Booth—the "Marshall"—and his wife Maud Charlesworth, who had an active independent role, presided over The Salvation Army in the U.S. during the period of its most rapid growth. The Army's evangelistic* crusade spread across the country, and the beginnings were made for the extensive system of social welfare activities for which the organization is so well known in the U.S. By all accounts the Ballington Booths were effective and popular leaders.

However, Ballington became estranged from his father over the issue of the Army's authoritarian international hierarchy, and in January 1896 the Ballington Booths resigned from The Salvation Army. Shortly thereafter they established the Volunteers of America,* an organization similar in form and purpose to The Salvation Army but with a more democratic structure. The Salvation Army leadership at first viewed the new organization as an unwelcome rival, but the two movements were eventually reconciled. The Volunteers of America, although always much smaller than The Salvation Army, developed an array of effective social welfare programs, especially among prisoners* and those recently released from prison.

See also SALVATION ARMY; VOLUNTEERS OF AMERICA.

BIBLIOGRAPHY. B. Booth, *The Prayer that Prevails* (1920); M. B. Booth, *Beneath Two Flags* (1889); *DAB* 2; E. H. McKinley, *Marching to Glory: The History of The Salvation Army in the United States, 1880-1980* (1980).　　　　E. H. McKinley

Booth, Catherine Mumford (1829-1890). Co-founder of The Salvation Army.* Born on January 17, 1829, in Derbyshire, England, in 1844 her family moved to London, where Catherine became an active lay worker in a Wesleyan* society. In 1855 she married William Booth,* a licensed preacher* in the Methodist* New Connexion. Ten years later the Booths established an evangelistic mission in London, which in 1878 became The Salvation Army.

Catherine was a woman of strong moral conviction and an exacting sense of personal integrity, but at the same time she was known for her kindness and thoughtfulness toward others. Widely read in the devotional* and popular theological works of the day, an energetic evangelist* and often original in her thinking, Catherine's interests and her compassion ranged freely over the contemporary scene. She was an early advocate for the humane treatment of domestic animals and a firm believer in women's rights to take roles equal to those of men in religious, social and political activities. Catherine's influence over her husband and the fledgling Salvation Army was very great. Her sympathetic knowledge of Quaker* theology, for instance, strengthened William's decision to abandon sacramental* observances in the Army when these proved confusing to new converts. The famous bonnet, too, was her inspiration. She was a gifted mediator at Army headquarters, a badly needed counter to William, who was often hurried and irascible in his dealings with their immediate circle.

The "Army Mother" profoundly affected the lives of her eight children, all of whom remained active in religious work until old age, five of them as Salvation Army officers, two of these as general. Kindly and patient to the end, Catherine died on October 4, 1890, after a long illness. Bereft of her companionship and counsel, William, who never fully recovered from his grief, increasingly occupied himself with travel and public speaking.

See also BOOTH, WILLIAM; SALVATION ARMY.

BIBLIOGRAPHY. F. de L. Booth-Tucker, *The Life of Catherine Booth,* 2 vols. (1892).

E. H. McKinley

Booth, Evangeline Cory (1865-1950). Salvation Army* leader. Born on December 25, 1865, she was the seventh child of William* and Catherine Booth,* founders of The Salvation Army. Christened "Eveline" and called "Eva" by her family, she adopted the more euphonious name of *Evangeline* in 1904. After directing Salvation Army operations in Canada from 1896 to 1904, Evangeline Booth became the third successive Booth child to be placed in command of the Army in the U.S. She served as national commander from 1904 to 1934, many times longer than any other officer in that position.

Flamboyant, melodramatic and strong willed, yet a capable administrator with the ability to attract and hold dedicated and efficient subordinates, Evangeline Cory Booth—the "Commander"—became famous. She remains the only Salvation Army officer to have been well known in the U.S. outside the ranks of the movement itself. During her long administration the Army gained prominence for its service to American troops in World War 1,* its campaigns to uplift homeless alcoholics, unwed mothers and neglected children in the 1920s and its widespread relief activities during the Depression.

Evangeline Booth was elected the fourth general of The Salvation Army in 1934 and returned to London. In 1939 she retired to her adopted homeland, the U.S., where she died on July 17, 1950.

See also BOOTH, CATHERINE; BOOTH, WILLIAM.

BIBLIOGRAPHY. *DAB* 4; *DARB;* E. H. McKinley, *Marching to Glory: The History of The Salvation Army in the United States, 1880-1980* (1980); *NAW* 1; *NCAB* B; M. Trout, *The General Was a Lady: The Story of Evangeline Booth* (1980); P. W. Wilson, *General Evangeline Booth of The Salvation Army* (1948).   E. H. McKinley

Booth, Maud Charlesworth (1865-1948).

Leader in The Salvation Army* and cofounder of Volunteers of America.* Born in Limpsfield, Surrey, England, Maud grew up in an Anglican* home, the daughter of an Anglican clergyman,* Samuel Charlesworth. Much to her father's displeasure, she joined The Salvation Army in her teens, and at sixteen accompanied Catherine Booth, the eldest daughter of Army founders William* and Catherine Booth,* to France and Switzerland. There she faced persecution and arrest while helping to establish a foothold for the work of The Salvation Army.

Maud married Ballington Booth,* the second son of William and Catherine Booth, and in 1887 the Ballington Booths were sent to the U.S. as the National Commanders of The Salvation Army in America. Both were indefatigable leaders, he using his administrative and preaching* skills, she publicizing the work of the Army through her writing and speaking, raising money, winning friends and assuming leadership of an Auxiliary League which enlisted both spiritual and financial support from people interested in the work of the Army. Maud Booth was also in charge of what was referred to as the slum work, and she visited prisons.

Both the work of the Army and the number of Salvation Army officers increased during the tenure of the Booths as National Commanders. However, all was not well. Both Ballington and Maud disagreed with William Booth, the general of the international Salvation Army, over the autocratic governance of the Army. They subsequently resigned on January 31, 1896, and in March of that year founded the Volunteers of America, with Ballington assuming the title of general.

The Volunteers, similar to The Salvation Army in purpose but more democratic in organization, engaged primarily in social ministries, the most notable being a ministry to prisoners. After Ballington Booth's death in 1940, Maud Booth assumed the title of general, and served in that capacity until her death on August 26, 1948.

BIBLIOGRAPHY. M. Booth, *Beneath Two Flags* (1889); E. H. McKinley, *Marching to Glory: The History of The Salvation Army in the United States, 1880-1980* (1980).   R. J. Green

Booth, William (1829-1912).

English evangelist* and founder of The Salvation Army.* Born on April 10, 1829, in Nottingham, the son of respectable but insolvent parents, Booth was forced to find work as a pawnbroker's apprentice, first in Nottingham and later in London. Intelligent and introspective, he was converted* at age fifteen and became an enthusiastic part-time evangelist. In 1852 Booth became a licensed Methodist* minister,* accepting pastoral appointments within a branch of that denomination* until 1861 when he resigned to devote himself to the work of an independent evangelist.

Booth married Catherine* Mumford in 1855 and the couple had eight children, all of whom not only survived infancy but lived to old age. Catherine, an independent-minded and energetic person, deserves credit with William for the success of the spiritual enterprises they founded together. The first of these was the Christian Mission, opened in London's East End in 1865.

Acting on what seemed a momentary impulse, William Booth altered the wording of the mission's annual report in 1878 in order to describe the work as "a Salvation Army." In fact, Booth and his closest advisors had been dissatisfied with the mission's organization for some time. The new name was a catalyst. An authentic military structure was now installed, with "General" William Booth at the apex. Catherine became the "Army Mother," and all eight children were eventually given high rank in the new organization. A complete and often colorful array of military trappings was added over the next two years. The new movement spread rapidly, and within ten years of the name change The Salvation Army was widely established throughout the British Isles, in the United States, Canada, Australia and Europe.

William Booth was single-minded in his zeal for lost souls, whose plight he imagined and described in graphic terms. He subordinated everything to the work of evangelism, including normal family relationships. His children were expected to think of him as "General," rather than as father and, influenced by Catherine, he streamlined the Army's theology* to better serve its spiritual warfare. The emphasis was on saving souls and on guiding converts into that second work of grace that Wesleyans* call "sanctification,"* by which one experiences God's love as the guiding force of one's life. Everything else in the way of doctrine or practice was simply jettisoned—especially if, like sacramental* observances, these things were confusing or divisive.

Booth created, piecemeal over many years, an elaborate system of social relief partly for the same reason: charity speeded the work of evangelism among the poor by showing them that Salvationists took Christianity seriously. In addition, acts of kindness to the poor were commanded by Christ himself, ending further argument. The General's complete social relief scheme was made public in 1890, when his book *In Darkest England and the Way Out* was published in Britain and the United States. In both its evangelistic activities and in its charitable operations, William and Catherine believed the Army was fulfilling what they saw as its unique ministry: to save souls among those parts of the population that other Christian workers seemed unable to reach.

Like many another zealot, Booth was less successful in some of his personal associations than in his public ministry. A troubled sleeper afflicted with poor digestion, Booth was a difficult guest and often irascible in his dealings with his immediate circle. His relationship with the leaders of the American branch of the movement was strained in the early years, leading to schisms within the movement in 1894 and 1896.

The General's zeal for souls, his moral courage and his compassion for the urban poor among whom he lived his entire life, however, were genuine and exemplary. The movement he founded bore the imprint of his dramatic personality, even in the most distant outposts. The rank and file, who knew nothing of his administrative difficulties, were deeply impressed with the force of his vision for lost souls. Undeterred by chronic illness, Booth was active in public ministry almost until his death on August 20, 1912. As a symbol he was, and is, revered by Salvationists. The movement he founded remains an important force for spiritual and social redemption in many parts of the world.

See also BOOTH, CATHERINE; SALVATION ARMY.

BIBLIOGRAPHY. H. Begbie, *Life of William Booth: The Founder of The Salvation Army,* 2 vols. (1920); S. J. Ervine, *God's Soldier: General William Booth,* 2 vols. (1935); G. S. Railton, *The Authoritative Life of General William Booth, Founder of The Salvation Army* (1912).   E. H. McKinley

Booth-Tucker, Frederick St. George de Lautour (1853-1929) and Emma Moss Booth-Tucker (1860-1903). National commanders of The Salvation Army in America.* The son of a British colonial officer in India, Frederick Tucker took a leave of absence from his civil service position in India, traveled to London, and joined The Salvation Army. Given the rank of major, he held seven appointments, culminating in 1882 when he sailed back to India to begin the work of The Salvation Army there, a task he accomplished in spite of opposition from the government, imprisonment, persecution and even the death of his first wife.

Emma, the second daughter of William* and Catherine* Booth, founders of The Salvation Army, became a Salvation Army officer. She was the principal of the first training home for women officers in 1880, and was the first to inaugurate what was termed the slum work of The Salvation Army, whereby the workers would live among the poorest of the urban slum-dwellers while ministering to them physically and spiritually.

Emma Booth and the then Commissioner Tucker were married on April 10, 1888. The Booth-Tuckers—William Booth insisted on a hyphenated name for his three married daughters to insure equality with their husbands, retain personal identity and provide for equal rank and authority—received many appointments, including a time of service in India. The title of consul was bestowed on Emma in 1895.

The Booth-Tuckers were sent in 1896 as the national commanders of The Salvation Army in America, which was in disarray due to the resignations of Ballington* and Maud Booth.* Frederick and Emma did not possess the charisma of their predecessors, but were determined, practical and tireless leaders and administrators. They regained the confidence of the general public, consolidated the finances of the Army and greatly increased the social ministry of the Army, especially in the area of prison ministry and in the erection of orphanages and three farm colonies.

While returning from an inspection of the farm colony in Fort Amity, Colorado, Emma Booth-Tucker was the only fatality of a train accident on October 28, 1903. The inconsolable Frederick remained as national commander only until November of 1904. He returned to further assignments in London, remarried and retired from active service in 1926.

BIBLIOGRAPHY. E. M. Booth-Tucker, *Heart Messages* (n.d.); F. Booth-Tucker, *The Consul: A Sketch of Emma Booth-Tucker* (1903); *DAB* I; H. Williams, *Booth-Tucker, William Booth's First Gentleman* (1980). R. J. Green

Borden, William Whiting (1887-1913). China Inland Mission* missionary* to Muslims. Born into a wealthy Chicago family, Borden came to Christ while a young boy under the ministry* of Reuben A. Torrey,* pastor of Moody Church. A concern for the spiritual need of the people in other countries was awakened in Borden's heart by a lengthy trip round the world when he was sixteen. The following year, 1909, he entered Yale University.* Inheriting great wealth (he was a millionaire at age twenty-one), Borden gave generously to many causes, one of which was the Yale-Hope Mission in New Haven, established through his personal efforts and gifts.

Spiritually mature beyond his years, he was appointed a director of the Moody Bible Institute* and the National Bible Institute of New York, and he was also a council member of the China Inland Mission (CIM). While at Princeton Seminary* he was active in the Student Volunteer Movement,* and his life was strongly influenced by John R. Mott,* Robert E. Speer* and Samuel Zwemer.* Burdened for the Muslims of northwest China, Borden joined the CIM in 1912 and sailed for Egypt to study Arabic in Cairo en route to China. His untimely death on April 9, 1913, from cerebrospinal meningitis was widely mourned. In his will he left almost $1 million to Christian causes. The legacy of total dedication and self-sacrificial living of William Borden had a lasting influence on countless Christians.

BIBLIOGRAPHY. Mrs. H. Taylor, *Borden of Yale '09* (1926). D. J. Michell

Born Again. Taken from Jesus' words in John 3:7, "You must be born again" (or "anew" or "from above"), this term has acquired a broad and imprecise usage in general American discourse. It has come to mean any Christian who exhibits intensity or overt self-identification or a keen sense of divine presence, or one who attributes causation to God for events in personal life or in the historical and natural processes.

In the understanding of American Christians, *born again* is associated with revivalism* or any conversionist* form of Protestantism.* It describes the direct experience of a person in a notable single event or a specifiable period when that person shifts his or her life focus from any other center to Jesus Christ. It is as if that person had undergone a personal microchronic passage from B.C. to A.D. Whenever used, it bespeaks an earnest, outspoken and transformed Christian and refers to churches that preach* that message.

S. S. Hill

Bosworth, (F)red (F)rancis (1876-1958). Early Pentecostal* healing* evangelist.* Bosworth spent part of his youth in John Alexander Dowie's* church in Chicago, Illinois, and eventually joined Dowie's utopian city of healing, Zion, Illinois. Baptized in the Spirit* when Charles F. Parham* brought Pentecostalism to Zion in September 1906, Bosworth, ostracized for his beliefs, left Zion and by 1910 had founded a church in Denver, Colorado. In 1912 he sponsored a six-month series of meetings led by healing evangelist Maria B. Woodworth-Etter,* thus propelling her into the Pentecostal limelight. Bosworth went on to establish a successful independent healing ministry in the post-World War 1* era, attracting large crowds in major cities throughout America. He also pioneered in radio evangelism, founding the National Radio Revival Missionary Crusaders in Chicago.

Bosworth was an early leader of the emerging Assemblies of God,* but in 1918 he led a small schism, affirming the minority viewpoint that glossalalia* was just one of many initial evidences of the Holy Spirit baptism. He became associated with the Christian and Missionary Alliance.* As did all healing evangelists, Bosworth suffered financial hardship in the 1930s. He retired, but during the post-World War 2* healing revival, he joined the William Marrion Branham* team and functioned as a revered advisor to younger evangelists. Bosworth's teachings on faith healing made him an important precursor to the faith movement,* so prominent in contemporary Pentecostalism.* The last few years of his life were devoted to mission* work in Africa.

BIBLIOGRAPHY. E. M. Perkins, *Fred Francis Bosworth: His Life Story* (1927); C. D. Weaver, *The Healer-prophet, William Marrion Branham: A Study of the Prophetic in American Pentecostalism* (1987). C. D. Weaver

Bouchard, Claude Florent (1751-?). French Catholic* priest* in Boston. A native of Craon, France, ordained* in 1777, Bouchard was assigned to the French fleet operating in American waters in aid of the Revolution. After deserting in October 1788, he began an unauthorized ministry* as pastor of the School Street Church in Boston under the pseudonym Abbé de la Poterie. Not until after he had offered his first Mass* on November 2, 1788 did he seek canonical permission from John Carroll,* bishop* of Baltimore. Though confirmed in his pastorate by Carroll, Bouchard rapidly became controversial. His accumulation of huge debts, his aristocratic and pretentious airs and his habit of praying for the king of France at Mass* alienated his parishioners. When the archbishop* of Paris learned of his desertion, he notified Carroll that he had suspended Bouchard. Carroll, in turn, notified Bouchard that he was sending the Rev. William O'Brien, pastor in New York City, to investigate the state of affairs in Boston. Bouchard responded by denouncing Carroll in a vitriolic 1789 pamphlet entitled *The Resurrection of Laurent Ricci; or a True and Exact History of the Jesuits.* Faced with legal action for nonpayment of debt, Bouchard left Boston for Canada in 1790. His date of death is unknown.

BIBLIOGRAPHY. J. Hennesey, *American Catholics* (1981); J. T. Ellis, *Catholics in Colonial America* (1965). L. R. Riforgiato

Boudinot, Elias (Galagina) (c. 1802-1839). Tribal leader and publisher among the Cherokee Indians. Born near Rome, Georgia, as a young man he was sent to study at the Foreign Mission School at Cornwall, Connecticut. While at the school he was converted* to Christianity and also took the name Elias Boudinot from a patron of the school. He was to become widely influential as a Christian leader among his tribe. After his schooling in New England, which included a year at Andover Theological Seminary* (1822-1823), he returned to Georgia. Working with the missionary* Samuel A. Worcester,* he translated a variety of religious and educational literature into the Cherokee language, including portions of the Bible.* In 1828, at the direction of the Cherokee National Council, Boudinot began publication of *The Cherokee Phoenix,* the first Native American newspaper. When the removal controversy engulfed the Cherokees, Boudinot advocated emigration to the West as the most prudent alternative. In 1835 he signed the removal agreement (The Treaty of New Echota), thus earning the wrath of the party of Cherokees determined to resist removal. In June 1839, shortly after he had moved to the Indian Territory, he was murdered by embittered opponents of the treaty.

See also MISSIONS TO NATIVE AMERICANS, PROTESTANT.

BIBLIOGRAPHY. *DAB* I; *DARB;* T. Perdue, ed., *Cherokee Editor: The Writings of Elias Boudinot* (1983); R. H. Gabriel, *Elias Boudinot, Cherokee, and His America* (1941); *NCAB* 19.

M. S. Joy

Bounds, Edward McKendree (1835-1913). Methodist* minister* and devotional writer. Born in Shelby County, Missouri, Bounds studied law and was admitted to the bar at the age of twenty-one. Three years later he began his pastoral ministry at Monticello, Missouri. While serving at Brunswick, Missouri, at the start of the Civil War,* he was taken into custody because he would not swear allegiance to the federal government. In 1863 he secured his release from detention in Memphis, Tennessee, and made his way to join the Confederate forces in Mississippi, where he was appointed chaplain of the Fifth Missouri Regiment. He served in that capacity until he was taken prisoner at Franklin, Tennessee, near the end of the War.

After the War, Bounds served pastorates in Tennessee and Alabama. In 1875 he was appointed to St. Paul's Methodist Church in St. Louis, Missouri, and later briefly served as pastor of the First Methodist Church in the same city. Later he served as editor of the *St. Louis Christian Advocate* for eight years and as associate editor of the *Nashville Christian Advocate* for four years. Bounds taught a doctrine of entire sanctification* as a distinct second work of grace. He spent the last seventeen years of his life in Washington, Georgia. There he wrote most of his devotional* books, such as *Purpose in Prayer* (1920) and *The Necessity of Prayer* (1929), which continue to appear around the world in numerous new editions to the present time.

BIBLIOGRAPHY. H. W. Hodge, "Introduction" in E. M. Bounds, *Purpose in Prayer* (1921).

M. E. Dieter

Bourget, Ignace (1799-1885). Catholic* bishop* of Montreal. Born near Quebec City, Bourget studied theology* and taught at the Seminaire de Nicolet for three years. In 1821 he was appointed secretary to the first Bishop of Montreal. His indefatigable zeal, administrative ability and Christian dedication made him virtually indispensable in the developing diocese and commended him to his superiors. As an ambitious young man, he had a vision for the place of the Roman Catholic Church in Canadian life and particularly the life of French Canada. At the same time, living in Montreal, with its powerful Anglo-Saxon commercial community, he was aware of the threat of Protestantism and of various forms of liberal thought. As a result he was drawn to ultramontanism,* which saw the Catholic answer to the modern world to lie in a Romantic* reassertion of the high Middle Ages, with papal authority* and Thomistic theology and philosophy to the fore.

Installed as co-adjutor bishop while still in his

thirties, and consecrated* as bishop in 1840, he made the diocese* of Montreal the dynamic center of Canadian ultramontanism. A large company of men and women were brought from the religious orders* of France to engage in parish, educational and social ministries. The percentage of the population attending church regularly increased significantly. Bourget also insisted that the Church had authority* in all areas of life where Christian doctrine* and morals were at stake. He did not hesitate to attack those who did not share his vision, all the way up to the archbishop of Quebec, Elzear Taschereau,* where he met his match. Although Bourget resigned in 1878, as a result of apparent defeat, he nonetheless was highly successful, for he did more than any other individual to make Francophone Quebec an unofficial theocracy,* a situation that would continue until the Quiet Revolution of the 1960s.

BIBLIOGRAPHY. *DCB* XI.

I. S. Rennie

Bourne, Hugh (1772-1852). Cofounder of the Primitive Methodist Church.* Born at Stoke-on-Trent, England, Bourne was a Wesleyan Methodist who was influenced by the American Methodist evangelist* Lorenzo Dow.* Dow advocated American-style camp meetings* during his trip to Britain in 1805-1807 and inspired Bourne to hold a camp meeting at Mow Cop in the summer of 1807, which succeeded sufficiently to warrant repetition. It also aroused opposition; the Wesleyan Methodist Church forbade its ministers to promote these American-style phenomena. Bourne rejected the prohibition, was excluded by the Wesleyan Conference, and with William Clowes founded the Primitive Methodist Church in 1811. In 1829 the Conference, with Bourne as its leader, initiated an ill-conceived mission to America. By 1840, the American group formally severed its connections with Britain. Four years later the British Conference appointed the retired Bourne as its "adviser" to the work in Canada. He included the U.S., but his visit to New York caused additional tensions; Bourne tended to be more autocrat than adviser. He left for England after only seven months in New York.

BIBLIOGRAPHY. H. B. Kendall, *The History of the Primitive Methodist Church* (1900); J. T. Wilkinson, *Hugh Bourne* (1952).

M. R. Fraser

Bowne, Borden Parker (1847-1910). Methodist* philosopher. Born at Leonardville, New Jersey, Bowne studied modern languages and philosophy at the University of the City of New York (B.A., 1871). Following a brief Methodist pastorate at Whitestone, New York (1872-1873), Bowne studied at the universities of Paris, Halle and Göttingen (1873-1875) and returned to teach at his alma mater, serve as religion editor of *The Independent* and receive his M.A. (1875-1876). In 1876 he joined the faculty at Boston University, where he was to stay for thirty-five years (1876-1910).

As the head of a prestigious philosophy department and an effective teacher, Bowne exerted a considerable influence on his contemporaries, including Edgar S. Brightman* and Albert C. Knudson.* His philosophy increasingly centered on the role of personality and self-image in one's religious make-up and expressions. One term Bowne developed for this idea was *transcendental empiricism,* to indicate a reality beyond the apprehension of the senses.

Though an ardent exponent of free will, Bowne shunned evolutionary thought and adhered to a conservative christology.* But his promotion of intuition and his metaphysic known as "personalism," as well as his insistence on open inquiry into even the most controversial of subjects troubled some conservatives. His own Methodist denomination* tried Bowne for heresy* in 1904 on the grounds of his liberal* views. His acquittal was something of a victory for the modernists* in Methodism.

Bowne's numerous publications, including *Studies in Theism* (1879); *Metaphysics* (1882); *The Theory of Thought and Knowledge* (1897); *The Immanence of God* (1905) and *Personalism* (1908), were significant and creative contributions to modern philosophical theology. His thought anticipated Freud on the importance of personality and Einstein on the relativity of time and space, but always in the context of the religious significance of these concepts. Bowne's career is an example of late nineteenth- and early twentieth-century efforts to respond to social Darwinism and industrialization from a positive, modern Christian perspective.

BIBLIOGRAPHY. *DAB* I; *DARB*; F. J. McConnell, *Borden Parker Bowne, His Life and His Philosophy* (1929); *NCAB* 11; C. B. Pyle, *The Philosophy of Borden Parker Bowne* (1910).

C. P. Dawson

Boyce, James Petigru (1827-1888). Southern Baptist* educator, theologian* and seminary* founder. Born in Charleston, South Carolina, Boyce was educated at Charleston College, Brown University* and Princeton.* Princeton professor Charles Hodge* helped shape Boyce's own appreciation for Reformed* theology. His conversion* to Christianity in 1846 led him to religious studies and the decision to enter the ministry.* After serving as pastor of First Baptist Church, Columbia, South Carolina, and as professor of theology at Furman University, in 1859 Boyce helped to found the Southern Baptist Theological Seminary in Greenville, South Carolina. He served as professor and chairman of the seminary faculty until his death in 1888. Boyce was chief fund raiser for the seminary and a proponent of theological education for all Southern Baptist ministers. Under his guidance the fledgling seminary survived the Civil War* years and a move to Louisville in 1877. Boyce's moderate Reformed theology left its imprint in the seminary's doctrinal statement, "Abstract of Principles," and in his book *Abstract of Systematic Theology* published in 1887. Boyce was also president of the Southern Baptist Convention 1872-1879 and 1888.

BIBLIOGRAPHY. J. A. Broadus, *Memoir of James Petigru Boyce* (1893); *DAB* I.   B. J. Leonard

Bradbury, William Batchelder (1816-1868). Sunday-school-tunes composer and compiler, music publisher and piano manufacturer. Born into a musical family in York, Maine, Bradbury studied with Lowell Mason* at Bowdoin Street Church, Boston, and the Boston Academy. He taught in Maine and New Brunswick and then became organist at Baptist Tabernacle, New York City (1841), and began teaching and promoting Mason's public-school music approach. He studied in England and Germany (1847-1849)—where he saw Mendelssohn, Liszt and Schumann—and returned to compose, publish and hold musical institutes with George F. Root,* Thomas Hastings and Mason. His "Golden" series (1861-1867) of songs sold over three million copies. Bradbury set the texts of such popular lyricists as Fanny J. Crosby.* His publishing firm, which specialized in Sunday-school music books, later became Biglow & Main, and his Bradbury Piano Company was later absorbed by Knabe. Bradbury tunes which are still familiar are "Bradbury" (Savior, Like a Shepherd), "He Leadeth Me," "Jesus Loves Me," "Olive's Brow" ('Tis Midnight), "Sabbath" (Holy Is the Lord), "Sweet Hour of Prayer," "The Solid Rock" and "Woodworth" (Just as I Am).

BIBLIOGRAPHY. *DAB* I; *New York Musical Gazette* Obituary (December 1867-June 1868); A. B. Wingard, "The Life and Works of William Batchelder Bradbury" (unpublished dissertation, Southern Baptist Seminary, 1973).
                                                R. J. Stanislaw

Bradford, William (1590-1657). Governor of Plymouth Colony and historian. Born in Yorkshire, England, while still in his teens he absorbed the teachings of religious dissenters called "Separatists" who met in the neighboring home of Elder William Brewster.* Unlike the Puritans who sought to reform the Church of England,* the Separatists believed that the church was so hopelessly apostate* that they refused to acknowledge its authority* in any form. For this hostility, Separatists were persecuted and many, including Bradford, fled to Leyden, The Netherlands, in 1609. While there, the Separatists were free to worship* as they pleased, but they feared that their children would soon lose all contact with English ways. Consequently, when the possibility of New World settlement arose, Bradford and other Separatist leaders embarked on the Mayflower in 1620.

Within a year of the "Pilgrim"* settlement of Plymouth Colony, Bradford was elected governor and served in that capacity for thirty years, until his death in 1657. As governor, Bradford saw to the defense of the colony and established a close alliance with the neighboring Puritans* of Massachusetts Bay. At the same time, he resisted the absorption of Plymouth Colony into Massachusetts Bay. Although Pilgrims and Puritans were similar in questions of doctrine* and church government,* they could not agree on their relationship to the Church of England and so remained separate throughout the seventeenth century.

Besides acting as governor of Plymouth Colony, Bradford served as chief chronicler and historian of the first settlements. His manuscript *History of Plymouth Plantation* was written between 1630 and 1651 and is preserved at the Massachusetts Historical Society. It stands as one of the greatest chronicles of New World settlement in North America. The document is remarkable not only for the information it supplies about civil and economic settlement, but also for the point of view, which is emphatically theocentric and providential in its interpretation of historical events. Although written in the plain style for which the Puritans and Separatists were famous, it stands as the most profound testimony to the Congregational* vision and sense of destiny that prompted their New World settlement.

BIBLIOGRAPHY. *DAB* I; *DARB;* G. D. Langdon, Jr., *Pilgrim Colony: A History of New Plymouth, 1620-1691* (1966); S. E. Morison, ed., *Bradford's Of Plymouth Plantation* (1952); *NCAB* 7.
                                                H. S. Stout

Bradley, Preston (1888-1983). Unitarian* minister* and civic leader. Bradley grew up in Linden,

Michigan, and studied at several colleges in the state without completing a degree. Drawn to the ministry, he went to Chicago in 1911 to study at Moody Bible Institute* and became pastor of a Presbyterian* church. He severed his relations with both in 1912 and founded the People's Church, which he led until semi-retirement in 1968. Preaching in halls and theaters, he built a huge following, which in 1926 erected its own Uptown auditorium-playhouse. His optimistic theism stressed human goodness, progress, openness to science, as well as interfaith and interracial understanding. He styled himself a heretic who disdained the traditions and creeds* of organized religion. He was a pioneer in religious radio broadcasting, long-time director of the Chicago Public Library, member of the Chicago Commission on Human Relations, founder of the Izaak Walton League and citizen-delegate to the United Nations's founding conference in 1945.

BIBLIOGRAPHY. P. Bradley (with H. Barnard), *Along the Way: An Autobiography* (1962); D. R. Chandler, *The Reverend Dr. Preston Bradley: The Official, Authorized Biography* (1971).

J. H. Dorn

Bradstreet, Anne (c. 1612-1672). Puritan* poet. Born Anne Dudley and married to Simon Bradstreet when she was sixteen, Anne immigrated with her husband and parents to Massachusetts Bay with the Winthrop party in 1630. The Bradstreets settled first at Ipswich, where she initially rebelled at her new and harsh environment. Nevertheless, she adjusted and, as a consequence of her husband's leadership in the colony, came to enjoy the company of Massachusetts's most cultured society. The family moved in 1644 to North Andover where, despite continuing health problems, she gave birth to eight children.

Her poetry, written in the midst of demanding domestic duties, reveals a warm Puritan piety that accepted the joys and trials of life as from the hand of a sovereign and loving God. Her lyrics frequently expound the beauty and wonders of the natural world through which she perceived the hand of God. The satisfactions of religious experience and the domestic pleasures of home, children and marital love also are expressed in a style that reflects her reading of poets such as Edmund Spenser, Philip Sidney and John Donne. She was the first poet in the colonies to have her work published, when her first volume of poetry, *The Tenth Muse* (1650), was issued in London without her knowledge through the efforts of her brother-in-law, the Reverend John Woodbridge. However, it was not this bulky first work but her less pretentious poems concerning the familiar objects of her daily life, published later, which have won her a place in literary history. Her poetry revealed much of the inner workings of early Puritan New England society and earned for her the distinction of being America's first noteworthy poet.

BIBLIOGRAPHY. A. Bradstreet, *The Works of Anne Bradstreet in Prose and Verse,* ed. J. H. Ellis (1867); H. Campbell, *Anne Bradstreet and Her Time* (1890); *DAB* I; J. K. Piercy, *Anne Bradstreet* (1965); M. C. Tyler, *A History of American Literature during the Colonial Period* (1949).

The Editors

Brainerd, David (1718-1747). Presbyterian* missionary* in the Middle Colonies. Born in Haddam, Connecticut, and left an orphan at the age of fourteen, Brainerd seemed destined for a life as a Connecticut farmer, working land that he had inherited. But in 1739 he had a conversion* experience and enrolled at Yale College* with aspirations for the Congregational* ministry.* Brainerd emerged as one of the New Light* leaders of the Great Awakening* at Yale, but he was dismissed from the college in 1742 for reputedly saying that a tutor had no more grace than a chair.

Nevertheless, Brainerd continued to study for the ministry,* received a license* to preach,* accepted appointment as a missionary of the Society in Scotland for Propagating Christian Knowledge in 1742 and was ordained* by the Presbytery* of New York in 1744. Between 1743 and 1747, Brainerd served as a missionary to Indians in New York, Pennsylvania and New Jersey. His most significant achievement as a missionary occurred near Trenton, New Jersey, between 1745 and 1746. There he led a revival* among small bands of Delaware Indians, baptized thirty-eight converts and formed a church. Brainerd described his success in his *Journal,* which was published in 1746.

On a visit to New England in 1747, Brainerd became seriously ill from the tuberculosis that had afflicted him for years. He died in Northampton, Massachusetts, having been nursed by his fiancée, Jerusha, daughter of his Northhampton friend and mentor Jonathan Edwards.* Brainerd left behind his diary which contained a detailed account of the emotional and physical hardships he experienced during the four years he spent as a missionary. Edwards fashioned the diary into a heroic memoir and inspirational guidebook, which he published in 1749. As a result, Brainerd's life continued to instruct and inspire his missionary successors.

BIBLIOGRAPHY. *AAP* 3; *DAB* I; *DARB;* J. Conforti, "David Brainerd and the Nineteenth-Century Missionary Movement," *JER* 5 (1985): 309-329; Edwards, *Life of David Brainerd: The Works of Jonathan Edwards,* ed. N. Pettit, vol. 7 (1984); *NCAB* 2.   J. Conforti

Branham, William Marrion (1909-1965). Healing* evangelist.* The post-World War 2* healing revival* in Pentecostalism* began in the ministry* of William Branham, an independent so-called "Holy Ghost" Baptist* minister* from Jeffersonville, Indiana. In 1946 Branham claimed that an angel commissioned him to be a prophet with the message of divine healing. From 1946 to 1955 Branham conducted a healing ministry that only Oral Roberts* could match. The Pentecostal masses revered his legendary healing gifts, the ability to detect diseases by the vibration of his hand and the ability to discern the secrets of a person's heart.

As healing revivalism transformed into the broader charismatic movement,* the unsophisticated Branham did not readily adapt. Attempting to cope with declining popularity, Branham increasingly asserted doctrinal revelations regarding the end-time message of God. The most controversial revelation was his claim to be the end-time prophet to the Bride of Christ. Since his death in 1965, Branham's followers have partially or totally deified him and have given his sermons scriptural status, the voice of God to this last generation.
See also FAITH HEALING; PENTECOSTALISM.

BIBLIOGRAPHY. D. E. Harrell, *All Things Are Possible* (1975); C. D. Weaver, *The Healer-Prophet, William Marrion Branham: A Study of the Prophetic in American Pentecostalism* (1987).
                                         C. D. Weaver

Brant, Joseph (Thayendanegea) (c. 1743-1807). Mohawk Indian statesman. As a young man, Brant was sent in 1761 to Moor's Charity School at Lebanon, Connecticut, directed by Congregationalist* missionary* Rev. Eleazar Wheelock.* While there he embraced Christianity* (c. 1763) and became interested in its spread among his people. Staunchly loyal to the British crown during Pontiac's Rebellion (1763), he fought with a band of loyalist Indians against the insurgent tribes. The Rev. John Stuart,* who came to the Mohawk country in 1770, was instrumental in leading Brant into the Anglican* church. Brant assisted Stuart in learning the Mohawk language and in translating parts of the Bible* and other religious literature. During the American Revolution* he played an

important role in keeping the Mohawks loyal to the Crown and fought in several actions with and for the British, gaining a reputation as a warrior that has led some biographers to question his Christian profession. After the Revolution he led a band of Mohawks to emigrate to Canada, settling at Brantsford, Ontario.

BIBLIOGRAPHY. *DAB* I; I. T. Kelsay, *Joseph Brant, Seventeen Forty-Three to Eighteen Seven: Man of Two Worlds* (1984); J. O'Donnell, "Joseph Brant," *American Indian Leaders: Studies in Diversity,* ed. R. D. Edmunds (1980).   M. S. Joy

Brattle, William (1662-1717). Harvard* academic and Congregational* minister.* Brattle, a member of Harvard College's class of 1680, served the school as tutor through much of Increase Mather's* long tenure as absentee president. An independent thinker whose interest in astronomy won him induction into the Royal Society in 1713, he prepared a text on Cartesian logic that remained in use at Harvard as late as 1765. Although Brattle was in most respects a loyal son of the Massachusetts Congregational establishment, his catholic spirit and enthusiasm for Anglican* works of theology* smoothed the path for a number of students who subsequently entered the Church of England. Installed in 1696 as pastor of the Cambridge church, Brattle was among the first local Congregational clergy* to dispense with the traditional requirement that applicants for admission to communion make a public relation of their religious experience* (*See* Conversion Narratives) and submit to a vote of the membership,* in favor of a system of private examination by the pastor and silent assent by the congregation. Brattle lent aid to his older brother Thomas Brattle, John Leverett* and others active in the 1699 founding of the Brattle Street Church in Boston, bringing this and other innovations to the seat of Puritan* orthodoxy.*

BIBLIOGRAPHY. *AAP* 1; *DAB* I; S. E. Morison, *Harvard College in the Seventeenth Century,* 2 vols. (1936).   G. W. Harper

Bray, Thomas (1658-1730). Anglican* minister* and promoter of missionary* and philanthropic* causes. Born in Marton, Shropshire, Bray studied at Oxford, earning his B.A. (1678) at All Souls College, his M.A. (1693) at Hart Hall and his B.D. and D.D. (1696) at Magdalen College. He served several charges in Shropshire and Warwickshire from 1682 to 1695, when Henry Compton, bishop of London, made him commissary to Maryland (active 1695-1704). Bray was actually in Maryland for only three months during 1700, living his last thirty-five years in Warwickshire and London, where he was rector of St. Botolph Without, Aldgate (1706-1730). Nevertheless, he continued to support the Anglican cause in America as well as various good causes in London.

Bray succeeded in securing the establishment of the Church of England in Maryland in 1702 (but failed in his plea for a bishop there) and near his life's end influenced the creation of a debtors' colony in America (Georgia). Moreover, through personal financial sacrifice and aided by wealthy patrons, he launched three organizations which still exist and had a major impact on the American colonies. Parsons there commonly being too poor to own many books, Bray set up the Society for Promoting Christian Knowledge* (SPCK) in 1699 as a major agent for founding over seventy libraries (provincial, parochial and lay), some quite large, from Newfoundland to the Carolinas, and especially in Maryland. The Society for the Propagation of the Gospel in Foreign Parts* (SPG), founded in 1701, mainly supplied clergy and funds to extend the Church of England in the colonies. Finally, Dr. Bray's Associates (1724) aimed, against great odds, to convert and educate the Native Americans and African-Americans, through catechists* or missionaries, books and schools.

BIBLIOGRAPHY. *DAB* I; *DARB*; B. C. Steiner, ed., *Rev. Thomas Bray: His Life and Selected Works* (1901); H. P. Thompson, *Thomas Bray* (1954); J. C. Van Horne, ed., *Religious Philanthropy and Colonial Slavery: The American Correspondence of the Associates of Dr. Bray, 1717-1777* (1985).

E. W. Kennedy

Brébeuf, Jean de (1593-1649). French Catholic* missionary* and martyr. Born in France, Brébeuf was ordained* a Jesuit* priest* in 1622. He arrived in Quebec in 1625 to begin missionary work among Native Americans allied with New France. He soon began his main work among the Hurons near Georgian Bay, Lake Huron. The capture of Quebec by the English in 1629 forced his return to France, but he rejoined the Hurons in 1634. Injured in 1641, Brébeuf had to retire to Quebec, but in 1644 he went back to Huronia to stay. The more powerful Iroquois, envious of the position of the Hurons in the fur trade, attacked them in the 1640s. In 1649 the Iroquois seized Brébeuf and other missionaries and tortured them ferociously. The end of the Huron* mission and nation, however, marked the beginning of a dramatic spiritual advance among them and neighboring tribes. Brébeuf left behind reports in the Jesuit

Relations, as well as other writings, notably the beautiful "Huron Carol." He was canonized* with seven companion martyrs in 1930 and with them was named patron saint* of Canada in 1940.

BIBLIOGRAPHY. R. G. Thwaites, ed., *The Jesuit Relations,* vols. 8 and 10 (1897); R. Latourelle, *Brébeuf* (1958).   J. G. Stackhouse

Breck, James Lloyd (1818-1876). Episcopal* missionary.* Born in Philadelphia County, Pennsylvania, on June 27, 1818, Breck was educated at William Augustus Mulhenberg's* Flushing Institute, Flushing, New York, and graduated from the University of Pennsylvania in 1838. He studied at the General Theological Seminary, New York City (1838-1841), and there was influenced by the high church* principles of the Tractarian Movement.* Breck determined to give his life to three goals: (1) missionary work in the West; (2) the establishment of a theological seminary* in the West; and (3) the revival of a disciplined religious community life. He was ordained* deacon* by Bishop* Henry U. Onderdonk* of Pennsylvania on July 4, 1841, and with two other graduates of General Seminary headed west to establish a center of missionary activity in the newly opened Territory of Wisconsin.

On October 9, 1842, Bishop Jackson Kenyer of Indiana and Missouri ordained him priest* at Duck Creek, Wisconsin, in the midst of the Oneida Indians. Breck and his associates made Nashotah their base of operations and in 1842 established their theological school named Nashotah House. At Nashotah House, Breck focused on the regular recitation of the canonical hours,* manual labor and missionary activity. In 1850 he moved to Minnesota and worked among the Chippewa Indians, establishing educational and missionary centers at Crow Wing and Leech Lake. While Breck continued to cherish the ideal of an order of celibate* clergy* living in community under a religious rule, he eventually gave up the ideal for himself and on August 11, 1855, married Jane Maria Mills, one of his assistants. In 1857 he settled at Faribault and in 1858 founded the Seabury Divinity School as well as schools for boys and girls. After nine years at Faribault, the "apostle of the wilderness" moved to California and settled at Bernica. Again he followed his usual plan and established St. Augustine's College, with a grammar school and divinity school attached. There he worked until his death on March 30, 1876. No priest did more for the Episcopal Church in the West than Breck.

BIBLIOGRAPHY. C. Breck, ed., *The Life of the Reverend James Lloyd Breck, D.D., Chiefly from Letters*

Written by Himself (1883); *DAB* II; *DARB;* W. P. Haugaard, "The Missionary Vision of James Lloyd Breck in Minnesota," *HMPEC* 54 (1985): 241-251; T. I. Holcombe, *An Apostle of the Wilderness: James Lloyd Breck, D.D., His Missions and His Schools* (1903).   D. S. Armentrout

Breck, Robert (1713-1784). Congregational* minister.* Controversy followed Breck from his youth. He was dismissed from Harvard College* in 1729 on moral grounds, but upon his repentance and after much urging from his father, the College granted his degree in 1730. Breck took his M.A. in 1733 and began preaching* in the Scotland District in Connecticut. His ideas that the good heathen might be saved* and that some portions of the Scriptures* are not inspired shocked orthodox* hearers. This prompted an interrogation from Thomas Clap,* the future president of Yale,* and marked the beginning of the "Breck Affair." Breck, who was outraged but unpersuaded, denounced Clap, who later refused to recommend Breck for a pastorate in Springfield. In response, Breck persuaded leading Boston ministers to sign a certificate of his orthodoxy. Jonathan Edwards* wrote a defense for the Hampshire Association's effort to block Breck's settlement. After a series of bizarre events, including Breck's arrest, he was ordained* in 1736. In the years following the "Breck Affair," Breck and Edwards clashed, and in 1750, when Edwards was in controversy with the Northampton Church, Breck represented the majority which voted to dismiss him.

BIBLIOGRAPHY. C. K. Shipton, *Sibley's Harvard Graduates,* vol. 8 (1951).   S. D. Crocco

Breckinridge, Robert Jefferson (1800-1871). Presbyterian* theologian.* Born near Lexington, Kentucky, Breckinridge graduated from Union College in Schenectady, New York, practiced law and served in the Kentucky legislature. After a little theological study at Princeton,* he became pastor* of Second Church, Baltimore (1832-1845). From there he became president of Jefferson College in Pennsylvania (1845-1847) and later pastor of First Church, Lexington, Kentucky, and served as state superintendent of public instruction (1847-1853). Breckinridge founded Danville Seminary in Kentucky, where he served as professor of theology* for the remainder of his career (1853-1869).

As editor of the *Baltimore Literary and Religious Magazine* (1835-1841) and *Spirit of the XIX Century* (1842-1843), he became known as a controversial churchman. He was an outspoken oppo-

nent of slavery *(see* Abolition Movement), intemperance *(See* Temperance Movement), universalism,* Sabbath* desecration and Roman Catholicism.* Within his own church he initiated the Act and Testimony (1834), a statement of the Old School* party in the Presbyterian Church, which led to the denomination's division in 1837. Although he sided with the North in the Civil War* and in the division of the Old School Presbyterians in 1861, his views in favor of the parity of ministers* and ruling elders* were very influential in Southern Presbyterianism.* Breckenridge's major theological contribution was a systematic theology* in two volumes, *The Knowledge of God, Objectively Considered* (1858) and *The Knowledge of God, Subjectively Considered* (1859).
See also AUBURN DECLARATION; OLD SCHOOL PRESBYTERIANS.

BIBLIOGRAPHY. *DAB* I; *Encyclopaedia of the Presbyterian Church in the U.S.A.,* ed., A. Nevin (1884); E. C. Mayse, "Robert Jefferson Breckinridge: American Presbyterian Controversialist," (Unpublished Ph.D. dissertation, Union Theological Seminary in Virginia, 1974).   A. H. Freundt

Brenneman, John M. (1816-1895). Mennonite* Church minister* and bishop.* Brenneman was ordained* as a Mennonite Church minister in Fairfield County, Ohio, in 1844 and as a bishop of that conference in Franklin County, Ohio, in 1849. In 1855 he moved to Allen County, Ohio, where he lived for the rest of his life. Despite his almost complete lack of formal education, Brenneman was an influential leader in the conference and helped to make Allen County a prominent Mennonite center. He traveled extensively, maintaining contact with Mennonites in isolated communities throughout the West and was influential in the development of Sunday schools* within the Mennonite Church. Known as a skillful mediator, he assisted in the resolution of numerous church controversies. He wrote several widely read booklets, including *Christianity and War* (1863) and *Pride and Humility* (1867).

BIBLIOGRAPHY. J. C. Liechty, "Humility: The Foundation of Mennonite Religious Outlook in the 1860s," *MQR* 54 (1980): 5-31; J. Umble, "The Allen County, Ohio, Mennonite Settlement," *MQR* 6 (1931): 81-109.   K. Enns-Rempel

Brent, Charles Henry (1862-1929). Episcopal bishop* and ecumenical* pioneer. Born in Ontario and educated at Trinity College, Toronto, an Anglican* institution of strongly high-church* orientation, upon ordination* he entered the

Episcopal Church* in the U.S. and was an incumbent in Boston. American missions* flooded the Philippines after the American takeover of 1898, and in 1901 Brent was elected by the Episcopal Church as its first missionary* bishop to the country. In keeping with his theological presuppositions, he felt that converts should not be sought from Roman Catholicism,* so he concentrated on American, British and Chinese expatriots, as well as missions to the Muslims and animists.

Brent was an active participant in the famous Edinburgh Missionary Conference of 1910, expressing in his own person the shift of much missionary leadership to those who were not of an evangelical* position. Ill health forced him to leave the Philippines in 1917, and he subsequently was appointed bishop of western New York. In 1926 he was given episcopal oversight over the American Episcopal congregations in Europe. His vision and energy made him part of the Faith and Order movement, and he was elected president of the first World Conference on Faith and Order held in Lausanne, Switzerland, in 1927. The Conference was concerned with the doctrinal and corresponding ecclesiological issues which divided the some-ninety Protestant* denominations represented. Brent's missionary concern was evident in the Conference's concentration on the message of the church to the world, as was his high churchmanship in the central position given to the subjects of apostolic succession* and the sacraments.* His published works include *The Mind of Christ in the Church of the Living God* (1908) and *The Mountain of Vision* (1918).

See also ECUMENICAL MOVEMENT.

BIBLIOGRAPHY. *DAB* 1; A. C. Zabriskie, *Bishop Brent, Crusader for Christian Unity* (1948).

I. S. Rennie

Bresee, Phineas Franklin (1838-1916). Founder of the Church of the Nazarene.* Born and raised in the Burned-Over District* of western New York, Bresee was converted* in a Methodist* meeting in 1856. He moved to Iowa and was accepted "on trial" as a Methodist itinerant preacher.* His gifts, energy and ministerial success were rewarded with preferment. In 1883 flooding ravaged a mine in which he had held and sold stock. Bankrupt and embarrassed, he moved from Iowa to the pastorate of the Los Angeles First Methodist Church. Many leading laypersons* in his congregation professed to be sanctified* and in time Bresee joined them.

In 1895 Bresee and J. P. Widney started the Church of the Nazarene. Opposing the tide of increasingly luxurious churches, they proposed a denomination* with churches furnished to welcome the poor and in which holiness* would be preached. The work expanded and in 1908 several of the groups within the Holiness Movement* joined together at Pilot Point, Texas, to form the Pentecostal Church of the Nazarene (*Pentecostal* was dropped in 1919). Bresee became general superintendent and held the position until his death.

BIBLIOGRAPHY. D. P. Brickley, *Man of the Morning* (1960); E. A. Girvin, *Phineas F. Bresee: A Prince in Israel* (1916); T. L. Smith, *Called Unto Holiness* (1962). M. R. Fraser

Brethren in Christ Church. A small American denomination* with Anabaptist,* Pietistic* and Wesleyan* Holiness* roots. The Brethren in Christ emerged from the pietistic revival* movements in Lancaster County, Pennsylvania, during the latter years of the eighteenth century. The founders (among them Jacob Engle*), largely Anabaptist in background, experienced conversion* in meetings held by German Reformed minister* Philip Otterbein* and Mennonite* minister Martin Boehm.* Their newfound pietism, in addition to their growing conviction that baptism* should be by immersion, led them to form their own fellowship around 1778. While the group referred to itself as "Brethren," others, attempting to distinguish them from other Brethren* groups in the area, called them the Brethren by the River (Susquehanna) or River Brethren. During the Civil War* the leadership formally registered the group as Brethren in Christ. From their base in Pennsylvania, members spread to Canada (beginning in 1788), to the Midwest (by the 1840s) and, by the early 1900s, to California. These areas remain the centers of the Brethren in Christ Church.

By 1900 the Brethren in Christ had been deeply influenced by the American Holiness Movement, and in 1936 established Roxbury Holiness Camp, the first of four such camps now operated by the denomination. In 1887 a denominational paper, the *Evangelical Visitor,* was established, and in 1909 the first of four schools, Messiah Bible School and Missionary Training Home (now Messiah College, in Pennsylvania), was founded. In addition, the Brethren in Christ were active in Sunday-school work and protracted revival meetings. Their missionary* work, first begun in Africa and India, is now carried out on all continents except Australia.

Beginning in the late 1940s the Brethren in Christ moved closer to the conservative, evangelical* mainstream of American religious life as they dropped requirements for plain dress and adopted a more ecumenical spirit by allowing open communion. By 1949 they were members of the National Association of Evangelicals* and in 1950 joined the Christian Holiness Association.* They retain such historic Anabaptist emphases as obedience, brotherhood and peace, and are active members of the Mennonite Central Committee.* In 1987 there were 200 congregations in Canada and the U.S., with a combined membership of nearly 18,000. The congregations are divided into six conferences, each headed by a bishop.* A governing body, the General Conference, meets biannually.

See also OLD ORDER RIVER BRETHREN.

BIBLIOGRAPHY. C. O. Wittlinger, *Quest for Piety and Obedience: The Story of the Brethren in Christ* (1978). E. M. Sider

Brett, Pliny (fl. 1805-1840). Reformed Methodist* Church leader. Brett first itinerated* "on trial" in 1805 in the New England Conference of the Methodist Episcopal Church,* becoming a deacon* in 1808 and an elder* and "supernumerary" in 1810. The bishop* appointed him to the smaller circuits.* He reported his only great increase in 1812 after he had served one circuit for three years. After this he was moved to a smaller circuit. He, with some lay* preachers and laity, ceased to itinerate after the 1813 Conference because they were opposed to the arbitrary nature of episcopal* government. They formed the Reformed Methodist Church (RMC) in 1814. The new Methodist body kept much of the Methodist Episcopal Church structure but was congregational* in polity* and emphasized divine healing* and the attainability of entire sanctification.* Brett remained in the RMC until the late 1830s when he led a large group into the Ohio Conference of the recently formed Methodist Protestant Church in which he exercised no important leadership role.

BIBLIOGRAPHY. F. E. Maser and G. A. Singleton, "Pliny Brett and the Reformed Methodist Church," in *The History of American Methodism*, ed. E. S. Bucke (1964). M. R. Fraser

Breviary. A term referring primarily to the Roman Breviary, or divine office,* which contained the canonical hours,* composed of prayers,* psalms, scriptural readings and patristic lessons to be recited daily by the clergy* and certain nonordained religious* in the Latin church. It developed in the tenth and eleventh centuries by combining and abridging various office books into a single volume for use in special circumstances. At first the Latin term *breviarium* meant an index of texts, but it came to denote this single volume. Later, portable breviaries developed, particularly for members of the mendicant orders. In the twelfth century, the Franciscan* friars spread a shortened version of an office approved by Innocent III for the Roman curia. This became the basis for the 1568 Breviary of Pius V, revised by later popes, but which has now been superseded by the Liturgy of the Hours* (1971), whose reform was mandated by the Second Vatican Council* (1962-1965).

BIBLIOGRAPHY. P. Salmon, *The Breviary through the Centuries* (1962); R. Taft, *The Liturgy of the Hours in East and West* (1986).

J. B. Ryan

Brewer, Grover Cleveland (1884-1956). Church of Christ* preacher.* Graduating from Nashville Bible School (now David Lipscomb* College) in 1911, he began a ministry* in Chattanooga and then went on to several other successful ministries. He was a masterful orator, writer and preacher. He has been considered one of the most influential second-generation leaders in the noninstrumental Church of Christ* during the first half of the twentieth century.

Brewer engaged in numerous debates, including with individuals from the instrumental Christian Churches on the use of musical instruments in worship.* He insisted that the noninstrumental Churches of Christ were not a denomination.* Brewer preached in some of the largest congregations of the Churches of Christ and helped that group achieve numerical growth after their separation from the instrumental Christian Churches. He also helped establish their exclusivist attitude which prevailed in the first half of the twentieth century.

BIBLIOGRAPHY. C. G. Brewer, *Autobiography of G. C. Brewer* (1957). J. B. North

Brewster, William (c.1564-1644). Elder* of Plymouth, Massachusetts. In 1580 Brewster matriculated at Peterhouse College, Cambridge, but he did not remain long enough to take a degree. Brewster's father, an official for the Anglican Church,* secured a position for his son as a servant for diplomat William Davison, who took Brewster with him on a mission to the Low Countries in 1585. When his father died in 1590, Brewster assumed his post as assistant to the archbishop* and postmaster of Scrooby. It was there that he fell in with the Separatist congregation that would eventually settle Plymouth.

With the High Commission Court threatening prosecution of nonconformists, Brewster attempted in 1607 to escape to Holland with a number of other Separates but was captured and held in prison. After his release the following year, he managed to reach Leyden, where he became an assistant to the Rev. John Robinson, taught Latin and English and became somewhat notorious for printing works by Puritan* theologians. At Leyden he also became elder of the Pilgrim* church, a position he was to hold for the rest of his life.

In 1620 Brewster sailed on the *Mayflower* and played a significant role in establishing Plymouth Colony, in governing the church and in providing spiritual guidance for the colonists. Since Plymouth had no settled minister until 1629, Brewster, as the only university-educated person in the colony, assumed virtually all pastoral duties except administering sacraments.* In keeping with the Puritan belief in lay* prophesying, Brewster conducted services, prayed and preached* twice every Sabbath to the satisfaction and edification of his brethren. William Bradford stated that Brewster "did more in this behalf in a year, then many that have their hundreds a year doe in all their lives."

BIBLIOGRAPHY. W. Bradford, *Of Plymouth Plantation*, ed. S. E. Morrison (1952); *DAB* II; *DARB*; G. D. Langdon, *Pilgrim Colony: A History of New Plymouth, 1620-1691* (1966); *NCAB* 7; A. Steele, *Chief of the Pilgrims: The Life and Time of William Brewster* (1857). K. P. Minkema

Briand, Jean-Olivier (1715-1794). First Roman Catholic* Bishop* of Quebec following the British conquest of New France. A native of Brittany, Briand was educated at the Seminaire de Saint-Brieuc and ordained* priest* in 1739. Arriving in Quebec in 1741 to serve as a canon, he soon became the secretary and principal advisor to Bishop Pontbriand, a position he filled for nearly twenty years. Briand's greatest challenges, however, came as a result of the British victories over the French in North America during the Seven Years' War. He was appointed vicar general of Quebec immediately following Montcalm's loss to Wolfe in September 1759. Pontbriand died the following June, and three months later all of Canada surrendered into British hands.

Left without a bishop, cut off from France, and uncertain of its relationship with Protestant Britain, the church was in a precarious position. Although he was not consecrated* bishop until 1766, Briand assumed the leadership of the Canadian church at this critical point. His actions ensured its survival.

In accomplishing this Briand fostered a close and amicable relationship with successive British governors, particularly James Murray and Guy Carleton. He sought to safeguard the rights of the church and prevent undue civil interference in its affairs, while at the same time remaining loyal to the British authorities. Under his direction the bulk of the clergy* supported the British cause during the American Revolution.*

BIBLIOGRAPHY. J. S. Moir, *The Church in the British Era* (1972); *DCB* IV. R. W. Vaudry

Briant, Lemuel (1722-1754). Congregational* minister.* Born in Scituate, Massachusetts, Briant graduated from Harvard* in 1739 and took his M.A. in 1742. After preaching* in several Massachusetts churches, he accepted a call to the North Church of Braintree in 1745. Briant's tenure as a pastor there was dominated by the controversy that followed his sermon, "The Absurdity and Blasphemy of Depreciating Moral Virtue" (1749). Irritated by the insistence of the New Lights* that the righteousness of the unregenerate was but "filthy rags," Briant used this sermon to announce his "common sense," or Arminian,* views on human nature. In the face of measured questions Briant angrily denounced his critics with *ad hominum* arguments and satire. A series of moral improprieties on Briant's part hampered his defenders, but before matters could come to a head, he fell into ill health, asked to be dismissed from his pulpit and died a year later.

BIBLIOGRAPHY. C. K. Shipton. *Sibley's Harvard Graduates,* vol. 10 (1958). S. D. Crocco

Bridgman, Elijah Coleman (1801-1861). First American missionary* to China. A graduate of Amherst and Andover Seminary* (1829), Bridgman was sent to Canton, China, by the American Board of Commissioners for Foreign Missions* in 1830. His years at Canton (1830-1847) were chiefly distinguished by his editorship of *The Chinese Repository,* a monthly magazine begun in 1832 which did much to enlighten foreigners on the China coast and in the West about China. He wrote several pieces in Chinese, the most important of which was a long geographical history of the U.S., published in 1838. In 1844 he assisted the American legation to China under Caleb Cushing. After 1847 Bridgman lived in Shanghai, where as a missionary elder statesman he devoted his time mainly to Scripture translation until his death. But he remained a frequent contributor to *The Chinese Repository* until it ceased publication in 1851.

BIBLIOGRAPHY. *DAB* II; F. W. Drake, "Protestant

Geography in China: E. C. Bridgman's Portrayal of the West," in *Christianity in China: Early Protestant Missionary Writings,* ed. S. W. Barnett and J. K. Fairbank (1984).   D. H. Bays

Bridgman, Eliza Jane Gillet (1805-1871). Episcopal* educator and missionary* to China. Born in Connecticut and confirmed in the Protestant Episcopal Church* after an 1821 conversion* experience, Eliza moved to New York City as a teacher and became principal of a girls' school. When the church changed its policy against unmarried female missionaries, she was one of the first three appointed. She arrived in Hong Kong in 1845, met and married Congregationalist* Elijah Coleman Bridgman,* and worked on a variety of educational projects under the American Board of Commissioners of Foreign Missions.* Using native teachers she founded a day school for girls in Shanghai and authored *Daughters of China* (1853) from her diary. Widowed in 1861, she wrote her husband's biography (1864) and then joined the North China Mission at Peking. There, with her own funds, she opened Bridgman Academy, which eventually became the Women's College of Yenching University. Returning to Shanghai in 1868, she spent her final years developing a new girls' school.

BIBLIOGRAPHY. *NAW* 1.   K. K. Kidd

Briggs, Charles Augustus (1841-1913). Biblical scholar and Presbyterian* minister.* A native of New York City, Briggs was educated at the University of Virginia (1857-1860), Union Theological Seminary in New York* (1861-1863) and the University of Berlin (1866-1869). In 1874, after brief service as a Presbyterian pastor,* he accepted a call to Union Theological Seminary in New York where, in 1876, he assumed the chair of Hebrew and Cognate languages.

In 1880 Briggs became co-editor, with Archibald A. Hodge* of Princeton Seminary, of the newly founded *Presbyterian Review.* Before long the *Review* proved to be a source of profound tension as Briggs's higher-critical views conflicted sharply with the more traditional Princeton doctrine of Scripture.* This, combined with differences over proposed Presbyterian confessional revision, led to the dissolution of the journal in 1889.

Throughout the 1880s Briggs published works which championed the higher-critical method and questioned the orthodoxy* of Princeton Theology.* Despite strong opposition to these positions in the church, it was Briggs's inaugural address, "The Authority of Holy Scripture" (1891), deli-

vered upon his induction into the chair of biblical studies at Union, which precipitated one of the most famous heresy trials* in American religious history.

In a polemical tone Briggs denied the verbal inspiration, inerrancy* and authenticity of Scripture, appeared to place the authority* of reason and the church on a par with the Bible* and defended the doctrine of progressive sanctification* after death. As a result, the 1891 General Assembly* vetoed Briggs's professorial appointment, the 1892 Assembly specifically endorsed the doctrine of biblical inerrancy and the 1893 Assembly suspended Briggs from the ministry. In addition, the controversy occasioned the divorce of Union Seminary and the Presbyterian Church.

Briggs retained his position at Union and, in 1898, entered the priesthood of the Episcopal Church.* A growing concern for church union* led him to resign his chair in 1904 to teach symbolics and irenics. Briggs authored over twenty books, including *General Introduction to the Study of Holy Scripture* (1899). Together with F. Brown and S. R. Driver he edited *A Hebrew and English Lexicon of the Old Testament* (1906), which is still in use today, and served as one of the original editors of the prestigious *International Critical Commentary.*

See also BIBLICAL INTERPRETATION; FUNDAMENTALIST-MODERNIST CONTROVERSY; HERESY TRIALS; PRINCETON THEOLOGY.

BIBLIOGRAPHY. *DAB* II; *DARB;* R. T. Handy, *A History of Union Theological Seminary in New York* (1987); L. Loetscher, *The Broadening Church: A Study of Theological Issues in the Presbyterian Church Since 1869* (1954); M. G. Rogers, "Charles Augustus Briggs: Heresy at Union," *American Religious Heretics,* ed. G. H. Shriver (1966); *NCAB* 7.

B. J. Longfield

Bright, William ("Bill") Rohl (1921-). Founder and president of Campus Crusade for Christ International.* Born in the small Oklahoma town of Coweta, Bright graduated from Northeastern State College, Oklahoma (B.A., 1943). Eager for financial success, he moved to Los Angeles and successfully established Bright's California Confections, a company marketing fancy foods through exclusive shops and department stores. There he became associated with Hollywood's First Presbyterian Church, and through the influence of the church's director of Christian education,* Henrietta Mears,* Bright in 1945 made a promise to follow Jesus Christ. This commitment led him to Princeton Theological Seminary.* However, business responsibilities eventually forced him to leave Princeton and return to California, where he entered the first class of Fuller Theological Seminary* in 1947. Bright, always torn between evangelism* and seminary studies, departed from Fuller in 1951 without graduating.

Within a few months of leaving Fuller, Bright followed his calling to go out into the world and win students to Christ by selling his confection business and renting a house one block from the University of California at Los Angeles. A board of directors was established, and Campus Crusade for Christ came into existence in 1951. Within a few months, 250 students had committed their lives to Christ, and by the following year the movement had spread to other prominent West Coast colleges and universities. From this base of college campuses, Bright expanded Campus Crusade into an international movement operating in approximately 150 countries. Under his leadership the organization clearly reflects his evangelical* point of view.

In nineteen books and booklets, Bright has presented a theology* grounded on two basic ideas: (1) people should accept Jesus Christ as Lord and Savior; (2) Christians should be filled and guided by the Holy Spirit in a life of love and service. His basic approach to evangelism has been summed up in his popular "Four Spiritual Laws."* Beyond these key ideas, his theology is relatively free of dogmatism and legalism,* and has proven attractive to people from diverse religious traditions and cultures. As the leader of an international organization, Bright has been called upon to preach in Christian churches in the Soviet Union, and in 1974 he participated in the Lausanne International Congress on World Evangelism.* Because of his accomplishments, Bright has received several honorary doctorate degrees from colleges in the U.S. and Korea.

BIBLIOGRAPHY. B. Bright, *Come Help Change the World* (1979); R. Quebedeaux, *I Found It! The Story of Bill Bright and Campus Crusade* (1979).

K. L. Staggers

Brightman, Edgar Sheffield (1884-1953). Personalist philosopher and liberal* Methodist* theologian.* Born in Holbrook, Massachusetts, the only child of a Methodist minister,* Brightman graduated from Brown University (B.A., 1906; M.A., 1908) and took graduate degrees from Boston University (S.T.B., 1910; Ph.D., 1912) and was ordained* a Methodist minister in 1912. After studying at the Unversities of Berlin (1910-1911) and Marburg (1911-1912), he taught philosophy at Nebraska Wesleyan University (1912-1915) and ethics and religion at Wesleyan University in Connecticut (1915-1919). In 1919 he became professor of philosophy at Boston University, holding the Borden Parker Bowne Chair of Philosophy from 1925 until his death in 1953.

Despite frequent physical illnesses Brightman was a prolific scholar and a major spokesperson for the philosophical movement known as Boston Personalism. Personalism, as developed by Borden Parker Bowne* and then Brightman, is idealism with an empirical cast. It is a philosophical system in which persons (or selves) are the sole or dominant metaphysical realities, as well as the only ultimate intrinsic values. Brightman's method is properly called rational empiricism. His personal religion combined empirical testing and mystical contemplation.

While convinced of the truth of the Christian faith, he learned much from other religions and particularly from Hinduism through his good friend Swami Akhilananda. There was for him no conflict between religion and philosophy. All he demanded was that every aspect of experience, including the religious, be included and tested before final judgments about truth were made. His philosophy led him to a concern for social issues reflected by his membership in the Methodist Federation for Social Action, the Committee on Peace through Justice, the American Civil Liberties Union, and by his support of conscientious objectors. Brightman was attacked by the conservative wing of the Methodist Church and blacklisted for his liberal leanings.

Among Brightman's published works are *The Problem of God* (1930), *The Finding of God* (1931), *Is God a Person?* (1932), *Personality and Religion* (1934), *The Future of Christianity* (1937) and *A Philosophy of Religion* (1940). The principal innovation of Brightman's metaphysics and philosophy of religion was his finite theism.* According to this view, the perfectly good will of God must act within the limitations of God's own nature, described as "the Given." Even though self-limited, God's purposes are never finally defeated but gradually overcome evil at progressively higher levels, using even the worst of tragedies as instruments of progress. God and the world are alike seen as growing. Brightman believed that the pain and sorrow in the world were both quantitatively and qualitatively beyond adequate explanation by those theists who believe God's power unlimited.

BIBLIOGRAPHY. *DAB* 5; *DARB*; J. J. McLarney, *The Theism of Edgar Sheffield Brightman* (1936); *NCAB* 41.

J. C. Brown

Broad Church. A term referring to a party within the Anglican Church* that has interpreted the Christian faith in its broadest and most inclusive sense. The origins of the movement are associated with men such as Thomas Arnold (1795-1842), the famous headmaster of Rugby School, and Renn D. Hampden (1793-1868), fellow of Oriel College, Oxford. The movement originally emphasized a strong sense of morality, but a toleration of a variety of theological views. It was relatively unconcerned about ritualism and the issues that divided high church* and low church.* In America the movement was inspired by English writers such as Frederick D. Maurice (1805-1872) and is associated with the Memorial Movement* of William A. Muhlenberg.* Today the term is seldom used, and the theological descendants of the movement, known as "modernists"* in years past, are more commonly called "liberals."*

See also ANGLICANISM; HIGH CHURCH; LOW CHURCH.

BIBLIOGRAPHY. E. C. Chorley, *Men and Movements in the American Episcopal Church* (1946); R. B. Mullin, *Episcopal Vision/American Reality* (1986).   R. Webber

Broaddus, Andrew (1770-1848). Baptist* pastor* and associational leader. Born in Caroline County, Virginia, Broaddus rarely ventured outside his native state. He was largely self-educated, but his father, John Broaddus, probably tutored him for a time. Though his family was of Episcopal* background, Andrew came under the influence of Theodore Noel, pastor of the Upper King and Queen Baptist Church, by whom he was baptized (1789) and ordained* (1791). A good number of children were born of four marriages, and Broaddus was severely criticized for his third marriage to the sister of his deceased wife.

Broaddus served as pastor of several rural churches in Virginia, including Salem (from 1820) and Upper King and Queen (from 1827). His son and grandson succeeded him at Salem, providing a continuous ministry for over a century. An active leader and often moderator of the Dover Association, Broaddus resisted views of Alexander Campbell* and his followers in associational conferences, numerous articles and a book entitled *The Extra Examined* (1831). Regarded as a superb preacher* and biblical expositor,* he declined invitations from influential city churches and remained a rural pastor.

A frequent contributor to the *Religious Herald* and author of several books, Broaddus may be best remembered for three collections of hymns: *Collection of Sacred Ballads* (1790); *The Dover Selection of Spiritual Songs* (1828); and *The Virginia Selection of Psalms, Hymns, and Spiritual Songs* (1836). A few of his own compositions appear in these works.

BIBLIOGRAPHY. *AAP* 6; J. B. Jeter, *The Sermons and Other Writings of the Rev. Andrew Broaddus with a Memoir of His Life* (1852); J. B. Taylor, *Virginia Baptist Ministers* (1860).

C. L. Howe

Broadus, John Albert (1827-1895). Seminary professor and Southern Baptist* minister.* Reared in Virginia in a home marked by a high degree of culture and spiritual devotion, Broadus was converted at sixteen years of age. Following his graduation from the University of Virginia in 1850 (M.A.), he became a tutor in Latin and Greek at the university while serving as pastor* of the Baptist church of Charlottesville. Later Broadus became one of the four original faculty members of the Southern Baptist Theological Seminary, originally established at Greenville, South Carolina, in 1859. For the next thirty-six years (1859-1895) he served as professor of New Testament interpretation and homiletics, interrupted only by the seminary's closure during the Civil War* when he served a stint as chaplain* in Lee's army. After the war he and his colleagues reopened the seminary, which later moved to Louisville, Kentucky, in 1877. There Broadus was to serve for several years as president of the seminary (1889-1895).

Of his numerous books, pamphlets and tracts, he is best known for his introduction to homiletics* *On the Preparation and Delivery of Sermons* (1870), which became a textbook in many denominational seminaries and remains in print even today. His *Commentary on the Gospel of Matthew* (1886) was esteemed for its careful scholarship in its day, and his *Harmony of the Gospels* (1893) was to achieve a long and distinguished reputation. In 1889 he delivered the Yale* Lectures on Preaching, the first Southern Baptist to do so. Known for his biblical scholarship and homiletical skills, Broadus was invited to serve on other theological faculties, but he was consistently loyal to his calling of nurturing a blend of scholarship and erudition in the Southern Baptist ministry.

BIBLIOGRAPHY. *DAB* II; *DARB; ESB* 1; W. A. Mueller, *A History of Southern Baptist Theological Seminary* (1959); *NCAB* 18; A. T. Robertson, *Life and Letters of John A. Broadus* (1901).

W. R. Estep

Brook Farm (1841-1847). Nineteenth-century transcendentalist* community in West Roxbury,

Massachusetts. In April of 1841 George Ripley* and seventeen others formed the Brook Farm Institute of Agriculture and Education. Its purpose, according to Ripley, was "to insure a more natural union between intellectual and manual labor; to combine the thinker and the worker, as far as possible, in the same individual; to guarantee the highest mental freedom, by providing all with labor adapted to their tastes and talents . . . to prepare a society of liberal, intelligent, and cultivated persons, whose relations with each other would permit a more wholesome and simple life than can be led amidst the pressure of our competitive institutions."

The community attempted to give form to the philosophy of many members of the Boston Transcendentalist Club, which rejected Enlightenment* empirical philosophy and what the Transcendentalists perceived to be its disintegrating effects on the social order. The community listed among its residents and visitors the leading figures of the New England Renaissance: Ralph Waldo Emerson,* Henry David Thoreau, Nathaniel Hawthorne,* Bronson Alcott and others. The community had a profound effect upon two individuals who would later convert to Catholicism*: the author and philosopher Orestes Brownson* and Isaac Hecker,* one of the chief founders of the Paulist* order.

In 1844 Brook Farm was reorganized according to the theories of French reformer Charles Fourier. Never able to become economically solvent, it was dissolved in 1847 after a fire destroyed the main building.

See also ROMANTICISM, CATHOLIC; TRANSCENDENTALISM.

BIBLIOGRAPHY. L. Swift, *Brook Farm: Its Members, Scholars, and Visitors* (1900); J. Myerson, *Brook Farm, An Annotated Bibliography and Resource Guide* (1978).   J. Farina

Brooke, John (d.1707). Anglican* missionary* in the Middle Colonies. John Brooke, an Anglican clergyman* who had served as the curate of Ardsley, Wakefield, England, came to Hemsted, New York, in 1705 to serve as a missionary for the Society for the Propagation of the Gospel.* In that same year, however, he transferred his efforts to Elizabethtown, New Jersey, where he gathered a sufficient number of worshipers to begin construction of a church building (1706). He also preached* at seven other locations in the same general area.

In November of 1705 Brooke met with thirteen other Anglican clergy in Burlington, New Jersey, to sign a letter asking the Church of England for a

suffragan bishop.* It may have been at that time that Brooke met Thoroughgood Moor, a clergyman who was jailed soon after by Governor Cornbury for criticizing the governor's transvestism and for refusing Communion to his lieutenant governor. Brooke helped Moor escape from jail (1707) and embarked for England with him. Both men drowned, however, before they reached their destination.

BIBLIOGRAPHY. E. L. Pennington, *Apostle of New Jersey: John Talbot* (1938).   R. W. Prichard

Brookes, James Hall (1830-1897). Presbyterian* minister.* Born in Pulaski, Tennessee, the son of a minister, Brookes was raised by his mother after his father died when Brookes was only three. After attending Stephenson Academy in Ashewood, Tennessee, in 1851 he matriculated as a junior into Miami University in Oxford, Ohio. Brookes attended Princeton* Seminary during the 1853-1854 term but was unable to finish his studies because he lacked funds. Nevertheless, he was ordained* on April 20, 1854, by the Miami Presbytery* and moved to Dayton, Ohio, to begin his first pastoral charge. In 1858 he accepted a call to the Second Presbyterian Church of St. Louis, and six years later he accepted a call to the Sixteenth & Walnut Street Church, which had been organized by 149 former members of Second Church. There he remained until his retirement. Brookes served as a commissioner to the General Assembly in 1857, 1880 and 1893 and was stated clerk of the Missouri Synod* in 1874.

Brookes is best known for his wide ministry as a conference speaker and was one of the founders of the Niagara Bible Conference,* which he presided over until his death. He was also active in the International Prophetic Conferences held in 1878 and 1886. As an author he was prolific, writing seventeen books, dozens of sermons and pamphlets, over 250 tracts and many articles. From 1875 until his death he was editor of the *The Truth,* an influential premillennial* journal that assailed liberals and encouraged conservatives in their battle against Protestant apostasy. As a dispensational* premillennialist Brookes was instrumental in promoting the view that Christ might return at any moment. Among the most notable of his disciples was C. I. Scofield,* who would later edit the influential *Scofield Reference Bible.*

See also NIAGARA CONFERENCES.

BIBLIOGRAPHY. *NCAB* 5; D. R. Williams, *James H. Brookes* (1897).   P. C. Wilt

Brooks, Phillips (1835-1893). Episcopalian*

[191]

preacher* and bishop.* Of Congregational* and Unitarian* lineage, Phillips Brooks was born in Boston on December 13, 1835. Raised an Episcopalian, Brooks graduated from Harvard* (1855), failed at teaching, and was ordained to the ministry* (1859) following studies at Virginia Theological Seminary. Two pastorates in Philadelphia—Church of the Advent (1859-1862) and Holy Trinity (1862-1869)—established his reputation as a premier preacher. An imposing presence (six feet four inches, three hundred pounds), Brooks was attractive, well read and capable of impressive oratory and rapid delivery (213 words a minute). He was the embodiment of his own belief that "preaching is the bringing of truth through personality." His eulogy "Character, Life, and Death of Mr. Lincoln," delivered on Independence Day,* 1865, brought Brooks to national attention.

In 1869 Brooks returned to his native Boston to become rector of Trinity Episcopal Church and presided over its relocation and reconstruction following the Great Boston Fire of 1872. Though a minister in a liturgical denomination, Brooks won his reputation as an orator and author in such works as *Lectures on Preaching* (1877), *The Influence of Jesus* (1879), *The Candle of the Lord* (1881), *Sermons Preached in English Churches* (1883), *Twenty Sermons* (1886), *Lectures on Tolerance (1887), The Light of the World* (1890) and *The Law of Growth* (1902). His Christmas carol, "O Little Town of Bethlehem," composed for Sunday-school* children (1865-1866), remains popular to this day. Preeminently a pastor, Brooks declined a chaplaincy* at Harvard (1881) and an episcopacy* in Pennsylvania (1886), but accepted election in 1891 as bishop of Massachusetts. A broad church* evangelical* of wide sympathies, his installation was opposed by conservatives and Anglo-Catholics alike. His death on January 23, 1893 deprived America of a creative and energetic preacher who was able to make the gospel come alive and instill in his listeners a sense of the presence of God.

BIBLIOGRAPHY. R. W. Albright, *Focus on Infinity* (1961); A. V. G. Allen, ed., *Life and Letters of Phillips Brooks,* 2 vols. (1900); *DAB* II; *DARB;* W. Lawrence, *The Life of Phillips Brooks* (1930); *NCAB* 2.   C. G. Fry

Brown, Arthur Judson (1856-1963). Presbyterian* clergyman,* mission* executive. Born in Holliston, Massachusetts, Brown's family moved to the West after the death of his father. Brown attended Wabash College and Lane and McCormick theological seminaries. In 1883 he was

ordained* by the Presbyterian Church in the U.S.A.* and served churches in the West and Midwest. In 1895 the Board of Foreign Missions called him to be an administrative secretary, and he served the Board until 1929. Brown traveled extensively for his denomination,* guided by his belief in the missionary character of the church, the necessity for Christian cooperation and the call to Christian witness in both word and deed. He was a proponent of self-governing, self-supporting and self-propagating churches around the world.

Brown was a leader and participant in numerous ecumenical* endeavors, including the Ecumenical Missionary Conference (New York, 1900), the World Missionary Conference (Edinburgh, 1910) and the International Missionary Council formed in 1921. He contributed to the development of the World Council of Churches.* Brown was drawn into public affairs on various occasions, notably as a member of the Hoover Relief Committee for Europe (1915) and the American Committee on Religious Rights and Minorities (1920). He was also a long-time member of the Church Peace Union.* As an author, he interpreted the missionary enterprise through his sixteen books and many reports and pamphlets, including *One Hundred Years: A History of the Foreign Missionary Work of the Presbyterian Church in the U.S.A.* (1936). Brown died at the age of 106.

BIBLIOGRAPHY. A. J. Brown, *Memoirs of a Centenarian,* ed. W. N. Wysham (1957); R. P. Johnson, "The Legacy of Arthur Judson Brown," *IBMR* (April 1986):71-75.   J. M. Smylie

Brown, Phoebe Hinsdale (1783-1862). Hymn-* writer and essayist. An orphan raised by relatives, Phoebe Hinsdale had only three months of schooling at the age of eighteen; at that time she learned to read and write. Married to Timothy H. Brown, a house painter, she lived in Connecticut and Massachusetts, writing for Congregationalists* there. Her essays were serialized in the New Haven *Religious Intelligencer* (1816-1837). Two didactic novels, *Village School* and *The Tree and Its Fruits,* claim to be drawn "from real life." The 1835 advertisement for *The Tree* says "vice is spreading at a fearful rate, and almost unresisted over our land—multipling and boasting its victims, the author hopes [that] the living and uncontaminated may be warned, and the plague stayed." Her stories traced the evils of drinking and gambling; many of her hymns paralleled those themes or are devotional* in tone. Brown's hymns were often reprinted. Four, including "I Love to Steal Away" and "Welcome, Ye Hopeful Heirs of Heaven," a song for new converts, were published in *Village Hymns* (1894), compiled by A. Nettleton.

BIBLIOGRAPHY. *DAB* II; C. W. Hughes, *American Hymns Old and New: Notes on the Hymns* (1980); F. J. Metcalf, *American Writers and Compilers of Sacred Music* (1925). R. J. Stanislaw

Brown, Charles Reynolds (1862-1950). Congregational* minister* and educator. Born in Bethany, West Virginia, Brown was raised in an atmosphere of religious instruction and devotion* on a farm in Washington County, Iowa, where the family had moved in 1866. Graduating from the University of Iowa (B.A., 1883; M.A., 1886), Brown first considered a law career but decided on the ministry and in 1886 entered Boston University's School of Theology (S.T.B., 1889; S.T.D., 1922). His first pastorate was the Methodist Episcopal* Wesley Chapel in Cincinnati, but three years later he became a Congregationalist and moved to Winthrop Congregational Church in Boston. In 1896 he accepted a call to First Congregational Church in Oakland, California, where he was to remain for nearly fifteen years. During those years he also was a guest lecturer in ethics at Stanford University (1899-1906) and served as president of the board of trustees of Mills College in Oakland. In 1905-1906 he delivered the Beecher Lectures at Yale,* published as *The Social Message of the Modern Pulpit* (1906).

In 1911 Brown became dean of the Yale University Divinity School,* a post he held until his retirement in 1928. Brown's tenure at Yale was marked by increased student enrollment as well as a growth in faculty and funding. For eleven years he served as pastor* of the University Church, but his travels took him to numerous pulpits, college chapels and lecture halls. In 1924 he was voted one of the twenty-five "foremost living American preachers." Brown exercised an enormous influence in mainline* Protestant* churches on behalf of theological liberalism* during the first half of the twentieth century through his distinguished career as a teacher, preacher and administrator, and through his thirty-nine published books.

BIBLIOGRAPHY. C. R. Brown, *My Own Yesterdays* (1931); *DAB* 4; E. D. Jones, *The Royalty of the Pulpit: A Survey and Appreciation of the Lyman Beecher Lectures on Preaching Founded at Yale Divinity School, 1871* (1951).

D. G. Reid

Brown, Francis (1849-1916). Old Testament scholar and president of Union Theological Seminary (New York).* Born in Hanover, New Hampshire, Brown graduated from Dartmouth* in 1870, and Union Theological Seminary in 1877. After two years in Berlin, he became an instructor at Union and in 1890 professor of Hebrew and cognate languages. He was the first to teach Akkadian in America. Brown served as editor-in-chief of the *Hebrew and English Lexicon of the Old Testament* (1907). He became president of Union in 1908. Brown was a charter member of the Society of Biblical Literature* (1880) and served as the society's president (1895-1896).

Brown became enmeshed in the controversies surrounding Charles A. Briggs* over higher criticism. He stood by Briggs and approved the severing of Union from the Presbyterian Church.* Brown remained a Presbyterian and was a leader among the liberals* who approved such critical positions as the Graf-Wellhausen documentary hypothesis and that biblical revelation is located in religious ideas, not in historical details. Despite his liberal identity, Brown's posture was mediating. His chief contribution to scholarship was Semitic lexicography, and his lexicon remains a standard reference work in its field.

BIBLIOGRAPHY. *DAB* II; L. A. Loetscher, *The Broadening Church* (1954); H. P. Smith, "Francis Brown—An Appreciation," *American Journal of Semitic Languages and Literature* (1917).

T. H. Olbricht

Brown, George (1818-1880). Canadian politician and founder of the Toronto *Globe*. Born at Alloa, Scotland, and educated in Edinburgh, Brown immigrated to New York City in 1837 with his father, Peter. In 1843 they moved to Toronto, where they established the *Banner*, a religious paper which added considerable weight to the cause of the Free Church of Scotland in Canada. The following year they established a second, more political, journal, the *Globe*, which became the most powerful newspaper in British North America.

Having entered the Parliament of the United Province of Canada for the first time in 1851, Brown was a major force in politics over the next fifteen years. He spoke for the interests of many Protestants* in Canada West (now Ontario) in his opposition to perceived Roman Catholic* aggression and French-Canadian domination of the political union. He was also an indefatigable worker for the federal union of all British North American provinces, which resulted in the formation of the Dominion of Canada in 1867. He was also a warm supporter of the temperance,* Sabbatarian* and antislavery movements.* He died May 9,

1880, after having been shot by a disgruntled former *Globe* employee.

BIBLIOGRAPHY. *DCB* X.   R. W. Vaudry

Brown, John (1800-1859). Militant messianic abolitionist.* A Connecticut native reared in a Calvinist* home, Brown was taught not only to fear and obey God but also to be kind to African-Americans and oppose slavery as a sin against God. During the 1820s and 1830s, he actively assisted runaway slaves on the Underground Railroad and advocated African-American education. By the 1850s he grew convinced that only violent action would end the wrong of slavery. Having joined the antislavery forces in Kansas in 1855, Brown led a band of guerrillas in the 1856 Pottawatomie massacre in which five proslavery settlers were killed.

In early 1857 Brown gained financial and moral support from six Northeastern abolitionists for his plan to incite an insurrection among the Southern slaves. These "Secret Six" shared his belief that the slave question could not be settled through peaceful means. For Brown the only recourse left was a massive slave uprising which would bring God's judgment upon unrepentant Southerners. Furthermore, he was convinced that God had anointed him to be the agent of this purging of the nation's sin. At a meeting of blacks and whites in Canada in 1858, he set up a provisional government for the South, with himself as commander-in-chief.

On October 16, 1859, Brown and his raiders took control of the federal armory at Harper's Ferry, Virginia (now West Virginia). However, the slaves of the area failed to rally to his cause, and the following day he was overpowered by U.S. Marines. Hanged for treason against the state on December 2, Brown became a martyr to the antislavery cause and a symbol of Northern conspiracy to the South. Questions remain as to his sanity, but he saw clearly that his actions would provoke a crisis in which the North would put an end to slavery on the battlefield.

BIBLIOGRAPHY. *DAB* II; S. B. Oates, *To Purge This Land with Blood, A Biography of John Brown* (1970); J. Rossbach, *Ambivalent Conspirators: John Brown, The Secret Six and a Theory of Slave Violence* (1983).   M. S. Shanaberger

Brown, Morris (1770-1849). African-American Methodist* minister.* A free African-American from Charleston, South Carolina, Brown was the second bishop of the African Methodist Episcopal Church (AME) from 1820 until his death. Licensed* in the Methodist Episcopal (ME) Church, he was an early leader of the African Church in Charleston—a movement encouraged by Bishop Francis Asbury* for African-American Methodists. By 1816, when African Methodists separated from the ME Church, Brown's congregation numbered 1400 members. Despite missing the organizing conference in Philadelphia, he was ordained* deacon* in 1817 and elder in 1818. White Charlestonians opposed Brown's church, jailing its leaders for breaking laws regulating African-American religious services. By 1822, however, the church had grown to 2,000 members.

Public reaction to the Denmark Vesey* plot of 1822 forced the congregation to disband, and Brown moved to Philadelphia. Brown served churches and assisted Bishop Richard Allen* until 1831. During his tenure as bishop, the church moved into Canada and the Midwest, sponsored its first periodical, *The A. M. E. Church Magazine,* and achieved international attention at the Evangelical Alliance* in London in 1846. Described as a preacher* with an earnest and direct style and as a capable administrator, Brown was active in the Vigilance Committee of Philadelphia—a public arm of the Underground Railroad. An itinerant bishop, in 1844 he was stricken with illness at a church conference in Toronto and remained infirm much of the rest of his life.

BIBLIOGRAPHY. R. R. Wright, *The Bishops of the A. M. E. Church* (1963).

W. B. Gravely and P. Strom

Brown, (R)obert (R)oger (1885-1964). Christian and Missionary Alliance* pastor*, district superintendent and radio preacher. Born in western Pennsylvania and educated at the Missionary Training Institute (now Nyack College and Alliance Theological Seminary), Brown served as pastor to congregations in Beaver Falls, Pennsylvania; Chicago, Illinois; and Omaha, Nebraska. In 1920 he was appointed superintendent of the Western District and subsequently transferred the district office from Chicago to Omaha, where he began the Omaha Gospel Tabernacle in 1923. Brown served the Christian and Missionary Alliance as a member of the Board of Managers from 1925 to 1960 and founded the Bible and Missionary Conference Center at Okoboji Lakes, Iowa, in 1935.

At the annual General Council he championed established policies and procedures and there directed his own creation, the Sunday-afternoon missionary* rally with its parade of furloughing missionaries in national costume. This procession, followed by a call for missionary volunteers, was adopted by many local missionary conferences* across the country.

To those outside his own group Brown was best known for his radio ministry, "World Radio Chapel." Broadcasting over WOW in Omaha, Brown began this ministry in 1923, the same year he opened the Omaha Gospel Tabernacle. At one point the program reached over a half million listeners in the Midwest. An early pioneer in religious broadcasting, his radio ministry continued through 1964, probably the longest sustained religious broadcast to that time.

See also CHRISTIAN AND MISSIONARY ALLIANCE; ELECTRONIC CHURCH.

BIBLIOGRAPHY. R. L. Niklaus, J. S. Sawin, S. J. Stoesz. *All for Jesus: God at Work in the Christian and Missionary Alliance over One Hundred Years* (1986). H. B. Shelly

Brown, William Adams (1865-1943). Presbyterian* educator and theologian.* Born into a prominent New York family, Brown was educated at St. Paul's School (Concord, New Hampshire) and received a B.A. from Yale College* (1886), where he also received an M.A. in economics (1888). At Union Theological Seminary* in New York he studied with Charles Briggs* and Philip Schaff* (B.D., 1890). Upon graduation he attended the University of Berlin for two years and there was greatly influenced by Adolph von Harnack (1851-1930) and indirectly by the thought of Albrecht Ritschl (1822-1889). Eventually he was to receive his Ph.D. from Yale (1901), but upon returning to New York he began teaching at Union Theological Seminary where he spent his entire career, most significantly as professor of systematic theology* (1898-1930) and research professor in the field of applied Christianity (1930-1936).

Throughout his career Brown was a strong advocate of theological liberalism* and was particularly concerned with the relationship between the historical and the absolute in Christianity. In *The Essence of Christianity* (1906) he argued that the absolute was to be found in the person of Jesus Christ as revealer of divine sonship and human brotherhood. His Ritschlian sympathies led him to emphasize the importance of the ethical aspect of Christianity in reforming the social order, and he was a strong defender both of the Social Gospel* and the importance of religion in undergirding liberal democracy.* Brown was also actively involved with the Federal Council of Churches,* the Faith and Order movement and other ecumenical* outreaches.

BIBLIOGRAPHY. W. A. Brown, *A Teacher and His Times* (1940); *DAB* 3; *DARB;* S. McC. Cavert and H. P. van Dusen, eds., *The Church through Half a Century: Essays in Honor of William Adams Brown* (1936). R. B. Mullin

Brown University. An institution of higher education founded by colonial Baptists.* Founded at Warren, Rhode Island, the College of Rhode Island was a Baptist response to earlier collegiate formation. Concern over the initial charter presented to the legislature, which seemed to vest control in Congregationalist* interests, led to a revised charter in 1764, which placed the institution squarely in Baptist hands.

From its beginnings the college espoused principles of religious freedom.* No religious tests were required of either students or faculty and, by 1770, Jews were also allowed as students, though Roman Catholics,* deists* and atheists were still proscribed. All of the school's presidents, however, were Baptist ministers until well into the twentieth century.

In 1765 James Manning,* a Baptist minister, was appointed as first president, and the first class was graduated in 1769. The college moved to Providence in 1770. In 1776 the last commencement until after the Revolutionary War* was held. Subsequently, the college was used as a barracks and hospital by the Continental and French armies, and badly damaged. In the 1780s a lack of students and funds created additional problems. In gratitude for a $5,000 gift from Nicholas Brown, an alumnus, the name of the college was changed to Brown University in 1804.

Academically, Brown reached its nineteenth-century apex during the innovative presidency of Francis Wayland.* Among his accomplishments were the introduction of a largely elective curriculum and a program of instruction which allowed students to finish in three years. Women were first admitted in 1891. The university has offered graduate instruction since 1897 and grants degrees through the doctoral level.

BIBLIOGRAPHY. W. C. Bronson, *The History of Brown University, 1764-1914* (1914).

F. M. Perko

Brownlow, William Gannoway (1805-1877). Controversial Methodist* preacher,* journalist and governor of Tennessee. Orphaned at an early age in east Tennessee, Brownlow eventually became a Methodist circuit rider* in southern Appalachia. From the 1830s until his death he maintained a pugnacious career as a religious and political journalist. He engaged in the intense denominational* rivalries of the trans-Appalachian South, especially in his accusations and rebuttals directed toward the Presbyterian* journalist F. A. Ross and the Baptist* journalist J. R. Graves.* Because of his intense nativism* and anti-Catholicism, he became a prominent Southern leader in the Know-Nothing Movement. At the end of the Civil War* his staunch Unionism led to his appointment as governor of Tennessee. Through the influence of his office he continued his attacks on former Confederates, especially those from other denominations who had provided leadership to the Rebel cause. His popular appeal faltered after the war.

BIBLIOGRAPHY. *DAB* II; E. M. Coulter, *William G. Brownlow: Fighting Parson of the Southern Highlands* (1937). M. G. Bell

Brownson, Orestes Augustus (1803-1876). Preacher,* author, editor and Catholic* lay* apologist.* Born in Vermont, Brownson's early years were influenced by New England Puritanism* and his adolescent years by the religious revivals* of upstate western New York. To attain some stability in his spiritual life, he embraced Presbyterianism* at age nineteen but later rejected its Calvinist* emphases. In 1826 he was licensed as a Universalist* preacher in New Hampshire and edited one of their publications *The Gospel Advocate.* Then followed a period of radical humanism as he joined the Workingmen's Party to work for social reform in 1829-1830. After reading William E. Channing's* *Likeness to God,* Brownson renewed his religious life. Throughout the 1830s he intertwined his spiritual quest with a passion for social reform. He edited *The Philanthropist,* became a Unitarian* preacher and frequently contributed to Unitarian journals. He was also influenced by Transcendentalism.*

Finding New England Unitarianism staid, he founded his own Church of the Future in Boston and developed his spiritual vision in a book called *New Views of Christianity, Society and the Church* (1836). To forge links between American democracy* and religion, he edited his own *Boston Quarterly Review* (1838-1842). Therein he advocated the re-election of Martin Van Buren as U.S. president, published his Marxist-like *Essay on the Laboring Classes* (1840) and developed P. Leroux's ideas on communion of life. In 1843-1844 he began to see the Catholic Church as the only church capable of providing the spiritual power for social reform. Accordingly he was baptized* a Roman Catholic by Bishop* Fitzpatrick of Boston in October 1844.

Writing in his own *Brownson's Quarterly Review*

(1844-1864; 1873-1875), Brownson defended Catholic doctrine* against Protestant* thinking, such as the Mercersburg* theology* and even certain Catholic writers such as John Henry Newman (1801-1890) of England, whose views on the development* of dogma* Brownson found dangerous and unorthodox. Against the Know-Nothings and other nativist* groups, Brownson argued for the compatibility between Catholicism and American democracy* and asked Catholic immigrants* to integrate themselves both into American political institutions and the native American Catholic Church. However, since American democracy could find its true basis only in Catholicism, he advocated America's conversion* to the Catholic faith. As a consequence of his doctrine of the supremacy of the spiritual (the Catholic Church) over the temporal (the State), he argued for the supremacy of the Pope,* not only in spiritual matters but even in temporal matters, insofar as the latter touched on spiritual concerns.

When Pius IX* published *Quanta Cura* and the accompanying *Syllabus of Errors* (1864), Brownson ceased publishing his liberal *Review* and became more conservative, both doctrinally and politically, in his later years. When he resumed his *Review* in 1873, he focused his attention on defending the authority of the Pope. In that same year Brownson finished his lifelong effort to develop a sound objective basis for God's existence, published as his *Essay in Refutation of Atheism.* He died three years later in Detroit; he was buried at University of Notre Dame* in Indiana.

BIBLIOGRAPHY. O. A. Brownson, *Works,* ed. H. F. Brownson, 20 vols. (1882-1887); *DAB* II; *DARB;* R. M. Leliaert, "The Religious Significance of Democracy in the Thought of Orestes A. Brownson," *The Review of Politics* 38 (1976):3-26; R. M. Leliaert, "Brownson's Doctrine of God: The Catholic Period," *The Thomist* 40 (1976):571-603; *NCAB* 7; T. R. Ryan, *Orestes A. Brownson: The Pope's Champion in America* (1984); A. M. Schlesinger, Jr., *Orestes A. Brownson: A Pilgrim's Progress* (1939). R. M. Leliaert

Brunner, (H)einrich Emil (1889-1966). Swiss Reformed* dialectical* theologian.* Born in Winterthur, Switzerland, Brunner studied at the universities of Berlin and Zurich, receiving his Th.D. from the latter in 1913. Following a brief pastoral career he occupied the chair of systematic* and practical theology at the University of Zurich (1924-1955).

Neo-orthodoxy* was a prominent Protestant theological movement from the late 1930s to the late 1950s, and began as an attempt to return to the teachings of the early Reformers, especially their insistence on grounding Christian faith in an historical revelation. The representatives of this new theology were convinced that liberal* Protestantism had surrendered to relativism in theology (what Brunner termed *historicism*).

It was Brunner who first introduced neo-orthodoxy to the English-speaking world, spending more time in England and the U.S. than did any other European representative of the movement. He was visiting professor of theology at Princeton Theological Seminary in 1938-1939; and more than twenty of his books were translated into English, usually only a few years after they appeared in German. This factor, in contrast to the relatively late appearance of Barth's works in English translation, also facilitated the influence of Brunner on American theology. His major works included: *The Mediator* (1927; ET 1934); *The Divine Imperative* (1932; ET 1937); *Revelation and Reason* (1941; ET 1947); and his three-volume *Dogmatics* (1946-1960; ET 1949-1962).

Although frequently associated with Barth,* Brunner developed his theology independently. A major point of difference between the two theologians is their respective attitudes toward philosophical anthropology and the philosophy of religion.* Barth recognized little of value in these disciplines, while Brunner regarded them as necessary. Brunner contended that there must be a point of contact between revelation and reason. He even held that there was a natural knowledge of God that was drawn from the "orders of creation."

Another prominent motif in Brunner's theology, influenced by Søren Kierkegaard* and the Jewish philosopher Martin Buber (1878-1965), was his concept of revelational truth as "personal encounter." The specific quality of biblical revelation is that God comes to one as "absolute subject." Consequently, special revelation is not the communication of facts but God's disclosure of himself. God encounters one interpersonally through an inwardly transformative event. Revelation is the inner change by which the recipient of the revelation makes the surrender of faith. This notion led Brunner to deny that the content of revelation can be expressed in propositional form. Dogma is simply a human reaction to revelation.

Despite his negations of the historic orthodox* view of biblical revelation, Brunner did help restore to modern theology a sense of the transcendent reality of God and the personal commitment demanded by faith. Almost an entire generation of theological students in America received their basic training in some type of reaction to Brunner's theological system, as a whole or in part.

BIBLIOGRAPHY. J. E. Humphrey, *Emil Brunner* (1976); C. Kegley, ed., *Theology of Emil Brunner* (1962).
J. F. Johnson

Brush Arbor. Overhanging tree branches sheltering the main area of a camp meeting* site. Camp meetings, which originated in 1800, were usually held in wooded groves, cleared in the center to accommodate a preaching* platform and rows of plank benches, with tents pitched on the periphery. The brush arbor consisted of trees surrounding the cleared area, shorn of limbs to a height of ten or twelve feet and forming a natural canopy which created a cathedral-like effect. After the middle of the nineteenth century, as more and more camp meetings adopted permanent locations with fixed buildings, the brush arbor waned in significance.
W. G. Travis

Bryan, Andrew (1737-1812). Pioneer African-American Baptist* minister.* Born in slavery at Goose Creek, South Carolina, Bryan was brought to a plantation near Savannah, Georgia. Near the age of thirty-five he was converted* to Christianity by George Liele,* who evangelized along the coastal plantations. Beginning his own ministry, Bryan and his brother, Sampson, were brought before city authorities and whipped for refusing to discontinue their work. He and his followers were forbidden to hold services at night, but they were able, with owners' permission, to meet during the day, and Bryan's master opened his barn at Brampton for their use. In 1788, Abraham Marshall, a white Baptist minister, accompanied by Jesse Galphin (or Jesse Peter), a African-American associate, visited the congregation. After examination they baptized forty to sixty people and ordained* Bryan—an early, if not the first, ordination of an African-American. The First Colored, later African, Baptist Church erected its first building in 1794, and the membership grew to 850 by 1802. After purchasing his freedom Bryan was able to extend his ministry, organizing a Second African Baptist Church with Henry Francis, a slave, as pastor. He then went on to organize a Third Church in another part of town. Widely known by Baptists in England and in North America, Bryan died in October 1812, active in the ministry until the end of his life.

BIBLIOGRAPHY. J. M. Simms, *The First Colored Baptist Church in North America* (1888); M. Sobel, *Trabelin' On: The Slave Journey of an Afro-Baptist Faith* (1979).
W. B. Gravely and C. White

Bryan, William Jennings (1860-1925). American editor, politician and anti-evolutionary leader. He was a three-time candidate for president of the U.S., and secretary of state under Woodrow Wilson.

Raised in Illinois of Bible*-reading parents, Bryan attended school at Illinois College (B.A., 1881) and was admitted to the bar in 1883. He practiced law in Illinois and Nebraska and in 1891 went to Washington for the first time as a thirty-year-old congressman from Lincoln, Nebraska. From 1894 to 1896 he also served as editor of the Omaha *World-Herald*. Bryan adopted the populist creed of the agrarian Midwest that characterized the progressive movement in the region during the decades prior to World War 1.* He was soon catapulted into the national political arena.

The hottest election issue in 1896, backed by farmers, was the addition of cheap money (silver) to the American currency. At the Democratic convention Bryan supported silver by delivering his famous "Cross of Gold" speech, "You shall not crucify mankind upon a cross of gold." Although only thirty-six years old, Bryan won the presidential nomination, but he lost to William McKinley* and sound money in the election.

Chosen as the Democratic nominee in 1900 and again in 1905, he lost both elections. In 1912 Woodrow Wilson's election brought Bryan to the State Department. Bryan negotiated a series of arbitration treaties with thirty countries, but the crisis of 1914, marked by the sinking of the *Lusitania,* brought a conflict within the administration over the use of the treaties. Bryan resigned in June 1915.

The end of Bryan's political career opened the door for his reforming and religious leadership. He soon threw himself into the prohibition* cause and played a significant role in securing the passage of the Eighteenth Amendment outlawing alcoholic* beverages across the country after January 1920. The 1920 census, however, revealed that for the first time in American history the majority of the population was living in urban centers. The Eighteenth Amendment had no sooner become law than it was flouted openly. Traditional standards of morality seemed to be crumbling. Bryan saw one of the causes of this moral decline in Darwin's conception of man's origin.

In the spring of 1921, Bryan issued a series of attacks on evolution that instantly placed him in the forefront of fundamentalist* forces. The most important of these was his lecture "The Menace of Darwinism." Morality and virtue, he argued, are dependent on religion and a belief in God, and anything that weakens belief in God weakens man and makes him unable to do good. The evolutionary theory robs man of his major stimulus to moral living.

Bryan's last great battle, the Scopes Trial,* was the consequence of a Tennessee law prohibiting the teaching of evolution by a public-school* teacher. A young high-school biology teacher in Dayton named John Scopes was charged with violating the law. He was defended by Clarence Darrow, a well-known lawyer, while Bryan joined the prosecuting team. Darrow argued that nothing less than intellectual freedom was on trial and succeeded in getting Bryan himself on the stand, using Bryan's testimony as evidence of fundamentalist stupidity. Scopes was found guilty and fined a token sum, but Bryan and fundamentalists were ridiculed throughout the country. Five days after the trial, Bryan passed away.

See also SCOPES TRIAL.

BIBLIOGRAPHY. P. E. Coletta, *William Jennings Bryan: Political Evangelist, 1860-1908* (1964); *DAB* II; *DARB*; P. W. Glad, *The Trumpet Soundeth: William Jennings Bryan and His Democracy, 1896-1912* (1960); L. W. Levine, *Defender of the Faith* (1965); *NCAB* 19.   B. L. Shelley

Bryant, William Cullen (1794-1878). Poet and editor. Born in Cummington, Massachusetts, Bryant was raised in a religious and cultured environment. After one year at Williams College (1810-1811), Bryant was forced to leave school for financial reasons. To support himself he prepared for a law career, was admitted to the bar in 1815 and practiced law, unhappily, for the next ten years. His heart was in poetry. As early as 1808, when Bryant was thirteen, his first poem—"The Embargo," a castigation of President Thomas Jefferson*—appeared in print. Three years later he composed the first draft of his best-known poem, "Thanatopsis." Six years later it was published in the *North American Review,* bringing national recognition to the young poet. In 1821 he married Francis Fairchild and read the Phi Betta Kappa poem, "The Ages," at Harvard.* That same year he published a volume entitled *Poems,* which included the final version of "Thanatopsis," along with "To a Waterfowl," "The Yellow Violet" and other lyrics. Bryant was established as America's finest poet.

In 1825 he went to work for the *New York Review.* Two years later he moved on to the *New York Evening Post,* where he became editor and part owner, positions he maintained for the rest of his life. His liberalism caused him to break with the Democrats, become a Republican and an ardent abolitionist.* In another change, Bryant rejected Puritanism* for Unitarianism.* Many of his poems deal with nature, in which he saw the presence of God. His popularity as a poet and his use of religious themes contributed in a subtle way to the influence of Unitarianism in nineteenth-century America.

BIBLIOGRAPHY. W. C. Bryant, *The Complete Poems of William Cullen Bryant* (1894); *DAB* II; A. F. McLean, *William Cullen Bryant* (1964); A. Nevins, *The Evening Post: A Century of Journalism* (1922). D. B. Chesebrough

Buchman, Frank Nathan Daniel (1878-1961). Founder and director of Moral Re-Armament.* Born in Pennsburg, Pennsylvania, Buchman attended Muhlenberg College (B.A., 1899) and studied at Mt. Airy Seminary (1899-1902). He served as a Lutheran* minister* at Overbrook, Pennsylvania (1902-1905), director of a Lutheran settlement house in Philadelphia (1905-1909), secretary for the YMCA* chapter at Pennsylvania State College (1909-1915) and a lecturer in personal evangelism* at Hartford Seminary (1916-1921).

A brilliant organizer, tireless promoter, charismatic leader and insightful counselor, Buchman founded a controversial religious movement in 1921 that for more than forty years had significant worldwide impact. Known successively as The First Century Christian Fellowship, the Oxford Group Movement and Moral Re-Armament, Buchman's movement eventually spread to more than sixty countries. The primary goal of the movement was to help individuals develop a deep spiritual commitment within the context of their own religious traditions. Concentrating its efforts on reaching students, intellectuals, the wealthy and influential political and labor leaders, the movement sponsored "house parties" which emphasized discussion, meditation, testimonies and public confession of sin.* In addition, a traveling team of "lifechangers" and sophisticated use of films, drama and literature, especially books written by Buchman, won many to the movement.

In 1930 Buchman renamed his movement Moral Re-Armament and changed its focus to promoting moral awareness and peace among nations. During the international crises of the summer of 1939, he worked diligently to convince European leaders of his principles for peace and British statesmen of his appeasement policy. The failure of appeasement brought discredit upon Moral Re-Armament, but during World War 2* the movement's many patriotic efforts, especially in England and America, helped it to regain a more favorable image.

Buchman continued to direct Moral Re-Armament until his death in 1961, but his movement never again reached the same level of influence it had during its first two decades.

See also MORAL RE-ARMAMENT.

BIBLIOGRAPHY. F. Buchman, *Remaking the World* (1949); *DAB* 7; P. Howard, *Frank Buchman's Secret* (1961); P. Howard, *The World Rebuilt: The Story of Frank Buchman* (1951); G. Lean, *On the Tail of a Comet: The Life of Frank Buchman* (1985); *NCAB* B. G. S. Smith

Buckley, William (F)rank, Jr. (1925-). Conservative Catholic* editor, author and political activist. Born in New York City, Buckley received his early education in France and England, where he attended exclusive Roman Catholic private schools. After graduating from Millbrook School, a prep school in upstate New York (1943), Buckley spent a half year at the University of Mexico (1943-1944) before serving in the U.S. Army (1944-1946). Buckley then attended Yale University* (B.A., 1950), where he distinguished himself in debate and was an instructor in Spanish (1947-1951).

Buckley achieved his first notoriety with the publication of *God and Man at Yale* in 1951. His critique of what he perceived as the anti-religious and collectivist teachings of Yale faculty triggered a firestorm of controversy. After a year as a C.I.A. agent in Mexico and further writing, Buckley launched *National Review* in 1955. The biweekly journal, he said, stood "athwart history, yelling 'Stop' " when few were inclined to do so. It has become the most important publication on the American right, with a circulation of around 100,000.

In 1960 he helped organize Young Americans for Freedom to train and educate young conservatives. The following year he helped found New York's Conservative Party, the vehicle for his unsuccessful (13.4 per cent of the vote) mayoral candidacy in 1965 and his brother James's 1970 election to the U.S. Senate.

His syndicated newspaper column, "On the Right," began in 1962 and has been carried by over 300 newspapers; in addition, many of his collected columns have been published by G. P. Putnam. Adding another medium in 1966, he launched his television interview program, "Firing Line," in New York and saw the Public Broadcasting Service pick it up in 1971, making him a national media celebrity. With *Saving the Queen* in 1976, Buckley began writing spy thrillers that drew upon his own experience and have proven effective propaganda for his conservative ideas. He is conservatism's

[199]

intellectual Renaissance man.

Buckley, who has defined conservatism as "tacit acknowledgement that all that is finally important in human experience is behind us," has been, according to Arthur Schlesinger, Jr., "the scourge of American liberalism." A staunch Roman Catholic, a laissez-faire capitalist, an anti-Communist and an outspoken defender of traditional values in private and social morality, Buckley has been a major force in the post-World War 2* resurgence of conservatism in the U.S.

BIBLIOGRAPHY. J. B. Judis, *William F. Buckley, Jr.: Patron Saint of the Conservatives* (1988).

J. R. M. Wilson

Buhlmaier, Marie (1859-1938). Baptist* home missionary.* Born in Heilbronn, Germany, Buhlmaier came to the U.S. with her family in 1868. With only three years of schooling, she had to go to work at age ten. Confirmed* in the Lutheran* Church in 1873, she was baptized* into the German Baptist Church the same year. At fifteen she became a church worker for the First Baptist Church of Harlem, New York. In 1893 she became a missionary to German immigrants in Baltimore for the Home Mission Board of the Southern Baptist Convention. A gifted speaker, she also wrote *Along the Highway of Service* (1924).

N. A. Hardesty

Bultmann, Rudolf Karl (1884-1976). German biblical scholar and theologian.* Born in Wiefelstede, Bultmann graduated from the *Gymnasium* of Oldenburg in 1903 and did undergraduate work at the universities of Tübingen, Berlin and Marburg under the distinguished theologians and biblical scholars of his day (1903-1906). Encouraged to pursue further studies, Bultmann completed his doctoral degree at the University of Marburg (1910) and later served as an instructor at the university (1912-1916). He was then assistant professor at Breslau (1916-1920) and in 1920 became full professor at Giessen but stayed only one year. In 1921 he returned to Marburg to serve the rest of his career as professor of New Testament and early Christian history (1921-1951). After retiring he remained in Marburg until his death twenty-five years later.

Bultmann is most widely known for his program for "demythologizing"* the New Testament. Defining myth as the attempt to objectify powers that cannot be objectified, as in the case of angels, demons, heaven and a heavenly redeemer, Bultmann called for a hermeneutic that would interpret the mythically conveyed truth of the New Testament into terms meaningful to modern people. In this sense he distinguished himself from nineteenth-century liberal theologians who had attempted to find the historical Jesus behind what they believed were the eschatological and mythical trappings of the Gospels—a Jesus whose moral teachings could give shape and substance to liberal Christianity.

Bultmann's own investigation of the New Testament was guided by form criticism, a method he was instrumental in developing. His research into the synoptic Gospels yielded little reliable information about the historical Jesus and much that reflected the faith of the early Christians as it grew out of their subjective and visionary experiences of the resurrected Christ. Jesus, the Jewish eschatological teacher, had been transformed by the early church into the heavenly Lord, modeled after the gnostic heavenly redeemer.

But this paucity of reliable information about the historical Jesus did not trouble Bultmann. Heavily influenced by the existentialism of his Marburg colleague Martin Heidegger (1899-1976), Bultmann interpreted the Christian message in terms of the Word of God that addresses moderns in their scientific and technological quest for security. To seek a historical Jesus was to abandon faith and engage in a quest for security and freedom apart from God. Reflective of an inauthentic existence at best, theologically speaking, it was a quest for knowledge of Christ after the flesh (2 Cor 5:16) rather than an encounter with the Word that calls men and women to meaningful existence. Thus he wedded a call to existential freedom with a modern rendition of the Lutheran* doctrine of justification* by faith alone.

This perspective was profoundly human-centered rather than God-centered. Bultmann was not only able to give a fresh alternative to the dilemma of the liberal quest for the historical Jesus, but also to provide a recasting of the Christian message that was attractive to many modern intellectuals who were troubled by the erosion of the foundations of their faith in the face of biblical criticism and lived in an age that raised new and troubling questions about the meaning of human existence.

Bultmann's influence in America spread largely through his writings, which in turn attracted students to Marburg from the U.S. Bultmann's *The History of the Synoptic Tradition* (1921) did not appear in English translation until 1963, though its influence was felt in the scholarly world long before then. *Jesus and the Word* (1926) appeared in English in 1934 and helped introduce his method and thought to America. In 1951 he traveled to the U.S. and gave the Shaffer Lectures at Yale* Divinity School and the Cole Lectures at Vanderbilt University, as well as lecturing at several other leading American divinity schools. These lectures were published in the popular introduction to his thought, *Jesus Christ and Mythology* (1958). A number of other significant works eventually found their way into English, including *The Gospel of John: A Commentary* (1941; ET 1971); *Theology of the New Testament,* 2 vols. (1948-1953; ET 1951, 1955) and the partially translated *Kerygma and Myth* (1948-1955; ET 1953-1962). In addition, some of his American students became leading New Testament scholars and further promoted his views.

Bultmann's influence among biblical scholars and theologians of the latter half of the twentieth century has been second to none. Yet his synthesis of literary-critical method, religious-historical approach and philosophical interpretation has gradually eroded. New discoveries and insights into the world of Judaism and Hellenistic religion have severely undercut Bultmann's view of the shape of Hellenistic religion and its influence on New Testament writers. By the 1980s a new generation of scholars was more optimistic about clarifying its picture of the historical Jesus against the background of a newly enhanced understanding of first-century Judaism. Moreover, Bultmann's individualistic existential interpretation of the New Testament lost much of its impact during the 1960s, when societal upheaval turned the attention of the churches to social issues and a world-formative Christianity.

See also BIBLICAL INTERPRETATION; EXISTENTIALISM, CHRISTIAN.

BIBLIOGRAPHY. S. M. Ogden, *Christ Without Myth* (1962); T. F. O'Meara and D. M. Weiser, eds., *Rudolf Bultmann in Catholic Thought* (1968); N. Perrin, *The Promise of Bultmann* (1969); R. C. Roberts, *Rudolf Bultmann's Theology* (1977); J. M. Robinson, *A New Quest of the Historical Jesus* (1963); W. Schmithals, *An Introduction to the Theology of Rudolf Bultmann* (1968).

D. G. Reid

Burial Hill Declaration. A summary statement of belief issued by Congregationalists* meeting in a national council in Boston, June 14-24, 1865, the first denomination-wide doctrinal statement since 1649. The earlier meeting produced the Cambridge Platform,* a declaration of Reformed* (Calvinist) principles. The "Burial Hill Declaration," read on June 22 at the famous Pilgrim* burial site in Plymouth, was a short affirmation of evangelical* beliefs, with strong statements upholding

congregational polity* and a plea for unity among Protestant* denominations.* Significantly, after much debate on the matter, the "Declaration" omitted specific reference to Calvinism, whose long-time influence was waning as Congregationalism underwent theological change in the nineteenth century.

BIBLIOGRAPHY. G. G. Atkins and F. L. Fagley, *History of American Congregationalism* (1942).

W. G. Travis

Burke, Edmund (1753-1820). First Catholic* vicar apostolic of Nova Scotia. Born in Maryborough, Ireland, and educated at the University of Paris, Burke was ordained* priest* in 1775 or 1776. He was a pastor* in County Kildare until 1786, when he left for Quebec. After teaching mathematics and philosophy at the Seminaire de Quebec for five years, he returned to the pastorate and served two parishes* on Isle d'Orleans before assuming responsibility for missions* in the province of Upper Canada (including the western posts in Michigan and Ohio until 1796). He remained in Upper Canada until 1801, when he moved to Halifax and assumed the position of vicar general of Nova Scotia (under the jurisdiction of the bishop* of Quebec). Under his leadership Nova Scotia became a vicarate apostolic in 1817 which removed it from Quebec's jurisdiction. He became its first incumbent with the title of bishop of Sion and vicar apostolic of Nova Scotia, having been consecrated in 1818. Burke was active in promoting the Roman Catholic interest in Nova Scotia. He was involved in defending his church and faith in exchanges with the Anglican* Bishop Charles Inglis* and with others like Robert Stanser (Anglican) and Thomas McCulloch (Presbyterian*).

BIBLIOGRAPHY. *DCB* V; J. S. Moir, *The Church in the British Era* (1972). R. W. Vaudry

Burke, John Joseph (1875-1936). Catholic* publisher and founder of the National Catholic Welfare Conference.* Born in New York City, the son of a horseshoer, Burke grew up as a parishioner in St. Paul the Apostle Church, the mother-church of the Paulist* community. There the young man saw and heard Father Isaac Hecker,* founder of the Paulists, who lived at the church rectory until his death in 1888. Burke was educated at St. Francis Xavier College in New York, and like his older brother, Thomas, joined the Paulist community. His further education was at Catholic University of America,* and he was ordained* in 1899.

Burke served on the *Catholic World* as assistant editor in 1903 and was its editor from 1904 to 1922.

He helped found the Catholic Press Association in 1911 and was director of what is now called the Paulist Press. His major contribution, however, was organizational. In 1917 he founded and was director of the Catholic War Council, established to coordinate services to Catholics in World War 1.* After the war, the Council continued as the National Catholic Welfare Council. In 1922 it became the National Catholic Welfare Conference, coordinating Catholic activities in the U.S. Burke served as general secretary of the administrative board of the Conference until his death. His vision of the importance of such an organization as the NCWC was confirmed at Vatican II,* and the format and operation of the Conference has served as a model for more than fifty other national hierarchies. His broad record of public service, diplomacy and ecumenical* leadership earned him the admiration of many political and church leaders of his time. He was made a monsignor in 1936, and he died in Washington, D.C., on October 30 of that year.

BIBLIOGRAPHY. *DAB* I; J. B. Sheerin, *Never Look Back: The Career and Concerns of John J. Burke* (1975).
R. Van Allen

Burned-Over District. An area located in New York State, bounded by the Catskill Mountains on the east and the Adirondock Mountains on the north and known for its concentration of religious experimentalism. The district was populated in the early nineteenth century by New England settlers who brought with them an experimental approach to religious practices and reform objectives. They were contemporaries of the Age of Jackson and contributed to the cultural history of that era. The variety of religious experimentation was evidenced by the presence of Mormons,* spiritualists, Shakers,* abolitionists,* perfectionists* and the sexual communitarians of Oneida.*

Charles G. Finney,* the most famous revivalist* of that era, referred to the area as a "burnt district" which had been the scene of frequent revivals of religion. Although born in Connecticut in 1792, Finney was taken by his parents into the area along the path named by Whitney Cross as the "psychic highway." Finney put his own mark on the Burned-Over District by reconstructing Calvinism to fit his own revivalistic objectives, fashioning a theology that blended with the ideals of Jacksonian America and introducing a series of "new measures"* that provided a means for the excesses that characterized some movements during that time. Though Finney eventually moved out of the Burned-Over District, the path he blazed through the area was later followed by Dwight L. Moody,* Billy Sunday* and others in the revival tradition.

BIBLIOGRAPHY. C. C. Cole, Jr., *The Social Ideas of the Northern Evangelists, 1826-1860* (1954); W. R. Cross, *The Burned-Over District: The Social and Intellectual History of Enthusiastic Religion in Western New York, 1800-1850* (1950).
J. E. Johnson

Burton, Ernest Dewitt (1856-1925). Baptist* biblical scholar and president of the University of Chicago. Born in Granville, Ohio, Burton graduated from Denison University (B.A., 1876) and as a young man taught school in Michigan and Ohio, after which he studied for the ministry* at Rochester Theological Seminary (B.D., 1882). At twenty-seven, he was elected to the chair in New Testament at Newton Theological Institute (1883). It was, however, at the reorganized University of Chicago that Burton made his major contribution. In 1892 he became the head of the department of New Testament and early Christian literature. In this capacity he edited *Biblical World* and the *American Journal of Theology* and wrote widely in the New Testament field. Upon Harry Pratt Judson's retirement in 1923, Burton became president of the University (1923-1925).

Few writers surpassed Burton's usefulness in producing New Testament scholarship. He was among the first to develop the field of biblical theology* as an historical discipline, presenting the thesis that the books of the Bible* represent an historical process. He paid particular attention to the environment of the biblical writers and the context of extra-canonical literature. With E. J. Goodspeed, Burton edited *Harmony of the Synoptic Gospels* (1920), and he organized *A Sourcebook for the Study of the Teaching of Jesus in Its Historical Relationships* (1923) which provided a new approach to the contemporary quest for a unified life of Christ. Burton's work in the New Testament paralleled that of William R. Harper* in Old Testament and Semitics and Shailer Mathews* in historical theology in the well-known Chicago School* of religious studies.

BIBLIOGRAPHY. T. W. Goodspeed, *Ernest Dewitt Burton* (1926); *DAB* II.
W. H. Brackney

Bushnell, Horace (1802-1876). Congregationalist* theologian* and pastor.* Born in Bantam, Connecticut, Bushnell was educated at Yale College* (B.A., 1827) and studied for the bar at the Yale Law School (1829-1831). Converted* in the revival* of 1831, he entered the Yale Divinity

School (B.D., 1833) where he studied under Nathaniel W. Taylor,* the famous champion of the New Divinity (*See* New Haven Theology). Bushnell rejected Taylor's defense of theological systems by formal logic, and turned instead to reading Samuel Taylor Coleridge, whose "intuitive" *Aids to Reflection* opened to him "a range of realities in a higher tier." In old age he stated that he owed more to Coleridge's book than to any other save the Bible.*

In 1833 Bushnell was ordained* pastor* of the North (Congregational) Church in Hartford, Connecticut, where he remained until the end of his pastoral ministry in 1859. Bushnell was not a popular preacher, and his lack of success in effecting conversions abetted his search for a new system that would transcend the Old School*/New School* debates then exercising New England Congregationalists by offering a theology* that would "comprehend, if possible, the truth contended for in both."

In 1847 Bushnell published *Christian Nurture,* a landmark work in American theology whose "environmental," non-revivalist approach to religious nurture advised that "the child grow up a Christian, and never know himself as being otherwise." This covert attack on revivalism* as a source of church growth had decisive long-term effects for American religious history—turning the attention of the churches toward the training of the young and offering a theological rationale for the burgeoning Sunday-school movement.* It also served as a seminal theological prolegomenon to the Social Gospel* Movement by bolstering a growing confidence in the redemptive potentialities of the world.

In 1849 Bushnell adumbrated his mature theological system in *God in Christ,* whose preliminary "Dissertation on Language" offered the poetical key to his entire method. All religious language, he asserted, including that of the creeds, must be understood as poetical and not literal. Spiritual realities could not be precisely expressed in formal linguistic statements, for words were "suggestive" of religious truth but could never be definitive. Such an understanding of religious language discredited all theological attempts at exact system building, and almost immediately involved Bushnell in charges of heresy* brought against him in the General Association of Congregational Ministers in 1850. Bushnell retained his pulpit, despite the conservative outcry, and the "Dissertation" achieved something like canonical status among later Protestant* modernists,* who drew extensively on Bushnell's hermeneutical argument for changing the language of doctrine in order to conserve the "essential meaning" of religious symbols.

Bushnell's 1858 treatise on *Nature and the Supernatural* (in which he argued that science and religion, like reason and faith, constituted the "one system of God") was widely influential among a younger generation of ministers troubled by the new scientific discoveries of the nineteenth century. *The Vicarious Sacrifice* (1866) advanced an equally influential "moral influence" theory of the atonement* among liberal Protestants. Bushnell is thus often likened to Coleridge or Schleiermacher, battling the dry rationalism of Protestant scholasticism and restating religious truths in terms of human experience. More than any other single thinker, Bushnell laid the intellectual foundations for American Protestant modernism and the Social Gospel.

BIBLIOGRAPHY. W. S. Archibald, *Horace Bushnell* (1930); M. B. Cheyney, *Life and Letters of Horace Bushnell* (1880); B. M. Cross, *Horace Bushnell: Minister to a Changing America* (1958); *DAB* II; *DARB*; W. A. Johnson, *Nature and the Supernatural in the Theology of Horace Bushnell* (1963); T. T. Munger, *Horace Bushnell: Preacher and Theologian* (1899); *NCAB* 8.   M. S. Massa

Bushnell, Kathryn (1856-?). Physician and temperance* reformer. Born in Peru, Illinois, Bushnell was educated at Northwestern University in Evanston, Illinois, and the Chicago Woman's Medical College, from which she received the degree of M.D. Bushnell spent several years in China as a medical missionary. She returned to the U.S. and established a medical practice in Colorado and was drawn into the Social Purity department of the Women's Christian Temperance Union* as a full-time evangelist* in 1885. She helped to expose the abuse of young women lured to the Wisconsin wineries by the promise of work. Her interest in the well-being of young women also led to the establishment of the Anchorage Mission in Chicago, a rescue home for women and girls. In 1891 she began to lecture on behalf of temperance around the world, carrying with her Frances Willard's* Polyglot Petition to the rulers of the world, asking for their cooperation in eliminating opium and liquor traffic. As a result of her influence, the Indian government passed legislation protecting certain rights of native women.

BIBLIOGRAPHY. F. Willard and M. Livermore, *A Woman of the Century* (1893).

B. J. MacHaffie

Buswell, (J)ames Oliver, Jr. (1895-1977). Presbyterian* fundamentalist* educator and organizational leader. Born in Mellon, Wisconsin, Buswell was educated at the University of Minnesota (A.B., 1917), McCormick Theological Seminary (B.D., 1923), the University of Chicago* (M.A., 1924) and New York University (Ph.D., 1949). Ordained* in the Presbyterian Church, U.S.A.* in 1918, he ministered* as an Army combat chaplain* (1918-1919), in a Presbyterian church in Milwaukee (1919-1922) and a Reformed* church in Brooklyn (1922-1926). Buswell was dismissed from the Presbyterian ministry in 1936 for his involvement with a fundamentalist Presbyterian mission board. He subsequently served with several separatist Presbyterian denominations. He was the author of eleven books and dozens of articles, his most significant contribution being *A Systematic Theology of the Christian Religion*, 2 vols. (1962-1963).

As president of Wheaton College* (Illinois) from 1926 to 1940, Buswell developed the school into a rapidly growing, academically respected, strategic fundamentalist center. After leaving Wheaton, Buswell taught at Faith Theological Seminary in Wilmington, Delaware (1940-1947); was president of the National Bible Institute in New York City and its successor, Shelton College in New Jersey (1941-1955); and taught at Covenant College (1956-1964) and Covenant Theological Seminary (1956-1970) in St. Louis.

A creative developer of conservative Protestant institutions, a distinguished teacher of theology and an ecclesiastical controversialist, Buswell's legacy included a vision for a vigorous evangelical* intellectual witness and a series of ecclesiastical separations. Both of these helped to shape the "neo-evangelical"* movement that some of Buswell's star pupils led in the 1950s and 1960s.

BIBLIOGRAPHY. *Presbyterion: Covenant Seminary Review* 2:1-2 (1976): J. Oliver Buswell, Jr. Commemorative Issue.   J. A. Carpenter

Butler, Elizur (1794-1857). Medical missionary* among the Cherokee Indians. Born at Norfolk, Connecticut, Butler was sent in 1821 by the American Board of Commissioners for Foreign Missions* to work among the Cherokee in Georgia. He worked at the Brainerd Mission from 1821 to 1824 and at the Haweis Mission from 1824 to 1831. When Georgia, seeking more control over the Indian tribes within its borders, ordered all whites residing among the Indians to swear allegiance to the state, Butler and Samuel Worcester* refused to comply. They were arrested, convicted and in September 1831, were sentenced to four years in prison. Their case was appealed to the

U.S. Supreme Court *(Worcester v. Georgia, 1832),* where the state law was held invalid. Both men were released from prison in January 1833, and Butler returned to his mission work, accompanying the Cherokees when they were forced to remove to the Indian Territory in 1838. There he worked at the Park Hill Mission and the Fairfield Mission and was steward of the Cherokee Female Seminary at Park Hill from 1850 until his death.
See also NATIVE AMERICAN INDIANS, MISSIONS TO.

BIBLIOGRAPHY. R. S. Walker, *Torchlight to the Cherokees: The Brainerd Mission* (1931); W. G. McLoughlin, "Civil Disobedience and Evangelism Among the Missionaries to the Cherokees, 1829-1839," *JPH* 51 (1973):116-139.   M. S. Joy

Buttrick, George Arthur (1892-1980). Congregational* preacher* and theologian.* Born and raised in Northumberland, England, where his father was a pastor* in the Primitive Methodist Church,* Buttrick underwent a personal religious experience* during his grade-school years. During his youth he rebelled against the rigid conservatism and organization of the family's denomination,* and with his father's help found his way into the care of the Congregational Church and one of its pastors, John Gardner.

After completing high school in Yorkshire, Buttrick sought a career in the British Civil Service, but he did not pass the qualifying exam. Feeling led toward ordained* ministry,* he enrolled in a Congregational seminary* at Lancashire and took his degree with honors in philosophy in 1915. He took only a minimal amount of work in homiletics* and none at all in theology—both areas where he would distinguish himself in later life. His seminary studies were interrupted by a brief period of service as a military chaplain* during the early days of World War 1.* A lung infection ended his career as a chaplain,* and a physician recommended that upon graduation from seminary he leave the damp English climate for America.

Through the assistance of John Gardner, who had also come to the U.S., Buttrick accepted a call to become pastor of the First Congregational Church in Quincy, Illinois. The following year, 1916, he married Gardner's daughter, Agnes. In 1918 he became pastor of the First Congregational Church of Rutland, Vermont, and then in 1921 moved to the First Presbyterian Church of Buffalo, New York. At age thirty-four, Buttrick was named in 1927 to succeed Henry Sloane Coffin* as pastor of Madison Avenue Presbyterian Church, the largest church of its denomination in New York City.

In his twenty-seven years at Madison Avenue,

Buttrick distinguished himself in his preaching and writing. Known in some circles as "the preacher's preacher," he twice delivered the Lyman Beecher* Lectures on Preaching at Yale* and taught homiletics for two decades at Union Theological Seminary, New York.* He served as president of the Federal Council of Churches,* and he was general editor of *The Interpreter's Bible* (12 vols., 1952-1957) and *The Interpreter's Dictionary of the Bible* (4 vols., 1962).

In 1954, Buttrick went to Harvard* as Plummer Professor of Christian Morals and Preacher to the University. He retired in 1960, served as a visiting professor at several theological schools, and settled in Louisville, Kentucky, where he died in 1980.

BIBLIOGRAPHY. J. Sittler, "George Buttrick: A Tribute and Reflection," *CCen* 97 (April 16, 1980):429-430. W. B. Lawrence

C

Cabrini, Francesca Xavier (1850-1917). Catholic* saint* and founder of the Missionary Sisters of the Sacred Heart. Born at Sant' Angelo Lodigiano in Lombardy, Italy, Francesca Cabrini was the youngest of thirteen children of Agostino, a prosperous farmer, and Stella (Oldini) Cabrini. She completed normal school with the Daughters of the Sacred Heart at Arluno, earning a diploma with highest honors in 1870. A smallpox victim in 1872, she was rejected, perhaps because of health, as a candidate for the Daughters of the Sacred Heart and the Canossians of Crema.

Francesca then spent two years teaching in the village school of Vidardo when the pastor,* Antonio Serrati, persuaded her to take over the direction of an orphanage in his new parish of Codogno in 1874. There she attempted to form the staff into a religious community and made vows on September 14, 1877. When the orphanage closed in 1880, Francesca and seven companions moved to an abandoned Franciscan friary in Codogno, where the Missionary Sisters of the Sacred Heart was founded November 14, 1880. Witnessing the growth of the new institute in Italy, Bishop* Scalabrini of Piacenza and Pope* Leo XIII directed Francesca toward the Italians in America. Relinquishing her dream of going to China, she arrived in New York March 31, 1889, with six sisters.

Mother Cabrini's work in the U.S. coincided with the era of massive Italian immigration.* She provided evangelization through catechetical* instruction, prison work,* orphanages and schools in New York, Brooklyn, Denver, Los Angeles, Chicago, New Orleans, Seattle, Philadelphia, Scranton and Newark. Headquarters were established on Jesuit* property at West Park, New York, and with sharp business acumen she succeeded in establishing Columbus Hospitals in New York (1892), Chicago (1905) and Seattle (1916). She extended her prodigious efforts to South America as well as Europe and the U.S., crossing the ocean thirty times. In 1909 Francesca Cabrini became a U.S. citizen. She died in Columbus Hospital in Chicago at sixty-seven years of age, and in 1946 she was canonized,* the first American citizen to be declared a saint.

BIBLIOGRAPHY. *DAB* II; *DARB;* P. D. Donato, *Immigrant Saint: The Life of Mother Cabrini* (1960); T. Maynard, *Too Small a World: The Life of Francesca Cabrini* (1945); *NAW* 1; *NCAB* 27; *NCE* 2.   P. Byrne

Cadbury, Henry Joel (1883-1974). New Testament scholar, Quaker* historian and humanitarian worker. Born in Philadelphia, Pennsylvania, and educated at Penn Charter School, Haverford College (B.A., 1903) and Harvard* University (M.A., 1904; Ph.D., 1914), Cadbury taught biblical literature at Haverford (1910-1919), Andover Seminary* (1919-1926) and Bryn Mawr College (1926-1934), and lectured at the Quaker School of Graduate Study (1954-1972). In 1934 he was named Hollis Professor of Divinity at Harvard Divinity School (1934-1954).

Cadbury became a leading New Testament scholar in America, specializing in Luke-Acts. He was on the translation team for the Revised Standard Version of the New Testament (published 1946) and produced numerous scholarly books and articles on the New Testament, including *The Making of Luke-Acts* (1927) and *The Book of Acts in History* (1955). His interest in Quaker history resulted in a number of essays, as well as *John Woolman in England* (1971). An ardent humanitarian, he worked for peace and academic freedom and was chairman of the American Friends Service Committee for twenty-two years. In 1947 he received the Nobel Peace Prize on behalf of the Society.

BIBLIOGRAPHY. *DARB.*   W. A. Cooper

Cadman, Samuel Parkes (1864-1936). Congregational* minister.* The English-born Cadman grew up in the coal-mining region of Shropshire near the Welsh border, the son of a lay* preacher* who contracted for the right to work proprietors' mines. His childhood was saturated with the Bible,* poetry and John Bunyan's works, and at sixteen he experienced a powerful conversion,* which led to his own licensing* as a Wesleyan* Methodist* lay preacher in 1884 and a degree in theology* and classics from Richmond College, London, in 1889. He then immigrated to New York and served churches in Millbrook and Yonkers and the Metropolitan Temple in New York City. Becoming a Congregationalist, Cadman led Brooklyn's Central Church from 1900 to his death, making it one of the leading churches in the U.S.

Cadman was an evangelical* liberal* who interpreted Darwin's work and contemporary biblical scholarship* sympathetically and stressed the themes of divine Fatherhood, human brotherhood and the kingdom of God* with a christocentric focus. *Charles Darwin and Other English Thinkers* (1911), *Imagination and Religion* (1926) and *The Christ of God* (1929) were especially important among his many books. He was acting president of Brooklyn's Adelphi College from 1911 to 1913. Prominent in ecumenical* circles, he participated in the Open and Institutional Church League* in the 1890s, was president of the Federal Council of Churches* (1924-1928) and chaired the American section of the Stockholm Conference on Life and Work (1925). From 1928 to his death he reached a national audience as the Federal Council's radio preacher over NBC on Sunday afternoons. His own denomination* elected him moderator of its National Council in 1934.

BIBLIOGRAPHY. *DAB* 2; F. Hamlin, *S. Parkes Cadman: Pioneer Radio Minister* (1930); H. S. Leiper and E. D. Staples, *S. Parkes Cadman: A Great Churchman and Christian* (1967).

J. H. Dorn

Cahensly, Peter Paul (1838-1923). German Catholic lay* leader. An officer in the St. Raphaelsverein, an organization founded in 1871 for the care of German Catholic immigrants, Cahensly sought to protect the faith of the immigrants to the U.S. by preserving their ethnic identity. In 1890 he and fifty other members of the European boards of directors of the St. Raphaelsverein from seven nations petitioned Pope Leo XIII* for (1) separate parishes* for each nationality in America; (2) the appointment of priests* of the same nationality as the parishioners; (3) parochial schools* where the immigrants' mother tongue would be taught; and (4) representation of each of the immigrant nationalities in the American hierarchy. The petitioners' position, known as "Cahenslyism," was opposed by most American bishops* as based on unfounded allegations of pastoral neglect of the immigrants, leading to the fragmentation of the

Church in the U.S. and hindering the assimilation of the immigrants into American society. The Vatican did not act on the petition.
See also IMMIGRATION AND ETHNICITY, CATHOLIC.
BIBLIOGRAPHY. C. J. Barry, *The Catholic Church and German Americans* (1953).

J. T. Connelly

Cain, Richard Harvey (1825-1887). Black Methodist* minister,* editor and politician. The son of a Cherokee mother and African-American father, Cain was born in Greenbriar County, Virginia. His family moved to Ohio, where he worked on steamboats before being converted* in 1841. The Methodist Episcopal Church licensed* him to preach* three years later in Hannibal, Missouri. Dissatisfied in that denomination,* he joined the African Methodist Episcopal* (AME) Church, served several charges and studied at the denomination's new school, Wilberforce, in Ohio. Ordained* deacon* in 1859 and elder* in 1862, he was pastor* in Brooklyn during the Civil War.* At its close, he became a distinguished preacher-politician in South Carolina. As presiding elder, he organized AME churches among the freed people, was an editor of the *South Carolina Leaders* and *The Missionary Record,* headed Emmanuel AME Church in Charleston, and ran successfully for state office and for the U. S. Congress (1872-1874, 1876-1878). Cain was a member of South Carolina's convention of 1868, which included universal manhood suffrage for the first time in a state constitution.

Throughout Reconstruction, Cain sought to obtain land for the freed people. In Congress he spoke eloquently for civil rights, supported women's suffrage* and endorsed selling public lands to fund education. Retiring from politics, he was elected bishop,* serving in Louisiana and Texas. A founder and second president of Paul Quinn College, he also presided over AME annual conferences back East. He was still active in the episcopacy at his death.

BIBLIOGRAPHY. *DAB* II; R. R. Wright, *The Bishops of the A.M.E. Church* (1963).

W. B. Gravely and P. R. Strom

Caldwell, David (1725-1824). Presbyterian* minister,* educator and physician. A Scotch-Irish immigrant to Pennsylvania, Caldwell studied at the College of New Jersey* (B.A., 1761) and moved to Guilford County, North Carolina, in the 1760s. There he founded his Log College* in 1767 and become pastor of the Buffalo and Alamance churches in 1760. He tried unsuccessfully to avert the Battle of Alamance in 1771, and served in the North Carolina constitutional convention of 1776. Although his support of the Revolution* caused Lord Cornwallis to put a price on his head, after the Battle of Guilford Courthouse (1701) Caldwell, a self-taught physician, helped the British physician tend the wounded. He later discovered that the British army had ransacked his house and farm, destroying all of his papers. After the war he devoted himself to his school, his church and his farm. He served as a delegate to the state convention that refused to ratify the U.S. Constitution and was offered, but declined, the presidency of the University of North Carolina. He continued teaching and ministering into the late 1810s.

BIBLIOGRAPHY. E. W. Caruthers, *A Sketch of the Life and Character of the Rev. David Caldwell* (1842); B. P. Robinson, "David Caldwell," *Dictionary of North Carolina Biography* 1:300-302, ed., W. S. Powell (1979).   T. T. Taylor

California, Christianity in. California has had a significant influence in the shaping of American culture, including American Christianity. The Christian faith, in the form of Roman Catholicism,* was first brought to California during the era of Spanish control. The first permanent colony in California was established at San Diego in 1769 with the collaboration of the Franciscans* under Junipero Serra.* Between 1769 and 1823 a total of twenty-one missions were established in a chain extending nearly five hundred miles up the Pacific coast (*See* Missions to North America, Spanish). Following Mexico's independence from Spain, the missions were secularized in 1833, a well-intended project that unfortunately proved detrimental to Native Americans and the Church. The Catholic Church in California generally fell into decay during the last years of the Mexican period, prior to American seizure of California in the Mexican War (1846-1847).

The gold rush which began in 1848 attracted thousands of adventurers who eventually settled in the area. Protestant* ministers, recognizing the spiritual needs of the region, soon arrived and began established churches. The first Protestant congregation was established in San Francisco in 1848, but within four years the city boasted twenty-two Protestant, six Catholic and two Jewish congregations. In that year the first Roman Catholic archbishop* was appointed to that city. Though the churches grew, their attempts to enforce New England and Midwestern traditionalism did not make strong headway in the face of the independent Westerners who were more attracted to unor-

thodox religious movements such as Spiritualism, Unitarianism* and Seventh-day Adventism.* It was not until the years following 1880 that Protestants began to establish a strong constituency in Southern California. From within Southern California Methodism* came one Holiness* group that would eventually join with other similar movements to become the Church of the Nazarene.*

During the first quarter of the twentieth century, Southern California gained wide acclaim for its mild and healthful climate. This attraction, along with the lure of inexpensive housing, drew both solid citizens and unusual cultists who expected a new lease on life in the Promised Land. Coming to California in this era were such diverse religionists as the Methodist fundamentalist* and radio-preacher Robert P. Shuler* and evangelist Billy Sunday,* joined by Yogi mystics, palm readers, rainmakers, Hindu fakirs and a wide variety of occultists.* The Bible Institute of Los Angeles (now Biola University) was established in 1908 under the leadership of Lyman Stewart,* largely out of concern that theological ignorance and error were widespread. Stewart also was instrumental in publication of *The Fundamentals,* a series of books setting forth and defending conservative Christian doctrines.

The 1908 Azusa Street Revival* in Los Angeles was a significant event in the birth of the Pentecostal Movement.* Later the dynamic and independent Pentecostal Aimee Semple McPherson* would play a significant role in the development of Christianity in California. In 1923 she founded Angelus Temple, the beginning of the Foursquare Gospel Church.* With a flair for the unusual and dramatic, she attracted Californians to a gospel characterized by showmanship, vigorous evangelism* and aid to the sick and needy. Mrs. McPherson was also an early radio evangelist, using the airwaves effectively for twenty years from her pulpit at Angelus Temple. By the time of her death in 1944, the denomination had approximately four hundred churches nationwide.

Orthodox Christianity in California was threatened by rival movements such as Theosophy. A notable instance was Katherine Tingley's theosophical community at Point Loma near San Diego, which lasted from 1900 until her death in 1929. A rival theosophical community was established near Santa Barbara. New Thought and Christian Science* also enjoyed popularity from around the turn of the century. By 1906 California had the nation's sixth-largest population of Christian Scientists. On the broader religious front, California contributed the concept of the cemetery as a park where the living might enjoy art and landscape and funerary inscriptions employing the theme of family reunion in heaven.

While California has earned a reputation for tolerance of religious movements and ideologies that would have embarrassed much of the rest of the nation, traditional Christianity has thrived as well. Since World War 2,* California—and the Los Angeles area in particular—has produced a number of "super churches." Often situated on large campuses and encompassing thousands of members, these evangelical churches frequently emphasize biblical preaching. One super church that has catered to Southern California's love affair with the automobile is Robert Schuller's* Garden Grove Community Church, whose Crystal Cathedral accommodates both walk-in and drive-in worshipers. Schuller has also restated the gospel in terms gauged to reach the unchurched. More recently California's churches have seen a trend toward crosscultural Christian ministries among the region's growing ethnic populations.

Among the other notable movements of recent decades have been the Jesus Movement,* arising out of the counterculture of the late 1960s and early 1970s; the 1968 founding in Los Angeles of the Metropolitan Community Church—the first of a nationwide fellowship of gay churches; the birth of the charismatic movement* through individuals as diverse as Dennis Bennett, rector of St. Mark's Episcopal Church in Van Nuys (1959); and the efforts of Southern-California dairyman Demos Shakarian,* the founder of the Full Gospel Business Men's Fellowship*; and, more recently, the Vineyard Christian Fellowship, a nationwide movement emphasizing healing and "power evangelism" and originating from John Wimber's Yorba Linda congregation. In religion as in other aspects of American life, California has gained a reputation as a trendsetting region.

BIBLIOGRAPHY. A. Rolle, *California, A History* (1987); W. Bean, *California, An Interpretive History* (1978); J. Caughey and L. Caughey, *California Heritage* (1966); S. S. Frankiel, *California's Spiritual Frontiers: Religious Alternatives in Anglo-Protestantism, 1850-1910* (1988); F. J. Weber, *The Pilgrim Church in California* (1973); F. J. Weber, ed., *The Religious Heritage of Southern California: A Bicentennial Survey* (1976).

A. M. Carden

Callahan, Patrick Henry (1866-1940). Catholic* layman.* Born in Cleveland, Ohio, the son of Irish immigrants,* Callahan was educated at Spencerian Business College. Callahan prospered

as a leader in the paint and varnish business in Louisville from the 1890s until his death. A devout Catholic, he actively participated in the affairs of the Church. During World War 1* he initiated a crusade for religious toleration that consumed much of his time in the years ahead. He bravely confronted such organizations as the Ku Klux Klan.* While Callahan adamantly defended the tenets of Catholicism, he often took his own co-religionists to task for not always adhering to his ideas of American civil religion.*

As president of the Louisville Varnish Company, Callahan directly applied his religious beliefs to the workplace. With the collaboration of Monsignor John A. Ryan,* he inaugurated a successful profit-sharing plan in 1912 that survived the pressures of the Great Depression.* After the turn of the century, Callahan became increasingly active in politics, though he never considered running for office. He employed the "Callahan Correspondence," a mimeographed series of communications with leading political, religious and business figures, to influence public opinion. Using the honorary Kentucky title of *Colonel,* he gained entry to political and religious circles in the South because of his unbending support of Prohibition.* In 1928 he broke with the Democratic Party and stoutly opposed the candidacy of Governor Al Smith.*

Callahan's life serves as a model for the archetypal progressive, owing to the constancy of his political, economic, social and religious ideals. He counted among his friends such diverse personalities as William Jennings Bryan* and H. L. Mencken.

BIBLIOGRAPHY. *DAB* 2; W. E. Ellis, "Catholicism and the Southern Ethos: The Role of Patrick Henry Callahan," *CHR* 69 (1983):41-50.

Wm. E. Ellis

Calvert, Cecilius (1606-1675). Catholic* colonizer of Maryland. Born in London in 1606, Cecilius, or Cecil, was the eldest son of George Calvert,* Baron of Baltimore in Ireland. On his father's death in 1632, Cecilius succeeded to the title. He immediately began to realize his father's dream of establishing a colony in America as a refuge for his fellow Catholics. On November 22, 1633, Calvert dispatched to Maryland two ships, the Ark and the Dove, with between 200-300 settlers aboard, the majority of them Protestant.* Among these were the Jesuit* priests* Andrew White* and John Altham* accompanied by a lay* brother* Thomas Gervase.

Determined to avoid religious strife in the new

colony, Cecilius instructed his brother Leonard Calvert,* whom he had appointed governor, that all settlers were to be granted religious liberty. He invited the Society of Jesus to care for the spiritual needs of Maryland's Catholics provided they construct self-supporting missions,* land for which they would obtain from him. When the Jesuits insisted on their right to acquire unlimited land grants as gifts from the Indians, Cecilius pressured the Jesuit General to order his subjects to conform to proprietary law and to grant the proprietor a veto over missionaries* assigned to the colony.

During the English Civil War Maryland was seized by Virginia Puritans* who expelled Governor Leonard Calvert. He regained control of the colony but died shortly thereafter in 1647. To defuse religious tension Cecilius appointed as governor a Protestant, William Stone, in 1648. When Charles I was executed in January 1649 and the Commonwealth created, Calvert wrote "The Act Concerning Religion," adopted by the colony on April 21, 1649, which was designed to allay Puritan suspicions and save his proprietorship. Though Virginia Puritans again seized Maryland in 1655, it was returned to him in 1658. Calvert died in London on November 30, 1765.

See also CALVERT, GEORGE; COLONIAL CATHOLICISM; TOLERATION, ACT OF.

BIBLIOGRAPHY. W. H. Browne, *George Calvert and Cecilius Calvert: Barons of Baltimore* (1890); *DARB;* J. T. Ellis, *Catholics in Colonial America* (1965); *NCAB* 7; *NCE* 2.   L. R. Riforgiato

Calvert, Charles (1637-1715). Third Lord Baltimore, last Catholic* proprietor of Maryland. The oldest son of Cecil* and Anne (Arundel) Calvert, Charles Calvert served as governor of Maryland from 1661 to 1684 and became proprietor upon the death of his father in 1675. His arbitrary style of government, through a mainly Roman Catholic oligarchy, raised religious tensions and offended the sensibilities of the largely Protestant* colony. During Calvert's trip to England in the 1680s to defend his charter, the Glorious Revolution occurred. The subsequent revolt in Maryland by the Protestant Associates in 1689 concluded with Maryland as a royal colony and the establishment of the Church of England* there in 1702. Though Charles Calvert retained his property rights, he did not regain his proprietorship. However, his son, Benedict Leonard Calvert, conformed to Anglicanism* in 1713. Maryland once more became a proprietary colony after the death of Charles Calvert on February 20, 1715.

BIBLIOGRAPHY. L. G. Carr and D. N. Jordan,

Maryland's Revolution of Government, 1689-1692 (1974); *DAB* II; J. D. Krugler, " 'With Promise of Liberty in Religion': The Catholic Lords Baltimore and Toleration in Seventeenth-Century Maryland, 1634-1692," *MHR* 79 (1984):21-43.

T. E. Buckley

Calvert, George (1580-1632). British Catholic* colonizer in America. The child of Catholic parents who were outwardly forced to conform to the Anglican* Church because of the penal laws, George Calvert was tutored by an Anglican clergyman* and graduated from Trinity College in 1597. He then entered a political career serving as secretary, then clerk, of the privy council. In 1609 he was elected to Parliament where he became a staunch defender of King James I. James knighted him in 1617 and, in 1619, appointed him one of the principal secretaries of state for the realm. From 1621 to 1624 he again served in Parliament. He was made first Baron of Baltimore in County Longford, Ireland in 1625, about the time he publicly professed his Catholicism, and continued to serve the new king, Charles I, as a member of his privy council. However, Calvert's interests were increasingly turning to colonization as a means of providing fellow Catholics with refuge from England's penal laws.

In 1620 he purchased from the Virginia Company a Newfoundland plantation he called Avalon on which, in 1623, he established the settlement of Ferryland. Calvert and his family visited the colony in 1628 but found the climate cold and inimical to settlement. He now asked Charles I for another, warmer land grant in Virginia which was given in 1629. Charles, however, bowing to the outrage of the Virginia Company, rescinded the grant. Instead he offered Calvert land north of the Potomac, beyond the domains of the Virginia Company, which was to be named Maryland in honor of his wife, Queen Henrietta Maria. George Calvert died on April 15, 1632 before the actual charter was issued, so it fell to his son Cecilius* to found the new colony.

See also COLONIAL CATHOLICISM; CALVERT, CECILIUS.

BIBLIOGRAPHY. W. H. Browne, *George Calvert and Cecilius Calvert: Barons of Baltimore* (1890); *DAB* II; J. T. Ellis, *Catholics in Colonial America* (1965).   L. R. Riforgiato

Calvert, Leonard (1610-1647). First colonial governor of Maryland. Born the second son (Cecilius* being the eldest) of George Calvert, first Lord Baltimore, Leonard, with his father and brothers, converted* to Roman Catholicism.* In 1632, shortly before his death, George Calvert* obtained a charter from Charles I for the proprietary colony of Maryland. His eldest son, Cecil, inherited the title and the proprietorship. When the first colonists were dispatched in November 1633, the second Lord Baltimore appointed his brother Leonard as governor, with instructions to maintain a policy of toleration for all Christians. In Maryland Governor Calvert strongly supported the Jesuit* missionaries'* efforts to convert the Native Americans, struggled to maintain peace between Catholics and Protestants* and met repeated challenges to his authority. At the outbreak of the English Civil Wars, Puritans* he had welcomed to the colony seized control, forcing him in 1644 to flee to Virginia's Governor William Berkeley for protection. Two years later he returned to Maryland with an armed force and repossessed the government. He died there on June 9, 1647.

BIBLIOGRAPHY. H. H. Browne, *George Calvert and Cecilius Calvert, Barons of Baltimore* (1890). T. E. Buckley

Calvinism. A doctrinal tradition originating with the Reformer John Calvin (1509 1564) and providing the foundational theology* of the Congregational,* Reformed* and Presbyterian* churches in America. Calvinism begins with the fundamental principle of the sovereign majesty of God and, consequently, emphasizes his exclusive initiative in salvation.* Otherwise known as Reformed theology (to be distinguished from Lutheran* theology, which also originated with the Reformation), Calvinism as it came to America was defined by the tradition's classic confessions such as the Belgic Confession (1561), the Heidelberg Catechism (1563), the Thirty-Nine Articles* of the Church of England (1562, 1571), the Canons of the Synod of Dort (1619) and the Westminster Confession of Faith* (1647).

Adhering to the fundamental Reformation principle of *sola Scriptura,* Calvinism claims to derive its doctrines entirely from Scripture.* Calvin and his successors have believed that Scripture—not reason or church tradition—is the fully trustworthy revelation from God and the only reliable foundation for Christian faith and practice. Hence, even Calvinistic doctrinal statements are only binding inasmuch as they reflect the clear teaching of Scripture.

The Synod of Dort (1618-1619) clearly defined in five points the salvific implications of Calvinism over against Arminianism.* These five points, which some scholars believe oversimplify the richness of Calvinist theology and the variety of its historic formulations, nevertheless provide a helpful summary: (1) humanity is by nature totally depraved and unable to merit salvation; (2) some people are unconditionally elected by God's saving grace; (3) God's atonement* in Christ is limited in its efficacy to the salvation of the elect; (4) God's transforming grace, ministered by the Holy Spirit, is irresistible on the part of humans; (5) the saints must persevere in faith to the end, but none of the elect can finally be lost. Calvinism at its best has grounded all of these doctrines in the person and work of Christ, but a logical deductivism has at times influenced the tradition.

The doctrine of the sovereignty of God not only shapes Calvinism's understanding of redemption, but its perspective on creation, history, politics and life in general. Thus the Calvinist world view has frequently inspired its adherents to engage culture and transform all of life under the mandate of the sovereign rule of God. In addition, Calvinism in America, particularly in its Puritan* strain, has frequently been wedded to a philosophy of history known as covenant theology.* This philosophy—encompassing both the sacred and profane, the seed of Adam and the seed of Christ—was to pose its own problems for Calvinist thought and church life (*see* Half-Way Covenant).

The most pressing questions within Calvinism in America have revolved around the twin issues of human responsibility and divine sovereignty as they relate to the Fall and redemption. These issues, originally pastoral concerns brought into focus by the Great Awakening,* set the theme for theological and philosophical reflection and discussion from Jonathan Edwards* through the New England Theology* of the nineteenth century. The followers of Edwards debated and refined Edwards's speculative metaphysic. They were opposed by the Old Calvinists, who called these followers of Edwards "New Divinity Men." The Old Calvinists, in their uneasiness over revivalism, maintained the pre-Awakening Calvinism of the Puritan establishment. Relatively uninterested in the finer points of systematic theology,* they stood for the Puritan covenant theology of the past that had assured a stable orthodox community.

But the movement within Calvinism to modify its understanding of human responsibility and allow for a greater freedom of the will in responding to conversionist preaching, provided a theological basis for many American Calvinists to participate in the First and Second Great Awakenings and in American revivalism in general. Among Presbyterians, however, the Princeton Theology* of the mid-to-late nineteenth century was the most resistant to the modified Calvinism. The Princeton Theology has had a continued influence on conservative Presbyterians and other evangelical Calvinists of the twentieth century.

In whatever form it has taken, Calvinism has been a dominant shaping force in American Protestantism and has had a strong influence not only on Congregationalists,* Presbyterians* and Continental Reformed bodies, but on many Anglicans,* Baptists* and independent churches. But denominations such as the Reformed Church in America* and the Christian Reformed Church,* as well as a few Presbyterian bodies such as the Orthodox Presbyterian Church* and the Presbyterian Church in America,* would claim to be the faithful conduits of Calvinist orthodoxy in American religious life today.

See also COVENANT THEOLOGY; ELECTION; PREDESTINATION; REFORMED TRADITION, THE.

BIBLIOGRAPHY. J. H. Bratt, ed., *The Heritage of John Calvin* (1973); B. Kuklick, *Churchmen and Philosophers* (1985); J. H. Leith, *Introduction to the Reformed Tradition,* rev. ed. (1981); J. T. McNeill, *The History and Character of Calvinism,* rev. ed. (1967); W. S. Reid, ed., *John Calvin: His influence in the Western World* (1982); B. B. Warfield, *Calvin and Augustine* (1956); D. F. Wells, ed., *Reformed Theology in America* (1985).

The Editors

Cambridge Platform (1649). Written codification of New England Congregational church government.* Responding to English requests for a definitive statement of the principles of New England Congregationalism,* the Massachusetts General Court convened the Cambridge Synod in 1646. The Synod,* consisting of lay* and clerical* delegates elected from churches throughout New England, met three times in the next two years before agreeing upon a formal platform of church discipline.* The completed *Cambridge Platform,* written largely by Dorchester pastor Richard Mather,* offered a detailed description of, and biblical justifications for, the practices and government of New England churches. This system of church government differed little from the "mixed" form of church order described by Puritan* theorists, in which the government of local, independent churches was shared by church members and church officers. The elders published the *Platform* in 1649 and read it aloud before each congregation. Individual congregations voted to ratify the document as the true form of church government drawn from the Word of God.

Originally intended as a nonbinding description

of church practices, the *Platform* soon came to be regarded as a higher law that bound ministers* and congregations alike to its precepts. Ministers reminded their flocks that the "Congregational Way" distinguished New Englanders as a unique people of God and warned them never to lose sight of the duties and precious liberties guaranteed in the *Platform.* By the beginning of the eighteenth century, Massachusetts Congregationalists regarded the *Platform* as their constitution, a term they frequently used to describe the document. Lay and clerical violations of the *Platform* became a common source of church disputes through the rest of the colonial period. Despite a number of changes in church practices and a gradual decline in the significance of church government, the *Cambridge Platform* continued to serve as a fundamental statement of Congregational practice well into the nineteenth century.

BIBLIOGRAPHY. W. Walker, *The Creeds and Platforms of Congregationalism* (1960); H. S. Stout, *The New England Soul* (1986).

J. F. Cooper

Cameron, Robert (c. 1845-c. 1922). Canadian Baptist* minister* and prophetic writer. A Baptist minister from Brantford, Ontario, Cameron was a prominent figure in the Niagara Bible Conference,* who first embraced and then rejected strict dispensationalism's* doctrine of a secret and imminent return of Christ before the tribulation of the last days. In 1884 he questioned the increasing dominance of this pretribulation view at the conference, maintaining his own posttribulation premillennial* eschatology.*

Despite differences over eschatology, Cameron worked closely with A. J. Gordon,* an historicist premillennialist. Following Gordon's death, Cameron took over from him the editorship of *The Watchword,* a leading millenarian journal. He cooperated with James H. Brookes,* the dispensationalist who edited another prophetic magazine, *The Truth.* Following Brookes' death, Cameron purchased this journal and merged the two publications to form *The Watchword and Truth.* In 1902 he published a strong attack on the pretribulationist view, which led to an aggressive assertion of the full dispensational position by opponents. Cameron expounded his millenarian views in two books *The Doctrine of the Ages* (1896) and *Scriptural Truth about the Lord's Return* (1922).

BIBLIOGRAPHY. E. Sandeen, *The Roots of Fundamentalism* (1970). D. M. Lewis

Camp Meeting. An outdoor revival* meeting,

inter-denominational in origin, during which the participants came prepared to encamp at the meeting site for several days. While outdoor preaching* was a feature of the Great Awakening* and early American Methodism,* the camp meeting proper developed in Kentucky under the auspices of Presbyterian revivalists.* The first of these was at Gasper River in Logan County (July 1800), led by James McGready,* followed by Cane Ridge* in Bourbon County (August 1801), directed by Barton W. Stone.* These meetings, and others which quickly followed, shaped the "Great Revival" and Protestant development in the trans-Allegheny West for several decades.

The natural outdoor setting, the break from the routines of home and farm life, the social and community nature of the event, the exhortations of backwoods preachers—all combined to produce a flood of zealous emotionalism that came to be characteristic of frontier religion.* Critics considered camp-meeting revivalism to be false religion and a delusion that promoted excess and schism. Defenders believed that camp meetings exhibited a genuine and "blessed revival of religion." These two views have yet to be reconciled. Clearly, thousands were reached by the gospel, yet some denominations (particularly the Presbyterians) became seriously divided.

By the mid 1840s Baptists* and Presbyterians had abandoned camp meetings in favor of "protracted" revival services held inside church buildings. Methodists, on the other hand, institutionalized the meetings, planning every detail, even to the point of constructing permanent meeting sites. Some of these later developed into Chautauqua*-style gatherings or family resort centers. In the later nineteenth century the camp meeting became a significant feature of the Holiness* revival movement.

See also FRONTIER RELIGION; REVIVALISM, PROTESTANT.

BIBLIOGRAPHY. J. R. Boles, *The Great Revival, 1787-1805* (1972); D. Bruce, *And They All Sang Hallelujah: Plain-Folk Camp Meeting Religion, 1800-1845* (1974); C. A. Johnson, *The Frontier Camp Meeting* (1955).   D. B. Eller

Campaign for Human Development (1969). An organization launched by the National Conference of Catholic Bishops* (NCCB) to combat poverty and racism through fund-raising and educational programs. The Campaign for Human Development (CHD), originally called the National Catholic Crusade Against Poverty, has its immediate origins in a resolution adopted by the NCCB on November 14, 1969, in which the NCCB

made a commitment to raise 50 million dollars to subsidize self-help projects for the poor and educational projects to promote solidarity between the poor and the non-poor. CHD represents the NCCB's response to the Catholic Church's growing awareness of its responsibility to the poor, underscored by *The Pastoral Constitution on the Church in the Modern World,* published by the council fathers at Vatican II* and by the Latin American bishops who met at Medellin, Colombia, in 1968. It was also a response to indigenous American problems which exploded in the 1960s, especially the urban violence of 1967 and 1968, which focused unprecedented public attention on the relationship between racism and poverty.

A hallmark of CHD's approach to the problems of poverty and racism has been its increasing support of the kind of community organizations associated with the name of Saul Alinsky from the 1940s onward. By the early 1980s, seventy-eight per cent of CHD's grants went to grassroots community organizations. CHD has also nurtured collaboration between whites and ethnic-racial minorities and between urban and rural constituencies. On the diocesan* and parish* level, CHD has been involved in social-justice education programs and worked in conjunction with adult spirituality* programs such as RENEW.

BIBLIOGRAPHY. *Daring to Seek Justice: The Story of the Campaign for Human Development* (1986).
          D. Campbell

Campanius, John (Johan) (1601-1663). Swedish Lutheran* minister* and missionary.* A graduate of the University of Uppsala, Campanius ministered in his native Sweden for all but five years of his adult life. In 1643 he and his family accompanied Johan Printz, New Sweden's first governor, to America, where he ministered to the colony's Swedish, Finnish and German settlers in the Delaware River area. He also collected astronomical and meteorological data and information on local flora and fauna, and worked among the Delaware Indians (who called him *big mouth* because he had so much to say). He prepared a vocabulary of local Native American tribes and translated Luther's Shorter Catechism into the Lenape language. (Charles XI published the catechism in 1696 and sent 500 copies to America in 1697.) The Campanius family returned to Sweden in 1640, where Campanius served congregations in Frosthult and Hernevi until his death in 1663. Some of his papers, edited by his grandson, Thomas Campanius, appeared in *A Short Description of the Province of New Sweden* (Stockholm,

1702; Philadelphia, 1834).

BIBLIOGRAPHY. A. Kastrup, *The Swedish Heritage in America* (1975); E. C. Nelson, ed. *The Lutherans in North America* (1975).

T. T. Taylor

Campbell, Alexander (1788-1866). One of the founders of the Restoration Movement* in America. Born near Ballymena, County Antrim, Ireland, Campbell grew up in Ireland and was educated by his father, Thomas,* a Scotch-Irish Seceder Presbyterian* minister.* Besides his general studies in classics, literature, philosophy and religion, Alexander was introduced to the works of John Locke.

In October 1808, Alexander, his wife and children set out for America; but, thwarted by a shipwreck, he took the opportunity to spend ten months at the University of Glasgow, where he studied the Greek New Testament, literature, logic, French and experimental philosophy. While there he was also impressed by a Scottish movement, based on the teaching of James and Robert Haldane, which promoted a return to primitive Christianity as revealed in the New Testament.

In September 1809, Alexander arrived in Pennsylvania where he found his father, who had emigrated from Ireland in 1807, had withdrawn from the Presbyterians after being censured for his open Communion* practices and disagreements over Calvinist* doctrine.* Thomas had also been disturbed by the petty denominational* quarrels, and in August of 1809 he had formed a fellowship called the Christian Association of Washington, a local association of believers distinguished only by their geographical location. The younger Campbell, having come to much the same conclusions as his father, started the Brush Run Church and on May 4, 1811, with Thomas as elder, Alexander was ordained* to preach.

By the fall of 1813 the Brush Run Church, convinced that immersion was the only proper form of baptism,* was welcomed into the Redstone Baptist Association. Alexander spent the next several years itinerating throughout Ohio, Indiana, Kentucky, Tennessee and West Virginia and making converts. Throughout his travels he emphasized a Christianity that recaptured the essence of New Testament faith and life, free from denominational and creedal restrictions and ecumenical* in its acceptance of all who confessed Jesus as Savior and had been baptized by immersion. Drawing largely from Baptists and others who were open to his basic revivalistic emphases, Campbell formed groups of believers who called themselves "Disciples of Christ"* and were known to outsiders as "Campbellites."

Campbell found debate to be congenial to his task of spreading his message of authentic Christianity. Whether the subject be baptism, Christian evidences (with Robert Owen* in 1829) or Roman Catholicism* (with Archbishop Purcell* in 1837), Campbell was an able frontier spokesman for the truth of the gospel. But his reputation was not limited to the frontier. In 1847 he traveled abroad, preaching and teaching in several of the leading cities of Europe. Two successive monthly journals, *The Christian Baptist* (1823-1830) and *The Millennial Harbinger* (1830-1866), contributed to make the Disciples of Christ the fastest growing religious movement in nineteenth-century America (growing from 22,000 adherents in 1832 to nearly 200,000 by 1860). In 1840 Campbell chartered Bethany College in Bethany, Virginia (now West Virginia), to provide a more learned ministry for his growing movement. There he served as president (1840-1860).

The affiliation between Campbell's Brush Run Church and The Redstone Baptist Association lasted until 1825 when they broke from the Association over its adherence to the Philadelphia Confession of Faith. While the Campbellites and the Baptists agreed on many issues (e.g., the authority of the Bible,* the autonomy of local congregations, believers' baptism by immersion), the Campbellites could not accept the use of creedal statements and disagreed over the purpose of baptism, the frequency of the Lord's Supper, the operation of the Holy Spirit in conversion* and requirements for church membership.*

On January 1, 1832, a group of 12,000 Disciples and 10,000 of Barton W. Stone's* group known as "Christians" came together for a meeting in Lexington, Kentucky. Within a few years the two groups were joined to form the Christian Church (Disciples of Christ),* although nearly half of Stone's total movement distrusted the Campbellite formulation of baptism and did not join in the union.

Campbell published an English translation of the New Testament (1827) and authored several books, including *Psalms, Hymns and Spiritual Songs* (1834); *The Christian System* (1839) and *Christian Baptism* (1854). His theology,* with its emphasis on the simplicity of New Testament Christianity, free from the accretions of history and tradition, was a theology readily wedded to the ethos of the American frontier.* The Bible provided the only authority* for restoring simple evangelical* Christianity, and this principle in turn protected individual freedom of opinion. Scripture was not only the final authority in matters of faith and practice, it was also to be the guarantor of individual freedom in religious, personal and ethical* matters. These emphases, along with his willingness to synthesize the best thought of his day with the Christian revelation and his concern for applying biblical truth to the ethical issues, made his movement a vital force in American religion.

See also CAMPBELL, THOMAS.

BIBLIOGRAPHY. *DAB* II; *DARB;* J. R. Kellems, *Alexander Campbell and the Disciples* (1930); T. L. Miethe, *The Philosophy and Ethics of Alexander Campbell* (1984); *NCAB* 4; R. Richardson, *Memoirs of Alexander Campbell,* 2 vols. (1897).

T. L. Miethe

Campbell, Thomas (1763-1854). Cofounder, with his son Alexander Campbell,* of the Restoration Movement.* Born in County Down, Ireland, and raised an Anglican,* Campbell graduated from the University of Glasgow in 1786 and became a minister* in the Seceder Presbyterian* Church of Scotland. Campbell continued his theological education by enrolling in a theological school run by Anti-Burgher Presbyterians. But Campbell was increasingly disturbed by the divisions among Scottish Presbyterians* and, at the cost of his health, worked tirelessly for unity.

In April 1807, on the advice of his physician, Campbell set sail for America. Settling in Pennsylvania, Campbell soon came into conflict with fellow Presbyterians over matters of Calvinist* doctrine* and the administration of the Lord's Supper.* In 1809 Campbell finally withdrew from the Presbyterians and founded a fellowship called the Christian Association of Washington, named after Washington County, Pennsylvania. The purpose of the Association was to promote biblical Christianity and Christian union, its sole creed being "Where the Scriptures speak, we speak; where the Scriptures are silent, we are silent."

The founding document of the movement, Thomas Campbell's *Declaration and Address,* was written in September 1809 and consisted of thirteen propositions grouped around three concepts: (1) the sinfulness of divisions within the body of Christ; (2) the sufficiency of the Bible* as the only standard for doctrine; (3) the necessity of love and forbearance as essential manifestations of Christian spirit. Joined in that same year by his able son Alexander, the two Campbells went on to found the Brush Run Church. As the movement grew Thomas handed the leadership over to Alexander and spent several restless years living

and teaching in Ohio; Pittsburgh, Pennsylvania; and Burlington, Vermont. He died in Bethany, West Virginia, at the age of ninety and is remembered as the founder of the movement that would issue in the churches now known generally as the Churches of Christ* or Disciples of Christ.*

See also CAMPBELL, ALEXANDER.

BIBLIOGRAPHY. A. Campbell, *Memoirs of Elder Thomas Campbell,* 2 vols. (1861); *DAB* II; *DARB;* L. G. McAllister, *Thomas Campbell: Man of the Book* (1954). T. L. Miethe

Campbell, Will D. *See* COMMITTEE OF SOUTHERN CHURCHMEN.

Campus Crusade for Christ International. An evangelistic* organization. Campus Crusade was founded in 1951 on the campus of the University of California at Los Angeles by a former businessman and seminarian, William ("Bill") R. Bright.* The organization is committed to fulfilling the Great Commission of spreading the gospel throughout the world, particularly among college students. An important tool for evangelization is a well-known booklet, entitled *Have You Heard of the Four Spiritual Laws?* that serves as a guide for converting people to Jesus Christ. Emphasizing commitment rather than doctrine,* Campus Crusade is ecumenical* in spirit, with many religious denominations* represented on its staff.

In 1962 the headquarters for Campus Crusade was moved to a former luxury hotel complex at Arrowhead Springs near San Bernardino, California. From this location, direction is given to the 16,000 staff and volunteer members working in approximately 150 countries and ministering to such diverse groups of people as college students, athletes, high-school students, businessmen, military personnel and prison inmates. The organization has also been involved in high-profile evangelistic work, such as Explo '72, that attracted 85,000 Christians to Dallas, Texas; Explo '74, that attracted 1.3 million people to Seoul, Korea; and Explo '85, that involved an eighteen-satellite hookup with 600,000 Christians at 100 different locations throughout the world. Other prominent ministries of Campus Crusade include the International School of Theology and New Life Training Centers.

BIBLIOGRAPHY. B. Bright, *Come Help Change the World* (1979); R. Quebedeaux, *I Found It!; The Story of Bill Bright and Campus Crusade* (1979).

K. L. Staggers

Campus Ministries. Christian organizations and

movements founded to nurture Christian faith in college students and to influence the direction of higher education.* Higher education began as a religious movement in America. In 1636 Puritans* founded Harvard College* in Cambridge, Massachusetts, to train ministers* and other elites who would provide religious leadership in the new colony. Harvard was closely associated with the church, and ministers were always appointed as president. Harvard was not unique in its initial purpose. Yale,* Princeton* and a host of lesser colleges were founded with a similar vision in mind.

Over time, however, nearly all of these schools became secularized,* drifted from the original vision of their founders and loosened or severed their ties to organized religion. Religion began to function on campuses as little more than an academic discipline. The addition of such new fields of study as sociology, psychology and anthropology further relativized traditional religion. The emergence of state colleges after the Civil War* and the modern university in the late nineteenth century necessitated the creation of complex administrative structures and increased the momentum toward greater academic specialization, thus making religion ever more marginal in academic life.

The advent of campus ministries can be understood largely as a response to these developments. The early evangelical* student movement became the first model of what is known today as campus ministries. Many colleges had become inhospitable to Christianity. Small groups of Christians began to meet in secret to support one another, pray for revival* and plan strategies for evangelism.* The famous Haystack Prayer Meeting* near Williams College in 1806 provided a major impetus for the worldwide Protestant missionary movement.*

By the late nineteenth century these small campus groups and organizations, founded to nurture devotional life, stimulate theological thinking, evangelize the unreached or uncommitted, and pursue such worthy causes as abolition* and temperance,* had spawned many larger organizations, such as the YMCA,* the YWCA* and the Student Volunteer Movement,* which began at a conference in Northfield,* Massachusetts, in 1886 under the leadership of Dwight L. Moody.* John R. Mott* also emerged as a giant leader in the movement. From 1899 to 1914 the SVM sent out 4,500 missionaries. The World's Student Christian Federation* was founded in 1895. The enormous influence of these organizations continued well into the twentieth century. Several of them merged

in 1934 to form the National Intercollegiate Christian Council.

Large university churches were also started in the nineteenth century to cultivate religious life on secular campuses. Though churches have been closely associated with academic institutions from the beginning of American history, these churches were founded with the intention of evangelizing and training students who would otherwise lack Christian influence. Their pastors were (and still are) noted for being great preachers and intellectuals. These churches have often provided important services to college students, such as counseling, small groups, Christian education* and hospitality.

At the turn of the century, some denominational leaders, concerned about the students who were being lost to the faith at state colleges and universities, organized student foundations and commissioned pastors to become campus ministers. The first foundation was organized at the University of Illinois in 1907. Over time such groups as the Disciples Student Fellowship and the United Student Fellowship of the United Church of Christ* were founded. Originally intended to keep students within the orbit of particular denominations, these ministries now provide a vast number of services to university campuses—small-group Bible studies,* religious education, worship,* political activism, counseling, ecumenical activities and service projects. Many of these foundations merged together to form the National Student Christian Council (1944) to strengthen their work and develop deeper ecumenical ties. This federation of denominational campus ministries merged later with the Student Volunteer and Interseminary Movement to form the National Student Christian Federation (1959). The Roman Catholic Church started similar ministries in its Pax Romana and Newman* clubs, and Jewish groups in America founded the World Union of Jewish Students.

The emergence of neo-evangelicalism* in the 1940s introduced a new kind of campus ministry, the parachurch* organization. Groups like Inter-Varsity Christian Fellowship,* Campus Crusade for Christ* and the Navigators* were founded in the 1940s and 1950s as an alternative to mainline campus ministries. They represent a "back to the basics" philosophy. Eschewing politics, they concentrate on devotional life, fellowship,* evangelism* and missions.*

See also AWAKENINGS, COLLEGE.

BIBLIOGRAPHY. G. L. Earnshaw, ed., *The Campus Ministry* (1964); C. P. Shedd, *The Church Follows Its Students* (1938); L. A. Cremin, *American Edu-*

cation: The National Experience (1970); K. Underwood, ed., The Church, the University, and Social Policy (1969); J. E. Cantelon, A Protestant Approach to the Campus Ministry (1964).

G. L. Sittser

Cana Conferences. Spiritual and educational program for Roman Catholic* married couples. The Cana Conference movement traces its beginnings to family renewal days conducted by Rev. John Delaney, S.J., in New York City in 1943 and a retreat* held in St. Louis during October 1944, conducted by Rev. Edward Dowling, S.J., in honor of our Lady of Cana. The conferences originated as a day of joint spiritual renewal* for Catholic married couples, during which they were instructed on the proper supernatural dignity and sacramentality of Christian marriage and included a renewal of their wedding vows.

Many Americans in the post-World War 2* era believed that the American family was in crisis, due largely to the effects of widespread secularism* in American society. The Cana movement and the Christian Family Movement,* both of which shared many of the same leaders and participants, sought to renew the Catholic family and to use a revitalized Catholic family life to combat secularism and eventually effect a Christian reconstruction of American society.

Cana and the Christian Family Movement helped lay the basis for the active and varied family-life ministries of the Church in the Post-Vatican 2* period and inspired related activities such as pre-Cana conferences for couples preparing for marriage and Cana Clubs, gatherings of groups of Catholic couples. Cana was among the first national-level American Catholic social movements in which laypersons were instrumental.

BIBLIOGRAPHY. J. M. Burns, "American Catholics and the Family Crisis, 1930-1962: The Ideological and Organizational Response" (unpublished Ph.D. dissertation, University of Notre Dame, 1982); A. H. Clemens, The Cana Movement in the U.S. (1953).

D. L. Salvaterra

Canadian Baptist Federation. A loose confederation of four autonomous Baptist Conventions/Unions. The founding denominations are: The United Baptist Convention of the Maritime (now Atlantic) Provinces (560 churches, 62,000 members); the Baptist Convention of Ontario and Quebec (382 churches, 46,000 members) and the Baptist Union of Western Canada (162 churches, 21,000 members). In 1970 the Union d'Eglises baptistes françaises au Canada, or Union of

French Baptist Churches in Canada (22 churches, 1,200 members), joined the Federation. Previously known as the Baptist Federation of Canada (1944), the Federation has held its current name since 1983.

Atlantic Baptists trace their history to the late 1800s when British Empire Loyalists emigrated following the American Revolution.* Growth attributable to the Alline* revivals and Free Will Baptist* missionary enterprise eventually resulted in an Arminian* stream which coalesced with Calvinistic* Baptists to form the United Baptist Convention of the Maritime (now Atlantic) Provinces in 1905-1906. The Baptist Convention of Ontario and Quebec (1888) was organized in Upper and Lower Canada by Baptist emigrants from Britain and the U.S., the majority of them Particular Baptists.* Baptist witness in Western Canada began in Manitoba in 1873 through the initiative of Ontario missionaries, and in British Columbia in 1875 with American Baptist support. In 1907 to 1909 four provincial conventions founded the Baptist Union of Western Canada. The Union d'Eglises baptistes françaises au Canada (1969) is the indigenous product of the historic Grand Ligne Mission. Canadian Baptists support four theological colleges, one junior college and two lay* training institutes.

In the 1840s and in the decade of the 1900s, attempts were made to unite Baptists in Canada. However, it was only in 1944, in Saint John, New Brunswick, that the Federation emerged as a national coordinating agency. The structure is presbygational, with a twenty-six member council nominated by the convention/unions, but it is consental in practice. An inspirational Triennial Assembly elects officers but lacks legislative or fiscal authority. In the 1920s the fundamentalist-modernist controversy produced schisms from the Baptist Convention of Ontario and Quebec as well as the Baptist Union of Western Canada. In 1965 the resulting communions organized a second indigenous Baptist denomination, the Canada-wide Fellowship of Evangelical Baptist Churches.

The Canadian Baptist Federation, through its Canadian Baptist Relief and Development Fund, cooperates with the Canadian Baptist Overseas Mission Board and numerous relief agencies overseas. In Canada the Federation serves as the voice of Canadian Baptists before governments, and it provides ministerial support services and limited publication assistance. The Federation's headquarters are in Mississauga, Ontario.

BIBLIOGRAPHY. H. Renfree, Heritage and Horizon: The Baptist Story in Canada (1988); E. Levy,

The Baptists of the Maritime Provinces, 1753-1946 (1946); S. Ivison and F. Rosser, *The Baptists in Upper and Lower Canada before 1813* (1946); J. E. Harris, *The Baptist Union of Western Canada* (1976); E. A. Therrien, *Baptist Work in French Canada* (1954). W. E. Ellis

Canadian Council of Churches. An ecumenical organization founded in 1944 as a national expression of the worldwide ecumenical movement.* In its origin the Council reflected the spirit of cooperation and the institutional sense of need engendered by World War 2.* It was developed by the major Protestant* denominations* as a consultative body to help coordinate the growing number of cooperative ventures in the fields of social service, religious education,* evangelism* and overseas missions.*

Although the Canadian Council of Churches works closely with the World Council of Churches,* it has never achieved the prominence or influence that the National Council of Churches* has in the U.S. or even the British Council of Churches in the United Kingdom. This may in part be explained by the denominational success and spirit of self-sufficiency of the 1950s, the strong sense of heritage within the Canadian churches and the fallout from the failure of union negotiations between the United Church of Canada* and the Anglican Church of Canada,* the two largest members of the Council. After 1975 an attempt was made to develop a more comprehensive body which the Roman Catholics* would join, but this became unnecessary when the Roman Catholic Church joined the Council as an associate member in 1985.

The present membership includes the United Church of Canada, the Anglican Church of Canada, the Presbyterian Church in Canada,* the newly united Evangelical Lutheran Church in Canada, the Baptist Convention of Ontario and Quebec *(See* Canadian Baptists), a number of the Eastern and Orthodox* churches, the Disciples of Christ,* the Quakers,* and two Communions which hold membership in the Evangelical Fellowship of Canada* as well—The Salvation Army* and the Reformed Church in America.* At present the public profile of the Council suggests that its main concern is with justice and peace issues, although it continues to press for greater convergence among its members and to encourage church unions wherever possible.

See also CHURCH UNION MOVEMENTS; ECUMENICAL MOVEMENT; ECUMENICITY; NATIONAL COUNCIL OF CHURCHES; WORLD COUNCIL OF CHURCHES.

BIBLIOGRAPHY. J. W. Grant, *The Church in the Canadian Era* (1972). I. S. Rennie

Candler, Warren Akin (1857-1941). Bishop,* educator and leader of the Methodist Episcopal Church,* South. Born in Villa Rica, Georgia, Candler attended Emory College and in 1875 joined the North Georgia Conference. In 1888 he was elected president of his alma mater, serving there until his election as bishop in 1898.

Candler was a conservative leader in a time of transition. He bitterly opposed the efforts to reunify the Southern and the Northern Methodist Churches.* He also cautioned the Church against political involvements, a stance in sharp contrast with the inclinations of most of Methodism, even Southern Methodism during the later years of his life. Though he was a strong supporter of Methodist missions, his greatest contributions were in the area of education. He and his family were influential in moving Emory College to Atlanta as Emory University in 1914. He became chancellor of the new school and served until 1921. Later, the school of theology was named in his honor.

BIBLIOGRAPHY. M. K. Bauman, *Warren Akin Candler, the Conservative as Idealist* (1981); *DAB* 3; A. M. Pierce, *Giant Against the Sky: the Life of Bishop Warren Akin Candler* (1948).
M. E. Dieter

Cane Ridge Revival. Largest and most famous camp meeting* of the Second Great Awakening.* Barton W. Stone, after investigating reports of religious revivals* in western Kentucky, laid plans for a "sacramental meeting" at his Cane Ridge meeting house* (Presbyterian) in Bourbon County, Kentucky, near the county seat of Paris. The revival scene that took place during August 1801, defies objective description. Some have considered it the greatest outpouring of the Holy Spirit since Pentecost.

The crowd, variously estimated at between ten and twenty-five thousand, began to gather on Friday afternoon. Crude preaching* platforms were hastily constructed in the rough clearing. Presbyterian, Baptist* and Methodist* preachers forgot sectarian distinctions. They labored simultaneously through daytime heat and by the light of campfire, graphically portraying the evils of hell* and glory of personal redemption. Within the crowds—tense with excitement and expectation, and near exhaustion—all manner of emotionalism broke loose. Stone detailed six types of bodily agitations or "exercises" that seemed to have touched many: "falling," "jerks," "dancing," "barking" (a form of the jerks), "running" and "singing."

After six or seven days of virtually continuous noise and chaos, the course of Protestantism* in the West was forever changed. The spiritual fires from Cane Ridge touched off waves of camp-meeting revivalism* that lasted for years. Through these events Western churches, particularly those in the Midwest and upland South, were revitalized and thousands of the unchurched were brought into the fold of organized religion.

BIBLIOGRAPHY. J. R. Boles, *The Great Revival, 1787-1805* (1972); R. McNemar, *The Kentucky Revival* (1807); B. W. Stone, "A Short History of the Life of Barton W. Stone," in J. R. Rogers, *The Cane Ridge Meeting-House* (1910).

D. B. Eller

Cannon, James, Jr. (1864-1944). Methodist* bishop* and temperance* advocate. Born in Salisbury, Maryland, Cannon was educated at Randolph-Macon College in Virginia (A.B., 1884), Princeton Theological Seminary* (B.D., 1888) and Princeton University* (M.A., 1890), Cannon was admitted by the Virginia Conference as a minister* in 1888. Advancement in the church began with his appointment in 1894 as principal of Blackstone (Virginia) Female Institute, which prospered under his nearly twenty-five years of leadership. Editorship of denominational and temperance newspapers from 1894 to 1912 brought attention to both Cannon and his ideas. As bishop (1918 to 1938), he undertook episcopal duties in the South and Southwest; supervised missionary* activities in Mexico, Cuba, Brazil and the Congo; and chaired the Commission on Temperance and Social Service.

Along with deep ties to the South and to Southern Methodism, Cannon had national, ecumenical* and international interests. He sought to unify American Methodists and to encourage greater cooperation among American Christians through the Federal Council of Churches.* He was one of the few American churchmen to participate in all the major ecumenical streams that joined to form the World Council of Churches* in 1948. In 1919, he helped to organize the World League Against Alcoholism, which sought to bring about a "dry" world.

Closely associated with the national Anti-Saloon League* almost from its inception, he organized a state league in Virginia in 1901 and served as superintendent from 1910 to 1920. Almost single-handedly he persuaded Virginia politicians and voters to adopt statewide prohibition in 1914. As chairman of the National Legislative Committee of the national League, he played a vital role in the framing and ratification of the Eighteenth Amendment. During the 1920s, he was the leading lobbyist for the "dry" cause in Washington, D.C.

The Democratic Party's nomination of Al Smith,* the "wet" governor of New York, for president convinced Cannon that the Eighteenth Amendment faced a serious challenge. His leadership of the Anti-Smith Democrats played a major role in the defection of four Southern states which had voted for Democratic presidential nominees since Reconstruction.

Cannon's political participation aroused powerful opposition, and within a year he faced charges ranging from flour hoarding during World War 1* to adultery and misuse of campaign funds. Officially, guilt was never established, but Cannon's reputation was damaged, and he never regained the power he once held.

BIBLIOGRAPHY. J. Cannon, Jr., *Bishop Cannon's Own Story,* ed. R. L. Watson, Jr. (1955); V. Dabney, *Dry Messiah: The Life of Bishop Cannon* (1949); *DAB* 3; *DARB; NCAB* 35.

G. F. Goodwin

Canon. A religious standard or list. The word *canon* is used in various ways, all of which derive from its ancient root meaning "a measuring rod," which set a fixed quantity. A canon may be a church regulation, usually decreed by a council and listed in the "canon law."* *Canon* also names the unchanging core of the liturgy,* like the Sanctus and Jesus' words from the Last Supper. Some persons are titled *canon,* usually cathedral* priests* who perform regular services. *Canon* also is the list of officially recognized, or "canonized,"* saints.

The most common American usage speaks of the Bible* as the canon because it is the authoritative, established collection of writings recognized as God's word. For most Christians, this collection was defined before A.D. 400, although Protestants* and Catholics* disagree somewhat about the exact composition of this list. Recent American scholarship has devised "canonical hermeneutics" as an alternative to historical-critical method; it represents a post-critical attempt to interpret biblical texts in relationship to their setting within the canon of Scripture.

BIBLIOGRAPHY. F. F. Bruce, *The Canon of Scripture* (1988); J. A. Sanders, *From Sacred Story to Sacred Text* (1987).

P. D. Steeves

Canon Law. In its most general sense the term refers to the various laws and prescriptions issued by ecclesiastical authority* for the governance of a given church. Canon law, in that sense, distinguishes itself from civil law which issues from secular government.

In the Roman Catholic* Church the first code of canon law was promulgated in 1917 as a distillation of all of the earlier laws which had been part of the church's tradition for centuries. The code applied only to the Latin rite* of the church (the Eastern rites* were to have their own code). In 1959 Pope John XXIII* announced that the code was to be revised. The new code was promulgated by Pope John Paul II* in 1983. The new code abrogates previous legislation and stands as the law for the Latin rite of the Roman Catholic Church.

The code consists of 1,752 canons divided into seven books of varying length. Book one treats general norms in canon law. Book two, entitled "The People of God," sets out the rights and obligations of both clergy* and laity.* It specifies papal,* episcopal* and parochial rights and obligations as well as rules for the various religious orders* of the church. Book three, on the teaching office of the church, treats the preaching* ministry* of the church, missionary* activities and Catholic education. Book four concerns the worship* of the church in its sacramental* and nonsacramental forms. Book five discusses the temporal goods of the church. Books six and seven treat sanctions and legal processes in the church.

BIBLIOGRAPHY. *The Code of Canon Law* (1983).
L. S. Cunningham

Canon of the Mass. Also called the Eucharistic* Prayer, it is the fixed formula found in the Roman Catholic* liturgy* (with variations it is also central to Orthodox,* Anglican* and other liturgically oriented churches) that is proclaimed by the priest* after the offerings of the gifts of bread and wine. The central focus of the Canon—meaning in this case a fixed prayer—is the formula of consecration: This is my body; this is my blood. The Canon ends with the great Amen. Immediately after, the Communion* begins with the recitation of the Lord's Prayer.

There are various forms of the Canon or Eucharistic Prayer (known as the Anaphora* in the Eastern churches) that have come down through history. Four canons are in current use in the Roman Catholic church, with elements going back to the so-called Canon of Hippolytus, which was in use in Rome in the very early third century.

The Protestant* Reformers, with the exception of the English reformer Thomas Cranmer (1489-1556), rejected the Canon of the Mass nearly in its entirety, preferring a simple narration of the institution of the Lord's Supper* and a prayer for its worthy reception.

See also MASS.

BIBLIOGRAPHY. G. Dix, *The Shape of the Liturgy* (1945); R. C. D. Jasper and G. J. Cuming, eds., *Prayers of the Eucharist: Early and Reformed* (1980). L. S. Cunningham

Canonization. The term used by Roman Catholics* to describe the formal procedures and process by which a deceased man or woman is defined and declared a saint* gloriously reigning in heaven, someone whose memory should be kept by the whole church and to whom prayers may be directed. Early Christian piety included a lively sense of the presence and power of angels and of deceased men and women who had died for their faith as martyrs or who had lived in heroically holy fashion. As early as the fourth century there is evidence of public church honors given to "confessors," those who had survived persecution and torture without denying Christ.

Between the sixth and tenth centuries local churches identified and venerated increasing numbers of holy men and women. These, although deceased, were kept in memory and prayed to as if they still walked among the living in the community. Local bishops* were obliged to exercise some control over this neighborhood enthusiasm, but this proved inadequate to prevent abuses, invention of fake martyrdoms and exaggerations of piety. At the end of the eleventh century local bishops' rights to authorize such veneration were restricted. In 1588 the papacy established an agency, the Congregation of Rites, to receive petitions for papal canonization. In 1634 Pope* Urban VII removed the rights of local bishops to authorize beatification* (meaning the public veneration of someone by a particular region or religious order*) or canonization (the authorization for public veneration by the entire church).

Today a regular process has been established for gathering data about a would-be saint. A local bishop can begin the investigation, the results of which go to the Congregation of Rites (now renamed Congregation for the Causes of Saints) which can then launch a full investigation using its own appointed judges. If the results of the investigation are positive, the candidate may be declared "blessed," and venerated in a local church or religious order. Except for martyrs, two authenticated miracles ascribed to his or her intercession after death must be proven in order for the subject to be beatified. Further distinctly different miracles must be attested before the subject is canonized, receiving the title "Saint."

See also BEATIFICATION; SAINTS, CULT OF THE.

BIBLIOGRAPHY. P. Molinari, "Canonization of Saints," *NCE* 3.   B. Moran

Capers, William (1790-1855). Methodist* missionary* and bishop.* Born in South Carolina of Huguenot* ancestry, Capers rose to prominence as a Methodist clergyman.* A series of religious experiences* in 1808 called him to the ministry, where he joined others opposed to human bondage. By 1830, however, Capers defended slavery. As this issue festered, he earnestly tried to prevent the North-South schism which split his denomination in 1844.

Eloquence and dedication brought Capers influence in his church and throughout the South. He rode numerous circuits,* supervised missions to the Creek Indians, represented his church in Great Britain, occupied prominent pulpits in South Carolina and Georgia, edited the *Southern Christian Advocate* and traveled extensively as a bishop of the Methodist Episcopal Church, South (1846-1855). But Capers was proudest of his missionary work among plantation slaves. He convinced many masters to accept this mission and in the course of his ministry he reached African-Americans on hundreds of plantations and contributed to the system of oral instruction by authoring a catechism* and book of sermons.*

BIBLIOGRAPHY. *AAP* 7; *DAB* II; D. G. Mathews, *Slavery and Methodism: A Chapter in American Morality, 1780-1845* (1965); W. M. Wightman, *Life of William Capers, D.D.* (1858).

D. B. Touchstone

Capital Punishment. Execution carried out under authority of the law as the penalty for crime. Capital punishment in America has been characterized by three major trends: (1) limiting the types of crimes for which execution is permitted; (2) the unsuccessful effort to have capital punishment declared unconstitutional; and (3) the development of standards for imposing the death penalty.

As the result of both legislative and executive action (beginning in colonial times) and more recent Supreme Court rulings, the crimes for which execution may be imposed have been narrowed to those resulting in death of the victim. While the constitutionality of the death penalty for any crime has been hotly litigated since the mid-1960s (e.g., *Furman* v. *Georgia,* 1972; *Gregg* v. *Georgia,* 1976; *Coker* v. *Georgia,* 1977; *McClesky* v. *Kemp,* 1987), the Supreme Court has upheld the sanction for

murder, but has required states to provide rational, objective standards for imposing it.

American Christians have taken one of three general positions on the issue. Some, including William Penn,* founder of colonial Pennsylvania, have argued that when the Old and New Testament are considered together, a moral imperative against the use of the death penalty emerges. Virtually every mainline* denomination* currently takes this position.

Others, including the Puritans,* have held that Scripture* offers at least a moral imperative, if not an outright mandate, for states to administer the death penalty. This is the prevailing view of contemporary evangelicals* and fundamentalists.* While the Old Testament law provided for the execution of those who committed any of at least eighteen different crimes, most Christian advocates of the death penalty (taking their authority from Gen 9:6) focus on the crime of murder.

A third view is that the death penalty is neither mandated nor prohibited but is a permitted sanction so long as biblical conditions are met. The rationale for this position is that while the Old Testament provides for the death penalty, the examples of murderers who were not executed (e.g., Moses and David) undermine the position that capital punishment is required. The death penalty is therefore permitted, but only when biblical principles concerning its application have been met. These include proportionality (Ex 21:23-25); intent (Num 35:22-24); due process (Deut 17:8-9; Num 35); individual responsibility (Deut 24:16); fairness, regardless of the wealth or class of the accused (Num 35:29-31; Ex 23:6-7); reluctance to execute (Ezek 33:11); and certainty of guilt (Deut 17:6; Num 35:30).

Interestingly, these principles are strikingly similar to the issues raised before the Supreme Court in the last two decades. The Court has ruled that the death penalty for rape is "grossly disproportionate and excessive punishment" (*Coker* v. *Georgia,* 1977). It has decided that actual intent need not be proven if the accused had a major role in the crime and exhibited "reckless indifference to human life" (*Tison* v. *Arizona,* 1987). The lack of adequate due process protections led the Court to strike down all existing death penalty statutes (*Furman* v. *Georgia,* 1972), with new death penalty procedures upheld as constitutional four years later (*Gregg* v. *Georgia,* 1976). The racial inequities in imposing the death penalty were a major reason for the *Furman* decision, but evidence that those who kill whites are eleven times more likely to be executed than those who kill blacks was ruled irrelevant unless racial discrimination in the particular case can be proven (*McClesky* v. *Kemp,* 1987). Mandatory death penalty statutes were declared unconstitutional as failing to allow evidence of mitigating circumstances (*Woodson* v. *North Carolina,* 1976).

BIBLIOGRAPHY. H. A. Bedau, ed., *The Death Penalty in America* (1982).   D. W. Van Ness

Capitalism and Christianity. The Protestants* who settled the thirteen original colonies, and whose influence was normative for what eventually became the U.S., included many merchants. Although in colonial times churches still imposed certain restrictions on economic activity, mostly stemming from medieval ideas about the use of wealth, on the whole Christianity and the capitalist system grew together on American soil.

The rise of industrialism and the concomitant institution of the corporation presented the churches with a new challenge in the half-century before the Civil War.* For the most part leading clergy were supporters of the capitalist system. Their support stemmed mainly from a philosophical acceptance of the economic theory of laissez faire, by which economic activity operates according to certain impersonal laws, and participants in such activity must enjoy maximum freedom to pursue their goals. Such views were commonly propounded in textbooks of ethics and of political economy, many of them written by clergy.

Occasionally, radical ideas in one area spilled over into others. For example, the Unitarian* Theodore Parker,* a leading crusader to abolish slavery, was also a socialist of sorts. However, liberal* theology,* as in the most famous preacher of the day, Henry Ward Beecher,* often included some version of laissez faire, if only because the latter economic philosophy also called itself liberal because of its emphasis on personal freedom. The theological liberals' optimistic view of human nature tended to give them an equally optimistic view of the existing social and economic order.

In the late nineteenth century the Gospel of Wealth* had a wide following in the churches, according to which the pursuit of wealth was a divine command, although the wealthy were also expected to patronize worthy social causes. The Presbyterian* layman* Andrew Carnegie was its virtual embodiment.

However, the excesses of industrial capitalism inevitably gave rise to criticisms of the system, including support for labor unions (almost universally condemned by churchmen earlier in the century) and demands that government intervene

in the economy to correct glaring abuses. Rarely, however, did clergy or other prominent Christians espouse socialism* or any other program which challenged the basic right of private property. A partial exception was the religious support—some of it from Catholic* priests*—given to Henry George's "single tax" movement, which was regarded by critics as confiscatory of wealth. Until well after the turn of the century, the debate within American Christianity was not over the legitimacy of the capitalist system itself but over its abuses and how they should be corrected.

The Social Gospel Movement,* flourishing from about 1885 to 1915, argued passionately that there was a direct moral and religious duty to work for such correction. The movement had born tangible fruit by World War 1,* when many of the leading Protestant denominations had established national offices concerned with social issues, almost always supporting "progressive" causes. So did the Federal Council of Churches,* the earliest national Protestant ecumenical federation. But socialists as such continued to be a small minority within the churches, for the most part occupying fringe positions.

Economic issues had been particularly acute for the Catholic Church because the vast majority of its American members were of the working classes. Taking their lead from Pope Leo XIII,* who in 1891 issued a famous letter on capital and labor, *Rerum Novarum,* the American bishops generally favored labor unions and movements of economic reform. In 1919 the Bishops' Program of Social Reconstruction* gave official support to a basically progressive economic policy. However, as with Protestantism, Catholic social thought* firmly upheld the sacredness of private property.

Between 1920 and 1940 most American churches moved to the left on such issues, to the point where some liberal Protestants (e.g., the journal *The Christian Century**) gave at least cautious support to the Communist experiment in the Soviet Union. During the 1930s the liberal churches overwhelmingly supported the New Deal, as did the most influential Catholic spokesmen, such as John A. Ryan,* head of the bishops' social-action office in Washington.

Criticism of this liberalism came sometimes from the left (e.g., the Fellowship of Socialist Christians, which included Reinhold Niebuhr,* among others) and sometimes the right—the newly militant fundamentalist* movement within Protestantism tended on the whole to be strongly procapitalist and critical of the New Deal.

In the period after 1945, mainstream religious

opinion in the U.S. tended to accept the basic soundness of the American capitalist system, while also assuming the essential rightness of liberal programs of reform. Militant defenders of laissez faire tended to be limited to the fundamentalist* wing of Protestantism and a few Roman Catholics.

The 1960s saw a resurgence of social radicalism in the churches, including expressions of admiration for Marxist regimes in various parts of the world, use of Marxist analysis in criticizing American capitalism and renewed calls for some form of socialism. Some of this institutionalized itself in the social-action departments of the National Council of Churches* and the various Protestant bodies. The 1985 Catholic bishops' statement on the economy was considerably more critical of capitalism than the bishops had ever been previously, although the right of private property was still affirmed.

Coincident with the presidency of Ronald Reagan,* there were also counter-movements by Christians (Peter Berger, Michael Novak) to defend the capitalist system, albeit not usually in terms of a philosophy of unrestricted laissez faire.

See also SOCIALISM, CHRISTIAN.

BIBLIOGRAPHY. A. I. Abell, *American Catholicism and Social Action* (1960); C. H. Hopkins, *The Rise of the Social Gospel in American Protestantism, 1865-1915* (1940); H. F. May, *Protestant Churches and Industrial America* (1949); R. M. Miller, *American Protestantism and Social Issues, 1919-1939* (1958); D. J. O'Brien, *American Catholics and Social Reform* (1968). J. F. Hitchcock

Cardinal. A member of the Sacred College of Cardinals, the chief Roman clergy.* The term originally applied to any clergyman permanently attached to a church. It later became the common designation for clergy attached to a central or episcopal* church, an ecclesiastical *cardo* (Latin, "hinge"); but during the Catholic Reformation it was restricted to the clergy in Rome. Roman cardinals, from the early Middle Ages, were deacons,* priests* or neighboring bishops* who formed the pope's* consistory, advising him and helping him administer the church. In 1568 the number was fixed at seventy, but John XXIII* removed the upper limit, and there are now more than one hundred. Since 1962 all have been raised to the episcopacy. They reside in Rome (unless away on special duties or as bishops of foreign dioceses); they head up curial offices, Roman congregations and church commissions; and (unless they are over eighty years of age) they vote to appoint a successor to a deceased pope, a privilege they have exercised since the Third Lateran Council (1179). J. G. Stackhouse

Carlsson, Erland (1822-1893). Swedish-American Lutheran* pastor* and home missionary.* Born in Elghult, Smoland Province, Sweden, Carlsson graduated from Lund University (1840) and was ordained* a Lutheran minister* in 1849. After serving parishes in Sweden, he immigrated to the U.S. in 1853 and became pastor of the newly founded Swedish Evangelical Lutheran Immanuel Church in Chicago. There he served the teeming multitudes of Swedish immigrants* then pouring into or through that booming frontier metropolis. His effectiveness is shown by the phenomenal growth of the congregation during his pastorate (1853-1875). Carlsson held a second pastorate in Andover, Illinois (1875-1887), and helped organize congregations in Illinois, Indiana and Minnesota.

One of the founding fathers of the Evangelical Lutheran Church, or Augustana Synod (1860), he was also involved in founding the Swedish Lutheran Publication Society (later called the *Augustana Book Concern*) and the Augustana Hospital in Chicago. Carlsson was elected to the first board of directors of the Augustana College and Seminary, and served as its chairman for many years. In addition to serving as treasurer and business manager of the school (1806-1809), he also served his church in a variety of other boards and committees. In 1887, Carlsson retired to his farm near Lindsborg, Kansas, because of ill health, and died there in 1893.

BIBLIOGRAPHY. E. Lindquist, *Shepherd of an Immigrant People* (1978). J. W. Lundeen

Carman, Albert (1833-1917). Canadian Methodist* leader. Born in the Methodist heartland of eastern Ontario, Carman was raised in the Methodist Episcopal Church,* which represented more fully than any branch of Canadian Methodism the Wesleyan* heritage mediated through the dynamism of American frontier* revivalism.* As principal of the denominational* educational institution, Albert College, Belleville, he made his reputation as a teacher, administrator and preacher.* In 1873 he was made bishop,* and in 1884, with the final union of Canadian Methodism, he became general superintendent.

A steadfast nineteenth-century evangelical,* he brought to his new position a deep concern for piety* and holiness,* as well as churchmanship, evangelism,* social concern and postmillennial* hope. With the opening of western Canada to agricultural settlement, he sought to mobilize

Methodism to meet the opportunity, while he was also concerned to lead the church in its ministry to the eastern industrial proletariat. Carman was also interested in interchurch cooperation and even potential union, seeing this as the likely way to stem the flood of Roman Catholicism* and Christianize Canada.

Remaining as superintendent* until 1915, he was caught in the theological conflicts of the era. In 1899 and 1907 his opposition forced Old Testament scholar G. B. Workman to be relieved of his post in two Methodist institutions, and in 1909 he engaged in an unsuccessful controversy with George Jackson of Victoria College, Toronto. He was convinced that the suspicions of supernaturalism evident in so much of biblical criticism (*See* Biblical Interpretation) were undercutting the roots of Christianity, eroding conversion* and Christian life and destroying the hope of Church Union* between the Methodists and Presbyterians.*   I. S. Rennie

Carmelites. A family of Roman Catholic* religious orders* with a common origin. The original Carmelite order began during the Crusades in Palestine on Mt. Carmel (c.1154) as the "Brothers of the Blessed Virgin Mary of Mount Carmel." It received its first official rule from Albert of Jerusalem in A.D. 1209 and official ecclesiastical approval from Pope Honorius III in 1226. From there it spread as one of the mendicant orders, emphasizing a life of seclusion with abstinence,* fasting* and silence as the chief ways of attaining the highest goal, that of union with God through prayer.* Traditionally the Carmelites minister through preaching,* teaching and writing.

By the sixteenth century the Carmelite order had allowed certain relaxations of the original discipline. Under two of its most celebrated members, St. Teresa of Avila (1515-1582) and St. John of the Cross (1542-1591), a reform was undertaken and a parallel order was created, the "Order of Discalced Brothers of the Virgin of Mary of Mt. Carmel." In addition to going barefoot (discalced), the new order distinguishes itself through greater discipline and more rigorous spiritual exercises. There is also a female counterpart of Carmelite nuns, who remain permanently cloistered and emphasize contemplative prayer.

BIBLIOGRAPHY. P. T. Rohrback, *Journey to Carith: The Story of the Carmelite Order* (1966).
                                    W. Corduan

Carnegie Council on Ethics and International Affairs. An interfaith organization seeking to relate religion and ethics to international affairs. Founded as the Church Peace Union in 1914 with a gift of $2 million from Andrew Carnegie, the organization was an early expression of interfaith cooperation between Protestants,* Catholics* and Jews. The leaders of this union, such as Charles S. McFarland and Frederick Lynch, tried to consolidate the peace ideals of all the major faiths, but the coming of World War 1* destroyed this vision. The Union was forced by this development to direct its resources into the funding of peace-education campaigns, and it also became an information center for ministers* and teachers. Despite the fact that it supported groups that engaged in political activity to promote peace, the Union insistently maintained the position that it was not a political-pressure group but an opinion-forming agency. By 1961 it was called the Council On Religion and International Affairs, adopting the current designation in 1986. In its efforts to relate religion and ethics to international affairs, it sponsors lectures and seminars and publishes newsletters and books on peace.

BIBLIOGRAPHY. C. DeBenedetti, *Origins of the North American Peace Movement 1915-1929* (1978).   R. G. Clouse

Carnegie Hall Conference (November 15-21, 1905). Also known as the Interchurch Conference on Federation, it led to the establishment of Federal Council of Churches of Christ in America* (FCC) in 1908. The National Federation of Churches and Christian Workers, an association of ecumenically minded Christians, directed Elias B. Sanford* in 1902 to organize a conference of official denominational* representatives. Under the chairmanship of William H. Roberts, the meeting convened in New York's Carnegie Hall, with representatives from twenty-nine Protestant denominations attending. Discussion centered around common interests, such as evangelism,* missions* and education, as well as social and international problems. The conference adopted a "Plan of Federation" which proposed the formation of the FCC with a constitution where theological differences were overlooked and cooperation between autonomous denominations emphasized. To bring the FCC into being, approval of the "Plan" was required by two-thirds of the denominations in attendance. Sanford was made corresponding secretary for the purpose of gaining this approval.

BIBLIOGRAPHY. S. M. Cavert, *The American Churches in the Ecumenical Movement, 1900-1968* (1968); E. B. Sanford, ed., *Church Federation:*

Interchurch Conference on Federation (1906).

B. V. Hillis

Carnell, Edward John (1919-1967). Evangelical* theologian* and educator. Born in Antigo, Wisconsin, Carnell grew up in a Baptist* parsonage. He attended Wheaton College* (B.A., 1941), where he was influenced by Gordon H. Clark, a Christian rationalist dedicated to the defense of orthodoxy.* Carnell received his seminary education at Westminster Theological Seminary (Th.B., Th.M., 1944) and concentrated on apologetics under Cornelius Van Til.* He later studied at Harvard University* (Th.D., 1948), writing his dissertation on the theology of Reinhold Niebuhr.* His second doctorate, in philosophy, came from Boston University (Ph.D., 1949), where he studied under E. S. Brightman* and wrote his dissertation on "The Problem of Verification in Søren Kierkegaard."*

In 1945 Carnell commenced his teaching career at Gordon College and Divinity School as professor of philosophy and religion. Three years later (1948) he moved to California to join the faculty of the newly founded Fuller Theological Seminary.* During his nineteen years at Fuller, he served in several positions. He was president of the school from 1954 to 1959 and at the time of his death was professor of ethics and philosophy of religion.

Carnell became one of the leaders in the intellectual awakening of conservative evangelicalism in America after World War 2.* His influence was extended through nine books. *An Introduction to Christian Apologetics* (1948) argued that Christianity satisfies the demands of reason, while two later books, *Christian Commitment* (1957) and *The Kingdom of Love and the Pride of Life* (1960), broadened his apologetic* to include "knowledge by acquaintance."

BIBLIOGRAPHY. R. Nelson, *The Making and Unmaking of an Evangelical Mind: The Case of Edward Carnell* (1988); J. A. Sims, *Edward John Carnell: Defender of the Faith* (1979); G. M. Marsden, *Reforming Fundamentalism: Fuller Seminary and the New Evangelicalism* (1987).

B. L. Shelley

Carrick, Samuel (1760-1809). Presbyterian* minister* and college president on the Tennessee frontier.* Carrick was born in York (now Adams) County, Pennsylvania, but as a youth moved to the Shenandoah Valley in Virginia. A member of the first graduating class of Liberty Hall Academy, he was ordained* to the Presbyterian ministry* in

1783. During the next few years he began occasional missionary* tours into the Tennessee country and in 1791 settled near the forks of the Holston and French Broad rivers, establishing Lebanon Church. One year later he organized a congregation at nearby Knoxville, the newly established capital of the Tennessee territory.

In 1793 Carrick opened in his home a seminary,* offering instruction in ancient languages, English, geography, logic and philosophy. In 1794 the school was chartered as Blount College, a nondenominational school named in honor of the territorial governor, Carrick becoming its president. The college admitted young women to its classes and was arguably the first such coeducational institution in America. During its first years enrollments were low and finances uncertain, and in 1807 the institution was renamed East Tennessee College to take advantage of a promise of Congressional land-grant support. After the Civil War* it would become the University of Tennessee. Carrick died unexpectedly in August 1809 and was memorialized in the *Knoxville Gazette* as "a much-needed man of culture in a pioneer community, a gentleman of commanding appearance, of great urbanity."

BIBLIOGRAPHY. *AAP* 3; *DAB* II; W. H. Foote, *Sketches of Virginia, Historical and Biographical* (1856); E. W. Crawford, *An Endless Line of Splendor* (1983).

W. J. Wade

Carroll, (B)enajah (H)arvey (1843-1914). Southern Baptist* pastor,* educator and controversialist. Born in Mississippi, Carroll received formal education at Baylor University (then Waco University). During the Civil War* he served in the Texas Rangers as well as in the Confederate army. After the war he served various Baptist* churches in Texas, including First Baptist Church in Waco (1871-1899). In 1899 he became corresponding secretary for the Texas Baptist Education Commission. During the years 1872-1905 he taught theology* at Baylor and then organized Baylor Theological Seminary in 1905. In 1908 the seminary was chartered as Southwestern Baptist Theological Seminary and moved to Fort Worth in 1910. Carroll was president of the seminary until his death in 1914. A popular preacher,* Carroll was an able spokesman for Southern Baptist doctrine* and polity, promoting evangelism* and attacking heresy.* Largely self-educated, he wrote extensively, with some thirty-three volumes published.

BIBLIOGRAPHY. R. A. Baker, *The Southern Baptist Convention and Its People, 1607-1972* (1974); W. W. Barnes, *The Southern Baptist Convention,*

1845-1953 (1954); J. M. Carroll, *Dr. B. H. Carroll, the Colossus of Baptist History* (1946).

B. J. Leonard

Carroll, Charles (1737-1832). Roman Catholic* patriot and U.S. Senator. Born in Annapolis, Maryland, on September 19, 1737, Carroll was educated in Jesuit* schools in Maryland and France. After law studies in France and England, he returned to Maryland in 1768. Because English law barred Catholics from a legal career, Carroll became a planter at his Maryland estate, Carrollton Manor, where he amassed a fortune that made him one of the wealthiest men in the colonies.

Carroll first ventured into public life in 1773 when he defended against Daniel Dulany the principle of no taxation without representation. With his cousin Rev. John Carroll,* later archbishop* of Baltimore, and Benjamin Franklin, he traveled to Canada in a futile effort to secure its support for the American Revolution.* A delegate to the Maryland Convention (1776), he sought to pass the resolution to bring about Maryland's separation from England, thus bringing it into line with the other colonies.

Elected to the Continental Congress in 1776, he was the first to sign the Declaration of Independence, doing so on Maryland's behalf. His leadership and risk-taking for the cause of independence encouraged American Catholics to give their overwhelming support to the Revolution. He retired from Congress in 1778 when elected to the Maryland Senate. After supporting ratification of the Constitution he was elected to the U.S. Senate in 1789. In 1792 he returned to the Maryland Senate until he retired from public life in 1800. He died on November 14, 1832, the last surviving signer of the Declaration of Independence.

BIBLIOGRAPHY. *DAB* II; T. O. Hanley, *Charles Carroll of Carrollton: The Making of a Revolutionary Gentleman* (1984); E. H. Smith, *Charles Carroll of Carrollton* (1942).   L. R. Riforgiato

Carroll, Daniel (1730-1796). Catholic* congressman. Born in Upper Marlboro, Maryland, on July 22, 1730, Daniel was the older brother of Archbishop* John Carroll.* After studying in Flanders, he returned to Maryland, married a cousin, Elizabeth Carroll, and amassed a fortune as a tobacco planter and merchant. An early champion of colonial independence, Carroll was elected to the Maryland Senate and Council (1777-1780). From 1780 to 1784 he sat in the Continental Congress as a member of Maryland's delegation. Carroll attended the Constitutional Convention in

Philadelphia in 1787-1788 and campaigned for ratification of the Constitution by his native state. He served a single term in the United States Congress (1789-1791) as a representative from Maryland, closing out his public life (1791-1795) as a member of a congressionally appointed commission mandated to select a site for the new federal capital. He was influential in the choice of the Potomac location where Washington, D.C. was constructed, within whose boundaries he owned land.

BIBLIOGRAPHY. *DAB* II; M. V. Geiger, *Daniel Carroll: A Framer of the Constitution* (1943).

L. R. Riforgiato

Carroll, John (1735-1815). First Roman Catholic* bishop* in the United States. Born in Upper Marlboro, Maryland, fourth of seven children (including Daniel Carroll, Jr.,* signer of the U.S. Constitution), Carroll's family was well-to-do, despite colonial penal laws against Roman Catholics. His father, Irish immigrant Daniel Carroll, Sr., owned tobacco plantations and an export-import business. His mother, Eleanor Darnall, belonged to an old Maryland Catholic family and was educated in France. Through her John was related to the major Maryland Catholic families, including the Charles Carrolls.*

After two years at a primary school run illegally by English Jesuit* priests* at Bohemia Manor near the head of the Chesapeake Bay, he enrolled (1748-1753) at the emigré English Jesuit college at St. Omer in French Flanders. Entering the Jesuit order in 1753, he studied at seminaries* in Watten (France) and Liege and Ghent (Belgium). Ordained* a Roman Catholic priest in 1761 (some sources: 1769), he taught at Liege and Bruges and twice traveled through Europe as a tutor before the suppression of the Jesuit order by Pope Clement XIV in the summer of 1773 changed the course of his life.

Returning to Maryland in 1774, he did pastoral work in what is now the District of Columbia and on the northern neck of Virginia. In early 1776, on behalf of the Continental Congress, he accompanied his cousin Charles Carroll of Carrollton and Benjamin Franklin on an unsuccessful mission to Montreal to seek Canadian support for the American Revolution.* After independence Carroll led the reorganization of the Roman Catholic Church in the United States. Benjamin Franklin recommended him to Rome, and he was named in 1784 superior of the American mission.* Elected bishop of Baltimore by the clergy* in 1789, he was ordained bishop in 1790 and promoted to archbishop* in 1808.

Carroll saw the Roman Catholic Church as a communion of basically self-governing national churches which chose their own bishops, presenting their names to the pope* for confirmation, and educated their own clergy. At various times Carroll advocated use of vernacular languages in the Mass* and a lay* role in choice of pastors,* although later conflicts weakened his resolves along these lines. He accepted the pope as head of the universal church and Rome as its center, but he understood church unity less in terms of governmental control from Rome than of shared belief and practice. Papal infallibility,* not defined as Roman Catholic dogma* until 1870, was for him a freely debated question; for definitive teaching he looked rather to ecumenical councils ("pope and council, received by the church").

Carroll strongly supported separation of church and state* and religious toleration. While he resisted state control of the church, he advocated cooperation between religious and civil spheres as well as among people of differing religions. He was deeply convinced that the "freedom and independence acquired by the united efforts and cemented by the mingled blood of Protestants and Catholics" should be shared equally by all. Carroll was a strong advocate of education for men and women. He founded the academy which became Georgetown University and served on the boards of several secular colleges. He was the chief patron of Matthew Carey's 1789-1790 edition at Philadelphia of the Douai-Rheims English translation of the Bible.*

See also COLONIAL CATHOLICISM.

BIBLIOGRAPHY. *DAB* II; *DARB;* P. Guilday, *The Life and Times of John Carroll, Archbishop of Baltimore, 1735-1815,* 2 vols. (1888); J. Hennesey, "An Eighteenth Century Bishop: John Carroll of Baltimore," *AHP* 16 (1978):171-204; A. M. Melville, *John Carroll of Baltimore: Founder of the American Catholic Hierarchy* (1955); *NCAB* 1; *NCE* 3; J. G. Shea, *The Life and Times of the Most Rev. John Carroll* (1888); T. Spalding, "John Carroll: Corrigenda and Addenda," *CHR* 71 (1985):505-518.

J. Hennesey

Carter, James Earl, Jr. (1924-). Businessman, farmer, statesman, Baptist* layman and thirty-ninth U.S. president. Born in Plains, Georgia, Jimmy Carter (as he preferred to be known) was the eldest of four children of James Earl and Lillian Gordy Carter. He grew up near Plains, where his father both farmed and operated a small country store. He was appointed to the U.S. Naval Academy in 1942; graduated in 1946; married his hometown sweetheart, Rosalynn Smith, shortly thereafter; and spent the next seven years in the U.S. Navy. However, in 1953, following the death of his father, he resigned his commission and returned to Plains to take over the family farm.

After a successful stint as a businessman-farmer and considerable experience in local politics, Carter in 1962 ran a successful campaign for election to the Georgia State Senate, where he served two terms (1963-1967). In 1966 he unsuccessfully sought the Georgia governorship, but in 1970 he won election to that office. On completing his term as governor in 1975, Carter began to run for the presidency. On most issues, his campaign was built on moderate positions, and he set a moral tone for the election by promising never to lie to the American people and to institute a compassionate and responsible government. This gained him the support of many people who were looking for a change in leadership after the Vietnam War, the Watergate Scandal and the ignominious resignations of Vice President Spiro Agnew and President Richard Nixon.* Despite the fears aroused by the fact that he was a self-acknowledged evangelical* Christian, a Southerner and a nonestablishment outsider, he won the presidency in 1976.

Carter's administration (1977-1981), like his earlier legislative and gubernatorial career, received mixed reviews. He never was able to seize the economic initiative in domestic affairs, and the country suffered increasing inflation, unemployment and federal deficits during his tenure in office. He succeeded in some matters, such as civil-service reform, environmental legislation and in getting a significant portion of his energy program through Congress.

In foreign affairs, Carter inaugurated full diplomatic relations with the People's Republic of China in 1979; persuaded Israel and Egypt to sign the Camp David peace accord in March 1979; and tried, with limited success, to establish human rights as a basic tenet of American policy. He signed the SALT II Treaty in 1979 but failed to secure Senate ratification. His successful push for confirmation of the Panama Canal treaties in 1977 was criticized by the political right as a sell-out of American interests; he received little support for his boycott of the 1980 Summer Olympic Games in Moscow in retaliation for the 1979 Soviet invasion of Afghanistan; and his handling of the Iran Hostage Crisis in 1979-1980 was perceived as bungled by many Americans.

Much of the 1980 presidential campaign was

played out under the cloud of the hostage problem, and Carter was criticized by his Republican opponent, Ronald Reagan,* for ineptitude and a lack of leadership. In addition, many evangelicals who had supported Carter in 1976 drifted away to the Reagan camp. Reagan was swept into office in a landslide victory.

In 1981 Carter returned to Plains, where he wrote his memoirs; oversaw the development of his presidential library in Atlanta; taught and lectured on public affairs in various universities around the country; worked in his local Baptist church; served as a special envoy to various Latin American countries; and promoted Habitat for Humanity, a Christian organization that provides low-cost housing for the poor.

Having burst onto the national stage in 1976, the much-ballyhooed "Year of the Evangelicals," Carter displayed a combination of straightforwardness, an aura of moral rectitude that exemplified traditional values and a transparently authentic religious faith that struck the right note for the time. Carter was perhaps the most dedicated Christian ever to occupy the White House and, along with Abraham Lincoln* and Woodrow Wilson,* he was certainly one of the most theologically perceptive. Conversant with the work of such noted theologians as Reinhold Niebuhr* and Søren Kierkegaard,* Carter also was steeped in the teachings of the Bible. He had professed faith in Christ in 1935 at age eleven, and he had been baptized and become a member of a Southern Baptist* church shortly thereafter. A Sunday-school* teacher since 1936 and a deacon* since 1958, sometime in late 1966 or early 1967, following his defeat in his first try for the governorship of Georgia, he experienced a spiritual crisis which led to a rededication of his life to Christ and eventually to a commitment to fulfill his Christian vocation through politics.

Carter thus brought with him to the presidency a faith which was an integral part of his personal identity. On church-state* issues, for example, he adhered to the traditional Baptist insistence on a high wall of separation, even refusing to hold worship* services in the White House. His Baptist faith also taught him that Christians are on earth to serve; thus he considered himself, as president, the First Servant of the nation. His personal style—marked by enormous self-discipline, a commitment to hard work, orderliness and fiscal responsibility—largely reflected his evangelical world view. His dedication to social justice also flowed from his Christian faith. Most of all, his biblical faith dictated restraint in the use of power.

Essentially Niebuhrian in his understanding of the complexity of ethical issues, Carter's "Christian realism" sometimes led him to appear to be indecisive because he understood the irony of how humans are often in the most danger of being wrong when they think they are absolutely right. He frequently cited a paraphrase of Niebuhr when articulating his own political philosophy: "The sad duty of politics is to establish justice in a sinful world."

The supreme irony of Carter's presidency may have been the reaction to his energy address, known as "the malaise speech," delivered in prophetic civil religion* language on national TV in July 1979. The president used the occasion to talk of a national moral and spiritual crisis, and to call on his fellow Americans to repent of the sins of materialism and consumptionism and to be prepared to sacrifice in order to resolve the energy crisis and restore national vigor. Carter's loss in the 1980 election was, in part, a reflection of public rejection of his prophetic civil religion in favor of Reagan's politics of nostalgia for a bygone era of respected might and limitless plenty.

BIBLIOGRAPHY. J. T. Baker, *A Southern Baptist in the White House* (1977); J. Carter, *A Government as Good as Its People* (1977); J. Carter, *Keeping Faith: Memoirs of a President* (1982); J. Carter, *Why Not the Best?* (1975); W. L. Miller, *Yankee from Georgia: The Emergence of Jimmy Carter* (1970); R. B. Flowers, "President Jimmy Carter, Evangelicalism, Church-State Relations and Civil Religion," *JCS* 25 (Winter 1983):113-132; E. C. Hargrove, *Jimmy Carter as President* (1988); R. G. Hutcheson, Jr., *God in the White House* (1988); R. L. Maddox, *Preacher at the White House* (1984); R. V. Pierard and Robert D. Linder, *Civil Religion and the Presidency* (1988); W. G. Pippert, ed., *The Spiritual Journey of Jimmy Carter* (1979); G. Smith, *Morality, Reason, and Power: American Diplomacy in the Carter Years* (1986); D. Winter, "The Carter-Niebuhr Connection," *National Journal* 10 (February 4, 1978):188-192.   R. D. Linder

Cartwright, Peter (1785-1872). Methodist* frontier preacher.* Born in Amherst County, Virginia, Cartwright moved with his family to Kentucky in 1790, where Peter spent his adolescent years as a young tough in Rogue's Harbor, Logan County. Although he had little formal education, the religious instruction from his Methodist mother eventually led to a camp-meeting* conversion* in 1801. He immediately joined the Methodist Episcopal Church, receiving an exhorter's license* in 1802 and becoming a traveling preacher in 1803. Referring to himself as "God's plowman," Cartwright, who mastered the "extempore style," preached an average of more than a sermon a day for the first twenty years of his ministry. With a keen wit, an uncompromising devotion to Christ and church, and a rugged physical constitution, his colorful exploits soon became well known throughout the American frontier.

Ordained* deacon* in 1806 by Francis Asbury,* and elder in 1808 by William McKendree,* he served as a circuit rider* until 1812 when he was appointed presiding elder,* overseeing churches in the Wabash District (1812) and Green River District (1813-1816). After four more years as a circuit rider (1816-1820) and two more years as the presiding elder of the Cumberland District (1821-1823), he was transferred to the Illinois Conference, where he remained for the rest of his life.

During Cartwright's nearly fifty years in Illinois, he was a presiding elder for most of those years, a delegate to every General Conference of the Methodist Episcopal Church and twice a member of the Illinois Legislature. He was defeated in his bid for Congress by none other than Abraham Lincoln.* He strongly opposed slavery and championed the cause of Methodist colleges (in spite of his own lack of academic training). He feared no mortal and died, honored and revered by the church, on September 25, 1872, in Pleasant Plains, Illinois.

BIBLIOGRAPHY. P. Cartwright, *Autobiography of Peter Cartwright,* ed. C. L. Wallis (1956); P. Cartwright, *Fifty Years as a Presiding Elder,* ed. W. S. Hooper (1871); *DAB* II; *DARB;* H. Grant, *Peter Cartwright, Pioneer* (1931); *NCAB* 6; P. Watters, *Peter Cartwright* (1910).   R. G. Tuttle

Carver, (W)illiam (O)wen (1868-1954). Southern Baptist* pastor,* professor and missiologist.* Born in Tennessee, Carver graduated from Richmond College, Richmond, Virginia (M.A., 1891) and the Southern Baptist Seminary, Louisville, Kentucky (Th.M., 1895; Th.D., 1896). After serving several pastorates in Virginia, Tennessee, and Kentucky, Carver joined the faculty of the Southern Baptist Theological Seminary in 1896. In 1899 he offered the seminary's first course in missions* and comparative religion. In 1900 he became head of the missions department, a position he held until his retirement in 1943.

Carver helped to establish the Woman's Missionary Union Training School at Southern Baptist Seminary in 1907. In 1953 the School's name was changed to the Carver School of Missions and Social Work. An ecumenical* churchman, Carver sought to interpret the Baptist missionary imperative within the mission of the whole church. He published twenty books, many of which helped shape Southern Baptist theology* of missions in the twentieth century. These include *Missions in the Plan of the Ages* (1909) and *Christian Missions in Today's World* (1942).

BIBLIOGRAPHY. W. O. Carver, *Out of This Treasure* (1956); C. U. Littlejohn, *History of the Carver School of Missions and Social Work* (1958).

B. J. Leonard

Cary (Carey), Lott (c.1780-1828). African-American Baptist* missionary. Born a slave in Charles City County, Virginia, Cary worked in Richmond tobacco warehouses. After hearing a sermon on John 3:16, he was converted* in 1807 and swore off "profanity and intoxication." Cary joined the biracial First Baptist Church, learned to read and write, and became a lay preacher.* Officially licensed* in 1813—the year he also bought his freedom—Cary helped found the Richmond Baptist Missionary Society, which, with the American Colonization Society* (ACS) and the Triennal Convention* of Baptist churches, authorized in 1819 his trip to Africa. Accompanied by another African-American Baptist, Colin Teague [Teage], Cary surrendered leadership in The First Baptist Church of Richmond to go to Sierra Leone early in 1821. His farewell sermon on Romans 8:32 advocated the missionary cause.

Early in 1822 the colonists moved to found the colony of Liberia. Over the next six years Cary lost his wife, survived a conflict with Jeduhi Ashmun (the white agent of the ACS), gave military and administrative leadership to the colony and became a lay medical practitioner. Ordained* before his departure for Africa, he established churches and schools among the local inhabitants. An explosion during one of several conflicts with local tribes took Cary's life in November 1828. African-American Baptists in America sixty years later named its foreign missionary organization for Cary.

BIBLIOGRAPHY. M. M. Fisher, "Lott Cary, The Colonizing Missionary," *JNH* 7 (1922):380-418; W. A. Poe, "Lott Cary: Man of Purchased Freedom," *CH* 39 (1970):49-61.

W. B. Gravely and D. Nelson

Case, Shirley Jackson (1872-1947). Baptist* New Testament scholar. Born in New Brunswick, Canada, Case was educated at Acadia University (A.B., M.A.) and Yale* Divinity School (B.D., Ph.D.), then became professor of New Testament and early church history at the University of Chicago Divinity School* (1908-1938) and dean after 1933. Case refined the "socio-historical-environmental" method of the Chicago School,* which viewed religious movements and theology mainly as products of their social settings. Contrary to the views of A. Schweitzer, Case believed that he could find the historical Jesus and contended that the Jesus of history was in fact the Christ of faith (*The Historicity of Jesus,* 1912; *Jesus: A New Biography,* 1927). In his study of Christian origins he emphasized the importance of understanding the social environment of early Christians over analyzing the documents of the New Testament (*The Evolution of Early Christianity,* 1914) and viewed the development of theology as "transcendental politics." Thus Case stood midway between skeptics who accounted for Christianity's emergence without a historical Jesus and conservatives who viewed Christian origins in purely supernaturalistic terms.

See also CHICAGO SCHOOL OF THEOLOGY.

BIBLIOGRAPHY. *DAB* 4; W. Hynes, *Shirley Jackson Case and the Chicago School: The Socio-Historical Method* (1981).

T. P. Weber

Cashwell, Gaston Barnabas (1826-1916). Pentecostal* pioneer in the South. Born in Sampson County, North Carolina, Cashwell was a minister* of the Methodist* Episcopal Church, South, until under the influence of A. B. Crumpler* he joined the Pentecostal Holiness Church (then called the Holiness Church of North Carolina) in 1903. When the Pentecostal movement erupted with the Azusa Street* (Los Angeles) revival* of 1906, Cashwell attended the meeting and spoke in tongues. He returned to his home in Dunn, North Carolina, and led a month-long revival which drew many Holiness* ministers into the Pentecostal ranks. Accounts of the "Dunn meeting" spread quickly, and Cashwell subsequently engaged in a preaching* tour of the South from 1907 to 1909. Among his converts were J. H. King and A. J. Tomlinson,* leaders of the Fire-Baptized Holiness Church and the Church of God* in Cleveland, Tennessee. These two Holiness bodies and Cashwell's Pentecostal Holiness Church joined the Pentecostal movement as a result of his preaching. In 1909 Cashwell left the Pentecostal Holiness Church and later attempted to disavow his pivotal role in the spread of Pentecostalism. Nevertheless, Cashwell was regarded as the "Pentecostal apostle to the South."

BIBLIOGRAPHY. V. Synan, *The Holiness-Pentecos-* *tal Movement in the United States* (1971); V. Synan, *The Old-Time Power* (1973).

C. D. Weaver

Catechetics, Catholic. The teaching and explanation of the Catholic* faith primarily to children, Native Americans* and African-American slaves. The context and teachers of catechetics varied with circumstances. In colonial America it was customary for a Catholic priest* to instruct children in the catechism* after Sunday Mass.* Since priests were frequently not available, there is evidence that at least some Catholics gathered in groups and said some prayers,* and then one or more of the parents instructed the children in their catechism.

By the 1820s it is clear that Catholics followed their Protestant fellow-citizens in opening Sunday schools,* where priests, seminarians, nuns* and lay* men and women taught the lessons in a parish context. While full-time Catholic schools included catechism as a matter of course, it was not until the late nineteenth century, after the 1884 decision to push ahead with a separate school system, that catechetical activity became centered in the full-time Catholic schools and was taught on a daily basis primarily by teaching nuns. While the Sunday schools continued to serve students not in Catholic schools, a Vatican-inspired, twentieth-century movement known as the Confraternity of Christian Doctrine* (CCD), brought a renewed effort, especially in the 1930s, to reach out to these children, frequently during release-time from public schools, where local law allowed.

After Vatican II* ended in 1965, when the number of nuns, and consequently Catholic schools, had declined significantly, much of the "religious education," as it was then called, was back in the hands of the laity in once-a-week parish classes. A new emphasis on the religious education of adults also appeared during this time, at first as a way to explain the changes taking place as a result of the Council, and then as a means of reaching children by informing their parents.

A large number of catechisms have been used by American Catholics, but a few have been particularly influential, especially as source books for the many others. The most significant in this regard was *A Short Abridgement of Christian Doctrine,* sometimes called the "Carroll Catechism," first published in the U.S. around 1780 as a reprint of a British catechism of the same name. This small book, along with another British catechism produced by Bishop James Butler, were the primary catechisms in use prior to about 1829, but even after that they continued to have influence by their incorporation into later catechisms, especially *A*

General Catechism of the Christian Doctrine, prepared by order of the First Plenary Council of Baltimore in 1852, and the Third Plenary Council of Baltimore's *A Catechism of Christian Doctrine* (1885), which dominated the scene for some sixty years. The catechisms were generally in question-and-answer form, although several featuring historical narrative were also used, beginning with the publication of Fleury's *Short Historical Catechism* in 1813. The inclusion of prayers and liturgical* explanations were not uncommon additions to this basic pattern.

In spite of all of the variations in content and format, and the large number of different catechisms in use, Catholic catechisms had a remarkably consistent content. In one way or other, the so-called Apostles' Creed functioned as the main framework for the content of the catechisms, whether doctrinal or historical in nature. In the main points of the sections on faith, the first point raised was usually the end of the human person, followed by discussion of God as one and triune; the creation of the world; a fall; a restoration by the life, death and resurrection of Jesus; the Church; and an eschatology focused on eternal life. Understanding the world in this way, young Catholics were led to interpret their situations as fallen and, short of God's intervention, hopeless and headed for eternal suffering. Christ's redemption, begged for in prayer, especially the Lord's Prayer, and received in the seven sacraments* of the Church, made possible the keeping of the commandments, meaning the Ten Commandments and those of the Church, which would lead to salvation after death. A comparison of these Catholic catechisms with those used by New England Puritans,* such as the *Shorter Westminister Catechism** or John Cotton's* *Spiritual Milk for Boston Babes,* shows remarkable similarity in framework and ethical teachings, although, as one would expect, there are differences reflecting Reformation disputes.

The Second Vatican Council* had a profound impact on Catholic catechetics. The older format of memorizing questions and answers gave way to a more biblical and liturgical catechesis which is not merely comprised of formulas about God. God is portrayed as loving and revelation as interpersonal communion with God. The world-and-self-denying Augustinianism* used to interpret the creed* was replaced with a generally more positive, Enlightenment*-inspired interpretation of the human condition and of the possibilities for improvement in the social and economic order, as is reflected in the American Catholic bishop's *Sharing the Light of Faith: National Catechetical Directory for Catholics of the United States* (1979).

BIBLIOGRAPHY. C. J. Carmody, "The Roman Catholic Catechesis in the United States, 1784-1930: A Study of Its Theory, Development, and Materials" (unpublished Ph.D. dissertation, Loyola University, Chicago, 1975); R. G. Bandas, *Catechetical Methods: Standard Methods of Teaching Religion* (1929); M. K. Oosdyke, "The *Christ Life Series* in Religion: Liturgy and Experience as Formative Influences in Religious Education" (unpublished Ph.D. dissertation, Boston College, 1987). T. E. Wangler

Catechisms, Protestant. A summary of Christian beliefs, usually set out in questions and answers to make doctrine* more pedagogically accessible. Protestant catechisms often express the theological content of a doctrinal confession* or standard in simpler terms, for those without theological training. Beginning with a brief introductory summary of what it means to be a Christian, they usually move to a practical exposition of the Apostles' Creed, the Ten Commandments, the Lord's Prayer and the meaning of the Sacraments.* Often, there is a larger catechism for adults and a shorter one for children. Catechism classes are the traditional context in which a catechist* instructs confirmands (*See* Confirmation*) or baptismal candidates in the worship,* doctrine and life of the church.

Luther's Catechisms, the Reformed* Heidelberg Catechism, the Episcopal* "Church Catechism," the Presbyterian* Westminster Catechisms,* and the Methodist* Catechisms carried great theological and practical authority* when brought to America by its settlers and immigrants. They were often the primary means of Christian education* until the Sunday-school movement.* Even after this, they remained popular on the American frontier, since they could be used in small groups without elaborate organization. Individual pastors and teachers also produced catechisms of their own for use in training congregations or students. These might be printed for use on a wider scale by others. An important use of private catechisms was in educating Southern slaves.

In contemporary American churches, catechisms are less strictly used and followed in preparing confirmands or candidates for membership.* This is largely due to a growing preference for more flexible and experiential educational approaches. However, catechisms are recently receiving renewed attention for their value as clear, accessible and existentially relevant statements of the beliefs of the Christian traditions which they represent.

BIBLIOGRAPHY. P. Schaff, *The Creeds of Christendom*, 3 vols. (1877); T. F. Torrance, *The School of Faith* (1959); A. C. Repp, Sr., *Luther's Catechism Comes to America* (1982); J. Westerhoff and O. C. Edwards, *A Faithful Church; Issues in the History of Catechesis* (1981). P. W. Butin

Catechist. A teacher who systematically instructs students in Christian doctrine,* usually by means of a catechism.* In traditional catechesis, the catechist teaches sequentially through each question and answer of the catechism, explaining and expanding upon the meaning and personal application of the answers. These are then memorized as the chief preparation for confirmation,* baptism* or public profession of faith for admission to active church membership.* Once memorized, the catechism is often formally recited before the church's leaders or the entire congregation, with the catechist prompting the student through the catechism's questions.

Normally the catechist is a pastor* or lay* officer of the church to which the candidate belongs. The term may also be used more technically to refer to (1) Roman Catholic lay teachers; or (2) indigenous believers on the mission* field who instruct new believers. P. W. Butin

Cathedral. A church, usually in a major city, containing the throne or seat (Latin, *cathedra*) of a bishop,* and therefore the central church of a diocese* or archdiocese.* Cathedrals are usually maintained by religious groups, such as the Roman Catholic* and Episcopal* churches, that adhere to the apostolic succession* of bishops. The term may also be used metaphorically to characterize an unusually large or important church, such as Robert Schuller's* Crystal Cathedral in Garden Grove, California (1980). Prior to World War 2* most American cathedrals were Gothic in style, but contemporary modes are now usual, such as St. Mary's Catholic Cathedral (San Francisco, 1971). Cathedrals such as St. Patrick's in New York (Roman Catholic; 1858-1979); St. John the Divine, also in New York (Episcopal; begun 1892); and the Washington Cathedral (Episcopal; begun 1907) are vast in scale, lavish in art and ornament, and symbolic of their traditions.

See also ARCHITECTURE, CHURCH.

BIBLIOGRAPHY. L. Cook, *St. Patrick's Cathedral* (1979); E. H. Hall, *The Cathedral Church of St. John the Divine* (1916). P. W. Williams

Catholic Action. A term used to designate both a concept and an organization of laity,* it has a variety of meanings, depending upon the decade and the region to which reference is made. The term is a literal translation from the Italian *Azione Cattolica,* a specific national organization which strove in the 1920s and 1930s to establish better relations between the Church and the Italian government. Pope Pius XI* gave *Catholic Action* its classical definition in 1922 as "the participation of the laity in the apostolate* of the Church's hierarchy." His successor, Pius XII,* acknowledged "a regrettable and rather widespread uneasiness which arises from the use of the term 'Catholic Action,' " because it had developed both a specific referent (tightly structured organizations with overt episcopal support) and a general connotation (all Catholic lay activity on behalf of the gospel). To complicate matters further, the term *lay apostolate* entered Catholic parlance in the 1950s.

The type of Catholic Action which developed in the U.S. originated with Canon Joseph Cardijn of Belgium, whose work Pius XI regarded as a model of Catholic Action and whom Pope Paul VI* elevated to the College of Cardinals in 1965. "Jocism" sought to Christianize economic and social institutions through a technique expressed in the formula "Observe, judge, act" applied in small groups in a specialized or like-to-like apostolate. Priests* such as Reynold Hillenbrand,* Donald Kanaly, Louis Putz and John Egan, and Chicago laymen James O'Shaughnessy and Edward Marciniak, among many others, established Catholic Action groups in Catholic high schools and colleges, edited journals on labor and politics, and formed groups such as the Catholic Labor Alliance, the Catholic Interracial Council, the Cana Conference,* the Young Christian Students, the Young Christian Workers and the Christian Family Movement.* These grass-roots movements trained Catholics to influence the worlds of labor, race relations, marriage and family life, and local economics. These movements served as a vital complement to the more highly centralized and officially sponsored organizations like the National Councils of Catholic Men* and Women* and the Confraternity of Christian Doctrine.*

Although Pius XI saw the layman as an extension of the priest* and the priest as "the soul of Catholic Action," the pioneers of the movements which developed in the U.S. in the 1940s and 1950s recognized a clear distinction between the realm of the priest and the layperson, and resisted attempts to "clericalize" the laity. The proper arena of lay activity, they maintained, is in the world outside the church, not in the sanctuary. But in the

1970s and 1980s, the advent of lay ministry eclipsed Catholic Action in the U.S. by centering lay activity in the parish rather than the workplace. Theology of the laity after Vatican II* (1962-1965) emphasized the commission each Christian receives in baptism,* rather than at the hands of the bishop* in holy orders, as the basis for apostolic service.

BIBLIOGRAPHY. D. J. Geaney, "Catholic Action," *NCE* 3; D. J. Geaney, *Emerging Lay Ministry* (1979); T. Hesburgh, *The Theology of Catholic Action* (1946); M. Quigley, Jr., and E. Connors, *Catholic Action in Practice* (1963).

R. S. Appleby

Catholic Association for International Peace. *See* PEACE MOVEMENT, CATHOLIC.

Catholic Biblical Association of America. A Catholic society of biblical scholars. On January 18, 1936, Archbishop Edwin V. O'Hara* of Kansas City-St. Joseph, Missouri, chairman of the American Bishops Committee on the Confraternity of Christian Doctrine* (CCD), convened a meeting of Catholic biblical scholars in Washington, D.C. Bishop O'Hara saw the need for a new English translation* of the Bible* to enrich catechetical* instruction, preaching* and adult discussion. The Rev. Romain Butin proposed that the plan be expanded to include a permanent society of Catholic biblical scholars. This plan was implemented, and the first general meeting of the Catholic Biblical Association (CBA) convened in October 1937.

Because of tensions between scholarship and popularization, the CBA gradually came to hold its meetings separately from CCD, the latter having a Sunday-school* orientation. The fundamental goal of the CBA is to "devote itself to the scientific study of the Bible . . . in conformity with the spirit and instructions of the Catholic Church." The CBA has produced *The New American Bible* (Confraternity Version), publishes the *Catholic Biblical Quarterly* and helped launch *The Bible Today.* The one-hundred active charter members in 1937 were all ordained priests* in the Roman Catholic Church. In 1947 the first woman, Kathryn Sullivan, became a full active member. William Foxwell Albright,* a Protestant,* was voted an honorary member in 1944, but active membership was opened to non-Catholics only in 1962. In 1984 Paul J. Achtemeier became the first Protestant to be voted president of the CBA. In the late 1980s CBA had over eight hundred active members, including priests, religious* and laity*—as well as some Protestant and Jewish members. The income of CBA, gained through royalties from *The New American Bible,* is annually tithed for donations to the poor. Today the organization represents the state of contemporary biblical scholarship, where divisions lay less along denominational lines than over the acceptance or rejection of historical-critical methodologies.

BIBLIOGRAPHY. F. S. Rossiter, "Forty Years Less One, An Historical Sketch of the C.B.A. (1936-1975)," *CBQ* Supplement (July 1977):1-14; D. Senior and C. Stuhlmueller, "American Catholicism and the Biblical Movement," in M. Glazier, ed., *Where We Are: American Catholics in the 1980's* (1985).

R. Van Allen

Catholic Foreign Mission Society of America (Maryknoll Missioners). An American congregation of diocesan priests* dedicated to foreign missions.* The Maryknoll Missioners were founded in 1911 by two diocesan priests, Thomas F. Price from Wilmington, North Carolina, and James A. Walsh* from Boston, Massachusetts. They had spent months soliciting the patronage of significant members of the hierarchy, and because they intended their society to be the official American Catholic outreach to the foreign missions, they sought and received the approval of the Apostolic Delegate* and the entire U.S. hierarchy at their annual meeting in 1911. Pius X* officially permitted the Society to begin on June 29, 1911.

The congregation was patterned on the Foreign Missionaries of Paris; they were diocesan priests who did not take religious vows but an oath to serve in the missions and be faithful to the Society. The first Maryknoll missionaries went to China in 1918. Within fifteen years they opened other missions in Manchuria, Korea, the Philippines, Hawaii and Japan. When many missionaries had to be repatriated during World War 2,* they opened missions in Latin America (1942) and Africa (1946). In 1987 they served in twenty-seven countries.

The congregation experienced a rapid growth after their founding, and by 1965 there were 1,240 members. Afterwards they suffered the same losses as other congregations and in 1987 numbered only 792. On principle, they do not recruit men in the countries in which they serve. From their origin they have been active in mission education through their journal, *Field Afar* (later called *Maryknoll*), and Maryknoll Publications, now known as Orbis Press.

BIBLIOGRAPHY. G. D. Kittler, *The Maryknoll*

Fathers (1961); A. J. Nevins, *The Meaning of Mary-knoll* (1954).   L. Nemer

Catholic Peace Fellowship. *See* PEACE MOVEMENT, CATHOLIC.

Catholic University of America. The only university belonging to the Catholic hierarchy of the U.S., Catholic University of America (CUA) was incorporated in the District of Columbia in 1887 and granted a charter to confer pontifical degrees by Pope Leo XIII* in 1889. Governance is by a board of trustees consisting of the nation's cardinals* and residential archbishops,* the chancellor (ex officio, the archbishop of Washington), rector* and elected bishops,* priests* and laypersons.

Action to found the University was first taken at the Third Plenary Council of Baltimore (1884) and Bishop John J. Keane* of Richmond was named as first rector in 1886. Despite opposition, the University opened in 1889 with a total faculty of twelve. In that same year the Paulists* became the first of many religious communities to establish a house of studies near the University. Initially the new institution offered only advanced degrees in ecclesiastical disciplines for clergy.* Within a few years it had broadened to offer graduate instruction in secular subjects, a Catholic analog to the recently founded Johns Hopkins (1874) and Clark (1889) universities. Financial difficulty led to authorization by Pope Pius X* of an annual public collection for the University in 1903, as well as the introduction of lay* undergraduate education in 1905. It has, however, maintained its predominantly graduate character.

Presently the University consists of ten schools (theology,* philosophy, canon law,* civil law, arts and sciences, education, social service, engineering and architecture, music and nursing) along with an undergraduate college of arts and sciences. Although nearly half of the American Catholic hierarchy are alumni, over eighty per cent of the faculty and seventy-five per cent of the students are lay.

BIBLIOGRAPHY. P. H. Ahern, *The Catholic University of America, 1887-1896* (1949); C. J. Barry, *The Catholic University of America, 1903-1909* (1949); P. E. Hogan, *The Catholic University of America, 1896-1903* (1949).   F. M. Perko

Catholic Worker. Lay* Catholic* movement. Founded during the depth of the Great Depression* by Dorothy Day* and Peter Maurin,* the Catholic Worker encourages lay Catholic initiative in changing the social order and helping its victims. The Catholic Worker gives meals, clothing and shelter to the needy on New York City's Lower East Side where the movement began, and in satellite houses throughout the U.S., as well as in England, Canada, Australia and Mexico. This responsibility to care for others is rooted in a literal interpretation of the gospel command to love one's neighbor. The poor are understood to be ambassadors of Christ, persons with inherent dignity, who need not uplift themselves as a condition for receiving help.

As an intentional community, with volunteers drawn from all walks of life, the Catholic Worker movement views itself as a prophetic leaven for church and society, calling people to the essential teachings of Christ. Followers practice voluntary poverty and some Catholic Worker groups have founded farming communes in an effort to provide meaningful employment and to supply produce to urban soup lines. The movement's emphasis on small communities has led to its characterization as a Christian anarchist movement.

The movement presents its ideas in a penny paper, *The Catholic Worker,* and at public round-table discussions where topics such as spirituality,* psychology, alternative economics and anarchism are addressed. Advocating nonviolent solutions to social problems and international conflicts, the Catholic Worker was the first Catholic pacifist* movement to emerge in the U.S. At first controversial, its pacifism has become more acceptable to nuclear-age Catholics.

See also DAY, DOROTHY.

BIBLIOGRAPHY. A. Klejment and A. Klejment, *Dorothy Day and The Catholic Worker: A Bibliography and Index* (1985); M. Piehl, *Breaking Bread: The Catholic Worker and the Origin of Catholic Radicalism in America* (1982); N. L. Roberts, *Dorothy Day and the "Catholic Worker"* (1985).   A. Klejment

Catholic Youth Organization. Catholic* archdiocesan youth organization founded in 1930 in Chicago by Auxiliary Bishop* Bernard Sheil.* Drawing upon his experiences as a prison chaplain* and convinced that there was no such thing as a "youth problem," only the "normal problems of youth," Sheil founded the Chicago Catholic Youth Organization during the years of the Great Depression* primarily to help young people avoid a life of crime. Using Catholic parishes as the basis for organizing its activities and setting up clubs according to age groups, the organization developed a variety of services to help poverty's children form Christian living habits. Although these programs were intended to promote the spiritual, mental, cultural and physical development primarily of Catholic young people, many of the activities were open to all, regardless of creed. Many dioceses* across the nation set up similar youth services, some of them in imitation of the Chicago models.

Catholic Youth Organization has also referred to diocesan youth services that in 1937 began to affiliate with the National Council of Catholic Youth in the National Catholic Welfare Conference,* Washington, D.C. This was to promote authorized diocesan youth organizations and to train Catholic leaders in "authentic Catholic Action* in conformity with the directions of the Holy Father and the America Hierarchy." Church renewal following the Second Vatican Council* reshaped Catholic Action and de-emphasized national affiliation, thus encouraging dioceses to develop Catholic Youth Organizations according to specific needs.

See also SHEIL, BERNARD JAMES.

BIBLIOGRAPHY. *The National Catholic Almanac* (1941); R. L. Treat, *Bishop Sheil and the CYO* (1951). J. W. Evans

Cauthen, Baker James (1909-1985). Southern Baptist* missionary,* educator and missions executive. Born in Huntsville, Texas, Cauthen was licensed to preach at age sixteen and ordained* in 1927. He received his education from Stephen F. Austin College (B.A., 1929), Baylor University (M.A., 1930) and Southwestern Baptist Theological Seminary (Th.M., 1933; Th.D., 1936).

While serving as pastor of the Polytechnic Baptist Church, Fort Worth (1933-1939), he was also professor of missions at Southwestern Seminary (1935-1939). Offering themselves as missionaries, he and his wife served in China from 1939 to 1945. He was then elected secretary for the Orient, (1945-1953) and executive secretary of the Foreign Mission Board of the Southern Baptist Convention (1954-1979). His service in the calling of missions encompassed more than forty-six years.

With a longer tenure than any of his seven predecessors as head of the mission board (twenty-six years), Cauthen led Southern Baptists in building one of the largest missionary forces among Protestant denominations,* from 908 missionaries in 1954 to 3,008 in 1979, located in ninety-four countries. Missions funding grew from $6.7 million (1954) to $76.7 million (1979).

Cauthen challenged Southern Baptists, "God has not given us our current resources that we may use them upon ourselves." His goal was 5,000 missionaries in 125 countries by A.D. 2000, with 10,000 lay volunteers. He urged major thrusts into urban areas and among students; increases in overseas churches; leadership training; greater use of media; more attention to health care, disease prevention, world hunger and disasters. His vision and achievements earned him the honor of a missionary statesman.

BIBLIOGRAPHY. J. C. Fletcher, *Baker James Cauthen: A Man for All Nations* (1977).

W. M. Patterson

Cavadas, Athenagoras (1885-1962). Greek Orthodox* bishop* and educator. Destined to spend most of his career in the shadow of his namesake, Athenagoras Spyrou, Cavadas was one of the most gifted and energetic of Greek clergymen in America. An abbot and academic dean in Greece before accepting to serve as a roving evangelist* in the U.S., he proved effective in healing the strife in the Greek-American community and stemming the tide of innovationism. In 1937 he organized the Greek Orthodox preparatory theological school Holy Trinity in Pomfret, Connecticut (renamed Holy Cross and relocated in 1947 to Brookline, Massachusetts), molded its program in the monastic style rather than the ivy league, and served as dean and professor of dogmatics.* After a stint as chancellor of the archdiocese,* he was advanced to the episcopacy* in 1938, and he served ten years as bishop of Boston. Twice he was named *locum tenens* in expectancy of succeeding as archbishop,* but was passed over and reassigned to Germany and later England, where he died, a good deal disillusioned, as archbishop of Thyateira and former president (1951-1954) of the World Council of Churches.*

BIBLIOGRAPHY. G. Poulos, *Footsteps in the Sea: A Biography of Archbishop Athenagoras Cavadas* (1979). P. D. Garrett

Cavanaugh, John Joseph (1899-1979). Catholic educator. Although too poor to finish high school, Cavanaugh persuaded the man for whom he was named, John W. Cavanaugh, president of the University of Notre Dame,* to hire him as his secretary in 1917 and then to give him a scholarship to Notre Dame. He graduated in 1923 as president of his class and went to work for the Studebaker Corporation, where he became an executive within two years.

Cavanaugh joined the Congregation of Holy Cross* in 1925, received an M.A. in English from Notre Dame (1927), and was ordained* priest* in

1931. After taking an advanced degree in theology* at the Gregorian University in Rome (1933), Cavanaugh returned to Notre Dame to become prefect of religion, or director of campus ministry.* Appointed assistant superior of the Holy Cross Priests and Brothers in the United States in 1938, he also became vice president of Notre Dame in 1940. In 1946, Cavanaugh was named Notre Dame's fourteenth president.

Cavanaugh presided over the transition of Notre Dame from an enclosed compound with most of the students living on campus to an institution seeking integration into post-World War 2 American society. He reorganized the structure of the university, encouraged new programs in teaching and research, and laid the foundation for the fund-raising machinery which would build an endowment and make expansion and development possible. Forced to resign as president in 1952 by the tenure requirements of church law, Cavanaugh served in a number of capacities, including campus ministry at St. Mary's College at Notre Dame. He was an unofficial chaplain* to the family of President John F. Kennedy.

BIBLIOGRAPHY. T. Stritch, "A Hero of Transition," *Notre Dame Magazine* (Feb. 1980) 3-5; T. Hesburgh, "Eulogy for Rev. John J. Cavanaugh, C.S.C.," *Notre Dame Report* (Jan. 1980) 230-232.

J. T. Connelly

Caven, William (1830-1904). Canadian Presbyterian* leader. Born in the southwest of Scotland, his faith and life were nurtured among the Seceders or United Presbyterians, who had left the Church of Scotland in the eighteenth century in order to preserve their evangelical* witness. At seventeen he migrated with his family to the Galt area of Ontario, began studies soon after at the Secession Seminary in London, Ontario, and then pastored for over a decade. In 1861 the Free Church and Secession joined in Ontario and Quebec to form the Canada Presbyterian Church.* Its theological institution was Knox College, Toronto, and Caven was appointed to its Chair of Exegetical Theology in 1865, having personal responsibility for instruction in Old and New Testament. He was to remain there for the remainder of his life, becoming principal in 1873.

Caven was a typical nineteenth-century evangelical Presbyterian of the Secession heritage, akin in his outlook to James Orr (1844-1913) of Glasgow. He was staunchly conservative, yet without confessional rigidity; greatly interested in social questions of a moral kind; thoroughly committed to missions* and fearful of church and state too

readily transgressing each other's boundaries. An active churchman, he was moderator of the Canada Presbyterian Church in the year prior to the Presbyterian union of 1875. Though Caven was interested in church union,* prompted in measure by the fear of Roman Catholicism,* it was not to be had at the expense of a large measure of doctrinal consensus. A number of his writings were posthumously published under the title *Christ's Teaching Concerning the Last Things* (1908), one article of which, "The Testimony of Christ to the Old Testament," was included in *The Fundamentals** (1910-1915).

BIBLIOGRAPHY. J. A. Macdonald, "A Biographical Sketch" in W. Caven, *Christ's Teaching Concerning the Last Things* (1908). I. S. Rennie

Celebrant. The principal minister* who presides at the Eucharist.* In the early church the celebrant was normally the bishop* assisted by members of his presbytery* or local clergy.* Later in the East, the role of celebrant was frequently assigned a single priest, but under the presidency of the bishop; while in the West, the various eucharistic ministries were often performed by a single priest unassisted by other ministers. Characteristic of modern practice are the recent (post-Vatican II*) restoration of the practice of concelebration* (the eucharistic rite performed by several priest celebrants under the presidency of the presiding celebrant) and renewed emphasis on ministerial roles other than that of the presiding celebrant.

BIBLIOGRAPHY. A. A. King, *Concelebration in the Christian Church* (1966). C. Waddell

Celebritism, Christian. The practice of elevating certain well-known Christians to celebrity status, often in both Christian and secular communities. Celebritism is not new. In the New Testament Simon the Magician claimed to be "somebody great" (Acts 8:9, RSV) and attempted to purchase the Holy Spirit's power. In early church history the desert fathers, hermits and stylites were famous for their piety* and sought out for their counsel. By the Middle Ages the church often promoted certain celebrated individuals such as Thomas Becket, whose relics and shrine at Canterbury were the object of great devotion. The medieval papacy also attained a particular celebrity status, elements of which continue to enhance the stature of the Roman Catholic* pope. In some sense, the pope remains the world's most famous Christian person.

American Christianity also knows its share of celebrities. Many flamboyant preachers* and evangelists became famous (or infamous) in the larger society. The colorful oratory of the colonial evangelist George Whitefield* made him a popular figure (Ben Franklin loved to hear him preach). Evangelist Dwight L. Moody* and singer Ira Sankey* were so popular that their pulpit chairs and other personal articles were sold to admiring fans at the end of revival campaigns. Caricatures based on the career of baseball player/evangelist Billy Sunday* are evident in such popular literary works as Sinclair Lewis's *Elmer Gantry* and Carl Sandburg's poem "To a Contemporary Bunk Shooter." Likewise, the adultery trial and acquittal of prominent New York pastor Henry Ward Beecher* made newspaper headlines across the country.

The rise of the broadcast media increased the fame of numerous radio and television preachers, musicians and writers. Billy Graham* has become one of the most famous Protestant* preachers of the twentieth century and a confidant to numerous political leaders. Television contributed significantly to Christian celebritism through the so-called electronic church.* Evangelical preachers such as Jerry Falwell,* Pat Robertson,* Oral Roberts,* Robert Schuller,* Jim and Tammy Bakker* and Jimmy Swaggert,* became media personalities in American culture. Scandals involving some television preachers merely increased their fame. Contemporary Christian recording artists represent yet another group of prominent celebrities. The Christian book publishing industry has fortified the status of individuals through advertising and promoting books by or ghost-written for celebrities. Most devout believers would agree that celebrity status requires great responsibility of all who bear it.

BIBLIOGRAPHY. W. McLoughlin, *Modern Revivalism* (1959); J. K. Hadden and C. E. Swann, *Prime Time Preachers* (1981).

B. J. Leonard

Cell Group. A small group of individuals gathered into a particular unit of a larger organizational structure, similar to the way many cells join together to make a body. Often the cell group is formed around a common purpose or task, and the membership is determined by a willingness to adopt a common discipline or pattern of study and action. The term itself is not biblical, but it suggests a tie to the monastic tradition of historic Christianity. In North America, small-group meetings of religious persons, such as the Methodist* "class meetings," existed from the latter part of the eighteenth century onward. However, the term *cell group* was not common until the twentieth century when it appears simultaneously in political,

religious and psychological contexts.

T. R. Albin

Chafer, Lewis Sperry (1871-1952). Presbyterian* minister,* popular conference speaker and founder of Dallas Theological Seminary.* Born into the home of a Congregational* pastor* in Rock Creek, Ohio, Chafer was raised in a stable home which was sadly disrupted by the death of his father in 1882. Under the painstaking care of his mother, Chafer and his brother and sister were educated at nearby New Lyme Institute and Oberlin College,* where he studied for three semesters in the Conservatory of Music.

In the early 1890s he supplemented the family's income by joining Arthur T. Reed, an evangelist with the YMCA* in Ohio, as his advance man and baritone soloist. His marriage* in 1896 to Ella Loraine Case (whom he had met during his Oberlin years) brought a career change. He briefly settled in the Painesville Congregational Church, Ohio, as assistant pastor to Perry Wayland Sinks and formed his own evangelistic team (he preached, Loraine played the organ, and they sang). In 1899 Chafer became an assistant in the First Congregational Church, Buffalo, New York, and was there ordained* into the Congregational ministry in April 1900.

In early 1901 Chafer's center of activity shifted to Northfield,* Massachusetts, where he purchased a farm, traveled widely in evangelistic work during the winters and assisted in the music ministry of Dwight L. Moody's* famous summer conferences. His encounter, in the fall of 1901, with C. I. Scofield, who was teaching in the Northfield Training School, redirected his life once again. Thoroughly enamored by Scofield's teaching abilities and seemingly clear explanation of the Bible,* Chafer's life was shaped by his newly found mentor. Though he taught in Moody's two schools at Northfield in the area of music, Chafer, sensing an almost parental affection from Scofield, relocated in the New York City area in 1915. He became an extension teacher for Scofield's Bible correspondence school and traveled extensively throughout the South. In 1907 he transferred his ministerial credentials to the Presbyterian Church in the U.S.*

Through his Northfield contacts and his broad exposure through Bible conferences, Chafer gained prominence in the Bible conference movement.* He eventually conceived the idea of founding a theological school that would combine the standard elements of seminary education with the distinctives of the Bible institute* and Bible conference movements (i.e., premillennialism,* Keswick Theology* and extensive instruction in the contents of the English Bible). While pastoring Scofield's former church in Dallas, Texas (renamed in 1922 the Scofield Memorial Church), and directing a mission Scofield had established in 1890 (the Central American Mission), Chafer founded the Evangelical Theological College in 1924 (since 1936, Dallas Theological Seminary) and served as its president and professor of systematic theology* until his death.

Within the emergent evangelical*/fundamentalist* movement of the early twentieth century, Chafer emerged as a champion of the premillennial and dispensational* segment. In addition to numerous books, which include *Satan: His Motive and Methods* (1909), *True Evangelism* (1911), *The Kingdom in History and Prophesy* (1915), *Salvation* (1917), *He That Is Spiritual* (1918), *Grace* (1922) and *Major Bible Themes* (1926), he published his magnus opus, a multi-volume *Systematic Theology,* in 1948. His books reflect the emphasis of his various ministries: gospel preaching, the spiritual life and eschatology.*

BIBLIOGRAPHY. J. D. Hannah, "The Social and Intellectual History of the Evangelical Theological College" (unpublished Ph.D. dissertation, University of Texas at Dallas, 1988).

J. D. Hannah

Chamberlain, Jacob (1835-1908). Dutch Reformed* missionary* to India. Born in Sharon, Connecticut, and raised in Hudson, Ohio, Chamberlain graduated from Western Reserve College in 1856 and studied theology* at Union Theological Seminary,* New York, and the Dutch Reformed Theological Seminary in New Brunswick, New Jersey. Following his seminary graduation, he studied medicine at the College of Physicians and Surgeons in New York City. On taking his medical degree in 1859, he was ordained* a missionary by the Reformed Protestant Dutch Church (now the Reformed Church in America*). In April 1860 he arrived at the site of his life's work, the Arcot Mission in the Madras Presidency of South India.

After studying Tamil and then Telugu, he engaged in extensive evangelistic tours. Utilizing his medical skills, he established two hospitals which ministered to thousands of Indians. As a linguist he was instrumental in producing a Telugu translation of the Bible.* His concern for the education of Christian leaders led in 1887 to his founding at Madanapalle what is reputed to be the first theological seminary on the mission field. There he taught and later served as principal from 1891 to

1902. Chamberlain also worked to unify the Presbyterian* and Reformed churches in India and played a principal role in the establishment of the Reformed Synod of South India in 1902, of which he was elected the first moderator.

Afflicted by recurring illness, he was forced to spend a total of more than ten years in America and the West, an opportunity he took to promote the cause of missions. His writings include: *The Bible Tested in India* (1878); *The Religions of the Orient* (1896) and *The Kingdom in India, Its Progress and Its Promise* (1908). In 1878 his denomination* honored him by making him president of the General Synod of the Reformed Church in America. He died on March 2, 1908, at his home in Madanapalle in South India.

BIBLIOGRAPHY. H. N. Cobb, "A Biographical Sketch," in J. Chamberlain, *The Kingdom in India: Its Progress and Its Promise* (1908); *DAB* II; *Missionary Review of the World* (August 1908).

D. G. Reid

Channing, William Ellery (1780-1842). Unitarian* minister* and theologian.* Born in Newport, Rhode Island, Channing graduated from Harvard College* in 1798 and served as a tutor in Richmond, Virginia (1798-1800). He assumed the pastorate at the Federal Street Church in Boston in 1803 and held it until his death. It fell to Channing to define the liberal movement in New England Congregationalism* that came to be known as Unitarianism. Channing's difficulties in accepting orthodox* Calvinism* began early in his life, but it was not until 1815 that he emerged as the key spokesman for the liberals, with *A Letter to the Rev. Samuel C. Thacher.* Responding to the criticism of the emerging Unitarian movement from the orthodox spokesmen Jedidiah Morse* and Jeremiah Evarts, Channing launched a defense of liberalism that became the theological basis of the American Unitarian Association,* which was formed in 1825. In *Unitarian Christianity* (1819), he accepted the name *Unitarian* for the liberal movement, and the sermon* marks a key point in the liberals' growing conception of themselves as a separate religious community.

Always frail of health, Channing withdrew gradually from an active pastorate at the Federal Street Church, but his work gained increasing influence during his life, as he became a public conscience for New England liberalism. As his theology developed through such important sermons and lectures as *The Evidences of Revealed Religion* (1821), *Likeness to God* (1828), *Spiritual Freedom* (1830) and *Self-Culture* (1838), Channing argued that every individual possessed an innate spiritual potential and that the religious life consisted in the cultivation of that potential.

Likeness to God, a sermon which anticipated some of the themes of the later Transcendentalist Movement,* is his most radical statement of the divine potential of the individual. There Channing argued that a growing "likeness to God" was the object of human life, a concept which stood as an explicit rejection of the Calvinist doctrine of innate human depravity. Channing's theology of spiritual self-culture, which depicted human spiritual potential aspiring toward a benevolent God, became the hallmark of nineteenth-century Unitarianism. The stylistic eloquence of his preaching and important literary essays such as "Remarks on National Literature" (1830) also exerted an important influence on the formation of American literature. Much of Channing's later work was devoted to causes of social justice, as is seen in *Slavery* (1835), an important early indictment of the slavery system. His last work, the *Address at Lenox* (1842), was aimed at further awakening the anti-slavery sentiment in New England.

BIBLIOGRAPHY. *AAP* 8; J. W. Chadwick, *William Ellery Channing; Minister of Religion* (1903); C. Forman, " 'Elected Now by Time,' " in C. C. Wright, ed., *A Stream of Light* (1975); *DAB* II; *DARB;* A. Delbanco, *William Ellery Channing: An Essay on the Liberal Spirit in America* (1981); *NCAB* 5; D. M. Robinson, "The Legacy of Channing," *HTR* 74 (April 1981):221-239.   D. M. Robinson

Chapel. A place of worship,* often small, for a special group or purpose. Some chapels, such as *lady chapels* dedicated to the Virgin Mary,* are found adjoining the main sanctuary or along the aisles of churches or cathedrals.* Others may be contained within a larger institutional structure, such as a convent, dormitory, hospital, prison or even an airport. Still others, such as college and preparatory school chapels, may be free-standing or part of a complex of adjoining structures and provide a central focus for a self-contained community. Family chapels, such as that of the architect Ralph Adams Cram in Sudbury, Massachusetts, are unusual in America. (Cram was America's outstanding designer of chapels, primarily for the Episcopal Church.*) Chapels at older American campuses—Harvard,* Princeton,* Bowdoin, Chicago,* Duke—are fine examples of Gothic or Georgian revival styles, while Eero Saarinen's Kresge Chapel at the Massachusetts Institute of Technology (1955) is of striking contemporary design.

BIBLIOGRAPHY. P. V. Turner, *Campus* (1987); *The Work of Cram and Ferguson, Architects* (1929).   P. W. Williams

Chaplain. A priest* or minister* who performs pastoral duties for special groups and in non-church, though sometimes church-related, institutions. The first chaplains were appointed to minister to bishops* or royalty, carrying out their duties in the "chapels"*—private churches—of these elites. In more recent times, however, the work of the chaplain has been applied to the ministry of clergy* who serve institutions separate from local churches.

The chaplaincy in America began in the military —the army in 1776, the navy in 1794. The military chaplaincy* gradually evolved until, by the period of the Civil War,* chaplains had officer status, wore regular uniforms and were required to be ordained.* Roman Catholic chaplains began to serve in 1824; Jewish chaplains in 1917. By 1860 chaplains were allowed to conduct services according to their own denominational* standards. The first army and navy chiefs of chaplains were appointed in 1920 and 1917 respectively. The military chaplaincy has become very prominent in the twentieth century, due in part to two world wars and the influence of ecumenical organizations like the Federal Council of Churches.*

Like military chaplains, college chaplains began to gain prominence in the late nineteenth century. Before the Civil War the vast majority of colleges in America were church-related. It was assumed that administrators and professors would take an interest in the spiritual needs of students. But when criteria for selecting faculty, presidents and trustees changed, the religious life of many colleges and universities was entrusted into the hands of chaplains. At denominational colleges such chaplains are now responsible to conduct chapel services, teach the theological distinctives of their heritage and nurture the religious life of students, often through counseling and social activism. Chaplains on university campuses carry out similar duties, with the added responsibility of working cooperatively with a wide variety of religious groups.

The work of the chaplaincy has proliferated in the twentieth century as institutions, once controlled by churches and clergy, have become increasingly secular. Many of these institutions now allow for official religious influence through the work of chaplains. The U.S. Senate, for example, employs a chaplain, who cares for the religious needs of the senators and their families. Many state governments also have chaplains who pray at the beginning of legislative sessions and organize religious activities for legislators. Hospital chaplains bring comfort to patients and their families by leading religious services, visiting and counseling patients, and working cooperatively with medical professionals. Prison* chaplains nurture religious life among inmates, administer programs for rehabilitation, organize worship,* support the families of inmates and function as mediators between inmates and prison officials. Industrial chaplains provide religious assistance and counseling for employees of large corporations. Chaplains for athletic teams organize team worship services, prayer meetings and Bible studies* for professional athletes. Thus chaplains in modern American society establish connections between the church and secular spheres of society, providing opportunities for the Christian faith to influence public life.

The popularity of chaplains in American institutions raises at least two important questions. First, chaplains have sometimes found themselves caught between obedience to their religious tradition and loyalty to the institutions they serve. In such cases the priestly witness of the Christian faith has often taken precedence over the prophetic, especially in the case of military, industrial and sports chaplains. Second, chaplains have often had an ambiguous and ambivalent relationship with the organized church. Though ordained, they do not normally serve a local church. Their peculiar status as clergy answerable to both denomination and secular institutions has sometimes created conflicts of interest and conviction.

BIBLIOGRAPHY. H. G. Cox, ed., *Military Chaplains* (1971); A. R. Appelquist, ed., *Church, State and Chaplaincy* (1969); K. R. Mitchell, *Hospital Chaplain* (1972); B. E. Eshelman, *Death Row Chaplain* (1962); L. E. Holst and H. P. Kurtz, eds., *Toward a Creative Chaplaincy* (1973).

G. L. Sittser

Chaplain, Military. Chaplains have been part of Western armies since the fourth century and were transplanted to America with the earliest settlers. They served on a regular basis with colonial militias and under the leadership of George Washington* and, with the approval of the Continental Congress, became a fixed part of the Revolutionary Army and of later federal forces in the years since the adoption of the Constitution in 1789. The Army chaplaincy, founded July 29, 1775, is the second-oldest branch of that service, just behind the infantry. The Navy has used chaplains since November 26, 1775, and the Air Force

authorized them on May 10, 1949. They remain a regular and valued part of those services.

Chaplain duties have been shaped by the mission of the military and distinctive conditions existing within it. Chaplains serve both as staff officers and as religious leaders, responsible for religion, morale and morals. They conduct services of worship,* administer rites and sacraments* consistent with their own faith groups, and provide a full range of religious activities. By regulation, they serve the entire military population and not just members of their own denomination.* Encouraged to minister* where members of the nation's military forces are working or fighting, the chaplaincy is a highly mobile ministry.

The military receives its chaplains through the recruiting efforts of forty-seven separate ecclesiastical endorsing agencies representing 120 denominations. These endorsing agencies certify a candidate's qualifications and may also withdraw its endorsement if it sees fit, insuring that chaplains are authentic representatives of their own denominations and not advocates of some civil,* established or military religion. Prior to endorsement, clergy* must meet military requirements of age, clerical status, physical condition, educational level and security clearance. The Department of Defense, for example, requires an educational level of at least a Master of Divinity or an equivalent degree or three resident years of graduate-level study in theology* or related subjects. Each service maintains a chaplain school where new chaplains receive initial and continuing training in military subjects.

Like other officers, chaplains wear uniforms and bear rank (although they have only supervisory rather than command authority) and are evaluated on their work. Significantly, however, they are always addressed as "chaplain" rather than by their rank. Unlike other officers, they have a dual accountability both to their own religious group and to their military superiors.

Since the end of World War 2,* chaplains have been leaders in initiating and supporting military relief measures, working against drug abuse, supporting efforts to end racial and sexual discrimination and laboring in interfaith cooperative ventures.

BIBLIOGRAPHY. *History of the Chaplain Corps, U.S. Navy* (1985); R. J. Honeywell, *Chaplains of the United States Army* (1958); D. B. Jorgensen, *Air Force Chaplains, 1947-1960* (1961).

C. B. Currey

Chapman, John Wilbur (1859-1918). Presbyterian* pastor* and evangelist.* Born in Richmond,

Indiana, Chapman studied at Oberlin College* in Ohio (1876-1877) and graduated from Lake Forest College in Illinois (B.A., 1879). While attending Lane Seminary in Cincinnati, Ohio (B.D., 1882), Chapman was licensed by the Presbytery of Whitewater in April 1881. His first charge was a two-church circuit, consisting of a rural church in College Corner, Ohio, and a village church in Liberty, Indiana. In subsequent years he served the Old Saratoga Dutch Reformed Church of Schuylerville, New York (1883-1885), the First Dutch Reformed of Albany (1885-1890), Bethany Presbyterian of Philadelphia (1890-1893, 1896-1899) and Fourth Presbyterian of New York (1899-1902). After 1890 Chapman became increasingly involved in evangelistic endeavors and assisted Benjamin F. Mills,* a close friend from college days, in the Cincinnati-Covington and Minneapolis campaigns of 1892, and Dwight L. Moody* in the Chicago World's Fair campaign of 1893.

In 1901 Chapman was appointed corresponding secretary of the Presbyterian General Assembly Committee on Evangelism, where he came in contact with John H. Converse, president of Baldwin Locomotive Works, to whom Chapman acknowledged a great debt, not only for his financial support but for his zeal for lay* evangelism.* After 1903 Chapman devoted himself full-time to evangelistic work. Teamed with musician Charles Alexander,* he conducted meetings across the United States and around the world, with outstanding success in Boston (1909) and Chicago (1910). Chapman introduced the method of the simultaneous campaign into urban evangelism. In addition to the central meeting, numerous other meetings would take place in various parts of a target city, using evangelists and musicians to attract and influence people of various classes.

Chapman was also the first director of the Winona Lake Bible Conference in Indiana. He was the author or editor of thirty books and many tracts and pamphlets. In addition, he authored several hymns* and gospel songs* and compiled a number of hymn books. In 1917 he was elected moderator of the Presbyterian General Assembly.* After his term as moderator he served his denomination* with the National Service Commission and the New Era Forward Movement. Chapman died after emergency surgery on Christmas Day, 1918.

BIBLIOGRAPHY. *DAB* II; *DARB;* J. C. Ramsey, *John Wilbur Chapman: The Man, His Methods and His Message* (1962); D. E. Soden, "Anatomy of a Presbyterian Urban Revival: J. W. Chapman in the Pacific Northwest," *AP* 64 (1986): 49-57.

P. C. Wilt

Chappell, Clovis Gillham (1882-1972). Methodist* minister.* Born in Flatwoods, Tennessee, about sixty miles from Jackson, Chappell attended Duke University (1902-1903) and Harvard University* (1904-1905). In 1908 he was ordained* a minister in the Methodist Episcopal Church, South, and began his ministry in Texas. After pastorates in Oklahoma, Washington, D.C., and Tennessee, in 1932 he became the pastor of First Methodist Church in Birmingham, Alabama. He was pastor of St. Luke's Methodist Church, Oklahoma City (1936-1941); Galloway Memorial Methodist Church, Jackson, Mississippi (1941-1945); and First Methodist Church, Charlotte, North Carolina (1945-1949). Chappell was an outstanding preacher,* widely known for his biographical sermons in which he concentrated on biblical characters. Over thirty volumes of his sermons have been published. In a *Christian Century* poll he was named one of the ten most effective preachers of his time.

D. S. Armentrout

Chapter. Term used of various clerical bodies. The term arose from the meeting of monks* to hear a chapter of their rule or of Scripture read. It then began to designate the meeting itself, which often would include an address from the abbot, resolution of monastery business, etc., and finally to designate the monks themselves in their corporate capacity. By extension, meetings of monks at the provincial level or of the whole order became known as "provincial chapters" or "general chapters." The term has been used in still another way, to designate monks or canons* who are charged, under the administration of the dean, with the maintenance and worship* of a cathedral* or collegiate church. The rectangular (or, occasionally, polygonal) meeting houses erected for these groups are called "chapter-houses" or (rarely nowadays) "chapters." J. G. Stackhouse

Charismatic Movement. The classical Pentecostal movement* usually traces its origin to New Year's Day, 1901, when Agnes Ozman* first spoke in tongues in Charles F. Parham's* Bible school in Topeka, Kansas. The movement that ensued was ridiculed by many outsiders as the religion of the economically deprived, the socially disinherited, the psychologically abnormal and the theologically aberrant. However, by the 1960s many sociological, psychological and theological theories had given way under the increasing evidence that Pentecostals were becoming middle class and educated. At the same time, their characteristic teachings were gaining acceptance among Chris-

tians within mainline* Protestant* denominations,* as well as the Catholic Church.* As the
national media publicized this new movement,
American Christians began to grapple with a
phenomenon that would come to be known as the
charismatic, or neo-Pentecostal, movement.

Charismatic Roots. Just as the nineteenth-
century healing* movement helped mold the
Pentecostal movement, similar dynamics are
evident in the origins of the charismatic movement. One of the earliest Protestant precursors to
the charismatic movement was the International
Order of St. Luke the Physician. By 1947 this
organization, consisting of physicians, ministers*
and laypersons,* was promoting "the restoration of
the Apostolic practice of healing as taught and
demonstrated by Jesus Christ." While embracing
Christians from a variety of traditional churches,
the majority of the society's officers were Episcopalian.* Although this group did not endorse the
fledgling Protestant charismatic movement in the
1960s, it unconsciously played a role in founding
the movement. The importance of healing to the
wider charismatic movement would later be
observed in the ministries of Episcopalian Agnes
Sanford, founder of the School of Pastoral Work,
and the Catholic* monk* Francis MacNutt.

Undoubtedly the most prominent figure in
founding the charismatic movement was the
Southern California dairyman Demos Shakarian.*
As founding president of the Full Gospel Business
Men's Fellowship International* (1953), his efforts
were the catalyst for the Pentecostal experience
penetrating the mainline Protestant and Catholic
churches. Revered as a patriarch of the movement,
he stands alongside Oral Roberts* and David
DuPlessis*—classical Pentecostals who would
each contribute to the growth of the movement
among mainline clergy and laity.

Mainline Protestant Charismatics. In 1960
independent and isolated Protestant charismatic
groups realized they were not alone, and the
nation's religious observers came to recognize that
a new and vital religious movement had been
born. The most newsworthy event was the resignation of Dennis Bennett, rector of St. Mark's Episcopal Church in Van Nuys, California. Bennett had
experienced the baptism in the Spirit* the previous
year, under the influence of a local group of
charismatic laypeople. Within a year, under his
leadership more than 100 others had received the
baptism and spoken in tongues.* Under increasing
pressure from his superiors, Bennett resigned his
parish in 1960 and accepted a reassignment to a
languishing parish in Seattle. Bennett's case

received national attention.

These events gave rise to the influential *Trinity*
magazine that eventually reached an international
audience. Many Protestant charismatics predated
Bennett, and among the better known are Alexander Boddy (1854-1930), James Brown (1912-
1987), Gerald Derstine, John Osteen, Tommy
Tyson, Harald Bredensen and Pat Robertson.*
Robertson's role as founder and head of the
Christian Broadcasting Network has made him an
imposing international figure, but he was just one
on a long list of individuals who gained Pentecostal experiences but retained enough influence
within their church traditions not to join the
Pentecostal movement.

The early 1960s witnessed the movement's
spread into every major stream of traditional
Protestantism. An Assemblies of God* minister,
Ralph Wilkerson, founded the Melodyland Christian Center, a large charismatic congregation that
hosted numerous conferences and supported
various educational ventures. A parachurch organization known as Women's Aglow gained widespread influence. Larry Christenson became a
prominent Lutheran* charismatic, and his church,
the American Lutheran Church,* along with the
Lutheran Church in America,* became fertile ground
for charismatics. The leadership of the Lutheran
Church—Missouri Synod,* on the other hand,
solidly resisted any incursion of the charismatic
movement.

The major Presbyterian* denominations felt the
effects of the movement. The charismatic experience of George C. "Brick" Bradford, Robert C.
Whitaker and Louis Evans, Jr., would be repeated
throughout the United Presbyterian Church
(U.S.A.).* The American Baptist Church had Kenneth Pagard and others, but the Southern Baptist
Convention has yet to concede much influence to
charismatics within its ranks. The United Methodist
Church has been home for vibrant charismatics
like Robert G. Tuttle, Jr., and James Buskirk.

All of these denominations have a sizable
charismatic constituency served by their respective
charismatic organizations employing a full-time
staff, hosting numerous conferences and publishing a considerable literature. Similar fellowships
may be found in the United Church of Christ,* the
Church of Christ* and the Mennonite Church.*
Denominational responses to the movement and
organizations have been both critical and constructive and are compiled in K. McDonnell's *Presence,
Power and Praise* (1980).

Non-Aligned Charismatics. Though the term
independent is spurned by charismatics that are

not aligned with a traditional denomination, it is in fact their theological, personal and social independence that accounts for their separate identities. In this segment of the movement, the trend is toward denominationalism rather than the celebrated ecumenicity of the charismatic movement as a whole.

The movement has produced several megachurches, including Charles Green's Word of Faith Temple in New Orleans, Louisiana; Lester Sumrall's Cathedral of Praise in South Bend, Indiana; Wally and Marilyn Hickey's "Happy Church" in Denver, Colorado; Billy Joe and Sharon Daugherty's Victory Christian Center in Tulsa, Oklahoma; Ron Tucker's Grace World Outreach Center in Maryland Heights, Missouri; and John and Anne Gimenez's Rock Church in Virginia Beach, Virginia. Among the most prominent individual ministries are those of Kenneth Hagin, headquartered in Tulsa, Oklahoma, and Kenneth Copeland of Fort Worth, Texas—both identified with the faith movement.*

In its embryonic stage this denominationalism led to the controversial Discipleship/Shepherding Movement* of the 1970s, centered in the ministries of Derek Prince, Charles Simpson, Don Basham, Bob Mumford and Ern Baxter—collectively known as the Christian Growth Ministries. Originally headquartered in Fort Lauderdale, Florida, they led an authoritarian movement marked by charismatic emphases and a high regard for mutual accountability. A by-product of this movement has been the fledgling denomination known as Covenant Churches.

Though their circumstances vary, a number of groups are taking on increasingly denominational characteristics. These would include Chuck Smith's Calvary Chapels, Bob Weiner's Maranatha Christian Churches, Larry Lea's Churches on the Rock and John Wimber's Vineyard Christian Fellowships. Among the leading charismatic parachurch organizations are Youth With A Mission* and Bethany Fellowship. Three umbrella organizations bringing together many national charismatic leaders are the Network of Christian Ministries, National Leadership Conference and Charismatic Bible Ministries. Other noteworthy groups include the Jews for Jesus,* Orthodox Spiritual Renewal and the Wesleyan Holiness Charismatic Fellowship. Many of these ministries have sizable television enterprises that are either broadcast over network television or have their own cable system, as in the case of Trinity Broadcasting Network. A plethora of books and periodicals are published within the movement, the most influential magazine being *Charis-*

ma, published by Stephen Strang Ministries.

Protestant Charismatic Beliefs. A variety of doctrinal formulations have arisen within the movement, few of them articulated as theology and many of them subject to rapid change. Generally speaking, charismatics in mainline Protestant churches have retained many of the major distinctives of their tradition. The greatest doctrinal variety is found among the non-aligned ministries, fellowships and churches.

In general, Arminianism* has made deep inroads into many charismatic groups, and eschatologies* focused on Christ's imminent return find numerous adherents. Most christologies* are traditional, with the exception of the recurring Spirit christologies, and almost all devotees are classical Trinitarians. Worship* services center on praise and blessing. Some, but not all, charismatics are fervent Zionists.* Women are prominent within the movement, but few women have been given significant authority. Political and social activism does not characterize the movement at large.

Typically middle class and higher in social standing, charismatics are frequently well educated, yet seldom theologically literate. They are avid proponents of inner healing and consider spontaneous, revelational prophecy* a commonplace. Their doctrinal centerpiece remains baptism in the Spirit. Most leaders readily equate their experience with that of classical Pentecostals, but have disavowed the older Pentecostal formulas of two or three so-called works of grace, with tongues-speech as the initial evidence of baptism in the Spirit. In reality, however, there is considerable pressure for communicants to "move up higher" spiritually and not be satisfied until they have spoken in tongues.

The Catholic Charismatic Movement. An indirect result of the extensive changes arising from Vatican II,* the Catholic charismatic movement is perhaps the most remarkable segment of the large charismatic movement. Catholic historians and theologians* are careful to point out that the movement is not new to Catholic history. However, in more recent times, the Cursillo Movement* was foundational for the specific events that took place in 1967 at Pittsburgh's Duquesne University, a Catholic University under the direction of the Fathers of the Congregation of the Holy Spirit. A group of Duquesne students on a spiritual retreat experienced the baptism in the Spirit.

The movement spread to the University of Notre Dame* and then Michigan State University in 1968, where a weekend conference gave birth to a number of early leaders in the movement and

[243]

made Ann Arbor the most prominent center of Catholic charismatic activities. The movement rapidly diversified, and various headquarters opened up across the nation. Especially prominent are the Pecos Benedictine* Abbey, the University of Steubenville and the Southern California Renewal Center. Numerous communities were founded, including the Word of God, now known as Sword of the Spirit, in Ann Arbor, Michigan; People of Praise in South Bend, Indiana; Servants of the Lord in Minneapolis, Minnesota; and Mother of God in Gaithersburg, Maryland.

The movement has enjoyed official encouragement, beginning with the 1969 report by the Committee on Doctrine submitted to the Catholic Bishops of the U.S.A., the response of Pope Paul VI* in 1973, and the more recent encouragement of Pope John Paul II.* Prominent leaders in the movement include theologians Donald Gelpi, Kilian McDonnell, Simon Tugwell, George T. Montague, F. A. Sullivan, Herbert Muhlen and Peter Hocken. There are television celebrities like John Bertolucci and Mother Angelica, along with specialized ministries such as FIRE, SHARE, LAMP, Calix, Centurions and Families in Christ. The *New Covenant* magazine is the most widely distributed periodical among the movement's adherents.

In the first decade of the Catholic movement, a number of Catholics who received the Pentecostal experience joined Protestant churches. While a small percentage of Catholics have joined Pentecostal churches, a few notable Pentecostals have become Roman Catholics. But by the 1980s it was apparent that Catholic charismatics had found a home within their Church. Ecumenical* efforts range from the Vatican-approved dialog with classical Pentecostals to cooperation between Protestant and Catholic charismatics on the grassroots level. Pentecostal scholars have also benefited from the theological reflection of Catholic theologians regarding the person and work of the Holy Spirit.

Catholic theologians are by no means unanimous regarding the meaning of Spirit baptism, but the prevailing opinion seems to be that, regardless of temporal discontinuity, Spirit baptism is related to Christian initiation, whether that be defined as water baptism,* confirmation* or some other experience. They uniformly deny any graduated experience of the Spirit's work and resist the idea that tongues-speech is the initial evidence of Spirit-baptism. On a practical level, however, a larger portion of Catholic charismatics claim to have spoken in tongues than any other segment of the modern charismatic movement.

In 1977 approximately 45,000 to 50,000 Pentecostals and charismatics gathered in Kansas City to celebrate their oneness in Christ and exalt Jesus as Lord. Pentecostals were the least in evidence, with Catholic charismatics constituting the largest single group. In 1985 the conference steering committee decided to sponsor two more major conferences in the U.S. The first, held in October 1986, was the Leader's Congress on the Holy Spirit and World Evangelization. Drawing 7,500 participants, it was a more theologically diverse group than those gathered at the 1977 meeting. The July 1987 congress in New Orleans drew up to 35,000 participants for five days of charismatic celebration and an emphasis on the challenge to extend the movement across the world before the advent of the next millennium. Toward that goal, a Congress was scheduled for August 1990 in Indianapolis and a World Leader's Congress to be held at Brighton, England, in July 1991.

BIBLIOGRAPHY. J. T. Connelly, "Neo-Pentecostalism" (unpublished Ph.D. dissertation, University of Chicago, 1977); D. L. Gelpi, *Pentecostalism: A Theological Viewpoint* (1971); M. Harper, *Three Sisters* (1979); C. Hummel, *Fire in the Fireplace* (1978); K. McDonnell, ed., *Presence, Power, Praise: Documents on the Charismatic Renewal,* 3 vols. (1980); G. T. Montague, *The Holy Spirit* (1976); E. D. O'Conner, *The Pentecostal Movement to the Catholic Church* (1974); R. Quebedeaux, *The New Charismatics II* (1983); K. Ranaghan and D. Ranaghan, *Catholic Pentecostals Today* (1984); T. A. Smail, *The Forgotten Father* (1980); R. Wild, *The Post-Charismatic Experience* (1984); J. R. Williams, *The Gift of the Holy Spirit Today* (1980).

H. D. Hunter

Chase, Philander (1775-1852). Episcopal* bishop* and missionary.* A descendant of New England Puritan* stock, Chase grew up a Congregationalist* on a New Hampshire farm. Upon attending Dartmouth College* (B.A., 1795), he discovered the *Book of Common Prayer* and became an avid Episcopalian. Following his ordination,* he became a most energetic missionary,* traversing over 4,000 miles in New York State during a year and a half. His early work also saw him journey to New Orleans (1805-1811) to establish an Episcopal parish which was the first Protestant church there. Returning to New England, he became rector of Christ Church, Hartford, in 1811. Chase remained in this comfortable station only until 1817, when he again traveled west to found the diocese of Ohio and become its first bishop (1818-1831).

An adept fund raiser, he sailed to England to persuade Lord Kenyon and other aristocrats to endow a theological school and college for Ohio. Out of his efforts grew Kenyon College and a diocesan seminary* which gained the active support of Senator Henry Clay. Chase left Ohio in the wake of a controversy over his autocratic rule of these institutions. Undaunted, he soon embarked on his last great enterprise, the founding of the Illinois diocese, where he served as bishop (1835-1852). Illinois was more sparsely populated than Ohio, and here his efforts to create an institution of higher learning met with less success. Jubilee College lasted only about two decades, expiring shortly after the Civil War.*

Throughout his career, Chase was able to brave financial hardship and sustain his pioneering work due to his resourcefulness as a commercial farmer. He effectively combined the hearty self-reliance of the frontiersman with the evangelistic fervor of the missionary.

BIBLIOGRAPHY. *AAP* 5; P. Chase, *Reminiscences of Bishop Chase, an Autobiography* (1848); *DAB* II; *DARB;* L. C. Smith, *The Life of Philander Chase* (1903).   S. E. Berk

Chauncy, Charles (1589-1672). Puritan* pastor-scholar and second president of Harvard College.* Born in England and educated at Cambridge, Chauncy early distinguished himself as a scholar of Greek and Hebrew, and later as a minister of the gospel. His allegations of "heresy"* and "idolatry" within the Church of England,* however, got him into trouble with Archbishop Laud. Imprisoned, he was forced to recant, an act for which his conscience convicted him throughout the rest of his life.

Eventually silenced and condemned despite his recantation, Chauncy immigrated to Plymouth, Massachusetts, in 1638, and three years later he became the settled pastor at Scituate. In 1654 he succeeded Henry Dunster* as president of Harvard College and served in that post for seventeen years, until his death. A stringent Calvinist,* Chauncy nevertheless differed from his Puritan colleagues in his support of the practice of immersing, rather than sprinkling, infants presented for baptism.* Nevertheless, contemporaries and later historians esteemed him as an administrator, scholar and pastor. By most accounts he was unusual in his ability to balance erudition with plain, accessible preaching.* His extant writings include more than twenty-five sermons and a tract written against the proceedings of the 1662 Synod that produced the Half-Way Covenant.*

BIBLIOGRAPHY. *AAP* 8; *DAB* II; S. E. Morison, *Harvard College in the Seventeenth Century* (1936).   E. C. Nordbeck

Chauncy, Charles (1705-1787). Boston* minister* and Arminian* theologian.* Born on January 1, 1705, Chauncy stepped into a distinguished Boston lineage. His great-grandfather, also named Charles Chauncy,* was the second president of Harvard College,* serving from 1654 to 1672. His father, a merchant, died in 1711, leaving him in the care of his mother. Chauncy prepared for college at Boston Latin School and then attended Harvard, from which he graduated in 1721. After reading theology, he was called by the First Church in Boston, which ordained* him in 1727. He served the church until his death.

The early years of Chauncy's ministry were uneventful, and he developed a reputation as an erudite but dull preacher* of orthodox* doctrines. The advent of the Great Awakening,* however, divided New England Congregationalism* into New Light* (pro-revival) and Old Light* (anti-revival) wings. Chauncy initially approved of the spiritual renewal the revival* brought, but he soon grew concerned about the emotional excesses that he found in the behavior of some of its partisans, who were moved by their preachers to cry out and faint at meetings. Between 1742 and 1745 Chauncy led the Old Lights in resisting the revival. In *Seasonable Thoughts on the State of Religion in New-England* (1743), a 400-page volume written after he had made a 300-mile tour of New England, New York and New Jersey, Chauncy catalogued what he considered to be the revival's worst consequences.

Although *Seasonable Thoughts* was a polemic, in many of his later works Chauncy resumed the scholarly tone that ordinarily characterized his sermons and other writings. His subsequent publications placed him in the forefront of the liberal, or Arminian, movement which became increasingly apparent within New England Congregationalism after mid-century. In common with other Arminians, Chauncy preached the benevolence of God and the importance of human reason to a sincere conversion* experience. He also shared their view, in opposition to the Calvinist* doctrine of predestination,* that a sinner could enhance his chances for salvation* through moral conduct and spiritual self-development. Reasoning from his belief in God's benevolence, Chauncy eventually became convinced of the doctrine of universal* salvation, a view he promoted in several publications, notably *The Benevolence of the Deity* and *The Mystery Hid from Ages* (both published

[245]

posthumously in 1784).

A man of strong beliefs, Chauncy was often involved in controversy. Two such events occupied much of the final quarter-century of his life: the effort to resist an Anglican* episcopate in the American colonies and the American Revolution,* which he strongly supported. Chauncy first argued the invalidity of episcopal* ordination in 1732 when his brother-in-law converted* to Anglicanism and took holy orders. A massive manuscript that he prepared at the time remained unpublished until 1771, however, when in response to plans for a colonial bishop,* it appeared as *A Compleat View of Episcopacy*. Chauncy recognized connections between the proposed episcopacy and royal measures to strengthen the imperial system. His ardent support of the revolutionary cause throughout the 1760s and 1770s grew out of his conviction that British religious and political activities threatened American liberties.

BIBLIOGRAPHY. *AAP* 8; *DAB* II; E. M. Griffin, *Old Brick: Charles Chauncy of Boston, 1705-1787* (1980); C. Lippy, *Seasonable Revolutionary: The Mind of Charles Chauncy* (1981); C. K. Shipton, *Sibley's Harvard Graduates,* vol. 6 (1942); C. C. Wright, *The Beginnings of Unitarianism in America* (1955). C. E. Wright

Cheney, Charles Edward (1836-1916). Second bishop* of the Reformed Episcopal Church.* After ordination* to the priesthood* of the Episcopal Church* in 1860, he became the first rector of Christ Church, Chicago. He was at once embroiled in the contest then being waged in the Episcopal Church between evangelicals* and the Tractarian Movement,* and in 1869 he was placed on trial by his bishop, H. J. Whitehouse, for deliberately omitting the liturgical* declaration of "regeneration" in the order for baptism.* Although condemned by the diocesan* court, the sentence was declared invalid by the Supreme Court of Illinois, and his subsequent deposition from the ministry* by Bishop Whitehouse in 1871 has since been acknowledged to have been without proper foundation.

Cheney joined the Reformed Episcopal Church upon its organization in 1873 and was consecrated a missionary* bishop. He organized the Synod* of Chicago in 1875 and served as presiding bishop from 1876-1877 and again from 1887-1889. However, he resigned all of his ecclesiastical posts, except the bishopric of Chicago, in 1897 in protest against regulations restricting the use of liturgical vestments. His lectures, *What Reformed Episcopalians Believe* (1888), are a concise statement of

Cheney's views of the issues raised by the Tractarian Movement in America.

BIBLIOGRAPHY. *DAB* II; R. H. Longmire, "Charles Edward Cheney, Bishop of the Reformed Episcopal Church" (S.T.M. thesis, Lutheran Theological Seminary, Philadelphia, 1965); E. C. Chorley, *Men and Movements in the American Episcopal Church* (1946). A. C. Guelzo

Cheverus, Jean Lefevre de (1768-1836). First Roman Catholic* bishop* of Boston. Born in Mayenne, France, and ordained* in Paris in 1790, Cheverus fled to England in 1792 because he refused to support the Civil Constitution of the Clergy. In 1796, he immigrated to the U.S. at the urging of François Matignon, a former seminary teacher who had left France to serve as parish priest* in Boston. Accepted for pastoral work by Bishop John Carroll,* Cheverus began ministering to Passamaquoddy Indians in Maine and Catholics in the Boston area. In 1808 the Vatican appointed him head of the newly created diocese* of Boston, which encompassed all of New England. As bishop, Cheverus continued to foster better relations with the dominant Protestant* majority, counting William Ellery Channing* and Edward Everett as close friends. When he was recalled to France in 1823 to serve as bishop of Montauban, 226 non-Catholics in Boston, including Elbridge Gerry, Daniel Webster and Josiah Quincy, signed a petition to the King of France declaring that Cheverus was "a blessing and treasure in our social community which we cannot part with." Cheverus became archbishop of Bordeaux in 1826, and Pope Gregory XVI named him a cardinal* in February 1836.

BIBLIOGRAPHY. *DAB* II; A. J. Hamon, *Life of the Cardinal de Cheverus* (1839); A. M. Melville, *Jean Lefevre de Cheverus, 1768-1836* (1958). W. P. Leahy

Chicago Declaration of Social Concern. An evangelical declaration of commitment to social involvement. A landmark document, the Declaration manifested to evangelicals, the greater church and society that a new period of evangelical* social involvement had arrived. The statement was formed and signed at a Thanksgiving workshop coordinated by Ronald J. Sider in November 1973. The diverse fifty-three original signers included senior neo-evangelical* leaders, but many were younger or represented different evangelical traditions. The Declaration attracted wide recognition in the secular and religious press.* Two further implementing workshops were also held in

Chicago in 1974 and 1975. Two organizations, the Evangelical Women's Caucus and Evangelicals for Social Action, originated in these meetings. Proclaiming the power of Christ to provide freedom from sin,* the Declaration confessed racial and economic injustice, nationalism, materialism, militarism, maldistribution of resources, domination by males and passivity by women. The primary drafters of the statement were William Pannell, Jim Wallis and Stephen Mott, who reworked a manuscript prepared by Paul Henry.

BIBLIOGRAPHY. R. J. Sider, ed., *The Chicago Declaration* (1974). S. C. Mott

Chicago School of Theology. A theological movement centered at the Divinity School of the University of Chicago. In its early years, from its founding in 1892 to the mid-1920s, three central motifs characterized the Chicago School: a sociological orientation, use of the historical-critical method and an appropriation of pragmatism as developed by William James* and, especially, John Dewey.

Faculty members Shailer Mathews* and Shirley Jackson Case* saw Christianity as a social movement whose origins and development were to be studied by the methods of secular historical criticism. Edward Scribner Ames* viewed religion as one of humanity's many ways of adapting to its environment, the real meaning of religious doctrines and practices being located in the specific functions which they perform. This focus on the practical, utilitarian and adaptive nature of religion led the Chicago School to an appreciation of the theory of evolution. In its focus on the empirical, concrete, practical and functional aspects of religion, the Chicago School showed that it emerged out of the same cultural background as American fundamentalism* which, in its appeal to the people in the pew, also emphasized the practical and functional value of religion for daily life—without appropriating the theory of evolution.

The Chicago School could not avoid the question of whether Christianity, however defined and modified in the interests of modernity, is true. Both Gerald Birney Smith* and George Burman Foster* wrestled with this question. Foster as early as 1906 was struggling with the possibility of the Death of God,* as well as experimenting with concepts of God which stressed God as Cosmic Process as opposed to the supernatural, timeless and perhaps static deity of the Christian tradition.

In the 1920s, Henry Nelson Wieman* introduced the empirical metaphysics of Alfred North White-head to the Divinity School (*see* Process Theology). The newer members of the Divinity School faculty found Whitehead's metaphysics to be no less empirical than Dewey's pragmatism and yet conceptually more powerful as a means of articulating Christianity in the modern world. At Chicago the movement called process theology took on a public and self-conscious identity.

Of all the theologians of the Chicago School, perhaps no one was more focused on Whitehead's philosophy as the basis for Christian theology than Bernard M. Loomer (1912-1985), who became dean of the Divinity School a few years after completing his dissertation at Chicago on the implications of Whitehead's philosophy for theological method. As dean he organized the entire curriculum around process thought and in so doing firmly identified the Chicago School with process theology.

But even during the peak of process theology's dominance in the Chicago School, most of the Chicago theologians employed additional resources beyond Whitehead's philosophy. During his later years Wieman moved away from the more speculative aspects of Whitehead's philosophy, as did Loomer. Daniel Day Williams,* while clearly centered in process theology, nonetheless tried to remain open to the concerns of neo-orthodoxy.* Bernard E. Meland (1899-) had the goal of deepening the rather naive and superficial optimism of traditional liberalism by attending carefully to the "dimensions of depth" in human experience as revealed by modern psychology, physics and social analysis, as well as by the endless tragedies of the twentieth century. Charles Hartshorne (1897-) produced his own version of process philosophy, which incorporated more rationalistic and idealistic elements than Whitehead's version.

The addition of Paul Tillich* to the Divinity School faculty, first on a part-time basis in 1955 and full-time in 1962, signaled the end of the dominance of pragmatism and process thought at Chicago. Tillich brought with him his own rather European theological method. In the 1960s, several new appointments to the faculty completed the transition to a more pluralistic methodology and thus marked the end of the Chicago School. However, professors in historical theology at Chicago had been maintaining contacts with alternative types of Christian theology, including those based on revelation and on the Bible as a sacred text.

While the Chicago School no longer exists as a clearly demarcated movement, it continues its influence in the growth of process theology throughout the U.S. Many of the leading process theologians, such as John Cobb, Jr. (1925-), and Schubert Ogden (1928-), graduated from the Divinity School at the height of its commitment to process theology.

See also HARPER, WILLIAM RAINEY.

BIBLIOGRAPHY. C. H. Arnold, *Near the Edge of Battle* (1966); L. E. Axel, *God or Man at Chicago: The Chicago School of Theology* (1975); W. E. Dean, *American Religious Empiricism* (1986); W. J. Hynes, *Shirley Jackson Case and the Chicago School* (1981); B. E. Meland, "Introduction: The Empirical Tradition in Theology at Chicago," in *The Future of Empirical Theology,* ed. B. E. Meland (1969); C. Peden, *The Chicago School* (1987).

S. T. Franklin

Chicago-Lambeth Quadrilateral. Seminal and authoritative document of four articles held by the Episcopal Church* and the worldwide Anglican Communion* as a minimal basis for any discussions that may lead to church unity. Originating in *The Church Idea* (1870) of William Reed Huntington,* the Quadrilateral was adopted by the American Episcopalian bishops* in 1886 and, after some revision, by the Lambeth Conference* of 1888.

Its four articles affirm: (1) the Holy Scriptures as "the rule and ultimate standard of faith"; (2) the Apostle's and Nicene Creeds as "the sufficient statement of the Christian faith"; (3) the sacraments* of Baptism* and the Lord's Supper* ministered with "Christ's words of institution" and "the elements ordained by Him"; and (4) the "historic episcopate, locally adapted in the methods of its administration." Originally conceived as a starting point from which other matters in dispute might then be discussed, the four points have sometimes been misinterpreted as a goal in themselves constituting a sufficient basis for reunion.

Although the Quadrilateral's influence in the ecumenical movement* has been great, its fourth point has been the subject of continual controversy and varying interpretations. It did not achieve a reunification of American churches, as was originally intended, but it did inaugurate for Anglicans a new era of ecumenical discussion and gradually increasing cooperation. Reaffirmed by subsequent Lambeth Conferences, it has been the basis for all Anglican unity negotiations with non-episcopal churches, and it remains the ecumenical position of the worldwide Anglican Communion of Churches today.

BIBLIOGRAPHY. *Book of Common Prayer* (1979):876-878; J. F. Woolverton, "Huntington's Quadrilateral—A Critical Study," *CH* 39 (1970):198-211; J. R. Wright, *Quadrilateral at One Hundred* (1988).

J. R. Wright

Child Evangelism Fellowship. An international evangelistic* organization working with children. Jesse Irvin Overholtzer, founder of Child Evangelism Fellowship, directed his ministry* to the spiritual needs of children after reading a statement from one of Charles Haddon Spurgeon's sermons: "A child of five, if properly instructed, can as truly believe and be regenerated as an adult." Overholtzer first led a child to Christ in 1916 and for the next 14 years pursued a children's ministry through the Christian Training Association, a program of adult leadership training and children's Bible* classes.

In the 1930s, Overholtzer left California to administer a training school in Chicago, where he felt the call of God to begin a worldwide evangelistic ministry to children. A national committee was formed and a prayer offered that "every child . . . have a chance to accept Christ." Child Evangelism Fellowship was officially organized May 20, 1937.

The ministry began with an extended bus tour to the major cities of the U.S. and Canada. Committees were formed, directors appointed, and training schools begun. The International CEF Institute opened in Dallas in 1945. CEF originally focused on children's Bible classes (later known as Good News Clubs) and through its fifty-year history had added prayer programs, "Radio Kids Bible Club," a magazine (*Evangelizing Today's Child*), summer programs, an Overseas Summer Missions program for college students, a radio program called "Here's How" to train adults, a children's television program ("The Treehouse Club"), telephone outreach (Tel-A-Story), video training and a summer camping program. The CEF home office is located in Warrenton, Missouri, and serves 850 U.S. staff workers, 180 missionaries and 600 nationals and missionaries sent from countries other than the United States.

BIBLIOGRAPHY. *50 Years—Still Sharing the Vision* (1987).

B. E. Brown

Children, Christian Ministries to. The nature of Christian ministries* to children has paralleled historical shifts in attitudes toward children. Whereas Christianity was an integral part of childhood in seventeenth-century Puritan* New England, the impact of industrialization, urbanization and immigration* in subsequent centuries has served to institutionalize responsibility for religious training.

The Puritan ministry to children was focused within the family and church. Parents taught their own children to read the Bible* and to memorize the catechism.* New England Puritans viewed the establishment of public schools as part of their ministry to children because the ability to read God's Word increased the possibility of salvation.* In other parts of the New World, Christianity was encouraged among slave children, and mission* schools were established for Native American children. Apart from schools, institutions specifically designed for children were rare, except as a means of caring for the destitute.

As more non-Puritans settled in America, the impact of Puritan ideas was diffused. The early republic and Jacksonian eras brought the creation and democratization of religious organizations. The Sunday-school movement* was established to supplement church preaching*; and many church colleges* were founded, in part to offset the impact of Enlightenment* thought on the young.

Early nineteenth-century revivals* and reform movements* prompted the formation of religious organizations which would address societal ills. Nineteenth-century immigration created the need for more orphanages and almshouses. Of the numerous Christian organizations in the "Benevolent Society," many were directed toward children—for missions, evangelism* and morality, as well as social welfare.

Late nineteenth-century Christian ministries to children were typified by the example of the Student Volunteers for Foreign Missions,* which not only reaffirmed Christian principles but also motivated young people to spread the gospel throughout the world. The Protestant* emphasis on voluntary organizations and on crusades was exemplified in one of the early parachurch* organizations, the YMCA.* The Sunday-school movement and the Christian Endeavor* groups made conscious attempts to counter the secularization of society. Part of the rationale for the temperance movement* was the impact of alcoholism on children. Organizations like The Salvation Army* and urban rescue missions* evangelized and cared for poor children and also offered religious alternatives to secular youth clubs like the Girl Scouts.

Twentieth-century ministries to children have burgeoned and continue to respond to changes in society. Christian parachurch organizations address issues such as abortion* and homosexuality,* as well as providing for children's social welfare, religious education within the church and Christian-oriented private schooling as an alternative to public education. Christian youth groups apply biblical principles to contemporary problems such as divorce, drug abuse and teen suicide, as well as addressing issues such as self-esteem and sexuality. In addition to encouraging Bible study,* Christian ministries often adapt their methodologies to compete with the trend toward entertainment in secular society. Almost all ministries are age-specific and highly organized in order to fit the fast-paced age of advanced industrialized society in the U.S. Thus, over time, Christian ministries to children have reached a broader spectrum of the population and have become more systematic in their approach.

See also CATHOLIC YOUTH ORGANIZATION; CHILD EVANGELISM FELLOWSHIP; CHRISTIAN SERVICE BRIGADE; CHRISTIAN ENDEAVOR SOCIETY; EPWORTH LEAGUE; SUNDAY-SCHOOL MOVEMENT; YOUNG LIFE; YOUTH FOR CHRIST.

BIBLIOGRAPHY. R. H. Bremner, ed., *Children and Youth in America: A Documentary History,* 3 vols. (1971, 1974); R. W. Lynn and E. Wright, *The Big Little School: 200 Years of the Sunday School* (1980).   L. Schneider

Children of God. *See* FAMILY OF GOD.

China Inland Mission. *See* OVERSEAS MISSIONARY FELLOWSHIP.

Choir. Any group musical performance, such as a male chorus, a brass ensemble or bells; usually a mixed choral group singing in four parts. Choral singing is as ancient as written music. Most choral literature is sacred because until the twentieth century it was associated nearly exclusively with churches.

Choirs in America grew out of the singing school movement of both colonial New England and the frontier West. English and German choral traditions influenced nineteenth-century expansion as community choirs grew along with church and school music. Trained singers and the opportunity to lead in hymns and other worship brought the choir together in a special section of the church—often at the front. Choir repertoires are as varied as the tastes of churches and schools. Choirs perform gospel songs,* hymn arrangements, anthems and large works.

BIBLIOGRAPHY. E. A. Wienandt, *Choral Music of the Church* (1965).   R. J. Stanislaw

Chornock, Orestes (1883-1977). Metropolitan* of the American Carpatho-Russian Orthodox Greek Catholic Diocese of the U.S.A., bishop* of Agathonikia. Born in Ortutova, Prjasevska Rus (Southeastern Czechoslovakia), he attended the Presov Theological Academy and was ordained* a priest* of the Greek Catholic Church in 1906. In 1908, with his wife, Pani Yolanda, he immigrated* to the U.S. and served in several parishes.*

Like other graduates of Presov, he stressed the Eastern orientation of the Greek Catholic Church, following what he perceived to be the true spirit of the Union of Uzhorod (1646). That union permitted Carpatho-Russians, while being united with the Roman Catholic Church,* to maintain their liturgical* customs, have married priests and elect their own bishops. Thus, when the Vatican* issued the decree *Cum Data Fuerit* (1929), requiring Greek Catholic clergy* in America to be celibate, he protested. As a result, he was suspended by the Carpatho-Russian Bishop Takach in 1931. For the next four years, he led the fight to uphold the Uzhorod Union for the American Church, serving on the Committee for the Defense of the Eastern Rite (KOVO). In 1936, with this situation unresolved, "anti-celibacy" forces met in Pittsburgh to form a new Greek Catholic Diocese and chose Father Orestes to be its administrator until a suitable bishop could be elected.

After the death of Father Orestes's wife in 1937, the National Religious Convention met and elected Father Orestes to be bishop of the new diocese. With his selection, all ties with Rome and the Union of Uzhorod were severed. The Carpatho-Russian Diocese turned to the Patriachate of Constantinople and petitioned to be brought into the Orthodox Communion. After the petition was approved, Father Orestes went to Constantinople, where he was consecrated* bishop and given the titular see of Agathonikia on September 18, 1938. The next day, the Carpatho-Russian Greek Catholic Diocese of the Eastern Rite of the U.S.A. was canonized as a diocese of the Ecumenical Patriarchate by Patriarch Benjamin I.

In the years that followed, Father Orestes's ministry focused on establishing the means by which the survival and growth of the Diocese would be insured. In this endeavor, he was actively involved in the founding of the American Carpatho-Russian Youth Organization (1947), along with the establishment of Christ the Saviour Seminary (1951) at Johnstown, Pennsylvania. For his long years of service to the Diocese, he was elevated to the rank of metropolitan in 1965.

BIBLIOGRAPHY. L. Barriger, *Good Victory: Metropolitan Orestes Chornock and the American Carpatho-Russian Orthodox Greek Catholic Diocese* (1985); Archimandrite Serafim, *The Quest for Orthodox Church Unity in America* (1973).

C. M. Elliott

Choruses. A general term given to simple, usually four-line, gospel songs which repeat text, tune or both so that they can be learned by rote. Although the genre originally was a refrain, such as the "Hallelujah" or "Bound for the Kingdom" closing lines of early nineteenth-century African-American or white spirituals, the style quickly stood alone as a musically simple setting of an easily remembered text.

Designed to be quickly learned, choruses are usually short-lived—except for sentimental favorites. A few, such as "Jesus Loves the Little Children" or "For God So Loved the World," have become standards.

The broad term now includes the "worship music" of charismatic* improvisation, group singing at popular Christian entertainers' concerts or mini-hymns learned by rote in liturgical traditions, as well as songs used in children's worship and instruction. R. J. Stanislaw

Chrism. The early Christian name (from the Greek, *chrisma,* meaning "anointing") for a mixture of olive oil, balsam and (in Eastern Christianity) perfumes used sacramentally* and liturgically.* Its early Christian use is witnessed to by Church Fathers. Anointing was primarily related to the sacrament of chrismation or confirmation,* and to the consecration of church buildings. The Eastern Orthodox* and Roman Catholic* Churches hold that the sacrament conveys the strength and gift of the Holy Spirit, completes the baptismal cleansing and grants full layperson status to those anointed with it. In both Churches, the bishop* is involved, either directly or indirectly. The Orthodox anoint newly baptized infants; the Roman Catholics anoint older children as part of confirmation rites. Among the Orthodox, this sacrament is also used to receive converts who have been previously baptized in the name of the Holy Trinity in other churches and apostates returning to Christianity.

BIBLIOGRAPHY. G. W. H. Lampe, *The Seal of the Spirit* (1951); A. Schmemann, *Of Water and the Spirit* (1974). S. S. Harakas

Christian. Believers in Christ were first called Christians (*christianos*) in Antioch of Syria (Acts 11:26). What the term intended to convey is uncertain, but the Greek papyri provide some help. There, a comparative form is *kaisarianos,* a slave or soldier of the divine Caesar; *christianos*

then would signify a slave or soldier belonging to the divine Christ. Such persons are bought with a price (1 Cor. 6:19, 20) and are "born again" or "born from above" (John 3:7) through faith in Christ (John 3:16; Eph. 2:8, 9).

After the Roman Empire became officially Christian and started to persecute pagans, the church was filled with the unconverted as membership requirements declined. As barbarians moved into the West and Muslims conquered the East, the Christian enclave shrunk. With the establishment of the Holy Roman Empire after 800, all of Europe gradually became officially Christian. People were baptized as infants, confirmed and grew up as Christians, never knowing anything else. Russia also became officially Christian after Vladimir's conversion in 988. During the Middle Ages, until Luther began the Protestant* Reformation in 1517, a Christian was a Roman Catholic* or Eastern Orthodox* person who was a member of the institutional church. In Reformation lands, after the initial emphasis on the conversion* experience to become a Christian, established Lutheran,* Reformed* and Anglican* churches arose; and a Christian again tended to be one who was baptized and confirmed and grew up in the church.

With the English colonization of North America, there was initially among the Puritans an emphasis on the necessity of a conversion experience to become a Christian. But this emphasis waned with succeeding generations and the establishment of the Congregational Church in nine of the thirteen colonies. New England Congregationalists* were baptized in the church and later "owned the covenant." Anglicans were baptized in the church and subsequently confirmed. Some dissenting groups required evidence of the new birth* for church membership* and a claim to the title "Christian." The Great Awakening* of the eighteenth century and the Second Great Awakening of the nineteenth century emphasized the need for spiritual new birth to be a real Christian. Today's mainline denominations do not require prospective members to witness to having experienced a new birth. Historically speaking, they have been influenced by Horace Bushnell's* theory of Christian nurture,* which maintained that children should grow up in a Christian home as children of the covenant, never knowing they were anything but Christian.

In North America today, a Christian is often regarded as someone who belongs to a Christian church or practices the ethic of Christ. However, those within the evangelical tradition and its sphere of influence, continue to maintain that a true Christian is a person who has experienced a turning point in their life in which they committed themselves to Jesus Christ. A 1982 Gallup Survey found that thirty-eight per cent of Americans attested to having had a "born again" experience.

H. F. Vos

Christian Action. *See* FELLOWSHIP OF SOCIALIST CHRISTIANS.

Christian and Missionary Alliance. Evangelical* denomination* with strong emphases on overseas missions* and personal holiness.* The century-long history of The Christian and Missionary Alliance (C&MA) is essentially the story of a parachurch* organization evolving into a denomination.

The founder of the movement, A. B. Simpson,* was a Canadian-born Presbyterian* minister.* As pastor of a well-to-do church in New York City, Simpson began to gather like-minded people with a burning interest in evangelism,* world missions and a deeper Christian life. After leaving his prestigious parish Simpson began a number of ministries: the Gospel Tabernacle, a nondenominational church (1881); the Missionary Training Institute (now Nyack College, 1882); the Christian Alliance (1887) and the Evangelical Missionary Alliance (1887).

The Christian Alliance was envisioned by Simpson as a broad fellowship of Christians who, while retaining membership in their denominations and individual churches, would gather for fellowship and mutual encouragement. This ecumenically spirited fellowship focused on themes such as "The gospel of full salvation* and present and complete sanctification"* and "the provision Christ has made in the Gospel for our physical redemption through divine healing."* The Evangelical Missionary Alliance was the missionary arm of this parent organization. Its role was to promote missions and send missionaries around the world. In 1897 the two alliances amalgamated into one organization, the Christian and Missionary Alliance.

The primary institutions of the movement were branches, local gatherings of people from varying churches and denominations, as well as national conventions of the various branches. Simpson had never intended to start new churches or a new denomination. But over the years this parachurch organization began to look more and more like a denomination. Many branches became actual churches, and people associated with the movement began churches which they designated as Christian and Missionary Alliance. By the 1960s its leadership had acknowledged that it was indeed a denomination.

Today the worldwide constituency of the Alliance is approximately two million members and adherents in over forty countries. As of 1986 there were 1,214 overseas missionaries. In 1986 the U.S. constituency included 1,691 churches and 238,734 members and adherents (130,116 members and 108,618 adherents). The U.S. headquarters for the Alliance is in Nyack, New York. The denomination owns and operates three colleges (Nyack College, Simpson College in San Francisco, and St. Paul Bible College in Minnesota) and Alliance Theological Seminary in New York, while the Canadian schools are Canadian Bible College and Canadian Theological Seminary in Regina, Saskatchewan.

The doctrinal statement of the C&MA includes such themes as the inerrancy* of Scripture, sanctification* as both a crisis and a progressive experience, physical healing* and the imminent and premillennial* return of Christ (*see* Eschatology). *See also* SIMPSON, A. B.

BIBLIOGRAPHY. D. Hartzfeld and C. Nienkirchen, *The Birth of a Vision* (1986); R. Niklaus, J. Sawin and S. Stoesz, *All for Jesus* (1986); A. W. Tozer, *Wingspread* (1943).

D. P. Hollinger

Christian Booksellers Association. A retail management organization. Christian Booksellers Association, headquartered in Colorado Springs, Colorado, was organized in 1950 to service the specific needs of Christian bookstore owners and managers. It is the vehicle for uniting over 3000 Christian bookstores in the U.S., nine International Chapters and over 650 suppliers. The goal of the organization is "accomplishing ministry through retailing . . . getting the Christian product off the shelf and into the hands of people who need it." Media exposures are employed to increase public awareness of the bookstores' offerings for help in private lives and public ministries.

Members of the CBA benefit from the organization's management training, technical business advice, advertising assistance, insurance programs and computer information. CBA conventions provide opportunities to view products, talk with suppliers, order merchandise, attend workshops and exchange ideas with other Christian booksellers. Practical help is also provided through a number of publications. *The Bookstore Journal,* a monthly trade journal, provides industry news, informational articles, supplier advertising and best-seller lists. CBA also publishes a Suppliers Directory and an organization newsletter.

BIBLIOGRAPHY. J. P. Dessauer et al., *Christian Book Publishing and Distribution in the United States and Canada* (1987).

B. E. Brown

Christian Camping. Christian camping has been defined as an experience in guided Christian living in the out-of-doors. Its uniqueness as an agency of Christian education* is in the combination of a round-the-clock living experience in a group setting of peers with qualified leadership in the out-of-doors, especially the world of nature. Dr. Charles Eliot, former president of Harvard,* expressed the opinion that "the organized summer camp is the greatest contribution America has made to education."

The antecedents of Christian camping may be found in the frontier camp meeting,* the educational assemblies (such as Chautauqua), Bible conference* grounds, the appeal of outdoor adventure associated with the Civil War* and the exploration of the West, and the ardor of evangelical* men and women who creatively evangelized* and discipled youth.

The first church camp was led by Reverend George Hinckley in Rhode Island in 1880. Prior to this, Frederick and Abigail Gunn operated a school camp in 1861 and Dr. Joseph T. Rothrock conducted a private health camp in 1876. In 1881 Ernest B. Balch organized a pioneer camp in which campers contributed to its operation. The worldwide YMCA* camping movement had its inception with Sumner F. Dudley's Camp Bald Head in 1885. Dr. Luther and Charlotte (Vetter) Gulick, children of missionaries and authorities in health, education and recreation, operated a family camp in 1887 and held the first girls camp in 1888. They helped found the Campfire Girls in 1912.

In 1907 Robert Baden-Powell set up a trial camp in England and authored *Scouting for Boys* in 1908. Ernest T. Seton helped organize the Boy Scouts of America in 1910. This movement helped to popularize camping as a character-building ally to the home, school and church. Its *Manual* has long been a valued resource in campcraft and camping skills.

Camping in the early decades was largely agency-related. These camps were in large measure Christian in aim, program and staff. After camping moved from its dominant Christian character to a broader educational and social institution, evangelical church-related camps developed. This happened between the two world wars and increasingly after the second war.

The camping industry and profession is served by the American Camping Association (ACA), originating in the Camp Directors Association of America in 1910. ACA has 5,500 members serving 6,000 camps. They estimate upwards of 10,000 camp programs (not properties) currently serving four million children and youth in the summer and nine million children, youth and adults per year throughout the U.S. Christian Camping International (CCI) is an alliance of twelve camping associations around the world, with 900 member camps in CCI-USA organized into six regions and twenty-five sections. There are 550 CCI-related camps outside the U.S.

The camping associations publish journals, hold conventions, establish standards and accredit camps. In the late 1980s the camping movement faced the challenges of plateaued enrollment by using trained volunteers, appealing to specialized camping needs, and developing partnerships with churches to help them accomplish their objectives.

BIBLIOGRAPHY. E. Eells, *History of Organized Camping: The First 100 Years* (1986); C. V. Anderson, "Camping History," *An Introduction to Christian Camping,* ed. W. Graendorf and L. Mattson (1979).
C. V. Anderson

Christian Century, The. An ecumenical* Protestant* journal of news and opinion. *The Christian Century* began publication in 1884 as the *Christian Oracle,* published by the Disciples of Christ.* The magazine was renamed *The Christian Century* in 1900 and began to achieve prominence in 1908 when Charles Clayton Morrison* became editor. Morrison expanded the focus and audience of the journal, dropping its denominational affiliation in 1916 and calling his effort "An Undenominational Journal of Religion." It is now described as "An Ecumenical Weekly."

Through its history *The Christian Century* has reflected and communicated the social and theological agenda of mainline* American Protestantism. While the journal has often extended its view beyond this focus, it has primarily served as a forum for the debate and discussion of the causes and concerns of its principal audience, Protestant clergy* and lay* people in the mainline denominations. Over the years the most important of these causes and concerns have included the Social Gospel,* the ecumenical movement* and other attempts at Christian unity, pacifism,* prohibition,* liberal* theology* and civil rights.* Many of the leading figures in American Protestantism have contributed to the journal, as contributing editors, reviewers, writers or participants in the long-running series spotlighting theological development over the decades, "How My Mind Has Changed." As in the past, subjects addressed in the pages of the magazine today include politics, ethical questions, the arts and literature, news of the secular and religious worlds, liturgy* and worship,* and theology. The journal continues today to provide an accurate picture of the contemporary mainline American Protestant community, in both its unity and its diversity.

BIBLIOGRAPHY. L. Delloff, "C. C. Morrison: Shaping a Journal's Identity," *CCen* 101 (January 18, 1984):43-47; L. Delloff, "The Century in Transition: 1916-1922," *CCen* 101 (March 7, 1984):243-246; D. Peerman, "Forward on Many Fronts: The Century 1923-1929," *CCen* 101 (June 6-13, 1984):595-600; M. E. Marty, "The Protestant Press: Limitations and Possibilities," in *The Religious Press in America,* ed. M. Marty, J. G. Deedy, Jr., D. W. Silverman and R. Lekachman (1963).
W. A. Silva

Christian Church (Disciples of Christ). A denomination* arising out of the Restoration Movement.* The Christian Church (Disciples of Christ) traces its roots to the Restoration Movement of the early nineteenth century, arising out of the 1831 merger between Barton W. Stone's* "Christians" and Alexander Campbell's* "Disciples" to form the Christian Church/Disciples of Christ. By the end of the nineteenth century the movement represented the fastest growing religious body in America and, until overtaken by the Mormons* well into this century, the Christian Church (Disciples of Christ) was the largest indigenous American religious body.

Originally the movement was marked by two distinctive goals: to restore simple evangelical* Christianity and to unite all truly Christian churches and denominations under the Lordship of Jesus Christ and the authority of Scripture. But from the beginning of the movement, these dual emphases were held in tension. Although this fellowship of Christian Churches was one of the very few American religious bodies that did not split during the Civil War,* the tension between primitivism and inclusivism had begun to fracture the movement by the late nineteenth century. By 1906 the U.S. Religious Census could distinguish between the more traditional Churches of Christ and the more liberal and inclusivist Disciples of Christ. This distinction was sealed in 1927 by the formation of the North American Christian Convention* by the conservative Independents (*See* Christian Churches/Churches of Christ [Independent]).

Over most of its history the Christian Church

(Disciples of Christ) have maintained the practices common to most Restoration churches: the local autonomy of individual congregations, the plurality of elders,* Communion* every Sunday* and baptism* by immersion for the remission of sins as a condition for church membership.* Today, however, most congregations practice open membership and accept non-immersed believers into fellowship as full members. Disciples continue to claim the Restoration tradition of having "no creed but Christ" and "no book but the Bible," but many do so within the context of modern biblical criticism. Thus, doctrines of Christ's virgin birth, his pre-existence, his sinlessness and his deity are not requirements for church membership.

In the twentieth century the Christian Church (Disciples of Christ) gradually recognized its denominational nature and took its place among mainline* Protestant* denominations. Today the Disciples have a regional and national structure. Always proponents of ecumenism,* the Disciples were active in the founding of the Federal Council of Churches* as well as the World Council of Churches* and are members of the Consultation on Christian Union.* During the past twenty-five years the Disciples, as have many mainline denominations, have experienced a numerical decline. In 1986 their national office reported 4,227 congregations in North America, with a total membership of 1,111,357 (a decline of 106,390 from the membership recorded in their 1980 *Year Book & Directory*). *See also* CHRISTIAN CHURCHES/CHURCHES OF CHRIST (INDEPENDENT); CHURCHES OF CHRIST (NONINSTRUMENTAL); RESTORATION MOVEMENT.

BIBLIOGRAPHY. W. E. Garrison and A. T. DeGroot, *The Disciples of Christ: A History* (1958); L. G. McAllister and W. E. Tucker, *Journey in Faith: A History of the Christian Church (Disciples of Christ)* (1975); K. L. Teegarden, *We Call Ourselves Disciples* (1975).   T. L. Miethe

Christian Church (Disciples of Christ) in Canada. A denomination* in the Restoration* tradition. The Disciples in Canada trace their origins to two separate streams of missionary enterprise. In the Maritimes some emigrants from Scotland with Presbyterian,* Scottish Baptist* and (Robert) Haldane Society roots determined to follow strict New Testament polity and practice. This resulted in establishment of the first Canadian congregation at Cross Roads, Prince Edward Island, in 1810-1811 by Alexander Crawford (1789-1827). Elsewhere in the Canadian colonies, Congregations sprang up through contact with followers of the Christian Movement founded by Barton Stone*

(1804), or with "Reforming Baptists," later known as Disciples of Christ, led by Thomas* and Alexander Campbell.* The two movements coalesced in 1832, and Disciples churches appeared in Ontario (c. 1820) and in Western Canada (1881).

The early Disciples were New Testament restorationists who espoused frontier ecumenism,* eschewed creedal* tests and practiced congregational* polity. Arminian,* post-millennial* and revivalistic,* most forwarded the "five finger" plan of salvation* (faith, repentance, confession [of faith], baptism* and the gift of the Holy Spirit) introduced by an associate of the Campbells, Walter Scott.*

Disciples congregations are led by elders* and deacons,* and their clergy* are ordained* by one of the thirty-five regions. They observe the Lord's Supper* weekly and believers' baptism by immersion. Historically their congregational polity militated against centralization, but communication through journals such as *The Christian Gleaner* (c. 1833), Halifax, and the *Gospel Vindicator* (1837), Cobourg, eventually led to the formation of "co-operations" or associations of churches. In 1922 an All-Canada Committee came into being. Regional papers united to become *The Canadian Disciple,* and in 1927 the short-lived College, Churches of Christ in Canada was incorporated. Disciples are charter members of the Canadian Council of Churches* (1944), and they joined the World Council of Churches* (1948). They were formal participants in the ill-fated General Commission on Church Union (1973) with the United and Anglican churches.

In response to the restructuring of the denomination in 1968, about one-third of the churches ceased association. Two major schisms have taken place from the Disciples. In the nineteenth century, regional and theological tensions in the U.S. gave rise to the Churches of Christ (non-instrumentalists).* Later protests over theological liberalism* and social action led to organization of the North American Christian Convention* (1927), popularly known as the Christian Churches.* Both groups are relatively significant in Canada. In 1987 the Disciples had nine churches in Atlantic Canada, seventeen in Ontario and eleven in Western Canada, with a membership of 4,700.

BIBLIOGRAPHY. R. Butchart, *The Disciples of Christ in Canada since 1830* (1949); W. E. Garrison, *The Disciples of Christ: a History* (1958); W. E. Tucker and L. G. McAllister, *Journey in Faith* (1975); General Commission on Church Union, *Plan of Union and By-Laws* (1973).

W. E. Ellis

Christian Churches/Churches of Christ (Independent). An association of churches arising out of the Restoration Movement.* The Christian Church/Churches of Christ (Independent) traces its roots to the Restoration Movement of the early nineteenth century, arising out of the 1831 merger between Barton W. Stone's* "Christians" and Alexander Campbell's* "Disciples" to form the Christian Church/Disciples of Christ.

While never intending to become a denomination*—they referred to themselves as a "Brotherhood," a cooperative association of like-minded congregations—nevertheless tensions between strict and progressive restorationists did become apparent by the end of the nineteenth century. By 1906 the U.S. Religious Census had recognized a distinction between more strict Churches of Christ and the Disciples of Christ. In 1927 a group that could not support the educational, missionary and evangelistic programs of the United Christian Missionary Society and objected to the liberalism* of the International Convention of the Disciples, met in Memphis to form the North American Christian Convention.* Not intending to withdraw from the Brotherhood, these conservatives, or "Independents" as they were called, developed a direct-support missionary program, Christian service camps and several educational institutions, the most prominent being Cincinnati Bible Seminary and Lincoln Christian College and Seminary. In the late 1960s conservative leaders made a concerted effort to have all independent congregations withdraw their names from the Disciples of Christ *Year Book,* a published list of local congregations within the Brotherhood.

The Christian Church/Churches of Christ have always had much in common with the mainstream of evangelicalism,* particularly in their understanding of Scripture* as a divinely inspired and sufficient revelation and in their opposition to theological liberalism.* However, they have also remained insulated from the controversies over issues such as millennialism,* perfectionism* and glossolalia* that have marked the larger evangelical tradition in America. Doctrinally, the Independents have also been distinguished by their belief in the necessity of baptism* by immersion for the remission of sins as a condition for church membership* (in obedience to what they believe to be the injunction of Acts 2:38). But in recent years there has been a growing tension within the churches over the theology of baptism. While some suggest a theology approximating baptismal regeneration, others, still maintaining a high view of baptism, stop well short of making water

baptism regenerative. According to the *Directory of the Ministry of the Christian Churches and Churches of Christ,* in 1986 they had 5,671 congregations and a total membership of 1,074,834.

See also CHRISTIAN CHURCH (DISCIPLES OF CHRIST); CHURCHES OF CHRIST (NONINSTRUMENTAL); RESTORATION MOVEMENT.

BIBLIOGRAPHY. L. Garrett, *The Stone-Campbell Movement: An Anecdotal History of Three Churches* (1981); J. D. Murch, *Christians Only: A History of the Restoration Movement* (1961); and M. W. Randall, *The Great Awakenings and the Restoration Movement* (1983).   T. L. Miethe

Christian Connection. An association of restorationist* groups of the nineteenth century. At the beginning of the nineteenth century, there were a number of "primitivist" movements within American Christianity. Coming from a variety of different backgrounds, these were all concerned with restoring the original church of the apostles as depicted in the New Testament. The three major components were the movements associated with James O'Kelly* in Virginia-North Carolina, Abner Jones* and Elias Smith in New England and Barton W. Stone* in Kentucky. About half of the Stone movement did not stay with the Connection, however, preferring to follow Stone into union with the followers of Alexander Campbell* and eventually becoming the Christian Churches,* Churches of Christ* or Disciples of Christ.*

The Christian Connection established its national headquarters in Dayton, Ohio, but in 1931 it merged with the Congregational Church.* In 1957 this body in turn united with the Evangelical and Reformed Church to become the United Church of Christ.* A few churches refused to merge, however, and still maintain a separate identity.

BIBLIOGRAPHY. N. Summerbell, *History of the Christian Church . . . to 1870* (1873).

J. B. North

Christian Education. The intentional and organized efforts to teach the Christian faith, its methods of reflection and action and lifestyle. In the mid nineteenth century, churches began to use the phrase *Christian education* to refer to their practice of religious instruction. Earlier efforts of formal church education in the U.S. had consisted of catechetical* instruction led by pastors.* With the rise of the public school and increasing religious diversity, churches took on the responsibility for religious instruction.

Denominations* influenced by the Sunday-school movement,* including the Methodists,* Baptists* and Congregationalists,* used the Sunday school as a primary means for teaching the content of the Bible,* as well as their specific denominational distinctives. Around these efforts were organized corporate worship,* family devotions,* mission* agencies, church publishing* and Christian higher education.* These emphases and institutions united with the general Anglo-Protestant American culture to provide a comprehensive system of education. Other religious bodies, such as the Catholic Church* and a variety of Lutherans,* had the additional concern of preserving their ethnic* identities and built their educational programs around parochial schools.* Thus nineteenth-century Christian education took place in either the dominant Protestant*-evangelical* culture or a school and neighborhood subculture.

With the increased religious pluralism* and secularism of the twentieth century, mainline* Protestant churches could no longer rely on the influence of Protestant American culture to support Christian education. As a result of their search for a more effective means of Christian education, the Religious Education Association* was founded in 1903. Seeking to integrate religion and public education, it helped establish programs of religious education in colleges and seminaries.* In turn, the profession of director of religious (or Christian) education* was founded. Practical efforts were made to develop comprehensive church schools integrating parish programs such as Sunday school, vacation Bible school, youth leagues and adult groups. During this period, Roman Catholic education continued to center on the parochial school, yet new attention was given to the Confraternity of Christian Doctrine* (CCD) as an effort to expand parish programs of education for children and adults.

With the Great Depression,* the efforts of religious education were challenged, both in terms of their effectiveness and their theology.* Again, within mainline Protestant churches a Christian education movement emerged that continued to define the field until the mid 1960s. Based on neo-orthodox* theology, this movement sought to focus on Christian theology and the special role of the church as agent in faith formation.

Today many educators are concerned about the function of Christian education within the plurality of educational influences present in American culture. For many smaller ethnic churches, as well as evangelical denominations, a close-knit community life provides a comprehensive system of education, much like a subculture. Large urban evangelical and fundamentalist churches often support a complex educational program led by several full-time ministers of Christian education, each responsible for a particular age group. In some cases these programs include pre-school, primary and secondary education on the church campus. These efforts are supported and serviced by a host of parachurch organizations. Many mainline Protestants and Roman Catholics feel a greater conflict between their faith and their openness to modern American culture. Though their educational structures are in some ways similar to those of the distinctively evangelical churches, they see their task as implementing a variety of strategies in a program that will both form the faith of their members and influence the culture at large.

See also CATECHETICS, CATHOLIC; CATECHISM; CATECHIST; SCHOOLS, PROTESTANT DAY; CHRISTIAN NURTURE; PAROCHIAL SCHOOLS, ROMAN CATHOLIC; SUNDAY-SCHOOL MOVEMENT.

BIBLIOGRAPHY. D. C. Wyckoff, ed., *Renewing the Sunday School and the CCD* (1986); J. Seymour, R. O'Gorman and C. Foster, *The Church in the Education of the Public* (1984).

J. L. Seymour

Christian Endeavor Society. An evangelical* and interdenominational youth ministry.* Founded in 1881 in Portland, Maine, by Congregationalist* minister Francis E. Clark,* Christian Endeavor quickly became a big success and was evangelicalism's first interdenominational youth ministry. By the late 1880s, over a half-million members could be found in seven thousand local societies. Under Clark's able leadership, the movement organized nationally (United Christian Endeavor Society, 1887) and internationally (World's Christian Endeavor Union, 1895) and published its own magazine, *Christian Endeavor World.*

Christian Endeavor's motto was "For Christ and the Church," and its purpose was to incorporate young people into the total life of the local church and prepare them for future leadership. To join, young people pledged themselves to lead a Christian life, pray* and read the Bible* daily, and attend all the services of the church. Each society was organized into various committees (lookout, prayer meeting, social, missionary,* etc.) to maximize participation and training opportunities. Though the movement was thoroughly evangelical, each local society reflected the distinctives of its church and denomination.*

When numerous denominations organized their

own youth ministries, Christian Endeavor experienced declining support in the U.S., though more recently the movement has had renewed success in the Third World. In the late 1980s societies could be found in seventy-eight nations, with over two million members.

BIBLIOGRAPHY. F. E. Clark, *The Christian Endeavor Manual* (1925); W. Shaw, *The Evolution of an Endeavorer* (1924).

T. P. Weber

Christian Family Movement. A Catholic Action* organization for married couples. When first introduced into the U.S., Catholic Action tended to organize men and women in separate groups. At a 1946 meeting in Wilmette, Illinois, at the home of Patrick Crowley, a Chicago attorney, and his wife, several married couples decided to experiment with a form of Catholic Action that consisted of units or cells comprised of husbands and wives working together on the parish level to christianize family life and to create communities supportive of Christian family life. A publication, *Act,* was launched to promote an exchange of ideas and information.

In 1947, the pioneer couples group met in South Bend, Indiana. The name, Christian Family Movement, was first proposed in a 1948 *Act* article. In 1949, at the first national meeting of CFM couples at Childerley Retreat House in Wheeling, Illinois, a National Coordinating Committee was set up under the chairmanship of the Crowleys. The first overseas unit was started in Lima, Peru, in 1951. By 1963, there were more than 40,000 active CFM couples in the U.S. and Canada. In 1968, CFM became ecumenical.* The International Confederation of Christian Family Movements embraces a worldwide membership.

A typical CFM group consists of five or six couples from the same parish or neighborhood who meet regularly in one another's homes. The group follows a program of prayer, discussion and action based on the "observe, judge and act" technique of Catholic Action. The couples in the group work to educate themselves to better their own family situation and to ameliorate the conditions of family life in their milieu. Program and materials are prepared and distributed by a national office.

BIBLIOGRAPHY. J. Burns, "American Catholics and the Family Crisis, 1930-1962: the ideological and organizational response" (unpublished Ph.D. thesis, University of Notre Dame, 1982); M. Quigley, Jr., and E. Connors, *Catholic Action in Practice* (1963).   J. T. Connelly

Christian Front. A nativistic* American fascist organization. The Christian Front was organized by the Catholic* priest,* Father Charles E. Coughlin,* who had built up a popular following as a "radio priest," broadcasting from Royal Oak, Michigan. Capitalizing on the economic distress of the Depression* years, Father Coughlin attacked both the international banking community and the Communists.* Calling for an American version of fascism as a bulwark against godless Communism and Jewish interventionism, Coughlin turned against the New Deal and organized a Social Justice Movement and helped organize the Union Party opposition to Roosevelt in 1936.

Following Roosevelt's decisive victory in 1936, Coughlin reorganized his Social Justice Movement into the Christian Front. By then, left with only the most virulent and fanatical of followers, the Christian Front resorted to baiting Jews, Communists and labor unions. The Front published a directory of non-Jewish merchants in portions of New York City, and its members abused and physically attacked Jews in the streets. Harshly anti-Semitic* and anti-Communist, Coughlin continued to publish his paper *Social Justice,* often borrowing directly from the Nazi World Press Service, even to the point of reprinting the notorious forgery, *The Protocols of Zion.* Abandoned by most Catholic as well as Protestant supporters, discredited by the antics of the group and restricted by a new code for broadcasters, the Front was in its death throes by late 1940.

See also COUGHLIN, CHARLES EDWARD.

BIBLIOGRAPHY. C. E. Coughlin, ed., *Social Justice* (July 1939); S. Marcus, *Father Coughlin: The Tumultuous Life of the Priest of the Little Flower* (1973); W. Stegner, "The Radio Priest and His Flock" in *The Aspirin Age,* ed. I. Leighton (1929).
J. De Vries

Christian Holiness Association. Association of Holiness churches,* originally known as the National Campmeeting Association for the Promotion of Christian Holiness. In 1867 Methodist* ministers* John S. Inskip,* John Allen Wood, George Hughes, Bishop* Matthew Simpson* and others were the primary figures at a camp meeting* in Vineland, New Jersey, called to promote the doctrine of holiness* (also known as "entire sanctification,"* Christian perfection* or the "second blessing"*). Impressed by the success of the meeting, these ministers organized the National Campmeeting Association for the Promotion of Christian Holiness in its aftermath, with Inskip serving as president until 1884.

In its early years the Association was a close-knit circle of Methodist revivalists who served as pastors during the winter months. They owned no property or facilities, but convened revival* meetings when invited by local, state or district camp meeting* committees. These committees often were part of state or local holiness associations, the organization of which had been encouraged by the National Association. Between 1867 and 1883 some fifty-two meetings were held in such places as Asbury Grove, Massachusetts; Mannheim, Pennsylvania; and Des Plaines, Illinois.

The Association began as an evangelistic* organization with the special task of restoring what it regarded as John Wesley's* teaching on Christian perfection. Camp meeting revivalism was the Association's principal method. However it also published books and periodicals in support of the Holiness cause. From 1870 to 1959 the Association published the *Christian Witness and Advocate of Bible Holiness,* its principal periodical.

In 1971 the group changed its name to the Christian Holiness Association. By this time it had evolved into an association of Holiness churches and later sponsored its own scholarly fellowship, the Wesleyan Theological Society. More conservative members of the Association expressed their growing dissatisfaction with relaxed discipline by forming, after 1955, the Interdenominational Holiness Convention.

See also HOLINESS CHURCHES AND ASSOCIATIONS; HOLINESS MOVEMENT.

BIBLIOGRAPHY. C. E. Jones, *A Guide to the Study of the Holiness Movement* (1974); C. E. Jones, *Perfectionist Persuasion: The Holiness Movement and American Methodism* (1974); T. L. Smith, *Called Unto Holiness* (1962). M. D. Strege

Christian Literature Crusade. A nondenominational foreign missionary* and literature-distribution agency. Christian Literature Crusade (CLC) had its roots in the Christian bookstore ministry of Kenneth and Bessie Adams, which they established in Colchester, England, in 1939. During the next two years they developed close ties with Norman P. Grubb and the Worldwide Evangelization Crusade. In 1941 these pioneers responded to wartime literature shortages by launching the Evangelical Publishing House, which was renamed Christian Literature Crusade in 1945. CLC initiated its work in North America with the opening of offices in Toronto, Ontario, and Rochester, New York, in 1947. Further ventures soon followed in Australia, Europe, Africa, Latin America and the Far East.

This faith mission* has focused primarily on the distribution of evangelical* Christian literature and Bibles* through bookstores, book tables, bookmobiles and door-to-door selling. In addition, agency growth has involved the auxiliary activities of printing, publishing and translating. CLC also has nurtured a cooperative relationship with other missions to assist in evangelism* and church planting.

Today CLC operates in forty-five countries on all continents, supported by over 600 workers representing forty different nationalities. The American branch reports an annual income of almost a quarter million dollars and a full-time overseas staff of seventeen. Robert J. Gerry currently directs the mission from its headquarters in Fort Washington, Pennsylvania. CLC communicates with its constituency through its *Floodtime* magazine. Affiliations include the Evangelical Foreign Missions Association* and the Christian Booksellers Association.*

BIBLIOGRAPHY. K. R. Adams, *The Foolishness of God* (1981). J. A. Patterson

Christian Methodist Episcopal Church. An African-American Methodist* denomination.* Formally organized in 1870 by the remaining African-American members of the Methodist Episcopal Church, South (MECS),* the Colored Methodist Episcopal Church (CME)—its official name until 1954—was the fourth African-American denomination to separate from biracial, but proscriptive, connections in nineteenth-century American Methodism. The product of both the Southern Methodist program to evangelize* the slaves and the African-American initiative to embrace the Christian faith despite the social system of slavery, the CME Church evolved at local and annual conference levels, beginning in 1867. The members of the CME had refused to join the African Methodist Episcopal* (AME) and African Methodist Episcopal, Zion* (AMEZ) denominations, or the Northern-based Methodist Episcopal Church as it returned to the South after the Civil War.* Cooperating with their former masters, they adopted the theology* and polity* of the MECS and received title to church property from white trustees. Disavowing political activism during Reconstruction, the new church had, and has kept, a Southern base in Tennessee. Its first seven bishops* were born in slavery.

Accompanying Southern African-Americans as they migrated North, the CME Church expanded to eighteen Northern and Western states. The denomination authorized an order of deaconesses* in

1894, channeled the energies of female members into the Women's Missionary Council in 1918 and opened ordination* to women later in the century. It supported a number of church schools in the South, including Paine, Lane, Texas, Miles and Mississippi Industrial colleges, and the Phillips Theological Seminary, now part of the Interdenominational Theological Center in Atlanta. Its denominational paper, *The Christian Index,* is the second-oldest continuing African-American religious periodical in the country.

In this century the CME Church has moved into the mainstream of African-American social and political involvement, with public condemnations of lynching, cooperation with the civil rights* programs, and participation in the Social Gospel* orientation of the Federal (later National*) Council of Churches.* The denomination has also been active in world Methodist organizations and ecumenical discussions, the Consultation on Church Union* (1967) and merger proposals with the AME and AMEZ churches.

Numbering more than 300,000 members, the CME Church is organized into thirty-eight annual conferences in thirty-four states, besides conferences in Ghana and Nigeria and missions in Haiti. It adopted a constitution in 1975, continuing its Women's Connectional Council from 1937 and the presiding responsibilities for bishops over boards of finance, publication services, missions, Christian education, evangelism, lay activities and personnel services, plus a dozen other committees and commissions.

BIBLIOGRAPHY. O. H. Lakey, *The History of the CME Church* (1985); C. H. Phillips, *The History of the Colored Methodist Episcopal Church in America,* 3rd. ed. (1925). W. B. Gravely

Christian Nationals Evangelism Commission. In 1943, the China Native Evangelistic Crusade (CNEC) was established by North American businessmen with the purpose of training and supporting Chinese evangelists.* Within the next several years, several training institutes were established and by the early 1950s they were supporting 150 Chinese. The coming of Communism to power forced the mission to focus its efforts first on nearby Asian countries, and then on a global ministry. Consequently, the name was changed to Christian Nationals Evangelism Commission. CNEC retained its vision of using Western funds (including support from Britain and Australia) to assist strategic ministries that would otherwise be hampered for lack of finances. Individuals are not supported directly, but only through local

organizations with strong national boards, thereby affirming indigenous principles. By the mid-1960s some 200 workers were supported. By the late 1980s some eighty organizations (embracing hundreds of workers) in forty countries on all continents were in varying degrees supported by CNEC. Many ministries that were formerly funded by CNEC are now self-supporting.

D. G. Tinder

Christian Nurture. The instilling of Christian beliefs, devotion,* character and lifestyle through intentional and sustained participation in the caring community of the church, through the agency of the Holy Spirit. The concept was proposed by Horace Bushnell* in the mid-nineteenth century as an alternative to the revivalistic* and conversion*-centered approach to the Christian life so influential in that period. Bushnell rejected the idea that people "are to grow up in evil, and be dragged into the church by conquest." Instead, he emphasized the role of the Christian family* and church environment in shaping a baptized child of Christian parents to "grow up as a Christian, and never know himself as otherwise." Bushnell did not regard humanity as essentially good but emphasized rather that in the context of the baptismal covenant, a child's sinful tendency should be confronted and reoriented from the earliest possible opportunity.

"Christian nurture" as a paradigm for Protestant* Christian education* was most influential from the end of World War 2* to the mid-1960s. By this time, many who supported the revivalistic approach had left the mainline* churches to form their own denominations.* Christian nurture in this period actually combined Bushnell's suggestions with the educational theory of John Dewey, in order to emphasize the shaping role of participation in the faith community as the key dynamic of Christian education.

BIBLIOGRAPHY. H. Bushnell, *Christian Nurture* (1861); L. J. Gable, *Christian Nurture through the Church* (1955); R. C. Miller, *Christian Nurture and the Church* (1961); A. J. Myers, *Horace Bushnell and Religious Education* (1937).

P. W. Butin

Christian Reformed Church in North America. A small Reformed* denomination,* principally of Dutch descent, centered in the American Midwest. The Christian Reformed Church (CRC) grew out of the later (1840s-1920s) wave of Dutch immigration* to the United States. Although the first arrivals affiliated with the Reformed Church in

America,* some seceded in 1857 to form the "True Dutch Reformed Church." The group became a viable enterprise only around 1880 with the resurgence of Dutch immigration* and a second defection from the Reformed Church in America, this time over the issue of Freemasonry.

For the next fifty years, the church, now called the Christian Reformed Church, continued this strategy of absorbing the disaffected (in New Jersey) and the recently immigrated (extending to the West Coast). It moved into Canada with the post-World War 2 Dutch migration there, so that Canadians constitute over a quarter of its current membership (310,000, including baptized children, in 875 congregations). More recent additions have come from outside the Dutch circle, consisting of many African-Americans but largely Korean-Americans.

While the language change from Dutch to English was completed in the 1930s, the CRC has been consistently defined by traits from its Netherlandic past. It stresses (1) heartfelt conversion* and piety,* although cast in covenantal* rather than revivalistic* terms; (2) confessionalism* and orthodoxy,* as set by its three standards—the Belgic Confession, the Heidelberg Catechism and the Canons of Dort; and (3) Christian cultural engagement. The latter emphasis was enunciated by the Dutch Neo-Calvinist forebear Abraham Kuyper* and is exemplified in the denomination's* longstanding Christian day school* system, as well as its academic and political leadership in recent American evangelicalism.*

BIBLIOGRAPHY. J. D. Bratt, *Dutch Calvinism in Modern America* (1984); P. De Klerk and R. R. De Ridder, eds., *Perspectives on the Christian Reformed Church* (1983); J. H. Kromminga, *The Christian Reformed Church* (1949).

J. D. Bratt

Christian Schools. *See* SCHOOLS, PROTESTANT DAY.

Christian Science. An indigenous American religion noted for its theory and practice of religious healing.* Christian Science was born in 1866 when Mary Baker Eddy's* spontaneous recovery from a severe injury authenticated her discovery that reality is completely spiritual and evil—as well as sickness and death—is only an illusion. There is no reality except Mind and Spirit. The result is that the essential orthodox* Christian doctrines of creation, fall and redemption are denied. Her understanding of the mind-body relationship and her healing techniques owed much to the principles of homeopathy and the practice of Phineas Parkhurst Quimby.* Given the authority Eddy's teachings and personality have exerted and continue to exert on the movement, Christian Science would not have come to exist without her.

Despite Eddy's teaching and the publication of her textbook of Christian Science, *Science and Health* (1875), to which *Key to the Scriptures* was added in 1883, Christian Science grew slowly. When in 1879 she and her followers organized the first Church of Christ, Scientist, in Lynn, Massachusetts, they numbered only twenty-seven. She moved her headquarters to Boston and in 1881 chartered the Massachusetts Metaphysical College to educate practitioners in Christian Science healing. All Christian Scientists practice healing by "demonstrating" over (curing) "false claims" (sickness and sin), but some devote themselves professionally to full-time service as practitioners. Although dramatic physical cures attract the most public attention, healing may involve simply a process of growth and enlightenment that slowly transforms a person into the spiritual image of God's ideal. Christian Science church services do not permit preaching, but are carried out by first and second readers who read selections from Scripture and from *Science and Health.*

The early Boston years proved rocky as influential former students, such as Emma Curtis Hopkins,* Luther M. Marston and Ursula N. Gestefeld, questioned Eddy's originality and prophetic authority* and left the movement to disseminate their own brand of Christian Science or to join New Thought. In an effort to define orthodox Christian Science, Eddy in 1883 established and edited the monthly *Journal of Christian Science* (renamed the *Christian Science Journal* in 1885) and encouraged the formation of a National Christian Scientist Association in the spring of 1886. She also invited the graduates of her Normal Classes to move across the country, teaching, healing and establishing institutes of healing and instruction.

In 1892 she established a central church organization, the Mother Church, in Boston and appointed a board of directors to oversee its affairs and implement her instructions to organize evangelistic lectures and monitor educational standards. Through lectures and class instruction key individuals such as Augusta Stetson, Edward Kimball, Carol Norton and Bicknell Young exerted a lasting influence over Christian Science practice and the interpretation of Eddy's writings. Six years later Eddy founded the Christian Science Publishing Society to spearhead worldwide evangelism through the printed word, including *The Christian*

Science Monitor (1908). These missionary activities enhanced the growth of Christian Science, spreading it to Europe and the Orient by the early twentieth century. Membership exploded from only 8,724 in 1890 to about 55,000 (seventy-two per cent of whom were women) by 1906, and the U.S. Government Census of 1936 reported 268,915 Christian Science adherents. Although no more recent statistics are available because Eddy forbade their publication, local churches now number about 3,000 worldwide, with the vast majority of Christian Scientists, including practitioners (currently about 2,884), still in the U.S.

Generally, Christian Scientists have gained legitimacy in American society, but their distinctive practices of physical healing still bring them their greatest public attention and create some of their most difficult legal challenges.

BIBLIOGRAPHY. C. S. Braden, *Christian Science Today: Power, Policy, Practice* (1969); S. Gottschalk, *The Emergence of Christian Science in American Religious Life* (1974); R. Peel, *Mary Baker Eddy,* 3 vols. (1966-1977); R. B. Schoepflin, "The Christian Science Tradition," in *Caring and Curing: Historical Essays on Health, Medicine, and the Faith Traditions,* eds. R. L. Numbers and D. W. Amundsen (1986).

R. B. Schoepflin

Christian Service Brigade. An international discipleship program for boys. In 1937, Joseph Coughlin, a Wheaton College* student, volunteered to teach a Sunday-school* class of sixth-grade boys. Sensing that his students needed additional training beyond the classroom, he developed a weekly boys' club program of games and Bible study* which focused on Christian service. Coughlin recruited several other college students to begin similar groups in the Wheaton area. In 1940, a board of directors was established to guide the fledgling ministry of Christian Service Brigade (CSB).

Not long after, Herbert J. Taylor,* founder of the Christian Workers Foundation, took an interest in the work of Brigade, providing financial and organizational assistance. Brigade grew slowly during the 1940s and early 1950s, but experienced fifteen subsequent years of rapid growth. CSB expanded into forty-five states and nine Canadian provinces, and organized centers to service local churches participating in its program. A separate Canadian Brigade organization developed, opening an office in Burlington, Ontario, in 1963. In the 1960s, Brigade established a national training center and expanded into fourteen countries. CSB has attempted to counter numerical decline in the 1970s and 1980s with the addition of programs for primary-age boys and their fathers, small churches, fathers with daughters, single-parent families and urban black churches. In 1982 CSB became the official youth program of the Church of God,* based in Cleveland, Tennessee.

Today, CSB is headquartered in Carol Stream, Illinois. Over 2,000 churches across North America conduct some form of the Brigade program, with over 50,000 boys and 10,000 men participating in weekly activities. The purpose of CSB remains the same—"to train men to cultivate friendships with boys and prepare them for future leadership in their families, churches, and communities."

BIBLIOGRAPHY. P. H. Heidebrecht, *The Brigade Trail: 50 Years of Building Men to Serve Christ* (1987). B. E. Brown

Christian Social Union (1891-1911). An Episcopal organization concerned with social questions. Modeled on an English organization of the same name, the Christian Social Union (CSU) was organized by Robert A. Holland, an Episcopal minister of St. Louis, Missouri. Its peak membership was about 1,000 in ten chapters and included over thirty bishops, but also a number of leading Christian socialists such as William Dwight Porter Bliss,* Philo Sprague and Vida Scudder. Its most prestigious lay officer was Richard T. Ely,* the economist.

In 1894 the CSU changed its name to the Church Social Union, but changed it back again in 1897. For a time it was affiliated with the larger Church Association for the Advancement of the Interests of Labor (CAIL), but the latter was too controversial for an organization that took pains to insist that "the Union has no program and no doctrine" other than "to claim for the Christian Law the ultimate authority to rule social practice." To fulfill its goals the CSU encouraged sermons and lectures on, and investigations of, social conditions in major U.S. cities; published over 100 pamphlets on such topics as "The Church's Duty to the Immigrant," "The Church and the Wage-Earner," "The Church and the Negro" and "The Church and Current Standards of Commercial Life;" and organized CSU groups in colleges and seminaries.

In 1910 the Episcopalians' General Convention voted to appoint a permanent Commission on Social Service, and the CSU disbanded.

BIBLIOGRAPHY. *Christian Social Union Publications,* n.s., no. 2 (1908). J. C. Cort

Christian Socialist Fellowship. A voluntary

society promoting Christian socialism.* The late nineteenth-century Social Gospel* Movement, with its emphasis upon building a Christian social order in the United States, gained support among some Christians for socialism as a means of improving human society. An 1872 Christian Labour Union and an 1889 Society of Christian Socialists were early attempts to provide a Christian solution for the growing problems of an industrializing America.

The Christian Socialist Fellowship of 1906 grew out of *The Christian Socialist,* a journal begun in 1903 in an attempt to reconcile socialism and Christianity. The journal, edited by the Rev. Edward Ellis Carr, an ex-Methodist* and member of the Socialist Party, and supported by radical Christians, argued that socialism was a necessary economic expression of the Christian life and that the goal of industrial democracy* was one Christians should support. It further advised the Socialist Party not to ignore Christianity. The Christian Socialist Fellowship, which grew out of these efforts, affiliated with the Socialist Party and helped produce the nearly one million votes for Eugene U. Debs in the 1912 presidential race against Roosevelt, Taft and Wilson. The activities of Christian leaders in the Party, such as the Presbyterian* Norman Thomas, also grew out of the kind of Christian support advocated by the Christian Socialist Fellowship. The Society, however, died in the anti-Socialist climate produced by the First World War.*

See also CHRISTIAN SOCIALISM.

BIBLIOGRAPHY. R. T. Handy, "Christianity and Socialism in America, 1900-1920," *CH* 21 (1952):39-54; C. H. Hopkins, *The Rise of the Social Gospel in American Protestantism, 1865-1915* (1940). J. De Vries

Christianity Today. The leading evangelical* periodical. The launching of *Christianity Today* (CT) in 1956 was largely the initiative of Billy Graham* and his father-in-law, L. Nelson Bell.* CT was aimed at ministers and thoughtful laymen, especially those who were holding forth, or could be won back to, the historic faith within the major denominations. At the same time it attempted to foster a broader sense of church and social responsibility for independent evangelicals and to let liberals and secularists see that orthodoxy* did not entail obscurantism. Bell served as CT's executive editor (1956-1973) and Carl F. H. Henry* as editor-in-chief (1956-1968). An influential supporter and board member until his death in 1971 was multimillionaire oilman J. Howard Pew.*

As a biweekly (now eighteen times yearly)

journal of evangelical opinion and religious news, CT consciously pitted itself against the prestigious liberal weekly *Christian Century,* and it soon succeeded in overtaking the *Century* in paid subscribers and in becoming the most widely quoted religious journal in the secular press. CT's circulation of about 160,000 (which it still maintains) was maintained for many years by free distribution to many ministers and the seminarians it was trying to influence, a practice that was discontinued in 1967. Under Harold Lindsell's editorship (1968-1978) efforts were made to broaden its paying readership while re-enforcing its theological stance. In 1977 CT relocated from Washington, D.C., to the Chicago suburb of Carol Stream, near Wheaton, Illinois, the headquarters of many evangelical agencies and institutions. In more recent years, under the direction of Harold Myra, CT has broadened its appeal to evangelical laypeople and added other publications, including the quarterly *Leadership* (begun 1980) which thoughtfully addresses practical ministerial concerns and has a circulation of 80,000 paying subscribers.

More than any other evangelical periodical, CT has reflected and reported the evangelical resurgence of the second half of the twentieth century. Politically, prior to the Reagan era, CT's stance has generally been to the right of the national center, and it was clearly to the right of the theological and ecclesiastical mainstream in America, though many fellow conservatives found its tone too moderate and irenic.

BIBLIOGRAPHY. C. F. H. Henry, *Confessions of a Theologian* (1956); R. B. Fowler, *A New Engagement: Evangelical Political Thought, 1966-1976* (1982). D. G. Tinder

Christmas. The festival observed on December 25 celebrating the nativity of Jesus Christ. The date for the celebration does not in any way accurately mark the birthdate of Jesus, and at least two explanations for the date are offered. The festival may represent a Christian appropriation of a "Birthday of the Invincible Sun" instituted at Rome on this day in A.D. 274 by the emperor Aurelian, and the influence of Constantine is often cited in favor of such borrowing from pagan culture. The Christian festival may antedate Constantine's conversion and mark the date nine months after March 25, a date already assigned to Christ's crucifixion and to his conception at the Annunciation to Mary. Sources from the fourth and following centuries support the latter explanation, but the coincidence with the traditional winter solstice date surely influenced the popularity of Christmas and the manner of its celebration.

Both the northern European and North American custom of exchanging gifts at Christmas and the Mediterranean, and the Latin American custom of exchanging gifts on Epiphany* are possibly related to pre-Christian celebrations at the close of the year. The celebration of Christmas has sometimes been opposed as pagan by religious leaders. New England Puritans* considered Christmas "popish" idolatry, and the Massachusetts General Court in 1659 passed an act against its celebration, though the law was repealed in 1681. At least since the mid-nineteenth century the celebration has gained in popularity so that today it extends well beyond Christianity itself. German Christmas customs, such as the Christmas tree, were brought to America by nineteenth-century immigrants and are now firmly established in North American culture.

BIBLIOGRAPHY. A. A. McArthur, *The Evolution of the Christian Year* (1953); T. J. Talley, *The Origins of the Liturgical Year* (1986).   T. J. Talley

Christmas Conference. The organizing meeting of American Methodism.* Ordained* as Anglican* priests,* John* and Charles Wesley, founders of Methodism, opposed separation from the Church of England. Especially difficult in the colonies, between the Declaration of Independence (1776) and the ratification of the Constitution (1787), was the plight of Methodists who were cut off from the Lord's Table* because most of the Methodist immigrants favored independence for the colonies.

Always the pragmatist, John Wesley "allowed" the Christmas Conference of 1784 to be called and recognized the ordination* of Thomas Coke* and Francis Asbury* as the first independent ecclesiastical leaders of Methodism. Convening in Baltimore's Lovely Lane Chapel on December 24, 1784, the Conference acted to establish Coke and Asbury as spiritual leaders, declared the new denomination* to be an episcopal* church, established its clergy* as traveling preachers, defined local congregations, outlined a circuit* structure and made a commitment to Wesley's ideal of spreading scriptural holiness,* if not to his actual leadership.

BIBLIOGRAPHY. E. S. Bucke, ed., *The History of American Methodism,* 3 vols. (1964); F. A. Norwood, *The Story of American Methodism* (1974).

P. A. Mickey

Christology. A technical theological term for the doctrine of Christ, usually consisting of carefully

formulated statements describing his person and nature. The earliest American Christologies were basically orthodox* and Chalcedonian in their expression. The Puritans,* like their reforming forebears, shared with Roman Catholics,* whether they be French or Spanish, the creedal definitions of Christ and his nature formulated by the early church. But while Catholic Christology in the New World was to remain relatively unchanged in its formal expressions, at least until the Second Vatican Council,* the Protestant* understanding of Christ was subject to various influences. For the most part the story of American Christology has unfolded in dialog with orthodoxy as it was transmitted through the Puritan* tradition, both with occasional fresh influences from the intellectual centers of Europe.

Jonathan Edwards,* representing the tradition of English Puritanism transplanted in the New World, stood in the orthodox tradition as he spoke of Christ in terms of the great distance between God and humanity. Because Christ was both God and man, he could bridge that gap as the covenanted mediator. For Edwards the Incarnation emphasized Christ's glory, majesty and equality with God on the one hand, and his humility, meekness and reverence toward God on the other.

Unitarianism. The first major threat to orthodox Christology in America was Unitarianism.* Beginning in New England as early as 1710, some Congregationalists* began to reject the deity of Christ and thus also the Trinity. By 1750 this view had become quite widespread among the Congregational pastors in the Boston area. The best known and most influential of these was William Ellery Channing.*

While Channing did not call himself a Unitarian, not wishing to be identified with particular parties, he held that Jesus was the perfect manifestation of God to humanity, though not God incarnate. Although he emphasized the humanity of Jesus, he held to the pre-existence and sinless perfection of Christ, as well as the authenticity of his miracles and resurrection. Thus, his nephew and biographer William Henry Channing referred to him as an Arian rather than a Unitarian. Other eighteenth-century Unitarians, however, such as the more radically rationalistic Joseph Priestley,* rejected the deity of Christ in no uncertain terms, though even he maintained the authenticity and importance of Jesus' miracles and resurrection.

Christology and Liberal Protestantism. In the late-nineteenth and early-twentieth century, Protestant liberals* began to redefine the nature of Christ. While many of them continued to use the term *divinity* to speak of Christ, the word took on new meaning and nuance. To some the divinity of Christ was a matter of degree—something Christ held in common with other humans, but which he possessed to a greater degree than they.

Most liberals treated Jesus as central to Christian faith. He was the founder of Christianity, the one who supremely defined it by his teachings. But liberalism tended to be averse to metaphysics and questions about Jesus' nature and being. Horace Bushnell,* the nineteenth-century father of American Protestant liberalism, viewed religious language as metaphorical and evocative rather than logical and abstract. This approach, prompted by New England romanticism* and German idealism, was to shape the emerging contours of Protestant liberal Christology. More interested in Jesus' acts and teachings, liberals studied the humanity of Jesus, what he said, what he did and how he set an example for Christian living.

This movement was given further definition by the late-nineteenth-century quest for the historical Jesus. Influenced in part by imported German biblical criticism, theologians distinguished between "the religion *of* Jesus" and "the religion *about* Jesus." Liberals believed that the church in its Christological formulations, and even to some degree in the Christology of the apostle Paul himself, had constructed a complex theological view of Christ on the basis of Greek metaphysics. It was necessary to get behind this construction to the real person and teachings of Jesus. Having accomplished this, they found that Jesus had called people to believe *with* him, rather than *in* him. Consequently, authentic Christianity should not require belief in statements *about* Christ's deity, but call for an imitation of his humanity.

Some liberals, however, retained this emphasis on following Jesus the man, without abandoning belief in his uniqueness. The Baptist* theologian* William Newton Clarke* believed in Jesus' supernatural birth, miracles, sinlessness and bodily resurrection. Yet, he sought the divinity of Jesus "not in the metaphysical constitution of his being . . . but in character worthy of God."

American liberal theology was in some ways a blend of two streams of German liberalism, that which derived from the thought of Friedrich Schleiermacher (1768-1832), which stressed feeling as piety and that which was influenced by Albrecht Ritschl (1822-1889), which emphasized ethical activity. Thus, American liberalism thought of Jesus both as the supreme example of devotion to God and as a teacher and practitioner of ethics. Although Albert Schweitzer's (1875-1965) *The*

Quest for the Historical Jesus (1906; ET 1909) showed that liberalism had reconstructed Jesus in its own image, the effect of his teaching was somewhat slow in reaching American theological circles.

To some extent it could be argued that any twentieth-century crisis in Christology related to the issue of the deity of Christ. Many who subscribed to the divinity of Jesus had in mind a characteristic or set of characteristics by which he differed from other humans only in degree, not in kind. Thus, in using the term *divinity,* Harry Emerson Fosdick* meant that God had revealed himself and was at work in Jesus. This did not prevent his being an example for humanity, however. If he were merely human, he could not serve as an example because then he would have to be a genius, a superior person, whom ordinary individuals could not emulate. Because he did what he did by the power of God working in him, however, he could serve as an example, for that God also works within men and women.

Orthodoxy, Neo-Orthodoxy and the New Quest. Because the reference to Christ's divinity had been so generalized, it became increasingly important for conservatives to be able to affirm the deity of Christ in an unequivocal fashion. This was to say that Jesus was God in the same way in which the Father was God, in a way that has not been true of any other person who has walked upon the earth. The litmus test for orthodox Christology was found in the doctrine of the virgin birth, a doctrine deemed so essential that it became one of the traditional tenets defended in *The Fundamentals* (1910-1915). Generally speaking, anyone who believed in the virgin birth of Christ almost assuredly believed in a qualitatively unique deity of Christ. While the virgin birth was only mentioned in Matthew and Luke and alluded to in Isaiah, conservatives believed it was the clear teaching of Scripture and an important christological datum. It also stood in contradiction to purely naturalistic conceptions of religion and reality. Perhaps the most notable defense of the virgin birth by an American Protestant was made by the Princeton Seminary* New Testament scholar and apologist* J. Gresham Machen* in *The Virgin Birth of Christ* (1930).

In some cases, however, the humanity of Jesus, if not rejected in theory, was neglected in practice. In emphasizing the deity of Christ, the historical Jesus was somewhat neglected by the neo-orthodox* movement. In their case, and even more so in the followers of Rudolf Bultmann,* there was a conviction that the search for the historical Jesus had failed or would inevitably fail. However, the "New Quest for the Historical Jesus," a movement begun in Germany in the 1950s and imported to America largely through James M. Robinson's *A New Quest of the Historical Jesus* (1959), though more modest in its endeavor than the original quest for the historical Jesus, renewed scholarship's concern for the real human side of Jesus and his self-understanding.

Late-Twentieth-Century Christologies. The late-twentieth century has seen several attempts to recast Christology into terms responsive to the needs of the age. In recent years a significant development in American theology has been the secularization of theology. Challenged by the reality of secularism and intrigued by the German theologian and martyr Dietrich Bonhoeffer's* references to "Christian worldliness," some theologians turned to the world as a source of truth and have tended to make secularism the sphere of theological discourse. The most extreme branch of this movement flowered briefly in the mid-1960s as the Death of God Theology,* or Christian Atheism.

While this distinctively American theology came in several varieties, perhaps the best known was that of Thomas J. J. Altizer. Emphasizing that God had been progressively giving up his transcendent or "primordial" status and becoming immanent in the world, Altizer maintained that the process had been completed in Jesus. Jesus is the culmination, not the whole, of the process of reincarnation. From Jesus, however, this incarnation has spread outward throughout the entire human race. We serve Jesus by serving our fellow humans, for Jesus is to be found behind the mask of the other person's face, a fulfillment of Matthew 25:40. In Altizer's theology it is not proper to refer to Jesus as "Lord," for that carries connotations of a uniqueness of deity. Rather, as the one who exemplifies for us the identification with and concern for the world, he might better be called "leader."

Existential* theology has also produced a significant redefinition of Christology in the twentieth century. Paul Tillich,* a German theologian who came to the U.S. during the early days of the Nazi regime, developed his theology around the concept of God as the Ground of Being, the force or cause of being for all that is. New Being is the overcoming of the estrangement of finite beings. When Christ died upon the cross, he became transparent to the Ground of Being. He is, therefore, the New Being, the answer to the human existential predicament and the means of partici-

pating in the New Being.

Process theology,* a movement that has been particularly influential among America's academic theologians, has also given rise to a distinctive Christology. In process thought, reality is not seen as fixed, rather it is characterized by process, change and relationship. God is active in every event of history, and in this sense every event is an incarnation and none exclusively so. Consequently, many process theologians find it difficult to speak of the uniqueness of Jesus and tend to speak of the degree to which Jesus fulfilled or actualized God's purpose. Yet John Cobb, utilizing a Logos Christology, can describe Jesus as the most complete incarnation of the Logos, making him unique. His life was so fixed on God's immanence that it was, in the words of John Cobb, "coconstitutive of his selfhood."

Since the early 1970s various forms of liberation theology* have arisen, the one most indigenous to America being black theology.* Its leading and in some ways most radical spokesperson has been James Cone.* Cone aligns his black theology quite closely with the black power movement, and sees Christ's message as being the complete emancipation of African-American people from white oppression by any means necessary. Christ is seen as supporting black power. To consider him non-black would be as wrong as considering him non-Jewish in the first century. Other African-American theologians, such as Deotis Roberts and Major Jones, consider this overstated and as parochial as a yellow or white Christ. Roberts looks for reconciliation, not warfare, between the races.

Another distinctly twentieth-century type of Christology is found among feminist theologians, ranging from the more radical thought of Mary Daly (1928-) to the less radical views of Rosemary Radford Ruether (1936-). Feminist Christologies tend to emphasize Jesus' attitudes toward and treatment of women. They tend to minimize belief in his deity, which they identify with patriarchalism.

American Roman Catholic theology prior to the Second Vatican Council* (1961-1965), held the same orthodox view of Jesus Christ that was found throughout Roman Catholicism worldwide. Vatican II opened the possibility of a greater variety of positions on doctrinal matters. American Catholic theologians then focussed much of their attention first upon the nature of the church, and then upon the person of God. More recently Christology has come in for more concentrated attention. Although differing in many ways, the theologies of Leslie Dewart, Gregory Baum, Avery Dulles and, most radically, David Tracy, all interpret doctrine in a more contingent, relative, existential and subjective fashion than had traditionally been characteristic of Catholic theology. Tracy, for example, speaks of an inclusivist Christology in which Jesus as the Christ is the Christian's expression of understanding the God who is present to all humanity at every time and place. The story of Jesus is the illuminating symbol for a religious understanding of existence.

BIBLIOGRAPHY. T. J. J. Altizer, *The Gospel of Christian Atheism* (1966); L. J. Averill, *American Theology in the Liberal Tradition* (1967); H. Bushnell, *God in Christ* (1849); J. B. Cobb, *Christ in a Pluralistic Age* (1975); D. W. Ferm, *Contemporary American Theologies: A Critical Survey* (1981); J. G. Machen, *The Virgin Birth of Christ* (1930).   M. J. Erickson

Church. Historically, the Christian church is a community founded on the teachings of Jesus Christ and striving to bear witness to Christ's gospel in its worship* and faith, work and memory. Theologically, the church is a spiritual communion of the whole people of God. It is rooted in the ancient covenant with Israel and the divine promise to deliver God's people. To use the imagery of the apostle Paul, the church is the body of Christ and Christ is the head of his body. Without Christ there is no church. The church, therefore, is an incarnate community of those who receive the Word of God in Jesus Christ and seek to express that Word in their own lives through the power of the Holy Spirit.

The New Testament, which informs the Christian understanding of the church, speaks of it as a living organism of persons closely related to Christ and to one another. Likewise, the New Testament provides important images by which the church has come to understand its life. These include people of God (2 Cor 6:16-18), body of Christ (Rom 12:5; Eph 4:12), household of faith (Gal 6:10, Eph 2:19) and fellowship of the Holy Spirit (2 Cor 13:14; Phil 2:1).

Christian history reflects diverse interpretations of what the church is and how it should be organized. Roman Catholics* unite around apostolic authority* based on Scripture* and church tradition mediated through the bishops* (the episcopacy*), and ultimately the bishop of Rome, the pope (*See* Collegiality). With Vatican II* the identification of the church with the papacy (*See* Ultramontanism) and the institution was rejected in favor of an understanding of the church as a mystery and sacrament subsisting in the Catholic

Church and serving as a witness to the world. The Orthodox* and Anglican* traditions also stress the role of the episcopacy* in defining the truly apostolic church, though Anglicans vary widely in their interpretation of the significance of the episcopacy as a mark of the true church.

The churches of the Reformation reasserted the Scripture as the true measure of apostolicity. The true church was to be distinguished by the faithful preaching* of the Word, the proper celebration of the sacraments* and the exercise of church discipline.* The Reformed Tradition* generally favors a presbyterian* form of church order represented in pastors,* teachers,* deacons* and elders.* Congregationalists* and Baptists* emphasize the authority of Christ as expressed through the congregation.

In America the quest for the truly apostolic church has frequently been dominated by a primitivism* which attempts to bypass the centuries of church history and tradition and recapture the ancient order of things as it was experienced in the early church and recorded in the New Testament. For some this impulse has self-consciously led to separatism,* and for others, such as the churches of the Restoration Movement,* it has been conceived as a nondenominationalism.

In America the denomination* became an important means of organizing church life for local, regional and international endeavors. Denominations helped institutionalize missionary* and other humanitarian efforts, while providing programs linking local congregations. This denominational identity has sometimes fostered competition between groups. Consequently, the word *church* in popular parlance frequently means a denomination such as "the Methodist Church" or "the Lutheran Church."

In the popular mind *church* has often become associated with buildings, programs and services provided to a specific constituency in a particular geographical location. Through ecumenical relationships—both formal and informal—churches and denominations may reassert their essential unity in Christ, while recognizing, and even celebrating, their historical, liturgical* and ecclesiastical diversity.

See also CHURCH GOVERNMENT; CULT; DENOMINATIONALISM; SECT; VOLUNTARYISM.

BIBLIOGRAPHY. A. Dulles, *Models of the Church* (1978); H. Küng, *The Church* (1967); P. Minear, *Images of the Church in the New Testament* (1950); L. Newbigen, *The Household of God* (1957).   B. J. Leonard

Church and State, Separation of. In the American experience, separation of church and state is the exclusion of civil authority from religious affairs and the institutional independence of organized religion from government sanction or support. The American tradition in church and state, the nonestablishment of religion and the free exercise of religion, represented on behalf of the founding fathers a bold experiment unparalleled in human history. Not until the twentieth century were the American guarantees of the First Amendment* constitutionally and unequivocally enunciated anywhere else in the world. The uniqueness of this American tradition in church and state is of profound importance in understanding both the nation's political and religious history.

At the time of the adoption of the First Amendment, separation of church and state was seen as the legal arrangement by which religious liberty,* the cornerstone of the Bill of Rights, was to be ensured. More than three-quarters of a century ago, David Dudley Field, one of America's greatest jurists of the nineteenth century, declared that the separation of church and state in America was the "greatest achievement ever made in the cause of human progress." "If we had nothing else to boast of," Field wrote, "we could lay claim with justice that first among the nations we of this country made it an article of organic law that the relations between man and his Maker were a private concern, into which other men have no right to intrude."

At the time of the nation's founding, an establishment* of religion was both practically and ideologically an impossibility if a sense of nationhood and the ideal of *E Pluribus Unum* were to be realized. Not only was religious pluralism* rampant throughout the colonies, but the vast majority of the population in each of the colonies was unchurched, a population described as "the largest proportion of unchurched in Christendom." While some form of religious establishment in the New World followed the patterns of the Old, in at least nine of the thirteen colonies, there was no pattern of uniformity among the colonies regarding a religious establishment.

With independence, there was a move on the part of religious dissenters throughout the states to bring an end to religious establishment and the privileges that it assumed. By the time of the nation's founding, religious freedom was eloquently championed by religious and political leaders alike. For both theological and political reasons, it was argued, religion should be free of the state, and government should be denied the right of jurisdiction over religion, a view that was widely shared by the Founding Fathers. As James Madison* wrote, "The religion . . . of every man, must be left to the conviction and conscience of every man. . . . We maintain, therefore, that in matters of religion no man's right is [to be] abridged by the institution of civil society; and that religion is wholly exempt from its cognizance." Or as one renowned minister, Isaac Backus,* expressed it: "The free exercise of private judgment, and the unalienable rights of conscience, are of too high a rank and dignity to be submitted to the decrees of councils, or the imperfect laws of fallible legislators."

While disestablishment did not take place in all the states until some decades later, disestablishment and provisions for guarantees of the free exercise of religion clearly prevailed in a majority of the states by the time of the Constitutional Convention of 1787. Delegates to the Convention were well aware of the persecution of dissenters and nonconformists earlier in the colonies and in England. With the vast majority of the population without any church affiliation, it was to be expected that the unchurched, too, could be counted on to favor no establishment of religion, that is, a secular state without religious tests for office. There was now growing recognition that a person's religious opinions were not in any way to be related to the exercise of one's civil liberties.

The only reference to religion in the original Constitution, Clause 3 of Article VI, is written in the form of an unequivocal prohibition on giving any consideration to religion in determining one's qualifications for public office: "No religious test shall ever be required as a qualification to any office or public trust under the authority of the United States." While the adoption of this prohibition applied at this time only to federal office, not state or local, the adoption of this provision precluded the possibility of any church-state union or the establishment of a state church in the absence of any religious test for public office. Article VI not only removed the basis for any preferential treatment of one religion over another for holding public office, but it also denied the right of any preferential status of religion over nonreligion in matters of one's political participation in the life of the Republic.

From dissenters, especially Baptists,* Presbyterians,* Methodists,* Unitarians,* Deists* and Quakers,* among others, came the demand in the form of a Bill of Rights to guarantee the separation of church and state and to provide some explicit assurance of the free exercise of religion. Consequently, an establishment of religion, at least on a national level, was expressly prohibited by Congress on September 25, 1789, with the adoption of the First Amendment, which begins with the words: "Congress shall make no law respecting as establishment of religion or prohibiting the free exercise thereof." Ratification came in 1791.

As with the ratification of Article VI, the First Amendment did not mark an end to state laws of religious tests for public office, so ratification of the First Amendment did not end state churches since Article VI and the religion clauses of the First Amendment of the Constitution originally applied only to the federal elections and the federal government respectively. Only after the ratification of the Fourteenth Amendment in 1868, followed by a lengthy history of "incorporation," were the religion clauses of the First Amendment specifically incorporated into the Fourteenth Amendment and, thus, applied to the states. Nonetheless, most of the states came specifically to forbid religious tests as a qualification for public office and, almost without exception, even more explicitly than the federal Constitution, to guarantee religious liberty and to deny financial aid in any form to any religious group.

The First Amendment rests upon the concept of a secular state, in which government is denied jurisdiction over religious affairs, and upon the recognition of America as a pluralistic society, in which "the free exercise of religion" is assured to all religions equally under the law. The American concept of the secular state is not born out of hostility toward religion, for hostility toward religion is irreconcilable with the very nature of the secular state, and therefore has been so declared as irreconcilable with the American tradition in church and state. America is a secular state, a free society, in which neither religion nor irreligion enjoys any official status, but one in which the attitude of government toward religion is, in the words of the Supreme Court, one of "benevolent neutrality." As the separation of church and state is regarded as the guarantee of religious liberty, so the secular state is the legal basis of the pluralistic society.

Because of separation of church and state, in America the state knows neither *churches** nor *sects,** as the terms are used historically in Europe, but only *denominations,** a distinctly American term. Government is not competent and has no authority to judge which religions are churches and which are cults,* or which religions are true and which are false, any more than it can determine which religions are good and which are bad. In the words of the Supreme Court, "The law

knows no heresy,* and is committed to the support of no dogma,* the establishment of no sect" (*Watson v. Jones,* 1872). No religious group is to be the object of privilege or discrimination under the law. So long as one's free exercise of religion does not infringe on the rights of others, or contravene the just civil laws of the state, or threaten public health and order, both the rights of religious dissent and the free exercise of that dissent are guaranteed to all citizens.

While the phrase, "separation of church and state," does not appear in the Constitution, ever since the *Everson v. Board of Education* (1947) the phrase has been used repeatedly by the Supreme Court to define the Establishment Clause. The American separation principle, as embodied in the First Amendment, is not a negative or sterile concept—something to be likened more to the image of the Berlin Wall than to a democratic* society. Like all phrases applied to dynamic principles in history, the phrase "separation of church and state" is not entirely satisfying. The phrase has meant, and does mean, far more than the sum total of its parts. Church-state separation has not meant, at least historically, the separation of religion and politics or the denial of the right of the churches to be involved in the body politic, a right acknowledged by the U.S. Supreme Court in *Walz v. Tax Commission of the City of New York* (1970). As applied to the Establishment Clause, it does mean the institutional separation of the direct and official functioning of the church from the direct and official functioning of the state.

There can be little question, from a historical point of view, but that religious liberty finds its fullest expression where the church is not legally dependent upon the state for its sanction and support. To suggest that separation of church and state may be achieved so long as no one church enjoys special privileges and all denominations are treated impartially, is to fail to understand the historical meaning and significance of the Establishment Clause of the First Amendment in the light of the American experience.

See also FIRST AMENDMENT.

BIBLIOGRAPHY. W. S. Hudson, *The Great Tradition of the American Churches* (1953); A. W. Johnson and F. H. Yost, *Separation of Church and State in the United States* (1948); L. W. Levy, *The Establishment Clause: Religion and the First Amendment* (1986); L. Pfeffer, *Church, State, and Freedom* (1967); F. Sorauf, *The Wall of Separation: The Constitutional Politics of Church and State* (1976); A. P. Stokes, *Church and State in the*

United States, 3 vols. (1950); J. E. Wood, Jr., ed., *Religion and the State* (1985).

J. E. Wood

Church Government: Congregational. Congregationalism is a Protestant* tradition of ecclesiology and church government maintaining that local congregations, consisting of men and women who acknowledge the Lordship of Jesus Christ and seek his will, can minister* and govern themselves through congregational vote, covenant and participation. The congregational tradition was brought to America by the Puritans* and may be defined with a phrase drawn from colonial America: turning "the meeting house into a throne room."

The "throne room" speaks of the congregational ideal of recognizing Jesus Christ as head of the church. Authority* belongs to Jesus Christ and is not found in any earthly ecclesiastical authority external to a particular body of believers. The local body of believers is autonomous of any ecclesiastical structure and seeks God's guidance by reading, hearing and interpreting the Bible,* along with seeking through prayer the continual guidance of the Holy Spirit.

The phrase *meeting house* speaks of the gathering of a local body of believers who mutually govern and minister to one another as a manifestation of Christ's church. Although a unanimous "sense of the meeting" (as in the Friends' tradition) would be the ideal form of government, the process is usually a democratic voting procedure using a "Rule of Order," with the majority vote prevailing. Minority and dissenting opinions are respected, with the due consideration that "more light" may be shed on an issue.

Pastors, as well as church members elected to boards of deacons* and elders,* councils and committees, are to minister to the congregation as servants. In America a supplemental congregational tradition of ruling elders, set out in the Cambridge Platform* of 1648, was influential well into the nineteenth century. The ordained ministry is revered but has "no power of government" (Boston Platform, 1865). Local church government may entail a moderator and other church officers.

Congregationalists often form larger fellowships and denominational structures beyond the local church. These structures are intended to aid in larger ministries, but they do not rule over or speak for the local church. The local church calls its own pastor,* while associations or conferences cooperate with the local church in the ordination* and installation with "ministerial standing"—a status held and granted by the denomination. Congrega-

tional government is used not only by churches directly in the congregational tradition, but is also practiced by Baptists,* independents, churches in the Restoration* tradition and many other denominations standing in the Free Church* tradition.

See also CONGREGATIONALISM; NEW ENGLAND WAY; PURITANISM.

BIBLIOGRAPHY. G. G. Atkins and F. L. Fagley, *History of American Congregationalism* (1942); R. S. Paul, *Freedom with Order, The Doctrine of the Church in the United States* (1987); United Church of Christ, *Constitution* (1961) and *Manual on Ministry* (1988); O. E. Winslow, *Meeting House Hill, 1630-1783* (1952).

L. E. Wilshire

Church Government: Episcopal. A form of church government distinguished from presbyterian* and congregational* forms insofar as local churches are subject to the more or less monarchical authority* of a bishop* (derived from the Greek *episkopos,* meaning "overseer"). Roman Catholics,* Orthodox* and Episcopalians* maintain the doctrine of apostolic succession,* sometimes referred to as the "historic ministry," signifying that the episcopacy derives in direct line from the beginnings of Christianity and is indispensable to the church. Through the sacrament* of orders, conferred by the imposition of a bishop's hand on the head of a candidate, the powers of the episcopal office are transmitted from generation to generation.

The liturgical ceremony is often referred to as consecration* and, apart from emergency conditions, is administered by at least three bishops. The new bishop thus receives the authority to teach, to sanctify and to govern. It is the prerogative of the bishops to teach authoritatively the meaning of Christianity and its application to contemporary society. Invested with the fullness of the priesthood, they are also responsible for leading the faithful to holiness through prayer,* baptism,* the Eucharist* and other sacramental experiences. To this end they establish subordinate ministers* by ordaining priests* and deacons,* thus bestowing a share in their own powers.

Unlike in many civil societies, the governing role is not separated into a separate executive legislature and judiciary. Bishops exercise the three functions with varying degrees of independence according to the canons of each denomination.* Circumstances sometimes require that a bishop have a special assistant—an auxiliary or coadjutor bishop. Both receive episcopal consecration (ordination*) and are thus full-fledged bishops, though they do not possess a diocese* in their own right. The coadjutor differs from the auxiliary in that the coadjutor has the right to succeed as the ordinary bishop of the diocese.

Roman Catholic. At least every three years the bishops of an ecclesiastical province or archdiocese* meet to compile a list of priests considered suitable for the episcopacy. The list is then sent to Rome. Whenever a diocesan bishop or coadjutor is to be appointed, the papal representative in the U.S. (*See* Papal Nuncio/Pro Nuncio) secures nominations from the archbishop* and the other bishops of the province concerned. After extensive investigation through a series of questionnaires, the representative forwards to Rome a list of three candidates in order of preference. If an auxiliary bishop is to be named, the bishop requesting the assistant submits three nominations to Rome. The Congregation for Bishops (a bureau in the Roman curia) studies the materials and makes its own recommendation to the pope,* who actually makes the choice. Every bishop, upon reaching the age of seventy-five, must proffer his resignation.

The diocesan bishop has extensive powers. He appoints all the pastors and diocesan officials as well as assigns every priest belonging to the diocese. For a good reason he can remove or transfer any of his appointees. In certain matters he needs the consent of the college of consultors and of the finance council. Every diocese is obliged to have a tribunal which acts in the bishop's name; in practice it deals almost exclusively with marriage nullity cases. All the bishops in the U.S. belong to the National Council of Catholic Bishops,* which has its headquarters in Washington, D.C. The Conference meets at least once a year to set policy. Under certain limited conditions it is empowered to enact uniform legislation for all Catholics. It can determine, for example, the age at which confirmation* is to be received.

Orthodox. The archbishop and the bishops in the Greek Orthodox Church are appointed by the synod in Constantinople (Istanbul) presided over by the ecumenical patriarch.* The Orthodox Church in America provides that the Diocesan Assembly, composed of equal numbers of clergy and lay* delegates, nominate a candidate for the office of diocesan bishop to be submitted for approval to the Holy Synod. The Holy Synod consists of all the diocesan bishops of the (American) Church. If it finds the candidate unacceptable, it will make its own choice. Auxiliary bishops are "nominated by the bishop of the diocese in which they are to serve, with the agreement of the Diocesan Council, and are canonically elected by

the Holy Synod." One of the diocesan bishops is elected Metropolitan of All-America and Canada; "he enjoys primacy being the first among equals." The Holy Synod is the supreme canonical authority in the Church.

Episcopalians. The bishop is elected by a convention of all the clergy and lay representatives of the parishes of the diocese which the bishop is to head. The election must be approved by a majority of the bishops and of the standing committees of the other dioceses in the U.S. If needed, a diocesan bishop may be aided by a coadjutor bishop who has the right of automatic succession, or by a suffragan bishop (an *auxiliary bishop,* in Roman terminology). These bishops must be elected and approved by the other bishops and standing committees. The diocesan bishop does not appoint pastors but must accept the choice of the parish vestry.* No pastor can be removed without the bishop's acquiescence. A bishop must retire at age seventy-two.

The presiding bishop of the Church is elected at a General Convention by the House of Bishops* subject to the approval or veto of the House of Deputies.* Upon assuming office, the bishop gives up the former diocese to live at Dover House near Greenwich, Connecticut, and assumes the throne in the cathedral* at Washington, D.C.

Methodist Churches. Although Methodists do not regard the episcopacy and apostolic succession as essential to the Church or as an order different from that of elder, they do consider it to be scripturally warranted, and American Methodists accord bishops a key role. Bishops are elected by jurisdictional conferences composed of equal numbers of ministerial and lay delegates. The Council of Bishops is made up of all the bishops of the United Methodist Church*; it meets at least once a year and plans for the general oversight and promotion of the temporal and spiritual interests of the entire Church. Bishops have the right to appoint ministers to the local churches after consultation with the district superintendents and representatives from the congregation.

BIBLIOGRAPHY. J. A. Coriden, T. J. Green and D. E. Heintschel, eds., *The Code of Canon Law: A Text and Commentary* (1986); D. J. Constantelos, *Understanding the Greek Orthodox Church: Its Faith, History, and Practice* (1982); H. Harper, *The Episcopalian's Dictionary* (1974); F. D. Leete, *Methodist Bishops* (1948). J. E. Lynch

Church Government: Presbyterian. A form of church government consisting of a graduated series of councils from the congregational to the national level. Presbyterians view church* government, along with the civil magistry, as a gift from God. It is always subordinate to, and for the service of, the gospel and the ordering of the faith and life of the Christian community. Although not priestly in character, it is never merely functional or for the sake of convenience. Rather, government expresses several principles which Presbyterians find in the Scriptures*: (1) that Jesus Christ is the head of the church; (2) that the church is one, holy, catholic and apostolic; (3) that the government of Christ's body is best manifested primarily through councils, rather than through bishops* or congregations; (4) that such government should guarantee the parity of the clergy* and (5) that the laity* should participate in the government of the Christian family.

In the U.S., Presbyterianism is organized under a presbyterium, a graduated series of councils, first under the local church session* of laity, men and women, moderated by the pastor*; presbyteries,* made up of several congregations and composed equally of clerical and lay representatives from sessions; synods,* larger regional bodies with similar representatives; and a General Assembly,* a national body made up of clergy and lay commissioners from the presbyteries. Because American Presbyterianism developed from the bottom up, with the organization of the first presbytery in 1706 and the first General Assembly in 1789, presbyteries have claimed and have exercised great authority and power among Presbyterians, for example, ordaining clergy, male and female, and exercising supervision of congregations. The General Assembly has legislative, judicial and executive authority and power given to it by the presbyteries, especially to review the actions of lower governing bodies.

Congregations elect their own ministers under presbytery advice and consent, as well as other officers called elders* and deacons* who are ordained* by the congregation. Pastors, who are members of presbyteries, have responsibility for the ministry of the Word and sacraments. Elders have responsibility for the general oversight of the faith and life of congregations, while deacons exercise a ministry of compassion within and outside the congregation. Church property is held by trustees for the whole church in conformance to the laws of the states in which congregations are located. Moderators preside over these upper three councils for a period of one year, assisted by stated clerks. Between the yearly meetings of the General Assembly, the work of the whole denomination is carried on by agencies (e.g., boards, committees, etc.), whose work includes domestic and international mission, education (including the training of ministers), discipleship within the larger society, administration of pension and foundation funds under policies set by the General Assembly.

BIBLIOGRAPHY. J. T. McNeill, *The History and the Character of Calvinism* (1954); *The Constitution of the Presbyterian Church in the United States of America* (1956); *Constitution of the Presbyterian Church (U.S.A.)* (1983). J. H. Smylie

Church Growth Movement. A missiological* movement founded by Donald A. McGavran* and characterized by a pragmatic approach to planting and nurturing the growth of churches, based on a systematic analysis of growing churches.* McGavran, a missionary to India, founded the Institute of Church Growth at Eugene, Oregon, in 1959. In 1965 the Institute became a part of Fuller Theological Seminary's* School of World Mission, with McGavran serving as dean.

The Church Growth Movement arose in response to the crisis in missions,* especially after World War 2.* McGavran's seminal work, *The Bridges of God—A Study in the Strategy of Missions* (1955), introduced the concept of "people movements" as the key to mission strategy. This concept may be traced to the pioneering work of J. Waskom Pickett,* who studied the phenomenon and wrote *Christian Mass Movements in India* (1933). Subsequently, Pickett and McGavran collaborated on further research projects in India. The term *mass movement* was superseded by *people movement*.

Noting that most growth in the new churches resulted where a group of people together made the decision to become Christians, McGavran shaped the cornerstone of his theory of mission, the homogeneous unit principle. A homogeneous unit was "simply a section of society in which all the members have some characteristics in common." Since people prefer to come to faith without crossing linguistic or cultural barriers, mission strategy should focus on discrete groups and be timed to meet a people's openness to the gospel.

Emphasizing the Great Commission (Mt 28:18-20) as the foundation for mission, McGavran has distinguished between the "discipling" and "perfecting" tasks of the church, warning of the inherent tendency of the church to give priority to perfecting, while neglecting the discipling of those who have never heard the gospel. The movement has elaborated a methodology for surveying and analyzing people groups, using the tools of the social sciences, in order to determine their readiness to receive the Christian message. At the International Congress on World Evangelism,* held at Lausanne, Switzerland, in 1974, McGavran introduced the concept of the world's "hidden peoples" as a further refinement. More than 16,000 "hidden" or "unreached" groups have been identified.

McGavran and certain of his associates have emphasized the importance of taking a pragmatic approach in working out mission strategy. Arguing that unproductive efforts ought to be abandoned, they have recommended that each mission effort be subjected to the question: Is this resulting in the planting of new churches, and are these churches growing through the winning of people who have never heard the gospel?

Response to the Church Growth Movement has been most positive among evangelicals.* In addition to Fuller's School of World Mission, which has trained hundreds of students from all parts of the world, most evangelical seminaries* in North America have been influenced by the movement's concepts. The movement has made the most influential contribution to mission strategy since World War 2 for several reasons: (1) it has systematically and persistently scrutinized the conduct of missionary work with a view toward improvement; (2) it has emphasized the importance of measurable results; (3) it has kept in focus the unfinished task of evangelizing the unreached; (4) it has taken an optimistic view of how the task can be completed.

BIBLIOGRAPHY. C. H. Kraft, *Christianity and Culture* (1979); D. McGavran, *The Bridges of God* (1955); D. McGavran, *How Churches Grow* (1959); D. McGavran, *Understanding Church Growth* (1970, 1980); W. R. Shenk, ed., *Exploring Church Growth* (1983); A. R. Tippett, ed., *God, Man and Church Growth* (1973).   W. R. Shenk

Church Membership. Two different traditions of church membership have characterized Christianity in America, an inclusive and an exclusive tradition. The former carried over from European Christendom the concept of the church being coextensive with the territory—that is, that everyone located geographically within a parish* is eligible for baptism,* which signifies membership in the church. The exclusive tradition confined church membership to those who could give a credible profession of faith, sometimes requiring evidence of internal regeneration* along with knowledge of saving doctrine* and a morally upright life. The latter nevertheless sometimes included children of believers as also "within the covenant." Such children were eligible for baptism although not admitted to the Lord's Supper* or

other functions of full membership until they made their own professions of faith. The eventual separation of church and state* in the context of American religious pluralism* meant that each denomination had to rely on evangelism* for church membership. This fact contributed to the revivalism* which came to characterize much of American religion.

The Massachusetts Bay Colony in its nonseparating Congregationalism* produced the distinctive situation of an established church* which nevertheless made profession of an experience of regeneration a requirement for church membership. This limitation of membership to "visible saints" led to pressures resulting in the Half-Way Covenant* of 1662, which allowed those who were not guilty of heresy* or scandal (though unable to profess experience of regeneration) to have their children baptized. Even so, the majority of the population in early eighteenth-century America were not church members.

During the Great Awakening,* Jonathan Edwards* broke with the Half-Way Covenant in insisting that one must be genuinely converted* to have access to the sacraments* and the privileges of church membership. It has been estimated that during the Second Awakening* the number attending church was three times greater than the number of actual church members.

By the early twentieth century, however, membership requirements in mainline* denominations were less demanding. The Presbyterian* J. Gresham Machen* could complain in *Christianity and Liberalism* (1923) of "the admission of great companies of persons who have never made any really credible confession of faith at all and whose entire attitude toward the gospel is the very reverse of the Christian attitude."

BIBLIOGRAPHY. E. S. Morgan, *Visible Saints: The History of a Puritan Idea* (1963); R. G. Pope, *The Half-Way Covenant: Church Membership in Puritan New England* (1969); E. B. Holifield, *The Covenant Sealed: The Development of Puritan Sacramental Theology in Old and New England* (1974).   W. S. Barker

Church Missionary Society. An evangelical* voluntary missionary* organization within the Church of England. The Church Missionary Society (CMS) was founded in 1799 as part of the first phase of the modern Protestant missionary movement. Since the Church of England has never had an official missionary society, CMS began as, and continues to be, a voluntary society* within the Church. During the nineteenth century it was the largest English missionary society and was looked to as the leader in missionary thought and practice. During the twentieth century, while it has not retained such a unique position, it has nonetheless continued as a large and important part of the English missionary scene.

The work of the CMS in North America was restricted almost entirely to ministry among Canada's native peoples. This involvement began in 1822 when the Reverend John West* was appointed to work among the Native Americans of Red River (Winnipeg). As the century progressed the CMS missionaries labored around Hudson's Bay, across the northern prairies and then up into the Northwest Territories and the Yukon. In addition to the missionaries, a remarkable number of outstanding native clergy* and laity* emerged. Missionary bishops* were also associated with CMS, and none more heroic than the Apostle of the North, William Carpenter Bompas,* who with his wife from 1874 to 1906 continually chose the most distant and difficult fields until they finally arrived on the shores of the Arctic Ocean.

The work on the West Coast began with the arrival of the lay missionary William Duncan,* who at Metlakatla near Prince Rupert developed a famous Christian village where the church was larger than any comparable building west of Chicago and north of San Francisco. Early in the twentieth century the CMS began to retire from Canada, believing that Canadian Anglicans should take the lead.

BIBLIOGRAPHY. E. Stock, *A History of the Church Missionary Society,* 3 vols. (1899).

I. S. Rennie

Church of England. *See* ANGLICAN CHURCH.

Church of God in Christ, Mennonite. A small conservative Mennonite* denomination.* The group was founded by John Holdeman,* who left the main body of Mennonites when they failed to ordain* him. Holdeman began preaching* on his own in 1859 and formed his own following.

Self-educated, fluent in English and in German, and able in Dutch and Greek, Holdeman studied the writings of Dirk Philips and Menno Simons, as well as the Dutch martyrology the *Martyrs Mirror* and the Eighteen Articles, the Dutch Mennonite confession of faith (1632). Holdeman became a firm adherent of the traditional Mennonite practice of maintaining a strictly disciplined church, including the shunning of excommunicated members. He also emphasized the new birth, the ministry of the Holy Spirit and strict separation from the world. Holdeman's followers were drawn from the Mennonite Church, as well as the Dutch Mennonite immigrants who had lived a few generations in Russia before coming to America. To this day the group is often referred to as the Holdeman Mennonites.

Like the Mennonite Church, they baptize only those who can claim repentance from sin, and faith in Christ. All oaths are refused and the ethic of nonresistance is strictly adhered to. The Church, the body of Christ, is to be holy, as its Lord is. As a symbol of nonconformity the men wear a neatly trimmed beard and no ties; the women wear full dresses, plain in character and without ornamentation. All jewelry is shunned. Higher education is not permitted. The Holdeman Mennonites are found mostly in North America and number about 12,000 baptized members in some 100 congregations.

BIBLIOGRAPHY. C. Hiebert, *The Holdeman People* (1971). J. C. Wenger

Church of the Brethren. Founded in 1708 by Alexander Mack* and seven others in Schwarzenau/Eder, Germany, as an Anabaptist*/pietist* sect,* by 1719 persecution had forced a group to immigrate to Pennsylvania under the leadership of Peter Becker.* It was not until 1729 that Mack arrived in Germantown, along with a group he had led to Holland in 1720, and assumed leadership of the Brethren in America. By the late eighteenth century the Brethren had followed the westward movement and settled in eastern Missouri, and by the mid-nineteenth century they could be found on the Great Plains and West Coast. By 1948 the Brethren had become an ecumenically* oriented Free Church* known for its service outreach and peace emphasis. In 1986 the Church of the Brethren had about 170,000 adult members in over 1,000 congregations in the U.S., with a rapidly growing daughter church in Nigeria (c. 40,000 members) created by missions efforts. Congregations in other former mission areas have joined united churches in India, China and Ecuador.

Called an historic Peace Church since 1935, Brethren organized in 1941 a service committee that developed worldwide activity in relief and rehabilitation programs. Among the Brethren-initiated projects that found interdenominational support were the Christian Rural Overseas Program (CROP), Heifer Project International and International Christian Youth Exchange (ICYE).

Brethren resist creedal statements but accept basic Protestant* doctrines. In patterning church life after the early Christians, they practice several ordinances.* These include: believer's baptism* by threefold immersion (earning them the nickname "Dunkers"); the love feast (following Jn 13), incorporating a time of examination, foot washing,* a fellowship meal and partaking of bread and cup; affirmation instead of oathtaking; and the laying on of hands. Brethren teach a simple, nonconforming way of life; until 1911 the church required a prescribed plain dress.

Brethren polity combines congregational* and presbyterian* elements, with an authoritative annual conference. Staff workers located at Elgin, Illinois, and New Windsor, Maryland, carry out church programs under the direction of an elected General Board. The denomination was a charter member of the National Council of Churches of Christ* in 1950 (having joined the Federal Council* in 1941) and of the World Council of Churches* in 1948.

See also FREE CHURCH TRADITION IN AMERICA.

BIBLIOGRAPHY. D. F. Durnbaugh, ed., *The Brethren Encyclopedia* (1983); D. F. Durnbaugh, *The Brethren in Colonial America* (1967); D. F. Durnbaugh, ed., *Church of the Brethren: Yesterday and Today* (1971); R. E. Sappington, *Brethren Social Policy, 1908-1958* (1961).

D. F. Durnbaugh

Church of the Nazarene. A denomination originating from the union of several religious bodies with roots in the nineteenth-century Holiness Movement.* Consonant with its origins, the Church of the Nazarene* emphasizes the doctrine* of entire sanctification* as a second definite work of grace subsequent to conversion* and advocates a disciplined lifestyle for its members reflecting "holiness of heart and life."

The Church of the Nazarene began in the U.S. as a result of the proliferation of independent Holiness associations, missions and churches during the second half of the nineteenth century and early part of the twentieth century. Eventually, a "union movement" favoring a national Holiness church arose among some of these bodies, encouraged notably by Phineas F. Bresee,* a former Methodist* pastor* and presiding elder who organized the first group to use the name Church of the Nazarene in Los Angeles in 1895. Bresee's group, and a group of Holiness churches in the East, the Association of Pentecostal Churches in America, united in Chicago in 1907 to form the Pentecostal Church of the Nazarene. This body subsequently united in 1908 with the Holiness Church of Christ, a Southern group, at Pilot Point, Texas. The name remained Pentecostal Church of the Nazarene for a time, but in 1919 the term *Pentecostal* was dropped due to its association with tongues speaking,* a practice not endorsed by the Church of the Nazarene. After 1908 the church continued to grow through numerous accessions of Holiness groups in North America and the British Isles, as well as through an aggressive evangelistic* and missionary* program.

Doctrinally the Church of the Nazarene has been shaped most by that branch of the Christian tradition associated with John Wesley* and his Methodist movement. Wesley's teaching, especially his doctrine of Christian perfection,* was central to the Holiness Movement out of which the Church of the Nazarene arose. Fifteen Articles of Faith in the *Manual* summarize the essential teachings of the church. Among these are belief in the "plenary inspiration of the Holy Scriptures" which "inerrantly reveal the will of God concerning us in all things necessary to our salvation"; belief that through grace all persons who will may "turn from sin to righteousness" and "believe on Jesus Christ for pardon and cleansing from sin"; and belief in entire sanctification as "that act of God, subsequent to regeneration,* by which believers are made free from original sin,* or depravity, and brought into a state of entire devotement to God, and the holy obedience of love made perfect," an act "wrought by the baptism with the Holy Spirit." Divine healing* is affirmed although not to the exclusion of medical means. Both infant and adult believer's baptism* are provided for, and belief in the Second Coming of Christ is held to be essential to Christian faith.

The *Manual* of the church also contains "General" and "Special Rules" according to which members pledge themselves to "feeding the hungry, clothing the naked, visiting the sick and imprisoned, and ministering to the needy" as well as "avoiding evil of every kind," including profaning the Lord's Day; using alcohol, tobacco or drugs; the "indulging of pride in dress or behavior"; and "entertainments which are subversive of the Christian ethic."

The Church of the Nazarene combines elements of congregational,* episcopal,* and presbyterian* forms of government. Local churches retain considerable congregational autonomy while at the same time they are subject to oversight by both district superintendents and general superintendents. Ultimate authority in the church is held by the general assembly, an elected body of both lay* persons and clergy* which meets usually every four years. In addition, a general board of both clergy and lay people elected by the general assembly oversees the work of the church in the time between general-assembly meetings.

Strongly committed to world missions* from its beginning, the church now has work in over eighty world areas, with an international membership of 874,000 distributed throughout nearly 9,000 congregations (as of 1988). With international headquarters in Kansas City, Missouri, the church operates a publishing house, a graduate theological seminary, nine liberal-arts colleges in the U.S. and Canada and two colleges in Europe, as well as numerous schools, hospitals and clinics in various other parts of the world.

BIBLIOGRAPHY. J. F. Parker, *Mission to the World* (1988); W. T. Purkiser, *Called unto Holiness, the Second Twenty-Five Years* (1983); T. L. Smith, *Called unto Holiness, the Story of the Nazarenes: The Formative Years* (1962); *Manual of the Church of the Nazarene.*   H. E. Raser

Church of the New Jerusalem. A religious body founded on the spiritual teachings of Emanuel Swedenborg. The Swedish scientist Emanuel Swedenborg (1688-1772) claimed to have had a revelation that enabled him to communicate with the world of spirits and angels. During his various communications with that world, he claimed to have learned the secrets of the universe. Swedenborg accepted a canon of twenty-nine books of the Old Testament and five books of the New and attempted to move beyond their literal and historical meaning to extract their spiritual or allegorical meaning. He seems to have denied the orthodox doctrine of the Trinity (teaching that God is one in three principles, each of which are manifest in Jesus Christ), original sin,* the vicarious atonement* and the bodily resurrection; but some individual congregations of the church do not appear to be quite so unorthodox.

Based on the teachings of Swedenborg, Robert Hindmarsh launched the New Jerusalem Church in London in the 1780s, and churches were established in England, Sweden, Germany and North America. The churches exist in three main bodies today: the General Conference in England, The General Convention of the New Jerusalem in the U.S.A. and the General Church of the New Jerusalem, which in 1890 broke from the parent group in the U.S.A.

The General Convention had 1,820 members in thirty-one societies in 1985 and maintains a theological school at Newton, Massachusetts. The General Church had 3,297 members in 1985, meeting in twenty-one organized circles and fifteen organized groups. It maintains a theological school, a college and a secondary school, and its headquarters are at Bryn Athyn, Pennsylvania. The General Convention has self-regulating societies holding services based on the *Book of Worship* of the Convention. There is an annual meeting. It subscribes to the belief "that there is one God, in whom there is a Divine Trinity; and that He is the Lord Jesus Christ" and "that saving faith is to believe on Him." The General Church accepts the full authority* of the writings of Swedenborg and has no fixed constitution. Church organization is based on "essential unanimity" in free council and assembly. Both U.S. branches have pastors. There is a Swedenborg Foundation in New York City which distributes the writings of Swedenborg, published in thirty volumes. Swedenborg's followers have included William Blake and Helen Keller, and his teachings influenced the work of Coleridge, Balzac and others.

BIBLIOGRAPHY. I. Jonsson, *Emanuel Swedenborg* (1971); H. Keller, *My Religion* (1972); C. O. Sigstedt, *The Swedenborg Epic* (1952); S. M. Warren, *A Compendium of Swedenborg's Theological Writings* (1974).   H. F. Vos

Church of the United Brethren in Christ, The. An evangelical* denomination* with roots in German-American revivalism.* The Church began in 1800 as a result of the preaching of Martin Boehm* and William Otterbein* among Germans in Pennsylvania, Maryland and Virginia. Methodist* in doctrine,* church government* and practice, it followed a *Discipline* patterned on the Methodist *Discipline.* The denomination split in 1889, primarily over proposed constitutional changes permitting members to join lodges and secret societies. The majority, or "new constitution," group joined with the Evangelical Church in 1946 to become the Evangelical United Brethren Church. That body then merged with the Methodist Church in 1968 to form the United Methodist Church.*

The continuing Church of the United Brethren in Christ (Old Constitution) retains its Methodist heritage, with a belief in the Trinity, the deity, humanity and atonement* of Christ and a lifestyle that forbids alcoholic beverages,* membership in secret societies and engaging in aggressive (but not defensive) war. Its form of government follows that of the Methodist Church, and both men and women can be ordained to the ministry. The denomination maintains a college and Graduate School of Christian Ministries in Huntington, Indiana, and supports missionary ventures in Sierra Leone, Jamaica, Honduras and Hong Kong. Evangelical* in orientation, the Church holds membership in the National Association of Evangelicals.*

[275]

In 1987 the denomination claimed 26,869 members in 256 churches.

BIBLIOGRAPHY. B. Behney and P. Eller, *History of the Evangelical United Brethren Church* (1979); J. S. O'Malley, *Pilgrimage of Faith: The Legacy of the Otterbeins* (1973); J. S. O'Malley, *Touched by Godliness: Bishop John Seybert and the Evangelical Heritage* (1985). H. F. Vos

Church Peace Union. *See* CARNEGIE COUNCIL ON ETHICS AND INTERNATIONAL AFFAIRS.

Church Union Movements. North American denominationalism* was the result of a combination of factors that existed on the vast frontier of the newly discovered continent. Though most religious thinkers, past and present, acknowledge that the testimony of the Christian faith involves a unity of witness not always evident in denominationalism, few denominations were willing to actively seek union for that reason alone. More practical issues, such as foreign missions, acute social problems or the availability of resources in times of economic depression, usually were the stimuli for any serious movements toward unity. When unifying movements did occur, they ranged from cooperative ventures between denominations to full organic union, though the latter were much more rare.

In the U.S. before 1800, men like Henry M. Muhlenberg* and Michael Schlatter* tried to unify religious bodies of similar ethnic background. After 1800, specific concerns brought individuals and denominations together in voluntary societies* such as the American Board of Commissioners for Foreign Missions* (1810), the American Bible Society* (1816) and the American Temperance Society* (1826). The formation of the YMCA* (1851), the World Student Christian Federation* (1895) and the Student Christian Movement* (1858) are other examples of cooperative ventures resulting from areas of shared concern. Also active in the nineteenth century were American ecumenists like Samuel Schmucker* (Lutheran*), Alexander Campbell* (Disciples of Christ*), William Reed Huntingdon* (Episcopalian*) and Elias B. Sanford* (Congregationalist*) who, together with academics like Philip Schaff,* laid the intellectual groundwork for ecumenical undertakings such as the Evangelical Alliance* of 1867.

In twentieth-century America, ecumenical cooperation across denominational lines increased. In order to exert a more effective influence on the moral and social condition of the people, over thirty denominations formed the Federal Council of Churches* (FCC) in 1908. FCC leaders were instrumental in organizing the World Council of Churches* in 1948, which emphasized "unity in diversity." Denominations concerned that the FCC was so involved in matters of social concern that the salvation* of the individual was being neglected, formed the National Association of Evangelicals* in 1942.

Organic unions among American denominations also became more frequent in the twentieth century. In 1930 the American Lutheran Church* was formed from the unification of three major Lutheran bodies. Having the same polity but different historical antecedents, the Congregational Churches and Christian Churches (General Convention) joined to become the Congregational Christian Churches in 1931. Of the same ethnic background but different religious heritage were the Reformed Church in the United States and the Evangelical Synod of North America, which united in 1934 to become the Evangelical and Reformed Church. In 1957 the Evangelical and Reformed Church united with the Congregational Christian Churches to form the United Church of Christ.* Social problems, such as racial discrimination, continued to plague denominations in their merger attempts; for example, the Methodist* Church was formed in 1939 from the merger of three Methodist groups, even though this union excluded all black Methodist denominations.

In Canada, denominational mergers occurred earlier in the nation's history as this country's great expanses and sparse population, particularly in the West, necessitated a coordinated effort in the mission field. In 1875 a Presbyterian* union was effected; in 1884, the Methodist Church of Canada became the largest Protestant church in Canada and in 1893, the Anglicans* united under the banner of the Church of England in Canada. The broadly based, and perhaps most spectacular, interdenominational union on the continent took place in Canada when the Presbyterian, Methodist and Congregational bodies, concerned about developing missions in western Canada, merged in 1925 to become the United Church of Canada.*

In the rural areas of the U.S. and Canada, a community church movement sprang up during the 1930s as individual congregations, frustrated by the delays of denominational leaders in effecting organizational union, merged with other congregations in order to better serve the local community. After the mid-1930s, when economic hardships were not nearly as severe and the modern ecumenical spirit was successful in forging major denominational unions, this community church movement lost its momentum.

In the last half of the twentieth century, the ecumenical spirit has become even more pervasive as denominations seem more willing to discuss organic union. In 1962 a Consultation on Church Union* began between major American denominations, with three Canadian churches active as observers. Though the momentum behind these discussions has died, dialogs between pairs of churches continue (i.e., Anglican and Catholic,* Lutheran and Reformed*). Denominational families are also making an effort to consolidate their resources in organizational mergers; for example, The United Presbyterian Church in the U.S.A.* merged with the Presbyterian Church in the U.S.* to become the Presbyterian Church (U.S.A.)* in 1983, and three major American Lutheran denominations merged in 1988 to form the Evangelical Lutheran Church in America.* While it is doubtful that the current ecumenical spirit will ever produce a completely united Christian church on earth, the challenges of increasing secularization and pluralism,* to name just two, have encouraged continuing cooperation and movement toward union among North American denominations.

BIBLIOGRAPHY. S. M. Cavert, *The American Churches in the Ecumenical Movement: 1900-1968* (1968); R. E. Richey, *Denominationalism* (1977); W. G. Rusch, *Ecumenism: A Movement Toward Church Unity* (1985).   B. V. Hillis

Church World Service.
Ecumenical relief agency. Founded in 1946 by the Federal Council of the Churches of Christ in America* (FCC), the American Committee of the World Council of Churches,* and the Foreign Missions Conference of North America,* the Church World Service (CWS) was to integrate church organizations initiated to meet the needs of refugees and other war-sufferers. Historian Merle Curti called it the "first fully unifying and coordinating instrument for overseas relief in the history of American Protestant* and Orthodox* churches." CWS became a part of the National Council of the Churches of Christ in the USA* (NCCC) when that organization succeeded the FCC in 1950. A reorganization in 1964 united it with the Division of Foreign Missions to form the Division of Overseas Ministries; in 1985 CWS became an independent division. Over thirty Protestant and Orthodox churches support the agency in its worldwide mission to "carry on works of Christian mercy, relief, technical assistance, rehabilitation, and interchurch aid."

Since 1949 its major fund-raising appeal has been "One Great Hour of Sharing," which reaches congregations across the U.S. Its funding makes up more than eighty per cent of the NCCC budget. CWS is noted for its prompt aid to victims of disasters, wars and other social disturbances and has assisted thousands of refugees to resettle in North America. Headquarters are in the Interchurch Center in New York City, with a branch office in Elkhart, Indiana, and field offices overseas. Centers at New Windsor, Maryland, and other places receive and send material aid, medicines and other supplies. Other agencies, such as the Christian Rural Overseas Program (CROP), work under the CWS umbrella.

BIBLIOGRAPHY. H. E. Fey, *Cooperation in Compassion: "The Story of Church World Service"* (1966); J. H. Haines, *A World Without Hunger* (1980); P. Romanofsky, ed., *Social Service Organizations,* vol. 1 (1978).   D. F. Durnbaugh

Churches of Christ (Non-Instrumental).
A brotherhood of churches spawned by the nineteenth-century Restoration Movement.* The Churches of Christ, first recognized as a distinct group in the 1906 federal census, tend to be the most conservative of the three groups (including the Disciples of Christ* and the Christian Churches*) arising out of the Restoration Movement.

The Churches of Christ retain Restorationist motifs from early stages of the movement, which according to Alexander Campbell's* *Millennial Harbinger* (1850) were: (1) Scripture* as the sole authority; (2) Christ as Messiah and Savior; (3) the ancient church order; (4) the authority* of the Messiah and apostles, as opposed to the Old Testament; and (5) cooperation among the churches. The ancient order entailed congregational independence, believer's baptism* by immersion, weekly observation of the Lord's Supper,* teaching elders* and traveling non-salaried evangelists.* Theological formulations not found in Scripture (e.g., Calvinism,* Arminianism,* Trinitarianism and Unitarianism*) were to be avoided. The proponents were strongly anti-creedal, arguing that creeds* generated schisms in the body of Christ. John Locke and the Scottish Enlightenment deeply influenced the leaders, who opposed unusual manifestations of the Holy Spirit in any form. Early preachers* castigated the Westminster Confession* for its distinctive Calvinistic tendencies and "metaphysical" language, but agreed with about eighty per cent of the conclusions, even though they did not admit as much.

The controversies leading to the 1906 separation

were over state and national mission societies and over musical instruments in worship*; the Churches of Christ were opposed to both practices. The Civil War* added to the cultural aspects of the division. The Disciples tended to become more ecumenical while the Churches of Christ saw themselves as outsiders both to American religion and society, controverting Christian history beyond New Testament times. Leaders among the Churches of Christ were Tolbert Fanning* and David Lipscomb* of Nashville, Tennessee, and Austin McGary of Austin, Texas.

Small factions have occurred over issues such as plural Communion cups, premillennialism* and the disbursement of church funds to parachurch ministries. Lectureships,* journals and universities stimulate brotherhood cohesiveness. Leaders now tend to be more grace-oriented than in former times. There are over 13,000 autonomous congregations making up the Churches of Christ, with a membership of over 1,600,000. Eighty per cent of them live two hundred miles on either side of a line drawn from Chattanooga, Tennessee, to El Paso, Texas.

BIBLIOGRAPHY. E. West, *Search for the Ancient Order,* 4 vols. (1949-1988); R. Hooper, *Crying in the Wilderness: A Biography of David Lipscomb* (1979); M. Lynn, ed., *Where the Saints Meet* (1987).
T. H. Olbricht

Churches of God. Because it is a generic term, any religious organization can choose the words *Church of God* as its title, and over 200 religious groups and countless independent storefront congregations in America have adopted it. Use of this name became popular in the late nineteenth century because of its biblical basis and its universal nature. The majority of Churches of God are Holiness* or Holiness/Pentecostal.* There are, however, several small Adventist* groups that have the name Church of God. The Worldwide Church of God* founded by Herbert Armstrong,* initially a pastor in the Church of God (Seventh Day), has achieved notoriety but is not representative of other Churches of God. This article will discuss the major Christian denominations* that go by this name.

Church of God (Anderson, Indiana). The Church of God (Anderson) is the largest of the Holiness groups bearing the name. Daniel Sydney Warner* experienced sanctification* in 1877 and was disfellowshipped a year later from the General Eldership of the Church of God in North America because of his emphasis on entire sanctification. He then joined an offshoot of this group, the

Northern Indiana Eldership of the Church of God, which was open to Holiness teaching. When this group refused to adopt Warner's proposal to ban both pastoral licenses* and church membership,* he announced his freedom from all sects* and was joined by five other individuals. This action, in October 1881, is generally considered the beginning of the Church of God. Persons from various denominations heeded Warner's call to reject sectarianism and "come out" from them.

Warner opposed all forms of ecclesiastical organization, including formal church membership, arguing that only God knows who the true Christians are. Ordination* was simply a recognition of the reception of a divine call to preach and would be granted by a committee of state or regional pastors. This emphasis on the guidance of the Holy Spirit accounts for the fact that women have always been ordained by the movement.

Development of the Church of God was hindered by its opposition to organization. Gradually, the group has accepted the argument that while the Church itself cannot be organized, it is expedient to organize the work of the Church. Currently, nine agencies serve this function. A General Ministerial Assembly, begun in 1917 and renamed the General Assembly,* consists of ministers and some laypeople.* It cannot speak for the whole movement, so its resolutions are not binding. Each congregation is independent and calls its own pastor.

The Bible* serves as the group's creed and is regarded as infallible in matters of faith and life. The doctrines of holiness and unity were the major theological themes of the new movement. Initially, the group was known as church of God, with a lowercase *c* to indicate its inclusion of all Christians. The early leaders insisted they were restoring primitive* Christianity rather than founding a denomination. The group continues to reject a denominational designation, preferring to be called a movement. Arminian* in orientation, the Church teaches faith healing* and a doctrine of the Second Coming of Christ unaccompanied by a millennium.* Three ordinances* are practiced: baptism* by immersion, Communion,* which is open to all believers, and foot washing.*

The *Gospel Trumpet* (renamed *Vital Christianity* in 1962) has provided a vital function in the growth of the Church, supplemented by itinerant preachers, called "flying messengers," during the early years of the movement. Since 1906 the *Gospel Trumpet* has been published in Anderson, Indiana, which in turn became the national headquarters for the Church of God. While congregations primarily emerged in rural areas, at least forty-five missionary* homes operated in urban areas between 1890 and the early 1920s. These homes served as training centers and provided experience in urban ministries. Realizing the need for formal education for pastors, Anderson Bible Training School (now Anderson University) opened in 1917. The School of Theology was added in 1950. The Church supports several colleges in the U.S.

The Missionary Committee, established in 1909, by 1987 could count 229,258 adherents in sixty-two countries outside the U.S. Since 1947 the movement has sponsored the Christian Brotherhood Hour, a radio program broadcast in the U.S. and abroad. In 1987 there were 100,662 adherents in 2,296 congregations in the U.S.

Church of God (Cleveland, Tennessee). The Church of God (Cleveland, Tennessee) is the oldest Pentecostal Church in the U.S. In 1886 eight people formed the Christian Union in Tennessee with the goal of restoring primitive Christianity, promoting Holiness doctrine and uniting all denominations. The Christian Union chose Richard G. Spurling, Jr., as its pastor. The Church joined with another group in North Carolina in 1896. Church members first spoke in tongues* at services near Camp Creek, North Carolina, in 1896 under the ministry of W. F. Bryant, a layperson.

Originally opposed to organization, the group adopted a simple plan of government in 1902 to guard against fanaticism. At that time, it adopted the name The Holiness Church at Camp Creek, abandoning its mission to bring all denominations together. The group endured, despite early persecution from mobs who threw rocks at members' houses, burned churches and whipped members.

Ministers met yearly in various churches as a general assembly from 1906 until 1916 when an auditorium in Harriman, Tennessee, was purchased for this purpose. In 1920 a new auditorium was built in Cleveland, Tennessee, and while the general assembly has met in various locations since 1934, the general headquarters remain in Cleveland. As the Church grew, so did the organization, and the office of general moderator was established in 1909, renamed general overseer a year later. The duties of this position included the appointment of pastors. State overseers were first appointed in 1911. A Council of Twelve, established in 1917, assists the general overseer and plans the agenda for the general assembly of pastors. All ordained ministers meet prior to the general assembly and discuss issues presented by the Council of Twelve. Their recommendations are generally accepted by the entire general assembly.

Originally decrying creeds, in 1948 the Church formulated a Declaration of Faith affirming belief in the verbal inspiration of the Bible, the premillennial* Second Coming of Christ and divine healing. Three ordinances, baptism by immersion, the Lord's Supper and foot washing are practiced. The Church has maintained its Holiness doctrine of sanctification but believes that this experience is followed by the baptism of the Spirit,* evidenced by speaking in tongues.

Ordained ministers were called bishops* until 1948. Women serve as evangelists* and preachers* but are not ordained. Since 1910 the *Church of God Evangel* has been the official organ of the Church. In 1910 the Church of God established its Bible Training School, which was relocated in Cleveland, Tennessee, in 1947, and is now known as Lee College. The Church also sponsors three Bible colleges. Over the years the Church of God has experienced numerous splits resulting in several independent groups, also bearing the name Church of God. In 1987 there were 505,755 members in the U.S. worshiping in 5,346 churches.

Church of God of Prophecy. Ambrose J. Tomlinson* joined the Church of God (Cleveland, Tennessee) in 1903 and was the body's first General Moderator. As the years passed, Tomlinson assumed increasing leadership until 1923, when the Church impeached him on fifteen charges, including disloyalty, usurpation of authority and misappropriation of funds. Relieved of his duties, Tomlinson founded a rival Church in Cleveland, Tennessee, known as Tomlinson Church of God. At his death in 1943 the Church split into two factions, headed by Tomlinson's sons.

Milton R. Tomlinson led the group, now known as the Church of God of Prophecy, which maintained its headquarters in Cleveland, Tennessee. In 1987 membership in the Church of God of Prophecy was 73,952. The Church of God of All Nations is a splinter movement which separated from the Church of God of Prophecy in 1957 under the leadership of G. R. Kent.

Homer A. Tomlinson assumed responsibility for the other group which emerged from the Tomlinson Church of God. He chose the title Church of God and established headquarters in New York. When he died in 1960 the headquarters relocated in Huntsville, Alabama. Membership in this denomination was 75,090 in 1980.

Church of God in Christ. The Church of God in Christ, with headquarters in Memphis, Tennessee, is the largest African-American Pentecostal group in the world. Its founder was Charles H. Mason* who was licensed* by the Missionary Baptist

Church* in 1893. Claiming to experience entire sanctification that same year, he was expelled by the Baptists.* In 1895 Mason and Charles P. Jones* founded the Church of Christ (Holiness) U.S.A., a group emphasizing entire sanctification. Mason also began a congregation in Lexington, Mississippi, in 1897, which he called the Church of God in Christ as a result of his conviction that this was the appropriate biblical name.

In 1907 Mason traveled to Los Angeles to witness the Azusa Street* revival,* and there he first spoke in tongues. During the general assembly of the Church of Christ (Holiness) U.S.A., Mason introduced the new Pentecostal doctrine. The non-Pentecostal faction, led by Jones, withdrew and retained the name Church of Christ (Holiness) U.S.A. The majority remained with Mason who, along with D. J. Young, called together African-American preachers who believed in speaking in tongues. Meeting in Memphis, Tennessee, in August 1907, they organized themselves as a general assembly of the Church of God in Christ. Mason was elected to serve as the general overseer, and Young became editor of the group's newspaper, *Whole Truth.*

From its inception the Church has been governed by a council of apostles and elders, in keeping with its understanding of the governance of the New Testament church. Emphasis is placed on the role of the Holy Spirit in directing the leadership. As general overseer and chief apostle, C. H. Mason maintained full control over the Church. He appointed overseers for the various jurisdictions, as well as heads of the national departments. After his death in 1961, the issue of authority* preoccupied the Church. In 1968, a constitutional convention decided that a general board of twelve bishops, elected for a four-year term by the general assembly, would oversee the work of the Church. The general assembly would also elect a presiding bishop and two assistants. The Church of God in Christ engaged in its first general election that same year. As a result of this change in policy, fourteen bishops of the Church withdrew and organized the Church of God in Christ (International) in 1969 with headquarters in Kansas City, Missouri.

The Church of God in Christ is Trinitarian and premillennialist.* The Church believes in divine healing and that tongues is a gift for all Christians, not just an elite few. Baptism is by immersion, and the Church practices Communion and foot washing. Church members engage in an active worship style that includes dancing and shaking, practices they defend on biblical grounds. The Church of God in Christ sponsors Saints Junior College in Lexington, Mississippi. In 1979 there were reportedly 420,000 members in 4,100 churches.

Church of God (Seventh Day). Adventists who refused to endorse Ellen White's* visions and writings departed from her church in 1858 and organized the General Conference of the Church of God in 1884. "Seventh Day" was added to the name in 1923, reflecting their observance of the Sabbath on the seventh day of the week. The Church's offices were in Stanberry, Missouri, until 1950, when they relocated to Denver. A rival faction, keeping the same name, established headquarters in Salem, West Virginia, in 1933. Most members of the Church in Salem reunited with the Denver group in 1949, but a small number with the same name are still headquartered in Salem. The Denver group reports a membership of 5,830.

BIBLIOGRAPHY. B. L. Callen, ed., *The First Century* [Church of God (Anderson, Ind.)], 2 vols. (1979); C. W. Conn, *Like a Mighty Army: A History of the Church of God, 1886-1976* [Church of God (Cleveland, Tennessee)] (1977); C. W. Conn, *Where the Saints Have Trod: A History of Church of God Missions* [Church of God (Cleveland. Tenn.)] (1977); J. G. Melton, *The Encyclopedia of American Religions,* 2nd ed. (1987); J. O. Patterson et al., *History and Formative Years of the Church of God in Christ* (1969); J. Stone, *The Church of God of Prophecy: History and Polity* (1977).

S. C. Stanley

Circuit Rider. A term peculiar to early American Methodism,* it describes those preachers who were responsible for the spiritual well-being of local churches or societies that banded together for the purpose of pastoral supervision. The early Methodist preachers were appointed to circuits, some of them as large as states, and paid a price for the faithfulness of their labors. Of the circuit riders who died before 1847, nearly half died before the age of thirty. Two-thirds died before completing twelve years of service, and half of those before completing five years of service. On particularly stormy nights on the American frontier, a favorite cliché was: "nothin' out but crows and Methodist Preachers."

The circuit riders were not all out of the same mold. Some were fairly well-educated, according to the standards of the day; some were not. A few were married; most had little or no personal wealth. The message of the circuit rider was, on the whole, true to the gospel, spoken first to awaken and then to convert* and sanctify* through faith in Jesus Christ by the power of the Holy Spirit.

BIBLIOGRAPHY. D. Byrne, Jr., *No Foot of Land: Folklore of American Methodist Itinerants* (1975); W. D. Smithers, *Circuit Riders of the Big Bend* (1981).   R. G. Tuttle

Civil Religion. A scholar's term which embodies and describes a religio-political phenomenon considered by anthropologists, sociologists and historians to be as old as organized human communities. Civil religion is a way of thinking which makes sacred a political arrangement or governmental system and provides a religious image of a political society for many, if not most, of its members. Also called civil, public, political or societal religion or public piety, civil religion is the general faith of a state or nation that focuses on widely held beliefs about the history and destiny of that state or nation. It is a religious way of thinking about politics which provides a society with ultimate meaning (thus making it a genuine religion) which, in turn, allows a people to look at their political community in a special sense and thus achieve purposeful social integration. In short, it is the social glue which binds a given society together by means of well-established ceremonies—rituals, symbols, values—and allegiances which function in the life of the community in such a way as to provide it with an overarching sense of spiritual unity. Therefore, it is not a particular or specific religion or expression thereof, but is of such a nature that those who hold specific beliefs can read into it whatever meaning they choose. Civil religion has no formal organization and no central authority, yet it can be highly institutionalized in the collective life of a society.

The traits commonly associated with civil religion appeared as far back as classical antiquity when each Greek city-state had its own official gods and civic dogmas and in which the citizenry regularly affirmed their public faith by means of collective ideas, sentiments and ceremonials. Plato even developed the outline of a civil theology in *The Republic* in the fourth century B.C. The Romans had a more highly developed civil religion which centered on the person of the emperor, who functioned as both the chief priest of the state cult and as an object of worship. However, it was Jean-Jacques Rousseau who actually coined the term in his *Social Contract* (1762) when he identified civil religion as something which could deal with religious pluralism* and at the same time cement people's allegiances to civil society, thereby achieving and ensuring social peace. In the Western world in modern times, civil religion has developed along Rousseauean lines, especially in terms of his insistence that it be kept general with simple, positive beliefs. The more recent popular use of the term and the ensuing debate over its conceptual utility was inaugurated in 1967 by the publication of sociologist Robert N. Bellah's seminal essay entitled "Civil Religion in America."

The modern American civic faith developed from English civil religion, especially as understood by the early Puritan* settlers of New England. First England, then New England and finally the new American nation, came to see itself as "God's New Israel" and a "covenanted people" with a special mission and destiny "under God." It was John Winthrop,* first governor of Massachusetts, who, in 1630, spoke to the Puritans of their divinely appointed task to build a "city upon a hill." Situated in the American wilderness, they were to serve as a godly model for the remainder of the world. In this way a powerful image was fastened on the people who eventually created the American nation and gave it a collective identity. The Mayflower Compact, the Declaration of Independence, the Constitution and, later, Lincoln's Gettysburg Address, became the sacred scriptures of the new public faith. Just as the colonies saw their own church covenants as vehicles of God's participation in history, so these public documents became the covenants which bound the people of the nation together in a political and religious union and secured for them God's blessing, protection and summons to fulfill their historic mission.

In addition, during the first hundred years of nationhood American civil religion developed its own system of worship—that is, special ceremonies, holidays and symbols which fused piety and patriotism and melded God and country. For example, the most prominent of the civil religion holidays have come to be Memorial Day,* the Fourth of July, Thanksgiving Day* and, more recently, Martin Luther King, Jr.,* Day, each designed to promote public expressions of faith in the chosen nation. Themes of death, sacrifice and rebirth were introduced into America's public faith with the coming of the Civil War* (1861-1865) and the presidency of Abraham Lincoln,* expressed vividly in Lincoln's "Gettysburg Address" (1863) and his subsequent martyrdom. In the same vein, the Lincoln Memorial in Washington has become a national temple before which more recent ceremonies of civil religion have been performed, such as King's "I Have a Dream" speech in 1963 and Billy Graham's* Honor America Day address in 1970.

America's civil religion was undergirded from

the beginning by the support of its dominant religious faith, evangelical* Christianity, and intellectual community, the members of which were mostly steeped in Enlightenment* thought. These two sometimes-antagonistic socio-ideological components of early U.S society were able to join in affirming civil religion because of their desire for national well-being and unity and because civil religion was, by nature, general. An unspoken, informal understanding kept the civic faith general enough to accommodate both fervent evangelicals and less fervent deists* (both groups believed in God) while the intellectuals (e.g., Franklin, Jefferson) were willing to allow the dominant evangelical religious consensus to establish the civic values of the new nation. This arrangement was confirmed and strengthened by the Second Great Awakening* of the early nineteenth century, which gave the U.S. a basically evangelical orientation. The momentous decision of the founders to separate the institutions of church and state* and to prohibit any kind of religious establishment made some kind of civil religion highly likely. Evangelical Christianity supplied the social glue which made it possible.

However, the increasing religious pluralism of the U.S. in the twentieth century made it necessary, by definition, to enlarge the spiritual canopy of American civil religion to accommodate, first, the great influx of Roman Catholic* Christians at the turn of the century, then the growing importance in national life of adherents to Judaism in the first half of the century and, finally, the large numbers of immigrants of other religious faiths (e.g., Muslims, Buddhists, Hindus) in the last half of the century. Over the years the American civic faith has grown conceptually from evangelical Protestantism-in-general, to Christianity-in-general, to the Judeo-Christian* tradition, to theism-in-general.

Historically speaking, some forms of civil religion have emphasized the Deity and others the nation itself as the ultimate transcendent reference point of highest loyalty and final judgment. These two varieties of public faith have been apparent throughout Western history and, generally speaking, have been supported by what scholars have identified as prophetic and priestly civil religion, respectively. Both have been present in America, with the prophetic form dominating the scene from the foundation of the republic until the mid-twentieth century and the priestly variety prevailing in the last half of the century. In prophetic civil religion the president often leads the nation in evaluating the country's actions in relation to the will of the Almighty, thus correcting the idolatry of

religious nationalism and calling the nation to repent of its corporate political sins. In sum, he acts as prophet of the national faith. In priestly civil religion the president often makes the nation itself the ultimate reference point in evaluating national activities and leads the people in affirming and celebrating the nation while he glorifies the national culture and strokes his political flock. In short, he acts as the high priest of the civic faith.

In any case, since the inception of the republic, the president has been the foremost representative of civil religion in the U.S. In the context of a population that is increasingly more diverse religiously and culturally, an office that is increasingly more influential politically and a nation that is increasingly more powerful militarily, the person of the president has become increasingly more important religiously. In the last half of the twentieth century, the religious dimension of political leadership in America has become more apparent and the president's role as "spiritual father of his people" accentuated.

Modern American civil religion, therefore, is an alliance between religion and politics which transcends separation of church and state and permeates every level of national life. As such, it rests on a politicized ideological base: (1) there is a God; (2) his will can be known and fulfilled through democratic procedures; (3) America has been God's primary agent in modern history; and (4) the nation is the chief source of identity for Americans in both a political and religious sense. According to this world view, Americans are God's chosen people, a New Israel which made the exodus to the Promised Land across the sea and became a "city on a hill," a light to the nations proclaiming the message of democracy as the socio-messianic doctrine that will lead the human race to freedom, prosperity and happiness.

Evidence of the civil faith includes the biblical imagery and references to Almighty God and Providence that have pervaded the speeches and public documents of the nation's leaders from earliest times, the trappings of religious celebration at presidential inaugurations, the religio-political symbolism of much of the architecture of the nation's capital, patriotic songs in church hymnals,* the display of the nation's flag in church sanctuaries, the celebration of national holidays in which themes of "God and country" are skillfully blended, the inclusion of *under God* in the Pledge of Allegiance and, above all, the national motto "In God We Trust."*

Civil religion has been and continues to be both a concept and an issue in American political and religious life and reveals something of the religious nature of the American political system and of the office of the American presidency. Its supporters point out that it contributes significantly to the formulation of a national identity, helps hold an increasingly pluralistic society together and provides (especially in its prophetic form) a context within which political responsibilities can be examined and judged. Its critics stress that in the hands of unscrupulous politicians it too often and too easily has become a useful tool to promote partisan political programs at home and an adventurous foreign policy abroad and to sanctify all sorts of political skulduggery in high places.

Historical American civil religion continues to challenge Christians to sort out the sometimes conflicting, sometimes complementary, dimensions of public religion and personal faith, and to make necessary distinctions between the national mission and the Great Commission. Most important, a knowledge of the existence and nature of civil religion will force followers of Jesus Christ to make conscious choices concerning the proper relationship of the Christian faith, especially in its catholicity, to the political culture of the day.

See also CHURCH AND STATE, SEPARATION OF; PUBLIC POLICY, CHRISTIANITY AND.

BIBLIOGRAPHY. R. N. Bellah and P. E. Hammond, *Varieties of Civil Religion* (1980); R. N. Bellah and W. G. McLoughlin, eds., *Religion in America* (1968); C. Cherry, *God's New Israel: Religious Interpretations of American Destiny* (1971); J. M. Cuddihy, *No Offense: Civil Religion and Protestant Taste* (1978); R. T. Handy, *A Christian America: Protestant Hopes and Historical Realities,* 2nd ed. (1984); W. Herberg, *Protestant-Catholic-Jew,* rev. ed. (1960); S. E. Mead, *The Nation with the Soul of a Church* (1975); M. A. Noll, N. O. Hatch and G. M. Marsden, *The Search for Christian America* (1983); R. B. Pierard and R. D. Linder, *Civil Religion and the Presidency (1988);* A. J. Reichley, *Religion in American Public Life* (1985); R. E. Richey and D. G. Jones, eds., *American Civil Religion* (1974); E. L. Tuveson, *Redeemer Nation: The Idea of America's Millenial Role* (1968); J. F. Wilson, *Public Religion in American Culture* (1979).

R. D. Linder

Civil Rights Movement and the Churches.

The Civil Rights Movement (1954-1966), the struggle for equal civil rights for African-American people in America, was one of several events that culminated in the convulsive decade of the 1960s. Although most churches entered the civil rights struggle late and with reservations, their beliefs were basic to the moral premises of the movement. Traditional patterns of segregation within churches remained, but the theology* and social conscience of American churches were significantly modified by the Civil Rights Movement.

During the decade following the 1954 Supreme Court* decision that overturned the "separate but equal" approach of the earlier *Plessy vs. Ferguson* decision (1896), American churches remained essentially passive toward civil rights. In predominantly white churches, traditional segregationist and racist attitudes prevailed, especially in the South. Although churches typically opposed racial violence and officially hailed the *Brown vs. the Board of Education* decision, the idea of racial equality was alien to many accepted beliefs and practices.

Thus the original impetus for civil rights activism came from outside the institutional church. Even in African-American churches there were barriers to direct involvement by clergymen.* Many decades of passivity were difficult to overcome, although many African-American lay parishioners and clergymen were members of the National Association for the Advancement of Colored People (NAACP), Congress of Racial Equality (CORE) and other minority advocacy organizations. It was the Montgomery bus boycott and the rapid development of other centers of nonviolent activism in places like Tallahassee, Mobile, Birmingham and Nashville that spurred the increased involvement by African-American pastors in the movement.

A significant historical event for the movement was the creation of the Southern Christian Leadership Conference* (SCLC) in 1957, led by Dr. Martin Luther King, Jr.,* pastor of the Dexter Avenue Baptist Church in Montgomery. The Conference was to provide the movement with both leadership and a framework for collective action. Based largely in local churches, the SCLC drew upon the traditional linkage of religion and liberation indigenous to African-American experience. It also attracted the unprecedented grassroots support that produced the campaigns in Birmingham, St. Augustine and Selma between 1963 and 1965 and enabled the Civil Rights Movement to attract a national support network. By then a growing number of white clergy* and lay persons* were actively involved in the movement. Some, including the Rev. James Reeb and the Rev. Bruce Klunder, lost their lives for the sake of the movement.

The increased activism by churches in the mid-1960s was actually the fourth major phase of their advocacy for civil rights in America. The first was during the abolitionist era preceding the Civil War,* and the next significant watershed was just after World War 1,* when the widespread racial violence of 1917-1919 triggered the involvement of a number of church-related organizations, such as the Commission on Interracial Cooperation (1919) and denominational service and missionary* organizations. Methodist* women were distinctive between the wars for their commitment to racial justice. But while Methodists, Baptists,* Presbyterians,* Catholics* and Episcopalians,* among others, decried the racism and violence of this period, they did not de-segregate their seminaries or most of their local congregations.

After World War 2* the third juncture was reached. The plight of returning African-American soldiers and their families attracted further church involvement in civil rights. The double victory over both National Socialism abroad and racism at home proved elusive, leaving many African-Americans without adequate housing or jobs and eliciting sympathy from churches. Direct involvement by churches, however, remained limited, and clergy who took strong stands in their behalf were at some professional risk. By the mid-1950s few structural changes had occurred and segregationists frequently appealed to the Bible* for justification of their position. White citizens' councils, and even the Ku Klux Klan, had members who were active in churches. Nevertheless, the pendulum was swinging. Overt public violence in Birmingham (1963) and Selma (1965) had a marked impact on churches. Martin Luther King, Jr., wrote his "Letter from a Birmingham Jail," not only countering the criticisms by a group of white Jewish and Christian clergymen, but also emphasizing Christian responsibility toward civil and human rights. The passage of the 1964 Civil Rights Act added momentum to the movement.

The peculiar problems and contributions of churches in the area of civil rights derived from the nature of the church itself. As African-American churches became the single most decisive factor in the nonviolent Civil Rights Movement, white congregations and clergy wrestled with the tension between their support of law and order and the direct action taken by movement leaders. Equally problematic was the apparent contradiction between the churches' message of love and their de facto segregation. But as time passed, church courts, assemblies and ministerial associations reflected the progress of civil rights in America. Presbyterians created a Commission on Religion and Race in 1963, and in 1965-1966 Prince A.

Taylor, Jr., became the first African-American person to head the Methodist Council of Bishops. Episcopalians created the Episcopalian Society for Cultural and Racial Unity and by 1967 had established the Convention Special Program. Roman Catholics enlarged their already extensive programs in civil and human rights advocacy, as did several other church structures.

Most churches, whether African-American or white, remained separate. African-American churches wanted to retain their distinctive identity, and demographics also contributed to the pattern of separate congregational existence. In some ways dialog across denominational and racial lines increased. This was one of the most important results of the Civil Rights Movement for American churches. In retrospect it can be seen that religious faith was crucially important for the Civil Rights Movement. And in turn the progress of the movement exposed racism to a sharper theological critique, providing the historical context within which the beliefs and practices that had maintained segregation for centuries could be re-examined.

See also BLACK RELIGION; BLACK THEOLOGY; KING, JR., MARTIN LUTHER; SOUTHERN CHRISTIAN LEADERSHIP CONFERENCE.

BIBLIOGRAPHY. A. Fairclough, "The Preachers and the People: The Origins and Early Years of the Southern Christian Leadership Conference," *JSH* 52 (1986):403-440; C. E. Lincoln, *The Black Experience in Religion* (1974); A. D. Morris, *The Origins of the Civil Rights Movement: Black Communities Organizing for Change* (1984); H. M. Nelson, "Ministerial Roles and Social Actionist Stance: Protestant Clergy and Protest in the Sixties," *ASR* 38 (1973):375-386.   T. R. Peake

Civil War and the Churches. The middle years of the nineteenth century marked a traumatic convulsion for America's churches quite as much as for the nation at large. For decades a conflict over slavery had been simmering as an inner civil war within the churches, and three major denominations broke into sectional factions several years before the eruption of the shooting war. The churches' equivocal response to the moral dilemma posed by a system of human bondage in a professedly free republic both confirmed and hardened the alienation between North and South by inflaming the rhetoric of pro- and antislavery* polemics, setting an early example of sectional division, exacerbating the sense of moral outrage that each section felt against the other, and assuring their respective constituencies of God's blessing on their partisan cause. When armed hostilities began in 1861, most churches North and South offered massive support to their side in the conflict. Their behavior before and during the war led to a long-lasting legacy of suspicion and bitterness between the sections.

Pro- and Anti-slavery Forces. In the Revolutionary* and Early National periods, when exalted ideas of liberty and human equality occupied many Americans' minds, several church bodies issued strong proclamations against slavery. A typical statement came from the General Assembly of the Presbyterian Church,* which in 1818 denounced slavery as "a gross violation of human nature . . . utterly inconsistent with the law of God . . . totally irreconcilable with the spirit and principles of the Gospel of Christ," and declared it the duty of all Christians "as speedily as possible to efface this blot on our holy religion and to obtain the complete abolition of slavery throughout christendom, and if possible throughout the world." Actual emancipations by church members, however, were few. Slaveholders resisted efforts to tamper with "the peculiar institution," and soon even the formal proclamations softened or ceased altogether.

Abolitionist* activity increased sharply after 1830, and whatever success it may have had among Northern church members, its main effect in the South was to harden support for slavery. Prominent Southern churchmen developed a biblical and religious argument to fortify the South's faith in the rightness of the slavocracy. They maintained that Abraham and the patriarchs held slaves with God's approval, Jesus lived in a world where slavery was an accepted social reality and never spoke a word against it, New Testament writers issued specific instructions for master-slave relationships, and Paul sent a converted runaway back to his Christian master. The argument concluded that slavery was a religious good because it brought benighted heathens to a Christian country where they could hear the gospel for the saving of their souls— something that might never have happened in Africa. Such claims became the regulating dogmas of Southern society, and, repeated with increasing confidence and stridency, they conditioned Southerners to regard as erroneous and even infidel all attacks on their social system or their Christianity.

As Northern church folk mounted their "evangelical war against slavery," increasingly bitter conflict in the national church bodies pointed to the day when Christian community would break down. Antislavery activities collided head-on with the proslavery apologetic, while denominational*

bureaucrats struggled to maintain the ecclesiastical peace by suppressing all discussion of the issue. But the conflict proved to be irrepressible, and the large evangelical* denominations divided along lines that would increasingly mark the division between slaveholding and nonslaveholding sections of the United States. These schisms, as many contemporaries noted, presented an ominous threat to the future of the federal Union. Occurring in organizations that together enrolled the vast majority of church members in the country, and even more importantly, in influential bodies that embraced nationwide constituencies, the sundering of the denominations became both portent and catalyst for the disuniting of the U.S.

Divided Churches. The first rupture came in 1837, when the Presbyterian Church in the U.S.A.* divided as a result of a dispute in which sharply differing attitudes toward slavery figured significantly, if not decisively. Old School Presbyterians,* led by Princetonian* traditionalists, were becoming increasingly restive over the revivalistic* activities and interdenominational alliances of the New School,* whose strength centered mainly in the North and Old Northwest. At the General Assembly* of 1837, the Old School marshalled a majority to vote for ousting four New School synods,* thus dividing the Presbyterian Church almost in half. Although the break was not strictly along a North-South line, most of the Southern delegates sided with the Old School. Their theological affinities clearly inclined toward the Old School, but the Southerners were also unhappy with the aggressive abolitionism they saw in the New School. In return for assurances that all discussion of slavery in the General Assembly would cease, they voted with the Old School to exscind the New School synods. A few Southern presbyteries* sided with the New School on the ground that the exscinding action had been unconstitutional, but after enduring for twenty years a rising tide of antislavery in the "Constitutional Assembly" (as the New School body called itself), they withdrew in 1857, completing the North-South division of the Presbyterian Church.

Methodists* had regularly expressed disapproval of slavery since 1784, when they formally organized their denomination in America. But whatever antislavery rules Methodists enacted were never to be enforced any "farther than is consistent with the laws of the states" in which slaveholding members resided. The question was left to local option, whereby each annual conference* would formulate its own rules in reference to slavery. Antislavery activists in the North brought their concerns to the national meetings—the quadrennial General Conference—where their "agitation" discomfited the Southern delegates. As elsewhere, centrist ecclesiocrats tried to suppress discussion for the sake of peace and unity, but the controversy continued to swirl throughout the denomination. A sizable defection of abolitionist Methodists occurred in 1843, when Orange Scott* organized the Wesleyan Methodist Church,* and the following year matters came to a head in the General Conference. A Southern bishop, James O. Andrew,* had become "connected with slavery." After two weeks of debate, the conference voted along manifestly sectional lines that Andrew must "desist from the exercise of his [episcopal] office so long as this impediment remains." The Southerners promptly withdrew, and the next year they organized the Methodist Episcopal Church,* South, as a proslavery denomination.

Baptists* had no single national judicatory; their strict congregational* polity allowed only single-purpose societies for missionary* and related endeavors. Leaders of these societies ruled repeatedly that consideration of slavery was not among the objects for which their organizations existed. Abolitionists formed the American Baptist Anti-Slavery Convention, which at its first meeting in 1840 admonished Baptists in the South that unrepentant slaveholders were unfit for Christian fellowship. Southerners replied with a threat to "cut off their benevolent funds to the general Baptist agencies, and, if necessary, to separate from them altogether." As tension mounted, in 1845 Alabama Baptists asked the Foreign Mission Board point blank whether it would appoint a slaveholder who was otherwise qualified for missionary service. The Board, most of whose members resided in the North, wriggled all around the question but finally replied in the negative: "We can never be a party to any arrangement which would imply approbation of slavery." Baptists in Virginia promptly issued a call for a consultative convention to consider forming a new missionary organization, and the result was the Southern Baptist Convention.* Its first president, William B. Johnson,* explained at the outset that Southern Baptists were now free "to promote slavery" along with various other objects.

A Divided Nation. The Southern members of the three denominations that divided over irreconcilable views of slavery represented ninety-four per cent of the churches of the South: Methodists had forty-five per cent; Baptists, thirty-seven per cent; and Presbyterians, twelve per cent. Because these schisms represented such an ominous division of

the nation—before 1844, for example, the Methodist Episcopal Church was the largest national organization in the United States besides the federal government—observers from all quarters feared the possibly fateful consequences to political union. Even the advocates of division in the affected denominations warned that what they were doing could lead to national disaster.

Presbyterian William S. Plumer predicted in 1837 that the dividing of his church would lead to the rending of the star-spangled banner; then "the hostile forces will be marshalled against each other, and the Potomac will be dyed with blood." Methodist Thomas Crowder declared in 1844 that if Bishop Andrew were deprived of his episcopal authority, "the division of our Church may follow—a civil division of this great confederation may follow that, and then hearts will be torn apart, master and slave arrayed against each other, brother in the Church against brother, and the North against the South—and when thus arrayed, with the fiercest passions and energies of our nature brought into action against each other, civil war and far-reaching desolation must be the final results."

Following the Presbyterian and Methodist schisms, a Baptist editorialist surveyed the fracturing of his own denomination and asked sadly: "If the Baptists, unmindful of their duty to Christ and their country, shall bite and devour one another, and array themselves into two great parties, the Northern and the Southern, what conservative principles, what salt of the earth will be left to restrain and modulate the madness of political strife and ambition and save from ruin our Republic?"

The sundering of the churches evoked similar forebodings from a wide spectrum of public figures. A Kentucky editor wondered, "Who can expect that our country will remain united when the bonds of religious concord are broken?" Reflecting on the organization of the Southern Baptist Convention and the Methodist Episcopal Church, South, the Charleston (S.C.) *Mercury* observed grimly: "In this contest of religions, we have an entire and remediless severance of the Union—a division that henceforth creates in the two most numerous denominations of the country *a Northern and a Southern religion* . . . a dissension that turns one of the strongest bands of the political union into a destroying sword."

Senator Henry Clay of Kentucky brooded over the church schisms, calling them "the greatest source of danger to our country." Senator John C. Calhoun of South Carolina, whom some charged with encouraging the divisions at the time of their occurrence, later spoke somberly of the looming political consequences. His last speech in the U.S. Senate, given on March 4, 1850, noted that the national denominations "together formed a strong cord to hold the whole Union together." After the bonds of ecclesiastical unity were broken, Calhoun feared that the continuing agitation over slavery would "finally snap every cord, when nothing will be left to hold the States together except force." Such dire predictions seem in retrospect extraordinarily prescient readings of contemporary events.

Several smaller denominations, which because of their size and/or regionally concentrated memberships had not figured largely in national public affairs during the antebellum period, reinforced the growing sectional estrangement. Congregationalists,* clustered mainly in New England, condemned both slavery and the "wicked rebellion" which sought to perpetuate it. The Society of Friends,* who had worked out their antislavery position before the end of the eighteenth century and maintained it in the face of rising sectional conflict, furnished many leaders to the abolitionist crusade. Old School Presbyterians avoided schism up to the outbreak of war, but when the General Assembly finally declared loyalty to the Union, the Southern members withdrew and formed their own church. Episcopalians,* Lutherans* and Roman Catholics* maintained official silence on slavery until political rupture and war forced them into temporary sectional divisions supporting their respective governments. The Disciples of Christ,* centered largely in the border regions of Kentucky and Tennessee, heeded Alexander Campbell's* teaching that one's view of slavery was a matter of private opinion, not faith. Their members based their sectional loyalties on other considerations, and Disciples were found on both sides of the conflict.

As the Civil War began, a Presbyterian Southerner commented that the secession of the Southern churches was the indispensable precondition for the disruption of the Union. "Much as is due to many of our sagacious and gifted politicians, they could *effect nothing* until the religious union of the North and South was dissolved, nor until they had received the *moral support and co-operation of Southern Christians.*"

Southern preachers* denounced with increasing stridency the "rationalism and infidelity" that underlay the "meddling spirit" of Northern churches. They supported the Confederacy by encouraging men to join the army, preaching that God favored their cause and doing all in their power to maintain Southern morale. Pastors* served as volunteer chaplains* to the troops, holding revivals* in the camps and promising the young fighters that if they were killed in battle they would go immediately to heaven. The chairman of the Military Commission in the Confederate House of Representatives testified that "the clergy have done more for our cause than any other class. . . . Not even the bayonets have done more."

Yankee Protestants were equally fervent for the Northern crusade. They preached with apocalyptic thunder that the Union was God's cause. They ministered through the U.S. Christian Commission* to the soldiers, whom they regarded as God's instruments in trampling out the grapes of divine wrath against the sinful South. The Roman Catholic archbishop of New York, at President Lincoln's* request, made a goodwill tour of Europe, while many other church leaders were active in behalf of the Union.

The Enduring Legacy. The Civil War, and the controversies that preceded it, set Northern and Southern Christianity on divergent courses. The proslavery apologetic hardened into a rigid biblicism that relied on the literal language of selected proof texts unrelieved by any awareness of changed historical circumstances. The antislavery attack, drawing on ideas like the requirements of Christian love and the spirit of Jesus, flowered into a progressive type of interpretation that gave more weight to the principles of Christianity. Northerners rejected a religion that refused to allow the leaven of the gospel to spread throughout the society, producing freedom and the application of the Golden Rule to all of life's relationships, while Southerners condemned as infidel those who rejected the strict construction of the Bible, the constitution of the church. At the close of the war, Southern preachers denied that they had been wrong on slavery and acquiesced in the mysterious working of Providence, convinced that suffering for the right is the supreme test of faith, while Northern preachers hailed the military outcome as irrefutable evidence of the rightness of the antislavery crusade and the sanctity of the Union— attitudes that Robert Penn Warren called, respectively, "The Great Alibi" and "The Treasury of Virtue."

Denominations that had not been torn apart by the slavery controversy reunited easily after the war. Northern Episcopalians meeting in national convention in 1862 called the complete roll and marked the Southern deputies unavoidably absent; after the war the Southerners readily accepted a warm invitation to return. But all such reunions

[287]

Denominational Divisions over Slavery and the Civil War

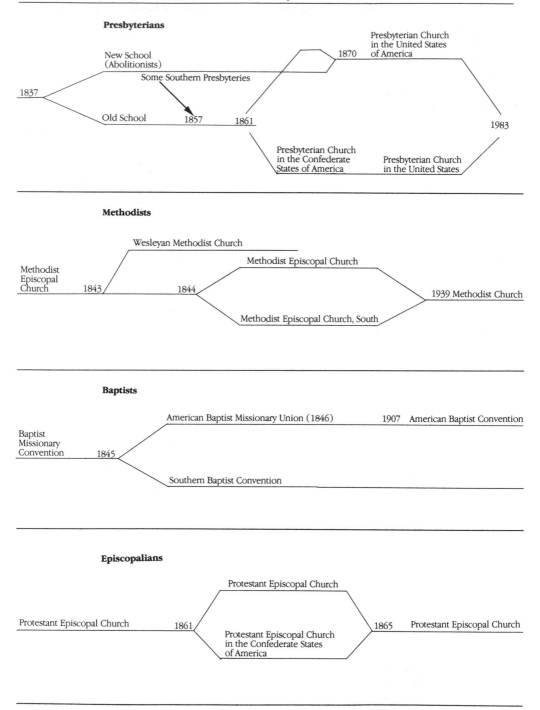

Presbyterians

Presbyterian Church
in the United States
of America

New School
(Abolitionists)

Some Southern Presbyteries

1870

1837

Old School   1857   1861

1983

Presbyterian Church
in the Confederate
States of America

Presbyterian Church
in the United States

Methodists

Wesleyan Methodist Church

Methodist Episcopal Church

Methodist
Episcopal
Church   1843   1844

1939 Methodist Church

Methodist Episcopal Church, South

Baptists

American Baptist Missionary Union (1846)   1907   American Baptist Convention

Baptist
Missionary
Convention   1845

Southern Baptist Convention

Episcopalians

Protestant Episcopal Church

Protestant Episcopal Church   1861

Protestant Episcopal Church
in the Confederate States
of America

1865   Protestant Episcopal Church

involved only a minority of the Southern churches. The denominations that had divided before the war invested themselves so heavily in the sectional conflict that postwar reconciliation became next to impossible.

The Southern factions especially regarded reunion as undesirable and worked assiduously to reinforce the regional self-consciousness of Southerners as "a different people," while their Northern counterparts increasingly occupied themselves with urban social problems, mass revivalism and church extension in the West. Northern and Southern Methodists remained apart until 1939. Presbyterians began coming back together only in the 1970s, and the reunion of white Baptists remains as remote as ever. The predominantly African-American denominations grew rapidly as a result of massive withdrawals of former slaves from white-controlled churches, and having long ago achieved organizational maturity and moderate financial strength, they seem destined to continue separate existence into the foreseeable future.

Perhaps the most significant religious legacy of the Civil War is the impetus it gave to civil religion.* Sometimes called the "spiritual center" of the nation's history, the war exposed the flaws in America's earlier claim to be "God's New Israel," a special people with a divinely ordered destiny. In restoring the "broken covenant" under a president who believed profoundly that God had brought the whole nation under judgment in order to cleanse it and reclaim it for its mission under God, the argument goes, Americans could continue to think of themselves as a chosen people with a special purpose in history. Lincoln himself, assassinated on Good Friday, became a Christ-figure in the national mythology; and his agony in preserving the Union as the "last, best hope of earth" was taken as a symbol of the redemption of the "Redeemer Nation" through a baptism of blood. Robert E. Lee* came to be honored in the North as a national hero, while Southern choirs learned to sing with fervor the "Battle Hymn of the Republic," originally a Union crusader's song. In the late twentieth century, as the nation continues its struggle to achieve the ideals of unity, freedom and equality, the nineteenth-century "time of testing" furnishes many clues to the meaning of "one nation under God."

BIBLIOGRAPHY. C. C. Goen, *Broken Churches, Broken Nation: Denominational Schisms and the Coming of the American Civil War* (1985); D. R. Jones, *The Sectional Crisis and Northern Methodism: A Study in Piety, Political Ethics, and Civil Religion* (1979); J. W. Jones, *Christ in the Camp, Or,*

Religion in Lee's Army (1888); J. R. McKivigan, *The War Against Proslavery Religion: Abolitionism and the Northern Churches, 1830-1865* (1984); S. E. Mead, *The Lively Experiment: The Shaping of Religion in America* (1963); J. H. Moorhead, *American Apocalypse: Yankee Protestants and the Civil War, 1860-1869* (1978); L. Moss, *Annals of the United States Christian Commission* (1868); J. W. Silver, *Confederate Morale & Church Propaganda* (1967); H. S. Smith, *In His Image, But . . . : Racism in Southern Religion, 1780-1910* (1972); R. P. Warren, *The Legacy of the Civil War* (1983); C. R. Wilson, *Baptized in Blood: The Religion of the Lost Cause, 1865-1920* (1980); W. J. Wolf, *The Almost Chosen People: A Study of the Religion of Abraham Lincoln* (1970).   C. C. Goen

Clap, Thomas (1703-1767). Congregational* minister* and president of Yale College.* A Harvard* graduate (1722), Clap was ordained* pastor* in Windham, Connecticut, in 1726. Clap assumed leadership of Yale College as rector* in 1739 and president in 1745 under the new charter which was one of his administrative reforms. An Old Light,* Clap was repelled by the Great Awakening's* emotional excess, and opposed the methods of George Whitefield* and Jonathan Edwards.* His expulsion of evangelical* student David Brainerd* created a furor. But as the pro-revivalist wing moderated in the 1750s and Old Lights tended toward Arminianism,* Clap joined the evangelicals.* Controversy swelled when Clap abandoned college participation at New Haven's First Church and began preaching himself at the college in 1753 and then established the Church of Christ at Yale. His methods of insuring Calvinist* orthodoxy* created bitterness. Power politics involving Clap, the Connecticut General Assembly, tutors and rebellious students wore him down. He retired in 1766 and died soon thereafter. Among his works are *The Religious Constitution of Colleges* (1754) and *The Annals or History of Yale College to the Year 1766* (1766).

BIBLIOGRAPHY. *AAP* 1; *DAB* II; F. B. Dexter, *Biographical Sketches of the Graduates of Yale College With Annals of the College History* (1885-1912).   C. E. Hambrick-Stowe

Clark, Francis Edward (1851-1921). Congregationalist* minister* and founder of the Christian Endeavor Society.* Born Francis Edward Symmes in Quebec, he was orphaned at age eight, moved to Massachusetts and took his uncle's name. After graduating from Dartmouth* (1873) and Andover Theological Seminary* (1876), Clark became pastor* of the Williston Congregational Church in Portland, Maine, where in 1881 he organized the "Williston Young People's Society of Christian Endeavor" to incorporate young people into the life of the church. The movement spread quickly. Within six years, there were over a half million "Christian Endeavorers" in 7,000 local societies. In 1883 Clark became pastor of Phillips Congregational Church in Boston, but resigned in 1887 to devote himself full-time to the movement.

Christian Endeavor became American evangelicalism's* first national and interdenominational youth ministry. Clark consolidated his work in the U.S. by founding the United Christian Endeavor Society in 1887 and then traveled the world to establish new societies, which he organized into the World's Christian Endeavor Union in 1895. To bind the Society together, Clark edited *Christian Endeavor World* and wrote thirty-seven books on Christian Endeavor and youth ministry. Shortly after his death, a convention of the World's Christian Endeavor Union drew delegates from over forty countries.

BIBLIOGRAPHY. F. E. Clark, *Christian Endeavor in All Lands (1906); DAB* II. T. P. Weber

Clark, Gordon Haddon (1902-1986). Calvinist* philosopher. Born in Philadelphia, Clark graduated from the University of Pennsylvania (B.A., 1924) where he also did his graduate work in philosophy (Ph.D., 1929). During his years as a graduate student and for several years thereafter, Clark was an instructor (1924-1936) at the University of Pennsylvania and at the nearby Reformed Episcopal Seminary (1932-1936). He also studied at the Sorbonne in Paris during 1931. In 1936 he was a visiting professor at Wheaton College,* Illinois, where he joined the faculty the following year. There Clark had a decisive influence on the minds of a number of future evangelical* intellectual leaders, most notably Edward J. Carnell* and Carl F. H. Henry.*

Within a fundamentalist* institution that had not yet achieved intellectual depth, Clark stood out as a profound and rigorous thinker whose philosophical rationalism challenged both modernism* and the unexamined thoughts of students raised on popular fundamentalism. For these students, Clark provided their first encounter with an intellectually respectable Christianity. But however much devotion he evoked from his students, Clark's Calvinism was an intolerable challenge to the Arminianism* that prevailed on Wheaton's campus, and at the end of the 1942-1943 school year, Wheaton's

president V. Raymond Edman* let him go. By 1945 Clark was teaching on the faculty of Butler University in Indianapolis, Indiana, where he came to chair the department of philosophy for twenty-eight years. From that secular campus he continued to exert a notable influence on the evangelical intellectual world, and the Reformed sector in particular, through over thirty publications. Most notable were: *A Christian Philosophy of Education* (1946); *A Christian View of Men and Things* (1951); and his history of western philosophy, *Thales to Dewey* (1956). In the early years of *Christianity Today,* he served as a contributing editor.

During the hiatus between Wheaton and Butler, Clark sought ordination* in the Orthodox Presbyterian Church.* Having passed the examinations and having received ordination, Clark's ordination was challenged on doctrinal grounds having to do with Clark's understanding of the role of logic—particularly the law of contradiction—in theology* and apologetics.* This conflicted with the presuppositionalism* of Cornelius Van Til* and his definition of the incomprehensibility of God, which was influential within that denomination. The controversy, which was long remembered on both sides, ended when Clark left the denomination and joined the Reformed Presbyterian Church. Nevertheless, the wider evangelical intellectual world tended to concur with Carl Henry's assessment that Clark was "one of the profoundest evangelical Protestant philosophers of our time."

BIBLIOGRAPHY. R. H. Nash, ed., *The Philosophy of Gordon Clark* (1968). D. G. Reid

Clark, William Smith (1826-1886). Educator and administrator. Graduating from Amherst College in 1848 with high academic honors, Clark went to Germany (Göttingen) for advanced study (Ph.D, 1852). He returned to his alma mater and taught with distinction for fifteen years, except for two years of military service during the Civil War* (1861-1863). He was influential in the founding of Massachusetts Agricultural College (MAC) and served as its first president. In 1876 the government of Japan engaged Clark to help in establishing an agricultural college in Sapporo, the capital of Hokkaido. The school that resulted (Sapporo Agricultural College) was modeled after MAC and developed into what is now Hokkaido University.

An earnest Christian and a former colonel in the Union Army, Clark insisted on rigorous standards and the teaching of the Bible* as a textbook in ethics. This deeply impressed the students who came from a Samurai background. Clark was only in Japan eight months, but before he left he drew up a "Covenant of Believers in Jesus," which all of his students signed. Clark is still widely remembered in Japan for his influence on Japanese Christianity and for his parting words to his students, "Boys, be ambitious!"

BIBLIOGRAPHY. *DAB* II; J. M. Maki, "Clark, William Smith," vol. 1, *Kodansha Encyclopedia of Japan,* 9 vols. (1983).   W. N. Browning

Clarke, James Freeman (1810-1888). Unitarian* transcendentalist* minister.* Born in Hanover, New Hampshire, Clarke was educated at Harvard* (B.A., 1829; B.D., 1833). While ministering in a small Unitarian congregation in Louisville, Kentucky (1833-1840), Clarke edited the monthly *Western Messenger* (1836-1839) and formulated his antislavery* views. In 1840 he returned to Boston, where he organized the Church of the Disciples and began to put his broader religious ideas into practice, later publishing a sermon on the new church's "principles" and "methods."

Along with Charles Frederic Hedge, Clarke represented a more institutionalist point of view within the transcendentalist, or "New School,"* movement. While many of the best-known transcendentalists were known for their opposition to traditional organized Christianity, Clarke and Hedge were active reformers within the church. They theorized about a democratic,* reformist "Church of the Future." It was to be an eclectic combination of what Clarke considered the best elements in Catholicism,* Protestantism,* Unitarianism, transcendentalism and humanitarian reformism.

Believing strongly in the American egalitarian ideal, Clarke committed himself to thorough democratization, incorporating broad-based lay* participation in the entire scope of church life. So much did he accomplish in this endeavor that in the 1850s, while he was on a three-year sick leave, the congregation thrived under lay leadership. Clarke's church was also flexible in its requirements for membership, making such ordinances* as baptism* and Communion* optional. After 1867 Clarke served as an adjunct to the faculty of the Harvard Divinity School. As minister, Harvard educator and church reformer, Clarke had a strong impact on nineteenth-century Christian liberalism.*

BIBLIOGRAPHY. A. S. Bolster, Jr., *James Freeman Clarke: Disciple to Advancing Truth* (1954); *DAB* II; *DARB;* E. E. Hale, ed., *James Freeman Clarke: Autobiography, Diary, and Correspondence* (1891); *NCAB* 2; J. W. Thomas, *James Freeman Clarke:*

Apostle of German Culture in America (1949).
          S. E. Berk

Clarke, John (1609-1676). Baptist* minister,* co-founder of Rhode Island Colony and advocate of religious freedom.* Clarke was born in Suffolk County, England, and while his educational experience remains unknown (he may have studied at the University of Leyden), he was well versed in theology,* languages and medicine. Emigrating to Massachusetts Bay in 1637, Clarke championed the cause of Anne Hutchinson* in the antinomian controversy.* Searching for refuge from persecution, Clarke and several other settlers, with the help of Roger Williams,* purchased land from the Indians on the island of Aquidneck in Narragansett Bay, where they established the town of Portsmouth in 1638. By 1639 he had helped found Newport on the land now renamed Rhode Island. Clarke became the minister of the local congregation which became identified as a Baptist church by 1644. A Calvinist* by persuasion, Clarke led the congregation in professing Particular Baptist* beliefs.

In 1651, while leading a prayer meeting* in the home of a blind Baptist by the name of William Witter in Lynn, Massachusetts, Clarke and two young men, John Crandall and Obadiah Holmes,* were arrested and imprisoned for conducting an unauthorized worship* service. Sentenced to be fined or whipped, Clarke's fine was paid, but Holmes was publicly flogged. Out of this experience Clarke published in England an account of his persecution in the Massachusetts Bay Colony entitled *Ill Newes from New England, or a Narrative of New England's Persecutions* (1652).

In 1652 Clarke traveled with Roger Williams to London in an attempt to secure a new charter for Rhode Island Colony. While Williams returned to Rhode Island in 1654, Clarke remained in England until he succeeded in securing a charter from Charles II in 1663. Not only did the charter confirm their right to the land but it gave the colonists permission to attempt "a lively experiment" in which they could enjoy complete religious liberty.* *Ill Newes* had done much to secure British sympathy for the Rhode Island colonists.

After his return from England in 1664, Clarke was elected to the General Assembly (1664-1669) and was later elected to three terms as deputy governor (1669-1672). Throughout his years in the colony he served as pastor of the Newport Baptist Church while practicing medicine to support himself. Both Clarke and Williams shared the same convictions regarding religious liberty and the separation of church and state,* though Clarke was more influential in the development of the Baptists in the colony.

BIBLIOGRAPHY. *AAP* 6; T. W. Bicknell, *Story of Dr. John Clarke* (1915); *DAB* II; *DARB;* E. S. Gaustad, *Baptist Piety* (1978); *NCAB* 7; W. Nelson, *The Hero of Aquidneck and Life of Dr. John Clarke* (1938). W. R. Estep

Clarke, Sarah Dunn (1835-1918). Cofounder of Pacific Garden Mission.* Born in Cayuga County, New York, Sarah Dunn taught school in her native New York and in Iowa before moving to Chicago, where she began a visitation program among the poor and in 1869 started a mission Sunday school.* She married Colonel George R. Clarke, a Civil War* veteran and in 1873 envisioned a mission among Chicago's poor. But it was four years before her husband shared her goal. The mission they established was the second rescue mission in the U.S. In 1880 the mission relocated and became known as the Pacific Garden Mission.

"Mother" Clarke was involved in every facet of the mission's operation. She advertised meetings by distributing cards, and those who attended the mission received a heartfelt welcome from her. She shared the gospel of salvation, working at the altar with seekers. One of her converts was Billy Sunday.* She also supervised discipline for the first twenty-seven years and never missed a meeting. Clarke remained involved in the mission's work until injured in an accident in 1912.

BIBLIOGRAPHY. C. F. H. Henry, *The Pacific Garden Mission* (1942). S. C. Stanley

Clarke, William Newton (1841-1912). Baptist* minister* and theologian.* Born in Cazenovia, New York, Clarke graduated from Madison (now Colgate) University and Theological Seminary in New York. He pastored Baptist churches in Keene, New Hampshire (1863-1869); Newton Center, Massachusetts (1869-1880); and Montreal, Quebec (1880-1883). He then taught New Testament interpretation at the Baptist Theological School in Toronto (1883-1887). After a brief pastorate in Hamilton, New York (1887-1890), he became professor of theology* at Colgate Theological Seminary (1890-1908), where he became a leader in the New Theology.*

Unable to use any available textbook, Clarke wrote America's first systematic theology* from a liberal* perspective (*An Outline of Christian Theology,* 1898). Following Friedrich Schleiermacher (1768-1834), he believed that the starting point for theology was "religious sentiment," not the irreducible facts of Scripture. Since all theology grew out of religious experience,* all the world's religions contain some truth. He rejected older views of biblical inspiration and condemned orthodoxy's* "proof-texting" method. He claimed to take the Bible "as it is" and argued that the Scriptures should inspire theology, not be its source (*The Use of the Scriptures in Theology,* 1905, and *Sixty Years with the Bible,* 1912).

Though his *Outline* included traditional categories, he often replaced technical terms with simpler, more dynamic ones and redefined historic doctrines in accordance with his scientific and critical approach to the Bible. Underlying his method was the assumption that the ultimate arbiter of theological truth was the Holy Spirit working in individuals, culture and all humanity. Clarke also showed a keen interest in foreign missions,* as evidenced in *A Study of Christian Missions* (1900). Rejecting traditional motives for saving the lost, he suggested that missionaries should call the world to Christ and Christian civilization because of their superiority over other alternatives.

BIBLIOGRAPHY. E. S. Clarke, *William Newton Clarke* (1916); *DAB* II; *DARB; NCAB* 22.

T. P. Weber

Classis. Originally designating a class or division in Roman society according to property and taxation, among North American churches with *Reformed* in their title (e.g., Reformed Church of America* and Christian Reformed Church*), *classis* refers to an organizational unit within the church's governmental structure. A number of churches in a limited geographical area are grouped into a classis. The classis functions in a supervisory capacity over the churches and ministry* in its area. The classes are in turn responsible to the synod.* All of the ministers of the area and one elder* from each consistory (the ruling board in each particular church) form the membership of the classis. The classes usually meet individually two or three times per year. The classis and the presbytery* of Presbyterian* bodies are similar structures.

M. D. Floding

Clayton, Thomas (?-1699). Pennsylvania Anglican.* In 1695, twelve years after the founding of Philadelphia, the first efforts were made to erect a building for members of the Church of England.* This was the beginning of Christ Church. In 1698 Dr. Henry Compton, Bishop of London with responsibility for the American colonies, sent the Rev. Thomas Clayton to be its first rector.* Clayton was thus the first rector in Pennsylvania, and within two years Clayton had increased the membership of the church from about fifty persons to 700. Clayton worked hard to convert the Quakers* to the Church of England by addressing their yearly meeting and by open debate. His efforts were successful, and reference is made by George Keith in his journal to "the considerable number of converts to the Church from Quakerism" that "the Rev. Mr. Clayton had baptized." Church of England members in Maryland were critical of Clayton's efforts at proselytizing. In 1699 he died "of a contagious distemper caught in visiting the sick," that is, yellow fever.

BIBLIOGRAPHY. W. S. Perry, *The History of the American Episcopal Church, 1587-1883,* 2 vols. (1885); S. F. Hotchin, *Early Clergy of Pennsylvania and Delaware* (1890).   D. S. Armentrout

Clearwaters, Richard Volley (1900-). Baptist* preacher* and educator. Born in Wilmot, Kansas, Clearwaters graduated from Moody Bible Institute (1924) and went on to graduate from Northern Baptist Theological Seminary (Th.B., 1928; B.D., 1931). He also attended Kalamazoo College (B.A., 1930) and the University of Chicago Divinity School (M.A., 1931). Clearwaters served churches in the Northern Baptist Convention, becoming pastor of Fourth Baptist Church, Minneapolis, Minnesota (1940-1982). He was president of the Iowa Baptist Convention (1937-1939) and served on the board of trustees of Northern Baptist Theological Seminary.

Apart from his pastoral ministry, Clearwater served as dean and professor of practical theology of Northwestern Theological Seminary and then, in 1956, became founder and president of Central Baptist Seminary in Minneapolis, Minnesota, which was housed in his church. He also founded and served as first president of Pillsbury Baptist Bible College, Owanatonna, Minnesota. He received honorary degrees from Northern Baptist Theological Seminary, San Francisco Conservative Baptist Theological Seminary and Bob Jones* University.
          E. L. Towns

Clergy. Persons ordained* by a denomination* or local church to serve as priests* or ministers.* Roman Catholic,* Eastern Orthodox* and Episcopal* churches emphasize the distinction between clergy and laity* more sharply than many Protestant* traditions. Lutheran* and Reformed* bodies nevertheless have required clergy for administration of the sacraments.* Free Church,* Pentecostal* and other nonliturgical traditions have differentiat-

ed less between clergy and laity, although the role of pastor* is important in most groups. Secular considerations, such as requirements of the Internal Revenue Service and social security, have also served to determine clerical status.

BIBLIOGRAPHY. H. R. Niebuhr and D. D. Williams, eds., *The Ministry in Historical Perspectives* (1981); D. S. Schuller et. al., eds., *Ministry in America* (1980).   C. E. Hambrick-Stowe

Clergy Reserves. Lands in Upper and Lower Canada allotted by the Constitutional Act of 1791 "for the support and maintenance of a Protestant* clergy."* The reserves amounted to one-seventh of the whole. Proceeds went to the Church of England,* the one established Protestant church, until the mid nineteenth century. By then, the Church of Scotland had claimed a share as a church co-established with the Church of England in the Empire. Most other denominations* (notably the Methodists* and Baptists*), believing that the government should support *no* church directly, wanted the lands secularized. And many people saw the scattered reserves simply as an impediment to settlement and communication. Lord Durham reported that these concerns were one cause of the Upper Canadian Rebellion of 1837. A compromise was worked out in 1840 in which the proceeds of past sales of the reserves were divided among the Churches of England, Scotland, Rome and the Wesleyan Methodists, and the proceeds of future sales were to be divided among other denominations. The matter surfaced again as an important political issue within a decade, however, and in 1854 the reserves were secularized entirely.
          J. G. Stackhouse

Cleric. A member of the clergy*; one ordained* by a church* to serve as minister* or priest.* Associated most strongly with transplanted hierarchical European state churches, such as the Roman Catholic,* Eastern Orthodox* and Episcopal* churches. In these traditions distinctive clothing—such as a clerical collar—serve to identify the cleric in public.   C. E. Hambrick-Stowe

Clericalism. The rule or influence of clergy* in church* and society. Authority* varies with church polity,* ranging from government by bishops* or elders* (presbyters) to congregationalism,* with authority vested in the people (though early Congregational New England is often linked with clericalism). In most traditions lay* boards of trustees at least share authority. The charismatic religious leader endowed with spiritual, ecclesiastical and even political power is also a common figure. Although Alexis de Tocqueville* wrote, "the American clergy stands aloof from public business" (*Democracy in America*, 1835), many have brought the gospel into political and economic spheres. Black ministers, serving as the voice of the community, have naturally sought election to public office. With the Constitution's establishment clause, Americans are uneasy about clergy and political power.

BIBLIOGRAPHY. A. M. Greeley, *Priests in the United States* (1972); H. B. Hicks, Jr., *Images of the Black Preacher* (1977); D. S. Schuller et. al., eds., *Ministry in America* (1980).

C. E. Hambrick-Stowe

Clough, John Everett (1836-1910). Baptist* missionary* to India. Born in western New York, Clough graduated from Upper Iowa University in 1862, was ordained* two years later and went to India to serve in the Telegu Mission. He settled in Ongole, Madras Presidency, in 1866 and promptly founded a church* as he ministered among the outcaste Madigas. His relief work during the terrible famine of 1876-1878 was much respected among the people, and after assuring himself of the sincerity of their conversion,* he and his assistants baptized some 9,000 persons in a six-month period as his influence spread among 400 villages. His congregation totaled 21,000 members five years later, before it was divided for sake of convenience. He became well known at home through his reports and addresses while on furlough, and he contributed to the growing popularity of foreign missions.* He retired in 1905 and died five years later in Rochester.

BIBLIOGRAPHY. J. E. Clough, *Social Christianity in the Orient* (1901); E. R. Clough, *John E. Clough* (1902); *DAB* II. R. T. Handy

Cobbs, Nicholas Hamner (1796-1861). Episcopal* bishop.* Born in Bedford County, Virginia, Cobbs was educated in a neighborhood old-fields school. At age seventeen he began to teach in his native county. Although his family was Anglican,* the Episcopal Church had not survived disestablishment in much of southwestern Virginia, and Cobbs attended Presbyterian* services. Becoming interested in theology* and church history, he gradually read himself into the Episcopal Church.

Confirmed* and ordained* deacon* on the same day in 1824 and ordained to the priesthood* in 1825, Cobbs devoted weekdays to schoolteaching and evenings and weekends to preaching* in houses and schools. A zealous missionary,* he established Episcopal churches not only in his native county but also in four adjoining counties in southwestern Virginia. In the 1830s he was Episcopal chaplain* to the University of Virginia. From 1839 to 1843, he served as rector of St. Paul's Church, Petersburg, Virginia, leaving it to be rector of St. Paul's Church, Cincinnati, Ohio. In 1844 he was elected and consecrated* first Episcopal bishop of Alabama.

Humble, earnest and so rustic as a young man that William Meade* viewed him on their first meeting as "another clog upon the Church," ironically, Cobbs guided the small diocese of Alabama into growth. Although the evangelicalism* of Virginia influenced him throughout his life, he subsequently combined high* and low* church emphases in a way that many thought paradigmatic of Anglicanism. A slave owner, he nevertheless opposed secession. He died in Montgomery just before Alabama seceded.

BIBLIOGRAPHY. G. White, *A Saint of the Southern Church* (1897); W. C. Whitaker, *History of the Protestant Episcopal Church in Alabama, 1763-1891* (1898); K. L. Brown, *Hill of the Lord* (1979).

D. L. Holmes

Cody, John Patrick (1907-1982). Catholic* archbishop* of Chicago (1965-1982). Born in St. Louis, Cody was educated for the priesthood in Rome at the North American College* and the Appolinaris (Ph.D., 1928; S.T.D., 1932; J.C.D., 1938) and was ordained* there in 1931. The following year he served as assistant rector* of the North American College and then as personal secretary to Archbishop John Glennon of St. Louis until the latter's death in 1946. Cody was consecrated auxiliary bishop* of St. Louis in 1947, named bishop of St. Louis, Missouri, in 1955 and bishop of Kansas City in 1956. In 1961 he was named coadjutor* archbishop of New Orleans, becoming archbishop of New Orleans in his own right in 1964. In 1965 he was transferred to Chicago and named a cardinal* in 1967.

Cody earned a reputation for racial liberalism in New Orleans by working for the desegregation of that city's parochial schools,* but he angered liberal Catholics in Chicago by closing many inner-city schools for financial reasons. Prodded by the Association of Chicago Priests, Cody established a clergy* personnel board, a mandatory retirement age and extensive insurance and pension plans for priests.* His secretive and authoritarian administrative style, however, neutralized much of these policies' effects and led to continuing controversies with the clergy. The United States attorney investigated Cody's financial affairs, but no charges were laid and the investigation was dropped after his death in 1982. Perhaps his most permanent legacy was the decision not to build Catholic schools in new suburban parishes. This retrenchment in the nation's largest parochial school system is not likely to be reversed.

BIBLIOGRAPHY. C. W. Dahm and R. Ghelardi, *Power and Authority in the Catholic Church: Cardinal Cody in Chicago* (1982); "Cardinal Keeps Chicago See in Forefront," *The New World* (July 1, 1977):1-29.   E. R. Kantowicz

Coe, George Albert (1862-1951). Professor of religious education. Born in Mendon, New York, the son of a Methodist* minister, Coe graduated from the University of Rochester (B.A., 1884), where he developed a commitment to scientific inquiry. While pursuing further studies at the Boston University School of Theology (S.T.B., 1887; M.A., 1888), Coe rejected the orthodoxy* of his youth. In 1888 he began teaching at the newly opened University of Southern California and concurrently completed his doctoral work at Boston University (Ph.D., 1891). In 1893 he became professor of philosophy of religion* at Northwestern University, Evanston, Illinois, and there published *The Spiritual Life: Studies in the Science of Religion* (1900), in which he applied psychology to questions of religious experience* and conversion.* In 1909 he became professor of religious education and psychology of religion at Union Theological Seminary, New York,* and in 1922 became professor at Teachers College, Columbia University.*

Coe was the leading theorist in liberal* religious education during the first half of the twentieth century. In 1903, he addressed the first meeting of the Religious Education Association* on the subject of "Salvation by Education." He appealed to Horace Bushnell's* theory of Christian nurture,* arguing that people could be educated into Christian faith with no need for religious conversion.* Drawing on John Dewey's pragmatism and the social Darwinism of his time, Coe proposed a reconstructionist theory of religious education where teacher and student reconstructed Christianity according to the truth of their personal experiences, resulting in a practical faith beneficial to both individuals and society. His pervasive emphasis on human relationships is reflected by his definition of Christian education* as "the systematic, critical examination and reconstruction of relations between persons, guided by Jesus' assumption that persons are of infinite worth, and

by the hypothesis of the existence of God, the Great Valuer of Persons." In his old age Coe embraced the Marxian ideal of a classless society and attracted the attention of the House Committee on Un-American Activities.

BIBLIOGRAPHY. *DAB* III; K. O. Gangel and W. S. Benson, *Christian Education: Its History and Philosophy* (1983); *Religious Education* (March-April 1952).   B. E. Brown

Coe, Jack (1918-1957). Pentecostal* healing* revivalist.* Born in Oklahoma City, Coe was abandoned by his parents and raised in an orphanage. Characterizing his early life as "deep in sin," Coe received a miraculous healing while serving in the army during World War 2* and felt called to the ministry.* Ordained* by the Assemblies of God* (1944), his dynamic revivalist style led to a tent ministry by 1947, in what was reputed to be the world's largest "gospel tent." When the nationwide healing revival of 1947-1952 began, Coe was already a prominent figure. Brash and explosive, Coe attracted large numbers from the lower class, including blacks, and was second only to Oral Roberts* in the movement's leadership.

Expelled from the Assemblies of God in 1953 for reason of his extreme independence and practices, Coe established an independent ministry and in 1954 opened his Dallas Revival Center. He had a limited, short-lived television ministry, but his *Herald of Healing* reached a circulation of 250,000 in 1956. Two crises curtailed Coe's ascendancy. In February 1956, while preaching in Miami, Florida, Coe was arrested for practicing medicine without a license and released on $5,000 bond. His two-day trial led to the case being dismissed. But in December of 1956 he was diagnosed as having polio. When Coe died in 1957 his wife, Juanita, continued his ministry, though she gradually shifted her priorities to missions and a children's home.

BIBLIOGRAPHY. D. E. Harrell, *All Things Are Possible* (1975).   H. D. Hunter

Coffin, Henry Sloane (1877-1954). Presbyterian* minister* and educator. Born in New York City, Coffin was educated at Yale,* Edinburgh, Marburg and Union Theological Seminary (New York).* Following his ordination* in the Presbyterian Church in the USA* (1900), he founded and served in a Presbyterian mission in the Bronx. After pastoring the Bedford Park Presbyterian Church (1900-1905), he was called to the prestigious Madison Avenue Presbyterian Church in New York City (1905-1926), where he became known as one of America's great preachers.* During his pastorate at the Madison Avenue Church he also served as professor of practical theology at Union Theological Seminary, where he eventually served as president and professor of homiletics* (1926-1945).

Throughout his career, Coffin championed liberal* causes of one kind or another. He opposed preparedness and the American entry into World War 1* and become a liberal leader during the fundamentalist-modernist controversy* within the Presbyterian Church. As a signer of the "Auburn Affirmation"* (1924), he advocated an "inclusivist" church and protested what liberals believed was the fundamentalist* assault on the denomination's unity and liberty. In the heated General Assembly* of 1925 he defended the New York Presbytery's refusal to require candidates for ordination to adhere to all the doctrinal standards of the church. Calling himself an "evangelical liberal," Coffin attempted to find a mediating position between extreme conservative and liberal factions in the Presbyterian Church of his day.

Always the committed churchman, Coffin worked to make Union Seminary a training ground for pastors as well as scholars. He became well known as a liturgist (*The Public Worship of God*, 1946), a hymnologist (*Hymns of the Kingdom*, 1910) and an ecumenist,* and served as moderator of the Presbyterian Church in the USA in 1943-1944.

BIBLIOGRAPHY. *DAB* 5; *DARB; NCAB* E; M. P. Noyes, *Henry Sloane Coffin: The Man and His Ministry* (1964).　　　　　　T. P. Weber

Coffin, Levi (1789-1877). Quaker* merchant and president of the Underground Railroad. Born to a North Carolina Quaker family, at age seven he witnessed a chain gang of black slaves, a beating and other cruelties which instilled in him hatred for the institution of slavery and its degrading influences, though his Southern upbringing always fostered in him an empathy for slave owners.

Levi and his cousin Vestal Coffin initiated the Underground Railroad in 1819. The Coffin family, as did many other Southern Quaker families, migrated to Indiana in order to get away from slavery. Levi Coffin's house in Old Newport (now Fountain City), where Coffin resided from 1826-1847, was dubbed the "Grand Central Station of the Underground Railroad" by frustrated slave hunters. By the time of the Emancipation Proclamation,* he had aided 3,000 slaves on their way to freedom.

In 1847 Coffin moved to Cincinnati to manage a wholesale business dealing in "free goods." He searched the South for goods and produce which were not dependent on slave labor and made these available to Northern merchants. His Cincinnati home continued as a refuge for fugitive slaves. The "Eliza" of Harriet Beecher Stowe's* *Uncle Tom's Cabin* was a slave Coffin hid in his home after she had escaped Kentucky with her baby, having crossed the Ohio River on ice floes. Coffin later supplied Stowe with the details.

Following the Civil War,* Coffin helped organize the Western Freedman's Aid Society, which was devoted to alleviating distress among the freed slaves. In 1864 he went to England and raised over $100,000 for the Western Freedman's Aid Societies.

BIBLIOGRAPHY. L. Coffin, *Reminiscences of Levi Coffin* (1876); *DAB* II; *DARB*.　　R. E. Selleck

Coffman, John S. (1848-1899). Pioneer Mennonite* Church evangelist.* In 1875, after a brief stint as a schoolteacher, Coffman was ordained* in Virginia as a minister of the Mennonite Church. In 1879 he became assistant editor of the *Herald of Truth* in Elkhart, Indiana. During this time he wrote Sunday-school* material, collaborated on the writing of the Mennonite Church Confession of Faith of 1891 and was president and tract editor of the Mennonite Book and Tract* Society. Coffman also helped organize Elkhart Institute, the forerunner of Goshen (Indiana) College. But Coffman's greatest contribution was as an evangelist. Despite resistance to evangelistic techniques by fellow Mennonites, Coffman's gentle style and tact helped break down opposition to such work within the conference. His first evangelistic series was held in Kent County, Michigan, in 1881, and he continued such meetings until his premature death at age fifty.

BIBLIOGRAPHY. M. S. Steiner, *John S. Coffman: Mennonite Evangelist* (1903); John Umble, "John S. Coffman as an Evangelist," *MQR* 23 (1949):123-146.　　　　　　K. Enns-Rempel

Coffman, (S)amuel (F)rederick (1872-1954). Canadian Old Mennonite* bishop* and educator. Coffman was born in Virginia, the son of Mennonite minister John S. Coffman,* but his family moved to Elkhart, Indiana, in 1879. After high school he worked with a Mennonite publishing firm, and in 1894 he began attending Moody Bible Institute* in Chicago. Ordained* in 1895, he served as an itinerant evangelist* until 1901 when he and his bride settled permanently in Vineland, Ontario. Coffman became a Mennonite bishop in the Niagara District in 1902. From 1903 he served on the executive committee of the Ontario Mennonite Conference. From 1907 to 1948 he was the (first) principal of Ontario Mennonite Bible School in Kitchener.

Coffman was one of Ontario's most influential Mennonites in the first half of the twentieth century. In 1922 he helped persuade the Canadian government to reverse its 1919 ban on Mennonite immigration* and worked hard to deal with the 1923 influx of Russian immigrants. Theologically a conservative, Coffman opposed liberalism* but eschewed the tone and temper of militant American fundamentalism.*

BIBLIOGRAPHY. U. Bender, *Four Earthen Vessels* (1982). D. M. Lewis

Coke, Thomas (1747-1814). Methodist* bishop.* Born in Brecon, Wales, Coke earned a Doctor of Laws degree from Oxford before being ordained priest in the Church of England (1772), only to be turned out of his parish for Methodist sympathies. In 1776, Coke offered his services to John Wesley,* who used him extensively in drafting deeds and documents, anticipating the organization of the Methodists in both England and America. (In Wesley's later years, Coke was his most trusted companion.) Appointed superintendent of the London circuit in 1780, Coke's skills were soon put to work in Ireland (he chaired in 1872 the first Irish Conference) and America, where his contribution was most crucial. In 1784 Coke was ordained* by Wesley as the first bishop (or superintendent, as preferred by Wesley) for the American Methodist Episcopal Church which would be organized later that year. Over the next thirty years Coke made nine trips across the Atlantic.

Coke's first journey to America was in response to an appeal from American Methodists for ordained clergy* to administer the sacraments* among the societies that were virtually without ministerial leadership. Coke immediately joined with Francis Asbury* (the only English missionary to remain in America during the Revolution*) to establish the Methodist Episcopal Church at the well-known Christmas Conference* of 1784. Coke ordained Asbury deacon,* elder* and superintendent on successive days. He presented the founding documents provided by Wesley, which were approved and instituted. Coke then proceeded to stir the waters on both sides of the Atlantic by referring to Anglican bishops as immoral or unconverted and strongly criticizing—true to the spirit of Wesley—American slavery.

Coke's second journey to America (1787) found the American Methodists moving away from the direct rule of Wesley and during his next three visits (1789, 1791, 1792) saw them challenging even Asbury's authority* as inconsistent with the independent spirit of a new Republic. During the first General Conference (1792), Coke observed the first split among American Methodists, as James O'Kelly* withdrew over the issue of ministerial right of appeal regarding ecclesiastical appointments.

During Coke's last four visits (1796-1797, 1797, 1800, 1803), he sensed that the American church was no longer in need of English supervision, so he returned to England, where his influence remained considerable until his death. Imbued with a missionary* spirit, Coke planted churches and societies around the world, sometimes at considerable personal expense. On May 3, 1814, he died on board a ship headed for Ceylon and was buried in the Indian Ocean.

BIBLIOGRAPHY. *AAP* 7; W. A. Candler, *The Life of Thomas Coke* (1923); *DAB* II; *DARB; NCAB* 10; S. Sowton, *Thomas Coke* (1956); J. Vickers, *Thomas Coke: Apostle of Methodism* (1969).

R. G. Tuttle

Coker, Daniel (born Isaac Wright) (1780-1846). African Methodist Episcopal* minister.* Born a slave in Maryland, Coker ran away as a youth to New York State, where he was ordained* a Methodist* deacon* by Bishop Francis Asbury.* Upon returning to Maryland Coker purchased his freedom and taught in a church school for many years. He assumed leadership of the African Bethel Church in Baltimore, organized after he and other members withdrew from Sharp Street Church. Coker organized the first school in Baltimore for African-American children and published what is believed to have been the first pamphlet written by a African-American man in America. He was one of the few literate ministers involved in the early African-American independent church movement. Working closely with Richard Allen* in Philadelphia, Coker became one of the founders of the African Methodist Episcopal Church in 1816. He was elected the first bishop of the new denomination,* but for reasons unknown declined to assume the office. In 1820 he left America to conduct missionary* work in Africa, where he died after organizing several churches in Liberia and Sierra Leone.

BIBLIOGRAPHY. H. V. Richardson, *Dark Salvation: The Story of Methodism As It Developed Among Blacks in America* (1976).

M. R. Sawyer

Cole, Nathan (1711-1783). Lay* leader of the

separatist* movement in New England. Cole was a Connecticut farmer who experienced an evangelical* conversion* as the result of George Whitefield's* visit to Middletown in 1740. This experience induced him to question the common Congregational* practice of extending Communion* to the unconverted, leading in turn to his separation from the Kensington Church in 1747. Cole led a small dissenting group for a few years, but their inability to secure a minister caused the abandonment of this effort, and in 1764 Cole joined Ebenezer Frothingham's* separatist congregation. The following year he composed his apologia and spiritual autobiography, *The Spiritual Travels of Nathan Cole*, which contains the famous account of his journey to hear Whitefield. Though *Spiritual Travels* was never published during Cole's lifetime, it was only one of a number of controversial works that he produced, among which was a defense of his 1778 rejection of paedobaptism and subsequent acceptance of the Baptist* faith.

BIBLIOGRAPHY. M. J. Crawford, "The Spiritual Travels of Nathan Cole," *WMQ* 33 (1976): 89-126.
R. M. Payne

Coleman, Alice Blanchard Merriam (1858-1936). Home missions leader. Born in Boston, she graduated from Bradford Academy (1878). Her father worked for the Boston City Missionary Society, and in 1879 she became involved in the Women's Home Missionary Association of the Congregational* Church. In 1886, under the influence of A. J. Gordon,* Coleman joined his Clarendon Street Baptist Church. On June 30, 1891 she married Georgia William Coleman, a deacon* and Sunday-school* superintendent of the church. She was president of the Woman's American Baptist Home Mission Society from 1890 to 1909. After it merged with Chicago's Woman's Baptist Home Mission Society in 1920, she was president of the national organization until 1928. She was founder and first president of the ecumenical Council of Women for Home Missions (1908-1916). She also served as a trustee of Gordon College.

BIBLIOGRAPHY. *NAW* 1. N. A. Hardesty

Colgate, William (1783-1857). Manufacturer, philanthropist* and Baptist* layman.* Born in Kent, England, in 1795 Colgate's father moved the family to Baltimore, Maryland. William went to work at the age of fifteen and by 1804 was employed in New York City by a tallow chandler. By 1806 he had established his own tallow business which proved very successful. By the 1840s he had

begun to manufacture soap and other toiletries, and his new plant in Jersey City had become an acknowledged leader in the industry.

A Baptist, Colgate had determined to give at least ten per cent of each year's net earnings to charitable and religious causes—an amount he frequently doubled or tripled. He gave generously to Madison University (later known as Colgate University) and helped found several Bible societies,* including the American Bible Society* and the American and Foreign Bible Society. In 1838, having rejected sectarianism as inconsistent with the nature and progress of Christianity, he organized a new religious society, not bound by any creed.*

BIBLIOGRAPHY. *DAB* II; W. W. Everts, *William Colgate, the Christian Layman* (1881).
D. G. Reid

Collect. A short, structured public prayer* which follows a distinctively formalized pattern. The collect form consists of: (1) an address to God; (2) a clause appealing to an attribute or saving act of God; (3) the petition; (4) a statement of the divine purpose for which the prayer is intended; and (5) a conclusion with a doxological, Christological or Trinitarian orientation.

Originally, as a Western Catholic* phenomenon, collects concluded a unit of worship.* They have been widely adapted for weekly use in various American Protestant* churches which often prescribe one for each worship service of the church year.* In Protestant use, a collect may open worship, precede the reading of the Word or conclude either the processional, the sharing of greetings, an improvised general prayer or the service of Communion.*

BIBLIOGRAPHY. P. Cobb, "The Liturgy of the Word in the Early Church," in *The Study of Liturgy,* ed. C. Jones et al. (1978). P. W. Butin

College of New Jersey. *See* PRINCETON UNIVERSITY.

College of Rhode Island. *See* BROWN UNIVERSITY.

Collegiality. The principle that the church* is a communion (college) of local churches which make up the church universal. In Roman Catholic* ecclesiology, collegiality applies to the bishops* as a college which possesses authority* in union with and under the pope* (*Dogmatic Constitution on the Church,* 1964, no. 22). Collegiality is exercised in ecumenical councils and synods* of bishops.* In practice collegiality is a mode of decision making which emphasizes collaboration, not only between pope and bishops but at all levels of the church, whether national episcopal* conferences, diocesan pastoral* councils or parish* councils.

BIBLIOGRAPHY. R. P. McBrien, "Collegiality: The State of the Question," in *The Once and Future Church,* ed. J. A. Coriden (1971).

A. M. Clifford

Colonial Catholicism. Catholicism came to North America with the three major colonial powers: England, France and Spain. In the French and Spanish domains, the union of church and state* and the privileged position enjoyed by Catholicism assisted that church's growth and development (*see* Missions, French; Missions, Spanish). But Catholics in the English colonies were generally subject to severe civil penalties. Though Catholics could be found in Massachusetts, New York, New Jersey and Virginia, they formed visible communities only in Pennsylvania and Maryland.

The first English Catholics settled in Maryland, a proprietary colony established in 1634 by the Calvert family. While the Calverts wished primarily to make Maryland a successful commercial venture, as converts to Catholicism they were interested also in a refuge for their coreligionists. Realizing that an exclusively Catholic settlement was an impossibility, they determined on a policy of toleration for all Christians. Appointing his brother Leonard* as governor, Cecil Calvert,* second Lord Baltimore, instructed him to maintain religious harmony between Catholics and Protestants.* Quarrels over religion were to be avoided and the Catholic Mass* was to be said privately.

Two Jesuit* priests,* Andrew White* and John Altham,* accompanied the first settlers, and from the outset Catholics formed a significant minority in a religiously pluralistic* society. The upper class of gentlemen was mainly Catholic, and Catholics dominated the colonial offices. Faced with growing pressure from the Protestant majority in the colony, the Catholic-controlled Maryland Assembly in 1649 passed a Toleration Act,* guaranteeing religious toleration for all Christians. This law was repealed in 1654 when the Puritans* seized control of the colony. About the time of the Stuart restoration in 1660, Lord Baltimore regained his proprietorship and toleration resumed; but following the Glorious Revolution of 1688, Maryland became a royal colony, and the Church of England was established in 1702. The assembly instituted a harsh penal code. Catholics were not permitted to hold office or vote, and could only worship* privately.

Despite discrimination, the Catholic population gradually increased from almost 3,000 in 1708 to 20,000 by 1755. They included a gentry class composed of families (such as the Carrolls, Neales and Brookes), small planters, subsistence and commercial farmers who lived off the land, some tenant farmers and slaves. Their spiritual support came from the Jesuit priests, who operated a number of farms (seven by the time of the Revolution*) that provided bases for an itinerant clergy.* In time these farms became centers for stable congregations which began to exhibit the features of a parish* church. In addition, Franciscan* and secular* (diocesan) priests also worked in the colony at different times. During the eighteenth century, Maryland Catholics produced numerous vocations* to the priesthood and religious life. Thirty-six men became Jesuits, and at least that many women entered European convents of Benedictines,* Poor Clares, Carmelites, Dominicans* and Augustinians.* Though the sons and daughters of well-to-do families were usually sent to English Catholic schools in Flanders for their education, Jesuits operated schools for brief periods at St. Mary's City and Newtown Manor in the seventeenth century and at Bohemia Manor in the 1740s.

While Maryland Catholicism was overwhelmingly English and rural, an urban, ethnic Catholicism was located in Pennsylvania. German and Irish Catholics were among the earliest settlers in Philadelphia. The first permanent Catholic chapel,* St. Joseph's, was erected there in 1733. Catholics were tolerated, though they could not hold public office. A special census in 1757 listed 1,365 Catholics over the age of twelve, of which seventy per cent were German speaking. German Jesuits rode circuits through southeastern Pennsylvania and western Jersey.

New York briefly enjoyed religious toleration during the proprietorship of the Duke of York (James II) who had converted to Catholicism in 1672. Under the administration of Catholic Governor Thomas Dongan,* Jesuits opened a chapel and a school for the small Catholic community. But Leisler's rebellion in 1689 ended toleration, Catholicism was proscribed, and the Jesuits were driven from the colony.

After the suppression of the Society of Jesus by Pope Clement XIV in 1773, the twenty-three Jesuits active in Maryland and Pennsylvania regrouped as secular priests and continued their ministry.* Other American Jesuits, studying or working in Europe, returned home including John Carroll,* destined to become the first Catholic bishop in the

U.S. At the time of the Revolution, most colonial Catholics allied themselves with the country party and the revolutionary cause. They were led by Charles Carroll* of Carrollton, who attended the First Continental Congress in Philadelphia, signed the Declaration of Independence, and was the first Catholic to hold political office in Maryland since the seventeenth century.

See also ROMAN CATHOLICISM.

BIBLIOGRAPHY. J. T. Ellis, *Catholics in Colonial America* (1965); J. P. Dolan, *The American Catholic Experience* (1985); J. D. Krugler, "Lord Baltimore, Roman Catholics, and Toleration: Religious Policy in Maryland during the Early Catholic Years, 1634-1649," *CHR* 65 (1979):49-75.

T. E. Buckley

Colporteur. Itinerant hawkers of religious tracts and books in nineteenth-century America. The idea and the term were borrowed from France. The word *colporteur* refers to the pack a peddler carried (*porter*) over his shoulder or neck (*col*). The chief American promoter of the colportage system was the American Tract Society* (ATS). The ATS launched its "colporteur enterprise" in 1841 with two paid agents assigned to Kentucky and Indiana. Within ten years, the society had more than 500 colporteurs at work, mainly in the frontier regions of the West and South. Other societies and churches also sent brigades of colporteurs to the Western frontier. But as community churches sprang up along with towns and villages in the West, the need for itinerant lay* agents declined. By 1900 the ATS employed only fifty-four colporteurs. Thus, colportage largely disappeared in America, along with the frontier itself.

BIBLIOGRAPHY. E. S. Gaustad, ed., *The American Tract Society Documents, 1824-1925* (1972).

D. P. Nord

Columbia University. Educational institution with colonial Anglican* roots. Kings College, later called Columbia University, opened in New York City in 1754 with Samuel Johnson,* a clergyman, as its first president. Its first site was the schoolhouse vestry of Trinity Church in lower Manhattan. Throughout much of its early history, Anglicans struggled with Presbyterian* and secular interests for control. The institution which emerged was the result of an alliance between Anglican clerics and the city's mercantile and legal elite. The final charter of Kings College created an interdenominational board which was lay-controlled and included a number of public officials. Anglican interests did, however, tend to predominate, with

about two-thirds of the members of the early boards being Anglican laymen.*

In 1776 the college was dispersed as a result of the Revolutionary War* and its buildings turned over to the Continental Army. It remained closed until 1784, when its name was changed to Columbia and governance power was vested in the newly formed New York State Board of Regents. By a legislative act in 1787, however, direct control passed once again into the hands of a private board of trustees. In 1857 the college moved to more spacious quarters in midtown Manhattan. Continued growth resulted in its final move to a 28.5-acre campus in Upper Manhattan.

The first of Columbia's postgraduate units was the school of medicine, established in 1767. Under the leadership of presidents Frederick A. P. Barnard (1864-1889), Seth Low (1889-1901) and Nicholas M. Butler (1902-1945), graduate and professional education expanded to include such schools of philosophy and business, as well as the affiliated College of Pharmaceutical Sciences and Teachers College. In 1912 Columbia was officially recognized by the state as a university. Enrollment presently averages around 17,000 students.

BIBLIOGRAPHY. J. W. Burgess, *Reminiscences of an American Scholar: The Beginnings of Columbia University* (1934); D. C. Humphrey, *From Kings College to Columbia, 1746-1800* (1976).

F. M. Perko

Columbian Catholic Congress. National conference of Catholic* laity.* In November 1889, a congress of Roman Catholic laymen met in Baltimore to celebrate the centenary of the establishment of the first diocese* in the U.S. and the dedication of the Catholic University of America* in Washington, D.C. The second Catholic Congress of the U.S. was held in Chicago, September 4-6, 1893. It was organized to coincide with the Columbus Exposition and World's Fair of that year which commemorated the four-hundreth anniversary of the discovery of America by Europeans.

The papers delivered dealt with three topics: the social question as outlined in Pope Leo XIII's* encyclical letter, *Rerum Novarum**; Catholic education; and the independence of the Holy See. Archbishop Patrick A. Feehan* of Chicago opened the Congress. Prominent American Catholic laymen presided at the sessions, and distinguished prelates and lay leaders from the U.S. and abroad addressed the delegates.

BIBLIOGRAPHY. *Progress of the Catholic Church in America and the great Columbian Catholic Congress of 1893* (1897). J. T. Connelly

Columbus, Christopher (1451-1506). Sailor, chartmaker, navigator and discoverer of the New World. Born in Genoa, Italy, and reared in a pious Catholic* family, Columbus remained a devout Catholic all his life, in fortune and misfortune. Without formal education, he learned, beyond his native Genoese dialect, Castilian Spanish, Portuguese and Latin. His self-education included wide-ranging reading as well as expertise in chartmaking and navigation.

Columbus was obsessed with the idea of finding a westward sea route to Asia. To secure funding for this project, he and his brother, Bartholomew, spent eight years petitioning the crowns of Portugal, Spain, England and France. Finally, in 1492 Queen Isabella of Spain reversed her previous refusals and granted the necessary funds. Between 1492 and 1504 he made four voyages, always convinced he was headed for the Asian Indies, but always landing in Caribbean America, land heretofore unknown to Europe. As an administrator of the colonies resulting from his voyages, Columbus was less successful than he was as the navigator of the voyages. However, given the strangeness of this New World, Columbus certainly deserved less harsh treatment than he received at the end of his life, when he died alone and forgotten. Through one of the strangest quirks in history, even the New World he discovered was not named after him. In 1507, through the efforts of an obscure landlocked cleric in the Vosges Mountains, Martin Waldseemuller, and the instantaneous influence of the newly invented printing press, the New World was named after Amerigo Vespucci, who had discovered South America in 1501.

Columbus himself was a strong-willed, ambitious, industrious, bold and above all pious person, whose religious devotion* and practice usually surpassed that of all his companions, including the monks and priests.* Although the pursuit of "God and Gold" may not inaptly describe the ambitions of his voyagers, for Columbus personally the emphasis was clearly on God. In American history the Anglo-Puritan* "Errand in the Wilderness" is a well-known motif. "The conversion to our Holy Faith" of millions of pagans in Asia was equally the errand of Columbus, however much gold the Spanish monarchs may have expected and been promised. This emphasis is highlighted in Columbus's baptismal geography— San Salvador, Trinidad, Santa Maria. . . . This unbounded optimism even led Columbus to describe the native people as "much inclined to conversion to our holy faith," although subsequent missionary efforts did not confirm this inclination on the part of the native inhabitants. Columbus established the first church in the New World on Isabella (Haiti), where the first Mass* was celebrated on January 6, 1494, the first baptism* on September 21, 1494.

Columbus is a hero not only to sailors and navigators, but especially to American Catholics, who used him as an inspiration and patron on their own errand in the wilderness of the New World, especially in their efforts to establish themselves socially and religiously. These efforts were seen most clearly in their combat against the Nativist* anti-Catholicism which they experienced from their beginnings in Maryland and throughout American history. Thus, the largest mutual-benefit societies among Catholics have been the Knights of Columbus* for men and the Daughters of Isabella for women. Curiously, no serious effort has been made to promote the cause of Columbus's sainthood.

BIBLIOGRAPHY. S. Madriaga, *Christopher Columbus* (1967); S. E. Morrison, *Admiral of the Ocean*, 2 vols. (1942); S. E. Morrison, *European Discovery of America*, 2 vols. (1971).   R. L. Kress

Commission of the Churches on International Affairs. Ecumenical* agency seeking Christian solutions to international problems. At a conference in Cambridge, England, in August 1946, Christian clergy* and lay experts in international affairs met under the auspices of the provisional World Council of Churches,* the International Missionary Council, and the American Commission on a Just and Durable Peace to organize the Commission of the Churches on International Affairs (CCIA). It was to discover and proclaim a Christian approach to post-War international problems, apply it to immediate issues and educate the churches. Its founders hoped that a permanent agency representing many of the great Christian denominations would have a greater influence on international affairs than had the churches acting separately in the 1930s. When the World Council of Churches was formed in 1948, the CCIA became its official, but nearly autonomous, agency under the guidance of its first chairman, Sir Kenneth Grubb, a British layman,* and director, Otto Frederick Nolde, an American Lutheran* clergyman. They directed studies of long-term problems and counseled governments to forego violence, seek mediation and use the services of the United Nations. The CCIA is given substantial credit for the religious-freedom clause in the Universal Declaration of Human Rights (1948).

In 1968, the CCIA's autonomy was reduced, and two years later the announcement by the World Council that it was financially assisting organizations combating racism, some of which used violence, provoked internal and external criticism. During the 1970s, the increased representation of Third World countries on the CCIA led to more controversial decisions, but by the 1980s the CCIA appeared to be following a less contentious course.

BIBLIOGRAPHY. O. F. Nolde, "Ecumenical Action in International Affairs," *A History of the Ecumenical Movement,* ed. H. E. Fey, vol. 2 (1970).

G. F. Goodwin

Committee of Southern Churchmen. A small nondenominational Christian service network based in Nashville and led by Will D. Campbell. The Committee of Southern Churchmen emerged in 1963-1964 from the dormant Fellowship of Southern Churchmen.* The latter Fellowship was virtually disbanded by the late 1950s, save for the efforts of Will D. Campbell and others to maintain some continuity. By 1964 they had formed the new Committee of Southern Churchmen, a smaller and more conservative group headed by a board of one hundred. Campbell and the Committee of Southern Churchmen shared certain basic concerns with Walter Rauschenbusch* and the early Social Gospel Movement,* but with a more Barthian* view of the limitations imposed by human sinfulness on any social reform effort. The Committee continued the racial justice emphasis of the late Fellowship of Southern Churchmen and its board members participated in the Birmingham, St. Augustine, Selma and other major Southern nonviolent campaigns of the 1960s.

More of a nonmembership network than an organization, the Committee worked behind the scenes to promote causes viewed as derivative from the biblical theme of reconciliation. During the Vietnam War* period the Committee aided draft evaders and anti-war protesters, as well as ministering to prisoners and others in need. From 1975 to 1983 Campbell published a theological journal known as *Katallagete—Be Reconciled,* carrying articles by writers such as Thomas Merton,* Walker Percy and Vincent Harding. Theologically, the journal mirrored the Committee's emphases upon sin, reconciliation and service, as well as its criticism of aspects of mainstream church policies. Evangelism,* prophetic social criticism and promotion of a Christocentric human community are basic to the Committee of Southern Churchmen's perspective.

BIBLIOGRAPHY. W. D. Campbell, *Race and the Renewal of the Church* (1962); W. D. Campbell and J. Y. Holloway, *Up to Our Steeples in Politics* (1970); R. F. Martin, "Critique of Southern Society and Vision of a New Order: The Fellowship of Southern Churchmen, 1934-1957," *CH* 52 (1983):66-80.

T. R. Peake

Common Sense Philosophy. *See* SCOTTISH REALISM.

Communion of Saints. The universal fellowship* of Christians and the solidarity they have with one another. The term stems from the Apostles' Creed, "I believe . . . in the communion of saints." While it is not, strictly speaking, a biblical phrase, the concept is suggested by New Testament texts (e.g., Jn 14:6-24; 17:20-26; 2 Cor 13:13; Eph 2:18; 4:12; 1 Jn 1:3) indicating Christians have intimate fellowship with God and with one another through their union in Christ and by the power of the Holy Spirit. In this broad sense, "saints" describes all Christians. Some Christians believe that their "communion" or fellowship is most tangibly expressed through the celebration of the Lord's Supper,* and the phrase "communion of saints" can also be translated "communion of holy things" to describe the church as a sacramental* community.

The earliest attestation of the phrase stems from writings of the mid fifth century which identify "saints" as those martyrs and faithful confessors of Christ who have gone on to paradise. Hence, Roman Catholics use the phrase, "the communion of saints," to describe the fellowship of all members of the triparte church—triumphant in heaven, expectant in purgatory and militant on earth. Where the Catholic Church had formerly placed much emphasis on invoking the saints, Post-Vatican II* expressions use the phrase to stress the fellowship members enjoy in the life of the Church. Protestants also use the phrase to describe the fellowship Christians have with one another as they are formed together into one body by the Spirit of God. Sectarian and separatist* groups have occasionally used the phrase to designate themselves as the true church.

See also ALL SAINTS DAY; SAINTS, CULT OF THE.

BIBLIOGRAPHY. S. Benko, *The Meaning of Sanctorum Communio* (1964); L. Cunningham, *The Meaning of Saints* (1980). J. R. Tyson

Communion Table. The table on which the elements of bread and wine rest during the Eucharist* and from which Holy Communion is distributed. The table is often ornamented with a text taken from the narrative of the Last Supper. Although writers of the patristic period used the term *table* interchangeably with *altar,* the sixteenth-century reformers found the term *altar* redolent of the theology* of eucharistic sacrifice and systematically replaced that term with such expressions as *table, holy table* or *table of the Lord.* They often took care to set up a table in another part of the church so as to discourage any confusion with the old altar. Modern altars (so designated) often take the form of a table.

BIBLIOGRAPHY. C. E. Pocknee, *The Christian Altar* (1963).　　　　　　　　　　T. J. Talley

Community of True Inspiration. *See* AMANA CHURCH SOCIETY.

Concelebration. The practice of reciting the central prayer* of the Christian Eucharist* by a number of presiders simultaneously at the same altar.* Some claim that concelebration was the normal practice of the early church, when the bishop* was the principal celebrant assisted by a college of presbyters in each local Christian community. In any case, concelebration was discouraged as the Church progressively moved toward requiring all priests* to say Mass daily. Gradually this daily Mass obligation was fulfilled by private Masses, each priest praying the Eucharist at a different altar. In the Eastern Orthodox* churches, concelebration remained the usual practice, since only one Eucharist was allowed to be celebrated at any one church on a given day.

Among Roman Catholics since Vatican II,* there has been an attempt to recover concelebration as a remedy for the excessive privatization of the Mass. The practice of concelebration can also occasionally be found within some Protestant* denominations,* especially among those American Episcopalians* influenced by nineteenth-century Tractarianism.*　　　　　　　　　　　S. J. White

Conciliar Tradition, American. Ancient Christian tradition traced the origin of holding councils or synods* to decide doctrinal or disciplinary questions to the meeting of apostles and elders at Jerusalem (Acts 15:1-29; Gal 2:1-10). General, or ecumenical, councils began with Nicaea (A.D. 325) and in Roman Catholic* usage have continued to Vatican Council II* (1962-1965). Roman Catholics also hold conciliar-type meetings on other levels: synods (the clergy* and representative laity* of an individual diocese,* together with the bishop*), provincial councils (bishops of dioceses grouped

in a church province, with the metropolitan archbishop* presiding) and plenary councils (bishops of several provinces, usually but not always from a single nation, with a bishop chosen by them but approved by Rome presiding).

Canon 443 of the 1983 Code of Canon Law provides for attendance at such "particular" councils of certain categories of clergy and of representative lay men and women, as well as of guest-observers who need not be Roman Catholics. In a reform decree dated 1563 the Council of Trent had ordered that church provinces hold councils every three years, but the rule was poorly observed, and in 1858 Pope Pius IX* lengthened the time span to every twenty years. The 1983 code encourages provincial and plenary councils as "necessary . . . advantageous . . . opportune," but sets no time schedule for them, and they have not been a feature of late twentieth-century Catholicism, in which alternative forms of assembly, such as conferences of national bishops, are preferred.

During the nineteenth century the Roman Catholic Church in the U.S. held three plenary councils and thirty-one provincial councils, one-quarter of all those in the whole church. The American councils responded to the free environment of the U.S. by collaborative action to adapt to the nation's political and social culture. They drew upon a colonial and federal experience of an autonomous and familial church.

Beginnings in Baltimore. The structured Roman Catholic Church of the U.S. is descended from the church community begun in 1634 in Maryland. For 150 years, until John Carroll's* appointment as superior of the missions in 1784, Jesuit* priests managed church affairs in Maryland and Pennsylvania with only nominal supervision by a bishop in London and occasional contacts with Rome through the provincial superior of the Jesuit order in England. Save for a few German Jesuits among the Pennsylvania Dutch, priests and laity belonged to the tiny minority of English "papists," which had a strong tradition of independent-minded priests and influential lay leaders. In America hostility to the office of bishop had kept both Anglicans and Catholics from establishing the position. In 1765 a petition against such a project was made by 265 Maryland lay Catholics. Even after independence, American priests meeting at Whitemarsh Plantation near Bowie, Maryland, organized finances and church structure and adopted rules for the life and accountability of the clergy before they voted for establishment of a diocesan bishop.

With the creation in 1789 of the diocese of Baltimore, the clergy chapter which had met at

Whitemarsh lost official status. Bishop John Carroll held two meetings during his twenty-six-year tenure as leader of the American church: a synod of priests in 1791 and, after his diocese was divided, an informal session in 1810 with three of the new suffragan* bishops. The War of 1812 delayed more formal proceedings, and it was 1829 before the first provincial council of Baltimore* was held.

Chief proponent of introducing the conciliar system was Bishop John England* of Charleston, South Carolina, whose diocese in the Carolinas and Georgia was governed according to a constitution adopted in 1823 and with the advice of consultative conventions composed of houses of clergy and representative laity. The diocesan convention system died with Bishop England in 1842, but his influence continued in the councils of Baltimore, the first seven of which (1829-1949) were, in effect, national councils, while that of 1846 was technically international, since the missionary* bishop for the Republic of Texas attended. A second church province was begun in 1846 with Oregon City as its center, and St. Louis became an archdiocese* in 1847, but the seventh provincial council of Baltimore (1849) proceeded as planned and its legislation was effective nationally.

The archbishops of Baltimore presided at all these councils. Their chief result was to fix the pattern of a church firmly dominated by bishops. Lay trustees* of church holdings and discontented priests were brought under control, and little provision was made for consultation in church decision making. The councils and the pastoral letters* they issued in the name of the attending bishops dealt largely with internal church matters. Except to protest the civic loyalty of Roman Catholics in the face of nativist* attacks, they avoided topics of national interest like slavery and abolition,* although they did express concern for the problems of the papacy* in its struggles with the growing Italian national movement. Other subjects discussed included the division of dioceses and provision of bishops, recruitment and education* of priests and members of religious orders*, church schools* (see Parochial Schools) and religious books, missionary* work among native Americans and the freed slaves in Liberia, control of church property, and evangelization.*

Three nationwide plenary councils (1852, 1866, 1884) were also held at Baltimore, with the archbishop of Baltimore in each instance named by the pope as apostolic delegate* and president. Their legislation, binding on all U.S. dioceses,

reinforced general Roman Catholic doctrinal and disciplinary norms. The 1866 council attempted to adapt to the American scene some of the strictures contained in Pope Pius IX's 1864 syllabus of errors, a listing of condemnations reflecting the situation of the church in Europe. Encouragement was given to opening seminaries* and staffing diocesan offices and to the operation of separate schools on all levels. Uniform laws governing church marriages* were adopted. The 1884 plenary council insisted that every parish open a parochial grade school; it also authorized the beginning of the Catholic University of America,* which opened in 1889. All legislation of the councils of Baltimore was subject to review in Rome before it took effect in the church in the U.S. These reviews provided Roman officials with the opportunity to insist that practice in the U.S. conform to universal church norms.

Provincial councils have been infrequent, and there has been no plenary council since 1884. The archbishops of the U.S. met annually after 1890 until World War 1,* and a more formal organization developed from the National Catholic War Council, organized to coordinate church cooperation in providing social services in the 1917-1918 war effort. The War Council, a heavily lay-staffed operation, marked the first substantial cooperation of an official Roman Catholic entity with similar efforts of other church groups. Reorganized as the National Catholic Welfare Conference* (NCWC), with a Washington secretariat and the nation's bishops meeting annually under its aegis, the conference provided an umbrella for national Catholic organizations and was used as a vehicle for statements on major social issues.

Modern Conciliar Tradition. In 1966, after the Second Vatican Council encouraged establishment of permanent bishops' conferences, the National Council was succeeded by the National Conference of Catholic Bishops* (NCCB), with the U.S. Catholic Conference* (USCC) as its operational arm. The generally liberal democratic cast of the USCC staff has drawn fire from right-wing Catholics for the orientation of many of its projects and pronouncements. Two pastoral letters issued by the bishops on war and peace (1983) and on the economy (1986) sparked lively debate.

American bishops attended the First* (1869-1870) and Second* (1962-1965) Vatican Councils, where their approach was primarily pastoral and pragmatic. At Vatican I most saw definition of papal primacy and infallibility* as unnecessary and potentially harmful to interreligious relations at home; several objected strenuously that the doctrines were not in the tradition. At Vatican II American Catholics, as well as guest observers from several U.S. religious traditions, made substantial contributions to documents on ecumenism* and relations with non-Christians. American Jesuit John Courtney Murray* was a principal author of the conciliar declaration on religious liberty.*

Since 1967 bishops from the U.S. have participated actively in the series of international synods of bishops held in Rome. Less successful have been efforts to incorporate laity and priests in collegial meetings. A proposal in 1970 for a national pastoral council* came to nothing; the 1976 "Call to Action" conference, part of an ambitious bicentennial project, fell prey to special-interest coups and had little impact. While in technical terms the Catholic Church in the U.S. has an impressive conciliar record, it has yet to develop broader sharing of responsibility with all its members.

See also BALTIMORE, COUNCILS OF; NATIONAL CATHOLIC WELFARE CONFERENCE; VATICAN I; VATICAN II.

BIBLIOGRAPHY. P. Guilday, *A History of the Councils of Baltimore 1791-1884* (1932); J. Hennesey, "Councils of Baltimore," *NCE;* J. Hennesey, "Councils in America," *A National Pastoral Council Pro and Con* (1971); J. Hennesey, "The Baltimore Conciliar Tradition," *Annuarium Historiae Conciliorum* 3 (1971):71-88.

J. Hennesey

Cone, James Hal (1938-). African-American theologian.* Born in Fordyce, Arkansas, Cone graduated from Philander Smith College (B.A., 1958) and Garrett Theological Seminary (B.D., 1961) and did graduate work at Northwestern University (M.A., 1961; Ph.D., 1965). After academic appointments at Philander Smith College (1964-1966) and Adrian College (1966-1969), in 1969 Cone joined the faculty of Union Theological Seminary,* New York. Since 1977 he has been Charles A. Briggs* Professor of Systematic Theology at Union. He is a member of the African Methodist Episcopal Church.*

Cone is widely considered to be the originator of the contemporary expression of black theology,* one of the very few authentically indigenous American theological movements. His writings, among which are *Black Theology and Black Power* (1969); *A Black Theology of Liberation* (1970); and *God of the Oppressed* (1975), are recognized as near-normative formulations of the concepts central to black theology. Viewing black theology in conjunction with African-American history and black power, he writes: "Black theology places our

past and *present* actions toward Black liberation in a theological context, seeking to create value-structures according to the God of Black freedom."

Cone is extensively indebted to Karl Barth's* Christocentric theology, an influence that may be seen in the foundational role Jesus' proclamation of release to the captives (Lk 4:18-19) plays in his own theological formulations. Furthermore, the discernable relationship in the Old Testament between the spiritual, economic, political and social dimensions of human existence (pre-eminently illustrated in the exodus event), figures significantly in Cone's contention that the Bible* unmistakably witnesses to God's commitment to the poor and the oppressed. Cone maintains that in twentieth-century America, Christ would identify with blackness—the most effective symbol of that divine commitment.

Cone's theses have been widely debated by other African-American scholars. James Deotis Roberts, on the one hand, insists that to be Christian, black theology must speak of reconciliation between races as fervently as it does of liberation for African-American people. Cain Felder, on the other hand, laments Cone's failure to espouse violence as an option in the struggle for freedom. As a result of these debates and ongoing dialog with Latin American theologians of liberation,* feminist theologians and black scholars from Africa and the Caribbean, Cone's position continues to evolve and mature. More recently he has spoken of having developed a more inclusive perspective on social problems, enabling him to recognize a close interconnection between racism, sexism, imperialism and monopolistic capitalism. From this perspective he is critical of his earlier near-exclusive concern for the race issue (*My Soul Looks Back,* 1982).

Cone continues to pursue his major thesis that liberation of the oppressed is inherent in the gospel message. He remains a powerful voice calling the church at large into dialog regarding the issue of liberation.   V. A. Cruz

Confession of 1967. Most recent theological standard of the Presbyterian Church (USA).* At the one hundred seventieth General Assembly* (1958) which merged the United Presbyterian Church of North America and the Presbyterian Church in the USA, a committee was commissioned to draft a brief contemporary confession* of faith. In 1965 the committee presented a draft of the Confession, along with a proposal to create a Book of Confessions, to the General Assembly. A revised draft of the Confession was submitted in

1966. By June 1967 the Confession of 1967 had been ratified by all but 19 (who rejected it) of 184 presbyteries. The Confession and Book of Confessions was accepted by the 1967 General Assembly.

Its preface acknowledges the historical particularity of all creeds* and singles out eight earlier church statements to serve with it as the theological guides of the Church. The Confession's overriding theme is Christian reconciliation, the "peculiar need" of its generation. Four contemporary situations are pinpointed as urgently requiring such reconciliation, that is, the discrimination dividing the family of humanity, conflict between nations, "enslaving poverty" in an affluent world, and male-female relations. The Confession regards the Bible as "the witness without parallel," yet in the "words of men" and so approachable only "with literary and historical understanding." It also notes that the Church universal organizes its ministry with a variety of acceptable forms, though the presbyterian polity* is especially suited to promote "the responsibility of all members for ministry," to foster "the organic relation of all congregations in the church," and to protect against "exploitation by ecclesiastical or secular power and ambition."

Conservatives resisted the Confession on a number of counts, including what they determined to be a weakening of the orthodox* view of the authority* of Scripture* and the deity of Christ, an absence of reference to the virgin birth, a discarding of the doctrine of predestination* and a possible compromise of Presbyterian polity. Questions were also raised regarding the role of the church as an agent of reconciliation in the social and political arena.

BIBLIOGRAPHY. E. A. Dowey, Jr., *A Commentary on the Confession of 1967 and an Introduction to the "Book of Confessions"* (1968); J. B. Rogers, *Presbyterian Creeds: A Guide to the Book of Confessions* (1985). M. J. Coalter

Confessionalism. The practice of defining a religious body's faith and identity by reaffirming historical creeds* and confessions of faith. In addition to the ancient ecumenical creeds, the Lutheran* and Reformed* bodies of Europe ascribed to their own confessions. The historic Lutheran bodies have ascribed to the confessions making up their Book of Concord (1580). The Dutch Reformed have adhered to the Heidelberg Catechism, The Belgic Confession and The Canons of Dort. Presbyterians and, to a lesser degree, Congregationalists, have held to the Westminster Confession of Faith.*

The issue of confessions and confessionalism became particularly acute during the eighteenth and nineteenth centuries when the historic Protestant denominations were challenged by the rise of liberalism* on the one hand and revivalism* on the other. For example, during the Great Awakening,* the Scottish and Scotch-Irish Presbyterians,* known as the "Old Side,"* responded to revivalism by enforcing the Adopting Act* (1728-1729), which stipulated the degree of confessional subscription to the Westminster Confession required by candidates for ordination, and by requiring that revivalist Log College* graduates submit their credentials to a synodical reviewing committee before licensure and ordination. The nineteenth-century Princeton Theology* again maintained a confessional orthodoxy in the face of Arminianism,* revivalism and liberal innovation.

Lutherans also fought a battle for the constitutive elements of their tradition. In the New World they too were faced with the conversionist orientation of evangelical* Pietism* or revivalism. In this new environment some Lutherans continued to maintain a conservative confessionalism while others, like the groups that later became the Lutheran Church in America, learned to adapt to their new environment and combine confessionalism with Pietism.

The most popular forms of American Protestantism have been conversionist rather than confessional, oriented toward a direct personal experience of God rather than subscription to a creed.

The Editors

Confessor. A person, usually a priest,* to whom one confesses sin. When the early Christian communities suffered severe persecution, the title "confessor" was given to those who despite great suffering did not deny their Savior and their faith. Those who did were called "lapsed" and were often excluded from their local churches as a result. A custom arose whereby the lapsed might be reintroduced to their local churches by asking the confessors to intercede for them. When the early Roman persecutions subsided, the title of confessor was later used to describe outstanding Christians whose lives were models for others. In more modern times, Catholics and others use the title to designate the priest to whom one confesses one's sins. The meaning is that the confessor's own life and wisdom are such that he can be a confidant, trusted advisor or spiritual guide.

BIBLIOGRAPHY. E. Day, "Confessor," *NCE;* J. Sudbrack, *Spiritual Guidance* (1983).

B. Moran

Confirmation. A post-baptismal sacrament* or rite of prayer* and ecclesiastical laying on of hands,* and sometimes anointing.* Reflecting its uncertain origin, confirmation has been associated variously with (1) the reception, strengthening, sealing, gifts or anointing of the Spirit (Orthodox,* Catholic,* high Anglican*); (2) the fulfillment and appropriation of baptism* and preparation for the first reception of Holy Communion* (Catholic, Anglican, Lutheran*); (3) the increasing of sanctifying grace to equip the baptized believer to faithfully live the Christian life (Catholic); (4) the personal affirmation and confession of faith required for active church membership* (traditional American Protestant*); and/or (5) the ordination* of the laity* for service in the world (recent Protestant).

Confirmation seems to have grown out of chrismation rites (the making of the sign of the cross on the forehead with oil) associated with the reception of the Spirit, which were part of baptism in the early church. In Eastern Orthodoxy this connection is still maintained. Perhaps due to the requirement that it be administered by a bishop,* Western confirmation gradually became more clearly distinct from baptism in the Middle Ages. In the Reformation it was associated with the baptized child's need for catechetical instruction before assuming the full responsibility of adult church membership (*See* Catechism; Catechist). Since then it has commonly been administered to older children or teens in Western churches.

In most American denominations there is widely acknowledged uncertainty as to the contemporary role of confirmation in Christian nurture* and worship.* This has led to a re-emphasis on: (1) personal public reaffirmation of the baptismal covenant in its call to lifelong discipleship; (2) the Spirit's strengthening and bestowal of gifts for witness and service; (3) extensive catechetical training through both experiential and more traditional educational approaches; and (4) thorough integration into the worship, fellowship and service of the larger community of faith.

BIBLIOGRAPHY. J. D. C. Fisher, *Confirmation, Then and Now* (1978); K. B. Cully, ed., *Confirmation Re-Examined* (1982); D. G. Bloesch, *The Reform of the Church* (1970). P. W. Butin

Confraternity of Christian Doctrine. A Catholic association concerned with the religious education of Catholics, particularly youth who do not attend a Catholic elementary or high school. Originating in 1905, the Confraternity of Christian Doctrine (CCD) evolved as the primary means of providing formal religious education* through the local parish* for millions of American Catholics, from preschool children to adults. To counteract the lack of religious training, Pope Pius X* ordered every parish to establish a CCD unit which would enlist the help of lay* persons, trained and guided by clergy,* who would conduct religious education classes for an hour or two weekly as well as in summer vacation schools. It was not until the 1930s, however, that the U.S. Catholic Church began to develop its CCD national movement. In 1935 a national center, under Archbishop* Edwin V. O'Hara,* was established as a bureau of the National Catholic Welfare Conference* and a first national Catechetical Congress was held at Rochester, New York.

Catechetical* materials and texts for teaching are produced through the auspices of the national CCD Center for use by parishes and dioceses.* Traditionally, the Baltimore Catechism and its revised version, with their question-and-answer formats, have provided the foundational texts for CCD teachers. In recent years, scriptural and liturgical materials have gained more attention and use as a result of the emphases of Vatican II.* Although its organizational strengths and effectiveness differ from parish to parish and diocese* to diocese, the CCD has, more than any other vehicle for service, afforded lay persons an opportunity to participate in the church's educational ministry prior to Vatican II.

BIBLIOGRAPHY. J. E. Kraus, "Confraternity of Christian Doctrine," *NCE* 4; J. B. Collins, *The Kerygmatic Renewal and the CCD* (1962).

M. L. Schneider

Congregation for Divine Worship. Catholic* administrative body. Formerly known as the Congregation of Sacred Rites, the Congregation, consisting of a cardinal* prefect and a number of other prelates and based in the Vatican, has two functions. It is responsible for the supervision of the liturgy* of the Catholic Church, including all ceremonies, rites and celebrations of the church, with the object of ensuring that the sacred rites and ceremonies are carefully observed in all that pertains to the worship of the Latin Church. In this capacity, it approves of liturgical service books and also has jurisdiction over any new liturgical offices and calendars. It resolves any doubts which may arise regarding liturgical matters. A recent important task of this body was the revision of the liturgy, as ordered by Vatican II* in 1963. Its second function pertains to the beatification* and canonization* of specific individuals. It investigates the background of candidates for sainthood, and based on its research, including that of the "Devil's Advocate," it recommends candidates to the pope* for beatification or canonization.

BIBLIOGRAPHY. F. R. McManus, "Rites, Congregation of," *NCE* 12.　　　　C. E. Ronan

Congregation for the Doctrine of the Faith.

The name applies to a Catholic agency, formerly known as the Holy Office and located in the Vatican, whose task is to assist the pope* and the whole church in preserving the integrity of doctrines* concerning faith and morals.

While it is the responsibility of local pastors,* bishops* and national groupings of bishops to oversee and promote sound doctrinal teaching, a need for a church-wide office was felt at the time of the Protestant Reformation. Pope Paul III established what is considered the earliest permanent structure in 1542, a Roman commission composed of six cardinals,* called the Congregation of the Roman and Universal Inquisition, or the Holy Office. The pope saw this originally as a temporary agency with the task of maintaining and defending the integrity of faith until the reform Council of Trent* was organized. The Holy Office had the power to investigate, call witnesses and punish deviants.

After the Council of Trent, the Roman Holy Office continued in existence, not to be confused with the Spanish Inquisition, an agency of the Spanish crown first established to detect Jews and Muslims suspected of false conversions. Pope Paul VI* in 1965 renamed the office Congregation for the Doctrine of the Faith and reformed its procedures. The pope is at the head but assisted by a presiding cardinal and ten others. This group can be enlarged, depending on needs, to include an international body of consultors.

Pope Paul VI's mandate to the Congregation for the Doctrine of the Faith makes the promotion of authentic Christian teaching a priority. The agency is also supposed to alert the church to errors. Therefore it can examine new teachings and make judgments about books and authors. In matters of faith and morality, this Congregation can issue various types of decisions, some relating to individual authors, others providing directives for the whole church.

BIBLIOGRAPHY. U. Beste, "Doctrine of the Faith, Congregation for the," *NCE* 4.　　B. Moran

Congregation of Holy Cross. Roman Catholic*

religious order. Founded in 1837 by Basil Moreau, a priest* of the diocese* of Le Mans, France, the Congregation of Holy Cross is a union of two previously existing institutes, the Brothers of St. Joseph and the Auxiliary Priests of Le Mans. The new community's center was at Sainte-Croix (Holy Cross), a suburb of Le Mans, from which it took its name. An institute of women, the Marianite Sisters of Holy Cross, was added in 1841. At the insistence of the Vatican, the women were reorganized in 1857 as an autonomous institute.

In 1841, seven members, under the leadership of Edward F. Sorin,* were sent to work in the diocese of Vincennes, Indiana. Their first permanent foundation was at Notre Dame, Indiana, in 1842, where they opened a school. It was chartered in 1844 as the University of Notre Dame du Lac (*See* University of Notre Dame). Long active as educators, the congregation started or took on the direction of seven other colleges and universities in the U.S.: St. Joseph's College, Cincinnati, Ohio (1871-1920); University of Our Lady of the Sacred Heart, Watertown, Wisconsin (1872-1912); St. Edward's University, Austin, Texas (1876-); Holy Cross College, New Orleans, Louisiana (1879-1912); University of Portland, Portland, Oregon (1901-); King's College, Wilkes-Barre, Pennsylvania (1946-); and Stonehill College, North Easton, Massachusetts (1948-). In addition, the community directs more than twenty high schools and serves more than thirty-five parishes in the U.S.

As of 1986, the congregation numbered 1,922 members, more than eighty-five per cent of whom were in the U.S. and Canada. The community is also established in France, Italy, Bangladesh, India, Brazil, Chile, Haiti, Peru, Ghana, Kenya, Liberia and Uganda.

BIBLIOGRAPHY. E. and T. Catta, *Basil Anthony Mary Moreau* (1955); A. Hope, *Notre Dame One Hundred Years* (1943).　　　J. T. Connelly

Congregation of Sacred Rites. *See* CONGREGATION FOR DIVINE WORSHIP.

Congregation of the Missionary Society of St. Paul the Apostle. An officially recognized association of Roman Catholic* priests* and seminarians. Popularly called "Paulists," the Congregation was founded in 1858 in the state of New York by Isaac Thomas Hecker.* Raised as a Protestant,* Hecker made a spiritual quest in late adolescence that led him to become a Catholic at age twenty-five. In 1849 Hecker joined the Redemptorist* religious order* and was ordained* a priest.* He and four other Redemptorist priests, also converts* to Catholicism, engaged in preaching* and teaching, primarily among Catholic German immi-

grants.* However, differences in goals brought Hecker and his friends into conflict with the Redemptorists and in 1858, with papal approval, they established the Congregation of the Missionary Society of St. Paul the Apostle. Convinced that fair-minded people would be attracted to Catholicism if it were explained properly, Hecker and his companions began this task. In 1865 Hecker began publishing *Catholic World* (now *The New Catholic World*), and in 1866 he founded a publishing house, now known as the Paulist Press.

After Hecker's death in 1888, the Paulists grew and established bases for their work from coast to coast in the United States and Canada. Men joining the Paulist Fathers receive theological training and live by a constitution which governs their work, their use of money and their living arrangements. Recent reassessment of Hecker's hopes and aims has led the Paulists to affirm three main emphases for their lives and work: (1) reconciliation of Catholics alienated from the church; (2) evangelism*—bringing gospel truth to the people, institutions and cultures of North America; and (3) ecumenism,* the search for the unity God wills for the church. Members now number about 230 and work in parish* settings as well as in universities, the media, information centers, ecumenical ventures and evangelism.

See also HECKER, ISAAC THOMAS.

BIBLIOGRAPHY. V. F. Holden, *The Yankee Paul, Isaac Thomas Hecker* (1958); J. Farina, *An American Experience of God, the Spirituality of Isaac Hecker* (1981); J. McSorley, *Isaac Hecker and His Friends* (1951).   B. Moran

Congregational Home Missionary Society.
See AMERICAN HOME MISSIONARY SOCIETY.

Congregationalism.
A Protestant* tradition of ecclesiology and church government,* Congregationalism maintains that local congregations, consisting of men and women who acknowledge the Lordship of Jesus Christ and seek his will, can minister* and govern themselves through congregational vote, covenant and participation. Congregationalists view this polity* as a more complete fulfillment of the Reformation principle of the priesthood of all believers.* Although there are specific Congregational denominations,* this type of church government can also be found in many other churches and denominations in America, particularly among Baptist* and independent churches. This article will focus, however, on historic Congregationalism in America and its present manifestation in the United Church of

Christ* and the smaller Congregational fellowships and denominations.

Historic Congregationalism came to America with the Separatist* Pilgrims* of Plymouth and the Puritans* of the Massachusetts Bay Colony. Congregationalism originated in English Puritanism, being the more radical wing of a Reformed* movement that believed it impossible to renew the Church of England* from within. Choosing rather to form "gathered" congregations bound by a covenant between God and believers, these nonconformists came into conflict with the Anglican Church, including Anglicans of Puritan persuasion. By 1608 a group of Separatists had taken refuge from persecution at Leiden in the Netherlands. In 1620 a band of Pilgrims settled in Plymouth, Massachusetts. In 1629, the nonseparatist English Puritans, fleeing persecution under Archbishop William Laud (1573-1645) in England, established settlements around Boston, Massachusetts. These American Puritans ordained* their ministers* congregationally, even when the latter had already been ordained episcopally in England. In the rigorous living conditions of New England, the two groups found themselves cooperating with each other and agreeing on the central points of Calvinism* as it was mediated by the English Puritan divines.

From 1646 to 1648 the religious leaders of New England met several times in a synod* at Cambridge, Massachusetts, and there decided to accept the Westminster Confession of Faith* as their doctrinal* statement. They also drafted and adopted the "Platforme of Church Discipline"—better known as the "Cambridge Platform"*—defining their polity.* Codifying the "mixed" polity of Puritan theorists, they described a government of local, independent churches that was shared by church members and church officers. It is the earliest document setting forth American Congregational faith and church government and served as the constitution of the "Congregational Way" well into the nineteenth century.

The Great Awakening,* which peaked in the years 1740-1742 and spread thoughout the colonies, had a great impact on New England Congregationalism. On the one hand there was the revival* of a heart-felt religion that was profoundly evangelical* in character. The Congregationalist minister and theologian* of the movement, Jonathan Edwards,* was perhaps the greatest intellect early American Congregationalism produced, and he set the agenda for the tradition of New England Theology* that was carried on well into the nineteenth century. On the other hand, a significant number of Congregational clergy* opposed the revivals, and a rift developed that was to seriously divide Congregationalism into liberal and evangelical wings and profoundly affect American religious and political life in general.

This liberalism, centered in eighteenth-century Boston, was fueled by Enlightenment* ideas and manifested itself first in a liberalized Calvinism and then in an Arian or Socinian view of the person of Christ. The chief leaders of this movement were the Congregational ministers Charles Chauncy* and Jonathan Mayhew.* The appointment of Unitarian Henry Ward* to the chair of divinity* at Harvard* in 1803, the publication of William E. Channing's* manifesto, *Unitarian Christianity,* in 1819 and the Dedham Decision* of 1820 in which the Massachusetts Supreme Court awarded the property of a Trinitarian congregation to a Unitarian parish, were all landmarks in the gradual move toward the founding of a separate American Unitarian Association* in 1825.

In the nineteenth century, Congregationalism was again influenced by theological liberalism, the leading voice being that of Congregational minister Horace Bushnell,* called by some "the father of American religious liberalism." His controversial views on the Trinity, the atonement,* conversion* and the nature of religious language were widely influential, first in the seminaries* and then in the pulpits. Other influential liberal ministers of late nineteenth-century Congregationalism were Henry Ward Beecher* and Washington Gladden,* the latter developing Bushnell's romantic notions of evolutionary progress into the Social Gospel.* Liberalism has continued to hold a prominent place in twentieth-century Congregationalism, though in recent decades it has traded its earlier optimism for a more chastened mood.

Although the modified Calvinism of colonial times was intentionally left behind by the Congregational mainstream, evangelicals* and evangelical theology has maintained a presence within Congregationalism. The Congregational "Burial Hill Declaration"* (1865) proclaimed, "With the whole church we confess the common sinfulness and ruin of our race, and acknowledge that it is only through the work accomplished by the life and expiatory death of Christ that believers in Him are justified before God, receive the remission of sins, and through the presence and grace of the Holy Comforter are delivered from the power of sin and perfected in holiness." These beliefs are echoed in the contemporary United Church of Christ's Statement of Faith (1959) when it speaks of confessing a belief in God who seeks "in holy love to save all people from aimlessness and sin" and in Jesus Christ "conquering sin and death and reconciling the world to Himself." Although a minority, evangelical churches and individuals continue within contemporary Congregational fellowships and denominations, with notable evangelical leaders such as Harold John Ockenga* (1905-1985) and theologian Donald G. Bloesch (1928-) representing this tradition.

Concern for the proclamation of the gospel has always been present in Congregationalism, and early Congregational Puritans were concerned to take the gospel to the Native American population. The Protestant foreign-mission movement* in America arose among Congregationalists when in 1810 the American Board of Commissioners for Foreign Missions* was organized. In 1812 the Board sent out five missionaries, two of whom had dedicated themselves to missionary service in the "Haystack Prayer Meeting"* of 1806. While the Board was originally predominantly Congregational, a number of other Reformed* denominations used it until they had formed their own agencies.

In 1801, under the Plan of Union,* Congregationalists cooperated with Presbyterians* in frontier missionary work. Finding that Congregationalism was being swallowed up in Presbyterianism, however, the Congregationalists repealed the agreement at the Albany Convention of 1852. One of the fruits of this earlier cooperative spirit was the American Home Missionary Society,* which was established in 1826 in conjunction with the Presbyterians, but after 1861 became the church planting agency of the Congregational churches. In 1846, the American Missionary Association* was established. Committed to evangelism* to non-whites and strongly abolitionist,* after the Civil War* it carried out a noble effort to educate former slaves. Currently the United Church of Christ carries out its mission work through the Board of World Ministries and the Board of Homeland Ministries, the successors of the earlier boards, along with mission work done by the other Congregational denominations and fellowships.

Feeling the need to organize and work with each other in wider ministries, American Congregational churches from their inception have formed fellowships beyond the local church. Starting first with the colonial consociations and associations, by 1822 the first state conference was held in Maine. In 1871, the National Council of Congregational Churches was formed, serving the interests of the churches in national, international and other delegated tasks. In 1913, meeting in Kansas City, the National Council was given a broader mandate in the work of the Church. A general secretary was chosen to represent the churches before other groups. The present United Church of Christ actively continues programs and agencies on a national level.

In the late nineteenth century, Congregationalists began to consider whether their fellowship might not extend beyond their National Council. As early as 1871 the National Council at Oberlin produced a "Declaration on the Unity of the Church" and began consultations with other denominations, many of which were unsuccessful. Two consultations did, however, lead to later developments. Talks with a Restorationist* group, the Christian Connection,* were carried out in 1890 and again in 1923, finally leading to a merger of the two bodies in 1931 when they formed the General Council of Congregational and Christian Churches.

In 1938 a union of the General Council of Congregational and Christian Churches with the Evangelical and Reformed Church was proposed, but it was not until 1957 that a body of delegates from both denominations, meeting at Cleveland, Ohio, elected a constitutional committee. In July 1961, in Philadelphia, a constitution was adopted and the United Church of Christ was established. Consultations with the Disciples of Christ,* which broke down in 1895, were again revived in 1977. In the late 1980s the two denominations were actively exploring avenues of cooperation.

Congregational polity continued to be modified as it developed in American history. The "Statement of Congregational Principles" or "Boston Platform" (1865) superseded the Cambridge Platform and proclaimed three affirmations: (1) the local church derives its power and authority* directly from Christ; (2) there must be duties of respect and charity included in a communion of churches; and (3) the ministry implies "no power of government." In contemporary practice, ministers are ordained and installed by the local church but "ministerial standing" is held by associations (sometimes by conferences) which cooperate in the ordination or installation. Organizations beyond the local church (associations, conferences, general synod) speak for themselves but not for the local churches. The constitution and bylaws of the United Church of Christ further define this relationship of both mutual cooperation and congregational independence.

Other Congregational churches and fellowships of churches in the Congregational tradition continue to exist apart from the United Church of Christ. These have either remained independent or have joined the loose fellowships of the National Association of Congregational Churches (noted for its "referendum council" which allows local churches to modify any act of national bodies) and the Conservative Congregational Christian Conference* (noted for its mutual confession of a more comprehensive and conservative doctrinal statement). The United Church of Christ, along with these other fellowships, have appropriated, each in its own way, various strands of historic American Congregationalism.

BIBLIOGRAPHY. G. G. Atkins and F. L. Fagley, *History of American Congregationalism* (1942); D. Horton, *The United Church of Christ: Its Origins, Organization and Role in the Church Today* (1962); M. L. Starkey, *The Congregational Way: The Role of the Pilgrims and Their Heirs in Shaping America* (1966); W. W. Sweet, *The Congregationalists* (1939); W. Walker, *The Creeds and Platforms of Congregationalism* (1893).

L. E. Wilshire

Congress of National Black Churches. Black ecumenical* organization. The Congress of National Black Churches (CNBC) was formed in December 1978 by black churchmen and scholars participating in a Consultation on Interdenominational Dialogue in Atlanta, Georgia. An African Methodist Episcopal bishop,* John Hurst Adams, was the first chairman. The name of the organization denotes a continuing forum for leaders of black denominations* with national constituencies. Presently, member denominations are the African Methodist Episcopal Church,* African Methodist Episcopal Zion Church,* Christian Methodist Episcopal Church,* Church of God in Christ,* National Baptist Convention of America* and Progressive National Baptist Convention, Inc.

CNBC is distinctive among black ecumenical organizations in that the conciliar model brings together the top ecclesiastical authorities of the major denominations. Like other black ecumenical efforts, however (e.g., National Conference of Black Christians, Partners in Ecumenism, National Black Evangelical Association*), CNBC is concerned with neither doctrinal conformity nor structural merger, but with cooperative social and economic action to empower the black community. Convocations are held annually. Program activities are administered through seven task forces: Theological Education, Evangelism in the Black Perspective, Stewardship of Black Resources, Communications, Human Development and Social Concerns, Public and Higher Education, and International Affairs. The dominant emphasis is on economic institution-building, including collective insurance, purchasing, banking and community development programs. The Congress Press is a commercial publishing venture based on a coalition of the six individual denominational presses. Other priorities are training and education of black clergy* and support of the black family. National offices are maintained in Washington, D.C.

BIBLIOGRAPHY. M. R. Sawyer, "Black Ecumenism: Cooperative Social Change Movements in the Black Church" (unpublished Ph.D. dissertation, Duke University Divinity School, 1986).

M. R. Sawyer

Connecticut Missionary Society. Early nineteenth-century organization that funded missions to the American West. Founded in 1798 by the General Association of the Congregational* Church, the Connecticut Missionary Society was the largest and most expansive of the New England missionary organizations established in the early nineteenth century in response to growing concern about the moral fate of the Western territories. Although chartered with the dual purpose of evangelizing the Native Americans and establishing churches in the new American settlements, the Society concentrated its efforts on American settlers.

The first missionaries were sent on four- to eight-week tours, preaching* the gospel and distributing thousands of religious books and tracts.* Although initiated by the Congregationalists, under the Plan of Union* (1801), the majority of Western churches adopted Presbyterian* status, and many others retained a hybrid or "presbygational" polity. The Western Reserve of Connecticut was an area of early concern. Joseph Badger, the first missionary to Ohio, described a strenuous year of itinerant preaching among sparsely settled communities in his *Memoir of Joseph Badger* (1851). Other notable missionaries included Timothy Flint and Salmon Giddings, whose travels in 1815-1816 in Missouri represented the western terminus of the Society's efforts. The Society gradually adopted a circuit-style organization out of a desire to cover more effectively the expanding Western territories, and thereafter it funded settled ministers* who preached to a number of churches on a semi-regular basis. In 1826, in keeping with a widespread effort to nationalize missionary resources and prevent the duplication of efforts, the Society became an auxiliary of the American Home Missionary Society.*

BIBLIOGRAPHY. C. B. Goodykoontz, *Home Missions on the American Frontier* (1839); K. S.

Latourette, *The Great Century* (1941); W. W. Sweet, *Religion on the American Frontier, 1783-1840,* 4 vols. (1946). L. F. Maffly-Kipp

Connelly, Cornelia Augusta Peacock (1809-1879). Roman Catholic* convert,* founder of the Society of the Holy Child Jesus. Born in Philadelphia, Cornelia received an excellent education. Her marriage in 1831 to Pierce Connelly, an Episcopal* priest,* produced five children, and in 1834-1835 both Connellys converted to Catholicism. As a result of Pierce's decision to become a Catholic priest, Cornelia professed a solemn vow of chastity in Rome, June 18, 1845. Although she thought of establishing a religious* congregation in America, Cornelia was persuaded by Nicholas Wiseman to open the first Convent of the Holy Child in Derby, England, in 1846.

Pierce, having taken the children and left the Catholic Church, in 1848 instigated the sensational case of "Connelly vs. Connelly," an appeal for the restoration of conjugal rights, which was finally dismissed in 1858. Despite this trial and long years of dispute over the constitutions of the new Society, Cornelia succeeded in establishing a religious order* which provided teacher training and first-rate education for all classes, as outlined in her *Book of the Order of Studies in Schools of the Society of the Holy Child Jesus* (1863). Upon her death at St. Leonard's-on-Sea, near Hastings, there were houses of her congregation in England, the United States and France. The cause for her canonization* was introduced in 1959.

BIBLIOGRAPHY. *DAB* II; C. McCarthy, *The Spirituality of Cornelia Connelly: In God, For God, With God* (1986); *Positio: Documentary Study for the Canonization Process of the Servant of God, Cornelia Connelly (neé Peacock), 1809-1879* 3 vols. (1983). P. Byrne

Conner, Walter Thomas (1877-1952). Baptist* theologian* and educator. Born in Rowell, Arkansas, Conner lived most of his life in Texas. Ordained* in 1899, he attended Simmons College and graduated from Baylor University (A.B., 1906), Baylor Theological Seminary (Th.B., A.M., 1908), Rochester Theological Seminary (B.D., 1910) and Southern Baptist Theological Seminary (Th.D., 1916; Ph.D., 1931). He studied briefly at the University of Chicago.*

Conner served as pastor of several small churches, but his greatest contributions came through thirty-nine years of teaching (1910-1949) at Southwestern Baptist Theological Seminary. A frequent contributor to theological journals, a popular teacher and a dedicated scholar who stayed abreast of theological developments, Conner published fifteen books, including: *A System of Christian Doctrine* (1924); *Revelation and God* (1936); *Christian Doctrine* (1937); *The Faith of the New Testament* (1940); *The Gospel of Redemption* (1945); *The Work of the Holy Spirit* (1949); and *The Cross in the New Testament* (1954), edited by Jesse J. Northcutt.

Strongly influenced by professors John S. Tanner at Baylor, Augustus H. Strong* at Rochester and E. Y. Mullins* at Southern, Conner took a conservative but progressive approach to theology.* He essentially set forth a strong Christocentric theology rooted in the incarnation and atonement. He viewed Scripture* as authoritative for faith and practice but defended no fixed view of inspiration. Through his teaching and writing he shaped the theology of thousands of Southern Baptists, becoming one of the most influential and respected Southern Baptist theologians of the twentieth century.

BIBLIOGRAPHY. S. A. Newman, *W. T. Conner: Theologian of the Southwest* (1964); J. J. Northcutt, "Walter Thomas Conner, Theologian of Southwestern," *SwJT* 9:1 (Fall 1966):81-89.

C. L. Howe

Conscience. A human faculty or capacity used in judging how to live morally. Puritan* anthropology assumed with Medieval thinkers that the human personality was composed of five "faculties," one of which was the conscience. For them conscience functioned in a mechanical fashion, sorting out moral issues and providing solutions to them. Consciences had to be trained and pastors had many "cases of conscience" which they used in training their parishioners' consciences.

At the time Puritans settled New England there were two important views of how conscience functioned. William Perkins,* a leading seventeenth-century Puritan divine, argued that conscience had to be informed through instruction and left free to decide right and wrong for itself. This he understood to be a proper stance in light of Scriptural teachings on Christian freedom. His student, William Ames,* took a different view, arguing that moral issues had one and only one answer. The Winthrop* party that settled in Boston followed Ames's view, effectively arguing that no such thing as "freedom of conscience" existed. This was evident in Winthrop's words to the antinomian* Anne Hutchinson*: "Your conscience you must keep or it will be kept for you."

In time, however, most Puritan settlers in America followed Perkins's view of freedom (liberty) of conscience—Roger Williams* being a prominent example. Following the Perkins-Williams tradition, James Madison argued for liberty of conscience in Congressional debates on the First Amendment* to the Federal Constitution. Others opposed him, arguing for mere toleration of conscientious dissent. Madison's view prevailed, as is evident in the religion (conscience) clause of the First Amendment.

Throughout the nineteenth century the concern for freedom of conscience remained within the context of Christian thought. During the twentieth century, however, public discourse regarding conscience has left its Christian heritage and become increasingly individualistic and relativistic.

BIBLIOGRAPHY. L. J. Van Til, *Liberty of Conscience: The History of a Puritan Idea* (1972); E. S. Morgan, *Roger Williams: The Church and State* (1967).

L. J. Van Til

Consecration. The act by which a person, a place or an object is set apart for holy use by ritual words and gestures. In Christian terminology, consecration generally denotes three more specific actions of the church. At the Lord's Supper, the eucharistic bread and wine are consecrated, in the Catholic tradition to become the presence of the body and blood of Jesus Christ for the Christian community. Some traditions have referred to the central prayer* of thanksgiving over the bread and wine as the "prayer of consecration," but the most recent revisions of liturgical texts have abandoned this term, since it tended to imply that the recitation of particular words constituted an isolated moment at which consecration occurred. Secondly, the term *consecration* has been applied to the rites by which certain individuals, traditionally bishops* and abbots, but now also missionaries* and other church workers, are inducted into office. And finally, church buildings, furnishings and musical instruments are dedicated for use in the worship* of God by rites of consecration.

S. J. White

Conservative Baptist Association of America. An association of approximately 1,200 Baptist* churches, chiefly in the Northern and Western areas of the U.S. Organized in Atlantic City, New Jersey, in 1947, the association is closely allied with the Conservative Baptist Foreign Mission Society; the Conservative Baptist Home Mission Society; Southwestern Bible College in Phoenix, Arizona; and three theological seminaries: Denver Seminary (Denver, Colorado), Western Seminary (Portland,

Oregon) and Eastern Conservative Baptist Seminary. The seven organizations constitute the Conservative Baptist "Movement." Total membership of the churches in the association is approximately 230,000, but thousands more in other congregations, providing financial support for the missions and schools, add to the total strength of the movement.

Conservative Baptists prefer to speak of their *movement* rather than their *denomination** because the CBA creates only a loose affiliation for its churches. Unlike most denominations, it has no unified budget for its cooperating agencies. Each of the schools and mission societies has its own budget and board of directors. Structurally, then, Conservative Baptists operate more as cooperating interdenominational agencies than as a traditional denomination.

The association emerged from the fundamentalist-modernist controversy* within the Northern (now American*) Baptist denomination. As early as 1921 conservative pastors within the convention attempted to establish doctrinal standards for the missionary* agencies of the Northern Baptist Convention. But several votes at annual conventions (1922-1925) proved fruitless. Then, in 1943, after renewed but unsuccessful attempts to create theological tests for the Northern Baptist missionary program, several hundred conservative churches formed the Conservative Baptist Foreign Mission Society. Pastor Richard Beal at the First Baptist Church of Tucson, Arizona, and Pastor Albert Johnson at Hinson Baptist Church in Portland, Oregon, assumed the leadership in this action.

The conservative association of churches was organized when it became apparent, at the Northern Baptist Convention meeting at Grand Rapids, Michigan (1946), that the older convention would not tolerate a competing missionary agency within its structures. In the following years hundreds of Northern Baptist churches left their national convention to join the conservatives. In Minnesota and Arizona, conservatives even captured the state conventions of the denomination.

Conservative Baptist agencies grew rapidly during the first fifteen years of independent ministry, but in the late 1950s internal conflict developed over acceptable affiliations outside the movement. The vast majority of Conservative Baptist churches cooperated with other denominations and parachurch* agencies in the National Association of Evangelicals,* and specifically with the Billy Graham Association.* A militant minority within Conservative Baptist circles, however,

insisted that such cooperation was dangerous and to be avoided. These were the fundamentalists* within Conservative Baptist circles. After seven years of intense debate over separation,* the militant minority, consisting of about 200 churches, found a new home in fundamentalistic circles.

During the 1970s Conservative Baptist schools and mission agencies shared in the resurgence of evangelicalism,* highlighted by the election of Jimmy Carter* to the presidency. In more recent years Conservative Baptists have supported annually nearly 1,000 career and short-term missionaries through their foreign and home missionary societies, and have enrolled over 1,000 students in their three seminaries.

BIBLIOGRAPHY. B. L. Shelley, *A History of Conservative Baptists* (1971); B. L. Shelley, *Founded on the Word, Focused on the World: The Story of CBFMS* (1978); A. W. Wardin, Jr., *Baptists in Oregon* (1969).

B. L. Shelley

Conservative Congregational Christian Conference. An evangelical* association of Congregational* churches. This group of churches and ministers* was organized in 1948 in order to provide a fellowship for evangelical churches and ministers who did not wish to become a part of the emerging United Church of Christ,* which brought together the General Council of Congregational and Christian Churches and the Evangelical and Reformed Church (1957). The Conservative Congregational Christian Conference arose out of an earlier fellowship formed in 1945 to maintain a biblical witness within the General Council of Congregational and Christian Churches. This fellowship itself had come out of an informal association of evangelicals which had existed within the regular Congregational denomination since the 1930s.

The Conference describes itself as a "fellowship of churches" and affirms its commitment to five principles in Congregationalism: (1) the necessity of a regenerate church membership*; (2) the authority of the Holy Scriptures; (3) the lordship of Christ; (4) the autonomy of the local church; and (5) the voluntary fellowship of believers. It subscribes to a seven-article statement of faith. In recent years a number of evangelical Bible* or community churches with congregational polity have joined the Conference, and in the late 1980s there were 170 churches and a total membership of approximately 29,000.

L. E. Wilshire

Consistent Calvinism. *See* HOPKINS, SAMUEL; NEW ENGLAND THEOLOGY.

Constantinides, Michael (1892-1958). Greek Orthodox* bishop.* A graduate of the Ecumenical patriarchate's Theological School on Halki and one of the last students of the Russian Theological Academy in Kiev before the Bolshevik Revolution of 1917, Constantinides' early ministry was exercised in war-ravaged Asia Minor following World War 1.* From 1927 to 1933 he was assigned to the Greek Orthodox Cathedral in London, England, and represented both the Ecumenical patriarchate and the Orthodox Church of Greece at various early ecumenical* gatherings, including Lausanne (1927) and Edinburgh (1937), and was present at Lambeth (1930). In his later years the challenge of Christian union continued to inspire him, and he represented the patriarchate at the first meeting of the World Council of Churches* in Evanston* (1954). During this period he translated several classics of Orthodox spirituality* into English.

Consecrated* metropolitan* of Corinth in 1939, he saw his flock through the horrible years of World War 2* and the Greek Revolution before being sent to New York in 1949 to succeed the newly enthroned Ecumenical Patriarch Athenagoras* as archbishop* of America. His nine-year tenure was marked by taking measures to stabilize the Archdiocese's finances and to promote the Hellenic spirit in parish* schools and through the founding of such organizations as the Greek Orthodox Youth of America (GOYA) and St. Basil's Academy (for orphans). Forever faithful to his love of the printed word, he founded the bilingual *Orthodox Observer* to serve as the diocesan newspaper.

BIBLIOGRAPHY. I. Konstantiknides, "Michael Constantinides," *Religious and Ethical Encyclopedia* 8 (1966):1213-1216 (in Greek).

P. D. Garrett

Constructive Theology. A theological movement which emerged in the mid-1970s. The movement originated with members of the Workshop on Constructive Theology. This group was formed in an attempt to promote collaborative work among systematic theologians* and to define issues that could benefit from their cooperative efforts. The group initially met in Nashville, Tennessee, with support from Vanderbilt University, but in 1978 its sponsorship was assumed by the Institute for Ecumenical and Cultural Research in Collegeville, Minnesota. Among the most prominent theologians included in the group were Edward Farley, Julian Hartt, Peter Hodgson, Sallie McFague, John Cobb, Langdon Gilkey, Gordon Kaufman, David Tracy, Schubert Ogden and Walter Lowe.

The perspective which unites the members of this movement is that theology, for all of its reliance on tradition, is a *constructive* project. At the heart of this contention is the view that the Scriptures* of the Old and New Testaments, along with their doctrinal interpretations, no longer occupy an indispensable place of authority* for Christian faith and practice. Since there is no longer any real consensus about the substance of Christian theology, what had previously been set down in the tradition cannot be taken for granted. Theology must be reshaped to meet the needs of the modern world. As applied to specific Christian doctrines, this means for example, that the doctrine of creation must be made consistent with the contemporary view of an open universe rather than the closed universe of religious and scientific tradition. The doctrine of the Christian life must be reconstructed so as to appeal to an environmental consciousness. The concept of God is a human construct like all other concepts and images and must, therefore, be recast so that it holds together contemporary patterns of human experience. The treatment of these and other Christian doctrines demonstrates that the primary problem with which constructive theology is dealing is the problem of theological method.

BIBLIOGRAPHY. P. Hodgson and R. King, *Christian Theology: An Introduction to Its Traditions and Tasks* (1985); G. Kaufman, *Theology for a Nuclear Age* (1985). J. F. Johnson

Consubstantiation. The doctrine* which teaches that the substance of the bread and the substance of the body are coexisting in the consecrated host at the Lord's Supper.* Using the Aristotelian terms of substance as opposed to the accidence of appearance, this doctrine is an alternative to transubstantiation,* which holds that the substance of the bread is wholly changed into the body of Christ, while retaining the accidence of the outward appearance of bread.

This doctrine is often erroneously described as the Lutheran* position on the real presence of Christ in the sacrament* of the altar,* but it is specifically rejected by the Lutheran confessions and all of the early Lutheran theologians,* who used the formula that Christ is really present "in, with and under" the bread but refused to speculate about the manner of Christ's presence or the relation between the substance of the bread and the substance of Christ's body. To such speculation, Luther said, "What does it matter? It is enough that it is a divine sign, in which Christ's flesh and blood are truly present—how and where, we leave to Him."

Lutheran theology,* following Luther, has always insisted that Christ's words "This is my body" be taken seriously, though how that can be true remains a mystery. The Zwinglian view that Christ's body is really present only in heaven and that his presence in the sacrament of the Lord's Supper is only a representation, was rejected by Luther at the Marburg Colloquy and has been by Lutheran theologians ever since.

See also LUTHERAN TRADITION.

BIBLIOGRAPHY. J. T. Mueller, *Christian Dogmatics* (1934); H. Sasse, *This Is My Body* (1957); H. Schmid, *The Doctrinal Theology of the Evangelical Lutheran Church* (1889).

J. D. Sutherland

Consultation on Church Union. A movement toward church union among mainline* U.S. churches. The Consultation on Church Union (COCU) grew out of a proposal for a united church "truly catholic, truly evangelical, and truly reformed" inspired by a sermon preached by Eugene Carson Blake* at Grace Cathedral (Episcopal), San Francisco, on December 4, 1960. In 1962, representatives from four churches gathered in Washington, D.C., for the first COCU plenary and established commissions to deal with the issues which effect reconciliation: faith, order and polity,* liturgy* and sacraments,* sociological and cultural factors, organization and power structures. These commissions and future plenaries produced *Principles of Church Union* (1966), which revealed a consensus on the issues of Scripture* and tradition; the threefold ministry* of bishops,* presbyters* and deacons*; the faith of the church and the sacraments*; *A Plan of Union for the Church of Christ Uniting* (1970), which tried to express this common vision of church in a new shape, but was judged by many to be too bureaucratic; and two ecumenical liturgies (1968, 1984) which have been used widely and with approval by the churches.

In recent years the nine COCU churches—African Methodist Episcopal,* African Methodist Episcopal Zion,* Christian Methodist Episcopal,* Christian Church (Disciples of Christ),* Episcopal,* International Council of Community Churches, Presbyterian (USA),* United Church of Christ* and United Methodist*—have submitted a theological text, *The COCU Consensus* (1984), to the assemblies of the churches for official reception.

At the seventeenth plenary in 1988 COCU called upon these churches to affirm "covenanting," a new concept of visible union which will draw them into new relationships made genuine by eight acts: mutually and publicly recognizing each as true churches; mutually recognizing each other's members and baptism*; claiming the theological consensus; sharing an inclusive life across racial and social barriers; mutually recognizing and reconciling ordained ministries; regularly celebrating eucharistic* fellowship; engaging in common mission* and evangelism*; and forming national, regional and local "covenanting" councils. A definitive plan, "Churches in Covenant Communion: The Church of Christ Uniting" (1989), now stands before the churches. COCU is seeking a renewed, comprehensive church in "sacred things," not a merger of existing organizations. Hopeful though problematic, COCU represents predominantly African-American churches and predominantly white churches seeking to overcome racism, sexism and nationalism and to express a truly inclusive church in which ethnic and cultural diversity is celebrated yet brought into communion.

See also BLAKE-PIKE UNITY PROPOSAL; CHURCH UNION MOVEMENTS; ECUMENISM.

BIBLIOGRAPHY. *Consultation on Church Union, 1967* (1967); P. A. Crow and W. J. Boney, *Church Union at Midpoint* (1972); P. A. Crow, *A Bibliography of the Consultation on Church Union* (1967); G. L. Hunt and P. A. Crow, eds., *Where We Are in Church Union* (1965). P. A. Crow

Contraception. See BIRTH CONTROL.

Conversion. In its most basic sense, conversion means a turning from one way of life to another. For Christians it is a turning from sin* to a new life in Christ, an experience of the saving power of God. While most American religious traditions agree on the need for conversion, they frequently differ on the nature of conversion itself. Some groups stress the gradual nature of salvation* as a process nurtured by the church through instruction, worship* and sacraments.* Certain groups—Baptists,* Pentecostals* and other evangelicals*—emphasize conversion as a powerful and more immediate experience of God's transforming grace. Some, Methodists,* Presbyterians* and others, combine elements of both.

In America the theology* and process of conversion evolved with the nation itself. Early colonial

Puritans* frequently viewed conversion as an extended process of spiritual struggle as the individual waited on God's irresistible grace. As Calvinists,* they believed that God alone was the author of conversion, offering it only to those elected* to salvation before the foundation of the world.

Nineteenth-century evangelicals shortened the conversion process considerably, putting greater emphasis on individual free will and immediate regeneration.* Conversion was for all who would come to Christ by repentance and faith. Revivalists* such as Charles G. Finney* and Dwight L. Moody* developed various "new measures"* and methods for introducing individuals and mass audiences to conversion. The preaching* of the need for conversion has led to numerous awakenings in which large numbers of persons were introduced to Christian faith.

See also NEW BIRTH; RELIGIOUS EXPERIENCE.

BIBLIOGRAPHY. J. Brauer, "Conversion: From Puritanism to Revival," *JR* (1978); B. J. Leonard, "Getting Saved in America: Conversion Event in a Pluralistic Culture," *RE* (1985): 111-127; E. S. Morgan, *Visible Saints* (1963).   B. J. Leonard

Conversion Narratives. Speeches given before the congregation for admission to full membership.* One of the distinguishing marks of colonial New England church polity* was the practice of testing applicants for full membership. The most important ingredient in this examination process was the conversion* narrative, or relation, which was a short speech describing the narrator's experience of grace. Though practice varied from church to church, the relation was usually rendered extemporaneously before the congregation, which could ask questions of the individual during the relation. If they judged that the speaker was a recipient of grace, the candidate was recommended for membership.

In practice, the narrative followed a prescribed pattern, with the individual describing how God had taken the individual from sinfulness, through the various steps of conversion, to regeneration. Religious practices, or "means," such as reading the Bible,* praying,* hearing sermons,* reading religious literature and receiving counsel from family, friends and pastor were mentioned. The Puritans* believed that conversion was for the most part a gradual process and that it was through these means of grace that regeneration came. Thus, the narrator was expected to deliver his speech in these terms.

See also CONVERSION.

BIBLIOGRAPHY. P. Caldwell, *The Puritan Conversion Narrative* (1985); G. Selement and B. Woolley, *Thomas Shepard's Confessions* (1981).
                                        K. P. Minkema

Conwell, Russell Herman (1843-1925). Inspirational lecturer and writer, Baptist* pastor.* Born near Worthington, Massachusetts, Conwell attended Wilbraham Academy and Yale College* (1860-1862) before enlisting in the Union Army during the Civil War.* He graduated from Albany Law School in 1865 and worked as a lawyer and traveling journalist. Among his legal clients was Mary Baker Eddy,* founder of Christian Science.*

In 1882 Conwell became pastor of The Baptist Temple in Philadelphia. By 1893 the church had over 3,000 members, a new building with a gymnasium and reading rooms. It also had a large Sunday school* and two hospitals, making it the largest Protestant church in America. Conwell founded Temple University when he began teaching evening classes for workers who desired an education but could not afford it. In 1969 the Conwell School of Theology, associated with Temple University, merged with Gordon Divinity School to form the Gordon-Conwell Theological Seminary.

Conwell wrote over thirty inspirational books but is best remembered for "Acres of Diamonds," the sermonic lecture he delivered over 6,000 times nationwide. Contemporaries believed he "addressed more people than any man of the past century." The central theme of "Acres of Diamonds" summarizes Conwell's message: It is one's Christian responsibility to become wealthy in order to help the cause of Christ. Like Andrew Carnegie's* "Gospel of Wealth," the rich were to be wise stewards. Unlike Carnegie, Conwell announced wealth was available to all—there were "acres of diamonds" in everyone's own back yard.

Conwell echoed a long tradition, dating back to Puritanism,* of popular religious notions concerning success, health and wealth. His popularization helped mold twentieth-century expression of these ideas by religionists like Bruce Barton,* Norman Vincent Peale* and Robert Schuller,* as well as entrepreneurs such as W. Clement Stone (founder of *Success Magazine*).

BIBLIOGRAPHY. D. W. Bjork, *Victorian Flight: Russell Conwell and the Crisis of American Individualism* (1979); A. R. Burr, *Russell H. Conwell and His Work* (1926); R. H. Conwell, *Acres of Diamonds with His Life and Achievements by Robert Shackleton* (1943); *DAB* II; *DARB; NCAB* 3.
                                        J. R. Wimmer

Cook, David C. (1850-1927). Sunday-school* curriculum author and publisher. Born in New York, Cook was a Methodist layman who sold sewing machine accessories before becoming a publisher. Beginning at age seventeen, he remained active in teaching and organizing mission* Sunday schools throughout his life. Because of the need for inexpensive curriculum materials for mission schools, he, with his wife, Marguerite, produced *Our Sunday School Quarterly.* After its success, he founded in 1875 the David C. Cook Publishing Co. in Lake View, Illinois (moving it to Elgin, Illinois, in 1882), where his Sunday-school publications expanded.

Cook led Sunday-school educators in attending to the needs of different age levels, producing age-graded curricula, developing the I.A.H. (I Am His) Circles for youth and promoting the adult Bible class movement. He attended to the needs of special Sunday schools, producing a comprehensive set of resources for rural Sunday schools as well as resources for mission Sunday schools. Interested in encouraging improvement in classroom and Sunday-school organization, he produced resources like the "Officers' Quarterly" and "Sunday School Executive." An innovator, he wrote a set of resources related to the educational theories of John Dewey. For example, Cook utilized a plan in which ethical issues were discussed, integrating both Bible study* and conflicting opinions.

A pioneer in his field, Cook became a national and international leader in the Sunday-school movement. The publishing firm bearing his name continues as a leader in the field of Christian educational curriculum publishing.

BIBLIOGRAPHY. D. C. Cook, *Memoirs: David C. Cook, The Friend of the Sunday School* (1928).

J. L. Seymour

Cook, Joseph (Flavius Josephus) (1838-1901). Congregationalist* lecturer. The only child of a prosperous upstate New York farming family, Cook was educated at Yale* (1858-1861), Harvard* (B.A., 1865) and Andover Seminary* (B.D.,1868). In the 1870s he was catapulted into international prominence as a popular spokesman for the concerns of American Protestantism.* Riding the crest of nineteenth-century America's regard, Cook combined talent, study, travel, patriotism, incredible diversity and an imposing rhetoric into a successful career as a lecturer. With the Boston Monday Lectures as an institutional fixture for almost a quarter-century, he had a firm basis for launching national and worldwide lecturing tours and nurturing an even greater reading public

through the printed dissemination of his addresses—first in syndication via newspapers and then in the eleven-volume *Boston Monday Lectures* (1877-1888).

Cook was an early advocate for social reform in industrializing America. Primarily, however, he used his lectures as a forum to attempt the reconciliation of orthodox* Christianity with other pressing issues of modernity—especially Darwinism.* Though fellow orthodox reconcilers such as Asa Gray* and George F. Wright* winced at Cook's extravagant apologetic* claims and liberal* religionists bristled, Cook's drawing power remained strong. Nonetheless, he was not successful in defending Edwards A. Park's* "Consistent Calvinism" against the inroads of liberalism within Congregationalism. By the time of his death, therefore, Cook's image was no longer that of a progressive thinker but an "obstructionist conservative."

BIBLIOGRAPHY. J. T. Cumbler, *A Moral Response to Industrialism: The Lectures of Reverend Cook in Lynn, Massachusetts* (1982); *DAB* II; *DARB*; *NCAB* 2; S. R. Pointer, "Joseph Cook—Apologetics and Science," *AP* 63 (1985): 299-308; S. R. Pointer, *The Perils of History: The Meteoric Career of Joseph Cook* (1981).

S. R. Pointer

Cooke, Terence James (1921-1983). Archbishop* of New York. Born in a slum tenement in New York City, Cooke was educated in local parochial schools.* He studied for the priesthood in Cathedral College and St. Joseph's Seminary and was ordained a priest* in 1945. In 1947 he was sent to the Catholic University of America* to study social work (M.A., 1949). Between 1949 and 1954 he directed the youth activities of Catholic Charities in New York, was an assistant at a church in Manhattan, and taught a course in social work at Fordham University. A gifted fund raiser and administrator, in 1957 Cooke was appointed to the chancery office of the Archdiocese of New York as personal secretary to Cardinal Spellman.* Cooke became vice-chancellor in 1958 and chancellor in 1961 and supervised all construction within the archdiocese.

Ordained* bishop* in 1965 and appointed vicar general of the archdiocese, he was given charge of one of the six administrative divisions within the archdiocese. This involved visiting parishes and attempting to stem the flight of affluent parishioners to the suburbs. He was also active in promoting the training of bilingual parish priests, especially in Spanish-English. After Spellman's death in 1967, Cooke was appointed archbishop in 1968. Although known as an enlightened conservative in matters of doctrine, most notably supporting Pope

Paul's* encyclical* on artificial birth control *(See Humanae Vitae)*, he was considered a liberal in his stand on racial, economic and social issues. During his term in office, the New York Archdiocese was the richest Catholic diocese in the U.S., its net worth, including all buildings, estimated at over $500,000,000.

BIBLIOGRAPHY. *Current Biography* (1968, 1983). C. E. Ronan

Cooper, Samuel (1725-1783). Calvinist Boston preacher. Born in Boston to the Reverend William and Judith Sewell Cooper, Samuel was a lifelong resident of Boston. After graduating from Harvard College* he began a forty-year career as pastor of Brattle Street Church in 1743. He was chosen co-pastor in a dying request from Brattle Street Church's pastor, Benjamin Coleman. Contemporaries regarded Cooper as an able and eloquent preacher.* In 1773 he oversaw the erection of a new church building, which was acknowledged to be the most expensive and attractive church in Boston. Cooper actively supported the American Revolution* and was a friend of John Adams and Benjamin Franklin. Through them he met many foreign dignitaries. He was also active in civic affairs, helping raise money for Harvard's library. He declined the presidency of Harvard in 1774.

BIBLIOGRAPHY. *AAP* 1; *DAB* II; S. K. Lothrop, *A History of the Church in Brattle Street, Boston* (1851). L. J. Van Til

Copley, Thomas (Philip Fisher) (c. 1595-1652). Jesuit* missionary* in Maryland. Born in Madrid, Spain, of an English family exiled by Elizabeth I, Copley entered the Society of Jesus, where he was ordained.* In 1637, he sailed to Maryland as a missionary. After serving at Saint Inigoes, he was appointed second superior of the Maryland Jesuits. During his tenure in office he fought bitterly with Governor Leonard Calvert* over the obligation of the Jesuits to conform to the proprietor's charter, specifically in land acquisitions. Calvert insisted the Society acquire land only from the proprietary government at a ratio of two thousand acres for each five men brought to the colony by a gentleman adventurer. Copley upheld the right of the Society to accept unlimited gifts of land from the Indians. The Jesuit General settled the dispute in 1643 by ordering the Society to obey Maryland's secular law. In 1645 William Claiborne, who had invaded Maryland and driven Governor Leonard Calvert from the colony, arrested Copley along with Andrew White.* In England Copley was tried and acquitted of violating the penal law.

Deported to the Netherlands, Copley re-entered Maryland in 1648 where he labored, sometimes under the pseudonym Philip Fisher, until his death in 1652.

BIBLIOGRAPHY. *DAB* II; J. Hennesey, *American Catholics* (1981); J. T. Ellis, *Catholics in Colonial America* (1965). L. R. Riforgiato

Corcoran, James Andrew (1820-1889). Catholic theologian* and educator. Born in Charleston, South Carolina, Corcoran was sent to Rome to study in 1833 at the age of fourteen. He was ordained* on December 21, 1842, the first native of South Carolina to become a priest.* After receiving his S.T.D. from the College of Propaganda, he returned to Charleston (1843) where he taught at the Charleston Seminary and was rector* of the cathedral.* Corcoran's reputation as a theologian was earned in his role as secretary for the Eighth Baltimore Council* of 1855 and his similar work for the Ninth Council. He later served as secretary-in-chief for the Plenary Councils at Baltimore in 1866 and 1884.

In 1868 Corcoran was sent to the Vatican as the sole representative of the U.S. archbishops* on the preparatory commission for Vatican I.* Joining the preparations that were already three years underway, Corcoran found himself disagreeing with many of the decisions that had already been made. Most pointedly, he concluded that some of the proposed canons would condemn the accepted American political doctrine of the separation of church and state.* Regarding the issue of papal infallibility,* he was an inopportunist, maintaining that the proposed definition was untimely and suggesting a compromise that would define the doctrine indirectly.

On his return to America, Corcoran became professor of theology at St. Charles Seminary, Philadelphia, where he remained until his death. In 1884 he was made a domestic prelate. Although he did not write any notable works, he served as editor of the *United States Catholic Miscellany* (1848-1861) and was founding editor of the *American Catholic Quarterly Review* (1876-1889). With Augustine F. Hewit* and Patrick N. Lynch,* he edited *The Works of the Rt. Rev. John England*, which was published under the name I. A. Reynolds (5 vols., 1849). An American-born theologian, Corcoran served with distinction as both pastor and theologian. In his later years he was invited to join the original faculty of the Catholic University of America,* but his advanced age forced him to decline.

BIBLIOGRAPHY. *DAB* II; J. J. Keane, "Monsignor

Corcoran," *American Catholic Quarterly Review* 14 (1889):738-747; *NCE* 4.   D. G. Reid

Corpus Christi, Feast of. A festival in the Roman Catholic* church year* celebrating the presence of Christ in the Eucharist.* Corpus Christi, literally the Body of Christ, now known as the Solemnity of the Body and Blood of Christ, celebrates the Eucharist, or Lord's Supper,* whose institution is celebrated on Holy Thursday. This feast is clearly the result of particular events in the life of the Church. In theology* great emphasis was placed on the real presence of Christ in the consecrated* bread and wine. In piety,* as the frequency of Holy Communion decreased, greater emphasis was placed on the veneration and adoration of Christ really present in the consecrated bread and wine, both during and outside the Mass* itself. This was in keeping with the development which regarded the Mass as an allegorical dramatization of the passion of Christ, which one attended and observed, rather than a sacramental action in which one participated.

The feast originated in Liege about 1209 and was prescribed for the whole Church by Pope Urban IV in 1264, but was widely celebrated only after 1317. From the fourteenth century the procession with the Blessed Sacrament assumed an increasingly important role. The host was carried in procession either through the whole town or the church grounds or, as in the case of Louisville, Kentucky, at Churchill Downs. The feast is celebrated on Thursday of the first week of Pentecost.*

BIBLIOGRAPHY. P. Parsch, *The Church's Year of Grace,* 5 vols. (1862).   R. L. Kress

Corrigan, Michael Augustine (1839-1902). Archbishop* of New York. Born in Newark, New Jersey, the fifth of nine children born to his Irish-immigrant* parents, in 1859 Corrigan graduated from Mt. St. Mary's College in Emmitsburg, Maryland. He was then sent by his bishop to the North American College* in Rome, where in December 1859 he was one of the school's original twelve students. He was ordained in 1863, after completing his theological courses at the College of Propaganda. In 1864 he completed his S.T.D. and returned to Newark to become professor of dogmatic theology and sacred Scripture at Seton Hall College and Seminary, where he eventually succeeded Bernard J. McQuaid* as president (1868-1876). In 1868 he was named vicar general and as such administered the diocese* while Bishop Bayley attended Vatican I* (1870) and later was translated to Baltimore. He was consecrated* bishop* of Newark on May 4, 1873, by Archbishop McCloskey.* As bishop he focused attention on the plight of Italian immigrants and promoted the founding of parochial schools,* orphanages and hospitals.

On October 1, 1880, Pope Leo XIII* named Corrigan titular archbishop of Petra and coadjutor to succeed Cardinal McCloskey of New York. In this new role Corrigan carried responsibilities for preparing and conducting the fourth provincial council of New York (1883) and represented McCloskey at the Third Plenary Council of Baltimore* (1884). On May 4, 1886, he was formally installed as archbishop of New York, following McCloskey's death in October 1885.

Corrigan's greatest difficulty came in his efforts to put into effect the Baltimore Council's decree requiring the establishment of a church school in every parish. This decision was strongly opposed by Edward McGlynn,* whom Corrigan was forced to remove from his parish in 1887. This and succeeding events in the "McGlynn Affair" cast a shadow over Corrigan's public image, even though Corrigan did not carry a personal grudge against McGlynn and presided over his requiem Mass* (1900). A vigorous conservative, Corrigan opposed the Knights of Labor,* Catholic membership in secret societies and the so-called heresy* of Americanism.* But history has remembered him as a masterful administrator and builder who greatly increased the number of churches, priests, schools and charitable institutions in his diocese. Under his leadership the progressive St. Joseph's Seminary in Dunwoodie, Yonkers, New York, was established.

BIBLIOGRAPHY. R. E. Curran, *Michael Augustine Corrigan and the Shaping of Conservative Catholicism in America, 1878-1902* (1978); *DAB* II; J. M. Farley et al., eds., *Memorial of the Most Rev. M. A. Corrigan (1902); NCE* 4.

D. G. Reid

Cotton, John (1584-1652). Seventeenth-century Puritan* minister* and spokesman for New England Congregationalism.* Born in Derby, England, Cotton was educated in Puritan doctrine,* church practice and preaching* style at Trinity and Emmanuel Colleges at Cambridge University. Cambridge ministers William Perkins* and Richard Sibbes were particularly influential in shaping Cotton's thought and religious experience.* In 1612 he was ordained* vicar of St. Botolph's Church in Boston, Lincolnshire, where over the course of twenty years he earned a reputation as a great and learned preacher. In 1630 Cotton preached his famous farewell sermon, *God's*

Promise to His Plantation, to the passengers of the ship *Arbella,* justifying their departure for Massachusetts Bay and urging them to reform the practices of the Church of England.* Called before the High Commission for nonconformity in 1633, Cotton himself departed for the New World, where he became teacher of the First Church of Boston.

The most eminent minister in Massachusetts, Cotton's evangelical* preaching sparked a large number of conversions* within the first two years of his arrival. Many of his Boston congregation, including Anne Hutchinson,* believed that Cotton's conversion*-oriented exhortations and emphasis on justification* by faith alone contradicted the doctrine of other ministers, who stressed the importance of good works in addition to saving grace. Citing Cotton's sermons and probably enjoying his tacit approval, Hutchinson initiated the "Antinomian controversy"* of 1636-1638. Cotton at first dismissed the significance of the differences before belatedly clarifying his views. His public statements in support of orthodoxy* were prerequisite to ministerial unity and Hutchinson's banishment.

Cotton may justly be considered the father of early New England Congregationalism. Though ministers agreed upon most of the larger principles of church government,* many practical questions concerning baptism,* election of officers and other church procedures remained unresolved during the first years of settlement. Church authorities frequently looked to Cotton to turn to the Scriptures* for answers to such problems and, according to Roger Williams,* most "could hardly believe that God would suffer Mr. Cotton to err." Churches probably began to require conversion as a condition for church membership* at Cotton's suggestion.

Cotton spent much of his later life defining and defending New England Congregationalism in tracts* that explained New England church practices and offered biblical justifications in support of the system. His most important works included: *The Keyes of the Kingdom of Heaven* (1644), *The Way of the Churches of Christ in New England* (1645) and *The Way of the Congregational Churches Cleared* (1648). Many of Cotton's writings were directed to an English audience, skeptical of Congregationalism's success in the New World. Appropriately, Cotton also played a major role in the construction of the Cambridge Platform* of church discipline and wrote the preface to the finished document. Cotton fell mortally ill in 1652; a comet, or "attendant to the seven stars," admirers observed, "continued all that while and until his burial . . . then disappeared."

BIBLIOGRAPHY. *AAP* 1; *DAB* II; *DARB;* E. H. Emerson, *John Cotton* (1965); *NCAB* 7; L. Ziff, *The Career of John Cotton* (1962).   J. F. Cooper

Coughlin, Charles Edward (1891-1979). Radical Roman Catholic* priest* and radio preacher,* Father Coughlin was born in Hamilton, Ontario, and educated at St. Michael's College, University of Toronto (Ph.D., 1911). He was ordained* (1916) and taught philosophy and English at Assumption College, Sandwich, Ontario. This was followed by pastorates in Detroit, Kalamazoo and North Branch, Michigan. In 1926 he was sent to found a parish at Royal Oak, Michigan, where he established the Shrine of the Little Flower, remaining there until 1966. Coughlin began an effective radio ministry in 1926 in an effort to explain Roman Catholicism after the Ku Klux Klan burned a cross in the churchyard of his church.

By 1930 he had turned from strictly religious topics and had begun to promote political views on radio, first over Detroit's radio station WJR and later on the CBS network, where he reached an estimated forty million listeners. His preaching was characterized by anti-Communism* and anti-Semitism, and in time he became pro-Nazi. In 1934 Coughlin organized the National Union for Social Justice and through the magazine *Social Justice* (1936) was able to promote his views. By 1936 Coughlin was in open opposition to Roosevelt and New Deal politics and reorganized the National Union for Social Justice into the Christian Front.* Perceiving what he called a British-Jewish-Roosevelt conspiracy, Coughlin vehemently opposed the entry of the United States into World War 2.* Coughlin was eventually forced off the air by church authorities and his magazine put out of print (1942). He spent his last years in seclusion, occasionally writing tracts denouncing communism and Vatican II.*

See also CHRISTIAN FRONT.

BIBLIOGRAPHY. *DARB;* W. Stegner, "The Radio Priest and His Flock," in *The Aspirin Age,* ed. I. Leighton (1929); S. Marcus, *Father Coughlin* (1973); C. J. Tull, *Father Coughlin and the New Deal* (1965).   R. L. Petersen

Council on Religion and International Affairs. *See* CARNEGIE COUNCIL ON ETHICS AND INTERNATIONAL AFFAIRS.

Counsels of Perfection. There are three so-called counsels of perfection (also called evangelical counsels): poverty, chastity and obedience.

Christian tradition teaches that this is a threefold remedy for a threefold obstacle. The author of the First Epistle of John refers to this threefold obstacle as "all that is in the world, the lust of the flesh and the lust of the eyes and the pride of life" (1 Jn 2:16, RSV). These three tendencies are the obstacles in life to the perfection of love. They represent fundamental weaknesses in human nature which, if left unattended, have the power of keeping the soul separated from God.

According to Thomas Aquinas, perfection is nothing other than the love of God and of neighbor. However, in practice, it consists in observing God's commandments, the most important of which is love, and secondarily in the counsels which are directed toward love inasmuch as they remove the obstacles that hinder its practice. A person may take vows of chastity, poverty and obedience. In this case chastity fosters an undivided love of God, poverty sets the heart free to love God, and obedience subjects the will to God.

Individuals, particularly members of Catholic religious orders,* may bind themselves by vows to a life of poverty, chastity and obedience. But the counsels are by no means the property of religious or spiritual elite. The spirit of the vows may be observed according to one's station in life. Thus, husband and wife may exemplify the spirit of chastity in their marriage by avoiding lust so that they do not turn each other into sexual objects. By the spirit of poverty, a person might avoid the dangers of materialism. Through the spirit of obedience, one may submit with docility to God or those superiors in whom they see an image of God.

BIBLIOGRAPHY. R. J. Foster, *Money, Sex and Power* (1985); A. Tanquerey, *The Spiritual Life* (1961). D. T. DeMarco

Covenant Theology. A doctrine* or system of theology* explaining the relationship between God and mankind in terms of a compact, or covenant; also called federal theology. Theologians* who have taught the covenant doctrine have based it on biblical themes, especially God's covenant with Israel as recorded in the Old Testament.

Although the concept of covenant is ancient, the rigorous development of an overall, systematic covenant theology grew out of the Protestant* Reformation. The concept of a "covenant" (Latin, *foedus,* from which is derived "federal theology"), as it was generally understood at the time of the Reformation, meant a compact between two or more parties by which they solemnly obligated

themselves to each other to accomplish a particular task. This concept was utilized as a theological construct by sixteenth-century Reformed* theologians, particularly John Calvin (1509-1564), Ulrich Zwingli (1484-1531) and Johann Heinrich Bullinger (1504-1575). Anabaptists* also developed a doctrine of covenant, primarily referring to the union of believers with each other.

Reformed covenant theology has taught that God offers grace and salvation* to mankind. To those who by faith accept God's offer of salvation—on his terms—he assuredly grants salvation. Thus, mankind gains assurance from its covenant relationship with God. Although there are many variations, theologians have discerned three covenants in Scripture: The Covenant of Works (offered to Adam, which he failed); the Covenant of Grace (offered after the Fall of Adam, again to Abraham and renewed in Christ); and, for some theologians, the Covenant of Redemption (the eternal promise of God's salvation underlying the Covenant of Grace).

The covenant approach to theology strongly affected English Puritanism, and through Puritanism's influence in the New World, came to have a significant influence in America. One of the trademarks of Puritan theology, it is evident in the writings of such Puritan giants as William Perkins, Dudley Fenner, Richard Sibbes, John Preston,* William Ames* and the separatist* Robert Browne. The appeal of the covenant among Puritans of England and America was varied, but most noteworthy was its rational and easily understood organizational structure. Moreover, the doctrine offered absolute assurance of God's eternal graciousness. Moreover, since many English and American Puritans were involved in the commercial and political world with its many "compacts" and "contracts," the preacher's use of "covenant" contextualized theology in terms of their everyday world and spoke to them in a special way. Although Puritans did not invent covenant theology, they did make good use of it.

The writings of William Ames, the English Puritan theologian and university professor, were an important means for spreading the covenant method of theology in both England and America. His *Medulla Theologiae* (1627, known in many English editions as *The Marrow of Sacred Divinity*) and his *De Conscientia* (1630) present nearly the entire scope of theology within the framework of covenants. In dealing with "intelligent creatures" (i.e., man and woman), God governs in a moral, intelligible way through covenants. "This covenant is, as it were, a kind of transaction of God with the creature whereby God commands, promises, threatens, fulfills; and the creature binds itself in obedience to God so demanding." First God covenanted with Adam in the covenant of creation (the covenant of works); he offered Adam, the public person, a bargain or conditional covenant, saying: "Do this and you will live; if you do it not you shall die." Adam failed, but then in the very dawn of human history (Gen 3), God made his second covenant, the unconditional covenant of grace. The history of the new covenant is the story of salvation.

Not all theologians developed the covenant idea in exactly the same way as Ames, but his exposition illustrates the main lines of the doctrine. Although European rather than American, Ames helped to mold American Puritan thought and he was one of the forerunners of American Congregationalism.* Many American settlers praised him as the "learned doctor," and his *Medulla* and *De Conscientia* had a wide readership, with the *Medulla* long serving as a textbook at Harvard* and Yale.*

Through the English Puritan writers, covenant theology entered New England Congregationalism. American versions of it can be found in the writings of John Cotton,* Thomas Hooker,* Thomas Shepard,* Peter Bulkeley and many others. Scottish Presbyterians* also brought their distinctive covenant doctrine to America. Another source of the covenant ideal is the *Westminster Confession of Faith** (1647), a theological creed* revered by Congregationalists, Presbyterians* and Baptists* in both England and America. Outside of the Reformed tradition, however, the covenant concept was not nearly as prominent. Some Anabaptist groups, namely Amish,* Hutterites* and Mennonites,* drew upon their own understanding of covenant in forming communal and mutual aid groups.

Covenant Theology and the Church. Although rooted in theological speculation, the covenant ideal had many applications in America. American Congregationalists wanted to organize churches* pleasing to God and free from all episcopal* trappings. From the individual covenant of grace, they deduced the corporate church covenant, whereby the believers would band together to carry out their covenant responsibilities. According to Perry Miller,* the church covenant "was held to be a miniature edition of the divine covenant." The local congregation was to be composed only of truly godly people, so-called visible saints. To gain membership* in the church, the Christian believer had to testify to his or her faith and conversion;

moreover, the believer promised to covenant with fellow believers in fruitful church fellowship.* A congregation was "a society of believers joined together in a special bond. . . . This bond is a covenant." A very early American version of the church covenant at Salem, Massachusetts, read: "We Covenant with the Lord and one another; and doe bynd ourselves in the presence of God, to walke together in all his waies, according as he is pleased to reveale himself unto us in his Blessed word of truth."

This type of covenanted church had been occasionally practiced in English churches in the Netherlands before 1620. It functioned, to an extent, surreptitiously in England, and then became the norm for American Congregationalist churches. In addition to the Salem covenant, other church covenants were enacted very early at Charleston (1630) and at Watertown (1630).

When religious zeal waned, as it did within a few decades, the problem of maintaining pure, saintly churches became a dilemma. Many respectable citizens, baptized* as infants into the church, could not as mature persons point to a particular experience of true conversion.* Thus, they were not allowed to take up active membership in the church. To solve this dilemma, the New England Congregationalists created the policy of the Half-Way Covenant* (1662). This allowed persons without, or unassured of, conversion to have a minimal "half-way" participation in the church, including baptism for their children. Regarded as a compromise measure, the Half-Way Covenant was, nevertheless, accepted as a practical solution in a society no longer in tune with the ideological fervor of its founding fathers.

Covenant Theology and Public Life. Just as God had covenanted with mankind in salvation and in gathering churches, so groups within society were to covenant with one another as they carried out their ordinary affairs. In fact, the seventeenth century was an age of compacts, contracts and secular covenants, through which the public business was transacted. Theological covenants and social-political covenants sprang out of the same milieu in America, and overlapped with one another. The Mayflower Pilgrims* formed themselves into a "civil Body Politick" by means of a covenant, the Mayflower Compact* (1620). Roger Williams* founded Providence in Rhode Island by a compact (1636); the Fundamental Orders of Connecticut (1639) created government by covenant, and such practice prevailed throughout the towns of New England.

In a larger sense, the Puritan leadership envisioned the entire people of Christian New England as forming a covenanted people in compact with God, a kind of national covenant. They were a New Israel. Governor John Winthrop* preached a sermon on shipboard while sailing to America, in which he promised that by "mutual consent" they would establish their own "due form of Government both civil and ecclesiastical." The founding of America, in Puritan eyes, was a mission world witness accomplished by covenant. "Thus stands the cause between God and us; we are entered into Covenant with him for this work. . . . We shall be as a City upon a Hill" (1630). Covenant theology was one important ingredient, although not the only one, in developing the American ideal of political compact and contract, so prominent in its great public documents. H. Richard Niebuhr* has suggested the likelihood of an enduring connection between "The Idea of the Covenant and American Democracy."

The reign of covenant theology began to fade in the late eighteenth century; its greatest day was in the early history of America. Nevertheless, the covenant ideal, with its teaching about mutual obligation and communal responsibility, continued to influence American life, although in ever more secularized forms. Moreover, the pervasive ideal that America has a moral mission in the world, beyond the mundane, owes much to covenant theology.

See also Half-Way Covenant; Manifest Destiny; New England Theology; New England Way.

BIBLIOGRAPHY. S. E. Ahlstrom, *A Religious History of the American People* (1972); P. Y. De Jong, *The Covenant Idea in New England Theology, 1620-1847* (1945); P. Miller, *The New England Mind: The Seventeenth Century* (1939); H. R. Niebuhr, "The Idea of Covenant and American Democracy," *CH* 23 (1954):126-135; R. G. Pope, *The Half-Way Covenant* (1969); W. Roth and R. R. Ruether, *The Liberating Bond: Covenants—Biblical and Contemporary* (1978); K. L. Sprunger, *The Learned Doctor William Ames* (1972).

K. L. Sprunger

Cowley Fathers. *See* SOCIETY OF ST. JOHN THE EVANGELIST.

Cowman, Lettie Burd (1870-1960) and Charles Elmer Cowman (1864-1924). Missionaries* to Japan and founders of OMS International.* Lettie Burd Cowman was raised in Thayer, Iowa, and Charles Cowman was born in Toulon, Ilinois. Childhood sweethearts, they married on June 8, 1889. Charles, a telegraph operator for Western

Union, was transferred to Chicago as traffic chief shortly after their marriage and later advanced to division wire chief. In December 1893 Lettie was converted* in Chicago's Grace Methodist Episcopal Church. A month later Charles experienced conversion after a meeting in the same church situated next door to Moody Bible Institute.* On September 3, 1894, in Moody Church Lettie and Charles heard A. B. Simpson,* founder of the Christian and Missionary Alliance,* speak and both dedicated themselves to missionary service.

Although Charles first applied to the Methodist* Board, he later felt called to go to Japan by faith and without board or denominational backing. This conviction led to the founding of OMS International, then known as The Oriental Missionary Society. The Cowmans sailed for Japan on February 1, 1901. Together they labored in Japan and Korea until ill health forced Charles to leave Japan on November 3, 1917. Charles suffered a heart attack in September 1918, and for the next six years continued in poor health, finally dying on September 25, 1924.

For nearly sixty years Lettie Cowman played a crucial role in OMS International. President of the mission for twenty-one years, her speaking and writing gave her worldwide influence. She is best known for her devotional book *Streams in the Desert* (1925), compiled during her husband's illness. It is the all-time best seller among devotional books, with more than three million copies in print in English and more than a dozen foreign languages. In her last years Lettie Cowman concentrated on promoting the Every Creature Crusade evangelism* method conceived by her husband in the Great Village Campaign in Japan. She died on Easter, April 17, 1960, at 90 years of age.

BIBLIOGRAPHY. L. Cowman, *Charles E. Cowman* (1939); B. H. Pearson, *The Vision Lives* (1961).

E. N. Hunt

Craig, John (1710-1774). Pioneer Presbyterian* minister* in western Virginia. Originally from Northern Ireland, Craig attended Edinburgh University in Scotland and immigrated to Maryland in 1738. Licensed* by the presbytery* of Donegal, Pennsylvania, in August 1738, he served as a supply preacher* in Opequhon, Irish Tract and other places in western Virginia. In September 1740 he was ordained* and went on to organize the Augusta Stone Church and Tinkling Spring Presbyterian Church. Craig's parish extended over more than six hundred square miles at first, and today thirteen Presbyterian churches owe their origin to his missionary* activity. Retiring from Tinkling

Spring in 1754, Craig continued to serve the Augusta Church until he died. One of the early bearers of confessional Calvinism* in colonial America, he sided with the Old Side* in the split of 1741, and with Samuel Davies* he helped form a distinctive American Presbyterian consciousness.

BIBLIOGRAPHY. H. A. White, *Southern Presbyterian Leaders* (1911). L. B. Weeks

Cramp, John Mockett (1796-1881). Canadian Baptist* leader and educator. Born in the Baptist parsonage at St. Peter's, Ramsgate, England, to Thomas and Rebecca Cramp, John was educated at Stepney College, Regents Park. Between 1818 and 1844 he had pastorates at Dean Street Chapel, Southwark, St. Peter's and Hastings. A prolific writer, he published thirty-five works as well as hundreds of articles and edited the *Baptist Magazine* (1825-1828). He was president of the English Baptist Union (1837-1838).

After serving as president of Canada Baptist College, Montreal (1844-1849), Cramp edited several papers and in 1851 became president of Acadia College, Wolfville, Nova Scotia. "The Second Founder" of the College, he rebuilt its financial and faculty resources between 1851 and 1869. He taught every subject at some time at the College, while preaching* every Sunday, writing and maintaining a massive correspondence. He became a Maritime Baptist leader and also gave direction to the temperance* and education causes. His best-known work was his *Baptist History from the Foundation of the Christian Church to the Close of the Eighteenth Century* (1868), which was translated into German. As an educator, denominational leader and historian, he shaped a generation of Maritime Baptist scholars and pastors as he helped integrate the British and American traditions.

BIBLIOGRAPHY. *DCB XI.* R. S. Wilson

Crapsey, Algernon Sidney (1847-1927). Episcopal* priest.* Born in Fairmount, Ohio, Crapsey studied at St. Stephen's College, Annandale-on-Hudson, New York (now Bard College) from 1867 to 1869 and received his B.D. from the General Theological Seminary, New York. From 1872 to 1879 he was on the staff of Trinity Church, New York, as assistant minister* at St. Paul's Chapel. In June 1879, Crapsey became the rector* of St. Andrew's Church, Rochester, New York, where he worked with Walter Rauschenbusch.* He remained there until 1906.

Crapsey's orthodoxy* was unquestioned until 1905, when he published *Religion and Politics,* in which he argued for social reform and a symbolic interpretation of the creeds.* In 1906 at a heresy* trial he was accused of denying the doctrine of the Trinity and Jesus Christ's divinity, virgin birth, conception by the Holy Spirit and resurrection. On December 4, 1906, Bishop William Walker of western New York deposed him from the ministry. Crapsey died in Rochester on December 31, 1927.

BIBLIOGRAPHY. A. S. Crapsey, *The Last of the Heretics* (1924); H. M. Jason, Jr., "Algernon Sidney Crapsey: Heretic at Rochester," in *American Religious Heretics,* ed. G. H. Shriver (1966).

D. S. Armentrout

Crawford, Alexander (c.1785-1828). Pioneer Baptist* preacher on Prince Edward Island. Born on the island of Arran, Scotland, Crawford joined the Baptistic Haldane Movement (1800) and attended the Haldane brothers' seminary in Edinburgh, following them when they became Baptists (1808). Alexander and Jane Crawford immigrated to Yarmouth, Nova Scotia, in 1810. There he taught school but found little fellowship with the local revival-oriented Baptists led by Henry Alline's* disciple, Harris Harding. Crawford visited Prince Edward Island (1812), where he performed the first adult believer's baptism* and founded a Baptist Church at Three Rivers, Montague. In 1815 he moved to Prince Edward Island where he taught school in Charlottetown. In 1818 he settled on a farm in Tryon and served as an itinerant preacher.* He helped found churches at Three Rivers, Tryon, East Point, Lot Forty-Eight, Cross Roads and Belfast. Because he believed that prayer,* praise, reading of Scripture,* salutation, breaking of bread, offering, exhortation and discipline should be observed every Sunday by believers only, he did not join the local churches. He published his views on baptism in *Believer Immersion as Opposed to Unbeliever Sprinkling* (1827). Both the Baptists and the Disciples of Christ* look to him as their founding father on Prince Edward Island.

R. S. Wilson

Crawford, Florence (1872-1936). Founder of the Pentecostal* Apostolic Faith movement. While attending the Azusa Street revival* of 1906, Crawford experienced her baptism in the Holy Spirit.* In her own words, "A sound like a rushing, mighty wind filled the room, and I was baptized with the Holy Ghost and fire. Rivers of Joy and love divine flooded my soul." Crawford also testified to speaking "in another language" and being healed, an experience that prompted her to begin an itinerant ministry of Pentecostal evangelism* that took her to Washington, Minnesota and Canada before she established her headquarters in Portland, Oregon, in 1907.

There she founded a large city mission center which included two auditoriums accommodating more than three thousand people. Under her leadership the movement adopted a strict lifestyle code with regulations against so-called worldly amusements, stylish clothing, short hair for women and remarriage for divorced persons. Members were also required to separate from all other religious groups. This issue of religious separation,* as well as the female leadership of the movement, led to a split in 1919 when many of the pastors in the movement departed to form The Open Bible Standard Churches. While the Apostolic Faith movement continued to grow after her death, it has, because of its exclusivism, remained on the fringe of evangelical* and Pentecostal* circles.

BIBLIOGRAPHY. *A Historical Account of the Apostolic Faith* (1965); R. B. Mitchell, *Heritage and Horizons: The History of Open Bible Standard Churches* (1982).   R. A. Tucker

Crawford, Percy B. (1902-1960). Evangelical* youth minister,* educator and broadcaster. Born in Minnedosa, Manitoba, Crawford was converted* at Church of the Open Door, Los Angeles (1932), and educated at Biola, UCLA, Wheaton College* (B.A., 1929), Westminster Theological Seminary (Th.B., 1932) and University of Pennsylvania* (M.A., 1932). He received the D.D. from Bob Jones* University in 1940. Crawford married Ruth Duvall, a talented vocalist and pianist who assisted in his radio and television ministry.

Crawford was a significant figure in pre- and post-World War 2 fundamentalism* and evangelicalism. In 1930 he launched the Saturday-night youth rallies which became the foundation for the later Youth for Christ* rallies. In 1931 he began one of the first national Christian radio broadcasts, the Young People's Church of the Air, which was heard on 450 stations on the Mutual and American Broadcasting networks. In 1950 he started broadcasting the first fundamentalist coast-to-coast television program with a Sunday-night audience in the millions. In addition, Crawford established the Pinebrook Bible Conference in Stroudsburg, Pennsylvania, and in 1938 The King's College, in Briarcliff Manor, New York. His largest in-person audience was 70,000 people gathered at Chicago's Soldier Field for the first anniversary of the Chicagoland Youth for Christ on May 30, 1944.

BIBLIOGRAPHY. B. L. Shelley, "The Rise of Evangelical Youth Movements," *FH* 18 (January 1986): 47-63.   H. F. Vos

Creation Science. During the early 1920s, advocates of creation science gained visibility through their antievolution articles in the *Princeton Theological Review,* a major evangelical* journal that had carried articles mildly supportive of evolution.* In 1926 George McCready Price typified the evolutionary principle of uniformity as "essentially pagan or atheistic" and declared the literal creation of all the primal types as recorded in Genesis 1 to be the only fact needing to be dealt with by modern science.

Price, a Seventh-Day Adventist,* had been trained as a schoolteacher but soon turned his attention to the study of science and biblical creation. In 1902 his *Outlines of Modern Science and Modern Christianity* appeared. *The New Geology* (1923) gave him national prominence among evangelicals as he declared Darwinism to be "a most gigantic hoax." William Jennings Bryan* also helped translate the antievolution mood into a movement. He launched a nationwide crusade against Darwinian biology as he attributed to it a variety of evils ranging from German militarism to seared consciences.

Creationists gained prominence in the well-publicized Scopes Trial* of 1925. Bryan's victory in prosecuting John Scopes for teaching human evolution in a public school* sharpened the creationist agenda: Whoever was not for the antievolution cause, was against it. This new movement represented a fundamental break with the approach to evolution by mainstream evangelicalism of the nineteenth century.

In the 1930s theologian Floyd Hamilton's writings marked a shift in emphasis. He first cataloged problems in evolutionary biology and geology. He then concluded that if the evolutionary hypothesis has no foundation in fact, special creation is the only alternative left.

In recent decades civil engineer Henry Morris, a close friend of Price, spearheaded the modern creationist revival. With theologian* John Whitcomb he published *The Genesis Flood* in 1961. As an alternative to evolutionary theory it offers a creationism holding that the universe is about 10,000 years old; all basic kinds of living things were created in six twenty-four-hour days and the geological data can be explained by a worldwide flood. In 1972 the Institute for Creation Research was formed, with Morris as president. Two years later he edited *Scientific Creationism* (1974), which asserts that "evolutionist teaching is not only harmful sociologically, but it is false scientifically and historically." The scientific theory of evolution is consistently linked, and often identified, with a philosophy of evolutionism.

The public school edition of *Scientific Creationism* deals with the creation-evolution question from a strictly scientific point of view without reference to the Bible or other religious literature. The general edition adds a chapter that "places the scientific evidence in its proper Biblical and theological context." Its literalistic interpretation of Genesis 1 requires the "special creation and formation of all things in a period of six (twenty-four-hour) days" with an "appearance of age." Alternative interpretations—such as theistic evolution, progressive creation, day-age and framework views—are rejected. A second edition of the two books appeared in 1985.

In 1981 Arkansas Act 590 legislated the teaching of "creation science" alongside evolutionary theory to provide a "balanced treatment." A year later the law was ruled unconstitutional on the basis that an essentially religious statement was being promoted as science, a view vigorously opposed by creation-science adherents.

See also DARWINIAN EVOLUTION AND THE AMERICAN CHURCHES; SCIENCE AND CHRISTIANITY.

BIBLIOGRAPHY. F. Hamilton, *The Basis of Christian Faith* (1927); D. N. Livingstone, *Darwin's Forgotten Defenders* (1987); H. M. Morris, *History of Modern Creationism* (1984); H. M. Morris, ed., *Scientific Creationism* (1974); R. Numbers, "Creationism in 20th-Century America." *Science* 218 (1982):534-44.　　　　C. E. Hummel

Creationism. *See* CREATION SCIENCE.

Creed. A confession of adherence to selected essentials in the Christian faith. A term derived from the Latin *credo (I believe* or *I trust)*, creeds have been used for many purposes: to confess the faith of a Christian individual or group (most commonly in corporate worship); to teach the young or prospective church members; to hear or test the beliefs of candidates for baptism,* confirmation* or ordination*; to clarify the meaning of Scripture*; to provide a basis for founding or uniting churches; to enable one church group to commend itself to others; to warn against error; to highlight essential (often neglected) beliefs that speak to new situations; to unite churches in response to common danger; and to proclaim judgment and hope to the world.

Since no statement of any length can adequately present all the essentials of the Christian faith, the church has many creeds, some of which have gained wide authority* from ecclesiastical action and/or enduring popularity. Such authority, however, varies with the denomination.* Churches in the Restoration* tradition,* for instance, are bound by "no creed but Christ." Churches in the Mennonite,* Brethren* and Baptist* traditions also resist creedal statements, while nineteenth-century liberal* theologians* saw their faith as founded not on creeds of doctrine, but on religious experience* and sentiments. A creed can be brief or lengthy, spontaneous or formal, oral or written, the work of an individual or a group, a direct statement or a series of questions and answers. The earliest Christian creed may be embedded in the New Testament (e.g., Rom 10:9). Most widely known are the Apostles' Creed and the Nicene Creed. Twentieth-century American examples are the Methodist Social Creed* (1908), adopted by the Federal Council of Churches* in 1912, and the Statement of Faith of the United Church of Christ* (1959).

BIBLIOGRAPHY. J. H. Leith, *Creeds of the Churches* (1963); P. Schaff, *Creeds of Christendom*, 3 vols. (1877); W. Walker, *The Creeds and Platforms of Congregationalism* (1893).

R. M. Healey

Cridge, Edward (1817-1913). Bishop* of the Reformed Episcopal Church.* Born in Bratton Fleming, Devonshire, and educated in St. Peter's College, Cambridge, Cridge immigrated to Canada under the sponsorship of the Hudson Bay Company in 1854 to become rector of the Victoria (British Columbia) District Church. He was made dean of Victoria and rector* of Christ Church Cathedral in 1865, but his years as dean were marred by his growing unhappiness with the influence of Tractarianism* in the Anglican Church in Canada.* A confrontation with George Hills, the bishop of Columbia, was precipitated over a sermon preached by the bishop's archdeacon, and in November, 1874, Cridge and half the Cathedral* congregation seceded and joined the evangelical* Reformed Episcopal Church. Actions to retain control of the Cathedral property failed (the decision, *Bishop of Columbia v. Cridge* 1 B.C.R., [Pt. 1] 5, was a landmark case in Canadian church-state jurisprudence), and Cridge instead built the Church of Our Lord in Victoria in 1876.

Cridge remained rector of the Church of Our Lord until his retirement in 1902. He was consecrated* a missionary* bishop of the Reformed Episcopal Church in 1876 for a proposed "Missionary Jurisdiction of the Pacific," but in fact he proved unable to organize more than a few short-lived parishes on the West Coast.

BIBLIOGRAPHY. A. D. Price, *A History of the Reformed Episcopal Church, 1873-1902* (1902); A. C. Guelzo, *The First Thirty Years: A Historical Handbook for the Founding Years of the Reformed Episcopal Church, 1873-1903* (1986).

A. C. Guelzo

Criswell (W)allie (A)mos (1909-). Southern Baptist* minister.* Born in El Dorado, Oklahoma, Criswell escaped early family poverty and graduated magna cum laude from Baylor University in 1931. He continued his education at Southern Baptist Theological Seminary in Louisville, Kentucky, where, after six years, he earned his Th.M. (1934) and his Ph.D. (1937). Author of nearly fifty books, Criswell is considered one of the most influential fundamentalist* ministers in the latter half of the twentieth century. The hallmark of Criswell's theology* is his belief that the Bible* is inerrant,* as expressed in his book *Why I Preach That the Bible Is Literally True* (1969).

After pastoring in Chicasha (1937-1941) and Muskogee (1941-1944), both in Oklahoma, the thirty-four-year-old Criswell accepted the August 1944 call of First Baptist Church of Dallas. An expository* preacher, Criswell places great emphasis on evangelism.* During his more than forty-four years of strong conservative leadership, the church has grown nearly fourfold, to a membership,* on paper at least, of around 26,000. His sermons are broadcast live over radio and television throughout the Southwestern region of the U.S. In the late 1960s his influence in mainstream Southern Baptist life reached its height when he served two years as president of the Southern Baptist Convention. More recently, he has spoken as an advocate for the "Inerrancy Party" within Southern Baptist life.

BIBLIOGRAPHY. B. Keith, *W. A. Criswell: The Authorized Biography* (1973); C. A. Russell, "W.A. Criswell: A Case Study in Fundamentalism," *RE* 81 (1984):107-131; M. G. Toulouse, "W.A. Criswell," in *Twentieth Century Shapers of American Popular Religion,* ed. Charles H. Lippy (1989).

M. G. Toulouse

Crittenton, Charles Nelson (1833-1909). Businessman, evangelist* and philanthropist.* Born in Henderson, Jefferson County, New York, Crittenton attended local schools and began his career in a village store. He later moved to New York City and eventually established a highly

succesful drug company. Crittenton experienced a dramatic conversion* in 1882, which soon rechanneled his efforts from business into evangelism in urban slums. His first such effort convinced him that he should work to provide practical assistance to the destitute persons to whom he was witnessing.

On New York City's Bleeker Street, he opened a mission and home for women that became the mother home of the Florence Crittenton missions (named after the daughter whose death had precipitated his conversion). After guiding that mission for six years, in 1850 he launched in California the twin national ministries of welfare and evangelism that were to occupy the final quarter century of his life. Among the most active of American evangelists during that era, he held services in cities across the country, characteristically beginning a "Florence Mission" with the help of converts and other supporters. His chain of mission homes for women, which held its first national convention in 1857, numbered forty-five by 1855 and more than seventy by the time of his death. Crittenton served on the board of the National Gospel Mission Union and was active in other welfare and evangelistic organizations.

BIBLIOGRAPHY. C. Crittenton, *The Brother of Girls; The Life Story of Charles N. Crittenton* (1910); *DAB* I; C. Edholm, *Traffic in Girls and Florence Crittenton Missions* (1893); *The Florence Crittenton Magazine* (1899-1909); N. Magnuson, *Salvation in the Slums* (1977).

N. A. Magnuson

Cronyn, Benjamin (1802-1871). First Anglican* bishop* of Huron (Canada West, now Ontario). Born in Kilkenny, Ireland, Cronyn was educated at Kilkenny College and Trinity College, Dublin (B.A., 1822; M.A., 1825; D.D., 1855). While a deacon* he served as a curate in Lancashire, England, before being ordained* priest* in 1827, whereupon he was appointed to a parish* in Longford, Ireland. In 1832 he immigrated to London, Upper Canada, where he remained for the rest of his life. In 1857, when the diocese* of Huron was formed out of that of Toronto, Cronyn was elected as its first incumbent, defeating A. N. Bethune, the favored candidate of Bishop John Strachan* of Toronto. His election by the clergy* and laity* of the diocesan synod* was the first of its kind in the Church of England.*

Cronyn's evangelicalism* involved him in further controversies with high-churchmen* like Strachan and George Whitaker, provost of Trinity College, Toronto. In 1860 Cronyn was forthright in declaring his suspicions of the teaching of Whitaker and Trinity. Because of his opposition to Trinity and the need for additional clergy,* Cronyn took steps toward establishing a theological* college in his own diocese. Huron College was accordingly opened in 1863.

BIBLIOGRAPHY. *DCB* X.   R. W. Vaudry

Crosby, Thomas (1840-1914). Canadian Methodist* missionary* to British Columbia. Born in Yorkshire, England, Crosby came to Ontario with his parents in 1856. In 1862 he began teaching Indians in a Methodist mission school at Nanaimo on Canada's West Coast. In 1869, two years before his ordination,* he took charge of the Methodist missions to the Indians in southern British Columbia. Crosby married a clergyman's daughter in 1874, the same year in which he moved to Port Simpson to establish mission stations in central and northern British Columbia.

Crosby's work had a strong emphasis on material and cultural improvement: European housing and industrial undertakings marked the Indian communities that he touched. He was the first to include medical work as part of the Methodist Episcopal missions in Canada. Crosby was honored in 1907, the year of his retirement, with a D.D. from Victoria University in Toronto. In the same year, he published *Among the An-ko-me-nums or Flathead Tribes of Indians of the Pacific Coast.*

BIBLIOGRAPHY. T. Crosby, *Up and Down the North Pacific Coast by Canoe and Mission Ship* (1914); O. J. Smith, ed., *Men of God* (1971).
                              B. A. McKenzie

Crosby (Van Alstyne), Fanny Jane (1820-1915). Gospel song* writer, musician, preacher* and evangelist.* Born in Putnam County, New York, Crosby was blind from the age of six weeks, due to a physician's mistreatment. Raised in a religious environment, she memorized Scripture and poetry, and was able to recite the first four books of both the Old and New Testaments by age ten. Entering the New York School for the Blind in 1835, she went on to teach at the school from 1848 until her marriage to Alexander Van Alstyne in 1858. She was known by the public as "Mrs. Crosby" for the rest of her life.

Her first publication was *The Blind Girl and Other Poems* (1844), but she would eventually establish the style of poetry which still characterizes gospel songs, and her prolific output of hymn* texts made her familiar to an entire generation. Traveling, preaching and witnessing brought her

into contact with many Christian leaders and public figures.

Her texts, written in her own name or under numerous pseudonyms, were set to music by the most popular American tunesmiths of the century, including Ira D. Sankey,* but she asked only about two dollars for each hymn and deliberately lived a frugal life. The author index of any contemporary evangelical* hymnal is testimony to her influence. "True hymns," she said, "make themselves." "I never undertake a hymn without first asking the good Lord to be my inspiration." Among her thousands of familiar hymns and gospel songs are: "All the Way My Saviour Leads Me"; "Blessed Assurance"; "I Am Thine, O Lord"; "Jesus, Keep Me Near the Cross"; "Rescue the Perishing"; "Tell Me the Story of Jesus" and "To God Be the Glory." The collection of Crosby's papers are held at the Lincoln Center Music Division of the New York Public Library.

BIBLIOGRAPHY. F. J. Crosby, *Fanny Crosby's Life Story* (1903); F. J. Crosby, *Memories of Eighty Years* (1906); *DAB* II; *NAW* 1; B. Ruffin, *Fanny Crosby* (1976).   R. J. Stanislaw

Croswell, Andrew (1708-1785). Itinerant* Congregational* preacher* and radical supporter of the Great Awakening.* A Harvard* graduate of 1728, Croswell was ordained* at Groton, Connecticut, in 1738. Influenced by George Whitefield* and his followers, he began in 1742 to itinerate and promote revivals.* His unorthodox methods, including the use of children and African-Americans in the pulpit, swiftly made him a controversial figure, while his outspoken criticism of Old Lights* (as well as moderates like Jonathan Edwards*) earned him a reputation for extremism. In 1746 he resigned his church, without advice of ecclesiastical council, to itinerate full-time, but within two years he was settled at what became Eleventh Church in Boston. Throughout most of his life he remained a much-published controversialist. He engaged in newspaper and pamphlet wars over most of the religious and secular debates of his day, ranging from justification* by faith to the slave trade and cruelty to animals. Ostracized by many of his peers in Boston, Croswell pastored a church that had dwindled to just seven members at the time of his death.

BIBLIOGRAPHY. C. K. Shipton, *Sibley's Harvard Graduates,* vol. 8 (1951).   E. C. Nordbeck

Crowell, Henry Parsons (1855-1944). Manufacturer and Christian philanthropist.* Crowell was president of Quaker Mill (1881-1891); general manager and president of American Cereal (1891-1944); president and chairman of the board of Quaker Oats (1922-1942); chairman of the board of Cleveland Foundry, later, Perfection Stove Company (1888-1944); and owner of Wyoming Hereford Ranch. Influenced by Dwight L. Moody* during Moody's visit to Cleveland in 1873, Crowell later insured the financial survival of Moody Bible Institute,* serving as chairman of the board from 1902 to 1944 and influencing its theological development. He was chairman of the Layman's Evangelistic Council in Chicago, which sponsored crusades by R. A. Torrey,* Gipsy Smith* and Billy Sunday.* A leader of the Committee of Fifteen (1915-1944), he lobbied for laws against commercialized prostitution and other vice. A longtime Presbyterian, Crowell contributed to the publication of *The Sunday School Times* and *The Fundamentals.* He left the Presbyterian Church in 1943 over the issue of liberalism.

BIBLIOGRAPHY. R. E. Day, *Breakfast Table Autocrat: The Life Story of Henry Parsons Crowell* (1946).   D. D. Bundy

Crucifix. A cross bearing the figure of Christ. Traditionally, the image on the cross (usually called by the Latin term *corpus*) takes one of two forms. The more common is the suffering Christ of the crucifixion, stripped and showing the marks of the passion: a wound in the left side, a crown of thorns and the marks of scourging. The other image used is that of the victorious Christ, standing upright, fully robed and reigning in glory from the wood of the cross.

During the Middle Ages, the crucifix, along with other religious images, came to have very extensive devotional* use. Many of the Reformers of the sixteenth century, fearing idolatry, dispensed of all such devices, and the crucifix disappeared from Protestant* homes and churches. In the nineteenth century, those American Episcopalians* who were influenced by English Tractarianism* began to reinstate the crucifix as a liturgical furnishing, causing bitter debate within the Episcopal Church. More recently, with concern over idolatry abated, some American Protestants are regarding the crucifix more sympathetically, as a valid way of calling to mind the events of the Passion.

S. J. White

Crummell, Alexander (1819-1898). Episcopal* minister* and missionary* to West Africa. Born a free African-American in New York in 1819, Crummell attended primary school in New York and later New Hampshire, and completed a rigorous classical curriculum at Oneida Institute in 1837. When he was denied admission to the leading seminary* of the Episcopal Church, General Theological Seminary, on account of race, Crummell studied privately in Boston. He became an Episcopal priest* in 1844.

Denied a parish in Providence, Philadelphia, Boston and New York, Crummell left for England in January 1848. In England, he raised funds, lectured for the abolitionist movement* in the U.S., and received his B.A. from Queen's College in February 1853. On June 24, 1853, Crummell and his family set sail for Monrovia, Liberia. He remained in Africa for twenty years, returning to the U.S. in 1872 to become rector* of St. Luke's Episcopal Church in Washington, D.C., from 1873 to 1894. Crummell spent the final years of his life as president and one of the founders of the American Negro Academy. He died on September 10, 1898.

Alexander Crummell dedicated his life to the liberation of African-American people in the U.S. and in Africa and became one of the earliest leaders of the Pan-African movement. A scholar, activist, missionary and minister, Crummell believed that unity among African-American people was a necessary ingredient for the unity of all humankind. He lectured and wrote about the responsibility of the black intelligentsia and the Christian church to provide the organizational infrastructure and philosophical foundation for the liberation of black people.

BIBLIOGRAPHY. *DARB; NCAB* 5; G. U. Rigsby, *Alexander Crummell: Pioneer in Nineteenth-Century Pan African Thought* (1987).

L. J. Edwards

Crumpler, (A)bner (B)lackman (1863-1952). Holiness* evangelist.* A pioneer leader of the Holiness Movement in North Carolina, A. B. Crumpler was born near Clinton in Sampson County in 1863. As a youth he entered the ministry* of the Methodist Episcopal Church, South.* In 1890, during a district conference at Bismarck, Missouri, under the preaching* of the noted Southern evangelist Beverly Carradine, Crumpler claimed the experience of entire sanctification,* which proved to be the turning point of his life. Beginning in 1896 he itinerated as an evangelist in Sampson, Duplin and Wayne counties, North Carolina, and on May 15, 1897, organized a state Holiness association at Magnolia.

Attacks on worldlings, tobacco users, and bishops* put Crumpler on a collision course with the church. On October 12, 1899, he was charged with "immorality" for having conducted a revival* meeting over the objections of the minister in charge of the circuit.* Though acquitted, he left the Methodist Episcopal Church, South, and later that month founded the Holiness Church at Goldsboro. From 1900 to 1908 Crumpler's *Holiness Advocate* drew sharp distinctions between the editor's teachings on holiness, healing* and right conduct and those of opponents.

Crumpler inspired demonstrative worship* and deep loyalty, and was elected convention president of the first nine years of the church's existence. In 1907, despite his disapproval, almost the entire ministerium was swept into the Pentecostal* camp under G. B. Cashwell.* Nevertheless, the convention unanimously re-elected Crumpler as president. He then withdrew and returned as a layman* to the Methodist Church. Thereafter, Crumpler practiced law in Clinton, emotionally distant from both his Methodist Holiness and glossolalic children. He died there in 1952.

BIBLIOGRAPHY. J. E. Campbell, *The Pentecostal Holiness Church, 1898-1948: Its Background and History* (1951). C. E. Jones

Crusade Evangelism. *See* MASS EVANGELISM.

Culbertson, William (1905-1971). Bishop* of the Reformed Episcopal Church* and president of Moody Bible Institute.* A native of Philadelphia, Culbertson graduated from the Theological Seminary of the Reformed Episcopal Church in Philadelphia in 1927 and entered the ministry* of the Reformed Episcopal Church. After serving briefly as rector* of Grace Church, Collingdale, Pennsylvania (1927-1930) and St. John's-by-the-Sea, Ventnor, New Jersey (1930-1933), he became rector of the Church of the Atonement, Philadelphia (1933-1942), and in 1937 was elected bishop for the New York and Philadelphia Synod of the Reformed Episcopal Church. His reputation as a preacher* and his longstanding interest in Christian education* led to an invitation in 1942 to become dean of education at Moody Bible Institute in Chicago. In 1948 he was elected president of the Institute, a position he held until 1970.

Culbertson published little apart from his sermons that appeared in various periodicals, though he was in great demand as a missionary* and evangelistic* speaker. He repudiated liberal* theology and called for strict separation* from liberal church bodies, and vigorously promoted dispensationalism.* Out of the pulpit, Culbertson was reticent and deliberate, but he proved to be a successful administrator who preserved the idea of the Bible institute* as a viable evangelical* educa-

tional entity apart from the college or seminary.* He modernized the informal, lay-oriented curriculum of Moody Bible Institute and transformed it into a degree-granting institution, while at the same time maintaining its doctrinal fundamentalism* and emphasis on practical churchmanship.

BIBLIOGRAPHY. W. W. Wiersbe, *William Culbertson: A Man of God* (1974); R. A. Acker, *A History of the Reformed Episcopal Seminary, 1886-1964* (1965). A. C. Guelzo

Cullis, Charles (1833-1892). Physician and faith healer.* After study at the University of Vermont, Cullis established a lucrative medical practice in Boston. A devout Episcopalian* inspired by Wesleyan/Holiness* spirituality,* Cullis established a home to care for the "Indigent and Incurable Consumptives." Its success required several moves to larger quarters. Cullis became famous for his efforts in "Faith Cures through Prayer" and worked diligently to promote that perspective around the world. He organized a mission society, "Faith Missions at Home and Abroad" with Methodist* theologian* Daniel Steele as a trustee. An influential publisher through his Willard Tract* Society, which by 1872 had distributed over 500,000 items free of charge, Cullis published his own books as well as books of authors advocating Wesleyan/Holiness higher life* and faith healing. Cullis founded periodicals, such as *Times of Refreshing* (1869), *The Word of Life* (1873) and *Service for Jesus* (1885), that achieved wide circulation. He influenced William E. Boardman,* Carrie J. Montgomery,* John A. Dowie* and, through them, the larger Keswick,* Wesleyan/Holiness and Pentecostal* movements around the world.

BIBLIOGRAPHY. W. E. Boardman, *Faith Work Under Dr. Cullis in Boston* (1874); *DAB* II; W. H. Daniels, *Dr. Cullis and His Work: Twenty Years of Blessing in Answer to Prayer* (1885).

D. D. Bundy

Cult. Although widely used by scholars, journalists and the public, the term lacks precise definition. Its meaning varies according to the constituency and frame of reference of the user. In journalistic and popular usage the term often carries pejorative and sensational connotations and is associated with curious and unconventional belief and behavior.

Social and behavioral scientists define cults as religious groups lying outside the American religious mainstream, incorporating beliefs and practices in tension with the dominant culture. Within this context cults represent a radical religious innovation within American society. They are new religious movements, as distinguished from sects* which have a prior tie with another religious organization and church and have shown greater accommodation toward dominant cultural and social realities. Cults may either originate in the host society (as did Mormonism,* Christian Science* and Scientology) or be imported from another religious culture (as were the Unification Church,* the Hare Krishnas and the Baha'i Faith).

Evangelical* Christians tend to define cults as religious groups which deviate significantly from orthodox* Christianity. This theological focus emphasizes analysis of the truth claims of any given group in light of traditional Christianity and its historic interpretation of the Bible.
See also SECT.

BIBLIOGRAPHY. R. Enroth et al., *A Guide to Cults & New Religions* (1983); J. G. Melton, *Encyclopedic Handbook of Cults in America* (1986); R. Stark and W. S. Bainbridge, *The Future of Religion* (1985).

R. Enroth

Cumberland Presbyterian Church. Presbyterian* denomination* with churches predominantly in the South and West. An outgrowth of the frontier revivals* of 1800 in Kentucky, this denomination originated on February 4, 1810 in Dickson County, Tennessee, with the formation of an independent Cumberland Presbytery by Finis Ewing,* Samuel King and Samuel McAdow. This followed a lengthy controversy between the more Arminian* and revivalist elements of Cumberland Presbytery and the Presbyterian Church in the U.S.A.* over subscription to the Westminster Confession's* teaching on predestination,* educational requirements for ministers* and the extent of synodical* authority over presbyteries.*

The Church enjoyed rapid growth on the frontier with the establishing of the Cumberland Synod in 1813 and the formation of a General Assembly* in 1829. Growing fivefold between 1835 and 1860, the predominantly rural denomination established congregations from Pennsylvania to California. The Civil War* did not result in a formal split. Following the revision by the Presbyterian Church in the U.S.A. of the Westminster Confession's teaching on divine sovereignty, a merger of the two denominations was approved in 1906. A continuing Cumberland Presbyterian Church was perpetuated, however, by a sizable minority which feared that doctrinal* harmony between the two churches had not been achieved.

Standing self-consciously between Calvinism* and Arminianism, Cumberland Presbyterians have held to a "medium theology" which affirms an unlimited atonement,* universal grace, conditional election,* the eternal security* of the believer and the salvation of all children dying in infancy. The denomination lists 831 churches with a membership of 98,829. It supports Bethel College in McKenzie, Tennessee, and Memphis Theological Seminary. Close ties are maintained with the predominantly African-American Second Cumberland Presbyterian Church, which subscribes to the Cumberland Presbyterian confessional standards.

BIBLIOGRAPHY. B. M. Barrus, M. L. Baughn and T. H. Campbell, *A People Called Cumberland Presbyterians* (1972); T. H. Campbell, *Studies in Cumberland Presbyterian History* (1944).

W. B. Evans

Cummins, George David (1822-1876). Founding bishop* of the Reformed Episcopal Church.* A native of Delaware, he was educated at Dickinson College, Pennsylvania (M.A., 1844), and then entered the Protestant Episcopal Church in the U.S.A.* and was ordained* deacon* in 1845 and priest* in 1847. Between 1846 and 1866 he served a succession of important parishes* in Baltimore, Richmond, Washington and Chicago, until being elected assistant bishop of Kentucky.

As bishop, Cummins's principal inspiration was the catholic evangelicalism* of William A. Muhlenberg.* This brought him into opposition to high church* ideas concerning the exclusive validity of Episcopal ordinations and to the influence of the Tractarian Movement* in the Episcopal Church. In October 1873 he was a major participant in the convention of the Evangelical Alliance* in New York City, and on October 12 he participated in an ecumenical communion service in connection with the Alliance. This action was censured by Henry C. Potter, bishop of New York, in a public letter on November 5. In response, Cummins resigned his office on November 10, 1873, with the intention of transferring his episcopate to "another sphere." A "Call to Organize" a new Episcopal church was issued by Cummins on November 15, and on December 2, 1873, he presided over a meeting of eight clergymen and twenty lay leaders who organized the Reformed Episcopal Church in New York City. His leadership of the new church was cut short by his untimely death less than three years later. A posthumous collection of *Sermons* was published in 1884.

BIBLIOGRAPHY. B. A. Aycrigg, *Memoirs of the Reformed Episcopal Church* (1880); A. M. Cummins, *Memoir of George David Cummins, D.D.* (1878); *DAB* II.

A. C. Guelzo

Curate. The word *curate* is derived from the Latin *cura,* meaning "care," and *curator* which means "one who takes care of." In French a *curé* is a rector,* parson or parish* priest.* Originally it meant any clergyman* or ordained* person. Under the system of "provision" in the Middle Ages, the pope* could nominate persons to a vacant see. These persons were called vicars. When vicars were absent a temporary priest would be named to the benefice, and these were called curates-in-charge. In English practice, the term *curate* has been reserved for the assistant to a rector. The term is used primarily by the Episcopalians,* Roman Catholics* and the Orthodox.* Most Protestant* groups do not use the term.

D. S. Armentrout

Curse of Ham. An argument used to justify slavery, based on Noah's curse of Canaan, the son of Ham. American expressions of the argument focused on Genesis 9:18-27. After the flood, Noah drank too much wine and fell asleep naked inside his tent. Ham, one of Noah's sons, looked upon his father's nakedness and went out to tell his brothers, Shem and Japheth. They covered Noah while looking the other way. When Noah awoke from his stupor, he cursed Canaan, son of Ham, declaring that he would be the lowest of slaves to his brothers. Writers in the antebellum South used the philological argument that Japheth's name could mean "whiteness" and Ham's name "dark," "hot" and "black." Thus Japheth and Ham were identified as the ancestors of the white and black races, respectively. The story was used by proslavery advocates not only to explain why the Negro race was black but also to legitimize their enslavement.

The textual basis for the utilization of the curse as an explanation for blackness and slavery goes back to Hebraic literature between A.D. 200 and 600. The writings of St. Jerome and St. Augustine refer to the curse in connection with slavery in the abstract but not with blacks. The story was used by Christians in the sixteenth century to explain the Negro's blackness. In America the use of the story can be traced to the beginning of the eighteenth century. After 1830 the story became one of the most popular defenses of slavery. It was used by clergy* representing various denominations:* Baptist,* Methodist,* Presbyterian,* Episcopalian,* Roman Catholic,* Congregational* and German Reformed.*

BIBLIOGRAPHY. W. D. Jordan, *White Over Black, American Attitudes toward the Negro, 1550-1812* (1977); T. V. Peterson, *Ham and Japheth, The Mythic World of Whites in the Antebellum South* (1978).

D. B. Whitlock

Cursillo. A twentieth-century Catholic* movement emphasizing spiritual growth within small groups. Cursillo has its origins in an effort to mobilize Spanish youth in organized Catholic Action* during the Franco regime. The workshops ("little courses in living Christianity"), originally designed as spiritual preparation for a youth pilgrimage to the shrine of St. James of Compostela in 1948, became the prototype for the world-wide Cursillo movement by the late 1950s. The first Spanish-speaking Cursillo in the U.S. took place in Waco, Texas, in 1957. The first English-language Cursillo was held in San Angelo, Texas, in 1961. The movement grew rapidly in the U.S. during the 1960s, and by 1965 it was organized along national lines. By 1985 the national office reported that roughly 600,000 had participated in Cursillos in the U.S.

Individuals become involved in the movement by participating in a Cursillo, an intense, single-sex weekend experience which includes a series of lectures *(rollos)* delivered by trained leaders and punctuated by opportunities for individual and group response. The weekends result in the formation of small groups of *cursillistas* who share common interests, groups that meet weekly to build upon the spiritual renewal and sense of community achieved through the initial Cursillo. Through Cursillo, members of the Catholic laity* have become involved in a wide spectrum of grassroots spiritual and social movements. Although the Cursillo movement is not formally linked to the Catholic charismatic movement,* the Cursillo movement—especially the National Cursillo Convention held in 1966—was an important catalyst in the growth of the Catholic charismatic renewal in the U.S.

BIBLIOGRAPHY. G. P. Hughes, "Cursillo Movement" *NCE* 17; M. Marcoux, *Cursillo: Anatomy of a Movement* (1982).

D. Campbell

Cushing, Richard James (1895-1970). Cardinal* of Boston. Born in Boston in 1895, Cushing attended Boston College (1913-1915) and graduated from St. John's Seminary, Brighton, Massachusetts (1921). While still a seminarian he developed a strong interest in the foreign missions.* As a diocesan priest* (ordained 1921) that work was closed to him, but after a short period in pastoral work he served in the Boston office of the Society for the Propagation of the Faith,* an international organization which raised funds for the missions.

Cushing was extremely successful in that work, a success reflected in his appointment as auxiliary bishop* of his native city in 1939. Five years later he was appointed archbishop, succeeding Cardinal William O'Connell.*

Archbishop Cushing was in almost every way a complete contrast to his rather aristocratic predecessor. Possessed of a gruff voice, he was habitually informal and breezy and always identified with his working-class Irish origins. He was regarded as an outstanding administrator who not only presided over a major see but raised millions of dollars for numerous charities. His special interests were the missions and retarded children, but his gifts—often unpublicized—went to a wide variety of causes.

A long-time friend of the Kennedy family, Cushing offered the invocation at John F. Kennedy's* presidential inauguration in 1961, and officiated at his funeral two years later. Politically, the archbishop appeared to be a bundle of contradictions. He was a long-time member of the National Association for the Advancement of Colored People and was strongly in favor of labor unions. But his anti-Communism* also made him an outspoken supporter of Senator Joseph McCarthy and of the John Birch* Society. These apparent inconsistencies stemmed from the fact that he seldom held a systematically thought-out position but usually reacted to events and to people on the basis of intuition and feeling, considering himself a man of the heart rather than of the head.

Passed over twice by Pius XII,* he was one of the first group of cardinals appointed by John XXIII* in 1958. At the Second Vatican Council* he complained that he could not follow the Latin speeches and stayed away from many of the sessions. However, he spoke out strongly on behalf of ecumenism* and religious liberty.* Even before the Council he had been a kind of instinctive ecumenist, frequently visiting Jewish synagogues and Protestant* churches. He had a special affection for Jews and publicly denounced anti-Semitism.

Like many bishops, he seemed uncertain of his own positions in the confusion which followed Vatican II and seemed once again often to take contradictory positions. He retired in 1970 and died later the same year.

BIBLIOGRAPHY. (Anon.), *The World's Cardinal* (1964); J. H. Cutler, *Cardinal Cushing of Boston* (1970); *DARB;* J. Dever, *Cushing of Boston* (1965); J. H. Fenton, *Salt of the Earth: An Informal Portrait of Richard Cardinal Cushing* (1951).

J. F. Hitchcock

Cutler, Timothy (1684-1765). Anglican* rector* in Boston. Cutler graduated from Harvard College* (B.A., 1701) and served as pastor* to the Congregationalists* in the Stratford, Connecticut, area (1710-1719) before becoming rector* at Yale* in 1719. There his exposure to the works of seventeenth-century Anglican* divines helped persuade him and several colleagues (including Samuel Johnson) that neither presbyterian* ordination* nor congregational polity* were valid. In 1722 Cutler, along with Samuel Johnson and Daniel Brown, defected to Anglicanism,* a move that permanently shocked the Congregational establishment and paved the way for Anglican growth in Puritanism's back yard.

Upon returning from England as an ordained* Anglican priest* and as the recipient of an honorary doctorate from Oxford University, Cutler immediately began his long pastorate in Boston. He quickly established himself as a formidable controversialist in conflicts with the colony's Congregationalists and as the city's leading spokesperson for Anglican prerogatives. An early colonial exponent of Arminian* rationalism, Cutler's sermons reflected a large debt to Lockean epistemology and Newtonian cosmology. Such a theology* gave him little sympathy for the religious enthusiasm of the Great Awakening* in general and of fellow churchman George Whitefield* in particular. Little wonder, then, that with Cutler's natural appetite for controversy, he would devote much of his later career to combatting what he called the "madness" of revivalism.* For more than forty years (1723-1765), Cutler staunchly defended Anglicanism as rector* of Boston's Christ Church (Old North Church). Yet throughout his lifetime he was best known in colonial New England as the central figure in the so-called Yale apostasy of 1722.

BIBLIOGRAPHY. *AAP* 5; *DAB* III; *DARB;* R. E. Daggy, "Education, Church and State: Timothy Cutler and the Yale Apostasy of 1722," *JCS* 13 (1971): 43-69; D. Huber, "Timothy Cutler: The Convert as Controversialist," *HMPEC* 44 (1975):489-96.

R. W. Pointer

Cuyler, Theodore Ledyard (1822-1909). Presbyterian* minister* and author. Born in Aurora, New York, Cuyler studied at Princeton University (B.A., 1841). The following year, while on a trip to Europe, he visited Wordsworth, Dickens and Carlyle, a description of which is found in his *Recollections of a Long Life* (1902). After graduating from Princeton Theological Seminary (B.D., 1846), he was licensed* and ordained* into the

Presbyterian ministry. From 1846 to 1860 he pastored churches in New Jersey and Ohio, prior to beginning a thirty-year pastorate at the Lafayette Avenue Presbyterian Church in Brooklyn, New York City. In 1890 he became pastor emeritus and continued preaching,* lecturing and writing.

During his extended years of service in Brooklyn, Cuyler became one of New York City's most popular preachers. His sermons were forceful and evangelical* in tone. He wrote incessantly for the religious press, compiling over four thousand articles and twenty-two books, many of which were translated into Dutch, Swedish and other foreign languages.

BIBLIOGRAPHY. *DAB* III; *Lafayette Avenue Church: Its History and Commemorative Services, 1860-1885* (1885). R. R. Mathisen

D

Dabbs, James McBride (1896-1970). Southern Presbyterian* civil rights* advocate. Born in Hayesville, South Carolina, and reared on a large cotton plantation, Dabbs attended the University of South Carolina, Clark University and Columbia University.* After teaching briefly, Dabbs farmed for a living and wrote about the South until his death. A fervent Christian, he brought faith to bear on issues of importance for the region. His books include: *The Southern Heritage* (1958), *Who Speaks for the South* (1964) and *Haunted by God* (1972).

Dabbs helped form the Fellowship of Southern Churchmen* and served as president of the Southern Regional Council, a civil rights organization. Theologically, Dabbs reiterated classic themes of Reformed tradition*: the sovereignty of God over the affairs of the world, the universality of human sinfulness, the need for Christian proclamation of the gospel, and the responsibility of Christians for others in every aspect of life.   L. B. Weeks

Dabney, Robert Lewis (1820-1898). Southern Presbyterian* theologian* and educator. Born in Louisa County, Virginia, Dabney studied at Hampden-Sydney College (1836-1837). Following a stint as a schoolteacher (1838-1839), he continued his education at the University of Virginia (M.A., 1842) and Union Theological Seminary, Virginia (1846). Dabney began his ministerial career as a rural missionary* but soon became pastor of Tinkling Spring Church, Virginia (1847-1853), and headmaster of a classical academy. In 1853 Hampden-Sydney awarded him an honorary doctorate, and he was called to Union Seminary (then located at Hampden-Sydney) as professor of church history and polity.* From 1859 to 1883 he taught theology* and simultaneously served much of that time as co-pastor of Hampden-Sydney College Church (1858-1874). A respected churchman, Dabney was elected moderator of the Southern Presbyterian General Assembly* in 1870. In 1883 Dabney left Virginia for health reasons and became professor of philosophy at the University

of Texas (1883-1894), where he helped found the Austin Theological Seminary and also served on its faculty (1884-1895). By 1890 Dabney was in ill health and had suffered a total loss of his eyesight, yet always a man of intense energy and conviction, he continued to lecture.

Prior to the Civil War* Dabney opposed secession, but he soon became a strong advocate of the Southern cause. When war interrupted his academic profession, Dabney served as a chaplain* (1861) in the Confederate army and, in 1862, as an officer under General T. J. (Stonewall) Jackson.* A loyal Southerner to the end, Dabney never wavered from his belief that the cause of the South was right and would eventually be vindicated. Embittered by Reconstruction policies, he vigorously opposed reunion with the Northern Presbyterians. Despite his regional loyalties, he was, nevertheless, a perceptive social critic of post-Civil War industrialized capitalism, secular materialism and a powerful centralized government.

A man of wide and detailed learning, Dabney taught with great intensity and clarity of insight and was recognized as the leading Southern Presbyterian theologian after the Civil War. His theology was the moderate but consistent Calvinism* of the Westminster Confession* and Catechisms and was comparable to other nineteenth-century Old School* Presbyterian theologians such as Charles Hodge* of Princeton.* Like the Princeton theologians, Dabney was influenced by the Scottish Common Sense* philosophy, but he avoided speculation and deplored some of the traditional theological distinctions, regarding them as over-refinements and undue subtleties.

Dabney's style was terse, powerful and fresh. Interested in practical matters, he was concerned to apply Christian faith not only to religious topics but also to moral and social philosophy. Because of his willingness to wrestle with difficult theological issues and make his own critical observations, some have regarded Dabney's systematic theology as more profound than that of Charles Hodge. His many writings include: *Life and Campaigns of*

Lieut-General Thomas J. Jackson (1866), *A Defense of Virginia, and Through Her of the South* (1867), *Sacred Rhetoric* (1870), *Systematic and Polemic Theology* (1871), *The Sensualist Philosophy of the Nineteenth Century* (1875), *Christ Our Penal Substitute* (1897), *The Practical Philosophy* (1897) and articles on a wide range of topics in *Discussions* (4 vols., 1890-1897).

As a defender of the South and its institutions, Dabney's influence for most of his lifetime did not extend outside of his region. At war with most of the developments of the latter half of the century and inflexible in resisting change, he lived to see many of the issues he had championed fall from favor within his denomination.* Recent reprints of several of his books have given him a larger reading public than he enjoyed even during his lifetime.

BIBLIOGRAPHY. *DAB* III; *DARB;* T. C. Johnson, *The Life and Letters of Robert Lewis Dabney* (1903); D. F. Kelly, "Robert Lewis Dabney" in *Reformed Theology in America,* ed. D. F. Wells (1985); *NCAB* 2; D. H. Overy, *Robert Lewis Dabney: Apostle of the Old South* (1967).

A. H. Freundt

Dagg, John Leadley (1794-1884). Baptist* minister,* educator, theologian.* Born at Middleburg, Virginia, the oldest of eight children, he was baptized* in 1812 by the Ebenezer Baptist Church and ordained* in 1817. Although his formal education was limited, Dagg possessed genuine intellectual gifts and a strong desire to learn. Thus, other than having six or seven years of formal schooling, he was largely self-taught in his mastery of Latin, Greek, Hebrew and higher mathematics.

Dagg served several churches in Virginia and for nine years (1825-1834) was pastor of the Fifth Baptist Church in Philadelphia. However, because of difficulty with his throat, he withdrew from the pastorate and thereafter gave himself to teaching, educational administration and writing. He first became head of the Haddington Institution near Philadelphia and then the Alabama Female Athenaeum in Tuscaloosa in 1836. From 1844 to 1854 he was president of Mercer University in Penfield, Georgia. He remained there as professor of theology* until 1856.

During his years as an educator Dagg wrote essays dealing with the ordinances and with the Bible: *An Essay in Defence of Strict Communion* (1845), *A Decisive Argument against Infant Baptism* (1849) and *Origin and Authority of the Bible* (1853). His more influential books on theology were written after his retirement: *A Manual of Theology* (1857), *A Treatise on Church Order* (1858), *The Elements of Moral Science* (1860) and *The Evidences of Christianity* (1869). Through these volumes he became recognized as a theologian and exerted wide influence on his former students and other Baptists. Whether writing or teaching, Dagg's aim was to assist in the preparation of ministers. His theology may be described as essentially biblical and moderately Calvinistic,* and it earned him the reputation as the pioneer Baptist theologian in America.

BIBLIOGRAPHY. *DAB* III; R. G. Gardner, "John Leadley Dagg," *RE* 54 (1957): 246-263.

W. M. Patterson

Daggett, Naphtali (1727-1780). Congregational* minister,* professor of divinity* at Yale College.* Born in Attleboro, Massachusetts, Daggett graduated from Yale in 1748, studied theology* and was ordained* in 1751 as pastor of the Smithtown Presbyterian* Church on Long Island. In 1753 he married Sarah Smith. In 1756, President Thomas Clap,* in the interest of moving Yale in a New Light* direction, named Daggett the college's first professor (heretofore instruction was by tutors and president) and pastor to students. Daggett served as acting president from 1766 to 1777. Though known as a dull teacher and preacher (nicknamed "Tunker" on campus), Daggett established the college on a firm institutional footing. An ardent patriot, during the Stamp Act crisis he wrote the incendiary "Cato Letters" in the *Connecticut Gazette* and in 1779 was captured as he helped defend New Haven against British attack. His numerous books include: *The Great and Tender Concern of Faithful Ministers for the Souls of Their People, Should Powerfully Excite Them Also to Labour After Their Own Salvation* (1770).

BIBLIOGRAPHY. B. M. Kelly, *Yale: A History* (1974); F. B. Dexter, *Biographical Sketches of the Graduates of Yale College With Annals of the College History* (1885).

C. E. Hambrick-Stowe

Dake, Vivian Adelbert (1854-1892). Free Methodist* pastor and founder of the Pentecost Bands. Dake attended Chili Seminary and University of Rochester. Influenced by William Taylor* and Benjamin Titus Roberts,* he promoted faith missions* and an ascetic lifestyle. On this model, the first Pentecost Band, a team of youth devoted to short-term evangelistic and missionary endeavors, was organized in Mankato, Minnesota (1882), and took permanent form in Parma, Michigan (1885). Denominational* efforts to restrict the independent faith missions led the Bands to work outside the church. The Bands were active in evangelism* and social reform in the U.S., India, Europe and Caribbean. Dake also traveled to Europe where he met with various higher life* groups. He died in Sierra Leone. After his death, the Pentecost Bands continued, but most Bands eventually joined Wesleyan/Holiness* or Pentecostal churches.*

BIBLIOGRAPHY. T. H. Nelson, *Life and Labors of Rev. Vivian A. Dake, Organizer and Leader of Pentecost Bands* (1894); I. D. Parsons, *Kindling Watch-Fires, Being a Brief Sketch of the Life of Rev. Vivian A. Dake* (1915).   D. D. Bundy

Dallas Theological Seminary. A professional graduate-level institution, training men and women for ministry.* In the fall of 1924 Dallas Seminary, then called the Evangelical Theological College, began with thirteen students in rented quarters in South Dallas, Texas. It was the fulfillment of the aspirations of Lewis Sperry Chafer,* an Ohioan who had traveled extensively, beginning in the 1890s as an evangelist's assistant, then an evangelist* and eventually as a popular Bible* teacher.

Through his travels and conversations with numerous pastors and colleagues, Chafer had become convinced that an entirely new departure was needed in the preparation of godly servants for the ministry.* The standard theological curriculum had three glaring deficiencies: a neglect of an intensive study of each book of the Bible, a general failure to foster the spiritual development of each student (particularly in the principles and interpretative insights associated with the Keswick* and Northfield Conferences*) and the absence of the teaching of dispensationalism* and premillennialism,* which he felt singularly provided insights for understanding and unfolding the Scriptures. In essence, the school sought to institutionalize the theological distinctives of the Bible conference movement.*

After two years the school was moved to its permanent location at Swiss and St. Joseph avenues, where it initially occupied the former mansion of one of the pioneers of East Dallas, William H. Gaston. By the late 1930s, with the ravages of the Great Depression* behind it, the seminary began to emerge into a place of increasing prominence in the evangelical* community. Symbols of this were the acquisition in 1933 of *Bibliotheca Sacra,* a time-honored theological journal, the shift in 1936 to a four-year Th.M. program from the three-year Th.B. and a name change in 1936. Shifting theological currents and alignments in the 1930s

and 1940s (i.e., the rise of liberalism* in the mainline* Northern denominations and a growing hostility to the Bible conference distinctives in others) caused the institution's graduates to join the independent church movement. Consequently, the school has become a major training center for the nondenominational, or separatist,* evangelical movement in America.

In 1952, with the passing of Chafer, John F. Walvoord was named president and remained so until 1986 when Donald K. Campbell became the institution's third president. During the former's tenure, the seminary emerged from numerical obscurity to become an important training school for the professional evangelical ministry. In the late 1980s the seminary had a faculty of over seventy and a student body of over 1,500 men and women.

BIBLIOGRAPHY. J. D. Hannah, "The Social and Intellectual Origins of the Evangelical Theological College" (unpublished Ph.D. dissertation, University of Texas at Dallas, 1988).

J. D. Hannah

Damien, Father (Joseph de Veuster) (1840-1889). Missionary*-priest* to the Lepers of Molokai. Born in Tremloo, Belgium, Joseph followed his brother into the Congregation of the Sacred Hearts of Jesus and Mary (Picpus Fathers) at Louvain in 1859 and was professed in 1860. In March 1864 he arrived in Hawaii and was ordained* there May 21. For eight years he worked as a missionary priest on the island of Hawaii. In 1873, in response to a request of the Vicar Apostolic, he began to work among the lepers of the Hawaiian island Molokai. He cared spiritually not only for Catholics but for all, nursing them and building homes and seeking goods for them, in addition to forcefully establishing some moral discipline. In 1884 he was declared a leper. After death his reputation was attacked, drawing a forceful response from Robert Louis Stevenson. His body was returned to Belgium in 1936. A petition for his canonization* was made in 1962.

BIBLIOGRAPHY. G. Daws, *Holy Man: Father Damien of Molokai* (1984); P. de Veuster, *Life and Letters of Father Damien* (1889).

L. Nemer

Dana, James Dwight (1813-1895). Geologist and mineralogist. Born in Utica, New York, the son of a saddler and hardware merchant, Dana studied under Benjamin Silliman* at Yale.* Following his graduation in 1830, he worked as an assistant in Yale's chemical laboratory and coedited the *American Journal of Science* with Silliman. In

1837 he published his *System of Mineralogy* and the following year departed with the Wilkes expedition (1838-1842) which took him around the world and gave him the experience and knowledge that would contribute to his becoming America's foremost geologist. Prior to departing, however, he underwent a conversion* to evangelical* faith.

In 1855 he became Silliman Professor of Natural History at Yale and the following year engaged in a major controversy with classicist Tayler Lewis* of Union College. The essence of their theological disagreement was that Lewis argued that scientific theory was transitory and should not affect biblical interpretation, while Dana argued that science informed biblical interpretation. Dana, though uniformitarian in his geology, believed that entire species were periodically destroyed and replaced by a higher divine creation. This led him initially to disagree with Darwin's *Origin of the Species* (1859) and its assumption of linear evolution. Nevertheless, by 1883 he had, with qualifications, accepted Darwin's principle of natural selection. Humans, he argued, were derived from a lower species, albeit by a special work of divine creativity.

Dana did not find these views incompatible with his evangelical faith and his understanding of Scripture. Along with Asa Gray* of Harvard* and George Wright* of Oberlin,* Dana was an influential force in advocating a theistic Darwinism among evangelicals of the late nineteenth century.

See also DARWINIAN EVOLUTION AND THE AMERICAN CHURCHES.

BIBLIOGRAPHY. *DAB* III; D. G. Gilman, *The Life of James Dwight Dana* (1910); D. N. Livingstone, *Darwin's Forgotten Defenders* (1987); W. F. Sanford, Jr., "Dana and Darwinism," *Journal of the History of Ideas* 26 (1965):531-546.

D. G. Reid

Danforth, Samuel (1626-1674). Puritan* minister.* Born in England, Danforth was brought to America in 1634 by his father after the death of his mother. Soon his father also died, and thereafter he lived with the Reverend Thomas Shepard.* After graduating from Harvard College* in 1643, he became a pastor of the Roxbury Church in 1650. Danforth married the daughter of the Reverend John Wilson in 1651. He also spent some time with the Reverend John Eliot* as a missionary to Native Americans in the region. He served as a fellow of Harvard and became an accomplished preacher. Several of his sermons and essays were published after his death. Danforth's election sermon of May 11, 1670, "A Brief Recognition of New England's Errand into the Wilderness," has provided historians of New England Puritanism with a useful metaphor by which to describe the Puritan mission in America.

Like many other New England preachers, Danforth took a deep interest in astronomy. Cotton Mather reported that Danforth's published astronomical description of the great comet of 1665 (*An Astronomical Description of the Late Comet or Blazing Star*) was widely appreciated. Danforth interpreted the comet as portending death.

BIBLIOGRAPHY. *AAP* 1; C. Mather, *Magnalia Christi Americana,* vol. II (1702).

L. J. Van Til

Darby, John Nelson (1800-1882). British promoter of ecclesiastical separatism* and dispensational* premillennialism.* Born in London, England, of wealthy Irish parents and named in honor of Admiral Lord Nelson, Darby graduated from Trinity College, Dublin, Ireland (1819), as a classical gold medalist. After a brief time as a lawyer—and in the context of a religious conversion*—he entered the ministry* of the Church of England* in 1825 as a deacon* and eventually became a tireless, enormously successful parish* priest* in County Wicklow, Ireland.

Darby rapidly became disenchanted with what he perceived as the lifeless formalism of state-church religion. Beginning in 1827 he found a spiritual oasis in a gathering of people meeting in Dublin for simple worship,* Bible* instruction, and the breaking of bread without ecclesiastical ritual or ministerial hierarchy or statecraft. Leaving the Church of England in 1831, he joined others of like sympathies in Plymouth, England, where they spawned a remarkably influential movement known as the Plymouth Brethren.*

The Brethren excelled in the study of Scripture,* godly living and missionary* zeal. The theological innovations of the movement were in two areas: ecclesiology and eschatology.* While the Brethren typically shunned a professional ministry* and made the Lord's Table the focus of their meetings, along with Bible teaching, Darby stressed the idea that organized Christianity was corrupt and strenuously called for ecclesiastical separation. Growing out of his ecclesiological pessimism was Darby's unique view of prophetic events that involved a new perspective and interpretation of Scripture which would come to be known as dispensationalism. In the period between 1827 and the disruptive clash with B. W. Newton over the doctrine* of the secret rapture* in 1845, Darby developed his distinctive views through prophetic conferences and Bible study. As the dominant leader among the Brethren, Darby shaped their prophetic perspective.

After 1837, when he went to Lausanne, Switzerland, Darby traveled extensively, spreading his ideas throughout the expanding Brethren movement. Between 1859 and 1874 he made seven visits to Canada and the U.S. Though dismayed by the reluctance of American clergymen to accept his ecclesiastical separatism and pessimism, his prophetic ideas influenced men such as Dwight L. Moody* of Chicago, A. J. Gordon* of Boston and James H. Brookes* of St. Louis. In addition to Darby's writings and public ministry, Americans read other prominent Brethren writers such as William Trotter, C. H. Mackintosh and William Kelly.

Out of this collective influence emerged the Bible conference movement* in America after 1870. Through the periodic prophetic conferences and the annual Niagara Bible Conference,* directed by James H. Brookes and A. J. Gordon, premillennialism gained an ever-increasing constituency. The culminating impact can be seen in William E. Blackstone's* *Jesus Is Coming* (1878) and in Cyrus I. Scofield's* immensely popular Scofield Reference Bible,* which was published in 1909. Darby's teachings deeply influenced the rise of the separatist fundamentalist* movement in America early in the twentieth century.

BIBLIOGRAPHY. E. Sandeen, *The Roots of Fundamentalism: British and American Millenarianism, 1800-1930* (1970); C. Bass, *Backgrounds to Dispensationalism (1960)*; H. A. Ironside, *An Historical Sketch of the Brethren Movement* (1942).

J. D. Hannah

Dartmouth College. An American college with roots in the Great Awakening.* Dartmouth developed from Moor's Indian Charity School begun by Eleazar Wheelock* in 1754 in Lebanon, Connecticut. Gradually more white students enrolled than Native Americans, and Wheelock relocated the school in Hanover, New Hampshire, with the new state charter naming it Dartmouth College. Like Princeton,* Brown* and Rutgers,* its birth was inspired by the Great Awakening. The original sponsors were pro-revival Congregationalists* who were dismayed with the disdain expressed toward emotional religion at the older Congregational colleges, Harvard* and Yale.*

In 1815 an internal power struggle between President John Wheelock, son of the founder, and the absentee board of trustees led Wheelock to seek the support of the New Hampshire state legislature which had granted the original charter half a century earlier. When the Republican-controlled government, which sided with Wheelock, sought to bring the college more directly under state control so as to better serve the needs of an increasingly democratic population, the trustees and the state went to court. The state Supreme Court in 1817 determined that Dartmouth was a public corporation and that its trustees were therefore responsible to the state legislature. The following year, however, the trustees, enlisting the counsel of alumnus Daniel Webster, gained a reversal of the decision in the famous U.S. Supreme Court case of *Dartmouth College* vs. *Woodward*.

The case established the sanctity of private property and contract rights in general, and for higher education specifically it clarified the distinction between private and public institutions, carefully protecting the former from state control. The decision contributed to both the burgeoning of denominational colleges in the generation following the Second Great Awakening* and to the removal of private colleges from access to public funding.

BIBLIOGRAPHY. L. B. Richardson, *History of Dartmouth College,* 2 vols. (1932).

W. C. Ringenberg

Darwinian Evolution and the American Churches. In 1896 Andrew Dickson White, president of Cornell University, published *A History of the Warfare between Science and Theology in Christendom.* No book has done more to instill in the public mind the conviction that science and theology are mortal enemies. That military metaphor continues to distort current views of the church's reaction to Darwin's theory of organic evolution.

Although Darwin was not the first to suggest the *possibility* of evolution, he presented a wealth of evidence to support a possible *mechanism,* the concept of *natural selection.* Darwin argued that over a long period of time a reduction and eventual elimination of the less favorable variations effect a gradual transformation of one species into another.

Darwin's controversial theory stirred passionate debate, but not along clearly drawn lines between scientists and theologians.* The situation was far more complex. Roman Catholic* theology* was largely able to see evolution as God's *modus operandi,* at least below the human level. Protestant* theologians of the nineteenth century had three major reactions to Darwin's teaching. Their concerns centered on the theory of evolution itself: its relationship to the Genesis account of creation, and its implications for the nature of human beings and for the belief in divine design.

Conservative anti-Darwinians relied on the observed design in nature to be a crucial argument for the existence of God. So they opposed the concept that natural selection could account for design in the organic world without recourse to divine activity. Zoologist Louis Agassiz* of Harvard* and geologist William Dawson* of McGill University waged a campaign against Darwin's theory, but the latter eventually saw that design could still be held within the evolutionary framework. Presbyterian* theologian Charles Hodge* would not accept a theistic evolution, although he allowed that others could do so and retain confidence in the Scriptures.* He vigorously attacked a Darwinism that taught natural selection without design.

Conservative Darwinians staked out a "middle ground" with confidence in both biblical theology* and evolutionary theory. Harvard botanist Asa Gray* and Yale* geologist James Dwight Dana* demonstrated that eminent scientists could coordinate biological evolution and an evangelical* faith. Princeton theologian Benjamin Warfield,* a champion of biblical inerrancy,* allowed that the theory could operate as natural law under the control of Providence. This group affirmed the biblical teaching that God's superintendence of his creation is continuous, not limited to special creative acts and miracles.

Liberal Darwinians vested nothing of importance in the historical accuracy of the Bible. The prosperity of the 1880s encouraged liberal theologians to interpret biological evolution in the light of Enlightenment* progressivism. Their progressionist philosophy went far beyond the competence of science and the content of biblical teaching.

Amidst these swirling cross-currents the most significant conflicts occurred, not between scientists and theologians, but within individual minds struggling to come to terms with new scientific discoveries. White's warfare model is not supported by the evidence; science and Christianity have not been enemies. Attempts to identify villains and victims have proved futile.

During the decades before 1920 the evangelical movement showed a surprising diversity of response to Darwin's theory of evolution. *The Fundamentals,* published in 1910, carried two anti-Darwin polemics, plus articles by George F. Wright* and James Orr* that distinguished be-

tween *evolution* as a scientific theory, which they could accept, and *evolutionism* as an unbiblical world view. In the 1920s, however, the lines quickly hardened in a shift from moderation to militancy.

See also CREATION SCIENCE; SCIENCE AND CHRISTIANITY.

BIBLIOGRAPHY. *The Fundamentals,* 12 vols. (1910); D. N. Livingstone, *Darwin's Forgotten Defenders* (1987); J. R. Moore, *The Post-Darwinian Controversies: A Study of the Protestant Struggle to Come to Terms with Darwin in Great Britain and America, 1870-1900* (1979); A. D. White, *A History of the Warfare between Science and Theology in Christendom* (1896).

C. E. Hummel

Davenport, James (1716-1757). Presbyterian* minister* and revivalist.* Great-grandson of the founding divine* of New Haven, John Davenport,* he graduated from Yale College* in 1732, an acknowledged prodigy who was prey to emotional instability. Ordained* in 1738 as pastor of a church in Southold, Long Island, he was deeply affected by the preaching of George Whitefield* in 1740 and the outbreak of the Great Awakening,* and abandoned his congregation to become an itinerant* revivalist. He conducted revival missions in New York and Connecticut, but his tendencies toward outlandish behavior, his extemporaneous preaching* and singing, and his refusal to cooperate with settled ministers raised serious opposition in his path.

His first major itinerating tour began in Stonington, Connecticut, in July 1741, and culminated in September at the Yale Commencement, where he whipped up feeling among the students against James Noyes, pastor of New Haven's First Church, and Thomas Clap,* rector of the College. After wintering in Long Island, he returned to minister in Connecticut. But the General Association had passed a strong resolution against itinerant preaching, and in June 1742, he was arrested in Stratford for disturbing the peace and was tried and deported back to Long Island.

Undaunted, he set out at once for Massachusetts, only to find that the Boston and Charlestown Clergy Association had resolved on July 1, 1742, to close their churches to his use. He responded by taking to the streets to preach, but in August the Suffolk County grand jury indicted him for slander, imprisoned him and deported him again to Long Island as insane. The following spring, he joined forces with a group of Separate* Congregationalists in New London, Connecticut. On March 6, 1743, he led a book-burning rally, but the incident cost him what little public respect he retained, and in July 1744, he broke down and published a series of *Confessions and Retractions.*

Though unrepresentative of the Great Awakening, his activities were seized upon by critics as examples of the logical conclusion of revivalist principles. He afterwards served several New Side* Presbyterian churches in New Jersey from 1747 until his death in 1757, and was elected moderator of the New Side Synod* in 1754.

See also DAVENPORT, JOHN.

BIBLIOGRAPHY. *AAP* 3; R. Bushman, ed., *The Great Awakening* (1970); *DAB* III; *DARB;* A. Heimert and P. Miller, eds., *The Great Awakening* (1967); H. S. Stout and P. Onuf, "James Davenport and the Great Awakening in New London," *JAH* 70 (1983):556-578; J. Tracy, *The Great Awakening, A History of the Revival of Religion in the Time of Edwards and Whitefield* (1841).

A. C. Guelzo

Davenport, John (1597-1670). Congregational* minister.* Educated at Oxford, Davenport found employment first as a domestic chaplain* and then was appointed curate of St. Laurence Jewry (1619) and vicar* of St. Stephen's, Coleman Street (1624), both in London. Drawn into association with the Puritans* in the 1620s, he was a shareholder in the Massachusetts Bay Company. These activities brought him the unwelcome attention of William Laud (1573-1645), the bishop of London, and when Laud became archbishop* of Canterbury in 1633, Davenport resigned his parish* and fled to Holland.

There Davenport accepted the co-pastorate of an exiled English congregation with a Presbyterian minister. But Davenport's Congregational persuasion led to a 1635 quarrel over the "promiscuous baptism'"* of infants, and in 1637 he returned to England, where he assisted in organizing a company of 250 settlers bound for New England. Arriving in Boston in the midst of the antinomian* crisis, he participated in the examination of Anne Hutchinson.*

In April 1638, Davenport and the settlers moved to Quinnipiac on Long Island Sound and organized the colony of New Haven. Elected pastor of the New Haven church, his ministry soon became noted for its strict Congregational practices. However, in 1662 a synod* of New England churches resolved, over Davenport's furious opposition, to relax restrictions on infant baptism and substitute the "Half-Way Covenant'"* as the basis of church membership.* He suffered a further disappointment in 1665, when the New

Haven colony was forcibly absorbed into the Connecticut colony. He resigned his New Haven pastorate in 1667 after being called as pastor of the First Church in Boston, but New Haven was reluctant to dismiss him and a large faction in Boston reluctant to receive him. He presided over the Boston church for only several months, dying on March 11, 1670. His apologetic for Congregational principles, *The Power of Congregational Churches Asserted and Vindicated* (1672), is a skillful defense of the New England Way.* He was also an early advocate of premillenial* eschatology.*

See also DAVENPORT, JAMES.

BIBLIOGRAPHY. *AAP* 1; *DAB* III; *DARB;* C. Mather, *Magnalia Christi Americana,* 2 vols. (1852); P. Miller, *Orthodoxy in Massachusetts* (1933); *NCAB* 1.

A. C. Guelzo

Davies, Samuel (1723-1761). Presbyterian* minister* and educator. Born in Delaware and of Welsh lineage, Davies grew up with parental expectations that he would serve the Presbyterian Church. After studying with Samuel Blair in Pennsylvania, he was licensed to preach* there in 1746 but soon moved to Virginia with his new bride, where he served as an evangelist* and organizer of dissenting congregations that had been meeting informally.

In Anglican* Virginia Davies had to overcome the suspicion and hostility of Anglican officials, who had the power to authorize and bar assemblies by religious dissenters. Soon he was conducting worship* services over a five-county area. In his struggle to gain licenses for his congregations, Davies became known as an advocate of civil liberties. Eventually, arguing that the Toleration Act* of 1689 applied to the colonies as well as the British homeland, Davies was able to secure enough toleration to allow open evangelism and organization of dissenting churches. For his own evangelical* zeal for preaching,* Davies gained the reputation of fomenting a Southern Great Awakening during colonial times.

Davies also conducted a successful campaign in England and Scotland in 1753-1755 for support in behalf of the fledgling College of New Jersey (later named Princeton University*). In 1755 he was instrumental in organizing the Presbytery of Hanover, the first in Virginia. Elected president of the College of New Jersey in 1759, Davies died eighteen months after taking office. A model preacher and intellectual leader, Davies has been remembered for his skill as an orator, his academic leadership at the College of New Jersey and as a champion of religious freedom* who helped break the grip of established* religion in the colonies.

BIBLIOGRAPHY. *AAP* 3; *DAB* III; *NCAB* 4; G. W. Pilcher, ed., *The Reverend Samuel Davies Abroad* (1967); G. W. Pilcher, *Samuel Davies: Apostle of Dissent in Colonial Virginia* (1971).

L. B. Weeks

Davis, John Merle (1875-1960). Missionary* and social researcher. The son of missionaries under the American Board of Commissioners for Foreign Missions,* Davis was the first foreign child born in the interior of modern Japan. Educated at Oberlin College* and Hartford Theological Seminary, Davis was for nearly twenty years the YMCA secretary in Japan (1905-1922). In 1925 he became the first director of the Institute of Pacific Relations. At the formation of the Department of Social and Industrial Research of the International Missionary Council (IMC), Davis was named director (1930-1946). His studies of Asian churches in preparation for the IMC Conference at Madras in 1938 called attention to social and economic environments as the "Fourth Dimension" of mission. Studies in Latin America and the Caribbean (1940-1943) led to formation of the United Andean Indian Mission. In 1946, he inaugurated a major study of African marriage customs. His book, *New Buildings on Old Foundations* (1946), distilled a decade of studies and publications.

BIBLIOGRAPHY. J. M. Davis, *John Merle Davis: An Autobiography* (1960). D. M. Stowe

Dawson, John William (1820-1899). Canadian geologist and principal of McGill University. Born in Pictou, Nova Scotia, Dawson was educated at Pictou Academy and the University of Edinburgh. He began a serious study of the geology of his native Nova Scotia in the 1840s, where he came under the influence of Charles Lyell. From 1850 to 1853 Dawson served as superintendent of education for Nova Scotia. He was appointed principal of McGill in 1855, a position he held until 1893. Under his leadership McGill was rescued from the brink of ruin and established as a world-class institution. In 1878 he was offered the chair of geology at Princeton, but he declined in order to remain in Montreal and serve the interests of Protestantism.*

Dawson was Canada's best-known scientist of the nineteenth century. He was the first president of the Royal Society of Canada and served as president of both the American Association for the Advancement of Science and the British Association. He was also Canada's most outspoken critic

of Darwinism.* He was a proponent of the "day-age theory" of creation and a firm believer in the harmony of science and Scripture (*See* Science and Christianity). Dawson wrote prolifically on both geology proper and on the relationship of Christianity to science. He also served as president of the Dominion Evangelical Alliance.

BIBLIOGRAPHY. C. F. O'Brien, *Sir William Dawson: A Life in Science and Religion* (1971).

R. W. Vaudry

Dawson, (J)oseph (M)artin (1879-1973). Southern Baptist* minister,* denominational* executive and advocate of civil liberty. Born in Corsicana, Texas, Dawson graduated from Baylor University in 1904 and later received honorary doctorates from Baylor (1916) and Howard Payne College (1936). Serving as pastor of several Texas churches, including thirty-five years at First Baptist Church, Waco, Dawson also participated in numerous aspects of Southern Baptist denominational life, such as the Convention's executive committee, its Relief and Annuity Board and the Baylor board of trustees.

Dawson was best known as an outspoken representative of the Baptist position on religious freedom, peace, social justice and civil liberty. He was the first executive director of the Baptist Joint Committee on Public Affairs, 1946-1953, an agency serving as a united lobby for various Baptist denominations in behalf of religious liberty* and separation of church and state.* Dawson was particularly concerned that Baptists know and understand their heritage as defenders of religious liberty. He wrote twelve books and innumerable articles on social issues and his book *Baptists and the American Republic* (1956) is a classic statement of the Baptist role in shaping the nation. The J. M. Dawson Institute of Church-State Studies at Baylor University is named in his honor.

BIBLIOGRAPHY. J. E. Wood, Jr., "The Legacy of Joseph Martin Dawson, 1879-1973," *JCS* 15 (1973):363-366.

B. J. Leonard

Day, Dorothy May (1897-1980). Journalist, social activist and cofounder of the Catholic Worker movement.* Baptized into the Episcopal* Church as a teen-ager, Day rejected bourgeois religion while studying at the University of Illinois, where she became a socialist. After plunging into radicalism and a bohemian lifestyle in Greenwich Village, she converted to Catholicism* in 1927. Still uncomfortable with mainstream Christianity's complacency toward an unjust social order, Day searched for ways to serve the poor that were compatible with her radical Christian social vision. She met Peter Maurin,* a like-minded street philosopher, and together they started the Catholic Worker. Day attributed the idea of the Catholic Worker to Maurin, but she actually oversaw the movement's day-to-day operations, including fundraising, serving soup and editing its paper, *The Catholic Worker*. Besides publishing Maurin's free-verse social thought and her own reflections on social justice, Day attracted such authors as Claude McKay, J. F. Powers, Catherine De Hueck Doherty, Helene Iswolsky, Thomas Merton* and Daniel and Philip Berrigan to contribute to the paper.

Under Day's leadership, the Catholic Worker's social activism ranged from picketing unfair labor practices to civil disobedience against government-mandated Civil Defense air-raid drills. She insisted on strict pacifism* during World War 2,* which led to the loss of some volunteers and many supporters. Day maintained her radicalism and pacifism even in the face of an FBI investigation of the group for possible subversiveness.

Much of Day's influence came from her writing. She wrote several books, mainly autobiographical, which recount the story of her conversion and the founding of the movement. *From Union Square to Rome* (1938) explains how Catholicism came to supplant her favored Communism* as a means toward helping the poor. Her best-known work *The Long Loneliness* (1952), a classic of conversion literature, has been reprinted in several foreign-language editions.

See also CATHOLIC WORKER.

BIBLIOGRAPHY. D. Day, *By Little and by Little: The Selected Writings of Dorothy Day*, ed. R. Ellsberg (1983); A. Klejment and A. Klejment, *Dorothy Day and "The Catholic Worker": A Bibliography and Index* (1985); W. M. Miller, *Dorothy Day: A Biography* (1982).

A. Klejment

Day Schools. *See* SCHOOLS, PROTESTANT CHRISTIAN DAY.

Deacon. In classical Greek the term *diakonos* meant a servant, especially one who performed the menial task of waiting on tables. The evangelists adopted this term when they recorded Christ's description of his own ministry and that of his disciples, "Whoever wants to become great among you must be your servant (*diakonos*)" (Mt 20:26; Mk 10:43). All Christian ministry, therefore, is to be *diakonia*.

Yet the church quite early began to designate

official *diakonoi*, or servants, whose role was to look after the basic needs of the community, to carry messages, to purchase food for the poor and to prepare a place for the celebration of the Lord's Supper.* Although the selection of seven men from the Church of Jerusalem (Acts 6) was not the formal institution of the ordained diaconate, yet this episode is quite legitimately seen as an example of, and as a model for, the diaconate of special service.

After the time of Constantine, the churches quickly grew in size and wealth. During the fourth and fifth centuries, the deacons became the powerful and influential administrators of these busy churches and were often chosen to fill the office of bishop* when that post became vacant. But in the Middle Ages the diaconate declined in importance, becoming a temporary stepping stone to the priesthood* in the Latin Church and a liturgical solemnity in the Greek Church.

In the post-Reformation churches, only Catholics,* Anglicans,* Swedish Lutherans* and Orthodox* have deacons who are ordained by a bishop through the laying on of hands.* In the Reformed tradition,* deacons are ordained by the pastor* and the elders* of the local congregation. Other Christian churches either have no office of deacon or use the title to designate laypersons with special administrative duties.

The Catholic Church in America, following guidelines established by Vatican II,* has recently restored the diaconate to its earlier status of an independent and permanent ministry in the church and has opened its ranks to married men. In addition to their liturgical duties, these deacons also have a special responsibility for works of charity.

BIBLIOGRAPHY. J. M. Barnett, *The Diaconate—A Full and Equal Order* (1981); E. P. Echlin, *The Deacon in the Church* (1971); *The Ministry of Deacons* (1965).

M. E. Hussey

Deaconess Movement. A Protestant* movement of single women who gave themselves to Christian service, ministering particularly to the sick, the dying and the disadvantaged. The precedent for this ministry is found in the early church where women such as Phoebe (mentioned in Rom 16:1) carried out a ministry of service (*diakonia*) within the congregation. It is uncertain whether the early church recognized an office of deaconess as it did the male diaconate.

The deaconess movement in America received its impetus from the European Lutheran* deaconess movement such as that of Kaiserwerth, Germany. In 1849 Theodore Fliedner, at the request of William Passavant,* brought four deaconesses to the U.S. and opened the Pittsburgh Infirmary in Pittsburgh, Pennsylvania. In May 1850 Katherine Louisa Marthens became the first consecrated* American deaconess. Several other Lutheran* denominations* established deaconess houses in the 1880s and 1890s. By 1855 Episcopalians* had founded a deaconess institution, St. Andrew's House, in Baltimore, Maryland. Other important early deaconess ministries were founded at Mobile, Alabama (1864); Brooklyn, New York (1872); and Louisville, Kentucky (1875).

The Methodist Episcopal Church, whose deaconess movement was to become the most prominent, did not begin until 1883, when the Woman's Home Missionary Society moved to start the first of many schools for preparing women home missionaries,* the Chicago Training School. But the office of deaconess—being part of a larger issue of the role of women's ministry within the Methodist Church*—was not sanctioned by the General Conference until 1888. In the ensuing decades deaconess leaders such as Lucy Rider Meyer* and Jane Bancroft Robinson would disagree over whether the movement should come under the jurisdiction of a denominational bureau (which did eventually take place in 1939) or remain autonomous under an agency such as the Womans' Home Missionary Society.

Many regarded the office of deaconess as a lifelong commitment of single women to provide a female ministry of nurturing and care giving to the church and to the world. Deaconesses frequently wore a distinctive dress of navy blue or black with a white collar and a black hat, and so were sometimes referred to as "Protestant nuns." They frequently ministered in urban settings among the poor immigrants* who were flooding the cities of late nineteenth-century America. In their efforts to creatively apply the message of the gospel to physical and spiritual needs of the cities, the deaconess movement reflected many of the same concerns of the Social Gospel Movement.* While the movement prospered from the 1880s until the early years of the twentieth century (with approximately one thousand Methodist deaconesses consecrated between 1887 and 1910), by the 1920s it had declined.

In 1957 there were reported to be 1,550 deaconesses in the U.S. and Canada, of whom 788 were Methodist; 416, Lutheran; 142, United Church of Canada*; 130, Episcopalian; and 74, United Church of Christ.*

BIBLIOGRAPHY. M. A. Dougherty, "The Method-

ist Deaconess, 1885-1906: A Study in Religious Feminism" (unpublished Ph.D. dissertation, University of California at Davis, 1979); L. Rider Meyer, *Deaconesses, Biblical, Early Church, European, American* (1892); C. De Swarte Gifford, ed., *The American Deaconess Movement in the Early Twentieth Century* (1987); S. M. Winter, "Deaconess," in *The Encyclopedia of the Lutheran Church,* ed. J. Bodensieck, vol. 1 (1965).

D. G. Reid

Death of God Movement. During the 1960s, several American theologians used the phrase *Death of God* to describe what they felt to be an important event in modern Western culture. Five authors are frequently identified as the primary figures in the Death of God movement. Each meant something quite different by the phrase *Death of God,* and they never constituted a self-consciously unified group. Some of them significantly altered their opinions in later years.

In 1961 Gabriel Vahanian (1927-) published a book entitled *The Death of God.* Vahanian believed that Western culture had lost its sense of the sacred. According to Vahanian, contemporary Westerners could find no sacramental significance to their lives, their personal existence revealed no transcendental purpose, and the history of their societies seemed void of any undergirding providence. For Western culture, therefore, God had died. Vahanian, however, refrained from concluding that God did not really exist. Rather he argued for a new cultural transformation—the creation of a post-modern culture—if the reality of God were to become viable for Westerners once again.

Paul M. van Buren (1924-) and William Hamilton (1924-) also stressed the loss of transcendence and the growth of secular modes of thought in Western culture. They placed more weight, however, on the normativity of modern culture and drew the conclusion that there was no God. The collapse of the sense of transcendence and the loss of the meaningfulness of the category of God among broad segments of Western culture was a central element in their understanding of the death of God. Nonetheless, precisely because modern Westerners no longer have God, they must attend to the human Jesus as a model of sacrificial love and practical ethics. The church as a human community would remain a central reality which even the most secularized person could affirm.

Thomas J. J. Altizer (1927-) developed the most idiosyncratic version of the Death of God. In dependence on Hegel, who held that the Universal must become specific and concrete, Altizer seemed to be teaching that God had once really existed, but that when he became incarnate in Jesus Christ he ceased to exist as a reality independent of the world.

The Jewish scholar Richard L. Rubenstein (1924-) argued that the Jewish holocaust* under the Nazis made it impossible to believe that God exists, that he had made a covenant with Israel or that there is any purpose to individual or social existence. The only meaning is the meaning which we ourselves make. Contemporary Jews must, therefore, band together to create their own culture.

The Death of God movement was a sensational event while it lasted, attracting the attention of the popular press and making the cover story of *Time* magazine. But it was not of enduring significance except as a reminder of the poverty of twentieth-century theologies that had lost their roots in Christian theism.*

BIBLIOGRAPHY. T. J. J. Altizer, *The Gospel of Christian Atheism* (1966); T. J. J. Altizer and W. Hamilton, *Radical Theology and the Death of God* (1966); L. Gilkey, *Naming the Whirlwind: The Renewal of God-Language* (1969); R. L. Rubenstein, *After Auschwitz* (1967); P. M. van Buren, *The Edges of Language* (1972); G. Vahanian, *The Death of God* (1961).   S. T. Franklin

Declension. A theory describing changes leading to the breakdown of Puritanism* in seventeenth-century New England. By the end of the seventeenth century, many pastors lamented a widespread spiritual deadness and loss of interest in the Holy Commonwealth. In their view, subsequent generations did not measure up to the piety* and dedication of the first generation, whose ability to point to visible evidence of their conversion* entitled them to the privileges of church membership.* Increased moral laxity in the community and lower standards for participation in the church, such as the Half-Way Covenant,* were seen as evidence of a spiritual decline. In this century, historian Perry Miller did much to popularize the theory. However, it has been criticized on the grounds that it idealizes the achievements of the first generation, exaggerates the effects of the Half-Way Covenant, and minimizes the role of increased economic prosperity and rising population in transforming New England Puritanism.

BIBLIOGRAPHY. P. Miller, *The New England Mind: The Seventeenth Century* (1939); R. G. Pope, "New England Versus the New England Mind: The Myth of Declension," *JSH* 1 (1969-1970):95-108.
                                                S. D. Crocco

Dederer, Anna (1902-1976). Missionary* to Micronesia. Born in Germany, Anna graduated from the Liebenzell Mission Seminary in 1929, served as an assistant pastor and then took nurse's training. In 1935 she was assigned by the Liebenzell Mission to be a nurse and church worker in the Mortlock Islands. Later she worked in the Girls Training School at Truk where she spent World War 2,* at times living in caves under American bombardment. In 1948 she accepted appointment by the American Board of Commissioners for Foreign Missions.* She studied at Andover Newton Theological School and was ordained* a Congregational* minister in Honolulu. Returning to Truk, she inaugurated a girls school which pioneered in vocational training. In 1954 she was assigned to Majuro in the Marshall Islands as a general missionary, and in 1958 became an American citizen. In 1963 she was assigned to Kusraie, giving general church leadership and focusing on work with youth and women. She retired in 1971.
                                                D. M. Stowe

Dedham Decision (1820). A court decision effectively ending the established* Congregationalism*—or "Church of the Standing Order"—of Massachusetts. In 1818 the pulpit of Dedham's First Church became vacant. Two-thirds of the parishioners* voted to call the liberal* minister* Alvan Lamson. In New England, however, few parishioners were actual church members, even though they were taxed to support the minister.* A majority of the orthodox church members*—the visible saints who had professed faith and owned the church covenant*—overruled the liberal parish* vote by eighteen to fourteen. Withdrawing from the parish, they took the church property with them. However, the dissenting minority of church members joined the parish majority who were not members, reorganized and sued to recover the church's property. In 1820 a Unitarian*-dominated Massachusetts Court ruled that title to all Standing Order property was vested in parishes, not in communicant membership. The parish had the right to call a minister of its choice and retain control of the church property. As a result of this decision, over 100 parishes became Unitarian, while orthodox* Calvinists* saw little reason to continue to support an established church. Calvinist* Congregationalists joined other dissenters to help demolish the Federalist Party and achieved official disestablishment in 1833. But for the Unitarians, the court decision became one more stone for the foundation of their emerging denomination.*

See also ESTABLISHED CHURCHES IN NEW ENGLAND.

BIBLIOGRAPHY. S. Haven, *A Statement of the proceedings in the First church, and parish in Dedham, respecting the settlement of a minister* (1819); L. W. Levy, *The Law of the Commonwealth and Chief Justice Shaw* (1957); *Eliphalet Baker v. Samuel Fales,* 16 Massachusetts 488 (1820).

M. B. Newell

DeHaan, (M)artin (R)alph (1891-1965). Author and radio preacher. Trained as a medical doctor, DeHaan established one of the most successful national radio and Bible literature ministries, Radio Bible Class, of Grand Rapids, Michigan. A powerful and persuasive Bible conference* speaker and engaging pulpiteer, he skillfully interpreted and explained Scripture* through analogies and anecdotes. DeHaan started a local radio ministry in the mid-1920s, and by the 1940s his gravelly voice was heard on several hundred stations in the U.S. and elsewhere. The ministry's daily devotional booklet, "Our Daily Bread," complemented the radio and Bible-conference* ministries of the energetic DeHaan. He authored twenty-five books, often dealing with his premillennial* view of the Second Coming and God's saving grace. A robust and rugged man, he possessed a keen mind and a photographic memory. Unlike many media preachers, he refused to solicit funds on the air or through the mail. Under the leadership of son, Richard, Radio Bible Class spawned "Day of Discovery," which became one of the ten highest-rated religious television programs in the 1980s.

BIBLIOGRAPHY. J. R. Adair, *M. R. DeHaan: The Man and His Ministry* (1969).

Q. J. Schultze

Deism. An Enlightenment* religion particularly influential during the late eighteenth century. Deism developed in Europe out of the context of the Enlightenment and became popular among some upper-class Americans at the time of the American Revolution. Although lending itself to a large variety of expressions, deism is essentially a rationalistic religion, which assumes that all men naturally possess the ability to know the universe's Deity through reason, and that the creator of the universe was a rational architect. Thus deism assumes a correspondence between the rational structure of the physical universe and the rational capacity of the human mind. Each person, therefore, knows or can know the physical universe by applying their rational capacity for understanding. As rational people come to know the physical universe, they also come to know its creator—the Deity. The knowledge of God came not through

Jesus Christ or the power of the Holy Spirit, nor were the Christian Scriptures* or church tradition necessary. God revealed himself in nature and through reason.

As an intellectual movement, deism stood between Renaissance humanism and the pure naturalism of Auguste Comte (1798-1857) or John Dewey (1859-1952). Like Renaissance humanism, deism focused on the glories of nature, especially human nature with its rational capacity. On the other hand, unlike Renaissance humanism it assigned God to the outer reaches of the universe, seeing him as only a beneficent, impersonal and artful creator. God was only marginally necessary. Naturalistic thinkers would go one step beyond deism and deny the existence of God altogether. Thus Comte created his "Religion of Humanity" which Dewey later embraced.

In the post-Revolutionary War era, individuals such as Ethan Allen* (*Reason the Only Oracle of Man,* 1784), Elihu Palmer* (*Principles of Nature,* 1801) and Thomas Paine* (*Age of Reason,* 1794-1796) disseminated deistic ideas. Palmer organized the "Deistical Society" in New York (1794) which published a weekly paper entitled *The Temple of Reason* (1800-1803), but his attempts to make deism an organized republican religion failed. Even in his own lifetime the resurgence of evangelical* religion was underway in a movement that would come to be known as the Second Great Awakening.* The most forceful deist of the period, Thomas Jefferson,* wed Enlightenment religion with the ideals of American democracy.* By 1810 deism had lost its momentum in its bid for becoming a popular religious option.

BIBLIOGRAPHY. C. A. Koch, *Religion of the American Enlightenment* (1933); H. F. May, *The Enlightenment in America* (1976).

L. J. Van Til

DeKoven, James (1831-1879). Episcopal* educator and ritualist leader. Born in Middletown, Connecticut, DeKoven graduated from Columbia College (1851) and the General Theological Seminary (1854). On being ordained* deacon* in 1854, he moved to Wisconsin where he became tutor of church history at Nashotah House seminary and also rector of the Church of St. John Chrysostom at nearby Delafield. In 1855 he was ordained priest* and later founded St. John's Hall, a preparatory school for ministerial candidates. This institution in 1859 was united with Racine College, where DeKoven became warden and remained until his death, devoting himself to the cause of Christian education.*

An advanced high churchman* and brilliant

orator, DeKoven was the acknowledged leader of the ritualist movement in the Episcopal Church after the Civil War.* In the General Conventions of 1871 and 1874, he stoutly opposed attempts to legislate ritual uniformity, defending Eucharistic* adoration and pleading for comprehensiveness in matters of doctrine* and worship.* This principle eventually won acceptance, though his controversial views at the time kept him from the episcopate,* an office to which he was nominated five times and once elected, only to be refused confirmation.* A man of vast learning and holiness of character, he is today commemorated in the calendar of the Episcopal Church.

BIBLIOGRAPHY. *DAB* III; F. C. Morehouse, *Some American Churchmen* (1892); T. C. Reeves, ed., *James DeKoven, Anglican Saint* (1978).

C. R. Henery

Democracy and Christianity in America.

Democracy and Christianity, especially in its Protestant* form, have mutually influenced each other in the U.S., exemplifying the close relationship between religious and political ideas in American culture. Democratic ideals have helped shape the expression of Christianity in America, and Christianity in turn—while certainly not the only shaping force—has contributed to the development of democratic government in the U.S.

One of the major ideas of Christianity which was expressed in American democracy was belief in the existence of fundamental law. Christianity teaches that there are fixed, or fundamental, laws ordained by God and that governments are instituted to safeguard these laws. This concept of fixed and immutable laws or principles was used as a defense against the claim to absolute and arbitrary authority* in government. The laws of God were judged superior to any human law, and the role of government was to enact legislation more closely approximating the moral laws of God. The Declaration of Independence refers to these fundamental laws as "the Laws of Nature."

Related to the concept of fundamental law is the idea of a written constitution guaranteeing the rights of individuals. When it was concluded that sovereignty resided in the people as a whole and not in the crown, it was deemed necessary to set forth in a written constitution the principles for governing. In order to protect the popular sovereignty and limit the powers of government, a written constitution had to be framed. As God's law was written, so the constitution should be written.

The existence of fundamental laws implies the right to resist any human authority that usurps the authority of God's law. It was on the basis of fundamental laws that the American colonists first attempted to justify their resistance to the existing authority, England. It was reasoned that when a sovereign fails to abide by the moral law of God, that sovereign ceases to have the right to rule and becomes a tyrant. The people are then morally obligated to resist, and if the sovereign persists in tyranny the people are morally obligated to rebel. Not to resist and rebel against an unjust sovereign was to commit sin.

The Christian view of the dignity and worth of every individual, created in the image of God, influenced American democracy. The Declaration of Independence states as a self-evident truth: "that all men are created equal." This does not mean that all men are created with the same potential, but that all men are equal before the law and should have the same opportunities. In the ensuing history of the nation the implications of this statement have gradually extended beyond white males to include women and non-whites.

While Christianity asserted the worth of each individual, it was the sixteenth-century Protestant Reformation which stressed this most clearly. Luther's great emphasis on the individual conscience and the fundamental Protestant doctrine of the priesthood of all believers* further clarified the worth of the individual. Since God respects each individual, people are to respect each other. All people are equal before the law, all persons are assumed innocent until proven guilty, all persons have the right to vote. The Christian rejection of the significance of human differences has influenced the democratic doctrine of equality.

Congregational church government,* with its stress on the autonomy of the local congregation, also shaped democracy in America. Congregationalist autonomy is built around the belief that true Christians should covenant* together regarding their beliefs, their worship* and their leadership. In Puritan* New England, Congregationalism came to be more than church polity, it spilled over into life in general and the concept of civil government. New England had entered into a covenant with God comparable to Israel of old. That covenant granted New Englanders certain liberties as well as stipulated certain conditions and responsibilities. Even the place of church and village government overlapped as colonists met in their meetinghouses on Sunday to worship and on occasional week days to carry out matters of government. In the end, the pattern of congregational government contributed to the shape of American democracy.

The Christian doctrine of original sin* also

contributed to American democracy. This realistic and uncomplimentary assessment of human nature implies that the exercise of power must be limited by constitutional restraints. The recognition of original sin is expressed in American democracy in the doctrine of the balance of powers of the executive, legislative and judicial branches of the government, and in the checks and balances of the Constitution. This creates a government of laws and not of men.

Protestant Christianity has also insisted on free and open discussion about God's revelation. The will of God is often discerned through the unfettered discussion of fallible people as they reflect on the truth of God's Word. In the church this process works best when minority voices are protected and heard. Likewise, freedom of speech became a cherished value in American life and essential to democratic government, which is government by discussion.

Democracy has also influenced American Christianity. While the doctrine of the priesthood of all believers has stressed the significance of the individual, the democratic idea has promoted the role of the laity* in the legislative councils of the churches. When the American churches were being organized during and after the Revolution,* laity were included in the church legislatures and given voice and vote. Even episcopal forms of church government reflected the American democratic experience, with the Protestant Episcopal Church instituting lay representation at every level of its government.* In this and other examples, democratic ideals contributed to the diminished clerical power in the American churches.

A significant dimension of the democratic experience is the separation of church and state,* the disestablishment of the churches (especially the Congregationalists in New England and the Anglicans* in the South), and the practice of religious liberty.* This meant that the American churches could no longer depend on the state for support and that they had to rely on their own resources. Democracy helped to make American churches voluntary associations dependent on voluntary contributions and volunteer workers. Even membership became a voluntary decision (*See* Voluntaryism).

This democratic situation also promoted the pluralism* which characterizes American Christianity. In a free democratic society of equals, many churches developed, and all are equal with regard to the civil government. While religious pluralism was a fact prior to the birth of the Republic, American democracy provided a legal basis for this pluralism and an environment for a stunning variety of religious bodies to grow and multiply. In the context of American democracy, churches were gradually transformed into a peculiarly American institution, the denomination—a voluntary association of like-minded persons. Thus, in America, an established church from Europe became one denomination among many.

While Christianity and democracy are not the same, they have often been confused in the course of American history. In the nineteenth century, the ideal of democracy, compatible as it is with Christian values, became inextricably intertwined with Christian faith and mission.* As home missionary organizations such as the American Sunday School Union* moved westward, they saw themselves as vehicles for Christian and democratic values. For the immigrant* Catholic* Church of the late nineteenth century, the challenge was to show its true enculturation by demonstrating that democracy was not an exclusively Protestant doctrine but was in harmony with Catholicism. In the end, democratic values profoundly shaped the life of the Catholic Church in the twentieth century. Thus in mutual relationship, Christianity has encouraged the democratic impulse, and democracy has helped shape American religious life.

BIBLIOGRAPHY. W. S. Hudson, "Theological Convictions and Democratic Government," *TT* 10 (1953):230-239; S. E. Mead, *The Lively Experiment* (1963); J. H. Nichols, *Democracy and the Churches* (1951); H. R. Niebuhr, "The Idea of Covenant and American Democracy," *CH* 23 (1954):126-135; W. Pauck, "Protestantism and Democracy," in *The Heritage of the Reformation* (1950); R. B. Perry, *Puritanism and Democracy* (1944).

D. S. Armentrout

Demythologization. Rudolf Bultmann's* 1941 essay, "New Testament and Mythology," spoke of demythologization (German, *Entymythologisierung*) as a method of interpreting the New Testament. His concern was to communicate the gospel of Jesus Christ to modern men and women who no longer believe in literal phenomena such as angels, demons and a heavenly redeemer, but regard them as mythical images from a pre-scientific world view. Bultmann argued that biblical myths are not to be ignored, as was done by many nineteenth-century liberals,* but interpreted as portrayals of a self-understanding. Biblical interpreters* must ask what this mythology points toward, what it says about God, the world and human existence. To explain the message of the Christian myth, Bultmann drew upon existential philosophy, especially that of his colleague Martin Heidegger (1889-1976). Bultmann maintained that only when texts are demythologized can one come to a faith decision and commitment to Christ who redeems individuals from self-centeredness and calls them to authentic existence in reliance on God's grace.

BIBLIOGRAPHY. R. Bultmann, *Jesus Christ and Mythology* (1958); R. Bultmann, *Kerygma and Myth,* ed. H.-W. Bartsch, 2 vols. (1953, 1962); J. Macquarrie, *The Scope of Demythologizing: Bultmann and His Critics* (1960).

D. K. McKim

Denominationalism. The word *denomination* is derived from a Latin word (*denominare*) meaning "to name." A denomination is an association or fellowship of congregations within a religion that have the same beliefs or creed,* engage in similar practices and cooperate with each other to develop and maintain shared enterprises. Similar religious groups like the many Baptist* bodies in the U.S. constitute a "denominational family."

There are such a wide variety of denominations that sociologists identify several subcategories, building upon the typology of Christian orientations—church, sect and mysticism—developed in Ernst Troeltsch's historical study, *The Social Teaching of the Christian Churches* (1912; ET 1931). Troeltsch viewed the church* as a universal body into which people are born. It tries to cover the whole life of humanity in society, and its clergy* convey Christ's saving work through proclaiming the Word and dispensing sacraments.* Sects* renounce the world, have a voluntary membership and insist that members experience a new birth and practice personal holiness.* They are dominated by lay* leadership and power. Mysticism* is a form of individualism that emphasizes inward spiritual experience, freely combines various Christian and other ideas, gives little attention to fellowship* and is inclined toward relativism. These types reflected the numerous movements, controversies and splinter groups that have been apparent ever since Christianity's beginning, especially in Europe. In effect, the politically established* religious bodies were churches; splinter groups and independent bodies were sects. Because they were dissenters from the church, sect members were maligned and many were persecuted.

Several American colonies followed the European example of having an established church, but when the new nation gained independence, none had sufficient power to become the dominant national religion. This contributed to the provisions for religious liberty* and the separation of church and state* guaranteed by the Bill of Rights of the U.S. Constitution. Both as cause and effect, it provided for the denominational pattern of tolerance and freedom for every religious group as long as it does not subvert the state or violate the rights of others. Immigrants* from nations with established Anglican,* Reformed,* Catholic,* Lutheran* or Orthodox* churches were no longer part of a dominant national religion but of only a minority religious body coexisting with hundreds of others. Since there was no established "church," "sects" could not be defined as splinters from it.

Religious bodies that accommodate themselves to the power structures and values of society came to be labeled by the term *denomination.* In contrast, sects are in tension with society, uphold differences from it, oppose it or separate themselves from it. The types overlap and merge into each other, for most denominations began as sects. Cults also overlap; they are either newly created religious innovations, imports from other cultural settings or groups formed by syncretistic merger and adaptation of elements from more than one religious tradition. The words *sect* and *cult* have negative connotations, so the more neutral label of *new religious movement* is now often used. All are included in American denominationalism.

Religious denominations are so significant in America that Andrew Greeley called it *The Denominational Society* (1972). He believes that people gain their sense of identity and meaning for life by belonging to one of the hundreds of available religious options. As self-definition and social location by nationality decrease, denominational identity increases, stimulating the vitality of American religion.

Denominational Statistics. The annual *Yearbook of American and Canadian Churches* provides statistics and directories on more than two hundred denominations, including three-fifths of the U.S. population and two-thirds of the people of Canada. The *Yearbook* is not a complete record of all religious bodies because independent congregations are not counted, many groups lack adequate records, and some refuse to provide data because the *Yearbook* is produced by the National Council of the Churches of Christ in the U.S.A.* Most omitted groups are small, but some large ones, like the Church of Christ, Scientist,* refuse on doctrinal grounds to report statistics.

Arthur C. Piepkorn's *Profiles in Belief* reports the theological and confessional commitments of more than 700 U.S. and Canadian denominations, and J. Gordon Melton's *Directory of Religious Bodies in the United States* (Garland, 1977) identifies 1,275. (His current count exceeds 1,500.) He defines a religious body as a church, denomination, sect or cult that meets three criteria: (1) seeking the chief religious loyalty of members; (2) having at least two congregations, or over 2,000 members who make a measurable impact on society through the mass media, or members from more than one state and beyond a single metropolitan area, or being at odds with most people in the nation (as in the case of some Satanic groups); and (3) promoting its particular views of faith.

As of 1980 David B. Barrett identified 20,800 Christian denominations worldwide and classified them into seven major blocs and 156 ecclesiastical traditions. He reported 2,050 "organized churches and denominations" in the U.S., with 385,000 congregations, 111,662,300 members and 160,918,000 affiliated people. Corresponding figures for Canada are 330 with 29,300 congregations, 10,610,000 members and 17,872,500 affiliates. However, the 2,050 include 32 archdioceses* and 134 dioceses* of the Catholic Church in the U.S., and Canada's 330 counts 18 Catholic archdioceses and 49 dioceses, 32 provinces and dioceses of the Anglican Church and 11 conferences of the United Church of Canada.*

The decennial Census of Canada asks questions on religion, and the U.S Census Bureau collected such data from the 1880s to 1946, publishing *Censuses of Religious Bodies* in 1906, 1916, 1926 and 1936. However, the data lack internal consistency and comparability, and it is almost impossible to correlate them with other census statistics. Because of mounting opposition both within and outside the religious community, the practice was discontinued. An experimental survey of U.S. religious preferences in 1957 was successful, but attacks upon the alleged invasion of privacy and religious liberty were so severe that most of the data were never reported, and the tentative plan to ask questions on religion in the Census of Population was dropped. In that survey 66.2 per cent of the population had Protestant preferences, 25.7 Roman Catholic, 3.2 per cent Jewish, 1.3 per cent some other religion, 2.7 per cent none, and only 0.9 per cent failed to report. Recent public opinion polls indicate that about 57 per cent of the U.S. adult population have Protestant preferences, 28 per cent Catholic, 2 per cent Jewish, 4 per cent other, and 9 per cent none; but only about 68 per cent claim to be church or synagogue members, and 40 per cent attend religious services in a typical week.

All religious statistics must be interpreted with caution. Criteria for and definitions of membership vary greatly from one religious body to another. Some count as members everyone who is in an ethnic* group associated with the church. Others count all baptized* persons, including infants, and still others only baptized believers, communicant members or members in good standing. Denominational records depend upon local reporting units with varying levels of care for keeping records up to date, so defectors, departed and deceased members may be included. A person may be on the records of two congregations, thus even of different denominations, and statistics for congregations affiliated with two denominations are reported by both. Instances of deliberate deceitfulness are rare, but errors from incompleteness, duplications, estimates and nonstandardized reporting are widespread.

Denominational Organization and Trends. The polity* of Christian denominations usually takes one of three forms. Episcopal government* consists of a hierarchy of top officials, with bishops* over dioceses, and clergy over parishes* and members; power flows from the top down, as in a monarchy. In congregational church government,* authority resides in the members of local churches and flows democratically from congregation to clergy and then to denominational agencies. Between these two forms is the presbyterian* form of church government modeled after aristocracies in which both congregations and the denomination are under the control of middle-level agencies. Mixed forms increasingly prevail, for American denominations are, as Ross P. Scherer put it, "open transformation systems." They must continually relate to an ever-changing environment, personnel changes, and accompanying negotiations and modifications of roles, rules and understandings.

The denominational structure of the nation is continually changing. New religious bodies frequently emerge and others disappear. Sociologists have found that the life cycle of a denomination typically includes development through stages of incipient sectarian organization, formal organization, maximum efficiency, institutional bureaucracy and finally, if no corrective action is taken, disintegration. From 1890 to 1906, 13.8 per cent of the bodies listed in the U.S. Census of Religious Bodies became defunct, compared to 8.8 per cent from 1906 to 1916 and 15.3 per cent from 1916 to 1926. Some disappeared, others were transformed into "new" bodies, and many merged with one another.

[351]

The growth rates of religious bodies are influenced by their values, goals and programs and by conditions and characteristics of society, including its composition by race, nationality, social class, sex and religious traditions. For several decades the theologically conservative Protestant denominations and those with strict membership standards have been growing, while most mainline* denominations have been declining. There is fluidity among church memberships as many move between congregations, often crossing denominational lines. Many clergy change denominations as well.

Scholars like H. Richard Niebuhr,* who value the organizational unity of Christians, interpret the proliferation of Christian denominations as an indication of moral failure, hypocrisy and scandal. The ecumenical movement* has tried to vanquish the struggles for power that divide and weaken Christianity, to achieve cooperation among denominations so that they will be more influential in society and even to build structural unity, as in the Consultation on Church Union* (COCU, since 1962). Others have tried to regain the unity that presumably existed in the New Testament church by drawing people out of denominations into the "true church." Their efforts to unite all Christians and defeat denominationalism by applying such labels as *Brethren, Church of God,* *Disciples of Christ,* *Restoration Movement* or *Bible Church* have instead been equivalent to founding additional new denominations.

The goal of organizational unity is opposed by many just as strongly as is the "melting pot" ideology that once dominated American ethnic policy. Those who are suspicious of large bureaucracies view denominations as positive results of practical social and institutional necessity working in a pluralistic society. A highly mobile population, a great diversity of races, social classes and other traits have even shaped Roman Catholicism into the social equivalent of numerous denominations.

Alongside the ecumenical movement are other tendencies toward Christian unity.* Cooperative evangelistic,* educational, social-action and service ministries are bringing evangelicals* together with fundamentalists,* charismatics* and other Christians. This "spiritual ecumenism" often is mediated through parachurch* organizations supported by individual Christians outside of denominational channels.

American Christianity shows greater vitality than that of most other nations. Religious diversity and competition have contributed to broader opportunities to satisfy people's spiritual needs and stronger efforts to recruit them for church membership and Christian ministries. Denominationalism does not necessarily violate the spiritual unity of the body of Christ. It is consistent with the competitive free enterprise system, the voluntary* principle of individual freedom and other liberties deeply engrained in American society.

See also MAINLINE DENOMINATIONS; PLURALISM, RELIGIOUS; VOLUNTARYISM.

BIBLIOGRAPHY. D. B. Barrett, ed., *World Christian Encyclopedia* (1982); S. E. Mead, *The Lively Experiment* (1963); J. G. Melton, *The Encyclopedia of American Religions,* 2nd ed. (1986); D. O. Moberg, *The Church as a Social Institution,* 2nd ed. (1984); H. R. Niebuhr, *The Social Sources of Denominationalism* (1929); A. C. Piepkorn, *Profiles in Belief,* 4 vols. (1977, 1978, 1979); R. E. Richey, ed., *Denominationalism* (1977); R. P. Scherer, ed., *American Denominational Organization* (1980); R. Wuthnow, *The Restructuring of American Religion* (1988).

D. O. Moberg

Deposit of Faith. Roman Catholics* understand the deposit of faith to be the entirety of those truths communicated explicitly or implicitly to the apostles by Jesus Christ, both in his earthly life and risen glory, during a distinct epoch, now closed, which is usually referred to as "the Apostolic Age." The church guards this deposit as a sacred trust and may not add to or subtract from it. This pious affirmation alone does not, however, address a number of complex questions which have recurred in the historical life of the church: By what processes are the implicit truths unfolded, clarified and defined? Is the expression of these truths in human language absolute or historically conditioned? If the latter, do the church's understanding, appreciation and appropriation of these truths develop or deepen over time? In other words, the concept of the deposit of faith is closely related in any given age to the opinions held concerning the development of doctrine* and the role and status of religious authority.*

Although used by Vincent of Lerins in the fifth century, the word entered theological parlance in the sixteenth century and was canonized by the First Vatican Council* which identified the deposit of faith with the revelation made known by God and handed down to the church through the apostles. This coincided with the nineteenth-century Vatican insistence that the faith is an "objective fact" independent of subjective human need, perception or preparation for it. The magisterium of the Church, composed of the bishops* in union with the pope,* was seen as the necessary guardian of such objectivity. In 1907 Pope Pius X* condemned the modernist notion that "the truths of the faith are not fallen from heaven."

This notion of the deposit as a closed and self-contained reality impervious to historical adaptation has been challenged since the nineteenth century by several Roman Catholic thinkers. Many of these have maintained that the deposit is meant to be a living and salvific reality for every age, and that the church preserves it by proclaiming it in such a way as to make present and meaningful its salvific efficacy. In short, the church guards the deposit most effectively by demonstrating its relevance to every age and mentality.

American Catholic thinkers participate in this ongoing discussion from the unique vantage as citizens of a religiously pluralist* and voluntarist* republic. In the age of Enlightenment* and evolutionary* thinking, Isaac Thomas Hecker,* founder of the Missionary Society of St. Paul the Apostle (Paulists),* imbued his writing on Catholic evangelization with the progressive, immanentist spirit of the age. He awarded greater importance to the inspiration of the Holy Spirit and individual religious experience* than to the traditional view of faith emphasizing dogma* and doctrine. In recent decades, several American Catholic theologians have responded to the spirit of the Second Vatican Council* by re-examining the notion of the deposit of faith. Perhaps the most sustained discussion of the topic is to be found in *The Survival of Dogma* (1973) by the American Jesuit* Avery Dulles.

See also DEVELOPMENT OF DOCTRINE.

BIBLIOGRAPHY. K. Adam, *The Spirit of Catholicism* (1929); P. F. Chirico, "Deposit of Faith," *NCE* 4; A. Dulles, *The Survival of Dogma: Faith, Authority and Dogma in a Changing World* (1982).

R. S. Appleby

Development of Doctrine. The problem of how Christian doctrine* develops over time has primarily been the concern of Catholic theologians.* Beginning in the thirteenth century, the word *infallibility* was first used of papal teaching, though the doctrine of papal infallibility* was not made an official doctrine until Vatican I. This understanding of the authority of Rome has stood in tension with the obvious fact that articles of faith have emerged in the dogmatic tradition which were not explicit in the primitive deposit of faith.* Protestants too have wrestled with this issue, though their emphasis on *sola scriptura* has generally focused their attention on the interpretation of Scripture and reconciling any new theological insights with their particular church creeds* and confessions. Theologians today may argue that some developments came about as the church moved into new cultural environments, while other developments arose as the ancient church responded to heresies by composing new doctrinal formulations. However, throughout much of church history Christian doctrine was believed to be a precise formulation of what the Church had always explicitly and consciously believed.

In the late nineteenth century the issue became particularly acute as a developmentalist world view took hold in Western thought and challenged traditional understandings of Christian doctrine. German philosophers such as G. F. W. Hegel (1770-1831) elaborated the idea of development and progress as the inner meaning of history, a concept supported by Darwin's theory of evolution* and Marx's theory of economics.

Christian theologians* responded in various ways. Some, labeled by Karl Rahner* as "dogmatic positivists," continued to hold an exclusively propositional concept of faith and understood development as a process in which revealed truth logically unfolds. Roman Catholic neo-scholastic* theologians of the late nineteenth century, for example, taught that propositions are formally revealed when they are contained, either explicitly or implicitly, in the verbal expression of primitive faith.

Transformists, influenced by German Pietists, argued that unchangeable doctrine is not the essence of Christianity. Revelation and faith are experiential, with revelation always at work in human experience, slowly creating, purifying and clarifying a consciousness of communion with God in the individual and in humanity. Propositional doctrines are creations of the mind inspired by faith and cannot contain the truth of revelation, which is beyond human expression. The continuity between contemporary faith and apostolic faith is not in doctrine but in inspiration.

This viewpoint is illustrated by Friedrich Schleiermacher (1768-1834), the seminal German liberal Protestant thinker of the modern era, who taught that Christianity consists in a participation by Christians in Christ's perfect experience of the redeeming love of the Father. As this participation increases and deepens, there occurs a slow transformation of the public norm of doctrine and behavior. Adolph von Harnack (1851-1930), another German theologian and church historian, reduced religion to an interior experience and Christ's original message to the eternity of the soul and the brotherhood of all people. All subsequent doctrinal development was, for Harnack, an inevitable but corrupting series of accretions. His contemporary, the Roman Catholic priest* Alfred F. Loisy (1857-1940), claimed in response that there is nothing in Christianity which is not historical and social. Doctrine is not the translation of revealed truth into human concepts but a mere symbolic construct which changes with the cultural environment.

In the U.S. these two schools frequently clashed. The modernist impulse in American Protestantism found articulation in the critical biblical theology* of Presbyterian* Charles Briggs* and Southern Baptist* theologian Crawford Toy,* both of whom viewed all religious expression, including creeds and dogmas, as substantially human and culturally conditioned. In the twentieth century, theologians such as William Adams Brown* and George A. Gordon,* among others, attempted to reformulate inherited doctrines to achieve a nondoctrinal and deculturized Christian message. A small movement of progressive American Catholic priests, including James Driscoll and Francis Gigot of Dunwoodie Seminary in New York, also dabbled in modernism* at this time, but were silenced by the "dogmatic positivists" in power at Rome.

In the 1970s and 1980s, American denominations have produced proponents of a neo-dogmatism resembling "dogmatic positivism." Protestant fundamentalists* have emerged as vehement critics of liberal interpretations of Christian doctrine and its development. Catholic traditionalists in the U.S. (*See* Neo-Conservative Catholicism), such as those in Catholics United for the Faith (CUFF), oppose what they see as the victory of the transformist school in the teachings of Vatican II.*

A third option, the theological theory of development, came to prominence in twentieth-century Catholicism as a reaction to the perceived deficiencies of both dogmatic positivism and transformism. Traced back to nineteenth-century Catholic thinkers such as J. S. von Drey (1777-1853) and Johann A. Möhler (1796-1838) of Tübingen, it introduces a supernatural factor that can only be accepted by faith and elucidated by theology. God not only gives to his church a doctrine of salvation* expressed in human words, but a light by which she enters into living communion with her Savior. This inner light does not reveal anything independent from God's publicly and prophetically revealed truth, but God continues to unveil truth through a historically conditioned process guided by the light of the Spirit. In the English-speaking world, John Henry Newman (1801-1890) is often associat-

ed with the view that development is a supernatural process in which new aspects of the mystery emerge from the unconscious idea or vision of faith but are apprehended in connection with explicit doctrine.

In the 1970s and 1980s, the American Catholic theologian David Tracy, among others, has absorbed the seminal insights of Paul Tillich,* Bernard Lonergan* and a host of others who have reflected systematically on the relationship between inherited formal expressions of faith and the wisdom of the contemporary age. Overall, the problem of the development of doctrine continues to be a problem for professional theologians. Many laypeople, whether Protestant or Catholic, earnestly believe that their church's doctrinal standards are modern equivalents to the faith of the apostles. This is particularly true of nonconfessional Protestant groups such as Baptists (*See* Landmark Movement) and churches of the Restoration movement* who profess "no creed but the Bible."*

BIBLIOGRAPHY. P. W. Carey, ed., *American Catholic Religious Thought* (1987); W. R. Hutchison, *The Modernist Impulse in American Protestantism* (1976); G. A. Lindbeck, "Doctrinal Development and Protestant Theology," in E. Schillebeeckx, ed., *Man as Man and Believer* (1967); J. H. Newman, *An Essay on the Development of Doctrine* (1845); P. Toon, *The Development of Doctrine in the Church* (1978); D. Tracy, *Blessed Rage for Order; The New Pluralism in Theology* (1979); J. H. Walgrave, *Unfolding Revelation* (1972).

R. S. Appleby

Dialectical Theology. A European theological movement during the 1920s, centering around Karl Barth* and Emil Brunner,* called dialectical or "crisis theology." Barth then was indebted to Søren Kierkegaard* and stressed the radical difference between God and sinful* humanity. In Jesus Christ, God is revealed as reconciler and in Christ, said Barth, "two worlds meet and go apart, two planes intersect, the one known and the other unknown." Christ faces humanity with "crisis," as it must turn either toward or away from the Word of God.

The theological method of dialectic—or statement/counterstatement—is how the judgment/grace in Jesus Christ is encountered. Only God-given faith can hold together both poles of the dialectic in the divine/human dialog to which the Scriptures witness. The paradoxical tension is crucial, for God's divine "Yes" can be heard only with God's "No." Since faith holds the paradox together, no human theological statements can ultimately be identified with divine truth.

Brunner, having studied in the U.S. and having taught at Princeton Theological Seminary* (1938-1939), was more influential than Barth in introducing dialectical theology to America, and his books were more rapidly translated and assimilated by Americans. The Great Depression* and the shattered hopes for world peace and democracy* made Americans more receptive to a message of "crisis" during the 1930s and 1940s. Dialectical thought could be found in the thought of theologians such as Douglas Horton,* Paul Tillich* and Reinhold Niebuhr.*

BIBLIOGRAPHY. H. E. Brunner, *A Theology of Crisis* (1929); A. I. C. Heron, *A Century of Protestant Theology* (1980); E. Jungel, *Karl Barth: A Theological Legacy* (1987); W. Lowrie, *Our Concern with the Theology of Crisis* (1932); J. M. Robinson, ed., *The Beginnings of Dialectical Theology,* vol. 1 (1968). D. K. McKim

Dickinson, Emily Elizabeth (1830-1886).

American poet. A shy recluse from Amherst, Massachusetts, Dickinson spent most of her life in her home and garden, yet the lines that she penned and stored there have made her one of America's foremost poets. Dickinson published only seven poems during her lifetime, despite the fact that she carried on a twenty-two-year correspondence with Thomas Wentworth Higginson, a poetry critic and her acknowledged "preceptor." Nevertheless, after her death, over 1,500 of her poems were found, and the true poetic genius of Emily Dickinson came to light. Her poetry is characterized by a remarkable economy of style, an intensified use of language, an absence of titles and an experimental use of punctuation. In terms of thematic material, her intense interest in death, immortality and nature led to a rather pronounced treatment of religious themes. For example, she often pictured death as a lover or friend in order to eliminate its horror.

Emily Dickinson's interest in religion was magnified by her admiration of the Reverend Charles Wadsworth. Their relationship is obscured and uncertain, but she probably loved him and he was at least a spiritual example to her. Nevertheless, despite her connection to Wadsworth and her concentration on religious themes in her poetry, Emily Dickinson spurned traditional Calvinism* and the institutional church, and she resisted pressure to join the church. She clearly sets forth her attitude toward organized religion in lines that exalt the experience of nature over church observance. Thus, the eccentric recluse from Amherst,

with her cryptic, lyrical lines, has become one of America's most famous poets—one who wrote about religious matters yet rejected traditional religious institutions.

BIBLIOGRAPHY. *DAB* III; T. Johnson, *The Complete Poems of Emily Dickinson* (1960, 1976); J. Leyda, *The Years and Hours of Emily Dickinson,* 2 vols. (1960); *NAW* 1; J. Pickard, *Emily Dickinson, An Introduction and Interpretation* (1967).

C. E. Ostwalt

Dickinson, Jonathan (1688-1747).

Presbyterian* minister* and theologian.* Born at Hatfield, Massachusetts, he graduated from Yale College* (1706) and studied theology* independently (1706-1708)* before becoming a pastor* and practicing medicine in Elizabethtown, New Jersey. There Dickinson was to minister the rest of his life (1709-1747).

In 1717 he persuaded his Congregational* church to join the Presbytery* of Philadelphia, where their pastor* would gradually exert his influence in shaping colonial Presbyterianism. A strong Calvinist,* he was nonetheless opposed to the rigid confessionalism* of Scotch*-Irish Presbyterians who wished to impose the Westminster Confession* and Catechism as a test of orthodoxy.* As a leader of the antisubscriptionists (*see* Subscription Controversy), Dickinson argued for the strict examination of the ministerial candidate's religious experience.* In the end he helped negotiate an uneasy peace through the Adopting Act* of 1729, which required ministerial candidates to accept the Westminster standards "as being in all the essential and necessary articles, good forms of sound words and systems of Christian doctrine, and . . . as the confession of our faith." The emphasis upon "essential" articles, as well as its allowance for mental reservations, marked a victory for Dickinson's party.

However, this victory was not to last. The Great Awakening* divided Presbyterians over the issue of revivalism* and drove the wedge deeper yet between subscriptionists and antisubscriptionists. Dickinson's sympathies were clearly with the New Side* Presbyterian revivalists. After failing to reconcile the parties at the May 1741 meeting of the Synod* of Philadelphia, Dickinson led in the formation of the rival Synod of New York (1745).

Dickinson provided colonial Presbyterians with leadership through several controversies: defending Calvinism against Arminianism* and Deism,* presbyterianism against episcopacy,* and Nonconformity against Anglicanism.* His published works included: *The Reasonableness of Christianity*

(1732), A *Display of God's Special Grace* (1742) and *Sermons and Tracts* (1793). His most famous work was *Five Points: The True Scripture-Doctrine Concerning Some Important Points of Christian Faith* (1741). Dickinson was arguably the most distinguished Presbyterian minister in the colonial period, with an international reputation as a theologian second only to Jonathan Edwards,* who like him defended the Great Awakening while criticizing revivalistic excesses.

In 1746 the College of New Jersey* was opened in his home. Established for the training of pro-revivalist ministers, Dickinson served as its first president (1746). He died before it moved to Princeton.

BIBLIOGRAPHY. *AAP* 3; H. C. Cameron, *Jonathan Dickinson and the College of New Jersey* (1880); *DAB* III; K. J. Hardman, *Jonathan Dickinson and the Course of American Presbyterianism, 1717-1747* (1971); *NCAB* 5.   A. H. Freundt

Diehl, Nona May (1894-1981). United Lutheran* missionary* leader. Born in York, Pennsylvania, she graduated from Goucher College in 1917 and pursued graduate work at the University of Pennsylvania and Columbia University. In 1927 she became secretary of the Women's Missionary Society of the United Lutheran Church, and later executive secretary. Under her leadership the organization brought new prominence to women's part in the missionary cause. The Women's Missionary Society supported schools and hospitals in Appalachia, as well as Africa, India and the Caribbean, and helped raise over $25 million for missions. Diehl wrote numerous pamphlets, articles for church publications, missionary literature and a standard work on the Women's Missionary Society, *United Lutheran Church Women: Heritage and History* (1981).

M. L. Bendroth

Dietz, Peter Ernest (1878-1947). Labor priest.* Born in New York City to Bavarian parents, Dietz attended St. Mary's College, North East, Pennsylvania; the College of St. Francis Xavier, New York; and St. Gabriel's College, Moedling, Germany. Following theological studies at St. Mary's Seminary in Baltimore, he was ordained* a priest for the diocese of Cleveland in 1904 and transferred to the archdiocese of Milwaukee in 1912.

Although he began and ended his priestly career in parish ministry,* between 1909 and 1922 Dietz was involved in attempts to develop the social ministry of the American Catholic Church. Thus, he devoted his energies to educating American Catholics in the social teachings of the Church, and to establishing ties with the American labor movement. Successively the social service editor for the *Central Blatt and Social Justice* (1909-1910) and the *Bulletin* of the American Federation of Catholic Societies (1911-1918), he also served as the secretary of the Federation's Social Service Commission, as well as its fraternal delegate to the American Federation of Labor (AFL).

To counteract socialist influence in the AFL, he joined with Catholic labor leaders to form the Militia of Christ for Social Service (1910), a Catholic organization for workers. With the backing of his allies in the labor movement, he founded the American Academy of Christian Democracy (1915) in Hot Springs, North Carolina, to provide training for Catholic social workers. Following its relocation to Cincinnati in 1917, the school evolved into an institute for industrial relations. Just as Dietz was finalizing plans to transform his school into a National Labor College, disagreements with Archbishop Henry Moeller of Cincinnati led to his return to Milwaukee. After twenty-four years as the pastor of St. Monica's Church, Whitefish Bay, Wisconsin, he died on October 11, 1947.

BIBLIOGRAPHY. A. I. Abell, *American Catholicism and Social Action* (1963); *DAB* II; M. H. Fox, *Peter E. Dietz, Labor Priest* (1953).

J. M. McShane

Diocesan Pastoral Council. An advisory group of clergy* and laity* to aid the bishop* in fulfilling his ministerial responsibilities. The canon law* of the Roman Catholic Church* requires such a council to be established in each diocese* "to the extent that pastoral circumstances recommend it" (canon 511). While it is up to the bishop to determine how the members are to be chosen, the council must reflect the population "with due regard for the diverse regions, social conditions and professions of the diocese" (canon 512). The Greek Orthodox* Archdiocese* of North and South America provides for a similar diocesan council. In the Orthodox Church in America, the diocesan council is the permanent body of diocesan administration. The Protestant Episcopal Church* at an annual diocesan convention elects a standing committee to advise the bishop between conventions. The Presbyterian* presbytery* and the Methodist* annual conference are themselves representative and collegial.

BIBLIOGRAPHY. E. F. Hemrick and M. P. Burke, *Building the Local Church: Shared Responsibility in Diocesan Councils* (1984).   J. E. Lynch

Diocese. A geographical area over which a bishop has jurisdiction. The English word *diocese* is derived from the Greek word *dioikesis,* meaning "housekeeping," "province" or "administration." The Latin word *dioecesis* was originally used in the Roman Empire for the area surrounding a city. Diocletian applied it to the twelve subdivisions of the empire. As the church spread out from the cities in the third and fourth centuries, it adopted the word for the area of a bishop's jurisdiction. In the U.S. the Episcopal,* Roman Catholic* and Orthodox* churches use the term for their main geographical units. These churches consider the diocese, not the congregation, as the primary ecclesiastical unit. Frequently dioceses are organized into provinces.   D. S. Armentrout

Disciple, Discipleship. In Christian usage a disciple is a follower of Jesus Christ, an adherent to the Christian tradition. *Discipleship* identifies the lifestyle or process whereby individuals or groups live out their understanding of what it means to be a disciple. The concept undergirding these terms is an ancient one and can be found in both the Old and New Testaments. At the end of his life, Jesus instructed his followers to go and make disciples of all nations (Mt 28:18-20).

Dietrich Bonhoeffer's* classic book *The Cost of Discipleship* (1937) has helped to shape the current usage of these terms, which tend to stress the cost and content of intentional obedience to Jesus and his teachings. However, modern American usage is far from consistent and any church member or practicing Christian may be called a disciple, regardless of the individual's own level of commitment or religious observance. Vatican II* introduced *discipleship* into official Roman Catholic* terminology, using *disciple* as a synonym for *Christian.* Some evangelical* Protestant groups, such as the Navigators,* have become well known for their practice of discipling new believers. Abuses of discipleship have also appeared in groups with an authoritarian orientation (*See* Shepherding Movement).

BIBLIOGRAPHY. A. Dulles, "Discipleship," *ER* 4.   T. R. Albin

Discipleship Movement. *See* SHEPHERDING MOVEMENT.

Discipline, Church. The church's efforts to rebuke, correct and reform its membership through the use of censures that range from admonition through suspension from the Lord's Supper* (and also from office for officeholders) to excommuni-

cation* or expulsion from the fellowship of the church.

Whereas Martin Luther had set forth only two marks of the true church—the true preaching* and hearing of the Word and the right administration of the sacraments,* the Reformed* and Presbyterian* tradition emphasized discipline along with these marks of the true church. The Anabaptist Tradition* placed even greater emphasis on discipline. The Anabaptist Schleitheim Confession of 1527, Article II, calls for a "ban" or excommunication of those who have fallen "into error and sin" to be carried out according to Jesus' instruction recorded in Matthew 18. By this means the church is kept pure.

The Puritans* brought to America a concern for discipline aimed at producing a purer visible church that would approach conformity with the invisible church. The Cambridge Platform* (1648) spelled out the manner of church government* through which such discipline was to be exercised. A new generation of New Englanders, including people who were without experience of conversion,* although not guilty of moral or doctrinal deviation, brought about the Half-Way Covenant* of 1662, which compromised church discipline. By the end of the seventeenth century, Solomon Stoddard* in Northampton, Massachusetts, was allowing the unregenerate to come to the Lord's Supper, which he used as a converting ordinance.*

Jonathan Edwards,* Stoddard's grandson and successor at Northampton, saw this practice as inconsistent with Scripture and sought to restore a biblical form of church discipline, allowing those with a credible profession of faith in Christ to participate in the Lord's Supper. This stand proved to be one cause of his ouster from that pastorate in 1750. Another preacher of the Great Awakening,* Theodorus J. Frelinghuysen,* could be said to have triggered revival* through exercising church discipline along with fervently preaching the need for repentance.

While certain periods of church history have seen oppressive measures of church discipline, churches in twentieth-century urban American society have tended toward the opposite extreme of neglecting church discipline except for the most obvious cases—usually of sexual sin.* The relative anonymity of urban life, the strong American impulse toward individualism,* the plurality of denominations competing for church members, the ethical relativism that has influenced even the churches and, in some cases, the questioning or rejection of biblical authority* are just some of the factors leading to this decline.

The goal of church discipline has ordinarily been threefold: the restoration of the sinner, the deterrence of other church members from such offenses and the honor of Christ as head of the church.

See also EXCOMMUNICATION.

BIBLIOGRAPHY. E. S. Morgan, *Visible Saints: The History of a Puritan Idea* (1963); W. Walker, *The Creeds and Platforms of Congregationalism* (1893); H. S. Smith, R. T. Handy and L. A. Loetscher, eds., *American Christianity: An Historical Interpretation with Representative Documents,* 2 vols. (1960-1963). W. S. Barker

Dispensationalism. A hermeneutical approach to the Bible* that became a movement within American evangelicalism* after the 1870s. The term originates from *oikonomeo* and its derivatives, which appear about twenty times in the Greek New Testament and mean "to manage, regulate, administer and plan the affairs of a household" (see Lk 16:1-2; Eph 1:10; 3:2, 9; Col 1:25). When used of God, the word refers to his sovereign plan for the world.

At the heart of dispensationalism is the dividing of all time into distinguishable economies (or dispensations) which are seen as different stages in God's progressive revelation. C. I. Scofield,* a leading exponent of dispensationalism, defined a dispensation as "a period of time during which man is tested in respect of obedience to some specific revelation of the will of God." Furthermore, "these periods are marked off in Scripture by some change in God's method of dealing with mankind. . . . Each of the dispensations may be regarded as a new test of the natural man, and each ends in judgment—marking his utter failure in every dispensation."

Though many Christians have used historical periodization, John Nelson Darby* (1800-1882) was the first to create a full-blown system of interpretation. An early leader of the Plymouth Brethren* in Great Britain, Darby was a futurist premillennialist* who believed that Christ will return before the millennium and that biblical prophecies of the last days were yet to be fulfilled. To these ideas Darby added a literalistic hermeneutic and the strict separation of Israel and the church.

Darby saw in Scripture* two totally distinct divine plans for history, one concerning an earthly people (Israel), the other a heavenly people (the church). God's plan for Israel was revealed through a series of covenants (Adamic, Mosaic and Davidic) which pointed to the establishment of a Messianic kingdom on the earth. But when Messiah came, Israel rejected him. God then postponed the kingdom, turned away from Israel and created out of the Gentiles a new people, the church. According to this postponement theory, God will not resume his dealings with Israel until he finishes building the church and raptures it to heaven. Then the "great parentheses" in prophetic time will end and the events of the last days will take place: the great tribulation, the rise of Antichrist and the false prophet, the battle of Armageddon, the Second Coming of Christ, the binding of Satan and the setting up of the millennial kingdom. Initially not all premillennialists accepted Darby's views. Especially controversial was his doctrine of the pretribulation rapture of the church, which split his own Plymouth Brethren.

Darby's dispensationalism came to America in the 1870s. During a series of preaching tours, Darby won over a number of influential evangelical pastors and teachers, including William E. Blackstone,* James H. Brookes,* James M. Gray* and C. I. Scofield. Dispensational views spread into conservative evangelicalism through the Bible and prophetic conference* movement (*see* Niagara Conferences), the Bible institutes,* a number of influential journals and, most importantly, The Scofield Reference Bible* (1909, revised 1967). Scofield identified seven dispensations (innocence, conscience, human government, promise, law, grace and kingdom) and articulated what became the standard dispensational approach in America. Though rejected at first by many conservatives, by the 1920s it eclipsed other kinds of premillennialism and became closely identified with the fundamentalist* movement, thanks to able teachers like Arno C. Gaebelein,* Harry A. Ironside* and Lewis S. Chafer,* who founded Dallas Theological Seminary* in 1924 and wrote the movement's most influential *Systematic Theology* (1947).

In the 1980s dispensationalism finds able defenders in John F. Walvoord, Charles C. Ryrie and J. Dwight Pentecost, all from Dallas Theological Seminary, and is the most common view of eschatology taught in fundamentalist schools and churches.

See also APOCALYPTICISM; ESCHATOLOGY; FUNDAMENTALISM; PREMILLENNIALISM; SCOFIELD REFERENCE BIBLE.

BIBLIOGRAPHY. C. B. Bass, *Backgrounds to Dispensationalism* (1960); C. N. Kraus, *Dispensationalism in America* (1958); C. C. Ryrie, *Dispensationalism Today* (1965); E. R. Sandeen, *The Roots of Fundamentalism* (1970). T. P. Weber

District. A sub-unit of the Methodist* annual conference.* Districts are organized to carry out the programs of the conference and the general church, to promote good will in the local area and to provide for initial screening of candidates for ordination.* Their chief spiritual overseer is the district superintendent.

In 1878 *The Discipline* called for the district conference to be composed of all of the preachers* in the district, both traveling and local (including superannuated preachers). Representative laymen* were to participate as determined by the annual conference.

It was the duty of the district to inquire after the spiritual state, the attendance of ordinances* and the social meetings of the church, including its missions* activities and Sunday schools.* It was also responsible for financial systems, upkeep of real estate, accurate records of quarterly conferences, election of representatives to the annual conference and, above all, for the "religious exercises, such as preaching,* prayer-meetings,* love-feasts, and the administration of sacraments."

In the earlier days of Methodism, due to the limitations of travel and communication, the districts and their superintendents were much more autonomous than they are today.

P. A. Mickey

Divine, Major J. ("Father Divine") (c. 1880-1965). African-American cult* leader. Believed to have been born George Baker on Hutchinson's Island, Georgia, Divine and his wife, after various encounters with charismatic religious figures, purchased a house in Sayville, Long Island, in 1919. There they began to shelter and feed the destitute. The movement grew rapidly and moved to Harlem in 1933 and in 1942 established its headquarters on an estate outside Philadelphia. "Peace Mission Kingdoms," organized on a communal basis, were established in other states and countries as a result of Divine's speaking engagements and weekly magazine, *New Day*. The movement was known for the social services it provided to the needy, its strict moral code, claims of healings, emphasis on racial equality and fierce loyalty to Father Divine, who proclaimed himself God. Divine developed vast business holdings but never made public the details of his wealth. He claimed twenty million followers, though two million may be closer to reality. Present-day followers numbering in the thousands are concentrated in New York, New Jersey and Philadelphia, where Divine moved in 1942 to avoid legal entanglements in New York.

BIBLIOGRAPHY. *DARB;* R. A. Parker, *The Incred-* ible Messiah: The Deification of Father Divine (1937); R. Weisbrot, *Father Divine* (1983).

M. R. Sawyer

Divine Office. *See* LITURGY OF THE HOURS.

Divinity. A term frequently used prior to the twentieth century to refer to the study of theology or the "science of divine things." Derived from the Latin *Divinitatem* or "godhead," the term could also refer to the quality of being divine as well as to God himself. In preparing for the Protestant ministry, a young man might "study divinity" under a learned minister* or theologian* (or "divine," as they were sometimes called). When Protestant* seminaries* (a term which prior to the nineteenth century seems to have been used exclusively of Roman Catholic institutions for the training of priests) arose in America in the early nineteenth century, these institutions were frequently called *divinity schools*. The term is preserved in some contemporary institutions with nineteenth-century heritages (e.g., Yale* Divinity School) and has occasionally been adopted by seminaries of more recent founding (e.g., Trinity Evangelical Divinity School). These institutions formerly gave degrees entitled *Bachelor of Divinity* (B.D.)—renamed *Master of Divinity* (M.Div.) around 1970—and *Doctor of Divinity*.

The Editors

Divino Afflante Spiritu. Encyclical* promoting biblical studies.* Issued by Pope Pius XII* in September 1943, it commemorated the fiftieth anniversary of Pope Leo XIII's* encyclical *Providentissimus Deus* of 1893. Both encyclicals promoted biblical studies and outlined a proper approach for Catholic biblical scholars. Pius wished to encourage a renewed study of Scripture in the midst of the chaos of World War 2,* as well as point to the progress in modern biblical scholarship which might advance Catholic understanding of God's purposes as revealed in Scripture.*

Affirming the juridical authority and long-standing position of the Latin Vulgate for the Catholic Church, he nevertheless encouraged Catholic scholars to base their study on the Hebrew and Greek manuscripts, making use of the tools of text criticism. The heart of the encyclical detailed recent advances in scholarship and called upon Catholic scholars to take full advantage of them. Calling for "literal interpretations" in keeping with the original intent of the authors, he discouraged clever figurative explanations. Moreover, he urged a theological interpretation that would move beyond strictly scholarly concerns.

Assuring scholars that recent advances in biblical interpretation had added to the understanding of Scripture, rather than undermining its authority, he impressed upon biblical scholars the sacredness and significance of their calling. Freed from the constraints of the past, they were to pursue their studies with a moderate critical freedom. The result was a renaissance of Catholic biblical scholarship in which Catholic scholars began to share the same critical concerns and tools of other Western biblical scholars. This movement came to full fruition after the decree on Divine Revelation passed by Vatican II.*

BIBLIOGRAPHY. W. M. Abbott, "Pius XII's Encyclical on Bible Study," *Bible Today* (1963):439-443; C. Carlen, ed., *The Papal Encyclicals, 1740-1981,* vol. IV: 65-79 (1981); T. A. Collins and R. E. Brown, "Church Pronouncements," in *The Jerome Biblical Commentary,* ed. R. E. Brown et al. (1968); G. P. Fogarty, *American Catholic Biblical Scholarship: A History from the Early Republic to Vatican II* (1989); R. B. Robinson, *Roman Catholic Exegesis since Divino Afflante Spiritu: Hermeneutical Implications* (1988).   D. L. Salvaterra

Divorce. See MARRIAGE AND DIVORCE.

Dixon, (A)mzi (C)larence (1854-1925). Baptist* pastor* and evangelist.* Born in Shelby, North Carolina, Dixon attended Wake Forest College (B.A., 1875) and studied theology* for six months under John A. Broadus* at the Baptist Seminary in Greenville, South Carolina. Following several early pastorates in North Carolina (Bear Marsh and Mount Olive, 1874-1875; Chapel Hill and Ashville, 1876-1882), Dixon became pastor of Immanuel Baptist Church in Baltimore (1882-1890). During this period Dixon became a popular Bible conference* speaker in America and England (he traveled as a delegate to the 1889 World's Sunday School Convention in London), and his reputation as an effective evangelist spread. In 1893, while pastor of the Hanson Place Baptist Church in Brooklyn (1890-1901), he preached with Dwight L. Moody* in Moody's World's Fair evangelistic campaign.

After pastoring the Ruggles Street Church in Boston for several years (1901-1906), Dixon was called as pastor to Moody's Chicago Avenue Church in Chicago (1906-1911). However, his most prestigious pulpit was Spurgeon's Tabernacle in London, where he pastored from 1911 until 1919. A committed churchman, Dixon headed the London Baptist Association from 1915 to 1916 and attended Baptist World Congresses in London in

1905 and in Stockholm in 1923. Returning from London in 1919, Dixon spent several years in an itinerant evangelistic and Bible* teaching ministry across the U. S. During this time he lectured for several months at the Bible Institute of Los Angeles and conducted a preaching tour of mission stations in Japan and China. His last pastorate was at University Baptist, Baltimore (1921-1925).

Dixon was a staunch fundamentalist* and premillenialist,* an opponent of Darwinism* and biblical criticism.* His most noteworthy contribution to the fundamentalist cause was his role as the first executive secretary and editor of *The Fundamentals,* a twelve-volume defense of the basic doctrines of conservative orthodoxy* published between 1910 and 1915. Dixon oversaw the publication of the first five volumes of that series. Above all of his accomplishments, Dixon regarded his first love as evangelism.

BIBLIOGRAPHY. H. C. A. Dixon, *A. C. Dixon, A Romance of Preaching* (1931); *NCAB* 39.
P. C. Wilt

Doak, Samuel (1749-1830). First Presbyterian* minister* to settle in Tennessee. Born in August 1749 to Scotch-Irish immigrants* of Augusta County, Virginia, Doak sought an education, following a profession of religion at age sixteen, and offered to surrender his patrimony for the privilege. He graduated from the College of New Jersey* in 1775, studied theology* under John Blair Smith and William Graham and was ordained* by the Hanover Presbytery. Shortly before 1780 he removed to the frontier settlements along the Holston River in northeastern Tennessee, establishing the first Presbyterian congregations in that territory. Settling in Washington County, Tennessee, Doak founded Martin Academy in 1785, chartered ten years later as Washington College and the first institution of higher learning west of the Appalachians. In 1818 Doak moved once more to Greene County where, with his son Samuel, Jr., he founded Tusculum Academy and College near Greeneville. A man of sober and even grave disposition, Doak was nevertheless irenic, and the early success of Presbyterianism in east Tennessee is largely attributable to his skill and indefatigable labors. In the New Divinity* controversies, he was a vigorous leader of the orthodox* party.

BIBLIOGRAPHY. *AAP* 3; J. E. Alexander, *A Brief History of the Synod of Tennessee* (1890); *DAB* III.   W. J. Wade

Doane, George Washington (1799-1859). Episcopal* bishop* of New Jersey. Born in Trenton, New Jersey, Doane graduated from Union College, Schenectady (1818), and studied at the General Theological Seminary, New York (1820-1821). Bishop John Henry Hobart* of New York ordained* him deacon* on April 19, 1821, and priest* on August 6, 1823, and Doane began his ministry as Hobart's assistant at Trinity Church, New York.

From 1824 to 1828 Doane was professor of rhetoric and belles-lettres at Washington (Trinity) College, Hartford, Connecticut. In 1828 he became assistant minister at Trinity Church, Boston, and in 1832 its rector.* On October 3, 1832, the Diocese of New Jersey elected him its second bishop, and he was consecrated* on October 31, 1832, at St. Paul's Chapel, New York, by Presiding Bishop William White.*

While bishop, Doane served as rector of St. Mary's, in Burlington, New Jersey, and was a leading promoter of the missionary movement and a founder of Episcopal schools. He preached the sermon at the consecration of the first missionary bishop of the Episcopal Church, Jackson Kemper, in 1835 and founded St. Mary's Hall for girls in 1837 and Burlington College for men in 1846. Doane was a high churchman* and supported the Tractarian Movement,* editing the first American edition (1834) of John Keble's *Christian Year.* He was also a hymnwriter (not to be confused with William H. Doane) and for a time edited the *Episcopal Watchman,* the *Banner of the Cross* and the *Missionary.*

BIBLIOGRAPHY. *DAB* III; W. C. Doane, *The Life and Writings of George Washington Doane,* 4 vols. (1860-1861). D. S. Armentrout

Dock, Christopher (c.1690-1771). Colonial Mennonite* schoolmaster. A native German, Dock apparently taught school in Germany before 1714. From about 1718 to 1728 he taught at Skippack, Pennsylvania, in the heart of the Franconia Mennonite Conference, north of Philadelphia. For several years he farmed but then returned to full-time teaching at Skippack and nearby Salford until the day of his death. Dock is best known for his *Schulordnung* ("School-Management"), written in 1750 (published in 1770), the earliest known essay in North America on the theme of pedagogy. He also published several other articles that reveal the customs and practices of the Colonial Pennsylvania Germans, giving careful attention to artwork (*Fraktur-Schriften*) and to singing. He composed at least seven hymns. Of gentle and loving character, Dock viewed teaching as a divine calling and gave his pupils individualized instruction, building

in them character and godliness.

BIBLIOGRAPHY. *DAB* III; G. C. Studer, *Christopher Dock; Colonial Schoolmaster; The Biography and Writings of Christopher Dock* (1967).

L. Gross

Dogma, Dogmatic Theology. The truths and systematic presentation of those truths which all Christian believers are obligated to accept, particularly within a Roman Catholic* context. The word *dogma* is derived from the Greek word *dokeo,* which refers to something which "appears" to be true, but in ecclesiastical practice it has come to stand for those items of belief which to a Christian are necessarily true. These are the points of doctrine which are essential to Christianity. Apart from believing in them, one cannot be Christian; thus their denial constitutes heresy.* Included in these beliefs are such essential doctrines as the deity of Christ.*

In Roman Catholic theology what constitutes dogma is defined by the teaching office of the Church primarily through ecumenical councils* and the pope.* Dogma is recognized by the fact that it was revealed by God in the apostolic era and maintained by tradition throughout the history of the Church. Thus no dogma can be created or negated; it can only be accepted or ignored. A dogmatic theology collects and expounds on the Church's dogma by recognizing levels of importance, implications and corollaries.

An unsettled question concerns those beliefs held as dogma which are either not explicitly taught in Scripture or for which no strict logical derivation from Scripture can be deduced (e.g., the assumption of Mary*). Modern Roman Catholic theology has largely followed the lead set by John Henry Newman in proposing an organic development of dogma.* Under this model all dogmatic truths are implicitly contained in apostolic tradition, but need not be made explicit until much later in the history of the Church. This notion was at least partially absorbed into the Second Vatican Council.*

In contemporary theological discussion in America, much has been made of the fact that not everything promulgated by the teaching office of the Church is necessarily dogma. Thus, many theologians hold that it is legitimate to disagree with the Church on some recent teachings on sexual morality without losing one's standing in the Church, a latitude that would not be possible on doctrinal matters which are pronounced as essential for belief (*de fide*).

See also CONGREGATION FOR THE DOCTRINE OF THE

FAITH; MAGISTERIUM OF THE CHURCH; SYSTEMATIC THEOLOGY.

BIBLIOGRAPHY. "Dogmatic Constitution on Divine Revelation" (*Dei Verbum*) in *Documents of Vatican II,* ed. A. P. Flannery (1975); J. H. Newman, *Essay on the Development of Christian Doctrine* (1845).   W. Corduan

Dominicans. Catholic* mendicant religious order.* In 1805 four Dominican friars set out from Maryland to establish in frontier Kentucky a new American province of their worldwide Order of Preachers. They had come from the Dominican province in England with the same mission for which St. Dominic had founded the order in 1216: to proclaim the Word of God through preaching and teaching, sustained by fraternal apostolic life in community. Their leader was Edward Dominic Fenwick,* an American, who with the others had conducted a college in Belgium (Holy Cross*) and planned to do the same in Maryland. Instead, they made their foundation in Kentucky in response to an urgent call for priests, conveyed by Bishop John Carroll,* and issued by Catholic settlers in Kentucky.

Near the village of Bardstown the four Dominicans established in 1806 their church, college and preaching center under the patronage of St. Rose of Lima. They were soon joined by sons of the pioneers, who asked to join the order. From their priory they fanned out on horseback, often riding alone through the wilderness and clearings to reach the settlers in Kentucky and then Ohio and Tennessee. As the population grew and the numbers of Dominicans increased, they founded parishes and colleges in the heartland of the nation from the Canadian border at Mackinac to Louisiana, and eastward to Washington, D.C., and New York. When California became a state, Dominicans went there immediately after the first gold miners. The order has continued to expand in numbers and ministries throughout the nation and to peoples of Asia, Africa and South America. Today nearly 1,000 friars, organized into four provinces, continue the work of their pioneer members in the U.S.

Foundations of Dominican Sisters began in the U.S. soon after that of the friars. In 1822 nine young women, experiencing the spiritual needs of their people in Kentucky, formed there the first American community of Dominican Sisters. From the Bardstown area they went out to proclaim the gospel by teaching and healing the sick. As young women asked to join them, they formed new communities to reach people in many towns and cities. There are now forty congregations of Dominican Sisters serving in the U.S., each having many branch communities. Their members count more than 11,000 women engaged in education, social service, health care and many other means of proclaiming the gospel.

A place for women in the Order of Preachers was not only anticipated by its founder but initiated by him in the founding of monasteries of contemplative nuns* who would support the ministry of the Word through their lives of prayer.* The first such monastery was founded at Prouille in southern France in 1206. The first in the U.S. was founded in 1880 by American and French nuns in Newark, New Jersey. Other women founded monastic communities in various states and foreign countries (e.g., Kenya and Pakistan). The number of contemplative Dominican monasteries in the U.S. today totals nineteen.

For more than seven centuries lay* men and women have been welcomed to membership in the Dominican family, to partake in the apostolic life and mission of the order by means of study, prayer and various types of ministry. The first American chapter of lay Dominicans was formed in the mid-nineteenth century. Today more than 3,000 members are identified with chapters throughout the United States.

BIBLIOGRAPHY. *"To Gladly Learn . . ."* : *A Bibliography Related to Dominican Life in the United States* (1985); V. O'Daniel, *The Dominican Province of Saint Joseph* (1942); W. A. Hinebusch, "Dominicans," *NCE* 4; S. Torvend, ed., "Dominic and His Family," *U.S. Dominican* 6.1 (Fall 1986); J. B. Walker et al., "Dominicans—Sisters," *NCE* 4.

M. N. McGreal

Dominion Theology. *See* RECONSTRUCTIONISM, CHRISTIAN.

Dongan, Thomas (1634-1715). Catholic* governor of colonial New York. Born in Ireland of a distinguished Catholic family, Dongan served in the English army and later held the position of Lieutenant Governor of Tangiers. The Duke of York appointed him governor of New York in 1682. He arrived there the next year and, following the Duke's instructions, convened an assembly which adopted a "Charter of Liberties." Religious toleration* for Christians was included, but Dongan insisted that Jews also be enrolled as freemen and given licenses to trade. Although the charter was disallowed after the Duke became James II, the clause on religious freedom was allowed to stand.

Dongan worked to establish the boundaries of

New York and maintain them against the threat from the French and their Iroquois allies. After he was succeeded as governor by Sir Edmund Andros in 1688, Dongan retired to Long Island until Leisler's rebellion forced him to flee to England. He succeeded his brother as Earl of Limerick in 1698, but as a Catholic his lands were forfeited. He died in London on December 14, 1715.

BIBLIOGRAPHY. *DAB* III; J. T. Ellis, *Catholics in Colonial America* (1965); J. H. Kennedy, *Thomas Dongan, Governor of New York, 1682-1688* (1935). T. E. Buckley

Dooyeweerd, Herman (1894-1977). Dutch Calvinist* philosopher. A foremost Christian philosopher of the twentieth century, Dooyeweerd developed the core ideas of Dutch neo-Calvinism into a wide-ranging, tightly argued, well-nuanced system, known as the philosophy of the cosmonomic idea. Dooyeweerd spent his entire academic career (1926-1965) at the (Calvinist) Free University of Amsterdam, where he had received his doctorate in 1917 and in whose environs he had been born and raised.

Dooyeweerd's North American influence rose with the post-1945 Dutch immigration to Canada and the subsequent building there of political, labor and especially academic (the Institute for Christian Studies in Toronto) institutions bearing his inspiration. In this context "Dooyeweerdian" implies the conviction that religion is at the heart of *every* human enterprise; that Christians are called above all to forceful, reformatory social-cultural engagement; that these efforts are to be guided by God's creation ordinances or norms more than by the Bible* alone; and that human activity and natural being are to be respected and encouraged in all their diversity. His ideas have been made available to English readers in *A New Critique of Theoretical Thought* (4 vols., 1953-1958); in *The Twilight of Western Thought* (1960); and *Roots of Western Culture* (1979).

BIBLIOGRAPHY. L. Kalsbeek, *Contours of a Christian Philosophy* (1975); C. T. McIntire, ed., *The Legacy of Herman Dooyeweerd* (1986).

J. D. Bratt

Dorchester, Jr., Daniel (1827-1907). Methodist* minister* in New England. Born in Duxbury, Massachusetts, the son of Methodist minister* Daniel Dorchester, Sr., young Daniel attended Norwich Academy and Wesleyan University, leaving the latter in 1847 because of ill health. The university later granted him an M.A. in 1856 and a D.D. in 1874. Dorchester served as a minister in the

Providence Conference of the Methodist Episcopal Church until 1855, when he was elected state senator from Mystic, Connecticut. Received into the New England Conference in 1858, Dorchester held a number of pastorates and served on three occasions as presiding elder before his retirement in 1895. In 1882 he was elected to the Massachusetts legislature and seven years later, in 1889, was appointed Commissioner of Indian Education by President Harrison. While serving in this capacity, Dorchester played a significant role in the government's decision to retract federal funding of sectarian (mainly Catholic*) Native American institutions. A prolific writer, Dorchester wrote many influential books, including *Problem of Religious Progress* (1881); *History of Christianity in the United States* (1888); *The Liquor Problem in All Ages* (1884); and *Romanism versus the Public School System* (1888). Dorchester was a leader in the temperance movement* and a powerful advocate of the burgeoning Social Gospel.*

BIBLIOGRAPHY. *DAB* III. B. K. Turley

Doremus, Sarah (1802-1877). Founder and first president of the Woman's Union Missionary Society of America.* Doremus, the wife of a wealthy New York businessman, was informed by missionary* David Abeel, a fellow member of the Reformed Church in America,* of the need for single women to minister* to Asian women who were inaccessible to male missionaries.* In response Doremus organized what was to become the first of more than forty female missionary agencies founded between 1860 and the turn of the century. Setting aside denominational* considerations, she called on women from other churches to aid her, and in 1861 they sponsored their first missionary, a Baptist* named Sarah Marston, for service in Burma. In addition to foreign missionary outreach, Doremus was involved in urban* ministries. She was the first director of the Women's Prison Association and founded or directed several other humanitarian organizations to aid the urban poor.

BIBLIOGRAPHY. R. P. Beaver, *American Protestant Women in World Mission* (1980); C. Van Liere, "Sarah Doremus: Reformed Church Saint," *The Church Herald* (October 4, 1985).

R. A. Tucker

Dougherty, Dennis J. (1865-1951). Catholic* cardinal.* Born in the coal region of Ashland, Pennsylvania, to a large Irish immigrant family, Dennis picked coal as a boy. At the age of fourteen he entered St. Mary's College in Montreal, Canada, and two years later transferred to St. Charles

Borromeo Seminary in Overbrook, Pennsylvania. After studying at the North American College* in Rome, he received his D.D. and was ordained* there in 1890. Years later Dougherty remarked, "After God I owe what I am to the Holy See." He returned as a professor to St. Charles Seminary, where he taught a wide range of subjects, including dogmatic theology.*

In 1903, Dougherty was appointed bishop* of Nueva Segovia, Luzon, the first American bishop to the Philippines. There he crushed a schism led by Padre Gregorio Aglipay, and in 1908 Dougherty was transferred to Jaro, on the Philippine island of Panay. Eight years later he was installed as bishop of Buffalo, New York, where he united the various national groups and revitalized the Catholic school system. In 1918 he was the first native son to become archbishop* of Philadelphia. Three years later he was the fifth American named a cardinal. Calling himself "God's bricklayer," he vastly extended the facilities of his archdiocese where, among other institutions, he created a unique system of free high school education for all Catholic teens. He served as president of the National Commission for Colored People and Indians for almost two decades and considered the work of Mother (now Saint) Katharine Drexel* "the crowning glory of the diocese." In a surprising move, Dougherty gave public support for the Equal Rights Amendment in 1945. He was a crusader for temperance,* anti-Communism* and morality in the motion picture industry. He died on the 61st anniversary of his ordination.

BIBLIOGRAPHY. *DAB* III; H. J. Nolan, "Cardinal Dougherty: An Appreciation," *RACHAP* 62 (1951): 135-141; H. J. Nolan, "The Native Son," in *The History of the Archdiocese of Philadelphia*, ed. J. F. Connelly (1976).   M. M. Reher

Douglass, Frederick Augustus Washington Bailey (1817?-1895). Ex-slave, orator, journalist and abolitionist.* Born a slave in Talbot County, Maryland, Douglass spent his early life moving between Talbot County and Baltimore, working as a house servant and ship caulker. Douglass learned to read with the aid of his slave owner's wife and thereafter improved his skills by using the Bible* and the *Columbian Orator*. In 1838 Douglass escaped to freedom and settled in New Bedford, Massachusetts, where, at the encouragement of William Lloyd Garrison,* he became a speaker for the Massachusetts Anti-Slavery Society. An outspoken advocate for the abolition* of slavery and for temperance* and women's rights, Douglass lectured widely in America and abroad, edited four

newspapers, and wrote three autobiographies in support of such causes. He also served under Presidents Hayes and Garfield as the marshal and recorder of deeds for the District of Columbia. Douglass's crowning achievement was his 1889 appointment as the minister-resident and consul-general to the Republic of Haiti in President Benjamin Harrison's administration. Douglass was a scathing critic of what he called the "Christianity of this land," which hypocritically professed a gospel of grace and brutally held and abused African-American slaves. In contrast to this religion, he wrote, "I love the pure, peaceable, and impartial Christianity of Christ."

BIBLIOGRAPHY. J. W. Blassingame, ed., *The Frederick Douglass Papers*, 3 vols. (1985); D. J. Preston, *Young Frederick Douglass: The Maryland Years* (1980); B. Quarles, *Frederick Douglass* (1948).   M. C. Bruce

Doukhobors (Dukhobors). A mystical, communal Christian sect* with Russian origins. Derived from *Dukhobortsy,* Russian for "spirit wrestlers," the word was first applied in a pejorative sense and later adopted by a mystical, pacifist, communal sect of Christians appearing around 1740 in the Kneiper River region of the Ukraine. Dissenting from the Orthodox Church,* they taught that the "inner light" or voice of God, what they also identified as the "Christ Spirit," inhabited all things and persons. Hence, they denied the authority* of the Church,* took an anarchist position toward government, embraced pacifism* and eventually became vegetarians.

Doukhobors reject the authority of the Bible,* revere Christ as a sinless person and recognize God as present in fullest power in other persons. They accept the Ten Commandments but hold that if individuals follow their "inner light," law and secular government are unnecessary. Doukhobors are a communal society, worshiping in meetings called *sobranyas.* Their only symbols are salt, water and bread. Psalms, meditations and hymns,* orally transmitted in the "Living Book," transmit their doctrine, history and culture. Doukhobor leaders are revered as persons having a "magnified" spark of the Divine.

Sporadic persecution in Russia during the nineteenth century led to several deportations, and in 1898, with the assistance of Count Leo Tolstoy and English Quakers,* 8,000 Doukhobors immigrated to Canada. In 1903 they were joined by their dynamic leader, Peter Vasilevich Verigin (1859-1924), who had been in Siberian exile. Known as the Christian Community of Universal Brotherhood, most settled in communities in Saskatchewan on land received as individual homesteads under the Dominion Lands Act (1873). At first the Canadian government granted military exemptions and educational concessions, but in 1905 they were required to take a prescribed oath of allegiance to the crown as a condition of transfer of title to their land. Their resolute refusal resulted in eviction. Finally, in 1908, Veregin led the majority to the Kootenays in British Columbia, where 6,000 settled communally on property privately purchased.

Assimilationist pressures in Canada gave rise early on to the accommodationist Independent Doukhobors. In 1902 a reactionary splinter group of radical millennarians arose called "The Sons of Freedom." In protest of state-imposed education and taxation, this group has occasionally resorted to arson, bombing and parading naked. Their indebtedness led the government of British Columbia to foreclose on their land in 1939. Since World War 2,* violence and civil disobedience by a small minority have led to unwarranted prejudice against law-abiding Doukhobors.

In 1930 there were 10,000 Doukhobor descendants, and in 1987 an estimated 34,000, half of whom continue to speak Russian and remain religiously active. The majority, the "Orthodox," or Union of Spiritual Communities of Christ (USCC), are led by John J. Verigin, great-grandson of Peter Vasilevich Verigin.

BIBLIOGRAPHY. G. Woodcock and I. Avakumovic, *The Doukhobors* (1968); H. B. Hawthorn, ed., *The Doukhobors in British Columbia* (1955); K. J. Tarasoff, *A Pictorial History of the Doukhobors* (1969); M. Krisztenovich, *A Doukhobor Bibliography* (1970, 1972, 1973). W. E. Ellis

Dow, Lorenzo (1777-1834). Itinerant evangelist.* Born in Connecticut, Dow was converted* through the ministry* of Methodist* elder* Hope Hull in 1791. By 1794 he declared a call to preach,* but because of his mannerisms and his asthma, the Methodist church did not appoint him until 1798. His zeal and his eccentricity soon earned him the name "Crazy Dow." His health failing him in 1799, he sailed to Ireland. His last Methodist appointment was on his return in 1801, but after six months he sailed to Georgia. He spent the rest of his life in ceaseless travels throughout the U.S., Canada and Great Britain, his peculiarities, prescience, directness and powerful preaching attracting large crowds. A great advocate of the camp meeting,* he was a catalyst in the formation of the Primitive Methodist Church* in England. Unwilling to accept a regular itinerancy, Dow nevertheless remained essentially true to Methodist doctrine. A variety of his writings were published in *The Life, Travel, Labors, and Writings of Lorenzo Dow* (1856).

BIBLIOGRAPHY. *DAB* III; J. Kent, *Holding the Fort* (1978); C. C. Sellers, *Lorenzo Dow* (1928). M. R. Fraser

Dowie, John Alexander (1847-1907). Healing* evangelist* and founder of religious colony. Born in Edinburgh, Scotland, Dowie was a Congregational* pastor* in Australia from 1872 to 1877. A serious plague during those years led him to discover divine healing. After he began to pray for parishioners, it is reported, no more died. Dowie made healing a focus of his ministry in 1883 when he founded the Free Christian Church in Melbourne. Immigrating to America in 1888, he settled in Chicago in 1890.

Dowie continued to proclaim his message of divine healing and suffered bitter persecution from doctors (Dowie opposed all medicine) and the press—but this only increased his following. In 1896 he founded the Christian Catholic Church in Chicago, and by the autumn of 1899 it had grown to several thousand members. Dreaming of a Utopian colony, Dowie bought six thousand acres of land forty miles north of Chicago and unveiled his plans for Zion City on New Year's Day, 1900. Thousands moved to the city under Dowie's theocratic leadership. In June 1901 Dowie declared himself to be Elijah. This claim and the financial disaster into which he led his city caused his popularity to wane. A stroke paralyzed Dowie in September 1905, and in 1906 other Zion leaders stripped him of his rule. The church and the city continued under his successor, Glenn Voliva, though eventually the theocratic laws were repealed. Despite his ignominious end, Dowie directly influenced many healing evangelists of early Pentecostalism.*

BIBLIOGRAPHY. G. Lindsay, *John Alexander Dowie* (1951); D. E. Harrell, *All Things Are Possible* (1975). B. Barron

Doxology. An ascription of praise offered to God in Christian worship.* The term comes from the Greek roots *doxa* and *logia* ("words of glory"). In the broadest sense, Christians strive to make not only worship, but also theology* and life itself, a doxology.

Specifically, American Protestants* speak of "the Doxology," referring to the response "Praise God from whom all blessings flow. . . ." Written by

Thomas Ken around 1700, it is often sung in worship to the tune "Old One Hundreth" as the offering of the people is presented to God.

More technically, the term may refer to the lesser doxology, denoting the short response also known as the Gloria Patri ("Glory be to the Father . . ."), sung in many Protestant worship services following the declaration of pardon for sin, and added to the end of chanted psalms and canticles in both the Eastern and Western liturgical* traditions since the early church. In liturgical churches (Roman Catholic,* Episcopal,* Lutheran*), the "greater doxology" ("Glory to God in the highest") is sung in eucharistic* celebrations.

BIBLIOGRAPHY. J. A. Jungmann, *The Mass of the Roman Rite,* vol. 2 (1961); G. Wainwright, *Doxology: The Praise of God in Worship, Doctrine, and Life* (1980).   P. W. Butin

Dreher, Godfrey (1789-1875). Lutheran* minister,* evangelist.* A patriarch of South Carolina Lutheranism, Godfrey Dreher (or Drehr) was born in Irmo, South Carolina. Self-educated, Dreher was licensed* to preach* by the North Carolina Synod in 1810 and ordained* in 1812. An ardent evangelist, Dreher served a great number of congregations, including the Lexington congregations of St. Peter's (1810, 1837-1851), Nazareth (1827-1828), Zion (1810-1854) and St. John's (1831?); St. Peter's (1833-1852) at Piney Woods, St. Michael's (1814?) and Bethlehem (1810?-1851) at Irmo; Sandy Run (1824-1826) at Swansea; St. Paul's (1832-1851) at Gilbert; Mt. Calvary (1833) at Johnston; Bethlehem (1829-40?) and Cedar Grove (1852-1854), both at Leesville; and St. John's (1850?) at Pomaria.

Dreher was a prime mover of the South Carolina Synod (1824) and was its first president and its treasurer (1825-1834). Active in education, Dreher promoted Sunday schools* and sat on the Board of the Lutheran Southern Seminary (1831). His confessionalism* caused him to oppose revivalism,* the General Synod,* and synodical connectionalism. As early as 1824 Dreher considered, along with other regional Lutherans, the formation of a separate synod from the North Carolina Synod. Following the "Dreher Controversy" (1834-1837)—a conflict involving the Synod and Dreher's neighboring pastors—Dreher became an independent Lutheran minister. In 1852 Dreher's congregations associated with the like-minded Tennessee Synod, though Dreher himself remained independent.

BIBLIOGRAPHY. G. Dreher, *Journal of Rev. Godfrey Drehr, 1819-1851,* ed. B. H. Holcomb (1978);

A History of the Lutheran Church in South Carolina (1971).   C. G. Fry

Drexel, Katharine (1858-1955). Heiress, founder of the Sisters of the Blessed Sacrament for Indians and Colored People. Katharine was born in Philadelphia, the second daughter of Francis Anthony Drexel of the prominent banking family, and Hanna Jane Langstroth, a Quaker,* who died five weeks after Katharine's birth. In 1860 Drexel married Emma Bouvier, who bore him a third daughter. The girls were educated by tutors and extensive travel in the U. S. and Europe. A strong sense of social responsibility was inculcated through the charitable practices of Mrs. Drexel, who distributed aid to the poor three times weekly from her home, and by the habitual philanthropy of the Drexel family.

Upon the death of Emma Drexel in 1883 and of Francis in 1885, the daughters inherited an estate of over $14 million, which they decided to use in line with their parents' concern for Native Americans and African-Americans. In 1887 Katharine asked Pope Leo XIII* for missionaries to Native Americans,* but he challenged her to become one herself. As a result, she determined to found a new order for that purpose. Katharine made her novitiate with the Sisters of Mercy* in Pittsburgh, Pennsylvania, professing vows as a Sister of the Blessed Sacrament for Indians and Colored People on February 12, 1891.

Headquarters of the new congregation were established at Cornwells Heights, Pennsylvania; its first project, begun in 1894, was St. Catharine's School for Pueblo Indians in Santa Fe, New Mexico. Katharine Drexel served as superior general of the order until her health failed in 1937. She established numerous missions and schools for African-Americans and Native Americans, including, in 1915, Xavier University of New Orleans, the only Catholic college established for African-Americans in the U.S. When her two sisters died childless, Mother Katharine's congregation received the total income for the Drexel estate until her death at Cornwells Heights at ninety-six years of age. The Sisters of the Blessed Sacrament, devoted entirely to African-Americans and Native Americans, then numbered over 500. The cause for Katharine Drexel's canonization* was introduced in 1964, and she was beatified in 1988.

BIBLIOGRAPHY. K. Burton, *The Golden Door, the Life of Katharine Drexel* (1950); *DAB* 5; C. M. Duffy, *Katharine Drexel: A Biography* (1966); *NAWMP.*   P. Byrne

DuBose, William Porcher (1836-1918). Episcopal* theologian.* Born near Winnsboro, South Carolina, he graduated from the Military College of South Carolina (Citadel) in 1855 and in 1859 received his M.A. from the University of Virginia. In October 1859 he entered the diocesan seminary* at Camden, South Carolina, but in 1861 withdrew to enter the military service of the Confederacy. Ordained* deacon* by Bishop Thomas F. Davis on December 13, 1863, at Grace Church, Camden, he served the remainder of the War as a chaplain.* Bishop Davis ordained him priest* on September 9, 1866, at St. John's, Winnsboro, South Carolina, where DuBose began his parochial ministry. On January 1, 1868, he became rector* of Trinity Church, Abbeville, South Carolina, and July 12, 1871, he became chaplain at the University of the South, in Sewanee, Tennessee, where he remained until his death on August 18, 1918. During those years he served as dean of the School of Theology (1894-1908).

DuBose's theological position developed out of early evangelical* convictions into a liberal Catholicism, stressing the incarnation and evolution.* While Christ was the particular incarnation of God, all of humanity shares in a generic incarnation. His position was articulated in six major books. *The Soteriology of the New Testament* (1892) presents his incarnational understanding of Christ as our representative, and *The Ecumenical Councils* (1896) treats his Christology and defends the full humanity of Jesus Christ. *The Gospel in the Gospels* (1906) treats the Christ of the synoptic Gospels, and *The Gospel According to St. Paul* (1907) is his treatment of the Epistle to the Romans. *High Priesthood and Sacrifice* (1908) is an exposition of Hebrews, and *The Reason of Life* (1911) concentrates on the Johannine interpretation of the gospel. *Turning Points in My Life* (1912) is autobiographical and personal. Largely uninfluential in his own day, his intellectual creativity has since been recognized, and he has been called the American Episcopal Church's greatest theologian.

BIBLIOGRAPHY. D. S. Armentrout, *A DuBose Reader: Selections from the Writings of William Porcher DuBose* (1984); T. D. Bratton, *An Apostle of Reality: The Life and Thought of the Reverend William Porcher DuBose* (1936); *DAB* III; *DARB;* W. P. DuBose, *Unity in the Faith,* ed. W. N. Pittenger (1957); *NCAB* 18.   D. S. Armentrout

DuBourg, Louis William Valentine (1766-1833). Catholic* educator and bishop.* Born in Cap Français, Santo Domingo, DuBourg moved at the age of two with his family to Bordeaux, France.

After college studies with the Jesuits,* he entered the Seminary of St. Sulpice at Issy. Following ordination* in 1788, he directed a minor seminary* at Issy. Forced by the Revolution to flee from France, DuBourg made his way first to Spain and then to the U.S. In Baltimore he did some tutoring, became a priest of St. Sulpice* and began ministering to the African-American refugees from Santo Domingo. In 1796, Bishop John Carroll* appointed DuBourg president of Georgetown College, where he served for two years. Friction with the board of trustees prompted him to resign, and he next attempted to begin a college in Cuba. When that was unsuccessful, he returned to Baltimore in 1799 to found St. Mary's Academy (or College), which flourished until 1852. During his twelve years as president, he had the college chartered as a university, was involved in the founding of Mount St. Mary's College at Emmitsburg and brought Elizabeth Seton* to Baltimore to begin a school and a religious sisterhood.

In 1812, Bishop Carroll sent DuBourg to New Orleans as the administrator of the Diocese* of Louisiana and the Floridas. He struggled there with entrenched forces and with the problems of the War of 1812. Appointed the diocese's bishop in 1815, he was consecrated in Rome and spent the next two years recruiting help from the Vincentians, the Jesuits and the Religious of the Sacred Heart (under Mother Rose Philippine Duchesne*). For several years he lived in St. Louis, but then returned to New Orleans from 1820 to 1825. He resigned his see in 1825 and returned to France. There he served for some years as bishop of Montauban and for his final months as archbishop of Besançon.

BIBLIOGRAPHY. *DAB* III; A. M. Melville, *Louis William DuBourg,* 2 vols. (1986).

J. W. Bowen

Duchesne, Rose Philippine (1769-1852). Pioneer, missionary,* founder of the Society of the Sacred Heart. Born in Grenoble, France, of a prestigious family, Philippine was the second of eight children of Pierre François Duchesne and Rose Euphrosine Perier. Given an extraordinary education by governesses and tutors, she entered the Visitation Monastery of Sainte-Marie-d'en-Haut in 1788. When the Revolution dispersed the nuns,* she returned home and spent the next ten years in charitable activities. Following a failed attempt to restore her Visitation community, in 1804 Philippine joined the Society of the Sacred Heart, founded in 1800 by St. Madeleine Sophie Barat for the education of girls.

Though longing for missionary life, Philippine spent fourteen years in administrative positions of her order in France. At the invitation of Bishop Du Bourg, in 1818 Philippine and four other nuns left for St. Louis, Missouri. Relegated to the villages of St. Charles and Florissant by Du Bourg, the nuns established a novitiate, boarding academy, free school and a short-lived school for Native American girls. Lacking pupils, the institutions did not flourish until, under Bishop Rosati, the Religious of the Sacred Heart moved to St. Louis where they attracted daughters of the most prominent pioneer families. In 1821 they established academies at Grand Coteau and in 1825 at St. Michael's, Louisiana.

Mother Duchesne spent over thirty years in the Sacred Heart schools in the St. Louis area. She insisted on high standards of education but also on rigid adherence to French custom and discipline. Coupled with her inability to speak English, this occasioned much criticism. Her ardent nature, however, endeared her to intimates. At seventy-two, she fulfilled her lifelong desire of working among the Native Americans. In 1841 at Sugar Creek, Kansas, she accompanied others of her order as they joined a Jesuit* mission to the Potawatomi. Among the Catholic Potawatomi she was known as "the Woman-Who-Prays-Always." She died at St. Charles at eighty-three. Although Philippine Duchesne considered her own work a failure, in 1918 the Historical Society of Missouri named her the greatest benefactor among the state's pioneer women, and in 1940 she was beatified* by Pius XII.*

BIBLIOGRAPHY. L. Callan, *Philippine Duchesne, Pioneer Missionary of the Sacred Heart, 1769-1852* (1957); L. Callan; *DAB* III; *DARB;* M. Erskine, *Mother Philippine Duchesne* (1926); *NAW* 1.

P. Byrne

Duffy, Francis Patrick (1871-1932). Catholic* military chaplain.* Born in Cobourg, Ontario, and educated at St. Michael's College in Toronto, Duffy entered St. Joseph's Seminary in Troy, New York, in 1894, and was ordained* a priest* in Cobourg in 1896. He taught philosophy at the seminary in Dunwoodie, New York, until 1912. Editor of the *New York Review* between 1905 and 1908, he also wrote for several major Catholic journals. In 1914 he became chaplain of the 69th regiment of the New York National Guard and was stationed at the Mexican border until being shipped to France in 1917. Duffy became the best-known American chaplain in World War 1,* participating in all major battles in which his unit was engaged. For his

bravery he was decorated with the French *croix de guerre* and the U.S. Distinguished Service Cross, and was made an officer of the French Legion of Honor. His experiences in France are told in his book, *Father Duffy's Story* (1919). In the presidential campaign of 1928, he helped prepare Governor Alfred E. Smith's* reply to charges that American Catholics were not loyal citizens.

BIBLIOGRAPHY. *DAB* 1; F. D. Cohalan, "Duffy, Francis Patrick," *NCE* 4.

C. E. Ronan

Dukhobors. *See* DOUKHOBORS.

Dulles, John Foster (1888-1959). U.S. secretary of state and Presbyterian* layman. Born in Washington, D.C., John Foster Dulles grew up in a Presbyterian manse in Watertown, New York, where he early learned to appreciate the importance of religious convictions. His father, Allen Macy Dulles, a respected liberal* Presbyterian minister, practiced a home devotional* life emphasizing for his children the importance of a pious and educated commitment to the principles of Scripture.*

Named valedictorian at his graduation from Princeton University* (1908), Dulles also earned the highest honors in the philosophy department, including a scholarship to the Sorbonne where he studied briefly with philosopher Henri Bergson. Upon his return from France, he studied law at George Washington University Law School and took the New York State bar exam in 1911. He accepted a job as a law clerk with the Wall Street law firm of Sullivan and Cromwell, and by the time he was thirty-nine he had become head of the firm. In 1917 he accepted an assignment by President Woodrow Wilson to Central America, the beginning of a career in public service that climaxed in his role as secretary of state (1952-1959) under the Eisenhower* administration.

Throughout these years, Dulles remained active in the life of the church. Not only did he serve as an elder* in his local congregation in 1924, representing the New York Presbytery, he argued Harry Emerson Fosdick's* case before the Presbyterian General Assembly.* This brought him into direct confrontation with William Jennings Bryan.*

Dulles worked in ecumenical* church circles as well. Beginning in 1921, he became closely associated with the Federal Council of Churches of Christ in America* (the predecessor to the National Council of the Churches of Christ*). His most significant contribution to ecumenical Protestantism* resulted from his leadership as chair of the Commission on a Just and Durable Peace. Formed by the Federal Council of Churches in 1941, during World War 2,* the Commission was to mobilize Christian support for a peace consonant with Christian principles. Among its members were notable church leaders such as John R. Mott,* Reinhold Niebuhr,* Charles Clayton Morrison* and Harry Emerson Fosdick. Dulles served as chair for the full five years of the commission's work. The commission's influential support for the development of a United Nations organization marks an important point in American Protestantism.

BIBLIOGRAPHY. *DAB* 6; J. M. Mulder, "The Moral World of John Foster Dulles," *JPH* 49 (Summer 1971):157-182; R. W. Pruessen, *John Foster Dulles: The Road to Power* (1982); M. G. Toulouse, *The Transformation of John Foster Dulles: From Prophet of Realism to Priest of Nationalism* (1985).

M. G. Toulouse

Duncan, William (1832-1918). Anglican* lay* missionary* in British Columbia and Alaska. A Yorkshire schoolteacher, William Duncan was sent by the Church Missionary Society* (CMS) in 1856 to evangelize* and teach the Tsimshean Indians at Fort Simpson, British Columbia. Horrified by pagan rituals and cannibalism in their villages and their degradation in white townships, Duncan embarked on a plan to create a self-supporting Christian community for the Tsimshean. In May of 1862, Duncan and fifty followers settled at Metlakatla and built a model Victorian town and light industry that became the showpiece of all CMS missions.

For the first fifteen years, Metlakatla received the full support of church and government. However, Duncan's autocratic leadership, based on his conviction that the Tsimshean were unable to function as responsible Christian adults, eventually led to hostile clashes with Bishops Ridley and Hills and the CMS, from which Duncan resigned in 1881. With presidential agreement, in 1887 Duncan and 800 Tsimshean Indians settled at New Metlakatla on Annette Island (near Ketchikan, Alaska). Duncan died there in 1918, but the fish cannery and community still exist.

BIBLIOGRAPHY. J. Usher, *William Duncan of Metlakatla: A Victorian Missionary in British Columbia* (1974).

R. H. Chilton

Dunkers. *See* EPHRATA SOCIETY.

Dunster, Henry (1609-1659). First president of Harvard College.* Born in Bury, England, Dunster graduating from Magdalene College, Cambridge University (B.A., 1630; M.A., 1634), and returned to Bury as schoolmaster and curate (1634-1640). Dunster immigrated to Boston in 1640, where New England magistrates and ministers* immediately elected him president of Harvard College, which had languished since opening its doors in Cambridge in 1638.

Dunster established the academic curriculum (modeled on Cambridge, Oxford and Edinburgh), completed buildings, raised funds, secured the college charter (1650), attracted students and taught full-time (his specialty was oriental languages; instruction was in Latin). The primary purpose of the college was to educate future clergy,* but magistrates and other civic leaders were trained as well. Dunster oversaw New England's publishing enterprise, as Anglo-America's first printing press operated in his own home. Dunster married twice, first in 1641 to widow Elizabeth Glover, from whose husband the college inherited the press, and afterwards, in 1644, to another Elizabeth.

Heretofore an orthodox* Puritan* Congregationalist,* Dunster came to the opinion through study that infant baptism* was without scriptural warrant. Refusal to bring his son, born in 1653, to the Cambridge church for baptism caused a controversy which drove him from office. College and civil officials, esteeming him highly and striving to persuade him to abandon or at least keep to himself his Baptist* views, treated him honorably during an amazingly gradual dismissal period. Although he suffered a formal "public admonition" for the disturbance, neither side harbored animosity. Dunster lived out his years as minister* in relatively liberal Scituate, Plymouth Colony.

BIBLIOGRAPHY. *AAP* 1; J. Chaplin, *The Life of Henry Dunster* (1872); *DAB* III; *DARB;* S. Dunster, *Henry Dunster and His Descendants* (1876); *NCAB* 6.

C. E. Hambrick-Stowe

Du Plessis, David (1905-1987). Leader of charismatic movement.* For his contributions as the premier spokesman of the charismatic movement, David du Plessis is known as "Mr. Pentecost." A South African native, he served as a pastor and the general secretary of the Apostolic Faith Mission Church in South Africa. In 1947, du Plessis was the organizing secretary of the World Pentecostal Fellowship (now the World Pentecostal Conference*). After coming to the U. S. in 1949, he affiliated with the Assemblies of God.*

Unique among Pentecostals,* du Plessis was a zealous ecumenist.* In 1936 Smith Wigglesworth, a revered British healing* evangelist, prophesied that du Plessis would take the Pentecostal message to all denominations.* He attended each assembly of the World Council of Churches* from its second meeting in 1954 until his death, and he was the only Pentecostal invited to attend the third session of Vatican II* in 1964. Du Plessis served as the co-chair of the International Roman Catholic/Pentecostal Dialog from 1977 to 1982, and in 1987 he helped sponsor the first formal meeting of Pentecostals and the Faith and Order Commission of the National Council of Churches.* Called a "WCC gadfly" by *Christianity Today*,* du Plessis' fellow Pentecostals criticized him for compromising with modernism* and ecumenical apostasy.* The Assemblies of God revoked his ministerial credentials in 1962 but restored them in 1980.

Throughout the 1960s and 1970s, "Mr. Pentecost" served as a catalyst for the spread of the charismatic movement, speaking at hundreds of gatherings. In 1974 a poll by seven church magazines called him one of the eleven most influential Christians in the world. For his work with Catholics, in 1983 Pope John Paul II* gave du Plessis the "Good Merit" medal for excellent "service to all Christianity." Du Plessis was the first non-Catholic to ever receive the honor. Du Plessis spent his later years at Fuller Theological Seminary* and founded its David du Plessis Center for Christian Spirituality (1985).

BIBLIOGRAPHY. D. J. du Plessis, *Simple and Profound* (1986); D. J. du Plessis, *The Spirit Bade Me Go* (1970); *DPCM*; B. Slosser, *A Man Called Mr. Pentecost* (1977).   C. D. Weaver

Durham, William (1873-1912). Pentecostal* leader. A native of Kentucky, Durham's earliest religious associations were among Baptists,* with whom he associated from 1891. While in Minnesota in 1898, he embraced Holiness* teaching. Shortly thereafter he entered the ministry,* eventually serving as pastor of a small mission in Chicago known as the North Avenue Mission. Attracted to Los Angeles by reports of Pentecostal revival,* he attended services at the Azusa Street Mission,* a widely heralded, rundown building sometimes called the "cradle of American Pentecostalism." There on March 2, 1907, he experienced Spirit baptism.* On returning to Chicago, he made his mission an important local Pentecostal center and issued a monthly magazine *The Pentecostal Testimony*. Criticizing Holiness teaching on instantaneous sanctification* and promulgating a baptistic view of progressive sanctification, which he called "the finished work of grace," Durham was largely responsible for forging a non-Wesleyan view of sanctification as an option for Pentecostals. Today

his views on the subject are best represented by the Assemblies of God.* The target of much criticism, Durham moved much of his work to Los Angeles after 1910. He died of pneumonia in Los Angeles on July 7, 1912.

BIBLIOGRAPHY. *The Pentecostal Testimony* (July 1912).   E. L. Blumhofer

Dutch Reformed. *See* REFORMED CHURCH IN AMERICA.

Dutton, Anne (1692-1765). English evangelical* author. From youth Dutton was nurtured in evangelical Christianity by her parents and a series of ministers.* After her first husband died, she married Benjamin Dutton, a clothier and Baptist* preacher* in Gransden, Huntingdonshire. Dutton's first publication in 1734 was a poetic description of God's complete plan of salvation* for humanity. By 1747, when Benjamin Dutton was drowned, she had published over a dozen pieces of devotional* literature, many of them written anonymously. She also edited *The Spiritual Magazine* and carried on an extensive correspondence with revivalist* George Whitefield,* who encouraged her writing and admired her devotion to the evangelical cause. During the Great Awakening,* she wrote pastoral letters to a widening circle of American converts, including a group of slaves in South Carolina.

BIBLIOGRAPHY. J. C. Whitebrook, *Anne Dutton: A Life and Bibliography* (1921); S. Stein, "A Note on Anne Dutton, Eighteenth-Century Evangelical," *CH* 44 (1975):485-491.   B. J. MacHaffie

Dwight, Louis (1793-1854). Prison reformer.* Born in Stockbridge, Massachusetts, Dwight graduated from Yale* (1813) and from Andover Seminary* (1819). Though ordained,* his preaching was limited, due to weak lungs. As an agent for the American Bible Society,* he visited many prisons in the U.S. and was appalled at the abuses and inhumane conditions that existed. He became the secretary and manager of the Boston Prison Discipline Society and was instrumental in having the Auburn System of cell blocks and group labor replace the Pennsylvania System of solitary confinement and solitary labor. This reform made U.S. prisons a model for the rest of the world. Dwight published nearly thirty annual reports for the Discipline Society, which are valuable primary sources on prison reform.

BIBLIOGRAPHY. H. E. Barnes, *The Evolution of Penology in Pennsylvania* (1927).

D. B. Chesebrough

Dwight, Timothy (1752-1817). Congregational* clergyman,* theologian,* poet and educator. Born in Northampton, Massachusetts, and grandson of Jonathan Edwards,* Dwight was educated at Yale College.* At commencement in 1771, Dwight delivered his first public address: *A Dissertation on the History, Eloquence and Poetry of the Bible.* The Yale Corporation elected him tutor, and Dwight began experiments in Yale's curriculum, stressing classics and poetry. With fellow tutors and several students, Dwight founded the "Connecticut Wits," the first American school of literary criticism. Dwight joined the military chaplaincy* in 1777, and during the American Revolution* he produced some of his best poetic work, including his massive poem, *Conquest of Canaan* (1785).

After the Revolution,* Dwight obtained additional theological training from his uncle, New Divinity* pastor Jonathan Edwards, Jr.* In 1783, Dwight became pastor of the Congregational Church at Greenfield, Connecticut. During this period he began several of his important works: a series of doctrinal sermons entitled *Theology, Explained and Defended* (1818-1819), the poems "Greenfield Hill" (1788) and "The Triumph of Infidelity" (1788), and his four-volume travelog, *Travels in New England and New York* (1821-1822). In 1795 Dwight accepted an invitation to become the president of Yale College, a post he held until his death in 1817.

Soon after he became president, Yale College experienced a series of small revivals.* In his *Autobiography* (1865), Lyman Beecher,* one of Dwight's most promising proteges, argued that these revivals stemmed from Dwight's aggressive preaching against French Enlightenment infidelity that was popular among Yale students. Until recently, many historians have taken Beecher's partisan account at face value and have credited Dwight with the first revival of the Second Great Awakening.* However, more recent studies of these revivals at Yale, and of New England as a whole, suggest that the Yale awakenings were a product and not the cause of the larger religious movement known as the Second Great Awakening.

Timothy Dwight has very often been described as a member of the New Divinity* movement headed by Samuel Hopkins* and Joseph Bellamy.* Indeed, some elements of Dwight's theology—especially his teaching on original sin,* disinterested benevolence and the Half-Way Covenant*—closely resemble New Divinity ideas. A close examination of Dwight's theology, however, reveals the he was suspicious of both the method and the conclusions of these "consistent Calvinists."* Whereas the New Divinity theologians stressed the role of logic, Dwight erected his theology on the conviction that unbounded reason inevitably produced theological distortions. In the face of the New Divinity's stress on divine omnipotence in evangelism,* Dwight elevated the utility of human activity in the conversion* process.

A traditionalist in theology and politics, Dwight supported Federalist attempts to protect the Connecticut Congregationalist churches from disestablishment* at the hands of Jeffersonian Baptists.* His interest in this political issue earned him the mock title, the "Pope of Federalism." Little evidence survives to suggest that Dwight wielded great political power. His Federalist views found their greatest expression in his literary works, which look backward to the Puritan* images of the city on a hill and the errand into the wilderness, and forward to a vision of American harmony, in which a moderate Calvinist ethos would prevail.

BIBLIOGRAPHY. *AAP* 2; S. E. Berk, *Calvinism Versus Democracy: Timothy Dwight and the Origins of Evangelical Orthodoxy* (1974); J. A. Conforti, *Samuel Hopkins and the New Divinity Movement: Calvinism, the Congregational Ministry, and Reform in New England Between the Awakenings* (1981); C. C. Cunningham, *Timothy Dwight, 1752-1817, A Biography* (1942); *DAB* III; R. D. Shiels, "The Second Great Awakening in Connecticut: A Critique of the Traditional Interpretation," *CH* 49 (1980):401-415.   J. R. Fitzmier

Dyer, Mary (c.1605-1660). Quaker* martyr in Boston. Mary Dyer probably came from the Barret family in Essex, England, was raised in London, served at Court and married William Dyer of Somerset. About 1835 he settled as a milliner in Boston, Massachusetts, and she became a friend of Anne Hutchinson.* The Dyer's stillborn deformed baby, regarded by some as a "monster," was blamed by John Winthrop* on Anne Hutchinson's teaching on free grace. In 1638, when Hutchinson was excommunicated from the Boston church and joined Roger Williams* in Rhode Island, Mary Dyer remained a sympathetic friend. Shortly thereafter the Dyers were themselves excommunicated, and they moved to Rhode Island. In 1651 they sailed to England to help in a dispute between Roger Williams and William Coddington.

William returned to America in 1653, while Mary remained in England, where she became a Quaker. Convinced that she must testify to her new faith, in 1656 she returned to the New World with a group of ten Quakers who sailed to New York and traveled overland to carry God's warning to intolerant Massachusetts. Mary was imprisoned in Boston, released through the efforts of her husband, expelled from New Haven in 1658 and expelled from Boston again in the summer of 1659. In September 1659, Mary returned to Boston with Quakers William Robinson and Marmaduke Stephenson of Yorkshire. While Robinson and Stephenson were executed, Mary Dyer was reprieved on the gallows. She returned the next year and died June 1, 1660, on Boston Common, where "she did hang as a flag," near where her statue now stands. When the news reached England, King Charles II banned further executions of Quakers in Massachusetts.

BIBLIOGRAPHY. E. Burrough, *A Declaration of the Sad & Great Persecution* (1660-1661); E. Bishop, *New England Judged* (1661); H. Barbour and A. O. Roberts, eds., *Early Quaker Writings, 1658-1700* (1973); *DAB* III; *DARB; NAW* 1; *NCAB* 11.   H. S. Barbour

E

Easter. An annual celebration of the resurrection of Jesus Christ. The precise origin and development of the celebration of Easter remain obscure, though it is likely that the early church annually celebrated the event of Christ's resurrection as a parallel to the Jewish Passover celebration. The gospels relate that it was during the Passover season that Christ died and rose from the dead. This connection with Passover is the origin of another ancient name for Easter, *Pascha*, derived from the Greek equivalent of the Hebrew name for the festival. The Council of Nicea in 325 decreed that Easter should be celebrated on the first Sunday after the vernal equinox, but the dating of Easter continued to be a matter of controversy within the church.

The celebration of Easter developed as part of a liturgical* complex including the events of Holy Week* and the preparatory period of Lent.* Churches with a strong liturgical tradition reflect in their worship the drama of Christ's movement toward the cross and the climax in the victory of the resurrection. From as early as the third century, new adult converts kept expectant vigil throughout Saturday night, were baptized early on Easter morning and then received their first Communion. The celebration of Easter has included the use of light—traditionally candles—to symbolize theophany and the triumph of Christ over darkness.

The practice of the vigil continues in liturgical church traditions, with the so-called Paschal Vigil capping the Easter *triduum* or three days of services. The service consists of Old Testament lessons mixed with psalms and prayers.* More recently, the baptismal* liturgy has been replaced by a renewal of baptismal vows. Easter Communion, or Eucharist* is an important occasion in most church traditions, and for those who only rarely take Communion it is frequently viewed as obligatory.

In the Greek Orthodox* Church, individuals greet one another on Easter with the words "Christ is risen," to which they receive the response "he is risen indeed." The Orthodox celebrate Saturday evening with a candlelight procession outside the church. On entering the church the pealing of bells marks the beginning of the Easter Morning Prayer, which is followed by the Eucharist.

In America, evangelical* and other Protestant* churches frequently hold Easter sunrise services in addition to their regular worship. These early-morning gatherings are usually held outdoors in a park setting. Larger ecumenical gatherings may be hosted by a local ministerial association and are held in open stadiums or other large outdoor gathering places. These services include the joyous singing of hymns celebrating the resurrection, the reading of the resurrection account from one of the gospels, prayers and preaching.*

Easter is also an occasion for wearing new clothes and a traditional time for the extended family to gather and share a meal, typically including ham. The celebration of Easter, at least for Anglo-Saxons, originally seems to have supplanted a pagan celebration of Spring. With the growth of religious pluralism* and secularism* in American culture, vestiges of the original pagan celebration—such as the fertility symbols of eggs and rabbits—have provided a popular alternative theme of celebration. Inevitably, this has eroded the formerly dominant Christian interpretation of the day.

BIBLIOGRAPHY. F. X. Weiser, *The Easter Book* (1954); F. X. Weiser, *Handbook of Christian Feasts and Customs* (1958).   The Editors

Eastern-Rite Catholics. Churches from the Eastern Orthodox* tradition that have returned to the Catholic Church,* yet retain their own liturgies,* canon law* and customs.

Attempts at the reunion of the Christian churches of the East and of the West usually ended in failure, especially in the centuries immediately after the mutual excommunications of 1054. Later, political necessity forced Emperor Michael VIII Palaeologus to seek the help of the Western powers for the support of Byzantium at the Council of Lyons (1274). Subsequently this agreement was revoked by the new pope in Rome, Martin V (1281-

[373]

1285); in the East its acceptance was forced, and it was soon repudiated by Michael's son, Andronicus II. The Council of Florence, after long negotiations, issued a bull of reunion, *Laetentur Coeli,* on July 6, 1439, but the Greek signatories began to deny the reunion as soon as they arrived in their home environment. Yet all these attempts at union were not futile because they kept the idea of union alive in Christian consciousness.

Sometimes referred to with the more pejorative term *Uniates,* historical developments have led several of these Eastern-rite bodies to seek communion with the Roman Catholic Church. The Second Vatican Council's "Decree on the Catholic Eastern Churches" (*Orientalium Ecclesiarum,* November 21, 1964) significantly affirmed the place of these Eastern churches with their distinctive rites and practices within the Roman Catholic Church. Within the Roman curia they organized under the Congregation for the Eastern Catholic Churches. In the U.S. there are Armenians, Chaldeans, Italo-Greeks, Maronites,* Melkites, Romanians, Syrians, Russian and Ruthenian or Ukrainian Catholics.* All but the Maronites have counterparts in Eastern Orthodoxy.

BIBLIOGRAPHY. D. Attwater, *The Catholic Eastern Churches* (1935); R. G. Roberson, *The Eastern Christian Churches: A Brief Survey* (1986).

T. F. Sable

Easton, Burton Scott (1877-1950). Episcopal* priest* and New Testament scholar. After studying at the University of Göttingen (1894), Easton earned a Ph.D. in mathematics at the University of Pennsylvania (1901), where he taught until 1905. While teaching, he earned his bachelor of divinity at the Philadelphia Divinity School (1906) and was ordained* a priest in the Episcopal Church (1905). Easton's background in mathematics brought clarity and method to his biblical scholarship. He taught New Testament at Nashotah House, Wisconsin (1905-1911), and Western Theological Seminary, Chicago (later known as Seabury-Western), until 1919, after which he moved to the General Theological Seminary as professor of the literature and interpretation of the New Testament until his retirement in 1948.

In addition to serving as president of the Society of Biblical Literature* (1931), Easton helped found the *Anglican Theological Review* (1918) and remained one of its editors until his death. However, he is primarily remembered for his work on Jesus and the Gospels, seen in his magnum opus, *The Gospel According to St. Luke* (1926). In *The Gospel before the Gospels* (1927), he provided the first full-length critical appraisal in English of New Testament form criticism, a movement which began to affect American theology in the 1920s.

BIBLIOGRAPHY. F. C. Grant, "The Life and Work of Burton Scott Easton," *ATR* 35 (1953):147-161.

S. Meier

Eaton, Nathaniel (c.1609-1674). First master of Harvard College.* Born in Coventry, England, the son of the Reverend Richard Eaton, Nathaniel attended Trinity College, Cambridge, and also spent some time studying in the Netherlands under William Ames,* the outstanding Puritan theologian* of his day. In 1637 he immigrated to Massachusetts Bay, where in 1638 he was named the first master of the infant Harvard College. But as Cotton Mather* observed, he "marvelously deceived the expectations of good men concerning himself, for he was fitter to be master of a Bridewell than a College." He not only was guilty of beating a student with a heavy club but of allowing his wife to serve the students moldy bread and mackerel "with their guts in." Worse, she deprived them of their beer for up to ten days at a time. Eaton was removed from his position, fined and excommunicated by the church. He fled to Virginia and eventually returned to England where he became vicar* of Bishop's Castle, Shropshire, in 1661, and rector* of Bideford, Devonshire, in 1668. He died in 1674, a prisoner for debt in King's Bench Prison, Southwark.

BIBLIOGRAPHY. *DAB* III.

R. L. Troutman

Eaton, (T)homas (T)readwell (1845-1907). Southern Baptist* pastor* and editor. Born in Murfreesboro, Tennessee, Eaton taught for five years at Union University, a local Baptist college where his father served as president. In 1881, after pastoring churches in Tennessee and Virginia, he became pastor of Walnut Street Baptist Church in Louisville, Kentucky. In 1887 he took on the additional responsibility of editing the Kentucky Baptist newspaper, *The Western Recorder.* Eaton served in both of these capacities until death. As editor of *The Western Recorder,* Eaton increasingly gained a reputation as the successor to J. R. Graves* in the Landmark Movement.* His powerful journalistic influence forced W. H. Whitsitt* to resign as president of Southern Baptist Seminary in Louisville. Whitsitt's assertion that Baptists began in seventeenth-century England undercut the Landmark notion of an unbroken succession of Baptists since the early church. The fall of Whitsitt demonstrated both the influence of Eaton and the strength of Landmarkism among Southern Baptists.

M. G. Bell

Ecumenical Movement. The name given in modern times to the concerted drive toward the attainment or restoration of unity among Christians and their communities throughout the world.

Americans on the World Scene. By way of persons and events America has made many contributions of varied importance to the global ecumenical movement. As early as 1747, Jonathan Edwards* struck the authentic missionary* and eschatological note of ecumenism* in his *Humble Attempt to Promote Explicit Agreement and Visible Union of God's People in Extraordinary Prayer for the Revival of Religion and the Advancement of Christ's Kingdom on Earth Pursuant to Scriptural Promises and Prophecies Concerning the Last Time.* In 1867 an American branch of the Evangelical Alliance* was formed, and the Alliance's annual Week of Prayer, together with the Octave of Prayer for Unity from the very different quarter of the Roman Catholic* Graymoor Community under Paul Wattson (1863-1940), has helped to establish the Week of Universal Prayer for Christian Unity now sponsored by both the World Council of Churches* (WCC) and the Roman Catholic Church.

The American Methodist* layman* and ecumenist John R. Mott* was chairman of the Student Volunteer Movement* (with its watchword "The evangelization of the world in this generation") and founder of the World's Student Christian Federation* (1895). He presided at the International Missionary Conference of Edinburgh (1910), from which the twentieth-century ecumenical movement is conventionally dated, and remained active until the foundation of the WCC in 1948.

The bishops* of the Protestant Episcopal Church,* in their Chicago Quadrilateral* of 1886 (turned by the bishops of the worldwide Anglican communion* into the Lambeth Quadrilateral of 1888), in effect set the agenda for much work in Faith and Order until today: (1) the sufficiency of Scripture*; (2) the ancient creeds* (Apostolic and Nicene); (3) the dominical sacraments* (baptism* and the Lord's Supper*); and (4) the historic episcopate.* Charles Henry Brent,* the Canadian-born bishop of western New York, figured prominently in the early history of the International Faith and Order Movement, a tributary of the WCC since 1948.

Moreover, North America has hosted two assemblies of the WCC: The Second Assembly of the WCC took place in Evanston,* Illinois, in 1954

("Jesus Christ the Hope of the World"), and the Sixth in Vancouver* in 1983 ("Jesus Christ the Life of the World"). Since so much of the dynamic of ecumenism consists in meeting, the location of encounters can be important.

American churches and theologians* also played an important part in the preparation of the WCC Faith and Order Lima document, *Baptism, Eucharist and Ministry* (1982). The Louisville consultation of 1979 was important for the progress there registered between adherents of infant and adult baptism. Evaluations of the WCC document have ranged from *Catholic Perspectives on BEM* (ed. M. A. Fahey, 1986) to *Baptism and Church: A Believers' Church Vision* (ed. M. D. Strege, 1986) and *Orthodox Perspectives on BEM* (ed. G. Limouris and N. M. Vapori, 1985). The pluralism of American church life is also making the U.S. a valuable testing-ground for the WCC project "Towards the Common Expression of the Apostolic Faith Today."

Catholic contributors to the ecumenical movement have included the noted American theologian John Courtney Murray,* who greatly influenced the Vatican II* *Declaration on Religious Liberty,* and Thomas F. Stransky and John Long, who were important in the early years of the Roman Secretariat for Promoting Christian Unity. The ecclesiological writings of the Jesuit* Avery Dulles are always ecumenically sensitive.

A contemporary Lutheran* theologian, Yale's George A. Lindbeck, has for ten years chaired the joint study commission of the Lutheran World Federation* and the Roman Catholic Church. The Lutheran-Catholic dialog* in the U.S. has produced some of the best doctrinal work of any bilateral dialog in the world: "The Status of the Nicene Creed as Dogma of the Church" (1965); "One Baptism for the Remission of Sins" (1966); "The Eucharist as Sacrifice" (1967); "Eucharist and Ministry" (1970); "Papal Primacy and the Universal Church" (1974); "Teaching Authority and Infallibility in the Church" (1980); and "Justification by Faith" (1983). Concomitant scholarly studies have been *Peter in the Church* (1973) and *Mary in the Church* (1978).

The American Scene Then and Now. In 1838 the Lutheran Samuel Simon Schmucker* issued a *Fraternal Appeal to the American Churches with a Plan for Catholic Union on Apostolic Principles.* His proposed confederated American Protestant Church would have been based on twelve articles common to the main Reformation confessions. In his *America* (1855), the Swiss Reformed* historian and theologian Philip Schaff* commented that the

U.S. offered "a motley sampler of all church history, and the results it has thus far attained." He envisaged America as a "Phoenix grave not only of all European nationalities, but also of all European churches and sects, of Protestantism and Romanism. . . . Out of the mutual conflict of all something wholly new will gradually arise." In the 1930s Dietrich Bonhoeffer* could still observe wryly that "it has been given to the Americans less than any other nation of the earth to realize on earth the visible unity of the Church of God" (*No Rusty Swords,* 1965). In his later years Schaff clearly favored a federal view of Christian unity (e.g., *The Theology for our Age and Country,* 1872; *The Reunion of Christendom,* 1893).

In 1908 the Federal Council of the Churches of Christ in America* was founded. Its constitution spoke of "united service for Christ and the world," "devotional fellowship and mutual counsel," and "a larger combined influence for the Churches of Christ in all matters affecting the moral and social condition of the people." The theme of cooperative agency for the sake of a Social Gospel* has remained predominant in the successor organization, the National Council of Churches* (1950), in which the original Protestants of the Federal Council were joined by the Orthodox.* Today, participation in local councils of churches sometimes extends to Roman Catholics.

In the historically less complicated Canadian situation, Methodists, Congregationalists* and the majority of Presbyterians* entered the United Church of Canada* (1925), although union with the Anglicans* still tarries. The nearest thing to a cross-confessional union in the U.S. has been the joining of the Congregationalists with the Evangelical and Reformed in the United Church of Christ* (1957). Even within confessional families, unions have been complicated or prevented by racial and ethnic factors. The reunion of Methodism from the North and South was attained in 1939 and enlarged by the Evangelical United Brethren to form the United Methodist Church* (1968); but the three black Methodist denominations (African Methodist Episcopal*; African Methodist Episcopal, Zion*; Christian Methodist Episcopal*) continue. The Presbyterians from the North and South were reunited in the Presbyterian Church U.S.A.* (1987), but the Reformed churches of Dutch origin continue as separate denominations. The Evangelical Lutheran Church of America* gathered most Lutherans together in 1988, but the Missouri* and Wisconsin* Synods maintain a separate identity on account of their more conservative interpretation of Lutheranism.*

Since 1962 the most comprehensive project has been the Consultation on Church Union.* Methodist, Presbyterian, Episcopalian and UCC theologians have largely agreed on an "emerging theological consensus" (1976, revised 1980), but the original "plan of union" (1970) has now been transmuted into a proposal for "covenanting toward unity" (1984), which would allow for local symbiosis within a national framework of mutual denominational recognition. A definitive plan, "Churches in Covenant Communion: The Church of Christ Uniting" (1989), now stands before the churches. Meanwhile, the Episcopal Church and the Evangelical Lutherans have enjoyed since 1987 a limited inter-communion between themselves. Other bilateral relations remain at an early stage of tentative dialog, such as the Southern Baptists* with Roman Catholics and Greek Orthodox.

E Pluribus Unum? While competition has tended to recede in favor of cooperation, the generally increasing friendliness of the larger U.S. churches toward one another has still not produced Schaff's "phoenix." Several impeding factors exist.

First, the varied ethnic and confessional origins of the citizenry have favored denominationalism* as a characteristically American phenomenon. A tolerant pluralism* has seemed the condition of religious liberty* and civil harmony. But the continuing divisions at the level of doctrine* and church government* leave the separate denominations short of the unity in belief and life which belongs to a classical Christian understanding of the church.

Second, even if remaining matters of faith and order could be settled, there are understandable doubts about the wisdom of a super church conceived on the lines of a big-business merger and administered by a national bureaucracy. Many might prefer the more decentralized vision of Richard Norris—a network of dioceses, each embracing a variety of geographical, cultural and confessionally reconciled parishes.

Third, many denominations know internal tensions over the degree and manner in which the gospel is to be adapted to contemporary cultural circumstances. Conservatives note that liberals have tended to win out in previous mergers (e.g., the Trinitarian name is now officially under threat in both the United Church of Canada and the UCC). Serious ecumenism has always entailed a struggle for unity in the truth of the gospel.

Fourth, most profound are the differences in ecclesiological vision as to what really constitutes, or would constitute, the unity of Christians and of the church. Further theological work would need to develop acceptable models of unity.

BIBLIOGRAPHY. *Confessing One Faith: A Guide for Ecumenical Study* (1988); A. Dulles, *Models of the Church* (1974); A. Dulles, *A Church to Believe In* (1982); A. Dulles, *The Catholicity of the Church* (1985); J. W. Grant, *The Canadian Experience of Church Union* (1967); T. D. Horgan, ed., *Apostolic Faith in America* (1988); C. H. Hopkins, *John R. Mott, 1865-1955: A Biography* (1979); "Issues in Southern Baptist-Roman Catholic Dialogue," *RE* (Spring 1982); *Journal of Ecumenical Studies* (1964-); *Midstream* (1961-); R. A. Norris, "What is 'Church Unity'?" in *One in Christ* 18 (1982):117-130; R. E. Richey, ed., *Denominationalism* (1977); R. Rouse et al., ed., *A History of the Ecumenical Movement*, 2 vols. (1967, 1970); G. Wainwright, *The Ecumenical Moment* (1983).

G. Wainwright

Ecumenism. Derived from the Greek *oikoumene,* meaning the inhabited earth, ecumenism refers to the efforts of Christians and their communities to live in such unity that they may with one heart and one voice glorify the God and Father of our Lord Jesus Christ (Rom 15:5-6), and by their witness bring the world to believe in the divine mission of the Son (Jn 17:21).

In recent American usage, *ecumenical* is sometimes opposed to *evangelical.** But the falsity of this opposition is revealed when it is noted that (1) the modern ecumenical movement was evangelistic* and missionary* in its very origins; (2) *evangelical* is properly no more a party word than *catholic* or *orthodox;* (3) modern ecumenism is no liberal* Protestant* preserve but has from the start engaged the classical churches of the Reformation, then the Orthodox* and finally the Roman Catholic Church.*

The ambiguities in ecumenism derive fundamentally from different conceptions of Christian unity. Adapting a typology proposed by Avery Dulles, we may distinguish five ecumenical visions:

(1) Substantialist. Certain indispensable elements of faith and life abide in the church, more or less closely identified with one's own community. By a principle of "economy," the Orthodox Church* may sometimes recognize others as Christians outside its own fullness. In communities beyond its own boundaries the Roman Catholic Church recognizes the presence of the Scriptures,* baptism* and the faith it signifies, and (in some cases) episcopal succession* and the Lord's Supper*; but, says Vatican II,* these belong by right to the one true Church of Jesus Christ which "subsists in" the Roman Catholic Church. Strictly understood, this still implies an "ecumenism of return."

(2) Invisibilist. Some claim that all true Christians are spiritually united in Christ, whatever their denominational* allegiance. This is inadequate insofar as it minimizes the scandal of visible disunity.

(3) Episodic. Church "occurs" whenever the pure Word is preached* and the sacraments* rightly administered. This minimizes the institutional continuity of the church, and particularly the need for a teaching office to safeguard doctrine.*

(4) Eschatological. True church unity will not be achieved until the eschaton. Too strong an emphasis on future unity may provide an alibi for failures to recognize or achieve what is given, possible or required in the present.

(5) Pragmatist. Here the desire is for cooperation in witness and social action. This, however, carries in fact certain doctrinal and institutional presuppositions and implications. A rounded ecumenical vision and praxis will need to incorporate the positive points of all these partial descriptions of the conditions for the unity of Christians and the church.

BIBLIOGRAPHY. A. Dulles, "The Church, the Churches, and the Catholic Church," *TS* 33 (1972):199-234; S. C. Neill, *The Church and Christian Union* (1968); W. A. Visser't Hooft, "The Word 'Ecumenical'—Its History and Use," in *A History of the Ecumenical Movement,* vol. 1 (1517-1948), ed. R. Rouse and S. C. Neill (2nd edn. 1967).

G. Wainwright

Eddy, (G)eorge Sherwood (1871-1963). YMCA* secretary for Asia. Born into a Congregational* family in Leavenworth, Kansas, Eddy attended the Student Volunteer Movement* summer meeting before his last year at Yale* and was inspired by the teaching of Dwight L. Moody.* After attending Union (New York)* and Princeton* seminaries,* Eddy took a one-year assignment with the YMCA in New York City. In 1896, under the persuasion of John R. Mott,* Eddy sailed to India to be the national secretary for the YMCA. This began Eddy's long career, both with the YMCA and in close association with Mott. In 1911 Eddy became the secretary for Asia, working without salary and relying on the family fortune.

Eddy described his life as moving from personal to shared to social religion. In his early years he was primarily, with Mott and Robert E. Speer,* an evangelist* to students in Asia. Eddy led evangelistic campaigns in Japan, China, India, Russia, Turkey and Egypt between 1907 and 1948. His perspective on the Christian faith was greatly* altered by two world wars. During World War 1 both the British and American Armies hired Eddy to speak to troops on topics of religion and morality. Eddy's commitment to social religion increased through the writings of Walter Rauschenbusch* and Reinhold Niebuhr.* Ecumenical in spirit, through his writings (over thirty books) and speaking, Eddy was a self-appointed ambassador for both personal and social salvation.

BIBLIOGRAPHY. G. S. Eddy, *Eighty Adventurous Years: An Autobiography* (1955); G. S. Eddy, *A Pilgrimage of Ideas* (1934). S. Sunquist

Eddy, Mary Baker (Glover, Patterson) (1821-1910). Founder of Christian Science.* Born in Bow, New Hampshire, Mary Morse Baker studied at Sanbornton Academy, New Hampshire (1842), and with the healer Phineas P. Quimby* in 1862 and 1864. Eddy's sudden recovery in 1866 from severe neck and back pain followed her discovery of the key to Jesus' healing miracles and signaled to her a divine calling. She embarked on a career of healing and teaching that culminated in the establishment of the Christian Science movement.

In 1875 Eddy published the first edition of the Christian Science textbook *Science and Health,* which went through numerous editions in her lifetime and bears the strong imprint of her experiences with homeopathy, mesmerism, Quimbyism and Victorian Christianity. Eddy founded the Massachusetts Metaphysical College in 1881 to educate students in the theory and practice of Christian Science healing and encouraged graduates to spread her teachings and establish professions as religious healers. She focused her own efforts on teaching, writing and organizing her followers.

Eddy taught a radical idealism. Only God, his manifestations and synonyms that express the completeness of his nature exist; all else, especially body, matter, death, error and evil are merely illusions. Healing is the experience of physical and spiritual wholeness that follows from a recognition of these truths.

Much of Eddy's life was fraught with controversy as she struggled to ensure the future of Christian Science while defending herself against charges of plagiarism and immorality. The 1870s and 1880s proved especially difficult, leading her in 1889 to retreat from public life for nearly three years. On her return she managed the complete reorganization of her movement and charted its future

course. Her final years saw her parrying public attacks from Mark Twain and the press and struggling with the pains and maladies of old age while still shepherding her adoring flock.

BIBLIOGRAPHY. *DAB* III; *DARB*; D. Meyer, *The Positive Thinkers: A Study of the American Quest for Health, Wealth and Personal Power from Mary Baker Eddy to Norman Vincent Peale and Ronald Reagan* (1988); *NAW* 1; *NCAB* 3; R. Peel, *Mary Baker Eddy*, 3 vols. (1966); J. Silberger, Jr., *Mary Baker Eddy: An Interpretive Biography of the Founder of Christian Science* (1980).

R. B. Schoepflin

Edman, Victor Raymond (1900-1967). Missionary,* college professor and president. Born in Chicago Heights, Illinois, Edman served in the U.S. Army Medical Corp in France and Germany during World War 1* (1918-1919). Educated at the University of Illinois (1919-1921), Nyack ·Missionary Training Institute (1921-1922) and Boston University (A.B., 1922-1923), he served as a missionary in Ecuador to Quechua Indians from 1923 to 1928. When tropical disease forced him to return home in 1928, he became pastor of the Christian and Missionary Alliance* Tabernacle in Worcester, Massachusetts (1929-1935). Earning a Ph.D. in Latin American history at Clark University in 1933, he taught history and missions at Nyack Missionary Institute (1935-1936).

In 1936 he moved to Wheaton College* to become professor of political science (1936-1940) and then president (1940-1965) and chancellor (1965-1967) of the college. Under his leadership the college gained North Central Association accreditation and undertook a building program. Edman was a member of the Billy Graham* Evangelistic Association* board of directors and a global traveller. He wrote over twenty books, mostly devotional, including *Disciplines of Life* (1948), *Delights of Life* (1954), *Finney Lives On* (1950), *They Found the Secret* (1960), and his more scholarly *Light in the Dark Age* (1949). He was editor of the *Alliance Witness* (1965-1967) and for many years wrote a personal-advice column in *Christian Life* (1951-1966).

BIBLIOGRAPHY. E. E. Cairns, *In the Presence of the King* (1972); V. R. Edman, *Out of My Life* (1961). E. E. Cairns

Education, Protestant Theological. American graduate theological education, in its modern form, emerged in the early nineteenth century. Before then ministerial trainees who acquired a formal education usually studied in one of the

Eastern undergraduate colleges or with a practicing minister in one of the Western theological academies or "log colleges."* The nearest colonial equivalent to the modern contemporary seminary program was the arrangement whereby some college graduates, especially at Harvard* and Yale,* remained for a period of months or years to "study divinity*" independently with the president or theology* professor while perhaps serving as a college tutor or schoolteacher.

Andover (Massachusetts) opened in 1808 as the first major theological seminary. It came into existence as an expression of protest by the evangelicals* of New England against the growing influence of Unitarianism,* especially at Harvard where within a two-year period Unitarian Henry Ware* became professor of theology and Samuel Webber, a virtual Unitarian, gained appointment as president. Other seminaries appeared soon thereafter, including Princeton* (Presbyterian,* 1812), Bangor (Congregational,* 1814), Auburn (Presbyterian, 1818), Harvard (Congregational/Unitarian, 1819), Yale (Congregational, 1822), Protestant Episcopal (1823), Union of Virginia (Presbyterian, 1824), Lancaster (German Reformed,* 1825), Lutheran (1826) and Newton (Baptist,* 1825). By 1860 there were a total of sixty seminaries This rapid increase occurred because of a growing sense of the inadequacy of the informal apprentice system, the desire for regionally trained clergymen* in the expanding frontier* and the fact that the Second Great Awakening* (1800-1835) had greatly stimulated both the supply of and demand for ministerial candidates.

During the four decades before the Civil War,* seminary enrollment grew twice as fast as did the general population, reaching a figure of 2,000 by 1860. Only three schools (Andover, Princeton and Union of New York,* the institution founded cooperatively in 1836 by Congregationalists and Presbyterians as a part of their Plan of Union*) attracted enrollments as high as 100. Most of the seminaries were affiliated with the Congregational, Presbyterian, Reformed, Episcopal,* Lutheran and Baptist denominations.*

Pioneering seminaries Andover and Princeton introduced a curricular structure which provided the model for later nineteenth-century schools and, to a large extent, for present-day curriculum. The three-year course of study included major work in biblical literature, including the Hebrew and Greek texts; Christian theology, including natural theology; practical theology, or the study of the practice of ministry, including sermon preparation, delivery and church history. Subsequent curricular reforms of the basic pre-ministerial program have been only modifications or enlargements of this basic pattern. No other professional curriculum has remained so completely intact for so long.

The seminary record has changed in other ways, however. The major innovation between 1860 and 1890 was the addition of over twenty-five new seminaries founded by denominations associated with the new immigrant* groups, mostly German and Scandinavian, and located mostly in the Midwest. In these schools only gradually did the language of instruction move from the native languages to English.

The most significant period of change in seminary history occurred during the generation following 1890. The faculty became increasingly professional, the curriculum adapted somewhat in reflection of the desire of the church to minister to a broader range of human needs: the new liberal* theology affected the approach to biblical and theological instruction and the belief system underlying it. Gradually the faculty, especially in the older schools, became less dominated by the older veteran ministers and became increasingly comprised of younger, well-trained scholars fresh from graduate programs and with specialized training and research interests.

The increasing abilities of the faculty, combined with the growing ability and size of the student enrollees (average school enrollment which had been twenty-five in 1860, grew to fifty in 1900 and seventy-five in 1920), the increasing popularity of an elective curriculum, as well as the increased interest of the church in the Social Gospel,* Christian education,* and foreign missions,* encouraged the seminaries to develop larger faculties (the average faculty grew from three in 1860 to seven in 1910, with a high of twenty-one in the latter year) and teach a broader curriculum. Therefore new courses, although still within the traditional fourfold curricular division, began to appear in such areas as Christian sociology, ethics,* religious education, missions, oriental languages and comparative religion.

Most significant of all, the seminaries, influenced by the German universities where many of the influential faculty had studied, began to cast doubt on the supernatural elements of the Christian faith. Such liberal thought was especially prominent at Harvard, Yale, Union (New York) and Chicago,* but its influence did not become widespread until the middle generation of the twentieth century, when the Great Depression* and the advent of the nuclear age led to more somber theological systems, such as neo-orthodoxy* and existentialism.*

The period since 1960 has witnessed sharp shifts in enrollment patterns. The overall enrollment has nearly doubled, primarily because of large growth in the conservative seminaries. Today a clear majority of the largest seminaries are evangelical or orthodox* in nature. Older or second-career students and women are enrolling in unprecedented numbers, with women now comprising over one-fourth of the enrollees in accredited schools. Another major change is the increase in the number of curricular options. Between 1969 and 1980 the percentage of students enrolling in the traditional pre-ministerial program declined from eighty per cent to fifty-four per cent; the rest concentrated their studies in areas such as Christian education, social ethics, psychology,* urban* ministries and theology, and earned academic degrees rather than a professional degree. Even the recent change in name for the traditional ministerial degree from the Bachelor of Divinity (B.D.) to the Master of Divinity (M.Div.) is indicative of the effort of the seminaries to become increasingly like the graduate schools.

Since at least 1918 there has been an organized form of inter-institutional cooperation among seminaries. In that year President A. Lawrence Lowell of Harvard called a conference of the North American theological schools, which organized and met regularly until 1936 when it became an accrediting association, the American Association of Theological Schools. ATS, as it is now known, presently includes about 200 U.S. and Canadian institutions as members with about one-fourth of these being non-Protestant. After the Second Vatican Council* of the 1960s, membership was opened to Roman Catholic,* Eastern Orthodox* and Jewish institutions.

The Canadian experience in theological education, while in many ways parallel to that of its southern neighbor, differs markedly from the U. S. in its relationship to the general pattern of graduate education. Whereas in the U. S. some seminaries have developed as schools within a university—usually a private university complex (e.g., Chicago, Duke, Harvard, Southern Methodist, Vanderbilt, Yale)—and others have established affiliate relationships (e.g., cross- registration, cooperative use of libraries) with universities, nevertheless the typical seminary has been a self-standing institution.

The Canadian record has been different, partly because its smaller population base made it less possible to consider establishing many autono-

mous units and partly because of the influence of the English university model. Therefore most Canadian theological colleges and seminaries have been federally related or affiliated with a university and more completely supported by public funds than has been the case in the U. S.

See also BIBLE INSTITUTES AND SCHOOLS; HIGHER EDUCATION, CATHOLIC; HIGHER EDUCATION, PROTESTANT; SEMINARIES, CATHOLIC DIOCESAN.

BIBLIOGRAPHY. H. F. Day, *Protestant Theological Education in America: A Bibliography* (1985); R. T. Handy, "Trends in Canadian and American Theological Education, 1880-1980: Some Comparisons," *TheolEd* 18 (1982):175-218; R. W. Lynn, "Notes Toward a History: Theological Encyclopedia and the Evolution of Protestant Seminary Curriculm, 1808-1868," *TheolEd* 17 (1981):113-144; N. A. Naylor, "The Theological Seminary in the Configuration of American Higher Education: The Ante-Bellum Years," *History of Education Quarterly* 17 (1977):17-30; G. G. Winkelman, "Polemics, Prayers, and Professionalism: The American Protestant Theological Seminaries from 1784 to 1920," (unpublished Ph.D. dissertation, State University of New York at Buffalo, 1975).

W. C. Ringenberg

Edwards, Jonathan (1703-1758). Colonial Congregational* preacher* and theologian.* Born in East Windsor, Connecticut, and educated at Yale College* (B.A., 1720; M.A., 1722), Edwards apprenticed for two years under his grandfather, Solomon Stoddard,* who had a powerful ministry, and in 1729 became the sole preacher of the Congregational Church in Northampton, Massachusetts.

Edwards's reputation as an influential preacher was fixed in 1734-1735 when a sermon on justification* caused a widespread awakening among his congregation. Edwards published a description of the Northampton conversions in *A Faithful Narrative* in 1737, which turned out to be a pattern for revivals* that swept through the colonies in the next few years. His congregation encouraged him to publish some of the more effective sermons, and in 1738 the Five Discourses, headed by *Justification by Faith Alone,* were widely received in England and America.

The notoriety of Edwards's preaching* and writing on revivals placed him in the forefront of American Christianity just prior to the Great Awakening.* When George Whitefield* first visited America, he made the effort to visit with Edwards. While the two had vastly different preaching styles, their concern for the new birth* was similar, and Edwards acknowledged that he had not seen the

"Grand Itinerant's" equal among preachers. Edwards's preaching style was even-tempered and intellectually demanding, based more on the use of fully written sermon notes than the extemporaneous passion of Whitefield's open-air, itinerant style. For all their differences, both generated highly emotional responses.

Edwards continued to preach in Northampton and yet became active in publishing defenses of the religious revivals seen in the colonies. *The Distinguishing Marks* was distributed in 1741 after Edwards had delivered the controversial address at the Yale College graduation. The defense of the results of the revivalists' activities as a true work of the Spirit of God established Edwards as the leading spokesman against those established Old Light* clergy* who found the revivals disruptive and too emotional.

Edwards revised and refined his arguments for the Awakening in *Some Thoughts Concerning the Revival,* published in 1743. He was reacting to those who were overzealous in favor of the revival and those who opposed it outright. In that work Edwards masterfully intertwined the experiences of his wife, Sarah, as proof that the Awakening was not a result of superstition or antinomian tendencies in the church, but of the supernatural grace of God.

Edwards's preaching continued to be his vehicle of expression in the 1740s. In 1741 he delivered his most famous sermon, *Sinners in the Hands of an Angry God*—perhaps the most famous sermon in American religious history. Throughout his career Edwards penned over 1,200 sermons, of which only a small percentage were published. Still, the sermons lived on through the theological treatises which grew out of his preaching and were widely disseminated to churchmen and scholars alike. The *Treatise on Religious Affections* was published in 1746 and served as further evidence of Edwards's intellectually demanding style and resolute determination to defend the centrality of the "affections" in religious experience.

By 1748 Edwards found himself in conflict with his congregation because he wished to exclude from Communion* those who had not experienced conversion. This controversy dated back to the Half-Way Covenant* of 1662 and the open Communion of Solomon Stoddard when tests for Communion were eliminated. Left without a pulpit by 1750, Edwards accepted a call to a Native American mission in Stockbridge, Massachusetts, where he spent more time writing than preaching. His two major treatises, *Freedom of the Will* (1754) and *Original Sin* (1758), were written while in Stockbridge. The College of New Jersey* (later Princeton College) called Edwards as its president in 1758, but he died of a smallpox inoculation several weeks after moving to his new appointment. Edwards's contribution placed him in the ranks of the greatest American theologians. Through them he became a renowned American colonial figure with Cotton Mather* and Benjamin Franklin.

See also AWAKENING, THE GREAT; NEW ENGLAND THEOLOGY.

BIBLIOGRAPHY. *AAP* 1; A. V. G. Allen, *Jonathan Edwards* (1889); C. C. Cherry, *The Theology of Jonathan Edwards* (1966); *DAB* III; *DARB*; P. Miller, *Jonathan Edwards* (1949); *NCAB* 5; O. E. Winslow, *Jonathan Edwards* (1940).

J. H. Edwards

Edwards, Jonathan, Jr. (1745-1801). Congregational* theologian* and president of Union College. The ninth child and namesake of colonial New England's most brilliant theologian, Jonathan Edwards, Jr. was born in Northampton, Massachusetts, in 1745. He graduated from the College of New Jersey (Princeton*) in 1765 and spent the next year studying theology* with his father's closest disciples in New England. Licensed* to preach* in 1766, Edwards returned to Princeton to serve as a tutor for a year. He then accepted a call from the White Haven Church in New Haven, Connecticut, and was ordained* in 1769.

Edwards' clerical career followed the model that his father and his father's New Divinity* ministers provided for him. He published theological treatises and essays dealing with the doctrinal and ecclesiastical problems that preoccupied the Congregational* ministers of his day. Actively engaged in reform efforts, he published an important antislavery* tract, *The Impolicy of the Slave Trade and Slavery* (1791). In addition, he was committed to missionary* work, and he was the individual chiefly responsible for the famous Plan of Union* (1801)—a cooperative missionary endeavor between New England Congregationalists and Mid-Atlantic Presbyterians* that was designed to bring Christianity to the rapidly developing Western frontier.*

Edwards remained in New Haven until 1795, when a series of disputes over theological and ecclesiastical issues led to his dismissal from the White Haven Church. Within several months he was installed in a new pastorate in Colebrook, Connecticut. From this small western Connecticut town he was summoned to the presidency of Union College in Schenectady, New York, in 1799.

He died two years later.

BIBLIOGRAPHY. *AAP* 1; *DAB* III; *DARB*; T. Edwards, "Memoir of His Life and Character" in *The Works of Jonathan Edwards . . . Late President of Union College*, ed. T. Edwards, 2 vols. (1842); R. L. Ferm, *Jonathan Edwards the Younger, 1745-1801* (1976); *NCAB* 7.   J. A. Conforti

Edwards, Morgan (1722-1795). Baptist* preacher,* evangelist,* historian and educator. Born in Trevethin, Wales, of Anglican* parents, Edwards was educated at Bristol Baptist College (1742-1744). After becoming a Baptist at age sixteen, he began ministering in Lincolnshire (1744-1751); Cork, Ireland (1751-1760); and Sussex (1760-1761), although he was not ordained until 1757. Edwards subscribed to the Particular Baptist* London Confession of 1689.

On the recommendation of John Gill, he served for ten years as pastor of the Philadelphia church, beginning in 1761. Immediately assuming an active role in the Philadelphia Baptist Association,* Edwards served as clerk, moderator, evangelist and historian. During the Revolutionary War* he came under sharp criticism and travel restrictions for his Tory views, being perhaps the only Baptist leader holding such views at the time. Edwards left the Philadelphia church in 1781, in part for "using intemperately an antidote" and in part for his friendship with the universalist* Elhanan Winchester,* whose views Edwards did not share.

Edwards's travels for the Philadelphia Association provided the opportunity to collect the historical information later published in his valuable *Materials Towards a History of the Baptists* (2 vols., 1770-1792), used since his time by historians of the era. His concern for an educated American Baptist clergy were fulfilled, with the aid of James Manning* and Hezekiah Smith,* in the founding of Rhode Island College (Brown University*). Edwards traveled through the North and in England, preaching and soliciting funds and books for the college. He also petitioned the Massachusetts delegates to the Continental Congress in support of the separation of church and state.*

BIBLIOGRAPHY. *AAP* 6; D. H. Ashton, "Morgan Edwards, First Historian of American Baptists," *Chronicle* 14 (April 1951):70-79; *DAB* III; T. B. McKibbens and K. L. Smith, *The Life and Works of Morgan Edwards* (1980).   L. W. Hähnlen

Edwards, Sarah Pierpont (1710-1758). Puritan* minister's wife,* early worker in women's ministries. Born in New Haven, Connecticut, Sarah Pierpont came from an aristocratic Puritan lineage.

Her father, the Reverend James Pierpont, was pastor* of First Church, in New Haven, and was a founder of Yale College.* Her mother was Mary Hooker, daughter of the Reverend Samuel Hooker of Farmington, Connecticut. Raised in a cultured and pious* household, Sarah had a deep—almost mystical—spiritual experience as a youth that well prepared her for her future ministry.

On July 20, 1726, at the age of seventeen, Sarah married Jonathan Edwards* and was immediately thrust into pastoral ministry when her husband became the assistant to his grandfather, Solomon Stoddard,* who had served in the Congregational church in Northampton for more than a half century.

Like many wives of Puritan divines, she viewed her marriage and ministry as a true partnership. A picture of Puritan piety,* Sarah was known for her beauty, wit and hospitality. Her religious enthusiasm and flair for fashion were criticized, as was the fact that six of her eleven children were born on the Sabbath (assumed by many to be the same day of the week on which they were conceived), but she was secure in her calling and worked tirelessly in church ministry. With her husband's blessing, she was active in women's ministries at a time when it was considered improper.

Her husband's forced removal from the Northampton church was a demoralizing blow to her, but far more devastating was his subsequent death, as well as the death of her daughter, Esther Burr (mother of the famous Aaron Burr), both from smallpox inoculations. Sarah died of dysentery six months later in Philadelphia.

See also EDWARDS, JONATHAN; EDWARDS, JONATHAN, JR.; MINISTER'S WIFE.

BIBLIOGRAPHY. E. D. Dodds, *Marriage to a Difficult Man: The "Uncommon Union" of Jonathan and Sarah Edwards* (1971); J. Edwards, *The Works of President Edwards,* ed. S. E. Dwight (1830); *NAW* 1; O. E. Winslow, *Jonathan Edwards, 1703-1758* (1940).   R. A. Tucker

Edwardseanism. *See* NEW ENGLAND THEOLOGY.

Eells, Cushing (1810-1893). Congregational* missionary* to the Oregon Territory. Born in Blandford, Massachusetts, Eells attended Williams College and East Windsor Theological Seminary (Hartford Seminary). In 1838, he and his new wife, Myra Fairbank Eells, were assigned by the American Board of Commissioners for Foreign Missions* to the new mission to the Native Americans of the Oregon Territory. At Tshimakain, northwest of Spokane, Eells and Elkaniah Walker established a mission among the Spokane Indians. They endured hard winters and experienced little success. After the 1847 massacre of missionary Marcus Whitman* and his family at Waiilatpu, Eells and his family fled to the Willamette Valley of Oregon. There he pursued educational endeavors, directing the Oregon Institute of Salem (Willamette University). After Washington was reopened to settlement in 1859, Eells established a school at Waiilatpu as a memorial to Whitman. Whitman Academy (Whitman College) opened in 1866, with Eells serving as principal from 1867 to 1869. Between 1869 and his death in Tacoma in 1893, Eells continued his tireless itinerant missionary work throughout the state, establishing churches and promoting educational activities.

BIBLIOGRAPHY. C. M. Drury, *Marcus and Narcissa Whitman and the Opening of Old Oregon*, 2 vols. (1973); M. Eells, *Father Eells or The Results of Fifty-five Years of Missionary Labors* (1894).

L. F. Maffly-Kipp

Eisenhower, Dwight David (1890-1969).

Soldier, statesman, thirty-fourth U.S. president and inspirational leader of American civil religion.* The third of seven sons, Eisenhower was born in Denison, Texas, during a two-year interlude there (1889-1891) after the Eisenhowers had moved from Pennsylvania to Kansas in 1878. He was named by his mother, Ida Stover Eisenhower, after the greatest evangelist* of the day (Dwight L. Moody*) and his father (David).

Back in Kansas, young Dwight (or "Ike," as he became known locally) grew to manhood in Abilene in an intensely devout, but somewhat erratic, religious home. His grandfather Jacob Eisenhower and his uncle Abraham Lincoln Eisenhower had been preachers in the River Brethren denomination, a branch of Mennonites,* now known as the Brethren in Christ.* However, Ida Eisenhower turned increasingly to the Jehovah's Witnesses* after 1900, and her husband eventually followed, without enthusiasm. Nevertheless, the Eisenhower home all during Ike's youth emphasized traditional evangelical* Mennonite values: fear of God, reverence for the Bible,* respect of individual free choice in matters of faith, nonviolence and personal integrity. Life on the Kansas frontier also added habits of independence and self-reliance.

The family's modest circumstances and the parents' willingness to leave religious and vocational choices to their children led young Dwight to accept appointment to West Point in 1911. After his graduation from the military academy in 1915

and marriage to Mary (Mamie) Doud in 1916, Eisenhower embarked on a competent but routine military career which kept him in virtual obscurity until America's entry into World War 2* in 1941.

Ike's rise to fame in the war was meteoric. A lieutenant colonel in 1941, he was a five-star general in 1945. As supreme commander of the Allied Expeditionary Forces in Europe, he brilliantly led the most powerful military organization ever assembled. Following the war, Eisenhower served in succession as U.S. military Chief of Staff (1946-1949), president of Columbia University* (1949-1950) and supreme commander of NATO forces (1950-1952).

Recruited as the Republican candidate for president in 1952, the enormously popular war hero with the charismatic smile won a landslide victory in that year and again in 1956. As president (1953-1961), Eisenhower brought the Korean War (1950-1953) to a speedy conclusion, developed a doctrine of containment in dealing with world Communism, resisted and finally overcame McCarthyism, began the process of integration of the nation's public schools in response to the 1954 Supreme Court decision ordering desegregation, attempted to moderate the Cold War and, in his farewell address to the nation, issued a prophetic warning against the growing power of "the military-industrial complex" at home and abroad.

Eisenhower's religious pilgrimage was as striking as it was unusual. Raised in a devout home, he turned from his parents' nonviolent faith to a military career. Before World War 2 he was largely indifferent to religion and only occasionally attended nondenominational military chapel* services. However, the pressures and consequences of command in battle revived the dormant faith of childhood and brought an increasingly spiritual dimension to what had become an often-profane military experience.

As president, he took the unprecedented measure of personally composing a prayer* to read at his first inaugural address, and on February 1, 1953, the second Sunday after his inauguration, he made a public profession of faith and was baptized,* being received into membership at the National Presbyterian Church in Washington, D.C. Thus, he became only the second president in history to join a church while in office (Calvin Coolidge, who became a member of a Congregational* church, was the other.) As chief executive, Eisenhower frequently spoke about religious values, unsuccessfully attempted to make the annual National Day of Prayer a major ceremony, signed an act making "In God We Trust"* the national motto in

1956, established the practice of opening cabinet meetings with silent prayer, innovatively employed Congregationalist minister Frederick E. Fox as special presidential assistant for religious matters, joined the International Council for Christian Leadership in inaugurating on April 5, 1953, the Presidential Prayer Breakfast* (now the well-established National Prayer Breakfast) and in general promoted civil religion. Critics dubbed the Eisenhower years an unctuous period of "piety along the Potomac," while supporters, including many evangelicals and Catholics,* hailed his public advocacy of religion as the prescription to society's ills and a guarantee of democracy's* survival.

The Eisenhower presidency brought with it not only a rebirth of Eisenhower's personal faith but also a renewal of America's civil religion. Perhaps Ike's most enduring legacy was his rejuvenation of the nation's public faith, which has continued strongly into the last decade of the twentieth century. Today, the Eisenhower Chapel in Abilene, Kansas, stands as yet another enduring shrine of American civil religion.

BIBLIOGRAPHY. S. E. Ambrose, *Eisenhower,* 2 vols. (1983-1984); K. S. Davis, *Soldier of Democracy: A Biography of Dwight Eisenhower* (1945); M. D. Gustafson, "The Religion of a President," *CCen* 136 (April 30, 1969): 610-613; P. Hutchinson, "The President's Religious Faith," *CCen* 121 (March 24, 1954):362-369; J. C. Juhnke, " 'One Nation Under God': Religion and the American Dream," *Mennonite Life* 38 (December 1983):23-26; W. L. Miller, *Piety Along the Potomac* (1964); R. V. Pierard and R. D. Linder, *Civil Religion and the Presidency* (1988).   R. D. Linder

Elaw, Zilpha (c.1790-c.1850). Methodist* Episcopal exhorter and preacher.* Born in Pennsylvania to free and pious African-American parents, Zilpha was hired out to a Quaker* family at age twelve. She attended Methodist meetings in her late teens, and joined the church in 1808. In 1810 she married nonbelieving fuller Joseph Elaw and moved to New Jersey; there, to his dismay, she became active in the church and began attending camp meetings.* In 1817 Zilpha felt herself sanctified* and called to exhort from house to house. When her husband died in 1823, she worked to pay off debts and then felt called to an itinerating ministry. In 1828 she left her daughter behind and began a dangerous but very successful tour of the slave states, preaching without license* or official sanction, and without regard to race, class or denomination.* She toured the Northern states from 1830 to 1838 and returned to the South in 1839. In 1840 she sailed for England and preached there until 1846, when the record ends with her plans to return home.

BIBLIOGRAPHY. Z. Elaw, *Memoirs of the Life, Religious Experience, Ministerial Travels and Labours of Mrs. Zilpha Elaw . . .,* in *Sisters of the Spirit,* ed. W. L. Andrews (1986).

K. K. Kidd

Election. As a biblical term *election* refers to God's choosing a particular people to receive his salvation* from sin,* guilt and condemnation. Classic Pauline passages teaching this doctrine* are to be found in Ephesians 1 and Romans 9. The Westminster Confession of Faith* of 1647, which expressed this doctrine for American Presbyterians,* Congregationalists* and the large number of Baptists* who were represented by the Philadelphia Confession of 1707, declared in Chapter III, 5: "Those of mankind that are predestinated unto life, God, before the foundation of the world was laid, according to his eternal and immutable purpose, and the secret counsel and good pleasure of his will, hath chosen in Christ, unto everlasting glory, out of his mere free grace and love, without any foresight of faith or good works, or perseverance in either of them, or any other thing in the creature, as conditions, or causes moving him thereunto; and all to the praise of his glorious grace."

This was in accord with the Calvinistic* teaching of the sovereignty of God's grace in unconditional election as set forth by the Synod of Dort in 1619 in answer to the five articles of the Arminian* *Remonstrance* of 1610, which taught that God's election was conditional, based on foreseen faith and perseverance.

Puritanism* in both England and America wrestled with the question of how one can be assured of salvation since it is based alone on the grace of God in the Holy Spirit's work of regeneration,* producing faith and repentance. In New England the majority of Puritan leaders favored a scheme of steps of preparation for grace, whereby an individual might gain assurance of salvation.* "Preparationism," by focusing on the subjective experience of salvation, helped open the way for increasing Arminianism in the eighteenth century. Such leaders of the Great Awakening* as Jonathan Edwards* and George Whitefield,* however, were Calvinists who reasserted the traditional understanding of God's sovereignty in election.

In the nineteenth century the New School* theologians like Congregationalist* Nathaniel

Taylor* again accommodated orthodox* Calvinism to meet the needs of the revivals* of the Second Awakening.* Baptists* also were divided between Particular* (Calvinistic) and General* (Arminian) Baptists.

By the twentieth century, revivalism's emphasis on freedom of the will and the individual's role in making a decision for Christ had caused Arminianism to prevail in America over the Calvinistic understanding of unconditional election. The Pentecostal Movement,* for example, was resistant to the doctrine of predestination.*

BIBLIOGRAPHY. G. M. Marsden, *The Evangelical Mind and the New School Presbyterian Experience, A Case Study of Thought and Theology in Nineteenth-Century America* (1970); P. Schaff, *The Creeds of Christendom,* 3 vols. (1877).

W. S. Barker

Electronic Church. The *electronic church* is a term used loosely by the media and scholars to refer to a wide variety of religious broadcasting styles and organizations. Usually mainline* Protestant* and Roman Catholic* broadcasters are not included, even though they have sponsored well-known national programs. Since 1980 the term has referred increasingly to prominent television programs produced by independent Protestant evangelists* from Pentecostal,* charismatic,* fundamentalist* and evangelical* traditions.

Although the term is new, the motivations and attitudes animating the electronic church are rooted deep in the American cultural and religious experience. American Protestants have always shaped the gospel to the latest media, from the spoken proclamations of early American itinerant evangelists to the printed pronouncements of nineteenth-century religious periodicals. The electronic church is the most recent attempt by conservative Protestants in the U.S. to fashion the gospel for the latest media technologies—broadcasting, satellites and cable television.

Electronic evangelism began in the 1920s with the rapid development of radio broadcasting. Churches* and evangelical educational institutions were among the first radio station owners and operators. However, few religious stations survived the growing cost of broadcasting as well as federal regulatory policies which discriminated against the licensing of noncommercial stations. Evangelicals responded by purchasing time on commercial stations and paying the bills with contributions from listeners. Evangelicals learned early how to create interesting and entertaining programming to garner audiences and elicit listener contributions.

During the 1930s and 1940s, Charles E. Fuller* and Walter A. Maier* successfully built radio audiences in the millions, proving that it was possible to finance national paid broadcasts. Fuller's independent "Old-Fashioned Revival Hour" was a folksy combination of live music,* preaching* and listener letters. Maier's program resembled the more traditional preaching style of his supporting denomination, the Lutheran Church—Missouri Synod.* Both programs were evangelistic, and both stressed the fundamental truths of Scripture* in the face of an increasingly secular culture.

In the 1950s various evangelists began experimenting with paid television broadcasts. Tulsa evangelist Oral Roberts* even tried prime-time variety shows featuring his family and various entertainers. Roman Catholic Bishop* Fulton J. Sheen* probably had the largest audience of any regular religious program during the decade, but his success has been overshadowed in recent years by the prominence of evangelical television preachers.

As the costs of television time rose significantly during the 1960s, television evangelists looked for formats which would attract larger audiences. Some broadcasters continued airing worship* services and revival meetings. Among them was Billy Graham,* who never took on the staggering costs of a national, weekly television show. Others, such as Rex Humbard, imitated popular nonreligious broadcasts, especially musical and variety shows.

The electronic church emerged slowly in the 1970s and 1980s as a hodgepodge of different program styles and evangelistic strategies, from the old-style revivalism of Jimmy Swaggart* to the charismatic talk-show formats of the "700 Club" and the "PTL Club." It was characterized less by a type of program than by a faith in the power of mass communications technologies to Christianize the nation and even the world. Some television evangelists, including Jerry Falwell* and James Robison, addressed current political issues and established specific political agendas on their programs. During most of the 1980s Falwell led the Moral Majority,* a political organization espousing conservative causes. Pat Robertson* left the "700 Club" in 1987 to run for the Republican nomination for president of the U.S.

Most electronic preachers were more interested in spreading the gospel than wielding political power. But media evangelism generally reached Christian audiences rather than the unsaved. Surveys of new church members showed repeatedly that only a small percentage of converts were influenced directly by television evangelism. One-to-one friendship evangelism remained the most effective and efficient means of sharing the faith and building local congregations. Television was far more successful at "confirming" beliefs than "converting" them.

Nevertheless, some churches gained members from viewers who transferred from one congregation to another. Mainline Protestant congregations lost the most, while various charismatic churches were the major gainers. The Assemblies of God* grew partly because of the programming of Swaggart, Robertson and Jim Bakker,* as well as dozens of successful local programs. Television's visual appeal heightened the dramatic presentations of charismatic preachers, who took naturally to the new medium. Older Protestant traditions established in an age of print were weak competition for the experiential worship of Pentecostals and charismatics. As the 1980s drew to a close, the latter traditions dominated religious television. The largest daily audience ("700 Club") and weekly audience (Jimmy Swaggart) of religious programs were Pentecostal. Even in Canada the major religious satellite television program ("100 Huntley Street") was charismatic.

In 1987 religious broadcasting was shaken by the public revelation that Jim Bakker of the "PTL Club" had committed adultery and received an annual salary of over $1 million. Donations to nearly all of the major television ministries quickly declined, and many religious broadcasters called for higher standards of accountability among television preachers. The major trade association, National Religious Broadcasters* (NRB), adopted new ethical guidelines. Nevertheless, it was still clear that self-regulation of the electronic church was merely an ideal that could not be strictly enforced by either the government or the NRB.

The PTL scandal brought to public attention the fact that television ministries were multi-million-dollar organizations dependent on viewers for their livelihoods. Annual budgets of the largest ones exceeded $100 million, and weekly expenses topped $1 million. As the cost of television time escalated in the 1980s, often religious broadcasters became significant deficit spenders, regularly appealing to supporters for emergency funds to stay on the air. They also turned to various professional marketing firms to design effective direct-mail fund-raising appeals. Toll-free telephone lines and free gifts offered over the air enabled some televangelists to compile valuable viewer lists.

Meanwhile, the number of religious broadcast stations grew rapidly in the 1980s. Religious radio expanded at the rate of one new station every week, while television added a new station every month, over 200 nationally in 1987. Nearly all of the television stations were operated as nonprofit organizations selling time to national evangelists. Religious radio was more diverse, featuring everything from music to talk shows and daily Bible studies.* The potential audience for religious cable television also increased quickly as urban areas in the U.S. and Canada were wired. The Roman Catholics and the Southern Baptists* started their own satellite broadcasting systems, as did numerous independent evangelical organizations.

Although the electronic church became a familiar part of the Protestant landscape in North America, it continued to elicit criticism even from within evangelicalism. A major study of the impact of religious broadcasting found that it does not substitute for church attendance for most viewers and that program contributors also give to their local congregations. But the most delicate and significant question remained unanswered: Is the electronic church changing the character of American Christianity? The history of religious media would suggest a positive reply; the circuit rider, the revival campaign and the printed tract* influenced religious styles and sensibilities in their days. But the impact of electronic evangelism largely remains a mystery understood only through the anecdotal evidence of supporters and critics.

Clearly the electronic church is not merely an evangelical or even solely a religious phenomenon. It is an American phenomenon which combines marketing, mass communication, celebrity promotion and religious language and imagery. Where the Christian faith leaves off and American culture takes over is difficult to determine. In the end, however, there is little doubt that much of the criticism of the electronic church is also criticism of American popular culture in the late twentieth century.

BIBLIOGRAPHY. J. H. Ellens, *Models of Religious Broadcasting* (1974); R. Frankl, *Televangelism* (1987); G. Gerbner et. al., *Religion and Television* (1984); G. H. Hill and L. Davis, *Religious Broadcasting, 1920-1983: A Selectively Annotated Bibliography* (1984); P. G. Horsfield, *Religious Television* (1984); Q. J. Schultze, "The Mythos of the Electronic Church," *Critical Studies in Mass Communication* 4 (1987):245-261; Q. J. Schultze, "Evangelical Radio and the Rise of the Electronic Church, 1921-1948," *Journal of Broadcasting and the Electronic Media* 32 (1988):289-306.

Q. J. Schultze

Eliot, John (1604-1690). Puritan* minister,* missionary,* linguist and Bible* translator. Born in Widford, Hertfordshire, England, Eliot graduated from Jesus College, Cambridge, in 1622. Having come under the influence of Thomas Hooker* while teaching at Hooker's school in Little Baddow, Essex, Eliot embraced Puritan tenets and was forced to flee to Massachusetts in 1631. The next year Eliot was installed as teacher of the church in Roxbury, a position he held until his death. A gifted linguist, Eliot prepared an Algonkian catechism* (1654) and grammar (1666), as well as Algonkian translations of the Westminster* Larger Catechism (1669) and both Old (1663) and New (1661) Testaments, the latter two together constituting the first edition of the Bible printed in North America.

Eliot's pioneering evangelism* among Native Americans, for which he was hailed as "Apostle to the Indians," motivated the establishment in 1649 of the Society for the Propagation of the Gospel in New England* to supervise and finance his own and other such ministries. From small beginnings, by 1674 Eliot had gathered converts into fourteen self-governing communities of "praying Indians,"* with a total population of about 3,600. Although King Philip's War* (1675-1676) dealt a near-fatal blow to these villages, they maintained a tenuous hold on life through the early decades of the eighteenth century. Eliot's other published works include the *Bay Psalm Book* (1640), a metrical edition of the Psalter prepared in conjunction with Richard Mather* and Thomas Welde that was the first book printed in New England, *A Harmony of the Gospels* (1678), and *The Christian Commonwealth* (1659), a political treatise suppressed by the Commonwealth of Massachusetts for its republican sympathies.

BIBLIOGRAPHY. *AAP* 1; D. Chamberlain, *Eliot of Massachusetts* (1928); *DAB* III; *DARB*; *NCAB* 2; W. E. Thwing, *A History of the First Church in Roxbury, Massachusetts, 1630-1904* (1908); O. E. Winslow, *John Eliot: "Apostle to the Indians"* (1968). G. W. Harper

Elliott, Stephen, Jr. (1806-1866). Episcopal* bishop.* Born into an influential and scholarly South Carolina family, Elliott attended Harvard* for a year and graduated from South Carolina College in 1825. While practicing law, he underwent an evangelical* conversion* and was ordained* in 1835 into the Episcopal ministry.* He taught and served as chaplain* at South Carolina College until 1841, when he was elected and consecrated* the first Episcopal bishop of Georgia.

Elliott extended the size and influence of the Episcopal Church until it ranked as the fifth-largest denomination* in Georgia by the Civil War.* He was especially concerned with ministry to slaves.

A scholarly evangelical, eloquent speaker and amateur horticulturalist, Elliott succeeded Bishop William Meade* in 1862 as presiding bishop of the Protestant Episcopal Church in the Confederate States of America. A supporter of the Confederacy who became increasingly saddened by the war, he took a leading role in reuniting the separated Northern and Southern dioceses of the Episcopal Church after its conclusion. He died suddenly in Savannah in 1866.

BIBLIOGRAPHY. T. M. Hanckel, *Sermons by the Rt. Rev. Stephen Elliott with a Memoir* (1867); H. T. Malone, *The Episcopal Church in Georgia, 1733-1957* (1960). D. L. Holmes

Ellyson, Edger P. (1869-1954). Minister,* theologian* and a founder of the Church of the Nazarene.* A Quaker* minister and headmaster of the Friends' Bible School in Marshallstown, Iowa, in 1907 Ellyson accepted a call to succeed A. M. Hills* as president of Peniel College in Greenville, Texas. His long-standing sympathies with the Holiness Movement* and his work at the college led Ellyson to the historic conference at Pilot Point, Texas, where the Church of the Nazarene was born in 1908. He was elected a general superintendent of the Church and spent the next three years visiting, evangelizing* and organizing the far-flung congregations of the new Church, as well as filling the presidency of Peniel College. The next decades were full of service as Ellyson served presidencies at Pasadena College and Olivet Nazarene College. An influential leader in the Church of the Nazarene's educational endeavors, Ellyson laid out the plans for the Nazarene Board of Education, served as chief editor for the denomination's Sunday-school* publications (1923-) and chaired the committee that revised the Nazarene Manual of discipline* in 1924.

Ellyson's *Theological Compend* (1908) was the first systematic theology* produced by the American Holiness Movement. It emphasized the basic themes of Holiness theology and provided the foundation upon which later theologians like A. M. Hills and H. Orton Wiley* built.

BIBLIOGRAPHY. T. Langford, *Practical Divinity* (1962); T. Smith, *Called unto Holiness* (1962).

J. R. Tyson

Ely, Richard Theodore (1854-1943). Economist. Born in Ripley, New York, to a Presbyterian* family, Ely was educated at Dartmouth,* Columbia, Halle and Heidelberg (Ph.D in economics under Karl Knies). He was professor of political economy at Johns Hopkins (1881-1892) and then the University of Wisconsin. Ely introduced in America the German "historical" school of economics, emphasizing the social, cultural and political factors that shaped economic systems, rather than classical theories which stressed universal laws.

An Episcopal* layperson* and a central figure in the growth of the Social Gospel movement* during the 1880s, Ely was a popular speaker at Chautauqua* and other conferences and held leadership roles in many organizations, including the Christian Social Union, the American Institute of Christian Sociology and the American Economic Association, which he founded. His books on economics and Christianity were widely read, especially by ministers,* and included *Social Aspects of Christianity* (1889) and *Ground Under Our Feet* (1938).

He emphasized the ethical function of economics, and tried to use the discipline to improve society. An important theme in his writing was "social solidarity," which encouraged cooperation and self-sacrifice over competition and individualism.* He often said that the Christian life demanded love of God and neighbor (theology* dealt with the first and sociology with the second), and he believed that churches* and seminaries* should be equally concerned with both topics.

BIBLIOGRAPHY. *DAB* III.   L. M. Japinga

Emancipation Proclamation. On September 22, 1862, President Abraham Lincoln* proclaimed that on January 1, 1863, "all persons held as slaves within any state or designated part of a state, the people whereof shall then be in rebellion against the United States, shall be then, thenceforward, and forever free." Although the proclamation freed no slaves directly, since the states to which it applied were outside the federal government's control, its practical effect was to transform the Civil War* from a struggle to preserve the Union into a crusade for human freedom. As a wartime strategy, it deprived the South of much of its labor force and brought blacks to enlist in the Union armies; as a diplomatic move, it exposed the South as fighting to maintain an institution that the rest of Western civilization had renounced and discouraged European nations from recognizing the Confederacy; as a humanitarian gesture, it excited black hopes and encouraged antislavery* advocates. Frederick Douglass called it "the greatest event in our nation's history."

Northern church leaders had long been pleading for such a measure, and Lincoln had received many petitions from Quakers,* evangelicals,* Unitarian-Transcendentalists* and others, urging him to proclaim emancipation. On September 13, 1862, the president told a delegation of churchmen from Chicago: "It is my earnest desire to know the will of Providence in this matter. And if I can learn what it is I will do it!" Jubilant celebrations on New Year's Day 1863 testified to the faith of many that God's will indeed had been done. New School* Presbyterians* rejoiced in the "wonder-working providence of God, by which military necessities become the instruments of justice in breaking the yoke of oppression." The Reverend Jeremiah E. Rankin preached to the United Congregational churches in Lowell, Massachusetts, that God "made the proclamation of freedom to the oppressed a military, as it was in the nature of things, a moral necessity." Among the Northern denominations, only Episcopalians* and Roman Catholics* failed to issue a public endorsement of emancipation.

The Southern reaction was harshly negative. On September 27, 1862, Lt. Charles C. Jones, Jr., wrote to his father, Charles C. Jones, Sr.,* an influential Presbyterian minister, that he regarded Lincoln's proclamation as "a most infamous attempt to incite flight, murder, and rapine on the part of our slave population." The elder Jones agreed, as did all of his Southern coreligionists. In April 1863, ninety-six ministers from eleven denominations issued an "Address to Christians Throughout the World," declaring that abolitionism was "an interference with the plans of Divine Providence," predicting that Lincoln's proclamation would lead to "the slaughter of tens of thousands of poor deluded [black] insurrectionists," and condemning the measure as "repugnant to civilisation [sic] . . . and in no proper sense an act of mercy to the slave, but of malice toward the master."

The Emancipation Proclamation was given permanent force by the Thirteenth Amendment, ratified in December 1865: "Neither slavery nor involuntary servitude . . . shall exist within the United States, or any place subject to their jurisdiction." But neither document dislodged the racism embedded in American society, and chattel slavery was replaced by a rigid pattern of racial segregation North and South that would prove extremely difficult to overcome.

See also CIVIL WAR.

BIBLIOGRAPHY. J. H. Franklin, *The Emancipation Proclamation* (1963); J. H. Moorhead, *American Apocalypse: Yankee Protestants and the Civil War,*

1860-1869 (1978); R. E. Beringer et al., *Why the South Lost the Civil War* (1986).

C. C. Goen

Embury, Philip (1728-1773). Methodist* minister.* Born in Ballingrane, Ireland, Embury was baptized a Lutheran* but came under Methodist preaching* and on Christmas* 1752 he experienced conversion* and soon became a Methodist class leader and preached locally. By 1758 he was proposed as an itinerant* minister, though he evidently did not carry out any extensive ministry and continued his trade of carpentry. On November 17, 1758, he married Margaret Switzer and in June 1760 they immigrated to America, arriving in New York on August 11. There he continued his trade, taught school, joined the Lutheran Church* and was apparently passive with regard to his earlier Methodism.

In 1766, his cousin Barbara Heck, disturbed by the spiritual condition of her fellow immigrants, prevailed on Embury to preach lest "we shall all go to Hell, and God will require our blood at your hands." Embury's first sermon was to a group of five gathered in his own home, but the congregation grew to fill a rented room, then a sail-rigging loft and finally the Wesley Chapel erected on John Street and dedicated in October 1768. Released from his duties by Methodist missionaries, in 1770 he moved to what is now Washington County, New York, where he continued to work and preach, establishing the first Methodist society north of New York City at Ashgrove. Embury was the first Methodist preacher in North America, though he was not an official minister.

BIBLIOGRAPHY. *AAP* 7; *DAB* III; *DARB; NCAB* 3.

D. G. Reid

Emerson, Ralph Waldo (1803-1882). Transcendentalist* essayist and poet. Born in Boston, Emerson came from a family with a tradition of intellectual and moral leadership reaching back to the Puritan* origins of New England. Just as his father had rejected orthodox* Calvinism* in favor of the liberal Unitarian* ministry, young Waldo, after three years as a Unitarian* minister, rejected what he called the "corpse-cold" rationalism of Unitarianism in favor of that New England variation of European Romanticism* called Transcendentalism.*

Emerson rejected the specific miracles atributed to Christ, preferring the antinomian belief that all life is a miracle and that God dwells in all nature and in every human heart, where he can be reached through intuition. Unable to tolerate Calvinism's emphasis on original sin,* yet frustrated by Unitarianism's inability to embrace life with enthusiasm, Emerson found in romanticism a language with which to celebrate the Spirit without what he called the "Hebraic mythology" of Christianity. Beginning with *Nature* in 1836, he argued for the primacy of Spirit over the legal rigidity of the law. "The moral law," he wrote, "lies at the center of nature and radiates to the circumference." Thus, in his 1838 "Divinity School Address," he told the students of Harvard* to bypass the "myths" and "idioms" of Christianity, which "have usurped the place of his truth." Instead, he referred them to the "intuition of the moral sentiment" and called on them to "dare to love God without mediator or veil."

Although they angered many, Emerson's essays and lectures inspired generations of churched and unchurched Americans. "I was simmering, simmering, simmering," declared the poet Walt Whitman. "Emerson brought me to the boil." Henry Ward Beecher* adapted Emerson's idea to his own Congregational* theology* and preached* a romantic Christianity emphasizing the indwelling love of Christ that became a dominant strain in American religion. Even such businessmen as John D. Rockefeller were inspired by Emerson's call for "self-reliance." Emerson's seemingly spontaneous free-verse poetry has been called the fountain of much of American poetry, including that of today.

Although he left the church and Christian doctrine to do so, Emerson carried what he considered the essential message of Christianity to a broader audience with remarkable success. In the words of Octavius Frothingham,* Emerson "simply claimed for all men what Protestant Christianity claimed for its elect."

BIBLIOGRAPHY. G. W. Allen, *Waldo Emerson: A Biography* (1981); *DAB* III; *DARB;* R. W. Emerson, *The Collected Works of Ralph Waldo Emerson* (1971); *NCAB* 5; S. Whicher, *Selections from Ralph Waldo Emerson* (1957); J. Porte, *Representative Man* (1979).

D. R. Williams

Emerson, William (1769-1811). Unitarian* minister.* Born in Concord, Massachusetts, the son of the minister William Emerson and his wife, Phebe (Bliss), he graduated from Harvard* in 1789, taught school for two years, studied theology* for a few months at Cambridge and then, in 1792, was ordained* a minister of the Unitarian Church at Harvard. In 1799 he accepted a call to the First Church of Boston, a position he held until his death. Emerson was heavily involved in various civic and literary pursuits. He was chaplain* of the state senate, overseer of Harvard College, a member of the Massachusetts Historical Society, editor of the *Monthly Anthology* (precurser of *The North American Review*) and founder of the Anthology Club, from whose collection of books grew the Boston Athenaeum Library. He authored *An Historical Sketch of the First Church of Boston* (1812), edited a volume of psalms and hymns, and published several sermons and discourses. In 1796 he married Ruth Haskins. The Emersons had eight children—among them the noted essayist Ralph Waldo Emerson.*

BIBLIOGRAPHY. R. L. Rusk, *The Life of Ralph Waldo Emerson* (1949); J. McAlear, *Ralph Waldo Emerson: Days of Encounter* (1984).

D. B. Chesebrough

Emmons, Nathaniel (1745-1840). Congregationalist* minister* and theologian.* Born in East Haddam, Connecticut, Emmons graduated from Yale College* in 1767 and studied theology* under Nathan Strong* and John Smalley,* two of the ablest advocates of the New Divinity.* He was called to the Congregational Church of Franklin, Massachusetts, in 1773 and served there until ill health compelled his retirement in 1827.

Emmons quickly acquired a reputation for being the most radical of the New Divinity Men. In the interests of preaching consistent Calvinism,* he followed Joseph Bellamy* and Samuel Hopkins* in advocating a governmental theory of the atonement, and followed Jonathan Edwards* in teaching both the moral inability of sinners to repent and the natural blameworthiness of those who do not.

In a further reflection of Edwards, he also dismissed the need to speak of an underlying "nature" or "substance" and described human self-consciousness in phenomenological terms as a continuous creation of God. As such, he held that original sin lay not in a natural inheritance of Adam's nature or a federal imputation of Adam's sin, but solely in the conscious "exercises" of the sinner. He concluded from this that the proximate cause of sinning must be God, who "produces those moral exercises in their hearts, in which moral depravity properly and essentially consists." Nevertheless, God's causality of sin was not a physical compulsion on the sinner, and "the divine influence upon the heart, in producing volitions, does not imply compulsion on the part of God, nor destroy liberty on the part of man." This last conclusion distanced him from the mainstream of the New Divinity and made him notorious as the author of the "Exercise Scheme."

Emmons was also renowned for personally training eighty-seven students for the ministry during his fifty-five-year pastorate in Franklin, in which he also saw substantial revivals* of religion in 1784, 1794 and 1809. He was also one of the founders of the Massachusetts Missionary Society and its president for the first twelve years of its existence. For a time he edited the *Massachusetts Missionary Magazine* (which later became the *Missionary Herald*). Emmons was an ardent supporter of the American Revolution,* a pronounced anti-Masonist* and an early abolitionist.* He published numerous sermons, and between 1800 and 1826 his sermons appeared in two separate sets. From 1842 to 1845 Jacob Ide published Emmons' sermons, arranged as a systematic theology* in six volumes, with a seventh issued in 1850.

BIBLIOGRAPHY. *AAP* 1; *DAB* III; *DARB*; B. Kuklick, *Churchmen and Philosophers: From Jonathan Edwards to John Dewey* (1985); E. A. Park, *Memoir of Nathaniel Emmons* (1861); H. B. Smith, "The Theological System of Emmons," in *Faith and Philosophy,* ed. G. L. Prentiss (1877); *NCAB* 5.

A. C. Guelzo

Empirical Theology. Early twentieth-century theologians* who sought a new departure for theology consistent with modern methods of thinking, especially as found in the empirical sciences, were termed *empirical theologians.* Theology was the search for pragmatic religious truth that finds its validity in its practical workableness. These theologians appealed to common human experience and current scientific knowledge. Gerald Birney Smith* of the University of Chicago* wrote in 1916, "Modern religious thinking is learning to draw its inspiration from the world in which we live."

Empirical theology was a type of liberal* theology termed *modernistic liberalism.* Authority did not rest in the historic Christian tradition, but traditional Christian symbols were reinterpreted in ways intelligible and meaningful for the scientific industrial age. There were variations, but empirical theologians were heavily influenced by the pragmatism of John Dewey* (1859-1952) and the current emphases on empirical data for the study of history and sociology. Adherents believed that the Christian tradition must be recast if the Christian faith was to survive in the twentieth century against atheism and humanism.

The empirical theology movement developed strongly at the University of Chicago Divinity School under the influence of Shailer Mathews,* who emphasized a socio-historical approach to Christianity. Henry Nelson Wieman* combined a value-centered religion with an empirical method and a naturalistic world view. *Theology as an Empirical Science* (1919) by Douglas Clyde Macintosh* of Yale was the classic statement of the movement and stressed that God is known through the experience of the moral transformation of the self. The movement was later sharply attacked by Reinhold Niebuhr* and H. Richard Niebuhr.*

BIBLIOGRAPHY. K. Cauthen, *The Impact of American Religious Liberalism* (1962); D. G. Peerman and M. E. Marty, eds., *A Handbook of Christian Theologians* (1965); W. R. Hutchison, *The Modernist Impulse in American Protestantism* (1976).

D. K. McKim

Endecott, John (c.1589-1665). Political and military leader of Massachusetts Bay Colony. Endecott was appointed the first governor of Massachusetts Bay, serving from 1628 to 1630, when he was succeeded by John Winthrop.* Thereafter, he served as governor in 1644, 1649, 1651-1653 and 1655-1665; deputy governor from 1641 to 1642 and assistant from 1630 to 1639. He also commanded an expedition against the Pequot Indians in 1636.

Endecott's leadership was characterized by his rigid principles and discipline, as seen in his belief that women should wear veils. He led the force that cut down the Maypole and broke up Thomas Norton's settlement at Mt. Wollaston. The banishment of John and Samuel Browne for their allegiance to the Church of England* illustrated his intolerance of nonconformity to New England practices. His suspicion of symbols and ceremonies prompted him in 1631 to cut out the cross from the English ensign, but the court was lenient since it was judged that he performed the act out of "tenderness of conscience."

BIBLIOGRAPHY. *DAB* III; E. Morgan, *The Puritan Dilemma* (1958); J. Winthrop, *The History of New England from 1630-1649,* ed. J. Savage, 2 vols. (1825-1826); A. Young, *Chronicles of the First Planters of the Colony of Massachusetts Bay* (1846).

K. P. Minkema

Engel, Jacob (1753-1833). One of the founders of the Brethren in Christ Church.* The son of Uhlrich Engel, a Swiss Mennonite,* Jacob Engel immigrated* with his family to the U. S. in 1754. Jacob eventually obtained land along the Susquehanna River and settled near Marietta in Lancaster County.

Engel was strongly influenced by the pietistic* revival* movement, a contemporary feature of Lancaster County life, and it may have been in one of these meetings that he experienced a crisis conversion.* Clearly this new-found pietism made Engel and others of his group dissatisfied with their Mennonite background. On the other hand, the emphasis their Mennonite heritage placed on obedience and peace made it difficult for them to become part of pietistic groups, which seemed concerned with the conversion experience alone. The tension created by this situation led Engel and others with similar views to organize their own group, known first as River Brethren but legally, since the Civil War,* as Brethren in Christ.

Engel was the most prominent figure in this movement, and he continued his leadership until his death. Thus, when members of the group began moving to what is now the province of Ontario, Engel made at least one trip on horseback to organize them and to provide a continuing contact between the separated churches.

BIBLIOGRAPHY. C. O. Wittlinger, *Quest for Piety and Obedience: The Story of the Brethren in Christ* (1978).

E. M. Sider

England, John (1786-1842). Catholic* bishop* of Charleston. Born in Cork, Ireland, England received his early education in one of the Protestant* schools there. In 1802 he entered St. Patrick's College Seminary in Carlow to prepare for ordination* to the priesthood, which he received in 1808. After ordination* he began his ministry in Cork, where he worked to reform Catholic life by publishing texts on spiritual life and educational reform, establishing a society for the improvement of education, building a nondenominational school for the poor and working for prison reform.

England irritated many of the Cork gentry when he supported the Irish peasants against their landlords. During the peak of the veto controversy (1813-1816), he became proprietor and editor of the *Cork Mercantile Chronicle* and forcefully advanced the anti-veto cause by advocating religious and civil liberty, separation of church and state* and voluntaryism.* England's education and his Irish experiences made him sympathetic to the republican and Enlightenment* values of his day.

In 1820 Rome appointed England to be the first bishop of Charleston, South Carolina, because many in the newly created diocese had asked for an Irish bishop, and some had suggested England because of his sympathies with American ideals. England was consecrated bishop in 1820 and immediately went to his diocese, which included the states of Georgia, North Carolina and South Carolina.

From 1820 to 1842, England not only served the small Catholic community in his diocese* but also became the leading Catholic apologist in the U. S.. Through the episcopal* government of his diocese, public lectures throughout the nation and the press,* England tried to help Catholics identify themselves as Catholics and Americans. The central focus of his ministry was to establish not only the compatibility of, but also the similarity between, American republicanism and Catholicism.

England created a constitutional form of government for his diocese that was modeled upon the federal Constitution. The diocesan constitution stipulated that a convention of clergy* and elected lay* representatives meet annually to discuss the spiritual and material welfare of the diocese and to make laws that would govern the church's temporalities. He also established the first American Catholic newspaper, the *U.S. Catholic Miscellany,* to disseminate foreign and national news and to defend Catholicism and helped organize the conciliar* form of government at the national level.

England's accommodationist stance toward American culture helped him define Catholic identity within that culture, but it also made him an uncritical advocate of most American values and institutions. Although personally his views were antislavery,* he supported slavery until it could be removed by proper constitutional means.

BIBLIOGRAPHY. P. Carey, *An Immigrant Bishop: John England's Adaptation of Irish Catholicism to American Republicanism* (1982); *DAB* III; *DARB*; J. England, *The Works of the Right Reverend John England,* ed. I. A. Reynolds, 5 vols. (1849); P. Guilday, *The Life and Times of John England,* 2 vols. (1927); *NCAB* 5. P. W. Carey

Enlightenment Catholicism. Enlightenment Catholicism* refers to the Christian rationalism and republicanism that arose during early antebellum American Catholicism, between the publication of John Carroll's first apologetical tract and the death of John England.

American Catholic thought and ecclesiastical structures were in continuity with the Catholic tradition as defined by the Council of Trent (1542-1565),* but problems created by the Age of Reason and the American Revolution* encouraged some antebellum American Catholics to accommodate Catholicism to Enlightenment ideals. Such accommodation had both the benefit of communicating Catholic values in terms that were intelligible to the age and the danger of confusing Catholic values with those of the age.

In the realm of thought, the American Catholic Enlightenment emphasized harmony and order in the universe, the role and capacity of reason in understanding both the created and revealed orders and the rights of individual conscience in society and in Christianity. Enlightened Catholics also asserted that the American values of religious freedom,* separation of church and state,* voluntaryism* and republican political theory were historically and theoretically compatible with the Catholic tradition.

The primary issue in American Catholic thought, as is evident in apologetical literature, was not the question of establishing the grounds for the possibility or necessity of revelation and Christianity but of vindicating the reasonableness of Catholicism. Catholic apologists* (and their Protestant neighbors) accepted what they called the "fact of revelation" and therefore saw little need of demonstrating the grounds of revealed religion. Catholics were preoccupied, instead, with constructing responses to the nativist* and Protestant charge that Catholicism represented mental slavery. Catholic apologists insisted that within Catholic tradition the individual, created in the image of God, had the right and duty to exercise his reason to discover the truth. They maintained that reason was capable of uncovering the "fact" of supernatural revelation and of demonstrating, through historical investigation, the divine establishment and authority of the Catholic Church. Submission to authoritative Catholic teachings, therefore, was reasonable and free because it was based upon rational inquiry of evidence.

In the realm of polity, Enlightened Catholics adopted some elements of republican constitutionalism at the congregational, diocesan* and national levels. Congregational lay* trustees* advocated a constitutional separation of powers within parishes that acknowledged the laity's* control over temporal affairs and the clergy's* over spiritual. This division of powers provided the laity with significant involvement in congregational life, matching their participation in the American political process.

At the diocesan level, only two bishops* instituted forms of government that reflected the values of republican constitutionalism. Bishops John Carroll* of Baltimore and John England* of Charleston divided powers and allowed for a maximum amount of participation in the decision-making process of ecclesiastical government.

Episcopal* councils governed the church at the national level and even these ancient forms of government, American Catholic apologists argued, were constitutionally limited forms of authority. Although episcopal authority was constituted by divine, not human, election (and therefore it was not republican in origin), it was clearly defined and limited by revelation, tradition and canon law.* Bishops, moreover, ruled by written legislation, not by personal whim or arbitrary edict.

It is difficult to say how widespread the American Catholic Enlightenment was. The values of the Enlightenment certainly influenced the thought and writings of John and Charles Carroll,* John England and a number of clerical and lay trustees. Although the Catholic Enlightenment did not endure much beyond the early antebellum period, it did have some lasting effects upon American Catholicism. Throughout the nineteenth and well into the twentieth century, American Catholics continued to emphasize the compatibility of Catholicism and American republican values: the fascination with reason, emphasis upon freedom, values of constitutionalism, respect for religious pluralism and enthusiastic acceptance of American political arrangements. As an intellectual movement, however, the Catholic Enlightenment gradually came to an end in the 1840s when the Romantic* impulse replaced it as a mode of thought for explicating the Catholic tradition to the American people.

See also ENLIGHTENMENT, PROTESTANT.

BIBLIOGRAPHY. P. Carey, ed., *American Catholic Religious Thought* (1987); J. P. Chinnici, "Politics and Theology: From Enlightenment Catholicism to the Condemnation of Americanism," Cushwa Working Paper Series (Spring 1981); J. Hennesey, "An Eighteenth Century Bishop: John Carroll of Baltimore," *AHP* 16 (1978):171-205.

P. W. Carey

Enlightenment Protestantism. The Enlightenment was an intellectual movement that stressed reason as the way to truth, a world based on perfectly ordered natural laws and a self-confident and optimistic belief in human ability to make progress. The epoch is also frequently called the Age of Reason because reason was understood to be the path to providing the true understanding of man, society, the world and God. Truth, it was believed, had been obscured by revelation and dogma,* but at last people could be enlightened through reason, science and education. The intellectual and religious implications of the Enlightenment were profound, constituting a massive shift in Western thought.

The Enlightenment began in England, spread to Europe (especially France) and flourished in America (c.1750-1800) as the new nation was forming. It followed the Great Awakening* (1740-1760) and preceded the era of romanticism* (1800-1850). It was not a mass movement but was advocated by an influential elite group of writers. American Enlightenment thought relied heavily on European writers, including Isaac Newton (1642-1717), John Locke (1632-1704), David Hume (1711-1776) and Voltaire (1694-1778). American religious Enlightenment ideas were influenced by the British writers John Tillotson (1630-1694), John Toland (1670-1722), Matthew Tindal (c.1656-1733) and John Ray (c.1627-1705).

Restructuring a Reasonable Religion. Enlightenment thinkers believed that the basic ideas of religion could be derived from reason alone. Religion is embedded in nature, and unaided reason can determine its major tenets; hence, the idea that religion is natural or rational. Enlightenment writers taught that reflection leads to three essential religious ideas. First, influenced by Newton's mechanistic view of the universe (reflected in his *Principia,* 1687) they suggest that God is chiefly a great designer who created the world and devised natural laws for its perpetual motion. Second, people everywhere experience the sense of obligation or ethical demands toward neighbors. Conscience* forbids killing, adultery and stealing. Proper treatment of others is what pleases God, not a particular manner of worship* or a collection of doctrinal statements. Ethics* was, in fact, the core of rational religion. Benjamin Franklin, one of America's best-known rationalists, described religion in terms of thirteen virtues in his *Autobiography* (1791). Third, because of the sense of right and wrong, it is reasonable to conclude that there will be an afterlife in which right and wrong will be rewarded and punished. Thus there is an attempt to reduce religion to its simplest and most permanent features.

Taken together these three ideas comprise the essential teachings of rational religion. Cotton Mather's* *Reasonable Religion* (1700) and Experience Mayhew's *Discourse Showing That God Dealeth With Men As Reasonable Creatures* (1720) were early American reflections on these themes. But rationalist ideas were to powerfully influence some leading Congregationalist ministers at mid-century, notably Charles Chauncy,* who wrote *Five Dissertations* (1758), and Jonathan Mayhew,* whose ideas were published in *Seven Sermons* (1749).

Religious teachings of the Enlightenment challenged traditional Christianity at several points: (1) Scripture* had always been considered the authority* for truth in classic Protestantism,* but for Enlightenment thinkers reason is the primary source of knowledge. John Locke's *Essay on Human Understanding* (1690) emphasized new approaches to knowledge which stressed sensation and experience combined with reason. Revelation through Scripture was useful for the rationalist, but it was not to be accepted if it went contrary to reason.

(2) God is creator, but the doctrine of the Trinity is contrary to reason and therefore must be abandoned. The notion of the active providence of God also was diminished.

(3) Jesus taught the ethical norm Christians should follow, but his divinity must be rejected since the notion that he is "fully God, fully man" is contrary to experience and reason (*See* Christology). Atonement* comes through the moral influence of the teachings and deeds of Jesus, not through God requiring his death.

(4) Because of a strong belief in causality, miracles, which were understood as interruptions of natural law, were considered impossible. David Hume's *Philosophical Essays* (1748) was especially influential on this issue. Thomas Jefferson's* *The Life and Morals of Jesus* (1819) recorded the teachings of Jesus but eliminated the miracles. Apologists* had used miracles for centuries as proofs of the truth of Christianity; now those events and the Bible which recorded them were called into question.

(5) Enlightenment religion provided an alternative to Calvinism* in American Protestantism. It began with the assumption of human free will and challenged Calvin's teaching on original sin,* limited atonement and predestination.* Calvinism was widely modified or abandoned by American Protestants in the nineteenth century.

These criticisms originated from within the Christian community in a sustained questioning of the authority of Scripture and of traditional doctrines amounting to a radical departure in religious thought. So pivotal were its theological ideas that many interpreters suggest that the Enlightenment closed the Medieval era and began modernity. These concepts shaped American deism* and Unitarianism* and raised important questions for all Christian traditions.

Organizing and Disseminating Reasonable Religion. Ethan Allen,* Elihu Palmer* and Thomas Paine* clearly articulated the ideas of American deism. Deism was not a denomination, but rather a system of religious thought. Ethan Allen, Revolutionary War* hero, published *Reason the Only Oracle of Man* (1784). He defended reason as the only path to truth and attacked the authority of the Bible and intellectual oppression by the clergy.* He denounced Calvinism, arguing that it destroyed free will. Elihu Palmer, in *Principles of Nature* (1801), argued that God's greatest creation is man's reason. This capacity allows man to free himself from superstition. He also repudiated Calvinism. Palmer worked to disseminate the ideas of deism, organizing the Deistical Society in New York (1794). Its stated purpose was the destruction of superstition and fanaticism and the promotion of virtue through education, science and religious liberty. The society sponsored a weekly paper, *The Temple of Reason* (1800-1803), and Palmer lectured extensively, especially in New York and Philadelphia, the center of the American Enlightenment. Thomas Paine's *Age of Reason* (1794-1796) attacked the teachings of Christianity, particularly the notion of a written revelation. In addition, Benjamin Franklin, John Adams, Thomas Jefferson and others adopted deist ideas. But Paine's work alarmed many readers, prompting countless replies, and organized deism lost momentum after 1810.

The Enlightenment produced British apologists whose writings were enormously influential in America. Joseph Butler's (1692-1752) *Analogy of Religion* (1736) was considered a major defense against infidelity. William Paley's (1743-1805) *Christian Evidences* (1794) set forth his celebrated watchmaker argument for the existence of God. Thomas Reid (1710-1796) founded a rational philosophical system called Common Sense Realism,* in which he emphasized that the universe is intelligible and that people have the capacity to make "common sense" moral judgments. His views were transmitted by John Witherspoon* through his *Princeton Lectures* (1795) and were widely accepted in nineteenth-century American Protestantism.

Two denominations* grew out of rational religion: (1) American Unitarianism (1825) stressed the oneness of God. The first Unitarian church was King's Chapel, Boston, pastored by James Freeman. Joseph Priestly* and William Ellery Channing* were influential in the formation of this denomination. (2) The Universalists* (1790), led by John Murray* and Hosea Ballou,* whose *Treatise on Atonement* appeared in 1805, believed that because God's nature is benevolent, God will eventually redeem everyone.

Thomas Jefferson was the most influential American rationalist. He, like Voltaire and other Enlightenment thinkers, was a strong advocate of a government which protected the liberties of the people, including religious liberty. He thought this goal could best be achieved by separation of church and state*—an idea set forth in the First Amendment* of the U.S. Constitution (1789). The new pattern of church-state relations, shaped in the American Enlightenment era, conferred on American Protestantism her most characteristic patterns of expression: voluntaryism* and denominationalism.*

See also ENLIGHTENMENT CATHOLICISM.

BIBLIOGRAPHY. E. Cassirer, *The Philosophy of the Enlightenment* (1951); P. Gay, *The Enlightenment: The Rise of Modern Paganism* (1966); C. A. Koch, *Religion of the American Enlightenment* (1933); B. Kuklick, *Churchmen and Philosophers* (1985); H. May, *The Enlightenment in America* (1976); C. C. Wright, *The Beginnings of American Unitarianism* (1955). W. L. Pitts

Ephrata Society. Colonial Pietist* community founded by Johann Conrad Beissel.* A baker by trade, the mystically inclined Beissel immigrated to Pennsylvania in 1720 from the Palatinate (Germany) in search of spiritual peace.

Beissel joined the German Baptist Brethren (Dunkers) in 1724 and was soon placed in the ministry.* His emphasis on personal revelation, Sabbath*-day worship* and other issues, however, resulted in his leaving the Brethren within a few years. In 1732 a small group removed to remote Lancaster County where the semi-monastic Ephrata community was formed. Three categories of membership soon evolved: celibate brothers, celibate sisters and married householders (who practiced continence). Numerous beliefs and practices continued to be held in common with the Dunkers, including three-fold immersion baptism,* nonresistance and a love feast with foot washing.* During the 1750s, when the society was at its height, membership was approximately two hundred.

Ephrata was an important force in colonial Pennsylvania cultural life. Several architecturally distinctive buildings were constructed. The printing press, beginning about 1743, rivaled that of other colonial printers. A classical academy was begun in 1740. Music, mystical*/devotional* writing and Fraktur also flourished. In addition, the community operated extensive agricultural enterprises.

Among Ephrata's most noted converts was the Reformed pastor and scholar John Peter Miller,* who assumed leadership upon Beissel's death. Miller did not have Beissel's vision or charisma, and a steady decline soon set in. Celibate orders ceased in 1814, although a small, nonmonastic group has survived as the German Seventh-Day Baptist* Church.

BIBLIOGRAPHY. E. G. Alderfer, *The Ephrata Commune. An Early American Counter Culture* (1986); *Chronicon Ephratense* (1786, 1889); J. E. Ernst, *Ephrata, A History* (1963); F. Reichmann and E. E. Doll, eds. *Ephrata As Seen by Contemporaries* (1953). D. B. Eller

Epiphany. A festival on January 6 celebrating, in Western liturgical* churches, the visit of the wise men to the newborn Jesus in Bethlehem (Mt 2:1-12). In early Eastern church tradition this festival celebrated both the nativity and the baptism of Jesus, a custom retained by the Armenian Church* today. Other Eastern churches eventually adopted the Western celebration of the nativity on December 25, and those churches have since celebrated only the baptism of Jesus in the Jordan on January 6. At Rome the nativity story was divided between the two dates, December 25 and January 6, putting the visit of the magi on the later date. The old understanding of *epiphany* as the manifestation of God in human form thus became limited to "the manifestation of Christ to the Gentiles." Gaul combined the traditions, celebrating the magi, the baptism and the miracle at Cana. Today Western liturgical churches observe the baptism of Christ on the Sunday after Epiphany.

BIBLIOGRAPHY. A. A. McArthur, *The Evolution of the Christian Year* (1953); T. J. Talley, *The Origins of the Liturgical Year* (1986).

T. J. Talley

Episcopacy. A term referring to the office of bishop,* a body of bishops in a church or geographical region, or the form of polity* comprising the three orders of bishop, priest* and deacon.* The word itself is derived from the Greek *episkopos,* meaning overseer, and has its Christian source in the New Testament. Though the pattern of episcopacy in the New Testament is unclear, by the end of the second century, a threefold ministry centering on the episcopal office had emerged as the normative order and so remained until the Reformation. In the Anglican,* Old Catholic, Orthodox* and Roman Catholic* traditions, episcopacy is still the accepted form of church order, being regarded as a continuation of the apostolic faith and practice of the primitive church. Among various Protestant* churches in North America, the title *bishop* is applied to those exercising specific ministerial oversight as chief executive or pastor. These churches, with the exception of the Moravian Brethren,* do not claim a formal, historic episcopal succession.

See also CHURCH GOVERNMENT: EPISCOPAL.

C. R. Henery

Episcopal Church. *See* PROTESTANT EPISCOPAL CHURCH IN THE U.S.A.

Epp, Theodore Herman (1907-1985). Religious broadcaster. Epp studied at Bible Institute of Los Angeles; Hesston College, Kansas; and Southwestern Baptist Theological Seminary. He served as a Mennonite* pastor in Goltry, Oklahoma (1932-1936); a church planter in Kansas (1936-1938); a part-time assistant to radio evangelist T. Myron Webb in Enid, Oklahoma; and a pastor in Kingman, Kansas (1938-1939). In 1939 Epp moved to Lincoln, Nebraska, to begin his radio ministry, Back to the Bible Broadcast, which grew to include more than 600 stations. He published seventy books and two periodicals: *Good News Broadcaster* (1942-1985), which became *Confident Living* (1986-) and *Young America* (1946), which was renamed *Young Ambassador* (1946-1986) and later *T. Q.: Teen Quest* (1986-). A founder of National Religious Broadcasters* (1944), Epp was named "Man of the Year" (1968) by the Nebraska Association of Broadcasters. Back to the Bible Missionary Agency (1952-), renamed International Ministries, supports missions around the world. The ministry also sponsored the Back to the Bible Correspondence School (1960-1985; renamed "Self-Study Course," 1985-1987).

BIBLIOGRAPHY. T. H. Epp, *45 Years of Adventuring Faith: The Back to the Bible Story* (1984).

D. D. Bundy

Epworth League (1889-1930). Methodist* youth organization. The product of a fusion of five Methodist young people's groups, the Epworth League, organized under the direction of Jesse L. Hurlbut and C. A. Littlefield, in Cleveland, Ohio, in 1889. Named for the place of John Wesley's* birth, the objectives of the new organization included the promotion of "an earnest, intelligent, practical, and loyal spiritual life in the young people of our church. . . ." The Methodist Church in Canada and the Methodist Episcopal Church, South, both organized Leagues in 1890. The Epworth Leagues stressed the importance of church loyalty, Christian education, commitment to Methodist missions, and spiritual and social development.

After receiving official sanction from their respective General Conferences, League membership expanded rapidly. With a combined circulation of over 125,000 in 1894, the official League organs—*Onward* (the Epworth League in Canada), the *Epworth Herald* (the M. E. Church), and the *Epworth Herald* (the M. E. Church, South)—were among the largest denominational publications in the world of that day. An important aspect of the Epworth League was the Sunday-evening devotional meeting. Because these gatherings were usually held exclusive of the evening church service, pastors frequently complained that the local chapters exhibited too much autonomy, and that many youths attended the League meetings instead of the services of the church. The 1924 General Conference of the M. E. Church and the 1930 Conference of the M. E. Church, South, voted to dissolve the League by placing its work under the auspices of a Youth Division within the educational structure of the church.

BIBLIOGRAPHY. J. F. Berry, "The Story of the Epworth League," in *The Story of Methodism,* ed. A. B. Hyde (1894). B. K. Turley

Erb, Paul (1894-1984). Mennonite Church* educator and journalist. Erb's career in the Mennonite Church began as an educator, serving as a professor of English at Hesston College (Kansas) from 1918 to 1941 and Goshen College (Indiana) from 1941 to 1945. He achieved his greatest influence as editor of the *Gospel Herald,* the organ of the Mennonite Church, from 1944 to 1962. Known as a diplomat and mediator during years of considerable change and conflict in the Mennonite Church, perhaps his most outstanding contribution in this regard was his *The Alpha and The Omega* (1955), which had a calming effect on an otherwise fierce conference debate over eschatology.* Erb generally identified with the rising Mennonite intellectuals of his time, most notably Harold S. Bender* and Guy F. Hershberger. As editor of the *Gospel Herald,* he helped gain acceptance in the conference for their ideas.

BIBLIOGRAPHY. K. Enns-Rempel, "Paul Erb: Mennonite Diplomat," (unpublished M.A. thesis, University of California—Riverside, 1984).

K. M. Enns-Rempel

Erdman, Charles Rosenbury (1866-1960). Presbyterian* clergyman and educator. Born in Fayetteville, New York, the son of premillenialist* leader William J. Erdman,* Charles Erdman was raised in a New School* Presbyterian environment. After graduating from Princeton University* and Princeton Theological Seminary,* Erdman served churches in Overbrook and Germantown, Pennsylvania. In 1906 he assumed the chair of practical theology at Princeton Seminary, which he held until his retirement in 1936. He pastored the First Presbyterian Church of Princeton from 1924 to 1934.

In 1925, at the height of the fundamentalist-modernist controversy* in the Presbyterian Church, Erdman won election as moderator of the General Assembly.* Though a self-described fundamentalist,* he believed that the unified evangelical* mission of the church was more important than precise doctrinal agreement. At a crucial moment in the General Assembly, when fundamentalists were apparently succeeding in forcing liberal Presbyterians into doctrinal conformity, Erdman referred the issue to a committee and so broke the momentum of the fundamentalist exclusivists. Erdman was also a major voice for inclusivism in an extended feud among Princeton faculty that led to the reorganization of the Seminary and the exodus of some faculty to form Westminster Theological Seminary in 1929. He also sat on the Presbyterian Board of Foreign Missions from 1906 to 1942 and was president of the Board from 1926 to 1940. Erdman authored over thirty books, most of which were biblical commentaries, and contributed to *The Fundamentals.** He numbered Woodrow Wilson,* Grover Cleveland and Billy Sunday* among his friends.

BIBLIOGRAPHY. *DAB* 6; C. T. Fritsch et. al., "In Memoriam," *PSB* 54 (1960):36-39; L. Loetscher, *The Broadening Church: A Study of Theological Issues in the Presbyterian Church since 1869* (1957).

B. J. Longfield

Erdman, William Jacob (1834-1923). Presbyterian* pastor and Niagara Conference* speaker. Born in Allentown, Pennsylvania, Erdman was educated at Hamilton College and Union Theological Seminary.* He was ordained* in the First Presbyterian Church of Philadelphia in 1860 and ministered in a number of Presbyterian and Congregational* churches in Ontario, Minnesota, New York, Michigan, Indiana and Boston. Most notable was his association with Dwight L. Moody* and his ministry in Moody's Chicago Avenue Church (1875-1878).

Erdman was a premillennialist* and closely associated with the Niagara Conference. He was often featured as a Bible expositor at the conference and served as its secretary throughout its entire existence. He was also a consulting editor for the *Scofield Reference Bible.** Erdman wrote several books, many pamphlets and scores of articles in religious and Bible study journals. His son, Charles R. Erdman,* was a professor at

Princeton* Theological Seminary and a controversial figure in the fundamentalist-modernist debate* within the Presbyterian Church.

BIBLIOGRAPHY. E. R. Sandeen, *The Roots of Fundamentalism* (1970).

P. C. Wilt

Esbjorn, Lars Paul (1808-1870). Swedish Lutheran* pastor,* missionary* and educator. Born in Delsbo, Helsingland Province, Sweden, Esbjorn graduated from Uppsala University. Ordained* a Lutheran minister in 1832, he served congregations in his home province until 1849 when he immigrated to the U.S. and made his home in Andover, Illinois. There, and in Princeton, he organized Swedish Lutheran congregations, which he served as pastor (1849-1856). At the same time he traveled to many other new Swedish settlements, organizing at least thirty-four other congregations. In 1856 he moved to Springfield, Illinois, to serve as theological mentor for the Scandinavian students at the newly founded Illinois State University, established by the Lutheran synods* in Illinois.

Becoming dissatisfied with the doctrinal laxity of both the school and its supporting synods, in 1859 he abruptly withdrew with his students to Chicago, causing the secession of the Swedes and Norwegians to form their own Scandinavian Evangelical Lutheran Augustana Synod of North America (later known simply as the Augustana Synod or Church). The new church body adopted Esbjorn's splinter school, christening it "Augustana Seminary," the direct ancestor of what later became Augustana College and Theological Seminary in Rock Island, Illinois. Returning to Sweden in 1863, Esbjorn served as rector* of the Oester Wohla parish in Uppland Province until his death in 1870.

BIBLIOGRAPHY. S. Ronnegard, *Prairie Shepherd* (1952).

J. W. Lundeen

Eschatology. Traditionally, eschatology is the doctrinal study of last things (from the Greek *eschata*) and may refer either to the fate of individuals (death, resurrection, judgment and afterlife) or to events surrounding the end of the world. In America, when tied to expectations of a coming millennium, such concerns have produced powerful movements with significant religious and social effects.

Millennial Types. Broadly speaking, Christian millennialism is the belief, deeply rooted in Revelation 20, that there will be a long period of unprecedented peace and righteousness closely associated with the Second Coming of Christ. Historically, Christians have divided themselves into three groups, depending on whether they expect a literal millennium on the earth and where they place Christ's return in relation to it.

Premillennialists* take Revelation 20 quite literally and expect the Second Coming of Christ to occur before the millennium. In order for the kingdom to come, there must be a radical break with the current age, which is marked by corruption and apostasy. After a series of cataclysmic events (wars, natural disasters, the preaching of the gospel to all nations, a regathering of Israel, the rise of Antichrist, a great apostasy, the tribulation and the battle of Armageddon), Christ will return, raise the Christian dead, bind Satan, eliminate evil, set up his kingdom and, with the help of his resurrected saints, rule over a thoroughly revitalized and reformed world. After a thousand years, Satan will be loosed to foment one last but short-lived rebellion against God, who will crush the revolt, resurrect the non-Christian dead for judgment and finally establish a new heaven and earth.

Postmillennialists* believe that the kingdom of God is already in the world and is now being extended through the preaching* of the gospel and the work of the Holy Spirit. Thus, as more individuals are converted and apply their principles to society, the current age will undergo gradual transformation until it becomes essentially Christianized. During this millennium, which may last longer than a thousand years, evil will be reduced to a minimum and a majority of the world's people will turn to Christ. After this spiritual golden age, Christ will return, raise and judge the dead and inaugurate the eternal age to come. Postmillennialists understand Revelation 20 more figuratively than do premillennialists, arguing that it describes either the reign of Christ in human hearts or events that have already taken place in the early days of the gospel's advance.

Amillennialists* (literally, "no-millennialists") do not expect a literal millennium of any kind on the earth. They neither believe that Christ will return to destroy the hopelessly corrupt current age nor that it will be gradually transformed into the millennium. They hold that good and evil will grow together in the world until the end and that the kingdom of God is already spiritually present in those who have personally accepted Christ's rule. Thus amillennialists believe that Revelation 20 describes the current reign of saints who have died and gone to be with Christ in heaven or his present reign in human hearts. The only perfect kingdom they expect is the new heaven and earth that will be established after Christ's Second Coming, when the dead have been raised and God's judgment executed.

At different times and to different degrees, American Christians have adhered to all three millennial types or felt free to alter them in various ways. In fact, it is often difficult to classify American groups as pre-, post-, or amillennial because such movements tend to ignore the categories of systematic theology. Nevertheless, millennial ideas have had their consequences. Because amillennialists view the millennium as having no material expression this side of the new creation, their views tend to need no institutional expression. But pre- and postmillennialists have frequently translated their beliefs into powerful and popular movements which have affected American society.

Movements. America has been fertile ground for millennialism. At times these hopes have been directly tied to the nation itself. Some Christian millennialists have seen America as the location of the future golden age or at least a crucial instrument of its coming somewhere else. Others have secularized millennial ideas and applied them to American expansion and institutions or equated them with ideas of human progress. More negatively, some have used millennial expectations to condemn America and predict its coming judgment.

America's earliest settlers were mostly Protestants,* who brought with them distinctly Protestant eschatological views. Though nearly all of the magisterial reformers (e.g., Luther and Calvin) rejected the apocalyptic* millennialism of Protestant radicals, they significantly reinterpreted the amillennialism which had prevailed since Augustine. For them the Antichrist in biblical prophecy was the papacy, the fall of Babylon began with the Protestant Reformation and the great tribulation was Catholicism's persecution of the evangelical* gospel. Such views encouraged a more literalistic understanding of prophecy and unintentionally led some to expect an earthly millennium.

During the Puritan* Revolution in England, many accepted the views of Reformed theologians Johann H. Alsted (1588-1638), Joseph Mede (1586-1638), and Thomas Goodwin (1600-1680), who argued for such a literal kingdom. Among their more radical followers were the Fifth-Monarchy Men who wanted to adopt Old Testament Law and create a holy commonwealth in England before the Second Coming. When Cromwell's government failed and the monarchy was restored by the Stuarts, premillennialism was generally discredited, though it continued in the writings of Isaac Newton (1642-1717), Johann A. Bengel (1687-1752) and Joseph Priestley.*

Such radical notions were rare among those who

settled America, but many Puritans did have millennial expectations. They believed that they were on an "errand into the wilderness" and that their "city set upon a hill" might be God's last chance to establish a thoroughly Christian society. As long as they kept their special covenant with God, the "lively experiment" would prosper and flourish. Increasing pluralism in New England dashed the hopes of most Puritans, though some still held on to the views of Richard Baxter (1615-1691), expressed in *The Glorious Kingdom of Christ, Described and Clearly Vindicated,* that the kingdom would grow in stages until it encompassed the whole world.

Such postmillennial optimism acquired a powerful spokesman in the middle of the eighteenth century. Bolstered by the commentaries of the Anglican Daniel Whitby and his own experience in the Great Awakening* in the 1730s, Jonathan Edwards* argued in his *History of the Work of Redemption* (1739) that God intended to establish an earthly millennium through the success of the gospel. Because of the recent "surprising work of God" in the colonies, Edwards believed that the golden age was imminent and would probably begin in America.

By the mid-1800s Edwards's postmillennialism was accepted by most American evangelicals. Leaders like Lyman Beecher* and Charles Finney* combined postmillennialism, revivalism* and perfectionism* in their effort to Christianize the nation through various religious and political reform movements.* Beecher and Finney were so confident in these measures that in the late 1830s they predicted that the millennium was imminent. In many cases it was difficult for such postmillennialists to separate their millennial hopes from national aspirations. Thus postmillennialism could be used to justify Manifest Destiny,* the Mexican War, the North's victory in the Civil War,* the subjugation of Native American tribes and, at the end of the century, American imperialism.

Sometimes difficult to categorize according to millennial types were the communal* or utopian experiments which occurred in the late eighteenth and early nineteenth centuries. In 1774 Mother Ann Lee* and eight followers emigrated from England and set up the United Society of Believers in Christ's Second Coming, which was also known as the Millennial Church or, due to their distinctive worship practices, the Shakers.* Earlier Mother Lee had visions that at the Second Advent Christ would come in the form of a woman. Quickly the Shakers concluded that Mother Lee was the prophesied female incarnation and that they were the advance

guard of the rapidly approaching millennium. In 1776 the Shakers started a number of socialistic Christian communities, which at their height in the 1830s numbered about six thousand people at nineteen sites. Initially the Shakers grew rapidly by recruiting converts from the Second Great Awakening,* but because Mother Lee's visions also mandated celibacy, growth could not be sustained.

Another communal experiment with millennialist overtones was the Oneida Community under John Humphrey Noyes.* Following a rather typical evangelical upbringing, Noyes became convinced that the Second Coming had taken place in A.D. 70 and that the only thing preventing the establishment of an earthly kingdom was the lack of Christian love. Building on popular views of Christian perfectionism, Noyes started a community near Putney, Vermont, in 1838. His practice of "complex marriage," based on the belief that in the kingdom all men would be married to all women, forced them in 1848 to relocate to Oneida in western New York, where the community eventually became better known for its commercial success. Though prophetic speculation was never primary in Noyes' thinking, his utopianism had millennialist underpinnings.

Likewise in the early nineteenth century, millennial views played prominent roles in the rise of restorationist movements, which held that after centuries of distortion, the pure and primitive gospel of the New Testament church had been recovered. Alexander Campbell,* a founder of the Disciples of Christ* (*See* Restoration Movement), named his journal *The Millennial Harbinger,* so manifesting his hope that the restored gospel would bring in a golden age for the church and the world.

Less optimistic were the Mormons,* whose restorationism was more premillennial. Founded by Joseph Smith* in 1830 on the basis of revelations received in the 1820s, the Church of Jesus Christ of Latter-Day Saints believed that God had re-established the true gospel in anticipation of the Second Coming of Christ. On the basis of an 1831 revelation, Smith declared that Christ would shortly return to establish a new Zion in Jackson County, Missouri. Smith produced a plan for the city with the new temple in its center and advised Mormons to be ready to move there in preparation for Christ's return. However, Mormons were soon driven from Missouri by persecution and eventually settled in Utah, where they established a temporary Zion. Shortly before his murder, Smith received other revelations that seemed to move the Second Coming into the 1880s or beyond, though they still maintained that the New Jerusalem would be in Missouri.

At about this same time others were adopting premillennial views. The violence of the French Revolution and widespread political upheaval revived a more apocalyptic outlook, which liked to speculate about the signs of the times and the fortunes of the Jews. America's most famous antebellum premillennialist was William Miller,* a Baptist* preacher from Vermont. Using "millennial arithmetic," Miller predicted that the Second Coming would occur in 1843-1844. Millerism grew throughout the 1830s but fell into disarray when Christ did not arrive on October 22, 1844, as Miller finally prophesied. Following this failure, known as the "Great Disappointment," most Millerites gave up their views, but many others found explanations for the failed prophecy and formed the Advent Christian Church and the larger Seventh-Day Adventist Church.* The latter became closely identified with the prophetic revelations of Ellen G. White* after the Civil War and some distinctive dietary practices considered eccentric by most evangelicals.

The Civil War was a watershed for American millennialism. That national disaster, together with the unprecedented pressures of immigration, urbanization and industrialization destroyed the earlier optimism that had reigned in nineteenth-century America. Popular postmillennialism waned, though most historians see in the rise of the Social Gospel Movement* during the 1880s a continuation of postmillennialist zeal. It must be noted, however, that many Social Gospelers were not millennialists per se but derived their faith in human progress from evolutionary thought and theological liberalism.*

At the same time that postmillennialism was in decline, a new kind of premillennialism became popular. Dispensationalism,* developed in the 1830s in England by John Nelson Darby,* came to America in the 1870s and found its way into a sizable segment of evangelicalism through Bible and prophetic conferences,* the Bible institutes* and later the *Scofield Reference Bible* (1909). Dispensationalism was distinctly different from earlier premillennialism in that it had a new hermeneutic and a novel chronology of the end-times, including the controversial pretribulation rapture of the church. After World War 1,* dispensational premillennialism became almost indistinguishable from militant fundamentalism,* thanks to promoters like Arno C. Gaebelein,* Harry A. Ironside,* Lewis S. Chafer* and C. I. Scofield.*

While dispensationalists worked hard to maintain evangelical orthodoxy, other premillennialist groups departed from it. The Jehovah's Witnesses,* founded in the 1870s by Charles T. Russell* and subsequently led by Joseph F. Rutherford,* adopted an Arian christology, taught that Christ spiritually returned to earth in 1914 and is presently building a theocratic kingdom through the Watch Tower Society and predicted an imminent battle of Armageddon. Unlike some other American millennialists, Jehovah's Witnesses foresaw the destruction of an unrepentant America. In more recent times, Witnesses have become known for their strict pacifism,* their refusal to take blood transfusions, their door-to-door proselytism and a number of well-publicized failed prophecies.

Since the 1970s, millennial movements have had a new lease on life. Dispensationalism had a surge of popularity thanks to the writings of Hal Lindsey, whose *Late Great Planet Earth* (1970) was the decade's best-selling book, and its acceptance by President Ronald Reagan,* whose foreign policy, his opponents feared, was greatly influenced by dispensationalism's view of a fast-approaching Armageddon. Likewise, postmillennialism had a revival in segments of American evangelicalism in the Reconstructionist movement.* Advocates such as Rousas J. Rushdoony, Greg L. Bahnsen and Gary North have predicted a coming golden age brought about by religious revival and strict conformity to biblical law (which they call "theonomy"), especially in the areas of economics and social policy, including the penalty of capital punishment for homosexuality, as well as apostasy and the reintroduction of their notion of biblical slavery. Though Reconstructionists tend to be nebulous about their political program, they often align themselves with the New Christian Right.

Social Effects. The social ramifications of these millennial views are significant and often predictable. Since postmillennialists expect religious revival and social reform to succeed in transforming the world, as a rule they support programs of social change. The followers of Finney engaged in antislavery* campaigns and other reform efforts before the Civil War, and the Social Gospelers found common cause with the progressive movement, which brought major changes to American society in the period of 1900-1920. Similarly, because they look at the current age as hopelessly doomed, premillennialists as a rule do not engage in long-term programs for social betterment, but rather emphasize the need to evangelize* before the Second Coming.

But these generalizations often need careful

qualification. Some postmillennialists opposed the abolition of slavery, while others refused to accept the Social Gospel's plan to revamp the American social structure. Likewise, not all premillennialists have totally disavowed political involvement. Some joined with Social Gospelers at the turn of the century to minister in the cities, while others became active participants in the Prohibition Movement.* More recently, in their efforts to make America a Christian nation, postmillennial Reconstructionists are often indistinguishable from premillennial fundamentalists in their support of antiabortion* legislation and prayer-in-school* constitutional amendments.

Nor is it completely warranted to label postmillennialism as optimistic and premillennialism as pessimistic. Premillennialists have often claimed that they are supremely optimistic because in their view the coming golden age cannot be deterred or delayed by human faithlessness or procrastination. At Christ's coming the millennium will be instantaneously achieved. Thus it might be safer to regard both millennial views as basically optimistic, while recognizing that they differ substantially on the means that will be used to bring in the millennium. Furthermore, it is not correct to say that only premillennialists care about saving souls while postmillennialists care more about saving society. Throughout most of the nineteenth century pre- and postmillennialists worked side by side to make it the so-called great century for foreign missions.*

Nevertheless, after noting such important exceptions, it is still safe to conclude that historically the Christian social conscience and commitment to social righteousness have tended to atrophy during times of premillennialist ascendency. People who believe that nothing can be done to alter the present age's rendezvous with the Antichrist and total apostasy generally do not waste their energy trying to change things in the meantime. By World War 1, most premillennialists had decided to leave social involvement to postmillennialists and theological liberals and concentrate on evangelism. Not until the 1970s have premillennialists like Jerry Falwell,* Tim LaHaye, Pat Robertson* and others been willing to re-evaluate their social responsibility.

See also AMILLENNIALISM; APOCALYPTICISM; DISPENSATIONALISM; FUNDAMENTALISM; POSTMILLENNIALISM; PREMILLENNIALISM.

BIBLIOGRAPHY. R. G. Clouse, ed., *The Millennium: Four Views* (1977); E. S. Gaustad, ed., *The Rise of Adventism* (1974); R. T. Handy, *A Christian America* (1971); G. M. Marsden, *Fundamentalism*

and American Culture (1980); H. R. Niebuhr, *The Kingdom of God in America* (1937); M. J. Penton, *Apocalypse Delayed: The Story of Jehovah's Witnesses* (1985); R. V. Pierard, *The Unequal Yoke* (1970); T. L. Smith, *Revivalism and Social Reform* (1955); E. L. Tuveson, *Redeemer Nation* (1980); T. P. Weber, *Living in the Shadow of the Second Coming* (1979).   T. P. Weber

Established Churches in New England. Churches enjoying privileged status. After the reign of the Roman emperor Constantine in the early fourth century, Christianity generally enjoyed the status of an "established" church, receiving support and protection from the state. The English society from which the leaders of the first generation in New England came was no exception. The ruling monarch served as "Supreme Governor" of the Church of England*; he or she appointed the bishops* who presided over the dioceses* into which the country was divided. A diocese was further subdivided into many parishes,* each with its own minister* responsible for worship* services. The state prohibited any competition for its established church, and it levied taxes to support the parish minister and maintain the church buildings.

While New Englanders paid lip service to the authority* of king and bishops when they founded their own churches, the locus of authority in each congregation was the body of communicant members. As soon as a town was settled, prospective church members were expected first to gather together and satisfy one another that they were saints eligible for full communion, then to covenant together to form a church and finally to call a minister.

Yet this "gathered" church polity* did not entirely displace the tradition of establishment. Within the boundaries of a New England town, the church functioned like an English parish. No religious competition was allowed. The town government assessed all taxpayers for support of the minister and maintenance of the meetinghouse, and everyone was expected to attend services, whether or not they had joined the church.

Requirements for church membership* were stringent. Not only did would-be saints have to demonstrate knowledge of doctrine and blameless behavior, they also had to make a verbal "relation" of their experiences of saving grace to the other members (*See* Conversion Narrative). Those who had satisfied these requirements could become a close-knit and mutually supportive group of insiders, but resentment inevitably arose from outsiders who were excluded from full membership in the church but were nevertheless required to support it. In many towns outsiders made up a significant percentage of the population; Dedham, Massachusetts, for example, numbered only about half its adult males as church members by 1662. How long could the churches legitimately remain established under those circumstances?

Other challenges to the New England establishment arose as towns grew. Those who settled on the edges of towns often wished to form their own churches rather than make the long trip to the old meetinghouse, but members of the original church were not always willing to recognize the aspirations of the new settlers or to lose their support. Severer tensions accompanied the revivals* of the early 1740s. Exposure to a charismatic revivalist frequently convinced New Englanders that their own minister lacked saving grace and that the members of their own churches were incapable of recognizing a true saint. Large factions might withdraw from communion to form a separatist* church of their own. Not only did these separatist churches and their ministers receive no support from the town government, but that government continued to assess separatists for the support of the church they had repudiated.

By the end of the eighteenth century, competitors to the established congregational churches dotted the New England landscape: Baptists,* Shakers,* Anglicans, Quakers* and even Universalists.* But the establishment hung on well into the nineteenth century. Not until 1818, when a coalition of Baptists, Methodists,* Anglicans and Jeffersonians controlled the ballot box, did Connecticut completely disestablish its churches. New Hampshire followed a year later. The last legally privileged churches in New England, those of the Commonwealth of Massachusetts, were not disestablished until 1833.

See also TOLERATION, ACT OF; ANGLICANISM.

BIBLIOGRAPHY. E. S. Morgan, *Visible Saints: The History of a Puritan Idea* (1963); O. E. Winslow, *Meetinghouse Hill, 1630-1783* (1972); K. A. Lockridge, *A New England Town: The First Hundred Years* (1970); D. D. Hall, *The Faithful Shepherd: A History of the New England Ministry in the Seventeenth Century* (1972); W. Walker, ed., *The Creeds and Platforms of Congregationalism* (1960); L. Ziff, ed., *John Cotton on the Churches of New England* (1968).   L. B. Tipson

Eternal Security. The belief that a person who has been truly justified* by faith in Christ has eternal salvation* and cannot lose it. Sometimes

termed *absolute final perseverance,* this doctrine affirms that Christians ". . . are shielded by God's power until the coming of the salvation that is ready to be revealed in the last time" (1 Pet 1:5). Based on texts such as Romans 8:30, John 10:28 and Philippians 1:6, it is an integral part of a Calvinistic* doctrine of salvation which affirms predestination,* unconditional election* and irresistible grace.

Eternal security found classical expression in the disputes between the Dutch Remonstrants, whose fifth Arminian Article (1610) affirmed that election was conditional and that salvation could be lost, and the Canons of Dort (1618), which took the opposite view in both respects. The doctrinal standard of many English-speaking Calvinists, the Westminster Confession of Faith* (1647), affirms that the elect "can neither totally nor finally fall away from the state of grace; but shall certainly persevere therein to the end, and be eternally saved."

American Puritans,* like Jonathan Edwards,* embraced final perseverance because of the immutability of God's decree of election. On the frontier, Wesleyan* Arminians,* like circuit-riding Bishop* Francis Asbury,* found Presbyterians* and Baptists* stoutly defending eternal security and assailing the doctrine of conditional election. As revivalism* swept America in the First and Second Great Awakenings,* the New Divinity* of Samuel Hopkins's* *System of Doctrines* (1793) sought to reconcile God's sovereignty and human agency without sacrificing the consistent Calvinism of his forefathers. The Methodist* Nathan Bangs* rejected Hopkins's unconditional election and final perseverance in works like *The Errors of Hopkinsianism* (1815). These disputations continued into the second and third generations as Hopkins's students Ebenezer Fitsch and Nathaniel Taylor,* both of Yale,* jousted with Wilbur Fisk* of Wesleyan University. Fisk's *The Calvinistic Controversy* (1837) showed that the basis of the argument remained unchanged. Popular revivalism, as manifested in Charles Finney's* "New Measures,"* opted for a doctrine of salvation that saw Christian life as "a state of trial" or "probation" which included the possibility of falling from grace.

Classical Calvinistic affirmations of eternal security continued in Princeton theologians* such as Charles Hodge* and Benjamin B. Warfield.* The *Systematic Theology* of Baptist theologian Augustus Strong* supported the doctrine; while Methodist theologians like William Burton Pope* and John Miley* argued against it from biblical passages warning of the dangers of falling away (e.g., Ezek

7:20; 1 Cor 9:27; Heb 6:4-6) and from the Wesleyan belief that divine grace enables as well as cooperates with the response of human wills.

See also ASSURANCE OF SALVATION.

BIBLIOGRAPHY. W. Fisk, *The Calvinist Controversy* (1835); R. Gromacki, *Is Salvation Forever?* (1981); C. Hodge, *Systematic Theology,* 3 vols. (1872-1873); I. H. Marshall, *Kept by the Power of God* (1969); J. Miley, *Systematic Theology* (1892-1894). J. R. Tyson

Ethics, Catholic Personal. Ethics in Catholic thought is distinguished from mores, morals, meta-ethics and moral theology.* Mores are actual behavior patterns approved by a social group. Morals are principles specifying right and wrong behavior. Ethics is the philosophical science of moral principles. Meta-ethics examines the criteria of meaning in ethical statements. Moral theology is based on faith in divine revelation and is the study of ethics from the viewpoint of God's law. In practice, the Catholic tradition has usually joined philosophy and theology, reason and faith, while clearly distinguishing them in theory.

Traditionally, ethics has been divided into three parts: (a) social ethics* (how we should treat each other); (b) personal or individual ethics* (what sort of individuals we should be); and (c) meta-physical ethics (what is the *summum bonum,* the greatest good or ultimate end). The first deals with rights and duties to others; the second with virtues* and vices of the soul (moral character); and the third with goods and ends, especially the final end. C. S. Lewis* aptly compares these three to three parts of a fleet's sailing orders: (a) how to cooperate and not damage each other; (b) how each ship should stay shipshape; and (c) why the whole fleet is at sea at all, that is, what its mission is. Typically modern ethical philosophies, except for the existentialists, concentrate on (a), less on (b) and hardly ever on (c), which raises ultimate metaphysical and theological questions.

The relation between individual and social ethics in Catholic tradition is neither the Machiavellian extreme of a double standard, whereby social ethics is divorced from the standards of individual ethics and reduced to power and pragmatism, nor the Platonic extreme of a perfect parallel between the two. As an example of this non-parallelism, a recent American bishops' pastoral letter on war and peace called pacifism "an honorable option" for *individuals,* while the just-war theory has always held that the *state* is obligated to use force when necessary to defend its citizens against unjust aggressors.

The relationship between God and ethics can be approached through Dostoevski's words, "If God does not exist, everything is permissible." Some atheists like Nietzsche and Sartre accept this dictum and reject all objective morality because they reject God. But Buddha, Plato and other pagan moralists seem to refute this dictum by knowing much about morality but little about God. Catholic ethics resolves this dilemma by holding that God is in fact the ultimate ground of morality (though human nature is the proximate ground), but that many can and do know morality (the effect) without knowing God (the cause). Though God's existence and some of his attributes can in principle be known by reason alone, this is relatively rare (as in Aristotle), while everyone has a conscience, that is the ability to know moral good and evil by reason (i.e., wisdom or understanding).

Natural Law. Natural Law is perhaps the most important and distinctively Catholic ethical teaching, though a few secular thinkers (such as Mortimer Adler) and a good number of Protestant thinkers (such as C. S. Lewis) also embrace the idea, which was held by nearly all pre-modern thinkers. Aquinas defined a law as "an ordinance of reason promulgated for the common good by one who has care of a community." Three kinds of law are distinguished: (a) eternal law (God's nature and will); (b) natural law (human reason's participation in eternal law, aware of the laws of human nature as designed by God); and (c) human posited or manmade law. The distinction between (b) and (c) corresponds to that between mores and morals, between the legal and the moral. Ethical positivism denies categories (a) and (b).

When modern Americans hear the word *natural* they think of the "birds and the bees" because, to modern science, nature is simply the actual, observable physical universe. But in Catholic philosophy, the term *natural* has a broader meaning, as when certain acts are called "unnatural" not because they are nonphysical but because they violate human nature. *Natural* in *natural law* also means that this law is known naturally, innately or instinctively (though not by biological instinct).

Can Natural Law change? Like Catholic dogma,* Catholic ethics can develop, as a plant grows, but the growth is organic, from within, an unfolding of what was already present implicitly. Natural Law can change (as Aquinas puts it) "by addition but not by subtraction." For example, adultery, abortion,* divorce,* homosexual* acts and artificial contraception,* once known to be wrong by nature, cannot ever become right. But new insight into new realities (e.g., nuclear versus nonnuclear war, or reasonable interest on money versus usury) can generate new moral principles on top of the old.

Two modern additions to Catholic Natural Law ethics, approved by recent popes* and Vatican II,* are a greater emphasis on the rights of individual conscience and on the intrinsic value of each person. Principles are now usually seen as necessary to preserve and respect persons rather than for their own sakes. Just as the proper object of faith is God, not creedal propositions which only specify faith, so the proper object of moral fidelity is God and neighbor. Principles specify how to faithfully love them. Neither of these two new emphases is wholly new. For example, Aquinas taught that it is always a mortal sin to act contrary to your conscience. But both are widely felt to be more necessary today to combat both the totalitarian Eastern and the hedonistic Western attacks on the dignity of man.

Application of Moral Law. The three moral determinants or factors that cause any freely chosen human act to be morally good or evil are: (a) the moral nature of the act itself as specified by the moral law; (b) the intention or motive of the actor; and (c) the circumstances, or situation. Legalism judges morality by (a) alone, subjectivism by (b) alone, and relativism by (c) alone.

Natural Law specifies (a), but must be applied to ever-changing and multifarious circumstances ([c]) by a prudent and well-intentioned individual ([b]). Though the principles of Natural Law are unchanging and universal, the applications of them are not. Nearly all Catholic ethicists agree with both these points, but conservatives emphasize the first and liberals the second.

Catholic ethics traditionally distinguishes four levels of moral absoluteness: (1) the ultimate axiom of morality, "do good, not evil"; (2) the "primary principles of the Natural law" (e.g., "thou shalt not kill"); (3) the "secondary (derivative) principles of the Natural Law" (e.g., antiabortion); and (4) the application of these principles to concrete situations (e.g., is a hysterectomy to save the life of a pregnant cancer patient allowed?).

The principle of double effect deals with the latter situation: If you foresee that an action will have two effects, one good and one bad, it is moral to perform it only if all five of the following conditions are met: (1) it is not an intrinsically evil act; (2) the bad effect is a byproduct, not the means to the good effect; (3) the bad effect is not intended; (4) there is no other way to get the good effect; and (5) the good outweighs the evil.

Proportionalism, popular among some American Catholic ethicists but never approved by the magisterium,* says in effect that (5) alone is sufficient to justify an act.

Love is the centerpiece of Catholic ethics rather than justice or law (two classical foci) or rights or duties (two modern foci). Love (Greek *agape,* Latin *caritas*) is defined unsentimentally as an unselfish willing of good to another. But this must be the other's true good, which entails the need for a knowledge of human nature, the Natural Law and the *summum bonum.* Thus intellect should inform the will, and emotions follow. Unhealthy emotions are usually regarded as symptoms of moral fault but are not, as such, morally good or evil.

Merit* is viewed by Catholics as a corollary of justice: morally good acts merit, or deserve, praise and reward; evil ones merit blame and punishment. Both God and nature attach rewards and punishments to deeds. For example, eating poison kills you, and final impenitence damns you. The Reformation controversy over whether good deeds merit salvation was clouded by misunderstandings. The Council of Trent, as did Aquinas, taught that no merit or salvation could ever be had without God's grace. But Catholic theologians* meant by salvation the whole process of justification* *and* sanctification,* and taught that our grace-enabled but freely chosen good deeds did have merit with God toward our salvation. Protestants, on the other hand, taught Luther's doctrine of justification by faith alone, a doctrine which Pope John Paul II* recently affirmed before German Lutheran bishops as Catholic doctrine also. Catholic theologians did not teach that people could buy their way into heaven simply by doing enough good deeds, though this view (technically a heresy) was popularly believed in Luther's day and still is by many poorly educated Catholics.

Revelation, Tradition and Reason. Catholic ethics is more traditional and less individualistic than Protestant ethics because of the Catholic emphasis on the authority of the church as a single worldwide community stretching back in time to Christ. Contributing to this tradition, like tributaries to a river, are both divine revelation and human reason. Revelation includes (1) the Word of God in person—Christ; (2) the Word of God in writing—the Scriptures; and (3) the teaching of the body of Christ—the church. The church is both mother and teacher in her officially formulated creeds defined *ex cathedra* and infallible, as well as in her ordinary teachings, which are not infallible but authoritative, like those of a wise mother. Reason includes (1) objective reason, the intelligible nature of things; (2) the individual's native power of intelligence; and (3) the written works of great thinkers and saints, especially Aquinas and Augustine, who is the chief common source for both Catholic and Protestant philosophers.

The authority of the teaching church and the unchangeableness of her moral teachings have increasingly been challenged by "dissenters" within the church, especially by European and American theologians in the years since Vatican II* and especially in areas of sexual morality (abortion, contraception, homosexual acts, premarital sex and divorce). All the popes since John XXIII* have used a less scholastic and more personalistic method, language and premises, but arrived at the same conclusions as the traditional moral teachings. These are unchangeable because they are based on natural law and on the teachings of Christ and the apostles, which the church has no authority to change. The Vatican's declaration in 1986 that theologians like Catholic University's* Professor Charles Curran (who dissent from essential church teachings, such as the intrinsic wrongness of abortion and homosexual acts) are not authentic Catholic theologians, is motivated by "truth in labeling" to protect her consumers (students) and by charity.

BIBLIOGRAPHY. St. Thomas Aquinas, *Summa Theologica*, I-II; E. Gilson, *Moral Values and the Moral Life* (1931); B. Häring, *The Law of Christ*, 3 vols. (1966); D. Von Hildebrand, *Christian Ethics* (1953); J. Maritain, *True Humanism* (1941); K. Woltiya, *Love and Responsibility: The Acting Person* (1981). P. J. Kreeft

Ethics, Protestant Personal.

Christian personal ethics is concerned with how one conducts one's life in the family, in the workplace and in the community, and it touches on issues of honesty, sexuality, the use of force and influence, and the management of resources. What is distinctive about Protestant* approaches to moral choice in the personal realm? There are significant differences in method between Protestant personal ethics and Roman Catholic* and Orthodox approaches. Catholic ethics recognizes two sources of moral knowledge, revelation and reason as it discerns the natural law. This gives it greater access to the results of philosophical reflection and to the Christian ethical tradition. By contrast, the Scriptures* are the primary focus in Protestant thinking. Theological ethicist James M. Gustafson notes that the Protestant tradition has always been characterized by "a return to Scripture directly and immediately." Gustafson regards as "the major differ-

ence" between Protestant and Roman Catholic thought the Protestant affirmation of a strict adherence to *sola scriptura*,* that Scripture alone is the normative guide for life, however much that principle might be stretched as application is made to contemporary issues.

Protestants not only emphasize Scripture but insist on individual freedom of interpretation and reject the tradition of detailed interpretation of quasi-legal ethical principles known as casuistry. Protestant ethics gains much of its diversity from the absence of a central church *magisterium*,* or teaching authority, employed by the Roman Catholic tradition.

Protestant personal ethics is, in a word, conservative. Protestants have tended to be absolutistic in their rejection of lying, extramarital sexual expression and homosexuality.* In addition, there has been a strain of thinking that is strongly suspicious of luxury, ostentatious display, and worldly ambition and gain. For the Protestant, all of life is lived unto God, and a final account will be given to him for every "deed done in the flesh." Even in its conservatism, however, Protestant ethics differs from Catholic ethics in that it does not ordinarily appeal to natural law. In the twentieth century most Protestants gave up their opposition to artificial birth control.* But Catholics were prevented from doing so by their teaching magisterium which maintains that artificial contraception is seriously against nature. Similarly, Protestants have come to accept sex practices in marriage* that Catholics still regard as seriously unnatural and immoral. Even in their opposition to homosexuality, Protestants rely almost exclusively on exegesis* of relevant biblical texts rather than an appeal to natural law.

The Protestant emphasis on Scripture as the authoritative source of ethical thinking was tested in this century when the fundamentalist-modernist controversy* erupted over the inspiration and ultimately the normative force of Scripture. Fundamentalists* saw Scripture as a set of propositional truths, of theological and ethical absolutes, which could be applied straightforwardly to present-day moral controversies. The liberal* factions within Protestantism tended to move toward what conservatives and even moderates regarded as relativism, consequentialism and situationalism.

As a result of this schism, fundamentalist and evangelical* Christianity felt itself shut out of the corridors of power in American society and began to emphasize personal ethics to the virtual exclusion of social ethics.* Liberal Protestant Christianity, on the other hand, led by Walter Rauschenbusch,* Reinhold Niebuhr* and others, focused on the social mission of the church. To the liberal, fundamentalists and evangelicals were obscurantists and withdrawn, while the latter group maintained that the liberals had sold out the Christian message for a "Social Gospel."* It was not until the post-war period that writers such as Carl F. H. Henry* would gain a hearing for a more positive evangelical social ethic with books such as *The Uneasy Conscience of Modern Fundamentalism* (1948).

If the liberal Protestant might be faulted for drifting into relativism and expediency, the life of the fundamentalist and evangelical left little room for experimentation and possible error. In this century evangelical personal ethics has devised rigid guidelines to cover virtually every area of life. Whereas their nineteenth-century forebears combined opposition to alcoholic* beverages and other "vices" with a positive thrust to shape society more in line with kingdom values, the less optimistic evangelicals of this century have developed legalistic* codes to govern their behavior even as they have expected the rest of society to slide into degradation. Traditional prohibitions against drinking, dancing, card playing, the use of tobacco and theater-going have persisted to the present day, joined by injunctions against newer temptations such as radio, television and motion pictures. Even styles of hair and dress came to be regulated. The effect of this almost Talmudic legalism on the Christian liberty so prized by Protestants was obvious, and it gave rise to what Edward J. Carnell* called a "cultic" faith. Nonetheless, it also tended to preserve a strong sense of evangelical belonging amidst the tumultuous social changes of this century. As these prohibitions lose their grip on newer generations of evangelicals, some have speculated that the sense of evangelical identity will be lost.

Evangelicals today display more diversity than in recent years. In issues such as women's roles and equality, the moral acceptability of homosexuality, the permissibility of abortion* and other issues, evangelicals argue positions undreamed of in past generations.

See also ETHICS, CATHOLIC PERSONAL.

BIBLIOGRAPHY. C. E. Curran, "Christian Ethics," *EncyR* 3:340-348; J. M. Gustafson, *Protestant and Roman Catholic Ethics* (1978); H. R. Niebuhr, *Christ and Culture* (1951). D. B. Fletcher

Ethnicity. *See* IMMIGRATION AND ETHNICITY.

Eucharist, Holy Communion or Lord's Supper. A liturgical* act utilizing bread and wine (or grape juice) and celebrating the death of Christ. Instituted by Christ at the Last Supper, this liturgical act is nearly universally celebrated by Christians, but its practice and meaning are by no means uniform and constitute one of the most divisive issues in the history of the church. In the pluralistic environment of American denominationalism,* it is understood as either a sacrament* or an ordinance, and is called by a variety of terms including: Mass,* Eucharist, Holy Communion, Lord's Supper, Sacrament of the Altar.

The four major sacramental traditions in North America are the Roman Catholic,* Eastern Orthodox,* Episcopal* and Lutheran.* Roman Catholics usually use the term *Mass* and believe that the elements of bread and wine are in their underlying reality changed into the body and blood of Jesus Christ. This doctrine, called *transubstantiation,* was promulgated by the Fourth Lateran Council in 1215. The Catholic understanding of the Mass as a eucharistic sacrifice was defined by the Council of Trent (1562). In recent years the doctrine has been restated by some Catholic theologians in order to avoid conflict with the once-for-all character of Christ's death, but the doctrine of the Mass remains a sensitive issue in Catholic-Protestant dialog. The Mass is always celebrated on Sundays and major feast days. Usually only baptized Catholics may receive the Sacrament, and a Catholic must receive it at least once a year. The Mass is the central rite of Catholic worship.*

The Eastern Orthodox Churches call the seven sacraments by the term *mysteries,* and the Holy Communion is referred to as *the Divine Liturgy.* Eastern Orthodoxy teaches that after the prayer of consecration* the bread and wine have become the body and blood of Christ, but the way this happens is a mystery. Immediately after receiving baptism* and chrismation (confirmation*), the new member, regardless of age, receives Holy Communion. The sacrament is administered by giving the communicant a piece of consecrated bread in a spoonful of consecrated wine from the chalice. Eastern Orthodox Christians are required to receive Holy Communion at least four times a year.

The Episcopal Churches, especially the Episcopal Church in the U.S., usually use the term *thanksgiving* for the Eucharist and teach that Jesus Christ is present in the meal. Christ's presence is affirmed but not explained. Bread and wine are used, and the 1979 *Book of Common Prayer* assumes a celebration every Sunday. In many parishes* all ages receive the Sacrament.

Lutherans usually refer to the meal as *Holy*

Communion and teach the real presence—Christ's body and blood are present "with, in and under" the bread and wine (*See* Consubstantiation). Some Lutherans have Holy Communion every Sunday, but a majority celebrate it on the first Sunday of the month. Most Lutheran bodies do not commune infants.

Presbyterian,* Congregational* and Reformed* Churches follow the teachings of John Calvin (1509-1564) and reject the doctrine of the presence of Christ's body. They teach that, during the Lord's Supper, Christ's body remains in heaven, but his spirit is in the meal and the faithful communicant receives Christ spiritually. While Calvin insisted on a weekly celebration, most churches in the Calvinist tradition have a monthly celebration.

Methodist* and Baptist* churches have traditionally called the meal *the Lord's Supper* and regarded it as a memorial recalling the death and sacrifice of Jesus, and stimulating faith and piety. It is more of a representative fellowship meal than a sacrament, and bread and grape juice, not wine, are used. Some, following the Reformer Ulrich Zwingli (1484-1531), suggest that the bread and grape juice signify or represent the body and blood of Christ. However, in recent years United Methodists and some within the American Baptist Churches, USA, have adopted a more sacramental understanding of the Lord's Supper as they have moved in the direction indicated by the ecumenical document *Baptism, Eucharist and Ministry* (1982).

Churches in the Restorationist* tradition (Disciples of Christ,* Christian Churches* and Churches of Christ*) celebrate the Lord's Supper weekly with bread and grape juice distributed to members seated in their pews. Like Baptists, they understand the meal as a memorial of the death of Jesus.

Many other American denominations do not emphasize the Eucharist and many understand it as nourishing only in a symbolic sense. The Salvation Army does not observe it at all.

See also SACRAMENTS AND ORDINANCES.

BIBLIOGRAPHY. *Baptism, Eucharist and Ministry* (1982); R. C. D. Jasper and G. S. Cuming, *Prayers of the Eucharist: Early and Reformed* (1975); J. A. Jungman, *The Mass of the Roman Rite: Its Origins and Development* (1956); H. T. Lehmann, ed., *Meaning and Practice of the Lord's Supper* (1961); B. Thompson, *Liturgies of the Western Church* (1962). D. S. Armentrout

Eucharistic Congress. *See* INTERNATIONAL EUCHARISTIC CONGRESS (XXVIII).

Eucharistic Devotions. Those acts of homage and adoration rendered by Roman Catholics* to the true presence of Jesus Christ under the eucharistic* elements of bread and wine. There have been a large number of such devotions* in the Roman Catholic Church, most of them developing either in the medieval period or in the period of the Catholic Reformation as a countersign to the eucharistic theology of the Protestant Reformation.

Some of the more common devotions range from the private act of praying before the tabernacle containing the eucharistic elements in a church to such public manifestations as the Feast of Corpus Christi* with its public processions or large gatherings at eucharistic congresses to honor Jesus Christ sacramentally* present. Somewhere between those poles would be such acts as blessing congregations with the Holy Eucharist (called Benediction of the Blessed Sacrament) or the exposure of the Eucharist in a receptacle, called a monstrance or ostensorium, for the adoration of the faithful. It was a pious custom in many Catholic parishes to do this for a fixed period on an annual basis; this devotion was known simply as "Forty Hours."

Since Vatican II* there has been a move to rethink such devotions in light of the centrality of the liturgy* in the life of the church, but their legitimacy is maintained in light of the Church's teaching of the real presence of Christ.

BIBLIOGRAPHY. C. Jones et al., *The Study of Liturgy* (1978). L. S. Cunningham

Euthanasia. The deliberate killing of a human being, either by acts of omission or commission, where the alleged intent is the benefit of the one being killed. Often referred to as "mercy killing," it is usually directed at the physically or mentally handicapped, the chronically ill or the elderly. Discussion of the issue is often confused by the terms used: "active" and "passive" euthanasia are sometimes distinguished, but the critical issue is intent, not method. The withdrawal of medical treatment when the pain and burden inflicted by the treatment itself outweighs its benefits to the patient (referred to as "extraordinary" or "heroic" means) is not euthanasia.

The Judaeo-Christian* tradition always condemned euthanasia; the movement to legalize it is a twentieth-century phenomenon, with agitation for it beginning in America in the 1930s. Starting in the 1960s bills were introduced in a number of state legislatures to legalize it. The case of Karen Ann Quinlan (1975) brought to the fore the issue of the removal of life-support systems from patients where the treatment was not itself painful or injurious. By the mid 1980s courts were permitting the withdrawal of food and water, causing the death of patients by dehydration and starvation. Allowing handicapped infants to die by withholding either food and water or necessary medical treatment had also become widespread. A case in Bloomington, Indiana (1972), caused a furor and led to the promulgation by the Reagan Administration of the "Baby Doe Regulations." Overturned by the courts, Congress in 1984 passed the Child Abuse Amendments to replace them.

The growing practice of euthanasia sparked the collaboration of pro-life and handicapped persons' rights activists, and in the late 1980s religiously oriented pro-life activists were realizing that their commitments must extend beyond the issue of abortion* to include euthanasia and other movements threatening the sanctity of human life.

BIBLIOGRAPHY. G. Grisez and J. M. Boyle, *Life and Death with Liberty and Justice: A Contribution to the Euthanasia Debate* (1979); D. J. Horan and D. Mall, *Death, Dying and Euthanasia* (1980); P. Ramsey, *The Patient as Person* (1970).

K. M. Cassidy

Evald, Emmy Carlsson (1857-1946). Lutheran missionary* leader. Evald is best known for helping to organize the Woman's Home and Foreign Missionary Society of the Augustana Lutheran Church (later Lutheran Church Women of the Lutheran Church in America) in 1892, and serving as its first president, a post she held for forty-three years. Under her gifted leadership the organization became "one of the greatest success stories in the history of the Augustana Church." Twenty-five years after its inception, the missionary society had raised nearly $200,000 and supported doctors, teachers, nurses, missionaries and evangelists* in China, India, Africa and Puerto Rico. Until 1920 the Women's Missionary Society budget was greater than that of the entire denomination.* In Chicago, Evald helped found the Augustana Hospital in 1884 and Lutheran Women's League. She was also a charter member of the International Suffrage Association and appeared before the Illinois State Legislature and U.S. Congress to promote the cause.

BIBLIOGRAPHY. G. Hall, *The Missionary Spirit in the Augustana Church* (1985); G. E. Arden, *Augustana Heritage* (1963). M. L. Bendroth

Evangelical Alliance. One of the earliest attempts to bring about Protestant* cooperation. The Evangelical Alliance was formed in London in 1846 at a large convention at which more than fifty

evangelical* groups from Europe and America were represented. America's participation in the organization was fostered by Samuel S. Schmucker* of Gettysburg Theological Seminary, who had published a *Plan for Protestant Union* in 1838. He proposed the formation of a group which, while respecting denominational* differences, would permit all American Protestants to agree to a common creed* and practice intercommunion.

Nothing came of his idea then, but eight years later seventy-five American clergymen* journeyed to London to participate in the founding of the Evangelical Alliance. The American group came mostly from the seaboard states and from the Reformed* denominations. The individuals gathered in London agreed to a very broad creedal basis, but no long-range program was established for the future. When English and American delegates engaged in discussions about the morality of slavery, a great controversy developed that ruined the Evangelical Alliance as a worldwide organization. The outcome was a consensus that each nation represented should form its own Evangelical Alliance.

The Evangelical Alliance in the U.S. was formed in 1867, being active in furthering numerous cooperative enterprises. Several national conferences were called, in Pittsburgh (1875); Detroit (1877); St. Louis (1879); Washington (1887); Boston (1889); and at the Columbian Exposition in Chicago in 1893. Probably the greatest of the meetings was held in New York in 1873, a conference to which all the European branches of the Alliance were invited to send representatives. By 1900 the influence of the Evangelical Alliance was waning in America, and in 1908 it was followed by the Federal Council of Churches in Christ in America.*

In surveys of American history the diversity of American religious life rather than its unity is stressed. In the early years of the nineteenth century, however, unity prevailed as a strong theme and carried over into the remainder of the century. Organizations like the American Tract Society,* American Bible Society,* American Sunday School Union* and the American Home Missionary Society,* to name a few, were supported by clergy and laymen* in many different denominations. Christians in various denominations also joined together in their attack on several notable evils, including intemperance, slavery, war and dueling. Thus America's participation in the London conference in 1846 was the one additional step taken which some Christian leaders hoped would result in the formation of a society uniting all Protestants. The strength of anti-Catholicism and nativism* were also significant in these efforts toward unity.

From its beginning in 1867, the Evangelical Alliance in the U.S. sought to demonstrate that evangelical identity and spiritual unity undergirded religious diversity. Evangelicals also desired to show the superiority of a democratic* society, but the great gap between the elites of the Alliance and the masses of the population mitigated against the very unity sought by the organization. By the end of the century, it was clear that the goals of the Alliance could not be accommodated to the contemporary individualism* of laissez faire economic and social philosophies.

BIBLIOGRAPHY. P. D. Jordan, *The Evangelical Alliance for the United States of America, 1847-1900* (1983).   R. R. Mathisen

Evangelical Alliance Mission, The. An evangelical* foreign mission* society, originally known as the Scandinavian Alliance Mission. The Mission was founded by Fredrik Franson,* a Swedish-born immigrant who was converted* in the U.S. and commissioned to ministry by the Moody* Church in Chicago. Challenged by Hudson Taylor's call for 1,000 missionaries for China, Franson determined to seek out at least one hundred volunteers. In October of 1890 he began a Bible* and training course for young people in Brooklyn, New York (the Mission dates its founding to that event), and a short while later organized a mission board in Chicago. Many of the churches* to which he appealed for personnel and money had no organized missionary program, so the mission was designed to combine their efforts with those of interested individuals in a cooperative outreach. A majority of these churches and individuals being of Scandinavian background, the early name of the organization was The Scandinavian Alliance Mission of North America. Not until 1949 was the name changed to The Evangelical Alliance Mission (TEAM).

TEAM is primarily committed to ministries of evangelism,* church planting and church development, but has initiated and maintained supporting ministries in medicine, linguistics, literature, education, Christian camping and radio. In 1987 there were approximately 929 full-time and 150 short-term missionaries working on twenty-nine fields and a home staff of ninety-nine. In North America the mission maintains an office in Regina, Saskatchewan, and a home office in Carol Stream, Illinois. It is a member of the Interdenominational Foreign Mission Association* and publishes *TEAM Horizons* and *Wherever* magazines.

BIBLIOGRAPHY. V. Mortenson, *Light is Sprung Up* (1965); V. Mortenson, *This is TEAM* (1973); D. Pape, *Branch of His Planting* (1962); E. P. Torjesen, *A Study of Fredrik Franson* (1984).

D. J. Hesselgrave

Evangelical Church. *See* GERMAN-AMERICAN REVIVALISM; UNITED METHODIST CHURCH.

Evangelical Covenant Church of America. A Free Church* denomination.* Founded in Chicago in 1885 as the Swedish Evangelical Mission Covenant of America, the Evangelical Covenant Church of America traces its roots back to the pietistic* revivals* in eighteenth- and nineteenth-century Sweden. Dissatisfied with what they viewed as the formalism and lack of spiritual warmth of the state Lutheran* Church of Sweden, groups of "mission friends" began to meet in conventicles in which leaders would direct small groups in prayer,* singing and explication of Scripture.* After immigration to America, the connections with the Lutheran Church became more and more tenuous, until finally on February 20, 1885, the new denomination was formed.

Rather than formulate a new creed,* the founders of the church determined that the final authority* of Scripture, along with affirmations of the historic creeds of the church, particularly the Apostles' Creed, would define the group. The Evangelical Covenant Church of America has been described as evangelical,* but not exclusive; biblical, but not doctrinaire; traditional, but not rigid; and congregational,* but not independent. The Reformation doctrine of justification* by grace through faith has been regarded as fundamental to the dual tasks of evangelism* and Christian nurture.

The Church is governed by the annual meeting of ministers* and laypersons* who serve as delegates from the churches. An executive board elected by the annual meeting implements its decisions. There are eleven geographical districts governed by superintendents who, among other duties, guide local churches in their calling of ministers. Publications by the denomination are the monthly *Covenant Companion* and the quarterlies *Covenant Quarterly* and *Covenant Home Altar.*

The headquarters of the denomination are in Chicago, where also are located the Swedish Covenant Hospital School of Nursing and North Park College and Theological Seminary. The

Evangelical Covenant Church also supports a Bible institute* in Canada and Minnehaha Academy in Minneapolis. Mission fields are in Africa, Alaska, China, Ecuador, Colombia, Japan, Mexico and Thailand. In the late 1980s the church had 86,079 members in 570 churches.

BIBLIOGRAPHY. D. C. Frisk, *Covenant Affirmations* (1981); K. A. Olsson, *By One Spirit* (1962).

S. R. Graham

Evangelical Fellowship of Canada. A national fellowship of Canadian evangelicals.* The Evangelical Fellowship of Canada (EFC) began in 1964 in Toronto as a fellowship of pastors* serving in both mainline* and uniformly evangelical denominations.* Defending orthodoxy* and encouraging evangelism* were central concerns, but committees were formed also for social action, education, spiritual life and inter-church relations. Affiliated with the World Evangelical Fellowship,* the EFC has directed the Canadian division of World Relief. A magazine, *Faith Today,* has brought Christian opinion on current events and news of evangelical ministries in Canada to a national audience. Since 1975 seminars have sought to strengthen church leadership. With the appointment of Brian C. Stiller as its first full-time executive director in 1983, the EFC has grown rapidly. By the late 1980s it included more than twenty denominations and an aggregate membership of more than one million. It also has responded to political issues, notably on those related to the new constitution, freedom of religion and family life.

BIBLIOGRAPHY. J. G. Stackhouse, Jr., "Proclaiming the Word: Canadian Evangelicalism since the First World War" (unpublished Ph.D. dissertation, University of Chicago, 1987). J. G. Stackhouse

Evangelical Foreign Missions Association. A fellowship of eighty-seven evangelical* missionary* organizations which either send missionaries or directly support the North American missionary endeavor.

The history of the Evangelical Foreign Mission Association (EFMA) is intricately intertwined with that of the National Association of Evangelicals* (NAE). When the NAE was formed in 1944 as an expression of cooperation by evangelical denominations, churches and individuals, there was an immediate recognition that denominations had missions departments that were not in touch with each other in any specific way.

Clyde W. Taylor,* having returned from missionary service in Colombia, South America, with the Christian and Missionary Alliance,* became chairman of a missions committee of NAE and moved to Washington, D.C., to serve the interests of missions. Taylor called a conference of missions which brought together thirty-nine agencies. A core group drawn from these agencies moved quickly to form the Evangelical Foreign Missions Association, which organized during a meeting held on September 19-20, 1945, at the LaSalle Hotel in Chicago, Illinois. There were fourteen charter members.

Taylor became its first executive secretary, a post he held until December 1974, when he was succeeded by Wade T. Coggins, a Christian and Missionary Alliance missionary who had served in Colombia. Coggins has continued to lead as executive director.

Missionary News Service (MNS) was instituted in 1954 as a twice-monthly service to member missions and other subscribers. In 1963 the EFMA and the Interdenominational Foreign Mission Association* formed a joint publishing arm called Evangelical Missions Information Service, which started *Evangelical Missions Quarterly* and later *Pulse.* Missionary News Service was integrated into Evangelical Missions Information Service in 1970.

Since its formation in 1945, EFMA has been a voice for mission concerns, providing a channel for cooperation and many services, including conferences, seminars, workshops, publications, government liaison and visa procurement. The EFMA is controlled by a board of directors composed of missions leaders elected at the annual convention and financed by its member missions. Its constituent members in 1986 had 12,564 missionaries serving in more than 130 countries.

See also INTERDENOMINATIONAL FOREIGN MISSION ASSOCIATON. W. T. Coggins

Evangelical Free Church of America. An evangelical* denomination* with roots in the Scandinavian free church* movement. Born out of revival among the scattered immigrants who had left the Lutheran* State Church in Scandinavia to come to America, the denomination dates officially to a conference of free churches* held in Boone, Iowa, in 1884. In 1950 the Evangelical Free Church of America (Swedish) and the Evangelical Free Church Association (Norwegian-Danish) merged into the present body, The Evangelical Free Church of America.

Committed to the absolute authority of the Scriptures* and the premillenial* and imminent return of the Lord, the EFCA statement of faith clearly enunciates the cardinal doctrines of the church but allows latitude in what it regards as "non-essentials to salvation," such as Calvinism* and Arminianism,* baptism,* spiritual gifts and eschatological* details compatible with premillennialism. The term *Free* indicates a congregational* form of government wherein individual churches hold title to property as well as decide and govern their own affairs.

In the late 1980s there were approximately 1,000 Evangelical Free Church congregations in the U.S. and Canada with an active membership of 100,000. The U.S. and Canadian bodies maintain a fraternal relationship, with each publishing a separate edition of the official organ, *The Evangelical Beacon,* and sharing one overseas mission board overseeing over 400 missionaries on fourteen foreign fields. The denomination operates Trinity Evangelical Divinity School and Trinity College in Deerfield, Illinois, as well as Trinity Western University in Langley, British Columbia.

BIBLIOGRAPHY. C. B. Hanson, *What It Means to Be Free* (1988); A. T. Olson, *This We Believe* (1961); A. T. Olson, *The Search for Identity* (1980).   C. B. Hanson

Evangelical Friends Alliance. An organization of evangelical* Friends* churches. Formed in 1965, the Alliance united Friends who had been influenced by evangelicalism. Appealing to the evangelical roots of Quakers in the seventeenth century, they include the Evangelical Friends Church, Eastern Division, which in the early nineteenth century came to include the Gurneyites,* the evangelically inclined followers of Joseph John Gurney.* The Gurneyites eventually adopted revivalistic* methods and the pastoral system of ministry rather than the traditional Quaker system of untrained and unsalaried itinerants.* In the late nineteenth century they were influenced by the burgeoning Holiness Movement.*

The Evangelical Friends have attracted evangelical congregations of Friends from across the U.S. and now consists of four regional yearly meetings or districts. The Alliance supports Malone College in Canton, Ohio, an institution originally founded by Walter and Emma Malone* in 1892 as the Christian Workers Training School.

The Editors

Evangelical Liberalism (1880-1930). A Protestant movement, also termed *New Theology* or *Progressive Orthodoxy.* During the first two decades after the Civil War,* American Protestants* experienced serious challenges to their way of looking at the world. German scholarship reached American seminaries* and encouraged the development of historical criticism of both Scripture* and doctrine.* Further, many American intellectuals accepted evolution* as a scientific account of humanity's origins and were using it to undergird a belief in progress as the key to understanding history. In response to these academic developments, many Protestant theologians* began to devise a "New Theology" or "Progressive Orthodoxy." These thinkers attempted a synthesis between the old faith and the new scientific thought, hoping to preserve the main lines of Christian orthodoxy* in an expression more suitable for modern times.

Evangelical liberalism represented a transformation of Calvinistic* orthodoxy, even though it retained the traditional theological language. Its theologians stressed human goodness rather than original sin,* emphasized an ever-present God of love without much mention of a transcendent God of wrath and punishment, focused on religious experience over correctness of doctrine and shared an optimistic belief that human actions would eventually overcome human need and culminate in the kingdom of God.* Above all, these progressive theologians made Christ the center of their theology by featuring the relevance of his life as both model and source for the ethical and religious life of humanity. For them, Christ-centered beliefs about reality were substantiated by the practical results of Christian experience.

The movement's most popular representatives were preachers like Henry Ward Beecher,* Phillips Brooks,* Lyman Abbott* and Harry Emerson Fosdick.* Its theologians were found in American seminaries where their work generally escaped public awareness. Included among them were George Harris,* William Newton Clarke,* Theodore Munger,* William Adams Brown,* A. C. Knudson* and Eugene W. Lyman.* Evangelical liberalism's more thoughtful social critics were Washington Gladden* and Walter Rauschenbusch.*

See also LIBERALISM/MODERNISM, PROTESTANT.

BIBLIOGRAPHY. K. Cauthen, *The Impact of American Religious Liberalism* (1962); B. Kuklick, *Churchmen and Philosophers* (1985); D. D. Williams, *The Andover Liberals: A Study in American Theology* (1941).   M. G. Toulouse

Evangelical Lutheran Church in America. The largest Lutheran* denomination* in America. The Evangelical Lutheran Church in America (ELCA) was organized April 20-May 3, 1987, in Columbus, Ohio, and officially born on January 1, 1988. It represents the merger of three Lutheran bodies: the Lutheran Church in America* (2.9 million members), the American Lutheran Church* (2.3 million members) and the Association of Evangelical Lutheran Churches* (110,000 members). The ELCA has its central office in Chicago. The 5,307,000 members and 11,174 churches are divided into 65 geographical synods grouped into nine regions.

See also LUTHERAN CHURCHES.

BIBLIOGRAPHY. T. W. Nichol, *All These Lutherans: Three Paths Toward a New Lutheran Church* (1986). The Editors

Evangelical Lutheran Church in Canada. The largest Lutheran* body in Canada. The Evangelical Lutheran Church in Canada (ELCC) is the product of a number of mergers, most of which took place in the U.S.A. Because Canadian Lutheranism has had close links with the U.S., both official and unofficial, these unions were experienced north of the border as well.

The first phase of ELCC came into being in 1960 and had three components. The largest constituent was the Canadian district of the American Lutheran Church,* which was largely in Eastern Canada and predominantly of German origin. It had originally been part of the Ohio Synod, which was long known for its robust theological conservatism and its keen sense of Lutheran distinctiveness.

The next element, and almost as large, was the Canadian district of the Evangelical Lutheran Church, which existed in Western Canada. This body was primarily Norwegian and represented the powerful evangelical movement which had developed in the homeland during the nineteenth century. While professing full loyalty to the Lutheran confessions and form of worship,* there was a great deal of active lay* involvement; prayer* meetings and evangelistic* services were commonplace, and Christian discipline frequently expressed itself most visibly in total abstinence from alcoholic* beverage and the shunning of dancing. This segment brought a developed infrastructure, with a Bible college, a junior college and a seminary.

The smallest component was the Canadian section of the Danish United Evangelical Lutheran Church. Together these became the Canadian district of the American Lutheran Church and was known as the Evangelical Lutheran Church of Canada.

In 1967 the second phase of ELCC came into operation as in Canada's Confederation year it became autonomous. The third phase occurred in 1985, when the Evangelical Lutheran Church of Canada joined with the Canadian district of the Lutheran Church in America, retaining autonomy and being known as the Evangelical Lutheran Church in Canada.

BIBLIOGRAPHY. G. O. Evenson, *Adventuring for Christ: The Story of the Evangelical Lutheran Church in Canada* (1974). I. S. Rennie

Evangelical Mennonite Brethren Conference. See FELLOWSHIP OF EVANGELICAL BIBLE CHURCHES.

Evangelical Presbyterian Church. See REFORMED PRESBYTERIAN CHURCH.

Evangelical Protestant Church of North America. See UNITED CHURCH OF CHRIST.

Evangelical Theological Society. An organization of North American theologians* and Bible scholars. On December 27 and 28, 1949, the first organizational meeting of the Evangelical Theological Society (ETS) took place in Cincinnati, Ohio. Earlier in the year members from the faculty of Gordon Divinity School had sensed the need to establish a society in which scholars from various denominational* backgrounds might unite to defend the doctrine of the inerrancy* of Scripture* and promote conservative biblical scholarship. At Cincinnati a constitution was drawn up which included the doctrinal basis for the society [Article 3]: belief in the inerrancy of the Bible* in the original autographs. The Society began to hold annual meetings, sponsored the publication of several works of evangelical scholarship and in 1958 launched its own journal, the *Bulletin of the Evangelical Theological Society,* later known as the *Journal of the Evangelical Theological Society.*

In the 1970s and 1980s, as debates ensued in the broader evangelical community regarding the meaning and normative character of biblical inerrancy for evangelical self-identity, ETS witnessed a series of cases in which the views of a number of its members were assessed in relation to their conformity with the doctrinal basis of the Society. Despite occasional tensions within the Society, ETS has remained for some four decades a society of healthy theological discussion and exploration in the context of a firm commitment to the truthfulness of Holy Scripture.

BIBLIOGRAPHY. M. A. Noll, *Between Faith and Criticism* (1986); J. Wiseman, "Index to the Bulletin/Journal of the Evangelical Theological Society, Volumes 1-25, 1958-1982," *JETS* (28:5) 1985:5-24. J. D. Woodbridge

Evangelical United Brethren Church. *See* UNITED METHODIST CHURCH.

Evangelical United Front. A network of benevolent societies formed by Protestants* to define America in Christian terms. The republican philosophy of the new nation called for a virtuous, self-reliant citizenry. But the social disruption, political bickering and rapid western settlement of the early years raised fears about the future. Beginning in 1816, Protestant leaders in the Northeast founded over one hundred interdenominational, voluntary societies* to foster religion, morality and education, the pillars of a Christian republic. The movement combined republican philosophy with the millennialism* of the Second Great Awakening,* which accorded America a special role in the imminent establishment of the kingdom of God.*

Among the best-known societies were the American Bible Society* (1816), American Tract Society* (1825), American Sunday School Union* (1824), American Education Society* (1816), American Home Missions Society* (1826) and the American Temperance Society* (1826). The effort declined by the 1840s with the growth of denominational* concerns, religious division and the financial impact of the Panic of 1837.

BIBLIOGRAPHY. C. I. Foster, *An Errand of Mercy: The Evangelical United Front* (1960); R. L. Handy, *A Christian America: Protestant Hopes and Historical Realities* (1971). G. W. Carlson

Evangelicalism. A movement in North American Christianity that emphasizes the classical Protestant* doctrines* of salvation,* the church and the authority* of the Scriptures,* but in the American context it is characterized by stress on a personal experience of the grace of God, usually termed the *new birth** or *conversion.** Estimates of evangelical strength in the U.S. and Canada run as high as fifty million, making it one of the major expressions of Christianity in North America.

Evangelicalism has been shaped by three significant periods of modern Christianity: first, the Protestant Reformation of the sixteenth century and especially its expression in English Puritanism*; second, the evangelical revivals* of the eighteenth century and third, the conservative reaction to modern America in the twentieth century, often called fundamentalism.*

The Protestant Reformation, 1517-1560. The Protestant Reformation, the sixteenth-century challenge to traditional Roman Catholicism,* was the first movement to shape the character of American evangelical Christianity. In the genera-

tion between 1520 and 1560, the Reformation assumed four major expressions: Lutheran*; Reformed,* or Calvinistic; Anglican*; and Anabaptist,* forerunners of modern Baptists* and Mennonites.*

These early Protestants denied that they were starting a new church. The Reformation, they said, was simply a rediscovery of the gospel within the historic Catholic tradition. The earliest generations of Protestantism had no thoughts of challenging the doctrines of Jesus Christ, the Holy Trinity, the universal sinfulness* of humans, the resurrection of the body and the life to come. As a result, much of what American evangelicals believe about God, Jesus Christ, humanity, sin and the eternal world, they owe to this Catholic tradition. They do not hesitate to confess, with other Christians, the Apostles' or the Nicene Creeds.

The Protestant Reformation, however, was in a special way a restatement of the gospel. While Martin Luther, John Calvin, Menno Simons and scores of other Protestant Reformers did not challenge the orthodox* tradition of early Christianity, they did call into court the medieval doctrines of salvation and the church. Their answers to four traditional Catholic questions created the division between the evangelical Protestant and the Catholic branches of Christianity that continues to this day.

These four questions were: what must a person do to be saved? where does religious authority lie? what is the church? and what is the essence of Christian living?

To the first question the Roman Catholic Church answered, justification* before God comes by a combination of faith and good works. The Protestant Reformers, however, answered the question in a sharply different way. They said that a person is justified in God's sight through faith in the Lord Jesus Christ alone. While good works are the fruit of this relationship, they are incapable of obtaining it.

To the second question—where does religious authority lie?—the Roman Catholic Church answered that Christians find out what they must believe and how they must live from the sacred institution established by Jesus Christ on Peter and his successors, the bishops* of Rome. Protestant Reformers, however, said that Christians find all truth necessary for their faith and behavior in one source, the Bible,* the written Word of God (*See* Sola Scriptura).

To the third question—what is the church?—the Roman Catholic Church answered that the true church is that sacred hierarchical and priestly

[413]

institution that Jesus Christ founded on Peter, the first pope, and on the apostles, the first bishops.

The Protestant Reformers responded differently. The true church, they said, is not a sacred hierarchy. It is a community of faith in which all true believers share the priestly task (*See* Priesthood of Believers), not with some physical sacrifice but with spiritual ones of praise, gifts and service to God and one another.

In response to the fourth question—what is the essence of Christian living?—the Reformers swept aside the Catholic argument for monasticism and taught instead that the essence of Christian living lies in serving God in one's calling whether in secular or ecclesiastical life. All useful callings are equally sacred in God's eyes.

Today, the Roman Catholic Church no longer condemns the Reformers, and many Protestants no longer accept the Reformation explanation of the gospel. But these basic questions and their answers explain why at the time of the Reformation the term *evangelical* was used to designate Lutherans and their attempt to renew the church on the basis of the authoritative Word of God, and why still later it was applied collectively to Lutheran and Reformed communions in Germany. Today many American Christians in Lutheran and Reformed churches continue in the tradition of this Reformation restatement of the gospel.

The Evangelical Revivals, 1720-1860. During the seventeenth century the vigorous defense of the gospel in the Protestant Reformation was replaced by an unyielding spirit of Protestant orthodoxy. Calvinists argued about God's eternal decrees and Lutherans about the presence of Christ in the Lord's Supper.* Throughout northern Europe Protestantism was legal, acceptable, orthodox and generally lifeless. Justification by faith was a doctrine to debate more than a life to experience.

A series of renewal movements, however, changed the face of traditional Protestantism and gave fresh meaning to the term *evangelical.* As a result of these awakenings, *evangelical* came to mean "born again"* Christianity, the experience of the Holy Spirit in a life-changing way.

The first of these revivals was a movement in Germany termed *Pietism.* Sparked in the late seventeenth century by Lutheran pastor Philipp Jacob Spener and the Lutheran professor of Hebrew, August Hermann Francke, Pietism stressed heartfelt faith through Bible study,* prayer* and mutual care within the church. The Pietists admired Luther and tried to return to his original emphasis on the gospel. They argued, however, that the state church in Germany was little help in

this spiritual venture. The state church, they said, had preserved Luther's doctrine of justification by faith by freezing it in creedal statements. What men and women needed most was the regenerating life of the Spirit; they needed to experience justification personally.

In northern Germany Pietism spread under Count Nicholas von Zinzendorf's* leadership by energizing a refugee group from Moravia called the Moravian Brethren.* In other areas of Europe Pietism blended with the Anabaptist tradition to produce the Mennonite and German Brethren* bodies we know today. But perhaps its greatest contribution to evangelicalism was through its influence upon John Wesley.*

From the Moravians, Wesley discovered that justification by faith could be an instantaneous experience. On May 24, 1738, at a Moravian meeting in Aldersgate Street, London, Wesley felt for the first time in his life that he did trust in Christ alone for salvation. A short time later, when he entered the open fields near Bristol to preach to 3,000 people, he found his life's calling as the most prominent spokesman for England's greatest spiritual awakening.

The American colonial counterpart of the Methodist* revival in the British Isles was the Great Awakening.* The revival appeared first in the 1720s as a series of regional awakenings. But under the incendiary preaching* ministry of John Wesley's friend George Whitefield,* the regional revivals merged into a Great Awakening that continued until the American Revolution. Most of the preachers of the Great Awakening freely confessed their admiration for their Puritan fathers, the leaders of the renewal movement within the Church of England that had shaped British life a century earlier.

Puritans originally stood for a life-transforming experience of the gospel that would be reflected in the structures of the church and the state. The revivalists of the Great Awakening, like the Puritans, preached the necessity of an invisible transformation of the soul, but they no longer dreamed of establishing a holy commonwealth as the Puritan Fathers did.

The evangelical call for an instantaneous conversion to Christ continued through the nineteenth century in camp meetings* and revivals and classrooms all across America. Evangelicals formed an alliance with American republicanism to claim the American wilderness for a "Christian America." Through educators such as President Timothy Dwight* of Yale,* and revivalists such as Charles Finney* at Oberlin* and circuit-riding* preachers such as Peter Cartwright,* evangelical Christianity emerged as the dominant faith in America before the Civil War.*

It echoed in ten thousand classrooms when a million McGuffey* Readers opened for the daily reading lesson. And when the slavery crisis plunged the nation into its bloodiest conflict, interpreters of the war, including President Abraham Lincoln,* turned to the evangelical themes of judgment, suffering and atonement* to explain the nation's tragedy.

William G. McLoughlin has dared to say that the story of American evangelicalism during the nineteenth century is the story of America itself. As motivation and rationale, "evangelical religion lay behind the concept of rugged individualism* in business enterprise, laissez faire in economic theory, constitutional democracy* in political thought, the Protestant ethic in morality, and the millennial hope in the manifest destiny* of white, Anglo-Saxon, Protestant America to lead the world to its latter-day glory."

The Fundamentalist Movement, 1920-1960. During the critical years between the Civil War and World War 1,* evangelicalism was dethroned as the reigning religious perspective of American society. The most highly publicized symbol of this overthrow was the famous Scopes Trial* in Dayton, Tennessee, fought over the teaching of evolution in America's public schools.*

The explanation of this struggle and evangelicalism's place in twentieth-century America lies in the fears and reactions of conservative evangelicals in the face of the rapid changes that swept over America after the Civil War. The changes were breathtaking in their speed and wide-ranging in their impact. We may focus on the three that troubled evangelical Protestants the most.

The first change was in the make-up of American society. Prior to the Civil War, America was largely a rural and small-town country, sympathetic with evangelical Christianity. After the war, however, millions of immigrants* streamed into Ellis Island in New York Harbor. Many of these were professing Roman Catholics, Lutherans and Jews, none of whom shared the Puritan and revivalistic traditions of American evangelicals. In three short decades these immigrations changed the face of religion in America.

Millions of these immigrants settled in the burgeoning cities of the nation: New York, Chicago, Boston, Philadelphia and St. Louis. That is where America's short-term future lay. Political power, ethnic pluralism, industrial strength, media coverage and liberal lifestyles were all concentrated in the cities. Many evangelical Protestants caught a glimpse of the future and were troubled by what they saw: the end of evangelical social dominance in America.

The next change in America was a shift in the way people thought about reality. The most dramatic illustration of this was the Scopes Trial, but the conflict of popular philosophies was rooted in the ideas of Charles Darwin's *The Origin of Species* (1859). The book's doctrine of evolution* did not directly challenge the evangelical understanding of God and creation, but popular speculation about its meaning tended to discount the traditional explanation of the origin of life and the personal God behind the universe. Everywhere, it seemed, men and women thought in terms of process, progress and evolution; no longer in terms of creation, miracles and new birth.

The third significant change was centrally religious. In the theological schools and Christian liberal arts colleges, professors in increasing numbers accepted a new approach to the Bible termed *higher criticism.* This was an attempt to employ the so-called scientific methods of literary investigation in the study of the Bible. The fundamental presupposition of this approach was that the Bible was a piece of literature like any other ancient document, nothing more. It was filled with the myths and folklore and religious insights of an ancient people, just as other books of the times.

Conservative Protestants saw clearly the damaging consequence of this new discipline. It undercut the special revelation in the Bible; it left the Christian minister without a supernatural gospel to preach; and it provided no basis for the evangelical experience of the new birth.

The first three decades of the twentieth century brought a bitter conflict that historians call the Fundamentalist-Modernist Controversy.* Those in traditional Protestant denominations* who welcomed the fast-paced changes in American society and tried to adapt the Christian faith to these changes were called "modernists."* They tried to retain the traditional Protestant hold on America by modifying the traditional doctrines of the Christian faith in order to reconcile them with science, evolution and religious pluralism.* The fundamentalists resisted changes in American society and defended a supernatural Christianity by emphasizing an infallible Bible and Jesus Christ as the divine Savior. This threw them into conflict with American society and made them appear outdated and irrelevant.

In the leadership of most traditional denominations, "modernist" thinking prevailed and fundamentalists were forced either to remain in their denominations and give passive support to denominational programs or to separate from their denomination and throw their support to independent parachurch* ministries.

The years after World War 2* saw a dramatic turn-around. In the judgment of many conservative Protestants, fundamentalism had reached unacceptable positions in its resistance to American culture. Harold John Ockenga,* Carl F. H. Henry,* Bernard Ramm and other heirs of fundamentalism questioned the movement's tendency to justify denominational separatism,* social and cultural irresponsibility, and anti-intellectualism.

The creation of the National Association of Evangelicals* in 1943 gave these questioning conservatives a new forum for cooperation. *Christianity Today,* founded in 1956, helped forge a broadly based coalition of evangelicals. And Fuller Theological Seminary,* founded in 1947, led scores of evangelical schools into a new quest for academic excellence. At the center of most of this new vitality was the extensive ministry of evangelist* Billy Graham.* Each of his crusades mobilized support from a broadly based evangelical constituency. In the 1960s a related movement, the charismatic movement,* added new vitality to American evangelicalism. By 1976 this new coalition of evangelicals gained national attention when Southern Baptist* Jimmy Carter* was elected president of the U.S.

The precise boundaries of contemporary evangelicalism in North America are hard to identify. Since it is composed of a host of small denominations and parachurch ministries, historians tend to speak of "mosaics" and "kaleidoscopes" when they try to describe it. Within a broad unity based on commitment to the Bible as its religious authority and on the gospel of Christ's saving work as the church's central message, we can identify at least seven evangelical traditions of faith:

1. Evangelicals in the Reformation tradition, primarily Lutheran and Reformed Christians

2. Wesleyan* evangelicals, such as the Church of the Nazarene*

3. Pentecostal* and charismatic evangelicals, such as the Assemblies of God*

4. Black evangelicals, with their own distinctive witness to the gospel

5. The counterculture churches (sometimes called Peace Churches), such as the evangelical Quakers* and Mennonites

6. Several traditionally white Southern denominations, led by the Southern Baptists

7. The spiritual heirs of fundamentalism found in independent churches and many parachurch agencies.

Perhaps the best summation of evangelical convictions in recent years is found in the covenant signed by about three thousand evangelicals who gathered at Lausanne, Switzerland, in July 1974 for the Lausanne Congress on World Evangelization.* This covenant describes what twentieth-century evangelicals believe and what they hope to do in the world.

See also FUNDAMENTALISM; NEW EVANGELICALISM.

BIBLIOGRAPHY. D. W. Dayton, *Discovering an Evangelical Heritage* (1976); D. E. Harrell, Jr., *Varieties of Southern Evangelicalism* (1981); J. D. Hunter, *American Evangelicalism* (1983); G. M. Marsden, *Fundamentalism and American Culture* (1980); G. M. Marsden, *Reforming Fundamentalism* (1987); G. M. Marsden, ed., *Evangelicalism and Modern America* (1984); W. G. McLoughlin, ed., *The American Evangelicals, 1800-1900* (1968); L. I. Sweet, *The Evangelical Tradition in America* (1984); J. D. Woodbridge, M. A. Noll, N. O. Hatch, *The Gospel in America* (1979).

B. L. Shelley

Evangelism and Evangelists. In the New Testament, evangelism is the spread of the gospel, or good news, by means of proclamation or announcement. The New Testament Greek verb *euangelizomai* means to announce the *euangelion,* or good news. New Testament evangelism is defined by its content or *message,* and not by its *methods* or *results.*

An evangelist is the person who carries out evangelism, proclaiming the good news of Jesus Christ. Though the word *evangelist* is a common term in American Christianity, it appears only three times in the New Testament. In each case the Greek word *euangelistes* refers to one who is called and empowered by God to proclaim the good news of Jesus. In North America the term *evangelist* has most often been used of mass evangelists in the revivalist tradition.

The message and methods of evangelism have evolved along with the nation. With the Great Awakening* arose the itinerant* evangelists, exemplified by George Whitefield, who were freed from the constraints of a settled ministry. Typically young and operating outside ecclesiastical sanctions and the familiar setting of the meeting house,* they depended on their ability to establish rapport with their audiences and proclaim a simple gospel message calling for new birth.* The Methodists* adopted the model of the itinerant preacher* and evangelist and made it an institution of the American frontier. Known as circuit riders,* the effectiveness of these evangelists was exemplified in figures such as Francis Asbury* and Peter Cartwright.*

In the Reformed* tradition, evangelists were trained in the methods of revivalism by William and Gilbert Tennent* at their "Log College,"* and were prepared to preach at any time and at any place. In the early nineteenth century, evangelistic camp meetings* served both social and spiritual needs and were a unique contribution of the American frontier to the history of evangelism. With a settled frontier, evangelism became institutionalized, particularly in the South, where evangelists held occasional or yearly preaching services known as "revivals."*

During the nineteenth century, revivalists and evangelists such as Charles G. Finney* and Dwight L. Moody* preached in churches, though they eventually moved to larger public facilities to accomodate the crowds. This tradition of the evangelistic preacher would continue through individuals such as R. A. Torrey,* Billy Sunday,* Modecai Ham* and Billy Graham.* Today, the tradition of mass evangelism has been adapted to the electronic medium by the so-called "televangelists." The effectiveness of these evangelists throughout American history is best measured by their ability to speak the simple but profound truth of the gospel in the language of everyday experience.

Since World War 2,* there has been an increasing emphasis on evangelism that is more personal, relational* and dialogical, as opposed to the approach of preaching. Personal evangelism, small-group evangelism and other such methods have become more common and have been extensively used by parachurch* groups. Denominational proponents of personal evangelism, such as Methodist layperson* Harry Denman, have also emphasized the role of average Christians in evangelizing through personal relationships.

The American experience has shaped a twentieth-century evangelistic message that is decidedly personal and individualistic—an offer of personal salvation* and a call for individual repentance and holiness. Known as "personal evangelism," its techniques are taught in many fundamentalist* and evangelical* Bible schools,* churches and parachurch* groups. In the twentieth century, with the rediscovery of the eschatalogical nature of the Christian gospel and the development of both liberation* and radical evangelical theologies, some have reclaimed the social, political and even cosmic dimensions of the Christian faith. This has

resulted in a call to radical obedience and discipleship* in response to an evangelistic message encompassing the broader issues of life and faith. *See also* REVIVALISM.

BIBLIOGRAPHY. M. Arias, *Announcing the Reign of God* (1985); C. H. Dodd, *The Apostolic Preaching and Its Developments* (1936); P. Little, *How to Give Away Your Faith* (1986); A. C. Outler, *Evangelism in the Wesleyan Spirit* (1971); J. R. W. Stott, "The Biblical Basis of Evangelism," in *Let the Earth Hear His Voice,* ed. J. D. Douglas, (1975); M. Taylor, *Exploring Evangelism* (1964); J. Wallis, *The Call to Conversion: Recovering the Gospel for These Times* (1981). V. W. Baker

Evangelism-in-Depth. A strategy for comprehensive evangelization* of a particular nation or region. Formulated by the American missionary,* R. Kenneth Strachan,* director of Latin America Mission,* it was first implemented in Nicaragua in 1960. The plan was subsequently put into operation in many other countries of Latin America, Africa and North America. In Africa it was known as New Life for All.

Noting a low level of evangelistic passion on the part of many churches at a time of rapid population growth, political unrest and mounting social needs, Strachan studied the writings of British missiologist* Roland Allen (1868-1947) and contemporary examples of both effective evangelization and stagnation. He identified a theorem: "The expansion of any movement is in direct proportion to its success in mobilizing its total membership in continuous propagation of its beliefs." Strachan thereby shifted emphasis to indigenous resources—rather than a foreign agency—and the local congregation and individual members. Evangelism-in-Depth encouraged cooperation by all Christians of a region or nation in each campaign.

BIBLIOGRAPHY. Latin America Mission, *Evangelism-in-Depth* (1961); G. W. Peters, *Saturation Evangelism* (1970); W. D. Roberts, *Revolution in Evangelism* (1967); R. K. Strachan, *The Inescapable Calling* (1968). W. R. Shenk

Evans, Evan (1671-1721). Anglican* clergyman* and missionary* to Welsh immigrants. Born in Carnoe, Montgomery County, Wales, he was educated at Oxford (B.A., 1695) and in 1700 was sent by the bishop* of London to serve as rector* of Christ Church, Philadelphia. There he had an immensely successful ministry* for the next eighteen years, preaching* not only at Christ Church, but also at Chester, Chichester, Concord, Oxford,

[417]

Perkiomen and New Castle. In addition to influencing the building of several other churches, his ministry to the Welsh immigrants of Pennsylvania is credited with retaining many of them within the Anglican fold. In addition, his warm piety* won many Quakers* to the Anglican Church. Though he attempted to secure a bishop for the American Church, he was unsuccessful.

In 1714 he accepted an appointment as a missionary to Welshmen under the auspices of the Society for the Propagation of the Gospel.* Continuing to serve at Christ Church until 1718, he then resigned his work in Pennsylvania and moved to serve the Spesutia congregation in St. George's Parish, Maryland.

BIBLIOGRAPHY. *AAP* 5; *DAB* II; L. C. Washburn, *Christ Church, Philadelphia* (1925).

D. G. Reid

Evans, James (1801-1846). Methodist* missionary,* linguist and inventor. In 1823 Evans left England and came to Upper Canada, becoming a schoolteacher at the Rice Lake Indian School. There he developed a written language, based on phonetic speech, for the Ojibway pupils. Ordained* as a Methodist* minister* in 1833, he was appointed general superintendent of the Northwest Indian Methodist Missions in 1840.

Founding a mission at Rossville, near Norway House, Evans created a written language consisting of fifty symbols based on the spoken syllabic language of the Cree. Using scrap material, he built the first printing press in the Canadian Northwest and published collections of hymns* and prayers,* as well as the Scriptures,* in Cree. This system of syllabic symbols has been successfully adapted for use with other Native American and Inuit languages and is still taught today.

Provoked by his persistent criticism of Hudson's Bay Company's policies regarding the liquor trade and Sunday* observance, opponents laid false charges of immoral conduct against Evans in 1845. He was recalled to England where he died in November 1846.

BIBLIOGRAPHY. J. Evans, *Letters of Rev. James Evans, Methodist Missionary* (1932); E. R. Young, *The Apostle of the North: James Evans* (1899).

R. H. Chilton

Evans, William (1870-1950). Evangelical* Bible* teacher and theologian.* A native of Liverpool, England, Evans immigrated to the U. S. in 1889 and graduated from Moody Bible Institute* in 1892. He received the B.D. at the Chicago Lutheran Seminary and was awarded the Ph.D. from the Chicago

Theological Seminary in 1914. After serving pastorates in Goshen, Indiana (1895-1897), and Wheaton, Illinois (1897-1900), Evans taught biblical studies at Moody Bible Institute (1901-1915) and simultaneously pursued graduate studies. Following his time at Moody, he served as associate dean of the Bible Institute of Los Angeles for three years (1915-1918).

From 1918 until his death, Evans was a director of World Bible Conferences, spending most of his time traveling and lecturing. He made numerous trips to Palestine, as well as missionary tours to Africa and Asia. Considered one of the outstanding Bible teachers of his time, in 1906 he was awarded a D.D. from Wheaton College* (Illinois) and in 1943 a Litt.D. from John Brown University. His extensive writings included *The Book of Books* (1902), *Personal Soul-Winning* (1910), *The Great Doctrines of the Bible* (1912) and *From the Upper Room to the Empty Tomb* (1928).

BIBLIOGRAPHY. *NCAB* 40.

D. G. Buss

Evanston Assembly. Second assembly of the World Council of Churches* (WCC) at Evanston, Illinois, on August 15-31, 1952. Meeting under the Christological* theme "Christ—the Hope of the World," 1,500 participants, including 500 delegates from 163 Protestant* and Orthodox* churches (as compared to 150 at the Amsterdam Assembly in 1948), tried to declare Christian faith and hope to a post-War, secular world. Contrasting views about hope were articulated in plenary papers by Edmund Schlink (Germany) and Robert L. Calhoun (U.S.), both reflecting an ongoing debate between American and European theologians.* Schlink envisaged hope in its eschatological expression, while Calhoun declared that hope lies in the possibility of social and moral improvements in the world made real by faith in, and practice of, the gospel of the kingdom.

The substance of Evanston came in the work of six sections focused on Christian unity, evangelism,* social ethics,* peace and international affairs, racial issues and the laity. Among those playing key roles at Evanston were: W. A. Visser 't Hooft (the WCC's first general secretary), Bishop George K. A. Bell (Church of England), Bishop J. E. Lesslie Newbigin (Church of South India), Franklin Clark Fry* (Lutheran Church in America*), D. T. Niles (Methodist from Sri Lanka), Orthodox theologians Georges Florovsky* (Russian Orthodox Church in the USA) and Hamilcar S. Alivisatos (Orthodox Church of Greece), Josef Hromadka (Czech Brethren), Kathleen Bliss (Church of England).

Evanston also debated the contrasts between

Christianity in capitalist* and Marxist societies, and for the first time the racist policies of apartheid in South Africa. Of particular interest to the delegates and the American press was the presence of fifteen delegates from churches in Marxist-controlled countries. Roman Catholics* were banned from coming in any capacity by Cardinal Stritch,* Archbishop of Chicago. The Evanston Assembly revealed a World Council of Churches willing to address the tough spiritual questions of the 1950s and to seek in its membership to stretch across the political, cultural and confessional divisions in the world. P. A. Crow

Evening Service. Church services held in the evening. The historic roots of the evening service go back to Jewish practice (Ex 29:39; Ps 141:2) and early Christian continuance of temple worship (Acts 2:46; 3:1). From antiquity the practice of praying at dawn and sunset has been observed, with other hours of prayer* added to constitute the canonical hours. Lutherans* of the early sixteenth century observed two vernacular services of prayer: morning and evening. This practice is reflected in the Anglican* *Book of Common Prayer** (1549) which incorporated service of Matins and Evensong.

In colonial America the Puritan* practice of two Sunday services differed from the Anglicans, being held in the afternoon so that members could return home before dark. The spiritual awakenings of the eighteenth and nineteenth centuries gave rise to the revivalistic* tradition that undergirds the evangelistic nature of many evening services in the twentieth century. In the evangelical* Protestant tradition, evening services tend to be informal and evangelistic, with a broader range of congregational participation. American revival services would often begin on Sunday evening, continue throughout the week, and conclude the following Sunday evening.

The reasons for the declining number of evening services are no doubt complex, but they do seem to coincide with the onset of modern urban living. In recent decades the competition from the entertainment industry in the form of radio, television, theatre and video has eroded the appeal of evening services that once provided a welcome diversion from the tedium of life. T. R. Albin

Evensong. *See* VESPERS.

Evolution. *See* DARWINIAN EVOLUTION AND THE AMERICAN CHURCHES.

Ewart, Frank (1876-1947). Oneness Pentecostal* minister. An Australian who had immigrated to Canada in 1903, Ewart was a Baptist minister who turned Pentecostal in 1908. Expelled from his Baptist church in Portland, Oregon, Ewart moved to Los Angeles, where he became William H. Durham's* pastoral assistant. Ewart succeeded Durham as pastor when Durham died in 1912.

In 1913 Ewart participated in the Pentecostal camp meeting* in Los Angeles that sparked an intense interest in the definitive biblical formula for water baptism.* In April 1914, Ewart preached a sermon that led him and Glenn A. Cook to rebaptize* each other on April 15, 1914, in the name of Jesus. Though their doctrine* was not confessedly Unitarian* at first, their understanding that true baptism was in the name of Jesus alone (excluding *Father* and *Holy Spirit,* which were only titles for Jesus Christ, the one person of the godhead), led to a rejection of Trinitarian theology. Ewart represented this doctrine at the 1916 general council of the Assemblies of God,* which resolved the matter with a clear Trinitarian statement. Thereafter Ewart became affiliated with the General Assembly of the Apostolic Assemblies which, for a brief time, joined together with the Pentecostal Assemblies of the World. He would become one of the stalwarts of Oneness Pentecostalism and contribute specifically to the church now known as the United Pentecostal Church.*

BIBLIOGRAPHY. F. J. Ewart, *The Phenomenon of Pentecost* (1975); D. A. Reed, "Origins and Development of the Theology of Oneness Pentecostalism in the United States" (unpublished Ph.D. dissertation, University of Notre Dame, 1974). H. D. Hunter

Ewer, Ferdinand Cartwright (1826-1883). Anglo-Catholic* preacher* and theologian.* Born into a prominent Unitarian* family in Nantucket, Massachusetts, Ewer joined the Episcopal Church* prior to entering Harvard College* in 1844. There he became a religious skeptic and abandoned his intention to study for the ministry. Determined on graduation to settle in California, he pursued a career first as a civil engineer and then as a successful journalist. On recovering his faith some time later, he applied for holy orders, and was ordained* deacon* in 1857 and priest* in 1858. He soon afterward was named rector of Grace Church, San Francisco, but ill health prompted his removal to New York City in 1860.

There he served as assistant to Thomas Gallaudet* at St. Ann's Church for the deaf, until he was called to the rectorship of Christ Church in

1862. From this parish* he achieved wide fame as a gifted preacher and emerged as the foremost apologist* for Anglo-Catholicism, although his ritual practices aroused much hostility and led to his resignation in 1871. Followed by several former parishioners, he at once founded St. Ignatius' Church as a seat of Catholic* teaching and worship,* and where he was rector* until his death. His chief works include: *The Failure of Protestantism* (1868), *Catholicity in Its Relationship to Protestantism and Romanism* (1878) and *The Operation of the Holy Spirit* (1880).

BIBLIOGRAPHY. *DAB* III; M. Dix, "Ferdinand C. Ewer, Priest and Doctor," *ACR* 42 (1883):511-529.
C. R. Henery

Ewing, Finis (1773-1841). Principal founder of the Cumberland Presbyterian Church.* Born into a Presbyterian* family in Virginia, Ewing moved to Logan County, Kentucky, in 1795 and was converted during the Great Revival under the exhortations of Southern Presbyterian leader James McGready.* He was ordained* to the Presbyterian ministry* by pro-revivalists, though his education and theological convictions did not qualify him in the eyes of anti-revival Presbyterians.

In 1810, while in the throes of a lengthy dispute between revival* and anti-revival Presbyterians, Ewing and two others started the Cumberland Presbyterian Church. The primary cause of the schism was the revivalists' moderating the Calvinism* of the Westminster Confession* in order to give greater place to the human will in conversion. Ewing was one of the chief proponents of this modified Calvinism which, in a number of parallel forms, became the new evangelical* orthodoxy* of the Second Great Awakening.*

Ewing published his views in *A Series of Lectures on the Most Important Subjects of Divinity* (1827). He held that God offers himself to all humanity through rational law, and not to a limited elect* through seemingly arbitrary and inscrutable decrees. In keeping with the growing democratic* ideals of the new nation, he emphasized that God gives every person full opportunity to repent. Ewing added an egalitarian frontier* note to a developing New School* Presbyterianism, modifying predestinarian* Calvinism in order to make it compatible with the frontier camp meeting.* The Cumberland doctrine fit well with the pragmatic revivalism of Charles G. Finney* and the benevolent movement that played such a strong role in antebellum evangelism.

BIBLIOGRAPHY. B. M. Barrus, M. L. Baughn, T. H. Campbell, *A People Called Cumberland Presbyte-*

rians (1972); *DAB* III; E. T. Thompson, *Presbyterians in the South,* vol. 1 (1963).
S. E. Berk

Excell, Edwin Othello (1851-1921). Gospel singer, songwriter and publisher. Born in Stark County, Ohio, he married Jennie Bell in 1871 and was converted* soon thereafter in a Methodist* revival,* where he had been engaged to lead the singing. In 1883 he moved to Chicago, where he associated for a time with B. F. Jacobs* and W. B. Jacobs in promoting Sunday schools.* Excell conducted the music at numerous conventions and Chatauquas.* Establishing a music publishing company in Chicago, he issued more than ninety books of gospel songs.* Excell became best known for his work with evangelist Sam P. Jones,* with whom he traveled for more than twenty years. Excell wrote more than 2,000 gospel songs, including "Since I Have Been Redeemed" and "Count Your Blessings." He died on June 10, 1921, in Louisville, Kentucky, where he was assisting Gipsy Smith* in an evangelistic meeting.
M. E. Dieter

Excommunication. Censure barring a Christian from the privileges and rights of church membership.* Excommunication is practiced, at least in theory, by nearly all Christian churches, although its definition and application vary widely. Warrant for excommunication comes from the New Testament, where we read that church members, warned twice about unrepented sin, are to be treated "as Gentiles" (Mt 18), driven out of the church (1 Cor 6) or handed over to the devil (1 Tim 1).

In Roman Catholic* canon law,* all excommunicated persons may not lawfully administer or receive the sacraments* and, though legally deprived of fellowship, need not be expelled if they violate the censure. Those excommunicated by the holy see, however, lose all office, rank, stipend, dignity, privilege and fellowship.

Most mainline* Protestant* denominations* rarely practice excommunication. The reasons are varied and complex. Situated in the mainstream of American society, they tend to reflect the diversity, social habits and moral posture of the culture. Not as clerically controlled and hierarchical as Roman Catholicism, they are less likely to enforce ecclesiastical censure. Tolerance tends to be valued above doctrinal or moral conformity.

Evangelical* Protestant churches are more apt to practice excommunication, due to their moral conservatism and rigorous biblicism. Strict allegiance to orthodoxy* makes them more vigilant of waywardness.

Religious sects* in America are the most likely to practice excommunication. The high level of commitment among their members, the greater strictness of their moral codes and doctrinal creeds, and the often unchecked authority of their leaders create conditions favorable to successful censure. Their tendency to label other churches as apostate makes it more difficult for excommunicated members to find fellowship elsewhere.

Competition among church bodies in America, social mobility, the threat of litigation, the value placed upon tolerance and the popularity of therapeutic psychology make the consistent practice of excommunication particularly difficult in the modern American church.

See also DISCIPLINE, CHURCH.

G. L. Sittser

Exegesis. Exegesis is the practice of discovering the meaning of a text in its original cultural, historical, literary and theological contexts. It is to be distinguished from hermeneutics, which is the theory of interpretation. An exegete is one who engages in exegesis, usually with some skill.

While exegesis may be applied to any text, in American religious usage the object of exegesis is usually the Hebrew or Christian Bible.* While exegetical methods have varied over the centuries, the most prominent exegetical tradition in America's religious history was shaped by the Reformation principle of literal and grammatical (rather than allegorical, anagogical or mystical) interpretation, as well as the Renaissance humanists' revival of Western classical languages and the study of ancient texts. Whether guided by theological,* pastoral or pietistic* interests, exegesis in this tradition has tended to be descriptive of the canonical text.

Yet the late nineteenth century saw the introduction of a historical and critical methodology. Imported primarily from German universities and often based on rationalistic, anti-supernatural presuppositions, this approach to exegesis tended to interpret the biblical text in the same way scholars would interpret any ancient text. This historical-critical method, resisted by fundamentalists* past and present and cautiously appropriated by some modern evangelicals,* has profoundly shaped biblical exegesis as it is practiced both within the academic study of religion and American mainline churches.* Recently, some biblical scholars from within the historical-critical tradition have attempted to redirect Christian biblical exegesis to its proper task of interpreting the Bible as Holy Scripture. This so-called canonical criticism has placed an emphasis on the meaning of biblical texts within their canonical settings.

The practice of exegesis begins by defining the boundary of a passage and its actual wording. A text may then be examined in terms of its original grammatical, historical, literary and religious contexts. In modern critical exegesis a conscious attempt is made to uncover not only the originally intended meaning of a text (or an oral tradition preserved within a text) but subsequent meanings and layers of interpretation introduced by later editors and compilers as they restated the biblical tradition within new historical contexts. Generally speaking, Christian exegetes through the centuries have agreed that their proper goal is restating the meaning of a text for their contemporary situation. Most Protestants, holding to the Reformation principle of *sola scriptura,* maintain the ideal that Christian theology and preaching should be derived from sound biblical exegesis.

See also BIBLICAL INTERPRETATION.

BIBLIOGRAPHY. G. Fee, *New Testament Exegesis* (1983); R. M. Grant and D. Tracy, *A Short History of the Interpretation of the Bible* (1984); M. Noll, *Between Faith and Criticism* (1986).

D. G. Reid

Existentialism, Christian. Christian existentialism stresses the role of human experience in discovering truth. Søren Kierkegaard,* the Danish philosopher whose writings inspired the movement, maintained that truth cannot be found by means of detached intellectual reasoning. It must be personally appropriated and demands the involvement and commitment of the whole self. Within the context of Christian faith, Kierkegaard argued, this means that one cannot become a Christian apart from a "leap of faith." By such a "leap," an individual accepts God's claim on his or her life and embraces the Christian gospel, with all its ethical demands for obedience to God. This frees the person to an open future in which the responsible self discovers Christian truth in encounter and action.

While existentialism as a secular or atheistic philosophy was developed by Martin Heidegger (1889-1976) and Jean-Paul Sartre (1905-1980), many of Kierkegaard's philosophical and theological insights were adopted by Karl Barth* and other theologians who promoted dialectical, or crisis, theology during the 1920s. Existential themes continued to emerge in the thought of continental philosophers and theologians such as Karl Jaspers*

(1883-1969), Gabriel Marcel* (1889-1973), Nicolai Berdyaev* (1874-1948), Dietrich Bonhoeffer,* Rudolf Bultmann* and Paul Tillich.* These and contemporary American theologians have shaped Christian existentialism, yet the existentialist impulse has also been especially strong in the arena of Christian ethics.*

Apart from the writings of Kierkegaard himself, Christian existentialism was imported into America through the writings and influence of theologians such as Karl Barth and Emil Brunner.* Both stressed the dialectical nature of theology as it encounters truth in paradox, exemplified in God, the "totally other," becoming flesh in Jesus Christ. The eminent American theologian, Reinhold Niebuhr,* acknowledged the importance of Kierkegaard and Brunner in shaping his own view of the Fall.

German immigrant theologian Paul Tillich, who taught at Union Theological Seminary (New York),* Harvard University* and the University of Chicago* (1933-1965), was deeply influenced by Kierkegaard. Led to a "full acceptance of existential philosophy," he referred to existentialism as "the good luck of Christian theology." Tillich sought to reinterpret all of Christian theology by means of existential categories.

Rudolf Bultmann, the widely influential German biblical scholar, was indebted to Heidegger's philosophy of the quest for authentic existence. In his famous program of demythologizing* the New Testament, Bultmann sought to retranslate the mythical language of Scripture into existential language that would be meaningful for modern men and women. Through his writings and visits to America, his approach to the New Testament as both critical historian and existential theologian was to leave a distinct impression on twentieth-century American theology.

Other influences can be observed in individuals such as the British theologian John Macquarrie (b. 1919), who was professor of systematic theology* at Union Theological Seminary, New York, and developed an existentialist approach to systematic theology. American Catholic theology has been significantly influenced by the continental Jesuit* theologian Karl Rahner,* who appropriated elements of Heidegger's existentialism.

Existentialist ethics seeks an alternative to legalism in making ethical decisions. Scriptural injunctions to love as the fulfillment of the Law (e.g., Mt 22:34-40) provide the source and norm for Christian action. Christian behavior is rooted in "the trans-moral conscience" (Tillich), "an ethic without laws" (Paul Ramsey), an "ethic of 'crea-

tivity' " (Berdyaev) or "responsivity" (H. Richard Niebuhr*). Existential ethics stresses the freedom by which laws are transcended through creative action. Situation ethics, popularized by British theologian John A. T. Robinson (1919-1983) and Joseph Fletcher, and the contextual ethics associated with H. Richard Niebuhr and Paul Lehmann, focus on the norm of love and a response to what God is doing in the world. They reject appeals to law as a norm, while stressing an immediate, concrete and personal encounter with God's command. While existential themes have had a significant influence on twentieth-century American theology, perhaps the most lasting impact it has had on the churches is in the realm of ethics.

BIBLIOGRAPHY. A. Cochrane, *The Existentialists and God* (1956); J. Macquarrie, *An Existentialist Theology* (1955); J. Macquarrie, *Existentialism* (1972); D. E. Roberts, *Existentialism and Religious Belief* (1957).

D. K. McKim

Expositor. An expositor defines and explains the meaning of a biblical text, whether in a classroom, from a pulpit, over electronic media or in published popular or scholarly commentary. In expository preaching* a text rather than a topic determines the preacher's theme and conclusion. An expository sermon is usually based on a biblical passage several verses in length but can be limited to a single phrase. For example, an expository sermon on Psalm 1 might develop the contrast between the righteous person who prospers in verses 1-3 and the wicked person who perishes in verses 4-6.

A popular preaching method in America since the days of the Puritans,* it has flourished in the evangelical* tradition where the centrality of Scripture is promoted in Christian worship* and piety.* In some circles extended series of sermons covering lengthy biblical passages or books of the Bible* are particularly favored. In some cases this form of preaching can barely be distinguished from a lecture. Among America's distinguished expository preachers have been Cotton Mather,* John A. Broadus,* Andrew Blackwood* and Donald G. Barnhouse,* whose radio exposition of Romans was in its eleventh year at the time of his death.

BIBLIOGRAPHY. A. W. Blackwood, *Expository Preaching for Today* (1953); J. A. Broadus, *On the Preparation and Delivery of Sermons* (1870); D. T. Holland, *The Preaching Tradition* (1980).

J. E. Stanley

Extreme Unction, Sacrament of. One of the traditional seven sacraments* of the Roman Catholic Church,* it is more commonly called today the Sacrament of the Anointing of the Sick. Both the Constitution on the Liturgy and the Constitution on the Church, which are documents from Vatican II,* insist that this sacrament is not to be reserved for those who are on the point of death but for those who are ill, so that the church might recommend to the Lord, who suffered and died for his people, that he might bring relief and salvation to the sufferer.

The justification for the anointing of the sick derives from the church's desire to be faithful to the admonition of James 5:14-16. The historical development of this sacrament in the tradition of the church has been a long and complex one, but it was only in the early Middle Ages that the anointing became identified with the dying. The medieval theologian Peter Lombard (d. 1160) seems to have coined the phrase "extreme unction" (*extrema unctio*). It was only in this century that theologians began to insist that the sacrament was more appropriately linked to illness rather than death. One development from this shift has been the development of anointing services during the church's liturgy for all the sick of the parish.

Technically speaking, the last sacramental gesture which the church offers the dying person is Holy Communion* which, when given in those circumstances, is called *viaticum* (from the Latin meaning to "carry with you on the Journey"). The complex of rites by which a priest confesses a person, anoints the person, gives the person Communion and prays with the person during a serious illness is often called "The Last Rites."

BIBLIOGRAPHY. W. H. Abbott, ed., *The Documents of Vatican II* (1966); B. Cooke, *Sacraments and Sacramentality* (1983); J. Martos, *The Doors of the Sacred: A Historical Introduction to Sacraments in the Catholic Church* (1982).

L. S. Cunningham

F

Faith Healing. A practice, particularly associated with the Pentecostal* and charismatic* movements, based on the belief that Jesus' promise of healing recorded in Mark 16:18 is for every generation of believers.

The post-apostolic church continued the tradition of first-century believers by teaching and practicing a healing ministry to the sick. Irenaeus, Justin Martyr and Tertullian viewed passages such as Mark 16:15-18 and James 5:14-16 as the church's mandate to pray for the sick in expectation of their healing. In the third century Gregory Thaumaturgus or "Wonder Worker" (c.213-c.270) was credited with many miracles, among them healings. However, evidence indicates that by the ninth century prayers for the sick had fallen from regular practice.

By the twelfth century in Italy the Waldensians were practicing faith healing, and the sixteenth-century Protestant Reformation brought with it a revival of prayers for the sick. Luther himself believed in praying for the sick and later Protestant groups continued this apostolic practice, including the Brethren,* Mennonites,* Quakers,* Moravians* and Wesleyans.*

The Catholic Church* has maintained the Sacrament of the Anointing of the Sick* since the eleventh and twelfth centuries, with healings reportedly taking place. However, in popular medieval thinking the sacrament* was regarded as a preparation for death (extreme unction*) rather than a sacramental means of healing grace. Other means of miraculous healings have been recognized by the Catholic Church, whether they take place by means of sacramentals* such as prayers or blessings, by healing power associated with places such as Lourdes, France, or as a result of prayers to a saint.* Certain individuals within the Catholic tradition, such as Francis of Assisi, Bernard of Clairvoux and Patrick of Ireland were credited with the spiritual gift of healing.

The Nineteenth Century. While reports of healings have accompanied revivals and awakenings throughout the history of the Christian church, the present-day faith-healing movements look to the late nineteenth century for their immediate antecedents. By that time Europeans had already seen a revival of faith healing in such figures as Dorthea Trudel of Switzerland, Johannes Blumhardt and Otto Stockmayer of Germany and William Boardman* in England.

This new wave of interest in faith healing eventually influenced the American revival* tradition. By the late nineteenth century, religious figures such as Charles Cullis, Carrie Judd Montgomery,* Maria B. Woodworth-Etter,* A. B. Simpson,* A. J. Gordon,* R. A. Torrey,* John Alexander Dowie* and R. Kelso Carter were teaching and practicing faith healing in America. But among these practitioners there were differences in interpretation and practice of healing. While some taught that healing is part of the atonement* and as readily available to believers as salvation, others reasoned that healing is a mercy available as a result of Christ's atonement but not a guarantee of physical well being. The latter group looked to the resurrection for the fullness of healing. On the other hand, conservative theologians, particularly those of a dispensationalist* persuasion, maintained that the gift of healing had ceased with the apostolic age.

J. A. Dowie, an emigrant from Australia, held the most radical view of faith healing. Teaching that medicine and faith healing were incompatible, his theocratic community of Zion, Illinois, banned the medical profession—including veterinarians—from practicing within the city.

Much more moderate were the views of A. B. Simpson,* a former Presbyterian* pastor who claimed to have been healed of a heart condition. His writings contained numerous teachings on faith healing, and Simpson founded the Christian and Missionary Alliance* on the "four-fold gospel" of Christ as Savior, Sanctifier, Healer and Coming King. But Simpson believed that the sick should receive prayer in a private place such as a "faith home," a hostel-like refuge for the ill. In his opinion, parading the sick through public prayer lines amid loud prayers and outbursts of emotion was more like a circus than a venue fit for divine healing. Others, like healing revivalist Maria B. Woodworth-Etter,* held meetings in which people fell to the sawdust floor as they received prayer for their afflictions.

The 20th Century. At the turn of the century, individuals within the Holiness Movement,* as well as isolated evangelicals,* were reporting divine healings. Yet the rise of Christian Science* and Pentecostalism* caused some to withdraw from faith healing for fear of being associated with these new movements or extremists such as Dowie. The Pentecostal Movement in particular, a near cousin to the Holiness Movement, was making faith healing an important part of its teachings and practices. Charles F. Parham,* William J. Seymour,* Florence Crawford* and others believed it was God's will that anyone who was sick should be healed. If healing grace was in the atonement—and they believed it was—people should expect to be healed by faith just as they had been saved by faith.

The unfortunate result of this doctrine was that those who prayed for the sick often placed the total responsibility for successful healings on the afflicted. If the sick were not healed it was because they lacked faith—leaving them to feel guilty, sinful and unworthy of God's favor. Many preachers later modified their views and admitted they did not understand why everyone was not healed. This attitude is more prevalent today among faith healers.

Prior to World War 2* evangelists such as Aimee Semple McPherson,* Raymond T. Richey, F. F. Bosworth,* Charles S. Price,* A. H. Argue,* and three Englishmen, Smith Wigglesworth, and Stephen and George Jeffreys, held salvation-healing meetings and attracted crowds numbering in the thousands. But the following and impact of these healing evangelists could not be compared with the new wave of faith healers who burst on the scene following World War 2. Most prominent among these new salvation-healing evangelists were William M. Branham* and Oral Roberts.* They were followed by figures such as Kathryn Kuhlman,* A. A. Allen,* T. L. Osborn, Jack Coe,* Gayle Jackson, O. L. Jaggers.

Dozens of giant revival tents sprung up across the American religious landscape, particularly in the South. The accent in these revivals was unashamedly placed on healing miracles. Personal appearances were important in creating a following (or "partners," as they were called), and the more successful evangelists utilized the medium of radio and television to reach the masses. But with this newfound popularity came criticism. Critics claimed that if anyone were healed, the illness was psychosomatic rather than organic. Healing evangelists were commonly charged with fraud, greed and moral failure. By the 1960s the charismatic movement had begun to surface in mainline* denominations, bringing faith healing a newfound respectability. Catholic charismatics rediscovered the power of their church's ancient tradition of prayer for the sick, as evidenced in Father Francis MacNutt's book *Healing* (1974).

The 1970s saw the birth of the "Word" or "Faith" movement,* a blend of charismatic and classical Pentecostal teachings, including a radical view of health and wealth as the rightful blessings of faith. Teaching their followers to claim healing and prosperity rather than *ask* God for it, the movement has created more controversy than the salvation-healing movement of the 1950s and is rejected as extremist by many traditional Pentecostals.

In 1982 many evangelicals were surprised to learn healing miracles had found their way into the curriculum of one of the tradition's foremost institutions, Fuller Theological Seminary* in Pasadena, California. A center of progressive but generally Reformed* evangelical thought since its founding in 1947, the seminary's respected School of World Mission had offered a well-attended course entitled "Signs, Wonders and Church Growth." Accompanying its more academic study of the subject were "practical sessions" in which exorcism and healings were recorded in the classroom.

While the course was discontinued in 1986 due to faculty controversy over its place in the seminary curriculum, its public profile caused many evangelicals to reassess their beliefs and attitudes toward faith healing. A parallel and equally controversial development has been the growth of the Vineyard Fellowship. Founded by John Wimber, a charismatic pastor and former instructor of the Fuller Seminary course, the movement consists of a nationwide network of congregations emphasizing the miraculous gifts of the Spirit.

See also CHARISMATIC MOVEMENT; FAITH MOVEMENT; PENTECOSTAL MOVEMENT.

BIBLIOGRAPHY. D. Dayton, "The Rise of the Evangelical Healing Movement in Nineteenth Century America," *Pneuma* I (1982):1-18; C. Farah, Jr., *From the Pinnacle of the Temple* (1980); A. J. Gordon, *The Ministry of Healing* (1881); D. E. Harrell, Jr., *All Things Are Possible* (1975); M. T. Kelsey, *Healing and Christianity in Ancient*

Thought and Modern Times (1973); F. MacNutt, *Healing* (1974); B. B. Warfield, *Counterfeit Miracles* (1918). W. E. Warner

Faith Missions Movement. Arising from the founding of the China Inland Mission by Hudson Taylor in 1865, the faith missions movement in North America has grown to include at least 15,000 missionaries representing more than seventy-five different agencies.

Despite its British origin in the person of Hudson Taylor, the movement rapidly took hold in North America, with the founding of missions such as the Christian and Missionary Alliance* (1887), the Evangelical Alliance Mission* (1890), the Central American Mission (1890), the Sudan Interior Mission* (1893) and the Africa Inland Mission* (1895). From its beginnings this movement has been almost exclusively evangelical, and its development closely parallels that of the Bible institutes* and colleges in North America, from which the majority of its recruits have come.

One of the most distinctive features of faith missions is their financial philosophy which, operating in faith that God will provide, generally does not guarantee salaries for missionaries. Faith missions will generally refrain from directly soliciting funds, but application of this philosophy ranges from a policy of simply stating a need, to not publicly revealing the needs of missionaries. This same "faith" principle has also characterized the personnel policies of these missions, whose members have often taken great personal risks for the sake of the gospel.

See also MISSIONS, EVANGELICAL FOREIGN.

BIBLIOGRAPHY. J. H. Kane, *Faith Mighty Faith: A Handbook of the Interdenominational Foreign Mission Association* (1956); R. A. Tucker, *From Jerusalem to Irian Jaya: A Biographical History of Christian Missions* (1986).

G. R. Corwin

Faith Movement (Word Movement). A movement arising within charismatic* Christianity during the early 1970s stressing the power of faith in obtaining the divine blessings of physical health and financial prosperity.

Kenneth Hagin (1917-), the acknowledged patriarch of the movement, began his ministry career in 1934 after reportedly experiencing a miraculous healing* of a heart condition. It was not until the late 1960s that he became established, and by the early 1970s he had achieved recognition within Pentecostal* circles. Now based in Tulsa, Oklahoma, he and his son, Kenneth Hagin,

Jr., have distributed over thirty million copies of their books. Their Rhema Bible Training Center has branches in South Africa and Australia.

Other leaders of the faith movement include popular television evangelist Kenneth Copeland and his former assistant, Jerry Savelle, both of Fort Worth, Texas; Fred Price, pastor of a large church (over 14,000 members in 1985) near Los Angeles, California; retired farmer Charles Capps of England, Arkansas; Bob Tilton, pastor and founder of World of Faith Satellite Network of Dallas, Texas; Marilyn Hickey in Denver, Colorado; and Lester Sumrall in South Bend, Indiana.

The first of the movement's three main emphases is that physical health is always the will of God, as assured by Jesus' atonement (Is 53:4-5; Mt 8:17; 1 Pet 2:24), and can be claimed by faith. Medicine is not discouraged, except in extreme and isolated cases (faith teachers actively support Christian hospitals), but divine healing and perfect health are considered preferable to medical treatment. Lack of faith is held to be the main obstacle to receiving healing; but ignorance, unbelief and a lack of forgiveness are also cited. The faith movement shares its emphasis on healing with all of Pentecostalism but gives greater assurance that healing is guaranteed.

Second, the faith movement's emphasis on prosperity seems to have been influenced by Oral Roberts* who, while not fully identified with the movement, has close doctrinal and personal ties with many faith teachers. Quoting 3 John 2, the faith movement teaches that God wants his people to prosper in every area of life and often focuses on financial prosperity in particular. Kenneth Copeland cites Mark 10:29-30 as evidence that one can believe for a literal "hundredfold return" on one's "investments" (i.e., contributions) in Christian ministries. Usually faith teachers are less bold, stating that God wants believers to prosper so that they can concentrate on serving God rather than attending to their own needs.

Third, drawing primarily from the writings of E. W. Kenyon,* the faith movement teaches that God's promises are obtained through positive confession—a positive statement of confident faith. Positive confession based on God's Word guarantees results—so assuredly so that faith teachers (appealing to Mk 11:22-24) thank God for answering prayer, even before the answer is manifested. Praying a second time for the same need is often seen as showing lack of faith in the first request.

The movement has spread largely through independent charismatic churches, many of them founded by Rhema graduates. Praised by some for encouraging victorious living and unquestioning trust in God's promises, critics have accused the movement of a "charismatic humanism" in which believers expect results by positive confession—a spiritualized "American dream" which inflicts guilt and confusion on sick and physically handicapped followers—and of favoring speculation and "revelation knowledge" over sound biblical interpretation.*

Furthermore, some have questioned the fundamental orthodoxy* of the more extreme faith teachers for teaching: the intrinsic power of words spoken in faith; "spiritual laws" to which even God is subject and which believers can manipulate; the possibility of redeemed believers becoming "gods" equal or nearly equal in power to the earthly Jesus; and that Jesus "died spiritually" when crucified and went to hell until he was "born again" in the resurrection.

BIBLIOGRAPHY. B. Barron, *The Health and Wealth Gospel* (1987); C. Farah, Jr., *From the Pinnacle of the Temple* (1980); D. E. Harrell, Jr., *All Things Are Possible* (1975); D. R. McConnell, *A Different Gospel* (1988).   B. Barron

Falckner, Justus (1672-1723). Lutheran* pioneer pastor* and hymnwriter. Born in Reinsdorf, Saxony, Germany, where his father and grandfather had been Lutheran pastors, Falckner was trained under pietist* influences at the University of Halle. He came to America in 1700 with his brother Daniel as a land agent for the Frankfort Land Company in Pennsylvania.

In 1703 Falckner was persuaded by the Swedish Lutheran Provost Andrew Rudman to accept a call to serve the Lutheran Church in New York. Ordained* by the Swedish Lutheran pastors of Pennsylvania and New York (the first Lutheran ordination* of record in America), for two decades he served a parish extending from Perth Amboy, New Jersey, in the south, to Albany, New York, in the north. After the death of Joshua Kocherthal,* the pastor who had led 2,000 Palatinate Germans to the Hudson Valley, Falckner also served as pastor to that large and scattered colony.

Falckner composed a number of German hymns, the best known of which has been translated into English as "Rise, Ye Children of Salvation." He also was one of the first to urge the introduction of organs for use in worship* in America. In 1708 he published the first theological work issued by Lutherans in America, a textbook on Christian doctrine, with special emphasis on the errors of Reformed* theology. Falckner is

remembered for his tireless and varied contributions to the establishment of German Lutheranism in Pennsylvania.

BIBLIOGRAPHY. D. W. Clark, *The World of Justus Falckner* (1946); *DAB* III; E. C. Nelson, ed., *The Lutherans in North America* (1975).

J. D. Sutherland

Falwell, Jerry (1933-). Fundamentalist* Baptist* pastor,* television evangelist* and founder of the Moral Majority.* Born in Lynchburg, Virginia, Falwell was converted* to Christian faith in 1952 through the influence of radio preacher Charles E. Fuller* and his popular program "Old-Fashioned Revival Hour." That same year Falwell entered Baptist Bible College in Springfield, Missouri, graduating in 1956. The school is closely related to the Baptist Bible Fellowship,* a loose-knit fellowship of independent, fundamentalist Baptist churches.

In 1956 Falwell founded the Thomas Road Baptist Church with thirty-five members meeting in a recently vacated building of the Donald Duck Bottling Company. By the 1980s the church had grown to a membership of over 18,000. Falwell soon began weekly radio broadcasts of church services. In 1968 the church began taping services for television. These programs were later called "The Old-Time Gospel Hour." In 1972 Falwell established the Lynchburg Christian Academy to provide education for children through grade twelve. In 1971 he formed Liberty Baptist College as a Christian undergraduate institution.

Long known among independent Baptists as a popular preacher and church-growth expert, Falwell gained national attention first as a prominent television evangelist and then as founder of the Moral Majority. From his media pulpit Falwell frequently addressed a variety of moral and social issues, setting forth his opposition to abortion* and the Civil Rights Movement* and his support for prayer* and Bible* reading in the public schools. The Moral Majority, founded in 1979, included a legislative lobby, educational activities and a political-action agency for promoting conservative moral and political concerns. Throughout the 1980s Falwell remained a leading spokesman for conservative views in both church and state. In 1987 Falwell resigned from the presidency of the Moral Majority in order to devote more time to his Lynchburg ministries. On June 10, 1989, he announced the dissolution of the Moral Majority, stating that it had fulfilled its goal of establishing the Religious Right* in the public arena.

As a fundamentalist Christian, Falwell stresses

the classic doctrines* of fundamentalism (biblical inerrancy,* the virgin birth, bodily resurrection, sacrificial atonement* and premillennial* return of Christ). As an independent Baptist he emphasizes personal regeneration,* baptism* by immersion, local church autonomy and missionary* outreach. His earlier concern for the doctrine of separation*—avoiding denominational or ecumenical* involvement—was moderated somewhat in his political involvements. Falwell remains one of the most prominent and controversial proponents of evangelical* fundamentalism and conservative politics in American religious life.

See also MORAL MAJORITY; NEW RELIGIOUS RIGHT.

BIBLIOGRAPHY. F. Fitzgerald, "A Reporter at Large," *The New Yorker,* May 18, 1981; J. Falwell, *Strength for the Journey* (1987); J. K. Hadden and C. E. Swann, *Prime Time Preachers* (1981).

B. J. Leonard

Family, Christian. The family as an entity and the role of its individual members changed dramatically from the seventeenth to the twentieth centuries. Primarily in response to the Industrial Revolution, the family experienced fragmentation of time and space, if not of spirit.

Seventeenth-century New England Christian families were influenced by the Puritans's* strong commitment to the family, and by the necessity of working together to survive in a somewhat hostile environment. Work and leisure were shared by both sexes and all ages, and divorce was virtually nonexistent. Although family and community cohesion dwindled as Puritan homogeneity broke down over subsequent generations, eighteenth-century colonial America was nevertheless influenced by Puritan tenets: devotion to family members, dedication to God and his church, wholehearted support of education as a stepping-stone to salvation,* commitment to the community, and recognition of the value and responsibility of the individual.

Although children were clearly important, they were not perceived as experiencing psychological stages and consequently did not receive the type of attention given to the twentieth-century child. Puritan discipline was based on a belief in original sin,* and thus the child's will had to be broken. Although Puritan discipline was firm, parents administered it with a clear message of love.

Late eighteenth-century European Enlightenment* thought affected American childrearing practices by emphasizing the concept that human nature is basically good. Consequently, discipline took the form of "moral suasion," and by the late

nineteenth century, psychology* also affected childrearing approaches. Christian families countered some of the secularizing trends by touting Horace Bushnell's* childrearing manual *Christian Nurture,* and by promoting Christian principles in the public schools.

The Industrial Revolution raised the general standard of living. However, it also drew the workers out of the home and into an environment in which they worked with and for strangers. The middle-class family's focus on survival diminished; work and leisure activities became increasingly structured and male and female roles more clearly defined, as a separation of spheres occurred.

To offset the impersonal nature of these changes, late nineteenth-century families romanticized home life and childrearing, and the "cult of true womanhood" was promoted. Although the shift was subtle, family training increasingly emphasized morality and values such as thrift and purity, more than specifically Christian beliefs. Christian families, especially those affected by revivalism,* attempted to counter this trend and purify the larger society through reforms and crusades.

The twentieth-century-family structure has faced the challenges of materialism, world wars,* the Great Depression,* more women working outside the home, and an apparent increase in secularization. Christians have responded in diverse ways: some hoping to strengthen the family's commitment to faith through Christian schools* or home schooling; some becoming more active in church and parachurch* efforts to ease problems such as divorce and substance abuse; and some seeking a re-emphasis on Christian principles through public policy.* Although Christians often express concern about the status of the family, there are also signs of its enduring strength. Since the late 1940s Catholics* and others have participated in a form of Catholic Action* known as the Christian Family Movement.* Since the 1970s evangelical* parachurch agencies have given increasing attention to the family, the most notable effort being James Dobson's California-based Focus on the Family.

BIBLIOGRAPHY. C. N. Degler, *At Odds: Women and the Family in America from the Revolution to the Present* (1980); E. S. Morgan, *The Puritan Family,* rev. ed. (1966); L. W. Rosenzweig and P. N. Stearns, *Themes in Modern Social History* (1985); J. Sommerville, *The Rise and Fall of Childhood* (1982).

L. Schneider

Family Life Division of the United States Catholic Conference. Prompted by Pope Pius

XI's* 1930 encyclical* letter on marriage and family life, *Casti Conubii,* a Family Life Section was established in 1931 in the Social Action Department of the National Catholic Welfare Conference* (NCWC). Organized under Rev. Edgar Schmiedeler, OSB, its director until 1956, this office was to "assist, stimulate and coordinate all Catholic family life activities" in the U.S. It sought to provide Catholic groups with ideas, resources and literature, but was to undertake no direct action itself. From 1940 to 1968, it was known as the Family Life Bureau. When the NCWC was reorganized as the U.S. Catholic Conference* in 1968, it became the Family Life Division in the Department of Education.

Among its projects were an annual Catholic Conference on Family Life, begun in 1933, the publication of a journal, *Family Digest,* and the initiation of marriage-preparation courses in Catholic high schools and colleges.

BIBLIOGRAPHY. J. Burns, "American Catholics and the Family Crisis, 1930-1962: the ideological and organizational response" (unpublished Ph.D. thesis, University of Notre Dame, 1982).

J. T. Connelly

Family of Love. A cultic* group arising from the Jesus Movement* of the 1960s. Founded in 1968 by David Berg in southern California, the movement has been known as Teens for Christ, Revolution for Jesus, Children of God and, since 1983, the Family of Love. It emerged during the Jesus Movement era and soon became identified as the most radical of the Christian hippie groups. Preaching* an apocalyptic* gospel and attacking the established institutions of conventional America, especially the church, Berg became known to his youthful followers as God's "End-Time Prophet." Communal in nature, the group is organized into colonies and has spread throughout the world. It has appealed to thousands of young people through its music, its sense of family and its unique form of mission—one which includes a sexual dimension.

The Children of God, originally an ultrafundamentalist sect,* devolved into a sex cult, as its leader, affectionately known as Moses David or "Mo" to his followers, promoted a form of religious prostitution known by members as "Flirty Fishing." Children of God colonies became centers of various forms of deviant sexual practices, including child-adult contact. Teaching as well as practical directives of all types were communicated to "disciples" via numerous "Mo Letters," from Berg who became increasingly mysterious and reclusive. Many of the Mo Letters also revealed the

spiritism and other forms of occultism* with which Berg was preoccupied. He regularly claimed to receive messages from spirit guides.

The Family of Love is an example of the cultic extremism which emerged from the context of rapid social and cultural change characterizing American society in the 1960s. They represent Jesus People gone cultic.

BIBLIOGRAPHY. D. Davis, *The Children of God: The Inside Story* (1984); R. Enroth et al., *The Jesus People* (1972); R. Enroth, *Youth, Brainwashing and the Extremist Cults* (1977); W. D. Pritchett, *The Children of God/Family of Love: An Annotated Bibliography* (1985).

R. Enroth

Fanning, Tolbert (1810-1874). Church of Christ* preacher* and editor. Born in Tennessee, Fanning spent his entire life in that state. He was converted* at age seventeen and immediately began preaching,* and though his first efforts were weak, he became as powerful in speech as he was imposing in presence—all six feet, six inches and two hundred and forty pounds of him. Besides preaching, Fanning's life work represents two of the major emphases of Christian Churches* and Churches of Christ—education* and publications.

In 1844 he founded Franklin College in Nashville and conducted it until the Civil War.* In 1855 he began editing the *Gospel Advocate,* but the paper lapsed during the War and was restarted with David Lipscomb* in 1866. Initially Fanning accepted the practice of organized missionary* societies, but by the 1850s he was convinced that they were improper means for the churches. His resistance to such societies continues as a distinctive feature of Churches of Christ.

BIBLIOGRAPHY. *DAB* III; E. I. West, *The Search for the Ancient Order,* vol. 1 (1949).

J. B. North

Farley, John Murphy (1842-1918). Cardinal* and fourth archbishop* of New York. Born in County Armagh, Ireland, Farley immigrated to New York in 1864 under the sponsorship of his maternal uncle who wished to educate him for the priesthood. There he entered Fordham College as a junior, followed by studies at Joseph's Seminary, Troy, New York, in 1865-1866. In 1866 he was sent to the North American College,* Rome, and on June 11, 1870, he was ordained* priest.* Returning to New York he became curate of St. Peter's parish, Staten Island (1870-1872), and then became secretary to Cardinal John McCloskey.* This was the beginning of an administrative career in the archdiocese* of New York which led from secretary (1872-1884) to vicar general (1891-1902) and finally archbishop of New York (1902-1918). Farley received a series of papal honors, ultimately crowned by the title of cardinal priest on November 27, 1911.

A learned man himself, he took particular interest in education, and under his leadership parochial schools* in the archdiocese doubled in number. He supported the Catholic University of America,* took an active interest in his own archdiocesan St. Joseph's Seminary and opened a minor seminary, Cathedral College, in 1903. A patron of the original *Catholic Encyclopedia,* his own scholarly pursuit resulted in two books, *The History of St. Patrick's Cathedral* (1908) and *The Life of John Cardinal McCloskey* (1918). Farley's career, much of which was spent in association with Cardinal McCloskey and Archbishop Michael A. Corrigan,* was characterized by a pastoral care dominated by his cautious and peace-loving nature.

BIBLIOGRAPHY. *DAB* III; M. J. Lavelle, "John Cardinal Farley, Archbishop of New York," *American Ecclesiastical Review* 60 (1919):113-125; *NCE* 5; A. J. Shipman, *His Eminence, Cardinal Farley* (1912).   D. G. Reid

Fast Days. A day devoted to abstinence from physical nourishment as a sign of penitence and dependence on God. Fasting appears to some extent in all religions, although in America government appeals for observance of fast days have led to much controversy. The fast day was an English Puritan* response to the Anglican* holy days, instituted in New England by either civil or ecclesiastical authority. Plymouth Colony observed the first such day in 1636. The other Puritan colonies followed suit and imposed fines on those who recreated or labored on government-appointed fast days. A fast day could be precipitated by celebration (dedicating a meetinghouse) or, more frequently, by a disaster (war, drought, plague or earthquake). In the latter case, the minister would deliver an "occasional sermon"* diagnosing the spiritual condition of the people and prescribing "repentance and reformation."

During the Revolutionary era, other colonies proclaimed fast days, and special days for "publik humiliation, fasting and prayer" were set aside by the Continental and Confederation Congresses. In 1798 John Adams made the first attempt to appoint a fast day under the Federal Constitution, arousing significant political opposition. Undeterred, Adams proclaimed a second fast in 1799. His successor, Thomas Jefferson,* balked at the practice as an

intrusion of the state into private religious matters, but Madison proclaimed a national fast at the urging of Congress during the War of 1812. No further attempts were made at government sponsorship of fasting until Henry Clay introduced a resolution in 1832 to appoint a fast in response to a cholera epidemic. Clay's attempt was a political move aimed at embarrassing Andrew Jackson, and it caused acrimonious debate in Congress. Presidents Tyler and Taylor, hoping to avoid similar problems, couched their fast-day proclamations in the form of official recommendations. In 1860 the Supreme Court held that all governmental fast-day proclamations were simply recommendatory and thus non-compulsory. Nonetheless, Lincoln* approved Congressional fast declarations during the Civil War,* and as late as 1918 Woodrow Wilson* acted with Congressional approbation in proclaiming a national fast.

BIBLIOGRAPHY. W. D. Love, *The Fast and Thanksgiving Days of New England* (1895); A. P. Stokes, *Church and State in the United States,* 3 vols. (1964).   R. M. Payne

Father. A form of address usually used by Catholic laity to address a priest.* Early Christians frequently called their spiritual leaders *father. Abba,* a child's word for *father* in Aramaic, is the root of *abuna,* a title for bishops* and priests among Arabic-speaking Christians, and of *abbot,* the title for the superiors of Catholic* monasteries. *Papas,* a child's word for *father* in classical Greek, is the root of *pope,* a title given to all bishops from the third to the fifth century, after which it was reserved for the bishop of Rome. In the Middle Ages *father* became the general form of address for monks and friars.

In fairly recent times, *father* has become the common form of address for all Catholic priests in English-speaking countries. This custom apparently began in Ireland and, as a result of Irish immigrations, spread to the U.S., where it became firmly established during the second half of the nineteenth century. It became widespread in England around 1880, largely due to the encouragement of Cardinal Henry Manning. Since 1900 many priests of the Anglican Communion* have also adopted the title.

Some American Protestants,* especially fundamentalists,* strongly object to this title, appealing to Jesus' words: "Do not call anyone on earth 'father,' for you have one Father, and he is in heaven" (Mt 23:9).   M. E. Hussey

Feast of Circumcision. This feast has been celebrated on January 1, the eighth day after

Christmas,* since the sixth century, in Gaul and Spain; since the eleventh century, in Rome; and then throughout the Eastern and Western Church. The developed liturgy* includes four motifs: (1) the New Year; (2) the octave of Christmas (all major feasts came to be celebrated for a period of eight days); (3) the circumcision of Jesus; (4) Mary* as the Virgin-Mother of God *(theotokos)* and also as the figure of the church, insofar as human believers share in making Jesus known to others. Recently a fifth motif has been added, and this day is celebrated as a day of world peace.

In the Roman Catholic Church* this has been a holy day of obligation. The texts of the liturgy reflect the development of this feast, which also reflects the spirit of the Eastern Church and liturgy, and its emphasis on *theiosis,* the divinization or deification of man, in contrast to the Western Church's emphasis on redemption from sin: God became man in order that man might become God. This is brilliantly presented in the first antiphon for vespers,* which also sums up the entire feast: "O admirable exchange *(commercium)!* The creator of mankind took to himself a human body and deigned to be born of a Virgin, and, becoming man without man's concurrence, bestowed on us all his divinity."

BIBLIOGRAPHY. P. Parsch, *The Church's Year of Grace,* 5 vols. (1962). R. L. Kress

Feasts of the Church. Except for a few Christian groups (such as the Adventists), the principal feast day of all Christian churches is the Lord's Day—Sunday.* Within the cycle of the year, however, most denominations designated special feasts connected with the life of Christ (such as Easter* or Christmas*) or Sundays which are given over to a special emphasis: Mission* Sunday or Reformation Sunday.

The more liturgically* oriented church bodies have a much more elaborate cycle of feasts. In the Roman Catholic Church,* for instance, the calendar is divided into the temporal cycle and the sanctoral cycle. The temporal cycle celebrates the saving mission of Christ, beginning with his promised coming (Advent* season culminating in Christmas); his manifestation as Savior (the Epiphany* season); followed by Lent* and Holy Week,* which culminates in Easter. Easter is recognized as the major feast of the temporal cycle in both Western and Eastern Christianity. After Easter, the gift of the Spirit is celebrated in Pentecost.* The Sundays that follow are called "ordinary time" until the cycle begins again with Advent.

The sanctoral cycle, by contrast, celebrates the feast days of the Blessed Virgin,* the apostles and the other saints.* Some of these feasts are celebrated by the whole church, while others are feasts peculiar to a given region or nation or even a particular monastic* or religious order.*

The feast days of the church were, in an earlier time, closely connected with the passing of the secular year. In modern cultures there are echoes of that closeness in the nearly universal practice of observing the Christmas Season or the more regional observances of feasts like Mardi Gras* (literally "Fat Tuesday"—the last day before the Lenten fast) or the feast days of Saint Patrick and Saint Valentine, which have now become largely secular celebrations.

See also CHRISTIAN YEAR.

BIBLIOGRAPHY. A. Adam, *The Liturgical Year* (1981); O. Casel, *The Mystery of Christian Worship* (1962). L. S. Cunningham

Federal Council of Churches. Ecumenical* association of denominations* studying and acting upon matters of social importance. Three years after the Carnegie Hall Conference* (1905), the founding convention of the Federal Council of Churches (FCC) was held December 2 8, 1908, in Philadelphia. Thirty-three denominations, numbering 18 million American Protestants, constituted the initial membership.

Organizers such as Elias B. Sanford* and William K. Roberts were aware that any doctrinal prerequisite could deter denominations from joining. Only the preamble to the constitution contained any hint of doctrinal conformity; it proclaimed that the FCC was "to manifest the essential oneness of the Christian churches of America in Jesus Christ as their divine Lord and Savior." Similarly, the full autonomy of member denominations was not to be limited by common forms of government or of worship*; rather the FCC could only counsel and recommend to its member churches. With these guidelines, the FCC's stated purposes were more easily obtained: namely, "to express the fellowship and catholic unity of the Christian church" and "to secure a larger combined influence for the churches of Christ in all matters affecting the moral and social condition of the people, so as to promote the application of the law of Christ in every relation of human life."

The FCC demonstrated its early and continuing concern with social issues by establishing a Commission on Church and Social Service in 1908. In 1912, the Social Creed of the Churches,* addressing the problems of the industrial era, was adopted . Conservatives such as Carl McIntire* were critical of the FCC for its preoccupation with social issues and its lack of emphasis on individual redemption. After 1932 these conservatives were joined by those who thought the FCC was leaning too much toward communism.

Some of the FCC's most obvious efforts occurred during and after the world wars. As World War 1* escalated, FCC support of the Allied position increased. In 1917 the General Wartime Commission of the Churches* was formed by the FCC to provide military chaplains.* Under the leadership of Robert E. Speer* and William A. Brown,* this Commission also actively campaigned for the rights of African-American soldiers. The same work was carried out by the FCC-sponsored General Committee on Army and Naval Chaplains during World War 2.* But throughout World War 2* the Council held out the goal of world peace, exemplified in establishing a Commission on a Just and Durable Peace under the leadership of John Foster Dulles* in 1941. Studies in 1946 regarding American/Soviet relations and the use of the atom bomb demonstrate how this attitude continued into the postwar years.

Several Eastern Orthodox* churches joined the FCC in 1938. As a leader in ecumenical relations, the FCC was able to lend its expertise and moral support to establishing of the World Council of Churches* in 1948. In 1950 the FCC merged with thirteen other interdenominational agencies to become the National Council of Churches.*

See also ECUMENICAL MOVEMENT; ECUMENISM.

BIBLIOGRAPHY. S. M. Cavert, *The American Churches in the Ecumenical Movement, 1900-1968* (1968); J. A. Hutchison, *We Are Not Divided* (1941); C. S. Macfarland, *Christian Unity in the Making* (1948); E. B. Sanford, *Origin and History of the Federal Council* (1916).

B. V. Hillis

Fee, John Gregg (1816-1901). Abolitionist* minister* and founder of Berea College. Born and raised in Kentucky, Fee spent most of his life in that state, working for educational and various antislavery causes. After graduating from Augusta College (1842), he began his study at Lane Theological Seminary, which was already well known as an abolitionist center through the efforts of Theodore Weld.* Two years later he was consecrated* to the abolitionist cause after having prayed* these words: "Lord, if needs be, make me an Abolitionist." Later that year he was rebuffed by his slaveholding parents in his attempt to convert them to his antislavery position.

Fee established and labored in two antislavery

churches in Kentucky, during which time he was shot at, clubbed and stoned. In 1853 he started the Berea Union Church after having given a series of antislavery sermons in the area. Two years later he founded an abolitionist school, now known as Berea College. He consistently acted with an intensity of moral purpose in joining conversion* and Christian commitment to socially relevant causes.

BIBLIOGRAPHY. *DAB* III.   R. R. Mathisen

Feehan, Patrick Augustine (1829-1902). First Catholic* archbishop* of Chicago (1880-1902). Born in County Tipperary, Ireland, Feehan was educated at the Maynooth College Seminary and then called to America by Archbishop Peter Kenrick* of St. Louis, where he was ordained* in 1852. Serving as a seminary* professor and then a pastor* in St. Louis, he was consecrated* bishop* of Nashville in 1865.

When Chicago was raised to the rank of an archdiocese* in 1880, Feehan became that city's first archbishop. He devoted most of his time and energy in Chicago to "brick and mortar" activities, establishing a total of 140 new parishes. He also founded St. Mary's Training School, an orphanage and industrial school in Des Plaines, Illinois. Feehan's last years were marked by a sharp dispute between Irish-born and American-born Irish priests. The foreign-born Irish nationalists believed Feehan relied too heavily on American-born advisors, and they tried to block the appointment of Peter Muldoon as Feehan's auxiliary bishop.* Rome excommunicated one of the nationalist leaders in 1901 and appointed Muldoon auxiliary, but the controversy prevented Muldoon from succeeding Feehan, who died in 1902.

BIBLIOGRAPHY. *DAB* III; *DARB;* C. J. Kirkfleet, *The Life of Patrick Augustine Feehan* (1922); *NCAB* 9; C. Shanabruch, *Chicago's Catholics* (1981).   E. R. Kantowicz

Feeney, Leonard (1898-1978). Jesuit* poet and controversialist. Born in Lynn, Massachusetts, Feeney joined the Jesuits in 1914 and studied at Woodstock College, Maryland; and Weston College, Massachusetts. After completing the Jesuit course of studies, Feeney gained fame in the 1930s as the author of "Catholic verse." His inspirational poetry became a staple of Catholic* primary and secondary schools, and his collection of stories on Catholic themes, *Fish on Fridays,* became a best seller in 1934. Feeney was elected president of the Catholic Poetry Society in 1940, and as literary editor of *America* magazine he became a highly visible presence on the lecture circuit.

In 1943 Feeney was sent to the St. Benedict's Center in Cambridge, Massachusetts, where his "Thursday night lectures" quickly gained a large following and numerous converts at Harvard University.* By 1946, however, Feeney began teaching an absolutist/rigorist interpretation of the ancient church doctrine* "outside the church there is no salvation." Feeling that too many "loopholes" had been created by twentieth-century theologians, Feeney taught that the orthodox* Catholic position was that anyone not in communion with the Bishop of Rome was damned. Feeney's much-publicized preaching* of this interpretation, as well as his denunciations of Harvard professors by name, quickly made his doctrinal crusade front-page news in the national press.

In 1949 the Vatican's Holy Office officially condemned Feeney's interpretation of church doctrine, but Feeney's refusal to submit to religious superiors led to his dismissal from the Society of Jesus and to his excommunication* from the Catholic Church in 1953. Although officially reconciled to the Church in 1972, Feeney is never known to have recanted his position and his unreconciled followers—the Slaves of the Immaculate Heart of Mary—continue to teach his rigorist interpretation. The "Boston Heresy Case" had made Feeney the most publicized heretic in American Catholic history.

BIBLIOGRAPHY. C. Clarke, *The Loyolas and the Cabots* (1951); R. Connor, *Walled In: True Story of a Cult* (1979). M. S. Massa

Fellowship of Evangelical Bible Churches.

Formerly Evangelical Mennonite Brethren Conference, the Fellowship of Evangelical Bible Churches (FEBC) was organized in 1889 as a schism among Mennonites who emigrated from Russia to the U. S. in the 1870s. Led by Isaac Peters of Henderson, Nebraska, and Aaron Wall of Mountain Lake, Minnesota, the conference was a product of pietist* and evangelical* influences within traditional Mennonite communities. An emphasis on individual morality and personal salvation, coupled with openness to Sunday school,* evangelistic* meetings and foreign missions* typified the conference from its beginning. In recent years the conference has identified more closely with its pietist/evangelical heritage than its Mennonite doctrinal roots, to the point that it dropped the word *Mennonite* from its name in 1987.

The current name is the conference's fourth. Begun as the Conference of United Mennonite Brethren of North America, it changed its name in 1917 to the Defenseless Mennonite Brethren in Christ of North America. In 1937 it became known as the Evangelical Mennonite Brethren Conference. From 1953 to 1962 the FEBC was loosely affiliated with the Evangelical Mennonite Church through The Conference of Evangelical Mennonites. Membership is roughly 4500 in thirty-six congregations in the U. S., Canada, Paraguay and Argentina (1986). FEBC headquarters are in Omaha, Nebraska. The conference organ, founded in 1910 as *Evangelisationsbote,* has been published as *Gospel Tidings* since 1943.

BIBLIOGRAPHY. C. Redekop, "The Embarrassment of a Religious Tradition," *Mennonite Life 36* (1981):17-21; G. S. Rempel, ed., *A Historical Sketch of the Churches of the Evangelical Mennonite Brethren* (1939). K. M. Enns-Rempel

Fellowship of Grace Brethren Churches. A

conservative Brethren denomination.* Although related to other evangelicals* and fundamentalists,* the Grace Brethren differ from them in their emphasis on a peculiar observance of the Lord's Supper* which includes the love feast* and the service of foot washing.* Other distinctive practices include anointing* the sick with oil (according to Jas 5) and refraining from amusements considered to be worldly. The Brethren also practice adult baptism* by triple forward immersion.

The Grace Brethren grew from a division that occurred at Ashland College and Seminary in 1937. As a result of this controversy, they emphasize congregational* church government. Despite this local autonomy the churches maintain a close relationship through annual district and national conferences where both lay* and ministerial* delegates vote on issues that concern the membership. There are also independent corporations that manage cooperative endeavors such as Home Missions, Foreign Missions and Grace Theological Seminary and College (Winona Lake, Indiana).

The church is characterized by a conservative social and political outlook and a sincere desire to share the gospel with unbelievers. This has led to an emphasis on missions* both at home and abroad. A life of service to God in active Christian work is constantly presented to young people. Among the Brethren leaders that have gained a reputation in the larger evangelical community are Louis Bauman,* Alva McClain,* Herman Hoyt and John Whitcomb. As the church has grown it has attracted many members from other traditions, and this has resulted in a decline in certain historical Brethren attitudes such as refusing to bear arms, take oaths and engage in lawsuits. In 1986 the group had a membership of 41,249 in over 300 congregations, most heavily concentrated in California, Ohio and Pennsylvania.

BIBLIOGRAPHY. R. G. Clouse, "Fellowship of Grace Brethren Churches" in *Meet the Brethren,* ed. D. Durnbaugh (1984); H. A. Kent, *Conquering Frontiers* (1972).

R. G. Clouse

Fellowship of Reconciliation. Nondenominational Christian pacifist* and social-reform organization. The American branch of the Fellowship of Reconciliation (FOR) was organized in November 1915, in Garden City, Long Island, at a meeting of a group of Quakers,* Social Gospel* ministers* and leaders of the YMCA.* The Fellowship was originally founded in Great Britain in 1914. Convinced that war violated Christian principles, FOR opposed war preparation and American intervention in World War 1.* When military conscription was enacted after war was declared in 1917, FOR sought exemption for conscientious objectors.

FOR leaders soon concluded that the war was not an aberration; rather it logically followed from existing social and economic ills. Therefore, the committed Christian pacifist must also seek social justice and economic redistribution. By the war's end, FOR had become a meeting place for left-wing reformers attracted to pacifism and Christian pacifists who now recognized the need for wide-ranging social and economic change. This alliance could have changed the FOR's Christian, non-violent orientation. However, in the late 1920s, its executive board reaffirmed the need for a Christian perspective to solve social and economic problems. In 1933 it refused to sanction violence, even to achieve social and economic reforms.

FOR was the most intellectually vibrant pacifist organization of the interwar period, and A. J. Muste's appointment as executive secretary in 1940 led to an additional innovation—the adoption of non-violent direct action as a weapon for reform. In 1942 Chicago FOR members organized the Congress of Racial Equality, which pioneered the use of this technique in the postwar crusade for black civil rights.* Active in the anti-Vietnam War* movement of the 1960s and 1970s, the FOR has recently campaigned for arms limitation and eventual disarmament.

BIBLIOGRAPHY. C. R. Marchand, *The American Peace Movement and Social Reform, 1898-1918* (1972); C. Chatfield, *For Peace and Justice: Pacifism in America, 1914-1941* (1971).

G. F. Goodwin

Fellowship of Socialist Christians. Organized in 1932 in the crisis of the Great Depression,* the Fellowship of Socialist Christians was to develop critical socialist theory and action. The Fellowship's guiding spirit was Reinhold Niebuhr,* for whom it served as a chief outlet for action from 1934 to the end of the decade. It sought to develop Christian social theory in order to critique capitalist individualism* while rejecting the secularism and reductionism of Marxism. The relationship between Christianity and Marxism was to be a discriminating one, while recognizing that Marx correctly saw the need for social control of the means of production and the necessity of social struggle. To indicate the priority of commitment to Christian faith, the title *Socialist Christians,* intentionally reversed the usual order *Christian Socialists.*

The journal *Radical Religion* (1935) (later named *Christianity and Society* [1940-1956]) was the Fellowship's primary activity in the 1930s. The members supported programs of social change, particularly interracial projects empowering laborers in the rural South. To fund the projects during the early years (until 1937), a progressive, self-imposed limitation on personal consumption was adopted (whereupon the membership dropped from 500 to 100). During World War 2* there was a shift from the critique of capitalist democracy* to its defense against the barbarism of fascism. The critical attitude toward Marxism increased.

The group was renamed Frontier Fellowship in 1948 in order to distinguish its concerns from Stalinism, the problems of which were seen to be rooted in Marxist illusions. The Fellowship still saw socialization of the forms of property that grant social power as one method of bringing economic power under control. The group was again renamed Christian Action in 1951, and in it socialist concepts were even less present.

BIBLIOGRAPHY. R. W. Fox, *Reinhold Niebuhr* (1985); R. Niebuhr, "Why a New Quarterly?" *Radical Religion* 1, 1 (Autumn 1935):3-5; P. Tillich, E. Helmann and R. Niebuhr, "The Second Focus of the Fellowship," *Christianity and Society* 15, 1 (Winter 1949/50):19-22.

S. C. Mott

Fellowship of Southern Churchmen. A non-denominational Christian social reform organization. Founded at a conference of some eighty people in Monteagle, Tennessee, in May 1934, it was known first as the Conference of Younger Churchmen. The Fellowship combined prophetic radicalism, neo-orthodoxy* and a strong sense of Christian vocation in supporting labor unions, tenant farmers and minorities during the post-

Depression period. Led by Howard Kester, the Fellowship attracted foundation funds and prominent participants and speakers like Reinhold Niebuhr,* Clarence Jordan,* Nelle Morton, Benjamin E. Mays, and Sadie and Neal Hughley.

Just before its decline in the late 1950s, the Fellowship shifted its primary focus to the intensifying Civil Rights Movement.* One of its leading members, Will D. Campbell, participated in the conferences in Atlanta and New Orleans that created the Southern Christian Leadership Conference* in 1957. Different in key respects from most civil rights advocacy groups, the Fellowship of Southern Churchmen envisaged a higher level of human community than one merely guaranteeing civil rights. The Fellowship was scattered by the late fifties but was revived and reorganized in 1964 as the Committee of Southern Churchmen.*

BIBLIOGRAPHY. A. P. Dunbar, *Against the Grain: Southern Radicals and Prophets, 1929-1959* (1981).   T. R. Peake

Feminism, Christian. A movement for women's equality rooted in Scripture and Christian faith. The seeds of American Christian feminism were planted in Europe centuries ago. Christian humanist, Desiderius Erasmus (c. 1469-1536) stressed women's right to education, including Bible reading. Though most Reformation Protestants still barred women from church leadership, radical Puritan* groups in seventeenth-century England granted women more freedom. Congregationalist* women voted in church; Baptist* women publicly confessed their faith; Quaker* women preached.* (Quaker Margaret Fell wrote *Women's Speaking Justified,* the first such document by a woman.) Most colonial American women preachers were Quakers. John Wesley,* the founder of the Methodists,* believed lay* women could receive an extraordinary call of God to publicly testify and pray. Soon women on both sides of the Atlantic served as Methodist class leaders.

In America, Christian feminism mobilized in the climate of nineteenth-century revivalism* where the Spirit's call, not necessarily ordination* or education, qualified one to preach. Evangelist Charles Finney's* "new measures"* allowed women to speak in the presence of a gathering of men. Later, women like Phoebe Palmer* gained national fame in the mid nineteenth-century Holiness Movement.* African-American revivalist Amanda Smith* effectively preached abroad and epitomized the courage of African-Americans who overcame the double barriers of race and sex.

Religious freedom* and disestablishment in America contributed to new denominations* which were able to utilize women however they chose. Free-Will Baptists* had female preachers as early as 1797 (Sally Parsons) and 1819 (Clarissa Danforth). Congregationalists, setting aside Antoinette Brown* for the ministry in 1853, became the first U.S. denomination to fully ordain a woman. Methodist Holiness churches often utilized women as preachers. The first American women's rights convention in 1848 occurred at a Wesleyan Methodist chapel in Seneca Falls, New York. By 1900 Unitarians* and Universalists* had ordained about seventy-five women.

Temperance,* abolition* and women's suffrage* helped spur Christian feminism. Abolitionist Sarah Grimké* (*Letters on the Equality of the Sexes,* 1837) saw links between the misuse of Scripture* to endorse slavery and the demand for female submission. Frances Willard's* Women's Christian Temperance Union* put socially concerned women in pulpits. The post-Civil War rise of female foreign missionaries meant women now studied Bible and theology* in training schools (*See* Women's Missionary Movement). Even early fundamentalists* often endorsed female public ministry. Bible institutes* trained women (often barred from seminary*) as evangelists,* pastors* and Bible teachers.

Diversity marks twentieth-century feminism. Early Pentecostals* (e.g., Maria Woodworth-Etter* and Aimee Semple McPherson*) and charismatics (e.g., Kathryn Kuhlman*) continued the tradition within Methodist-Holiness churches of advocating women's public ministry. All of the Protestant mainline* denominations now ordain women to the ministry. Evangelical* feminists officially organized in 1973 to form the Evangelical Women's Caucus. Post-Vatican II* American Catholics increasingly question female exclusion from the priesthood.*

A number of women have taken prominent theological roles both within the churches and the academe. Feminist theology—critical theological reflection carried out from a distinctly feminine perspective—has become a recognized theological movement among both Protestant and Roman Catholic theologians. Rosemary Radford Ruether and Elizabeth Schussler Fiorenza have achieved prominence within this diverse movement that in some expressions has become confessedly non-Christian.

Christian feminism was never uniquely American. Catherine Booth* of The Salvation Army in Britain, Pandita Ramabai in India and Catherine Juell in Scandinavia each preached in the context of revivalism. Nor was the movement unified; feminists still debate priorities and strategies. But it was rooted in biblical Christianity: women created equally in God's image, made one in Christ through redemption, fully gifted by the Spirit for service. Such liberating theology continues to fuel Christian feminists in America as they enter the twenty-first century.

See also INCLUSIVE LANGUAGE MOVEMENT; ORDINATION OF WOMEN; WOMEN'S SUFFRAGE.

BIBLIOGRAPHY. C. De Swarte Gifford, ed., *Women in American Protestant Religion, 1800-1930,* 36 vol. reprint collection (1987); R. R. Ruether and R. S. Keller, eds., *Women and Religion in America,* 3 vols. (1982-1986); *Women and the Church in America: Microfiche Collection,* American Theological Library Association (1985); N. A. Hardesty, *Women Called to Witness: Evangelical Feminism in the 19th Century* (1984).

J. R. Hassey

Fenwick, Benedict Joseph (1782-1846). Second Catholic* bishop* of Boston. Born near Leonardtown, Maryland, a member of a well-known Catholic family in Maryland and a graduate of Georgetown College, Fenwick entered the Jesuit* order in 1806 and was ordained* in 1808. He spent the next nine years in New York City, working as a pastor, helping found a college called the New York Literary Institute and serving as a diocesan* administrator. In 1817, Jesuit superiors appointed Fenwick president of Georgetown College and pastor of Holy Trinity Church; but within a year he was sent to Charleston, South Carolina, to end schisms there. He worked as vicar-general of the Charleston diocese from 1820 to 1822, when he rejoined the administration at Georgetown. The next year Fenwick was transferred to southern Maryland to be a pastor.* In January 1825, he became president of Georgetown again; but four months later, Pope Leo XII* approved his selection as bishop of Boston. As head of the Boston diocese until 1846, he contended against anti-Catholicism, started new parishes to care for the growing Catholic population and established a diocesan newspaper. Fenwick founded the College of the Holy Cross in 1843, the first Catholic college in New England.

BIBLIOGRAPHY. *DAB* III; R. H. Lord et al., *History of the Archdiocese of Boston,* vol. 3 (1945); J. M. McCarthy, ed., *Memoirs to Serve for the Future* (1978).

W. P. Leahy

Fenwick, Edward Dominic (1768-1832). Dominican* missionary* bishop* and founder of the

first province of Dominicans in the U.S. Born in Maryland of a colonial family whose forebears had sailed from England in Lord Calvert's* ships in 1634, Fenwick studied at the English Dominican-run Holy Cross College in Belgium. In 1790 he entered the English province of the Order of Preachers, or Dominicans. Returning to the U.S. in 1804, in 1806 he established a province of the Order on the Kentucky frontier near Bardstown. In the same area, in 1822, he encouraged the formation of the first community of American Dominican Sisters by daughters of the pioneers who had migrated from Maryland.

Meanwhile, in 1821 Fenwick was named the first bishop of Cincinnati, with responsibility for the spiritual welfare of Catholics in the vast area north to Canada and west across Lake Michigan to the upper Mississippi River. Bishop Fenwick was especially mindful of the tribes of Native Americans, to whom he sent such devoted missionaries* as Samuel Mazzuchelli* and Frederic Baraga. He sought justice for the tribes and planned for their adult education as well as schools for their children.

On a long, difficult journey from Mackinac Island back to Cincinnati in 1832, Bishop Fenwick fell victim to the rampant cholera epidemic and died in Wooster, Ohio, on September 26. He was buried in Cincinnati, where many mourned him as the "apostle of Ohio."

BIBLIOGRAPHY. V. F. O'Daniel, O.P., *Edward Dominic Fenwick, O.P., Founder of the Dominicans in the United States* (1920).

M. N. McGreal

Ferrill, London (Loudin) (?-1854). African-American Baptist* minister. Born a slave in Hanover County, Virginia, at the age of eleven Ferrill was rescued from drowning, an event precipitating his religious conversion.* As a young man he gained a reputation as an unordained slave preacher, claiming fifty converts. Freed upon the death of his owner, Ferrill moved with his wife to Lexington, Kentucky. There he began to compete with an older African-American free-lance preacher named "Old Captain." Ferrill, however, sought the sanction of the white First Baptist Church which sponsored his ordination* and the membership of his First African Church in the Elkhorn Association in 1822. Thirty years later, still an auxiliary of the white Baptists, the congregation was the largest in the state, numbering 1,820 members. Respected by whites and especially by younger African-Americans, Ferrill became a man of wealth and fame, even drawing a salary from the city because of his influence over his own people. Adapting to the circumstances of the upper South, Ferrill performed slave marriages with the stipulation "until death or distance do them part," and he left behind a prayer, blessing "the white people who have always treated me as though I was a white man." His pastorate of thirty-two years ended at his death, October 12, 1854.

BIBLIOGRAPHY. W. J. Simmons, *Men of Mark* (1887); M. Sobel, *Travelin' On: The Slave Journey of an Afro-Baptist Faith* (1979).

W. B. Gravely and C. White

Fideism. An epistemological perspective emphasizing the priority of faith (Latin, *fides*) over reason in religious knowledge. Fideists maintain that religious truth is apprehended by faith rather than evidential reasoning or rational arguments. Fideism can also be used in a pejorative sense, referring to perspectives stressing the role of faith at the expense of reason. A classic case of extreme fideism is Tertullian's statement, "I believe because it is absurd." Vatican I's* *Dogmatic Constitution on Faith* in effect did away with fideism in Catholic thought by declaring that unaided natural reason could comprehend God's existence and nature.

A milder form of fideism, while remaining firm in subjugating natural reason's capacity in the religious realm, attempts to develop the unique logic of faith. Augustine, Anselm and Karl Barth* advocated such a primacy of faith. Among American Reformed* thinkers, the apologetics* of Cornelius Van Til* has often been called fideistic. It is, however, the diminution of reason which normally evokes the use of the term. Thus, it is meant to imply an extreme subjectivity or solipsism equivalent to irrationalism in religious knowledge.

A. A. Glenn

Fielde, Adele (1839-1916). Baptist* missionary* to China. As a young woman Fielde became engaged to a Baptist missionary candidate to Siam. She agreed to marry him and join him in Southeast Asia, but upon her arrival in Siam in 1865, she was informed that he had died. Fielde stayed and conducted missionary work for several years, until she was dismissed from the mission for unbecoming conduct—dancing and card-playing with members of the diplomatic community.

On her return trip to America she visited China, where she caught the vision for missionary work among Chinese women. Pleading with her directors to be reinstated, in 1872 she returned to China and began training Chinese women to become

Bible women—lay* Bible teachers and assistants to missionaries. She organized a school, wrote textbooks, taught classes and conducted field training. During her twenty-year term of service she trained some five hundred women to evangelize and train their own people. After she retired from active missionary service, she resigned from the Baptist mission board and began a career of research and writing.

BIBLIOGRAPHY. F. B. Yoyt, " 'When a Field was Found Too Difficult for a Man, a Woman Should Be Sent': Adele M. Fielde in Asia, 1865-1890," *The Historian* (May 1982). R. A. Tucker

Fifield, James William, Jr. (1899-1977). Congregational* minister.* Born in Chicago, Fifield received his education at Oberlin,* the University of Chicago* and Chicago Theological Seminary. He served the East Church of Grand Rapids, Michigan (1924-1935), and the First Church of Los Angeles (1935-1967), making the latter the world's largest and wealthiest Congregational church. A controversial libertarian conservative, he founded Spiritual Mobilization in 1935 to rally the clergy* to resist collectivism, including the New Deal. Its monthly *Faith and Freedom* (1949-1960) spread his anticommunist* views. He condemned the Yalta agreements, was a board member of the American China Policy Association, organized in 1946 to promote aid to Chiang Kai-Shek and supported Senator Joseph McCarthy. Claiming it would jeopardize Congregational independence, he opposed the Congregational merger with the Evangelical and Reformed Church in 1957 to form the United Church of Christ* and led a secession to create the National Association of Congregational Christian Churches.

BIBLIOGRAPHY. R. G. Davis, *Light on a Gothic Tower* (1967); R. L. Roy, *Prophets of Discord: A Study of Organized Bigotry and Disruption on the Fringes of Protestantism* (1953).

J. H. Dorn

Fillmore, Myrtle Page (1845-1931) and Charles Sherlock Fillmore (1854-1948). Co-founders Unity School of Christianity.* Myrtle (Mary Caroline) Page was born in Pagetown, Ohio, into a Methodist* family. After studying at Oberlin College,* she was licensed as a teacher in 1868 and for a short time operated her own private school. Charles was born in St. Cloud, Minnesota (then part of the Northwest Territory), and though his mother was a devout Episcopalian,* Charles had little exposure to formal religion. His education consisted of tutoring by a frontier teacher. A hip injury in 1864 left him with a withered leg. Charles held various jobs, including railroad freight inspector, mule-team driver, assayer and real-estate salesman. Charles and Myrtle met in Denison, Texas (1876), and married in Clinton, Missouri (1881). For several years (1881-1884) they resided in Pueblo, Colorado, before finally settling in Kansas City, Missouri. Before founding Unity they were active in the temperance movement* and attended Methodist and Episcopal* churches.

For several years Myrtle was afflicted with tuberculosis. During the years 1886-1888, after hearing New Thought teaching from a disciple of Emma Curtis Hopkins,* E. B. Weeks, Myrtle began to experience a healing from the disease. Out of this the basic insight was born that as a child of God she was entitled to health. God could overcome evil and sickness and bring physical restoration. Charles, who gradually came to accept the truth of his wife's insight, experienced the gradual healing of his crippled leg. Both healings were instrumental in the birth and development of what came to be known as the Unity School.

Charles was a prolific writer, having authored thirteen books and numerous pamphlets, and interpeted the metaphysical basis of the movement. Myrtle, on the other hand, was the inspirational force in the early days of the movement, carrying on a ministry of prayer for those in need of healing. Though the Fillmores incorporated many aspects of orthodox* Christianity, their basic emphasis was on the necessity of obeying the divine laws by right thinking and right living, being unified with the Christ mind in prayer and thereby receiving the benefits of health and prosperity. Myrtle subscribed to a view of reincarnation. Through the dissemination of their writings, the movement spread and eventually took on a sectarian character. The Unity School of Christianity was founded in 1889 and by the 1930s was flourishing. Myrtle died on October 6, 1931, at Unity Village, Missouri. After Myrtle's death, Charles remarried (1933). His second wife (Cora Dedrick) had little impact on the movement. Charles died at Unity Village on July 5, 1948.

BIBLIOGRAPHY. H. D'Andrade, *Charles Fillmore: Herald of the New Age* (1974); *DAB* 4; *DARB;* J. D. Freeman, *The Story of Unity* (1978); *NAW* 1; *NCAB* B; T. E. Witherspoon, *Myrtle Fillmore: Mother of Unity* (1977).   D. deChant

Finley, James Bradley (1781-1856). Itinerant Methodist* minister.* Finley's father, a Princeton*-educated Presbyterian* clergyman,* started several churches in Kentucky. He freed the family slaves on religious grounds and early showed his sympathies for Methodists. James received a classical education in his father's academy and pursued the study of medicine until his desire to be a backwoods farmer won out. In August 1801, he visited a previous church of his father's at Cane Ridge,* Kentucky, witnessed the great camp meeting, and was converted on the way home. Resisting a call to preach, he reverted to his old life until he nearly shot his brother by accident in 1808. Both soon professed and entered the Methodist ministry.

He succeeded in every circuit he served, spending most of his fifty ministerial years in Ohio. In 1816, Bishop McKendree* put him in charge of the Ohio district, which extended from western New York and Pennsylvania throughout Ohio. Six years later, leading citizens in Detroit petitioned the bishops to allow Finley to be stationed in Detroit, but McKendree returned him to a highly successful ministry among the Wyandot Indians of Ohio. That mission ended when the government coerced the tribe to sell their land. In the General Conference of 1844, controversy arose concerning the slaves of Bishop Andrews and his wife. Finley proposed a motion that called for the bishop to "desist from the exercise of this office so long as the impediment remains." That motion passed and became the catalyst for the sectional split of the Methodist Episcopal Church. Finley authored several books which give unique information about early Methodism in the West.

BIBLIOGRAPHY.   *DAB* III; J. B. Finley, *Autobiography* (1853).   M. R. Fraser

Finley, Samuel (1715-1766). New Side* Presbyterian* evangelist* and fifth president of the College of New Jersey (later Princeton).* Born in Ireland, Finley was a pious, intellectually precocious youth who immigrated to Philadelphia at age nineteen. He probably attended William Tennent's* "Log College"* in Neshaminy, Pennsylvania, and thus cast his lot with those Presbyterians who became supporters of the Great Awakening* and favored an active, "experimental" piety.* In 1742 he was ordained* and enjoyed success as an itinerant* evangelist in the middle colonies, despite one foray into Connecticut where he was arrested for vagrancy. In 1744 he accepted a call to Nottingham, Maryland, and there remained for seventeen years, founding his own small but distinguished academy to prepare young men for the Presbyterian ministry.* As a scholar, teacher and one of the most successful and respected of the New Side Presbyterians, Finley was a logical choice for the presidency of the College of New

Jersey, chartered in 1746 as a successor to Tennent's primitive college. Finley served from 1761 to 1766, his term (like those of his four predecessors) cut short by death. Although he published several sermons and essays, Finley left no significant theological work of any size.

BIBLIOGRAPHY. *AAP* 3; A. Alexander, *Biographical Sketches of the Founder and Principal Alumni of the Log College* (1845); *DAB* III.

E. C. Nordbeck

Finney, Charles Grandison (1792-1875). Leading revivalist* of the nineteenth century. Finney, who would one day be known as the "Father of Modern Revivalism," was born in Warren, Litchfield County, Connecticut, the seventh child of farming parents, Sylvester and Rebecca (Rice) Finney. With land increasingly scarce and costly in Connecticut, in 1794 the Finneys joined with many other young families in the great westward migrations of post-Revolutionary America. Settling in Hanover (now Kirkland), Oneida County, New York, following a brief stay in the village of Brothertown, Charles first attended a nearby common school, then the Hamilton Oneida Academy in Clinton. While there, he came under the influence of Principal Seth Morton, who taught the popular, six-foot-two-inch Finney the basics of classical education, singing and the cello.

In 1812 Finney returned to Connecticut to attend the Warren Academy in preparation for further studies at Yale College.* Persuaded against attending Yale, Finney then spent two years teaching in New Jersey. In 1818 his mother's illness forced him to return to New York, where he began the study of law, entering the office of Judge Benjamin Wright in Adams as an apprentice. Although it is uncertain whether or not Finney was formally admitted to the bar, he did regularly argue cases in the local justice's court of Adams.

Finney's remarkable religious conversion* on October 10, 1821, however, dramatically changed the direction of his life. Leaving a promising legal career, claiming he had been given "a retainer from the Lord Jesus Christ to plead his cause," he sought entry into the Presbyterian* ministry.* Taken under care by the St. Lawrence Presbytery (June 25, 1823), he studied theology* with George Gale, his Princeton*-trained pastor in Adams; was licensed* to preach on December 30, 1823; and was subsequently ordained* on July 1, 1824. Hired by the Female Missionary Society of the Western District, he began his labors as a missionary* to the settlers of upstate New York in the spring of 1824.

Under his preaching,* a series of revivals broke out in a number of little villages throughout Jefferson and St. Lawrence counties, places such as Evans Mills, Antwerp, Brownville and Gouverneur. By 1825 his work had spread to the towns of Western, Troy, Utica, Rome and Auburn. These so-called Western revivals (centered in Oneida County) in which Finney exercised "new measures"* such as the anxious seat,* protracted meetings, allowing women to pray in public and the like, brought Finney national fame.

Not all were pleased with his success. Yale-trained revival leaders such as Lyman Beecher* and Asahel Nettleton,* troubled by false reports of alleged excesses, joined with other evangelical* leaders from the Northeast at the village of New Lebanon in the summer of 1827 to discuss their differences. It was at that meeting that Finney emerged as the new leader of evangelical revivalism. This leadership was consolidated during the years 1827-1832 as Finney's revivals swept urban centers such as New York City, Philadelphia, Boston and Rochester. Although Finney was involved in promoting revivals throughout his lifetime, even traveling to England for that purpose in 1849-1850 and again in 1859-1860, these early years were the high water mark of his revival career.

Forced in 1832 to curtail his travels, having contracted cholera in addition to the recurrent respiratory illnesses that troubled him throughout most of his lifetime, he became pastor of the Chatham Street Chapel (Second Free Presbyterian Church) in New York City. He subsequently held pastorates at the Broadway Tabernacle of New York City (1836-1837) and the First Congregational Church of Oberlin, Ohio (1837-1872). In 1835 he accepted an appointment as professor of theology at the newly formed Oberlin Collegiate Institute in Ohio (now Oberlin College*). He later served as president of Oberlin College from 1851 until 1866.

Theologically, Finney can best be described as a New School* Calvinist.* His preaching and teaching—always pointed and dramatic—stressed the moral government of God, the ability of people to repent and make themselves new hearts, the perfectibility of human nature and society, and the need for Christians to apply their faith to daily living. For Finney, this included the investment of one's time and energy in establishing the millennial* kingdom of God on earth by winning converts and involving oneself in social reform* (including antislavery,* temperance* and the like).

Throughout his lifetime, Finney produced a variety of books, sermon collections and articles. Among the more important were his *Lectures on*

Revivals of Religion (1835), a kind of manual on how to lead revivals. He wrote: "It [a revival] presupposes that the church is sunk down in a backslidden state, and a revival consists in the return of the church from her backslidings, and in the conversion of sinners. . . . A revival is nothing else than a new beginning of obedience to God." His *Lectures on Systematic Theology* (1846) reflect his special brand of "arminianized Calvinism." And his *Memoirs* (1876) recount his remarkable involvement in the great revivals of the first half of the nineteenth century.

BIBLIOGRAPHY. R. Carwardine, *Transatlantic Revivalism; Popular Evangelicalism in Britain and America, 1790-1865* (1978); *DAB* III; *DARB;* R. A. G. Dupuis and G. M. Rosell, eds., *The Memoirs of Charles G. Finney* (1989); K. J. Hardman, *Charles Grandison Finney (1792-1875): Revivalist and Reformer* (1987); W. G. McLoughlin, Jr., ed., *Lectures on Revivals of Religion* (1960); *NCAB* 2.

G. M. Rosell

Fire-Baptized Holiness Movement. An early radical Holiness* Movement characterized by "third blessing" theology.* By the late nineteenth century, Iowa had become the strongest state organization of the National Campmeeting Association for the Promotion of Holiness,* a movement generated in the 1860s to restore attention to Wesleyan* "second blessing"* theology.* In 1895 Benjamin Hardin Irwin* of Lincoln, Nebraska, a member of the Iowa Holiness Association, founded the Fire-Baptized Holiness Church. Irwin, an attorney, had left law practice to become a Baptist* preacher.* Influenced by the Iowa Holiness Association, Irwin became an ardent advocate of a crisis experience of sanctification* subsequent to new birth.* His reading of the British Methodist John Fletcher (1729-1785), who spoke of a "baptism of burning love," led him to believe in a "third blessing," a "baptism with the Holy Ghost and fire." This distinction between an experience of sanctification and a subsequent baptism of the Spirit* prepared the way for the modern Pentecostal* revival.

Irwin traveled widely, first throughout the Midwest, later the South, propagating his views. His meetings were marked by considerable emotional display, reminiscent of the earlier Cane Ridge,* Kentucky, camp meetings.* Some who received the baptism reported seeing balls of fire and feeling a burning sensation within. Irwin's evangelistic activity led to the formation of state Fire-Baptized Holiness associations, beginning with Iowa in 1895. Associations were organized in Kansas, Oklahoma and Texas. In 1898 Irwin formed the Fire-Baptized Holiness Association of America at Anderson, South Carolina, naming himself general overseer. By mid-year, additional state associations had been formed in Florida, Georgia, North and South Carolina, Virginia, as well as two Canadian provinces. A publication, *Live Coals of Fire,* was initiated as the official voice of the movement in 1899 and published in Lincoln, Nebraska.

Irwin's teachings, largely rejected by the National Association as the "third blessing heresy," nonetheless received considerable response through the rural Midwest and the South, with thousands reporting a "baptism of fire." This movement furnished the climate out of which the modern Pentecostal movement came. Agnes Ozman,* first person to receive the Pentecostal experience in Topeka, in Parham's Bible school, was a member of Irwin's group. Irwin was removed from leadership for "open and gross sin" in 1900. Joseph Hillery King,* a Methodist, succeeded Irwin. In 1907 the Pentecostal experience of Spirit baptism was introduced into the Fire-Baptized Holiness Church through G. B. Cashwell,* and in 1908 the church changed its official doctrinal statement to include a Pentecostal view of tongues.*

In 1911 the movement was absorbed by merger with the Pentecostal Holiness Church of North Carolina, a church originally organized as the Pentecostal Holiness Church by A. B. Crumpler* at Goldsboro, North Carolina, on November 4, 1898. A third body, the Tabernacle Pentecostal Church located in South Carolina, merged with the Pentecostal Holiness Church in 1915 and adopted the name of the latter body. In 1975 the name was changed to International Pentecostal Holiness Church, and in 1980 there were 110,000 members.

An African-American branch of the church peaceably withdrew from the Fire-Baptized Holiness Church in 1908 and is now known as the Pentecostal Fire-Baptized Holiness Church of God of the Americas, headquartered in Atlanta, Georgia. A white group, known today as the Pentecostal Fire-Baptized Holiness Church, withdrew from the Pentecostal Holiness Church in 1916 out of a desire for stricter dress and lifestyle standards. It is headquartered in Toccoa, Georgia, and is one of the smallest Pentecostal denominations in the U.S.

BIBLIOGRAPHY. A. Beacham, Jr., *A Brief History of the Pentecostal Holiness Church* (1983); J. Campbell, *The Pentecostal Holiness Church, 1898-1948* (1951); D. W. Dayton, *Theological Roots of Pentecostalism* (1987); C. E. Jones, *A Guide to the*

Study of the Pentecostal Movement, 2 vols. (1983); V. Synan, *The Holiness-Pentecostal Movement in the United States* (1971). W. W. Menzies

First Amendment to the Constitution. The First Amendment, or Bill of Rights, protects the most treasured rights of U.S. citizens—freedom of religion, speech, press and the right to peaceably assemble and petition. These rights have become so central and controversial that, with one exception, there have been more Supreme Court cases on the First Amendment than any other part of the Constitution. Invariably the courts and scholars insist that a proper judicial interpretation, especially the clause on religious freedom, the Christian's most treasured legacy, must be based on the history of the First Amendment and the intent of the Framers.

For a number of reasons the fifty-five Framers decided *not* to include a Bill of Rights in the original constitution (1787). First, many Framers held a religious-covenant notion of rights. Rights, like freedom of religion and speech, came from the original covenant between God and man. These God-given, unalienable rights were never created by political documents, although their prior existence had been recognized as early as the English Magna Carta (1215). Since the federal government was a government of limited powers, all rights not expressly excluded were reserved for its citizens. Second, it would be redundant for the federal constitution to also list rights. By 1787 twelve different states had drafted fifteen full-bodied constitutions, most of which included a list of rights. Third, it seemed wise to defer to state authority. For example, some states wrote constitutions endorsing religious pluralism;* others retained established churches.* The Framers had no desire to meddle with regional differences or preferences.

It was primarily pressure from antifederalists, citizens who disliked the federal constitution, that caused the First Congress (1791) to consider 210 suggested amendments which James Madison* distilled down to our present Bill of Rights.

See also CHURCH AND STATE, SEPARATION OF.

BIBLIOGRAPHY. R. A. Wells and T. A. Askew, eds., *Liberty and Law: Reflections on the Constitution in American Life and Thought* (1987).

D. E. Maas

Fisher, George Park (1827-1909). Congregationalist* clergyman* and Yale* church historian. Born in Wrentham, Massachusetts, Fisher studied at Brown University, Yale Divinity School, Auburn

Theological Seminary and Andover Theological Seminary.* Rooted in the later New England theology* as a student of Nathaniel William Taylor* at Yale and Edwards Amasa Park* at Andover Seminary, Fisher joined the Yale Divinity School faculty in 1854 after two years' study in Germany. There he served nearly fifty years as both professor (1854-1901) and later as dean (1895-1901). A leading American exponent of the Tübingen school of historical criticism, Fisher served as president of both the American Society of Church History* and the American Historical Association. Of liberal* theological leaning, he epitomized the effort of church historians to be impartial in judgment and to apply to the history of Christianity the same methodology as would be applied to any social institution. Among his many scholarly works are *The Reformation* (1873), *The Beginnings of Christianity* (2 vols., 1877), *History of the Christian Church* (1887), *History of Christian Doctrine* (1896) and the edited *Unpublished Essay on the Trinity* of Jonathan Edwards (1903). His *Discussions in History and Theology* (1880) appraises the most significant American orthodox* theologians* and their controversies.

BIBLIOGRAPHY. *DAB* III; F. H. Foster, *A Genetic History of the New England Theology* (1907).

C. H. Lippy

Fisher, Henry L. (1874-1947). Bishop* of the United Holy Church of America.* Born in Salisbury, North Carolina, in 1874 and a member of the African Methodist Episcopal Zion Church,* Fisher moved to Wilmington, North Carolina, where in 1892 he heard the preaching of holiness* from the Reverend Elijah Lowney, a Methodist* preacher at the Sam Jones Tabernacle. Fisher became associated with the United Holy Church of America, a predominantly African-American Holiness denomination, and quickly proved to be an effective evangelist.* In 1904 he was called to pastor at the Durham Tabernacle. His outstanding work in Durham led to the renaming of the church in his honor.

Fisher was without a doubt the single most influential individual in the United Holy Church of America during its early development. Following rather undistinguished predecessors, Fisher was elected to the office of president in 1916 and served with distinction until his death in 1947. Consecrated* a bishop* in 1924, Fisher traveled throughout the U.S. and beyond, preaching holiness,* establishing convocations and promoting missions.* In the early 1930s Bishop Fisher traveled to New York to gather members of the United

Holy Church who had migrated there, and along with others he founded the New Covenant Temple in that city.

Highly esteemed for his powerful preaching and endearing fatherly ways, Fisher was often referred to affectionately by members of the church as "Dad." In addition, he was greatly respected and quite influential among other church leaders of his time. The structure he gave the organization has remained essentially intact, and the growth and development under his administration has remained the measure of leaders who succeeded him.

BIBLIOGRAPHY. H. L. Fisher, *The History of the United Holy Church of America, Inc.* (1945); W. C. Turner, Jr., "The United Holy Church of America," (unpublished Ph.D. dissertation, Duke University, 1984). W. C. Turner

Fisher, Mary (1623?-1698). Quaker* traveling preacher.* As a servant in the home of Richard Tomlinson at Pontefract, Yorkshire, Mary and the whole family became convinced Quakers in 1631. With other early Quaker preachers of inner self-judgment, she was imprisoned at York in 1652 and whipped at Cambridge in 1653. Sailing via Barbados, she and Ann Austin* became the first Quakers to set foot in Boston. There they were jailed and their 100 Quaker books burned by the hangman. Mary preached in the West Indies in 1631 and returned to England, setting out in December with five others on a mission to Jerusalem. Two of the party were imprisoned by the inquisition in Rome, but Mary set out with Beatrice and John Buckley to visit the Sultan at Adrianople, who courteously heard Mary Fisher's message "from the great God." Safely returning to England, in 1662 she married Quaker sea captain William Bayly, raised three children, and after his death at sea in 1678 married John Cross with whom she sailed to South Carolina. There she, and later her granddaughter Sophia Hume, became pillars of the tiny Charleston Quaker Meeting.

BIBLIOGRAPHY. W. C. Braithwaite, *The Beginnings of Quakerism,* rev. ed. (1961); R. M. Jones, *The Quakers in the American Colonies* (1966); *NAW* 1. H. S. Barbour

Fisk, Pliny (1792-1825). Pioneer missionary* to the Near East.* Born in Shelburne, Massachusetts, Fisk graduated from Middlebury College and Andover Seminary* (1818) and served briefly as agent of the American Board of Commissioners for Foreign Missions* in Georgia. With Levi Parsons he embarked November 3, 1819, on the first American mission to the Near East, commissioned by the American Board to explore "What good can be done? By what means?" First based at Smyrna, Parsons went to Jerusalem, hoping to reach some of the thronging pilgrims there while Fisk stayed on, studying and officiating as British chaplain* until January 1822. After Parsons's return and death at Alexandria, Fisk was joined at Malta by Jonas King. They toured Upper Egypt, crossed the Sinai Desert and reached Jerusalem in April 1823. He visited Lebanon, returned to Jerusalem and then went to Beirut where he died of a fever. His extensive journal and correspondence helped lay the foundation for a very large mission.

BIBLIOGRAPHY. *AAP* 1; A. Bond, *Memoir of the Rev. Pliny Fisk, A. M.* (1828).

D. M. Stowe

Fisk, Wilbur (1792-1839). Methodist* minister* and educator. Born in Battleboro, Vermont, Fisk attended the University of Vermont (1812-1813) and graduated from Brown University* with honors in 1815. Three years later he became the first college graduate to enter the Methodist itinerancy* in New England. The Methodist Church recognized his gifts and his piety,* and he served as the presiding elder of Vermont (1823-1825), delegate to the General Conference (1824, 1828, 1832), principal of Wilbraham (Wesleyan) Academy in Massachusetts (1825-1830) and the first president of Wesleyan University in Connecticut (1830-1839). His commitment to that institution led him to decline several other significant appointments, including bishop of the Methodist Episcopal Church.*

Fisk spoke and wrote on behalf of missions* and temperance* and against Calvinism* (*Calvinistic Controversy,* 1835) and universalism.* While not pro-slavery, he objected to the methods of abolitionists.* He was the first American Methodist theologian* to achieve recognition outside of his denomination.

BIBLIOGRAPHY. *AAP* 7; *DAB* III; *DARB;* J. H. Holdich, *The Life of Wilbur Fisk* (1842); *NCAB* 3; G. Prentice, *Wilbur Fisk* (1890).

M. R. Fraser

Fiske, Fidelia (1816-1864). Missionary* to Persia. Born in Shelburne, Massachusetts, Fiske was a student and then a teacher at Mt. Holyoke Female Seminary, where she was deeply influenced by the founder, Mary Lyon.* In 1843 she was sent by the American Board of Commissioners for Foreign Missions* to its Nestorian Mission in Persia. For fifteen years she headed the school for girls at

Oroomiah, which became a center for religious revival among women of the Nestorian community. Poor health impelled her return to the U.S. in 1858, where she invested much time and energy in volunteer service at Mt. Holyoke. Her remarkable personal qualities enabled her to make a notable impact in Persia in her relatively limited term of service. She was largely responsible for the publication *Woman and Her Saviour in Persia* (1863), assisted in preparing *A Memorial of Mt. Holyoke Seminary* and at the time of her death was working on "Reminiscences of Miss Mary Lyon."

BIBLIOGRAPHY. *DAB* III; D. T. Fisk, *The Cross and the Crown* (1869); *NAW* 1.

D. M. Stowe

Five Point Deliverance. A doctrinal* statement adopted in 1910 by the Presbyterian Church (USA)* for licensing ministerial candidates. The Deliverance was an integral part of a fifty-year struggle over revision of the creedal foundation (The Westminster* Standards) and control of the denomination.* Conservatives opposed liberal efforts to make the church more inclusive in theology by requiring ministers* to subscribe to biblical doctrines which were deemed "essential and necessary": (1) the inspiration and inerrancy* of Scripture*; (2) Christ's virgin birth; (3) Christ's death as a "sacrifice to satisfy divine justice"; (4) Christ's bodily resurrection; (5) Christ's performance of miracles during his earthly ministry.

The Five Points expanded the Portland Deliverance of 1892 to encompass other doctrines which liberals challenged. Conservatives viewed the Five Points, which were similar to fundamentalist* doctrines of the early twentieth century, as a minimum platform necessary to keep the denomination tied to its evangelical* Calvinist* theology.* Liberals* challenged the Five Points in the Auburn Affirmation* (1924) and overturned them at the 1925 General Assembly.

BIBLIOGRAPHY. L. A. Loetscher, *The Broadening Church* (1954). W. A. Hoffecker

Flaget, Benedict Joseph (1763-1850). First bishop* of Bardstown (Louisville), Kentucky. Born in France, Flaget entered the seminary* at Clermont and in 1783 joined the Society of St. Sulpice,* a community of diocesan priests which conducted seminaries in France. After ordination* to the priesthood,* he taught theology* at Nantes. Flaget left France in 1792 to teach at the newly established St. Mary's Seminary in Baltimore. He later spent two years as a missionary* to Vincennes, Indiana, taught briefly at Georgetown College, and

finally returned to St. Mary's. Despite Flaget's protests, the Vatican in 1808 named him as bishop of the newly created diocese* of Bardstown, Kentucky. He was consecrated* by Archbishop* John Carroll* in 1810.

His diocese covered most of the U.S. beyond the Alleghenies, and there Flaget would spend the next forty years in tireless missionary activity. Within a few years he had convoked a diocesan synod, established St. Thomas Seminary and authorized the foundation of two communities of religious women, the Sisters of Charity of Nazareth and the Sisters of Loretto. Church and schools went up rapidly and in 1819 Flaget consecrated John Baptist David as coadjutor bishop to assist him in the diocese.

Flaget received two more coadjutors* in following years, and his diocese was divided eleven times as Catholicism developed in the West. In 1835 he visited Rome and then spent two years in France at the request of Pope Gregory XVI, speaking on behalf of the Propagation of the Faith,* to recruit missionaries and raise funds. In response to Flaget's request, the Vatican moved the diocese from Bardstown to Louisville in 1835. He died there on February 11, 1850, widely respected for his administrative skill and personal holiness.*

BIBLIOGRAPHY. *DAB* III; *DARB; NCAB* 6; J. S. Schauinger, *Cathedrals in the Wilderness* (1952); M. J. Spalding, *Life, Times and Character of the Right Reverend Benedict Joseph Flaget* (1852).

T. E. Buckley

Fleming, Paul William (1911-1950). Founder of New Tribes Mission. Fleming was influenced in his view of missions* and evangelism* by Paul Rader* at Chicago Gospel Tabernacle. In 1937 Fleming went to Malaya, where he endeavored to reach the Sakai tribe. When malaria forced him to return to the U.S., he traveled from church* to church raising money and volunteers for tribal work. In 1942 he recruited Cecil Dye from the Saginaw (Michigan) Bible Tabernacle, and Dye led a small band of eight adults and six children to Bolivia. The New Tribes Mission was thus formed. One year later the five men disappeared in the Bolivian jungle, leaving only the women and children. In 1943 Fleming formed the New Tribes Institute in Chicago for the training of missionary personnel. Fleming edited the magazine *Brown Gold,* starting in 1943, and set up a jungle-training camp in California in 1944 for missionaries. In 1950 Fleming was killed when a mission plane he was riding in went down in the Grand Teton Mountains of Wyoming.

BIBLIOGRAPHY. J. D. Johnson, *God Planted Five Seeds* (1966).   W. A. Detzler

Florovsky, Georges Vasilievich (1893-1979).

Russian Orthodox* theologian.* Educated in the secular sciences, law and humanities in prerevolutionary Russia and in his emigration, Florovsky was middle-aged when he began to study of the fathers of the church at St. Serge Orthodox Theological Institute in Paris. He quickly became a leader of the "Parisian School" of emigre Russian theologians, but dissented from its romantic spirit of religious renaissance, looking instead for a "return to the Fathers" and the spirit of Christian Hellenism. A neo-patristic synthesis underlies all his major writings, *The Eastern Fathers of the Fourth Century* (1931), *The Byzantine Fathers of the Fifth-Sixth Centuries* (1933) and *The Ways of Russian Theology* (1937).

Ordained* to the priesthood* in the jurisdiction of the Ecumenical Patriarchate, Florovsky traveled widely across Europe and attended most of the early pan-Orthodox and ecumenical* meetings. In 1948 he immigrated to America and became a professor at St. Vladimir's Orthodox Theological Seminary in New York. He served as dean from 1950 to 1955, recruiting fellow Parisians to bolster the faculty, and bringing the message of Orthodox Christianity to the campuses of Columbia University,* Union Theological Seminary* and Boston University. He founded *St. Vladimir's Theological Quarterly*. After leaving St. Vladimir's, Florovsky taught dogmatic theology at Harvard* Divinity School and history at Princeton University* while remaining active in the ecumenical movement.

BIBLIOGRAPHY. G. Williams, "George Vasilievich Florovsky: his American career," *GOTR* 11 (1965):7-107; W. Visser t'Hooft, "Fr. Georges Florovsky's Role in the Formation of the WCC," *SVTQ* 23 (1979):135-138.

                                        P. D. Garrett

Flower, Joseph James Roswell (1888-1970).

Assemblies of God* founder and leader. Born the first of three children of devout Canadian Methodist* parents, as a young teenager Flower moved with his family to John Alexander Dowie's* community, Zion City, Illinois. Disillusioned by some of Dowie's radical claims (he called himself both Elijah the Restorer and an apostle), the family moved to Indianapolis, where Flower read law with a local lawyer. In 1907 he identified with a newly formed Pentecostal* group that had been part of the local Christian and Missionary Alliance* branch. The next year Flower began to edit a

monthly paper, *The Pentecost,* as well as to travel in evangelistic* ministry. On June 1, 1911, in Indianapolis he married Alice Marie Reynolds. Six children, all of whom became ordained* Assemblies of God ministers,* were born into their home.

In 1912 and 1913 the Flowers lived in Plainfield and attended a short-term Bible school called Gibeah, directed by David Wesley Myland.* From June 1913, they issued the first Pentecostal weekly magazine, *The Christian Evangel.* In 1914 Flower participated in the convention in Hot Springs, Arkansas, which organized the General Council of the Assemblies of God. From 1914 until his retirement in 1959, he served that organization for multiple terms in various offices. The Flowers turned over their weekly paper to the General Council; it became the forerunner of the *Pentecostal Evangel,* the largest weekly religious publication in America today.

Flower served the denomination as office editor (1914-1916); missionary secretary (1919-1925); eastern district official and pastor, Scranton, Pennsylvania (1925-1935); assistant general superintendent (1931-1937); and general secretary (1935-1959). He was influential in organizing the National Association of Evangelicals,* as well as encouraging Assemblies of God participation in that and other evangelical groups. Flower was also active in community affairs in Springfield, Missouri, where he served several terms on the city council. He also taught occasionally at Central Bible Institute (Springfield, Missouri). For the forty-five years he served the denomination in various executive capacities, Flower's name was synonymous with the Assemblies of God.

BIBLIOGRAPHY. C. Brumback, *Suddenly from Heaven* (1961); *DPCM*; A. R. Flower, *Grace for Grace* (1962).   E. L. Blumhofer

Font. *See* BAPTISMAL FONT.

Foote, Julia A. J. (1823-1900).

African Methodist Episcopal Zion* exhorter and preacher.* Born in Schenectady, New York, to parents who had purchased their freedom, Julia went to work at ten years of age for a white family willing to help her attend school. She worked and studied for two years, then moved with her family to Albany. Converted at age fifteen, Foote joined an African Methodist Episcopal* Church, and claimed an experience of sanctification.* At the age of eighteen, she married a sailor, George Foote, and moved to Boston, where she joined an African Methodist Episcopal Zion Church, began promoting sanctification and was ultimately ejected from the congregation. Her husband was outraged by her behavior but was often at sea and could not stop her from exhorting and preaching as an itinerant. She held meetings in upstate New York, Ohio, Michigan and Canada. Eventually recognized by her church, she became her denomination's* first female deacon* in 1894, and was ordained* its second woman elder* in 1900.

BIBLIOGRAPHY. J. A. J. Foote, "A Brand Plucked from the Fire; An Autobiographical Sketch" in *Sisters of the Spirit,* ed. W. L. Andrews (1986).

K. K. Kidd

Foot Washing. A religious rite, regarded as either an ordinance or sacrament,* practiced by a number of American church groups. Denominations* practicing foot washing (known also as pedilavium) base their observance of the rite on the words of Jesus in John 13:14, its presence in the early church (1 Tim 5:10), and its practice, especially on Maundy Thursday, by various groups throughout church history. Apart from adherence to New Testament practice, theological reasons for the rite have ranged from a belief in its being a sacrament for the remission of sins to a belief in its value in instilling Christlike humility in the believer.

In America the practice of foot washing has been particularly associated with German pietist* and Anabaptist* denominations such as the Church of the Brethren.* However, the rite can also be found in groups as diverse as the Seventh-Day Adventists,* Pentecostal* and Holiness* churches, the Churches of God* (General Conference), a number of Southern Baptist* groups and the Roman Catholic Church* (on Maundy Thursday). In several denominations the issue of whether or not to wash feet has been controversial enough to split congregations. R. Kern

Ford, Gerald Rudolph (1913-). Thirty-eighth U.S. president and devout Episcopalian* churchman. Born in Omaha, Nebraska, and christened Leslie Lynch King, Jr., Ford's parents divorced when he was two, after which his mother moved to Grand Rapids, Michigan, remarried, and gave her son the name of his stepfather, Gerald R. Ford. After earning a B.A. from the University of Michigan (1935) and an LL.B. from Yale University* Law School (1941), Ford served four years as an aviation officer in the U.S. Navy during World War 2.* Elected to Congress in 1948 as a Republican from the Grand Rapids area for the first of thirteen times, he rose to be House Minority Leader in 1965, a position he held until 1973. He married

Elizabeth Bloomer Warren in 1948, and they eventually became the parents of four children, one of whom (Michael, b. 1950) became a Presbyterian* minister.*

On December 6, 1973, Ford was sworn in as vice president of the U. S., the first and only individual in American history to be chosen under a provision of the Twenty-fifth Amendment to the U.S. Constitution rather than as the result of a national election. Ford was also the first person to occupy the White House without being elected either president or vice president, succeeding Richard M. Nixon* on August 9, 1974. Each event resulted from one of the worst scandals in American political history: the first from the forced resignation of Vice President Spiro T. Agnew after he pleaded *nolo contendere* to a charge of income tax evasion, and the second from the Watergate Affair, which ultimately led to Nixon's resignation.

A conservative on domestic issues and an internationalist in foreign affairs, Ford's administration was characterized by unusual openness and integrity. Although he had been a faithful churchgoer of many years' standing who periodically ushered, served on parish committees, taught Sunday school* and occasionally preached,* it was a spiritual reawakening credited to the ministrations of evangelist* Billy Zeoli in 1971 which led Ford to give public testimony of his faith in Christ as Savior after that date. As president, he was widely known as a thoughtful man of prayer* whose public addresses often reflected both his personal faith and his civil religion.*

Ford became the Republican nominee for president in 1976, only to lose to fellow-evangelical* Jimmy Carter* in a close race. His retirement years have been devoted to serving on corporate boards, lecturing on public affairs and supporting charitable causes.

BIBLIOGRAPHY. J. F. TerHorst, *Gerald Ford and the Future of the Presidency* (1974); J. C. Hefley and E. E. Plowman, *Washington: Christians in the Corridors of Power* (1975); B. Zeoli, *God's Got a Better Idea* (1978); G. R. Ford, *A Time to Heal* (1979); R. G. Hutcheson, Jr., *God in the White House* (1988). R. D. Linder

Ford, Reuben (1742-1823). Baptist* pastor* and apologist for religious liberty.* Converted* in 1762 under George Whitefield,* Ford began his career as a lay exhorter.* He was baptized* in 1769 and two years later established and was ordained* by the church at Goochland, Virginia. Ford also assisted in the founding of Licking Hole Church and served the Dover Association as its clerk for thirty years. Additionally, much of his career was spent clarifying church-state relations through his contacts with Patrick Henry,* Thomas Jefferson* and James Madison. Ford contributed to the Baptist cause in Virginia, both directly and indirectly, in the elimination of compulsory tax support for the clergy* (1776), the guarantee of religious freedom (1785), and the return of glebe lands* to the public domain (1799). He also played a major role in the union of the Separate* and Regular* Baptists in 1787. Ford contributed to Baptist liturgy* by writing a service for the solemnizing of marriage, based on the Book of Common Prayer.*

BIBLIOGRAPHY. R. B. Semple, *History of the Baptists in Virginia,* rev. ed. (1972).

L. W. Hähnlen

Foreign Missions Conference of North America. Interdenominational cooperative mission bodies. On January 12, 1893, some seventy-five persons (including such leaders as John R. Mott,* Robert E. Speer* and J. Campbell White*), representing twenty-one mission boards and committees, plus the YMCA,* the American Bible Society* and the Committee on Co-operation of the Presbyterian Alliance, met in New York to discuss topics of mutual concern. From 1895 these meetings were held annually, and in 1911 the meetings became known as The Foreign Missions Conference of North America (FMC), with fifty-two member societies. The 1917 meeting was attended by 287 delegates representing 100 missions agencies.

In 1950 the FMC voted to become a constituting member of the National Council of the Churches of Christ in the U.S.A. as its Division of Foreign Missions (DFM-NCCCUSA). (The Canadian agencies withdrew to form the Department of Overseas Missions of the Canadian Council of Churches, though some remained as consultative members.) When the FMC joined the National Council of Churches, it had ninety-eight charter member agencies. Partly as a result of mergers, those numbers had decreased to fifty-one full and eleven associate agencies by 1965 when the DFM and the Central Department of Church World Service were integrated to become the Division of Foreign Ministries. The decline in member agencies was paralleled by a gradual decline in the number of associated overseas missionaries—a decline which began in the early 1960s and has continued since that time. In 1985 there were 4,349 missionaries associated with the department.

BIBLIOGRAPHY. H. C. Jackson, "The National Council of the Churches of Christ in the U.S.A.,

Division of Overseas Ministries" in *The Encyclopedia of Modern Christian Missions,* ed. B. L. Goddard (1967); *Mission Handbook, North American and Protestant Ministries Overseas,* 13th ed., eds. S. Wilson and J. Siewert (1986).

D. J. Hesselgrave

Fosdick, Harry Emerson (1878-1969). Liberal* Baptist* preacher.* Born in Buffalo, New York, Fosdick was educated at Colgate University (B.A., 1900), where he was mentored by William Newton Clarke,* the foremost Baptist liberal theologian* of the period. Fosdick later referred to Clarke as his "spiritual godfather" and translated Clarke's teachings into his own famous phrase: "We must distinguish between abiding experiences and changing categories." Fosdick subsequently studied at Union Theological Seminary,* New York, and Columbia University.* At Union he was influenced by the writings of Walter Rauschenbusch* on the Social Gospel.*

Ordained* to the Baptist ministry, Fosdick's first pastorate was Montclair Baptist Church, Montclair, New Jersey (1904-1915), where he came to be known as an outstanding preacher. During 1918 he served as a chaplain* in France, and then became Pulpit Minister at First Presbyterian Church, New York City (1918-1925).

There he gained national attention on May 21, 1922, when he preached his most famous sermon, "Shall the Fundamentalists Win?" Ivy Lee, a Presbyterian layman, published and distributed the sermon under the title "The New Knowledge and the Christian Faith." The sermon was intended as a plea for greater tolerance and understanding between fundamentalists* and liberals. But Fosdick identified three central issues where fundamentalists needed to be more tolerant. He suggested that belief in the virgin birth was unessential, belief in the inerrancy* of the Bible* was incredible to the modern mind and the literal Second Coming of Jesus Christ was outmoded and needed rethinking. Fosdick alerted fundamentalists that they could not "drive out from the Christian churches all the consecrated souls who do not agree with their theory of inspiration" and concluded by encouraging Christian fellowship that is "intellectually hospitable, open-minded, liberty-loving, fair, tolerant." The sermon made Fosdick the focal point of controversy within the Presbyterian Church of the U.S.A. In 1924 he was asked to become a member of the Presbyterian Church*; however, being a Baptist minister, he declined, thereby resigning his ministry at First Presbyterian Church.

At the urging of James C. Colgate* and John D. Rockefeller, Jr., Fosdick became pastor of Park Avenue Baptist Church (1925-1930). By 1930 the congregation had erected a new building named Riverside Church. Fosdick insisted that the ministry of Riverside Church be non-sectarian. The program was one of Christian personalism, a people-centered ministry emphasizing personal spiritual growth and social consciousness. Riverside Church developed a large church school and nursery school, and provided playground and gymnasium facilities for young people. A department of social service was organized to help find jobs for those hurt by the economic Depression.* Between 1930 and 1935 some seven thousand unemployed individuals found work through the church. Organizations such as the Riverside Symphony Orchestra, the Business and Professional Women's Club, the Riverside Guild (which served more than three hundred teen-agers) and the Riverside Men's Class were established.

In addition, Fosdick was a renowned pulpiteer and for years preached his message of Christian personalism to millions of listeners via a radio program entitled "National Vespers." His writing ministry also reached millions through works such as *The Meaning of Prayer* (1915), *The Meaning of Faith* (1917), *The Meaning of Service* (1920) and *The Modern Use of the Bible* (1924). Throughout much of his ministerial career (1908-1946), Fosdick was also professor of practical theology at Union Theological Seminary. He retired from Riverside in 1946 but maintained an active role within the causes of world peace and racial justice.

BIBLIOGRAPHY. *DAB* 0; *DARB;* H. E. Fosdick, *The Living of These Days: An Autobiography* (1969); R. M. Miller, *Harry Emerson Fosdick: Preacher, Pastor, Prophet* (1985); *NCAB* E.

C. W. Whiteman

Foster, Frank Hugh (1851-1935). Theologian* and historian. Educated at Harvard* (B.A., 1873), Andover Theological Seminary* (B.D., 1877) and the University of Leipzig (Ph.D., 1882), Foster taught at the U.S. Naval Academy (1874), Middlebury College (1882-1884), Oberlin College* (1884-1892), Pacific Seminary (1892-1902), Olivet College (1904-1925) and again at Oberlin (1925-1933).

Foster began his career as a defender of the consistent Calvinism* of his mentor, Edwards Amasa Park.* By the time he concluded his most important and best-known work, *A Genetic History of the New England Theology* (1907), Foster had divested himself of any loyalty to his old creed,*

and had become a radical naturalist dedicated to a thorough critique of authoritarianism in religion. His later articles and monographs display a polemical modernism* which utilized merciless rational and logical analysis of traditional Christianity, particularly indicting a habitual inattention to what he considered the central importance of scientific advances. Foster's analysis of the history of ideas in American theology marked an advance over contemporary sentimentalism and denominational allegiances. His published works include: *The Seminary Method of Original Study in the Historical Sciences* (1888); *Christian Life and Theology* (1900); *The Life of Edwards Amasa Park* (1936); and *The Modern Movement in American Theology* (1939). His *Genetic History of the New England Theology* remains the standard work on the subject.

BIBLIOGRAPHY. *DAB* 1.

K. S. Sawyer

Foster, George Burman (1858-1918). Baptist* theologian* and educator. One of the seminal thinkers of the late nineteenth century, Foster was a West Virginia native who first sought training for pastoral ministry and later turned to scholarship and teaching in philosophy and theology.* For most of his career he taught systematic* theology or philosophy of religion* at the University of Chicago* (1895-1910). Given the rising reputation of the Chicago school of theological studies, Foster had a broad influence on philosophical approaches to religion and on the next generation of theologians.

Foster accepted the socio-scientific approaches to religion and the Bible,* which his Chicago colleagues pursued with vigor. As a theologian, Foster insisted on separating the theological authority* of the Christian faith from the evolution of the Christian religion. In his major work, *The Finality of the Christian Religion* (1906), he argued that Jesus, as the archetype of love for others, possessed the ultimate spirit of Christianity, as he placed absolute value on persons rather than on society or predisposed moral codes.

A theological modernist,* Foster frequently debated more orthodox* opponents and suffered bitter attacks from fundamentalists.* Because of his convictions about the necessity of religion for human nature and the importance of a personal faith, he was continuously engaged in the central discussions of his era. Moreover, few teachers enjoyed the long-term student influence which Foster did in his twenty-three years at Chicago.

BIBLIOGRAPHY. K. Cauthen, *The Impact of American Religious Liberalism* (1962); *DAB* III; A.

Gragg, *George Burman Foster, Religious Humanist* (1978). W. H. Brackney

Four Spiritual Laws. Formulated by William ("Bill") R. Bright,* the founder of Campus Crusade for Christ,* the Four Spiritual Laws were designed to be a tool for evangelism* among college students. These laws, supported by Bible* verses and diagrams, provide a step-by-step approach for converting* an individual to Christianity. In 1965 the Four Spiritual Laws were printed in a tract* entitled *Have You Heard of the Four Spiritual Laws?* Since that time, an estimated one billion copies have been printed and distributed around the world in every major language. The Four Spiritual Laws are as follows: (1) God loves people and has a plan for each person's life; (2) Because people are sinful and separated from God, they are incapable of knowing God's love and plan; (3) Only through Christ can people experience God's love and plan for life; (4) Each individual must accept Jesus Christ as Lord and Savior in order to receive salvation* and God's love.

BIBLIOGRAPHY. B. Bright, *Come Help Change the World* (1979); R. Quebedeaux, *I Found It! The Story of Bill Bright and Campus Crusade* (1979).

K. L. Staggers

Foursquare Church. *See* INTERNATIONAL CHURCH OF THE FOURSQUARE GOSPEL.

Fox, George (1624-1691). Founder of the Religious Society of Friends* (Quakers). Born in England, Fox reached maturity during great political, social and religious upheaval. Charles I had been beheaded, Oliver Cromwell became Lord Protector, and the Rule of the Saints began. Puritans* struggled for reform of the Anglican Church,* while many, frustrated with the pace of reform, launched separatist groups such as the Baptists* and Congregationalists.*

Fox was nearly driven to despair with the question of where infallible religious authority* was to be found. He steeped himself in Scripture, spending many lonely hours meditating and reading the Bible.* He visited renowned teachers, but none could satisfy his tormented mind, and many seemed to profess far more than they actually possessed of the Christian life. Finally, when he had lost all hope in human teachers and his own efforts, Fox heard the words "there is one, even Christ Jesus, who can speak to thy condition." This experience assured Fox of the sufficiency of Christ's spiritual presence and drove him to travel throughout England and abroad, preaching and

organizing Friends of Truth that responded to his newly found message.

Fox's influence in America was primarily indirect through the religious movement that he founded. He visited America during the years 1672-1673, traveling up and down the Atlantic seaboard visiting Quaker settlements between Portsmouth (New Hampshire) and Cape Hatteras (North Carolina). His visit strengthened American Quakerism. Fox also collected information regarding a potential haven for Quakers and other persecuted groups. He conveyed this information to William Penn,* who was granted the colony of Pennsylvania in 1681. The Quaker "Holy Experiment" in Pennsylvania was to prove immensely influential upon the course of the developing nation.

See also FRIENDS, THE RELIGIOUS SOCIETY OF.

BIBLIOGRAPHY. *DARB;* G. Fox, *The Journal of G. Fox* (1694); R. M. Jones, *George Fox: Seeker and Friend* (1930); *NCAB* 7; V. Noble, *The Man in Leather Breeches: The Life and Times of George Fox* (1953). R. E. Selleck

Foxe's Book of Martyrs. A Protestant* martyrology influential among colonial Puritans.* Written by John Foxe (1517-1587), the book recounts the lives and deeds of Protestant reformers and martyrs in the years prior to and including the reigns of the English monarchs Henry VIII (1509-1547), Edward (1547-1553) and Mary (1553-1558). Foxe published the first edition of his work in 1563 under the title of *Acts and Monuments,* following the ascendancy of Elizabeth I (1558-1603) to the throne. The fact that it went through seven editions by 1684, despite its length of some 2,000 pages, is an indication of its profound influence on the English mind and subsequently on the American Colonies.

The reason for this influence is to be found in Foxe's effort to place Protestant martyrdom within the context of an elaborate interpretation of history. Foxe espoused a postmillenial* interpretation of history which identified the period of one thousand years spoken of in the book of Revelation with the history of the Church from Constantine to the fourteenth century. He identified the period of the Antichrist with the period beginning with the Catholic Inquisition and persecution of the pre-reformers. The martyrdom of Protestants was dramatized as a spiritual warfare of the elect, who were sustained by a confident expectation of the final triumph of the forces of Christ over those of the Antichrist and the inauguration of a new age.

Among Puritans in England and the New England colonies, this providential conception of history served as the inspiration for the belief that the English people were themselves an "elect nation" with a special role to play in God's redemptive plan. *Foxe's Book of Martyrs* was, for example, the literary model for Cotton Mather's* *Magnalia Christi Americana* (1698), which offers the same vision of holy history as a war between the saints and the Antichrist and describes New England as having a unique part in the final victory of the saints. Scholars have traced the influence of this historical vision on the New England mindset in the years leading up to the American Revolution.

BIBLIOGRAPHY. W. Haller, *Foxe's Book of Martyrs and the Elect Nation* (1963); L. Trinterud, ed., *Elizabethan Puritanism* (1971); J. W. Davidson, *The Logic of Millenial Thought: Eighteenth Century New England* (1977). R. P. Hesselgrave

Franciscans. A common designation for various religious communities professing to live according to the ideals of Francis of Assisi (d. 1226). Most often the term refers to his brotherhood, the Friars Minor. These "Lesser Brothers" strive to live according to the gospel by creating a fraternity of mutual care, deepening personal prayer to unite themselves to the Spirit of God, renouncing possessions to identify with the poor and outcast of society, and preaching* to all a message of conversion* and peace. Disagreements over the concrete realization of these goals led to a division of the Order by 1528, resulting in three autonomous branches: the Observant, Conventual and Capuchin friars.

Franciscans, who had always cultivated popular preaching and missionary* activities, took an active role in evangelizing the Americas under the patronage of the Catholic colonial powers. Observant friars came to the Spanish settlement in Florida in 1573, eventually building up a network of forty-four missions, with 30,000 Christian Native Americans. These gradually were abandoned with the British occupation of the area, the last friars leaving in 1763. Other large mission areas were developed in New Mexico (1598), Texas (1716) and California (1769), the latter under the leadership of Junipero Serra.* However, by the time these territories came under U.S. control in 1848, virtually all mission activity had ceased, due to the secularizing policies of the Mexican government. Franciscans had also been active in the French colonies, Observants ("Recollects") in Canada and the Great Lakes from 1615 to 1763, and Capuchins in Louisiana from 1722 to 1803.

Franciscans were reintroduced to America in 1844, when Austrian friars volunteered to minister to German Catholics in Cincinnati. Other missions soon followed, and by 1870 there were flourishing foundations of all three branches of the Order. Due to the needs of the church, North American Franciscans became heavily involved in parochial* and educational ministries, in addition to their traditional preaching activity. In 1987 there were 2,600 Observants (today known simply as Franciscans), 950 Capuchins and 790 Conventuals in the U.S.

Francis, with his disciple Clare, also founded an order of women dedicated to contemplative prayer. These "Poor Clares" came to America in 1875, eventually founding twenty-five monasteries. Finally, there were also many lay* people inspired by Francis, who wished to follow his ideals in the midst of secular life. Some members of this "Third Order" (especially women), dedicated to various charitable works such as care of the sick and education, often banded together to form religious communities. Over forty congregations of Franciscan women, presently numbering almost 30,000 sisters, have played a prominent role in the development of American Catholicism since 1950. *See also* MISSIONS TO NORTH AMERICA, FRENCH; MISSIONS TO NORTH AMERICA, SPANISH.

BIBLIOGRAPHY. W. J. Short, *The Franciscans* (1988); F. Morales, *Franciscan Presence in the Americas* (1983). D. V. Monti

Franson, Fredrik (1852-1908). Evangelist* and missionary* statesman. Immigrating to Nebraska in his teens, Franson was converted at the age of twenty and moved to Chicago where he was deeply influenced by Dwight L. Moody,* whose methods of evangelism* he adopted. Franson became the pre-eminent evangelist and revivalist* to the late-nineteenth-century Scandinavian communities of the north-central and western U. S.

Impressed by Hudson Taylor's appeal for 1,000 missionaries to go to China, Franson challenged the Scandinavian communities to foreign missions.* He was so successful in this venture that he is credited with founding some nineteen or twenty missionary societies in Europe and the U. S. The Evangelical Alliance Mission (TEAM)* is the most notable mission agency owing its origin to Franson. As a churchman Franson organized many congregations, considering the work of evangelism incomplete if a church was not established. Considered the founder of the Mission Covenant Church in Norway, he contributed to the founding of the Baptist General Conference,* The Evangelical Covenant of America* and the Evangelical Free Church of America.*

[449]

BIBLIOGRAPHY. O. C. Grauer, *Fredrik Franson: Founder of the Scandinavian Alliance Mission of North America* (1939); E. P. Torjesen, *Fredrik Franson, A Model for Worldwide Evangelism* (1983); D. B. Woodward, *Aflame for God* (1966).   C. B. Hanson

Free African Society. Early African-American voluntary association. Resisted both by white Methodist* authorities and some prominent African-Americans in their efforts to form a religious society with its own meetinghouse, Philadelphia Methodist ex-slaves Richard Allen* and Absalom Jones organized in April 1787 the Free African Society. Initially a mutual-benefit association which offered assistance to morally upright, dues-paying members and their families in the event of sickness or death, the Society increasingly assumed religious functions and reorganized itself during 1791-1792 as "the Elders and Deacons of the African Church." Methodist Allen, alienated from the Society early in 1789 over its developing Quaker* tendencies, was disappointed again in 1794 when the initially nondenominational successor group voted to become St. Thomas African Episcopal Church, the first African-American Episcopal congregation in the U.S. Jones became the pastor of this church, while Allen founded the first African-American Methodist congregation, Bethel African Methodist Episcopal Church (1794). *See* AFRICAN METHODIST EPISCOPAL CHURCH.

BIBLIOGRAPHY. W. Douglass, *Annals of the First African Church in the United States, Now Styled the African Episcopal Church of St. Thomas, Philadelphia.*   D. W. Wills

Free Church Tradition in America. The term *free church* emerged in nineteenth-century England among non-Anglican denominations as a more positive self-description than *Nonconformist, Dissenter* or even *Protestant.** Emphasizing the principled separation from the established church,* the term denoted a voluntary covenanting of believers in self-supporting and self-regulating gathered churches.

In America the term was popularized by Franklin H. Littell, who traced its origin to the Anabaptists* of the Reformation era and emphasized the contributions of the tradition to modern society. The role of the laity,* religious liberty,* ethical emphasis and missionary* zeal, he reasoned, all find their bases in the free churches. The free church tradition became widely recognized in ecumenical* dialog, not only through Littell's advocacy but also through the writings of Angus Dun and Leslie Newbigin. The term has been widely used in North America since the 1950s.

Since the term *free church* has been used with a variety of meanings, some prefer the term *Believers Church* (coined by Max Weber) as a more precise alternative. Since 1967 a series of study conferences in the U. S. and Canada have employed this term as a focus for deliberations. Nevertheless, the attractiveness of *free church* has resulted in its continued use to designate voluntary church bodies that formally reject governmental affiliation. Most of these groups are congregational* in polity, have a flexible style of worship,* promote the role of the laity, practice baptism* of believing adults and favor scriptural authority* above tradition.

Although many American denominations are derived from continental free churches, they can be categorized into several church families. These include: (1) radical reformers; (2) Brethren; and (3) pietists. The Waldensian Church, originating in the late twelfth century and sometimes called the "Mother of the Reformation," persists in Italy and Latin America, but only a small number of its congregations were planted in the U. S. through immigration of Italian Waldensians. Furthermore, a number of Lutheran* and Reformed* church groups in Europe took on free church status (occasionally adopting the name as well) to preserve their doctrinal independence in the face of government pressure. Although some immigrated to North America, they fundamentally differ in theology and practice from the religious bodies customarily regarded as free churches.

Radical Reformers. Alongside mainstream Lutheran and Reformed churches emerged reformers dedicated to a more radical revision of church life. Called Anabaptists (rebaptizers) because they rejected infant baptism and practiced baptism of covenanting believers—and hence the rebaptism* of those who had been baptized as infants—by 1525 they had appeared in various parts of Europe. Several influences, both religious and social, nurtured this movement: (1) Christian humanism with its concern for biblical study and ethical conduct; (2) peasant protest against unjust taxes and lost rights; (3) renewal movements among monastic orders; and (4) Protestantism itself. Anabaptists often understood themselves as uncompromising disciples of the Protestant reformers, determined to complete the reform of doctrine by reformation of life. Although considered political and economic revolutionaries by authorities, Anabaptists taught nonresistance (biblical pacifism*) and submission to the state as long as it did not demand actions contrary to the plain teachings of Scripture.*

Anabaptists were bloodily suppressed by Catholics* and Protestants alike. Many were executed, others survived only by living quiet lives in isolated communities. The earliest free development of this tradition took place in the Netherlands, where the movement took the name "Mennonite,"* after Menno Simons, a former Catholic priest who became a leader of the movement after 1536. In the late seventeenth and early eighteenth centuries, many Mennonites, leaving Switzerland and the Palatinate, migrated to America with Pennsylvania as their favored destination.

The Mennonite Church,* or "Old" Mennonite Church, is the largest of the Mennonite denominations in America. Having grown out of the Palatinate and Swiss Mennonites who immigrated to America before the Revolutionary War,* their numbers were supplemented by later immigrants from Europe. For decades a withdrawn, agricultural, German-speaking minority in America, the Mennonite Church experienced a remarkable renewal in the twentieth century with a recovery of the Anabaptist vision.* Reaching out in mission efforts both at home and abroad, it has become a multi-ethnic church.

The smaller General Conference Mennonite Church,* founded in 1860, was the consolidation of three Mennonite associations (representing Ontario, Ohio, Iowa, Illinois and eastern Pennsylvania) and attracted many late-nineteenth-century Russian, Swiss, Polish and German Mennonite immigrants. The Mennonite Brethren Church of North America* traces its origins to a revival that took place in a nineteenth-century Russian Mennonite community. Facing the prospect of mandatory military service under the Czar, they immigrated to North America in the 1870s, settling mostly in Kansas, Nebraska, Minnesota and the Dakotas. Closely linked with the Mennonites is the Brethren in Christ Church,* also called "River Brethren." It originated around 1780 out of a revival* movement among Pennsylvania Mennonites. All of these groups also have strong contingents in Canada, where recent nationalistic influences brought into existence independent institutions.

Two other Anabaptist-derived movements garner wide attention for their determinedly nonconformist ways; these are the Amish* and the Hutterian Brethren.* The Hutterites immigrated to South Dakota in the 1870s to escape military conscription in the Ukraine while the Amish, a Mennonite faction, emigrated in the eighteenth and nineteenth centuries from Germany, Switzerland, Russia and Holland. The Amish and Hutterites differ principally in the Hutterite dedication to communitarian life. Although the Amish reside within limited geographical areas and support one another closely, they live in separate nuclear families. Hutterite families, on the other hand, are organized into communal groups. In the twentieth century the Hutterian Brethren were augmented by a union with the Society of Brothers, a commune organized in Germany in 1920 by Eberhard and Emmy Arnold. This branch of the Hutterites currently has four colonies in the U. S. and one in England.

A related but non-Anabaptist body is the Schwenkfelder Church,* which takes its name from Kaspar von Schwenkfeld, a contemporary and one-time colleague of Martin Luther, whose followers migrated to Pennsylvania in 1734.

Brethren. Initiated as a merging of Pietist and Anabaptist strands in 1708 in central Germany, Brethren emigrated to America after 1719. Known colloquially as "Dunkers" because of their practice of baptizing believers by threefold immersion, the movement experienced its first schism in 1728-1732 when the Ephrata Community* was organized by Johann Konrad Beissel.* Although communalism in Ephrata and its daughter colony Snow Hill (Quincy, Pennsylvania) died out in the nineteenth century, a small church body persists in the late 1980s as the German Seventh-Day Baptist Church.

From 1881 to 1883 the Brethren suffered a three-way split: the conservative element seceded to form the Old German Baptist Brethren ("Old Orders"), the progressives organized as the Brethren Church (Ashland, Ohio), leaving the larger middle party, known after 1908 as the Church of the Brethren. This body endured another division in 1926 when the Dunkard Brethren withdrew over the issues of mandatory dress codes and higher education. In 1939 a split through the middle of the Brethren Church (Ashland, Ohio) resulted in the mission-oriented Fellowship of Grace Brethren Churches* (Winona Lake, Indiana).

Pietists. Pietism* was a renewal movement beginning among late-seventeenth-century German Lutheran and Reformed Churches seeking to inculcate true piety in individual believers. Although the Moravian Church* originated in the fifteenth century, it experienced pietistic revitalization in 1727 under Count Zinzendorf.* The church was noted for its missionary zeal, ecumenical initiatives, thorough organization and musical accomplishments. Moravians founded several colonies in America, notably in Bethlehem, Pennsylvania, and Winston-Salem, North Carolina, which served as bases for its American religious and cultural development.

Whereas the Moravians imported their early communal organization from Europe, the Community of True Inspiration became fully communal only upon its immigration to America. Founded in 1714 in the Wetteravian area of Germany, the Inspired were noted for their belief in latter-day prophecy. They settled first on a former Indian reservation near Buffalo, New York, in 1843-1844; but they moved on to found seven thriving colonies in Iowa (the Amana Church Society*) in 1854-1855. There they persisted in their communal existence until 1932, when a free-enterprise economy was instituted.

Two remaining continental free churches stem from Scandinavia. The Evangelical Covenant Church* developed from pietist Bible study* conventicles in nineteenth-century Sweden. After participants immigrated to the U. S., they formed a separate denomination in the 1880s. First called the Swedish Evangelical Mission Covenant Church, by 1957 it was known as the Evangelical Covenant Church of America.* A similar group, the Evangelical Free Church of America,* was formed in 1950 when two independent Scandinavian bodies of pietist derivation united. As with the Evangelical Covenant Church, the Evangelical Free Church is keenly mission-minded.

Although religious bodies in all three categories have distinctive heritages and character, they share common adherence to the free church tradition. Some participate actively in the ecumenical movement, seeking to bring their testimony to the larger Christian community; others seek to be faithful witnesses to the gospel of Jesus Christ as individual churches. Together, they make significant contributions to church and society.

See also ANABAPTIST TRADITION AND VISION; MENNONITE CHURCHES; PIETISM.

BIBLIOGRAPHY. D. F. Durnbaugh, *The Believers' Church: The History and Character of Radical Protestantism* (1968); C. J. Dyck, ed., *An Introduction to Mennonite History* (1967); F. H. Littell, *The Origins of Sectarian Protestantism* (1964) (originally published as *The Anabaptist View of the Church and The Free Church* [1952]); F. E. Stoeffler, ed., *Continental Pietism and Early American Christianity* (1976). G. Westin, *The Free Church Through the Ages* (1958).

D. F. Durnbaugh

Free Methodist Church of North America.
The Free Methodist Church of North America was

founded in 1860 by the union of two unsuccessful reform movements in the Methodist Episcopal Church. Laity* expelled from a local church in Illinois under the leadership of J. W. Redfield were joined by ministers* expelled from the Genessee annual conference in New York under the leadership of Benjamin T. Roberts.* The group added the word *Free* to its name to show that it stood for free pews,* freedom for the slaves and freedom in worship.* Its doctrine* and government were like the Methodist Church except that it expressly taught the possibility of entire sanctification,* and included an equal number of lay and ministerial representatives in every decision-making body. Today the church remains close to its theological roots and supports a vigorous missions program. In 1987 there were 1,048 churches and over 72,000 members in the U.S., with at least as many members in other countries. The denominational headquarters are in Winona Lake, Indiana.

BIBLIOGRAPHY. L. R. Marston, *From Age to Age a Living Witness* (1960). C. E. White

Free Will. *See* PREDESTINATION.

Free Will Baptists. Formed in the eighteenth century in opposition to Calvinist* predestination* among Regular Baptists,* Free Will Baptists (often written *freewill*) arose in this country from two streams. Paul Palmer* formed General Baptist churches in North Carolina in the 1720s. These churches held a doctrine of "free will," that is, freedom of any to believe in Christ, as opposed to the Calvinist doctrine of predestination of the "elect" to salvation.* In time most of these early "Freewillers" succumbed to intense proselytism of the Regular (Calvinist) churches of the Philadelphia Baptist Association.*

In 1780 another stream of Free Will Baptists arose in New England, led by Benjamin Randall.* Converted* in George Whitefield's* revivals,* Randall joined the Baptists in 1776 but broke with them in 1779 over predestination. In 1780 he formed a church of seven members at New Durham, New Hampshire, the first of many Free Will Baptist churches in New England. In time the Calvinism of Regular Baptists moderated, diminishing the justificaton for Free Will Baptists. In 1911 most Free Wills in the North merged into the Northern Baptist Convention.*

Remnants of the Palmer and Randall lines reestablished contact, and in 1935 representatives from both groups met in Nashville, Tennessee, to form the National Association of Free Will Baptists (NAFWB). They adopted a confession of faith in

1935, and established a college in Nashville in 1942. The Free Wills are distinguished from other Baptists by their intense conservatism, centralized organizational structure and the practice of foot washing.* In 1981 the NAFWB reported 216,848 members in 2,479 churches. The United American Free Will Baptist Church (1867) and the General Conference of Original Free Will Baptists (1962) represent smaller groups with similar emphases. *See also* BAPTIST CHURCHES.

BIBLIOGRAPHY. *A Treatise on the Faith of the Free Will Baptists* (1834); W. F. Davidson, *The Free Will Baptists in America, 1727-1984* (1985).

H. L. McBeth

Freed, Arvy Glenn (1868-1931). Church of Christ* educator, preacher* and debator. In 1889, after graduating from Valparaiso University, Freed went to preach and teach in Tennessee. In 1895 he became president of what was then called West Tennessee Christian College in Henderson. Controversy over the use of musical instruments in worship* and the support of missionary societies divided the local church in 1905, causing Freed to leave the college. For a brief period he was president of a college in Texas, but he returned to Henderson in 1907. There he joined a former student, Nicholas B. Hardeman,* in establishing a new school called National Teachers' Normal and Business College, which eventually became Freed-Hardeman College. Freed continued in Henderson until 1923, when he became vice president of David Lipscomb College in Nashville, a position he still held at the time of his death.

Freed was an outstanding preacher and debator, receiving many invitations to hold meetings and debate. He was not, however, considered a great orator. He was highly regarded as a preacher, but his real influence was in education. At his death, *The Nashville Tennessean* described him as an outstanding religious and educational leader, "a mental and spiritual giant."

BIBLIOGRAPHY. J. M. Powell and M. N. H. Powers, *N.B.H.: A Biography of Nicholas Brodie Hardeman* (1970).

L. B. Sullivan

Freeman, Hobart (1920-1984). Cult* leader. Born in Louisville, Kentucky, Freeman was converted* in 1952 while living in Florida; completed his studies at Georgetown College, Kentucky; and was ordained* by a Baptist* congregation. He studied theology* at Southern Baptist Theological Seminary, leaving with two degrees in 1959. After earning a doctorate at Grace Theological Seminary, Winona Lake, Indiana, in 1961, Freeman taught in

the seminary's Old Testament department, having joined the Fellowship of Grace Brethren Churches* in 1960. He was dismissed from his post and from the church early in 1963 for promulgating extreme antidenominational views.

Freeman then began a house church in Winona Lake, and after 1972 he was associated with the charismatic* "Glory Barn" near North Webster, Indiana. In 1978 Freeman left to establish the "Faith Assembly" near Warsaw, Indiana. This movement grew rapidly, attracting many young couples who gladly accepted Freeman's eloquent teachings. Followers were placed under strict discipline and allowed no contact with outside influences. A large meeting hall was constructed in Wilmot, Indiana, for the 2,000 members. Freeman's most controversial tenet involved faith healing,* rejecting all use of traditional medicine. Some ninety persons, primarily children, were said to have died as a result, leading to prosecution beginning in 1982. Freeman died of bronchopneumonia and heart failure in December 1984, free of medication. Faith Assembly continued to operate after his death.

BIBLIOGRAPHY. B. Barron, *The Health and Wealth Gospel* (1987); J. J. Davis [four-part series on the Faith Assembly], *Warsaw* (Ind.) *Times-Union* (September 1983).

D. F. Durnbaugh

Frelinghuysen, Theodorus Jacobus (1691-c.1747). Dutch Reformed* minister* in New Jersey. Frelinghuysen, educated at the University of Lingen and influenced by pietistic* followers of Gisbertus Voetius, served two pastorates in the lowlands before immigrating to America. When Frelinghuysen arrived in New York in 1720, his contumacious behavior immediately aroused the suspicions of the Dutch ministers there. A fervent pietist, Frelinghuysen chided his clerical colleagues for their personal vanity and for their use of the Lord's Prayer in worship.*

Frelinghuysen quickly settled in the Raritan Valley of New Jersey, where he enjoyed considerable success among the Dutch. He flouted ecclesiastical conventions and excoriated the Dutch Reformed hierarchy back in Amsterdam for failing to send pietist ministers* to the New World. In New Jersey, his pietistic scruples demanded the exclusion of "sinners" (i.e., the unconverted) from the Lord's Table, but his rather arbitrary enforcement of that discipline provoked bitter recriminations from some of the more affluent church members, who published an extensive bill of particulars, called the *Klagte,* against him. Frelinghuysen, however, refused to relent, sometimes taunted his ecclesiastical opponents and, though plagued by recurrent, debilitating bouts of mental illness, continued to demand high standards of morality from his congregants.

Frelinghuysen's evangelical fervor and his itinerancy contributed to the onset of the Great Awakening* in the Middle Colonies. Gilbert Tennent,* who often shared Frelinghuysen's pulpits, acknowledged that Frelinghuysen had taught him much about piety and revival, and both Jonathan Edwards* and George Whitefield* spoke highly of Frelinghuysen's ministry. Among his contributions to the Dutch Reformed Church in America was his effort to establish greater autonomy by seeking approval from the Classis of Amsterdam for the organization of a coetus in America. The coetus was approved in 1747, but Frelinghuysen did not live to see the fruit of these labors.

BIBLIOGRAPHY. *AAP* 9; R. H. Balmer, "The Social Roots of Dutch Pietism in the Middle Colonies," *CH* 53 (1984):187-199; *DAB* IV; *DARB; NCAB* 12; J. R. Tanis, *Dutch Calvinistic Pietism in the Middle Colonies* (1968). R. H. Balmer

Friar. A member of one of the mendicant orders of Roman Catholicism.* Various orders of friars (or "brothers," from the Latin *frater* and the French *frere*) were established in the high and later Middle Ages. These groups were distinguished from monastic orders chiefly by their initial reliance on begging for support (hence "mendicant orders") and by their active work in the world, whether in education, poor relief, missionary* work and other ministries. The four chief orders were recognized in the thirteenth century and are sometimes distinguished by the color of their habits: the Franciscans,* or Friars Minor ("Grey Friars"); the Dominicans,* or Preachers ("Black Friars"); the Carmelites ("White Friars"); and the Augustinians.* J. G. Stackhouse

Friends, The Religious Society of (Quakers). The Society of Friends was one of many religious groups which arose from the ferment of the English Puritan* revolution. The movement dates its origin from 1652 when George Fox,* standing atop Pendle Hill, received a vision of "a great people to be gathered" in Northwest England. The nickname "Quaker," originally used in 1647 of a sect of women in England who reportedly shivered and shook in religious excitement, was first used in 1650 to describe the Friends because they too were known to tremble when they fell under the power of God. "Friends" or "Society of

Friends" is the preferred title.

From his early years Fox had thirsted after the divine life but was tormented by temptation and despair. Living during a time of upheaval, he faced religious plurality* and political upset. In place of the one holy catholic church there were now many; and in the political arena, England's Charles I had been beheaded, and Parliament had taken control of the government. Amidst this turmoil Fox undertook a troubled quest for infallible religious authority.* Earnestly studying the Scriptures* for long hours and lonely days, walking about through long and restless nights, he sought the Lord in great agitation of soul. Having met the most renowned religious teachers of his day, he found them not to possess in themselves what they preached* to others. When he had despaired of all human help, he heard a voice which said, "There is one, even Christ Jesus, who can speak to thy condition." Through this experience Fox came to trust the immediate spiritual presence of Jesus Christ above every outward form and human teacher.

The burden of Fox's preaching was to turn every person to the Light of Christ within. Fox's doctrine of the Light, or Spirit of Christ, made him slightly more optimistic about human nature than the Puritans. Nevertheless, the Light was not natural in the sense of being an inherent part of man, such as conscience, nor was it merely the spiritual side of human nature. The Light was the transcendent God perceptibly breaking into human consciousness.

Fox taught that both Spirit and Scripture spoke with one voice, but that the Scripture could only be properly understood and applied by one who stood in right spiritual relationship with God. Resolute in his deprecation of bibliolatry, he tirelessly stressed that the Scriptures are not the Word of God but rather point to him that is, Jesus Christ. Consequently, Quakers came to esteem Scripture for self-examination and as a test of morals and doctrine, but always placed them under the authority of the living Christ.

Fox taught that only obedience to Christ could make one a true Christian. Biblical proficiency was insufficient. True worship meant quiet waiting on the Spirit of God and could not be produced by human will. Trained choirs,* glorious architecture* and religious art* were all condemned as mere gratification of sensual desires. True worship* was to apply oneself in silence directly to Jesus Christ to receive his grace and know his will.

Fox refused to participate in war or to take an oath because he understood these to be prohibited by the Sermon on the Mount, and he believed that the Spirit always speaks in harmony with Christ's teachings as recorded in Scripture. These views have caused Quakers considerable difficulties throughout the past three centuries. Many seventeenth-century Quakers were imprisoned for refusing to take oaths. In America, Quakers have suffered for their pacifist* stance during every war since the colonial period, often being accused as traitors.

Fox was not a trained theologian and so never produced a systematic account of his views. His *Journal* (1694), however, is a religious classic. It was Robert Barclay's *Apology for the True Christian Divinity* (1676) that was to become the most systematic and authoritative account of Quaker theology, though its purpose was polemical. On the other hand, William Penn's *No Cross No Crown* (1682) laid the basis for Quaker ethics. This ethic was symbolized in the Quaker custom of plain dress—an attempt to deny the vanity and wanton extravagance of keeping up with worldly fashion. Always alert to the pretensions of social custom, Quakers also adopted the use of *thee* and *thou* to address singular persons—a protest against the seventeenth-century practice of addressing one's social betters in the plural *you,* but one's inferiors with the singular "thou." Quakers argued that such distinctions merely flattered sinful pride, which was the greatest obstacle to genuine conversion. For the same reasons they disused other civilities such as "doffing the hat."

Almost immediately after the movement was born, Quakers began immigrating to America. Perhaps the first Quakers to arrive in the colonies were Mary Fisher* and Ann Austin,* who arrived from Barbados in Boston in July 1656. Imprisoned and suspected of witchcraft, within five weeks they were shipped back to Barbados. Two days after they had left, a ship carrying eight Quakers arrived in Boston to the same welcome. Barred from Boston, by August 1657 a number of Quakers had found a more tolerant home in Rhode Island. Yet their intentions were missionary, and by 1660 their persistent efforts had won many converts in southern Massachusetts, as well as inciting the ire of Puritan authorities. Between 1659 and 1661 four Quakers were hung from the gallows in Massachusetts.

When William Penn,* the most prominent Quaker in American history, received a charter for his colony of Pennsylvania in 1681, it immediately became a haven for persecuted Quakers and other religious groups. The colony thrived under religious tolerance and set a persuasive example for the developing nation. Indeed, many features of Pennsylvania's government were incorporated into the Constitution and Bill of Rights. But developments in Pennsylvania were not wholly pleasing to Quakers, and during the 1750s they withdrew from the government rather than be compelled to appropriate money for a militia to fight the Native Americans.

Exhausted by seventeenth-century persecutions, colonial Quakers began to turn inward. Taking advantage of stable social conditions, they carved farms, homes and businesses out of the wilderness. The bright flower of eighteenth-century American Quakerism was John Woolman.* Woolman, who was critical of his co-religionists' preoccupation with business, purposely cut back his own mercantile activities when they began to take up the energy and attention which he felt should be reserved for serving God.

Woolman, sensitive in conscience, early recognized the evils of slavery (*See* Abolition Movement). Asked to write a will involving the transfer of a slave as a piece of property, he became troubled. Gradually he came to the conclusion that slavery was wrong and that the only remedy was to grant slaves their freedom. Woolman believed this to be the only conclusion consistent with the love of God manifested in Jesus Christ. Through patient dedication, Woolman brought the Society of Friends to recognize and condemn the evil of slavery. A gentle reformer, he always showed love to the slaveholder, seeking to gain his soul rather than his condemnation. After 1776 it was no longer permissible for a Quaker to own a slave.

Woolman's efforts were exerted almost entirely within the Society of Friends. Woolman's associate in antislavery work, Anthony Benezet,* succeeded in convincing John Wesley* and Thomas Clarkson of the evils of slavery. If Benezet had not convinced non-Quakers of the evils of slavery, Woolman's accomplishment would have been a relatively minor event. But when Wesley, Clarkson and William Wilberforce became interested in abolition, it marked the beginning of a battle which did not relent until the slaves in the British Empire and America were set free.

The nineteenth century compelled American Quakers to respond to the forces of the Enlightenment,* revolution, revivalism,* the expanding frontier, abolition* and women's rights. The flush of revolutionary ardor and the exaltation of free thought over against Scripture and religious authority captured the imagination of Elias Hicks* and resulted in the Hicksite schism of 1827-1828. The remaining body of orthodox Friends regrouped only to be torn again over responses to the evangelical* revivals. This resulted in three major groups: Hicksites,* Gurneyites* and Wilburites. The Hicksites equated the Light with reason, disparaged the deity of Christ,* his substitutionary atonement,* biblical authority, mission* activity, most evangelical* philanthropies* and cooperation with other denominations.*

The Gurneyites derived their designation from their adherence to the teachings of the British Quaker banker and minister Joseph John Gurney,* a close associate with William Wilberforce, Thomas Clarkson and Thomas Fowell Buxton in the British anti-slavery movement. Gurney's sister was the prison reformer Elizabeth Fry, whose fame in the nineteenth century approached that of Queen Victoria. An excellent speaker and writer, Gurney attempted to provide a fresh understanding and defense of Quaker theology, and he and his followers were orthodox regarding the authority of Scripture, the deity of Christ and the significance of his death and resurrection for the forgiveness of sins. Gurney himself defended the traditional Quaker style of silent worship, without benefit of prepared sermon,* hymns* or paid clergy*; but his followers on the American frontier gradually adopted these innovations.

The Wilburites took their name from the New England Quaker schoolteacher John Wilbur.* Wilbur was also orthodox in his belief in the deity of Christ and the significance of his death on the cross. He feared, however, that Gurney was placing too much stress on biblical authority and losing the traditional Quaker reliance on the immediate presence of Christ. Wilbur believed the newly instituted practice of family Bible reading and prayer to be "will worship." Having no tolerance for revivalism and its practices, he once retrieved a Quaker child from a revival and rebuked the parents for not being more vigilant. Wilbur, like Hicks, sought to preserve the separation between Quakers and other denominations and stiffly opposed cooperative benevolent associations. The Wilburites did their best to preserve seventeenth century Quakerism in every detail as they understood it, but they failed to recognize that early Quakers were not bent on conserving a tradition; they had sought to carry the gospel throughout the earth.

Many nineteenth-century Quakers provided leadership for the abolitionist movement, including the poet John Greenleaf Whittier.* Whittier shared the management of the American Antislavery Society's office with Charles Finney's* convert Theodore Dwight Weld.* Other Quaker abolition leaders included the president of the Underground Railroad, Levi Coffin,* and the early feminists and abolitionists Angelina and Sarah Grimke.*

Quakers, believing that the gift of ministry is not distributed according to gender, have fostered female leadership since the movement's earliest days. Fox's first convert was a woman, and Quakers have had women preachers ever since. The role of Quaker women was fostered by separate business meetings for women, established to allow them to manage their affairs free of male domination. This group of women, grown accustomed to equality and the exercise of independent thought, provided a disproportionate number of women's rights leaders, including Lucretia Mott,* Abby Kelly, Susan B. Anthony* and Alice Paul.

Though presently numbering only 112,000 members in the U.S., there is as much theological diversity among American Quakers as there is among Protestants generally. The Evangelical Friends Alliance* includes 25,500 members. Their congregations have pastors, are theologically conservative evangelicals and use music and prepared sermons in their worship services. Friends General Conference is the liberal wing and includes 17,400 members. Worship in these meetings is generally silent and without reliance upon paid leadership or prepared messages. Friends United Meeting, which roughly corresponds theologically to mainline Protestantism, includes 43,400 American members. Almost all of these congregations have pastors. Some Yearly Meetings hold dual membership in Friends United Meeting and Friends General Conference. The number of members of Yearly Meetings with joint membership is 17,400. Another 6,700 American Quakers belong to congregations that are unaffiliated with any of these major bodies. The Conservative Friends are the smallest group, comprising 1,670 members. As a remnant of the Wilburites, they share many of the attitudes and attributes of Old Order Mennonites and Old German Baptists. Including all of these groups, there are about 1,000 Quaker congregations in the U.S.

BIBLIOGRAPHY. M. H. Bacon, *The Quiet Rebels: The Story of the Quakers in America* (1969); M. H. Bacon, *Mothers of Feminism: The Story of Quaker Women in America* (1986); H. Barbour and A. Roberts, eds., *Early Quaker Writings, 1650-1700* (1973); R. C. Braithwaite, *The Beginnings of Quakerism* (1912, rev. 1955); R. C. Braithwaite, *The Second Period of Quakerism* (1919, rev. 1961); R. M. Jones, *The Quakers in the American Colonies* (1911); E. Russel, *The History of Quakerism* (1942).   R. E. Selleck

Frontier Fellowship. *See* FELLOWSHIP OF SOCIALIST CHRISTIANS.

Frontier Religion. A term loosely applied to popular Protestantism* of the Second Great Awakening* as it developed in the trans-Allegheny West during the first decades of the nineteenth century. In this context the frontier is not viewed so much as unsettled territory as it is a process. Beginning with the Atlantic coast and moving westward, pioneers found it necessary to accommodate to the natural environment and harsh conditions of frontier life. As a result of coping with these factors, their values and institutions, including religious faith and church life, were somehow supposedly transformed or changed into new expressions and forms.

This thesis, based on the ideas of Frederick Jackson Turner (1861-1932), has undoubtedly been overstated by church historians such as William Warren Sweet.* There is little agreement among scholars on the role that a continuously moving frontier had on organized religion. Denominations* active in America's westward movement have been alternatively described as democratic and autocratic. Faith itself has been viewed as individualist* and conformist; and worship* forms as promoting schism and promoting unity. Moreover, there was an unmistakable continuity between frontier religion and the creeds* and religious institutions dominant on the Atlantic coast, even in Europe. It was the character of religion in the West that was different.

Some broad generalizations may be made. First, popular religion was decidedly evangelical,* emotionally intense, often individualistic and anti-intellectual. These characteristics are best illustrated by camp meeting* revivalism,* particularly the great Cane Ridge revival* of 1801, and the experiences of dedicated backwoods preachers, such as Methodist* Peter Cartwright.* Cartwright's "muscular Christianity" was equally adept at fighting sin among frontier ruffians as well as in other denominations.

Second, those denominations which used Western revivalism and best adapted to frontier conditions reaped the most benefits in terms of expansion and growth. With few exceptions, the shape of America's denominational life in 1900 was a result of the foundations laid in the Midwest between 1800 and 1830. Two of the most successful evangelical churches were the Baptists* and Methodists. The "farmer-preacher" system of the Baptists allowed leadership to be developed locally. The Methodist circuit rider* covered a vast

territory, thus allowing churches to be organized in the most remote areas. By contrast, important colonial churches who failed to appropriate these techniques (e.g., Anglicans,* Congregationalists*) expanded slowly.

A third characteristic of frontier religion was its plurality and the opportunity it provided for experimentation. Although many equated millennial* hopes with America's destiny, there was no orthodox* theology.* The adoption of the Constitution insured that there was no official ("established"*) church. These factors, coupled with the availability of land, privacy and relaxed social constraints, allowed all sorts of different faiths to develop. Communitarian* societies, such as the Shakers,* Zoar Separatists, Rappites of New Harmony,* Amana* Inspirationists and later the Hutterites* flourished. New churches, such as the Mormons* and Disciples of Christ* were able to successfully test their ideas. Competition among frontier religious groups was colorful if not friendly.

Although the census department officially closed the frontier in 1890, the religious diversity and individualism nurtured on the frontier have continued to shape American church life.

See also CAMP MEETINGS; REVIVALISM, PROTESTANT; SECOND GREAT AWAKENING.

BIBLIOGRAPHY. R. H. Gabriel, "Evangelical Religion and Popular Romanticism in the Early Nineteenth Century," *CH* 19 (1950):34-47; P. G. Mode, *Frontier Spirit in American Christianity* (1923); T. S. Miyakawa, *Protestants and Pioneers* (1964); W. W. Sweet, *Religion in the Development of American Culture* (1952, 1963); W. W. Sweet, ed., *Religion on the American Frontier, 1783-1850,* 4 vols. (1931-1946); L. B. Wright, *Culture on the Moving Frontier* (1955).   D. B. Eller

Frost, Henry Weston (1858-1945). Mission society* director. Born in Detroit, Frost was reared in New York City and educated at Princeton.* After college he joined his father's oil production business, working in Attica, New York (1880-1888). In 1904 he was ordained* in the Presbyterian Church.* Frost established the American branch of the China Inland Mission (Overseas Missionary Fellowship*) and at first served as secretary of the Mission (1889-1893) and later was home director at Philadelphia (1893-1919). As a Presbyterian and a dispensationalist,* Frost was sought after as a Bible conference* speaker. He was also a prolific author, producing numerous pamphlets, books of poetry, devotional books and missionary works. Among his best-known writings are *Heart Songs*

(1917), *Men Who Prayed* (1914), *Matthew 24 and Revelation* (1924), *Outline Bible Studies* (1925), *Effective Praying* (1926) and *Little Sermons from the Pentateuch* (1928). He was also a contributor to *The Fundamentals* (1910-1915).

BIBLIOGRAPHY. F. H. Taylor, *"By Faith"; Henry W. Frost and the China Inland Mission* (1938).

W. A. Detzler

Frost, James Marion (1848-1916). Southern Baptist* pastor* and Sunday School* Board executive. Born and raised in Georgetown, Kentucky, the son of a pastor, Frost graduated from Georgetown College and was ordained,* having accepted the pastorate of First Baptist, Maysville, Kentucky, on the same day in 1870. Frost served a succession of churches in Kentucky, Virginia and Alabama.

Frost captured the attention of Southern Baptists in 1890 by announcing, through the *Religious Herald* and other Baptist papers, that he would propose forming a denominational* Sunday School Board to the upcoming Southern Baptist Convention. Then pastor of Leigh Street Baptist Church in Richmond, Virginia, Frost discovered strong opposition to his resolution from many Baptist editors and pastors. The Convention in Fort Worth, Texas, set up a Sunday School Committee instead of the Board. However, at the next Convention (1891) in Birmingham, Alabama, Frost made a similar proposal that was adopted without debate after a heated discussion in committee.

The Board was established in Nashville, Tennessee, and Frost, after much persuasion, consented to lead the enterprise as secretary. Eighteen months later he resigned to become pastor of First Baptist, Nashville, but returned in 1896 to lead the Board for two decades. Under his leadership the Board gained denominational confidence, developed into publishing curriculum materials and books, and launched programs designed to strengthen Sunday schools and the denomination. In time the Board produced income for the Convention and served as a source of unity for the entire denomination. Today the Board is the largest denominational publishing agency in the world.

BIBLIOGRAPHY. R. Baker, *The Story of the Sunday School Board* (1966); J. M. Price, *Baptist Leaders in Religious Education* (1943).

C. L. Howe

Frothingham, Ebenezer (1719-1798). Congregational* Separatist.* Frothingham was the leading apologist of the pro-revival Separatists or, as they preferred, "Strict Congregationalists," of the Great Awakening.* While pastor of the Wethersfield-Middletown separate church in Connecticut (1747-1788), he wrote two significant works. *The Articles of Faith and Practice* (1750) was the first comprehensive treatment of Separate beliefs, particularly the new birth,* regenerate church membership* and the ability to determine the church's membership and select its officers without outside interference. The second work, *A Key to Unlock the Door* (1767), was an apology for absolute religious liberty, arguing that liberty of conscience was the inalienable, unalterable right of every person. This apology was the strongest plea for religious liberty* by a dissenter in Connecticut and helped effect some toleration in 1771. During his early ministry, Frothingham considered becoming a Baptist.* In his later years, however, he became a fierce opponent of the Baptists, especially Isaac Backus,* over the question of infant baptism.*

BIBLIOGRAPHY. C. C. Goen, *Revivalism and Separatism in New England, 1740-1800: Strict Congregationalists and Separate Baptists in the Great Awakening* (1962); M. L. Green, *The Development of Religious Liberty in Connecticut* (1905).

C. D. Weaver

Frothingham, Octavius Brooks (1822-1895). Unitarian* minister.* Frothingham's ministry from 1847 to 1879 in New England and New York City marked a transition in Unitarianism. Frothingham guided the "deChristianization" of a large segment of that movement through the founding of the Free Religion Association.

Born in Boston and educated at Harvard College* (1843) and Harvard Divinity School (1846), Frothingham became pastor of North Church in Salem, Massachusetts, in 1847. In 1855 he moved to Jersey City, New Jersey, to become pastor of the Unitarian Society and in 1859 became pastor of New York City's Third Unitarian Society. Later called the Independent Liberal Church, the congregation flourished until it was disbanded in 1879, and Frothingham retired to his native Boston and a life of writing.

Frothingham's religious beliefs became increasingly unorthodox throughout the 1860s when he began to describe himself as a "theistic* humanist." He criticized the revivals* of Henry Ward Beecher* and Dwight L. Moody* and accused Christianity of becoming "institutionalized." Frothingham's arguments that the Bible* was not divinely inspired and that Jesus was a good leader but not God, effectively alienated a large segment of Unitarians and created a split among them. He helped found the Free Religion Association, served as its president (1867-1878), contributed articles to its journal, *The Index,* and published *The Religion of Humanity* (1872) as a primer of the movement.

Known as the "historian of Transcendentalism,"* Frothingham wrote his classic work, *Transcendentalism in New England* (1876), and biographies of Theodore Parker,* George Ripley,* William Henry Channing and Garrit Smith, as well as a study of Boston Unitarianism. Though not widely remembered today, his contemporaries regarded Frothingham as one of America's best preachers* and the leader among religious thinkers of his day.

BIBLIOGRAPHY. S. E. Ahlstrom, "Introduction" in O. B. Frothingham, *Transcendentalism in New England* (1965); J. W. Caruthers, *Octavius Brooks Frothingham, Gentle Radical* (1977); *DAB* IV; S. A. Eliot, ed., *Heralds of Liberal Faith,* 3 vols. (1910); O. B. Frothingham, *Recollections and Impressions, 1822-1890* (1891).   C. P. Dawson

Fry, Franklin Clark (1900-1968). Lutheran* leader and ecumenist.* Born in Bethlehem, Pennsylvania, and raised in Rochester, New York, Fry graduated from Hamilton College in Clinton, New York (1921), and Lutheran Theological Seminary, Philadelphia (1925). He then undertook further study in Greece. He held pastorates in Yonkers, New York, and Akron, Ohio. His successive service to Lutherans at large tasks revealed his gifts. As president of the United Lutheran Church in America (1944-1962) and of the consolidated Lutheran Church in America* (1962-1968), he linked confessional* loyalty and ecumenical endeavor, emphasizing the oneness of Christ's church. A founder of the Lutheran World Federation* (1947), Fry was president from 1957 to 1963 and headed Lutheran World Relief from 1945 to 1968.

As vice chairperson of the Central Committee of the World Council of Churches, followed by two terms as chairperson (1948-1968 combined), he was fair, forthright and influential. In the National Council of Christian Churches' constitution (1950), Fry secured the inclusion of a Trinitarian "evangelical and representative principle" as a guide to membership and participation. Fry had rapport with the Eastern Orthodox* as well as with the Vatican Secretariat for Promoting Christian Unity. To many he was "Mr. Protestant." With his family roots in the colonial era, Fry personified a fuller Lutheran participation in American religious life.

BIBLIOGRAPHY. R. H. Fischer, ed., *Franklin Clark Fry: A Palette for a Portrait, Lutheran Quarterly Supplement,* vol. XXIV (1972); *Mr. Protestant: An Informal Biography of Franklin Clark Fry* (symposium) (1960).   E. T. Bachmann

Fulford, Francis (1803-1868). Anglican* bishop* of Montreal. Born in Sidmouth, England, and educated at Oxford, Fulford was ordained* in 1828. Fulford arrived in Canada in 1850 as first Lord Bishop of Montreal and became Primate of All Canada a decade later. Widely respected because of his gifts as a conciliator, he worked to establish links between the Church of England and the Protestant Episcopal Church* in the U.S. A sympathizer with the Tractarian Movement,* he died just before a crucial synod* on ritualism, where failure to achieve the reconciliation he had hoped for between the evangelicals* and Anglo-Catholics* contributed to the polemical distancing of the two parties in Canada. His major publication was entitled *The Progress of the Reformation in England* (1841).

BIBLIOGRAPHY. *DCB* IX.   P. D. Airhart

Full Gospel Business Men's Fellowship International. A lay* organization within the charismatic* movement. The Full Gospel Business Men's Fellowship International (FGBMFI) is a nondenominational association of charismatic businessmen who emphasize fellowship* and world evangelism,* being united in their belief in the full gospel (salvation,* divine healing,* Spirit baptism* accompanied by the sign of speaking in tongues* and the imminent personal return of Jesus).

The founder and president of the FGBMFI is Demos Shakarian.* An active supporter of the post–World War 2* Pentecostal healing* revival, he helped sponsor Oral Roberts's* 1951 Los Angeles campaign. Shakarian told Roberts of his desire to organize Pentecostal businessmen to spread the full gospel, and Roberts agreed to speak at an initial meeting. The first chapter developed out of that meeting in 1952. Roberts and other evangelists encouraged the creation of new chapters. In turn, the success of the FGBMFI gave the healing revival impetus. The journal *Voice,* initiated in 1953 and edited by Pentecostal leader Thomas Nickel, gave the revivalists extensive coverage. Originally viewed with suspicion by Pentecostal denominational leaders, the FGBMFI represented a subtle laymen's rebellion by a new elite of young entrepreneurs who were excluded from denominational decision making.

In the 1960s and 1970s, the FGBMFI functioned as the institutional cohesion for charismatic renewal. Along with Roberts and David du Plessis,* the FGBMFI was largely responsible for the spread of the full gospel message into the mainline* denominations and its acceptance by thousands of successful American middle-class non-Pentecostals. Chapter meetings emphasize the financial successes of Spirit-filled businessmen and, in the 1980s, have re-emphasized healing as the key to a lay-led "end-time" revival. By 1987 there were 3,000 chapters with 700,000 participants in ninety-three countries.

BIBLIOGRAPHY. S. Durasoff, *Bright Wind of the Spirit: Pentecostalism Today* (1972); D. Shakarian, *The Happiest People on Earth* (1975); D. E. Harrell, Jr., *Oral Roberts: An American Life* (1985).

C. D. Weaver

Fuller, Charles E. (1887-1969). Radio evangelist* and cofounder of Fuller Theological Seminary.* Fuller grew up in a Christian home in Southern California. Graduating from Pomona College in 1910, he entered the family orange-growing business. After his conversion* in 1916 under the ministry of evangelist Paul Rader,* Fuller studied for three years at the Bible Institute of Los Angeles. While there he came under the influence of R. A. Torrey.* In 1920 he began teaching an adult Bible* class in the Placentia Presbyterian Church, but after a few years he resigned from the elders* board, apparently dissatisfied with the social emphasis of the church. The Bible class continued, however, and in 1925 Fuller was ordained* to serve Calvary Church, which grew out of the Bible class. He served the church as pastor until 1932.

While serving at Placentia, Fuller launched a radio ministry which led to his international influence. His early program called "The Pilgrim's Hour" aired on seven stations in Southern California. In 1937 he moved to a national audience with his "Old Fashioned Gospel Hour." Starting with the Mutual Broadcasting System, he later moved to the Columbia Broadcasting System. By 1939 the program reached an estimated 10 million listeners on Sunday evenings. During World War 2* Fuller launched live broadcasts from the Municipal Auditorium in Long Beach. Several thousand people, including many military personel, filled the auditorium every Sunday.

In 1947 Fuller joined Harold John Ockenga,* pastor of Park Street Church in Boston, in founding Fuller Theological Seminary in Pasadena, California.

BIBLIOGRAPHY. D. P. Fuller, *Give the Winds a Mighty Voice* (1972); G. M. Marsden, *Reforming Fundamentalism: Fuller Seminary and the New Evangelicalism* (1987); W. M. Smith, *A Voice for God: The Life of Charles E. Fuller* (1949).

B. L. Shelley

Fuller, Richard (1804-1876). Prominent Baptist* pastor* and leader in the formation of the Southern Baptist Convention.* Born into a wealthy family in South Carolina, Fuller was educated at Harvard.* In 1847 he came to Baltimore as a pastor, where he served for the rest of his life. Raised in the South and educated in the North, his situation in Baltimore gave him a rare perspective on the national tensions leading up to the Civil War.*

In 1844 Fuller entered a journalistic debate over slavery with Francis Wayland,* who was then president of Brown University. Out of this debate came his defense of slavery, *Domestic Slavery Considered as a Scriptural Institution* (1845). Fuller was active in the denominational life of the newly formed Southern Baptist Convention, serving as president of the Convention for two years, preaching the first annual sermon in 1846 and avidly supporting theological education* for all ministers.

BIBLIOGRAPHY. *DAB* IV; J. H. Cuthbert, *Life of Richard Fuller* (1879).

M. G. Bell

Fuller, Samuel (?-1632). Deacon and physician of Plymouth, Massachusetts. Described by Plymouth governor William Bradford* as a "tender hearted man," Fuller was among those who wanted John Lyford, who had plotted against Bradford, to be readmitted to church communion after his censure in 1624. As Plymouth's surgeon, Fuller was sent in 1630 to offer medical assistance against the infectious fever, scurvy and other diseases plaguing the settlers of Massachusetts Bay. His services, and, more importantly, his explanations of Plymouth's separatist church polity* to the leaders of the Bay, were of signal importance in establishing religious ties between the two colonies. Fuller has been inaccurately accredited with persuading the Bay ministers of the correctness of Congregationalism.* It is more likely that he provided some practical recommendations, based on Plymouth's experience, to people who were already theoretically convinced of non-separating Congregationalism.

BIBLIOGRAPHY. "Bradford's Letter Book," *Collections* of the Mass. Hist. Soc., 3 (1794):25-75; W. Bradford, *Of Plymouth Plantation,* ed. S. E. Morrison (1952).

K. P. Minkema

Fuller Theological Seminary. A leading seminary* in the evangelical* renaissance following World War 2.* Fuller was founded in Pasadena, California, in 1947, primarily through the efforts of radio evangelist* Charles E. Fuller* and Boston pastor* Harold John Ockenga.* They envisioned a school that could effectively engage modern theological scholarship, further world-wide evangelism and reform some of strict fundamentalism's* most unattractive elements. The founding faculty consisted of Carl F. H. Henry* in theology,* Wilbur Smith* in apologetics,* Everett Harrison* in New Testament and Harold Lindsell in church history and missions.* Ockenga served as president *in absentia* from Boston. Fuller's faculty grew and eventually included some of evangelicalism's most distinguished scholars: George E. Ladd,* Edward J. Carnell,* Paul K. Jewett, William S. LaSor, Geoffrey W. Bromiley and Ralph P. Martin.

From the beginning Fuller's standing within fundamentalism was precarious. At a time when the lines between fundamentalism and evangelicalism were indistinct, the seminary increasingly was identified with the "new evangelicalism"* (Ockenga's term), which criticized fundamentalism for its anti-intellectualism, separatism,* combativeness and predictable unwillingness to address social and political issues. During the 1950s and 1960s the seminary experienced internal division and external attacks over a variety of issues, including eschatology,* apparent openness to neoorthodoxy,* and some of the faculty's refusal to hold a strict separatist line. These problems were aggravated by a persistent problem in leadership. After serving seven years as a nonresident president, Ockenga was succeeded by Carnell (1954-1959), who was temperamentally ill-suited for such a position. Securing a replacement for Carnell proved to be difficult because the school was deeply divided into conservative and progressive camps over the inclusion of biblical inerrancy* in the seminary's statement of faith.

In the end, the opponents of inerrancy won and David Hubbard became president in 1963. Under his leadership, Fuller has become the undisputed leader in progressive evangelicalism. In the 1960s Schools of Psychology and World Mission were established; and new seminary programs attracted women and minorities in unprecedented numbers. Thanks to Hubbard's ability to develop a new constituency from mainline* evangelicals and Pentecostals,* by the 1980s Fuller had become the largest nondenominational seminary in the U.S.

BIBLIOGRAPHY. G. Marsden, *Reforming Fundamentalism: Fuller Seminary and the New Evangelicalism* (1987). T. P. Weber

Fundamental Theology. The systematic reflection on the possibility and legitimacy of Christian theology prior to revealed doctrinal content, not to be confused with fundamentalist* theology, which concerns itself with a particular expression of the essential doctrines of orthodox Protestant* Christianity. Fundamental theology has been a particular concern of modern Roman Catholic* theologians* such as Karl Rahner.*

Fundamental theology can be understood as a part of natural theology.* It attempts to demonstrate certain truths without reference to what is revealed to the church* in Scripture.* Its basic premises come from the world at large and from within the human person. Fundamental theology may lead to truths such as the existence of God, the possibility of revelation and the possibility for human beings to hear and understand revelation—truths held in common with dogmatic theology.* This is not only expected, but intended by those who do fundamental theology.

Fundamental theology is apologetic* in nature. It can be a part of the defense of Christian theology over against other revelation claims or against modern nonreligious thought forms. But its posture need not be confrontational. It can also be designed as a project of self-conscious legitimization of Christian theology within contemporary philosophies. As such it is considered an essential first step to any modern theologizing.

Fundamental theology has become increasingly anthropocentric. Whereas older apologists tended to begin with the world order as a whole, modern Roman Catholic thinkers have tended to concentrate on an existential dimension within the human person as a ground for divine revelation. Thus Karl Rahner argued that the possibility of human knowledge presupposes a grounding of the human spirit in the transcendent.

Protestantism has frequently suffered from an aversion to natural theology. But it also has had a strong apologetic interest, much of which can be aligned with fundamental theology. Insofar as Protestants have concerned themselves with the philosophical categories facilitating theology, they can be said to have contributed to fundamental theology.

BIBLIOGRAPHY. W. Corduan, *Handmaid to Theology: An Essay in Philosophical Prolegomena* (1981); G. O'Collins and R. Latourelle, *Problems and Perspectives of Fundamental Theology* (1980); K. Rahner, *Foundations of Christian Faith* (1978). W. Corduan

Fundamentalism. A movement organized in the early twentieth century to defend orthodox* Protestant* Christianity against the challenges of theological liberalism,* higher criticism of the Bible,* evolution* and other modernisms* judged to be harmful to traditional faith.

Changing Interpretations of Fundamentalism.
Until recently most historians viewed fundamentalism in terms of cultural lag or social displacement. In the 1930s Stewart G. Cole and H. Richard Niebuhr* saw the fundamentalist-modernist controversy* as the religious side of a much larger urban-rural conflict, with fundamentalists as provincial people from small towns and the countryside standing in opposition to more progressive and sophisticated city dwellers. During the 1950s Norman Furniss and Ray Ginger defined fundamentalism primarily in terms of its pervasive anti-intellectualism, as seen in its opposition to evolution and other kinds of modern thought. In the early 1960s Richard Hofstadter suggested that the movement was rooted in a so-called status anxiety brought on by a loss of power, influence and respect in society.

By the late 1960s historians had begun looking at fundamentalism as a bona fide religious, theological and even intellectual movement in its own right. Paul Carter challenged the older consensus by showing that instead of being anti-intellectual, fundamentalists were simply intellectual in a way different than their opponents. In 1970 Ernest R. Sandeen argued that twentieth-century fundamentalism grew out of a nineteenth-century alliance between the Calvinist* orthodoxy of Princeton Seminary* and millennialism.* The most sophisticated thesis to date has been offered in George M. Marsden's *Fundamentalism and Modern Culture* (1980). Defining fundamentalism as "militantly anti-modernist Protestant evangelicalism,"* he showed how a number of older evangelical movements joined forces to mount a new and rather distinctive crusade against various perceived threats.

Such shifts in historiography suggest that fundamentalism should be seen as a rather distinctive modern reaction to religious, social and intellectual changes of the late 1800s and early 1900s, a reaction that eventually took on a life of its own and changed significantly over time. In fact, one can detect five distinct but overlapping phases in the history of American fundamentalism.

Forming Conservative Coalitions, 1875-1900.
After the Civil War* various intellectual, social and religious changes undermined the foundations of the Evangelical Empire. The so-called higher criticism of the Bible* (*See* Biblical Interpretation) cropped up in many seminaries* and called into question traditional views of biblical accuracy and authority.* Darwinism and the new geology won rapid acceptance in scientific and educational circles and made many doubt older views of creation. The new social sciences of psychology,* sociology and comparative religions undercut confidence in the uniqueness of Christian religious experience* and the finality of the Christian faith. Large numbers of Catholic* and Jewish immigrants* threatened to change forever the balance of power in American religious life; while urban overcrowding and labor problems made many evangelicals feel that they were losing control.

Many Protestants adjusted to these challenges by adopting a New Theology* which not only welcomed biblical higher criticism and evolutionary thought but undertook a program of modernizing traditional doctrine. Many others developed a Social Gospel* which tended to emphasize saving society over saving souls. On the other hand, most conservative evangelicals found such adjustments unacceptable. They feared that older meanings were being eliminated by the newer definitions and that the church's primary calling (evangelism*) was being neglected. In some cases conservatives tried to stem the tide through well-publicized heresy trials* of suspected liberal seminary professors. More common, however, were the attempts to shore up traditional beliefs and practices and to create new coalitions of conservative groups.

Theologians Benjamin B. Warfield* and Archibald A. Hodge* of Princeton Seminary increased confidence in the Bible with their doctrine of biblical inerrancy.* Dwight L. Moody* brought together large numbers of Baptists,* Presbyterians* and Congregationalists* with his new style of urban revivalism.* Others doubled their efforts in foreign missions.* A. J. Gordon* and R. A. Torrey* joined with others from the Methodist* tradition to push varieties of Holiness* doctrine. Dispensationalists* spread a new kind of premillennialism,* which gained popularity in many circles. Though they often differed, these conservatives built bridges and engaged in many cooperative efforts. They built Bible institutes,* where the old doctrines were protected and promoted, and they gathered in summer Bible conferences,* where traditional evangelicalism was extolled. Such associations cut across denominational* lines and provided the personal and organizational framework for a more self-conscious fundamentalism later on.

Finding a Fundamentalist Agenda, 1900-1920.
During this period conservative evangelicals continued to consolidate by identifying the issues around which they were willing to do battle,

articulating a core of non-negotiable beliefs and developing a stronger sense of mutual identity.

Scores of conservative evangelicals from America and Europe contributed to a series of twelve volumes called *The Fundamentals** (1910-1915) in order to identify and overcome what was wrong with modern religion and society. They criticized Romanism, Mormonism,* Christian Science,* atheism, spiritualism, modern philosophy and socialism. But they most objected to liberal theology, German higher criticism, Darwinism and their underlying naturalistic assumptions that led to the rejection of the inspiration of the Bible and the supernaturalistic basis of Christianity. For the most part *The Fundamentals* were scholarly, well-reasoned, carefully nuanced and polite. In time, however, fundamentalists learned to narrow their list of concerns and become more militant in their approach.

Conservatives also articulated their non-negotiable doctrines during this period. This process began much earlier in the Bible conference movement, where evangelicals from a variety of backgrounds decided to spell out the doctrinal basis of their cooperation. In 1878 leaders of the Niagara Bible Conference* issued the "Niagara Creed," which listed fourteen "fundamentals of the faith." By the early twentieth century, conservatives were reducing them even further. In 1910 the General Assembly of the Northern Presbyterian Church affirmed five essential doctrines (*See* Five Point Deliverance) which, it believed, had come under attack: the inerrancy of the Bible, the virgin birth of Christ, his substitutionary atonement,* his bodily resurrection and his miracles. By the time these essentials were reaffirmed in 1916 and 1923, conservative Presbyterians believed that they were the *sine qua non* of Christianity. Other conservatives drew up their own lists. When William Bell Riley* organized the World's Christian Fundamentals Association* in 1919, its statement of non-negotiables added one about Christ's Second Coming, in deference to its substantial premillennialist clientele.

Such list-making meant that conservatives were ready to rally around a rather short and specific set of doctrinal fundamentals. Evidently, the terms *fundamentalist* and *fundamentalism* were first coined in 1920 by Curtis Lee Laws* in his *Baptist Watchman-Examiner.* By then fundamentalism was a self-conscious movement with a well-defined enemy and a list of non-negotiables. World War 1* helped sharpen its focus. To a large extent fundamentalists blamed the war on the effects of German higher criticism and the wide-spread acceptance of evolutionary thought. In order to save Christian civilization and stem the cultural crisis, such errors needed to be purged from society, starting with the evangelical denominations.

Battling Modernism in the Public Arena, 1920-1935. During the 1920s and early 1930s fundamentalists engaged in a series of public disputes in order to purge liberals from the evangelical denominations and took action to eliminate the teaching of evolution in the public schools.

Struggles between fundamentalists and modernists occurred in the Methodist Episcopal Church,* the Protestant Episcopal Church,* the Disciples of Christ* and the Southern Presbyterian Church;* but the fiercest battles were waged in the Northern Baptist* and Presbyterian denominations. Shortly before the 1920 Northern Baptist Convention in Buffalo, conservatives organized the "Fundamentalist Fellowship"* in order to draw attention to the spread of liberalism in Northern Baptist schools and mission agencies. Irritated by the overt modernism of people like Harry Emerson Fosdick,* they called for investigations of all Baptist institutions and tried to get the Convention to adopt a binding statement of faith, which they hoped would eliminate modernists from the church. But they were consistently outmaneuvered by liberals who convinced other moderates and conservatives that the fundamentalists wanted to destroy Baptist "soul liberty" and make the church less inclusive. A more militant group, the Baptist Bible Union,* was organized in 1923; but it too failed to bring changes and threatened to disrupt the Convention permanently.

Northern Presbyterians also experienced heated public debates in the 1920s. In 1923, the same year that the General Assembly reaffirmed the five essentials, Professor J. Gresham Machen* of Princeton Seminary published *Christianity and Liberalism,* in which he argued that because of its radically different assumptions, liberalism was not Christianity at all. Liberals countered by issuing the Auburn Affirmation* (1924), in which they made a clear distinction between the facts of religion and the theological theories developed to explain them and called for an inclusive church in which doctrinal differences could be tolerated. In 1925 fundamentalists failed in their attempt to censure the New York Presbytery for ordaining candidates who denied some of the five essentials, and by 1927 the General Assembly voted that the essentials were no longer binding. When Princeton Seminary, the traditional bastion of Calvinist orthodoxy, was reorganized in order to bring it in line with the church's theological diversity, Presbyterian fundamentalists withdrew, founded Westminster Theological Seminary (1929) and began making plans to form their own church.

Fundamentalists also battled modernists outside the churches, especially in the crusade to make it illegal to teach evolution in the public schools.* The World's Christian Fundamentals Association and the Anti-evolution League mobilized their forces and succeeded in getting legislation passed in a number of states. But the undisputed leader of the popular anti-evolution crusade was William Jennings Bryan,* Presbyterian layman and three-time Democratic candidate for president. In the Scopes Monkey Trial* in Dayton, Tennessee (1925), defense attorney Clarence Darrow humiliated Bryan, and as a result fundamentalism was held up to public ridicule. By the early 1930s their early successes were also rolled back.

During this period, then, fundamentalists failed in their attempts to rid their churches of modernism and the schools of evolution. Consequently, there was a division in their ranks between moderate fundamentalists who wanted to stay in the churches and find other ways to bring about change and the more militant fundamentalists who were ready to go their own way.

Establishing New Institutions, 1930-1950. Having failed in their two crusades, many fundamentalists decided to start institutions of their own. The fundamentalism of the 1930s and 1940s had become increasingly alienated, separatistic and divisive. Unable to get control of the older denominations, they also found it nearly impossible to get along with each other.

By the early 1930s the more militant fundamentalists decided that "come-outism" was their only alternative. Militant members of the Baptist Bible Union left the Northern Baptist Convention in 1932 to form the General Association of Regular Baptist Churches;* while members from the more moderate Fundamentalist Fellowship stayed in the Convention until 1947 when they formed the Conservative Baptist Association.* Fundamentalist Presbyterians organized the Orthodox Presbyterian Church* (1936) and then two years later had to establish the Bible Presbyterian Church* when they disagreed on the acceptability of premillennialism. In the South controversial Baptist preacher Frank Norris* started the World Baptist Fellowship* in the mid 1930s and then saw it split into the Baptist Bible Fellowship* in the late 1940s. In addition, literally thousands of independent Baptist* and Bible Churches* were founded during these decades.

Equally important was the vibrant subculture that separatistic fundamentalism created for itself. Because they were unwilling to associate with people who differed from them, fundamentalists had to build their own schools,* publishing houses and mission agencies. Thus while mainline denominations were experiencing a religious depression in the 1930s, fundamentalists enjoyed a binge of institution-building. They continued or founded their own Bible conferences and Bible institutes and even engaged in their own brand of ecumenism.* As an alternative to the World Council of Churches,* militants under Carl McIntire* founded the American Council of Christian Churches* (1941), while moderates founded the slightly less separatistic National Association of Evangelicals* (1942). In all of these endeavors, fundamentalists were always careful not to cooperate with so-called compromisers or soft conservatives who were not as separatistic or militant as they were.

Clearly fundamentalism changed its identity during this phase of its history. Many who called themselves fundamentalists in the 1920s became unacceptable in the 1930s when they refused to leave their churches and become more militant. Separatistic* fundamentalism also became more demanding and selective in its doctrine and behavior patterns. For example, in the 1920s simple belief in the Second Coming of Christ qualified as a fundamental, but in the 1930s one might have to believe in Christ's pretribulational and premillennial Second Coming (*See* Eschatology) to be considered a fundamentalist. Indeed, a person's spiritual condition was often judged on the basis of conformity to certain religious and social practices. As a result, fundamentalism became identified in the public mind with anti-intellectualism, combativeness, extremism and what was viewed by many as a "paranoid" style.

Rebuilding and Regrouping, 1945-1980s. After World War 2,* fundamentalists continued to change. Many were not happy with what had happened to their movement in the 1930s and began working for a revival in their own ranks. In the late 1940s a number of younger fundamentalists who had secured graduate educations in top universities created a new fundamentalism. Harold J. Ockenga* called for a "new evangelicalism"* devoid of fundamentalism's shortcomings. Carl F. H. Henry* criticized fundamentalism for its anti-intellectualism, divisiveness, lack of social conscience and uncritical alliance with political conservatism. Edward J. Carnell* scorned the movement's obscurantism and challenged it to engage modern thought. Even some fundamental-ist "old-timers" supported such changes. Charles E. Fuller,* pioneer in religious broadcasting, donated money for the founding of Fuller Theological Seminary (1947), which hoped to achieve intellec-tual respectability. Other evangelicals founded *Christianity Today** as the journal for the new movement and looked to the leadership of a young evangelist named Billy Graham.* This neo-evangelicalism demonstrated considerable vitality and produced many new parachurch* organiza-tions such as Youth for Christ,* Campus Crusade for Christ* and Young Life.*

Militant fundamentalists were not happy with these developments. They looked on the new evangelicals as defectors and compromisers who were too willing to cut doctrinal corners and associate with people from apostate denomina-tions. In response, the militants boycotted Billy Graham, avoided any connection with fundamen-talist institutions that had been contaminated by neo-evangelicalism and became even more suspi-cious of each other.

But even separatistic fundamentalists could not avoid change. By the 1970s they had identified new enemies and supported new causes. They organized to oppose secular humanism,* the decline of traditional values, feminism, legalized abortion,* homosexuality* and the elimination of prayer from the public schools.* They even revived their old anti-evolution crusade by sponsoring legislation to provide equal time for what they called "creation science"* in the public schools. But entering the political process raised new questions. To what extent should Jerry Falwell's* Moral Majority* and other organizations of the New Christian Right include nonfundamentalists in their programs? Some militants, such as those at Bob Jones* University, condemned such coopera-tion and labelled political activists like Falwell as "pseudo-fundamentalists."

By the 1980s fundamentalism was more divided than ever. Militants still argued over the limits of separatism and fretted over how many of their own had moved toward neo-evangelicalism. More moderate evangelicals became equally concerned about the growing diversity in their ranks over biblical inerrancy, Christian feminism,* charismat-ic* gifts and political involvement.

Despite these differences new alignments seem to be emerging. Fundamentalists in the Southern Baptist Convention* recently organized to exclude so-called moderates from places of denomination-al power. Equally important was the new middle ground that moderate fundamentalists and more

conservative evangelicals have been exploring. While the most militant fundamentalists keep moving to the right, and left-wing evangelicals are heading back toward the mainline churches from which fundamentalism arose in the first place, fundamentalists and evangelicals closer to the center appear to be experimenting with new alliances which may give the fundamentalist tradition a new opportunity to affect American society in significant ways.

See also EVANGELICALISM; FUNDAMENTALIST-MODERNIST CONTROVERSY; NEW EVANGELICALISM.

BIBLIOGRAPHY. D. O. Beale, *In Pursuit of Purity* (1986); J. Falwell, ed., *The Fundamentalist Phe-nomenon* (1981); N. F. Furniss, *The Fundamental-ist Controversy, 1918-1931* (1954); L. Gasper, *The Fundamentalist Movement, 1930-1956* (1963); J. D. Hunter, *American Evangelicalism* (1983); G. M. Marsden, ed., *Evangelicalism and Modern America* (1984); G. M. Marsden, *Fundamentalism and American Culture* (1980); G. M. Marsden, *Reforming Fundamentalism* (1987); C. A. Russell, *Voices of American Fundamentalism* (1976); E. R. Sandeen, *The Roots of Fundamentalism: British and American Millenarianism, 1800-1930* (1970); D. F. Wells and J. D. Woodbridge, eds., *The Evangelicals* (1977). T. P. Weber

Fundamentalist Baptist Fellowship. A move-ment of conservatives in the Northern Baptist* Convention. In 1921 a group that came to be called the "Fundamentalist Fellowship" sought to rid Northern Baptist Convention schools of liberal* teachers. Meeting prior to the national conference of the Convention, they planned a strategy for imposing their views on the denomination* as a whole. To this end they prepared a confession of faith known as The Goodchild Confession, based on the Philadelphia and New Hampshire Confes-sions.* Their plans were shattered, however, by alternate committee reports and parliamentary maneuvers. In 1922 the denomination affirmed the New Testament as their only rule of faith in order to avert the adoption of a fundamentalist state-ment. Fundamentalists could muster only one-third of the voting participants for their doctrinal standard.

The Fundamentalist Fellowship never again had the opportunity to capture the Convention or put their policies into effect. Several smaller groups emerged from the Convention in the late 1920s, but the Fundamentalist Fellowship itself stayed within the denomination until the 1940s. In 1943 the fundamentalists, in protest of the policies of the Convention's foreign mission society, organized the Conservative Baptist Foreign Mission Society and laid the foundation for the Conservative Baptist* movement. A separatistic* wing among the conservatives continued the critical influence of the Fundamentalist Fellowship until 1965 when it withdrew and adopted the name *Fundamental Baptist Fellowship*. Offices for the Fellowship were in Chicago until 1970, when for the next two years it was located in Denver. In 1972 it moved back to Chicago.

BIBLIOGRAPHY. G. M. Marsden, *Fundamentalism and American Culture* (1980); B. L. Shelley, *A History of Conservative Baptists* (1981).

E. L. Towns

Fundamentalist-Modernist Controversy. The fundamentalist*-modernist* controversy was an extended conflict in the Protestant* churches and American society at large between religious liberals, who sought to preserve Christianity by accommodating the traditional faith to modern culture, and militant theological conservatives, determined to save evangelical* Christianity and American civilization from the advances of modernism and Darwinism.*

In 1865 most Americans thought of their country as a Christian nation and looked on evangelical Protestantism as the national religion. Though the evangelical establishment was marked by denominational* rivalries and marred by divisions between Northern and Southern churches, it demonstrated an impressive unity of beliefs and values. In the years between the Civil War* and World War 1,* this consensus dissolved. Differing responses to the profound intellectual and social changes of the late nineteenth and early twentieth centuries produced sharp divisions in American Protestantism which, in the wake of World War 1, erupted in the fundamentalist-modernist controversy.

A revolution in thinking challenged traditional Christianity in the years after Appomattox. The publication of Charles Darwin's *Origin of the Species* in 1859 and the subsequent rise of evolutionary philosophy attacked dearly held beliefs about the accuracy of the Bible* and God's providential design. Additionally, changes in the study of history, sociology, psychology* and world religions and the Bible* questioned the possibility of absolute religious and moral truth. Profound social changes added to the cultural turbulence. Immense immigration,* rapid urbanization and industrialization, and the gradual secularization of society all presented formidable challenges to America's churches.

Evangelical Protestants responded to these changes in different ways. Many, accepting the advances in science,* history and biblical studies, set out to save Christianity by adjusting the traditional faith to modern intellectual trends. These liberals, or so-called modernists, built on the foreign philosophical tradition of Immanuel Kant (1724-1804) and German Idealism and the religious thought of Friedrich Schleiermacher (1768-1834) and Albrecht Ritschl (1822-1889). In addition, they were heavily influenced by Unitarianism,* Transcendentalism* and the religious thought of Horace Bushnell.* By the 1880s an identifiable movement known as the "New Theology" had arisen. Pastors such as Theodore Munger* and theologians like William Newton Clarke* worked to accommodate the old faith to new ways of thinking. By the end of World War 1 liberals were well entrenched in the major Northern denominations,* dominating perhaps half of the seminaries* and a third of the Protestant pulpits.*

Liberal theology placed particular stress on the idea of divine immanence. Enamored of evolutionary thought, modernists insisted that God revealed himself through the progress of history. This affirmation led to an optimistic world view manifested in an irrepressible faith in the goodness and freedom of mankind and the inevitable movement of history toward the fulfillment of the kingdom of God* on earth.

Experience provided the final religious authority for modernists. Doctrines* were seen as tentative and historically conditioned accounts of unchanging religious feelings. This emphasis allowed liberals to endorse wholeheartedly the findings of biblical higher criticism. Since the Bible was only an historically limited record of the progressive self-revelation of God to Israel, historical or scientific difficulties could be overlooked as anachronistic expressions of abiding religious experience.*

Finally, ethics* became the test of religious truth. In liberal circles concern for life here eclipsed interest in the life hereafter. The divinity of Jesus was commonly attributed to his ethical and religious perfection, and the church was understood to be an agency for moral action and development. Many liberals, insisting that the purpose of Christianity was to transform society into God's kingdom, became vocal proponents of the Social Gospel.*

While liberals were making peace with modernity by adjusting Christianity to culture, some conservatives engaged in theological innovations that would influence the fundamentalist movement of the 1920s. Most significant was the development of dispensational* premillennialism,* primarily by the Englishman John Nelson Darby.* Popularized in America by Bible and prophecy conferences,* the *Scofield Reference Bible** (1909) and numerous Bible institutes,* dispensationalism was a complex method of literal biblical interpretation that divided history into seven eras, each marked by a different covenant between God and humanity. According to this scheme, the present age was destined to irreversible spiritual decline that would end only with the supernatural personal return and millennial reign of Christ. The dispensationalist view of the Bible as divinely inspired and without error found contemporary scholarly support in the doctrine of scriptural inerrancy* formulated by nondispensationalist Presbyterian* conservatives, most notably Benjamin B. Warfield,* at Princeton Theological Seminary.*

Another conservative development that affected fundamentalism was the Keswick Holiness Movement.* The Keswick teaching, a brand of Calvinistic* holiness* imported from England, emphasized a personal experience of "consecration," followed by a filling with the Holy Spirit for a life of service. By the early twentieth century, Keswick holiness, which was popularized by many of the conferences, institutes and publications that promoted dispensationalism, had become an influential force among numerous theological conservatives.

Around the turn of the century, conservative Protestants began to forge alliances to defend supernatural Bible-based Christianity against the advances of the more naturalistic liberal theology. The clearest manifestation of this nascent coalition was the publication of twelve paperback volumes entitled *The Fundamentals** (1910-1915). The essays in these works addressed diverse topics, but almost all contributors defended the authority of the Scriptures against the claims of modern science and higher criticism. While the coalition behind *The Fundamentals* adumbrated the postwar conservative alliance, the essays were notably free of the militancy that would characterize fundamentalism in the 1920s.

In the heat of the cultural crisis that gripped America after World War 1, fundamentalism emerged as a distinct movement and the long-developing differences between liberals and conservatives exploded in the fundamentalist-modernist controversy. Modernists, more aggressive and influential than ever, and fundamentalists, sure that liberal theology and Darwinism were undermining Christianity and American civiliza-

tion, squared off for battle. As the controversy intensified, theological moderates moved to one extreme or the other, polarizing church and society. In 1920 the conservative Curtis L. Laws* coined the term *fundamentalist* to describe those willing "to do battle royal for the Fundamentals." Eventually, the term *fundamentalist* came to refer to militantly antimodernistic Protestant evangelicals in general.

Fundamentalists and modernists fought on two fronts: the churches and the culture at large. In the major denominations and their mission* fields, conservatives sought to halt liberalism by requiring subscription to traditional doctrines of supernaturalist Christianity, such as the inerrancy of Scripture, the virgin birth, substitutionary atonement,* bodily resurrection and miracle-working power of Christ and premillennialism. In *Christianity and Liberalism* (1923), J. Gresham Machen* articulated the conservative claim that modernism was not Christianity and that liberals, therefore, ought to withdraw from the churches. Liberals, led by Harry Emerson Fosdick* and Shailer Mathews,* insisted that they were evangelical Christians and appealed to the American sense of liberty and tolerance. Denominational battles were especially intense among the Northern Baptists,* Northern Presbyterians and Disciples of Christ,* where both modernism and fundamentalism had strong and vocal representation. The Episcopalians* and Northern Methodists,* dominated by moderates and liberals, experienced minor skirmishes. Most Southern denominations, controlled by conservatives, remained relatively calm. By 1926 the liberal appeal to tolerance had, essentially, succeeded. To the dismay of the fundamentalists, the churches refused to drive modernists from their ranks.

In the culture generally, a variety of interdenominational groups, such as the World's Christian Fundamentals Association,* and a host of fundamentalist stars—William Bell Riley,* John Roach Straton* and J. Frank Norris*—led by three-time presidential candidate William Jennings Bryan,* sought to save American civilization from the effects of Darwinism. Many conservatives had concluded that German military atrocities, biblical higher criticism, modernist theology and the revolution in morals of the twenties were all directly attributable to the spread of atheistic evolutionary philosophy. Darwinism, by sanctioning the law of hate, paralyzed the Christian conscience and threatened American democracy.* To halt this apostasy a number of Southern states had, by the mid-1920s, passed laws banning the teaching of organic evolution in the public schools. This movement resulted in the famous Scopes trial* of 1925 where Bryan and agnostic lawyer Clarence Darrow faced off amidst a carnival atmosphere in Dayton, Tennessee. Though John Scopes was convicted of teaching biological evolution in a local school, the Eastern press coverage, which characterized fundamentalists as ignorant hicks, and Bryan's simplistic defense of the Bible under Darrow's cross-examination, did irreparable damage to the fundamentalist cause. With Bryan's death five days after the trial, fundamentalism lost its most conspicuous leader. In the culture at large, as in the churches, the controversy wound down after 1926.

Fundamentalism and modernism underwent significant changes after 1930. Conservatives, enjoying impressive gains both inside and outside of the major denominations, regrouped and emerged later in the century as evangelicals and fundamentalists. Liberals responded to the challenges of the Great Depression,* growing international tensions and neo-orthodoxy* by abandoning their sanguine view of humanity and history. Nevertheless, the battles of the 1920s had profoundly altered the shape of American Protestantism. Henceforth, divisions between conservative and liberal Christians would far overshadow differences based on formal denominational ties.
See also EVANGELICALISM; FUNDAMENTALISM; HERESY TRIALS; LIBERALISM/MODERNISM, PROTESTANT.

BIBLIOGRAPHY. S. E. Ahlstrom, *A Religious History of the American People* (1972); W. B. Gatewood, Jr., ed., *Controversy in the Twenties; Fundamentalism, Modernism, and Evolution* (1969); W. R. Hutchison, *The Modernist Impulse in American Protestantism* (1976); G. M. Marsden, *Fundamentalism and American Culture: The Shaping of Twentieth-Century Evangelicalism, 1870-1925* (1980); E. R. Sandeen, *The Roots of Fundamentalism: British and American Millenarianism, 1800-1930* (1970); F. M. Szasz, *The Divided Mind of Protestant America: 1880-1930* (1982).

G. M. Marsden and B. J. Longfield

Fundamentals, The. A twelve-volume paperback series, published between 1910 and 1915, containing essays testifying to the truth of traditional Protestant* orthodoxy.* *The Fundamentals,* usually regarded as a signal of the beginning of the organized fundamentalist movement, was one of the sources for the movement's name. The project was the idea of a wealthy California oilman, Lyman Stewart,* who financed it with the help of his brother Milton.* When the volumes were completed, the Stewarts sent out some three million

individual volumes free to Protestant religious workers all over the English-speaking world. Amzi C. Dixon,* who edited the first five volumes, was followed by Louis Meyer and Reuben A. Torrey,* who completed the task. In addition, Torrey edited a four-volume edition published in 1917. All these editors were involved in the dispensational* premillennial* movement, though that doctrine was not conspicuous in this publication. The authors of the essays were mostly respected Bible teachers. A few were widely recognized conservative Protestant scholars, such as Benjamin B. Warfield* and James Orr of Scotland. Not all the authors were dispensationalist. Rather, they were chosen to present a united conservative "testimony to the truth" (as the subtitle to the volumes put it).

Of the ninety articles bound in twelve volumes (bearing no systematic organization), about one-third defend the Bible,* usually against higher criticism. Another third are either presentations of basic doctrines or general apologetic* works. The rest include personal testimonies, practical applications of Christian teaching, appeals for missions* and evangelism,* as well as attacks on various "-isms." Some of the articles had been published previously.

The essays were generally moderate in tone and a mix of both scholarly and popular interests and styles. Those on the inspiration of Scripture were all written by dispensationalists who defended biblical inerrancy.* Other authors, however, were known not to take a strict inerrantist view. Though essayists were critical of Darwinism,* some left room for limited theistic evolution. A number of the essays taught Keswick* holiness* doctrines. The central themes of the volumes, however, were that conservative evangelical* Protestantism could be defended on two major counts. First, its affirmations of miraculous divine interventions—as expressed in fundamental doctrines such as the inspiration of Scripture, the incarnation, the miracles and the resurrection—were fully compatible with modern science and rationality. Second, the testimony of personal experience was also important in confirming Christian belief.

The Fundamentals represented an early stage in emerging fundamentalism, an alliance of a variety of conservatives alarmed particularly over the spread of false doctrines. After the 1920s fundamentalism generally became more militant. Eventually, when in the 1940s and 1950s the main part of interdenominational fundamentalism broke between "neo-evangelicals"* and stricter separatist dispensationalists, that split reflected a tension that had been present in the alliance that *The Funda-*

mentals helped forge.

See also FUNDAMENTALISM; FUNDAMENTALIST-MODERNIST CONTROVERSY.

BIBLIOGRAPHY. G. M. Marsden, *Fundamentalism and American Culture: The Shaping of Twentieth-Century Evangelicalism* (1980); E. R. Sandeen, *The Roots of Fundamentalism: British and American Millenarianism, 1800-1930* (1970); W. R. Hutchison, *The Modernist Impulse in American Protestantism* (1976). G. M. Marsden

Funerals. A ceremony customarily performed to mark the death of a person and to dispose of the body in a respectful manner. Historical records and archaeological evidence suggest that all societies have developed funeral rituals, sometimes elaborate and mostly religious. Contemporary American funeral rites and customs vary greatly from one part of the country to another, yet there are common elements, particularly among Christian communities. It is generally believed that the funeral provides comfort and reassurance for the bereaved, helping them to accept the reality and finality of death.

Christian burial practices evolved out of the customs of Judaism, but emphasized reverence for the body as "the temple of the Holy Spirit" and the positive message of the resurrection. Christians abandoned Jewish practices of extended wailing, often carried out by hired professional mourners. In Christian funerals there is normally a triumphant note of celebration based on Christ's victory over the grave.

Modern funerals are frequently conducted in mortuaries or funeral homes, but since the publication in 1963 of *The American Way of Death* by Jessica Mitford, there seems to be a trend to return funeral services to the church. A few groups (such as Roman Catholic* nuns*) retain the historic Christian practice of preparing their own dead for burial, but generally professional morticians are retained to perform this service and other necessary legal matters, such as securing death certificates. Embalming is an established custom in Western society. Embalming makes possible the display of the body for a few days prior to burial. However, some see the practice of embalming and display of the deceased as a part of the denial of death.

The funeral service itself consists of the reading of Scripture,* music, sometimes the singing of a hymn,* an obituary and a brief pastoral sermon. In a funeral of an outstanding Christian, there are often eulogies or brief testimonials by family members or close associates of the deceased. Traditional funeral processions have been abandoned for the most part, except in the death of a state or military officer. The committal service at the grave is brief, consisting of a scriptural passage and the committal proper.

Christian funeral rites are seen as instrumental for bereaved families to express their grief and accept their loss, and for friends to demonstrate their love and respect.

BIBLIOGRAPHY. P. E. Irion, *The Funeral* (1966); E. N. Jackson, *The Christian Funeral* (1966).

J. E. Means

Funk, John Fretz (1835-1930). Mennonite* leader. Born in Bucks County, Pennsylvania, Funk studied for a brief period at Freeland Seminary (now Ursinus College). From 1857 to 1867 he worked in a lumber business in Chicago. In 1858 he was converted* in a Presbyterian* revival and was later influenced by Dwight L. Moody.* Baptized* in the Mennonite Church in 1860, he was ordained* in 1865. In 1867 he moved to Elkhart, Indiana, where he continued the printing and publishing business he had begun in Chicago.

An innovator within his denomination,* Funk was nevertheless conscious of the need to conserve the deep historical tradition of his forebears. In 1864 he successfully launched *Herald of Truth* (which merged in 1908 with *Gospel Witness* to form *Gospel Herald*), the denomination's first periodical in both German and English, and his Mennonite Publishing Company published many standard Mennonite works in English translation. Through his influence Mennonites were introduced to methods such as Sunday schools* and evangelism.*

During the period of c.1870 to 1900, Funk was the outstanding leader of the Mennonite Church. He was influential in settling Russian Mennonites in the U.S. and Canada and instrumental in helping the church move from a German-speaking immigrant church to a predominantly English-speaking church that was increasingly at home in America.

BIBLIOGRAPHY. H. K. Gates et al., *Bless the Lord O My Soul* (1964); A. C. Kolb, "John Fretz Funk, 1835-1930: An Appreciation," *MQR* VI (1932):44-55, 250-263; *ME* 2; K. Schnell, "John F. Funk, 1835-1930, and the Mennonite Migration of 1873-75," *MQR* XXIV (1950):199-229. L. Gross

Furman, Richard (1755-1825). Early eighteenth-century Baptist* leader in the South. Considered the most important Baptist leader of the antebellum South, Richard Furman was converted in 1771 by the revivalistic* Separate* Baptists. The "boy evangelist" began preaching at age sixteen and was pastor of the High Hills of Santee Church, in South Carolina, from 1774 to 1784 and First Baptist, Charleston, the most prominent Baptist church in the South, from 1787 until his death.

Furman was a pioneer denominational statesman. He was the first president of the Triennial Convention,* the first national body of Baptists in America (1814-1820); the first president of the South Carolina Baptist Convention, the first state convention of American Baptists (1821-1825) and for more than twenty-five years the moderator of the Charleston Baptist Association. In addition, Furman was most responsible for developing the organizational concepts that prevailed in the creation of the Southern Baptist Convention* (1845). Opposed to separate societies, in 1817 Furman convinced the Triennial Convention to support ministerial education* in addition to missions.* Although this plan later was discarded, the South Carolina State Convention was organized along Furman's plan of a centralized convention which supported multi-benevolence.

Having had little formal education himself, Furman was the "apostle of education" among Baptists in the South. In 1790 he led Charleston Baptists to set up an education committee and personally directed the work for thirty-four years. Furman's 1817 plan of education, adopted by the Triennial Convention, led to the formation of Columbian College (George Washington University). Furman University, the first Baptist college in the South, was named in his honor.

A leading advocate of religious liberty in colonial South Carolina, Furman was also an aristocratic slave owner who, in 1822, wrote the classic Southern biblical defense of slavery.

BIBLIOGRAPHY. H. T. Cook, *A Biography of Richard Furman* (1913); *DAB* IV; *DARB; NCAB* 12; J. A. Rogers, *Richard Furman: Life and Legacy* (1985).   C. D. Weaver

G

Gaebelein, Arno Clemens (1861-1945). Fundamentalist* Bible* teacher and editor. Born in Thuringia, Germany, Gaebelein immigrated to the U. S. in 1879. After receiving a call to preach* in the early 1880s, he became an avid student of the Bible* and ancient languages. He served as an assistant at the German Methodist Episcopal Church in New York City and was ordained* in 1885. Following successful Methodist* pastorates in Maryland, New York and New Jersey, in 1894 he joined the Hope of Israel Mission in New York City and founded *Our Hope,* a magazine dedicated to Jewish missions* and prophetic study. In 1899 he left the Mission to devote his full time to writing and conference speaking.

Gaebelein was a leading figure in the growth of American dispensationalism* and fundamentalism. Adopting dispensational premillennialism* in the late 1880s, he soon became one of its most articulate advocates. He was a regular speaker at Bible and prophetic conferences,* a consulting editor of the *Scofield Reference Bible* (1939) and a prolific author on prophetic issues. Gaebelein frequently speculated about current events as "signs of the times" and believed that civilization was in irreversible decline. Especially interested in the Jewish people, he used *Our Hope* to condemn anti-Semitism and promote the role of the Jews in the events surrounding the Second Coming. Nevertheless, his *Conflict of the Ages* (1933) drew a connection between the international Communist conspiracy and an apostate Jewish minority.

Gaebelein was a forerunner of the militant fundamentalism that emerged after World War 1. In 1899, believing the Methodist Church to be apostate, he left that church and promoted ecclesiastical separatism* long before it became fashionable among other conservative evangelicals.

BIBLIOGRAPHY. A. C. Gaebelein, *Half a Century: The Autobiography of a Servant* (1930); D. A. Rausch, *Arno C. Gaebelein* (1984).   T. P. Weber

Gailor, Thomas Frank (1856-1935). Episcopal* bishop.* Born in Jackson, Mississippi, Gailor attended Racine College, Wisconsin (1873-1876), where James DeKoven, a leading Anglo-Catholic,* taught. After graduating from the General Theological Seminary, New York (S.T.B., 1879), he began his ministry at Messiah Church, Pulaski, Tennessee. On May 15, 1882, he became professor of ecclesiastical history at the School of Theology, The University of the South, Sewanee, Tennessee. Over the years Gailor became synonymous with The University of the South and the diocese* of Tennessee. From August 6, 1890 to July 27, 1893, he was vice-chancellor of the University, and from June 23, 1908 until his death he was chancellor, the only person to hold both of these positions. On July 25, 1893, he was consecrated assistant bishop of Tennessee and become the third bishop, on February 15, 1898, when Bishop Quintard* died. From October 1919 until December 31, 1925, he was president of the National Council of the Episcopal Church. Gailor died on October 3, 1935.

BIBLIOGRAPHY. D. S. Armentrout, *The Quest for the Informed Priest: A History of the School of Theology* (1979); *DAB* 1; T. F. Gailor, *Some Memories* (1937).   D. S. Armentrout

Gallicanism. A complex doctrine with origins from as early as the eighth or ninth centuries concerning the proper relationship between the papacy and the French Church. It stressed the limitation of papal power, the authority of the king and a wide role for councils of the Church. It had counterparts in Febronianism and Josephinism which sought similar ends in the German states and the Holy Roman Empire respectively.

In North America the clearest expression of Gallicanism was found in the colonial government of New France, which both supported the Catholic Church and simultaneously sought to limit its political power and direct some of its affairs. Even after the British conquest of Quebec (1760), Gallicanism persisted among some sections of the clergy* and the population, largely as resistance to the claim of papal infallibility.* The triumph of Ultramontanism* over Gallicanism was sealed by

[471]

the declaration of papal infallibility by the First Vatican Council* (1869-1870).

See also PAPACY AND U.S. CATHOLICS; ULTRAMONTANISM.

BIBLIOGRAPHY. C. J. Jaenen, *The Role of the Church in New France* (1976).

K. M. Cassidy

Gallitzin, Demetrius Augustine (1770-1840). Pioneer Catholic missionary* in Maryland and Pennsylvania. Born at The Hague, Holland, the son of a Russian prince, Demetri Gallitzin, and Amalia von Schmettau, daughter of a Prussian field marshall, Gallitzin was raised in the Russian Orthodox* Church, and he converted to Roman Catholicism* as a young man. On a trip to the U.S. in 1792, Gallitzin entered St. Mary's Seminary in Baltimore and was ordained* in 1795, the first priest* to receive all his training and orders in the U.S.

After missionary work in Maryland, he established a Catholic community at Loretto in Cambria County, Pennsylvania. There he built a church and, by selectively selling tracts of land he had purchased, gathered Catholic settlers around his colony. Although considered several times for possible bishoprics, Gallitzin declined. It was just as well. Despite his missionary zeal, certain personal eccentricities and frequent financial problems made him a less than apt candidate. He died at Loretto on May 6, 1840.

BIBLIOGRAPHY. *DAB* IV; D. Sargent, *Mitri; or, the story of Prince Demetrius Augustine Gallitzin, 1770-1840* (1945). T. E. Buckley

Gambrell, James Bruton (1841-1921). Southern Baptist* pastor,* editor and denominational* leader. Born in South Carolina and raised in Mississippi, Gambrell served in the Confederate army. After marrying Mary T. Corbell in 1864, the couple settled in Mississippi. Ordained* in 1867, he served churches at West Point and Oxford before becoming editor of the *Baptist Record* in 1877, a position he held for fifteen years. Gambrell then became president of Mercer University (1893-1896) before moving to Texas in 1896 as superintendent of missions. He became editor of the *Baptist Standard* in 1910 and four years later was elected executive secretary of the Texas Convention. Gambrell also served four terms as president of the Southern Baptist Convention (1917-1921) and died a few months after returning from a visit with European Baptists. Known for his practical wisdom and keen wit, Gambrell stressed cooperation within Southern Baptist life and isolation from ecumenical* involvement.

BIBLIOGRAPHY. B. J. Leonard, "The Southern Baptist Denominational Leader as Theologian," *BHH* 16 (1980):23-32, 61, 63; E. C. Routh, *Life Story of Dr. J. B. Gambrell* (1929).

C. L. Howe

Gannett, Ezra Stiles (1801-1871). Unitarian* minister* and denominational* statesman. Born in Cambridge, Massachusetts, and named for his maternal grandfather, Ezra Stiles,* Gannett graduated from Harvard College* (B.A., 1820) and Harvard Divinity School (1823). He was ordained* in 1824 and served as an associate of William Ellery Channing,* pastor of Boston's Federal Street Church. Gannett continued as the church's sole pastor after Channing's death in 1842, supervising its 1859 relocation to Arlington Street in the newly developed and fashionable Back Bay. Gannett, a leader in the 1825 founding of the American Unitarian Association* (AUA), served as the AUA's secretary from 1825 to 1831 and as its president from 1847 to 1851. Gannett was also a prime mover in the 1834 organization of the Benevolent Fraternity of (Unitarian) Churches,* serving as its first secretary and, from 1857 to 1862, as its president. His published works include: *Atonement* (1839), *Righteousness: the Central Principle of Christianity* (1842) and *The Essential in Christianity* (1847).

Although Gannett was an eloquent foe of slavery, his rejection of the methods of the abolitionists* led to sniping from Theodore Parker* and other Unitarian radicals. Gannett, a conservative whose preaching stressed the primacy of faith in Christ, opposed the Transcendentalists'* efforts to reduce Unitarianism to a species of ethical humanism.

BIBLIOGRAPHY. *DAB* IV; W. C. Gannett, *Ezra Stiles Gannett: Unitarian Minister in Boston, 1824-1871* (1875). G. W. Harper

Gano, John (1727-1804). Baptist* pastor, itinerant* evangelist* in the South, Revolutionary War* chaplain.* Born of Huguenot* and English stock in Hopewell, New Jersey, Gano was converted* in his early youth. After study with Presbyterian* pastors, including one of the Tennents,* he became a Baptist and was immersed, joining the Hopewell church. His call to the ministry* confirmed, Gano was ordained* in 1754 and conducted a missionary* tour of the South. His longest pastorate was in New York City (1762-1787), interrupted by service as chaplain in the New York Brigade, where he served with George Washington. It was popularly believed that Gano baptized Washington,* but there is no evidence of this having taken place. While in New York, Gano served as a Regent of the University of New York and a Trustee of Kings College* (Columbia). He was also associated with the new College of Rhode Island* (Brown), addressing the commencement in 1771. In 1788 Gano left New York for Kentucky, settling as pastor at Town Fork, near Lexington.

In 1754 Gano began a series of trips into the South as an evangelist of the Philadelphia Association,* distinguishing himself as a warm-hearted preacher* and peacemaker among the struggling churches. He was instrumental in establishing and reorganizing churches conforming to the Regular* Baptist (Calvinist) order.

BIBLIOGRAPHY. *AAP* 6; L. C. Barnes, *The John Gano Evidence of George Washington's Religion* (1926); *DAB* IV; J. Gano, *Biographical Memoirs of the Rev. John Gano of Frankfurt, Written by Himself* (1806). L. W. Hähnlen

Garden, Alexander (1685-1756). Anglican* leader in colonial South Carolina. Alexander Garden arrived in South Carolina in 1720 to serve Saint Philip's Church in Charleston, where he was elected rector* in 1725. A strong personality and a natural leader, Garden was appointed commissary for the Carolinas in 1728. Able to control his clergy* while at the same time maintaining harmony among them, Garden created an effective working arrangement between the clergy and political leaders of the colony, improved relations with the laity,* moved the provincial Anglican Church toward more independence from England, opposed pluralism and significantly strengthened Anglicanism* in the Carolinas. Garden created the first ecclesiastical court in South Carolina history and made a much-publicized attack on George Whitefield* regarding his views on the nature of regeneration.* Garden established the Charles Town Negro School for the purpose of instructing young slaves. His position as commissary ended in 1748. He resigned as rector of Saint Philip's in 1753 and died in 1756.

BIBLIOGRAPHY. *AAP* 5; S. C. Bolton, *Southern Anglicanism: The Church of England in Colonial South Carolina* (1982). N. L. Erickson

Garfield, James (1831-1881). Twentieth president of the U.S. and first chief executive openly to confess that he had been "born again."* Garfield rose to the presidency from humble beginnings in Ohio, having been born in a log cabin near Cleveland on November 19, 1831. His father died in 1833 and left his mother to raise Garfield and three siblings. Shortly before his father's death, Garfield's parents had joined a Disciples of Christ* church and embraced its teachings. Thus, Garfield's mother reared her children to revere the Bible* and exposed them widely to Disciples preaching* and hymn*-singing.

According to his own account, his conversion* occurred on March 4, 1850, when he was "buried with Christ in baptism* and arose to walk in newness of life." There followed a Renaissance-like young manhood as Garfield worked as a farmer, a canal-barge deckhand, schoolteacher, carpenter, lawyer, soldier and politician. During this period, a serious illness led him to consider higher education, and he briefly attended both a Baptist* academy and Hiram College, eventually graduating from Williams College in 1856.

In 1861 he entered the Union army as a lieutenant colonel and by 1863 had risen to the rank of major general. In 1862 he was elected to the U.S. House of Representatives as a Republican, and took office in 1863 after resigning his commission. He served in the House until 1880 when he was elected U.S. Senator from Ohio. However, before he could take his seat, a deadlocked Republican national convention nominated Garfield on the 36th ballot as a compromise candidate for the office of president of the U.S. Winning comfortably, Garfield took office on March 4, 1881, only to be shot four months later by a deranged lawyer and disappointed federal office seeker named Charles J. Guiteau. After a lingering illness and much pain, Garfield died on September 19, 1881, a little more than seven months after taking office.

Garfield's religion deeply affected his general outlook on life. A lay* preacher* in early life, he gradually abandoned the church pulpit for the political podium. At first he was mainly a Disciples partisan but as he grew older, especially after his experience at Williams College, he became more appreciative of the views of other Christians. During his distinguished career in Congress, he became a favorite of evangelicals* and enjoyed their heavy support during the presidential election of 1880. His inaugural address illustrates his civil religion,* and his replies as president to disappointed Disciples' office-seekers who thought their day had finally come shows that he intended to be a religiously nonpartisan chief executive. Garfield was both a devout and scholarly politician and often reflected on the relationship between religious commitment and political participation. Although his presidency was too brief to yield extensive change, his efforts eventually resulted in broad civil-service reform—hastened in part by his tragic assassination.

BIBLIOGRAPHY. T. C. Smith, *The Life and Letters of James Abram Garfield*, 2 vols. (1925); V. B. Hampton, *The Religious Background of the White House* (1932); W. W. Wasson, *James A. Garfield: His Religion and Education* (1952); J. M. Taylor, *Garfield of Ohio: The Available Man* (1970).

R. D. Linder

Garnet, Henry Highland (1815-1882). Presbyterian* preacher* and abolitionist* orator. Born in slavery on a Maryland farm, at age nine Garnet fled to New York City, along with his parents and sister. Three years later slavecatchers invaded Garnet's home, destroyed the family's household possessions and forced the family to split up. His parents and sister only narrowly escaped being returned to slavery. Garnet was educated in New York City schools operated by African-American Presbyterian ministers and in abolitionist-sponsored academies in New Hampshire and New York.

Ordained in 1842, he served Presbyterian churches in Troy, New York; Stirling, Jamaica; New York City; and Washington, D.C. Involving himself with the politically active wing of the anti-slavery movement, he campaigned at various times for the Liberty, Free Soil, and Republican Parties prior to 1865. In 1843, in his most famous speech, Garnet exhorted slaves not to submit voluntarily to the degradation of bondage. Instead, he said, "let your motto be resistance! resistance! RESISTANCE!" During the Civil War,* Garnet helped to recruit African-American troops. In 1881 Garnet accepted an appointment as U.S. minister to Liberia, and he died shortly after his arrival there.

BIBLIOGRAPHY. *DAB* IV; J. Schor, *Henry Highland Garnet: A Voice of Black Radicalism in the Nineteenth Century* (1977). S. W. Angell

Garrettson, Freeborn (1752-1827). Itinerant* Methodist* minister.* Born to an affluent family in Hartford County, Maryland, Garrettson was converted in his early twenties under the preaching* of Francis Asbury.* Joining the Methodists, he freed his slaves and started an itinerant ministry in 1775. Garrettson traveled widely, and his message of Christian perfection,* pacifism* and aggressive abolitionism* provoked life-threatening opposition as well as imprisonment. Nevertheless, his evangelistic* efforts resulted in the founding of new churches in New York. In 1784, when Thomas Coke* came with instructions from John Wesley* to organize the American Methodist Church, Garrettson summoned ministers to the Christmas Conference* of 1784.

Garrettson volunteered for mission work in Nova Scotia. After three years the Conference unanimously voted to make him a bishop* over that work, only to inexplicably table the motion. His diplomatic skill and republican tendencies offset Asbury's autocratic bent. Although Garrettson always favored broader representation in the Church, he opposed splits. In 1792 he appealed to William McKendree* (successfully) and James O'Kelly* (unsuccessfully) to remain in the Church (*see* O'Kelly Schism). He thought presiding elders* should be elected rather than appointed by the bishop and that each annual conference should have its own bishop. Unlike most of his colleagues, he married. Catherine Livingstone belonged to a wealthy and influential New York family. Settling (1800) in Rhinebeck, New York, they became known for their hospitality and philanthropy.* The first to push Methodism beyond the Alleghenies, apart from Asbury, Garrettson was the most important figure in early American Methodism.*

BIBLIOGRAPHY. *AAP* 7; *DAB* IV; *DARB*; R. D. Simpson, *American Methodist Pioneer* (1984); N. Bangs, *The Life of the Rev. Freeborn Garrettson* (1830); *NCAB* 10. M. R. Fraser

Garrigus, Alice Belle (1858-1949). Pentecostal* evangelist.* Born in Rockville, Connecticut, Garrigus attended Mount Holyoke Female Seminary for three years, after teaching in rural schools. Leaving the college in 1881, she returned to teaching for a time. In 1891 she accepted a position as a worker in a home for poverty-stricken women and children. After moving to New Hampshire in 1897, she traveled as an itinerant* preacher* until her decision to go as a missionary to Newfoundland. Arriving in St John's in 1910, she oversaw the organization of Bethesda Mission, which later became part of the Pentecostal Assemblies of Newfoundland. She is thus credited with founding the Pentecostal movement in Newfoundland. In addition to articles and sermons for denominational publications, she wrote the essay on Pentecostal work for Joseph R. Smallwood's *Book of Newfoundland.*

BIBLIOGRAPHY. B. K. Janes, *The Lady Who Came*, 2 vols. (1982-1983). P. D. Airhart

Garrison, James Harvey (1842-1931). Disciples of Christ* editor. Born in Missouri, Garrison enlisted in the Union Army in 1861 and served four years. After the war he attended Abingdon College in Abingdon, Illinois, a Disciples of Christ institution. Raised a Baptist,* Garrison joined the Disciples of Christ while at Abingdon, attracted by their plea for Christian unity.

Graduating from college in 1868, he became associate minister* of a Disciples church in Macomb, Illinois, and junior editor of a journal published by the minister. This was the beginning of what would be an editorial career. Garrison soon merged the paper, *The Gospel Echo,* with other papers, and by 1882 he was editing his *Christian-Evangelist* in St. Louis. Among Disciples' papers Garrison's (25,000 in 1884) was second only to the *Christian Standard* in circulation, and by 1907 it would take the lead. He remained editor of the *Christian-Evangelist* until his retirement in 1912.

Garrison was a moderate in a time of great change within the Christian Churches* and Disciples of Christ. A theological conservative, he was nevertheless open to scholarly opinion regarding higher criticism. He opposed "open membership," the receiving of unimmersed persons into the membership of Christian Churches, but he did not make it a test of his fellowship with other leaders of the Disciples churches. He also supported the involvement of the Disciples in the Federal Council of Churches.* Garrison became one of the pre-eminent elder-statesmen among the Christian Churches and helped lead them into national recognition.

BIBLIOGRAPHY. *DARB*; J. H. Garrison, *Memories and Experiences, A Brief Story Of a Long Life: An Autobiography* (1926); *NCAB* 18; W. E. Tucker, *J. H. Garrison and Disciples of Christ* (1964).

J. B. North

Garrison, William Lloyd (1805-1879). Reformer and journalist. Because his father deserted his family when William was three years old, young Garrison had a meager education. At age thirteen he was apprenticed to the editor of the Newburyport, Massachusetts, *Herald* under whom he developed into a skilled compositor and writer. Upon the completion of his apprenticeship in 1826, he became editor of the local *Free Press,* which failed after a short time. In 1828 he met Benjamin Lundy, a Quaker* who influenced Garrison in beginning a lifetime of antislavery activity. On July 4, 1829, in Boston's Park Street Church, he delivered the first of his numerous public speeches against slavery.

The indifference of many clergymen* to the slavery issue brought him into open conflict with orthodox* churches. He eventually denied the plenary inspiration of the Bible* and was openly unorthodox, as evidenced by his keen interest in phrenology, clairvoyance and spiritualism. Though espousing peaceful means to his antislavery goals, he was uncompromising and inflammatory, often antagonizing even his friends.

BIBLIOGRAPHY. *DAB* IV; A. H. Grimke, *William Lloyd Garrison, The Abolitionist* (1891).

R. R. Mathisen

Garvey, Marcus (Mosiah) (1887-1940). African-American nationalist and founder of the Universal Negro Improvement Association. Born and educated in St. Ann's Bay, Jamaica, from 1904 to 1911 Garvey worked as a journalist in Kingston, Jamaica, and traveled throughout Central America organizing migrant West Indian workers. Inspired by Booker T. Washington's *Up From Slavery,* in 1914 Garvey formed the Universal Negro Improvement Association (UNIA), an organization modeled after Washington's Tuskegee Institute and designed to promote education, self-help and racial solidarity among African-American people. Garvey moved the organization to the U.S. in 1916 and lectured in African-American churches throughout the country to gain a wider audience and financial support.

By 1918 a widely circulated newspaper, the *Negro World,* and numerous UNIA branches enabled Garvey to finance his ill-fated Black Star Line Steamship Corporation, a business venture financed entirely by black stockholders. Garvey also organized the first International Convention of the Negro Peoples of the World and issued a Declaration of the Rights of the Negro Peoples of the World. Yet by 1922, rising criticism of Garvey's black nationalism and allegations of mail fraud brought him into conflict with the U.S. Government. In 1925 Garvey was tried and sentenced to five years in the Atlanta Penitentiary, where he remained until President Coolidge commuted his jail term and deported him to Jamaica in 1927. Garvey's attempts to organize the movement outside America met with little success, and he died in 1940 at the age of fifty-two.

Garvey's religious view was that African-American people needed to conceive of God as black rather than white and so undo the oppression of European theology over blacks. These ideas were given institutional support when he established the African Orthodox Church* with UNIA chaplain* and former Episcopal* priest* George A. McGuire* as its first bishop.* Convinced that no white man would die on a cross for blacks, the church's art featured a black Christ, a black Madonna* and black angels and saints. In his religious views Garvey was a forerunner of some late twentieth-century black theology* and the

Black Muslim religion.

BIBLIOGRAPHY. *DAB* 2; *DARB*; R. A. Hill, ed., *The Marcus Garvey and Universal Negro Improvement Association Papers*, 6 vols. (1983); T. Martin, *Marcus Garvey, Hero: A First Biography* (1983).

M. C. Bruce

Gay, Ebenezer (1696-1787). Early Arminian* and "patriarch" of Unitarianism.* Born in Dedham, Massachusetts, Gay graduated from Harvard* (B.A., 1714) and settled as pastor at Hingham, Massachusetts, in 1717. Despite his theological unorthodoxy and Tory sympathies, he retained that post for the extraordinary duration of seventy years. Even prior to 1750, Gay was articulating those distinctly non-Calvinist views that later were designated "Unitarian"—by repute the first person in New England clearly to do so. Already an Arminian and an Arian, Gay opposed the Great Awakening* of the 1740s, with its Calvinist* reassertion of God's power and humanity's powerlessness. He objected to creeds,* confessions and all rules of faith that are of "human prescription" and spoke out against religion that emphasized sectarian peculiarities rather than those more significant matters on which all might agree.

In 1759, Gay delivered the prestigious Dudleian lecture at Harvard. Speaking on "Natural Religion, as Distinguished from Revealed," he exemplified the "supernatural rationalism" that was characteristic of evolving liberalism.* Natural religion, he argued (i.e., those truths which the unassisted human reason can establish, such as the existence and attributes of God), and revealed (i.e., biblical) religion do not contradict, but confirm and strengthen each other. First it is necessary to prove, through reason, the existence of God, and only then can persons truly believe that God has provided them with a revelation, or understand the divine meaning of its texts. Gay's generally moderate tone and his pastoral charge in a commercial center where liberalism flourished kept him out of trouble. Nevertheless, as one no longer able to accept either the seemingly arbitrary, inscrutable deity of the Calvinists nor their assumptions of a humanity utterly depraved and corrupt, Gay represents the front lines of change in the transition between seventeenth-century Puritanism* and nineteenth-century liberalism.

BIBLIOGRAPHY. *AAP* 8; *DAB* IV; R. J. Wilson III, *The Benevolent Deity: Ebenezer Gay and the Rise of Rational Religion in New England, 1697-1787* (1984); C. C. Wright, *The Beginnings of Unitarianism in America* (1955). E. C. Nordbeck

Geddie, John (1815-1872). Canadian missionary* to the South Seas. Born in Banff, Scotland, Geddie immigrated with his parents to Nova Scotia, Canada. He received his academic preparation and theological education at Dalhousie College and was ordained* by the Presbyterian* Church of Nova Scotia. Motivated by his parent's piety he pursued mission service, though he had to stir other Presbyterians to support foreign missions* while he was a pastor in Cavendish and New London, on Prince Edward Island.

Having studied printing and medicine, he and his family sailed for the South Seas in 1840 and finally settled on Aneitium Island in the New Hebrides. There, despite harassment, he won the confidence of the people and their leader by learning the language and ministering through word, print and medicine. Finally, in 1854 the whole population became Christian. When at home on furlough in the 1860s, he was honored with a doctorate by Queen's University at Kingston and appointed moderator of the Synod* of the Presbyterian Church, although he declined the responsibility. He died while on a trip to Melbourne, Australia, in 1872, where he was guiding his translation of part of the Old Testament through the press.

BIBLIOGRAPHY. G. Patterson, *The Life of John Geddie* (1882). J. H. Smylie

General Assembly. Central governing body of the Presbyterian churches. Rapid growth and geographical expansion in the eighteenth century led to poor attendance at the Presbyterians' yearly synod,* which was unable to meet the increasing demands of larger numbers of churches. In response, church authorities began a movement in the mid-1780s to revise the governmental structure of the organization. In contrast to the previous arrangement, where representatives of several presbyteries* met in the yearly synod, the new system created sixteen presbyteries, four synods and one General Assembly. The General Assembly, which included delegates from each of the presbyteries, ruled on appeals from the synods and served as a unifying force in the church. Though modeled after the General Assembly in the Church of Scotland, the American version was carefully checked and restrained; any innovations suggested by the General Assembly required the consent of a majority of the presbyteries.

BIBLIOGRAPHY. L. J. Trinterud, *The Forming of an American Tradition* (1949).

J. F. Cooper

General Association of Regular Baptist Churches.

An association of fundamentalist* Baptist* churches. The General Association of Regular Baptist Churches (GARBC) was founded at the final meeting of the Baptist Bible Union* in May 1932. The objectives of the GARBC were to (1) create an association of churches rather than a convention; (2) uphold the conservative Baptist New Hampshire Confession of Faith (1833) with a revised premillennial* stance in the article on eschatology*; and (3) work separately from the Northern Baptist Convention,* promote missionary spirit, and assist churches in securing fundamentalist* pastors.

The GARBC early came under the guiding influence of Robert T. Ketcham (1889-1978), who was elected vice president (1933), president (1934) and editor of *The Baptist Bulletin* (1938). He served as national representative from 1948 to 1960. In 1934 a council of fourteen (enlarged to eighteen in 1972) elected delegates from Association churches was established to carry out directives voted on by the churches at the annual meeting. At this same time the GARBC adopted a policy concerning approval of education and mission organizations. Each organization seeking approval must submit an annual request for approval, thereby allowing the GARBC opportunity to withdraw approval from those organizations not meeting GARBC standards. Today the GARBC approves seven colleges and seminaries, five mission agencies and several social programs. The Regular Baptist Press was begun in 1950 to carry out the publication needs of the GARBC, particularly *The Baptist Bulletin.*

Theologically, the issues of separation* and eschatology have been distinctive of the GARBC. Regarding separation, the Association advocates "obedience to the Biblical commands to separate ourselves unto God from worldliness and ecclesiastical apostasy" (2 Cor 6:17; Rom 16:17). On the issue of eschatology, the GARBC believes in the premillennial return of Christ, rapture* of the church, the great tribulation and Christ's establishment of the millennial kingdom (1 Thess 4:13-18; Dan 9:25-27; Rev 20).

In the late 1980s the GARBC had 1,591 fellowshiping churches with a total membership of 220,517.

BIBLIOGRAPHY. J. M. Stowell, *The Background and History of the General Association of Regular Baptist Churches* (1949); J. M. Murdoch, *Portrait of Obedience: The Biography of Robert T. Ketcham* (1979). C. W. Whiteman

General Baptists.

Those Baptists named for their adherence to the Arminian* doctrine of general atonement,* which claims that Christ died for all persons. Their first church was gathered by John Smyth in 1608/1609 and Separatists* who had followed him in exile to Amsterdam. When Smyth sought closer ties with local Mennonites,* Thomas Helwys led a schismatic group to Spitalfields (London), where they planted the first Baptist church in England (1612). Growing to forty-seven churches by 1650, General Baptists formed a national general assembly by 1654 and issued the Standard Confession (1660) and the Orthodox Creed (1678). Their earliest American churches resulted from schisms in Particular-General churches: Providence (1652), Newport (1665) and Swansea (c.1680). Also known as Six-Principle Baptists, they held Arminian doctrine, opposed singing in worship, and required hands to be laid upon new converts.

General Baptists formed what is perhaps the first (temporary) Baptist association in America (c.1670) and the first Baptist churches in New York (1714), Virginia (1714) and North Carolina (1727). Suffering from doctrinal ambiguity, diminishing evangelism,* hesitancy to organize, untrained ministers* and proselytizing by Regular* Baptists, they were almost extinct by 1800. A new movement, led by Benoni Stinson after 1822, culminated in formation of the General Association of General Baptists (1870). With headquarters at Poplar Bluff, Missouri, it covers sixteen Midwestern states, publishes *The General Baptist Messenger,* supports Oakland City (Indiana) College and maintains boards for home and foreign missions, ministers' aid, publications, education and women's work. In 1987 there were 879 American churches with 73,515 members, and 14,820 members overseas.

BIBLIOGRAPHY. T. A. Laslie, *Laslie's History of the General Baptists* (1938); O. Latch, *History of the General Baptists* (1954); B. R. White, *The English Baptists of the Seventeenth Century* (1983). J. T. Spivey

General Conference Mennonite Church.

The second-largest organized body of Mennonites* in North America. The General Conference Mennonite Church (GCMC) was organized in 1860 as an agency for Mennonite denominational unity, mission* work, Christian education* and publication. Its progressive agenda attracted Mennonite congregations who were becoming Americanized and wanted to move beyond Mennonite traditionalism, legalism and separation from the world. The Conference holds to traditional Anabaptist*-Mennonite teachings, including nonresistance. It does not have an official creed* and follows a congregational* polity.

The GCMC embraces greater cultural variety than other Mennonite bodies. The first congregations were of Swiss and south-German background, located in Pennsylvania and the Midwest. In the 1870s, 1920s and 1940s, numerous congregations of immigrants of Dutch extraction, who had immigrated to Russia and Eastern Europe, and then to the U. S., joined the Conference. Most of the later immigrants came to Canada, where about forty-three per cent of the Conference's membership lives. In recent decades the congregations have undergone a major shift from rural areas to small towns and to urban centers.

Early GCMC mission work produced congregations in India, China and among the Cheyenne, Arapahoe and Hopi Indians. A major expansion in mission after World War 2* led to additional work in Japan, Taiwan, Colombia and in other countries of Africa and Latin America. The GCMC has contributed to the international relief and service ministries of the Mennonite Central Committee,* as well as to institutions for health care for the aged, to mental health facilities, church camping, mutual aid, disaster service and related activities.

The GCMC seminary is in Elkhart, Indiana. The Conference is also indirectly related to eight Bible institutes and to colleges in Bluffton, Ohio; North Newton, Kansas; Winnipeg, Manitoba; and Waterloo, Ontario. The publishing arm of the Conference is Faith and Life Press, Newton, Kansas, where the denominational headquarters are also located. The GCMC has 66,000 baptized members.

See also ANABAPTIST TRADITION AND VISION; MENNONITE CHURCHES.

BIBLIOGRAPHY. H. P. Krehbiel, *History of the Mennonite General Conference,* 2 vols. (1898, 1938); S. F. Pannabecker, *Open Doors, A History of the General Conference Mennonite Church* (1975); R. J. Sawatsky, *Authority and Identity, The Dynamics of the General Conference Mennonite Church* (1987).

J. C. Juhnke

General Conference of German Baptist Churches. *See* NORTH AMERICAN BAPTIST CHURCHES.

General Conference of Mennonite Brethren Churches of North America. A Mennonite* denomination* growing out of Mennonite immigrants* from Russia and Crimea. Between 1874 and 1884 it is estimated that approximately 18,000 Mennonites immigrated from Russia to North America. Among these immigrants were some 200 families affiliated with the Mennonite Brethren Church, a group founded in Russia in 1860, who settled in Kansas, Nebraska, Minnesota and the Dakota Territory. These congregations organized themselves as a General Conference in 1879. In 1909 the General Conference was subdivided into three district conferences. Today there are five district conferences in sixteen states and six provincial conferences in seven Canadian provinces. In 1985 membership stood at 24,500 in Canada and 17,200 in the U.S. In 1960 the Krimmer Mennonite Brethren Conference merged with the Mennonite Brethren, adding approximately 1,600 members to the Conference roles.

The Conference supports an extensive foreign mission program, with missionaries in more than twenty countries. The Conference seminary is Mennonite Brethren Biblical Seminary in Fresno, California, and several other colleges and Bible institutes* are operated by various district conferences. The official publications of the Conference are: *The Christian Leader* (U.S.), the *Mennonite Brethren Herald* (Canada) and *Le Lien* (Quebec). A scholarly journal entitled *Direction* is published twice yearly by the General Conference. The Mennonite Brethren Conference is a member of the National Association of Evangelicals* and Mennonite Central Committee.*

BIBLIOGRAPHY. J. H. Lohrenz, *The Mennonite Brethren Church* (1950); J. A. Toews, *A History of the Mennonite Brethren Church: Pilgrims and Pioneers* (1975).

K. M. Enns-Rempel

General Confession. A corporate or personal act of repentance. In the liturgical* practice of many churches, an order for confession to be said by the whole congregation, often with the pastor* or minister,* is incorporated into services of worship* on regular or particular occasions. It usually consists of a confession of sin* in general terms, a petition for forgiveness, and a prayer for grace to amend one's life. This set form of public confession in the Anglican *Book of Common Prayer** is traditionally called the general confession. In the Roman Catholic Church* the term is also applied to a private confession in which sins committed in one's life, or a considerable part of it, are again confessed. Such a confession is customarily made when serious doubt exists as to the validity of previous confessions or when someone is preparing to enter a new state of life, as in the case of ordination* or religious profession.

C. R. Henery

General Council of Cooperating Baptist Missions of North America. *See* BAPTIST MID-MISSIONS.

General Missionary Convention and the Baptist Board for Foreign Missions. *See* AMERICAN BAPTIST BOARD OF INTERNATIONAL MINISTRIES.

General Synod. An early Lutheran* denomination.* Organized in 1820, the General Synod brought together regional Lutheran synods identified with Pennsylvania, North Carolina, Maryland and Virginia. The strong leadership of Samuel Simon Schmucker* enabled the Synod to survive the loss of the Pennsylvania Ministerium in 1823, to establish a theological seminary* at Gettysburg in 1826, and to encompass by 1860 two-thirds of the Lutheran congregations in America. Hoping to blend the Synod with the mainstream of evangelical* Protestantism,* Schmucker advocated the use of revivalist* methods and compromise of Lutheran sacramentalism.* But mounting opposition to such an "American Lutheranism" led to schism, and in 1867 the creation of a separate General Council. Southern constituents also withdrew during the Civil War,* reorganizing themselves in 1886 as the United Synod in the South. Reunion of all these groups occurred in 1918 with the formation of the United Lutheran Church in America. The legacy of the General Synod is reflected in the commitment of today's Evangelical Lutheran Church in America* (ELCA) to ecumenism.*

BIBLIOGRAPHY. E. C. Nelson, ed., *The Lutherans in North America* (1975); F. K. Wentz, *Pioneer in Christian Unity: Samuel Simon Schmucker* (1967).

J. T. Diefenthaler

General Synod of the Associate Reformed Presbyterian Church. A small Presbyterian* denomination.* Deriving mainly from Scottish* seceder heritage, the Associate Reformed Presbyterian Church (ARPC) members immigrated to the American colonies in the 1700s. The seceders formed the ARPC in 1782 through union with Reformed, or covenanting, Presbyterians. The new church grew to establish four synods* by 1803, and in 1804 the first general synod was formed. Controversies over exclusive psalm-singing, closed Communion and church government* led eventually to synodical defections and to the merger that began the United Presbyterian Church in 1858. Only the Synod of the Carolinas and a very small Associate Church minority remained outside the union.

The Synod of the Carolinas continued the heritage of the ARPC. It grew slowly due to internal conflict and migration of its anti-slavery members to the North. In 1837 Erskine College was established, in part to train pastors. Erskine Seminary was founded in 1858. Growth was stabilized, in part due to home mission emphases sometimes involving a colonizing method whereby a part or the whole of a congregation would move to a new settlement. Known as the Associate Reformed Presbyterian Church since 1858, in 1935 the term *General Synod* was added (GS, ARPC).

Genuine piety,* an increasing emphasis on local church government and allegiance to the Westminster* standards—maintained with varying degrees of firmness—characterize the GS, ARPC. Exclusive psalm singing became optional in 1946. Statistics for 1987 indicated that the GS ARPC had 177 churches and 32,289 members.

BIBLIOGRAPHY. R. A. King, *A History of the Associate Reformed Presbyterian Church* (1966); R. Lathan, *History of the Associate Reformed Synod of the South* (1882); L. Ware, *The Second Century: A History of the Associate Reformed Presbyterians, 1882-1982* (1983).

J. H. Hall

General War-Time Commission of the Churches. An interdenominational agency organized in response to World War 1.* In May 1917, with the encouragement of the federal government, the Federal Council of the Churches of Christ in America* organized the General War-Time Commission of the Churches to coordinate the wartime activities of the Protestant* denominations* and such interdenominational agencies as the YMCA.* At the time, no effective military or civilian agencies existed to minister* to the armed forces. The Commission gained the right to approve and train chaplains.* It also distributed Bibles* and religious tracts* as part of its missionary* efforts in training camps and maintained recreational facilities. Federal Council leaders hoped that the Commission's activities would make the Protestant churches a more potent religious force during and after World War 1.* Its work did raise the prestige and influence of the Federal Council; government officials cooperated willingly with the Commission because they welcomed the moral and spiritual tone it added to the war effort. To critics, the disavowal of pacifism* which the creation of the Commission represented and its enthusiastic cooperation with the war effort reflected a moral blindness that effectively destroyed the Protestant churches as independent critics of wartime policy and actions.

BIBLIOGRAPHY. J. A. Hutchison, *We Are Not Divided* (1941).   G. F. Goodwin

Gerhart, Emanuel Vogel (1817-1904). German Reformed* theologian. After graduating from Marshall College in Mercersburg, Pennsylvania (1838), and Mercersburg Theological Seminary* (1841), Gerhart pastored a German Reformed congregation in Gettysburg, Pennsylvania (1843-1849), and then worked briefly as a missionary* among German immigrants* in Cincinnati. For the next five years he served as president and professor of theology* at his denomination's Heidelberg College in Tiffin, Ohio. From 1855 to 1866 he was president and professor of moral philosophy at the newly merged Franklin and Marshall Colleges in Lancaster, Pennsylvania. Gerhart then accepted a position as professor of systematic* and practical theology at the Reformed Church Seminary in Lancaster. While teaching there from 1868 to 1904, he contributed many articles to periodicals and for several years helped edit the *Mercersburg Review.* His theological contribution is seen in his *Philosophy and Logic* (1891) and two-volume *Institutes of the Christian Religion* (1891, 1894). Along with Philip Schaff* and John W. Nevin,* Gerhart helped shape the direction and theology of the German Reformed Church during the second half of the nineteenth century.

BIBLIOGRAPHY. *DAB* IV.   G. S. Smith

German Baptist Brethren. *See* EPHRATA SOCIETY.

Gibbons, James (1834-1921). Catholic vicar apostolic of North Carolina, bishop* of Richmond and archbishop* of Baltimore. Born in Baltimore, Gibbons moved with his parents to Ireland at the age of three. He returned to the U.S. at age nineteen and worked as a grocery clerk in New Orleans before entering seminary.* Ordained* from St. Mary's Seminary in 1861, he spent the next four years in pastoral service in the Catholic archdiocese* of Baltimore. In 1865 he became secretary to the archbishop, Martin J. Spalding.* The next year he became assistant chancellor and helped Spalding prepare for the second plenary council of Baltimore* in 1866. Two years later he was made a bishop and given pastoral care over the newly created vicariate apostolic of North Carolina. In 1870 he was the youngest bishop to take part in the First Vatican Council.*

Gibbons became bishop of Richmond in 1873 and in 1876 published his best-known work, *Faith of Our Fathers,* a popular presentation of Catholicism based on his near-decade of pastoral experience in the South. Translated into six European languages, it became one of the most widely used expositions of Catholicism in the nineteenth century. In 1877 Gibbons succeeded James Roosevelt Bayley* as archbishop of Baltimore. As the church of John Carroll,* the first American Catholic bishop, Baltimore held a certain place of honor among American sees. Prior to the establishment of the apostolic delegate* in 1893, it was the Vatican's custom to carry on general business with the Catholic Church in the U.S. through the archbishop of Baltimore. At the age of forty-three, Gibbons inherited this mediating role of representing the Catholic Church in the U.S. to the Vatican and the Vatican to his fellow bishops.

In 1884 Gibbons successfully presided over the third plenary council of Baltimore. Named a cardinal* in 1886, he found himself in the midst of the controversies which split the hierarchy and the Catholic community during the last two decades of the nineteenth century. His authentic devotion to American ideals led him to sympathize with the Americanist* party. In Rome, on March 25, 1887, he preached a courageous sermon praising the benefits the church derived from the American separation of church and state.*

In February of that same winter which he spent in Rome with John Ireland,* John Keane* and Denis O'Connell,* Gibbons made the contribution for which he is perhaps best remembered. He presented the Vatican with a document, probably written by Keane and Ireland, arguing that the Knights of Labor* ought not be condemned as a secret society in the U.S. This request gained a reversal of two previous Roman condemnations of the Knights, many of whose U.S. members were Catholics. Gibbons's efforts were not always so successful. During the Americanist controversies, both sides accused him of uncertainty and vacillation. Pope Leo XIII* addressed his letter condemning Americanism, *Testem Benevolentiae,* to Gibbons, and the latter's reply denied that anyone in the U.S. held the reproved doctrines.

Gibbons's last decades as a bishop were more peaceful than his first. He had become a kind of civic symbol of the compatibility of Catholicism and American institutions and presided over the founding of the two episcopal bodies, the National Catholic War Council (1917) and the National Catholic Welfare Conference* (1919), which would eventually evolve into the present National Conference of Catholic Bishops.* In 1917 Theodore Roosevelt could describe him as occupying the position of being "the most respected, and venerated and useful citizen of our country." He is perhaps the best-known Catholic bishop in U.S. history.

BIBLIOGRAPHY. *DAB* IV; *DARB*; J. T. Ellis, *The Life of James Cardinal Gibbons,* 2 vols. (1952); *NCAB* 29; A. S. Will, *The Life of Cardinal Gibbons,* 2 vols. (1922).   W. L. Portier

Gideons International. A voluntary organization devoted to the worldwide distribution of Scripture.* The Gideons grew out of a meeting in the fall of 1898 between John Nicholson and Samuel Hill at the Central Hotel, Boscobel, Wisconsin. The following year (1899), together with W. J. Knights, these businessmen formed an association of traveling business and professional people. Throughout its history the association has been comprised mainly of laypeople dedicated to evangelism,* chiefly through the distribution of Scripture.

Originally known as the Christian Commercial Travellers Association of America, they became best known as the "Gideons." The name was taken from the Old Testament story in Judges 7 of Gideon leading a band of Israelites to victory over the Midianites with no more than torches and pitchers. This is represented in the Gideons' emblem of a two-handled pitcher with a torch.

The Gideons began distributing the Bible* in 1908, placing Scripture in hotel rooms, hospitals, prisons and schools, and engaging in personal evangelism. The Gideons today have more than 20,000 members active in at least seventy-five countries. Millions of Bibles and New Testaments in many languages have been distributed since 1908. In the late 1980s it was estimated that the Gideons distribute one million Scriptures worldwide every forty-six days. In addition, hundreds of services are conducted by the Gideons every year in missions, penal institutions, senior citizens' homes and other centers. The work is financed primarily through voluntary offerings from private individuals and from churches. The organization publishes a monthly magazine, *The Gideon.*

BIBLIOGRAPHY. K. A. Palmer, *Kenyon Palmer's Scrapbook* (1952); P. A. Westburg, *Then Stood Every Man in His Place* (1959).

D. Ewert

Gilkey, Langdon Brown (1919-). Theologian.* Born in Chicago, the son of Charles W. Gilkey, then pastor of Hyde Park Baptist Church and later (1928) the first dean of the University Chapel of the University of Chicago,* Gilkey's early home environment was both theologically and politically liberal. In the spring of his senior year (1940) as a philosophy student at Harvard, Gilkey, who had become increasingly oriented toward naturalism and humanism, experienced a conversion. Urged by his father, Gilkey went to hear Reinhold Niebuhr* preach in the Harvard chapel. The two sermons he heard on that April Sunday broke through his humanism and introduced him in a new way to both the estranged character of human existence and to a God transcendent to the fallen world "and yet seeking to bring it back to its true self and all of us to our true selves."

This Niebuhrian conversion was further solidified by the events of the next five years. In the summer of 1940 Gilkey went to Peking to teach English language at Yenching University. When the war with Japan began in December 1941, he was first placed under house arrest (until March 1943) and then placed in a civilian internment camp in Shantung Province (until August 1945). This experience of life in internment, autobiographically accounted in *Shantung Compound* (1966), convinced Gilkey of the profound relevance of moral awareness, spiritual self-understanding and trust in God for personal and communal life.

On returning to the U.S., Gilkey began graduate studies at Union Seminary,* New York, under Reinhold Niebuhr and Paul Tillich.* His thesis at Union addressed the doctrine of creation in relation to the metaphysical theories of Alfred North Whitehead and F. H. Bradley. After teaching at Vassar College (1951-1954) and Vanderbilt Divinity School (1954-1963), Gilkey in 1963 moved to the Divinity School of the University of Chicago. In 1976 he was appointed to the Shailer Mathews* Chair in Systematic Theology at Chicago and retired from full-time teaching in the spring of 1989.

Gilkey's theology is self-consciously contextual, dealing with issues that socio-historical experience has forced on him. As with Tillich, his theological method strives for a correlation between the message of the gospel and the contours of present cultural existence. His introduction to systematic theology, *Message and Existence* (1981), is both a Christian reflection on contemporary existence and a reinterpretation of the symbols of that faith in a manner relevant to modern experience.

Gilkey has addressed an astounding breadth of contemporary issues, but his central concern has been to develop a theology of culture. His first book, *Maker of Heaven and Earth: A Study of the Christian Doctrine of Creation* (1959), defended the doctrine against its cultural critics and illustrated its illuminative power and relevance to existential questions of meaning, purpose and evil, scientific questions about the intelligibility of our world, and philosophical questions of the nature of time and the possibility of a Christian metaphysics. In *How the Church Can Minister to the World without Losing Itself* (1964), Gilkey addressed the secularization of the church and advocated a "relevant transcendence."

The major theological issue of the 1960s, posed by the Death of God movement,* maintained that in a secular culture any language about God is unintelligible and therefore meaningless. In response to this challenge, Gilkey wrote his prolegomenon to any future theology, *Naming the Whirlwind: The Renewal of God Language* (1969). Gilkey argued that a phenomenological analysis of the very contours of modern secular experience discloses *within* that experience a dimension of ultimacy that can only be adequately thematized by recourse to religious language. In *Religion and the Scientific Future* (1970), Gilkey established that even modern science is rooted in myths, theories and attitudes that can only be understood as ultimate or religious in character. This argument was brought to its completion in part one of *Reaping the Whirlwind: A Christian Interpretation of History* (1976), where Gilkey disclosed a dimension of ultimacy in the very structure of historical and political experience.

The purpose of this prolegomenal argument is not only to provide theology with a reflective foundation but to disclose the fundamental religious substance or world view of modern culture. Throughout his career he has argued that modernity as a cultural epoch and as a cultural experiment in history is in decline (*Society and the Sacred: Toward a Theology of Culture in Decline,* 1981). In his anecdotally reflective account of his testimony on behalf of the ACLU at the 1981 "Creationist Trial" at Little Rock, Arkansas (*Creationism on Trial: Evolution and God at Little Rock,* 1985), Gilkey not only evaluated creation science,* but addressed the problems of the establishment of science in Western culture and the inevitable appearance of pseudo-science in this time of decline.

Gilkey is perhaps the best example of the combined influence of Tillich and Niebuhr in American theology, combining Tillich's method of correlation and philosophical insight with Niebuhr's sober assessment of modern culture and employment of traditional Christian symbols.

BIBLIOGRAPHY. A. Evory, ed., "Gilkey, Langdon B," in *Contemporary Authors,* New Revision Series (1982):183-184; L. B. Gilkey, "Introduction. A Retrospective Glance at My Work," in *The Whirl-*

wind in Culture: Frontiers in Theology—In Honor of Langdon Gilkey, eds. D. W. Musser and J. L. Price (1988); T. E. Hosinski, "Experience and the Sacred: A Retrospective Review of Langdon Gilkey's Theology," *RSR* 11, 3 (July 1985):228-235; J. Shea, *Religious Language in a Secular Culture: A Study in the Thought of Langdon Gilkey* (1976); B. J. Walsh, *Langdon Gilkey: Theologian for a Culture in Decline* (1990). B. J. Walsh

Gillespie, Eliza (Mother Angela) (1824-1887). Educator and superior of the Sisters of the Holy Cross. Descended from an old American family and educated at the Visitation Convent near Washington, Eliza Gillespie joined the Sisters of the Holy Cross at Bertrand, Michigan, in 1853. As Sister Mary of St. Angela, her superior, Edouard Sorin,* sent her to France to make her novitiate. In 1855 she became directress of the new St. Mary's Academy for women at Notre Dame.* In 1857 she became the first sister to be elected superior of the Sisters of the Holy Cross, who were centered at Notre Dame, an office she held until 1860.

When Governor Morton of Indiana asked for nuns to serve as nurses in the military hospitals during the Civil War,* Sorin sent Mother Angela to supervise the work. By war's end, eighty Sisters of the Holy Cross had served in eight hospitals and on two hospital ships.

In 1860 Mother Angela had begun editing and publishing the *Metropolitan Readers,* a graded literature series, and when Sorin founded the weekly *The Ave Maria* in 1866, she was the unofficial editor during the first year. She again served as superior of her community from 1862 to 1865 and from 1867 to 1882 and was influential in the separation of the Holy Cross Sisters in the U.S. from the mother house in France in 1869. Under her leadership her order expanded its educational and medical ministry in America, opening forty-five foundations, including three hospitals.

BIBLIOGRAPHY. *DAB* I; A. S. McAllister, *Flame in the Wilderness: Life and Letters of Mother Angela Gillespie* (1944); *NAW* 2. J. T. Connelly

Gillis, James Martin (1876-1957). Catholic* preacher,* editor and author. Born in Boston, Gillis was educated at the Boston Latin School; St. Charles College, Baltimore; and St. John's Seminary, Boston. He joined the Paulists* in 1898 and was ordained* in 1901. He continued his study of theology* at Catholic University of America* (S.T.L., 1903). Gillis was novice master and professor at St. Paul's College, Washington, D. C. (1907-1910), and was then involved in parish* mission preaching until 1922 when he succeeded John J. Burke* as editor of the *Catholic World. False Prophets,* the first of his six books, was published in 1925. In 1928, he began a widely syndicated column, and from 1930 to 1941 he appeared on "The Catholic Hour" radio program. In 1948 he resigned as editor of *Catholic World.*

Gillis was outspoken and controversial, writing his editorials in the first person and avoiding what he called "that pompous 'we'." An early critic of Mussolini, he was also a vigorous critic of Franklin Delano Roosevelt, whose thirteen years as president he described as "disastrous." Eleanor Roosevelt was also no favorite of Father Gillis. Beset by illness during the last years of his life, he died in New York on March 14, 1957.

BIBLIOGRAPHY. *DAB* 6; J. M. Gillis, "Valedictory," *The Catholic World* 167 (September 1948):481-490; J. F. Fainley, *James Gillis, Paulist* (1958).

R. Van Allen

Gladden, Solomon Washington (1836-1918). Congregationalist* minister.* Born in Pottsgrove, Pennsylvania, to schoolteacher parents, Gladden grew up on a farm near Owego, New York. After working as a printer's apprentice, he studied at Williams College (B.A., 1859). He then taught school and studied divinity* privately under Moses Coit Tyler, entering the ministry* in 1860. Gladden served churches in Brooklyn, New York (1860-1861); Morrisania, New York (1861-1866); North Adams, Massachusetts (1866-1871); Springfield, Massachusetts (1875-1882); and Columbus, Ohio (1882-1914). He was religion editor of *The Independent* in New York from 1871 to 1875.

Gladden wrote over thirty-eight books, including *Applied Christianity* (1886), *Social Salvation* (1902), *The Christian Pastor and the Working Church* (1907) and *The Church and Modern Life* (1908). In these and numerous articles Gladden tried to apply Christian theology* to the everyday problems of life in an increasingly industrial and urban society. Profoundly influenced by Horace Bushnell's* writings and friendship,* Gladden advocated a liberal* Christianity from early in his ministry. Gladden was a popular writer and speaker and lectured widely, becoming one of the most influential clergymen* of his day. His memorable hymn,* "O Master, Let Me Walk with Thee," still holds a revered place in many Protestant hymnals.

While he was not a systematic thinker, he was concerned to bring Christianity to bear on all areas of life, including the so-called secular issues of race, labor, politics, taxation and sectarianism. Emphasizing the corporate and social implications

of Christian faith, he argued that Christians were to be interdependent and responsible to others, rather than exclusively concerned with individual salvation.* Gladden addressed many industrial problems and encouraged cooperation between labor and capital, and over the years he became increasingly critical of the American free enterprise system. He served on the Columbus City Council from 1900 to 1902, demonstrating his belief that Christians can and should be involved in issues related to the infrastructures and administration of the city. Above all, he stressed the importance of character and urged people not to segregate religion from their work week, but to act morally and justly in all aspects of their lives. Remembered as the father of the Social Gospel,* Gladden's efforts were a significant force in awakening Protestants to the needs of society and the claims of the kingdom of God.*

BIBLIOGRAPHY. *DAB* IV; *DARB*; J. H. Dorn, *Washington Gladden: Prophet of the Social Gospel* (1966); W. Gladden, *Recollections* (1909); R. D. Knudten, *The Systematic Theology of Washington Gladden* (1968); *NCAB* 10. L. M. Japinga

Glebe Lands. Wherever the Anglican Church* was formally established* during the colonial period, legislative provision set aside farm lands (glebes) together with homes, barns and slaves for the support of the clergymen* and their families. At the time of the Revolution* this property was usually transferred to the possession of the Protestant Episcopal Church* in the new republic. Only in Virginia was there a major campaign, guided by the Baptists,* to seize this property. The 1798 legislature revoked all former grants to the Episcopal Church, and a further law in the 1801 assembly provided for the confiscation and sale of the glebe lands.

BIBLIOGRAPHY. G. M. Brydon, *Virginia's Mother Church and the Political Conditions Under Which It Grew,* 2 vols. (1947, 1952).

T. E. Buckley

Glossolalia. *See* TONGUES, SPEAKING IN.

Glover, Goodwife Ann (d. 1688). Colonial Catholic executed for witchcraft.* An Irish Catholic woman living in Boston, she was a casualty of the witchcraft hysteria that swept Massachusetts Bay Colony in the late seventeenth century. After she rebuked one of the daughters of John Goodwin for falsely accusing her own daughter of theft, the four Goodwin children began to exhibit signs of "bewitchment." They purred, barked and feigned choking; the oldest girl was struck senseless in the presence of the Westminster Assembly's *Catechism* and other orthodox* literature. Cotton Mather* studied the case and published a widely read account, *Late Memorable Providences Relating to Witchcraft and Possessions* (1689), arguing that the strange behavior was proof of demonic power at work. The children accused Goody Glover, a "wild Irish woman" who could recite the Lord's Prayer in Latin but not in English, of bewitching them. The magistrates executed her for witchcraft in 1688.   M. L. Bendroth

Glover, Robert Hall (1871-1947). Missionary* educator and statesman. Born and educated in Canada, Glover was trained in both medicine and theology* before his appointment to service in China with the Christian and Missionary Alliance* in 1894. He was named foreign secretary for the China Inland Mission* (CIM) in 1913 and taught missions at Moody Bible Institute* from 1921 to 1926. Returning to the CIM in 1926, he became the home director in 1930. Glover's thirteen years in this position coincided with the addition of 500 new members and 100 stations to the mission.

In response to the heavy toll of persecution and martyrdom that missionaries in China suffered at the time, Glover wrote an apologetic entitled "Shall Suffering and Danger Halt Our Missionary Work?" Drawing on the precedents of the early church found in the Acts, Glover noted that the apostolic church, "far from being dismayed by suffering, regarded it as something to be expected and [to] rejoice in." His enduring contribution to the missionary enterprise was his survey text *The Progress of World-Wide Missions* (1924), based on his lectures at Moody. Widely used in the preparation of missionaries, his book was translated into several languages and in 1960 was revised by J. Herbert Kane in tribute to its author's comprehension and insights.

BIBLIOGRAPHY.   H. Taylor, *"By Faith"; Henry W. Frost and the China Inland Mission* (1938).

        E. A. Wilson

God. *See* THEISM.

God's Will. An expression derived from Scripture* referring to the work of God in both creation at large and in the lives of individual men and women. It is composed of two aspects: God's immutable plan, which cannot be frustrated (Acts 2:23; Eph 1:11) and his desired wish involving the cooperation of individual people (Eph 5:17; 1 Thess 4:3). Another way to phrase this distinction is to denote the former as God's sovereign or determined will and the latter as his moral will.

The expression *God's will* is often used by evangelical* Christians to refer to God's guidance and plan for the lives of individuals. Among young people it is used most frequently when referring to the choice of a career or a marriage partner, and for this reason it is a popular subject in youth meetings and rallies. This usage reflects the biblical passages where God's will is implicitly related to the issues of guidance and decision making. Believers often refer to this by using the phrase "finding God's will," thus communicating the necessity of placing God at the center of life.

Some Christians who use this phrase believe that there is an individual blueprint or plan for each Christian, which can and must be discovered in order for God's will to be fulfilled. Christians of this persuasion often view the relationship between God's will and human decision making as a mysterious and even mystical affair. As a form of piety, it was enunciated within the Puritan* tradition, shaped by nineteenth-century revivalism* and transmitted through Holiness* and Keswick* piety to twentieth-century fundamentalism* and evangelicalism.

Like much Christian thinking on the subject, it draws a close correlation between an individual's communion with God and God's leading. Evangelicals of the twentieth century sometimes speak of Bible verses "given" to them during study or devotional reading of the Scriptures. These verses are often alleged to speak precisely to decisions or issues they face and provide divine direction. At times believers will "put out a fleece" (as Gideon in Judg 6:36-40) as a litmus test of God's will, in which a less significant request is to be granted or denied by God as a sign of his direction in a matter of greater consequence. Others will speak of doors of opportunity being opened or shut in answer to prayer.

In Pentecostal* and charismatic* circles it is customary for people to speak of a variety of means of divine direction, the outstanding feature being direction given through visions, prophecies and auditory experiences in which individuals and groups receive precise guidance from God. This tradition of divine guidance draws its inspiration from the Hebrew prophets and the experiences of the apostles of the early church.

Another view of divine leading is also found among Christians, drawing its inspiration from the wisdom literature of the Bible, as well as biblical promises of Christ's presence and the aid of the Spirit. Unpersuaded that Scripture indicates God has an individualized plan that each believer must discover, they hold that knowing God's will is neither mysterious nor mystical. For them, God's will requires Christians to understand biblical principles, make good and wise decisions and to live obediently and draw upon the Spirit's wisdom in each situation. This approach has been adopted by many evangelicals in recent years.

BIBLIOGRAPHY. M. B. Smith, *Knowing God's Will* (1979); G. Friesen, *Decision Making and the Will of God* (1981); D. Willard, *In Search of Guidance* (1983).   S. A. Wenig

Goetschius, John Henry (1717-1774). Dutch Reformed* minister* in Middle Colonies. When the seventeen-year-old John Henry Goetschius arrived in Philadelphia in 1735, he immediately began preaching in various churches in the Delaware Valley. After the presbytery* of Philadelphia denied him ordination* because of his lack of learning, he studied with Peter Henry Dorsius in Bucks County and was later ordained* by Dorsius, Gilbert Tennent* and Theodorus Jacobus Frelinghuysen.*

Both the Classis of Amsterdam and most of the Dutch Reformed ministers in the Middle Colonies had opposed Goetschius's ordination because of his pietist* leanings and his schismatic tendencies. In 1740, however, amidst the Great Awakening,* Goetschius managed to secure an appointment among the Dutch churches on Long Island, where his tenure was marked by bitter contention and, eventually, an ecclesiastical investigation into his probity and his practice of barring congregants from Holy Communion.* Goetschius reluctantly submitted to an ordination examination and transferred to the Dutch church at Hackensack, New Jersey, where he served until his death.

BIBLIOGRAPHY. *AAP* 9; R. H. Balmer, *"A Perfect Babel of Confusion"* (1989); *DAB* IV; H. G. Hageman, *Two Centuries Plus* (1984).

R. H. Balmer

Goforth, Jonathan (1859-1936). Canadian Presbyterian* missionary.* Raised in the Presbyterian* heartland of western Ontario, upon his conversion* in 1877, Goforth devoured the writings of Robert M. McCheyne, Charles H. Spurgeon and the Puritans.* Soon after he heard the famous missionary George Leslie Mackay, who was home from northern Taiwan, Goforth committed himself to evangelistic* missionary* service. While studying at Knox College, Toronto, he engaged in intense evangelistic activity in the poorest and most sordid parts of the city. In 1888 he and

his bride, a cultured artist, left for China, where for years their ministry would be centered in Honan.

Goforth was a deeply spiritual person and a man of iron determination and indefatigable activity. Theologically a Calvinist,* he learned premillennialism* at the famous Niagara Bible Conference.* Goforth regarded Hudson Taylor as a mentor in the Spirit, while Charles Finney's* writings encouraged the development of his evangelism into mass revivalism.* For years the Goforth family lived lives of almost constant itinerant evangelism, a ministry* that widened after his leadership in the Manchurian Revival of 1907. When he was on furlough his powerfully direct preaching style made him one of the best-known missionaries of his generation. Goforth's book, *By My Spirit* (1912), recounted the revivals in China and helped promote the cause of missions in China.

A strenuous opponent of theological liberalism* wherever he encountered it, he refused to enter the United Church* in 1925 and in his old age pioneered work for the Presbyterians in Manchuria. Appropriately, his funeral service was held in Knox Presbyterian Church, Toronto, where he and his wife had been married and first sent on their way to China and where he had found constant sympathy and support.

BIBLIOGRAPHY. R. Goforth, *Goforth of China* (1937); A. Austin, *Saving China: Canadian Missionaries in the Middle Kingdom, 1888-1959* (1986).   I. S. Rennie

Good Friday. The Friday before Easter* and an important Holy Week observance. Since the early days of Christianity, Good Friday has been a time of somber reflection, penance and meditation. In Roman Catholic* tradition the Mass* is not celebrated on that day nor on Holy Saturday. Bells are not sounded, organs are not played, and black is the liturgical color of the day. Many churches drape the altar area in black. Particular attention is given to the Stations of the Cross, reflections of certain events along Christ's way to Calvary.

Many Protestant* churches also observe Good Friday with special services and memorial observances focusing on the crucifixion. Some schedule meditations on the "Seven Last Words" from the cross or other pascal themes. On Good Friday evening many churches observe the Lord's Supper,* while others use the Tenebrae service centered on the theme of light and darkness. Some evangelical* churches produce dramas which re-enact the Last Supper and the betrayal of Jesus.

B. J. Leonard

Goodell, William (1792-1867). Pioneer missionary* in Turkey. Born into a family of modest means in Templeton, Massachusetts, Goodell put himself through Phillips Academy, Dartmouth College* and Andover Seminary,* graduating from the latter in 1820. After serving as agent of the American Board of Commissioners for Foreign Missions* in the middle and Southwestern states and visiting the Cherokee and Choctaw missions, he embarked for Malta in December 1823. Periods of service at Beirut and Malta were followed by an assignment to inaugurate a mission at Constantinople in 1831. He was a leader among the men of the American Board's Near East Mission in whom the Earl of Shaftesbury discerned a "marvellous combination of common sense and piety." His good humor, tact and persuasiveness were legendary. He translated the Bible* from Hebrew and Greek into Armeno-Turkish. Returning to America in 1865, he died in Philadelphia after two active years there.

BIBLIOGRAPHY. *DAB* IV; W. Goodell, *The Old and the New, or The Changes of Thirty Years in the East* (1853); E. D. G. Prime, *Memoirs of Rev. William Goodell, D.D.* (1891).   D. M. Stowe

Goodpasture, (B)enjamin (C)ordell (1895-1977). Church of Christ* editor and evangelist.* Born to a Christian family in Livingstone, Tennessee, Goodpasture was baptized* at age fourteen and began preaching* when he was seventeen. In 1918 he graduated from Nashville Bible School (now David Lipscomb College). Later other colleges honored him with honorary degrees.

As a preacher he served churches in Alabama and Tennessee before undertaking a ten-year ministry in Atlanta, Georgia. In 1930 he moved to Nashville to become minister of the Hillsboro Church of Christ. He continued in that position until 1951. He was considered an outstanding preacher and was invited to hold many gospel meetings. In 1939 he became editor of *The Gospel Advocate,* a journal that among Churches of Christ is called "The Old Reliable." He continued in that position until his death. In addition to being an editor, Goodpasture authored two books, *Biographies and Sermons of Pioneer Peachers* (1954) and *Sermons and Lectures* (1964). It was as an editor that Goodpasture achieved his greatest influence. His moderate stance on most matters of controversy was considered a strong force for stability within the denomination.*

BIBLIOGRAPHY. J. E. Choate, *The Anchor That Holds: A Biography of B. C. Goodpasture* (1971).
                    L. B. Sullivan

Goodrich, Chauncey (1836-1925) Missionary* to China. Born in Hinsdale, Massachusetts, Goodrich graduated from Williams College and Andover Theological Seminary.* He was ordained* in 1865 as a missionary of the American Board of Commissioners for Foreign Missions* and sailed for Peking. He was the first preacher at Tungchow (1866) and settled there in 1873 as dean of Gordon Memorial Theological Seminary. In 1905 that school became part of North China Union Theological College; it moved to Peking and Goodrich moved with it. He was deeply involved from the beginning with the creation of a Union version of the Bible* in *baihua* (common speech Mandarin), chairing the translation committee from 1908 until the Bible appeared in 1919. His ten-thousand-character Chinese-English dictionary (1891) was a standard for many years. Goodrich collaborated with an American Board colleague, Henry Blodget, in publishing an early and widely used Chinese hymnal (1872). When he died in Peking, the *Missionary Herald* (December 1908) noted his "sixty years of service on the field spent in scholarly work, in song, and in just loving people."   D. M. Stowe

Goodspeed, Edgar Johnson (1871-1962). Baptist* New Testament scholar and Bible translator. Born in Quincy, Illinois, Goodspeed was raised in the suburbs of Chicago, where his father was a Baptist minister. Goodspeed graduated from Denison University (B.A., 1890) and then went to Yale to study Hebrew and Semitic languages (1890-1891) under William Rainey Harper. Shortly after Harper became the first president of the University of Chicago, Goodspeed followed him there, enrolling first in the Divinity School (B.D., 1897) and then in the University (Ph.D., 1898). His father, Thomas Goodspeed, was a founding trustee and fund raiser for the University of Chicago. When Goodspeed completed his graduate work, Harper sent him to Europe for two years of study. There Goodspeed studied under Harnack at the University of Berlin, visited the major universities of Germany and England, and toured the important sites of the Mediterranean world. In Egypt he visited the camps of Flinders Petrie and Bernard P. Grenfell and Arthur S. Hunt, collaborating with the latter in their publication of *The Tebtunis Papyri,* part II (1907).

On his return to America in 1900, Goodspeed began teaching New Testament at the University of Chicago, where he would spend his entire career. An industrious scholar, he rose rapidly through the academic ranks and succeeded Ernest D. Burton as chairman of the New Testament department (1923-1937). Under his leadership the department became a center for New Testament manuscript and textual studies.

As a Bible translator Goodspeed first published *The New Testament: An American Translation* (1923), a work that received praise and established him not only as a translator but also as a popular communicator of scholarship. He was a member of the New Testament translation committee for the Revised Standard Bible, and after retiring in 1937 he published *The Apocrypha: An American Translation* (1938) and, with J. M. P. Smith, *The Complete Bible: An American Translation* (1939). In *The Meaning of Ephesians* (1933), he argued that Ephesians was written as an introduction to the collection of Paul's letters. One of his prized manuscript discoveries—a Byzantine manuscript containing prints from the thirteenth century—was published as *The Rockefeller McCormick New Testament,* 3 vols. (1932). Perhaps one of the most prolific and versatile American New Testament scholars of the twentieth century, his other publications included *An Introduction to the New Testament* (1937), *A History of Early Christian Literature* (1942) and *How to Read the Bible* (1946). Ten years after retiring from Chicago, Goodspeed moved to Southern California, where he continued his writing and was a popular lecturer at the University of California at Los Angeles and Scripps College, Claremont. A lifelong Baptist, he regarded the church—and particularly the Baptist Church—as his second home.

BIBLIOGRAPHY. J. H. Cobb, *A Biography and Bibliography of Edgar Johnson Goodspeed* (1948); J. Cook, *Edgar Johnson Goodspeed: Articulate Scholar* (1981); E. Goodspeed, *As I Remember* (1953).   J. E. Stanley

Gordon, (A)doniram (J)udson (1836-1895).
Baptist* minister* and missions* leader. After completing his education at Brown University* and Newton Theological School, Gordon became, in 1863, the pastor* of the Jamaica Plain Baptist Church in Massachusetts. In 1869 he became pastor of the Clarendon Street Church in Boston, where he labored until his death.

In the twenty-five years that Gordon pastored the Clarendon Street Church, he was to transform it into one of the leading missions-minded* churches in America and a leading fundraiser for Baptist foreign missions. But the church's mission involvement was not limited to overseas. In 1877 Dwight L. Moody* held a revival* near the church, which inspired the congregation to minister to alcoholics, the homeless and other needy people in Boston. Gordon himself began the Boston Industrial Temporary Home as a social service for unemployed men.

The last decade of Gordon's life brought an increased devotion to foreign missions. Active in the American Baptist* Missionary Union, Gordon played a key role in the ABMU's adoption of the British Livingstone Inland Mission as its Congo mission in 1884. In 1888 he was elected chairman of the ABMU's executive committee. As chairman of the ABMU, Gordon guided the denomination's* missions for seven years. His other mission activity included attendance at the London Centenary Conference in 1888 and associate editorship of *The Missionary Review of the World.* Above all of these efforts, Gordon is best remembered for founding, in 1889, the Boston Missionary Training School, the forerunner of Gordon College and Gordon-Conwell Theological Seminary.

Gordon was a prolific writer on Christ's Second Coming. In 1878 he founded *The Watchword,* a journal to help believers "looking for that blessed hope, and the glorious appearing of the great God and our Saviour Jesus Christ." Works on spirituality and theology included *Ecce Venit—Behold He Cometh* (1889), *The Holy Spirit in Missions* (1893), *How Christ Came to Church* (1893) and his most famous book, *The Ministry of the Spirit* (1894).

Well known for his emphasis on the Holy Spirit and his advocacy of faith healing,* Gordon was also a leading evangelical* supporter of women's suffrage* and of women's work in the Prohibition Movement.* In 1894 he wrote "The Ministry of Women" in defense of women's right to preach,* prophesy and teach men in the church. From its opening, the Boston Missionary Training School had a majority of women students studying to be missionaries,* evangelists* and city workers. Gordon received heavy criticism for supporting "short-cut" training for ministry, but he encouraged the multiplication of Christian workers by any means so as to prepare for Christ's Second Coming. Despite denominational ties, he supported the emerging Bible schools* and faith missions* of the 1890s.

A close associate of evangelist Dwight L. Moody, Gordon was a leader in the emerging fundamentalist* movement as it was exemplified in the Niagara* and prophetic Bible conferences.* Gordon was one of the most influential evangelicals of the late nineteenth century, and his popularity permitted him to bridge the ranks of separatist fundamentalists and denominational loyalists. After his death, friends renamed his missionary training school in his honor.

BIBLIOGRAPHY. *DARB;* E. B. Gordon, *Adoniram Judson Gordon: A Biography* (1896); *NCAB* 11; D. L. Robert, "The Legacy of Adoniram Judson Gordon," *IBMR* 11 (October 1987):176-181; *The Watchword* 1878-1895; C. A. Russell, "Adoniram Judson Gordon: Nineteenth-Century Fundamentalist," *ABQ* 4 (March 1985):61-89.

D. L. Robert

Gordon, Charles William (1860-1937). Canadian novelist and Social Gospel* activist. Born in Glengarry County, Canada West (now Ontario), Gordon was educated at the Universities of Toronto and Edinburgh, and at Knox College, Toronto. He was ordained* as a minister* of the Presbyterian Church in Canada* in 1890, and served as a missionary* near Banff, Alberta, before being called in 1894 to St. Stephen's Presbyterian (later United) Church in Winnipeg, Manitoba, where he remained for the rest of his life. In 1921 he was elected moderator of the General Assembly of the Presbyterian Church in Canada. He was an advocate for the movement which united the Congregationalists,* Methodists* and approximately two-thirds of the Presbyterians in 1925 as the United Church of Canada.* As a Social Gospel activist Gordon was involved with such issues as immigration, temperance,* moral reform and industrial relations. Under the pseudonym "Ralph Connor," Gordon was the most popular Canadian writer of his generation. He wrote some twenty-six novels, the best known of which are *The Sky Pilot* (1899) and *The Man from Glengarry* (1901).

BIBLIOGRAPHY. J. Grant, "Charles William Gordon" in *The Oxford Companion to Canadian Literature,* ed. William Toye (1983); J. S. Moir, *Enduring Witness: A History of the Presbyterian Church in Canada* (1974).

R. W. Vaudry

Gordon, George Angier (1853-1929). Congregationalist* preacher* and theologian.* Born in Aberdeenshire, Scotland, Gordon immigrated to the U.S. in 1811 and, reversing the usual sequence, studied for the ministry at Bangor Theological Seminary (1874-1877) and at Harvard College* (1878-1881). Gordon's exposure at Bangor to the incarnational theories of British theologians F. D. Maurice (1805-1872) and Frederick W. Robertson (1816-1853) and, at Harvard, to George Herbert Palmer (1842-1933) and William James,* profoundly shaped the message and approach of his later career. In 1881 Gordon became pastor of the Second Congregational Church in Greenwich,

Connecticut, from which he was called to Boston's Old South Church in 1884.

From his prestigious pulpit on Boston's Copley Square, Gordon reigned for over two decades as one of the most visible and outspoken leaders of the "New Theology"*—a modernist theological movement—especially after publishing two significant works in 1895. *The Gospel for Humanity,* Gordon's "mission sermon" before the annual meeting of the American Board of Commissioners for Foreign Missions,* proved to be the pivotal event in elucidating one of the most important and hard-fought modernist programs—that of defining an "exportable Christianity," a faith stripped of Western "cultural accretions" for interaction and competition with other world religions in the mission field. Likewise, *The Christ of Today* (1895), Gordon's most important and influential theological work, enunciated and popularized a "Progressive Orthodoxy" that combined an emphasis on divine immanence within human culture, an incarnational Christology, and an assertion of human free agency, into an "experiential Christianity" defined as a progressive encounter between persons in history rather than a creed* or doctrinal set of beliefs.

BIBLIOGRAPHY. *DAB* IV; *DARB*; *NCAB* 22.

M. S. Massa

Gordon, Samuel Dickey (1859-1936). Devotional writer. Born and educated in Philadelphia, Gordon was involved in various parachurch* organizations, chief among which was the YMCA. For ten years he served as an assistant secretary and later state secretary of the YMCA. Following his years with that organization, he initiated a ministry* of preaching* and lecturing on religious issues in the U.S. Beyond American shores he traveled for four years in Europe and the Orient, where he conducted Bible conference* and missionary conventions. He is probably best known for the more than twenty devotional books he wrote in the later years of his life. Each was entitled "Quiet Talks," most notable of which was *Quiet Talks on Power* (1901), *Quiet Talks on Prayer* (1904) and *Quiet Talks on Jesus* (1906). These books were widely used by clergy* and lay leaders alike, as well as by the common person in the pew.

R. R. Mathisen

Gorton, Samuel (c.1592-1677). New England religious radical. From 1637 until his departure for England in 1644, Gorton was at the center of a series of controversies in Massachusetts and Rhode Island. Fined and banished from Boston in 1637, he lived for short times near Portsmouth, Providence, Pawtuxet and Shawomet. From Shawomet he was seized and brought back to Boston where he was imprisoned in 1643 for being an enemy of "all civil authority among the people of God." Released in 1644, he spent four years in England before returning to Shawomet, which he renamed Warwick. He lived peacefully for the rest of his life, preaching and serving in several civil offices, including representative to the assembly. His difficulties in New England stemmed in part from his promulgation of the radical ideology of John Saltmarsh (c.1612-1647), prominent English radical of the time. His doctrine* of the indwelling Spirit resembled that of the Quakers,* and he manifested the same anticlericalism* and confidence in lay exhorting* as did they. His followers called themselves Gortonites well into the 1700s.

BIBLIOGRAPHY. P. F. Gura, *A Glimpse of Sion's Glory: Puritan Radicalism in New England, 1620-1660* (1984). T. T. Taylor

Gospel Hymns and Songs. The musical term *gospel* refers to a range of styles which grew from the popular-based music* used in American camp meeting* revivals* of the early nineteenth century and the Sunday-school movement* tunes of the late nineteenth century. The tradition has parallels in popular church music throughout the history of the church, such as the New Testament "spiritual songs" (Eph 5:19; Col 3:16), the hymns of early church evangelists, the *Laude* of St. Francis and the Dissenter's hymns of Isaac Watts.

Gospel hymns are personal expressions of faith. Characteristically, they are strophic with a refrain, rhythmic (often accompanied in the "gospel piano" style), popular and easily learned. They often function as a theological shorthand, instructing Christians in the basics of the faith. They may also serve as an evangelistic tool, as in the case of the hymns of Charles and John Wesley,* the black and white spirituals of the Second Great Awakening,* the black spirituals* of the Reconstruction period, the ballads of Ira Sankey,* the choirs of Charles Alexander,* the songleading of Homer Rodeheaver,* the group sing-alongs of Cliff Barrows, the "singing in the spirit" of charismatics* and the present-day concert tours of Christian celebrity* entertainers.

Gospel music's style moved from the folk music of the early nineteenth century (captured in four-shape shape-note tunebooks for singing schools) to commercial single-composer music later in the century (e.g., George F. Root and Philip P. Bliss*), to this century's divergent forms of black gospel,

hillbilly or country and even secular tin pan alley. Since the 1940s, gospel music has become a type of commercial Christian music, dominated by a few publishing houses (Word, Sparrow, Alexandria, Lexicon, Manna, Lillenas, Benson, Broadman, Singspiration, Hope, Gentry, Glorysound, Lorenz) and the traveling entertainers who write, perform and record gospel songs—now known as contemporary Christian music. An informal network of Christian radio programming supplements the tastemaking.

In the church, current gospel music is largely a performer-audience phenomenon. Congregations have difficulty learning rock-based tunes and publishers of pop-oriented group songs have yet to find effective distribution methods. Many evangelical* and charismatic* churches use overhead projections or even rote learning (the nineteenth-century approach) to add a few new gospel songs to the congregation's repertoire. Some standard songs, such as the choruses of William Gaither or the songs of Ralph Carmichael, are included in non-denominational hardcover hymnals.

If the past is any measure of the future, churches will continue to need and use music that is accessible, straightforward and popularly based. Gospel hymns of the future will undoubtedly take many forms as they respond to popular culture.

See also HYMNS, HYMNALS; MUSIC, CHRISTIAN.

BIBLIOGRAPHY. R. Anderson and G. North, *Gospel Music Encyclopedia* (1979); *Bio-Bibliographical Index of Musicians in the United States of America Since Colonial Times,* 2nd ed. (1956); D. P. Ellsworth, *Bibliography to Christian Music in Contemporary Witness* (1980); D. P. Hustad, *Jubilate! Church Music in the Evangelical Tradition* (1981); E. Routley, *The Church and Music* (1967, 1978); S. Sizer, *Gospel Hymns and Social Religion* (1979). R. J. Stanislaw

Gospel Missionary Union. Evangelical* foreign missionary* society. In 1889 at a YMCA* Bible conference* near Ottawa, Kansas, James H. Brookes* and Irish missionary H. Grattan Guinness challenged the audience with the missionary needs of the Sudan. Among those who responded was a young man of great promise, Will Mitchell. On the same day, however, Mitchell was drowned. The tragedy made a great impression upon everyone in attendance, including the secretary of the Kansas State YMCA, George S. Fisher, who subsequently visited YMCAs in Kansas and the surrounding area, pleading for missionary candidates for Sudan and other needy countries.

Since the policy of the International Committee

of the YMCA did not permit it to undertake direct missionary activity, the leaders of the new movement organized the World's Gospel Union in Topeka in 1892, with A. E. Bishop, R. A. Torrey* and George Fisher serving as executives. The group had already sent missionaries to Sierra Leone in 1890, and within two years of its formation they had sent a small group to Morocco. Within the next twenty-five years missionaries were sent to Ecuador, Colombia and the French Sudan (now the Mali Republic). Work was confined to these four fields until 1950, after which a number of new fields were added, including others in Central and South America.

In the late 1980s the Gospel Missionary Union consists of 391 full-time and 130 short-term missionaries from the U.S. and Canada working in nineteen countries, primarily in evangelism,* church planting and leadership development. The mission headquarters are in Kansas City, Missouri, and its official publication is *The Gospel Message*.

BIBLIOGRAPHY. C. P. Chapman, *With the Bible Among the Andes* (n.d.); F. Drown and M. Drown, *Mission to the Headhunters* (1961); B. J. Nickel, *Along the Quichua Trail* (n.d.); D. P. Shidler, *Exploits of Faith* (1982).   D. J. Hesselgrave

Gospel of Wealth. *See* WEALTH, GOSPEL OF.

Gould, Thomas (?-1675). Early colonial Baptist* pastor* from Boston. Gould (Goold) first came to notice through his association with Henry Dunster,* ousted president of Harvard College* (1654), over the issue of infant baptism.* In 1655, under the influence of Dunster and convinced of the error of the practice, Gould refused to have his first child baptized. Gould separated himself from the Charlestown church and met with other Baptist dissenters in his home, being charged in 1665 with schism. With others, in 1666, he was fined and required to post bond; failing to pay they were imprisoned. When the desired conformity to church law was not secured, Gould left for Noddle's Island (East Boston). Despite continuing threats of persecution, Gould ministered to the Baptists of the area. A modest permanent meetinghouse was erected in 1678 in Boston.

BIBLIOGRAPHY. I. Backus, *History of New England with Particular Reference to the Denomination of Christians Called Baptists* (1796); A. H. Newman, *A History of the Baptist Churches in the United States* (1894).   L. W. Hähnlen

Grabau, Johannes Andreas Augustus (1804-1879). Lutheran* pastor,* teacher, writer and synodical leader. Born at Olvenstadt, near Magdeburg, Germany, Grabau was educated at Halle and, after a brief period as a teacher, was ordained* in 1834. He served the St. Andrew Church, Erfurt, where he was twice imprisoned for not complying with the practices of the United (Lutheran and Reformed) Church of Prussia. Bound by conscience to the Lutheran Confessions, Grabau and 1,000 sympathizers immigrated to the U.S. in 1839.

Settling in Buffalo, New York, Grabau founded the Martin Luther Seminary (1840) where he served as president and major professor. Grabau gathered the Synod of the Lutheran Church Emigrated from Prussia (Buffalo Synod) in 1845. As editor of *Die Wachende Kirche* and senior minister of Trinity Lutheran Church, Buffalo, Grabau showed himself an exponent of Old Lutheranism and a vigorous polemicist. A major controversy occurred with C. F. W. Walther* and the Lutheran Church-Missouri Synod* over the issue of church and ministry,* with Grabau advocating a high church* or hierarchical position. Following Grabau's death on June 2, 1879, the Buffalo Synod drew close to the Ohio and Iowa Synods, merging with them in 1930 to form the American Lutheran Church.*

BIBLIOGRAPHY. P. H. Buehring, *The Spirit of the American Lutheran Church* (1940); *DAB* IV; J. A. Grabau, *Lebenslauf des ehrwuerdigen J. An. A. Grabau* (1879).   C. G. Fry

Grace, Charles Manuel ("Sweet Daddy") (1881-1960). Founder and bishop* of United House of Prayer for All Peoples. Born Marcelino Manuel de Graca in the Cape Verde Islands, "Sweet Daddy" Grace (an assumed name) worked as a cook, dishwasher and sewing machine salesman before founding his United House of Prayer for All Peoples. His first church may have been opened as early as 1921 in New Bedford, Massachusetts, but his first success occurred when he opened a branch in Charlotte, North Carolina, in 1926. The church prospered, growing to include 375 branches from coast to coast and about 25,000 members by the time of his death.

The flamboyant Grace sported a mustache, shoulder-length hair, jewels and five-inch-long fingernails painted red, white and blue. His appeal was greatest among urban African-American women. The core of Grace's ministry was his alleged gift of healing. His touch was said to cure numerous diseases, such as colds, stomach upset and infertility. "Daddy Grace" tea, coffee, soaps, hand creams and other products were also reputed to have miraculous healing powers. The worship* style in his churches, influenced by Pentecostalism,* incorporated singing, shouting, dancing, testifying and speaking in tongues.* While Grace acknowledged that he was only a servant of God, he also claimed that "God poured his own love into one man and Daddy Grace is the only man with that love."

The Internal Revenue Service accused him of tax evasion, and he was eventually forced to pay $125,000 in back taxes. After Grace's death in Los Angeles in 1960, Walter McCullough was elected bishop and held the church together, but he did not claim all of Grace's powers.

BIBLIOGRAPHY. *DARB*; A. H. Fauset, *Black Gods of the Metropolis: Negro Religious Cults of the Urban North* (1970); A. Poinsett, "Farewell to Daddy Grace," *Ebony* 16 (April 1960):25-34.

S. W. Angell

Grace Brethren. *See* FELLOWSHIP OF GRACE BRETHREN CHURCHES.

Grady, Henry Woodfin (1850-1889). Editor and layman in Methodist Episcopal Church,* South. Born in Athens, Georgia, after the Civil War,* Grady graduated from the University of Georgia and studied law at the University of Virginia. Grady's interest in journalism led him to secure a loan enabling him to purchase a fourth interest in Atlanta's *Constitution* in 1879. Through his efforts the paper attained great influence in the Southeast, a position it retains to this day. Grady took the vanguard in championing worthy social issues, such as the problem of racism. His views were at times controversial, but his sincere intention and godly Christian character were widely regarded. As a member of First Methodist Church in Atlanta, he also championed the social views of the church, particularly prohibitionism.* Through his efforts, impetus was given to the renewal of spirit in the churches and culture of the post-bellum South.

BIBLIOGRAPHY. *DAB* IV; F. Norwood, *The Story of American Methodism* (1974).

J. S. O'Malley

Graham, Isabella Marshall (1742-1814). Pioneer of organized charity and Sunday schools.* Born and educated in Scotland, she married and moved to Canada, but returned to Scotland in 1773 as a widow with four children. After three years of debasing poverty, she founded a small school and began organizing ways to help others. In 1789, encouraged by John Witherspoon,* she came to America, opened a school for girls in New York

City and continued her philanthropy.* With her daughter Joanna Bethune* and friends Sarah Hoffman and Elizabeth Seton,* she founded one of America's first organized charities—the Society for the Relief of Poor Widows with Small Children. Under her leadership this prototypal female society began several innovative programs, including two of America's earliest Sunday schools. In later years, Graham sought to meet the needs of a wider range of women and children. Pessimistic about social reform, she remained hopeful about the impact of early instruction.

BIBLIOGRAPHY. J. G. Bethune, *The Life of Mrs. Isabella Graham* (1839); *DAB* IV; *NAW* 2.

K. K. Kidd

Graham, William (Billy) Frank (1918-). International evangelist.* Born near Charlotte, North Carolina, Graham was raised in a moral home atmosphere by his church-going parents, dairy farmer William Franklin and Morrow Coffey Graham. At age sixteen Graham was converted to Christ during an evangelistic campaign led by Mordecai F. Ham,* a hard-driving evangelist. In 1936 Graham began classes at Bob Jones* College, Cleveland, Tennessee, but transferred to Florida Bible Institute in Tampa in January of 1937. When a young woman broke an engagement with him, Graham felt deeply troubled. He was also struggling with a call to a preaching ministry. One evening in March, 1938, on the eighteenth green of a golf course near the Bible Institute, Graham surrendered himself to a life of gospel preaching.*

Between 1940 and 1943, Billy Graham attended Wheaton College,* Wheaton, Illinois. There he met Ruth Bell, the daughter of Dr. and Mrs. Nelson Bell,* Presbyterian* missionaries* to China. The couple was married in 1943. Following a brief pastorate, Graham became an evangelist for Youth for Christ* in 1944-1945, an organization recently formed by Torrey Johnson. In 1946-1947, he made two trips to England for evangelistic tours, the first with Torrey Johnson, the second with Cliff Barrows. He also served as the president of Northwestern Bible College in Minneapolis, Minnesota, for a time (1947-1951).

Graham's evangelistic efforts in Los Angeles (1949) brought him to national attention. Just before the campaign, he had experienced doubts about the full authority of Holy Scripture.* At Forest Home Camp, he committed himself completely to a belief that the Bible* is the very Word of God. Thereafter he became even more determined to preach what "the Bible says." The Los Angeles Crusade seemed to be winding down until

William Randolph Hearst gave the order to his newspaper people to "puff Graham." Suddenly, the crusade was the subject of numerous newspaper articles, and Graham appeared on the front pages of *Time, Newsweek* and later *Life* magazines.

In 1950 he founded the Billy Graham Evangelistic Association* and "The Hour of Decision" went on the air on November 5 of that year. Graham continued to preach in crusades, often making allusion to the threat of communism. In 1954 the Graham team ministered in England with remarkable results. This crusade ushered Graham onto the international stage. In those years he published two important books, *Peace with God* (1953) and *The Secret of Happiness* (1955). In 1956 he was a major force in establishing the publication *Christianity Today.** Graham's stature within American society led him to become an unofficial spiritual advisor and confidant to many U.S. presidents, beginning with Dwight D. Eisenhower.*

Criticism began to mount regarding the evangelist's positive stance on co-operative evangelism—meaning Graham's policy of working cooperatively with non-evangelical, mainline* churches. This criticism came to a head in the summer of 1957 in the wake of the New York Crusade —one of the first nationally televised crusades. A number of fundamentalists* broke with Graham because they believed that "decision cards" were not necessarily going to conservative churches for the follow-up of converts and that the evangelist gave too prominent a position to Protestant liberals* during the crusade.

Graham became involved in launching a number of important congresses on evangelism: Berlin (1966), Lausanne* (1974) and Itinerant Evangelists (1983, 1986). These congresses encouraged Christian leaders from many nations to pursue world evangelization.

Characterized by sterling integrity and a genuine humility, Graham has weathered criticism by not responding to it and has remained one of the most respected public figures of his generation and the most influential evangelical of the twentieth century. He has preached the gospel to more people than any evangelist in the history of the church, reaching nearly one hundred million individuals in person and untold numbers by radio and television throughout the world. During his meetings two million individuals have come forward in response to his invitation* to accept Christ.

See also BILLY GRAHAM CENTER; BILLY GRAHAM EVANGELISTIC ASSOCIATION; REVIVALISM, PROTESTANT.

BIBLIOGRAPHY. M. Frady, *Billy Graham, A Parable of American Righteousness* (1979); W. G. McLoughlin, *Billy Graham, Revivalist in a Secular Age* (1960); R. V. Pierard, "Billy Graham and the U.S. Presidency," *JCS* 22 (1980):107-127; J. Pollock, *Billy Graham, The Authorized Biography* (1966); J. Pollock, *Billy Graham, Evangelist to the World: An Authorized Biography of the Decisive Years* (1979).
J. D. Woodbridge

Grail, The. An international Catholic* laywomen's movement. The Grail has its origins in the Women of Nazareth, a spiritual movement (or apostolate*) established by a Dutch Jesuit,* Jacques van Ginneken, in 1921. In May 1940 two European Grail leaders, Lydwine van Kersbergen and Joan Overboss, aided by Bishop Bernard Sheil* of Chicago, established the Grail's first American headquarters at Doddridge Farm in Libertyville, Illinois. The Grail offered specialized programs for young Catholic women, designed to heighten their awareness of the integral relationships between their spiritual lives, their work (especially rural women's work) and communal worship* in the liturgy.* These courses, offered at Grailville, the Grail's new headquarters near Loveland, Ohio, from 1944 on, touched the lives of countless Catholic women who stayed for a few weeks, a summer or a year.

During the 1950s Grail volunteers established "city centers" in Detroit; Cincinnati; Lafayette, Louisiana; and New York City, where they supported the movements for civil rights* and urban renewal, and worked in Catholic college chaplaincies.* In 1950 Grailville opened a School of Missiology. During the 1960s members of the Grail reassessed their movement in the light of Vatican II* and the ecumenical movement.* They launched Semester at Grailville in 1967, a program in which college students combined academic work with community involvement. In 1969 they admitted their first Protestant* member. By sponsoring the "Women Exploring Theology" conference held at Grailville in 1973, the Grail expressed its commitment to nurturing new theologies which take feminist* concerns seriously.

BIBLIOGRAPHY. A. V. Brown, *The Grail Movement in American Catholicism, 1940-1975* (1988); A. V. Brown, "The Grail Movement to 1962," *USCH* 3 (1983):149-166.
D. Campbell

Grant, Frederick Clifton (1891-1974). Episcopal* priest* and biblical scholar.* Ordained* in the Anglican* Church after preparing for the ministry at Nashotah House (1909-1911) and General Theological Seminary (1913), Grant served as curate and rector in two parishes in Illinois (1917-1924), during which time he earned a Th.D. at Western Seminary (1922). After teaching as professor of systematic theology at Berkeley Divinity School (1926-1927), Grant served as president of Western (later Seabury-Western) Seminary (1927-1938) until he became professor of biblical theology* at Union Seminary,* New York, where he served until his retirement in 1959.

In addition to being editor of the *Anglican Theological Review,* Grant is primarily remembered for his critical studies in the Gospels, as well as his investigation of the Jewish and Hellenistic backgrounds of the New Testament. These interests are exemplified in his numerous writings, including *Economic Background of the Gospels* (1926) and *Ancient Judaism and the New Testament* (1959). He also served on the translation committee of the Revised Standard Version of the Bible.

S. Meier

Grant, George Monro (1835-1905). Canadian Presbyterian* educator. Born in a Scottish immigrant community in Nova Scotia, Grant's early experiences of warring religious factions gave him a deep hostility toward any form of sectarianism. In 1853 Grant went to study at the University of Glasgow, returning home in 1861 as an ordained Church of Scotland missionary.*

Grant was deeply influenced by the Scottish thinkers John Caird (1820-1898) and Edward Caird (1835-1908), as well as by the English philosopher T. H. Green (1836-1882), all of whom stimulated his interest in Kantian and Hegelian philosophy. German biblical scholarship also influenced him, as did romantic idealists like Coleridge and Carlyle. In 1877 he became principal of Queen's University in Kingston, Ontario, and had a powerful impact on fellow Presbyterian clergy* through an annual theological conference* held at Queen's.

Relentlessly optimistic, Grant pioneered the Social Gospel* in Canada and interpreted the Christian message in terms of active social service, moral elevation and opposition to secularism.* A popularizer rather than a systematic thinker, he was arguably the most influential Canadian clergyman in the last two decades of the nineteenth century.

BIBLIOGRAPHY. W. L. Grant and F. Hamilton, *Principal Grant* (1904). D. M. Lewis

Graves, James Robinson (1820-1893). Southern Baptist* preacher,* editor and publisher who led in the formation of the Landmark Movement.* Born into a Congregational* family in Vermont, he joined a Baptist congregation at age fifteen. Growing up in a poor farming family, Graves received little formal education. However, he applied himself diligently to private studies and became a schoolteacher, finding work first in Kingsville, Ohio (1840-1842), and then in Jessamine County, Kentucky (1842-1843). In 1842 he was ordained* into the Baptist ministry and preached in Ohio for a short period (1843-1845) before taking a teaching position in Nashville, Tennessee, in 1845.

Soon after moving to Nashville, Graves became pastor of a church; and by 1848 he was the editor of *The Tennessee Baptist.* His chief contribution to Baptist life and history was through his career in journalism. By the eve of the Civil War,* *The Tennessee Baptist* had the largest circulation (13,000 in 1859) of any denominational paper in the South. Not only did it serve the Baptists of Tennessee, it was also the denominational* journal for Mississippi, Louisiana, Arkansas and most of the lower Mississippi Valley. Graves also formed a publishing company which became one of the most influential and prolific religious presses* in the South during the second half of the nineteenth century.

During the decade before the Civil War, Graves became the dominant figure of a developing movement in Baptist life known as Landmarkism.* In 1851 he convened a meeting at Cotton Grove, Tennessee, that formulated the chief tenets of the movement, the foundational premise being the sole validity of Baptist churches as true churches of Christ, joined in unbroken succession since the New Testament era. Throughout the latter half of the nineteenth century, Landmarkism became the most potent force in the Southern Baptist Convention, especially in the old Southwest. The sectarian tendencies of the movement continue to characterize many aspects of Southern Baptist life, particularly in rural churches of the mid South and the lower Mississippi Valley. Graves' book *Old Landmarkism: What Is It?* (1880) is a classic pronouncement of this doctrine.

BIBLIOGRAPHY. *DAB* IV; *DARB*; O. L. Hailey, *J. R. Graves, Life, Times and Teaching* (1929); J. E. Tull, *Shapers of Baptist Thought* (1972). M. G. Bell

Gray, Asa (1810-1888). Harvard* botanist. Educated as a medical doctor, Gray's long career as a professor at Harvard (1842-1873) allowed him to specialize in his first love, botany. There, in respectful rivalry with Louis Agassiz, Gray championed a new empirical approach to science that made him (and not Agassiz) receptive to Darwinism.* Despite the Unitarian* environment at Harvard, Gray persisted in a tolerant but firm orthodox* Congregationalist* faith. Thus, in *Darwiniana* (1876) and other writings, Gray served as the leading American advocate for a theistic interpretation of Darwinism, in contrast to Darwin's own religious views and to the materialistic, naturalistic world view of other Darwin supporters (e.g., T. H. Huxley, Herbert Spencer).

The pre-eminent American botanist of the nineteenth century, Asa Gray's career combined an outstanding scientific reputation with an evangelical* Christian faith. He employed both in his efforts to urge the compatibility of theism with Charles Darwin's biological theory of evolution on the basis of natural selection.

BIBLIOGRAPHY. *DAB* IV; A. H. Dupree, *Asa Gray* (1959); D. N. Livingstone, *Darwin's Forgotten Defenders* (1987); J. R. Moore, *The Post-Darwinian Controversies* (1979). S. R. Pointer

Gray, James Martin (1851-1935). Reformed Episcopal* clergyman* and first dean and president of Moody Bible Institute.* Born in New York City, Gray was ordained* in 1877 in the Reformed Episcopal Church. He briefly served the Church of the Redemption, Greenpoint, New York (1878), the Church of the Cornerstone, Newburgh, New York (1879) and the First Reformed Episcopal Church, Boston (1880-1892). He was elected to the lectureship in English Bible at the Theological Seminary of the Reformed Episcopal Church in Philadelphia in 1892.

Gray first became associated with Dwight L. Moody* in 1893, when he began preaching at Moody's Northfield, Massachusetts, summer conferences. In 1904 he was selected as the first dean of the Moody Bible Institute* in Chicago, a position which he held until his death (his title was changed to president in 1925). Gray was chiefly responsible for the sharpening of the Institute's conservatism after Moody's death, especially during the fundamentalist-modernist controversies* of the 1920s. Devoted to the study of the Bible* and the defense of its verbal inspiration, he was one of the contributors to *The Fundamentals*™ (1910-1915). Gray also infused the Institute with his interest in dispensationalism* and was one of the seven editors of the *Scofield Reference Bible* (1909).

As a teacher and administrator, Gray was involved in every aspect of the Institute's life—overhauling and professionalizing the music

curriculum (he authored a number of hymns), participating in the organization and licensure of the Institute's first radio station, editing the Institute periodical, *Moody Bible Institute Monthly,* from 1907 until 1935, and introducing so-called synthetic Bible study* as a means of studying the Bible as an organic whole. Gray was also instrumental in the organization of the Evangelical Teacher Training Association in 1931.

BIBLIOGRAPHY. *DARB*; G. A. Getz, *MBI: The Story of Moody Bible Institute* (1969); W. M. Runyan, *Dr. Gray at Moody Bible Institute* (1935).

A. C. Guelzo

Great Awakening. Although the term *Great Awakening* was not used by eighteenth-century Americans, it soon came into use by historians to describe a unique wave of intercolonial religious revivals* that peaked throughout many of the colonies in the years 1740-1742. Historians described these revivals as a "Great Awakening" because they saw in those revivals novel qualities that would transform pulpit and pew in early America and that would mark the beginning of popular evangelicalism* in the American churches.

Religious revivals *per se* were not new to the eighteenth century. Indeed, since the land's first settlement, religious revivals were common occurrences. In every generation, large numbers of people (generally young adults) would experience conversion* in a concentrated period of time and enter into full church membership.* In the wide-open spaces of the New World, religious revivals functioned not only as momentous personal and spiritual experiences, but also as primary organizing devices that would bring individuals voluntarily together into a coherent community. Puritanism* itself can be considered as a great religious revival that began through the preaching* of the Word in England and traveled like fire through the towns and villages.

What then was different about the religious revivals that peaked in 1740 in conjunction with the preaching tour of England's famed revivalist George Whitefield*? First was the difference of expanse. For the most part, pre-1740 revivals were local affairs that took place within insular towns that often had little contact with one another. Occasionally outbursts of piety* and mass conversion would spill over into nearby towns—particularly in the Connecticut River Valley where Solomon Stoddard* and his grandson Jonathan Edwards* encouraged regional revivals—but they never encompassed an entire colony or group of colonies.

The second difference was in leadership. As local affairs, most revivals before 1740 were conducted by local pastors who saw in the revivals a means for reasserting their spiritual leadership and drawing their people closer together in spiritual harmony. Rarely in America would these local revivals get out of hand and move in directions the ministers* were unable to channel. There was a certain predictability and solace to these revivals, which generally occurred as large numbers of young people began having families of their own and thinking more seriously about their spiritual responsibilities. Invariably these influxes of young people were cause for unreserved celebration and happiness.

Much of this localism and harmony changed dramatically with the speaking tour of the Anglican itinerant George Whitefield. Despite Whitefield's youth (he was only twenty-four), he attracted crowds of such unprecedented size and enthusiasm that he became known as the "Grand Itinerant." First in the fields of England, and then in Scotland and America, crowds materialized out of nowhere to hear him speak in the most stirring terms about the "New Birth."* Although nominally an Anglican,* Whitefield deliberately minimized his connections to that church and spoke of his ecumenical hopes for a "revival of true and undefiled religion" in all religious groups. Promote revival he would, though in a "catholick spirit" that was decidedly Calvinist* in tone and aimed especially at listeners who would be moved by the rhetoric of total human depravity and supernatural grace. Such listeners existed in the Southern and, to a greater extent, in the Middle Colonies (especially among Presbyterians* in Pennsylvania and New Jersey), but nowhere were they more concentrated or receptive than in New England. There, in 1740, Whitefield would realize his greatest triumph as an itinerant* preacher in America.

So great was Whitefield's influence that local revivals sprang up throughout the colonies. Many of the elderly were "confirmed" in their faith, but the youth were especially moved to "Prayer and reading Books of Piety." To document this surge in popular piety, Boston's chronicler Thomas Prince* began America's first religious magazine—*The Christian History*—which collected and transmitted ministerial reports of revival as they occurred throughout the Christian world.

Through Whitefield's example many uneducated itinerant preachers surfaced in colonial America, and with their ministries there appeared unprecedented conversions *and* unprecedented controversy. Earlier revivals fostered corporate unity and stability because local ministers were able to retain their singular, unitary voice in the pulpit. But when competing speakers appeared—often from out-of-town—presenting their own schemes for "true religion" and urging listeners to separate from their local churches, unity broke down, placing established ministers in the position of defending their right to speak alone for God in public assembly. In New England, where the fires of revival burned hottest, the most notorious instance of discord and separatism* occurred when the itinerant James Davenport* led a group of New London men and women out of the established church* onto the town wharf where they proceeded to place all the great works of Puritan authors in a bonfire and burn them.

By 1743 America's clergy* were evenly split over whether the revivals were a work of God or a work of the devil. The wild accusations and theatrical antics of itinerants like James Davenport or his uneducated imitators did not instigate these divisions so much as they fixed them into opposing camps. While both sides opposed the extremes for promoting lay itinerancy and open separation, they did so for very different reasons. Opponents of the revivals, led by Boston's Charles Chauncy,* detected symptoms of mental illness throughout the ranks of their "enthusiastic" opponents, which Davenport exhibited in acute form. Supporters of the revivals, led by Northampton's Jonathan Edwards, thought Davenport was deranged and not typical of the revival impulse.

The revivals, Edwards insisted, did not have to lead to separations and discord, nor were impassioned calls for an immediate conversion experience necessarily a form of madness or hysteria. Rather, such behavior reflected "a divine and supernatural light" at work in the community. By stating their cases for and against the revivals in such extreme, polemical terms, Chauncy and Edwards made it nearly impossible for their supporters to speak with each other. Earlier generations of ministers had their debates and personality conflicts, but never before had they become the public spectacle they now were as a result of their voluminous writings and sermons for and against the revivals. To survive, the established churches in America had to achieve a rough clerical concord. If the ministers could not achieve perfect harmony, they would at least have to agree upon a common set of assumptions large enough to accommodate divergent emphases and orientations around the "head" and "heart." Opposing points of view could not be stated in extreme terms of salvation* or damnation. But in 1743 the long record of accommodation that had existed before the revivals was broken, and the results were cataclysmic.

By refusing to recognize the legitimacy of opposing views, the established American ministry temporarily lost the public trust. Once substantial numbers of ministers were labeled "unconverted" or "antinomian,"* congregations everywhere faced the terrifying prospect that their ministers—historically the prime bulwark against divine desertion—might indeed be wolves in sheep's clothing. With these developments in mind, the Great Awakening may be designated the most critical period of colonial America's intellectual and religious history. Nothing in the Glorious Revolution of 1688 came close to wreaking the internal havoc created by the ministers themselves in the midst of their heated debates. Nor would any event tip the balance of religious authority in America so firmly and decisively in the laity's direction. Suddenly it was the people—guided by their self-made leaders—who had to take responsibility for their religious lives to retain God's special favor for America.

What neither supporters not opponents of the new revivals recognized was that in publicly dividing themselves the decision for or against the revivals was no longer theirs to make. In the vacuum of leadership created by clerical discord, congregations and their lay officers made decisions for themselves. In this sense the Great Awakening represented a crucial index of democratization that would lead to the creation of "evangelical" religious movements, whose authority emerged from beneath, among ordinary people, rather than in Old World fashion from the top down.

Yet if the Great Awakening promoted discord and democratization in social and political terms, it also represented a profound spiritual movement that produced America's greatest "theologian of the heart"—Jonathan Edwards. Through his numerous treatises and printed sermons, Edwards taught a generation of evangelical ministers how to articulate their extemporaneous sermons in glowing terms that warmed the hearts of their listeners. His two most famous students—Samuel Hopkins* and Joseph Bellamy*—remained lifelong adherents of the "Edwardsean" theology (See New England Theology) and transmitted it to their postgraduate students, who in turn filled pulpits throughout New England and on the Southern and Ohio frontier. All these speakers absorbed evangelical concerns with the New Birth and, in Hopkins's

words, "a Disinterested Supream Regard to God the Attendant of True Grace." They taught that the most important quality of religious life was a direct "Experimental, Saving Knowledge" of God imparted by the Holy Spirit through evangelical preaching. Such knowledge was available to all and brought with it the responsibility to speak out and testify, regardless of social class or education. Thus alongside the social legacy of the mid-century revivals was a spiritual legacy that has endured in American religion and made the Great Awakening "great."

See also NEW LIGHTS; OLD LIGHTS; REVIVALISM; SECOND GREAT AWAKENING.

BIBLIOGRAPHY. E. S. Gaustad, *The Great Awakening in New England* (1957); C. C. Goen, *Revivalism and Separatism in New England, 1740-1800: Strict Congregationalists and Separate Baptists in the Great Awakening* (1962); P. Miller and A. Heimert, eds., *The Great Awakening: Documents Illustrating the Crisis and its Consequences* (1967); H. S. Stout, *The New England Soul* (1986).

H. S. Stout

Great Depression, The Churches and the.

The Great Depression of the 1930s marks a distinctive period in American church history. The economic upheaval and its contrast to the relative prosperity of the 1920s adversely affected the life of most churches. Church budgets became strained as members' incomes declined and charity needs increased. Massive relocation of persons in search of livelihood (such as dust-bowl migrations from the Midwest to the Pacific Coast) altered the geographic and demographic characteristics of some denominations.* Whereas most large denominations struggled to maintain their membership size and financial stability, churches of the more traditionally disinherited (such as black congregations), plus the aggressively fundamentalist* Holiness* and Pentecostal* churches, grew notably.

Distinctions among Protestants widened, moreover, as they responded to the liberal New Deal social programs identified with President Franklin D. Roosevelt. Opposition from the extreme right came from such widely followed personalities as Frank Buchman* (Moral Re-Armament Movement*) and evangelist*-journalists Gerald B. Winrod* (*The Defender* magazine) and Gerald L. K. Smith* (*Liberation* magazine). In contrast, the liberal* and Social Gospel* traditions found revival in movements associated with such leaders as activists Benson Y. Landis,* Harry F. Ward and Francis J. McConnell, preachers Ernest Fremont

Tittle* and Harry Emerson Fosdick,* and laywomen Helen Barrett Montgomery* and Lucy Waterbury Peabody. *The Christian Century** emerged as the primary periodical of liberal Protestant ecumenical* commentary, while the Federal Council of Churches* strengthened its position as facilitator of interdenominational cooperation. A variety of nondenominational movements also helped Protestants respond to the economic crisis: the National Religion and Labor Foundation, the Fellowship of Socialist Christians,* the United Council for Christian Democracy,* the Christian Social Action Movement and others.

A distinctively new Protestant thrust, however, critiqued both reactionary conservatism and idealistic liberalism. Largely an intellectual movement within academic circles, but with widespread influence, the "crisis theology" and "social realism" of Neo-Orthodoxy* sought to recover Reformation Protestant identity within the modern world. In conversation with a company of post-World War 1* European scholars (i.e., Karl Barth,* Rudolf Bultmann,* Emil Brunner,* Karl Holl, Anders Nygren), the leading American theologians included Walter Lowrie,* Douglas Horton,* Wilhelm Pauck,* Paul Tillich,* H. Richard Niebuhr* and Reinhold Niebuhr.* Their scholarly social-historical-theological endeavors, moreover, brought them into creative interaction both with New Deal policies and with religious intellectual creativity within the Jewish and Roman Catholic* traditions.

Much of the remarkable new vitality and renewal of twentieth-century American Roman Catholicism in matters of theology* (Neo-Thomism*) and liturgy* (led by Virgil Michel*), biblical and historical scholarship, and ministries of the laity* took place during the post-World War 2* years, leading to the dramatic changes following Vatican II.* During the 1930s decade of economic depression, however, these developments were anticipated by a fresh Catholic expression of social thought,* organization and action within the civil order that marked the continuing Americanization of the Church. The strong showing of New York's Catholic Governor, Alfred E. Smith, in the 1920 U.S. presidential campaign (won by Herbert Hoover), despite widespread anti-Catholic sentiment, demonstrated the growing political strength of Catholic citizens. After 1932 the New Deal program received large (though critical) Catholic support, while Catholics were appointed to key advisory and formal positions in the Roosevelt administration.

The papal encyclical* *Quadragesimo Anno** (1931), plus such strong social-economic reform statements by the American bishops* through the Social Action Department (*See* Bishop's Program of Social Reconstruction) of the National Catholic Welfare Conference* (led by Monsignor John Ryan,* "The Right Reverend Mr. New Dealer") as "Organized Social Justice" (1936) presented the Church's dominant social teachings applied to contemporary problems. Catholic social commentary appeared regularly in such journals as *America, Guildsman, Commonweal* and *Catholic World.* In 1937 the Association of Catholic Trade Unionists was formed to support union objectives and promote Catholic social teachings. Among dissenting conservative voices was that of reactionary Charles Coughlin,* the "Radio Priest" who moved away from a liberal social justice advocacy to oppose New Dealism with racist and anti-Semitic overtones. A popular radical "leftist" social thrust emerged among the laity with the Catholic Worker Movement,* led and personified primarily by the journalist Dorothy Day,* featuring Houses of Hospitality offering "works of mercy" in urban slum areas, rural farm communes, nonviolent "direct action" participation in labor and other protests, and *The Catholic Worker* newspaper of social commentary.

World War 2 brought an end to the Great Depression and fueled revolutionary social forces on a global scale. The American churches emerged from the experience with a chastened and more mature determination to engage the modern social-intellectual-technocratic world with effective Christian faith and order, life and thought.

BIBLIOGRAPHY. S. E. Ahlstrom, *A Religious History of the American People* (1972); P. A. Carter, *The Decline and Revival of the Social Gospel, 1920-1940* (1956); D. B. Myer, *The Protestant Search for Political Realism, 1919-1941* (1961); D. J. O'Brien, *American Catholics and Social Reform: The New Deal Years* (1960); M. Piehl, *Breaking Bread: The Catholic Worker and the Origins of Catholic Radicalism in America* (1982).

E. G. Ernst

Greater Europe Mission. Evangelical,* nondenominational mission* agency. The Greater Europe Mission (GEM) was founded by Robert P. Evans, a World War 2* Navy chaplain* who, while in a French hospital recovering from injuries he suffered during the Normandy invasion, became aware of the spiritual needs of the European continent. Subsequent service with Youth for Christ* led him to believe that the best way for North Americans to help would be to start more schools that would train Europeans to evangelize* and disciple* their own peoples.

In 1949 Evans moved with his wife to Paris and founded European Bible Institute as the first ministry of GEM, a nondenominational, North American-staffed and supported mission. By the mid-1960s there were ninety missionaries. Evans continued as the European director of GEM through 1985. The Paris venture (which moved in 1960 to Lamorlaye) was the first of ten schools, each having the long-range goal of becoming a European-led, staffed and supported institution. They are located in Austria, France, West Germany, Greece, Italy, Portugal, Spain, Sweden and Belgium. In addition, seminary*-level schools were founded in West Germany (1974), Belgium (1979) and Tyndale Seminary in the Netherlands (1985), the latter being an international, English-language school following the North American pattern.

More than 2,000 Europeans have been trained at GEM schools and more than 700 are currently in residence, with many more in extension programs. In most countries, GEM maintains the only nondenominational Bible institute* or seminary. Soon after its founding, GEM realized that North Americans could also help plant evangelical churches in Europe, but so far only a few churches have become fully self-supporting. Nevertheless, church planting has become an increasing emphasis, especially in cooperation with existing European groups. Currently nearly half of GEM's some 250 missionaries serving in Europe are involved more with evangelistic than educational ministries.

BIBLIOGRAPHY. R. P. Evans, *Let Europe Hear* (1963); A. V. Koop, *American Evangelical Missionaries in France, 1945-1975* (1986).

D. G. Tinder

Greek Orthodox Archdiocese of North and South America. The largest Orthodox* jurisdiction in the U.S. In 1768 a colony containing many indentured servants who were Greek Orthodox from the Ottoman Empire was established near St. Augustine, Florida, and from 1794 missionaries* from the Orthodox Church of Russia were at work in Alaska. However, the actual growth of Orthodox Christianity in the U.S. began to occur in the years following the American Civil War.* Under the direction of Orthodox merchants, diplomats and immigrants of various ethnic backgrounds, early parishes* were established in New Orleans in 1864, San Francisco in 1867 and New York City in 1870.

The growth in the number of parishes serving the specific needs of Greek Orthodox in America took place in the wake of the massive influx of immigrants from Greece and Asia Minor between the years 1880 and 1920. By this time there were about 150 parishes located throughout the U.S. These early parishes were served by priests* who came to this country with the approval of their ecclesiastical superiors either in the Patriarchate of Constantinople or in the Church of Greece. Throughout this early period there was no resident Greek Orthodox bishop* to unify or to direct the parishes in accordance with canon law.*

The patriarchate of Constantinople affirmed its ecclesiastical authority* over the Orthodox in America in 1908 but at the same time, perhaps due to political developments in the Balkans, temporarily transferred the authority to organize the Greek-American Orthodox parishes to the Church of Greece. In 1918 Metropolitan Meletios (Metaxakis)* of Athens came to America with plans to organize the parishes into an archdiocese. In 1921 the Greek Orthodox Archdiocese was formally incorporated in New York during the second visit of Metropolitan Meletios. In the same year he was elected patriarch of Constantinople. One of his first acts was to reverse the decision of 1908 and restore jurisdiction of the Orthodox in America to the Patriarchate of Constantinople.

In 1922 the Archdiocese of North and South America was canonically established, thereby sanctioning the earlier civil incorporation, and Archbishop* Alexander (Demoglou) (1876-1942) was elected as its first archbishop, with his see in New York. Other bishoprics were established in Chicago, Boston and San Francisco. While Meletios may have envisioned a unified archdiocese uniting all Orthodox parishes in the Americas, the particular needs of the Greek immigrants precluded this possibility.

In the wake of the wars in the Balkans, the Greek immigrants in America were deeply divided over political differences between the Royalists and the Republicans in their mother country. These differences often manifested themselves within the parishes. When Metropolitan Athenagoras (Spyrou)* of Kerkyera (Corfu) was elected as the new archbishop in 1930, his principal task was to bring unity to the Greek Orthodox in America. During his eighteen years as archbishop, Athenagoras succeeded in uniting the parishes and in establishing a college and theological school, an orphanage, a national church magazine and a national association of women known as the Philoptochos Society. He also encouraged greater unity among all the Orthodox jurisdictions in America. Athenagoras was elected the Patriarch of Constantinople in 1948.

During the period from 1949 to 1958, when Archbishop Michael (Konstantinides or Constantinides*) served as head of the Archdiocese, important demographic changes began to take place: new parishes were established in the suburbs, the majority of the members were now persons born and raised in the U.S. and not all were of Greek ethnic background. Reflecting these developments, there was a growing desire for a national youth organization and for church-school programs and religious literature in the English language. There were also those who called for the greater use of English in liturgical services. This development, however, did not take place formally until the mid-1960s.

Known for his special interest in ecumenical relations and social concern, Archbishop Iakovos* (Coucouzis) has headed the Archdiocese since 1959. It now consists of about 500 parishes and claims two million communicants throughout the U.S., Canada and Central and South America. In addition to the archdiocesan see, there are ten dioceses headed by a bishop. Clergy* and lay* representatives meet biannually. The entire Archdiocese is a province of the Patriarchate of Constantinople. As its exarch in the Americas, Iakovos also presides over the Standing Council of Canonical Orthodox Bishops,* which brings together the presiding hierarchs from nine other Orthodox jurisdictions. Theologians* of the Archdiocese are active in bilateral dialogs, in the National Council of Churches* and in the World Council of Churches.* The Archdiocese is a major sponsor of missionary work in Africa, Korea and Indonesia.

BIBLIOGRAPHY. M. Efthimiou, ed., *A History of the Greek Orthodox Church* (1984); F. Litsas, ed., *A Companion to the Greek Orthodox Church* (1984); G. Papaioannou, *From Mars Hill to Manhattan* (1976).   T. E. FitzGerald

Green, William Henry (1825-1900). Presbyterian* theologian.* Educated at Lafayette College (A.B., 1840) and Princeton Theological Seminary* (1846), Green joined the Princeton faculty in 1851, beginning a career of teaching in Old Testament and Semitic studies. He wrote extensively and almost exclusively in his field of specialization and until his death was chairman of the Old Testament section of the committee that produced the American Revised Version (1901) of the Bible. In 1868 he was elected president of Princeton University* but declined to accept. In 1891 he served as the moderator of the General Assembly* of the Presbyterian Church in the U.S.A.*

Like his other "Old" Princeton colleagues, he was firmly committed to the divine inspiration and inerrancy* of Scripture.* He was resolute in his opposition to the mounting influence of biblical criticism* in America. Among his contemporaries he took the lead in refuting the documentary hypothesis of the origin of the Pentateuch. These emphases were reflected in his two-volume *General Introduction to the Old Testament* (1898) and *The Higher Criticism of the Pentateuch* (1895).

BIBLIOGRAPHY. *DAB* IV; M. Noll, *Between Faith and Criticism* (1986); "The Jubilee of Prof. William Henry Green," *PPR* 7 (1896) 507-521.
R. B. Gaffin

Grellet, Stephen (1773-1855). Quaker* minister,* missionary* and evangelical* social reformer. Born in Limoges, France, Grellet studied at the College of the Oratorians in Lyon but became disenchanted with Roman Catholicism.* A refugee of the French Revolution, Grellet escaped imprisonment and fled via Amsterdam and Guyana, arriving in New York in 1795.

Grellet was greatly influenced by his reading of William Penn's *No Cross, No Crown* and converted to Quakerism while listening to Deborah Derby of Coalbrookdale, England. Joining the Friends* in 1796, he became a missionary. Grellet's missionary journeys extended from Haiti to Scandinavia, Russia, the Mediterranean and all of Europe, with the lone exception of Denmark. By the end of his career he had stood before most of the crown heads of Europe, pleading the cause of the poor, the sick and the imprisoned. His concern for the women prisoners of London's Newgate Prison prompted Elizabeth Fry to begin her prison-reform work. Grellet's concern for the young people living in London's streets prompted the first sociological investigation of juvenile delinquency.

Grellet became one of America's greatest Quaker leaders. Most English-speaking people have heard his famous prayer: "I expect to pass through this world but once. Any good, therefore, that I can do, or any kindness that I can show to any fellow creature, let me do it now. Let me not delay it nor neglect it, for I shall not pass this way again."

BIBLIOGRAPHY. W. W. Comfort, *Stephen Grellet* (1942); *DAB* IV; B. Seebohm, ed., *Memoirs of the Life and Gospel Labours of Stephen Grellet* (1860).   R. E. Selleck

Grenfell, Wilfred Thomason (1865-1940). Missionary* to Labrador. Born in England and trained as a physician at London Hospital and London University, Grenfell was influenced to become a medical missionary by a Dwight L.

Moody* campaign.

After five years ministering to deep-sea fishermen across the Atlantic, he visited Labrador in 1892 and resolved to devote his life to alleviating the misery of the poor folk there. Beyond numerous persons converted or strengthened in the faith, his over forty years of labor produced six hospitals, seven nursing stations, four hospital ships, four boarding schools, twelve clothing-distribution centers, about a dozen cooperative stores, a cooperative lumber mill, a dry dock and a YMCA/YWCA. He also developed cottage industries and directed the first mapping of the Newfoundland coast. Grenfell's books and his visits to Britain, Canada and the U. S. raised funds for the mission and brought him acclaim. Among other honors, he was awarded Oxford's first honorary M.D. in 1907 and was knighted in 1927.

BIBLIOGRAPHY. W. T. Grenfell, *A Labrador Doctor* (1920); J. L. Kerr, *Wilfred Grenfell: His Life and Work* (1959). J. G. Stackhouse

Griffin, Edward Dorr (1770-1837). Congregational* minister* and president of Williams College. The son of a prosperous Connecticut farmer, Griffin graduated from Yale* with honors. He began studying law but turned to theology* after suffering a major illness in 1791. He held Congregational pastorates in New Salem and New Hartford, Connecticut, as well as in New Orange and Newark, New Jersey. At the opening of trinitarian Andover Seminary* in 1808, Griffin became professor of pulpit eloquence. In that same year, Union College conferred on him the D.D.

From 1811 to 1814 he served as pastor* of Park Street Congregational Church in Boston and built its reputation as a bulwark of trinitarian theology. His doctrinal series on total depravity, regeneration,* election* and perseverance, delivered in the winter of 1812-1813, was published as *Park Street Lectures.* In February 1812, Griffin assisted at Salem in the ordination of the first overseas missionaries of the American Board of Commissioners for Foreign Missions* to Asia. In his final years he effectively served as president of Williams College (1821-1836), where he enlarged the curriculum and injected evangelical* fervor.

BIBLIOGRAPHY. P. Cooke, *Recollections of Rev. E. D. Griffin* (1855); *DAB* IV; H. C. Englizian, *Brimstone Corner: Park Street Church* (1968); W. B. Sprague, *Memoir of the Rev. Edward D. Griffin, D.D.* (1839); *NCAB* 6. D. G. Buss

Grimké, Sarah Moore (1792-1873) and Angelina Grimké Weld (1805-1879). Quaker* abolitionists* and women's rights activists. Born into a wealthy slaveholding family in Charleston, South Carolina, the sisters' abolitionist convictions took root after they left the Episcopal Church to become Quakers and became members of Philadelphia's antislavery Quaker community in the 1820s. In 1836 they moved to New York and began a career mobilizing women for the abolitionist cause.

Angelina's popular tract, *An Appeal to the Christian Women of the South* (1836), was widely read in the North and publicly burned in Charleston. She addressed the first Anti-Slavery Convention of American Women in 1837. In 1838, in Massachusetts, she became the first woman to address an American legislature. The Grimké sisters, with their plain Quaker bonnets and their firsthand testimonials of slavery, became popular public speakers, touring New England as agents of the American Anti-Slavery Society in 1837. In response, however, the Massachusetts General Association of Congregationalist* Ministers* issued a pastoral letter condemning the unfeminine practice of platform oratory. Sarah responded with a lengthy biblical defense, *Letters on the Equality of the Sexes, and the Condition of Women* (1838).

Convinced that abolitionism and women's rights were inseparable humanitarian causes, the sisters remained loyal to William Lloyd Garrison's radical, broad-based American Anti-Slavery Society when the movement split over the issue in 1839. Angelina married the prominent abolitionist Theodore Weld* in 1838. After the wedding, the sisters settled into domestic life, and their public career faded somewhat, although they assisted Weld in his monumental and sensational survey of *Slavery As It Is* (1839).

BIBLIOGRAPHY. C. H. Birney, *The Grimké Sisters: Sarah and Angelina Grimké* (1885); *DAB* IV; *DARB*; B. G. Hersh, *The Slavery of Sex: Feminist-Abolitionists in America* (1978); G. Lerner, *The Grimké Sisters from South Carolina* (1967); K. D. Lumpkin, *The Emancipation of Angelina Grimké* (1974); *NCAB* 2; *NAW* 2. M. L. Bendroth

Griswold, Alexander Viets (1766-1843). Episcopal* bishop* of the Eastern Diocese.* Born in Simsbury, Connecticut, the son of Elisha and Eunice Viets Griswold, Griswold was raised an Episcopalian. He was educated by his uncle, Roger Viets, rector at Simsbury. In 1785 he married Elizabeth Mitchelson, which prevented him from entering Yale* as he had planned. Until 1794 he cultivated a small farm and read law. In that year he presented himself for orders and began serving as lay-reader* at three small churches in Litchfield

County, Connecticut. He was ordained* deacon* on June 7, 1795, at Stratford, by Bishop Samuel Seabury* and took charge of the churches at Plymouth, Harwinton and Litchfield. On October 1, 1795, at St. Matthew's, Plymouth, he was ordained priest* by Bishop Seabury.

In 1804 he became the rector of St. Michael's Church, Bristol, Rhode Island. Outside of Connecticut the Episcopal Church was not strong in New England, and on May 29, 1810, at a convention in Boston, representatives of the Church in New Hampshire, Vermont, Massachusetts and Rhode Island organized the Eastern Diocese, and on May 31 they elected Griswold to be its bishop. He was consecrated* at Trinity Church, New York, on May 29, 1811, by Bishop William White* of Pennsylvania and so became the first and only bishop of the Eastern Diocese. He continued to serve as rector at Bristol until 1830, when he took charge of St. Peter's Church, Salem, Massachusetts. In 1835 he resigned this charge and devoted himself wholly to his episcopal work. On the death of Bishop White, he became the fifth presiding bishop of the Episcopal Church, serving from July 17, 1836, until his death at Boston on February 15, 1843. After Griswold's death the Eastern Diocese, having grown under his care, was divided into five dioceses.

Griswold is credited with recreating the Episcopal Church in New England, outside of Connecticut, following the Revolutionary War.* A number of his sermons and addresses were published. Perhaps his most significant work was *The Reformation, A Brief Exposition of Some of the Errors and Corruptions of the Church of Rome* (1843), which expressed his concern about the progress of the Oxford Movement. As a moderate evangelical* he stressed the teachings of the gospel rather than the distinctive doctrines of the Episcopal Church.

BIBLIOGRAPHY. *AAP* 5; *DAB* IV; *DARB*; W. W. Manross, "Alexander Viets Griswold and the Eastern Diocese," *HMPEC* 4 (1935):13-25; *NCAB* 4; J. S. Stone, *Memoir of the Life of the Rt. Rev. Alexander Viets Griswold* (1844).

D. S. Armentrout

Grundtvig, (N)ikolai (F)rederik (S)everin (1783-1872). Danish Lutheran* theologian,* hymnwriter and minister.* Nikolai was the youngest of Pastor Johan Ottosen and Catherine Marie (Bang) Grundtvig's four children. He received his divinity degree from the University of Copenhagen (1803). Religious crises punctuated Grundtvig's theological development. In *The Rejoinder of the Church* (1825), he set out his position which gave

authority* to the Apostles' Creed over the Bible* and emphasized baptism* over conversion*—a view that alienated him from pietistic Lutherans. His positive view of the relation of Christianity to secular culture was evident in his interest in Norse and Anglo-Saxon literature and his efforts on behalf of folk schools. He is also well known as a hymnwriter and poet. The Christianity of those influenced by Grundtvig was characterized by "joy of life, openness and freedom." Though he never visited America, Grundtvig exerted his influence in American religion primarily among Lutheran "happy Danes" (Danish Evangelical Lutheran Church in America), though it was also felt in some Norwegian-American Lutheran circles.

BIBLIOGRAPHY. N. L. Jensen, ed., *A Grundtvig Antholoy* (1984); G. E. Arden, *Four Northern Lights: Men Who Shaped Scandinavian Churches* (1964).

L. D. Lagerquist

Gulick, Orramel H. (1830-1923). Congregational* missionary* to Japan. Born in Hawaii to one of the pioneer missionaries who had helped convert* the whole leadership of the islands, Gulick served there for some time and then in 1869 was assigned with his wife to Japan by the American Board of Commissioners for Foreign Missions.* His language instructor became, in 1872, the first Japanese Protestant* martyr, when officials learned of his faith. The Gulicks settled in Osaka in 1873, where two years later he started Japan's first Christian periodical, the eight-page *Shichi Ichi Zappo* (*Weekly Miscellany*), which initiated a vigorous tradition of Christian journalism. After a number of postings in Japan, Gulick was reassigned to Hawaii in 1894, where he finished sixty years of evangelistic work. His nephew, Sidney Gulick, became well known for his books about Japan and in particular for his efforts to ameliorate worsening relations between America and Japan right before World War 2.*

BIBLIOGRAPHY. O. Cary, *History of Christianity in Japan,* vol. 2 (1909); W. T. Thomas: *Protestant Beginnings in Japan* (1959).

J. F. Howes

Gunsaulus, Frank Wakeley (1856-1921). Congregational* minister,* author and educator. Born in Chesterville, Ohio, Gunsaulus graduated from Ohio Wesleyan University (1875). Ordained* a Methodist* minister (1875), he preached a circuit of Methodist churches until 1879, when he entered the Congregational ministry. The publication of *The Metamorphoses of a Creed* (1879) marked his transition toward theological liberalism.* Moving to Chicago after several eastern pastorates, he gained national renown at Plymouth Congregational Church (1887-1899) and the nondenominational Central Church (1899-1919), which met in Louis Sullivan's Auditorium. A sermon at Plymouth on how he would use a million dollars led Philip D. Armour to found the Armour (later Illinois) Institute of Technology, over which Gunsaulus presided from 1893 till his death. A great orator, he was preacher at the Congregational National Council (1895) and gave the Beecher Lectures at Yale* Divinity School (*The Minister and the Spiritual Life,* 1911). A lover of art, music and books, he used the proceeds from lectures for collections left to the Chicago Art Institute and University of Chicago.

BIBLIOGRAPHY. E. Bancroft, *Dr. Gunsaulus: The Citizen* (1921); *DAB* IV.   J. H. Dorn

Gurney, Joseph John (1788-1847).

Quaker* leader, banker and philanthropist.* Born in Norwich, England, a descendant of Quaker theologian* Robert Barclay, as a young man Gurney spent a short period at Oxford University. In 1818, at age twenty-nine, he became a recorded Quaker minister.*

Gurney's theology was evangelical* in orientation, and it stressed the authority of the Scriptures* and the importance of Christ's atonement.* While he adopted many elements from evangelical revivalism,* promoting Bible study* and evangelism,* he did so without sacrificing such traditional Quaker doctrines as pacifism,* plain dress and worship* in silence.

In 1837 Gurney undertook a three-year trip to North America and the West Indies, visiting numerous Quaker meetings, holding a religious service attended by President Van Buren and members of Congress in the U.S. Capitol, and lobbying hard but unsuccessfully with Henry Clay and John Calhoun to bring about an end to slavery* in the U. S. But American Quakers became embroiled in bitter disputes over his theology and ecumenical activities, resulting in schisms in New England and Ohio (Orthodox) Yearly Meetings in 1845 and 1855, after Gurney had returned to England (*See* Gurneyites).

In his home country Gurney was a patron of the British and Foreign Bible Society, a member of the nonconformist Lancastrian school movement and an associate of William Wilberforce in the British antislavery movement. His sister was the prison reformer Elizabeth Fry. As a banker and a humanitarian, Gurney had a broader appeal than many of his co-religionists and was able to commend a warm Quaker spirituality to many who could not accept the sectarianism of traditional Quakers. Gurney, the leading evangelical Quaker theologian of the first half of the nineteenth century, was to leave his impression upon a segment of the Quaker tradition now best represented in the Evangelical Friends Alliance and the Friends United Meeting.

See also FRIENDS, SOCIETY OF; GURNEYITES.

BIBLIOGRAPHY. D. E. Swift, *Joseph John Gurney: Banker, Reformer, and Quaker* (1962).
                                        S. W. Angell

Gurneyites.

A branch of the Religious Society of Friends* (Quakers). Gurneyites were those Quakers who derived their designation from the British Quaker minister,* banker and abolitionist,* Joseph John Gurney,* who paid an influential visit to America in 1837-1840. A descendant of the seventeenth-century Quaker theologian Robert Barclay, Gurney was easily the most theologically astute Quaker after Barclay. Providing his contemporaries with fresh interpretations of basic Quaker doctrines, he sparked a great revival of interest in Bible study* and religious and philanthropic* work of all kinds.

Gurneyites were sympathetic to Protestant evangelicalism* and eventually adopted revivalistic* methods and the pastoral* system. Previously Quakers had relied on itinerant, untrained and unsalaried ministers (though their expenses were paid). Modern descendants of the Gurneyites are included in the Evangelical Friends Alliance and Friends United Meeting which, between them, include 69,000 of the total 112,000 American Quakers.

BIBLIOGRAPHY. E. Russell, *The History of Quakerism* (1942).   R. E. Selleck

Guyart, Marie de l'Incarnation (1599-1672).

Pioneer Ursuline* missionary* and mystic. Born at Tours, France, Marie was the fourth child of Florent and Jeanne (Michelet) Guyart. Although she desired to be a nun, she submitted to her parents' wishes and in 1617 she married Claude Martin. At twenty she was a widow with an infant son, Claude.

The first of her mystical experiences occurred in 1620, and the account of her interior life, considered a spiritual classic, is found in her *Relations* of 1633 and 1654. In 1631 she entered the Ursuline Order at Tours, taking the name of Marie de l'Incarnation. With two other nuns* and their lay* benefactor, Madeleine de la Peltrie, she departed for Canada in 1639. When they arrived on August 1, the Ursulines immediately received both French and Native American girls in a school conducted in their two-room home.

At Quebec Mere Marie built a European-style monastery and recruited French nuns for the first institute for women's education in Canada. She assiduously studied native languages and edited catechisms in Huron and Algonquin, as well as an Algonquin dictionary. Although her linguistic works are lost, her spiritual writings have been preserved, chiefly through the efforts of her son and first biographer. Her correspondence provides important sources for the early history of Canada. In 1980 she was beatified* by John Paul II.*

BIBLIOGRAPHY. M. de l'I. Guyart, *Ecrits spirituels et historiques,* ed. A. Jamet (1929); G. M. Oury, *Marie de l'Incarnation, 1599-1672,* 2 vols. (1973). P. Byrne

H

Haas, Francis Joseph (1889-1953). Catholic labor priest* and bishop* of Grand Rapids. Born of Irish and German parentage in Racine, Wisconsin, the second of seven children, Haas attended parish* and public schools in Racine and then transferred to St. Francis Seminary in Milwaukee and was ordained* a priest in 1913. He received a Ph.D. in sociology from The Catholic University of America* in 1922, studying under Fathers John O'Grady and John A. Ryan* and publishing a dissertation on collective bargaining procedures in the men's garment industry. He was then assigned to the faculty of St. Francis Seminary, was director of the National Catholic School of Social Service in Washington from 1931 to 1935, rector* of St. Francis Seminary from 1935 to 1937 and dean of the School of Social Science at Catholic University from 1937 to 1943. In 1943 he was named bishop of Grand Rapids, Michigan.

A staunch supporter of organized labor and of government assistance to the poor, Haas was appointed to numerous government positions during the New Deal years of Franklin Roosevelt. He was a member of the Labor Advisory Board of the National Recovery Administration, the National Labor Board and the Wisconsin Labor Relations Board, and he was chairman of the Fair Employment Practices Committee in 1943. As Special Commissioner of Conciliation for the Department of Labor, he mediated some of the nation's most nettlesome strikes during that turbulent period.

Liberal in political and economic matters, Haas was conservative theologically. He was comfortable with traditional Church teachings and structures, saw no need for major change and was unhesitatingly loyal to the Holy See. His episcopal* administration was traditional rather than innovative, and he inaugurated an extensive building program to keep pace with the expanding Catholic population of Grand Rapids. Even as bishop he continued his work in labor relations and civil rights, and at his death on August 29, 1953, he was revered by many as "the big friend of the little guy."

BIBLIOGRAPHY. F. J. Kennedy, "Bishop Haas," *The Salesianum* 39 (1944):714; T. E. Blantz, "Francis J. Haas: Priest and Government Servant," *CHR* 57 (1972): 571-592; and T. E. Blantz, *A Priest in Public Service: Francis J. Haas and the New Deal* (1982).   T. E. Blantz

Hague, Dyson (1857-1935). Canadian Anglican* minister.* Born in Toronto, Hague attended the University of Toronto and Wycliffe College. After his ordination* in 1883, he was rector* of a number of Anglican churches, including St. James' Cathedral in Toronto. From 1897 to 1901 he was professor of apologetics,* liturgics* and pastoral theology* at Wycliffe College, Toronto. He published several books on the English Reformation, notably *The Church of England before the Reformation* (1897) and *The Story of the English Prayer Book* (1926). His extensive writings also included books and pamphlets, and a contribution to *The Fundamentals* (1910-1917), establishing him as one of the most influential evangelicals* within the Church of England and a leader of Canadian fundamentalism.*   P. D. Airhart

Haldeman, (I)saac (M)assey (1845-1933). Baptist* pastor.* Born in Concordville, Pennsylvania, Haldeman received his education at West Chester Academy and was ordained* to the Baptist ministry* in 1870. After serving Northern Baptist churches in Chadds Ford, Pennsylvania (1871-1875), and Wilmington, Delaware (1875-1884), he was called to the First Baptist Church of New York City, where he remained until his death nearly fifty years later.

Because Haldeman was an outstanding pulpit orator, his parishioners often found standing room only at the rear of the church. Haldeman was deeply commited to the fundamentalist* crusade against "worldliness" in any of its forms but especially the theater. As a dispensationalist* he had radical views of cultural pessimism. In *The Signs of the Times* (1910), he provided a popular reading of prophecy and current events, indicating that the end of history was near. Haldeman had no time for reform movements, arguing that such efforts were like setting staterooms in order as the ship sinks.

Haldeman was also active in the fundamentalist-modernist controversy,* contending with fellow Baptists Cornelius Woelfkin, Harry Emerson Fosdick* and Walter Rauschenbusch.* He authored scores of books and pamphlets, most of which were derived from sermons preached in his church. In 1909 William Jewel College conferred on him an honorary degree of D.D.

BIBLIOGRAPHY. G. Marsden, *Fundamentalism and American Culture* (1980); *NCAB* 15.

P. C. Wilt

Hale, Edward Everett (1822-1909). Unitarian* minister, author and reformer. Hale was born into a prominent Boston family, his father being the editor of a Whig newspaper, the *Daily Advertiser.* His mother, a writer, named her son for her brother, Edward Everett, a minister, orator and politician. Though Hale inclined to enter the ministry* after his graduation from Harvard* in 1839, he worried that the clerical profession might restrict his interests and delayed his ordination* until 1846, when he settled at the Church of the Unity in Worcester, Massachusetts. During his pastorate, he opposed slavery by sponsoring Northern settlers to Kansas. In 1856, he moved to the South Congregational Church in Boston, where he remained until his retirement in 1899.

Hale was exceedingly active in ecclesiastical, political, social and literary affairs. Though he admired Emerson,* Hale was a moderate Unitarian who helped found the National Conference of Unitarian Churches, in 1865, to restrict the influence of Transcendentalism* and later forms of religious radicalism. He served on the Sanitary Commission* during the Civil War* and later acted as chaplain* of the U. S. Senate (1903-1909). Among many causes, he worked for African-American education, Native American rights and the Associated Charities of Boston. He was a prolific author of fiction and historical works, and edited *Old and New* (1869-1874), a journal of religion and culture. One story, *Ten Times One Is Ten* (1870), inspired the establishment of "Lend a Hand" clubs nationwide that aimed to promote benevolence. He was best known for his patriotic story, *The Man Without a Country* (1863). Hale's career epitomizes the way nineteenth-century liberal Protestants* adapted secular means to apply religious principles to social issues.

BIBLIOGRAPHY. *DAB* IV; E. E. Hale, *The Works of Edward Everett Hale,* 10 vols. (1898-1901); E. E. Hale, Jr., *The Life and Letters of Edward Everett Hale,* 2 vols. (1917); J. Holloway, *Edward Everett Hale; A Biography* (1956).

A. C. Rose

Hale, Sarah Josepha Buell (1788-1879). Magazine editor. Born in Newport, New Hampshire, and educated at home, Sarah Buell taught school until she married David Hale, a lawyer, in 1813. When he died in 1822 she was left with five children and so began a literary career. While working in a milliner's shop, she published moderately successful novels and poems (including "Mary's Lamb") until in 1827 she moved to Boston to become editor of the *American Ladies' Magazine.* In 1837 she became editor of *Godey's Lady's Book,* based in Philadelphia. As editor of *Godey's* from 1837 to 1877, Mrs. Hale became the popular arbiter of feminine taste. In her editorials she articulated a genteel feminism, arguing that women, gifted with superior piety* and tact, possessed a primary calling to the home and not to the public realm. But Hale championed the cause of women's education as a means of fulfilling their high calling and encouraged careers for women in education, foreign missions* and medicine. She served as an officer in the Woman's Union Missionary Society and the Ladies' Medical Missionary Society of Philadelphia.

BIBLIOGRAPHY. *DAB* IV; *NAW* 2.

M. L. Bendroth

Half-Way Covenant. Modified colonial Congregational* church membership* requirements. By 1636 New England Congregationalists agreed that only "elect"* or regenerate individuals merited church membership. Only these church members, in turn, were allowed to present their children for baptism.* Within a few years, however, the elders faced an unforeseen corollary to the question of baptism. What was the status of a child whose parents had been baptized in infancy but had never experienced conversion* upon attaining adulthood? Did the children of baptized but unregenerate parents retain a right to baptism? Nearly all of the ministers assembled at the Cambridge Synods of 1646-1649 agreed on the need to extend baptism to this group, but a minority of dissenters prevented the elders from adding the provision to the *Cambridge Platform* (1649) of church government.*

With each passing year the issue became more acute, as increasing numbers of baptized but unregenerate parents came before their churches and, citing the ministers' own justifications and conclusions, demanded baptism for their new-borns. The ministers recognized that eventually they would have to make another attempt to alter church procedures. They responded in 1656 by assembling seventeen clergymen in Boston to debate the issues. Their conclusion, *A Disputation concerning Church-Members and their Children in Answer to XXI Questions,* published in London in 1659 and commended to the churches by the General Court, contained a full endorsement of what opponents later derisively labeled the "Half-Way Covenant."

Under its provisions, the innovation allowed unregenerate children of regenerate parents to baptize their offspring, providing they led an upright life and agreed to own the church cove-nant before the assembled congregation. As adults, all "half-way" members assumed the responsibili-ties of mutual watchfulness incumbent upon those engaged in the church covenant, but did not enjoy the privileges of voting or participation in the Lord's Supper* unless they experienced conver-sion and became full members. The measure thus brought the children under church discipline* without corrupting church purity. These same principles were reaffirmed in a much larger assembly of ministers and lay delegates which convened in Boston at the "Half-Way Synod" of 1662.

Despite these ministerial pronouncements, lay opposition initially prevented most churches from implementing the Half-Way Covenant. A small but influential group of clergymen, led by New Haven pastor John Davenport,* pointed out that for decades ministers had warned churchgoers to avoid sinful "innovations" in church practice and to adhere to the letter of the *Cambridge Platform.* The Half-Way Covenant clearly represented a departure from standard New England practices. Eventually nearly every church in New England adopted the Half-Way Covenant. But as late as 1700, one-fifth of the churches in Massachusetts still refused to practice the measure, and some held out until the 1730s. Though most church-goers favored the change, disputes over the innovation sometimes became ferocious, leading, for example, to formal separations in the First Churches of Hartford and Boston, the most impor-tant churches in the colonies of Connecticut and Massachusetts. Indeed, no previous question of church order or doctrine had so badly divided ministers and laypeople.* The issue would surface again during the Great Awakening* and in the celebrated dispute between Jonathan Edwards* and his Northampton congregation.

See also CHURCH MEMBERSHIP; COVENANT THEOLOGY; DISCIPLINE, CHURCH; NEW ENGLAND WAY.

BIBLIOGRAPHY. R. Pope, *The Half-Way Covenant* (1969); E. S. Morgan, *Visible Saints: The History of a Puritan Idea* (1963); P. Miller, *The New England Mind: From Colony to Province* (1953); W. Walker, *The Creeds and Platforms of Congregationalism* (1960). J. F. Cooper

Hall, John (1829-1898). Presbyterian* preach-er.* Born in County Armagh, Ireland, of Scotch-Irish descent, Hall received his education at the Royal College, Belfast, graduating in 1845, and received his theological training at the Irish Presbyterian General Assembly's seminary, gradu-ating in 1849. From 1849 to 1852, he was a "Student's Missionary" and temperance advocate in County Connaught, Ireland. In 1852, he became pastor of First Presbyterian Church of Armagh, remaining there until 1858, when he moved to Mary's Abbey Presbyterian Church in Dublin. Hall remained in Dublin until 1867, when as a fraternal delegate to the General Assembly of the Presbyte-rian Church in the United States,* he received a call to the Fifth Avenue Presbyterian Church in New York City. It grew to become the largest congrega-tion in the city, and Hall remained there until his death.

Hall was a gifted preacher, but he was especially noted for his pastoral labors, including an exten-sive program of regular visitation to each family in his large congregation. His theology* was conser-vative, which led to opposition from a minority in his church during his latter years. In 1875 he delivered Yale's* Lyman Beecher Lecture, pub-lished as *God's Word Through Preaching* (1875). From 1882 to 1891 he was chancellor of the University of the City of New York. Hall published a number of his sermons and several other devo-tional books, and was a regular contributor to religious periodicals.

BIBLIOGRAPHY. *DAB* IV; T. C. Hall, *John Hall, Pastor and Preacher* (1901).

J. R. Wiers

Hallelujah. An expression of praise to God used formally and informally in numerous Christian traditions. The word literally means "praise ye Yah," and is translated to mean "praise the Lord" or "praise God." It appears throughout the Psalms, particularly Psalms 111—117, indicating wide usage in Hebrew liturgy. The "Alleluia" was used early in the church as a hymn of praise and celebration. In many Protestant* churches, partic-ularly in America, *hallelujah* is used as a spontaneous expression of praise, adoration or spiritual ecstasy. In numerous evangelical* traditions it is a favorite response of the newly converted and other members of the worshiping community.

B. J. Leonard

Hallinan, Paul John (1911-1968). Archbishop* of Atlanta. Born in Ohio and educated at Notre Dame University* (B.A., 1932), Hallinan entered St. Mary's Seminary in Cleveland and was ordained* a priest* in 1937. He was involved in pastoral work in Cleveland until 1942, when he became a chaplain* in the U.S. Army. Serving in the Far East until 1945, he earned a Purple Heart. On return to his diocese* he became archdiocesan director of the Newman Clubs,* served as chaplain at Western Reserve University and became national chaplain of the Newman Clubs in 1952. Ordained bishop of Charleston, South Carolina, in 1958, he became the first Archbishop of Atlanta when it became an archdiocese in 1962. Hallinan was active in efforts to end racial segregation in the South. A supporter of the ecumenical movement,* he also welcomed the liturgical changes approved by Vatican II.*

C. E. Ronan

Ham, Mordecai Fowler (1877-1961). Fundamentalist* Baptist* evangelist* and pastor.* Reputed to be a descendant of a line of Baptist ministers* going back to Roger Williams,* a claim that cannot be proven, Ham was born in Allen County, Kentucky. After attending Ogden College in Bowling Green, Kentucky, he pursued a business career in Chicago (1897-1900). He left business to enter the ministry in Bowling Green and was ordained* in 1901.

Concern for evangelism led him into a life of itinerant ministry through the Southern U.S., holding city-wide meetings. At the close of his ministry, he claimed one million converts, including Billy Graham* who had made a decision at the Charlotte, North Carolina, meetings in 1934. Ham utilized the radio extensively in gaining publicity for his campaigns. He left his evangelistic campaigns for a brief term as pastor of the First Baptist Church of Oklahoma City (1927-1929) and later served as president of the Interdenominational Association of Christian Evangelists (1936). He campaigned fervently against evolution* and communism,* as well as liquor interests in the South. In 1935 he was awarded a doctor of divinity degree by Bob Jones College.

BIBLIOGRAPHY. E. E. Ham, *50 Years on the Battle Front with Christ: A Biography of Mordecai F. Ham* (1950). R. T. Clutter

Hamlin, Cyrus (1811-1900). Missionary* educator in Turkey. Born in Waterford, Maine, and a graduate of Bowdoin College (1834) and Bangor Theological Seminary (1857), Hamlin had the Yankee gifts of enterprise, ingenuity, grit and determination in pre-eminent measure. Sent to Constantinople in 1839 by the American Board of Commissioners for Foreign Missions,* he opened Bebek Seminary with a general course and Protestant* religious emphasis. He made his own teaching apparatus for science and later developed extremely successful workshops (sheet-metal working, rat-trap making, a bakery) by which his mostly poor students could earn their own keep. Breaking with the Board over its insistence on education in the vernacular only, in 1859 he became the founding president of Robert College (today University of the Bosphorus). In 1877 he became professor of theology* at Bangor Seminary, and in 1880 president of Middlebury College, where he remained until 1885.

BIBLIOGRAPHY. *DAB* IV; C. Hamlin, *My Life and Times* (1893). D. M. Stowe

Hammet [Hammett], William (d. 1803). Founder of the Primitive Methodist Church.* Ordained* by John Wesley* in 1786 to work in Newfoundland, storms drove Hammet's ship to Antigua. Hammet was successful in St. Christopher, but he exhausted himself in a repressive Jamaica. In 1791 Thomas Coke* took him to Charleston to rebuild his strength. Hammet preached* ably at the Methodist* conference, and local Methodists petitioned Francis Asbury* to appoint Hammet to Charleston. Asbury refused the "unprecedented" challenge to the nascent itinerant system. Hammet then built Trinity Church, dividing the Methodist society in Charleston. He published several attacks against Asbury and Coke and, having split Nassau Methodism, named the first American Methodist schism the Primitive Methodist Church (not to be confused with the later denomination of that name). Taking upon himself the power of appointment, he set up a triennial conference. Hammet rejected previous principles, became a slaveholder and, according to Lorenzo Dow,* died drunk. In America, the Primitive Methodist Church did not survive his death, although it continued at least two decades in Nassau.

BIBLIOGRAPHY. E. S. Bucke, ed, *The History of American Methodism* (1964). M. R. Fraser

Hammond, Lily Hardy (1859-1925). Southern Methodist* advocate of interracial justice. Born in Newark, New Jersey, Lily Hardy was educated at private schools in Norfolk, Virginia, and Brooklyn, New York. She married John Dennis Hammond, a minister,* in 1879 and moved to the South. Working within the Southern Methodist Church, she founded the social service department of the Women's Missionary Council and promoted its programs.

Hammond addressed issues of racial discrimination, mob violence, labor peonage and poverty, arguing that social problems must be viewed in light of Christian precepts. She wrote several books, including *In Black and White* (1914) and *In the Vanguard of a Race* (1922). While Hammond's opinions, in many respects, were more enlightened than those of the society in which she lived, she was content with a separate-but-equal policy toward African-Americans.

BIBLIOGRAPHY. *DARB.*   S. C. Stanley

Hardeman, (N)icholas (B)rodie (1874-1965). Church of Christ* evangelist,* educator and debater. Born and educated in Tennessee, Hardeman is considered one of the builders of the Church of Christ in the South. He began preaching as a young man, holding gospel meetings across the country. He is best known for the "Tabernacle Meetings" he held in Nashville's Ryman Auditorium between 1922 and 1942. These meetings made Hardeman's reputation as an evangelist. The newspapers carried the text of his sermons which were later published in a series called Tabernacle Sermons.

As art educator Hardeman taught in the public schools and served as a county superintendent of public instruction. In 1908 he and A. G. Freed founded a college in Henderson, Tennessee, that in 1919 became known as Freed-Hardeman College. The college pioneered the effort among Churches of Christ to teach the Bible as part of a liberal arts education. He served as vice president until 1925 and as president until his death. Hardeman also held public debates with Baptists* and Methodists* on baptism* and church polity* and with Christian Church (Disciples)* preachers on the use of musical instruments in worship.*

BIBLIOGRAPHY. J. M. Powell and M. H. Powers, *N.B.H.: A Biography of Nicholas Brodie Hardeman* (1970).   L. B. Sullivan

Hargis, Billy James (1925-). Fundamentalist* evangelist.* Born in Texarkana, Texas, Hargis was ordained* by an independent Christian Church in 1943. He was the pastor* of several churches until 1948, when he founded The Church of the Christian Crusade in Tulsa, Oklahoma. Hargis's motto became "For Christ and Against Communism." He

identifies Communism,* the United Nations and politically liberal Americans as anti-Christian. He advocates limited government, free enterprise and a restoration of Christian principles at all levels of American society. Hargis preaches* over radio and television, and publishes a monthly periodical entitled *The Christian Crusade Newspaper.* He is the author of several books on Communism. His church supports mission activity among Native Americans in the Southwest and provides aid to homeless children in other countries. In 1975 Hargis founded the Billy James Hargis Evangelistic Association.

BIBLIOGRAPHY. J. H. Redekop, *The American Far Right: A Case Study of Billy James Hargis and Christian Crusade* (1968).   W. M. Ashcraft

Harkness, Georgia (1891-1979). Methodist* theologian* and ecumenist. Born in Harkness, New York, Harkness was converted and joined the Methodist Church in 1905. After college she taught high school until she responded to an article in *The Christian Advocate* describing a new profession for women in religious education. While she attended Boston School of Theology, Edgar S. Brightman* challenged her to devote her life to teaching religion. Following his advice, her career led her successively to Elmira College for Women (1923-1937), Mt. Holyoke College (1937-1939), Garrett Biblical Institute (1939-1950) and Pacific School of Religion (1960-1974).

In 1924 she traveled to Europe in the company of E. Sherwood Eddy,* Kirby Page,* Reinhold Niebuhr* and Ernst Fremont Tittle,* initiating her commitment to the ecumenical* and peace movements. She attended the Madras Conference (1938) and the Amsterdam and Evanston* meetings of the World Council of Churches* in 1948 and 1954. From 1936 on, she participated in a theological discussion group, meeting twice a year with America's most prominent theologians in attendance.

Harkness's devotional autobiography, *Grace Abounding* (1969), demonstrates how her poetry, hymns and prayers reflect her theology. "Hope of the World," "Tell It Out with Gladness" and "God of the Fertile Fields" are three of her many hymns. From 1939 through the early 1940s, she suffered from overwork, insomnia and acute depression. In response to this difficult season of her life, she wrote *The Dark Night of the Soul* (1945).

Harkness was a twentieth-century pioneer, both as a woman theologian and in her service to the Methodist Church. She was ordained* a deacon* in the Troy Conference of the Methodist Church in

1926 but, valuing her association with the laity,* declined ordination when the opportunity arose thirty years later. At the 1937 Oxford Conference on Life and Work, she gave a four-minute speech on the place of women in the church. At the Amsterdam Conference (1948), Karl Barth* challenged her statement that men and women are equal before God, and a lively exchange ensued, in which Harkness quoted Galatians 3:28.

Harkness was a prolific writer, publishing thirty-six volumes in her lifetime. Yet she always wrote for the average layperson, attempting to present theology in everyday terms.

BIBLIOGRAPHY. *NAWMP.* J. E. Stanley

Harper, Frances Ellen Watkins (1825-1911). African-American writer and reformer. Born free in Baltimore, Maryland, in 1825 and orphaned at an early age, Harper grew up under the abolitionist* influence of her aunt and uncle. She left her studies at her uncle's school at age thirteen to work as a household servant in Baltimore. Well-read and self-educated, she left domestic work to teach school before she finally became a dedicated lecturer for the antislavery movement in 1854. Employed by the Maine Anti-Slavery Society, Frances Harper delivered lectures throughout the Northern United States and Canada from 1854 to 1860.

Frances Harper integrated her careers as lecturer, poet, novelist and abolitionist. As the nation's most popular African-American poet of the late nineteenth century, her lectures featured her abolitionist poems, such as "The Slave Auction," "The Slave Mother" and "Bury Me in a Free Land." Dedicated to the cause of freedom and equality, she contributed the extra income from the sale of her publications to the Underground Railroad. After her husband of four years died in 1864, she continued her work as a lecturer to freed slaves and white audiences in the South at the end of the Civil War.*

In 1871 Frances Harper settled in Philadelphia with her daughter. An active speaker for the Women's Christian Temperance Movement,* Frances Harper organized Sunday schools* and educational programs as the organization's Superintendent for Colored Work. Faced with discrimination within the suffrage* and temperance movements,* she helped African-American women organize an independent, autonomous movement in 1896—the National Association of Colored Women—and remained active in the organization until her death in 1911.

BIBLIOGRAPHY. Hazel V. Carby, "Introduction,"

in *Iola Leroy* by F. E. W. Harper (1987); D. Sterling, ed., *We Are Your Sisters: Black Women in the Nineteenth Century* (1985); G. Lerner, ed., *Black Women in White America: A Documentary History* (1973). L. J. Edwards

Harper, William Rainey (1856-1906). Baptist* Old Testament scholar and founding president of the University of Chicago.* Born in New Concord, Ohio, Harper received the B.A. from Muskingum College at the age of fourteen (1870). He was admitted to the Yale* Ph.D. program and received the degree at age eighteen (1875). In 1876 he became a tutor at Denison University and three years later, in 1879, he became an instructor in Semitic languages at Baptist Union Theological Seminary, Morgan Park, Illinois, where he also received the B.D.

Harper developed a correspondence course in Hebrew and soon had more than three thousand students enrolled. He was very active in the Chautauqua movement, serving for some years as president of the college of liberal arts. He also published several books and started two journals: *Hebrew Student* and *Hebraica.* In 1886 he began teaching Semitics at Yale* Divinity School where he became known nationally as a teacher, lecturer and editor. Harper was chosen by John D. Rockefeller to be the founding president of the University of Chicago (1892), and in a short time he created a major comprehensive research university. Because of his own interests, biblical studies flourished at the new institution, and Harper continued teaching full time while serving as president.

As a scholar Harper's greatest contribution lay in his promotion of the study of Hebrew. The materials he prepared were inductive and sound, and were successful both from the standpoint of motivation and insight. Aside from his many handbooks and articles, he published a major commentary in the prestigious International Critical Commentary series, *Critical and Exegetical Commentary on Amos and Hosea* (1905). Theologically, Harper was a liberal* and adamant in insisting on a modern critical approach to Scripture* and the freedom of the Chicago faculty to teach whatever they judged right and true. Yet he remained a loyal churchman, active in the Chicago Baptist Minister's Conference and a frequent speaker in churches.

BIBLIOGRAPHY. *DAB* IV; T. W. Goodspeed, *William Rainey Harper* (1928); F. W. Shepardson, *The Biblical World* (March 1906); R. J. Storr, *Harper's University: The Beginnings* (1966); J. P. Wind, *The*

Bible and the University: The Messianic Vision of William Rainey Harper (1987).

T. H. Olbricht

Harris, George (1844-1922). Congregational* minister* and theologian.* Born in East Machias, Maine, Harris graduated from Amherst College (B.A., 1866) and from Andover Theological Seminary* (B.D., 1869). After pastoring High Street Congregational Church in Auburn, Maine (1869-1872), and Central Congregational Church, Providence, Rhode Island (1872-1883), he became professor of Christian theology* at Andover (1883-1899), where he succeeded Edwards Amasa Park.* He later became president of Amherst College (1899-1912).

At Andover, Harris was a part of the "new theology," or "progressive orthodoxy" (*See* Evangelical Liberalism), that was being shaped by the faculty and was soon disseminated through the *Andover Review* (1884). Harris's part in this and other faculty publications (such as *Progressive Orthodoxy,* 1886, and *The Divinity of Jesus,* 1893) was largely anonymous. When heresy charges were brought against him and four other faculty members in 1886, the case against him and three others was dismissed. Harris's interests were more in the realm of ethics and society, as evidenced by his *Moral Evolution* (1896) and *Inequality and Progress* (1897).

BIBLIOGRAPHY. *DAB* IV; D. D. Williams, *The Andover Liberals* (1941). D. G. Reid

Harris, Merriman Colbert (1846-1921). Methodist* missionary* to Japan and Korea. Born in Ohio and educated in Allegheny College, Harris enjoyed an illustrious career that included work with east Asians in Hakodate, Tokyo, Seoul and San Francisco. At the Sapporo Agricultural College, soon after his arrival in Japan, Harris baptized the young students who later became known as the "Sapporo Band." They included Nitobe Inazo, whose distinguished career included service as the undersecretary of the League of Nations, and Uchimura Kanzo, now remembered as Japan's most profound Christian thinker. Between 1904 and 1916 Harris served as bishop, first in Japan and then in Korea. His endorsement of Japan's colonial development of Korea led to several official Japanese decorations. Though Uchimura disagreed with Harris's approval of Japanese actions in Korea, he wrote in his tribute after Harris's death that "probably no missionary to Japan . . . is remembered by Japanese with greater respect or affection." Harris wrote three books about Japan and its

Christianity, and his wife published pioneer translations of Japanese literature.

BIBLIOGRAPHY. *DAB* IV; J. F. Howes, "Merrimen Colbert Harris," *Kodansha Encyclopedia of Japan,* ed. G. Itasaka (1983). J. F. Howes

Harris, Samuel (1814-1899). Congregational* theologian.* Born in East Machias, Maine, Harris graduated from Bowdoin College (B.A., 1829), where he studied under Longfellow. After serving as principal of Limerick Academy (1833-1834), he studied theology at Andover Theological Seminary* (1835-1838) and then was principal of Washington Academy in his hometown (1838-1841). In 1841 he was ordained a Congregational minister* and then served churches in Conway (1841-1851) and Pittsfield (1851-1855), Massachusetts, before turning to an academic career. From 1855 to 1867 he was professor of systematic theology* at Bangor Seminary, Maine, and was then called to be president and professor of mental and moral philosophy at Bowdoin College. In 1871 he became Dwight Professor of Systematic Theology at Yale* Divinity School, where he remained until he resigned in 1895. Harris published very little until 1883, when *The Philosophical Basis of Theism* appeared, followed by *The Self-Revelation of God* in 1887.

BIBLIOGRAPHY. *DAB* IV; B. Kuklick, *Churchmen and Philosophers* (1985). D. G. Reid

Harrison, Everett Falconer (1902-). Presbyterian* clergyman and biblical scholar. Born to missionary* parents serving in Alaska, he was raised in the course of his father's later prestigious pastorates in Seattle, Washington; St. Louis, Missouri; and Minneapolis, Minnesota. Harrison received his education at the University of Washington (B.A., 1923), the Bible Institute of Los Angeles, Princeton University* (M.A., 1927), Princeton Theological Seminary* (Th.B., 1927), Dallas Theological Seminary* (Th.D., 1939) and the University of Pennsylvania (Ph.D., 1950). He taught at Dallas Theological Seminary from 1927 to 1947, though he took two extended leaves. The first (1930-1932) was to teach at the Hunan Bible Institute, Changsha, China (the fulfillment of an undergraduate vow when in the Student Volunteer Movement*), and during the second (1940-1944) he pastored the Third Presbyterian Church in Chester, Pennsylvania, while doing graduate studies in Hellenistic Greek at the University of Pennsylvania.

In 1947 he became a part of the original faculty of Fuller Theological Seminary* in Pasadena,

California, and served as professor of New Testament until his retirement in 1973. His major publications include *Introduction to the New Testament* (1964) and *A Short Life of Christ* (1968). He served as an editor of the *Wycliffe Bible Commentary, Baker's Dictionary of Theology* and the revision of *The International Standard Bible Encyclopedia,* as well as on the translation committees of two Bibles, the New American Standard Version and the New International Version. In both institutions he distinguished himself by his godly demeanor and the academic brilliance which characterized his defense of traditional evangelical* views.

BIBLIOGRAPHY. G. Marsden, *Reforming Fundamentalism* (1987); M. Noll, *Between Faith and Criticism* (1986). J. D. Hannah

Hartshorne, Charles. *See* PROCESS THEOLOGY.

Harvard University. First institution of higher education founded in North America. The Puritan* founders of the Massachusetts Bay Colony were unusually well educated as well as unusually devout, and, therefore, they waited only six years after arriving in the New World before establishing Harvard College (1636) to train their future ministers* and other gentlemen. No other American college appeared until the very end of the seventeenth century when the Anglicans founded William and Mary* (1694) in Virginia and the conservative Congregationalists began Yale* (1701) in Connecticut. These institutions and most other eighteenth- and nineteenth-century colleges followed many Harvard precedents, including: (1) feeding, housing and supervising the students; (2) establishing student religious societies; (3) charging the students only part of the cost of their education and employing college agents to raise the balance of the operating funds; and (4) placing major curricular emphasis on ancient languages, rhetoric, philosophy and mathematics.

Even within the last century Harvard has continued to lead the nation in curricular planning. Under President Charles Eliot (1869-1909), the university moved away from the traditional prescribed classical course of study to an elective curriculum that allowed the students to choose from a broad variety of courses those which best met their vocational and personal needs in an increasingly industrial and pluralistic society. Most colleges followed the Harvard example so that by 1940 the average college offered a curriculum that was only forty per cent prescribed. Under Eliot's successor, Abbott Lawrence Lowell (1909-1933),

Harvard once again led the nation in curricular organization, this time by adopting general education and major requirements to balance the freedom of election.

The intellectual base of American higher education gradually changed from Christian theism* to secularism during the late nineteenth and early twentieth centuries. Harvard was the early leader in this process already in the early nineteenth century as it moved from Calvinism* to Unitarianism* en route to secularism. The shift was most clearly evident in the installment in 1805 of the liberal and later Unitarian theologian Henry Ware* as the successor to the Hollis chair of divinity* vacated by the death of the Old Calvinist* theologian David Tappan.* Theists responded by founding Andover Theological Seminary,* but under the presidency of John Kirkland,* Harvard gradually (beginning with the 1816 founding of the Society for the Promotion of Theological Education in Harvard University) established its own Divinity School (with Divinity Hall completed in 1826). This helped ensure the stability of Unitarianism as a denomination.*

Today Harvard continues its premier reputation in higher education. It holds an endowment of over $1 billion and maintains the largest university library in the world (over 10 million volumes). *See also* EDUCATION, PROTESTANT THEOLOGICAL.

BIBLIOGRAPHY. S. E. Morison, *Three Centuries of Harvard, 1636-1936* (1936); C. Wright, "The Election of Henry Ware: Two Contemporary Accounts, Edited with Commentary," *Harvard Library Bulletin* 17 (1969):245-278.

W. C. Ringenberg

Hasselquist, Tufve Nilsson (1816-1891). Pioneer Swedish-American Lutheran* pastor, church president, educator and journalist. Born in Ousby, Scandia Province, Sweden, Hassellquist graduated from Lund University and was ordained* a Lutheran minister* in 1839. After serving several parishes in Sweden, he immigrated* to the U.S. in 1852, served as pastor in Galesburg, Knoxville, Paxton and Rock Island, Illinois, and was one of the organizers of the Scandinavian Evangelical Lutheran Augustana Synod (Church) in 1860. He was elected president of the denomination,* serving in the decade 1860-1870. He was also elected president and theological professor of the denomination's infant Augustana College and Theological Seminary. Under his leadership it moved from Chicago to Paxton, Illinois, and finally, in 1877 to Rock Island, Illinois, where it developed into a fully accredited four-year college with a graduate department of theology.* He was also the founder and publisher in 1855 of the first Swedish-American newspaper, *Hemlandet, det Gamla och det Nya* (*The Homeland, the Old and the New*), which later under other editors developed into *Hemlandet,* the longest-lasting and most widely read secular Swedish-language newspaper in America, and also into *Augustana,* the official journal of the Augustana Church, published until 1962. In all these ways he became the single most influential figure among nineteenth-century Swedish-Americans.

BIBLIOGRAPHY. O. F. Ander, *T. N. Hasselquist* (1931); *DAB* IV.   J. W. Lundeen

Hatcher, William Eldridge (1834-1912). Baptist* minister and editor. Born and raised in Virginia, Hatcher attended the schools of Bedford County prior to studying at Richmond College (B.A., 1858). After graduating in 1858, he accepted a call to the Baptist Church in Manchester, Virginia. In 1867 he became pastor of Franklin Square Baptist Church in Baltimore, but in 1868 returned to Virginia to become pastor of First Baptist of Petersburg. In 1875 he assumed the pastorate of Grace Street Church in Richmond, where he remained for twenty-six years (1875-1901). Hatcher maintained a variety of other activities during his pastoral career. From 1882 to 1885 he was editor of, and a frequent contributor to, the *Religious Herald.* In 1888 he went to Europe where he visited numerous preacher friends, including Charles Spurgeon. In 1899 he championed the cause of William H. Whitsitt,* the Southern Baptist Theological Seminary professor who fell into controversy because of his criticism of the popularly held view that Baptist churches and believer's immersion had been maintained in unbroken succession throughout church history. Hatcher was instrumental in arranging for Whitsitt's call to Richmond College. A gifted preacher and master pulpiteer, Hatcher was known in the South for his leadership in Baptist circles.

BIBLIOGRAPHY. *DAB* IV; E. B. Hatcher, *Wm. E. Hatcher* (1915); W. E. Hatcher, *Along the Trail of the Friendly Years* (1910).   R. R. Mathisen

Hatfield, Mark Odom (1922-). Christian politician. Born in Dallas, Oregon, as the only child of Baptist* parents, Hatfield's father was strongly religious, and his mother was a staunch Republican who wanted her son to be involved in politics. After graduating from high school, he studied political science at Willamette University for three years and received a degree in 1943. From 1943 to 1945 he served in the U.S. Navy and was one of the first Americans to enter Hiroshima after the nuclear attack. After the war he studied at Stanford University (M.A., 1948), doing a thesis on the labor policies of Herbert Hoover's administration. Hatfield taught political science at Willamette University (1949-1956) and at the same time was elected to the Oregon state house, where he served until his election to the state senate in 1954.

During his tenure in the state legislature, Hatfield made a decision to serve Christ through the political process. He served as secretary of state of Oregon (1957-1959) and then as governor of the state (1959-1967) until winning the election for U.S. senator in 1966. As a maverick Republican senator with liberal social concerns, he sought to bridge the gap between his evangelical* Christian faith and the world of politics by stressing compassion in government policy. This led Hatfield to be an advocate for America's poor as well as a leading critic of the Vietnam War*—the latter proving to be an unpopular stand in the eyes of many of his fellow evangelicals. He is the author of several books and articles dealing with politics and Christianity, including *Conflict and Conscience* (1971) and *Between a Rock and a Hard Place* (1976).

BIBLIOGRAPHY. R. Eells and B. Nyberg, *Lonely Walk; The Life of Senator Mark Hatfield* (1979).

K. L. Staggers

Haury, Samuel S. (1847-1929). First missionary* sent by the North American Mennonites.* Born in Bavaria, Germany, Haury immigrated to America with his parents in 1856 and settled near Summerfield, Illinois. He attended Wadsworth Seminary (1868-1871) and then studied theology* in Barmen, Germany, graduating in 1875. Haury began medical studies at Jefferson Medical College, in Philadelphia, but was forced to drop out because of illness.

Experiencing a call to mission work, Haury first considered Indonesia and then Alaska as potential mission fields. However, in 1880 he and his wife, Susannah (Hirschler), decided instead to begin mission work within the Arapaho tribe in Indian Territory (now Oklahoma), where they served for seven years under the mission board of the General Conference Mennonite Church. Haury then completed medical school in 1889 and practiced medicine, first in Moundridge, Kansas (until 1894), then in Newton, Kansas (1894-1913), and finally in Upland, California, where he died in 1929. Convinced that Mennonites were occupied with "nonessentials and insignificant things," Haury wished to recall his church to "the new birth and the spread of the kingdom of God."

BIBLIOGRAPHY. J. C. Juhnke, *A People of Mission* (1979); *ME* 2. L. Gross

Haven, Gilbert (1821-1880). Methodist Episcopal* bishop* and abolitionist.* Born at Maldon, Massachusetts, Haven was converted during his student days at Wesleyan Academy in Wilbraham, Massachusetts, and he graduated from Wesleyan University (B.A., 1846). After serving as a professor of Greek and German and later as principal in the seminary at Amenia, New York, he was ordained* a member of the New England Annual Conference in 1851.

Ten years later, after serving five pastoral appointments in his home conference, Haven became a chaplain* in the Eighth Massachusetts Regiment of the Union army. Following the Civil War,* he was elected editor (1867-1872) of *Zion's Herald,* where he developed further his reputation as an abolitionist by championing equality between the races. These convictions brought him into disrepute with his constituents during his period of service as bishop of the Atlanta, Georgia, area in 1872. Committed to missions, he was actively involved in planting Methodism in Mexico (1873). During a missionary visit to Liberia in 1876, he contracted a fever, to which he succumbed in 1880, while living in his hometown of Malden, Massachusetts

His published writings, including books and pamphlets, provided him a forum for articulating his progressive views. In addition to his radical stand on abolition and racial equality, he was an early supporter of civil rights, prohibition,* women's suffrage* and lay representation in the conferences of his denomination. He was forthright in championing his social views, even in hostile settings, and sought to base them on Scripture* and the Wesleyan tradition.*

BIBLIOGRAPHY. *DAB* IV; *DARB;* W. H. Daniels, ed., *Memorials of Gilbert Haven* (1880); W. Gravely, *Gilbert Haven: Methodist Abolitionist* (1973); *NCAB* 13; G. Prentice, *The Life of Gilbert Haven* (1883). J. S. O'Malley

Haviland, Laura Smith (1808-1898). Quaker* abolitionist* and underground railroad conductor. Born in Kitley Township, Ontario, Canada, Haviland grew up in Niagara County, New York. Though she was raised a Quaker, she left the faith of her youth for evangelical* revivalism.* In 1825 she married a Quaker farmer, Charles Haviland, Jr., and in 1829 they moved to Michigan Territory from New York. There she helped organize, with Elizabeth M. Chandler, the first antislavery association in Michigan. Her abolitionist activities embarrassed the conservative Society of Friends, so she withdrew and joined the Wesleyan Methodists.* She did not rejoin the Friends until 1872. The Havilands established the River Raisin Institute in 1837, which accepted students regardless of race or sex. Working with the Underground Railroad she assisted runaway slaves along the route from Cincinnati to Windsor, Canada. She also taught in several African-American schools and spoke publicly against slavery. During the Civil War* she worked at army hospitals and prisons and assisted freed slaves in the South. After the war she undertook relief efforts in the South and Kansas, working as an agent for the Freedmen's Relief Association and the American Missionary Association.*

BIBLIOGRAPHY. L. S. Haviland, *A Woman's Life Work: Including Thirty Years Service on the Underground Rail Road and In the War* (1881); *NAW* 2. S. C. Stanley

Hawaweeny, Raphael (1860-1915). First Orthodox* bishop* ordained* in America. A native of Damascus, Syria, he was educated at the Patriarchal Theological School in Constantinople and at the Theological Academy at Kiev, Russia. There in 1894 he was appointed professor of Arabic language and literature. Following his ordination as a priest,* he came to New York in 1895 to serve the growing numbers of Arab Orthodox there and in other cities along the East Coast. He published a Book of Services in Arabic in 1898. On March 12, 1904, he was ordained as the bishop of Brooklyn by Archbishop Tikhon* at St. Nicholas Church in that city. Having special responsibility for the Arab Orthodox immigrants, Bishop Raphael served as a vicar* to Tikhon in the North American Mission directed by the Holy Synod of the Church of Russia. He founded the magazine *Alkalemat,* later known as *The Word.* There were about thirty Orthodox parishes serving about 25,000 Arab immigrants at the time of his death. They were usually referred to as Syrian Orthodox.

BIBLIOGRAPHY. C. J. Tarasar and J. H. Erickson, eds., *Orthodox America, 1794-1976* (1975). T. E. FitzGerald

Hawthorne, Nathaniel (1804-1864). New England fiction writer. The son of a sea captain in Salem, Massachusetts, Hawthorne captures in his fiction the themes and atmosphere of Puritan* New England while simultaneously pointing the American mind toward the ambiguities and complexities of the later nineteenth and twentieth centuries. His own life reflected the tensions of a once predominantly Christian culture facing numerous changes. His traditional collegiate education at Bowdoin College was balanced by numerous opportunities for rambles and forays into the wilderness. Hawthorne's internal search for perfection in art was caught in the necessities of making a living. His strong desire for seclusion and retirement was modified by close friendships with political leaders like Franklin Pierce (1804-1869) and literary luminaries like Henry Wadsworth Longfellow (1807-1882) and James Russell Lowell (1819-1891).

Hawthorne's literary reputation rests on five novels and numerous short stories and sketches. Among the novels, *The Scarlet Letter* (1850) and *The House of the Seven Gables* (1851) retain their early popularity while his first novel, *Fanshawe* (1828), is seldom read and the last two, *The Blithesdale Romance* (1852) and *The Marble Faun* (1860), are studied primarily by specialists. In *The Scarlet Letter* and *The House of the Seven Gables*, Hawthorne explores the themes which possessed his imagination and permeated the short stories as well: the horror of secret sin; the sacredness of the human heart; the consequences of a sinful past (especially the Puritan past) on the present; the inevitability of the loss of innocence; and the impact of pride and selfishness on the human personality.

Between 1830 and 1852, Hawthorne produced about one hundred tales and sketches, mostly anonymously in newspapers, magazines and gift books. Some of these pieces appeared later in *Twice-Told Tales* (1837), *Mosses from an Old Manse* (1846), and *The Snow-Image and Other Twice-Told Tales* (1852). These anthologies contained most of the stories prized by readers of short fiction today: "The Minister's Black Veil," "My Kinsman, Major Molineux," "Young Goodman Brown," "Rappaccini's Daughter" and "The Great Stone Face."

BIBLIOGRAPHY. F. C. Crews, *The Sins of the Fathers: Hawthorne's Psychological Themes* (1966); R. Stewart, *Nathaniel Hawthorne: A Biography* (1948); H. H. Waggoner, *Hawthorne: A Biography* (1948).   J. E. Barcus

Hayes, Patrick Joseph (1867-1938). Cardinal* archbishop* of New York. The son of immigrant Irish parents, Hayes was born in New York City on November 20, 1867. He received his early education at LaSalle Academy and Manhattan College. Following seminary studies at St. Joseph's Seminary (Troy, New York) and the Catholic University of America,* he was ordained* a priest* in 1892.

Following his return to New York, Hayes spent eight years in urban ministry before being named both chancellor of the Archdiocese of New York and president of Cathedral College in 1902 by John Cardinal Farley.* As a result of his performance in these posts, he was made an auxiliary bishop* of New York in 1914. The following year he became pastor of St. Stephen's Church in New York City.

During World War 1* Hayes assumed two additional, more nationally oriented, positions. In 1917 he was made a member of the Administrative Committee of the newly formed National Catholic War Council* (NCWC). In the same year, he was appointed the first bishop-chaplain* of the Military Ordinariate. Although he resigned from the NCWC in 1919, he remained the bishop-chaplain until his death.

Following the death of Cardinal Farley, Hayes was named archbishop of New York in 1919. In 1924 he was made a member of the College of Cardinals. A retiring, pastoral man, Hayes avoided involvement in national affairs. Within his own diocese* he devoted most of his energies to the works of charity and social welfare. As archbishop he overhauled the organizational apparatus of Catholic Charities, stressed the need for professional training for Catholic social workers, and instituted an annual appeal to raise money for the increasingly sophisticated and ambitious program of Catholic relief services. His successful reforms in this area earned for him the epithet "The Cardinal of Charity."

BIBLIOGRAPHY. J. B. Kelly, *Cardinal Hayes* (1940); *DAB* 2; G. P. Fogarty, *The Vatican and the American Hierarchy from 1870 to 1965* (1985).
                                          J. M. McShane

Haygood, Atticus Greene (1839-1896). Methodist Episcopal,* South, bishop,* editor and educator. Born in Watkinsville, Georgia, Haygood graduated from Emory College (B.A., 1859) and was admitted to the Georgia Conference. He pastored until 1870 when he was elected Sunday-school* secretary and editor of Sunday-school publications for the denomination.* He later served as president of Emory College (1875-1884) and was editor of *The Wesleyan Christian Advocate* (1878-1882). Elected bishop in 1882, he declined the office.

At Emory, Haygood's innovative educational philosophy aroused controversy. He introduced practical courses such as bookkeeping and telegraphy into the Emory curriculum, and his interest in the education of African-Americans brought opposition. In 1884 he resigned the presidency of the college to take up full-time duties as agent for the Slater Fund—a foundation established to encourage education for African-Americans in the South (*See* Black Colleges). Haygood contributed significantly to the establishment of Paine College in Augusta, Georgia, and his book on African-Americans education, *Our Brother in Black: His Freedom and Future* (1881), was one of the period's most influential works on African-American education.

After a brief but failed effort to establish a new university for women in Sheffield, Alabama, Haygood was again elected bishop in 1990. Accepting the ordination, he resigned his agency with the Slater Fund and took up residence in Los Angeles (1890-1893), where he worked to establish the churches on the West Coast.

BIBLIOGRAPHY. *DAB* IV; *DARB;* E. F. Dempsey, *Atticus Green Haygood* (1940); H. W. Manny, *Atticus Greene Haygood: Methodist Bishop, Editor and Educator* (1965); *NCAB* 1.

M. E. Dieter

Haygood, Laura Askew (1845-1900). Methodist* educator and missionary* to China. Born in Watkinsville, Georgia, Haygood grew up in Atlanta where her family was active in the Methodist Episcopal Church, South. One of her brothers was Atticus Greene Haygood,* who would become a prominent bishop of the Methodist Episcopal Church, South. Laura graduated from the Wesleyan Female College at Macon in 1864, and returned to Atlanta following the Civil War* to begin a long career as an educator. She was active in church work of all kinds, and when asked to locate a woman to organize the church's outreach to the women of Shanghai, she could find no one more qualified than herself. The Woman's Board of Foreign Missions appointed her to the task in 1884. She organized extant day schools, launched new programs and in 1896 became the director of all Women's Board work in China. Among her many achievements was the McTyeire Home and School in Shanghai, a girls' school which also served as a training center for new missionaries. She was widely revered and after her death a school, built in Soochow on the McTyeire model, was named in her honor.

BIBLIOGRAPHY. O. E. and A. M. Brown, *The Life and Letters of Laura Askew Haygood* (1904); J. Cannon, *History of Southern Methodist Missions* (1926); *DAB* IV; *NAW* 2. K. K. Kidd

Hays, Lawrence Brooks (1898-1981). Lawyer, congressman and Southern Baptist Convention*

president. Raised in Russellville, Arkansas, and a graduate of the University of Arkansas (1919) and the Law School of George Washington University (1922), Hays married Marion Prather in 1922. For two decades thereafter he practiced law in Russellville and Little Rock, engaged unsuccessfully in political campaigns for governor and congressman, and filled several appointive posts in his native state. From 1943 to 1959 he served as U.S. congressman from the fifth district of Arkansas.

An active advocate of civil rights for all citizens, Hays opposed the views of Governor Orval Faubus during the school desegregation crisis in Little Rock (1958), which brought his defeat for re-election by a strong segregationist candidate. President Dwight D. Eisenhower* appointed him to the board of the Tennessee Valley Authority (1959-1961), after which he served as a special presidential assistant for President John F. Kennedy* (1961-1963) and President Lyndon B. Johnson (1963-1964).

Hays maintained an active church involvement throughout his career. He was president of the Southern Baptist Convention for two terms (1957-1959) and a vice president of the National Council of Churches* (1969). He directed the Ecumenical Institute at Wake Forest University for five years (1969-1974) and published several books, including *The Baptist Way of Life* (1963), with John Steely, and his autobiography, *Politics Is My Parish* (1981). C. L. Howe

Haystack Prayer Meeting (1806). Founding event of the American foreign missionary movement.* In 1806 students at Williams College, in Massachusetts, were overtaken by a thunderstorm during their regular prayer meeting, and they took shelter under a haystack. Present at this meeting were Samuel J. Mills, Jr.,* James Richards, Francis Robbins, Harvey Loomis, Gordon Hall, Luther Rice* and Byron Green. From the group was formed the Society of the Brethren (1808), which took as its motto, "We can do it if we will." Later, at Andover Seminary,* the group was joined by Adoniram Judson,* Samuel Newell and Samuel Nott, Jr. In 1810 Judson, Mills, Newell and Nott presented an appeal for missionary action to the General Association of the Congregational Ministers in Massachusetts. Consequently, in 1810 the American Board of Commissioners for Foreign Missions* was formed. W. A. Detzler

Haywood, (G)arfield (T)homas (d. 1931). Oneness Pentecostal* minister.* Born in Greencastle, Indiana, Haywood grew up in a Christian home in Indianapolis. Another African-American, Henry Prentiss, introduced him to Pentecostalism, and by 1908, Haywood was pastoring an African-American Assemblies of God* congregation in Indianapolis that would grow to over 450 members. When Glenn A. Cook* visited his church in January 1915, heralding the new "oneness" doctrine of a baptism* in "Jesus only," Haywood and his congregation were rebaptized according to the new formula. As a respected minister of one of the largest churches in the Assemblies of God, Haywood attracted the attention of denominational leaders, who attempted to dissuade him from following the new doctrine. But Haywood was resolute and under his persuasive leadership a number of other African-American Pentecostal ministers and congregations joined the Oneness Movement. When the movement merged with the Pentecostal Assemblies of the World in 1917, Haywood became secretary. The fledgling denomination was racially integrated for a time, largely as a result of the temporary transmigration of white ministers from the Assemblies of God. Haywood continued to pastor his church until his death in 1931. He edited the periodical *The Voice in the Wilderness* and composed some hymns. Among his published works was *Before the Foundation of the World* (1923). A cartoonist in his earlier years, Haywood was well known for his charts and illustrations depicting spiritual truths.

BIBLIOGRAPHY. M. E. Golder, *History of the Pentecostal Assemblies of the World* (1973); M. E. Golder, *The Life and Works of Bishop Garfield Thomas Haywood (1880-1931)* (1977).

H. D. Hunter

Healy, James Augustine (1830-1900). Catholic* bishop* of Portland, Maine. Born on a plantation near Macon, Georgia, the eldest son of Irish-born Michael M. Healy and Georgia-born mullato slave Eliza, James and his nine siblings were slaves according to state law. Sent at age seven to Quaker* schools in New York and New Jersey, at fourteen he attended Holy Cross College. Baptized* a Catholic there, he graduated in 1849, after which he entered the Sulpician* Seminary in Montreal and then transferred to the Sulpician Seminary at Issy, France. Ordained* priest in Paris on June 10, 1854, he returned to the U.S. to serve in the Diocese of Boston, where he labored in various capacities as bishop's secretary, chancellor, cathedral* rector,* director of orphanages and pastor of St. James, Boston, New England's largest parish.

Consecrated* on June 2, 1875, the second bishop of Portland, Maine, he established sixty parishes, eighteen schools and several welfare institutions. A gifted administrator and eloquent preacher, Healy was the first priest and the first bishop in the U.S. with African ancestry, yet ironically he declined to identify personally or publicly with the African-American community.

BIBLIOGRAPHY. A. S. Foley, *Bishop Healy: Beloved Outcaste* (1954); J. T. Skerrett, Jr., " 'Is There Anything Wrong with Being a Nigger?' Racial Identity and Three Nineteenth Century Priests," *Freeing the Spirit* 5 (1977):27-37.

M. J. McNally

Heaven and Hell. The final states of everlasting bliss for the righteous (those saved) and of everlasting torment for the wicked (those lost or damned). The traditional Christian doctrines of heaven and hell, while formally accepted by most North American believers, are increasingly slighted or reinterpreted, or both, except among fundamentalists* and other conservatives.

Contemporary Christians, unlike their forebears, rarely write hymns* about the sweet by and by (including reunion with family and friends) or preach* hellfire-and-brimstone sermons. Missionary* evangelism,* to snatch souls as brands from the burning, is less predominant now than a century ago, even among evangelicals. Not as many are eager to die for their country, secure in the hope of a better life hereafter. Belief in retributive justice is waning, not only in penology (e.g., the decline of capital punishment) but in theology* (the decline of the doctrine of hell).

The Puritan concept of heaven as expressed in Richard Baxter's *Saints' Everlasting Rest* (1649) was theocentric and otherworldly, with worship the pre-eminent activity. During the eighteenth century a more material concept of heaven began to gain currency, with human love and progress characterizing life in the new order. This anthropocentric view became more prominent in the nineteenth century, with depictions of family reunions, creative activity and spiritual growth filling out the popular concept of heaven.

Although the heavenly hope continues as a common theme at funerals,* most theological schools emphasize the biblical, Hebrew beliefs in the future resurrection of the body and in the unity of the person, while they question so-called Greek soul-body dualism, the immortality of the soul and a conscious, disembodied, "intermediate state" between death and the resurrection. Also, much recent theology has accented God's love, and sometimes human goodness, at the expense of such traditional teachings as judgment, wrath, propitiation, reprobation and hell. Finally, post-Kantian agnosticism* about nonmaterial reality has tended to erode belief in angels and demons, heaven and hell, and even a transcendent God.

Thus, contemporary Christian scholars often stress as a substitute for the old hope of heaven (and fear of hell), the biblical promise of "a new heaven and a new earth" (Rev. 21:1), sometimes linked with a horizontal gospel focusing on this-earthly weal or woe (i.e., heaven and hell here and now). Even many evangelicals are preoccupied with contemporary themes such as ecology, bodily healing, human potential, liberation of the poor and the oppressed, and the whole social, political and economic domain. This-worldliness is increasingly eclipsing other-worldliness.

Late-twentieth-century reinterpretations of heaven and hell commonly view the biblical imagery nonliterally and emphasize the Gospel of John's perspective that eternal life and death are already present in this life. An evangelical picture of heaven—or as some would prefer, God's new world—is dominated by the overwhelming reality of the triune God, the absence of all negative influences (e.g., evil, suffering, death, insecurity), a heightened sense of community (e.g., the recognition of loved ones), continuity with this world's culture, activity and worship.*

Hell is now usually interpreted as endless, self-chosen separation from the presence of God. Some would recognize degrees of punishment. Universalism,* the view that sooner or later all will be saved, has gained ground among more liberal Christians who, in an ever-shrinking world, have entered into dialog with other world religions, but it is usually rejected by evangelicals. But the doctrine of conditional immortality or annihilationism—the view that God condemns the wicked to nonexistence—has recently won support among some evangelicals.

BIBLIOGRAPHY. C. S. Lewis, *The Great Divorce* (1946); C. McDannell and B. Lang, *Heaven: A History* (1988); G. Rowell, *Hell and the Victorians . . .* (1974); S. H. Travis, *Christian Hope and the Future* (1980); D. P. Walker, *The Decline of Hell* (1964). E. W. Kennedy

Heck, Barbara Ruckle (1734-1804). Mother of American Methodism.* Born Barbara Ruckle in Ireland, where she was part of a colony of German refugees from the Palatinate, in 1760 she married Paul Heck and with him and her cousin Philip Embury* immigrated to New York. There, in 1766, she stirred up Embury, who had been converted in

1752 as a result of hearing John Wesley,* to recover his role as class leader and local preacher* and to organize the Methodists there into a class. According to a story which survives in several versions, Heck came upon a card game. She swept the cards from the table into her apron and then into the fire, and hastened to Embury's home to demand that he begin conducting regular Methodist meetings without delay. Despite Embury's protests that there was no proper meetinghouse, Heck remained adamant and instructed Embury to conduct services in his own home if nothing else was available. The next day the first Methodist meeting in New York was held. Two years later Heck herself whitewashed the walls of the first Methodist chapel in America—Wesley Chapel on John Street.

In 1770/1771 the Hecks moved to Camden in the upper Hudson Valley and established another Methodist society. In 1774, being Loyalists in sympathies, they moved to Sorel near Montreal and later to Augusta Township in Upper Canada (Ontario), where they again formed a Methodist society.

BIBLIOGRAPHY. G. L. Caddel, *Barbara Heck: Pioneer Methodist* (1961); *DAB* IV; *NAW* 2; *Methodism* (1858); W. H. Withrow, *Barbara Heck: A Tale of Early Methodism* (1895).

J. C. Brown

Hecker, Isaac Thomas (1819-1888). Catholic* priest,* missionary,* journalist and founder of the Missionary Society of St. Paul the Apostle (Paulist Fathers).* The son of a Methodist* mother, Hecker was among the most influential and well-known American converts to Catholicism in the nineteenth century. Born in New York City, he went through a period of searching that led him into an examination of Jacksonian politics, Mormonism,* progressive Unitarianism* and Transcendentalism.*

In 1844, after six months at Brook Farm* and a brief sojourn at Bronson Alcott's Fruitlands, he converted to Catholicism. In this he was influenced by his reading of Continental Romantics* such as Victor Cousin and by the apologetical work of the German theologian J. A. Moehler. Hecker joined the Redemptorist* order and was ordained* to the priesthood* in 1849. During the early 1850s, he and three other American-born converts carried on a series of parish missions,* the success of which encouraged them to form plans for a mission band dedicated to work with non-Catholic Americans.

After a protracted struggle that led to his expulsion from the Redemptorists and the nullification of that expulsion by Pope Pius IX,* he founded the Paulist Fathers in 1858. He went on to become an internationally known figure for his fresh presentation of Catholicism as a religion best suited for the demands of modern democratic society. In 1857 he had authored his first book, *Aspirations of Nature,* followed two years later by *Questions of the Soul.*

The 1860s were the high point of his active ministry, during which he founded *The Catholic World* magazine and the Catholic Publication Society, which later became the Paulist Press. As a missionary he toured the country, giving parish missions to Catholics and lecturing to non-Catholics, often on the lyceum circuit.

In 1870 he attended the First Vatican Council,* where he was among the inopportunists on the question of papal infallibility.* After the definition was made, however, he accepted it rather easily and, in fact, used it to bolster his contention that the time was ripe for the Catholic Church to emphasize the harmony of inner workings of the Holy Spirit in the soul with its work in the Church and society. It was that synthetic vision, refined by his reading of Jesuits Louis Lallemant and J. P. de Caussade that became the preoccupation of his later life.

In 1872 his labors were inhibited by the onset of chronic leukemia, which plagued him until his death. In an effort to regain his health, he toured Europe between 1873 and 1875, making the acquaintance of European Catholic liberals. In 1875 in Italy he composed his call to worldwide social and spiritual renewal: *The Exposition of the Church and the Age.* Returning to New York he lived out his final thirteen years severely enfeebled by his disease but engaging in limited editorial work and taking a minimal role in the governance of his community. After his death his ideas became the center of the Americanist controversy* of the late 1890s.

BIBLIOGRAPHY. *DAB* IV; *DARB;* W. Elliott, *The Life of Father Hecker* (1891); J. Farina, *An American Experience of God: The Spirituality of Isaac Hecker* (1981); J. Farina, ed., *Hecker Studies: Essays on the Thought of Isaac Hecker* (1983).

J. Farina

Heidelberg Catechism. A German Reformed* catechism* published in 1563. Frederick William III, elector of the Palatinate, commissioned the principal formulators of the Heidelberg Catechism, Casper Olevianus (1536-1585) and Zacharius Ursinus (1534-1583), to create a work that would bridge the divisions between Lutheran,* Calvinist*

and Zwinglian disciples during the Reformation. The historian Max Goebel characterized the resulting catechism* as a harmonious blend of "Lutheran inwardness, Melanchthonian clearness, Zwinglian simplicity, and Calvinistic fire."

Divided into three parts which parallel the path to salvation,* the catechism begins with humanity's misery and guilt before the unreachable perfection of God's law. It then focuses on redemption through Christ's suffering and resurrection for all who repent and accept him. Christ's exemplary righteousness and sacrificial satisfaction for manifold human transgressions are emphasized along with the doctrine of providence. But the catechism avoids discussion of predestination,* reprobation and limited atonement,* and recognizes in the Lord's Supper* both the Zwinglian recall of Jesus' suffering on humanity's behalf and the mystical union of the earthbound redeemed and the ascended redeemer found in Calvin's theology.* The catechism concludes with a section on the human joy and gratitude arising from the reception of divine grace. It acknowledges good works as the fruits of saving faith, views the Ten Commandments as a summary of the ethical Christian life and declares prayer the "chief part of the gratitude which God requires."

This catechism was the first Protestant confession to be brought to America by Europeans (1609). It has been the most widely accepted doctrinal standard among Reformed denominations in America up to the present day. It is one of several creedal statements accepted by the Presbyterian Church (USA)* and one of three Reformed creeds accepted by the Reformed Church in America* and the Christian Reformed Church.*

BIBLIOGRAPHY. P. Schaff, *A History of the Creeds of Christendom* (1877); J. W. Nevin, *History and Genius of the Heidelberg Catechism* (1847); Z. Ursinus, *Commentary on the Heidelberg Catechism,* trans. G. W. Williard (1954).

M. J. Coalter

Hell. *See* HEAVEN AND HELL.

Helm, Lucinda Barbour (1839-1897). Methodist* missions* leader and reformer. Born near Elizabethtown, Kentucky, one of eleven children of John Helm, a lawyer, and Lucinda Hardin Helm, Helm was known for her tact, judgment, cheerfulness, practical good sense and loyalty to friends and church. An early Sunday-school* worker and teacher of black and white children, she shifted her energies to the newly formed Woman's Foreign Missionary Society (WFMS) in 1876.

Helm's work with the Society led her to write for the *Woman's Missionary Advocate* and other church publications on foreign and home missions, as well as edit leaflets published by the WFMS. Helm is best known for her work in conceiving and organizing the Woman's Department of the Board of Church Extension, serving as its general secretary from 1886 to 1890. During that period the WFMS became the Woman's Parsonage and Home Mission Society. She served an additional quadrennium as general secretary of this organization, resigning in 1894 to devote more time to the organization's journal, *Our Homes,* for which she had served as editor from its inception in 1892. Even in death she served the mission cause, leaving money in her will for a cottage to be built at Sue Bennett Memorial School in London, Kentucky. Helm was a tireless worker until the day of her death. The last text marked in her Bible,* November 12, 1897, was "I must work the works of him that sent me, while it is day, the. night cometh when no man can work."

BIBLIOGRAPHY. A. W. Alexander, *The Life and Work of Lucinda B. Helm* (1898); N. D. Tatum, *A Crown of Service: A Story of Woman's Work in the Methodist Episcopal Church, South, from 1878-1940* (1960). J. C. Brown

Hemmenway, Moses (1735-1811). Old Calvinist* minister.* Born in Framingham, Massachusetts, Hemmenway graduated from Harvard College* in 1755. A staunch Whig, he spent more than fifty years as pastor of the First Church in Wells, Maine. He was a friend and correspondent of his Harvard classmate President John Adams. Hemmenway's biographers delight in telling of his unassuming character, love for children and obliviousness to formalities of dress and custom. He was a capable classicist and biblical scholar, and although he was not known as a great preacher,* his lengthy sermons were scholarly and eloquent. Francis Turretin (1623-1687), John Owen (1654-1706) and Jonathan Edwards* were Hemmenway's favorite authors, and he brought to them an irenic spirit for which he was much beloved by his fellow Congregational* ministers.

Ironically, Hemmenway is remembered today for writings which took on an uncharacteristically polemical cast after he was attacked by New Divinity* Calvinists. Hemmenway was drawn into controversy when in 1767 he published *Seven Sermons, On the Obligation and Encouragement of the Unregenerate, to labour for the Meat which endureth to everlasting Life.* Here he encouraged the unconverted to draw on an inherent, natural,

nonsalvific goodness and build a foundation for receiving saving grace, should it be granted. Samuel Hopkins,* however, accused him of attributing genuine moral goodness, however qualified, to the unconverted sinner's desires, thereby soothing the sinner's conscience rather than convicting it of sin.* Nathaniel Emmons* simply dismissed Hemmenway's nuanced *A Discourse Concerning the Church* (1792) as Stoddardism (*See* Stoddard, Samuel). In spite of these controversies, Hemmenway was a strong voice for infant baptism,* and against Arian, Socinian and universalist* tendencies in New England.

BIBLIOGRAPHY. *AAP* 1; C. K. Shipton, "Moses Hemmenway," in *Sibley's Harvard Graduates,* vol. XIII (1965). S. D. Crocco

Henkel, Paul (1754-1825). Lutheran* evangelist.* Born in Howan County, North Carolina, Henkel grew up a frontiersman in what is now West Virginia, though he was the grandson of Anthony Jacob Henkel (1663-1728), the court chaplain to Duke Maurice of Saxony. A cooper by trade, Henkel was familiar with the rigors of frontier life, including Native American warfare.

In 1776 he heard evangelist George Whitefield,* experienced the New Birth,* and resolved to be a preacher.* Self-trained and self-supporting, Henkel was licensed* in 1783 and ordained* in 1792 by the Pennsylvania Ministerium.* Preaching in both German and English, Henkel became an itinerant evangelist to Virginia and West Virginia, North and South Carolina, Tennessee, Kentucky, Ohio and Indiana. A prolific promoter of Lutheranism, Henkel fathered three synods* (North Carolina, 1803; Ohio, 1818; and Tennessee, 1820) and six sons who entered the ministry: Solomon, a publisher of religious literature; Philip, who conducted protracted meetings* in Tennessee; Ambrose, a pastor* and publisher in Virginia; Andrew and Charles, ministers* in Ohio; and David, who served in Kentucky and Indiana.

Together with his son Ambrose, Henkel operated a press in New Market, Virginia, which for years was the only Lutheran publishing house in the U.S. Henkel supplied material for publication, including a German (1810) and English hymnbook (1816), a German catechism* (1814) and, in both English and German, a work on *Baptism and the Lord's Supper* (1809). Committed to a fervent confessionalism* and an ardent evangelicalism,* by the time of his death on November 27, 1825, Paul Henkel was recognized as one of the major founders of Lutheranism in America.

BIBLIOGRAPHY. *AAP* 9; *DAB* IV; *DARB;* G. E.

Lenski, "Henkel Family," *The Encyclopedia of the Lutheran Church,* ed. J. Bodensieck (1965); B. K. Pershing, "Paul Henkel, Frontier Missionary," *LCQ* 24 (1934):125-151.   C. G. Fry

Hennepin, Louis (c.1626-1705). Priest,* Recollet,* missionary,* explorer and historiographer of New France. Belgian by birth but French by education, much of Hennepin's life was spent in an environment of intrigues and secret plots.

In May 1675 he left for New France (*See* French Missions to America) on the same ship as the Cavelier de la Salle. Upon arrival in Canada Hennepin lost no time in getting to work. He gave the Advent and Lent* sermons at the Hotel-Dieu of Quebec at Bishop Laval-Montmorency's* invitation and went through the St.-Lawrence countryside preaching the gospel. Beginning in 1678 he accompanied Cavelier de la Salle on explorations of the West. As a part of La Salle's advance guard, he helped map and explore much of the upper Mississippi. Hennepin soon returned to Europe and published his *Description de la Louisiane* (1683). The work was an unqualified success, and Hennepin became a celebrity overnight, with readers hungering for exotic stories and descriptions of America.

For a time the Recollet's name was honored, but for reasons still unknown, Hennepin suddenly fell into disgrace and was expelled from the province of Artois. A fearless disseminator of the faith but also an independent person, he more than once antagonized La Salle, provoked dissension among the civil authorities and made enemies of the Jesuits.* In Canada he administered the sacraments* without the bishop's authorization. In his day Louis Hennepin was the most fashionable of popular authors, but he was not always careful about details and at times exaggerated. He remains a key figure in the early exploration of the Mississippi and through his writing popularized America in Europe.

BIBLIOGRAPHY. J. Delanglez, *Hennepin's Description of Louisiana* (1941); J. R. Rioux, "Louis Hennepin," *DCB.*   D. A. Scalberg

Henry, Carl (F)erdinand (H)oward (1913-). Evangelical* theologian.* Born in New York City to German immigrant parents, Henry grew up in Central Islip, Long Island. An early interest in journalism led him to report high-school events for *The Islip Press* and, following graduation, take a job as a full-time reporter. At the age of nineteen he was given the editorship of the *Smithtown Star.* In the summer of 1933, Henry made a conscious commitment to Jesus Christ. Henry decided to attend Wheaton College* in Illinois, an institution that shaped many leaders of post World War 2 evangelicalism.

Following graduation from Wheaton (B.A., 1938), Henry attended Northern Baptist Seminary in Chicago while simultaneously studying in Wheaton's newly established graduate program in theology. He received the M.A. from Wheaton in 1941 and the Th.D. from Northern Baptist in 1942 (with his dissertation published as *Successful Church Publicity: A Guidebook for Christian Publicists,* 1943). During those years he married (1940) Helga Bender, the daughter of Baptist missionaries to the African Cameroons, was an instructor at Northern Baptist and was ordained to the Baptist ministry (1941). He and Helga wrote *A Doorway to Heaven* (1942), a history of the Pacific Garden Mission.* But his first significant book was *Remaking the Modern Mind* (1946), which pointed to the poverty of modern Western culture and challenged Christians to engage in the task of rebuilding a Christian mind that would serve the future. Meanwhile, during his summers Henry was teaching at Gordon College and doing Ph.D. studies in philosophy at Boston University, where in 1949 he would defend his dissertation before Albert C. Knudson* and Edgar S. Brightman* (later published as *Personal Idealism and Strong's Theology,* 1951).

In 1948 Henry moved to Pasadena, California, to be part of the original faculty of Fuller Theological Seminary,* an institution established to engage modern theological scholarship, further worldwide evangelism and reform some of the unattractive elements of fundamentalism. Henry's *The Uneasy Conscience of Modern Fundamentalism* (1947) was a manifesto calling for Christians to develop a comprehensive world view that would encompass all of life, including its social and political dimensions. For many evangelical intellectuals of the post-war era, Henry's book was a decisive influence in awakening their social conscience and overcoming their separatist tendencies.

Henry's years at Fuller were busy and satisfying, and they increasingly established him as an intellectual spokesperson for the emerging new evangelicalism. But by 1955 Henry was being invited by Billy Graham* and L. Nelson Bell* to become editor of a new magazine projected for publication, *Christianity Today.* The magazine was intended to give the evangelical community an alternative voice to the mainline *Christian Century.* Beginning with a one-year leave of absence from the seminary in 1956-1957, Henry moved to Washington, D.C., to launch the magazine and eventually severed his ties with Fuller. Under his leadership, *Christianity Today* came to surpass the *Century,* with over 150,000 paid subscribers by December 1967.

Henry's great success as an editor brought international recognition. Besides his numerous speaking engagements and invitations to other positions of evangelical leadership, he had opportunity to interview theologians such as Karl Barth,* Emil Brunner,* Rudolf Bultmann* and Paul Tillich,* and was himself interviewed by *Time, Newsweek,* the *New York Times* and radio broadcasts. Among his many other involvements were the chairmanship of the World Congress on Evangelism* (Berlin, 1966) and the presidency of the Evangelical Theological Society* (1967-1970). Henry remained editor until July 1, 1968, when he was released. His departure seems to have been based on misunderstandings between him and the executive committee, but most particularly with the politically conservative financial backer of the magazine, J. Howard Pew.* While Henry officially resigned, he regarded it as "involuntary termination after twelve years of sacrificial labor."

Following an interim period of study and research at Cambridge University (1968-1969), Henry began publishing his major six-volume theological work *God, Revelation and Authority* (1976-1983), which defended biblical theism, the full authority and inerrancy of Scripture, and the necessity of intelligible supernatural revelation for meaningful theological discourse. On his return to the U.S. he accepted a position at Eastern Baptist Theological Seminary, where he taught from 1969 to 1974 while carrying on wide-ranging speaking commitments. In 1974 he became lecturer-at-large for World Vision,* a position that allowed him to continue his writing and engage in an international speaking ministry. His retirement since 1978 has continued to bring him numerous speaking and writing opportunities, including the presidency of the American Theological Society in 1979-1980. He continues to serve as the senior statesman of the new evangelicalism.

BIBLIOGRAPHY. G. Fackre, "Carl F. H. Henry," in *A Handbook of Christian Theologians,* ed. D. G. Peerman and M. E. Marty (1984); C. F. H. Henry, *Confessions of a Theologian* (1986); G. M. Marsden, *Reforming Fundamentalism* (1987); B. Patterson, *Carl F. H. Henry* (1984).

D. M. Roark

Henry, Patrick (1736-1799). Revolutionary statesman and governor of Virginia. Born at Studley, Hanover County, Virginia, Henry is best known as an orator, an opponent of the ratification of the Constitution and a five-term governor of Virginia. Considerably less is known about his religious views. His father, John, belonged to St. Paul's, the local Anglican church,* where young Patrick's paternal uncle was rector* and where Patrick was undoubtedly instructed in the catechism.* His mother, Sarah, embraced Presbyterianism* following her conversion* during the Great Awakening* in the 1740s.

During his teen-age years Patrick reportedly accompanied his mother to many a service at the Fork Church Presbyterian meetinghouse, in Hanover County, where Samuel Davies,* one of the greatest preachers of his time, was the stated pastor. Despite Davies's sermons and his mother's earnest pleas, Patrick continued steadfast in the Anglican faith. His brother-in-law Col. Samuel Meredith observed that he "was through life a warm friend of the Christian religion." Henry reportedly was so pleased with Soame Jenyn's *Internal View of the Christian Religion* that he had several hundred copies printed and distributed at his own expense during his second term as governor. Nevertheless, as he approached the end of his life he was alarmed at the realization that the deists* claimed him as one of their own. In a letter to one of his daughters, he confided: "Such a thought gives me much pain. I find much cause to reproach myself that I have lived so long, and have given no decided and public proof of my being a Christian." Henry died at his "Red Hill" plantation on the Staunton River on June 6, 1799.

BIBLIOGRAPHY. M. C. Tyler, *Patrick Henry* (1887); H. Mayer, *A Son of Thunder* (1986).

R. L. Troutman

Hepburn, James Curtis (1815-1911). Pioneer Protestant* missionary* to Japan. Born in Milton, Pennsylvania, of Scotch-Irish and English ancestry, Hepburn was brought up by earnest Christian parents. He graduated from the College of New Jersey (now Princeton University*) in 1832 and received an M.D. from the University of Pennsylvania in 1836. He practiced medicine for several years and married in 1840. Accompanied by his wife, he served as a medical missionary between 1841 and 1845, first in Singapore and then in Amoy (now Xiamen), China.

Because of poor health, the Hepburns returned to New York, where Hepburn practiced medicine until they went to Japan in 1859. Upon arrival in Kanagawa, near the present port of Yokohama,

Hepburn immersed himself in the study of the language. Soon he opened a dispensary and while carrying on medical work, also trained young Japanese men in medical science and taught English and mathematics. He was one of the founders of what is now Meiji Gakuin University. Hepburn became proficient in Japanese at all levels of usage.

This facility enabled him to make contributions in Japan that rivaled even his medical work. He compiled the first Japanese-English dictionary, had a key role in translating the Bible* into Japanese and produced a Bible dictionary in Japanese. He used and popularized a system of romanizing Japanese which, in modified form, is still in use today.

BIBLIOGRAPHY. *DAB* IV; W. E. Griffis, *Hepburn of Japan* (1913); E. R. Beauchamp, "Hepburn, James Curtis," *Kodansha Encyclopedia of Japan* (1983).   W. N. Browning

Heresy Trials (1878-1906). A series of ecclesiastical and civil trials within Protestant* denominations* aimed at checking the inroads of theological liberalism.* The Congregationalists* and Baptists,* with their loose form of denominational government, offered few barriers to the spread of liberalism. At Andover Seminary* the board of visitors dismissed Egbert C. Smyth, but appeals carried the case to the Supreme Court of Massachusetts where, in 1892, the court voided the action. Among Baptists, conservatives gained the dismissal of Ezra P. Gould from Newton Theological Seminary in 1882 and Nathaniel Schmidt from Colgate in 1896, but by the outbreak of World War 1* all the Baptist seminaries in the North were in the liberal camp.

While the Methodists* had better structures for addressing liberalism, their tests of fellowship tended to stress morality rather than doctrine.* In 1904, when charges of denying the inerrancy* of Scripture* were leveled against Hinkley G. Mitchell at Boston University's School of Theology, and then against Bordon P. Bowne,* the General Conference of 1908 called a halt to any further heresy proceedings and relieved the bishops of the responsibility for investigating false teaching in Methodist schools.

The most publicized heresy trials were in Presbyterian ranks in the North. As early as 1874 Francis L. Patton* of McCormick Theological Seminary lodged charges against David Swing,* pastor of the Fourth Presbyterian Church in Chicago. The local presbytery* acquitted him of the charges, but when Patton threatened to appeal the verdict, Swing resigned his pastorate and established an independent congregation. The following decade saw the dismissal of several other ministers on doctrinal grounds, including William C. McCune of Cincinnati; W. W. McLane of Steubenville, Ohio; and J. W. White of Huntington, Pennsylvania.

The rise to prominence of the issues of biblical inerrancy and the historical accuracy of the Scriptures sparked the two most celebrated cases of heresy, brought against Charles A. Briggs* at Union Theological Seminary* in New York and against Henry Preserved Smith* at Lane Theological Seminary in Cincinnati. In 1891 Briggs, in an address at Union, vigorously condemned the "dogma of verbal inspiration" taught at Princeton Seminary.* Conservatives were so angered that they filed charges of heresy against him in the presbytery of New York. The presbytery acquitted Briggs of the charges, but the General Assembly set aside the verdict and suspended Briggs from the ministry. The seminary, however, severed its connection with the denomination and retained Briggs.

During the trial, Smith spoke in Briggs's defense and was soon charged and convicted of heresy on similar grounds by the presbytery of Cincinnati. The General Assembly upheld the decision. Smith was dismissed from Lane, but Union offered him a position in New York. Both men left the Presbyterian Church. Briggs became an Episcopalian* and Smith, a Congregationalist.

BIBLIOGRAPHY. W. R. Hutchison, *The Modernist Impulse in American Protestantism* (1976); L. A. Loetscher, *The Broadening Church* (1957); M. A. Noll, *Between Faith and Criticism: Evangelicals, Scholarship, and the Bible in America* (1986); G. H. Shriver, ed., *American Religious Heretics* (1966).
                                                    B. L. Shelley

Herman, Saint (c.1756-1836). First Orthodox* saint canonized* in America. Little is known of the life of the Monk Herman before he entered the monastic life in the Holy Trinity/St. Sergius Cloister near present-day Leningrad. There and in the more stringent Valamo Monastery where he transferred in 1778, he gained a reputation for introspection and simplicity. It seemed out of character for such an ascetic to volunteer for the team recruited to engage in mission* in the newly discovered waters of Alaska, but on Kodiak Island Herman proved himself the mission's most steadfast and important member.

His refusal to accept ordination,* claiming his unworthiness, effectively limited his role as an active missionary, but his patience with the foibles of others enabled him to serve as peacemaker between his idealistic brothers and the rapacious civil authorities. When the head of the mission, Fr. Ioasaf Bolotov, left for Russia in 1794, Herman was given preference over his ordained comrades to provide interim leadership. Following Bolotov's death, Herman was given the office outright. The remaining missionaries retired home, leaving him alone to instruct the natives in the rudiments of Christianity and practical living skills, twice from ignominious exile on Spruce Island.

More than anything else, Herman lived a life of simplicity and holiness which attracted others. Thirty years after his death, followers began to collect stories about him and about reputed miracles, and by 1900 he stood among the candidates for canonization in the Russian Church. The Bolshevik Revolution prevented such action in the land of his birth, but the Russians in diaspora several times came close (in 1936, 1953 and 1957), being prevented only by their lack of ideological unity. When ultimately in 1970 Herman was glorified as the New World's first Orthodox saint, it was in two parallel ceremonies—one on Kodiak Island by the newly independent Orthodox Church in America and another in San Francisco by the Russian Orthodox Church* Outside of Russia.

BIBLIOGRAPHY. R. Pierce, ed., *The Russian Orthodox Religious Mission in America, 1794-1837* (1978); M. Oleksa, ed., *Alaskan Missionary Spirituality* (1987).   P. D. Garrett

Herron, George Davis (1862-1925). Radical social prophet. Born in Indiana, limited in formal education, Herron worked as a printer and editor. In 1883 he entered the Congregational* ministry, served a number of congregations as he studied on his own, became known through publishing books of his sermons and addresses and was granted an honorary D.D. in 1892. Drawn to the early Social Gospel Movement,* the next year he was named as professor of applied Christianity at Iowa (later Grinnell) College, Iowa, and quickly attained a national following through his lectures and writings as the central figure in the controversial "Kingdom Movement."

Against the background of the labor strife, financial panic, drought and depression of the early 1890s, the Movement gained a wide hearing in the churches and won many to social Christian views. But as Herron moved steadily toward a more radical position, in both his theology* and social teachings, he lost most of his support in the churches. In 1900 he left the college, became a conspicuous figure in the organization of the American Socialist Party the following year and was divorced, remarried and deposed from the ministry. He then lived abroad as a leader in socialism until disillusioned by its tolerance for Germany. During World War 1* he became prominent again as a diplomatic agent of the Wilson* administration and interpreter to Europe of Wilson's war and peace aims. He died in Munich in 1925.

BIBLIOGRAPHY. M. P. Briggs, *George D. Herron and the European Settlement* (1932); *DAB* IV; R. T. Handy, "George D. Herron and the Kingdom Movement," *CH* 19 (1950):97-115.

R. T. Handy

Hewit, Augustine Francis (1820-1897). Cofounder of the Paulists.* Descended from illustrious New Englanders, Hewit was born in Fairfield, Connecticut, the son of Congregationalist* minister* Nathaniel Hewitt and Rebecca Hillhouse. He was educated at Phillips Academy, Amherst College and the Theological Institute of Connecticut (later Hartford Theological Seminary), where he read church history avidly. Influenced by the Tractarian Movement,* he left the Congregationalists and entered the Episcopal Church,* and was ordained* a deacon* in 1843. Three years later Hewit became a Catholic* and was ordained priest* in 1847 by Ignatius Reynolds, second bishop of Charlestown, South Carolina. Hewit taught in the seminary founded there by Bishop John England* and collaborated in editing his works for publication. Attracted to the Redemptorists* by John N. Neumann, Hewit was professed in 1850. Eight years later he, Isaac Hecker* and three other converts, were dispensed from their vows to establish the Paulists.

For almost forty years, Hewit contributed richly to the life of the young community and to Catholic letters. He wrote the first rule, educated the candidates and served as theologian* at the Second Plenary Council of Baltimore.* He frequently contributed articles to the *American Catholic Quarterly Review* and to the *Catholic World,* established in 1865 by Hecker. Hewit was assistant editor and became chief editor after Hecker's death in 1888. He was elected second superior of the Paulists in 1889. That year the Catholic University of America* opened and Hewit temporarily took the chair of church history and moved the Paulist house of studies to the campus. He established the Columbus Press (1891), now Paulist Press, began missions* to non-Catholics (1893), sent the Paulists to San Francisco (1894), and founded the Catholic Missionary Union (1896). He was given honorary doctorates by

Amherst and the Holy See.

BIBLIOGRAPHY. *DAB* IV; A. F. Hewit, *Memoir of the Life of the Rev. Francis A. Baker* (1889); J. P. Flynn, *The Early Years of Augustine F. Hewit, CSP* (1945); J. McSorley, *Father Hecker and His Friends* (1953). M. M. Reher

Hickok, Laurens Perseus (1789-1888). Congregational* theologian* and philosopher of religion.* Born in Bethel, Connecticut, Hickok was educated at Union College (B.A., 1820) and studied theology* under Bennet Tyler.* Hickok was ordained* in 1823 and ministered* at Kent (1823-1829) and Litchfield (1829-1836), Connecticut, before serving as a professor of theology at Western Reserve (1836-1844) and Auburn (1844-1852) seminaries. In 1852 he returned to Union, first as vice president and professor of mental and moral philosophy and later as president (1866-1868). After resigning from Union, he retired in Amherst, Massachusetts, where he continued his writing.

Hickok was one of several late nineteenth-century Congregationalists who drew on German thought, particularly Kant, in order to form a philosophical foundation for Calvinism* which he called "constructive realism." In his most significant work, *Rational Psychology* (1849), he argued that sense and understanding could apprehend objects, though only their primary qualities (such as substance and cause) were real and independent of mind. Secondary qualities (such as color) were mental. God, who is above the senses and understanding, could be apprehended by a third mental faculty, reason. He concluded that Calvinism was consistent with reason. His other writings include: *Creator and Creation* (1872) and *Humanity Immortal; or, Man Tried, Fallen and Redeemed* (1872). While some acclaimed him as having achieved the height of speculative thought, his critics charged him with being an idealist and even a pantheist.

BIBLIOGRAPHY. *DAB* V; B. Kuklick, *Churchmen and Philosophers* (1985).

D. G. Reid

Hicks, Elias (1748-1830). Farmer and leader of the Hicksite* schism among the Religious Society of Friends (Quakers).* Born in a Long Island Quaker farming community, Hicks came of age during the waning years of Quaker quietism.* From 1774, when he underwent a religious crisis, until his death in 1830, Hicks devoted himself to serving Quaker communities as far afield as Virginia, Indiana and Canada, covering over forty

thousand miles in his itinerant ministry.

Quakers had always stressed the Light of Christ as the continued presence of the historic Jesus Christ. With Hicks the Light came to be equated with the native rational capacity of the virtuous, naturally pure farmer, unburdened with the taint of unearned wealth, fine education or delicate manners. Religious authority for earlier Quakers had been grounded in an interplay between spiritual illumination and scriptural authority.* Hicks asserted that the common man's subjective rational capacity was primary. Hicks found Christ's atonement* for sin to be unreasonable. He believed that, at best, Christ's death achieved satisfaction only for the sins of his Jewish contemporaries. For Hicks salvation depended solely upon obedience to the inward Light.

In the age of rising Jacksonian democracy, Hicks represented the great commoner, who earned his living by the sweat of his brow and sought to throw off the yoke of wealthy Quaker bankers and industrialists with strong British ties who dominated Quaker leadership.

A liberal in his stress on reason, Hicks was a quietist in other respects. He opposed the development of the Erie Canal, claiming that if God had wanted a river flowing across northern New York, he would have put one there. He also opposed cooperative philanthropic* associations. Some of his discourses are recorded in *A Series of Extemporaneous Discourses* (1825).

See also FRIENDS, THE RELIGIOUS SOCIETY OF; HICKSITES.

BIBLIOGRAPHY. *DAB* V; *DARB*; E. Hicks, *Journal of the Life and Religious Labours of Elias Hicks* (1832); B. Forbush, *Elias Hicks: Quaker Liberal* (1956); *NCAB* 11. R. E. Selleck

Hicksites. A branch of the Religious Society of Friends (Quakers).* Hicksites derive their designation from the Long Island farmer and Quaker minister Elias Hicks.* Earlier Quakers had used *Light* as a term synonymous with *Holy Spirit*. With Hicks, the Light, as the autonomous and natural reason of the common laboring man, was exalted to primary authority. Among those views which Hicks found unreasonable was Christ's substitutionary death on the cross and his physical resurrection.

Hicks opposed missions,* Bible societies,* public schools, cooperative charitable and reform* activities and industrial developments such as the Erie Canal. He was much admired by that sort of democratic American individualism* that Walt Whitman celebrated in his poetry.

Hicks led a schism among American Quakers

which began in Philadelphia in 1827-1828. Modern Hicksites compose the Friends General Conference with a membership of 25,000. They maintain the traditional silent worship service but have abandoned any sort of designation of those who are especially called to public ministry.*

See also FRIENDS, THE RELIGIOUS SOCIETY OF; HICKS, ELIAS.

BIBLIOGRAPHY. R. W. Doherty, *The Hicksite Separation* (1967). R. E. Selleck

Higginson, Francis (1588-1630). Teacher of Salem, Massachusetts. A graduate of Emmanuel College, Cambridge (B.A., 1609; M.A., 1613), Higginson served for a time as curate of the Claybrooke parish in Leicester. But he soon demonstrated Puritan* tendencies by examining people before admitting them to Communion.* He eventually converted to Puritanism under the influence of Arthur Hildersham and Thomas Hooker.* Though silenced for nonconformity, he remained very popular amongst his parishioners, who employed him periodically as a lecturer.

While waiting to be haled before the High Commission Court, the agents of the New England Company contacted Higginson. He, with a number of his former congregation, consented to emigrate. They departed in May 1629, and arrived in New England on June 29. His journal of the voyage is extant, as is his *New England's Plantation* (1630) describing New England's geographical and climatological conditions, as well as the state of its settlements.

On a fast day, July 30, 1629, after seeking advice from representatives of Plymouth, the settlers of Salem appointed by ballot Higginson as their teacher and Samuel Skelton* as pastor. The church covenant* composed by the pair established Salem as the first non-separating congregational* Puritan* church in New England. The covenant instituted the practice of allowing into Communion only those who could prove sound doctrinal knowledge and an experience of grace, thereby setting the precedent for New England orthodoxy.

BIBLIOGRAPHY. *AAP* 1; *DAB* V; *DARB;* T. W. Higginson, *Life of Francis Higginson* (1891); C. Mather, *Magnalia Christi Americana* (1702); *NCAB* 1; P. Seaver, *The Puritan Lectureships* (1970); A. Young, *Chronicles of the First Planters,* Collections of the Mass. Hist. Soc., 1 (1792):117-124.

K. P. Minkema

High Church. A term referring to individuals and congregations within the Anglican Church* who interpret the episcopate,* priesthood* and Book of Common Prayer* in a Catholic* sense, stressing the continuity of the Anglican Church with Catholic Christianity. High churchmen are followers of the Tractarian* or Oxford Movement (1833-1845) led by John Henry Newman and Edward Pusey in England, standing in the tradition of William Laud (1573-1645), the archbishop* of Canterbury, who advocated a high view of the church,* ministry,* worship* and sacraments.* In America the influence of the movement reached a peak during the 1840s and 1850s and resulted in a number of ecclesiastical trials of bishops,* as well as secessions of Anglicans to Roman Catholicism (See Ives, Levi Silliman). The Sunday* service of the high church tradition took on a ceremonialism very similar to the Roman Mass.* The influence of the movement may also be seen in Gothic church architecture.*

See also ANGLICANISM; BROAD CHURCH; LOW CHURCH; TRACTARIANISM.

BIBLIOGRAPHY. E. C. Chorley, *Men and Movements in the American Episcopal Church* (1946); R. B. Mullin, *Episcopal Vision/American Reality* (1986). R. Webber

Higher Christian Life. A late-nineteenth century Protestant* movement emphasizing experiential holiness* as a distinct work of grace clearly distinguishable from justification.* The yearning for a higher spirituality has given birth to a number of diverse movements in the history of the church. The Higher Christian Life Movement, with its cornerstone of experiential holiness, originated among North American Protestants and was eventually to move worldwide by means of the British Keswick Movement.

In North America the Movement had predecessors such as* Charles G. Finney,* who developed a Reformed* version of perfectionism*; the Methodist* Timothy Merritt, who edited *The Guide to Christian Perfection*; Methodist Phoebe Palmer,* who developed a theology* of the experience of "second blessing"*; and Asa Mahan,* an associate of Finney who later modified his Oberlin* perfectionism to reflect Higher Life emphases. The common thread running through these individuals and their theologies of sanctification* was the pursuit of personal holiness. This pursuit was part and parcel of the nineteenth-century camp-meeting* revival movement. In many cases they reflected the Wesleyan* teaching of perfection and entire sanctification, but even when the terminology was not Wesleyan, the pursuit of holiness remained their goal.

The figures most prominently associated with

the phrase *Higher Christian Life* are William E. Boardman,* a Presbyterian* minister* who in 1859 published *The Higher Christian Life;* the husband-wife team of Robert Pearsall Smith,* who wrote *Holiness Through Faith* (1870); and Hannah Whitall Smith,* who published the immensely popular *The Christian's Secret to the Happy Life* (1875). Hannah Smith in particular was influenced by Quaker* theology. The basic theology expressed by these leaders was that while justification* by faith brought cleansing from the guilt of sin,* sanctification by faith brought cleansing from the power of sin and, consequently, a happy, or higher, Christian life. While differences existed between proponents, such as whether sanctification came through a crisis experience, they agreed that sanctification was realized by a second act of faith which delivered the Christian from an endless round of sinning and repenting. In this way they were able to introduce perfectionism to non-Methodists who would have found the language of perfectionism distasteful.

In a Victorian age when there were not many certainties left to which the common person could cling, the proponents of the higher Christian life offered the certainty of individual salvation and personal holiness through the witness and power of the Holy Spirit. Although the Keswick* Convention in England chose to emphasize suppression rather than cleansing or freedom from sin, the annual meetings in the English Lake District, which have continued into the twentieth century, are a reflection of the Higher Christian Life Movement. The ideas became common among many evangelicals of the twentieth century and formalized in the doctrinal positions of several so-called Holiness denominations in America.

See also HOLINESS MOVEMENT; PERFECTIONISM; SANCTIFICATION; VICTORIOUS CHRISTIAN LIFE.

BIBLIOGRAPHY. J. Abbott, "The Higher Christian Life," *Bibliotheca Sacra and Biblical Repository* XVII (July 1860):508-535; D. W. Dayton, ed., *The Devotional Writings of Robert Pearsall Smith and Hannah Whitall Smith* (1984); D. W. Dayton, ed., *The Higher Christian Life: A Bibliographical Overview* (1984); M. E. Dieter, *The Holiness Revival of the Nineteenth Century* (1980); D. W. Frank, *Less Than Conquerors* (1986); C. E. Jones, *The Perfectionist Persuasion* (1974); B. B. Warfield, *Perfectionism,* 2 vols. (1931). W. S. Gunter

Higher Education, Catholic. The system of colleges and universities operated by or connected with dioceses* or religious orders* of the Roman Catholic Church* in the U.S. Catholic higher education in the U.S. began after American independence from Great Britain. Catholic colleges were not founded in colonial America for two chief reasons: (1) the legacy of virulent anti-Catholicism from English culture led to a number of legal and social disabilities, including proscriptions on Catholic schooling at all levels; and (2) the small Catholic population was dispersed throughout the mid-Atlantic states.

The New Republic: Birth. Colonial Catholics of higher social standing sent their youth to England or the Continent for their university education. Consequently, when American Catholics did begin to found colleges, lacking indigenous educational models and traditions, they turned to the Continent. But it would be some time before Catholics had a large and stable population, well enough educated to profit from higher education. For this reason, earlier colleges faced enrollment and financial constraints. Until well into the nineteenth century, Catholic colleges were very small, strongly denominational,* in perennial financial straits and geared to produce classically educated young men fit to study for the priesthood.* But in these respects they resembled most other American colleges in the early nineteenth century. Their most obvious difference was their institutional structure and, in the long term, their persistence in retaining these early features long after many other American colleges had undergone dramatic change during the mid nineteenth century.

The denominational influence was felt most strongly in the relationship between colleges and diocesan authorities. Until the mid nineteenth century Catholic colleges were generally founded by bishops* in order to provide pre-seminary training in philosophy, classical languages and literature. Bishops were eager to sponsor colleges because they wanted to solve the practical problem of a perpetual shortage of priests and seminarians. They were also interested in educating a cultured elite who would represent Catholicism in the face of a growing hostility. Colleges served a defensive and apologetic* purpose as intellectual centers from which Catholic doctrine might be diffused.

Georgetown, the first American Catholic college, was founded by America's first Catholic bishop, John Carroll.* Typical for its period, it served as a model for many later Catholic educational institutions. Although it opened in 1791, Georgetown did not grant any degrees until 1817. Its curriculum and operating principles were influenced by traditional European practices, particularly those of the Jesuit* order, of which Bishop Carroll was a member. Renowned as educators since the late sixteenth century, the Society of Jesus had a distinctive educational system called the *ratio studiorum,* and Georgetown operated according to a modified version of it. This system called for a structure essentially different from the typical American college, since this continental tradition combined both secondary and collegiate studies in the same institution.

Georgetown took students at an early age, usually after they had completed the equivalent of a modern elementary education, and trained them in Latin grammar and eloquence of expression. The curriculum was completed by moral studies. Student life and discipline in the antebellum American Catholic college differed little from that found in Catholic seminaries.* Faculty and administration were both drawn from the religious orders* which operated the colleges; they were exclusively male clerics and seldom had extensive formal training in their teaching fields.

Late Nineteenth Century: Growth. Beginning in the mid nineteenth century, many changes took place which eventually transformed the Catholic college. European Catholic immigrants* settled in urban areas. Their arrival transformed Catholicism into the largest religious denomination in the U.S., and in turn contributed to the greatest growth of Catholic higher education as new colleges proliferated. Catholic higher education tended to follow the immigrant settlement patterns and took on an urban character.

In addition, religious orders took on an ever-greater role in Catholic higher education, with the result that diocesan influence waned. Only a few present-day institutions have retained diocesan affiliations, most Catholic colleges and universities being affiliated with a particular male or female religious order. The role of religious orders brought about a diversity and decentralization in American Catholic higher education, as each order implemented its own educational practices and traditions and supplied faculty and administrators from within its own ranks. The Jesuits, to this day the leading Catholic religious order in higher education, have tended to found their educational institutions in urban areas. Dozens of other religious orders have founded and supported institutions of higher education, but their schools have generally continued to be small, financially precarious, and dedicated to educating seminary candidates as well as a class of elite Catholic intellectuals.

The one institution which departed dramatically from this pattern was the Catholic University of America.* Founded in 1889 as a graduate institution of research in theology and related studies, it was modeled after the University of Louvain in Belgium and remains as the only pontifical university in the U.S. This unique status means that it is chartered by the papacy* and authorized to grant pontifical degrees: the licentiate (S.T.L.) and doctorate (S.T.D.). For several decades after its founding, it remained the only American Catholic institution seriously committed to graduate studies, scholarship and scholarly publishing—characteristics reflecting the influence of non-Catholic higher education.

The rest of Catholic higher education was slow to respond to these influences of the general revolution in American higher education, but Catholic University eventually validated and promoted them among other Catholic colleges and universities. Though Catholic University supplied the graduate training for scores of Catholic college professors over the next several decades, it never achieved the success its founders envisioned. Jointly sponsored and financially dependent upon all the bishops and dioceses of the U.S., it suffered from those bishops that preferred to invest their resources in their own diocesan institutions. In addition, in the 1890s Catholic University became a center of Americanism.* This ensuing controversy split the American church along liberal and conservative lines. In the eyes of conservatives, Catholic University was associated with dangerous liberal Americanist views. Pope Leo XIII's* condemnation of Americanism and Pope Pius X's* condemnation of modernism* combined to restrain creative Catholic scholarship for many decades to come.

The Early Twentieth Century: Consolidation. The intellectual philosophy undergirding Catholic higher education in the early decades of the twentieth century was based on the view that the Catholic Church was the one true church, the trustee of a sacred legacy of divine wisdom passed down from the apostolic age. The mission of a college or university was to transmit this body of truth to future generations and develop its implications for Catholics. The vocation of a scholar was not to find new truth but to transmit and defend revealed truth. In the neo-scholasticism* of the early twentieth century, Catholic schools and scholars found a coherent and cohesive intellectual basis for their work. They formed their own learned societies, published their own journals and monographs, founded their own university presses, and eventually instituted graduate and doctoral programs in the pursuit of neo-scholastic scholarly excellence. In so doing they took the outward forms of the university revolution and adapted them to their own apostolic and devotional* purposes.

Structurally, Catholic colleges also underwent change. Foundations, accrediting agencies, federal and state educational agencies, as well as scholarly and educational associations shaped the institutions by their professional and national standards, defining college structures and curriculum. In order to gain accreditation, grants or recognition from the non-Catholic educational institutions and accrediting bodies, Catholic higher education had to adjust. They did so by detaching the preparatory or high school departments from their collegiate operations, by accepting the definition of a college as a four-year course of study, by bringing their curriculum into closer step with non-Catholic curricula, by upgrading their faculties and by instituting graduate programs.

But while Catholics were rebuilding their colleges and universities, student life and discipline remained resistant to change. Student organizations and activities in the early twentieth century reflected the dominant devotional character of pre-conciliar Catholicism. Devotional life and athletics flourished, while academic life continued to center around the mastery of revealed truth expressed through neo-scholasticism.

Post-World War 2: New Identity. In the 1950s the post-World War 2* enrollment boom brought Catholic institutions stable enrollment and financial bases. For the first time, Catholic higher education had a cadre of Catholic leaders committed to academic excellence. In part this was due to a wave of self-criticism within the Catholic academic community. Initiated by Msgr. John T. Ellis and picked up by others, Catholics were charged with failing to contribute their portion to the intellectual and cultural life of the nation. The chief explanation was found in Catholic anti-intellectualism, a mentality largely based on their unquestioning obedience to authority.*

During the 1960s Catholic higher education not only faced the student unrest and reaction against authority generally associated with that decade, it also faced the far-reaching changes associated with Vatican II.* Catholic higher education reflected the uncertainty and uneasiness accompanying the dissolution of the apparently cohesive world view of pre-conciliar Catholicism. If the church no longer represented absolute certainty and if, as Vatican II seemed to teach, a new role was to be given to the laity,* then a whole new approach to authority was conceivable. In turn, this would call for a new identity and purpose for Catholic higher education.

Cultural assimilation and socioeconomic progress were combining to make third-generation American Catholics similar to other Americans in most respects, not least in their attitudes toward freedom and authority. Record enrollments supplied the financial means for dramatic improvements in Catholic higher education. During the 1960s Catholic colleges numbered over 300, with an enrollment of over 400,000 students. More importantly, the larger schools reached substantial enrollment levels, allowing for significant improvements in quality.

Curricular revision, including the elimination of traditional courses, took place at many institutions. Faculty and administrative posts were increasingly filled by lay people as religious vocations declined and large numbers of sisters, priests and brothers left their orders and dioceses. Lay people were actively sought and hiring was done on the basis of professional qualifications, rather than religious vocation. These new faculty members and administrators often had degrees from prestigious non-Catholic universities and brought with them vastly different attitudes toward church authority. They eased the transition to greater lay representation on the boards of trustees and distanced themselves and their institutions from the official church.

By the 1970s and early 1980s, the better Catholic colleges and universities resembled their non-Catholic counterparts in more ways than they differed. Ownership and administration had passed from priests or religious, with little training beyond philosophy or theology, to professionally trained men and women. Faculties conducted their teaching, research and writing in accordance with professional and disciplinary norms, rather than by the standards dictated by their local bishop or religious superior. Academic freedom was jealously guarded, even in the face of accepted church teachings.

Apart from the likelihood that they would identify themselves as Catholic, in intellectual ability and socioeconomic background, Catholic student bodies became virtually indistinguishable from non-Catholic student bodies. Their Catholic sensibilities, shaped largely or solely in the post-Vatican II church, were vastly different from devotionally pious pre-conciliar students. Many of these new students had studied in Catholic parochial schools,* which had also become very similar to their non-Catholic counterparts.

As Catholic institutions receive more government, foundation and corporate funding, a kind of de facto secularization has set in. Conditions for funding have sometimes involved assurances that there will be no clerical or doctrinal interference in the execution of programs. An implicit recognition of this secularization has come from several court rulings stating that government funding for Catholic higher education has not violated First Amendment* provisions since Catholic institutions are civil corporations, are run by lay boards and benefit society as a whole. The increased role of the laity, the waning of a traditional Catholic identity, and de facto secularization have promoted academic progress, but they have also left Catholic educational institutions with an unresolved identity crisis.

Catholic college presidents, the International Federation of Catholic Universities, the Association of Catholic Colleges and Universities (formerly the college and university department of the National Catholic Educational Association) and episcopal supporters both within and without the National Conference of Catholic Bishops* have clearly articulated the need for autonomy from church authority, the importance of academic freedom and the primary goal of academic excellence.

In the face of uncertainty regarding the role of Catholic dogma in their colleges and universities, many leaders in Catholic higher education have redefined their role in terms of confronting the modern world as signs of Christianity and of serving society by exploring and applying Christian principles of peace and justice. This new identity has only recently begun to take shape and its ultimate direction is yet unclear. Adjusting to this new agenda, student life is now less characterized by devotion and more by social activism, with an emphasis on peace* and justice.

Recently, some elements of traditional Catholicism have come to the fore, raising issues of church authority. Catholic educational leaders and others have come to recognize the distinctive nature of Catholic higher education in the U.S. Not only is it the largest system of its kind in the world, it has traditionally had less formal ties to the institutional church and tended not to have been canonically* erected or administered. Moreover, due to American pluralist* democracy,* government interference is unlikely, due not only to First Amendment guarantees, but also to the fact that Catholic institutions continue to comply with the standards of accrediting agencies, educational associations and similar regulatory bodies.

One of the chief concerns has been the revision of the Code of Canon Law,* both before and after its promulgation in 1983. Of special concern are the canons (807-814) dealing with Catholic colleges and universities. American Catholic educators have lobbied to change the wording of the relevant canons, with some success. Failing to gain all they sought, they are attempting to gain exemption for American institutions. Reasoning from the uniqueness of American Catholic higher education, they argue that full compliance with canons designed for vastly different countries and cultures holds potential dangers for Catholic higher education in the U.S. Full compliance could jeopardize accreditation status, government or foundation funding, the institutions' ability to attract and retain first-rate faculties and ultimately undermine their academic excellence and autonomy.

The well-publicized case of Charles E. Curran of the Catholic University of America is an example of a tenured professor of moral theology whose views on certain moral questions were not in complete compliance with church teachings. Suspended from his professorship in August 1986, he appealed the action through university and ecclesiastical channels. His case has raised the questions of whether civil law could be invoked and the larger issue of the legal status of Catholic colleges and universities in the U.S., the status of faculty and administrators and the proper relationship between American Catholic higher education and the Vatican.

In 1987 there were 238 Catholic colleges and universities in the U.S., enrolling a total of 556,337 students. This can be compared to approximately one decade earlier, when 251 institutions enrolled a total of 422,243 students. In the decade prior to that, there were over 300 institutions enrolling approximately 400,000 students. Thus, while enrollments have increased, the number of institutions has declined. The remaining institutions are generally stronger and bear a greater likeness to their non-Catholic counterparts than they did in the past. In all likelihood this trend will continue. But Catholic colleges and universities in the U.S. are faced with the challenge of maintaining and improving their academic standing, while shaping their identity between the forces of Catholic magisterium and academic freedom.

See also CATHOLIC UNIVERSITY OF AMERICA; NORTH AMERICAN COLLEGE, THE PONTIFICAL; NOTRE DAME, UNIVERSITY OF; SEMINARY, CATHOLIC DIOCESAN.

BIBLIOGRAPHY. F. L. Christ and G. E. Sherry, eds., *American Catholicism and the Intellectual Ideal* (1961); P. A. Fitzgerald, *Governance of Jesuit Colleges in the United States* (1984); A. F. Greeley, *The Changing Catholic College* (1967); R. Hassenger, ed., *The Shape of Catholic Higher Educa-*

tion (1967); N. G. McCluskey, *The Catholic University: A Modern Appraisal* (1970); M. Oates, *Higher Education for Catholic Women: An Historical Anthology* (1987); E. J. Power, *Catholic Higher Education in America: A History* (1972).

D. L. Salvaterra

Higher Education, Protestant. From the 1636 opening of Harvard,* the first American college, until the late nineteenth century, Christian higher education, almost without exception, was synonymous with American higher education in general. Most colleges, including the state universities, operated as Protestant institutions. The last century has been different, for with the development of a more pluralistic society, the modern concept of separation of church and state, as well as secular thought patterns among American intellectuals, the Christian liberal-arts college and its educational philosophy have become merely one option among many in the panorama of American higher education.

The colonial colleges were few in number and, like most other seventeenth- and eighteenth-century American institutions, reflected the existing British cultural patterns. Harvard* (Puritan*/Congregational*), William and Mary* (Anglican*), Yale* (Congregational), Princeton* (New Light* Presbyterian*), Columbia* (essentially Anglican), Pennsylvania* (essentially secular), Brown* (Baptist*), Rutgers* (Dutch Reformed*) and Dartmouth* (New Light Congregational) in their organization and philosophy showed the influence of Cambridge, Oxford and the dissenting academies in England, and Edinburgh and Aberdeen in Scotland. Cambridge and Oxford were the primary models, and the colonial colleges imitated them in several ways: religious groups largely controlled the institutions; the curriculum was narrow; the students resided as well as studied on the campus; higher education was primarily for the elite; and the primary purpose was to teach youthful minds, rather than discover new knowledge.

Both in the late colonial period and the early to mid-nineteenth century, revivalism* was a major factor in motivating religious leaders to found new colleges. Zeal created by the First* (1730s-1740s) and the Second (1800-1835) Great Awakenings* led to the founding of Princeton, Brown, Rutgers and Dartmouth in the mid-eighteenth century and to the single most prolific period of college founding in American history: the second generation of the nineteenth century.

Not only was revivalism important in giving birth to colleges, but it also was a major means of stimulating the spiritual development of the students, especially during the nineteenth century. Although the college leaders were Christian in orientation, the majority of the students were not, and the periodic revival served as the most effective method for bringing a large number of students to Christian conversion. Therefore, the nineteenth-century colleges played a larger role in evangelizing their students than do contemporary Christian colleges, with their higher percentage of Christian students. Although revivalism was very significant in the U. S. colleges, it was not prominent in the Canadian schools, except at the nineteenth-century Methodist colleges, such as Albert and Victoria.

Frequently revivalism combined with the frontier movement as a stimulant to college founding. As the population moved westward, many institutions came into existence because community leaders were anxious to work with the denominational* leaders in beginning new institutions. While the religious factor may have loomed large in the motives of the ministers,* it was only one of several factors influencing the community leaders who desired the prestige, cultural advantages and stimulus to economic and population growth which a new college could bring. Especially noteworthy as mid-nineteenth-century college founders were the Baptists and Methodists* who joined the Presbyterians and Congregationalists as the four denominations sponsoring the greatest number of colleges by 1860.

In the older colleges, the curriculum was much more limited and the extracurricular much more closely correlated with the curriculum than has been the case in the past century. Students who began college in the same year enrolled in the same classes together for four years. The curriculum emphasized the study of ancient languages and mathematics, with only limited attention given to science. Frequently the most stimulating courses were those in philosophy and religion, usually taught by the president to the senior class and identified, variously, as mental, moral and intellectual philosophy; evidences of Christianity; logic; and ethics. These courses usually gave major attention to the social sciences as well as philosophy and religion.

The literary society was by far the most influential social activity in the pre-Civil War college; it may also have been the leading intellectual one as well. On each campus the students divided into two or more societies, which fervently competed with one another in debate and oration contests, building library collections and furnishing halls.

They found their society libraries invariably more accessible and sometimes better equipped than the main college library.

After the Civil War,* Christian higher education became increasingly available to youth other than the relatively affluent, mainline Protestant, white young men that had populated the old-time colleges. A few white women and blacks enrolled in college before the Civil War, but the many new black colleges and women's colleges founded by Christian denominations and individuals, and the new land-grant colleges founded by individual states for youth with agricultural and mechanical interests, represented the first significant democratization of higher education. Adding further to the broadening spectrum in Christian higher education were the colleges begun by such late-nineteenth-century immigrant groups as the Scandinavian Lutherans,* the Dutch Reformed, the German Brethren* and Mennonites.*

The democratization of higher education led to curricular reform. The old heavily classical curriculum may have worked well when most college students were preparing to be preachers,* teachers, lawyers and doctors, but the new students in an increasingly industrial society had broader interests. By 1900 many colleges allowed their students to choose from elective courses for at least fifty per cent of their curriculum. One significant consequence of the new elective system was that colleges began to offer systematic courses in biblical literature. The increasingly specialized curriculum was possible only because the instructors were becoming better trained in the old European and the new American graduate schools.

The pivotal event in all of American higher education was the movement toward secularization which began in the late nineteenth century. Before this intellectual revolution, nearly all college instructors and other leading thinkers accepted Christian theism* or at least a supernatural world view. Today, even at many church-related colleges, secular modes of thought dominate over the Christian understanding of truth. The transition occurred gradually but broadly in many disciplines, including biblical interpretation,* theology,* philosophy, sociology, psychology,* economics and, particularly, the biological and physical sciences, as American intellectuals, following the lead of their European counterparts, began to embrace logical positivism as the new approach to truth, and relativism as the new value system. In general the major state universities and some of the elite private institutions led the secularization movement in the late nineteenth century. They were followed by the state colleges and more of the elite private schools. After the First World War,* most colleges of the major denominations began to be affected. Today, the continuing Christian colleges reflect a minority view within the intellectual community.

Not since the skeptical 1790s, on the eve of the Second Great Awakening, had the Christian colleges experienced the degree of discouragement that they encountered during the second quarter of the twentieth century, for added to the mounting secularization was the impact of the nation's worst economic crisis, the Great Depression.* Frequently the continuing Christian colleges were less affluent than the secularizing ones and thus more vulnerable to the effects of the Depression. Yet most survived, and by the 1940s the Christian college movement was beginning to recover. Although the movement toward secularization continued, the stimulus of war production ended the Great Depression, and the GI Bill brought a record number of enrollees of all types.

This recovery process has continued steadily in the last three decades until today the Christian colleges are stronger than they have been at any time since the secular revolution. This recovery has come because of a combination of factors: the decline in the number of colleges to begin the secularization process, the increasing affluence of society in general, the development of government-based student-aid programs for students in private as well as public institutions, the increasing popularity of attending college and cooperative efforts such as the Christian College Coalition that have allowed the Christian colleges to achieve greater influence and increased public awareness of their growing quality and clearly defined goals. At present the avowedly Christian liberal arts colleges (exclusive of the Bible colleges*) number perhaps 200. These include some of the colleges affiliated with the mainline* denominations—especially the Baptist and Lutheran groups, the colleges affiliated with the small evangelical* denominations and the independent evangelical institutions.

The Canadian record in church-sponsored higher education differs from the U. S. pattern in several ways. It developed more slowly, with only a few colleges (mostly Anglican) operating for a very limited number of students before 1830. Then in the generation before the Confederation (1867), the church college achieved its maximum influence with the founding of Acadia, Victoria, Queen's, Bishop's, Mount Allison, Knox, St. John's, Trinity, Albert, Huron, Morrin and Queen's Newfoundland. The process of secularization began earlier and extended more completely in the Canadian schools than it did south of the border. Already by 1867 King's Fredericton, King's Toronto and McGill had ceased to be church colleges. Gradually over the next century most of the others dropped (or greatly loosened) their denominational connections and affiliated with the growing public universities. A combination of financial pressures, smallness of size and increasing acceptance of secular thought patterns made it difficult for the church colleges to retain their independent status. By the mid-1960s only four church-related colleges—Acadia (Baptist), Bishop's (Anglican), Mount Allison (Methodist) and Waterloo Lutheran—continued independent of university affiliation; and except for the Bible colleges, there existed very few evangelical institutions (e.g., Waterloo Lutheran, Conrad Grebel, Regent), whether independent or university-affiliated.

See also BIBLE INSTITUTES AND SCHOOLS; SEMINARIES, CATHOLIC DIOCESAN; HIGHER EDUCATION, CATHOLIC; THEOLOGICAL EDUCATION, PROTESTANT.

BIBLIOGRAPHY. A. F. Holmes, *The Idea of a Christian College* (1975); D. C. Masters, *Protestant Church Colleges in Canada* (1966); M. A. Noll, "Christian Thinking and the Rise of the American University," *CSR* 9 (1979); M. M. Pattillo and D. M. MacKenzie, *Church Sponsored Higher Education in the U. S.* (1966); W. C. Ringenberg, *The Christian Colleges: A History of Protestant Higher Education in America* (1984); F. Rudolph, *The American College and University: A History* (1962); C. P. Shedd, *Two Centuries of Student Christian Movements* (1934). W. C. Ringenberg

Hildebrand, Henry (1911-). Canadian Bible College* pioneer. Born in a Mennonite* farming community in southern Russia, Hildebrand's family immigrated to Canada and settled in a Mennonite community in Winkler, Manitoba, in 1925. Converted at the age of seventeen, Hildebrand's early faith was nurtured in the Mennonite Brethren Church.* He trained for three years at Winnipeg Bible College, where he was influenced by premillennial* dispensationalism.*

During the early 1930s he worked as an itinerant evangelist* on the Canadian prairies. In so doing, he established contacts with people who later played key roles in Briercrest Bible College, which Hildebrand organized in 1935 near Caronport, Saskatchewan. He served as its president and principal until 1977.

In the wake of a revival* on the Canadian prairies (which was at its peak between 1937 and 1945), Briercrest grew to be one of Canada's largest Bible colleges, with a strongly dispensational and faith-missions* orientation. Hildebrand's Mennonite background and his role in mainstream fundamentalism* enabled many in the Canadian Mennonite community to emerge from their ethnic isolation and move away from some Mennonite distinctives.

BIBLIOGRAPHY. H. Hildebrand, *In His Loving Service* (1985). D. M. Lewis

Hillenbrand, Reynold Henry (1904-1979). Seminary* rector,* liturgical pioneer and social activist. Born in Chicago, Hillenbrand entered Quigley Preparatory Seminary in Chicago in 1920 and St. Mary of the Lake Major Seminary in 1924. Ordained* to the priesthood by George Cardinal Mundelein* September 21, 1929, he completed doctoral work at St. Mary of the Lake (S.T.D., 1930). During a year of study in Rome, Hillenbrand came into contact with papal social teaching enunciated in Pius XI's* encyclical* *Quadragesimo Anno.**

When Hillenbrand returned to an America convulsed by the Great Depression, the papal teaching on social reconstruction seemed timely and imperative and became the wellspring of Hillenbrand's ideology and activity. Back in Chicago he served as a professor at Quigley Seminary and as the head of the Archdiocesan Mission Band. In 1936 he was appointed as the second rector of St. Mary of the Lake Seminary. His years as rector (1936-1944) allowed him to deepen his interest in the cause of liturgical renewal, which he saw as intimately connected with the cause of social reconstruction. He enthusiastically implemented many of the liturgical innovations suggested by reformers such as Virgil Michel, O.S.B.* Hillenbrand also took a leading role in the formation of the National Liturgical Conference in 1943. Linking the liturgy* with social action compelled Hillenbrand to teach classes on the social encyclicals and bring activists such as Dorothy Day,* Catherine DeHueck, Francis Haas* and Robert Lucey to speak to the seminarians. In addition, he was extensively involved with labor unions and the sponsorship of labor schools for the growing number of unskilled laborers being organized by the C.I.O. in Chicago.

His lifelong interest was the Specialized Catholic Action (*See* Catholic Action) work of Canon Joseph Cardijn of Belgium—a successful cell technique of Christian action drawing small groups of students and workers together to effect change in the social order. Hillenbrand soon established Specialized Catholic Action cells in the Chicago Archdiocese and his name was synonymous with this work in the U.S.

In 1944, when he was made pastor of Sacred Heart Parish in Hubbards Woods, his interests in liturgy and the social apostolate did not flag. His parish became a showplace of liturgical renewal* and his concern for Specialized Catholic Action continued to keep him busy as chaplain* to the Young Christian Students and Young Christian Workers as well as providing important leadership to the popular Christian Family Movement (CFM).* Hillenbrand suffered a serious car accident in 1949 which impaired his health and to some degree his spirit, but he kept at his work with CFM until he retired in 1970. Hillenbrand's work at St. Mary of the Lake inspired a generation of seminarians to embrace liturgical reform and social action.

BIBLIOGRAPHY. D. M. Robb, "Specialized Catholic Action in the United States, 1936-1949: Ideology, Leadership, and Organization" (unpublished Ph.D. dissertation, University of Minnesota, 1972); D. J. Geaney, O.S.A., "The Chicago Story" *Chicago Studies* 2 (Winter 1963):287-300.

S. M. Avella

Hillis, Newell Dwight (1858-1929). Congregationalist* clergyman* and pulpiteer. Born in Magnolia, Iowa, Hillis, at the age of seventeen, joined the American Sunday School Union* (ASSU) and spent approximately five years organizing Sunday schools* and ASSU churches in Nebraska, Utah and Wyoming. After graduating from Lake Forest College, Illinois (B.A., 1884), he attended McCormick Theological Seminary (B.D., 1887).

Following Presbyterian* ordination* on May 1, 1887, Hillis pastored the First Presbyterian Church, Peoria, Illinois (1887-1890), followed by First Presbyterian Church, Evanston, Illinois (1890-1894). He then became pastor of the independent Central Church, Chicago (1894-1899), where he established his reputation as a preacher* and lecturer. In 1899 he moved to the Plymouth Church of Brooklyn, New York (1899-1924), where he followed in the line of distinguished preachers Henry Ward Beecher* and Lyman Abbott.*

Hillis became an immensely popular preacher in both the U. S. and Great Britain. As a well-read and cultured pulpiteer, he developed a style which was described as "brilliant, original and pictorial." But Hillis's influence moved well beyond the pulpit. He developed an interest in urban planning and preached on the subject, and his illustrated lecture "A Better America" was used by the U. S. Government during and following World War 1. During the years 1914-1917, Hillis spoke in 250 cities across the nation, encouraging the country's early entrance into the war and favoring a plan to exterminate the German people.

Hillis authored about twenty-five books, including *Great Books as Life Teachers* (1899), *Great Men as Prophets of the New Era* (1922) and *A Man's Value to Society* (1896), as well as a compilation, *Lectures of Henry Ward Beecher* (1913). For many years his sermons were transcribed and published in Chicago and Brooklyn newspapers (1,000 sermons in twenty-five years). In addition, his travels and lectures continued unabated for many years, often averaging one hundred lectures in a year.

BIBLIOGRAPHY. R. H. Abrams, *Preachers Present Arms* (1933); *DAB*.

V. D. Macleod

Hills, Aaron Merritt (1848-1935). Church of the Nazarene* theologian.* Educated at Oberlin College* and the Yale* Divinity School, Hills was for twenty years the pastor of Congregational* churches at Ravenna, Ohio; Pittsburgh, Pennsylvania; and Springfield, Missouri. At Oberlin, Hills became greatly interested in Christian holiness* through the influence of Charles G. Finney* and during his later pastorates increasingly identified with the Holiness Movement.* He labored for several years as an evangelist* and during this period professed the Holiness Movement's cardinal experience of "entire sanctification."*

Hills was subsequently founding president of three Wesleyan*-Holiness colleges: Texas Holiness University (Greenville, Texas), now part of Southern Nazarene University (Bethany, Oklahoma); Central Holiness College in Iowa; and Illinois (now Olivet) Nazarene University. He also taught theology* at Asbury College and Bethany Nazarene College but was associated longest with Pasadena College (Nazarene) in California, where he taught from 1916 until 1932. Hills wrote nearly thirty books, including biographies of leaders in the Holiness and temperance* reform movements. The most notable are *Holiness and Power* (1897), a widely influential book in the Holiness Movement of its day, and *Fundamental Christian Theology,* 2 vols. (1931), the first Nazarene systematic theology.

BIBLIOGRAPHY. A. M. Hills, Collection of the Nazarene Archives; *Herald of Holiness* (July 2, 1951):4.

R. S. Ingersol

Himes, Joshua V. (1805-1895). Early Adventist* preacher* and leader of the Millerite movement. Himes was pastor of Boston's Chardon Street Chapel, a Christian Connection* church with close ties to various reform movements including abolitionism,* pacifism* and temperance.* He was a close friend and supporter of abolitionist William Lloyd Garrison.* In 1839 he accepted the views of William Miller* regarding the immediacy of Christ's Second Coming, which Miller calculated would occur sometime between 1843 and 1844. Through Himes's promotional skills, Miller, an obscure Baptist* preacher from New York, became a nationally known figure. Himes established several Millerite publications, including the *Signs of the Times,* founded in Boston in 1840; the *Advent Herald*; and a hymnal, *The Millennial Harp.* Chardon Street Chapel became a center of the Millerite movement. As Miller's millennial speculations failed to occur, Himes tried to rally the faithful through new calculations and publications. Ultimately he left the movement and became an Episcopal* priest* in the Dakotas.

BIBLIOGRAPHY. *DAB* V; G. Land, ed., *Adventism in America* (1986). B. J. Leonard

Hispanic Churches in America.

The Hispanic churches in America consist primarily of Catholics* and Protestants,* although there is a growing number of Hispanic adherents to other religious sects. Traditionally, active Catholics and Protestants have each made up about ten per cent of the Hispanic population. The remaining eighty per cent has been considered to be nominal Catholics who do not participate in the institutional life of the Church. During the 1970s an estimated five million Hispanics joined Protestant churches. During the late 1980s Hispanic Catholics were defecting from their mother church to Protestant bodies at the rate of approximately 60,000 per year. An estimated seventy per cent of the Hispanic population remained Catholic and of the remaining thirty per cent, an estimated twenty-two per cent were Protestant, with Pentecostal* groups showing the largest gains.

Despite their differences of faith and practice, the Protestant and Catholic Church have a remarkably similar history in their efforts and success among Hispanics. In their public and formal religious involvements, Hispanic Catholics and Protestants have faced similar issues.

Notwithstanding the true Christian commitment and heroic efforts of the early Spanish missions,* the overall experience of the Hispanic churches in North America has been one of spiritual neglect and one with the lowest involvement in the activities of the Christian church. This condition of indifference is rooted in historical, ethical and ecclesiastical antecedents, first in Latin America

and more recently in America. The establishment of structures of dependence that have had a long and serious impact on the Hispanic church, took place during the initial contacts between the church and the existing pre-Columbian cultures.

For Protestants the major thrust began in the early 1800s when mainline* denominations such as Presbyterians, Methodists and Baptists sent missionaries to evangelize the existing Hispanic populations then concentrated in the American Southwest and in the Caribbean islands of Puerto Rico and Cuba. In spite of the resistance by Anglo-Saxon colonists and the paternalism and incipient racism among some of the missionaries themselves, a number of churches were planted among the Hispanic population.

The efforts and results of the so-called missionary phase were very similar in all denominations. As Hispanics grew in numbers they were allowed to form separate congregations, conferences,* presbyteries* and conventions. But this segregated stage was short-lived as it gave way to an integrated form of polity which all but absorbed the Hispanic churches. In the late twentieth century a new stage of self-determination and liberation is now beginning to stir among Hispanics.

Hispanic Catholics faced a similar situation. When the present Southwest was annexed to the U.S. in the mid-nineteenth century, the Catholic Church within the region was in a state of near collapse. In Latin America a long tradition of Spanish colonialism and a long-standing conflict between the Church and state left a divided and weakened Church. Founded not on the basis of instruction and conviction but on the presence of social and religious customs, artifactual medals, holy pictures and fiestas, Hispanics brought with them to America a religious indifference. For decades they were essentially the religious serfs of a European immigrant church.

Unlike other immigrant groups in America, the Hispanic Church—Catholic and Protestant—remains today a religiously impoverished church among an economically deprived people. Hispanics were left without the succor the churches had given to earlier arrivals. Poverty, population shifts, inadequate clergy, patronizing missionary attitudes and inconsistent stands on social issues are just some of the factors that have retarded the assimilation of Hispanics into the churches.

The demands for assimilation have been stronger in religion than in any other aspect of Hispanic-American life. Historically, Hispanics have not wanted to give up their ethnic distinctives, wishing instead to have them accepted by the churches.

Differences such as emphasizing the heart over the mind, ardor over order, the right to remain different over the demand to assimilate represent some basic cultural traits of Hispanics. They have led to a duality within the Church—an institutional Church versus a folk Church.

Reminiscent of the sixteenth century when the symbolism of the Virgin of Guadalupe opened up a new possibility for racio-cultural dialog, a new openness began taking place within the Catholic Church during the 1960s. By the mid-seventies, a Secretariat of Hispanic Affairs had been appointed, and the first Hispanic archbishop* had been named. In the 1980s a series of "Encuentros" were held, dealing with relevant Hispanic issues. In 1983 a "Pastoral Letter on Hispanic Ministry" was issued to emphasize the need for trained leadership and ministry to serve Hispanics. The *Comunidades Ecelsiales de Base* (base communities) are offering the laity a new opportunity for involvement in the Church. Hispanic leadership continues to make progress in penetrating the mainstream of church hierarchy.

Outside the mainstream of American Protestantism, Pentecostals have been making the largest gains among Hispanics. Pentecostalism has a particular appeal to Hispanic ideology and tugs at the heart strings of Hispanics as it presents a God who accepts Hispanic passion and idiosyncrasies. Although similar to fundamentalist* churches in their regard for Scripture* and their anti-Catholic persuasion, Pentecostals offer the empowerment and ownership which Hispanics have historically sought in their institutions. The Pentecostal emphasis on the power and freedom of the Spirit is a refreshing option to the initial cultural barriers and traditional structures of dependence imposed by the historic mainstream churches. Pentecostals emphasize the participation of all believers and introduce a new type of theology that is practical and transforming. The nature of the Pentecostals's success in reaching Hispanic culture has not yet been understood and appropriated by many churches that continue to seek the spiritual and religious involvement of the growing Hispanic population in America.

As the Hispanic presence continues to grow in the U.S., the Hispanic Christian—and increasingly Protestant—population will continue to grow. As Hispanics take an active part in *their* churches, they will undoubtedly bring a new vitality to an increasingly multi-ethnic American church.

BIBLIOGRAPHY. T. Weyr, *Hispanic USA: Assimilation or Separation* (1988); H. J. Abramson, *Ethnic Diversity in Catholic America* (1973); L. Grebler, J.

Moore and R. Guzman, *The Mexican-American People, The Nation's Second Largest Minority* (1970).   J. Miranda

Hitchcock, Edward (1793-1864). Congregationalist* layman and geologist. Born in Deerfield, Massachusetts, and raised in a family of slender means, Hitchcock was largely self-taught. As principal of Deerfield Academy (1816-1819), he developed an interest in botany and mineralogy, which he zealously pursued on his own. In his faith Hitchcock moved from the Unitarian* affiliation of his youth to a Congregationalist orthodoxy* and then prepared for a career in pastoral ministry. While studying for the ministry at Yale* (1820), he became associated with Benjamin Silliman* as student and friend, and Hitchcock distinguished himself as Silliman's prize pupil. In 1825 poor health forced Hitchcock to leave the pastorate and accept a position at Amherst College in Massachusetts. For almost four decades he served there as professor (1825-1845; 1854-1864) or as president (1845-1854), distinguishing himself as an eminent geologist in his own right.

Hitchcock's geological work was a conscious attempt to reveal (usually through analogical means) the evidences of God in nature. His appointment at Amherst (ultimately as professor of natural theology and geology) reflected his era's conviction regarding the compatibility of natural theology and the natural sciences—leading to what has been called the "doxological" usage of science.

A prolific writer, Hitchcock advocated in perhaps his best work, *The Religion of Geology* (1852), the "restitution" or "re-creation" theory to account for the earth's antiquity and the truthfulness of Genesis one. That theory (earlier proposed by Thomas Chalmers and William Buckland) allowed the earth's entire geological record to be assigned to a prior creation (as inferred from Genesis 1:1-2). Not disposed to endorse any evolutionary scheme, Hitchcock's work argued for the complementarity of Christian faith and science, even if the latter required accepting an old earth.

See also SCIENCE AND CHRISTIANITY.

BIBLIOGRAPHY. T. D. Bozeman, *Protestants in an Age of Science* (1977); *DAB* V; *DARB*; H. Hovenkamp, *Science and Religion in America 1800-1860* (1978); D. N. Livingstone, *Darwin's Forgotten Defenders* (1987); *NCAB* 5.

S. R. Pointer

Hobart, John Henry (1775-1830). Episcopal* bishop* and controversialist. Graduating from what is now Princeton University* in 1793, he studied for the priesthood* under William White.* Hobart served briefly in churches in Pennsylvania and New Jersey before moving to New York in 1801, where he quickly became an important figure in the church there. He was elected assistant bishop in 1811 and became bishop of the diocese* of New York in 1816. During his career he was a vigorous champion of the high church* (*See* Tractarian Movement) vision of Episcopalianism, often characterized by his motto "evangelical faith and apostolic order." In numerous tracts and books, such as *A Companion for the Altar* (1804), he emphasized the value of the liturgy* and forms of the Episcopal Church.*

He furthermore stressed the differences between his church and the other Protestant* communities, particularly over the issue of apostolic succession*—or the claim that the Christian ministry can only rightfully be derived from the apostles through a continuing succession. Hobart claimed that apostolic succession was a necessary mark of a true church. These views naturally provoked strong controversy from other Protestants. Hobart's most famous work, *An Apology for Apostolic Order and Its Advocates* (1807), is a fruit of such controversy. Opposition to his views similarly emerged within the Episcopal Church and spawned a clash between high church and low church* (evangelical) parties. Hobart was also an active missionary,* preaching as far west as Michigan. Through his labors he did much to extend the Episcopal Church. Hobart's thought and labor made him one of the most important figures in the revitalization of the Episcopal Church in America after the Revolutionary War.*

BIBLIOGRAPHY. *AAP* 5; E. C. Chorley, *Men and Movements in the American Episcopal Church* (1946); *DAB* V; *DARB*; R. B. Mullin, *Episcopal Vision/American Reality* (1986); *NCAB* 1; R. W. Wertz, "John Henry Hobart, 1775-1830; Pillar of the Episcopal Church" (unpublished Ph.D. dissertation, Harvard University, 1967).

R. B. Mullin

Hocking, William Ernest (1873-1966). Philosopher of religion* and critic of Protestant* foreign missions.* Born in Cleveland, Ohio, Hocking received both M.A. and Ph.D. degrees from Harvard University.* On graduating from Harvard he taught philosophy at Andover Theological Seminary,* University of Southern California and Yale* (1908-1914). He then became a professor of philosophy at Harvard, where he remained until becoming professor emeritus in 1943. Hocking's philosophic

position was in the idealist tradition in modern philosophy which he identified as "Objective Idealism." His major philosophic works include: *The Meaning of God in Human Experience* (1912), *Human Nature and Its Remaking* (1918), *The Self: Its Body and Freedom* (1928), *Types of Philosophy* (1929), *Living Religions and World Faith* and *Science and the Idea of God.*

Hocking's political and ethical activities extended his influence beyond the community of professional philosophers. He took an active role in seeking the U.S.'s acceptance of the League of Nations in the 1920s and 1930s. Later he actively supported the United Nations and other political and ethical causes.

Hocking's major contribution to missions involved his service as chairman of the Commission of Appraisal of the Laymen's Foreign Missions Inquiry* which visited American Protestant missions* in India, Burma, China and Japan in 1931. In 1932 the Commission published its findings as *Rethinking Missions: A Laymen's Inquiry after One Hundred Years* (1932). Hocking served as editor of the report and wrote its controversial "General Principles" section. The *Inquiry* criticized much of the Protestant missionary effort and argued for the continuation of missions along the following lines. First, missions ought to emphasize social effort, through medicine and other techniques, apart from evangelism.* Second, missionaries should seek to link their faith with whatever common features they find in non-Christian religions. The aim ought to be cooperation rather than conversion.* Third, there ought to be greater unity in missionary activity both between missions and with members of other religions. The ultimate goal ought to be an international fellowship in which each religion would find its appropriate place. In the eyes of its critics, the *Inquiry* expressed a viewpoint fundamentally different from that of nineteenth-century missions and of the 1910 Edinburgh Conference. In *Living Religions and a World Faith* (1940) and *The Coming World Civilization* (1956), Hocking stated his belief in the Incarnation, the resurrection and Trinity, and asserted that Christianity was best fitted to be the world religion.

BIBLIOGRAPHY. K. S. Latourette, "Re-thinking Missions After Twenty-Five Years," *IRM* 46 (1947): 164-170.

G. J. Bekker

Hodge, (A)rchibald (A)lexander (1823-1886). Princeton* theologian.* Born the eldest son and successor of Princeton theologian Charles Hodge,* he was educated at Princeton* (1841) and

Princeton Seminary* (1846) and came to defend Calvinist* theology and its world view in the tradition begun by Archibald Alexander* after whom he was named. Upon graduating from seminary, Hodge and his family went to Allahabad, India, as Presbyterian missionaries. Forced to return for reasons of health, Hodge was a pastor in Maryland, Virginia and Pennsylvania for several years (1851-1862). In 1864 he became professor of systematic theology at Western Theological Seminary, Allegheny, Pennsylvania, and in 1878 accepted the chair of didactic and exegetical theology at Princeton Theological Seminary, a position he held until his death in 1886. Though his teaching at Princeton lasted but ten years, his writings reflect the warm evangelicalism* which nourished Princeton's stout theology, conservative Presbyterianism's resistance to all attempts to revise the Westminster Confession of Faith* and a breadth of vision extending to America's political and social milieu.

His *Life of Charles Hodge* (1880) was not merely an adulatory biography of his father. It reveals characteristics of evangelical piety* that motivated all Princetonians—the role of conversion* in religious experience* and the necessity of balancing a vital devotional life with orthodox* doctrinal belief. In *Outlines of Theology* (1878), accounts of his popular preaching on doctrinal themes, Hodge responded to liberals* who used a naturalistic world view to interpret Scripture.* To critics who claimed contradictions existed in the biblical text and between the Bible and what scientists have found in nature, the younger Hodge made explicit Princeton's doctrine of plenary and verbal inspiration. The Bible* is inerrant in its original autographs and infallible in what it teaches. While difficulties in interpretation and apparent irreconcilable statements exist, no proved discrepancies have been found. Since God's works in nature and his Word are both revelation, scientific research can never ultimately conflict with biblical teaching. Hodge reaffirmed his views on inerrancy in an article, "Inspiration," written with Benjamin B. Warfield* in 1881 for the *Presbyterian Review.* His denomination adopted Princeton's view of the Bible as its official teaching in the Portland Deliverance* (1892), which figured in three heresy trials,* and the Five Point Deliverance* (1910), which influenced the fundamentalist-modernist debate.*

After the Civil War,* Hodge led evangelical resistance against secularists who mounted a campaign to alter the religious basis for American public life. In 1877, at the First General Council of the World Alliance of Reformed Churches, he denounced attempts to replace biblical theism* with naturalism as the philosophical foundation of education, law, politics and other public institutions. Arguing against secularist claims that religion applies only to private morality and that public life should be neutral, Hodge contended that God held both nations and individuals accountable for implementing biblical principles in public life. He belonged to the National Reform Association* whose aim was to amend the preamble to the Constitution to acknowledge the authority* of Jesus Christ over the U.S. government. Hodge believed church and state should be separate, but as an ardent postmillenialist* he also thought religion must be closely integrated into American political, economic and social institutions. The sovereignty of God requires believers to bring all aspects of human society into conformity with God's righteous laws.

In *Popular Lectures on Theological Themes,* published posthumously in 1887, Hodge called for a revitalization of Calvinism. He contended that only the Reformed world view, because it seeks the glory of God in all areas of life, is sufficiently broad to provide a biblical basis for the family, law, education and economics, and that only it prevents them from being drastically reinterpreted by secularists.

See also PRINCETON THEOLOGY.

BIBLIOGRAPHY. *DAB* V; L. A. Loetscher, *The Broadening Church* (1954); M. A. Noll, *The Princeton Theology, 1812-1921* (1983); G. S. Smith, *The Seeds of Secularization* (1985); C. A. Salmond, *Princetonia: Charles and A. A. Hodge* (1888).

W. A. Hoffecker

Hodge, Charles (1797-1878). Princeton* theologian.* Born in Philadelphia, Pennsylvania, Hodge studied at Princeton* College (1815), where he was converted* during a revival,* and Princeton Seminary (1819). A committed disciple of Archibald Alexander,* Hodge was to faithfully transmit his teacher's tradition of defending Reformed* orthodoxy* by combining a firm grasp of Calvinist* theology,* undergirded by a fervent evangelical* piety,* with a rigorous adaptation of Scottish Common Sense Philosophy.*

Troubled by his lack of knowledge of contemporary theological scholarship, Hodge left after four years of teaching biblical literature at Princeton Seminary (1822-1826) to study in German institutions from 1826 to 1828. While in Europe Hodge encountered remnants of Pietism* at Halle, post-Kantian philosophy, the speculative theology of Friedrich Schleiermacher (1768-1834) and reports of revivals in Eastern European countries. He returned to Princeton intellectually and morally prepared to defend orthodoxy and preserve piety as hallmarks of his theology and to contend against theological innovation and its practical consequences.

In an era when theological ideas powerfully influenced American culture, Hodge became the central figure in one of the most prestigious graduate schools of the country. Under his leadership the *Biblical Repertory,* later renamed the *Princeton Review,* became a respected theological journal renowned for its staunch support of Old School* Calvinism. As editor until 1872, Hodge propagated the Princeton position on prominent national and denominational events such as the Presbyterian schism of 1837 and subsequent reunion in 1868. Conservative Presbyterians eagerly awaited his yearly assessment of the General Assembly.* Hodge also contributed lively and insightful intellectual comment on European and domestic theological discussions. He defended an authoritative Bible* and a Reformed perspective of its teaching when theological and cultural tides were shifting toward Arminian,* revivalist and Unitarian* views. His statement that "a new idea never originated in this Seminary" reflects Princeton's adamancy in maintaining confessional orthodoxy in the face of liberal* innovation.

To the challenge of German biblical criticism, Hodge advocated a verbally and plenarily inspired Scripture. In response to Nathaniel W. Taylor's* New Haven Theology* of moral government, Hodge defended the corporate solidarity of the human race, human inability apart from grace and Christ's substitutional atonement.* And to Charles G. Finney's* new measures* and Edwards Amasa Park's* theology of feelings, Hodge proposed a lively but subdued religious experience founded on objective Calvinist theology.

Hodge's publications spanned several disciplines. His books include: commentaries on Ephesians (1856), Romans (1836) and 1 (1859) and 2 (1857) Corinthians; *What Is Darwinism?* (1873), an attack on Darwin's evolutionary theory, natural selection and denial of design in nature; and *The Way of Life* (1841), a layman's theology published for the American Sunday School Union* stressing internal evidences and a pious appropriation of Christian truth). Hodge's most enduring work is his three-volume *Systematic Theology* (1872-1873). His definition of theology as an inductive science in which theologians gather facts from the Bible to construct an objective system of truth reflects nineteenth-century-American preoccupation with scientific method. But Hodge attempted to balance both head and heart in his theology by emphasizing the internal work of the Holy Spirit, who illuminates revealed truth to the mind of the believer.

As the most prominent American Presbyterian theologian of the nineteenth century, Hodge trained more than two thousand students in the Princeton theology from 1822 to 1878.

BIBLIOGRAPHY. *DAB* V; *DARB*; A. A. Hodge, *The Life of Charles Hodge* (1880); W. A. Hoffecker, *Piety and the Princeton Theologians* (1981); *NCAB* 10; M. A. Noll, *Charles Hodge: The Way of Life and Selected Writings* (1987); M. A. Noll, *The Princeton Theology, 1812-1921* (1983); C. A. Salmond, *Princetonia: Charles and A. A. Hodge* (1888).

W. A. Hoffecker

Hodge, Margaret E. (1869-1943). Presbyterian* foreign missions* leader. Elected a member of the Philadelphia branch of the Woman's Board of Foreign Missions (Presbyterian Church in the U.S.A.*) in 1899, Hodge served as president from 1910 to 1917. In 1917 she became executive secretary of the denomination's* six regional women's foreign mission boards, and three years later, president of the Woman's Board of Foreign Missions, which consolidated all six groups. Hodge was a forceful advocate for women's interests after the denomination reorganized its mission boards in 1923, absorbing the independent Woman's Board into its own Board of Foreign Missions. As a vice president of the new organization, she voiced the growing discontent of Presbyterian women, co-authoring with Katherine Bennett an influential report on the "Causes of Unrest Among Women in the Church" (1927). Hodge also served on two specially appointed committees to respond to the report, where she and Bennett pressed the denomination to consider wider equality for women in all aspects of church life.

BIBLIOGRAPHY. L. A. Boyd and R. D. Brackenridge, *Presbyterian Women in America* (1983).

M. L. Bendroth

Hogan, William (1788-1848). Schismatic Catholic* priest.* A native of Limerick, Ireland, Hogan entered seminary* in 1813 but disciplinary violations the next year resulted in his suspension. Eventually ordained* for the diocese of Limerick, he immigrated* to the U.S. in 1819 and obtained a pastoral assignment in Albany from the bishop* of New York. In 1820 Hogan moved to St. Mary's Church in Philadelphia, though without the approval of his bishop in New York. He soon became a favorite of influential parish* members, including some trustees, partly because of his personality and preaching* ability. But others, especially clergy,* viewed him with suspicion, noting that he had left New York without permission, did not live in the existing parish rectory and acted imprudently at times.

Shortly after Henry Conwell became head of the Philadelphia diocese* in late November 1820, Hogan criticized his new bishop in a sermon. In reaction to that incident and other negative reports about Hogan, Conwell revoked Hogan's faculties to function as a priest in his jurisdiction. But Hogan refused to accept Conwell's decision and received strong support from parish members. In 1821 the trustees of St. Mary's elected Hogan pastor,* barred Conwell from the church (the cathedral* of the diocese) and declared that they had the right to name their own pastors and bishop. Conwell subsequently responded by declaring the dissident parishioners to be schismatics and by excommunicating Hogan. The conflict was not completely resolved for a decade. Hogan left Philadelphia in 1823, but he attempted to return to St. Mary's the next year. Eventually, he married twice and became a lawyer. He also worked as a newspaper editor in Boston, served as American consul in Cuba in 1843, and toured the U.S. giving anti-Catholic lectures.

BIBLIOGRAPHY. M. J. Griffin, "The Life of Bishop Conwell," *RACHSP* 24-29 (1913-1918); F. E. Tourscher, O.S.A., *The Hogan Schism* (1930).

W. P. Leahy

Hogan Schism. A division within the Catholic diocese of Philadelphia (1820-1831). The conflict began in December 1820, after the new bishop,* Henry Conwell, for moral and disciplinary reasons, revoked permission for William Hogan,* a popular pastor at St. Mary's Church, to act as a priest* in his diocese.* Tensions escalated after Hogan refused to reform as demanded by his bishop and received strong support from influential parishioners. To advance the crisis, in 1821 the parish trustees elected Hogan to be pastor and prohibited their bishop from using the church (the diocese's* cathedral*); they proclaimed that congregations had the right to select their own priests and bishops. Faced with a direct challenge to his authority* and longstanding Church policy, Conwell responded by excommunicating Hogan and by declaring that St. Mary's was no longer an authorized place of worship* for Catholics. Conwell and the trustees worked out a compromise in

1826, but the Vatican* repudiated the agreement the next year and removed Conwell from administrative control of the diocese. The schism finally ended in 1831 when the new bishop, Francis Kenrick,* prevailed against the trustees.
See also TRUSTEEISM.

BIBLIOGRAPHY. F. E. Tourscher, O.S.A., *The Hogan Schism* (1930); P. Carey, *People, Priests and Prelates: Ecclesiastical Democracy and the Tensions of Trusteeism* (1987).

W. P. Leahy

Hoge, Moses Drury (1819-1899). Southern Presbyterian* preacher.* Born at Hampden-Sydney, Virginia, Hoge's father was a Presbyterian minister* and his grandfather, Moses Hoge, was the president of Hampden-Sydney College (1807-1820). Most of his early childhood was spent in Ohio. Hoge attended Hampden-Sydney College, graduating with distinction in 1839, and Union Theological Seminary of Virginia, graduating in 1843. He went to First Presbyterian Church of Richmond, Virginia, as assistant to William S. Plumer. When a mission church (Second Presbyterian) was started in 1845, Hoge became the pastor, remaining there until his death in 1899. During the Civil War* he was a volunteer chaplain* to the Confederate soldiers stationed nearby, often preaching to large crowds.

Hoge was an extremely able speaker, and his church became one of the largest and most influential Presbyterian churches in all the South. In addition to his pastoral labors, he was involved in running the Union blockade during the Civil War to procure Bibles* from England. He was also moderator of the General Assembly, a delegate to the Evangelical Alliance* and a delegate and key speaker at the Alliance of Reformed Churches in Scotland. An orthodox* Calvinist,* he worked hard for reconciliation with the Northern Church. Hoge defended the orthodoxy of the Northern Church against those who used charges of heterodoxy as the main reason for the continued existence of the Southern Church.

BIBLIOGRAPHY. *AAP* 3; *DAB* V; P. H. Hoge, *Moses Hoge, His Life and Letters* (1899); J. M. Wells, *Southern Presbyterian Worthies* (1936).

J. R. Wiers

Holdeman, John (1832-1900). Founder of the Church of God in Christ, Mennonite.* After a series of conversions* and visions, beginning at age twelve, Holdeman had another conversion, was baptized* and joined the Chester Mennonite* congregation in Wayne County, Ohio, in October

1853. With his baptism, Holdeman also developed a conviction that God had destined him for the ministry.*

Extensive reading in early Mennonite sources convinced Holdeman that the Mennonite Church of his day had fallen into "decay," having departed from such teachings of the fathers as opposition to holding of civil office, stylish dress and worldly amusements, and the enforcement of church discipline.* In April 1859 he organized the church referred to popularly as the Holdeman Mennonites. It fused conservative Mennonite practices with what Holdeman had apparently learned from the revivalism* of John Winebrenner.* Winebrenner's influence had taken root in Wayne County through meetings in 1833 and was perpetuated in a church of Mennonite converts located a mile from the Chester congregation.

Although Holdeman traveled widely, preaching to other Mennonites, for the first dozen years his membership* consisted mainly of family members. After Mennonite immigrants* from Russia began arriving in 1874, a group of *Kleine Gemeinde* in Manitoba and a group in the Lone Tree community of McPherson County, Kansas, left leaderless by the death of Tobias A. Unruh,* joined Holdeman's new church. Membership jumped from under 150 to more than 500. In 1883 Holdeman moved with most of his congregation to Jaspar County, Missouri. He spent his last three years among his people in McPherson County. Among Holdeman's writings were: *The Old Ground and Foundation* (1863) and *A History of the Church of God* (1876).

BIBLIOGRAPHY. C. Hiebert, *The Holdeman People: The Church of God in Christ, Mennonite, 1859-1969* (1973); T. F. Schlabach, *Faith, Peace, Nation: Mennonites and Amish in 19th Century America,* Mennonite Experience in America, vol. 2 (1988). J. D. Weaver

Holiness. In Christian theology* the term *holiness* first of all describes God's unblemished moral character and majesty. Objects, institutions and people may be holy inasmuch as they are consecrated to God, separated from that which is unclean and renewed for holy use. But in each case their holiness is derivative from God. For the people of God, *holiness* may describe either the condition of being holy or the process by which a person is brought to that state. Three general approaches to holiness can be identified within the Christian traditions that have flourished in America.

Sacramental* holiness, emphasized in the Roman Catholic Church* and by certain high church* Anglicans,* is premised on the holiness of the church, inasmuch as it has been granted by God the deposit of faith, the ministry of the gospel and the sacraments. The Holy Spirit, working through the church and the ministry of the sacraments, conveys grace and cleanses believers from unrighteousness, making them holy, though not perfectly so. Upright Christians may continue in venial sins, as opposed to mortal sins. The Catholic Church teaches that final holiness may be obtained by the purgation of sin after death, aided by the prayers and good works of the faithful still on earth.

Positional holiness, espoused by those in the Reformed tradition,* emphasizes the status of holiness before God for those that have been justified* by faith. They enjoy an assured position of holiness "in Christ," though by human nature they remain sinful. Holiness cannot be fully realized in this life, but it is to be sought after through progress in piety and the sanctifying work of the Holy Spirit. This tradition greatly shaped the course of American religion through the influence of the Puritans.*

The quest for personal holiness characterizes churches of the Holiness* or Wesleyan* tradition. While they acknowledge the Reformed doctrine of justification by faith and a believer's positional holiness before God, they emphasize the possibility of attaining personal holiness by the recreative and sanctifying work of the Holy Spirit. Depending on the group, they may maintain that entire sanctification may be had either in an instantaneous experience or through a process of growth in holiness. The growth and development of this tradition was a distinctive contribution of the American religious experience.

In each of these three traditions, biblical themes of consecration, separation and renewal are maintained as expressions of a relationship with God in Christ. In some traditions the consecration is liturgically* enacted. For the Puritans, separation was conceived in terms of moral distinction, whereas for others, like the Shakers,* it implied physical separation from society. Christians of the Reformed and Catholic traditions both hold that sanctification is a process, the goal of which cannot be obtained in this life, though they often sharply disagree over the means by which it is obtained. Others, like Wesleyans and Nazarenes,* hold to the possibility of being freed from all sin in this life, possibly even in a moment.

The theology of John Wesley provided the foundation for the emergence of a distinctive holiness theology in nineteenth-century America.

Wesley described "Christian perfection"* as a fundamental change in the motivational center of a person. Since Wesley believed that only a "willful transgression of a known law of God" should properly be called "sin," he allowed that Christian perfection implied victory over all sin because the love of God purified and filled one's life. Wesley's emphasis on "holiness of heart and life" was readily received and embodied in the Holiness Movement which swept across American Christianity.

See also HOLINESS MOVEMENT; PERFECTIONISM; SACRAMENTS AND ORDINANCES; SANCTIFICATION.

BIBLIOGRAPHY. C. Hodge, *Systematic Theology,* 3 vols. (1871-1872); C. G. Finney, *Lecture on Systematic Theology,* 2 vols. (1846-1847); C. E. Jones, *The Perfectionist Persuasion: The Holiness Movement and American Methodism* (1974); J. Peters, *Christian Perfection and American Methodism* (1956); O. Wiley, *Christian Theology* (1940).

J. R. Tyson

Holiness Churches and Associations. The quest for unity is a recurring theme in the history of the Holiness Movement.* John Wesley,* the Movement's forefather, fostered holy living through pietist* cell groups. Likewise, collective spirituality* (or social holiness) was emphasized in American Methodism* from the 1830s on by Phoebe Palmer* of New York City, in whose weekly Tuesday Meetings a large segment of the American Holiness Movement was born. After the Civil War,* associations emerged as enlarged means for pursuing "unity in holiness," while in the 1880s the rise of Holiness sects* added new dimensions to the impulse. Twentieth-century Holiness denominationalism* developed from sectarianism, assuming a dominant role in the Movement's search for unity in holiness.

Early Associations. A vital relationship exists between Holiness associations and churches, since the former encouraged cells, or "bands," that sometimes evolved into congregations, giving rise to new sects. The first, most influential and longest continuing association was organized in 1867 at Vineland, New Jersey, as the National Camp Meeting Association for the Promotion of Holiness,* known popularly as the National Holiness Association (NHA) until 1971, when officially it became the Christian Holiness Association. Its principal founders (John Inskip, John A. Wood and Alfred Cookman) were Methodist clergy,* and its early strength was in the Northeast.

In spite of a regional and Methodistic character, the NHA was the archetype that inspired a large network of regional, state, county and local Holiness associations that operated as independent entities. Among these were the Western Holiness Association (1872) in Illinois, the Iowa Holiness Association (1879), the Holiness Association of Texas (1901) and the Holiness Union (1904) in the Southeast. Leaders of county and local associations were sometimes lay—even female—and generally were less loyal to Methodism than counterparts in the NHA. In this diffusion and democratization of leadership lay the roots of sectarian dissent.

Sectarian Heyday. The Holiness Movement began losing cohesion in the 1880s. Its sectarian heyday (1880-1910) was followed by a period of merger and consolidation and then, after mid-century, by new sect formation in reaction to cultural accommodations.

Several early sects combined Wesleyan-Holiness theology with stress on the restoration of "true church order." These include the Church of God* (Anderson, Indiana) launched in 1881 by Daniel Sidney Warner*; the Church of God (Holiness) begun in 1883 under A. M. Kiergan; the Holiness Church (c.1883) in Southern California, which restricted membership to the "wholly sanctified"; and the New Testament Church of Christ (1894) in the South. A leading text representing this linkage of "true holiness" and restorationist* ecclesiology was *The Divine Church* (1891) by John P. Brooks of the Church of God (Holiness).

Other groups arose that were congregational* in polity* but not committed to a rigid doctrine of "true church order." Still others, though democratic in spirit, accepted superintending authority* and a more structured polity. Among these: the Alliance of the Reformed Baptist Church of Canada (1888); the West-Coast-based Church of the Nazarene (1894), organized by Phineas F. Bresee*; the Metropolitan Church Association (1894) of Chicago; the Pentecost Bands (1895), later the Missionary Bands of the World; the Fire-Baptized Holiness Church* (1895), organized by Benjamin H. Irwin*; the Association of Pentecostal Churches of America (1896), of New England and the Mid-Atlantic States; the International Holiness Union and Prayer League (1897), later the International Apostolic Holiness Church, led by Martin Wells Knapp; the Pentecostal Alliance (1898), later Pentecostal Mission, begun in Nashville by J. O. McClurkan; the predominantly African-American Church of God in Christ* (1898), started by Charles H. Mason* and C. P. Jones*; the Missionary Church Association (1898), founded in Berne, Indiana; the Holiness Church of North Carolina

(1898), organized by A. B. Crumpler*; the Independent Holiness Church (1901), in Texas led by C. B. Jernigan; the Pillar of Fire Church (1901), led by Alma White*; the African-American Church of Christ (Holiness) (1907), organized by C. P. Jones; and the Churches of Christ in Christian Union (1909). These were Wesleyan-Holiness in character, but A. B. Simpson* formed the Christian and Missionary Alliance* (1887) around Keswick*-Holiness thought, stressing a second work of grace as an enduement of spiritual power rather than Wesleyanism's emphasis on purity of heart.

Other Traditions. The Holiness Movement also affected existing Methodist and non-Methodist groups. The Wesleyan Methodist Church (1843) and the Free Methodist Church* (1860) originated over other points of dissent but were participants in the holiness revival by the 1880s. The Salvation Army,* organized in England (1865) by William Booth,* was in America by 1880, becoming active in the holiness revival. The Brethren in Christ,* a blend of Anabaptism* and early American Pietism,* responded favorably to the holiness crusade, adopting its view of personal sanctification.* Holiness thought also spread in nineteenth-century Quaker* circles and was a factor in the creation of the Association of Evangelical Friends (1947), now the Evangelical Friends Alliance.*

Consolidation. Two other factors shaped the mosaic: "unitive holiness," which was increasingly important to leaders pondering the limited ability of regional bodies to carry out a mission to the world, and the rise of Pentecostalism.*

The Church of the Nazarene* and the Wesleyan Church* best represent the consolidations of the twentieth century. The former was created in 1907 and 1908 when three regional bodies united, forming the Pentecostal Church of the Nazarene. Due to earlier regional mergers, six pre-existing bodies were actually incorporated, including the Church of the Nazarene (West), the Association of Pentecostal Churches of America (East), and the Holiness Church of Christ (South), the latter created by merger (1904) of the New Testament Church of Christ and the Independent Holiness Church. Nazarenes later absorbed the Pentecostal Mission (in 1915) and groups in Britain and Canada, including (in 1955) the Gospel Workers of Canada (est. 1918). The present Wesleyan Church resulted from the 1968 merger of Wesleyan Methodists with the Pilgrim Holiness Church. Wesleyan Methodists had received smaller entities before then, including the Alliance of the Reformed Baptist Church of Canada in 1966. The Pilgrim Holiness Church was home for at least eight

previously separate groups, principally the International Apostolic Holiness Church but also the Pilgrim Church of California (1917) and the Holiness Church.

Pentecostalism created churches that are both Wesleyan-Holiness *and* Pentecostal in emphasis. These embrace three works of grace (conversion,* entire sanctification and Baptism of the Spirit*). Leading representatives today are the Pentecostal Holiness Church (1911), formed by merger of The Fire-Baptized Holiness Church and the Holiness Church of North Carolina; the Church of God (Cleveland, Tennessee),* whose history as a Holiness body dates to 1886; and the Church of God in Christ.* There is little interaction between these and non-Pentecostal Holiness churches. Indeed, to avoid popular identification as a "tongues-speaking" church, the Pentecostal Church of the Nazarene dropped *Pentecostal* from its name in 1919.

Contemporary Associations. Following the shift from "Holiness Movement" to "Holiness churches," the National (now Christian) Holiness Association (CHA) changed from a Methodist body into an ecumenical one. The CHA presently lists nineteen denominations as affiliated or cooperating members, representing over 1.5 million constituents in the U.S. and Canada. This includes the major Wesleyan-Holiness denominations (except Holiness-Pentecostal ones), among them the Church of the Nazarene, with 541,000 members (figures are for the U. S. and Canada); The Salvation Army, with 535,000 members; the Church of God (Anderson, Indiana),* with 192,000 members; the Wesleyan Church, with 114,000 members; and the Free Methodist Church of North America, with 79,000 members. These bodies are international, in character, with larger worldwide memberships. The Wesleyan Theological Society is a CHA-related scholarly society.

Reaction to changing behavioral standards and "worldly" trends within older Holiness denominations led to organization of the Inter-Denominational (now Inter-Church) Holiness Convention as a fellowship of conservatives in 1952. Membership is individual and congregational, not denominational. Similar concerns have led to minor schisms in the larger churches, creating more than thirteen new bodies between 1955 and 1970, including the Bible Mission Church (1956), the Allegheny Wesleyan Methodist Connection of Churches (1966), and the Bible Methodist Connection of Churches (1966). Members of these bodies tend to cooperate with the IHC, as do those in some older but smaller groups such as the

Church of God (Holiness).

BIBLIOGRAPHY. M. E. Dieter, *The Holiness Revival of the Nineteenth Century* (1980); C. H. Jacquet, Jr., *Yearbook of Canadian Churches* (1988); C. E. Jones, *A Guide to the Study of the Holiness Movement* (1974), C. E. Jones, *Perfectionist Persuasion: A Social Profile of the National Holiness Movement within American Methodism, 1867-1936* (1974); J. G. Melton, *Encyclopedia of American Religions,* 2nd ed. (1987); A. C. Piepkorn, *Profiles in Belief,* vol. 3 (1979); H. E. Schmul and E. Fruin, *Profile of the I. H. Convention* (n.d.).

R. S. Ingersol

Holiness Movement. The Holiness Movement grew from seeds planted in the 1830s, although it did not take definite institutional form until after the Civil War.* It emphasized the complete sanctification* of Christian believers, often, though not always, conceiving of it as something like a second conversion* experience, instantaneous and dramatic. A variety of terms was used to describe this "deeper work" beyond conversion, including "entire sanctification," "Christian perfection," "the second blessing," "the higher Christian life,"* "the rest of faith" and "full salvation." The Movement drew support from persons of many different ecclesiastical traditions and denominations,* although Methodists* were always prominent among its leaders. At first more or less tolerated, if not actually embraced warmly by the existing churches, many Holiness advocates eventually came into open conflict with denominational leaders. This led by the 1880s and 1890s to the founding of numerous independent Holiness churches, many of which have continuing histories to the present.

Pre-Civil War Beginnings. The immediate antecedents of the Holiness Movement lie in pre-Civil War American revivalism* and the growing influence of Methodism over American Protestantism* in the early decades of the nineteenth century. The revivalism associated with the Second Great Awakening* helped to create a religious climate in which the power and active presence of God in the world and in Christian believers' lives were expected—and perceived—on every hand. A religious optimism mirrored and contributed to the broad optimism in American social, political and economic life in this same period. Revivals of religion encouraged Christians to believe in great spiritual possibilities, including the full perfection of individuals and society. As a result several varieties of perfectionist* teaching had sprung up by the 1830s and 1840s.

One influential center of perfectionist thought grew up at Oberlin College.* Sponsored mostly by New School* Presbyterians* and Congregationalists,* Oberlin after 1835 became a hotbed of social, educational and religious innovation. Perfectionist thought there was championed notably by Charles G. Finney* and Asa Mahan,* among others. Both were active in revivals in the 1820s and early 1830s, and their religious views were greatly affected by this experience. Both were also influenced by the theology of Nathaniel William Taylor,* who was modifying traditional Calvinist* orthodoxy* by stressing the moral ability of human beings and virtually doing away with the concept of inherited depravity.

Already incipient perfectionists when they arrived at Oberlin (Mahan in 1834, Finney in 1835), their union enabled them to sharpen their focus and clarify their ideas. In late 1836 and early 1837 they entered together into an extended period of study and reflection, emerging from this period as fully convinced perfectionists. Finney's *Lectures to Professing Christians* (1837), which were delivered and then serialized in the *New York Evangelist* at this time, gave considerable space to the matter of sanctification or "perfect sanctification." Mahan soon systematized his ideas in print in *The Scripture Doctrine of Christian Perfection Illustrated and Confirmed* (1839). Also in late 1838 they launched the periodical *The Oberlin Evangelist* mainly as a forum for Holiness teaching. Finney further emphasized the theme by unfurling a banner over his revival tents proclaiming "Holiness unto the Lord."

Crucial to the full conversion of both Mahan and Finney to perfectionist teaching was their exposure to Methodist literature during the winter of 1836-1837. They consulted John Wesley's *Plain Account of Christian Perfection,* the Bible* commentaries of English Methodist Adam Clarke and John Fletcher's *Last Check to Antinomianism* (often identified as the *Treatise on Christian Perfection*). These were the very same sources read by American Methodists. And from them Methodists learned that Christians could experience a "deeper work" of God's grace subsequent to conversion which, while not freeing them from the temptation to commit sin, gave them ability to resist temptation and thus live a life governed by a perfect intention to please God and do good to humankind. Preaching this optimistic gospel of "perfect Love," Methodism grew in America from a handful of small societies modeled on the work of John Wesley in England into the largest Protestant denomination in the country. Methodism's obvious success opened doors for its theology and methods, with the result that many American churches began to absorb aspects of Methodist piety,* and some new groups formed along Methodist lines (e.g., the Evangelical Association and the United Brethren; *see* German-American Revivalism).

In the flush of its greatest success, however, American Methodism developed an intense anxiety over its identity. Symbolic of its unique identity for many Methodists was the Wesleyan doctrine of Christian perfection. John Wesley himself had declared this the "grand depositum" entrusted by God to the care of the Methodists and the doctrine was a hallmark of early American Methodist preaching. As Methodism grew from a collection of small bands of persons earnestly seeking "Holiness of heart and life" to a far-flung, thriving denomination, however, new challenges and needs sometimes displaced Christian perfection from the center of Methodist life. Concern over this surfaced as early as the first decades of the nineteenth century, and by the 1830s many Methodist leaders were echoing the pastoral address to the 1832 general conference which asked Methodists, "Why . . . have we so few living witnesses that 'the blood of Jesus Christ cleanseth from all sin?' " and urged on them renewal of the pursuit after perfect love. Before long, special meetings, books and periodicals were promoting a revival of "second blessing Holiness" among Methodists.

One of the most effective of the Methodist promoters of Holiness was laywoman Phoebe Worrall Palmer.* Daughter of a prominent New York Methodist family and wife of well-to-do physician Dr. Walter C. Palmer (1804-1883), she became an articulate spokesperson for "the way of Holiness." An extensive preaching* ministry* took her to churches and camp meetings across the U.S., Canada and Britain. Over the span of three decades, she authored numerous books, beginning with *The Way of Holiness* (1843), and between 1864 and 1874 she edited the periodical *The Guide to Holiness.* But perhaps most significant was her leadership of the Tuesday Meeting for the Promotion of Holiness, a "social religious gathering" in New York City which for more than sixty years helped shape the views of many ministers and lay* people both inside and outside of Methodism.

Palmer's work grew out of an intense personal religious pilgrimage which was capped in 1837 by an act of entirely devoting herself to God, which resulted in her full sanctification. Benefitting much from the spiritual counsel of her sister, Sarah Worrall Lankford,* she joined her in promoting Holiness among a group of women—later women and men—which met on Tuesday afternoons to pray,* study the Bible* and share accounts of religious experience.* When Sarah moved in early 1840, Phoebe became the acknowledged leader, presiding for more than thirty years over this group which sometimes reached several hundred in attendance, included prominent Methodists and non-Methodist religious leaders of the day, and spawned hundreds of similar gatherings throughout North America and some other parts of the world. Palmer herself considered this meeting to be the "nursery" of the Holiness Movement.

Whereas Finney at Oberlin blended Wesleyan perfectionism with the "new measures"* revivalism which he pioneered among Presbyterians and Congregationalists, Phoebe Palmer blended new measures revivalism with the Wesleyan perfectionism she absorbed from her Methodist heritage. The ingredients were the same in each case, but the mixture was slightly different. Both stressed the obligation of Christians to be fully sanctified. Both taught that Christians could experience full sanctification through willing the complete consecration of themselves to God. And both expected fully sanctified Christians to express their total devotion to God and God's will through constant efforts to preach the gospel, feed the hungry, clothe the naked, and generally alleviate human suffering and promote the welfare of humankind. Palmer, however, emphasized the instantaneous "second conversion" aspect of full sanctification, while Finney tended to see it as more of a gradual process. Also, Finney defined full sanctification, or holiness, in terms of perfect obedience to the moral law, while for Palmer it was more a matter of perfect submission to the divine will. In practice the differences were minimal, however, with Oberlin perfectionists mixing easily with Methodist perfectionists inspired by Palmer and together stimulating a quest for holiness throughout much of American Protestantism on the eve of the Civil War.

The Post-Civil War Holiness Crusade. The Civil War brought the first phase of the Holiness Movement to an end. The division and distraction the war occasioned, as well as the exhausting moral debate over slavery leading up to it, combined to sap the Movement's momentum and at the same time to undermine the fortunes of organized religion generally. Desiring to revive the sagging fortunes of the quest for holiness, a group of ministers met two years after the war's end to organize a camp meeting* for promoting holiness, a perfect vehicle they thought for generating new interest in the higher Christian life. This would be like the popular camp meetings of the day, except that almost all preaching and activity would have as its explicit aim the full sanctification of those who were already Christian believers.

This first "general camp meeting" (as distinguished from the usual district or conference camp meetings sponsored by many Methodist districts and conferences) for the promotion of holiness was held in the Methodist village of Vineland, New Jersey, in July 1867. Among its sponsors were William Bramwell Osborn (1832-1902), Methodist presiding elder of southern New Jersey; John Inskip (1816-1884), a prominent Methodist pastor entirely sanctified through the influence of Phoebe Palmer; and Mrs. Harriet Drake, a Methodist lay woman who underwrote half the expenses of the meeting. Pleased with the results of their efforts, the sponsors met near the close of the camp and organized the National Campmeeting Association for the Promotion of Holiness,* electing Inskip as its president. The purpose of the new group was simply to organize and promote subsequent Holiness camp meetings, although its activities eventually came to include a publishing arm (National Publishing Association for the Promotion of Holiness) and a foreign missionary arm (National Holiness Missionary Society—precursor of today's World Gospel Mission). The camp meetings were so popular that the association very soon began sponsoring several meetings each summer in different locations rather than only one.

This new development significantly changed the course of the Holiness Movement. It gave the Movement an organizational center it had not previously had. In 1874 Phoebe Palmer died, and in 1875 Finney died. A new generation of leaders emerged to direct the quest for full sanctification, largely through the National Campmeeting Association and the host of state, regional and local Holiness organizations which it spawned. The latter were not formally affiliated with the national organization, but they modeled themselves after it, employed the Holiness evangelists it endorsed and generally cooperated with it in promoting the higher Christian life. Both the national association and the numerous regional, state and local associations were interdenominational, but often dominated by Methodists. After the Civil War Holiness preaching and teaching in America increasingly came to be defined by, and identified with, the activities of the new organizations.

In time the National Holiness Association* (as the Campmeeting Association came to be known) and the various independent organizations it had encouraged took somewhat different paths. Always the preserve of Methodists loyal to their denomination, the national association fought the strong tendency of organized "Holiness work" to move beyond the orbit of the existing churches. On the other hand, regional, state and local Holiness associations often became quasi-churches as members zealously found outlets for expressing their "entire devotion to God" through evangelistic meetings, prayer groups, Holiness papers, downtown city missions and organizations to deal with social problems such as homes for "fallen women" and orphanages. These groups were strongest in the Midwest and Southwest, where they were geographically distant from eastern seats of power. They were typically led by younger, often rural-bred leaders, who had a smaller stake in existing denominations, and they were often more truly interdenominational than the national association. Such groups became the breeding ground for "come-outism," as the movement to form independent Holiness churches was known.

A series of General Holiness Conventions commencing in 1877 provided a forum for both denominational loyalists and "come-outers" within the Holiness Movement. Promoted first by Methodist loyalists who petitioned the bishops of the Methodist Episcopal Church to call a conference on Holiness, thus demonstrating that church's commitment to Christian perfection—when Methodist officials declined to cooperate, the conventions were actually organized by the national association working together with some of the regional Holiness groups. National association leaders hoped to harness these meetings to the cause of denominational loyalty and interdenominational cooperation and tried to control the proceedings accordingly. Come-outers helped to sway participants to their view. Neither side was fully successful, although the cause of "come-outism" did prosper significantly during the period in which the conventions were held.

About the time the Holiness Movement entered this phase of its development in the U.S., its influence was spreading to the British Isles. American Holiness evangelists like Charles Finney and Phoebe and Walter Palmer had preached there occasionally in the 1840s, 1850s and 1860s, but it was not until the 1870s that an organized movement emerged. This was due largely to the work of the American husband and wife team of Robert Pearsall Smith* and Hannah Whitall Smith,* who visited Britain from 1873 to 1875. They were central figures in the Oxford Union Meeting for the Promotion of Scriptural Holiness held in 1874 and a similar gathering held at Brighton in 1875.

These were not unlike the American Holiness camp meetings, and they gave a central focus to higher life activity in Britain. This was made permanent with the founding of the Keswick* Convention in 1876, a higher life institution which continues to the present, convening yearly in the English Lake District. Representatives of various religious bodies in the British Isles participated in these meetings and embraced perfectionist teaching. The Movement was not dominated by Methodists, however, as it was in the U.S. As a result, Keswick Holiness thought developed a distinctive coloring which owed more to the Calvinist* tradition than to the Arminian* strain in Wesleyan thought. Keswick teachers taught that the second blessing* "suppressed" rather than eliminated the inclination to sin in the Christian believer, and that the chief result of the "deeper work" of divine grace was not purity of heart and intention so much as it was power for service to God and fellow human beings.

Keswick teaching was eventually imported to the U.S. in the 1880s and 1890s via the celebrated Northfield Conferences* organized by Dwight L. Moody.* Moody, who was preaching in England when the Oxford and Brighton conferences were held, was attracted to higher life teaching and regularly invited prominent British higher life teachers to his conferences when these began in 1880. In this way a broad spectrum of American Protestants who esteemed Moody were exposed to one variety of Holiness teaching. As a result Keswick teaching blended with Oberlin and Methodist perfectionism, strengthening the perfectionist strain already present in American Protestantism.

Separation. By the 1880s and 1890s large numbers of Holiness advocates had become alienated from their churches. Opposition of ecclesiastical officials to the highly independent and rapidly multiplying Holiness associations and bands led to tension and conflict. Changing patterns of worship* in some large urban churches disappointed recent arrivals from small towns and farms who were more accustomed to revival or camp meeting-style religion. The growing influence of theological liberalism and modernism* in many denominations symbolized to some a further drift away from "old time religion." And, of course, the Holiness association had a way of developing a life of its own, finally siphoning the energies of its supporters off from their denominations. All this came together to create a climate which was right for separation.

Beginning in 1881 with Daniel Sidney Warner's*

Church of God* (now Church of God, Anderson, Indiana), the Holiness Movement began to produce numerous independent churches. By the end of the century, the Church of God was joined by such groups as the Association of Pentecostal Churches in America, the New Testament Church of Christ, the Church of the Nazarene, the Hephzibah Faith Missionary Association and the Missionary Church Association. Several of these groups united over time under the name the Church of the Nazarene,* thus becoming the largest of the new denominations produced by the Holiness Movement. Several other churches already in existence also came to identify themselves as "Holiness churches" and to associate themselves with the new groups. These included, among others, The Salvation Army,* the Wesleyan Methodist Church, the Free Methodist Church,* the Brethren in Christ Church* and the Evangelical Friends.*

Holiness and Pentecostalism. By promoting entire sanctification the Holiness Movement helped to make possible the rise of Pentecostalism* in the early twentieth century. But a significant factor during the second half of the nineteenth century was the growing popularity in Holiness circles of using the term *baptism of the Holy Spirit* or *baptism with the Holy Spirit* to describe the "deeper work of grace," or "second blessing," of entire sanctification. This term was embraced by Wesleyan, Oberlin, and Keswick segments of the Movement alike, and the biblical account of the gift of the Spirit to the early church on the Day of Pentecost became an important resource for preaching and teaching Holiness. In time some within the Holiness Movement began to identify speaking in tongues as the outward sign of receiving the baptism with the Spirit. This new teaching led to a fracture in the Movement and the emergence of still more new churches in the years following the 1906 Azusa Street Revival* in Los Angeles, an event generally regarded as the beginning of the modern Pentecostal Movement.

BIBLIOGRAPHY. D. W. Dayton, ed., *"The Higher Christian Life": Sources for Studying the Holiness, Pentecostal and Keswick Movements,* 48 vols. (1984-1985); D. W. Dayton, *Theological Roots of Pentecostalism* (1987); M. E. Dieter, *The Holiness Revival of the Nineteenth Century* (1980); C. E. Jones, *A Guide to the Study of the Holiness Movement* (1974); C. E. Jones, *Perfectionist Persuasion: The Holiness Movement and American Methodism, 1867-1936* (1974); J. L. Peters, *Christian Perfection and American Methodism* (1956); T. L. Smith, *Revivalism and Social Reform in Mid-Nineteenth-*

Century America (1957); V. Synan, *The Holiness-Pentecostal Movement in the United States* (1971).

H. E. Raser

Holmes, Obadiah (c.1607-1682). Colonial Baptist* minister.* Born near Manchester, England, Holmes immigrated to Massachusetts in 1638. The following year he and his family settled in Salem where he joined the Congregational* Church and worked as a glassmaker. In 1645 he moved to Rehoboth in Plymouth Colony and quickly became critical of church practices. When he became a Baptist in 1650, the Rehoboth church excommunicated him and the Plymouth General Court indicted him. As a result, he moved his family to Newport, Rhode Island, where he joined the Baptist Church pastored by John Clarke.*

In 1651 Holmes, Clarke and John Crandall traveled to Massachusetts Bay Colony to help a blind and aged fellow Baptist. But they were promptly arrested in Lynn, then put on trial in Boston for promoting Anabaptism.* The trio was fined and ordered to leave the colony, but when Holmes refused to comply, he was imprisoned and eventually "well whipped" in public. After his release, he returned to Newport, where he was ordained* to the ministry* (1652) and served the church as pastor* for nearly thirty years.

Holmes's greatest legacy was his *Last Will and Testimony* (1675), which remains the best example of Baptist theology,* preaching* style, piety* and family life to come out of the seventeenth century.

BIBLIOGRAPHY. E. S. Gaustad, ed., *Baptist Piety: The Last Will and Testimony of Obadiah Holmes* (1978). T. P. Weber

Holocaust and the American Churches. The Holocaust (*Shoah*) refers to the colossal tragedy of the attempted annihilation of European Jewry at the hands of the Nazis. During the twelve years of the Third Reich (1933-1945), under the despotic leadership of Adolf Hitler, six million Jews were killed. Countless others also suffered persecution, imprisonment, dehumanization and death—including Protestant* pastors* and laity,* Catholic* priests,* Jehovah's Witnesses,* gypsies, Slavs, political opponents, homosexuals and the intelligentsia—but by far the most harrassed, persecuted, humiliated and murdered people were the Jews in Germany and the occupied territories.

During this crisis the publications of the American churches, for the most part, sought to keep their constituents informed of the Nazi treatment of the Jews. One detailed study of fifty-two Protestant journals prior to *Kristallnacht* (November 9-10, 1938)—the date when Nazi terror was let loose against hundreds of synagogues and Jewish-owned businesses—shows that more attention was given to the Jews who had become Christians. After 1938, however, much greater attention was given to the plight of all Jews living in Nazi-controlled lands. Journals such as *The Christian Century, The Gospel Messenger, The Churchman, The Sunday School Times, American Commonwealth, Our Hope, Moody Monthly, The Presbyterian* and several denominational organs, conveyed specific reports of the discriminatory laws, the deportations, the ghettos, the massacres, the gas chambers, the death camps and the medieval experiments. Consequently, it could be said that "American Protestant Christians who read the periodicals even minimally could not plead ignorance or say that they had little or no knowledge about what was happening to Jews under the Nazis" (R. W. Ross).

The responses of the American churches proved, however, to be totally inadequate and ineffective. The national climate affected by depressed economic circumstances, isolationist attitudes, persistent anti-Semitism and persistent skepticism about the reports from Nazi-occupied territories pervaded both Protestant and Catholic churches. Official responses varied among the mainline* bodies, covering a spectrum from ignoring the magnitude of the crimes being committed to passionate concern. A number of Christian leaders voiced publicly their revulsion of Nazi actions, among them Harry Emerson Fosdick,* Francis J. McConnell,* Ernest Fremont Tittle,* Ralph W. Sockman,* William T. Manning, S. Parkes Cadman,* Allan Knight Chalmers, Oscar Blackwelder and Reinhold Niebuhr.*

In 1939 fifty-three clergy, both Catholic and Protestant, presented a petition to the White House urging Congress and the president to seek legislation that "would offer sanctuary to German refugee children." They, together with such bodies as the Federal Council of Churches,* the American Friends Service Committee* and several other key church leaders, supported the Wagner-Rogers bill in the U.S. Congress. The bill would have authorized the admission of 20,000 children from Germany or German-controlled areas over a two-year period. In spite of the support by an impressive array of church supporters, the bill failed to pass.

American churches did respond, albeit too little and too late, to the refugee crisis created by the turmoil in Europe. A refugee rescue program was launched in 1939 by the Federal Council of Churches, directed by Charles S. Macfarland.

Contacts were made with hundreds of congregations and community federations of churches, encouraging the foundation of refugee/resettlement channels. A Catholic Committee for Refugees was likewise organized in 1939 by the American Catholic bishops. It is estimated that between 1933 and 1945 about 250,000 refugees found refuge in the U.S., many of them aided by the churches.

In summary, although one can recount responses of the American churches to the Holocaust —published reports in journals, a few denominational and ecumenical public statements, attempts now and then to influence political leaders, assistance to fleeing refugees— it would be difficult to dispute the conclusion of a renowned Holocaust scholar: "At the heart of Christianity is the commitment to help the helpless. Yet, for the most part, America's Christian Churches looked away while European Jews perished" (D. Wyman).

BIBLIOGRAPHY. G. Greenberg, "American Catholics During the Holocaust," in *Simon Wiesenthal Center Annual* 4, ed. S. Milton and H. Friedlander (1986); W. E. Nawyn, *American Protestantism's Response to Germany's Jews and Refugees (1933-1941)* (1981); R. W. Ross, *So It Was True: The American Protestant Press and the Nazi Persecution of the Jews* (1986); D. S. Wyman, *The Abandonment of the Jews: America and the Holocaust, 1941-1945* (1984); D. S. Wyman, *Paper Walls: America and the Refugee Crisis, 1938-1941* (1985); J. D. Hegel, *A Church Come of Age: American Lutheranism and National Socialism* (unpublished Ph.D. dissertation, Lutheran School of Theology, Chicago, 1988).   F. B. Nelson

Holy Name Society. A Roman Catholic* spiritual group encouraging reverence for the name of Jesus. A Dominican* friar, Diego of Victoria, established the "Confraternity of the Name of God" in fifteenth-century Spain, and the Society was officially approved by Pope Pius IV a century later.

Parish* units long flourished in the U.S. and Canada. Papal permission obtained in 1896 allowed diocesan bishops* to form a Holy Name group in any American Catholic parish.* The growth of the Society in the U.S. owes much to the work of Dominican Father Charles H. McKenna. Before he died in 1917, the Society existed for men in thousands of American parishes. By 1963, at about the height of the Society's activities, membership numbered five million worldwide, including some women.

The primary purpose of the Holy Name Society has always been that of devotion to the name of Jesus. An important secondary aim, however, has been its members' sanctification.* When Catholics observed a fast from the midnight preceding Sunday morning Mass,* the Society encouraged its members to receive Holy Communion in a body at Sunday* Mass once a month. Accompanying "communion breakfasts," often with guest speakers, were popular social and educational events in many parishes. After the relaxation of the stricter fast regulations (1953) and with increasing numbers of Catholics receiving Holy Communion each Sunday, this feature of the Society gradually declined. For decades, rallies, parades, "holy hours" of prayer and other devotions also strengthened the religious base from which members were directed toward various forms of parish service.

Since Vatican II,* the Holy Name Society in America has been joined, and often supplanted, by many other groups which further the mission and spirituality* of parishes.

BIBLIOGRAPHY. V. F. O'Daniel, *Very Rev. Charles Hyacinth McKenna, O.P., P.G., Missionary and Apostle of the Holy Name Society* (1917).

G. P. Evans

Holy Office. *See* CONGREGATION FOR THE DOCTRINE OF THE FAITH.

Holy Orders. Catholic* term for the sacrament* of the priesthood. Holy Orders (derived from the Latin *ordo*) is the proper name for that sacrament commonly referred to as the sacrament of the priesthood. The difference in terminology is significant. *Priesthood* tends to connote the cultic, emphasizing liturgical* worship* and temple. *Ordo* refers to the arrangement of individual members within a common unity on the basis of their mutual relationship to a beginning, an end, a purpose and each other. In the history of the Roman church, a special role has been performed by priests and bishops* who, having received the sacrament of holy orders, promote this orderliness.

BIBLIOGRAPHY. R. Kress, *The Church: Communion, Sacrament, Communication* (1985).

R. L. Kress

Holy Rollers. A derisive term, dating from the early twentieth century, used to describe groups who gave extreme emotional expression to their faith. The term included ecstatic activity, such as trances, jumping up and down (hence also "Holy Jumpers") and rolling on the floor. At first used of Pentecostals,* eventually the term was applied to any who were accused of extreme emotionalism in religious meetings. After World War 2* the term gradually fell into disuse and is little heard today.

W. G. Travis

Home Missions Council. Interdenominational network of home mission agencies. Organized in 1908 under the chairmanship of Charles L. Thompson,* the purpose of the Home Missions Council (HMC) was to promote fellowship, conferences and cooperation among Christian organizations doing missionary work in the U.S., Canada and their dependencies. The ecumenical concern was evident in the HMC's close relationship to the Federal Council of Churches of Christ in America* and the Council of Women for Home Missions. Although each council retained its autonomy, each hoped that mutual re-enforcement and a unified program of service would enhance the churches' ability to proclaim the gospel, plant new churches and renew existing ones.

In field studies and publications the HMC's interest was the proper distribution of resources and the adoption of the most effective methods for evangelism. Two significant gatherings sponsored by the HMC were the Church Comity Conference (January 1928) and the North American Home Missions Congress held in Washington, D.C. (December 1930).

The HMC continued to grow until the early 1930s when it served as agent for forty-two Protestant home mission boards and societies, representing twenty-seven denominations. The Great Depression,* however, brought the Council's activities to a virtual standstill, and the changing theological climate led to the withdrawal of numerous agencies. By 1933 the number of boards represented by the HMC had dropped to thirty-one. In 1940 the HMC and the Council of Women for Home Missions were merged to form the Home Missions Council of North America, which in turn was incorporated into the National Council of Churches* as the Division of Home Missions.

BIBLIOGRAPHY. R. T. Handy, *We Witness Together: A History of Cooperative Home Missions* (1956); *North American Home Missions Congress, Washington, D.C., Dec 1-5, 1930. Reports of Commissions, Addresses and Findings* (1930).

E. Rommen

Homecomings, Church. A Southern tradition of reunion of present and former members of a local congregation, usually celebrated annually on a designated Sunday.* Typically the celebration begins with morning worship,* followed by a "dinner on the grounds" and concludes in the afternoon with congregational singing and "special music" in the Southern Gospel* style. Primarily an event with rural origins, most homecomings occur in late July or early August, a time originally designated because the crops were laid by.

In the South, church homecomings have great sentimental value because of the interrelatedness of church, community and family in rural areas. The event not only allows church members to celebrate their spiritual heritage, it also provides a setting for families and members of a bygone community to reminisce. Because many rural churches are surrounded by a cemetery, the occasion frequently provides an opportunity for rituals of respect at the graves. Today, the homecoming provides a link to the unique cultural values of the rural South.

BIBLIOGRAPHY. G. K. Neville, "Homecomings," *ERS.*

M. G. Bell

Homiletics. The study of the content, manner and method of preaching.* Preaching has been central to the Christian faith from the church's inception. Homiletics has followed accordingly, as preachers have reflected on the act of preaching and tried to teach the art of preaching to others.

Homiletics has had a rich history in the American church. The Puritans* revered preaching and, embracing the "plain style" of their English counterparts, produced several generations of great preachers, including Jonathan Edwards.* In the nineteenth century Charles G. Finney* and Dwight L. Moody* became the master technicians of revivalist* preaching, and prominent Protestant pastors like Phillips Brooks* and Henry Ward Beecher* became pulpit giants and educated a generation of preachers through their teaching and writing. In the twentieth century two cultural movements have had significant impact on homiletics: the advent of radio and television, and the influence of liberal* theology. The former has tended to transform preaching into a form of entertainment; the latter has tended to alter the traditional message of preaching. A third movement—the popularity of African-American preaching—has demonstrated the importance of passion and protest in the pulpit. Perhaps the greatest example of this homiletical model has been Martin Luther King, Jr.*

Homiletics has traditionally maintained a creative tension between the authority* of the Bible* and the ethos of culture. Homiletics is the discipline which enables the preacher to understand the text, discern the spirit of the times and bring the two together. The study of the Scriptures, organization of the sermon, application to the congregation, method of delivery and character of the preacher are important aspects of homiletical study.

Certain trends in modern American culture have made preaching a complex and strategic discipline of study. Doubts about the authority of traditional biblical language, the moral failure of clergy and the apparent popularity of emotive, moralistic and authoritarian styles of preaching have raised new issues that homiletics has had to address.

See also EXPOSITOR; PREACHING.

BIBLIOGRAPHY. F. B. Craddock, *Preaching* (1985); J. R. W. Stott, *Between Two Worlds* (1982).

G. L. Sittser

Homosexuality and the Churches. Until the latter half of the twentieth century, the American churches gave little public attention to the phenomenon of sexual attraction and sexual behavior between members of the same sex. The traditional view of most ecclesiastical bodies condemned homosexuality, finding justification for the condemnation in natural law* and in such biblical texts as Genesis 19:4-11; Leviticus 18:22; 20:13; 1 Corinthians 6:9; 1 Timothy 1:10; and Romans 1:27.

The first sign of a re-evaluation of the issue appeared in 1955 with the publication in England of *Homosexuality and the Western Christian Tradition* by Rev. Derrick Sherwin Bailey, an Anglican* priest. Bailey challenged the Church's traditional view with current findings from the behavioral sciences and a reinterpretation of relevant biblical passages. His work broke ground for a number of studies published in the U.S. which were sympathetic to gay and lesbian concerns from a religious point of view, beginning with H. Kimball Jones's *Toward a Christian Understanding of the Homosexual* (1966).

In 1964 four homophile organizations and two Methodist* agencies came together in San Francisco to hold a Consultation on the Church and the Homosexual. These meetings resulted in the creation of the pioneering Council on Religion and the Homosexual, whose primary objective was "to promote continuing dialogue between the religious community and homosexuals." Such dialog soon became increasingly heated throughout the nation: Five years later the "Stonewall Riots" in Greenwich Village launched the gay/lesbian liberation movement, which during the seventies confronted the churches openly with demands for full acceptance of homosexual orientation and practice.

In 1969 the Universal Fellowship of Metropolitan Community Churches (UFMCC) was founded by the Rev. Troy D. Perry, a former minister of the Church of God (Cleveland, Tennessee)* who had been asked to leave the denomination* because of his homosexual orientation. The UFMCC, affirming homosexuality as a gift of God and welcoming both homosexual and heterosexual Christians into its fellowship, grew quickly in the following two decades to include over 100,000 members in more than 150 congregations throughout the world. Nevertheless, in 1983 the new denomination was denied membership in the National Council of Churches.*

Perry's views, published in the book *The Lord Is My Shepherd and He Knows I'm Gay* (1972), were soon echoed in similar statements by professional therapist Ralph Blair (*An Evangelical Looks at Homosexuality,* 1977), psychotherapist and former Jesuit* John J. McNeill (*The Church and the Homosexual,* 1978) and others. Blair also organized a parachurch* group in 1976, called Evangelicals Concerned, to help evangelical* Christians integrate their faith with their homosexuality.

Meanwhile, inside the traditional churches, lesbian and gay advocacy groups began forming to lobby for full acceptance of homosexual Christians within the church. In some denominations their presence stimulated the formation of opposing caucuses. At the same time, "ex-gay" Christians began to organize in parachurch groups such as Homosexuals Anonymous and Exodus International. Their goal was to help homosexual Christians live celibately and, when possible, achieve sexual reorientation.

The discussions in the churches resulting from the conflicting concerns of these groups have focused primarily on three issues: the moral status of homosexual orientation and behavior; the ordination* of homosexuals; and civil-rights legislation for the homosexual community. Heated debates, carried on most visibly in the central legislative bodies of the denominations, have raised questions about the meaning of relevant biblical passages, the adequacy of the natural law tradition and the validity of behavioral-science data with regard to the causes of homosexuality and the possibility of sexual reorientation.

The results of these debates are still uncertain, though a number of churches have issued official statements regarding the issues involved. Responses range widely, from the approval of ceremonies for joining same-sex couples by the Unitarian-Universalist Association,* to the severe condemnations of homosexuality and statements of opposition to homosexual civil rights which have been issued by several Southern Baptist* state conventions. Most denominations, however, have followed a typical pattern of response: Studies submitted by church agencies or church-appointed task forces are sympathetic to gay and lesbian concerns, but majority opposition to such studies within the central legislative bodies results in an official reaffirmation of more traditional positions.

Among the American and Canadian denominations issuing such statements, most have gone on record as: supporting civil rights for the homosexual community; opposing homosexual practice, though recognizing that sexual orientation is rarely chosen; calling for ministry* to lesbians and gays; and denying ordination to self-affirming, practicing homosexuals. Even so, within some of these same churches a few openly homosexual clergy remain in ministry, and networks of individual congregations publicly welcome practicing homosexuals into the life of the church.

Within the Catholic Church,* some theologians* have called for full acceptance of committed, loving, same-sex relationships, and a few clergy have celebrated Mass for chapters of Dignity, the Catholic gay/lesbian advocacy group. The increasing number of AIDS cases among priests, and well-publicized instances of homosexual child abuse by some clergy, have focused attention as well on the existence of ordained, practicing homosexuals in the church. Nevertheless, the "Letter to the Bishops on the Pastoral Care of Homosexual Persons," issued by the Congregation for the Doctrine of the Faith in 1986, reaffirmed the Vatican's position that the homosexual inclination is "an objective disorder" and that homosexual behavior is immoral.

Even so, as in nearly all the American churches, the debate is not likely to end soon. Reinterpretations of biblical content and authority,* conflicting evidence from the behavioral sciences, and the range of experiences among homosexuals themselves are all contributing to a controversy which will not easily be resolved.

BIBLIOGRAPHY. T. F. Hewitt, *The American Church's Reaction to the Homophile Movement* (unpublished Ph.D. dissertation, Duke University, 1983); J. Boswell, *Christianity, Social Tolerance, and Homosexuality: Gay People in Western Europe from the Beginning of the Christian Era to the Fourteenth Century* (1980); R. T. Barnhouse, *Homosexuality: A Symbolic Confusion* (1977); H. Thielicke, *The Ethics of Sex* (1964); R. Scroggs, *The New Testament and Homosexuality: Contextual Background for Contemporary Debate* (1983).

T. P. Thigpen

Homrighausen, Elmer George (1900-1982).

Reformed* pastor* and educator.* Born in Wheatland, Iowa, Homrighausen graduated from Lakeland College, Wisconsin, before studying at Princeton Seminary (B.D., 1924). He served pastorates of the Evangelical and Reformed Church in Illinois and Indiana, and studied at the University of Dubuque. In 1938 he was called to Princeton Seminary and became Thomas Synnott Professor of Christian Education. He was dean of the seminary from 1955 to 1965 and retired in 1970. Homrighausen also briefly taught at the University of Dubuque, Occidental College and Butler University. He served as director of the National Council of Churches's* Department of Evangelism and in 1948 took leave of his seminary teaching to organize a European evangelistic campaign for the World Council of Churches.*

An early, enthusiastic supporter of Karl Barth's* theology, Homrighausen helped introduce Barth's early thought to American theologians. In the 1930s he was a co-translator of Barth and Eduard Thurneysen's sermons *Come Holy Spirit* (1933), as well as Barth's *God's Search for Man* (1935) and the later *God in Action* (1963). While in 1935 he suggested several reasons why America was not yet ready to embrace Barth's thought; by 1963, the year after Barth's visit to America, he had become convinced that America's attitude toward Barth had changed. Homrighausen's own books included *Current Trends in Theological Thought* (1937), *Let the Church Be the Church* (1940) and *I Believe in the Church* (1951).

BIBLIOGRAPHY. D. N. Voskuil, "America Encounters Karl Barth, 1919-1939," *FH* 12 (1980):61-74; D. N. Voskuil, "America Protestant Neo-Orthodoxy and Its Search for Realism (1925-1939)," *Ultimate Reality and Meaning* 8 (1985):277-287.

D. K. McKim

Hooker, Thomas (1586-1647). Puritan* minister,* theologian* and political theorist. Born in Marfield, Leicestershire, England, Hooker in 1608 graduated from Emmanuel College, Cambridge, the quintessential Puritan educational establishment, receiving the A.M. from that institution in 1611. Having attracted a considerable following as lecturer at St. Mary's, Chelmsford, and hence the notice of the authorities, in 1630 he was summoned to appear before King Charles I's High Commissioners. Hooker first fled to Holland but subsequently returned to England and finally opted to immigrate to Massachusetts, arriving in Boston in 1633 on the same ship that carried John Cotton.*

Having settled the next year as pastor* of the

church in Newtown (present-day Cambridge), Hooker in 1636, against the wishes of the Massachusetts authorities, led his congregation in an exodus to the banks of the Connecticut River, founding the town of Hartford. Hooker's political perspective, sharply distinguishing as it did between the national (religious) covenant* and all civil covenants, was reflected in Connecticut's Fundamental Orders of 1638, which refused to make church membership* a prerequisite for the franchise, as was the pattern in Massachusetts.

Hooker, the leading theoretician of New England preparationism, clashed with Cotton over the order of salvation* in the antinomian controversy* of 1637 to 1638. Hooker's mature views on church government* found expression in his enormously influential *Survey of the Summe of Church Discipline* (1648). Among his other significant publications are *The Unbeleevers Preparing for Christ* (1638) and *The Application of Redemption* (1656), developing the idea of preparation for conversion,* and *The Soules Effectuall Calling* (1637) and *The Soules Exaltation* (1638), on the theme of union with Christ.

BIBLIOGRAPHY. *AAP* 1; S. Bush, Jr., *The Writings of Thomas Hooker: Spiritual Adventure in Two Worlds* (1980); *DAB* V; *DARB*; *NCAB* 6; F. C. Shuffelton, *Thomas Hooker, 1586-1647* (1977).

G. W. Harper

Hoover, James Matthew (1872-1935). Methodist* missionary* to Southeast Asia. Born in Greenvillage, Pennsylvania, and graduating from the State Teachers College in Shippensburg, Hoover taught school for nine years before going to Malaya as a missionary of the Methodist Episcopal Church (1899). There he served in the Anglo-Chinese school in Penang and later was appointed to a similar post in Sibu, Sarawak (Borneo).

Using Foochow Chinese persons as teachers and evangelists,* he established more than forty churches and schools, mainly along the Rajang River, accomplishing a high degree of self-support through better methods of farming and marketing. He introduced to Sarawak the bicycle, motor launch, machinery for rice mills and ice-making, electricity for churches and hospitals, new medical techniques, modern export-import procedures and wireless telegraphy. Upon Hoover's death from cerebral malaria, the British "White Rajah," Sir Charles Brooke, conferred upon him the highest honors and ordered Sarawak's flag to be flown at half-mast and all schools to be closed.

BIBLIOGRAPHY. E. T. Cartwright, *Tuan Hoover of Borneo* (1938); *DAB* 1. J. T. Seamands

Hoover, Willis Collins (1856-1936). Methodist* missionary* and founder of the indigenous Chilean Pentecostal* movement. Born in Freeport, Illinois, Hoover earned a medical degree (M.D., 1884) and as a youth felt called to South America. Hoover began his missionary career in 1889 as a teacher in northern Chile and in 1902 became pastor of a Methodist church in Valparaiso, Chile. Estranged from his fellow missionaries, due in part to his emphasis on the Wesleyan* doctrine of sanctification,* Hoover became impressed with reports of the recent revivals in Wales, India and the U.S. and led his church in intense, protracted meetings that produced unusual emotional expressions. Further estranged from his colleagues, Hoover and as many as six hundred Chileans, left the Methodist Church to form in 1910 the parent organization of the contemporary movement, the Pentecostal Methodist Church (Iglesia Methodista Nacional). At the time of his death his churches had a membership equal to the combined total of all other Chilean Protestant groups. But during his declining years, Hoover faced the problem of transferring leadership that for so long had depended on his personal influence.

BIBLIOGRAPHY. J. B. A. Kessler, Jr., *A Study of the Older Protestant Missions and Churches in Peru and Chile* (1967). E. A. Wilson

Hopkins, Emma Curtis (1853-1925). Leader of New Thought. Emma Hopkins received instruction in Mary Baker Eddy's* December 1883 Boston class and rapidly assumed leadership responsibilities in the Christian Science* movement. After a short stint as editor (1884-1885) of the *Christian Science Journal,* Hopkins broke with Eddy and joined another former Eddy student, Mary Plunkett, to establish the Emma Hopkins College of Christian Science (1886) in Chicago (renamed Christian Science Theological Seminary in 1887). Through this institution her lectures and publications such as her journal, *Christian Metaphysician* (1887-1897), Hopkins taught a brand of Christian Science that freely borrowed from a variety of the world's mystical and religious traditions. Eddy denounced such eclecticism, but religious healers who formed New Thought found it invigorating. Hopkins's lecturing took her from Chicago to both coasts, and she gained a widespread reputation among religious healers as the "teachers' teacher," influencing, among others, Ernest Holmes, founder of Religious Science; Charles and Myrtle Fillmore,* who established the Unity School of Christianity*; and Malinda E. Cramer and Mona L. Brooks, cofounders of Divine Science. In her later years she retired to publish her major work, *High Mysticism* (1920-1922), and conduct private healing lessons.

BIBLIOGRAPHY. C. S. Braden, *Spirits in Rebellion: The Rise and Development of New Thought* (1963); *DARB*; *NAW* 2.   R. B. Schoepflin

Hopkins, John Henry (1792-1868). Episcopal* bishop.* A convert to the Episcopal Church, Hopkins was both bishop of the diocese* of Vermont (from 1832) and a prolific controversialist. His fundamental argument was that religious doctrine be grounded on Scripture,* as interpreted through the witness of the primitive church.

In *The Primitive Church* (1835) he employed this claim to defend Episcopal doctrine against Protestant* critics, while he used the same criterion to oppose in the 1840s the theological tendencies of the Tractarian Movement.* During the 1850s and 1860s, he attacked the abolitionist movement* on the same grounds, that it was an innovation unsupported by either Scripture or tradition. His anti-abolitionist writings stirred up much controversy during the Civil War.* Hopkins's aesthetic interests came to expression in his *Essay on Gothic Architecture* (1836), the first American treatment of the topic. Despite his anti-Tractarian convictions, Hopkins was always willing to distinguish between questions of doctrine and practice, and in *The Law of Ritualism* (1866), he supported the adoption of practices such as eucharistic vestments and incense.

BIBLIOGRAPHY. *DAB* V; J. H. Hopkins, Jr., *A Life of the Late Right Reverend John Henry Hopkins . . . by One of His Sons* (1875); C. F. Sweet, *A Champion of the Cross* (1894); R. B. Mullin, *Episcopal Vision/American Reality* (1986).

R. B. Mullin

Hopkins, Mark (1802-1887). Moral philosopher and president of Williams College. Born in Stockbridge, Massachusetts, the great-nephew of renowned theologian* Samuel Hopkins,* Mark Hopkins graduated from Williams College (B.A., 1824). After serving as a tutor at Williams for two years, he began studying medicine at the Berkshire Medical Institute (1829), intent on practicing in New York. When his former professor of moral philosophy died, Hopkins was offered the post, which he accepted (1830-1836). He remained at Williams until his death. Ordained* to the Congregational* ministry* in 1836, the year he became president of Williams (1836-1872), Hopkins served as pastor of the college church for over half a century and also as president of the American Board of Commissioners for Foreign Missions* for

thirty years (1857-1887).

While keenly interested in both law and medicine, Hopkins's first loves were philosophy and theology.* He was convinced that those religious and philosophical truths that stood the test of time provided sufficient answers to all facets of human life. Hence he stood in opposition to many of the intellectual currents of his day, including transcendentalism* and nascent Darwinism.* His own convictions were based on the firm belief that God had ordained a rational end for all beings and that the intellect, the sensibilities and the will were all parts of a whole. Thus the educational enterprise was one of molding virtuous character as much as sheer intellectual endeavor. Never a great scholar or thinker, Hopkins was a gifted teacher, skilled at persuading students of the rationality of his own positions and earning their lasting respect.

BIBLIOGRAPHY. *DAB* V; *DARB*; J. H. Denison, *Mark Hopkins: A Biography* (1935); *NCAB* 6; F. Rudolph, *Mark Hopkins and the Log* (1956).

C. H. Lippy

Hopkins, Samuel (1721-1803). Congregational* clergyman* and theologian.* Born in Connecticut and trained at Yale College,* Hopkins was profoundly influenced by the preaching of Jonathan Edwards.* After graduation from Yale, Hopkins lived and worked in Edwards's Northampton "school for the prophets," an informal seminary in which Edwards tutored students in his unique brand of pro-Awakening* Reformed* theology. Hopkins became one of Edwards's closest friends and most influential disciples and spent his entire career in the ministry. He served churches in what became Great Barrington, Massachusetts, and later in Newport, Rhode Island.

With his colleague Joseph Bellamy,* another of Edwards's proteges, Hopkins helped to shape a highly nuanced version of Edwards's theology. Within a decade of Edwards's untimely death in 1758, Hopkins and Bellamy began to systematize and extend the religious thought that Edwards had formulated in his *Freedom of the Will* (1754), *Original Sin* (1758) and the posthumous *Nature of True Virtue*. By the final decades of the eighteenth century, Hopkins and Bellamy had won a group of some sixty like-minded ministers to their way of thinking. This first indigenous school of American Calvinism* has borne a plethora of names: *Edwardseanism, Consistent Calvinism, Hopkinsianism* and *New Divinity Theology*. Although *New Divinity*   is the most common name, it was first used as a term of derision. As early as 1765, traditional Old Calvinist ministers complained that Hopkins's radical departure from standard Reformed doctrine represented an altogether "new" system of divinity.

The most distinctive features of Hopkins thought—his teaching on the radical corruption of humanity and the nature of regeneration—are contained in his *System of Doctrines* (1793). Taking Edwards's lead, Hopkins taught that sin, though not transmitted to humanity via the imputation of Adam's guilt, is manifested in selfishness or inordinate self-love. Hence, for Hopkins, the "sincere" unregenerate seeker-after-righteousness is ultimately motivated by wicked self-interest. This notion led Hopkins and other New Divinity theologians to declare the liabilities facing unregenerate persons who actively used the means of grace in their search for salvation. Opponents of New Divinity theology, such as Ezra Stiles,* worried that such a deprecation of the means of grace would lead to the notion that the "unregenerate man had better be killing his father and mother than praying for converting grace."

However severe Hopkins's teaching on selfishness appeared to his opponents, he balanced his system with a unique understanding of the nature of genuine Christian virtue. Working from Edwards's notion of virtue as "benevolence to Being in general," Hopkins argued that the center of regeneration lay in the convert's new access to "disinterested benevolence." Despite opponents' fears that Hopkins's hyper-Calvinistic metaphysics would lead people away from righteous social action, just the opposite occurred. Seeing the heart of Christian virtue as selflessness—disinterested charity for all of God's creation—Hopkins erected a Calvinistic apologia for social reform. In the era when Arminian* perfectionist* theologians were developing their popular rationale for social action, Hopkins coupled disinterested benevolence and an optimistic post-millennial* eschatology,* and became one of New England's earliest and most vocal abolitionists.*

BIBLIOGRAPHY. *AAP* 1; W. Breitenbach, "Unregenerate Doings: Selflessness and Selfishness in New Divinity Theology," *American Quarterly* 34 (1980):479-502; J. A. Conforti, *Samuel Hopkins and the New Divinity Movement: Calvinism, the Congregational Ministry, and Reform in New England Between the Great Awakenings* (1981); *DAB* V; *DARB*; *NCAB* 7; E. A. Park, *Memoir of the Life and Character of Samuel Hopkins* (1854); S. West, *Sketches of the Life of the Late Samuel Hopkins* (1805). J. R. Fitzmier

Hopkinsianism. *See* HOPKINS, SAMUEL.

Horner, Ralph Cecil (1853-1921). Father of the Canadian Holiness Movement.* Born in Quebec, Horner experienced "entire sanctification" in the 1870s and soon began preaching* with strong emotional appeal. He attended Victoria College in Cobourg, near Toronto (1883-1885), studied rhetoric in Philadelphia (1885-1886) and was ordained* in 1887 by the Montreal Conference (Methodist*). Horner rejected a standard circuit to continue evangelistic* campaigns marked by conversions,* sanctifications,* slayings in the Spirit and speaking in tongues.*

Deposed as a Methodist minister* in 1895, he organized the Holiness Movement Church and became its first bishop.* The majority of Horner's support came from the Ottawa Valley, but there was also significant interest in western Canada and Michigan. When Horner's leadership was challenged in 1916, he formed the Standard Church of America. The small, 1,600-member Holiness Movement Church joined the Free Methodists* in 1958, while the slightly larger Standard Church still exists as a small body.

BIBLIOGRAPHY. S. D. Clark, *Church and Sect in Canada* (1948). B. A. McKenzie

Horton, Douglas (1891-1968). Congregational* leader and advocate for Christian unity.* Born in Brooklyn, New York, Horton studied at Princeton University (B.A., 1912); New College, Edinburgh; Mansfield College, Oxford; University of Tübingen; and Hartford Theological Seminary (B.D., 1915). He received honorary degrees from numerous institutions and was ordained* as a Congregational minister in 1915. After serving churches in Middletown, Connecticut; Brookline, Massachusetts; and Chicago, Illinois, he was named minister and secretary of the General Council of Congregational Christian Churches (1938-1955). Throughout the years Horton taught at a number of seminaries,* including Newton, Chicago and Union (New York).* From 1955 to 1959 Horton was dean of the Harvard* Divinity School.

Horton was an active proponent of the merger of the Congregational Christian Churches with the Evangelical and Reformed Church, leading in 1957 to the creation of the United Church of Christ.* He served on the General Committee of the World Council of Churches* and, from 1957 to 1963, chaired its Faith and Order Commission. As representative of the International Congregational Council, Horton served as an official Protestant* observer at Vatican II.* Among Horton's important publications are his translation of a volume of sermons by Karl Barth*—the first appearance of

Barth in English—published as *The Word of God and the Word of Man* (1928), an important study of congregational church polity, and *Toward an Undivided Church* (1967).

BIBLIOGRAPHY. L. H. Gunnemann, *The Shaping of the United Church of Christ* (1977).

W. A. Silva

Horton, (T)homas (C)orwin (1848-1932). Minister and cofounder of the Bible Institute of Los Angeles (now known as Biola University). Born in Cincinnati, Ohio, Horton attended Farmer's College at College Hill, Ohio, for one year and went on to become a successful businessman by age twenty-seven. Turning to Christian work, he served as YMCA* secretary in Indianapolis (1876), later serving in that same position in St. Paul, Minnesota, and Dallas, Texas (1904-1906). Horton spent some time at Hope Presbyterian Church in St. Paul, apparently as an evangelist.* Ordained* into the Presbyterian* ministry in 1884, Horton soon went to Philadelphia to serve as associate pastor with dispensationalist* and missions leader A. T. Pierson* at Bethany Presbyterian Church (1885-1889). He then pastored the First Congregational Church (1900-1903) of Dallas, Texas (later called Scofield* Memorial Church). In 1906 Horton moved to Los Angeles, where he would remain for the rest of his career.

In 1906, while serving at Los Angeles's Immanuel Presbyterian Church, he founded the Fishermen's Club. Established to train laymen* in Bible* and evangelism,* the club eventually became an international organization. His wife, Anna (Kingsbury), founded the Lyceum Club for women. Horton's most significant educational contribution was his founding of the Bible Institute of Los Angeles in 1908 (now Biola University in La Mirada, California). With the financial backing of oilman and Christian layman Lyman Stuart,* Horton founded and served as the superintendent of the school, which was established to prepare young people for Christian service.

During his years in Los Angeles, Horton remained an active minister and served for several years as associate pastor of the Church of the Open Door (1915-1924). As a leading dispensational premillennialist,* Horton organized the Southern California Premillennial Association. He published several popular Christian books, including *Personal and Practical Christian Work* (1922) and the *Potency of Prayer* (1928). He also served as editor of two periodicals: *The King's Business* (1910-1925) and *Fishers of Men* (1930-1932).

BIBLIOGRAPHY. "Daddy Horton," *Fishers of Men*

(April-June 1932):1-15; J. O. Henry, "Black Oil and Souls to Win", *The King's Business* (February 1958):10-41.

D. G. Buss

Horton, Walter Marshall (1895-1966). Neo-orthodox* theologian.* Born in Somerville, Massachusetts, Horton was educated at Harvard* (B.A., 1917); Union Theological Seminary, New York* (B.D., 1920; S.T.M., 1923); and Columbia University (M.A., 1920; Ph.D., 1926). He also studied at the Sorbonne, University of Strasbourg and the University of Marburg. Ordained* a Baptist* minister* in 1919, Horton began his teaching career at Union Theological Seminary, New York (1922-1925), but soon moved to Oberlin College Graduate School of Theology, where he spent the rest of his career as Fairchild Professor.

Horton began his active professional career amidst the transition from liberal* thought to Neo-orthodox or, as in the title of his book, *Realistic Theology* (1934). In 1931 he published *A Psychological Approach to Theology* in which he analyzed religious experience in terms of its behavioral dimensions, integrating moral values and human development with traditional theological doctrines such as theism,* sin,* salvation* and human destiny. Always aware of the limitations of psychology,* Horton attempted thus to reconnect theology and the sciences in the wake of the disintegration of the liberal tradition after World War 1.* He is rightly regarded as a parent of the field of pastoral psychology.

Later, in the 1950s, Horton made a second important contribution in creating an ecumenical* theology (*Christian Theology: An Ecumenical Approach,* 1955). Determining denominational* theological education and theologies to be inadequate, he found in the universal necessity of religion and the commonality of Christian doctrinal expression a need for a more universal Christian faith. He believed, for instance, that the Christian unity of the Roman Catholic Church,* together with the Christian liberty* of Protestantism,* provided a unique model for an historically valid ecumenical theology. A friend of Paul Tillich* and Gustaf Aulén, Horton was also a leading advocate of the role and work of the World Council of Churches.* As one of the first proponents of the psychological basis for theology and as a vigorous advocate of an ecumenical approach to theological inquiry, Horton broke new ground in twentieth-century American theology.

BIBLIOGRAPHY. "The Man of the Month," *Pastoral Psychology* VII:6 (November 1956).

W. H. Brackney

Hospice. Wholistic care for the terminally ill and their families. The term *hospice,* derived from the Latin *hospes,* meaning primarily a host and secondarily a guest, in medieval times signified a place of shelter for travelers on difficult journeys or pilgrimages. The hospice of today is a skilled community dedicated to: enabling the terminally ill (those whose life expectancy is measured in months or weeks) to experience the fullest possible quality of life before their death; making the patient-family the primary focus of concern; and supporting the family in its bereavement.

Various models of hospice care have been developed, including hospices operated as independent units, hospices associated with a hospital (or, rarely, a total hospital functioning as a hospice), hospices linked with nursing homes and hospices administered from a central facility but sending care teams directly into the homes of the terminally ill.

At the turn of the century three refuges for the dying existed in London, England, one of them being St. Joseph's Hospice founded by the Irish Sisters of Charity. There Dr. Cicely Saunders's research in the 1950s led to the founding of the well-known St. Christopher's Hospice in Sydenham, near London, in 1967. St. Christopher's provided the model for certain American hospices, such as Hospice, Inc., of New Haven, Connecticut.

Certain essential characteristics mark a hospice, despite differences between programs. A hospice program is autonomous and centrally administered; and it coordinates both out- and inpatient services. The patient and family constitute the primary unit of care. To provide a wholistic program of physical, emotional, psychological and spiritual care, as well as symptom control, hospices often employ physician-directed interdisciplinary teams. Nurses provide constant on-call clinical services, and other professionals, such as social workers or the clergy, are called upon as needed. Trained volunteers are essential to the hospice program and provide such nonclinical services as transportation, shopping, recreation and companionship. Certified hospices generally provide support during bereavement.

BIBLIOGRAPHY. P. M. DuBois, *The Hospice Way of Death* (1980); S. Stoddard, *The Hospice Movement: A Better Way of Caring for the Dying* (1978). R. M. Leliaert

Hostetter, (C)hristian (N)eff, Jr. (1899-1980). Brethren in Christ* bishop* and educator. Born in Lancaster County, Pennsylvania, Hostetter grew up in a Brethren in Christ home and graduated from Messiah College in 1922. For the next twelve years he was pastor of the Brethren in Christ congregation at Refton, Pennsylvania. In 1934 he became president of Messiah College and served in that role until 1960.

Hostetter was also active in his denomination as an evangelist,* board member and moderator (four times) of General Conference, the denomination's governing body. From 1936 to 1957 he was bishop of the Grantham District.

Outside his denomination he was active in the National Association of Evangelicals,* serving two terms on its board of administration, and from 1959 to 1967 as chairman of that organization's World Relief Commission (later Organization). But his most significant work outside his denomination was done with the Mennonite Central Committee,* on which he served from 1948 to 1967, the last fourteen as its chairman.

BIBLIOGRAPHY. E. M. Sider, *Messenger of Grace: A Biography of C. N. Hostetter, Jr.* (1982).
E. M. Sider

Hotovitzky, Alexander (c.1870-c.1935). Russian Orthodox* priest.* Hotovitzky arrived in America fresh out of seminary, one of Bishop Nicholas Ziorov's finest recruits—honest, idealistic and deeply religious. He married* in the U.S., was ordained,* and quickly became the trusted advisor of all the East Coast Orthodox clergy.* As editor of and primary writer for the Russian-American *Orthodox Messenger,* his was a major voice in the Church. He led the battle against the Unia and rampant American russophobia, and championed evangelistic* outreach to an American-grown materialistic. He spearheaded the Mission's charitable programs, served as its de facto English-language spokesman and, after Fr. Alexis G. Toth's* death in 1909, as the de facto dean of American clergy. In 1914 he returned home to Russia to serve under his former bishop* in America, Tikhon Bellavin,* and was caught in the thick of the Bolshevik Persecution of Christianity. Twice in the 1920s and 1930s he endured exile but avoided rumored show trials. Finally, at some point after a 1935 sentencing, he was executed by a Soviet firing squad, the date and place of his martyrdom not having been preserved.
P. D. Garrett

Houghton, William Henry (1887-1947). Fundamentalist* Baptist* minister* and president of Moody Bible Institute.* Born in South Boston, Massachusetts, Houghton was educated in Boston and Providence, Rhode Island. In 1901, at the age of fourteen, he was converted* in an evangelistic meeting in Lynn, Massachusetts. In his earlier years he pursued an interest in music and drama, but in 1909, under the preaching of a Nazarene* pastor, he was convicted of his life of disobedience, gave up his stage career and soon enrolled in Eastern Nazarene College. After no more than six months at college (c.1910), he was invited by Reuben A. Torrey* to be his evangelistic and Bible conference* song leader. Torrey looked after his further instruction in the faith and served as his mentor in succeeding years.

Houghton was ordained* a Baptist minister in 1915 and served churches in Canton (1915-1917), New Bethlehem (1918-1922) and Norristown (1922-1924), Pennsylvania. During his years at Bethlehem, he published some successful tracts and began a short-lived periodical *The Baptist Believer*, at Norristown he increasingly became involved in evangelistic endeavors. An evangelistic campaign in Ireland in 1924 was followed by further successful pastorates at the Baptist Tabernacle in Atlanta, Georgia (1925-1930), and Calvary Baptist Church in New York City (1930-1934), where he succeeded John Roach Straton.* Finally, in 1934 he became president of Moody Bible Institute,* where he succeeded James M. Gray.*

At Moody he built up the faculty and student body (from 848 in 1934 to 1,428 in 1945) and edited and expanded the circulation of *Moody Monthly* (from 35,000 in 1934 to 75,000 in 1945). Houghton, with Irwin A. Moon, initiated the idea of a periodic meeting of Christians involved in science, which eventually became the American Scientific Affiliation. Moon carried out a novel form of evangelism called "sermons from science," which under Houghton's leadership become the Moody Institute of Science. A passionate leader and tireless worker, Houghton's years at Moody were a significant chapter in the institution's life. Houghton died in Los Angeles after several months of coronary problems.

BIBLIOGRAPHY. W. M. Smith, *A Watchman on the Wall: The Life Story of Will H. Houghton* (1951). D. G. Reid

House Churches. Gatherings of believers held in the home of a Christian individual or family. The group might be as small as two or three family members, or large enough to include the extended family and as many others as the facility can accommodate.

House churches have existed from the time Christianity began and the apostle Paul frequently wrote letters to "the church in your house" (Rom 16:5; 1 Cor 16:19; Philem 2). From the second century A.D. onward, house churches were gradually replaced by special structures erected for Christian worship* whenever financial resources and local regulations allowed. This held true for most religious groups during the colonization and settlement of North America as well.

On the American frontier a devout husband or wife might conduct some form of simple worship service in the family home on a regular basis. In general, these home gatherings involved singing, Scripture* reading, prayer* and a brief devotional thought or reading from a religious text. When there were a sufficient number of believers in the area to invite a traveling preacher to conduct services, the members would begin to make plans to build a special structure for public worship (and often education as well). Frequently the same structure would function as the town hall, the local school and the place for Sunday services.

Americans have always valued religious freedom, and the twentieth century has given rise to a number of new independent groups and house churches. Contemporary house churches are not limited to any particular theological tradition—they may be Calvinists* or Arminians,* liberals* or conservatives, Holiness,* Pentecostal* or charismatic.* In some cases they are temporary arrangements in the course of establishing a new congregation with a new church building; in other cases they represent a quest for intimacy and community that members have not found in a large church. Some groups, such as the Old Order River Brethren,* regard the house church as the biblical model for Christian community and worship and refuse to use church buildings.

BIBLIOGRAPHY. P. A. Anderson, *The House Church* (1975); T. E. Barlow, *Congregational House Churches* (1978).

T. R. Albin

House of Bishops. The national legislative body of the Episcopal Church* in the U.S. is the General Convention, a representative body that meets every three years. It is, like the U.S. Congress, a bicameral legislative body, consisting of a House of Deputies* and a House of Bishops. Each bishop*— diocesan, coadjutor, suffragan, assistant, active and retired—has a seat and vote. The House of Bishops chooses one of the bishops to be the presiding bishop of the Episcopal Church. During the years when the General Convention does not meet, the House of Bishops meets but cannot pass legislation. Periodically the House of Bishops issues a pastoral letter. D. S. Armentrout

[557]

House of Deputies. The national legislative body of the Episcopal Church in the United States* is the General Convention, a representative body that meets every three years. It is, like the U.S. Congress, a bicameral legislative body, consisting of a House of Bishops* and a House of Deputies. Each diocese* elects four ordained* persons, presbyters* or deacons,* canonically resident in the diocese, and four lay* persons, in good standing in the diocese but not necessarily domiciled in the diocese. When the general convention meets, the House of Deputies elects a president and vice president, who shall be of different orders, and who serve until the next General Convention. Female lay deputies were approved in 1967 and seated for the first time at the General Convention of 1970.   D. S. Armentrout

Howe, Julia Ward (1819-1910). Unitarian* author and social reformer. Born in New York City, one of seven children of a wealthy banker, Samuel Ward, and Julia Cutter, Julia Ward married Samuel G. Howe of Boston in 1843. Samuel was a man already involved in many reform causes, including the establishment of the Perkins School for the Blind. Together they edited the *Commonwealth,* an abolitionist* newspaper. Though she was the mother of six children, Julia published several volumes of poetry, essays and drama, but her chief fame came from a single poem, "The Battle Hymn of the Republic" (set to the tune of "John Brown's Body"), which she composed in Washington in 1861 after she had visited a Union Army camp. Published in February 1862 in the *Atlantic Monthly,* the poem brought her instant acclaim.

After the war and her husband's death in 1876, she was active in reform causes as president of the American Woman Suffrage Association and the American Branch of the Women's International Peace Association. A Calvinist* in her early years, Howe was increasingly attracted to Unitarianism after moving to Boston in the 1840s, and she regularly attended James Freeman Clarke's* Church of the Disciples. She supported the ordination of women* and frequently preached in Unitarian pulpits. In the end she preached a gospel of culture to a society she believed had grown neglectful of basic American values. At her funeral Samuel A. Eliot, president of the American Unitarian Association,* gave the eulogy and 4,000 people sang the "Battle Hymn of the Republic" at Boston's Symphony Hall.

BIBLIOGRAPHY. D. P. Clifford, *Mine Eyes Have Seen the Glory: A Biography of Julia Ward Howe* (1979); *DAB* V; *NAW* 2; L. E. Richards and M. H. Elliot, *Julia Howe,* 2 vols. (1915).

R. R. Crocker

Howell, (R)obert (B)oyte (C)rawford (1801-1868). Southern Baptist* pastor* and denominational* leader. Born in North Carolina and raised an Episcopalian,* Howell became a Baptist* in 1821. After attending Columbia College, Washington, D.C., he entered the ministry, first as a pastor* and later as a home missionary.* In 1835 Howell became pastor of First Baptist Church, Nashville, Tennessee. That same year he began publication of *The Baptist,* a monthly periodical addressed primarily to Baptist churches in Tennessee.

Howell was one of the leading figures in the formation of the Southern Baptist Convention in 1845 and was its second president. A proponent of theological education* among Baptists, he was instrumental in the founding of various Baptist institutions, including the Southern Baptist Seminary (1859). Howell also addressed numerous controversies in Southern Baptist life and is best known for his opposition to the movement called Old Landmarkism* and its effort to trace Baptist churches directly to New Testament times. He wrote numerous books on Baptist history and theology; among them are *The Cross* (1854), *The Early Baptists of Virginia* (1876) and *The Evils of Infant Baptism* (1854).

BIBLIOGRAPHY. J. W. Barton, *Road to Augusta: R. B. C. Howell and the Formation of the Southern Baptist Convention* (1976); *DAB* V.

B. J. Leonard

Hughes, John Joseph (1797-1864). Roman Catholic* prelate and controversialist. A native of County Tyrone, Ireland, Hughes immigrated to the U.S. in 1817. In 1820 he began studies under the Sulpicians* at Mount Saint Mary's Seminary, Emmitsburg, Maryland, and was ordained, October 15, 1826, in Philadelphia, where he served as pastor* and fiery apologist. In 1838 he became coadjutor* to New York's Bishop* John Dubois, whom he succeeded in 1842. He was named New York's first archbishop* in 1850.

Hughes was an aggressive prelate and created a centralized diocesan* authority that also maintained its Roman identity. He halted lay* trustees'* attempts to republicanize Roman Catholic polity and ensured the diocese's twenty-two new parishes* came under episcopal* control. He also founded St. John's College, later Fordham University (1841), laid the cornerstone for St. Patrick's Cathedral (1858) and established St. Joseph's Seminary in Troy (1862).

Despite his autocratic style Hughes was popular among his predominantly immigrant community because he promoted American Catholic aspirations in the face of nativist* hostility. His lectures, sermons* and newspaper articles proclaimed Roman Catholicism to be the moral foundation for the American social order. In the face of the 1844 Native American and 1854 Know Nothing threats against Catholics, Hughes remained undaunted, calling upon his flock to defend themselves and their churches. His protest against Protestant*-controlled public schools moved the state to legislate secular education (1842) and won the commitment of Catholics to parochial schools.*

Hughes enjoyed national prominence. His rhetorical skill gained him an invitation to speak before Congress (1847) and even a request from Secretary of State William H. Seward to represent the Union before Pius IX* and Napoleon III (1861). He died in New York City.

BIBLIOGRAPHY. *DAB* V; *DARB;* L. Kehoe, ed., *Complete Works of the Most Reverend John Hughes, First Archbishop of New York,* 2 vols. (1865); John R. G. Hassard, *Life of the Most Reverend John Hughes, First Archbishop of New York* (1866); *NCAB* 1; R. Shaw, *Daggar John: The Unquiet Life and Times of Archbishop John Hughes of New York* (1977).   S. Y. Mize

Huguenots. The popular name for the Calvinist* French Protestants,* officially the Reformed* Church of France. An epithet of uncertain origin, it most probably is a French corruption of the German word *Eidgenossen* ("confederates"), the term applied by the cantons of the Swiss Confederation to themselves. Or, as some scholars have argued, it perhaps refers to a legendary King Hugon whose spirit was thought to haunt a part of Tours where Protestants met secretly in the early years of the movement. In any event, in the sixteenth and seventeenth centuries, the word was often used to describe the French Protestants as both a religious movement and a political faction.

Under the intellectual and spiritual leadership of their exiled countryman, John Calvin, and with the help of missionary pastors dispatched from Geneva, the French Protestants grew rapidly in numbers from about 1540 to 1560. During these decades, many French nobles, including the powerful House of Bourbon, embraced the evangelical* Calvinist faith and began to fuse the movement with political goals. While most of them were sincere in their conversion,* they also found in Calvinism an ideology useful for influencing public opinion and an ecclesiastical structure

beneficial for raising money and mustering troops. Efforts to suppress the French Reformed Church led to a series of ferocious, complex and inconclusive Wars of Religion in France between 1562 and 1598. A resolution of the civil conflict came when the Huguenot leader Henry of Navarre, of the House of Bourbon, succeeded to the throne as Henry IV (1589-1610), declared himself a Catholic, and in 1598 issued the Edict of Nantes granting the Protestants religious toleration, full civil liberties, control of the education of their children, and the right to fortify certain Protestant towns. In many ways, it allowed the Huguenots to exist as a "state within a state."

However, during the reigns of the next two kings these rights would be undone. Their military and political prerogatives were removed under Louis XIII (1610-1643), beginning under the direction of Cardinal Richelieu (minister, 1624-1642), then almost completely in 1629, following the Protestant defeat at La Rochelle. The Huguenots' religious rights were gradually withdrawn early in the reign of Louis XIV (1643-1715) and abolished completely in 1685 with the revocation of the Edict of Nantes. With Protestantism made illegal in almost all of France, over 400,000 of the more than two million Huguenots immigrated to Prussia, the Netherlands, Switzerland, the British Isles and North America.

A Huguenot presence had actually been established in America more than a hundred years before the revocation of the Edict of Nantes. In 1562 Admiral Gaspard de Coligny, a high-ranking Protestant government official in France, sent Jean de Ribault with thirty Huguenot families to establish a settlement. They built a town at a place they called Port Royal, near present-day Charleston, South Carolina. But the colony disintegrated when de Ribault was hastily called home because of the outbreak of the first of the religious civil wars. Two years later, Coligny sent René de Laudonnière with about two hundred Huguenots to colonize the same general area. They founded Fort Caroline near the mouth of the St. Johns River, not far from the modern city of Jacksonville, Florida, but in 1565 the settlement was annihilated by a Spanish strike force from St. Augustine, with only about thirty survivors returning to France.

Huguenot immigration* to British North America between 1565 and 1685 consisted mostly of families and small groups, probably numbering no more than 5,000 in all and coming mainly by way of the Netherlands and England. Several French Protestants were among the passengers on the *Mayflower* when it arrived at Plymouth in 1620.

[559]

The following year Huguenot Philippe de la Noye arrived at Plymouth, anglicized his name to Philip Delano, became a leading Massachusetts merchant and eventually the ancestor of President Franklin Delano Roosevelt. In 1623 the ship *Nieuw Nederlandt* deposited some thirty Huguenot families in what is now Connecticut, Delaware and New York. In 1626 Peter Minnewit (Pierre Minuit), a ruling elder* in the Reformed Church, bought Manhattan Island from Native Americans and established New Amsterdam. Later, in 1652, a Huguenot named Isaac Bethlo emigrated from Calais to New Amsterdam, bestowed his anglicized name upon Bedloe Island where the Statue of Liberty now stands. In like manner, others came in the pre-1685 period—to Massachusetts, Virginia, Maine, Pennsylvania, South Carolina and New York (especially New Paltz, 1677).

In the sixty-five years following the revocation of the Edict of Nantes in 1685, about 15,000 more Huguenots immigrated to America. Most of them settled in and around Charleston where they became a major force in South Carolina life, but large numbers also landed in Pennsylvania, Virginia, New York, Rhode Island and Massachusetts. The story of Huguenot community migration to America came to an end when in 1712 Madame Marie Ferée led a group of her co-religionists to found a plantation in Lancaster County, Pennsylvania. Though small in numbers, the Huguenots wielded a considerable influence in colonial life because most of them were merchants, bankers, skilled craftsmen or members of the legal and medical professions. They also dotted the landscape of fame in America with French Huguenot surnames: Paul Revere, John C. Fremont, Matthew Vassar, James Bowdoin, Thomas Hopkinson Gallaudet, Henry D. Thoreau, Henry W. Longfellow and John G. Whittier, to name a few.

The story of the Huguenots in America constitutes one of the great mysteries of ethnic refugee assimilation in American history. Like so many other immigrants in the colonial period, they came to find religious freedom and to better themselves economically, and they clustered together in rural New England, New York and South Carolina as well as in urban Boston, New York City and Charleston. However, by 1750, as a group, they had largely disappeared into the larger Anglo-Saxon culture and assimilated almost flawlessly into Protestant America, contrary to the normal pattern that sustained immigrant identity (*See* Immigration and Ethnicity, Protestant).

It may be that assimilation occurred easily because the Huguenots did not immigrate en masse but in a steady flow of individuals and families over a long period. Also, they may have been especially eager to forget their recent grim past in France. Moreover, most of the American-bound Huguenots migrated by way of another country which, in turn, helped to make their second adjustment more quickly. In addition, there appears to have been a lack of the clerical and lay leadership and practical churchmanship necessary to sustain their collective religious identity in the New World. Further, many French Protestant refugees proved susceptible to Anglican* overtures in the colonies because of Anglican kindnesses toward Huguenot refugees in London and to immigrant congregations in America. Perhaps most of all, the very fact that the Huguenots' primary identity was religious rather than French allowed them to assimilate more easily and more rapidly into the evangelical Protestant ethos of colonial America.

BIBLIOGRAPHY. J. Butler, *The Huguenots in America* (1983); J. G. Gray, *The French Huguenots* (1981); R. M. Kingdon, *Geneva and the Consolidation of the French Protestant Movement* (1967); R. M. Kingdon, "Why Did the Huguenot Refugees to the American Colonies Become Episcopalian?" *HMPEC* 49 (1980):317-335; G. E. Reaman, *The Trail of the Huguenots in Europe, the United States, South Africa and Canada* (1963).

R. D. Linder

Humanae Vitae. An encyclical letter of Pope Paul VI* (July 25, 1968) on the topic of birth control.* The context for the encyclical is the twentieth-century debate over the nature and purpose of Christian marriage. Some Catholics in Western countries such as the U. S., while not denying that in God's plan (Gen 1:28) procreation is an essential dimension to marriage, desired greater emphasis than before on married love as likewise being essential (Gen 2:18).

With the development and mass marketing of the birth control pill, Catholics in the U. S. debated whether traditional Catholic opposition to contraception was a matter of revealed truth or an application based on abiding Christian principles, subject to change with circumstances. Many expected the Second Vatican Council* (1963-1965) to address the issue. Instead, in June 1964, Paul VI created a special commission of experts to study the disputed questions. Vatican II's *Pastoral Constitution on the Church in the Modern World* had treated marriage and family at length (pars. 47-52) but avoided the issue of artificial contraception. On June 26, 1966, the papal commission made its report. While strongly rejecting arbitrary contraception, it advocated leaving decisions about how to achieve responsible parenthood in the context of fruitful married life to the consciences of Christian parents.

Published two years later, *Humanae Vitae* rejected this report's conclusions. The text is divided into thirty-one numbered paragraphs in three parts. Part I (pars. 1-6) reviews new questions raised by recent social changes and some of the reasons offered for a change in the Church's position. Part II (pars. 7-19) spells out the pope's teaching, based on the principle that married love cannot be isolated from the responsibility of parenthood—a responsibility given to men and women as ministers of God's own plan. The claim is not that the mere physical ordering of things is inviolable. Rather, this specific physical ordering is generative of human life. Only God, not humans, has dominion over human life.

From this the pope concludes that every act of marital intercourse must remain open to the possibility of procreation. This is not to deny the inherent worth of all such acts, whether they issue in procreation or not. Rather, it means that "regulating birth is wrong when it involves directly some interruption of the procreative process once begun." This rules out direct abortion, sterilization and all actions which "stop the natural effect of any marriage act," done before, during or after the act. Explicitly rejected is the view expressed in the Commission's theological report that "contraceptive actions are allowed within married life that is considered fruitful as a whole" (par. 14). Therapy for organic difficulties, without direct contraceptive intent, is allowed, as is spacing children for responsible parenthood by use of "natural rhythm." This entails accurate determination of when ovulation has occurred and sexual abstinence during the wife's fertile period. Part III (pars. 19-31) acknowledges the difficulty of this teaching but reiterates the belief that the Church cannot change God's law. The discipline involved will require God's help.

Because of the widespread controversy and public dissent attending its publication, some have interpreted it as a kind of turning point in U.S. Catholic history, dividing so-called liberals and conservatives. Its impact on the Catholic Church in the U.S. is still a matter of debate.

See also BIRTH CONTROL; ETHICS, CATHOLIC PERSONAL.

BIBLIOGRAPHY. P. Harris et al., *On Human Life, An Examination of "Humanae Vitae"* (1968); R. A. McCormick, *Notes on Moral Theology, 1965 Through 1980* (1981); C. Curran, ed., *Contraception: Authority and Dissent* (1969); G. Grisez, *Contraception and the Natural Law* (1964).

W. L. Portier

Humanism. *See* SECULAR HUMANISM.

Humbard, Alpha Rex Emmanuel (1919-). Televangelist* and pastor.* Born in Little Rock, Arkansas, the son of a traveling evangelist,* Rex Humbard was introduced to the methods of revivalism* at an early age. While working in his family's crusade ministry, Humbard met Maude Aimee Jones, whom he married in 1942. Together they traveled with Humbard's family until they finally settled in Akron, Ohio (1952), where Humbard established a church which would eventually become known as the Cathedral of Tomorrow. The Cathedral was also the home base of a television ministry featuring a nondenominational Sunday-morning service.

Though Pentecostal in background, Humbard has not promoted Pentecostal* doctrine* and experience, though he has placed moderate emphasis on healing through prayer* and anointing with oil. Maude, a successful gospel singer, has been a regular part of the television ministry. The show was carried over network stations during the late 1960s and early 1970s and enjoyed great success. Questions regarding Humbard's handling of funds arose in 1973 and clouded the ministry for some years, but Humbard has been widely regarded as a successful pioneer in the field of television ministry.

BIBLIOGRAPHY. D. E. Harrell, Jr., *All Things Are Possible* (1975); R. Humbard, *Miracles in My Life* (1971).

D. G. Reid

Hunt, Robert (c.1568-1608). First Anglican* priest* in America. Hunt attended Magdalen Hall, Cambridge (B.A., 1592; M.A., 1595), and was vicar of Reculver, Kent (1592-1602), and in 1602 became the vicar of Heathfield in Sussex. Captain Edward Wingfield, first president of the Virginia Company, named Hunt the chaplain of the Company's 1607 expedition to Jamestown. On the voyage and after the landing, Hunt was the peacemaker of the expedition. On their first Sunday* in Virginia, May 14, 1607, Hunt held a service—the first Anglican service in the New World—and from then on he led morning and evening prayer, preached* two sermons each Sunday and presided at Holy Communion* every three months. The first celebration of Holy Communion of which record is made was July 1, 1607, the third Sunday of Trinity. A fire in January 1608 destroyed the church

[561]

and all of Hunt's books and other possessions. He died shortly prior to June 12, 1608.

BIBLIOGRAPHY. *DAB* V; C. W. F. Smith, "Chaplain Robert Hunt and His Parish in Kent," *HMPEC* 26 (1957):15-33.   D. S. Armentrout

Huntington, Frederic Dan (1819-1904). Unitarian* minister,* convert* to theism* and first Protestant Episcopal Bishop of central New York. Born in Hadley, Massachusetts, the son of an orthodox* Congregational* clergyman,* Huntington was educated at Amherst College (B.A., 1839) and Harvard* Divinity School (B.D., 1842). While at Harvard, Huntington developed a lifelong interest in social Christianity through his prison work, and a love of high-church* liturgy* through working at King's Chapel, Boston. In 1842 Huntington was ordained* as pastor* of the South Congregational Church (Unitarian) in Boston, from which pulpit he preached* a distinctive "evangelical Unitarianism." From 1845 to 1858 he served as editor-in-chief of the *Monthly Religious Magazine.*

In 1855, Huntington became the first incumbent of the Plummer Professorship of Christian Morals, making him preacher to Harvard College. A spiritual struggle ensued, reflected in his articles in the *Religious Magazine.* In 1860, having accepted a Trinitarian theism,* the deity and redemptive work of Christ, as well as the doctrine of apostolic succession,* he resigned his professorship at Harvard—one of the most famous conversions in Harvard College history. In 1861 he was called as first rector* of Emmanuel Church (Episcopal), Boston, and was ordained an Episcopal priest.* In 1869 he was elected first bishop of central New York and relocated to Syracuse, New York. Among his writings are: *Christian Believing and Living* (1859) and *Christ in the Christian Year and in the Life of Man,* 2 vols. (1878-1881). As bishop, Huntington continued to apply Christian priniciples to social problems, and in this respect he was a forerunner of the Social Gospel Movement.*

BIBLIOGRAPHY. *DAB* V; *DARB*; A. S. Huntington, *Memoir and Letters of Frederic Dan Huntington* (1906); G. C. Richmond, *Frederic Dan Huntington* (1908); *NCAB* 3.   M. S. Massa

Huntington, William Reed (1838-1909). Episcopal* priest,* ecumenical* leader and liturgical* reformer. Born in Lowell, Massachusetts, Huntington was educated at Harvard* (B.A., 1859), and he studied theology* with Frederic Dan Huntington* (1859-1862) while serving as an instructor in chemistry at Harvard (1859-1860) and curate* at Emmanuel Church in Boston (1861-1862). In 1862 Huntington became rector* of All Saints' Church in Worcester, Massachusetts (1862-1883), and later of Grace Church, New York City (1883-1909). For many years he was the most influential member of the House of Deputies of the Episcopal Church's General Convention.

Huntington's seminal work, *The Church Idea* (1870), set forth the basis for the reunification of the church and was the major source of the fourfold Anglican* basis for discussion of church unity known as the Chicago-Lambeth Quadrilateral.* The spirit of his work continued in the ecumenical movement* of the twentieth century. Huntington's experience and skills as a liturgist were brought to bear on the 1892 revision of the Episcopal Church's *Book of Common Prayer,* which owes more to him than to any other single person. He also revived the order of deaconesses* in the Episcopal Church.

For twenty-two years a trustee of the Cathedral of St. John the Divine in New York City, Huntington originated the iconographic plans of the Cathedral. The Cathedral's Chapel of St. Ansgar (consecrated 1918) is a memorial to him. July 27 is a feast day in his honor in the calendar of the *Book of Common Prayer* of the Episcopal Church in the U.S.A.

BIBLIOGRAPHY. *DAB* V; *DARB*; C. J. Minifie, "William Reed Huntington and Church Unity," *HMPEC* 35 (1966):155-166; *NCAB* 38; J. W. Suter, *Life and Letters of William Reed Huntington: A Champion of Unity* (1925).

J. R. Wright

Huron Mission. During the middle decades of the seventeenth century, the outstanding French missions* were those of the Jesuits* among the Hurons. A semi-agricultural people, the Hurons were a fairly compact group living in villages, some of which were fortified, mostly between Lake Simcoe and Georgian Bay in modern Ontario. Though they belonged to the widespread Iroquoian family, they were held in bitter enmity by the Iroquois proper. In 1639 the Hurons were said to number twenty thousand.

Jesuit contacts with the Hurons had begun in 1626 when Jean de Brebeuf* had lived in the Huron country. In 1634 Champlain induced a group of Hurons on a trading visit to Quebec to take back some Jesuits to reside with them. At the head of this mission was Brebeuf. The Hurons, looking to their own background for a parallel, regarded the Jesuits as professionals in magic, holding them responsible for crop failures and epidemics, and praising them when crops were abundant. The progress of the Jesuit mission, however, was fairly rapid; and before long a number of converts were gathered. During the initial years baptisms were limited to children and the dying. Not until 1637 was the first able-bodied adult baptized.

In 1640 a college and seminary for Huron children was established at Quebec. But the disasters of war brought an early and tragic end to the mission. The Iroquois had obtained firearms from the Dutch traders in New York. Strengthened by this superior equipment, they fell upon the Hurons. As the attacks of the Iroquois increased from 1645 to 1648, many of the Hurons became more responsive to the missionaries. In their desolation and despair many Hurons came to the missionaries for relief, and in some towns Christians increased to a majority. The Jesuits, remaining by the Hurons and striving to nerve them to resistance, lost several priests in the conflict. In 1649 Brebeuf himself was tortured and martyred at the hands of the Iroquois. Most of the surviving Hurons fled, some were taken captive, but a few were led by the Jesuits to Quebec and given a permanent settlement in the vicinity. However, the distinctive Huron mission was terminated.

See also MISSIONS TO NORTH AMERICA, FRENCH.

BIBLIOGRAPHY. F. M. Gagnon, *La conversion par l'image* (1975); W. Jury and E. M. Jury, *Sainte-Marie Among the Hurons* (1954); K. E. Kidd, *The Excavation of Ste. Marie I* (1949). D. A. Scalberg

Hutchinson, Anne Marbury (1591-1643).

Puritan* Massachusetts religious dissenter. Born in Alford, England, Hutchinson immigrated to Massachusetts in 1634, shortly after the arrival of Boston minister John Cotton,* whom she had regarded as her spiritual leader in England. A member of Boston's First Church, in 1635 she began holding weekly meetings in her home, elaborating on Cotton's sermons. From her own theological perceptions and those of Cotton, she began to question the doctrine of other Massachusetts preachers. Particularly at issue was whether "good works" provided evidence of salvation.* Hutchinson insisted that God granted salvation to whomever he pleased, and human actions could in no way influence his decision nor help establish proof of election.* The established ministers, she believed, placed too much emphasis upon deeds. So began the celebrated Antinomian* crisis in Massachusetts Bay.

Initially, Hutchinson enjoyed the tacit support of Cotton, the most prestigious minister in the colony. By the fall of 1636, growing numbers found themselves in agreement with her heretical* doctrines. Eventually, Hutchinson won over nearly the entire Boston First Church. Her supporters often disrupted church meetings, condemning the orthodox* ministers who, they declared, preached a "covenant* of works." Alarmed at the divisions in Boston and neighboring towns, a convocation of ministers met in Cambridge in August 1637, to define and confute Hutchinson's heretical opinions.

Armed with the ministers' pronouncements, the civil arm tried and banished Hutchinson and three of her supporters for "traducing the ministers." John Cotton belatedly condemned Hutchinson's views and in March of 1638, the Boston First Church unanimously excommunicated her. Hutchinson shortly left for Rhode Island and later moved to Long Island Sound, where she was killed in an Indian uprising in 1643.

See also ANTINOMIANISM.

BIBLIOGRAPHY. *DAB* V; *DARB*; D. D. Hall, *The Antinomian Controversy, 1636-1638: A Documentary History* (1968); E. Battis, *Saints and Sectaries; Anne Hutchinson and the Antinomian Controversy in the Massachusetts Bay Colony* (1962); *NAW* 2; *NCAB* 9.

J. F. Cooper

Hutterites (Hutterian Brethren). A communal

form of sixteenth-century Anabaptism* that has survived and flourishes in North America. Hutterite origins may be traced to Moravia, where persecuted Anabaptists from Switzerland and Tyrol found refuge in the mid 1520s. Jacob Wiedemann gathered these early pacifist dissenters into a fellowship at Austerlitz in 1528, where they practiced a "community of goods" (according to Acts 2:44-47). A few years later Jacob Hutter (martyred in 1536) reorganized the unstable and struggling group into the movement that still bears his name. Somewhat later Peter Riedemann published a *Confession of Faith* (1540), a statement that has since become the accepted authority for Hutterite faith and practice. Distinctive features of Hutterian life include believer's baptism,* nonresistance, separation of church and state,* distinctive dress and communitarian* living.

The Hutterite colonies in Moravia experienced a "golden age" during the mid sixteenth century but were harshly persecuted and suppressed by the Counter-Reformation. A few refugees were able to remove to Hungary and Rumania, and eventually further east to the Ukraine (1756). When privileges granted by the Tzarist government were withdrawn

[563]

in 1870, three colonies immigrated to the U.S. from 1874 to 1877. Because of unfavorable treatment by the military during World War 1,* most of the Hutterites moved to Canada (1918), although many later returned to the U.S. There are over 300 communities with about 30,000 members, primarily in the U.S. and Canada. Four Bruderhof communities founded by Eberhard Arnold (Society of Brothers, 1920) were reunited with the older Hutterians in 1972.

BIBLIOGRAPHY. *Chronicle of the Hutterian Brethren,* vol. 1 (1987); J. A. Hostetler, *Hutterian Society* (1974); P. Riedemann, *Confession of Faith: Account of Our Religion* (1970).

D. B. Eller

Hymns, Hymnals. In 1640 the first book printed in North America for the English-speaking colonies was "The Bay Psalm Book."* It gave the Old Testament psalms in rhymed, metrical and literal-as-possible (but awkward) English translations for use in Puritan* worship.* The book, refined by Henry Dunster* in 1651, went through more than twenty editions in over a century.

In the eighteenth century, tunebooks served singing schools as instruction manuals. Their number and content increased after mid century. Typically they were oblong in shape and contained an introduction to the rudiments of music followed by an anthology of metrical psalms, hymns, fuguing tunes (psalm and hymn tunes with imitative sections) and anthems. Oliver Holden's tune "Coronation" first appeared in his tunebook, *Union Harmony* of 1793. Shape-note books in the fasola tradition were also issued in an oblong shape. The most widely used of these, B. F. White's and E. J. King's *Sacred Harp,* is still in print. It was first published in 1844 and revised many times thereafter.

Benjamin Franklin reprinted Isaac Watts's hymns as early as 1729, but it was not until after the Revolution* that Watts was generally embraced in the churches. Then, altered versions for the American scene became popular under the title of their editors, like "Barlow's Watts" and "Dwight's Watts." John* and Charles Wesley's *Hymns and Sacred Poems* of 1739 were reprinted in Philadelphia in 1749, and in 1784 John Wesley himself prepared a hymnal for America as a safeguard on the excitable American scene; but American Methodists* did not always follow his lead.

In the early nineteenth century the Methodists often joined others in using anonymous publications, with choruses fashioned from Watts which responded to the immediacy of revivalism,* but they cared little about quality. Asahel Nettleton's* *Village Hymns for Social Worship* assembled in 1824 as a supplement to Watts, and Joshua Leavitt's *The Christian Lyre* of 1831 also addressed this need. Both had a wide influence, and the latter was the first American hymnal to join tunes with the texts. Lowell Mason* and Thomas Hastings criticized *The Christian Lyre* and in 1832 fashioned the less emotional, more "chaste" *Spiritual Songs for Social Worship* to counteract it. Gospel hymns became popular anyway. Beginning in 1875 Ira D. Sankey* collaborated successively with Philip P. Bliss,* James McGranahan and George C. Stebbins* to publish in 1895 the 739 selections of *Gospel Hymns Nos. 1 to 6 Complete.*

Throughout the nineteenth century, denominations* produced hymnals. At mid century Henry Ward Beecher* initiated the *Plymouth Collection of Hymns and Tunes* for his own Plymouth Congregational Church in Brooklyn. Lowell Mason had championed congregational singing, but his reforms yielded more trained choirs* and professional quartets than hearty singing from the people. Beecher set out to change that. His church's hymnal attempted a variety of texts and music and was the first American church hymnal to print the tunes with the music. This attempt, and especially the English *Hymns Ancient and Modern* of 1861 from the Oxford movement,* became the model of the twentieth-century American hymnal.

Around the 1940s various denominations produced hymnals, each with its own denominational flavor, but usually in an ecumenical* mold that included classic metrical psalms and hymns; translations from the Latin and German heritage; sometimes with Gregorian and chorale tunes; and hymns with high art, social, ethical and patriotic themes, from Unitarian* or nondenominational sources from the end of the nineteenth century. The classic hymnal of this group was the Episcopal *Hymnal 1940.*

Forty years later another set of denominational books was produced, including *The Lutheran Book of Worship,* the Episcopal* *Hymnal 1982,* the Roman Catholic* *Worship III,* and *Rejoice in the Lord* for the Reformed Church in America*— edited by the foremost twentieth-century hymnologist, Erik Routley. Editors of all these publications had to struggle with language. King James English was often updated to avoid archaisms. Battle symbolism drew heated debate. Discriminatory language, especially with reference to sex, created ferment. Avoiding the generic use of words like *man* and *his* became commonplace for most contemporary hymn writers (*See* Inclusive Language Movement), but editors of classic hymn texts were hard-pressed to make suitable alterations. The problem became even more acute and yielded considerably less consensus when applied to language about God.

See also MUSIC, CHRISTIAN.

BIBLIOGRAPHY. L. F. Benson, *The English Hymn* (1915); F. J. Metcalf, *American Psalmody* (1968); H. W. Foote, *Three Centuries of American Hymnody* (1940). P. Westermeyer

I

Iakovos, Archbishop (Demetrios Coucouzis) (1911-). Greek Orthodox* archbishop* of North and South America. Born on the Turkish island of Imbros, Archbishop Iakovos studied in the Patriarchal Theological School of Halki, graduating in 1934, when he also was ordained* a deacon.* Invited to the U.S. in 1939 to serve on the faculty of Holy Cross Greek Orthodox School of Theology, then located in Pomfret, Connecticut, he was ordained to the priesthood in 1940.

From 1942 to 1954 Coucouzis was dean of the Annunciation Cathedral in Boston, Massachusetts, when he was elected titular bishop of Melita, and until 1959 served as the personal representative of the ecumenical patriarch at the World Council of Churches* in Geneva. In 1959 he was elected archbishop of North and South America. He pioneered the reorganization of the Greek Orthodox archdiocese with a new constitution. Numerous new departments, notably the offices of communications, missions, stewardship, ecumenical affairs and church and society, were established.

From 1959 to 1968 Archbishop Iakovos was a co-president of the World Council of Churches. He founded and serves as chairman of the Standing Conference of Canonical Orthodox Bishops in the Americas. He marched with Martin Luther King* in Selma and has frequently written and spoken on behalf of human rights and is a critic of abortion* and capital punishment. He has also sought to promote peaceful relations between Greece and Turkey, contributing significantly to the 1988 meeting in Davos, Switzerland, of the prime ministers of the two nations. He has been awarded numerous honorary doctoral degrees and other awards in the U.S. and abroad.

BIBLIOGRAPHY. Archbishop Iakovos, with W. Proctor, Jr., *Faith for a Lifetime: A Spiritual Journey* (1988); G. Poulos, *Breath of God: A Biography of Archbishop Iakovos* (1984). S. S. Harakas

Icon. A painting on a flat surface depicting a person or event venerated as holy in the Eastern Orthodox Church.* The majority of icons depict the Lord Jesus* Christ. Other subjects include the Virgin Mary,* John the Baptist, the apostles, angels, Old Testament characters and saints* of the Orthodox Church.

Icons are used in the corporate worship of the Eastern Orthodox Church and are prominently displayed in church buildings. The iconostasis is a wall covered with icons separating the sanctuary from the nave. Believers display devotion by genuflecting, kissing, incensing and lighting candles before icons, which are considered channels of grace and miracles. However, a distinction is made between the honor given to the saints and the worship that belongs to God alone.

The representation of the subjects is non-realistic. The eyes, nose and ears are drawn larger than life to depict the increased spiritual sensitivity of the saint. The use of light in the icon is designed to portray the divine presence. Certain icons are believed to have been painted by a miraculous appearance of the saint so that the image actually reflects the heavenly prototype. Icons are not signed, nor can the artist substantially change the icon. Painting icons is a spiritual work requiring the consecration of artist and materials.

The iconoclastic controversy (725-842) focused on the veneration of images. Various emperors enforced an anti-image policy while popular devotion* supported the use of icons. Iconodules claimed that the incarnation reversed the Mosaic prohibition against images. The victory of the icon worshipers over the icon breakers is celebrated by the Eastern Church on the first Sunday* of Lent* as the "Feast of Orthodoxy."

BIBLIOGRAPHY. C. D. Kalokyris, *The Essence of Orthodox Iconography* (1971); E. J. Martin, *A History of the Iconoclastic Controversy* (1930); V. Lossky and L. Ouspensky, *The Meaning of Icons* (1982). J. J. Stamoolis

Illinois Band (Yale Band). A group of Yale* students who on February 21, 1829, formally pledged to establish a seminary* and plant churches* in Illinois. Original members were Theron Baldwin, John F. Brooks, Mason Grosvenor, Elisha Jenney, William Kirby, Julian M. Sturtevant and Asa Turner, Jr. Eight more joined later. All became Congregational* ministers,* and many associated themselves with the American Home Missionary Society.* Of the original seven, all but Grosvenor, who actually founded the group, went to Illinois within the next few years and began to build on the work of itinerant missionary John M. Ellis, with whom Grosvenor had corresponded originally. Sturtevant opened the seminary, Illinois College, on January 4, 1830, at Jacksonville with nine students. Baldwin, the moving spirit behind the group, pastored and helped found Monticello Female Seminary near Alton in 1838. After pastoring eight years at Quincy, Turner left for Iowa, was later joined by eleven Andover* students (the Iowa Band), and founded what is now Grinnell College in 1848. The Illinois Band was responsible for the rapid spread of Congregationalism in Illinois and strongly influenced the abolitionist* and temperance movements* there.

BIBLIOGRAPHY. J. R. Willis, *God's Frontiersmen: The Yale Band in Illinois* (1979); J. M. Sturtevant, *Julian M. Sturtevant: An Autobiography* (1896).

M. B. Newell

Immaculate Conception. A teaching of the Roman Catholic Church* that the Blessed Virgin Mary,* by a singular grace and privilege of God, through the merits of her son Jesus Christ was preserved from the stain or effects of original sin* from the first moment of her conception by her parents.

Two church councils, Ephesus (A.D. 431) and Chalcedon (A.D. 451), defending the belief that Jesus was divine, spoke of the Blessed Virgin as "Mother of God," or God-bearer (*theotokos*). While Christians before this had long appreciated Mary's special character, these councils gave new impetus to the veneration of Mary. Well before the eleventh century, Christians in several countries were celebrating a feast of Mary's conception.

Catholicism holds that over time Christians guided by the Holy Spirit can sometimes see fuller implications in the deposit of faith* given in Scripture* and handed down by valid apostolic tradition. Could this doctrine be among them? While many Catholic scholars and theologians had no difficulty with prayers to Mary (*See* Marian Devotions), declaring her sinless or venerating her as a key figure in God's plan for salvation, some had serious problems with the view that she was preserved from the first moment of life from the effects of original sin.

Spirited debates over many years gave way to a consensus, which enabled Pope Pius IX* to declare this official Catholic teaching in 1854. Biblical faith confesses that we are all born with a propensity to sin. The Catholic Church teaches that Mary was prepared especially for motherhood of a unique order by an advance blessing: freedom from this sinful tendency. This singular grace does not mean Mary was free of temptation nor that she was exempt from the struggles all Christians face in their journey of faith. In Catholic theology the doctrine of the Immaculate Conception flows from the central teaching that Jesus is both divine and human, redeemer of all.

See also ASSUMPTION OF MARY; MARIAN DEVOTIONS; MARIOLOGY.

BIBLIOGRAPHY. A. Stacpoole, ed., *Mary's Place in Christian Dialogue* (1982); B. Buby, *Mary, the Faithful Disciple* (1985); A. J. Tambasco, *What Are They Saying About Mary?* (1984).

B. Moran

Immigration and Ethnicity, Catholic. All nations include immigrants in their population, but no nation can match the U.S. in the size and diversity of its immigrant population. This was as true in the 1980s as it was in the 1890s. Such diversity first became apparent in the nineteenth century when a major migration of people took place in Europe. Between 1820 and 1920 over fifty-two million people left Europe. They traveled to many different nations, but the bulk of them, about thirty-four million, immigrated to the U.S. These newcomers came from every country in Europe and belonged to a variety of religious traditions. Both Jews and Christians, Protestants* as well as Catholics,* they permanently altered the religious landscape of the U.S.

Two Waves of Immigration, 1820-1920. Two major waves of immigration from Europe took place between 1820 and 1920. In the first wave, 1820-1860, most immigrants came from Germany and the British Isles, with Ireland numbering more immigrants than England, Scotland and Wales combined. The next wave of immigration began in the 1880s and lasted until the outbreak of World War 1.* These immigrants came from quite different parts of Europe than their predecessors in the mid-nineteenth century. Numerous Italians immigrated at this time; Polish, Hungarian, Czech, Slovak, Ruthenians, Slovenians and numbers of other people from Eastern Europe streamed into the U.S. In response to the influx of so many immigrants, various denominations* began to establish foreign-language churches, and mission-ary* efforts among immigrant communities became commonplace.

The 1916 census of religious bodies included a lengthy section on the use of foreign languages in the churches, and it not only revealed how ethnically diverse the American religious pantheon had become but also the great cultural diversity of peoples gathered in the nation's churches. Of the 200 denominations studied in 1916, 132 of them reported a part or all of their congregations using a foreign language; a total of forty-two different languages were in use in these churches. Just among Roman Catholics, twenty-eight foreign languages were spoken; Methodists* reported twenty-two different languages in use. Immigration had clearly affected numerous denominations, but the one group most closely identified with the phenomenon of immigration in the nineteenth century was the Roman Catholic Church.

Changing Demographics. Immigration changed the Catholic Church in a number of ways. First of all, it altered the ethnic mix of the people. In the early-nineteenth century most Catholics were of Irish or Anglo-American descent, with some German and a large number of French clergy.* By the end of the century Catholics came from as many as twenty-eight different countries; the largest immigrant groups were the Irish, German, Italian and Polish. They accounted for almost seventy-five per cent of the total Catholic population in 1916. Among the clergy the Irish dominated to such an extent that two of every three bishops in 1900 were of Irish descent. Immigration also put an indelible urban stamp on American Catholicism. In 1800 most Catholics lived in the South, in Maryland or Kentucky. By 1900 most of them lived in cities scattered throughout the East and Midwest, the economic core of the nation that stretched from St. Paul, Minnesota, to New York City. As a result of immigration the number of Catholics increased substantially so that by 1850 the Catholic Church had become the largest single denomination in the country, and it has retained that distinction ever since.

Each immigrant group established its own community in the city. The Germans flocked to Little Germany, the Italians to Little Italy, and so on. The sounds, the sights and the smells of these immigrant neighborhoods were reminiscent of the old country. Even though most immigrant neighborhoods were made up of a number of ethnic groups, each group stayed within the cultural boundaries of its own community. They lived in their own world and seldom interacted with people from a different ethnic background. As a result, inter-ethnic marriages were most uncommon, whereas inter-ethnic rivalries became quite ordinary. A key institution in these neighborhoods was the church.

Ethnic Churches. One of the first major acts of a settled immigrant community was to organize a religious society of some type. It was generally a mutual-aid society that provided sickness and death benefits, or a devotional confraternity that honored a favorite saint* of the old country. Once established, the society then became the catalyst for the building of a church. Money was collected, land purchased, plans for the church building discussed and the church itself built. In all of this activity, which generally went on for several months, the lay people were the major actors. If clergy were available who spoke the language of the people, they would have an important role in these activities. Most often, however, such clergy were not available; only later, when the laity* had launched the parish,* would the clergy emerge on the scene at the invitation of the people or of the local bishop.*

These churches, at first modest wooden structures but eventually transformed into large stone buildings, were museums of the Old World. Their design and ornaments brought back memories of the old country. When services took place in these immigrant churches, the music* and rituals, spoken in the language of the people, heightened this sense of Old-World religion. The key element in all of this was language. This was the cement that held the community together, and anything that threatened the survival of the mother tongue was judged to be destructive of the community. The reason for this was the close bond between language and faith. To many immigrants the loss of language meant the loss of faith. The Germans were so convinced of this that the slogan "language saves faith" became their battle cry for cultural survival. Other groups were equally adamant and coined similar slogans.

Ethnic Schools. A key institution in the immigrant neighborhood was the school. Since the public school was permeated with the ethos of American Protestantism, immigrant Catholics, led by such churchmen as Archbishop John Hughes* of New York and Archbishop John B. Purcell* of Cincinnati, launched a crusade on behalf of the Catholic parochial school.* The clergy enthusiastically backed this crusade, and so did many of the laity. One reason was that such schools were judged to be, in the words of the 1852 Baltimore church council,* "indispensable for the security of faith and morals among Catholic children." Another reason was that the parish school was viewed as a key agent in the effort to maintain the culture of the old country. In the immigrant neighborhood the elementary school was a culture factory that kept alive the memory of the past through history and language. The key to their existence was the availability of sisters, women religious,* who shared the language and culture of the people and were able to pass this heritage on to the young children. Some groups put more emphasis on the parish school than others. Germans, French Canadians and the Polish were the most enthusiastic in this regard, with the Italians and Mexicans manifesting the least enthusiasm for parochial schools.

Ethnic Societies and Organizations. In some communities the church and the school were just the beginning of an extensive institutional complex. It was not unheard of to have a large Polish or German congregation supporting a hospital and orphanage, as well as numerous societies that appealed to the needs of various age groups. Such communities were a church within a church, where the immigrant pastor often presided with papal-like authority.*

The parish and the school provided the organization that immigrant Catholics sought at the neighborhood level. Beyond the neighborhood and the city were national organizations. Through their annual conventions they provided a forum for discussion as well as support for a particular ethnic group's needs in both the church and the nation. The more noteworthy of these groups were men's fraternal societies, such as the German Central Verein, the Polish Roman Catholic Union of America and the Irish Ancient Order of Hibernians. These societies sought to keep alive both ethnic pride and the Catholic heritage.

To maintain harmony and unity in the midst of so many culturally different and intensely nationalistic groups was a difficult balancing act for the Catholic bishops who presided over the immigrant Church. Nonetheless, they did succeed. Minor squabbles took place at the neighborhood level where one ethnic group would try to lord it over another. But such conflicts were short-lived. At the national level two major schisms did take place involving the Polish and the Ukrainians. Both dissident groups did break from the Roman Catholic Church; the Polish formed their own church, the Polish National Catholic Church, and the Ukrainians joined the Russian Orthodox Church.* Different understandings of authority in the Church was a key reason for these schisms, but

cultural differences fueled the conflicts.

Immigration laws passed in the 1920s altered the future of the Catholic Church in the U.S. Henceforth, European immigrants would no longer set the agenda for the American Church. Since then a new wave of immigration, at first Hispanic and then Asian, has presented a new set of challenges for the descendants of the immigrants as the twentieth century draws to a close.

BIBLIOGRAPHY. J. P. Dolan, *The American Catholic Experience: A History from Colonial Times to the Present* (1985); R. A. Orsi, *The Madonna of 115th Street: Faith and Community in Italian Harlem, 1880-1950* (1985); J. J. Parot, *Polish Catholics in Chicago, 1850-1920* (1981); C. Shanabruch, *Chicago's Catholics: The Evolution of an American Identity* (1981).   J. P. Dolan

Immigration and Ethnicity, Protestant. As a nation of immigrants, the U. S. contains in microcosm the religious and cultural diversity (*See* Pluralism, Religious) of the world's peoples. Ethnic pluralism is the hallmark of American society. Ethnicity (from the Greek word *ethnos,* meaning nation or peoplehood) is the socialization process by which individuals inherit a sense of identity and common culture from their national, religious or racial group. Ethnic identity and religion are inextricably linked. As H. Richard Niebuhr* recognized, "Perhaps religion is as often responsible for ethnic character as the latter is responsible for faith." Swedish and German Lutherans,* Dutch Reformed,* Swiss Mennonites,* Russian Hutterites,* Scottish Presbyterians,* Cornish Methodists,* French Huguenots,* Moravian Brethren* and New England Congregationalists* are examples of immigrant groups in which ethnicity and religion are mutually reinforcing.

Ethnicity and Identity. Because ethnicity and religion are so intertwined, scholars recognize that in some societies distinctive faiths may provide the source for ethnic identity, just as distinctive peoples may in other societies develop unique religious beliefs and practices. The religious aspect of ethnicity varies. For state-church adherents like the German Lutherans, Dutch Reformed, Swedish Lutherans and English Episcopalians,* a shared nationality, language and homeland may overshadow religious beliefs and practices as the source of ethnicity. For religious dissenters however, like the Huguenots, Amish,* Quakers* and Hutterites, religious beliefs are their very reason for existence and survival.

From the time of the Protestant* Reformation, every Western European nation had a state church, dictated by the monarch. "He the ruler, his the religion"; and "religious uniformity in a civil commonwealth" were unquestioned dicta. Anabaptist* dissenters, at great cost, first challenged these axioms during the Reformation era, but the national churches held firm until the democratic revolutions of the late eighteenth century undermined their authority and that of their monarchs.

Thus, in 1815 at the dawn of the great century of immigration, religious uniformity within European nations had broken down. According to Sydney Ahlstrom,* European Protestants had accommodated themselves ecclesiastically in five major ways: national church loyalists, disciplined or incipient sectarians, Free Church* adherents, pietistic* dissenters and nominal secularists. The immigrants brought each of these perspectives to America. Views of church governance, religious practices and theological beliefs were carried over along with their cultural baggage. But in the open, competitive environment of American religious life, where churches were voluntary* associations financially dependent on their members and free of government restraint, immigrant churches faced conflicting pressures—to differentiate themselves from or to conform to mainline* Protestantism.

Self-Preservation and Accommodation. Initially, the desire for self-preservation was overriding, especially for non-English-speaking groups who faced nativist* attacks. Hostility bred fear and withdrawal. "In isolation is our strength," declared immigrant church leaders. Preserving the mother tongue and Old Country customs and practices in church, school and family was deemed to be essential. These immigrant groups fostered Christian day schools,* promoted economic exchange within the group and waged bloc voting in public elections. Ethnicity and religion had merged into one force for survival. The sense of peoplehood that the group brought with them to the hostile environment of America was reinforced and in some cases awakened for the first time.

But eventually, usually by the second generation, the forces of Americanization pressed immigrant churches to choose between accommodation or extinction. In order to survive and thrive, the immigrant churches borrowed methods, theologies and organizational structures from the dominant native Protestant churches—Congregational, Presbyterian and Methodist. Pragmatic methods of revivalism,* a theology of individualism,* congregational* forms of church governance, and above all, the adoption of the English language in worship* for the sake of the young people became appealing if not mandatory re-

forms. Language change, which was the source of great controversy and anguish in every immigrant church, symbolized accommodation, and this carried into all aspects of life—church, home, school and work.

Protestant immigrant churches thus gradually became less ethnically homogeneous and more integrated into the melting pot of native Protestant America, at the same time that the long dominant Protestants were distinguishing themselves from rising Catholics* and Jews. As the mother tongue gave way to English among second generation Protestant immigrants, they preserved their unique identity by clinging all the more strongly to the historic doctrines of the faith. Many third generation immigrants, however, again sought to revive the waning ethnic heritage.

The social revolution of the 1960s brought about a renewed sense of ethnic identity that surprised those who had assumed that such primal, tribal ties had long lost all significance in a modern, liberal society. Church leaders were also chagrined that Christians who professed belonging to the "holy catholic church" should proudly proclaim their particularistic ethnic roots. As the editor of the Christian Reformed Church's* weekly publication, *The Banner,* declared on the editorial page (Jan. 11, 1981), "It's time to burn the wooden shoes," dramatically illustrating his point with a colorful cover photograph of a pair of wooden shoes engulfed in flames.

Ethnocentrism and chauvinism may have no place in the Christian church, but ethnic differentiation may be necessary for the mental and emotional health of many members. As Catholic sociologist, Father Andrew Greeley, has explained: "Diversity may lead to hellish miseries in the world but without the power to diversify and to locate himself somewhere in the midst of the diversity man may not be able to cope with the world at all." Many people need a sense of peoplehood and desire to find it in an ethnically homogeneous inner life of church and family. Approximately three-fourths of the American people can give an ethnic identification and two-thirds specify a primary ethnic identity. Cultural and religious pluralism is thus one of the most important legacies of immigration in America.

Sanctuary and Community. Christian beliefs and churches also had a direct bearing on the success of immigration. Religious convictions undergirded immigrants in their crises as "strangers in a foreign land." Churches served as agencies of the transplanting process. The influence was also reciprocal—immigrants effected the churches as well. Europeans who left their motherland for America inevitably faced cultural dislocation in the new country. Their self-esteem was threatened, they felt lost and adrift, and they were usually unable to communicate until they gained a rudimentary use of the English language. The churches were their sanctuary, their home away from home. The pastors* dispensed spiritual sustenance, fellow believers gave acceptance and encouragement, and their God gave strength in adversity. In short, immigrants with a meaningful Christian faith held more realistic expectations and were better able to cope with the problems of immigration.

The role of the church differed, depending on whether immigrants settled in colonies or scattered and dispersed themselves. Colonies surrounded the newcomers with compatriots and enabled them quickly to re-establish churches, schools, shops, businesses and social clubs. This supportive cocoon, in which churches played a refugee function, enabled immigrants to adjust gradually in the new land or even to remain isolated altogether, relying on the children to reach out or break out. In colonies such as the Dutch in Michigan and Iowa, the church, an Old-Country replica, was the focal point of community life; pastors stood between the people and the outside world, filtering information and interpreting it for them.

Protestant churches, with their emphases on the sermon, made language more important than in Catholic worship based on the Latin liturgy. Dutch Catholic immigrants could worship effectively in a German Catholic parish in America, whereas Dutch Calvinist immigrants could not do so in a Presbyterian church. Non-English-speaking Protestant immigrants thus assimilated more slowly than Catholic immigrants or English-speaking Protestants.

Immigrants who wished to take the fast track to Americanization refused to settle in the colonies or they departed as soon as possible. These assimilators usually joined indigenous Protestant churches, often Presbyterian congregations if they were of Reformed background or American Lutheran congregations if they hailed from Lutheran lands. The transcultural Christian heritage that was stressed in these churches helped immigrants to leave their former identity and to adopt the new one.

In Protestant immigrant families, the parents have a high degree of loyalty to the church. But their children may suffer from the dislocation caused by immigrating and defect to indigenous churches or leave the Christian faith altogether, particularly when a transplanted church resists language change and cultural adaptation for too long. For the families who remain attached, however, the grandchildren identify as strongly with the church as the first generation, and this has given immigrant churches a renewed vitality in the third generation.

See also ASIAN-AMERICAN PROTESTANTS; HISPANIC CHURCHES; IMMIGRATION AND ETHNICITY, CATHOLIC; REVIVALISM, GERMAN-AMERICAN; SCOTTISH PRESBYTERIANS.

BIBLIOGRAPHY. H. J. Abramson, "Religion," in *Harvard Encyclopedia of American Ethnic Groups,* ed. S. Thernstrom et al. (1980):869-879; A. M. Greeley, *Ethnicity in the United States* (1974); M. E. Marty, "Ethnicity: The Skeleton of Religion in America," *CH* 41 (1972):5-21; H. R. Niebuhr, *The Social Sources of Denominationalism* (1929); T. L. Smith, "Religion and Ethnicity in America," *AHR* 83 (1978):1155-1185; H. S. Stout, "Ethnicity: The Vital Center of Religion in America," *Ethn* 2 (1975):204-224; R. P. Swierenga, "Local-Cosmopolitan Theory and Immigrant Religion," *JSocH* 14 (1981):113-135.   R. P Swierenga

Imprimatur. Translated as "it may be printed," this Latin phrase signifies a Roman Catholic* bishop's* permission for publication of a book by a Catholic author. Though it indicates that the content does not contradict official Catholic doctrine, an *Imprimatur* does not approve theological opinion, technical format or the literary value of the work. According to Canon Law* (1983), this consent is required for translations of Scripture* (covering the accuracy of translation and orthodoxy* of accompanying explanations), liturgical books* and catechisms* and theological textbooks. Given by the bishop of the author's or publisher's diocese,* the *Imprimatur* (specifying the name of the bishop, place and date) is usually printed on the book's copyright page. Rooted in magisterial obligations to promote authentic statements of faith for the Church, censorship of books prior to publication became a standard practice after the proliferation of books subsequent to Gutenberg's invention of the moveable typeset press (c.1439) and after the diffusion of the Reformers' writings in the sixteenth century.

BIBLIOGRAPHY. D. H. Wiest, *The Precensorship of Books: A History and a Commentary* (1953); J. A. Coriden, "The End of the *Imprimatur,*" *Jurist* 44 (1984):339-356.   G. L. Sobolewski

In God We Trust. National motto. In 1865, at the instigation of Secretary of the Treasury Salmon P.

Chase, legislation was passed which authorized, but did not require, the placement of "In God we trust" on certain U.S. coins. An 1873 law reaffirmed the procedure. In 1908 legislation required the phrase to be placed on all coins on which it had previously been inscribed. Gradually, by administrative decision, the words were put on all denominations of coins. Finally, legislation in 1955 required the phrase on all U.S. coins and, for the first time, paper money. In 1956 Congress made the phrase the national motto and in 1962 the words were inscribed above the Speaker's desk in the House of Representatives' chamber.

The inspiration for the phrase seems to have come from the last stanza of the "Star Spangled Banner," which contains the words "And this be our motto—'In God is our trust,'" although Secretary Chase chose the actual words. The motivation for adopting the phrase was a national crisis: in the nineteenth century, the hostility between the States; in the twentieth, the perceived advance of Communism.* Sponsoring legislators used the rationale that the phrase expressed the nation's "spiritual way of life." They agreed with Secretary Chase's opinion: "No nation can be strong except in the strength of God or safe except in His defense." The legislators intended the national motto to be a reminder to Americans of our freedoms and a way to preserve them.

See also CIVIL RELIGION.

BIBLIOGRAPHY. A. P. Stokes and L. Pfeffer, *Church and State in the United States,* vol. 3 (1950); U.S. Congress, House, Committee on Banking and Currency, *Providing that All United States Currency and Coins Shall Bear the Inscription 'In God We Trust,'* 84th Cong., 1st sess., May 26, 1955, Rept. 662; U.S. Congress, Senate, Committee on the Judiciary, *National Motto,* 84th Cong., 2nd sess., July 20, 1956, Rept. 2703.

R. B. Flowers

Inclusive Language Movement. A movement to make the language of worship,* Scripture* and Christian education* materials more inclusive in terms of gender, race and ability. The idea first emerged among public-school educators concerned that the exclusive use of male terms gave students the message that women were excluded from various professions and roles, and that the use of illustrations containing no people of color encouraged racial discrimination. McGraw-Hill was the first publisher to issue inclusive language guidelines for its writers, and other textbook publishers followed suit.

In the church the movement promotes more inclusive language about both people and God because the exclusive use of male terms makes it difficult for many women and men to read Scripture or relate to God. For example, in the New Testament the word *adelphoi* is translated into English as *brothers,* whereas it originally included men and women. The terms *'adam* and *enosh* in Hebrew and *anthropos* in Greek are translated *man* when they are more general terms for *person* or *people.* Scripture speaks of God using both female and male images (see Num 11:12; Deut 32:18; Ps 22:9-10; 131:2; Prov 1:20; 4:5-6; 9:1; Is 46:3-4; 49:15; 66:7-9; Jn 3:5).

Within worship, proponents of inclusive language have suggested using either plural terms for people or both male and female pronouns; a variety of scriptural titles and descriptions of God; illustrations which include people of both genders, all ages, races, classes and physical conditions. Various church bodies have issued reports, guidelines and study guides on the topic (e.g., the United Methodists' *Words That Hurt, Words That Heal*). Many denominations are also revising hymnals* and liturgical texts to be more inclusive.

BIBLIOGRAPHY. T. Emswiler and S. Emswiler, *Women and Worship,* rev. ed. (1984); T. Emswiler and S. Emswiler, *Wholeness in Worship* (1980); N. A. Hardesty, *Inclusive Language in the Church* (1987); C. Miller and K. Swift, *Words and Women* (1977); National Council of Churches, *Inclusive Language Lectionary* (1983, 1984, 1985).

N. A. Hardesty

Independence Day (July 4). The day commemorating the signing of the Declaration of Independence, drafted in 1776 by Thomas Jefferson,* with assistance from Benjamin Franklin and John Adams. It expressed the belief that all people are endowed by their Creator with inalienable rights, and demanded that Great Britain recognize the independence of the colonies. Although actually adopted by the Continental Congress assembled in Philadelphia on July 2, the *Congressional Journal* indicated the date was July 4. Observed by some states as early as 1781, nationalization of Independence Day occurred in 1826, the year in which both Jefferson and Adams died on the fourth of July. Celebrations of Independence Day vary, but most observe John Adams's suggestions for the first anniversary: parades; band concerts; patriotic shows of red, white and blue; ringing of bells and fireworks. Speakers will often invoke themes of American civil religion,* and ministers,* particularly conservative Protestants,* will frequently eulogize the faith of the nation's Founding Fathers.

BIBLIOGRAPHY. C. Cherry, "Two American Sacred Ceremonies: Their Implications for the Study of Religion in America," *AQ* 21 (1969):739-754. A. M. Clifford

Independent Fundamental Churches of America. An organization of independent fundamentalist* churches and agencies. The Independent Fundamental Churches of America (IFCA) began out of a desire to unite fundamentalists across denominational* lines. Several leaders had been a part of the American Council of Undenominational Churches but wanted to create an organization for fundamentalists within denominations.

In 1930 thirty-nine men met with William McCarrell, pastor of the Cicero Bible Church, Cicero, Illinois. Others present were: J. Oliver Buswell, Jr,* Martin R. DeHaan,* Wendell P. Loveless, William L. Pettingill* and John F. Walvoord. Out of this group there were twelve Congregationalists,* three Presbyterians,* nineteen Independents,* one Baptist* and four with no denominational identification. Together, they began the IFCA.

The present bylaws state that the purpose is to unify those that have "separated from denominations which include unbelievers and liberal teachers" and to encourage one another in world evangelism.* There are sixteen points to the doctrinal statement, including the verbal, plenary inspiration of the Bible; Christ's virgin birth, deity, sinless life, atoning death and bodily resurrection; and Christ's premillennial,* pretribulational return. It also includes statements opposing ecumenism,* ecumenical evangelism, neo-orthodoxy* and neo-evangelicalism.*

The group grew slowly at first and reported only thirty-eight churches in 1935, with a membership of 550. Today, there are 1,600 individual members, 707 churches, twenty-three church-extension organizations, seven schools, five camps and conferences, twenty home-mission agencies, three foreign-mission agencies and one Christian home. The official publication of the IFCA is a bimonthly journal, *The Voice,* and the denomination's headquarters are in Westchester, Illinois.

BIBLIOGRAPHY. G. W. Dollar, *A History of Fundamentalism in America* (1973); J. O. Henry, *For Such a Time as This, A History of the Independent Fundamental Churches of America* (1983). C. E. Hall

Index of Forbidden Books. An alphabetical catalog specifying books Roman Catholics* could not publish, read, defend, retain or sell. The *Index Librorum Prohibitorum* was issued by the Vatican from 1559 to 1966. Evolving from magisterial concerns to protect the faith and morals of the Church, the Index emerged during Catholic reaction to the Reformation and from a constant history of Christian censorship that includes the first formal condemnation of a book with the Council of Nicea's injunction against Arius's *Thalia* (325) and the Ephesians's book-burning in Acts 19. Twentieth-century editions and periodic supplements were compiled and enforced according to Canon Law* (1917) and contained only those books judged to be most pernicious. The final edition in 1948 listed approximately 4,100 entries and specified five titles from four American authors, including John William Draper's *History of the Conflicts Between Religion and Science* (1874).

BIBLIOGRAPHY. R. A. Burke, *What Is the Index?* (1952); J. M. Pernicone, *The Ecclesiastical Prohibition of Books* (1932). G. L. Sobolewski

Individualism. The concept of individualism gained currency in America after the publication in 1835 of Alexis de Tocqueville's* *Democracy in America.* "Individualism," he wrote, "is a novel expression, to which a novel idea has given birth." He defined it as the tendency of Americans to sever themselves from the larger society and draw apart into smaller circles defined by family and friendship, and he feared that eventually it would destroy the virtues of American public life. From its inception, therefore, the term bore negative connotations. Even Ralph Waldo Emerson,* the foremost proponent of individuality and self-reliance in American letters, equated individualism with the vice of egotism. Religious writers appropriated the term and expanded its meaning in discussions of four topics: the church,* doctrinal* authority,* the economic order and psychological well-being.

In the early nineteenth century a number of theologians* argued that American Protestants,* formed by revivalistic* piety,* had lost the traditional sense of the church as a corporate organism. The Catholic writer Orestes Brownson* accused them of counterposing individual preferences to the rightful authority of the church. The Reformed* theologian John Williamson Nevin* saw the problem as a Protestant inclination to define the church as the product of individual experiences, whereas he argued in his treatise *The Anxious Bench* (1843) that "individual Christianity is the product, always and entirely, of the church." When Horace Bushnell* published his expanded version of

*Christian Nurture** (1861), he complained that an ideology of individualism had led countless Protestants to view the church as a mere collection of units.

Other theologians debated the principle of "private judgment" in the interpretation of Scripture* and the formation of doctrine. Almost all American Christians opposed Thomas Paine's* deistic* claim that his own mind was his church, but Protestant theologians normally insisted on the right of private judgment in the interpretation of Scripture. A few warned, however, that they were overstating the point. Nevin argued that the refusal to acknowledge a controlling authority beyond the individual mind when interpreting Scripture promoted sectarian disunity, and he urged that Protestants use tradition and the creeds* as a check on private interpretation. Several studies have drawn attention to the persistent tendency of American Christians to combine belief in Christian doctrine with an affirmation of other ideologies, ranging from New Thought and spiritualism in the nineteenth century to astrology or existentialism* in the twentieth. Wade Clark Roof and William McKinney observed in the 1980s a growing inclination of Americans to select aspects of a religious tradition, discard the rest, and recast their religious identity according to individual preferences.

The primary debate over individualism resulted from the need to redefine the relationship between Christianity and the social order after the maturing of industrial capitalism* in the late nineteenth century. The businessman Andrew Carnegie expressed a widespread cultural assumption when, in his famous essay "Wealth" (1889), he argued that individualism was the foundation of the modern economic order and civilization. He acknowledged that competition could be "hard for the individual," but he contended that only a rugged economic individualism could ensure the future progress of the race. Carnegie was appropriating, though revising, an older form of utilitarian individualism associated with Thomas Hobbes that viewed human life as an effort by individuals to maximize their self-interest.

Carnegie's doctrine had proponents within the churches, but a number of theologians warned against its perils. While defending the sacredness of the individual, they argued, in the words of the Boston preacher George A. Gordon,* that a "wanton wealthy individualism is drawing near its end." They observed not only that individuals were linked to each other through their relations to past generations, social institutions and a common language and culture, but also that economic individualism threatened to produce social disorder and flouted the Christian ethical precept of care for the neighbor. Walter Rauschenbusch,* speaking for proponents of the Social Gospel,* criticized both a religious individualism that narrowed its concern merely to the salvation* of isolated souls and an economic individualism that ignored social obligations. Both forms of individualism, he charged, overlooked the prophetic tradition and obscured Christ's proclamation of the kingdom of God.*

Sociologists of religion and culture have recently observed that individualism remains a powerful ideology in America and that it has now assumed new forms. They distinguish the older economic individualism from an expressive individualism that exalts the goal of self-fulfillment. As early as 1909 the philosopher Josiah Royce* replied in his *Philosophy of Loyalty* to "the partisans of individualism" who sought only "the completest possible self-development and the fullest self-expression" for private selves. But expressive individualism proved to be increasingly attractive in American culture. Some argue that it permeates current understandings of religious faith, leading many to value Christian teachings only insofar as they promise richer forms of self-realization for autonomous individuals. The result is a private and instrumental faith that devalues the corporate practices and disciplines of the congregation as well as the ethical responsibilities that have traditionally defined Christian commitment.

To the extent that the concept of individuality has functioned to safeguard the inherent dignity of the human person, American Christians have affirmed it. The notion of individualism, however, has carried other connotations, and throughout American history many Christians have found it problematic.

BIBLIOGRAPHY. R. N. Bellah et al., *Habits of the Heart: Individualism and Commitment in American Life* (1985); W. C. Roof and W. McKinney, *American Mainline Religion: Its Changing Shape and Future* (1987); A. de Tocqueville, *Democracy in America* (1835). E. B. Holifield

Indulgence. Release from temporal punishment for sins* already forgiven. This Catholic* doctrine teaches that after a forgiven sinner receives justification* through Christ's sacrifice, purification from sin's corruption (sanctification*) comes through the sacrament of reconciliation* (penance). By indulgence, the Church accepts good works of charity or devotion in lieu of such discipline. Indulgences, whether partial or full (plenary), are based on the treasury of satisfaction (or merit*) of Christ and the saints.* They may be granted for oneself or for souls in purgatory.* Cross commercialization of indulgences contributed to igniting the Lutheran* Reformation, and it has been condemned by both Protestants* and Catholics. Since Vatican II* the Church's teaching on indulgences has been carefully guarded so as to remove them from the center of Catholic piety,* and though still granted, popular interest in it has substantially decreased. The doctrine remains a significant issue in the contemporary Lutheran-Roman Catholic dialog.*

See also MERIT; PURGATORY.

BIBLIOGRAPHY. C. J. Peter, "The Church's Treasures (*Thesauri Ecclesiae*), Then and Now," *TS* 47 (1986):251-272.   P. D. Steeves

Inerrancy Controversy. One of the most vexing controversies within conservative Protestantism* since World War 2* has focused on the doctrine of biblical inerrancy. In 1949 the Evangelical Theological Society,* which gathered academics from various denominational* backgrounds, established as its doctrinal basis the inerrancy of the Bible* in the original autographs. In the 1950s fundamentalists,* most evangelicals,* and for that matter most Roman Catholics,* upheld the inerrancy of the Bible.* By this they meant that the Bible, when correctly interpreted, is "truthful," regardless of the topic it broaches, whether in the area of doctrine* and ethics,* or history and the natural world.

As late as 1975 Martin Marty observed that evangelicals and fundamentalists viewed biblical inerrancy as one of their essential doctrines. A year later, however, Harold Lindsell published *The Battle for the Bible* (1976), in which he chronicled what he believed were defections from the doctrine of biblical inerrancy at evangelical colleges and seminaries.* In the late 1950s a small number of evangelical scholars had become uncomfortable with the doctrine, believing that the Bible does in fact contain material errors. They claimed that the doctrine's defenders often practiced a particularly wooden ("literal") exegesis* and relied on deductive logic rather than an inductive study of the texts of Scripture to prove their case.

In 1967 Fuller Theological Seminary* removed the doctrine of biblical inerrancy from its Statement of Faith. In response to Lindsell's book, Jack Rogers of Fuller edited *Biblical Authority* (1977) and later with Donald McKim wrote *The Authority and Interpretation of the Bible: An Historical Approach* (1979). In the latter volume the authors argued that the doctrine of biblical inerrancy had

been created in the last decades of the seventeenth century. In 1980 George Marsden proposed that the doctrine had been greatly shaped by the commitment of professors at Princeton Theological Seminary* to Common Sense* philosophy and that its particular late nineteenth-century configuration became a defining characteristic of fundamentalism. Critics of the doctrine essayed to demonstrate that Christians of earlier centuries had believed in the Bible's infallibility defined as its capacity to lead us to salvation and right living but not in its inerrancy.

As a foil for these developments, conservatives in the Lutheran Church—Missouri Synod,* who favored the doctrine of inerrancy, gained control of their denomination* in the 1970s. In the same decade the International Council of Biblical Inerrancy was established to defend the doctrine. This council held a series of academic and lay* conferences and commissioned a series of volumes. It drew up "The Chicago Statement on Biblical Inerrancy" (1978), which was published in the volume *Inerrancy* (1979). This statement represented for large numbers of evangelicals a responsible exposition of the doctrine. In other publications, scholars such as J. I. Packer, Kenneth Kantzer and D. A. Carson argued that the doctrine of biblical inerrancy, carefully defined, represents what the Bible teaches about itself and what the "central tradition" of the Christian churches has maintained. In the late 1980s conservatives in the Southern Baptist Convention* met with success in their attempt to gain control of the convention. They were determined to bring the doctrine of biblical inerrancy back into more prominence in Southern Baptist seminaries. Thus the debate regarding biblical inerrancy showed few signs of slackening at the end of the 1980s.

BIBLIOGRAPHY. N. Geisler, ed., *Inerrancy* (1979); H. Lindsell, *The Battle for the Bible* (1976); G. Marsden, *Reforming Fundamentalism* (1987); J. Rogers, ed., *Biblical Authority* (1977); J. Rogers and D. McKim, *The Authority and Interpretation of the Bible: An Historical Approach* (1979); J. D. Woodbridge, *Biblical Authority: A Critique of the Rogers/McKim Proposal* (1982).

J. D. Woodbridge

Ingersoll, Robert Green (1833-1899). Agnostic controversialist. Born in Dresden, New York, Ingersoll's father, a Congregational* and Presbyterian* minister,* imparted a stern Calvinist* world view to his son. Migrating to Illinois as a young man, Ingersoll began a legal practice and served as the state's attorney general. Following a brief stint as a Union officer in the Civil War* and an unsuccessful attempt to win a seat in Congress, Ingersoll moved to Washington, D.C., in 1879 to expand his practice and promote his irreligious views.

Ingersoll's greatest notoriety resulted from his frequent and highly popular lectures in which he promoted "freethinking." He rejected any attempt to harmonize evolution* and Christianity and asserted that the "Garden of Eden is an ignorant myth." Though he recognized the ethical authenticity of Jesus Christ, Ingersoll advocated a thoroughgoing scientific skepticism which was summarized in his self-constructed creed: "I believe in Liberty, Fraternity, and Equality—the blessed Trinity of Humanity; I believe in Observation, Reason, and Experience—the blessed Trinity of Science; I believe in Man, Woman, and Child—the blessed Trinity of Life and Joy."

With his wit and charm Ingersoll's lecture series drew audiences rivaling those of Mark Twain. Disarming critics with his impeccable manners and personal ethic, he pressed his case for individualism in the face of constraining Calvinism. Through extensive public appearances and correspondence (filling twelve published volumes), Ingersoll posed the period's most visible and potent arguments for freethinking and against orthodoxy.* Known by religious contemporaries as "the great agnostic," Robert Green Ingersoll rode the late nineteenth-century tide of Darwinian evolutionary* naturalism to challenge orthodox* churches and Christianity in general.

BIBLIOGRAPHY. C. H. Cramer, *Royal Bob: The Life of Robert Green Ingersoll* (1952); *DAB* V; *DARB*; O. Larson, *American Infidel: Robert G. Ingersoll* (1962); *NCAB* 9.   C. P. Dawson

Inglis, Charles (1734-1816). Anglican* bishop* of Nova Scotia. Born in Ireland and educated at Oxford University, Inglis came to the American colonies in 1757 as a teacher. After working for a year in Pennsylvania, he was ordained* in England, then returned to North America. First serving as a missionary* in Delaware, he soon became assistant rector at a church in New York City. His Loyalist sympathies made public in a pamphlet published in 1776 drew hostile responses from American patriots, some of whom burned his church a year later. Leaving the Middle Colonies in 1783 for a brief sojourn in Nova Scotia, he departed for England in 1784. When he returned to North America in 1787, it was as the first bishop appointed to a colony by the Church of England. As bishop of Nova Scotia (which at that time included jurisdiction over the Maritime provinces, New-

foundland and the provinces later named Ontario and Quebec, as well as Bermuda), he used his position to foster loyalty to the established church and British political traditions.

BIBLIOGRAPHY. R. V. Harris, *Charles Inglis* (1937); J. W. Lydekker, *The Life and Letters of Charles Inglis* (1936); *DCB* V.

P. D. Airhart

Institutional Church Movement. A turn-of-the-century effort by Protestant* Social Gospel* leaders to regain ground the church* had lost in the city, and particularly among the laboring poor. Pioneered by William A. Muhlenberg* and Thomas K. Beecher, the first significant expression of this idea was William S. Rainsford's St. George's Episcopal Church in New York, beginning in 1882. Rainsford began by eliminating pew rents* and then sought to expand the use of the church building to each day of the week. By the 1890s, Institutional Church programs included banks, game rooms, youth clubs, soup kitchens, kindergartens, deaconess homes, gymnasium classes, employment services, food and clothing dispensaries, sewing and cooking classes, clinics, hospitals and colleges—one of the more famous being Temple University in Philadelphia.

Examples of Institutional Churches in the 1890s included Berkeley Temple (Congregational*) in Boston; Baptist Temple in Philadelphia; Metropolitan Temple (Methodist*) in New York City; the People's Temple (Congregational) in Denver; the Ninth Street Baptist Church in Cincinnati; and the Markham Memorial Presbyterian* Church in St. Louis. The Institutional Church movement consolidated in 1894 with the establishment of the Open and Institutional Church League* to coordinate various programs and to pursue interdenominational cooperation. In New York City, the Protestant Episcopal Church* was reportedly well organized along institutional church lines.

BIBLIOGRAPHY. R. D. Cross, ed., *The Church in the City, 1865-1910* (1967); C. H. Hopkins, *The Rise of the Social Gospel in American Protestantism, 1865-1915* (1940); J. H. Dorn, "Religion and the City," in *Urban Experience,* ed. R. A. Mohl and J. F. Richardson (1973).

C. E. Stockwell

Interchurch World Movement. A short-lived ecumenical movement.* The first meeting of the Interchurch World Movement (IWM) was held in New York on December 17, 1918, in response to a call from the Board of Foreign Missions of the Presbyterian Church in the U.S.A.* to plan a united drive for world evangelism* and reform. At this meeting, 135 church and agency leaders, flushed with a post-World War 1* vision of a united church uniting a divided world, adopted a program of scientific surveys, education and publicity in preparation for a massive fund drive in 1920. The overambitious goal was $336,777,527. Despite a slick publicity effort for the "biggest business of the biggest man in the world," the IWM fell far short of its financial target. This failure, together with a lack of clearly stated objectives and confusion regarding the IWM's relationship to the denominations* it claimed to represent, contributed to the Movement's demise in the summer of 1920. Despite this, many took hope from the spirit of cooperation generated by the visionary ideals of the Movement.

BIBLIOGRAPHY. E. G. Ernst, *Moment of Truth for Protestant America: Interlude Campaigns Following World War I* (1974). B. V. Hillis

Interdenominational Foreign Mission Association of North America.
A fellowship and accrediting agency for nondenominational faith missions.* The Interdenominational Foreign Mission Association (IFMA) began in 1917 through the efforts of several mission societies committed to world evangelization, including the South Africa General Mission (now Africa Evangelical Fellowship), the China Inland Mission (now Overseas Missionary Fellowship*), the Central American Mission (now CAM International), and the Africa Inland Mission.* China Inland Mission's Henry W. Frost* was selected as the first president. As the organization experienced steady growth, it developed doctrinal, spiritual, ethical and financial standards for membership, which have helped to identify missions that merit the support of a conservative evangelical* constituency. In 1949 the IFMA opened an administrative office in Ridgefield Park, New Jersey, and in 1957 appointed J. O. Percy as its first full-time executive secretary.

The IFMA provides important information services for its members, particularly through books, pamphlets and the *IFMA News,* a quarterly established in 1955. It also sponsors mission conferences, several of which have been held in conjunction with the Evangelical Foreign Mission Association* (EFMA). The IFMA and the EFMA also cooperate through joint committees and the Evangelical Missions Information Service, which publishes the *Evangelical Missions Quarterly* and *Pulse.*

Today almost one hundred mission groups from the U.S. and Canada are affiliated with the IFMA.

These agencies represent over 8,000 missionaries from North America and another 3,000 from other nations. The IFMA is now based in Wheaton, Illinois, and Edwin L. Frizen, Jr., serves as executive director.

BIBLIOGRAPHY. W. T. Coggins and E. L. Frizen, Jr., eds., *Reaching Our Generation* (1982); J. H. Kane, *Faith Mighty Faith* (1956).

J. A. Patterson

International Bible Reading Association.
An organization established to encourage personal Bible reading and study. Founded in England in 1882 by the National Sunday School Union, the International Bible Reading Association (IBRA) was the inspiration of Charles Waters, a bank manager and member of Charles Spurgeon's Metropolitan Tabernacle and the IBRA's first secretary. Its first publication was a series of Bible readings coordinated with the International Sunday School Lessons. Its membership, which had increased in three years to 100,000, by 1900 had risen to 750,000, and in 1917 the London Sunday School Union, with which the association was affiliated, claimed the organization had one million readers in nearly one hundred countries.

In the late nineteenth century the association spread rapidly beyond England's shores, to Australia (1882), New Zealand and Canada (1883), the U.S. (1885) and numerous other countries. In 1890 members supported a Sunday-school* missionary* to India, thus establishing the IBRA Missionary Fund. The organization continues to publish daily Bible notes, along with reading aids for children, young people and adults.

BIBLIOGRAPHY. E. Rice, *The Sunday School Movement 1780-1917 and the American Sunday School Union, 1817-1917* (1917).

R. R. Mathisen

International Bible Society.
A society distributing Scripture* worldwide. The International Bible Society (IBS) is an outgrowth of the New York Bible Society,* which was established in 1809. In 1967, under the leadership of its executive secretary, Y. R. Kindberg, the New York Bible Society undertook the financial sponsorship of the New International Version of the Bible which was eventually published in 1978. In the process of publishing this version, the New York society became the International Bible Society (IBS).

Although it changed its headquarters from New York City to East Brunswick, New Jersey, it regards itself as standing in continuity with the parent society and counts 1809 as the year of its beginning. In 1988 the IBS decided to relocate once again and now has its headquarters in Colorado Springs, Colorado. Financial reasons played into the decision to relocate, but the Society also wanted to be more centrally located and close to a number of evangelical* organizations. The New York Bible Society will continue to function as an affiliate.

Whereas the NYBS, to begin with, limited itself largely to the New York City area and to the immigrants coming to America from around the world, its focus soon broadened. Today the Society, under its new name, provides Scripture for evangelism worldwide. In 1984 the Society celebrated 175 years of ministry. In 1908 the Society allocated a thousand dollars for the publication of one Asian translation. In the 175 years since 1809 the Society has distributed 130 million Bibles, New Testaments and Scripture portions around the world. Through association with the Wycliffe Bible Translators,* it has published Scripture in over 350 tribal languages in the past decade alone. Today it is involved in projects in ninety-nine different languages in thirteen countries. In the 1986/1987 fiscal year the IBS was able to provide 25 million Scriptures to believers and seekers around the world.

Bibles are made available to churches, prison inmates, school children, university students and evangelical agencies at home and abroad. The Society's stated purpose is to lead men and women, young people and children to a life-changing faith in Jesus Christ through the translation, publication and distribution of the Word of God. Although the greatest efforts are concentrated on countries overseas, the homeland has not been abandoned. The IBS supplies Bibles for prisons, hospitals and hotels, and maintains a full-time staff of evangelists in New York City.

BIBLIOGRAPHY. D. J. Fant, *The Bible at Work in New York* (1965). D. Ewert

International Church of the Foursquare Gospel.

Pentecostal* denomination.* The International Church of the Foursquare Gospel grew out of Pentecostal evangelist* Aimee Semple McPherson's* Angelus Temple in Los Angeles.

McPherson, a young widow and successful Pentecostal evangelist, arrived in California in 1918 with her two children, Roberta and Rolf. Though associated with the Assemblies of God,* her ministry* was largely interdenominational until she founded the Foursquare in 1927. In California she attracted thousands to her meetings, which, under her flamboyant leadership, offered salva-

tion,* prayer for the sick, baptism in the Holy Spirit,* speaking in tongues* and a concern for the needy.

In 1923 the 5,300-seat Angelus Temple was completed and a Bible school* to train ministers* and missionaries,* Lighthouse International Foursquare Evangelism (L.I.F.E.), was opened in 1925. The church went on the air with its own radio station, and Angelus Temple became a dynamic center of Pentecostal worship* and ministry.

The "Foursquare Gospel" was derived from the four-faced figures of Ezekiel 1 which McPherson reported seeing in a vision in 1921. The faces (a man, a lion, an ox and an eagle) were interpreted as the fourfold gospel of salvation, baptism in the Holy Spirit, divine healing and the Second Coming of Christ. These tenets placed the church in the mainstream of the Pentecostal Movement. Yet the church holds to a progressive view of sanctification,* rather than the Wesleyan* perfectionism.

Church growth in the 1920s was spectacular but then leveled off until about 1970. The charismatic renewal* in mainline* denominations prompted further growth, and by 1985 the church had expanded to more than 1,200 local congregations. In 1987 the largest Foursquare Church in the U. S. was the Church on the Way in Van Nuys, California (more than 6,000 members), pastored by Jack Hayford. Total church membership in 1985 was 181,594 in the U. S., with 863,642 members in other countries. The denomination publishes a monthly periodical, *Foursquare World Advance*.

Foursquare is a charter member of the National Association of Evangelicals* and the Pentecostal Fellowship of North America.* The church was organized with an essentially episcopal* polity.* Rolf McPherson, who succeeded his mother as president at her death in 1944, was scheduled to retire from that position in 1988.

BIBLIOGRAPHY. L. Thomas, *Storming Heaven* (1970); A. S. McPherson, *The Story of My Life* (1951); K. Kendrick, *The Promise Fulfilled* (1961); V. Synan, "Fulfilling Sister Aimee's Dream," *Charisma* (July 1987). W. E. Warner

International Congress on World Evangelization (Lausanne, Switzerland, 1974).

A ten-day conference attended by 3,700 representatives from 150 nations to consider world evangelization by the year A.D. 2000. With its theme "Let the Earth Hear His Voice" the meeting has been called the most global and representative such undertaking to date. Financial assistance to Third-World participants ensured representation of world evangelical leadership. The plenary sessions presented leading figures in evangelism,* while small-group workshops addressed specific theological and methodological concerns. In addition, participants met by nation to coordinate efforts to reach their own populations. Agreement on some issues, like the authority* of the Scripture,* was evident from the outset, as was the wide range of cultural and ecclesiastical diversity among the conferees.

The Congress, which Honorary Chairman Billy Graham called a "congress of ideas," provided ample room for debate. The term *delegate* was avoided so that participants would not appear to speak for their respective communions. The notion of an international center for evangelization, raised informally, was dismissed by speakers who favored a decentralized effort to increase awareness and commitment in every country and denomination. To this end the Congress produced a Covenant, a statement on the primacy of evangelism drafted by the British churchman John R. W. Stott, as well as the organization for continuing discussions at the regional and national levels. A major concern of the Congress, the relationship between social action and evangelization, was not resolved, although discussion supported social action that originated in evangelization. The Congress also stressed the continuing strategic need for crosscultural missionaries,* tending to dismiss the then-highly publicized demand for a moratorium on Western missionaries, in the light of increasing world need and the sparse resources of many overseas churches.

BIBLIOGRAPHY. J. D. Douglas, ed., *Let the Earth Hear His Voice* (1975); K. Kantzer, "Revitalizing World Evangelism: The Lausanne Congress Ten Years Later," *CT* 28 (1984):10-12; D. McGavran, "A New Age in Missions Begins," *Church Growth Bulletin* 11 (1974): 407-410; C. P. Wagner, "Lausanne Twelve Months Later," *CT* 19 (1975):961-963.   E. A. Wilson

International Council of Biblical Inerrancy. *See* INERRANCY DEBATE.

International Council of Christian Churches. A separatist* fundamentalist* association of churches. After World War 2* there were many conservative Protestants* who were concerned about what they regarded as a growing apostasy in American mainline* churches. Among those were Carl McIntire* of the Bible Presbyterian Church* in Collingswood, New Jersey. In August 1948 he organized the International Council of Christian Churches (ICCC) to offset the influence of ecumenism.* The first meeting was held in

Amsterdam just preceding the charter meeting of the World Council of Churches* in that same city.

In a resolution adopted at the first meeting, the purpose of the ICCC was "to protest against the tenets of modernism* and to proclaim the doctrines of the faith of the Reformation." The contention was that the World Council supported the admission of the Roman Catholic* and Orthodox* Churches and advocated a "radical pacifism* . . . on the road to creating a super-church."

There are two types of membership in the ICCC. One is a constituent membership for national church bodies or associations of churches. The other is a consultative membership (without a vote) for local churches not belonging to any denomination* affiliated with the Council. In addition, provision is made for membership by missionary* societies, Bible leagues, schools, etc. No group belonging to the World Council can be a member of ICCC. At least every five years, a plenary congress is held.

In America much of the message of the ICCC is spread by the affiliate organization, the American Council of Christian Churches,* and by McIntire's national radio program, the "Twentieth Century Reformation Hour," as well as a newspaper, the *Christian Beacon.* In 1987 the ICCC had 424 denominations in ninety-seven countries. The American headquarters are in Collingswood, New Jersey.

See also AMERICAN COUNCIL OF CHRISTIAN CHURCHES; FUNDAMENTALISM.

BIBLIOGRAPHY. C. McIntire, *Modern Tower of Babel* (1949); E. Jorstad, *The Politics of Doomsday, Fundamentalists of the Far Right* (1970); G. W. Dollar, *A History of Fundamentalism in America* (1973).   C. E. Hall

International Council of Religious Education. An interdenominational religious education* organization. The International Council of Religious Education (ICRE) was formed in 1922 as a merger of the International Sunday School Association* and the Sunday School Council of Evangelical Denominations. It was the leading voice in religious education in North America until 1950, when it merged with other denominational* agencies to form the National Council of Churches.*

In 1928 the ICRE established the Educational Commission to begin developing a detailed curriculum guide to aid denominations in creating curricula in accordance with the contemporary trends in educational thought. This guide became the ICRE's source of greatest impact on local church ministry. It included a statement of educational principles, a description of educational experiences, a list of comprehensive objectives and specific age-group objectives. The comprehensive objectives of the Council were: a consciousness of one's relationship to God, an appreciation of Jesus Christ, the development of Christlike character, "the ability and disposition" to help construct a Christian social order, participation in the church, a Christian life philosophy, and "the assimilation of the best religious experience of the race, pre-eminently that recorded in the Bible*'" as a guide for daily living. Later the ICRE added the establishment and nurture of the family to its list of educational objectives.

The International Council of Religious Education emphasized the value of integrating research and thought in secular education with Christian thought and practice in educational ministry. This emphasis by the Council contributed greatly to the professionalism of education in the church.

BIBLIOGRAPHY. C. B. Eavey, *History of Christian Education* (1964); M. J. Taylor, *Religious Education* (1960).   B. E. Brown

International Eucharistic Congress (XXVIII). A Catholic* devotional event celebrated in Chicago in 1926. Started in France in 1881, the Eucharistic Congress was a biannual gathering to honor Christ in the Blessed Sacrament. Usually held in traditionally Catholic countries, this pilgrimage had come to the New World only once before, to Montreal in 1910. George Cardinal Mundelein* of Chicago convened the twenty-eighth congress in his city in order to highlight the rapid growth of Catholicism in the U. S.

About a million pilgrims converged on Chicago from June 20 to 24, worshiping in area churches and in the lakefront Soldier Field. The Congress climaxed with an outdoor procession on the final day at Mundelein's newly built St. Mary of the Lake Seminary. The Chicago Congress succeeded in gaining publicity for American Catholicism, but many Protestants reacted negatively to the pomp and display. This may have contributed to the uneasiness they felt when a Catholic Al Smith* ran for president two years later.

BIBLIOGRAPHY. M. Fairman, "Twenty-Eighth International Eucharistic Congress," *Chicago History* 5 (1976-1977):202-212; E. R. Kantowicz, *Corporation Sole: Cardinal Mundelein and Chicago Catholicism* (1982).   E. R. Kantowicz

International Federation of Gospel Missions. *See* INTERNATIONAL UNION OF GOSPEL MISSIONS.

International Missionary Council. An ecumenical missionary organization. A direct outgrowth of the World Missionary Conference at Edinburgh in 1910, the International Missionary Council (IMC) was organized in 1921 under the leadership of John R. Mott,* chairman, and Joseph Oldham and A. L. Warnshuis, secretaries. It was constituted by several missionary* councils and national organizations from North America and Europe, but also represented groups in China, Japan, India, Burma and Ceylon. It sought to stimulate thinking and research on issues of mission; to help coordinate the activities of the national organizations and their member societies, encouraging united action; to stimulate support of religious freedom, including missionary work; and to encourage international and interracial justice. It also published the *International Review of Missions.*

While the Council did not attempt to determine doctrinal issues, its theological consensus included a recognition of the obligation to proclaim the gospel in all the world and a common loyalty to Jesus Christ confessed as the Son of the living God.

The IMC's first conference was held in Jerusalem in 1928. Half of the 250 delegates were from Asia, Africa and Latin America, making it the first truly global meeting of Christians in history. The 1938 meeting near Madras brought together 471 men and women from sixty-nine countries. Resisting some prior calls for syncretism, the IMC reaffirmed the authority of Scripture* and the truth and grace of God in Jesus Christ. The 1947 meeting called for "Partnership in Obedience," and in 1952 it challenged its members to rethink the nature of the missionary task in a revolutionary world. The IMC merged with the World Council of Churches* in 1961, becoming its Commission on World Mission and Evangelism.

See also MISSIONS, PROTESTANT MAINLINE FOREIGN.

BIBLIOGRAPHY. H. E. Fey, ed., *A History of the Ecumenical Movement, 1948-1968* (1970); W. R. Hogg, *Ecumenical Foundations* (1952); S. C. Neill, and R. Rouse, eds., *A History of the Ecumenical Movement, 1517-1948* (1967).

P. E. Pierson

International Sunday School Association. A nondenominational Sunday-school* agency. Although the International Sunday School Association (ISSA) was formally named in 1905, it had existed since 1860 as the National Sunday School Convention system, the organization responsible for popularizing the Sunday school and producing the International Uniform Lesson curriculum. The leadership of these conventions, primarily laity,* sought to avoid conflict with denominations over the control of the Sunday school. When the ISSA was incorporated in 1907, conflict did ensue. However, its resolution resulted in a new consensus for religious education and the merger in 1922 of the ISSA with the Sunday School Council of Evangelical Denominations to form the International Sunday School Council of Religious Education (renamed in 1924 the International Council of Religious Education*). The council continued until 1950, when it became the Division of Christian Education of the National Council of Churches in Christ in the U.S.A.*

See also SUNDAY SCHOOL MOVEMENT.

BIBLIOGRAPHY. *Organized Sunday School Work in America, 1908-1911* (1911); *Organized Sunday School Work in North America, 1918-1922* (1922); R. W. Lynn, *The Little Big School* (1980).

J. L. Seymour

International Union of Gospel Missions. An association of urban rescue missions. The International Union of Gospel Missions (IUGM) was begun in 1913 as a continuation of the National Federation of Gospel Missions (NFGM), an organization that had built on informal structures that had been developing for more than two decades. Central to this developing cooperation (from the 1870s to 1906) were Jerry McAuley* and S. H. Hadley,* superintendents of what is probably the first modern rescue mission, New York City's Water Street Mission.* The IUGM, from its inception partially operating through a growing number of districts (thirteen listed in 1964) that were themselves active cooperative bodies, recorded thirty mission superintendents among its charter members in 1913. The total of member missions increased to 124 in 1923, 215 in 1946 and approximately 250 by the 1980s. Until the 1920s the rescue missions generally offered wide-ranging emergency assistance to the very poor, but they have since diversified their services, and now serve the needy through at least forty different programs.

See also RESCUE MISSION MOVEMENT.

BIBLIOGRAPHY. W. E. Paul, *The Romance of Rescue* (1948); C. Y. Furness, *Gospel Rescue Mission Update* (1987); N. A. Magnuson, *Salvation in the Slums: Evangelical Social Work, 1865-1920* (1977).

N. A. Magnuson

InterVarsity Christian Fellowship. An evangelical interdenominational organization working with Christian student groups in North American universities and colleges. The movement began in Great Britain, where four Christian unions (or campus chapters) united in 1873 to form the Medical Prayer Union. The Cambridge Inter-Collegiate Christian Union began in 1877, and from there the ministry* spread to other schools. In 1919 the first annual InterVarsity conference was organized to promote evangelical* and missionary* activities in other colleges.

InterVarsity work began in Canada in 1928, and six years later C. Stacey Woods,* an Australian, assumed leadership of the Canadian ministry. In 1939 he helped to organize the Michigan Christian Fellowship at the University of Michigan. The next year Herbert Taylor,* an American businessman, convinced the Canadian board that an American office should be opened in Chicago. The move became official in 1941, when the Canadian board appointed eight staff workers for the U.S., and Stacey Woods as the general secretary. Within a year forty-one chapters were linked to the U.S. ministry.

By 1986 InterVarsity Christian Fellowship was ministering to 27,200 students on 750 campuses in all fifty states. The most visible ministry of the movement is the huge Urbana Missionary Conference* which meets every three years during the Christmas holiday break at the University of Illinois at Urbana, Illinois, and attracts as many as 18,000 students. Another ministry, InterVarsity Press, publishes a steady stream of books integrating the Christian faith and contemporary thought.

BIBLIOGRAPHY. D. M. Howard, *Student Power in World Evangelism* (1970); B. L. Shelley, "The Rise of Evangelical Youth Movements," *FH* 18 (1986):47-63; C. S. Woods, *The Growth of a Work of God* (1978).

B. L. Shelley

Ireland, John (1838-1918). Archbishop* of St. Paul. Born in Burnchurch, near Kilkenny, Ireland, of artisan parents, John Ireland immigrated with them to Burlington, Vermont, in 1849. After a move to Chicago in 1851, they finally settled in the frontier village of St. Paul, Minnesota, in 1852. Educated in local primary schools, he attended St. Mary's College in Chicago, where the priests recognized his brilliance and devotion to the Church. He studied for some time at the College of Meximieux, Diocese of Belly, France, and was ordained* a priest* in 1861. Ireland then became the assistant at the cathedral* in St. Paul. During the Civil War* he became chaplain* (1862) to the Fifth Minnesota Regiment, serving under William Rosecrans at Corinth, Mississippi. After catching a fever at Vicksburg, he resigned his post in 1863.

Ireland returned to St. Paul, becoming pastor of the cathedral in 1867, and in 1869 he attended the First Vatican Council.* A leader in the Irish-American Temperance Society, he incurred the wrath of German-Americans. In 1875 the pope named him bishop* co-adjutor of St. Paul, and in 1884 the outspoken priest became bishop. When St. Paul became an archdiocese in 1888, he became archbishop. Ireland's life centered on Catholic reform, as he worked to bring Catholics to the West, supported Catholic education, defended labor organizations and worked with the Roosevelt wing of the Republican Party. He served as long-time vice president of the National Conference of Charities and Correction.

In 1876 Ireland founded the Catholic Colonization Society, with the belief that Catholics would thrive in the new Western agrarian environment as opposed to their miserable lives in Eastern ghettos. His speculation in Western lands for Irish settlement often left him in debt. As an educator Ireland established St. Thomas Seminary, St. Thomas College and, in 1894, St. Paul Seminary. His greatest educational accomplishment was to assist in the founding of The Catholic University of America,* traveling to Rome to argue the case for the American Catholic school system. He also defended the Faribault plan for mixed public and parochial schools,* with public investment in education and Church influence in religious instruction.

Ireland's greatest struggle for American Catholics was in the Americanist* movement, which eventually caused him much trouble with Rome. He desired to stop foreign influence on American Catholics, to teach English exclusively in American schools and to turn immigrant* Catholics into American nationalists. He had a major influence on the *Catholic World,* as that magazine resisted the appointment of foreign-speaking prelates being sent to the U.S. Ireland also lobbied the U.S. Congress in opposition to foreign interference in American politics. Again, in the political arena he fought with President Benjamin Harrison over the treatment of Catholic Native Americans, spoke at the Republican National Convention in 1896 where he condemned Bryanism, and became a close ally of Progressive Republicans. Ireland also wanted the Catholic Church and the Congress to support the Knights of Labor* as a legitimate force in the American economy and society. During World War 1* he befriended France and desired to keep Midwestern German Catholics loyal to the American cause. This frank exponent of a mainstream middle-class Catholic-American people succumbed to old age in 1918.

BIBLIOGRAPHY. J. Ireland, *The Church and Modern Society* (1896); *DAB* V; *DARB*; D. J. Dease, *The Theological Influence of Orestes Brownson and Isaac Hecker on John Ireland's Americanist Ecclesiology* (unpublished Ph.D. dissertation, The Catholic University of America, 1978); T. T. McAvoy, *The Formation of the American Catholic Minority, 1820-1860* (1967); J. H. Moynihan, *The Life of Archbishop John Ireland* (1953); *NCAB* 9.

J. L. Wakelyn

Ironside, Henry ("Harry") Allen (1876-1951). Fundamentalist* Bible* expositor. Born in Toronto of parents who were involved in the Plymouth Brethren* movement, Ironside experienced conversion* at age fourteen, became a Salvation Army* officer two years later, and served for three years at various posts in California. After struggling with the Army's Wesleyan* doctrines of sanctification,* Ironside resigned and spent several months in rest and study. He joined the Plymouth Brethren in 1896 and began a preaching* and teaching ministry. Helen Schofield, another former Salvation Army officer, became his wife in 1898 and they settled in Oakland in 1900.

Ironside's fame as a Bible teacher, evangelist* and author grew steadily, but his only pastorate, at the Moody Memorial Church in Chicago from 1930 to 1948, brought him to the center of the fundamentalist network and the peak of his influence. Although his formal education ended with grade school, Ironside read widely in history, literature, philosophy, theology* and biblical studies. His theology was dispensational,* as was common in Brethren circles. Adept at publishing his sermons and lectures, Ironside eventually wrote forty-six books and thirty-one pamphlets. By 1946 nearly one million of these had been sold.

His lively style and clear-cut interpretations frequently made Ironside the final authority* on the sacred text in fundamentalist pulpits and Bible-study* circles. Recent conservative biblical scholarship has eclipsed Ironside's work, but evangelicals' demand for his lively and assertive Bible exposition continues. As of 1986, three dozen of Ironside's titles were still in print.

BIBLIOGRAPHY. *DAB* 5; E. S. English, *H. A. Ironside, Ordained of the Lord* (1946); H. A. Ironside, *Random Reminiscences from Fifty Years of Ministry* (1939); E. Reese, *The Life and Ministry of Harry Ironside, 1876-1951* (1976).

J. A. Carpenter

Irwin, (B)enjamin (H)ardin (b.1854). Holiness* evangelist.* Born near Mercer, Missouri, at the age of nine Irwin moved to Tecumseh, Nebraska, where in early manhood he practiced law and served as pastor* of the Mount Zion Baptist Church. In 1891 this lifelong Baptist* came into contact with Wesleyan* teaching, claimed entire sanctification* and became, he said, a "John Wesley Methodist." Reports in the Holiness papers from 1893 to 1895 indicate that Irwin was itinerating as an evangelist,* preaching to largely Methodist Episcopal* congregations in Iowa, Nebraska, Kansas, Oklahoma Territory and Colorado. He adopted the theory of John Fletcher, Wesley's coworker, that the full baptism of the Holy Spirit* might require effusions of the Spirit beyond entire sanctification, a belief confirmed to him at Enid, Oklahoma, on October 23, 1895.

There, in response to a "very furnace of intense desire," he in a vision saw "a cross of pure transparent fire," which was followed by a burning spiritual experience of "rest in a measureless ocean of pure living fire." Proclamation of the baptism of fire, the so-called third work heresy, cost Irwin the friendship of Holiness editors in Chicago, Louisville and Philadelphia, and Holiness support within establishment Methodism. Fire Baptized associations were organized in Iowa, Kansas, Oklahoma, Texas, Georgia, Florida, North Carolina and South Carolina, and in Ontario and Manitoba in 1897 and 1898. The introduction of experiences subsequent to fire, symbolized by dynamite, by lyddite and by selenite and oxydite, combined to alienate all but the most entranced of his followers.

Irwin inspired deep loyalty, drawing into his movement a scattering of radical former Episcopal Methodists, Wesleyan Methodists, Quakers* and River Brethren* from a geographical area coincident to that of political Populism. In 1898 at Anderson, South Carolina, he organized the Fire Baptized Holiness Association of America and was made general overseer for life. On October 6, 1899, he issued the first number of *Live Coals of Fire,* the official organ of the new body.

Both the journal and the tenure of the general overseer were cut short, however, by an announcement in 1900 in H. C. Morrison's* *Pentecostal Herald,* that Irwin had been seen on an Omaha street drunk and smoking a cigar. The *Christian Witness* reprinted the item under the caption: "Whisky Baptized." Soon thereafter he divorced his wife and married a younger woman. In 1907 Irwin appeared with her as a coworker in Pentecostal* missions in Oakland and San Francisco. His career after that time is uncertain.

BIBLIOGRAPHY. M. H. Schrag, "The Spiritual Pilgrimage of the Reverend Benjamin Hardin Irwin," *Brethren in Christ History and Life* 4 (1981): 3-29, 89-121; C. C. Fankhauser, "The Heritage of Faith: An Historical Evaluation of the Holiness Movement in America" (unpublished M.A. thesis, Pittsburg State University, Kansas, 1983):121-144.   C. E. Jones

Itinerancy. The practice of preaching* on an irregular basis to randomly visited pulpits or parishes.* Traditionally, preachers were called to serve the pulpit of a specific congregation. Once installed in that place, the preacher stayed. A departure from this typically English and Puritan practice began at about the time of the Great Awakening in America. This new practice, called *itinerancy* by its opponents, grew up among relatively untutored preachers of the New Light* movement.

Itinerant preachers moved about calling for revivals,* and preaching in an extemporaneous style that established a special rapport with their audiences and appealed to the heart over the mind. In so doing they were creating a new social context for preaching and a new form of mass communication. Their activity evoked hostility among established preachers, who in many cases understood them to be a threat to their own ministries. Some itinerants did criticize settled ministers in public, the best example being Gilbert Tennent's* controversial sermon on "The Danger of an Unconverted Ministry." Whereas settled ministers had a certain aristocratic authority over their congregations, itinerants earned their right to be heard by attracting the voluntary attention of people who gathered to hear them outside the established institution of the meetinghouse. The most famous eighteenth-century itinerant preacher in America was the Englishman George Whitefield.*

BIBLIOGRAPHY. H. S. Stout, *The New England Soul* (1986).   L. J. Van Til

Ives, Levi Silliman (1797-1867). Episcopal* bishop* and Roman Catholic* apologist. Born in Connecticut, Ives moved while still young to Turin in upstate New York. In 1816 he began to study at Hamilton College, intending to enter the Presbyterian* ministry,* yet he left within a year. By 1819 he had abandoned the Presbyterian for the Episcopal Church and studied for the priesthood* under Bishop John Henry Hobart,* who instilled in his student an attraction for high church* theology.* After ordination* to the priesthood in 1823, he served in a number of churches in Pennsylvania and New York until his election in 1831 as second bishop of the diocese* of North Carolina.

The establishing of church schools and religious work among the slave community were two of Ives' major concerns. As a result of his work among the slaves, Ives, though a Northerner, became an apologist for Southern slavery and incurred sharp criticism from the English bishop and abolitionist* Samuel Wilberforce.

Ives strongly supported the Oxford Movement's* attempt to reclaim the Catholic heritage of his church. At Valle Crucis in western North Carolina, he established (1847-1848) a religious brotherhood, the Order of the Holy Cross, whose teachings and practices provoked great alarm within his diocese. Ives suppressed the brother-hood but for a number of years publicly vacillated as to the legitimacy of practices such as auricular confession* and prayers for the dead.* Finally, while in Rome in December of 1852, Ives resigned his episcopate and entered the Roman Catholic Church. He recorded his reasons in *Trials of a Mind* (1854). For the rest of his life he taught at various Catholic institutions and involved himself in philanthropic labors, particularly the Catholic Male Protectorate for destitute children.

BIBLIOGRAPHY. *DAB* V; *DARB*; M. De L. Haywood, *Lives of the Bishops of North Carolina . . .* (1910); J. O'Grady, *Levi Silliman Ives: Pioneer Leader in Catholic Charities* (1933).

R. B. Mullin

J

Jackson, Jesse Louis (1941-). Minister,* political activist and presidential candidate. Born to a woman who later married, Jackson grew up in a stable upper-lower-class family in Greenville, South Carolina. He graduated from North Carolina Agricultural and Technical College (B.A., 1964), where he was a star athlete and a participant in civil-rights activities. He attended Chicago Theological Seminary, which he left one semester prior to graduation to work with Martin Luther King, Jr.* In 1968 he was ordained* (Progressive National Baptist Convention). In 1966 he became head of Operation Breadbasket in Chicago and, in 1971, founded Operation PUSH (People United to Save Humanity) and some satellite organizations to deal with problems of African-American unemployment, poverty and educational opportunity. In the late 1970s, as the result of working for an African-American candidate for the mayor of Chicago, Jackson turned his attention to politics.

In 1984 Jackson became the first African-American candidate for the presidency of the U.S. Although a Democrat, he based his candidacy on the "Rainbow Coalition," that is, the political support of African-Americans, Hispanics, women, Native Americans, gays and others who had traditionally been politically disenfranchised. He won enough delegate support in the primary elections to address the Democratic National Convention, where he made an impassioned plea for a new order of politics to change the effects of the Reagan* years and be more concerned for the poor of America and the world. In 1988 he pursued the same themes with more effectiveness and appealed to enough white voters to be considered a serious candidate for the presidency. At the Democratic National Convention he lost the nomination to Massachusetts Governor Michael Dukakis. Jackson's principal political liability was strained relations with the Jewish community because of a remark perceived to be anti-Semitic, a pro-Arab position on Middle East problems and his friendship with Black Muslim leader Louis Farrakhan.

His critics accused him of producing more rhetoric than results in either civil rights or political activities, of being opportunistic, and of invoking the name of Martin Luther King, Jr., and manipulating African-American concerns for his own aggrandizement. But all acknowledged that he was a political phenomenon of great importance in the 1980s.

BIBLIOGRAPHY. J. Jackson, *Straight from the Heart,* ed. R. D. Hatch and F. E. Wains (1987); T. H. Landess and R. M. Quinn, *Jesse Jackson and the Politics of Race* (1985); A. L. Reed, Jr., *The Jesse Jackson Phenomenon* (1986); B. Reynolds, *Jesse Jackson: The Man, The Movement, The Myth* (1985); E. Stone, *Jesse Jackson* (1984).

R. B. Flowers

Jackson, Samuel Macauley (1851-1912). Presbyterian* educator and author. Born in New York City, where his father was an Irish-immigrant* businessman, Jackson was educated at the College of the City of New York, graduating with distinction in 1870. He studied theology* at Princeton Theological Seminary* (1870-1871) and Union Theological Seminary of New York* (1871-1873), where Philip Schaff* and Henry Boynton Smith* awakened his interest in church history. Following his graduation, he did further study at the Universities of Leipzig and Berlin in Germany (1873-1876). During this period, he also traveled in Palestine.

Returning to the U.S., Jackson was ordained* and served as pastor* of the Presbyterian Church in Norwood, New Jersey (1876-1880). Finding himself unsuited to the pastoral ministry because of his retiring temperament, he became involved in charitable work and historical scholarship. He served on the board and held positions with such organizations as the Charity Organization Society and the Prison Association of the State of New York, but his most famous work was as associate editor or editor of such reference works as the *New Schaff-Herzog Encyclopedia of Religious Knowledge* (1907-1911), *A Dictionary of the Bible* (1880) and *Johnson's Universal Cyclopedia* (1893-1895, 1897). He also edited and contributed the volume on Zwingli to the series Heroes of the Reformation (1899). In 1895 he became professor of church history at New York University, where he remained until 1912.

BIBLIOGRAPHY. *DAB* V. J. R. Wiers

Jackson, Sheldon (1834-1909). Presbyterian* missionary* to frontier West and Alaska. Born in Minaville, New York, Jackson attended Union College in Schenectady (B.A., 1855) and Princeton Theological Seminary* (B.D., 1858). Influenced by the revival* of student interest in missions* during the fall of 1857, Jackson applied for overseas work with the Presbyterian Church and was appointed by the foreign board to teach Choctaw Indians at Spencer Academy in the Indian Territory. Unhappy, both because of health problems and his desire to preach* more, Jackson was reassigned under the home board to La Crescent, Minnesota (1858).

From 1859 until 1869 Jackson labored in western Wisconsin and southern Minnesota, beginning his long career of pioneering Presbyterian work on the Western frontier. During this period he helped organize twenty-three churches and secured twenty new ministers from seminaries* in the East. By 1869 Jackson had worked to secure a call from the Synod* of Iowa to superintend their work. Later the Board appointed him to oversee the Presbyterian work from Canada to Mexico and from Nebraska to Nevada. In 1877 he began superintending work in Alaska.

Jackson's consistent concern for the social improvement of people, both native and settler, led to his 1879 appointment by the U.S. Government to head a special commission "to investigate the conditions of the natives in S.E. Alaska." In 1884 he was appointed the first superintendent of public instruction for Alaska, a post he held until his death in 1909. Despite the federal government's early reticence, Jackson raised funds and personally directed the introduction of domestic reindeer from Siberia to Alaska (1891) to prevent either the starvation or forced removal of the Eskimos to reservations.

Sheldon Jackson, known as the "Bishop of All Beyond" (or "Apostle to Alaska"), was tireless in his efforts to establish the American frontier as a Christian society. His pioneering efforts often caused friction with his own church and government, but these efforts also founded over 150 churches, Westminster College in Salt Lake City, the *North Star* newspaper in Sitka, Alaska (1887), The Alaska Society of Natural History and Ethnology (1887) and The Women's Executive Committee of Home Missions (1878, later called The Women's Board of Home Missions).

BIBLIOGRAPHY. A. K. Bailey, "Sheldon Jackson: Planter of Churches," *JPHS* 27 (1948):120-148, 193-214; *JPHS* 28 (1949):21-40; *DAB* V; *DARB*; J. A. Lazell, *Alaska Apostle* (1960); *NCAB* 9; R. L. Stewart, *Sheldon Jackson* (1908). S. Sunquist

Jackson, Thomas Jonathan ("Stonewall") (1824-1863). Confederate general and Presbyterian* layman.* Born in Clarksburg, Virginia (now West Virginia), Jackson barely passed the entrance examination at West Point, though he achieved seventeenth place in his graduating class (1846). He was an officer in the Mexican War, where he first exhibited his military talents. In 1851 he began a ten-year position as an instructor at the Virginia Military Institute. During this decade he married Elinor Judkin (1853), who died the following year in childbirth. In 1857 he married Mary Anna Morrison.

Sometime after the Mexican War he began a serious study of religion, beginning with Roman Catholicism,* then developing a private code of morals and finally affiliating with the Presbyterian Church in 1851. Religion became an important aspect of his life, and Southern preachers often referred to him as a "prophet-warrior." He consistently observed the Sabbath* and was in the habit of rising for prayer several times during the night on the eve of battle. A personal friend of Southern Presbyterian divines* such as Robert L. Dabney* (who served on Jackson's staff) and Thomas E. Peck, he frequently sought their company and enjoyed discussing theology.*

During the Civil War* Jackson distinguished himself as an outstanding Confederate officer. At the first battle of Bull Run, his stout resistance to Union advances earned him the nickname "Stonewall." Other battles that gave evidence of his tactical genius were the Seven Days' Battles, the Shenandoah Valley Campaign, Cross Keys, Port Republic, the second battle of Bull Run and Fredericksburg. In the Battle of Chancellorsville, he was caught in the confused fire of his own men on May 2, 1863. His left arm was amputated, and he began to improve. Then pneumonia set in, and he died on May 10. His dying words were: "Let us cross over the river, and rest under the shade of the trees." General Lee mourned the loss of his "right arm."

BIBLIOGRAPHY. *DAB* V; R. L. Dabney, *Life of Lieut.-Gen. Thos. J. Jackson,* 2 vols. (1864-1866); G. F. R. Henderson, *Stonewall Jackson and the American Civil War,* 2 vols. (1898); J. P. Smith, *Religious Character of Stonewall Jackson* (1897);

F. E. Vandiver, *The Mighty Stonewall* (1957).

D. B. Chesebrough

Jacobs, Benjamin Franklin (1834-1902). Sunday-school movement* leader. Born in New Jersey, Jacobs spent most of his life in Chicago. A Baptist* layman,* produce dealer and real estate entrepreneur, Jacobs served throughout his life as a Sunday-school superintendent. Locally he helped organize a mission Sunday school, the Chicago YMCA* and city and state Sunday-school associations. Nationally, he was the organizing genius of the national Sunday-school convention system and the uniform lesson curriculum system, serving both on the convention executive committee and the lesson committee. Jacobs had a vision of uniting churches around the world through weekly study of the same Sunday-school lesson. Internationally, he helped to found the World's Sunday School Convention System in 1889, serving on its executive committee as both a president and U.S. secretary.

J. L. Seymour

Jacobs, Henry Eyster (1844-1932). Lutheran* theologian* and historian. Born in Gettysburg, Pennsylvania, Jacobs graduated from Gettysburg College and Seminary and served as a pastor in Allegheny, Pennsylvania. His academic career began as an instructor at Thiel Hall, followed by professor of classics at Gettysburg College and professor of systematic theology* at the Lutheran Theological Seminary in Philadelphia (1883-1932). There he also served as dean (1894-1920) and president (1920-1928).

Among his scholarly contributions were: *A History of the Evangelical Lutheran Church in the United States* (1893) in the American Church History Series, *The Elements of Religion* (1896), *Martin Luther* (1898), *A Summary of the Christian Faith* (1905) and *The Lutheran Encyclopedia* (1899) which he edited with J. A. W. Haas. Jacobs, through his historical studies and translations from the German, provided a bridge by which English-speaking Lutherans could understand their Continental roots. At the same time his firm rootage in Gettysburg—even during the Civil War*—provided a bridgehead on American soil. He was a key figure in the confessional* and liturgical renewal and reunion of Lutherans. His gift of teaching and longevity combined to interpret his field to generations of laity and ministerial students.

BIBLIOGRAPHY. H. E. Horn, ed., *Memoirs of Henry Eyster Jacobs: Notes on a Life of a Churchman* (1974).

H. E. Horn

James, William (1842-1910). Philosopher and psychologist of religion. Born in New York City, James studied at Harvard* (1861-1863) and received an M.D. from Harvard Medical School in 1869. James's career as professor at Harvard (1872-1907) led him through a varied intellectual pursuit in the areas of physiology, psychology* and philosophy. He is best known as an advocate of pragmatism, a distinctively American philosophical school, and as a founder of the field of the psychology of religion. His work in both areas gave support to liberal trends in American Protestantism,* particularly liberalism's* emphasis on the role of feeling in religion and its hesitancy to regard religious claims as absolutes.

James was intent on combining social scientific method with an appreciation of human day-to-day experience and in 1876 started the first psychology laboratory at Harvard to give his work a scientific basis. He was convinced that any analysis of religious belief had to begin with the subjective experience of individuals. As a result, he took seriously the accounts individuals gave of personal religious experience and attempted to understand and interpret them. His Gifford lectures at Edinburgh (1901-1902) appeared as the *Varieties of Religious Experience* (1902), one of the first systematic attempts to analyze religious experience* since the time of Jonathan Edwards.* James argued forcefully for the integrity of a range of types of religious experience (the "once born" and "twice born" were his two main categories), although it is clear that he had a personal affinity for mystical experience—a direct, intuitive encounter with the Divine that transformed the way one viewed all reality. His intrigue with mysticism* led to a continuing interest with psychic phenomena.

Religious belief for James was true not because of its metaphysical claims but because of its consequences for human behavior and conduct. Truth, then, was not an absolute, but rather an attribute that ideas acquired as individuals exercised their right to believe. Since he thought different beliefs provided different individuals with a viable way to understand their experience, a relativism often associated with liberalism was a hallmark of James's thinking. This same emphasis carried over into his constructive philosophy. His book, *The Will to Believe* (1897), contained the core of the theories of pragmatism and pluralism that marked James's later philosophical work.

BIBLIOGRAPHY. J. S. Bixler, *Religion in the Philosophy of William James* (1926); *DAB* V; *DARB*; H. M. Feinstein, *Becoming William James* (1986); G. E. Myers, *William James: His Life and Thought*

(1986); *NCAB* 18; J. D. Wild, *The Radical Empiricism of William James* (1980).

C. H. Lippy

Janes, Leroy Lansing (1837-1909). Independent evangelist* to Japan. Born and raised in rural Ohio, Janes matured in a society dominated by the concerns of evangelical* Protestantism.* He graduated from West Point in 1861 and immediately served in the Civil War.* Post-War duty on the West Coast led him to resign from the army and accept an invitation to teach in Japan, where officials desired a military man to teach Western techniques. Here Janes led a group of students—later known as the "Kumamoto Band"—to conversion.* Some of its members became leaders in the Congregational Church* and its educational institutions; others played distinguished roles in secular society. Janes's years in Kumamoto (1871-1876) proved the high point of his career. He taught a second time in Japan after a period in the U.S. but left after a few years, disillusioned. Though he died in impoverished obscurity, the members of the Kumamoto Band retained their loyalty, helped him and informed others of his deeds. A trunkful of unpublished manuscripts reflect his enthusiasms and disappointments.

BIBLIOGRAPHY. F. G. Notehelfer, *American Samurai: Captain L. L. Janes and Japan* (1985).

J. F. Howes

Jansen, Cornelius (1822-1894). A leader of the Mennonite* immigration from Russia to the U.S. in the 1870s. Jansen moved from Prussia to Berdyansk, Russia, in 1856, exporting wheat and serving as a local Prussian consul. In the 1860s Jansen and his friend Leonard Sudermann* were among those who quickly came to believe that new laws threatened the Mennonites' century-old exemption from military service and other privileges. Writing to various American Mennonite leaders for information, Jansen became an ardent advocate of immigration to North America, for which he was expelled from Russia in March 1873. The family reached Berlin (now Kitchener), Ontario, in August 1873. The following year they moved to Mount Pleasant, Iowa, and in 1876 to Beatrice, Nebraska, which became their permanent residence.

Jansen and his son Peter worked tirelessly for immigrants, raising money, securing homes in the Midwest and petitioning the U.S. government. Their efforts included a visit to President Ulysses S. Grant, which led to a chance meeting with Gen. George A. Custer, with whom they chatted in German. Jansen published a number of pamphlets on pacifism,* the occasions for civil disobedience, religious freedom* and ecumenical* relationships.

BIBLIOGRAPHY. G. E. Reimer and G. R. Gaeddert, *Exile the Czar: Cornelius Jansen and the Great Mennonite Migration, 1874* (1956); P. Jansen, *Memoirs of Peter Jansen* (1921); G. Leibbrandt, "The Emigration of the German Mennonites from Russia to the United States and Canada in 1873-1880, I, II," *MQR* 6.4 (Oct. 1932):205-226 and 7.1 (Jan. 1933):5-41.

J. D. Weaver

Jarratt, Devereux (1733-1801). Anglican* revivalist* of the Great Awakening.* Born in Virginia and raised a nominal Anglican, Jarratt was converted to evangelical* faith under Presbyterian* influences. But preferring the catholicity of Anglicanism,* Jarratt traveled to London in 1762 to be ordained* an Anglican priest.* Returning to Virginia in 1763, Jarratt began his thirty-eight years (1763-1801) of ministerial service in Bath Parish, Dinwiddie County, Virginia.

Jarratt was to play a leading role in the Southern Awakening. From 1764 to 1772 he led a revival among Southern Anglicans, itinerating* extensively throughout Virginia and North Carolina and organizing religious societies. In 1773 Jarratt joined forces with the Methodists,* a cooperation that climaxed in the revival of 1775-1776, the so-called Methodist phase of the Southern Awakening. Together with Archibald McRoberts, Jarratt's ministry represented an evangelical Anglican counter-awakening to the revival that was spreading among Presbyterians* and Baptists* in Virginia. His own account of the revival is found in "A Brief Narrative of the Revival of Religion in Virginia. In a letter to a Friend."

Jarratt was opposed by his fellow-Anglican ministers who regarded him as a dissenter and a fanatic. By his own admission, Jarratt's emphasis on the perils of hellfire and the need for personal, heartfelt religion was a reaction against the innocuous homilies on moral virtue pronounced by "velvet-mouthed" Anglican ministers. Intolerant of those who disagreed with him, Jarratt felt isolated within his own denomination. When the Methodists separated from the Anglicans in 1784, Jarratt, who had hoped they would be an instrument for continued revival within Anglicanism, bitterly attacked their itinerant preaching and religious societies. Although he occasionally cooperated with the Methodists in his latter years, Jarratt's autobiography, *The Life of Devereux Jarratt* (1806), revealed an enduring bitterness and sense of isolation.

BIBLIOGRAPHY. *AAP* 5; *DAB* V; *DARB;* W. M. Gewehr, *The Great Awakening in Virginia, 1740-1790* (1930); D. L. Holmes, "Devereux Jarratt: A Letter and a Reevaluation," *HMPEC* 47 (1978):37-49; *NCAB* 10.   C. D. Weaver

Jefferson, Charles Edward (1860-1937). Congregationalist* minister.* Born in Cambridge, Ohio, Jefferson attended Ohio Wesleyan University (B.S., 1882) and served as a superintendent of public schools at Worthington, Ohio (1882-1884). In 1884 he entered law school at Boston University, but under the influence of Boston's pulpit prince Phillips Brooks,* he decided to study divinity instead, graduating from Boston University in 1887 (S.T.B.). Ordained* that same year, he became pastor at Central Congregational Church in Chelsea, Massachussetts (1887-1898). In 1898 he moved to Broadway Tabernacle in New York City, where he was to remain until his retirement in 1930.

Jefferson became known as a lucid thinker who expressed the gospel in a clear, passionate yet conversational pulpit style. Theologically a liberal evangelical,* Jefferson could stress orthodox doctrines such as the deity of Christ, as he did in *The Character of Jesus* (1908); yet he was comfortable with the modern critical approach to the Bible,* as he demonstrated in *Cardinal Ideas of Isaiah* (1925).

In 1910 Jefferson delivered the Lyman Beecher* Lectures at Yale,* published as *The Building of the Church* (1910). He authored numerous books, many of them collections of his sermons. His ministry was marked by a warm regard for the Puritan* tradition as well as a concern to communicate the gospel in terms understood by his contemporary world. His passion for social justice was expressed in his preaching as well as his involvement in the Church Peace Union.* On his presence and bearing, a New York newspaper described him as "austere, a Puritan, and given to setting up exacting standards for those who would follow the great Galilean."

BIBLIOGRAPHY. *DAB* 2; C. E. Fant and W. M. Pinson, *20 Centuries of Great Preaching* (1971); E. D. Jones, *The Royalty of the Pulpit* (1952); W. Shepherd, *Great Preachers as Seen by a Journalist* (1924); F. K. Stamm, *The Best of Charles E. Jefferson* (1960).   D. Macleod

Jefferson, Thomas (1743-1826). Principal author of the Declaration of Independence, Enlightenment* philosopher, diplomat, statesman and third U.S. president. Born in Albemarle County, Virginia, Jefferson graduated from the College of William and Mary* (1762), was admitted to the Virginia bar in 1767 and became a distinguished lawyer. Already the inheritor of a considerable landed estate from his father, Peter Jefferson, he doubled the size of his holdings by a happy marriage to widow Martha Wayles Skelton on January 1, 1772.

Jefferson served the province and commonwealth of Virginia and the young American republic for almost forty years as a public official. He wrote the main draft of the Declaration of Independence (1776) and the Virginia Statute of Religious Freedom (adopted 1786). Believing that the government was not being conducted in the spirit of 1776, he turned against the administration in Washington's* second term and remained in opposition during John Adams's presidency (1897-1801). In the process he became the head of the first left-of-center political party in American history, the Republicans (later the Democratic-Republicans, and eventually the Democrat Party). His election as president in 1800 and again in 1804 furthered the development of political democracy and checked in the U.S. the tide of political reaction then sweeping the Western world.

On leaving the presidency, he retired to his estate of Monticello near Charlottesville. A distinguished architect and naturalist, a remarkable linguist, a noted bibliophile and the principal founder of the University of Virginia (chartered 1819), he was the chief patron of learning and the arts in this country in his generation. With the possible exception of Benjamin Franklin, he was the closest American approximation of "the universal man."

In many ways, Jefferson was a living paradox. Widely hailed as a "man of the people," he was a person of wealth and a natural aristocrat. Highly tolerant of the views of others, he was highly intolerant of those he believed unfaithful to republicanism. An individual who kept his personal opinions concerning religion to himself, Jefferson was often charged with being "an infidel and atheist" and was well known for his insistence on a thorough-going separation of church and state.* In reality, he was one of the most thoughtfully religious men ever to occupy the White House.

Baptized* an Anglican* as an infant, Jefferson took great pains as an adult not to identify as a communicant of any denomination.* He never acknowledged membership in any church, yet insisted on calling himself a Christian, even though he was most certainly what might be described as a conservative deist.* Unlike Thomas Paine,* who attacked all sects,* Jefferson attacked none, and he contributed to many churches. But he was bluntly anticlerical and opposed authoritarianism in clergy* as well as kings.

In private correspondence with friends, he revealed that he believed in God and immortality but was unitarian* in theology,* though he seldom used that term. He revered Jesus as a great teacher and thought his doctrines were the road to true happiness. On the other hand, he could not accept Jesus' deity and rewrote the New Testament in his spare time, stripping it of all supernatural elements. This *Jefferson Bible,* as it is popularly known (he called it *The Life and Morals of Jesus of Nazareth*), remained unpublished until 1928. In short, his was an Enlightenment form of "republican religion" which stressed human reason and natural law rather than supernatural revelation or mystical faith.

Jefferson's well-known republicanism and anti-clericalism did not endear him to establishmentarian evangelicals* like the Congregationalists* of New England nor to most Anglicans and Catholics.* In addition, his strong advocacy of the separation of church and state alienated these same elements but attracted the support of many other evangelicals, especially the Baptists.* Jefferson's famous affirmation of the intent of the founders to establish "a wall of separation between Church and State" was contained in a letter to the Danbury Baptist Association of Connecticut in 1802 in response to a letter from them expressing concern that an established church in their state still limited genuine religious liberty there.

His views on clericalism and church-state relations and his republicanism led many orthodox* Christians, especially in New England, to attack him when he stood for president in 1796, 1800 and 1804. Religion became a major issue in a presidential campaign for the first time in 1800 when Jefferson was attacked as an atheist,* infidel and enemy of Christianity, and evangelicals were warned that they would have to hide their Bibles if he became president.

As president, Jefferson clearly articulated in his two inaugural addresses and many public speeches that he believed in God, valued piety* for its civic utility, and accepted the basic framework of American civil religion.* Both his presidential words and deeds and his philosophical writings revealed that he also believed in the self-perfectibility of humanity and thus the perfectibility of society through enlightened progress. These ideals and his determination to destroy artificial privilege of every sort, to promote social mobility and to make way for a natural aristocracy of talent and

virtue which would provide leadership for a free society, led Saul Pandover to call him "the St. Paul of American democracy." With a superb sense of timing, he died at Monticello on July 4, 1826, just hours before John Adams, on the fiftieth anniversary of the Declaration of Independence.

BIBLIOGRAPHY. H. W. Foote, *Thomas Jefferson: Champion of Religious Freedom, Advocate of Christian Morals* (1947); S. E. Mead, "Thomas Jefferson's 'Fair Experiment' Religious Freedom," *Religion in Life* 23 (1954):566-579; S. K. Padover, ed., *Thomas Jefferson on Democracy* (1967); M. D. Peterson, *Thomas Jefferson and the New Nation* (1970); H. S. Commager, *Jefferson, Nationalism, and the Enlightenment* (1975); S. C. Pearson, "Nature's God: A Reassessment of the Religion of the Founding Fathers," *Religion in Life* 46 (1977): 152-165; C. Mabee, "Thomas Jefferson's Anti-Clerical Bible," *HMPEC* 48 (1979):473-481; D. Malone, *Jefferson and His Times,* 6 vols. (1948-1981); C. B. Sanford, *The Religious Life of Thomas Jefferson* (1984). R. D. Linder

Jehovah's Witnesses. A religious body originating with Charles Taze Russell,* also known as The Watchtower Bible and Tract Society of New York, Inc. The movement grew out of an independent Bible study* started in Pittsburgh by Charles Taze Russell in 1870 and acquired its present name in 1956. Russell, who had privately studied Scripture* for years and come to radical Adventist* conclusions, soon became the group's pastor and in 1876 began the publication of a small magazine, *Zion's Watchtower,* which eventually became today's *Watchtower* (over 18 million copies published bimonthly in 106 languages). Russell's organization became the Zion's Watch Tower Tract Society in 1884, and in 1909 he moved its headquarters to Brooklyn, New York, where it has remained. The original theology* of the movement was worked out by Russell in his seven-volume *Studies in the Scriptures* (1886-1917), which over the years has sold millions of copies. The final volume appeared a year after Russell's death and led to a schism in the organization.

Most of Russell's followers joined J. F. Rutherford, to form the Millennial Dawnists, who adopted the name Jehovah's Witnesses in 1931. A smaller group rejected Rutherford's leadership and became the Dawn Bible Student's Association and in the late 1980s had a membership of about 60,000. During the same period the Jehovah's Witnesses proper reported around 2,842,531 members worldwide with over 800,000 in North America. Following Rutherford's death the movement was led by

Nathan H. Knorr,* who was succeeded by Frederick W. Franz (1893-).

Theologically the Witnesses are confusing, due to their lack of a well-defined systematic theology* and frequent, though officially unacknowledged, changes in their teachings. In many respects, however, they resemble traditional Roman Catholicism* rather than Protestantism* because of their understanding of doctrinal and ecclesiastical authority,* which is the key to their theology.

From at least 1895 onwards "Pastor Russell," as he is known, functioned more as a prophet than pastor.* His prophetic office was given official recognition as a result of challenges to his authority by dissident members in 1895. At that time his wife, Maria Russell, answered her husband's critics by arguing that he was the "faithful and wise servant" of Matthew 24:45. This notion was later applied to Russell's successors, and to the leadership of the Witnesses collectively, to give the group a doctrinal stance almost identical to the magisterium* of Roman Catholicism. Equally important for the development of authority has been the role of tradition, ascribed first to Russell and then to his successors as the medium through which Scripture is to be interpreted, thus indicating a form of apostolic succession.* Similarly, the spiritual obedience demanded by the leadership of the Witnesses is like the Roman Catholic understanding of the pope's ability to speak *ex cathedra*. Finally, the authority of the leadership is bound together by an understanding of progressive revelation whereby the leadership receives both direct revelation from God and an authoritative understanding of Scripture through their function as the "faithful and discreet slave," which is a prophetic class within the organization.

The early works of Russell were characterized by a rationalism and the occasional use of typology and allegory. Since Russell, the leadership has concentrated more on typology and allegory. While the movement constantly expresses a strong formal hostility to biblical criticism, which is seen as evidence of the apostasy of established churches, it has been quick to follow Russell's lead in using the results of biblical criticism to discredit orthodox* interpretations of Scripture.

Theologically the Witnesses deny orthodox teachings about the person and work of Christ, arguing that Jesus was "a god" who died on a "torture stake" as a ransom to the devil. Their Christology* is thus pseudo-Arian, emphasizing Jesus as the "Second Adam" who was essentially a perfect man. Baptism* and the Lord's Supper* are not sacraments.* Baptism, by total immersion, is a "witness" to God which all members must undergo. In addition there is a "baptism into Christ" which consecrates the 144,000 (see Rev 7 and 14) elect believers who will attain heavenly glory. The Lord's Supper is an annual feast which can only be fully participated in by those Witnesses who know themselves to be among the 144,000 who represent the totality of Christians who go to be with Christ. According to the society's statistics there were 9,601 of these "blessed" individuals alive in 1981. By contrast, most Witnesses have to be content with eternal life on earth.

Three other doctrines form an essential part of Witness doctrine and have brought them notoriety. First is their eschatology* which, due to their habit of setting dates—Russell himself maintained that Christ had spiritually returned to earth in 1874 and would begin his visible reign in 1914—has repeatedly proved false. Second, their belief in the sacredness of life and refusal to imbibe blood in any form has led to a rejection of both military service and blood transfusions. Third, the preaching work whereby Witnesses are expected to proclaim their gospel as a means of obtaining salvation by works has made their presence known in many North American communities. In recent years the movement has been split by schisms and continual accusations of harsh treatment meted out to ex-members. During the 1930s and 1940s the Witnesses fought and won many court cases, forty-three in the U.S. Supreme Court,* in the interest of their religious freedom.*

BIBLIOGRAPHY. H. Botting and G. Botting, *The Orwellian World of Jehovah's Witnesses* (1984); M. J. Penton, *Apocalypse Delayed; The Story of Jehovah's Witnesses* (1985); A. Rogerson, *Millions Now Living Will Never Die: A Study of Jehovah's Witnesses* (1969).   I. Hexham

Jeremiad. A sermon of woe and promise, deriving its name from the Old Testament prophet Jeremiah. The Jeremiad originated with the Puritans* and was based on a belief in a previous golden age from which subsequent generations had dangerously departed. Focusing attention on contemporary moral failure and natural disasters, the Jeremiad attempted to create an anxiety that would lead the audience to reform and renewal of the covenant.

While the sermon explicitly warned of God's punishment, this threat was perceived as God's loving antidote to spiritual complacency. Its purpose was to redirect God's wayward people toward the fulfillment of their corporate destiny and guide them individually toward salvation.*

The sermon was structured in a three-part format. First, a precedent from Scripture was given that established God's demands for his people. Second, a series of denunciations were made, demonstrating how the people had violated their covenant with God. Finally, a reassuring prophetic vision was proclaimed that unveiled the promise of God's blessing upon his repentant people. The Jeremiad was preached as an occasional sermon* given on public occasions, such as election days and days set aside by the civil authorities for fasting, prayer or thanksgiving.

See also OCCASIONAL SERMON; PURITANISM.

BIBLIOGRAPHY. S. Bercovitch, *The American Jeremiad* (1979); E. Emerson, *Puritanism in America, 1620-1750* (1977); P. Miller, *Errand into the Wilderness* (1956); H. S. Stout, *The New England Soul* (1986). S. A. Wenig

Jessup, Henry Harris (1823-1910). Presbyterian* missionary* to the Near East. Born in Montrose, Pennsylvania, Jessup was educated at Yale College* and Union Theological Seminary,* New York. Ordained* in 1855 by the Presbyterian Church in the U.S.A.,* he was sent to Syria by the American Board of Commissioners for Foreign Missions* (ABCFM) and arrived in Beirut in 1856. For thirty years he was pastor of the Syrian church in that city and head of its school. Jessup became fluent in Arabic, and his ministry led him to associations with the journal *El-Neshrah,* a hospital for the emotionally disturbed and the Syrian Protestant College, now known as the American University of Beirut. Although best known for his *Fifty-three Years in Syria* (2 vols., 1910)—a history of the mission as well as an autobiography—he also wrote concerning Arab women, Arab family life and the relations between Greek Christians and Protestant missions. The Board of Foreign Missions of the Presbyterian Church in the U.S.A. took over the work of the ABCFM in 1870. In 1884 the general assembly* of that denomination elected Jessup moderator when he was in the U.S. on furlough.

BIBLIOGRAPHY. *DAB* V; H. H. Jessup, *Fifty-Three Years in Syria,* 2 vols. (1910); J. H. Smylie, "Henry Harris Jessup: Mission in the Land of the Bible," in *Go Therefore, 150 Years of Presbyterians in Global Mission,* ed. J. H. Smylie et al. (1987).

J. H. Smylie

Jesus Christ. *See* CHRISTOLOGY.

Jesus Movement. Christian countercultural youth movement of the late 1960s and early 1970s.

Parallel to the counterculture movement of the late 1960s and early 1970s, a new counterculture spirituality* emerged on the American religious landscape. It was variously called the Jesus movement, the Jesus revolution, or the Jesus people movement. Participants were sometimes labeled *Jesus freaks* because of their former status as drug users ("drug freaks") and street people. But not all Jesus people were once drug users or "hippies." Many came from mainstream Christian churches and found those churches less fulfilling and less exciting than the new Christian counter-cultural groups.

The Jesus people phenomenon must be viewed in the context of the changing American culture of the decade of the sixties. It was a period of transition, protest, uncertainty and social upheaval. It witnessed the emergence of the hippie as a new social type. The contemporary youth culture experimented with psychedelic drugs, sought to expand their consciousness via Eastern/occult religion and ideologically opposed the established social institutions, including the church. The so-called flower children were characterized by idealism, long hair and rock music. They were cynical about the prospects of effecting change within "the system." The secular counterculture valued subjectivity and experience, depreciated history and reacted against the prevailing scientism and technology of Western society. In pursuit of happiness and life purpose, urban-based counter-culturists adopted the Aquarian Age motif, which implied a social utopianism.

Out of this social and cultural matrix, the Jesus people movement developed during the late 1960s. It was an unorganized, diverse movement consisting of many widely scattered subgroups. Despite its diverse natures the Jesus people shared common interests and certain basic concerns. Above all, the Jesus movement was characterized by its intense evangelistic zeal and emphasis on experience. Feelings rather than doctrine were stressed. Like the secular counterculture, the Christian counterculture was marked by expressions of protest and alienation against established, mainstream religion. The music of the movement—Jesus rock—expressed young people's frustration with traditional religious forms. Jesus people held anti-intellectual and anti-cultural views of the world. Many, though not all, elements of the Jesus movement were charismatic* in orientation. Services were intense and emotional. An apocalyptic* fervor suffused the movement, influenced greatly by Hal Lindsey's book *The Late Great Planet Earth.* Mainstream Christians were frustrated by their simplistic mentality.

The symbols and slogans of the movement reflected the influence of the larger secular counterculture, but they also revealed the unique themes of the Jesus people. The visual and musical art of the movement evidenced the spontaneity, subjectivity and faddishness of the subculture. Events like beach baptisms* and Jesus concerts received wide media coverage. Jesus people typically carried huge Bibles,* had long hair and wore unconventional clothes. There were Jesus coffee houses, Jesus newspapers and Jesus bumper stickers proclaiming "Have a Nice Forever." The slogan "One Way!" could be heard and seen everywhere, accompanied by the sign of a finger (beside the cross) pointing upward.

Prominent periodicals of the movement included the *Hollywood Free Paper,* associated with Duane Pederson, and *Right On!* published by the Christian World Liberation Front of Berkeley, California. Personalities linked with the movement included Larry Norman, Chuck Girard, Arthur Blessit, Jack Sparks and Chuck Smith.

As the faddish elements and excessive emotionalism of the movement waned and as the teen-age participants matured into early adulthood, the Jesus movement tended to dissolve in two directions. One segment, consisting of groups like the Children of God,* The Way and the Alamo Christian Foundation, became increasingly authoritarian and assumed cultic* characteristics. Such groups became even more estranged from both the religious community and the larger society. Another segment of the Jesus people drifted toward more conventional evangelicalism.* This segment is represented by churches like Calvary Chapel (Orange County, California) and the Christian World Liberation Front, the latter organization giving birth to both *Radix* magazine and the Spiritual Counterfeits Project, an evangelical counter-cult ministry.

The Jesus people, as a sociologically distinct movement, revitalized segments of evangelicalism through its music,* its informal worship* style and its ability to retain young people of more conventional church background within the Christian community. It provided an alternative community for many young adults who had already been disillusioned by drugs, radical politics or Eastern mysticism. Some of these "Jesus freaks" eventually burned out and became dropouts from religion. Others married, raised families and drifted into established denominational* and fundamentalist* churches. For these, the Jesus movement was a mechanism for reintegration and resocialization

into mainstream American life.

BIBLIOGRAPHY. R. S. Ellwood, *One Way: The Jesus Movement and Its Meaning* (1973); R. Enroth, E. Ericson and C. B. Peters, *The Jesus People* (1972); L. D. Streiker, *The Jesus Trip* (1971).

R. Enroth

Jeter, (J)eremiah (B)ell (1802-1880). Southern Baptist* pastor,* editor and denominational* leader. Born in Bedford County, Virginia, Jeter was converted* and baptized* during a local revival* in 1821 and soon began to preach.* Although he was self-taught as a minister,* Jeter was a very effective pastor of several large churches, including the First Baptist Church, Richmond, Virginia, where he served for more than thirteen years.

Jeter was also a leading denominational activist. He was involved in the organization of the Baptist General Association of Virginia, attended meetings of the Triennial Convention and was present at the formation of the Southern Baptist Convention in 1845. Jeter opposed the efforts of the anti-missionary* forces among the Baptists and served as the first president of the Foreign Mission Board of the Southern Baptist Convention (1845-1849).

In his later years Jeter purchased and edited the *Religious Herald,* an influential Virginia Baptist paper. He was an ardent if amiable controversialist, and although he had a personal aversion to slavery,* he defended it on the basis of biblical precedent. Jeter also wrote a popular refutation of the views of Alexander Campbell,* *Campbellism Examined* (1855). Jeter was a strong supporter of Richmond College and served, at the time of his death, as president of the board of trustees of the Southern Baptist Theological Seminary.

BIBLIOGRAPHY. *DAB* V; W. F. Hatcher, *Life of J. B. Jeter* (1887); J. B. Jeter, *Recollections of a Long Life* (1891). T. F. George

Jewish-Christian Dialog. The general climate of Christian-Jewish relations in America until the middle of the twentieth century was stormy. In the last few decades, however, more positive changes have taken place between synagogue and church than in the entire period since these bodies irreversibly split following the biblical period. Several major factors have contributed to this rapid shift in perspective: an increased awareness of the long history of anti-Semitism; the impact which the Holocaust* bears (1933-1945) on the world's conscience; the remarkable birth of the state of Israel (1948); ecumenical* endeavors stressing mutual recognition and reconciliation; a growing respect for religious pluralism*; acknowledgment of the need to dispel faulty images and popular stereotypes of the other group; and renewed interest in exploring a common Hebrew heritage.

This new understanding between Christians and Jews has been fostered through a variety of means: through numerous books, publications and media presentations; through courses, seminars, conferences and dialog groups; and through various programs sponsored by national organizations such as the Anti-Defamation League, American Jewish Committee and National Conference of Christians and Jews.*

Mainline* liberal* Protestants* were the first major group with which the Jewish community in America entered serious dialog. This came about largely through the pioneering efforts of such leading interfaith voices as Martin Buber, Abraham Heschel and Marc Tanenbaum. Because many liberal Protestant groups espouse revisionist theologies and do not generally engage in proselytism of Jews, from the outset fewer theological obstacles have had to be worked out between both groups. Lack of strong support for Israel, however, is yet a major tension in the current dialog.

Among Catholics,* the work of Pope* John XXIII* in calling together Vatican II* (1963-1965) has done more to eradicate Catholic-Jewish misperceptions than any other single force. In section four of the 1965 Vatican II decree *Nostra Aetate* ("In Our Times"), issued by Pope Paul VI,* the church's Jewish ancestry and spiritual debt to Judaism is freely acknowledged. In addition, the charge of deicide is denounced and all anti-Semitism decried.

Evangelical*-Jewish dialog did not begin to take serious shape until the mid-1970s. Since then a growing rapport, based on mutual understanding, has continued to develop. Israel's unstable position in the Middle East has led Jews to value the solid support of Israel often given by evangelicals. Other important issues frequently found on the Jewish dialog agenda with evangelicals are missionizing, the Hebrew-Christian movement (*see* Jewish Christians) and the relation of religion to politics with special reference to the rise of the new Religious Right.* Evangelicals have tended to center their dialog agenda more on biblical and theological themes.

In recent years major denominations,* such as the Episcopal Church,* the Presbyterian Church U.S.A.,* and the United Church of Christ,* have developed statements on Judaism and the Jewish people. Other Christian groups are planning the same. In this regard an important resource in helping to shape current Christian thinking on the

Jewish people is the National Workshop on Christian-Jewish Relations, the largest and most comprehensive ongoing conference in Christian-Jewish relations in the U.S.

BIBLIOGRAPHY. D. A. Rausch, "Chosen People: Christian Views of Judaism Are Changing," *CT* 32, no. 14 (1988):53-59; A. J. Rudin, "Protestants—Those Liberals, Those Evangelicals," *Present Tense* 11, no. 4 (1984):16-19; M. R. Wilson, "An Evangelical View of the Current State of Evangelical-Jewish Relations," *JETS* 25 (1983):139-160; M. R. Wilson, "Changing Christian Perceptions of Jews in America," *Jews in Unsecular America,* ed. R. J. Neuhaus (1987):20-40.   M. R. Wilson

Jewish Christians (or Messianic Jews). Jews converted* to Christianity. The terms *Jewish Christian* or *Messianic Jew* refer broadly to people of Jewish birth who convert to Christianity. These individuals typically insist that their conversions do not invalidate their Jewishness and that they have actually become more aware of their traditional heritage after their acceptance of Christ as the Jewish Messiah. Many insist on distinguishing between Jewish Christians and Messianic Jews, though the difference is largely a matter of emphasis.

Few Jewish Christians lived in the U.S. until Jewish immigration began en masse in the 1880s. Louis Meyer, a German Jewish immigrant and well-known mission researcher, estimated that between 1870 and 1900 American churches baptized* 4,000 Jews. In 1903 Meyer spearheaded an attempt to organize an alliance of converts to represent their mutual interests before American churches. Though all in attendance agreed on the need for unity, doctrinal differences prevented any formal arrangement. This was only achieved in 1915 when several Jewish-Christian missionaries organized the Hebrew Christian Alliance for the purpose of strengthening fellow converts in the Christian faith, evangelizing* other Jews and serving as an aid to American churches in accomplishing these goals.

These years witnessed the first debate between Hebrew Christians and Messianic Jews. In 1915 most converts came from Orthodox Judaism. A few, calling themselves Messianic Jews, wished to continue following the Mosaic Law as a cultural practice only, not as a means of salvation. Most converts disagreed and adopted the Hebrew Christian position which emphasized their freedom from these rituals. Messianic Judaism attracted few followers until the early 1970s when, as a result of the so-called Jesus Revolution,* a significant number of young Jews converted to Christianity. For them, Messianic Judaism represented less a commitment to Orthodoxy than a link to their heritage. In 1975 a majority voted to change the Alliance's name to "Messianic Jewish Alliance." Four years later thirty-three leaders founded the Union of Messianic Congregations as a loose federation of individual worshiping bodies. In distinction from Jewish Christians who associated themselves with traditional churches, the Union sponsored "messianic congregations," which employed Jewish symbols and liturgy in an attempt to maintain their culture.

BIBLIOGRAPHY. D. A. Rausch, *Messianic Judaism: Its History, Theology, and Polity* (1983); H. J. Schonfield, *The History of Jewish Christianity* (1936); B. Z. Sobel, *Hebrew Christianity: The Thirteenth Tribe* (1974). J. H. Warnock

Jews, Christian Missions to. Christian missions to Jews began in the U.S. in 1816 with the arrival of Joseph S. C. F. Frey from England. A German-born Jewish Christian, Frey helped found the London Society for Promoting Christianity Amongst the Jews, and envisioned the establishment of a similar mission in the U.S. In 1820 he organized the American Society for Meliorating the Condition of the Jews. For the next forty years this agency existed precariously, first attempting to colonize converted European Jews in Pennsylvania and then sponsoring missionaries in American cities. The Society claimed fifty converts in the 1850s, its most successful decade.

A few denominational efforts followed the American Society's demise. Small Baptist* and Presbyterian* missions existed in antebellum America. The Church Society for Promoting Christianity amongst the Jews, operated as an auxiliary of the Protestant Episcopal Church,* maintained schools and mission centers in Jewish neighborhoods and claimed about 100 converts between 1878 and 1904 when it ceased operations.

Since the turn of the century, dispensationalists* have shown the greatest interest in evangelizing Jews. Inspired by the model of faith missions* then operating overseas, several small, independent ministries began work in the Jewish areas of American cities. Few of these ministries employed more than five workers, and most received their funding directly from individual Christians rather than from denominations. Prior to World War 1,* the Chicago Hebrew Mission provided the model for all American societies. It operated schools for Jewish children, engaged in open-air preaching in the summers, opened reading rooms to attract inquirers, and utilized converted Jews

as its principal missionaries.

With the growth of liberal* theology* and ecumenicism* following World War 1,* American Christians lost a good deal of interest in evangelizing Jews. The Holocaust,* which afflicted European Jewry during the Second World War,* further weakened their commitment to Jewish missions, so that until the Jesus Movement* of the 1970s the field received little attention. At that time many young Jews became Christians and formed the nucleus of both a rejuvenated missionary effort and an ambitious attempt to found "messianic congregations" of converted Jews.

See also JEWISH CHRISTIANS; JEWS FOR JESUS.

BIBLIOGRAPHY. N. T. Ammerman, "Fundamentalists Proselytizing Jews," in *Pushing the Faith: Proselytizing and Civility in a Pluralistic World,* ed. M. E. Marty and F. E. Greenspahn (1988); J. H. Cohn, *I Have Fought a Good Fight; The Story of Jewish Mission Pioneering in America* (1953); M. Rosen with B. Proctor, *Jews for Jesus* (1974); H. J. Schonfield, *The History of Jewish Christianity* (1936). J. H. Warnock

Jews for Jesus. A term referring to both a contemporary movement of young Jews to Christianity and a missionary* sending agency. The movement began in the late 1960s with the so-called Jesus Revolution,* a revival that took place in the youth counterculture. By 1973 enough Jews had accepted Christianity that both the Christian and the Jewish communities noticed the phenomenon, and the subject of evangelizing the Jewish population became a key issue in discussions between Jewish and Christian leaders.

Jews for Jesus as an organization grew out of this revival when Moishe Rosen, a career missionary with the American Board of Missions to the Jews,* relocated to San Francisco in 1970. After some success in his ministry, in 1973 he and a few followers incorporated Jews for Jesus as an independent evangelistic agency. Known initially for their assertive "confrontation evangelism," group members also sought to demonstrate that accepting Christianity did not entail an automatic rejection of their Jewish heritage. To this end they continued to participate in Jewish community life and causes while at the same time vigorously maintaining their Christian beliefs.

Annually since 1974, Jews for Jesus has conducted "witnessing campaigns" in New York City in which staff workers and volunteers distribute tracts and employ open-air preaching* and drama as a means of contacting potential converts who then receive follow-up visits by staff workers. The organization is also noted for its distinctive Jewish gospel music, which sets biblical passages to Jewish-style melodies. Recently, it has made extensive use of evangelistic advertisements in national magazines and newspapers.

BIBLIOGRAPHY. M. Rosen with B. Proctor, *Jews for Jesus* (1974); J. G. Lipson, "Jews for Jesus: An Illustration of Syncretism," *Anthropological Quarterly* 53 (April 1980):101-110.

J. H. Warnock

Jogues, Isaac (1607-1646). Jesuit* missionary* and martyr.* Born in Orleans, France, Jogues entered the Society of Jesus in 1625 and was educated in philosophy and theology at La Fleche (1626-1629) and Paris (1633-1636). Shortly after his ordination* in 1636, Jogues began his decade of missionary work among the Huron* Indians in Canada.

Jogues made several journeys into the interior of North America and was the first white man to see Lake George, which he named Saint-Sacrement. In 1640 Father Jerome Lalement* entrusted Jogues with the building of a central residence for missionaries at Sainte-Marie. A year later Father Jogues and his assistant had pushed as far west as the Sainte-Marie Falls (Sault Ste. Marie), where they were warmly welcomed by the local Indians. In June 1642 Jogues was designated by Lalement to accompany a trading convoy to Quebec. On the return trip the canoes were ambushed by a party of Iroquois. After a brief exchange of gunfire, Jogues, several Frenchmen and some Hurons were carried off as prisoners into Mohawk territory and put to the most appalling tortures: floggings, bitings, mutilations, strippings, forced marches and insults. Jogues bore this torment with extraordinary fortitude.

Motivated by a desire for martyrdom and a zeal to minister to the tortured captives, Jogues admitted to casting himself into the hands of the Iroquois of his own free will. Kept under constant threat of death until 1643, he was rescued by the Dutch and sent to France, only to return to Quebec in 1644. Despite the torment he had suffered, he eagerly sought from his superiors the privilege of devoting himself to evangelizing* the Iroquois. After a brief ministry at Montreal, which allowed him to compose the account of his captivity and travels in upper New York, Jogues was authorized to take part in a peace mission in 1646. Taken prisoner by the Iroquois at Ossernenon (Auriesville, New York), Jogues was killed by a hatchet blow to the head. Known for his great piety* and vivid spiritual writing, his self-sacrifice stimulated

and inspired the cause of French Canadian missions.*

See also MISSIONS TO NORTH AMERICA, FRENCH.

BIBLIOGRAPHY. *DAB* V; *DARB;* J. A. O'Brien, *The American Martyrs: The Story of the Eight Jesuit Martyrs of North America* (1953); F. X. Talbot, *Saint Among Savages: The Life of Isaac Jogues* (1935); R. G. Thwaites, ed., *The Jesuit Relations,* vol. 28 (1898). D. A. Scalberg

John XXIII (1881-1963). Pope.* Born Angelo Giuseppi Roncelli, the child of peasants from Sotte il Monte, near Bergamo, Italy, he spent his early career in his home diocese.* After a brief time in Rome (1920), he served Vatican* diplomacy for nearly thirty years—in Bulgaria (1925), Turkey and Greece (1934) and as nuncio in France (1944)—until becoming cardinal* and patriarch of Venice (1953), and pope (1958). Considered a caretaker, he surprised everyone by convening all the bishops of the Church in the Second Vatican Council* (1962). He asked the first session of Vatican II (1962-1963) to initiate the "aggiornamento"* of the Church, and he enabled the progressive figures in the Council to undertake the task. He died before the second session began, but he opened a new period in the Church, in America as elsewhere.

His impact on America was magnified by the coincidence of the first Catholic president, John F. Kennedy,* elected by Catholic and African-American voters (1960). He named an American, Elizabeth Seton,* to the roll of the blessed (1959), saying that American Catholics had reached "full maturity." Two of his encyclicals,* *Mater et Magistra* (1961) on social issues, and *Pacem in Terris* (1963) on human rights and peaceful coexistence between the U.S. and the Soviet Union influenced public discourse in America. He reversed Vatican policy toward non-Roman Catholics and established the Secretariat for Christian Unity (1960) to work with them; made dramatic overtures to Anglicans* (1960), the Orthodox* (1961), and the World Council of Churches* (1961); and brought observers from eighteen non-Roman Catholic churches into Vatican II.

BIBLIOGRAPHY. E. E. Y. Hales, *Pope John and His Revolution* (1965); E. C. Bianchi, *John XXIII and American Protestants* (1968).

C. T. McIntire

John Birch Society. Far-right political society. Founded in 1959 by Robert Welch, a retired candy manufacturer, it was named after Captain John M. Birch, a Baptist* missionary* and Army Air Force officer killed by the Chinese Communists in 1945. Birch became a Cold War hero and an illustration of the tyranny of communism. The Society was a leader in American secular far-right politics in the 1960s and 1970s. It was firmly controlled by Welch, who espoused an anti-statist and conspiratorial view of American politics. He called for the removal of the U.S. from the United Nations; demanded the impeachment of Chief Justice Earl Warren; and charged Presidents Eisenhower,* Truman and Roosevelt with being agents of the Communist party.

For much of the 1960s the John Birch Society played a major role in defining the far-right agenda: boycott of UNICEF, restoration of prayer* in the public schools,* opposition to civil-rights legislation and elimination of the welfare state. Welch predicted that America would soon fall to the Communist conspiracy because the educational and economic elite were Communists or Communist sympathizers. Although the society is not explicitly Christian, it attempts to gain support from the religious community. Members consider themselves to be "men and women of integrity and purpose" who are committed to "building rededication to God, to family, to country and to strong moral principles."

Located in Belmont, Massachusetts, the Society publishes the magazine *The New American* (formerly *American Opinion*). Congressmen Lawrence McDonald (D.-Georgia) and John Rousselot (R.-California) have been members of the John Birch Society and articulated its agenda. At its peak, the Society is estimated to have had a membership of about 100,000. Robert Welch died on January 6, 1965, in Winchester, Massachusetts.

BIBLIOGRAPHY. L. DeKoster, *The Christian and the John Birch Society* (1966); B. R. Epstein and A. Forster, *Report on the John Birch Society, 1966* (1966); R. Welch, *The Blue Book of the John Birch Society* (1961).   G. W. Carlson

John Paul II (1920-). Pope. Born in Wadowice near Krakow, Poland, Karol Wojtyla broke the cycle of Italian popes. Educated in theology* and philosophy, a poet and actor, he was a professor of theology and ethics in Poland before becoming auxiliary bishop* of Krakow (1956), archbishop* of Krakow (1963) and a cardinal* (1967). He was active on the progressive side of Vatican II,* and consistently promoted the implementation of its decrees in Poland. He brought with him to the papacy his experience of affirming the Catholic identity of a predominately peasant and working-class church in Poland in distinction from the ethos of the Communist Polish government. Wojtyla became Pope John Paul II in 1978. He has combined relentless concern for the poor and laboring people with opposition to liberation theology* and Marxism, and has joined devotion to Church renewal with a rigorous defense of the Church tradition.

On his papal journeys to the U.S. and Canada, he has enhanced the prestige of the Catholic Church through his evident charisma and integrity. He also aroused hostility among priests,* religious and women when he emphasized obedience and celibacy among clergy,* flatly rejected the ordination of women,* and strictly upheld Church teaching against contraception,* divorce,* abortion* and homosexuality.* He appeared to stifle creative theology by his support of Church measures against theologians Edward Schillebeeckx, Leonardo Boff, Hans Küng* and the American Charles E. Curran. At the same time, he has helped give new recognition to the Hispanic* Americans who were fast becoming the majority of the American Church.

BIBLIOGRAPHY. P. Johnson, *Pope John Paul II and the Catholic Restoration* (1981); M. Malinski, *Pope John Paul II, the Life of Karol Wojtyla* (1979); J. V. Schall, *The Social Thought of John Paul II* (1981); G. H. Williams, *The Mind of John Paul II* (1981).

C. T. McIntire

Johnson, Carrie Parks (1866-1929). Methodist* advocate of human rights for women and minorities in the South. A native of Georgia, Johnson's family included several ministers* of the Methodist Episcopal Church,* South. Graduating from LaGrange College (1883), frail health prevented her from pursuing her ambition of becoming a missionary* to China. She later married a Methodist minister, Luke Johnson. Her work in that denomination's* Woman's Home Missionary Society and Woman's Missionary Council began in 1899 and was highlighted by her forceful crusade for lay representation for women in the conferences and councils of her church. In 1922 she became a delegate from the North Georgia Conference to the first General Conference to include women delegates. In 1922 she also became the director of the Commission on Interracial Cooperation, leading a concerted opposition to mob violence and lynching, practices common to the period. In this regard she anticipated legislative changes in these areas that would occur in the decades following her death.

J. S. O'Malley

Johnson, Charles Oscar (1886-1965). Baptist* minister.* Born in Tennessee and educated at Carson Newman College in Jefferson City (B.A., 1910) and Southern Baptist Theological Seminary (Th.M., 1920), Johnson was ordained* a Baptist minister in 1909. In 1910 he began the first in a series of pastorates that took him to Baptist churches in Newport Beach (1910-1911) and Los Angeles (1911-1915), California; Campbellsburg, Kentucky (1915-1920); and Tacoma, Washington (1920-1931). Johnson's final pastorate was at Third Baptist Church, St. Louis, Missouri (1931-1958), which under his leadership grew by over 10,000 members.

During his years in St. Louis, Johnson was president of the Metropolitan Church Federation (1936) and served on the city school board (1946-1949). In addition to serving as first vice-president of the Southern Baptist Convention* and president of the Northern Baptist Convention, he was president of the Baptist World Alliance* (1947-1952). Johnson spent the final years of his career as a faculty member of Berkeley Divinity School in California (1958-1960). His sermons* were published in five volumes (1953-1958).

B. A. McKenzie

Johnson, Samuel (1696-1772). Anglican* minister,* philosopher and president of King's College.* Born in Guilford, Connecticut, Johnson graduated from Yale* (B.A., 1714), where he also served as a tutor (1716-1719). His Congregational* pastorate in West Haven, Connecticut (1720-1722), gave him easy access to Yale's library, where his reading in church history and theology* worked a change in his convictions. Johnson left the Congregational Church in 1722, joining Timothy Cutler* in an apostasy that scandalized the New Haven community. Receiving holy orders in the Church of England, he returned to America and served successively with the Society for the Propagation of the Gospel* as a missionary rector* in Stratford, Connecticut (1723-1754), as president of King's College (1754-1763) and again as Stratford's rector (1764) until his death in 1772. A friend of George Berkeley, he wrote extensively, if not brilliantly, on idealist philosophy. His *Elementa Philosophica,* published by Benjamin Franklin in 1752, was the first philosophy textbook published in America and secured his position as the second-most important philosophical mind in colonial America. As the unofficial leader of New England's Anglicans, he led them in numerous public controversies, as in his criticisms of strict Calvinism* and the Great Awakening,* and in his advocacy of bishops*

for the American colonies. Among his more important theological works were *Letters to His Dissenting Parishioners* (1733-1737) and *Aristocles to Authades* (1745-1747).

BIBLIOGRAPHY. *AAP* 5; P. N. Carroll, *The Other Samuel Johnson: A Psychohistory of Early New England* (1978); *DAB* 10; *DARB;* J. J. Ellis, *The New England Mind in Transition: Samuel Johnson in Connecticut, 1696-1772* (1973); S. Johnson, *Samuel Johnson: His Career and Writings,* ed. H. Schneider and C. Schneider, 4 vols. (1929); *NCAB* 6.

T. T. Taylor

Johnson, William Bullein (1782-1862). Southern Baptist* minister* and leader. Born on John's Island, South Carolina, Johnson had little formal education but was self-educated—even in law. In 1814 he was awarded an honorary M.A. by Brown University. After his conversion* in 1804, Johnson became convinced he should enter the ministry.* He was ordained* in 1806 and became pastor* of Eutaw Baptist Church.

Throughout Johnson's several pastorates, he maintained an active interest in education, serving as headmaster of a number of schools and chancellor of the Johnson Female University (1853-1858). He was also one of the founders of Furman Academy and Theological Institution (later Furman University), from which would come the Southern Baptist Theological Seminary.

His interest in Baptist missions* led him to suggest the first meeting of the General Baptist Missionary Convention, which was held in Philadelphia. As a result of this meeting, the Triennial Convention* was formed, of which he served as president from 1841 to 1844. When a number of Baptists in the South decided it best to separate from the General Missionary Convention and the American Baptist Home Mission Society, Johnson led in organizing the Southern Baptist Convention and devised a plan incorporating the associational structure of cooperation rather than the society plan followed in the North.

According to this plan, the Southern Baptist Convention would meet every three years, just as the General Convention did. Originally there were only two boards, a foreign and a home mission board, to which other boards could be added. Johnson has somewhat inaccurately been called the "Father of the Southern Baptist Convention," but there is little doubt that he was the major architect of the Southern Baptist Convention and was its most important spokesman as well as its first president.

BIBLIOGRAPHY. R. A. Baker, *The Southern Baptist*

Convention and Its People, 1607-1972 (1974); *DAB* V; *ESB* 1. W. R. Estep

Joliet (or Jolliet, Jollyet), Louis (c.1645-1700). French-Canadian explorer and entrepreneur. Recognized as the co-discoverer of the Mississippi River with Father Jacques Marquette,* Joliet, a Quebec-born Jesuit,* achieved distinction in several fields. After training for the priesthood, he became the first Canadian to study music in France. A classics scholar and teacher at the Jesuit college in Quebec, Joliet left the priesthood in 1667 in favor of fur-trading and exploration.

The existence of the Mississippi was no mystery when Joliet began his famous expedition from Michilimackinac in May 1673. On the advice of Jean Talon, Louis de Buade (Count of Frontenac), the colonial governor, ordered Joliet, in company with Marquette from the Jesuit Mission at St. Ignace, to find and follow the river to its mouth in the hope of discovering a route to the Orient. The seven-man expedition reached the Mississippi via the Wisconsin River on June 15, and traveled 1,650 miles by canoe as far as the confluence of the Arkansas River. Turning back for fear of attack, the expedition never reached the mouth of the Mississippi but established that it flowed into the Gulf of Mexico, not the Pacific Ocean as hoped. Unfortunately, the records of their five-month expedition were lost on the return trip to Quebec, when the canoes capsized and several members of the party were drowned.

Joliet led further expeditions for the colonial government in 1679 (Hudson Bay) and 1694 (Labrador Coast), although most of his life was spent in the fur trade and in operating fisheries at Mingan and Anticosti islands. He was appointed hydrography master at Quebec in 1692 and king's hydrographer in 1697. Despite his achievements and international reputation, Joliet died in obscurity and poverty in 1700.

BIBLIOGRAPHY. *DAB* V; J. Delanglez, *Life and Voyages of Louis Jolliet (1645-1700)* (1948); E. Gagnon, *Louis Jolliet* (1902).

R. H. Chilton

Jones, Abner (1772-1841). Pioneer leader of the Christian Connection.* Born in rural New England and converted* to the Baptists* at age twenty, Jones began preaching* but soon came to have doubts about the validity of the Baptist name, their teaching on predestination* and their organization of churches under the control of Baptist associations. In 1801 he established a new congregation in Lyndon, Vermont, under the simple title of "Christian Church." The Bible was to be the only rule of faith and practice, and the congregation had no attachment to any higher body.

By 1804 he had been joined by Elias Smith, another former Baptist preacher. Together these men developed a whole movement of Christian churches, known as the Christian Connection.* Jones never occupied an official position of leadership within the group. He made his living by teaching school and practicing medicine, but his major interest was in ministry,* evangelism* and his reform movement.

See also RESTORATION MOVEMENT.

BIBLIOGRAPHY. *DAB* V; A. Jones, *Memoirs of The Life and Experiences, Travels and Preaching of Abner Jones* (1842). J. B. North

Jones, Bob, & Family. Robert R. "Bob" Jones, Sr. (1883-1968); Robert R. "Bob" Jones, Jr. (1911-); Robert R. "Bob" Jones, III (1939-). Fundamentalist* educators.

Bob Jones, Sr., was converted at age eleven in a rural Alabama Methodist* Episcopal, South, church in which he was licensed* to preach* at age fifteen. He attended Southern University (Birmingham) (1900-1902) and became a renowned evangelist.* His fight against modernism,* and what he judged to be sinful social practices convinced him of the need for conservative religious educational institutions. He founded Bob Jones College in St. Andrews Bay, Florida, in 1926. It collapsed during the Great Depression* (1933), and he subsequently moved Bob Jones College to Cleveland, Tennessee, where it prospered until 1947. Finding it impossible to purchase land for expansion of facilities, he sold the campus to the Church of God (Cleveland) as a new site for that denomination's Lee College.

Bob Jones University moved to Greenville, South Carolina, in 1947. Fearing regulation and scrutiny by government and secular educators, Bob Jones University has remained outside the regular U.S. educational system and is unaccredited. It has sought to remain uncompromisingly apart from modernism. It remained racially segregated until it lost a U.S. Supreme Court* case in 1983.

Bob Jones, Jr., graduated from Bob Jones College and the University of Pittsburgh, and became acting president (1932-1947) and then president of Bob Jones College (1947-1971). As an evangelist, he pioneered in the use of commercial-quality radio, television and film for evangelistic work. A student of Shakespeare, he sought to make the university a center for Christian fine arts, and the university's Art Gallery of Religious Paintings has received international recognition.

Fear of compromise on theological and social issues caused the Jones family to break relations with Youth for Christ,* the National Association of Evangelicals* and the new evangelical* movement. More dramatic was the break with the Billy Graham Evangelistic Association.* Most of the leaders, including Billy Graham,* T. W. Wilson, Cliff Barrows and Grady Wilson, attended or graduated from Bob Jones University. However, the ecumenical cooperation fostered by the Billy Graham Crusades, the encouragement of converts to attend nonfundamentalist churches and the acceptance of the Revised Standard Version of the Bible* were considered intolerable compromises by the Jones family. When Bob Jones, Jr., denied Graham permission to hold meetings on campus, Nelson Bell* attacked the Joneses in *Christianity Today.* John R. Rice,* in defense of the Joneses, responded in the *Sword of the Lord* against the "modernistic" Graham Crusades. The controversy marked a major split between evangelicals and fundamentalists.

Bob Jones III served Bob Jones University as assistant dean of men (1960-1961), professor of speech (1961-1962), assistant to the president (1962-1963) and vice president (1963-1971) before succeeding his father as president of the university in 1971. He has continued the tradition of militant fundamentalism and as leader, as their motto proclaims, of "The World's Most Unusual University."

BIBLIOGRAPHY. G. W. Dollar, *A History of Fundamentalism in America* (1973); R. K. Johnson, *Builder of Bridges: The Biography of Dr. Bob Jones, Sr.* (1969); "Text of the U. S. Supreme Court Decision: *Bob Jones University* v. *United States* and *Goldsboro Christian Schools, Inc.* v. *United States,* Argued 12 October 1982—Decided 24 May 1983," *JCS* 25 (1983):605-628.   D. D. Bundy

Jones, Charles Colcock, Sr. (1804-1863). Presbyterian* minister.* Born into a prominent family in Liberty County, Georgia, and educated at Andover* and Princeton Theological* seminaries, Jones entered the ministry in 1830. He served the First Presbyterian Church of Savannah (1831-1832), taught ecclesiastical history and church polity* at Columbia Theological Seminary in South Carolina (1837-1838; 1848-1850) and was corresponding secretary of the Board of Domestic Missions of the Presbyterian Church in Philadelphia (1850-1853). But Jones is best known as the devoted "Apostle to the Blacks."

Although he impugned slavery while studying in the North (1825-1830), upon returning to his family's plantations, Jones joined Southern clergy-

men* in biblically defending the "peculiar institution." Despite ill health, he developed a system for evangelizing* slaves and convinced masters in Liberty County and throughout the South to adopt it. Jones wrote such widely used texts as *A Catechism of Scripture, Doctrine and Practice . . . for the Oral Instruction of Colored Persons* (1837, 1843), *The Religious Instruction of the Negroes in the United States (1842)* and *A History of the Church of God* (1867). Jones did not view his mission as a threat to the institution of slavery, believing that slaves must be transformed into a "civilized people" before they could commend themselves to their masters as worthy of freedom. *See also* MISSIONS TO THE SLAVES.

BIBLIOGRAPHY. E. Clarke, *Wrestlin' Jacob: A Portrait of Religion in the Old South* (1979); D. G. Mathews, "Charles Colcock Jones and the Southern Evangelical Crusade to Form a Biracial Community," *JSH* (1975):299.   B. Touchstone

Jones, Clarence Wesley (1900-1986). Pioneer missionary* broadcaster. Born in Sherrard, Illinois, Jones graduated from Moody Bible Institute* in 1921 as class president and valedictorian. Together with Lance Latham, Merrill Dunlop, Carlton Booth and his brother, Howard Jones, Clarence Jones assisted Paul Rader* at the Chicago Gospel Tabernacle. There, during the 1920s, Jones founded the AWANA ("Approved Workmen Are Not Ashamed") youth program—what is today a large national nondenominational youth program. In 1928 he undertook an exploratory journey to South America, with a view to the establishment of a radio station. At the invitation of Reuben Larson, Jones moved to Quito, Ecuador, in 1930. On Christmas Day, 1931, radio station HCJB ("Heralding Christ Jesus' Blessing") commenced broadcasting. In 1940, with the assistance of Robert G. LeTourneau,* a 10,000-watt transmitter was erected. Now the combined power of HCJB transmitters totals more than one million watts. After retiring in 1961 Jones traveled extensively promoting Christian radio. In 1975 he became the first inductee into the National Religious Broadcasters'* Religious Broadcasting Hall of Fame.

BIBLIOGRAPHY. C. Jones, *Radio: The New Missionary* (1946); L. Neely, *Come Up to This Mountain: The Miracle of Clarence W. Jones and HCJB* (1980).   W. A. Detzler

Jones, (E)li Stanley (1884-1973). Methodist* missionary* to India. Born in Maryland, Jones attended Asbury College in Wilmore, Kentucky (B.A., 1906). While at Asbury, he felt called to missionary work. Ordained* as a Methodist minister,* in 1907 he departed for Lucknow, India, as a missionary with the Methodist Episcopal Church.* In Lucknow he first worked with lower-caste Indians but gradually felt drawn to work with the educated higher castes, as well as student groups. In 1911 he moved to Sitapur, where he also married Mabel Lossing.

An innovator in his approach to missions, Jones founded Christian ashrams (retreat centers for study and meditation) to share Christ with higher-caste Hindus, the most famous ashram being in Sal Tal, India. He also utilized round-table conferences, as illustrated in his *Christ at the Round Table* (1928), gathering groups of fifty persons for informative presentations of Christ, followed by discussion. These and other approaches of witness to non-Christian Indians he described in his best-selling *The Christ of the Indian Road* (1925). Written in haste during one of his trips to America, the book sold over 600,000 copies and brought him international recognition in the West. In America, as well as Asia, he was an immensely popular preacher* and lecturer. In 1938 he toured the U. S., speaking for a university mission sponsored by the Federal Council of Churches.*

Jones was a hopeful ecumenist* and envisioned a single worldwide united church governed by local congregational* polity.* Likewise, as a spokesman for world peace, he argued for a world government. Concerned by the rising specter of war in the Pacific, Jones, along with Toyohiko Kagawa of Japan, worked unsuccessfully behind the scenes to prevent the outbreak of World War 2.*

Jones authored many books and articles, including his autobiography, *A Song of Ascents* (1979). His commitment to his missionary calling was dramatically underscored when he was elected bishop of the Methodist Episcopal Church in 1928. Jones resigned the next day, saying "I am called to be an evangelist and a missionary."

BIBLIOGRAPHY. W. K. Anderson, ed., *Christian World Mission* (1946); E. S. Jones, *The Contribution of E. Stanley Jones* (1973); E. S. Jones, *Selections from E. Stanley Jones* (1972).

J. E. Stanley

Jones, John William (1836-1909). Baptist* minister,* Confederate soldier and author. Born, raised and educated in Virginia, Jones graduated from the University of Virginia and later studied at Southern Baptist Theological Seminary. Soon after his ordination* in 1860, he was appointed a missionary* to China by the Southern Baptist denomination. His departure was delayed, how-

ever, by the outbreak of the Civil War.* When Virginia seceded, he enlisted as a private in the Confederate army. He saw service in the ranks for a year, and then did duty as both regiment chaplain* and missionary chaplain. In his volume *Christ in the Camp* (1877), he recorded the history of the famous revival services which swept through Lee's army during the winter of 1862/63.

During the years following the war, he held several pastorates, served as chaplain of Washington College, and was an agent for the Southern Baptist Theological Seminary in Louisville. Though ill health afflicted him in his latter years, he continued to write, lecture and labor in various ways so as to keep alive interest in the history of the Confederacy.

BIBLIOGRAPHY. *DAB* V. R. R. Mathisen

Jones, Rufus Matthew (1863-1948). Quaker* mystic,* philosopher, educator and humanitarian. Born in South China, Maine, Jones was educated at Moses Brown School, Haverford College (B.A., 1885), the University of Pennsylvania (1893-1895) and Harvard* University (1900-1901); he also pursued advanced study in Germany. Jones taught school at Providence, Rhode Island (1887-1889), and then served as principal of Oak Grove Seminary in Vassalboro, Maine (1889-1893). The major portion of his career was spent at Haverford College, where he was professor of philosophy for over forty years (1893-1934). A popular college and university lecturer, his many contributions were recognized by thirteen honorary degrees.

Jones served the Friends by editing *The American Friend* (1894-1912) and was active in the formation of the Five Years Meeting of Friends (now Friends United Meeting). In 1917 Jones helped found the American Friends Service Committee* and served as its chairman for many years. He was a prime mover of other Quaker enterprises, including Pendle Hill Study Center, Friends Fellowship Council, Wider Quaker Fellowship and Friends World Committee for Consultation. Ecumenically he was actively involved with the foreign missionary movement.*

Jones' scholarly work was done on the Quakers and Continental mystics, and he was coauthor and editor of the Rowntree Quaker history series. He authored approximately fifty books and more than 600 articles; among them were *Studies in Mystical Religion* (1909); *The Later Periods of Quakerism* (1921); *Pathways to the Reality of God* (1931) and *The Testimony of the Soul* (1936). Through his writings Jones interpreted the Quaker ideal of the inner life to a broad spectrum of the American religious public.

BIBLIOGRAPHY. *DAB* 4; *DARB;* D. Hinshaw, *Rufus Jones: Master Quaker* (1951); *NCAB* 38; E. G. Vining, *Friend of Life: The Biography of Rufus Jones* (1958).   W. A. Cooper

Jones, Samuel ("Sam") Porter (1847-1906). Methodist* minister* and evangelist.* Born in Chambers County, Alabama, Jones moved with his family to Cartersville, Georgia, when he was nine years old. There he was educated by private tutors and in boarding schools. After serving in the Confederate army in the Civil War,* he was admitted to the Georgia bar in 1869. His addiction to alcohol* ruined his law practice, but in 1872 he was converted* to Christianity and was admitted to the ministry of the Methodist Episcopal Church, South, in the same year. From 1872 to 1880 he held several pastorates, after which he was agent of the North Georgia Conference Orphan's Home (1880-1892). While serving in that capacity he met T. DeWitt Talmage,* who invited him to conduct a revival* meeting in Brooklyn. This was the start of a new ministry in evangelism which took him to every major city in the North and South.

As an evangelist his delivery and mannerisms were direct and controversial. In his effort to reach the common people, he used blunt, homespun language which some considered irreverent. Nevertheless, his effectiveness as an evangelist earned him the title "The Moody of the South." In an era when rapid urbanization brought social change and tension, Jones took an absolutist stand on the issues and urged his audiences to resist the advances of alcoholism, profanity, gambling and Sabbath breaking.

BIBLIOGRAPHY. *DAB* V; *DARB;* W. Holcomb, *Sam Jones* (1947); L. M. Jones, *The Life and Sayings of Sam P. Jones* (1906); *NCAB* 13.
R. R. Mathisen

Jordan, Clarence (1912-1969). Founder of Koinonia Farm. Born in Talbotton, Georgia, Jordan studied agriculture at the University of Georgia (B.S., 1933), but resigned his ROTC commission to become a licensed Baptist* minister.*

While studying at Southern Baptist Theological Seminary (Th.M., 1936; Ph.D., 1939), Jordan developed strong convictions in favor of pacifism,* racial equality and communal living. As director of Sunshine Center in Louisville, he was among the earliest white clergy to minister to inner-city blacks. In 1942, in company with Martin English, Jordan founded Koinonia Farm on 400 acres near Americus, Georgia. The farm was established as a

racially integrated witness of Christian community, brotherhood and peace. Koinonia (Greek for *fellowship*) taught local farmers scientific techniques and prospered until its opposition to the postwar draft and racial prejudice brought its members expulsion from the Rehobeth Baptist Church in 1950.

For a decade after 1956 Koinonia suffered from an economic boycott as well as physical violence by its opponents. Jordan's response to the segregated South was his Cotton Patch Version of the New Testament, published in four volumes (1968-1973)—the New Testament translated into Southern vernacular and setting. In 1968 Jordan and Millard Fuller reorganized Koinonia Farm as Koinonia Partners, noted for its Fund For Humanity that provides non-interest capital for low-cost housing.

BIBLIOGRAPHY. J. Hollyday, "The Legacy of Clarence Jordan," *Sojourners* 8 (December 1979):10-19; D. Lee, *The Cotton Patch Evidence: The Story of Clarence Jordan and the Koinonia Experiment* (1971).   D. E. Pitzer

Jowett, John Henry (1864-1923). English Congregationalist* minister.* Born in Halifax, Yorkshire, Jowett was educated at the University of Edinburgh (1883-1887) and at Oxford (1888-1889). In England he served at St. James Congregational Church, Newcastle-on-Tyne (1889-1895), and Carr's Lane, Birmingham (1895-1911), before coming to New York's Fifth Avenue Presbyterian (1911-1918). Prior to coming to New York, he had visited the U. S. in 1909 and had been a prominent speaker at the Northfield Conference* of that year.

In his day Jowett was reputed to be one of the greatest evangelical* preachers. His sermons were noted for their expository style and their emphasis on the doctrine of grace. While in America he presented the Lyman Beecher* Lectures at Yale Divinity School* (1911-1912), published as *The Preacher: His Life and Work* (1912). Returning to England, Jowett succeeded G. Campbell Morgan* at Westminster Chapel, London (1918-1922).

BIBLIOGRAPHY. A. Porritt, *J. H. Jowett* (1925); C. Fant and W. Pinson, *Twenty Centuries of Great Preaching* (1971); H. Davies: *Varieties of English Preaching, 1900-1960* (1963).   D. Macleod

Judeo-Christian Tradition. A religious and political slogan which has played a critical role in defining the spiritual ideology of the U.S. since World War 2. It was during the 1930s that *Judeo-Christian* came to be used by the political Left to signify the religious inheritance of the West, for at the time "Christian" had become a political code word for fascism and anti-Semitism (e.g., Father Coughlin's* Christian Front*). The idea was to extend an umbrella of common spirituality to a threatened Jewish population. During the War, the Judeo-Christian tradition served in America as a mobilizing slogan for the Allied cause. Once the War was over, it played a similar role in the rhetorical arsenal of anti-Communism.

What theological substance the concept had came from Reinhold Niebuhr* and his followers, who emphasized the "Hebraic" character of Christianity over against "Hellenic" influences. They saw the tradition less as a set of specific doctrines and moral ordinances than as a shared prophetic view of God and God's relationship to humankind. This interpretation drew criticism from some Roman Catholics,* who rightly saw it as hostile to their natural-law* theology, and from some Jews, who deemed it threatening to their distinctiveness. Only in the late 1960s, however, did the Judeo-Christian tradition fall into serious disfavor.

Arthur Cohen's book *The Myth of the Judeo-Christian Tradition* (1969) asserted that Christians and Jews shared only a tradition of mutual enmity, and went so far as to blame the mythical tradition's proponents for fostering Nazism. Meanwhile, for the culturally avant-garde, the concept came to symbolize conventional bourgeois morality. It was in conflict with this latter view that the Judeo-Christian tradition was reclaimed in the late 1970s by the Christian Right*—above all by Jerry Falwell's* Moral Majority* organization, which sought an ecumenical image for itself. Although the concept threatened to become merely a code word for "family values," by the end of the Reagan* era it seemed to have regained favor across a broad religio-political spectrum.

Since it burst upon the scene, the Judeo-Christian tradition has functioned more as a rallying cry than as an identifiable piece of religious common ground. Scholars have not interested themselves in trying to determine what features of Jewish and Christian history might actually constitute a Judeo-Christian tradition as such. Useful in polemic, the phrase is most meaningful for what it discloses about the spiritual politics of the U.S. in the latter part of the twentieth century.

See also CIVIL RELIGION.

BIBLIOGRAPHY. M. Silk, *Spiritual Politics: Religion and America since World War II* (1988).

M. Silk

Judson, Adoniram (1788-1850). Pioneer mis-

sionary to Burma. Born in Malden, Massachusetts, the son of a Congregational* minister, Judson graduated from Brown University (B.A., 1807) and underwent a profound spiritual experience while attending Andover Seminary* (B.D., 1810). He participated in the formation of the nation's first foreign missionary agency, the American Board of Commissioners for Foreign Missions* and was among the first contingent to go overseas. Judson, with his bride, Ann Hasseltine Judson,* sailed for India in 1812. En route they became convinced of the correctness of the doctrine of baptism* by immersion, and were baptized shortly after their arrival in Calcutta. Their consequent disassociation from the ABCFM led to the organization of the American Baptist Missionary Union and their expulsion from India.

Circumstances led to their taking up work in Rangoon, Burma, where Judson, despite restrictive government policies, succeeded in gathering a small group of converts while beginning the difficult task of mastering the language and translating the Scriptures.* In 1824, at the age of thirty-six, he was imprisoned when war broke out between England and Burma. For twenty-one months he suffered intolerable confinement and deprivation, facing the possibility of imminent death and knowledge of his wife's hardships, including the unattended birth of their child, smallpox and severe tropical fevers. Ann Judson died in 1826, not long after Judson's release. In 1834 Judson married Sarah Boardman Judson,* the widow of a colleague, but she died in 1845 after having contributed significantly to the monumental translation and literary work that became Judson's legacy to the church in Burma. In 1846 he married a young writer, Emily Chubbuck, whom he had selected as biographer of Sarah Boardman Judson. Emily sailed with him to Burma in that same year and survived him by only a few years.

Not returning to the U.S. until thirty-three years after the beginning of his missionary career and having sustained such hardship and loss in pursuit of his calling, Judson became an inspiring example of missionary sacrifice and dedication for several generations of young people. The concrete results of his work were no less impressive, as he left a flourishing church of 7,000 members and more than 100 national ministers among both the Burmese and the tribal peoples of the country that has continued in unbroken succession since his death.

BIBLIOGRAPHY. *AAP* 6; C. Anderson, *To the Golden Shore: The Life of Adoniram Judson* (1956); *DAB* V; *DARB; NCAB* 3; R. Torbet, *Venture of Faith* (1955); F. Wayland, *A Memoir of the Life and*

Labors of the Rev. Adoniram Judson, 2 vols. (1853).

E. A. Wilson

Judson, Ann Hasseltine (1789-1826). Baptist* missionary* to Burma. Born in Bradford, Massachussetts, she was educated at a local academy where, on July 6, 1806, she was converted* to an evangelical* faith. Shortly thereafter she joined the Congregational Church.* A schoolteacher until she married (February 5, 1812) Adoniram Judson,* they departed shortly thereafter as missionaries to India. Ann Judson was the first woman to leave America as a missionary, a move regarded by her family and friends as wild and romantic.

Though she was the wife of the renowned American missionary, she served with distinction as a missionary in her own right. Committed to foreign missions prior to her marriage, she insisted that her going abroad in 1812 was not influenced by her love for a man—"an attachment to an earthly object"—but was prompted by an "obligation to God with a full conviction of its being a call." When her husband decided to become a Baptist* enroute to India, Ann did not relinquish her own Congregational ties without some hesitation.

Forced to depart from India, the Judsons settled in Burma, where Ann quickly learned the language and soon began teaching Burmese women and doing translation work. Her most important contribution to missions was her personal writing. Her account of their years in Burma, *A Particular Relation of the American Baptist Mission to the Burman Empire* (1823), was published on her brief return visit to America due to an illness (1822-1823). Her surviving letters and a portion of her journal, published in her memoirs, provided insight and inspiration to a generation of Americans whose knowledge and commitment to overseas missions was very limited. Her gripping accounts of the problems of Burmese women made a heart-rending appeal for women's work. An inhospitable climate, childbirth and her husband's extended imprisonment took a severe toll on her health; and she died of a tropical fever at the age of thirty-six, after only thirteen years of missionary service.

See also JUDSON, ADONIRAM; JUDSON, EMILY CHUBBUCK; JUDSON, SARAH HALL BOARDMAN.

BIBLIOGRAPHY. *AAP* 6; C. Anderson, *To The Golden Shore: The Life of Adoniram Judson* (1972); J. J. Brumberg, *Mission For Life: The Story of the Family of Adoniram Judson* (1980); *DAB* V; E. D. Hubbard, *Ann of Ava* (1913); J. D. Knowles, *Memoirs of Mrs. Ann H. Judson* (1831); *NAW* 2.

R. A. Tucker

Judson, Emily Chubbuck (1817-1854). Popular author and missionary.* Born into a poor family, Emily began work in the Hamilton, New York, woolen mills at age ten. In 1840 a friend recommended her to the Utica Female Seminary, where she was granted a scholarship and hired to teach composition. After hours she wrote for publication under the pen name Fanny Forester. Adoniram Judson* saw her work and selected her to write the biography of his recently deceased second wife, Sarah Hall Boardman Judson*; they met, were soon married and sailed for Moulmein, Burma, in July 1846. On the mission field, Emily wrote Sarah's biography, supervised domestic matters and nursed others while fighting her own illness. Adoniram and a newborn son died in April 1850, and poor health forced Emily to return home in 1851. She published three final books and assisted Francis Wayland* with his biography of Judson, hoping to earn money for the care and education of her five stepchildren and daughter. She died of tuberculosis at age thirty-six.

BIBLIOGRAPHY. *DAB* V; A. C. Kendrick, *Life and Letters of Mrs. Emily C. Judson* (1860); *NAW* 2.

K. K. Kidd

Judson, Sarah Hall Boardman (1803-1845). Missionary* to Burma. Born in Alstead, New Hampshire, Sarah married George Dana Boardman* on July 4, 1825, and that year sailed with him to Calcutta, India, as missionaries to Burma. In Calcutta they began studying the Burmese language and in April 1827, they moved to Amherts, the British capital of Burma. Subsequently they moved to Maulmain and finally to Tavoy in 1828, where she established a girl's school and worked on the Talaing translation of the New Testament, the first Burmese translation of the Bible.

Upon the death of her first husband in 1831, Sarah decided to remain in Burma with her son, the only one of her three children to have survived the hardships. During the ensuing years she is reported to have made many journeys into the interior, accompanied by converts of the Karen people and addressing large gatherings. In 1834 she married Adoniram Judson* and returned with him to Maulmain. There she continued her translation work and published several tracts and small books, including a portion of *Pilgrim's Progress* and Mr. Boardman's "Dying Father's Advice." That year she also completed her translation of the New Testament, which was partially published in 1838, followed by the complete version by Haswell in 1847. In 1845, her health impaired, she and her husband embarked for the U.S. She died en route on September 3, 1845, and was buried on the island of St. Helena.

BIBLIOGRAPHY. *DAB* V; *NAW* 2; A. Wilson, *Ann H. Judson and Mrs. Sarah B. Judson, Missionaries to Burmah* (1852); W. N. Wyeth, *Sarah B. Judson: A Memorial* (1889).   E. Rommen

Jurisdictional Conference. An organizational body within the United Methodist Church* with responsibilities within a large geographic region of the church. In the merger of 1939 that created The Methodist Church, five jurisdictions were established, dividing the country into five geographical regions. A sixth, the central jurisdictional conference, overlapped the five and was the organizational unit for African-American Methodists. The jurisdictional system was a compromise effort to enable the Methodist Episcopal Church, South, and the African-American Methodists across the country to maintain a degree of independence from the Methodist Episcopal Church (North). This hotly contested division continued until the 1968 merger of Evangelical United Brethren and Methodist churches. In 1962 the central jurisdiction was abolished.

Equal numbers of clergy* and lay* delegates are elected by the annual, missionary and provisional annual conferences to be a part of the jurisdictional conference. Meeting times and places are determined by the council of bishops.* The principal function of the jurisdictional conference is the election of bishops, who generally serve in the jurisdiction out of which they were elected.

P. A. Mickey

Justification. Derived from the Pauline epistles, especially Galatians and Romans, and generally understood to be a term that arose within a judicial context as a statement of a person's just status before a court, justification has been closely associated with the doctrines of divine grace and human faith in describing what God does for and to believers in Jesus Christ.

Justification became a major emphasis of Martin Luther, for whom it was "the article for the standing or falling of the church," a rallying center of the Protestant Reformation, and hence a crucial issue in dispute between Protestants* and Roman Catholics,* beginning in the sixteenth century. The magisterial Reformers held that sinners are declared or reckoned to be righteous as God's free gift by the imputation of the righteousness of Christ and through faith. Hence to be justified is to have a new standing before God, not a new nature. This teaching found its way to the English colonies in North America, especially through the Puritans.*

The fathers of the Council of Trent (1547), on the other hand, held that sinners are made righteous by the infusion of God's justice through Christ's merits so that believers are justified to the extent that they are, in Protestant terms, sanctified. Moreover, individuals cannot be certain that they are justified, and they can cease to be justified. Such conciliar teaching was brought by Roman Catholics to North America.

Post-Reformation distinctions regarding justification arose in Europe and were also carried across the Atlantic. These differences pertained to whether one is passive or active in being justified (Calvinists* of the Synod of Dort vs. Arminians* respectively), how justification is to be related to eternity as well as time (eighteenth-century English hyper-Calvinists), and whether the dissimilarities are to be downplayed and the similarities emphasized between justification, forgiveness, reconciliation and adoption (Albrecht Ritschl, 1822-1889).

Among the Puritans, Thomas Hooker* taught that the preparation of the heart for Christ (sanctification*) constitutes the basis for assurance of having been justified, while John Cotton* held, at least after coming to New England, that faith alone is the basis for assurance. Jonathan Edwards* related justification to covenantal theology* in that Christ, as the elect's federal representative, made available through his death his imputed righteousness, and the Presbyterian theologian Charles Hodge* expounded the same declarative and imputational position. America's noted German Reformed* theologian and church historian Philip Schaff* considered justification by faith the "material principle" of the Protestant Reformation, the "formal principle" being that the Scriptures* are "the pure and proper source as well as the only certain measure of all saving truth."

Outside of the Reformed tradition, Methodist* theologians (e.g., Thomas O. Summers, Henry C. Sheldon) retained the distinction between justification and sanctification but in the sense that the former is the objective work and the latter the subjective. In contrast to Calvinists, Methodists have held to an Arminian view that the gift of justification is extended to all and not limited to a select number of elect. This has also been true of the Holiness* and Pentecostal* traditions as a whole, though the emphasis is placed on the second blessing*—the deliverance from the present power of sin. There have been some notable variations, such as Holiness theologian W. B. Godbey (1833-1920), who held an eccentric view affirming that all humans are justified prior to physical birth so as not to be born as sinners. Pentecostal theologians such as Myer Pearlman (1898-1943) could affirm that justification is declarative and imputed to the believer.

A further variety of views may be seen in the Mennonite* (e.g., Daniel Kauffman*) emphasis on justification joined with the necessity of obedience and Baptist* theologian Walter T. Conner's* contention that justification should be coupled with and not set over against regeneration.* From a sectarian perspective, Latter-day Saint* theologian James E. Talmage labeled justification by faith a "pernicious doctrine."

Lutherans* in the U.S., who maintain that justification is a singular act by which the righteousness of Christ is imputed to the believer, had to cope with Tübingen professor Karl Holl's (1866-1926) contention that Luther actually taught that sinners are "made righteous" as well as "declared righteous." On the other hand, German biblical scholar Rudolf Bultmann regarded his program of demythologizing* as a radical application of the Lutheran doctrine of justification by faith: "Like the doctrine of justification, de-mythologizing destroys every longing for security." In the mid-twentieth century, justification by faith was said to be strange and unintelligible to modern people—even Protestants (Paul Tillich*)—while others claimed that justifica-tion continues to answer a central human question (Henry P. Hamann).

Lutheran and Roman Catholic theologians in the U.S., who engaged in intensive dialog (1978-1984) on justification (*See* Lutheran-Catholic Dialog), have reached remarkable agreement regarding justification. They concluded that "our entire hope of justification and salvation rests on Christ Jesus and on the gospel of God's merciful action in Christ," and hence "we do not place our ultimate trust in anything other than God's promise and saving work in Christ. This excludes ultimate reliance on our faith, virtues or merits, even though we acknowledge God working in these by grace alone."

BIBLIOGRAPHY. H. G. Anderson et al., eds., *Justification by Faith: Lutherans and Catholics in Dialogue VII* (1985); A. B. Crabtree, *The Restored Relationship: A Study in Justification and Reconciliation* (1963); J. Edwards, *Justification by Faith Alone* (1843); A. E. McGrath, *Iustitia Dei: A History of the Christian Doctrine of Justification,* 2 vols. (1986); J. Reumann, *Righteousness in the New Testament* (1982); P. Schaff, *The Principle of Protestantism* (1845); G. H. Tavard, *Justification: An Ecumenical Study* (1983).

J. L. Garrett

K

Kauffman, Daniel (1865-1944). Mennonite* leader and theologian.* Born in Juniata, Pennsylvania, Kauffman grew up in Morgan County, Missouri, and attended Missouri State University. He taught school in Missouri for several years (1883-1897) and in 1890 was converted under J. S. Coffman.* Ordained* in the Mennonite Church in 1892, he became a bishop in 1896.

Kauffman was the leading spirit within the Mennonite Church from c.1898 to 1930. He made his mark as a theologian with his *Manual of Bible Doctrines* (1898), one of his many books, and as a church leader in the creation of the Mennonite General Conference (of the [old] Mennonite Church). The latter was for Mennonites a new approach to denominational* structures. Kauffman was also editor of the official denominational paper, *Gospel Herald* (1908-1943).

His doctrinal approach emphasized a "true orthodox evangelical faith," to be expressed in modest, indeed uniform, dress for all church members, along with proper Christian demeanor and conduct in all areas of life. With the coming of World War 2,* new forces were to bring Kauffman's doctrinal era to an end. For most Mennonites, the ahistorical era of Kauffman was transformed into a more traditional Mennonite approach to Christianity, including both faith and history as the essence of Mennonite faith.

BIBLIOGRAPHY. L. Gross, "The Doctrinal Era of the Mennonite Church," *MQR* 60 (1986):83-103; *ME* 3.   L. Gross

Keach, Elias (1667-1701). Baptist* minister* in middle colonies. The son of the famous London Baptist pastor Benjamin Keach, Elias, unordained, arrived in Philadelphia in 1686/87, dressed in the black coat and white collar of a minister.* The pretension succeeded and Elias was asked to preach.* Seized by conviction, the young pretender stopped his sermon and confessed his sin.* Keach sought the spiritual aid of Thomas Dungan of Cold Spring, who counseled and baptized him. Returning to Pennepek he gathered a small church, constituted in 1688. From Pennepek he traveled to Trenton, Philadelphia, Middletown, Cohansey, Salem and other small communities, preaching to groups of English, Irish and Welsh settlers. According to Morgan Edwards,* these churches met in "General Meetings" held twice a year due to the distance separating this Baptist community. When numbers were sufficient a church was gathered in each location. Contact between the churches of the area was maintained, evolving into the Philadelphia Association of Baptists,* formally established in 1707. Their doctrine and practice was that of the English Particular Baptists.* Called "the chief apostle of the Baptists in these parts" by Edwards, Keach returned to England in 1692.

BIBLIOGRAPHY. T. Armitage, *A History of the Baptists,* 2 vols. (1892); M. Edwards, *Materials Towards a History of the Baptists,* 2 vols. (1770-1792).   L. W. Hähnlen

Keane, John Joseph (1839-1918). Roman Catholic prelate and founder of Catholic University of America.* Born in Ballyshanon, Donegal, Ireland, Keane, at nine, immigrated with his family to the U.S. He graduated from St. Charles' College, Maryland (1862), and St. Mary's Seminary, Baltimore (1866), and was ordained* to the priesthood in 1866. For the next twelve years Keane served as a parish* priest* in Washington, D.C. (1866-1878), after which he was appointed the fifth bishop* of Richmond (1878-1888).

The works and interests which would occupy the rest of his life emerged during Keane's years in Washington: temperance, Protestant-Catholic relations, the black apostolate and the education and formation of youth. From his friend, the aging Isaac Hecker,* he learned the devotion to the Holy Spirit which would be at the heart of his interior life and the sense of providence which would anchor his theology.* From 1887 until the Vatican's censure of Americanism* in 1899, Keane worked closely with John Ireland* and Denis O'Connell* at the center of the Americanist Movement. He had come to believe in American Catholicism's providential mission* to the church universal. With its arrangement of separation of church and state* and its promise for Christian reunion, America would lead the church into the modern age.

Keane is best remembered as the founding rector* (1889-1896) of the new Catholic University of America, for which he recruited a distinguished international faculty. His beliefs about American messianism influenced his public behavior as rector as well as his involvement in the controversies of the day. He played a major role in 1887 in preventing a Vatican condemnation of the Knights of Labor,* in organizing Catholic participation in the 1893 Parliament of Religions* in Chicago and in advocating rapid assimilation for German immigrants.* But his identification with the progressive party in these and other disputes led to his removal as rector in 1896, after which he spent four years in a kind of ecclesiastical limbo at Rome.

As a man of deep faith, Keane accepted, in exemplary Christian fashion, his exile in Rome as well as his partial rehabilitation as archbishop* of Dubuque (1900-1911). An energetic pastor,* a popular speaker and a prolific writer, Keane was one of the most visible Catholic figures of his day and left behind a bibliography of more that 230 publications.

See also AMERICANISM.

BIBLIOGRAPHY. P. H. Ahern, *The Life of John J. Keane, Educator and Archbishop, 1839-1918* (1955); J. P. Chinnici, *Devotion to the Holy Spirit in American Catholicism* (1985); *DAB* V; *DARB; NCAB* 6; T. E. Wangler, "Emergence of John J. Keane as a Liberal Catholic and Americanist," *AER* 166-167 (1972):457-478; "A Bibliography of the Writings of Archbishop John J. Keane," *RACHSP* 89 (1978):60-73.   W. L. Portier

Keeble, Marshall (1878-1968). African-American evangelist.* Born in Rutherford County, Tennessee, Keeble attended churches associated with the Church of Christ,* the conservative wing of the Restorationist Movement.* Manufacturing buckets and soap for a living, Keeble eventually opened a grocery store. Around 1900 he began preaching* part-time, and twenty years later he became a full-time evangelist. Though he held revivals* throughout the U.S., he spent most of his time in the Southeast. As many as 350 congregations, mostly African-American churches in the South, trace their origins to his evangelistic efforts, and approximately 30,000 people were baptized* by him. Keeble was an ardent controversialist, always ready to vindicate in debate his church's doctrines on matters such as adult baptism. He was a conserva-

tive on racial matters, avoiding direct challenges to Southern segregation. In 1962 and 1966 he conducted evangelistic campaigns in Nigeria, Ethiopia and several Asian countries. Deeply moved by his encounter with his African roots, he helped raise funds for Nigerian hospitals and was delighted to be made an honorary chief of a Nigerian tribe.

BIBLIOGRAPHY. J. E. Choate, *Roll, Jordan, Roll: A Biography of Marshall Keeble* (1968); B. C. Goodpasture, ed., *Biography and Sermons of Marshall Keeble, Evangelist* (1931).   S. W. Angell

Kehuckee Baptist Association. Baptist* antimissionary* group in North Carolina. Baptist churches were formed along Kehuckee Creek in North Carolina by the 1740s and in 1769 formed their own association. In 1803 the Kehuckee Association declared itself in favor of missions,* though some churches in the association opposed organized missions for theological and methodological reasons. Churches in the Chowan area split off from the association in 1805 to form their own association, leaving most of the remaining churches in the Kehuckee group opposed to missions. In 1826 the Kehuckee Association voted to "discard all Missionary Societies, Bible Societies, and Theological Seminaries, and the practices heretofore resorted to form their support, in begging money from the public." Thereafter *Kehuckeeism* became a synonym for anti-missions among Baptists. In 1878 remnants of the Kehuckee Association formed the Kehuckee Primitive Baptist* Association.

BIBLIOGRAPHY. L. Burkitt and J. Read, *A Concise History of the Kehuckee Baptist Association* (1850); G. W. Paschal, *A History of North Carolina Baptists* (1930).   H. L. McBeth

Keith, George (1638-1716). Quaker* teacher and controversialist. Born in Aberdeenshire, Scotland, Keith was educated in philosophy, theology* and mathematics at the University of Aberdeen (M.A., 1685), and there became a lifelong friend of Robert Barclay.* Both men became "convinced" Quakers in the 1660s, traveling with George Fox* and William Penn* to visit potential Quakers in Holland and Germany in 1677. During the persecution of all Nonconformist worship* in England and Scotland in 1662-1685, Keith was imprisoned in 1664, 1667 and 1675. He wrote tracts such as *Immediate Revelation . . . not Ceased* (1668) on Quaker doctrines later developed by Barclay and Penn. Keith moved to London in 1670 and with Barclay was influenced by the ideas of new Friends, including Henry More (1614-1687) the Cambridge Platonist and the Countess of Conway. Penn and Barclay invited him in 1684 to survey a boundary between West and East New Jersey as they respectively organized the settling of those two colonies. In 1689 Keith became a schoolmaster in Quaker Philadelphia.

In 1691 Keith was accused by local Quakers of preaching salvation* through the historical death of Christ independently of Christ within. He in turn wrote tracts* on the dispute, organized a faction of followers as "Christian Quakers" and was "disowned" by the Philadelphia Yearly Meeting. He returned to England in 1693. The London Yearly Meeting, after failing to mediate the dispute or persuade Keith to patience, also "disowned" him and his splinter Meeting in Turners Hall. Keith's concern for the Bible* and the historic Christ took him into the Church of England,* where he was ordained* a priest* in 1702 and sent him back to America to reconvert the Quakers. He made little headway and became priest of an English parish* church for the last decade of his life (1706-1716).

BIBLIOGRAPHY. *AAP* 5; *DAB* V; *DARB*; J. W. Frost, ed., *The Keithian Controversy in Early Pennsylvania* (1980); E. W. Kirby, *George Keith* (1942).

H. Barbour and J. W. Frost

Kellogg, John Harvey (1852-1943). Physician and health reformer. Born in Michigan, Kellogg grew up in a Seventh-Day Adventist* family. After attending Russell Trall's Hygieo-Therapeutic College and the University of Michigan, he completed his medical education at Bellevue Hospital Medical College, where he received his M.D. in 1875.

The following year, Kellogg became superintendent of the Seventh-Day Adventist Western Health Reform Institute, later Battle Creek Sanitarium, in Michigan. Here he sought to combine reform or sectarian medicine with the best of orthodox medical practice. Kellogg advocated "biologic living," which included a vegetarian diet, and promoted his ideas through lectures and books. He also invented corn flakes and various meat substitutes.

Kellogg came into conflict with the Adventist Church and was disfellowshipped from the denomination* in 1907. He maintained control over Battle Creek Sanitarium, until financial problems led to its sale in 1942.

BIBLIOGRAPHY. *DAB* 3; R. W. Schwarz, *John Harvey Kellogg, M.D.* (1981). G. Land

Kellogg, Samuel Henry (1839-1899). Presbyterian* missionary* and pastor.* Born at Quoque,

Long Island, Kellogg received his early education at home, except for about six months at Haverstraw Mountain Institute. He briefly attended Williams College in 1856 and graduated from Princeton College in 1861 with high honors. Completing his studies at Princeton Seminary* in 1864, he was ordained* a missionary to India on April 20, 1864. Kellogg spent nearly a decade in India, mostly at the Theological School at Allahabad.

In 1875 he completed a monumental grammar of the Hindi language. Following the death of his wife, Antoinette (Hartwell) Kellogg, in 1876, he returned with his four children to America and remarried in 1879. Kellogg served as pastor of the Third Presbyterian Church in Pittsburgh and as professor of systematic theology at Western Seminary in Allegheny, Pennsylvania (1877-1885). From 1886 to 1892 he was pastor of St. James Scare Presbyterian Church in Toronto. In 1892 he returned to India to assist in revising the Hindi Old Testament. He died there, following a bicycle accident, on May 3, 1899.

An accomplished linguist as well as a missionary, Kellogg authored nine books and numerous pamphlets and articles in scholarly journals. He was a member of the American Society of Orientalists as well as the Victoria Institute of England and an associate of the Philosophical Society of Great Britain.

BIBLIOGRAPHY. *DAB* V; A. H. H. Holcomb, *Men of Might in India Missions* (1901). P. C. Wilt

Kelpius, Johannes (1673-c.1708). Communitarian mystic. A native of Transylvania, a student of Jacob Boehme and a brilliant scholar, Kelpius accepted the millenarian* view of Johann J. Zimmerman and became one of the forty scholars and mystics who, under the leadership of Zimmerman, set sail for Pennsylvania where they would await Christ's return. Before the group embarked, Zimmerman died and Kelpius became the leader of the party. Arriving in Philadelphia in 1694, they settled along Wissahickon Creek near Germantown. Devoted to an ascetic lifestyle, Kelpius himself lived in a cave, while many others in the community built cave-like huts.

Scanning the heavens with their astronomical instruments, they watched for the first sign of Christ's return. Meanwhile they shared their spiritual vision with others, engaged in teaching children and, with their herbal medicines, helping the sick. Attracting the attention of the surrounding populace, they became known as the Society of the Woman in the Wilderness (Rev 12:6), while members of the group referred to themselves as the Contented of the God-Loving Soul. When Christ did not return as expected, the group lost some of its cohesiveness, finally disbanding with Kelpius's death. Later Rosicrucians were to claim them as the first of a series of Rosicrucian councils in America.

BIBLIOGRAPHY. *DAB* V; D. F. Durnbaugh, "Work and Hope: The Spirituality of the Radical Pietist Communitarians," *CH* 39 (1970):72-90; A. Steinmetz, "Kelpius, The Hermit of Wissahickson," *AGR* 7 (1941): 7-12.   M. H. Schrag

Kennedy, John Fitzgerald (1917-1963). First Roman Catholic* president of the U.S. Born in Brookline, Massachusetts, Kennedy's ancestry was entirely immigrant Irish, his father, Joseph P. Kennedy, was a wealthy businessman and Harvard* graduate, and his mother, Rose Fitzgerald Kennedy, was the daughter of a powerful Boston mayor. Joseph Kennedy believed that, since his sons would have to compete in the secular world, they should attend the best secular schools. John Kennedy spent only one year in a Catholic school and then attended Choate, an elite preparatory school, and Harvard (B.A., 1940), later doing graduate work at the London School of Economics. Following a distinguished World War 2* record in the Navy, he was elected to the U.S. House of Representatives from Massachusetts in 1946 and to the U.S. Senate in 1952.

For the most part his early political career conformed to what might have been expected of a Boston Irish Catholic. He introduced legislation authorizing federal aid to private schools, and he was strongly anti-Communist, giving some support to Senator Joseph McCarthy of Wisconsin. When Kennedy announced his candidacy for president in 1960, he was opposed by many Democratic liberals who considered him too conservative.

The first Catholic to run for the presidency since Alfred E. Smith* in 1928, he encountered strong opposition because of his religion, some of it from secularists, some from Protestants* and Jews. The Episcopal* Bishop James A. Pike* wrote a book titled *A Roman Catholic in the White House?* and the suitability of a Catholic was openly questioned by Norman Vincent Peale.*

Kennedy was advised on this matter by the Catholic journalist John Cogley, who later became an Episcopalian. On numerous occasions, but especially in a meeting with the Houston Ministerial Alliance, Kennedy explained that his religion was a purely personal affair and that he would not allow religious considerations to dictate his conduct as president. By the end of the campaign,

most of the public opposition on this score had dissipated.

Friends such as Paul Fay described Kennedy as only nominally Catholic, with a superficial knowledge of his faith and no great degree of piety.* As president he reversed some of his earlier positions, such as federal support for private schools, and gave at least lukewarm support to Supreme Court* decisions forbidding prayer* and Bible reading in the public schools.* Another friend, Benjamin Bradlee, said that shortly before he was assassinated Kennedy said privately that he favored the legalization of abortion.*

Kennedy's response to the religious issue in 1960 became a model for a number of later politicians, both Catholic and Protestant. It left unanswered, however, the question to what degree a public official should follow the dictates of a religiously formed conscience, and it left the way open for a purely secular approach to public policy. Kennedy was buried with full Catholic rites following his assassination in 1963.

BIBLIOGRAPHY. B. Bradlee, *Conversations with Kennedy* (1975); J. M. Burns, *John Kennedy* (1960); *DAB* 7; P. B. Fay, *The Pleasure of His Company* (1966); L. H. Fuchs, *John F. Kennedy and American Catholicism* (1967); N. A. Schneider, *Religious Views of President John F. Kennedy* (1965).

J. F. Hitchcock

Kenrick, Francis Patrick (1796-1863). Roman Catholic* prelate and scholar. Born in Dublin, Ireland, in 1815 Kenrick left home to enter Rome's College of the Propaganda and was ordained* April 2, 1821. From Rome he went to Bishop* Benedict Flaget's* Kentucky diocese,* where he served as a St. Joseph Seminary professor, a pastor* and eventually a controversialist against local Protestants.*

Kenrick, consecrated* bishop on June 6, 1830, became coadjutor to Philadelphia's Bishop Henry Conwell, whom he succeeded in 1842. His leadership was immediately tested by trustees of St. Mary's Church, who refused to recognize episcopal* parish* appointments until Kenrick's 1831 interdict which, in effect, ended trusteeism* in Philadelphia. A more severe trial was the nativist* rioting of May and July 1844, that left churches razed and several Catholics dead. Kenrick fled the city during the May riots, closed churches and condemned retaliation. He demanded—with no result—civil payment for the damages.

Kenrick also pursued scholarly interests. Encouraged by the Oxford Movement,* he called the American Episcopalian* hierarchy to unite with

Rome. This effort inspired his books on papal primacy and justification. Among his other writings were his four-volume *Theologia Dogmatica* (1834-1840) and the three-volume *Theologia Moralis* (1841-1843)—used in American seminaries for twenty-five years—and his revision of the Douai Bible* (1849-1850).

Kenrick contributed to the American episcopacy's national efforts. He composed the pastoral letters of Baltimore's Sixth (1846) and Seventh (1849) Provincial Councils.* After being appointed Baltimore's archbishop* in 1851, he convened the First Plenary Council (1852). The archbishop also collected the American hierarchy's opinions on the Immaculate Conception* (1853) and attended the dogma's* promulgation in Rome (1854). Kenrick's final challenge was the Civil War.* His scholastic approach, placing national stability above slavery's abolition* and states' rights, antagonized both sides. He died in Baltimore during the conflict.

BIBLIOGRAPHY. *DAB* V; H. J. Nolan, *The Most Reverend Francis Patrick Kenrick, Third Bishop of Philadelphia, 1830-1851* (1948); J. J. O'Shea, *The Two Kenricks* (1904). S. Y. Mize

Kenrick, Peter Richard (1806-1896). First Roman Catholic* archbishop* of St. Louis. After ordination* to the priesthood* in 1832 in Ireland, Kenrick immigrated to Philadelphia, where his brother, Francis Patrick Kenrick,* was the bishop* of the diocese.* Peter became rector* of the cathedral,* president of the seminary* and vicar general. In 1841 he was named coadjutor bishop of the diocese of St. Louis, and archbishop in 1847. During the Civil War* he refused to allow the U.S. flag to be flown from the cathedral. After the Civil War, when Missouri adopted the Drake constitution, which forbade any clergyman* from solemnizing marriages or preaching* without first taking an oath of loyalty to the state, Kenrick won an appeal of the case at the U.S. Supreme Court.* Kenrick was an important member of the minority party at the First Vatican Council* in Rome that opposed the definition of papal infallibility* on the grounds that the bishops of the world would have to concur with any pronouncement for it to be considered infallible.

BIBLIOGRAPHY. *DAB* V; P. K. Hennessy, "Infallibility in the Ecclesiology of Peter Richard Kenrick," *TS* (1984) 45:702-714.

T. F. Sable

Kenyon, (E)ssek (W)illiam (1867-1948). Pastor,* radio preacher and author. Born in Saratoga County, New York, and converted to Christ as a teenager, Kenyon attended Emerson College of Oratory in Boston, where he probably came into contact with the metaphysical thought systems (often described as New Thought) that influenced his theology.* After founding a Bible school* and pastoring* several churches in New England, he moved to Los Angeles in 1923. There he was a pioneer in radio ministry. In 1931 he moved to Seattle, founding a Baptist* church and a morning radio program.

The pithy, somewhat disjointed style of his fifteen books stressed the power of words spoken in faith and the supremacy of a so-called revelation knowledge over knowledge obtained by the senses: "A strong confession [of positive faith] . . . brings God on the scene." "Faith counts the thing done before God has acted. That compels God's action."

Kenyon was not widely known during his lifetime, but his teachings on faith, healing,* positive confession, revelation knowledge, and the godlike spiritual power available to "new creation" believers have directly influenced Kenneth Hagin, Kenneth Copeland, and other leaders in the Pentecostal* faith movement.*

BIBLIOGRAPHY. J. Matta, *The Born-Again Jesus of the Word-Faith Teachings* (1987); D. R. McConnell, *A Different Gospel* (1988). B. Barron

Kerygmatic Theology. A mid-twentieth-century emphasis, associated with Rudolf Bultmann,* grounding theology* in the New Testament proclamation of Jesus as the Christ rather than in the historical figure of Jesus of Nazareth. Kerygmatic theology takes as its starting point the New Testament *kerygma* (from the Greek word meaning "preaching" or "what is preached"); that is, the proclamation of the early Christian community recorded in the Gospels that Jesus is the Christ, and that in his life, death and resurrection God's redemptive purposes for humankind are accomplished.

Some biblical scholars early in the twentieth century posited that the Gospel accounts of the life of Jesus are actually confessions of faith by the early Christian community, not factual records providing accurate details of Jesus' life. Consequently, theological attention turned from the quest for the historical Jesus and toward the contemporary elaboration and understanding of the kerygma—the message proclaimed in the Gospels about Jesus Christ and the fulfillment in him of God's gift of salvation to humanity.

The most important figure in the development and expression of kerygmatic theology was the

German theologian and New Testament scholar Rudolf Bultmann. Bultmann asserted that the only valid subject for Christian theology (as distinct from historical-critical inquiry) is the Christ of faith confessed by the early Christian community and not the historically inaccessible figure of Jesus of Nazareth. Kerygmatic theology focuses on the figure of Christ, whose significance as a heavenly redeemer was couched in the world view of the first century.

For Bultmann this kerygma had to be demythologized* in order to arrive at its essence, which in turn could be meaningfully expressed today in existentialist terms. This approach was adopted in some form by a wide variety of American theologians and theological movements of the mid-twentieth century, primarily because it freed faith in Jesus Christ from dependence on the results of historical research. More recently, however, Bultmann's view has been criticized from the standpoint of both philosophy and biblical criticism. During the late 1950s and 1960s some of his students, most notably Ernst Käsemann in Germany and James M. Robinson in America, became convinced of a continuity between the historical Jesus and the Christ of the Kerygma and pursued a "new quest" for the historical Jesus. More recently New Testament scholars have tried to understand Jesus within the Jewish environment of his day and theologians have pursued more direct lines between the Jesus of history and the Christ of faith.

BIBLIOGRAPHY. C. E. Braaten and R. A. Harrisville, *Kerygma and History* (1962); ed. H. W. Bartsch, *Kerygma and Myth* (1961); J. M. Robinson, *A New Quest of the Historical Jesus* (1959).

W. A. Silva

Kester, Howard Anderson ("Buck") (1904-1977). Congregationalist* minister* and social activist. Born in Martinsville, Virginia, Kester attended Lynchburg College and Vanderbilt University (B.D., 1931). Ordained* in 1936, he served as youth secretary (1927-1929) and Southern secretary (1929-1934) of the pacifistic Fellowship of Reconciliation.* He then worked independently under the auspices of the Fellowship of Southern Churchmen,* doing grass-roots work on racial and economic issues. He helped found Friends of the Soil and the Southern Tenant Farmers Union, as well as investigated lynchings and racial unrest for the NAACP. In 1931 he ran for Congress in Tennessee on the Socialist party ticket. From 1943 to 1947 he was principal of Penn Normal Industrial and Agricultural School. He served as secretary of the Fellowship of Southern Churchmen from 1952 to 1957, and then as a college professor and administrator.

L. M. Japinga

Keswick Movement. An evangelical* movement stressing personal holiness* commonly disseminated through summer conferences and Bible schools* in North America. The Keswick teaching had its genesis in the writing and speaking ministries of three Americans: William E. Boardman* and the husband-wife team, Hannah Whitall* and Robert Pearsall Smith.* In 1843, as a young Presbyterian* grocer in Potosi, Illinois, Boardman began seeking the experience of sanctification.* After reading the testimonies of Charles G. Finney* and Asa Mahan,* he and his wife found "rest of heart in Jesus for sanctification." After study at Lane Theological Seminary, Boardman found his mission in life as an advocate of the "Higher Christian Life."* In 1859 his book *The Higher Christian Life* was published and spread his views to thousands. The book led to his attendance at various Holiness conferences.

In the late 1860s Pearsall Smith and his wife, Hanna Whitall Smith, also began traveling in the interest of Holiness. A businessman by vocation, Smith, along with his wife, had come to faith in Christ in 1858, eight years after their marriage. With the passing of years, however, both became dissatisfied with their spiritual experience. A change came in 1867 when Mrs. Smith learned through a Methodist* dressmaker about an experience called the "second blessing"* which brought a believer "victory." As a consequence, she soon found deliverance from sin's guilt and power. She then introduced her husband to "the secret of victory."

The Smiths began to propagate their views through magazines, books and Holiness meetings. In London, during Dwight L. Moody's* 1873 campaign, the Smiths joined Boardman for a series of breakfasts designed to promote Holiness. By this means 2,400 ministers heard their message. A series of conferences followed at the Broadlands estate of W. Cowper-Temple, at Oxford and at Brighton.

Under the inspiration of the Oxford meetings, Canon T. D. Harford-Battersby arranged for an open-air conference in his parish.* Keswick, located about twenty-five miles from Carlisle, became the center of Holiness teaching in England and gave its name to the movement. The first conference, in July 1875, came only three weeks after the huge Brighton Convention. Annual conferences at Keswick followed.

The Keswick teaching rejected the traditional evangelical teaching that a believer can be justified in a moment but then the process of sanctification must proceed by inward struggle and strife. Keswick offered instead deliverance from the power of sin through faith in Christ the Victor. Keswick speakers often urged their listeners to yield and trust Christ in an instant, but maintained that the believer's tendency to sin was not extinguished but merely counteracted by living victoriously in the Spirit. This life in the Spirit equips believers for service—thus the movement has maintained an emphasis on evangelism* and missions.*

Largely through Moody's Northfield Conferences in Massachusetts, the Keswick teaching spread throughout the U.S. and Canada, and captured many evangelical Bible schools and missionary agencies. The birth of the American Keswick organization came in 1913 when Robert C. McQuilkin,* later president of Columbia Bible College, invited a group of young people from Philadelphia to a conference at Oxford, Pennsylvania, to hear Henry W. Frost,* the home director of the China Inland Mission,* and W. H. Griffith-Thomas,* a frequent speaker at Keswick conferences. The next year the conference met at Princeton, New Jersey, but in 1923 it moved to its permanent home at Keswick Grove, New Jersey.

BIBLIOGRAPHY. S. Barabas, *So Great Salvation: The History and Message of the Keswick Convention* (1952); J. C. Pollack, *The Keswick Story* (1964); B. B. Warfield, *Perfectionism,* 2 vols. (1931). B. L. Shelley

Ketcham, Robert Thomas (1889-1978). Fundamentalist* Baptist* minister.* A native of Nelson, Pennsylvania, Ketcham lacked a college and seminary education but pastored Baptist churches in Roulette (1912-1915), Brookville (1915-1919) and Butler (1919-1923), Pennsylvania; Niles (1923-1926) and Elyria, Ohio (1926-1932); Gary, Indiana (1932-1939); and Waterloo, Iowa (1939-1948).

He entered the fundamentalist-modernist controversy* in the Northern Baptist Convention (NBC) through the circulation of more than 200,000 copies of his pamphlet, *A Statement of the First Baptist Church of Butler, Pennsylvania, with reference to the New World Movement and the $100,000,000 Drive* (1919). A member of the Baptist Bible Union,* Ketcham withdrew from the NBC in 1928 and became president of the newly formed Ohio Association of Independent Baptist Churches. He led in the development of the General Association of Regular Baptist Churches

(GARBC),* serving as vice president (1933) and president (1934-1938). He was National Representative of the GARBC (1948-1960), editor of the *Baptist Bulletin* (1948-1955) and National Consultant to the GARBC (1960-1966). Diagnosed as suffering with conical cornea in 1913, he was near blindness throughout his ministry.

BIBLIOGRAPHY. J. M. Murdoch, *Portrait of Obedience* (1979); R. Rayburn, "The Outworking of Obedience," *The Baptist Bulletin* 31:10 (March 1966):9-12. R. T. Clutter

Key, Francis Scott (1780-1843). Author of "The Star Spangled Banner," Episcopal* layman and Sunday-school* statesman. Born in Maryland, Key attended St. John's College, Annapolis, where he later studied law. Opening a practice in 1801, he eventually moved to Georgetown, Washington, D.C.

During the War of 1812 Key was sent to obtain the release of Dr. William Beanes, who had been seized by the British and was held aboard the fleet in Baltimore's harbor. Key, detained on an enemy vessel, was compelled to witness the bombardment of Fort McHenry, one of the defenses of Baltimore. Overcome by anxiety and fearful the city would fall, he saw the American flag illumined by bomb explosions during the night. By the light of dawn, seeing that the flag still flew, he penned the words to the "The Star Spangled Banner." Published in the Baltimore *American* on September 21, it became the U.S. national anthem in 1931.

Less known is Key's work in the Sunday-school movement. From his office in Washington, D.C., Key commuted home each weekend to Baltimore, Maryland, where he taught a large Sunday-school class of over 400 men. One of the founders of the American Sunday School Union* in 1824, he served on its board and presided over the 1830 Sunday-school meeting in Washington, D.C., that launched the Mississippi Valley Campaign, one of the most aggressive Sunday-school outreach programs ever conceived. Key envisioned establishing within two years a Sunday school in every town in an area which covered 1,300,000 square miles and had a population of four million. The anticipated budget for the project was $40,000.

Key was active in getting many people interested in the enterprise, including members of Congress, a justice of the Supreme Court and his friend Senator Daniel Webster. The Mississippi Valley Enterprise ultimately involved a variety of voluntary organizations and took fifty years to complete. In all there were 61,297 Sunday schools organized with 407,244 teachers and 2,650,784 pupils. A million books were placed in Sunday-school libraries and 80 to 100 missionaries were employed each year in the project. A total of $2,133,364.13 was ultimately invested in the missionary project.

BIBLIOGRAPHY. *DAB* V.   E. L. Towns

Key 73. An effort by American evangelicals* to "call our continent to Christ" in the year 1973. The program, sparked by a 1967 *Christianity Today* editorial, was sponsored by over 130 denominations* and religious organizations. Eschewing doctrinal* divisions in favor of the common concern to present the gospel message to as many people as possible, the program was nevertheless unable to enlist separatist* fundamentalists* because of its ecumenical nature. Leaders sought to awaken local congregations to their calling to evangelize* and to mobilize local churches in carrying out the year-long endeavor. Prayer* meetings, Bible studies* and lay* witness programs were organized. Specific plans were made to develop vacation ministries, summer leisure programs with children, spontaneous evangelism, hymn* contests and art festivals—all outside the traditional forms of evangelism. Churches were encouraged to implement those evangelistic efforts which best fit their specific needs and contexts. Although results were mixed, Key 73 represented an important attempt at grass-roots cooperation among evangelicals in America.

BIBLIOGRAPHY. *Key 73 Congregational Resource Book* (1973).   B. J. Leonard

Kierkegaard, Søren Aabye (1813-1855). Danish philosopher. Born and educated in Copenhagen, Denmark, Kierkegaard studied for ordination* in the Danish Lutheran Church but was never ordained. Given to deep melancholy and introspection, Kierkegaard lived much of his short life withdrawn from society, writing on philosophical, aesthetic and theological topics. Having undergone a deep religious experience in 1848, Kierkegaard began to reflect on the radical difference between authentic Christianity and that of the Danish state church. His later writings are characterized by the themes of personal authenticity, the profound distinction between God and humanity, and the need for a personal, subjective engagement with truth, which can be known only indirectly and dialectically.

Kierkegaard's influence was not felt in America until the century after his death. Intellectually, Kierkegaard stood behind the development of existentialism which, through its many facets, emphasizes the priority of existence over essence. This philosophical movement has been one of the major currents of twentieth-century thought, particularly through the period 1920-1960. Christian existentialism* is the appropriation of Kierkegaard's insights for Christian theology* and ethics,* stressing human experience, freedom and the commitment of faith. Existentialism was late in coming to North America, partially because it presupposed a certain anxiety that was lacking in American culture until the 1930s, when the Depression* and the shattered hopes of world peace and democracy* began to take effect. During the 1940s Walter Lowrie's* English translations of Kierkegaard's works helped introduce Americans to Kierkegaardian thought.

Elements of Kierkegaard's theological approach are found in some leading European theologians who greatly affected American theology. Karl Barth's* early dialectical* theology was heavily indebted to Kierkegaard's contention that Christianity was absolutely paradoxical since its central tenet was that God has appeared in the flesh in Jesus Christ. But Kierkegaard's influence could also be detected in Paul Tillich's* view of humanity's existence as estrangement, Emil Brunner's* understanding of the personal nature of truth and Rudolf Bultmann's* emphasis on the decision of faith. The Catholic* theologian Karl Rahner* echoed Kierkegaard's concerns when he stressed the human recipient of Christian revelation. And America's own Reinhold Niebuhr* showed his indebtedness to Kierkegaard in his discussions of "anxiety." But while Kierkegaard received a sympathetic reading among theologians broadly understood as neo-orthodox,* the conservative evangelical* response during the 1940s and 1950s was mixed, ranging from the stringent critique of existentialism by the Reformed* apologist* Cornelius Van Til* to the critical appreciation by theologian Edward J. Carnell.*

BIBLIOGRAPHY. E. J. Carnell, *The Burden of Søren Kierkegaard* (1965); M. J. Heinecken, "Søren Kierkegaard," in *A Handbook of Christian Theologians,* eds. M. E. Marty and D. C. Peerman (1984); S. Kierkegaard, *A Kierkegaard Anthology,* ed. R. Bretall (1946); W. Lowrie, *Kierkegaard* (1938).

D. K. McKim

King, Jonas (1792-1869). Pioneer missionary* to the Near East and Greece. Born in Hawley, Massachusetts, King graduated from Williams College (1816) and Andover Theological Seminary* (1819), and then engaged in two years of home missionary work and private study. In 1821 he was appointed professor of Oriental languages at the newly established Amherst College. While studying Arabic in Paris, he was asked by Pliny Fisk* to join him in surveying missionary opportunities in the Near East. Local solicitation for his support led to the formation of the Paris Evangelical Missionary Society. From 1822 to 1827 he observed and did missionary work in Palestine, Lebanon and Syria. After returning to the U.S. he agreed in 1828 to accompany a shipment of relief supplies to Greece. In 1829 he was reappointed by the American Board of Commissioners for Foreign Missions* and in 1831 settled in Athens for thirty-eight years of pioneer missionary work, with occasional tours in Europe, the Levant and America. King published extensively in Greek, and helped establish a number of schools. His special contribution was the translation of the Bible* into Armeno-Turkish.

BIBLIOGRAPHY. *DAB* V; F. E. H. Haines, *Jonas King, Missionary to Syria and Greece* (1979).

D. M. Stowe

King, Joseph Hillary (1869-1946). Holiness* and Pentecostal* leader. Born in Anderson County, South Carolina, King's family moved to Franklin County, Georgia, in 1885. There he was converted* in a Methodist* camp meeting* (1885) and soon embraced the doctrine and experience of entire sanctification.* Although he had only eighteen months of formal elementary education, King decided to prepare for the ministry by enrolling as a theology* student at the U. S. Grant University in Chattanooga. Eventually, this was to make him one of the better-educated leaders of the early Pentecostal Movement. After several years as a Methodist pastor* in north Georgia, in 1898 King became vice-president of come-outist Benjamin Irwin's* fledgling Holiness group, the Fire-Baptized Holiness Church.* In 1900 he succeeded Irwin as president following Irwin's departure under a cloud of "open and gross sin."

In 1908, King embraced Pentecostalism and brought the Fire-Baptized Holiness Church with him into the Pentecostal Movement. In 1911 it merged with the Pentecostal Holiness Church, and the newly formed Pentecostal denomination* established its headquarters in Franklin Springs, Georgia. King became general superintendent of this group in 1917 and in 1937 was consecrated* its first bishop. King's *From Passover to Pentecost* (1914) was as an early and influential defense of the Pentecostal Movement.

BIBLIOGRAPHY. J. C. Campbell, *The Pentecostal Holiness Church, 1898-1948* (1951); J. H. King, *Yet Speaketh: The Memoirs of the Late Bishop Joseph H. King* (1949).

E. L. Blumhofer

King, Martin Luther, Jr. (1929-1968). African-American Baptist* minister* and civil rights* leader. Born and raised in Atlanta, Georgia, King experienced the restrictions of segregation throughout his youth. The son and grandson of Baptist ministers, he himself chose a career in the ministry while a student at Morehouse College (B.A., 1948). He then studied for the ministry at Crozer Theological Seminary (B.D., 1951) and did graduate studies in systematic theology at Boston University (Ph.D., 1955).

In 1954 he became pastor of Dexter Avenue Baptist Church in Montgomery, Alabama. A year later he gained national acclaim as president of the Montgomery Improvement Association and the leader of the Montgomery bus boycott. It was during this first major campaign of the modern Civil Rights Movement that King developed his philosophy and tactic of nonviolent protest to bring about social change. Following the boycott, King became associate pastor of his father's church, Ebenezer Baptist, in Atlanta. In 1957 King participated in the Prayer Pilgrimage to Washington, D.C. The same year he became president of the newly organized Southern Christian Leadership Conference* (SCLC), which served as the coordinating body for local protests and affiliates across the South. Two primary objectives of SCLC were desegregation of public accommodations, and voter education and registration of African-Americans. Major campaigns led by Dr. King included the Albany, Georgia, movement in 1962; the Birmingham protest in 1963; and the Selma to Montgomery march in 1965. These events, along with the 1963 March on Washington, contributed to passage of the 1964 Civil Rights Act and the 1965 Voting Rights Act. In 1964 King was named the Nobel Peace Prize recipient.

Recognizing that civil rights statutes were of limited meaning to the poor, after 1965 King turned his attention to economic inequities, particularly in Northern urban areas. His Chicago campaign of 1966 served mainly to reveal the complexity and intransigence of economic problems. King is perhaps best known for his 1963 "I Have a Dream" speech, which reflected the goal of integration, the ideology of reform and the strategy of moral persuasion that characterized the first phase of the Civil Rights Movement. His 1967 "Beyond Vietnam" speech, in which he denounced the Vietnam War,* linking the issues of poverty, racism and militarism, is reflective of his movement to a more radical critique of the structures of American society in the last three years of his life. In 1968 King began organizing a Poor People's Campaign to bring together a coalition of impoverished whites and ethnic minorities to lobby the federal government for an "Economic Bill of Rights." His outspokenness on international issues of peace and imperialism earned him the enmity of many former supporters, while intensifying the opposition long waged against him by the FBI and others. He was assassinated on April 4, 1968, while in Memphis, Tennessee, to support striking garbage workers. King authored five books: *Stride Toward Freedom* (1958), *Strength to Love* (1963), *Why We Can't Wait* (1964), *Where Do We Go from Here: Chaos or Community?* (1967) and *Trumpet of Conscience* (1968). His birthday, observed on the third Monday in January, became a national holiday in 1986.

BIBLIOGRAPHY. *DARB*; D. J. Garrow, *Bearing the Cross: Martin Luther King, Jr. and the Southern Christian Leadership Conference, 1955-1968* (1986); D. L. Lewis, *King: A Biography,* 2nd ed. (1978); S. B. Oates, *Let the Trumpet Sound: The Life of Martin Luther King, Jr.* (1985).

M. R. Sawyer

King Philip's War (1675-1676). The most bloody and destructive Native American war of the seventeenth century. King Philip became the leader of the Wampanoag tribe in 1662 and unlike his father, Massasoit, who befriended the Pilgrims,* Philip deeply resented the power of the English and the expansion of their settlements, believing their attempts to civilize and Christianize Native Americans were primarily designed to gain military allies. Following the execution of three Native Americans for the murder of one of missionary* John Eliot's* "praying Indians," Philip and his warriors began looting houses in the town of Swansea in June of 1675. The New England Confederation declared war but was initially hampered by poor commanders and lack of unity. The violence spread, leaving little of New England untouched. Both Native Americans and whites were fighting with guns, and the resulting brutality was unparalleled in the New England experience. Philip was finally captured and killed on August 12, 1676, when, according to Richard Hutchinson, "the Providence of God wonderfully appeared."

By the war's end, more than a dozen towns were almost completely destroyed, and several thousand people had died. In Massachusetts alone two thousand people were on public relief, and the war expenses were estimated by the colonies at one hundred thousand pounds. For Native Americans, the war meant utter destruction. In addition to loss of life, there were numerous restrictions on freedom of movement, residence and right to own arms. Many were sold into slavery, including Philip's nine-year-old son. While there continued to be skirmishes on the frontier, King Philip's War ended the Native American menace in southern New England and opened a vast area to white settlement.

After the war there was little hope that Christian missions would save the Native Americans. The New England Company still provided funds for the effort, but little more was accomplished. New Englanders had their illusions of a wilderness Zion shattered, and many believed that the war was God's way of punishing them for befriending Native Americans and being too easy on the heretics in their midst. According to John Fiske, "The Puritan, who conned his Bible so earnestly, had taken his hint from the wars of the Jews, and swept his New English Canaan with a broom that was pitiless and searching." While some Puritans* did stiffen their resistance to heresy, forced population movements into Rhode Island and Maine broadened the vision of many, and Puritan society began losing its narrow parochialism.

BIBLIOGRAPHY. T. Church, *The History of Philip's War, Commonly Called the Great Indian War of 1675 and 1676* (1716); W. Hubbard, *A Narrative of the Troubles with the Indians in New-England* (1677); D. E. Leach, *Flintlock and Tomahawk: New England in King Philip's War* (1958); C. H. Lincoln, ed., *Narratives of the Indian Wars, 1675-1699* (1913). N. L. Erickson

Kingdom of God. The biblical term *kingdom of God* has taken on various meanings in American religious history. H. Richard Niebuhr's* *The Kingdom of God in America* (1937) concluded that the idea of the kingdom of God had been "the dominant idea in American Christianity," but it had meant different things in different eras. In the colonial period it meant "sovereignty of God," in the age of revivals it meant "reign of Christ," and in the late nineteenth and early twentieth centuries it meant "kingdom on earth." Right or wrong, Niebuhr's analysis shows that trends in American religion can be traced through the nuances of this term. The concept of the kingdom often reflects attitudes toward the church, toward the American nation and toward future expectations.

For the nonseparating Puritans* of the Massachusetts Bay Colony, as exemplified by Governor

John Winthrop* or Boston minister John Cotton,* the term *kingdom of God* represented not only an internal lordship over the individual conscience, as it did for Roger Williams,* but an external sovereignty of God over corporate society, whether in the church or in the civil sphere. By the era of the Great Awakening* the individual, internal sense of the term was receiving greater emphasis. Jonathan Edwards's* own conversion occurred in connection with his meditation on 1 Timothy 1:17: "Now unto the King eternal, immortal, invisible. . . ." His sense of the sovereignty of God produced in him an internal sweetness that inspired his revivalistic preaching and his teaching of love as the essence of true virtue.

During the nineteenth century, revivalists* of the Second Awakening* and those who followed extended the sense of the reign of Christ through love to active social reform. Charles G. Finney* launched a "benevolent empire" to apply to society the moral principles of "God's government." By the beginning of the twentieth century, Christocentric liberals* such as William Newton Clarke* and William Adams Brown* were developing the concept of the kingdom of God in a two-fold sense: as the community of the redeemed and as the purpose of history.

The social application of the gospel stressed by liberalism* was further enunciated by the Social Gospel Movement,* fathered by Washington Gladden* and articulated most clearly by Walter Rauschenbusch.* In contrast to the evangelical* emphasis on individual response to the reign of Christ, Social Gospelers stressed the corporate or organic sense both of the kingdom of God and of sin* as it is found in the structures of society. As Rauschenbusch was ministering in the "Hell's Kitchen" area of New York City, the concept of the kingdom of God struck him "as a new revelation." As he later wrote in *A Theology for the Social Gospel* (1917), "If theology is to offer an adequate doctrinal basis for the social gospel, it must not only make room for the doctrine of the Kingdom of God, but give it a central place and revise all other doctrines so that they will articulate organically with it." Contrary to the optimism prevalent at the turn of the century, he saw juxtaposed to the kingdom of God a "kingdom of evil" in society.

Among evangelicals at the turn of the century, postmillennialists* tended to identify advancement of the kingdom with social and cultural progress, whereas premillennialists* tended to be pessimistic about secular culture and to view the kingdom as coming visibly only with the return of Christ. For the latter, the kingdom in this age was conceived of primarily in spiritual terms, advanced through evangelism* and missions.* Nevertheless, for American evangelicals of all types, there was a tendency to relate positively toward America as God's instrument for bringing moral and social improvement and for spreading the gospel around the world.

Thus the kingdom of God for some came to be so closely identified with the American nation that it served as a basis for civil religion* in the U.S. Such American values as democracy,* liberty, equality and capitalism* were associated with Christian virtues and were exported together as the kingdom in some foreign missions work. Particularly characteristic of American Christianity was a stress on the kingdom at the expense of the institutional church. In the context of religious pluralism* fostered by the separation of church and state,* the kingdom concept extended over denominational* boundaries and laid stress on the church as invisible rather than visible. Typical of numerous parachurch* organizations, many a Protestant Christian college* adopted some variation of the motto "For Christ and His Kingdom."

Late-twentieth-century evangelicalism has sought anew to apply the gospel to social and political concerns, recognizing the relevance of the petition in the Lord's Prayer, "Thy kingdom come. Thy will be done in earth, as it is in heaven" (Mt 6:10, KJV).

BIBLIOGRAPHY. J. H. Moorhead, "Theological Interpretations and Critiques of American Society and Culture," in *Encyclopedia of the American Religious Experience,* ed. C. H. Lippy and P. W. Williams (1987); H. R. Niebuhr, *The Kingdom of God in America* (1937); T. L. Smith, *Revivalism and Social Reform: American Protestantism on the Eve of the Civil War* (1957); M. E. Marty, *Righteous Empire: The Protestant Experience in America* (1970); M. Marsden, *Fundamentalism and American Culture; The Shaping of Twentieth Century Evangelicalism, 1870-1925* (1980).

W. S. Barker

Kings College. *See* COLUMBIA UNIVERSITY.

Kingsbury, Cyrus (1786-1870). Missionary* educator among the Cherokee and Choctaw Indians. Born at Alstead, New Hampshire, Kingsbury was educated at Brown University* and Andover Theological Seminary.* In 1816 he was ordained* to the ministry* and was sent by the American Board of Commissioners for Foreign Missions* to establish mission schools among the Indians of the Five Civilized Tribes in the Southeast.

In 1817 he established the Brainerd Mission among the Cherokee near Chattanooga, Tennessee. In June 1818 he and his family moved to Mississippi where he founded the Eliot Mission on the Yazoo River, and two years later the Mayhew Mission, both among the Choctaws. Kingsbury remained there until 1830, when the Choctaws sold their Mississippi lands to the federal government and moved west to Arkansas. For the next several years, Kingsbury worked at various places among the Osage, Creek, Cherokee and Choctaw tribes and in 1836 moved to the Pine Ridge Mission near Ft. Towson in the Indian Territory, where the Choctaws were settling after being pushed west once again. There he worked among Native Americans for the remainder of his life.

BIBLIOGRAPHY. R. S. Walker, *Torchlights to the Cherokees: The Brainerd Mission* (1931); W. G. McLoughlin, *Cherokees and Missionaries, 1789-1839* (1984).   M. S. Joy

Kino, Eusebio Francisco (1645-1711). Jesuit* missionary to the American Southwest. Born to a family surnamed *Chino* in Segno, Italy, he devoted himself to missions* following an answered prayer to St. Francis Xavier. Joining the Society of Jesus, he studied in several German cities. Excelling in mathematics, he hoped to use his skills in China, where Jesuit scholars fused scientific expertise with missionary endeavors. In 1678, however, he was assigned by lot to a Mexico mission, and (after a two-year delay in Spain) sailed from Cadiz to Vera Cruz, landing in Mexico in 1681.

The following year he joined the Atondo expedition to Baja (lower) California, serving as royal cosmographer during its 1683 exploration; he then stayed to help establish Jesuit missions in the area. Drought closed the missions in 1685, and Kino (he changed the spelling of his name in Mexico) returned to Mexico City. In 1687 he went to Pimeria Alta, astradle today's Mexico-U.S. border, where he thereafter labored, becoming renowned as the "Apostle of Sonora and Arizona." Establishing his headquarters in Mission Dolores, he founded missions in various river valleys, ranging as far north as San Xavier del Bac, just south of present-day Tucson. He baptized approximately 4,500 Pima Indians and helped launch a cattle industry for the region.

Kino explored north and west to the Gila and Colorado rivers, drafting maps which facilitated subsequent Spanish penetration of this region. He proved Baja California to be a peninsula, not an island, and encouraged Jesuits to re-establish missions there in 1697 by supplying cattle as well as useful maps and encouragement. Kino died in Magdalina, where he had gone to dedicate a chapel.

See also MISSIONS TO NORTH AMERICA, SPANISH.

BIBLIOGRAPHY. H. E. Bolton, ed., trans., *Eusebio F. Kino: Historical Memoir of Pimeria Alta*, 2 vols. (1919); H. E. Bolton, *Rim of Christendom: A Biography of Eusebio Francisco Kino* (1936); *DAB* V; F. J. Smith et al., eds., *Father Kino in Arizona* (1966).   G. A. Reed

Kirk, Edward Norris (1802-1874). Congregationalist* evangelist* and pastor.* Born in New York City, Kirk graduated from the College of New Jersey* (B.A., 1820) and went on to study law in New York (1820-1822). However, his conversion* turned his attention to the ministry,* and he returned to Princeton to study at the seminary* (1822-1826).

Six years later he became pastor of the Fourth Presbyterian* Church in Albany, New York, a congregation organized in response to his revival* messages. Within eight years, over 1,000 new members had been added. But amid this success Kirk went to Great Britain where his protracted meetings enhanced his reputation as a polished and powerful preacher* and opened the door for evangelistic campaigns in several major Eastern cities upon his return to America. His success in Boston led to the formation of Mt. Vernon Congregational Church, where he pastored from 1842 to 1871. During his long ministry there, and even before, Kirk combined his evangelism* with antislavery,* temperance,* educational and other reform* activities, personally embodying the strong links between revivalism* and social reform within antebellum evangelicalism.*

Proof that nineteenth-century revivalism was as popular in urban* as in rural areas, Kirk's evangelistic preaching held great appeal for middle class Presbyterians* and Congregationalists in cities on both sides of the Atlantic Ocean. Kirk tailored the "new measures"* revivalism of Charles G. Finney* to fit the urbane tastes of his audiences in Boston, New York and London. In so doing, he made revivalism far more respectable and set the stage for the businessmen's-style evangelism of his most famous convert, Dwight L. Moody.*

BIBLIOGRAPHY. R. Carwardine, *Transatlantic Revivalism: Popular Evangelicalism in Britain and America, 1790-1865* (1978); *DAB* V; *DARB*; D. O. Mears, *Edward Norris Kirk* (1877); *NCAB* 6; T. L. Smith, *Revivalism & Social Reform: American Protestantism on the Eve of the Civil War* (1957).   R. W. Pointer

Kirkconnell, Watson (1895-1977). Linguist, poet, Milton scholar and university president. His translation and publication of elegies from forty different languages (*European Elegies,* 1928) immediately established Kirkconnell's reputation as one of the foremost translators in the Western world and began a lifelong interest in the poetry of other countries. His work as translator led him to investigate and encourage Canadian literature written in other than French and English, championing Canadian multiculturalism. His translations, original poetry, reviews and articles constitute a bibliography of massive proportions.

In 1948 he became president of Acadia University, a Baptist* institution in Wolfville, Nova Scotia. He led the successful struggle in that province for government funding for universities, funding that guaranteed Acadia's survival and expansion in the 1960s. One of the most prominent Baptist laymen in the country, he was one of the key founders of the Baptist Federation of Canada* in 1944.

BIBLIOGRAPHY. W. Kirkconnell, *A Slice of Canada: Memoirs* (1967); J. R. C. Perkin and J. B. Snelson, *Morning in His Heart; The Life and Writings of Watson Kirkconnell* (1986).

B. M. Moody

Kirkland, John Thornton (1770-1840). Unitarian* minister* and Harvard* president. Born near Little Falls, New York, to missionaries* to the Oneida Indians, Kirkland graduated from Harvard in 1789. He went to Stockbridge to study divinity with Stephen West* but was repelled by West's Hopkinsian views. Returning to Harvard he tutored and continued his studies and was influenced by reading the Unitarian Joseph Priestley.* In 1794 he was ordained,* having already been called as pastor of New South Church, Boston, in 1793. There he won the younger generation away from "French infidelity" through logical, intelligent, attractive sermons and led them painlessly toward Unitarianism without even mentioning the term. When the Harvard presidency became vacant in 1810, Kirkland, the ideal gentleman scholar, was chosen for the post without opposition. Loved by students, his tenure marked the emergence of Harvard as a true university, with new law and divinity* schools. In 1819, with money raised for new professorships in divinity, a "Faculty of Theology" was officially recognized, and by 1826 a new Divinity Hall had been constructed. Declining enrollment, due to a Calvinist campaign against the new influences at Harvard, and loss of public funds when Massachusetts voted Republican in 1824, drove Kirkland to resign in 1828.

BIBLIOGRAPHY. *AAP* 8; *DAB* V; S. E. Morison, *Three Centuries of Harvard, 1636-1936* (1936).

M. B. Newell

Knights of Labor. The first national labor union and focus of a controversy among Catholics* in the late nineteenth century. Founded as the first national labor union (1869) by Uriah Stevens, the Knights of Labor had a majority of immigrant* Catholic members and after 1878 was headed by a Roman Catholic, Terrence Powderly, the four-term mayor of Scranton, Pennsylvania. Unions customarily used secrecy to protect their memberships and often took their rituals and trappings from secret societies like freemasonry. Pope Leo XIII's* encyclical* *Humanum Genus* (1884) opposed secret societies. This factor, in addition to questions raised about Powderly's ideological leanings despite his public repudiation of socialism* and radicalism, made the Knights suspect by a large portion of the American Roman Catholic hierarchy. Bishop James A. Healey* of Portland, Maine, excommunicated those who belonged to the Knights of Labor.

In 1884 Canadian archbishop Elzear A. Taschereau* obtained a condemnation of the Knights of Labor from Roman Church authorities. The American archbishops at their annual meeting in 1887 voted ten to two against such a condemnation being applied to the U.S.. Bishops James Gibbons,* John Ireland* and John Keane* warned the Roman authorities in a separate letter that the condemnation of the Knights would be a tragic loss. Vatican officials agreed, provided that any reference to communism* or socialism was eliminated from the Knights's constitution. In the larger Americanism* controversy, this decision was regarded as a victory for those within the American Catholic Church who wished to accommodate their Church to American culture.

See also RERUM NOVARUM.

BIBLIOGRAPHY. H. J. Browne, *The Catholic Church and the Knights of Labor* (1949).

T. F. Sable

Knorr, Nathan H. (1905-1977) Leader of Jehovah's Witnesses.* Born in Bethlehem, Pennsylvania, Knorr graduated from Allentown High School in 1923. In that year he began working in the Watchtower Society's publishing office, becoming director in 1934. Knorr had considerable managerial skills, and in 1942 he succeeded Joseph F. Rutherford* as president of the Jehovah's Witnesses. Knorr worked hard to improve the education of members, beginning the Kingdom Ministry

School to help Witnesses carry out missionary activity. He also enlarged the group's program of international conferences. His final years were marked by the expectation and disappointment surrounding the prediction that the Second Advent would take place in 1975.

BIBLIOGRAPHY. J. Penton, *Apocalypse Delayed: The Story of Jehovah's Witnesses* (1985).

I. Hexham

Knox, John (c.1817-1892). Disciples of Christ* pioneer on Prince Edward Island. Born and educated in Edinburgh, Scotland, Knox trained as a medical doctor in London before going to Charlottetown, Prince Edward Island, as an Anglican* missionary* in 1841. Upon arrival, however, he changed his views on baptism.* Knox was baptized* by immersion and moved to Albany, New York, where he pastored a Baptist* church. He returned to the Island in 1842 but only after being deeply influenced by the ideas of men like Barton W. Stone* and Alexander Campbell,* who believed that they were restoring the church to its original New Testament simplicity. In theory this meant a rejection of all credal statements and church structures.

Knox soon emerged as the leader of a small group of like-minded believers associated with Campbell's Disciples of Christ. For about forty years he pioneered the Disciples' work in Canada's Maritime Provinces. A powerful preacher,* Knox did much to establish his denomination* in the area. In 1881 deteriorating eyesight forced him to give up his itinerant preaching, and he returned to medical practice in Charlottetown.

BIBLIOGRAPHY. R. Butchart, *The History of the Disciples of Christ Since 1830* (1949).

D. M. Lewis

Knubel, Frederick Hermann (1870-1945). Lutheran* Church president. Born in Manhattan, the son of immigrant parents, Knubel switched from business to ministry,* attending Gettysburg College (1893) and Seminary (1895) and Leipzig University (1895-1896). A New York City pastorate (1896-1918) revealed his gifts of leadership, and his guidance of the wartime Lutheran Commission on Soldiers' and Sailors' Welfare made him known nationally. Elected president of the new United Lutheran Church in America (ULCA), his twenty-six-year tenure helped consolidate this largest and, by antecedents, oldest North American Lutheran body. With Charles M. Jacobs of the Philadelphia Seminary, Knubel formulated the ULCA "Washington Declaration" (1920)—a position on confes-

sional* unity and interchurch relations eventually taken by most other American Lutherans. Knubel helped found the National Lutheran Council* (1918), and the Lutheran World Convention (1923), guiding the latter's American Section (1937-1944). He also fostered Lutheran participation in the Faith and Order movement and proposed (1938) that the movement adopt a proportionate confessional representation for Lutherans and others in the assembly and central committee of the nascent World Council of Churches.*

E. T. Bachmann

Knudson, Albert Cornelius (1873-1953). Methodist* Old Testament scholar and theologian.* Born in Grandmeadow, Minnesota, Knudson graduated from the University of Minnesota (B.A., 1893) prior to studying for the ministry at Boston University (S.T.B., 1896). He then did graduate work in Europe at the universities of Jena and Berlin (1897-1898) and was awarded the Ph.D. by Boston University (1900). Knudson began his career teaching church history at Denver University (1898-1900) and then taught philosophy and English Bible at Baker University (1900-1902) and Allegheny College (1902-1906). In 1906 he returned to Boston University, where he would spend the remainder of his career, first as professor of Hebrew and Old Testament exegesis* (1906-1921) and then as professor of systematic theology* (1921-1943) and dean of the School of Theology (1926-1938).

Knudson published several books on the Old Testament, the best known being *The Religious Teaching of the Old Testament* (1918). His principal contribution developed later in his career as he turned his attention to systematic theology and the problem of relating metaphysics to religious knowledge. Deeply influenced by Boston University's Borden P. Bowne,* Knudson emphasized the personalist themes of the immanence of God, an understanding of God in terms of personal categories, and religious knowledge as a fundamental and valid aspect of human experience. His systematic and speculative thought was published in *The Philosophy of Personalism* (1927); *The Doctrine of God* (1930); *The Doctrine of Redemption* (1933); and *The Validity of Religious Experience* (1937). In his teaching and writing he became an important advocate of personalism in pre-World War 2 Protestant* liberalism.*

BIBLIOGRAPHY. *DARB.* The Editors

Kohlmann, Anthony (1771-1836). Jesuit* priest* and vicar general of the diocese* of New

York. Born in Kaiserberg, Alsace, Kohlmann completed theological studies in Friburg, Switzerland, and was ordained* a priest in 1796. A member of the Fathers of the Sacred Heart for nine years, in 1805 he was admitted to the Society of Jesus and entered the Jesuit novitiate at Dunaburg, White Russia. After one year he was dispatched to the Jesuit mission in the U.S. and completed his novitiate training at Georgetown College.

In 1808 he was assigned to New York City, where he became both the pastor* of St. Peter's Church and the vicar general of the newly erected diocese of New York. Following the death of Bishop Luke Concanen, he assumed the additional title of apostolic administrator of the diocese. During his tenure as vicar he laid the cornerstone and oversaw the construction of Old St. Patrick's Cathedral and founded both the New York Literary Institution (1808-1815) and an Ursuline academy for girls (1812).

Kohlmann's involvement in a celebrated 1813 case concerning the secrecy of the confessional brought him wide recognition. Used as an intermediary by a penitent to make restitution for a theft, Kohlmann was summoned to court and asked to reveal the name of his penitent. Citing the seal of confession, he refused to answer. Although the district attorney wished to drop the case, Kohlmann and his supporters, eager to establish a precedent, insisted that the case be heard. The Court of General Sessions, presided over by Mayor DeWitt Clinton, ruled in Kohlmann's favor. Subsequently the state of New York recognized the confidentiality of the confessional.

Following his return (1815) to Washington, Kohlmann served as master of novices, president of Georgetown and superior of the American Jesuits. In 1824 he was made a professor at the Gregorian University in Rome, where the future Pope Leo XIII* was one of his students. He died on April 11, 1836, while on the staff of the Church of the Gesu in Rome.

BIBLIOGRAPHY. F. X. Curran, *The Return of the Jesuits* (1966); L. J. Kelly, "Fr. Charles Neale and the Jesuit Restoration in America," *Woodstock Letters* 72 (1943):21-33; 116-147; 243-263.

J. M. McShane

Konstantinides, Michael. *See* CONSTANTINIDES, MICHAEL.

Krauth, Charles Philip (1797-1867). Lutheran* church leader and theologian.* Initially preparing for a medical career at the University of Maryland, he studied for the Lutheran ministry* and was ordained* by The Evangelical Lutheran Synod of Maryland and Virginia in 1821. Krauth became professor of biblical literature at the Lutheran Seminary in Gettysburg, Pennsylvania, in 1833 and served as the first president of Pennsylvania College (later called Gettysburg College) from 1834 to 1850. He returned to the faculty of the seminary* in 1850 and taught biblical philology and church history until his death. He was an editor of two influential Lutheran periodicals, *The Evangelical Lutheran Intelligencer* and *The Evangelical Review.*

Krauth, like his son, Charles Porterfield Krauth,* was a staunch defender of strict Lutheran confessionalism* within the General Synod of the Evangelical Lutheran Church in the United States and was its president in 1848. He fostered a Lutheran self-consciousness which helped prevent a collapse of Lutheranism into American sectarianism.

BIBLIOGRAPHY. *DAB* V; A. Spaeth, *Charles Porterfield Krauth,* 2 vols. (1898). J. F. Johnson

Krauth, Charles Porterfield (1823-1883). Lutheran* clergyman,* theologian* and educator. Born in a Lutheran manse at Martinsburg, Virginia (now West Virginia), Krauth was the son of Charles Philip Krauth,* an eminent leader of American Lutheranism* who in 1834 became president of the Lutheran college at Gettysburg, Pennsylvania. At the age of sixteen young Krauth graduated from the college over which his father presided and two years later (1841) from the seminary at Gettysburg. Owing in part to his academic surroundings, Krauth became a serious student and a bibliophile. He eventually collected fifteen thousand rare books in his personal library.

In 1842 he was ordained* to the Lutheran ministry.* Over the next several years (1841-1855) Krauth ministered at churches in Canton and Baltimore, Maryland, as well as Shepherdstown, Martinsburg and Winchester, Virginia. He then served pastorates in Pittsburgh (1855-1859) and Philadelphia (1859-1861). During this time Krauth began an intensive study of German theological literature virtually unknown among native American Lutherans. Of particular interest to him were the Lutheran dogmaticians and the confessional* standards of the sixteenth and seventeenth centuries. Krauth's translation and publication in the *Evangelical Review* of a portion from Heinrich Schmid's *Doctrinal Theology* in 1849 reflected his growing preference for conservative Lutheran theology.* This development in Krauth's thought coincided with the Great Immigration* of the 1840s and 1850s which brought close to one million Germans to America, among them many conservative Lutherans.

In the crisis that developed out of the increasing tension between native and European Lutheranism, Krauth became a spokesman for the conservative or European theological position. In 1861 he resigned as the pastor of St. Mark's Church in Philadelphia to become editor-in-chief of the *Lutheran and Missionary*. His writings not only revived conservative Lutheranism and secured a place for it in the American church but reflected his great gifts as a scholar. Krauth's intellectual abilities were recognized first by the Lutheran Church when he became the first professor of systematic* theology in 1864 at the newly formed theological seminary in Philadelphia.

From 1866 to 1868 Krauth served as a trustee of the University of Pennsylvania. In 1868 he joined the faculty to teach moral and intellectual philosophy, and in 1873 he was elected vice-provost. Krauth also played an important role as a member of the American Revision Committee of the Old Testament from 1871 until his death. Even though his activities outside the church increased, Krauth continued to work on behalf of conservative Lutheranism. In 1882 he became the editor-in-chief of the newly established *Lutheran Theological Review,* a journal expressing the conservative theological position of the Lutheran seminary at Philadelphia.

Krauth's chief literary contribution was *The Conservative Reformation and its Theology* (1871). A collection of essays and reviews written to express and defend confessional Lutheranism, it summed up Krauth's own theology and influenced many American Lutheran ministers. Sadly, Krauth died in Philadelphia before he could undertake a contemplated and partially researched biography of Luther.

BIBLIOGRAPHY. *DAB* V; *DARB; NCAB* 1; A. Spaeth, *Charles Porterfield Krauth,* 2 vols. (1898, 1909).							D. G. Hart

Kugler, Anna Sarah (1856-1930). Lutheran* medical missionary* to India. Born in Ardmore, Pennsylvania, the second of Charles and Harriet (Sheaff) Kugler's six children, Anna's education began at public school and included time at a Quaker* school. As a child she was inspired by a Baptist* missionary to consider a missionary career. In preparation she attended the Woman's Medical College of Pennsylvania, graduating in 1879. In 1883 Kugler went to Guntur, India, under the auspices of the General Synod (Lutheran) and its Women's Missionary Society. Despite her appointment as a teacher, Kugler equipped herself for medical work, which she commenced upon her arrival. Official medical work among Indian women began in 1885 when the Lutheran Women's Missionary Convention appointed Kugler as medical missionary and authorized collection of money for a women's dispensary (1893) and hospital (1898). Kugler's medical skill and regard for Indians won their respect. She died in the hospital she founded and which now bears her name.

BIBLIOGRAPHY. A. S. Kugler, *Guntur Mission Hospital* (1928); *NAW* 2.			L. D. Lagerquist

Kuhlman, Kathryn (1907-1976). Healing* evangelist.* Growing up in Concordia, Missouri, Kuhlman had an intense religious experience* at the age of thirteen and dropped out of high school at the age of sixteen to begin an itinerant preaching* ministry* that took her to Idaho and the Midwest.

In 1933 she came to Denver for a two-week revival* which was so successful that she settled there and founded the Denver Revival Tabernacle. In 1938 she married traveling evangelist Burroughs Waltrip, a decision that forced her to leave her Denver ministry. When she left him in 1944 she resumed her career as an evangelist. In 1946 she experienced the baptism of the Holy Spirit.*

Kuhlman moved to Franklin, Pennsylvania, where she ran revival meetings and hosted a radio show. In the spring of 1948 two spontaneous healings occurred during the course of her preaching and caused her to turn her attention to healing ministry. In 1950 she moved to Pittsburgh, where her meetings, theatrical but not fanatical, earned favorable treatment from both the media and church leaders. She freely admitted that not all were healed under her ministry, saying "only God knows" why not. From 1955 to 1975 she held meetings in the auditorium of the Carnegie Library.

During the 1960s her ministry expanded to include national and international appearances, a weekly television program on CBS, as well as regular services in Pittsburgh, Ohio, and Los Angeles. Two of her books, *I Believe in Miracles* (1968) and *God Can Do It Again* (1969), were immensely popular, the former selling millions of copies. Kuhlman was never directly associated with the Pentecostal Movement* and disapproved of the techniques of many healing evangelists. Along with Oral Roberts,* she was primarily responsible for bringing respectability to healing revivalism in North America.

BIBLIOGRAPHY. J. Buckingham, *Daughter of*

Destiny (1976); D. E. Harrell, *All Things Are Possible* (1975); H. K. Hosier, *Kathryn Kuhlman: The Life She Led, the Legacy She Left* (1976); A. Spraggett, *Kathryn Kuhlman: The Woman Who Believes in Miracles* (1970).   B. Barron

Kuhn, Isobel Miller (1901-1957). Missionary* to China. A Canadian, Kuhn attended Moody Bible Institute* when she was in her twenties and then joined the China Inland Mission (now Overseas Missionary Fellowship*) in 1928. She and her husband, John Kuhn, were assigned to work among the ethnic minorities of Yunnan Province in southwest China. From 1929 to 1950, with the exception of the World War 2* years, the Kuhns worked among the Lisu tribe. Forced to leave China after the Communist revolution, they continued work among tribal groups in northern Thailand. Isobel returned to the U.S. with cancer in 1954. In the period before her death, she wrote several inspirational accounts of mission work among the Lisu, including *Stones of Fire* (1960); *Ascent to the Tribes* (1956) and *Green Leaf in Drought* (1957). A popular writer among evangelicals,* some of her books sold over 100,000 copies and did much to familiarize the Christian reading public with her mission's work among the Lisu and other tribal peoples.

BIBLIOGRAPHY. C. Canfield, *One Vision Only: Biography of Isobel Kuhn* (1959).

D. H. Bays

Küng, Hans (1928-). Swiss Roman Catholic* theologian.* Educated at the Gregorian University in Rome and the Catholic Institute in Paris, since 1960 he has been associated with the University of Tübingen, where since 1963 he has directed the Institute for Ecumenical Research. One of his first books compared the positions of Karl Barth* and Catholics such as Aquinas on the topic of justification* (*Justification,* ET 1965), and he was a strong voice at the Second Vatican Council,* urging Catholic participation in ecumenical* efforts to reunite the church.

Küng's early works concentrated on ecclesiology. In 1970 he published a book questioning traditional Catholic claims for infallibility* (*Infallible?,* ET 1971). This book was a major reason for a Vatican censure in 1979 that took away his right to teach as an official Catholic theologian.

Küng has taught in the U.S. at the University of Michigan, and several of his books have been very influential, especially the translations of *On Being a Christian* (ET 1977), *Does God Exist?* (ET 1980) and *Eternal Life?* (ET 1984). Liberal Roman Cath-

olics have viewed him as a champion of religious liberty and theological freedom against restrictive Roman authorities, while Protestants have welcomed his ecumenical openness. In recent years Küng has broadened his ecumenism to include non-Christian religions, interesting himself in dialog with Muslim, Buddhist and Hindu views (*Christianity and World Religions,* ET 1986). Again and again, Küng has been at the forefront of new theological concerns.

BIBLIOGRAPHY. H. Haring and K.-J. Kuschel, eds., *Hans Küng: His Work and His Way* (1979); C. M. LaCugna, *The Theological Methodology of Hans Küng* (1982); R. Nowell, *A Passion for Truth* (1981).   J. T. Carmody

Kurtz, Benjamin (1795-1865). Lutheran* pastor,* editor and advocate of social reforms. Born in Harrisburg, Pennsylvania, Kurtz was closely identified with Samuel S. Schmucker* in the founding of Gettysburg Lutheran Seminary. As a Baltimore pastor he became the influential editor (1833-1861) of the *Lutheran Observer,* an English-language weekly through which Kurtz entered stridently into the many issues of the day within the nation and his church, advocating the use of the English language, religious revival* methods, the causes of temperance,* antislavery* and Christian unity among evangelicals.* Under Kurtz's editorship the pages of the *Lutheran Observer* were influential in defending the theological position that had prevailed in earlier decades among American Lutherans, a position that fell short of complete subscription to the Augsburg Confession. Several journals emerged in opposition to the *Observer* in order to promote more conservative theological postures. Kurtz founded the Missionary Institute, which later became Susquehanna University.

BIBLIOGRAPHY. E. C. Nelson, ed., *The Lutherans in North America* (1975); A. R. Wentz, *A Basic History of Lutheranism in America* (1964).

F. K. Wentz

Kuyper, Abraham (1837-1920). Dutch Calvinist* theologian* and statesman. Born in Massluis, the Netherlands, Kuyper was brought up in an orthodox* Reformed* household, his father being a minister in the Reformed Church. A brilliant student, Kuyper took both his undergraduate and doctoral degrees (in theology) at Leyden (1855-1862) and served for several years as a minister* in the Reformed Church. By the 1870s Kuyper was deeply involved in politics and the growing Dutch Neo-Calvinist Movement (1875-1925).

As founder and leader of this wide-ranging movement, Kuyper worked to mobilize the conservative Reformed sector of the Dutch population against the theological and cultural modernism* ascendant at the time. This required the development of a Calvinistic "world and life-view," which Kuyper advanced through his voluminous writings; and of a full set of separate institutions through which the Reformed could take forceful action. To this end Kuyper helped found a Calvinistic newspaper, university, labor union and political party, the latter's success bringing him the prime ministership of the Netherlands from 1901 to 1905.

Kuyper's influence in North America has descended chiefly along Dutch immigrant lines, especially those connected with the Christian Reformed Church.* In the U. S. the strategy of separate institutions went forward only in the educational realm, but there it has produced a full system of Christian schools* and concerted leadership in Christian scholarship nationwide. Kuyper's Canadian descendants have had some success as well in labor and politics. Kuyper's legacy consists chiefly in a presuppositionalist* approach to philosophy and apologetics* and in the drive to engage every domain of society and culture from a distinctly Christian point of view. Cultural analysis accordingly aims at uncovering the world view behind a movement or text, while social engagement proceeds under a principled pluralism toward a biblical concept of justice, out of the conviction that Christian models in both realms offer the best solution to modern problems.

BIBLIOGRAPHY. J. D. Bratt, *Dutch Calvinism in Modern America* (1984); D. W. Jellema, "Abraham Kuyper's Attack on Liberalism," *Review of Politics* 19 (1957):472-485; A. Kuyper, *Lectures on Calvinism* (1898).   J. D. Bratt

Kyle, Melvin Grove (1858-1933). Presbyterian* fundamentalist* educator and biblical archaeologist. Born in Cadiz, Ohio, Kyle graduated from Muskingum College (1881) and Allegheny Theological Seminary (1885) before entering the Presbyterian ministry. In 1908 Kyle began his long tenure as professor (-1922), and then president (1922-1930) at Xenia Theological Seminary (located at Xenia, Ohio, and later at St. Louis, Missouri). Kyle brought the seminary into national prominence by his archaeological research, writing and training of scores of fundamentalist Presbyterian pastors. During this most productive period of his life, Kyle helped to found the Bible League of North America, was a prominent speaker on the

Winona Bible Conference circuit, was active in establishing the League of Evangelical Students (a forerunner of InterVarsity Christian Fellowship*), and encouraged the support of fundamentalist missions under the umbrella of the Bible Union.

Following the lead of his friend and fellow archaeologist George F. Wright, Kyle edited (1922-1933) the respected theological journal *Bibliotheca Sacra* just prior to its 1934 removal to the new dispensationalist* seminary in Dallas, Texas (*See* Dallas Theological Seminary). Kyle was also known for his books and articles, most notably for his contribution to *The Fundamentals* (1910), entitled "The Recent Testimony of Archeology to the Scriptures." He asserted that archaeology is "exactly in harmony" with the biblical narrative and believed that the eventual collation of archaeological evidences would discredit Wellhausen's documentary hypothesis and all higher criticism.   D. M. Strong

Kynett, Alpha Jefferson (1829-1899). Methodist* minister* and temperance* advocate. Born in Adam County, Pennsylvania, Kynett spent his childhood in Ohio, Indiana and Iowa. Though his formal education was limited, Kynett studied on his own and at the age of twenty-two became a minister in the Methodist Episcopal Church. During his career as a minister Kynett worked at the highest levels of his denomination* to increase lay* participation, particularly by women. Having pushed for the formation of the Church Extension Society, he served as its secretary from 1867 until his death. The organization assisted more than 11,000 churches, particularly in the West, to construct and enlarge church buildings.

Like so many reform-minded evangelical* Protestants* of his generation, Kynett sought to destroy the liquor traffic. In 1892 he organized in his denomination the Committee of Temperance (later renamed the Board of Temperance, Prohibition, and Public Morals), and Prohibition campaigns in Ohio and Pennsylvania acquainted him with the political power of the liquor industry; yet he concluded that a political party, even the Prohibition Party, could not unite the temperance forces. Only a single-issue organization, capable of uniting temperance advocates across party and denominational lines, had any chance of success. His first effort in this direction came in 1893 with the formation of the Ohio Interdenominational Christian Temperance Alliance. He was the primary figure behind the calling of a national convention in Washington, D.C., in December 1895, which organized the Anti-Saloon League.* Although a founder of the organization that came to dominate the temperance movement, he died before he could contribute to that achievement.

BIBLIOGRAPHY. K. Austin Kerr, *Organized for Prohibition: A New History of the Anti-Saloon League* (1985); *DAB* V.

G. F. Goodwin

L

LaBerge, Agnes N. Ozman (1870-1937). Pentecostal* evangelist.* Born in Albany, Wisconsin, Ozman moved with her family in 1871 to a Nebraska homestead. Ozman and her five siblings were raised in the Methodist Episcopal Church.* As a young adult Ozman became involved in various interdenominational settings. She attended several Bible institutes* and worked as a home missionary* in Kansas City before deciding in the fall of 1901 to attend Charles Parham's* fledgling Bible institute in Topeka.

On the evening of January 1, 1901, in an atmosphere permeated by emphasis on the Holy Spirit and charged with expectation, Parham laid hands on Ozman and prayed that she would receive the baptism with the Holy Spirit* in response, Ozman spoke in tongues.* Her experience convinced others that they had rightly believed that such speech should uniformly attest Spirit baptism.* Ozman's experience has been touted as having proved the truth of Parham's assertion from this perspective, her tongues speech became the basis for the emergence of a distinct Pentecostal Movement* in American religion.

Ozman parted company with Parham early in 1901 and worked as a city missionary in Omaha. She did not share her experience in Topeka with others until 1906, when word of the Azusa Street* revival reached her in Omaha. In 1911 she married a Pentecostal evangelist, Philemon LaBerge. The couple worked as evangelists among struggling congregations. Agnes LeBerge died in Los Angeles, California.

BIBLIOGRAPHY. A. O. LaBerge, "History of the Pentecostal Movement from January 1, 1901," (Typescript, Assemblies of God Archives, n.d.); R. M. Anderson, *Vision of the Disinherited* (1979).

E. L. Blumhofer

Lacombe, Albert (1827-1916). Catholic* missionary.* Born in Lower Canada (Quebec), Lacombe was ordained* to the priesthood* in 1849 as a member of the Oblate order. He was one of the first Roman Catholic missionaries to the Northwest, accompanying members of the Hudson's Bay Company. Working primarily with the Blackfoot Indians in the region that is now Alberta, he traveled widely and established many churches and schools. He was instrumental in the success of Canada's westward expansion after Confederation, persuading the Blackfoot to allow the Canadian Pacific Railroad to be built across their territory.

BIBLIOGRAPHY. K. Hughes, *Father Lacombe, the Black-Robe Voyageur* (1911).

P. D. Airhart

Ladd, George Eldon (1911-1982). Evangelical* New Testament scholar. Born in New Hampshire, Ladd was converted in 1929 under the preaching ministry of a woman graduate of Moody Bible Institute.* Graduating from Gordon College of Theology and Missions (B.Th., 1933), he was ordained* a Northern Baptist* minister* and continued his theological studies at Gordon Divinity School while pastoring a church in Gilford, New Hampshire. Following a pastorate in Montpelier, Vermont (1936-1942), Ladd served as minister of Blaney Memorial Church in Boston. Resuming his studies, he took up graduate work in classics, first at Boston University and then at Harvard,* where he completed his Ph.D. under Henry J. Cadbury* in 1949.

Ladd joined the faculty of Fuller Theological Seminary* in 1950. His thirty years at Fuller were characterized by hard work, well-reasoned but passionately held views and a driving, Socratic classroom style. Beyond the classroom he was to have a profound impact on a generation of evangelical biblical scholars. In *The New Testament and Criticism* (1967), he moved evangelical biblical interpretation beyond the horizons of defensive fundamentalism,* accepting the positive gains of modern critical method while challenging the negative results of critical scholars on their own ground.

Books such as his *Crucial Questions about the Kingdom of God* (1952) established his reputation among conservatives as a proponent of classic

[626]

premillenialism* rather than dispensationalism.* His *Jesus and the Kingdom* (1964), later republished as *The Presence of the Future* (1974), was intended to bring him the cherished recognition of the broader community of biblical scholars. Unfortunately, while the book won him prestige within the evangelical community, it was severely criticized from without. His later work, *A Theology of the New Testament* (1974), became a benchmark of evangelical New Testament scholarship in America.

BIBLIOGRAPHY. D. A. Hubbard, "Biographical Sketch of Appreciation," in *Unity and Diversity in New Testament Theology,* ed. R. A. Guelich (1978); M. A. Noll, *Between Faith and Criticism* (1986); G. M. Marsden, *Reforming Fundamentalism* (1987).

D. G. Reid

LaFarge, John (1880-1963). Jesuit* editor and pioneer for interracial justice. Born in Newport, Rhode Island, LaFarge graduated from Harvard* in 1901 and the University of Innsbruck in 1905. That same year he was ordained* and entered the Society of Jesus.* From then until 1926 he took additional academic and spiritual training while serving as college teacher, prison and hospital chaplain,* and, for fifteen years, missionary* in rural Maryland. From 1926 until his death, he served in various editorial capacities at the Jesuit weekly *America* and was editor-in-chief from 1944 to 1948.

In 1926 LaFarge also founded the *Interracial Review,* a publication of the Catholic Layman's Union—black Catholics who met regularly with LaFarge to study race relations and develop programs of spiritual formation. The group arose from LaFarge's conviction that the most effective way to develop lay apostles was by sharing faith, professional interests and problems during prayerful retreats.* In 1934 the Union also launched the first Catholic Interracial Council, which, joined by thirty-nine other organizations in 1958, set up the National Catholic Conference for Interracial Justice. LaFarge also served as first chaplain in St. Ansgar's Scandinavian Catholic League, the Catholic Association for International Peace and the National Catholic Rural Life Conference, as well as various national commissions. LaFarge lectured in U.S. and French universities and published books on social justice, including *Inter-racial Justice* (1937), *No Postponement* (1950), *The Race Question and the Negro* (1953) and *The Catholic Viewpoint on Race Relations* (1956). He was the chief Catholic spokesperson for the the Civil Rights Movement.

BIBLIOGRAPHY. *DAB* 7; *DARB;* J. LaFarge, *The Manner Is Ordinary* (1954); J. LaFarge, *Reflections on Growing Old* (1973); *NCAB* 49.

J. W. Evans

Laity. A term normally referring to people in the church who are not ordained* clergy.* *Laity* finds its root meaning in the Greek word *laos* which refers simply to "the people," although in the New Testament it may refer to the church as the people of God.

In the American religious experience there stands at one end of the spectrum the traditional Roman Catholic* distinction between the baptized* laity and those in the clerical state who participate in the church's hierarchy. At the other end, groups like the Brethren* argue that there is no distinction to be made between lay and clergy.* All believers are priests before God.

Since the colonial period lay leadership has characterized the American church. In many cases, particularly on the Western frontier, congregations were formed and maintained by clergy-recruited lay leaders. Given these circumstances the laity exercised a decisive voice in the life of the church. As the Lutheran* pastor Henry M. Muhlenberg* noted in his *Journals,* "everything [is dependent] on the vote of the majority." This spirit of lay leadership and initiative provided the impetus for a variety of voluntary societies in the nineteenth century and the parachurch* movement in the twentieth century.

See also LAY MOVEMENT, MODERN CATHOLIC; LAY PEOPLE, PROTESTANT. M. D. Floding

Lalemant (L'Allemant), Gabriel (1610-1649). Jesuit* missionary* martyr in Canada. Born of Parisian nobility, Father Gabriel Lalemant, whose two uncles, Charles and Jérôme,* held important Jesuit positions in New France, began his brief but famous missionary career in 1646 along the St. Lawrence River. In the summer of 1648 he moved to Sainte-Marie-des-Hurons and, in 1649, was sent to assist Father Jean de Brebeuf* at the nearby Saint-Louis mission. The great Jesuit plan to establish a Christian Huronia (*See* Huron Mission) failed when the Iroquois began their campaign to eliminate the Hurons in 1642. With English and Dutch support, they reached Saint-Louis on March 16, 1649, overpowered the Huron defenses and took their prisoners, including de Brebeuf and Lalemant, to Saint-Ignace. The priests were stripped, tied and beaten, had their nails removed, and were roasted alive. De Brebeuf lasted only four hours, whereas Lalemant survived until the following day. The bones of the priests were recovered to Quebec in 1650, where they were venerated as relics. Lalemant was subsequently canonized* by Pope Pius XI* on June 29, 1930.

See also MISSIONS TO NORTH AMERICA, FRENCH.

BIBLIOGRAPHY. E. Kenton, ed., *Black Gown and Redskins* (1954); F. Parkman, *The Jesuits in North America* (1900); R. G. Thwaites, ed., *The Jesuit Relations and Allied Documents* (1954).

R. H. Chilton

Lalemant, Jérôme (Achiendassé) (1593-1673).

Jesuit* missionary* and superior in New France. Born in Paris and trained for the Jesuit priesthood at Clermont, Lalemant gained a wide reputation for his creative administrative ability. Arriving at Quebec in 1638, he was appointed De Brebeuf's successor at the Mission to the Hurons at Sainte-Marie.

Lalemant's strategy to strengthen the work was twofold: he built a huge, fortress-like mission house (Sainte-Marie-des-Hurons) as the focus of missionary expansion; and he created an order of skilled lay workers, called *donnés*. He hoped to extend the missions westward to create a Christian Huronia, but the subsequent extermination of the Hurons by the Iroquois (1642-1649), including the martyrdom of several Jesuits (among them Lalemant's nephew Gabriel*), destroyed that vision forever.

As Superior in New France (1645-1650 and 1659-1673), Lalemant initiated a great resurgence in missions and was highly respected for his skills, devotion to the poor, personal piety* and discretion. While at Quebec, he was appointed vicar general to the archbishop of Rouen, the highest clerical position in New France at that time.

See also HURON MISSION; MISSIONS TO NORTH AMERICA, FRENCH.

BIBLIOGRAPHY. *DCB* I; T. J. Campbell, *Pioneer Priests of North America,* vol. 2 (1908); H. H. Walsh, *The Church in the French Era* (1966).

R. H. Chilton

Lalor, Teresa (1769-1846).

Roman Catholic* foundress of Order of Visitation. Born in Ireland, Lalor achieved an early reputation for unusual piety* and assisted her local bishop* in founding a community of Presentation nuns.* Family disapproval forced her to immigrate to the U.S. with her sister in 1794. Once in Philadelphia, Lalor and two shipboard friends sought out the Reverend Leonard Neale, a man of intelligence and perception, for spiritual guidance. With his help the three established an unofficial religious community. In 1798 the women moved to Washington, D. C., after Neale became president of Georgetown College. In 1816, with his help, their growing community of thirty-five women won the approval of Rome to become fully accredited Visitation nuns, with Teresa as superior. She held the post until 1819, after which she established other houses in Mobile, Alabama; St. Louis, Missouri; Baltimore, Maryland; and Brooklyn, New York. Mother Teresa and Archbishop* Neale are considered cofounders of the Order of the Visitation in the U.S.

BIBLIOGRAPHY. J. B. Code, *Great American Foundresses* (1968); *DAB* IX.

M. L. Bendroth

Lambeth Conference.

Assembly of Anglican* bishops representing the Anglican Communion.* In 1865 unfavorable publicity about a dispute between South African prelates Robert Gray and John Colenso prompted the synod* of the Anglican Church in Canada to request that Archbishop of Canterbury Charles Longley summon an international convocation of Anglican bishops. Langley agreed, inviting bishops to meet in 1867 at Lambeth Palace, his official residence. Sixty-seven of the 144 Anglican bishops attended. American presiding bishop (1865-1868) John Henry Hopkins,* who had proposed such a gathering in an 1851 letter, was among the active participants. Those who attended found the conference valuable enough to warrant subsequent meetings. These have been held in every decade since, with one exception caused by World War 1.*

While individual national churches that make up the Anglican Communion are not bound by the recommendations of the conferences, the deliberations of the body do strongly affect the decisions that national churches make for themselves. The Episcopal Church* in the U.S., for example, opened reception of the Eucharist* to unconfirmed baptized persons after the bishops at Lambeth 1968 declared that baptism* was a sufficient qualification for reception.

The Lambeth Conference has also been an important forum in which Anglicans have discussed the ordination of women.* Conferences have taken note of the ministry of women as deaconesses* (1897, 1920 and 1930), priests (1948, 1968 and 1978) and bishops (1988). The decisions of Lambeth—particularly the 1888 Quadrilateral Statement—have also affected Anglican participation in the ecumenical movement.*

See also CHICAGO LAMBETH QUADRILATERAL.

BIBLIOGRAPHY. S. C. Neill, *Anglicanism* (1958);

A. M. G. Stephenson, *Anglicanism and the Lambeth Conferences* (1978).   R. W. Prichard

Lamy, John Baptist (Jean Baptiste) (1814-1888). First Catholic* archbishop* of Santa Fe, New Mexico. Born in Lempdes, France, Lamy was ordained* to the priesthood in 1838. A year later he responded to an invitation to do mission work along the Ohio River. Following the Mexican War, whereby the U.S. gained possession of new lands in the West, in 1850 Lamy was appointed vicar apostolic of New Mexico.

After a perilous journey by way of New Orleans, Lamy arrived in Santa Fe and assumed jurisdiction of a vast territory, including eastern Colorado and most of Arizona as well as New Mexico. The Hispanic people and priests* resented the U.S. conquest, but Lamy diplomatically worked to unite his people and priests.

In 1852 he attended the First Plenary Council of Baltimore* and also recruited six Sisters of Loretto in Kentucky to start a school in Santa Fe. On July 29, 1853, he was consecrated* bishop* of Santa Fe, becoming archbishop in 1875.

Lamy unified and expanded the Catholic Church in New Mexico, preaching* and traveling as well as overseeing his diocese.* By 1865 there were 100,000 Catholics under his jurisdiction, and many churches and schools (including a seminary*) had begun to prosper. Whereas there were only ten priests in New Mexico in 1850, there were thirty-seven by 1865, six of them natives ordained by Lamy himself. Lamy died in Santa Fe, New Mexico.

BIBLIOGRAPHY. W. Cather, *Death Comes for the Archbishop* (1927); A. Chavez, *Archives of the Archdiocese of Santa Fe, 1678-1900* (1957); *DAB* V; R. J. DeAragon, *Padre Martinez and Bishop Lamy* (1978); P. Horgan, *Lamy of Santa Fe: His Life & Times* (1975); W. J. Howlett, *Life of Rt. Rev. Joseph P. Machebeuf* (1908); L. H. Warner, *Archbishop Lamy: An Epoch Maker* (1936).

G. A. Reed

Landis, Benson Young (1897-1966). Congregationalist,* social activist and researcher. Born near Coopersburg, Pennsylvania, Landis was educated at Moravian College (A.B., 1918), Teachers College, Columbia University (M.A., 1923) and Columbia University (Ph.D., 1927). He was part of the survey staff of the Interchurch World Movement* (1920-1921), managing editor of *The Christian Work* (1921-1923), editor of *Rural America* (1923-1941) and associate secretary for the Federal Council of Churches' Department of Research and Education (1923-1946). He later held a similar position with the National Council of Churches.* Landis conducted surveys and research in industrial, social and moral issues and was particularly interested in rural and agricultural problems. He served on numerous committees and was a prolific author, perhaps best known for his book on Franklin D. Roosevelt's New Deal, *The Third American Revolution* (1933).

L. M. Japinga

Landmark Movement. A nineteenth-century Baptist* movement in the South asserting the sole validity and unbroken succession of Baptist churches since the New Testament era. This exclusivistic ecclesiology arose among Baptist churches in the South during the mid nineteenth century and was linked with the concept that the church is always a local and visible institution. In the latter half of the nineteenth century, Landmarkism made deep inroads in the Southern Baptist Convention,* affecting concepts of missions,* ordination,* ordinances* and even eschatology.*

Landmarkers refused to be involved in cooperative ventures with other Baptist churches—mission societies included. Their ecclesiology made them question the validity of transferring church membership by letter, a practice common among many Baptist churches but seen as a violation of the rights of the local church by Landmarkers. Most important was the proper baptism by immersion of believers who had confessed their faith. Baptisms by immersion not performed under the auspices of a Baptist church were not true baptisms but "alien immersions."* Access to the Lord's Supper* was protected by the practice of "closed communion," allowing only baptized members of a given local church to participate in its celebration.

The dominant figure behind the movement was James R. Graves,* who was perhaps the most influential Baptist clergyman* in the nineteenth-century South. Graves found two strong allies in James M. Pendleton* of Kentucky and A. C. Dayton of Mississippi. Together the three were known by their followers as the "Great Triumvirate." Although the movement actually began in the late 1840s with Graves' appointment as editor of *The Tennessee Baptist,* Pendleton coined the term *Landmark* in an essay he wrote in 1854, which Graves published under the title *An Old Landmark Re-set.*

Today Landmarkism continues to show residual strength through the localism of many Southern Baptist churches. Shortly after the turn of the present century, the Landmark movement gave rise

[629]

to a splinter group which is represented today by the American Baptist Association* and the Baptist Missionary Association of America.

BIBLIOGRAPHY. J. R. Graves, *Old Landmarkism: What Is It* (1880); J. M. Pendleton, *An Old Landmark Re-set* (1854); H. Wamble, "Landmarkism: Doctrinaire Ecclesiology among Baptists," *CH* 33 (1964):429-447.   M. G. Bell

Lankford, Sarah Worral. *See* PALMER, SARAH WORRAL LANKFORD.

Lard, Moses E. (1818-1880). Disciples of Christ* minister* and editor. Born in Tennessee, Lard moved to Ray County, Missouri, in 1829. At the age of seventeen he taught himself to write. Entering Bethany College in 1845, the college founded by Alexander Campbell* in 1841, he graduated with honors. He returned to Missouri, serving churches until the Civil War.* Lard rapidly became a leading minister among the Disciples and was selected by Campbell to respond to Jeremiah B. Jeter,* the Baptist* controversialist who in 1855 published a popular refutation of Alexander Campbell's views. Fleeing Union sentiments, he moved to Canada and then Kentucky. In Lexington he commenced *Lard's Quarterly* (1863-1868), thereafter editing the *Apostolic Times.*

Lard took a moderate position among Disciples, halfheartedly approving mission societies, but opposing creeds,* open communion, instrumental music and a settled ministry. Theologically he was more venturesome, being a pacifist* and arguing against everlasting punishment, for which he was charged with universalism.* As a writer and preacher* he was clear, vital and eloquent, even though sometimes disputatious. Twentieth-century Disciples historians characterize him as extremely conservative.

BIBLIOGRAPHY. *DAB* V; W. T. Moore, *The Living Pulpit of the Christian Church* (1869).

                                T. H. Olbricht

Larkin, Clarence (1850-1924). Baptist* pastor* and author. Born in Chester, Pennsylvania, Larkin briefly worked in his father's feed store before becoming a bank clerk. While a clerk he became involved in the YMCA,* through which he was converted.* He was confirmed* in the Episcopal Church.* Larkin enrolled in the Polytechnic College of Philadelphia, from which he received a degree in mechanical engineering (1873). After a short employment at a shipyard, he became supervisor and instructor at the Pennsylvania Institution for the Blind, where he served for three years prior to entering into the business field. While serving in secular occupations, he taught Bible* classes.

At the age of thirty-two Larkin joined the Baptist Church and was ordained* two years later. He pastored at Kennett Square and Fox Chase, Pennsylvania. He is included in the list of signers of the call for the fundamentalist* pre-convention meeting of the Northern Baptist Convention in 1920 at Buffalo, New York. Subsequent to his ordination Larkin became a premillennialist* and published books on prophetic themes. Utilizing his background as an engineer, Larkin included his numerous memorable charts, many illustrating prophetic themes. His books include *Dispensational Truth* (1920), *The Book of Revelation* (1919) and *The Book of Daniel* (1929).   R. T. Clutter

Larsen, Peter Laurentius (1833-1915). Lutheran* minister and college president. Born in Norway, the eldest of Capt. Herman and Elen Else Marie (Oftedahl) Larsen's nine children, Laurentius received his theological training at Christiania (Oslo) University (Candidate in Theology, 1855). To assume a pastorate in Wisconsin he immigrated* in 1857. For two years he served as the Norwegian (Lutheran) Synod's representative on the faculty of Concordia Seminary. Controversy (in part over slavery) prompted the Synod to found its own school, Luther College. Larsen was appointed president (1861-1902), but also served as professor, pastor, editor and synodical officer. In these capacities he advocated both orthodox* Lutheran doctrine and careful attentiveness to the American setting which became his home. Larsen's influence was carried by many of his students who became pastors and teachers. He first married Karen Radine Neuberg (1855), and following her death he married Ingeborg Astrup (1871). Most of Larsen's twelve children had careers in education or the church.

BIBLIOGRAPHY. *DAB* VI; K. Larsen, *Laur. Larsen: Pioneer College President* (1936).

                                L. D. Lagerquist

Lartigue, Jean-Jacques (1777-1840). First Roman Catholic* bishop* of Montreal. Born in Montreal, Lartigue studied law before embarking on a clerical career. He was ordained* priest* in 1800 and acted as secretary to Bishop Pierre Denaut of Quebec until 1806. He then joined the Sulpician* order and served as vicar of Notre-Dame de Montreal until 1819. In 1820 when Bishop Plessis attempted to subdivide the diocese* of Quebec, Lartigue was given episcopal* jurisdiction over the district of Montreal, and was accorded the title of Bishop of Telmesse en Lycie—a controversial appointment. The British authorities would not publicly acknowledge him as bishop, and the Sulpicians, as seigneurs and vicars of Montreal, refused to submit to his authority.* This latter dispute reflected Gallican*-Ultramontane* tensions and was not settled until about 1836. Lartigue was appointed bishop of Montreal in 1836 at a time when the political situation in Lower Canada was reaching critical proportions. The bishop took a firm stand in opposition to the *Patriotes* and their liberal and republican ideas. He enjoined obedience and submission to the rule of law, and when rebellion occurred in 1837-1838 he stood firmly against it.

BIBLIOGRAPHY. J. S. Moir, *The Church in the British Era* (1972); F. Ouellet, *Lower Canada 1791-1840: Social Change and Nationalism* (1980).

R. W. Vaudry

La Salle, René Robert Cavalier Sieur de (1643-1687). French explorer of North America. Born into a wealthy middle-class family in Rouen, La Salle studied at the local Jesuit* college and, at his father's urging, entered the Society of Jesus as a novice. He left the order, however, at age twenty-two, apparently because his independent nature resisted their tight discipline.

In 1666 he went to New France where he became interested in exploring the interior and joined several such ventures, the first in 1669. In 1672 he and the new governor, Frontenac, began planning a great French empire based on the Western territories. The two men shared a dislike for the Jesuits and invited the Franciscans* to minister to the white settlements along the Saint Lawrence River and serve as chaplains* to the military posts in the West.

In 1679 La Salle led an expedition into Lake Michigan and central Illinois. In 1682 he went through the Illinois territory and down the Mississippi to the gulf, the first white man to do so. Here he claimed the entire Mississippi River Valley for the King of France, naming it Louisiana in his honor.

When Frontenac was replaced by a new governor sympathetic to Jesuit suggestions, La Salle lost his position. A return to France restored the king's favor and gave him command of a colonizing expedition to the lower Mississippi. However, the group missed the mouth of the Mississippi and landed in Texas. Here La Salle could not control his men, and he was soon killed in a mutiny. With his death ended French Franciscan plans for an

increased activity in New France. Their future included little more than serving as chaplains at the Western military posts.

BIBLIOGRAPHY. *DAB* VI; J. T. Ellis, *Catholics in Colonial America* (1965); F. Parkman, *LaSalle and the Discovery of the Great West* (1879).

J. B. North

Lathrop, John (d. 1653). Puritan* minister* and English Congregationalist* leader. Lathrop was one of three pastors of a church of Congregational independents founded in London in 1616. Henry Jacob, the church's founder, left for America in 1624, and Lathrop, "a Preacher in Kent," succeeded him as pastor. In 1634 Lathrop and some thirty followers also immigrated to the colonies. His successor was Henry Jessey. The church was thus known as the Jacob-Lathrop-Jessey Church. Lathrop was described as "a man of tender heart and a humble and meek spirit." During his pastorate, the London church dismissed several factions which moved toward Baptist* views.

BIBLIOGRAPHY. L. McBeth, *The Baptist Heritage* (1986).

B. J. Leonard

Latin America Mission. A service agency to extend and assist the evangelical* church* in the Spanish-speaking republics. Founded in 1921 by Protestant* missionaries* to Argentina Harry and Susan Strachan, Latin America Mission (LAM) attempted to replace the slow-moving approaches to evangelism* then in use. The Strachans undertook aggressive, concentrated efforts in fourteen of the twenty Hispanic-American republics in the next decades, conducting meetings in tents, theaters and parks, and using innovative techniques like popular music, handbills and fireworks to attract audiences. By the 1930s a training school that later became the Seminario Bíblico Latinoamericano was founded, along with a central church and a clinic and orphanage in San José, Costa Rica. In later years youth and student ministries were added, as well as a literature division and a radio station.

Administrative oversight of LAM was assumed by R. Kenneth Strachan at the death of his father in 1945. Raised in Costa Rica and trained at Princeton Theological Seminary,* Kenneth Strachan was an aggressive, visionary leader. Observing the rapid growth of Marxists and sectarian groups, he concluded that a common denominator of their effectiveness was their ability to mobilize the common people. Out of concern for the awakening masses, Strachan developed Evangelism-in-Depth* in the 1960s. From Nicaragua, Costa Rica and Guatemala, these concerted efforts at turning every believer into an evangelist were extended throughout much of Latin America. In 1971 LAM took an additional innovative step by creating the Community of Latin American Evangelical Ministries (known by its Spanish acronym, CLAME), turning control of the mission's nearly twenty agencies over to national leadership. LAM, the parent organization, retained its function of fund raising and personnel recruitment, its 175 missionaries often working under contract to other missions or engaging in so-called tentmaking ministries in which mission work is combined with full-time vocational employment.

BIBLIOGRAPHY. D. M. Howard, "Mission with a Vision," *Latin America Evangelist* 66 (1986):4-5; W. D. Roberts, "CLAME's First Five Years; A Case Study in Partnership," *Latin American Evangelist* 57 (1977):2-5; W. D. Roberts, *Strachan of Costa Rica* (1971); W. M. Nelson, *Protestantism in Central America* (1984).　　　E. A. Wilson

Latin Rite. The term *rite* here refers primarily to the whole way of being a particular Christian church. In summary, this includes the church's liturgical* rites, legal code and spiritual heritage. In this sense, the Latin Rite is distinguished from the Eastern Rites,* all of which have their own distinct way of being a Christian church. The Latin Rite has its center of unity in the church at Rome, overseen by the bishop* of Rome, the pope,* considered under his title of patriarch of the West. Hence it is also called the Roman Rite.

In the development of rites, the root principle of diversification was especially geopolitical. The rite grew out of a major geographical center that enjoyed a sphere of influence in neighboring regions. With political changes in the Roman Empire, the Latin Rite developed its own distinctiveness, especially with the Peace of Constantine (337), while remaining heir to many influences. When Charlemagne (814) introduced the Roman liturgical books* and customs into his empire, they in turn received Gallo-Frankish additions. The Council of Trent (1545-1563) ushered in a period of uniformity in doctrine and liturgy that endured down to the Second Vatican Council (1962-1965), which introduced a whole program of liturgical reform, a new code of canon law* (1983) and a reorientation of many of the rite's spiritual emphases.

Since it is not liturgical language that makes the rite, in the U.S. and Canada and throughout the world, Latin Rite liturgies are in the vernacular, although they are translated from typical editions

in Latin. With its spread throughout Western Europe and from there to the Americas, Asia and Africa, the Latin Rite is the largest and most widespread of the canonical rites within the Catholic Church.

BIBLIOGRAPHY. A. Caron, "Latin Rite," *NCE* 8; E. E. Finn, *These Are My Rites* (1980).

　　　J. B. Ryan

Latitudinarianism. A term used to describe the beliefs of a prominent group of Anglican* divines in the late seventeenth and early eighteenth centuries. As followers of the Cambridge Platonists, they held reason in high regard and were broadly Arminian* in outlook. Reacting against the dogmatic Calvinism* of the Puritans* and the liturgical* practices of the high church,* they sought a common ground between Anglicans, Presbyterians* and Nonconformists. They developed a tolerant approach to religion based on a narrow core of fundamental doctrines and a common morality. While Scripture* remained their chief authority, they maintained that reason and revelation must both be used to establish truth. They were theologically ambiguous but possessed a strong ethical emphasis, which constantly stressed man's moral responsibility.

Moderate in tone, they were acutely interested in science and attempted to reconcile the church to new developments in the contemporary intellectual environment. They represent a transitional phase between the embittered struggles over religious authority in the seventeenth century and the unquestioning reliance on rationalism in the eighteenth. By the latter part of the eighteenth century, their religious views had veered toward various forms of Unitarianism.* In America, King's Chapel of Boston was known for its latitudinarianism and was influential in encouraging a trend toward Christian rationalism, and eventually Unitarianism, that became more acceptable in revolutionary New England.

BIBLIOGRAPHY. G. R. Cragg, *The Church and the Age of Reason* (1960); F. W. P. Greenwood, *History of King's Chapel in Boston* (1863); N. Sykes, *Church and State in England in the XVIIIth Century* (1934).　　　S. A. Wenig

Latourette, Kenneth Scott (1884-1968). Distinguished scholar of Asian and missions history. Born in Oregon City, Oregon, Latourette was educated at Linfield College (B.S., 1904) and Yale University* (B.A., 1906; M.A., 1907; Ph.D., 1909), where his involvment with the Student Volunteer Movement* led him to a brief term of missionary service in China (1910-1912). Returning in ill health after two years, he turned to an academic career, first at Reed College (1914-1916), then at Denison University (1916-1921), and finally as professor of missions and Oriental history at Yale Divinity School. There he taught for thirty-two years, retiring near his seventieth year, in 1953, after having contributed a prodigious volume of publications to his two areas of major interest. His works have reportedly sold more than a million copies, including histories of China and Japan that by the 1940s had established him as a foremost Asian scholar. He held honorary doctorates from seventeen universities, including Oxford, Yale and Princeton.* His professional achievement was recognized by his selection as president of the American Historical Association, the American Society of Church History and the American Baptist Association.

Latourette's view of Christian history, presented in his presidential address to the American Historical Association and dispersed in his histories, is well illustrated in two monumental series, *History of the Expansion of Christianity* (7 vols., 1937-1945) and *Christianity in a Revolutionary Age: A History of Christianity in the Nineteenth and Twentieth Centuries* (5 vols., 1958-1962). Placing the church in the context of unfolding historical developments, Latourette perceived God's work in the world through human institutions. History moves toward the realization of human redemption in sometimes fitful expansions and contractions, but always with assurance of ultimate triumph, with the Christian faith, rather than the church, as the focus. Latourette's objectivity and comprehensiveness have brought him acclaim, while his optimism and confidence have sometimes been considered unduly sanguine and rational, given the tragedies of human history his generation witnessed.

BIBLIOGRAPHY. S. Bates, "Christian Historian, Doer of History. In Memory of Kenneth Scott Latourette, 1884-1968," *IRM* 58 (1969):317-326; W. C. Harr, ed., *Frontiers of the Christian World Mission Since 1938: Essays in Honor of Kenneth Scott Latourette* (1962); W. A. Speck, "Kenneth Scott Latourette's Vocation as Christian Historian," *CSR* 4 (1975):285-299.   E. A. Wilson

Laubach, Frank Charles (1884-1970). Congregationalist* missionary.* Born in Pennsylvania, Laubach was educated at Princeton and Columbia (Ph.D., 1915) universities, and Union Theological Seminary,* New York. He entered missionary service in the Philippine Islands in 1915, begin-

ning a career that was to take on an increasingly worldwide focus. In the late 1920s he initiated the two major emphases of his long career. The first was an experiment in prayer—the practice of the presence of God. The second, a literacy work among the underprivileged people of the world, he began on the Philippine island of Mindanao in 1929. He developed the approach "Each One Teach One," which came to be known as the Laubach Method. With a program that soon expanded to other countries, he was eventually responsible for the creation of literacy primers for approximately three hundred languages and dialects in more than one hundred countries. Laubach authored more than thirty books on a variety of subjects, including *Prayer, the Mightiest Force in the World* (1951); *The World Is Learning Compassion* (1958) and *Toward World Literacy* (1960).

BIBLIOGRAPHY. F. Laubach, *Letters by a Modern Mystic* (1937); F. Laubach, *Thirty Years with the Silent Billion* (1960); D. Mason, *Frank C. Laubach* (1967); H. M. Roberts, *Champion of the Silent Billion* (1961).   N. A. Magnuson

Lausanne Congress on World Evangelism. *See* INTERNATIONAL CONGRESS ON WORLD EVANGELIZATION.

Laval de Montmorency, François Xavier (1623-1708). First bishop* of Quebec. Born in France and ordained* in 1647, Laval was nominated by the Jesuits* to head the church in New France (Quebec). Despite opposition from other religious orders* and those who wished state control of the colonial church, Laval was appointed apostolic vicar in 1658 through the aid of the queen-regent. Until Quebec became a diocese* in 1674, Laval held episcopal status as bishop of Petraea.

In 1659 Laval became a member of the Quebec Council, where he opposed the governor and others who sought to control the church. Although willing to compromise on financial matters (the size of tithes), Laval was steadfast on religious and moral issues. Discipline of clergy* was removed from lay* hands by establishing church courts to try clerics. Despite protest, Laval departed from the French custom of giving clergy permanent parish postings, and thereby he was able to replace priests* whenever necessary and to direct parish tithes to the Seminaire de Quebec (now Laval University) which he founded in 1663 as a theological school.

Laval established a strong, centralized church,

but the French king protected the Sulpician* and Franciscan* orders to prevent Laval's power from being total. Laval's development of a strong church structure independent of the French crown and of a Canadian clergy (through the seminaire) enabled the Roman Catholic Church to hold its own after British conquest. It also contributed to the Ultramontane* Movement in Quebec during the nineteenth century.

BIBLIOGRAPHY. A. L. de Brumath, *Bishop Laval* (1906); A. Vachon, *François de Laval* (1980).

B. A. McKenzie

Laws, Curtis Lee (1868-1946). Baptist* clergyman* and editor. Born in Loudoun County, Virginia, Laws graduated from Crozer Theological Seminary (1893) and served important pastorates in Baltimore, Maryland (1893-1908), and Brooklyn, New York (1908-1913), before assuming the editorship in 1913 of the Baptist weekly newspaper, the *Watchman-Examiner*. When he took over the paper, it enjoyed the widest circulation of any Baptist periodical in the North, and he used its columns to advance his evangelical* orthodox* Baptist principles.

As an editor, Laws favored a restoration of historic Baptist identity, affirming the authority* of Scripture,* the autonomy of local congregations and a mission imperative for all Christians. He rejected contemporary popular labels like *landmarker,* conservative* or *premillennialist* as being rigid or carrying historical disadvantages. Instead, in an editorial in 1920, he coined the name *fundamentalist* for those "who still cling to the great fundamentals and who mean to do battle royal for the faith." In his later years, Laws helped to organize The Eastern Baptist Theological Seminary in Philadelphia, and the Association of Baptists for World Evangelism,* both loyal to the Northern Baptist Convention but founded on clearly evangelical bases. As pastor,* editor and denominational* leader, Laws was a prominent leader of the conservative reaction to modernism* in the Northern Baptist Convention from 1920 through the 1940s.

BIBLIOGRAPHY. W. H. Brackney, *The Baptists* (1988); J. W. Bradbury, "Curtis Lee Laws, D.D., L.L.D.: An Appreciation," *Watchman-Examiner* XXXIV:29 (July 18, 1946).   W. H. Brackney

Lay Movement, Modern Catholic. The modern American Catholic* lay movement cannot be portrayed as a consistent, organized movement unified by a consensus on goals and values. Nevertheless, there has been a protracted (and not

always self-conscious) effort on the part of a certain cadre of non-ordained American Catholics to gain autonomy and equality within their Church, an effort which has been more visible in some periods than in others. Three periods in which lay aspirations were especially prominent were: the lay renaissance (c.1889-1894), the 1930s and the 1960s.

During the first period Catholics who had functioned as leaders in a broad array of Catholic social and educational movements on the regional and national level and enjoyed the support of liberal bishops, launched the lay congress movement. At congresses held in Baltimore (1889) and Chicago (1893), and at a parallel series of congresses for black Catholics* convened between 1889 and 1894, non-ordained Catholics took a critical look at their Church and proposed future changes. The congress movement disappeared in the second half of the 1890s, however, when its episcopal allies turned their attention elsewhere.

The 1930s witnessed an upsurge in lay social activism—a shift which was prompted both by the socioeconomic problems of the Depression* and by a growing awareness of three European Catholic movements: the papal call for lay participation in Catholic Action* movements led by the hierarchy, the Liturgical Movement* and the theology* of the Mystical Body of Christ.* Catholics of the 1930s and 1940s joined a variety of lay movements which sought to remake American society in the image of Christ. Some clergy-led organizations, such as the Jesuit* Daniel A. Lord's* Sodality of Our Lady and the network of youth movements organized by Bishop Bernard J. Sheil* in Chicago, were designed to nurture the laity's leadership skills and their sense of responsibility for their church and their society. Smaller communal movements, such as Dorothy Day's* Catholic Workers* (1933) and Catherine de Hueck's Friendship House (1938), provided alternative models for young people seeking spiritual growth and a life of service. The Christian Family Movement* (1949) suggested a whole new level of commitment possible for Catholic married people of the post-war era.

Although they were not aimed explicitly at achieving equality and autonomy for the non-ordained, the lay movements of the 1930s and 1940s produced a whole new generation of educated, self-conscious lay people who were already asking fundamental questions about their relative position in the Church on the eve of the Second Vatican Council.* In the wake of the Council, the laity found new opportunities for spiritual growth and leadership, such as in Cursillo,* the charismatic* renewal and on the parish councils.* In 1967 lay leaders assembled in St. Paul, Minnesota, formed the National Association of Laymen (NAL) and expressed their concerns about urban problems, racism, nuclear arms and women in the church. The spectrum of issues addressed by the NAL underscores a salient characteristic of the post-Vatican II lay movement: its polarization. Since the emergence of officially sanctioned lay ministries in the early 1970s, the polarizations among the American laity have intensified, and the preparations for the Synod on the Laity held in Rome in 1987 did little to mitigate this situation.

See also LAY PEOPLE, PROTESTANT.

BIBLIOGRAPHY. D. Callahan, *The Mind of the Catholic Layman* (1963); R. D. Cross, *The Emergence of Liberal Catholicism in America* (1958); L. Doohan, *The Laity: A Bibliography* (1987); D. J. Thorman, *The Emerging Layman* (1965).

D. Campbell

Lay People, Protestant. Throughout the history of American religion, Protestant* lay people have played an exceptionally active role. In so doing they have realized the vitality of the Protestant doctrine of the priesthood of all believers* and the national doctrine of democratic* equality.

During the colonial period (1607-1789), lay people had considerable control over religious life in the Protestant colonies. In the Anglican* colonies a shortage of clergy* promoted the role of laity, and the vestries* tended to dominate church life. A shortage of clergy gave rise to the hiring of lay readers.* Presbyterian* elders* were leading laymen and deacons* who exercised a lay ministry of caring for the poor. New England Congregationalism* theoretically made only a functional distinction between clergy and laity. The laity exercised considerable power in calling and ordaining* their pastor, as well as in determining his salary. Learned ministers, on the other hand, occupied a prominent social position that was threatened by Baptist and pietist lay exhorters.*

Those groups coming out of the radical or left wing of the Reformation, such as the Mennonites* and Friends,* also stressed the role of lay people and reduced the role of the clergy. Their position was not that there were no clergy but that there were no laity—that is, all church members were ministers. Most Reformation groups insisted that every Christian is a priest because of his or her baptismal ordination. (*See* Priesthood of Believers.)

The Great Awakening* (1720-1760), the first period of American revivalism,* spelled a pro-found victory for the role of the laity, especially among the Baptists* and Methodists.* The revivalism of the period focused criticism on the "unconverted ministry" and placed religious initiative in the hands of the laity. The established Congregational ministers of New England could no longer assume the authority and sanctity of their ministerial office. Ministerial authority also depended on the voluntary trust and support of their congregations who were frequently made up of an informed and assertive laity. This democratizing of the churches was to contribute to the birth of democracy* within the nation as a whole.

During the Revolutionary War era (1775-1800), the churches were disestablished and religious liberty* was guaranteed. This made all the churches voluntary associations (denominations*) and promoted lay activity and control. Laymen were included in the legislative councils, and their financial contributions were the major form of support.

The nineteenth century experienced several revivals which greatly increased church membership.* The Arminian* theology* of the Second Great Awakening* and of Charles G. Finney,* with its emphasis on free will, made salvation* available to all. Especially significant were the voluntary associations which cut across denominational lines and were basically lay movements. The Sunday-school movement* was the greatest of these voluntary associations and began as a lay movement that was opposed by many clergy. To this day the Sunday school remains a major dimension of lay ministry.

Another significant development of the nineteenth century was the activity of lay women. Lay women taught in the Sunday schools and worked in other voluntary associations. They were the backbone of the missionary societies, both foreign and domestic (*See* Missionary Movement, Women's), and of the temperance movement.* Frequently excluded from leadership roles in their local congregations, women exercised their ministries in missionary and temperance organizations.

Lay activity reached something of a climax in the early twentieth century with the organization of the interdenominational Laymen's Missionary Movement* in 1906 and the Men and Religion Forward Movement* in 1911. The latter was an interdenominational campaign to win 3 million Americans to the church.

After World War 2* there was a resurgence of lay activity, which has been called a "lay renaissance." It began in Europe after the physical and moral destruction of the war and was centered in the evangelical academies and the German *Kirchentag*, which was a lay rally, and gradually spread to the U.S. This lay renaissance stressed that the laity are the church and that authentic lay ministry is not ministry to the church but ministry in and to the world.

After 1948 the World Council of Churches* (WCC) became the major supporter of lay ministries to the world. The Second Assembly of the WCC at Evanston,* Illinois, in 1956, stated in its report "The Laity—the Christian in His Vocation": "The real battles of the faith today are being fought in factories, shops, offices, and farms, in political parties and government agencies, in countless homes, in the press, radio, and television, in the relationship of nations. Very often it is said that the Church should 'go into these spheres'; but the fact is that the Church is already in these spheres in the persons of the laity." The laity were viewed as the "salt of the earth," scattered and penetrating the world.

The ministry of the laity is rooted in the sacrament* of baptism* by which God calls persons into the life and fellowship of the church and into service in the world. Lay ministry is not what a Christian goes out and does, but it is what Christians do when they go out. Lay ministry is how Christians enact what it means to be God's people in the world. A primary means of carrying out lay ministry is through one's vocation.* Protestant laity have frequently found reassurance in Luther's words: "The housemaid on her knees scrubbing the floor is doing a work as pleasing in the eyes of Almighty God as the priest on his knees before the altar saying the Mass."

See also LAY MOVEMENT, MODERN CATHOLIC.

BIBLIOGRAPHY. H. Kraemer, *A Theology of the Laity* (1958); R. J. Mouw, *Called to Holy Worldliness* (1980); S. D. Neill and H.R. Weber, *The Layman in Christian History* (1963); H. R. Weber, *Salty Christians* (1963). D. S. Armentrout

Lay Reader. A licensed unordained worship* leader in the Episcopal Church.* The office of reader as an unordained liturgical* ministry is encountered as early as *The Apostolic Tradition,* a Roman Church order of the early third century. By the early medieval period this and other such ministries were considered to be minor orders,* but all minor orders were discontinued in churches of the Protestant* Reformation, as also in the Roman Catholic Church,* since 1972. In the Church of England laity* have been admitted to the conduct of non-sacramental services since 1866, and such lay readers are regulated by the

Canons of 1969, from which date women also have been admitted to the office. In the American Episcopal Church the licensing of lay readers is regulated (Title III, Canon 2) and provision is also made for lay eucharistic* ministers* (Canon 3). In most liturgical churches in this country today, lay persons are allowed to read certain of the Scripture* lessons in public worship without formal license. The Roman Catholic Church, in addition, regulates readers as an unordained ministry since 1972 (Paul VI, *Ministeria quaedam*).

T. J. Talley

Laying on of Hands. A religious rite in which the imposition of hands suggests consecration, blessing and invocation of the Holy Spirit. The New Testament evidences three main usages of the rite: healing,* ordination* or setting apart for service and communication of the Holy Spirit, often in conjunction with Christian baptism.* In the Roman Catholic* tradition laying on of hands is associated with infant baptism, confirmation,* ordination and extreme unction;* in each case it is a sign of invocation and communication of the Holy Spirit. In a less formal sense imposition of hands upon the head or shoulders of a parishioner often accompanies the reception of a priest's* blessing. Among many Protestants, laying on of hands is associated principally with ordaining ministers* or commissioning Christian workers. In some groups, like General Six-Principle Baptists* of Rhode Island, laying on of hands is a rite which occurs after baptism to symbolize the impartation of the Holy Spirit. Among Pentecostal* Christians the imposition of hands is a rite distinct from water baptism, in which a believer is baptized with the Holy Spirit and receives spiritual gifts like the ability to speak in tongues.* J. R. Tyson

Laymen's Foreign Missions Inquiry (1930-1932). An inquiry into missions* conducted by prominent Protestant* laypersons.* Following the International Missionary Council* meeting at Jerusalem in 1928, a number of American lay* supporters of missions became concerned over the apparent wane in support for foreign missions. They felt that a reappraisal of mission motives and methods was in order. As a result of a proposal originally put forward by the Northern Baptists,* an inquiry was inaugurated, financed by John D. Rockefeller, Jr. A Board of Directors composed of laymen from the Northern Baptist, Congregational,* Dutch Reformed,* Presbyterian Church in the U.S.A.,* Methodist Episcopal,* Protestant Episcopal* and United Presbyterian communions was constituted.

The Inquiry was confined to missions connected with churches in Burma, China, India and Japan, and a team of researchers was sent to each of these countries. The collected information was then turned over to a Commission of Appraisal headed by William E. Hocking* of Harvard* University. After about nine months of visiting the four countries and conducting its study, it framed its report, which was published as *Re-thinking Missions* (1932). This was supplemented by later publications based on the work of the researchers and the Commission of Appraisal.

The report advocated greater autonomy for the churches in Asia, a strengthening of theological education, greater cooperation and unity and a unified administration of missions at the "home base." Most controversial was the liberal attitude toward non-Christian religions and the proposal that Christian missions re-enforce the nobler aspects of other religions rather than seeking to convert their adherents. The latter proposal was due largely to Hocking's leadership and helped evoke the response of Dr. Hendrik Kraemer at Tambaram in 1938, where he insisted on the uniqueness of the Christian faith (*The Christian Message in a Non-Christian World,* 1938).

BIBLIOGRAPHY. K. S. Latourette, "Re-thinking Missions After Twenty-Five Years," *IRM* 46 (1947):164-170.   D. J. Hesselgrave

Laymen's Missionary Movement. An interdenominational program to raise funds for Christian missions.* First proposed by John B. Sleman of Washington, D.C., a participant in the Student Volunteer Movement,* the Laymen's Missionary Movement was formally organized in New York City. In the next few years committees of lay leaders were organized to ascertain the amounts of missionary contributions in their respective communities and elicit higher levels of commitment through educational presentations. Such meetings, often conducted as a banquet, were held throughout Canada in 1908 and in seventy-five cities in the U.S. the next year. Dramatic increases in missions receipts after 1906 seem to document the movement's effectiveness. Between 1907 and 1909 Presbyterian* giving increased by 240 per cent, Methodist* by 166 per cent and Baptist* by 265 per cent. Total missionary giving for American denominations* increased from $8,980,000 in 1906 to $45,272,000 in 1924.

BIBLIOGRAPHY. G. S. Eddy, *Pathfinders of the World Missionary Crusade* (1969); J. R. Mott, *The Decisive Hour of Christian Missions* (1910).
                    E. A. Wilson

Leachman, Emma (1868-1952). Southern Baptist* social ministries pioneer. A native of Washington County, Kentucky, Leachman attended the Central Teachers College in Indiana. In 1904 she was appointed as the city missionary* in Louisville under the Kentucky State Mission Board. She was closely associated with the Woman's Missionary Union Training School, which was organized in Louisville in 1907. There she taught applied methods in city missions and exerted a formative influence over a generation of students. In 1912 she became director of the Good Will Center, an inner-city settlement house which served as a missions workshop for the students.

In 1921 "Miss Emma" was appointed as the first general field worker of the Home Mission Board of the Southern Baptist Convention. In this capacity she traveled widely throughout the South enlisting support for city missions projects and promoting the cause of Christian social ministries among churches, associations and denominational leaders. She retired from the Home Mission Board because of failing health in 1940. Many of the goals for which Emma Leachman worked are now advanced through the Social Ministries Department of the Home Mission Board and the W. O. Carver* School of Church Social Work at the Southern Baptist Theological Seminary.

BIBLIOGRAPHY. C. U. Littlejohn, *History of the Carver School of Missions and Social Work* (1958); *ESB* 11.   T. F. George

League for Social Reconstruction. Canadian social reform organization arising out of the Great Depression.* The League was established in Toronto and Montreal, Canada, in 1931-1932 by a group of academics, businessmen and ministers,* many of whom had close ties to the Social Gospel Movement* in Canadian Protestantism.* Acutely sensitive to the suffering caused by the Great Depression and highly critical of monopoly capitalism,* League members demanded an economy and society which served "the common good rather than private profit." They called for nationalization of large corporations and banks, the cooperative organization of agriculture and publicly funded health and welfare benefits for Canadians—all to be achieved, however, by democratic means.

Frank Underhill, first national president and a University of Toronto professor, intended the League to be the Canadian equivalent of the British Fabian Society. Its members played a major part in the organization, in 1932, of the Canadian Commonwealth Federation (CCF), the predecessor of the present-day New Democratic party. Underhill and Harry Morris Cassidy wrote the Regina Manifesto, the platform issued by the CCF in 1933. The coming of World War 2* and the growth of the CCF diminished the significance of the League, and it disbanded in 1942. It played a major role in shaping socialist thought in Canada. As well, it served as a way station for a number of Canadian reformers as they moved from a Social Gospel background to a more secular orientation.

BIBLIOGRAPHY. M. Horn, *The League for Social Reconstruction* (1980). G. F. Goodwin

Leavell Family. Landrum Pinson (1874-1929); Frank Hartwell (1884-1949); Roland Quinche (1891-1963). Eight of the nine sons of George Washington and Corra Alice Berry Leavell of Oxford, Mississippi, served Southern Baptist Churches* and agencies. Landrum, the oldest, was educated at the University of Mississippi (1899) and Southern Baptist Theological Seminary. After engaging in Sunday-school* work for several years, he became (1907) the first secretary of the Baptist Young People's Union (BYPU). His *B.Y.P.U. Manual* (1907) became the standard guide for this organization. When this work was incorporated into the Sunday School Board (1918), he directed the department and edited much of the literature.

Frank also graduated from the University of Mississippi (B.S., 1909) as well as Columbia University (M.A., 1925). Mississippi College (1935) and Baylor University (1945) conferred him honorary doctorates. After almost a decade as secretary of the Georgia BYPU, he became the executive leader of the Inter-Board Commission, which was responsible for student work of the Southern Baptist Convention. When this assignment was given to the Sunday School Board (1928), Frank directed their Department of Student Work. He stressed student conferences and the election of state student directors. He also led the Youth Committee of the Baptist World Alliance* for almost two decades and edited or authored about a dozen books.

Roland also attended the University of Mississippi (B.A.; M.A., 1914) and Southern Baptist Theological Seminary (Th.M., 1917; Th.D., 1925). He served in France for two years (1917-1919) with the YMCA.* For the next two decades he was pastor of churches, mostly in Mississippi and Georgia, before becoming the first superintendent of evangelism* for the Home Mission Board (1937-1942). A pastorate (1942-1946) in Tampa, Florida, was followed by his election as president of the New Orleans Baptist Theological Seminary (1946-

1958). He strengthened the faculty and curriculum of this institution and moved the campus to its present location. Roland published fifteen books, including *Evangelism, Christ's Imperative Commission* (1951).

BIBLIOGRAPHY. C. H. Leavell, ed., *Genealogy of the Nine Leavell Brothers of Oxford, Mississippi* (1957); *ESB* 2. C. L. Howe

Lectionary. A regular cycle of assigned Scripture* readings to be used in worship* on specific occasions. Contemporary lectionaries commonly include four readings for each Sunday service: Old Testament, Psalms, New Testament (Epistle, Acts, or Revelation) and Gospel.

Generally, a lectionary is planned by a group of denominational* or ecumenical* representatives, pastors and scholars. Its use is recommended or required for each congregation of that fellowship. It provides for the systematic coverage of a large portion of the Bible* over a cycle which may vary from one to four years or even more. Readings are normally chosen according to the church year, so that the gospel text is central, with other readings selected to illuminate the meaning of the gospel passage. Many lectionaries also include *lectio continua:* continuous reading of portions of a book of the Bible in its original sequence. Lectionaries have sometimes been modified to give prominence to particular theological issues. A controversial example is the *Inclusive Language Lectionary* (1983), which gives prominence to feminist concerns.

Long an established part of the higher liturgical traditions, lectionaries are now recognized for their ecumenical and liturgical value by many Protestant* bodies as well. Ecumenical cooperation in sermon preparation and discussion of texts has become widespread in the 1980s with the advent of the new *Common Lectionary,* which has been adapted from the Roman Catholic* lectionary. It is now recommended for use in Episcopal,* Lutheran,* Presbyterian,* Congregational,* Methodist* and various other traditions. Increasingly, music,* sermon* and worship planning resources are being developed around this system.

BIBLIOGRAPHY. H. T. Allen, *A Handbook for the Lectionary* (1980); R. C. D. Jasper, ed., *The Calendar and the Lectionary* (1967); J. F. White, *Introduction to Christian Worship* (1980).

P. W. Butin

Lectureships. Annual gatherings of members of the Churches of Christ.* Churches of Christ are committed to rigorous congregational independence, but function as a brotherhood cultivated through nonofficial journals and publishers, schools, colleges and universities, and lectureships which the latter conduct. The lectureships feature sermons and classes for inspiration, motivation and information. The speakers and teachers are the best known as well as promising younger men and women. In addition there are meetings and exhibits representing colleges, mission efforts, nonofficial benevolent organizations and other parachurch* activities, as well as publishers who display and sell books, manuals and journals.

The most influential and largest (15,000) lectureship meets annually at Abilene Christian. Other major lectureships are held at Pepperdine, Freed-Hardeman, David Lipscomb, Harding, Oklahoma Christian and Lubbock Christian. The 1970s saw the rise and decline of evangelistic, or soul-saving, workshops conducted by churches, the largest being Garnett Road of Tulsa, Oklahoma.

BIBLIOGRAPHY. W. S. Banowsky, *Mirror of a Movement* (1965).   T. H. Olbricht

Lee, Ann (Mother Ann) (1736-1784).

Shaker* leader. Born in Manchester, England, the second of eight children, to a blacksmith father (John) and a pious mother, Lee remained illiterate all her life. Lee worked in a textile factory and as a cook. In 1758 she joined a group of millenialists,* led by Quakers* Jane and James Wardley, but did not assume leadership until after her unenthusiastic marriage (1762) to blacksmith Abraham Standerin (Stanley) and the births and deaths of their four infants. She became convinced this was divine punishment for "concupiscence" and began proclaiming celibacy as the way to salvation.*

In 1770, possibly during a prison term for her Shaker "Sabbath disturbing," Lee had a vision of her union with Christ. Further revelation convinced her that the group should go to America. Eight Shakers went with her (1774), including her husband and some relatives. In New York, Lee's husband deserted her, so she joined the others at Niskeyuna (Watervliet), New York.

Mother Ann was revered by the community for her prophetic powers, healings, ecstatic singing and praying.* Previously in England, and also during missionary ventures through New England, the group suffered repeated, severe physical persecution by local inhabitants. Lee died in 1784 as the result of injuries sustained in one such episode.

Through prolonged reflection on Lee's role and progressive theological elevation, a belief arose among Shakers that she was the second coming of Christ in female form. This belief was held most strongly during the Shaker spiritual revival, known as "Mother Ann's Work," that occurred over fifty years after her death (c. 1837-1847).

BIBLIOGRAPHY. E. D. Andrews, *The People Called Shakers: A Search for the Perfect Society* (1953); *DARB; DAB* VI; F. W. Evans, *Ann Lee* (1858); *NAW* 2; S. Y. Wells, ed., *Testimonies of the Life, Character, Revelations and Doctrines of Our Ever Blessed Mother Ann Lee* . . . (1816).

L. A. Mercadante

Lee, Daniel (1807-1896).

Methodist* missionary* to Oregon. Commissioned as a member of the New Hampshire Conference by the Foreign Missionary Society, Lee was sent in 1834 as a missionary to the Native Americans of Oregon, where he worked under the supervision of his uncle, Jason Lee.* Lee's party left Independence, Missouri, on April 28, 1834, accompanying a party of fur traders to the Willamette Valley in Oregon. There Daniel took part in building the mission, and he was given primary responsibility for opening a second mission in 1838 at The Dalles on the Columbia River. His successful mission there was terminated after five years (1843) because of the poor health of both Daniel and his wife. After returning to New England, Lee published, with J. H. Frost, *Ten Years in Oregon* (1844), which served to awaken the interest of the church in the Oregon mission. In his later years he served pastorates in New England and the Midwest.

BIBLIOGRAPHY. F. Norwood, *The Story of American Methodism* (1974).   J. S. O'Malley

Lee, Jarena (1783-c.1850).

African Methodist Episcopal* exhorter and preacher.* Born in New Jersey to free parents, Lee was hired out as a maid at the age of seven. She moved to Philadelphia in 1804, and was converted* under the ministry* of Richard Allen.* She experienced sanctification* a few months later, but when she heard the call of God to preach in 1809, Allen told her that the Methodist Church only permitted women to exhort. In 1811 she married a pastor, Joseph Lee, and moved to Snow Hill. There she bore six children, lost all but two, and returned to Philadelphia after her husband died in 1818. She reached an understanding with Allen (by then bishop of the African Methodist Episcopal Church) and began preaching as an itinerant in 1819—a work she continued tirelessly, despite obstacles, for more than thirty years. She joined the American Antislavery Society in 1840, and was active in the movement for women's full access to the pulpit.

[639]

Nothing is known of her life after 1849.

BIBLIOGRAPHY. J. Lee, *The Life and Religious Experience of Jarena Lee*, in *Sisters of the Spirit*, ed. W. L. Andrews (1986); D. A. Payne, *History of the African Methodist Episcopal Church* (1891).

K. K. Kidd

Lee, Jason (1803-1845). Methodist* missionary* to the Pacific Northwest. The son of a Revolutionary War* soldier, Lee was born in Vermont and converted* in a Methodist revival* in 1826. After preparing for the ministry at Wilabraham Academy in Massachusetts, he ministered in a church in Stanstead, Massachusetts (1830-1832). Appointed by the Missionary Society of his church to lead a party to the Flathead country, Lee and his party, including his nephew Daniel Lee, traveled to the Oregon Territory in 1834, accompanying a party of fur traders. He traced his burden for this mission back to an inquiry about the "white man's religion" that had come from four Northwest Indians who had traveled to St. Louis in 1831.

Lee is credited with preaching* in 1834 the first Protestant* sermon* delivered west of the Rocky Mountains. The Flathead mission was abandoned after their arrival, and a mission was established in the Willamette Valley, ten miles northwest of present-day Salem, Oregon. Despite difficulties in communication and the devastation of Native Americans due to illnesses, the Oregon Institute was founded in 1842, becoming the basis for the first collegiate institution in the Far West, Willamette University. Lee also took an active role in promoting U.S. territorial claims to the area over those of Britain. Although this position brought him into dissension with other missionaries, who objected to his church and to the settlement of the boundary dispute is widely recognized.

BIBLIOGRAPHY. *AAP* 7; C. J. Brosnan, *Jason Lee, Prophet of the New Oregon* (1932); *DAB* VI; F. Norwood, *The Story of American Methodism* (1974). J. S. O'Malley

Lee, Jesse (1758-1816). Methodist* preacher.* Born in Prince George County, Virginia, Lee was converted* just before the outbreak of the American Revolution.* Joining the Methodist Society in 1774, in 1777 he became a class leader, exhorter and local preacher in North Carolina. In 1780, while preaching in North Carolina, Lee was drafted into the army, only to be jailed for refusing to bear arms. There he preached and sang to the guards and other soldiers. He was convinced to consent to unarmed duty as a wagon driver until his

honorable discharge four months later.

Lee received his first appointment as a circuit rider* in North Carolina and Virginia in 1783. Francis Asbury,* whom Lee met in 1785, soon recognized his gifts and graces and took him as a traveling companion for three years. Lee then heard of the low state of religion in New England and in 1790—the year he was ordained* deacon* and elder* by Asbury on successive days—he preached on Boston Common. His influence continued to spread throughout New England for over a decade.

After losing a close vote for bishop* in 1800, in 1801 Lee returned to Virginia where he remained for fourteen years, during which time he was elected chaplain* of the U.S. House of Representatives (1809), and of the Senate (1814) and published the first *History of Methodism in the United States* (1810).

An imposing man, Lee weighed 250 pounds, and as a preacher he was clear and practical, with a quick and persuasive wit. Lee died September 12, 1816, in Maryland, where he had moved the previous year. Perhaps next to Francis Asbury in his influence on early Methodism, Lee is regarded as the father of Methodism in New England.

BIBLIOGRAPHY. *AAP* 7; *DAB* VI; *DARB*; L. Lee, *The Life and Times of the Reverend Jesse Lee* (1848); M. Thrift, *Memoir of the Reverend Jesse Lee* (1923). R. G. Tuttle

Lee, Robert (E)dward (1807-1870). Confederate general, commander of the Southern armies. His father, "Light-Horse Harry" Lee, had been a famed cavalry officer in the Revolutionary War* and a governor of Virginia. His mother, Ann Hill Carter, also came from prominent Virginia stock. The Lee family was Episcopalian* and maintained a family life characterized by Christian piety.* Lee graduated second in his class at West Point (1829). In 1852 he began a three-year term as superintendent at West Point. Lee had already proven his military skills in the Mexican War (1846-1848) and would do so again in the suppression of John Brown's slave insurrection at Harper's Ferry (1859).

The coming of the Civil War* posed a dilemma for Lee. He loved the Union and opposed slavery and secession, but he could not betray his native Virginia. Given command of the Army of Northern Virginia on June 1, 1862, Lee, though always outnumbered, won strategic victories in the Seven Days' Battles (June 25—July 1, 1862), the Second Battle of Bull Run (August 29-30, 1862) and the Battles of Fredericksburg (December 13, 1862) and Chancellorsville (May 1-4, 1863). The tide of the war changed when Lee was defeated at Gettysburg (July 1-3, 1863). The South was already nearly defeated when he was appointed general-in-chief of the Confederate armies early in 1865. Lee surrendered to Grant on April 9 at Appomattox Courthouse.

After the war, Lee became president of Washington College (later Washington and Lee University) where he proved to be a progressive educator. A devout Episcopalian, Lee was low church* in his orientation, although he was not a controversialist in matters of doctrine* or churchmanship. Even as a military man he was known for keeping the Sabbath and calling for days of prayer* and fasting.* Throughout the South, Lee was esteemed as a Christian knight and was often compared to Christ.

BIBLIOGRAPHY. *DAB* VI; C. Dowdy, *Lee* (1965); C. Dowdy and L. Manarin, eds., *The Wartime Papers of Robert E. Lee* (1961); D. S. Freeman, *R. E. Lee,* 4 vols. (1935).   D. B. Chesebrough

Lee, Robert Greene (1886-1978). Southern Baptist* minister.* Born in a sharecropper's cabin in South Carolina, Lee felt called to preach* when converted* at the age of twelve, but family hardship delayed his education at Furman University until 1909 to 1913. Lee served seventeen short pastorates before going in 1927 to Bellevue Baptist in Memphis, Tennessee. When he retired from there in 1960, he had received 24,071 new members, 7,649 by baptism.* His ministry was marked by an evangelistic* emphasis in every church activity and by strong pastoral leadership. A master of alliterative sermons, he published fifty volumes of them and delivered one, "Payday Someday," 1,275 times. Though admired by separatist* fundamentalists,* he was a loyal Southern Baptist, serving as president of the Tennessee Baptist Convention (1932-1936) and the Southern Baptist Convention (1948-1950). Based on a national poll of Protestant ministers, *The Christian Century* (April 19, 1950) featured Bellevue as one of twelve "Great American Churches."

BIBLIOGRAPHY. P. Gericke, *The Preaching of Robert G. Lee* (1967); J. E. Huss, *Robert G. Lee: The Authorized Biography* (1967).

J. H. Dorn

Legalism. The act of putting law above gospel by establishing requirements for salvation* beyond repentance and faith in Jesus Christ. Legalism reduces the broad, inclusive and general precepts of the Bible* to narrow and rigid codes. Ultimately,

it creates a system that obligates God to bless those who have proven themselves worthy. It thus tends to underestimate both the sinfulness* of humanity and the holiness* of God.

The problem of legalism is well attested to in the New Testament when Jesus accused the Pharisees of making the "tradition of the elders" more authoritative than the truth of God. They neglected justice and righteousness in their obsession with modes of purification and Sabbath regulations. The apostle Paul combatted legalism too, opposing the Judaizers who undermined the gospel by requiring gentile converts to be circumcised. Paul argued that faith alone was sufficient for salvation. Christ came, he said, to break down the dividing wall between Jew and Gentile and thus erase any distinctions that made one group feel superior to another.

The concept of legalism is complex, however, because the Christian faith does not altogether dismiss the requirements of obedience to law. Indeed, law has always played an important, albeit complex, role in the Christian faith. If legalism has been abhorred in the history of the church, so has license. Churches have tried to strike a balance between the two. There are many examples in history. Roman Catholics* elaborated a complex code of canon law* in the twelfth century. Calvinists* emphasized the "third use of the law" for the believer's life of faith, and even Lutherans argued that law, while playing no role in the believer's relationship with God (except to convict of sin), was useful in guiding Christian behavior for the sake of one's neighbor.

The relationship of law and gospel, legalism and license, has caused problems in American Christianity. It has always been an open question to determine exactly what constitutes legalism in America. No religious group in America has been entirely free from it. Roman Catholics sometimes err on the side of ritual legalism. Catholic theology tends to stress the efficacy of the sacraments, and Catholics can be assured of salvation through baptism* and communion. Catholic ritual can thus become a substitute for vital faith in Jesus Christ.

American fundamentalists* gravitate toward moral and doctrinal legalism. They try to separate from the world by forbidding drinking, card playing, movie attendance and dancing. Furthermore, they stress doctrinal purity by drawing particular attention to doctrines such as the virgin birth, the substitutionary atonement,* the premillennial* return of Christ and the inerrancy* of Scripture, making them theological essentials.

Pentecostals* are sometimes guilty of experiential legalism. Pentecostals believe that true Christians, though saved only through Jesus Christ, must also receive the baptism of the Holy Spirit,* which occurs in a separate experience after conversion* and is usually accompanied by speaking in tongues.*

Many mainline* Protestants* lean toward political legalism. Justice and liberation become as important as, if not synonymous with, the gospel itself. Their bias toward left-wing ideology is as errant as the fundamentalists' capitulation to right-wing politics.

When these ritualistic, moral, doctrinal, experiential and political propensities are forced to become Christian essentials, they undermine the once-for-all work of Christ and alienate other Christians who approach the Christian faith from a different, though equally legitimate, perspective. The Christian antidote to legalism is, as Reinhold Niebuhr* suggested, to recognize that believers are fallen creatures and must, therefore, in humility, stay close to the cross.   G. L. Sittser

Leiper, Henry Smith (1891-1975). Missionary* and ecumenist.* Born in Belmar, New Jersey, Leiper was educated at Amherst College, Columbia University and Union Theological Seminary,* New York. He was ordained* by the Presbyterian Church in the U.S.A.* in 1915 and pastored a Presbyterian church for a short while, though he later became a Congregationalist* (1922). After doing relief work in Siberia, Leiper served as a missionary with the American Board of Comissioners of Foreign Missions* in China (1918-1923). He was also a pastor in Paris to Americans living abroad. Leiper's interests led him to increasing involvement in national and world ecumenical agencies. He was foreign secretary of the Federal Council of Churches* (1930-1948) and associate general secretary of the World Council of Churches* (1938-1952). Leiper wrote *World Chaos or World Christianity* (1938) and edited a survey of the contemporary state of the church entitled *Christianity Today* (1947). He also wrote on racism, nationalism and church-state relations.

BIBLIOGRAPHY. W. J Schmidt, *What Kind of a Man? The Life of Henry Smith Leiper* (1986).

J. M. Smylie

Le Jeune, Paul (1591-1664). Jesuit* missionary* and superior in New France. Born into a Protestant Huguenot* family in France, Le Jeune became a Roman Catholic* at sixteen, trained as a Jesuit at La Fleche and Clermont, and taught in France before his appointment as superior of the Jesuit Missions in Quebec in 1632. There he completely rebuilt the Quebec mission after its demise under English rule. He also initiated Native American-language study for missionaries and established schools, seminaries and hospitals for Native Americans to assist in their settlement.

Le Jeune was responsible for creating the *Jesuit Relations,* a collection of annual reports and articles begun in 1632 to raise French support for the missions. In terms of the interest in New France and the missions which the *Relations* evoked, his influence while superior, editor and regular contributor was substantial. They are recognized as the most reliable, comprehensive and accurate historical documents of the period in New France. Replaced as superior in 1639, Le Jeune worked as a missionary for ten years before his recall to France as *procureur* of Jesuit missions to Canada and edited the *Relations* until shortly before his death in Paris in 1664.

BIBLIOGRAPHY. F. Parkman, *The Jesuits in North America* (1900).   R. H. Chilton

Leland, John (1754-1841). Baptist* preacher* and religious libertarian. Reared in Massachusetts as a Congregationalist,* Leland was nurtured by Scripture* and Bunyan's *Pilgrim's Progress* from an early age. At the age of eighteen he underwent conversion* and was baptized* by Wait Palmer, a Baptist minister. Leland felt called to devote himself to the ministry* and was licensed* to preach two years later.

By 1777 he and his new bride had arrived in Anglican* Virginia where he was to spend fourteen years pastoring a number of small Baptist churches (e.g., those located at Mt. Poney, Orange and Louisa) and serving as an itinerant evangelist.* Leland's ministry was carried out in the midst of hostility—Baptist preachers had been imprisoned, mobs had broken up worship services, and churches had been shut down by local magistrates—and challenges from his Baptist brethren, who questioned the regularity of his ordination.* The latter obstacle was overcome in 1786 when Leland was ordained again, this time with the proper "laying on of hands." In the end Leland, a leading Separate Baptist,* became a member and spokesman of the General Committee composed of Separate and Regular Baptists.*

Through his preaching, writing and personal friendship with Thomas Jefferson* and James Madison,* Leland exercised notable influence in the struggle to disestablish the Anglican Church and establish religious liberty. The General Committee, of which he was a part, repeatedly circulated petitions to the House of Burgesses for the redress of grievances. Leland led the Baptists in support of Jefferson's bill establishing religious liberty* in Virginia. Leland-led Baptists also rallied the support of the Presbyterians, Mennonites and others to defeat the General Assessment Bill which the established* church was attempting to promote in the House of Burgesses. Finally, Leland, like Isaac Backus,* proposed a Bill of Rights to the Constitution and apparently refused to support James Madison's candidacy for Virginia's ratifying convention without assurance from Madison that he would personally see to it that such a Bill of Rights was forthcoming once the Constitution was ratified.

In 1792 Leland moved back to Cheshire, Massachusetts, where he spent his next fifty years in itinerant ministry that took him throughout New England, as well as on several return trips to Virginia. In Massachusetts and Connecticut he again championed religious freedom and the separation of church and state,* serving in the Massachusetts House of Representatives from 1811 to 1813. In addition to his political tracts and articles on behalf of religious liberty, Leland also wrote as many as twenty-one hymns.*

BIBLIOGRAPHY. *AAP* 6; L. H. Butterfield, *Elder John Leland, Jeffersonian Itinerant* (1953); *DAB* VI; *DARB;* J. M. Dawson, *Baptists and American Republic* (1956); *NCAB* 5. W. R. Estep

Lenski, (R)ichard (C)harles (H)enry (1864-1936). Lutheran* minister* and biblical scholar. Born in Prussia, Lenski immigrated to America in 1873 and studied at Capital University in Columbus, Ohio. He was ordained* to the ministry in 1887 and served pastorates in Maryland and Ohio until 1911. He then joined the theology faculty of Capital University and taught there until his death. Lenski's writings included *The Epistle Selections of the Ancient Church* (1935) and *The Gospel Selections of the Ancient Church* (1936). His most influential work, however, was his eleven-volume commentary series, The Interpretation of the New Testament (1932), which remains in print and is still used in a number of evangelical* and Lutheran seminaries in America. J. F. Johnson

Lent. A six-week period of spiritual preparation prior to Easter.* The practice may have begun in the early church with baptismal candidates undergoing a forty-day period of preparation prior to their baptism* at Easter. The period eventually came to last six weeks (beginning on Ash Wednesday). Those doing penance initially joined the

baptismal candidates in spiritual discipline and in time the season became a period of spiritual devotion for the church as a whole.

The season is characterized by penitence and in the early centuries of the church a fast was observed that allowed only one meal a day, to be taken in the evening. The theme of penitence has been reflected in the Lenten liturgy of the Catholic Church* with a special Mass* assigned to each day of Lent and the omission of the Gloria and Alleluia. Personal spiritual discipline and attention to devotional practices such as prayer is encouraged, as is abstinence from festivities and almsgiving.

Lent has continued to be observed in the Anglican* tradition and was particularly encouraged by the Tractarians* of the nineteenth century. It is observed by Lutherans* and, more recently, other Protestant* denominations affected by the liturgical movement* have incorporated it into their church year.* A variety of prayer books and daily devotional readings, as well as collections of Lenten sermons, have been published for both Catholics and Protestants.

See also MARDI GRAS.

BIBLIOGRAPHY. T. J. Talley, *The Origins of the Liturgical Year* (1986). The Editors

Leo XIII (1810-1903). Pope. Leo, elected pope in 1878, deeply influenced the growth of the Catholic Church* in the U.S. During his pontificate, the Catholic population grew tremendously, owing largely to European immigration.* By 1884 there were 12 million Catholics in the U.S. in a total population of 76 million. Although the U.S. Church was still looked on as a mission church during the pontificate of Leo, it was removed from that status in 1908.

Between the Second Baltimore Plenary Council of 1866 and 1883, various problems had arisen within the American Church demanding the attention of the hierarchy. The impetus for a council came chiefly from the bishops of the Midwest. In 1883 the U.S. archbishops were called to Rome to plan the assembly. Archbishop James Gibbons* was appointed to preside, although it was originally planned to send an Italian archbishop as apostolic delegate* for that purpose. The decrees of the Third Baltimore Council (meeting November 9 to December 7, 1884) embraced topics such as the education of Catholic youth, erection of parochial schools,* church property and divine worship.* Committees were also created to arrange for the setting up of a Catholic University* (a project receiving Pope Leo's full support) to prepare what eventually became the

Baltimore Catechism and to provide for missions to the Native American and African-American communities.

Leo's pronouncements on capital, labor as well as other social issues were set forth in his well-known encyclical *Rerum Novarum,** in which he supported the working classes and labor unions. He refrained from condemning the Knights of Labor* in the U.S. on the advice of Cardinal Gibbons. When Secretary of State John W. Foster invited papal participation in the Columbian Exposition of 1893 in Chicago, Leo obliged by loaning valuable documents and by sending a personal representative, Archbishop Francesco Satolli,* to the Exposition.

When a permanent Apostolic Action in the U.S. was created (January 1893), Satolli was appointed the first apostolic delegate. By this appointment, Leo aimed at assisting the bishops in settling problems that arose in the American Church. In 1895 Leo sent his first encyclical* to the American Church, *Longinqua Oceani,** in which he praised the prosperity of the Church and the freedom it enjoyed. Shortly thereafter, in the late 1890s, the crisis of Americanism* developed. Its doctrines held that the Church should modify certain doctrines for the purpose of gaining more converts and to keep in step with modern civilization. The matter was settled in Leo's letter to Cardinal Gibbons, *Testem Benevolentiae** (1899), which condemned these tenets—tenets which Gibbons insisted no educated American Catholic ever held. In the twenty-fifth year of his pontificate, the American bishops sent a letter of congratulations to Leo, and he responded in 1902 with a warm letter in which he stated that he always cherished the devotion of American Catholics.

BIBLIOGRAPHY. J. T. Ellis, *The Life of James Cardinal Gibbons, Archbishop of Baltimore, 1834-1921* (1952); T. T. McAvoy, C.S.C., "Leo III and America," in *Leo III and the Modern World,* ed. E. T. Gargan (1961); *NCE* 8.

C. E. Ronan

LeTourneau, Robert Gilmour (1881-1969). Protestant layman, educator and industrialist. Born in Richfield, Vermont, LeTourneau had little formal education. After several years running a garage (1917-1929), he founded his own company, R. G. LeTourneau, Inc., over which he served as president (1929-1969). An inventor, LeTourneau specialized in heavy machinery used to clear and build roads. A layman* in the Christian and Missionary Alliance* and a popular speaker among evangelicals,* he combined business and missions

by setting up companies in Peru and Liberia to develop natural resources, provide employment for nationals and provide a means of evangelism.* In 1946 LeTourneau founded and generously endowed a school to train students in mechanical and industrial arts, LeTourneau College in Longview, Texas.

BIBLIOGRAPHY. A. W. Lorimer, *God Runs My Business: The Story of R. G. LeTourneau* (1941).

E. E. Cairns

Leverett, John (1662-1724). Massachusetts lawyer, political leader and president of Harvard College.* After graduating from Harvard College (B.A., 1680; M.A., 1683), Leverett worked for fifteen years as fellow and tutor while Increase Mather* served as president from Boston. Though orthodox* in matters of theology,* Leverett had liberal opinions regarding liturgy* and church membership.* With William and Thomas Brattle,* he formed Boston's new Brattle* Street Church in 1699 as a "broad and catholick" alternative to orthodox Congregationalism.* The Mathers succeeded in removing Leverett from his Harvard post in 1700.

Leverett went on to practice law, enter politics and be appointed judge. After the Mathers lost control of the corporation, he was elected, though not without controversy, Harvard's first non-clerical president in 1707. He led the college in an entirely new direction, introducing Anglican* divinity,* broader readings in secular literature and a freer style of campus life. In 1721 he established the Hollis professorship of divinity, notably free from a required test of orthodoxy. In the wake of further conflict with Cotton Mather,* Samuel Sewell* and other orthodox political leaders, Leverett died unexpectedly.

BIBLIOGRAPHY. *DAB* VI; S. E. Morison, *Harvard College in the Seventeenth Century,* 2 vols. (1936); J. L. Sibley, *Biographical Sketches of Harvard University,* vols. 1-4 (1873-1885).

C. E. Hambrick-Stowe

Lewis, (C)live (S)taples (1898-1963). British scholar, writer and Christian apologist.* Born in Belfast, Northern Ireland, Lewis received most of his education in England. He studied first at Malvern and then at University College, Oxford, where his education was interrupted by service in World War 1.* After the war he took a double First in English and *Literae Humaniores* at University College and then stayed on at Oxford where he was a fellow in English Language and Literature at Magdalen College (1925-1954). From Oxford,

Lewis moved to Cambridge University where he served as professor of Medieval and Renaissance English (1954-1963).

Lewis's enormous reputation stems largely from his extensive list of publications. A poet, essayist, novelist, literary historian and critic as well as Christian apologist, Lewis published thirty-nine books, 125 essays and pamphlets, sixty-eight poems, three dozen book reviews, two short stories, and edited or wrote prefaces to eleven other volumes. His fame was further enhanced by his popular BBC radio broadcasts on Christianity during World War 2,* as well as his numerous public lectures and sermons.

Though Lewis never visited North America, he has had an immense impact on North American Christians. Over three dozen of his titles are available, with over forty million copies in print, making him the best-selling Christian author of all time and perhaps the most frequently quoted in sermons, lectures, books and articles. The list of people who claim to have become Christians or have been aided in their spiritual growth because of his books is seemingly endless.

Lewis's extraordinary influence can be explained, in part, by the size and diversity of his publication list. His writings include the popular *Chronicles of Narnia* for young people, as well as a space trilogy for adults. These volumes, including *The Lion, The Witch and the Wardrobe* (1950), and *Perelandra* (1943), as well as such fictional works as *The Screwtape Letters* (1942) and *The Great Divorce* (1945), have touched countless lives by opening people's imaginations to spiritual reality. Former doubters and seekers who are more inclined to nonfiction testify to the impact of encountering such tightly reasoned apologetic works as *Mere Christianity* (1952) and *Miracles* (1947). Finally, Lewis's spiritual autobiography, *Surprised by Joy* (1955), has pushed many an agnostic and atheist toward the Christian faith.

Besides pointing nonbelievers to Christ, Lewis's books are frequently used to instruct believers in the essentials of the faith and in matters of Christian conduct. Volumes typically used in church classes and adult study groups are: *The Four Loves* (1960), *Letters to Malcolm: Chiefly on Prayer* (1964), *Reflections on the Psalms* (1958), *The Weight of Glory* (1962) and *The World's Last Night and Other Essays* (1960). Christians have also found Lewis's letters instructive. Several volumes have been published, including: *Letters of C. S. Lewis* (1966), *Letters to an American Lady* (1967) and *Letters to Children* (1985).

Lewis's vast impact is due not only to the variety of his writings but also to his willingness to confront difficult questions. Never one to sidestep tough issues such as pain, evil and death, Lewis directly and intelligently grappled with these topics and made them themes for books such as *The Problem of Pain* (1940) and *A Grief Observed* (1961).

Although Lewis predicted that interest in his books would disappear within five years after his death, in the late 1980s, a quarter century after he was laid to rest, interest in his works continues to grow.

BIBLIOGRAPHY. R. L. Green and W. Hooper, *C. S. Lewis: A Biography* (1974); W. Griffin, *Clive Staples Lewis: A Dramatic Life* (1986); C. Walsh, *The Literary Legacy of C. S. Lewis* (1979).

L. W. Dorsett

Lewis, Edwin (1881-1959). Methodist* theologian.* Born in Newbury, England, Lewis was sent as a British Methodist missionary to Labrador at the age of nineteen. Lewis was later educated at New York State College for Teachers (A.B., 1915) and studied theology at Drew Theological Seminary (B.D., 1908; Th.D., 1918). While a graduate student at Drew, Lewis began to teach, which led to his career as professor of theology at Drew Theological Seminary from 1916 to 1951.

In the 1920s Lewis's theology reflected the evangelical* liberalism* which prevailed in mainline* Protestantism.* Thus in his first major work, *Jesus Christ and the Human Quest* (1924), he sought to construct a Christology* based on the philosophy of personal idealism. However, toward the end of the decade, he became disenchanted with his theological position because of his growing concern over the spread of naturalistic thinking within liberalism and the effect of liberal theology on missionary expansion.

At the time, Lewis was being influenced by the theology of Karl Barth* and above all was engaged in his own rediscovery of the Bible* through his labors as co-editor of the *Abingdon Bible Commentary* (1929). The result was a radical reorientation in his thinking "from philosophy to revelation" and from this emerged Lewis's most influential work, *A Christian Manifesto* (1934). There he passionately urged American Protestantism to return to the beliefs of the historic faith in supernaturalism, radical human sinfulness and the reality of incarnation and atonement.* Lewis's last major work, *The Creator and the Adversary* (1948), adopted a modified dualism as a solution to the problem of evil, again reflecting the continuing development of his thought. Lewis's shift from liberalism to neo-orthodoxy* was the most prominent example within American Methodism of a movement that was taking place in American theology as a whole.

BIBLIOGRAPHY. S. A. Seamands, *Christology and Transition in the Theology of Edwin Lewis* (1987). S. A. Seamands

Lewis, Tayler (1802-1877). Biblical scholar. Born in Northumberland, Saratoga County, New York, Tayler graduated from Union College in 1820 and went on to study law. After several years of law practice (1825-1833), he taught in academies in Waterford and Ogdensburg (1833-1838) until in 1838 he was appointed professor at the University of the City of New York. In 1850 he returned to Union College, first as professor of Greek and later as professor of oriental languages and biblical literature.

One of Lewis's chief interests was the relationship between science and religion, particularly regarding creation. The publication of his book *The Six Days of Creation* (1855) resulted in a four-part response from Yale* geologist James Dwight Dana,* to which Lewis offered his rejoinders. Lewis's chief contention was that biblical interpretation need not be harmonized with scientific theories that were notably defective and subject to change. Dana, on the other hand, believed that science could inform the Christian understanding of Scripture.*

BIBLIOGRAPHY. *DAB* VI; M. B. Sherwood, "Genesis, Evolution, and Geology in America before Darwin: The Dana-Lewis Controversy, 1856-1857," in *Toward a History of Geology,* ed. C. J. Schneer (1969). D. G. Reid

Liberal Catholic Church. A religious movement based on Theosophy and founded in Great Britain. The Liberal Catholic Church was founded by James Ingall Wedgwood in London in 1916. In addition to Wedgwood, the church recognizes Charles W. Leadbeater as its cofounder. Its historical and theological roots can be traced to the Old Catholic Church, from which it emerged; the Anglican Church,* with which its early leaders were formerly affiliated; but most significantly the Theosophical Society, whose mystical* tradition it adapted to Catholic ritual. Of the cofounders, Leadbeater had the greatest impact in the development of the church through his authorship of the movement's foundational theological document, *The Science of the Sacraments.*

The church's international headquarters is in London, and membership in America probably numbers no more than a few thousand. The church was established in the U.S. in 1919. Its first regionary (chief) bishop was Irving Steiger Cooper (1882-1935). Today there are about eighty priests* and deacons* active in America and about forty established churches. The regionary bishop of the U.S. resides in Chicago, and the movement's U.S. headquarters are in Ojai, California. Congregations are generally quite small. Priests receive no salary and collect no fees for administering the sacraments*; all are required to hold secular jobs. The church has no formal ties with Theosophy, although the intellectual and spiritual linkage is recognized.

The Science of the Sacraments offers a carefully structured reinterpretation of the traditional Catholic sacraments based on the spiritual assumptions of Theosophy and Leadbeater's own clairvoyant insights. Although the church affirms complete freedom of belief for its followers, in practice it represents a Theosophical reading of orthodox* Catholicism based on Leadbeater's theology. Central to this theology are the sacraments and especially the Eucharist,* which functions to focus and release spiritual energy in and through the congregation. Notable doctrinal positions include belief in: (1) the innate divinity of humanity; (2) reincarnation and denial of hell*; (3) spiritual masters (saints) which spiritually interact with humanity; (4) Christ as divine messenger, historically manifested through others in addition to Jesus; and (5) the necessity of an exclusively male clergy.

BIBLIOGRAPHY. F. S. Mead, *Handbook of Denominations in the United States,* rev. ed. S. S. Hill (1985); W. J. Whalen, *Minority Religions in America* (1981). D. deChant

Liberalism/Modernism, Protestant (c. 1870s-1930s). A late nineteenth- and early twentieth-century movement seeking to preserve the Christian faith by adjusting traditional Christianity to developments in modern culture.

Liberalism, in the general sense of a movement desiring freedom from tradition, has been a recurring impulse throughout the history of Christianity. Within American Protestantism* the term *liberalism* or *modernism* refers more precisely to a theological movement in the late nineteenth and early twentieth centuries which sought to save Christianity from the assault of contemporary intellectual developments by accommodating the traditional faith to modern culture.

American modernists received inspiration from European sources in the philosophy of Immanuel

Kant (1724-1804), as well as the religious thought of Friedrich Schleiermacher (1768-1834) and Albrecht Ritschl (1822-1889). Closer to home, liberals found precedent in the theology of Unitarianism,* Transcendentalism* and Horace Bushnell.* Bushnell was perhaps the most important precursor of the religious liberals who followed later in the century. In *Christian Nurture* (1847), *God in Christ* (1849) and other works, he developed many of the themes that came to dominate modernism: the immanence of God, the importance of Christian experience, the necessity of doctrinal revision and the poetic nature of religious language.

In the decades after the Civil War,* profound intellectual and social changes rocked the United States. The publication of Charles Darwin's *Origin of Species* in 1859 and the consequent spread of evolutionary* thought challenged cherished notions about the Bible's accuracy and God's providential design. Developments in the disciplines of biblical studies,* history, psychology,* sociology and comparative religions led to a relativistic view of truth which added to the forces threatening Victorian orthodoxy. Unprecedented social changes further aggravated the cultural turmoil. Massive immigration,* rapid industrialization, skyrocketing urban growth and the gradual secularization of society resulted in pervasive tensions in American society.

The new intellectual and social trends nourished the liberal impulse in America which, by the 1880s, had given rise to an identifiable movement known as the New Theology or Progressive Orthodoxy. Two Connecticut pastors, Theodore Munger* and Newman Smyth,* gave early and eloquent testimony to this movement. Munger, in *The Freedom of Faith* (1883), and Smyth, in *Old Faiths in New Light* (1878) and *The Orthodox Theology of Today* (1881), sought to reconcile the old faith and the new knowledge.

By the first decade of the twentieth century, William Newton Clarke* of Colgate Seminary and William Adams Brown* of Union Seminary, New York, had systematized the New Theology in popular texts. Despite efforts by many of the major denominations to arrest the progress of the New Theology, the most famous of which was the Charles Briggs* heresy trial* in the Presbyterian Church* (1893), liberalism enjoyed rapid gains throughout the Northern churches. By 1920 liberals dominated perhaps half of the country's Protestant seminaries* and publishing* houses and a third of the Protestant pulpits.* While the diverse nature of liberalism makes it difficult to define,

certain prominent principles and themes allow a fairly clear description of the movement.

An emphasis on the immanence of God in nature and history held a central place in the liberal impulse. Turning a theistic trick on Darwinism, the pre-eminent idea of the age, modernists argued that God was present in and revealed through the progress of history and the evolution of culture. God worked in the world through natural laws, not by miraculous intervention in the natural order. Traditional distinctions between the supernatural and natural, church and world, were rejected in favor of a stress on the unity of the sacred and the secular. God was not external to the world but permeated all of life.

This affirmation naturally lent a roseate glow to the liberal world view. The freedom and ability of mankind were emphasized; humans were the fundamentally good, infinitely valuable children of God. Sin* was not a radical disjunction between God and humanity but merely a matter of ignorance or bestial remains that could be corrected by Christian education. The significance of the incarnation, therefore, lay not in Jesus' death on the cross as a vicarious sacrifice for the sins of the world but in the Master's revelation of the worth of human personality and the power of love. History, though perhaps marred by minor detours, demonstrated a steady and inevitable progress toward the historical realization of the kingdom of God.*

Following the lead of Schleiermacher and Bushnell, liberals contended that experience and feeling, not creeds or doctrine, provided the foundation of Christianity. The ultimate authority for faith was the self-evidencing testimony of the heart to the individual believer. Liberals insisted that Christianity was a growing and changing life rather than a static creed,* ritual or organization. Doctrines, which were nothing more than the tentative and historically limited expressions of abiding religious sentiment, necessarily required periodic reformulation to adjust to the ever-expanding knowledge of mankind. Modernists thus deplored the continuing division of the church over anachronistic doctrinal disputes and became enthusiastic supporters of efforts for ecclesiastical reunion.

The modernist emphases on progress and experience were manifested in the liberal understanding of the Scriptures* as an account of the advancing religious consciousness of the Hebrew people fulfilled in the life of Jesus. The Bible was not a repository of inerrant* history and doctrine but an historically conditioned norm of religious experience* to be interpreted and reproduced in light of the progress of culture. This belief allowed liberals to embrace the results of historical criticism and the natural sciences without worry. If modern Christians had difficulty with the resurrection, the virgin birth or the miracles of Jesus, they need only realize that these categories were but outmoded expressions of unchanging religious consciousness.

For modernists, ethics replaced doctrine as the theological centerpiece. The value and truth of religion was demonstrated by the moral impact it had on individuals or society. Concern for this world overshadowed interest in the life hereafter. This stress on morals was nowhere clearer than in the liberal view of Jesus which often attributed his divinity to his ethical and religious excellence. Modernists distinguished the religion of Jesus, which emphasized the tender, loving nature of God, the value of human personality and the triumph of God's kingdom in the world, from the religion about Jesus, often condemned as metaphysical and dogmatic. The mission* of the church was to help bring in the kingdom of God through religious education and social reform.

Although most liberals agreed on the importance of ethics,* they possessed differing opinions on the proper implementation of Jesus' commands. Some liberals, like the pulpit giants Henry Ward Beecher* and Phillips Brooks,* stressed personal rather than corporate morality. Proponents of the Social Gospel,* disturbed by the cultural upheaval created by the rapid urbanization and industrialization of the late nineteenth century, took a different tack. Washington Gladden,* generally considered to be the originator of the Social Gospel, insisted that the ethics of Jesus applied not just to the individual but to economic and political structures as well. The most articulate spokesman of this movement was Walter Rauschenbusch* of Rochester Theological Seminary who, in his work *A Theology for the Social Gospel* (1917), gave the Social Gospel a realistic tenor by adding the concept of the kingdom of evil to the common liberal concept of the kingdom of God on earth. In 1908 the Federal Council of Churches* adopted a "Social Creed of the Churches,"* giving the Social Gospel Movement the official endorsement of the major denominations.

Having reached its zenith by the 1920s, liberalism found itself assaulted by fundamentalists on the right and scientific humanists on the left. Both argued that modernism was not Christianity and demanded that liberals make a clean and honest choice between the orthodox faith and humanism.

Modernists like Harry E. Fosdick,* pastor of the Riverside Church in New York City, and Shailer Mathews,* dean of the Divinity School of the University of Chicago,* responded by insisting that liberals were evangelical Christians and that modernism provided the only real option to unbelief in the modern world. Nevertheless, the crises of World War 1,* the Great Depression* and the rise of totalitarianism in Europe posed serious problems for a movement based on a belief in ineluctable human progress. By the 1930s neo-orthodoxy* was challenging American modernism on yet another front. While neo-orthodox thinkers accepted the results of historical criticism, they rejected the modernist emphases on the immanence of God, the goodness of mankind and the upward movement of history. Liberals, unable to withstand these attacks, executed a strategic retreat.

Although most modernists felt compelled to modify or reject their optimistic view of humanity and human history, many refused to renounce their belief in the immanence of God. As Sydney Ahlstrom* noted, liberals played an important educative role by leading "the Protestant churches into the world of modern science, scholarship, philosophy, and global knowledge." The most persistent legacy of modernism to American Protestantism was its insistence that Christian theology acknowledge and exploit the inevitable involvement of religion and culture. Though liberalism, by its very nature, was constantly changing, it continued to be a major force in old-line Protestant denominations.*

See also FUNDAMENTALISM; FUNDAMENTALIST-MODERNIST CONTROVERSY; HERESY TRIALS; MODERNISM, CATHOLIC.

BIBLIOGRAPHY. S. E. Ahlstrom, *A Religious History of the American People* (1972); S. E. Ahlstrom, *Theology in America: The Major Protestant Voices from Puritanism to Neoorthodoxy* (1967); L. J. Averill, *American Theology in the Liberal Tradition* (1967); K. Cauthen, *The Impact of American Religious Liberalism* (1962); W. R. Hutchison, ed., *American Protestant Thought in the Liberal Era* (1968); W. R. Hutchison, *The Modernist Impulse in American Protestantism* (1976); D. D. Williams, *The Andover Liberals: A Study in American Theology* (1941). B. J. Longfield

Liberation Theology. Liberation theology was introduced to North Americans with the English translation of Gustavo Gutierrez's *A Theology of Liberation* in 1973. As a movement for both the reform of theology* and a Christian commitment to radical social change, liberation theology has had a profound influence on theology in North America and elsewhere.

Historical Roots. In the early 1960s some Latin American theologians saw the need for a theological response to widespread conditions of poverty and injustice. Their concerns took a relatively consistent theological shape which made a strong impact on the Roman Catholic Church* at the Second General Conference of the Latin American Episcopate (CELAM), held in Medellin, Colombia, in 1968. At that conference the current historic situation in Latin America was recognized as one of oppression, poverty and liberation. The church was called to denounce the oppression and side with the forces struggling for liberation.

The bishops at Medellin recognized and encouraged the development of "base communities," small groups of Christians gathered together for Bible study,* prayer* and reflection on the gospel in their context. These groups have become the major vehicle for the spread of liberation themes beyond academic circles. By 1980 there were as many as 100,000 base communities meeting in Latin America. Nevertheless, liberation theology remains controversial in the Roman Catholic Church, with strong opposition from some of the Latin American Church hierarchy.

Liberation theology quickly spread to the Protestant Church in Latin America, with similar controversy. Conservative Christians sometimes saw it as undermining the spiritual message of the gospel. Jose Miguez Bonino of Argentina became the most prolific and articulate Protestant advocate of the new way of "doing" theology.

Since becoming a North American and worldwide movement in theology, liberation theology has appealed primarily to people committed to addressing situations of economic, racial and sexual exploitation. In the U.S. liberation theology may be divided into three major streams: (1) white, male liberation theologians, among whom Robert McAfee Brown and Frederick Herzog are prominent; (2) feminist liberation theologians, among whom Rosemary Radford Ruether and Elizabeth Schussler Fiorenza are well known; and (3) African-American liberation theologians (*See* Black Theology), among whom James H. Cone* and Gayraud S. Wilmore are recognized leaders. In addition to these major streams, the influence of liberation theology can be seen in the writings of Asian-American,* Native-American and Hispanic-American* church leaders.

Liberation Method. Liberation theology employs a method whose principal source is not reason (as in natural law* theology), nor tradition (as in many institutions), nor the Bible* (as in evangelicalism*), nor the voice of the Spirit (as in some charismatic* circles), nor social analysis (as in some liberal* circles), but in a Christian praxis which enlists all of the above.

Liberation theologians argue that praxis—the unity of theory and practice in a concrete historical situation—is the starting point for theology. Theology is seen as the second step. First we must have a fundamental commitment to the poor and/or oppressed that is expressed in the way we live. According to Luis Segundo, this is a biblical preunderstanding of the Bible itself. Theology is the reflection on our experience of committed action in light of the Bible.

For North American feminist theologians, the emphasis on praxis has taken the form of a focus on women's experience as a starting point for theological reflection. Solidarity with women in their oppression, both past and present, leads to the experience of empowerment—the unified will to resist sexism in all its forms.

Orthodoxy* gives way to orthopraxis. Liberation theology reflects a revolution in the way theology has traditionally been conceived. In the Western world, theological debates have largely focused on correct doctrine or orthodoxy: What is true? What does it mean? What are its implications? While some liberation theologians are remarkably orthodox, they deny that orthodoxy is the measure of theological adequacy. Instead, the verification of a theological position depends on its conformity to the actual process of liberation that God is bringing about in the world. In practice this means that theology is measured by orthopraxis—by whether or not it leads to concrete action designed to liberate people from their oppression.

African-American and women theologians question the legitimacy of any orthodoxy that perpetuates a slave mentality. They call for true faith to resist the unjust structures which concentrate power in the hands of white males. A group in the U.S. known as the Evangelical Women's Caucus has explicitly sought to unite a conservative theology with "biblical feminism."

Ideology is inherent in all theology. Liberation theologians employ a "hermeneutic of suspicion" by which they look for the basic ideological commitments implicit in every theology. Karl Marx used the term *ideology* in a negative sense as a tool of bourgeois society to cover the reality of capitalism.* Liberationists use it in a neutral sense as a commitment to a way of understanding the world implicit in all thought.

Most Latin American liberation theologians

utilize Marxism as an ideological system which accurately exposes the reality of class conflict and oppression in their countries. They see Marxism as an irreplaceable tool for a "scientific" understanding of poverty in Latin America. Most North American liberation theologians have downplayed the role of Marxism in their theology, either because it is seen as marginally relevant in the North American context, or because it raises so many complex negative emotions.

Feminist theologians see patriarchy as the dominant ideology of a male-oriented society. They have effectively applied the hermeneutic of suspicion to historical, literary and biblical studies to uncover patriarchal attitudes which demean or ignore women.

Similarly, African-American theologians point out the pervasive existence of racism in a white-dominated society. They call for the ideology of inferiority and subservience to be replaced in the black community by a African-American identity that takes pride in its African roots and present accomplishments.

Liberation Themes. Several themes have come to characterize liberation theology:

1. God is on the side of the poor and the oppressed. The Bible reveals a God of justice who acted to liberate his oppressed people from slavery in Egypt. The God of the Bible hates oppression and acts in history to liberate people from injustice.

2. Jesus, the supreme revelation of God, identified with the poor, denounced economic and sexual oppression, and took on the suffering of the world in order to set it free.

3. Authentic faith includes the practice of liberation. This must include more than words, more than charity. Love must act to overcome the conditions of injustice.

4. The church is called to be a prophet against social injustice. The church must denounce oppression, whatever its form.

5. Conflict is necessary. Violence is inherent in unjust structures. As long as there are oppressors and oppressed there will be conflict. Christians must side with the oppressed. Most liberation theologians do not rule out the possibility that in extreme situations violent revolution may be necessary. However, of North American liberationists, only African-American theologians have conceded the possibility of redemptive violence. Many feminist theologians are pacifists.

6. Reform is not enough. Reform movements are too often co-opted by the ruling class. Revolution (preferably nonviolent) is necessary because the structures of power must be changed.

7. History is an indivisible unity. There is no dichotomy between the history of spiritual salvation and the history of material liberation. While all political movements are limited and flawed, authentic liberation from all kinds of bondage, both personal and social, are part of God's plan for the ultimate triumph of the kingdom of God.

BIBLIOGRAPHY. L. Boff and C. Boff, *Introducing Liberation Theology* (1987); J. M. Bonino, *Doing Theology in a Revolutionary Situation* (1975); J. H. Cone, *A Black Theology of Liberation,* 2nd ed. (1986); B. W. Harrison, *Making the Connections: Essays in Feminist Social Ethics* (1986); L. Scanzoni and N. Hardesty, *All We're Meant to Be* (1974).

B. T. Adeney

Liberty, Christian. Christian freedom from the necessity of good works and religious practices, particularly regarding their necessity for salvation.* The Protestant* Reformers affirmed Christian liberty, often in Pauline terms (Gal 3; Rom 3:21-31), as a corollary to justification* by faith alone. A Christian is set free *from* sin, death and the curse of the Law. But there is also a sense in which saving faith is not *alone,* since it extends beyond itself in concern for others. Thus, a Christian is also set free *for* being a new creature, a different person.

Martin Luther captured well the dialectical character of *The Freedom of a Christian* (1520) when he wrote: "A Christian is perfectly free, lord of all, subject to none. A Christian is a perfectly dutiful servant of all, subject to all." Luther's conception of Christian liberty includes freedom of both deed and conscience, granted through salvation by faith. Yet it is all predicated by the attitude of a "dutiful servant" because genuine faith is active in love.

John Calvin combined the two sides of Christian liberty with his ideal of a Christian commonwealth wherein activities like drunkenness, brawling, dancing, usury and dishonoring the Sabbath were controlled by civil law. Calvin's conception of a committed covenant community ordered for the spiritual improvement of all, continued in American Puritanism.* While salvation was based on God's gracious election,* the quest for purity was guided by community standards that demonstrated their election and safeguarded the credibility of their witness. In the Wesleyan tradition* sanctification* was associated with similar proscriptions which, while they did nothing to save one's soul, enabled the believer to enjoy both the "form and power of godliness." The Wesleys's *General Rules of the United Societies* (1743) urged members of

Methodist* classes to "avoid evil of every kind," including matters like "drunkenness, buying or selling spirituous liquors, or drinking them," and "laying up treasure on earth."

In American revivalism* the Puritan vision of a godly commonwealth was expanded to encompass the nation, and infused with the Wesleyan conception of sanctification, linking stewardship of the human body with a mandate to reform society through the prohibition* of alcohol, tobacco and unholy practices. The temperance movement,* which became a landmark of evangelical idealism, was born in the early 1830s during Charles Finney's* revivals in the "Burned-Over District"* of western New York. Churches that were significantly influenced by the great revivals, such as the Baptists* and various Holiness* churches, incorporated into their standards for church membership* prohibitions against alcohol, profaning the Lord's Day and various indications of worldliness (such as extravagant attire or dancing).

Following the Pauline injunction, " 'Everything is permissible for me'—but not everything is beneficial" (1 Cor 6:12), many contemporary evangelicals* have continued to set limits on their Christian liberty in order to produce a lifestyle that is reflective of the gospel, conducive to sanctification and motivated by concern for the "weaker brother" who may be harmed by an irresponsible use of a Christian's liberty (1 Cor 8).

See also ALCOHOL, DRINKING OF.

BIBLIOGRAPHY. W. R. Cross, *The Burned-Over District* (1950); A. C. Piepkorn, *Profiles in Belief,* 4 vols. (1977-1979). J. R. Tyson

License. Licensing to preach* is an early stage of ministerial ordination* in many Protestant* churches, particularly in the Free Church* tradition.* Evident in many American churches since the nineteenth century, licensing is an early stage of recognition for those who demonstrate ministerial gifts. On the Western frontier many itinerant* preachers were licensed as a way of monitoring their behaviors and giving them a certain credibility as they practiced their skills. After a period of probation, licensed candidates might then be considered for ordination. In many denominations*—such as the Baptists*—licensed persons may, given congregational approval, perform most ministerial functions. B. J. Leonard

Liele, George (c.1750-1820). African-American Baptist* preacher.* Born a slave in Virginia, Liele was taken by his master to Burke County, Georgia, where he was converted* to Christianity in 1772. In 1775 he was ordained* to work as a missionary* among slaves on surrounding plantations. Among those he converted were David George and other slaves of George Calphin, who ran a Native American trading post at Silver Bluff on the South Carolina side of the Savannah River. David George was designated to minister* to Silver Bluff Baptist Church, now regarded as the oldest African-American church in America. Liele, considered the first formally ordained African-American minister in America, was freed by his master to carry out his ministry. The attempted re-enslavement of Liele following his master's death was prevented by a British officer in Savannah, where Liele preached for the three years of the British occupation during the Revolutionary War.* Among the slaves baptized by Liele was Andrew Bryan* who, in 1788, organized the First African Church of Savannah. In 1783 Liele accompanied the British to Jamaica, traveling as an indentured servant to pay his passage. After securing his freedom in 1784, he obtained permission to preach in Jamaica, becoming the first African-American foreign missionary.

BIBLIOGRAPHY. E. A. Holmes, "George Liele: Negro Slavery's Prophet of Deliverance," *Foun* 9 (1966):333-345; C. G. Woodson, *The History of the Negro Church* (1921). M. R. Sawyer

Lifting of Hands. A gesture of worship* generally, though not exclusively, associated with charismatic and Pentecostal Christianity. Finding biblical precedent primarily in the Psalms (63:4; 134:2) and 1 Timothy 2:8, charismatics raise their hands during periods of prayer, singing or corporate praise. The gesture is one of joy and exuberance but also of gratitude, devotion or surrender to God, the object of worship. In traditional churches where lifting of hands is not a common practice, this nonintrusive, yet immediately noticeable, behavior is often the initial cause of conflict between those who appreciate charismatic styles of prayer and praise and those who prefer more reserved forms of worship. In charismatic and Pentecostal churches, on the other hand, lifting of hands is so normal as to have become in effect a Pentecostal ritual, especially since those not raising hands in praise stand out as different and may be perceived as more subdued or less worshipful.

B. Barron

Limbo. In Roman Catholic* theology,* the region or state proximate to heaven (*limbo* is from the Latin word for "edge" or "border") in which reside departed souls who do not enjoy the beatific vision but do not suffer any other privation. Two kinds of

[651]

limbo are distinguished: the *limbus patrum,* or limbo of the Old Testament believers, and the *limbus infantium,* the limbo of unbaptized infants. The origin of the idea can be traced with confidence only as far back as the high Middle Ages: the word is not used either by Scripture* or the church fathers. Some theologians have seen the Old Testament believers as entering heaven with Christ (as in 1 Pet 4:6). As for the latter group, Augustine believed that the souls of unbaptized infants went to hell, thereby implicitly denying the idea of limbo. Most theologians of the high Middle Ages (notably Thomas Aquinas), on the other hand, defended the view which came to predominate, that these souls went to an intermediate state in which they were deprived of supernatural blessing (since baptism was understood to be essential to full salvation) but enjoyed full natural happiness. Only one official Roman Catholic document speaks of limbo, the bull of Pius VI, *Auctorem Fidei* (1794), and even this leaves open the question of limbo's very existence. Since 1900, some theologians have suggested that God's universal salvific will extend to these souls and have therefore denied the existence of limbo altogether.

J. G. Stackhouse

Lincoln, Abraham (1809-1865). Lawyer, statesman, political theologian and sixteenth U.S. president. Born in modest circumstances in a log cabin near Hodgenville, Kentucky, on February 12, 1809, Lincoln spent his early years on the brink of poverty as his restless pioneering family made repeated fresh starts in Kentucky, Indiana and Illinois. During his youth he worked periodically as a surveyor, farmhand, ferryman and storekeeper, and during the Blackhawk War of 1832 served as a captain in the Illinois militia. He was postmaster at New Salem, Illinois, from 1833 to 1836, while he studied law. He moved to Springfield in 1837, where he opened a law office and gained a reputation as a trial attorney. He soon became involved politically, serving in the Illinois legislature as a Whig from 1835 to 1843 and the U.S. House of Representatives from 1847 to 1849 when he chose not to seek re-election. Lincoln wed Mary Todd on November 4, 1842, after a stormy courtship which presaged a difficult marriage.

Lincoln continued his political interests and in 1856 joined the newly formed Republican Party. Two years later he stood for the U.S. Senate but lost out to incumbent Stephen A. Douglas. However, his many speeches and debates during the 1850s made him a national figure, and in 1860 he won the Republican nomination for president on the

third ballot. Judged by its consequences, the election of 1860 was the most momentous in American history. The issues were so important that the losing side felt it could not abide by the results. When Lincoln won a bitter four-sided race, the South withdrew from the Union and civil war ensued.

He thus entered office at a critical juncture in U.S. history, the Civil War* (1861-1865), and died from an assassin's bullet at the war's end before the greater implications of the conflict could be resolved. Even though relatively unknown and inexperienced when elected president, he soon proved to be a consummate politician. Above all, he was firm in his convictions and dedicated to the preservation of the Union.

More has been written about Lincoln, including his religion, than about any other president. Although not particularly religious as a young man, Lincoln became increasingly thoughtful about spiritual matters during his last years. Like many aspects of his life, Lincoln's religious development appears paradoxical. On the one hand, during his youth he appears to have rejected his parents' Baptist* faith and the various other expressions of evangelical* Christianity which permeated the frontier during the heyday of the Second Great Awakening.* On the other hand, he never discarded the teachings of the Bible* as he understood them. The Bible was probably the only book his family owned, and his abundant use of scriptural quotations in his later writings shows how earnestly he must have studied it.

Lincoln's religious reflections were intensified when he lost one of his four sons in 1850 and a second in 1862, and when his highstrung wife suffered a nervous breakdown shortly thereafter. Further, the complex problems and human slaughter of the war years drove him to spend increasing amounts of time in Bible study* and prayer.* It was also during the war that he regularly began to attend the New York Avenue Presbyterian Church and to take counsel from its pastor, Dr. Phineas D. Gurley, and from Methodist* bishop Matthew Simpson,* both of whom were evangelicals.

However, it was not Lincoln's personal faith but rather his public religion which grew from it that profoundly affected the course of American history. According to historian Sidney Mead, Lincoln was "the most profound and representative theologian of the religion of the Republic," and William Wolf and Elton Trueblood cite the president from Illinois as the theologian* of American destiny. Sociologist Robert Bellah claims that Lincoln represented civil religion* at its best and that the

Civil War leader was "the man who not only formulated but in his own person embodied its meaning for America."

Lincoln, as heir of the Puritans,* was convinced that the U.S. was more than an ordinary nation, that it was a proving ground for the idea of democratic government. He was the person most responsible for fusing the dominant evangelical-biblical religion of his day with democratic ideals and for creating a civil-religion version of the old Puritan quest to build a "city upon a hill." Moreover, he came to believe that he was leading a struggle to preserve "the last best hope of earth." He argued that the Union should be preserved because it was a republic based on propositions which championed human freedom and that as long the nation allowed human beings to be held in chains, it mocked the sacred founding document which proclaimed that "all men are created equal." In order to preserve the chosen nation, Lincoln called for removing this inconsistency between belief and practice by freeing the slaves. Therefore, in his speeches to Congress and in the Gettysburg Address (1863), he expounded the public faith, explaining that the war was an effort to preserve both the Union and the American experiment in democracy in order that the nation's God-given mission in the world might continue. This was the theological meaning of the conflict.

In the meantime, the president called for the nation to repent of the sin of slavery and to make certain that they were on God's side in the struggle between good and evil in the world. He also argued that the bonds of religious faith were needed to hold the country together, especially once the war ended and reunification took place. Thus, in clear and eloquent language—especially in his Second Inaugural Address of 1865—Lincoln preached a prophetic civil faith which acknowledged that "the Almighty has His own purposes" and that the nation stood under judgment. Awareness of human limitations, Lincoln thought, should check human pride and encourage a spirit of humility and charity. Little wonder that many scholars have regarded him as "our most religious president," a veritable unbaptized saint in the White House.

Lincoln's assassination on April 15, 1865, made him a redeemer-savior-martyr figure and created a new focus of American civil piety. He thus joined George Washington* as the second great hero of the public faith. Much of this deification of the fallen president was metaphorical, but the legend was based on a considerable body of fact. Political and religious feeling were blended in one majestic figure who might be either admired as a hero or invoked as a god. With the war ended and the question of slavery resolved, the civil religion of Abraham Lincoln—with malice toward none, with charity for all—provided a shared outlook which facilitated national reconciliation. It assured a war-weary people that they had not fought in vain and promised that the new society could be qualitatively better than what had existed before.

BIBLIOGRAPHY. W. E. Barton, *The Soul of Abraham Lincoln* (1920); A. V. House, "The Genesis of the Lincoln Religious Controversy," *Proceedings of the Middle States Association of History and Social Science Teachers* 36 (1939):44-54; E. D. Jones, *Lincoln and the Preachers* (1948); L. Lewis, *Myths After Lincoln* (1929); S. E. Mead, "Abraham Lincoln's Last Best Hope of Earth: The American Dream of Destiny Democracy," *CH* 23 (March 1954):3-16; R. Niebuhr, "The Religion of Abraham Lincoln," *CCen* 82 (February 10, 1965):172-175; M. A. Noll, "The Perplexing Faith of Abraham Lincoln," *CT* 29 (February 15, 1985):12-16; S. B. Oates, *With Malice Toward None: The Life of Abraham Lincoln* (1977); R. V. Pierard and R. D. Linder, *Civil Religion and the Presidency* (1988);J. G. Randall and R. N. Current, *Lincoln the President,* 4 vols. (1945-1955); C. Sandburg, *Abraham Lincoln,* 6 vols. (1926-1939); B. P. Thomas, *Abraham Lincoln* (1952); D. E. Trueblood, *Abraham Lincoln: Theologian of Anguish* (1973); W. J. Wolf, *Lincoln's Religion* (1970).   R. D. Linder

Lind, Jenny (Goldschmidt) (1820-1887).

Swedish soprano and philanthropist* who toured America from 1850 to 1852. Born out of wedlock in Stockholm, Sweden, Johanna Maria Lind had an abiding faith in God instilled in her by her Lutheran grandmother. At age nine, her voice won her a place in the Theatre School for Girls of the Stockholm Royal Theater. Within ten years she was Sweden's premier opera and concert coloratura.

Lind's Christian faith was nondenominational, though she preferred Swedish Lutheran churches and small chapels where the "pure gospel" was preached. In 1849 her religious convictions forced her to give up dramatic opera; she continued as a concert singer. In 1850, when her career was at its height, P. T. Barnum offered Lind a 150-concert tour throughout the eastern U.S. She accepted, hoping to raise funds for her charitable enterprises before retiring from the stage.

Barnum's shrewd and energetic advertising made New Yorkers breathless for Lind's arrival. Over 30,000 admirers met Lind's ship, and the first concert ticket sold at auction for $225. Each concert included "I Know That My Redeemer Liveth," which was the message in song Lind liked most to give. Lyman Abbot* wrote, after hearing Lind sing the piece, "It is impossible to doubt the Resurrection while she sings it. She seemed a celestial witness. . . ."

Lind demonstrated her Christian charity through actions as well as song. Believing her art was God's instrument by which she could reach out to others, Lind used the proceeds of her performances primarily to benefit private individuals, institutions, struggling churches and causes. Lind's visit was the catalyst for the American people to discover in themselves a taste for good music. Toward the end of her tour, Lind married her piano accompanist, Otto Goldschmidt. They settled in England, where Jenny lived a quiet life as a wife and mother of three.

BIBLIOGRAPHY. P. T. Barnum, G. Bryan, eds., *Struggles and Triumphs; The Life of P. T. Barnum, Written by Himself,* 2 vols. (1927); G. D. Shultz, *Jenny Lind: The Swedish Nightingale* (1962); I. Wallace, *The Fabulous Showman; The Life and Times of P. T. Barnum* (1959).

L. M. Davis

Lindsay, Gordon (1906-1973) and Freda Schimpf Lindsay (1916-). Charismatic* mission* strategists and leaders of the healing* movement. After a youth spent in the communitarian experiments of John Alexander Dowie's* Zion City, Illinois, and Finis E. Yoakum's (1851-1920) Pisgah Grande, California, Lindsay was converted* by Charles Parham* in Portland, Oregon. Lindsay worked with John G. Lake's evangelistic campaigns and, during 1948, with William Branham.* Returning to Portland, Oregon, in 1946 he married Freda Schimpf, a Foursquare Gospel Church* member and graduate of Aimee Semple McPherson's* L.I.F.E. Bible College. After a pastorate in Ashland, Oregon, Lindsay began publishing from Dallas, Texas, the influential magazine *Voice of Healing* (1948-1967) as an effort to coordinate the work of the healing evangelists. He also operated an organization by the same name (with both the magazine and organization renamed Christ for the Nations in 1967).

By the mid-1950s Lindsay had turned his attention to missions, and in 1961 he founded the Native Church Crusade, which has supplied Third World church-building programs. As theologian* and historian of the healing movement, Lindsay wrote over 250 books. Through his Native Literature Work, millions of pieces of literature have been distributed throughout the world. In 1970 he

opened Christ for the Nations Institute (CFNI) as a center of theological and spiritual formation for the charismatic and Pentecostal* movements. After Gordon's death in 1973, Freda Lindsay was elected president of CFNI, and under her leadership the Institute has experienced growth.

BIBLIOGRAPHY. G. Lindsay, *The House the Lord Built* (n.d.); G. Lindsay, *The Gordon Lindsay Story* (n.d.); F. Lindsay, *My Diary's Secrets* (1976); F. Lindsay, *Freda* (1987); D. E. Harrell, *All Things Are Possible. The Healing and Charismatic Movements in Modern America* (1975).

D. D. Bundy

Lipscomb, David (1831-1917). Church of Christ* preacher* and editor. Born in Tennessee, Lipscomb received his education at Franklin College (1846-1849) in Nashville under the direction of Tolbert Fanning.* For years he made his living farming near Nashville, but he began preaching in the mid 1850s. At the conclusion of the Civil War,* Lipscomb determined to reactivate the *Gospel Advocate,* with the help of its former editor, Fanning. The paper appeared in its new form on January 1, 1866, sympathetic to the South and reflecting the more conservative viewpoint of the Southern Churches of Christ. Consequently, the paper took a firm position against the use of organized missionary* societies, as well as the use of musical instruments in worship* services. The *Gospel Advocate* became the leading paper among the Southern churches of the Restoration Movement,* a position it still maintains today.

In 1891 Lipscomb founded Nashville Bible School to continue the work of Fanning's earlier Franklin College and provide an education for young men who wanted to enter the ministry. After his death, this school became David Lipscomb College. In 1906 Lipscomb corresponded with the director of the U.S. Census Bureau, leading to a separate listing of the noninstrumental Churches of Christ in recognition of their distinction from the instrumental Christian Churches, the Disciples of Christ,* a distinction that continues to the present. Lipscomb and the *Gospel Advocate* were major factors in both creating and maintaining the separation.

BIBLIOGRAPHY. *DARB;* R. E. Hooper, *Crying in the Wilderness: A Biography of David Lipscomb* (1979); E. I. West, *The Life and Times of David Lipscomb* (1954). J. B. North

Litany. A form of liturgical* prayer. Derived from the Greek *litaneia* (to petition on someone's behalf), a litany is a form of alternating prayer in which a leader voices petitions and the people affirm these with a short, repeated refrain (e.g., *Leader:* "We pray for the peace of the world." *People:* "Lord, hear our prayer."). Its primary purpose is to enable the people to participate actively together in expressing corporate prayers.

The pattern of the Christian litany seems to come from the worship* of ancient Israel (cf. Ps 136). By the fourth century, litanies were used in Christian churches, beginning in the East and spreading rapidly to the West. Protestant litanies have been in continuous use since the time of Luther. But it is still in Eastern Orthodoxy* that litanies have the most comprehensive role.

A litany may express prayers of confession, intercession, praise or thanksgiving. It can be said or sung. Sometimes the congregation repeats the same phrase throughout. In other cases a particular refrain is repeated several times and then a new one is used as the content of the petitions changes. Major American denominations* have used litanies for the corporate confession of sin, the general intercessory prayer of the church, the liturgical review of the Ten Commandments or the Beatitudes, the prayers for Christian unity, world peace, or the nation and for ordination,* baptism,* marriage* and funeral* services.

BIBLIOGRAPHY. C. Jones et al., *The Study of Liturgy* (1978); J. A. Jungmann, *The Mass of the Roman Rite* (1955); C. Kucharek, *The Byzantine-Slav Liturgy of St. John Chrysostom* (1971).

P. W. Butin

Literature, Christianity and. The interaction between Christianity and American literature has been both subtle and complex. Even in the early years of the new republic, when many of the settlers held firm commitments to Christianity, St. Jean de Crèvecoeur, an astute observer of the experiment in democracy,* predicted that religious indifference would predominate. He wrote, ". . . all sects are mixed as well as all nations; thus religious indifference is imperceptibly disseminated from one end of the continent to the other; . . . where this will reach no one can tell, perhaps it may leave a vacuum fit to receive other systems." The history of the interaction of Christianity and literature in America is, therefore, both a fulfillment of de Crèvecoeur's prophecy and a refutation of it. As the influence of religious dogma declined and Puritanism* waned while industrialism surged, the literature reflected the loss of faith in creeds,* but the best creative minds continued throughout the nineteenth and twentieth centuries to wrestle with religious issues.

Many of the early settlers, especially in New England where Puritanism dominated, viewed literature and all of the arts with suspicion unless they were employed didactically for the faith. In spite of the appreciation that great European reformers like Calvin had for artistic endeavor, among many adherents to the stricter sects, the arts were viewed with skepticism because the Roman Catholic Church* had supported strong appeals to the senses. Another ambiguity grew out of the frank commercialism and special pleading that marked early American writing, for explorers, settlers and adventurers found it advantageous to encourage additional settlers and to console the remnant in the New World by appealing to Providence. Thus, from its beginnings, American literature experienced an uneasy alliance with Christianity.

The Seventeenth Century. Among early seventeenth-century New England writers, two prose writers and two poets deserve special notice. The prose of William Bradford* and Roger Williams* receive high marks. Bradford began *Of Plymouth Plantation* in 1630, but three-fourths of the book was written between 1645 and 1650. Since Bradford had been involved in the events surrounding the founding of Plymouth since 1605, his account is intriguing, but it also reflects the concerns of a leader who regrets evidences of disintegration which were besetting the colony. Roger Williams, having fled the Massachusetts Bay settlement whose leaders found him divisive, took refuge with the Narragansett Indians, and secured a sanctuary for all who found Massachusetts Bay intolerable. Williams's commitment to religious liberty* included toleration of Quakers,* Baptists,* Jews and Native Americans. These principles were expressed in his *A Key into the Language of America* (1643) and especially *The Bloody Tenet* (1644), in which he attacked the "soul killing" requirement of religious conformity.

Although *belles-lettres* did not rank particularly high among the Puritans and Separatists,* the early colonists produced two poets of note, Anne Bradstreet* and Michael Wigglesworth.* Having received an education in England much superior to that of most young women contemporary with her, Bradstreet immigrated to New England with her husband and continued her habit of writing poetry. Although she may have preferred her long devotional poems, contemporary readers find her lyrics celebrating life and death, personal loss and fear of the unknown more compelling. *The Tenth Muse* (1650), the first published volume of poetry written by a settler in the English colonies, ap-

[655]

peared in London without her permission.

The Day of Doom (1662) by Michael Wigglesworth, was the New World's first best seller. It sold 1,800 copies in the first year and was frequently committed to memory, all 224 eight-line stanzas. Although readers in all periods may have been most interested in the poem's vivid picture of hell* and damnation, the poem also traces an ordered world and the hope of life eternal for the regenerate.

Among the next generation of authors, Edward Taylor* stands out. Practically unknown until the 1930s when his poetry was discovered in the Yale University* Library, Taylor now receives acclaim as the first major American voice in poetry. Educated in part at Harvard,* he spent his life pastoring in western Massachusetts. His poems capture many Puritan themes, but his poetic voice is both genuinely New World and Old World. Echoes of the English metaphysical verse of Donne and Herbert are evident in Taylor's love of puns, paradoxes and extravagant comparisons. His finest efforts are found in *Preparatory Meditations,* poems evidently related to his preparation of sermons for monthly communion* services.

The Eighteenth Century. In the eighteenth century, two major prose writers reflect the growing tensions between Christianity and life in the developing colonies: the Puritan Jonathan Edwards* and the Quaker John Woolman.* Edwards's efforts were monumental and worthy of perhaps the finest intellect the New World has produced. Committed to orthodox* Christianity but learned in the philosophy of Locke and the development of philosophy after Locke, Edwards sought to revive the fervor of the early Puritans in the descendants he pastored. Although he is best known for the startling imagery and inexorable logic of the sermon "Sinners in the Hands of an Angry God," the popularity of this one piece does not do justice to either Edwards's intellect or his goal. His *Personal Narrative* ("An account of his conversion, experiences, and religious exercises, given by himself") better represents Edwards's attempt to renew American Christianity by calling his parishioners to an experiential knowledge of Christian doctrine justified by an underpinning of Lockean philosophy and psychology.

John Woolman, a Quaker reared in New Jersey, reflects another dissenting tradition in colonial America. *The Journal of John Woolman* recounts the spiritual pilgrimage of a man dedicated to living out his Christian principles consistently. In this journal (which has never been out of print since it first appeared in 1774), Woolman traces the personal conflict between the Quaker call for simplicity and the effect of trade and materialism on the spiritual life. He deliberately chose to limit his mercantile interests and activities in order to concentrate on developing his inner resources. And, when he came to recognize that slavery contradicted the essence of the gospel, he refused even to produce a bill of sale which would, in effect, make him an accomplice to slavery. A man of integrity, compassion and honesty, he expressed himself in a simple, elegant prose style which still captures the hearts and minds of his readers.

Although the founding fathers of the U.S. continue to be praised for their religious faith, evidence of their commitment to deism* rather than to orthodoxy is overwhelming, if they express any deep religious commitment at all. Both Thomas Jefferson* and Benjamin Franklin were excellent stylists, and both are read and studied, but primarily for their influence on the character of the new nation, not for their exploration of Christian themes. Both men, however, defended vigorously the individual's right to worship*—or not to worship. But de Crèvecoeur would have found in Franklin and Jefferson evidence for his prediction that American society would become increasingly secular.

The Nineteenth Century. The finest literary artists of the first half of the nineteenth century document both the accuracy of de Crèvecouer's prophecy and its weakness. William Cullen Bryant,* Ralph Waldo Emerson,* Nathaniel Hawthorne,* Henry David Thoreau* and Herman Melville (1819-1891) represent the flowering of literature in America. Although not one affirmed orthodox Christianity, all five possessed the religious imagination. And their minds, as revealed in their literature, were teased by religious questions.

William Cullen Bryant's poetry, infused with moral earnestness and vague religious language, earned him considerable acclaim in his own day. Two of his poems, "To a Waterfowl" and "Thanatopsis," are still read. Both reflect Bryant's faith in a distant providence that makes all things right, though the journey is solitary and death inevitable.

Emerson, Hawthorne and Thoreau, all products of New England culture, engaged in religious and philosophical quests which gave direction to American intellectual inquiry throughout the nineteenth century. Within several years of his ordination to the ministry, Emerson announced his inability to participate in the Lord's Supper.* German higher criticism, the influence of Coleridge and Carlyle, and the sway of Unitarianism* had culminated in a radical new perspective. In subsequent years Emerson lectured and preached and published essays which became the new scriptures for the Transcendentalists.* Although loosely organized and unable to agree on many tenets, members of The Transcendental Club, mostly intellectuals who lived in or near Concord, Massachusetts, found in Emerson's *Nature* (1836) and his other essays a pattern for coping with the intricacies of nineteenth-century living.

Emerson's neighbors, Thoreau and Hawthorne, participated in the intellectual renaissance sparked by Emerson's ideas. Thoreau's account of his life in a cabin on property owned by Emerson near Walden Pond earned for Thoreau a key position in American letters. Concerned about growing materialism and the concomitant failure of Americans to nurture spirituality,* Thoreau set out to awaken the American conscience. His tool was *Walden* (1854). Retaining Puritan zeal and concern for the health of the soul, Thoreau attempted to renew the American mind and spirit in a highly critical age. For Thoreau, like Emerson and their counterparts in England—Wordsworth and Carlyle, the central questions of how to live were not being addressed adequately either by a moribund orthodoxy or a decadent materialism.

No other American writer carried the burden of his Puritan heritage the way Nathaniel Hawthorne did. A descendant of one of the judges in the Salem witch trials,* Hawthorne was obsessed with the weight of guilt and the difficulty of attaining redemption in the ambiguous realities of human existence. Extraordinarily conscious of the corrosive influence of hidden sin and the devious character of the human heart, Hawthorne dissects relationships and individuals, revealing the horror beneath the skin. In addition to his two great novels, *The Scarlet Letter* (1850) and *The House of Seven Gables* (1851), Hawthorne's best short stories ("The Minister's Black Veil" and "Rappaccini's Daughter") trace these themes in eloquent detail and startling candor.

Herman Melville, friend and admirer of Hawthorne, sums up the tensions of the nineteenth-century intellectual. Sensitive to the claims of Christianity and frustrated by the failure of Christians to live their faith, Melville's greatest novels, *Mardi* (1849) and *Moby Dick* (1851), weave metaphysical speculation, ironic contemplation and verbal ingenuity into engrossing tapestries. *Mardi* continues to baffle and intrigue Melville fans; *Moby Dick* is the cornerstone of Melville's reputation. In this novel of whaling and seamanship, Melville poses the significant dilemmas about

the nature of the universe, any controlling powers in the universe and man's inability to define finally his own role in the universe.

Among nineteenth-century poets, Walt Whitman (1819-1892) and Emily Dickinson* take first place. Although both poets support de Crèvecoeur's prediction that Americans would grow more diffident to organized religion, Whitman and Dickinson struggle with spiritual issues. Whitman's social concerns, his dedication to artistic integrity and his commitment to illuminating the American experience are evident in his extensive revisions of the poems in *Leaves of Grass* (first published in 1855). And supporting these questions is Whitman's refusal to deny the primacy of the spiritual.

In contrast to Whitman, Emily Dickinson, the Belle of Amherst, lived a reclusive life. Although in her last years she seldom, if ever, left her house or yard, like Thoreau she traveled much in her mind and art. She too strove to discover whether life was worth living. During her lifetime only seven of her poems appeared in print and not until the 1955 edition of her poems were readers aware of her achievements. As did Melville, Dickinson probes the essential questions of human existence: fate, human responsibility, consciousness and the vagaries of divine intervention.

The Twentieth Century. Twentieth-century American literature, a rich lode of artistic endeavor, again reflects the complex interaction of Christianity and American thought. To be sure, the quest for new and more satisfactory expressions of Christianity carries over from the previous century. But a more scathing and ironic picture of Christianity appears in the work of Mark Twain (1835-1910). Other artists, such as Wallace Stevens (1879-1955), accept the dissolution of old intellectual structures, including Christianity, and strike out in search of new myths and ordering devices. Finally, in the aftermath of two world wars, artists like T. S. Eliot (1888-1965) and Flannery O'Connor* affirm and proclaim a renewed faith in Christian certainties.

Best known as a humorist and chronicler of life on the Mississippi River, as in *The Adventures of Huckleberry Finn* (1883), Twain explores the dark side of Christianity as well. Many of his characters, Miss Watson, for example, exhibit a venial pride in their own superiority and righteousness. Twain's exceptional ability to hone language to a deadly point allows him to unmask the fraud unmercifully—whether the person be religious or nonreligious. In Twain's later years, his stories and essays take on an even more ironic and dark character as he struggles in his own life to deal with the death of loved ones and financial reverses. His story "The

Man Who Corrupted Hadleyburg," concludes ironically, and perhaps bitterly, the town's citizens having passed through severe trials to little effect. Twain stands as the fountainhead of a twentieth-century tradition in American literature marked by skepticism and even cynicism. In poems like "Richard Cory" and "Miniver Cheevy," Edward Arlington Robinson (1869-1935) traces the lives of individuals who live and die ingloriously in a cold, brutal and tainted world.

On the other hand, some tough-minded artists of the twentieth century forged new and alternate strategies for coping with the loss of faith. Among these, the poet and business executive Wallace Stevens (1879-1955) stands pre-eminent. Recognizing that traditional Christianity possessed little intellectual or emotional power over the lives of twentieth-century people, Stevens dared to suggest that the poet may be responsible for creating new myths which would speak to the modern mind. In poems like "Sunday Morning," he develops a vivid contrast between the old faith of a "silent Palestine,/ Dominion of the blood and sepulchre" and the vibrant celebration of life by the woman in a peignor enjoying "coffee and oranges in a sunny chair." In his struggle to find an order both beyond and within the lived realities of the twentieth century, Stevens practiced his craft and earned his position as a first-rank poet. In his art and his life, he lived out the stresses of modern life.

A third and powerful tradition in the twentieth century is the affirming faith forged by T. S. Eliot (1888-1965) and Flannery O'Connor. Reared a Unitarian and educated at Harvard, T. S. Eliot sailed eastward and found his refuge in England and a visible expression of Christianity in the Anglican* tradition. His poem "The Wasteland" (1922) focused on the decline of Western civilization and the impoverishment of the modern spirit. The post-World War 1 generation found in "The Wasteland" the definitive statement about Western man's predicament. In two other poems, "The Journey of the Magi" and "Ash Wednesday," Eliot portrays the difficult path which man's search for faith must take in this iron age. When Eliot turned to Christianity in "The Four Quartets" (1943), many of his critics and admirers found little to praise in this vision of a renewed orthodoxy. Still Eliot's newfound faith intrigued and inspired a whole generation of artists and readers who began to rethink the claims of orthodoxy.

The Georgian fiction writer, Flannery O'Connor, grappled to express the Christian vision in forms acceptable to the modern mind. An acute observer of human beings and a devout Catholic believer as well, O'Connor was never overcome by rampant hypocrisy nor was she prey to easy religion. In her stories and novels she confronts the invidious darkness of the human heart and the decay of modern civilization by underscoring verbally the evil in all of its grotesque horror. Nevertheless, in "A Good Man Is Hard to Find" and "Good Country People," she uncovers an unshakeable faith in the grace that enlivens and the Light that drives out shadows.

The twentieth-century American literary scene neither completely fulfills nor denies de Crèvecouer's prophecy of religious diffidence in America. Growing secularism* and coarse materialism call all values into question. But even in the darkest visions, such as Twain's and Robinson's, there is a yearning for a lost cause. Artists like Wallace Stevens struggle to find or to create new certainties in an unstable but brilliantly beautiful world. Finally, Eliot and O'Connor, all too aware of the course of Western civilization, rediscover in the Christian world view viable alternatives to despair and disillusionment.

BIBLIOGRAPHY. H. S. Commager, *The American Mind: An Interpretation of American Thought and Character since the 1880's* (1950); J. D. Hart, *The Oxford Companion to American Literature,* 5th ed. (1983); M. J. Herzberg, *The Reader's Encyclopedia of American Literature* (1962); L. Howard, *Literature and the American Tradition* (1960); F. O. Matthiesson, *American Renaissance* (1968); M. McGiffert, *Puritanism and the American Experience* (1969); P. Miller, *The New England Mind: The Seventeenth Century* (1939); P. Miller, *The New England Mind: From Colony to Province* (1952); E. S. Morgan, *Visible Saints: The History of a Puritan Idea* (1963); V. L. Parrington, *Main Currents in American Thought: An Interpretation of American Literature from the Beginnings to 1920,* 3 vols. (1987); M. C. Tyler, *A History of American Literature,* 2 vols. (1878).

J. E. Barcus

Liturgical Art. Liturgical art is that art which serves the worship,* or devotional,* life of the Christian community. It forms a separate category within religious art in general, which is simply art with some religious theme or subject matter regardless of its use.

Liturgical art may take any one of a number of forms. It may be an element within the fabric of the church building itself (*See* Architecture, Church), such as stained glass or woodcarving. It may be devotional icons,* paintings or statuary. But more strictly, the arts that are liturgical are those that have actual use in services of corporate worship. These would include decorative bookbinding for Bibles,* gospel books and lectionaries, metalwork for candlestands and processional crosses, textile art for vestments, banners and paraments, and the actual liturgical furnishings themselves: the altar,* pulpit, lectern, baptismal font* or organ case.

In the earliest period of American colonization, liturgical art reflected the varied artistic and liturgical traditions of the new settlers. Spanish missionaries* in the Southwest and Spanish colonists in Florida had carried with them the painted devotional statuary and elaborate metalwork, textiles and woodcarving which had been popular in seventeenth-century Spain. In certain areas of New Mexico, indigenous styles of art were also influential in the furnishing and decoration of mission churches.

Because of the fear of idolatry, Puritan* colonists in New England eschewed visual representations of religious subjects in their meetinghouses and churches, and even the image of the cross was suspect because of medieval devotional abuses related to it. But the simplicity and elegance of the liturgical furnishings themselves, and especially the ornamentation of the pulpit, can be properly understood as a form of Puritan liturgical art. This emphasis on dignified simplicity continued through the eighteenth century, not only among Puritans, but also among Lutheran,* Quaker,* Methodist* and Presbyterian* inhabitants of America.

Beginning in the nineteenth century, several forces conspired to change the direction of liturgical art in the U.S. Massive waves of Roman Catholic,* Lutheran and Orthodox* immigration introduced into the American liturgical art scene fresh infusions of the European artistic vocabulary. For Roman Catholics, this meant increased realism and sentimentality in the choice and depiction of religious subjects. In addition, just as liturgy had become increasingly privatized, liturgical art had come to be increasingly devotional in character and directed mainly toward engendering pious emotions. Medieval romanticism* and the revival of the Gothic style affected not only the design of nineteenth-century church buildings, but also of vestments, liturgical furnishings and statuary. At about the same time, the introduction of mass-production techniques allowed for the wide distribution of manufactured images and liturgical furniture, the quality of which was often quite poor. By the end of the nineteenth century, the Gothic Revival had given a medieval look to the liturgical art of nearly every mainstream denomination* in the U.S.

The twentieth century, however, saw the coalition between the liturgical movement,* with its emphasis on the centrality of corporate worship rather than private devotions, and proponents of well-designed and crafted art for liturgical use. Many of the pioneers of American liturgical renewal, in both Roman Catholicism and Protestantism alike, were also strong advocates of contemporary style as the fittest artistic and architectural expression of a reformed liturgy. The quarterly magazine *Liturgical Arts,* published from 1931 to 1972, had wide influence among those planning and designing houses of worship, and by mid-century many had begun to see liturgical art as an integral and necessary part of the environment for worship and not simply as a diverting accessory. Where once it had been condemned as "blasphemous" or "atheistic," modern art began to be widely employed in the service of Christian worship.

The practical needs of a rapidly expanding American suburbia has also had an effect on the direction of liturgical art in the late-twentieth century. The production and distribution of catalog furnishings, textiles and devotional items has led to a substantial reduction in the quality and diversity of art forms for the church, and those artists who wish to undertake liturgical commissions have not been particularly successful in convincing churches that works of art are a necessity to the healthy worship life of a community.

In recent years a renewed theological emphasis on the function of symbols and images in religious life has led many denominations back to a serious consideration of liturgical art. Now that the fear of idolatry has abated, many Reformed* traditions, previously shy of the extensive use of liturgical art, have rediscovered that the visual environment can be an essential support for the message of the gospel proclaimed in Christian worship.

BIBLIOGRAPHY. J. Dillenberger, *The Hand and the Spirit: Religious Art in America, 1700-1900* (1972); *Liturgical Arts* (1931-1972); T. G. Simons, *The Ministry of Liturgical Environment* (1984).

S. J. White

Liturgical Books. Service books used in the public worship* of several American liturgical traditions. Liturgical books function with varying degrees of authority.* For Roman Catholics,* use of approved books is mandatory in most forms of public worship; for Lutherans* and Episcopalians,* the forms of public worship are in prescribed books which are normally used; and for United Methodists* and Presbyterians,* liturgical books provide forms for public worship but use, while common for the sacraments,* is not enforced on congregations. Thus, although these books contain many of the same types of services, the degree of use may vary considerably.

The Roman Catholic liturgical books were all revised after the Council of Trent (1545-1563) except for dioceses* and orders that could prove two hundred years of continuous use. The Roman books include: breviary (daily prayer, 1568); missal (mass,* 1570); martyrology (deeds of saints, 1584); pontifical (bishop's rites, 1596); *caeremoniale episcoporum* (bishop's rules, 1600); and ritual (pastoral offices, 1614). For four hundred years changes were minimal and translations often forbidden. After the Second Vatican Council* massive changes occurred in all the Roman liturgical books. These changes included a new missal (1970), individual portions of the ritual and pontifical in the 1970s, the liturgy of the hours* (breviary) in the early 1970s and *caeremoniale* and book of blessings in the 1980s. The recent process of revision and translation is nearly complete as of 1988.

Similar drastic revisions have occurred in many Protestant* churches. Among Lutherans, the process has been complicated by the variety of Lutheran denominations in North America, largely concentrated now in the Evangelical Lutheran Church in America,* whose service book is the *Lutheran Book of Worship* of 1978, supplemented by *Occasional Services* (1982). It was preceded on an experimental basis by the ten-volume Contemporary Worship series. The Lutheran Church—Missouri Synod* produced its own liturgical book, *Lutheran Worship,* in 1982. In common with previous Lutheran books, these volumes combine liturgical texts, service music* and hymnal.* Previous landmarks were Missouri Synod's *The Lutheran Hymnal* (1941) and, for a variety of other Lutheran bodies, *Service Book and Hymnal* (1958), which in turn replaced for many the *Common Service Book* (1918). An earlier landmark was the "Common Service" (1888), and there were various nineteenth-century service books in German and other North-European languages.

The service books of the Episcopal Church have been the *Book of Common Prayer** (BCP) and various hymnals. The first American prayer book, approved in 1789, was a revision of the English BCP of 1662 and also contained a metrical psalter and some hymns. After nearly a century in use, the prayer book was next revised in 1892, but hymnals had meanwhile emerged as separate entities, especially in 1871, 1874 and 1892. A standard music edition, *The New Hymnal,* appeared in

1918, followed a decade later by the 1928 BCP. The rapid liturgical changes after Vatican II produced a series of trial-use service books, The Prayer Book Studies series (1950-1976), leading to the present BCP, given final approval in 1979. The very popular *The Hymnal, 1940* has recently been replaced by *The Hymnal, 1982.* The *Book of Occasional Services* (1979) provides services for special occasions.

Methodist services were part of the Methodist *Discipline* until 1968 and could be revised every four years. In 1945 the first *Book of Worship* appeared and was replaced by the second in 1965. Hymnals have been used ever since John Wesley* published the first American hymnal in 1737. In this century *The Methodist Hymnal* was revised in 1905, 1935 and 1966. A new edition, *The United Methodist Hymnal,* was expected in 1989. The rapid changes after Vatican II, influencing even Protestant liturgies, are reflected in a seventeen-volume series, the Supplemental Worship Resources (1972-1988). Much of this material will find a place in the new hymnal and is already found in the *Book of Services* (1985). *An Ordinal* was approved in 1980.

The various Presbyterian bodies have operated under the general supervisions of a series of the *Directory for Public Worship,* the most recent of which was expected to be approved in 1989. A series of hymnals have been provided by various Presbyterian denominations, the most recent being the *Worshipbook* (1972), *The Hymnbook* (1955) and *The Hymnal* (1933). In 1906 northern Presbyterians approved a *Book of Common Worship* for "voluntary use." This was revised in 1932 and 1946 and still remains in use in some churches. The service portion of the *Worshipbook* (1970) marks the beginning of recent revision. This has accelerated in the 1980s in the Supplemental Liturgical Resources series, of which five volumes were in print as of 1988. Others will appear in time, with the possibility of a new service book sometime in the early 1990s.

Other recent service books include the United Church of Christ* *Book of Worship* (1986), *Rejoice in the Lord* (1985) of the Reformed Church in America,* and *Psalter Hymnal* of the Christian Reformed Church* (c.1988).

BIBLIOGRAPHY. J. F. White, "Sources for the Study of Protestant Worship in America," *Worship* LXI (1987):516-533.   J. F. White

Liturgical Commissions. Organizations within many American denominations,* regional bodies or local churches that work for the promotion of good liturgical practice. Many of the national liturgical commissions produce publications and conduct workshops and seminars to stimulate developments in thought and practice. Among Roman Catholics,* the Bishops' Committee on the Liturgy is the national organization, responsible to the National Conference of Catholic Bishops.* Diocesan* liturgical commissions relate to the Federation of Diocesan Liturgical Commissions. Individual parish churches may have similar groups to guide local worship.* The Episcopal Church* has a Standing Liturgical Commission and diocesan commissions are represented in the Association of Diocesan Liturgy and Music Commissions. Some parishes* have liturgy committees. Lutheran* liturgical revision was done in the 1970s by the Inter-Lutheran Commission on Worship, now defunct. United Methodist* work is headed on the national level by the Section on Worship of the Board of Discipleship, while worship commissions may function on the annual conference and local church levels. There is a Fellowship of United Methodists in Worship, Music and Other Arts. Presbyterians have a national staff in the Theology and Worship Ministry Unit, and the Presbyterian Association of Musicians is a volunteer organization. Several ecumenical groups also exist: The Commission on Worship of the Consultation on Church Union,* the Consultation on Common Texts and the English Language Liturgical Consultation, all producing various publications.

J. F. White

Liturgical Movement. A movement to reform the Roman liturgy* and thereby renew the attitude of the faithful toward worship and its relationship to the Christian life. The modern liturgical movement had its origin in the French Benedictine* monk, Prosper Guéranger (1805-1875), who sought to purify Catholic* religiosity of its popular or culturally derived liturgical and devotional elements by following the Romantic* impulse and Catholic ultramontanism* in a return to the Middle Ages and the Roman liturgy.* By the late nineteenth century this movement was extended by Guéranger's fellow Benedictine Dom Lambert Beauduin (1873-1960) from monastic and academic circles to a popular movement designed to involve the laity* in an intelligent participation in the sacramental mysteries of the Church—the "democratization" of the liturgy, as Beauduin referred to it. In the early twentieth century Pope Pius X* pointed the way toward liturgical renewal in urging more frequent reception of the Eucharist* and the restoration of Gregorian chant for the universal church.

In North America one can find only occasional early proposals reflecting what would later be identified with the liturgical movement. John Carroll,* first Catholic bishop* of the U.S., hoped for a liturgy in the vernacular rather than the Latin language, and he allowed the publication of liturgical books with English translations in parallel columns next to the Latin. Bishop John England* of Charleston, South Carolina, published an English translation of the Roman Missal in 1822, but questions were raised about the appropriateness of this development, and in 1851 the Roman Congregation of Rites* ruled that the ordinary of the Mass* ought not to be translated into the vernacular, although this position was relaxed after 1877.

The Rev. Alfred Young, C.S.P. (1831-1900) began in the 1870s to urge and arrange congregational participation in the music* at St. Paul's parish in Manhattan. And the American Catholic hierarchy, at the Second and Third Plenary Councils of Baltimore* in 1866 and 1884 respectively, urged that Gregorian chant be taught in Catholic schools. The latter Council also ordered the publication of a *Manual of Prayers for the Use of the Catholic Laity* (1889), which drew almost all of its material from the Roman Missal, the Roman Breviary and the Roman Ritual. The purpose of this publication was to balance the widespread, Romantic-inspired devotionalism, including a deep civic and domestic piety,* of the mid-nineteenth century. The project failed in this objective (*See* Piety, Popular Catholic), and thus there remained need for liturgical reform.

Dom Virgil Michel,* a Benedictine monk of St. John's Abbey, Collegeville, Minnesota, who learned of the liturgical movement while living in Benedictine monasteries in Europe, became the center of the movement in North America. After returning to the U.S. in 1926, he began the journal *Orate Fratres,* which continues to be published as *Worship* magazine, and the Liturgical Press to disseminate liturgical reform. Inspired by the influence of modern biblical and patristic study, Michel began with the conception of the Church as the mystical Body of Christ,* which in sacramental ritual expresses the sacrificial worship of Christ and the Church on earth.

This mystical dimension of the reform stood in contrast to a more juridical view of the Church as the community of the faithful under the authority of the hierarchy, and even the older religious view of a worshiping risen Christ in union with the heavenly communion of saints and the Church on earth. For the reformers the ritual of the earthly

Church was thus the visible expression of Christ's worship, and the mission of the Church, including for Michel the social apostolate, was the visible expression of Christ's love for the world. Following from this perspective the ideal was to involve the laity as much as possible in the liturgy by the introduction of the dialog Mass, in which the laity would respond to the prayers of the priest, engage in community singing and use the Missal in vernacular translation to follow the ritual.

The first National Liturgical Day was held on July 25, 1929, and the first liturgical week in 1940, two years after Michel's premature death. Other figures, such as Msgr. Martin Hellriegel of St. Louis; Rev. Gerald Ellard, S.J., of St. Mary's, Kansas; Msgr. William Busch of St. Paul, Minnesota; Rev. Godfrey Diekmann of Collegeville, Minnesota; Rev. William J. Leonard, S.J., of Boston; and Sister Jane Marie Murray, O.P., of Grand Rapids, Michigan, who worked with Michel in producing a series of textbooks for Catholic schools (the Christ-Life series), based on the liturgical movement, played leadership roles in spreading the reform.

There were frequent disputes surrounding the liturgical reform movement, especially in its tendency to downplay the popular devotions, and thus Pius XII* found it necessary to issue an encyclical,* Mediator Dei, on the matter in 1947. There he encouraged active participation in the liturgical movement, while also blessing the non-liturgical devotions. A year later he proceeded to create a Liturgical Commission which, throughout the decade of the 1950s, worked to revise the Easter Vigil and Holy Week services, and to initiate other reforms. During this period progressive Catholics used the English Missal at Mass, responded to the priest in Latin and sang the Mass, frequently in chant.

The Second Vatican Council, in its Constitution on the Sacred Liturgy, incorporated in its recommendations many of the earlier proposals of the liturgical movement. It encouraged full participation on the part of the laity and thus introduced the vernacular language and a simple and clear liturgy designed to educate the faithful. The increased use of Scripture* in the liturgy was emphasized, the Divine Office* and liturgical calendar were ordered revised and restored, and the common celebration of vespers* on Sundays* was encouraged. Gregorian chant, referred to as having "pride of place," was to be returned to popular use, although contemporary sacred music was not excluded. While some of these ideals have been realized, such as the active participation of the laity, others (such as the restored use of the calendar, Sunday vespers and Gregorian chant) have not found wide acceptance. The absence of reference to the devotions in the Constitution on the Sacred Liturgy, so vigorously defended in Mediator Dei, has meant their demise in many Catholic communities. Ultimately, the liturgical movement was not limited to the Catholic Church, but spilled over into a liturgical renewal in mainline* Protestant* churches.

BIBLIOGRAPHY. J. Hall, "The American Liturgical Movement: The Early Years," Worship 50 (1976):472-489; C. Last, Remembering the Future: Vatican II and Tomorrow's Liturgical Agenda (1983); E. B. Koenker, The Liturgical Renaissance in the Roman Catholic Church (1954); P. B. Marx, Virgil Michel and the Liturgical Movement (1957).

T. E. Wangler

Liturgies in America. Among the forms of public worship* in America, there are a wide variety of liturgical traditions, each with distinctive characteristics. They include several traditions of the Eastern (Orthodox or Oriental) churches and eight Western traditions ranging from Roman Catholic* to Quaker.* The term liturgical tradition denotes a definite body of inherited patterns of worship practices and understanding of such practices. Most Christian worship in America has been historically shaped within a single tradition, although such traditions frequently interact. Within each tradition there are ethnic and cultural styles (e.g., frontier Reformed* practice or the worship of black Methodists*).

The Eastern Tradition. The various Eastern liturgical traditions are represented by several Orthodox* and Oriental churches and by Eastern-rite* Roman Catholics. Although some smaller bodies follow liturgical traditions established in Egypt or West Syria as early as the fourth century, the majority of American Eastern Christians use the Byzantine rite or Liturgy of St. John Chrysostom, with the Liturgy of St. Basil substituted on certain occasions in the liturgical year.

Particular problems among the Eastern churches have revolved around the question of how much adaptation is permissible without compromising Orthodox worship.* Translation into the vernacular has been accomplished in most instances while other adaptations (mostly westernizations), such as congregational seating, mixed seating, pipe organs, stained glass and women in choirs, are still debated. Ceremonial (actions) and rites (texts) are carefully guarded in order to remain faithful.

The Roman Catholic Tradition. In the Roman Catholic tradition, developments have taken quite different forms. After the Council of Trent (1545-1563), a period of rubricism began, in which the ideal was liturgical uniformity throughout the world on the basis of standard Roman service books, all in Latin. For four centuries, the Congregation of Sacred Rites (1588) (*See* Congregation for Divine Worship) enforced global uniformity. Such centralization was useful in America during the period of Catholic immigration* in creating a sense of unity. The liturgical movement* in the U.S. had its real beginning in 1926, two years after the end of mass immigration. Its leaders were predominantly Midwesterners of German background: Virgil Michel,* Martin Hellriegel (1890-1981), H. A. Reinhold (1897-1968), William Busch (1892-1971), Michael Mathis (1885-1960) and Gerald Ellard (1894-1963).

Broadly speaking, the movement had a Benedictine* phase which lasted until the end of World War 2* and stressed a recovery of lost treasures and a Protestant* phase which emphasized the vernacular, simplification of rites, preaching* and congregational hymnody. Both facets became part of the worldwide liturgical agenda after the "Constitution on the Sacred Liturgy" was promulgated during Vatican II* in 1963. This has led to wholesale reform of liturgical books, new emphasis on Scripture* and preaching in the Mass,* some moves toward decentralization of liturgical decisions, and above all, an emphasis on increased participation by the laity.*

The Lutheran Tradition. The Protestant traditions emerge from the same background of late medieval worship in western Europe as the Roman Catholic tradition does, and they retain various elements of that matrix in varying degrees. Most conservative was the Lutheran tradition which came to America from various European countries. At times, Lutheran worship on the East Coast seemed to be evolving toward the patterns of American Free Church* worship and in danger of losing distinctive Lutheran services and hymnody. A fresh influx of Germans in the nineteenth century helped to move Lutheran worship in a more conservative direction. As a consequence, much of the nineteenth-century movement was in the line of restoring authentic Lutheran liturgies.

The same period saw new forms of Americanization, especially worship in English, and a wide acceptance of English hymnody. Much effort has been concentrated in the twentieth century toward bringing the various Lutheran bodies together. Joint service books have helped accomplish this, culminating in the *Lutheran Book of Worship* (1978). This represents the triumph of much of the

agenda of the modern liturgical movement: renewed emphasis on the lectionary, a richer church year, daily prayer, a particular stress on baptism* and more frequent celebrations of the Eucharist.*

The Reformed Tradition. The Reformed tradition reflects the contributions of such European Reformers as John Calvin (1509-1564), Ulrich Zwingli (1484-1531), Martin Bucer (1491-1551) and John Knox (1513-1572). Although, in its origins, this tradition used fixed liturgies and Calvin advocated a weekly Eucharist, much was to change in America. Free Church worship of the frontier, with its strong emphasis on music* and preaching, both leading to personal conversion,* had a profound impact on the Reformed tradition. Charles G. Finney,* ordained* as a Presbyterian,* came to be the most persuasive advocate of this revivalistic approach to worship.

Two German Reformed theologians, John Nevin* and Philip Schaff,* advocates of the so-called Mercersburg Theology,* strongly opposed subsuming worship under the heading of revivalism.* But theirs was a minority voice and most Presbyterian worship became indistinguishable from that of American Free Church congregations. A few smaller Reformed churches still refuse to use any hymnody but the psalter. Gradually, in the twentieth century, service books have been introduced but their use remains voluntary. The effects of the liturgical movement have brought widespread use of the lectionary* and liturgical year and fuller sacramental life.

The Anglican Tradition. The focus of the Anglican tradition is the *Book of Common Prayer** (BCP) first revised in America in 1789. Sunday* worship in the colonial period later usually consisted of morning prayer, litany* and first part of the Lord's Supper.* The Eucharist was celebrated rarely and then with a minimum of ceremonial procedure. A major change occurred in the nineteenth century as a result of the Catholic revival in the Church of England. Controversies arose over the use of medieval ceremonial procedure, more frequent eucharistic celebrations, and a higher doctrine of the sacraments.* The Episcopal Church had managed to remain the least affected by the prevailing American Free Church worship. Now the distinctions became even more accentuated.

Recent decades have seen an American Episcopal liturgical movement gather strength since World War 2 and culminate in a new BCP (1979) and *Hymnal* (1982). A much greater variety of liturgical practices is now accommodated. The Eucharist has replaced morning prayer as the principal Sunday service in many parishes.

The Free Church Tradition. The dominant liturgical tradition in American Protestantism is the Free Church tradition. Historically it has several roots, the earliest being the radical reformation of the continent, represented in America by such groups as the Mennonites.* The English Puritans* rebelled against those elements of ceremonial procedure and theology* in the English BCP which they found unscriptural. The third root is the churches of the American frontier, where Disciples of Christ* sprouted and Baptists* came to flower. The frontier gave a distinctive stamp to much of this worship in its basically pragmatic approach to worship—it was shaped to do something useful, namely make converts.

It is characteristic of this tradition that historic practices are not considered of great moment, but everything is subject to the scrutiny of God's Word. This rigorous biblicism came in time to be replaced by pragmatic norms. The ordering of worship is left to each congregation to determine, in order best to suit its own needs. Thus prayer is usually ex tempore with little need felt for set forms.

The most radical tradition of all is the Quaker, which originated in England among the followers of George Fox.* It involved worship in which the Holy Spirit speaks directly to the congregation through individuals. So-called will worship—worship prepared in advance—is avoided. Worship is conducted under the prompting of the Spirit, who is equally accessible to all, men or women, free or slave.

In the nineteenth century, Quakers in the Midwest frequently adopted Free Church patterns of worship, utilizing paid clergy. Thus while the original form of "unstructured" worship remains virtually unchanged in many congregations (particularly on the East Coast), structured worship with preaching and hymnody is common, although without visible sacraments.

The Methodist Tradition. The eighteenth century saw the origins of the Methodist tradition. A key factor was John Wesley's* pragmatic traditionalism. In trying to minister to unchurched masses, Wesley preferred to use traditional means, both those in current use but also some long disused, such as the love feast (agape), watchnight (vigil) and covenant renewal (renewal of vows). A major factor in the Wesleyan movement was the introduction of popular hymnody, largely at the hands of Charles Wesley (1707-1788). The Wesleyan movement, unlike most, has stressed both fervent preaching and a strong sacramental life (*See* Wesleyan Tradition).

The latter was largely lost in American Methodism,* together with Wesley's liturgy, the *Sunday Service* of 1784. Under the leadership of Francis Asbury,* American Methodism largely reflected the patterns of the frontier Free Church, using set forms from what came to be known as the "Ritual" only for the sacraments. Recent years have shown signs of moving in a more Wesleyan direction, with greater attention to fixed forms and sacramental worship.

The Pentecostal Tradition. The birth of Pentecostalism* coincides with the beginning of the twentieth century. It is essentially unstructured worship, left to the spontaneous guidance of the Spirit. This can take many forms: hymn singing, praying, preaching and speaking in tongues.* Originating among the economically deprived, many of its emphases have spilled over into the charismatic movement.* In recent years both charismatic and Pentecostal worship has had an appeal to people of traditions accustomed to structured worship. Thus there are charismatic services among Roman Catholics, Episcopalians and other mainline* Christian groups.

African-Americans have played a major role in the shaping of the Pentecostal tradition ever since its origins. They have also developed distinctive styles of worship in each of the other Western traditions. Hispanics,* Native Americans and Asian Americans* are now doing the same.

As worship traditions mature, they seem more willing to recognize the values of other worship traditions and to borrow from them. Thus, spontaneous prayer appears in Episcopal services and set forms attract some Free Church people. Greater variety seems to be evolving within each tradition, yet without abandoning its distinctive characteristics.

See also Worship: Eastern Orthodox; Worship: Protestant; Worship: Roman Catholic.

Bibliography. D. Adams, *From Meetinghouse to Campmeeting* (1981); G. J. Cuming, *A History of Anglican Liturgy,* rev. ed. (1982); F. Hall, ed., *Quaker Worship in North America* (1978); J. Melton, *Presbyterian Worship in America* (1967); W. J. Hollenweger, *The Pentecostals* (1972); L. D. Reed, *The Lutheran Liturgy,* rev. ed. (1959); W. N. Wade, "American Methodist Worship" (unpublished Ph.D. dissertation, University of Notre Dame, 1981). J. F. White

Liturgy of the Hours. Also known as the Divine Office, the term refers to the public celebration of prayer, distinct from the Eucharistic liturgy (Mass*) in the Roman Catholic Church.* Since Vatican II*

the Office has been revised and is now celebrated in the vernacular. Since 1970 its name has been changed to "Liturgy of the Hours" and is considered the official public prayer and praise of the Church, keyed to times of the day, days of the week and seasons of the year.

While the Divine Office is most commonly celebrated in monastic* and religious houses, cathedrals where there are resident canons and by the ordained* clergy* who are bound to its private recitation, it has become once again a prayer of the Catholic Church for the Church by laity.* Many laypeople in different walks of life pray the Psalms, supplemented by intercessory prayer, hymns and scriptural selections, usually in the morning and the evening.

The ancient church knew two public prayer services, one at morning and the other at evening. Those services have also been known as Lauds and Vespers or, in the Episcopal Church,* as Morning Prayer (or Morning Song) and Evening Prayer (or Evensong). The monastic orders developed a more detailed round of public prayer, which was seen as one of their primary duties.

The *Rule of Saint Benedict* prescribed prayer at punctuated periods during the day. There was to be a period of prayer at long before the dawn (called Vigils or Matins) and seven periods (see Psalm 119:164) during the day. The names and approximate times of these services are: Lauds (before dawn); Prime (the first hour of the day); Terce (the third hour, roughly 9:00 A.M.); Sext (the sixth hour, at noon); Nones (the ninth hour, at 3:00 P.M.); Vespers (in the early evening) and Compline (the last service before retirement). This pattern, with variations, has persisted to the present day. Some monastic houses, for example, follow a usage even older than the Benedictine model with nightly vigils and three offices at dawn, noon and in the evening.

The offices of the Liturgy are made up of the Psalms interspersed with readings from the Scriptures, with the whole introduced and concluded by hymns and canticles. The Office is so arranged that the entire psalter is sung during the course of a week. The Liturgy of the Hours is either recited or sung according to chant tones, depending on the capacities and customs of each place.

Contemporary Catholic publishers provide the full liturgy of the hours in a set of volumes, as well as abbreviated versions in a range of styles and sizes.

See also CANONICAL HOURS; LITURGIES.

BIBLIOGRAPHY. P. Bradshaw, *Daily Prayer in the Early Church* (1982); T. Fry and I. Baker, ed., *The Rule of Saint Benedict* (1982); K. Irwin, *Liturgy, Prayer, and Spirituality* (1984); C. Jones, G. Wainwright and E. Yarnold, eds., *The Study of Liturgy* (1985).

L. S. Cunningham and B. Moran

Livermore, Mary Ashton Rice (1820-1905). Temperance* and women's suffrage* leader. Born in Boston, Massachusetts, Livermore experienced conversion* at the age of fourteen. As a child she liked to preach* and, after reading *Foxe's Book of Martyrs,* play "martyr." Her father, a strict Baptist* deacon,* had devised a plan for reading through the Bible* in one year, which Mary followed from age seven through age twenty-three. She attended and taught at Charlestown Female Seminary, a Baptist school. In 1845 she married Universalist* minister* Daniel Livermore. They had three daughters. In 1857 they moved to Chicago, where she became involved with the Sanitary Commission* during the Civil War.*

Livermore became convinced that women needed the vote to fight poverty, drunkenness and sexual exploitation, so she convened Illinois's first suffrage convention in 1868 and became president of the Illinois Woman Suffrage Association. She also served in 1869 as vice president and from 1875 to 1878 as president of the American Woman Suffrage Association. She moved back to Boston in 1870 to merge her paper, the *Agitator,* with Lucy Stone's* *Woman's Journal.* Livermore was its editor until 1872. She helped found the Massachusetts Woman Suffrage Association, serving as president (1893-1903), and also served as president of the Massachusetts Women's Christian Temperance Union* (1875-1885). Between 1872 and 1895 she lectured from coast to coast on women's suffrage and temperance. After her retirement from the lecture circuit and her husband's death in 1899, she turned to spiritualism.

BIBLIOGRAPHY. *DAB* VI; M. Livermore, *The Story of My Life* (1897); *NAW* 2; F. Willard, *Woman and Temperance* (1883). N. A. Hardesty

Livingston, John H. (1746-1825). Dutch Reformed* minister* and president of Queen's (Rutgers) College.* Born in Poughkeepsie, New York, Livingston graduated from Yale* College (B.A., 1762) and studied law for several years (1762-1764) before choosing to enter the ministry. He elected the Dutch Reformed Church over the Presbyterians and the Anglicans because he aspired to heal some of the divisions that had plagued the Dutch through much of the colonial period. Livingston graduated from the University of

Utrecht (S.T.D., 1770), passed his ordination examination before the Classis of Amsterdam in 1769 and returned to New York City the next year to become the second English-speaking minister in the churches there.

An ardent Patriot during the Revolution, Livingston became an ecclesiastical peacemaker, assisting an ethnic church in finding its new identity and status in the emerging republic. In 1784 he was elected professor of theology by his Dutch Reformed colleagues. For many years he conducted classes in theology and divinity, in addition to his pastoral duties in New York. From 1810 to 1825 he served as president of Queen's College in New Brunswick, New Jersey, where he also institutionalized the seminary (known today as New Brunswick Theological Seminary) he had begun during his pastorate in New York.

BIBLIOGRAPHY. *AAP* 9; E. T. Corwin, *Manual of the Reformed Church in America, 1628-1902* (1902); *DAB* VI; *DARB*; A. Gunn, *Memoirs of the Rev. John H. Livingston* (1829); *NCAB* 3.

R. H. Balmer

Loehe, Johannes Konrad Wilhelm (1808-1872). German Lutheran* pastor,* writer and pioneer in mission* work. Educated in theology* at Erlangen and Berlin, he was pastor in the village of Neuendettelsau from 1837 until his death. Reacting to the rationalism of the Enlightenment,* Loehe was part of the Lutheran Awakening that stressed a return to the Lutheran Confessions, a renewed appreciation of liturgy* and the office of pastor.*

In response to the pleas of pastors working among the German immigrants in North America, he recruited and trained hundreds of "Christian emergency pastors" to work among the settlers and to evangelize* the Native Americans. In 1843 Loehe published a paper on behalf of America's needs, *Kirchliche Mitteilungen aus und ueber Nordamerika.* In 1846 he founded a seminary which trained American Lutheran pastors under the direction of Wilhelm Sihler. Working with the immigrant groups, he helped lay the foundations of the Lutheran Church—Missouri Synod and, later, the Iowa Synod, though he never left Germany.

BIBLIOGRAPHY. E. C. Nelson, ed., *The Lutherans in North America* (1980); J. L. Schaaf, *Wilhem Loehes Relations . . .* (1961).

J. D. Sutherland

Log College. Colonial school for training Presbyterian* ministers* in the revivalist* tradition. The Log College was a small school founded and run by the Rev. William Tennent* in Neshaminy, Pennsylvania, during the 1730s and 1740s, the purpose of which was to train men for the Presbyterian ministry. Tennent, himself a Presbyterian minister, had tutored his four sons in theological matters through the early 1720s and had apparently been sufficiently successful to attract others to his tutelage. Historical accounts differ over when this informal tutoring became formalized as the Log College, some sources placing the date as early as 1726, others as late as 1735.

Tennent's work produced severe criticism within the Presbyterian Synod,* which officially sought to restrict the influence of Tennent and his pro-revival theological perspective by voting in 1738 to require that any ministerial candidate who did not have a degree from a New England college or a European university would have to submit to a special examination by the Synod. This was clearly an attack on the Log College and precipitated an intensifying theological struggle within the Presbyterian Church. The result was the Old Side*-New Side* split in 1741. The Log College continued to turn out New Side-type Presbyterian ministers until the early 1740s when, with Tennent's increasing age and frailty, it ceased to function. The college was exceptionally influential in the crucial formative years of the Presbyterian Church, and while there was no formal institutional continuity, the spiritual legacy of the Log College was continued by the College of New Jersey (Princeton),* which was founded in 1746 by men either trained at or influenced by the Log College.

BIBLIOGRAPHY. A. A. Alexander, *The Log College* (1851); T. C. Pears, Jr., and Guy S. Klett, "Documentary History of William Tennent and the Log College," *Journal of the Department of History* (The Presbyterian Historical Society) XXVIII (1950): 37-64; 105-28; 167-204; L. J. Trinterud, *The Forming of an American Tradition: A Re-Examination of Colonial Presbyterianism* (1949).

S. T. Logan

Lonergan, Bernard J. F. (1904-1984). Canadian Catholic* theologian.* A native of Canada, Lonergan joined the Jesuits* after high school and studied at Heythrop College, London, before going to the Gregorian University in Rome to study theology. Ordained in 1936, Lonergan stayed on at Rome to earn a doctorate in theology with a dissertation on operative grace according to Thomas Aquinas. He then taught philosophy and theology in Canada (1940-1953) and the Gregorian University in Rome (1953-1965). After a lung operation in 1964, he spent the remainder of his career in research, writing and occasional lecturing, first at Regis College in Toronto (1965-1975) and then at Boston College (1975-1983).

Lonergan's main contribution was to bring Thomistic thought into dialog with modern science and propose a new method for doing theology. His work *Insight* (1957) elaborated a cognitional theory and metaphysic based on the act of understanding. *Method in Theology* (1972) proposed an eightfold collaboration of the different functional specialties that his cognitional theory revealed: research, interpretation, history, dialectic, foundations, doctrines, systematics and communications.

Followers of Lonergan have acclaimed him as a new methodological master, doing for his age what Aristotle and Francis Bacon had done for theirs. His theory of consciousness stays close to experience and is both complex and subtle. Lonergan provides for experience, understanding, judgment and decision. He distinguishes such realms as common sense, theory, art and prayer. The power of his method comes from inviting readers and students to appropriate their own consciousness—to learn how they make meaning in different realms. Because meaning is common to all lives, Lonergan's work is thoroughly ecumenical.

BIBLIOGRAPHY. F. E. Crowe, *The Lonergan Enterprise* (1980); H. Meynell, *An Introduction to the Philosophy of Bernard Lonergan* (1976); D. Tracy, *The Achievement of Bernard Lonergan* (1970).

J. Carmody

Long, Ralph H. (1882-1948). Lutheran* minister* and director of the National Lutheran Council.* Born in Ohio, Long served pastorates in Ohio and Pennsylvania before becoming stewardship secretary of the Lutheran Joint Synod of Ohio and then for eighteen years director of the National Lutheran Council (1930-1948). This Council, begun in 1918, was the chief agency of cooperation for a majority of the Lutherans of North America. War and post-War emergencies had given it vitality, uniting Lutherans for action. By 1930 the enthusiasm was seriously eroded, the budget reduced, and there was talk of disbanding. Long's vigorous leadership not only rescued the Council during the financially precarious Depression* years, but also provided stable programming in such areas as continuing common Lutheran publicity, stewardship education, study of social issues, coordination of Lutheran welfare agencies and the beginning of a radio ministry. In the emergencies of World War 2,* the Council blossomed, proving

highly effective under Long's wise direction.

BIBLIOGRAPHY. F. K. Wentz, *Lutheran in Concert* (1968); E. C. Nelson, ed., *The Lutherans in North America* (1975). F. K. Wentz

Longinqua Oceani. A. papal encyclical* by Pope Leo XIII* to the bishops* of the U.S., January 6, 1895. It mixes warm praise for "the young and vigorous American nation" and its burgeoning Catholic Church,* with pointed warnings about separation of church and state* and heavy emphasis on the role of the recently (1893) appointed apostolic delegate.*

While acknowledging the happy effect that the "equity" of U.S. laws had on the growth and prosperity of the Catholic Church, the pope cautioned American Catholics against the conclusion "that in America is to be sought the type of the most desirable status of the Church, or that it would be universally lawful or expedient for State and Church to be, as in America, dissevered and divorced." The Church would be even more prosperous, he thought, if it "enjoyed the favors of the laws and the patronage of public authority." This disturbed the Americanists.* It contradicted their hope that American-style separation of church and state could strengthen the Church's embattled position in Europe. At a time when the anti-Catholic American Protective Association was growing, they had apprehensions about the possible effects of these remarks on non-Catholics.

The pope went on to note his own contributions to American Catholicism, singling out his support for learning, as witnessed by the establishment of The Catholic University of America* in 1889, and his improvement of "methods of managing church affairs," a reference to the apostolic delegate. His description of the delegate as "one who should represent our person" signals the belated arrival on American shores of the effects of the nineteenth-century trend to Roman centralization in Catholic affairs. It sent a clear message to the bishops, who almost unanimously opposed the delegate's establishment. Fears that the delegate might obstruct the bishops' exercise of their office were dismissed as "unjust and baseless." Rather, the pope warned the feuding bishops not to obstruct each other. He addressed a few concluding remarks to various issues of the day, chief among them the labor question. In general this encyclical can be read as a warning shot which halted the Americanist party's advance and marked the beginning of its decline.

See also AMERICANISM; APOSTOLIC DELEGATE.

BIBLIOGRAPHY. J. T. Ellis, ed., *Documents of*

American Catholic History (1962); S. J. Thomas, "The American Press and the Encyclical *Longinqua Oceani,"* JCS 22 (1980):475-485.   W. L. Portier

Loras, Jean Mathias Pierre (1792-1858). First Catholic* bishop* of Dubuque, Iowa. A native of France, Loras came to America in 1829 as a priest* in the Mobile diocese.* In 1837 he became the bishop of the Dubuque diocese.

The vast area encompassed by the new diocese—most of the present states of Iowa and Minnesota—was virtually empty. Loras set out to people these prairies with Catholic settlers. Using money received from Europe, he purchased thousands of acres of cheap government land which would later serve as the sites of parishes* and other religious institutions. To attract Catholics to Iowa, Bishop Loras wrote letters to Catholic newspapers inviting German and Irish immigrants to come to his diocese.

Loras's success is illustrated by statistics. In 1839, when he first reached Iowa, Loras found four priests, three churches and a few scattered congregations. In 1858, at the time of his death, his diocese contained fifty churches, thirty-seven priests, two congregations of Sisters and a Trappist* monastery.

BIBLIOGRAPHY. *DAB* VI; M. E. Hoffmann, *Church Founders of the Northwest* (1937).

T. Auge

Lord, Daniel Aloyisius (1888-1955). Roman Catholic* writer, composer and playwright. Born in Chicago, Lord was educated at St. Ignatius College (present-day Loyola University) and St. Louis University. He entered the Society of Jesus* in 1909 and was ordained* a Catholic priest* in 1923. He was instrumental in reviving the Sodality of Mary, a Jesuit organization for the spiritual* formation of the laity,* and became its national director in the U.S. in 1925. From 1925 to 1948 he also served as editor of *The Queen's Work,* the Sodality's magazine, and opened its pages to an analysis of social issues. In 1928 Lord organized the first national Leadership School for lay Catholics and in 1931 the national Summer School of Catholic Action, which had held 190 sessions by 1963. In 1943 he became director of the Jesuits' Institute of Social Order.

Lord authored some thirty books, almost 300 pamphlets, sixty-six booklets, fifty plays, twelve musicals, six pageants, a syndicated column, "Along the Way" and 900 transcripts for radio presentation. He gave technical advice to movie producers (e.g., Cecil B. De Mille) and was coauthor of the original Motion Picture Code.

BIBLIOGRAPHY. D. A. Lord, *Played By Ear: The Autobiography of Rev. Daniel A. Lord, S.J.* (1956).   J. T. Connelly

Lord's Day Act. Canadian federal act regulating Sunday activities. Introduced by the government of Prime Minister Wilfrid Laurier and passed by the Parliament of the Dominion of Canada in 1906, the Lord's Day Act came into effect March 1, 1907. It sought to limit work, commerce, pleasure traveling and games and public performances on the Lord's Day. The act provided for prosecutions (at the discretion of the Provincial Attorneys-General) and the levying of fines against offenders. Also included in its provisions was a list of twenty-four exemptions considered to be "Works of Necessity and Mercy," ranging from those connected with divine worship* and the care of the sick to various industrial processes. Prior to this, colonial and provincial governments had enacted their own laws regulating Sunday activities, but recent court decisions had challenged the constitutionality of many of these and had necessitated a federal law. Subsequently, provincial governments were permitted to formulate their own Sunday laws, thus in effect opting out of some of the provisions of the federal act. Much of the initiative behind the enactment of this law came from the Lord's Day Alliance (established 1888) under the direction of the Rev. J. G. Shearer, but support from organized labor and Catholic* bishops* was important in securing its passage. The 1906 Lord's Day Act was repealed in 1985.

BIBLIOGRAPHY. *The Revised Statutes of Canada, 1906* (1907); *Report on Sunday Observance* (for the Federal Minister of Justice) (1976).

R. W. Vaudry

Love Feast. A worship* practice based on a shared common meal. The Love Feast is a distinctive communal meal and service based on the New Testament *agape,* or love meal. European Pietism* revived the ancient practice, and it became part of the worship of Mennonites,* Brethren* and Moravians.* Through Moravian influence, the practice was adopted by John Wesley* and the early Methodists.* Today, the Love Feast is particularly associated with the Church of the Brethren and the Moravians. The Love Feast includes the traditional Communion meal (bread and wine) as a memorial rite and as the climax of the feast, but the Love Feast is not limited to the broken bread and the wine used to celebrate the memory of Christ's death. It may also include washing each other's feet (*See* Foot Washing) as a re-enactment of

Christ's servitude, and the agape meal, which is a simple meal taken communally as a demonstration of Christian love within the community. The Love Feast has been utilized by some within the ecumenical movement* as a means of demonstrating Christian unity.

BIBLIOGRAPHY. F. Baker, *Methodism and the Love-Feast* (1957); F. W. Benedict, *Brethren Love Feast* (1967); D. F. Durnbaugh, ed., *The Brethren in Colonial America* (1967).

C. E. Ostwalt

Lovejoy, Elijah Parish (1802-1837). Presbyterian* minister* and abolitionist* martyr. Born in Albion, Maine, into a Congregational* minister's family of Puritan* heritage, Lovejoy attended Waterville (now Colby) College and then journeyed west to teach school in Missouri. Settling in St. Louis in 1827, he bought into and began editing a local newspaper.

The seeds of faith and his later radical abolitionism were planted when Lovejoy experienced conversion* under the preaching of an antislavery evangelist,* David Nelson. Deciding to enter the ministry, Lovejoy attended Princeton Seminary* and then returned to St. Louis, where he was called to edit a Presbyterian newspaper. Lovejoy initially devoted far more space to attacking Roman Catholics,* Baptists* and "Campbellites"* than slaveholders.

Gradually Lovejoy grew convinced of the evils of slavery and moved toward the radical position of immediate abolition. Increasingly unwelcome in St. Louis, in 1836 he moved his paper to Alton, Illinois, where he again met with hostility. Mobs destroyed his press on three occasions, and Lovejoy, who had defended a black man burned at the stake by a mob, was accused by a judge of inciting slaves to revolt. Ever more outspoken in his condemnation of slavery, he portrayed a host of slaveholders' abuses and accused them of raping slave women as a matter of course. He was finally shot down in an encounter between his small band of followers and a mob seeking to burn down his warehouse. An early and well-publicized abolitionist martyr, Lovejoy in his death played a notable role in galvanizing antislavery sentiment.

BIBLIOGRAPHY. *DAB* VI; M. L. Dillon, *Elijah P. Lovejoy, Abolitionist Editor* (1961); F. H. Dugan, "An Illinois Martyrdom," *Papers in Illinois History and Transactions* (1938); J. C. Lovejoy, *Memoir of the Rev. Elijah P. Lovejoy* (1970).

S. E. Berk

Low Church. A term referring to individuals and congregations within the Anglican Church* who interpret the episcopate,* priesthood* and Book of Common Prayer* from a distinctly Protestant* point of view. The term, originally used of eighteenth century latitudinarians, or liberals,* was later used of eighteenth-century Anglican evangelicals* to distinguish them from high-church* Anglicans who interpreted the episcopate, priesthood and Book of Common Prayer in a Catholic sense. *See also* ANGLICANISM; HIGH CHURCH.

R. Webber

Lowrie, Walter (1868-1959). Episcopal* minister* and Kierkegaard* scholar. Born in Philadelphia, Lowrie was educated at Princeton University.* From 1907 to 1930 he was rector* of Saint Paul's American Church in Rome. A theological liberal,* Lowrie was deeply influenced by his reading of German dialectical theologians and began reading the Danish philosopher Soren Kierkegaard in German translation. Lowrie's own writings covered a variety of Christian topics and thinkers, including a most favorable interpretation of the Barthian movement (*see* Barth, Karl) published in 1932. At the age of sixty-five Lowrie taught himself Danish and embarked on a study and translation of Kierkegaard's works. In 1938 Lowrie published his two-volume biography, *Kierkegaard,* and in 1942 his *A Shorter Life of Kierkegaard.* Lowrie translated fourteen of Kierkegaard's works into English and during the 1930s and early 1940s, when interest in Kierkegaard among English speakers had not yet developed, Lowrie himself paid to have the books published. Among these translations were Kierkegaard's *Christian Discourses (1940); Fear and Trembling* (1941); *The Sickness Unto Death* (1941); *Concluding Unscientific Postscript* (with David F. Swenson, 1941); *Attack Upon Christendom* (1944); *Either/Or* (vol. 2, 1944); *The Concept of Dread* (1944) and *On Authority and Revelation* (1955). Lowrie's scholarly efforts contributed significantly to the discovery and influence of Kierkegaard among American theologians in the post-war period.

BIBLIOGRAPHY. H. T. Kerr, ed., *Sons of the Prophets* (1963).

D. K. McKim

Loy, Matthias (1828-1915). Lutheran* minister,* theologian* and educator. Born near Harrisburg, Pennsylvania, Loy learned the printing trade as a young man. In 1847 he moved to Ohio and prepared for the ministry at the Lutheran Seminary in Columbus, Ohio. After serving a pastorate in Delaware, Ohio (1849-1865), Loy was called in 1865 to be professor of theology* at the Lutheran seminary in Columbus, where he served until his retirement in 1905. During and after his tenure Loy was the leading theologian and churchman of the Evangelical Lutheran Joint Synod of Ohio and Adjacent States.

As a theologian Loy authored *The Doctrine of Justification* (1869), *Essay on the Ministerial Office* (1870), *Christian Prayer* (1890), *The Christian Church* (1896), *The Augsburg Confession* (1908) and several books of sermons. He also edited the *Lutheran Standard* (1864-1891) and founded and edited the *Columbus Theological Magazine* (1881-1888). He was president of the Joint Synod of Ohio (1860-1878, 1880-1894); president of Capital University, Columbus, Ohio (1881-1890); and a participant in the founding of the General Council in 1866, although his church body did not affiliate with it. A leader along with C. F. W. Walther* in the organization of the Lutheran Synodical Conference in 1871, he reluctantly led the Joint Synod of Ohio's withdrawal from that body in 1881 as a result of a dispute over predestination.* Loy died in Columbus, Ohio.

BIBLIOGRAPHY. *DAB* VI; M. Loy, *Story of My Life* (1905); C. G. Fry, "Matthias Loy: Ohio Lutheran Educator," *Ohio History* 76 (1967):183-201; D. L. Huber, *Educating Lutheran Pastors in Ohio* (1988).

J. L. Schaaf

Loyalist, United Empire. *See* ANGLICANISM; REVOLUTION, AMERICAN.

Lutheran Church in America, The. The largest Lutheran* denomination* prior to its merger to form the Evangelical Lutheran Church in America (ELCA). The lineage of the Lutheran Church in America* (LCA) reached back to Henry Melchior Muhlenberg,* who arrived in Pennsylvania in 1742 and worked to gather Lutheran immigrants and to plant the Lutheran Church. A nineteenth-century leader, Samuel Simon Schmucker,* the first professor at historic Gettysburg Seminary, did most to Americanize this branch of Lutheranism, and was accused of over-adaptation to Protestantism by his right-wing foes. His movement, focused in a General Synod* (begun in 1820) inspired a reaction in a General Council, formed in 1867.

These "General" bodies began to collaborate in publishing books of liturgy and hymnals and in 1918 formed the United Lutheran Church in America (ULCA), which also brought in a smaller United Synod South (formed in 1863). Subsequently, the ULCA attracted the Slovak Zion Synod (in 1920), the Icelandic Synod (joined in 1940), the (Finnish) Suomi Synod (which worked in

close concert with but did not join the ULCA), and one of two Danish groups, the American Evangelical Lutheran Church. Larger than these was a group of Swedish heritage, a vital body called The Augustana Synod, whose merger with the ULCA in 1962 was the largest force behind the creation of the Lutheran Church in America out of the old ULCA and some other bodies. When the LCA merged to form the ELCA in 1987, it brought with it 2.9 million members.

Like all Lutherans in America, the members of this body would be classed as theologically conservative, but they were the most moderate and, to the ultra-orthodox, represented the Lutheran "left." The LCA was fully involved with the National Council of Churches* and the World Council of Churches,* and this ecumenical* engagement often led it to be typed most easily as part of "mainstream Protestantism."* While truly a national body, much of its constituent strength was in the East.

BIBLIOGRAPHY. E. C. Nelson, ed., *The Lutherans in North America* (1975); A. C. Piepkorn, *Profiles in Belief,* vol. 2 (1978). The Editors

Lutheran Churches in America. The vast majority of Lutherans in America are members of three bodies: the recently formed (1988) new merger called the Evangelical Lutheran Church in America (with about 5.5 million members at the time of merger); the Lutheran Church—Missouri Synod* (about 2.6 million members); and the Wisconsin Evangelical Lutheran Synod* (400,000 members).

Lutheran Diversity. It was not always so. Lutherans in America have been noted for their existence in a great number of small and independent bodies. From time to time they have formed cooperative groups, but never have these solely included Lutherans.

There are still a number of very small independent, unlinked churches. Brief mention of some of these must suffice: the (Finnish) Apostolic Lutheran Church of America (1929), the Church of the Lutheran Brethren (1900) and the Church of the Lutheran Confession (1961). The largest of any of these groups has only 11,000 members, and these groups are not in communion with each other, with any other Lutheran groups or with Christians beyond Lutheranism. They exist either as legacies of an ethnically divided Lutheranism or as ultra-conservative splits off other bodies, designed to perpetuate some theological point or to represent some residue of controversy. They have no impact on the rest of Lutheranism.

The largest, most dispersed and most complex of the Lutheran Churches in America is the Evangelical Lutheran Church in America, constituted at Columbus, Ohio, in 1987 and born officially on January 1, 1988, with headquarters in Chicago. It has three main components, each of which bears tracing by anyone who would understand the Lutheran Churches in America.

It should be said that the prior great diversity of Lutheran churches resulted from two factors. First, immigration.* Lutherans arrived from Germany, Norway, Sweden, Denmark, Finland and Iceland, where there were established* state churches, as well as from Baltic and Central European nations, over more than a three-century period. These European churches had virtually no contact with each other until the twentieth century; they had known separate development since their formation, usually in the sixteenth century. Mere immigration was complicated also by doctrinal differences. Many of the immigrant groups represent "free" (non-established), schismatic or sectarian movements that resulted from revivalist* or pietist* movements in Europe and had not been in contact with each other. Still others were expressions of extremely conservative "confessionalism,"* which meant that they adhered to sixteenth-century Lutheran creeds* or confessions and resisted modern rationalism or forced movements of union with Reformed* churches in parts of Germany.

These differences based on ethnicity,* European provenance, diverse motives for migrating, isolation in America and often almost sectarian definition once in America, accounted for the crazy-quilt pattern behind the churches that came together in the Evangelical Lutheran Church in America (to say nothing of those that did not join it).

The Lutheran Church in America. The largest component was the Lutheran Church in America* (LCA), the result of a merger in 1962. Like all Lutherans in America, the members of this body would be classed as theologically conservative, but they were the most moderate and, to the ultra-orthodox, represented the Lutheran "left." The LCA was fully involved with the National Council of Churches* and the World Council of Churches,* and this ecumenical* engagement often led it to be typed most easily as part of "mainstream Protestantism."* While truly a national body, much of its constituent strength was in the East.

The patriarch of the LCA bodies (and, it might be said, of Lutheranism in general) was Henry Melchior Muhlenberg,* who arrived in Pennsylvania in 1742 and worked to gather Lutheran immigrants and to plant the church. A nineteenth-century leader, Samuel Simon Schmucker,* the first professor at historic Gettysburg Seminary, did the most to Americanize this branch of Lutheranism and was accused of over-adaptation to Protestantism by his right-wing foes. His movement, focused in a General Synod* (begun in 1820), inspired a reaction in a General Council formed in 1867.

These "General" bodies began to collaborate in publishing hymnals and books of liturgy; and in 1918 they formed the United Lutheran Church in America (ULCA), which also brought in a smaller United Synod South (formed in 1863). Subsequently the ULCA attracted the Slovak Zion Synod (in 1920), the Icelandic Synod (joined in 1940), the (Finnish) Suomi Synod (which worked in close concert with, but did not join, the ULCA), and one of two Danish groups, the American Evangelical Lutheran Church. Larger than these was a group of Swedish heritage, a vital body called the Augustana Synod, whose merger with the ULCA in 1962 was the largest force behind the creation of the Lutheran Church in America out of the old ULCA and some other bodies.

The American Lutheran Church. The second large native body in the formation of the ELCA was the American Lutheran Church.* While it too had a national presence, its concentration of power tended to be west of the LCAs, in the Upper Midwest, where it had headquarters in Minneapolis. Its historic components were mainly nineteenth-century arrivals to America, and they tended to stress a blend of both confessionalism and pietism that often found the ancestors of the LCA to be too "worldly," too adapted to the American Protestant ethos.

In 1818 congregations in Ohio formed the Joint Synod of Ohio; in 1845 a Buffalo Synod organized to serve congregations further north, while in the Midwest in 1854, the Iowa Synod took shape. (It should be noted that almost never did these state identifications mean that a church was confined to the particular state). This Iowa Synod gave expression to the impetus of a great German leader, Wilhelm Loehe,* who had a missionary's* eye for the need to support immigrant churches in America.

Further south, Lutherans in Texas German settlements had formed a Texas Synod in 1851, while among the contentious Norwegian groups (at one time one was called the Anti-Missourian Brotherhood), the most powerful came to be the Evangelical Lutheran Church, heir to what had been several distinct and reasonably vigorous separate bodies at the turn of the century. Meanwhile the more pietistic Danish bodies, nicknamed the "gloomy" Danes (over against the more worldly "happy" Danes that went into the LCA) formed the United Evangelical Lutheran Church in 1896, another component in the eventual American Lutheran Church.*

Many of these groups through the years worked to establish good relations and possible merger with the Missouri Synod, but efforts at concord always broke down, often in the midst of acrimony over theological differences that, to non-Lutherans, looked minute. Therefore in 1930 four synods, Ohio; Iowa; Buffalo (New York) and Texas formed an "old" American Lutheran Church. Finally in 1960 this church merged with the chiefly Norwegian-backgrounded ELC to produce the "new" American Lutheran Church that lasted until 1988.

The Association of Evangelical Lutheran Churches. The third bent in the ELCA was the Association of Evangelical Lutheran Churches. While the other two brought 2.9 and 2.3 million members to the merger, the AELC had only 110,000 members in 272 congregations. These congregations had left the Missouri Synod after an ultra-conservative element took over leadership of the latter body in 1969. The conservatives set out to bring the moderates into line or to purge them, an activity that led to the formation of a celebrated "Seminex," a "Concordia Seminary in Exile," which represented the large majority of faculty and students of Missouri's flagship Concordia Seminary in St. Louis. The AELC always described itself as a kind of holding or lifeboat operation on the way to merger with ALC or LCA, with whom it had theological sympathies. It turned out that, in the end, it merged with both of these to form the ELCA.

Lutheran Church—Missouri Synod. During all this merging activity, the Missouri and Wisconsin Synods went their ways. The historic name for the former was the Evangelical Lutheran Synod of Missouri, Ohio, and Other States, but the word *German,* part of the title at the time of formation in Chicago in 1847, was dropped in World War 1, and in its centennial year the official name became the Lutheran Church—Missouri Synod. The majority of its members never were in Missouri, but it acquired this name because its headquarters and major seminary and publishing house were in St. Louis and because its ancestry was a group of Saxon immigrants that came to Perry County, Missouri, in 1839.

The coming of this first group set much of the tone for the subsequent conservative body. The original leader, Martin Stephan,* who left the immigrants in disgrace soon after arrival, was replaced by Carl F. W. Walther,* who joins Muhlenberg and Schmucker among the shapers of American Lutheranism. Walther, who reacted against nineteenth-century German Lutheran rationalism and who had to convince the Missouri Saxons that they were truly a "church," stressed extreme seventeenth-century-style orthodoxy.* He rejected "unionism," which to him meant not only not praying and worshiping with other Protestants but also with Lutherans who were not in perfect doctrinal accord with Missouri. A theologian of note, Walther picked up some elements of Luther, particularly the theme of rightly distinguishing "law" from "gospel," and helped give birth to a vital movement of conservatives.

Throughout his career he was engaged in some efforts at concord and many expressions of controversy with almost all other kinds of Lutherans. While many of these controversies (over the role of laity,* over the nature of divine election*) came largely to be forgotten, Walther's heirs in the twentieth century were concerned to make biblical inerrancy* a major theme, one that they found understressed in the rest of Lutheranism.

The Missouri Synod Lutherans came to be known distinctively not only for their standing apart but because they established a very extensive network of elementary and secondary parochial schools,* one of the most elaborate outside Catholicism.* The parish schools at first were to help perpetuate the German language as a contributor to orthodoxy*; later they served, as in Catholicism, as an alternative to corrosive contact in public schools. Eventually the schools came to be rather open expressions of Lutheran life and acquired a good reputation also among non-Lutherans who patronized them.

The Missouri Synod between the 1930s and 1960s kept making moves that did not wholly discourage the American Lutheran Church and even became a vigorous if often critical partner in the Lutheran Council in the U.S.A.* It was during these mid-century years that Missouri saw its greatest vitality and growth, while incorporating a moderate and an ultra-conservative party. After the latter established itself in leadership, the Synod became increasingly wary about other Lutheran ties.

Wisconsin Evangelical Lutheran Synod. However tentative its inter-Lutheran engagements had been, these did serve to antagonize the Wisconsin Evangelical Lutheran Synod (WELS), usually simply called the Wisconsin Synod, though it was not confined to Wisconsin; indeed, its 415,000 members are in congregations in fifty states and

Lutheran Churches

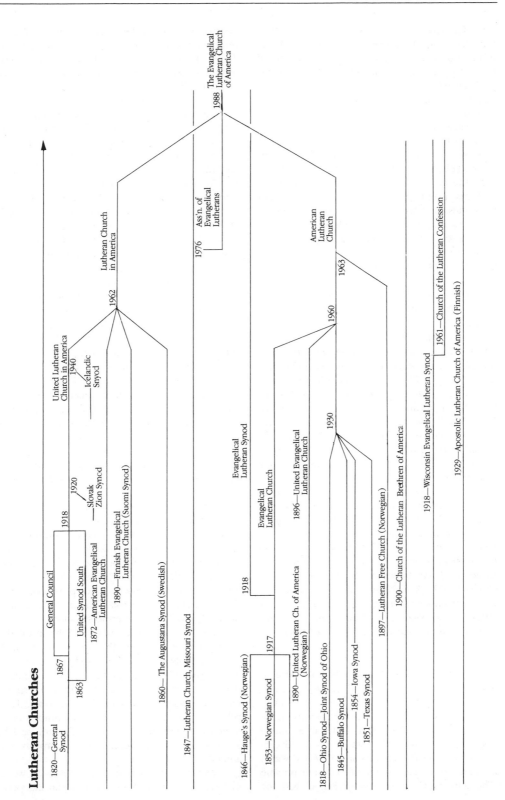

three Canadian provinces. When formed in 1850 the ancestor of the current WELS was a moderate group, but since 1917, when it absorbed several other Upper Midwest synodical groups, it has prided itself in being the most conservative sizable Lutheran group. It had ecumenical relations with no one.

The history of the Lutheran churches in America, then, has been a history of immigrations, doctrinal controversies and mergers down to the three main groups (ELCA, LC—MS and WELS). This history has seen the churches leaving behind many ethnic customs, non-English languages and European memories. They have become thoroughly at home in America but in their "evangelical Catholicism" tend to see themselves situated somewhat independent of both mainstream and Reformed evangelical* Protestantism. They differ from the former in their confessionalism and from the latter in their consistent practice of infant baptism* and their belief in "the Real Presence" of Christ in the Lord's Supper.*

See also LUTHERAN TRADITION.

BIBLIOGRAPHY. G. E. Arden, *Augustana Heritage: A History of the Augustana Evangelical Lutheran Church* (1963); W. A. Baepler, *A Century of Grace: A History of the Missouri Synod, 1847-1947* (1947); R. J. Jalkanen, ed., *The Faith of the Finns: Historical Perspectives on the Finnish Lutheran Church in America* (1972); J. M. Jensen, *The United Evangelical Lutheran Church: An Interpretation* (1964); J. Knudsen, *The Formation of the Lutheran Church in America* (1978); C. P. Lutz, ed., *Church Roots: Stories of Nine Immigrant Groups That Became the American Lutheran Church* (1985); F. W. Meuser, *The Formation of the American Lutheran Church: A Case Study in Lutheran Unity* (1958); E. Mortensen, *The Danish Lutheran Church in America: The History and Heritage of the American Evangelical Lutheran Church* (1967); E. C. Nelson and E. L. Fevold, *The Lutheran Church among Norwegian-Americans* (1960); T. W. Nichol, *All These Lutherans: Three Paths Toward a New Lutheran Church* (1986).

M. E. Marty

Lutheran Church—Missouri Synod, The. A large Lutheran* denomination* of German background. On April 26, 1847, a group of German-American pastors* and their congregations organized the German Evangelical Lutheran Synod of Missouri, Ohio, and Other States. The word *German* was dropped from the name in World War 1, and in its centennial year the official name became "The Lutheran Church—Missouri Synod" with the

"Missouri" recalling the original German-Lutheran immigrants who came to Perry County, Missouri, in 1839. The denominational headquarters, major seminary and publishing house are also located in St. Louis, Missouri.

The original immigrants included in the Missouri group had immigrated* in 1838 under the leadership of Martin Stephan.* Stephan and his group had left Saxony in protest against the rationalism that had infiltrated the German Lutheran Church, as well as the Prussian Union which had forced a merger of Lutheran and Reformed* Churches. Congregations in Michigan and Indiana were founded by German Lutheran missionaries* sent by the Franconian confessional Lutheran pastor Wilhelm Loehe.* All of these groups had been influenced by conservative pietism,* as well as the revival of Lutheran confessionalism* in early nineteenth-century Germany.

Under the leadership of its first two presidents, Carl F. W. Walther* (president, 1847-1850; 1864-1878) and F. C. D. Wyneken (president, 1850-1864), the Synod developed a strong defense of its biblical theology, anchored in the sixteenth-century Lutheran confessions of the Book of Concord, and its congregational* polity.* This polity led to disputes with German Lutherans and with other German-American Lutherans, including the Buffalo Synod of Johannes A. A. Grabau* and the Iowa Synod, founded by other disciples of Loehe.

These disputes and related doctrinal discussions led the Synod to arrange a series of free conferences (1856-1859) and colloquies (1866-1867), out of which came the organization of the Evangelical Lutheran Synodical Conference, an organization in which the Missouri Synod took the lead until its dissolution of the Conference in 1967. In its early years the Conference was rent by a dispute over predestination* (1879-1883), in which the Missouri Synod, accused of "crypto-Calvinism," defended Luther's understanding of the unconditional election* of believers to salvation.

Under Walther, Wyneken, H. C. Schwan (1819-1905; president, 1878-1899) and Franz Pieper* (president, 1899-1911), the Synod trained pastors who organized German immigrants into congregations and created the largest single German Protestant denomination in North America. This religious subculture met German immigrants' needs through effective pastoral care; parish schools; and, in larger cities, hospitals, orphanages and other social services.

In 1893 the Synod began foreign mission work in India. Mission work in China, begun independently by a synodical college professor E. L. Arndt, was incorporated in the Synod's program in 1917. Rapid expansion of foreign missions took place after World War 2.* In 1987 the Synod was involved in denominational or cooperative mission outreach in thirty-five nations on four continents.

The leaders of the Synod early recognized that the immigrant church would have to acculturate, though of all the major Lutheran denominations, it has retained its ethnic identity the longest. In 1875 an English-language conference was organized. In 1891 it became a separate synod, rejoining as a district of the Missouri Synod in 1911. Persecution of German-Americans during World War 1 hastened the acculturation process. Under the presidencies of Frederick Pfotenhauer (1859-1939; president, 1911-1935) and John W. Behncken (1884-1968; president, 1935-1962), the Synod turned to outreach into the mainstream of American life through evangelism, publishing, radio and television, aided by two auxiliary organizations, the Lutheran Laymen's League (organized 1917) and the Lutheran Woman's Missionary League (organized 1942).

Two long-related churches, the Finnish-descended National Evangelical Lutheran Church (organized 1898) and the former Slovak Evangelical Lutheran Church (organized 1902), were assimilated into the LCMS in 1964 and 1971 respectively.

During the 1960s and early 1970s, tensions arose over the proper interpretation of the Synod's traditional confessional stance. Controversy centered around issues of biblical interpretation and authority, as well as ecumenical relationships with other Lutheran and non-Lutheran denominations. The controversy culminated in 1974 during the presidency of J. A. O. Preus (president, 1969-1981), when the majority of students and faculty at Concordia Seminary, St. Louis, walked out and formed the Christ Seminary-Seminex and the Association of Evangelical Lutheran Churches. The group comprised four per cent of the Synod's membership.

The Synod trains pastors in two seminaries: Concordia in St. Louis, Missouri (founded 1839), and Concordia in Fort Wayne, Indiana (founded 1846). It also offers college-level programs at more than a dozen campuses, chiefly for the training of parish schoolteachers and for preparing men for seminary study. These colleges have expanded into general liberal arts colleges since 1970.

In the 1980s, under the presidency of Ralph A. Bohlmann, the Synod continues its commitment to a strict interpretation of the Lutheran confessions,

a strong educational program at every level and a firm commitment to evangelism and missions. In 1986 the membership numbered 2.7 million, making it the second-largest Lutheran denomination in the U.S.

See also LUTHERAN CHURCHES; LUTHERAN TRADITION.

BIBLIOGRAPHY. W. O. Forster, *Zion on the Mississippi, The Settlement of the Saxon Lutherans in Missouri, 1839-1841* (1953); F. D. Lueking, *Mission in the Making, The Missionary Enterprise among Missouri Synod Lutherans, 1846-1963* (1964); C. S. Meyer, *Moving Frontiers, Readings in the History of the LCMS* (1964); C. S. Meyer, *Log Cabin to Luther Tower, Concordia Seminary 1839-1964* (1965); M. L. Rudnick, *Fundamentalism & the Missouri Synod* (1966). R. A. Kolb

Lutheran Council in Canada. A cooperative organization of Lutheran* denominations* in Canada. The story behind the Lutheran Council in Canada (LCC) goes back at least to 1940, when the Canadian Lutheran Commission for War Service was begun. Joint work in home mission was projected in 1944 and plans for a Canadian Lutheran Council (CLC) materialized in 1952. Paralleling these developments was Canadian Lutheran World Relief (CLWR, 1946). Its resettlement of post-War displaced persons and others involved extension to Europe and cooperation with governmental agencies as well as with the Lutheran World Federation* based in Geneva. Embracing these and other functions, The Lutheran Council in Canada was formed in 1967 and relocated in 1985 from Winnipeg to Toronto. At the time of its formation, the LCC included such activities as missions, chaplaincies, social service, public relations, theological studies and work among university students and faculty. It serves the participating church bodies in their dealings with the federal government (Ottawa) and in their ecumenical interests of nationwide scope—most of which have an organizational base in Toronto. The LCC has contributed significantly to the growth and unity of the Lutheran constituency and to its cooperation with other Canadian communions.

As the movement for Lutheran union has advanced, the LCC has diminished. Its functions have been assumed by the now two major bodies: the Evangelical Lutheran Church in Canada, launched in 1985, and the Lutheran Church-Canada, which expects to be autonomous from its parent, Lutheran Church-Missouri Synod,* in 1989. For Canada's 300,000 Lutherans (gathered in 1,050 congregations, and served by approximately 720 parish pastors), the LCC in decline—paradoxically— holds the promise of still fuller church union.

See also LUTHERAN CHURCHES IN AMERICA.

BIBLIOGRAPHY. N. J. Threinen, *Fifty Years of Lutheran Convergence: The Canadian Case Study (1919-1969)* (1983). E. T. Bachmann

Lutheran Tradition in America. The churches and culture derived from northern Europe and transplanted to the United States make up a religious tradition that has had considerable influence on the nation.

The very concept of European transplantation is of considerable importance, because in the Scandinavian nations or in the parts of Germany from whence the vast majority of the American Lutheran ancestry derives, Lutheranism was the dominant, established,* state-supported religion. In America, while it has attracted millions of participants, Lutheranism has been a minority in a culture more shaped by Reformed* Protestantism,* Roman Catholicism* and the religious ethos of the Enlightenment.* The act of surviving and prospering in such an environment has led to considerable adjustment and adaptation.

Three Theological Motifs. Doctrinally, the Lutheran tradition in America has perpetuated the historic outlook of its European ancestry. In the eyes of great numbers of its articulators, at the heart of this theological tradition are three great motifs of the sixteenth-century Reformation led by the German Martin Luther, after which the movement of churches is named.

The first of these is *sola gratia,* the concept that a person is saved (from sin,* eternal death, the devil) solely by the divine initiative, which reaches a person as an act of grace or unmerited favor. Second is *sola fide,* which means that the bond between God and the redeemed is formed entirely by faith. This faith means trust in the promises of God, reliance on the trustworthy character of God and a willingness to forgo all notions of a claim upon God that a person merits because of his or her spiritual, intellectual or moral achievements.

Associated with this combined central notion that one is "saved by grace through faith" is another accent, *sola scriptura.* This means for the Lutheran tradition in America that the canonical books of the Bible* are the only source and norm for Christian teaching. Negatively it means that Lutherans are not to base any essential teaching on any source that does not itself derive from the clear witness of Scripture. Positively it means that this tradition has a very high view of biblical authority, setting the Scriptures qualitatively apart from all other writings.

There have been controversies over the nature of this biblical authority. Many theologians argue that the claim of Scripture on the hearts and minds of the faithful results from the fact, as Martin Luther had said, that the Bible "presses Christ," or "is the cradle in which Christ lies." This means that the Holy Spirit brings one to faith, and because of this Christ-centered trust in God, one accepts the full authority of the Bible, the unique and "divinely inspired" witness.

Another strand of Lutheranism, influenced more by the surrounding Reformed evangelical* culture and more eager to resist the approaches of modern "higher criticism" of the Bible, stresses that this authority and the divine inspiration of the Bible center in the concept of the "inerrancy"* of the Bible. The source for this teaching in Lutheranism is less the writings of Martin Luther than the scholastic tradition of seventeenth-century Lutheranism. In that period, dogmaticians at German universities located the doctrine of Scripture at the beginning of their systems. In effect, they first witnessed to or set out to "prove" the inerrancy of the Bible as a kind of first principle, rather than to speak of it in connection with the doctrine of the Incarnate Word, Jesus Christ.

This choice by some Lutherans to stress the inerrancy of the Bible also in matters of historical and geographical detail, of concerns with scientific and natural matters, has led to disputes and even schisms within the tradition in America. Some Lutheran bodies, most notably the Lutheran Church—Missouri Synod* and the Wisconsin Evangelical Lutheran Synod*—which together make up about three of the more than eight million Lutherans in America—stand apart from the rest in large measure because of their insistence on inerrancy.

Confessionalism. If there are arguments over the nature of biblical authority (as there have seldom been over justification by grace through faith), so too there have been some differences over the nature of Lutheranism's "confessionalism."* When Lutherans speak of confessions and confessionalism in this context, they refer to the fact that their churches and members respond to the ecumenical creeds of the early Christian centuries and the formal writings of the Lutheran churches in the sixteenth century, writings that together make up *The Book of Concord* of 1580. Not all American Lutherans treat all the writings of this book equally. They are most concerned with Martin Luther's *Small Catechism* and *Large Catechism* and the decisive Augsburg Confession* of

1530, which they believe best condense and set forth the central themes of the faith.

To more moderate Lutherans, fidelity to these confessions is expected *quatenus,* in so far as they agree with Scripture. The more conservative groups, led and typified by the Missouri Synod, claim loyalty *quia,* because these writings agree completely with Scripture. This latter claim has not always led to literalism about interpreting these confessions. Thus the teaching that the Roman pope* is the "Antichrist" prophesied by Scripture is held to with less vigor, even by the Missouri Synod people, than it was by their ancestors in America or by Martin Luther, who introduced that interpretation of Scripture into the confessional tradition.

Lutheran Tradition/American Experience. Lutherans in America have adopted various polities.* In some European nations, particularly Sweden, bishops* are of the essence *(esse)* of the church, while elsewhere they have been seen as beneficial *(bene esse).* This means that in Sweden the bishops are seen to be in the Apostolic Succession,* whereas elsewhere they have belonged simply to the good order of church governance.

None of the groups that came to America retained the historic Episcopate and its accompanying claim of apostolic succession. However, for late twentieth-century Lutherans, particularly in the Evangelical Lutheran Church in America (formed officially in 1988), the leaders of the synods* and the highest elected officer of the whole body are called bishops. Lutheran polity in America has been quite varied. There is considerable accent on the powers and responsibilities of local congregations. Yet in the vast majority of the Lutheran bodies through American history, there has also been linkage with others, usually through synodical polity. Lutherans like to speak of "the priesthood of all believers" and to assure that the laity* has considerable voice in Lutheran affairs and especially in congregational and synodical life.

Geographically, Lutherans have been more at home in the American North than in the South. While they have never been established (by law) in and of the United States, there are particularly thick concentrations of Lutheran congregations in Pennsylvania and surrounding states where Lutherans have been at home in colonial times (*See* Pennsylvania Ministerium). In certain areas of the Upper Midwest, notably Minnesota, Wisconsin and the Dakotas, there have even been numerical and cultural dominances by Lutherans.

Lutherans have not made a cultural impact commensurate with their size in America in part because of their relatively late arrival on the American scene after the mid-nineteenth century; because most of them came speaking German or Scandinavian languages and not English; and because they inherited traditions of political passivity from Europe. They have perpetuated European traditions of loyalty to the government, a loyalty that was tested when those of German background were often accused of lack of enthusiasm for a war against Germany in 1917 to 1918. Few of them have risen to positions of political leadership until recent years.

Lutherans are at home with what Americans like to call "the separation of church and state,"* though such separation between civil and religious authority has not been characteristic of the largely Lutheran nations of Europe. In America they have not sought political versions of what H. Richard Niebuhr* calls "Christ transforming culture" and have generally resisted Social Gospel* language about "bringing in the Kingdom of God."* They are not progressives about the social and cultural orders, believing that the demonic pervades these orders and all structures of fallen human existence. They do believe, however, that Christians are called to responsibility and care for neighbors, to work for justice and to engage in acts of mercy in the human city.

The Lutheran tradition has been more at ease with cultural expression in the arts than it has been with identifying certain political and social movements as being especially God-pleasing. The Lutheran churches are "singing churches," inheriting as they do Martin Luther's love for music. Many of them have chosen in recent decades to express themselves through often excellent contemporary architecture.* They have established a considerable number of colleges where cultural expression and the liberal arts receive attention.

The Lutheran tradition in America goes back to colonial times, when Lutherans arrived in the middle colonies, especially to Pennsylvania, which was generally hospitable to the non-English-speaking immigrants. The majority arrived from Germany, portions of central Europe, the Baltic nations and especially Scandinavia, after the 1830s and beyond World War 2* when many displaced persons arrived. In recent decades Lutherans have made considerable effort to downplay their reliance on ethnic heritages and to be inclusive. The Evangelical Lutheran Church in America even established quota systems for many levels of representation and leadership to show its hospitality to a variety of ethnic and racial lineages.

Lutherans all proclaim that they are part of the "one, holy, catholic, apostolic church," and the Evangelical Lutheran Church in America is a vigorous participant in a variety of expressions of the modern ecumenical movement.* The tradition is thoroughly at home in America, and its perpetuators rarely look back for source, model or sustenance to the northern Europe from which their foreparents came.

See also LUTHERAN CHURCHES IN AMERICA; IMMIGRATION AND ETHNICITY, PROTESTANT.

BIBLIOGRAPHY. C. Bergendoff, *The Church of the Lutheran Reformation: A Historical Survey of Lutheranism* (1967); J. H. Groh and R. H. Smith, eds., *The Lutheran Church in North American Life* (1979); E. C. Nelson, *Lutheranism in North America, 1914-1970* (1972); E. C. Nelson, *The Rise of World Lutheranism: An American Perspective* (1982); E. C. Nelson, *The Lutherans in North America* (1975); R. W. Solberg, *Lutheran Higher Education in North America* (1985); J. H. Tietjen, *Which Way to Lutheran Unity?* (1966); R. C. Wolf, *Documents of Lutheran Unity in North America* (1966). M. E. Marty

Lutheran World Federation. A free association of ninety-nine Lutheran churches* from fifty countries. The Lutheran World Federation succeeded the Lutheran World Convention that met in 1923, 1929 and 1935 as a result of contacts made by American and European Lutheran leaders in post-World War 1* relief efforts. The Assembly meets every six years, and commissions function continuously from the headquarters in Geneva.

Cooperative theological study, exchange of scholars, and the translation and publication of important theological literature is done to cultivate Lutheran unity. International coordination of interchurch aid, service to refugees and other emergency work is the responsibility of the Department of Lutheran World Service. World missions* goals have expanded from care of orphaned missions and coordination of outreach to encouragement of Lutheran churches in Third World countries and aid to Lutherans behind the Iron Curtain. The Federation has no legislative authority but has served to unite fifty-four million of the world's sixty-eight million Lutherans in many cooperative endeavors.

BIBLIOGRAPHY. C. P. Lutz, *Abounding in Hope: A Family of Faith at Work through the Lutheran World Federation* (1985).

J. D. Sutherland

Lutheran-Catholic Dialog. Lutheran-Catholic dialog in the U.S. began in July 1965. Representatives are appointed by the United States Roman Catholic Bishops' Committee for Ecumenical and Interreligious Affairs and by Lutheran World Ministries (the United States National Committee of the Lutheran World Federation*). A Catholic* and a Lutheran* co-chairpersons have presided at virtually each of the biennial meetings.

Lutheran representatives have represented the three major Lutheran bodies in America: the Lutheran Church—Missouri Synod (LCMS),* the Lutheran Church in America (LCA)* and the American Lutheran Church (ALC).* With the merger of the last two named groups on January 1, 1988, into the Evangelical Lutheran Church in America (ELCA), arrangements have been made for continuing the same breadth of representation.

Seven rounds of theological discussion had been completed by 1987, and the eighth was in progress. Common statements resulting from each completed round have been published, together with some of the preliminary essays. Round I considered "The Status of the Nicene Creed as Dogma of the Church." Successive topics discussed in later rounds were: Round II, "One Baptism for the Remission of Sins"; Round III, "The Eucharist as Sacrifice"; Round IV, "Eucharist and Ministry"; Round V, "Papal Primacy and the Universal Church"; Round VI, "Teaching Authority and Infallibility in the Church"; and Round VII, "Justification by Faith." Round VIII considers Mary and the saints.

Though the dialog has been widely hailed by the press as an ecumenical breakthrough and celebrated by theologians for their depth of theological investigation, assessments differ on the degree of consensus achieved, and it remains unclear precisely for whom the participants speak. The published documents on justification by faith have been strongly criticized, and by some who would not be considered anti-ecumenical in principle. Conservatives on both sides have generally been more critical of the dialogs or given them little attention.

A significant issue in the recent merger discussions between the American Lutheran Church and Lutheran Church in America has been whether the future of Lutheranism lies in further overtures toward the Catholic Church or in further identification with mainline American Protestantism.

BIBLIOGRAPHY. P. C. Empie and T. A. Murphy, eds., *Lutherans and Catholics in Dialogue I-III* (n.d.); P. C. Empie and T. A. Murphy, eds., *Eucharist & Ministry* (1979); P. C. Empie and T. A.

Murphy, eds., *Papal Primacy and The Universal Church* (1974); P. C. Empie, T. A. Murphy and J. A. Burgess, eds., *Teaching Authority & Infallibility in the Church* (1978); K. G. Anderson, T. A. Murphy and J. A. Burgess, eds., *Justification by Faith* (1985).   H. D. Hummel

Lutheranism. *See* LUTHERAN TRADITION.

Lyman, Eugene William (1872-1948). Philosopher of religion and theologian.* Born in Cummington, Massachusetts, in a distinguished New England line, Lyman graduated from Amherst (B.A., 1894), where he was influenced by the personalistic idealism of Charles Edward Garman. After teaching Latin for two years, Lyman attended Yale* Divinity School (B.D., 1899), followed by two years of study (1899-1901) at the universities of Halle, Berlin and Marburg. Ordained* into the Congregational* ministry in 1901, Lyman in that year began teaching, first at Carleton College (1901-1904), followed by the Congregational Church College of Canada (1904-1905), Bangor Theological Seminary (1905 1913), Oberlin School of Theology (1913-1918) and finally Union Theological Seminary,* New York (1918-1940).

Raised in a family influenced by Horace Bushnell's* theology,* his own avid reading of Bushnell, Theodore Munger* and Washington Gladden,* as well as his study in Germany cemented him in the liberalism* of the Social Gospel* that dominated turn-of-the-century American Protestant thought. His *The Meaning and Truth of Religion* (1933), appearing the same year as Reinhold Niebuhr's* *Moral Man and Immoral Society,* argued for the role of intuition in grasping moral values and revealed truth and for viewing God as a cosmic, creative spirit.

BIBLIOGRAPHY. *DAB* 4; D. E. Roberts and H. P. VanDusen, eds., *Liberal Theology, An Appraisal: Essays in Honor of Eugene William Lyman* (1942);

W. K. Cauthen, *The Impact of American Religious Liberalism* (1962).   C. H. Lippy

Lyon, Mary (1797-1849). Founder of Mount Holyoke College. Born in Buckland, Massachusetts, Lyon spent the early part of her life attending and teaching in a variety of schools and academies in the western part of Massachusetts. Lyon taught at several schools, including the Adams Female Seminary in Londonderry, New Hampshire. Baptized in 1822, she joined the Congregational* church in Buckland. By 1828 she had devoted herself to teaching at Ipswich Female Seminary, but she resigned in 1834 in order to fulfill her vision of founding a residential seminary for young adult women. It was to be a permanent institution, established on a sound financial basis through the generosity of the "Christian public." In 1835 she helped found Wheaton Female Seminary in Norton, Massachusetts (now Wheaton College), but in 1836 she founded Mount Holyoke Female Seminary (Mount Holyoke College), which flourished under her inspired leadership. Lyon served both as a teacher and principal of the seminary, and her methods in both roles were innovative. The students performed their own domestic work and were taught a rigorous curriculum, which included science, mathematics, history and theology.* Discussion and questions replaced the customary rote memorization. Lyon's only book, *A Missionary Offering* (1843), was a plea for the missionary* cause. Her educational endeavors were motivated by the same spirit: Mount Holyoke was to carry forward "the salvation of the world" by preparing women to take part in the creation of a Christian America.

BIBLIOGRAPHY. *DAB* VI; E. A. Green, *Mary Lyon and Mount Holyoke* (1979); E. Hitchcock, *The Power of Christian Benevolence, Illustrated in the Life and Labors of Mary Lyon* (1858); *NAW* 2.
                    B. J. MacHaffie

M

Mabie, Henry Clay (1847-1918). Northern Baptist* pastor* and missionary* leader. Born in Belvedere, Illinois, Mabie was encouraged to go into the ministry by his British pastor, Charles Hill Roe, whose daughter he later married. After attending Chicago University and Seminary, Mabie served ably as pastor of Baptist churches in Rockford (1869-1873) and Oak Park (1873-1875), Illinois; Boston (1876-1879); Indianapolis (1879-1883); St. Paul (1885-1888); and Minneapolis (1889-1890). A strong supporter of the missionary cause among Baptists, he attended the World Missionary Conference in London in 1888.

In 1890 he was elected as the Home Secretary of the American Baptist Missionary Union (later called American Baptist Foreign Mission Society*). In this capacity he traveled extensively to mission sites around the world. Mabie was also a prolific writer and apologist for the missionary cause. Among his better-known books are: *The Meaning and Message of the Cross* (1906), *The Divine Right of Missions* (1908) and *The Task Worth While* (1910).

In matters of denominational controversy, Mabie sympathized with the fundamentalists* against the modernists* and protested the move toward centralization in the Northern Baptist Convention, which, he felt, undermined the voluntary character of the Missionary Union. In later years, Mabie lectured widely in Baptist colleges and seminaries* and served as sometime professor at Rochester Theological Seminary.

BIBLIOGRAPHY. H. C. Mabie, *From Romance to Reality* (1917). T. F. George

McAlister, Robert Edward (1880-1953). Canadian Pentecostal* leader. Born and raised in a Scottish immigrant family in Cobden, Ontario, in his early twenties, McAlister attended a Bible college* in Cincinnati, Ohio, and worked with the "Holiness Movement* Church." In 1906 he went to Los Angeles to investigate the Azusa Street* revival* and returned to Canada to promote Pentecostalism. He was involved in a revival in 1908 in the

Ottawa Valley and began publishing two short-lived religious journals.

One of the founders of the Pentecostal Assemblies of Canada* in 1919, he was its first general secretary-treasurer until 1937 and the founding editor (1920-1937) of *The Pentecostal Testimony,* the denomination's official organ. In the 1910s McAlister promoted the "Jesus Only" doctrine of Oneness Pentecostalism. The denomination* initially embraced this teaching, but in 1920, under pressure from the Assemblies of God (U.S.A.),* it repudiated the view.

BIBLIOGRAPHY. G. G. Kulbeck, *What God Hath Wrought* (1958); W. E. McAlister, "Called Home," *Pentecostal Testimony* 34 (November 1953):3.

D. M. Lewis

Macartney, Clarence Edward Noble (1879-1957). Fundamentalist* Presbyterian* preacher.* Coming from a line of Scottish Covenanters, Macartney entered the Presbyterian ministry* after earning degrees from the University of Wisconsin, Princeton University* and Princeton Theological Seminary.* He served churches in Patterson, New Jersey (1905-1914), Philadelphia (1914-1927) and Pittsburgh (1927-1953). In 1925 he declined an appointment to the chair of apologetics* at Princeton Seminary.

In 1922 Macartney led the conservative response to Harry Emerson Fosdick's* famous sermon "Shall the Fundamentalists Win?" and in 1924 won election as moderator of the General Assembly.* A steadfast opponent of liberal* theology,* he supported the formation of Westminster Theological Seminary after the Princeton reorganization in 1929. In the 1930s, when his most militant colleagues seceded, Macartney chose to maintain a conservative witness within the denomination.*

Macartney authored fifty-seven books, most of which were collections of sermons, and traveled widely at home and abroad. He was a vocal opponent of Sabbath* desecration, divorce, liquor and birth control.* Macartney was a popular lecturer and preacher at colleges and seminaries.*

BIBLIOGRAPHY. C. E. Macartney, *The Making of a Minister: The Autobiography of Clarence E. Macartney,* ed. J. C. Henry (1961); C. A. Russell, *Voices of American Fundamentalism: Seven Biographical Studies* (1976).

B. J. Longfield

McAuley, Jeremiah (1839-1884). Evangelist* and founder of New York's Water Street Mission.* Born in County Kerry, Ireland, McAuley was abandoned by his parents at age thirteen, and that same year he made his way to New York. Battling for survival in America's largest city, young McAuley spent four years in crime. He was arrested in 1857 for robbery and sentenced to fifteen years in the state penitentiary.

After five years in Sing Sing, McAuley was converted* to faith in Christ. Two years later (1864) the governor pardoned him. For the next few years the ex-convict held odd jobs and did the work of an evangelist. Then in 1872, with a financial stake from wealthy Christian friends, the thirty-three-year-old McAuley founded the Helping Hand for Men Mission on New York's Lower East Side, in the Bowery district. One of the first city rescue missions,* this institution, renamed Water Street Mission in 1876, became a model for similar facilities all over urban America.

In 1882 a second rescue mission, the Cremorne Mission, was opened in New York City. This facility and Water Street Mission gained national attention because of the effectiveness of the work. Christians throughout urban America learned about activities and ministries through "Jerry McAuley's Newspaper." One of the first mission newsletters, it became a model of its kind. McAuley died of tuberculosis in New York City at the age of forty-five.

See also RESCUE MISSION MOVEMENT; WATER STREET AND BOWERY MISSIONS.

BIBLIOGRAPHY. *DAB* VI; J. McAuley, *The History of a River Thief* (1876); N. Magnuson, *Salvation in the Slums: Evangelical Social Work, 1865-1920* (1977); R. M. Offord, *Jerry McAuley* (1907).

L. W. Dorsett

McAvoy, Thomas Timothy (1903-1969). Catholic* historian. Born in Tipton, Indiana, McAvoy graduated from Notre Dame (B.A., 1925) and joined the Congregation of Holy Cross* in 1925. After further studies at College of the Holy Cross, Washington, D.C., he was ordained* a Roman Catholic priest* in 1929. Assigned by his religious superiors in 1929 to organize The Catholic Archives of America at the University of Notre Dame, over the next forty years he supervised the cataloging and expansion of this collection. During that period he earned an M.A. (1930) from Notre Dame and a Ph.D. from Columbia Unversity (1940). A cofounder of *The Review of Politics,* McAvoy also taught history at Notre Dame from 1933.

As an historian of American Catholicism, McAvoy argued that U.S. Catholics were a minority group held together by a common faith and order of worship.* An amalgam of immigrants,* the Catholic minority had been influenced by an Anglo-American elite augmented over the years by American Protestant converts of English stock whose spirit and leadership enabled the Catholic Church to adapt to American culture. He is best known for *The Great Crisis in American Catholic History, 1895-1900* (1957) and *A History of the Catholic Church in the United States* (1969).

BIBLIOGRAPHY. J. D. Thomas, "A Century of American Catholic History," *USCH* 6 (1987): 25-50; F. J. Weber, "Thomas T. McAvoy, C.S.C.: Historian of American Catholicism," *Indiana Magazine of History* 44 (1968):15-24.

J. T. Connelly

McClain, Alva J. (1888-1968). Brethren* educator and theologian.* Born in Aurelia, Iowa, McClain moved west with his family to Arizona and California and settled in Sunnyside, Washington. Converted* in 1911 under the revival* preaching* of Louis S. Bauman,* he transferred from the University of Washington to the Bible Institute of Los Angeles (BIOLA). While there he attended Bauman's Long Beach church (1911-1915). While studying for a diploma in theology* (1917) at Xenia Theological Seminary, Ohio, McClain pastored churches in Clayton, Miamisburg and Dayton, Ohio. Ordained* to the ministry in 1917, he became pastor of the First Brethren Church in Philadelphia, Pennsylvania (1918-1923). While in Philadelphia, McClain became known as a spokesperson for the fundamentalist* wing of the Brethren Church, and taught at Philadelphia School of the Bible (1919-1923). In 1925 McClain returned to California to finish his college degree at Occidental College (1925). He then became a professor in the undergraduate seminary of Ashland College, Ohio (1925-1927), but soon returned to teach at BIOLA (1927-1929), while serving also as Minister of Education at the First Brethren Church of Long Beach.

Involved in the founding of the Brethren's Ashland Theological Seminary (1930), McClain spent several years as professor of theology, associate dean and dean of the seminary (1930-1937). Due to his desire for theological and social conformity to fundamentalist views, he came into conflict with the school's administration and was dismissed in June 1937. The following October, Grace Theological Seminary opened in Akron, Ohio, as another Brethren institution, with McClain as president and professor of theology. The existence of the two seminaries helped polarize the Brethren Church, resulting in a 1939 division along Grace and Ashland lines. Prior to 1939 he served two terms as moderator of the denomination. In 1939 Grace Seminary moved to Winona Lake, Indiana, and in 1948 Grace College was established. He resigned his position in 1962.

An advocate of dispensational* premillennialism,* McClain served as a member of the revision committee of the Scofield Reference Bible* (1954-1963). His writings include *Daniel's Prophecy of Seventy Weeks* (1940), *Law and the Christian in Relation to the Doctrine of Grace* (1954) and *The Greatness of the Kingdom (1959).*

BIBLIOGRAPHY. H. A. Hoyt, "McClain, Alva J.," *Brethren Encyclopedia,* Vol. 2; N. B. Rohrer, *A Saint in Glory Stands* (1986).   R. T. Clutter

McCloskey, John (1810-1885). First U.S. Catholic* cardinal* and archbishop* of the New York archdiocese. Born in Brooklyn, New York, the son of Irish immigrant parents, McCloskey became the first native of New York State to enter the diocesan priesthood. Educated at Mt. St. Mary's College and Seminary, he was ordained in 1834 and spent the next three years studying in Rome. Serving first as pastor of St. Joseph's Church, Sixth Avenue, in New York City, McCloskey became professor of philosophy at the first seminary* (Nyack, New York) of the diocese, and the first president (1841) of St. John's College (later to become Fordham University). He was instrumental in the conversion to Roman Catholicism of many prominent Americans: James Roosevelt Bayley* (1842), later archbishop of Baltimore; Isaac Hecker* (1844), later founder of the Paulists*; Clarence Walworth,* a prominent Paulist; and James McMaster (1845), editor of the *Freeman's Journal and Catholic Register.* After a stint as bishop of Albany, New York, he became archbishop of New York on May 6, 1864. A participant at Vatican Council I* in Rome (1869-1870), he was a member of the commission on discipline and opposed a definition of papal infallibility,* arguing that it was inopportune, though he later voted for the definition.

BIBLIOGRAPHY. *DAB* VI.   T. F. Sable

McCloskey, William George (1823-1909). First rector of the North American College, Rome, and bishop* of Louisville. Born in Brooklyn of Irish parentage, McCloskey was educated at Mt. St.

Mary's College and Seminary, Maryland, and ordained* priest* October 6, 1852. After nine years as rector in Rome (1859-1868), he was appointed to Louisville March 3, 1868, and began a career (1868-1909) marked by authoritarian rule and widespread clerical discontent. As bishop of the primal see of the Midwest and Upper South, he also alienated many of the religious communities within his jurisdiction, once placing a motherhouse under an interdict because of an insurance dispute. Even though he was an example of the growing "romanization" of the Catholic* Church in America in the nineteenth century, he at first considered the promulgation of papal infallibility* at the First Vatican Council* to be inopportune. Several appeals about his decisions were sent to Rome, and his actions overturned. He died as a senior member of the American Catholic hierarchy.

BIBLIOGRAPHY. C. F. Crews, *An American Holy Land: A History of the Archdiocese of Louisville* (1987); *DAB* VI.   C. F. Crews

McComb, Samuel (1864-1938). Clergyman* and pastoral counselor. Born in Londonderry, Northern Ireland, McComb studied theology* at Magee College in Londonderry and Oxford University. After a time in the pastoral ministry, McComb became professor of church history at Queen's University at Kingston, Ontario.

In 1905, McComb, who had an interest in psychology, joined Elwood Worcester* of the Emmanuel Church in Boston in a new effort to provide counseling to troubled individuals using a combination of contemporary psychological knowledge, a medical understanding of mental illness and liberal* Protestant theology. McComb became closely identified with this endeavor and collaborated with Worcester on several books, perhaps the most important of which was *Religion and Medicine, The Moral Control of Nervous Disorders* (1908). McComb was involved with the Emmanuel Movement until 1916 when he became rector of the American Episcopal Church in Nice, France. He died in Cheltenham, England, in 1938. *See also* PASTORAL CARE.

BIBLIOGRAPHY. E. B. Holifield, *A History of Pastoral Care in America* (1983); R. C. Powell, "Healing and Wholeness: Helen Flanders Dunbar (1902-59) and an Extra-Medical Origin of the American Psychosomatic Movement, 1906-1936" (unpublished Ph.D. dissertation, Duke University, 1974).   S. B. Thielman

McConnell, Francis John (1871-1953). Methodist* bishop.* Born in Trinway, Ohio, the son of a Methodist minister* who served nine parishes in seventeen years, McConnell was educated at Ohio Wesleyan and Boston University School of Theology (B.D., 1897) where he earned his Ph.D in philosophy under Borden Parker Bowne* (1899). He served churches in West Chelmsford (1894-1897), Newton Upper Falls (1897-1899), Ipswich (1899-1902) and Cambridge (1902-1903), Massachusetts, as well as Brooklyn, New York (1903-1909). In 1909 he became president of DePauw University, leaving that post in 1912 when he was elected bishop. As bishop he presided in Denver, Pittsburgh and New York (1912-1944).

McConnell was active in ecumenical affairs and was president of the Federal Council of Churches* (1928-1932). He was also interested in social reform and served as president of the Methodist Federation for Social Service, whose purpose, he said, was to raise disturbing questions—ahead of time. In 1919 he chaired a commission of the Interchurch World Movement,* which investigated the Steel Strike of 1919. The commission's report was largely supportive of the strikers.

McConnell wrote many books and articles on religion and public life. His ideas were not precise or systematic, but he stressed what he believed were practical, prudent, reasonable responses to the social issues of his time. Believing human nature to be basically wise, benevolent and unselfish, he thought it possible to gradually transform society into a Christian community.

BIBLIOGRAPHY. *DAB* 5; *DARB*; J. N. Hughley, *Trends in Protestant Social Idealism* (1948); F. J. McConnell, *By the Way* (1952); *NCAB* 15.

L. W. Japinga

McCorkle, Samuel Eusebius (1746-1811).

Presbyterian* minister* and educator. After graduating from the College of New Jersey (B.A., 1772), he prepared for the ministry with his uncle, Joseph Montgomery of Delaware and Pennsylvania, and thereafter served as pastor of Thyatira Church in Rowan County, North Carolina, and as a teacher at Salisbury Academy and his own Zion-Parnassus Academy. As a trustee at the young University of North Carolina, he tried unsuccessfully to mold that school in the likeness of John Witherspoon's* College of New Jersey.* In the 1790s he published doctrinal works on deism,* Communion,* Sabbath* observance, sacrificing and charity in order to raise funds for the University. He addressed broader social and political themes in *A Sermon On the Comparative Happiness and Duty of the United States Contrasted with . . . the Israelites* (1795), *The Work of God for the French Republic* (1798), and *True Greatness: A Sermon on the Death of Gen. George Washington* (1800). His cautious appraisals of the revivals* of 1802 were published by James Hall. His brother-in-law was the noted Federalist congressman John Steele.

BIBLIOGRAPHY. W. F. Craven, "Samuel Eusebius McCorkle," in *Princetonians, 1769-1775: A Biographical Dictionary,* ed. R. Harrison (1980); T. T. Taylor, "Samuel E. McCorkle and a Christian Republic, 1792-1802." *American Presbyterians: The Journal of Presbyterian History* 63 (1985):375-385.

T. T. Taylor

McCormick, Cyrus Hall (1809-1884).

Presbyterian* philanthropist.* Building on the labors of his father, Robert, a Virginia planter and mechanical genius, Cyrus invented the mechanical reaper in 1831, a machine which revolutionized farming in the American plains and made the U.S. the world's leading producer of wheat. His organizational and business skills enabled McCormick to accumulate a fortune through his manufacturing of reapers, headquartered in Chicago.

A devout Old School* Presbyterian layman,* McCormick used his wealth to fund educational enterprises, influencing Presbyterianism in both the North and South. His financial gift helped to establish a seminary* in Chicago in 1859, which eventually took his name. He also contributed significant sums to Washington and Lee University and Union Theological Seminary, both in Virginia. Under his control during the 1870s, *The Interior* of Chicago strongly promoted Presbyterianism in the old Northwest. Staunchly conservative, both theologically and socially, McCormick vigorously opposed efforts to depart from or modify Old School Calvinism* within American Presbyterianism.

BIBLIOGRAPHY. H. N. Casson, *Cyrus Hall McCormick: His Life and Work* (1909); *DAB* VI.

G. S. Smith

McCosh, James (1811-1894).

Presbyterian* minister,* philosopher and college president. Born in Scotland and educated at the universities of Glasgow (1824-1829) and Edinburgh (M.A., 1834), McCosh served as a Presbyterian minister from 1835 to 1852. As such, he sided with Thomas Chalmers and the insurgent evangelical party in the Disruption of 1843, leading to the creation of the Free Church of Scotland. The second phase of his career began in 1852 when McCosh became professor of logic and metaphysics at Queen's College in Belfast, Ireland (1852-1868). For the next sixteen years he was immersed in the leading philosophical debates of his age.

Widely regarded as the last major voice of the philosophical realism of the Scottish Enlightenment, McCosh attempted throughout his diversified career to fuse the best modern thinking with a lively evangelical* faith. Influenced by Sir William Hamilton's restatement of Scottish Common Sense Realism* in a neo-Kantian framework, McCosh's own "intuitional realism" labored to counteract German idealism, David Hume's skepticism and John Stuart Mill's sensationalism. His most significant contributions came in *The Intuitions of the Mind* (1860) and *The Scottish Philosophy* (1875).

McCosh's impact upon American Christianity became more direct after 1868 when he was appointed president of the College of New Jersey* and thus culminated his career in the U.S. During his two-decade tenure (1868-1888) at Princeton, he helped transform a fledgling, parochial college into a national university. Though McCosh was an early advocate in America for reconciling Christian orthodoxy* and Darwinism,* an ardent defender of revivalism* and a tireless academic reformer and administrator, his legacy, nonetheless, was not successful in preserving a role for Scottish realism among American intellectuals nor in maintaining Princeton's evangelical heritage.

BIBLIOGRAPHY. *DAB* VI; *DARB;* J. D. Hoeveler, Jr., "Evangelical Ecumenism: James McCosh and the Intellectual Origins of the World Alliance of Reformed Churches," *JPH* 55 (Spring 1977): 58-73; J. D. Hoeveler, Jr., *James McCosh and the Scottish Intellectual Tradition* (1981); *NCAB* 5; W. M. Sloane, ed., *The Life of James McCosh: A Record Chiefly Autobiographical* (1896).

S. R. Pointer

McCracken. Robert (J)ames (1904-1973). Baptist* preacher.* Born in Motherwell, Scotland, McCracken studied at the University of Glasgow (M.A., 1925; B.D., 1928). He then served the Marshall Street Baptist Church, Edinburgh (1928-1932), and the Dennistown Baptist Church, Glasgow (1932-1938), and taught systematic theology* at Baptist Theological College, Glasgow. In 1937 McCracken served as a delegate to the World Conference on Faith and Order at Edinburgh.

In 1938 he moved to Ontario and became professor of Christian theology and philosophy of religion at McMaster University, Hamilton, Ontario (1938-1946). In 1946 he succeeded Harry Emerson Fosdick* as minister of the Riverside Church, New York City, where he preached until he retired in 1967. During his time at Riverside, McCracken

taught homiletics at Union Theological Seminary in New York and delivered the Sprunt Lectures at Union Theological Seminary,* Virginia (1952), the Stone Lectures at Princeton Theological Seminary* (1954) and the Shaffer Lectures at Yale University* (1957).

Among his publications were: *Questions People Ask* (1951), *The Making of the Sermon* (1956), *Putting Faith to Work* (1960) and *What Is Sin? What Is Virtue?* (1966). As a preacher, McCracken brought to the American pulpit the gift of classic Scottish oratory combined with an emphasis on the biblical text.

BIBLIOGRAPHY. C. Fant and W. Pinson, Jr., ed., *20 Centuries of Great Preaching* (1971).

D. Macleod

McCulloch, Thomas (1776-1843). Canadian Presbyterian* minister,* educator and writer. Born and educated in Scotland, McCulloch was ordained* a Presbyterian minister in 1799 and sent as a missionary* to British North America in 1803. Settling in Pictou, Nova Scotia, he immediately turned his attention to education, deploring the low level of instruction available and the Anglican control of higher education in the colony. In 1816 he established his Pictou Academy, soon recognized as one of the finest schools in British North America. Here McCulloch took the first important steps to educate a native Presbyterian clergy* and laid the foundations of what would eventually become Pine Hill Divinity College (in Halifax, Nova Scotia). His pre-eminence as a teacher was recognized with his appointment in 1838 as the first principal of Dalhousie College.

Through the public press, McCulloch agitated for political reform and significantly influenced the direction of political change in the colony. In addition, he wrote extensively, using the pen to instruct and to promote social change. His best-known work, *The Stepsure Letters* established him as the founder of modern Canadian humor.

B. M. Moody

McDaniel, George White (1875-1927). Southern Baptist* preacher* and denominational* leader. Born in Texas, McDaniel received his formal education at Baylor University, in Texas, and the Southern Baptist Seminary, Louisville, Kentucky. Ordained* in 1899, he served as pastor of numerous Southern Baptist churches, including Gaston Avenue Baptist, Dallas, and First Baptist, Richmond, Virginia (1902-1927).

McDaniel was an active leader in denominational life, serving on numerous agencies and boards of trustees, including Richmond College and the Southern Baptist Seminary. He was also president of the Southern Baptist Convention and the Baptist General Association of Virginia. As a spokesman for his denomination, McDaniel opposed efforts to require Bible* reading in Virginia public schools (*See* Religion and Public Education). In 1926 the Southern Baptist Convention approved the "McDaniel Statement," which repudiated the theory of evolution* and declared humanity the unique expression of divine creation. All Southern Baptist seminary faculty members were required to subscribe.

BIBLIOGRAPHY. D. S. McDaniel, *George White McDaniel* (1928).   B. J. Leonard

McDowell, Henry Curtis (1894-). African-American Congregational* minister* and missionary* to Angola. Born in Epes, Alabama, McDowell was raised by his widowed mother in Meridian, Mississippi. McDowell attended Lincoln Normal School and Meridian Academy, and graduated with highest honors from Talladega College in 1915. After graduating from Talladega Theological Seminary in 1917, he was the pastor of First Congregational Church in Chattanooga, Tennessee, for one year. He and his wife received appointments as missionaries to Angola in 1919. In Angola he founded the Galangue Mission Station, which was fully staffed by African Americans until 1939. He and his wife worked there until 1937 when Henry McDowell became director of Lincoln Academy and pastor of the First Congregational Church in Kings Mountain, North Carolina. In 1944 he left Lincoln Academy to become pastor of Dixwell Avenue Congregational Church in New Haven, Connecticut. McDowell returned to Angola in 1947, and he retired from the mission field in 1959. In 1959 he founded the Church of the Open Door, in Miami, Florida, and was pastor there until he and his wife retired to Kings Mountain, North Carolina, in 1967.

BIBLIOGRAPHY. L. M. Johnson, "Missionary-Government Relations: Black Americans in British and Portuguese Colonies," in *Black Americans and the Missionary Movement in Africa*, ed. S. M. Jacobs (1982); J. T. Stanley, *A History of Black Congregational Christian Churches of the South* (1978).
                                                    L. J. Edwards

McGarvey, John William (1829-1911). Church of Christ* minister* and educator. Born in Kentucky, McGarvey spent his entire life there, except for the period 1846-1862. He attended Bethany College, studying under Alexander Campbell*

when that religious leader was at his prime. In 1862 he was called to be the minister of a church in Lexington to keep it from dividing under the pressures of the Civil War.* In 1865 he became one of the founding faculty members of the College of the Bible in Lexington, serving as president from 1895 until his death.

Though he accepted the use of missionary societies, McGarvey was a convinced non-instrumentalist who did not limit his fellowship to those of like persuasion. But when the teachings of higher criticism began to move into the Christian Churches, he used all the power of his teaching and writing to counter them. He wrote a number of significant books on biblical interpretation* and contributed a weekly column, "Biblical Criticism," to *The Christian Standard,* the most significant magazine among the Christian Churches at the time.

A cordial Christian gentleman, personally respected by friend and foe alike, McGarvey often dipped his pen in gall and vitriol. He was the acclaimed champion of the conservative position among the Christian Churches during his lifetime, but his bitter writings often inclined people to give the liberals* a hearing. Within six years after his death, liberal professors had replaced his teachings at the College of the Bible, indicating the continued polarization and future friction between conservatives and liberals within the Christian Churches.

BIBLIOGRAPHY. *DAB* VI; J. W. McGarvey, *Short Essays in Biblical Criticism: Reprinted from the Christian Standard,* 1893-1904 (1910); W. C. Morro, *"Brother McGarvey": The Life of President J. W. McGarvey of the College of the Bible, Lexington, Kentucky* (1940).   J. B. North

McGary, Austin (1846-1928). Church of Christ* preacher* and editor. Born in Texas, McGary served in the Confederate army during the Civil War* and then engaged in politics for almost fifteen years. Converted* in 1881, he soon began preaching,* quickly winning a reputation for being fiery, blunt and effective. In 1884 he began the publication of *Firm Foundation,* a monthly journal which became a weekly the next year.

McGary championed the theological position that baptism* is for remission of sins, and individuals being baptized must understand this at the time or the action is not valid. Specifically, this meant the rebaptism* of Baptists* who are not immersed on such an understanding. McGary's major editorial opponent was David Lipscomb,* editor of *The Gospel Advocate,* who felt McGary's position was too restrictive. This issue disturbed the Churches of Christ for some time, and it is still held to by the *Firm Foundation* and its constituency.

BIBLIOGRAPHY. E. I. West, *The Search for the Ancient Order, Volume II* (1950).

J. B. North

McGavran, Donald A. (1897-). Founder of the Church Growth Movement.* Born of missionary* parents in India, McGavran was educated at Butler College, Yale* Divinity School and Columbia University* (Ph.D.). He and his wife, Mary, served as missionaries in India (1923-1954) with the United Christian Missionary Society (Disciples of Christ*). There he held posts in education, administration and village evangelism.*

Becoming a mission administrator in 1933, McGavran noted that out of 145 mission stations in Central India, the number of believers in 135 was growing slightly or not at all, while in the other ten there was an increase of up to 200 per cent per decade. After studying the factors which led to church growth, he began to recommend a style of evangelism which used the natural familial and social "bridges" existing within the cultural networks of each society.

After leaving India he spent five years lecturing and doing further research on church growth in various countries. He became convinced that the major goal of missions was to establish churches in non-Christian segments of society. In 1961 he established the Institute of Church Growth, in Eugene, Oregon, and in 1965 became the founding dean of the School of World Mission and Institute of Church Growth at Fuller Theological Seminary,* Pasadena, California. He continued to teach until 1980.

McGavran developed his ideas in several important books, including *The Bridges of God* (1955); *How Churches Grow* (1959); and *Understanding Church Growth* (1970). For McGavran the central goal of Christian mission is to bring people to faith in Christ and gather them into growing and multiplying churches. His methodology relies heavily on research and the use of the social sciences, especially anthropology, to bring greater understanding of the culture and religious system of each people group.

See also CHURCH GROWTH MOVEMENT.

BIBLIOGRAPHY. T. Stafford, "The Father of Church Growth," *CT* 30 (February 21, 1986):19-23.

P. E. Pierson

McGee, (J)ohn Vernon (1904-1988). Radio evangelist.* Born and raised in the South, McGee received his B.D. from Columbia Theological Seminary in Decatur, Georgia, and a graduate degree from Dallas Theological Seminary* in Dallas, Texas. He was ordained* to the ministry* in 1933, serving Presbyterian* churches in the South until 1941, when he became the pastor of a Presbyterian church in Pasadena, California. During this pastorate he began a weekly radio program called "The Open Bible Hour." In 1949 McGee became the pastor of an interdenominational congregation, The Church of the Open Door, in Los Angeles, California. To increase church attendance, he began the radio program "Thru the Bible," teaching the books of the Bible* consecutively. Every five years he completed a series of programs from Genesis through Revelation. He retired from the pastorate in 1970 but continued to broadcast his Bible lessons as well as weekly sermons. Beginning in 1973, "Thru the Bible" was aired in Spanish over the transmitters of Trans World Radio. In the years following, McGee's program was broadcast in many other languages. His ministry has also provided tapes of his radio programs and Bible study books through the mail.

BIBLIOGRAPHY. J. V. McGee, *Through the Bible Radio Ministry, 40th Anniversary* (1981).

W. M. Ashcraft

McGiffert, Arthur Cushman (1861-1933). Congregational* church historian and educator. Born in Sauquoit, New York, McGiffert was educated at Western Reserve University (B.A., 1882) and Union Theological Seminary, New York* (B.D., 1885), and pursued graduate studies in Germany, France and Italy. He received the Ph.D. at the University of Marburg (1888) where he developed a close friendship with Adolf Harnack (1851-1930). McGiffert taught at Lane Theological Seminary from 1888 until 1893, when he succeeded Philip Schaff* as Washburn Professor of Church History at Union Theological Seminary, New York. Denominational heresy* charges following publication of *A History of Christianity in the Apostolic Age* (1897) led McGiffert from the Presbyterians* to the Congregationalists in 1900. As president of Union Seminary from 1917 until 1926, McGiffert sought closer association with Columbia University,* eased the seminary's financial plight through successful fund-raising and supervised the renovation of the curriculum. He served as professor emeritus at Union until his death in 1933.

Though Philip Schaff considered him to be his intellectual successor, McGiffert's methodological allegiances were with the scientific historians, and his clear theological convictions were with Adolf Harnack and Albrecht Ritschl (1822-1889) in the advancement of Protestant* liberalism.* In his polemics, McGiffert accused conservatives of too often skewing historical evidence in favor of creedal formulations, though McGiffert himself grafted liberalism to his historical studies, veering at the end of his life toward a modernistic functionalism which led him to deny any meaningful continuity in Christian history.

McGiffert's published titles included: *The Apostles' Creed* (1902); *Martin Luther* (1911); *The God of the Early Christians* (1924); and *A History of Christian Thought* (2 vols., 1931-1933). A prolific historian of Christian thought in translations, critical editions, as well as historical surveys, McGiffert's theological commitments and his prominent position at Union Seminary made him one of America's foremost advocates of theological liberalism over a forty-year career.

BIBLIOGRAPHY. *DAB* 1; *DARB*; *NCAB* 24.

K. S. Sawyer

McGlynn, Edward (1837-1900). Catholic* priest* and social reformer. The son of Irish immigrants, McGlynn attended public schools in New York City until he went to Rome at the age of thirteen to study for the priesthood* at the Urban College of the Propaganda. He earned a doctorate in divinity there, and after his ordination* in 1860 he returned to New York to be an assistant pastor. In 1866 McGlynn was appointed pastor of St. Stephen's, a working-class parish of 25,000 members which included many who were poor, unskilled and unemployed. His ministry influenced him to become a well-known advocate of social and economic reform. He established an orphanage that cared for over 500 children, but he resisted opening a parish school, convinced that the funds required for its construction and operation would be better spent for more pressing needs. In 1870 he created a sensation when he attacked public aid to all religious institutions as a violation of the separation of church and state.*

In the early 1880s, McGlynn became convinced that Henry George's single-tax theory offered a way of alleviating economic distress, and his campaigning for George in the 1886 New York mayoral race caused Archbishop* Michael Corrigan* to order McGlynn not to speak in favor of George at an upcoming public meeting. McGlynn felt he could not comply on such short notice, and Corrigan suspended him for two weeks. In early 1887, the archbishop removed McGlynn as pastor of St.

Stephen's, and the Vatican ordered him to disavow his support for George's land tax idea. McGlynn refused and was excommunicated until 1892 when Archbishop Francesco Satolli,* the Pope's personal delegate to the U.S. and four professors from Catholic University* judged that McGlynn's views did not violate Church teachings. In 1894 Corrigan appointed McGlynn to be pastor of a parish in Newburgh, New York, and he served there until his death.

BIBLIOGRAPHY. S. Bell, *Rebel Priest and Prophet: A Biography of Dr. Edward McGlynn* (1968); R. E. Curran, *Michael Augustine Corrigan and the Shaping of Conservative Catholicism in America, 1878-1902* (1978); *DAB* VI.

W. P. Leahy

McGready, James (c.1758-1817). Presbyterian* revivalist* and father of the frontier camp meeting.* McGready came from Scotch-Irish stock in Pennsylvania, but as a child he moved with his family to western North Carolina. Under a childhood diet of hard work and Calvinistic* doctrine, young James gave evidence of preaching* potential. A visiting uncle, impressed by these signs of ministerial calling, persuaded the family to send him back to Pennsylvania for theological studies (1787-1788) under a Princeton* graduate named John McMillan. Shortly after taking up his studies, McGready fell under a siege of smallpox and faced the question of his eternal destiny. He wrestled with it, and on the first Sunday after his recovery from smallpox, he was converted.* His zeal for revival may have been kindled during a visit to Hampden-Sydney College in Virginia. In 1788, when "about 30 years of age," he was licensed to preach in the presbytery* of Redstone, in western Pennsylvania.

Returning to North Carolina, McGready preached the wrath of God so vigorously that he ignited revival fires which drove penitents to faith in Jesus. One of these was Barton W. Stone,* who later led the famous Cane Ridge* camp meeting in Kentucky. McGready was also capable of provoking violent opposition. When he fled the area in 1796, a tale circulated that the suggestion that he move West had come from an anonymous letter written in blood.

He took up his new challenge in the southwestern corner of Kentucky, preaching to three small congregations at Red River, Gasper River and Muddy River. All three were in Logan County, notorious for its lawlessness. Surprisingly, however, the backwoodsmen responded enthusiastically to McGready's vivid preaching.

In July 1800 McGready helped shape the course

of American history. After an original revival at Red River, he decided to send out advance notice of the next Communion service at the Gasper River church. When the word spread through the settlements, scores of pioneers headed in wagons and on horseback for Gasper River, expecting to witness the work of God. They came from as far away as 100 miles, prepared to stay several days. This was probably the first camp meeting in American history, a religious service of several days' length held outdoors for people who had traveled some distance to attend. Such revivals spread to many other settlements throughout the South and Midwest. The most famous camp meeting was at Cane Ridge in Bourbon County, Kentucky in August 1801. Estimates of the size of the crowd range from 10 to 25 thousand. McGready's last days were spent preaching in northern Kentucky and southern Indiana.

BIBLIOGRAPHY. C. C. Cleveland, *The Great Revival in the West, 1797-1805* (1916); *DAB* V; *DARB*; C. A. Johnson, *The Frontier Camp Meeting: Religion's Harvest Time* (1955); B. A. Weisberger, *They Gathered at the River* (1978).

B. L. Shelley

MacGregor, James Drummond (1759-1830). Presbyterian* missionary* to the Maritime Provinces. MacGregor was raised in St. Fillans, Perthshire, Scotland, in a strict Antiburgher secessionist Presbyterian* family. He studied classics (Edinburgh University) and theology* and was ordained* by the Associate Presbytery of Glasgow. In 1786 he accepted a call to aid the struggling Highland Scottish Presbyterians of Nova Scotia and emigrated almost immediately. MacGregor settled at Pictou and, using that as his home base, he itinerated on numerous missionary trips. Thus he was the first Presbyterian minister to visit Prince Edward Island (1791), the Miramichi area of New Brunswick (1797) and Cape Breton Island (1798). Later journeys solidified this earlier Presbyterian work throughout the region. He was also instrumental in forming the Associate Presbytery of Nova Scotia in 1795 and, eventually, the united secessionist Presbyterian Synod of Nova Scotia in 1817, an independent judicatory autonomous of Scotland. MacGregor has consequently been dubbed "the father of Presbyterianism in the Maritimes." Besides his ecclesiastical work, MacGregor published a volume of sacred poems in Gaelic, denounced slavery and intemperance, encouraged improved agricultural and health-care methods, and assisted Thomas McCulloch* in the formation of Pictou Academy.

BIBLIOGRAPHY. *DCB* VI; G. Patterson, *Memoir of the Rev. James MacGregor, D.D.* (1859).

D. M. Strong

McGuffey, William Holmes (1800-1873). Professor of moral philosophy and author of readers for elementary schools. McGuffey was born near Claysville, Pennsylvania, but grew up near Youngstown, Ohio. He was educated by his mother, irregularly attended rural schools, and studied Latin with a Presbyterian* minister.* McGuffey was renowned for his prodigious memorization of Scripture* and literature. In 1818 he attended Old Stone Academy in Darlington, Pennsylvania, and then entered Washington College. On the way to his degree he taught intermittently, mostly in Kentucky. Graduating with honors in 1826, he became professor of languages at Miami University in Oxford, Ohio, and in 1832 head of the department of mental philosophy and philology. In 1836 he accepted the presidency of Cincinnati College, and while there helped found the College of Teachers, an association designed to promote public-school education, which as yet had not been legislated in most states, including Ohio and Kentucky. From 1839 to 1843 he was president of Ohio University, Athens, and from 1845 professor of moral philosophy at the University of Virginia.

McGuffey, a Presbyterian, was licensed* by his presbytery to preach* in 1829, but he never accepted a regular call. He took pride in the fact that he spoke extemporaneously, later declaring that he had preached more than 3,000 sermons without writing a single one.

McGuffey was best known as author of the Eclectic Readers. Published in six books from 1836 to 1857, some with Alexander, his brother, they sold an astronomical 122 million copies and helped shape the nineteenth-century American mind. McGuffey was immersed in the Scottish moral education typical of American educators of his epoch. These books included simple moral exhortations to industry, honesty and loyalty, as well as warnings against strong drink and exhortations on Sabbath keeping—values commonly espoused by the nineteenth-century Protestant consensus. The demand accrued from the rise of the public schools and the conviction that moral education of a nonconfessional character was an imperative aspect of the curriculum.

BIBLIOGRAPHY. *DAB* VI; M. Tope, *A Biography of William Holmes McGuffey* (1929); H. C. Minnich, *William Holmes McGuffey and the Peerless Pioneer McGuffey Readers* (1928); J. H. Westerhoff, *McGuffey and His Readers* (1978).

T. H. Olbricht

McGuire, George Alexander (1866-1934). Founder of the African Orthodox Church. Born on Antigua in the West Indies, McGuire immigrated to the U.S. in 1894 and became a priest* in the Protestant Episcopal Church,* remaining so until 1919. As an Episcopalian, he futilely advocated the consecration of African-American bishops* in order to speed missionary* work among African-Americans. By 1920 McGuire was active in Marcus Garvey's* African-American nationalist movement, the United Negro Improvement Association (UNIA). He became chaplain*-general of the UNIA, and wrote a catechism* and a book of ritual for it. In a 1924 speech, McGuire urged Garvey's followers to worship* a black Madonna and Christ. Meanwhile, after a brief affiliation with the Reformed Episcopal Church,* McGuire decided to found a new denomination,* the African Orthodox Church, an all-black body with a polity* and ritual similar to Episcopalianism. On September 28, 1921, McGuire was consecrated bishop by representatives of the Swedish Orthodox Church and American Catholic Church, both small schismatic denominations. Garvey disavowed any connection with McGuire's church, but many of the UNIA members joined it. By the time of McGuire's death in 1934, his church had approximately 30,000 members.

BIBLIOGRAPHY. R. K. Burkett, *Garveyism as a Religious Movement: The Institutionalization of a Black Civil Religion* (1978). S. W. Angell

Machen, (J)ohn Gresham (1881-1937). Presbyterian* clergyman,* New Testament scholar and educator. Born the second of three sons to a prominent Baltimore lawyer, Machen was reared in an Old School* Presbyterian home of genteel tastes. From his father Machen acquired an interest in classical literature and an appreciation for rare books. His mother catechized* her children and encouraged them to read English and French Victorian literature. Remaining in Baltimore for his undergraduate education, Machen majored in classics at the Johns Hopkins University and graduated in 1901. He stayed at Hopkins for another year to undertake graduate study with the renowned American classicist Basil L. Gildersleeve.

Uncertain about career plans, Machen enrolled at Princeton Theological Seminary* the following year, apparently deciding against a Ph.D. in the classics. At Princeton he earned a masters in philosophy (1904) from the University, while completing the requirements for the bachelor's of divinity at the Seminary (1905). There Machen was greatly influenced by the teaching and scholarly model of Benjamin B. Warfield.* Machen's interests in Greek literature, however, did not subside, and during his senior year at the seminary, he took New Testament electives with William Park Armstrong,* professor of New Testament. Recognizing Machen's abilities, Armstrong advised the young student to do advanced study in Germany. In the fall of 1905, Machen left to study at the German universities in Marburg and Göttingen. One year later he returned to Princeton to become an instructor in the New Testament department (1906-1914), a position which he held until his ordination,* at which time he became assistant professor.

Aside from some early studies of the birth narratives in the Gospels, the apostle Paul absorbed most of Machen's scholarly interests as a young man. After a year of service in the YMCA* during World War 1,* he devoted three years of research to *The Origin of Paul's Religion* (1921), a work intended to answer critics in establishing the continuity between Jesus and Paul. From his study of Paul, Machen returned to his early interest in the New Testament accounts of Christ's birth, with the publication of *The Virgin Birth of Christ* (1930). These studies were marked by the careful conservative scholarship that had typified the Princeton tradition, and the book was given careful attention by liberals* and conservatives alike.

Machen was best known for championing the cause of orthodoxy in the fundamentalist-modernist controversy.* Not only did his biblical scholarship provide a cogent defense of orthodox belief in the trustworthiness of Scripture; in *Christianity and Liberalism* (1923) Machen argued that liberalism and historic Christianity were two entirely distinct religions. The logic of Machen's opposition to liberalism led to confrontation both within Princeton Seminary and in the Presbyterian Church in the U.S.A. In 1929, when Princeton Seminary was reorganized to ensure a more inclusive theological spectrum, Machen and a core of conservative faculty members withdrew from Princeton to found Westminster Theological Seminary at Philadelphia.

With increasing suspicion of liberalism on the mission* field, Machen led other conservative Presbyterians in the formation of the Independent Board for Presbyterian Foreign Missions in 1933. When the General Assembly proscribed the Independent Board in 1934, Machen refused to sever his connections with this Board and was tried and suspended from ministry in the Presbyterian Church in 1935. After appealing the verdict in 1936, Machen played a central role in founding a new denomination, the Presbyterian Church of America (later the Orthodox Presbyterian Church*). On a trip to Bismarck, North Dakota, to rally support for the new denomination, Machen came down with pneumonia and died on January 1, 1937.

See also FUNDAMENTALIST-MODERNIST CONTROVERSY.

BIBLIOGRAPHY. DAB 2; DARB; G. M. Marsden, "J. Gresham Machen, History, and Truth," WmTJ 42 (1979):157-175; W. S. Reid, "J. Gresham Machen" in Reformed Theology in America, ed. D. F. Wells (1985); C. A. Russell, Voices of American Fundamentalism (1976); N. B. Stonehouse, J. Gresham Machen: A Biographical Memoir (1954).

D. G. Hart

Machray, Robert (1831-1904). Anglican* archbishop* of Rupert's Land. A native of Aberdeen, Machray left Scotland to attend Cambridge University and was ordained* in 1856. After serving parishes in England, he arrived in North America in 1865 to take up his appointment as bishop* of Rupert's Land, the large region of western Canada which later became the provinces of Manitoba, Saskatchewan and Alberta. In 1893 he was named first Primate of All Canada, thereby becoming archbishop of Rupert's Land, a position which he held until his death. Under his leadership, the Anglican Church linked its expansion in the West to the denomination's educational institutions, in particular St. John's College, Winnipeg. He guided the Anglican Church in its attempts to play a moderating role in the region's two major political controversies, the Riel affair and the Manitoba Schools question.

BIBLIOGRAPHY. R. Machray, Life of Archbishop Machray (1909).

P. D. Airhart

McIlvaine, Charles Pettit (1799-1873). Episcopal* bishop* of Ohio. Born in Burlington, New Jersey, McIlvaine's father was a lawyer and would later serve as a United States senator (1823-1826). Graduating from the College of New Jersey* in 1816, he then studied theology at Princeton and in private. He was ordained* deacon* by Presiding Bishop William White* on June 18, 1820, and priest by White on March 20, 1821. From 1820 to 1824 he was made rector of Christ Church, Georgetown, Washington, D.C.

In 1824 John C. Calhoun, the secretary of war and an attendant at Christ Church, appointed McIlvaine chaplain* and professor of ethics at West Point, where under his leadership a revival* broke out. One of the fruits of this revival was the conversion of Leonidas Polk,* later the first bishop of Louisiana. From 1827 to 1832 McIlvaine was

rector of St. Ann's Church, Brooklyn, and for part of that time professor of Christian evidences at the University of the City of New York. His lectures were published as The Evidences of Christianity (1832). On October 31, 1832, he was consecrated the second bishop of Ohio by Bishop White. As bishop he lived at Gambier, Ohio, the location of Kenyon College and its theological seminary (later called Bexley Hall), over which institutions he also served as president.

During his episcopate he was the leader of the evangelical* party in the Episcopal Church and an opponent of the Oxford Movement (See Tractarianism). His Oxford Divinity: Compared with That of the Romish and Anglican Churches (1841) condemned the Oxford leaders as unscriptural, contrary to the Thirty-Nine Articles* and leading Anglicans to Rome. He believed they substituted the Church for Christ and priests for the gospel. He refused to consecrate any churches with altars and defended his position in Reasons for Refusing to Consecrate a Church Having an Altar Instead of a Communion Table (1846). His evangelical position was also expressed in No Priest, No Sacrifice, No Altar but Christ (1850). In 1861 he was chosen by President Lincoln to go to England as an ambassador of good will at the time of the "Trent Affair." McIlvaine died at Florence, Italy, on March 12, 1873.

BIBLIOGRAPHY. W. Carus, Memorials of the Rt. Rev. Charles Pettit McIlvaine (1882); DAB VI; DARB; W. H. Hall, "Bishop McIlvaine, the Reluctant Frontiersman," HMPEC 44 (1975):81-96; NCAB 7; G. F. Smythe, A History of the Diocese of Ohio Until the Year 1918 (1931).

D. S. Armentrout

McIntire, Carl (1906-). Militant fundamentalist* and anti-Communist. Born in Ypsilanti, Michigan, the son of a Presbyterian* minister,* McIntire was raised in a devout Christian home. During his childhood the family moved to Durant, Oklahoma, where McIntire grew up. Graduating from Park College, Parkville, Missouri, in 1927, McIntire attended Princeton Theological Seminary,* where he was a devoted student of J. Gresham Machen.* When Machen and a group of conservatives left Princeton to form Westminster Theological Seminary in 1929, McIntire followed them and graduated from Westminster in 1931. McIntire was an ordained* minister of the Presbyterian Church in the U.S.A. until he was defrocked by his presbytery* in 1935 for his involvement in the conservative's Independent Board for Presbyterian Foreign Missions.

In 1936 McIntire joined Machen in the newly

founded church that eventually became known as the Orthodox Presbyterian Church.* Three years later, however, McIntire led a group that separated to form the Bible Presbyterian Church. Rigidly fundamentalist, McIntire and the Bible Presbyterians adopted dispensational* premillennialism,* proscribed all consumption of alcohol* and demanded strict separation from anyone not adhering to fundamentalist standards. The headquarters for this movement was Collingswood, New Jersey, where McIntire also pastored the local Bible Presbyterian Church, a congregation that numbered nearly 2,000 in the 1960s. McIntire, with Allan A. MacRae and J. Oliver Buswell, Jr.,* helped found the denomination's Faith Theological Seminary in 1937.

In 1941 McIntire founded the American Council of Churches* as a counter to the Federal Council of Churches,* which he considered too liberal. McIntire refused to join the National Association of Evangelicals,* organized the following year, because of what he considered its latitudinarian policies and its refusal to exclude members of the Federal Council. In 1948 he formed the International Council of Christian Churches* to provide an international association of like-minded fundamentalists. When the Revised Standard Version of the Bible was published by the National Council of Churches in 1952, McIntire opposed it through numerous "Back to the Bible" rallies.

Like Billy James Hargis,* McIntire became vociferous in his condemnation of Communism and his advocacy of patriotism during the McCarthy era, postures he maintained long after the Red Scare had dissipated. During the Viet Nam War* his group led repeated Marches for Victory in Washington, D.C., supporting the war effort. Through his "Twentieth-Century Reformation Hour," a daily half-hour radio broadcast begun in 1957, and his publication, *Christian Beacon* (1936-), McIntire disseminated his militant fundamentalism.

In 1963 McIntire purchased the Admiral Hotel at Cape May, New Jersey. Renaming it the Christian Admiral, he operated it as a Bible conference center and vacation hotel for his followers. There he also built Shelton College, a small Bible school. In 1971 he purchased a hotel and property at Cape Canaveral, Florida, which he also utilized for the same purposes and where he relocated Shelton College. By the 1980s, McIntire's extremist views had fallen somewhat out of favor, even among devoted fundamentalists, and his institutions, notably Shelton College in Cape May, New Jersey, had run afoul of tax officials in both New Jersey and Florida. McIntire, however, still claims the loyalty of a core of devoted followers.

See also AMERICAN COUNCIL OF CHRISTIAN CHURCHES; BIBLE PRESBYTERIAN CHURCH; INTERNATIONAL COUNCIL OF CHRISTIAN CHURCHES.

BIBLIOGRAPHY. L. Gasper, *The Fundamentalist Movement, 1930-1956* (1963); J. D. Woodbridge, M. A. Noll and N. O. Hatch, *The Gospel in America* (1979). R. H. Balmer

Macintosh, Douglas Clyde (1877-1948). Baptist* theologian* and educator. Born in Breadalbane, Canada, Macintosh was educated at McMaster University (B.A., 1903) and the University of Chicago (Ph.D., 1909). From his rural Canadian background Macintosh emerged to become one of America's leading philosophical theologians. Influenced by his mother's piety* and a familial connection with Wesleyan Methodism,* he remained devoted to a vital Christian experience, though his studies in theology and his three-decade teaching career at Yale* Divinity School identified him as a powerful thinker of liberal* Protestantism.*

Macintosh studied with significant theologians of his era, including George Herbert Mead and George Burman Foster,* and he also claimed an indebtedness to the German liberal theologian Albert Ritschl (1822-1889). Early in his career he attempted an empirical* theology in response to the skepticism and historical relativism of his contemporaries. In several major books he created a theology based on empirically verifiable knowledge in combination with other emerging sciences. He also envisioned a world which could be improved by good will and energetic human effort, and his doctrine of Christ stood apart from the *logical* essentials of Christian belief. Among his published works were *The Reasonableness of Christianity* (1928) and *Theology as an Empirical Science* (1919).

Beyond the classroom, Macintosh was remembered for his celebrated struggle to achieve U.S. citizenship. During World War 1,* he became a critic of U.S. military involvement and was subsequently denied the right to citizenship. The U.S. Supreme Court upheld the decision in 1931.

BIBLIOGRAPHY. *DAB* 4; *DARB*.

W. H. Brackney

Mack, Alexander (1679-1735). First Brethren* minister.* A native of Schriesheim, Germany, Mack was reared in the Reformed* faith. He became an active Pietist* and was forced to leave his home. In his refuge at Schwarzenau/Eder in Wittgenstein, Mack emerged as the "teacher of the word" of an

Anabaptist*/pietist community of eight persons founded in 1708. Outsiders called the group "New Baptists" because of their adoption of baptism* by immersion. They simply called themselves the "brethren" and looked to early Christianity as their model. Fervent evangelism* by Mack and other members led to the creation of daughter congregations in the Marienborn area (near Buedingen), in the Palatinate, in Krefeld (Lower Rhine), in Hamburg/Altona and in Switzerland. The original Schwarzenau congregation, with Mack as its leader, left Germany in 1720 for West Friesland, from where almost all members immigrated to Pennsylvania in 1729. There they joined an earlier (1719) emigration from Krefeld directed by Peter Becker.*

A schism led by Johann Konrad Beissel* confronted Mack on his arrival in Pennsylvania, and his efforts to reconcile the dissidents with the larger Brethren community failed. Mack died in 1735 as a much-respected figure among the German-speaking element in Pennsylvania. His son Alexander ("Sander") Mack, Jr., later became a Brethren elder* and their most prolific writer. Alexander Mack, Sr., was known for two publications: *Grundforschende Fragen* (*Basic Questions,* 1713) and *Rechte und Ordnungen* (*Rights and Ordinances,* 1715), both issued first in Germany and then later in several editions in America. The first published translation in English was in 1810, the most recent in 1958.

BIBLIOGRAPHY. W. G. Willoughby, *Counting the Cost: The Life of Alexander Mack, 1679-1735* (1979); D. F. Durnbaugh, ed., *European Origins of the Brethren* (1958); F. Ankrum, *Alexander Mack the Tunker and His Descendants* (1943).

D. F. Durnbaugh

Mackay, John Alexander (1889-1983). Presbyterian* clergyman,* missionary,* ecumenist and educator. Born in Inverness, Scotland, Mackay studied at the University of Aberdeen (M.A., 1912) and then traveled to America where he attended Princeton Theological Seminary* (B.D., 1915). The following year he studied at the University of Madrid, Spain, where he came under the influence of the great mystic and philosopher, Miguel de Unamuno.

In 1916 he was ordained* a minister* of the Free Church of Scotland and soon appointed an educational missionary by that church and sent to Lima, Peru, where he founded the Anglo-Peruvian College and served as its principal (1916-1925). From 1925 until 1932 Mackay served as a writer and evangelist for the South American Federation of the YMCA,* with occasional posts in Uruguay and

Mexico. In 1932 he returned to the U.S. to be secretary for the Latin America Division of the Board of Foreign Missions of the Presbyterian Church in the U.S.A.* A pioneer in the ecumenical movement,* Mackay was a central figure in founding the World Council of Churches* and chairman of the Joint Committee of the World Council of Churches and the International Missionary Council* (1948-1954).

In 1936 Mackay became president of Princeton Theological Seminary, where he served until 1959. At Princeton he was able to restore stability to a faculty that had recently undergone a struggle over fundamentalism* and the departure of the conservative element that formed Westminster Theological Seminary in 1929. During his years at Princeton, Mackay founded the theological quarterly, *Theology Today* (1944), for which he served as editor from 1944 to 1951. He also served as moderator of the General Assembly* of the Presbyterian Church in the U.S.A. (1953) and president of World Presbyterian Alliance (1954-1959).

Mackay authored several books, some of which were written in Spanish. His study of the spiritual history of Spain and Latin America was translated into English as *The Other Spanish Christ* (1933). Other publications included: *A Preface to Christian Theology* (1941), *God's Order* (1953) and *Ecumenics: The Science of the Church Universal* (1964).

BIBLIOGRAPHY. E. J. Jurji, ed., *The Ecumenical Era in Church and Society* (1959); *The Annual Obituary 1983* (1984).

D. Macleod

McKelway, Alexander Jeffrey (1866-1918). Southern Presbyterian* progressive and political activist. Although born in Pennsylvania, McKelway's family background and education (at Hampden-Sydney College and Union Theological Seminary in Richmond) were Southern. Following seminary, McKelway served as a Presbyterian pastor in North Carolina (1891-1897). He then became editor (1898-1905) of the *Presbyterian Standard,* the denomination's periodical in North Carolina. During this time he developed an interest in social-justice issues, particularly child-labor reform. Consequently, in 1909 McKelway moved to Washington to lobby for federal legislation under the auspices of the National Child Labor Committee. Soon McKelway became convinced that his fellow former Southerner, Presbyterian and moderate progressive Woodrow Wilson* would be well suited for the presidency.

When Wilson decided to run in 1912, McKelway urged him to state explicitly his progressivism in order to keep social reformers from voting for Theodore Roosevelt. When Wilson sought re-election in 1916, McKelway was even more involved, especially since the final drive for the passage of the federal Child Labor Bill coincided with the campaign. Several months before the election, McKelway persuaded Wilson to intervene with Congress on behalf of the legislation. After the bill's passage, McKelway turned his full energies toward the re-election campaign. He drafted the labor and welfare planks of the Democratic platform and founded the Democratic "Bureau of Education and Social Service," an organization which made direct appeals for Wilson to voters interested in social reform. McKelway was one of the few Southern churchmen whose concerns matched those of the Social Gospel* advocates of the North.

BIBLIOGRAPHY. B. J. Brandon, "A Wilsonian Progressive—Alexander Jeffrey McKelway." *JPH* 48 (1970):2-17; H. J. Doherty, "Alexander J. McKelway: Preacher to Progressive." *JSH* 24 (1958):177-190.   D. M. Strong

McKendree, William (1757-1835). First American-born bishop* in the Methodist* Episcopal Church and father of Western Methodism. Born in King William County, Virginia, McKendree was reared an Anglican* and joined a Methodist society sometime before 1777. Moving in and out of class meetings for ten years before his conversion* in 1787, he spent this time serving in the Revolutionary War* and was present at the surrender of Cornwallis at Yorktown. His religious turn at age thirty was soon recognized, and he was received on trial in the Virginia Conference in 1788. For six years he served on several Virginia circuits.* In 1792 he sided with James O'Kelly* (his presiding elder for four years) who was to split with the Methodists over the failure of a General Conference resolution allowing dissatisfied preachers to appeal their appointments. After just a year with O'Kelly's Republican Methodist Church and while traveling with Francis Asbury* and carefully examining the *Rules and Discipline* of the church drawn up by John Wesley,* McKendree became convinced that O'Kelly was in error.

Quickly reestablishing his Methodist Episcopal loyalties, McKendree served faithfully on circuits in Virginia until 1796, when he was appointed presiding elder. He continued to serve as presiding elder after moving from Virginia to the Kentucky District of the newly formed Western Conference (including Ohio, Kentucky, Tennessee, western Virginia and part of Illinois) in 1801. Here he did his pioneer work, combining extraordinary gifts of lively preaching and solid administration. McKendree, in effect, domesticated the high enthusiasm of the frontier camp meeting* and harnessed it to the establishment of churches, circuits and districts throughout the conference.

In 1808 McKendree became the third elected bishop for American Methodism. Commonly called Asbury's greatest successor, he made his most significant administrative mark by asking the advice of his presiding elders as to the appointment of preachers. In spite of Asbury's doubts, this eventually led to the formation of the "cabinet system" so prevalent today. During the years after Asbury's death (1816), McKendree's health broke under the strain of the added responsibility. Although he continued to travel over the connection, after 1820 his involvement lessened until his death in Tennessee on March 5, 1835.

BIBLIOGRAPHY. *AAP* 7; *DAB* VI; *DARB*; B. Fry, *The Lives of Bishops Whatcoat, McKendree, and George* (1853); R. Paine, *Life and Times of William McKendree* (1885); *NCAB* 10.   R. G. Tuttle

Mackie (Macky), Josias (John) (?-1716). Presbyterian* missionary* in Virginia. One of the first Presbyterian ministers* to come to America, little is known of his early life except that he originated from St. Johnstone, County Donegal, Ireland, the son of Patrick Mackie. He evidently had a classical education, since it is known that his library was particularly well stocked with Greek and Latin works for someone in the American wilderness. Mackie may have immigrated as early as 1684; definitely, he was in Virginia by 1692. In that latter year it is recorded that he received permission from the Commonwealth to preach at certain designated places. The locations Mackie selected to regularly conduct Presbyterian worship* were along the Elizabeth River in Norfolk and Princess Anne counties. As the pastor of these struggling dissenting churches, Mackie was probably the successor of Francis Makemie,* the early Presbyterian pioneer. Also following Makemie, Mackie was likely employed as a planter and merchant in order to supplement his meager resources as a pastor. Due to the long distance from any other Presbyterian support, Mackie's work was difficult and, by 1712, the Presbytery of Philadelphia (the nearest judicatory) reported that he was laboring under "melancholy circumstances." He died sometime in the autumn of 1716.

BIBLIOGRAPHY. *AAP* 3.   D. M. Strong

McKinley, William (1843-1901). Methodist* churchman, lawyer and twenty-fifth U.S. president.

Born in Niles, Ohio, McKinley was one of nine children of working-class parents. He grew up in Poland, Ohio, attended Allegheny College (1860-1861) and served with distinction as an officer in the 23rd Ohio Volunteer Infantry during the Civil War* (1861-1865). After the war he became a lawyer, settled in Canton, Ohio, married Ida Saxton in 1871 and launched a career in politics. He served in the U.S. House of Representatives from 1877 to 1883, and again from 1885 to 1891, where he became a powerful Republican leader and a national figure. With the wealthy Cleveland businessman Marcus A. Hanna as his chief advisor, the popular McKinley successfully campaigned first for governor of Ohio (1891 and 1893) and later for president of the U.S. (1896 and 1900).

The strengthening and expansion of presidential power so characteristic of the twentieth century began during McKinley's presidency (1897-1901). More important, he presided over the swift and decisive U.S. victory in the Spanish American War* (1898) which changed the traditional course of American foreign policy and launched the nation on nearly a century of imperialist ventures. He used his considerable managerial skills to secure Senate ratification of the Treaty of Paris (1899), pacified the Philippines and initiated civil governments in the dependencies taken from Spain (Cuba and Puerto Rico). Following the war, he joined the competition for markets in China and won agreement for an Open Door policy for Chinese trade. In domestic affairs, he pushed a higher protective tariff through Congress (1897), established the nation firmly on the gold standard and worked hard for societal harmony.

McKinley's evangelical Christian faith undergirded his political philosophy and provided him with his basic world view. He summed this up on May 26, 1899, while president. He wrote in his notebook: "My belief embraces the Divinity of Christ and a recognition of Christianity as the mightiest factor in the world's civilization." McKinley had been "born again"* at age ten during a revival* meeting and later joined a Methodist church. Regular in attendance the remainder of his life, he served at various times as a Methodist trustee and Sunday-school* superintendent. He also actively supported the YMCA* and the temperance movement* and was particularly interested in missionary* endeavors and world evangelization, while maintaining good relations with all religious communities. The McKinleys were regulars at Washington's Metropolitan Methodist Church and often entertained guests with Sunday-evening hymn* sings in the White House.

In 1898, when faced with the question of how to deal with the new territories seized from Spain during the war, McKinley utilized civil religion categories to justify America's new policy of overseas expansion. For the first time in U.S. history, the national mission came to include the awesome assignment of carrying Christianity and democracy* to the "benighted peoples" in the "uncivilized quarters of the world." Thus, McKinley tried, in part, to justify the acquisition of the Philippines by claiming that the U.S. was going to "Christianize" a native population, ninety per cent of whom were already Roman Catholics.*

His personal devoutness, his tender and patient care of his chronically invalid, epileptic wife, his public forgiveness of his assassin (a crazed anarchist named Leon Czolgosz), and the dignity of his lingering death (September 6-14, 1901) made McKinley extremely popular among churchgoing Americans. He died with the words of the hymn "Nearer My God to Thee" on his lips.

BIBLIOGRAPHY. P. W. Glad, *McKinley, Bryan and the People* (1964); L. L. Gould, *The Presidency of William McKinley* (1980); V. B. Hampton, *The Religious Background of the White House* (1932); M. Leech, *In the Days of McKinley* (1959); H. W. Morgan, *William McKinley and His America* (1963); R. B. Nye, *The Almost Chosen People* (1966); C. S. Olcott, *The Life of William McKinley,* 2 vols. (1916); R. V. Pierard and R. D. Linder, *Civil Religion and the Presidency* (1988).

R. D. Linder

McLaurin, John Bates (1884-1952). Canadian Baptist* missionary.* Born in India of Canadian Baptist missionaries, he received his high-school education in the U.S. and Canada and in 1905 graduated in engineering from McMaster University. In 1906 he began theological training at McMaster Divinity School.

Ordained* as a Baptist minister,* McLaurin was accepted in 1909 as a missionary in south India. There he exercised a remarkably effective ministry among Telugu-speaking people. He taught for a time at Ramapatnam Theological Seminary and later established the Jeevamruta Seminary in Kakinada. A strong advocate of turning over missionary functions to the indigenous church (especially the task of evangelism), McLaurin was critical of the physical and social distance between missionaries and their Indian colleagues. He supported ecumenical cooperation on the field.

McLaurin was one of Canada's best-known missionaries of the first half of the twentieth century. From 1939 until his death he served as the general secretary of the Canadian Baptist Foreign Mission.

BIBLIOGRAPHY. E. C. Merrick, *J. B. McLaurin: A Biography* (1955).   D. M. Lewis

McMaster, James Alphonsus (1820-1886).
Catholic* editor and controversialist. Born in Duanesburg, New York, the son of a Presbyterian* minister,* McMaster graduated from Union College, Schenectady, New York, and studied law at Columbia College, New York City. He studied for the Episcopal* priesthood* at General Theological Seminary at a time when both students and professors were watched for the "Roman" influences conveyed by the Tractarian Movement.* McMaster was forced to leave the seminary and eventually converted to Roman Catholicism under the tutelage of Bishop John McCloskey* and the Redemptorist priest Gabriel Rumpler. His attempt to become a member of the Redemptorist order was unsuccessful. Returning to New York City, McMaster began to work on the newspaper *The Freeman's Journal and Catholic Register.* By 1848 he was the sole owner and editor of the paper. During the Civil War* the paper was banned by the U.S. Postmaster as treasonable and seditious, and McMaster was imprisoned at Fort Lafayette for almost nine months. His attacks on Lincoln,* the American press, the public schools and free thought labeled him a "militant" in the eyes of many. His defense of the rights of American Catholic pastors earned him the opposition of many American bishops.*

BIBLIOGRAPHY. *DAB* VI; R. F. Trisco, "Bishops and Their Priests in the United States," in *The Catholic Priest in the United States,* ed. J. T. Ellis (1971).   T. F. Sable

McMaster, William (1811-1887).
Canadian Baptist* philanthropist.* Born in County Tyrone in Ulster, Ireland, McMaster was converted at ten years of age and joined the Baptist congregation in Omagh. The intense faith of the small Irish Baptist community, under the leadership of Alexander Carson, so formed McMaster that in spite of his later financial, political and social eminence, he never deviated from his earliest convictions. He immigrated to Toronto in 1833 and quickly became a partner in, and then sole proprietor of, a dry goods firm.

McMaster's entrepreneurial genius and canny Ulster approach soon made him one of the wealthiest men in Toronto. He held numerous business directorates in railways and insurance. In 1867, the year of Canadian Confederation, at a time in life when many might be slowing down, McMaster became a founding president of the Bank of Commerce, a position which he held for two decades, building it into one of the largest banks in the country. In the same year he was also appointed to the newly formed Canadian Senate.

McMaster was a leader in Toronto's original Baptist Congregation, having a great deal to do with the erection of its magnificent building on Jarvis Street in 1875. He helped found Woodstock College, the first Baptist college in Ontario in 1860, and was even more involved in moving the theological department to Toronto in 1881. In the year of his death, the whole institution moved to Toronto, where McMaster munificently contributed to land, building and endowment for what was named McMaster University.

BIBLIOGRAPHY. C. M. Johnston, *McMaster University,* 2 vols. (1976); *DCB* XI.   I. S. Rennie

McNicholas, John Timothy (1877-1950).
Catholic* archbishop* of Cincinnati. Born in Kiltimagh, County Mayo, Ireland, McNicholas's family immigrated* to Chester, Pennsylvania, in 1881. In 1894 McNicholas entered the Dominican* novitiate in Springfield, Kentucky, and took the religious name *John.* Ordained* to the priesthood* by Archbishop Henry Moeller on October 10, 1901, at the request of his superiors he was sent to the College of St. Thomas in Rome, where he studied Thomistic philosophy and theology.* Ambitious, shrewd and outspoken, McNicholas gained many friends in Rome.

After attaining the Lectorate in Sacred Theology, McNicholas returned to the U.S. and became a master of students at the Dominican Priory in Washington, D.C. In 1908 he was appointed to the head of the Holy Name Societies* and traveled extensively, building up the organization around the nation. In 1914 he became pastor* and prior of St. Catherine of Siena Church in New York. Two years later he was recalled to Rome to become an advisor to the Master General of the Dominicans. While in Rome he became a close confidant of Pope Benedict XV, who in 1918 appointed him the second bishop of Duluth, Minnesota. In 1925 he succeeded Archbishop Henry Moeller as the archbishop of Cincinnati.

In his twenty-five-year administration, McNicholas was especially interested in promoting Catholic education on every level and served as president-general of the National Catholic Education Association (1946-1950). He was highly influential in the affairs of the National Catholic Welfare Conference,* serving as chairman of the Department of

Education (1930-1935; 1942-1945) and as chairman of the administrative board (1945-1950). When confronted with the troublesome activities of Father Charles Coughlin,* McNicholas banned him from speaking in his archdiocese.

BIBLIOGRAPHY. *DAB* IV; M. E. Reardon, *Mosaic of a Bishop* (1957); S. M. Avella, "John T. McNicholas in the Age of Practical Thomism," *RACHSP* 97 (March-December 1986):15-126.

S. M. Avella

McNicol, John (1869-1956). Canadian Christian educator. Born and raised in a Presbyterian* home in Ottawa, McNicol graduated from the University of Toronto (B.A., 1891) and Knox College (B.D., 1895). Ordained* as a Presbyterian minister,* he pastored in the Ottawa valley. In 1902 he began teaching at Toronto Bible Training School (later known as Toronto Bible College and later still as Ontario Bible College). He served as its principal from 1906 to 1946.

McNicol was a scholar as well as educator and contributed an article to *The Fundamentals.** He sought to exercise an irenic influence among fundamentalists,* but his rejection of dispensational* premillennialism* proved to be a point of contention with some. An effective administrator, McNicol was greatly concerned with improving the college's curriculum and strengthening its faculty and developed a remarkably broad-based support constituency for the institution. He was also instrumental in the launching of the *Christian Evangel* and in 1944 published a four-volume work entitled *Thinking through the Bible.*

D. M. Lewis

McPherson, Aimee Semple (1890-1944). Pentecostal* evangelist* and founder of the International Church of the Foursquare Gospel.* Born Aimee Kennedy in Ontario, Canada, to a prosperous farm couple, James and Mildred Kennedy, McPherson embraced Pentecostalism in 1908 and married Robert James Semple, the evangelist who had converted her. Ordained* at William Durham's* North Avenue Mission in Chicago in 1909, Aimee and her husband left as missionaries* to China in 1910. Three months after their arrival, Robert died in Hong Kong. The next month (September 1910), their daughter, Roberta, was born. Early in 1911 Aimee returned to the United States, and on February 20, 1912, she married Harold McPherson. A son, Rolf, was born to them in March 1913.

Restless in the confines of her marriage and home, McPherson rediscovered her call to preach.*

In 1915 she left her husband, taking her children to her father's home in Ingersoll, Ontario. (Her mother, an occasional Salvation Army* lassie, shared her daughter's restlessness in traditional roles and left her husband for long periods to preach and later to assist her daughter.) That year McPherson gradually entered the world of itinerant evangelism. When her husband joined her and promised to assist her ministry, their future briefly seemed promising.

From 1916 to 1918 McPherson traveled up and down the East Coast of the United States, conducting huge tent crusades in which she promulgated Pentecostal doctrine and practiced faith healing,* usually by the laying on of hands. Everywhere she went, tumult followed. Dramatic and unpredictable, she proved exceptionally adept at transfixing her audiences as she recounted a simple, unsophisticated gospel message. While the content was ordinary, however, her delivery was not; crowds thronged to her meetings. In 1917 Aimee began to publish *Bridal Call,* a monthly magazine which she wrote, both to communicate her message and to report events in her meetings. From Maine to Florida she gained a public hearing for the Pentecostal message; and wherever she went, she strengthened both the visibility and the prospects of struggling Pentecostal missions.

In 1918 McPherson, now separated from Harold (they would divorce in 1921), took her two children and her mother on a transcontinental preaching tour which ended in Los Angeles. During the next five years, she crossed the U.S. eight times, conducting some forty revival crusades in tents, theaters and municipal auditoriums in large cities such as Philadelphia, Washington D. C., St. Louis and Denver. She held credentials from the Assemblies of God* from 1919 until 1922. In 1920 she also obtained a Methodist* exhorter's license,* and in 1922 she briefly joined Baptist* ranks in San Jose, California.

On January 1, 1923 she opened Angelus Temple, a 5,000-seat church in Los Angeles. She dedicated it as the Church of the Foursquare Gospel, referring to an inspiration she claimed to have had in Oakland in 1922. By this time she was an independent Pentecostal, preaching a baptism* with the Holy Spirit evidenced by tongues* speech as well as healing. The Foursquare Gospel focused on "the fourfold ministry of the Lord Jesus Christ" as Savior, Healer, Baptizer and Coming King. In 1927 she incorporated the International Church of the Foursquare Gospel. Her other ministries eventually included a radio station and a Bible institute* known as L.I.F.E. (Lighthouse of International Foursquare Evangelism).

The notoriety attached to her alleged kidnapping in 1926 was exacerbated by her marriage to David Hutton on September 13, 1931. Four years later they were divorced. McPherson died in 1944 in an Oakland hotel from an overdose of pills. Medical examiners ruled it accidental. By then her denomination* had some 400 churches in the United States and some 200 abroad, with an inclusive membership of 22,000. Her Bible institute had trained over 3,000 pastors, missionaries and evangelists, many of whom were women. Her son, Rolf, assumed leadership of the denomination.

See also INTERNATIONAL CHURCH OF THE FOURSQUARE GOSPEL

BIBLIOGRAPHY. *DAB* 3; *DARB;* A. S. McPherson, *This Is That: Personal Sermons and Writings* (1919); A. S. McPherson, *The Story of My Life* (1927); N. B. Mavity, *Sister Aimee* (1931); *NAW* 2; *NCAB* 35; L. Thomas, *Storming Heaven* (1970).

E. L. Blumhofer

McQuaid, Bernard John (1823-1909). Bishop* of Rochester, educator. The Manhattan-born son of Irish immigrants, McQuaid studied at Chambly College, Montreal (1839-1843) and St. Joseph's Seminary, Fordham, New York (1843-1848). In 1848 he was ordained* a priest* of the New York diocese* and named pastor* at St. Vincent's Church, Madison, New Jersey (1848-1853), where he opened New Jersey's first parochial school.* In the new diocese of Newark (1853), he became founding president of Seton Hall College and Seminary (1856) and diocesan vicar general (1866). Consecrated the first bishop of the diocese of Rochester, New York (1868-1909), he established there sixty-nine parishes,* several welfare institutions, two high schools and two seminaries.* A national publicist for parochial schools, he set up forty of them in his own diocese.

At the First Vatican Council* (1870), McQuaid had voted against the definition of papal infallibility.* However, on national issues where Catholicism and Americanism* overlapped, he was a staunch leader of the conservative bishops, taking a firm stand against Americanizers such as John Ireland,* John Keane* and Denis O'Connell.* Although a strong patriot, he believed that the Americanization of immigrants should be encouraged rather than forced. Imaginative and forceful, McQuaid, as a progressive conservative, exercised a moderating influence on the American church of his day.

BIBLIOGRAPHY. *DAB* VI; *DARB;* R. F. McNamara, *The Diocese of Rochester, 1868-1968* (1968); *NCAB* 12:141-142; F. J. Zwierlein, *Life and Letters of Bishop McQuaid,* 3 vols. (1925-1927).

R. F. McNamara

McQuilkin, Robert Crawford (1886-1952). President of Columbia Bible College and Bible conference* speaker. Born in Philadelphia, Pennsylvania, McQuilkin was converted* in the United Presbyterian Church.* Following high school, he worked at William Steele and Sons, Philadelphia, as a clerk and estimator (1902-1911). After a spiritual experience (1911) at the New Wilmington Missionary Conference, he became associate editor (1912-1917) of Charles G. Trumbull's* *The Sunday School Times* and married Marguerite Lambie (1912). Following his graduation from the University of Pennsylvania (1917), he studied theology* privately under Melvin G. Kyle,* professor of theology at Xenia Seminary and archaeological editor of *The Sunday School Times.*

McQuilkin was one of the initiators of the Victorious Life Conferences (1913-1923). First held at Oxford, Pennsylvania, for several years they were held at Princeton, New Jersey (1914-1918), before moving to Stonybrook, Long Island (1919-1922), and finally Keswick Grove, New Jersey (*See* Keswick Movement). McQuilkin became founding president of Columbia Bible School (1923-1952). Efforts to improve evangelical* education resulted in the Evangelical Teacher Training Association, with McQuilkin as president (1931-1941).

McQuilkin was active in missions, but his own attempt to become a missionary to Africa in 1917 was foiled by his inability to secure passage. The Victorious Life Conferences supported missionaries, including Ralph Norton of the Belgian Gospel Mission. McQuilkin also served as director of the Latin American Mission and the Mexican Indian Mission. In 1928 McQuilkin founded the Ben Lippen Conference Center in Asheville, North Carolina, and in 1940 the Ben Lippen School. Both became institutions of national importance. McQuilkin withdrew from the Southern Presbyterian Church* in 1951 and joined the Fellowship of Independent Evangelical Churches. Among his publications were: *Studying Our Lord's Parables* (1925); *The Baptism of the Spirit: Shall We Seek It?* (1935); *The Lord Is My Shepherd* (1938); *The Message of Romans: An Exposition* (1947); and *Victorious Life Studies* (1918). McQuilkin's role in promoting Victorious Life* teachings was to have a significant effect in shaping the spirituality* of a large sector of fundamentalism and evangelicalism.

BIBLIOGRAPHY. M. McQuilkin, *Always in Triumph: The Life of Robert C. McQuilkin* (1955).

D. D. Bundy

McTyeire, Holland Nimmons (1824-1889). Methodist* bishop* and founding president of Vanderbilt University. Born in Barnwell County, South Carolina, McTyeire graduated from Randolph-Macon College in 1844. He held pastorates in Williamsburg, Virginia; Mobile, Alabama; Demopolis, Alabama; Columbus, Missouri; and New Orleans. There he organized the New Orleans *Christian Advocate*. In 1858 he moved to Nashville to edit the official publication of the Methodist Episcopal Church, South, also called *The Christian Advocate*. When the publishing house was occupied by the Union Army during the Civil War,* he moved to Montgomery, Alabama. After the war he was instrumental in reorganizing the Methodist Episcopal Church, South, to include lay representation at Annual Conferences and the General Conference. Elected bishop in 1866, he aided in forming the new Colored Methodist Episcopal Church (CME).*

Through a family connection (McTyeire's wife, Amelia Townsend McTyeire, was a cousin of the second Mrs. Cornelius Vanderbilt), in 1873 McTyeire persuaded Vanderbilt to give $500,000 to create a university in Nashville aimed at healing sectional differences. Although a Methodist Central University had been planned, the New York shipping tycoon's money made the university a reality. Vanderbilt did not share the bishop's piety, but he admired McTyeire's entrepreneurial spirit and specified that McTyeire be president of the university. McTyeire ruled over the fledgling university until his death in 1889. The university separated from the Methodist Church after a bitter dispute in 1914. Among his writings was a *History of Methodism* (1884), which is notable for its treatment of slavery.

BIBLIOGRAPHY. P. K. Conkin, *Gone with the Ivy* (1985); *DAB* VI; J. J. Tigert, *Bishop Holland Nimmons McTyeire* (1955).

R. R. Crocker

Madison, James (1749-1812). First Protestant Episcopal* bishop* of Virginia. Cousin to the future U.S. President of the same name, James Madison was born in Virginia, attended the College of Willliam and Mary*, and was ordained* in England to the ministry in 1775. During the Revolution* he became president of William and Mary, a position he held until his death. An enthusiastic republican of the Jeffersonian school, Madison's interest in clerical duties was less marked. But after the death of the first bishop-elect, David Griffith, Madison accepted the episcopal nomination and was consecrated in London in 1790.

The new bishop initially busied himself in church affairs and took a leadership role in formulating the church's response to the Baptists'* assault on its glebe lands* in the 1790s. But his involvement in ecclesiastical business waned after 1800. Episcopal visitations ceased, and church conventions were rarely held. During his tenure, the Protestant Episcopal Church in Virginia reached its nadir.

BIBLIOGRAPHY. C. Crowe, "Bishop James Madison and the Republic of Virtue," *JSH* 30 (1964):58-70; *DAB* VI.

T. E. Buckley

Madonna. Artistic representation of the mother Mary with her child Jesus primarily through painting, sculpture, stained glass and medals. Depictions of the Madonna date from at least the art of the Roman catacombs. With the rise in Marian devotion during the Middle Ages, artists and architects strongly featured Mary and her child. Eastern iconographers produced Madonnas which were often decisive in converting whole areas to Christianity. In the West, great artists rendered the Madonna and Child, with some notable differences among artists, eras and schools. The Madonna theme, like others in religious art, responds to a yearning of some Christian believers for symbolic expression of sublime Christian truths that almost defy statement. In North America, recent Marian art can be found in the National Shrine of the Immaculate Conception, Washington, D.C., where Mary is honored not only as mother of the Lord but also under titles deriving from various nations and devotions.

BIBLIOGRAPHY. M. O'Carroll, "Art," "Theotokos," in *A Theological Encyclopedia of the Blessed Virgin Mary* (1985).

G. P. Evans

Magisterium. In the widest sense, the teaching authority of the whole church. In the Roman Catholic Church since the nineteenth century (Gregory XVI, Pius IX* and Vatican Council I*), *magisterium* applies to the authority* of the pope* and the college of bishops to teach on matters of faith and morals. Teaching authority is exercised at two levels: (1) as doctrine* infallibly proclaimed by definitive act in an ecumenical council or *ex cathedra* pronouncement by the pope, and as teachings consistently affirmed as necessary for salvation*; (2) as authoritative (non-infallible) teaching.

To infallible teachings, assent of faith (*assensus fidei*) is owed. To authoritative teaching, religious respect *(religiosum obsequium)* is due (*Dogmatic Constitution on the Church* [1964] #25 and *Code of Canon Law* [1983] #747—#755). There is considerable debate among Catholic Church hierarchy and theologians about what is included under infallible teachings consistently affirmed as necessary for salvation, how to interpret *religiosum obsequium* and what are the criteria for public dissent to authoritative (non-infallible) teaching. The debate became particularly acute in the U.S. after the Vatican disciplined moral theologian Charles E. Curran in 1986.

BIBLIOGRAPHY. J. A. Coriden, T. J. Green and D. E. Heintschel, eds., *The Code of Canon Law, A Text and Commentary* (1986); C. E. Curran and R. A. McCormick, eds., *The Magisterium and Morality* (1982). A. M. Clifford

Magnalia Christi Americana. A history of the churches of New England written by Cotton Mather.* Mather, then minister of the Second Church (Old North), Boston, started to write the *Magnalia* in 1693 and had largely completed it by 1697, though he did not send it to the printer for another three years. The formal title of the history is *Magnalia Christi Americana; or, The Ecclesiastical History of New-England From Its First Planting, in the Year 1620, Unto the Year of our Lord 1698, in Seven Books.* Published in London in 1702, the first American edition did not appear until 1820. When the first edition arrived from London, Mather was distressed to find many errors in the work, and issued a list of errata, which appears in some of the editions. The seven books deal with the following material: I. History of the Several Colonies of New England; II. Governors and Magistrates; III. Sixty Famous Divines; IV. Harvard University; V. Church Synods, Deliberations and Actions; VI. Divine Providences with Respect to Individuals; VII. "The Wars of the Lord": afflictions upon the church in New England. This vast record of New England's foundation was more than a chronicle—it invited readers to view New England's history as sacred history. It remains one of the most valuable resources for New England's civil and ecclesiastical history.

BY. D. Levin, *Cotton Mather* (1978); C. Mather, *Magnalia Christi Americana*, ed. T. Robbins and L. F. Robinson, 2 vols. (1853).

D. A. Weir

Mahan, Asa (1799-1889). First president of Oberlin College.* Reared in a Congregational* home, Mahan graduated from Andover Theological Seminary* in 1827. As pastor of the Sixth Presbyterian* Church in Cincinnati and a trustee of Lane Theological Seminary, he supported the abolitionist* "Lane Rebels." Mahan accepted the presidency of Oberlin (1835-1850) on the condition that the school be integrated. He was offered the position because the Lane Rebels insisted on it, because Finney was his friend and because the Tappan brothers'* funding for the struggling Oberlin depended on Mahan's appointment. Mahan continually advocated a realistic equity for women and African-Americans at Oberlin, an attainable Christian perfection* and Scottish Common Sense* philosophy. His changing understanding of these latter two issues parallels that of a large portion of nineteenth-century evangelicalism.* Mahan's tactlessness and some faculty and community dissent resulted in his resignation at Oberlin. He became president of Cleveland University and later Adrian College. In 1871 he joined the abolitionist Wesleyan* Methodist Church. Mahan's perfectionism, as it was developed at Oberlin, had emphasized the work of the Holy Spirit in granting believers entire sanctification. By 1870, when he published *The Baptism of the Holy Spirit,* his theology reflected the themes of the Higher Christian Life Movement,* and by the early 1870s he was being invited as a speaker to the British Keswick* meetings.

BIBLIOGRAPHY. *DAB* VI; E. H. Madden and J. E. Hamilton, *Freedom and Grace: The Life of Asa Mahan* (1982); A. Mahan, *Autobiography: Intellectual, Moral, and Spiritual* (1882); D. L. Dayton, "Asa Mahan and the Development of American Holiness Theology," *WTJ* 9 (Spring 1974):60-69. M. R. Fraser

Maier, Walter Arthur (1893-1950). Pioneer Lutheran* radio preacher.* Born in Boston, Maier was educated at Concordia Collegiate Institute, Bronxville, New York; Boston College (B.A. 1913); and Concordia Seminary, St. Louis, Missouri (1916). He was ordained* by the Lutheran Church—Missouri Synod* in 1917. Maier then began studies in Old Testament and Semitics at Harvard University,* receiving an M.A. (1920) and eventually a Ph.D. (1929) in Semitic studies. In 1920 Maier became executive secretary for his denomination's youth organization, the Walther League, and began his work as editor of *The Walther League Messenger.* While Maier left his position as executive secretary in 1922 to begin teaching Old Testament at Concordia Seminary, St. Louis, his involvement with the magazine, both as editor and contributor, continued throughout most of his career (1922-1945).

In 1930 Maier accepted an invitation from his denomination's Lutheran Laymen's League to speak on their fledgling radio program, "The Lutheran Hour." The program was suspended that year, but when it resumed in 1935 Maier became its regular speaker, a role he filled until his death. "The Lutheran Hour" eventually became the world's largest radio broadcast venture of its time, being aired over 1,200 stations world-wide in thirty-six languages with an estimated annual audience of two-thirds billion. Maier's messages were often characterized by denunciations of modernism, Communism and moral laxity; it reached an audience far broader than his denomination.

A prolific author, Maier published over twenty books, mostly sermon collections. Of his many popular titles, one was a widely read work on Christian marriage,* *For Better, Not for Worse.* He annually wrote a daily devotional guide, *Day by Day with Jesus.* His scholarly commentary on Nahum was published posthumously. He was much in demand as a speaker, not only for "Lutheran Hour" rallies but for various other religious and civic events.

Through his diverse and prominent ministries, many were brought to Christian faith. More than any other person in the 1930s and 1940s, Maier brought his church body to national attention.

BIBLIOGRAPHY. *DAB* 4; P. L. Maier, *A Man Spoke, a World Listened* (1963); M. L. Rudnick, *Fundamentalism and the Missouri Synod* (1966).

M. L. Rudnick

Mainline Churches. The term *mainline* seems to take its meaning from the traditional aristocratic community ("The Main Line") just outside Philadelphia, Pennsylvania, once served by the main line of the former Pennsylvania Railroad. The *Oxford English Dictionary* indicates that the first usage of the term *mainline* in connection with a railroad, occurred in 1841. However, the *OED*'s first reference to the term applied to "the mainline Christian churches" dates only from 1972. According to the evidence presented by the *OED*, the common use of the term *mainline churches* appears to have emerged in the youth counterculture of the 1960s and from there passed into widespread usage by journalists, social analysts and church historians in the 1970s.

Today, it is not always clear what is meant by the phrase *mainline churches.* For some it means only those churches or denominations most closely

associated with tradition and convention, that is, the unofficial Protestant establishment (i.e., Congregationalists,* Presbyterians* and Episcopalians*). To these may be added the less traditional denominations, such as Baptists,* Methodists* and Disciples,* who in the nineteenth and twentieth centuries eventually found acceptance in socially prominent communities. More recently, a broader definition has included Roman Catholics* and Jewish congregations.

In 1972 Dean M. Kelley categorized as "typically mainstream" twentieth-century denominations the Presbyterian Church in the U.S.,* Reformed Church in America,* Episcopal Church,* American Baptist Convention,* United Presbyterian Church,* United Methodist Church,* United Church of Christ,* along with Reform Jews, the Ethical Culture Society and the Unitarian-Universalists.* Newcomers to the mainstream were the Southern Baptist Convention,* Lutheran Church—Missouri Synod,* American Lutheran Church,* Roman Catholic Church, Conservative Jews and the Russian and Greek Orthodox.*

In 1973 Martin E. Marty identified what he called the "old dominion" denominations (meaning primarily Congregationalists, Presbyterians and Episcopalians) as the churches which "originally took responsibility for relating religion positively to culture" and which assumed "custodianship of the evangelical empire" in America. Three years later, in his *Nation of Behavers,* Marty devoted a chapter to "Mainline Religion," where he argued that the mainline is thought of as "standard brand religion," that is, "the traditional, inherited, normative, or median style of American spirituality and organization," over against "marginal" and/or "fringe" groups which historically have dotted the periphery of the religious landscape. He further defined as mainline those churches which have significant numbers, a proportionate share of the national citizenry's loyalties and attention, the ability to quicken curiosity, the power to provide people with a group or social identity, and the moral force to inspire stereotypical behavior patterns. This meant mainline Protestantism until well into the twentieth century when it came to include Catholicism and Judaism as part of the normative faith of an increasingly pluralist nation.

In 1987 Wade Clark Roof and William McKinney used the term *mainline* to refer to "religious groups that identify with and contribute to the definition of society's core values." For them, "to speak of a religious group as mainline is to acknowledge its place in the nation's religious establishment." Thus the distinction between mainline and non-mainline churches turns on whether a religious body accepts or challenges the core values of American culture.

Some contemporary scholars see Protestant mainline denominations as distinct from "evangelicals"* and "fundamentalists."* Richard J. Hutcheson, Jr., defines "mainline" churches as part of the "large historical denominations having membership reflecting great diversity, but leadership and official positions putting them generally in the liberal, ecumenically included and socially concerned wing of Christianity." However, this definition eliminates some mainline denominations on Kelley's list, and certainly would exclude many local congregations and individuals within denominations generally held to be mainline. This diversity within the membership of mainline denominations is one of the emerging characteristics of modern American religion. As Robert Wuthnow has argued concerning the American religious scene in the last half of the twentieth century, ". . . the division between religious liberals and conservatives is one that *cuts across* denominational lines, rather than pitting one set of denominations against another."

Nevertheless, many denominational leaders, as well as large segments of the clergy* and laity* in the older, generally acknowledged mainline denominations, have stood in a tradition largely shaped by theological liberalism. They are noted for their ecumenism,* their philosophy of Christian nurture* and their interest in community, national and international affairs. Other churches, not defining themselves as mainline, have stressed the doctrine of personal salvation,* along with church growth* through personal evangelism.* The declining membership of most contemporary mainline churches has been credited to the lack of a clearly defined gospel and active personal witness, though, as Roof and McKinney have argued, sociological factors may also be at work.

The difference between mainline churches and churches of an evangelical or fundamentalist persuasion may also be one of contrasting social agendas. However, since the 1970s a differentiation between mainline and evangelical or fundamentalist denominations on the basis of their involvement in social issues is no longer valid. With the recent social activism of evangelicals and fundamentalists, it may be more accurate to speak of a conflict of agendas. Old mainline churches continue to stress social issues such as civil and human rights,* nuclear disarmament and feminism,* while many evangelicals and fundamentalists offer the alternative agenda of the rights of the unborn (*See* Abortion), national defense, opposition to the Equal Rights Amendment, and prayer in the public schools.* With the rise of political conservatism in the 1980s, the older mainline churches, though continuing to exist, have ceased to be a dominant factor in American society. Americans at the close of the twentieth century may be witnessing the emergence of a new class of wealthy, socially prominent, evangelical/fundamentalist "mainline" churches. It remains to be seen what these new realities will mean in terms of religion and public life in America at the turn of the twenty-first century.

See also DENOMINATIONALISM.

BIBLIOGRAPHY. R. J. Hutcheson, Jr., *Mainline Churches and the Evangelicals* (1981); D. Kelley, *Why Conservative Churches Are Growing* (1972); M. E. Marty, *The Fire We Can Light: The Role of Religion in a Suddenly Different World* (1973); M. E. Marty, *A Nation of Behavers* (1976); R. J. Neuhaus, ed., *The Believable Futures of American Protestantism* (1988); W. C. Roof and W. McKinney, *American Mainline Religion; Its Shape and Future* (1987); R. Wuthnow, *The Restructuring of American Religion* (1988).   L. E. Wilshire

Major, Sarah Righter (1808-1884). Brethren* preacher.* As a young woman in her native Philadelphia, Sarah Righter felt a strong inward call to preach. Local Brethren ministers* invited her to preach in their congregations. However, in obvious reaction to her initiative, the denomination's* Annual Meeting in 1834 forbade women to preach, citing biblical testimony. In 1842 she married Thomas Major, a minister; they moved to Highland County, Ohio, where they raised a family. The Majors held many preaching missions in Ohio and Indiana, with Thomas commonly opening the meeting and then deferring to his wife, the better and more spiritual speaker. Where local opinion was against her open preaching, he invited her to lead in prayer. A church committee sent to silence her returned without completing its mission. One member said: "I could not give my vote to silence someone who could outpreach me." Despite the prejudice against her public ministry, she once preached at the Brethren Annual Meeting. Sarah Major was known as well for her strong interest in temperance* work, prison visitation and ministry to African-Americans.

BIBLIOGRAPHY. P. Brubaker, *She Hath Done What She Could: A History of Women's Participation in the Church of the Brethren* (1985); D. F. Durnbaugh, "She Kept on Preaching." *Messenger* (April, 1975).   D. F. Durnbaugh

Major Orders. Catholic* term for a set of offices or orders within the Sacrament* of Holy Orders. Originating in the divisions of church leadership in the early church, the Catholic Church has come to recognize bishops,* priests* and deacons* as "major orders" or offices.

The origin of the diaconate is traced to Acts 6:1-8, and 1 Timothy 3:8-10. Their earliest functions were practical concern for the poor, preaching,* baptizing and distribution of the Holy Eucharist.* Diaconate in the Roman Catholic tradition has been a step toward priesthood and in recent centuries reserved to celibate candidates for that order. In recent years diaconate is now open to married men interested in liturgical, pastoral and administrative work in the Church.

Priesthood has its origins in the cultic priesthood of the Jewish religion, and in the system of elders who governed towns and communities in apostolic times (1 Tim 5:17-20; Titus 1:6). In some places they were a collaborative team with an overseer-bishop. In other places they were helpers appointed and authorized by what scholars have called monarchical bishops.

Bishops (Greek, *episcopoi*) or overseers were originally leaders of the Christian communities and presiders at the Eucharist, but part of a college of presbyters. Particularly in the Roman Catholic tradition, bishops are seen as successors to the apostolic Twelve and collaborators with the Bishop of Rome. Bishops exercise supervision of a region called a diocese,* divided into sub-units of geography, termed *parishes.**

Current Roman Catholic organization and doctrine* regard the ministerial priesthood, as distinguished from the priesthood of all baptized* believers, as consisting of three orders: episcopate, presbyterate and diaconate. Each order is sacramental.

BIBLIOGRAPHY. R. McBrien, *Catholicism* (1981).

B. Moran

Makemie, Francis (c.1658-1708). Colonial Presbyterian* missionary* to America. A native of Ireland and educated in Glasgow, Makemie was ordained* as a missionary* by his Irish Presbytery* of Laggan in 1682. He arrived in America in 1683 and scattered records indicate he itinerated in Maryland, Virginia, New York, North Carolina and Barbados.

From there he served or founded churches on the eastern shore of Maryland and Virginia. Between 1692 and 1698, Barbados was his base. Returning to Virginia, he was licensed to preach there in 1699. He based his ministry in Accomack County, from which he also operated the mercantile trade that supported his ministry. From 1704 to 1705 he was in Britain to raise funds and recruit pastors for churches in Maryland. Makemie's greatest achievement as a founder of the Presbyterian Church in America was the organization of the Presbytery of Philadelphia in 1706.

In January 1707 Makemie was arrested for preaching without permission in New York and was held in custody until March of that year. At his June trial Makemie was acquitted on the ground that his license,* issued in Barbados and validated in Virginia, should have been recognized in all English territories. A significant case in the history of American religious toleration, Makemie's trial gained for the Presbyterians a reputation for upholding the rights of dissenting churches.

Though Presbyterian ministers had preceded Makemie in the American colonies, he has been called the "Father of American Presbyterianism." During his lifetime he was Presbyterianism's chief exponent, a defender of its faith and liberties, a founder of congregations and the chief organizer of the first American presbytery.

BIBLIOGRAPHY. *AAP* 3; L. P. Bowen, *The Days of Makemie* (1885); *DAB* VI; *DARB*; *NCAB* 11; I. M. Page, *The Life Story of Rev. Francis Makemie* (1938); B. S. Schlenther, ed., *The Life and Writings of Francis Makemie* (1971); J. H. Smylie, "Francis Makemie: Tradition and Challenge," *JPH* 61 (1983): 197-209.

A. H. Freundt

Malone, John Walter (1857-1935). Evangelical* Quaker* educator, publisher, industrialist and philanthropist.* Born in Clermont County, Ohio, Malone entered into business with his brothers in stone, railroad and oil enterprises in Cleveland, Ohio. In 1886 he married Emma Isabel Brown, and together in 1892 they founded the Christian Workers Training School in Cleveland, Ohio, known since 1956 as Malone College, now in Canton, Ohio (1957).

Malone was involved in a number of other Christian enterprises. He was publisher of *The Christian-Worker,* which he merged with the *Friends Review* (edited by Rufus Jones*) to found *The American Friend* in 1894, and in 1905 he founded *The Evangelical Friend.* His interest in missions led him to found an American Friends mission to India in 1892, today known as the *Bundelkhand Masihi Mitra Samaj* (The Bundelkhand Christian Friends Society), and in 1901 the Friends Africa Industrial Mission, today known as the East Africa Yearly Meeting of Friends. He also founded the Gospel Rescue Mission in Cleveland, which provided job training and other assistance to the poor, and the Children's Country Training Home, which cared for orphans and abused children. A dedicated philanthropist, Malone was known to have provided some 10,000 meals to homeless persons in one five-month period.

J. W. Oliver

Manifest Destiny. The term *manifest destiny* first appeared in an unsigned editorial article published in the July-August 1845 issue of *The United States Magazine and Democratic Review.* The article was subsequently associated with the editor of the magazine, John L. O'Sullivan. It stated that foreign governments were obstructing the annexation of Texas and trying to stop the fulfillment of our "manifest destiny to overspread the continent allotted by Providence for the free development of our yearly multiplying millions." The phrase became more widely known after it appeared in the *New York Morning News,* in an editorial dealing with the Oregon dispute. It was first used in Congress in a speech given by Representative Robert C. Winthrop, who claimed during the debate on the Oregon boundary that it was the Manifest Destiny of the U.S. to spread over the whole continent.

The idea certainly contributed to the war with Mexico. The rationale given for expansion was that the democratic* institutions forged by the Revolutionary generation and fine-tuned during the Jacksonian era were of such magnificent perfection that no boundaries could contain them. This was not viewed as imperialism but as a natural flow of providential institutions. The jingoists of the era, likewise, believed that it was manifestly destined for the U.S. to take over all of Mexico as a result of the American army victories. Indeed, the more ardent exponents envisioned American dominance from pole to pole. The routes West, notably the Oregon and California trails, were being referred to as "paths of empire." Native Americans felt the pressure of Manifest Destiny as much as any group. Their resistance to the westward advance by the whites placed them in the role of obstructing progress. Hence, the very harsh measures which were employed to subdue them were justified because the end result would assure the triumph of the theory.

The missionary* thrust which carried the Marcus Whitmans* and Jason Lees* to Oregon Territory paled in comparison to the "New Manifest Destiny" of the 1890s. God was called upon to open the doors to "foreign mission fields," using the diplomatic and military forces of the U.S. govern-

ment whenever necessary. President McKinley* justified the occupation of the Philippine Islands as a task thrust upon the U.S. by her destiny, and the native peoples became a subject of U.S. government foreign policy (*See* Spanish-American War).

All of this fostered an indigenous civil religion.* The U.S. was a providential kingdom whose destiny was manifest. Hence, civil religion became an important force in the unification of a pluralistic* nation. Civil religion could flourish in a formal religious manner or in secular patriotic form and both claim that the goal was a manifest destiny for America. Indeed, the words of the patriotic song "God Bless America" imply that the portion of the North American continent occupied by the U.S. is solely worthy of God's blessing.

BIBLIOGRAPHY. E. M. Burns, *The American Idea of Mission: Concepts of National Purpose and Destiny* (1957); F. Merk and L. B. Merk, *Manifest Destiny and Mission in American History* (1983).

J. E. Johnson

Manly, Basil, Jr. (1825-1892). Southern Baptist* educator, preacher,* organizer and hymnwriter. Born in South Carolina, Manly moved with his family to Tuscaloosa, Alabama, in 1837. Graduating from the University of Alabama (where his father was president) in 1843, he studied theology at Newton Theological Institute and Princeton Theological Seminary,* graduating from Princeton in 1847. Manly served as pastor of the prestigious First Baptist Church of Richmond, Virginia (1850-1854), but resigned in 1854 to become president of Richmond Female Institute.

In 1859 Manly was asked to compose an "Abstract of Principles" for the newly formed Southern Baptist Seminary. His effort reflects the moderate Calvinist approach to Baptist doctrine. Manly also joined the seminary faculty as professor of Old Testament interpretation. Except for a brief period as president of Georgetown College, Kentucky (1871-1877), Manly spent the remainder of his career at the seminary. Among Manly's publications were: *A Call to the Ministry* (1867) and *The Bible Doctrine of Inspiration* (1888). He was also a noted hymnwriter and, with his father, Basil Manly, Sr.,* compiled a collection entitled *Baptist Psalmody* (1850). Manly was also instrumental in the founding of the Sunday School* Board of the Southern Baptist Convention in 1863.

BIBLIOGRAPHY. *DAB* VI; L. Manly, *The Manly Family* (1930). B. J. Leonard

Manly, Basil, Sr. (1798-1868). Baptist* pastor,* educator and Confederate statesman. Born in

Chatham County, North Carolina, Manly attended the South Carolina College, graduating in 1821. He soon accepted the pastorate of the Edgefield Baptist Church, in South Carolina, and became known for his ability as a preacher.* In 1826 Manly became pastor of the First Baptist Church of Charleston, South Carolina, and remained there until 1837, when he became the second president of the University of Alabama, a position he held for eighteen years. In 1855 he returned to the pastorate, accepting the call to Wentworth Baptist Church of Charleston. Four years later he became state evangelist for Alabama Baptists and from 1860 to 1863 he was pastor of First Baptist Church, Montgomery, Alabama.

Manly was a strong supporter of the recessionist cause and a leader in the formation of the Southern Baptist Convention.* He was also a strong supporter of theological education and the formation of the Southern Baptist Theological Seminary.

BIBLIOGRAPHY. J. P. Cox, "A Study of the Life and Work of Basil Manly, Jr." (unpublished Ph.D. dissertation, Southern Baptist Seminary, 1954); *DAB* VI; L. Manly, *The Manly Family* (1930).

B. J. Leonard

Manning, James (1738-1791). Colonial Baptist* pastor* and first president of Rhode Island College. Born at Elizabethtown, New Jersey, Manning was converted in a Baptist church in his hometown and was subsequently ordained* by the church as an evangelist.* Manning attended the Hopewell Academy (1756-1758) and graduated from the College of New Jersey* (B.A. 1762; M.A., 1765). In 1764 he was asked by the Philadelphia Association* to assist in the founding of a college to train Baptist ministers. Manning settled in Warren, Rhode Island, where he founded a church and established a Latin grammar school. The college opened with one student, William Rogers, in 1765. In 1767 Manning founded the Warren Association, the first association of Baptists in New England. After resigning from the Warren church, Rhode Island College (later Brown University*) was moved to Providence, where Manning also assumed the pastorate of the Providence church. President Manning represented Rhode Island at the Continental Congress (1785-1786) and was influential in the ratification of the constitution of the new nation. In 1791 he argued in favor of free public schools.

BIBLIOGRAPHY. *AAP* 6; I. Backus, *History of New England Baptists,* rev. ed. (1871); *DAB* VI.

L. W. Hähnlen

Mardi Gras. A winter celebration marking the approach of Lent,* especially popular in New Orleans, Louisiana. Celebrated the Tuesday before Ash Wednesday,* the first day of Lent,* a period of preparation for Easter,* *Mardi Gras* (literally, "fat Tuesday"), also designates the entire period between Epiphany* and Ash Wednesday.

Lent is called the springtime of the church and a period of spiritual combat. For Western Christians this period became a season of festivity and partying. It combined a traditional nature feast, the celebration of the end of winter and beginning of spring, with a last celebration before the strenuous exercises of Lent. The nature feast included the *Narrenfest,* or Feast of Fools, when people dressed up in costumes and made fools of themselves. Rich foods are proper to Mardi Gras as both a winter fools' feast and preparation for Lent. Names like *Fat Tuesday, Pancake Tuesday, Fasching* (German) and *carnevale* (Italian) emphasize the approaching Lenten fast and abstinence from meat.

Shrove Tuesday highlights another dimension of the Tuesday itself, namely the custom of confession (receiving absolution in the sacrament* of penance*) in preparation for Lent. Whatever its later developments and current status in modern America, Mardi Gras itself should be understood as a religious celebration, not merely the preparation for a religious celebration. The feast of fools is an integral element of Mardi Gras and, theologically speaking, relativizes the seriousness of ordinary everyday life, and, indeed, of Lent itself. In the U.S., Mardi Gras is usually associated with the vigorous celebrating in New Orleans and among the Cajuns in Southwest Louisiana.

R. L. Kress

Marechal, Ambrose (1764-1829). Third archbishop* of Baltimore. Born in France, Marechal studied law before entering seminary.* After joining the Sulpicians,* a society of diocesan* priests,* he was ordained* at Bordeaux in 1792. He then came to America and ministered to Catholic communities in Maryland until 1799 when he began teaching, first at St. Mary's Seminary in Baltimore and later at Georgetown College. Recalled to France in 1803 by his Sulpician superior to work in seminary education there, he returned to the U.S. in 1811 as a theology* professor at St. Mary's Seminary. In 1817 he succeeded Leonard Neale as archbishop of Baltimore, with an ecclesiastical province encompassing the entire country.

Various problems made Marechal's tenure a stormy one. There were conflicts with the Jesuits* over Maryland property, ethnic* tensions between French priests and Irish immigrants,* and trustee* controversies over church management and the efforts of congregations in Charleston, Norfolk and elsewhere to hire clergymen* independent of the bishop. Wandering Irish priests troubled Marechal the most; a problem the Vatican exacerbated by appointing Irish bishops to the new dioceses of Richmond and Charleston. The archbishop concluded that one of the most pressing needs of the young American church was a native-born clergy.

Despite entreaties from Irish-born Bishop John England* of Charleston, South Carolina, Marechal refused to call a provincial council, convinced that it was unnecessary and reluctant to unite his suffragan* bishops or to foster the growing Irish influence in the rapidly developing church. In 1821 he presided at the dedication of the Baltimore cathedral* begun by Archbishop John Carroll* and designed by Benjamin Latrobe.

BIBLIOGRAPHY. *DAB* VI; *DARB*; J. Hennesey, *American Catholics: A History of the Roman Catholic Community in the United States* (1981); *NCAB* 9.   T. E. Buckley

Marian Devotions. Mary is honored among Roman Catholics* not only in the liturgy,* the Church's official prayer,* but also in extra-liturgical devotional* practices of individuals and groups. As forms of Christian worship,* Catholics believe that Marian devotions derive their origin and effectiveness from Christ, find complete expression in Christ and lead to the Father—through Christ and in the Spirit.

In the Church's liturgy, commemoration of Mary occurs in the Eucharistic* prayer at the heart of every Mass,* as well as in prayers and readings proper to special days celebrating aspects of Mary's role in God's plan of salvation. Even on other days, hymns,* antiphons, prayers and readings express veneration, remembrance or intercession of Mary.

Popular devotion to Mary has taken on many forms, according to circumstances of time and place, and amid different sensibilities and cultural traditions. The best-known form is the rosary,* a gospel-inspired meditation on central salvific events ("mysteries") in Christ's life. Each set of five mysteries spans a harmonious succession of ten "Hail Marys," preceded with the Lord's Prayer and concluded with the doxology to the Trinity. Strongly reliant on the "Hail Mary," the rosary displays a fundamental gospel theme: the Incarnation of the Word, contemplated at the decisive moment of the Annunciation to Mary. This is found also in the Angelus,* a longstanding devotional prayer for peace and safety which aims to sanctify times of the day.

Notable among other Marian devotions are novenas,* nine days of intercessory prayer, usually conveying a specific intention throughout. There are also cherished short prayers (e.g., "Memorare," "Regina Caeli"). Litanies* rhythmically alternate Marian titles with pleas for her prayers. Mary is often honored under any of her particular titles (e.g., "Help of Christians") or because of her occasional appearances reported throughout Christian history (e.g., Guadeloupe in Mexico, Lourdes in France). Shrines, medals, statues and paintings all orient devotees to Mary.

Catholics evaluate Marian extra-liturgical devotions according to their helpfulness for extending liturgical themes to both cognitive and affective dimensions of human life—but, most significantly, according to the fruit they bear in Christian discipleship.

BIBLIOGRAPHY. Pope Paul VI, *Devotion to the Blessed Virgin Mary* (1974).   G. P. Evans

Mariology. In post-Reformation Roman Catholic* theology,* Mariology emerged as the systematic study of Mary and, more precisely, as that part of theology treating her uniqueness. Today a preferable term is *theology of Mary,* which still highlights reflection on what Catholics understand to be her unique person, but always in light of the life, death and resurrection of her Son.

The New Testament portrait of the mother of Jesus is not uniform or extensive, but it is significant. Mary is a first-century Jewish woman with a central place among those redeemed in Christ because of her physical motherhood of Jesus and her faithful openness to the unfolding divine plan of salvation in Christ. She hears the word of God and keeps it.

Early Christians saw Mary as the new Eve, a type of the believing church. Mary's motherhood was emphasized in combatting heretical denial of Christ's humanity. Her perpetual virginity was stressed as the practice of celibacy increased. At the Council of Ephesus (431), the application to Mary of the title *Theotokos* ("God-bearer") both underscored Christ's divinity and accentuated Mary's distinctiveness. In the Middle Ages Mary's special place was furthered steadily, with lofty titles and roles attributed to her. Where Jesus was viewed as a stern and remote judge, Mary's role as a humane, approachable advocate of mercy came to the fore. When liturgy* and theology became remote from the experience of most people, devotion to Mary kept alive the good news of the gospel.

The Reformers honored Mary precisely as a model of faith; but they expressed disgust with

Marian devotional* practices, which they perceived as abuses. Their theology aimed to safeguard the absolute sovereignty of God in the work of redemption, and so it criticized Catholic insistence on Mary's mediating role in redemption. The Reformers viewed any mediatory role ascribed to Mary as detracting from the unique mediation of Christ.

Succeeding centuries brought intensification of Marian devotion among Catholics, while devotion to Mary greatly declined among Protestants. Mariology reached a peak among Catholics in the nineteenth and early twentieth centuries, with numerous congresses, journals and devotions.

In this period two longstanding Marian teachings were promulgated as dogmas: the Immaculate Conception* (1854) and the Assumption* (1950). The first teaches that Mary, from the first moment of her existence, was preserved from original sin* by God, through the foreseen merits of her Son. The second states that at the end of her earthly life Mary was assumed, body and soul, to heavenly glory.

Scriptural, patristic, liturgical and ecumenical renewal in Catholic theology of the early twentieth century contributed to the Second Vatican Council's* finely balanced consideration of Mary. Situated within a theology of the Church, the Council's Marian theology is founded on the doctrine of the communion of saints*: a familial bond of love endures among those, living and dead, who are united with Christ. Mary stands in solidarity both with Christ and his people. While she is distinct among other saints of Christ in her being pre-eminently the type of the Church, and for her being the paradigmatic disciple of Christ, she is one with the Church and has a subordinate role vis-a-vis that of Christ in redemption. Her mediation is the perfection of the mediation exercised by every member of Christ's body. Catholic theologians maintain that in view of conciliar teaching, Mary's mediation detracts from Christ's mediation no more than the priesthood of the faithful detracts from the one priesthood of Christ, or the goodness of Christians detracts from God alone being good.

The ecumenical movement has brought renewed and ongoing efforts to honor Mary in ways which contribute to, rather than detract from or compete with, an appreciation for God's salvation in Christ. Mainline churches of the Reformation tradition have given greater attention to Mary in recent years. Recent theology, particularly Liberation Theology,* has also stressed Mary's relationship to the poor and oppressed (Lk 1:46-55).

Contemporary theology's renewed appreciation of the role of the Holy Spirit has challenged the Catholic Church to show the relationship of Mary to the Spirit.
See also ASSUMPTION OF MARY; IMMACULATE CONCEPTION; MARIAN DEVOTIONS.

BIBLIOGRAPHY. H. Graef, *Mary: A History of Doctrine and Devotion,* 2 vols. (1985); E. A. Johnson, "Marian Devotion in the Western Church," in *Christian Spirituality: High Middle Ages and Reformation,* ed. J. Raitt et al. (1987); T. O'Meara, *Mary in Protestant and Catholic Theology* (1966); A. Tambasco, *What Are They Saying About Mary?* (1984); Vatican Council II, *Dogmatic Constitution on the Church,* chapter 8 (1965).

G. P. Evans

Marney, Carlyle (1916-1978). Southern Baptist* pastor.* A native of Harriman, Tennessee, Carlyle Marney took degrees from Carson-Newman College (1938) and the Southern Baptist Theological Seminary (Th.M., 1943; Th.D., 1946). He had an outstanding pastoral ministry in three notable churches: Immanuel Baptist Church, Paducah, Kentucky (1946-1948); First Baptist Church, Austin, Texas (1948-1958); and Myers Park Baptist Church, Charlotte, North Carolina (1958-1967). During the last decade of his life, he founded and directed the Interpreter's House at Lake Junaluska, North Carolina, a counseling and continuing-education center for pastors and laypersons.

Marney was recognized as one of the great preachers* of his day and was much in demand as a lecturer and conference speaker. Although he never severed ties with his Baptist heritage, Marney moved freely in wider ecumenical* circles. While he exerted a great influence on progressive pastors within the Southern Baptist Convention, he became increasingly alienated from the denominational* hierarchy.

Marney was a prolific author. Many of his books reflect his advanced ideas on social ethics* and pastoral psychology.* His writings include: *Beggars in Velvet* (1960), *Structures of Prejudice* (1961), *The Recovery of the Person* (1963) and *Priests to Each Other* (1974). In 1976 Marney was awarded the D.D. by Glasgow University.

BIBLIOGRAPHY. J. J. Carey, *Carlyle Marney: A Pilgrim's Progress* (1980); M. Kratt, Marney (1979). T. F. George

Maronite Catholics. Eastern-rite* Catholics* with origins in northern Syria. The Maronite Church traces its origins to the fourth century and to the monk Maron (d.423), who received a Greek and

Syrian literary education and went to Antioch to complete his studies. There he met and befriended John Chrysostom (c.344/354-407), who was soon to be the bishop of Constantinople. Centuries later, a community of Maronites grew up around the Monastery of Saint Maron on the banks of the Orontes River in northern Syria. Seeking to escape from the persecutions of the Caliphates of Damascus and Baghdad, Maronites began to seek refuge in the mountains of Lebanon. Although the Maronite Church never rejected the primacy of the Roman see, communication between the two churches was interrupted for centuries and only after 1182 and the advent of the Crusaders was Roman recognition of the Maronite rite restored.

Maronites had the same rights as Latins, and their own magistrates judged them according to their own customs and laws. The head of the Maronite Church began to use the title *patriarch* during the fifteenth century. The title became definitive in a bull of Pope Paul V in 1608. The Maronite Church is the only Eastern-rite Catholic church that does not have a parallel Orthodox hierarchy. The rite of the Maronite Church belongs to a group of Antiochene rites, and its liturgical language is West Syriac or Aramaic. The Maronites adopted more and more the use of Arabic as that language became the vernacular. Political and economic turmoil in the Middle East has caused the immigration of a large number of Maronites to the U.S. The Diocese of Saint Maron is located in Brooklyn, New York.

T. F. Sable

Marquette, Jacques (1637-1675). Jesuit* missionary* and explorer. The subject of historical controversy, Jacques Marquette was born into a distinguished family at Laon, France, and studied at the Jesuit college at Nancy before acceptance as a missionary to New France in 1666. His first post was at Trois-Rivieres where he became fluent in six Native American languages. With Father Claude Dablon, Marquette established a mission to the Algonquin tribe in 1668. Later he was to plant missions to the Ottawans and Hurons at Chequamegon Bay (1669) and to the Hurons at St. Ignace (1671). He died shortly after founding a mission to the Illinois in 1675.

From his strategic missionary post at St. Ignace (near Michilimackinac), Marquette was chosen to accompany Louis Joliet* on the expedition that discovered the Mississippi River and followed it to its mouth. Marquette was an obvious choice because of his knowledge of native languages and his desire to evangelize unreached Native Ameri-

cans. The seven-man party reached the Mississippi in June 1673 and charted its course as far south as the Arkansas River. Marquette used every encounter with new tribes of Native Americans to preach the gospel, in the course of which he also baptized* at least one child. In 1675 he returned to the Illinois Indians, preaching to over 2,000 Kaskaskians at Easter, but his health failed and he died on the return trip to St. Ignace.

Father Marquette's *Recit,* describing the Mississippi expedition in the first person, has been discredited in this century as an autobiographical account and is generally regarded as the work of Father Dablon. Popularized as a pioneer explorer, Marquette was a man of simple piety* who devoted his life to the evangelization and spiritual welfare of the Native Americans.

BIBLIOGRAPHY. *DAB* VI; *DARB; DCB* I; J. P. Donnelly, *Jacques Marquette* (1968); R. N. Hamilton, *Father Marquette* (1970); F. B. Steck, *The Jolliet-Marquette Expedition, 1673* (1928).

R. H. Chilton

Marriage and Divorce. The Christian concept of marriage is not monolithic, though many Christians would agree that it is a relationship ordained by God from the creation, in which a man and a woman leave their parents to join in exclusive, monogamous union in order to carry out the will of the Creator (Gen 2:18). This union is for life—that is, until the death of one of the marriage partners dissolves the union, in which case most Christians would regard remarriage of the surviving partner as permissible. Up until the late nineteenth century, individuals (usually men) who lived into old age had usually been married two or more times, having suffered the death of one or more spouses.

Theologically speaking, the role of marriage in the church is given special prominence, being given the status of a sacrament* or an ordinance.* The Eastern Orthodox* and Roman Catholic* churches regard marriage as one of the sacraments, though the Catholic tradition, under the influence of Augustine, has tended to see celibacy as a spiritual ideal and marriage as necessary for procreation and the curbing of lust. Protestant* churches have historically regarded marriage rather than celibacy as the ideal and have rejected its sacramental status in favor of an emphasis on its spiritual significance. For Martin Luther marriage was essentially a civil act in which all men and women participated and over which the church could only give its blessing in its ritual ceremony.

Whereas the Orthodox and Catholic marriage

rituals include Communion, the Reformers omitted this element and emphasized the biblical teachings about marriage. John Calvin emphasized a significant dimension to marriage when he recognized that its purpose was not only for procreation and to provide a remedy for lust, but its highest purpose was to form the most sacred relationship known to humanity. This included an emphasis on marriage as both physical and spiritual companionship. The New England Puritans,* who made up the first significant movement of European families to the New World, brought this Reformed view of marriage with them. In this manner they set a strong cultural tradition in which marriage came to be regarded as both a civil and a Christian ordinance or sacrament.

Colonial marriages were patriarchal, thus reflecting a strong Christian tradition that regards the husband as having headship over the wife, just as Christ is the head of the church. But with the rise of industrialization and urbanization in the late nineteenth century, women increasingly moved out of the home to participate in the work force and movements for social reform. Traditional family structures were inevitably altered, and male authority within the family was weakened. At the same time, parental control of children was weakened, and young people became more likely to marry out of romantic attraction than for economic or familial concerns. The increasing mobility of twentieth-century Americans, the loss of a sense of community and family structure, the growing acceptance of women in professional careers, and the shortening of child-bearing and child-rearing years have all contributed to a more egalitarian view of marriage. Marriage has increasingly become a voluntary relationship and, with the relaxing of civil laws, divorce has become an acceptable alternative to continuing a relationship that no longer satisfies either or both parties.

These and other social and cultural stresses have challenged the traditional Christian understanding of marriage as a lifelong spiritual and monogamous relationship requiring loyalty and commitment. Many American churches have been forced to re-evaluate their understanding of marriage on many fronts. Among more conservative bodies, this has led to controversy over the issue of male headship in marriage. They have had to ask whether or not the scriptural teaching has been correctly understood and, regardless of their conclusions, what the role of husband and wife should be, given the circumstances of modern urban life. Answers have ranged from a reassertion that the proper role of the wife is homemaker, to

a Christian definition of egalitarian marriage.

On another front, the Catholic Church has recently seen controversy over the requirement that priests* be celibate. In the Eastern Orthodox tradition, married priests have always been allowed, and in the early centuries of the Roman church, priests were permitted to marry. But the Roman priesthood was gradually limited to celibates. Since the 1960s an unprecedented number of men have left the priesthood, and for many a principal issue has been the requirement of celibacy. One cause of this frustration was the introduction by Vatican II* of a broader definition of lay* ministry which narrowed the distinction between the laity and the priesthood. This led many priests to question the necessity of a celibate life. Though the issue has continued to receive attention, the Church has not changed its law requiring priests to be celibate.

The issue of divorce has also taken a prominent place in church life. The sharp rise in the divorce rate among Americans, both churched and unchurched, has forced Christians to re-examine Scripture and tradition in order to understand the legitimate grounds for divorce—and remarriage—and the acceptance of divorced—and divorced and remarried—men and women into the church and its leadership.

The Roman Catholic Church continues to refuse to grant the dissolution of a consummated sacramental marriage bond, though an innocent spouse may terminate married life if the other partner is guilty of adultery or threatens the spiritual or physical well-being of any member of the family. The Orthodox Church grants the right of an innocent spouse to divorce and remarry in the case of a partner guilty of adultery and other types of misbehavior. There is no single mind among Protestants, though generally it may be said that mainline* Protestants accept divorce and remarriage for a variety of reasons, including incompatibility, and generally permit divorced and divorced and remarried people to be ordained* or continue in their ministry. The more conservative bodies have been less lenient toward divorce and generally counsel those seeking divorce to continue in their marriage and continue to seek reconciliation. These groups frequently bar divorced people from church leadership, whether as lay leaders or as ordained ministers.

Despite the changing concept of marriage in modern America, the majority of couples continue to prefer to be married in a church. This cultural preference for church weddings officiated by an ordained minister has been viewed by some clergy as an opportunity to bear witness to the transcendent meaning and purpose of the marriage covenant and its possibilities under God.

BIBLIOGRAPHY. C. N. L. Brooke, *Marriage in Christian History* (1978); R. Malone and J. R. Connery, eds., *Contemporary Perspectives on Christian Marriage* (1984); J. Meyendorff, *Marriage: An Orthodox Perspective* (1975); J. A. Mohler, *Love, Marriage, and the Family: Yesterday and Today* (1982). D. G. Reid

Marsh, James (1794-1842). Congregationalist* educator. Born in Hartford, Vermont, Marsh experienced a religious conversion* while a Dartmouth* student and abandoned an intended farming career to study for the ministry.* He was ordained* a Congregational* minister* in 1824, two years after completing a degree at Andover Seminary* (1822). His career, however, was spent in education rather than the church. After teaching Oriental languages at Hampden-Sydney College (1823-1826), he accepted the presidency (1826-1833) of the University of Vermont and remained there until his death, serving later as professor of moral and intellectual philosophy (1833-1842).

In Vermont, Marsh encountered the "new measures"* revivalism* of the Second Great Awakening* and became a strident critic of emotional excess in religious experience.* While not denying the role of emotion in religion, Marsh sought to balance intense personal experience with the "deliberative aspects of religion." An avid reader, Marsh was keenly interested in the critical method of biblical study* then being advanced in Germany and in Romanticism.* He turned away from the Scottish Common Sense realism* that had long provided philosophical support for American religious thought and found greater intellectual satisfaction with the Cambridge Platonists and related currents associated with Romanticism. His introductory essay to an edition of Samuel Taylor Coleridge's *Aids to Reflection* (1829) and his translation of J. G. Herder's *Spirit of Hebrew Poetry* (1833) both influenced the thought of the Transcendentalists,* especially Ralph Waldo Emerson.*

BIBLIOGRAPHY. *AAP* 2; *DAB* VI; *DARB*; M. H. Nicolson, "James Marsh and the Vermont Transcendentalists," *PR* 34 (1925):28-50; J. Torrey, *The Remains of the Rev. James Marsh With a Memoir of His Life* (1843). C. H. Lippy

Marshall, Andrew (?-1856). African-American Baptist* minister.* Born in slavery, Marshall was converted and nourished in the pioneering African-American Baptist ministry of his uncle, Andrew

Bryan,* in Savannah, Georgia. Succeeding him to the pulpit* of the First African Church in 1813, he developed a powerful and popular ministry for forty-three years. Once his congregation numbered nearly 2,800 members, but he lost the support of many of them in the 1830s when Marshall adopted Campbellite* theology.* Charged with antinomianism,* Marshall was opposed by a contingent of the congregation, which appealed to the Sudbury Baptist Association to put the church under the authority of the white Baptists of Savannah. By 1837 the schism was healed when Marshall renounced Alexander Campbell's teachings, and his popularity was restored. Having once been whipped for violating the laws of slavery, Marshall became a prosperous man and an astute leader among Southern African-American Baptists. His congregations held membership in biracial associations, the Savannah River and Sudbury, and his services became tourist attractions, earning inclusion in the travel sketches of European writers Fredrika Bremer and Charles Lyell.

BIBLIOGRAPHY. B. K. Lowe, *History of the First African Baptist Church* (1888); A. J. Raboteau, *Slave Religion* (1978).

W. B. Gravely and C. White

Marshall, Catherine Wood (1914-1983). Inspirational writer. Born in Johnson City, Tennessee, Catherine grew up in Presbyterian* manses in Canton, Mississippi, and Keyser, West Virginia. She graduated from Agnes Scott College in 1936. While in college she met Peter Marshall,* twelve years her senior and pastor of Westminster Presbyterian Church, Atlanta. They were married on November 4, 1936, and moved to Washington, D.C., where he became pastor of New York Avenue Presbyterian Church and chaplain* of the U. S. Senate. They had one son, Peter John. From March 1943 to the summer of 1945 Catherine was in bed with tuberculosis; she considered her disease spiritual as well as physical. When Peter died abruptly of a heart attack at the age of forty-six in January 1949, Catherine collected his sermons and prayers into *Mr. Jones Meet the Master,* which became an instant best seller. In 1951 she published a biography of her late husband entitled *A Man Called Peter.* The book was three years on the best-seller list and was made into a successful movie in 1955. Her other books included: *To Live Again* (1957); *Beyond Ourselves* (1961); a novel, *Christy* (1967); *Something More (1974); Adventures in Prayer* (1975); and *The Helper* (1978). On November 14, 1959, she married Leonard E. LeSourd, executive editor of *Guideposts* magazine, and became an editor of

[709]

the magazine herself in 1961. Together they published Chosen Books. She died March 18, 1983.

BIBLIOGRAPHY. C. Marshall, *Meeting God at Every Turn* (1980).   N. A. Hardesty

Marshall, Daniel (1706-1784). Separate Baptist* preacher* and revivalist,* organizer of the first Baptist church in Georgia. Born in Windsor, Connecticut, Marshall was a member the Congregational* church. Converted* in 1726, he served as a deacon* for twenty years. By 1744 Marshall seems to have begun to object to the doctrine of infant baptism,* and in 1745 he heard George Whitefield* preach. After the death of his first wife, Marshall married Martha Stearns, the sister of Shubal Stearns,* in 1747. By 1751 both Marshall and Stearns were convinced separatists.* Sometime in 1751/1752 Marshall, joined by his wife and children, began to travel south. Settling in Pennsylvania, they ministered among the Mohawks until difficulties preceding the French and Indian War forced him southward again. Arriving in Opekon (Winchester), Virginia, in 1754, Marshall found a Baptist church (Mill Creek) affiliated with the Philadelphia Association.* There he was baptized and licensed to preach, although his enthusiastic manner produced some complaints from the Regular Baptists.* Already middle aged, Marshall preached throughout southern Virginia and North Carolina, and eventually established the first Baptist church in Kiokee, Georgia, in 1772. In 1784 Marshall moderated the first meeting of the Georgia Baptist Association, consisting of six churches.

A man of simple natural gifts, yet a passionate and energetic evangelist,* Marshall, with Stearns, was responsible for rapid growth among the Baptists in Virginia and the Carolinas. Because of their emphasis on revivalistic evangelism, the Separate Baptists were suspected of Arminianism,* but it is more accurate to describe their theology* as a simple Calvinism* suited to the expanding Southern frontier.

BIBLIOGRAPHY. *AAP* 6; *DAB* VI; W. L. Lumpkin, *Baptist Foundations in the South* (1961); J. Mercer, *History of the Georgia Baptist Association* (1838).
L. W. Hähnlen

Marshall, Peter (1902-1949). Presbyterian* minister,* chaplain* of the U.S. Senate. Born in Coatbridge, Scotland, Marshall studied in Coatbridge Technical School and Mining College (1916-1921) and was a machine operator and foreman in a tube mill in Scotland until 1927 when he immigrated to the U.S. After about a year of employment spent largely in Birmingham, Alabama, he enrolled in Columbia Theological Seminary in Decatur, Georgia, graduating in 1931. Ordained* to the Presbyterian ministry that same year, he served pastorates in Covington (1931-1933) and Atlanta, Georgia, moving in 1937 to the 1,800-member New York Avenue Presbyterian Church in Washington, D.C. In that same year he became a U.S. citizen.

With a growing reputation as a fine preacher, in 1947 Marshall was elected chaplain of the U.S. Senate by the Republican majority, amidst charges of partisan politics. In that position he became widely known for his brief and memorable prayers. An eloquent speaker, whose sermons were marked by relevance to life, he made a special impact upon the large number of young people who attended his churches in Atlanta and Washington. His wife, Catherine Wood Marshall,* whom he married in 1936, authored his best-selling biography, *A Man Called Peter* (1951), and compiled several books of his sermons, among them *Mr. Jones, Meet the Master* (1949) and *John Doe, Disciple* (1963), as well as *The Prayers of Peter Marshall* (1954). Marshall died of a heart attack at the age of forty-six.

BIBLIOGRAPHY. C. W. Marshall, *A Man Called Peter; The Story of Peter Marshall* (1951).
N. A. Magnuson

Martin, (T)homas (T)heodore (1862-1939). Southern Baptist* evangelist.* A native of Mississippi and son of the celebrated preacher* Matthew Thomas Martin, T. T. Martin was one of the most popular and influential Southern Baptist evangelists in the first third of the twentieth century. A graduate of Mississippi College (1886) and the Southern Baptist Theological Seminary (1896), Martin first pastored churches in Kentucky and then Colorado, where he preached to miners in the open air.

Martin's full-time evangelistic ministry began in 1900. Most of his meetings were held in second-hand Barnum and Bailey circus tents, which seated 600-800 people. Focusing his sermons on the free offer of salvation by grace through faith, he stressed the sovereignty of God and the objectivity of his Word. He disapproved of sensational displays of religious feeling. Martin recruited and trained the Blue Mountain Evangelists, a team of gospel singers and preachers for which he booked revivals* throughout the country.

A strong fundamentalist* and anti-evolutionist (*See* Darwinism), Martin was a friend of William Jennings Bryan* and attended the Scopes Monkey

Trial* in 1925. An able controversialist himself, Martin attacked William L. Poteat, president of Wake Forest College, for his liberal theological teachings. At the same time, Martin was a loyal supporter of his denomination.* This led him to criticize his fundamentalist ally J. Frank Norris* for his attacks on the Southern Baptist Convention. Martin's favorite sermon was "Going to Hell in Droves." His writings include: *God's Plan with Men* (1912), *Redemption and the New Birth* (1913) and *Hell in the High Schools* (1923).

BIBLIOGRAPHY. J. F. Loftis, "Thomas Theodore Martin: His Life and Work as Evangelist, Fundamentalist, and Anti-Evolutionist" (unpublished Th.M. thesis, The Southern Baptist Theological Seminary, 1980); T. T. Martin, *Viewing Life's Sunset from Pike's Peak* (n.d.). T. F. George

Marty, Martin (1834-1896). Benedictine* abbot and missionary* bishop.* A Benedictine monk of the Swiss Abbey of Einsiedeln, Marty came to the U.S. in 1860 to serve as superior of the newly established monastic community of St. Meinrad, Indiana. He later became the first abbot of that community in 1871. In 1879 he was named bishop and vicar apostolic of the Dakota Territory. In 1889 he was made bishop at Sioux Falls, South Dakota, and in 1895 bishop of St. Cloud, Minnesota. Marty left his stamp on the American Catholic Church in the last half of the nineteenth century in a variety of roles. He was by turn a charismatic religious superior, an accomplished musician, a church historian, a theologian* and an innovative frontier bishop. Perhaps his most singular contribution was in the field of evangelization of the Native American, whose cause he championed as both religious pastor and political spokesman. He was also a leading advocate of missionary activity for American Benedictine monasteries. His own example of tireless service to the Sioux Indians and his extensive recruitment of Benedictine men and women to assist him in this venture are a lasting legacy of this activity.

BIBLIOGRAPHY. *DAB* VI; R. Karolevitz, *Bishop Martin Marty* (1890); J. Rippinger, "Martin Marty: Monk, Abbot, Missionary and Bishop," *ABR* 33:3-4 (1982):223-240; 376-393.

J. A. Rippinger

Maryknoll Missioners. *See* CATHOLIC FOREIGN MISSION SOCIETY OF AMERICA.

Mason, (C)harles (H)arrison (1866-1961). African-American Pentecostal* minister* and founder of Church of God in Christ.* Born on a farm near Memphis, Tennessee, Mason was the son of Jerry and Eliza Mason, farmers and members of a local Missionary Baptist* church. In 1878 the family moved to Plumersville, Arkansas. After a dramatic religious experience* in 1880, Mason was baptized by his brother, Nelson, pastor* of nearby Mt. Olive Missionary Church. Claiming a call to preach,* he obtained a local preaching license in 1893 from the Mt. Gale Missionary Baptist Church. He identified with a fledgling African-American Holiness Movement* in Arkansas the same year, claiming a sanctification* experience.

Mason had minimal formal education. In November 1893 he enrolled in the Arkansas Baptist College in Little Rock, where he stayed three months before abandoning schooling for itinerant preaching. In 1895 Mason met Charles Price Jones,* an African-American Baptist holiness preacher from Jackson, Mississippi, with whom Mason worked closely until 1907. The two conducted Holiness conventions and formed a loose network of sympathetic congregations which they called The Church of God in Christ. Their efforts were part of a broad restorationist* impulse in the religious culture. Jones wrote numerous songs that gradually won acceptance in Holiness and Pentecostal hymnals.

When he heard of the restoration of tongues speech* and other New Testament phenomena in a revival* on Azusa Street* in Los Angeles in 1906, Mason decided to examine this heralded restoration of the apostolic faith firsthand. He and Jones had previously agreed that believers should have three crisis experiences: conversion,* sanctification and Spirit baptism.* Shortly after his arrival at Azusa Street early in 1907, Mason became convinced that tongues speech should evidence Spirit baptism. In March 1907 he claimed his Spirit baptism. After five weeks imbibing Pentecostal teaching in Los Angeles, he returned to Memphis.

Jones disapproved of Mason's Pentecostal views, and the two parted company, with a majority of their followers supporting Mason. Mason's new doctrinal views identified him with the emerging Pentecostal Movement. He retained the name The Church of God in Christ and presided as bishop over a thriving constituency until his death in 1961. Mason was popular among white Pentecostals and was widely acclaimed within Pentecostalism for his spirituality.* The Church of God in Christ (with headquarters in Memphis) is the largest African-American Pentecostal denomination* in the U.S. Among American Pentecostal denominations, it is second only to the Assemblies of God* in worldwide constituency.

BIBLIOGRAPHY. L. J. Cornelius, ed., *The Pioneer: History of the Church of God in Christ* (1975); E. Lee, ed., *C. H. Mason, A Man Greatly Used of God* (1967); E. W. Mason, *The Man, Charles Harrison Mason* (1979).   E. L. Blumhofer

Mason, John Mitchell (1770-1829). Associate Reformed* minister* and educator. Born in New York City, the son of a Scottish Presbyterian* minister, Mason was educated at Columbia College (1789) and Edinburgh (1792). Mason pastored two Associate Reformed congregations in New York City (1793-1821). He delivered the municipal commemorative oration at George Washington's* death and ministered to the dying Alexander Hamilton after his duel with Aaron Burr.

In 1805 Mason established a biblical and theological school for training pastors of the Associate Reformed Synod. It was the prototype for the American seminary. He was its sole professor through its closing in 1821. Concurrently, he was a trustee and later provost (1811-1816) of Columbia College. He elevated its academic standards, enhanced its financial position, helped acquire the property for its present campus, and taught classics and apologetics.*

Mason helped found the New York Missionary Society (1790) and the American Bible Society* (1816). Many of his most influential writings were published a chapter at a time in the *Christian's Magazine* which he established and edited. *Letters on Frequent Communion* (1798), *Essays on the Church of God* (1807-1809) and *A Plea for Sacramental Communion on Catholick Principles* (1816) reflect his concerns for sacramental reform and Christian unity. Mason exemplified these convictions, practicing inter-communion with American Presbyterians,* working for the formal merger of his denomination* with the Presbyterian Church in the U.S.A.* and eventually joining the latter's Presbytery of New York during his presidency of Dickinson College in Carlisle, Pennsylvania (1821-1824).

BIBLIOGRAPHY. *AAP* 4; *DAB* VI; J. H. M. Knox, "John M. Mason. S.T.D.," *Columbia University Quarterly* 3 (Dec. 1901):26-34; F. D. McCloy, "John Mitchell Mason: Pioneer in American Theological Education." *JPH* 44:3 (1966):141-155; *Mason's Works,* ed. E. Mason, 4 vols. (1832); J. Van Vechten, *Memoirs of John M. Mason* (1856).
                    P. W. Butin

Mason, Lowell (1792-1872). Music educator, hymnwriter and composer. Born in Medfield, Massachusetts, his father and grandfather early New England settlers and musicians, Mason studied with his local schoolteachers and by age sixteen was leading a village choir and playing several instruments. Not intending to pursue music, he moved to Savannah, Georgia, where he worked as a bank clerk, continuing musical studies with F. L. Abel. Together they compiled the Handel and Haydn Collection (published by the choral society, but without Mason's name) which sold over 50,000 copies.

In 1827 Mason returned to Boston, where he became president of the Handel and Haydn Society and published extensively. Following study in Europe (the source of his school music ideas), he returned to bring experimental music education to Boston schools, eventually influencing the entire city and all of the eastern U.S.

Mason served as musician in Lyman Beecher's* church, directed many fine church choirs and composed or arranged hundreds of hymn tunes. Like his colleagues Thomas Hastings and William B. Bradbury,* Mason's practice was to adapt preexistent "classical" music and compose in that genteel style. His collections of hymns and anthems sold as many as 1,000,000 copies. Some of his memorable hymns are "When I Survey the Wondrous Cross," "Nearer My God to Thee" and "My Faith Looks Up to Thee."

BIBLIOGRAPHY. *DAB* VI; H. L. Mason, ed., *Hymntunes of Lowell Mason: A Bibliography* (1944); C. A. Pemberton, *Lowell Mason: His Life and Work* (1971).   R. J. Stanislaw

Mass, The. A term reflecting the Roman Catholic understanding of the Eucharist,* or Lord's Supper, the Mass is the sacramental* thanksgiving at the heart of the Church's existence, the memorial of Jesus' leave-taking and the sacrifice of Calvary.

The prevailing motif in Roman Catholic celebration of the Eucharist has been the representation of Jesus' sacrificial death. Without denying the other motifs, the Mass especially has served as a memorial of Jesus' self-gift on the cross, through which God has redeemed humankind. Believers were to unite themselves with this self-gift, not as though the Mass were redoing the sacrifice of Calvary, but as though it bore on their present lives, as though they had become contemporary with it.

The structure of the Mass has varied somewhat among the different rites of Roman Catholicism, and the Eastern* (Uniate) rites celebrate a eucharistic liturgy quite similar to the Divine Liturgy of Eastern Orthodox* Christians. But all of the liturgies, including the most influential Roman

Rite, have developed from Jewish precedents, blending music,* introductory prayers, petitions for purification, scriptural readings, frequently a sermon,* a consecration,* a Communion service and a leave-taking blessing. The word *Mass,* in fact, most likely comes from the act of being sent on mission and was conveyed in the centuries-old Roman Rite in its penultimate words: "*Ite, missa est*" ("Go, the mass is completed," or "Go, it is the sending forth").

The first portion of the traditional Roman Mass, sometimes called the Mass of the Catechumens, comprised the preliminary prayers, the scriptural readings and the sermon. Those who were being instructed in the faith could participate in these. However, they were deemed unprepared for the Mass of the Faithful, which began with the offertory (the presentation of the gifts of bread and wine, which symbolized the people's gift of themselves) and peaked in the consecration. The words of consecration were and still are the climax of a lengthy eucharistic prayer that assumes intimacy between God and the Church, God's people. Ultimately it is the intimacy of a shared life, since the Spirit of Christ and the Father makes all members of the Church children of God, partakers of the divine nature (2 Pet 1:4). The words of consecration repeat Jesus' identification of himself with the bread and wine: "This is my body. This is my blood." In receiving the consecrated bread and wine, believers receive Christ himself.

The traditional Catholic understanding of the consecration, as expressed at the Council of Trent, describes what happens in terms of transubstantiation*: what had been bread and wine in its substance becomes really and substantially the body and blood—the personal reality—of Christ. While the elements—the loaf or wafer and the liquid in the chalice—remain bread and wine in appearance, their significance and ultimate being now are those of Christ, of whom believers partake in eating and drinking them. Modern Catholic theology has stressed the shift in meaning and downplayed suggestions of the miraculous or magical. Although many American Catholics now are confused about the precise significance of the consecration, Catholic theology continues to find it important to affirm the real presence of Christ in the Mass.

Similarly, even though contemporary Catholic liturgists stress the motif of a celebratory meal that builds up the community, Catholic liturgical theology continues to affirm the motif of Christ's sacrifice. At Mass one encounters the personal, free act of self-giving love that was the historical crux of the drama of salvation. In going to his death out of love for the Father and human beings, Jesus once and for all reversed the law of sin and death that expressed human alienation. Catholics believe the Mass presents again this central act of salvation dramatically and sacramentally, enabling believers to experience its healing and nourishment.

See also EUCHARIST; LITURGY: ROMAN CATHOLIC; TRANSUBSTANTIATION.

BIBLIOGRAPHY. G. Dix, *The Shape of the Liturgy* (1945); J. A. Jungmann, *The Mass of the Roman Rite,* 2 vols. (1951); E. Schillebeeckx, *The Eucharist* (1968); M. Thurian, *The Eucharistic Memorial* (1961).   J. Carmody

Mass Evangelism. The act of proclaiming the gospel to a large audience with the intention of converting large numbers of people. A mass evangelist is usually an itinerant or visiting speaker who specializes in evangelistic ministry,* is gifted in expressing the gospel message in the language of the people and holds a series of meetings in one location before moving on. Mass evangelism is sometimes called "crusade evangelism" and is a part of the broader Protestant religious phenomenon known as "revivalism." Crusade evangelism involves a series of evangelistic services or rallies held in a large public facility such as a stadium or a convention facility. The services include singing, special music, personal testimonies by well-known personalities, preaching by the evangelist, including a presentation of the gospel and an invitation to Christian discipleship.* Crusades require extensive preparation and follow-up with those who respond to the gospel message. Mass evangelistic crusades are usually held in cooperation with churches in the geographical area within which the crusade is held, and volunteers are solicited from cooperating churches.

The phenomenon began in America with the Great Awakening* and the itinerant ministry of George Whitefield.* Whitefield's ministry took him outside the familiar confines of the meetinghouse and into the town commons, where people gathered in great numbers to hear the simple gospel message and the challenge to repent of their sins and experience the new birth.* Whitefield's outdoor meetings were attended by as many as 12,000 people at one time.

The method of mass evangelism was appropriated by Whitefield's successors, but the next outstanding leader and innovator in mass evangelism was the nineteenth-century revivalist Charles Finney.* Best remembered for his "new measures"*—including protracted meetings, forceful language and the "anxious bench"*—whereby he encouraged sinners to repent and come to Christ, Finney brought these methods to an urban environment. Other outstanding mass evangelists in American history have been Dwight L. Moody,* R. A. Torrey,* Billy Sunday* and Billy Graham.* Graham's evangelistic crusades have taken mass evangelism to an unprecedented level in numbers alone, speaking live to millions in a single campaign (e.g., an audience of 1,100,000 was reported in Korea in May 1973) and to many more through television broadcasts.

Many of those who have engaged in mass evangelism have also been instrumental in bringing about social reform. Both Finney and Moody believed that the conversion of as many people as possible was the avenue to true social reform. Finney was influential in broadening the support for the abolition* of slavery, and Moody was involved in the YMCA* and was concerned about the urban poor. Mass evangelism has also led to greater ecumenical* cooperation among Christians, and a greater concern for worldwide evangelism. While mass evangelism has received a great amount of bad press, particularly in a day when it has become more visible through its use of the electronic media of radio and television, mass evangelism has played a significant part in shaping religious as well as the ethical and political culture and commitments in the U.S.

See also BILLY GRAHAM EVANGELISTIC ASSOCIATION.

BIBLIOGRAPHY. D. Dayton, *Discovering an Evangelical Heritage* (1976); L. Ford, *The Christian Persuader* (1966); W. G. McLoughlin, *Revivals, Awakenings, and Social Reform* (1978); T. L. Smith, *Revivalism and Social Reform* (1976); M. Taylor, *Exploring Evangelism* (1964).

V. W. Baker

Massachusetts Proposals. An attempt by Massachusetts clergy* to revise Congregational church government.* In response to lay* disorder within local churches and clerical disagreements over church government, delegates from all five of Massachusetts's ministerial associations* met in 1705 to consider revisions of the Congregational Way. The *Proposals* that they adopted were written by Cotton Mather,* who aimed to strengthen the authority* of ministers.* The most important of the innovations concerned the creation of a standing council of ministers that would pass final judgments on all church disputes. The elders* also sought to make the decisions of synods* binding upon local churches. The *Proposals* stood to curtail lay initiative in church governance, and opposition

arose from lay people and several ministers. Ipswich pastor John Wise* attacked the proposals in his celebrated pamphlet, *The Churches' Quarrell Espoused,* and Cotton Mather's father, Increase,* also objected to them. Though they were never implemented in Massachusetts, they did serve as the basis for the Saybrook Platform* in Connecticut.

BIBLIOGRAPHY. W. Walker, *The Creeds and Platforms of Congregationalism* (1960).

J. F. Cooper

Massanet, Damián (c.1660-c.1710). Franciscan* missionary* to Texas. A Franciscan from Majorca, Massanet arrived in Mexico in 1683. He joined Alonso de León's 1689 expedition that sought to expel LaSalle from Texas and kept a log of the journey. The expedition found few Frenchmen, but a Texas Indian chief requested Spanish missionaries, so in 1690 Massanet and three Franciscans built the first Spanish mission* in Texas, San Francisco de los Texas, near the Neches River. Massanet then returned to Mexico and proposed a chain of eight missions for Texas. He recruited thirteen associates and, with the Terán de los Ríos column, retraced the *camino real,* planting a cross and saying Mass* in a Payaya Indian village on the banks of a stream he christened San Antonio de Padua. The missionaries at San Francisco de los Texas, however, faced growing Native American hostility, so in 1693 Massanet abandoned this earliest Spanish effort to missionize Texas.

BIBLIOGRAPHY. Fr. J. A. Morfi, *History of Texas, 1673-1779,* 2 vols. (1935); C. E. Castaneda, *Our Catholic Heritage in Texas, 1519-1936,* 7 vols. (1936-1950).

G. A. Reed

Massee, (J)asper (C)ortenus (1871-1965). Baptist* pastor* and evangelist.* Born in Marshallville, Georgia, Massee graduated from Mercer University (A.B., 1892) and spent one year at Southern Baptist Theological Seminary (1896-1897). Ordained* in 1893, he held pastorates in Kissimmee, Florida (1893-1896); Orlando, Florida (1897-1899); Lancaster, Kentucky (1899-1901); Mansfield, Ohio (1901-1903); Raleigh, North Carolina (1903-1908); Chattanooga, Tennessee (1908-1913); Dayton, Ohio (1913-1919); Brooklyn, New York (1920-1922); and Tremont Temple in Boston, Massachusetts (1922-1929). Following a successful pastorate in Boston, witnessing a growth of almost 2,500 members, Massee entered a Bible conference* and evangelistic ministry. In later years Massee lectured at Eastern Baptist Theological Seminary (1938-1941) and the Winona Lake

School of Theology (1947-1948).

Presiding at the fundamentalist* preconvention meeting at Buffalo, New York (1920), Massee was elected president of the Fundamentalist Fellowship* within the Northern Baptist Convention and called for an investigation of the orthodoxy* of Baptist colleges* and seminaries.* His lack of militancy in fundamentalist causes cost him the support of some of that faction, and he resigned his presidency in 1925. Weary of battles within the convention, in 1926 he called for a six-month truce for the sake of reconciliation, after which conflict diminished.

BIBLIOGRAPHY. C. A. Russell, "J. C. Massee, Unique Fundamentalist," *Foun* 12:4 (1969):330-356; C. A. Russell, *Voices of American Fundamentalism* (1976). R. T. Clutter

Masters, Victor Irvine (1867-1954). Southern Baptist* editor. Masters was born in Anderson County, South Carolina, and attended Furman University (B.A., 1888; M.A., 1889) and the Southern Baptist Theological Seminary (Th.M., 1893). In 1889 Masters was ordained* and spent one year pastoring* four rural Baptist churches in York County, South Carolina. After graduating from seminary,* Masters pastored Rock Hill Baptist Church, Rock Hill, South Carolina (1893), and Pocahontas Baptist in Pocahontas, Virginia (1894-1896). From 1896 to 1900 Masters was a field reporter for South Carolina's *Baptist Courier.* He then pastored three rural churches in Aiken County, South Carolina. In 1903 he returned to the *Baptist Courier* as an associate editor. Masters was part-owner and associate editor of South Carolina's *Baptist Press* (1905-1907); associate editor of the *Religious Herald* of Virginia (1908-1909); superintendent of publicity at the Home Mission Board of the Southern Baptist Convention (1909-1921); editor of the Board's journal, *The Home Field* (1909-1917); and editor of Kentucky's *Western Recorder* (1921-1942).

While at the Home Mission Board, Masters wrote six books on home mission work, appealing to Southern Baptists to Christianize America. Throughout his editorial career, Masters was especially concerned about the socio-economic and religious implications of the Catholic* presence, as well as the influx of immigrant* groups into America. In his editorials Masters warned Southern Baptists about the dangers of liberal* theology and the bureaucratization of their denomination.* Masters called for laws prohibiting the teaching of evolution* in public schools, vigorously opposed the presidential candidacy of

Alfred E. Smith in 1928 and was a strong supporter of Prohibition.* While Masters could at times be intensely critical of his denomination, he found a lifetime of service within it.

D. B. Whitlock

Mateer, Calvin Wilson (1836-1908). Pioneer Presbyterian* missionary* to China. Born near Harrisburg, Pennsylvania, Mateer attended Jefferson College (later Washington and Jefferson) and Allegheny (Western) Theological Seminary. Ordained* in 1861, he pastored a Presbyterian church in Delaware, Ohio (1861-1863), before sailing as a Presbyterian missionary to China in 1863. He spent his entire career in Shantung Province, north China, especially at Tengchow, where in the 1860s he established a boys' school which eventually became one of the best Christian colleges in nineteenth-century China. Mateer was a man of great energy, determination and all-around skill: a fine teacher and schoolmaster, he was also an indefatigable writer, organizer, publicist and promoter. His language texts were used for decades, and no school taught science better than did his. His strong personality made him a formidable adversary, however. After 1900 Mateer was a missionary statesman, well known among American Presbyterians as a successful missionary. His wife, Julia, was more visible than most missionary wives and was herself the author of several works in Chinese.

BIBLIOGRAPHY. *DAB* VI; D. W. Fisher, *Calvin Wilson Mateer, Forty-five Years a Missionary in Shantung* (1911); I. T. Hyatt, *Our Ordered Lives Confess: Three Nineteenth-Century American Missionaries in East Shantung* (1976).

D. H. Bays

Mather, Cotton (1663-1728). Puritan* minister* and theologian.* Born in Boston, the son of Increase Mather,* Cotton was descended from a distinguished line of Puritan ministers and was exceptionally precocious, graduating from Harvard College* in 1678. In 1680 he started preaching at Dorchester and Boston, and graduated M.A. from Harvard in 1681. In 1683 he was elected pastor* of the Second Church (Old North), Boston, where he was ordained* as a colleague of his father, who was the teacher. In 1690 he was elected a Fellow of Harvard College. In 1713 he was elected a Fellow of the Royal Society, London, and in 1724 he received the D.D. from the University of Glasgow. He continued as pastor of the Second Church until his death on February 13, 1728.

Cotton Mather wrote on a vast array of subjects, ultimately publishing 469 works. One of his claims to fame lies in the amount of writing that he did. He had an opinion on virtually everything that happened in New England during his adult lifetime. In the area of witchcraft, he published a treatise just before the Salem witch trials,* exploring the entire subject, and then later defended the use of spectral (unseen) evidence after the trials. In the area of history, he published the *Magnalia Christi Americana,** which was a history of the church in New England from 1620 to 1698. His interest in ethics led to *Bonifacius: An Essay Upon the Good . . .* (1720), while his interest in science led him to correspond with the Royal Society in London about natural phenomenon in New England. Mather's *The Christian Philosopher* was an attempt to reconcile theology* and natural science, while in 1721 he opposed medical authorities by supporting smallpox inoculation. In 1717 he called for toleration of other forms of Christianity in *Malachi, Or, The Everlasting Gospel. . . .* Mather also summarized the form of discipline used in the New England churches for one hundred years in the *Ratio Disciplinae Fratrum Nov. Anglorum,* while his *Manuductio ad Ministerium: Directions for a Candidate of the Ministry* gave advice to pastoral candidates. Besides these more famous publications, he wrote in the areas of biography, evangelism* of slaves, philosophy and biblical studies. His massive manuscript entitled *Biblia Americana,* a reference work covering the entire Bible,* remains unpublished to this day.

As a descendant of both the Mather and the Cotton family, Cotton Mather to some degree considered himself the preserver of a "priesthood" of New England pastoral leaders. Both his contemporaries and many historians have considered him to be overly pious, priggish and artificial at various junctures in his life. However, we are indebted to him for excellent insights on life in New England during the late seventeenth and early eighteenth centuries. He was a defender of the old ways of New England, but he nevertheless realized that New England was inevitably changing. He was a strong supporter of the new charter and the royal governor of Massachusetts Bay Colony, Sir William Phips (1692-1702), but after Phips departed Mather did not have the same amount of influence under Governor Joseph Dudley. Seeing changes in Harvard, he took great interest in the establishment of Yale College.*

BIBLIOGRAPHY. *AAP* 1; L. Boas and R. Boas, *Cotton Mather: Keeper of the Puritan Conscience* (1964); *DAB* VI; *DARB;* T. J. Holmes, *Cotton Mather: A Bibliography of His Works,* 3 vols. (1940); D. Levin, *Cotton Mather: The Young Life of*

the *Lord's Remembrancer, 1663-1703* (1978); R. Lovelace, *The American Pietism of Cotton Mather* (1979); C. Mather, *Diary of Cotton Mather,* ed. W. C. Ford (1911-1912); S. Mather, *The Life of the Very Reverend and Learned Cotton Mather, D. D.* (1725); R. Middlekauff, *The Mathers: Three Generations of Puritan Intellectuals, 1596-1728* (1971); B. Wendell, *Cotton Mather: The Puritan Priest* (1926). D. A. Weir

Mather, Increase (1639-1723). Puritan* minister,* theologian* and president of Harvard College.* Born in Dorchester, Massachusetts, the son of Richard Mather,* he received the B.A. from Harvard in 1656 and in 1657 went to visit his brother in Dublin, Ireland. In 1658 he graduated from Trinity College, Dublin, with an M.A. From 1658 to 1661 he served in various ministerial positions in England but then returned to New England. He was a delegate to the Half-Way Synod of 1662 (*See* Cambridge Platform), and in 1664 he became the teacher of the Second Church (Old North), Boston, where he remained until his death. In 1674 he was elected a Fellow of Harvard College, and eventually was elected president of Harvard (1685), a position he held until he was forced to resign in 1701. While president he supported the expansion of the study of science at Harvard, which would expand the scope of the school beyond being an institution of training for the Christian ministry. Between 1688 and 1692 he served the colony on a self-appointed mission to London to secure from the English court a new charter for the Massachusetts Bay Colony. He was successful in securing a new charter creating a royal province of Massachusetts (including Plymouth and Maine) under a crown-appointed royal governor. The new charter was highly controversial among the colonists, some of whom saw in it the end of the Puritan* theocracy.

Mather wrote 130 books and pamphlets covering a variety of subjects. He published a biography of his father in 1670, and after King Philip's War* was concluded he chronicled its history. In the 1680s he turned his attention to the doctrine of divine providence and its reconciliation with natural phenomenon. After the Salem witch trials* he wrote a tract rejecting spectral evidence as a means of identifying the guilty. After being forced to resign as president of Harvard, he published several jeremiads* about the decline of New England. Just before his death he published a tract in support of smallpox inoculation, an unpopular stance in his day. Increase Mather was a diligent opponent of Solomon Stoddard's* more liberal ways in western Massachusetts and was a defender of the older congregational way against the younger generations. He did not support the Half-Way Covenant* at first, opposing his father in the matter, but he later changed his mind, making his new opinion public in 1675 when he published two volumes defending the practice. Increase married Maria Cotton, daughter of the distinguished John Cotton.* Their son, Cotton Mather,* was to carry on the family name as a distinguished Puritan leader in Boston.

BIBLIOGRAPHY. *AAP* 1; *DAB* VI; *DARB;* M. Hall, *The Last American Puritan: The Life of Increase Mather* (1987); C. Mather, *Parentator: Memoirs of . . . Increase Mather* (1725); R. Middlekauf, *The Mathers: Three Generations of Puritan Intellectuals, 1596-1728* (1971); K. B. Murdock, *Increase Mather: The Foremost American Puritan* (1925); *NCAB* 6.   D. A. Weir

Mather, Richard (1596-1669). Puritan* minister* and defender of the congregational* form of church government. Mather was born in Lowtown, near Liverpool, England. He taught at Toxteth Park and later was minister there, his time being interrupted by a brief stay at Brasenose College, Oxford. Ordained* by the bishop of Chester in 1619, he was suspended for nonconformity in 1633. Immigrating to Boston, Massachusetts Bay Colony, in 1635, in 1636 he helped found the church of Dorchester, Massachusetts, where he was pastor until his death in April 1669. Mather assisted in producing *The Bay Psalm Book* (1637) but is best known for his defense of the congregational form of government in the 1640s, engaging in debate with Samuel Rutherford, the Scottish Presbyterian.* Between 1646 and 1648 he drafted a form of church government for the Massachusetts Bay Colony which, after modification by the Cambridge Synod, emerged as "The Cambridge Platform* of Church Government" (1648). In the late 1650s he was engaged in the baptismal controversy which engulfed New England. He actively participated in the Half-Way Synod of 1662, and wrote a tract defending the conclusions of the Synod. His journal gives an account of the crossing of the Atlantic Ocean in 1635. Richard Mather was the father of Increase Mather and the grandfather of Cotton Mather, both illustrious statesmen of New England Puritanism.

BIBLIOGRAPHY. *AAP* 1; B. R. Burg, *Richard Mather of Dorchester* (1976); B. R. Burg, *Richard Mather* (1982); *DAB* VI; I. Mather, *The Life and Death of That Reverend Man of God, Mr. Richard Mather . . .* (1670).   D. A. Weir

Mather, Samuel (1706-1785). Congregational* minister.* Born in Boston, the son of Cotton Mather,* Samuel Mather was to be the last of the Mather family to occupy a Boston pulpit. Graduating from Harvard College (B.A., 1723) and Yale College* (M.A., 1724 to 1725), he went on to study at the University of Glasgow (M.A., 1731) and the University of Aberdeen (M.A., 1762). Harvard College awarded him a D.D. in 1773. From 1724 to 1732 Mather was chaplain* at Castle William. In 1732 he became the assistant to Joshua Gee at Boston's Second Congregational Church and was then elected pastor* the next year, serving until 1741. A new church was established (Tenth Congregational Society of Boston), and he ministered there until his death in 1785. In 1729 he wrote the biography of his father, *The Life of the Very Reverend and Learned Cotton Mather D. D. and F. R. S. . . .* Samuel maintained the Mather tradition of a learned ministry and possessed a larger library than his father's—which was the envy of New England—but his influence was significantly less than his Mather forbears.

BIBLIOGRAPHY. *DAB* VI.   D. A. Weir

Mathews, Shailer (1863-1941). Baptist* educator, ecumenist* and spokesman for theological modernism.* Born in Maine, Mathews graduated from Colby College (B.A., 1884) and Newton Theological Institute (B.D., 1887) before studying briefly at Berlin University (1890-1891). He taught at Colby College (1887-1894) and the University of Chicago Divinity School* (1894-1933), where he served as professor and dean (1908-1933).

Mathews' *The Faith of Modernism* (1924) was American liberalism's most widely read book in the 1920s. It declared that "modernists as a class are evangelical* Christians . . . [who] accept Jesus Christ as the revelation of a Savior God." Their starting point is the "inherited orthodoxy,"* which Mathews identified as humanity's need for salvation* from sin* and death, the fatherly love and forgiveness of the Creator, Christ as the revelation of God and the means of salvation, the persistence of human life after death and the centrality of the Bible* as the record of divine revelation and as a guide for life. But Mathews believed that such convictions needed occasional, and even radical, restatement according to the latest scientific, historical and social standards in order to stay viable (*The Gospel and Modern Man,* 1910). When fundamentalists* and other conservatives claimed that Mathews's redefinitions departed from traditional Christianity, he accused them of undercutting the faith's relevance by holding to old patterns of thought.

[717]

Mathews also advocated the Social Gospel,* as in *The Social Teachings of Jesus* (1897) and *The Atonement and the Social Process* (1930). As an avid ecumenist and churchman, he was president of the Federal Council of Churches* (1912-1916) and promoted the formation of the Northern Baptist Convention,* of which he served as president in 1915.

See also CHICAGO SCHOOL OF THEOLOGY.

BIBLIOGRAPHY. C. H. Arnold, *Near the Edge of the Battle* (1966); *DAB* 3; *DARB;* W. R. Hutchison, *The Modernist Impulse in American Protestantism* (1976); S. Mathews, *New Faith for Old: An Autobiography* (1936); *NCAB* 11.

T. P. Weber

Matthews, Mark Allison (1867-1940). Fundamentalist* Presbyterian* minister* and civic reformer. Born in Calhoun, Georgia, Matthews attended Calhoun Academy and later graduated from Gordon County University (1887). He studied theology* privately under J. B. Hillhouse, professor at Calhoun Academy and minister of Calhoun's Presbyterian church. Converted* at thirteen, Matthews was ordained* at the age of twenty in the Presbyterian Church in the U.S.* (Southern). Following the sudden death of Hillhouse, Matthews succeeded him as pastor, remaining there for five years. He then pastored at Dalton, Georgia (1893-1896), and Jackson, Tennessee (1896-1902), before moving to First Presbyterian Church of Seattle, Washington (1901-1940).

A Calvinist* premillennialist,* Matthews eschewed professional evangelists,* serving as his own leader of revivals.* In 1917 he founded the Bible Institute of Seattle. Matthews founded the first church-owned and church-operated radio station in the country (KTW) and led in the founding of a major hospital which became affiliated with the Medical School of the University of Washington. His pulpit pronouncements on social issues were wide-ranging. He favored cremation of the deceased, supported socialized medicine and mandatory agricultural education for young men and argued that a coeducational institution ought to have at least one-third of its faculty comprised of "the brainiest women" available. At the same time he opposed the granting of suffrage* to women and their ordination to the ministry. As an American patriot, Matthews enthusiastically supported the First* and Second* World Wars, believing that neutrality was impossible. On one occasion he characterized Hitler as a madman and wrote him personally suggesting that he abdicate for the cause of world peace.

Matthews' Seattle congregation grew to become the largest Presbyterian church in the country (9,000 members) and, according to Matthews, the largest Presbyterian church in the world. Matthews combined in himself a personal pulpit flair, strong executive ability and a fundamentalist theology (save for his disbelief in hell* as a state or place of literal fire). He participated actively in the civic and political life of Seattle and was recognized for his contributions by a bronze bust erected in his honor.

BIBLIOGRAPHY. C. A. Russell. *Voices of American Fundamentalism: Seven Biographical Studies* (1976).

C. A. Russell

Mattson, Alvin Daniel (1895-1970). Lutheran* pastor* and theologian.* Born in Bloomington, Illinois, Mattson graduated from Augustana College, Rock Island, Illinois (1916), and from Augustana Theological Seminary (1919), later earning a M.S.T. and S.T.D. He did further graduate work in theology* at Yale University* and was ordained* by the Augustana Synod Lutheran Church in 1919. As a pastor he served congregations in Avoca, Dundee and St. James, Minnesota (1919-1924), and two rural churches near St. James: East and West Sveadahl (1924-1927). As a professor he taught at Upsala College in East Orange, New Jersey, and at Augustana College in Rock Island, Illinois (1928-1931). From 1932 until his retirement in 1967, he was professor of Christian ethics at Augustana Seminary.

Mattson remained essentially orthodox* in his theology but became a strong advocate of the social application of the gospel. His writings include *Christian Ethics* (1938) and *Christian Social Consciousness* (1953). He earlier had become a strong advocate of ministry in the small town and rural church, about which he wrote an extensive study in booklet form, *Town and Country Churches.* His ideas influenced a whole generation of pastors and the policies of the Augustana Synod and other Lutheran churches.

BIBLIOGRAPHY. G. L. Jackson, *Prophetic Voice for the Kingdom* (1986). J. W. Lundeen

Maundy Thursday. The designation given to the Thursday before Easter, marked by special observances during Holy Week in many Christian traditions. The name is taken from the Latin words *mandatum novum* (Jn 13:34), "a new command," and recall Jesus' washing the feet of his disciples. It also marks Christ's institution of the Lord's Supper* following the act of foot washing. The Council of Hippo (393) established its celebration in the church. In the Roman Catholic Church,* Maundy Thursday is marked by numerous practices, including the stripping of altars and the emptying of holy-water fonts. Church leaders— bishops* and abbots—wash feet. In St. Peter's Basilica, the pope also observes the practice. Many Protestant congregations administer Holy Communion on Maundy Thursday as a part of their Holy Week observances. Some Baptist groups practice foot washing* and serve the Lord's Supper on that day.   B. J. Leonard

Maurin, Peter (Pierre Aristide) (1877-1949). Sidewalk philosopher and cofounder of the Catholic Worker Movement.* Born into a large peasant family in Oultet, France, Maurin joined the La Salette Brothers but left before taking his final vows. He immigrated to Canada to farm with a partner and eventually settled in the United States after his friend's death. Shortly before the Depression, Maurin, who apparently slipped away from Catholicism,* underwent a conversion.* He now took no wages for his labor, only donations, and he began to synthesize the writings of Catholic theologians, novelists and other thinkers into a program of radical change which he called "the green revolution."

In 1932, at the suggestion of a Catholic editor, he sought out Dorothy Day,* a journalist and convert from Communism. At first only tolerant of the talkative, scruffy immigrant, Day was gradually won over to his program of radicalism based on an idealized view of medieval society. They founded the Catholic Worker, with its flophouses, farming communes and newspaper. Maurin's "easy essays," which were published in the paper, gained him disciples throughout the United States and Europe. He credited diverse writers for inspiration, including the English distributists, the French personalists, modern popes, Peter Kropotkin and Nicholas Berdyaev.

Maurin preached and lived voluntary poverty, believing that the industrial capitalist system and socialism were flawed in their inability to restore human dignity through materialism. Personally unencumbered by worldly goods and concerns, he was sometimes mistaken for a bum. Appearance aside, perhaps the most controversial aspect of Maurin's program for building a new society "within the shell of the old" was the establishment of farming communes, or "agronomic universities," where workers and scholars could practice subsistence farming and learn through experience and discussion. After a long and debilitating illness, Maurin died at the Catholic Worker farm in Newburgh, New York.

See also CATHOLIC WORKER; DAY, DOROTHY MAY.

BIBLIOGRAPHY. *DAB* 4; *DARB*; M. H. Ellis, *Peter Maurin: Prophet in the Twentieth Century* (1981); A. W. Novitsky, "Peter Maurin's Green Revolution: The Radical Implications of Reactionary Social Catholicism," *Review of Politics* 37 (1975):83-103; A. M. Sheehan, *Peter Maurin: Gay Believer* (1959).   A. Klejment

Maxwell, (L)eslie (E)arl (1895-1984). Founder of Prairie Bible Institute. Born in Kansas, Maxwell was exposed to Christianity only through relatives. After high school he went to live with an aunt who brought him to her Presbyterian* church, and he soon was converted.* Following his discharge from the U.S. Army after World War 1,* he enrolled at the short-lived Midland Bible Institute in Kansas City, a school founded by a former teacher at the Christian and Missionary Alliance's* Nyack College. This training, coupled with earlier experiences, impressed upon Maxwell his characteristic concerns for self-discipline in the cause of world evangelization.*

Upon his graduation in 1922, Maxwell answered a call for help from some farmers on the Alberta prairie. These men wanted Bible instruction for themselves and their families, and Maxwell headed north for a short-term stint with them to get a Bible school* founded. He stayed for the next sixty-two years, seeing Prairie Bible Institute in Three Hills, Alberta, become one of the largest and most influential Bible schools in the world. Combined with the attendance at its Christian high school, enrollment at the 130-acre campus hit a peak of 900 after World War 2. In keeping with Maxwell's evangelistic emphasis, close to 2,000 missionaries* went out from the school during his tenure.

Maxwell presided over the school until 1977 and stopped teaching only in 1980. He helped edit its periodical, *The Prairie Overcomer,* and wrote several popular devotional works, the most notable of which was *Born Crucified* (1945).

BIBLIOGRAPHY. W. P. Keller, *Expendable! With God on the Prairies, the Ministry of Prairie Bible Institute, Three Hills, Alberta, Canada* (1966).
                            J. G. Stackhouse

Mayflower Compact. A civil compact signed in 1620 by Puritan* separatists who were founding the Plymouth Colony in New England. The Mayflower Compact was the foundation for the state government of Plymouth, but not the church government.* The original document does not survive. The earliest surviving record of it is in

"Mourt's Relation" (1622), but no signers are listed. Nathaniel Morton gives the text and signers in *New England's Memorial* (1669). William Bradford,* in his manuscript "Of Plymouth Plantation, 1620-1647" (not published until 1856), gives the text of the Compact and a list of Mayflower passengers but does not list the Compact signers. The Mayflower Compact was written because of the need of the moment, the most immediate threat being the danger of disunity amongst the settlers as they began the settlement. Signed on November 11, 1620, it upheld total allegiance to King James I of Great Britain and acknowledges before God that the community has the right to enact laws and that the people must obey them. No details of civil government are given.

BIBLIOGRAPHY. W. Bradford, *History of Plymouth Plantation,* ed. S. E. Morison (1952); D. Heath, ed. *Mourt's Relation* (1963).

D. A. Weir

Mayhew, Jonathan (1720-1766). Congregational* minister.* Great-great grandson of the original Mayhew proprietors of Martha's Vineyard, Mayhew was descended from a family renowned for its Calvinist* missionary* work among the Nantucket and Vineyard Indians. But his father, Experience Mayhew, became disenchanted with Calvinism in the aftermath of the Great Awakening,* and Jonathan's education at Harvard* (A.B., 1744) disposed him to favor Unitarian* and Arminian* views. He was called in 1747 to the new and fashionable West Church in Boston, where he spent the remainder of his life.

Mayhew's theological views caused considerable controversy, especially when his *Sermons* (1755) defended a doctrine of free will on Scottish intuitionist grounds. He especially aroused the ire of the Edwardsean "New Divinity Men"* and engaged in sharp pamphlet wars with Samuel Hopkins* and J. Cleaveland. However, these exchanges were dwarfed by his strenuous attacks in 1763-1764 on Anglican* missionary efforts carried on in New England by the Society for the Propagation of the Gospel* and on the Stamp Act in 1765-1766.

Mayhew was more the bold and eloquent preacher* than the profound theologian,* and his *Seven Sermons* (1749) suggested that a rational Christianity ought to comprise no more than three propositions: that there is a natural difference between right and wrong, that men can naturally discern this difference and that they have a natural obligation to do so. His political Whiggism, derived from Locke, Harrington and other English Whigs and given its sensational form in his 1750 sermon *A Discourse Concerning Unlimited Submission,* united with his Unitarianism to place him securely in the mainstream of eighteenth-century Dissenter opposition to centralized government and religious authority.

BIBLIOGRAPHY. *AAP* 8; C. W. Akers, *Called Unto Liberty: A Life of Jonathan Mayhew, D.D.* (1964); A. Bradford, *Memoir of the Life and Writings of Rev. Jonathan Mayhew, D.D.* (1838); *DAB* VI; *DARB*; C. Rossiter, *Six Characters In Search of a Republic* (1953); C. Wright, *The Beginnings of Unitarianism in America* (1955).

A. C. Guelzo

Mayhew, Thomas (c.1620-1657). Congregational* missionary.* Son of the original patentee and governor of Martha's Vineyard, Mayhew was ordained* pastor of the small English Puritan* congregation on Martha's Vineyard in 1642. Reputed as a talented linguist, he quickly mastered the local Indian dialect and in 1644 began quietly evangelizing* individual Native Americans on the Vineyard. His first converts opened opportunities for Native American evangelism, and after the conversion* of the chiefs Myoxeo and Towanquatick, he was able to set up a regular preaching mission in 1647 for 282 adults, followed by a school in 1652. Support for the mission originally came from his own means, but he was soon able to attract attention in England by publishing an account of the mission, *The Glorious Progress of the Gospel* (1649), and in 1654 the mission was underwritten by the Society for the Propagation of the Gospel in New England.*

Mayhew sailed for England with a Native-American convert in 1657, but his ship was never heard from again. The mission was continued by his father and finally organized as a Congregational church in 1670. A cairn of stones was erected by Native Americans over the site of his farewell sermon, and replaced in 1901 by a permanent monument.

BIBLIOGRAPHY. *DAB* VI; C. Mather, *Magnalia Christi Americana,* 2 vols. (1702); A. T. Vaughan and E. W. Clark, eds., *Puritans among the Indians* (1981). A. C. Guelzo

Mays, Benjamin Elijah (1894-1984). African-American Baptist* minister,* educator and racial leader. Born in rural South Carolina to ex-slave parents, Mays studied at Bates College (B.A., 1920) and the University of Chicago (M.A., 1925; Ph.D., 1935). Ordained* to the Baptist ministry in 1921, Mays spent his early career pursuing intermittent graduate study, pastoring in Atlanta, teaching at Morehouse and South Carolina State colleges, serving the Urban League (Tampa, Florida) and the YMCA* among Southeastern African-American colleges, and directing a major sociological study of African-American churches. From 1934 to 1940 he was dean of Howard University School of Religion and until 1967 president of Morehouse College. From 1970 to 1982 he was chairman of the Atlanta Board of Education. A theological liberal* who authored several books and numerous articles, an internationally known churchman who held high office in the major ecumenical bodies and a nationally prominent leader in the struggle for racial justice, Mays was an important influence on Martin Luther King, Jr.*

BIBLIOGRAPHY. B. E. Mays, *Born to Rebel: An Autobiography* (1986); B. E. Mays and J. Nicholson, *The Negro's Church* (1933).   D. W. Wills

Mazzuchelli, Samuel (1806-1864). Dominican* missionary* to mid-America. One of the earliest Italian immigrants to the U.S., Samuel Mazzuchelli of Milano arrived in 1828 to answer the call for frontier missionaries and to remain for life. As he explained to the Milanese, "A Christian's native country is wherever God calls one." Ordained* in 1830 by his fellow Dominican, Bishop Edward Fenwick* of Cincinnati, he was sent to Mackinac Island, near Canada, to evangelize the vast territory west of Lake Michigan. From 1830 to 1836 he traveled through the roadless wilderness to reach the Native Americans, fur traders and soldiers who guarded the American forts from Sault Ste. Marie to the Mississippi River. Among the Menominee and Winnebago tribes, he shared their way of life and hardships, planned for their education in their own languages and sought justice for them from government officials. Among the settlers at Green Bay, in 1831, he directed the construction of the first church in Wisconsin, and the first of twenty-five churches which he would design and build in Wisconsin, Iowa and Illinois.

From 1836 to 1844 Mazzuchelli was assigned to the upper Mississippi Valley, to serve the settlers in the burgeoning towns of the lead-mine region from Prairie du Chien, south to Rock Island and Keokuk. He built Christian communities through preaching* and sacramental* ministry,* care of the sick and instruction. Having won the respect of all citizens, he was asked to be chaplain* of the first legislature of Wisconsin Territory in 1836.

The last twenty years of Samuel Mazzuchelli's life, 1844-1864, were centered in southwestern Wisconsin. At Sinsinawa Mound he founded a province of Dominican friars (1845), a college for men (1846) and a community of Dominican Sisters (1847). The first two projects did not last, but the Sinsinawa Dominican Sisters, formed of daughters of pioneers, grew steadily and have enrolled more than 3,000 women to the present. Mazzuchelli died from exposure in the course of his pastoral duties while serving as superintendent and teacher at the Academy of St. Clara in Benton, Wisconsin.

BIBLIOGRAPHY. S. Mazzuchelli, *The Memoirs of Father Samuel Mazzuchelli O.P.,* trans. M. M. Armato and M. J. Finnegan (1967); M. N. McGreal, *Samuel Mazzuchelli O.P.: A Kaleidoscope of Scenes from His Life* (1973).   M. N. McGreal

Meacham, Joseph (1741-1796). Shaker* leader. Born in Enfield, Connecticut, Meacham was the first American-born male converted to the United Society of Believers (Shakers). Meacham, an eloquent New Light* lay preacher,* in 1780 embraced Ann Lee's* (Mother Ann) simple, if severe, route to salvation*: a confession of sin and total repudiation of carnal thoughts and acts. Shortly after Lee's death, Meacham assumed leadership of the sect. In 1788 he initiated the gathering of Shakers at New Lebanon, New York. Father Meacham, who devised many Shaker bylaws and orders, modeled the Shaker family after the temple at Jerusalem. It contained three courts, including an inner sacred circle and a junior order, and an outer court to carry on business with the outside world. Before his death, eleven other Shaker settlements had appeared, primarily thanks to Meacham's personal efforts at promoting expansion. Through Meacham's leadership the followers of Ann Lee Stanley were molded into a viable communitarian venture.

BIBLIOGRAPHY. E. D. Andrews, *The People Called Shakers* (1953); J. M. Whitworth, *God's Blueprints: A Sociological Study of Three Utopian Sects* (1975).   J. M. Craig

Meade, William (1789-1862). Episcopal* bishop.* Descendant of a patrician Virginia family, Meade attended and graduated from Princeton* (1808) because of the concern of his evangelical* mother about the influence of deism* at the College of William and Mary.*

Entering the ministry of the Episcopal Church in Virginia at the low point of its existence in 1811, Meade devoted his life to the revival of the church of his forefathers. Except for the single year of 1819, when he served as national agent for the American Colonization Society,* he spent his entire career in Virginia. After notable service in Frederick and Fairfax parishes, he was elected assistant bishop of Virginia in 1829. In 1841 he succeeded the evangelical Richard Channing Moore* as bishop of Virginia.

A spartan, circuit-riding,* missionary*-minded Episcopal evangelical who was at once thoroughly Protestant* and loyally Anglican,* Meade placed a stamp that persists today on the Episcopal churches of Virginia. One of the principal American opponents of the Oxford Movement,* he was a leading figure in the evangelical party and a guiding spirit in the affairs of the Protestant Episcopal Theological Seminary in Alexandria, Virginia (founded 1823). He died in 1862, while serving as presiding bishop of the Protestant Episcopal Church in the Confederate States of America. Scholarly and prolific, he is best remembered for his *Old Churches, Ministers and Families of Virginia* (1857).

BIBLIOGRAPHY. *DAB* VI; J. Johns, *A Memoir of the Life of the Right Rev. William Meade* (1887); R. Nelson, *Reminiscences of the Rt. Rev. William Meade* (1873).   D. L. Holmes

Mears, Henrietta Cornella (1890-1963).

Presbyterian* Bible* teacher and pioneer in Christian education.* Born in Fargo, North Dakota, and educated at the University of Nova Scotia, Mears taught school in Minnesota and served as a Sunday-school* teacher at William B. Riley's* First Baptist Church in Minneapolis, where she saw her class of eighteen-year-old girls grow from five to five hundred.

In 1928 she moved to Southern California to become director of Christian education at Hollywood Presbyterian Church. Under her leadership the church's entire Sunday school* grew from 450 to more than four thousand in less than three years. A highly respected Bible teacher, Mears had a powerful impact on college-age young men and is said to have encouraged about five hundred men to enter the ministry—making her one of the most significant shapers of West Coast Presbyterianism. Among her proteges were Bill Bright,* founder of Campus Crusade for Christ;* Richard Halverson, chaplain* of the U.S. Senate; and Louis H. Evans, Jr., pastor of National Presbyterian Church, Washington D.C. Mears was also noted for her influence on Hollywood personalities such as Dale Evans and Roy Rogers.

Mears was cofounder of Gospel Light Publications (1933), the Hollywood Christian Group, as well as Forest Home, a Christian conference center in the San Bernardino Mountains. She never married, choosing rather to devote her entire life to her varied ministries. Though she did not openly espouse women's rights, she served as a strong role model for evangelical* women in ministry. The late Clarence Roddy, homiletics professor at Fuller Theological Seminary,* often referred to her as the best preacher in Southern California.

BIBLIOGRAPHY. E. M. Balwin and D. V. Benson, *Henrietta Mears and How She did It* (1966); G. M. Marsden, *Reforming Fundamentalism* (1987).

R. A. Tucker

Meckelenburg, Jan van (Megapolensis, Johannes) (1603-1669).

Dutch Reformed* Church cleric in New Netherland. Born in Koedijk, Netherlands, of Roman Catholic* parents, he converted* to the Reformed Church at age twenty-three and was disinherited. After serving several pastorates near Alkmaar, Holland, and marrying Machtelt Steengen, in 1642 he moved to Rensselaerswyck (now Albany) with his wife and four children. The devout and kindly dominie there struggled to build a vibrant congregation among lower-class farmers and artisans, and he carried the gospel to the neighboring Mohawk Indians after learning their language.

In 1649 Meckelenburg planned to return to the Netherlands, but Director-General Peter Stuyvesant* prevailed on him to accept the more prestigious pastorate of New Amsterdam. For three years he was the sole Dutch Reformed cleric in the entire colony. Meckelenburg established schools for religious instruction and prepared a catechetical* book. He is best known for the defense of the historic principle of "religious uniformity in a civil commonwealth," which in New Netherland protected the Reformed Church. But the colony's owners, the West India Company directors, wished to encourage colonization of foreigners and non-Reformed Hollanders. Meckelenburg and his associates thus lost the struggle for religious conformity, first against Lutherans* and then Quakers,* Jews and Jesuits.*

When the English fleet of conquest arrived in 1664, Meckelenburg prevailed on the fiery Stuyvesant to surrender and avoid unnecessary bloodshed, believing resistance to be futile given the weak defenses of the fort. The West India Company directors and his superiors in the Classis* of Amsterdam castigated him for being "chicken-hearted" and withheld his salary. The loss eventually totaled 2,000 guilders ($5,000). Meckelenburg died discouraged and in poverty six years after the English conquest, but his selfless service enabled the Reformed Church in America to survive its difficult beginnings.

BIBLIOGRAPHY. *AAP* 9; *DAB* VI; *DARB;* G. F. De Jong, "Dominic Johannes Megapolensis: Minister to New Netherland," *New York Historical Society Quarterly* 52 (1968):6-47; *NCAB* 12.

R. P. Swierenga

Megapolensis, Johannes. *See* MECKELENBURG, JAN VAN.

Melchite Catholics. Eastern-rite* Catholics* arising out of the patriarchates of Alexandria, Antioch or Jerusalem. Melchite (from the Syriac, or Arabic, word for "king" or "emperor") were given this name by the anti-Chalcedonian party because they adhered to the Christological position of the Byzantine emperor after the Council of Chalcedon (451). Until the 1300s the Melchites used the Antiochene rite. In the countryside the liturgy* was celebrated in West Syriac or Aramaic, and in the cities in Greek. With the advent of Islam, Arabic gradually replaced Syriac. In the course of the fourteenth century, the Byzantine rite replaced the Antiochene rite.

The Melchite faithful tried to preserve allegiance to both Rome and Constantinople. By 1724 renewed communication with Rome had resulted in the creation of a Catholic Melchite Church parallel to the Orthodox Melchite Church, although no formal written agreement of union was ever drawn up. The patriarch of Antioch, Maximos Mazloum (1833-1855), added the sees of Alexandria and Jerusalem to his title. Patriarch Maximos IV Sayegh (1947-1967) defended the traditions of the East in his patriarchate and at Vatican II* in Rome. Many Melchite Catholics immigrated to North and South America at the beginning of the twentieth century and formed two eparchies (dioceses*), in Newton, Massachusetts, and in Sao Paolo, Brazil.

T. F. Sable

Membership, Church. *See* CHURCH MEMBERSHIP.

Memorial Day (Decoration Day). A legal holiday in the U.S., first celebrated on May 30, 1868, in the North, when members of the Grand Army of the Republic decorated the graves of Union soldiers who died in the Civil War.* Since World War 1* it has become a day on which the U.S. honors the dead of all its wars. Observed on the last Monday in May since 1968, it is a sacred day in what has been called the "ritual calendar of American civil religion.*" Characteristic ceremonies include interdenominational memorial servi-

ces, parades and the decoration of graves with flags and crosses. National services are held at the Tomb of the Unknowns in Arlington, Virginia. Joining piety to patriotism, the day in effect serves to unite the living with the dead and integrate both with the will of the Deity and a sense of national destiny. Canada honors its war dead on Remembrance Day, which takes place on November 11, the anniversary of the armistice that ended World War 1* in 1918.

BIBLIOGRAPHY. W. L. Warner. *American Life: Dreams and Reality* (1962); C. Cherry, "Two American Sacred Ceremonies: Their Implications for the Study of Religion in America," *AQ* 21 (1969):739-754.

A. M. Clifford

Memorial Movement. The introduction of Anglo-Catholicism* into the Protestant Episcopal Church* in the 1840s provoked serious opposition from evangelical* Episcopalians. They considered its preoccupation with ritualism, sacramental* efficacy and the exclusive validity of episcopal ordination* (derived by apostolic succession*) to be an attempt to push the Church away from its Protestant identity and toward Roman Catholicism.* Resistance to the Anglo-Catholics found an important focus in William A. Muhlenberg,* who promoted his own "Catholic Evangelicalism" as a counter-poise to Anglo-Catholic influence.

On October 18, 1853, during sessions of the General Convention of the Episcopal Church, a *Memorial* drawn up by Muhlenberg and signed by eleven other Episcopal presbyters was presented to the House of Bishops.* It called for (1) the extension of episcopal ordination to non-episcopal clergy* who desired it; (2) the loosening of restrictions on "opinion, discipline,* and worship'"*; and (3) stronger ecumenical* ties with other Protestant denominations to effect "a Church unity in the Protestant Christendom of our land." In an *Exposition* of the *Memorial* in 1854, Muhlenberg reiterated his call for greater freedom in the use of the Book of Common Prayer* and more joint evangelical efforts with other churches, and attacked Anglo-Catholicism as a "delusion."

The House of Bishops formed its own committee to study the *Memorial,* and its report to the 1856 General Convention offered several minor concessions on liturgical freedom and offered to create a committee on church union. But none of the major proposals of the *Memorial* were adopted, and evangelical dissatisfaction eventually led to the formation by several of Muhlenberg's followers of the Reformed Episcopal Church* in 1873. In time, the discussions sparked by the *Memorial* bore fruit in several significant Episcopalian ecumenical initiatives, most notably the Chicago-Lambeth Quadrilateral* (1886-1888).

BIBLIOGRAPHY. W. A. Muhlenberg, *Evangelical and Catholic Papers,* ed. A. Ayres (1875); J. T. Addison, *The Episcopal Church in the United States, 1789-1931* (1951). A. C. Guelzo

Men and Religion Forward Movement.

An interdenominational campaign with a twofold goal: personal acceptance of Jesus Christ, and enlistment in the program of Jesus Christ. The movement was the brainchild of Harry W. Arnold, who had organized a successful statewide religious meeting in Maine. The efforts of Fred B. Smith then led to the organization of the ad hoc Committee of Ninety-seven, composed of ministers and social service workers from all over the country. They conducted extensive surveys in cities and used the information to set up a program covering six areas: Bible study,* boys' work, missions,* evangelism,* community extension and social service. Four teams of expert speakers then visited sixty cities to conduct eight-day meetings. The campaign reached 1.5 million people. It encouraged cooperation among churches and attempted to make religion efficient, meaningful and practical in the lives of men and boys.

BIBLIOGRAPHY. C. A. Barbour, ed., *Making Religion Efficient* (1912); *Messages of the Men and Religion Movement,* 7 vols. (1912).

L. W. Japinga

Mendicant Orders.

Religious communities, mainly Catholic,* emphasizing a vow of poverty. The term *mendicant* comes from the Latin *mendicare,* "to beg." Understanding the gospel call as a call to radical poverty, late twelfth- and early thirteenth-century religious groups sought to renounce all personal and communal property and subsist on begging and daily work while traveling and preaching repentance. Francis of Assisi (1182-1226) is the best-known founder of a mendicant order, the Franciscans.* Along with Dominic Guzman (1170-1221), founder of the Dominican* order, Francis stressed a love for "Lady Poverty" as the key to spiritual growth; leaving all possessions for the sake of the reign of God. The Franciscans and other mendicant groups were eventually forced by Rome to modify their radical poverty. They now own property and goods in common. They, like the Dominicans, have developed into large and differing groups, while retaining their basic charisma. Other mendicant orders include Augustinians,* Carmelites and Servites. Mendicant

priests,* brothers and sisters mainly engage in preaching,* teaching, nursing and social work.

BIBLIOGRAPHY. L. E. Boyle, "Mendicant Orders," *NCE* 9. M. L. Schneider

Mennonite Church/(Old) Mennonite Church.

As a North American body the Mennonite Church, frequently called the "Old" Mennonite Church (to be distinguished from Old Order Mennonites*), goes back to colonial times and the first major Mennonite immigration to Pennsylvania in 1683. Many waves of immigrations, especially from Switzerland, South Germany and Alsace brought Mennonites first of all to southeast Pennsylvania. Gradually, others came to Maryland, Virginia and the Carolinas, and later to Ontario, Ohio, Indiana, Illinois, Iowa and Kansas. Today Mennonites can be found in almost every province and state of Canada and the U.S.

Throughout the nineteenth century, members of the Mennonite Church were bilingual, with German being their main language. By about 1890 English began to displace the German. After 1890 the spirit of evangelical* revivalism* and the missionary outreach of the Western world renewed Mennonite interests in urban as well as overseas missions.* Mennonite interest in higher education also began about this time. From the 1890s to about 1950, a cultural conservatism developed which set the Mennonite Church apart culturally—in dress and other customs—from their contemporaries. This development contrasted with earlier Mennonites for whom simplicity in dress and life had meant avoiding extremes rather than wearing a peculiar garb. Both fundamentalism* and liberalism* also affected the Church during the first half of the twentieth century.

The change from German to the English language and the acceptance of many new ideas eroded the strong sense of continuity with the mainstream of the Anabaptist*-Mennonite tradition to the point that (Old) Mennonites were in danger of losing their historical rootedness. Hence the new quest for roots, begun in the 1920s at Goshen College (Indiana), perhaps best depicted in the book title *The Recovery of the Anabaptist Vision* (1957), was a necessary counterbalance in maintaining a Mennonite identity.

Since World War 2,* the once-rural Mennonites have become increasingly urbanized. The violence and upheavals of the 1960s throughout the Western world affected the Mennonite Church as well as all other segments of North American society. The traditional stand of nonresistance was thoroughly tested, and this time emerged substantially transformed, having taken into account the modern complexities of urbanized society. The world was again a place in which the Mennonite Church found itself involved.

Prior to 1860 there was no attempt to create a unified denominational structure for all North American Mennonites. But after the eastern Pennsylvania schism of 1847, "New Mennonites" came into being who in turn referred to the Franconia Conference of Mennonites as "Old Mennonites." The term *New Mennonites* was not used much beyond eastern Pennsylvania. In 1860 the "New Mennonites" helped to establish the denominational structure known as the General Conference Mennonite Church.* The term *Old Mennonites* was never an official term, although it was commonly used for purposes of identification. *Mennonite Church* was the unofficial designation prior to 1971, but since then it has become the official designation.

Today the Mennonite Church includes members from many cultures. Its structure includes a board of congregational ministries, of education, of missions, of mutual aid and a publication board. The Mennonite Church has a modified congregational* polity. The congregation is the locus of authority,* although congregations belong to conferences, which in turn relate to the Mennonite Church General Board. Conferences send delegates to the biennial Mennonite Church General Assembly to which the General Board is responsible. The Mennonite Church is the oldest and largest of the several organized Mennonite groups in North America, with an adult membership of over 100,000 (with approximately ten per cent of that number in Canada and ninety per cent in the U.S.).

BIBLIOGRAPHY. L. Gross, "The Mennonite Church" in *Mennonite World Handbook*, ed. P. N. Krehbiel (1978); H. S. Bender and C. H. Smith, eds., *Mennonite Encyclopedia*, 4 vols. (1956-1969); J. C. Wenger, *The Mennonite Church in America* (1966).   L. Gross

Mennonite Central Committee. The major North American Inter-Mennonite/ Brethren in Christ* relief, service and development agency. The Mennonite Central Committee (MCC) was formed in 1920 as a unified North American response to the famine in Russia which caused the starvation of Russian Mennonites and others.

Emergency relief has been an aspect of MCC work since 1920, as exemplified by its massive relief program following World War 2, the $320,944 material aid program in Vietnam (1976) and the

35,743 metric tons of food sent to twenty countries in 1985. Major refugee resettlement programs included moving 16,000 Russian Mennonites (in the 1930s and after World War 2) to Canada and South America and sponsoring thousands of refugees from Southeast Asia as they settled in North America. In addition, MCC workers have served in refugee camps around the globe. Mennonite Disaster Service responds with short-term volunteers and material aid in the wake of natural disasters.

Peacemaking, following the model and teaching of Jesus, has been a dynamic behind many MCC efforts. Since World War 2, MCC has enabled conscientious objectors to give a peace witness through alternative programs. In the 1980s MCC continued to work for peace and reconciliation through local programs, such as its 1986 efforts in Uganda, Nicaragua and the West Bank. In North America this vision is carried out through victim-offender programs and the Mennonite Conciliation Service.

Mennonite Mental Health Services has eight mental health centers in North America and Paraguay. Development projects have been undertaken in many parts of the world, and scores of teachers have been sent out. Through the Selfhelp Crafts program, MCC provides income for 30,000 families, as the products of people from thirty-five countries are sold in North America.

In 1986 the MCC had 1,010 workers serving in fifty-one countries working with a $25.8 million budget.

See also TRADITION AND ANABAPTIST VISION; MENNONITE CHURCHES.

BIBLIOGRAPHY. J. D. Unruh, *In the Name of Christ* (1952); C. J. Dyck, ed., *The Mennonite Central Committee Story,* 3 vols. (1980).
                                   M. H. Schrag

Mennonite Churches. There are twenty organized church bodies in North America in the Anabaptist* "believers' church" or "historic peace church" tradition. The term "Anabaptist" is derived from the Greek word *(anabaptizein)* meaning "to rebaptize" and is historically derived from the label given by opponents to the sixteenth-century movement known for its denunciation of infant baptism—just one feature of its vision of restoring the New Testament church in both essence and form. Neither Catholic* nor Protestant,* this radical or left wing of the sixteenth-century Reformation stressed pacifism,* separation of church and state,* church membership* of believing adults and the conviction that ethics* are an essential part of the gospel of Jesus Christ. The Anabaptist tradition has been conveyed through the Mennonites,* Amish* and Hutterites.*

The Anabaptist or Mennonite family of churches in North America constitutes a mosaic of cultural backgrounds and styles. They are named after Menno Simons (c. 1496-1561), a Dutch Anabaptist leader. Anabaptist-Mennonite teachings emphasize the church as a body of believers who make mature decisions to commit themselves as a body of believers to the discipline of the church. Mennonites believe that the state, ordained by God to maintain order in the world, has no authority in the realm of faith. Christians are to be disciples who follow the way of Jesus as revealed in Scripture,* including the commands to reject violence and the oath, and to serve humanity in humility and love. In the modern era of nationalism and militarism, Mennonite refusal of military service has replaced rebaptism as a touchstone of identity and conflict with the world.

Mennonitism in North America has a bipolar ethnic-cultural shape. The larger pole consists of groups which originated in the Swiss and South German wings of the Anabaptist movement and immigrated in small groups to America from 1683 into the nineteenth century. This Swiss-American pole was shaped by harsh and protracted persecution in Switzerland, by the Schleitheim Confession of 1527 which set forth a strict church-world dualism and by a schism between Amish* and Mennonites (1693-1697). The Swiss Mennonites who moved to William Penn's Holy Experiment in colonial Pennsylvania became a part of the Pennsylvania German culture. Their vanguard arrived aboard the Concord in Philadelphia on October 6, 1683. Under the leadership of Francis Daniel Pastorius,* they settled in Germantown. Further settlements north of Philadelphia in the Franconia area and westward in Lancaster County served as a Mennonite heartland, which even today has the largest concentration of Mennonites in North America. The Mennonite ethos of these communities, carried along to new settlements in Virginia, Maryland, Ontario, western Pennsylvania and the Midwest, emphasized the virtues of humility, yieldedness and simplicity. Organized groups with the largest numbers of Swiss-background members are the "Old" Mennonite Church* (which includes many members of Amish background), the Old Order Amish* and the Brethren in Christ.*

A second role of Mennonite culture in America consists of groups which originated in the Dutch and North German wings of the Anabaptist movement. Their ancestors migrated from the Nether-lands to Prussia, East Europe and Russia in the seventeenth and eighteenth centuries. During the 1870s, some eighteen thousand migrated to the North American frontier, including about ten thousand who settled from the Dakotas to Texas, and others who settled in Canada. During the 1920s and following World War 2, Mennonites emigrated from Russia, settling primarily in Canada.

The Dutch-Russian experience, while also marked by intense early persecution, benefited from relatively greater toleration and from opportunities for autonomous development, especially in the Ukraine. Mennonites of Dutch-Russian background tended to be less inclined toward separatism and more inclined toward positive involvement in local social and political affairs. At home and on the farm, they spoke a low-German dialect. In North America the largest concentrations of Dutch-Russian Mennonites are in central Kansas and in southern Manitoba. Groups with the largest numbers of Dutch-Russian background members include the Mennonite Brethren,* the Conference of Mennonites in Canada and the General Conference Mennonite Church.*

The traditionalist "Old Order" groups, the most visibly distinctive members of the Mennonite family, are of both Swiss and Dutch origin. The earliest records of Amish coming to America are for 1727 and then in increasing numbers to Berks, Lancaster and Chester counties of Pennsylvania, from where they followed the movement of westward migration. By 1822 they were also locating in Ontario, Canada. From 1850 to 1880 the pressures of cultural accommodation led to the separation of "Old Order Amish"* from the progressives. Most of the latter eventually joined the Mennonites. In 1988 Old Order Amish numbered approximately 35,000 baptized members in the U.S. with less than one thousand in Canada. In the early twentieth century smaller groups, such as the Conservative Amish Mennonite Church (1910) and the Beachy Amish Mennonite Churches (1927), broke off from the main body.

Old Order groups maintain a simple lifestyle and separation from the world by enforcing uniform standards of dress and by limiting acceptance of modern technology, such as radio, television, automobiles or other modern conveniences. These groups draw the line against modernity at widely differing points, but all are intent to maintain the positive and durable virtues of face-to-face fellowship, closeness to nature, meaningful labor and communities of compassion in a world of increasing individualism, materialism and

Mennonite Churches

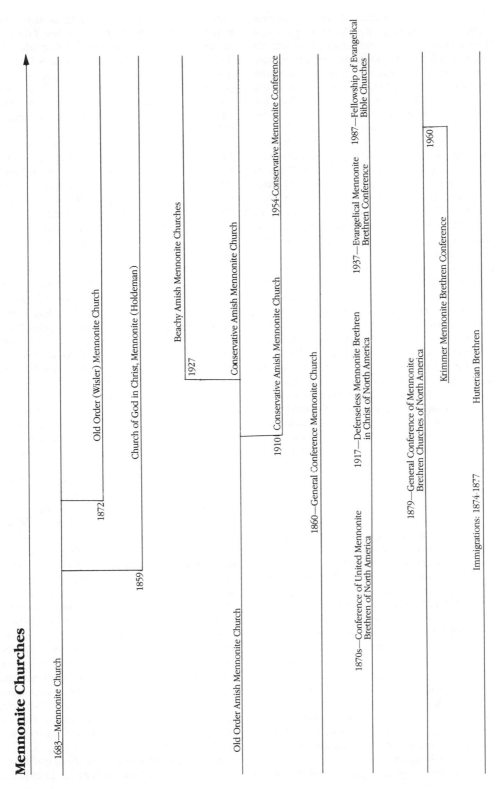

1683—Mennonite Church

1859

1872

Old Order (Wisler) Mennonite Church

Church of God in Christ, Mennonite (Holdeman)

Beachy Amish Mennonite Churches

1927

Conservative Amish Mennonite Church

1954-Conservative Mennonite Conference

Old Order Amish Mennonite Church

1910 Conservative Amish Mennonite Church

1860—General Conference Mennonite Church

1870s—Conference of United Mennonite
Brethren of North America

1917—Defenseless Mennonite Brethren
in Christ of North America

1937—Evangelical Mennonite
Brethren Conference

1987—Fellowship of Evangelical
Bible Churches

1879—General Conference of Mennonite
Brethren Churches of North America

Krimmer Mennonite Brethren Conference

1960

Immigrations: 1874-1877

Hutterian Brethren

alienation. Once considered declining remnants marked by "culture lag," the Old Order groups in the twentieth century have exhibited remarkable vitality and growth. The Old Order groups of Swiss-South German background include the Old Order Mennonites* and Old Order Amish. The Old Order groups of Dutch-Russian background include the Old Colony Mennonites in Canada and the Church of God in Christ Mennonites (Holdeman).*

The communitarian Hutterites,* also of Anabaptist origin, may be included in the category of Old Order groups. The descendants of Swiss, Tyrolean and Austrian Anabaptists who fled to Moravia beginning in 1527, their name comes from Jacob Hutter (? -1536) who joined the community in 1533 and became its leader until his death. In addition to Anabaptist and Mennonite doctrines, Hutterites stress community property and complete surrender to Christ in absolute trust. Having found temporary homes in various parts of Eastern Europe for three centuries, they migrated to the U.S. in 1874. Pressure to perform military service during World War 1* drove many to leave the Dakotas for the Canadian Midwest. Nonagricultural settlements have been established by "new" or nonethnic Hutterites, known as the Society of Brothers, in Pennsylvania, New York state and Connecticut. In the 1980s there were approximately 13,000 Hutterian Brethren in North America.

Most Mennonites in America have made more accommodations to North American society than have the Old Order groups. In the late nineteenth and the twentieth centuries, progressive Mennonites adopted the forms of church life and activity characteristic of evangelical* Protestant denominationalism.* One stage of this development was institutional. Mennonites established denominational boards and agencies to engage in tasks of Christian mission,* education, publication and benevolence. Stimulated by revivalism* and by the modern missionary movement, Mennonites sent out missionaries who planted churches in Asia, Africa and Latin America. These churches have grown rapidly and, given current trends, will outnumber the Mennonites of European background and culture in several decades. Beginning in the 1890s, progressive Mennonites also established schools and colleges, the oldest continuing colleges being Bethel, Kansas (1893), and Goshen, Indiana (1903). The colleges became centers of denominational activity, leading congregations into more professional patterns of ministry and educating thousands of youth for leadership within and beyond the churches.

Another stage of progressive Mennonite denom-

inational development was theological. Mennonite leaders sought to clarify and renew belief through historical study of Anabaptism. Cornelius H. Wedel* of Bethel College and Harold S. Bender* of Goshen College redefined the Anabaptist vision of community, nonconformity, discipleship and nonresistance in ways that preserved a distinctive biblical theology while making the case for greater involvement in the world. The call for "recovery of the Anabaptist vision" energized twentieth-century Mennonites and helped them see their tradition as a viable alternative to fundamentalism,* modernism* or other American Protestant options. Prominent Mennonite theologians today who have had influence in wider circles are Gordon Kaufman of Harvard* University and John Howard Yoder of Associated Mennonite Biblical Seminaries and Notre Dame.*

In recent decades progressive Mennonites have expanded their work and witness through more than sixty inter-Mennonite organizations for a wide range of cooperative activities, including mutual aid, museums, relief sales, historical projects and disaster service. The Mennonite Central Committee,* founded after World War 1* for international relief and service, has had a prominent role in this ecumenical* revival. A Mennonite World Conference holds major international meetings every five or six years and serves as a forum for multi-cultural fellowship and exchange of ideas. While progressive Mennonites have gradually set aside their ethnic distinctives of language and dress, Mennonite pluralism has increased at another level with the creation of congregations of Spanish, Asian, African and Native-American cultural background.

Each American war has brought its own test for Mennonite pacifism* or nonresistance. World War 1 was especially traumatic, as superpatriotic Americans accused the German-speaking Mennonites, who refused military service and were reluctant to buy war bonds, of treasonous identification with the German enemy. During World War 2* the Civilian Public Service System provided opportunities for conscientious objectors to do civilian work as an alternative to military service. Since the Vietnam War,* Mennonites have wrestled with the issues of war taxes and Selective Service registration in the context of increasing militarization and the nuclear arms race. In the 1970s and 1980s Mennonites have engaged in discussions with Catholic* and Protestant groups about the implications of the crisis of militarism for theologies of pacifism* and the just war.

American Mennonites have not been extensively involved in ecumenical associations. In 1912 the

General Conference Mennonite Church joined the Federal Council of Churches* but withdrew from membership in the face of the Protestant militarism in World War 1. Some Mennonite groups, including the Mennonite Brethren,* the Evangelical Mennonite Brethren, and the Evangelical Mennonite Church have been drawn to various levels of participation in the National Association of Evangelicals.* The Old Order groups participate selectively in inter-Mennonite activities but avoid wider associations.

In 1975 a thorough sociological survey of five Mennonite and Brethren in Christ groups (not including Old Order groups) showed that Mennonites were socially and theologically conservative compared to other American Protestants and to Catholics. In response to questions covering a liberal/orthodox* continuum of belief, ninety per cent or more chose the most orthodox options, a more conservative profile than general Protestants but less conservative than Southern Baptists.* Mennonites are also distinctively conservative on moral issues such as tobacco, alcohol,* dancing and sexual behavior. They are well above the Protestant average in church attendance, Sunday-school* involvement and levels of stewardship.

In 1984 a Mennonite world membership summary reported that there were 340,000 members in North America, about forty-seven per cent of the world Mennonite total of 730,000. The approximate membership of the largest Mennonite groups in North America is as follows: (Old) Mennonite Church,* 114,300; General Conference Mennonite Church (including Conference of Mennonites in Canada), 65,200; Mennonite Brethren, 40,200; Old Order Amish, 34,700; Brethren in Christ, 17,400; Hutterian Brethren, 13,200; Old Order Mennonite, 12,800; Church of God in Christ (Mennonite), 10,300.

See also AMISH; ANABAPTIST TRADITION AND VISION; CHURCH OF GOD IN CHRIST, MENNONITE; FELLOWSHIP OF EVANGELICAL BIBLE CHURCHES; GENERAL CONFERENCE MENNONITE CHURCH; GENERAL CONFERENCE OF MENNONITE BRETHREN CHURCHES OF NORTH AMERICA; MENNONITE CHURCH; OLD ORDER AMISH; OLD ORDER MENNONITES.

BIBLIOGRAPHY. C. J. Dyck, ed., An Introduction to Mennonite History (1981); J. H. Kauffman and L. Harder, Anabaptists Four Centuries Later (1975); P. N. Krehbiel, ed., Mennonite World Handbook 1984 Supplement (1984); R. K. MacMaster, Land, Piety, Peoplehood, The Establishment of Mennonite Communities in America, 1683-1790 (1985); C. H. Smith, The Story of the Mennonites, 5th ed., rev. (1981); N. P. Springer and A. I. Klassen, eds., Mennonite Bibliography, 1621-1961, 2 vols. (1977).   J. C. Juhnke

Mercersburg Theology. The Christocentric theological system developed after about 1836 at the German Reformed* seminary in Mercersburg, Pennsylvania, under the leadership of the theologian* John Williamson Nevin* and the church historian Philip Schaff.* Utilizing insights of the philosopher/psychologist Frederick A. Rauch,* Nevin and Schaff formulated a theological system based on the Incarnation and the continuation of the life of Christ in his church. This they hoped would be a corrective to the revivalism* and sectarianism that prevailed in mid-nineteenth-century American Christianity. Strongly influenced by the Romanticism,* idealism and Pietism* of the mediating (or evangelical*) school of German theology, they sought to make American Christianity more historical, in contrast to the neglect of the history of the church by many American denominations; more organic and churchly, in contrast to the revivalist focus on individual salvation*; more sacramental,* in contrast to the nearly total preoccupation of American ("Puritan"*) emphasis on the sermon; and more ecumenical,* in contrast to American sectarianism. On the other hand, the Mercersburg Theology emphasized development in doctrine and the value of the Protestant Reformation in contrast to both Roman Catholicism* and the Tractarian Movement.*

The doctrines of the movement were set forth in a journal created by Nevin and Schaff, the *Mercersburg Review*, as well as in major theological and historical works they produced. Nevin's most important works were *The Anxious Bench* (1843), a critique of new measures* revivalism, and *Mystical Presence* (1846), where he reaffirmed the Calvinistic doctrine of the spiritual presence of Christ in the Eucharist* against both Lutheran* and the more common memorialist ideas. Schaff contributed to the movement with his *Principle of Protestantism* (1845), a manifesto which pointed out weaknesses in American Christianity and emphasized the value of every era of church history, and *What Is Church History?* (1846) where he vindicated the concept of development in doctrine.

The movement may be divided into three periods of somewhat different emphases. The first (1836-1843), under the leadership of Rauch, emphasized philosophy. The second (1843-1858), comprising the main work of Nevin and Schaff, dealt with the church question. The third (1858-1866) dealt with questions of liturgy* and liturgical reform. The period of strongest influence in American theology was the second, while Nevin and Schaff worked together in Mercersburg. Nevin left Mercersburg in 1853 and Schaff moved to New York in 1865. After they left, a number of their students carried the standard of the Mercersburg Theology, but none of them had the creative gifts of the founders of the movement, and it gradually fell from prominence in American theology. There was renewed interest in the Mercersburg Theology in the 1930s due to widespread concern for the themes of Christocentrism and ecumenism.* The Mercersburg Theology continues to experience revivals of interest because of the continuing importance of the issues it addresses.

BIBLIOGRAPHY. L. J. Binkley, *The Mercersburg Theology* (1953); J. H. Nichols, ed., *The Mercersburg Theology* (1966); J. H. Nichols, *Romanticism in American Theology: Nevin and Schaff at Mercersburg* (1961). S. R. Graham

Meredith, Thomas (1795-1850). Pioneer Baptist* pastor,* educator and denominational* leader in North Carolina. Born in Bucks County, Pennsylvania, Meredith graduated from the University of Pennsylvania (A.M., 1819). Meredith moved to North Carolina in 1819, where he emerged as a leading voice among Baptists and was one of the founders of the Baptist State Convention of North Carolina in 1830, drawing up its constitution. He also wrote the address to the public to promote the new convention, explaining its twin objectives of Christian education* and missions.* Meredith helped form the Wake Forest Institute (now Wake Forest University) and served for many years on its board of trustees. In 1832 he launched the *Baptist Interpreter,* which changed its name to *Biblical Recorder* in 1835, and served as its editor until his death. At the state convention in 1838, Meredith introduced a resolution urging the formation of a "female academy." In recognition of his leadership, the Baptist school for women in North Carolina was in 1909 renamed Meredith College.

BIBLIOGRAPHY. G. W. Paschal, *A History of Wake Forest College* (1935); G. W. Paschal, *A History of North Carolina Baptists* (1930). H. L. McBeth

Merit. As both a theological concept and Roman Catholic* doctrine,* merit refers to a supernatural value assigned by God to a believer's good act. This reward can be an increase of grace on earth or an increase of glory in heaven. The concept evolves from an adherence to God's promise of reward for progress in Christian living (see Rom 2:1-11; 2 Tim 4:7-8), not from any belief in the inherent value of human action. Accordingly, meritorious actions must be divinely oriented and prompted, freely willed and morally good.

Theological avowal of merit occurred in early Christianity but was fully developed by medieval Scholastic theologians. The Scholastics posited that sinful persons are transformed by God's justifying grace and consequently are capable of a secondary influence on their salvation,* cooperating with God in various meritorious actions (e.g., prayer,* almsgiving) to grow in holiness. The Scholastics distinguished two kinds of merit according to the spiritual condition of the believer: *condign,* where an "equivalent proportion" exists between the believer's act and the reward; and *congruent,* where a "fitting proportion" exists between the act, executed by a believer in serious sin, and the reward given by God. The Protestant Reformers rejected any notion of salvific merit, asserting that justification* is based on the merits of Christ alone, effected through grace alone by faith alone. This justification is not enhanced by moral action. Believers are incapable of promoting their own salvation or that of others. Subsequently, Roman Catholicism recognized merit as a doctrine of the faith at the Council of Trent (Decree on Justification, January 13, 1547). The doctrine of merit has been discussed extensively in Protestant-Catholic dialogs, but it remains an unresolved theological difference between the Catholic Church and the churches of the Protestant Reformation.

BIBLIOGRAPHY. H. G. Anderson, ed., *Justification by Faith, Lutherans and Catholics in Dialogue* VII (1985); C. J. Peter, "The Church's Treasures (*Thesauri Ecclesiae*): Then and Now," *TS* 47 (1986):251-272; C. S. Sullivan, *The Formulation of the Tridentine Doctrine of Merit* (1959). G. L. Sobolewski

Merritt, Timothy (1775-1845). Methodist* Holiness* author and editor. Born in Connecticut, in 1796 Merritt was received on trial as a Methodist minister* in Maine. There he spent a large portion of his career, with the notable exception of two periods (1817-1819; 1825-1827) at the First Methodist Society of Boston. Merritt is best known for editing the Methodist periodical *Zion's Herald* (1831-1832), was assistant editor of the *Christian Advocate* and *Journal,* until relieved of his duties for publishing abolitionist* sentiments (1832-1836). A few years later he founded and edited the first Holiness periodical in America, the *Guide to Christian Perfection* (1839-1845), later known as the *Guide to Holiness* and purchased by Phoebe

Palmer* and her husband in 1865. Rarely original in his thinking, he often cited John Wesley* and John W. Fletcher (1729-1785) in his writings, as illustrated in his best-known work, *The Christian's Manual: A Treatise on Christian Perfection, with Directions for Obtaining That State* (1825).

Merritt was the first American Methodist to publish a sermon linking Christian perfection* with the baptism of the Spirit* (1821). His advocacy of this teaching so influenced Sarah Lankford Palmer* that when she testified to Spirit-baptism, she called him "Father Merritt" (1835). In the 1820s he spearheaded the democratic* movement to have an elected presiding eldership in Methodism, though the effort was frustrated. Merritt actively supported the Sunday school,* temperance,* missions* and abolition* movements and has some claim to being the "Father of the American Holiness Movement."

BIBLIOGRAPHY. E. S. Bucke, *The History of American Methodism* (1964).   M. R. Fraser

Merton, Thomas (1915-1968). Trappist* monk,* poet and spiritual writer. Born to artist parents in Prades, France, in 1915, and orphaned at age sixteen, Merton spent his youth in rootless travel, settling briefly in several locations in France and England, where he attended various schools. He won a scholarship to Cambridge (1933-1934), but his profligate and worldly lifestyle, with little time devoted to study, led to his dismissal after only a year. Moving to Douglaston, Long Island, to live with his mother's family, he finished his undergraduate studies in literature and poetry at Columbia University (B.A., 1937), where he also edited and wrote for student publications. Continuing his studies at Columbia (M.A., 1939), he participated for a time in a young communist organization before seeking instruction in the Catholic faith and being baptized* a Roman Catholic* in 1938.

Merton was deeply transformed by his conversion, and in 1941 he entered the Trappist (Cistercian) Abbey of Our Lady of Gethsemani near Bardstown, Kentucky, where he led a strict monastic existence while pursuing what he considered his true vocation, writing. In 1948 he began his ascent to worldwide fame with the appearance of his spiritual autobiography, *The Seven Storey Mountain,* which powerfully and popularly portrayed his conversion from worldliness to a life of contemplation. But Merton's fame as a writer caused problems with his religious superiors, many of whom regarded writing a suspect activity for a monk. Nevertheless, in the midst of opposi-

tion and the physical, mental and devotional rigors of Cistercian life, Merton went on to write hundreds of articles, as well as books of poetry, works on the spiritual life, mysticism* and contemporary problems such as violence, race relations, nuclear weapons and ecumenism.* Notable are *Ascent to Truth* (1951); *No Man Is an Island* (1955); *New Seeds of Contemplation* (1962); and *Faith and Violence* (1968).

After his ordination in 1949, Merton was assigned additional duties at Gethsemani, particularly as master of novices. Though the responsibility of preparing novices for ordination was demanding, Merton was popular with his charges, and the experience shaped some of his later writings. From 1965 until his death, Merton received permission to leave the corporate lifestyle and discipline of his community to live a solitary existence in an isolated hermitage located on the monastery grounds. A period of intense introspection, reading and contemplation, it deepened his spirituality* and led him to a more mystical experience and insights from Eastern religions. In 1968, on a tour of Asia to confer and exchange ideas with religious leaders and to address a conference on Asian Christian contemplation, which included Buddhist monks, Merton died by electrocution while bathing in Bangkok, Thailand. His experiences are recorded in his posthumously published *Asian Journal of Thomas Merton* (1973). An eloquent exponent of nonviolence and justice, a formidable critic of American materialism and secularism, and a sensitive spiritual writer and poet, Merton continues to have a significant impact on an elite, but ecumenical, cross-section of religious readers in America.

BIBLIOGRAPHY. *DARB*; J. T. Baker, *Thomas Merton: Social Critic* (1971); D. Q. McInerny, *Thomas Merton: The Man and His Work* (1974); M. Mott, *The Seven Mountains of Thomas Merton* (1984).   D. L. Salvaterra

Messianic Jews. *See* JEWISH CHRISTIANS.

Metaxakis, Meletios Emmanuel (1871-1935). Organizer of the American Greek Orthodox Church.* A native of Parsas, Crete, he studied theology in Jerusalem, where he was ordained* in 1894. Elected metropolitan* of Kition, Cyprus, in 1910, he was subsequently elected metropolitan of Athens and primate of the Church of Greece in 1918. He traveled to the U.S. in 1919 to organize the Greek Orthodox parishes which were divided by Old-World politics. Deposed from his see due to political pressure, he returned to the U.S. in

1921. While in the U.S., he was elected patriarch of Constantinople and became the last to serve under Ottoman rule. He restored the jurisdiction of the patriarchate over the Orthodox in Europe and America in 1922, which had been temporarily ceded to the Church of Greece in 1908, and established the Orthodox Archdiocese of North and South America, intending to unite all the Orthodox in the Americas. In the wake of political developments, Meletios resigned in 1923. He was elected patriarch of Alexandria in 1926. There he continued to have special interest in relations between Orthodoxy* and Anglicanism.* He had affirmed the validity of Anglican orders in 1922, an opinion not shared by all Orthodox churches.

BIBLIOGRAPHY. G. Bebis, "Metaxakis in Profile," in *A History of the Greek Orthodox Church,* ed. M. Efthimiou (1984).   T. E. FitzGerald

Methodist Churches. Churches which acknowledge their origins in a revival and reform movement begun by John Wesley* and his brother Charles in England in the eighteenth century. While studying at Oxford University, the Wesleys, George Whitefield* and others formed a "Holy Club" designed to foster greater Christian discipline, devotion* and concern for the poor. Fellow students derided them as "Methodists" because of their disciplined spirituality.* In 1735 the Wesleys accompanied James Oglethorpe* to the new colony of Georgia to minister to the natives and the settlers. Their experience there convinced them that the regimen they had established to save their souls and develop a holy life had failed them.

Upon their return to England three years later, they came to an evangelical* understanding of faith and justification* through the influence of Peter Bohler, a Moravian.* On May 24, 1738, John Wesley experienced an evangelical conversion,* writing that his heart "was strangely warmed" as he attended a service in a Moravian chapel on Aldersgate Street in London. Charles had experienced his own conversion several days before. Thus Methodism or Wesleyanism* was born with the founders' spiritual rebirth. Soon thereafter, they realized that purity of heart and perfection* in love, which they believed was the work of Christ promised to believers, came to them not by their own efforts but by faith, as in the case of justification. The tone of Methodism was set in their belief that through a second work of grace and continuing obedience in faith one could be freed from sin* and love God with the whole heart—even in this life. *Christian perfection,* perfect love, entire sanctification* or simply *holiness** became the terminology of choice

for a new experience of Christian living. John, the evangelist* and organizer, and Charles, the evangelist and hymnist, led the Wesleyan revival* and helped change the face of English society in the eighteenth and early nineteenth centuries. Across the Atlantic the movement shaped much of American religion in the nineteenth century and continues to influence contemporary Christianity and society.

Methodist theology* stands in the broad tradition of Christian orthodoxy.* More specifically, Wesleyanism is concerned with the doctrines of how a person may be saved, the nature of the life of God in the souls of men and women and how believers may bear Christian witness in the world. Wesley's theological sources, other than the final authority* of the Bible,* were more extensive than those used by the Reformed* traditions of his time. Patristic, Roman Catholic* and Eastern Orthodox* influences are evident in his teachings, especially in his doctrine of Christian Holiness. Nevertheless, Wesley believed that his theology still lay "within a hair's breadth of Calvinism." His adherence to scriptural authority and salvation* by faith alone and through Christ alone relate the movement intimately with the Reformed tradition.

Wesley's chief differences with that tradition centered in his understanding of the doctrine of the Holy Spirit and sanctification. Opposing the logic of the Calvinistic determinism of his day, he stressed the doctrine of prevenient and universal grace. God offered his saving grace in Jesus Christ to all persons and was continually seeking to bring everyone to the true knowledge of himself by the work of the Holy Spirit in the world. Everyone who believed on Jesus Christ was already predestined* in him to salvation. This is the evangelical Arminian* element in Methodism. Wesley's understanding of regeneration* and sanctification emphasized the actual change in the believer, not just a change in status before God. Righteousness was not just imputed but imparted and made real within them through the regenerating and sanctifying work of the Holy Spirit. The end of the process in this life was a perfection in God's own love which extended to fellow Christians and all neighbors— "faith working by love" in the here and now. For Wesley, a holiness that was not practical and social was no holiness at all. Wesley's chief contribution to the Christian church was his insistence that biblical Christianity must ultimately be tested by whether or not it restores the moral image of God in the lives of men and women, thus producing the Christian life promised and commanded in Scripture.

The message the Wesleys preached and sang proved an effective response to the onslaught of unprecedented religious and social change among the working classes of eighteenth-century England. Methodism has always had a note of strong ethical* and social concern in its Christian witness. This "optimism of faith," with its expectations for the work of God in the present life of the church and the world, evoked ardent responses from those who accepted and those who rejected it. Evangelical doctrine, effective organizational structures and pragmatic innovations in mass evangelism* contributed to the growth of the movement.

At first a movement within the Anglican Church,* Wesley organized into religious societies those who wanted to live this kind of Christianity. British Methodism did not separate from the Established Church until 1795. In British North America Methodism spread first through the efforts of migrating Methodists. In the 1760s the first congregations began to meet regularly in Virginia and New York, but growth was initially slow, not picking up until after the Revolutionary War.* Formal organization of an American Methodist church dates to the Christmas Conference* of 1784 in Baltimore, Maryland, when Francis Asbury* and Thomas Coke* were elected as the first two bishops.*

The Methodists were both significant participants and major beneficiaries of the Second Great Awakening* of the late eighteenth and the early nineteenth centuries. Under Asbury's able guidance, a corps of itinerant* preachers known as "circuit riders,"* ranged throughout a network of churches and preaching points across the ever-expanding frontiers of the new nation. By 1840 the Methodists had become the largest denomination* in America, outstripping the reigning colonial denominations—the Presbyterians,* Congregationalists* and Anglicans.* Methodists continued to outpace other Protestant churches until the mid twentieth century, numbering 5.7 million adherents in 1906 and over eight million adherents in roughly 40,000 congregations in 1946. Today, North American Methodist bodies manifest a variety of emphases in polity (from episcopacy* to congregationalism*) and doctrine (from liberalism* to evangelicalism* and traditional to Holiness) existing within the Wesleyan tradition, a feature common to Methodism worldwide.

The largest North American Methodist body is the United Methodist Church* (c.9,000,000 members). The denomination was formed in 1968 by the merger of the Methodist Church with the Evangelical United Brethren Church. The Methodist Church was itself the product of the 1939 merger of the estranged Methodist Episcopal Church and the Methodist Episcopal Church, South, the latter having separated in 1844 from the Methodist Episcopal Church over the slavery issue (*See* Civil War and the Churches). Nevertheless, when the two bodies joined in 1939, a minority known as the Southern Methodist Church refused to realign with the Methodist Church in the North because of the apostasy they perceived in that denomination. At the same time, the two northern and southern bodies were joined by the Methodist Protestant Church, which had formed in 1830 when about 5,000 members withdrew from the Methodist Episcopal Church over concern that democratic procedures and lay representation were being neglected by the parent body. The partner in the 1968 merger, the Evangelical United Brethren Church, had itself emerged from the 1946 union of the Evangelical Association and the Church of the United Brethren, both being associations of German-American revivalists*—Methodists rooted in the same revivals which had fostered mainline Methodism in nineteenth-century America.

The African Methodist Episcopal Church* (c.2,250,000 members) and the African Methodist Episcopal Zion Church* (c.1,250,000 members) represent the major branches of African-American Methodism in America. The Rev. Richard Allen* was instrumental in founding the African Methodist Episcopal Church after he and other African-Americans were refused equal access to the seating and sacraments* of the St. George's Methodist Church in Philadelphia, Pennsylvania, in 1787. The African Methodist Episcopal Zion Church resulted from the separation of African-American Methodists from the John Street Methodist Episcopal Church in New York City in 1796. The smaller Christian Methodist Episcopal Church* (c. 800,000 members), until 1954 known as the Colored Methodist Episcopal Church, was formed in 1870 by African-Americans leaving the Methodist Episcopal Church, South, after the Civil War.

The Primitive Methodist Church* is a very small evangelical body tracing its origins back to Connecticut-born Lorenzo Dow's* evangelistic efforts in England (1807), with the first American body forming around 1829. Its proposed merger into the Methodist Church in 1929 failed by only thirteen votes. The Free Methodist Church of North America* (c.75,000 members) and The Wesleyan Church* (c.110,000 members) are smaller, more conservative bodies. The Wesleyan Church resulted from the 1968 merger of the Wesleyan Method-

Methodist Churches

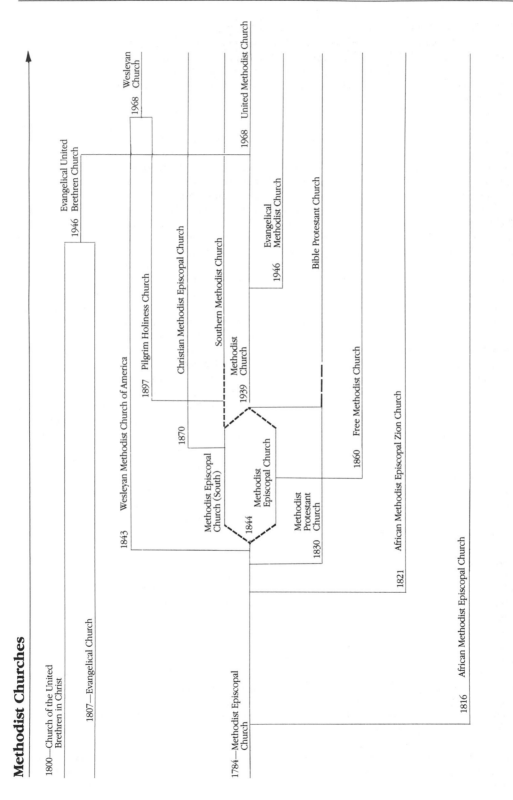

1800—Church of the United
Brethren in Christ

1807—Evangelical Church

1946 Evangelical United
Brethren Church

1968 Wesleyan
Church

1968 United Methodist Church

1843 Wesleyan Methodist Church of America

1897 Pilgrim Holiness Church

1870 Christian Methodist Episcopal Church

Southern Methodist Church

1939 Methodist
Church

Evangelical
Methodist Church

1946

Bible Protestant Church

1844 Methodist Episcopal
Church (South)

Methodist
Episcopal Church

1830 Methodist
Protestant
Church

1860 Free Methodist Church

1821 African Methodist Episcopal Zion Church

1784—Methodist Episcopal
Church

1816 African Methodist Episcopal Church

1829—Primitive Methodist Church

ist Church with the Pilgrim Holiness Church. Both the Wesleyan Methodists (1843) and the Free Methodists (1860) had left the pre-Civil War Methodist Episcopal Church because of the failure of the parent body to advocate the immediate abolition* of slavery, a cause they both espoused. The Pilgrim Holiness Church, on the other hand, was formed in 1897 by Methodists within the Holiness Movement,* who held to a doctrine of entire sanctification. Both the Free Methodists and Wesleyan Church are commonly known as Holiness churches because of their association with the Methodist Holiness revival of the nineteenth century.

As with the Pilgrim Holiness Church, a number of bodies, such as the Church of the Nazarene* (c.525,000 members), the Salvation Army* (c.435.000 members) and the Church of God* (Anderson, Indiana) (c.190,000 members), owe their existence to the Holiness Movement within the Wesleyan tradition. These Holiness bodies relate to one another through membership in the Christian Holiness Association,* which was founded as the National Holiness Association by a group of Methodist pastors* following the Civil War to promote a revival of Christian perfection within the American churches.

Many of the above bodies unite with other Methodist churches around the world in the World Methodist Council, which represents sixty-four member churches with fifty-four million adherents. The latter figure includes the membership of United churches, such as the United Church of Canada* (formed in 1925), which count former national Methodist churches in their constituencies.

See also REVIVALISM, GERMAN-AMERICAN; WESLEYAN TRADITION.

BIBLIOGRAPHY. E. M. Bucke, ed., *History of American Methodism* (1964); M. E. Dieter, *The Holiness Revival of the Nineteenth Century* (1980); *Encyclopedia of World Methodism* (1984); C. W. Ferguson, *Organizing to Beat the Devil* (1971); T. A. Langford, *Wesleyan Theology: A Sourcebook* (1984); F. A. Norwood, *The Story of American Methodism* (1974); H. V. Richardson, *Dark Salvation: The Story of Methodism as It Developed among Blacks in America* (1976); *World Methodist Council Handbook of Information, 1987-1991* (1987). M. E. Dieter

Metropolitan. An episcopal* title dating from the fourth century. In the early church, the title referred to the bishop* of a large city who exercised jurisdictional authority* over an ecclesiastical province corresponding to the geographic boundaries of a civil province. His duties included presiding at the local synod,* as well as interpreting and enforcing its rulings. Furthermore, he oversaw the canonical election of new bishops for the province. In the Americas, this original understanding is maintained by the Antiochean Orthodox Christian Archdiocese of North America, the Orthodox Church in America, the Bulgarian Eastern Orthodox Church, and the Russian Orthodox Church* Abroad, each of which is headed by a metropolitan. In Greek Orthodox* churches the title is used differently and can denote any bishop presiding over a diocese. Such is the case in the Greek Orthodox Archdiocese of North and South America, where the diocese of New Jersey is headed by a metropolitan.

BIBLIOGRAPHY. T. Ware, *The Orthodox Church* (1963); *Yearbook 1989: Greek Orthodox Archdiocese of North and South America* (1989).

C. M. Elliott

Meyendorff, John (1926-). Orthodox* theologian* and dean of St. Vladimir's Orthodox Theological Seminary. Born in France and educated at St. Serge Orthodox Theological Institute in Paris and the Sorbonne, Meyendorff early established himself as a patristic scholar and Byzantinist, and as an Orthodox spokesman in the mid-century encounter with French Roman Catholicism.* Ordained* to the priesthood* shortly before he immigrated to the U.S. in 1959, Meyendorff was one of the younger scholars recruited by Dean Georges Florovsky* in his efforts to strengthen the faculty of St. Vladimir's Theological Seminary in New York.

As professor of church history, patristics and canon law at the Seminary, professor of Byzantine history at Fordham University, lecturer at Dumbarton Oaks Center for Byzantine Studies, Washington, D.C., and as a much-demanded speaker and prolific writer, he further strengthened his academic reputation. In the mid-1960s he emerged as a leading clergyman in the Russian Orthodox Greek-Catholic Church of America (Metropolia), representing that body at ecumenical* gatherings and helping form its future as the Orthodox Church in America. From 1967 to 1976 he served as chairman of the Faith and Order Commission of the World Council of Churches,* and as chairman of the Department of External Affairs of the Orthodox Church in America and editor of its monthly newspaper, *The Orthodox Church,* from 1965 to 1984. He influenced change in many areas of the church's life, bringing to contemporary challenges the lessons of history. In 1983 he succeeded Alexander Schmemann* as dean of St. Vladimir's Seminary. Among his scholarly contributions have been *The Orthodox Church* (1962), *Orthodoxy and Catholicity* (1966) and *Christ in Eastern Christian Thought* (1975).

P. D. Garrett

Meyer, Albert Gregory (1903-1965). Cardinal* archbishop* of Chicago. Born in Milwaukee, Wisconsin, Meyer attended Old St. Mary's Grade School and Marquette Academy. Entering St. Francis Seminary in 1917, he completed the classics course in 1921. He was then sent to Rome for studies at the Urban College of the Propaganda with residence at the North American College.* Ordained* to the priesthood* on July 11, 1926, at the church of Santa Maria Sopra Minerva in Rome, he completed his theological studies in 1927 and received a doctorate in sacred theology (S.T.D.). In 1927 he began a course of studies at Pontifical Biblical Institute, graduating with a licentiate (S.S.L) in 1930. On returning to Milwaukee he was appointed to the chair of dogma* at St. Francis Seminary. He became rector of that institution in 1937. After World War 2,* his ecclesiastical promotions came at phased intervals. In 1946 he was nominated bishop of Superior Wisconsin and was consecrated* on April 11, 1946 by Archbishop Moses E. Kiley of Milwaukee. In 1953 he was appointed to the See of Milwaukee and five years later he was designated archbishop of Chicago. In the consistory of 1959 he was created a cardinal by Pope John XXIII.*

A reserved and even shy prelate, Meyer nonetheless presided over a period of rapid growth and institutional expansion of Catholic life in two major metropolitan centers of the Midwest. In Chicago especially, he met major urban problems head on, forcefully condemning racial discrimination in a famous address entitled "The Mantle of Leadership," in 1960, and hosting a major ecumenical conference on religion and race in January 1963. Moreover, he threw the prestige of his office and the financial resources of the archdiocese behind the community-organizing activities of Saul Alinsky.

His most significant contribution came as one of the intellectual leaders and spokesmen for the American bishops at Vatican II.* He aligned himself with the progressive faction at the Council and took firm stands in favor of modern biblical exegesis, episcopal collegiality* and against anti-Semitism. In a dramatic appeal to Pope Paul VI* during the third session of Vatican II (1964), he

forcefully urged the passage of a conciliar declaration in favor of religious liberty.* His premature death by a brain tumor on April 9, 1965, deprived the last session of the Council of his carefully reasoned interventions and his powerful voice in favor of conciliar-reform efforts.

BIBLIOGRAPHY. S. M. Avella, "Meyer of Milwaukee: The Life and Times of a Midwestern Bishop" (unpublished Ph.D. dissertation, University of Notre Dame, 1984); *DAB* 7; V. A. Yzermans, "The Reluctant Leader: Albert Cardinal Meyer, 1903-1965." *Chicago Studies* 5 (Spring 1966):5-24.

S. M. Avella

Meyer, (F)rederick (B)rotherton (1847-1929). Baptist* pastor,* Bible conference* speaker and writer. Born in London, Meyer was convinced from his childhood that he would be a preacher.* He graduated from London University (1869) and in his student days there served the Duke Street Baptist Church. Upon graduation he took the position of assistant pastor at Pembroke Chapel, Liverpool (1869-1872), after which he served as pastor at Priory Street Baptist Church, York (1872-1874); Victoria Road Baptist Church, Leicester (1874-1878); Melbourne Hall, Leicester (1878-1888); Regent's Park Chapel, London (1888-1892, 1909-1915); and Christ Church, Westminster Bridge Road, Lambeth (1892-1907, 1915-1920). Meyer served two terms as president of the National Free Church Council (1904, 1924) and one as chairman of the English Baptist Union (1906).

While at Priory Street Church in 1873, Meyer befriended Dwight L. Moody* and Ira D. Sankey,* who had arrived in England to minister but had found that the two men who had invited them had died. Invited to York, Moody found Meyer very helpful in getting his campaign started. This friendship resulted in Moody inviting Meyer to America in 1891, the first of twelve trips. He spoke at the East Northfield Summer Conference for two weeks and proved to be so popular that he was asked to give post-conference addresses. In one meeting at Northfield, J. Wilbur Chapman* was touched by Meyer's preaching* and testified later to a life-changing commitment made there.

Meyer's travels through America often proceeded at an exhausting pace. In one six-week tour he visited thirteen cities, covering 3,500 miles and delivering a hundred messages. In his last trip to America, at the age of eighty, his ministry extended over 15,000 miles. Prior to his coming to the U.S., his written works had received appreciative attention. His biographies of Bible characters gained great popularity, as did his expositional and devotional works.

BIBLIOGRAPHY. W. Y. Fullerton, *F. B. Meyer: A Biography* (1929); A. C. Mann, *F. B. Meyer: Preacher, Teacher, Man of God* (1929).

R. T. Clutter

Meyer, Lucy Jane Rider (1849-1922). Social worker and pioneer of Methodist* deaconess* movement. Born in New Haven, Vermont, Lucy was converted* in a Methodist revival* at age thirteen. She attended several colleges, including Oberlin* and Massachusetts Institute of Technology, and taught professionally. In 1885 she married Josiah Meyer and launched the Chicago Training School for City, Home and Foreign Missions, the center of her subsequent activities where more than 5,000 students were educated for missions and social work. In 1887 Meyer completed her M.D. at the Women's Medical College of Chicago and founded the first American "deaconess home" with single female students from the Training School who wanted to do social and medical work among Chicago's poor. Official Methodist sanction for deaconesses followed in 1888, and Meyer became a key figure in the movement as editor of *The Deaconess Advocate.* She worked tirelessly until 1917, and more than forty philanthropic organizations can be traced to her influence.

BIBLIOGRAPHY. I. Horton, *High Adventure: Life of Lucy Rider Meyer* (1928); *NAW* 2.

K. K. Kidd

Michaelius, Jonas (1577-?). Dutch Reformed* minister* in New Netherland. Educated at the University of Leiden and probably licensed* by the Classis* of Enkhuysen, Michaelius arrived in New Amsterdam on April 7, 1628, to become the first minister of the Dutch Reformed Church in America. Michaelius is best known for a rather lugubrious letter he sent to Adrian Smoutius in Amsterdam, dated August 11, 1628, which provides a glimpse into the early days of New Netherland.

Michaelius wrote of the death of his wife seven weeks after he had arrived in New Amsterdam. He reported that he had fifty Walloon and Dutch communicants at the first administration of the Lord's Supper* in New Amsterdam. Although he described the climate as "good and pleasant," Michaelius lamented the state of civil government, the barbarity of the natives and the lack of provisions. Michaelius left New Netherland several years later and in 1637 turned down an offer from the Classis of Amsterdam to return.

BIBLIOGRAPHY. E. T. Corwin, *Manual of the Reformed Church in America,* 5th ed. rev. (1922);

DAB VI; M. Kammen, *Colonial New York* (1975).

R. H. Balmer

Michel, Virgil George (1890-1938). Benedictine* leader of the liturgical movement.* Born in St. Paul, Minnesota, into a large, well-to-do and profoundly Christian family, George Michel's early education at St. John's Preparatory School and College, Collegeville, Minnesota, prepared him for entry into the novitiate of St. John's Abbey in 1909. Solemnly professed in 1913, and ordained* a priest* in 1916, Dom Virgil received a doctorate in English (1918) and a licentiate in theology* at the Catholic University of America* before enrolling at Columbia for courses in education. After teaching and filling various administrative positions at St. John's (1918-1924), Dom Virgil, still interested primarily in education and philosophy, pursued further philosophical studies, first in Rome and then in Louvain. Experience of the liturgical movement flourishing in Europe contributed to the crystallization of his mission as architect of the liturgical movement in the States, with St. John's as the center of its diffusion. The effectiveness of this apostolate* was ensured in part through the establishment of the Liturgical Press and of the movement's chief organ, *Orate Fratres* (later renamed *Worship*). As attested by his extensive bibliography devoted to liturgy,* social action, economics, education, philosophy and the arts, Dom Virgil envisaged ultimately a synthesis of the theological movement, the liturgical movement and the apostolate.

BIBLIOGRAPHY. *DAB* 2; P. B. Marx, *Virgil Michel and the Liturgical Movement* (1957).

C. Waddell

Midtribulationism. *See* RAPTURE OF THE CHURCH.

Miles, William Henry (1828-1892). Black Methodist* bishop.* Born into slavery in Springfield, Kentucky, Miles was released by his owner, Mary Miles, through her will. Joining the Methodist Episcopal Church, South, in 1855, Miles became a licentiate in 1857 and a deacon* in 1859. After the Civil War,* he briefly joined the African Methodist Episcopal Zion Church,* but, dissatisfied with the lack of support he received, he returned to the Methodist Episcopal Church, South. When the latter church allowed its remaining African-American members to form a separate denomination, Miles took part in the first General Conference of the Colored Methodist Episcopal Church* in 1870 and was elected one of its first two bishops. He sought, with mixed success, to recover for the

Colored Methodist Episcopal Church the property which the African Methodist Episcopal and African Methodist Episcopal Zion Churches had occupied since the Civil War. Miles was an enthusiastic supporter of the establishment of black colleges* such as Lane College in Jackson, Tennessee, and Paine Seminary in Augusta, Georgia. He died in Louisville, Kentucky, after twenty-two years as bishop.

BIBLIOGRAPHY. H. V. Richardson, *Dark Salvation: The Story of Methodism as It Developed Among Blacks in America* (1976).   S. W. Angell

Miley, John (1813-1895). Methodist* minister* and theologian.* Born in Butler County, Ohio, Miley graduated from Augusta College (B.A., 1834; M.A., 1837) and in 1838 became a minister in the Ohio conference of the Methodist Episcopal Church. After ministering in several Ohio churches, he moved to New York and for some time was pastor of Washington Square Church in New York City. In 1873 he accepted an invitation to fill the chair of systematic theology at Drew Theological Seminary. At Drew, Miley set about developing a Methodist Arminian* theology. In *The Atonement in Christ* (1879), he set forth a governmental theory of the atonement which opposed the limited atonement of Calvinist* theology. His two-volume *Systematic Theology* (1892, 1894) set forth a restatement of Methodist theology for his day. Both works became standard texts for Methodist students of theology.

BIBLIOGRAPHY. J. R. Joy, *Teachers at Drew* (1942).   D. G. Reid

Millenarian Movements. Groups that expect a period of unprecedented peace and righteousness upon the earth, usually associated with the return of Christ. Some of these groups, commonly called by the term *postmillennial,** believe that the present age will be gradually transformed into the millennium through natural means, such as religious revival* and social reform.* Others, usually termed *premillennial,* believe that the golden age will come only after the present age is destroyed through supernatural means, such as the Second Coming of Christ.

Postmillennial Movements. From the beginning, Americans have been susceptible to millenarian hopes. Puritans* believed that God had sent them on an "errand into the wilderness" to set up the ideal Christian church and commonwealth. Jonathan Edwards's* experience in the Great Awakening* led him to believe that the millennium was imminent and would begin in America. By

the early nineteenth century, most evangelicals had adopted similar postmillennial views and used them to Christianize America and the world. The revivals of the Second Great Awakening,* social reform movements in the Evangelical United Front* and new foreign mission* agencies grew out of the conviction that God would reward such effort by bringing in his kingdom.* Charles G. Finney,* the leading revivalist before the Civil War,* believed that the success of his work contributed significantly to the coming of the kingdom. In the 1830s he predicted that if believers continued to work diligently, the millennium might arrive in only three years.

Postmillennial views were harder to maintain after the Civil War, when mounting social, economic and religious crises made the arrival of the millennium seem less likely. However, postmillennial optimism and resolve can be detected in the Social Gospel Movement,* which remained vital from the 1880s to World War 1.* Though Social Gospelers still hoped for the coming kingdom, most thought in terms of the human progress extolled in Ritschl's liberal* theology and evolutionary* thought rather than the millennial views of Edwards or Finney.

In the 1970s and 1980s postmillennialism was revived in the Reconstructionist* Movement led by Rousas J. Rushdoony, Greg Bahnsen and Gary North. Unlike previous American postmillennialists, who tended to view the coming kingdom as compatible with democratic values and institutions, the Reconstructionists envision a more authoritarian world run according to biblical law (theonomy), which includes an expanded use of capital punishment and a "Christian economics," which includes the re-establishment of so-called biblical slavery.

Postmillennialism in America has been a rather diverse movement in the sense that its adherents have not founded separate churches or denominations.* Instead, they have come from many different groups to aid special causes or to organize cooperative efforts for revival, missions or reform.

Communities and Prophecies. On the other hand, some groups have been expressly established as harbingers of the coming millennium. The Shakers* believed that the Second Advent of Christ had already occurred in the person of their founder, Mother Ann Lee,* and in the 1770s set up a number of colonies as outposts of the developing kingdom. Their initial growth was short-lived, however, because Mother Lee's view of the millennium included strict celibacy for all Shakers. Along similar lines, John Humphrey Noyes* founded the

Oneida Community in the 1840s on the assumption that the Second Coming had taken place in A.D. 70 and the arrival of the kingdom hinged on the willingness of believers to live out the demands of Christian love, which included for Noyes the practice of "complex marriage," in which all men were married to all women.

The Mormons,* founded by Joseph Smith* in 1830, believed that God had restored the true gospel to them in anticipation of the Second Coming, which would be preceded by intense persecution and tribulation for the saints. On the basis of Smith's prophecies, they expected Christ to rescue them and then set up a New Jerusalem in Jackson County, Missouri. Armed with a detailed map of the new Zion, Smith called the Mormons to settle there. But when local people objected and drove them from Missouri, the Mormons eventually settled for a temporary Zion in Utah, where they still await the prophet's word to return to Jackson County.

Some millenarian groups have become famous for their failed prophecies. The Millerites were organized in the 1830s around the teachings of Baptist* preacher* William Miller,* who calculated Christ would return in 1843-1844. After Christ did not appear on Oct. 22, 1844, as Miller finally predicted, some of the Millerites formed new adventist churches. After the Civil War, the largest of these groups, the Seventh-Day Adventists,* rallied around the leadership of Ellen G. White,* whose prophecies included distinctive dietary practices. No longer interested in date setting, in the twentieth century the Adventists concentrate on missions and health care.

The Jehovah's Witnesses,* founded in the 1870s by Charles T. Russell,* predicted an imminent Battle of Armageddon and the establishment of a theocratic kingdom under the Watch Tower Society. But their prophecies concerning these and other events have consistently failed, including a prediction that the end of the world would occur in 1917. Today the Witnesses are best known for their door-to-door evangelism, refusal to take blood transfusions and total withdrawal from military and political life.

Dispensational Premillennialism. Given more to speculation about the "signs of the times" than date-setting are the dispensationalists,* whose teachings first came to America in the 1870s. Based on the views of England's John Nelson Darby,* this form of premillennialism teaches that following the "Rapture of the church," the Antichrist will be revealed and the great tribulation will take place. From the beginning, they have been especially interested in finding the fulfilment of biblical prophecies in contemporary events and in the fate of the Jews, who they expect will play a major role in the period surrounding the Second Coming. In the late 1800s dispensationalists founded Bible conferences* and institutes* to promote their views and engaged in revivalism and missions because they believed that the Rapture might be imminent. In the twentieth century they also figured prominently in the rise of fundamentalism,* thanks especially to the Scofield Reference Bible* (1909). More recently dispensationalism has been popularized in the writings of Hal Lindsey, whose *Late Great Planet Earth* became a best seller in the 1970s.

Unlike the pattern observed elsewhere, most American millenarian groups are not made up of the poor and disinherited who dream of the millennium because they have few hopes in this life. Some groups, such as the Mormons and to a lesser degree the Adventists, were alienated from the mainstream in the beginning but later found social acceptance. For the most part, postmillennialists were never on the outside, though they obviously wanted to change things. Even premillennialists, who theoretically must bemoan the corruption and hopelessness of the present age, have often enjoyed the good life along with everyone else.

See also AMILLENNIALISM; APOCALYPTICISM; ESCHATOLOGY; POSTMILLENNIALISM; PREMILLENNIALISM.

BIBLIOGRAPHY. L. Foster, *Religion and Sexuality: The Shakers, the Mormons and the Oneida Community* (1984); E. S. Gaustad, ed., *The Rise of Adventism in America* (1975); N. J. Penton, *Apocalypse Delayed: The Story of Jehovah's Witnesses* (1985); E. R. Sandeen, *The Roots of Fundamentalism* (1970); T. P. Weber, *Living in the Shadow of the Second Coming* (1979).

T. P. Weber

Millennial Church. *See* SHAKERS.

Millennial Dawnists. *See* JEHOVAH'S WITNESSES.

Miller, John Peter (1709-1796). Ephrata Society* leader. Born in Kaiserslautern, Germany, Miller studied theology* and law at the University of Heidelberg. The son of a German Reformed clergyman,* he was ordained* in Pennsylvania during 1730 and served several Reformed* congregations in present-day Lancaster County where he was known as a gifted pastor and theologian.* In 1735 Conrad Beissel* converted and rebaptized Miller and some of his parishoners to his mystical vision of the Christian life. Miller lived in the Protestant* monastic community in Ephrata, Pennsylvania, under the name Brother Jabez, and he cooperated with Brother Lamech in writing the *Chronicon Ephratense* (1786), a history of the community. He also translated the *Martyrs' Mirror* (1748) into German for publication at Ephrata. In 1746 Miller assumed responsibility for the economic activities of the commune, and after Beissel's death in 1768 he assumed Beissel's place within the community. Miller was less charismatic than his predecessor, and Ephrata's fortunes declined during his tenure, finally disbanding after his death.

BIBLIOGRAPHY. *DAB* VI; W. J. Hinke, *Ministers of the German Reformed Congregations in Pennsylvania and Other Colonies in the Eighteenth Century* (1951); J. F. Sachse, *The German Sectarians of Pennsylvania,* 2 vols. (1899-1900).

M. J. Coalter

Miller, Samuel (1769-1850). Old School* Presbyterian* minister.* Born near Dover, Delaware, where his father was a Presbyterian pastor,* Miller graduated from the University of Pennsylvania* in 1789. He served in the New York City Presbyterian collegiate pastorate (1793-1813), where he made his name with his 1,054-page *A Brief Retrospect of the Eighteenth Century* (1803) and his opposition to high church* episcopacy.* Soon elected moderator of the Presbyterian General Assembly* (1806), he was a founder of that denomination's* theological seminary at Princeton* (1812) and professor of ecclesiastical history and church government* there from 1813 until his death.

Miller's move from New York to Princeton coincided with his transition from a freedom-loving Jeffersonian democrat to an order-loving Whig conservative with little faith in the common man. His evolving view of the role of the ruling elder* and his growing fear of New England Theology* reflected this shift and helped nudge Princeton Seminary into Old School Presbyterianism in the 1830s.

BIBLIOGRAPHY. *DAB* VI; B. C. Lane, "Miller and the Eldership: A Knickerbocker Goes to Nassau." *The Princeton Seminary Bulletin* 6:3 (1985):211-224; S. Miller, *The Life of Samuel Miller . . . ,* 2 vols. (1869).

E. W. Kennedy

Miller, William (1782-1849). Baptist* lay* preacher who predicted the Second Coming of Christ around the year 1843. Born in Pittsfield, Massachusetts, Miller grew up in Low Hampton, New York. Largely self-educated, he married in 1803 and moved to Poultney, Vermont, where he

farmed and served as a sheriff and justice of the peace. During the War of 1812 he was an officer in the U.S. Army.

In 1816 Miller was converted from his earlier Deism* and began a systematic study of the Bible* in an attempt to answer the challenges of skeptics. In 1818, after focusing on Daniel 8:14 ("Unto two thousand and three hundred days; then shall the sanctuary be cleansed."), he concluded that Christ would return around the year 1843. This interpretation was based upon his understanding that the "cleansing" referred to the purification of the earth by fire, that a day equalled a year in prophetic reckoning and that the 2,300 days began with the decree of Artaxerxes in 457 B.C. to rebuild Jerusalem. In many respects, Miller's interpretation was similar to that developed by the British Albury Conferences between 1826 and 1828.

Miller restudied his conclusions for several years and in 1831 gave the first public presentation of his ideas. The following year he published eight articles in the *Vermont Telegraph* and a year later wrote a sixty-three-page pamphlet explaining his views. Between 1834 and 1839, aided by elaborate charts and his own gifts as a speaker, Miller gave many public lectures, some of which were published in his *Evidence from Scripture and History of the Second Coming of Christ, About the Year 1843* (1836).

In 1839, Joshua V. Himes,* a Christian Connection* minister in Boston, began promoting Miller and his ideas through papers such as *The Midnight Cry* and *Signs of the Times,* and became thereafter the primary influence on the developing Millerite movement. Papers, tracts,* books, camp meetings* and city-wide campaigns were utilized to spread the message of Christ's soon return and the Judgment Day.

By 1843 the movement began encountering opposition from the established churches and a separatist* impulse developed within it. Pressure from the movement also encouraged Miller to identify more precisely the date of Christ's coming. In January 1843, after studying Jewish calendars, he established the period from March 21 (later revised by some of his followers to April 18), 1843 to March 21, 1844 as the time of the Advent. With the passing of these dates, many in the movement adopted October 22, 1844, the Day of Atonement—put forward by Samuel Snow on the basis that the Day of Atonement was a type of the judgment—as the day of Jesus' return. But Miller did not accept this new date until October 6. After the failure of this latest calculation, Miller said that the mistake might have resulted from a manmade error in Bible chronology. Until his death in 1849, however, Miller retained his faith in Christ's imminent return.

Estimates of Miller's following vary considerably, most ranging between 30,000 and 100,000. While many in the movement returned to their former churches after 1844, several adventist churches took form. Of these groups, the Seventh-day Adventists* became the largest and most widespread.

See also MILLENARIAN MOVEMENTS; SEVENTH-DAY ADVENTISTS.

BIBLIOGRAPHY. D. T. Arthur, "Millerism," in *The Rise of Adventism*, ed. E. S. Gaustad (1975); S. Bliss, *Memoirs of William Miller* (1853); *DAB* VI; *DARB*; C. E. Hewitt, *Midnight and Morning: An Account of the Adventist Awakening and the Founding of the Advent Christian Denomination, 1831-1860* (1983); R. L. Numbers and J. M. Butler, eds., *The Disappointed: Millerism and Millenarianism in the Nineteenth Century* (1987); F. D. Nichol, *The Midnight Cry* (1944); *NCAB* 6; D. L. Rowe, *Thunder and Trumpets: Millerites and Dissenting Religion in Upstate New York, 1800-1850* (1985).

G. Land

Mills, Benjamin Fay (1857-1916). Evangelist.* Born in Rahway, New Jersey, the son of an Old School* Presbyterian* minister,* Mills was educated at Phillips Academy, Hamilton College and Lake Forest College (B.A., 1879). He was ordained* a Congregational* minister in 1878, and served churches in Cannon Falls, Minnesota, Greenwich, New York (1878-1884), and Rutland, Vermont (1884-1886). In 1887 he became an itinerant* evangelist. During the first five years of his ministry, he preached about the need for repentance and conversion,* while discouraging the vices of card-playing, intemperance and dancing. During this period he published *Victory Through Surrender* (1892).

In 1893, influenced by George Herron,* he began preaching a social gospel,* emphasizing the themes of brotherhood and the coming kingdom of God,* and encouraging churches and individuals in their responsibility to transform society and its institutions. Christian duty involved more than saving drunkards, dancers and card-players, Mills now believed. The church's business was to care for the poor and the public welfare, while speaking out against those who acquired wealth unjustly. Mills was one of few evangelists in the nineteenth century who tried to combine the messages of personal salvation* and social responsibility. Though his revivals were technically efficient (he

claimed to have spoken to five million and converted 200,000 in twelve years), he found that many churches were reluctant to accept his twofold message. In 1899 Mills withdrew from evangelistic work and became minister of the First Unitarian Church of Oakland, California (1899-1903). He later founded two independent religious/ethical organizations: the Los Angeles Fellowship (1904-1911) and the Chicago Fellowship (1911-1914). His publications from this period included *Twentieth Century Religion* (1898) and *The Divine Adventure* (1905). In 1915, disenchanted with liberal* religion, Mills reconverted to a more evangelical* faith and was received into the Chicago Presbytery.*

BIBLIOGRAPHY. *DAB* VII; *DARB*; J. J. Francis, ed., *Mills' Meetings Memorial Volume* (1892); W. G. McLoughlin, *Modern Revivalism* (1959); *NCAB* 14; H. Stauffer, *The Great Awakening in Columbus, Ohio* (1896).

L. M. Japinga

Mills, Samuel John, Jr. (1783-1818). Promoter of foreign missions.* Born the son of a Congregational* minister* in Torringford, Connecticut, Mills was converted during a revival* in 1801. He sold his farm and entered training for the ministry at Williams College, Massachusetts. While there he gathered spiritually sincere students to form the Society of the Brethren. Mills led the Haystack Prayer Meeting* (1806), which issued in the founding of the American Protestant missionary movement.* After graduation from Williams College (1809), Mills enrolled briefly at Yale,* where he met Henry Obookiah* from Hawaii. When Mills transferred to Andover Seminary* (1810-1912), Obookiah accompanied him and was there converted* to Christianity.

In 1810 Mills, together with Adoniram Judson,* Samuel Newell and Samuel Nott, Jr., petitioned the General Association of Congregational Ministers at Bradford, Massachusetts, to initiate foreign missionary activity. Later in that same year Mills helped form the American Board of Commissioners for Foreign Missions* (ABCFM). In 1812 Mills was licensed* to preach,* and that same year the ABCFM sent its first missionaries* to Calcutta. By 1821 the ABCFM had sent out eighty-one missionaries.

Mills was ordained* to the Congregational ministry in 1815 at Newburyport, Massachusetts. Between 1812 and 1815 he undertook two missionary journeys through the South and Midwest, distributing Scriptures, preaching and collecting information. In 1816 he became an agent of the School for Educating Colored Men and helped found the American Bible Society* (1816) and the United Foreign Missionary Society of the Presbyterian and Dutch Reformed Churches (1816). In 1817 the American Colonization Society* sent Mills to West Africa, where he purchased land for the founding of Liberia near Cape Mesurado. On the return voyage he died of an illness and was buried at sea.

BIBLIOGRAPHY. *AAP* 2; *DAB* VII; G. Spring, *Memoirs of the Rev. Samuel J. Mills* (1820); T. C. Richards, *Samuel J. Mills* (1906); J. Tracy, *History of the American Board of Commissioners for Foreign Missions* (1842). W. A. Detzler

Minister. As a noun, *minister* means an ordained* minister of the gospel; a member of the clergy,* as distinct from the laity.* Literally, the term means "a servant" and is derived from the vocabulary of the apostle Paul who described himself as "a minister of Christ Jesus to the Gentiles with the priestly duty of proclaiming the gospel of God" (Rom 15:16). The term is identified with the primitive church's offices of deacon* (often an office of lay leadership), elder* and bishop.* Ordained primarily as pastors,* evangelists* and missionaries,* ministers are also professors of theology,* denominational and mission board executives, military and hospital chaplains,* pastoral counselors, etc. The term is also used for some unordained workers such as ministers of music.

As a verb, *minister* means to proclaim the gospel; to engage in acts of Christian love and mercy, including visitation, physical assistance, prayer and spiritual counsel. American churches and Christians energetically establish charitable programs and institutions, believing that God calls all believers to minister to others in the name of Jesus Christ. According to Scripture the task of pastors, teachers and evangelists is "to prepare God's people for works of service" (Eph 4:12), or "ministry," as it is translated in the King James Version and Revised Standard Version.

BIBLIOGRAPHY. H. R. Niebuhr and D. D. Williams, eds., *The Ministry in Historical Perspectives* (1956); E. B. Holifield, *A History of Pastoral Care in America* (1983); D. S. Schuller et al., eds., *Ministry in America* (1980). C. E. Hambrick-Stowe

Ministerial Associations, Colonial. Regular meetings of the clergy* for mutual edification and the resolution of church matters. In the context of the congregational* order of colonial New England, meetings of ministers* were generally frowned upon because they implied clerical authority* over the rights of the local churches. However, by the late seventeenth century, Massachusetts clergymen formed scattered, unofficial associations that met by appointment several times a year. At these meetings, candidates were suggested for vacant pulpits, theological questions and current issues were debated, conflicts within the churches examined and recommendations tendered.

By the eighteenth century, Connecticut's associational system was more effective than that of Massachusetts, which was a royal colony. The Saybrook Platform* of 1708 established that ministers of each county would meet three times a year and that representatives from each county association would attend an annual general association. The roles of these associations were essentially the same as those of Massachusetts, though a further duty given to the Connecticut associations was to examine and approve candidates for the ministry. This function reflected the general intention of the New England associations to resolve disputes within the congregational system and to keep it doctrinally pure by ensuring the integrity of the ministerial office.

BIBLIOGRAPHY. D. C. Harlan, "New England Congregationalism and Ministerial Professionalism in the Eighteenth Century," *Bulletin of the Congregational Library* 34 (1983):4-18; A. Quint, "The Origins of Ministerial Associations," *Congregational Quarterly* 2 (1860):203-212.
K. P. Minkema

Ministerial Call. The divine call (vocation) to a person to be a priest* or minister of* the gospel, distinguishable from God's call of believers to salvation* and to be the church. The ministerial call is twofold. Evangelicalism,* which has marked nearly every branch of the church in America, including Catholicism, has insisted that those who wish to be ordained "must be called by God" (Heb 5:4). Church bodies responsible for approving candidates require testimony of Christian experience and a sense of personal call from God to ministry. Catholics also emphasize human choice, urging potential priests and nuns* to "make a vocation."

The ecclesiastical call follows the spiritual call. While for some so-called Spirit-led preachers* a personal call from God is sufficient for independent ministry, most have sought to serve within a particular church structure. In some denominations* bishops* ordain* clergy* for work within their boundaries and then assign them to charges, parishes* or special ministry. The term *ministerial* *call* is most commonly used by presbyterial* and congregationally* organized churches in which the local body selects and calls its own pastor. Clergy "receive" and "answer" calls to specific ministries.

BIBLIOGRAPHY. A. C. Piepkorn, *Profiles in Belief,* 3 vols. (1977-1979).   C. E. Hambrick-Stowe

Ministerial Privilege. Rights or favors accorded clergy* as part of their remuneration, in recognition of their role in society or by virtue of their responsibilities. As part of pastors' remuneration, churches often provide them with housing, fuel and sometimes furnishings. In colonies with established churches, certain land (glebe lands,* clergy reserves*) or taxes yielded income for the ministry,* though by the early 1800s salaries everywhere were raised by members' contributions. Parishioners also frequently give pastors food and other gifts. In recognition of their role in society, pastors sometimes receive clergy rates (on railroads, at hotels, etc.), discounts from merchants and free memberships in clubs. Physicians and attorneys have offered free or discounted services as professional courtesy. "Benefit of clergy," a medieval concept transferred briefly into some colonies, meant clerical immunity from criminal or civil prosecution. By virtue of their responsibilities, aspects of the ministry involve special privilege, notably confidentiality (priest-penitent privilege). "Freedom of the pulpit," the right to preach uncensored, is at least an ideal in some traditions.

By the late twentieth century many privileges had been abandoned by a secular, pluralistic society. Clergy themselves sought change, desiring home ownership and eschewing preferential treatment, though still qualifying for tax advantages such as the housing allowance.

C. E. Hambrick-Stowe

Minister's Wife. Martin Luther's marriage to Katherine von Bora in 1525 created one of the Reformation's most important legacies, the Protestant* parsonage. In American Protestantism, however, the role evolved considerably. Puritan* pastors* in New England expected little more than domestic and spiritual companionship from their spouses. In the nineteenth century, many ministers' wives took on the demands of their husband's careers in addition to their domestic responsibilities. While for some the demands of social and spiritual modeling were too exacting, many carved out a positive role that fit their individual personalities and gifts. Ministers' wives provided important leadership in women's missionary* (*See* Missionary Movement, Women's) and benevolent organizations, both in local parishes and nationally. Some, like Lydia Finney, wife of evangelist* Charles G. Finney,* used the position to establish independent careers. Many women, however, found parsonage life full of unsung sacrifices. As unsalaried martyrs to the whims of the congregation, or as the lonely wives of Methodist* itinerants,* they endured the burden of traditionalism, in which the minister's wife received personal criticism and financial hardship without complaint.

In the twentieth century the role of the minister's wife has endured special stress. A major study in 1959 found many parsonage wives "harried and distraught, overwhelmed and underpowered," stretched by contradictory social trends. Pressed by the social conservatism of the churches into a primarily domestic, companionate role, or pushed by the impetus of the women's movement into social and spiritual detachment from the congregation, in recent years ministers' wives have struggled to establish themselves in viable public ministry.

BIBLIOGRAPHY. L. Boyd, "Presbyterian Ministers' Wives—A Nineteenth-Century Portrait," *JPH* 59 (Spring 1981):3-17; P. Boyer, "Minister's Wife, Widow, Reluctant Feminist: Catharine Marshall in the 1950s," *Women in American Religion,* ed. J. W. James (1980); L. Sweet, *The Minister's Wife: Her Role in Nineteenth Century American Evangelicalism* (1983).   M. L. Bendroth

Minor Orders. Lesser degrees of ministry within the Roman Catholic* Church, below the major orders* of bishop,* priest* and deacon.* While the minor orders and their functions have varied somewhat, in recent centuries they have been ranks through which a man advanced to the Catholic priesthood. Though technically not a minor order, the ceremony of tonsure (shaving of a designated amount of hair from the head) marked a man's move from the laity* to the clergy.*

The next step and first minor order was that of acolyte, literally a "follower." As early as the third century, acolytes seem to have been bishops' couriers or messengers. More recently their work has consisted of helping carry lighted candles into the churches and preparing the wine and water for the Eucharist.*

The second minor order was the exorcist, a task rooted in biblical passages such as Mark 16:17. In early times the exorcist's task was daily prayer over adults preparing for baptism.*

The third minor order was that of lector, mentioned in Christian sources in the fourth century.

Responsible for proclaiming the sacred texts to the congregation, at times they offered a commentary on the reading. In some places they were responsible for the safekeeping of the sacred documents.

The fourth order, porter or doorkeeper, assumed responsibility for opening and shutting church and sacristy doors, ringing the bells to summon people to worship* and keeping the unworthy from entering.

The fifth order, sometimes considered a part of the sacrament of holy orders or a major order, was the order of sub-deacon, originally an assistant to the deacons. This order was abolished by Pope Paul VI's* reform of the orders in 1972. Exorcism as a separate ministry was suppressed. The order of porter was abolished as a sacred order, and lay people have been encouraged to do that which lectors, acolytes and porters used to do. Exorcism is reserved for the clergy.

See also MAJOR ORDERS.   B. Moran

Missiology, Protestant. The study of Christian mission. In 1867 Alexander Duff (1806-1878) gave his inauguration address at New College, Edinburgh, in the first endowed chair of missions. Carl H. Plath (1829-1901), from his position at the University of Berlin, launched efforts to establish chairs of missions in German universities. Rufus Anderson,* just retired as secretary of the American Board of Commissioners for Foreign Missions* (ABCFM), began an itinerating lecture career at Andover* and other theological seminaries.* Missions had become a part of European and North American academic studies.

Europe's attention focused on the university. And its goals were to gain public recognition and theological respectability for the study. The Germans in particular, and the Dutch and Scandinavian to a lesser degree, aimed at the creation of an exact science in the theological encyclopedia. Out of this approach came a methodological clarity and rigorous investigative discipline unmatched in North America. But its ties with the university left the study divorced from church life and practice.

History of North American Missiology. By contrast, North America's impetus for study came from the pressure of student enthusiasm. Samuel Mills,* whose appeal had played a leading part in the formation of the ABCFM in 1810, launched in 1811 the student-centered Society of Inquiry on the Subject of Missions. By 1857 there were seventy such societies around the country, pressing universities and seminaries to give academic attention to their missions concerns. In 1886 the Student Volunteer Movement* (SVM) came into being,

intensifying that pressure.

Missiology now began to make a reluctant appearance in the seminary and university programs of study. Part-time and special lectureships were initiated at such places as Yale,* Auburn, McCormick, Austin, Garrett and others. There were only three full professorships by 1910. Pragmatic pressures had their effect on teaching in North American schools. Missionary education, unlike that in Europe, was oriented to two goals: (1) to provide the beginnings of pre-field training for prospective missionary candidates; and (2) to encourage future pastors, then in training, to promote missionary concerns and support. The European gap between school and church was bridged by American enthusiasm. But the promotional and motivational flavor of the training then and now has often left North American studies without a strong analytical base. Relegated to a place in the practical theology curriculum, missions often has been the object of condescension by other faculty members working in the classic theological disciplines.

The twentieth century represents a checkered history, but progress is evident. By the early 1930s a survey of sixty-eight institutions disclosed twenty-four full-time and 109 part-time professors in the field. In 1950 there were a total of seventy-one professorships of missions in the world; no less than fifty-one of those were in the U.S. A 1985 survey of mission teaching in sixty-six North American seminaries noted that in eleven of the institutions missions had the status of a separate department. Fifty-five offered some type of course in missions and thirty-two reported an increase in the number of courses offered. Professional associations have been created to stimulate academic work—the Association of Professors of Missions (1950), the Association of Evangelical Professors of Missions (1965), the American Society of Missiology* (1973).

On the other hand, mainline* denominational* seminaries and university programs now find interest in missions waning, due to a decline in theological certitude and a growing openness toward religious tolerance and pluralism. Sensitive to the reality of a global church and issues of interchurch relations, such schools often question the crosscultural dynamic so key to missiology's self-understanding in the past.

By contrast, evangelical seminaries have experienced growing interest in missiological studies and a solid increase in the number of missions lectureships. Fuller Theological Seminary's* School of World Mission, founded in 1965, is the clear leader with twelve full-time faculty and 755 students enrolled in 1986.

But in the evangelical community too there are problems. The seminary has never been a major source of American missionary candidates, and that remains the case. Evangelical mission agencies continue to find the bulk of their recruits in Bible institutes* and colleges. Sadly, in such schools a less rigorous academic commitment and heavy faculty teaching schedules leave little hope for sophisticated missiological research.

Evangelical scholarship continues to be strong, even developing, in those areas of its traditional interests: evangelism, strategizing, church planting and church growth. And it shows new interest in the use of the social and behavioral sciences, as well as creativity in areas such as contextualization. Theological studies linking missions to contemporary biblical research in hermeneutics, the kingdom of God,* eschatology and church/world relations are relatively infrequent and unsophisticated. With some exceptions, evangelical scholarship is weakest in its research on world religions and questions relating to a Christian approach to non-Christian religious systems.

Current Missiological Questions. In the last three decades North American Protestant missiologists have not been able to agree on a definition of Christian mission or missiology. The sharp divisions between liberals and evangelicals continue to hinder open and fair listening on both sides. Stereotypes, however, seem to be decreasing, and a common agenda of issues, though differently perceived, seems to be emerging.

These issues can be summarized in terms of a number of relationships: between the nature of missiology and traditional theology, historical theology and socio-behavioral sciences; between the church's mission and the kingdom of God; between evangelism and social responsibility; between Western sending churches and the receiving churches that have now matured into sending churches; between Western contextualized theology and the developed and nascent contextualized theologies of the non-Western world.

See also AMERICAN SOCIETY OF MISSIOLOGY; MISSIONS, EVANGELICAL FOREIGN; MISSIONS, PROTESTANT MAINLINE FOREIGN; MISSIONS, ROMAN CATHOLIC FOREIGN.

BIBLIOGRAPHY. R. C. Bassham, *Mission Theology; 1948-1975: Years of Worldwide Creative Tension, Ecumenical, Evangelical and Roman Catholic* (1980); D. Bosch, "Mission and Evangelism: Clarifying the Concepts," *ZMR* 68 (1984):161-191; H. M. Conn, "The Missionary Task of Theology: A Love/Hate Relationship?" *WmTJ* 45 (1983):1-21;

H. M. Conn and S. F. Rowen, eds., *Missions and Theological Education in World Perspective* (1984); J. A. Scherer, "Missiology as a Discipline and What It Includes," *MissRev* 15 (1987):507-522.

H. M. Conn

Missionary, Missioner. A person actively engaged in a mission, particularly one sent by a church to carry the gospel to those who have not heard the message of Jesus Christ. Directed by the so-called Great Commission of Jesus (Mt 28:19-20), missionaries may serve as evangelists,* church planters, educators, medical doctors or in a variety of other capacities, but they are sent primarily to share the gospel with those who are at a cultural distance from their own background. In general, missionaries may be denominationally ordained* clergy,* members of a lay religious order or parachurch group,* or persons independently supported and motivated. Missionaries today are frequently trained in missiology* and cross-cultural communication, although Protestant mission agencies frequently utilize short-term missionaries who may be young people or lay people with little specialized training in missions. The earliest missionaries were those apostles and evangelists commissioned by the early church. Today, missionaries are sent by individual churches, conventions or societies.

J. M. Glass

Missionary Baptists. Two types of Baptists* employ the term *missionary* in opposite ways. The first type, influenced by Daniel Parker* and James R. Graves,* represents a resurgence of nineteenth-century Landmarkism.* Opposing any form of convention bureaucracy as a threat to local autonomy, it promotes missions* solely through individual churches. Their most conservative branch is the American Baptist Association* (ABA), the product of a merger (1924) between Samuel Hayden's Texas-centered Baptist Missionary Association and Ben Bogard's General Association of Arkansas Baptists. With headquarters in Texarakana, Texas, it recently listed over one million members and 3,570 churches in the U.S. and Canada. A progressive branch, which broke away from the ABA in 1950, is now known as the Baptist Missionary Association of America (BMAA). The center of BMAA unity is its seminary in Jacksonville, Texas. Listing 219,697 members and 1,487 churches in twenty-nine states in 1982, its main strength is still in the Southwest.

In contrast to the ABA and the BMAA, which have been caricatured as anti-missionary, the second type cooperates in conventions which allow them to be involved in more comprehensive mission activities and diverse programs. Many Southern Baptist churches still add "missionary" to their title in order to show this distinction. The Southern Baptist Convention* has drawn its strength from such missionary groups as the Texas Baptist State Convention (1848), which opposed Parker's anti-mission movement; the Baptist General Convention of Texas (1885), which resisted Hayden's "anti-convention" party; and the Duck River Baptist Association, which added *Missionary* to its name (1953) in order to distinguish itself from the "Separate" Duck River Baptists.

BIBLIOGRAPHY. *Encyclopedia of Southern Baptists,* 3 vols. (1958-1982); H. L. McBeth, *The Baptist Heritage* (1987).

J. T. Spivey

Missionary Bishop. A bishop appointed to serve in an area not yet organized as a diocese.* The eighteenth General Convention of the Protestant Episcopal Church* at Philadelphia (August 19—September 1, 1835) passed a canon which created the office of missionary bishop. The canon empowered the House of Bishops* to nominate and the House of Deputies* to elect missionary bishops to serve in the states and territories not organized as dioceses and in areas outside the U.S. The Board of Missions could request that missionary bishops be elected by the House of Bishops between General Conventions and approved by a majority of the standing committees of the dioceses. The first domestic missionary bishop was Jackson Kemper of Indiana and Missouri, and the first foreign missionary bishop was William J. Boone* of China.

D. S. Armentrout

Missionary Movement, Women's. A late nineteenth- and early twentieth-century American Protestant* movement to form women's missionary* societies for the sending of single women to foreign mission fields.

The women's missionary movement has been neglected by historians who have written at length about other related movements, such as the Student Volunteer Movement,* the faith missionary movement* and the laymen's missionary movement.* Yet, the women's missionary movement sustained more than forty mission agencies, mobilized tens of thousands of women on the home front and sent thousands of women overseas during the late nineteenth and early twentieth centuries. The underlying impulse behind the women's missionary movement was the rejection of single women for missionary service by existing mission boards. The need for women to reach their "heathen" sisters was widely acknowledged, but missionary wives were generally too burdened with domestic duties to adequately meet the need. The prospect of accepting women as missionaries in their own right, however, was not one most mission boards were prepared to deal with.

From the onset of the modern missionary movement, women had served faithfully in foreign service as missionary wives, but they had no authority or official ministry of their own and thus were not perceived to be in violation of the apostle Paul's reputed admonitions regarding women as ministers of the gospel. On the home front women were the backbone of mission support efforts involving prayer and finances, but there was a growing desire among many of them to become more personally involved. Many women found outlets in urban ministries,* and during the nineteenth and early twentieth centuries, hundreds of inner-city mission endeavors were founded by women. But by the middle of the nineteenth century, women were beginning to clamor for wider opportunities of service. Many single women felt the call of God as assuredly as did their male counterparts, but without a marriage partner of like commitment, they were barred from answering that call.

It was this obstacle which prompted the groundswell of devotion that became the women's missionary movement. Women banded together to form "female agencies" to send their sisters overseas. The first such organization was the Women's Union Missionary Society,* founded in 1861 by Sarah Doremus.* She had been advised of the need for women's work overseas more than two decades earlier by David Abeel, a missionary to China from her own denomination,* the Reformed Church in America.* He challenged her with a simple but stirring message from women in China: "O bring us some female men." Doremus was prepared to act immediately, but her vision was dampened by Rufus Anderson,* who was then foreign secretary of the American Board of Commissioners for Foreign Missions.* His long-standing opposition to single women in missions was well known, and since she was actively involved in support efforts for that mission, she deferred to his wishes. However, the needs of women in foreign lands continued to weigh on her conscience; and finally in 1860, she called together women from various denominations, and together they launched their mission endeavor by sending Sarah Marston, a Baptist,* to Burma.

The interdenominational character of this mission stymied its growth—not because women themselves objected, but because their own denominations opposed such ecumenical* efforts. Nevertheless, the mission grew and after two decades had supported more than one hundred missionaries on twelve stations. More significant was the influence this female agency had on women's missions in general.

Inspired by the success of the Women's Union Missionary Society, other women's societies were quickly formed along denominational lines, the Congregationalists* of New England being the first to take up the mantle. Rufus Anderson of the American Board had retired, and the new foreign secretary, N. G. Clark, was supportive of single women missionaries. He lent his support to their formation of the Women's Board of Missions, which was incorporated in 1869. Methodist* women were next to organize, and the Baptists followed in 1870. In the decades that followed, a new women's mission society was formed on an average of one each year.

Sending missionaries abroad was not the only goal of the women's movement. Education of women on the home front was also a top priority. It was this ideal that led to the formation of the Central Committee for the United Study of Foreign Missions, an interdenominational organization that published textbooks and established short-term educational programs. In thirty-eight years the Central Committee published more than four million texts for women and girls written on a wide variety of mission subjects. The Central Committee also set up summer schools across the country featuring courses in missions. By 1917 there were twenty-five such schools, with nearly twelve thousand women and girls enrolled.

The most prominent leaders of the women's missionary movement on the national scene were Lucy Peabody* and Helen Barrett Montgomery.* Both worked tirelessly to promote the jubilee celebration in 1910, recognizing the five decades of women's missionary work. Meetings were held throughout the country: forty-eight two-day celebrations in major cities and many one-day meetings in smaller communities, some of which brought together as many as four thousand participants. More than a million dollars were collected in offerings.

One of the greatest contributions of the jubilee celebration was Helen Barrett Montgomery's jubilee book, *Western Women in Eastern Lands* (1910). Summarizing the accomplishments of the previous fifty years, she wrote: "It is indeed a wonderful story. . . . We began in weakness, we stand in power. In 1861 there was a single missionary in the field. . . . in 1909, there were 4,710 unmarried women." She went on to enumerate the increase in numbers of women involved on the home front, from a few hundred to two million, and the increase in financial giving, from two thousand dollars to four million. But the greatest causes for celebration were the results overseas. The gospel had reached many regions of the world where women had never before had opportunity to hear, and nationals were playing a prominent role in the ministry. There were nearly six thousand Bible women and native helpers, in addition to some 800 teachers, 140 physicians, 79 nurses and 380 evangelists.

In the decades following the 1910 jubilee, the women's missionary movement declined. Denominational boards had begun to readily accept single women missionaries, and there was considerable pressure for women's societies to merge with their "parent" boards. Many women fought against these mergers, fearing the loss of female participation when their work was taken over by male-dominated boards. Despite their protests, the denominational boards prevailed, and, as was feared, the women lost their influence. The once-vibrant educational and publishing ventures of the women's missionary movement were also absorbed into the general boards and eventually abandoned altogether. Women continued to have a vibrant interest in missions, but their focus was turned more and more to the new faith missions rather than to the mainline denominational boards.

See also MISSIONS, EVANGELICAL FOREIGN; MISSIONS, PROTESTANT MAINLINE FOREIGN; MISSIONS, ROMAN CATHOLIC FOREIGN.

BIBLIOGRAPHY. R. P. Beaver, *American Protestant Women in World Mission* (1980); L. A. Cattan, *Lamps Are for Lighting: The Story of Helen Barrett Montgomery and Lucy Waterbury Peabody* (1972); H. B. Montgomery, *Western Women in Eastern Lands* (1910); P. R. Hill, *The World Their Household: The American Woman's Foreign Mission Movement and Cultural Transformation, 1870-1920* (1985).

R. A. Tucker

Missions, African-Americans and. African-Americans have been committed to the evangelization of Africa since the early nineteenth century. The earliest and most intensive denominational* expansion of African-American churches began in Liberia and Sierre Leone to provide organized churches for African-Americans who colonized West Africa. Paul Cuffee founded the Friendly Society of Sierre Leone in 1811 and resettled thirty families there in 1815. In the same year, Lott Carey* formed the Richmond African Baptist Missionary Society with William Crane, and by 1819 the American Colonization Society* and the Baptist Foreign Mission Board had accepted Lott Carey and Colin Teague as their first African-American workers. In 1821 Carey and Teague, appointed by the General Missionary Convention of the Baptist Church, settled in Sierre Leone with other former slaves from America. A year earlier, in 1820, Daniel Coker* had gone to Liberia under the auspices of the American Colonization Society. Committed to the evangelization of African peoples wherever they lived, African-Americans sent missionaries to the Caribbean as well. In 1827, Scipio Bean began mission work in Haiti for the African Methodist Episcopal Church.*

All three major African-American denominations expanded their foreign missions in Africa and the Caribbean after the Civil War.* The African Methodist Episcopal Church (AME) established its first African mission in 1885 in Sierre Leone. The expansion of the mission work in the Sierre Leone Protectorate in the 1880s and 1890s, both in the number of missionaries and churches, was largely due to the influence of Henry McNeal Turner,* elected AME bishop in 1880 and assigned to oversee the West African churches. As a supporter of colonization, vice president of the American Colonization Society and editor of the *Voice of Missions,* Turner initiated the expansion of AME missions to Liberia in 1891 and to South Africa in 1898. By 1900 the Sierre Leone and Liberia Conferences had a total of thirty missionaries. In 1917, the AME Church had a total of fourteen stations in Africa with thirty-five men, thirty-four married women and two unmarried women. Between 1928 and 1932 Bishop George Benjamin Young extended the AME church into Swaziland and Rhodesia. By 1934, the Gold Coast had nine AME churches and schools, and Nigeria had fifteen churches. The denomination now has foreign missions in South Africa, West Africa, the Caribbean, South America and India.

William W. Colley, who had worked as a missionary in Liberia from 1875 to 1879, organized the Baptist Foreign Mission Convention on November 24, 1880, in Montgomery, Alabama. Six missionaries were sent in 1883 and by 1895 a total of twelve missionaries had been sent to Liberia. In 1895, the American National Baptist Convention and the National Education Baptist Convention

combined to form the National Baptist* Convention (NBC). By 1900, the NBC had nineteen missionaries in Liberia and South Africa and twenty-five missionaries in 1906.

An independent African-American mission board was organized in 1897 at Shiloh Baptist Church, Washington, D.C., as the Lott Carey Baptist Foreign Mission Convention. The work began with a couple sent as missionaries to the Congo in 1901, and by 1923 the Lott Carey Convention had forty-three missionaries —thirty-one in Africa and twelve in Haiti. In 1925 the organization joined with the American National Baptist Convention and the National Baptist Educational Convention. By 1938 the National Baptist Convention had a budget of $40,051 for nine stations in Liberia, Nigeria, Nyasaland and South Africa. The National Baptist Convention now has missions in West Africa, Southern Africa, the Caribbean and South America. The denomination supports 912 foreign churches, as well as three elementary schools, three secondary schools, one seminary* and two hospitals.

The African Methodist Episcopal Zion Church* (AMEZ) Foreign Mission Department was founded in 1875. Rev. and Mrs. Andrew Cartwright started Liberia missions in 1876. In 1896 mission work was expanded to the Gold Coast by John Bryan Small and Thomas B. Freeman, who started an African secession from the British Methodist Church and other white churches. In 1906 the first African-American missionary, J. J. Pearce, went to the Gold Coast, and in 1909 W. E. Shaw went to the Cape Coast. To inform the membership of mission activities and raise funds, the periodical *Missionary Seer* was started in 1901. Bishop Alexander Walters was placed in charge of foreign work in 1903, and by 1924 the church had appointed its first resident African bishop.

The Nigerian Conference, begun in 1930 by Rev. J. Drybauld Taylor, had twenty-eight churches, eleven African ministers and 2,345 members by 1932. The denomination now has 1,104 places of worship,* 450 elementary schools, fifty secondary schools, three colleges, one hospital and two clinics.

Before the twentieth century, white mission boards used African-Americans extensively in African missions. From 1877 to 1900, 112 black missionaries worked for white denominations in Africa. By the twentieth century, most white denominations had either stopped employing African-Americans or had drastically reduced their numbers due to discrimination against African-Americans by white denominations and by colonial governments in Africa.

BIBLIOGRAPHY. C. C. Adams and M. A. Talley, *Negro Baptists and Foreign Missions* (1944); L. L. Berry, *A Century of Missions of the A.M.E. Church* (1942); S. M. Jacobs, ed., *Black Americans and the Missionary Movement in Africa* (1982); Tony Martin, "Some Reflections on Evangelical Pan-African-ism or Black Missionaries, White Missionaries and the Struggle for African Souls, 1890-1930," *Ufaha-mu* 1 (Winter 1971):77-92; W. Williams, *Black Americans and the Evangelization of Africa, 1877-1900* (1982). L. J. Edwards

Missions, Evangelical Foreign. Historically, America's own founding was motivated by themes associated with world missions. In the seventeenth century the largest transoceanic passage in all history was launched toward American shores. And, though migrant rather than missionary, the colonization was interpreted by its Puritan* minority as a chapter in the gospel epic of the transformation of the wilderness into the garden paradise of God.

Alexander Whitaker,* "Apostle to Virginia," reminded his readers in 1613 that they were planting the kingdom of God* in the New World. The royal charters of Virginia, Plymouth, Connecticut and Massachusetts Bay cited as a main objective the imparting of the gospel to heathen. The great seal of Massachusetts depicted a Native American uttering the Macedonian call, "Come over and help us."

Colonial Missions. This sense of divine destiny first crossed cultural barriers in the evangelization of Native Americans (*See* Missions to Native American). John Eliot,* known as the "Apostle to the Indians," joined others in speculating about the connection between the American tribes and Israel's ten lost tribes. But his overriding concern was the nearness of Christ's kingdom and the part the conversion* of Native Americans would play in the progress of the gospel. Clearly the first fullness of the Gentiles was being completed. Soon to follow would be widespread conversions of both Jews and Gentiles.

Typical of the period, Eliot believed Native Americans had to "be civilized ere they could be Christianized." And, in keeping with that aim, he developed a mission strategy of gathering "praying Indians" into "praying towns"* where they could be weaned from their radically heathen culture and instructed in the Christian faith. By 1671 Eliot had gathered some 3,600 converted Native Americans into fourteen "praying towns." He worked faithfully at training Native American pastoral leadership, enrolling a number of Native American youth at Harvard.*

Eliot's model of "praying towns" was used widely throughout New England. In fact, some suggest it may have provided a model for the development of the missionary compound when the American missionary movement turned its attention overseas. The response of Native Americans to the gospel grew. Just prior to the outbreak of King Philip's War* in 1675, the total number of Native American Christians may have approached 2,500, or twenty per cent of the native population. But the War aborted the movement. "Praying towns" became easy targets for Native American antagonists. Only four of the fourteen towns survived, and an estimated 5,000 Native Americans and ten per cent of the colonial forces were killed.

The years between 1675 and 1735 were no kinder to the missionary vision in America. A new organization, the missionary society, was appearing in the colonies. But enthusiasm for the task never seemed to reach below the administrative level. New England piety* was in decline. Even the missionary vision of colonial leaders such as Samuel Sewall (1652-1730) and Cotton Mather* did not fully blossom into writing until after 1700. And when it did, it was a call for repentance; a celebration of the past and not the present.

Revival and Mission. The Great Awakening* and the Second Awakening* transformed this situation. In the 1730s and 1740s, and again in the early nineteenth century, revival fires swept through the churches of New England and the South. A renewed emphasis was placed on the New Birth* and the need for a living, personal faith in Christ. New churches were organized, voluntarily supported, by those whose quickened enthusiasm was often unwelcome in the older churches.

Jonathan Edwards,* a participant and defender of the Great Awakening and a missionary to the Stockbridge Indians, returned again to the earlier Puritan* theology for his understanding of the revival.* Edwards had been deeply stirred by the vision of his prospective son-in-law, David Brainerd,* a young missionary who had expressed hope that the coming of God's glorious kingdom "was near at hand." Edwards married the two themes of mission and eschatology into a union that lasted for the next century and a half. The church's mission was to be a colaborer with God in the consummation of the work of redemption. It was a mission that was to convert men and women, sanctifying* them and bringing them to glorification. And it was a mission to bring to completion God's total providential design—a creation fully subject to its Creator.

Out of the fire of the Awakenings, the growth of the Christian community, and the disestablishment of state religion came two missionary ideas that would draw the attention of the new nation to the world outside its borders. The first was church planting by larger ecclesiastical bodies. Missions was no longer the exclusive work of special societies and boards of commissioners aimed at the conversion of the "heathen" Native Americans. The Awakening had shown that America's congregations were full of well-churched "heathen." Moreover, the geographical expansion of the frontier further underlined the need for evangelization of the white settlers.

This perspective did little to reawaken strong interest in the evangelization of Native Americans. Nor did the white Christian conscience seem any more deeply sensitized toward the plight of the African-American population (1,002,000 by 1800; 18.9% of the country's total population). A 1729 English law still guided the colonies, stating that baptism* of a slave offered no guarantee of emancipation. And those missionaries, such as the Anglicans,* who did evangelize African-Americans had little impact, due in part to the opposition of slave masters (*See* Missions to Slaves). The African-American church would emerge, but from within its own circles (*See* Black Religion).

The second missionary idea coming out of the revivals was a growing sense of obligation of the American church toward the world. As late as 1802, a "foreign missionary society" was thought of as a society located in Western Europe. And in 1810, when Samuel J. Mills* and his fellow students at Andover Theological Seminary* petitioned the General Association of Congregational* Churches to form a society for overseas mission, the issue was not whether the American churches would evangelize the heathen. The question they posed was "whether they ought to direct their attention to the eastern or western world."

But increasingly, American interests turned beyond its shores. Tracts* and sermons* were published issuing ardent missionary appeals. Evangelical* periodicals turned their attention to the task of global evangelization. New boards began to emerge, with a growing focus on overseas ministry. The first was the American Board of Commissioners for Foreign Missions* (ABCFM), organized in 1810 through the appeal of Samuel Mills. The movement grew. Large numbers of women's "auxiliaries," many to become boards themselves, were formed to supplement the male-dominated structures (*See* Women's Missionary

Movement). By the end of the Civil War,* a total of fifteen boards were serving the major denominations.

"The Great Century" of American Missions. One hundred years later, by 1910, the U.S. and Canada were fast becoming the dominant world force in missions. Their Protestant missionaries serving overseas totalled 7,219 (thirty-four per cent of the world total). Voluntary giving had reached $13 million per annum (forty-three per cent of the total world's contribution to missions of $30 million). The number of sending societies in the U.S. had grown from one in 1810 to ninety-six in 1910, with eleven closely associated organizations in Canada.

A striking part of this contribution came from North America's growing African-American church community and its pioneering concern for Africa (*See* Black Americans and Missions). White concerns for Africa remained minimal. As early as 1782, former slaves had sought to transplant their churches from Georgia and South Carolina to Nova Scotia, Sierra Leone, Jamaica and the Bahamas. In 1820 the American Colonization Society* supported Daniel Coker* (one of the founders of the African Methodist Episcopal Church*) and eighty-eight other African-Americans in planting congregations in Liberia. In the same year Lot Carey* and Colin Teague were sent to Liberia by the African-American Baptists of Richmond, Virginia. Between 1877 and 1900 three African-American churches, the African Methodist Episcopal Church, the African Methodist Episcopal, Zion,* and the National Baptist Convention,* overtook the white churches in their support of African mission work. They sponsored at least seventy-six missionaries on the continent, educated thirty African students for missionary work among their own people, and troubled white missionaries with slogans like "Africa for the Africans."

During the first half of the nineteenth century, India, Burma and Ceylon were the chief targets of American mission efforts overseas. Then followed Southeast Asia, West Africa, the southernmost tip of Africa, the Turkish empire and Hawaii. The missions in the Near East aimed at the revival of the ancient Eastern churches. By the end of the century, China had become the major American field, with the total North American evangelistic personnel in China reaching 1,784 by 1910. By that time Latin America had also been added to the list.

Missionary motivation shifted during the nineteenth century. The earlier eschatological theme of *gloria Dei* vanished. In its place, mission leaders like Rufus Anderson* of the ABCFM spoke of

The North American Protestant Missionary Movement

A Time Line of Representative Agencies and Organizations

1810	American Board of Commissioners for Foreign Missions (1810)
1814	Triennial Convention (later American Baptist Missionary Union, 1845; and American Baptist Foreign Mission Society, 1910)
1815	African Baptist Missionary Society
1832	Dutch Reformed Church
1833	Methodist Episcopal Church
1837	Presbyterian Church in the U.S.A.
1845	Southern Baptist Convention
1846	Methodist Episcopal Church, South
1860	Women's Union Missionary Society of America
1861	Women's Missionary Society of America
1861	Presbyterian Church in the U.S.
1865	China Inland Mission (now Overseas Missionary Fellowship; 1888 in North America)
1869	Women's Board of Missions (Congregationalist)
1875	African Methodist Episcopal Zion Church Foreign Mission Department
1880	Baptist Foreign Mission Convention
1886	Student Volunteer Movement for Foreign Missions
1888	Congo Balolo Mission (now RBMU International; American council established 1948)
1889	African Evangelical Fellowship
1890	Scandinavian Alliance Mission (now The Evangelical Alliance Mission)
1890	Central American Mission
1892	Gospel Missionary Union
1893	Foreign Mission Conference of North America
1894	American Board of Missions to the Jews

1895	Africa Inland Mission
1898	Sudan Interior Mission (now SIM International)
1901	The Oriental Missionary Society (now OMS International, Inc.)
1906	Layman's Missionary Movement
1910	National Holiness Missionary Society (now World Gospel Mission)
1914	South America Mission
1917	Interdenominational Foreign Mission Association of North America (IFMA)
1919	Pentecostal Mission in South and Central Africa
1919	Assemblies of God Missionary Department
1920	Mennonite Central Committee
1921	International Missionary Council (IMC)
1921	Latin America Mission
1927	Association of Baptists for World Evangelism
1931	Unevangelized Fields Mission (now UFM International)
1934	Wycliffe Bible Translators
1934	Slavic Gospel Association
1936	Student Foreign Missions Fellowship
1938	World Home Bible League
1942	New Tribes Mission
1945	Evangelical Foreign Mission Association (EFMA)
1946	World Literature Crusade
1947	Far Eastern Gospel Crusade (now SEND International)
1949	Greater Europe Mission
1950	World Vision International
1961	Youth With a Mission

[751]

obedience to Christ's Great Commission (Mt 28:18-20). During the half century from 1830 to 1880, mission theory and mission sermons spoke of obedience to Christ's "marching orders for the church"; to seek the salvation of souls, and so meet the world's greatest need.

In the late nineteenth and early twentieth centuries, still another motivation began to gain prominence. The earlier goal of promoting Christian civilization became detached from the fading Puritan* vision of mission as the spread of the kingdom of God. Fed by the rise of nationalism and a sense of America's Manifest Destiny,* liberal* writers like Horace Bushnell* spoke of America as "the brightest hope of the ages." Josiah Strong's* 1885 best-selling *Our Country,* saw God shaping Anglo-Saxon civilization as the die with which to stamp the earth. To avoid a national catastrophe arising from the evils of "Rum, Romanism and rebellion," a new Anglo-Saxon world empire must emerge. World missions would be the instrument for shaping that destiny.

At first associated with both liberal and evangelical Christians, this enthusiasm for Christian civilization's world conquest increasingly became a liberal theme. The Social Gospel* Movement gave it theological backing. Mission scholars like James Dennis, in his work *Christian Missions and Social Progress* (1897-1906), tried to root it in the history of missions. His three volumes heralded the progress missions had wrought in social change, civilization, moral improvement and economic betterment.

Evangelical enthusiasm was not dimmed by this narrowed humanitarian appeal. The end of the nineteenth century saw the genesis of the Student Volunteer Movement* (SVM) in 1886. Soon carried to Great Britain and Europe, it became the most effective recruiting arm of the western mission boards. By 1945, under its watchword, "the evangelization of the world in this generation," some 20,500 of its volunteers were serving overseas. When liberal theology and other factors led to the growing decline of the SVM in the years following 1920, evangelicals in 1936 formed the Student Foreign Missions Fellowship* (SFMF). The merger of SFMF with the InterVarsity Christian Fellowship* in 1945 inaugurated the regular triennial student missions conventions at Urbana,* Illinois. There the original intent of the SVM annual conventions, and their role as a recruiting center for missions, has been perpetuated.

The Twentieth Century. By 1924, there were a reported 14,000 North American foreign missionaries, joined by 15,000 from Great Britain and Europe. The century was to become, in the language of Stephen Neill, "beyond question the American century." By 1952 North American missionary personnel numbered more than 18,000 (fifty-two per cent of the world total). By 1985 career personnel from the continent reached an estimated 39,309, with an additional 27,933 serving as short-term missionaries. In 1985 they labored in 175 countries. The number of boards had grown from seventy-five in 1900 to 764 in 1985 (661 in the U.S. and 103 in Canada).

However, it is difficult to determine exactly how many missionaries are evangelicals. During the early part of the twentieth century, North American churches, unlike those in Great Britain and Europe, began to divide over the growing conflict between liberalism and historic Christianity. And, as the conflict widened, it divided mission boards and created new ones, with many evangelicals remaining with the older boards. Evangelical fears had already begun to create new educational models for missionary preparation by the early twentieth century. Bible institutes* were founded in reaction to the liberal domination of Christian institutions of learning. The flagship of them all, Moody Bible Institute,* had sent out over 5,200 missionaries by 1973.

Working in close tandem with the Bible institute movement was the Faith Mission* movement. Originating in the mid-nineteenth century, the early British models of these boards (China Inland Mission—now Overseas Missionary Fellowship,* 1886; Sudan Interior Mission—now SIM International,* 1898; Africa Inland Mission,* 1895) were founded to reach the untouched interiors of the great continents of Asia and Africa when older church boards were restricting their activities to the port cities. Nondenominational in character, they offered no guaranteed salaries and made no solicitation of funds. The appeal of "the regions beyond," their principle of "faith giving," and their interchurch structure made them particularly attractive to North American evangelicals who were struggling with liberalism.

In 1917 the Interdenominational Foreign Mission Association* (IFMA) was formed in the U.S. to accredit the evangelical character of these mission boards and provide limited cooperation among them. As of 1985, fifty-six boards in the U.S. and forty in Canada are members of the IFMA. An accrediting institution with similar purposes, the Evangelical Foreign Missions Association* (EFMA), was formed in 1945 as an affiliate of the National Association of Evangelicals.* As of 1985, eighty-three mission boards are members of the EFMA.

The two agencies serve a total of over 17,000 missionaries from North America.

Evangelicals associated with these groups, for the same theological motives that originally drew them together, continue to show only marginal interest in the expanding ecumenical movement and the World Council of Churches* (WCC) formed in 1948. Evangelicals often suspect the WCC of liberalism, universalism* and ambitions for a "superchurch." The perceived radicalization of the WCC in the 1960s has reinforced those concerns.

The years following World War 2* have brought change again. Europe has emerged as a prominent mission field, with 3,862 North American personnel (eleven per cent of the total) laboring there in the 1980s. The largest field is Latin America (11,196 North American missionaries), a continent virtually untouched by North American personnel in 1910.

Since 1968 growth has plateaued within the IFMA and the EFMA. The four largest North American evangelical boards are not affiliated with either group—the Southern Baptist Convention* (3,346 career missionaries in 1985); Wycliffe Bible Translators* (3,022); Youth with a Mission* (1,741); and New Tribes Mission (1,438).

North America's Pentecostal* churches and the charismatic* movement have had a growing impact on the evangelical foreign missions movement. In less than seventy-five years, for example, the Assemblies of God* has grown from approximately 300 people in 1914 to a worldwide membership of more than 14 million, including more than 1,400 missionaries and over 90,000 national ministers. Ignored by evangelicals until the 1970s, Pentecostals and charismatics have been increasingly accepted as part of the global evangelical movement.

New concerns have appeared on the evangelical mission agenda of the 1980s. Mission boards struggle over their relationships with the churches they have planted. A 1982 report lists over one billion, 500 million Christians in the world (thirty-two per cent of the world's population). North American missionaries ask how their mission boards should support these churches and what role they should play in planting new churches. What role should missionaries and mission boards play in the development of indigenous evangelical theology? As the world church faces its unique cultural and religious contexts, how will it preach the gospel in a way that is faithful to the Scriptures and to its particular settings? What is a mission board's responsibility toward the poor and oppressed? How should missionaries plant churches

in countries dominated by Muslim, Marxist or right-wing ideologies?

New methods and definitions of the missionary task are being explored by missiologists*: the contextualization of the gospel, the church growth movement,* the concept of unreached peoples and theological education by extension. Still awaiting renewed investigation is the neglected—but not forgotten—issue of the relationship between missions and the eschatological kingdom of God. Premillennialism* dominates much evangelical mission theology today. But debate goes on regarding its ability to speak to the relationship between evangelism and social responsibility.

See also MISSIOLOGY; MISSIONS, ROMAN CATHOLIC FOREIGN; MISSIONS, PROTESTANT MAINLINE, FOREIGN.

BIBLIOGRAPHY. R. P. Beaver, ed., *American Missions in Bicentennial Perspective* (1977); R. P. Beaver, "Missionary Motives through Three Centuries," in *Reinterpretation in American Church History,* ed. J. C. Brauer (1968); C. L. Chaney, *The Birth of Missions in America* (1976); P. R. Hill, *The World Their Household: The American Women's Foreign Mission Movement and Cultural Transformation, 1870-1920* (1985); W. R. Hutchison, *Errand to the World: American Protestant Thought and Foreign Missions* (1987); S. Neill, *A History of Christian Missions* (1964); W. L. Williams, *Black Americans and the Evangelization of Africa, 1877-1900* (1982); S. Wilson and J. Siewert, eds., *Mission Handbook, North American Protestant Ministries Overseas, 13th Edition* (1986).

H. M. Conn

Missions, Protestant Mainline Foreign. Rooted in earlier efforts to evangelize* Native American* peoples of North America, the American Protestant missions movement was influenced by European initiatives and strongly motivated by the Second Great Awakening.* In 1806 Samuel Mills* led a group of students at Williams College in what became known as the "Haystack Prayer Meeting,"* where they committed themselves to overseas missions. In 1810 the group, now at Andover Seminary,* proposed to the Massachusetts Congregational Association the formation of the American Board of Commissioners for Foreign Missions* (ABCFM). The ABCFM, composed at first of Congregationalists,* soon included Presbyterian* and Reformed* personnel.

Nineteenth-Century Triumphs. The first five missionaries and their wives sailed for India in 1812, but Adoniram* and Anne* Judson and Luther Rice* became Baptists* en route. While Judson began work in Burma, Rice returned to the U.S. to awaken

American Baptists to missions. The result was the formation of the Baptist Mission Board in 1814, the first general organization of Baptists in the U.S. Unlike the European mission societies, which were peripheral to the churches, most mainline* American efforts were pursued through boards organized by the denominations* under the principle that the church itself was responsible for missions. Thus the Old School* Presbyterians* withdrew from the ABCFM in 1837 and organized their own board. By mid century all of the churches which today would be considered mainline (Baptist, Congregationalist, Episcopal,* Disciples of Christ,* Lutheran,* Methodist,* Presbyterian and Reformed*) had their own mission boards. In 1865 fifteen boards and societies served the major denominations.

India, Burma and Sri Lanka (then known as Ceylon) were the major fields in the first half of the century, followed by Southeast Asia, West Africa, Turkey and Hawaii and several Latin American countries. But by 1900 China was the largest field. The first half century was a time of small beginnings, great sacrifices and many deaths. Nineteen-year-old Harriet Newell died in 1813, shortly after arriving in India with her husband. In 1834 two missionaries of the ABCFM were killed and eaten by Bataks in Sumatra. But languages were learned, Scriptures translated and small churches established. Then a series of events greatly stimulated new advances.

In 1858 a new wave of revivals began to sweep the U.S. (*See* Prayer Meeting Revival). New missionary societies were formed, many of them organized by women. Scottish missionary David Livingstone sparked new interest in Africa, Japan was opened to the West, and Korea was opened two decades later, while England's victory in the tragic Opium Wars opened China. Two other major developments were the establishment of the prototype of interdenominational faith missions,* the China Inland Mission* by J. Hudson Taylor in 1865, and the Student Volunteer Movement* initiated in 1886 and organized in 1888. The first would symbolize what was to become a growing divergence between mainline missions and those which were more conservative; the second would eventually motivate over 20,000 youth to enter mission service, most through the older boards. Thus the number of missionaries grew from less than 1,000 in 1890 to 9,072 in 1915.

For women the movement provided opportunities for service and leadership denied them at home (*See* Women's Missionary Movement). The first to go overseas were simply seen as wives of missionaries, but many, especially Anne Judson, powerfully inspired women at home. In 1827 the need to establish schools for girls led the ABCFM to send Cynthia Farrar, a single woman, to India. But the male-dominated boards were slow to respond to the commitment that women had long demonstrated and gave them no voice in making policies. Thus a number of women's boards were established in the last half of the century. Through them, as well as the older boards, women pioneered in education, medical work and in many cases evangelism.* In the 1920s most women's boards were merged with their denominationally sponsored counterparts, but integration did not take place among the Methodists until 1964.

The motivation for early missions was rooted in modified Puritan* theology. Samuel Hopkins's* concept that Christians were to be motivated by "universal disinterested benevolence" brought an altruistic emphasis and a world-embracing concern. Its negative side was an uncritical view of American culture, coupled with a sense of superiority and condescension. But the most important motive was the desire to obey the command of Christ and see him known and honored throughout the world. In addition, the church was seen as cooperating with God in the work of redemption which would eventually bring the millennium.*

Rufus Anderson,* ABCFM secretary from 1826 to 1866, focused on preaching* in order to bring people to God through Christ. Social service and civilizing motives were secondary. For him the goal was to establish indigenous churches, defined as self-supporting, self-governing and self-propagating. These would take responsibility for the evangelization of their own nations as mission organizations moved to other fields. The social consequences of Christianity would follow. At the same time educational institutions, from primary schools to universities, were established. Their goals were to train Christians for church leadership, imbue non-Christians with the spirit of Christian service, and evangelize. Medical missions were also established. By the end of the century James Dennis's lectures at Princeton Seminary,* pointed to Christian missions as the major factor in bringing social progress to Asia and Africa.

Twentieth-Century Crises. Growth was now rapid. In 1900 American missionaries (including approximately 400 from Canada) numbered 4,891, making up twenty-seven per cent of the world's Protestant missionary force. Almost all were from the mainline churches. The total grew to 7,219 in 1910, the year of the Edinburgh Conference, and 13,608 in 1925, making up forty-nine per cent of the world's total. That number included 2,588 missionaries unaffiliated with the mainline boards, indicating a growing trend. The period between World War 1* and World War 2* brought new problems. Complacency about Western Christian culture was shattered, questions were raised about the validity of missions, the return to normalcy encouraged isolationism, and the Great Depression* had serious economic impact.

But even more seriously, the theological consensus which undergirded nineteenth-century missions began to crumble. The greatest challenge came from the Laymen's Foreign Missions Inquiry* report, *Rethinking Missions,* issued by William E. Hocking* in 1932. It seemed to reject the uniqueness of Christ, suggesting that Christianity and other world religions should grow together toward a final world faith that would unite all persons. Most executives and missionaries, including Robert E. Speer* and Samuel Zwemer,* rejected that position and in their replies emphasized the finality of Jesus Christ. But the consensus was gone. The American preparatory volume for the 1938 conference of the International Missionary Council—the first worldwide ecumenical council of churches—focused entirely on social issues.

An important gain was a more positive attitude toward non-Western cultures. E. Stanley Jones,* a Methodist, advocated culturally appropriate methods to communicate the gospel in India. His colleague, J. Wascom Pickett,* took a positive attitude toward so-called mass conversions, or people movements, and stimulated the thinking of Donald McGavran.*

Developments after World War 2* brought massive shifts in the missionary enterprise. Missionaries soon returned to China, Japan and the Philippines. But the triumph of China's Communist revolution in 1949 brought about the expulsion of Westerners, engendering a great deal of pessimism about the future of missions. The end of political colonialism in Asia and Africa raised questions about both the possibility and advisability of the missionary presence in the light of rising nationalism.

Mainline missions now shifted their focus to relationships with the national or so-called younger churches. "Partnership in obedience" was the call. Some of these churches had administered their own affairs for decades; now missionaries and their institutions were put under their control as well. While this was a positive step, it introduced the danger of transforming missions into interchurch aid. This factor, plus excessive institutionalization, made new evangelistic initiatives difficult.

In the 1960s, as the churches became more aware of the problems in American society, the decline in mainline missions was accelerated. On the other hand the independent interdenominational missions and those of the newer evangelical* and Pentecostal* groups grew rapidly. The number of mainline missionaries, approximately 10,500 in 1925, fell to 6,800 in 1970 and 2,600 in 1985. During the same period the total of American Protestant missionaries rose from 13,100 to 37,803.

Overall Achievements. Despite its weaknesses the movement brought magnificent achievements. National churches now exist in nearly every nation in the world, many the result of American missions. Some are strong and growing, as in South Korea, where over twenty-five per cent of the population consider themselves Christian, while in some countries Christians are a tiny minority. In China, where the Protestant Church numbered a million in 1949, the government-recognized "Three Self" church now gathers four million members, while house fellowships may include many times that number. Protestant churches are growing rapidly in most Latin American countries (although most are Pentecostal), and churches of every type—mainline Protestant, Roman Catholic,* independent Protestant and Pentecostal—are growing rapidly in most of sub-Sahara Africa.

Medical and educational institutions have been established. The first schools and colleges to educate women in a host of countries were planted by American missions. The movement toward Christian cooperation and unity was stimulated and nurtured by the missionary movement. Part or all of the Bible* had been translated and published in over 1,000 languages by 1937, and an equal number since then. Perhaps most significant of all, many of the churches established by these missions are now sending their own missionaries to unreached peoples of different cultures within their own nations and beyond their borders. These include Presbyterians in South Korea, Baptists in Northeast India, Methodists in the Philippines and Lutherans in Ethiopia.

As the world missionary movement enters a new phase, the American mainline churches can look back and express gratitude for the achievements of this enterprise to which they have given so much. At the same time their future role is unclear. Can their traditional mission structures serve as adequate channels for the missionary service of the many within their ranks who still wish to obey the call to overseas mission?

See also MISSIONS, EVANGELICAL FOREIGN; MISSIONS, ROMAN CATHOLIC FOREIGN.

BIBLIOGRAPHY. R. P. Beaver, *American Protestant Women in World Mission* (1980); C. W. Forman, "A History of Foreign Missions Theory in America" in *American Missions in Bicentennial Perspective,* R. P. Beaver, ed. (1977); W. R. Hogg, "The Role of American Protestantism in World Mission" in *American Missions in Bicentennial Perspective,* R. P. Beaver, ed. (1977); W. R. Hutchison, *Errand to the World* (1987); S. C. Neill, *A History of Christian Missions* (1964); S. Wilson and J. Stewart, eds., *Mission Handbook,* 13th edition (1986).   P. E. Pierson

Missions, Roman Catholic Foreign. American Catholics* were serving in overseas missions before the U.S. was removed from the jurisdiction of the Sacred Congregation for the Evangelization of Peoples or for the Propagation of the Faith* (Propaganda) in 1908, but only after that can one refer to an American Catholic missionary movement. It developed slowly. The First American Catholic Missionary Congress, in 1909, focused principally on evangelization* and church development in the U.S.

The movement took two forms of expression: one of European origin and another of American origin. Older religious congregations of men (*See* Religious Orders, Men's) came from Europe to the U.S., recruited personnel, sent some of them overseas, eventually developed American provinces and thus brought the direction of American overseas personnel under the direction of American superiors. Examples of these are the Jesuits,* Franciscans,* Redemptorists,* Holy Cross Fathers* and Brothers and Divine Word Missionaries. Maryknoll, founded in 1911, was established as the American Foreign Mission Society* under the auspices of the U.S. hierarchy. In subsequent decades it also provided a substantial number of overseas personnel, never however as many as the Jesuits. Only in the late 1950s did diocesan* priests* begin to serve abroad in any number.

American women who belonged to older European religious congregations (*See* Religious Orders, Women's) also served overseas even before 1908, and afterwards followed the same pattern as the male congregations. The Maryknoll Sisters were founded in 1919 and soon began to provide the largest number of female personnel overseas. Even in 1960 they made up one-third of American Catholic women missionaries working in foreign missions, the others coming from eighty-six other institutions and provinces.

Beginning in the 1940s, lay* missionaries were recruited by societies of European origin. However, their number became significant only after 1960. American lay missionary organizations, such as the Association for International Development, in New Jersey; the Lay Mission-Helpers, in Los Angeles; and the Papal Volunteers for Latin America, were established between 1958 and 1960. Lay missionaries were most numerous between 1962 and 1974 and again more recently.

There have been two major thrusts in the American Catholic missionary movement. The first came after World War 1* when Rome was anxious to have more American leadership in the missions; between 1918 and 1941 over thirty mission territories were entrusted to the exclusive care of American missionaries, almost all of them in Asia. The second came after World War 2,* when Americans saw themselves needing to perform a task which Europe could no longer perform. However, with China closed after 1949, the thrust took them into South America and Africa, although the Philippines and Caribbean continued to be of special interest to American missionaries. This thrust which began in 1946 with 3,093 American personnel in overseas missions, peaked in 1968 with 9,655. Afterwards the numbers gradually decreased to 6,037 in 1986. During the peak years between 1962 and 1970, one in three Americans overseas was serving in Latin America.

All the religious congregations were under the direction of the Propaganda in Rome and, until 1950, for the most part worked independently of one another. In that year Rome approved the establishment of a Mission Secretariat under the director of the National Office of the Society for the Propagation of the Faith (SPF). Frederick McGuire, CM, was the executive secretary of the Office from its inception until its termination in 1969. For twenty years this Office gathered leaders of mission-sending societies in annual meetings to discuss issues such as publications, spiritual training, passports and shipping, and provided them with many services. The Secretariat was replaced in 1970 by the U.S. Catholic Mission Council, composed of seven representatives from bishops, religious men, religious women, laity and mission agencies. Joseph Connors, SVD, was the first executive secretary, with Anthony Bellagamba, ICM, succeeding him in 1976. In 1981 the structure was once more changed, due to the withdrawal of the Bishops' and Mission Agencies' representatives. The U.S. Catholic Mission Association was formed in 1982 with a Board of Directors representing men and women religious, as well as lay missionaries. Joseph Lang, MM, succeeded Bellagamba as executive secretary in 1985.

U.S. Catholic Overseas Personnel

Year	Religious Men	Diocesan Priests	Religious Women	Laity	Total
1940	?		?		2227
1944	1218	—	818	—	2036
1949	2375	—	1748	—	4123
1958	3496	19	2532	96	6124
1964	4300	80	3137	532	8126
1968	4877	282	4150	419	9655
1972	3816	246	3127	376	7934
1976	3652	193	2840	257	7010
1980	3342	188	2592	221	6393
1984	3152	187	2492	263	6134
1987	2964	200	2505	351	6073

Top Five Areas in Which U.S. Personnel Serve

1940: China (740); West Indies (267); Philippines (231); India (170); South America (154)
1954: West Indies (800); Pacific Islands (686); South America (654); Philippines (418); Africa (379)
1962: Philippines (647); Puerto Rico (571); Hawaii (466); Japan (427); Brazil (370)
1970: Puerto Rico (715); Brazil (699); Peru (693); Philippines (662); Japan (474)
1975: Philippines (526); Peru (492); Brazil (485); Japan (364); Puerto Rico (352)
1980: Brazil (465); Peru (436); Philippines (428); Japan (343); Puerto Rico (251)
1985: Peru (435); Brazil (430); Philippines (364); Japan (295); Mexico (214)

The missionary movement was generously supported financially by American Catholics through their contributions to the individual religious and lay societies and the Pontifical Aid Societies. After 1922 funds gathered by the latter societies were distributed by the Propaganda in Rome and were not restricted to Americans.

The Catholic Students' Mission Crusade (CSMC), founded in 1918 by Clifford King, SVD, and several friends, was a significant force in arousing interest in the missions. The organization's monthly magazine, *The Shield,* began publication in 1921 and reported on the activities of the various groups as well as providing mission information. By 1940 the CSMC had organized 800,000 high-school and college students to study and support the missions. But by the late 1960s the attitude toward missions had changed, and the CSMC came to an end.

Between 1948 and 1970 several attempts were made to further mission studies. In 1948 J. Franklin Ewing, S J, initiated a five-day Mission Institute at Fordham University to encourage dialog between missionaries and academicians; these encounters took place for five years. Between 1950 and 1981 the SPF published *Worldmission.* In 1958 the Catholic University of America began an academic program in missions studies, and from 1962 to 1970 Ronan Hoffman, OFM TOR, held the chair of Missiology at the Catholic University of America in Washington, D.C. All of these developments were paralleled by Protestant* and ecumenical* efforts to bring methodological and theological rigor to the investigation of Christian mission. Since 1972 the American Society of Missiology* has provided an ecumenical forum for mission studies.

BIBLIOGRAPHY. T. A. Breslin, *China, American Catholicism and the Missionary* (1980); M. A. Habig, OFM, "Who Was First?" *Worldmission* (Summer 1954) 5:55-78; H. J. D'Souza, "Origins of the Mission Secretariat," *Worldmission* (Fall 1957) 8:103-108; Bi-annual and annual reports on overseas American personnel occasionally published by the Catholic Students' Mission Crusade; the Mission Secretariat; the U.S. Catholic Mission Board and the U.S. Catholic Mission Association.

L. Nemer

Missions Conferences, Evangelical. Conferences convened to further the cause of the Christian world mission. Evangelical missions conferences take a variety of forms, but most can be categorized as either forums for discussing mission programs and policies or informative and inspirational meetings intended to enlist prayer and financial support, as well as to encourage new missionary candidates.

Local church missionary conferences are typically informative and inspirational. They tend to be annual events following any of a variety of schedules. The long-established pattern of week-long conferences with nightly meetings, however, seems to be giving way to weekend conferences or a month-long emphasis on missions with meetings, taking place over several Sundays. Conference programs generally consist of presentations and displays by furloughing missionaries and mission agencies supported by the church, as well as one or more keynote mission speaker. It has been estimated that roughly ten per cent of the churches in the U.S. carry on a missionary program including this kind of conference.

Perhaps the most famous ongoing evangelical missions conference is the Urbana Student Missions Missionary Convention,* held triennially at the University of Illinois at Urbana since 1948. Beginning with the quadrennial student conventions initiated by the Student Volunteer Movement* in 1891 and continued by that group until 1936, the model was resumed after World War 2 by the recently merged InterVarsity Christian Fellowship* and Student Foreign Missions Fellowship.* The first of these conventions took place in Toronto in 1946. Meeting for five days between Christmas and New Year's Day, the conference attracts hundreds of mission agencies and thousands of students, as well as missionaries, ministers and lay* people. The total attendance at the 1987 convention was about eighteen thousand five hundred.

A longstanding, but now somewhat fading, tradition among fundamentalists and evangelicals has been the Bible and missions conference centers combining scenic vacation opportunities with a regular schedule of inspirational Bible messages and missionary reports. Conference grounds such as Gull Lake, Winona Lake, Ben Lippen, Muskoka and American Keswick are outstanding examples. The increasing affluence, busyness and mobility of the American evangelicals, however, seem to be contributing to the decline of these mission's conferences.

Mission's conferences devoted to discussing programs and policies have been influential in shaping the course of the North American evangelical missionary movement. The Interdenominational Foreign Mission Association* (IFMA) and the Evangelical Foreign Mission Association* (EFMA) have sponsored joint triennial conferences since their first joint meeting at Winona Lake,

Indiana, in 1963. From that first gathering, the Evangelical Missions Information Service was born. Likewise, the 1971 gathering at Green Lake, Wisconsin, pioneered in discussing mission and church relationships overseas, as well as independent mission and church relationships in North America.

In addition to these joint meetings, the IFMA and EFMA hold annual meetings of their own, which include regional strategy sessions. Annual conferences are also held by independent and denominational mission associations in North America, as well as by groups such as the American Society of Missiology and the Association of Professors of Mission. Numerous other mission program and policy conferences take place on a more ad hoc basis. These would include the Regional Update Conferences of the IFMA/EFMA and similar gatherings sponsored by groups such as the Overseas Ministries Study Center, Missionary Internship, the Trinary Consultation Group (Moody Bible Institute,* Trinity Evangelical Divinity School and Wheaton College*) and the U.S. Center for World Mission.

See also MISSIONS, EVANGELICAL FOREIGN; URBANA STUDENT MISSIONS CONVENTIONS.

BIBLIOGRAPHY. D. M. Howard, *Student Power in World Evangelism* (1970); S. Wilson and J. Siewart, *Mission Handbook: North American Protestant Ministries Overseas,* 13th ed., rev. (1986).

G. R. Corwin

Missions to Alaska, Russian Orthodox. The initial introduction of the Orthodox* faith to the North American native population was the work of the Russian fur traders (*promyshlenniki*). The first recorded baptisms* were by Stefan Glotov, a layman, who landed on the Fox Islands of the Aleutian Chain in 1759. When the first contingent of missionaries arrived in 1794, they found many of the indigenous people already baptized into the Orthodox faith. One of the motives behind the religious activity of the *promyshlenniki* was pacification of the natives and assurance of their loyalty to their baptismal sponsors. The competition for native fur hunters to serve the Russians was intense, and those bound to specific Russians by baptism were loyal workers.

Gregorii Shelikov, founder of the Russian American Company, which was to control Alaska from 1799 to 1867, recruited the first missionaries, whose financial needs were to be met by the company. The mission was composed of ten monks from Valaam Monastery, Finland. Led by Archimandrite Ioasaph (Joseph), the group encountered violent opposition from the Russian colonists under company manager Alexander Baranov. The abuse by the fur traders of the native peoples and the introduction of disease had decimated the population. The missionaries became the defenders of the indigenous peoples, but the hardships and obstacles faced by the missionaries prevented the establishment of regular church life. The frustration was heightened when Ioasaph was drowned on his return voyage from Russia in 1799 after being consecrated* bishop* for Alaska. The episcopal see was left unfilled until 1840. Of the original group, the most lasting work was accomplished by Herman,* who founded a school and continued his work until his death in 1837. Herman was canonized* in 1970 as the first Orthodox saint* in America.

Missionary work proceeded more rapidly after the arrival in 1824 and 1825, respectively, of the priests John Venyaminov* and James Netsvietov. Veniaminov, a tireless worker, constructed places of worship,* devised an Aleut alphabet and translated portions of the Bible* and certain liturgical* texts, founded schools and visited his scattered parishioners. Netsvietov, the first Aleut ordained* to the ministry, also engaged in translation work and evangelization. When Veniaminov became Bishop Innocent (1840), he could fully implement his evangelistic strategy. At the time of the sale of Alaska, there were about twelve thousand Orthodox Christians in forty-three communities. In 1872 the episcopal see was transferred to San Francisco. Support for the Alaskan Orthodox Church continued to come from Russia until 1917.

BIBLIOGRAPHY. G. Afonsky, *A History of the Orthodox Church in Alaska* (1794-1917) (1977); H. Chevigny, *Russian America* (1979); M. Oleksa, *Alaskan Missionary Spirituality* (1987); B. S. Smith, *Orthodoxy and Native Americans: The Alaskan Mission* (1980).   J. J. Stamoolis

Missions to Native Americans, Protestant. The beginnings of the outreach to the native inhabitants of the Americas coincided with the emergence of the modern Protestant* missionary movement,* and the American mission provided inspiration and models for missions worldwide. Missions to Native Americans faced considerable difficulties, including the wide cultural and linguistic differences among the more than four-hundred tribes, the persistence of the missionaries' own cultural biases and the pressures of a relentlessly expanding white population which often demonstrated little sympathy for either Native Americans or the missionary task.

The earliest Protestant effort was begun by Thomas Mayhew, Jr.,* among Native Americans on Martha's Vineyard in 1642. John Eliot* began preaching among the Massachusetts tribe in 1646, and his Bible* translations* into their language were the first in North America. Other early works in the Northeast included John Sergeant's mission among the Housatonics at Stockbridge in western Massachusetts, begun in 1734, and the efforts of David Brainerd* in New Jersey (1742-1745). Eleazar Wheelock,* at Moor's Charity School in Lebanon, Connecticut, attempted a different approach when in 1743 he accepted Native American students into his boarding school where they could be educated in isolation from their traditional lifestyles. The boarding-school model was widely imitated, though later schools tended more to emphasize vocational training.

The Moravians,* or United Brethren, were generally considered the most successful of the early missionaries, but their works suffered tragic setbacks because of the international colonial rivalries of the era. David Zeisberger* led his Moravian Indian converts from their homeland in Pennsylvania westward through several successive resettlements in an attempt to avoid entanglement in the affairs of the warring colonial powers. Nevertheless, a band of ninety Moravian Indians was killed at Gnadenhutten, Pennsylvania, in 1782 by American colonists who suspected them of pro-British sympathies.

The end of the American Revolution* brought the withdrawal of missionary organizations based in Great Britain, but many new American denominational* and interdenominational societies were organized in the years 1787-1820. The most significant was the American Board of Commissioners for Foreign Missions,* founded in 1810. The greatest advances, which came in the years after the War of 1812, were in part results of the Second Great Awakening.*

Among the important missions of the early nineteenth century were those to the Five Civilized Tribes in the Southeast. The American Board began its work there in 1817 when Cyrus Kingsbury* established Brainerd Mission among the Cherokee. Methodists,* Baptists* and Presbyterians* also had significant missions in the Southeast. Mission work throughout the nation benefited from the Civilization Fund, which Congress established in 1819 to finance education and vocational training among Native Americans. Missions received monies from this fund for the operation of their schools, and for a time the works in the Southeast and the Old Northwest showed significant promise, until the government began to push the program of Indian Removal in the late 1820s.

While some missionaries vigorously opposed removal, others, such as the Baptist Isaac McCoy, favored removal as the most viable solution to the continued problem of white encroachment. McCoy envisioned a Native American state in the West where white settlement would not be allowed. Although new missions were established in the Indian Territory, removal had devastating effects upon the missionary enterprise. Yet by the mid-1830s, with the establishment of Jason Lee's* Methodist mission among Native Americans of Oregon's Willamette Valley (1834) and the American Board's mission to the Dakota on the Northern Plains (1835), Protestant missions had expanded throughout the nation. But later alterations in government policy again had great impact. In 1869 President Grant initiated his "Peace Policy" and invited churches to nominate men to serve as Indian agents. Thirteen denominations were given control over seventy-three agencies, only one denomination being allowed to work at each location. The government patronage thus provided was a great boost to the missions, but by the 1880s changing attitudes about such close church-state ties, combined with complaints from some denominations about exclusion from former fields, led to the end of the program.

Twentieth-century missions to Native Americans have seen many new developments. A 1925 survey reported a Native American Christian community of 35,000. The results seemed meager after nearly three centuries of labor, and many denominations abandoned the field or scaled back their efforts. Syncretistic religions, such as the Native American Church, and resurgent traditionalism provided continued challenges. Yet mission work among Native Americans continues and has expanded in some fields, such expansion often being the result of new works established by evangelical* and Pentecostal* bodies. A 1979 survey reported over two thousand Native American congregations, representing over forty denominations and many independent groups. The total Protestant community was estimated at 120,000.

BIBLIOGRAPHY. R. P. Beaver, ed., *The Native American Christian Community: A Directory of Indian, Aleut, and Eskimo Churches* (1979); R. P. Beaver, "The Churches and the Indians: Consequences of 350 Years of Missions," in *American Missions in Bicentennial Perspective,* ed. R. P. Beaver (1977); R. F. Berkhofer, Jr., *Salvation and the Savage: An Analysis of Protestant Missions and American Indian Response, 1787-1862* (1965);

H. W. Bowden, *American Indians and Christian Missions: Studies in Cultural Conflict* (1981); J. P. Ronda and J. Axtell, *Indian Missions: A Critical Bibliography* (1978). M. S. Joy

Missions to North America, French. French colonization, whether in Acadia,* Canada, Louisiana or the West Indies, was almost immediately followed by the outreach to indigenous peoples that was believed to be its ultimate justification. The first attempts in North America were exploratory and largely destitute of tangible results. After hasty baptisms* by a secular priest* in 1610, Jesuits* labored in Acadia from 1611 until their expulsion by the Virginian Samuel Argall in 1613. In 1615 Samuel de Champlain secured some Recollects, reformed Franciscans* who specialized in spiritual retreats, to serve his colony at Quebec. They quickly made contact with the Montagnais and Algonquins of the Saint Lawrence and the Hurons of the present Ontario, but found their resources inadequate and in 1625 invited the Jesuits to join them. Unsympathetic traders hampered these efforts, and an English occupation in 1629 practically undid them.

The return of French rule in 1632 and the appointment of sympathetic secular administrators made possible more systematic and sustained enterprises. Capuchins, who were Franciscans of unusual austerity, maintained a substantial, although little-known, mission in Acadia until another British incursion in 1654 compelled their return to France. Jesuits took over the Canadian field alone, reclaiming earlier missions and reaching out to neighboring peoples. Their most ambitious enterprise was among the Hurons, who were sedentary and thus available for constant instruction. Reopened in 1634, it employed by 1648 twenty-two priests and a number of voluntary assistants called *donnés.* Ursuline* nuns for teaching and Augustinians* who arrived at Quebec for hospital work in 1639 proved invaluable to the missions; in 1642 the foundation of Montreal as a religious colony provided a base deep in Native American territory. Under deep suspicion for a number of years of causing epidemics that decimated the population, the Jesuits had converted almost half of the Hurons when in 1650 Iroquois attacks wiped out both the mission and the nation.

Defeated in one enterprise, the Jesuits responded by reaching out to all accessible tribes: the Abenakis of Maine; the Chippewas or Ojibwas of Sault Ste. Marie; varied Algonkian and other peoples who had taken refuge from Iroquois attacks around the upper Great Lakes; the much-feared Iroquois themselves; the Illinois of the Mississippi; and even the Crees around James Bay. In 1725 they were made responsible for the Indian missions of Louisiana, and in the same period they accompanied exploring expeditions to the Canadian prairies. Meanwhile they had been joined by other agencies as collaborators and sometimes competitors. The Sulpicians,* a society of diocesan priests who took charge at Montreal in 1657, opened missions in Ontario and later in Acadia. The Recollects, returning in 1670 with official favor, were to be found mainly at military posts but also maintained missions in Acadia. Graduates of the seminary of Quebec, founded in 1663 in association with the Society of Foreign Missions in Paris, worked in Acadia and Louisiana, while the Seminary of the Holy Spirit provided a number of their seventeenth-century successors. Most of these agencies, along with Dominicans* and Carmelites, were also active in the French West Indies.

Despite this expansion, missionary outreach in the eighteenth century became more difficult both to sustain and to prosecute successfully. In France the Enlightenment* dampened religious zeal and discouraged missionary recruitment. On the frontier dissolute traders were a demoralizing influence, internecine warfare almost constant. Everywhere missions were drawn into the struggle for supremacy in North America. Mission Indians became indispensable allies of the French, while missionaries who saw in British domination a deadly threat to Native American souls willingly cultivated their martial spirit. The Treaty of Paris in 1763, which handed over Louisiana to Spain and Canada to Britain, resulted in the departure of French missionaries from the former and their gradual attrition through retirement and death in the latter. Little had been achieved in Louisiana, and beyond Acadia and the St. Lawrence there was a general collapse of Catholic practice.

The story of French missions in North America was by no means over. Priests fleeing revolutionary France, notably Sulpicians who maintained continuous ministries at Detroit and at Oka near Montreal, kept memories of earlier blackrobes alive and preserved a fund of missionary experience. During the early 1840s Bishop Ignace Bourget* of Montreal scoured Europe, seeking the help of religious orders. French Jesuits, arriving in 1842, concentrated on the Ojibwas of northern Ontario. Oblates of Mary Immaculate from Provence, who had preceded them by a year, became missionaries to the entire west and north of Canada and ultimately to Inuit as well as Indians. By 1874 French Benedictines were working among African-Americans at

Charleston, South Carolina, and in 1886 French Jesuits entered Alaska. Many of these and other missions were made possible by financial aid from the Society for the Propagation of the Faith,* a lay organization founded at Lyon in 1822. That more than half of the native population of Canada embraced Roman Catholicism is almost entirely the result of French missionary effort, and many missions in the U.S. can be traced to the same origin.

As pioneers in practically all areas in which they worked, French missionaries were obliged to devise new approaches or adapt familiar ones. Confronted by languages unrelated to any they knew, they reduced them to writing and composed grammars and dictionaries. Faced with the necessity of dealing with bands constantly on the move, they imported from France the brief but intensive annual "flying mission" and developed mnemonic devices for enabling Native Americans to follow the ecclesiastical calendar in the woods. At first, in line with official French policy, all missionaries attempted to assimilate native peoples as thoroughly as possible to European ways. Experience convinced the Jesuits in time that native peoples made better Catholics when insulated from close contact with French settlers, and the result was the formation of separate villages. Many of these innovations became standard practice in Roman Catholic missions, giving them a distinctive ambience in which intensive indoctrination was combined with considerable tolerance for traditional ways. Most conspicuously, French missions depended on a spirit of self-abnegation that welcomed martyrdom and was frequently rewarded by it. They were not all successful, but they inspired fervor in many Native Americans and sanctity in some.

See also MISSIONS TO NORTH AMERICA, SPANISH.

BIBLIOGRAPHY. J. Axtell, *The Invasion Within* (1985); C. J. Jaenen, *The Role of the Church in New France* (1985); J. G. Shea, *History of the Catholic Missions among the Indian Tribes of the United States, 1529-1854* (1973); R. G. Thwaites, *The Jesuit Relations and Allied Documents* (1954).

J. W. Grant

Missions to North America, Spanish. Spain quickly harvested the fruit of Christopher Columbus's* 1492 landfall, dispatching conquistadores, soldiers, settlers and missionaries* to secure the New World for the mother country. The conquistadores, searching for gold and silver, explored vast regions; subdued, enslaved and exterminated great numbers of Indian peoples; and then passed on. Soldiers built and maintained presidios to impose and enforce Spanish rule. More permanent settlers, granted large estates by the government, established a feudalistic encomienda system which, under the Laws of Burgos (1512) bound Native American laborers to the land. Yet adventurers, soldiers and settlers did not establish Spanish culture as effectively among the Native Americans as did missionaries—by and large Dominicans,* Franciscans* and Jesuits*—who everywhere accompanied the soldiers and established missions which converted,* Christianized and civilized the Native Americans who populated Latin and South America.

Columbus and his patroness, Isabella, envisioned missions as part of Spanish expansion. Pope Alexander VI, dividing the world between Spain and Portugal (1493-1494), asserted "the peaceful conversion of the native inhabitants should have primary consideration." So from the beginning Catholic missionaries served in the vanguard of Spanish exploration and settlement. At times, some of them defended Native American rights, routinely trampled by soldiers and settlers. The first priest* ordained* in the New World, Bartolomé de Las Casas, following the example of another Dominican, Antonio de Montesinos, in ardently championing Native American rights. Through prolific writings and public disputations in Spain, he ultimately elicited royal support for an essentially missionary approach to indigenous peoples, protecting them from legalized enslavement and securing their standing as fully human beings.

The first priests to enter what is today the U.S. were not missionaries but Catholic chaplains* who accompanied Hernando de Soto on his fruitless journey (1539-1540) from Florida to Louisiana. In 1539 a Franciscan, Fray Marcos de Niza, following reports of Cabeza de Vaca (a survivor of the Panfilo de Narvaez expedition), accompanied an abortive expedition into Arizona. Fray Juan de Padilla,* after accompanying Coronado's 1540 tour through much of the American Southwest, returned to the Native Americans of Quivira (in Kansas) where, in 1544, he became the first martyr on U.S. soil.

More permanent missionary endeavors took place between 1565 and 1769, as Spanish settlements appeared from the Atlantic coast across the Gulf states into the American Southwest and California.* Actual missions began with the establishment of St. Augustine, Florida (1565 or 1566), planted by Pedro Menendez de Aviles in response to abortive French settlements nearby. From this strong presidio, Spanish control and missions

extended to the north and west. Jesuit missions extended up the Atlantic coast as far north as Virginia, though Native Americans there resisted and repeatedly killed missionaries. Franciscans came to Florida in 1573, withdrew under intense persecution and then returned in the 1580s to remain until 1763. They too had difficulty reaching many Native Americans, and the missions remained rather small and inconsequential. A 1597 Indian revolt, though put down by Spanish soldiers, revealed the depth of native hostility toward all things Spanish. Since Spain never considered Florida a major region for exploitation or settlement, she invested few resources to maintain it, so long as it remained a buffer zone to the English and French to the north.

As in Florida, Spain planted missions on the Texas Gulf Coast mainly in response to a French threat. When news spread that La Salle had canoed down the Mississippi River in 1685, claiming the river's drainage basin for France, Spanish officials in Mexico dispatched missionaries to the Asinai Indians on the Nueces River in the 1690s. A 1702 revolt closed these missions, and the Spanish abandoned Texas for a decade. In 1715, however, French traders operating in eastern Texas drew the Spanish back, and missions were established among several tribes. To the west, guarding the route to Mexico, San Antonio was established in 1718, where the Franciscans built the largest Texas mission, San Antonio de Valero (better known as the Alamo) near the presidio.

Following Coronado's 1540 journey, which unearthed no gold or Native-American civilization worth exploiting, little Spanish activity took place in present-day New Mexico until 1598. Then the Council of the Indies, alarmed by reports of Francis Drake's Pacific landfalls and associated English land claims, ordered the viceroy of New Spain to take control of the area drained by the Rio Grande. Don Juan de Oñate, leading 129 soldiers and ten Franciscan friars, entered the region during the summer of 1598 and imposed Spanish rule. Most native Pueblo Indians submitted to Oñate, but the Acoma Pueblo resisted, killing thirteen Spanish soldiers. The next year an army returned and took the mesa, killing 800 Native Americans; captives were sentenced to twenty years of slavery; males over twenty-five had one foot amputated. Such brutality effectively established Spanish rule, but hardly opened Native-American hearts to the Franciscans's preaching, however sincerely it may have been done.

Indeed, missionaries often defended the New Mexico Indians, and the Franciscan superiors *(custos)* struggled with royal governors over Native American mistreatment. In 1635, Fray Alonso de Benevides successfully petitioned the Crown to end the *encomienda* system in New Mexico. Soon thereafter, however, colonists managed to wrest generous *repartimiento* grants from the government, with which they could force Native Americans to labor on their lands for specific periods of time.

In the religious realm the Franciscans could be somewhat paternalistic and dictatorial. Pueblo Indians resented them as well as the secular rulers. By 1630 Franciscans operated twenty-five missions, serving approximately sixty pueblos. The Catholic faith was embraced by numbers of Indians. But in 1680 an Indian revolt, orchestrated by Pope, a San Juan Pueblo Indian, forced the Spanish to abandon New Mexico. Priests as well as soldiers and settlers fled or were killed, and mission buildings were often demolished. Native Americans briefly restored their rule in the Rio Grande Valley.

Within a decade, however, Spanish columns pierced the Indian-held region, and in 1695 Don Diego de Vargas restored Spanish rule in Santa Fe. During the eighteenth century, Spanish interest and investment in New Mexico waned. By 1776 only twenty priests lived in the province, and many Pueblo people returned to their traditional religion—or mixed it with the Catholic faith.

Missions in present-day Arizona began when Mexican officials established the province of Primería Alta and gave Jesuits the task of establishing missions therein. The work began in the 1680s under the guidance of Eusebio Francisco Kino,* who built missions in Sonora, Mexico, and southern Arizona, including San Xavier del Bac, established in 1700 just south of today's Tucson. Pima and Papago Indians, living on rancherias along rivers in this arid region, responded somewhat favorably to Kino but rebelled against Spanish authoritarianism and revolted in 1695, killing missionaries and burning buildings. Jesuits patiently continued working in the region with only modest success thereafter, until their order was suppressed in 1767. Franciscans followed the Jesuits and similarly failed to thoroughly convert many of the intensely independent Pimas, much less the raiding Apaches.

Prodded by Russian movement down the Pacific Coast in the eighteenth century, Spain sought to shore up its land claim to present-day California. In 1750 Jesuits had effectively established missions in Baja (Lower) California. A large Native American population awaited in Alta (Upper) California. Fourteen Franciscans, led by Father Junipero

Serra,* joined Don Gaspar de Portola on an overland march which met two supply ships in San Diego on July 1, 1769. Here Father Serra established Mission San Diego, the first of nine California missions he would build, the first of twenty-one which ultimately stretched up the coast to San Francisco, spaced about a day's journey apart along El Camino Real.

Under the missionaries' direction, California Indians settled into mission compounds, worked the fields and built the structures which typified the California missions. Effectively managed, providing food and protection, the missions mixed appeal for a more secure and comfortable existence, spiritual instruction and consolation, with coercion and intimidation. Some 90,000 Native Americans were baptized* between 1769 and 1822, when the new nation of Mexico secularized the missions. In becoming "Mission Indians," they had lost their tribal identities. And as first Mexico, then the U.S., took control of California, the Mission Indians lost their lands and social structures which had become their way of life.

Despite two centuries of often-heroic missionary labors, from the Atlantic to the Pacific, across the southern tier of states, little today remains of the Spanish missions in the U.S. Only in a few Pueblos does the Catholic Church preserve its missionary investment. Elsewhere, primarily because the Native Americans themselves were largely destroyed or removed by the voracious Anglo-American frontier, Spanish Catholicism left few traces on Native American peoples.

See also MISSIONS TO NORTH AMERICA, FRENCH; MISSIONS TO NATIVE AMERICAN INDIANS, PROTESTANT.

BIBLIOGRAPHY. J. F. Bannon, *The Spanish Borderlands Frontier, 1513-1821* (1971); H. E. Bolton, "The Mission as a Frontier Institution in the Spanish-American Colonies," *AHR* 23 (1917-1918):42-61; H. E. Bolton, *The Spanish Borderlands* (1921); M. Geiger, *Franciscan Missionaries in Hispanic California, 1769-1848* (1969); C. Gibson, *Spain in America* (1966); L. Hanke, *Aristotle and the American Indians: A Study of Race Prejudice in the Modern World* (1959); E. H. Spicer, *Cycles of Conquest: The Impact of Spain, Mexico, and the United States on the Indians of the Southwest, 1533-1960* (1962). G. A. Reed

Missions to the Slaves. Efforts to evangelize* enslaved African-Americans in the antebellum South. White Christian clergymen* and philanthropic laymen* perennially expressed concern for the souls of slaves. Such a ministry* was much easier to propose than to perform, for slaveowners had extensive control over their bondsmen, and from colonial times through the early nineteenth century, they generally opposed schemes for slave conversion,* instruction and worship.* Many masters feared converted African-Americans would become unruly servants or might even demand freedom and equality. During the 1820s and 1830s Southern churchmen tried to allay these fears and to conform new missionary* activities to the accepted and staunchly defended social conditions of the South. They developed a strong biblical defense of slavery and pointed out its corollary: the Christian responsibility to bring slaves into the fold. Yet fears of slave uprisings and the clergy's history of opposition to human bondage still elicited skepticism.

Interest in missions to the slaves grew rapidly in the mid 1840s, following the North-South splits in the Methodist* and Baptist* churches (*See* Civil War). Disclaiming "any right, wish, or intention to interfere with the civil and political relation between master and slave," these new denominations joined other Southern Protestants* in advocating the benefits of evangelizing slaves: It would improve the master-slave relationship by showing the Christian duties of both parties, further owners' pecuniary interests by encouraging slaves to be honest and diligent, promote public safety by diverting the passions of African-Americans and refute abolitionist criticism by demonstrating that slavery in the South was indeed a Christian institution. Once masters trusted clergymen among their slaves and were convinced that religion supported rather than disrupted slavery, white-sponsored missions spread westward from the established, tidewater plantation societies.

The Methodist Mission to the Slaves began as a conscientious alternative to antislavery efforts within this denomination.* William Capers* led this successful movement, which put the most money and men into the field. Across the South, dedicated circuit riders* and missionaries sought permission from owners to meet with slaves. Then, using Capers's simple catechism,* they orally taught basic Christianity* to all ages. Converts often joined Methodist churches and attended services held for slaves on their plantations or in local churches. Baptists converted almost as many slaves as did the Methodists and probably accepted more into bi-racial congregations. In fact, African-Americans outnumbered whites in many prewar Southern Baptist* churches. Slaves liked the Baptist spirit of equality and spontaneity. Moreover, baptism* by immersion especially appealed to African-Americans, and African-American preachers

usually considered themselves Baptists.

Presbyterians,* though stereotyped as intellectual and self-righteous, also ministered successfully to slaves. They often cooperated with other churches, and ministers such as Charles Colcock Jones* and James H. Thornwell* were among the earliest and most articulate spokesmen for a Christian slave system. Jones wrote a popular catechism for colored persons and a book advocating the oral instruction of slaves. Pious laymen and clerics emphasized Sabbath schools in the Presbyterian ministry to slaves. Wealthy communicants gave the Protestant Episcopal Church* influence far beyond its small membership. Led by several strong bishops,* Episcopal planters incorporated religion into their operations on manor-like estates. Some large plantations boasted chapels* and even chaplains.*

Approved religious activities were often contrived and limited; a frequent sermon was "Servants Obey Your Masters." But African-Americans adapted Christianity to their needs of communal interaction, personal solace and emotional release. By 1861, the great majority of slaves were Christians, and Southern churches were the most integrated institutions in America. This diffuse mission was the only serious effort within the antebellum South to reform the slave system.

See also BLACK RELIGION.

BIBLIOGRAPHY. J. B. Boles, ed., *Masters and Slaves in the House of the Lord* (1988); E. Clarke, *Wrestlin' Jacob: A Portrait of Religion in the Old South* (1979); C. C. Jones, *The Religious Instruction of the Negroes in the United States* (1842); A. J. Raboteau, *Slave Religion: The "Invisible Institution" in the Antebellum South* (1978).

D. B. Touchstone

Missions-Minded Church. A term often used among evangelicals* to refer to a local church's* or denomination's* commitment to the worldwide missionary* task. The degree of commitment is normally measured in one or more of three ways: the amount of attention given to missions in the pulpit and educational ministries of the church, the proportion of the budget which goes to missions and the number of individuals from the church who serve in missions overseas. Of these three measures, the missions budget tends to be the most visible indicator available to those who use the term.

The budget is also important because of the use of the "faith-promise method" in many churches. This practice, begun in the early 1930s by Oswald J. Smith,* pastor of the Peoples' Church in Toronto, has since become common in evangelical churches across North America. By encouraging church members to make "faith-pledges" of what they believe God will enable them to give to missions in the coming year, missions awareness is heightened in local churches.

G. R. Corwin

Mitchell, Jonathan (1624-1668). New England Puritan* minister.* Born in Yorkshire, England, and brought to America by his parents in 1635, Mitchell graduated from Harvard College* in 1647 and was ordained* in 1650. Although called to succeed Thomas Hooker* at Hartford, he succeeded Thomas Shepard* at Cambridge, marrying Shepard's widow, Margaret. While in Cambridge he also served as a fellow of Harvard, engaging in a dispute with President Dunster* on the question of baptism.* Mitchell's more significant role among New England Puritans involved drafting the Half-Way Covenant* in 1662, he being its leading advocate. He argued that children of nonconfessing members in good standing could be baptized. Mitchell was regarded as a good preacher* by his contemporaries. Several of his sermons were published in London after his death, in 1668, at the age of forty-four.

BIBLIOGRAPHY. *AAP* 1; F. H. Foster, *A Genetic History of New England Theology* (1907); C. Mather, *Magnalia Christi Americana* (1702).

L. J. Van Til

Modernism, Catholic. The crisis over modernism in Roman Catholicism from approximately 1895 to 1910 was an attempt by alleged modernists to challenge the static character of Neo-Scholastic* theology* by introducing contemporary biblical scholarship and recent scientific developments into Catholicism, resulting in a less absolutist outlook on Catholic dogma.* Modernism was condemned by the papal decree *Lamentabili* and the encyclical* *Pascendi* in 1907, and brought to a halt by an anti-modernist oath prescribed in 1910. Modernism, never an organized movement, evolved as an intellectual orientation among various liberal Catholic priests and scholars in Germany, Great Britain, Italy and France, notably Baron Friedrich von Hügel (1852-1925), George Tyrrell (1861-1909), Maurice Blondel (1861-1949) and Alfred Loisy (1857-1940). Its complex roots included challenges to the Catholic Church to confront new philosophical movements, to re-evaluate the essentialist metaphysics of Thomism,* to embrace evolutionary* theory in biology and to examine the Church's changing role in the socio-political order. Modernists replaced the older Neo-Scholastic categories of thought with models of transcendence, immanence and experience.

Although some have claimed that modernism was primarily a crisis in European Catholicism, its effects were felt in the U.S. as well, especially when viewed in relation to the Americanist controversy. In 1899 Pope Leo XIII* had condemned the "heresy"* of Americanism,* whose principles were akin to those censured in the modernist crisis of 1907. The relationship of the two crises however, was contiguous rather than continuous. Americanism was rejected because it presumably asked the Church to update itself, to conform to modern civilization and to examine its dogma in light of current popular theories and methods. Leo XIII summarized five specific errors of Americanism in the apostolic letter *Testem Benevolentiae* of January 1899.

The Americanist crisis peaked during the controversy surrounding publication of a French biography of Isaac Hecker,* the American founder of the Paulist* order, yet the crisis had American roots in the disagreement among bishops* and clergy* over how active Catholicism should become in public life. The Americanists, following the pattern proposed by Hecker in the nineteenth century, stressed the social relevance of the Church and the compatibility of Catholicism and democracy.* The American and European conservatives, however, believed that the Americanists who had strayed from the faith in pursuit of Hecker's spirit of liberty had deserved the papal warning.

Modernism, like Americanism, was not a disciplined movement or a specific heresy, but rather a tendency or preference among liberal Catholics who claimed freedom of religious thought against the papal position that theological scholarship should be subject to the magisterium,* the teaching authority* of the Church. Modernists, like the Americanists, invoked scientific methods and developmentalist models for Scripture* and dogma in order to reconcile the results with prevailing notions of the absolute and incorruptible nature of Catholicism. Unlike Leo XIII's *Testem,* which ended the Americanist crisis, Pius X's* encyclical *Pascendi Dominici Gregis* (September 1907) did not condemn any particularly American ideas as "modernist." *Pascendi* constructed a definition of modernism which drew on ideas from the work of various, often disagreeing, modernists. Thus, although the papal attack was comprehensive, it was not wholly accurate or warranted. The Church rejected agnostic, immanentist and evolutionary doctrines and forbade the teaching of modernist approaches in Catholic seminaries* and schools. The papacy* reaffirmed its commitment to Thomism as the mandatory theology of the Church.

In the U.S. modernism was most nearly embodied at St. Joseph's Seminary, Dunwoodie, founded at Yonkers, New York, in 1896. In 1902 the faculty modernized the curriculum to reflect new biblical scholarship, with articles innovatively applying biblical criticism appearing in the bimonthly journal of the seminary, *The New York Review*. Despite a limited circulation, the *Review* was the closest American equivalent to modernism, and thus received a hostile reaction from the Vatican. The archbishop of New York closed down the *Review* in 1908, censored the priest sponsors and reorganized the seminary staff. Elsewhere in the Catholic community, two modernist priests were affected by the condemnation of 1907: William Sullivan left the Paulist order and renounced Catholicism to become a Unitarian*; John R. Slattery,* a Josephite, expressed frustration at the hierarchy's refusal to consider new insights in theology.

In Europe, Pius X's decrees led to excommunication of several modernists: Tyrrell in England, Loisy in France, Josef Schnitzer in Germany and Ernesto Buonaiuti in Italy. In America the condemnation of modernism stifled Catholic scholarship, increased Catholic doctrinal uniformity and centralized the power of the papacy.

On the whole, the modernist dispute, one of several in Roman Catholicism at the end of the nineteenth century, reflected the attempt of Catholic liberals to examine the Church's traditions and role in the modern world. Anti-modernism led to a conservative reassertion of papal authority and narrow standards of orthodoxy.* In America, the combined effect of the Americanist and modernist crises was to end a short, enthusiastic spell in Catholic intellectualism, and to push American Catholics into a period of intellectual retreat for the next half century until Vatican II.*
See also AMERICANISM.

BIBLIOGRAPHY. M. Gannon, "Before and After Modernism: The Intellectual Isolation of the American Priest," in *The Catholic Priest in the United States*, ed. J. T. Ellis (1971); J. J. Heaney, "Modernism," *NCE* 11; L. Kurtz, *The Politics of Heresy: The Modernist Crisis in Roman Catholicism* (1986); M. Reher, "Americanism and Modernism: Continuity of Discontinuity?" *USCH* 1 (1981): 87-103; A. Vidler, *The Modernist Movement in the Roman Church: Its Origins and Outcome* (1933).
P. M. Kane

Modernism, Protestant. *See* LIBERALISM/MODERNISM, PROTESTANT.

Monsignor. A form of address in the Roman Catholic Church* for all clerical officials of the papal retinue below the rank of cardinal.* The title comes from the Italian *Monsignore,* which is in turn derived from the French *Monseigneur.* The title is of French origin and was introduced into the papal court during the fourteenth century when the popes resided in Avignon. In the late nineteenth century, Pope Pius IX* began to appoint priests throughout the world as titular or honorary officials of the Roman curia. This was one way of increasing the prestige of the papacy within the Catholic Church in the wake of the Italian *Risorgimento* and the ensuing loss of the Papal States. Although they had no official duties, these honorary papal chamberlains, domestic prelates and prothonotary apostolics were entitled to be addressed as "Monsignor."

Robert J. Seton, the grandson of St. Elizabeth Ann Seton,* was appointed a papal chamberlain in 1866 and a prothonotary apostolic in 1867, the first American to receive these honors. By 1884 twelve Americans had been named monsignors and they were all invited to participate in the Third Plenary Council of Baltimore (*See* Baltimore Councils). The increasing bestowal of this honor soon made the title of Monsignor a familiar one in the American Catholic Church. The number of monsignors peaked at the time of the Second Vatican Council.* In the post-conciliar era, the glamour of honorary titles has faded and only a few American bishops currently continue to recommend priests for these titular papal offices.
M. E. Hussey

Moe, Malla (1863-1953). Pioneer missionary* to Swaziland. A missionary in southern Africa for fifty-four years with the Scandinavian Alliance Mission (now The Evangelical Alliance Mission*), Moe conducted a far-reaching evangelistic* program, established dozens of churches, trained national pastors* and served as an unauthorized bishop* throughout the region in which she worked. In 1927, at the age of sixty-five, Moe began a new ministry of evangelism, traveling from place to place in her "gospel wagon." Accompanied by a band of native helpers, she maintained a hectic preaching* schedule, often in areas where the gospel had never before been heard.

The founder of the Scandinavian Alliance Mission, Fredrik Franson,* was a strong supporter of women in ministry, but both African and missionary colleagues characterized her as domineering and difficult to get along with, despite her many accomplishments. Though active in ministry on the mission field, Moe was barred from speaking from the pulpit during furloughs in America because of her sex.

BIBLIOGRAPHY. M. Nilsen and P. H Sheetz, *Malla Moe* (1956). R. A. Tucker

Moffatt, James (1870-1944). Biblical scholar, church historian. Born in Glasgow, Scotland, Moffatt graduated in classics from the University of Glasgow (1889) and then prepared for the ministry* at the United Free Church College in Glasgow (1894). After ordination* (1896) in the Church of Scotland, Moffatt pastored two churches until 1915. While ministering* in his parish, Moffatt published several books which established him as a scholar, earning him the position of Yates Professor of Greek and New Testament Exegesis at Mansfield College, Oxford (1911-1915). After returning to serve for over a decade as professor of church history at the United Free Church College (1915-1927), he moved to America, where until his retirement in 1938 he was Washburn Professor of Church History at Union Theological Seminary (New York).*

Moffatt is most widely remembered for his translation* of the Bible,* designed to demonstrate graphically and simply to the layperson the contemporary scholarly understanding of the biblical text (NT 1913; OT 1924-1925). After retirement, much of his time was spent as the executive secretary to the committee which eventually produced the Revised Standard Version, where his influence, although less well known, was eventually more far-reaching than the Moffat Bible.

S. Meier

Moffett, Samuel Austin (1864-1939). Pioneer Presbyterian* missionary* to northern Korea. Born in Madison, Indiana, Moffett studied chemistry at Hanover College (A.B., 1884; M.S., 1885) and attended McCormick Seminary (B.D., 1888). Under the influence of the Young Men's Christian Association* (YMCA), Dwight L. Moody* and the Student Volunteer Movement,* Moffett committed his life to Christian missions in 1886. In 1889 Moffett sailed for Korea with the Presbyterian Mission Board, arriving in the port city of Chemulpo on his twenty-sixth birthday, Jan. 25, 1890.

By 1893 Moffett had moved to Pyongyang, the ancient capital city, and became, in effect, the first Protestant* missionary to take up residence in inland Korea. Initially Moffett met with violent opposition, but he immediately began catechism*

classes and by 1895 had purchased 110 acres inside the city, which soon became the theological and medical center of Presbyterian missionary labors in Korea. In large part because of Moffett's initiative, four Presbyterian churches formed in 1907 the Korean Presbyterian Church, with Moffett as its moderator.

Influenced by John L. Nevius,* American missionary to China, Moffett adopted Nevius' "three-self principle," concerned with building strong indigenous churches and well-trained leaders. In his forty-six years in Korea, Moffett cofounded Union Christian College (now Soong Jun University), founded the Presbyterian Theological Seminary and encouraged the young Korean Presbyterian Church to form its own mission board. For his foresight and ceaseless initiative in establishing new churches, Moffett's Korean friends named him "the Looking-up-the-Road Man." Forced out of Korea by the Japanese in 1936, Moffett died three years later in Monrovia, California.

BIBLIOGRAPHY. M. Seth, "The Looking-up-the-Road Man," *Presbyterian Life* 7 (July 24, 1954):10-13, 26; R. E. Shearer, *Wildfire: Church Growth in Korea* (1966). S. Sunquist

Montgomery, Carrie Judd (1858-1946). Pentecostal* minister* and editor. Born in Buffalo, New York, Carrie Judd was the fourth of eight children. Reared in the Episcopal Church,* as a young woman Judd claimed healing* from debilitating illness and began a life dedicated to Christian ministries in 1879. She was associated with the early efforts of Albert B. Simpson* in creating the Christian and Missionary Alliance.* She operated a faith home in Buffalo—one of many homes for healing established by Holiness* ministers and lay people during the late nineteenth century—and was widely acquainted with those who pursued a deeper Christian life. Her book, *The Prayer of Faith* (1880), circulated widely among the growing constituency interested in healing. In 1881 Judd began to publish *Triumphs of Faith,* a monthly interdenominational magazine devoted to the deeper life and divine healing.

On May 14, 1890, she married George Montgomery, a layman who had made a fortune in mining. They moved to Oakland, California, where for several years they worked with The Salvation Army.* Shortly after Pentecostal teaching was brought to California in 1906, the Montgomerys identified with Pentecostalism. George remained a layman, but Carrie was eventually ordained* by leaders of the Churches of God in Christ* in

January 1914. She joined the Assemblies of God* and was issued credentials as an evangelist on November 30, 1917. Until she died on July 26, 1946, she operated the Home of Peace, a missionary rest home, edited *Triumphs of Faith* and was the pastor of Beulah Heights Chapel in Oakland.

BIBLIOGRAPHY. C. J. Montgomery, *The Life and Teachings of Carrie Judd Montgomery* (1985).

E. L. Blumhofer

Montgomery, Helen Barrett (1861-1934). Biblical scholar and Baptist* denominational leader. Born in Kingsville, Ohio, Helen Barrett was a native of Rochester, New York. She began her career as a schoolteacher and moved into religious work with several agencies of the Northern Baptist Convention. Helen's marriage to businessman William A. Montgomery provided her with unique social and leadership opportunities, including friendships with Susan B. Anthony* and Frances Willard.* Helen herself actually pioneered several leadership roles, serving as the first female member of the Rochester city school board, the first woman president of a religious denomination* (the Northern Baptist Convention, 1921) and the first woman to prepare a translation of the entire New Testament into English.

In Baptist life she promoted international missions by traveling abroad extensively with her colleague Lucy W. Peabody* and by helping to organize permanent support groups like the World Wide Guild and the World Day of Prayer. A licensed minister, she was the chief catalyst in the unification of the Women's Baptist Missionary Societies of the East and West into a single agency in 1914. When faced with fundamentalist* reactions in the 1921 annual sessions of the Northern Baptist Convention, President Helen Montgomery characteristically reminded delegates of their denominational heritage and responsibilities in mission.

Identifying with the scholarly traditions of her father and brother, Montgomery finished her *Centenary Translation of the New Testament* in 1924. Her lively style, yet faithfulness to the original Greek, provided a popular study edition which has enjoyed seventeen printings. She dedicated her work to Judson Press and its heritage of Bible-translation work in missionary endeavor.

As a lecturer and writer in great demand among seminaries* and churches, Helen believed that cooperative denominational missions would kindle and revivify churches which were broken by theological strife. She often scolded pastors for being lukewarm toward missions and unaware of the global implications of the gospel.

BIBLIOGRAPHY. H. B. Montgomery, *Helen Barrett Montgomery, From Campus to World Citizenship* (1940); *NAW* 2.

W. H. Brackney

Moody, (D)wight (L)yman (1837-1899). Urban revivalist.* Born in Northfield, Massachusetts, Moody had little schooling or religious training, though his family had ties to the Unitarian Church.* At seventeen he left home for Boston to work in his uncle's shoe store. After being converted by his Congregationalist* Sunday-school* teacher, Edward Kimball, and joining the church, Moody moved to Chicago in 1856, where he became a successful shoe salesman.

In Chicago Moody joined Plymouth Congregational Church and rented four pews which he filled with business associates and others he had met on the city streets. In 1858 he started a Sunday school in the Chicago slums and two years later quit his business to devote himself fully to his religious pursuits. Declining combat for conscience's sake during the Civil War,* he did evangelistic* and welfare work with the U.S. Christian Commission.* In 1863 he expanded his Chicago Sunday school into the undenominational Illinois Street Church and in 1866 became president of the Chicago YMCA.* During this period Chicagoans often referred to him as "Crazy Moody" because of his enthusiastic and sometimes unconventional approach to evangelism.

After the Chicago Fire of 1871 destroyed his work, Moody tried his hand at revivalism in the British Isles, where he had a number of contacts through the international YMCA. Thanks in no small part to his chorister Ira Sankey,* Moody's evangelistic meetings caused a sensation. For two years (1873-1875) he preached* to enormous crowds in England, Scotland and Ireland and returned to the United States as a famous revivalist in high demand. From 1875 to 1879 Moody and Sankey conducted successful revivals in Brooklyn, Philadelphia, New York City, Chicago and Boston. From 1881 to 1884 he returned to Great Britain for meetings and then had similar successes in the United States and Canada from 1884 to 1891. During the 1893 Chicago World's Fair, he conducted a crusade that drew huge crowds.

Unlike many other revivalists of his time, Moody was concerned about education and founded a number of educational institutions. In 1879 he began the Northfield Seminary for girls and in 1881 the Mount Herman School for boys, both in his Massachussetts hometown. In 1880 Moody established the Northfield Conferences,* which met annually for many years. The conference in 1886 gave rise to the Student Volunteer Movement* for foreign missions, which adopted the motto "the evangelization of the world in this generation." In 1889 he assisted the Chicago Evangelization Society in starting a Bible institute, which took the name Moody Bible Institute after his death.

Moody brought a new level of sophistication and organization to urban* revivalism. Never a sensationalist, he was always modest and congenial; he looked and acted like the businessman he was. His sermons* were homey, engaging and sentimental, stressing the love of God over God's wrath. His message was simple and straightforward: ruin by sin, redemption by Christ and regeneration by the Holy Spirit. For his city-wide crusades, he mobilized the business community which brought new levels of managerial expertise and gave his meetings a middle-class ethos.

Moody was the first major American revivalist to adopt premillennialist* views: "I look upon this world as a wrecked vessel. God has given me a lifeboat and said to me, 'Moody, save all you can.' " Such beliefs spurred Moody and his followers on to greater evangelistic efforts, but they tended to lessen their interest in social issues. Though American evangelicalism was beginning to splinter over changing theology, Moody maintained friendships with liberals* but failed in his efforts to maintain unity through a commitment to evangelism. Though never ordained,* Moody preached to more people than anyone else of his time.

BIBLIOGRAPHY. *DAB* VII; *DARB;* J. F. Findlay, *Dwight L. Moody: American Evangelist, 1837-1899* (1969); S. M. Gundry, *Love Them In* (1982); W. G. McLoughlin, *Modern Revivalism* (1959); *NCAB* 7; J. Pollock, *Moody* (1963).　　　　　T. P. Weber

Moody Bible Institute. An evangelical* training institution originating in the late nineteenth century. Moody Bible Institute in Chicago has its roots in the Chicago Evangelization Society that was officially organized on February 5, 1887. However, a formal year-round Bible institute was not organized until the fall of 1889 and was called the Bible Institute for Home and Foreign Missions of the Chicago Evangelization Society. After Dwight L. Moody's death in December of 1899, the school was named Moody Bible Institute on March 21, 1900.

Moody Bible Institute became rather quickly an influential organization in the religious world. Several factors contributed to this success. Chicago was a strategic location. The Institute's objectives were practical and met a need for biblical training

because of the influence of liberal* theology on the traditional seminaries.* Moody himself had credibility, both in the U.S. and Great Britain, and he had the financial support of a core of well-to-do Chicago businessmen.

The Institute's ministries extended beyond the training school. Many people came to know it for its publishing efforts through Moody Press and *Moody Monthly.* It has been a forerunner in religious radio and in producing films that integrate science and Scripture.* Furthermore, its history reveals an innovative institution in the areas of curriculum development, including day-school, evening-school and correspondence-school programs and a specialized program for preparing missionary* aviation pilots.

Moody Bible Institute is also identified by historians as the mother of the Bible institute* movement. Though it was not the first Bible institute in America, it became the model for numerous other schools that patterned their curricula after it.

The Institute has also had a strong influence on the fundamentalist* movement. Its first presidents, Reuben A. Torrey* and James M. Gray* were both strong defenders of the authority* of Scripture in the wake of the theological liberalism that prevailed during the first quarter of the twentieth century. The Institute's leadership, however, has generally avoided the rather militant attitudes of some fundamentalist leaders and has maintained a friendship with those of various persuasions within evangelical* Christianity.

The Institute's contributions to conservative Christianity are extensive. It has produced more missionaries than any other single school. Furthermore, no less than five major Christian organizations were spawned at Moody Bible Institute: The Evangelical Teacher Training Association (1931), Scripture Press Publications (1934), The American Scientific Affiliation (1941), The Christian Booksellers Association* (1950) and Evangelical Literature Overseas (1953).

BIBLIOGRAPHY. G. A. Getz, *M.B.I.: The Story of Moody Bible Institute* (1969); D. M. Martin, *Moody Bible Institute: God's Power in Action* (1977).　　　　　G. A. Getz

Moon, Charlotte ("Lottie") Diggs (1840-1912). Southern Baptist* missionary* to China. Born and raised on a Virginia plantation, Moon graduated from Albemarle Female Institute in 1861 with a master's degree in classics. Following the Civil War* Moon pursued a teaching career in Georgia, but her heart was in foreign missions.* In

1873 she sailed for China where she initially taught in a children's school. Finding her life lonely and unfulfilling, she considered marriage as a solution to her problems but in the end broke an engagement to a brilliant missionary-minded young man because of his views on evolution.*

With that decision, Moon was determined to continue her mission in China and insisted that she be permitted to conduct the type of work to which she was called, that of evangelism and church planting. She wrote: "What women want who come to China is free opportunity to do the largest possible work. . . . What women have a right to demand is perfect equality." Despite her field director's initial opposition, she successfully conducted evangelistic work, and in 1889 her work in P'ing-tu was described as the Southern Baptist effort's "greatest evangelistic center in all China."

Moon identified closely with the Chinese people, and when a time of great famine inflicted devastation on her Chinese friends, she gave her own food supplies to needy families. She died of starvation on Christmas Eve 1912, an event that stirred the conscience of Southern Baptists at home. The Lottie Moon Christmas Offering for Foreign Missions, inspired by her in 1888 and so named in 1918, has since grown to the sum of tens of millions of dollars annually. She is often referred to as the "patron saint" of Southern Baptist missions because of the influence she had on missionary outreach and giving.

BIBLIOGRAPHY. C. B. Allen, *The New Lottie Moon Story* (1980); I. T. Hyatt, Jr., *Our Ordered Lives Confess: Three Nineteenth-Century American Missionaries in East Shantung* (1976); *NAW* 2.

R. A. Tucker

Moon, Sun Myung. *See* UNIFICATION CHURCH.

Moore, George Foot (1851-1931). Old Testament scholar. Born in Pennsylvania, Moore received much of his early education through private study and tutoring by his father, a Presbyterian* minister.* Graduating second in his class from Yale* (B.A., 1872), Moore studied for the ministry at Union Theological Seminary* (B.D., 1877) and received Presbyterian* ordination* (1878). After pastoring in Zanesville, Ohio (1878-1883), Moore became successively professor of Old Testament at Andover Theological Seminary* (1883-1902) and professor of the history of religion at Harvard* (1902-1928) until his retirement. At Harvard Moore served as a member of both the faculty of Arts and Sciences and the faculty of Divinity.*

Moore's numerous publications gained him international recognition as a critical scholar in Hebrew and Old Testament. His classic commentary on Judges was published early in his career (1895). Having studied and taught in Germany (1885; 1909-1910), Moore's work reflected German scholarship, which he was instrumental in introducing into America. In addition to serving as assistant editor of *The Andover Review* (1884-1903) and editor of *The Harvard Theological Review* (1913-1924), his publications on the Old Testament were complemented by significant contributions to the history of religions and early Judaism, as seen in his two-volume *History of Religions* (1913-1919) and the three volumes of *Judaism in the First Centuries of the Christian Era* (1927-1930). Moore's broad interests and expertise are likewise reflected in the societies which he served as president: the American Academy of Arts and Sciences, the Massachusetts Historical Society, the American Oriental Society and the Society of Biblical Literature and Exegesis.*

S. Meier

Moore, Joanna P. (1832-1916). Baptist* home missionary.* In 1863 Moore began her missionary career working in refugee camps for freed slaves under the American Baptist Home Missionary Society. In 1873 she moved to New Orleans and worked alongside the African-American Baptist churches there. The newly formed Woman's Baptist Home Missionary Society supported her with financial help and missionary assistants. Moore is rightly credited as a major figure in Baptist women's home missionary work; her efforts in establishing schools and missions around the South and enlisting black and white teachers and evangelists,* consistently enlarged the missionary society's vision and scope. In 1891, in Little Rock, Arkansas, she established a Training School for Mothers and the Fireside School, a correspondence curriculum she published in her magazine, *Hope.* Moore's goal was to strengthen African-American families through vocational and religious training and to encourage independent African-American efforts in higher education.

BIBLIOGRAPHY. J. Moore, *In Christ's Stead: Autobiographical Sketches* (1902); G. M. Eaton, *A Heroine of the Cross: Sketches of the Life and Work of Joanna P. Moore* (1920). M. L. Bendroth

Moore, Richard Channing (1762-1841). Episcopal* bishop* of Virginia. Born in New York City, Moore studied at King's College and then studied medicine under Dr. Richard Bayley, a New York physician. He practiced medicine for a while and at the age of twenty-two married Christian Jones of New York.

Moore became interested in Christianity* and decided to enter the ministry.* After preparation under Bishop Samuel Provoost* of New York, he was ordained* deacon* on July 15, 1787, at St. George's Chapel, New York, and priest* on September 19, 1787, at St. Paul's Chapel, New York. He was rector* of Christ Church, Rye, New York, for two years and then rector of St. Andrew's Church, Richmond, Staten Island, until 1809. In 1809 he became rector of St. Stephen's Church, New York. On May 5, 1814, the Diocese* of Virginia elected him its second bishop, succeeding James Madison,* and he was called as rector of Monumental Church, Richmond. He was consecrated on May 18, 1814, at St. James' Church, Philadelphia, by Bishop William White of Pennsylvania. Moore preached the sermon "The Doctrines of the Church" at the General Convention of 1820.

Though the Diocese of Virginia had languished since the Revolution,* it prospered under his leadership; churches were re-established, the number of clergy* increased and the Virginia Theological Seminary at Alexandria was founded in 1823. Moore died on November 11, 1841, on a visitation to Lynchburg, and was buried in Richmond. An evangelical* high churchman,* Moore stressed the divine origin of the church and its apostolic ministry, as well as justification* by grace and the necessity for revival.*

BIBLIOGRAPHY. *AAP* 5; L. L. Brown, "Richard Channing Moore and the Revival of the Southern Church," *HMPEC* 35 (1966):3-63; *DAB* VII; J. P. K. Henshaw, *Memoir of the Life of the Rt. Rev. Richard Channing Moore* (1843). D. S. Armentrout

Moorehead, William Gallogly (1836-1914).

Presbyterian* minister* and educator. Born near Rix Mills, Ohio, Moorehead graduated from Muskingum College and Xenia Theological Seminary. After ordination* in 1862 he served seven years in Italy as a missionary,* and then accepted the pastorate of First United Presbyterian Church, Xenia, Ohio. In 1873 he returned to Xenia Seminary as a professor of New Testament. He became president of the seminary in 1899 and would remain Xenia's president and professor until his death.

Moorehead was prominent among American premillennialists,* speaking frequently at Bible institutes* and Bible and prophecy conferences.* He also served as a long-time leader of the Niagara Conference.* In the 1890s he modified his eschatology,* joining some other Niagara leaders in asserting that the rapture of the church would occur after (as opposed to before) the tribulation. The theological conflict that ensued helped bring the Niagara Conferences to an end. Moorehead also wrote eight books, including a firm defense of the Mosaic authorship of the Pentateuch.

BIBLIOGRAPHY. E. R. Sandeen, *The Roots of Fundamentalism: British and American Millenarianism, 1800-1930* (1970); *Testimonial and Memorial to William Gallogly Moorehead, for Forty-One Years Professor in the Xenia Theological Seminary.* W. V. Trollinger

Moral Majority. A conservative political group formed in 1979 by Baptist* pastor Jerry Falwell.* The Moral Majority has been the most visible manifestation of the New Religious Right,* which seeks to root out secular humanism and restore Judeo-Christian* morality in society. The Moral Majority works to educate and mobilize conservative citizens (mostly Christian) to elect moral candidates to office, to eliminate such evils as abortion* and pornography and to influence a wide range of public policies through lobbying offices in Washington, D.C.

The organization claims to have about four million members, although that reflects the mailing list rather than dues-payers or active participants. The president of the Moral Majority from 1979 through 1987 was Jerry Falwell, pastor of a Lynchburg, Virginia, church and host of the religious television program "The Old Time Gospel Hour." The current president is Jerry Nims. The headquarters are in Washington, D.C., with a branch office in Lynchburg. The 1987 budget was approximately $8.4 million.

The majority of the supporters are white fundamentalist Christians living in rural areas and attending independent Bible churches. Falwell also claims that about thirty per cent of the members are Catholics,* drawn to the organization by its anti-abortion stance. The executive board of the Moral Majority has included such theologically and politically conservative leaders as Tim LaHaye, D. James Kennedy, Charles Stanley and Greg Dixon.

The Moral Majority was formed in June 1979 in response to the political activities of feminist* and homosexual* groups and in response to governmental decisions about abortion, religion in public schools* and regulation of private schools. Its political platform is staunchly conservative, supporting a human life amendment, prayer in public schools, stricter limits on pornography, free-enterprise economics, the death penalty, a strong defense and support for Israel. It opposes the Equal Rights Amendment, pornography, drug use, homosexuality, most government welfare programs, government regulation of private schools and disarmament.

To achieve these goals the Moral Majority has launched a vigorous education campaign involving frequent mass mailings, a newsletter called "The Moral Majority Report," sporadic radio and TV shows, and occasional rallies. In addition, state organizations have been set up in all fifty states, usually led by a fundamentalist* pastor.

The group's impact has been mixed. Although generally credited with registering two to three million new voters, the group has not been a major factor in election outcomes. They have been able to keep issues such as abortion and school prayer on the congressional agenda, but the measures have not passed. Local chapters succeeded in restricting pornography sales. Media coverage has been extensive, although usually unfavorable. There has been vehement criticism by liberals, who see the Moral Majority as violating the separation of church and state* by trying to legislate a sectarian morality. Although the group has been a significant participant in political debates, its base of support has not gone much beyond the limited and politically inexperienced segment of Christian fundamentalists.

On June 10, 1989, Jerry Falwell announced the dissolution of the Moral Majority, which would take place by August 31, 1989. Falwell maintained that the organization had fulfilled its goal of establishing the Religious Right within the public arena.

BIBLIOGRAPHY. J. Falwell, *Listen, America!* (1980); E. Jorstad, *The Politics of Moralism* (1981); R. Zwier, *Born-Again Politics* (1982).

R. Zwier

Moral Re-Armament. Movement to promote moral awareness and world peace. Founded by Frank Buchman* in 1938, the movement was to prevent war by promoting moral and spiritual awakening throughout the world. It is the direct successor to a worldwide crusade Buchman organized in 1921 called the First Century Christian Fellowship or the Oxford Group Movement, aimed to help individuals achieve dynamic religious experiences. Buchman renamed his movement and changed its purpose in response to the political and military tensions of the late 1930s.

Inaugurated in England in 1938 and in America in 1939, Moral Re-Armament sought to effect "personal, social, racial, national and supernational

change." While the First Century Christian Fellowship had primarily used small-group techniques to stimulate spiritual conversion* among people with power and prestige, Moral Re-Armament, during its early years, used extensive advertising campaigns and mass rallies in an attempt to influence public opinion and national values. Vigorously opposed to communism, the movement displayed friendliness to fascism. During World War 2* its leaders powerfully promoted patriotism among citizens of allied nations. In the U.S. the movement initiated the "You Can Defend America" campaign for total defense in 1940, opened a school for Home Defense in 1941 and organized a Midwestern industrial morale-building campaign in 1942.

Although the movement declined in popularity and influence as its founder's health deteriorated in the 1950s, it has continued to the present day. After Buchman's death in 1961, Peter Howard served as its leader until 1965. Since then a group of directors has administered the movement, which now has international centers in Japan and Switzerland. Its "Up With People" program has been very popular in the U.S.

BIBLIOGRAPHY. F. Buchman, *Remaking the World* (1961); B. Entwistle and J. M. Roots, *Moral Re-Armament; What Is It?* (1967); G. Lean, *On the Tail of a Comet: The Life of Frank Buchman* (1988).

G. S. Smith

Moral Theology. The term *theology** means a reasoned account about God. Christian theology in particular is a body of knowledge which rationally interprets, elaborates and ordains the truths of revelation. For the sake of clarification, Catholic theologians have contrasted moral theology with dogmatic* theology. Dogmatic theology deals with teaching—an impersonal and abstract body of knowledge passed down from one agency to another. Moral theology, on the other hand, deals with the goal of life and how it is to be achieved. Moral theology utilizes both revelation and reason. Therefore, it is not the same as faith, which accepts the revealed truths of God by an act of belief; nor is it the same as moral philosophy which attempts to derive and describe norms for human conduct on the basis of reason alone.

As a part of theology, moral theology is the study of God. But as "moral," it emphasizes the way a human being must live—with grace and virtue—in order to attain the presence of God, the proper end of every person's life. Thus, moral theology is concerned with virtue and goodness. It examines such factors as freedom, conscience, love, responsibility and law, and endeavors to apply general principles to particular, concrete decisions and intentions. This it does in order to help individuals with the details of day-to-day living so that they can better achieve the fullness of their humanity and live more worthily as creatures of God.

BIBLIOGRAPHY. Y. Congar, *A History of Theology* (1968); H. J. Gratsche ed., *Principles of Catholic Theology* (1981).

D. T. DeMarco

Moravian Church in America. Popular name for two provinces of the *Unitas Fratrum* (Unity of the Brethren) in the U.S. and Canada. Founded by followers of John Hus in 1457, the movement was renewed under the patronage of Count Nicholas Ludwig von Zinzendorf* in the 1720s. The first group of Moravians to settle in North America arrived in Savannah, Georgia, in 1735 under the leadership of Augustus G. Spangenberg.* In 1740 the colony relocated to Pennsylvania and in 1741 founded a settlement at Bethlehem. Early Moravian ministers itinerated among the Germans living in Pennsylvania, and under the leadership of David Zeisberger, carried out mission work among Native Americans. The now-famous settlement in Salem, North Carolina, was begun in 1753 under Spangenberg's leadership.

The Moravians experienced little growth until German immigrations in the nineteenth century, which resulted in congregations founded in Wisconsin, New Jersey, Minnesota and North Dakota. In the twentieth century Moravians have founded churches in Florida; Arizona; California; Georgia; Washington, D.C.; and Ontario, Canada. Administratively, the churches are divided into two provinces with headquarters in Bethlehem, Pennsylvania, and Winston-Salem, North Carolina. In 1986 the total membership was 77,012. Mission work on the North American continent is carried out in Alaska and Labrador, with foreign missions in Nicaragua, Honduras, Guyana, Eastern West Indies and Tanzania. The churches have adopted a conferential system of church government. The official denominational organ is the *North American Moravian.*

Moravian worship is semi-liturgical, with Scripture-based liturgies* and services for the church year. Emphasis is placed on congregational singing and an extensive treasury of early-American Moravian anthems and sacred songs. Chorale hymnody is characteristic, although other hymns* are freely used. Moravians are also known for their traditional Christmas Eve candle services, lovefeasts and Easter dawn services.

BIBLIOGRAPHY. M. Taylor and K. G. Hamilton, *History of the Moravian Church* (1967).

A. H. Frank

Moravians. A Protestant* tradition with roots reaching back to the *Unitas Fratrum* (Unity of Brethren). One wing of the "first Reformation" Hussite movement, sparked in Bohemia by Jan Hus (martyred 1415), was the separatist and pacifist Unity of Brethren, organized in 1457. The Unity and other non-Roman Catholic churches were all but destroyed in Czech lands during the Thirty Years War (1619-1648) and through repressive measures of the Counter-Reformation. After several decades of clandestine existence, a handful of Moravian refugees found toleration in 1722 on the estate of Count Nicholas Ludwig von Zinzendorf* (1700-1760) in lower Saxony. Their village—which integrated religious, civic and economic life—was named *Herrnhut,* and it soon attracted other religious dissenters.

Powerfully moved by the spirit of German Pietism,* the Herrnhut group resolved to "renew" the old Unity movement. The ministry was restored in 1735 when David Nitschmann* was ordained* in Berlin by the sole surviving bishop of the *Unitas Fratrum.* Zinzendorf gradually became drawn to this group, and although he never broke with official Lutheranism,* he became a "bishop" of the Herrnhut Moravians in 1737.

Zinzendorf and his associate, Augustus Gottlieb Spangenberg,* were responsible for settlement of Moravians in the American colonies. Successful towns on the Herrnhut model were built in Pennsylvania (Bethlehem, 1741; Nazareth, 1743; Lititz, 1757) and in North Carolina (Salem, 1766). Zinzendorf, however, failed in his dream of unifying all German-speaking Protestants in an ecumenical synod* (1741). Extensive Native American mission efforts were tragically doomed because of frontier wars between 1754 and 1813. Moravian contributions to American religious life have continued in areas of education, hymnody and church music.*

See also MORAVIAN CHURCH IN AMERICA.

BIBLIOGRAPHY. A. J. Lewis, *Zinzendorf, the Ecumenical Pioneer* (1962); J. Taylor and K. G. Hamilton, *History of the Moravian Church* (1967); J. R. Weinlick, "Moravianism in the American Colonies," in *Continental Pietism and American Christianity,* ed. E. F. Stoeffler (1976).

D. B. Eller

Morehead, John Alfred (1867-1936). Lutheran international churchman. Born in Pulaski County, Virginia, Morehead graduated from Roanoke

College (B.A., 1889) and Lutheran Theological Seminary, Philadelphia (1892). After six years in Virginia parishes, Morehead moved into a wider ministry, serving first as professor and president at Lutheran Theological Southern Seminary, Columbia, South Carolina (1898-1903), and then as president of Roanoke College, Salem, Virginia (1903-20). As a churchman he was an influential president of the United Synod South (1910-1914), and became a founder of the United Lutheran Church in America (ULCA, 1918). Widely respected for his farsighted guidance of international church relief efforts after World War 1,* he chaired the U.S. National Lutheran Council's* (NLC) European Commission among the needy overseas (1919-1922) and became executive director of the NLC itself (1923-1930). Morehead rallied churches in North America and Europe to form the Lutheran World Convention (LWC) (Eisenach, 1923), a landmark in Lutheran history, and presided over LWC affairs, including the assemblies in Copenhagen (1929) and Paris (1935). Firmly confessional, his compassion, resourcefulness and tireless service won him respect and affection even among leaders in postwar relief work like Herbert Hoover. Morehead's most quoted words opened doors: "We want to help each other."

E. T. Bachmann

Morehouse, Henry Lyman (1834-1917). Baptist* minister* and missionary* statesman. Born in Stanford, New York, Morehouse studied at the University of Rochester (1854-1858) and Rochester Theological Seminary (1861-1864).

He began his ministry in 1864 in East Saginaw, Michigan, as a missionary of the American Baptist Home Mission Society, later serving as pastor of the East Avenue Baptist Church, Rochester, New York (1873-1879). Morehouse served as the correspondence secretary (1879-1892; 1902-1917) and field secretary (1893-1902) of the American Baptist Home Mission Society, and was foremost in the founding of the American Baptist Educational Society (1888) which in turn prepared the way for the founding of the University of Chicago* (1890). He was also the author of Baptist Home Missions in America (1883). As the most prominent Baptist statesman in home missions of his day, he diligently sought to provide education for immigrants, Native Americans and African-Americans.

BIBLIOGRAPHY. L. A. Crandall, *Henry Lyman Morehouse* (1919); *DAB* VII; A. H. Newman, *A Century of Baptist Achievement* (1901).

J. M. Glass

Morgan, G. Campbell (1863-1945). Expository* preacher.* Born and raised in Gloucestershire, England, in a home which was first Baptist* and then Plymouth Brethren,* Morgan became a Congregationalist* minister.* His earlier orientation, however, provided him with commitments which were quickly being lost in mainstream English Nonconformity, such as the full inspiration and authority* of Scripture* and a sympathetic appreciation for evangelical* revival* and expository preaching. In a period in which topical and textual preaching were popular, Morgan gave himself to the consistent exposition of the books of the Bible.*

Although lacking in formal theological training, by applying his remarkable intelligence to serious biblical study and wide reading, he became one of the most famous preachers of his age in the English-speaking world. His exposition was based on careful exegesis, with a strong emphasis on both the immediate context and that of the whole of Scripture. With such a working knowledge of the Bible, he found within its pages almost all his illustrations. And with his deep devotional life and mellifluous voice, his preaching was the voice of God to many. For evangelicals he was an example of how incomparably rich and relevant ministry is that mines the Bible.

Morgan came to prominence as the Bible teacher *par excellence* for the converts of Dwight L. Moody* and those who came to Christ in the revivals of 1904 to 1910. His ministry combined the settled and the itinerant. His great pastoral ministries were at Westminster Chapel, London, where he served from 1904 to 1917 and again from 1933 to 1945, and where he would be succeeded by Martyn Lloyd-Jones. His itinerant ministry took place largely in North America, where he was first invited by D. L. Moody from 1897 as a regular speaker at his Northfield conferences.* From 1917 to 1932 he gave himself almost entirely to North America. He was also a contributor to *The Fundamentals* (1910-1915).

BIBLIOGRAPHY. J. Morgan, *A Man of the Word: Life of G. Campbell Morgan* (1951); D. M. Wagner, *The Expository Method of G. Campbell Morgan* (1957).

I. S. Rennie

Mormonism. A new religion founded in the nineteenth century by Joseph Smith.* The Church of Christ, which became The Church of Jesus Christ of Latter-day Saints, or Mormonism, was established on April 6, 1830, at Fayette, in the "burned-over district"* of upstate New York, by Joseph Smith, following the publication of *The Book of*

Mormon on March 26, 1830. Smith claimed to have derived the book from golden plates which he had discovered with the aid of the angel Moroni. He maintained that the plates were written in "Reformed Egyptian" which he had translated with the aid of the "Urim" and "Thummim"—two stones through which he viewed the writings. Proclaiming himself a prophet, Smith gathered about him a following of devoted disciples. In 1840 the Mormon apostle Orson Pratt* published an account of an encounter between Smith, God the Father and Jesus Christ, said to have taken place as early as 1820. Today the story of this "first vision" has become one the basic apologetic claims of Mormonism, although it rests on contradictory historical evidence.

The Book of Mormon, among other things, revealed America as a new land of promise and traced the fortunes of pre-Columbian immigrants to America: the Jaredites, Lamanites (Native Americans) and the Nephites. After numerous battles between these groups, the righteous Nephites had been reduced by the Lamanites to only Mormon and his son, Moroni, who buried their book in A.D. 384, awaiting the day when God would raise up their spiritual descendants.

From the beginning Smith strove to develop economically strong communities, a practice his successors continued with great success, making the economic base of Mormonism the source of its evangelism.* One of the early converts was Sidney Rigdon,* a Campbellite Restorationist* who had gathered a small community in Kirtland, Ohio. Rigdon and nearly all of his followers were baptized into the Mormon faith, and by 1831 Kirtland had become the first Holy City of Smith's new church. But by 1838 the Kirtland community had suffered economic collapse, and Smith fled with others to Missouri where the group faced repeated and violent conflict with local residents and civil authorities. Fleeing to Illinois, they established a settlement at Nauvoo, on the Mississippi River.

Smith's downfall came as a result of teachings about polygamy which he advanced as a secret ordinance.* Smith appears to have begun this practice as early as 1836 and to have married at least forty-nine women, including the wives of several of his disciples. His adulterous advances eventually provoked a strong reaction against his authority* and led four disillusioned converts to found the anti-Mormon newspaper *The Nauvoo Expositor,* which exposed his secret life and teachings. His brothers instigated a riot which destroyed the newspaper office. As a result, Smith and one brother, Hyrum, were arrested and held in the nearby Carthage jail, where they were murdered on June 27, 1844, by a lynch mob.

Following Smith's death his disciples split into over twenty-five different groups, all of which claimed to follow his *true* teachings. The main division was between those who followed his brother William, and eventually his son Joseph Smith III, and those who followed Brigham Young.* In 1847 Young led the Mormons on their famous migration to the Salt Lake area of what would become the state of Utah (1850).

Branches of Mormonism. Today the largest group is the Utah Mormons based in Salt Lake City. At the end of 1986 there were 3,708,000 Utah Mormons in North America and over 5,500,000 worldwide. They are distinguished by their acceptance of the leadership of Brigham Young and his successors. In 1847 they moved to Utah to openly practice polygamy. Stories about the hardships they endured during their early years are an important part of the apologetics of this group.

In 1890 the Utah Mormons officially abandoned polygamy on the advice of their president, Wilford Woodruff (1807-1898), in order to reach a political accommodation with the U.S. Government. But it was not until 1904 that they actually forbade their members to enter into new polygamous relationships. Before settling in Utah, Young seriously considered moving to Vancouver Island, Canada. Later, Mormon groups established themselves in Alberta, Canada.

The other main branch of Mormonism is the smaller Reorganized Church of Jesus Christ of Latter-Day Saints, with its headquarters in Independence, Missouri. This group was supported by Joseph Smith's legal wife, Emma, and legitimated its claims on the basis of lineal descent from Joseph Smith. In 1986 it had 205,025 members. From the beginning it completely rejected polygamy and even tried to claim that Joseph Smith had not practiced it. Theologically it is closer to orthodox* Christianity than the Utah Mormons.

In addition there are still several fundamentalist sectarian groups such as the Bickertonites, Strangites and Temple Lot Churches, which generally hold to the teachings of *The Book of Mormon* and early Mormon doctrines but reject later developments as unscriptural innovations. There are also numerous groups of Utah fundamentalists who continue the practice of polygamy and claim that the Utah Church hierarchy has deviated from its calling for pragmatic reasons. These groups usually exist under the leadership of a prophet. Mormon fundamentalist groups have around 25,000 followers.

Mormon Beliefs and Practices. Utah Mormonism is an indigenous religious movement that incorporates American values of self-reliance, pragmatism, progress and democracy.* It fits into the religious context of early nineteenth-century New England, which produced the Oneida Community and a host of other communal experiments based on a theology of human perfectibility and an implicit belief in the essential divinity of mankind.

The Book of Mormon is fundamentally an early-American romance based on the Bible,* and its theology appears to be essentially Christian. Utah Mormon missionaries stress the importance of the Bible and *The Book of Mormon* as sources for their beliefs, downplaying the role of continuing revelation characteristic of their Church. Yet in reality they read both the Bible and *The Book of Mormon* in light of later revelations given to Joseph Smith and successive prophets. These include *Doctrine and Covenants* and *The Pearl of Great Price,* as well as other revelations given to church leaders since Smith's death. In addition there is an extensive tradition about Joseph Smith and his successors which functions much like the *haddith* of Islam. Fundamentalist polygamist groups tend to follow Utah Mormons in their approach to revelation, while the other fundamentalist groups are more conservative, tending to accept *The Book of Mormon* and other revelations only in so far as they correspond to biblical teachings.

Structurally, Utah Mormon theology is held together by an evolutionary framework known as the doctrine of eternal progression. This belief is summed up by the phrase "As man is, God once was; as God is, man may become." Thus human destiny is to evolve to Godhood through obedience to the laws and ordinances revealed to the Utah Church. Spiritual progress is, however, conditional on choices made by the individual, making Utah Mormon theology an extreme form of Pelagianism. The doctrine of eternal progression also opens the door to Mormon polytheism and claims by Brigham Young and other early leaders that Adam was the God of this earth. An early account of the beliefs of the Utah Mormons, the closest to a systematic theology* produced by Mormons in the nineteenth century, is Parley P. Pratt's* *Key to the Science of Theology* (1855). The original text, republished by the Modern Microfilm Company, shows that significant, unacknowledged changes have been made to recent editions issued by the Utah Mormons.

Belief in pre-existent souls and the existence of various heavenly realms endow Utah Mormonism with a system of rewards which motivate individuals to participate in elaborate Temple ceremonies having a strong resemblance to Masonic ritual. In many respects these beliefs reflect early nineteenth-century views about science, Eastern religions, the influence of Emanuel Swedenborg, Masonic beliefs and New England folklore, including popular magic. Contrary to sensational claims by some evangelical* writers, there seems to be no evidence that Mormon temple rites involve explicit Satanism. In fact, such bizarre accusations are a serious impediment to a scholarly understanding of Mormonism by Christians.

Major intellectual problems have plagued Mormonism from its inception, although they seem to have had little effect on its growth. It is historically established that Joseph Smith practiced and taught polygamy, although the Reorganized Church continues to deny this. It is also clear that this doctrine was central to his entire theological system and is an "everlasting covenant" (*Doctrine and Covenant* Section 132). Nevertheless, the Utah Mormons abandoned the practice.

Joseph Smith clearly taught that African-Americans could not enter the Mormon priesthood—an office held by most male church members. Nevertheless, on September 30, 1978, President Spencer W. Kimball claimed to receive a revelation extending the priesthood to all male members. While this may be socially acceptable, it highlights the status of women in Mormonism as an inferior group, with their salvation depending on marriage and the spiritual status of their husbands.

Since *The Book of Mormon* first appeared, critics have alleged plagiarism. Moreover, critics of Utah Mormons claim that the church has repeatedly changed the wording of both *The Book of Mormon* and other revelations to suit its own purpose. A recent example of this can be seen in changes made to 2 *Nephi* 6, where God is said to promise to make certain Native Americans "a white and delightsome people." Since 1978 the wording has read *pure* instead of *white.* Critics allege that over 3,000 changes of this nature have been made to *The Book of Mormon* and thousands more to other Mormon revelations and recent editions of historical works where the original text contradicts the official position of Utah Mormonism.

Recently, serious historical doubts have been raised about the truthfulness of Joseph Smith, including conclusive evidence that he was convicted of treasure hunting with the implication of deliberate fraud. Evidence about his use of folk magic as well as doubts about his other claims have created problems for Mormon historians. Most devastating of all has been the discovery in

1967 of the papyri Smith claimed to translate as *The Book of Abraham*. This has proved to be an Egyptian death scroll, the text of which bears no relation whatsoever to Smith's translation.

Finally, from the beginning Christians have rejected Mormon claims to be a Christian church. Although most Mormons sincerely believe that they are Christians, the differences between the teachings of Utah Mormons and traditional Christianity are so great that it would more accurately be called a new religion. While Utah Mormons protest against Christian "intolerance," their own standard works, such as James E. Talmage's *Articles of Faith* (1962) and Bruce R. McConkie's *Mormon Doctrine* (1979), charge Christian churches with apostasy.

In the late twentieth century Mormonism remains a vigorous all-American religion which sociologist Rodney Stark believes will, on a conservative estimate, have over 200 million followers within one hundred years, given present growth rates. If Stark is correct, Mormonism has the potential to become the first world religion to emerge since the birth of Islam in the seventh century.

BIBLIOGRAPHY. R. L. Bushman, *Joseph Smith and the Beginnings of Mormonism* (1984); F. M. Brodie, *No Man Knows My History* (1971); J. Heinerman and A. Shupe, *The Mormon Corporate Empire* (1985); T. O'Dea, *The Mormons* (1964); B. H. Roberts, *Studies in the Book of Mormon* (1985); J. Shipps, *Mormonism: The Story of a New Religious Tradition* (1984); J. Tanner and S. Tanner, *The Case Against Mormonism*, 3 vols. (1968).

I. Hexham

Morris, Edward Dafydd (1825-1915). Presbyterian* pastor* and educator. Born in Utica, New York, Morris graduated from Yale* in 1849 and Auburn Theological Seminary in 1852. He pastored the Second Presbyterian Church of Auburn, New York (1852-1855), and the Second Presbyterian Church of Columbus, Ohio (1855-1867). In 1867 he moved to Lane Theological Seminary in Cincinnati, Ohio, teaching church history there until 1874 and theology* from 1874 to 1897. An evangelical,* ecumenical,* New School Calvinist,* Morris served as the moderator for the General Assembly of the Presbyterian Church in the U.S.A. (PC—USA) in 1875. Both his teaching and his many periodical articles and books—most importantly, *Theology of the Westminster Symbols* (1900), displayed the clarity of his thinking, the broad range of his interests, his irenic and friendly spirit and his fervent commitment to the theology and mission* of his denomination. Through his deep involvement in efforts to reunite the Old* and New Schools* of the PC—USA in the 1860s and to revise the Westminster Standards* in the 1890s, Morris substantially influenced this major American denomination.*

BIBLIOGRAPHY. *DAB* VII.   G. S. Smith

Morris, Lelia Naylor (1862-1929). Camp meeting* hymnwriter. Born in Pennsville, Ohio, Lelia Naylor and family moved to Malta in 1866 following her father's return from the Civil War.* After his death, she and her mother and sisters opened a millinery shop in McConnelsville. In 1881 she married Charles H. Morris; together they were active in the Methodist Episcopal Church* and its camp meetings.

Encouraged by H. L. Gilmore, she wrote over 1,000 revival* hymns* and gospel song* tunes. She composed on location in response to an occasion, such as this altar call* recounted by G. W. Sanville: "Mrs. C. H. Morris quietly joined [a woman of culture and refinement] at the altar, put her arm around her and prayed with her." The song "Let Jesus Come into Your Heart" came from her words spoken on that occasion. When blindness began to overtake her around 1913, she composed on an oversized blackboard. Some of her more enduring hymns are "Jesus Is Coming to Earth Again"; "Nearer, Still Nearer"; and "The Savior Has Come in His Mighty Power."   R. J. Stanislaw

Morris, Samuel (c.1700-1770). Revival* leader in colonial Virginia. In about the year 1740 Morris, an otherwise obscure layperson in Hanover County, Virginia, began a reading ministry in his home that attracted some followers and engendered a small evangelical* awakening among them. When the members of the group began to absent themselves from the services of the established* (Anglican*) church, they were summoned to appear in court and "declare their creed." At a loss to identify their faith, Morris suggested that they were "Lutherans"* because Luther's works had been among those from which he had read in their meetings. Shortly after their court appearance, the group affiliated with the New Castle (PA) Presbytery, although in lieu of a settled pastor Morris continued his reading ministry and began itinerating in neighboring areas. Often fined for his dissenting activities, in 1747 Morris helped obtain Samuel Davies* as pastor for his struggling congregation, thus grafting New Light* revivalism onto his indigenous evangelical movement and bringing the Great Awakening* into the South.

BIBLIOGRAPHY. S. Davies, *The State of Religion*

Among the Protestant Dissenters in Virginia (1751); W. M. Gewehr, *The Great Awakening in Virginia, 1740-1790* (1930).   R. M. Payne

Morrison, Charles Clayton (1874-1966). Disciples of Christ* clergyman* and editor of *The Christian Century.** Born in Harrison, Ohio, Morrison graduated from Drake University (B.A., 1898) and pastored Disciples congregations in Perry, Iowa, and Chicago and Springfield, Illinois. While in Chicago he studied philosophy at the University of Chicago. In 1908 he purchased and became editor of *The Christian Century,* a position he held until 1947.

Headquartered in Chicago, Morrison transformed *The Christian Century* from a financially struggling Disciples of Christ magazine to a highly successful "undenominational" journal which spoke for a large segment of liberal* American Protestantism.* Leading liberals wrote for the *Century;* but Morrison maintained a firm grip on editorial policy. Though never a strict pacifist,* Morrison opposed America's entry into both world wars. He championed the Social Gospel,* generally supported labor in disputes with management and criticized unbridled laissez-faire capitalism.* He favored national prohibition* and lamented the failure of the Eighteenth Amendment and the Volstead Act. On racial issues, he called for full equality for blacks, though occasionally accepting separate-but-equal treatment. He condemned anti-Semitism but opposed the Zionist Movement because it resisted assimilation and was politically disruptive. Along with most American Protestant leaders, he initially underestimated Hitler's genocidal policy against the Jews.

Morrison's magazine was a barometer of the American religious scene. As a spokesperson for liberalism, he applauded all efforts at church union,* condemned fundamentalism,* bemoaned neo-orthodoxy* and regretted the decline of optimism and the belief in progress. But he could also be critical of his own movement. By the 1940s, he too called for a "new liberalism."

See also CHRISTIAN CENTURY, THE.

BIBLIOGRAPHY. *DARB;* L. M. Delloff, "C. C. Morrison: Shaping a Journal's Identity," *The Christian Century* 101 (1984):43-47; *NCAB* 52; D. Peerman, "Forward on Many Fronts," *The Christian Century* 101 (1984):595-600.   T. P. Weber

Morrison, Henry Clay (1857-1942). Methodist revival preacher. Born in Bedford, Kentucky, Morrison was dedicated by his mother to the Christian ministry at a Methodist Quarterly meeting

when he was only three weeks old. Converted* at the age of thirteen, he was licensed* to preach* in 1878. Following his education at Ewing Institute in Perryville, Kentucky, and Vanderbilt University, where he studied for one year, he became a member of the Kentucky Conference of the Methodist Episcopal Church, South, receiving his elder's* order in 1887. During the prior decade Morrison served four circuits* and five stations in Kentucky. In 1890 he was granted a located relationship with his annual conference in order to pursue his calling to be a full-time evangelist.*

For the next two decades Morrison served with growing acclaim as an effective mass evangelist.* His audiences numbered in the thousands, and during his career it is estimated that he traveled 500,000 miles, preached 15,000 times and held 1,200 revivals. Although he won thousands of converts for Christ and the Church, denominational authorities accused him of violating Church law. He was acquitted of this charge at a Church trial in the Kentucky Conference in 1897. Despite the trial, Morrison retained sufficient standing in the Methodist Episcopal Church, South, to be elected as a delegate to five of their General Conferences.

In addition to the legacy of his converts, Morrison's ministry had a lasting legacy in the *Pentecostal Herald,* which he founded about 1890, and in Asbury Theological Seminary, which he founded in 1923 during the first of his two terms as president of Asbury College in Wilmore, Kentucky (1910-1925; 1933-1948). Through these channels he furthered the cause of the Holiness movement,* rooted in the Wesleyan tradition.*

A forceful, direct preacher of salvation in Christ, he preached a total of sixty-three years and wrote twenty-five popular books on the Christian faith. E. Stanley Jones* declared that "Morrison was one of the great men of the religious life of America, the last of the old Southern orators."

J. S. O'Malley

Morse, Jedidiah (1761-1826). Orthodox* Calvinist* opponent of Unitarianism.* Born in Woodstock, Connecticut, Morse graduated from Yale College* (B.A., 1783) and studied theology* under Jonathan Edwards,* Jr.,* and Samuel Wales (1783-1785). Morse then ministered* in Connecticut, Georgia and New Jersey before becoming pastor of First Congregational Church at Charlestown, Massachusetts (1789-1819). There in the Boston vicinity he became a persistent Trinitarian opponent of the emerging Unitarian Congregationalists.*

When the Hollis Chair of Divinity* at Harvard

College* became vacant, Morse urged the appointment of an orthodox* scholar to fill the post. The struggle ended with defeat in 1805, when the liberal party won the appointment of a Unitarian, Henry Ware.* This event was the impetus for establishing, in 1808, the Andover Theological Seminary,* an orthodox institution for the training of Trinitarian Congregational clergy.* Morse, along with Leonard Woods,* was instrumental in founding the seminary. Throughout the years 1805-1810, Morse attacked the Unitarians through the *Panoplist,* which he published and edited.

Morse also had other interests which won him recognition. His attention to geography and publications of maps and other literature in that field established him as the father of American geography. He also helped establish the New England Tract* Society (1814) and the American Bible* Society* (1816). His interest in missions,* inspired by his connection with Andover Seminary and its early student missionary* activity, led him to serve on the American Board of Commissioners for Foreign Missions.* After leaving his parish in 1819, he investigated for the government the condition of the Native American populations along the nation's borders.

BIBLIOGRAPHY. *AAP* 2; *DAB* VII; *DARB;* J. K. Morse, *Jedidiah Morse: A Champion of New England Orthodoxy* (1939); W. B. Sprague, *Life of Jedidiah Morse* (1874).   D. G. Reid

Mother Angela. *See* GILLESPIE, ELIZA.

Mott, John Raleigh (1865-1955). Leader in student work, missions* and ecumenical movement. Born in Livingston Manor, New York, and raised in Iowa in a devout Methodist* home, Mott was educated at Upper Iowa University (1881-1885) and Cornell University (Ph.B., 1888), where he became a leader in the YMCA.* Mott was among the one hundred volunteers for foreign missions at the 1886 Student Conference at Northfield, Massachusetts, led by Dwight L. Moody.*

In 1888 he became college secretary of the YMCA at a time when the association was aggressively evangelistic* and evangelical.* That same year he became chairman of the joint committee which organized the Student Volunteer Movement for Foreign Missions* (SVM) as the mission department of the student YMCA and YWCA. In this capacity he became an evangelist* to students, a mobilizer for mission and an advocate of Christian cooperation and unity. By the time he spoke for the last time at the SVM's 1951 convention, over 20,000 volunteers had gone to mission fields

through its work. Mott also led in the formation of the World Student Christian Federation* (WSCF). In 1895 he and his wife, Leila, traveled around the world for twenty months to consolidate and expand the federation—the embodiment of his dream of a union of Christian students of all nations. A lay* movement which began to include women in leadership, the WSCF produced many church leaders.

As one of the founders of the Foreign Missions Conference of North America* in 1893, Mott led the planning for the Edinburgh Missionary Conference of 1910, serving as its chairman and heading its continuation committee. An appointment by Woodrow Wilson* to the Root Mission to Russia in 1917 provided the opportunity to extend the ecumenical* network to Russian Orthodox* leaders. With his growing involvement in the ecumenical missions movment, Mott gave up the leadership of the SVM and WSCF in 1920, becoming the first chairman of the International Missionary Council* in 1921. In this capacity he traveled widely, encouraging the formation of approximately thirty national councils of churches. These encouraged comity agreements and other types of cooperation. In 1926 Mott became president of the World Alliance of YMCAs, leading its expansion into many countries and encouraging Roman Catholics* and Orthodox Christians to become members.

Called the "father" of the World Council of Churches,* Mott participated in each of the movements that led to its formation and was a friend of nearly all its early leaders, most of whom had come out of the various student movements. He served as one of six provisional presidents during its organizational phase and was named honorary president of the council when it was formed. Widely honored as a symbol of hope and unity after World War 2,* he was one of the recipients of the Nobel Peace Prize in 1946.

Theologically Mott could be termed an ecumenical evangelical. His spiritual formation was in a warm Methodist piety* with an emphasis on perfectionist* holiness.* In addition, he was influenced by Moody* and by a variety of other Christian traditions, including Eastern Orthodoxy.* Mott embraced the concerns of the Social Gospel* without losing his commitment to evangelism and missions. He was known as a man of prayer with a worldwide vision, a builder of organizations for unity and an outstanding fundraiser and administrator. But most of all, as he said in his last public appearance, "While life lasts, I am an evangelist."

BIBLIOGRAPHY. *DAB* 5; *DARB;* C. H. Hopkins,

John R. Mott (1979); C. H. Hopkins, "The Legacy of John R. Mott," *IBMR* (April 1981):70-73; B. J. Mathews, *John R. Mott: World Citizen* (1934); J. R. Mott, *The Evangelization of the World in This Generation* (1900); J. R. Mott, *Addresses and Papers of John R. Mott*, 6 vols. (1946-1947); *NCAB* 44.   P. E. Pierson

Mott, Lucretia Coffin (1793-1880). Quaker* minister* and social reformer.* Born on Nantucket Island, Massachusetts, young Lucretia Coffin attended Nine Partners Friends Boarding School near Poughkeepsie, New York. In 1911 she married James Mott, a teacher at the school. She came under the influence of Quaker minister Elias Hicks,* and by the time of the Orthodox-Hicksite* separation of Friends in Philadelphia in 1827, the Motts had moved there to enter the cotton and later the woolen business. While raising a family of six children, Lucretia Mott became active in the Friends ministry and through her life and work was a forerunner of modern liberal Quakerism. Lucretia Mott is best remembered as a social reformer in the causes of abolition* and women's rights. The Motts were among the founders of the American Anti-Slavery Society, and in the same year, 1833, Lucretia helped establish the Philadelphia Female Anti-Slavery Society. In 1840 she joined a delegation to the World Anti-Slavery Convention in London, where she was disenfranchised as a woman. By 1848 she, together with Elizabeth Cady Stanton,* had become active in the Women's Rights Convention at Seneca Falls, New York, and in 1870 was made president of the Pennsylvania Peace Society. In 1869 she gave the dedicatory address at the founding of Swarthmore College. After her death in 1880 she, along with Elizabeth Cady Stanton and Susan B. Anthony,* was immortalized in a sculpture in the crypt of the U.S. Capitol.

BIBLIOGRAPHY. O. Cromwell, *Lucretia Mott* (1958); *DAB* VII; *DARB*; L. C. M. Hare, *The Greatest American Woman: Lucretia Mott* (1937); A. D. Hollowell, ed., *James and Lucretia Mott: Life and Letters* (1844); *NAW* 2.   W. A. Cooper

Mount Hermon One Hundred (1886). Nineteenth-century student mission* movement. In July of 1886, evangelist Dwight L. Moody* sponsored a Bible* study conference for leaders of collegiate chapters of the Young Men's Christian Association.* Held at Moody's Mount Hermon School in Northfield, Massachusetts, the conference attracted 251 men from 87 colleges. The format of the conference included morning Bible classes conducted by Moody and other prominent evangelicals,* followed by afternoon recreation.

A small group of participants led by Robert P. Wilder,* a Princeton student, promoted interest in foreign missions by arranging a set of special meetings. At their request, missions advocate Arthur T. Pierson* encouraged students to evangelize the world in their own generation. On July 24, Wilder's group held the "meeting of ten nations" at which international students and the sons of missionaries appealed for missionaries to their own lands. After the meeting, conference participants prayed and struggled with the call to missionary service. One week later, by the last day of the conference, exactly one hundred students had dedicated themselves to be foreign missionaries.

The "Mount Hermon One Hundred" sent representatives to tour colleges to enlist further support for missions. Within two years, approximately five thousand students had signed a pledge declaring their intention to become foreign missionaries. In order to coordinate the movement, students founded in 1888 the Student Volunteer Movement* for Foreign Missions (SVM). John Mott,* one of the "Mount Hermon One Hundred," served as first chairman of the SVM. Under his leadership, thousands of students volunteered for mission service, thereby revitalizing general missionary interest across the U.S. and Canada.

BIBLIOGRAPHY. J. R. Mott, *The Student Volunteer Movement for Foreign Missions. Addresses and Papers of John R. Mott*, vol. I (1946); R. P. Wilder, *The Great Commission. The Missionary Response of the Student Volunteer Movements in North America and Europe; Some Personal Reminiscences* (1935).   D. L. Robert

Mountain, Jacob (1749-1825). Anglican* bishop* of Quebec. Born in England in Thwaite Hall, Norfolk, Mountain was ordained* in 1780. He became the first bishop of Quebec in 1793, a position which then included jurisdiction over the region later named Ontario. Assessing the religious conditions as deplorable, he was particularly critical of the Methodists,* whom he described as "ignorant Enthusiasts." He was unable to persuade the British authorities to establish the Church of England in the predominantly Roman Catholic* region and unsuccessful in persuading Catholics to accept the religious traditions of the Church of England. Both goals were impossible given the political realities of the period after the American Revolution,* when alienation of Catholics in Quebec might well have resulted in the region being added to the newly formed U.S.

BIBLIOGRAPHY. *DCB* VI; T. R. Millman, *Jacob Mountain, First Lord Bishop of Quebec: A Study in Church and State, 1793-1825* (1943).

P. D. Airhart

Mourner's Bench. In revival* meetings, a synonym for the "anxious bench" or altar,* the area at the front of a meeting place where persons went when responding to the altar call.* Though possibly originating in the eighteenth century, the term is common only from 1800. In camp meetings* the mourner's bench was the area just below the preaching* platform where unbelievers went to pray and agonize about (mourn over) their sinful condition. In churches* or tabernacles,* the mourner's bench was usually the first several rows at the front. Charles G. Finney* preferred the term anxious bench, a place where those anxious over their souls' condition would pray and be exhorted to change. Critics saw the mourner's bench as too public and appealing only to the impetuous—or implying immediate conversion*—but its use prevailed. Though the term faded in the twentieth century, the technique it embodied—asking potential converts to come forward—remained a staple in evangelistic* meetings.

W. G. Travis

Mowat, Oliver (1820-1903). Premier of the Province of Ontario and Presbyterian* layman. Mowat was born at Kingston, Upper Canada, and educated privately in that city. After studying law he was called to the bar in 1841 and practiced law in both Kingston and Toronto. He was appointed a Queen's Counsel in 1855 and was subsequently made a bencher of the Law Society of Upper Canada.

Mowat sat in the Parliament of the United Province of Canada (1857-1864), and with Liberal leader George Brown, he entered the Great Coalition of 1864. He temporarily abandoned his political career in 1864 when he was raised to the bench as Vice Chancellor of Ontario. He re-entered the political arena in 1872 as leader of the Ontario Liberal Party and as premier of Ontario. He continued as premier until 1896, one of the longest ministries in Canadian history.

Never an "ultra-Protestant," Mowat tried to steer the Liberal Party away from its earlier anti-Catholic tendencies, instead stressing Protestant*-Catholic* cooperation. In 1896 he entered Wilfrid Laurier's Dominion cabinet as Minister of Justice. In 1897 he was appointed Lieutenant-Governor of the Province of Ontario.

A lifelong Presbyterian, Mowat also served as president of the Evangelical Alliance* of Ontario, and as a vice president of the Upper Canada Bible Society. He was also the author of two brief pamphlets—*Christianity and Some of Its Evidences* (1890) and *Christianity and Its Influence* (1898).

BIBLIOGRAPHY. A. M. Evans, "Oliver Mowat: Nineteenth-Century Ontario Liberal," in Donald Swainson, ed., *Oliver Mowat's Ontario* (1972); H. J. Morgan, *The Canadian Men and Women of the Time: A Handbook of Canadian Biography* (1898).

R. W. Vaudry

Muhlenberg, Henry Melchior (1711-1787). Colonial Lutheran* minister* and patriarch of American Lutheranism. Born in Einbeck in the Duchy of Hanover, Germany, after attending local schools Muhlenberg enrolled at the University of Göttingen in 1735. In 1737 he entered the university's seminary* to prepare for the Lutheran ministry.* The following year (1738) Muhlenberg transferred to the pietistically* inclined University of Halle with the intention of training for the Jewish mission fields. While awaiting an opportunity to sail to Palestine, he assumed pastoral duties at Grosshennersdorf in 1739, after ordination* at Leipzig that same year.

On September 6, 1741, Gotthilf August Francke, director of the Halle Institute, presented Muhlenberg with a call to the United Congregations of Philadelphia, New Hanover and Providence in Philadelphia. Muhlenberg arrived in Philadelphia on December 1, 1742, only to find his pastorate occupied by a vagabond preacher, Valentine Kraft. After disposing of Kraft, Muhlenberg set about the task of creating a stable Lutheran organization. He was greatly aided in this task by his marriage, on April 22, 1745, to Anna Maria Weiser. A daughter of the influential Indian agent Conrad Weiser, she brought him the support of Pennsylvania's most powerful German families.

The church Muhlenberg envisioned stood midway between orthodoxy* and pietism and was adaptable to the American environment. To erect it he had to dispose of threats from both the left and right. The former was posed by the pretensions of the ultra-pietistic Count Nicholas Ludwig von Zinzendorf,* whose Moravian Church,* or *Unitas Fratrum,* was determined to create an interdenominational "Congregation of God in the Spirit." Posing as Lutheran ministers, the Moravians had captured congregations at Tulpehocken and Lancaster.

By 1748, by means of legal suits, Muhlenberg forced the Moravians out. The right wing was represented by the orthodox William Christopher

Berkenmeyer,* who was determined to keep his New York synod* (which included New Jersey) subservient to the church in Europe. Muhlenberg felt American Lutheranism* had to operate independently if it were to survive. Intervening in disputes between Lutheran congregations and Berkenmeyer in Raritan, New Jersey (1745); Rhinebeck, New York (1750); and New York City (1751), Muhlenberg brought them under his control, establishing himself as the dominant Lutheran clergyman* in America and making his ecclesiastical model normative.

In 1748 Muhlenberg created the Pennsylvania Ministerium* as the governing body of American Lutheranism. Though the laity* had a voice, his constitution made them subordinate to the clergy, thus solving the problem of voluntaryism* for Lutheranism. His liturgical schema insisted on conformity to a conservative, churchly liturgy,* thus preventing revivalism,* which Muhlenberg detested, from making inroads into the church.

Though he avoided overt political involvement, Muhlenberg did take covert positions. He supported the demands of the Paxton Boys in 1764 for the military protection of frontiersmen, many of whom were Germans, against Native-American attacks. A bitter opponent of the Quakers,* Muhlenberg helped rally German support around the proprietary party. When the Revolution* began, he resigned his pastorate at St. Michael's in Philadelphia and moved to rural Providence in an effort to avoid publicly taking sides. He did, however, support the movement for independence secretly and gave what aid he could to Revolutionary troops. His son Friedrich served in the Continental Congress. A second son, Peter,* was a general in the Continental Army. Both had been pastors and resigned their posts with Muhlenberg's blessing.

Appalled at the chaos resulting from the weakness of the government of the Articles of Confederation, Muhlenberg would have supported the Constitution. Before it could be submitted for ratification, however, he died at Providence on October 7, 1787.

BIBLIOGRAPHY. *AAP* 9; *DAB* VII; *DARB;* C. H. Glatfelter, *Pastors and People: German Lutheran and Reformed Churches in the Pennsylvania Field, 1717-1793* (1979); W. J. Mann, *Life and Times of Henry Melchior Muhlenberg* (1887); *NCAB* 5; L. R. Riforgiato, *Missionary of Moderation: Henry Melchior Muhlenberg and the Lutheran Church in English America* (1980); T. G. Tappert and J. W. Doberstein, eds., *The Journals of Henry Melchior Muhlenberg in Three Volumes* (1942-1958).

L. R. Riforgiato

Muhlenberg, John Peter Gabriel (1746-1807). Lutheran* clergyman,* military officer and politician. Born in Trappe, Pennsylvania, the eldest son of Henry Melchior Muhlenberg,* the patriarch of Lutheranism in America, he returned to the University of Halle in Germany for his theological education. Ordained* after his return to America in 1768, he served as assistant to his father in churches in New Jersey. In order to become a licensed* minister* in Virginia, he was reordained by the bishop* of London in 1772 and took charge of the church in Woodstock, Virginia.

In June 1775 Muhlenberg dramatically left his parish to join the Patriots in the Revolutionary War.* At the close of a Sunday sermon,* he proclaimed "there is a time to fight, and that time has now come." Stepping into the vestry he donned the uniform of an American officer and reappeared to enlist a number of his parishioners in the Continental militia. Muhlenberg went on to serve as a colonel of a German regiment he had raised. In 1777 he became a brigadier general in the Continental Army, and at Yorktown he commanded the first brigade of light infantry. After the war he served as vice president of Pennsylvania, three terms as a member of Congress, and in 1803 he became collector of the port of Philadelphia. *See also* MUHLENBERG, HENRY MELCHIOR.

BIBLIOGRAPHY. *DAB* VII; H. A. Muhlenberg, *The Life and Times of Major-General Peter Muhlenberg of the Revolutionary Army* (1849).

J. D. Sutherland

Muhlenberg, William Augustus (1796-1877). Episcopal* clergyman* and educator. Born in Philadelphia of Lutheran* parentage and raised an Episcopalian, Muhlenberg was ordained* by Bishop William White* as a deacon* in 1817 and priest* in 1820. After a brief and unhappy pastoral charge in Lancaster, Pennsylvania, he became rector of St. George's Church, Flushing, New York. There he opened the Flushing Institute in 1828 on the model of Dr. Thomas Arnold's Rugby School, and the Institute quickly became the basic pattern for the creation of church-related preparatory schools throughout the Episcopal Church.

Muhlenberg's concern for deepening the spiritual life of his students led him to espouse a "Catholic Evangelicalism,*" and in 1846, when he became rector of the Church of the Holy Communion in New York City, he introduced a number of ceremonial innovations in vestments and eucharistic* worship.* His interest in developing "Catholic Evangelicalism" at first made him congenial to the emergence of the Oxford or Tractarian Movement* in American Episcopalianism. But his reading of J. H. Newman's *Essay on the Development of Christian Doctrine* caused a deep revulsion against the Tractarians and returned him to "the solid rock of evangelical truth, as republished by the Reformers." In 1853 he was the leading figure in the Memorial Movement* which called on the House of Bishops* to grant greater liturgical* freedom to evangelicals in the Episcopal Church and to promote greater union with other Protestant* churches.

Muhlenberg was also deeply concerned with maintaining the visibility of the Episcopal Church in urban industrial areas, and he incorporated into the ministry of the Church of the Holy Communion a parish infirmary, an employment agency, an order of deaconesses,* rent-free pews* and day schools.* He was the prime mover in the founding of St. Luke's Hospital in New York City in 1858 and became its director in 1859. In 1870 he organized a cooperative industrial community on Long Island named St. Johnsland, where he died in 1877.

BIBLIOGRAPHY. A. Ayres, *The Life and Work of William Augustus Muhlenberg* (1880); *DAB* VII; *DARB; NCAB* 9; A. W. Skardon, *Church Leader in the Cities: William Augustus Muhlenberg* (1971).   A. C. Guelzo

Mullins, Edgar Young (1860-1928). President of Southern Baptist* Theological Seminary and professor of theology.* Born in Mississippi and reared in Texas, Mullins was encouraged by his father, a teacher and preacher, to secure a good education. Graduating from Texas A & M University (1879), he worked as a telegraph operator to secure sufficient means to study law. However, during a revival* meeting conducted by lawyer and evangelist* William Evander Penn, Mullins was converted.* He was later baptized* by his father on November 7, 1880.

Shortly afterwards he entered Southern Baptist Theological Seminary to prepare for the ministry (B.D., 1885). Mullins had intended to go as a missionary to Brazil, but upon a doctor's advice decided to stay and pastored a church in Harrodsburg, Kentucky (1885-1888). During that time he married Isla May Hawley of Louisville (1886). His next pastorate took him to Baltimore, Maryland (1888-1895), where he also studied at Johns Hopkins University (1891-1892). After serving a short time as associate secretary of the Southern Baptist Foreign Mission Board (1895-1896), Mullins served as pastor of the First Baptist Church at Newton Center, Massachusetts (1896-1899).

In 1899 Mullins was elected president of the

Southern Baptist Theological Seminary in Louisville, Kentucky, succeeding William H. Whitsitt,* who had resigned in the midst of a controversy. Mullins was superbly fitted for such a challenge. The situation stabilized, the controversy died down, and the seminary was soon prospering again. It was he who engineered the transfer of the campus from downtown Louisville to "The Beeches."

Equally important for Baptists was Mullins's work as a theologian. As seminary president and professor he was able to foster a new level of theological sophistication among Southern Baptist ministers. Thoroughly committed to the great verities of the Christian faith, his systematic theology *The Christian Religion in Its Doctrinal Expression and the Axioms of Religion* (1917), and other works such as: *Why Is Christianity True?* (1905), *The Axioms of Religion* (1908), *Baptist Beliefs* (1912) and *Christianity at the Crossroads* (1924)—promoted moderate Baptist views.

As a Southern Baptist statesman Mullins led the denomination between the shoals of controversy over evolution* and the rise of the fundamentalist* movement. Under his leadership a revised version of the New Hampshire Confession of Faith* was adopted, the first confession ever adopted by the Southern Baptist Convention. In a preface which became part of the revised confession adopted in 1925, Mullins and his committee defined the role and limitations of a confession of faith for Southern Baptists. The convention under Mullins's guidance rejected the evolutionary hypothesis as expounded by Charles Darwin and affirmed the supernatural nature of the Christian revelation, while emphasizing that the Bible was authoritative in "religious opinions" alone.

As a scholar, administrator and statesman Mullins was one of the most influential leaders among Southern Baptists in the twentieth century.

BIBLIOGRAPHY. *DAB* VII; *DARB;* S. D. Gaines, "Mullins, Edgar Young." *ESB* (1958); W. A. Mueller, *A History of Southern Baptist Theological Seminary* (1959); I. M. Mullins, *Edgar Young Mullins: An Intimate Biography* (1929); *NCAB* 21.

W. R. Estep

Mundelein, George William (1872-1939). Catholic* archbishop* of Chicago and first American cardinal* west of the Atlantic seaboard. Born in New York City, Mundelein was ordained* in Rome in 1895 and consecrated auxiliary bishop* of Brooklyn in 1909. In 1915 he was named third archbishop of Chicago, the youngest archbishop in America at the time.

Mundelein was a consolidating bishop who centralized the administration of his archdiocese* and set it on a firm financial footing, while tying it more closely to Rome. Noted as a fund raiser and financial manager, he cultivated wealthy Catholic businessmen, obtained large donations for building projects and raised large sums for the Vatican and the missions. He built the seminary* of St. Mary of the Lake, reorganized the Catholic school board and Catholic Charities of Chicago and brought the International Eucharistic Congress* to the city in 1926.

Pope Pius XI* named Mundelein the "first Cardinal of the West" in 1924. During the 1930s he was a confidant of President Franklin D. Roosevelt and one of the few outspoken supporters of the New Deal in the American Catholic hierarchy. Mundelein publicly defended the rights of labor unions and sponsored many social-action projects, directed by his auxiliary bishop, Bernard J. Sheil.* Both Mundelein's contemporaries and later historians agreed that he brought the Catholic Church to a new prominence in the U. S.

BIBLIOGRAPHY. *DAB* 2; E. R. Kantowicz, *Corporation Sole: Cardinal Mundelein and Chicago Catholicism* (1983); C. Shanabruch, *Chicago's Catholics* (1981).   E. R. Kantowicz

Munger, Theodore Thornton (1830-1910). Congregationalist* minister* and theologian.* Born in Bainbridge, New York, Munger was educated at Yale* College and Divinity School (B.A., 1851; B.D., 1855). Ordained* in 1856, he served in a series of Congregational churches in Massachusetts (1856-1869; 1871-1875), Rhode Island (1869-1871) and California (1875-1877) before being called to the prestigious pulpit of the United Church on New Haven Green, New Haven, Connecticut (1885-1900). Profoundly influenced by the progressive theologies of Horace Bushnell* and the British Anglicans F. D. Maurice (1805-1872) and Frederick W. Robertson (1816-1853), Munger became deeply involved during the 1880s in a liberalizing trend among American Protestant theologians. Generally labeled the "New Theology,"* this was a modernist movement that he himself defined as advocating a "larger and broader use of reason in religion . . . (seeking) to replace the excessive individuality of the old theology by a truer view of the solidarity of the race."

In 1883 Munger published *The Freedom of Faith,* generally considered the manifesto of the movement. In it he offered the liberal New Theology as a viable creed to ordinary believers who had been left bewildered by the onslaughts of Darwin, higher criticism and the new history on traditional doctrines. The book attracted wide attention in both America and Britain, and was described by Whittier as being as "refreshing and tonic as the north wind." Likewise, his 1899 theological biography *Horace Bushnell, Preacher and Theologian* is a masterpiece of its kind, offering a judicious and sensitive interpretation of a spiritual predecessor to whom he was much indebted, and from whom an entire generation of American Protestant thinkers learned the implications of Christianity for a Social Gospel.*

BIBLIOGRAPHY. B. W. Bacon, *Theodore Thornton Munger: New England Minister* (1913); *DAB* VII; *DARB; NCAB* 31.   M. S. Massa

Murphy, Edgar Gardner (1869-1913). Episcopal* priest* and social reformer.* Born in Arkansas, Murphy graduated from the University of the South in 1889 and studied for a year at New York's General Theological Seminary. In his last charge, in Montgomery, Alabama (1898-1901), he devoted himself to improving conditions in the industrializing New South. In 1900 he planned a Conference on Race Relations that gained attention for its airing of diverse racial views. He helped form both Alabama (1901) and national (1904) child labor committees, and his lobbying and publications aroused support for child-labor laws. Murphy's states'-rights views and concern about Southern reactions led him to resign in 1907 when the national body endorsed a federal bill. From 1901 until illness forced his retirement in 1908, he was secretary of the Southern Education Board. Rooted in nostalgia about the Old South and optimism about leadership from the "best people," his views were humane but paternalistic and consigned African-Americans to a long subordination.

BIBLIOGRAPHY. H. C. Bailey, *Edgar Gardner Murphy: Gentle Progressive* (1968); *DAB* VII; J. T. Kirby, *Darkness at the Dawning: Race and Reform in the Progressive South* (1972).

J. H. Dorn

Murray, John (1741-1815). Early Universalist* minister* and leader. Born in England, Murray grew up in Ireland, where he followed his father from Anglicanism* to Methodism.* After more religious questioning, he rejected the Calvinistic* belief in limited atonement* in favor of the doctrine of universal redemption of all humanity as preached by James Relly. Murray immigrated to America in 1770 and preached* as an itinerant until 1779, when he became minister of a congregation in Gloucester, Massachusetts, the first Universalist group in America to sign a covenant and build a meetinghouse. In 1788 he married Judith Sargent Stevens, an early advocate of women's rights. Murray served as minister of the First Universalist Church of Boston from 1793 until his death in 1815.

Murray's Universalism was well attuned to intellectual trends in Revolutionary America. Though he retained such traditional Calvinist* beliefs as man's fall, Christ's divinity, and God's Trinitarian nature, Murray's doctrine of universal salvation coincided with the republican commitment to equality. Moreover, he preached a form of Arminianism* by emphasizing man's ability to believe. Since Universalists had to fight for recognition as a dissenting sect, in states such as Massachusetts that retained an established* (Congregational) church, Murray defended congregational autonomy and freedom of conscience, as shown in *Some Hints Relative to the Forming of a Christian Church* (1791). Overall, Universalism was a loose religious alliance, with native and often rural roots (represented by Caleb Rich, Elhanan Winchester* and Hosea Ballou*), as well as British influences and urban forms associated with John Murray.

BIBLIOGRAPHY. *DAB* VII; S. A. Marini, *Radical Sects of Revolutionary New England* (1982); R. E. Miller, *The Larger Hope; The First Century of the Universalist Church in America, 1779-1870* (1979); J. Murray, *Letters and Sketches of Sermons,* 3 vols. (1812-1813). A. C. Rose

Murray, John (1898-1975). Presbyterian* theologian.* A native of Scotland, Murray studied theology at Princeton Theological Seminary (Th.M., 1927). In 1930, after fulfilling a commitment to teach one year at Princeton (1929-1930), he joined the faculty of the newly formed Westminster Theological Seminary, Philadelphia. There he taught systematic theology* until retirement in 1966. A minister in the Orthodox Presbyterian Church,* he was fully involved in the life of the Church on both sides of the Atlantic throughout his career. Following retirement, he preached and lectured extensively throughout Great Britain until shortly before his death.

In a remarkable way Murray combined a systematizing bent with superior exegetical gifts, fused by a deep piety.* Influenced especially by B. B. Warfield* and Gerhardus Vos,* he sought to apply the biblical-theological method and insights of Vos to systematic theology. While he did not produce a major work in systematic theology, his commen-

tary, *The Epistle to the Romans,* 2 vols. (1960, 1965) was well received. Through his lecturing and numerous books and articles (*Collected Writings of John Murray,* 4 vols., 1976-1983), he brought fresh exegetical depth to many areas of classical Reformed* theology, to which he remained firmly committed.

BIBLIOGRAPHY. I. H. Murray, "The Life of John Murray" in *Collected Writings of John Murray,* vol. 3 (1976). R. B. Gaffin

Murray, John Courtney (1904-1967). Jesuit* theologian* and expert on church-state* relations. Born in New York City in 1904, Murray entered the Jesuit order in 1920 and studied at Weston College (B.A., 1926) and Boston College (M.A., 1927). From 1927 to 1930 he taught at the Ateneo de Manila, Philippines. Returning from the Philippines in 1930, he continued his studies, first at Woodstock College (S.T.L., 1934) and later at the Gregorian University in Rome (S.T.D., 1937). He was ordained* a priest* in 1933. In 1937 he became professor of theology at Woodstock, where he remained until his death. Murray became one of the chief editors of the Jesuit journal, *Theological Studies* (1941-1967), and for a while was religion editor of *America* (1945-1946). He was visiting professor of medieval philosophy and culture at Yale* (1951-1952), a minor advisor to John F. Kennedy* in his 1960 presidential campaign, a consultant to the Center for the Study of Democratic Institutions of the Fund for the Republic and in 1966 was named director of the La Farge Institute.

Murray's interest in ecumenism,* the problems of being Christian in a secular society and his concern that McCarthyism would lead to a resurgence of nativism,* led him to investigate church-state issues and the compatibility of Catholicism with a secularized democratic* state professing religious freedom. His church-state views were based on a clear distinction between the state and society, maintaining the state to be one small part of the total society. Incompetent in matters of religion, the state's only role regarding religion was to guarantee the freedom for religion to operate and to prevent the establishment or favor of any one religion. Government is to serve society and maintain the common good in terms of law and order. Society is to promote the common good of all its members, not through government proper, but through unions, religious groups, professional associations, families and the myriad other groups which comprise society.

These views set him at odds with traditional

Catholic teachings. Integrism, the traditional Catholic approach to church-state issues, held that Roman Catholicism was the one true religion and in itself a true moral good. The state is obliged to promote the common good and therefore belief in the one true religion. Thus the ideal situation is one in which Catholicism is established as the state religion.

In the context of the McCarthyism of the early 1950s, Murray began publishing his views. This led to controversy with Catholic theologians associated with the *American Ecclesiastical Review* and with some Roman officials who felt he was minimizing the claims of Catholicism and, moreover, altering a centuries-old doctrine. Murray strongly believed that church teachings were historically and culturally conditioned, could evolve over time and that while teachings on church-state relations and religious freedom may have been proper at one time, they should no longer be considered the only approach.

By 1954 Murray's controversial views had led his Jesuit superiors in Rome to order him to refrain from addressing issues of church and state for several years. At the opening of Vatican II* in 1962, he was still held in disrepute among Roman officials and missed the opening of the Council. Cardinal Spellman* later invited him to serve as a theological advisor, and Murray was a chief architect of the Council's "Declaration on Religious Freedom" (*Dignitatis Humanae,* 1965). An unprecedented accomplishment for an American theologian, it brought an important change in the church's traditional view. Murray felt the political and legal systems in operation in the U.S. were fully compatible with Roman Catholicism, a view he developed at length in *We Hold These Truths: Catholic Reflections on the American Proposition* (1960).

BIBLIOGRAPHY. *America* (November 30, 1985); *DARB*; T. T. Love, *John Courtney Murray: Contemporary Church-State Theory* (1965); D. E. Pelotte, *John Courtney Murray: Theologian in Conflict* (1975)   D. L. Salvaterra

Music, Christian. Music associated with Christianity in North America is as diverse today as the various Christian groups which populate the landscape, but it began more narrowly with Puritan* psalmody in the seventeenth century, broadened to hymnody in the eighteenth century and was controlled by revivalism* in the nineteenth century. Only in the ecumenical* climate of the twentieth century did the hidden diversity become obvious.

Psalm Singing. In the late fifteenth and sixteenth centuries, Spanish* Catholic* culture left traces of music related to the Mass* in what was to become the Southwestern U.S., but the Calvinist psalm singing of the New England Puritans was far more influential. In worship* the people sang only rhymed metrical versions of the Psalms, in unison, without instruments or polyphonic choral settings.

Within a generation or two, the Puritans forgot many of their psalm tunes, and the pace of singing slowed. *Lining out,* a practice in which a clerk or precentor sang or read a line followed by the people's singing of that line, gradually became more popular. This call-response pattern and the slowed tempo encouraged individuals to improvise their own variations on the psalm tunes ever more loudly in an increasingly cacophonous sea of sound. Ministers like Thomas Walter found this "singing by rote" intolerable and began in the second and third decades of the eighteenth century to argue for a return to "regular singing." By 1800 the practice of "lining out" had died in New England and moved South, more of its own accord than by argument, but concern for "regular singing" helped to create singing schools.

Singing schools, important components of church and culture from the mid-eighteenth and well into the nineteenth century, gave students the rudiments of music reading and singing. Itinerant teachers, with their oblong tunebooks, moved beyond metrical psalms to hymns, fuguing tunes (psalm and hymn tunes with imitative sections) and anthems; stimulated the formation of choirs as well as an indigenous white "shape-note" hymnody; and used pitch pipes and bass viols which helped introduce instruments into worship services.

Organs. The first use of an organ in a North American church probably occurred in Philadelphia in 1703 at a Lutheran* ordination* where none of the Scandinavian and German participants had Puritan scruples about instruments in worship. It was 1713 before there was a permanent organ installation in a New England church, and that was in Boston's Anglican* King's Chapel. Not until 1770 did a Puritan church acquire an organ, though the Dutch Reformed in New York—also Calvinist psalm singers—had one by 1727.

Pipe organs were in use in the eighteenth century, especially among immigrant communities from Germany whose traditions were not controlled by metrical psalmody. David Tannenberg, for example, built exemplary organs for Moravian,* Lutheran* and German Reformed* churches in Pennsylvania and neighboring states.

In the nineteenth century the reed organ (or "pump organ") became popular. Pipe organs with romantic sounds, pneumatic levers and electric currents gradually replaced traditional mechanical-action instruments. Under the influence of Albert Schweitzer, the 1930s saw a return to a more classic organ voicing, with some builders returning to mechanical action instruments. Simultaneously, technological advances led to attempts at imitating the organ electronically. Eventually, electronic organs became popular and gave churches short-term, inexpensive substitutes for the pipe organ.

Hymn Singing. In the eighteenth century, outstanding English composers such as Isaac Watts and Charles Wesley produced freer versions of psalms and hymns. Instead of woodenly literal metrical psalms, there was now Watts' "Our God, Our Help in Ages Past" and Wesley's "Hark! The Herald Angels Sing." After the American Revolution,* New England Congregationalism* generally embraced Watts's hymns, but not without a struggle.

The Presbyterians engaged in the fiercest battle over the introduction of hymns. The more revivalist "New Side"* party and the more orthodox* "Old Side"* party were divided over the issue, the former using Watts and the latter holding firmly to psalms. The dispute continued into the nineteenth century when the Kentucky pastor Adam Rankin, intensely opposed to hymns, led some congregations into the Rankinite Schism.

Hymnody, continuing psalmody, singing schools, choirs and the birth of the republic in the latter half of the eighteenth century helped to produce native American composers like William Billings.* A tanner by trade, with no formal training but a consuming passion for music, Billings taught, composed, conducted and published music. Some musicians, such as Oliver Holden (whose tune "Coronation" is still used today) viewed the crudity of composers like Billings with suspicion.

Apart from the dominant Puritan tradition in American religion, other groups contributed to the diversity which would become apparent in the twentieth century. The Swedish Lutherans, for example, settling along the Delaware in 1638, maintained their high church liturgical* practices and music. In the Anabaptist tradition,* Mennonites* and Amish* used a sixteenth-century hymnal known as the *Ausbund*—a hymnal still used by the Amish today.

The Wissahickon Pietists, who followed Johann Kelpius* to America in 1694, were known for singing, playing musical instruments and compiling the first extant musical manuscript in the colonies, but they died out within a generation. Their spiritual successors, the Ephrata Cloister,* lasted until the first part of the nineteenth century. In 1732 they gathered around a German immigrant named Conrad Beissel* at Ephrata, near Lancaster, Pennsylvania, to form a celibate community of men and women. In addition to using German chorales and pietistic hymns, they composed both music and texts, which they copied onto beautifully illuminated manuscripts. Women formed the matrix of the choral group, which at its height rehearsed under Beissel for four hours each night and amazed visitors with its ethereal quality.

The Moravians,* another group of Pietists, but much closer to the Protestant mainstream, produced not only "trombone choirs" for which they are famous, but organ builders like Tannenberg and choral and instrumental music which they integrated into their worship services. Already in 1744 they had organized a *Collegium Musicum*. By 1800 it was performing works by Bach and Haydn.

Revivalism. In 1800, on the eve of the Second Great Awakening,* the hymnody of Watts had gained ascendancy, along with tunes from eighteenth-century England and from American composers like William Billings. Camp meetings required simpler choruses that throngs of people could learn quickly, however; and these were often fashioned from Watts. Sometimes they were little above the level of doggerel. Literary and musical quality did not always accompany the "mourning bench."* German Reformed and Lutheran bodies, struggling with English, were sometimes carried along by the spirit of revivalism and sometimes virtually lost their heritage. On the other hand, the experience produced a resurgence in some confessional churches and a sophisticated level of hymnological research among scholars like John W. Nevin,* Philip Schaff* and Frederic M. Bird.

A concern for quality found expression in Lowell Mason,* a Congregational choir director and organist who exerted one of the strongest musical influences in the nineteenth century. He helped organize the Boston Academy of Music in 1832, introduced the first official public school music program in the U.S. into the public schools of Boston, edited numerous collections of church music and composed many hymn tunes (such as "Bethany," "Olivet" and "Missionary Hymn").

Black Music. In their music blacks employed West-African idioms with syncopated moans, shouts, slides, hand clapping, foot stomping and dancing. African songs were used, but so were Protestant psalms and hymns with altered melodies, rhythms and texts.

The seventeenth and eighteenth centuries gave rise to an oral tradition which by the nineteenth century resulted in "spirituals." African-American spirituals combined African and American elements and characteristically employed simple verses and refrains sung alternately between soloist and people. They could be sorrowful, like "Nobody Knows the Trouble I've Seen," or jubilant, like "Didn't My Lord Deliver Daniel?" They expressed not only the faith and hope Christians have always sung about, but were also coded protests against white oppression. In the 1870s the Fisk University Jubilee Singers toured the country, singing choral arrangements of African-American spirituals. Since then black and white choirs have regularly programmed spirituals, arranged by Harry Burleigh, William Dawson and other composers.

In the early nineteenth century, African-Americans adopted the hymns of Isaac Watts, but integrated them into their oral tradition by lining them out and "blackening" their rhythmic and melodic characteristics. These "Dr. Watts hymns" reached their peak of popularity by 1875, but never displaced spirituals.

African-American gospel music, characterized by a raspy vocal quality, high registers and a vibrato calculated to be heard over loud and amplified instruments, appeared at the end of the nineteenth century. The style was influenced by the emotionally charged atmosphere of the Pentecostal* churches. When the Methodist* minister Charles Tindley began setting hymns after 1900, African-American gospel music entered the mainstream of African-American churches. Thomas A. Dorsey, who wrote "Precious Lord, Take My Hand," developed Tindley's style by using blues and ragtime melodic and harmonic patterns.

Other Spirituals. White spirituals, researched most notably by George Pullen Jackson, have their roots in the British Isles and represent an oral tradition transmitted through the New England singing-school instructors. The pentatonic tune "New Britain"—of unknown origin and associated with "Amazing Grace"—exemplifies the style. Tunes in this tradition are often "gapped" (with leaps in the melody). Traditional rules of Western harmony are not observed. These songs were recorded in oblong tunebooks by a "shape-note" system advanced most successfully in 1801 by William Smith and William Little. Notes were printed in shapes and called by the names *fa, sol, la* and *mi*—hence, this kind of singing was called "fasola." In the nineteenth century Lowell Mason and his brother Timothy and others in urban centers were embarrassed by these so-called buckwheat or dunce notes. They attempted to substitute the European do-re-mi system, and in time the "shape-note" system was to be found mainly in the rural South. "Singings" of this music, with its haunting, rustic contours, still go on today and have attracted the attention of modern composers.

Pennsylvania spirituals were at home among the more revivalistic German groups like the United Brethren and the Church of God.* They employed Pennsylvania Dutch words set to chorus-type gospel songs. The Shakers,* a communitarian group that produced yet another American spiritual, reached their zenith in the first half of the nineteenth century. Like the Puritans, they avoided harmony and instruments. Though they sometimes employed shape-notes, they characteristically isolated themselves from the surrounding culture with arcane notational systems and "unknown tongues." Daniel W. Patterson has compiled and discussed several hundred of the 8,000 Shaker songs, the most popular of which is probably "Simple Gifts," used by Aaron Copland in *Appalachian Spring.*

Unlike most of the other groups which grew up in the nineteenth century and then declined, the Mormons* have become an aggressive twentieth-century missionary* body. They have employed much of the Protestant tradition's hymnody and have established the well-known Mormon Tabernacle Choir in Salt Lake City, Utah. A distinctive contribution to American musical culture, the choir sings a variety of choral music on its radio programs, accompanied by fine organ music as well.

Gospel Hymnody. In the 1840s William Bradbury,* one of Lowell Mason's students, took the catchy tunes, rhythms and refrains of camp meeting songs and introduced them as Sunday-school* hymns. When adults sang them, they became known as gospel hymns.*

The evangelist* Dwight Moody,* along with his song leader, Ira D. Sankey,* made gospel songs popular. Much gospel-hymn activity centered around Chicago and what was to become the Moody Bible Institute.* Fanny Crosby* was an exception. Blind from birth, she studied and taught at the New York City School for the Blind. At the age of forty-four she began writing gospel songs, and by the time of her death had written more than 8,500 texts, including the popular "Rescue the Perishing." Tune writers like Bradbury set her texts, and Biglow and Main, the largest nineteenth-century publisher of gospel hymnody, published them.

In the twentieth century, gospel hymnody continued to accompany revivalism. Homer Rodeheaver* used it with evangelist Billy Sunday*; Charles Alexander* sang it with massed choirs in the campaigns of R. A. Torrey* and J. Wilbur Chapman*; and Cliff Barrows and George Beverly Shea used it with Billy Graham.* Gospel hymnody has been described by W. Wiley Hitchcock as "irresistible in its visceral appeal" at its best, and "embarrassingly trivial" at its worst.

Other Movements. Revivalism dominated much of the nineteenth century's religious music, but there were other movements as well. From the mid-nineteenth century until after World War 1,* hired professional quartets replaced larger choirs in many mainstream Protestant churches. The Episcopal* Church, stimulated by the Tractarian Movement,* reacted against this and developed vested choirs of boys and men. In the twentieth century almost all mainstream Protestant churches—even "nonliturgical" ones—formed choirs who wore robes and sang responses.

In Roman Catholic parishes, when German, Italian or Irish immigrants could afford it, they hired soloists to imitate the theatrical and operatic music they had heard in European churches. The boys' choir at the Church of St. Xavier in New York City was one of the few exceptions until John Baptist Singenberger founded the Caecilian Society in 1873. He attempted to reintroduce Gregorian chant and revive polyphony in place of operatic music. His influence was especially felt in parishes in Chicago, Cincinnati and Milwaukee. St. John's Abbey, a Benedictine* house founded in the middle of the nineteenth century in Collegeville, Minnesota, also nurtured chant and polyphony.

Ecumenicity. By the twentieth century, groups outside the once-dominant Puritan tradition had, along with the ongoing psalmody, hymnody and revivalism, created a rich ecumenical scene. Societies like the American Guild of Organists (1896) and the Hymn Society of America (1922) crossed denominational boundaries. Schools represented interests broader than a single denomination: the Department of Church Music at Northwestern University in Evanston, Illinois, founded by Peter Christian Lutkin shortly after 1896, reached beyond its Methodist roots; Westminster Choir College, founded by John Finley Williamson in 1926, appealed to "nonliturgical" churches and was not limited to its Presbyterian tradition; the School of Sacred Music at Union Seminary* in New York City, established by Clarence Dickinson in 1928, reflected a breadth of denominations in its practice, scholarship and student body.

The sharing sometimes resulted in loss. Eastern Orthodox* groups, for example, did not always maintain their rich unaccompanied choral tradition, but sometimes allowed Western practices and electronic organs to obscure their uniqueness. That loss was offset by the arrival of the composer Igor Stravinsky, who came to the U.S. at the outbreak of World War 2. His return to the Orthodox faith stimulated his *Mass,* which, with his *Symphony of Psalms,* is a monument of music in the Christian tradition.

Charles Ives is perhaps the most important of America's native-born composers of music with Christian themes. He took the musical materials of American Protestantism and wove them together in symphonic and choral music with typical twentieth-century techniques, like polytonality and tone clusters. Other important church musicians in the first half of the twentieth century included Horatio Parker,* who taught at Yale* and wrote *Hora Novissima;* the Englishman T. Tertius Noble, who served St. Thomas Church in New York City and wrote well-known harmonizations of hymn tunes; the Englishman Healey Willan, who worked at the Church of St. Mary Magdalene in Toronto and produced numerous choral and organ works; Leo Sowerby, who served St. James Episcopal Church in Chicago; Lynwood Farnam, who was an unusually gifted organ recitalist and teacher in Montreal, Boston and New York; and F. Melius Christiansen, who developed the St. Olaf Choir and wrote settings of chorales for it.

The music of Christians did not escape the turbulence of the 1960s and 1970s. Traditions came unglued. In 1973 the School of Sacred Music at Union Seminary closed its doors and signaled the end of an era. The Second Vatican Council* forced Roman Catholics to scramble for English texts with appropriate music but also set in motion new relationships for all Christian groups. Guitar music was ground out quickly and without much thought. Organs were turned off in some churches.

By the 1980s the many Christian traditions America has welcomed had re-established themselves, albeit along broader outlines. Organs were turned on again as the love affair with the guitar waned. Though church musicians and their churches were still involved at times in acrimonious musical rancor, the debates were usually limited to one church or denomination. Generally they learned together from a broad range of diverse musical and liturgical styles—Renaissance to contemporary compositions sung by excellent choirs; less-than-excellent music sung by poor choirs; superb organs and organists; poor organs and organists; varieties of ecumenical psalms, hymns and service singing in parishes with and without strong musical resources; ephemeral music related to a popular television commercial idiom; liturgical worship of the Eastern and Western traditions, with historic music; and charismatic* and Pentecostal worship with its characteristic improvisatory style. All this and more formed the broad ecumenical musical mosaic of the late twentieth century from which church musicians faced common problems—most of which related to language.

See also GOSPEL HYMNS AND SONGS; HYMNS, HYMNALS.

BIBLIOGRAPHY. G. Chase, *America's Music* (1987); L. Ellinwood, *The History of American Church Music* (1953); D. Hustad, *Jubilate! Church Music in the Evangelical Tradition* (1981); G. P. Jackson, *White Spirituals in the Southern Uplands* (1933); W. T. Marrocco and H. Gleason, *Music in America* (1964); P. Maultsby, *Afro-American Religious Music* (n.d.); O. Ochse, *The History of the Organ in the United States* (1975); D. W. Patterson, *Shaker Spirituals* (1979); P. Westermeyer, "Religious Music and Hymnody," *Encyclopedia of the American Religious Experience,* ed. C. H. Lippy and P. W. Williams (1987); D. Yoder, *Pennsylvania Spirituals* (1961). P. Westermeyer

Musical Instruments in Churches. Instrumental church music in the U.S. was slow to gain wide acceptance. Today's use of synthesizers, drums, guitars and prerecorded orchestras is a far development from the arguments in the colonies over the use of a "whistle" (the pitch pipe's contemptuous name in the era of William Billings*) to "set the tune" for unaccompanied psalm singing.

Organs. The Puritans's* confession of 1571 forbade the "intermingling of organs" and the Westminster Confession* prompted destruction of organs. Building upon their imported Protestant* traditions, early-American Lutherans* also sang in parts with little interest in organs. The Presbyterians* of Scotland and other Reformed* churches excluded instruments (and sang in unison since harmony was non-Calvinistic) until the mid-nineteenth century when "kists of whistles" (organs) were first permitted. The Lutheran* Pietist* Justus Falckner* was one of the first in America to urge the use of organs in worship.* But in 1711, when Boston's Thomas Brattle* bequeathed his imported organ to Brattle Street Church, it was refused and in the end went to the Anglican King's Chapel.

In 1883 F. L. Ritter wrote of "famous organ recitals at Grace Church" (New York). By 1900

W. S. Pratt could tell a McCormick Seminary (Chicago) audience that "the organ has always been recognized in the Christian Church as the sacred instrument par excellence," adding, "most churches have pipe organs or mean to have them."

Orchestral Instruments. European churches in the eighteenth century utilized some instruments to aid congregational singing. Orchestras were civic organizations and instrumentalists identified with the town as much as they did with the church. In America, too, accompanied major choral works were performed in churches and concert halls. The Moravian* Pietists were the most notable early promoters of musical instruments in worship, accompanying their singing with flutes, trumpets, violins, horns and, later, organs. New Englanders heard Handel and Haydn oratorios with musical accompaniment nearly as soon as Londoners. In 1831 the orchestra of St. Paul's Church (New York) played Beethoven's "Mount of Olives." N. D. Gould represented a continuing divergent view when in 1853 he stated that instruments "sink into insignificance" when compared with the human voice.

Today, rhythm and electronic instruments have found a place along with standard instruments. In many settings prerecorded accompaniments reduce the need for instruments. Except for a few denominations that retain the practice of unaccompanied singing (such as the noninstrumental Churches of Christ*), instruments are unquestioned, and published instrumental music is widely available. Instrumental parts can be purchased for most hymns and instrumental accompaniments for major choral works.

BIBLIOGRAPHY. P. L. Ritter, *Music In America* (1890); C. Sachs, *The History of Musical Instruments* (1940); H. R. Trobian, *The Instrumental Ensemble in the Church* (1963).

R. J. Stanislaw

Myers, Cortland (1864-1941). Fundamentalist* Baptist* pastor.* Born in Kingston, New York, Myers graduated from the University of Rochester (A.B., 1887) and Rochester Theological Seminary (1890). Ordained* in 1890, he pastored the First Baptist churches of Syracuse (1890-1893) and Brooklyn, New York (1893-1909); Tremont Temple in Boston, Massachusetts (1909-1921); and in 1921 became pastor of Immanuel Baptist in Pasadena, California. In 1918 he called attention to what he called "false teachers" and "false teachings" in Baptist colleges* and seminaries.* In that same year he signed the call for the Philadelphia Prophetic Convention, where he was one of the speakers. There he decried German rational theology* and claimed it was a contributing factor to World War 1.* Myers also warned of the dangers of foreign immigration to America. A supporter of the World's Christian Fundamentals Association* from its beginning, he signed the call for the preconvention meeting on Baptist fundamentals held in Buffalo, New York, in 1920, and addressed the participants in a talk entitled "Things Not Shaken." A commanding pulpiteer, Myers was known among fundamentalists for his outspoken criticism of modernism.   R. T. Clutter

Myland, David Wesley (1858-1943). Pentecostal* minister,* evangelist* and educator. Born in Canada, Myland grew up near Cleveland, Ohio, and was originally associated with the Methodist* Episcopal Church. Having experienced healing himself, he promoted healing and by 1890 had found more compatible fellowship in the Christian and Missionary Alliance* (1890). Myland held several positions with the Ohio district of the CMA, serving also as an evangelist, pastor* and editor of the *Christian Messenger.* After experiencing Spirit baptism* in November 1906, Myland's theology became more Pentecostal, and in 1912 he left the CMA when that body parted with the Pentecostal Movement. Myland founded Gibeah Bible School in Plainfield, Indiana, where he also taught (1912-1913) and formed the short-lived Association of Christian Assemblies. He next founded the Ebenezer Bible Institute in Chicago (1915-1918) and then taught at Beulah Heights Bible Institute in Atlanta, Georgia (1918-1920). Over the next twenty-three years, Myland pastored churches in Pennsylvania, Michigan and Ohio. Among his literary products was a hymn* book that included hymns "given to him in the Spirit."

The Latter Rain theology central to early Pentecostalism and responsible for a short-lived movement in the late 1940s owes at least some of its impetus to Myland's *The Latter Rain Covenant and Pentecostal Power* (1910). Myland used charts of rainfall in Palestine from 1861 to 1901 to show that rainfall was increasing in the Holy Land. From these data, he initially concluded that the Second Coming of Jesus Christ would occur shortly after 1906.

BIBLIOGRAPHY. A. A. Boddy, *Confidence* 6 (January 1913):16; J. K. Butcher, "The Holiness and Pentecostal Labors of David Wesley Myland, 1890-1918" (unpublished Th.M. thesis, Dallas Theological Seminary, 1982).   H. D. Hunter

Mystical Body of Christ. Roman Catholic* term describing the relationship of Christ and the church.* The term derives from the Pauline metaphor of Christ as head and the faithful as members of the body. The doctrine was clearly set forth by Pope Pius XII* in his encyclical *Mystici Corporis* (1943) and in the *Dogmatic Constitution on the Church* promulgated by the Second Vatican Council* in 1964 with the authority of Pope Paul VI.*

Theologians* over the last decades have tried to articulate the relationship between the graced bond of all believers in the body of Christ and the visible reality of the church as a social institution. The radical distinction between an invisible church of believers and a gathered visible church has never found favor in Roman Catholic circles. In the metaphor of the Mystical Body of Christ, theologians have a way of tempering the more sociological descriptions of the church as a perfect visible society favored by the polemicists and apologists of the post-Reformation era.

BIBLIOGRAPHY. H. Kung, *The Church* (1976); Emile Mersch, *The Whole Christ* (1981).

L. S. Cunningham.

Mysticism, Christian. Mysticism can be defined in general as an immediate link to the absolute. It is premised on the reality of an absolute which stands in distinction to the phenomenal world and on the possibility of humans realizing an immediate link with the absolute. What this absolute is, and how one can have the link to it, varies from tradition to tradition. More often than not, the absolute is considered divine; the link can be an identity, a union or perhaps simply an unmediated awareness. Phenomena which are frequently termed "mystical" in everyday language, such as visions or miracles, are only peripheral to mysticism per se.

There are many examples of mysticism within Christendom. Augustine and Thomas Aquinas are both said to have had mystical experiences. Perhaps the most extreme examples of Christian mysticism are the sixteenth-century mystics Teresa of Avila and John of the Cross, who divided the mystical experience into three stages: the way of illumination—the recognition of relationship to God; the way of purgation—the necessary cathartic preparation; and the way of union—oneness of the soul with Christ. Other forms of Christian mysticism are bountiful. Mysticism has not been a significant movement in American religion, due on the one hand to the pervasive influence of Reformed* Christianity which tended to emphasize the place of Scripture in Christian piety,* but also perhaps because of a native American pragmatism.

Nevertheless, there are some significant examples that can be cited, particularly some mystical elements within various American Christian traditions that have flourished from time to time.

Reformed Christianity was not without its mystical elements. What Perry Miller* identified in Puritanism* as "the Augustinian strain of piety" could lead a Puritan such as Thomas Hooker* to speak of the soul as made "to enjoy union with him [God], and communion with those blessed excellencies of his. . . ." Jonathan Edwards* could also voice a Reformed, but genuine, mysticism in his *Dissertation Concerning the End for which God Created the World* (1765). But for the most part, the magisterial reformers had the effect of driving mysticism into the sectarian groups of the Radical Reformation. An example of these groups is the Schwenkfelders* or "confessors of the Glory of Christ," who practiced a form of mysticism and settled in Pennsylvania in the 1730s.

One of the clearer examples of mysticism in American Christianity is found in a radical form of Puritanism, the Quakers* (Friends). A main tenet of this movement is the inward revelation of the Holy Spirit. In its earliest days, Quaker piety was christocentric, but in time much of the movement took on a quality of generic mysticism. According to traditional Quaker beliefs, the Holy Spirit presents direct knowledge from God to the believer in an unmediated way. Traditional Friends meetings are often spent in long silences, waiting for the Spirit to move.

A mystic strain can also be found in various branches of the Wesleyan Holiness Movement* in America. A typical feature of this movement has been the emphasis on feeling the presence of the Spirit in the life of the believer, an experience believed to assure an individual of salvation. Insofar as members of these groups rely on this direct awareness of the Spirit, they can be classified as mystical. In the twentieth century the Pentecostal* and charismatic* movements have oftentimes exemplified a mystical approach to Christianity. However, this is not true in cases where a preoccupation with the gifts of the Spirit has replaced awareness of the Spirit's indwelling.

Nineteenth-century romanticism* yielded a more eclectic form of nature mysticism in the Transcendentalists.* While not specifically Christian, the leaders of the movement, such as Ralph Waldo Emerson,* significantly influenced American religious thought. The romantic movement as a whole influenced Catholic piety by encouraging intuition and religious feelings as a means of apprehending God. This led to a renewal of mysticism among Catholics.

Contemplative theology, a strong tradition of mystical spirituality within Roman Catholic as well as Anglican* theology, emphasizes a deeper spiritual life with the goal of direct union of the human will with God. But in contemplative theology the spiritual disciplines of prayer, meditation and fasting are considered worthwhile, even apart from any direct realization of this goal. A recent and well-known representative of contemplative theology was the Trappist* monk Thomas Merton.*

Mystical movements continue to surface, sometimes self-consciously acknowledged as mystical, oftentimes as paths of spiritual renewal. A surge of interest in mysticism, mostly Eastern, was evident during the 1960s and 1970s. In some cases this has touched American Christianity in the form of a syncretistic appeal to Eastern mysticism as a source for the renewal of Christian mysticism.

In evangelical Protestantism the twentieth-century writer A. W. Tozer,* who emphasized direct encounter with God, could be described as a very understated and moderate mystic. On the whole, mystical movements tend to de-emphasize Scripture for the sake of private inner knowledge and thus tend to be incompatible with evangelicalism. Nonetheless, insofar as Christian mysticism calls attention to the reality of the supernatural presence of the Holy Spirit in the life of the believer, one can look for its manifestation wherever there is genuine renewal in American Christianity.

BIBLIOGRAPHY. L. H. Bridges, *American Mysticism* (1970); T. Merton, *The Seven-Storey Mountain* (1946); W. James, *The Varieties of Religious Experience* (1902); A. W. Tozer, *Man, the Dwelling Place of God* (1966); E. Underhill, *Mysticism* (1911).   W. Corduan

N

Narrative Theology. *See* SCRIPTURE.

Nation, Carry (or Carrie) Amelia Moore (1846-1911). Temperance* organizer and evangelist.* Born in Garrard County, Kentucky, Carry's childhood was unhappy, overshadowed by her mentally ill mother. In 1867 Nation married Charles Gloyd, a physician. The marriage was short and unhappy, due to Gloyd's alcoholism that presumably took his life within about a year, leaving Carry with a daughter. After his death Carry taught school in Holden, Missouri, until 1877 when she married David Nation, a lawyer, editor and sometime minister. In 1879 they moved to Texas, where he tried his hand at cotton farming and then law, while Carry managed a hotel. In 1889 they moved to Medicine Lodge, Kansas.

Vehemently opposed to strong drink, in 1892 Carry became involved in the Women's Christian Temperance Union,* and by 1899 she was active in crusading against saloons. Convinced that her work was divinely commissioned by God, she became known as an extreme prohibitionist,* who waged war against liquor by singing hymns, quoting Scripture* and smashing liquor bottles and saloon furnishings with her hatchet—a demonstration that on more than one occasion was followed by her arrest for disturbing the peace. An imposing presence, Carry stood nearly six feet tall and was unusually strong.

Much of Nation's activity was confined to Kansas—particularly Wichita, where she smashed the Hotel Casey barroom, and Topeka, where she demolished the Senate Saloon. As was true of other temperance leaders, she was involved in evangelistic* endeavors. She was a jail evangelist for the Women's Christian Temperance Union,* and her demonstrations against saloons were often accompanied by an evangelistic message. In addition to alcohol,* she opposed tobacco and immodesty of dress. In 1901 her second husband divorced her on grounds of desertion, and for the next few years her activities were primarily confined to the national lecture circuit, where she also sold her autobiography and signed autographs. In 1908 she made a lecture tour of Britain. In the end her public presence had deteriorated into a vaudeville-like show.

See also ALCOHOL, DRINKING OF; PROHIBITION MOVEMENT; TEMPERANCE MOVEMENT.

BIBLIOGRAPHY. *DAB* VII; C. A. Nation, *The Use and Need of the Life of Carry A. Nation* (1909); *NAW* 2; R. L. Taylor, *Vessel of Wrath: The Life and Times of Carry Nation* (1966).

R. A. Tucker

National Association of Evangelicals. A voluntary fellowship of forty-four member denominations* providing evangelical* identification for fifty thousand churches and over five million Christians. Through its commissions, affiliates and service agencies, the organization has a service constituency of approximately fifteen million.

The National Association of Evangelicals (NAE) had its beginnings in the New England Fellowship in 1929. Led by J. Elwin Wright and Harold J. Ockenga,* a nationwide co-operative vision gripped NEF leaders and a call went out for an exploratory meeting. At the Hotel Coronado in St. Louis, Missouri, April 7-9, 1942, 150 delegates assembled for the National Conference for United Action Among Evangelicals. A counterforce to the ecumenical Federal Council of Churches* was needed, without succumbing to the perceived divisive theological and political tendencies which would develop within the rival fundamentalist American Council of Christian Churches.* One year later, over one-thousand delegates representing fifty denominations met in Chicago for the history-making constitutional convention of what became the National Association of Evangelicals.

A seven-point doctrinal statement was adopted that has remained descriptive of evangelical faith. Under the banner of "cooperation without compromise," millions of conservative Protestants* find in the NAE their most satisfactory channel for inter-church cooperation without compromise of doctrinal convictions.

Numerous extensions of the NAE ministry were organized to address constituency concerns. The Office of Public Affairs was created in 1943 to represent evangelical interests in the nation's capital. For thirty-five years it was led by Clyde W. Taylor*; since 1978 Robert P. Dugan, Jr., has been director. Organization of the National Religious Broadcasters* and Chaplains Commission followed in 1944, and 1945 saw the beginnings of the Evangelical Foreign Missions Association* and World Relief, the humanitarian* arm of the NAE. Commissions on evangelism* and home missions,* Christian education,* evangelical churchmen, stewardship, higher education, social action, Hispanics,* and women play a key role in NAE activities.

Acknowledging its obligation to society and the world, the NAE has taken a firm stand relative to current issues. Through resolutions adopted at annual conventions, the Association speaks as directed by its constituent members on matters of common agreement. In the early years it spoke out against the evils of communism, abuses of church-state* separation, racism and growing secularism within the educational system. It was one of the first ecclesiastical organizations to take a formal stand against abortion,* and spoke out against pornography, drug abuse and other social evils. On international affairs, NAE has authored guidelines for studies on peace, freedom and security, and adopted resolutions on conflict areas such as South Africa and Nicaragua.

Leadership of the NAE is given by an executive committee led by a president who is elected for two-year terms at annual conventions, and an executive director. Dr. Billy A. Melvin has served as executive director since 1967. NAE headquarters are in Wheaton, Illinois.

BIBLIOGRAPHY. J. D. Murch, *Cooperation without Compromise* (1956); B. E. Shelley, *Evangelicalism in America* (1967). R. C. Cizik

National Baptists. Four predominantly African-American Baptist* denominations* have taken variations of the name *National Baptist:* the National Baptist Convention of the United States of America, Inc.; the National Baptist Convention of America; the National Baptist Evangelical Life and Soul-Saving Assembly of the USA; and the Progressive National Baptist Convention, Inc.

The National Baptist Convention of the United States of America, Inc. and the National Baptist Convention of America. The National Baptist Convention of the United States of America, Inc. is the largest African-American denomination in America and the world. Established in Atlanta, Georgia, on September 28, 1895, this event marked the successful merger of three separate Baptist organizations: the Foreign Mission Baptist Convention of 1880, the American National Baptist Convention of 1886 and the Baptist National Educational Convention of 1893. Under the leadership of Reverend Elias C. Morris (1855-c.1923), a former slave and Arkansas minister who served the Convention as president for twenty-eight years, the Convention created foreign missions, home missions and education boards, each of which corresponded to the three organizations that predated the formation of the Convention itself. In 1896 the Home Mission Board established a publishing house which it later, in 1898, had incorporated as the National Baptist Publishing Board. By 1958 the Convention had over 27,000 ministers, 26,000 churches, 5.5 million members and foreign missions in Africa, South America, India and numerous other parts of the world. In 1984 it numbered an estimated seven million members in over 30,000 congregations.

In 1915 the Convention divided into two separate organizations following a dispute over the ownership of the National Baptist Publishing Board. Under the leadership of Reverend R. H. Boyd, corresponding secretary of the Convention's publication board and a skillful businessman, the publishing house had become a highly successful business, raising over $2 million within the first ten years of its existence. Tensions emerged between Boyd and the Convention when the publishing house failed to donate its substantial funds to other denominational projects, or comply with the charter of the Convention. Attempting to establish its legal right to the publishing house, the Convention adopted a new charter, redefined the charge of the publishing board and incorporated itself as the National Baptist Convention of the United States of America, Incorporated. Boyd and his constituents rejected the new charter, withdrew the publishing house from the newly incorporated Convention and designated themselves the National Baptist Convention of America, Unincorporated. In 1956, approximately forty years later, this relatively new denomination claimed over 2.5 million members and over 11,000 congregations.

These two denominational organizations, the National Baptist Convention of the United States of America, Inc., and the National Baptist Convention of America, Unincorporated, continue to function as distinctive bodies well into the twentieth century, though they share basic Baptist theological beliefs such as the authority* of the Bible,* the

Lordship of Jesus Christ, the baptism* of believers, the separation of church and state,* and the autonomy of local church and state associations.

The National Baptist Evangelical Life and Soul-Saving Assembly of the United States of America. This body was founded in 1920 at Kansas City, Missouri, as an evangelical* and educational branch of the National Baptist Convention of America, Unincorporated. Organized by the Reverend Arthur Allen Banks, Sr., the Assembly remained a division of the National Baptist Convention until 1936, when it declared itself a separate denomination at a meeting in Birmingham, Alabama. Preaching the "Bible doctrine as announced by the founder of the Church, Jesus Christ," the Assembly dedicated itself to relief work, evangelism and charities. It also created a correspondence school offering doctoral and master's degrees and courses in evangelism, missions and the work of deacons* and laypersons.* In 1951 the Assembly, still separate from, yet on favorable terms with, the National Baptist Convention of America, Unincorporated, consisted of 264 churches, 58,000 members and 137 ministers.

The Progressive National Baptist Convention, Incorporated. This denomination emerged in 1961, following a five-year debate within the National Baptist Convention of the United States of America, Inc., over policies regarding the election of officers and the length of the Convention president's term in office. In 1957 Dr. J. H. Jackson, who had already served a four-year term as the Convention president, ruled against the 1952 policy restricting a president's term in office to four years. Many in the Convention, among them Dr. G. C. Taylor, felt that this was a return to practices that predated the 1952 policy when presidents served for life. This discontent led to heated debates at the 1960 Convention in Kansas City, Missouri, and an invitation from a Convention member, Dr. L. Venchael Booth of Zion Baptist Church in Cincinnati, Ohio, for all dissatisfied delegates to attend a meeting at his church. Thirty-three delegates from fourteen states attended that meeting and formed the Progressive National Baptist Convention, Inc.

Though there is little doctrinal disagreement between the Progressive Convention and its parent body, the two organizations do show dissimilarities at the level of organization. The Progressive Convention elects its officers every two years and limits the Convention president's term in office to eight years. In the late 1970s the Progressive Convention was composed of 487 churches and a membership of over 500,000. By 1984 it had approximately one million members

BIBLIOGRAPHY. J. G. Melton, *The Encyclopedia of American Religion,* vol. 1 (1978); O. D. Pelt, *The Story of the National Baptists* (1960); A. C. Piepkorn, *Profiles in Belief: The Religious Bodies of the United States and Canada,* vol. 2 (1978).

M. C. Bruce

National Black Evangelical Association. Black evangelical* ecumenical* organization. The National Black Evangelical Association (NBEA) was organized in 1963 as the National Negro Evangelical Association. The name was changed in 1973. Among its early participants was the well-known African-American evangelist* Tom Skinner, and the first president was William H. Bentley. NBEA's theology* is generally conservative, while political perspectives range from apolitical to nationalistic.

The primary function of NBEA is to enable African-American evangelicals trained in white institutions and identified with white denominations* to reclaim the heritage and traditions of the Black Church. Its purposes are twofold: to provide support and fellowship* for evangelicals involved in ministries* to urban* African-American communities, and to develop ministries embracing both social and spiritual concerns. The NBEA has addressed social concerns such as hunger, poverty, racism and militarism. It also actively challenges white evangelical bodies to be more responsive to the concerns and needs of the African-American community. Convocations are held annually, and a variety of programs are organized by individual commissions on theology, social action, family life, evangelism,* missions, education, women's ministry, youth ministry,* children's ministry* and pastoral leadership.

Membership, numbering approximately 500, consists of roughly equal numbers of clergy and laity in independent,* Bible,* Holiness* and Pentecostal* churches, as well as Methodist,* Baptist,* Presbyterian,* Mennonite* and Quaker* bodies. Approximately one third are women and one third white. National offices are in Portland, Oregon. Separate entities initiated by the NBEA have included the National Black Christian Students Conference, the Women's Consciousness Raising Seminar and the National Association of Christian Communicators.

BIBLIOGRAPHY. W. H. Bentley, *National Black Evangelical Association: Evolution of a Concept of Ministry* (1979); M. R. Sawyer, "Black Ecumenism: Cooperative Social Change Movements in the Black Church" (Ph.D. dissertation, Duke University, 1986).

M. R. Sawyer

National Campmeeting Association for the Promotion of Christian Holiness. *See* CHRISTIAN HOLINESS ASSOCIATION.

National Catholic Welfare Conference. A national coordinating body for American Catholicism,* headquartered in Washington, D.C. The National Catholic Welfare Conference (NCWC) began its life as the National Catholic War Council, founded at a meeting of 115 delegates from 68 American dioceses in August 1917. A Paulist* priest, John J. Burke,* spearheaded the Council's organization and placed it under the jurisdiction of an administrative board of bishops.*

During World War 1* NCWC provided material support to chaplains* and Catholic servicemen and cooperated with such groups as the YMCA,* the Salvation Army* and the Jewish Welfare Board in fund-raising efforts for homefront activities. After the war the NCWC reorganized as a permanent welfare council. It issued the "Bishops' Program on Social Reconstruction"* in 1919, a liberal statement on social and political matters authored by John A. Ryan.* The Vatican nearly dissolved the NCWC in 1921 to 1922, fearful of conciliar bodies that infringed on individual bishops' prerogatives, but the organization survived by changing its name from *Council* to *Conference.*

The NCWC played a twofold role, as an informational clearinghouse for American Catholic leaders and a Washington lobby to protect Catholic interests in the political arena. In 1966 the NCWC disbanded, bequeathing its two functions to successor organizations. The National Conference of Catholic Bishops* acquired the clearinghouse role and the United States Catholic Conference* undertook the lobbying task.

BIBLIOGRAPHY. M. Williams, *American Catholics in the War* (1921); E. K. McKeown, *War and Welfare: American Catholics and World War I* (1988); J. Hennessey, *American Catholics* (1981). E. A. Kantowicz

National Committee of Black Churchmen. *See* NATIONAL CONFERENCE OF BLACK CHRISTIANS.

National Committee of Negro Churchmen. *See* NATIONAL CONFERENCE OF BLACK CHRISTIANS.

National Conference of Black Christians. African-American ecumenical organization. The National Conference of Black Christians (NCBC) was formed by a group of radical African-American clergymen* in 1966 in response to the hostile reaction of liberal* white clergy to the call for "black power." Originally called the National Committee of Negro Churchmen, the organization was subsequently known as the National Committee of Black Churchmen, the National Conference of Black Churchmen and finally the National Conference of Black Christians.

NCBC's first public act was the publication of a full-page ad in the *New York Times* defending black power and signed by forty-eight prominent African-American church leaders. Its most active years were from 1966 to 1972, when program concerns included relations with Africa, economic development in urban areas and education. Its most important contributions, however, were in the development of black theology* under the leadership of Gayraud S. Wilmore. In 1969 NCBC issued what became the normative statement on black theology, defining it as "a theology of black liberation.*"

Annual convocations were held from 1967 to 1982, with membership peaking at 1,200, about eighty per cent of whom were clergy. A disproportionate number—about forty per cent—came from predominantly white denominations,* and sixty per cent from the historic African-American denominations. In addition to interpreting developments in the African-American community to the white church establishment, NCBC also sought to raise the consciousness of clergy and congregations within the institutional Black Church. Participation in NCBC declined in the early 1970s as black caucuses within the white denominations grew stronger and as social radicalism declined in the society-at-large. The NCBC has been inactive since 1984.

BIBLIOGRAPHY. G. S. Wilmore, *Black Religion and Black Radicalism,* 2nd ed. (1983); G. S. Wilmore and J. H. Cone, *Black Theology: A Documentary History, 1966-1979* (1979). M. R. Sawyer

National Conference of Black Churchmen. *See* NATIONAL CONFERENCE OF BLACK CHRISTIANS.

National Conference of Catholic Bishops. Ecclesiastical organization of the U.S. Catholic bishops* for the exercise of their joint pastoral ministry.* Founded in 1966, the National Conference of Catholic Bishops (NCCB) is the ecclesiastical counterpart of the bishops' civil arm, the U.S. Catholic Conference.* The NCCB was founded to replace the National Catholic Welfare Conference* (NCWC) (1922-1966), which grew out of the National Catholic Welfare Council (1919-1922) and was earlier known as the National Catholic War

Council (1917-1919).

The NCCB membership consists of every bishop and archbishop* in the U.S. and its territories and possessions. It maintains a headquarters in Washington, D.C. Under certain conditions the NCCB's authority is juridically binding on U.S. Catholics, but ordinarily it bears moral authority and serves a role of advocacy and leadership within the American Catholic community.

The administrative committee is composed of bishops, four elected episcopal* officers and a professional staff headed by a General Secretariat. In 1987 there were twenty-five standing and nineteen ad hoc committees dealing with matters as diverse as the Campaign for Human Development, the preparation of pastoral letters,* liturgical* and doctrinal regulations, ecclesiastical boundaries, the training and supply of priests* and female religious* and relations between the U.S. Church and the Vatican.* In recent years Archbishop John Quinn of San Francisco; John Cardinal Dearden, formerly of Detroit; Joseph Cardinal Bernardin of Chicago and Bishop Joseph Malone of Youngstown, Ohio, have been among the Conference's most prominent leaders. In 1987 Archbishop John L. May of St. Louis was president and chairman of the Administrative Committee.

BIBLIOGRAPHY. E. B. McKeown, "The National Bishops' Conference: An Analysis of Its Origins," *CHR* 66 (1980):565-583; C. J. Nuesse, "The National Catholic Welfare Conference," in L. J. Putz, ed., *The Catholic Church, U.S.A.* (1956).

D. L. Salvaterra

National Conference of Christians and Jews. A nonprofit civic organization of individuals committed to the advancement of understanding, dignity and justice among peoples of various religious, racial and socioeconomic backgrounds. The National Conference of Christians and Jews (NCCJ) began in 1928 as a campaign of good will. Among those instrumental in the founding of the NCCJ were Chief Justice Charles Evans Hughes; clergyman* S. Parkes Cadman*; Carlton J. H. Hayes, who served as first Catholic* co-chairman; Roger Williams Straus, first Jewish co-chairman; and Newton D. Baker, first Protestant* co-chairman. These and other leaders were outraged at the campaign of hatred directed toward a Catholic, Alfred E. Smith,* who was Democratic nominee for president. Furthermore, they were appalled at the hostility shown toward Catholics, Jews and African-Americans by the Ku Klux Klan, a very visible organization that had the support of millions. This social climate provided the catalyst for the modest beginning of the NCCJ. Today, as a strong national organization, the NCCJ has remained unchanged in its original purpose: the elimination of prejudice and discrimination.

A variety of programs are sponsored annually by the NCCJ. These include conferences, seminars and workshops which focus on study, analysis, experimentation, research, discussion, consultation, conciliation, teaching and shared experience. In recent years interfaith programming has included Christian/Jewish/Muslim dialog, a Christian study group on Judaism and the Jewish people, and an interseminary project involving professors and students from the major religious traditions. The NCCJ also works closely with Hispanics,* Asians* and other immigrant groups.

Community, ethnic and religious networks under Conference sponsorship aim at building understanding, cooperation and a workable pluralism among all peoples. Presently, more than seventy-five regional offices of the NCCJ assist in this effort.

BIBLIOGRAPHY. *The Directory of Religious Organizations in the United States,* 2nd ed., (1982); "Aims to Harmonize National Groups," *The New York Times* (Sunday, December 11, 1927):1.

M. R. Wilson

National Council of Catholic Men. A national federation of Catholic men's organizations. The National Catholic Welfare Conference* established the National Council of Catholic Men (NCCM) in 1920 to help promote Catholic* lay action through federating Catholic men's organizations at the parish,* diocesan* and national level. Recently, however, support for separate men's groups has been replaced by programs joining lay men and women to address issues affecting not only Catholics, but all persons. After 1980 the NCCM became dormant at the national level, having already merged many of its programs with the new national Secretariat of the Laity. NCCM's ministries are now part of the numerous social and educational projects sponsored by that office of the United States Catholic Conference.* Today, some Councils of Catholic Men still operate at the local level, and a titular national president exists.

NCCM sought to federate all the men's organizations in each Catholic diocese as participants in the lay apostolate.* In the 1960s approximately 10,000 men's societies with a total membership of about nine million were affiliated with the NCCM. A staff at the national office in Washington, D.C., oversaw its programs in several areas: spiritual and religious activities; communications, which established a branch office in New York City for radio and television broadcasts; civic and social action; public policy; family life; youth programs; and international affairs.

NCCM was especially effective in its ministry of the Catholic media and of lay development. As the agency responsible for all scheduled Catholic radio and TV programs, the NCCM "Catholic Hour," aired on NBC radio since 1930, attracted a large listening audience of Catholics and non-Catholics. Following Vatican II,* NCCM actively supported the development of lay expertise at the parish level through the newly regularized parish councils,* which sought to share the administration of parishes between the pastor and the lay council. NCCM produced publications to educate the laity, such as the highly successful "Program Manual for Parish Meetings," and offered intensive training courses for lay leaders in Scripture* and liturgy.*

In the wake of Vatican II, as before, NCCM performed valuable service in educating and motivating laymen to their potential as Christians living in the world. Outside the Catholic community, NCCM programs mobilized Catholic men's organizations to fight racism, anti-Catholic prejudice, obscenity and discriminatory practices in education and in employment.

See also LAY MOVEMENT, MODERN CATHOLIC.

BIBLIOGRAPHY. J. Hennessey, *American Catholics* (1981); M. H. Work, "National Council of Catholic Men," *NCE* 10.   P. M. Kane

National Council of Catholic Women. A national federation of Catholic* lay women's organizations. The National Council of Catholic Women (NCCW) is a federation of 8,000 Catholic Women's organizations from 123 dioceses in the U.S.* As a service agency, its programs extend from the parish level to diocesan, state, national and international programs. It is an affiliated organization of the National Council of Catholic Bishops* and the United States Catholic Conference.* NCCW is governed by a biennial convention which elects NCCW's officers. Its board of directors is comprised of its elected officers, six program chairmen and directors selected from American ecclesiastical provinces.

In 1919 when the American Catholic bishops* established the National Catholic Welfare Council,* they founded a Department of Lay Organizations, which in 1920 separated into the NCCW and the National Council of Catholic Men.* As the first national Catholic women's organization to represent women's societies, NCCW intended to unify the work of Catholic women in church, family and society, and to broaden the scope of women's service. The emergence of NCCW after World War 1* reflected the emerging Catholic middle class in America, as well as the general phenomenon of American women's organizations founded on a spiritual basis for social service. In 1926 NCCW affiliated with the World Union of Catholic Women's Organizations (WUCWO) and also founded the first residential school to train women in social service, called the National Catholic School of Social Service, and located in Washington, D.C. In 1947 the school was incorporated into the Catholic University of America.*

Highlights of NCCW programs during the 1930s and 1940s included an NBC radio series entitled "Call to Youth," voluntary organization work during World War 2,* and aid to children who survived the Holocaust.* In the 1950s and 1960s, NCCW expanded its international outreach to aid refugees in Hong Kong and Macau. Beginning in 1958 NCCW also supported Mother Teresa's clinic in Calcutta. Individual members sponsored children and orphans in Korea beginning in 1961, which initiated the "Help-a-Child" program. Today, these ongoing international service projects are designated as parts of the "Works of Peace" program. In the 1960s NCCW supported President John Kennedy's Commission on the Status of Women and joined with other women's groups in fighting poverty among young women. The result was a program called WICS, Women in Community Service.

Today, NCCW represents American Catholic women at national and international conferences. Current programs include a volunteer program called RESPITE, which provides services for the families of homebound elderly; a national drug and alcohol awareness day; antipornography efforts at community, state and national levels; programs to assist developing countries administered by Catholic Relief Services; and evangelization programs at the parish* and diocesan levels.

BIBLIOGRAPHY. J. Hennessey, *American Catholics* (1981); M. Mealey, "National Council of Catholic Women," *NCE* 10.   P. M. Kane

National Council of Churches of Christ in the U.S.A. A cooperative ecumenical* agency representing thirty-three denominations.* The National Council of Churches of Christ in the U.S.A. (NCCC) was founded in Cleveland, Ohio, on November 28—December 1, 1950, and was built on the cooperative foundations of the Evangelical Alliance* (1867) and the Federal Council of the

Churches of Christ in America* (1908).

In its beginnings the NCCC brought together twelve interdenominational agencies, including the Federal Council of Churches, the Foreign Missions Conference of North America,* the Home Missions Council of North America,* the International Council of Religious Education,* the United Council of Church Women, and other agencies related to education, stewardship and communications. Its charter membership was composed of twenty-nine denominations, with a combined membership of 33 million church members and 143,000 congregations. These churches, basing their covenantal life on "Jesus Christ as the divine Lord and Savior," included twenty-five Protestant* bodies and four Orthodox bodies. Forty years later its membership involved thirty-two churches with 40 million members, adding mainly Orthodox bodies. Most of the member bodies are the so-called mainline churches,* with the majority of Christian churches in the U.S. remaining outside the NCCC, especially the Roman Catholic,* Southern Baptist,* Lutheran Church—Missouri Synod,* as well as many Pentecostal,* Holiness,* evangelical* and fundamentalist* churches. Representatives of fundamentalism, such as Carl McIntire,* attacked the NCCC with vehemence, particularly during the 1950s.

Throughout its life the NCCC has sought to bring the implications of the gospel to the life and problems of the church and society. Through programs on evangelism,* Christian education,* foreign mission,* stewardship, justice and liberation, international affairs and Christian unity, the NCCC claims as one of its purposes the commitment "to assist the churches in self-examination of their life and witness." Its concern for international understanding and peace has been expressed in its witness to world order, in advocating nonmilitary solutions to tension between nations, and in developing pastoral relations with Christians in countries in Eastern Europe (especially the USSR), Vietnam and China. In the 1960s and 1970s the NCCC, alongside Roman Catholics and Jews, was a special catalyst in the Civil Rights Movement.* For several decades it has been a strong advocate against racism in the U.S., southern Africa and elsewhere. Its work of Bible* translation led to the publication of the Revised Standard Version (1952). It is the arena through which over 250 regional and local councils of churches jointly plan and communicate their work.

The NCCC's most far-reaching ministry is exercised through Church World Service (CWS), an international network of relief, development,

compassion and caring for refugees and other persons in political asylum. Funded largely by an annual offering known as "One Great Hour of Sharing" and by the projects of the regional offices of Christian Rural Overseas Program (CROP), CWS funds represent eighty-five per cent of the NCCC's budget.

In 1981 the NCCC restructured its work and redefined its constitutional nature from "a cooperative agency of the churches" to "a community of Christian communions which, in response to the gospel revealed in the Scriptures, confess Jesus Christ, the incarnate Word of God, as Savior and Lord." In the late 1980s the NCC faced a crisis, with contributions from its membership down fifty per cent from 1975 and its staff cut to 61, down from 187 two decades earlier. In general, this was attributed to the changing status of mainline churches in American culture. The national headquarters of the NCC is located at 475 Riverside Drive in New York City.

See also ECUMENICAL MOVEMENT; ECUMENISM; NATIONAL COUNCIL OF EVANGELICALS; WORLD COUNCIL OF CHURCHES.

BIBLIOGRAPHY. W. C. McKinney, *American Mainline Religion: Its Shape and Future* (1987); R. Wuthnow, *The Restructuring of American Religion* (1988).   P. A. Crow

National Holiness Missionary Society. *See* WORLD GOSPEL MISSION.

National Liberal League. Nineteenth-century association established to combat government promotion of Christianity. A key figure in the organization of the League was Francis Ellingwood Abbot, a Unitarian*-turned-nonsectarian and founder of the Free Religious Association, which advocated scientific theism, a rejection of all dogmatic authority and any reliance on Scripture* for truth about the world and God. Instead, truth was discovered through scientific investigation; an empiricism founded on Darwinian* naturalism. As editor of the *Index*, the mouthpiece for the Free Religious Association, Abbot propounded this extreme form of liberal* and scientific religion.

Opposed to all forms of traditional Christianity, Abbot formed the National Liberal League in 1869 to combat the conservative National Reform Association* which had as its goal a Christian preamble to the Constitution. With the support of the Free Religious Association and such luminaries as Frank Lester Ward and Robert G. Ingersoll,* the National Liberal League fought against any government promotion of Christianity, such as Sunday* observance laws, Bible* teaching in the public schools,* a federal law against obscenity in the mails and the promotion of religious festivals.

BIBLIOGRAPHY. J. C. Furnas, *A Social History of the U.S., 1887-1914* (1969):880-881; R. H. Gabriel, *The Course of American Democratic Thought,* 2nd ed. (1956):216-217.   J. De Vries

National Lutheran Council. A cooperative agency of eight Lutheran Churches* in the U. S. The National Lutheran Council was formed by eight Lutheran Churches (about two-thirds of the Lutherans in the U. S.) after their successful cooperation in ministry to servicemen during World War 1.* In its early years the Council was involved in relief efforts among European Lutherans distressed by war and postwar conditions. In the midst of postwar emotionalism, the Council provided a common voice against threatened legislation to abolish the use of a foreign language in the press, public worship and instruction of the young. The Council also undertook home mission programs in industrial centers, later adding ministries to students in non-Lutheran colleges, as well as ministries to military personnel, including endorsing chaplains.* Relief work, primarily through the agencies that became the Lutheran World Federation,* continued to be important.

After World War 2* the resettlement of refugees became a major emphasis. The Council adopted many of the world missions of European Lutheran Churches that had been orphaned by the disruptions of World War 2, providing staff and administration when German missionaries were interned by the allies. The Council was phased out when the Lutheran Council in the U.S.A.* was formed to include cooperation by the Lutheran Church—Missouri Synod,* as well as the NLC bodies.

See also LUTHERAN CHURCHES.

BIBLIOGRAPHY. R. W. Solberg, *As Between Brothers* (1957); F. K. Wentz, *Lutherans in Concert* (1968).   J. D. Sutherland

National Reform Association. Association founded to restore the U.S. to its Christian* foundation. Reflecting nineteenth-century evangelical* convictions that the U.S. had a messianic national mission in the world, a group of conservative evangelical Christians founded the National Reform Association in 1863. Determined to ensure a Christian America, in 1894 and 1910 they proposed an amendment to the Constitution which would include an acknowledgement of the sovereignty of God and the supremacy of biblical revelation. Their ultimate goal was to tie the republic and Christianity firmly together by means of a solid Christian preamble to the Constitution. The movement gained the support of many Presbyterians,* particularly the Old School* Presbyterian General Assembly* and the Methodist* General Council. Notable evangelicals such as Jonathan* and Charles Blanchard* were involved in the movement. The Association was opposed by the National Liberal League,* founded by Francis E. Abbot* and supported by Robert G. Ingersoll.*

Later, the National Reform Association did battle with Darwinism, and in the twentieth century it joined with a host of other fundamentalist* groups in seeking to uproot the doctrine of evolution* from public schools and colleges across the country. The Christian Amendment Movement, organized in 1946 and supported by the National Association of Evangelicals,* was a revival of the concerns of the National Reform Association.

BIBLIOGRAPHY. W. E. Garrison, *The March of Faith* (1933); *National Reform Convention, Proceedings, 1874* (1874); H. F. May, *Protestant Churches and Industrial America* (1963).
                                      J. De Vries

National Religious Broadcasters. Religious broadcasting in the United States began on January 2, 1921, with a program produced by Calvary Episcopal Church in Pittsburgh, Pennsylvania, and aired over KDKA. The oldest licensed radio station in the nation, KDKA had been on the air only two months. The growth of religious broadcasting led to the founding of National Religious Broadcasters (NRB) in 1943. The agency arose out of the National Association of Evangelicals* and presently is a member of that parent organization.

NRB was founded to defend freedom of access to the airwaves and to promote excellence in religious broadcasting. In the earlier years it was heavily involved in protecting the isolated broadcaster, but today it is aggressively engaged in support and enhancement activity (e.g., sponsoring workshops and research projects with the academic-communication community and striving to maintain adherence to the NRB code of ethics and the principles and guidelines for fund-raising, accounting and financial reporting).

In recent years the NRB has come of age. It is consulted regarding federal legislation on broadcasting and telecommunication, and for the last twenty years the president and vice president of the U.S. have appeared at its annual convention in Washington. Jimmy Carter,* Ronald Reagan* and George Bush have been especially active at these conventions. A congressional breakfast is also a regular event at the conventions.

As of 1988 the number of religious radio stations in the U.S. was 1,393 (out of a total of 9,000), and the number of religious television stations was 259. NRB organizational membership stands at 1,300. An executive director guides the organization on a day-to-day basis. Governing NRB is a one-hundred-member board of directors (elected annually), with its president and executive committee.

See also ELECTRONIC CHURCH.

BIBLIOGRAPHY. *Religious Broadcasting* magazine; B. Armstrong, ed., *Directory of Religious Broadcasting* (annual). H. F. Vos

Nativism. A form of American nationalism. Nativism has been defined by historian J. Higham as an "intense opposition to an internal minority on the ground of its foreign (i.e., 'un-American') connections." Its most powerful strain is anti-Catholicism. Other manifestations are a fear of foreign radicals and racial Anglo-Saxonism. Although nativism and anti-Catholicism are not synonymous (indeed, Catholics have been nativists), the two are usually linked and anti-Catholicism has tended to dominate the other nativist traditions.

Outbursts of anti-Catholic nativism have occurred in U.S. history whenever conditions of social and economic stress have conspired to arouse the deep-rooted suspicion that Catholicism is not compatible with American democratic institutions. The Alien and Sedition Acts of 1798 were largely a response to national fears over the French Revolution. After the colonial period, three main waves of anti-Catholic nativism surged through the land.

Nativism in its prototypical form arose in response to the massive influx of European immigrants* from 1830 to 1860. The term dates from this period. Nativist disturbances were concentrated in the urban centers of the Northeast where there were dense immigrant populations. After three incendiary sermons by Lyman Beecher,* whose 1835 *Plea for the West* likened the immigrant threat to the Mississippi Valley to an invasion of Egyptian locusts or northern barbarians, a mob burned the Ursuline* convent at Charlestown, Massachusetts, on August 11, 1834. Serious disturbances occurred in New York and fatal rioting in Philadelphia (1844) and Louisville (1855). In 1853 mobs protested the visit of papal diplomat Archbishop Gaetano Bedini. The Know Nothing Party, or American Party, reached the height of its political power in 1855, after which nativist concerns were overshadowed by the slavery issue.

Anti-Catholic propaganda during this period included bogus tales of sacerdotal lust and infanticide in Maria Monk's *Awful Disclosures of the Hotel Dieu Nunnery in Montreal* (1836) and W. C. Brownlee's biweekly *American Protestant Vindicator* (1834-1842).

The second wave emerged in the period of rapid growth, labor strife and economic difficulty during the decade of 1886-1896. The rural Midwestern American Protective Association (APA) revived anti-Catholic feeling by blaming hard times on Irish Catholic labor leaders and claiming to have uncovered a secret papal plot for Catholic rebellion and the massacre of American Protestants. Democrats were branded the party of "rum, Romanism and rebellion" and APA members pledged never to vote for a Catholic, hire one if Protestants were available or join Catholics in a strike.

The third wave, directed from rural areas against urban Catholic political power and new immigrant groups, erupted sporadically between 1905 and 1930 and embodied itself in such organs as *Tom Watson's Magazine* and the revived Ku Klux Klan.* Although legislative curbs on immigration during the 1920s put an end to one of the chief nativist irritants, New York Governor Alfred E. Smith* would still feel residues of anti-Catholicism in his 1924 and 1928 bids for the presidency. During the 1950s, Senator Joseph McCarthy, himself a latter-day nativist, occasioned new manifestations of anti-Catholicism from such sources as the recently (1947) founded Protestants and Other Americans United for Separation of Church and State. The popularity of Paul Blanshard's *American Freedom and Catholic Power* (1949) showed that suspicions about the patriotism of American Catholics were still very much alive.

To say that the election of John F. Kennedy* in 1960 and his subsequent assassination had destroyed anti-Catholicism as a force in American life would probably be overly optimistic. The endurance of phenomena such as Jack Chick Publications suggests that, given sufficient stimuli, anti-Catholic nationalism might resurface. Nativism in general has tended to give patriotism a needlessly narrow cast and has probably led Catholics to an insufficiently critical embrace of American civil religion.*

BIBLIOGRAPHY. R. Bellah and F. Greenspahn, eds., *Uncivil Religion: Interreligious Hostility in America* (1986); R. A. Billington, *The Protestant Crusade, 1800-1860, A Study of the Origins of American Nativism* (1952); J. Higham, *Strangers in the Land, Patterns of American Nativism, 1860-*

1925 (1963); A. L. Lichtman, *Prejudice and the Old Politics: The Presidential Election of 1928* (1979); A. Greeley, *An Ugly Little Secret* (1977).

W. L. Portier

Natural Law. Binding ethical* principles derived directly from an understanding of the world and particularly of human nature. Acceptance of the idea of natural law is found among both religious and nonreligious thinkers. Its main influence today stems from its expression by the Enlightenment* deists* who provided the intellectual basis for American constitutional democracy* and from its prominent role in Roman Catholic* theology* and ethics, especially Thomism.*

Ancient classical thought abounded with various versions of natural law. Greek thinkers such as Aristotle and the Stoics, as well as Romans such as Cicero, held to the notion that human beings are under a clearly discernible set of ethical prescriptions. Opinions varied as to whether these laws were originally decreed by deity. But what is telling for natural law theory is that, regardless of their origin, these laws can supposedly be discerned apart from any revealed divine commandments.

When the American founding fathers held it to be "self-evident" that all were created equal, they were in fact voicing the conclusions of a natural law theory. This particular strain of thought goes back to John Locke (1632-1704) and Thomas Hobbes (1588-1679), both of whom held (for differing reasons) that government is a natural outgrowth from a society's commitment to protecting the rights and security of the individual. This idea became embodied in the mythical notion of a social contract, according to which our forebears agreed to commit themselves to government which would ensure the maximum liberty and happiness of its citizens. This philosophy is directly reflected in the U.S. Constitution. The Preamble defines the republic as an expression of this social contract, and the Bill of Rights emphasizes that the citizens enjoy particular rights by virtue of their being members of the commonwealth.

Within a Christian context, the starting point for understanding natural law may be in Romans 2:15, where the apostle Paul speaks of the Gentiles as having the law "written in their hearts, their consciences . . . bearing witness." This idea has been minimized by many Protestants,* who emphasize human failure to live up to this law, but it has also become the background for Catholic thinkers such as Thomas Aquinas (1224-1274), who emphasize the reality and obligatory nature of this law.

Aquinas distinguished between various expressions of law, but all legitimate law is derived from the eternal law which has its origin directly in God. One expression of it is the divine law, viz., the directly revealed moral code, including the Ten Commandments. But alongside it, and in complete harmony with it, there is the natural law, which has been installed by God directly in his creation. In general this means that God has made the world in such a way that all things and acts have a purpose, and it is right to promote the divinely intended purpose and wrong to thwart it. But even more importantly, natural law ensures that what is properly human—rights, dignities, obligations—is seen as natural in each human person. Thus the natural law is said to parallel the second table of the Ten Commandments. Human political law must build on natural and divine law, which are both founded on the eternal law.

Catholic natural law theory has made itself felt prominently in twentieth-century America in the context of bioethical discussions. The Vatican has decreed in various encyclicals* (*Humani Generis,* 1950; *Humanae Vitae,* 1968) that natural law can be known by and is binding on all human beings. All forms of artificial birth control* are strictly forbidden because they run counter to natural reproductive purposes. In the abortion* controversy, it is held that all active taking of human life (the fetus) is wrong, even if it involves thereby allowing another human life (the mother) to die passively. On death and the dying, this position holds that extraordinary means to prolong life are not mandated. All such positions have in common the view that God's will should not be understood as ever going counter to the natural order of his creation.

BIBLIOGRAPHY. T. Aquinas, *Summa Theologica* I/II, q. 91-95; R. M. Lemos, *Hobbes and Locke: Power and Consent* (1978); *NCE* 10.

W. Corduan

Natural Theology. The attempt to discover truths about God by means of human reason or empirical observation, without recourse to supernatural revelation. The enterprise presupposes (1) that certain aspects of God's self-disclosure are available to all (general revelation), having been etched in creation and/or in the structures of the human person; and (2) that humans have the ability to perceive this revelation.

The concept originated in ancient Greek philosophy. It was brought into Christian tradition as early as the second century by the apologists who desired to relate the God revealed by Jesus to the Greek philosophical heritage. Many proponents, however, find a foundation for the enterprise in the Bible itself (e.g., Ps 19:1-6; Rom 1:18-20; 2:14-15). Its classic formulation is found in the work of Thomas Aquinas.

Natural theology has been significant in America, especially in the nineteenth century. It was an integral aspect both of conservative and of liberal* theologies. Although attacked by Karl Barth* and de-emphasized by existentialist* theologies, natural theology continues to be prevalent among evangelicals* and Roman Catholics.*

Of the topics investigated by natural theology, the demonstration of God's existence is historically most significant. Four proofs are most widely known: the ontological (the structure of human thought necessitates God's existence), the cosmological (the existence of the world requires a divine first cause), the teleological (the presence of design in the universe requires a divine architect) and the moral (the human sense of being morally conditioned or responsible requires a divine lawgiver). These proofs have been rejected by critics, either as containing logical fallacies or as leading to a philosophical construct rather than to the Christian God.

Four basic viewpoints concerning natural theology and its relation to general revelation predominate. (1) General revelation is the norm, so that all theology is in some sense "natural" (John Cobb); (2) general revelation mandates natural theology, although supernatural revelation is necessary to bring knowledge of saving truth (Thomas Aquinas); (3) general revelation is obscured by sin,* so at best only a limited natural theology may be developed (John Calvin); (4) revelation is present solely in Christ, eliminating both general revelation and natural theology (Karl Barth).

BIBLIOGRAPHY. B. Demarest, *General Revelation: Historical Views and Contemporary Issues* (1982); J. F. Donceel, *Natural Theology* (1962); E. L. Miller, *God and Reason* (1972).   S. J. Grenz

Navigators, The. Evangelical* discipleship* ministry. In 1933 Dawson Trotman* and his wife, Lila, began an evangelistic outreach to sailors based at San Pedro, California. Following his conversion Trotman had been active in the International Fishermen's Club founded by T. C. Horton.* Trotman incorporated the principles of Bible study* and Scripture memorization, prayer,* meditation and witnessing he had learned in the club, as well as what he had learned in his one year

at the Bible Institute of Los Angeles. Trotman's energy, magnetism, directness of manner and love for people helped his ministry grow, and he enlisted a cadre of associates. By 1944 the Navigators had spread into all branches of the United States military, with ministries in 450 Army camps and on 350 Navy vessels. Trotman communicated to the members through his publication, *The Log.*

Beginning in 1940 Trotman began stressing "one-on-one discipleship." Lorne Sanny, who joined the organization that year, developed follow-up materials for new Christians and later assisted Billy Graham* in using these for his crusades. In 1953 Trotman moved the headquarters from downtown Los Angeles to the Glen Eyrie estate at Colorado Springs, Colorado. Then in the summer of 1956, while rescuing a swimmer at the Navigator Conference at Schroon Lake in the Adirondacks, Trotman suffered a fatal cardiac arrest. Lorne Sanny led the organization until June 1986, when Jerry White became the general director.

The Navigators continue in their original purpose of discipling believers, having extended their outreach also to businesspeople, as well as college students on campuses across the U.S. and around the world. By 1986 the organization had expanded into sixty-three countries, twenty of which had their own boards. Of the 2,700 staff members, half were overseas nationals coordinating their efforts through the International Navigator Council that meets annually. NavPress, the publishing arm of The Navigators, publishes in the U.S., Singapore, Korea and Great Britain.

BIBLIOGRAPHY. B. L. Skinner, *Daws: The Story of Dawson Trotman Founder of the Navigators* (1974); D. Hoke, "Sketch of the Month," *His* (September 1944):24-27.   D. G. Buss

Nazarenes. *See* CHURCH OF THE NAZARENE.

Near East Relief. A national voluntary relief effort of the early twentieth century. The American Committee for Armenian and Syrian Relief, formed in 1915 to assist Christian Armenians expelled from the Ottoman Empire and famine victims in Syria, was reorganized in 1919 and given a congressional charter as Near East Relief. Initial support had come from Protestant* missionary* organizations which viewed the Armenians as victims of religious persecution, but emotional appeals to aid the "starving Armenians" and door-to-door solicitation convinced Americans of all persuasions to donate food, clothing and money. The federal government provided transportation, personnel and additional financial assistance. After 1919, Near East Relief aided Greek refugees from Asia Minor, those fleeing the Russian Revolution and disaster victims in Syria, Persia and the Caucasus. In the 1920s it tried to expand its role as a relief agency by developing public health centers, polytechnic schools and rural rehabilitation programs to bring about permanent change. These provided models for Point Four and other post-World War 2* aid programs.

The first large international relief effort voluntarily undertaken by the American people, Near East Relief and its predecessor distributed more than one hundred million dollars in relief, assisted over one million refugees and offered shelter to more than one hundred thousand orphans. In 1930 it became the Near East Foundation.

BIBLIOGRAPHY. R. L. Daniel, *American Philanthropy in the Near East, 1820-1960* (1970).

G. F. Goodwin

Needham, George C. (1846-1902). Evangelist* and Bible conference* leader. Born in Ireland, one of nine children, Needham entered business in Dublin but left after one year to enter evangelistic work. He traveled throughout Ireland and England, a part of the time in the company of Henry Grattan Guinness, a famous Irish evangelist and founder of Regions Beyond Missionary Union.*

Needham came to America in 1868. He made his home in Boston and considered A. J. Gordon* his pastor, but he spent most of his life in an itinerant evangelistic and Bible conference ministry. He wrote more than a dozen books, including biographies of Henry Moorhouse and Charles H. Spurgeon and *Street Arabs and Gutter Snipes* and *Arabs of the City,* the latter two dealing with the problems of children of the urban poor. Needham's solution was emigration from the cities along the lines promoted by Charles Loring Brace and the Children's Aid Society. He was a founder of the Niagara Bible Conference* and active in the early International Prophetic Conferences* which embraced premillennialism.*

BIBLIOGRAPHY. E. R. Sandeen, *The Roots of Fundamentalism* (1970). P. C. Wilt

Neo-Conservative Catholicism. In the late 1960s and early 1970s, a host of new conservative movements arose in reaction to what was perceived as wrong-headed developments in American Catholicism* following Vatican II* (1962-1965). Traditionalist Catholics, associated with Father Gommar De Pauw and the French Archbishop* Marcel Lefebvre, rejected as invalid the post-conciliar liturgical* reforms and emphasized the unalterable nature of the sacramental* tradition.

Other conservative groups—those associated with *The Wanderer,* Catholics United for the Faith and a host of other conservative lay* Catholic organizations—accepted the conciliar declarations and Vatican-initiated reforms but repudiated the liberal interpretations and abuses. They censured unauthorized liturgical experimentations, a resurgence of modernism* in catechetics,* a weakening of magisterial* authority,* the minimizing of the supernatural, a capitulation to secularity and modernity and the creation of an "illusion of pluralism" within the Church.

Neo-Conservative Catholics are primarily those intellectuals who are rooted in the liberal Catholic tradition, but are disillusioned with post-Vatican II liberalism. Although they recognize diverse approaches to common theological* problems, they demand that Catholic theologians* be explicitly faithful to historical orthodoxy* and the authoritative magisterium. They are particularly critical of the post-conciliar development of national episcopal conferences because they tend to increase nationalism and to de-emphasize universality. They also criticize liberal Catholic views of the economic order and support, instead, a form of democratic capitalism* that is founded on theological and moral values and has proven beneficial to the poor and marginal.

BIBLIOGRAPHY. W. D. Dinges, "Catholic Traditionalism in America: A Study of the Remnant Faithful" (unpublished Ph.D. dissertation, University of Kansas, 1983); J. Hitchcock, *Catholicism and Modernity: Confrontation or Capitulation?* (1983); M. Novak, *Confession of a Catholic* (1986). P. W. Carey

Neo-Orthodoxy. Protestant theological movement of the twentieth century. Neo-orthodoxy in America became an important force in the 1930s when a number of theologians* became increasingly dissatisfied and disillusioned with the liberal* theology in which they had been trained. As the works of Europeans such as Karl Barth* and Emil Brunner* became known, their views came to have an increasing effect on American theologians and in mainline* American churches. This influence was strongest from the late 1930s to the 1950s. After that, neo-orthodoxy still maintained a following, though its theological force among ministers and theologians abated.

Neo-orthodoxy is also sometimes called "neo-reformation theology," "neo-Calvinism" or "neo-liberalism." From one perspective, neo-orthodoxy was a rediscovery of central theological themes of the Protestant Reformation, so it represented an attempt to restate these doctrines in a contemporary fashion. Insofar as major proponents of neo-orthodoxy were Reformed,* as opposed to Lutheran,* in their commitments, the movement had a strong Calvinistic flavor. Since many American theologians identified with neo-orthodoxy were former theological liberals, there is also a sense in which the movement represented a renovation or revision of liberalism. Thus, a plurality of labels is appropriate. *Neo-orthodoxy* as a term designated a basic commitment to orthodox* doctrine as the normative expression of Christian faith. Some American theological conservatives, however, opposed the reformulations of neo-orthodoxy and stated that "neo-orthodoxy" was actually "no-orthodoxy."

The Failure of Liberalism. The beginnings of American neo-orthodoxy can be traced to the 1930s, when the full effects of World War 1,* coupled with the economic Depression* in America, began to take their toll on American theologians. These events led them to question and reject the basic tenets of liberal theology. Liberalism stressed a basic continuity between human beings and God. This orientation expressed itself in an emphasis on the immanence, rather than the transcendence, of God, the belief that humanity was inherently good and morally perfectible and thus the view that religious knowledge comes through the use of reason and religious experience.* Liberalism, therefore, was quite compatible with the empirical methods of natural science in which observation and experimentation were key ingredients.

From the liberal perspective, the Bible* was to be subjected to the latest in literary and historical research. It was regarded as the record of the religious experiences of ancient peoples which could be repeated again and again in each generation. The religious truths of these "abiding experiences" were always developing. The task of theologians was to construct categories to describe religious experience in light of contemporary science and culture. These perspectives of liberalism were influenced by the principles of continuity, autonomy and dynamism. In emphasizing these, the formative forces of liberal thought stood in dramatic contrast to traditional Christian orthodoxy.

The Swiss theologian Karl Barth was led to reject liberal theology through his renewed study of Scripture, first expressed in his *Commentary on Romans* (1919; 2nd ed., 1922). Barth, however,

was also shaken when his former theological professors, who had taught him the principles of liberal theology, uncritically supported the Kaiser's policies when World War 1 broke out. These included the historian of dogma, Adolf von Harnack (1851-1930), the major liberal theologian of the day. Harnack had popularized the views of Albrecht Ritschl (1822-1889) who, along with Friedrich Schliermacher (1768-1834), had laid the foundations of liberal theology.

The Influence of Karl Barth. Barth, along with Eduard Thurneysen (1888-1974), Friedrich Gogarten (1887-1967) and Rudolf Bultmann* (1884-1976), began what was known as "dialectical" or "crisis" theology. Directly opposing liberalism, they stressed the absolute contrast between the transcendent God and sinful humanity and emphasized God's initiative in revealing himself in Jesus Christ. The church, they maintained, bears witness to the Word of God in Jesus Christ and must maintain its distinction from the prevailing culture, challenging it with the Word. Barth saw his whole theological enterprise as undoing what Schleiermacher had done. For neo-orthodoxy the starting point of theology was God, as opposed to human experience which marked the beginning for liberalism.

Barth's colleagues eventually carved out their own theological paths. Gogarten joined with Bultmann, the renowned New Testament scholar, to promote his program of "demythologizing" the New Testament. This led them to conflict with Barth. Barth and Brunner initially joined in their opposition to liberalism, but they too were divided by an explosive controversy over Brunner's views on revelation and natural theology as he expressed them in *Nature and Grace* (1934). Barth's heated reply, *Nein!* (1934), maintained that the sole means of God's revelation is Jesus Christ and that there is no "point of contact" in humanity for God's saving action and revelation. Brunner's writings were not as extensive as Barth's, and English translations of his major works became available in America earlier than those of Barth. This factor, together with their less formidable size, helped Brunner's works reach a wider readership and play an early and significant role in shaping American neo-orthodox theology.

The American Movement. In 1939 *The Christian Century,** America's leading liberal theological journal, published a series of autobiographical reflections by American mainline church leaders. This series, known as "How My Mind Has Changed," has been an occasional feature of the journal ever since. The 1939 articles revealed a significant theological shift overtaking American theologians. Thirty-two of the thirty-four contributors noted the emerging "theology of crisis" proposed by Barth and Brunner. Throughout the 1930s books and articles by liberal Protestants questioned the viability of liberalism. Henry P. Van Dusen* wrote of "The Sickness of Liberal Religion" (1931), Wilhelm Pauck* asked "What Is Wrong with Liberalism?" (1935) and Henry Sloane Coffin* questioned "Can Liberalism Survive?" (1935). In 1935 Harry Emerson Fosdick* preached a sermon entitled "Beyond Modernism," which was published in *The Christian Century*. There he claimed the church must not accommodate itself to modern culture but challenge it.

Early neo-orthodox proponents in America included Walter Lowrie,* H. Richard Niebuhr,* Wilhelm Pauck, George W. Richards,* Edwin Lewis* and Elmer Homrighausen.* While they did not necessarily follow Barth's theological method, they did take note of Barth and his critique of liberalism. For instance, Reinhold Niebuhr,* in *Moral Man and Immoral Society* (1932), emphasized the neo-orthodox theme of the radical nature of human sinfulness and recognized the unrealistic optimism of Protestant liberalism, which was incapable of dealing effectively with the social conditions of the times. Later, however, Niebuhr joked that an even better title for his volume would have been *Immoral Man and Even More Immoral Society*.

For many of that era the events of world history, characterized by social upheaval, political instabilities and economic disasters, called for a more realistic assessment of the relationship between God and humanity. Kierkegaard's "infinite qualitative difference" between God and humanity was adopted by Barth and Brunner, who emphasized the "crisis" of the confrontation of a holy God with sinful humans. For them, God was the "Wholly Other" who revealed himself only in Jesus Christ, the Word of God. In Christ, God acted to transform human sinfulness by giving the gift of faith for salvation through the work of the Holy Spirit. The Bible was the witness to God's revelation in Christ.

Neo-orthodoxy came to prominence in the wake of World War 2.* During the 1940s and 1950s, neo-orthodoxy's realism was welcomed by many in mainline Protestant denominations.* As an alternative to liberalism and fundamentalism,* it offered a fresh means of hearing the gospel. By locating the focus of revelation in Jesus Christ, to whom Scripture witnesses, neo-orthodoxy seemed to offer a way of allowing the Bible to serve as a source of doctrine without demanding literary or historical perfection. Neo-orthodoxy was particularly strong in the Presbyterian Church in the U.S.A.* There it affected the church's ministers, its doctrinal deliberations and the church-school curriculum. The denomination's Princeton Theological Seminary,* under the leadership of John A. Mackay,* became a major center for neo-orthodox theology. The Confession of 1967,* adopted as part of the church's confessional standards, shows a number of neo-orthodox emphases.

However, as America moved into an era of progress and increasing prosperity in the decades following World War 2, neo-orthodoxy began to wane as a dominant theological force. Some have noted that whereas neo-orthodoxy had chastised liberalism for only reflecting its culture's optimism, neo-orthodoxy was reflecting its culture's despair. When America moved into better times, the appeal of neo-orthodoxy lessened. By the 1960s theology had become issue-oriented in response to powerful forces of secularism.* During the 1970s and 1980s process theology* and liberation theology* became major theological movements, gradually eclipsing the influence of neo-orthodoxy.

As a theological position, however, neo-orthodoxy maintains strong individual adherents. Its emphases on the transcendence of God coupled with a strong sense of human sin has been a part of many of the theologies of evangelicalism in America. In particular, a number of prominent American theologians have noted the impact of Karl Barth's theology on their own theological formation. In that sense, neo-orthodoxy still exerts an influence and its perspectives continue to shape American Christian thought.

See also LIBERALISM/MODERNISM, PROTESTANT.

BIBLIOGRAPHY. S. E. Ahlstrom, *A Religious History of the American People* (1972); S. E. Ahlstrom, "Continental Influence on American Christian Thought since World War I," *CH* 21 (1958):256-272; K. Cauthen, *The Impact of American Religious Liberalism* (1962); W. Hordern, *The Case for a New Reformation Theology* (1959); D. K. McKim, ed., *How Karl Barth Changed My Mind* (1986); D. N. Voskuil, "America Encounters Karl Barth, 1919-1939," *FH* 12 (1980):61-74; D. N. Voskuil, "American Protestant Neo-Orthodoxy and Its Search for Realism (1925-1939)," *Ultimate Reality and Meaning* 8 (1985):277-287. D. K. McKim

Neo-Thomism. A modern movement in philosophy and theology, largely among Roman Catholic* thinkers, which applies the thought of St. Thomas Aquinas (1224-1274) to current issues. All forms of Thomism hold in common: (1) a commitment to reason as an acceptable way of attaining some theological truths; (2) the finite being as open to God; (3) a philosophical psychology stressing the composite unity of body and soul; (4) an ethic based on natural law. (*See* Thomism.)

There are two distinct trends in twentieth-century Neo-Thomism, both manifesting themselves in North America. The revival of a very traditional interpretation of Aquinas has centered around figures such as Jacques Maritain (1882-1973) in Europe and Etienne Gilson (1884-1978), director of the Pontifical Institute for Medieval Studies in Toronto. This school of Thomism attempts to return to the thought of Aquinas himself as opposed to his later interpreters. Representatives embrace Aristotelian language, endorse a rigorous cosmological argument and generally hold to conservative theological formulations. Because their philosophical starting point is in the objective givenness of being, they may be referred to as "existential Thomists."

Another strain of Thomism is characterized by the belief that the best way to be faithful to Aquinas is not simply to repeat his ideas, but to philosophize the way he did, by creatively interacting with modern thought. Thus, thinkers such as Karl Rahner* and the Canadian Jesuit Bernard Lonergan* have achieved a version of Thomism which attempts to take seriously the contributions made by Immanuel Kant (1724-1804) and Kantian philosophy in general. The thought of Aquinas is seen as starting with the human subject and the categories of being. This brand of Thomism has also lent itself to synthesis with the existentialism* of Martin Heidegger (1889-1976) and others. Tending to de-emphasize the objective cosmological argument, it argues for discovering the need for God in the framework of the individual's subjective experience. Known as "transcendental Thomism," it is more adaptable to modern theological expressions.

Thomism has traditionally been at home within Roman Catholic theology. In its history of rising and waning popularity, it is currently on a downward trend. But now it is being propagated by some evangelical* thinkers, who have found it a valuable apologetic* tool.

BIBLIOGRAPHY. N. L. Geisler and W. Corduan, *Philosophy of Religion,* 2nd ed. (1988); E. Gilson, *The Christian Philosophy of St. Thomas Aquinas* (1956); B. J. F. Lonergan, *Insight: A Study of Human Understanding* (1957).

W. Corduan

Nettleton, Asahel (1783-1844). Congregation-al* clergyman* and conservative revivalist.* Born in Killingworth, Connecticut, Nettleton was first a farmer, but after his conversion* in 1801 he eventually enrolled in Yale (B.A., 1809) where he became a protege of Timothy Dwight.* Nettleton became interested in evangelism* during his postgraduate studies under Bezaleel Pinneo and volunteered for missionary* service. Although his poor health prevented travel abroad, Nettleton's gifts for ministry were quickly recognized. In 1811 he was ordained* by the Litchfield (Connecticut) Consociation, and for over a decade he served as an itinerant* revivalist in New England and New York.

Nettleton's sober methods of revivalism stood in stark contrast to the progressive "new measures"* of Charles G. Finney.* Nettleton and his colleague Lyman Beecher* feared Finney's increasing power and attempted to protect New England from the sensationalism associated with the frontier revivals* of the Second Great Awakening.* The confrontation between these conservative "Watchmen of the East" and the progressive Western revivalists issued in a conference held in New Lebanon,* New York, in July 1827. Eighteen notable evangelists of the Second Great Awakening attended, but to Nettleton's dismay, the conference served to unite the contending parties. As participants debated the virtues of the "new measures," a broad consensus about the nature and methods of revivalism emerged. Even Beecher, chief among the early critics of the Westerners' techniques, and formerly Nettleton's closest ally, was won over to the opposition. In 1833 Nettleton and other conservatives, notably Bennet Tyler,* founded the Theological Institute of Connecticut (later renamed Hartford Theological Seminary) to combat "new measures" revivalism and the increasingly progressive "New Haven theology"* of Yale's Nathaniel W. Taylor* and Lyman Beecher.

BIBLIOGRAPHY. *AAP* 2; *DAB* VII; *DARB*; W. R. Cross, *The Burned-Over District: The Social and Intellectual History of Enthusiastic Religion in Western New York, 1800-1850* (1950); B. Tyler, *Memoir of the Life and Character of Rev. Asahel Nettleton, D.D.* (1844).

J. R. Fitzmier

Nevin, John Williamson (1803-1886). Mercersburg* theologian* and controversialist. Born near Shippensburg, Pennsylvania, Nevin was raised and educated as a Presbyterian,* graduating from Union College (B.A., 1821) and Princeton Theological Seminary* (1826), where he studied with Charles Hodge,* and later replaced Hodge as instructor of Bible and oriental languages (1826-

1828). When Hodge returned from his studies in Europe, Nevin accepted a post at Western Theological Seminary near Pittsburgh where he taught for a decade. By 1840, when Nevin was called to Mercersburg Seminary of the German Reformed* Church, he had come strongly under the influence of the writings of German theologians such as Isaac A. Dorner (1809-1884) and Johann A. W. Neander (1789-1850). For a period of over three years, Nevin served as the sole professor at the Seminary while also holding (1841-1853) the position of president of Marshall College. With the added stimulus brought by the coming of Philip Schaff* to Mercersburg in 1844, the work of Nevin and Mercersburg Seminary began to rise in prominence in the larger theological world of the U.S.

Just one year earlier, Nevin had burst upon the American theological scene with his critique of American "new measures"* revivalism,* *The Anxious Bench* (1843). American revivalistic individualism* and sectarianism, said Nevin, violated a true sense of the church* and seriously devalued the sacraments.* As an alternative, he advocated a system of nurture based on catechetical* instruction. Nevin's fully developed understanding of the Lord's Supper* appeared in 1846 as *The Mystical Presence: A Vindication of the Reformed or Calvinistic Doctrine of the Holy Eucharist.* Nevin argued that the Reformed churches in America had lost the essential position of Calvin on the Eucharist* in favor of a Zwinglian memorialist doctrine.

From 1849 to 1852 Nevin served as primary contributor and editor of the *Mercersburg Review,* the chief organ for disseminating the Mercersburg Theology. During much of that period, Nevin and Schaff were involved in the often-acrimonious debates within the German Reformed Church over the relationship between Protestantism* and Roman Catholicism.* In his zeal to defend the Church of Rome against what he perceived to be unfair attacks by Protestants, and due to his own intensive study of the Church Fathers, Nevin developed deep sympathy for Roman Catholicism. Indeed, for a time in 1852 it appeared that Nevin might ally himself with the Church of Rome, but after a period of retirement and convalescence, Nevin emerged as a defender of Protestantism. Nevin lectured at Franklin and Marshall College from 1861 to 1866 and served as president of that institution from 1866 to 1876. The last decade of his life was spent in retirement.

Nevin's most important contributions to theology and church life in America were his critique of the "Sect spirit" and the excesses of revivalism, and

his emphasis on the importance of tradition and the church. He was one of the most influential and controversial figures in the German Reformed Church in America.

BIBLIOGRAPHY. T. Appel, *The Life and Work of John Williamson Nevin* (1889); *DAB* VII; *DARB*; *NCAB* 5; J. H. Nichols, *Romanticism in American Theology: Nevin and Schaff at Mercersburg* (1961).　　　　　　　　　　　　S. R. Graham

Nevius, John Livingston (1829-1893). Presbyterian* missionary* to China. Born near Ovid, New York, Nevius attended Union College, Schenectady, and Princeton Theological Seminary* (B.D., 1853) where he decided to become a missionary. Assigned to Ning Po, China, under the Presbyterian Mission Board, he was there for several years (1854-1859) and then spent a brief period in Japan (1859-1861) where he worked on a *Compendium of Theology* for the Chinese church. Two more terms were spent in Shantung Province at Tungchow (1861-1864) and Chefoo (1871-1893).

Nevius objected to the conventional practice of missions boards paying national evangelists for their services. On the occasion of a visit to Korea in the early 1880s, he formulated what he believed to be the biblical view of church planting based on 1 Corinthians 7:20, "Let every man abide in the same calling wherein he was called" (AV). Missionary churches should be self-supporting, self-propagating and self-governing units, Nevius concluded. His treatise, published in China in 1885, appeared in book form the following year and appeared in two successive editions by 1889. In 1890 missionaries in Korea invited Nevius as a consultant to review their field, after which the Korean Presbyterian Church experienced extraordinary growth. From 100 communicant members at that time, the church grew to 30,000 in 1910 and 100,000 in 1933. When his *Planting and Development of Missionary Churches* was issued in a fourth edition after World War 2,* the Korean Presbyterians reported 800,000 communicants.

Nevius also applied his principles with notable success in his work in central Shantung. Nevius' theories were made required study for missionary candidates and had an obvious influence on subsequent theories of church planting and growth. Despite the widespread acceptance of his methods, however, Nevius faced resistance from contemporaries who questioned the arbitrariness of paying foreign workers and insisting on self-support for national ministers, as well as the criticism that after Nevius left Shantung, the church there failed to exhibit the characteristics he expected. Later studies, moreover, suggest that rapid church growth in Korea has resulted as much from fortuitous circumstances as from the application of Nevius' methods.

BIBLIOGRAPHY. C. Clark, *The Korean Church and the Nevius Methods* (1930); *DAB* VII; H. S. C. Nevius, *The Life of John Livingstone Nevius* (1895). E. A. Wilson

New Age Movement. The 1980s in America witnessed a rising interest in the New Age Movement (NAM), an umbrella term referring to a spiritual movement involving a variety of individuals, events, organizations, ideas and practices. The unifying essence of these manifold movements is a pantheistic and monistic world view focused on the supposed unlimited powers of the unshackled self; its agenda is impelled by a messianic and millennial ideology (sometimes bostered by astrological anticipations) of a New Age of peace, light and love soon to break forth. New Age influences can be found in areas as diverse as medicine, psychology, science, politics, business and education.

The NAM is both eclectic and syncretistic, drawing on sources as diverse as Vedantic Hinduism, assorted varieties of spiritism and avant garde theories in quantum physics. It is best viewed not as a unified denomination,* sect,* cult* or conspiracy—although these factors are not lacking—but rather as a world view shifting away from both monotheism and atheistic materialism, and toward the "ancient wisdom" or "perennial philosophy" (A. Huxley) of various Eastern religions (e.g., Hinduism, Buddhism, Taoism, etc.), pre-Christian Western religions (e.g., Druidism), Christian heresies (Gnosticism, heterodox mysticism) and the occult (e.g., divination, magic, spiritism).

The NAM draws on these diverse sources and often filters them through American sensibilities. For instance, the Eastern doctrine of reincarnation has historically often been both fatalistic and pessimistic: one is consigned by karma to the wheel of suffering. When adapted to suit American tastes, reincarnation is viewed as a ticket to unlimited advancement.

Marilyn Ferguson, whose best-selling *The Aquarian Conspiracy* (1980) is a primary document of the NAM, notes that "the emergence of the Aquarian conspiracy [NAM] in the late twentieth century is rooted in the myths and metaphors, the prophecy and poetry, of the past."

The most recent historical roots of the NAM in America are traced to the counterculture of the 1960s, when a variety of non-Christian spiritual gurus, swamis and yogis established themselves as alternatives to the "establishment" religions of Christianity and Judaism. The "Asian invasion" (C. Raschke) was aided by Western countercultural critics such as Alan Watts (1915-1973), Theodore Roszak (1933-) and Timothy Leary (1920-), who rejected Christian orthodoxy* and embraced forms of non-Christian mysticism. Although by the late 1970s the cult explosion had lost much of its dynamism, the pantheistic/monistic world view of the Eastern emissaries had taken root in the culture, and it began to play a significant part in American experience. What was once seen as exotic and esoteric—such as yoga—came to be acceptable in the pluralistic smorgasbord of modern America.

Yet the counterculture's display of "alternative altars" (R. Ellwood), while dramatic, wasn't the first of its kind in America. In many ways the vagabond spirituality of the "beat generation" of the 1950s, spearheaded by the literary experiments of Allen Ginsberg (1926-) and Jack Keroac (1922-1969), primed the cultural pump. A century earlier other spiritual movements had challenged the Christian consensus. Although the American ethos has historically been predominately Christian, freedom of religion often provided an opportunity for diverse religious expression.

The New England Transcendentalist* movement (1836-1860), best known for the literary efforts of Henry David Thoreau (1817-1862) and Ralph Waldo Emerson* (1803-1882), opened the West to the mysticism of the East by rejecting Calvinism* and experimenting with orientalism. Emerson's poem "Brahma" is but one example.

The Spiritualist movement dates from about 1848, when the Fox sisters of New York claimed contact with the dead. Although the sisters later confessed to fraud, Spiritualism garnished a distinguished roster of believers, including Elizabeth Barrett Browning, Horace Greeley, Sir Oliver Lodge and Sir Arthur Conan Doyle, who subscribed to its generally pantheistic philosophy.

In 1875 the Theosophical Society was founded in New York City by Helena P. Blavatsky (1831-1891) and Col. Henry Olcott (1832-1907). Theosophy emphasized the teachings of "Ascended Masters" (contacted by Blavatsky) and a religious syncretism that was essentially a pantheistic monism hostile to Christian orthodoxy. Theosophy proved to be fertile soil for other esoteric movements such as Rudolf Steiner's (1861-1925) Anthroposophy and Alice A. Bailey's (1880-1949) Arcane School.

The New Thought,* or Mind Cure, movement of

the late nineteenth century also contributed to the erection of alternative altars, such as Christian Science,* Religious Science and the Unity School of Christianity*—all of which emphasized the unlimited powers of the unlocked mind, especially in relation to physical healing. These groups drew terminology and concepts from Christianity while denying orthodox doctrines such as sin,* the saving work of Christ and a literal heaven and hell.*

Eastern spirituality gained another American foothold at the World Parliament of Religions* at the Chicago World's Fair in 1893. Participants gathering from around the globe shared syncretistic assumptions and called for greater religious tolerance. The darling of the conference was the charismatic Swami Vivekananda (1863-1902), who later set up Vedantic societies in America.

Two theological liberals,* Teilhard de Chardin (1881-1955) from France and Paul Tillich* from Germany, also contributed to New Age sensibilities in America—Teilhard through his utopian evolutionary emphasis and Tillich through his theology of God as the impersonal "Ground of Being."

Modern evangelical* critics have voiced concern over the NAM's influence both inside and outside the church and have called for a better understanding and application of biblical orthodoxy. Some critics, taking an apocalyptic* view, have tended to limit their critique to labeling the NAM as the harbinger of Antichrist, while others have adopted an apologetic* for facing a rival world view. Theologically liberal respondents such as Harvey Cox (*Turning East,* 1977) have sometimes criticized aspects of the NAM but have been more willing to incorporate New Age elements into their theological understanding. In the 1980s the Dominican* priest Matthew Fox was teaching what he called "Creation Spirituality" in books such as *The Coming of the Cosmic Christ* (1988) and through his Institute in Culture and Creation Spirituality. Clearly a proponent of the New Age perspective, in October 1988 Fox was ordered silenced by the Vatican's Congregation for the Doctrine of the Faith.

BIBLIOGRAPHY. H. G. Cox, *Turning East* (1977); R. S. Ellwood, *Alternative Altars* (1979); M. Ferguson, *The Aquarian Conspiracy* (1980); D. R. Groothuis, *Unmasking the New Age* (1986); W. R. Martin, *Kingdom of the Cults* (1965); C. A. Raschke, *The Interruption of Eternity* (1980); C. T. Jackson, *Oriental Religions and American Thought* (1981).

D. R. Groothuis

New Birth. An experience of Christian conver-

sion* in which a person is born again,* being spiritually regenerated* by the work of the Holy Spirit. The term reflects the evangelical* emphasis on spiritual regeneration as the mark of a true Christian.*

The New Birth is synonymous with being "born again." Both terms are derived from John 3:3-8, which records Jesus' words to the Pharisee Nicodemus on the necessity of being "born again" in order to "see the kingdom of God." The concept of New Birth assumes a spiritual deadness to God that can only be remedied by God's Spirit recreating spiritual life. Because this spiritual deadness is the result of a sinful nature and sinful acts, the New Birth must be accompanied by the human response of faith and repentance of sin.*

The early Puritans* maintained true conversion to be the prerequisite for church membership,* and thus the New Birth became the goal of the periodic conversionist preaching directed toward New England's second and third generation of church attenders. The necessity of the New Birth was the hallmark of George Whitefield's* preaching throughout the period 1740-1760, and largely through his influence it became the overarching theme of the revivalist* preaching of the Great Awakening.* Jonathan Edwards,* also an advocate of the New Birth, speculated that the experience imparted a supernatural knowledge that was immediate, "not making use of any intermediate natural causes." However, with the Second Awakening of the nineteenth century came an emphasis on the proper environment and the role of the human will in achieving the New Birth. This Arminian* influence within evangelical revivalism came to replace the earlier prevailing Calvinist understanding of the New Birth. The New Birth has continued to be an essential element of evangelicalism in America, though today the experience is more frequently referred to as being "born again."

The Editors

New Divinity. *See* NEW ENGLAND THEOLOGY.

New England Theology (1750-1850). The Pietist* revivals* in New England, known as the "Great Awakening," shattered the harmony of the established Congregational* churches of Massachusetts, Connecticut and New Hampshire, reawakening questions that had lain unresolved from the inception of the New England Way* in the seventeenth century

New Divinity Men. The most visible party to emerge within Congregationalism was the Edwardseans, or New Divinity* Men, who took Jonathan

Edwards* as their leader and mentor. Edwards was vitally concerned to formulate a Calvinistic moral theology, and his major works—*Original Sin* (1758), *Freedom of the Will* (1754) and *True Virtue* (1765)—were largely intended to inhibit the influence of eighteenth-century secular and benevolist moral philosophy within Calvinism. Edwards regarded the experimental* piety* of the revivals as a practical corollary to his efforts, leading him to embrace the pietistic strain of Congregational ecclesiology and to provide a series of justifications for closed Communion and diminished sacramental* efficacy.

After Edwards's death in 1758, his work was carried on by his students, Joseph Bellamy,* Samuel Hopkins* and Jonathan Edwards, Jr. Bellamy's *True Religion Delineated* (1750) set up the basic platform of the New Divinity. The New Divinity Men developed many of Edwards's issues for the next generation, especially: (1) the restatement of Calvinism in its most extreme and provocative forms; (2) the justification of revivalism based on Edwards's reconciliation in *Freedom of the Will* of the "moral inability" of sinners to repent with their "natural ability" to do so; and (3) moral rigorism, especially seen in Hopkins's demand for ethics based on "disinterested benevolence."

The New Divinity Men also reflected many of Edwards's ambiguities as well, especially concerning: (1) a governmental view of the atonement*; (2) the understanding of faith in terms of infusion rather than imputation; and (3) the definition of personal identity. This last problem, which grew from difficulties in Edwards's immaterialist perception of the self, divided the New Divinity Men into the "Taste Scheme," which asserted the existence of an independent spiritual substance underlying each personality, and the "Exercise Scheme," which defined personal consciousness as purely the continuous immediate creation of God.

Old Calvinists. The second major grouping in post-Awakening Congregationalism was Old Calvinism or Old Lights,* which like Edwards wanted to preserve New England Calvinism, but more in terms of the pre-Awakening *status quo* than by means of revivals. They sharply repudiated Edwards's espousal of revivalism and his philosophical justifications for Calvinist theology. Philosophically, Old Calvinism was drawn to the moderate Enlightenment* and Scottish Common Sense* moral philosophy. Ecclesiastically, it preferred parish* nurture by "use of the means" (sacraments,* preaching*) rather than immediate conversion* as the entrance to church membership.* Their most visible symbol was the perpetuation of

the Half-Way Covenant.*

This brought them into conflict with the New Divinity at every major point and sparked several major controversies, especially James Dana's* attack on *Freedom of the Will* and Edwards's immaterialism in 1770 and 1773, and the debate between M. Mather and Bellamy over the Half-Way Covenant. Their most systematic thinkers were Moses Hemmenway,* Timothy Dwight* and, in the 1820s, Nathaniel W. Taylor,* who successfully provided an alternative framework to Edwards for understanding the operation of the will in Calvinist as well as intuitionist terms. Lyman Beecher* and Jedidiah Morse* also contributed anti-Unitarian* polemics and organized opposition to the influence of Deism* and church disestablishment.

The institutional stability of the Old Calvinists gave them a decided advantage over the New Divinity Men, and the rise of theological seminaries* after 1812 as the principal means of training clergy* enabled them to obtain a virtual monopoly of clerical education. Andover Theological Seminary* was organized in 1808 as a joint venture between New Divinity and Old Calvinists in Massachusetts, but the Old Calvinist influence eventually came to predominate. The organization of Yale* Divinity School in 1822 gave the Old Calvinists complete control of professional clergy education in New England. The last major conflict between the two parties—the "Taylor-Tyler" controversy—occurred after the delivery of Taylor's *Concio ad Clerum* at Yale in 1828. The remaining New Divinity forces, under Bennet Tyler,* organized their own small theological seminary in East Windsor, Connecticut (later known as Hartford Theological Seminary), and moved out of the mainstream of New England theology. Old Calvinism, always stressing institutional and philosophical adaptability, was itself changing by 1850, and Horace Bushnell's* *Christian Nurture* (1847) represents an important transition between Old Calvinism and New England liberal* theology.

Unitarianism. Unitarianism constituted a third major response within Congregationalism to the Awakening, in that the Awakening demonstrated to them the impracticality of Calvinism as a religion for enlightened men. They embraced, not the materialist determinism of English Unitarians like Joseph Priestley,* but a liberalized Calvinism that deleted original sin* and the atonement, and added Arian or Socinian views of the person of Christ. The most important leaders of the Unitarians were Jonathan Mayhew* and, toward the end of his life, Charles Chauncy.* In 1803 the Unitar-

[811]

ians captured the Hollis Chair of Divinity* at Harvard* with the installation of Henry Ware,* an event which generated ferocious controversy between Unitarian and Trinitarian Calvinists. Similar controversies were sparked by William E. Channing's* manifesto, *Unitarian Christianity* (1819), a vigorous attack on Calvinism which resulted in an important and extended debate between Leonard Woods* and Henry Ware (the "Wood 'n Ware" controversy*) in 1820. This was aggravated by the Dedham Decision* of 1820, in which the Massachusetts Supreme Court awarded the property of a Trinitarian congregation to the overwhelmingly Unitarian parish in which it was located. In 1825, 125 Unitarian congregations formed the American Unitarian Association,* and in 1865 a separate Unitarian denomination was finally organized. The Unitarians, however, were geographically restricted almost entirely to eastern Massachusetts, and while they commanded the loyalty of much of the upper class of Boston, they failed to spread beyond that circle to any appreciable degree.

Both the friends and the enemies of the Awakening suffered their own internal dissensions and schisms. Extreme proponents of the revivals erected a short-lived Separate Congregational association, as well as a number of radical sects such as the Free-Will Baptists,* Universalists* and Shakers.* The Unitarians were also shaken by the defection of Ralph Waldo Emerson* in 1832 and the subsequent development of Transcendentalism,* which rebelled against the restraints of Channing's more conservative Unitarianism. A brief flowering of Deism, as represented by Ethan Allen's *Reason, the Only Oracle of Man* (1784), effectively died out after 1800.

BIBLIOGRAPHY. G. N. Boardman, *A History of New England Theology* (1899); F. H. Foster, *A Genetic History of the New England Theology* (1907); S. E. Mead, *Nathaniel William Taylor* (1942); D. W. Howe, *The Unitarian Conscience* (1970); J. Conforti, *Samuel Hopkins and the New Divinity Movement* (1981); A. C. Guelzo, *Edwards on the Will: A Century of American Theological Debate* (1989); J. Haroutunian, *Piety Versus Moralism: The Passing of the New England Theology* (1932); B. Kuklick, *Churchmen and Philosophers* (1985); S. Marini, *Radical Sects of Revolutionary New England* (1981).

A. C. Guelzo

New England Way. The unique system of church government* that evolved in Massachusetts Bay in the 1630s. By 1649 the central tenets of the New England Way were complete and codified in the Cambridge Platform.* Central to that system of government was the desire to create churches that were both "pure" in membership* and powerful in directing the outward governance of the New England towns.

In striving to create pure churches (from which their label *Puritan* derived), the Puritans sought to make the "visible" church of Christ conform as closely as possible to the "invisible" church of God's elect.* In terms of church government, this ideal meant that before joining a church, prospective members had to testify to a work of divine grace in their lives. Only then could they seek membership in the local church.

Beyond the requirement of personal testimony, the Puritan Way of pure churches meant that power would be distributed among the membership in such a way that no individual or group, including elders,* pastors,* presbyteries* or synods,* could ever have unchecked authority* over the local congregation. Puritans reasoned that if the Bible* was to be a truly sovereign Word of God, then all human powers and institutions would have to be limited. In practice, this meant that all power was concentrated within the individual or "particular" congregation. Synods or presbyteries comprised of neighboring elders and ministers could "advise" particular congregations on questions of who should be their minister or how a particular issue should be resolved, but they could not compel the local church to do or say anything they did not will. Within particular congregations, moreover, power was distributed equally between the laity* and the elders and ministers such that each checked and balanced the other. Congregations alone called and ordained their ministers. But once ordained, ministers alone could speak for God in public assemblies, and the laity had to submit to their teachings. In cases of gross ministerial negligence or heresy,* congregations retained the power to remove their pastors from office.

By balancing church powers and limiting membership to visible saints, the Puritans hoped to maintain their purity in the manner of Old World "sects." But unlike those sects who enjoyed no temporal powers in England, the Puritans established their churches as the law of the land, much like the Church of England.* And here the coercive aspects of the New England Way became readily, even painfully, apparent. The New England Way was not a way of religious liberty* but of conformity to Puritan teachings. Inhabitants either conformed to their authority and teaching or they were banished. Local and provincial government existed explicitly to uphold the local churches through mandatory taxes and legislation derived from Puritan readings of Scripture.* Thus the government could and did enact laws making church attendance compulsory and establishing civil penalties for such crimes as idolatry, blasphemy, heresy, profanity or contempt of religious authority.

As a system of church government, the New England Way depended on a like-minded core of citizens. Such a way would have been impossible to institute in diverse Old World societies. But it was perfectly adapted to the circumstances of New World settlement in New England, and it survived intact throughout the colonial era.

BIBLIOGRAPHY. P. Miller, *Orthodoxy in Massachusetts, 1630-1650* (1933); E. S. Morgan, *The Puritan Dilemma* (1958).

H. S. Stout

New Evangelicalism. A movement among American conservative evangelicals* in the 1940s, 1950s and 1960s to reform fundamentalism* and restore evangelical Christianity's influence in modern life.

Harold John Ockenga,* the scholarly pastor* of Park Street Church in Boston, and the president of the newly founded Fuller Theological Seminary* in Pasadena, California, was probably the first to coin the term *new evangelicalism* in 1948. Ockenga called this movement "progressive fundamentalism with a social message." It appealed to many younger Northern fundamentalists who felt that their movement needed to be purged of its sectarian, combative, anti-intellectual and anticultural traits. They saw their work as a strategic part of a larger evangelical program of world evangelization and Christian cultural renewal.

Recent trends fortified their hopes. The National Association of Evangelicals,* founded in 1942, was mobilizing new cooperative ventures. The Youth for Christ* movement and Billy Graham's* rise to national fame lent momentum to the cause. And the many evangelicals who were now solidly established in the American middle class gave the new evangelicalism a constituency.

New evangelicalism as a concept and a movement was largely the work of theologians.* Harold Ockenga was its organizational leader, and Fuller Theological Seminary, the home of several of the movement's leading spokesmen, such as Carl F. H. Henry* and Edward J. Carnell,* was its early stronghold. Other important leaders emerged, including Baptist theologian Bernard Ramm, who had studied with Karl Barth*; Vernon Grounds of the Conservative Baptist* Seminary in Denver; and

several scholars at Wheaton College,* Illinois, notably Merrill Tenney and Kenneth Kantzer. Other centers of the new evangelicalism were Gordon (now Gordon-Conwell) Seminary; the Evangelical Theological Society*; and *Christianity Today,* a biweekly magazine founded in 1956 under the editorship of Carl Henry and with support from Billy Graham.

From this network emerged a strategy for regaining cultural influence. While Billy Graham and the growing parachurch* organizations fostered popular religious vitality, the new evangelical intellectuals sought to lead a broad evangelical coalition and shape the life of the mind. They hoped to sweep away the stigma of fundamentalism and recapture the influence that their nineteenth-century ancestors had enjoyed.

At the same time, the new evangelicals were committed to holding the fundamentalist line against liberal* theology. When militant fundamentalists accused them of doctrinal innovation, the new evangelicals countered that they were restoring fundamentalism's original spirit. New evangelical theology did resemble earlier fundamentalism. In particular, it made the inerrancy* of Scripture* the keystone of orthodoxy.*

The new evangelicals made some significant changes, however. Beginning with George Ladd's* *Crucial Questions about the Kingdom of God* (1952), many abandoned dispensational* theology and rejuvenated the ethically important idea of the kingdom of God's* partial realization in the present age. New evangelicals also tried several modern philosophical approaches to apologetics.* Bernard Ramm's *The Christian View of Science and Scripture* (1954) offered a similar rapprochement with modern science. And perhaps the most important change was a qualified acceptance of biblical criticism.*

By the mid-to-late 1950s, the new evangelicals were beginning to earn some of the recognition they craved. Their brightest intellectual star, Edward Carnell, was publishing his apologetics and voicing his opinions in outlets formerly limited to liberal Protestants. *Christianity Today* was developing a large readership and dispelling negative stereotypes, Billy Graham was a respected international celebrity.

But by the late 1960s, the new evangelicalism began to break apart. On the stormy cultural front, the new evangelicals' instinctive political conservatism no longer commanded a consensus. On the ecclesiastical front, the sheer diversity of evangelical movements and an increasing recognition of the range of options for evangelical faith and life destroyed the semblance of a unified coalition.

Faced with either the disintegration of the movement or perhaps its takeover by a growing "open evangelical" party, a group of conservatives, led by *Christianity Today* editor Harold Lindsell, made the inerrancy of the Bible the test of evangelical fidelity and waged open battle against the progressives. The result was further fragmentation. By the late 1970s and early 1980s, while evangelicals of many kinds flourished and influenced public affairs, the aging champions of the new evangelicalism spoke sadly of their failed dreams.

Yet their achievements were many. The new evangelical pioneers won some respect in the theological academy. They and their proteges produced a substantial body of biblical scholarship. The evangelical seminaries* they built are now among America's largest and most rigorous. A few evangelical professors now hold chairs at prestigious university divinity schools. In the arts and sciences, the evangelical college* network is prospering, evangelical scholars have multiplied many-fold, and a few have become leaders in their fields. Perhaps the new evangelical vision of "remaking the modern mind" was too triumphal, monolithic and presumptuous. But the result has been a growing commitment to scholarship as kingdom work and a determination to confront the problems of the modern world.

BIBLIOGRAPHY. M. Erickson, *The New Evangelical Theology* (1968); G. Marsden, *Reforming Fundamentalism* (1987); R. Nash, *The New Evangelicalism* (1963); M. Noll, *Between Faith and Criticism* (1986). J. A. Carpenter

New Hampshire Confession of Faith. A widely influential summary statement of Baptist moderate Calvinism,* originally drafted in 1833. In late eighteenth-century New Hampshire, support for the previously dominant rigid Calvinism was waning. On June 24, 1830, the state Baptist convention appointed a committee to prepare a declaration of faith and practice consistent with the more moderate views of the churches. The document, which was to have been completed by the following year, was revised by several drafting committees. It was finally approved by the convention board on January 15, 1833, and recommended to the churches for adoption.

After 1850 the Confession gained stature in the wider Baptist fellowship. It was disseminated by the publications of influential leaders, including J. Newton Brown, who had prepared the 1833 draft; the Landmark* Baptist James M. Pendleton*; and Edward T. Hiscox, author of a widely used Baptist

manual. During the 1920s the Confession became a point of tension among the Northern Baptists. An attempt by some fundamentalists to secure its adoption by the Convention was rejected as a move toward creedalism.* In 1933 a group of conservative churches withdrew from the Northern Convention to form the General Association of Regular Baptists* and adopted a premillennial* version of the Confession as their standard. The Southern Baptist Convention* used the Confession as the basis for a document published in 1923 under the title *Baptist Faith and Message*. This was later revised in 1963.

The Confession is organized according to the general pattern of the Reformed creeds. The subjects discussed follow the order: Scripture,* God, Fall, salvation* and sanctification,* church (including civil government) and last things. Readily evident is the attempt by its drafters to articulate a moderate Calvinism during an era of theological controversy. Calvinist emphases are present, but subdued, both in the order in which the articles appear and in the descriptions themselves. Election,* for example, is not described until article nine, after statements on the Fall and salvation. Salvation, according to the document, is prevented only by personal voluntary refusal and the perseverance of the saints means that only those who endure to the end are real believers.

The article on consummation is short and omits any reference to rapture,* tribulation or millennium.* The opening article contains what is now a classic Baptist statement concerning Scripture: "It has God for its author, salvation for its end, and truth, without any mixture of error, for its matter. . . ."

See also BAPTIST CHURCHES IN CANADA; BAPTIST CHURCHES IN U.S.A.

BIBLIOGRAPHY. E. T. Hiscox, *The Baptist Directory* (1876); W. L. Lumpkin, *Baptist Confessions of Faith* (1974); W. J. McGlothlin, *Baptist Confessions of Faith* (1911). S. J. Grenz

New Harmony. Site of Harmonist (1814-1824) and Owenite (1825-1827) utopian communities in southwest Indiana on the Wabash River. New Harmony was first the site of a utopian community founded by Swabian separatists from the established Evangelical Lutheran* Church in Württemberg, Germany. Members of the Harmony Society and followers of Johann Georg Rapp,* they advocated Pietism,* pacifism* and baptism* of believers, and opposed confirmation, Communion and oaths. Having immigrated to America around 1803, 1,200 followers had first settled in Harmony,

Pennsylvania. Eight hundred Rappites founded New Harmony in 1814.

The Rappite community practiced celibacy and a Christian communism modeled after the practice of the early church as it was described in Acts 2 and 4. All of this was carried out in preparation for the imminent return of Christ. New Harmony became an outpost of civilization as Rapp's followers cultivated 2,000 acres, built 180 buildings and operated a bank. They carried on trade with twenty-two states and ten foreign countries. Their school for both sexes, extensive library, original choral and instrumental music, town band and printing press (on which was printed Rapp's *Thoughts on the Destiny of Man* in 1824) made the town a cultural oasis. The community disbanded in 1824.

In 1825 New Harmony was purchased by Robert Owen,* a wealthy cotton manufacturer and social reformer from New Lanark, Scotland. Rapp and his disciples had moved to Pennsylvania to build Economy (now Ambridge). Owen invited the general public to join his model, non-sectarian Community of Equality in which communal living, science and education would free their minds and bodies, perfect their characters and become the foundation of a worldwide secular millennium. Through his partner, William Maclure, Owen attracted Pestalozzian educators, naturalists, geologists and other scientists. Their infant and cooperative industrial schools, among the earliest in America, and their scientific works printed on New Harmony's press attracted attention long after communal living was abandoned in 1827. The first geological surveys of Indiana and the Midwest were conducted from the New Harmony laboratories of David Dale Owen, Robert's son. Twenty-six historic buildings remain to this day.

See also MILLENARIAN MOVEMENTS.

BIBLIOGRAPHY. D. F. Carmony and J. Elliott, "New Harmony, Indiana: Robert Owen's Seedbed for Utopia," *Indiana Magazine of History* 76 (September 1900):161-261; D. E. Pitzer and J. Elliott, "New Harmony's First Utopians," *Indiana Magazine of History* 75 (September 1979):225-300. D. E. Pitzer

New Haven Theology. A modified Calvinism* defined primarily by Nathaniel W. Taylor* and developed by the faculty of Yale's* Divinity School from the early 1820s into the 1840s. This theological school of thought was also known as "Taylorism" after its chief spokesman, Nathaniel W. Taylor, who along with Eleazar T. Fitch (1791-1871) and Chauncey A. Goodrich* established the Theological Department at Yale* in 1822. From that platform, and under the banner of "Calvinist orthodoxy," Taylor and his colleagues combined a rationalistic system based on God's moral government and a "reasonable" revivalism* that appealed to the "common sense" of Jacksonian America.

As a young pastor at the First Church in New Haven, Taylor dedicated himself to promoting Connecticut revivalism with Lyman Beecher,* to improving on Jonathan Edwards's* famous analysis of the freedom of the will and to countering Samuel Hopkins's* view of a sinner's powerlessness before regeneration.* The major tenets of "Taylorism" were propounded in Taylor's "Man, A Free Agent Without the Aids of Divine Grace" (1818), Fitch's "Two Discourses on the Nature of Sin" (1826) and other signed and unsigned articles in the *Christian Spectator.* As Yale professors in the early 1820s, the New Haven theologians* helped lead the battle against Boston Unitarianism.* But by 1828 conservatives within their own coalition of Congregational* and Presbyterian* Calvinists had begun to challenge the innovations being taught at Yale—innovations the conservatives would decry as heresy* through the next decade. Taylor's *Concio ad Clerum* (1828) restated the New Haven position on original sin* and responded to the heresy charge. *Concio* began a series of works defending New Haven Theology that would culminate in the publication of Taylor's two volumes on *The Moral Government of God* in 1859, a year after Taylor's death and at least a decade after attention had shifted from Taylorism to Taylor's greatest student, Horace Bushnell.*

As Yale faculty members, the New Haven theologians formally endorsed the "substance" of orthodox* Calvinist doctrine as found in the Westminster Confession* and Connecticut's Saybrook Platform.* They affirmed God's sovereignty, human depravity, the sinner's responsibility for personal sin, the justification* by faith through Christ's atonement* and the necessity of the soul's regeneration* by the special influence of the Holy Spirit. But they discarded the "secondary doctrines" or "explanations" that had been attached to these articles of faith. God was indeed sovereign, they argued, but within an eminently rational system of moral government. God revealed his reasonable laws intelligibly and always abided by them himself. He governed free moral agents by motives rather than force. Human depravity, they also argued, was a fact: human beings, always and everywhere, sin.

But the theologians rejected the explanation of depravity that described Adam's sin being imputed to all his descendants, for it robbed individuals of their status as moral agents, made God the author of sin and simply defied "common sense." Human beings are born into the world not with a sinful nature, but with a morally neutral instinct for their own happiness (self-love). At the first moment of moral agency, people choose the world over the ultimate good, and self-love becomes selfishness. Taylor wrote that this first sin, like every subsequent one, was "a man's own act, consisting in a free choice of some object rather than God." Although it is certain that individuals will choose to sin, at every moment they have "the power to the contrary." Similarly, they have the power to effect their own regeneration, but lack the will to do so until the Holy Spirit makes its forceful appeal to their understandings. All of this, the New Haven theologians claimed, could still be called "Calvinism," but more importantly, it was the truth of the gospel confirmed by a person's reason, the "candle of the Lord."

BIBLIOGRAPHY. F. H. Foster, *A Genetic History of New England Theology* (1907); J. Haroutunian, *Piety Versus Moralism: The Passing of the New England Theology* (1932); B. Kuklick, *Churchmen and Philosophers: From Jonathan Edwards to John Dewey* (1985); S. E. Mead, *Nathaniel W. Taylor: 1786-1858: A Connecticut Liberal* (1942); E. A. Pope, "The Rise of the New Haven Theology," *JPH* 44 (1966):24-44.   C. Grasso

New Lebanon Conferences. The meeting convoked (July 18-26, 1827) in New Lebanon, New York, for the purpose of obtaining a consensus on appropriate methods in Calvinistic revivalism.* The occasion for the meeting was the denunciation by Asahel Nettleton* of the "New Measures"* being introduced by Charles G. Finney.* Although both Finney and Nettleton represented the New England Theology* and admired Jonathan Edwards's* model of revival, Nettleton urged restraint and cooperation by itinerant revivalists with local ministry, whereas Finney stressed that sinners could readily repent and encouraged revivalists to defy uncooperative ministers who resisted on predestinarian* or other grounds.

Although both sides, represented by eighteen Congregational* and Presbyterian* ministers (including Lyman Beecher*) agreed on the legitimacy and importance of Calvinistic revivals, there was considerable debate over the role of women in leading revivals, the propriety of itinerant revivalists defying the local ministry and the use of "audible groaning, violent gestures, and boisterous tones" as well as "irreverent familiarity with God"

in revival preaching. Most of these problems were understood to be directed at Finney's "New Measures." Contrary to some accounts, no debate over Calvinism itself took place. No binding conclusions could be reached by the Conference, and the failure of the Conference to restrain the "New Measures" signaled the decline of Nettleton's influence and the consequent rise to national prominence of Finney.

See also REVIVALISM, PROTESTANT.

BIBLIOGRAPHY. L. Beecher, *Autobiography,* 2 vols. (1865); C. G. Finney, *Memoirs of Rev. Charles G. Finney* (1876); "Minutes," *The Christian Examiner and Theological Review,* vol. 4 (1827).

A. C. Guelzo

New Lights. The term *New Light* emerged in New England during the Great Awakening* (1740-1743) to describe the evangelical* supporters of George Whitefield* and the mass revivals* he inspired. In confronting the question of whether the revivals were a work of God, New Lights argued strenuously in the affirmative. Far from threatening true religion, they insisted, the state of religion in New England was never healthier than when drenched by the "showers of converting grace" issuing from the revivals.

The New Light party of Congregational* ministers and churches could be found throughout New England, but they were especially strong in the rural and frontier regions where there were fewer settled churches. In Northampton, where the forces for revival were always strong, the pastor Jonathan Edwards* emerged as the pre-eminent champion of the New Light party. In defending the revivals Edwards shifted the focus of attention away from the head to the heart or the "affections." In place of what he believed to be the overly intellectualized faith of the Old Lights,* Edwards proposed a model of the faithful self that stressed the interconnections of thought and emotion so that neither existed prior to or without the other. For every word that signified an idea, Edwards believed there was an accompanying sentiment of love or hatred, so that it was impossible to think of reaching the head before the heart. In his classic *Treatise on the Religious Affections* (1746) Edwards asserted that: "All acts of the affections of the soul are in some sense acts of the will, and all acts of the will are acts of the affections." As such, true religious experience* involved a new "sense of the heart," transforming the individual from love of self to love of God.

Beyond his theological defense of the revivals, Edwards championed an extemporaneous, heartfelt style of preaching in the pulpit that generations of New Light ministers sought to emulate. Through his printed sermons and the "School of Prophets" established in his household, Edwards taught a generation of New Light ministers how to articulate their extemporaneous sermons in glowing terms that warmed the hearts of their listeners. His two most famous students—Samuel Hopkins* and Joseph Bellamy*—absorbed his teaching and passed it on to their students, who in turn filled pulpits throughout Connecticut and western New England. In that sense the Congregational New Light tradition lived on in American culture and went on to inform a broad segment of what would eventually become the American "evangelical" tradition. *See also* OLD LIGHTS.

BIBLIOGRAPHY. E. S. Gaustad, *The Great Awakening in New England* (1957). H. S. Stout

New Lights (Canada). Followers of the revivalist* Henry Alline* in Nova Scotia. Alline, the "Apostle of Nova Scotia" was born in Newport, Rhode Island, and moved to Nova Scotia with his parents in 1760. He underwent a conversion experience in 1775, and the following year he embarked on a lifetime of preaching, traveling throughout much of Nova Scotia and what later became New Brunswick, bringing his message of the necessity for a "new birth"* to the pre-Loyalist Yankees of the region. Though he organized only a small number of separate, but short-lived, congregations, his itinerant ministry and his writings exerted a profound affect on the religious life of the Maritimes and parts of northern New England. Alline sat lightly to formal ecclesiastical structures, holding together whatever organization there was by the force of his personality.

Largely self-taught, Alline drew particular inspiration from the writings of the English Non-Juror, William Law (1686-1761), and through Law, from the mystic Jacob Boehme (1575-1624). The result was a somewhat idiosyncratic mixture of mysticism,* asceticism and anti-Calvinist theology.*

In the years following his death, Alline's ecclesiastical and theological influence tended to run in two distinct directions. The Baptists* of the Maritimes absorbed most of the remaining New Light churches and, while rejecting much of his formal theology in favor of more Calvinistic* emphases, adopted what one historian has called Alline's "revivalistic paradigm." On the other hand, the New England Free Will Baptist* movement, under the leadership of Benjamin Randall,* built on the foundations of Alline's thought. In social terms, the Allinite revival has been seen as furnish-ing the Nova Scotian "Yankees" with a new identity in which they saw themselves, in Rawlyk and Stewart's phrase, as "A People Highly Favoured of God."

BIBLIOGRAPHY. J. M. Bumsted, *Henry Alline, 1748-1784* (1971); G. A. Rawlyk, "New Lights, Baptists and Religious Awakenings in Nova Scotia 1776-1843: A Preliminary Probe," *JCCHS* 25 (1983):43-73. R. W. Vaudry

New Measures. The style of revivalism* espoused by Charles G. Finney* which highlighted the place of human effort in obeying divine laws to promote religious awakenings.* Finney started his revivalist work in the "Burned-Over District"* of Western New York in the mid 1820s. Ordained* by the Presbyterians,* he had studied law. Since his primary purpose was multiple individual conversions, he used some highly criticized methods (or measures) to achieve results. Exerting direct and often public pressure on individuals, sometimes by name, he pressed for an immediate decision about conversion. Other innovations included sustained prayer, women praying in mixed groups, encouragement of lay* participation and the anxious bench.* These means reflected a conviction that it was possible for any human to choose to make a commitment by faith. Revival would occur whenever Christians utilized the proper God-given means. Influential laypersons supported Finney and his successful methods, but prominent clergymen Lyman Beecher* and Asahel Nettleton* confronted Finney in 1827. While Beecher (and many others) soon relented in their attack, Nettleton, who typified "old measures" revivalism with its emphasis on the divine initiative, never withdrew from his attack.

Finney did not invent these measures. For over two decades the Methodists had been using equivalent measures, adapting the measures used in the Cane Ridge* revival to both urban and rural settings with little controversy. In their case, the measures were compatible with their theology and mission.

BIBLIOGRAPHY. R. Carwardine, *Transatlantic Revivalism, Popular Evangelicalism in Britain and America, 1790-1865* (1978); K. J. Hardman, *Charles Grandison Finney, 1792-1875* (1987). M. R. Fraser

New Religious Right. The New Religious Right is a social, political and religious movement started in the late 1970s and reaching its peak during the early to mid-1980s. The core of the movement is a loose alliance of social and political groups, including most notably the Moral Majority,* led by Baptist* pastor Jerry Falwell.* Most supporters are fundamentalist* Christians with theologically and politically conservative views. The most important goal of the movement has been to attack the influences of secular humanism* in politics and society by restoring traditional moral views and lifestyles consistent with biblical prescriptions. Although the overall impact of the New Religious Right is the subject of widely varying interpretations, the most significant contributions have been the political mobilization of millions of conservative Christians and the inclusion of its major issues, such as abortion* and school prayer,* in the national political agenda.

The most prominent group within the movement has been the Moral Majority, founded in 1979 by Jerry Falwell, pastor of a Baptist church in Virginia and televangelist* on the "Old Time Gospel Hour." Several other political organizations have been part of the New Religious Right. They include Christian Voice, headed by Robert Grant, with Gary Jarmin as the Washington lobbyist; Concerned Women for America, under the leadership of Beverly LaHaye; the Freedom Council, formed by Pat Robertson,* who heads the Christian Broadcasting Network and who was an unsuccessful candidate for the Republican presidential nomination in 1988; the defunct National Christian Action Coalition, directed by William Billings; the Religious Roundtable, a loose coalition of group leaders organized by Ed McAteer; and an umbrella organization called the American Coalition for Traditional Values, formed by Tim LaHaye.

The size of the movement is subject to various interpretations. At its peak, the Moral Majority numbered about four million, while Christian Voice numbered 400,000, and the mailing list for Concerned Women for America numbered approximately 100,000. It is difficult to estimate size because most of the organizations do not have dues-paying members; the various estimates reflect mailing lists rather than active participants. Public-opinion surveys seeking to identify people who support the New Religious Right have shown that the movement appeals to rural, less-educated, white fundamentalist Christians who are members of independent Bible churches in the South and the Midwest.

The historical roots of the New Religious Right lay in the emergence of fundamentalism in the 1920s as a reaction to the modernism* that swept through mainline* Protestantism.* These fundamentalists tended to withdraw from the evils of society and worked to maintain theological purity in the churches. Gradually, however, various fundamentalist groups ventured into the political arena, motivated by such lifestyle issues as prohibition* and gambling and by the strong anti-Communism of the Cold War period.

The more recent stimulus for the movement lay in the perceptions of conservative fundamentalists that the U.S. was coming under the influence of liberal secularism, reflected in Supreme Court* decisions about prayer* and Bible* reading in public schools and about abortion, in the political demands of feminists and homosexuals, and in the efforts by government agencies to regulate Christian day schools.* The major goal of the movement is to restore traditional moral values to American society by rooting out secular humanism, an ideology that denies God and emphasizes human reason as the ultimate authority.

The movement is theologically conservative, with a strong commitment to the Bible as the infallible word of God. They claim that all people have sinned* against God's commands and must be saved* through the death of Jesus Christ. There is an emphasis on being born again* as evidence of repentance and conversion.* Lifestyle issues are important, as they try to live according to the clear principles of Scripture. Most are premillennialists* and dispensationalists.* Some are charismatics,* but most are not.

The political platform of these groups includes stands against abortion, the Equal Rights Amendment, homosexuality, pornography and greater government involvement in education and welfare. The groups strongly support prayer in public schools, free-enterprise economics, tax credits for private schools, gun control, capital punishment,* a strong national defense and support for the nation of Israel. The platform closely mirrors that of the Republican Party. What distinguishes the New Religious Right from other conservative movements is the breadth of issues covered; many of the earlier efforts were focused more narrowly on anti-Communism or on social issues, ignoring economics and education.

To achieve these goals the leaders developed a network of state and local organizations, usually led by conservative Christian pastors who would use their pulpits to encourage voter registration and to make pronouncements on moral and political issues. These local organizations worked to eliminate pornography, picket abortion centers and protect Christian day schools from government interference. Nationally, the movement supported the presidential candidacy of Ronald Reagan,* spawning such organizations as Christians for Reagan. In the congressional elections of the 1980s, some of the groups developed lists of liberal legislators targeted for defeat. Voters in these election districts were flooded with information about the secular liberalism of the incumbents. One organization, Christian Voice, distributed a Morality Report Card rating each member of Congress on the basis of a dozen legislative votes. In addition to these electoral activities, at least three of the groups (Moral Majority, Christian Voice and Concerned Women for America) established lobbying offices in Washington, D.C.

The strength of the New Religious Right has come from the entrepreneurial leadership of individuals such as Falwell, Robertson and the LaHayes. In addition, the close ties with religious broadcasters (Falwell's Old Time Gospel Hour, Robertson's Christian Broadcasting Network and the 700 Club program) have helped to reach an audience open to their conservative political and religious appeals. The organizations have also mastered the use of such information technology as direct mass-mailings to flood millions of homes with their literature. Unlike some new movements, the New Religious Right has understood the importance of grass roots or local organization, relying on a network of conservative churches already upset with the secularization of American society. Finally, the movement has derived strength from its impressive media visibility and from the intensity of its critics.

Critics of the New Religious Right, led by Norman Lear's People for the American Way and the American Civil Liberties Union, have argued against this mixing of religion and politics, claiming that such use of political power to force sectarian morality on society is a violation of the separation of church and state. They have perceived the movement as undermining the tolerant pluralism needed for democracy. The movement has also been criticized for being confrontational rather than cooperative and for being simplistic in its policy analysis. Others have seen the movement as an expression of civil religion,* which uses religious symbols and terminology to justify patriotic nationalism and to legitimize political stances that are essentially ideological rather than religious. Finally, some have claimed that the leaders have been selective in their use of Scripture* to support political stands and that the groups have ignored societal evils such as racism, poverty and pollution.

The total impact of the New Religious Right on American politics and society has not yet been determined. The groups have succeeded in edu-

cating and mobilizing a segment of the population that had been politically inactive; the most conservative accounts suggest that at least two million people have become registered voters as a result of these efforts. Although movement leaders claim credit for electing Ronald Reagan and a more conservative Congress, the election data suggest that the New Religious Right rode along on a tide of conservative attitudes among the electorate. The 1988 presidential election was divisive for the movement in that the charismatic segment supported the political aspirations of Pat Robertson, while others championed George Bush or Jack Kemp. The groups have not been successful in achieving their major legislative goals, such as a human life amendment and school prayer.

Several factors detract from the potential of the New Religious Right. First, it is trying to mobilize a group of people who have traditionally been reactionary and separatist.* Second, it has accumulated members and funds largely because of the heightened media visibility. With less coverage, it will be difficult to maintain the fervor of the constituency. Third, its leadership is not constant. Jerry Falwell, for example, decided in 1986 to devote more of his attention to his church in Virginia, and his departure has reduced the visibility and fund-raising ability of the Moral Majority. Pat Robertson failed to win the Republican nomination in 1988 because his support base was too narrow. Finally, fund raising for religious organizations dropped in the late 1980s, due to scandals plaguing Jim Bakker* and Jimmy Swaggert.*

BIBLIOGRAPHY. D. Bromley and A. Shupe, *New Christian Politics* (1984); G. Fackre, *The Religious Right and Christian Faith* (1982); J. Falwell, *Listen, America!* (1980); R. Liebman and R. Wuthnow, *The New Christian Right* (1983); R. J. Neuhaus, *The Naked Public Square* (1984). R. Zwier

New School Presbyterians. New School Presbyterianism was the prorevivalist version of nineteenth-century Presbyterianism* that had strong ties to New England Congregationalism* and for the middle third of the century existed as a separate denomination.* Its origins lay in the evangelical* awakening of the first third of the nineteenth century (*See* Second Great Awakening), especially enhanced by the Plan of Union* of 1801 that created a working alliance between Presbyterians and Congregationalists on the western frontier of upstate New York and the Midwest.

New School Presbyterianism, however, was not perceptively different from the broader evangelical movement that nurtured it until it was attacked by

Old School Presbyterians* in the 1830s. Until then, it was part of an evangelical phalanx that shared a common commitment to evangelism* through revivals* and to Christianizing America through moral reform.* Perhaps the best early representative of the New School spirit was Lyman Beecher.* His easy movement between Congregationalism and Presbyterianism, support of revivalism, moral absolutism in reforming the nation and relative laxity in adhering to the Westminster* Standards were all indicative of the New School mentality.

Growing apprehension among Presbyterians over the taint of heresy* because of the close connections with New England paved the way for denominational schism in 1837-1838. Initial theological concerns had been expressed regarding the innovations of Samuel Hopkins* ("Hopkinsianism"), but even more serious reservations were expressed over the revisions of Calvinist* orthodoxy* made by Nathaniel Taylor* (*See* New Haven Theology). Taylor's reinterpretation of original sin* and his affirmation of unregenerate man's "power to the contrary" in resisting sin and choosing good were alleged to be the source of infection in explaining New School doctrinal innovations. Thus, with the 1831 heresy trial* of New School Presbyterian minister Albert Barnes,* known as a social reformer and biblical commentator, open party warfare within the Presbyterian Church commenced.

Between 1831 and 1836 the Old School party brought heresy charges against Barnes (twice), George Duffield (1794-1868) and Lyman Beecher, only to have the defendants acquitted in each case. Frustrated, Old School partisans mustered a majority at the 1837 General Assembly* (*See* Auburn Declaration) where they abrogated the Plan of Union of 1801 and, making that action retroactive, thereby eliminated four synods* formed under the Plan. That action cut the strength of the New School in half. The 1838 General Assembly completed the schism by refusing to acknowledge the New School representatives from the deposed synods.

In assessing the causes of the division, allied theological differences seem to have been the primary issue, although the extent and the significance of the variance is debatable. New School toleration of theological diversity was certainly a reality, but it is questionable how prevalent the New Haven theology actually was among Presbyterians. Complicating the perceived theological issues, however, were other factors as well. Old School Presbyterians favored a stricter meaning of confessionalism* and a more rigorous polity for

exercising church discipline* than did their New School counterparts. Moreover, Old Schoolers were wary of Presbyterian participation in the Evangelical United Front* of voluntary societies* that functioned independently of the control of the institutional church. New School zeal for interdenominational cooperation and its endorsement of the theology and practice of revivalism, including even the "New Measures"* of Charles G. Finney,* also greatly troubled Old School Presbyterians. Finally, the vexing issue of slavery shaped the division, with New Schoolers being more ardently abolitionist* (but not uniformly so) than Old Schoolers.

From 1837 until the reunion in 1869, New School Presbyterians existed as a separate denomination. As such, a discernible shift in spirit occurred. Determined to prove their authenticity as Presbyterians, New Schoolers became more doctrinally vigilant (their 1837 Auburn Declaration became virtually a theological creed* and thus a check on further innovation), more distinctly Presbyterian and hence more narrowly denominational in their outlook. Cooperative ventures with Congregationalists steadily declined in the 1840s until the latter terminated the Plan of Union in 1852. New School independence of thought was sustained by its own theological periodicals (e.g., *American Biblical Repository, Presbyterian Quarterly Review* and the *American Presbyterian and Theological Review*) and ministerial leadership supplied by its own seminaries (e.g., Auburn, Lane and Union* in New York City). Henry Boynton Smith* established himself as a major American theologian and the pre-eminent leader of the New School.

The experience of the Civil War* tended to reverse the parochial tendencies of the previous decades as New Schoolers (along with many other Northern Protestants) tended to elevate the nationalist cause of preserving the Union to the sacred level of seeing the kingdom of God.* The war also hastened Presbyterian reunion as both sides realized that previous causes for separation had largely dissipated. When a compromise was reached concerning the meaning of subscription to the Westminster Confession, formal reunion became a reality in 1869.

New School Presbyterianism is significant for understanding nineteenth-century American culture because it was so very typical of it. By almost any indicator, the movement stood near the center of American culture, and its near fusion of Christian and American values contributed to both its success and its failure. More typically American in character and spirit than Old School Presbyterians, New Schoolers combined a pietist*/revivalist emphasis with the cultural mandate of making America a Christian nation. In the half century after reunion, however, these twin strands unraveled under the secularizing pressures of modern America. Thus, nineteenth-century New School Presbyterianism would have historical ties with both twentieth-century theological liberalism* and fundamentalism.*

See also OLD SCHOOL PRESBYTERIANS; REFORMED TRADITION; REFORMED AND PRESBYTERIAN CHURCHES.

BIBLIOGRAPHY. S. J. Baird, A History of the New School (1868); G. M. Marsden, "Reformed and American," in Reformed Theology in America, ed. D. F. Wells (1985); G. M. Marsden, The Evangelical Mind and the New School Presbyterian Experience (1970); G. M. Marsden, "The New School Heritage and Presbyterian Fundamentalism," WmTJ 32 (1970):129-147; L. A. Pope, "Albert Barnes, The Way of Salvation, and Theological Controversy," JPH 57 (1979):20-34.   S. R. Pointer

New Side Presbyterians. Revivalist party within eighteenth-century Presbyterianism. The first Presbyterian* clergy* in the American colonies were Scottish* and Scotch-Irish ministers sent to preach to Presbyterian immigrants* in Pennsylvania and Maryland. The insufficient numbers of these clergy compelled the Presbyterians to accept Congregational* clergy, principally from New England, who differed from the immigrant ministers* over the degree of adherence to the Westminster Confession of Faith.* The New Englanders were strongly influenced by continental Pietism* and their own Puritan* origins, regarding personal religious experience* rather than confessional* subscription as the primary qualification for church membership* and ordained* ministry.*

This resulted in conflict first in 1728-1729 over the Adopting Act,* which demanded strict subscription to the Confession and was resisted by the New Englanders led by Jonathan Dickinson.* Contention broke out anew in 1738 over the standing of candidates for ordination graduated from the Log College,* a strongly pietistic school operated by William Tennent* in Neshaminy, Pennsylvania, and in 1739 over the action of the New Brunswick, New Jersey, presbytery* in ordaining a Log College graduate, J. Rowlandson, without synodical review. Further strife was generated by Gilbert Tennent's* support of itinerant* evangelists* and lay* exhorters* who sometimes invaded the parishes* of settled ministers. Tennent justified these tactics in a sensational sermon* preached*

on March 8, 1740, in Nottingham, Pennsylvania, "The Danger of an Unconverted Ministry." There Tennent urged lay people to abandon "the ministry of Natural men" and follow the itinerants. The Synod* of Philadelphia censured Tennent, and in June 1741, Tennent's critics presented a "Protestation" which forced the withdrawal of Tennent and the New Brunswick presbytery from the Synod. The ejected members organized their own so-called New Side jurisdiction, which was joined by the Presbytery of New York in 1745 to form the New Side Synod of New York.

With the sympathetic interest of George Whitefield,* the New Side assumed a place in the overall Great Awakening* of the 1740s, and its influence was carried into Pennsylvania and Virginia by Samuel Finley,* Samuel Davies* and Samuel Blair.* A famous Indian mission* was undertaken in New Jersey and Pennsylvania under David Brainerd.* The work of the Log College was continued in Elizabethtown and Princeton, New Jersey, where the College of New Jersey (Princeton University*) was organized under Jonathan Dickinson and Aaron Burr.* Jonathan Edwards* was briefly the president of the College in 1758 and addressed the New Side Synod in 1752.

As early as 1742, Gilbert Tennent began to express regret that his actions had been so violent, and the publication of his Irenicum Ecclesiasticarum (1749) opened the way to restoration of fellowship between the New Side and Old Side* synods in 1758. But the tension between the confessional and Pietist factions in the Presbyterian Church remained apparent and surfaced again in the New School*—Old School* schism of 1837.

See also GREAT AWAKENING; NEW SCHOOL PRESBYTERIANS; OLD SCHOOL PRESBYTERIANS; OLD SIDE PRESBYTERIANS.

BIBLIOGRAPHY. A. Alexander, The Log College (1851); A. Heimert and P. Miller, eds., The Great Awakening (1967); G. S. Klett, ed., Minutes of the Presbyterian Church in America, 1706-1788 (1976).   A. C. Guelzo

New Theology. See EVANGELICAL LIBERALISM.

New York Bible Society. An early nondenominational society established for the local publication and distribution of Scripture.* Five years after the founding of the British and Foreign Bible Society (1804), the New York Bible Society (NYBS) came into being (1809). It was one of several regional Bible societies* that emerged shortly after the Philadelphia Bible Society (the oldest in America) was founded in 1808. A year after its inception, the

NYBS established its purpose to publish, purchase, sell, circulate and distribute the Bible (or parts of it) in any and all languages in and about the city and the harbor of New York. All copies of Scripture, published or distributed, were to be without note or comment.

In 1866 the Society was incorporated under the laws of the state of New York. Over the years the Society was financed by donations from churches and individuals, memorial gifts, bequests and annuities. In its prime, the NYBS distributed more than a million copies of Scripture in some seventy different languages annually. A sixty-member board, chosen by churches of any denomination* in the New York area, governed the Society.

From its inception the Society concentrated on providing the millions of immigrants* who landed in New York with the Scriptures in their mother tongue. It also reached out to the sailors and dockworkers of the city's harbor. Hospitals, hotels and other public institutions were supplied with Bibles. From time to time volunteers canvassed the entire city to make sure that every family had a Bible.

With the publication of the New International Version (1978), the NYBS gave birth to the International Bible Society.* This Society continues to have a ministry in New York City, and this local ministry, located on Lexington Avenue, is still called the NYBS, but operates independently of the International Bible Society.

BIBLIOGRAPHY. D. J. Fant, *The Bible at Work in New York* (1965). D. Ewert

New York Missionary Society. Interdenominational voluntary society* dedicated to the evangelism* of the American frontier.* Founded in 1796 by New York Presbyterian,* Baptist* and Dutch Reformed* clergy,* the New York Missionary Society was the first interdenominational missionary* association established in a new era of American benevolent activity. Following the Revolutionary War,* Protestant* denominations* devoted increasing attention to the moral condition of new settlements on the frontier. Unlike similar societies in Connecticut* (1798) and Massachusetts (1799), which concentrated on establishing churches for new settlers, the New York Society concentrated on its mission to Native Americans.

Encouraged by the success of British missionary activities in Africa, the Society labored both to convert and civilize the natives. Joseph Bullen, the first missionary sent to Native Americans by the Society, was cautioned that he was being sent to a people "covered with the gloom of ignorance, superstition, and barbarism." Aside from the primary concern to preach the gospel and baptize* converts, missionaries were advised to concentrate on teaching English to Native American children, in the hope that they would thereby "be gained over" to civilized life. The Society funded missionaries from Georgia to New England, often working in conjunction with other missionary organizations. By 1822 the growing interest in national consolidation of associational resources motivated the Society to merge with other New York home-missionary societies into the United Domestic Missionary Society. This move also highlighted the shift of focus from Indian missions to work among the growing numbers of immigrants* in western New York. In 1826 the United Domestic Missionary Society was the largest single participant in the formation of the American Home Missionary Society.*

BIBLIOGRAPHY. C. B. Goodykoontz, *Home Missions on the American Frontier* (1939); K. S. Latourette, *The Great Century* (1941); W. W Sweet, *Religion on the American Frontier: 1783-1840*, 4 vols. (1946). L. F. Maffly-Kipp

Newcomer, Christian (1749-1830). Missionary bishop* of the Church of the United Brethren in Christ. A Pennsylvania Mennonite* farmer, Newcomer experienced a conversion* under the German-American* revivalist* movement led by Philip William Otterbein* and Martin Boehm.* Called to preach,* he became a full-time itinerant preacher in 1777 and established circuits across the Allegheny Mountains in the Midwest and upper South. In 1813 he was ordained by Otterbein, shortly before the latter's death, and in that same year he was elected superintendent, or bishop, to succeed Boehm.

Newcomer served as an itinerant bishop, evangelist and organizer of annual and general conferences. Re-elected bishop every four years, his tireless itinerancy led him over 150,000 miles of circuit* trails between 1795 and his death at the age of eighty-one. As an author he sought to bring order to his frontier revival movement by writing disciplinary and doctrinal statements. As an ecumenist he unsuccessfully sought union with the Methodists. A staunch opponent of slavery, he provided moral guidance to the rapidly expanding United Brethren during the antebellum years.

BIBLIOGRAPHY. *DAB* VII; S. S. Hough, ed., *The Journal of Christian Newcomer* (1941); B. Behney and P. Eller, *History of the Evangelical United Brethren Church* (1979). J. S. O'Malley

Newell, Bertha Payne (1867-1953). Educator and social reformer. Born in Racine, Wisconsin, on January 20, 1865, Newell attended the University of Leipzig and the University of Chicago (Ph.B. in 1907). She was principal of the Froebel Kindergarten Training School in Chicago (1895-1899) and headed the Department of Kindergarten Education at the School of Education, University of Chicago (1901-1909). On August 2, 1909, she married William A. Newell, a minister* of the Methodist* Episcopal Church, South. Moving to North Carolina, Newell became active in the Woman's Missionary Council of her denomination, as well as in politics. She was director of the Commission on Interracial Cooperation (1931-1935) and its third vice-president (1933-1938). She served as secretary of the Association of Southern Women for the Prevention of Lynching (1931-1938) and was also active in the Federal Council of Churches* department of race relations (1927-1935) and department of social service (1929-1935), the Women's International League for Peace and Freedom, the North Carolina Interracial Commission, the National Women's Trade Union League and the National Council for Prevention of War.

BIBLIOGRAPHY. J. D. Hall, *Revolt Against Chivalry* (1979). N. A. Hardesty

Newell, Harriet Atwood (1793-1812). Pioneer missionary* to India. Born in Haverhill, Massachusetts, Harriet Atwood was converted* as a student at the Bradford Academy and joined the Congregational Church* in 1809. In 1810 she met Samuel Newell, a student at Andover Seminary.* She shared his interest in missions, and they were married on February 9, 1812. Ten days later they sailed for India with Adoniram* and Ann* Judson. Harriet and "Nancy" were the first American women commissioned for missionary work abroad. They arrived in Serampore in June, but were ordered to leave the country by the British East India Company. Harriet's health was poor, so the Newells took passage for the Isle of France. Harriet gave birth prematurely at sea, lost the baby, and died at Port Louis in November, barely nineteen years of age and the first American missionary to die in service on a foreign field. Her subsequent reputation as "protomartyr" spread widely, and many traced their missionary calling to her example.

BIBLIOGRAPHY. *NAW* 2; N. M. Ragland, *Leaves from Mission Fields; or Memoirs of Mrs. Harriett Newell . . .* (1900). K. K. Kidd

Newman, Albert Henry (1852-1933). Baptist* church historian and educator. Born in South Carolina, Newman was educated at Mercer University and Rochester Theological Seminary, excelling in Semitic languages and historical studies. In his seminary studies, Newman was a favorite of Augustus H. Strong,* and was offered his initial teaching position at Rochester. John A. Broadus* and Crawford H. Toy* also sought him for Southern Baptist Seminary, as did the Morgan Park Seminary in Chicago. To the surprise of many, in 1881 Newman accepted an appointment at what became McMaster University in Toronto, Canada (1881-1901). In 1901 he moved to Baylor University (1901-1908) and finished his career as dean and later professor of church history at Southwestern Baptist Theological Seminary (1908-1913).

Newman's scholarship explored a variety of topics from New Testament and patristic studies to modern Baptist life. In his *History of Antipaedobaptism* (1897), he traced precursors to Baptistic principles through examples of opposition to infant baptism in the early and medieval churches. His one-volume contribution on the Baptists to the American Church History Series in 1901 sounded a note of triumphalism for the once-despised frontier sect in early America. Newman's two-volume *Manual of Church History* (1903) was a standard textbook for the first half of the twentieth century among both Baptist and non-Baptist institutions. Newman was one of the premier church historians of the late nineteenth century and one of a few Baptist educators who rose above regional politics and served in Northern, Southern and Canadian institutions.

BIBLIOGRAPHY. J. M. Dawson, "Our Greatest Baptist Historian," *Watchman Examiner* (June 29, 1933); *DAB* 1. W. H. Brackney

Newman Movement. A Catholic student ministry movement inspired by the life and writings of John Henry Newman (1801-1890) to provide pastoral care and religious education on non-Catholic college and university campuses.

The movement developed in three stages. The first phase (1883-1908) was characterized by strong leadership from bishops* who cooperated with the professors, students and a few priests* in organizing the chaplain* movement in state universities. Some of these bishops authorized Catholic Halls for religious services and classes in religion.

The second phase (1908-1962) of the movement witnessed the rise of two student organizations, the Catholic Student Association of America

(1908-c.1918) and the Federation of College Catholic Clubs (c.1915), which became the National Newman Club Federation in 1938. These organizations sought to regain the earlier episcopal* leadership which was lost when the hierarchy decided to promote Catholic colleges. (*See* Higher Education, Catholic.) During this period the movement defended itself on two fronts: against secularism in education and against Catholic critics who questioned their presence on the campuses at all.

In 1962 the movement reached its third phase in the formation of the National Newman Apostolate, by which the Catholic hierarchy mandated "the work of the Catholic Church in the secular campus community." Since then the diocesan-centered approach to campus ministry has returned and the movement has been validated by the large numbers of Catholics attending public universities as well as by the reforms of the Second Vatican Council.

BIBLIOGRAPHY. J. W. Evans, *The Newman Movement: Roman Catholics in American Higher Education, 1883-1971* (1980).

J. W. Evans

Newton, Joseph Fort (1867-1950). Liberal* Protestant* preacher,* writer, ecumenist* and mystic.* Born in Decatur, Texas, Newton was raised in the Southern Baptist Convention.* In 1895 he entered the Southern Baptist Theological Seminary in Louisville, Kentucky, but departed in 1897 without graduating, frustrated over doctrinal disputes rampant in the denomination. Following a two-year pastorate at First Baptist Church, Paris, Texas, Newton left the Southern Baptist Convention, becoming pastor of the People's Church, a nonsectarian congregation in Dixon, Illinois. There he established his liberalism in a confrontation with evangelist* Billy Sunday.* In 1908 he moved to Cedar Rapids, Iowa, as pastor of the Liberal Christian Church. From there he was called in 1916 as pastor of the prestigious City Temple, London, a center of British Protestant nonconformity. The pulpit committee called Newton, sight unseen, after reading his prosaic sermons. Newton returned to America in 1919 as pastor of New York's Universalist Church of the Divine Paternity. In 1925 he became an Episcopalian,* serving as pastor of various Pennsylvania parishes, including St. Paul's, Overbrook, and St. Luke and the Epiphany, Philadelphia, until his death in 1950.

Newton was a curious combination of diverse ideals and ecclesiological practices. A popular preacher, he was widely known for his homiletical skills. Largely self-educated, he was a prolific writer, author of over twenty-five books and innumerable articles on various historical, theological and political subjects. A Christocentric liberal, he was also a political conservative. A self-styled mystic, his concern for direct encounter with the Divine provided continuity throughout his diverse denominational pilgrimage.

BIBLIOGRAPHY. *DAB* 4; B. J. Leonard, *Joseph Fort Newton: Minister and Mystic* (1975); J. F. Newton, *The River of Years* (1946). B. J. Leonard

Niagara Conferences. A series of summer conferences that served as the progenitor of Bible and prophecy conferences* in the U.S. and Canada. Organized by millenarians James Inglis and George C. Needham* in the late 1860s, the Believers' Meeting for Bible Study, as it was originally called, was first opened to the public in the mid-1870s. After being held at a variety of locations in the northern U.S., this interdenominational conference found a home at Niagara-on-the-Lake, Ontario, where it thrived from 1883 through 1897.

The annual conference generally consisted of a week of meetings. Eschewing traditional pulpit oratory, many of the speakers gave "Bible* readings," in which they would read a string of Scriptural passages relating to a particular word or topic (e.g., *grace*), with a minimum of additional comment. In 1878 James H. Brookes,* who presided over the Conference for more than two decades, constructed a fourteen-point "Niagara creed," which included the inerrancy* of the Bible and the "personal and premillennial* advent" of Jesus Christ. The latter was a favorite topic of Niagara Conference speakers, many of whom were dispensationalists,* and many of whom were involved in organizing the major prophecy conferences of the late nineteenth and early twentieth centuries.

Along with Brookes' death in 1897, a controversy over whether the rapture* of the church would occur *before* or *after* the "Great Tribulation" sent the Conference into rapid decline. The final meeting was held in 1900. But the spirit of Niagara lived on in the interdenominational and predominantly premillennialist fundamentalist* movement of post-World War 1* North America.

BIBLIOGRAPHY. L. D. Pettegrew, "The Niagara Bible Conference and American Fundamentalism," *Central Bible Quarterly* 19-20 (Winter 1976—Winter 1977); E. R. Sandeen, *The Roots of Fundamentalism: British and American Millenarianism, 1800-1930* (1970); T. P. Weber, *Living in the*

Shadow of the Second Coming: American Premillenialism, 1875-1982 (1979).

W. V. Trollinger

Niebuhr, (H)elmut Richard (1894-1962). Protestant* theologian.* Born in Wright City, Missouri, Niebuhr was the youngest son of German immigrant* Pastor Gustav and American-born Lydia Niebuhr. Niebuhr graduated from Elmhurst College (1912) and Eden Theological Seminary (1915). Ordained* in the Evangelical Synod of North America (1916), Niebuhr held a pastorate in St. Louis until 1918 when he began his academic career by teaching at Eden Theological Seminary (1919-1922). Niebuhr earned the B.D. (1923) and Ph.D. (1924) degrees from Yale* University Divinity School. He was president of Elmhurst College (1924-1927), dean of Eden Theological Seminary (1927-31) and professor of Christian ethics at Yale Divinity School, where he remained from 1931 until his death.

Niebuhr's broad interests included a lifelong concern for the relationship of the church and the modern world. He analyzed the sociological and historical roots of denominational divisions in *The Social Sources of Denominationalism* (1929). He studied the influence of the idea of the kingdom of God* on American culture in *The Kingdom of God in America* (1937). And his typology of church/world interaction in *Christ and Culture* (1951) has become a classic. From 1954 to 1955 Niebuhr directed a study of theological education in the U.S. and Canada, publishing the results with Daniel Day Williams* and James M. Gustafson. Niebuhr also figured prominently in the merging of the Congregational Christian* and the Evangelical and Reformed Churches that formed the United Church of Christ* in 1957.

Niebuhr's theological work centered on questions of unity and diversity, the shape of knowledge of objective truth in a relativistic framework and the nature of faith in modern life. Influenced by Jonathan Edwards,* William James,* Josiah Royce* and George Herbert Mead as well as Karl Barth,* Paul Tillich,* Albrecht Ritschl and Ernst Troeltsch, Niebuhr developed a cross-cultural theology that addressed the issues of his day: the fundamentalist-modernist debate,* World War 2* and the Cold War era.

In *The Meaning of Revelation* (1941), Niebuhr argued that knowledge of universal truth can be gained only partially through historical traditions. Revelation occurs within particular communities and is limited by historical relativism, yet what is revealed is universal and objective, the Sovereign God of history.

Niebuhr's *Radical Monotheism and Western Culture* (1960) was a theological response to pluralism and the problem of faith in the twentieth century. Beyond the many religions and centers of value held by humans is One God. Faith, a relation of trust and loyalty among the self, others and a common cause, should be directed toward that One. However, often faith in finite centers of value, such as capitalism,* American nationalism or church-centeredness, rivals genuine faith in God. Niebuhr attempted to focus on God as the object of faith and avoid absolutizing any relative conceptions of God by developing a confessional stance toward theology* and ethics.*

Niebuhr's postuhumous work, *The Responsible Self* (1963), outlined a dispositional ethic oriented toward God and communal life. Values are relational; ethical action is the response of a social self to a center of value in which one trusts and to which one is loyal. Natural humanity, sinful and fearful of death, develops an ethic of survival. Transformation to a life-affirming ethic can occur only as dependence upon God is recognized and the goodness of God is apprehended in all actions upon one. The "fitting response" results from learning to respond to God as friend in the inevitable ethical dilemmas of life.

BIBLIOGRAPHY. *DAB* 7; *DARB*; J. Diefenthaler, *H. Richard Niebuhr: A Lifetime of Reflections on the Church and the World* (1986); J. W. Fowler, Jr., *To See the Kingdom: The Theological Vision of H. Richard Niebuhr* (1974); L. A. Hoedemaker, *The Theology of H. Richard Niebuhr* (1970); *NCAB* 47; P. Ramsey, ed., *Faith and Ethics: The Theology of H. Richard Niebuhr* (1957).

F. S. Adeney

Niebuhr, Karl Paul Reinhold (1892-1971). Theologian and ethicist. Born in Wright City, Missouri, Niebuhr graduated from his denomination's Elmhurst College (1910) and Eden Seminary (1913) before attending Yale* Divinity School (B.D., 1914) and Yale University (M.A., 1915).

Reinhold Niebuhr and his younger brother and theological counterpart, Helmut Richard Niebuhr,* grew up in the Evangelical Synod of North America, a church tracing its origin to the Church of the Prussian Union in Germany, which combined Lutheran* and Reformed* congregations. It united with the Reformed Church in the United States in 1934 to become the Evangelical and Reformed Church, which in turn became part of the United Church of Christ* in 1957. Niebuhr's theology* shows the influence of both Reformed and Lutheran motifs, but the latter is dominant.

Niebuhr pastored Bethel Evangelical Church in Detroit, Michigan, for thirteen years, during which he wrote his first book, *Does Civilization Need Religion?* (1927). In 1928 he moved to Union Theological Seminary* in New York where he would spend the rest of his career, first as associate professor of philosophy of religion* (1928-1930) and then as professor of applied Christianity (1930-1960). He was the founder and editor (1941-1966) of *Christianity and Crisis,* a magazine bringing religion to bear on critical social issues. During his years at Union, Niebuhr wrote several significant books, including his highly influential *Moral Man and Immoral Society* (1932) and his two-volume theological exposition, *The Nature and Destiny of Man* (1941-1943).

Politically, Niebuhr was at first supportive of socialism and was a Socialist Party candidate for congressional office in 1930, but by 1940 he had come to favor the mixed economy of Franklin Roosevelt's New Deal. Theologically, he was deeply influenced by Social Gospel* liberalism,* but his theological reflection and pastoral experience in Detroit, where he gained firsthand experience with Ford auto workers involved in labor disputes, transformed his optimism into a "Christian realism." Increasingly pessimistic regarding human possibilities, Niebuhr began to see the hope of the world in the coming kingdom of God* which stands in judgment over all human endeavors and achievements. Love—no longer a simple possibility—became an "impossible possibility," breaking into human life in moments of faith and surrender but never as a political strategy. It is the supra-historical norm that guides us in our struggle for social justice.

Niebuhr sought to relate love and justice dialectically. Love represents both the fulfillment and negation of every stride toward a more just society. Yet all progress toward social justice invariably falls drastically short of the ideal of love, which sporadically appears in history but is never an ongoing reality in history. Whereas justice employs coercion, love represents suffering passivity, the power of powerlessness. The highest holiness is the holiness of God's love, which overcomes evil by bearing the pain of evil in vicarious identification with a suffering humanity.

Niebuhr's "Christian realism" seeks to unite the ultimate norm of pure love with the rational norm of justice in order to maintain social relevance. The Christian realist acknowledges the ambiguity and paradox in all human ethical decision making, poignantly aware that we are often confronted by two evils and must then choose the lesser in a spirit of penitence. Our hope is in the divine grace that enables us to live with our ambiguity rather than in human perfectibility.

While Niebuhr has often been associated with neo-orthodoxy,* his basic methodology remained liberal. He saw revelation as the inner awakening to the reality of suffering love, and theology as the elucidation of religious experience.* The Bible* is an indispensable aid in understanding the divine purpose in history but is not itself God's revelation to us in the form of human words. Jesus is the crowning exemplification of the moral ideal of sacrificial love but not God incarnate in human flesh.

Niebuhr is best understood as an apologetic theologian who sought to validate the claims of the Christian faith to the secular world. His apologetics proceeded by exposing the contradictions in human existence and showing that only the love of the cross, which represents the divine forgiveness, can be the answer to human sin and despair. *See also* NIEBUHR, HELMUT RICHARD.

BIBLIOGRAPHY. *DARB;* G. Fackre, *The Promise of Reinhold Niebuhr* (1970); R. W. Fox, *Reinhold Niebuhr: A Biography* (1986); G. Harland, *The Thought of Reinhold Niebuhr* (1960); R. Harries, *Reinhold Niebuhr and the Issues of Our Time* (1986); D. W. Kegley and R. W. Bretall, eds., *Reinhold Niebuhr: His Religious, Social and Political Thought* (1956); *NCAB* G; R. H. Stone, *Reinhold Niebuhr: Prophet to Politicians* (1972).

D. G. Bloesch

Niles, Samuel (1674-1762). Old-Light* Congregational* minister.* Niles was born on Block Island, where hardships created by French privateers in 1689 forced him to delay his education until 1696. When he graduated in 1699, he was the first Rhode Islander to receive a Harvard* degree. After ten years of missionary* work in Rhode Island, Niles was called to the South Church of Braintree, Massachusetts, where he remained until his death. Obstinate by nature, Niles took an active part in the religious controversies of his day. It is said that he rode a horse no one else could and to him "were brought for breaking all the rebellious colts and young religious innovators of Braintree." Niles is best known for his *Tristitiae Ecclesiarum* (1745) and *The Sentiments and Resolutions of an Association of Ministers* (1745), in which he attacked George Whitefield* and illiterate ministers. In 1757 Niles wrote a treatise in answer to J. Taylor's views on original sin (*The True Scripture-Doctrine of Original Sin Stated and Defended*). Niles's *A Summary Historical Narra-*

tive of the *Wars in New England* is a well-known non-religious account of the French and Indian War.

BIBLIOGRAPHY. *DAB* VII; C. K. Shipton, *Sibley's Harvard Graduates,* vol. IV (1933).

S. D. Crocco

Nixon, Richard Milhous (1913-). Thirty-seventh U.S. president. The son of Frank Nixon, from a conservative Methodist* background, and Hannah Milhous, from a devout Quaker* family, Richard was raised in his mother's faith and attended the East Whittier (California) Friends Church. From his upbringing he learned tolerance of other peoples, the importance of peace, the idea that God helps those who help themselves and a distaste for showing emotions and physically expressing feelings. Thus, his Quaker experience was a blending of private reserve and public confidence.

As a teen-ager, Nixon made an evangelical* profession in a Paul Rader* revival* and testified publicly to his faith at Christian Endeavor* youth meetings. At maturity he gave up most of his orthodox* beliefs, and his faith became essentially a generalized Protestantism,* with a decided emphasis on civil religion.* Although he continued to identify with his Quaker background, he rarely attended church during his years in Washington in Congress, as vice president and as president. His spiritual counselor was evangelist* Billy Graham,* who established a relationship with him in the early 1950s that lasted even after Nixon's fall from power. This endeared Nixon to the evangelical community, which firmly supported his presidential bids in 1960, 1968 and 1972.

The inaugural ceremony in 1969 was practically a worship* service, while his most controversial religious action was the holding of Sunday services in the White House; his critics accused him of functioning as the "high priest of American civil religion," and he articulated a civil theology whose central ideas were those of national spirit, the innate goodness of America and America's mission. Nixon exuded the image of a man of great faith through his speeches, with religious themes, appearances with religious leaders and involvement in prayer events. However, the Watergate tapes revealed his religiosity to be much less than his evangelical supporters had supposed, and they reluctantly repudiated the man in whom they had placed so much trust.

BIBLIOGRAPHY. S. E. Ambrose, *Nixon: The Education of a Politician, 1913-1962* (1987); C. P. Henderson, *The Nixon Theology* (1972); R. V.

Pierard and R. D. Linder, *Civil Religion and the Presidency* (1988).

R. V. Pierard

Nominal Christian. A term describing those who are Christian in name only, often used in a pejorative sense. The term *nominal Christian* describes members of the Christian community who are perceived as being Christian by name only or who barely meet the minimal requirements of Christianity. Thus, the term often operates as a critique of Christians outside any given group who appear to be superficial or "lukewarm" in their commitment to the Christian faith and lax in their observance of traditional Christian precepts. Christians who apply strict and observable criteria to judge the authenticity of faith use this phrase most often in polemical settings to describe and characterize other Christians who do not measure up to those strict standards of behavior and faith. In more careful usage it may serve to distinguish, for example, between those who loosely identify themselves with Christianity and those who are practicing Christians.

C. E. Ostwalt

Norelius, Eric (1833-1916). Pioneer Swedish Lutheran* minister.* Born in 1833 in Hassela, Helsingland Province, Sweden, Norelius immigrated to America in 1850. After studying at Capital University, Columbus, Ohio (1851-1856), he was licensed* as a lay* preacher* in 1855 by the Evangelical Lutheran Synod of Northern Illinois (to which Swedish and many Norwegian congregations and pastors then belonged) and was ordained* a Lutheran minister by that Synod in 1856. Upon ordination he became pastor in Attica, Indiana (1855-1856; 1858-1860).

In 1860, with his bride and much of the Indiana Swedish group, he moved to Minnesota, where he organized congregations in Red Wing, Vasa, Spring Garden and Goodhue, serving one or another of these until his retirement in 1915. In Minnesota he also founded the Vasa Children's Home, in 1865, and St. Ansgar Academy in Carver, Minnesota, in 1865. The latter grew into today's Gustavus Adolphus College, St. Peter, Minnesota. Norelius was editor of a number of short-lived Swedish-American journals. He was the first to publish a comprehensive history of the Augustana Church in his *De Svenska Luterska Forsamlingarnas och Svenskarnes Historia i Amerika,* vol. I (1890), based on his own recollections as well as on his collection of documents and source materials. Translated into English, it has been published as *The Pioneer Swedish Settlements and Swedish Churches in*

America, 1845-1860 (1984).

Norelius was the youngest of the founding fathers of the Evangelical Lutheran Augustana Church (Synod) and the only one of them educated and ordained on this side of the Atlantic. He was a long-time president of the Augustana Church (1871-1881; 1899-1911) and of its Minnesota Conference (1874-1881; 1899-1911).

BIBLIOGRAPHY. G. E. Arden, trans., *The Journals of Eric Norelius* (1987); E. Johnson, ed. and trans., *Early Life of Eric Norelius* (1934); E. Johnson, *Eric Norelius, Pioneer Midwest Pastor and Churchman* (1954). J. W. Lundeen

Norris, J. Frank (1877-1952). Fundamentalist* Baptist* minister.* Born in Dadeville, Alabama, the Norris family moved to Hubbard, Texas, when Frank was eleven years old. He graduated from Baylor University (B.A., 1903) and Southern Baptist Theological Seminary (1905), and was ordained* a Southern Baptist minister in 1899. His first pastorate was the McKinney Avenue Baptist Church in Dallas, Texas (1905-1908), which under his leadership grew from less than one hundred to over one thousand in attendance. As editor (1907-1909) of the Texas Baptist newspaper, *The Baptist Standard,* Norris became a public figure when he stopped race-track gambling at the State Fair. During those same years he worked with B. H. Carroll* to found Southwestern Baptist Seminary.

Norris served as pastor of First Baptist Church in Fort Worth, Texas (1909-1952), and in later years served simultaneously as pastor of Temple Baptist in Detroit, Michigan (1935-1948), commuting by air between the two churches. Both were large congregations for their day (memberships of 15,000 and 10,000 respectively) and were built around Norris's forceful personality, sensational tactics, soul-winning* fervor and conservative theological and political views. From 1939 to about 1950 Norris presided over Baptist Bible Seminary, an undergraduate Bible school* located in his Fort Worth church.

A leader among Southern fundamentalists, in 1917 Norris started a paper first called *The Fence Rail,* later *The Searchlight* (1921) and finally *The Fundamentalist* (1927). Exposing sin, criticizing the Southern Baptist Convention* and promoting the fundamentalist cause, he became known by many of his fellow Baptist ministers for his independent spirit and acrimonious behavior. He was expelled from the Pastor's Conference of Fort Worth (1914), the Tarrant County Baptist Association (1922) and the Baptist General Convention of Texas (1924). Norris supported the Baptist Bible

Union* until its collapse in 1932 and was an ardent supporter of the World's Christian Fundamentals Association* throughout the 1920s, hosting their annual meeting in 1923.

Norris was known for his anti-Catholic convictions, which led him in 1928 to campaign for Herbert Hoover and against the Catholic nominee for president, Alfred E. Smith.* Earlier, in July 1926, in the heat of anti-Catholic sentiments he had helped stir up in Fort Worth, Norris shot and killed a man who had entered his study to threaten him. Charged with murder, the jury found Norris "not guilty," believing he had acted in self-defense. Nevertheless, the incident gave Norris an unfavorable notoriety in the public eye. Yet among Southern fundamentalists he was regarded as a strong leader and champion of the truth.

BIBLIOGRAPHY. *DAB* 5; G. W. Dollar, *A History of Fundamentalism in America* (1973); C. A. Russell, *Voices of American Fundamentalism* (1976); M. G. Toulouse, "A Case Study in Schism: J. Frank Norris and the Southern Baptist Convention," *Foun* (1981):32-53. D. G. Reid

North, Frank Mason (1850-1935). Methodist Episcopal* minister* and ecumenist.* Born in New York City, North attended Wesleyan University in Middletown, Connecticut. For nineteen years (1873-1892) he served in various pastorates of the Methodist Episcopal Church (*See* Methodist Churches) in the New York area. As corresponding secretary of the New York City Church Extension and Missionary Society, for two decades he directed a network of metropolitan missions* and challenged the church to its urban responsibility. He was corresponding secretary (1912-1924) and secretary (1924-1928) for the Board of Foreign Missions of the Methodist Episcopal Church.

An ardent organizer and ecumenist, North had helped form the Methodist Federation for Social Service, as well as the Open and Institutional Church League,* one of the forerunners of the Federal Council of the Churches of Christ in America* (FCC). He helped draft the FCC's historic "Social Creed of the Churches"* and served as president of the Federal Council during the critical war years of 1916-1920. Attending the famous Edinburgh Missionary Council of 1910, he went on to serve on its continuation committee and chaired the drafting committee for the Constitution of the International Missionary Council* which was adopted in 1921. Today he is remembered as the author of the hymn* "Where Cross the Crowded Ways of Life."

BIBLIOGRAPHY. C. Lacy, *Frank Mason North: His*

Social and Ecumenical Mission (1967).

J. T. Seamands

North American Baptist Conference. A small Baptist* denomination with German ethnic background. The roots of the North American Baptist Conference lie in the nineteenth century in the concern felt by European and North American Christians for the spiritual welfare of German immigrants* to the U. S. and Canada. As a result, German-speaking Baptist congregations were founded in the East, Midwest and Province of Ontario, the oldest being the church founded in Philadelphia in 1843 by Konrad Anton Fleischmann (1812-1867). These scattered congregations eventually formed regional conferences to promote evangelization efforts. By 1859 the German Baptist Conference at Philadelphia could claim 2,600 members in sixty-one churches. In 1865 the General Conference of German Baptist Churches in North America was formed, the forerunner of the current triennial meeting.

A seminary (now North American Baptist Seminary, Sioux Falls, South Dakota) was begun in 1865, when August Rauschenbusch was invited to become the German faculty member at the Rochester Theological Seminary. In succeeding decades others, including his son, Walter Rauschenbusch,* joined the Rochester faculty. Both the school and the work in general were supported heavily by the English-speaking Baptists. Expansion into western Canada resulted in the founding of a second school (now North American Baptist College and Divinity School) in Edmonton, Alberta, in the mid twentieth century.

A transition to the English language was inaugurated early in the twentieth century. But subsequent increases in German immigration reaffirmed the need for continued ministry in that language. At the current time, however, English is the sole language of nearly all congregations.

From its inception the NAB Conference has been oriented to missions.* In the nineteenth century, support was directed toward Cameroon and Nigeria. Since World War 2* work in Japan, Brazil and the Philippines, as well as ethnic ministries in North America, have been added.

Membership totals about sixty thousand in over three hundred fifty churches, twenty-seven per cent of which are Canadian. The conference office is located at Forest Park, Illinois. A journal, the *Baptist Herald,* is published monthly.

See also BAPTIST CHURCHES; IMMIGRATION AND ETHNICITY, PROTESTANT.

BIBLIOGRAPHY. S. J. Grenz, *The Baptist Congrega-* *tion* (1985); *These Glorious Years: The Centenary History of German Baptists of North America, 1843-1943* (1943); F. Woyke, *Heritage and Ministry of the North American Baptist Conference* (1979).

S. J. Grenz

North American Christian Convention. The annual national convention of the Christian Churches/Churches of Christ,* first held in 1927. When theological liberalism* affected the Restoration Movement* in the early twentieth century, the conservatives left the existing agencies to the Disciples of Christ* and organized their own convention in 1927. Because of their strict congregational government,* the convention could not have authority,* so it remains simply an ad hoc gathering of members of the independent Christian Churches/Churches of Christ. There is an office located in Cincinnati, Ohio, simply to coordinate the planning of the annual conventions.

This convention has become the major assembly point for these Christian Churches/Churches of Christ who currently number about one million in total membership in about 5,700 congregations. These support about 1,500 missionaries, numerous colleges and benevolent institutions, but without any central structure. The convention passes no resolutions, conducts no votes and has no delegates. Approximately 20,000 people attend each year.

BIBLIOGRAPHY. J. D. Murch, *Christians Only: A History of the Restoration Movement* (1962); North American Christian Convention, *NACC: History & Purpose* (1973).

J. B. North

North American College, The Pontifical. A church residence in Rome, Italy, for American Catholic* secular priests* and seminarians attending the Roman theological universities. Pope Pius IX* founded it (1859) in a seventeenth-century monastery at Via dell 'Umilta, 30, entrusting its management to the U. S. bishops.* In 1884 Pope Leo XIII* accorded it the rank of "Pontifical" (i.e., papal). The College was forced to close in 1940 because of World War 2.* Expansion followed its reopening in 1948, and 1953 saw the dedication of a new facility within Vatican City. Since then the original building has housed the graduate department (est. 1933). In 1970 the College also launched an Institute for Continuing Theological Education.

The alumni list includes over two-thousand priests, over one hundred fifty bishops and more than a dozen cardinals.* As Rome's largest American Catholic center, the North American College has assisted countless American pilgrims and visitors. It has also played host to many notables, including seven U.S. presidents.

BIBLIOGRAPHY. R. F. McNamara, *The American College in Rome, 1855-1955* (1956).

R. F. McNamara

Northern Baptist Convention. *See* AMERICAN BAPTIST CHURCHES IN THE USA.

Northfield Conferences. A series of summer conferences founded by Dwight L. Moody* and held in Moody's hometown of Northfield, Massachusetts. Moody established the Northfield Conference in 1880 in order to provide laypersons* with Bible* instruction and an opportunity for spiritual renewal. While Moody strove to include a broad variety of speakers, certain themes dominated the Northfield meetings. In keeping with Moody's close contact with the Keswick* movement in England, one central emphasis was on the power of the Holy Spirit to lead believers toward a sanctified life. These conferences did much to popularize the Keswick version of Holiness* among American evangelicals.* Moreover, in keeping with Niagara* and similar conferences of the time, many speakers at Northfield strongly promoted premillennialism* and even dispensationalism.*

At first the Northfield Conference involved a single meeting for adults, but in time separate sessions were established for Christian workers, women and college students. At the first student conference, in 1886, approximately one hundred students pledged themselves to work on the foreign mission field. Over the next few years thousands of students signed the same pledge. This marked the beginning of the ambitious and influential Student Volunteer Movement,* which sought "the evangelization of the world in this generation."

The conferences were held in 1880 and 1881, and discontinued over the next three years while Moody was in England, resuming in 1885 on his return. The 1880s and 1890s were the heyday of the Northfield Conferences. When Moody died in 1899 the meetings continued, but without Moody's evangelical fervor and vision, the influence of the Northfield Conferences waned.

BIBLIOGRAPHY. J. F. Findlay, Jr., *Dwight L. Moody: American Evangelist, 1837-1899* (1969); S. N. Gundry, *Love Them In: The Life and Theology of D. L. Moody* (1976); E. R. Sandeen, *The Roots of Fundamentalism: British and American Millenarianism, 1800-1930* (1970).

W. V. Trollinger

Norton, Andrews (1786-1853). Unitarian* theologian.* Born in Hingham, Massachusetts, Norton came from a long line of learned New Englanders and studied at Harvard College* (B.A., 1804), where he also undertook graduate studies in theology (M.A., 1809). After one year of tutoring at Bowdoin College, he returned to Harvard, where he was to serve his academic career first as tutor (1811-1812), then as editor of the short-lived *General Repository and Review* (1812-1813), followed by lecturer and librarian (1813-1819) and finally professor of sacred literature (1819-1830). In 1830 he resigned from Harvard in order to devote his full time to study and writing.

Norton rejected trinitarian orthodoxy* and was one of the leaders in the founding of the American Unitarian Association* in 1825. In the years thereafter he found himself on the conservative wing of the Unitarians. Unlike other Unitarians, such as Theodore Parker,* who rejected biblical authority,* Norton accepted the gospel record as authentic and containing everything essential to true religion but reasoned that the trinitarian hermeneutic was flawed. Thus while espousing a liberal* theology, he retained confidence in the historicity and authority of Scripture at a time when European and American critics were calling both into question. Among his major theological works were *Statement of Reasons for Not Believing the Doctrines of Trinitarians* (1833), *The Evidences of the Genuineness of the Gospels,* 3 vols. (1837-1844), *Tracts Concerning Christianity* (1852) and *Internal Evidence of the Genuineness of the Gospels* (1855). For his efforts in maintaining a conservative Unitarianism, Norton became known as the "pope of Unitarianism."

BIBLIOGRAPHY. *AAP* 8; *DAB* VII; *DARB;* D. W. Howe, *The Unitarian Conscience: Harvard Moral Philosophy, 1805-1861* (1970); W. Hutchison, *The Transcendentalist Ministers: Church Reform in the New England Renaissance* (1959); W. Newell, "Andrews Norton," *Christian Examiner* 55 (November 1953):425-452; *NCAB* 17.   D. G. Buss

Norton, John (1606-1663). New England Puritan* minister.* Born at Bishop's Stortford, Hertfordshire, England, Norton was educated at St. Peter's College, Cambridge (B.A., 1624; M.A., 1627). Strongly attracted to Puritanism, he decided to immigrate to New England, arriving at Plymouth in 1635. Shortly thereafter he removed to Massachusetts Bay and became teacher in the church at Ipswich. He quickly assumed a position of leadership in the young colony, playing an important part in the antinomian controversy* and in drawing up the famous Cambridge Platform* of 1648. When John Cotton* died in 1652, Norton succeeded him as pastor of First Church, Boston. He was respected as a man with a brilliant mind, but in urging the death penalty for Quakers* and the expulsion of those who differed in matters of theology,* he revealed himself to be narrow-minded and intolerant, even by the standards of his day. In 1662 Norton journeyed to England as one of two agents chosen by the colony to present a petition to Charles II. The failure of the mission and his subsequent loss of popularity may have hastened his death in Boston on April 5, 1663.

BIBLIOGRAPHY. *AAP* 1; *DAB* VII.

R. L. Troutman

Notre Dame, University of. Catholic university. The University of Notre Dame du Lac was founded in 1842 by Edward F. Sorin* and a group of French missionaries belonging to the Congregation of Holy Cross.* Its original site was a mission founded by Theodore Badin,* the first priest* ordained* in the U.S. The school was chartered by the Indiana state legislature in 1844 and the first degree granted in 1849. Notre Dame offered only secondary and liberal arts education until 1865, when science courses were introduced. The school's programs in law (1869) and engineering (1873) were the first in any Catholic school in the country.

The late nineteenth and early twentieth centuries were a time of major growth for Notre Dame, both in size and academic reputation. John Zahm,* a noted scholar who became vice president in the late nineteenth century, began to emphasize research. Its structure, finances and curricula were reorganized, and educational standards were raised during the tenure of James Burns, who became president in 1919. A graduate school was begun in 1918 and a college of commerce (later, business administration) in 1920. In 1927 the secondary department was discontinued. The university's visibility and financial circumstances also were raised during the career of Knute Rockne, who came as a student in 1910 and remained as chemistry teacher and football coach until his untimely death in 1931.

Besides instructional programs through the doctoral level, Notre Dame currently sponsors a wide range of research institutes. These, along with its athletic and educational programs, have made it arguably the best-known Catholic university in America.

BIBLIOGRAPHY. T. J. Schlereth, *The University of Notre Dame* (1976). F. M. Perko

Novena. A Catholic* devotional practice of nine successive days of private or public prayer* to obtain some special grace. Modeled on the reputed nine days of prayer spent by the apostles in Jerusalem in preparation for the descent of the Holy Spirit at Pentecost (Lk 24:49; Acts 1:13-14), the medieval devotion* first appeared in Spain and France as a nine-day preparation for Christmas* (nine days corresponding to Jesus' nine months in Mary's womb). Popular piety* soon extended the practice to feasts of Mary* and of other saints* prized for their intercessory powers. Novenas are also celebrated in occasional circumstances of special need. C. Waddell

Novice. A candidate for the religious life as lived within a particular institute. All forms of religious life, whether Christian, pre-Christian or non-Christian, require a period of testing and formation before admission of a candidate to membership within the institute or community. In the Christian West, the year of testing prescribed by the sixth-century Rule of Benedict became generally normative, and eventually was made a condition for the validity of religious profession by the Council of Trent (1545-1563). Some institutes require a two-year novitiate. Under the guidance of a special director, and in a house properly designated for this purpose, the novices receive a comprehensive formation: prayer,* Scripture,* liturgy,* the spiritual life in general, with further instruction on the history, nature and spirit of the particular institute. C. Waddell

Noyes, John Humphrey (1811-1886). Perfectionist* and founder of the Oneida Community (1848-1881). Born in Brattleboro, Vermont, Noyes attended Dartmouth College* and graduated in 1830 at the age of nineteen, making him the youngest Dartmouth graduate to that date.

Converted in the revival* fires that scorched the "burned-over district"* of New York, Noyes forsook his brief venture into law (1830-1831) to study for the ministry* at Andover Theological Seminary* (1831-1832). After one year he transferred to Yale* Divinity School, but he was dismissed and had his ministerial license revoked in 1834 for declaring himself sinless. Noyes based this conviction on his belief that Christ had returned in A.D. 70 and had inaugurated a new age in which all believers experienced sinless perfection.

Unable to gain recognition among revivalist leaders, Noyes developed ever more radical theological and social theories rooted in perfectionism, revivalism, millennialism,* the Unitarian* socialism of Brook Farm* and eugenics. He implemented these independently of any church, establishing in 1844 a "biblical communism" (based on Acts 2; 4) at Putney, Vermont, for his disciples. In 1846 the group began its notorious practice of "complex marriage," made practical by "male continence" to prevent conception. A sign of the new dispensation, it was established to avoid the exclusivism and disharmony of marriage that was felt incompatible with perfection. Noyes announced on June 1, 1847, that the kingdom of God* had come. He moved his disciples to Oneida, New York, in 1848, after being indicted on adultery charges.

More than 300 Oneida perfectionists lived communally, shared mates, disciplined themselves by "mutual criticism," sought divine healing, prospered economically by making animal traps and created many cultural amenities. Noyes fathered nine children in their spiritualized human eugenics experiment, termed *stirpiculture*. By 1877 Noyes had relinquished leadership of the colony to a ruling committee (which soon abandoned the practice of "complex marriage"), and by 1879 pending legal action had caused him to flee to Canada, from which he never returned. Noyes's publications included *Bible Communism* (1848); *Salvation from Sin the End of Christian Faith* (1869); *History of American Socialisms* (1870) and *Male Continence* (1872).

After his departure Oneida members resumed conventional marriage and reorganized as a joint-stock company (Oneida Community, Limited) in 1880. Known today for the fine tableware of their later company, Oneida Silversmiths, Oneida descendants still occupy the community's huge Mansion House.

See also MILLENARIAN MOVEMENTS.

BIBLIOGRAPHY. M. L. Carden, *Oneida, Utopian Community to Modern Corporation* (1969); *DAB* VII; *DARB; NCAB* 11; G. W. Noyes, ed., *Religious Experience of John Humphrey Noyes* (1923); G. W. Noyes, *John Humphrey Noyes* (1931); R. D. Thomas, *The Man Who Would Be Perfect: John Humphrey Noyes and the Utopian Impulse* (1977). D. E. Pitzer

Nun. A popular term referring to any Catholic* or Anglican* woman who is a vowed member of a religious community. Technically, the term refers only to religious women under solemn (as opposed to simple) vows, who live a cloistered life of prayer* and self-denial in a monastery. The most common examples of cloistered nuns are the Catholic monasteries of Poor Clares and Carmelites. In distinction from sisters,* nuns are not engaged in active works of charity such as teaching and nursing. They are governed by rules of enclosure and generally support themselves through various small crafts and industries as well as retreat* work.

See also RELIGIOUS ORDERS, WOMEN'S.

M. L. Schneider

O

Oakes, Urian (c.1631-1681). Puritan* minister,* poet and president of Harvard College.* Born in England, probably in London, in 1631 or 1632, Urian Oakes immigrated to Cambridge, Massachusetts, with his parents in about 1640. In 1649 he was awarded the B.A. degree by Harvard College, and in 1650 he became a fellow there. Three years later he returned to England, becoming minister of Tichfield. After being silenced by the Act of Uniformity of 1662, he became headmaster of the Southwark Grammar School. With the abatement of persecution of dissenters, he organized a Congregational church at Tichfield.

In 1671 he returned to New England, having been called to the ministry of the Cambridge, Massachusetts, church, where he remained until 1675 when he became acting president of Harvard College. During his five-year stint as interim president, enrollment in the college fell to an all-time low, with only twenty-two students graduating during the period. He is perhaps best remembered for his one published poem, the "Elegie" on Thomas Shepard,* although a number of his sermons were published, including *New England-er Pleaded With* (1673), a vigorous defense of New England's first principles; *The Unconquerable, All-Conquering and More-than-Conquering Souldier* (1674), the first printed artillery election sermon; and *A Seasonable Discourse* (1682), his final fast sermon. He was appointed a censor of the Massachusetts press and in 1680, shortly before his death, was elected president of Harvard College.

BIBLIOGRAPHY. *AAP* 1; *DAB* VII; J. L. Sibley, *Biographical Sketches of Graduates of Harvard University,* vol. I (1873).   G. F. Moran

Oberholtzer, John H. (1809-1895). Mennonite* minister* and a founder of the General Conference Mennonite Church.* Born in Berks County, Pennsylvania, Oberholtzer began teaching in local schools at the age of sixteen. He later learned the locksmith trade and so supported himself through much of his life. In 1842 he became a minister in the Franconia Conference of the Mennonite Church, but was dissatisfied with some of the traditional Mennonite ways. His innovative attempts to initiate change (including Sunday school,* a written constitution and changes in the ministerial garb) met with resistance, resulting in the so-called Oberholtzer schism of 1847. A new group was founded—known as the New Mennonites—known after 1860 as the Eastern District Conference of the General Conference Mennonite Church. Here, Oberholtzer was finally able to establish a mutual-aid plan, a conference periodical, and the Sunday school. To some degree Oberholtzer was simply a Mennonite ahead of his time. Ultimately, most of his ideas found acceptance in the Franconia Conference, the very group that he left.

BIBLIOGRAPHY. "Oberholtzer Division Issue," *MQR* 46 (1972).   L. Gross

Oberlin College. An educational institution with roots in nineteenth-century evangelicalism.* In 1833 John J. Shipherd led a group of Eastern families in the establishment of a modified Christian communal society in Lorain County, Ohio. Shipherd envisioned his Oberlin community not as a conclave to retreat from the world but as a base for converting it. At the center of the communal enterprise was to be an institute which would train Christian teachers and preachers* who would go forth as evangelists.*

The school opened on December 3, 1833, with forty-four students, including fifteen females. It was not, however, until Shipherd attracted the "Lane Rebels" to Oberlin in the fall of 1835 that the school acquired its unique character. Lane Seminary of Cincinnati in the early 1830s had enrolled the largest theological class in the history of the country. Many were converts of evangelist Charles G. Finney,* and like him they sought to promote a socially sensitive evangelicalism. When most of the Lane faculty and trustees criticized the strong abolitionist* views of the majority of the students, the latter negotiated the transfer to Oberlin. Shipherd succeeded in recruiting them because he agreed to their terms: they would choose the Oberlin president, and African-American students would be admitted. The Lane transfers gave the school a direct association with Finney, the best-known evangelist of the Second Great Awakening,* and they brought to the school an intense crusading spirit of reform unmatched in American educational history. Oberlin became the abolitionist hotbed of the country. It also promoted women's rights, pioneering in awarding degrees to both white and African-American women.

After the presidency of Finney (1851-1866), Oberlin continued its social reform emphasis, but the motivation for it gradually changed from evangelical and Holiness* theology* to the newly developing liberal* Protestant* theology. By World War 1* probably no college more intensely emphasized the Social Gospel* ideals. Still later, the intellectually elite Oberlin students pursued knowledge primarily through secular patterns of thought.

BIBLIOGRAPHY. J. B. Barnard, *From Evangelicalism to Progressivism at Oberlin College, 1866-1917* (1969); R. S. Fletcher, *A History of Oberlin from its Foundation through the Civil War,* 2 vols. (1943).   W. C. Ringenberg

Oberlin Theology. The doctrine* of holiness* associated with Oberlin College* during the nineteenth century. "Oberlin perfectionism,*" the teaching that holiness consists primarily of the perfection of the will and is available to every Christian after conversion,* became associated with Oberlin primarily through the influence of Asa Mahan* and Charles G. Finney.*

Asa Mahan, the first president of the college when in 1835 it absorbed the "Lane Rebels" and was reorganized, was committed to a doctrine of perfectionism, which he described as holiness or the baptism of the Holy Spirit.* Relying on biblical passages such as 1 John 3:4, Mahan identified sin as lawlessness—voluntary, willful and conscious disobedience. Thus, holiness was understood primarily as a perfection of the will, although Mahan did not deny the Wesleyan* emphasis on the perfection of the heart—that perfect love by which the heart is cleansed of inbred sin.

Mahan maintained that perfection of the will is taught in Scripture,* and can be attained in this life by every Christian through "the provisions and promises of divine grace." Such grace did not diminish human action. As Mahan wrote in his *Scripture Doctrine of Christian Perfection:* "That we be in a perfectly sanctified and blameless state in regard to our wills, implies that the action of all

our voluntary powers be in entire conformity to the will of God."

Finney began his association with Oberlin College in 1835 as professor of theology,* and was the president of Oberlin from 1851 to 1866. His own growing belief in a biblical doctrine of holiness was confirmed through his reading of John Wesley's *A Plain Account of Christian Perfection.* However, like Mahan, Finney emphasized holiness as voluntary conformity of the human will to the will of God. This holiness was available through grace, and attainable by every Christian in this life. An immensely popular revivalist* and evangelist,* Finney used his revival meetings and his writings not only to convert sinners, but to build up the saints by preaching perfectionism.

Unlike those who advocated a private holiness, Oberlin theology was associated with social reform. Founded in 1833 as an abolitionist institution, Oberlin College continued in the forefront of the antislavery struggle, and under Finney's influence it became a hotbed of social reform and Christian activism. Committed to women's rights, Oberlin was the first coeducational college in America. Other aspects of social reform, such as the peace movement and an educational reform movement, were also identified with Oberlin. Zealous activism in society was regarded as both a natural expression of Christian conformity to the will of God for this world and a hopeful sign of the perfection God desired for society as well as the individual.

The activist environment of Oberlin did not foster unanimous agreement, and serious discussions arose over questions such as the relationship between God's grace and human action; perfection as process and perfection as dramatic "second blessing"*; perfection as sinlessness and perfection as perfect conformity to God's moral will; and the relationship between the perfection of the individual and the perfection of society.

Nevertheless, Oberlin made a distinctive contribution to nineteenth-century evangelicalism* and has proven significant for the ongoing discussion of the relationship between Christian theology and Christian living.

BIBLIOGRAPHY. W. G. Ballantine, *The Oberlin Jubilee, 1833-1883* (1883); D. W. Dayton, *Discovering an Evangelical Heritage* (1976); C. G. Finney, *Lectures in Systematic Theology* (1846); A. Mahan, *Scripture Doctrine of Christian Perfection* (1839).   R. J. Green

Oblate Sisters of Providence. The first congregation of African-American Catholic religious women. The community began as a response to the needs of the African-American refugees who fled to Baltimore from revolutionary Haiti and San Domingo in the 1790s. Out of a desire to provide an education for their children, several African-American women began a school near St. Mary's Seminary, Baltimore. The Sulpician* priest* James Hector Joubert (1777-1843) helped form them into a religious community. On July 2, 1829, Elizabeth Lange (the first superior), Marie Magdaleine Balas, Rosine Boegue and Almaide Duchemin (later to leave the community and found the Sisters, Servants of the Immaculate Heart of Mary) took their first vows. The Holy See approved their congregation in 1831. Their school flourished and became a center of worship* for the Baltimore African-American community until the death of Joubert. The congregation faced great opposition in pre-Civil War Baltimore until they came under the direction of Redemptorists* Thaddeus Anwander and John N. Neumann. Subsequently the Jesuits* and later still the Josephite Fathers played a part in their development.

In their century and a half of labor, the Oblates have expanded from St. Frances' Academy in Baltimore to other schools, orphanages, day-care centers and missions for African-Americans in a dozen different dioceses in the eastern half of the U.S. They served in Cuba until their expulsion in 1961, and in recent years have opened houses in Costa Rica. In 1988 they numbered about 165 members of African-American and other racial backgrounds.

BIBLIOGRAPHY. N. A. Chineworth, "Oblate Sisters of Providence," *NCE* 10; J. R. Meehan, "In the Days of Father Joubert," *The Borromean* 20 (1960):11-14. J. W. Bowen

Obookiah (Opukahaia), Henry (1792-1818). Hawaiian Christian and inspiration for the American Board's Sandwich Islands Mission. As a fifteen-year-old orphan, Opukahaia was taken from Honolulu to New Haven by a Yankee ship captain, where he was befriended by Samuel Mills* and other mission-minded students. Experiencing conversion* in 1812, he joined the church at Torringford, Connecticut, in 1815, and in 1816 became affiliated with the American Board of Commissioners for Foreign Missions.* The next year he was enrolled in the Foreign Mission School established at Cornwall, Connecticut, to prepare youth from heathen lands for service to their own people. He was a most effective advocate for the new cause of foreign missions: "It is truly astonishing to see what effects are produced on the feelings of the

people by seeing Henry, and hearing him converse. It opens the hearts and hands even of enemies." When he died of typhus in 1818, a *Memoirs of Henry Obookiah,* which became a best seller in New England, was published by Edwin Dwight. It inspired the organization of a mission which sailed in 1819 and became a formative influence in the history of Hawaii.

BIBLIOGRAPHY. E. Dwight, *Memoirs of Henry Obookiah,* ed. E. Wolfe (1968).

D. M. Stowe

O'Brien, John Anthony (1893-1980). Catholic* apologist* and journalist. Born in Peoria, Illinois, O'Brien studied at Holy Cross College, Worcester, Massachusetts, and St. Viator College, Bourbonnais, Illinois. Ordained* a priest* in 1916, O'Brien was assigned as chaplain* to the few Catholic students at the University of Illinois in 1918. When he resigned twenty-two years later, he left behind a church, a residence for 300 students and a program of religion courses accredited by the university. Strongly criticized by many Catholic educators and bishops for drawing Catholic students to state institutions, O'Brien argued that tens of thousands would do so anyway and that pastoral care should be provided for them.

In 1940 O'Brien moved to the University of Notre Dame* as research professor of religion and author-in-residence. Responsible for some forty-five books and countless pamphlets, his best-known work, *The Faith of Millions* (1938), was eventually published in ten languages. Neither a profound theologian* nor a creative thinker, O'Brien's interest and talent lay in making Catholic Christianity understandable to reasonably intelligent laypeople.*

BIBLIOGRAPHY. D. J. Thorman, "The Fabulous Father O'Brien," *Voice of St. Jude* (March 1960):34-38. J. T. Connelly

Occasional Sermon. Sermons delivered at times other than regularly scheduled Sunday sermons. Based on English experience, New England preachers continued the practice of delivering sermons on special occasions in the life of the colony. Election days were one of the most significant days for such sermonizing. Later, sermons were delivered on days of thanksgiving as well. Natural disasters also drove preachers to their pulpits with special messages, including a call for fasting. On these occasions, the preacher would likely argue that the disaster was a sign of God's disfavor due to sin. In New England, occasional sermons were delivered about six or seven times a year. Of the sermons that were published, most (by the Revolutionary era eighty-five per cent) were occasional sermons. Occasional, or special, sermons have continued into the twentieth century among some denominations.

BIBLIOGRAPHY. H. S. Stout, *The New England Soul* (1986).   L. J. Van Til

Occom, Samson (1723-1792). Native American* evangelist.* A Mohegan Indian born near New London, Connecticut, Occom converted to Christianity about 1740 during the Great Awakening.* Later (1743-1747) he studied at Moor's Charity School at Lebanon, Connecticut, where his success inspired his teacher, Eleazar Wheelock,* with the idea of training young Native Americans as evangelists. In 1759 he received ordination as a Presbyterian* minister.*

Occom became an influential preacher and tribal leader among Native Americans in the Northeast, traveling widely in southern New England, Long Island and the New York region. In 1764 he accompanied Nathaniel Whitaker on a successful two-year trip to England, raising funds for Wheelock's mission. After the American Revolution,* he led several of his followers from Connecticut to a new settlement, Brothertown, in western New York, hoping to avoid white encroachment. There he continued his evangelistic work until late in life. Although little is known about the doctrinal nature of his preaching, he was a highly esteemed orator and was perhaps the most significant Native American evangelist of his era.

BIBLIOGRAPHY. *AAP* 3; H. W. Blodgett, *Samson Occom* (1935); *DAB* VII; *DARB;* W. D. Love, *Sampson Occom and the Christian Indians of New England* (1899); L. B. Richardson, *An Indian Preacher in England* (1933).   M. S. Joy

Occultism. From the Latin word *occultus,* meaning "hidden," the occult refers to those practices and beliefs dealing with supernatural influences, agencies or phenomena which are concealed or hidden from the masses and available only to "the initiated." The occult is best understood as religion since its subject matter lies in the realm of the paranormal (powers that exceed normal human expectations) and the supernatural (that which is beyond the natural, beyond the realm of normal human experience) and because its main goals pertain to the discovery of "ultimate meaning." Most scholars include under the rubric of the occult such phenomena as clairvoyance, telepathy, precognition, psychokenesis, alchemy, divination,

dowsing, sorcery, necromancy, astrology, spiritualism and mediumship, palmistry, tarot card reading, numerology, crystal-gazing, "the second sight," phantoms and apparitions, poltergeist activity, lycanthropy, vampirism, voodoo, shamanism, Satanism, demonology, exorcism, witchcraft, mysticism,* faith healing* and the New Age Movement.*

The study of the occult is fraught with controversy and difficulty in that the credibility of some of these phenomena (e.g., alchemy, lycanthropy, vampirism) is dismissed out of hand by many scholars, while others, such as J. B. Rhine, subsume clairvoyance, telepathy and precognition under the heading of extrasensory perception (ESP). Moreover, some individuals and groups hotly dispute that they are a part of the occult at all. For example, white witches claim that they are members of an ancient pagan religion which predates Judaism and Christianity and that they practice only benign magic; and New Agers maintain they belong to a loosely structured network of organizations and individuals bound together by common values based on mysticism and monism and a common vision of a coming "new age" of peace and mass enlightenment. Still, they are also known to embrace sundry occult practices such as spirit channeling, psychic healing and crystal power. Further, some aspects of the occult—such as exorcism, mysticism and faith healing—overlap with and impinge upon Christian belief and practice.

Occultism has been present since ancient times and exists in some form in every culture. Western civilization has experienced two major outbreaks of occult activity: first in the Renaissance era (the fourteenth through the sixteenth centuries) and again in the twentieth century. In the late 1960s and 1970s, the media focused its attention on a resurgence of interest in magic, spiritualism, witchcraft, and neo-paganism in general, while in the 1980s it spotlighted the spread of Satanism and the New Age Movement. Historically speaking, the term *occult* has had a generally negative connotation in Western society. Modern scientists consider it regressive in that, according to the canons of science, no thing should be left hidden that can be discussed and understood. Christians historically have distrusted the occult and have regarded it as evil because of its inherent paganism, because many of its beliefs and practices are contrary to biblical teaching, because of biblical injunctions against participating in most occult activities, and because of the self-destructive nature of many occult practices.

See also SALEM WITCH TRIALS.

BIBLIOGRAPHY. M. Adler, *Drawing down the Moon: Witches, Druids, Goddess-Worshippers, and other Pagans in America Today,* rev. ed. (1986); R. Cavendish, *The Black Arts* (1967); R. Cavendish, *Man, Myth, and Magic,* 24 vols. (1970); H. Kerr and C. L. Crow, eds., *The Occult in America* (1983); A. Lyons, *Satan Wants You: The Cult of Devil Worship in America* (1988); J. W. Montgomery, *Principalities and Powers* (1973); E. Peters, *The Magician, the Witch and the Law* (1978); J. B. Russell, *The Devil* (1977); J. B. Russell, *A History of Witchcraft, Sorcerers, Heretics and Pagans* (1980); J. W. Sire, *The Universe Next Door,* rev. ed. (1988); K. Thomas, *Religion and the Decline of Magic* (1971); J. S. Wright, *Understanding the Supernatural* (1971). R. D. Linder

Ockenga, Harold John (1905-1985). Congregational* minister* and new evangelical* organizational leader. Born and reared in Chicago in a Methodist* family, Ockenga experienced a call to the ministry* as a teen-ager. He attended Taylor University, an evangelical* Methodist college in Indiana, graduated in 1927, and enrolled in Princeton Theological Seminary.* Ockenga was among the student followers of a militantly conservative faction of Princeton's faculty, led by J. Gresham Machen.* This group founded Westminster Theological Seminary in Philadelphia in 1929, and Ockenga graduated from Westminster the following year.

After pastoring two Methodist churches in New Jersey, Ockenga accepted an invitation in 1931 to assist an eminent conservative, Clarence Macartney,* who was pastor of the First Presbyterian Church of Pittsburgh. Later that year Macartney and Machen recommended Ockenga for the pastorate of the Point Breeze Presbyterian Church in suburban Pittsburgh. While at that church, Ockenga began graduate study in philosophy at the University of Pittsburgh, and eventually was awarded the Ph.D. in 1939. He also met Audrey Williamson on the Pitt campus; they were married in 1935.

In 1936, on the advice of Macartney and Machen, A. Z. Conrad, a fundamentalist* leader in Boston, chose Ockenga to succeed him as pastor of the Park Street Congregational Church. The young pastor's organizational gifts and scholarly preaching* made Park Street Church thrive and brought him leadership opportunities among evangelicals in New England.

Ockenga soon began to exercise his talents in wider circles. In 1940 and 1941, he and J. Elwin Wright, director of the New England Fellowship,

planned and promoted the National Association of Evangelicals,* of which Ockenga served as president from its founding in 1942 until 1944. Ockenga was invited in 1947 to be founding president of a new theological seminary in Pasadena, California, by the famous radio evangelist Charles E. Fuller.* As president *in absentia* from 1947 to 1954 and 1960 to 1963, Ockenga helped establish Fuller Theological Seminary* as the leading scholarly institution of the "new evangelical" movement— a movement to reform fundamentalism and develop a positive theological and cultural agenda.

Ockenga helped lead the evangelical resurgence in other ways as well. In January 1950, Park Street Church hosted an evangelistic campaign with a young evangelist* named Billy Graham.* It met with astonishing success, and later that year Graham and Ockenga toured New England on an extended preaching mission. Subsequently, as one of the organizers with Graham in the founding of *Christianity Today** in 1956, Ockenga helped provide the new evangelical movement with a national voice.

Ockenga's later years were less eventful, but he continued to provide steady guidance to the neo-evangelical enterprise. He remained the pastor of Park Street Church until 1969, and then became president of Gordon College and Divinity School. He later presided over the newly merged Gordon-Conwell Theological Seminary from 1970 until 1979. Ockenga also served *Christianity Today* as chairman of its board until 1981.

From the early days of the evangelical resurgence onward, Ockenga stressed the need for strong national leadership among evangelicals. And through four dynamic and often stormy decades, he practiced what he preached.

BIBLIOGRAPHY. H. C. Englizian, *Brimstone Corner: Park Street Church* (1968); H. Lindsell, *Park Street Prophet* (1951); G. M. Marsden, *Reforming Fundamentalism: Fuller Seminary and the New Evangelicalism* (1987).

J. A. Carpenter

O'Connell, Denis Joseph (1849-1927). Strategist and Roman agent for the American Catholic liberal party of bishops* in the late nineteenth century. Irish-born O'Connell studied for the priesthood in Rome and was ordained May 26, 1877. He served as rector of the North American College,* Rome (1885-1895) and of Catholic University of America* (1903-1909). His last post was shadowed by a financial crisis not of the rector's making; despite financial setbacks, he worked to make the institution an academy of the highest academic standards, even in the midst of the crisis over Modernism.* In 1909 O'Connell arrived in San Francisco as auxiliary* bishop and was appointed bishop of Richmond in 1912, a position he held until 1926, one year before his death.

O'Connell was allied with such American liberal prelates as James Gibbons,* John Ireland* and John Keane.* He sought greater control of church affairs by American leadership and a full participation by American Catholics in the institutions of national life, including the public schools.* A strong defender of the First Amendment,* he believed that Catholicism must adapt itself to new cultures and that in the U.S., Catholicism could reach a new and excellent expression. He supported the cause of the worker, the involvement of the nation in the Spanish-American War* as a herald of the victory of American freedom over European decadence, and the introduction of the apostolic delegate* to the U.S. in 1893 as a means which he mistakenly thought would influence the pope* in more liberal directions.

BIBLIOGRAPHY. G. P. Fogarty, *The Vatican and the Americanist Crisis: Denis J. O'Connell, American Agent in Rome* (1974). C. F. Crews

O'Connell, William Henry (1859-1944).

Cardinal* of Boston. Born in Lowell, Massachusetts, O'Connell studied for the priesthood* in Rome, where he was ordained* in 1884. While there he studied under Francisco Satolli,* who in 1892 became the first apostolic delegate* to the U.S. O'Connell was an assistant priest in the Boston archdiocese in 1895 when Satolli nominated him to be rector* of the North American College in Rome,* where O'Connell himself had studied.

During the 1890s there was tension between the Vatican* and some American bishops over what Pope Leo XIII* regarded as overly independent tendencies on the part of the bishops. O'Connell's appointment was part of a process whereby priests who strongly supported the pope were promoted to sensitive positions. In 1901 O'Connell was made bishop of Portland, Maine. In 1905—a rare thing for an American—he was sent on a papal diplomatic mission as papal legate to Japan. There he negotiated issues arising out of the recent Russo-Japanese War and laid the groundwork for the establishment of a Jesuit* university in Tokyo. The following year he became coadjutor bishop of Boston, with the right of succession, becoming archbishop* the following year. In 1911, at an unusually young age, he was made a cardinal.

For a quarter of a century O'Connell was the dominant figure in the American Catholic hierarchy, a status achieved both by his strong personality and his close Vatican connections. Considered autocratic by many, he had a firm sense of episcopal* authority.* He opposed, for example, the establishment of the National Catholic Welfare Conference* in 1919 on the grounds that no national body should claim to speak for all the bishops. As a cardinal he was entitled to vote in papal elections. However, he missed those of 1914 and 1922, because of the time required to travel to Rome. He finally participated in the election of 1939, when Pius XII was chosen.

Cardinal O'Connell was a cultured man who played and composed music. He was also a lover of art and a great builder of churches. In 1937 he was awarded an honorary doctorate from Harvard University.*

BIBLIOGRAPHY. R. H. Lord et al., *History of the Archdiocese of Boston*, 3 vols. (1945); W. H. O'Connell, *Recollections of Seventy Years* (1934); D. G. Wayman, *Cardinal O'Connell of Boston* (1955). J. F. Hitchcock

O'Connor, Flannery (1925-1964).

Catholic* southern fiction writer. A master of short fiction and a superb regionalist, Flannery O'Connor was born in Savannah and lived most of her life in Milledgeville, Georgia. Educated at Georgia College and then at the University of Iowa Writing Workshops, O'Connor considered leaving the South. Following a fellowship at Yaddo (the writer's colony in New York) and a long stay with friends in Connecticut, O'Connor returned to her family farm, Andalusia, near Milledgeville, stricken with disseminated lupus—an incurable, but treatable, disease. There, under the care of her mother, O'Connor practiced her devotion to her art and her Catholic faith while carrying on a voluminous correspondence with friends and readers. Weakened by the cortisone injections which controlled the disease, she succumbed in 1964 at the peak of her powers.

In her two novels, *Wise Blood* (1952) and *The Violent Bear It Away* (1960), and in her short stories, especially "A Good Man Is Hard to Find" (1955) and "Everything That Rises Must Converge" (published posthumously in 1965), O'Connor's vision of the human predicament is carefully delineated. Although she was a regionalist, sensitive to the nuances of speech and the religious and cultural conventions of the Deep South, she discovered in her characters universal dilemmas. A staunch apologist* for the Christian faith, she nevertheless struck out at facile formulations but nearly always found a supernatural grace operating in the midst of horror and degradation. Recognizing that the twentieth-century reader may be immune to the sins of the world, O'Connor employed the grotesque in order to ensure that darkness be "writ large." Never doubting the reality of her Christian faith and the Church which guarded and nurtured it, she nevertheless knew that the Christian artist faces a hostile world. "That belief in Christ is to some a matter of life and death has been a stumbling block for readers who would prefer to think it a matter of no great consequences," she once commented. In her finest short stories, "A Good Man Is Hard to Find," "Good Country People" and "Revelation," for example, O'Connor explored human motivations and Christian doctrine, without tripping over dogma and without compromising her goal of integrating Christian faith and her artistic vision.

BIBLIOGRAPHY. F. O'Connor, *The Complete Stories* (1971); F. O'Connor, *The Habit of Being: The Letters of Flannery O'Connor,* ed. Fitzgerald (1979); M. J. Freedman and L. A. Lawson, eds., *The Added Dimension: The Art and Mind of Flannery O'Connor* (1966). J. E. Barcus

Oglethorpe, James Edward (1696-1785). English philanthropist* and colonizer. The fifth son of a landed English family, Oglethorpe abandoned a military career when the Jacobian sympathies of his only surviving brother left him heir to the family estate. He entered public life and served as a Tory member of Parliament (1722-1754). In that capacity he took an active interest in debtors, seamen and prisoners.

By combining an undesignated charitable bequest with an existing fund for the instruction of African-Americans, Oglethorpe was able to raise the capital to create a colony (Georgia) to which English poor could be sent as an alternative to debtors' prison. George II approved a charter (1732), and Oglethorpe sailed with the first ship of settlers, arriving in 1733. With the exception of two return trips to England (1734-1735 and 1736-1738), he spent the next ten years as resident governor of the colony.

Oglethorpe's early years were devoted to shaping Georgia along more humane lines than those of existing colonies. He negotiated a treaty with Tomochichi and other Native-American chiefs, limited the importation of rum, forbade slavery and opened the colony to Scottish, German, Austrian and Swiss Protestants.* He appealed to the Society for the Propagation of the Gospel* for Anglican* clergy,* but also supported efforts to bring Presbyterian,* Lutheran* and Moravian* clergy. Oglethorpe's later years in Georgia (1736-1743) were preoccupied in protecting the colony from the Spanish. The colonists began to reverse his idealistic program, repealing, for example, his anti-rum (1742) and antislavery policies (1750). Oglethorpe returned to England, and in 1752 the crown claimed Georgia as a royal colony.

BIBLIOGRAPHY. L. F. Church, *Oglethorpe: A Study of Philanthropy in England and Georgia* (1932). R. W. Prichard

O'Gorman, Thomas (1843-1921). Catholic* bishop* of Sioux Falls, South Dakota. Born in Boston, O'Gorman was educated in Chicago, St. Paul (under John Ireland*) and at seminaries in Maximieux and Montbel, France. He was ordained* a priest* in 1865 and in 1877 joined the Paulists.* He later became (1885) the first president of the College of St. Thomas in St. Paul. Resigning after two years, he became professor of dogmatic theology, French and English for four years and, in 1890, professor of modern church history at the Catholic University of America,* where he actively supported the liberal policies of Americanists* during the controversies of late nineteenth-century American Catholicism. A close friend of Archbishop John Ireland, O'Gorman was consecrated bishop in 1896 and assigned the diocese* of Sioux Falls. During his twenty-six-year tenure, the Catholic foundation of his diocese expanded considerably and the Catholic population doubled. Author of *A History of the Roman Catholic Church in the United States* (1905), he was appointed a member (1902) of President William McKinley's* Taft Commission that dealt with Rome regarding the friars' land problem in the Philippines, an issue that was settled amicably in 1903.

BIBLIOGRAPHY. *DAB* VII. C. E. Ronan

O'Hara, Edwin Vincent (1881-1956). Catholic* archbishop* and rural sociologist. Born in Lanesboro, Minnesota, O'Hara was educated at St. Thomas College in St. Paul, Minnesota, and St. Paul Seminary. In 1905 he was ordained* priest* for the diocese* of Oregon City (now Portland), with his first assignment to the cathedral* in Portland. On returning to his diocese after a period of studies at the Catholic University of America,* he exhibited a great concern for social rights and played a major role in the enactment of the 1913 Oregon minimum-wage law. After service in World War 1,* he began to promote Catholic education in rural districts and became the first chairman of the Rural

Life Bureau of the National Catholic Welfare Conference* in 1920, a post he held until 1930. As chairman, he published *A Program of Catholic Rural Action* and *The Church and the Country Community* and also convened the first National Catholic Rural Life Conference in 1923.

When the Oregon school bill requiring attendance in the public schools was passed, he led the legal fight against it until it was declared unconstitutional by the U.S. Supreme Court.* In 1930 he was consecrated* bishop and assigned the diocese* of Great Falls, Montana. There he worked with over 130 parishes as well as with the Native-American tribes of his diocese. While in Great Falls he also formed the Confraternity of Christian Doctrine,* which later expanded into a national confraternity. In 1936 he organized a committee to discuss a revised English translation of the Scriptures.* In 1952 the Confraternity of Christian Doctrine brought out its first volume of the revised translation of the Old Testament. In 1939 he was appointed to the diocese of Kansas City, where he began an ambitious building program which consisted of the construction of forty-two churches, fourteen convents, sixteen grade schools, six high schools and two colleges. In 1954 he was appointed archbishop. A leading American proponent of the use of the vernacular in the liturgy,* he was largely responsible for the first approved English ritual that came out in 1954. He died in Milan, Italy.

BIBLIOGRAPHY. *DARB; NCAB* 43; J. G. Shaw, *Edwin Vincent O'Hara, American Prelate* (1957). C. E. Ronan

O'Hara, John Francis (1888-1960). Educator and cardinal* archbishop* of Philadelphia. Born in Ann Arbor, Michigan, O'Hara's father was American consul to Uruguay, and so he first attended the Jesuit college in Montevideo, Uruguay. Graduating from the University of Notre Dame (B.A., 1911), he did graduate studies at the Catholic University of America* and the Wharton School in Philadelphia. He was ordained* a priest* in the Congregation of Holy Cross* in 1916 and from then until 1945 served at the University of Notre Dame as prefect of religion (1917-1933), founder and later dean of the College of Commerce (1920-1924), vice president (1933-1934) and president (1934-1939).

In 1939 he was named auxiliary bishop* of the Military Ordinariate and in 1945 became bishop of Buffalo, New York. Promoted to Philadelphia in 1951 and named a cardinal in 1958, O'Hara developed Philadelphia's parochial* school system by building over sixty new schools and promoting

education for the mentally retarded.

BIBLIOGRAPHY. T. T. McAvoy, *Father O'Hara of Notre Dame, The Cardinal Archbishop of Philadelphia* (1967). J. W. Evans

O'Kelly, James (1757-1826). Methodist* minister* and leader of the O'Kelly schism.* Born in Ireland, O'Kelly immigrated to America in 1778 during the heat of the American Revolution.* In that same year he became a traveling preacher within the Methodist connection and was ordained* elder* during the organizing conference for the Methodist Episcopal Church in 1784. For several years O'Kelly was presiding elder of the South Virginia district, during which time he became enamored with the independent spirit of the Republic and the themes of freedom and equality. This led him to a confrontation with the church hierarchy which he feared was not in line with the American people.

In 1792, during the first General Conference of the Methodist Episcopal Church, O'Kelly instigated the first notable schism within Methodism. Challenging supposed ecclesiastical despotism, primarily on the part of Bishop Francis Asbury,* O'Kelly championed an opposition to episcopal* authority.* The resolution introduced during this conference has continued to be an issue among Methodists to the present. The motion stated that any preacher* dissatisfied with his appointment has the right of appeal, and with conference approval the bishop shall reappoint. When the motion was defeated, O'Kelly withdrew and the controversy continued (in spite of Asbury's attempts at reconciliation), culminating in the organization of the Republican Methodist Church soon afterward.

Although the Methodist Episcopal Church reported a loss of 8,000 members to the schism over the next six years, and several prominent preachers (including William McKendree* for just one year), O'Kelly, disappointed with the numbers joining his ranks, watched the movement dissipate into relative obscurity within twenty years. For all his limitations and frustrations, O'Kelly continued a long and honorable life as a minister of the gospel and died October 6, 1826, respected and even beloved by many throughout the church.

BIBLIOGRAPHY. J. Burnett, *Reverend James O'Kelly, A Champion of Religious Liberty* (n.d.); *DAB* VII; *DARB*; W. E. MacClenny, *The Life of Rev. James O'Kelly* (1910); *NCAB* 13.

R. G. Tuttle

O'Kelly Schism. A schism named for Methodist* preacher* James O'Kelly* whose attempt to restrict the authority* of bishops* caused the first major division in the American Methodist Church. In 1789 O'Kelly, who had been a circuit rider* in southern Virginia since 1778, became alarmed at the increasing authority of Bishop Francis Asbury.* Then, as now, the Methodist episcopacy* functioned with an appointment system in which a minister is sent to a charge at the discretion of the presiding bishop. O'Kelly sought to create a more democratic system of appointments.

The resolution he introduced at the 1792 General Conference* stated that "after a bishop appoints the preachers at conference to their several circuits, if anyone thinks himself injured by the appointment, he shall have liberty to appeal to the conference and state his objections: and if the conference approve his objections, the bishop shall appoint him to another circuit." But the motion was lost after a long and heated debate, and the authority of the bishop over appointments and therefore over the clergy* remained unlimited.

O'Kelly withdrew from the Methodist Episcopal Church,* taking with him a few influential clergy, including William McKendree* and as many as 8,000 members to form the Republican Methodist Church. The schism precipitated a tractarian warfare that lasted into the early nineteenth century. O'Kelly's views were ably expressed in tracts like *The Author's Apology for Protesting Against the Methodist Episcopal Government* (1798) and *A Vindication of the Author's Apology with Reflections on the Reply* (1801). Numerically strong in southern Virginia and North Carolina, a remnant of the church survived to reunite with the Methodist Episcopal Church in 1934. The O'Kelly schism was the first of many collisions between American democractic* ideals and Methodist episcopal polity.* It had the lasting effects of solidifying the power of the bishops and also forced the Methodist Episcopal Church to scrutinize and formalize its church discipline.*

BIBLIOGRAPHY. C. F. Kilgore, *The James O'Kelly Schism in the Methodist Episcopal Church* (1963); F. A. Norwood, "James O'Kelly, Methodist Maverick," *MH* (April 1966):14-28. J. R. Tyson

Old Calvinists. *See* NEW ENGLAND THEOLOGY.

Old Lights. The term *Old Light* emerged in New England during the Great Awakening* (1740-1743) to describe the socially and theologically conservative opponents of George Whitefield* and the mass revivals* he inspired. In judging the fruits of the revivals, Old Lights denied that the Great Awakening was a work of God, claiming instead

that it destroyed the peace and unity of the church by pitting enthusiastic lay* people and itinerant* preachers* against the established clergy* of New England.

The Old Light clergy could be found throughout New England but were especially strong around Boston where they were led by the clergyman Charles Chauncy.* To document the excesses of the revivals, Chauncy embarked on an exhaustive speaking tour of New England churches, drawing examples of ways in which the new revivalists replaced reasonable Christianity with a blind "enthusiasm" (literally, for Old Lights, a form of mental illness or madness). In his massive treatise, *Seasonable Thoughts on the State of Religion in New-England* (1743), Chauncy identified the New Light revival party with Anne Hutchinson* and other "Antinomians"* of the seventeenth century. There was no rational arguing with these people, he complained: "You had as good reason with the wind." In place of "raised Affections," he continued, an "enlightened mind" must always be the guide of those who would call themselves Christians.

Besides Chauncy and perhaps half of the Congregational* clergy in New England, strong support for the Old Light cause came from the colleges in Cambridge and New Haven. Following the publication of Whitefield's *Journal* in 1741, with its blunt criticisms of the colleges, the faculties of Harvard* and Yale* joined forces with Chauncy in opposing Whitefield and the revivals as forces disrupting the spirituality* and order of the settled churches. So extreme were the arguments from both Old Lights and New Lights, that it seemed for a time as though one could not be party to the opposition and be a Christian at the same time.

By 1744 New England's Old Light and New Light clergy recognized that their divisions were hurting themselves and their churches more than they were helping. In place of the heated rhetoric of 1742 and 1743, moderate clerical voices pleaded for moderation and tolerance. Thereafter doctrinal and rhetorical divisions between Old Light and New Light continued, but without the intolerance that marked earlier debates. Not until after the Revolution would the debates renew and lead to a permanent schism in New England Protestantism* between heart-centered "evangelicals"* and a head-centered rationalist religion.

BIBLIOGRAPHY. E. S. Gaustad, *The Great Awakening in New England* (1957). H. S. Stout

Old Order Mennonites. A broad term refering to independent conservative Mennonite* bodies that separated from the Mennonite Church* in a series of schisms from 1872 to 1901. These divisions often arose as a result of objections to innovations such as Sunday schools* and a perceived decline of traditional discipline in the Mennonite Church. Old Order Mennonites can be classified as (1) more progressive and (2) more conservative. In general, the progressive groups conduct their worship* services in English and drive cars; they are also free to use modern inventions such as the telephone. The more conservative groups often conduct their services in Pennsylvania German (a Palatine dialect) and drive horses and buggies.

Old Order Mennonites hold in high esteem Anabaptist forebears such as Dirk Philips (1502-1568), Menno Simons (1496-1561), Michael Sattler, and T. J. van Braght, author of the seventeenth-century Dutch martyrology, the *Martyrs Mirror* (1660). All groups use the 1632 Dordrecht *Confession of Faith*.

Old Order Mennonites baptize* individuals on confession of faith in Christ—an event usually occurring among young people in their late teens. Members refuse to swear oaths, even in court, but testify to the truth with a simple affirmation. They hold to nonresistance, and do not unite with secret orders. Generally, those who wish to attend college or university transfer their membership to the main body, the Mennonite Church. Old Order men typically work as farmers, carpenters and masons; the women are homemakers, nurses or schoolteachers. They shun political office.

Old Order Mennonites are chiefly centered in southeastern Pennsylvania, especially Lancaster County; Virginia, particularly Rockingham County; Ohio, in Holmes and neighboring counties; Indiana, especially Elkhart County; and Ontario, particularly Waterloo County. In Indiana, the progressive Old Orders are known as Wislers; in Lancaster County, as the Hornings (Weaverland Conference); in Indiana, the conservatives are known as the Old Orders; in Pennsylvania's Lancaster County, as the Wengers (Groffdale Conference). Old Order Mennonites number under 20,000 members in approximately 100 churches.

BIBLIOGRAPHY. C. J. Dyck, *An Introduction to Mennonite History* (1967); A. B. Hoover, *Jonas Martin Era* (1982); J. C. Wenger, *The Mennonites in Indiana and Michigan* (1961).

J. C. Wenger

Old Order River Brethren. A small Brethren denomination. The Old Order River Brethren withdrew from the larger River Brethren Church (now Brethren in Christ*) in the 1850s in order to maintain conservative standards. First identified as a separate group in York County, Pennsylvania, they became known by some as "Yorker Brethren." In the twentieth century they have centered around Franklin County and Lancaster County, Pennsylvania, and Dallas County, Iowa.

The Old Order River Brethren believe in the basic tenets of conservative Christianity, with a special emphasis on personal conversion,* repentance and obedience to God. Old forms of worship* are practiced, including traditional, slow tunes sung a cappella. Leadership is not salaried or formally trained, being selected from the congregation by majority vote. They do not have Sunday schools,* but every worship service features an "experience meeting" in which members present may give their personal testimony. Communion* is observed during a two-day "love feast," which includes feet washing.* Believer's baptism* is practiced by threefold immersion. Worship services have traditionally been held in members' homes and barns, but meeting houses, schools and other public buildings have also been used. The Old Order River Brethren believe in nonresistance and nonconformity to the world. They observe plain dress, and women wear head coverings and men grow beards. The smallest of the three groups of Old Order River Brethren use horse-drawn vehicles rather than cars. In 1987 there were 324 members of the Old Order River Brethren fellowships.

BIBLIOGRAPHY. M. S. Dietz, "The Old Order River Brethren," *Brethren in Christ History and Life* 6 (1983):4-34; S. E. Scott, "The Old Order River Brethren," *Pennsylvania Mennonite Heritage* 1 (1978):13-22. S. E. Scott

Old School Presbyterians. During the 1730s and 1740s several colonial denominations* suffered internal divisions over questions regarding the theological legitimacy and ecclesiastical propriety of the Great Awakening* in New England and the Middle Colonies. New England Congregationalism* was rent asunder as two parties—the "New Light" pro-Awakening party and the "Old Light" anti-Awakening group—sought to impose their respective views on the denomination. Colonial Presbyterians* were also of two minds about the Awakening. Under the leadership of Gilbert Tennent,* "New Side"* Presbyterians labored to advance the Awakening, against the objections of "Old Side"* traditionalists. Although the New Side—Old Side division nearly effected a permanent schism within colonial Presbyterianism, the contending parties were finally reconciled in 1758. The rapprochement favored the New Side party, who had consolidated their gains by installing a series of pro-Awakeners (Jonathan Dickinson,* Aaron Burr, Sr., Jonathan Edwards,* Samuel Davies* and Samuel Finley*) in the presidency of the fledgling College of New Jersey* at Princeton, New Jersey. Building on Princeton's* impressive New Side intellectual tradition, its next president, John Witherspoon,* made Princeton the center of Presbyterian thought in America.

Witherspoon's presidency effected a new balance in the New Side—Old Side animosities. A Scot, he represented thousands of Scottish and Scotch-Irish Presbyterians* who had immigrated* to the new nation long after the Awakening. These new Americans, accustomed to the more traditional Presbyterianism of the Kirk, rapidly became the dominant force in American Presbyterianism, and a gradual shift away from New Side sentiment took place.

This movement is best seen in the career of Archibald Alexander.* Raised in Virginia, Alexander served a Presbyterian church in Philadelphia, from where he successfully led the effort to form Princeton Theological Seminary* in 1812. As the Seminary's first professor, Alexander formed a distinct version of Presbyterian theology that found its genesis in older, European formulations of Calvinism. Alexander eschewed the nuanced American versions of Reformed* thought found in the Puritans* and their latter-day heirs, Jonathan Edwards and Nathaniel W. Taylor.* Using François Turretin's *Institutio Theologiae Elencticae* and demanding strict adherence to the Westminster Confession of Faith,* Alexander formed what became known as the "Old School" theology.*

Under Alexander's direction, and due in great measure to the efforts of his colleague Charles Hodge,* Princeton Seminary became the intellectual center of Old School Presbyterianism. The Old School opposed many of the popular emphases of nineteenth-century American Protestantism.* In matters ecclesiastical, the Old School affirmed Presbyterian polity* (with its hierarchical system of presbyteries,* synods* and general assemblies*) as the most accurate, biblical form of church polity. Old School theologians were assiduous in their opposition to several nineteenth-century attempts to unite American Presbyterians and congregationalists into a single ecclesiastical body. Nor were they interested in the myriad of interdenominational efforts (voluntary societies* concerned with abolition,* temperance* or foreign missions*) that

were popular in antebellum America. From the Old School perspective, such efforts threatened the purity* of the church,* and hence were suspect.

The Old School found the revival* tactics of the Second Great Awakening* similarly distasteful. As Charles G. Finney* promulgated his "new measures"* for evangelism,* and as Methodists,* Baptists* and some Presbyterians on the frontier experimented with camp meeting* revivalism, Old School thinkers criticized these new phenomena as doctrinally shallow. When Lyman Beecher* and Nathaniel W. Taylor formulated their "New Haven"* theology, largely in defense of the new revivalism, the Old School responded predictably. Princeton theologians decried Taylor's progressive view of human depravity as a heretical denial of the classic Calvinistic doctrine of the imputation of sin.* Beecher fared little better at the hands of the Old School. In 1835, after becoming president of Lane Theological Seminary, a Presbyterian institution in Cincinnati, he was tried and later acquitted on the charge that he had abandoned the central tenets of the Westminister Confession.

Despite the fact that Princeton Seminary served as the chief intellectual center of the Old School through much of the nineteenth century, many Old School congregations were located in slaveholding states. Conversely, much of the New School strength was located north of the Mason-Dixon line. In 1837 Old School forces managed to expel four Northern New School presbyteries from the denomination on theological grounds, an event that led to the creation of two competing denominations (*See* Auburn Declaration). Despite this apparent Old School victory, however, the tumultuous slavery issue continued to threaten the unity of both the Old School and the New School alliances. Notwithstanding strenuous efforts to maintain unity within each of the competing groups, the New School body divided over the slavery issue in 1857, and the Old School divided soon after Confederate forces attacked Fort Sumter in 1861 (*See* Civil War and the Churches). The New School-Old School schism in the North was healed during the period 1868-1870, while Presbyterians in the South reunited in 1864, facilitated by the crisis of the Civil War.*

See also New School Presbyterians; New Side Presbyterians; Old Side Presbyterians; Princeton Theology; Scottish Presbyterians.

Bibliography. S. E. Ahlstrom, *A Religious History of the American People* (1972); L. A. Loetscher, *A Brief History of the Presbyterians* (1978); E. T. Thompson, *Presbyterians in the South,* 3 vols (1973).   J. R. Fitzmier

Old Side Presbyterians. Conservative party within eighteenth-century Presbyterians. Presbyterianism was planted in the mid-Atlantic American colonies by Francis Makemie* in the 1690s. Although the original intention was to organize Scottish and Scotch-Irish immigrants* under an authoritative synodical* hierarchy, it proved difficult to recruit clergy* from Scotland or Ulster. However, when New England college graduates were ordained, they tended to import notions of congregational* polity* and pietist* evangelicalism* into the Presbyterian churches and rather loosely held to the political tenets of the Westminster Confession.* This posed a serious challenge to traditional Presbyterian order, especially after 1735, when William Tennent* organized a theological school, the "Log College,"* which espoused Pietist principles.

In an effort to preserve conservative Presbyterian order, the Scottish and Scotch-Irish clergy,* known as the "Old Side," responded to the New England influence by: (1) enforcing the Adopting Act* (1728-1729), which stipulated the degree of confessional subscription required by candidates for ordination; (2) requiring the Synod of Philadelphia in 1738 to state that Log College graduates submit their credentials to a synodical reviewing committee before licensure and ordination; and (3) censuring the New Brunswick, New Jersey, presbytery in 1739 for ordaining a Log College graduate, J. Rowlandson, in defiance of synodical authority.

These tactics provoked fiery protest from Gilbert Tennent,* but the Synod of Philadelphia responded by rebuking Tennent, and under the terms of a "Protestation," Tennent and the New Brunswick presbytery were ejected from the Synod. The New Side and Old Side factions then engaged in a protracted pamphlet war that gradually expanded to a debate over the merits of revivals,* itinerant* preaching* and the Great Awakening* of the 1740s. Significant spokesmen for the Old Side were Francis Alison* and John Ewing, who argued against the New Siders' "disorderly Way, contrary to all Presbyterian Rules," criticized the psychology of revival and attacked the New Siders' association with George Whitefield.* The Old Siders, however, were unable to compete against the greater zeal of the New Siders and the mobility of New Side itinerant preachers, and so Old Side arguments failed to win a popular following. An effort by Francis Alison to organize a rival theological school failed.

The New Side and Old Side jurisdictions were eventually reunited in 1758. Old Side principles continued to command significant loyalty within Presbyterian education, especially under John Witherspoon* at the College of New Jersey* (Princeton) after 1768 and under Archibald Alexander* at Princeton Theological Seminary* after 1812. They played an important, if not the dominant, role in the Old School*—New School* schism of 1837.

See also GREAT AWAKENING; NEW SCHOOL PRESBYTERIANS; NEW SIDE PRESBYTERIANS; OLD SCHOOL PRESBYTERIANS.

BIBLIOGRAPHY. L. Trinterud, *The Forming of an American Tradition: A Re-examination of Colonial Presbyterianism* (1949); C. Hodge, *The Constitutional History of the Presbyterian Church in the United States of America,* 2 vols. (1851).

A. C. Guelzo

Olney, Thomas (?-1682). Colonial Baptist* leader. Olney was one of several colonists who followed Roger Williams* from Salem to Providence, Rhode Island, in 1638 after Williams's banishment from Massachusetts Bay Colony. There he joined Williams at the first Baptist church established in America. Williams soon stepped down as pastor of that church, and Olney replaced him. Olney was involved in several religious and political disputes in the following decades. In the schism of 1652 he led the "Five Principle Baptists" against William Wickenden and his followers, who insisted on the practice of the laying on of hands for each member of a congregation. The division lasted seventy years. In 1655 Olney helped lead the opposition to Williams's militia training law on the grounds that military service violated the teaching of Scripture.*

BIBLIOGRAPHY. I. Backus, *A History of New England with Particular Reference to the Baptists* (1796); S. H. Brockunier, *The Irrepressible Democrat: Roger Williams* (1941).

T. T. Taylor

OMS International, Inc. A nondenominational mission* agency in the Wesleyan* tradition. OMS International, originally known as The Oriental Missionary Society, was founded in 1901 by Charles E. and Lettie B. Cowman.* The Cowmans, who were married in 1889, were converted* while attending special meetings at Grace Methodist Episcopal Church, adjoining Moody Bible Institute* in Chicago. In September 1894, at a missionary convention held at Moody Church, the Cowmans responded to a call for missionaries by A. B. Simpson.* While awaiting their acceptance by the Methodist* mission board, the Cowmans decided to "launch forth . . . quite apart from any missionary society, and trust Him for all." On February 1, 1901, the Cowmans sailed from San Francisco for Japan.

In Tokyo they teamed up with Japanese evangelist* Juji Nakada, whom they met when Nakada had come to Moody Bible Institute. Within six weeks of their arrival in Japan, the Cowmans and Nakada opened a Bible training institute and a gospel hall where in 10,000 consecutive nights more than 15,000 Japanese converted to Christianity. Missionary candidates, prayer* and financial support come from the U.S., Canada, Great Britain, Australia, New Zealand and South Africa. OMS is committed to evangelism, church planting and leadership training. From Japan the mission expanded to Korea, China and India, and today ministers in Asia, Latin America, Europe and the Caribbean with nearly 500 missionaries, over 2,000 organized churches and more than 4,000 national staff. The mission's headquarters is in Greenwood, Indiana.

BIBLIOGRAPHY. L. B. Cowman, *Missionary Warrior*, (1928). E. N. Hunt

Onderdonk, Benjamin Tredwell (1791-1861). Episcopal* bishop* of New York. Born in New York City, he was baptized at Trinity Church, where his father was a vestryman* from 1801 to 1832. Graduating from Columbia College in 1809, he studied theology* under Bishop John Henry Hobart,* who also ordained* him deacon* on August 2, 1812, at St. Paul's Chapel, and priest* on July 26, 1815, at Trinity Church, Newark, New Jersey. In 1813 he married Eliza Moscrop and from 1814 to 1835 served as assistant minister* at Trinity Church, New York.

Onderdonk served as professor of ecclesiastical history (1821-1822) and as professor of ecclesiastical polity and law (1821-1861) at the General Theological Seminary, New York. From 1816 to 1830 he was secretary of the Diocese* of New York. On November 26, 1830, he was consecrated the fourth bishop of New York at St. John's Chapel, New York, by Presiding Bishop William White.*

In November 1844 Onderdonk was presented for trial on the charges of immorality and impurity by Bishops William Meade* of Virginia, James Otey* of Tennessee and Stephen Elliott* of Georgia. On January 2, 1845, after a trial by the court of bishops, he was found guilty and suspended "from the office of a Bishop of the Church of God and from all the functions of the sacred ministry . . . and from all the exercise of his Episcopal and ministerial functions. . . ." Onderdonk tried until his death in 1861 to have the suspension remitted,

but failed. He, with his brother Henry Ustick Onderdonk,* was a high churchman* and an aggressive supporter of the Oxford Movement.* His only written works were addresses and pastoral letters.

BIBLIOGRAPHY. E. C. Chorley, "Benjamin Tredwell Onderdonk, Fourth Bishop of New York," HMPEC 9 (1940):1-51; DAB VII.

D. S. Armentrout

Onderdonk, Henry Ustick (1789-1858). Episcopal* bishop* of Pennsylvania. Born in New York City, Onderdonk graduated from Columbia College in 1805 and then studied medicine in London and Edinburgh, receiving his M.D. from the University of Edinburgh. He returned to New York to practice medicine and in 1814-1815 was associate editor of the *New York Medical Journal.* On April 15, 1811, he married Eliza Carter.

Onderdonk, following his younger brother Benjamin Tredwell Onderdonk,* studied for the ministry* under Bishop John Henry Hobart* of New York, who ordained* him deacon* on December 8, 1815, at St. Paul's Chapel, New York, and priest* on April 11, 1816, at Trinity Church, New York. From 1816 to 1820 he worked at Canandaigua, a missionary* frontier post in western New York. In 1820 he became the rector* of St. Ann's Church, Brooklyn. He was elected assistant bishop of Pennsylvania and was consecrated to that office on October 25, 1827, in Christ Church, Philadelphia, by Presiding Bishop William White.* When Bishop White died on July 17, 1836, Onderdonk became the second bishop of Pennsylvania.

Onderdonk was subject to a chronic intestinal disorder, and he became addicted to the brandy he used to relieve his pain. In 1844 he wrote to the House of Bishops* to confess his habitual use of alcohol,* tendering his resignation and asking for discipline.* His resignation was accepted, and he was suspended from "all public exercise of the offices and functions of the sacred ministry" and from the office of bishop. Two years before his death the suspension was removed. Onderdonk was an able writer, and among his major works were *Episcopacy Examined and Reexamined* (1835) and *Essay on Regeneration* (1835). He also wrote several hymns.*

BIBLIOGRAPHY. *DAB* VII.

D. S. Armentrout

Oneida Community. *See* NOYES, JOHN HUMPHREY.

Open and Institutional Church League, The. An interdenominational agency promoting broad access to churches. Founded in 1894 at the Madison Avenue Presbyterian Church in New York City, the purpose of The Open and Institutional Church League was to promote the practice of opening church buildings to all worshipers and encouraging congregational programs of Christian social service. Charles L. Thompson, pastor of Madison Avenue Presbyterian Church, wanted to break the practice of reserved pews for those who paid. The League supported "open" and "free pewed" sanctuaries. But for the League members, including Presbyterian,* Methodist,* Baptist* and Congregational* churches, this openness was symbolic of Christians who would apply Christian teachings and practice to everyday life.

In addition to Thompson, League leaders included Josiah Strong,* Elias B. Sanford,* Charles A. Dickinson and Graham Taylor.* These men viewed the fundamental aim of the League "to save all men and all of the men by days and all means to the great end of saving the world for Christ." For several years the League published *The Open Church,* a "magazine of Applied Christianity," and held small conferences in New York; Boston and Worcester, Massachusetts; and Hartford, Connecticut, focusing on the mission of the institutional church* in the community. The Open and Institutional Church League constituted a brief-but-important step toward federation and unity. Its pioneering ecumenical* actions found fruition in the National Federation of Churches and Christian Workers, a predecessor to the Federal Council of the Churches of Christ in America.*

BIBLIOGRAPHY. R. D. Cross, ed., *The Church in the City, 1865-1910* (1967); C. H. Hopkins, *The Rise of the Social Gospel in American Protestantism, 1865-1915* (1940). P. A. Crow

Opus Dei. A Catholic* organization nurturing lay* spirituality.* Opus Dei began on October 2, 1928, when a young Spanish priest,* Josemaría Escrivá de Balaguer (1902-1975), believed God was calling him to found an organization of Catholic laymen to foster the pursuit of sanctity in everyday life. Escriva preached a universal call to holiness, associating personal struggle with becoming a leaven of cheerful Christian life in all environments. On February 14, 1930, Escriva founded the Women's Branch of Opus Dei, and on February 14, 1943, he founded the Priestly Society of the Holy Cross. Headquarters for the movement was established in Rome in 1940.

After World War 2, Opus Dei spread throughout Europe and beyond. Father Joseph Músquiz (d. 1983) and a young physicist, Salvadore Ferigle, arrived in Chicago in 1949 to begin the apostolate* of Opus Dei in the U.S. Expansion to other cities followed in subsequent years, with centers established in several major U.S. cities. These centers offer spiritual direction and a program based on prayer and active appreciation for the sacraments as the catalyst for putting Christian ideals into practice in everyday life. Daily attendance at Mass,* regular spiritual reading and constant devotion* to Mary* are among the integral aspects of members' piety. The organization has grown steadily, with over 70,000 members worldwide, representing over eighty nationalities.

BIBLIOGRAPHY. R. Shaw, *Working for God the World Over* (1985); D. M. Helming, *Footprints in the Snow: A Pictorial Biography of Josemaría Escrivá the Founder of Opus Dei* (1986).

S. M. Kane

Order of Cistercians of the Strict Observance. *See* TRAPPISTS.

Ordination. The setting apart of some members by a church for ministerial* or priestly* leadership, usually by laying on of hands* and invocation of the Holy Spirit. It is considered a sacrament* in Catholic* and Eastern Orthodox* theology.* Ordination usually requires both a spiritual call from God and an ecclesiastical call, including the fulfillment of standards of training, doctrinal conformity and other institutional requirements. Most churches require those who administer the sacraments or ordinances* to be ordained. In liturgical denominations the primary purpose of ordination has been to place priests* at the altar* and among evangelical* Protestants* to provide preachers* of the gospel. Roman Catholic, Eastern Orthodox and most conservative Protestant churches ordain men only, while the ordination of women* in liberal and some Holiness* and Pentecostal* churches began within the last century.

In Baptist* and other groups with radical congregational* polity,* ordination is administered by the local church, though regional associations may be represented. Only in the earliest years of New England, however, was re-ordination practiced upon call to the pastorate of a different congregation. In presbyterial* denominations the regional body examines candidates and exercises authority to ordain. In episcopally* organized churches such as the Methodist,* Episcopal,* Lutheran,* Roman Catholic and Eastern Orthodox, the bishop* is required to administer the rite. Ordination has been for life, unless serious charges of heresy* or immorality were brought by appropriate church authorities.

Ordination by bishops reflects some sort of an understanding of a doctrine of apostolic succession,* based on an understanding of Peter as the first bishop (Mt 16:18). The unavailability of bishops to ordain hindered the growth of Episcopal and Methodist churches until they established stable constitutional structures after the American Revolution.* Congregational and presbyterial churches have interpreted Jesus' designation of Peter as foundational rock as a reference to his confession of faith, with apostolic succession passing through the whole church, which in turn ordains leadership. In the final decades of the twentieth century the Consultation on Church Union* has moved toward mutual reconciliation of ministries among nine covenanting denominations.*

Among American denominations, a variety of practices may be observed. Methodism provides for ordination in two stages, first as deacon* and then, after a probationary period, as elder.* Most Protestant groups understand ordination as admitting a person to the equivalent of the biblical office of elder. Some independent African-American congregations ordain local pastors with the title of bishop. Presbyterian churches also ordain lay* leaders, usually as deacons and lay elders. Churches with an episcopate do not re-ordain priests as bishops, but consecrate them as bishops.

Ordination as an ecclesiastical rite also constitutes entry into the profession. The church that recognizes a minister's or priest's ordination assumes responsibility for such matters as pensions, continuing education and ethical and doctrinal discipline. The highest standard of ethical conduct naturally is expected of ordained clergy (1 Tim 5:17-22; Titus 1:5-9). Some shortcomings which formerly ended careers, such as divorce, are increasingly tolerated. The issue of whether homosexuality* should disqualify ordination is debated heatedly in some churches. In Roman Catholicism celibacy has been understood not only as a means to free priests (and nuns*) for full commitment to ministry, but also to higher spirituality and status.

BIBLIOGRAPHY. *Baptism, Eucharist, and Ministry* (1982); see books of discipline or ministerial manuals of various denominations.

C. E. Hambrick-Stowe

Ordination of Women. Women have played an active and varied role as laypeople* within the church since Colonial days—and some women were ordained* by the mid-nineteenth century—but the general movement for the ordination of women in the American churches is a more recent development and has led to a variety of practices.

Proponents of women's ordination have frequently pointed to the New Testament precedent for women in leadership, arguing that the earliest church leadership was based on the use of charismatic gifts, not on gender. For example, 1 Corinthians 11:5 suggests that women prayed and prophesied alongside men. Appeal has also been made to evidence suggesting that early Christian women such as Priscilla (Acts 18:2, 18, 26; Rom 16:3; 2 Tim 4:19), Tryphena and Tryphosa (Rom 16:12), Euodia and Syntyche (Phil 4:2) and others evangelized with Paul.

As the church developed specific ministerial offices, women appear in positions of responsibility: Romans 16:1-2 seems to indicate that Phoebe was a deacon,* and 1 Timothy 3:11 may be speaking of women deacons rather than the wives of male deacons. Some read 1 Timothy 5:2-17 and Titus 2:3-5 as referring to women elders.* Both textual and artistic evidence from the early centuries of the church portray women as deacons, elders (or priests*) and bishops.* Church councils gradually legislated against women holding such offices, and scholars came to interpret 1 Corinthians 14:34-35 and 1 Timothy 2:11-12 as prohibiting the ministry of women. The Reformation did not change or challenge this.

In America, although women preachers were common among the Quakers,* early Methodists* and Free Will Baptists,* the first woman to be officially ordained in the U.S. was Antoinette Brown (Blackwell*), who in 1853 was ordained in a Congregational* church in South Butler, New York. The second woman to be ordained was Olympia Brown, a Universalist,* in 1863.

Groups such as the Unitarians,* Christian Church (Disciples),* the Wesleyan Methodist Church and Pilgrim Holiness Church (*See* Wesleyan Church, The), The Salvation Army* and others ordained women in the nineteenth century. The ministry of women was common, particularly among Holiness* churches because of their emphasis on perfectionism* and consequent restoration of men and women to a prefallen state. For women this meant release from their subordination to men—a result of the Fall—and participation in church leadership. Pentecostalism,* growing out of this tradition and emphasizing the outpouring of the Holy Spirit on men and women (Acts 2), inherited this emphasis on women's equality in church leadership. However, in the early twentieth century several factors, including a concern to protect the institution of the family and its traditional roles, led to a decline in the ordination of women among many conservative groups, including Pentecostals and evangelicals.*

In the mainline* U.S. denominations, the Methodists permitted the ordination of women as local preachers in 1924 and granted them full denominational ordination in 1954. The Presbyterian Church in the U.S.A.* allowed women to be ordained as deacons in 1922, as ruling elders in 1930, and as fully ordained ministers in 1956. In the South, the Presbyterian Church in the U.S.* followed in 1964. The American Lutheran Church* and Lutheran Church in America* ordained women in 1970, with the Episcopal Church* allowing women deacons* in 1970 and priests* in 1976. In Canada, The United Church of Canada* (uniting Methodists, Presbyterians* and Congregationalists) ordained women in 1936.

While individual Southern Baptist congregations have ordained women pastors, the Southern Baptist Convention* is on record as opposing the practice. The ordination of women is also opposed by most modern fundamentalist churches and denominations, and the issue was hotly contested among many evangelicals during the 1970s and 1980s. Neither the Roman Catholic* or the Orthodox* churches ordain women, arguing that the practice is not found in church tradition and that women cannot physically represent Christ.

BIBLIOGRAPHY. B. Clouse and R. G. Clouse, *Women in Ministry: Four Views* (1989); D. W. Dayton, *Holiness Tracts Defending the Ministry of Women* (1985); P. K. Jewett, *The Ordination of Women* (1980); W. Liefeld and R. Tucker, *The Ministry of Women* (1987); B. T. Roberts, *Ordaining Women* (1891); J. Weidman, ed., *Women Ministers: How Women are Redefining Traditional Roles* (1985). N. A. Hardesty

O'Reilly, John Boyle (1844-1890). Catholic* newspaper editor. Born at Douth Castle, Drogheda, Ireland, O'Reilly started working as a printer's apprentice in Drogheda in 1855 and eventually became a newspaper reporter in England. In 1863, sympathetic to Irish nationalism and attracted to the Fenian movement, he returned to his homeland hoping to contribute to the cause of Irish independence. He enlisted in the British army, intending to promote disloyalty and thus strike at English control of Ireland from within. Arrested in 1866, he was given a twenty-year prison term for rebellion and transported to Australia in 1868 to finish serving his sentence. But early the next year, he made a dramatic escape and reached the U.S.

aboard an American whaling ship.

In 1870 O'Reilly obtained a job with the Boston *Pilot* as a reporter and editorial writer. Within a few months he advanced to editor and eventually became a respected journalist and poet in the U.S., especially among Irish-Americans. His editorial positions drew from his own experiences and the writings of European Catholic reformers. Consistent with his past, he remained committed to the goal of an Ireland free from British control, but he also paid close attention to American issues. He favored the Democratic Party, championed social reform, advocated westward migration in order to alleviate labor problems. O'Reilly also attacked prejudice against Native Americans, Jews and African-Americans. He advised African-Americans to defend themselves against Jim Crow laws and lynchings, noting that no race had ever obtained fair treatment from Anglo-Saxons without fighting for it or being ready to fight.

BIBLIOGRAPHY. J. R. Betts, "The Negro and the New England Conscience in the Days of John Boyle O'Reilly," *JNH* 51 (1966):246-261; J. J. Roche, *Life of John Boyle O'Reilly* (1891); F. G. McManamin, *The American Years of John Boyle O'Reilly* (1959). W. P. Leahy

Orr, James (1844-1913). Scottish theologian* and apologist for orthodoxy.* Born in Glasgow, Scotland, Orr studied at the University of Glasgow and The Theological Hall of the United Presbyterian Church of Scotland. He then pastored in Hawick (1874-1891) before becoming professor of church history in the United Presbyterian Theological College (1891-1901) and professor of apologetics* and theology* at United Free Church College, Glasgow (1901-1913). He established himself as an expert in German philosophy and theology with the Edinburgh Kerr Lectures, published as *The Christian View of God and the World* (1893), and volumes on *The Supernatural in Christianity* (1894) and *The Ritschlian Theology and the Evangelical Faith* (1897). Essays entitled *The Bible Under Trial* (1907), *The Virgin Birth* (1907) and *The Resurrection of Christ* (1908) achieved his reputation as an orthodox* opponent of modernism.* These works, along with contributions to *The Pulpit Commentary,* made him known to conservatives in the U.S. and Canada, resulting in invitations to lecture at Chicago, Auburn, Princeton and Toronto. His last contribution as editor, *The International Standard Bible Encyclopedia* (4 vols., 1915), was a reference work of enduring value.

Because of his reputation as a defender of

orthodoxy, Orr was one of a small number of British theologians invited to participate in *The Fundamentals** project (1910-1915). He contributed essays on "The Virgin Birth of Christ" (vol. I), "Science and Christian Faith" (vol. IV), "The Early Narratives of Genesis" (vol. VI) and "Holy Scripture and Modern Negations" (vol. IX). Orr's background and scholarly erudition lent credibility to the endeavor, and his work made significant contributions to the issues and structures of fundamentalist apologetic in the U.S.

BIBLIOGRAPHY. E. R. Sandeen, *The Roots of Fundamentalism* (1970); G. G. Scorgie, "A Call for Continuity: The Theological Contribution of James Orr" (unpublished Ph.D. dissertation, University of St. Andrews, Scotland, 1986). D. D. Bundy

Orthodox Presbyterian Church. A small Presbyterian* denomination* with roots in the fundamentalist-modernist controversy.* The Orthodox Presbyterian Church (OPC) was founded on June 11, 1936, in the aftermath of the fundamentalist-modernist controversy* which in 1929 had seen a group of professors at Princeton Theological Seminary,* led by Dr. J. Gresham Machen,* leave that seminary to establish Westminster Theological Seminary.

Paramount among the reasons for that action was the conviction of Machen and his colleagues that Princeton and the Presbyterian Church (USA),* of which Princeton was the leading seminary, had departed from historic Christianity. The particular matters at issue were their adoption of a weak view of the authority* of Scripture* and rejection of significant doctrines* such as the virgin birth of Christ. The seven years between 1929 and 1936 saw increasing friction between the majority in the Presbyterian Church and the minority led by Machen, with the result being the foundation of a new denomination in June of 1936. Originally calling itself *The Presbyterian Church of America,* the new body was forced by court action to discontinue use of that name in 1939, and it adopted in its place the name *Orthodox Presbyterian Church.*

The OPC has, since its inception, been best known for its vigorous affirmation of the truths of historic Christianity and Reformed* orthodoxy* as they are expressed in the Westminster Confession of Faith* and catechisms.* The denomination utilizes three standing committees representing the fundamental emphases within the OPC: world missions,* home missions and Christian education.* In 1987 the OPC had over 18,000 communicant members in approximately 175 congregations

throughout the U.S.

BIBLIOGRAPHY. C. G. Dennison, ed., *The Orthodox Presbyterian Church, 1936-1986* (1986); C. G. Dennison and R. C. Gamble, eds., *Pressing toward the Mark: Essays Commemorating Fifty Years of the Orthodox Presbyterian Church* (1986); N. B. Stonehouse, *J. Gresham Machen: A Biographical Memoir* (1954). S. T. Logan

Orthodox Tradition. Christianity in America is frequently identified solely with either its Protestant* or its Roman Catholic* expressions. While Orthodoxy has had a presence in North America which reaches back to the late eighteenth century, insufficient attention has been given to this expression of Christianity. It cannot be included under the various groups of Christians whose history and theological perspectives are rooted primarily in Western Europe and were greatly affected both by the ecclesiastical trends of the Middle Ages and events of the sixteenth and seventeenth centuries. Indeed, since the time of St. Augustine in the West and the Cappadocian Father in the East, Orthodox Christianity has understood and celebrated the Christian faith in a manner which is distinctive: sometimes complementary to the Christian West and sometimes dramatically opposed to the Christian West.

The Orthodox in America have a strong sense of unity with the Orthodox in other parts of the world and claim that they live in continuity with those who have shared the same faith since the time of the apostles. While the Orthodox will frequently speak of "Greek Orthodoxy" or "Russian Orthodoxy," these designations generally refer to historic expressions of a particular liturgical,* spiritual* or theological nature and do not imply different doctrinal understandings. Although the faith of the Orthodox may be expressed in a wide variety of languages and through many different cultures, its fundamental affirmations remain unchanged. It is for this reason that the American Orthodox view themselves as members of the Church who profess the "faith of the Church" and therefore forcefully refuse to be identified with one "denomination"* among many.

Orthodox. By using the term *orthodox,* Orthodox Christians recognize two very important and interrelated affirmations describing their church and their faith. First, *Orthodox* means "true glory." The emphasis here is on the importance of worship. Orthodox believe that the glorification of God, especially as expressed in praise and thanksgiving, is the fundamental response both of each believer and of the Church to his mighty acts.

Giving glory to God is the purpose of life. Because of this, worship has a special importance for the Orthodox. It is in and through worship that the believer celebrates the actions of God in history, affirms his presence and enters into communion with him. It is an act of praise and thanksgiving which is meant to be expressed not only in the context of communal and personal prayer but also through all the relationships and responsibilities of life. It is an act which is meant to endure throughout eternity.

The central expression of community worship for the Orthodox is the Eucharist.* Within the context of the eucharistic celebration, the Church gathers through the activity of the Spirit to hear the Word of God with praise and to respond to it by offering the gifts of bread and wine in thanksgiving to the Father and in obedience to the command of the Lord. Believing that the Lord is present in the sanctified gifts, the Orthodox receive Holy Communion to deepen the bonds between themselves and Christ and among each other. The eucharistic celebration is a manifestation of the kingdom of God* in the present.

Closely associated with the Eucharist are a number of sacraments,* often referred to as "mysteries" because they manifest the presence of God with his people. Among these are baptism* and chrismation, usually administered to infants of believing parents, which mark a person's entrance into the Church. These and the other sacraments of marriage,* ordination,* reconciliation* and the anointing of the sick* serve to signify either the establishment of new relationships or the healing of old relationships within the Church. Every sacrament has a bearing on the bond of unity which exists among the believers as well as between the believers and the persons of the Trinity. Although the Orthodox frequently speak of seven sacraments, there has been a reluctance to number them formally and thereby neglect other ecclesiastical events which also have a sacramental character.

There is a close association between the worship of the Church and the faith of the Church. The Orthodox acknowledge the ancient Christian dictum: the rule of prayer is the rule of faith. This means that the faith of the Church is expressed in the prayers,* hymns* and ritual actions of her worship. And the worship of the Church nurtures the believers in the development of their faith.

The second meaning of *orthodox* is "true doctrine." The Orthodox believe that under the guidance of the Holy Spirit, the Church has proclaimed, preserved and taught the authentic Christian faith free from addition, diminution or distortion since the time of the apostles. The Orthodox believe that there is nothing in their body of beliefs which is contrary to truth or which inhibits genuine union with God. The Orthodox also believe that the faith affirmations of the Church are meant to guide the believer in living an authentic human life in fellowship with God and in service to others.

God: Unknown and Known. The Orthodox understanding of God and the human person is rooted in divine revelation. While not diminishing the value of human reason, the Orthodox hold that God is mystery who is impenetrable and wholly beyond the reach of the human mind. God is far beyond our meager attempts to prove his existence and our attempts to capture his reality in human words. The limited knowledge of God which we have, therefore, does not result chiefly from our human speculation but rather from the fact that God has chosen to reveal himself to us. The One who is beyond all and is the Creator of all has allowed himself to be known because of his love for his creation. As a result of this divine revelation, the Orthodox claim that human persons have the privilege of experiencing and knowing the one God as Father, as Son and as Holy Spirit.

In order to better express these convictions, the Orthodox make two important distinctions. First, they affirm that God in his *essence* remains forever beyond our understanding. There always remains an aspect of the divine reality which is unknowable. At the same time, it is God in his *energies* or *activities* that is knowable in a deeply experiential manner within the context of the faith community.

Secondly, with regard to the description of the Trinity, the Orthodox affirm that the Father, the Son and the Holy Spirit share a common reality which is usually referred to as the divine essence or substance (Greek, *ousia*). At the same time, the Father, the Son and the Holy Spirit are distinct persons (Greek, *hypostasis*). Each person is, however, intimately related to the other in a bond of love. Each shares in the presence and the activity of the other. Thus the Trinity is a communion of persons who give and receive love. In its doctrinal affirmations, the Orthodox Church does not seek to define God but rather to describe in limited human language the actions of God in history.

Jesus Christ. The Incarnation of God the Son in fulfillment of the will of the Father and through the power of the Holy Spirit is the very core event of the divine revelation. According to the Orthodox perspective, the revelation of God to the ancient

Israelites is fulfilled in the coming of Christ who is the promised Messiah. In Jesus Christ divinity is united with humanity in such a way that both maintain their own characteristics while at the same time being brought together in a single person, the God-man. Jesus Christ is consubstantial with the Father and the Spirit with regard to his divinity and consubstantial with us according to his humanity. Christ possesses in his humanity, therefore, not only a genuinely human body but also a genuine soul, mind and will. Any perspective that denies either the full divinity or the full humanity of Christ is vigorously opposed by the Orthodox.

The event of the Incarnation establishes a new relationship between God and humanity. This new relationship is vividly expressed in the earthly ministry of Christ. In his preaching and teaching Christ reveals the triune God and the theocentric nature of the human person. In his healings and exorcisms, and especially through his own death and resurrection, Christ proclaims the ultimate victory of God over every force of evil. From the Orthodox perspective, the person and the work of Christ are essentially one. Neither can be separated from the other in the process of salvation. Christ is the Savior precisely because he shares fully in our humanity and, thereby, unites it fully with divinity in a manner that maintains the characteristics of each.

The Orthodox believe that the principal task of the Holy Spirit since Pentecost is to manifest the risen Christ to persons in every age and in every place, and to enable them to share in the reality of his saving work. Redemption in Christ cannot be fully appreciated by each person apart from the sanctifying work of the Holy Spirit. Thus, the person of the Spirit is not subordinate to Christ nor are the actions of the Spirit inferior to that of Christ. Within the divine plan of salvation, both the Son and the Spirit work in harmony to accomplish the will of the Father, who desires that all be saved. Within the life of the church, the Holy Spirit unites persons to Christ, the risen Lord, who leads them to the Father.

The Human Person: The Icon of God. According-ing to the Orthodox perspective, the whole purpose of the Incarnation of the Son of God is to restore the human person and the entire creation to fellowship with God. From the very beginning, the human person was created in the "image and likeness of God" and given the vocation to live in fellowship with God. While sin distorted the relationship between the Creator and his human creation, it did not destroy the fundamental bond between the Father and his sons and daughters.

While the Orthodox recognize the tragic character of humankind's fall through an act of disobedience, the emphasis is always on the love and mercy of God, who could not abandon those whom he created in love. God, through many means, sought to call women and men back to an authentic human life lived in communion with him. With the coming of Christ, the will of the Father to heal and restore reaches a new level. Orthodoxy frequently affirms the ancient axiom: God became what we are so that we may become by grace what he is.

There are a number of important characteristics of the Orthodox understanding of salvation. First, salvation is viewed primarily in terms of sharing. Through the Incarnation God has shared fully in human life, thereby enabling humans to share fully in the divine life. Salvation is, therefore, both the gift of fellowship with the triune God and the process in which the human person responds freely to the reality of Christ and grows closer to God in love. Salvation involves the forgiveness of sins but is not limited to this alone. The term *theosis,* meaning "deification," is usually employed by the Orthodox to describe this process of sanctification* whereby the human person progresses toward God through a life of virtue rooted in a personal relationship with Christ. The human person is most fully human when he or she lives in communion with God. Theosis does not imply the destruction of the human person but the fulfillment. For those who are faithful, the process of deification begins in this life and continues in the life to come. The Virgin Mary,* honored as the Mother of God (*Theotokos*), and the other saints* bear witness to this reality.

Second, salvation is viewed by the Orthodox as being ecclesial. Human persons grow in the process of salvation within the fellowship of the Church. According to the Orthodox perspective, the Church is an integral part and expression of the divine plan of salvation. The Church was established by Christ in its most embryonic form with the call of the apostles, and it was enlivened by the Holy Spirit on the day of Pentecost. Within this unique community of faith, the members of the Church have the opportunity to cultivate a bond of love not only with each other but with the persons of the Trinity.

Third, salvation is cosmic. Human persons are not saved from the world but through the world. The soul is not saved independently from the body but rather together with the body. Both the body and the soul are meant to participate in the process of salvation. Far from rejecting the value of the body and the rest of the material creation, the Orthodox look on it as the work of God and as the medium through which God continues to reveal himself. The Orthodox believe that the entire created world participates in the restoration accomplished in and through the Incarnation. The ultimate transfiguration of the cosmos, which shall be complete only at the Second Coming, is already expressed in the bodies of holy men and women, in the Eucharist and the other sacraments, in the relics of the saints and in holy icons.*

Tradition and Scripture. Sacred tradition is the body of fundamental faith affirmations which have been handed down through the life of the Church under the guidance of the Spirit from the time of the apostles. Sacred tradition embodies the Orthodox understanding of God, the human person and the created world which are centered on divine revelation. Within the context of the believing community, these faith affirmations express themselves especially in the lives of faithful men and women, in the prayers of the Church, in the teachings of the Fathers, in the decisions of the seven ecumenical councils and in the Scriptures.*

The Orthodox have great respect for the Holy Scriptures. While encouraging the believers to read the Bible,* the Orthodox view it as the book of the Church. Both the Old Testament and the New Testament originated within the context of the believing community and can only properly be understood within the context of that community. For the Orthodox, therefore, the Scriptures are ecclesial in nature and cannot be appreciated apart from the greater tradition of the Church. Because of this, the Church, according to the Orthodox, is the guardian and ultimate interpreter of her Scriptures.

Councils and Creed. Only when the fundamental truths of the faith have been seriously threatened by false teachings has the Church acted to express formally an article of faith. For this reason, the decisions of the seven ecumenical councils of the ancient, undivided Church are highly honored. To these synods,* bishops* from throughout the world came in order to discuss disputed issues and to proclaim the true faith. The Orthodox believe that these councils did not create new doctrines but proclaimed in a particular place and in a particular manner what the Church has always believed. Because of this, the decisions of these councils had to be received by the whole body of the Church.

The Nicene Creed, formulated at the Council of Nicaea in 325 and the Council of Constantinople in 381, has been recognized since then as an authoritative expression of the fundamental affirmations of the faith. The Orthodox recite this creed at every baptism and every Eucharist. It also serves as a basis for Christian formation and education.

The Orthodox have high regard for those important teachers of the faith who are honored as the fathers and mothers of the Church. Counted among the saints of the Church, these persons lived lives of exemplary holiness and, with a thoroughgoing understanding of the Scriptures, bore witness to the authentic teachings of the faith, often in the face of heretical distortion and personal attacks.

Christian Divisions. While differences in theological emphasis were to be found in the early church, it was not until the Middle Ages that serious doctrinal questions, complicated by political and cultural differences, led to the gradual separation of Eastern churches centered about Constantinople and the Western churches centered about Rome. The year 1054 is frequently given as the date of the Great Schism, but historians now recognize that it was a gradual estrangement not completed until at least 1204. Chief among the doctrinal differences at that time were the papal claims of universal jurisdiction and the Filioque (Latin meaning "and from the Son") clause—which the Western Church had added to the Nicene Creed after the phrase: *The Holy Ghost . . . who proceeds from the Father.*

The Orthodox were not directly involved in the disputes of the Reformation and Counter-Reformation. Although some Orthodox theologians of the time were influenced by the terminology and issues of these disputes, the Orthodox generally viewed the debates as having a particular Western Christian character to them.

The Orthodox have always recognized the tragic character of Christian division and have been active in efforts to achieve unity through greater mutual understanding and agreement in doctrine. Orthodox theologians are active in a number of bilateral consultations as well as in the World Council of Churches* and the National Council of Churches.*

Orthodox Tradition/American Experience. Two significant events led directly to the formal establishment of Orthodox Christianity in North America. The first was a mission in Alaska* begun in 1794 under the direction of the Church of Russia. It was the largest and most fruitful mission to be established by the Church of Russia prior to the Bolshevik Revolution. While the influence of the Orthodox Church declined somewhat after the sale of Alaska to the U.S. in 1867, the pastoral and educational work of the Orthodox there remains sizeable even to this day.

The second event was the massive immigration of Orthodox, especially from Greece, Asia Minor, Russia, the Balkans and the Middle East, which took place especially in the late nineteenth and early twentieth centuries. The establishment of Orthodox parishes in most major cities resulted from the religious concerns of these immigrants. Most of these parishes served the needs of particular immigrant groups. While all the Orthodox immigrants shared the same faith, they had differences in languages, customs and liturgical practices. Often the disputes from the Old World also served to keep the various immigrant groups separated from one another.

Although the Church of Russia had established a diocese in North America as early as 1870, not all the immigrants accepted the authority of the Russian bishop. Rather, they looked to ecclesiastical authorities in their homelands to provide clergy and rudimentary direction. In the decades following World War 1,* a number of the autocephalous churches* acted to unite the parishes and to establish dioceses* in the U.S. While these organizations served the immediate needs of the immigrants, the proliferation of parallel and often competing jurisdictions in the same geographical territory was an anomaly in Orthodox polity.

In recent decades the reasons for the establishment of parallel jurisdiction have become less and less pronounced while at the same time cooperation has greatly increased. This has resulted from changing demographics, a greater sense of mission and the extensive use of English in liturgical services. Today nine of these jurisdictions are united under the aegis of the Standing Conference of Canonical Orthodox Bishops.* The majority of these jurisdictions remain directly associated with one of the fourteen autocephalous churches. The Greek Orthodox* Archdiocese is the largest of these. One jurisdiction, the Orthodox Church in America,* formerly the Russian Metropolia, received autocephalous status from the Church of Russia in 1970. This status, however, has not been recognized by all the other autocephalous churches.

Throughout the world the Orthodox are organized into fourteen autocephalous or autonomous churches containing over one hundred million members. These churches profess the same faith, although each is self-governing and often has its own particular liturgical customs. The archbishop of Constantinople, known as the ecumenical patriarch, is recognized as the first bishop of the Church and has responsibility for coordinating intra-Orthodox activities.

The Orthodox in America number about five million and are gathered into over 1,500 parishes. The members of these parishes come from a wide variety of racial, ethnic and religious backgrounds. There are several monasteries, two schools of theology, a college and a number of other schools and charitable institutions associated with the Church. In due course, it is expected that the various jurisdictions will be united into a single autocephalous church which will be officially recognized as such by the ecumenical patriarchate and the other autocephalous Orthodox churches.

See also ARMENIAN CHURCH IN AMERICA; AUTOCEPHALOUS ORTHODOX CHURCH; GREEK ORTHODOX ARCHDIOCESE OF NORTH AND SOUTH AMERICA; PIETY: POPULAR ORTHODOX; RUSSIAN ORTHODOX CHURCH IN AMERICA; SPIRITUALITY: ORTHODOX; SYRIAN ORTHODOX CHURCH OF ANTIOCH; WORSHIP: ORTHODOX.

BIBLIOGRAPHY. I. Bria, *Martyria and Mission* (1980); S. Harakas, *Let Mercy Abound: Social Concern in the Orthodox Church* (1982); V. Lossky, *The Mystical Theology of the Eastern Church* (1957); J. Meyendorff, *Catholicity and the Church* (1983); M. Oleksa, *Alaskan Missionary Spirituality* (1987); A. Schmemann, *For the Life of the World* (1973); C. J. Tarasar and J. H. Erickson, *Orthodox America: 1794-1976* (1975); A. Ugolnik, *The Illuminating Icon* (1989); K. T. Ware, *The Orthodox Church* (1984); K. T. Ware, *The Orthodox Way* (1979); J. Zizioulas, *Being as Communion* (1985).
T. E. FitzGerald

Orthodoxy. Theological beliefs judged to be essential to Christian truth. Derived from two Greek words (*orthos* and *doxa*), the term literally means "right opinion" and has come to refer to established beliefs or doctrines. In traditional Christianity the basis for orthodoxy is divine revelation, particularly in the Bible.* Christian confessions attribute varying amounts of authority to tradition, with Roman Catholics* seeing it as a further expression of revelation and Protestants* denying it direct authority, though usually agreeing that many traditional doctrinal formulations (e.g., early creeds) are biblically accurate.

There is no agreement regarding which beliefs actually constitute the content of orthodoxy, and no consensus is likely to come about for two reasons. First, different groups stress different beliefs as vital elements of their own traditions, which they regard as true Christianity. Second, different verbal expressions of doctrines sometimes make an accurate comparison between beliefs difficult. Nonetheless, within limits it is possible to identify a general body of traditional orthodoxy. Among others, this would include beliefs in the Bible as revelation; God as transcendent, immanent and trinitarian; Christ as divine and human; faith in Christ's atoning death as necessary for salvation; and the personal Second Coming of Christ. Evangelicals* and other conservatives would sharpen these beliefs considerably, while more liberal groups would provide flexible understandings insofar as they hold these beliefs at all.

Obviously the same precision or lack of precision accompanies attempts to identify deviations from orthodoxy. Deviations can be identified on two levels. The denial of a belief generally accepted as true can be characterized as error, which would not sever one's connection with Christianity. But the denial of a belief essential to Christianity—an explicit violation of orthodoxy—constitutes heresy* and places one outside of traditional Christianity.

BIBLIOGRAPHY. G. K. Chesterton, *Orthodoxy* (1909); J. J. Davis, *Theology Primer* (1981).

W. Corduan

Otey, James Hervey (1800-1863). Episcopal* bishop.* Born in 1800 into an influential planter family in Bedford County, Virginia, Otey graduated from the University of North Carolina in 1820. His family had no formal church ties. After serving for a term as tutor at the university, he taught school in Tennessee from 1821 to 1824 and in North Carolina from 1824 to 1825. His use of the *Book of Common Prayer** while leading religious exercises as a schoolmaster prompted him to seek baptism* and confirmation* in 1825 in the Episcopal Church.

Ordained* to the diaconate* in 1825 and to the priesthood* in 1827 by Bishop John Stark Ravenscroft,* Otey served parishes in Tennessee while continuing to teach school. When he was consecrated* bishop of Tennessee in 1834, the tiny diocese* consisted of only 200 communicants. Despite thirty years of energetic efforts, the diocese had increased to only about 1,500 communicants by 1860.

Although markedly influenced by Ravenscroft, Otey opposed the Oxford Movement.* Tolerant of other denominations,* he once declared that he was neither high* nor low* church. He was an influential and respected member of the Episcopal House of Bishops.* Always concerned with education, he helped to found seven schools, including The University of the South. He was unionist in sentiment prior to the Civil War* but died in Memphis in 1863 as a supporter of the Confederacy. At his direction his tombstone bears the following words: "First Bishop of the Holy Catholic Church in Tennessee. The blood of Jesus Christ cleanseth us from all sin."

BIBLIOGRAPHY. *DAB* VII; W. M. Green, *James Hervey Otey* (1885); A. H. Noll, *History of the Church in the Diocese of Tennessee* (1900).

D. L. Holmes

Otterbein, (Philip) William (1726-1813). German Reformed* pastor,* cofounder and bishop* of the United Brethren in Christ.* Born to Daniel and Henrietta Otterbein in Dillenburg, the county seat of Nassau, Germany, William, as well as his father and all five surviving brothers, prepared themselves for the German Reformed* ministry at the academy of Herborn (near Dillenburg), the intellectual center of German Reformed Pietism.* After his ordination* in 1749 and a brief pastorate at Ockersdorf, Otterbein became one of Michael Schlatter's* six recruits for service in the American colonies.

Arriving in the colonies in 1752, he served a series of German Reformed congregations, his last pastorate in Baltimore (1774-1813). During his early days in the colonies, he traveled widely under the auspices of the Coetus, the first supervising body of the German Reformed congregations in America, thus playing a role among the German Reformed somewhat similar to Henry Melchior Muhlenberg's* role among the Lutherans.*

While pastor at York, Pennsylvania, he met the Mennonite* Martin Boehm* who had developed the custom of holding evangelistic meetings *(Grosse Versammlungen)*, one of which was in progress in Isaac Long's barn. After the sermon, the learned Otterbein and the lay* preacher* Boehm, sensing a kinship of spirit, embraced each other, saying *"Wir sind Brüder"* ("We are brethren"). Subsequently, they engaged in preaching tours together. Out of their joint endeavors came the United Brethren in Christ in 1789.

At the newly formed group's first conference, both Otterbein and Boehm were elected bishops (1800). Thus during his later years Otterbein served in the dual relationship of bishop of the United Brethren in Christ Church and pastor of a Baltimore congregation loosely associated with the German Reformed Church. He died in 1813 and was buried in the churchyard of his church in Baltimore.

See also GERMAN-AMERICAN REVIVALISM.

BIBLIOGRAPHY. J. B. Behney and P. H. Heller, *The History of the United Brethren Church* (1979); A. C. Core, ed., *Philip William Otterbein: Pastor, Ecumenist* (1968); *DAB* VII; *DARB*; A. W. Drury, *The Life of Phillip William Otterbein, Founder of the United Brethren in Christ* (1884); *NCAB* 10; J. S. O'Malley, *Pilgrimage of Faith: The Legacy of the Otterbeins* (1973). F. E. Stoeffler

Outler, Albert Cook (1908-1989). Methodist theologian.* Born in Thomasville, Georgia, Outler was educated at Wofford College (B.A., 1928), Emory (B.D., 1933) and Yale* (Ph.D., 1938). In addition to serving pastorates in his home state, he taught theology at Duke University, Yale University and Southern Methodist University. A noted scholar in historical theology, he gained stature as an ecumenical* theologian who interpreted John Wesley* as a significant practical theologian with catholic breadth as well as evangelical* fervor. He placed considerable emphasis on the influence of patristic theologians upon Wesley, particularly in Wesley's doctrine* of soteriology.

Outler was active in the faith and order movement in the former Methodist Church and the World Council of Churches,* and he was vice chairman of the Fourth World Council of Faith and Order (Montreal, 1963). He was an observer at the Second Vatican Council,* served as a member of the General Conference of his denomination* and was a chairman of the Commission on Doctrine and Doctrinal Standards that was commissioned to develop the authoritative report on doctrine and doctrinal standards for the newly formed United Methodist Church* in 1968.

In addition to numerous publications in ecumenical, patristic, Wesleyan and systematic theology,* he served as president of the American Theological Society and the American Society of Church History. As a member of the editorial board of the Wesley Works Project, he also edited the sermons of John Wesley (volumes I and II). Throughout his life, he was influential as an interpreter of the significance of the Wesleyan tradition for the twentieth century.

J. S. O'Malley

Overseas Missionary Fellowship. An interdenominational and international faith mission.* The Overseas Missionary Fellowship (OMF) was founded in England as the China Inland Mission (CIM) in 1865 by James Hudson Taylor. Known as the "Father of the faith missions movement," Taylor's life and work led to the birth of some forty faith missions. Taylor pioneered the entry of Protestant missionaries to China's inland provinces, the adoption of native dress and the acceptance of single women and unordained men as missionaries. A distinctive of the mission from the very beginning was a financial policy based on prayer to God without any public or private solicitation of funds.

In the mission's first quarter-century, over 300 missionaries went from England to China. However, in 1888 the pattern of faith missions became international with the transplanting of the CIM to North America through the visit of Taylor to speak at the Niagara Bible Conference* and Dwight L. Moody's Northfield Conference at Northfield, Massachusetts. The first band of fourteen North American CIM missionaries sailed from Vancouver, British Columbia, for China in October 1888. Henry W. Frost* was appointed as the first North American director of the CIM, a position he held for forty years.

Some of the best-known American and Canadian missionaries in CIM's eighty-five years in China are William W. Borden,* John and Betty Stam,* and John and Isobel Kuhn.* When missionaries were forced to leave China in the early 1950s, the mission expanded to other countries of East Asia, including Japan, Hong Kong, Taiwan, Korea, Indonesia, Philippines, Singapore, Thailand, Laos and Kampuchea. The mission headquarters moved from Shanghai to Singapore.

In 1964 the mission became fully international, opening its doors to members of any race. Currently, about one-tenth of the one thousand members are from Asian backgrounds. Since its founding the mission has had seven general directors—D. E. Hoste of the "Cambridge Seven" succeeded Hudson Taylor and was followed by George W. Gibb, Bishop Frank Houghton, J. Oswald Sanders, Michael C. Griffiths and James Hudson Taylor III, the great-grandson of the founder and the first American to lead the mission.

BIBLIOGRAPHY. A. J. Broomhall, *Hudson Taylor and China's Open Century,* 6 vols. (1981-1988); Dr. & Mrs. H. Taylor, *By Faith: Henry W. Frost and the China Inland Mission* (1938); Dr. & Mrs. H. Taylor, *Hudson Taylor in Early Years; Hudson Taylor and the China Inland Mission,* 2 vols. (1911, 1918). D. J. Michell

Owen, Robert (1771-1858). British industrialist, social reformer and communitarian. Believing that man's character is formed by his environment, Owen pioneered free infant and adult education as well as advanced working conditions in his cotton-spinning town of New Lanark, Scotland. At New

Harmony,* Indiana (1825-1827), he experimented with education, science and communal living as means to create a model Community of Equality.

Replicated worldwide, such communities were to produce the New Moral World. The millennium* created by this secular process would be marked by freedom of thought; religious toleration; community of property; equality of the sexes and races; and happiness based on moral, physical and mental health. Owen was influenced by the utilitarian thought of his business partner, Jeremy Bentham. A universalist,* perceived by many as an atheist, Owen had a public debate on the merits of organized religion with Alexander Campbell* in Cincinnati in 1829. Later, Owen espoused spiritualism, labor unionism and the ideas which led to the cooperative movement in Britain.

See also NEW HARMONY.

BIBLIOGRAPHY. J. F. C. Harrison, *Quest for the New Moral World: Robert Owen & the Owenites in Britain and America* (1969).   D. E. Pitzer

Oxford Movement. *See* TRACTARIAN MOVEMENT.

Oxnam, Garfield Bromley (1891-1963). Methodist* bishop,* ecumenical* leader and advocate of social reform. Born in Sonora, California, Oxnam graduated from the University of Southern California (B.A., 1913) and completed his theological education* at Boston University (S.T.B., 1915) before being ordained* a Methodist minister* in 1916. He pastored first in Poplar, California (1916-1917), and then at the Church of All Nations in Los Angeles (1917-1927), during which time he also taught social ethics at the University of Southern California (1919-1923). After teaching one year at the Boston University School of Theology (1927-

1928), he accepted in 1928 the presidency of DePauw University in Greencastle, Indiana (1928-1936).

Oxnam's pastorate in Los Angeles had elicited his sympathy for the labor movement, and as a bishop from 1936 to 1960 (in Omaha, Boston, New York and Washington, D.C.), he supported movements for social justice. In 1953 he demanded and received a hearing before the House Committee on Un-American Activities, which had released documents alleging falsely that he was a Communist. The committee refused to apologize, but his testimony won widespread support, especially from within the Methodist Church. His book, *I Protest* (1954), recounted his conflict with the committee.

Devoted to the movement for Protestant unity, Oxnam served as the president of the Federal Council of Churches* (1944-1946), as an officer at the founding of the National Council of Churches* (1950) and as a president of the World Council of Churches* (1948-1957). Deeply interested in world missions* and an extensive traveler himself,* Oxnam originated the policy that every American Methodist bishop should visit at least one foreign field. He also promoted theological education. When he died, his ashes were buried in Oxnam Chapel of Wesley Theological Seminary, which he had helped move from Maryland to Washington, D.C.

BIBLIOGRAPHY. *Christian Advocate* (March 28, 1963); *DAB* 7; A. Godbold, "Oxnam, Garfield Bromley," *The Encyclopedia of World Methodism,* ed. N. B. Harmon, 2 vols. (1974).   E. B. Holifield

Ozman, Agnes. *See* LaBERGE, AGNES N. OZMAN.

P

Pacem in Terris. 1963 papal encyclical* on peace. When Pope John XXIII* was elected to the papacy* in 1958, the just-war doctrine was viewed as the normative position for Roman Catholics, and there was no proscription against war in any of the Church's teachings. In *Pacem in Terris* (Peace on Earth), a papal encyclical issued on April 11, 1963, Pope John XXIII moved in a pacifist* direction and repudiated war in the modern world. He stated that "in an age such as ours which prides itself on its atomic energy it is contrary to reason to hold that war is now a suitable way to restore rights which have been violated" (par. 127). In this statement, Pope John XXIII was condemning not only nuclear war but all war in the nuclear age. And by repudiating the suitability of war as a means of restoring violated rights, he brought into question the theory of the just war.

Building his arguments on the principles of the freedom of the individual and the validity of natural law, Pope John XXIII concluded that each individual is called forth to "observe, judge, act" because it is the individual acting for the common good that will bring forth peace. Thus *Pacem in Terris* stands with the rights of individual conscience, rather than the right of political force. According to *Pacem in Terris,* the primacy of the individual right and duty to work for peace is what ultimately informs and judges the actions of governments and organizations.

Many Catholics still support the just-war doctrine. Nevertheless, there is no doubt that the encyclical heralded a new approach in Catholic thought not just about war, but concerning peace. Pope John XXIII's challenge to Catholics remains clear; war is no longer a valid policy, and the burden is on each person to act as a peacemaker.

See also PEACE MOVEMENT, CATHOLIC.

BIBLIOGRAPHY. W. J. Gibbons, ed., *Pacem in Terris; Encyclical Letter of His Holiness Pope John XXIII* (1963); J. W. Douglass, *The Non-Violent Cross: A Theology of Revolution and Peace* (1968); T. A. Shannon, ed., *War or Peace? The Search for New Answers* (1982).   P. McNeal

Pacific Garden Mission. Evangelical* rescue mission* in Chicago. Founded by Sarah Dunn Clarke* and her husband, Colonel George Rogers Clarke, the Mission opened in Chicago on September 15, 1877. Originally called the "Clarke's Mission," the mission was a one-room facility amid brothels, saloons and gambling halls. Seating capacity was restricted to about forty persons, mostly down-and-outers who frequented the nearby Levee District.

In 1880 the Clarkes purchased the "Pacific Beer Garden," a notorious establishment noted for cheap beer and revelry. At the suggestion of Dwight L. Moody,* the facility was renamed the Pacific Garden Mission. Utilizing gospel meetings, a mobile gospel wagon, evangelistic* teams and services to meet a wide range of human needs, over the past century of ministry the mission has welcomed some six million persons. Among those converted have been Harry Monroe, a notorious Detroit counterfeiter; Billy Sunday,* a baseball player for the Chicago White Stockings, who would go on to be a noted evangelist*; and Mel Trotter,* a hobo who founded a similar mission in Grand Rapids, Michigan.

In 1922 the mission moved to a former brothel on State Street known as "The White House." In 1941 two buildings to the north were acquired and in 1955 the Loyal Hotel to the south was purchased. The current Pacific Garden Mission now has four buildings. In the World War 2* era several new ministries were begun under Superintendent Harry George Saunier (1902-), including the night shelter for the homeless, a shelter for women and a ministry to servicemen. After the War, the mission produced films and a radio broadcast known today as "Unshackled." In 1951, two medical students opened up a clinic, to which dentistry services have since been added. One of the most celebrated of the urban rescue missions in America, the Pacific Garden Mission has served as a model to many similar ministries across North America.

See also RESCUE MISSION MOVEMENT.

BIBLIOGRAPHY. J. R. Adair, *The Old Lighthouse:*

The Story of the Pacific Garden Mission (1966); C. F. H. Henry, *The Pacific Garden Mission* (1942); N. Magnuson, *Salvation in the Slums: Evangelical Social Work, 1865-1920* (1977).

C. E. Stockwell

Padilla, Juan De (c.1500-c.1544). Franciscan* missionary* and martyr. Born in Andalusia, Spain, as a youth Padilla was probably a soldier, but after joining the Friars Minor, he came to New Spain (c.1528), where he soon embarked on missionary ventures, serving as chaplain* in Nuño de Guzmán's expedition to Nueva Galicia and Culiacan (1529-1530).

Padilla sought to protect natives from exploitation and made many missionary journeys to reach them. He also established monastic communities and served as superior at Tulantzingo during the 1530s. In 1540, yearning to reach tribesmen described by Fray Marcos de Niza, Padilla joined the Coronado expedition. Marching on foot, always in the vanguard, Padilla stayed with Coronado until they reached Zuni; then he joined smaller detachments which reached the Moqui and Hopi pueblos (near the Grand Canyon), and then to pueblos on the Rio Grande. In 1541 he marched with Don Lope de Urrea to the Pecos and later joined Coronado in quest of the legendary "Quivara," which turned out to be primitive villages in Kansas.

Wanting to work with the Native Americans, Padilla remained in New Mexico when Coronado returned to Mexico. In 1542 he and a few companions returned to "Quivara," where he established a mission. The Native Americans nearby treated him well, but when he sought to do missionary work among a neighboring tribe, the Quiviras killed him, probably near Herington, Kansas.

BIBLIOGRAPHY. H. E. Bolton and T. M. Marxhall, *The Colonization of North America* (1935); H. E. Bolton, *Coronado on the Turquoise Trail* (1949); *DAB* VII.

G. A. Reed

Page, Kirby (1890-1957). Disciples of Christ* minister,* pacifist* and social activist. Born in Tyler County, Texas, and educated at Drake University, the University of Chicago, Columbia University and Union Theological Seminary,* Page was ordained in the Christian Church (Disciples of Christ)* in 1915. He served pastorates in Iowa (1912-1915), Chicago (1915-1916) and New York (1918-1921). During World War 1* he was secretary to G. Sherwood Eddy,* conducting evangelistic* campaigns in Europe and Asia. After 1921 he was a free-lance lecturer and political activist.

Page traveled extensively and wrote over two dozen books, including *War: Its Causes, Consequences and Cure* (1923) and *The Sword or the Cross* (1921). From 1926 to 1934 he edited *The World Tomorrow,* a pacifist journal, and in 1922 he helped organize the Fellowship for a Christian Social Order,* serving as its executive secretary. He was active in the Fellowship of Reconciliation* and many other organizations and committees. Page was an ardent pacifist and socialist.* He was critical of capitalism* (or individualism, as he called it), but equally critical of Marxism and Communism for encouraging class warfare and militarism. He believed that the teachings of Jesus must lead to a nonviolent, cooperative social order.

BIBLIOGRAPHY. C. Chatfield and C. DeBenedetti, eds., *Kirby Page and Social Gospel* (1976); J. N. Hughey, *Trends in Protestant Social Idealism* (1948).

L. W. Japinga

Paine, Robert Treat (1731-1814). Massachusetts politician and jurist. Born in Boston, Paine attended the Boston Latin School and Harvard College* (B.A., 1749). Having studied theology* after his graduation, he served for a time as a military chaplain* during the French and Indian War (1754-1763). Admitted to the Massachusetts Bar in 1757, Paine was associate prosecuting attorney in the "Boston Massacre" trial of 1768 and, from 1774 to 1778, a delegate to the Continental Congress. During his lengthy tenure (1777-1790) as attorney general of Massachusetts, Paine engaged in a protracted effort to prop up the state's tottering religious order, prosecuting a series of cases concerning nonpayment of taxes assessed for the support of established* parish* clergy.* A member of the committee that drafted the state constitution of 1778-1779, he fought to retain as much of the old religious establishment as possible. Paine, a staunch Unitarian,* made his last public appearance at the installation in 1814 of Edward Everett as minister to the Brattle St. Church.

BIBLIOGRAPHY. *DAB* VII; W. G. McLoughlin, *New England Dissent, 1630-1833: The Baptists and the Separation of Church and State* (1971).

G. W. Harper

Paine, Solomon (c.1700-1754). Separate* Congregational* minister.* Converted* in the course of a revival* that swept through Windham, Connecticut, in 1721, Paine ultimately became a leading speaker for strict Calvinistic* Congregationalism, helping to organize the colony's first and most important Separate Congregational church, at

Canterbury in 1744. Ordained* to the ministry in 1746, Paine was jailed for a time for daring to accept the pastorate of the Canterbury congregation in contravention of Connecticut law. Paine set himself against the Congregational religious establishment and its nascent Baptist critics with equal vigor, opposing as anti-Christ the standing order's alliance of church and state while moderating a series of ecclesiastical councils in 1751-1752 that first censured Isaac Backus* and finally stripped him of his ministerial credentials after his conversion to Baptist* views. Paine's published works include *A Short View of the Differences between the Church of Christ and the Established Churches in the Colony of Connecticut* (1752).

BIBLIOGRAPHY. W. G. McLoughlin, *New England Dissent, 1630-1833: The Baptists and the Separation of Church and State* (1971).

G. W. Harper

Paine, Thomas (1737-1809). Deist* and pamphleteer during the American and French revolutions.* The son of an English Quaker* corsetmaker, Paine was unable to find a suitable outlet in England for his talents as a debater; so he decided to try America. He quickly became well known in the colonies as a pamphleteer. Although Paine did not have an original mind, his pamphlets pioneered in simplifying complex issues for a mass audience. His best-remembered American pamphlet was *Common Sense.* Writing in early 1776, he summed up in clear language the best arguments for independence from Britain at a time when few were so bold as to advocate such a radical step.

Once the fighting began, Paine wrote a pamphlet he called *The Crisis* (1776). Designed to wake up Pennsylvanians to fight an approaching army of redcoats, it contained one of the memorable phrases of the American Revolution: "These are the times that try men's souls."

By the time the French Revolution broke out in 1789, Paine was back in England trying to sell a revolutionary prefabricated iron bridge he had invented. He soon attacked aristocratic and monarchical privilege and encouraged the establishment of a republic in England as well as France. Paine argued that aristocracy was a heavier financial burden on society than it was worth; better that the money be spent on educating citizens to become wise voters. These ideas, expressed in Paine's soul-stirring language, caused a sensation in England and France. Paine immigrated to revolutionary France to enjoy the adulation of radical revolutionaries there.

In France Paine continued to condemn aristocrat-

ic society, now focusing on the church. He regarded the church as nothing more than an agent of the old regime. In *The Age of Reason* (1794, 1796), Paine expressed his Enlightenment* deism* in his simple belief in the existence of God, the hope of happiness hereafter and the duties of establishing justice, mercy and the well-being of humanity. He described the institutional church as largely a means of keeping the masses subdued while providing a handsome means of income for the aristocracy. This argument went further than anyone had gone before: Voltaire had poked fun at the church, but Paine implied that it was an evil institution.

Revolutionary opinion and politics in France changed, and Paine's radical views became less popular. He returned to America in 1802, where he enjoyed the friendship of the deist Elihu Palmer.* Paine spent the last years of his life in poverty and ill health, sustained by the financial aid of a friend.

BIBLIOGRAPHY. H. H. Clark, "An Historical Interpretation of Thomas Paine's Religion," *University of California Chronicle* 35 (1933):56-87; *DAB* VII; *DARB; NCAB* 5; R. P. Falk, "Thomas Paine: Deist or Quaker?" *Pennsylvania Magazine of History and Biography* 62 (1938):52-63; S. Williamson, *Thomas Paine: His Life, Work and Times* (1973).

J. E. Mennell

Palm Sunday. The Sunday* before Easter,* celebrating Christ's entry into Jerusalem. A procession with palm branches down the Mount of Olives is reported at Jerusalem for this day in A.D. 383 by the pilgrim Egeria, and the custom spread slowly from there to Spain, Gaul and eventually Rome. In many Western churches this same Sunday is also known as Passion Sunday, the Gospel for the day being the Passion according to Matthew, Mark or Luke in the three years of the triennial lectionary.* The preliminary palm liturgy* includes the account of the entry into Jerusalem from the same Gospel, and is followed by a procession with palm branches and the singing of traditional hymns. In America today the palm liturgy is sometimes celebrated ecumenically at a single location, the members of the participating congregations processing to their several churches for the more restricted celebration of Eucharist.* Orthodox churches celebrate only Christ's entry into Jerusalem on Palm Sunday, beginning the week of the Passion on Monday.

BIBLIOGRAPHY. J. G. Davies, *Holy Week: A Short History* (1963). T. J. Talley

Palmer, Benjamin Morgan (1818-1902). Southern Presbyterian* pastor.* Born in Charleston, South Carolina, Palmer graduated from the University of Georgia (1838) and Columbia Theological Seminary (1841). He pastored congregations in Savannah, Georgia (1841-1843), and Columbia, South Carolina (1843-1856), in addition to teaching church history and polity at Columbia Theological Seminary (1853-1856). Palmer helped found *The Southern Presbyterian Review* in 1847 and thereafter was an editor and frequent contributor. In 1856 Palmer became the minister of the First Presbyterian Church of New Orleans, a position he held for more than forty-five years. Perhaps the most outstanding Southern pulpit orator during the years from 1850 to 1900, Palmer influenced Southern views of slavery, abolition,* the North, secession and many other matters. During the Civil War* he served as a minister to both the Army of the West and the Army of Tennessee.

Elected moderator of the first General Assembly* of the Southern Presbyterian Church after that body split from the Old School* Presbyterian Church in 1861, Palmer worked diligently for years to further its growth. Along with James Henley Thornwell,* he believed in the spirituality of the church, the doctrine that the institutional church is exclusively spiritual and as an organization should not take any political positions. Rejecting reunion with the Northern Church after the Civil War, he argued that it would bring ruin to Southern congregations. A social and theological conservative, Palmer opposed racial integration during Reconstruction, waged a campaign in New Orleans for strict Sabbath* observance and worked to keep his denomination from accepting theistic evolution,* a position espoused by James Woodrow* of Columbia Theological Seminary.

BIBLIOGRAPHY. *DAB* VII; T. C. Johnson, *The Life and Letters of Benjamin Morgan Palmer* (1906). G. S. Smith

Palmer, Elihu (1764-1806). Deist* preacher.* Born in Canterbury, Connecticut, Palmer graduated from Dartmouth College* in 1787 and studied theology* with John Foster at Pittsfield, Massachusetts. After only six months (1788-1789) as minister* at the Presbyterian* Church of Newtown, Long Island, Palmer left because the congregation rejected his unorthodox thinking. He moved to Philadelphia to join the Baptists* and finally the Universalists,* but his teaching against the deity of Jesus outraged his parishioners so that he had to leave town in 1791.

In 1793 Palmer studied law in Philadelphia, but after a yellow fever epidemic left him blind, he returned to preaching as a free-lance deist speaker. He settled in New York City, where he founded a deist society known successively as the Philosophical Society, the Theistical Society and the Society of the Columbian Illuminati. Palmer preached at this gathering every Sunday night, as well as to similar groups in other cities. As editor of two short-lived weeklies, *Temple of Reason* (1801-1803) and *Prospect: View of the Moral World* (1803-1805), he attempted to publish his ideas to a broader audience as well.

Palmer's religious views evolved into a militant, anti-Christian deism. He attacked the Bible* as immoral and claimed that Moses, Mohammed and Jesus "were all of them impostors; two of them notorious murderers in practice, and the other a murderer in principle." Joining his own form of natural religion and rationalism with ardent republicanism, Palmer's goal was the overthrow of both superstition and tyranny. The most complete statement of his thought appeared in his *Principles of Nature; A Development of the Moral Causes of Happiness and Misery among the Human Species* (1802).

BIBLIOGRAPHY. *DAB* VII; E. Palmer, *Posthumous Pieces . . . To Which Are Prefixed a Memoir of Mr. Palmer . . .* (1826). T. P. Thigpen

Palmer, Paul (?-c.1750). Colonial Baptist* preacher.* A native of Maryland, Palmer was baptized in the Welsh Tract Church, Delaware, and ordained* in Connecticut. Arriving in North Carolina about 1720, he married Joanna Peterson, a widow, and they had two children. After preaching for several years, he organized the first Baptist church in North Carolina (Chowan County) in 1727. His itinerant* preaching resulted in other new congregations. A notable convert was Joseph Parker, who also became a Baptist preacher. The first Baptist church in Maryland (1742) grew out of converts Palmer baptized at Chestnut Ridge. Arminian* in doctrine, Palmer was a major leader of the early General Baptists* in America. Neither the year of his birth or death is known, but he apparently died before 1754.

BIBLIOGRAPHY. H. L. McBeth, *The Baptist Heritage* (1986); G. W. Paschal, *History of North Carolina Baptists* (1930). W. M. Patterson

Palmer, Phoebe Worrall (1807-1874). Methodist* lay* revivalist,* feminist,* humanitarian and editor. Born in New York City, Phoebe Worrall, at the age of nineteen, married a New York physician, Walter C. Palmer. By 1835 she was active in a "Tuesday Meeting for the Promotion of Holiness"

at the home of her sister Sarah Worral Lankford (Palmer*), where she eventually assumed leadership and began to develop and popularize her modified version of John Wesley's* perfectionism,* or "entire sanctification."*

Based on Jesus' words that "the altar sanctifies the gift," she reasoned that if she "presented her body a living sacrifice" by "laying her all on the altar," God would make her holy. Her "altar theology" reduced the quest for sanctification to a simple three-step process: (1) consecrating oneself entirely to God; (2) believing God keeps his promise to sanctify what is consecrated; and (3) bearing witness to what God has done. Her theology was adopted by Holiness* denominations such as the Wesleyan Methodists, the Free Methodists* and the Church of the Nazarene,* as well as by the Salvation Army* and the Keswick Movement* in England.

In addition, Palmer popularized the idea that Pentecostal Spirit baptism* was available to every believer. While she instructed Christians to wait for "the promise of the Father" which would purify their hearts, empower their witness and revive their churches, she never spoke in tongues.* But her emphasis on Pentecost and Spirit baptism helped pave the way for the later emergence of the Pentecostal* and charismatic* movements in America. Palmer disseminated her ideas through her ten books, including *The Way of Holiness* (1845). In addition she edited the widely circulated magazine *Guide to Holiness* (1864-1874).

As a revivalist she participated in more than three hundred camp meetings* and revival campaigns across the U. S., Canada and the British Isles. Her ministry helped reintroduce the concept of lay ministry to the church and touch off the awakening of 1858 (*See* Prayer Meeting Revival) which eventually brought more than two million new members into the churches. This emphasis on lay ministry helped American revivalism make the transition from the small-town, clergy-centered campaigns Charles G. Finney* waged, to the lay-oriented, city-wide crusades Dwight L. Moody* led.

As a feminist she promoted the cause of women's ministries, both through example and her writings. Pioneer feminists Catherine Booth* of The Salvation Army and Frances Willard* of the Women's Christian Temperance Union, credited Phoebe Palmer with an important influence on their lives. As a humanitarian, she served on the board of the Ladies' Home Missionary Society of the Methodist Episcopal Church. She persuaded them to demolish the "Old Brewery" which dominated New York City's worst slum, the Five

Points; and to establish a home, school, workroom and chapel* in its place. This mission* house was one of Protestantism's first efforts to bring social reform* to urban America's rapidly expanding slums. Its ministry helped set the pattern for the social action of the churches for the remainder of the nineteenth century.

See also HOLINESS MOVEMENT.

BIBLIOGRAPHY. *NAW* 3; H. B. Raser, *Phoebe Palmer: Her Life and Thought* (1987); R. Wheatley, *The Life and Letters of Mrs. Phoebe Palmer* (1876); C. E. White, *The Beauty of Holiness: Phoebe Palmer as Theologian, Revivalist, Feminist, and Humanitarian* (1986). C. E. White

Palmer, Sarah Worrall Lankford (1806-1896). Methodist* laywoman.* Like her more famous younger sister, Phoebe Worral Palmer,* Sarah Palmer was a vigorous proponent of the doctrine of entire sanctification.* In 1836 she established the "Tuesday Meeting for the Promotion of Holiness" in her home in New York City. This meeting was held under the direction of her and her sister for more than fifty years. Each week leaders from several of America's evangelical* denominations, as well as about two hundred laypeople came together for Bible* reading, prayer* and personal testimony.* With its emphasis on the experience of entire sanctification and the equality of laypeople and clergy (whether men or women), it became the model for 238 similar meetings held around the world. Two years after Phoebe's death, Sarah married her brother-in-law and assumed her sister's place as editor of *Guide to Holiness.*

BIBLIOGRAPHY. J. A. Roche, *The Life of Mrs. Sarah A. Lankford Palmer* (1898); C. E. White, *The Beauty of Holiness: Phoebe Palmer as Theologian, Revivalist, Feminist, and Humanitarian* (1986). C. E. White

Palmyra Manifesto (1865). A call for reorganization of Southern Methodism* following the Civil War.* In June 1865 Andrew Monroe, district superintendent of the Kansas Mission District of the Methodist Episcopal Church, South, called a meeting of twenty-four preachers in full connection, about a dozen laymen and Bishop Hubbard H. Kavanaugh in the town of Palmyra, Missouri, to consider the status and future of the Methodist Episcopal Church, South. The Manifesto disavowed the slave issue as the only question separating the two Methodisms, asserted the integrity of the Methodist Episcopal Church, South, and urged that this integrity be preserved. The Manifesto ended, declaring that the Methodist Episcopal

Church, South, ardently desired to cultivate fraternal relations with "all evangelical* churches." The Methodist Episcopal Church, North, was included, but as one among many. The salient point was that the Church South, regardless of attacks made upon it and attempts to absorb it, was an honorable and dignified body and would remain so. It was not up for auction, and its members would not be treated as penitents or traitors. This strongly worded text was reprinted by a revived Southern press and spread rapidly, inspiring the Methodist Episcopal Church, South, to reorganize and grow.

BIBLIOGRAPHY. W. H. Lewis, *The History of Methodism in Missouri for a Decade of Years from 1860 to 1879* (1890); F. Norwood, ed., *Sourcebook of American Methodism* (1982).

J. C. Brown

Papacy and United States Catholics. Spain and France brought to their colonies the religion of the Catholic Reformation and counter-Reformation. It was papal in its theological insistence on the pope as head of the Church but in practice, strongly nationalistic. The state-controlled church institutions, such as the Inquisition in Louisiana, subsidized missionaries* and chose bishops.*

Loyalty to Rome distinguished English colonial* Catholics from the established church*; they were called "papists." But distance and only nominal European supervision led to an autonomous church style. Republican ideas during the American Revolution* led to demands for recognition as "an ordinary national church" in union with Rome but picking its own leaders and managing its own property and internal structures. Nineteenth-century immigration* diluted American Catholic national unity at the same time as events in Europe brought about a highly centralized Church centered on a monarchical pope. In Baltimore church councils* adopted uniform national rules approved by Rome; Rome discouraged other nationalist American ideas, such as the request that the archbishop* of Baltimore be "primate"* of the Catholic Church in America. American priests* became honorary members of the papal court ("monsignors"*); a college for U. S. seminarians opened in Rome (*See* North American College in Rome), and many of its alumni became bishops; a papal representative was named, first to the American Church (apostolic delegate,* 1893-1984) and then to the U. S. government (pro-nuncio,* 1984-).

Papal letters in 1895 (*Longinquae Oceani**) and 1899 (*Testem Benevolentiae**) discouraged specif-ically American religious approaches. Papal condemnation in 1907 of Catholic modernism* brought in its wake increased Roman supervision of doctrinal* teaching and church discipline.* In 1908 the Church in the United States ceased to be supervised by Rome's missionary department, the Congregation for Propagation of the Faith, but that simply meant that American dioceses* reported to other Vatican agencies.

Between the world wars and into the 1950s, American Catholics were known for unquestioning loyalty to the pope and for generous financial support of church projects. Vatican II* brought changes. Debate among bishops and theologians* spread to priests and people. Radical as well as conservative meanings were read into the council's teaching on the Church as people of God; the baptismal* priesthood of all believers*; collegial* responsibility; religious liberty* and freedom of conscience; ecumenical* relations with other Christian churches and approaches to non-Christians.

In 1968 Pope Paul VI reiterated in the encyclical* letter *Humanae Vitae** the negative views on artificial birth control* enunciated in the 1930 letter *Casti Connubii.* Dissent increased, since it had been known for a year that the pope's commission on the subject had recommended otherwise. While the bulk of practicing American Roman Catholics follow a middle way, vocal pro-papal and anti-papal elements now compete in a community no longer so uniform in belief and practice as it once was.

See also AMERICANISM; CONCILIAR TRADITION, AMERICAN; VATICAN—U.S. CATHOLIC CHURCH RELATIONS.

BIBLIOGRAPHY. J. P. Dolan, *The American Catholic Experience* (1985); G. P. Fogarty, *The Vatican and the American Hierarchy from 1870 to 1965* (1985); J. Hennesey, *American Catholics* (1981).

J. Hennesey

Papal Infallibility. A Roman Catholic* term refering to the pope's share in the general grace that preserves the Church from error. Catholic theologians* distinguish between *infallibility* and *indefectibility.* The former regards the ability of the Church to teach without error the truths necessary for salvation, while the latter regards the ability of the Church to triumph sufficiently over human weakness to witness effectively to salvation. Both gifts flow from the nature of the Church and, it is argued, were implied from apostolic times. The First Vatican Council* (1870) formally defined the pope's role and share in infallibility, but from the early centuries the Roman Church enjoyed pre-eminence in settling doctrinal disputes and the bishop of Rome had special prestige. The False Decretals of the ninth century taught that papal teaching was irreversible, while the term *infallibility* first appeared in the fourteenth century. Present-day Catholic theologians generally teach that the pope is preserved from error when teaching in union with the entire episcopate, in union with a General Council or alone *ex cathedra* (formally) on matters of faith and morals. It is not a personal gift of the pope and is in force most rarely. The two modern papal teachings usually considered to have been *ex cathedra,* and so infallible, are the definition of the Immaculate Conception* of the Virgin Mary (1854) and the definition of the Assumption* of the Virgin Mary (1950). In recent decades Catholic theologian Hans Küng* has questioned the doctrine of papal infallibility in *Infallible? An Inquiry* (1970), and the doctrine remains a controversial issue dividing Catholics and Protestants* in particular.

See also MAGISTERIUM.

BIBLIOGRAPHY. E. C. Butler, *The Vatican Council, 1869-1870* (1962); J. T. Ford, "Infallibility: Recent Studies," *TS* 40 (1979):273-305; E. J. Yarnold and H. Chadwick, *Truth and Authority* (1977). J. T. Carmody

Papal Nuncio/Pro Nuncio. An envoy accredited as the pope's* ambassador to the civil government of a particular country. When the ambassador is recognized as the dean of the diplomatic corps, he is given the title *nuncio,* otherwise he is known as *pro nuncio.* The *nuncio* or *pro nuncio* is distinguished from an *apostolic delegate,*who is a papal representative with an exclusively religious mission to the Catholic Church in a particular country.

The first permanent apostolic delegate to the U.S., Francesco Satolli,* was appointed in 1893 and took up residence in Washington, D.C. When in January 1984 the Vatican and the U.S. government established full diplomatic relations (*See* Vatican-U.S. Catholic Church Relations), a pro nuncio was named. In Canada the delegation in existence since 1899 became a pro nunciature in 1969. It is the responsibility of the papal representative to solicit nominations for the office of bishop,* to compile dossiers on the candidates and to forward his recommendations to Rome. He is further charged to promote ecumenism* with other Christian churches and to foster cordial dealings with non-Christian religions.

BIBLIOGRAPHY. L. de Echeverria, "The Pope's Representatives," *Concilium* 127 (1979):56-63. J. E. Lynch

Parachurch Groups (Voluntary Societies). Voluntary, not-for-profit associations of Christians working outside denominational* control to achieve some specific ministry* or social service. The prefix *para* comes from Greek and means "beside" or "alongside of." The term became popular in the 1960s as a designation for various groups which were not only "alongside" but also supportive of more basic institutions. Paramedics extended the services of medical professionals; paralegal workers supplemented the work of attorneys; and parachurch organizations, in theory, extended the ministries of institutional churches.

Ralph D. Winter, director of the U.S. Center for World Mission in Pasadena, California, has analyzed the relationship between parachurch groups and official church organizations. He uses the terms *sodality* and *modality* to designate the two forms of Christian organizations. *Sodality,* borrowed from Roman Catholicism,* stands for "a society with religious or charitable objects." *Modality* refers to the official governing structures of denominations.

Voluntary Societies and the Churches. Voluntary associations of Christians have existed alongside and within official church organizations since Christianity's earliest days. Within the Roman Catholic tradition sodalities have functioned within the official Church. The various priestly* and lay* religious orders* are the classic examples of sodalities. They are voluntary and self-governing associations operating under the general supervision of the hierarchy (the modality).

In mainline* Protestant* denominations, "coalitions" of liberal* Christians have usually not assumed the form of parachurch organizations because they have had no need to raise money directly from church members. A few exceptions to this general rule can be cited. The Witherspoon Society, for example, was formed by liberals in the United Presbyterian Church in the early 1970s to counter the influence of the Lay Committee and Presbyterians United for Biblical Concerns. In general, however, liberal organizations within the mainline denominations have had little need for parachurch structures because the denominational leadership has been in liberal hands.

Liberal versions of the large nondenominational parachurch organizations have also been almost nonexistent. The structures of the National Council of Churches* and World Council of Churches* form the interdenominational organizations through which liberals work together, but since these are funded through official denominational channels, they have no need for direct fund-raising among the mainline congregations.

Among evangelical* Christians, however, parachurch organizations have become the primary means of cooperative endeavor. The Billy Graham Evangelistic Association,* for example, has its own board of directors, headquartered in Minneapolis, Minnesota, which oversees an annual budget running into millions of dollars. Other evangelistic and youth organizations also have sizable budgets raised by mass mailings to families and individuals or by personal appeals from traveling staff members of the organizations.

Few, if any, of these parachurch organizations offer any significant opportunity for democratic* participation in the governance of the organization by the individual supporter. Many of them are "one-man" operations, and some have guarded their financial records from outside inspection. They follow a highly corporate style of operation much closer to the "big business" management model than to the traditional denominational structure. Examination of the names of the boards of directors of the larger evangelical agencies reveals considerable overlap. Some board members' names may appear on ten or more lists.

Evangelicals and Parachurch Structures. Extensive evangelical employment of parachurch structures in modern times is traceable to the vision of William Carey, the pioneer in modern foreign missions. When Carey wrote his *Enquiry into the Obligations of Christians* (1792), he asked, what would a trading company do to undertake a work in a distant territory? From this parallel he proposed the formation of a company of serious-minded Christians, laymen and ministers. The voluntary group should have a committee to collect and sift information, and to find funds and suitable missionaries to send to foreign lands.

The voluntary society, as it was often called, transformed nineteenth-century Christianity. It was instituted to meet a need rather than to satisfy some theological argument, but in effect it bypassed established church doctrines* and denominational structures. Individual Anglicans,* Baptists,* Congregationalists* and Methodists* could work together for defined purposes without raising the troublesome questions of dogma* or polity.* It also altered the power base of the churches by encouraging lay leadership among both men and women.

In the American context, where the separation of church and state* required all religious work to be conducted by voluntary means, the voluntary society seemed to be just what God intended. In the first half of the nineteenth century an alliance

of voluntary societies—missionary,* Bible,* educational and social-reform movements—tried valiantly to evangelize and Christianize the American wilderness. By participating in the work of the societies, the missionary enthusiast or the social activist who collected a penny a week or who distributed the missionary magazine participated fully in the work of the society. The American missionary Rufus Anderson* wrote in 1834: "It was not until the present century that the evangelical churches of Christendom were ever really organized with a view to the conversion* of the world."

Later, during the 1920s when the fundamentalist-modernist controversies* took place in the major denominations, conservative evangelicals came to rely even more heavily on voluntary societies (or parachurch agencies). The struggles for leadership within the denominations usually resulted in the repudiation of the fundamentalists.* When the fundamentalists withdrew from their traditional denominations, most of the denominations chose to adopt more liberal policies, and fundamentalists adopted independent parachurch agencies to fulfill their missions. Thus, contemporary parachurch organizations often provide channels for dissent and for alternative activities.

Many of today's evangelical parachurch agencies dwarf the parallel ministries in the major denominations. In addition to the Billy Graham Evangelistic Association, World Vision International,* Jerry Falwell's* various enterprises and Robert Schuller* Ministries support multi-million-dollar "empires." These are only the giant organizations that lead a host of smaller bodies. Sound estimates indicate that more than 10,000 groups now exist in the U.S.

When the charismatic movement* swept through the American churches in the 1960s, charismatic leaders added hundreds (perhaps thousands) of additional parachurch groups to the extensive number formed by fundamentalists and evangelicals. Parachurch structures allowed dynamic leaders freedom to rally followers and finances without the burden of denominational oversight or constraints. The most highly publicized of these ministries were television evangelists who raised millions of dollars each month during the 1980s through a variety of religious enterprises. But in 1987-1988, scandals surrounding televangelists Jim Bakker* and Jimmy Swaggart* raised troubling questions about the proliferation and financial accountability of parachurch ministries.

Significant Questions Some recent observers have questioned the wisdom of the continuing proliferation of parachurch groups in American evangelicalism. J. Alan Youngren, a consultant to several of the organizations, traced this proliferation, at least in part, to the American frontier spirit. Four characteristics of the frontier spirit, he said, tend to increase the enthusiasm for parachurch ministries: (1) less respect for tradition and traditional structures; (2) communalism—an attitude favoring the autonomy of one's own group; (3) self-reliance and independency; and (4) infatuation with almost anything new. Steeped in this frontier mentality, many parachurch leaders start their own works rather than join organizations already in existence.

The widespread questions about the financial practices of parachurch agencies led in the late 1970s to the formation of the Evangelical Council for Financial Accountability. One of its purposes was to encourage donors to demand financial disclosures from parachurch groups. Some groups changed their practices to conform to the Council's standards, but many others failed to join the Council because they refused to reveal their financial operations.

BIBLIOGRAPHY. S. Board, "The Great Evangelical Power Shift," *Eternity* (June 1979):17-21; E. J. Hales and J. A. Youngren, *Your Money/Their Ministry* (1981); R. G. Hutcheson, *Mainline Churches and the Evangelicals* (1981); H. A. Snyder, *The Problem of Wineskins* (1975); J. E. White, *The Church and the Parachurch* (1983); R. D. Winter, "The Anatomy of the Christian Mission," in *The 25 Unbelievable Years* (1970); J. A. Youngren, "Parachurch Proliferation: The Frontier Spirit Caught in Traffic," *CT* (November 6, 1981):38-41.

B. L. Shelley

Parham, Charles Fox (1873-1929). Founder of the Apostolic Faith movement and one of the founders of the modern Pentecostal Movement.* Born in Muscatine, Iowa, Parham suffered from ill health as a child and would suffer many bouts with rheumatic fever throughout his lifetime. During his studies at Southwest Kansas College (1890-1893), he wrestled with a ministerial call and, through a bout with rheumatic fever, came to believe in divine healing.* He began his ministerial career in the Methodist Episcopal Church,* but left the denomination* after 1895 to evangelize as an independent Holiness* preacher,* teaching sanctification* as a second work of grace, divine healing and the "third experience" of a baptism with the Holy Ghost and fire (*See* Baptism in the Spirit).

In 1898 Parham began publishing a bimonthly paper entitled *Apostolic Faith,* and established the

"Beth-el Healing Home" in Topeka to gather the sick for prayer.* A visit during the summer of 1900 to Frank W. Sandford's Holiness commune at Shiloh, Maine, introduced him to the idea of a "latter rain" premillennial* outpouring of the Spirit and reports of xenolalic experiences (miraculous speech in a foreign language) among missionaries. Later that year he founded the Bethel Bible School, near Topeka, with about forty students. After an extended Bible study* in December 1900, Parham and his students concluded that the initial evidence of the baptism with the Holy Spirit was speaking in tongues,* a conviction which became central in all of his subsequent teaching. (Parham himself believed that tongues should be authentic human languages.) Not long afterward (January 1, 1901), a student named Agnes N. Ozman* prayed for the experience and began speaking in tongues. Soon the other students and Parham himself were also practicing tongues-speech, and the school began attracting attention throughout the state. But by April of that year, the movement had lost its impetus, not to be regained until a revival that broke out in Galena, Kansas, in 1903.

Within seven years his loosely organized "Apostolic Faith Missions" had spread throughout the lower Midwest, attracting some 25,000 followers to the new Pentecostal doctrine. In 1905 he opened a Bible school in Houston, Texas, which served as the center of the movement in that region. There William Joseph Seymour,* an African-American Holiness preacher, was trained by Parham. Seymour carried the movement to Los Angeles in 1906 with the "Azusa Street Revival,"* where the worldwide Pentecostal Movement was launched.

By 1907, however, Parham had lost his leadership in Pentecostal circles, owing to charges of sexual misconduct and his espousal of British Israelism. He nevertheless continued as leader of a relatively small group of Apostolic Faith churches headquartered in Baxter Springs, Kansas.

BIBLIOGRAPHY. S. E. Parham, *The Life of Charles F. Parham, Founder of the Apostolic Faith Movement* (1930); C. F. Parham, *A Voice Crying in the Wilderness* (1902); V. Synan, *The Holiness-Pentecostal Movement in the United States* (1971).

T. P. Thigpen

Parish. An ecclesiastical territory over which a pastor* presides, in which usually one church exists and to which Christians living within that territory automatically belong. Used originally to refer to the district under the jurisdiction of a bishop,* it was eventually applied to subdivisions in a diocese.* Usually one church and pastor served the Christians of the parish. The Roman Catholic* parish system in America was not organized until after the Revolutionary War,* when America's first bishop, John Carroll* of Baltimore, instituted the parish system. This gradually evolved over the years from "mission churches" to territorial churches (officially constituted in 1908). Besides functioning as a local center for worship* and administration of sacraments,* the parish has also taken on a number of other important functions. For example, it has become a center for recreation, charitable activities, political involvement and education.

Catholic parishes have had to make significant adjustments in the last 100 years. Trustee* control of churches has given way to ecclesiastical control, a flood of Catholic immigrants* has led to the creation of "national parishes" which serve the needs of ethnic groups, and the growth of urban America has necessitated the development of urban parishes which address problems peculiar to urban America.

The parish system is well suited to a religious body like Roman Catholicism, which makes the primacy of the sacraments, episcopal government and the universal nature of the "one true church" its theological foundation. Some Protestant* denominations* also call their local churches *parishes*. But the multiplicity of denominations, the voluntary* character of Protestant religion in America and religious competitiveness in local areas has made the parish principle difficult to put into practice.

BIBLIOGRAPHY. C. J. Nuesse and Thomas J. Harte, eds., *The Sociology of the Parish* (1951); M. Bordelon, ed., *The Parish in a Time of Change* (1967); H. Rahner, ed., *The Parish* (1958).

G. L. Sittser

Parish Council. A consultative body composed of the clergy* and lay* representatives of a local congregation for the purpose of fostering parochial activity. While the canon law* of the Roman Catholic Church does not mandate such bodies (as it does in the case of parish finance councils), they are quite common in the U.S. and Canada. The Greek Orthodox Church of North and South America and the Orthodox Church in America* both require these councils. They are comparable to the vestry* (an American innovation) in the Episcopal Church,* to the administrative board in the United Methodist Church* and to the session* in Presbyterianism.* Most Protestant* churches have a board of some sort for setting policy and for administration at the local level. Its competence is usually greater in churches which do not have an episcopal* form of government.

BIBLIOGRAPHY. A. J. Lindgren and N. Shawchuck, *Management for Your Church* (1977).

J. E. Lynch

Parish Mission. A movement in the Roman Catholic Church* to cultivate religious devotion in the local parish.* The parish mission began after the Council of Trent to strengthen the faith of practicing Catholics and to win back those lost to Protestantism.* Jesuits* functioned as itinerant missionaries who visited dioceses* and parishes to renew the church. Though the movement waned in the latter part of the eighteenth century, it was revived again in the nineteenth century under the leadership of Pope Leo XII* and Pope Pius IX,* as well as a reconstituted Jesuit order. The movement sprang up again in the twentieth century. This modern version has emphasized parish renewal, as its predecessors did; but it has also stressed the sociological study of the parish and cooperation among priests,* pastors,* professors, nuns,* chaplains of Catholic Action* and laity.*

The parish mission movement was well suited for nineteenth-century American Catholicism. A decline in the number of priests, the low level of church life, the loss of Catholics to Protestantism, the lack of a strong organization and the voluntary* nature of American religion created conditions favorable for its development and growth. Though isolated parish missions sprang up before 1825, the movement spread rapidly after 1830. An influx of Redemptorists* and Jesuits, in addition to hierarchical and parish encouragement, caused the movement to flourish after 1840.

The parish mission was characterized by strong, often emotional, preaching of itinerant priests who, like their Protestant counterparts, preached a message of sin* and salvation* in revivalistic meetings; by its advocacy of social causes like temperance*; and by its emphasis on community cooperation and action. Adapting to the American environment, Catholics resorted to persuasion instead of coercion to revive the parish and to spread a popular piety* known as "devotional Catholicism." The modern charismatic movement* in American Catholicism is a contemporary example of the parish mission at work.

BIBLIOGRAPHY. J. P. Dolan, *Catholic Revivalism: The American Experience, 1830-1900* (1978); J.-F. Motte and M. Dourmap, *The New Parish Mission* (1962). G. L. Sittser

Park, Edwards Amasa (1808-1900). Congregational* minister* and theologian.* A graduate of Brown University* in 1826, Park studied theology under Leonard Woods* at Andover Seminary.* In 1831 he was ordained* pastor in Braintree, Massachusetts; and in 1833 he came under the influence of Nathaniel W. Taylor* of Yale.* In 1835 he began teaching mental and moral philosophy at Amherst College and moved to Andover in 1836 to become Bartlet Professor of Sacred Rhetoric. Park succeeded Woods as Abbot Professor of Christian Theology at Andover in 1847 and served as faculty president from 1853 until 1868.

Park identified himself with Jonathan Edwards,* and especially that strand of Edwardsean theology represented by the "Exercisers" among the New Divinity* Men and (as he believed) by Taylor. Although his celebrated address, "The Theology of the Intellect and that of the Feelings" (1850), attempted to offer a mediating position between the strict propositional dogmatics* of New England Calvinism* and the romantic non-syllogistic faith espoused by Horace Bushnell,* the general orientation of his theology was conservative and intellectualistic. He bitterly resisted the introduction of German biblical criticism and philosophy to Andover in the 1860s and 1870s, but upon retirement in 1880, he was unable to prevent Andover from falling into the hands of the "Progressive Orthodoxy"* represented by George Harris (1844-1922) and others.

For many years Park was the guardian of a substantial collection of the manuscripts of Edwards and wrote important biographical studies of Samuel Hopkins* and Nathanael Emmons* for editions of their collected works. In *The Atonement: Discourses and Treatises* (1859), he edited the most important New England writings on the subject. Many of his historical studies of the New England Theology* were published in various encyclopedias and in the quarterly *Bibliotheca Sacra,* which he edited from 1844 until 1884.

BIBLIOGRAPHY. A. C. Cecil, *The Theological Development of Edwards Amasa Park: Last of the "Consistent Calvinists"* (1974); *DAB* VII; F. H. Foster, *Life of Edwards Amasa Park* (1936).

A. C. Guelzo

Parker, Daniel (1781-1844). Baptist* preacher, antimissions* leader, founder of the Two-Seed-in-the-Spirit Predestinarian Baptists. Born in Virginia, reared in Georgia, Parker lacked formal education. Baptized* in 1802, he moved to Tennessee in 1803, where he was ordained* (1806) and served churches. In 1817 he moved to Crawford County, Illinois, where he published his antimission views:

A Public Address to the Baptist Society (1820), *The Second Dose of Doctrine on the Two Seeds* (1826), *Views on the Two Seeds* (1826), and a monthly paper, *The Church Advocate* (1829-1831). He also served as an Illinois state senator (1826-1827).

Although portrayed as totally unsympathetic toward missions,* his writings suggest opposition to missionary societies and schemes not under church control. The society plan of organization represented by the Baptist Triennial Convention* (1814) was not based on Scripture.* He was not opposed to "the spread of the gospel" or "itinerant preaching."

Parker's Two-Seed notion was based on Genesis 3:15. He concluded there are two kinds of progeny—one of God and one of Satan—the elect (God's children) and the non-elect (Satan's offspring). The former are predestined* to eternal life, the latter are not. The non-elect may respond to the gospel, but when they do not it is their rebellion which condemns them. Although they are "the seed of the serpent, yet they are human beings, and no less accountable to God."

In 1834 Parker moved to Texas with his congregation, the Pilgrim Predestinarian Regular Baptist Church, the first organized Baptist Church in Texas. His itinerant preaching produced nine other congregations. Parker's efforts touched Baptists in several states and resulted in the formation of a small antimission denomination. A man of great energy, natural ability and uncommon resourcefulness, he was vigorous in the pulpit in denouncing the society method of denominational organization and caused much dissension among Baptists on the frontier.

BIBLIOGRAPHY. *DARB; ESB* 2; O. M. Lee, "Daniel Parker's Doctrine of the Two Seeds," (unpublished Th.M. thesis, Southern Baptist Theological Seminary); H. L. McBeth, *The Baptist Heritage* (1986); A. C. Piepkorn, *Profiles in Belief,* vol. 2 (1978). W. M. Patterson

Parker, Horatio William (1863-1919). Composer, organist and music educator. Born to an old New England family, Parker studied piano and composition in his teenage years, convinced that "every man should contribute to the advancement of the human race." His extensive career covered two continents. In Boston, he studied with Chadwick, Emery and Orth; in Munich, Germany (1882-1885), with Rheinberger. Returning to the U.S., he taught at cathedral* schools and at the National Conservatory of Music.

Along with his position (1893) as organist at Trinity Church in Boston, Parker was a popular professor at Yale* (1894-1919), teaching such notables as Charles Ives. His wide interests, extensive vocabulary, bushy mustache and elitist attitude combined to make him a memorable personality. Parker's international honors included guest conducting in many European cities, the first honorary doctorate in music given to an American by an English university (Cambridge, 1902) and two $10,000 awards for the operas *Mona* (1912) and *Fairyland* (1913). Parker edited *The Hymnal Revised and Enlarged* (1903), which included his hymn tunes. His choral works included *The Lord Is My Shepherd, Morning and Evening Service* and *The Holy Child*. He was the most distinguished American composer of church music of his time.

BIBLIOGRAPHY. G. W. Chadwick, *Horatio Parker* (1921); *DAB* VII; D. S. Smith, "A Study of Horatio Parker," *Musical Quarterly* (April 1930).

R. J. Stanislaw

Parker, Isaac (1768-1830). Massachusetts politician and jurist. Born in Boston, Parker attended the Boston Latin School and Harvard College* (B.A., 1786 and the LL.D. *[honoris causa]* in 1814). After a term (1797- 1799) in the U.S. House of Representatives, Parker served first (1806-1814) as a judge of the Massachusetts Supreme Judicial Court and finally (1814-1830) as the Commonwealth's chief justice. A staunch Unitarian,* Parker strove to preserve at least a vestigial religious establishment* in his capacity as president of the Massachusetts Constitutional Convention of 1820. Ironically, the court's landmark ruling of the same year (*See* Dedham Decision) that members of a church might be overruled in the choice of a pastor by members of the associated parish (generally much larger and more liberal theologically) drove trinitarian Congregationalists* into an alliance with the Baptists* that doomed what remained of New England's standing order.

BIBLIOGRAPHY. D. W. Howe, *The Unitarian Conscience: Harvard Moral Philosophy, 1805-1861* (1970); W. G. McLoughlin, *New England Dissent, 1630-1833: The Baptists and the Separation of Church and State* (1971).

G. W. Harper

Parker, Theodore (1810-1860). Unitarian* minister* and radical theologian* of New England transcendentalism.* Born in Lexington, Massachusetts, Parker engaged in private study and passed all of the examinations at Harvard (1831), going on to graduate from Harvard* Divinity School in 1836. A man of prodigious learning and probing intellect, Parker flowed with some of the deeper philosophical currents of his day. The American historian Henry Steele Commager portrays him as an environmental determinist whose belief in human perfectibility reflected the "wonderful afterglow of the Enlightenment." Parker's thoroughgoing humanism pointedly illustrates transcendentalism's break with traditional Christian doctrine.*

Parker's theology was influenced by close contact with German idealistic philosophy and the emerging "higher criticism." His radical and controversial sermon, "A Discourse on the Permanent and Transient in Christianity" (1841) has a strong Hegelian flavor. Parker argued that the creeds,* confessions* and doctrines* of the Christian faith are merely imperfect human expressions, while true faith comes in using one's intuitive faculties to discern and follow the sublime ethics of Christ. Like Jefferson,* but in more idealistic terms, Parker attempted to distill an ethical naturalism from the miraculous basis of the New Testament. He refused to believe that Christianity is grounded in any special revelation or the deity of Christ. As does liberalism* at large, Parker rejected the notion that a corrupted humanity is in need of transformation by supernatural grace, or salvation through a divine messiah.

Parker lived out his ethical beliefs with great integrity. He was a courageous reformer who did not hesitate to speak from his convictions. A leading spokesman of the antislavery movement,* he saw slavery as a crime against nature. Resistance to such gross iniquities as the Fugitive Slave Law was a religious duty sanctioned by the higher law, which could be grasped intuitively. Parker gave his active support to nearly every reformist cause of antebellum America. He was one of the few clergy to speak out against the exploitive excesses of acquisitive capitalism.* Ethically and theologically, he anticipated the style and limitations of the Social Gospel.*

BIBLIOGRAPHY. H. S. Commager, *Theodore Parker, Yankee Crusader* (1936); *DAB* VII; *DARB*; J. E. Dirks, *The Critical Theology of Theodore Parker* (1948); *NCAB* 2; T. Parker, *Works,* Centenary Edition, 15 vols. (1907-1913).

S. E. Berk

Parochial Schools, Roman Catholic. Parish-supported Catholic, usually elementary, schools. The first Catholic schools in North America were established by Spanish* and French* missionaries* as early as the sixteenth century. John Carroll,* the first U.S. bishop,* was an early advocate of Catholic schools when Catholics comprised only about one per cent (in 1800) of the country's population.

Catholic schools began to increase in the 1840s, contemporary with the development of the common school of Horace Mann.* Their growth was spurred by conflicts over curriculum, textbooks, teachers and policymakers, which Catholic leaders viewed as being dominated by a pan-Protestantism.

From 1870 to 1920, the growth of the secular public school, coupled with heavy Catholic immigration,* contributed to the increase of Catholic parochial schools which were founded on ethnic* as well as religious bases. Buttressed by Vatican* pronouncements and episcopal* edicts, especially by the Third Plenary Council of Baltimore* in 1884, a relatively impoverished Catholic minority population strove to transmit their cultural heritage to their children via parish* (i.e., parochial) schools. It was during this period that the motto "Every Catholic child in a Catholic school" was coined. Though the Catholic elementary school population increased from 405,234 in 2,246 parochial schools to 1,701,219 in 5,852 parochial schools from 1880 to 1920, it has been estimated that, at their peak, Catholic elementary schools enrolled about one half of the eligible population.

Catholic secondary schools, most usually private or diocesan,* not parochial, paralleled the growth of the public high school in the twentieth century. Their proportionate enrollments, however, lagged far behind their elementary (parochial) counterparts.

In 1959 Neil G. McCluskey accurately noted that the Catholic position on education had remained substantially the same since 1840. Catholic schools, established to protect the faith and values of a besieged minority, had successfully fended off what was perceived as hostile schooling, whether emanating from Protestantism* or from the civil government.

Events of the 1960s produced substantial change and even turmoil over the Catholic parochial education. Spurred by Vatican II,* which tended to open the Church to the world, criticism of Catholic schools from within the Church mounted. Catholic school enrollment (K-12) began its precipitous decline from 5,574,354 in 1965 (when it made up about 90 per cent of church-affiliated, nonpublic-school enrollment) to 3,027,312 in 1983 (about 65 per cent of that enrollment). Religious personnel suffered a parallel decline. Priests,* brothers* and sisters* comprised 56.7 per cent of the staff of Catholic schools in 1968-1969, only 25.8 per cent in 1981-1982.

Beset by spiraling financial costs, a widely doubted rationale, teacher strikes, uncertain support from clergy and a sizeable population that was moving to the suburbs, Catholic parochial schools reached a low point in the 1970s. Supported by episcopal documents such as *To Teach as Jesus Did* (1976), and fortified with the findings of research, Catholic schools weathered that tumultuous decade. In the 1980s the schools still faced challenges such as serving the urban poor, avoiding elitism, finding adequate financing and maintaining their uniqueness as religious institutions. *See also* SCHOOLS, PROTESTANT DAY.

BIBLIOGRAPHY. H. A. Buetow, *Of Singular Benefit: The Story of U.S. Catholicism* (1970); R. D. Cross, "The Origins of Parochial Schools in America," *American Benedictine Review* 16 (1965):194-209. "Declaration on Christian Education" in *The Documents of Vatican II,* ed. Walter M. Abbott (1966); A. M. Greeley, W. C. McReady and K. McCourt, *Catholic Schools in a Declining Church* (1976); N. G. McCluskey, *Catholic Viewpoint on Education* (1959); N. G. McCluskey, ed., *Catholic Education in America: A Documentary History* (1964); M. P. Ryan, *Are Parochial Schools the Answer?* (1968). T. C. Hunt

Parrish, Sarah Rebecca (1869-1952). First woman missionary* medical doctor in the Philippines. Born in Bowers, Indiana, and orphaned shortly thereafter, Parrish later studied medicine. In 1906 she arrived in the Philippines under the Methodist* Episcopal Woman's Foreign Missionary Society. In 1908, using a donation of $12,000 from a Mr. D. S. B. Johnston of Minneapolis, Minnesota, Parrish established the still-functioning Mary Johnston Hospital in Tondo, Manila. In this hospital Parrish maintained high medical standards, insisting that all physicians associated with it hold membership in the American Medical Association and its Manila affiliate. In addition to her medical work, Parrish and the hospital were involved actively in evangelism.* Almost daily she displayed a new religious poster near the hospital's front gate for passersby to read. The hospital regimen included vesper* services and daily Bible lessons in the clinic.

In 1933, after twenty-seven years of continuous service in the Philippines, Parrish returned to the U.S. In retirement she maintained an active lecture schedule and wrote her memoirs, entitled *Orient Seas and Lands Afar* (1936). In 1950 Philippine President Quirino presented her with a medal of honor from the Civic Assembly of Women, commending her for her pioneer efforts in "bringing Christian love, healing, and enlightenment, and a better way of life" to the Philippines.

G. J. Bekker

[869]

Parsons, Henry Martyn (1828-1913). Canadian millenarian leader. Born in East Haddam, Connecticut, Parsons graduated from Yale College* (1848) and Connecticut Theological Institute (1854). He then served churches in Springfield and Boston, Massachusetts, and Buffalo, New York. In 1880 he accepted the pastorate of Knox Presbyterian Church in Toronto, a position he held until his death. Involved in Toronto social service, Parsons helped establish the Toronto Mission Union and served as a board member of the Toronto Home for Incurables.

Prominent in the millenarian movement, Parsons was a long-time leader of the Niagara Conferences.* He also helped organize and lectured at the 1885 Niagara Prophecy Conference, a crucial event in the spread of premillenialism* in Canada. In the same vein, Parsons was a board member of the Toronto Willard Tract Depository, a publishing company which promoted dispensational* premillenialism. He also wrote a number of books and articles, primarily on premillenialism, and served as an instructor at the Toronto Bible Training School.

BIBLIOGRAPHY. C. N. Kraus, *Dispensationalism in America: Its Rise and Development* (1958); R. G. Sawatsky, " 'Looking for that Blessed Hope': The Roots of Fundamentalism in Canada, 1878-1914" (unpublished Ph.D. dissertation, University of Toronto, 1986). W. V. Trollinger

Particular Baptists. Calvinistic* Baptists* with origins in English Puritanism.* English Particular Baptists, following the Calvinistic doctrine of predestination,* believed that God redeemed only "particular" individuals. This opposed the Arminian* concept of "general" redemption held by General Baptists* and many Anglicans.* They emerged from a Southwark (London) Puritan-Separatist congregation which Henry Jacob had gathered in 1616. Later known by the last initials of its first three pastors, Jacob, John Lathrop and Henry Jessey, the "JLJ" Church, which practiced infant baptism,* experienced several schisms. During Lathrop's pastorate, Samuel Eaton formed a strictly separatist church (1633), some of whose members were rebaptized probably because they rejected Anglican baptism as corrupt. In 1638 the first English Calvinistic Baptists began meeting when six members explicitly favoring believer's baptism left the JLJ Church.

By 1644 seven Particular Baptist churches in the London area were associating together. They issued The London Confession (1644) in order to distinguish themselves from General Baptists and

continental Anabaptists.* To defy increasing Anglican persecution and to show doctrinal solidarity with the Presbyterian*-Congregational* tradition, they expressed a heightened Calvinism in their Second London Confession (1677; 2nd ed. 1688; revised 1689). A revision of this by Benjamin and Elias Keach* became the first widely used Baptist confession in America. Here, later known as Regular Baptists* and led by the Philadelphia Association,* they modified the 1689 confession and produced the Philadelphia Confession (1742). With its softened Calvinism, this became the unifying doctrinal statement for most Baptists in America by 1800.

BIBLIOGRAPHY. T. Crosby, *The History of the English Baptists* (1738-1740); H. L. McBeth, *The Baptist Heritage* (1987); B. R. White, *The English Baptists of the Seventeenth Century* (1983).

J. T. Spivey

Passavant, William Alfred (1821-1894). Lutheran* minister,* editor and leading promoter of Lutheran home missions* and institutions of mercy. Born in Zelienople, Pennsylvania, of well-to-do immigrant parents, Passavant was educated at Jefferson College and at the Lutheran Seminary, Gettysburg, graduating in 1842.

Passavant labored fruitfully in a mission church in Canton, a suburb of Baltimore, and then at First English Lutheran Church, Pittsburgh. He was the driving force in founding the Pittsburgh Synod (1845). In 1848 he founded and edited a newspaper, *The Missionary.* In 1861 it merged with a Philadelphia paper to become *The Lutheran and Missionary,* with Charles Porterfield Krauth* and Passavant as coeditors. Visiting London and the Rhineland in 1846, he was inspired by Theodor Fliedner's deaconess* institute and by the German inner mission movement. On his return he founded the first American Protestant hospital in Pittsburgh (1849) and brought deaconesses from Germany to run it. In 1850 Passavant made the first of many trips to Chicago to establish contact with the Swedes and other Scandinavians who were pouring into the West. He became the outstanding Eastern Lutheran friend of these immigrants. In 1852 he founded his first orphanage in Pittsburgh and relocated it in Zelienople in 1853.

In the late 1840s, chiefly under Krauth's influence, Passavant espoused the trend toward "old Lutheranism," a conservative movement which found its norms in Lutheran orthodoxy.* Passavant became convinced that this "pure Lutheranism" furnished the best foundation for the works of Christian love.

In 1855 he resigned his pastorate to devote his full time to his many enterprises. In the next two decades, he founded almost a dozen congregations, three more hospitals and three more orphanages. He was the real founder of Thiel College, Greenville, Pennsylvania (1870), and of Chicago Lutheran Seminary (1891).

In the rupture of the Lutheran General Synod, Passavant was one of the chief founders of the conservative, trilingual General Council (1867). Through his synod, and later through the General Council, he helped organize home-missionary expansion into Texas, Ontario, Nova Scotia and the Upper Midwest, eventually reaching the Pacific coast. To promote these enterprises he founded another newspaper, *The Workman,* in 1881 and edited it until his death.

Passavant was a strong influence in the slow process of transforming Lutherans (particularly the nineteenth-century arrivals) from their defensive immigrant mentality into "a worshiping, witnessing, working church." He promoted and exemplified a Lutheranism committed to nurturing a devout Christian life, aggressive outreach through evangelism* and humanitarian service, and responsible citizenship in American and Canadian society.

BIBLIOGRAPHY. *DAB* VII; G. H. Gerberding, *Life and Letters of W. A. Passavant* (1906); R. H. Fischer, "New Light on Passavant and His Era," in *Lutheran Historical Conference Essays and Reports,* vol. 2 (1968):18-29.   R. H. Fischer

Pastor. A term describing the relationship between a minister* and his or her congregation. The term *pastor* is derived from the Latin word *passere,* meaning "to pasture" or "to feed" and in biblical terminology frequently refers to a shepherd caring for a flock and figuratively of a leader caring for followers. More specifically, Christ is called the Good Shepherd. In the New Testament, Ephesians 4:11 speaks of some individuals appointed "to be apostles, some to be prophets, some to be evangelists, some to be pastors [literally *shepherds*] and teachers." The term has come to describe the relationship between minister and congregation as that of shepherd and flock—a relationship that entails caring, loving and giving.

In many denominations the term is used as a synonym for *Reverend* and may be used as a form of address. Characteristically, it refers to a minister who is actively engaged in ministry to a congregation. The term is most frequently used by Protestants in referring to their minister, and many Roman Catholics* use it for parish priests. Multi-

staffed churches may distinguish the ranking of their ordained* ministers by titles such as senior pastor, associate* pastor and assistant* pastor. Some groups are critical of the term, however, since shepherding is a concept remote from modern urban life, and because it does not include the priestly and prophetic aspects of ministry. The term *pastoral theology* refers to the theological basis for pastoral ministry and theological reflection on that ministry.

BIBLIOGRAPHY. H. R. Niebuhr, *The Purpose of the Church and Its Ministry* (1956); T. C. Oden, *Pastoral Theology: Essentials of Ministry* (1983).   D. S. Armentrout

Patrick, Mary Mills (1850-1940). Missionary educator in Turkey. Born in Canterbury, New Hampshire, and raised on a farm in Iowa, Patrick was sent to Turkey in 1871 by the American Board of Commissioners for Foreign Missions.* She taught until 1876 in a school for Armenian girls at Erzrum in the interior and was then assigned to the Home School, which had been established in 1871 by the Woman's Board of Missions and had just moved to Scutari on the Asiatic side of Constantinople. Patrick was founder and first president of a successor institution, chartered in 1890 by the State of Massachusetts as the American College for Girls at Constantinople (rechartered in 1908, later integrated with the secondary section of Robert College, today's University of the Bosporus). She retired in 1924. Her Ph.D. dissertation at the University of Berne, Switzerland, was published as *Sextus Empiricus and Greek Empiricism* (1899). Other publications were *Sappho and the Island of Lesbos* (1912) and *The Greek Sceptics* (1929).

BIBLIOGRAPHY. *DAB* 2; H. D. Jenkins, *An Educational Ambassador to the Near East* (1925); *NAW* 3; M. M. Patrick, *Under Five Sultans* (1929).
D. M. Stowe

Patterson, Frederic William (1877-1966). Canadian Baptist* leader and university president. Patterson served as pastor of Baptist churches in his native New Brunswick and in Western Canada. In 1916 he became editor of the *Western Baptist* and in 1919 secretary of the Baptist Union of Western Canada. In 1922 he was appointed president of Acadia University, Wolfville, Nova Scotia, a Baptist institution founded in 1838. A remarkable fund raiser and organizer, he guided the institution through the turbulent period of the Depression* and World War 2,* retiring in 1948. During his presidency Acadia's enrollment expanded from 307 to 890. Patterson successfully trod a middle path between the pressures of his Baptist constituency and the increasing student demands for freedom from denominational* restrictions. After his retirement he continued to serve the university as fund raiser.

BIBLIOGRAPHY. W. Kirkconnell, *The Fifth Quarter-Century: Acadia University, 1938-1963* (1968); R. S. Longley, *Acadia University, 1838-1938* (1939). B. M. Moody

Patton, Francis Landey (1843-1932). Presbyterian* clergyman,* educator and theologian.* Never a citizen of the United States, Patton was born in Bermuda and died there in his ninetieth year. Before graduating from Princeton Theological Seminary* in 1865, he also attended Knox College in Toronto and the University of Toronto. In 1865 Patton was also ordained* and for the next seven years held pastorates in the vicinity of New York City.

Between 1872 and 1881 he served as professor of theology at the Presbyterian Theological Seminary of the Northwest (now McCormick Seminary) in Chicago. During these years Patton gained some national attention through his role as prosecutor in the heresy trial of David Swing.* Princeton Seminary hired him in 1881 to fill a recently endowed professorship in apologetics,* and in 1883 Patton took on the additional task of lecturing on ethics* at the College of New Jersey.* His career took an unexpected turn when the College chose Patton to follow James McCosh* as the president of the institution in 1888.

Even though Patton was known for his intellectual gifts as a defender of theism* and Christian ethics, as well as for his personal charm, many supporters of the College doubted his administrative abilities. He successfully restructured the College to become Princeton University in 1896 but was never comfortable with his administrative duties. As a result, he resigned in 1902 and nominated Woodrow Wilson* as his successor. In that same year, Princeton Seminary created the office of president. Patton assumed that position and continued to lecture on ethics in the University until he retired to his home in Bermuda in 1913. His publications included: *The Inspiration of the Scriptures* (1869); *A Summary of Christian Doctrine* (1898); and *Fundamental Christianity* (1926).

BIBLIOGRAPHY. *DAB* VII; *DARB*; *NCAB* 5. D. G. Hart

Pauck, Wilhelm (1901-1981). Theologian* and church historian. Born in Laaphe, Germany, Pauck

studied at the University of Berlin (1920-1922) and the University of Göttingen (1922-1923) under Adolf Harnack (1851-1930), Karl Holl (1866-1926) and Ernst Troeltsch (1865-1923), receiving the licentiate in theology in 1925. Arriving in the U.S. in 1925, he studied at the Chicago Theological Seminary for one year and began teaching there, becoming a full professor in 1931. In 1939 he began teaching at the University of Chicago Divinity School,* and in 1945 joined the faculty of Union Theological Seminary,* where he was Charles A. Briggs* Graduate Professor of Church History (1960-1967). The final years of his career were spent at Vanderbilt University (1967-1972) and Stanford University (1972-1981). A member of the Evangelische Kirche in Germany, in the U.S. he joined the United Church of Christ.*

Pauck was a distinguished scholar, who authored many historical and theological studies throughout a long teaching career in America. In "What Is Wrong With Liberalism?" (1935), he criticized aspects of liberal theology and in 1939 rejected Harnack's historicizing of the doctrine of the Trinity. But Pauck did not follow Neo-orthodoxy.* In *Karl Barth—Prophet of a New Christianity?* (1931), Pauck analyzed Barth's theology, but concluded, "We cannot go back behind Troeltsch, Harnack, Ritschl, and Schleiermacher. We can only go beyond them." Pauck continued to maintain the abiding values of liberal* theology. As a church historian he produced significant studies on the Reformation and the development of Protestant* theology. In commenting on Pauck's vocation, Jaroslav Pelikan remarked, "He has kept theologians historically aware and historians theologically responsible."

BIBLIOGRAPHY. S. W. Soper, *Men Who Shape Belief* (1955). D. K. McKim

Paul VI (1897-1978). Pope* from 1963 to 1978. Born as Giovanni Battista Montini in Concesio, near Brescia, Italy, he worked on the Vatican* staff for almost thirty years, including as assistant to Cardinal Eugenio Pacelli before and after Pacelli became Pius XII.* While archbishop* of Milan (1954), he became a confidant of John XXIII,* who named him cardinal* (1958).

Upon election as pope he pledged to bring the work of the Second Vatican Council* to completion. At the end he promulgated all the Vatican documents, including the Declaration on Religious Freedom, sponsored by the American bishops* and drafted by the American Jesuit,* John Courtney Murray.* Moreover, he created the post-council means to implement the documents and made himself an example in following them—celebrating Mass* in the vernacular and personally promoted relations with Anglicans* (1966, 1972), Orthodox* (1967) and the World Council of Churches.* He was the first reigning pope to visit the U.S. (1965).

The church revolution he made possible erupted within the American Church, transforming its liturgy,* self-identity, practices and priesthood.* His encyclicals* commending caution, especially *Sacerdotalis Coelibatus* (1967) enforcing priestly obedience and celibacy, and *Humanae Vitae* (1968) against all contraception (*See* Birth Control), provoked antagonism. Priestly and religious vocations declined sharply, and countless American Catholics found themselves disobeying the pope and lapsing from the Church. The American Church, together with the Dutch Church, was the leader of the new movement which resisted the pope. To aid him in meeting the crisis in America and elsewhere, he convened three world episcopal synods* in Rome.

BIBLIOGRAPHY. W. E. Barrett, *Shepherd of Mankind* (1964); J. G. Clancy, *Apostle of Our Time* (1963); *NCE* 11. C. T. McIntire

Paulists. *See* CONGREGATION OF THE MISSIONARY SOCIETY OF ST. PAUL.

PAX. *See* PEACE MOVEMENT, CATHOLIC.

Pax Christi. *See* PEACE MOVEMENT, CATHOLIC.

Paxson, Stephen (1837-1881). American Sunday School Union* missionary.* Paxson, an Illinois farmer, was born with a speech impediment and was later nicknamed "stuttering Stephen." Paxson had little formal schooling, but when he was thirty years old, his daughter, Mary, begged him to attend Sunday school and help her win a prize. He obliged. When he arrived, he was pressed into service to teach a class of boys. They read the Scripture, and he asked questions out of a book. Embarrassed that the boys knew more about the Bible than he did, Paxson read the Bible and eventually was converted. Wishing to minister in some capacity, he began to organize Sunday schools in his spare time. He became a missionary with the American Sunday School Union and continued to travel throughout Illinois and adjoining states. The many facets of his ministry included teaching, counseling, preaching, organizing and distributing tracts, books, Bibles and other materials.

Never daunted by bad weather, he often said, "A Sunday School born in a snow storm will never be scared by a white frost." His horse, Raikes, is said never to have passed a child without waiting for Paxson to stop and give out the gospel. In a leather-bound book he recorded the names of over 83,000 children he recruited for Sunday school.

Paxson often returned East to raise money for libraries that would be used to establish Sunday schools. The sophisticated audiences alternately wept and laughed as he spoke, never heeding his grammatical mistakes. They gave liberally, becoming a part of founding Sunday schools in log cabins, tobacco barns, taverns and dance halls. Paxson was credited with founding 1,314 new Sunday schools in over twenty years of labor.

BIBLIOGRAPHY. B. P. Drury, *A Fruitful Life: A Narrative of the Experiences and Missionary Labors of Stephen Paxson* (1882).

E. L. Towns

Payne, Daniel Alexander (1811-1893). African Methodist Episcopal* bishop,* educator and church historian. Born of free parents in Charleston, South Carolina, Payne was early impressed with the importance of education. In 1829 he began a small school in Charleston, where he taught (1829-1835) until state legislation forced it to close. Payne attended Lutheran Theological Seminary in Gettysburg, Pennsylvania (1835-1837), and though licensed* to preach by the Lutheran Church,* he served for two years as a Presbyterian* pastor* in Troy, New York (1837-1838). He then opened a school for African-American children in Philadelphia (1840-1842) . Under the influence of individuals in the African Methodist Episcopal Church (AME), he joined that body in 1841, securing appointment as a minister two years later. Payne was elected a bishop of the AME in 1852.

For twelve years thereafter he traveled around the country, establishing schools and otherwise promoting education among illiterate African-Americans. Payne's advocacy of an educated ministry and his criticism of religious practices among the lower classes met with much opposition. Nevertheless, the requirement that ministers be formally trained became official church policy. In 1863 he purchased Wilberforce University in Ohio, on behalf of the denomination, for $10,000, becoming the first president of a African-American institution of higher learning in the U.S. (*See* Black Colleges). He served in that capacity until 1876, during which time he also organized the South Carolina Conference which was instrumental in the expansion of the AME Church in the South following the Civil War.* Payne served as a delegate to the first Ecumenical Conference of the Methodist Episcopal Church in London in 1881, and participated in the World Parliament of Religions* in Chicago in 1893. Among his works are *Recollections of Seventy Years* (1888) and *History of the African Methodist Episcopal Church* (1891), a work he was commissioned to write by his denomination. Until his death Payne was recognized as the senior statesman of the AME Church.

BIBLIOGRAPHY. H. V. Richardson, *Dark Salvation* (1976); *DAB* VII; *DARB*; C. S. Smith, *The Live of Daniel Alexander Payne* (1894); J. R. Coan, *Daniel Alexander Payne: Christian Educator* (1935). M. R. Sawyer

Peabody, Andrew Preston (1811-1893). Unitarian* minister* and educator. Born in Beverley, Massachusetts, Peabody graduated from Harvard College* in 1826 (at the age of fifteen) and from Harvard Divinity School in 1832. He was ordained* in 1833 and became minister of the South Parish Unitarian Church in Portsmouth, New Hampshire, where he remained pastor for twenty-seven years. In 1853 Peabody began editing the *North American Review,* considered by many the finest scholarly journal of its time. Peabody eventually succeeded Frederic Dan Huntington* as Plummer Professor of Christian Morals at Harvard in 1860, and later served twice as acting president of the college.

Nicknamed "the College Saint" by his students, Peabody was remembered by his colleagues more for his warmth and pastoral concern than for his scholarship. Nevertheless, he wrote 1,600 pages of articles for the *North American Review* and more than 190 books and pamphlets. The wide range of his interests is suggested by a sample of his titles: *Lectures on Christian Doctrine* (1844); *Conversation; Its Faults and Its Graces* (1856); *Christianity the Religion of Nature* (1854); and *A Manual of Moral Philosophy* (1873).

BIBLIOGRAPHY. *DAB* VII; E. J. Young, *Andrew P. Peabody* (1896). T. P. Thigpen

Peabody, Francis Greenwood (1847-1936). Unitarian* minister* and professor of social ethics* at Harvard Divinity School. Born in Boston, Peabody was educated at Harvard College* (B.A., 1869), the Harvard Divinity School (A.M., S.T.B., 1872) and the University of Halle (1872-1873). After teaching for one year at Antioch College (1873-1874), he ministered* at the First Parish Unitarian Church in Cambridge, Massachusetts (1874-1879), and then began a career at Harvard

Divinity School (1880-1913) where he was first lecturer in ethics and homiletics (1880-1881), followed by professorships in theology* (1881-1886) and in Christian morals (1886-1913).

As a clergyman* Peabody observed that moral problems arose from social contexts. He taught that the minister was the natural leader for social reform and believed that the minister should be a mediator between class conflicts and an advisor to community charities. A theological liberal,* Peabody was influenced by the thought of Friedrich Schleiermacher (1768-1834). Nevertheless, the Bible* held a distinct place in the development of his ethical thought, as reflected in two of his books, *Jesus Christ and the Social Question* (1900) and *The Apostle Paul and the Modern World* (1927). Jesus, he wrote, was not a reformer but a revealer; he was an idealist with a vision, not an agitator with a plan of action. Peabody also believed economic justice was not enough in itself; he looked for the spiritual renewal of humanity. Though Peabody was a political conservative, he supported cooperatives, social insurance, scientific planning and enlightened philanthropy.* Similar to populists and the Social Gospel* leaders to which he was akin, Peabody was an advocate of organized labor, although he believed that labor practices should be governed by principles of Christian ethics. Neither an avid supporter of specific forms like the Institutional Church* nor a political or social activist, Peabody was more of a propagandist of ideas and morals.

BIBLIOGRAPHY. *DAB* 2; *DARB*; J. Herbst, "Francis Greenwood Peabody: Harvard's Theologian of the Social Gospel," *HTR* 54 (1961):45-69.

C. E. Stockwell

Peabody, Lucy Whitehead McGill (1861-1949). Baptist* missionary* and denominational* leader. Born in Belmont, Kansas, she became a schoolteacher at Rochester School for the Deaf (1879-1881) in Rochester, New York, before being appointed as a missionary to India by the American Baptist Foreign Mission Society. On her return to the U.S. in 1888, she became secretary of the Women's American Baptist Foreign Mission Society as well as its principal editor. In that capacity and with the support and resources of her spouse, Henry W. Peabody, she became a roving ambassador for missionary endeavor, particularly women's work.

Early in her career as a schoolteacher, Lucy had made the acquaintance of Helen Barrett Montgomery,* and the two planned and executed significant advances in Protestant* work. In 1913, for instance, they made an extensive tour of mission fields in India, China and Japan, out of which grew study guides on mission work, new funds for overseas women's colleges and a proposal for a World Day of Prayer. The latter began as a vigil involving over seventy countries.

Lucy Peabody possessed extraordinary skills in organization to coordinate several worldwide efforts. In 1912 she helped create the Federation of Women's Boards of Foreign Missions. Later in life, at the request of her son-in-law Raphael C. Thomas, who was a missionary in the Philippines, she organized within the Northern Baptist Convention* the theologically conservative Association of Baptists for World Evangelism.* This group did much to revive interest in overseas ministry during a period of doctrinal tension. Her enthusiasm for missions was shared in two books: *A Wider World for Women* (1936) and *Just Like You: Stories of Children of Every Land* (1937).

BIBLIOGRAPHY. L. A. Cattan, *Lamps Are for Lighting: The Story of Helen Barrett Montgomery and Lucy Waterbury Peabody* (1972).

W. H. Brackney

Peace Churches. A name first used in 1935 to refer to the Mennonites,* Friends* (Quakers) and Brethren,* who share a witness against war. Their nonresistant views have led them to cooperate in programs of reconstruction, relief and social justice. They were originally brought into contact with one another when Mennonites and Brethren settled in the Quaker colony of Pennsylvania. The influence of the Friends on the other two sects is apparent in their plain dress, simple style of meeting places and church organization.

These churches have consistently opposed violence in American life. They attempted to avoid hostilities with Native Americans through fair play and material assistance. During the Revolutionary War* they opposed armed rebellion and sought exemption from military duty. The Civil War* brought them together in petitioning both the Confederacy and the Union for relief from conscription. A comparable merging of interest took place at the time of World War 1.* During the interwar years several conferences of the pacifist churches were held. Structures were provided so that with the outbreak of World War 2* work camps could be established for conscientious objectors. After 1945 these groups cooperated in a massive effort to meet the relief demands of a war-torn world. The peace and material assistance program of the churches are carried on through the American Friends Service Committee* (founded 1917), the Mennonite Central Committee* (1920) and the Brethren Service Committee (1945). The cold war era prompted the Peace Churches to work toward reconciliation between the East and the West through cooperative programs and educational activities.

BIBLIOGRAPHY. R. H. Bainton, *Christian Attitudes toward War and Peace* (1960); P. Brock, *Pacifism in the United States from the Colonial Period to the First World War* (1968); P. Brock, *Twentieth Century Pacifism* (1970); R. G. Clouse, ed., *War: Four Christian Views* (1981).

R. G. Clouse

Peace Movement, Catholic. Prior to the 1960s Catholics* did not play a leading role in the American peace movement. The Roman Catholic Church was predominantly a conservative and patriotic body whose hierarchy sanctified the doctrine of a just war in its official Church teaching and imposed it on a largely compliant laity.*

In 1928 John A. Ryan* founded the first Roman Catholic peace organization in American history and called it the Catholic Association for International Peace (CAIP). Prior to World War 2* it had grown in size to 500 members. When the U.S. entered World War 2 in 1941, the organization sanctioned the actions of the government and declared that the nation was engaged in a just war. After the war, the CAIP declined in significance.

The first Catholic group in the U. S. to challenge the just-war theory was the Catholic Worker,* founded in 1933. Dorothy Day,* its co-founder, first proclaimed that the Catholic Worker Movement was pacifist during the Spanish Civil War and maintained this position during World War 2 and all subsequent wars. Very few Catholics adopted the Catholic Worker position.

On the eve of World War 2, PAX, an offspring of the Catholic Worker Movement, was formed. Its aim was to form a "mighty league of COs" (conscientious objectors). In 1940 PAX was reorganized and given a new name, the Association of Catholic Conscientious Objectors (ACCO). During the War, out of a total of 21 million Catholics, only 223 claimed IV-E Conscientious Objector status (i.e., objectors to military service); 135 were eventually classified IV-E—a great change from World War 1* when only four of the 3,989 conscientious objectors were Catholic. After World War 2 the ACCO ceased to function, believing that the Catholic Worker could adequately carry on its work and message. Another separate peace group was not formed until 1961 when a new organization, also called PAX, was formed.

In 1964 a Catholic peace group, the Catholic Peace Fellowship (CPF), was organized under the auspices of the Fellowship of Reconciliation* (FOR), the oldest nondenominational pacifist* peace group in America. This was the first time in American history that a Catholic peace group was organized on an ecumenical* basis. Daniel Berrigan and his brother, Philip, were mainly responsible for the formation of CPF. With the 1968 Vietnam War* draft board action in Catonsville, Maryland, these two brothers became the leading peace figures in the Catholic Left. From 1928 to 1969 Catholics had moved from a marginal status in the American peace movement to a position of central importance.

The Catholic peace movement of the 1960s coincided with two of the major forces of the century: Vatican II* and Vietnam. These two forces would cause the American Catholic Church to undergo an internal revolution that would alter its outlook on peacemaking for the rest of the century.

During the course of Vatican II, Pope John XXIII* issued his encyclical on peace, *Pacem in Terris*,* and at the council itself the bishops* debated the morality of nuclear war and the provisions for conscientious objection. The Catholic Worker and PAX sent a delegation of American pacifists to Rome to lobby on behalf of conscientious objection and opposition to all war. The delegation won the support of a few American bishops, like Fulton J. Sheen,* who wanted to outlaw all modern war. On the issue of conscientious objection, they were even more successful, with the result that Vatican II declared conscientious objection a legitimate and praiseworthy Catholic response to war. With the involvement of the U.S. in Vietnam underway, the impact of Vatican II was decisive in challenging Catholics with the issue of positive peacemaking.

The Catholic Worker, CPF, PAX, campus groups and thousands of Catholic individuals began to respond to the call of Vatican II. By 1969, 2,494 Catholics had received Conscientious Objector status among the 34,255 so classified. This was the single largest percentage of all American religious bodies. In November 1968 most of the American bishops had moved toward neutrality on the war and issued a pastoral, *Human Life in Our Day*. For the first time in U. S. history, the Catholic hierarchy declared that conscientious objectors, even selective conscientious objectors, have a basis for their position in modern Catholic teaching. By 1970 more Catholics than Protestants were calling for withdrawal from Vietnam. Finally, in November

1971 the bishops condemned the war in Vietnam as unjust.

With the end of U.S. involvement in Vietnam, the Catholic peace movement, like the American peace movement in general, entered a period of inaction. Nevertheless, because of the shift in official Catholic thought away from the just-war tradition toward an acceptance of pacifism and nonviolence as legitimate Catholic alternatives, more American Catholics were concerned about peace than ever before. Moreover, Catholic peace activists adopted a twofold campaign—they wanted to stop the U.S. government from pursuing its militaristic policies and convert the American Catholic Church to a pacifistic and nonviolent position. This campaign took many forms. The Berrigans founded a movement called "Plowshares," which performed direct actions against nuclear weapons; the Catholic Worker and the CPF continued in their pacifism and opposition to the draft; and a new group, Pax Christi, was formed in 1975.

The organization of Pax Christi was one of the most important developments in the post-Vietnam phase of the Catholic peace movement. Founded by Joseph Fahey, Dorothy Day, Tom Cornell, Eileen Egan, Gordon Zahn and others, the new peace organization was committed to making the Catholic Church an instrument of positive peacemaking by educating and converting individual Catholics to peace. Two bishops, Carroll T. Dozier of Memphis and Thomas J. Gumbleton of Detroit, agreed to act as moderators. While attempting to maintain a balance between all segments of the Catholic peace movement, Pax Christi/USA was primarily pacifist in orientation.

The conversion of the American Catholic Church into a force for peace is nowhere more clearly seen than in the direction taken by the National Conference of Catholic Bishops* (NCCB) since 1970. J. Bryan Hehir, more than any other individual within the administration of the NCCB, may be credited with this achievement. Hehir worked hard in the Call to Action Conference held in Detroit in 1976. This conference condemned not only the use or threatened use of nuclear weapons, but also their production and possession. In 1978 and 1979 he diligently worked on the draft that the bishops issued in support of the Salt II Agreement. His greatest achievement was his work in the 1983 pastoral letter issued by the American Catholic bishops, *The Challenge of Peace; God's Promise and Our Response*. This letter stunned people by its bold advocacy of peace and has been called "the most profound and searching inquiry yet conducted by any responsible collective body into the relations of nuclear weaponry, and indeed of modern war in general, to moral philosophy, to politics, and to the conscience of the national state."

For the first time in American Catholic history, in *The Challenge of Peace* the bishops have proclaimed pacifism and active nonviolence as means of Christian action as legitimate as military defense in the service of the nation. Thus, pacifism has been recognized as a legitimate option alongside the just-war theory in American Catholic theology of peace.

BIBLIOGRAPHY. P. F. McNeal, *The American Catholic Peace Movement, 1928-1972* (1978).

P. F. McNeal

Peale, Norman Vincent (1898-). Reformed Church of America* minister* and promoter of positive thinking. Born in Bowersville, Ohio, the son of a Methodist* circuit minister, Peale's childhood was spent in a number of Ohio towns. After graduating from Ohio Wesleyan University in 1920, Peale first pursued a career in journalism, but after becoming disenchanted with that field, he decided to prepare for the ministry. He began studying theology at Boston University in 1921, was ordained* in the Methodist Episcopal Church in 1922 and continued his studies while pastoring a small church in Berkeley, Rhode Island.

After graduating from Boston University in 1924 (B.S.T., M.A.), he was appointed to a small congregation in Brooklyn, New York, which by the time he left in 1927 had grown from forty to nine hundred members. His next pastorate, University Methodist Church in Syracuse, New York, also flourished under his preaching. In June 1930 Peale married Loretta Ruth Stafford, who would later be actively engaged in the numerous Peale enterprises. In 1932 he accepted a call to Marble Collegiate Church in New York City, a move that required him to join the Reformed Church in America. Peale spent the remainder of his career at Marble Collegiate. Founded by the Dutch in 1628, it is said to be the oldest Protestant church in continuous use in the U.S. On Peale's first Sunday scarcely two hundred parishioners attended, but by the 1950s he was regularly preaching to overflow crowds frequently numbering 4,000.

Peale's message has been a combination of psychological themes and therapeutic prescriptions drawn from his understanding of Scripture and cast in simple principles expressed in everyday language. Early in his ministry at Marble Collegiate, he had recognized a need for integrat-

ing psychiatry with ministry. With psychiatrist Smiley Blanton, he began a religio-psychiatric clinic at the church. These therapeutic themes are clearly evident in his early books, such as *The Art of Living* (1937), *You Can Win* (1939), *A Guide to Confident Living* (1948) and *The Art of Real Happiness* (1950). But his most famous book appeared in 1952—*The Power of Positive Thinking*—and within weeks was at the top of the *New York Times* best-seller list, where it stayed for about three years. The phenomenal success of the book brought Peale to national prominence. With numerous speaking engagements, a syndicated newspaper column entitled "Confident Living," and a broadening radio audience (a weekly program entitled "The Art of Living" was begun in 1935) over 125 NBC affiliates, his name became synonymous with the phrase *positive thinking*.

Other enterprises generated by Peale's ministry have been *Guideposts,* an inspirational monthly magazine that began shortly after World War 2 as a four-page leaflet and now has a wide distribution and an associated book club; the American Foundation of Religion and Psychiatry, which originated with his church's clinic; and the Foundation for Christian Living, which has been directed by Mrs. Peale and distributes copies of Peale's sermons, booklets and recordings. Peale published numerous additional therapeutic self-help books, as well as inspirational books on biblical topics.

A conservative Republican, Peale did not shy from opposing Roosevelt's New Deal, from pointing out the dangers of electing the Roman Catholic John F. Kennedy to the presidency, nor from standing by his close friend Richard Nixon through the Watergate scandals of the early 1970s. His support of traditional American values was accented by a famous article he wrote for *Reader's Digest:* "Let the Churches Stand Up for Capitalism" (1953).

Peale has been criticized for his message of "positive thinking." Many have viewed it as a religious pragmatism that dilutes Christian theology and promotes American doctrines of self-reliance and materialistic rewards. Peale clearly staked his own place in the tradition of American "harmonial religion," which Sydney Ahlstrom has defined as "those forms of piety and belief in which spiritual composure, physical health, and even economic well-being are understood to flow from a person's rapport with the cosmos." Arguably, the post-World War 2 economic affluence and the accompanying anxieties of modern urban living contributed to build a religious atmosphere primed to receive a gospel promising confident living and peace of mind. But whatever the reasons for his success, Peale became one of the most prominent religious figures of the post-war decades.

BIBLIOGRAPHY. *Current Biography* (1974):306-309; A. Gordon, *Norman Vincent Peale: Minister to Millions* (1958); D. Meyer, *Positive Thinkers: Popular Religious Psychology from Mary Baker Eddy to Norman Vincent Peale and Ronald Reagan* (1988); C. Westphal, *Norman Vincent Peale: Christian Crusader* (1964).

D. G. Reid

Peck, (E)dmund (J)ames (1850-1924). Anglican* missionary* to the Canadian Inuit. Following his conversion* in the Royal Navy, E. J. Peck was trained by the Church Missionary Society* and sent to work under Bishop Horden of Moosonee in 1876. For twenty years from his missions at Little Whale River and Fort George, Peck evangelized both Inuit and Native Americans along the eastern shore of Hudson Bay. In 1885, after several attempts, he reached the Inuit at Fort Chimo on Ungava Bay. Teaching them the Scriptures* in a language he had developed from James Evans's syllabic system, he established a Christian community at Ungava which flourished without missionary visitation for over fifteen years. In 1894, with J. C. Parker, Peck traveled to Blacklead Island in Cumberland Sound, from where he founded several thriving missions on Baffin Island with their own Inuit teachers.

For his translation of the Bible,* *Book of Common Prayer* and hymns,* Peck, who had received very little formal education, was awarded an honorary doctorate. A prolific writer, he is remembered especially for his *Eskimo Dictionary* and for forty-eight years of missionary work among the Inuit, during which he saw Christian missions established over the vast area of northern Canada.

BIBLIOGRAPHY. A. Lewis, *The Life and Work of E. J. Peck amongst the Eskimo* (1904).

R. H. Chilton

Peck, George (1797-1876). Methodist* minister,* educator, editor and author. Born of Puritan* ancestry, Peck and his family became Methodists, leading to George's conversion at fifteen and his license* to preach at nineteen. In 1818 he became a member of Genesee Conference, New York, beginning a career of nearly six decades in seventeen pastorates, as a presiding elder,* as the denominational book agent, as an editor of the *Methodist Quarterly Review* and of *The Christian Advocate* in New York. Four brothers accompanied him into the Methodist ministry. A tireless ecclesi-

astical leader, he was a delegate to thirteen sessions of the Methodist Episcopal General Conference and to the London meeting of the Evangelical Alliance* in 1846. Peck promoted educational causes in general and the conference's course of studies for preachers in particular. A writer of popular evangelical* theology,* he wrote on the topics of Christian perfection,* Universalism* and the nature of authority.* An early historian of Methodism, Peck wrote two conference histories; an autobiography; a biography of his brother, Bishop Jesse T. Peck; and a defense of Northern Methodism following the sectional division of the denomination in 1844-1845. During the Civil War* he published a volume of patriotic sermons. Retiring in 1873, Peck died on May 20, 1876, in Scranton, Pennsylvania.

BIBLIOGRAPHY. *DAB* VII; G. Peck, *The Life and Times of George Peck* (1874).

W. B. Gravely

Peck, John Mason (1789-1858). Baptist* missionary* to the Missouri Territory, journalist and educator. Born in Litchfield, Connecticut, Peck and his wife, Sally, moved to Greene County, New York, in 1811. There they left Congregationalism* for Baptist views and Peck began to preach* in small Baptist churches in upstate New York. In 1815 Peck met Luther Rice,* a traveling agent for the newly formed Baptist Triennial Convention,* who encouraged Peck's missionary interests.

The Pecks were appointed to the St. Louis area in 1817, where they established a mission to the Missouri Territory. Peck preached,* formed churches,* organized Sunday schools* (which were then new in America), taught school, formed women's "mite societies" to sponsor mission work, and distributed Bibles* and religious literature. In 1827 he founded Rock Springs Seminary, one of the earliest schools west of the Mississippi. In 1832 the seminary moved to Upper Alton, Illinois, and was renamed Shurtleff College in 1836. In 1829 Peck launched *The Pioneer,* the first of several papers he sponsored in the West. During the 1820s he advocated abolition* of slavery, tax-supported public schools and temperance* societies. Peck helped form the American Baptist Home Mission Society in 1832 and the American Baptist Historical Society in 1853. Peck's interest in stimulating immigration to the West is evident in two of his publications, *Gazateer of Illinois* (1834) and *A New Guide for Emigrants to the West* (1836). He was convinced that the West was a place where Christian institutions could nurture democracy.* Peck's fifty-three-volume diary was destroyed, but

Rufus Babcock* preserved much of it in preparing Peck's memoirs. Though he had scant formal schooling, in 1852 Harvard University recognized his substantial contributions in conferring on Peck an honorary degree.

BIBLIOGRAPHY. R. Babcock, ed., *Forty Years of Pioneer Life: Memoir of John Mason Peck* (1864); *DAB* VII; *DARB*; C. Hayne, *Vanguard of the Caravan: Life Story of John Mason Peck* (1931); M. Lawrence, *John Mason Peck: The Missionary Pioneer* (1940). H. L. McBeth

Peloubet, Francis Nathan (1831-1920). Congregationalist* minister,* Sunday-school* lesson writer and Bible commentator. Born in New York City, Peloubet was educated at Williams College (A.B., 1853) and Bangor Theological Seminary in Maine (B.D., 1857). Ordained* in 1857, Peloubet served churches in Cape Ann (1857-1860), Oakham (1860-1866), Attleboro (1866-1871) and Natick (1872-1883), Massachusetts. In 1874 he wrote a series of question books on the International Sunday School Lessons which soon after publication reached a circulation of 116,000 a year. In 1880 the questions became a quarterly, reaching a circulation of 150,000 a year. In 1875 Peloubet began editing *Select Notes on the International Sunday School Lessons* intended for Sunday-school teachers and advanced students. Published annually, he continued in this work for forty-five years (1875-1920). Much of that time he also wrote quarterly books for Sunday schools (1880-1919). By 1883 he had resigned his pastorate in Natick to devote all of his time to writing, settling in Auburndale, Massachusetts, from 1890 until his death. A prolific author, Peloubet edited *Select Songs* for Sunday schools, wrote biblical commentaries and revised *Smith's Bible Dictionary* (1912). A pioneer in the Sunday-school movement, Peloubet's pen fed the growing need for biblical instruction in the burgeoning institution.

BIBLIOGRAPHY. *DAB* VII. E. E. Cairns

Pemberton, Ebenezer (1704-1777). Congregational* clergyman.* Born into a minister's* family in Boston, Pemberton followed in his father's footsteps, graduating from Harvard College* in 1721, serving first as a military chaplain* and then entering the pastorate. He preached* from 1727 to 1753 in a New York Presbyterian church and then returned to Boston to assume the pastorate of the Middle Street Church. Pemberton's church was forced to close in 1775 because of revolutionary activity in Boston. He was among the most popular preachers of his day, but his reputation among American revolutionary patriots suffered because of his friendship with the royalist governor Thomas Hutchinson, a member of Pemberton's congregation. Several of Pemberton's sermons, both from New York and Boston, were published during his lifetime, including a series of messages entitled "Salvation by Grace through Faith."

BIBLIOGRAPHY. *AAP* 1; B. Bailyn, *The Ordeal of Thomas Hutchinson* (1974). M. A. Carden

Penance, Sacrament of. The approved name for the sacrament* which Roman Catholics* have popularly called "confession"* (or, technically, "Auricular Confession"), the ritual expression of a repentant heart. The Roman Catholic Church teaches that persons who have sinned after the first forgiveness of sins* through Baptism* are to acknowledge openly subsequent sins. They are to receive guidance from a priest,* ask for and receive forgiveness and perform some penance. When the sins in question are serious, knowingly and deliberately committed, a person is deemed to have separated himself from the body of Christ. For this reason the sacrament is required before being admitted to the Lord's Table, unless exceptional circumstances prevent it.

Scriptural passages such as James 5:16 and Matthew 18:15-18 lie behind the sacrament's long and varied history. A key influence on the practice of the sacrament has been the ancient monastic custom whereby a beginner in the spiritual life revealed his or her struggles and sins to more experienced monks* or nuns.* Another influence was the Church's public ritual of reconciliation for sinners guilty of three major, socially damaging sins: homicide, adultery and denial of Christ under persecution.

Since the Reformation, Catholic consciousness has focused on the confession—the audible listing of sins, their type and frequency—in the priest's private hearing. Sacramental reforms introduced by Vatican II* (1962-1965) have urged priests and penitents to interact in biblically richer ways, looking in greater depth at the underlying causes of sin and stressing God's acceptance and embrace of all in Jesus. Catholics believe the sacrament provides a heightened awareness of sin and gives help to believers in their need for continual conversion.

BIBLIOGRAPHY. R. Gula, *To Walk Together Again: the Sacrament of Penance* (1984); M. Hellwig, *Sign of Reconciliation and Conversion, The Sacrament of Penance For Our Times* (1984). B. Moran

Pendleton, James Madison (1811-1891). Baptist* pastor, professor and journalist. Born in Spotsylvania County, Virginia, and raised in Christian County, Kentucky, Pendleton attended an academy at Hokinsville, Kentucky. By the age of seventeen he had joined the Baptist Church and by nineteen (1831) he was licensed* and preaching.* He was ordained* a Baptist minister in 1833, but for several years he taught school and studied theology* privately.

Pendleton became one of the better-educated Baptist pastors in western Kentucky, and he was the first in his region to enter the professional ministry.* In 1837 he became pastor of First Baptist Church, Bowling Green, Kentucky. There he remained until 1857 when he became professor of theology at Union University, Murfreesboro, Tennessee. The following year he became a joint editor of *The Tennessee Baptist.*

Pendleton, along with A. C. Dayton and James Robinson Graves,* made up the "Great Triumvirate" of a Baptist ecclesiological movement known as "Landmarkism."* Pendleton coined the term "Landmark" in 1854 in an article Graves published as a tract entitled *An Old Landmark Re-Set* (1854). Both men were alarmed that Baptists were setting aside an old landmark of the faith by participating in pulpit exchanges,* union meetings and fraternal relations with other denominations.* Pendleton was recognized as the systematist of Landmarkism.*

Because of his Union sympathies, with the onset of the Civil War* Pendleton withdrew to the North. There he pastored a church at Hamilton, Ohio (1862-1865), and then Upland, Pennsylvania (1865-1883), where he also played a role in founding Crozer Theological Seminary. In 1883 he returned to Tennessee to live with his sons. Among his several publications were *Three Reasons Why I Am a Baptist* (1853), *Church Manual* (1867) and *Christian Doctrines* (1878).

See also LANDMARK MOVEMENT.

BIBLIOGRAPHY. *DAB* VII; J. M. Pendleton, *Reminiscences of a Long Life* (1891); J. H. Spencer, *A History of Kentucky Baptists* (1886).

M. G. Bell

Penn, William (1644-1718). Quaker* statesman and founder of Pennsylvania. Born in London, Penn's father, Admiral Sir William Penn, sent him from their Tower Hill home in London to learn the classics and courtly manners at Chigwell School, followed by studies at Oxford University (1660-1662), a Huguenot* academy in Saumur, France (1663-1664), and London law schools. While administering his father's Irish estate, however, his boyhood among Puritans* and an encounter with persecuted Irish Quakers led him to join the Quakers in rejecting the worldly Restoration-court values. Disowned by his father, Penn made himself spokesman for the Quakers in several debates with Anglican,* Puritan and Baptist* theologians.* He was put in prison for a mistaken charge of Unitarianism,* twice again for leading public Quaker worship.* His trial in 1670 established the rights of a jury to acquit him. In 1672 he married Gulielma, daughter of Mary Penington, and after her death married Hannah Callowhill of Bristol. In 1677 he visited Dutch and German Quakers and Princess Elizabeth of the Palatinate in the company of George Fox*, Robert Barclay* and George Keith.*

Penn was the Quakers' leader after their first two decades of radical witness and world challenge under George Fox. Avoiding sectarian isolation, he guided the movement through the Second Conventicle Act persecutions of 1670-1685 and the years of quiet after English toleration came in 1689. His attitudes to social reform and responsibility have characterized most Quakers to the present day. Of the many books he wrote in those years, the best known became the ethically challenging *No Cross, No Crown* (1669). In later years he wrote *Some Fruits of Solitude* (1693) and a summary of Fox's life and the Quakers' story. In all these and in huge tracts of theological debate such as *The Christian Quaker* (1673), Penn appealed to the moral lives and writings of pagans like Socrates and to the consciences of non-Quaker persecutors to verify the Quaker claim that the Spirit and Light of God speak in every human heart to teach saving truth that can be recognized in part by everyone.

Penn's trust in truth and human conscience undergirded his second major life work, as advocate of religious toleration.* He wrote tracts such as *The Great Case of Liberty of Conscience* (1670). He lobbied with princes and parliaments and in 1678-1679 campaigned actively—if vainly—for Whig candidates pledged to toleration. He was among the few Englishmen who trusted the promises of toleration made by his father's friend, the Catholic Duke of York, who later became James II. Penn spent some years in forced retirement after James's fall.

James's brother, Charles II, had opened for Penn his third career as the founder of colonies. In 1674 as a trustee for the bankrupt Quaker Edward Billing, Penn had helped to buy and settle the West and later East New Jersey colonies, whose model constitutions included religious toleration, civil rights and democratic government. In 1688 Charles

II repaid a debt to Penn's father by granting the larger, richer Pennsylvania territory across the Delaware. Penn proclaimed equal legal rights there for the Delaware Indians and toleration not only for Quakers but for persecuted Germans such as Mennonites. Penn's *Frame of Government* (1682) was at first oligarchic, but the later version in 1701 gave power to the popular assembly. Penn had sailed with his settlers to Pennsylvania in 1682, but disputes over boundaries and debts unpaid by his settlers took him back to England. He only resided in Pennsylvania during 1682-1684 and 1699-1701. In 1712 a stroke curbed his active life.

BIBLIOGRAPHY. *DAB* VII; *DARB;* M. B. Endy, Jr., *William Penn and Early Quakerism* (1973); W. T. Hull, *William Penn* (1956); C. O. Peare, *William Penn* (1956); W. Penn, *The Collected Works of William Penn,* ed. J. Beese, 2 vols. (1726).

H. S. Barbour

Pennington, (J)ames (W)illiam (C)harles (1809-1870).

African-American Presbyterian* minister.* Born into slavery, Pennington escaped as a young adult and after acquiring an education in Pennsylvania and New York taught school on Long Island and New Haven, Connecticut, where he also studied theology.* Ordained* by the Presbyterian Church, he served congregations in Newtown, Long Island (1838-1840); Hartford, Connecticut (1840-1847); and then at the First (Shiloh) Presbyterian Church in New York (1847-1855). A skilled and popular lecturer and preacher, Pennington was invited to Europe several times, where he spoke in London, Paris and Brussels. He served as a delegate to the World's Anti-Slavery Convention and the World's Peace Society in 1843, and in 1851 was awarded the doctor of divinity degree by the University of Heidelberg. He was an activist in the abolitionist* and Negro Convention movements, speaking out against slavery through his lectures, sermons, editorials and books, including his autobiography, *The Fugitive Blacksmith, or, Events in the History of James W. C. Pennington . . . formerly a Slave in the State of Maryland, United States.* He died of alcoholism in 1870.

BIBLIOGRAPHY. *DAB* VII; B. Quarles, *Black Abolitionists* (1969). M. R. Sawyer

Pentecost.

An annual commemoration of the descent of the Holy Spirit. The word *Pentecost* is derived from the Greek name for the festival, literally meaning "fifty days"—the time between the feast of Passover and the celebration of the wheat harvest. The New Testament states that the Holy Spirit came on the disciples of Jesus on the day of Pentecost (Acts 2:1-4), some time after Jesus had ascended into heaven (Acts 1:1-11). In the early centuries of the church, the celebration of Pentecost was not the celebration of the fiftieth day but the fifty days following the Pasch or Easter.* This period was characterized by the theme of joyous victory in which no fasting was allowed and kneeling in prayer* was forbidden.

Later Judaism associated Pentecost with the giving of the Law to Moses on Mount Sinai, and Christians since Augustine have noted the correspondence between the giving of the Law in the old covenant and the granting of the Spirit in the new. The harvest of wheat has also found correspondence in the harvest of the nations at Pentecost, and the festival has historically been the occasion for baptisms.* The Anglo-Saxon name for the occasion—*Whitsunday*—is derived from the fact that those baptized were dressed in white.

Pentecost is commonly celebrated by liturgical churches with the final lighting of the paschal candle, appropriate readings from the lectionary* and prayers.

BIBLIOGRAPHY. J. Gunstone, *The Feast of Pentecost* (1967). The Editors

Pentecostal Assemblies of Canada.

The largest Pentecostal* denomination* in Canada. The roots of the Pentecostal Assemblies of Canada lie in the evangelical* world of the nineteenth century, with particular strength in the evangelistic emphasis of revivalism* and missions,* often from a Wesleyan* and Holiness* perspective. To this was added a millennial* eschatology* whose pessimistic view of church and society in this age interpreted the feelings of many and produced dissatisfaction with the whole system of denominations.

Canadian Pentecostalism, along with its associates around the world, was a Christian renewal movement. It brought its pessimistic world view into harness with its renewal optimism by positing a brief Latter Rain before the Second Advent of Christ, in which the church would be restored to apostolic fullness. This meant the active presence among Christians of the gifts of the Holy Spirit as described in 1 Corinthians 12, particularly signified by the gift of tongues.*

The movement sprang up in Canada from 1906, with R. E. McAlister going to the Azusa Street* meetings in Los Angeles and returning with the Pentecostal message to the receptive Ottawa Valley, with its Holiness heritage. A. H. Argue,* a prominent businessman, went to William H. Durham's* church in Chicago and returned with the Pentecostal emphasis to Winnipeg, making it the seedbed not only of the Social Gospel* but also of much of Canadian Pentecostalism. Meanwhile, from about 1906 James and Ellen Hebden were building a Pentecostal base at their Toronto mission hall.

As the movement spread, some kind of organization became necessary. In 1919 the Pentecostal Assemblies of Canada (PAOC) was chartered. This dynamic renewal movement was fortunate in its first educational venture, for its principal was J. E. Purdie,* a well-trained evangelical Anglican,* who laid excellent theological foundations under much of the denomination. The Assemblies have become the fastest-growing form of Canadian Christianity, with the total number of members and active nonmembers in the late 1980s being 190,000. The Pentecostal Assemblies of Newfoundland maintains a separate legal existence, but the two denominations are usually considered as one. Together they number 225,000—over seventy per cent of all Canadian Pentecostals—with some three hundred twenty-five congregations responding to pluralistic Canada by worshiping in a language other than English.

BIBLIOGRAPHY. G. G. Kulbeck, *What God Hath Wrought: A History of the Pentecostal Assemblies of Canada* (1958).   I. S. Rennie

Pentecostal Churches. The Pentecostal Movement* that emerged in 1901 has spawned some 300 distinct American denominations.* Nonetheless, a majority of those who identify themselves as classical Pentecostals are adherents of one of seven denominations. While these share roots in the early twentieth-century revival, they differ in significant ways in polity,* doctrinal emphasis, racial composition, social class and regional appeal.

All classical Pentecostals have in common at least one conviction: conversion* to Christ should be followed by another intense experience of Spirit baptism.* This baptism, classical Pentecostals insist, should be evidenced by tongues speech.* Spirit-filled believers then expect to manifest one or more of the nine gifts of the Spirit listed in 1 Corinthians 12 and 14. The older Pentecostal denominations generally also affirm divine healing* and subscribe to a premillennial* eschatology.* The seven largest and most important are the Church of God* (Cleveland), the Pentecostal Holiness Church,* the Church of God in Christ,* the Assemblies of God,* the Pentecostal Assemblies of the World, the United Pentecostal Church* and the International Church of the Foursquare Gospel.*

Church of God (Cleveland). This body traces its roots to the formation of the Christian Union, a small restorationist,* come-outist congregation formed in the mountains of western North Carolina in 1886. In 1902, having identified with Wesleyan Holiness* teaching, the group changed its name to the Holiness Church. In 1903 an itinerant preacher, Ambrose Jessup Tomlinson,* joined the group. A strong restorationist conviction motivated him: He was certain the group constituted the true and final restoration of the church of God. Over the next few years Tomlinson articulated the message that shaped the movement: It was, he insisted, the exclusive true church. In 1907 the name of the movement was changed to Church of God.

In 1908 Tomlinson embraced Pentecostalism, spoke in tongues and identified his fledgling movement with Pentecostalism. Elected general overseer in 1909, he held that office until 1923. His authoritarian style gradually dissuaded his associates; accused of financial mismanagement, he was deposed in 1923. Lengthy court proceedings followed over the use of the name *Church of God.* In the end, two other Churches of God were spawned by Tomlinson's predicament: the Church of God of Prophecy (Cleveland, Tennessee), and the Church of God (World Headquarters) in Huntsville, Alabama. Under new leadership, the Church of God (now identified by the addition of the word *Cleveland*) grew rapidly.

The Church of God (Cleveland) is part of the Holiness family of Pentecostal denominations. It affirms the necessity of two crisis works of grace: conversion and sanctification.* It expects believers to have a third experience: an enduement with power, or baptism with the Holy Spirit, evidenced by tongues speech. Though not often practiced, foot washing* is endorsed as an ordinance* of the Church. Although Churches of God are found in many states, the denomination's strength remains where it has always been: in the South, especially Tennessee and North Carolina. It operates a four-year liberal arts college, Lee College, in Cleveland, Tennessee; the Church of God School of Theology (also in Cleveland); West Coast Bible College in Fresno; and Northwest Bible College in Minot, North Dakota. Pathway Press in Cleveland is the second-largest Pentecostal denominational publishing enterprise in the U.S. In 1986 the denomination reported 505,775 members in the U.S. The group established its first church in Canada in 1920, and in the late 1980s counted nearly 5,000 Canadian members.

International Pentecostal Holiness Church.

With headquarters in Oklahoma City, this Holiness-Pentecostal denomination also traces its roots to the Holiness revivals* of the late nineteenth century. The denomination was created by the amalgamation of several Holiness associations* whose constituencies were based in North and South Carolina—a segment of the Fire-Baptized Holiness Church,* the Pentecostal Holiness Church and the Tabernacle Presbyterian Church. Reflecting the Methodist* heritage of its early leaders, the Pentecostal Holiness Church retains the office of bishop* and is divided into conferences: general, annual, district and missionary. Its numerical strength remains concentrated in the Southeast and in Oklahoma. The denomination nurtured evangelist* Oral Roberts,* who later left it in the 1960s for other affiliations. It maintains two colleges: Emmanuel College in Franklin Springs, Georgia, and Southwestern Pentecostal Holiness College in Oklahoma City. It also operates Holmes Theological Seminary in Greenville, South Carolina. In 1980 the Church reported 110,000 members in the U.S.

Church of God in Christ. Whereas both of the above denominations are predominantly white and are dominated by white male leaders, the Church of God in Christ attracts primarily an African-American constituency. It, too, emerged from the Holiness Movement of the 1890s, although its direct roots are among Holiness Baptists* rather than in Methodism. The Church of God in Christ was formed as a result of the activities of two African-American Baptists, Charles Price Jones* and Charles Mason.* Devout restorationists, the two promoted conventions for the deepening of spiritual life and the restoration of New Testament Christianity. Their activities centered in Jackson, Mississippi, and in Memphis, Tennessee. They taught the necessity of two works of grace and discussed at length the nature and meaning of Spirit baptism.

Mason resolved the issue of Spirit baptism by identifying with Pentecostalism, accepting the teaching that tongues speech would always evidence the baptism with the Holy Spirit. Jones, who agreed that the experience was necessary, disagreed over evidential tongues, and the two parted company. Mason retained the name, The Church of God in Christ, and remained its bishop (or chief apostle) until his death in 1961. His Church evolved a complex episcopal* polity which differed sharply from the looser associational arrangements many early Pentecostals preferred. Although the Church holds to the typical Holiness-Pentecostal doctrines, some scholars claim that it is distin-

guished within the African-American religious community more by its music than by its message. It is more attuned to social problems than are most other Pentecostal denominations. By some disputed figures (3,709,661 members in 1982), the Church of God in Christ (with headquarters in Memphis, Tenn.) is the largest American Pentecostal denomination. It is certainly the largest predominantly African-American denomination and the second largest overall.

Assemblies of God. This group traces its origins to a 1914 camp meeting* in Hot Springs, Arkansas, where about 120 delegates responded to an invitation to discuss ways to address commonly perceived problems. The group resisted the idea that they were forming a denomination, and understood themselves as participants in a loosely structured fellowship. Serious doctrinal disagreements and rapid growth gradually resulted in tighter organization. The denomination combines aspects of congregational* and presbyterian* polity. Governed by a General Council composed of all ordained* ministers* which meets biennially, the Assemblies of God is divided into fifty-seven districts, each of which has its own district council, superintendent and presbytery.

The Assemblies of God was led by men and women who had already rejected Holiness teaching that sanctification should be accomplished in an instantaneous experience. It was the first, and has always been the largest, non-Wesleyan Pentecostal denomination. The division in Pentecostalism over the nature of sanctification was bitter, and the Assemblies of God developed in virtual isolation from other white Pentecostal groups until the World War 2* era. Since it was the first Pentecostal denomination created specifically as a Pentecostal denomination (rather than having become Pentecostal by adding Pentecostal views on Spirit baptism to an established belief system), it is significant that the Assemblies of God had a more widely scattered constituency than other early Pentecostal groups. For example, although the largest delegation at early General Councils came from Texas, the second-largest delegation was usually from California.

The Assemblies of God has historically been predominantly white, although it has growing Hispanic* and Korean constituencies. In the early 1940s, its leaders affiliated with the National Association of Evangelicals.* The Church of God (Cleveland) also affiliated at about the same time. Through the National Association of Evangelicals, evangelicals* influenced Pentecostal denominations far more extensively than Pentecostal leaders influenced evangelicals. The Assemblies of God also played a prominent role in creating the National Religious Broadcasters,* the Pentecostal Fellowship of North America* and the World Pentecostal Conferences.* It maintains a vigorous missionary program, supporting some 1,500 missionaries abroad. It supports four nationally sponsored educational institutions in the headquarters city of Springfield, Missouri: Central Bible College, Evangel College, Berean College (a nontraditional college) and the Assemblies of God Theological Seminary. In addition, it endorses district-sponsored colleges scattered across the country. In the late 1980s the denomination numbered over 2 million members in over 10,886 congregations throughout the U.S. It is the largest classical Pentecostal denomination in the world (over 13 million members in 1985).

Pentecostal Assemblies of the World. The early history of the Pentecostal Assemblies of the World parallels that of the Assemblies of God. The first influential "oneness" denomination, the Pentecostal Assemblies of the World attracted many of those who left the Assemblies of God in a heated doctrinal dispute in 1916. But the origins go back to 1913 and must be understood in the context of the general Pentecostal milieu. Early Pentecostals ardently expected the restoration of the apostolic faith. They pursued intense religious experiences* and celebrated the presence and rule of the Holy Spirit among them. Prone to new, updated revelations, they dreaded "missing God." The convergence of several circumstances and individuals at a large camp meeting near Pasadena, California, in 1913 provided a context for "revelations" that set in motion events that would deeply and permanently divide Pentecostals.

In a very real sense, those who accepted the revelations and consequent new teaching were more thoroughly Pentecostal than those who did not. Stressing the New Testament model, and especially Acts 2:38, proponents of oneness Pentecostalism urged the necessity of a three-stage conversion experience: repentance, baptism* in the name of Jesus, Spirit baptism evidenced by tongues. Like other radical restorationists before them, they had trouble with the doctrine of the Trinity. They opposed organization, assuming that the New Testament model mandated congregational polity. For about three years, they succeeded in permeating segments of non-Holiness Pentecostalism with their views, which demanded rebaptism. Their success within the Assemblies of God forced that denomination to draft a "Statement of Fundamental Truths" in 1916, thereby excluding non-trinitarians.

Some of the disaffected joined other oneness Pentecostals in the Pentecostal Assemblies of the World, an organization that centered in Indianapolis, where an African-American oneness Pentecostal G. T. Haywood* had a strong congregation. Until 1924 the Pentecostal Assemblies of the World was racially mixed. In 1924 a substantial white segment withdrew, with the separation primarily racially motivated. The Pentecostal Assemblies of the World is an African-American, non-Holiness, oneness Pentecostal denomination. It follows the oneness practice (drawn from the New Testament) of using wine rather than grape juice in the communion service. Its polity resembles that of Methodism. In 1987 the Church reported a worldwide membership of 500,000.

United Pentecostal Church International. White oneness Pentecostals who withdrew from the Pentecostal Assemblies of the World in 1924 formed an organization called the Pentecostal Church. A few years later other oneness congregations created the Pentecostal Assemblies of Jesus Christ. In 1945 these two united to form the United Pentecostal Church. With headquarters in the St. Louis suburb of Hazelwood, Missouri, the United Pentecostal Church has recorded impressive growth. The denomination operates a publishing house, several Bible institutes, a radio broadcast and a foreign missions* program that has been especially successful in South America. In general, the United Pentecostal Church has urged on its members a more rigorous code of social behavior than have other predominantly white Pentecostal denominations. Excluded because of its anti-trinitarianism from such associations as the National Association of Evangelicals and the Pentecostal Fellowship of North America, the United Pentecostal Church has developed in relative isolation from other Pentecostal denominations. In the late 1987 the denomination reported a membership of approximately 350,000 members in the U.S. and Canada.

International Church of the Foursquare Gospel. This body is the only sizable Pentecostal denomination that developed out of the ministry of a single charismatic individual. Aimee Semple McPherson,* the denomination's founder, was a gifted-though-controversial figure throughout her career as a religious leader. Reared under strong Salvation Army* influences, Aimee Kennedy embraced Pentecostalism in her hometown of Ingersoll, Ontario. While still a teen-ager, she married Robert Semple, the evangelist who converted her, and went with him as a missionary to China. Her dreams of missionary service cut short by his death, she returned to the U.S., where she married Harold McPherson. Restive in the role of wife and mother, she left Harold in 1917 to become an itinerant evangelist.

After months of conducting huge campaigns in tents,* municipal auditoriums and stadiums, McPherson migrated to Los Angeles and began constructing Angelus Temple, a 5,300-seat domed church that became her base of operations for the rest of her life. Meanwhile, she affiliated with the Assemblies of God in 1919. In 1921, during a campaign in Oakland, California, McPherson became fascinated by the prophetic vision of four faces recorded in Ezekiel 1. Understanding the four faces as types of the ministry of Christ, she began to call her message the "foursquare" gospel: Christ the Savior, Healer, Baptizer and Coming King.

In 1922 McPherson dropped her Assemblies of God credentials. She briefly held a Methodist exhorter's license* and a preaching license from a Baptist association in San Jose. From 1923, when she opened Angelus Temple, it became evident that her work would expand and that a new Pentecostal denomination would emerge. She opened L.I.F.E. Bible College on property adjacent to her church in 1925 and sent her students to evangelize at home and abroad. Despite the notoriety associated with her name after her disputed kidnapping in 1926 and her third marriage a few years later (she had been divorced from Harold), her efforts continued to grow. After her death, her son and successor, Rolf K. McPherson, continued his mother's tradition of strong, centralized control of the Church. He took steps to lead the denomination in the direction the Assemblies of God had taken. Under his leadership, the International Church of the Foursquare Gospel affiliated with the National Association of Evangelicals, the Pentecostal Fellowship of North America and the World Pentecostal Conference.

Although its polity differs sharply from that of the Assemblies of God, the International Church of the Foursquare Gospel resembles the Assemblies of God in doctrine and practice. It is a non-Holiness, trinitarian Pentecostal denomination. Like other major Pentecostal denominations, its eschatology is futurist, pretribulationist premillennialism. It supports foreign and home missions outreaches and has seen steady growth in recent years. In 1988 the Church reported 188,757 members in the U.S.

These are the largest and most visible of the hundreds of denominations in which Pentecostal views find expression. With the rest, these denominations attempt to assert that Spirit baptism is for all believers, not merely for a special few. They further believe that Spirit baptism initiates believers into a life which is for all Christians, a life in which the transforming power of the Spirit's felt presence makes the believer triumphant.

BIBLIOGRAPHY. S. M. Burgess et al., *Dictionary of Pentecostal and Charismatic Movements* (1988); J. T. Nichol, *Pentecostalism* (1966); W. Menzies, *Anointed to Serve* (1971); C. Conn, *Like a Mighty Army* (1955); V. Synan, *The Holiness-Pentecostal Movement in the United States* (1971). E. L. Blumhofer

Pentecostal Fellowship of North America. A fellowship of Pentecostal organizations. The Pentecostal Fellowship of North America (PFNA) was founded in 1948, a year after the Pentecostal World Conference* was formed in Zurich, Switzerland. Fellowship,* rather than amalgamation of denominations, has been the purpose of the PFNA.

Twenty-four Pentecostal organizations make up the PFNA and send representatives to the administrative board. The board meets each spring to plan fall meetings and conduct business relating to the PFNA and the Pentecostal World Fellowship. Meetings in the fall are conducted in various cities in Canada and the U. S., and until 1986 they were primarily preaching services open to the public. Due to dwindling interest, in 1986 the board changed the format of its annual fall meeting to include a leadership seminar during the day, and preaching at night. Since 1982 the PFNA records have been kept in the Assemblies of God Archives.

BIBLIOGRAPHY. "Minutes, PFNA Board of Administration and Annual Meetings" (1948-); W. W. Menzies, *Anointed to Serve* (1971); W. W. Menzies, *PFNA News* (1960-). W. E. Warner

Pentecostal Movement. A twentieth-century Christian movement emphasizing a post-conversion experience of Spirit baptism* evidenced by speaking in tongues.* Once considered a glossolalic aberrant within Holiness* revivalism,* the Pentecostal Movement has emerged as perhaps the single-most-significant development in twentieth-century Christianity. In contrast to the stigmatization of early adherents, contemporary Pentecostals bask in the light of a modern-day success story. Glittering "super churches," political clout and renowned (and sometimes notorious) media evangelists* now adorn a burgeoning movement that defies categorization and confounds census-takers. No one knows just how large the movement is, nor is there agreement even on who should be included in its ranks. Estimates of its size range from 10 to 29 million adherents in the U.S., and from 50 to over 250 million adherents worldwide. In 1988 researcher David B. Barrett reported 176 million Pentecostal church members worldwide, with over 22.5 million of these in North America and the largest proportion in the Third World.

Pentecostalism is sometimes divided into two branches: "classical Pentecostalism," indicating the movement's historic bodies; and "neo-Pentecostalism" or the charismatic* renewal, indicating more recent forms of Pentecostalism especially among the mainline* churches. The lines of demarcation are not always clear, and the rather cumbersome title *Pentecostal Movement* is often used for the branches collectively.

Beginnings. The Pentecostal Movement's origins lie in the ministry of an itinerant Holiness evangelist and faith healer, Charles F. Parham.* While superintending a small Bible school in Topeka, Kansas, Parham instructed his students to read Acts and to search for the "Bible evidence" of baptism in the Holy Spirit. The search met spectacular results when on New Year's Day 1901, a student, Agnes Ozman,* spoke in tongues. The experience of glossolalic baptism soon swept the school and convinced Parham that glossolalia was the "initial, physical evidence" of baptism in the Spirit, its inevitable accompaniment. This belief became the doctrinal hallmark of the Pentecostal Movement.

Parham proclaimed his discovery in revival meetings throughout the mid-section of the U.S., generating a small fellowship of churches dubbed the "Apostolic Faith Movement." But the most fortuitous transaction of Parham's ministry took place during a campaign in Houston, Texas. There a young African-American Holiness minister named William J. Seymour* came under his influence. After briefly assisting with Parham's Houston campaign, Seymour moved to Los Angeles. Within weeks Seymour's ministry there had sparked an impressive revival that would come to hold epochal status in Pentecostal history. Based in the Azusa Street Mission,* Seymour's revival became early Pentecostalism's most widely publicized center and sparked much of its early growth and expansion.

The broader historical context for Pentecostalism's emergence is found in the groundswell of restorationist* and millenarian* currents of the 1800s. But its immediate antecedent was the Holiness Movement. The first Pentecostals were drawn from Holiness ranks. Their message spread through Holiness channels and answered aspirations and expectations nurtured within the Holiness revival.

The Holiness Movement itself was a confederation of several trends within nineteenth-century evangelical* Protestantism,* including at least four major streams of thought. The first was the Wesleyan* concept of "entire sanctification,"* by mid-century seen as a second and distinct act of grace identified with baptism in the Holy Spirit. A second stream involved the "Reformed" or "Keswick"* emphasis on the "higher Christian life."* Sanctification here was seen as a progressive work continuing throughout mortal life, and Spirit baptism was viewed as a special enduement with power. The third and fourth streams issued from the Plymouth Brethren* doctrine of dispensational* premillennialism* and from the faith-healing* movement, which saw in Christ's atonement* a provision for physical as well as spiritual healing. One common current among these streams was a deep fascination with the experience of Spirit baptism, however it was defined. In this common emphasis Pentecostalism found its distinctive event.

Beliefs and Practices. The concept of Spirit baptism was familiar to Holiness revivalism, and glossolalia was not unknown, especially among more radical groups like B. H. Irwin's* Fire-Baptized Holiness Church.* Consequently, neither of these phenomena in and of themselves set Pentecostals apart from their Holiness kin. Glossolalia was certainly more common among Pentecostals, but their insistence that this was the normative and necessary sign of Spirit baptism is what distinguished them from the Holiness mainstream.

The centrality of "tongues" for early Pentecostals, however, has been overstated. Glossolalia was viewed as a sign of the movement's broader role in divine history, not as the primary article by which Pentecostals should define themselves. That basic self-understanding rested instead on two coinciding convictions. The first was a resolute certainty that Christ's Second Coming was imminent and that they were to be its heralds. The second conviction held that in the events unfolding among them, one witnessed the first enthralling showers of God's "latter rain." This understanding of a "latter rain" was based on the "former rain" and "latter rain" mentioned in Joel 2:28, the "former" being fulfilled at the Day of Pentecost (Acts 2) and the "latter" in the last days immediately before the Second Coming. This second fulfillment would usher in a full restoration of New Testament Christianity—complete with all of its signs and wonders. So restored, the church could sweep the world with one great and final revival before the Last Day.

Pentecostal doctrine soon consolidated around the "Four-Square Gospel," a term alluding to the city of Revelation 21:16. The cornerstones of this gospel were personal salvation* through faith in Jesus Christ, divine healing, the soon Second Coming of Christ, and Spirit baptism with the evidence of tongues. The movement's theological center lay in the first article and was expressed in a deeply pietistic, even mystical, devotion to Jesus Christ.

A rather surprising component in the belief system of most early Pentecostals was pacifism. Whether this was due more to Holiness precedents or to the Movement's straightforward biblicism is unclear. In any case, the view was predominant prior to World War 1.* At the War's outbreak some Pentecostals called for a "great peace council" at which they could collectively state their opposition to warfare. The council never materialized, but every major Pentecostal body has adopted a pacifist resolution at some point in its history. Most of these resolutions, however, have been changed in recent decades to reflect the general rejection of this position by subsequent generations. Although some Pentecostal denominations* are still officially pacifist, the doctrine is unevenly attended.

In ethical matters Pentecostals generally followed the rigorous asceticism of their Holiness heritage. Evangelists like Glenn Cook* raised occasional voices against legalism,* but a stern Holiness line typically prevailed. Pentecostals were inclined to ban such pernicious elements as chewing gum, neckties, soft drinks and short-sleeved dresses in addition to standard vices like tobacco, alcohol* and moving picture shows.

Worship. Pentecostal worship* impressed many outsiders as a frightening babel of ecstatic emotionalism. Unsympathetic accounts sometimes exaggerated the pandemonium, but Pentecostal services frequently involved a degree of "Holy Ghost bedlam" not suited to the faint of heart. The fundamental precept of Pentecostal worship was that the Holy Spirit alone should direct the order and conduct of a service. Prepared speeches, rehearsal and formality were censured as hindrances to the free operation of the Spirit. Often no speaker would be designated beforehand—with the expectation that the Holy Spirit would make the appointment at the proper time. Sermons were to be delivered extemporaneously as well, as the Spirit—not the note cards—gave the utterance.

Services were subject at any moment to outbursts of glossolalia or other charismatic phenomena. "Suddenly the Spirit would fall upon the congregation," wrote one early pioneer. "God himself would give the altar call. Men would fall all over the house, like the slain in battle." (F. Bartleman, *Azusa Street,* 59-60). In their determination to submit every detail of the congregation's worship to the spontaneous inspiration of the Holy Spirit, Pentecostals often disallowed song leaders and worship leaders in their services. The ideal service was that which moved from start to finish with no visible sign of any human leadership.

Because of such persuasions, early Pentecostalism was a preeminently participatory religion. Testimony,* song, sermon,* prophecy, prayer,* divine healing and glossolalic utterance were the potential domain of anyone present, and not the restricted privilege of a designated few. "The Lord was liable to burst through any one," recalled Frank Bartleman. "It might be a child, a woman, or a man. It might be from the back seat or from the front. It made no difference. We rejoiced that God was working" (Bartleman, p. 59).

This rejection of the customary infrastructures of worship order was matched by a corresponding rejection of ecclesiastical superstructures. Early Pentecostals evidenced a deep-seated aversion for "ecclesiasticism" with its creeds,* doctrines and denominations. Such antipathy derived from the belief that the structures and formalities of organized Christianity had both bound the Holy Spirit and tragically divided the body of Christ. The denial of these devices was theologically conceived of as a refusal to participate in the fragmentation of Christianity. They saw their own movement as a fresh, unencumbered expression of apostolic Christianity, one that would restore the faith to its original pristine unity.

Few of these concepts were altogether new, but they were practiced with an intensity, daring and missionary zeal that set Pentecostalism apart in degree, if not in kind.

Social Factors. The destitution of early Pentecostals has frequently been exaggerated. Recent studies suggest that most early Pentecostals were drawn from the blue-collar working class, not from the ranks of the truly disinherited. Nevertheless, the movement clearly thrived among the poor and marginalized members of society. It provided for them a uniquely affirmative environment unlike anything they would have been likely to find in the mainline churches of that day. In fact, early Pentecostals sometimes voiced a nascent "theology of the poor," interpreting their remarkable growth as a fruit of and a divine endorsement for the options they provided those on society's fringes.

Racial diversity was another trademark of early Pentecostalism, one that directly challenged prevailing societal norms. The West Coast missions in particular were known for a veritable smorgasbord of ethnic identities. Orientals,* Hispanics,* Scandinavian and Eastern European immigrants* worshiped alongside their African-American and Anglo-Saxon brothers and sisters. In light of this reality, conversion* to Pentecostalism sometimes required a conversion in social attitudes as well. Pressures to segregate took their toll within a few decades, however, and most of Pentecostalism today is segregated. In spite of this trend, integrated congregations have always existed within the movement, and slow-but-certain steps toward reintegration are beginning to be made.

Another noteworthy aspect of Pentecostalism consists in the role it has traditionally afforded women. Some of the movement's most prominent leaders have been women, indicating that Pentecostal churches clearly do not expect women to remain silent. Pentecostals rarely endorse the feminist agenda, however, and the role of women in leadership, while allowed, has been viewed with ambivalence. Nevertheless, the Pentecostal emphasis on inspiration and divine calling has traditionally led Pentecostals to override such injunctions as 1 Timothy 2:12 in favor of the obviously gifted woman.

The widespread conviction among early Pentecostals that the true source of every inspired utterance was the Holy Spirit, with the human as the passive vessel only, also helps to explain the frequent accounts of messages coming through children in early Pentecostal meetings. Such occurrences reinforced the conviction of early Pentecostals that they were being spontaneously led by the sovereign wind of the Spirit, which blew wherever it pleased.

Controversy and Schism. In its short history, the Pentecostal-charismatic movement has spawned as many as 300 denominations and organizations in the U.S. alone. While these bodies have sprung from a variety of causes, schism accounts for many of them. In some cases divisions that occurred in the movement's pre-organizational stages were later confirmed by denominational lines. This volatility demonstrates that, contrary to a popular conception, Pentecostals were concerned about doctrinal regularity. They did belittle "doctrine," but only because that particular term was identified with cold, dead denominationalism. Biblical truth was another matter altogether. When strong personalities, shaped by rigorist perfectionism* and fired with urgent millennial* expectation,

clashed over matters of interpretation, compromise was not an affordable luxury. The result was a remarkable predilection to splinter. Indeed, one of the great ironies of Pentecostalism consists in the fact that those who considered themselves to have rejected the ultimate source of Christian schism, "ecclesiasticism," were themselves so unrelentingly schismatic.

The earliest division within Pentecostalism traces to differences in practice between the "old" Apostolic Faith movement related to Charles F. Parham's ministry, and the "new" Apostolic Faith missions connected to William J. Seymour's Azusa Street revival. Parham-oriented saints considered the Azusa faithful to be undisciplined, given to emotional excess and fraught with doctrinal irregularity. West Coast Pentecostals were likely to regard the "old" Apostolics as unspiritual organizers with a jealous desire to claim the Azusa revival as their own.

By 1910 a dispute of more longstanding significance had erupted over the doctrine of sanctification. Most early Pentecostals adhered to the Wesleyan Holiness view of sanctification, defining it as a second, distinct work of grace subsequent to conversion. Conversion brought justification,* but sanctification completed the salvation process by eradicating the Adamic nature with its propensity to sin.* Pentecostals had simply expanded this two-step formula by crowning it with baptism in the Holy Spirit. Some Pentecostals, however, were not committed to this view. These non-Wesleyan, or "Reformed,"* Pentecostals soon rallied around the preaching of a powerful Chicago-based evangelist named William H. Durham.* Durham emphasized the "finished work of Calvary" and declared that Christ's atoning work on the cross had accomplished everything requisite to full salvation. Sanctification, he argued, was a progressive work, a process in which the believer learned to express outwardly what was already an inward reality. The dispute became particularly vicious, especially between Durham and such Wesleyan stalwarts as Parham and Florence Crawford.* When Durham died suddenly in July 1912, his death was celebrated by Parham as a divine vindication of the Wesleyan Pentecostal cause.

While the sanctification debate was still raging, an even more bitter controversy arose over the doctrine of the Trinity. In the spring of 1913 a camp meeting* was held near Los Angeles to foster unity among Pentecostal saints. One of the speakers noted that the Trinitarian formula for baptism given in Matthew 28 was not used by the apostles, who rather baptized "in Jesus' name." Following this observation one John G. Schaepe (1870-1939) announced a new revelation on the "power of the name of Jesus." Some interpreted this only as a correction in the baptismal liturgy,* but others took the revelation to a more striking conclusion. The two baptismal formulae were in fact identical, they argued, because the "name" of the Father, Son and Spirit is *Jesus*. This adoption of a Jesus-Unitarian theology, dubbed "Jesus-Only," "Oneness" or "Jesus-Name" doctrine, initiated what has become Pentecostalism's most deeply entrenched division (*See* United Pentecostal Church International).

Relations between Wesleyan and non-Wesleyan Pentecostals have greatly improved in the past few decades. Organizations like the Society for Pentecostal Studies and the Pentecostal Fellowship of North America* include members from both traditions and fraternal relations prevail on other fronts as well. Relations between Trinitarian and non-Trinitarian Pentecostals, however, are still characterized by acrimony and suspicion.

Organization. Early Pentecostal pioneers had taken pride in their movement's lack of ecclesiastical vestments. But this anti-formalism left them without effective structures for defining and defending normative doctrinal standards. The movement grew rapidly, and new converts often brought doctrinal idiosyncrasies with them. This, together with the openness of many Pentecostals to new revelation, produced a climate of instability. Circulating newspapers, scattered Bible schools,* camp meetings, popular leaders and a few loosely knit associations provided what continuity was to be had, but heterodox and eccentric impulses continued to flourish. By its second decade many had come to feel that the movement's credibility, if not its survival, demanded some level of organization. In addition to their concern for standards of doctrine and polity, such persons were distressed by haphazard missions strategies and felt that "association" (a term unencumbered with the negative freight *organization* bore for early Pentecostals) could remedy many of the movement's ills.

Although several small Pentecostal denominations were already in existence by 1911, these did not represent original attempts to organize independent Pentecostals. Rather, these were previously organized Holiness bodies that had converted wholesale to Pentecostalism. Tendencies toward organization within the Pentecostal Movement proper, however, had been seen in Parham's Apostolic Faith movement in the Midwest and in a similar fellowship, also called "Apostolic Faith,"

related to Florence Crawford's ministry in Portland, Oregon. In spite of his deep distaste for "denominationalism," practical concerns led Parham to appoint rudimentary offices and form an "association" among the congregations sympathetic to his message. Crawford's association simply tied her Portland congregation together with various satellite churches planted by her members. In addition to facilitating missions and evangelism,* the association published a newspaper for its members.

The most significant step toward formal organization, however, occurred in 1913 when Howard A. Goss (1883-1964) and Eudorus N. Bell,* concerned about the state of the movement and alienated from the Wesleyan emphasis of many within it, issued a call for like-minded ministers to gather the following spring in Hot Springs, Arkansas. Out of that conference in April 1914 emerged what would become the single largest Pentecostal denomination, the Assemblies of God.*

Vigorous opposition came from those convinced that this attempt to organize the revival would prove to be the first regrettable step back into ecclesiastical bondage. A more threatening conflagration erupted when, in response to the "Jesus-Name" debate, the young association published a "Statement of Fundamental Truths," which was immediately perceived by other Pentecostals as a forbidden "creed." The statement clearly affirmed the doctrine of the Trinity, and a large contingent of non-Trinitarians, including Goss himself, departed. Others of Trinitarian persuasion, distressed by the formulation of a "creed" and by the use of ecclesiastical force against the non-Trinitarians, left the denomination as well. In spite of its early woes, however, the Assemblies of God survived to set the trend for the movement as a whole.

After the Assemblies of God, a few denominations formed from an open appeal for independent saints to organize. Some developed around the ministries of charismatic individuals or influential congregations. Many emerged from schisms within other denominations or groups. Some grew from particularly successful revivals. Common regional, geographical and doctrinal factors contributed to the formation of others. But despite its obvious popularity, the trend toward organization has not been universal among Pentecostals. Thousands of independent Pentecostal congregations still shun traditional modes of affiliation, and the 1987 *World Christian Encyclopedia* estimated the number of independent Pentecostals worldwide at twenty million.

[889]

Growth and Expansion. The history of Pentecos-talism has been interspersed with periods of explosive numerical growth. The reasons for this growth are certainly complex but are related to a zeal for missions and personal evangelism virtually unmatched in twentieth-century Christianity. This was especially evident in the movement's early years. Urgent millennial expectation, "latter rain" theology and the profoundly transformational experience of Spirit baptism combined to produce an intensely evangelistic orientation. Almost every convert, if not engaged in full-time missions work, was at least committed to active personal evangelism. It was not uncommon for individuals to depart as missionaries to remote lands within days or weeks of their "baptism," often leaving with little or no financial support. By no later than 1908, dedicated messengers had covered North America and made inroads into Scandinavia, the British Isles, Western Europe, China, Japan, India, Africa, Australia and the Middle East. The emergence of denominations brought better organized and yet more successful mission strategies, sometimes sparking revivals in foreign lands that dwarfed the sending body in their size.

The medium of print has also been instrumental in the growth of Pentecostalism. In fact, it could be said that the movement was carried on the back of its printing presses. From the beginning Pentecostals were avid publishers, with scores of organizations and individuals producing newspapers to spread the Pentecostal message. Some of the notable original Pentecostal publications were: Carrie Judd Montgomery's* *The Triumphs of Faith* (1881, originally a Holiness publication), G. B. Cashwell's *The Bridegroom's Messenger* (1907), Florence Crawford's *Apostolic Faith* (1908, originally founded in 1906 by William Seymour), J. Roswell Flower's* *The Pentecost* (1908) and Aimee Semple McPherson's* *Bridal Call* (1917).

Popular mass-evangelists and faith healers have also played a significant role in the growth of Pentecostalism. Perhaps the most influential of the early revivalists were Maria Woodworth-Etter,* Aimee Semple McPherson and the British revivalist Smith Wigglesworth (1859-1947). Sister Aimee, founder of the International Church of the Foursquare Gospel,* was the most flamboyant of these and in that sense set the tone for those who followed. The middle decades of the century saw the rise of such prominent faith healers as A. A. Allen,* T. L. Osborn, Oral Roberts,* Kathryn Kuhlman* and Rex Humbard.* The mantle has now passed to the diversified televangelism ministries of men like Pat Robertson* and the recently compromised Jim Bakker* and Jimmy Swaggart.*

A controversial offshoot of the faith-healing tradition is the "faith movement,"* identified by what its critics term the "name it and claim it" doctrine. Built on the idea of "positive confession," apparently first developed by E. W. Kenyon,* the movement's chief leaders currently are Kenneth Copeland and Kenneth Hagin, with Hagin's Rhema Bible Training Center being its primary institution. "Faith confession" teaches that the prayer of faith is inevitably efficacious and that financial prosperity and physical well-being are divine promises to all who exercise the laws of faith.

The spread of Pentecostalism into the mainline denominations, known as the charismatic renewal (*See* Charismatic Movement), is one of the most remarkable and influential developments in recent church history. This new direction for Pentecostalism was signaled in 1951 with the formation of the Full Gospel Business Men's Fellowship, International (FGBMFI).* Sponsored by Demos Shakarian* and Oral Roberts,* the FGBMFI provided a dignified forum within which mainline clergy* and laity* could interact with white-collar Pentecostals. The Fellowship did much to break the stereotypical image of Pentecostalism as a haven for the poor and unlearned, and through its mediation many from historic Protestant denominations experienced Pentecostal baptism.

At the same time, other developments were contributing to the growing respectability of the Pentecostal Movement. David Du Plessis* was beginning his rise to prominence as a Pentecostal emissary to the ecumenical world. Henry P. Van Dusen,* in a 1958 *Life* magazine article, had described Pentecostalism as the "Third Force" in world Christianity. Since the 1940s Pentecostals had shared common cause with other evangelicals through the National Association of Evangelicals* and in 1960 Thomas Zimmerman, then superintendent of the Assemblies of God, was elected president of that body.

But the shot heard round the mainline Protestant world was fired in 1959 when Dennis Bennett, rector of St. Mark's Episcopal Church in Van Nuys, California, received his baptism in the Spirit. Generally viewed as the beginning of the charismatic movement, it differed from its classical parent in that it has either worked within existing denominational structures or outside of any denominational structures whatsoever. By the mid-1960s the movement had crossed into the Catholic Church. Ironically, the Pentecostal Movement—

historically plagued by bitter factiousness—through its offspring has become one of the most profoundly unifying forces of our time among lay Christians.

Even decidedly non-charismatic bodies have seen fit to place new emphasis on spiritual gifts, evangelism, personal salvation and enthusiasm in worship because of the Pentecostal-charismatic presence. In this respect Pentecostalism has changed the face of American Christianity. Researcher David Barrett has recently created a new category, "mainline third-wave neo-charismatics," to describe the 21 million non-charismatic American believers who nevertheless exhibit Pentecostal characteristics in their worship. On the other hand, as the charismatic renewal has charted new directions, classical Pentecostalism has undergone change as well. Traditional Pentecostals are exhibiting more liturgical order in worship. Members are climbing the socioeconomic ladder. Interest in higher education is on the rise, and ethical rigorism is on the wane. Mainstream values are being adopted by most, but many are expressing a new level of social awareness and concern.

Growth among classical Pentecostalism has kept pace with that of the charismatic movement, especially in the global perspective. Statistical nonchalance and diverse counting procedures make estimates problematic, but the number of adherents in the major Pentecostal denominations in the U.S. is approximately as follows:
Reformed (Non-Wesleyan) Pentecostal:
Assemblies of God 2,000,000
International Church of the Foursquare Gospel 180,000
Pentecostal Church of God 100,000
Wesleyan Pentecostal:
Church of God in Christ 1,500,000
Church of God (Cleveland, Tennessee) 500,000
Church of God in Christ, International 200,000
Pentecostal Holiness Church, Inc. 120,000
Oneness (Non-Trinitarian) Pentecostal:
United Pentecostal Church, International 500,000
Apostolic Overcoming Holy Church of God 75,000
Pentecostal Assemblies of the World 50,000
It should be noted that U.S. adherence often belies the overall size of groups with large international affiliates. A good example of this is the Assemblies of God, which in 1986 reported an additional 14 million followers worldwide using conservative counting procedures.

Conclusion. From its inauspicious beginnings almost a century ago, the Pentecostal Movement has become a worldwide force of the first magnitude. It bears the distinction of being the world's fastest-growing major religious movement and boasts eight of the world's ten largest congregations, including the largest, Paul Cho's 500,000-member Yoido Full Gospel Church in Seoul, Korea.

Pentecostalism has always been a diverse phenomenon, but the contemporary reality is especially so. To the labyrinthine complexities of classical Pentecostalism must be added the kaleidoscopic world of neo-Pentecostalism. Although few generalizations can span the vast body of contemporary Pentecostalism, threads of continuity can be seen in a frank openness to supernatural gifts in a natural world, in the presupposition of an intimately involved and personal deity and in a simple and faithful biblicism. Across the Pentecostal-charismatic spectrum, one finds the unwavering conviction that, in the words of historian Grant Wacker, the gospel is still true—"not the old-fashioned gospel of the nineteenth century, but the awesome, wonder-working gospel of the first."

BIBLIOGRAPHY. R. M. Anderson, *Vision of the Disinherited: The Making of American Pentecostalism* (1979); D. B. Barrett, ed., *World Christian Encyclopedia* (1982); F. Bartleman, *Azusa Street* (1925, 1980); N. Bloch-Hoell, *The Pentecostal Movement* (1964); S. M. Burgess and G. B. McGee, eds., *Dictionary of Pentecostal and Charismatic Movements* (1988); F. T. Corum, ed., *Like as of Fire* (1981); D. W. Dayton, *Theological Roots of Pentecostalism* (1987); W. J. Hollenweger, *The Pentecostals* (ET, 1972); C. H. Jacquet, Jr., ed., *Yearbook of American and Canadian Churches* (1988); B. F. Lawrence, *The Apostolic Faith Restored* (1916); R. Quebedeaux, *The New Charismatics II* (1983); V. Synan, ed., *Aspects of Pentecostal-Charismatic Origins* (1975); V. Synan, *The Holiness-Pentecostal Movement in the United States* (1971); G. W. Wacker, "The Functions of Faith in Primitive Pentecostalism," *HTR* 77:3-4 (1984):353-375.

R. G. Robins

Pentecostal World Conference. A loosely organized fellowship of Pentecostal* groups throughout the world. Although preliminary meetings had been held in Stockholm, Sweden, in 1939, it was not until after World War 2* that an international conference became a reality. A contributing factor in calling the meeting was to offer cooperative aid to victims of the War. A second purpose was to work together "in spreading the full Gospel testimony in every country." Although initiated by European Pentecostals, representatives from twenty countries—including the U.S.—helped in the organization of the fellowship.

The 1947 conference, which was held in Zurich, Switzerland, was not an organizational meeting, but the group did create an office in Basel, Switzerland, and made provisions to publish a quarterly review, *Pentecost,* with Donald Gee, an English Pentecostal, as editor. Two years later a second conference was held in Paris (1949), where a constitution was adopted. Since 1949 triennial conferences have been held throughout the world, including London (1952), Stockholm (1955), Toronto (1958), Jerusalem (1961), Helsinki (1964), Rio de Janeiro (1967), Dallas (1970), Seoul (1973), London (1976), Vancouver, B.C. (1979), Nairobi (1982) and Zurich (1985). A 1989 meeting was scheduled for Singapore. The Pentecostal Fellowship of North America* cooperates with the Pentecostal World Conference. An advisory committee for the fellowship plans the triennial meetings and other activities.

BIBLIOGRAPHY. D. J. Du Plessis, *A Brief History of the World Pentecostal Fellowship (c. 1951); D. Gee, ed., Pentecost: A Review of World-Wide Pentecostal Missionary and Revival News* (1947-1966); *World Pentecost* (1971-); W. W. Menzies, *Anointed to Serve* (1971).   W. E. Warner

Perfectionism. The doctrine that holiness* or perfect love, brought about by the grace of God through faith, is attainable by every Christian in this life and sets believers free from willful sin.* This doctrine grew out of the teaching of John Wesley,* who described it as "the grand *depositum* which God has lodged with the people called Methodist."

Wesley believed that the clear teaching of Scripture* was that spiritual growth after conversion* culminates in a second work of grace wrought instantaneously in the heart of the believer. By this work the believer is filled with perfect love. As the work of God, it was to be accepted by faith and confirmed in the individual by the witness of the Holy Spirit.

While actual sin is dealt with at conversion, the believer eventually finds himself or herself again opposing God. In sanctification* the believer is cleansed from inbred sin—the selfish intent of the heart which is the root of such opposition—and freed to act in conformity with the will of God. The believer may then live without conscious, intentional sin. The doctrine was expressed in Charles Wesley's verse, "O for a heart to praise my God; a heart from sin set free."

Wesley taught that this perfect love was Christian perfection rather than human perfection, and that the Christian in this life would never be free from temptation, physical ailment or a multitude of cares. Perfect love "does not exclude ignorance and error and a thousand infirmities." Neither does perfect love exclude the believer from the possibility of sin itself, since the human will, acting freely, could always rebel against God. Sanctification for Wesley was not sinless perfection. Nor, on the other hand, did sanctification preclude the possibility of continued growth in God's grace. The result of this perfection of love was to be manifested in all areas of life, including economic, social and political life. Wesley himself was a strong antislavery advocate, regarding the institution of slavery as nothing less than "that villainy of villainies."

Such perfectionist doctrine found its way into numerous groups in America outside the Methodist Church. It was associated with the Oberlin theology* of Asa Mahan* and Charles G. Finney,* the first two presidents of Oberlin College.* They taught a doctrine of perfectionism made possible by the baptism of the Holy Spirit, which empowered and perfected the will of the believer to act in conformity with the will of God. Though not denying Wesley's emphasis on perfect love as moral perfection, Oberlin theology emphasized perfection of the will—the voluntary and conscious actions of Christians. Just as individuals sin voluntarily, so they can be made perfect voluntarily. Such perfectionism also influenced personal and institutional commitments to reform causes such as abolitionism* and women's rights. These were not only manifestations of sanctified Christian living, but hopeful signs of a perfect social and moral order yet to come.

Many American Methodists continued to embrace Wesley's doctrine of perfect love and remained within Methodism specifically to bear witness to that doctrine. Some, however, parted company with the Methodist Episcopal Church, perceiving a declining interest among Methodists in the doctrine. Chief among the groups that withdrew were the Wesleyan Methodist Connection (1843) and the Free Methodist Church* (1860). Other denominations also arose, maintaining a doctrine of sanctification characterized by perfectionism. Among these were The Salvation Army,* beginning in England in 1865, and the Church of the Nazarene,* arising out of the Wesleyan* Holiness Movement* and founded in Texas in 1908. Phoebe Palmer,* an influential Holiness teacher of the nineteenth century, taught a radical perfectionism that maintained the present possibility of the eradication of sin for Christians. For some, this experience became associated with the themes of Pentecost and the enduement with power, thus paving the way for the emergence of the twentieth-century Pentecostal Movement and its emphasis on Spirit baptism and tongues as a third moment in Christian experience.

Several other small denominations and sectarian groups in America, some of them communitarian movements, were also built on a belief in both personal and social perfection. Often outside of Christian orthodoxy, they frequently reflected a confusing mixture of doctrinal and philosophical positions. Among these was John Humphrey Noyes,* who was influenced by a revival* in 1831 and learned theology under Yale's* Nathaniel Taylor.* Claiming sinless perfection for himself, he believed that his was the only gospel relevant for this dispensation. He also sought social perfection in the establishment of several small communitarian societies, the best known being that of Oneida, New York. These failed efforts, striving after the establishment of the millennium on earth, were a long way from the perfectionism taught by Wesley, Mahan or Finney. Nevertheless, they serve as a reminder of the several components of perfectionism and of the far-reaching influence of perfectionism in American Christianity and culture.

BIBLIOGRAPHY. C. G. Finney, *Lectures in Systematic Theology* (1846); C. E. Jones, *Perfectionist Persuasion: The Holiness Movement and American Methodism, 1867-1936* (1974); A. Mahan, *Doctrine of the Will* (1845); A. Mahan, *Scripture Doctrine of Christian Perfection* (1839); T. Smith, *Called Unto Holiness* (1962); B. B. Warfield, *Perfectionism,* 2 vols. (1931); J. Wesley, *A Plain Account of Christian Perfection* (1777).

R. J. Green

Perkins, William (1558-1602). English Reformed* theologian.* Perkins graduated from, was converted at,* and taught at Christ's College, Cambridge University. The University's most popular preacher of the day, scholars and plain townspeople alike flocked to hear his reasoned and passionate sermons. John Cotton* who became teacher of Boston's First Church as an unregenerate student was so conscience-stricken by Perkins's preaching* that he reports having secretly rejoiced at Perkins's death. Yet after his conversion Cotton emulated Perkins's message and style. An early biographer wrote, "An excellent Chirurgeon [surgeon] he was at joynting of a broken soul, and at stating of a doubtfull conscience." His "practical divinity" analyzed and preached a psychology of conversion upon which the ministry of New England's first generation was closely modeled.

Perkins defined theology* itself as "the science of living blessedly for ever." The Puritanism* which Perkins helped delineate was an experiential form of religion based on the primacy of God's action (as opposed to human effort) in salvation.* He protested liturgical formalities in the Church of England* and the theology of "semi-Pelagian Papists" in such works as his *Reformed Catholike* (1597) and *A Golden Chain* (1597), but held to the non-separatist position which informed the founders of Massachusetts Bay and Connecticut. His works, published individually and in massive collected editions, were reprinted through the seventeenth century and highly esteemed by Puritans as next to those of John Calvin. Among Perkins's students were John Robinson,* pastor of "Pilgrims"* in England and Holland before their departure for Plymouth Colony; and William Ames,* whose theological textbook was basic to ministerial education in seventeenth-century New England.

BIBLIOGRAPHY. P. Miller, *The New England Mind* (1939); N. Pettit, *The Heart Prepared* (1966); W. Haller, *The Rise of Puritanism* (1938).

C. E. Hambrick-Stowe

Permanent Deacon. In the early Palestinian churches the leaders were elders* or presbyters, and in the early gentile churches the leaders were bishops and deacons. Gradually, with the decline of Palestinian Christianity and the rapid growth of the gentile churches, there emerged the threefold order of bishops, presbyters and deacons,* which is clear in Ignatius of Antioch (d.117). In the Patristic period the office of deacon was normally held for life; that is, it was permanent. Later, in Roman Catholic* and Anglican* churches the diaconate become a first stage in preparation for the priesthood. Since Vatican II* the Catholic Church has given extensive consideration to the office of deacon, and permanent deacons have become widely recognized. They may baptize, give Communion,* assist at marriages,* and preside at funerals. Older married men can, in certain cases, become deacons, but younger men ordained as deacons are bound to celibacy. The Eastern Orthodox Churches* and the Episcopal Church also recognize permanent deacons as a full and equal order of ministry.*

BIBLIOGRAPHY. J. M. Barnett, *The Diaconate: A Full and Equal Order* (1981).

D. S. Armentrout

Perseverance of the Saints. *See* ETERNAL
SECURITY.

**Peter, Johann Friederich (John Frederick)
(1746-1813).** Moravian* minister* and composer.
Born in Heerendijk, Holland, after completing his
education Peter joined his father in America in
1769.

He taught in a boys' school at Nazareth, Pennsylvania, for one year and then served the Moravian
Church as diarist and pastor first at Bethlehem,
Pennsylvania (1770-1786), then from 1786 to 1793
at Hope, New Jersey; Lititz, Pennsylvania; Graceham, Maryland; and Salem, North Carolina. He
then returned to Bethlehem, where he lived out
his final years. Peter was the primary force in the
musical development of each of these communities.

Peter had copied musical works while in school
in Germany and brought his manuscripts to
America. His own musical works include six
quintets for strings, thought to be the earliest
preserved chamber music in America. His early
anthems were written for small choirs with strings
and organs, while his later works were written for
larger choirs, incorporating string and wind instrument parts. Peter composed a "Psalm of Joy" in
1783 for the first official celebration of July 4 in
Salem, North Carolina. In 1811 he directed a
complete performance of Haydn's *Creation* at
Bethlehem, with him at the organ. In all he
composed some eighty anthems noted for their
instrumental and vocal lines. The most notable of
the early American hymnwriters, Peter's work
exemplifies the important musical contribution
the Moravians made to American religious life.

BIBLIOGRAPHY. *DAB* VII; K. Kroeger, "Moravian
Music in America," *Unitas Fratrum* (1975); H. T.
David, *Musical Life in the Pennsylvania Settlements
of the Unitas Fratrum* (1959).   A. H. Frank

Peters, George Nathaniel Henry (1825-1909).
Lutheran* minister and biblical scholar. Born in
New Berlin, Pennsylvania, following studies at
Gettysburg College, Peters attended Wittenberg
University (1846-1850). Profoundly influenced by
the "American Lutheranism" of Samuel Simon
Schmucker,* Peters was ordained* by the Witten-
berg Synod and served congregations in Wood-
bury, Springfield, Xenia and Plymouth, Ohio. Poor
health forced him to take early retirement.

Peters turned to writing. His major work, *The
Theocratic Kingdom* (1883, 3 vols.), was praised by
the twentieth-century evangelical Bible teacher
Wilbur M. Smith* as "the most exhaustive, thor-

oughly annotated and logically arranged study of
Biblical prophecy that appeared in our country
during the nineteenth century." In 2,000 pages
Peters cited more than four thousand authors,
ancient and modern, indicating a complete mastery of the subject of eschatology.* Often ignored
by fellow Lutherans, Peters "lived and worked in
an oblivion that seems almost mysterious." At the
time of his death, October 7, 1909, at the age of 84,
Peters was virtually forgotten. The re-publication of
The Theocratic Kingdom in 1957 led to a rediscovery of his prodigious work.

BIBLIOGRAPHY. W. M. Smith, "Preface," in G. N.
H. Peters, *The Theocratic Kingdom* (1957).

C. G. Fry

Pettingill, William Leroy (1866-1950). Fundamentalist* Bible teacher, author and cofounder of
the Philadelphia School of the Bible. Born in New
York City, Pettingill was ordained* a Baptist*
minister* in 1899 and served at North Church,
Wilmington, Delaware (1903-1913). In 1914 he
assisted in founding Philadelphia School of the
Bible and was dean (1914-1928) under its president, C. I. Scofield.* Later he served as pastor of
First Church, New York City (1948-1950).

Throughout his life Pettingill championed the
fundamentalist* cause and for a time served as vice
president of the Independent Fundamental
Churches of America.* In his preaching, teaching
and writing, he promoted dispensational* premillennialism,* and was a popular speaker at Bible
and prophetic conferences.* As editor and author,
Pettingill founded two periodicals: *Serving-and-
Waiting* (1911) and *Just a Word* (1928). He was
one of the consulting editors for the Scofield
Reference Bible* and among his numerous works
were *God's Prophecies for Plain People* (1923), *By
Grace through Faith Plus Nothing: Simple Studies
in Galatians* (1938) and *Simple Studies in the
Revelation* (1916).

BIBLIOGRAPHY. S. G. Cole, *The History of Fundamentalism* (1931).   R. L. Petersen

Pew, John Howard (1882-1971). Industrialist,
Christian layman* and philanthropist.* Born in
Bradford, Pennsylvania, and educated at Shadyside
Academy, Grove City College and Massachusetts
Institute of Technology, Pew went to work for the
family-owned Sun Oil Company as an engineer,
though he quickly rose through the ranks to
become president in 1912. He continued in this
capacity for thirty-five years, responsive to the
interests of his employees and the rapidly changing American and international industrial econ-

omy. Upon resigning the presidency in 1947, Pew became board chairman of Sun Oil Company, director of Sun Shipbuilding and Dry Dock Company and director of the Philadelphia National Bank. However, he devoted much of his energy to his philanthropic interests.

Pew was a strong supporter of Christian and independent education, primarily Grove City College where he served as president of the board of trustees. His most significant religious role was in funding a number of Presbyterian,* fundamentalist* and evangelical* causes, where Pew's primary interest was in maintaining conservative Christianity and free enterprise in American society. These commitments led him to support causes as diverse as Carl McIntire's* International Council of Christian Churches* and the fledgling evangelical journal, *Christianity Today.* Evangelical leaders in the post-World War 2* era often sought Pew's funding for their enterprises but sometimes felt the constraints of the oil magnate's conservative theological and political views.

BIBLIOGRAPHY. G. M. Marsden, *Reforming Fundamentalism* (1987); M. Sennholz, *Faith and Freedom: The Journal of a Great American J. Howard Pew* (1975).   R. L. Petersen

Pew Rents. An annual fee that determined seating in a meetinghouse. In the colonial era, when a new meetinghouse was built, the location of a family's seat was determined by how much they had contributed to the building of the structure. If the meetinghouse presently in use was reseated, as was often done, parishioners were seated according to how much they had given to the annual ministerial rate, which was identified as the pew rent. Generally, families were seated in separate pews, and the closer the pew was to the pulpit, the higher their standing in the community. The social hierarchy was thus observed in the weekly communal setting, as affluent families could afford the choice and more expensive pews, and the poor had to content themselves with pews to the rear of the sanctuary. This practice was continued by some churches into the early nineteenth century.

BIBLIOGRAPHY. O. E. Winslow, *Meetinghouse Hill* (1952).   K. P. Minkema

Philadelphia Baptist Association. Oldest surviving Baptist* association in America. In Baptist polity,* an "association" is a regional grouping of churches designed for fellowship,* mutual guidance and cooperation in missions and other endeavors. As early as the 1640s Baptist churches in England formed such associations, whence the

pattern was brought to America. The Philadelphia Association was formed in 1707, with five cooperating churches, none of them more than a few years old. In 1742 the Association adopted the influential Philadelphia Baptist Confession of Faith and in 1764 sponsored the first Baptist college in America at Providence, Rhode Island (now Brown University*). The Association also sponsored an "evangelist* at large" to itinerate on the frontier, founding new churches. By the 1750s the Association extended from New England to the South, functioning essentially as a national body. It proved vastly influential upon Baptists in America through its confession,* moderate Calvinist* theology,* organizational pattern and missionary zeal.

BIBLIOGRAPHY. A. D. Gillette, ed., *Minutes of the Philadelphia Baptist Association from 1707 to 1807* (1851); Robert G. Torbet, *A Social History of the Philadelphia Baptist Associations, 1707-1940* (1944).   H. L. McBeth

Philadelphia College and Academy. *See* UNIVERSITY OF PENNSYLVANIA.

Philanthropy, Christian. Christianity inherited from Judaism its concern for the poor, the widow, the orphan and the stranger. Jesus' teaching and example raised charity to new intensity, with the cross becoming the supreme example of self-giving. No other religion places such stress on giving to others.

During the Middle Ages institutions developed within the church to care for the needy. Many of these were monasteries. Monastic life included renunciation of private property. St. Francis of Assisi especially exemplified self-giving service to outcasts of all types. In England, when Henry VIII disbanded the monasteries, the system of caring for the needy was thrown into chaos. The Elizabethan Poor Law was one response to the need. But also, the cultural expectation of *noblesse oblige* received new emphasis. Benevolent giving reached a unique intensity in English-speaking countries.

In America, philanthropic activity had to await a surplus of wealth in the colonies. The Puritan* conscience, while it drove people to labor, also pointed to the dangers of riches and stressed community responsibility. This intensified benevolent giving. By the eighteenth century Americans were following the British in philanthropy. Hundreds of voluntary associations were founded in the nineteenth century to meet every sort of specialized need, from reviving drowning victims to caring for the poor.

In the nineteenth century the Civil War* stimulated the rise of large philanthropic organizations such as the Christian Commission,* Sanitary Commission* and Western Sanitary Commission* which, with the financial support of numerous businessmen, came to the aid of Union soldiers and their families. In the era of Reconstruction, freedman's relief societies were organized to assist freed slaves. In what has been described as a "philanthropic revolution," citizens at all levels of society responded to the fund-raising efforts of churches, relief societies and organizations such as ladies' aid societies. One writer of the period estimated that wartime contributions by 1864, in the North alone, had totaled $212 million. This tremendous burst in philanthropic activity was to reshape the social reformers' vision of what was possible and open a new era in American philanthropy.

One of the more noticeable features of philanthropy in America has been the large contributions to various Christian causes and institutions coming from wealthy industrialists and businessmen such as Andrew Carnegie, John Wanamaker,* William Colgate,* John Price Crozer, Cyrus H. McCormick,* John D. Rockefeller and J. Howard Pew.* Numerous organizations, such as American Friends Service Committee,* Church World Service,* Catholic Relief Services and World Vision, International,* have played visible roles in providing channels for the public's response to human need in the twentieth century. While philanthropic efforts have rarely, if ever, equaled the needs, Christian philanthropy has regularly pioneered in social service and has sensitized the nation's conscience.

BIBLIOGRAPHY. L. P. Brockett, *The Philanthropic Results of the War in America* (1864); J. Leiby, *A History of Social Welfare and Social Work in the United States, 1815-1972* (1978); R. Niebuhr, *The Contribution of Religion to Social Work* (1932).

R. E. Selleck

Phillips, (W)illiam (T)homas (1893-1973). African-American Oneness* Pentecostal* preacher* and founding bishop* of the Apostolic Overcoming Holy Church of God. Phillips began his career as a preacher in the Methodist Episcopal Church.* In 1912, discouraged by the religious restrictions of the Methodist Episcopal Church, Phillips joined the Apostolic Faith Mission, where he began to study and preach the Holiness* doctrine of sanctification* and accepted Oneness Pentecostalism. Four years later, in 1916, Phillips organized the

Greater Adams Holiness Church, which in 1920 became the Ethiopian (renamed *Apostolic* in 1927) Overcoming Holy Church of God in Mobile, Alabama. Bishop Phillips emphasized the baptism of the Holy Spirit* and practiced divine healing,* foot washing,* holy dancing and water baptism* in the name of "Jesus only." Bishop Phillips, who served as the sole bishop of the church for fifty-seven years, died in 1973, leaving behind a sect of nearly 200 churches, 1,000 ministers and missionaries, and well over 12,000 members in the U.S. The church had also spread to the West Indies, Haiti and Africa.

BIBLIOGRAPHY. J. T. Nichol, *Pentecostalism* (1966); W. T. Phillips, *Excerpts from the Life of Rt. Rev. W. T. Phillips and Fundamentals of the Apostolic Overcoming Holy Church of God, Inc.* (1967).

M. C. Bruce

Philosophical Theology. The discipline of thought which attempts to demonstrate truths of God and religion by means of philosophical methodology. Philosophical theology does not seek to correlate revealed truths as do dogmatic or systematic theology.* Instead, it relies on a rational exploration of the issues. Philosophical theology need not be a natural theology,* which assumes a general revelation of God. Philosophical theology may operate apart from such a stipulation though it does not foreclose it.

The beginnings of philosophical theology may be traced to the pre-Socratic philosophers, each of whose first principle also had divine qualities. For example, Thales, who believed that all was water, also endowed water with the spiritual qualities of deity. Plato's speculative explorations, such as in the *Timaeus,* come under the heading of philosophical theology, as does Aristotle's argumentation for an unmoved mover. Philosophical theology continued throughout the Middle Ages under the aegis of natural theology. As the world of thought moved into the modern period, philosophical theology remained an important enterprise, but with a significant difference. The new critical spirit also made it possible to reach more critical conclusions. David Hume in particular must be mentioned as a philosopher who came to negative assessments on virtually all areas of philosophical theology.

Some of the more significant issues frequently addressed by philosophical theology are: (1) the relationship between faith and reason; (2) the meaningfulness of religious language; (3) the validity of religious experience*; (4) the existence of God; (5) the nature of God; (6) the possibility of divine revelation; (7) the rational tenability of the Incarnation; (8) the compatibility of evil with the existence of an all-good and all-powerful God; (9) the possibility of miracles; and (10) the religious basis for ethics.

In North America philosophical theology has been carried out within a number of schools of thought. Jonathan Edwards* himself was not disinclined toward philosophical matters with his own synthesis of the Platonic-Augustinian tradition and the Locke-Newtonian innovations of his day. Edwards came to the startling conclusion that God is identical with space and that empirical reality is produced by the mind of God.

Analytical philosophy is dominant in American universities today. In this broad tradition, which comprises approaches varying from the logical positivism of A. J. Ayer to the ordinary language philosophy of Ludwig Wittgenstein, questions of the meaning of religious language have dominated. Technical issues have been assessed on the basis of whether the language used is meaningful at all. Where meaningfulness has been allowed, the meaning of specific terms has been settled by observing their function within specific contexts of use, not in their reference to independent reality.

Pragmatism has been considered a uniquely American philosophy. Roughly speaking, in this tradition truth is determined by the practical consequences of a belief. Consequently, pragmatism has yielded relativism (William James*) and atheism (John Dewey).

Another American contribution to philosophical theology has been the process* thought of Alfred North Whitehead and Charles Hartshorne. In this system God is seen as a finite, changing being who influences the world only through moral persuasion. In the 1980s process thought was becoming increasingly influential in seminaries* and other theologically oriented schools. Finally, neo-Thomism* and Augustinianism* (in several variations) have continued to make their presence felt in the thought-world of philosophical theology. In these various schools classical and medieval categories continue to be applied to contemporary issues.

Philosophical theology holds an important place in American philosophical thought. It is unlikely that it will become less significant in the foreseeable future.

BIBLIOGRAPHY. J. D. Collins, *God in Modern Philosophy* (1959); B. Kuklick, *Churchmen and Philosophers* (1985); A. Flew and A. MacIntyre, eds., *New Essays in Philosophical Theology* (1955); T. V. Morris, *The Logic of God Incarnate* (1986).

W. Corduan

Philosophy of Religion. Philosophy of religion is the critical philosophical reflection on the claims of religion. Historically, philosophers have always been interested in questions of religion—particularly issues centered around the existence of God and how God might be known. Christian theologians,* on the other hand, have also had some relationship to philosophy, even when it has gone unacknowledged. Most theologians have been indebted in one way or another to philosophy and its categories, for one of the objectives of Christian theology* has been to apply the truths of Christianity to the problems and situations of each successive age. But the term *philosophy of religion* in its contemporary meaning is of relatively recent vintage, though arising from the Enlightenment* and first appearing in the title of German philosophical works of the late eighteenth and early nineteenth centuries.

Modern philosophers of religion try to ascertain the reasonableness of religious beliefs—a study that can be carried out by those both within and without a particular religious tradition. Strictly speaking, it is a discipline of philosophy, not theology. Among the classic questions philosophers of religion have considered are: Can belief in God be justified? Does the existence of evil negate theism*? Is religious language unique and special? What is the nature of revelation? How is reason related to faith? What are miracles? Is there life after death? The multiplicity and breadth of these questions mean that philosophers of religion have worked in numerous contexts and with the assistance of many academic disciplines.

The scope of philosophy of religion may be seen in its relation to other approaches to the study of religion. The phenomenology of religion asks what religion is or says but does not try to establish the truth of religious claims. Apologetics* is a believer's reasoned defense of a given religious faith. Systematic* theology articulates a faith from a confessional standpoint and applies it to the lives of its adherents. Philosophical theology (or natural theology*) attempts to discern what may be known about God apart from revelation or any faith commitment. But none of these disciplines focuses specifically on the truth and coherence of religious beliefs themselves. So contemporary philosophy of religion has fundamentally different aims from these other disciplines, yet it overlaps them in many significant ways. Historically speaking, the term has had various meanings, sometimes being used for what today's philosophers would call *metaphysics, philosophical theology* or even *religious philosophy.*

Major philosophers of the Enlightenment, faced with the problem of the reasonableness of religion, dealt with the truth of religion and came to differing conclusions. This is seen in alternatives offered by Hume's *Dialogues Concerning Natural Religion* (1779), Kant's *Religion Within the Limits of Reason Alone* (1793) and Hegel's *Lectures on the Philosophy of Religion* (1832; ET 1895). The latter presented religion as part of his overall philosophical idealism and sought to present a philosophically substantiated and credible version of the Christian faith.

American philosophers of religion have dealt with the same issues from within their own contexts. In the eighteenth century one of America's most acute philosophers of religion was Jonathan Edwards,* a Calvinist* minister* who was influenced by the philosophy of John Locke (1632-1704) and wrote major philosophical works from a strongly confessional standpoint. His most famous works were *Religious Affections* (1746), dealing with the nature of religious experience, and *Freedom of the Will* (1754). An important philosophical tradition for a variety of eighteenth- and nineteenth-century American evangelical* theologians was Scottish Realism or Common Sense philosophy.* While not strictly a philosophy of religion, it was an attempt to answer the issues raised by Enlightenment thinkers and served to establish the possibility and necessity of religious knowledge and theology.

For most of the nineteenth century, however, American academic philosophers followed the lead of Europeans, particularly German thinkers, both in their philosophy and in their analysis of religion. A "golden age" of American philosophy came in a blossoming of philosophical thought during the latter half of the nineteenth and the first third of the twentieth century. Philosophy provided ways of interpreting the advances of the new social sciences and gave promise of solving the problems of life in a way that theology formerly had tried to do. As Sydney E. Ahlstrom* put it, "indeed in certain quarters the 'philosophy of religion' was looked upon as the higher form of life into which theology and dogmatics had evolved. As at no other time in American history, philosophy was hewing wood and drawing water for the Church."

Major American figures in this period were Charles Pierce (1839-1916), William James,* Josiah Royce,* George Santayana (1863-1952), Alfred North Whitehead (1861-1947) and John Dewey (1859-1952). These philosophers propounded views of the nature of humanity and science, as

well as of the place of human beings in the cosmos. Thus their philosophical writings were religious in orientation. From their positions in philosophy departments in major American universities and through their writings in nonreligious journals of opinion, a philosophical approach to religion enjoyed a period of prominence in American intellectual life. But perhaps most influential in the American churches was the tradition of philosophic idealism known as "personalism" and promulgated first by Borden Parker Bowne,* and then systematized and developed by his students A. C. Knudsen* and Edgar S. Brightman,* all Methodists* who taught at Boston University. Bowne's philosophical legacy was to lay the foundation for Protestant liberalism.*

From the late 1930s through the 1950s there was a revitalization of American theology through the impetus of theologians such as Paul Tillich,* Reinhold Niebuhr* and Richard Niebuhr.* Of these, Tillich was the most philosophically oriented and sought to bring theology into dialog with other disciplines, especially philosophy. During this same period, Henry N. Wieman* represented the empirical tradition of American philosophy, arguing that religious truths could be empirically verified.

Since World War 2* the dominant philosophical approaches to religion in America have been existentialism,* phenomenology and analytic philosophy. Intense interest in the analysis of language is a chief characteristic of philosophy of religion today. This focus arose from the later works of Ludwig Wittgenstein (1889-1951), particularly his *Philosophical Investigations* (1953). Earlier, the logical positivism of the 1930s maintained that only a statement which could be empirically verified could be considered true or false. Thus, religious statements about God were nonsense because they could not be verified this way. Those who have sought to philosophically vindicate "God-talk" in this arena include John Hick and Frederick Ferre.

Process* philosophy and theology are contemporary movements which, out of their critiques of traditional theism, have raised provocative questions in the philosophy of religion. Whitehead's American pupil, Charles Hartshorne, has done significant work in this area, along with John B. Cobb, Lewis S. Ford and David Ray Griffin. A leading American philosopher of religion whose work spans a number of issues is Alvin Plantinga.

Roman Catholic* theology, because of its base in Thomism,* traditionally has been heavily influenced by the Aristotelian tradition. One central concern of this tradition is natural theology* or the arguments for the existence of God. In the nineteenth century, Vatican I* expressed the Roman Catholic position on the relationship of faith and reason and argued for a valid natural theology. In the 1960s Vatican II* approached issues of reason and revelation in a biblical-historical framework and moved away from a reliance on philosophical categories. Both councils have, in their times, greatly affected the relationship between philosophy and theology in American Catholicism.

BIBLIOGRAPHY. W. J. Abraham, *An Introduction to the Philosophy of Religion* (1985); D. Allen, *Philosophy for Understanding Theology* (1985); S. Cahn and D. Shatz, *Contemporary Philosophy of Religion* (1982); B. Kuklick, *Churchmen and Philosophers: From Jonathan Edwards to John Dewey* (1985); B. Kuklick, *The Rise of American Philosophy* (1977); B. Mitchell, *The Philosophy of Religion* (1971); H. N. Wieman, *American Philosophies of Religion* (1936).   D. K. McKim

Philpott, Peter Wiley (1865-1957). Fundamentalist* pastor* and preacher.* Born in Iona, Elgin County, Ontario, Canada, he was a direct descendant of John Philpott, the first person to live on the Talbot settlement in southwestern Ontario, and of Peter MacGregor, one of the founders of London, Ontario. Philpott's education was received in grammar school and at the School of Languages in Ontario. He received the honorary Doctor of Divinity degree from Wheaton College,* Illinois, in 1925. During World War 1* Philpott served as an active recruiter (1914-1917) and acted as a presiding judge over a Military Conscription Court (1917-1918). He was a trustee of Wheaton College and a president of African Inland Mission* for North America.

Earlier in life Philpott was a member of The Salvation Army* (1884-1894), serving in various places in Ontario. He was also an evangelist* for a two-year period (1894-1896). He is best remembered as the founding minister and leader of The Philpott Tabernacle, Hamilton, Ontario, Canada (1896-1922). During that time the membership of this nondenominational congregation grew from thirty-five persons to over 1,700. After leaving the Tabernacle, Philpott became pastor of the Moody Memorial Church in Chicago (1922-1929), during which time a new church building was erected at a cost of over one million dollars. From Chicago, Philpott went to Los Angeles, where he was minister of the Church of the Open Door (1929-1934). Thereafter, he continued to preach in numerous communities in Ontario. It is reported that during his lifetime he delivered over 22,000 sermons. Philpott died at his home in Toronto, April 1, 1957.

See also ASSOCIATED GOSPEL CHURCHES.

BIBLIOGRAPHY. *Hamilton Spectator* (April 1, 1957); *Hamilton Spectator* (April 2, 1957).
                                              C. A. Russell

Pickett, Jarrel Waskom (1890-1981). Methodist* missionary* to India. Born in Texas and educated at Asbury College, Wilmore, Kentucky, Pickett set sail in 1910 as a missionary to India under the auspices of the Methodist Episcopal Church. There he served with distinction for the next forty-six years as pastor,* evangelist,* superintendent,* editor of *The Indian Witness* and bishop* (1935-1956).

Pickett had a profound influence on many of India's political leaders, including Mahatma Gandhi, B. R. Ambedkar, Prime Ministers Jawaharial Nehru and Indira Gandhi. He promoted educational and medical institutions and the building of many village churches. He was instrumental in the founding of Leonard Theological College, Jabalpur, and the United Mission to Nepal. His most outstanding literary contribution, *Christian Mass Movements in India* (1933), made a profound impact on missionary Donald McGavran,* who later became the prophet of the Church Growth Movement.*

BIBLIOGRAPHY. J. W. Pickett, *My Twentieth-Century Odyssey* (1980).   J. T. Seamands

Pidgeon, George Campbell (1872-1971). Canadian church leader. Born in a Scottish community on the south shore of the Gaspé Peninsula in eastern Quebec, Pidgeon early absorbed the qualities of much of the late nineteenth-century evangelical* Presbyterianism* which would remain the hallmarks of his life and ministry.* He was conservative in theology,* stressed the element of personal decision, embodied piety,* gave leadership in movements of moral reform and sought cooperation among the churches. In a distinctly personal way, he was also a refined and gracious Christian gentleman.

Pidgeon graduated from Presbyterian College, Montreal, pastored in Quebec and Ontario, was professor of practical theology at Westminster Hall, Vancouver (1909-1915), and then came to his great ministry at Bloor St. Church, Toronto, in 1915, where he would remain until 1948. Toronto was one of the preaching* centers of the Protestant* world when Pidgeon arrived, but Pidgeon readily held his own. He spent a period as first convener of the Board of Moral and Social Reform of the

Presbyterian Church in Canada.*

In 1917 he became convener of the Board of Home Missions, with its particular responsibility for western Canada. The scarcity of population particularly impressed upon him the need of church union,* and in 1921 he became the convener of the committee working toward that end. He was chosen as moderator of the Presbyterian* General Assembly* in 1925, and when on June 10 of that year the Methodists,* the Congregationalists* and two-thirds of the Presbyterians joined to form the United Church of Canada,* he was chosen as moderator. His great and unrealized hope was that the union would bring revival* to Canada. Upon his retirement the tradition of Bloor St. changed radically with the coming of the brilliant theological liberal E. M. Howse.

BIBLIOGRAPHY. J. W. Grant, *George Pidgeon: A Biography* (1962).   I. S. Rennie

Pieper, Franz August Otto (1852-1931). Lutheran Church—Missouri Synod* theologian.* Born at Carwitz, Pomerania, Germany, Pieper immigrated to Wisconsin with his widowed mother and two brothers, August and Reinhold, who also became seminary professors. He studied at Northwestern College, Watertown, Wisconsin, and after graduation from Concordia Seminary, Saint Louis, in 1875, he held pastorates in Wisconsin before becoming a professor at Concordia in 1878.

Pieper served as president of Concordia Seminary from 1887 to 1931 and as president of the Lutheran Church—Missouri Synod from 1899 to 1911. As editor of the periodical *Lehre and Wehre* and author of tracts and books, he was involved in the theological controversies of his day among North American and German Lutherans, particularly over predestination.* His legacy is found above all in his three-volume *Christian Dogmatics,* published in German (1917-1924; ET 1950-1957), which summarizes the positions of the Missouri Synod and demonstrates both their origins in the theology of Lutheran orthodoxy* and the points at which they differ from the positions of contemporary schools of thought, above all the Erlangen School. Pieper ably defended the verbal inspiration of the Scriptures,* the vicarious atonement* of Christ and justification* through faith, in the context of his thoroughgoing review of the whole of Christian teaching. He opposed every doctrinal compromise. His approach reveals his strong concern for the practical application of theology to believers' lives.

BIBLIOGRAPHY. *DAB* VII; C. S. Meyer, *Log Cabin to Luther Tower* (1965).   R. A. Kolb

Piepkorn, Arthur Carl (1907-73). Lutheran* theologian.* Born in Milwaukee, Wisconsin, Piepkorn was educated in Lutheran Church—Missouri Synod schools, including Concordia Seminary in St. Louis (1928). His graduate study in the U.S. and abroad (including the American School of Oriental Research, Baghdad), earned him a Ph.D. from the University of Chicago (1932) in archaeology. From his parish pastorate he entered the military chaplaincy* early in World War 2.* Teaching at the U.S. Army Chaplain School in Cambridge, Massachusetts (1942-1950), he became its commandant. This exposure to American religious pluralism* gave his confessional* Lutheranism ecumenical* breadth.

Called to his seminary alma mater, Piepkorn became distinguished as Concordia's erudite professor of systematic theology* (1951-1973). A consultant to the Federal, later National Council of Churches* department of worship and the arts (1947-1960), he was much in demand for his breadth of learning and his evangelical* commitment. Early in the era of bilateral dialogs, he became a key member of the Lutheran-Roman Catholic dialog* (1965-1973). A perceptive thinker and stimulating teacher, he cast old formulations into fresh contexts, often to the dismay of traditionalists less versed in their own history. When the notorious conflict in the Missouri Synod debated the orthodoxy* of Concordia Seminary, Piepkorn felt himself deeply involved—and confident. His sudden death was seen as an early casualty of the schism leading to the formation of Seminex—Concordia Seminary in Exile—later renamed Christ Seminary.

Piepkorn's magnum opus was published posthumously and remains a standard reference work: *Profiles in Belief: The Religious Bodies in the United States and Canada,* 3 vols. (1977-1979). Here the full range of his scholarship and experience places even prosaic facts into the embracing context of Christ's church universal.

E. T. Bachmann

Pierce, Lovick (1785-1879). Methodist* minister* and presiding elder. Born in Martin County, North Carolina, Pierce grew up in Barnwell County, South Carolina. While he came under Baptist* influence during his earlier years, Pierce's family began attending the Methodist Church in 1803, and in 1804 he experienced conversion* under the preaching of a circuit rider.* Pierce entered the Methodist ministry in 1804 and was assigned a circuit in South Carolina and in 1806 was reassigned to the Apalachee circuit. In 1809 he married, and in that same year Francis Asbury* appointed Pierce as presiding elder of the Oconee District in Georgia. Elected to the first delegated Methodist General Conference in 1812, Pierce served as a delegate to every general conference between 1824 and his death in 1879.

Drafted for the War of 1812, Pierce was assigned as a chaplain* at Savannah. During the years 1815 to 1816, he studied medicine at the University of Pennsylvania* in order to serve as a preaching physician. The first general conference (1846) of the newly formed Methodist Episcopal Church, South, meeting in Petersburg, Virginia, selected Pierce as fraternal representative to the 1848 General Conference of the Northern Church. Pierce never attended the conference, however. Growing animosity over the issue of slavery continued to widen the chasm between the two denominations. The general conference refused to acknowledge the legitimacy of the Southern church nor would it recognize Pierce as a fraternal delegate. After the Civil War* the two churches established friendly relations, and the elderly Pierce was again elected to head the fraternal delegation for the Methodist Episcopal Church, South. Lovick Pierce was known as a stirring preacher, but his son George Foster Pierce (1811-1884) was to gain even greater fame among Southern Methodists as a preacher and church leader.

BIBLIOGRAPHY. H. Luccock and P. Hutchison, *The Story of Methodism* (1926); G. G. Pierce, *The Life and Times of George F. Pierce* (1888); J. P. Pilkington, "Pierce, Lovick," in N. B. Harmon, ed., *The Encyclopedia of World Methodism,* vol. II (1974). B. K. Turley

Pierce, Robert ("Bob") Willard (1914-1976). Evangelist* and founder of World Vision International.* Born in Fort Dodge, Iowa, Pierce's family moved to California in 1924, where Pierce attended public schools and Pasadena College. In 1937 Pierce began an evangelistic career that took him throughout California and later to Japan, Korea and the Philippines. He was ordained* in 1940 by the First Baptist Church of Wilmington, California, and served in the Los Angeles Evangelistic Center. Pierce was one of the early leaders of Youth for Christ International.*

In 1947 he made his first trip to Asia as a Youth for Christ evangelist. There, in the aftermath of World War 2, he was confronted with the immediacy of human suffering and need. His sensitivity to the needs he encountered marked a turning point in his life and led to the founding of World Vision International (1950). Pierce argued that "we must

first treat people's physical needs so we can then minister to their real (spiritual) needs." Using documentary films, radio and personal appearances to arouse an evangelical* social consciousness, Pierce raised hundreds of thousands of dollars for orphanages, hospitals, national pastors and missionaries. By 1965 over sixty-five thousand children in twenty countries were being supported.

Pierce was forced to resign his presidency of World Vision in 1967 due to failing health. However, several years later he founded a new ministry with the help of World Vision, the Samaritan's Purse, devoted to raising money for evangelism and relief in Asia. Pierce helped to give a vision of the gospel for the whole person to American evangelical Protestantism.

BIBLIOGRAPHY. M. P. Dunker, *Man of Vision, Woman of Prayer* (1980); R. Gehman, *Let My Heart Be Broken* (1960). R. L. Petersen

Pierson, Abraham (c.1645-1707). Congregational* minister* and educator. The son of a Puritan* minister, Abraham Pierson the elder, young Pierson graduated from Harvard College* in 1668. He became a pastoral colleague with his father at New Ark (Newark), New Jersey, where the elder Pierson had immigrated with a group of New Englanders unhappy with the liberalized church membership* policy of the Half-Way Covenant. At his father's death the son became the sole minister of the congregation, remaining until 1692, when he left over a difference of opinion regarding church government. Pierson favored a moderate presbyterian government, while the congregation favored congregationalism.* For the next two years (1692-1694) he served as pulpit supply in Greenwich, Connecticut, but in 1694 he accepted a call to Killingworth, Connecticut, where he remained until his death. Pierson was critical of directions taken by Harvard and become involved in the founding (1701) and early leadership of the Collegiate School in the Colony of Connecticut, later known as Yale College.* Pierson served as the first rector of the school, which he envisioned as committed to preserving the true Puritan heritage. Torn between his duties as a pastor and his interests in the new college, he died before resolving the dilemma.

BIBLIOGRAPHY. *AAP* I; T. Clap, *History of Yale College, 1700-1838* (1841); *DAB* VII.

A. M. Carden

Pierson, (A)rthur (T)appan (1837-1911). Presbyterian* minister,* mission* theorist and

Bible expositor. Born in New York City, Pierson attended Hamilton College (B.A., 1857) and studied theology at Union Seminary,* New York (B.D., 1860). His career as a Presbyterian minister first took him to Waterford, New York (1863-1869), to Fort Street Presbyterian Church, Detroit (1869-1882) and then briefly to Second Presbyterian Church, Indianapolis (1882-1883). Afterward he pastored the nondenominational Bethany Tabernacle in Philadelphia (1883-1889) and later served briefly at Spurgeon's Tabernacle in London (1891-1893).

The 1880s and 1890s were Pierson's most productive years as a mission theorist. As head of the missions committee of the Philadelphia Presbytery, he wrote "The Problem of Missions" in which he argued for Christian colonies of mission workers. In 1886 he wrote *The Crisis of Missions,* a best-selling book that put the issue of missions before the American people in a vivid way. Throughout his career he was to author over fifty books, five of which covered recent mission history and were entitled *The Miracles of Missions.* He became editor of *The Missionary Review of the World,* and in his twenty-five years of service he transformed it from a small venture into the major American missions periodical of the period, published monthly and surveying the work of all Protestant missions around the world.

Pierson delivered the Alexander Duff Lectures and the Nathan Graves Lectures—two of the major mission lectureships antedating the establishment of chairs of missions in theological seminaries. In speaking and writing, Pierson promoted the Student Volunteer Movement (SVM),* the Laymen's Missionary Movement* and women's work in missions (*See* Women's Missionary Societies). He helped to found the Africa Inland Mission* and addressed the ecumenical* missions conferences* of 1888 and 1900. In 1893 he succeeded A. J. Gordon* as president of Gordon's Missionary Training School, now known as Gordon College.

Pierson's greatest theoretical contribution to missions stemmed from his premillennialism.* In 1886 he delivered a speech at the International Prophetic Conference* entitled "Our Lord's Second Coming as a Motive to World-Wide Evangelization." In it he argued that the hope of Christ's Second Coming was the greatest motivation for world evangelization,* defined as offering the good news to every person. Pierson did not believe that the world would be converted before Christ returned, but that world evangelization was a prerequisite to his return. For Pierson, then, the motivating force of the SVM watchword (which

was credited to him)—"the evangelization of the world in this generation"—was its implicit belief that Christ would return once world evangelization was complete.

In his later years, Pierson's piety and biblical conservatism brought him into demand as a Bible expositor.* He spoke at new Bible training schools, such as Moody Bible Institute,* Biblical Seminary, Nyack Missionary Training Institute and "higher life"* gatherings, such as Keswick* conferences. He contributed to *The Fundamentals** and was an original editor of the Scofield Reference Bible.* Most of his later works were on biblical or spiritual themes.

In his lifetime Pierson was a controversial figure. His piety and premillennialism alienated some people, while his tendency to cooperate across confessional lines for the sake of world evangelization alienated others. And yet, Pierson was the leading American spokesman for foreign missions in the late nineteenth century. Under his influence men such as John Mott,* Robert Speer,* Samuel Zwemer,* Henry Frost* and many others were propelled into work for foreign missions. After he died, admirers established in his honor Pierson Bible College in Seoul, Korea.

BIBLIOGRAPHY. *DAB* VII; D. L. Pierson, *Arthur T. Pierson* (1912); *The Missionary Review of the World* (1886-1912); D. L. Robert, "Arthur Tappan Pierson and Forward Movements of Late-Nineteenth-Century Evangelicalism" (unpublished Ph.D. dissertation, Yale University, 1984); D. L. Robert, "The Legacy of Arthur Tappan Pierson," *IBMR* 8 (July 1984):120-125.

D. L. Robert

Pietism. Pietism is gradually coming to be seen as a clearly discernible religious movement which has left few aspects of world Protestantism* untouched. The term itself seems to have been used first in reference to the followers of the Lutheran* pastor* Philipp Jakob Spener (1635-1705) at Frankfurt am Main, Germany in 1674. Gradually, however, historians with a primary interest in religion as it is lived, felt the need to expand the concept to include developments in other Protestant circles which appear to parallel Spener's preoccupation with biblical piety.

Continental Pietism. Pietism as it is now widely understood has its roots both in the magisterial and radical phases of the Reformation, as well as in the emphasis on "godliness" of many Puritans.* It gradually comes into view in what is sometimes referred to as "precisianism" in the Reformed* churches of the Netherlands. Among the Dutch Reformed it was represented by men like Willem Teellinck (1579-1629); the scholarly Gysbertus Voetius (1509-1676); Jadocus van Lodensteyn (1620-1677); as well as the Brakels— Theodor Gerardi (1608-1669) and his son Willem (1635-1711). Among separatists with a Dutch Reformed background, mention should be made of the former Jesuit* Jean de Labadie (1610-1674) and his gifted disciple Anna Maria van Schurmann (1607-1678).

The outstanding representatives of Pietism among the German Reformed were Theodor Untereyck (1635-1693), who about the year 1665 began in Germany the institution of Pietist conventicles among the Reformed, and Friedrich Adolph Lampe (1683-1729), the widely read theologian* of the movement. The intellectual center of German Reformed Pietism was the academy at Herborn, near Dillenburg in the county of Nassau. Reformed Pietist circles were also found in German-speaking Switzerland, out of which came Johann Caspar Lavater (1741-1801), the later spokesman for Swiss pietist sentiments.

Lutheran Pietism arose in Germany, where its first signs became visible in the pastoral activity and much-treasured devotional works of Johann Arndt (1555-1621) and his followers. Philipp Jakob Spener has the distinction of having given the movement a program by publishing his famous *Pia Desideria* in 1675. August Hermann Francke (1663-1727) established the academic center of Lutheran Pietism at Halle in Saxony, infused it with its penchant for charitable endeavors, and gave it its vision of a world in need of vital Christianity. Johann Albrecht Bengel (1687-1752), the soul of Lutheran Pietism in south Germany, became its beloved and widely appreciated expositor of the Bible.* From Germany Lutheran Pietism reached the Scandinavian countries and was especially represented by the Norwegian lay* evangelist Hans Nielsen Hauge (1771-1824).

Distinct branches of Pietism were represented by Count Nikolaus Ludwig Graf von Zinzendorf* (1700-1760) and the Renewed Moravian Church,* as well as by radicals such as the irrepressible Johann Conrad Dippel (1673-1734), the historian Gottfried Arnold (1666-1714), the deeply spiritual Hochmann von Hochenau (1670-1721) and the community of believers who found refuge at Wittgenstein in Westphalia.

In general terms Pietism represents a reaction against the lack of religious fervor, the moral laxity, the tendency toward cultural accommodation and the interconfessional bickering of the representatives of orthodoxy* within the established Protestant communions. It laid stress on the religious renewal of the individual (New Birth*) as evidenced through a life of piety. Pietists were given to a more or less literal interpretation of Scripture,* guided by common sense, as well as a deep sense of Christian fellowship which minimized confessional, national and ethnic boundaries. As a result they were prone to hold conventicles, members of which were addressed as "brother" or "sister," irrespective of social class or church affiliation. They deliberately meant to fashion a lifestyle based on an ethic which they read out of the New Testament and which was in conscious opposition to the shallow folk religion widely encouraged by the religious establishments of their day. On the whole Pietism is a broader movement than evangelicalism—Pietism being inward-directed and not necessarily expansionistic as is evangelicalism.

In time Pietism influenced every facet of Protestantism—its theology,* its hymnody,* its worship* and its church life. It encouraged the devotional* study of the Bible in the churches as well as in the homes; it stimulated church attendance, awakened the desire to establish charitable and educational institutions, created an awareness of the need for both domestic and foreign missions,* held out the hope for ecumenical* relations and opened the way for lay participation in the life of the churches. Against this background its impact upon Protestantism in colonial America becomes apparent.

New World Pietism. From about 1710 to the time of the American Revolution,* succeeding waves of German immigrants* swelled the ranks of American settlers, many of them having had a Lutheran background. Because of the paucity of competent Lutheran clergymen* various appeals were made to charitable societies in the home country and in Britain to supply them. The most generous response to these appeals came from Halle. Hence Lutheran congregations shepherded by Halle-trained pastors and loosely supervised by Henry Melchior Muhlenberg,* who was in constant contact with Halle, soon outnumbered by far their antipietist colleagues. In 1748 they controlled the synod.*

Dutch Reformed Pietism in the colonies seems to have first taken root through the efforts of Guilliam Bartholf (1656-1726) in the eastern section of New Jersey. He had brought with him the Pietist legacy of Teellinck, Lodensteyn and the latter's pupil Jacobus Koelman (1630-1695). In 1720 Theodor J. Frelinghuysen,* a confirmed Pietist, arrived in America and presently took up his work in the Raritan Valley of New Jersey. Under his fervent preaching a revival* broke out which attracted the Tennants—William, Sr.,* and his son Gilbert.* This fused the Pietist impulse with Puritanism. The Dutch Reformed devotional works by the Brakels, by Koelman and especially by Abraham Hellenbroek (1658-1731), frequently translated into both German and English, were widely used in the homes of the early settlers.

Among the German Reformed the Swiss-born Michael Schlatter* and the Herborn-educated Philip William Otterbein,* both of Pietist persuasion, wielded considerable influence. In 1747 the former organized the Coetus (an organization representing twelve out of the thirteen German Reformed congregations) and the latter, after having long promoted the interests of the Coetus, finally became one of the two first bishops* of the United Brethren in Christ (1800).

Pietism was dominantly represented among the German-speaking religious groups who, because of past experiences, held themselves aloof from the "church people" (Lutheran and Reformed). Among them were the Mennonites,* many of whom were shaken out of their traditionalism by Martin Boehm* who, after a conversion experience typical of many Pietists (1758), used the device of the "big meeting" to reach the churched and the unchurched. In 1800 he, along with Otterbein, became a bishop of the United Brethren in Christ. Among them were also the various German-speaking Brethren bodies whose understanding of the gospel was heavily indebted to the radical Pietists at Wittgenstein, notably Hochmann von Hochenau. Especially notable among them was Alexander Mack, Sr.,* who constitutes a link between the Pietism of Wittgenstein and its American extension. Not to be forgotten here are the Moravians who established themselves in Georgia under the leadership of August Gottlieb Spangenberg* and in Pennsylvania. The Covenant groups of Scandinavian origin (See Evangelical Covenant Church of North America; Evangelical Free Church of America) who found a home in the Middle West also need to be mentioned, as do the settlers who came out of a German Pietist background in Russia.

In hope of escaping the corruptions of the world around them, some of the early Pietists in America established religious communities. Among them were the followers of Johannes Kelpius* on the banks of the Wissahickon, the followers of Conrad Beissel* at Ephrata, and the Moravians in Bethlehem—all of them in Pennsylvania. There were also the communities of Economy (Pennsylvania) and Harmony* (Indiana) founded by George Rapp,* as well as others.

In one way or another Pietism appears to have influenced most if not all Protestant groups in America, though the specific lines of development are only beginning to emerge. The link to Presbyterianism* through Frelinghuysen and the Tennants has already been mentioned. The link to the Methodist* bodies and their successors includes not only John Wesley's* indebtedness to the Moravians and to Bengel but also the contact with Pietists of early Methodist preachers in America, as well as the legacy of Otterbein and of Jacob Albright,* the founder of the Evangelical Association (See Revivalism, German-American). Neither did the various Baptist* groups remain untouched as is indicated by a study of the life of Isaac Backus.* Perhaps least understood at this time is the connection of Pietism with the churches of New England and with the Episcopalians,* though they, too, did not escape the revival fires in the engendering of which the role of Pietism must not be underestimated. Whether it was Pietism or Puritanism which dominantly shaped Protestant church life in North America, future historians will have to decide.

See also FREE CHURCH, TRADITION IN AMERICA.

BIBLIOGRAPHY. J. O. Bemesderfer, Pietism and Its Influence upon the Evangelical United Brethren Church (1966); M. G. Brumbaugh, A History of the German Baptist Brethren in Europe and America (1899); L. A. Drummond, "The Puritan-Pietistic Tradition: Its Meaning, History, and Influence in Baptist Life," RE 77 (1980):483-492; D. H. Durnbaugh, The Church of the Brethren Past and Present (1971); G. J. Eisenach, Pietism and the Russian Germans in the United States (1948); C. C. Goen, Revivalism and Separatism in New England, 1740-1800 (1962); F. Hale, TransAtlantic Conservative Protestantism in the Evangelical Free and Mission Covenant Tradition (1979); W. J. Hinke, Ministers of the German Reformed Congregations in Pennsylvania and Other Colonies in the Eighteenth Century (1951); J. L. Kincheloe, "European Roots of Evangelical Revivalism: Methodist Transmission of the Pietistic Socio-Religious Tradition," MH 18 (1980):262-271; W. G. McLoughlin, Isaac Backus and the American Pietistic Tradition (1967); J. S. O'Malley, Pilgrimage of Faith: The Legacy of the Otterbeins (1973); J. F. Sachse, The German Pietists of Provincial Pennsylvania, 1694-1708 (1895); F. E. Stoeffler, ed., Continental Pietism and Early American Christianity (1976); J. Tanis, Dutch Calvinistic Pietism in the Middle Colonies (1967).   F. E. Stoeffler

Piety: Popular Catholic. Indigenous or extra-sacramental religious behavior of Catholics. In addition to the normal Sunday* eucharistic* worship,* and the sacramental* rituals which generally signified major transitions in life, Catholics in the Middles Ages engaged in numerous devotions* and prayer* forms, generally the product of individual or group zeal. Much of this activity, frequently focused on local or national heroic figures, or saints,* was carried to colonial America, and formed the basis for naming towns, rivers and other geographical entities in a effort to sacralize this world in imitation of the heavenly communion of saints.* It would appear that in general, Native Americans liked the color, expressiveness and pageantry associated with these multiple forms of medieval piety.

The influence of the Enlightenment* cooled Catholic devotionalism, at least along the Eastern seaboard, and thus in the period just before and shortly after the American Revolution,* a rather plain Catholic religiosity, focused on Sunday and especially the Mass,* existed and was suitably housed in neo-classical churches with clear glass windows and only a crucifix* and two statues or pictures of saints as interior decoration. Still there was to be found in the early East Coast churches small associations which gave special honor to the Blessed Sacrament or the Holy Cross, as in Boston, or to St. Augustine in Philadelphia, or to the Virgin Mary* via the practice of the rosary,* as in Maryland.

This situation was radically altered, however, as a result of the Romantic* revolt which seems to have begun among American Catholics in the 1830s. An elaborate devotional revolution followed which altered not only architecture,* making Gothic popular again, but everything else as well. Ritual now expanded to include multiple devotions, with a corresponding expansion of prayer books, hymnals* and even churches, the interior decoration of which had to be able to accommodate multiple side altars* with statues of the objects of these devotions. The names assigned to the large number of new urban churches reveal as little else can the nature of the devotions introduced—*Immaculate Conception, St. Joseph, Holy Family, Holy Child, Precious Blood* and *Sacred Heart*. This network of devotional activity, set in the context of an industrializing nation, represents a vast quest for innocence, especially sexual innocence, or the innocence of those unjustly persecuted. It took social form in the enormous expansion of the number of those willing to take religious vows, and a special concern that family life be innocent and stable. This Romantic Catholicism lasted for well over a century.

In addition to this devotional dimension to mid-nineteenth-century popular Catholic piety, one can discern both a domestic and civic form as well. By the mid-nineteenth century, Romantic Catholicism, with its emphasis on innocent family life, witnessed the emergence of a subtle, and yet to be fully explored, domestic piety. Many Catholic homes, like Catholic churches, were separated from the workaday world by holy water fountains, used to cleanse those who entered. Morning and evening prayers were to be said, although, unlike prayers before and after meals, there does not seem to have been much emphasis on doing these as a family.

The meal setting was especially important, also, because the Friday and Lenten* meal restrictions were there shared by the family. The communal saying of the "Angelus"* prayer or the recitation of the rosary were certainly done in the home by nineteenth-century Catholics, but widespread family rosary saying would not develop until the mid-twentieth century. Certainly Christmas* and Easter* were celebrated as religious events in the home, and the feasts of patron saints of family members were celebrated with better food or morning Mass, as on Sundays. A good range of household religious iconography was listed as for sale in the Catholic press, and was presumably present in the home—statues, crucifixes, images of the sacred heart,* Angelus clocks, May flowers and many other items.

A civic religiosity was also in evidence. Special social and religious services on civic holidays, a prayer for political as well as ecclesiastical leaders at each Sunday Mass, the mythologizing of Catholic Christopher Columbus,* discoverer of the nation, the successful quest to have Columbus Day set aside as a state and national holiday, the formation of such groups as the Knights of Columbus or the Daughters of Isabella, and the yet-to-be-successful movement to arrange his canonization* as patron saint of the nation, reflect the hopes of Catholics to symbolically project their identity as Catholics and Americans. The depth of Catholic Americanization can be gauged by the widespread use of the American flag in Catholic ritual, and even, early in the twentieth century, the inclusion of the flag in the sanctuary of churches, not to mention the extensive inclusion of national symbols, heroes, hymns and curriculum in Catholic schools. In spite of this process, which was only one element in a vast symbolic network, Catholics remained culturally distinct from the nation until recently.

Vatican II,* emphasizing the Catholic liturgy,* a more personal Christian faith and concern for a better world, had the effect of significantly diminishing the devotional side of Catholic religiosity, including its closely allied sentiment of withdrawal from the world in the innocence of religious vows and stable family life. Since much of the domestic religiosity emphasized routine prayer, devotionalism and world-denying fasting,* it declined after the Council also. And Catholic reaction to the later stages of the Vietnam War* during the same decade led to a rejection of much of the symbolism of the nation while, ironically, Catholics accepted much of the culture of the nation, including its hope for a better world, democracy,* equal rights, conscience rights and sexual freedom. Extra-sacramental religious ritual among Catholics is now downplayed, except where ethnic* parish communities have kept them alive.

BIBLIOGRAPHY. T. E. Wangler, "Catholic Religious Life in Boston," in R. E. Sullivan, ed., *Catholic Boston* (1985); P. W. Williams, *Popular Religion in America* (1980); C. McDannell, *The Christian Home in Victorian America* (1986); A. Taves, *The Household of Faith: Roman Catholic Devotions in Mid-Nineteenth Century America* (1986).

T. E. Wangler

Piety: Popular Orthodox. Orthodox piety is a way of living and thinking marked by fidelity to liturgical, moral and devotional practices of the Orthodox Church* reaching back to apostolic times, such as almsgiving, prayer* and fasting (Mt 6:2-18). Its motivation is the fulfillment of God's will in all things and its goal is the sanctification* of all aspects of life according to the biblical commands to holiness* (1 Pet 1:15-16; cf. Lev 11:44; 19:2). As interpenetrating realities, Orthodox piety and Orthodox spirituality,* although formally distinguished, cannot be empirically separated, for they are at once deeply rooted in the same worship,* theology* and life of the Orthodox Church as an ongoing living community of faith and witness guided by the Holy Spirit.

Orthodox piety is distinctly corporate and liturgical* insofar as Orthodox life is practically dominated by corporate participation in the mysteries or sacraments* (unofficially listed as seven: baptism,* chrismation, Eucharist,* marriage,* confession, holy oil and holy orders*) and in numerous other liturgical services (such as vespers,* matins, blessing of the waters, service for the dead, memorials and special intercessory services to Christ, the Virgin Mary* and many saints*).

The entire church year* (from September to August), as it shapes the devotion of devout

persons, features established cycles of feasts and fasting periods, together with their related universal or local customs (e.g., the blessing of first fruits, such as grapes, on the Feast of the Transfiguration of Christ, which is celebrated on August 6). The greatest religious feasts focus on Christ, the Virgin Mary, the apostles, John the Baptist and the Prophet Elijah, as well as on great church fathers such as St. Basil the Great and popular saints such as St. Nicholas. The communion of saints* exercises a powerful influence on Orthodox life and gives it both corporate and otherworldly qualities. The personal life of an Orthodox reflects this liturgical and ecclesial spirit through daily prayer before icons,* use of candles and incense, blessing of homes and other properties, fasting on Wednesdays and Fridays, reading Scripture* and lives of saints, baking the offering bread for the Eucharist* and celebrating namedays on the feast of patron saints.

In the new urban American milieu, especially among the third and fourth generations of American-born Orthodox, a gradual dissolution of Orthodox piety is occurring due to acculturation—including secularism, work patterns and a weakening of the ethnic community. Thus worship is narrowed to Sunday*-morning services and occasional baptisms, marriages and funerals.* Religious feasts falling on weekdays may be passed over. Daily prayer, fasting and other devotional practices are often neglected. Birthdays instead of namedays are more often celebrated. The blessing of first fruits in urban settings is mostly ceremonial. One could therefore speak of a crisis in traditional Orthodox piety in America, but with paradoxical ramifications; on the one hand, certain popular superstitious elements are unconsciously being purged, but on the other hand, Orthodox identity seems to be fading. In a secular society the nurture of genuine Orthodox piety would seem to require effective catechetical* and renewal programs based on the power of the gospel, sound theology, a personal commitment to holiness, as well as new expressions of piety related to modern life.

BIBLIOGRAPHY. N. Arseniev, *Russian Piety* (1964); A. Coniaris, *Making God Real in the Orthodox Christian Home* (1977); A. Coniaris, *Introducing the Orthodox Church* (1982); T. Ware, *The Orthodox Church* (1963).

T. Stylianopoulos

Piety: Popular Protestant. A variety of beliefs and practices related to personal religious devotion and daily Christian living. A type of "peoples' theology" expressed in practical Christian experience.

Popular piety involves certain inner religious experiences* and outward observances which contribute to spiritual growth. The seventeenth-century movement known as Pietism* helped shape the way in which many Protestants understood the need for *praxis pietatis* (the practice of piety) in practical living. German pietists such as Philipp Jacob Spener (1635-1705) urged all Christians to move beyond the dogma* and ritual of the church to a personal experience of God through conversion,* Bible study,* prayer* and virtuous living. For these Pietists, mere beliefs about Christ were less significant than experience with Christ. All Christians were called to "practice the presence of God."

Classical Pietism fostered spirituality* through small groups gathered for devotional confession, prayer, fellowship and study of Scripture. Much Protestant piety continues to be nurtured in Sunday-school* classes and prayer groups, where personal relationships are encouraged. Private devotion to God became public through collective services of worship,* preaching* and evangelism.* Lutheran,* Episcopalian* and other more liturgical traditions provide opportunities for Christians to articulate and enact personal piety through the order and dignity of common prayer, litany* and sacrament.* In the Free Church tradition,* popular piety was influenced by the spontaneity of the revivalistic* tradition and the camp-meeting* experience.

During the nineteenth century, frontier camp meetings were the scene of dramatic conversion and exuberant religious "affections." Religious "exercises" led people to shout, sing, run, laugh and even jerk as evidence of their religious devotion. Through the influence of revivalism, "walking the aisle" in response to the invitation to Christian conversion became a significant evangelical ritual, an outward sign of an inward religious experience. Many frontier churches developed significant rituals which gave evidence of Christian commitment and community. These included the washing of feet,* the right hand of Christian fellowship, the fellowship meal and the testimony meeting,* as well as baptism* and the Lord's Supper.*

Music* is also an important element in popular piety, in which great truths of the faith are expressed in common song. America hymnody includes Reformation chorales, the Psalter, camp-meeting melodies, African-American spirituals, gospel songs* and Wesleyan hymns. In the African-American religious tradition in America, popular piety is intricately related to public worship, an experience often characterized by spirituals, powerful oratory and the famous "answering congregation," in which preacher and congregation carry on a dialog throughout the sermon.

The Holiness* and Pentecostal* traditions of the late nineteenth and twentieth centuries focused on the need for sanctification*—growing in grace beyond the initial conversion experience. Holiness Christians pursued the deeper Christian life in confession of sin* and Spirit baptism.* Building on this piety, Pentecostals view speaking in tongues* (glossolalia), healing* and other spiritual gifts as outward evidence of the baptism of the Holy Spirit. These diverse expressions of personal piety represent a powerful force in Christianity. They represent the many ways in which religious persons express their faith and translate complex dogma into personal religious experience.

See also SPIRITUALITY, PROTESTANT.

BIBLIOGRAPHY. D. G. Matthews, *Religion in the Old South* (1977); H. Dorgan, *Giving Glory to God in Appalachia: Worship Practices of Six Baptist Subdenominations* (1987); J. K. Hadden and C. E. Swann, *Prime Time Preachers* (1981).

B. J. Leonard

Pike, James Albert (1913-1969). Episcopal* bishop* of California. Born in Oklahoma City, Pike attended the University of California—Los Angeles (B.A., 1934; LL.B., 1936) and studied law at Yale* University (J.S.D., 1938). After a law career in Washington, D.C., and service in the U. S. Navy, he decided to enter the ministry. Bishop Angus Dun of Washington ordained* him deacon* on December 21, 1944, and priest* on November 1, 1946. Pike began his ministry as curate* at St. John's Church, Washington (1944-1946), and from 1947 to 1949 was rector* of Christ Church, Poughkeepsie, and chaplain* at Vassar College. In 1949 he became chaplain at Columbia University,* and in 1952, after graduating from Union Theological Seminary,* New York (B.D., 1951), he became dean of the Cathedral of St. John, New York City. On May 15, 1958, he was consecrated bishop of California by Presiding Bishop Henry Knox Sherrill. Pike retired as bishop in 1966 and became theologian-in-residence at the Center for the Study of Democratic Institutions, Santa Barbara.

From 1960 on Pike struggled to relate the gospel to modern realities. His departure from orthodoxy* began with an article entitled "Three-pronged Synthesis" in *The Christian Century* on December 21, 1960. He denied the historical virgin birth and claimed that "Joseph was the human father of Jesus." He challenged the historical development of the doctrine of the Trinity and stated: ". . . all the verbiage associated with the Trinity is quite unnecessary. . . . I can't see its permanent value." He called for "more belief, fewer beliefs."

In 1966 Bishop Henry I. Louttit of Florida presented five accusations against Pike, two of which were "holding and teaching publicly and advisedly, doctrines contrary to that held by this Church" and "conduct unbecoming a clergyman." The latter was based on his divorce and remarriage. The House of Bishops* censured him and stated: "His writing and speaking on profound realities with which Christian faith and worship are concerned are too often marred by caricatures of treasured symbols and at the worst, by cheap vulgarizations of great expressions of the faith." Pike was a prolific writer, but his more advanced views are best stated in *A Time for Christian Candor* (1964) and *What Is This Treasure* (1966). Following his son's suicide in February 1966, Pike ventured into spiritualism, which he defended in *The Other Side* (1968). He died from exposure, under mysterious circumstances, in the Israeli desert sometime between September 3 and 7, 1969.

See also BLAKE-PIKE UNITY PROPOSAL.

BIBLIOGRAPHY. D. K. Pike, *Search* (1970); W. Stringfellow and A. Towne, *The Bishop Pike Affair* (1967); W. Stringfellow and A. Towne, *The Death and Life of Bishop Pike* (1976).

D. S. Armentrout

Pilgrim Holiness Church. *See* WESLEYAN CHURCH.

Pilgrims. Plymouth colonizers and American saints. In 1820, on the bicentennary of the Pilgrims' landing at Plymouth in Massachusetts Bay, Daniel Webster's oratory celebrated "our homage to our Pilgrim Fathers, our sympathy in their sufferings, our gratitude for their labors, our admiration of their virtues, our veneration of their piety,* and our attachment to those principles of civil and religious liberty" which they embodied. In the early nineteenth century, with the 1820 publication of Cotton Mather's* hagiography of the Pilgrims in the first American edition of the *Magnalia,* Longfellow's and Heman's popular odes to the Pilgrims, the publication of Bradford's long lost *History of Plimouth Plantation,* and Abraham Lincoln's* 1863 declaration of a national Thanksgiving Day,* the Pilgrims ceased to be merely regional heroes and became national symbols of American principles and values.

The original Pilgrims, less educated and more rustic than the Boston Puritans,* had in England been members of the Separatist* Scrooby congregation which followed the religious radical Robert Browne (c.1553-1633) in his demand for a "Reformation without Tarrying for Anie." Refusing to conform to the established Church of England,* they were forced to flee to Holland. After twelve years in exile, worried that their children might cease to be English, they set sail for America. In 1620 the Mayflower dropped anchor in Plymouth, establishing the first permanent English colony in North America. William Bradford,* the first governor of the colony, kept a detailed history which has since become a classic of American literature. Today, reference to "the Pilgrims" is to these pious Christians who brought to the New World the first seeds of what would become the U.S.

BIBLIOGRAPHY. *Mourt's Relation* (1622); W. Bradford, *Of Plymouth Plantation,* S. E. Morison, ed. (1952); G. F. Willison, *Saints and Strangers* (1945).

D. R. Williams

Pioneer Clubs. International nondenominational weekday club and camping program for young people. Pioneer Clubs (formerly Pioneer Girls) integrates spiritual and personal development, and emphasizes evangelism and discipleship by giving young people opportunities to learn new skills, make friends with peers and adults and develop Christian values. Eighty-five denominations* sponsor the weekday club program in the U.S.

The ministry began in 1939 when a Wheaton College* student, Betty Whitaker, responded to the pleas of a girl named Harriet Breehm and her friends. The girls wanted a club in which to study the Bible,* learn new skills and have fun together, as their brothers were doing in the Christian Service Brigade* club led by Wheaton student Joe Coughlin. Whitaker began Girls' Guild, and soon other Wheaton coeds were leading Girls' Guild clubs in surrounding towns. In 1940 Camp Cherith was started as the summer extension of the club program.

In 1941, Carol Erickson reworked the program to become Pioneer Girls. As Wheaton students graduated, they took the fledgling program with them throughout the U.S. and to various foreign missions. With H. J. Taylor's* Christian Worker's Foundation helping to fund and advising the early organization, the program began to be offered through churches nationwide. In the years that followed, clubs and camps began in Canada, averaging a growth rate of one-third the U.S. ministry.

In 1981, under a new umbrella organization, Pioneer Ministries, Inc., the program expanded to include Pioneer Boys, and the club's name was changed to Pioneer Clubs. Clubs are now conducted for young people in kindergarten through twelfth grade (77,376 in the U.S. in 1987), led by adult volunteers (16,241 in the U.S. in 1987) in local churches (2,236 in the U.S. in 1987), with curriculum, training and resources provided by the Pioneer Clubs national headquarters in Wheaton, Illinois, and Pioneer Clubs, Canada, in Burlington, Ontario. In 1989 there were twenty-one U.S. and seven Canadian Camp Cherith camps.

BIBLIOGRAPHY. S. A. Robertson, "A Description of Pioneer Girls: An International Religious Club Program" (unpublished Ph.D. dissertation, Northern Illinois University, 1977).

L. M. Davis

Pioneer Girls. *See* PIONEER CLUBS.

Pitt, Robert Healey (1853-1937). Southern Baptist* pastor* and editor. Born in Middlesex County, Virginia, Pitt attended Richmond College (1873-1879). He was licensed to preach in 1875 and ordained* in 1877 at Walnut Grove, where he pastored his first church (1878-1879). Other pastorates included Venable Street, Richmond, (twice); Martinsburg, West Virginia; Barton Heights, Richmond and for eight years Ashland, Virginia. While he was pastor at Venerable Street, Pitt began his career at the *Religious Herald.* In 1906 he became owner and editor of the paper.

Pitt's editorials won him acclaim for his progressive social views and for his staunch defense of religious liberty. He was an advocate of temperance* and was a leader in the Anti-Saloon League.* Pitt vigorously opposed anti-evolution laws and compulsory daily Bible reading in public schools.* He opposed the presidential candidacy of Alfred Smith* in 1928 and expressed caution concerning America's entry into the League of Nations, since several of the participating nations were Roman Catholic.* In the 1920s, when fundamentalists* within the Southern Baptist Convention were advocating a more firm expression of doctrinal orthodoxy* within educational institutions, Pitt advised mutual respect and tolerance among differing Baptists. In 1925 Pitt refused to sign the report of the Southern Baptist Convention Committee on Baptist faith and message. He believed the report, which was adopted by the Convention, constituted a creedal* statement and would lead to division among Southern Baptists.

Pitt held important leadership positions, including president of the Virginia Baptist General Association, president of the Virginia Baptist

Education Commission, American Secretary of the Baptist World Alliance* and for forty years member of the Southern Baptist Foreign Mission Board.

BIBLIOGRAPHY. *ESB* 2.   D. B. Whitlock

Pius IX (1792-1878). Pope* from 1846 to 1878. Pius IX's pontificate was the longest in history and among the more controversial. Born Giovanni Maria Mastai Ferretti in Senigallia, near Ancona, Italy, his career traced a model profile, first as priest* (1819), then as archbishop* of Spoleto (1827), later of Imola (1832), next cardinal* (1840) and finally pope (1846). His interest in the Americas began during a diplomatic posting for the Church in Chile and Peru (1823-1825). As pope he devoted himself to missions,* including as in the U.S., then formally a mission field directly responsible to Rome.

His major project for America was the organization and spirituality of the Church, which, by virtue of the arrival of well over three million immigrants* from Ireland, southern Germany and other Catholic territories during his period, had doubled in size to become the largest single denomination.* He created new dioceses* at a rapid rate, named Archbishop James Gibbons* as the first American apostolic delegate,* approved the extension of religious orders* and encouraged the creation of colleges* and parochial schools.* He established the North American College in Rome* (1859) to train priests for America. In spite of this, however, the distance between him and the American Church widened. Support for the pope when his political rule over the Papal States collapsed (1858-1861) was weaker among American Catholics than elsewhere, and all of the nearly fifty American bishops at the first Vatican Council* (1869-1870) initially opposed the declaration of papal infallibility,* which the Council eventually approved.

BIBLIOGRAPHY. E. E. Y. Hales, *Pio Nono* (1956); *NCE* 11.   C. T. McIntire

Pius X (1835-1914). Pope* from 1903 to 1914. Born as Giuseppe Melchiorre Sarto in Riese, near Venice, Italy, he served as a priest* in the diocese* of Treviso (1858), bishop* of Mantua (1884), and cardinal* and patriarch of Venice (1893) before his election as pope. During his pontificate, close to five million Catholic immigrants* to the U.S., mostly from Italy, Poland and Mexico, consolidated the Roman Catholic Church's standing as the largest denomination.* The desperate economic conditions of the immigrants helped stimulate the pope to promote the rights of laboring people. At the same time, the immigrants constituted a huge conservative weight in favor of obedience to Rome, and the pope encouraged the adoption of Roman-style devotions among them. The pope's encyclical *Pascendi Dominici Gregis* (1907) condemned the predominantly French Catholic version of modernism* as a heresy. Although there were few, if any, real Catholic modernists in America, the act stifled the *Catholic New York Review* and effectively established Roman-oriented domination of Catholic intellectual life for two generations.

His reorganization of the Roman Congregation for the Propagation of the Faith* (1908) removed the American Church from mission status and granted it full recognition equal to the Church in France or Italy. He stated appreciation for the relative freedoms enjoyed by Catholics in America but declined to give President Theodore Roosevelt a papal audience (1910). His support for missions* included approval for the Maryknoll Fathers of the Catholic Foreign Mission Society of America* (1911), and his liturgical* reforms later had immense effect in America as elsewhere. He was canonized* in 1954.

BIBLIOGRAPHY. F. A. M. Forbes, *Life of Pius X* (1918); R. Merry del Val, *Memories of Pope Pius X* (1939); *NCE* 11.

C. T. McIntire

Pius XI (1857-1939). Pope* from 1922 to 1939. Born in Desio, near Milan, Italy, Ambrogio Damiano Achille Ratti earned three doctorates at the Gregorian University in Rome and undertook a career as a seminary* professor and scholar. For thirty years he served successively on the staffs of the Ambrosian Library in Milan (1888) and the Vatican Library (1911), where he became prefect (1914). He was nuncio* to Poland (1919) and became cardinal* and archbishop* of Milan (1921) before his election as pope.

His impact on the U.S. came partly through his emphasis on education for the priesthood* and on eucharistic renewal, symbolized by the International Eucharistic Congress in Chicago* (1928). His many social statements were extraordinarily influential, especially *Quadragesimo Anno** (1931), which, during the worst moment of the Great Depression,* criticized both capitalism* and socialism* and advocated a Christian reconstruction of society. The American bishops, through the National Catholic Welfare Conference,* promoted the encyclical* as did the new Association of Catholic Trade Unions, and the magazine *Commonweal.* Dorothy Day* supported it in the *Cath-*

olic Worker. The encyclical probably played a role in the massive Catholic votes behind Franklin Delano Roosevelt and the New Deal. His encyclicals on education (1929) and marriage* (1930) assisted the vast extension of Catholic schools. His statements against Fascism (1931, 1938), Nazism (1937) and Communism* (1937) indirectly threw papal support behind the U.S. and Britain as Europe drifted toward war. He opposed the Protestant ecumenical movement* (1928) and secured the Lateran Treaty with Italy (1929), which created the independent Vatican State.

BIBLIOGRAPHY. P. Hughes, *Pope Pius the Eleventh* (1937); R. Fontenelle, *His Holiness Pope Pius XI* (1938); *NCE* 0. C. T. McIntire

Pius XII (1876-1958). Pope* from 1939 to 1958. Born and educated in Rome, Eugenio Maria Giuseppe Giovanni Pacelli joined the staff of the Vatican's secretary of state (1901), and except for a few years teaching ecclesiastical diplomacy (1909-1914) remained in Vatican service until he became pope. He was nuncio* to Bavaria (1917) and Germany (1920), and became cardinal* (1929) and secretary of state (1930) to Pius XI. He had the major responsibility for handling or defining Vatican relations with the Hitler government before and during World War 2.* He has received thorough criticism for not doing enough for the Jews, an issue perennially debated.

He knew the U.S. well, having traveled extensively there in 1936, meeting bishops,* experiencing American Catholicism and dining with President Roosevelt. Upon becoming pope, he received the Episcopalian* Myron C. Taylor as Roosevelt's personal envoy to the Vatican (1939), and corresponded extensively with Roosevelt on war themes, generally supporting the American position against Hitler and Communism. President Truman's unsuccessful proposal to name Taylor as ambassador to the Vatican (1947) revived anti-Catholic fears. The American Catholic Church doubled in size again during his pontificate, making it by far the largest church in the country. Four of the pope's encyclicals were enormously influential in American Catholic life: *Mystici Corporis Christi* (1943) on the Church as a community, *Mediator Dei* (1947) on liturgical reform* and lay* participation, *Divino Afflante Spiritu* (1943) permitting critical biblical scholarship, and *Vegliare con Sollecitudine* (1951) against divorce and contraception.* He gave approval to Catholic discussion with the Protestant* ecumenical movement.*

BIBLIOGRAPHY. S. Friedlander, *Pius XII and the Third Reich* (1966); *NCE* 11. C. T. McIntire

Plan of Union. Congregational*-Presbyterian* alliance. Sealed in 1801, the Plan of Union formally united Presbyterians and Connecticut Congregationalists in efforts to evangelize* the western frontier. Close ties that had existed among the two groups for at least thirty-five years finally culminated in this Plan designed to foster joint action rather than needless conflict in the home missionary* enterprise. Specifically, it encouraged all missionaries toward mutual forbearance and a spirit of accommodation, allowed members of each persuasion in a frontier settlement to found separate or united congregations and permitted congregations to affiliate with either a presbytery* or a congregational* association.

In practice, the Plan contributed to the extension of evangelical* faith into America's interior as missionaries,* pastors* and teachers made their way west under its auspices. Institutionally, the Presbyterians benefited most, due to their greater denominational* consciousness and organizational assertiveness. Conversely, the New England Theology* tended to dominate the doctrinal sympathies of Union churches and pastors. Ironically, both developments contributed to the ultimate demise of the Plan.

On the one hand, Presbyterian Old School* conservatives came to oppose the alliance because it prevented exclusive Presbyterian control over missionary endeavors and more importantly, allowed for the influx of what they considered dangerous theological innovations from Congregationalists. When Old Schoolers gained control of the Presbyterian General Assembly in 1837 (*See* Auburn Declaration), they revoked the Plan of Union and even cut off four western synods which had developed from the union plan. On the other hand, Congregationalists eventually voided the accord at the Albany Convention of 1852 after becoming more denominationally self-conscious and realizing that Presbyterian gains had been made partially at their expense.

BIBLIOGRAPHY. G. M. Marsden, *The Evangelical Mind and the New School Presbyterian Experience* (1970); R. L. Ferm, *A Colonial Pastor: Jonathan Edwards the Younger* (1976); W. Walker, *A History of the Congregational Churches in the United States* (1894).   R. W. Pointer

Plessis, Joseph Octave (1763-1825). Roman Catholic* bishop* of Quebec. Born near Montreal, Quebec, Plessis studied for the priesthood* at Petit Séminaire de Québec and was ordained* in 1786. In 1792 he was assigned to the cure of Notre Dame at Quebec. Consecrated* as bishop in 1801, he succeeded to the position in 1806. Plessis was instrumental in ensuring the loyalty of the French Canadians to Britain during the War of 1812 with the newly formed American republic. His vigilance in reminding British authorities of "the French fact" contributed to what, in practice, amounted to the "co-establishing" of Catholicism and Anglicanism* in the province of Quebec, provoking a bitter response from the Anglican bishop, Jacob Mountain.* His administrative abilities and political instincts combined to make him Quebec's most influential Catholic leader in the early nineteenth century.

BIBLIOGRAPHY. *DCB* VI.   P. D. Airhart

Plockhoy, Pieter Cornelisz (c.1620-c.1700). Mennonite* religious and social reformer. Born in the Netherlands, Plockhoy was evidently affiliated with the Dutch Mennonites and was influenced by the Collegiants, an interchurch reform movement with close connections to Dutch Mennonitism. Later, in England, Plockhoy was active in reform movements during the latter part of Cromwell's government.

Plockhoy was concerned with the establishment of ideal communities in North America and appealed in part to the example of the sixteenth-century Moravian* Anabaptists* and Hutterites* to support his theories. In 1663 he established a small settlement in present-day Delaware, consisting largely of Dutch Mennonites, but the colony was destroyed in 1664 during the Anglo-Dutch war. Plockhoy continued to live in Delaware until the last years of his life, when he moved to the Mennonite settlement in Germantown, Pennsylvania.

BIBLIOGRAPHY. L. Harder and M. Harder, *Plockhoy from Zurik-zee: The Study of a Dutch Reformer in Puritan England and Colonial America* (1952); I. B. Horst, "Pieter Cornelisz Plockhoy: An Apostle of the Collegiants," *MQR* 23 (1949):161-185.

K. M. Enns-Rempel

Pluralism, Religious. Religious pluralism refers both to the wide diversity of religious groups in America and to the polity which grants them equal liberty.

The Fact of Religious Pluralism. Religious pluralism, then, has little to do with philosophical pluralism. The philosophical version contends that reality is ultimately made up of multiple substances, or that no single system of explanation or view of reality will suffice to explain all that exists. Such pluralism rules out monotheism. Religious pluralism is practically compatible with both philosophical pluralisms and monisms. Thus the late Jesuit* priest John Courtney Murray,* from within the Thomist* tradition, could even say that religious pluralism was "against the will of God." But he went on to assert that it *is* the human condition; it will not marvelously cease to trouble the human city.

The phenomenon of religious pluralism then appears to the eye of the observer who simply sees great numbers of religious groups, movements and options in American life. It is noncontroversial to report that well over two hundred denominations* share space in the yearbooks and 1,200 religious groups are alphabetized in a standard encyclopedia of American religion. They are simply there and have to be reckoned with. The Yellow Pages of any telephone book in the U. S. lists enough alternatives under "Churches" to counter anyone who feels uneasy referring to pluralism as merely a plurality of churches.

What begins to make some uneasy is the corollary notion that in the eyes of society and of a constitutional republic, the various churches within this pluralism are on a par with each other. There is no possibility of arguing successfully that one group, however numerically strong it may be, is normative and that all others are to be measured from it. Each member of the society is free to see his or her denomination, tradition and movement as the sole and final embodiment or statement of truth, but no nonmember need assent to the claim in order to be a fully functioning and honored member of the society.

Religious pluralism on the scale of diversity represented in the U. S. results from the peculiar circumstances of settlement, immigration* and stipulation of the terms of life in a republic. Many societies are essentially monolithic. That is, one religion has such dominance in numbers and in legal and other power that, to all extents and purposes, it has a monopoly. If members of other groups are there, they are there by the sufferance of the established or favored one or they survive because the monopoly has not yet efficiently broken them up or hounded them out. Even nations consisting of two or three religious blocks are not usually called pluralist. A country divided into Shi'ite and Sunni Muslims, with no other contenders present, would not be pluralist.

The Circumstances of Religious Pluralism. The first factor, then, in forming American religious pluralism was simply the attractiveness of the landscape and natural resources to millions of people who came, usually with intact religious communions or traditions enveloping or chartering them, from Europe and, to lesser extents, Africa and Asia. Neither the Catholics* after 1492, the Anglicans* after 1607, or the Separatist "Pilgrims"* or more conventional Puritans* after 1620 and 1630 intended to found a pluralist society that would welcome people who were not, religiously, of their kind.

In the course of time it was seen that monopolies could not hold and that dualities could be treacherous. The first permanent settlement, a Catholic one at St. Augustine, Florida, in 1565, soon found itself in a miniature holy war with Protestant* Huguenots who built a fort slightly north of them. Catholic Maryland and Anglican Virginia had skirmishes. In Massachusetts Bay, the always-irritating representatives of pluralism, the Quakers,* kept coming back to disrupt the establishment. Yet hanging Quakers, as Bostonians did Mary Dyer* in 1662, was an act that showed that opposition to pluralism on a total basis could be embarrassing and inconveniencing to communal life.

In New Netherland, particularly in the port of New Amsterdam, the unfolding of pluralism was dramatic. Ostensibly a trading-post becoming a colony with an established Reformed* Church on its Dutch parent model, New Amsterdam by 1654 had attracted Jewish refugees in a population that already numbered Catholics, Lutherans* and members of small sects.* Efforts to enforce uniformity were inconveniencing to the commercial aspect of the city.

If assent to pluralism was tardy and partial in southern colonies where Anglicanism was established, or in New England, where Congregationalism* knew legal privilege—it was elsewhere more hearty; indeed, the founders provided for it in several colonies, notably Rhode Island and Pennsylvania. The Baptist* pioneers in one and the Quakers in another, set out to attract and welcome people from the many groups that were harbingers of later pluralism. Maryland, a proprietary colony of convert-to-Catholicism Lord Baltimore, similarly made provision for varied religions. The process of seeing ships arrive with settlers who represented always one more religious group was the main contributor to the pluralist situation and the need to develop a pluralist polity.

This polity developed as a corollary of the forming of a federal union and the drafting of the cited States Constitution and the Bill of Rights. The Constitution is positively silent about religion and that silence suggested that religion, not being subject to constitutional law, is an independent and free source within the society. The First Amendment* goes further and draws a line of distinction between civil and religious power by keeping the Congress from making laws respecting an establishment* of religion. The vestigial establishments by then (1791) had become so broad and ineffectual that they were doomed, and pluralism became legitimated everywhere.

The invention of a polity for pluralism led to the informal encouragement of any number of practices that have made possible the functioning of a religiously vital society. For one thing, it led to what has been called "the voluntary* system," one which developed almost automatically into a religiously competitive one. Leaders and laity of existing groups set out to prosper and grow by attracting hitherto uncommitted or newly arriving people. Where no existing and adapting religious group was attractive to a substantial number of potential members, new religious forces took shape. Thus the northern and the southern branches of some churches—Baptist, Methodist, Presbyterian*—split over regional, racial and political matters, adding churches which had no integral theological rationale for separate existence. Or new groups like the Mormons,* Adventists* or Jehovah's Witnesses* sprang up to take up life in any ecological niches between existing groups. Citizens were free to choose between any of these, and many did; hence, pluralism developed.

The Problem of Religious Pluralism. The presence of so many competitive voluntary churches and of a polity which encouraged them, led to concern about pluralism. Thus John Courtney Murray spoke for citizens in a long tradition when he asked how many and what kinds of religious groups could a republic tolerate and still function. Such an assertion reflected an anxiety many citizens have always known about mere or utter pluralism. They posit the notion that a functioning society needs certain sets of values that historically have been associated with religion. The presence and legitimation of so many kinds of religion can lead to a loss of coherence for all taken together and of plausibility for any one taken in isolation.

Two major forces serve to mitigate concerns about hyperpluralism. The first is the combination of ecumenical* and interfaith movements. "Brotherhood Week" of the National Conference of Christians and Jews,* for instance, served to minimize the civil differences between groups that could not agree ultimately. They reduced the venom of competing groups, if not the number of them. In this tradition, what religious groups held in common was seen to be a contributor to civic virtue necessary in a republic; the peculiarities of the various religions were important to the members of each but ordinarily irrelevant to the functioning of the larger society.

The other mitigating factor was the rise of what in 1749 Benjamin Franklin called a "Publick Religion" or what Robert Bellah and many other scholars in the 1960s called a "Civil Religion."* This construct represented a kind of "sacred canopy," to use Peter Berger's terms, one that overarched the nonreligious and the diverse religious groups, at the expense again of some interest in the peculiarities of each group.

As what was perceived to be a decline in morals, consensus and public virtue occurred in the 1970s and 1980s, many concerned citizens decided that a strategy beyond interfaith amity and countering civil religion was necessary. Some of them, particularly religious conservatives in both Catholicism and Protestantism, began to address the "problem of pluralism" during a "values crisis" with a program that would seek more homogeneity, what the founders called more "sameness" throughout a diverse population.

This strategy called its advocates and adherents to contend for the privileging of a putatively coherent tradition, "The Judeo-Christian,"* to give stability to a society that lacked a single monolithic base. While some called for a constitutional amendment to that effect, when it became visibly unrealistic to hope for one, these advocates adjusted tactics and began to ask for the privileging of the teaching of this majority tradition over against the chaos of pluralism.

Just as pluralism is seen by many as a complicator of civil life, so others have seen it bewildering the individual situation. In Peter Berger's terms, there is in the modern world a "heretical imperative." This meant not only the privilege but the necessity to choose between meaning-systems or symbol-systems as being best connected with one's own striving for "ultimate concern." In this imperative, one may be quite eclectic, choosing elements from one portion of, say, the Judeo-Christian tradition and from a non-Western faith like Buddhism or Hinduism on the other.

While those concerned with coherence of society or meaning in the life of individuals fretted with the problems of pluralism, others set out to perpetuate it and cause it to prosper. They stressed the First Amendment, the Jeffersonian interpretation of a "wall of separation between church and state,"* and efforts to prevent any group from reaching majority or monopoly status. Their strategy consisted of court actions and forming groups that countered the power of large ones. Constitutionally proscribed when it came to criticizing or blocking such aggressive religious movements, their opponents began to rely on the arguments of pluralist pioneer James Madison. In *The Federalist Papers,* number ten, Madison, argued that one could not cut off factions and sects at their root. One could, however, seek to blunt their native effects by encouraging other jealous and competitive factions and sects and so block efforts at monopoly by anyone.

Meanwhile many citizens encouraged a mixture of vital nonreligious and sectarian forces that, taken together, still led to coherence in society but which also allowed for the prosperity of pluralism as the best alternative for a free society, an inevitable result of its peopling and a development of the freedom it would encourage.

See also CHRISTIANITY AND PUBLIC POLICY; CHURCH AND STATE, SEPARATION OF; CIVIL RELIGION; DENOMINATIONALISM; VOLUNTARISM.

BIBLIOGRAPHY. C. A. Albanese, *America: Religions and Religion* (1981); P. Berger, *The Sacred Canopy* (1969); C. H. Jacquet, Jr., ed., *Yearbook of American and Canadian Churches* (1988); R. McBrien, *Caesar's Coin: Religion and Politics in America* (1987); M. E. Marty, *Pilgrims in Their Own Land: 500 Years of Religion in America* (1984); M. E. Marty, *Religion and Republic: The American Circumstance* (1987); S. E. Mead, *The Lively Experiment: The Shaping of Christianity in America* (1963); J. G. Melton, ed., *The Encyclopedia of American Religions,* 2nd ed. (1986); J. C. Murray, *We Hold These Truths: Catholic Reflections on the American Proposition* (1960); J. F. Wilson, *Public Religion in American Culture* (1981).

M. E. Marty

Plymouth (Christian) Brethren. An independent, nondenominational, evangelical movement. Dissatisfied with the formalism, clericalism and spiritual dryness of many British churches in the early nineteenth century, Christians of various groups met for Communion,* prayer* and Bible teaching on a simple, "New Testament" pattern. With centers in Dublin and Plymouth (the latter association giving them the name they themselves do not use), the Brethren, or Christian Brethren, as some prefer to be called, developed into a separate movement by the 1830s.

The Brethren were united in the practice of weekly Communion and evangelical* on central points of doctrine, but the movement split in the 1840s over church discipline. Since then it has fragmented further, with two types dominating. One group ("Exclusive"), who welcome to Communion only members of their own churches, are assemblies in a Circle of Fellowship directed by leaders who make decisions for the constituent churches. The other, larger group ("Open") welcome all professing Christians to Communion and are autonomous assemblies who join in common projects (usually the sponsoring of Bible conferences,* camps* or missions*).

J. N. Darby,* an Exclusive leader, developed dispensationalism,* the theology most popular throughout the movement. Open Brethren emphasize evangelism* and missions, and have been influential in many evangelical organizations. Brethren do not observe a "clergy*-laity*" distinction but have recognized some believers as gifted and called to preach* and often have supported them in full-time itinerant Bible teaching or evangelism. Recently, some Open assemblies have called seminary-trained men as resident pastoral workers. There are 1,000 congregations with 60,000 members in the U.S., and 600 congregations with 30,000 members in Canada.

BIBLIOGRAPHY. R. McLaren, *The Origin and Development of the Open Brethren in North America* (1982); H. H. Rowdon, *The Origins of the Brethren* (1967). J. G. Stackhouse

Pocket Testament League. A nondenominational organization seeking to evangelize* through distributing the written Word of God. The inspiration for the founding of the League came from a thirteen-year-old British girl in Birmingham, England, who made it a practice to read the Bible* every day. Charles M. Alexander* and J. Wilbur Chapman,* through their evangelistic crusades in America, launched the organization on its worldwide mission in 1908. Today the ministry* of the Pocket Testament League, with headquarters in Lincoln Park, New Jersey, encircles the globe.

League evangelists often travel in modern panel trucks equipped with public-address systems, carrying out citywide campaigns. By proclaiming the Word of God orally and distributing the Scriptures,* in whole or in part, the League has reached a great many people around the world for Christ. Converts are encouraged not only to carry the Scriptures with them but also to read them every day.

During the last two world wars,* the League made special efforts to get the Scriptures into the hands of men and women in uniform. In 1949 it began to concentrate on the Far East. Through

[914]

General McArthur's encouragement, a nation-wide campaign in Japan led to the distribution of 11 million portions of the Bible in that country. Other countries, such as China, Taiwan, South Korea, the Philippines and Indonesia have also been penetrated by the League.

Since 1956 League evangelists have worked in European countries as well as in Africa. Beginning with Kenya, the work has spread to thirteen other African countries, with millions of Scripture portions distributed in many languages. In 1961 the League turned its attention to Latin America. The publication of the League is *World-Wide News.*   D. Ewert

Political Theology. The term *political theology* began to be used in the 1960s by theologians* who were committed to establishing explicit connections between theology* and politics. The primary impetus for these efforts came from Germany and Latin America, where the lessons learned during the struggle against Nazism took shape in the "theology of hope," and the question of the church's role in revolutionary settings stimulated the development of "liberation theology."* The representatives of these schools of thought have not merely argued that theology should begin to deal with political issues, or that theologians should pay more attention to matters of "practical application." They have meant to highlight the ways in which theology always is political in nature, even when it claims to be "apolitical"; the concepts and strategies preferred by Christians who think that they are remaining aloof from the political struggle, they argue, are themselves the elements of a theological way of thinking about political life. The question is not whether or not to have a political theology. All theology, they say, is political, even if the political perspective is not explicitly stated.

Sometimes the case for theology's close ties to a political agenda has relied on Marxist-type notions, as in the insistence that all power relationships (parent-child, bishop-priest, husband-wife) are political in nature (e.g., "sexual politics"). But the case is also made in less ideological terms. North American black theologians, for example, have pointed to the ways in which theologians of the past have sometimes systematically ignored such fundamental biblical themes as God's concern for the poor and the oppressed and the dangers of political and economic idolatry.

If political theology is thought of, not as the domain of thinkers who hold to a specific political perspective, but as theological reflection on the political dimensions of the Christian message, then North America has a long tradition of political theology, even before the term itself was imported from other places. Walter Rauschenbusch's* *A Theology for the Social Gospel* (1917) is a political theological classic, in which Rauschenbusch explores the social dimensions of various basic theological topics: doctrine of God, atonement,* the nature of the church,* eschatology* and so on. Reinhold Niebuhr,* who criticized what he saw as the overly optimistic tones of the earlier Social Gospel* movement, nonetheless carried on the theological discussion of political issues. Niebuhr had a significant influence in American public life during his career, which began in the 1930s. Indeed, the combined contributions of Rauschenbusch and Niebuhr set the basic agenda for the treatment of social concerns in the mainline* Protestant churches of Canada and the U.S. for many decades in the twentieth century.

Evangelical* Christians have sometimes been critical of the enterprise associated with political theology. They have argued that political concerns, while having an important place in the Christian life, are not a part of theology proper, which has to do in their thinking with reflection about God. In arguing in this manner, defenders of political theology have responded by pointing to the fact that the God of the Bible,* as a sovereign ruler who calls human beings to serve in the divine Kingdom,* has himself presented the gospel in overtly political terms. Nor is this, they argue, a matter of mere metaphor: the Bible is full of prayers* and hymns* and visions that have inescapably political content, all of which are proper items for theological treatment.

The political scope of the gospel has been recognized by a number of important strains within the evangelical tradition. New England Puritanism* was systematically political in its theologizing. The Puritans insisted that the righteous ordering of public life was an essential part of obedience to the conditions of the divine covenant.* The theocratic* vision of New England has been revived by the New Right* of the 1970s and 1980s.

Even dispensationalism,* which has been the quasi-official theology of much fundamentalism* in the U.S. and Canada, can be classified as a political theology. In the dispensationalist scheme God's political designs for the world are tied to the people of ethnic Israel; the gentile church is accorded a status that is more spiritual in nature. Dispensationalists have shown a strong interest in the political dimensions of Bible prophecy and

[915]

have been ardent supporters of the policies of the Israeli nation-state (*See* Zionism).

Traditional Roman Catholicism* has also actively pursued questions of political theology; political instruction has been viewed as an important dimension of the church's teaching office or magisterium.* The West German Catholic theologian Johann Baptist Metz has been the most prominent international proponent of political theology and was largely responsible for reviving the term in the 1960s. In the 1980s, the pastoral letter* on peace-making, issued by the U.S. Catholic bishops,* along with similar documents on economic policies formulated by the bishops of both the U.S. and Canada, have received much public attention, and have occasioned considerable ecumenical* dialog. They are yet another sign that political theology continues to be a lively area for Christian discussion in North America.

BIBLIOGRAPHY. G. H. Anderson and T. F. Stransky, ed., *Mission Trends, No. 4: Liberation Theologies in North America and Europe* (1979); J. B. Metz, *Theology of the World* (1969); L. S. Rouner, ed., *Civil Religion and Political Theology* (1986). R. J. Mouw

Polity. *See* CHURCH GOVERNMENT.

Polk, Leonidas (1806-1864). Episcopal* bishop.* The descendant on both sides of prominent families, Polk was born in Raleigh, North Carolina. His cousin was President James K. Polk. A concern for education, public service and military service ran through the family history. Leonidas himself early exhibited a strong concern for justice.

Little record appears to exist about his early education or contact with formal religion. From 1821 to 1823, while awaiting an appointment to the U.S. Military Academy, he attended the University of North Carolina, which his father had helped to found.

Appointed to West Point in 1823, he experienced three "lively" years. In 1826, under the influence of an evangelical* tract,* a work on Christian evidences by a British military writer, and a new chaplain,* Charles P. McIlvaine,* Polk experienced a religious conversion.* His public demonstration of Christian belief, followed by his baptism,* prompted the first religious revival in the academy's history.

Graduating from West Point in 1827, Polk soon resigned his commission to study for the Episcopal priesthood at Virginia Theological Seminary. Ordained* deacon* in 1830 and priest* in 1831, he served parishes* in Virginia and Tennessee before

being elected missionary bishop* of the Southwest in 1838. The jurisdiction—which embraced five states—proved impossible to supervise. Traveling 5,000 miles during his first five months as bishop, he spent only four of the first twenty-four months with his growing family. In 1841 Polk gladly accepted election as first bishop of Louisiana.

Under his leadership the small diocese* steadily grew. Polk's special concern for the conversion and religious instruction of slaves caused African-American communicants to outnumber whites. Less successful for financial reasons was his attempt to establish a paradigmatic sugar plantation in Louisiana that included religious instruction and humane treatment of the hundreds of slaves his wife had inherited. After 1855 he lived in New Orleans and divided his time between the demands of the diocese and the rectorship* of Trinity Church, New Orleans.

In 1856 Polk began planning and raising funds for a great Episcopal university that would rival Harvard* and Yale* and dissuade young Southerners from attending Northern colleges. The University of the South, he hoped, would mold an elite who alone could solve the South's distinctive problems and guide it into the gradual cessation of slavery. Led by Polk, James H. Otey* and Stephen Elliott,* nine Southern dioceses supported the university. In 1860 Polk laid the university's cornerstone in the mountain town of Sewanee, Tennessee.

At the outbreak of the Civil War,* Jefferson Davis offered Polk a military commission. Although a supporter of the American Colonization Society* and an advocate of gradual emancipation since his seminary days, Polk supported the right of the Southern states to secede and considered their cause sacred. After securing the approval of Bishop William Meade,* he "buckled the sword over the gown" and, in June 1861, accepted his commission as a major general. Having taken temporary leave from episcopal office, he limited his public performance of religious duties while in service.

Through 1864 Polk commanded the defenses of the Mississippi Valley, defeated Grant in a minor battle, led the 1st Corps of the Army of Tennessee in four battles and commanded the Confederate right wing at the battle of Chickamauga. In 1862 he was promoted to lieutenant general. During the Confederate retreat to Atlanta, while surveying Federal lines on Pine Mountain, Georgia, with two other generals (one of whom he had recently baptized), he was killed by a cannonball on June 14, 1864.

Popular with his troops, charming in conversation, deficient in business sense, commanding in presence and evangelical in religion, Polk was large both in physique and in vision. Although he was inconsistent in actions, he was far more sensitive to the moral problems of slavery than most white Southerners of his time. Ironically, he is better remembered for his death while serving the Confederacy than for his humanitarian efforts with Louisiana's African-Americans and his plans for the gradual removal of slavery from his native South. His publications consist of official addresses only.

BIBLIOGRAPHY. *DAB* VII; *DARB;* J. H. Parks, *General Leonidas Polk* (1962); T. Reilly, "Genteel Reform Versus Southern Allegiance," *HMPEC* 44 (1975):437-450. D. L. Holmes

Pontifical Biblical Commission. A committee of Roman Catholic* cardinals,* assisted by various experts, named to help the pope* guide Catholic biblical studies. The Commission was created by Pope Leo XIII* in 1902. Its inaugural mandate and grant of powers stressed that Catholic biblical scholarship should produce sound opinions in keeping with received faith yet remain open to progress achieved by new research. The original atmosphere in which the Commission worked was marked by fears of Modernism*—the movement to bring historical criticism and modern philosophy to bear on Catholic faith—which was condemned by Pope Pius X* in 1907. In its early years the Commission did business through *responsa*; answers to questions submitted to it. Later it regularly issued "instructions" or guidelines. In 1907 Pope Pius X declared that all Catholics were bound in conscience to submit to the decrees of the Commission.

Roman Catholic biblical studies entered a new era in 1947 with the issuance of Pope Pius XII's* encyclical* *Divino Afflante Spiritu,* which gave Catholic scholars the liberty to employ the findings of such new methods of biblical research as the criticism of genres and textual traditions. Since that time the Commission has served mainly as an organ for Rome's reservations and advice about scriptural scholarship. American and European Catholic scholars now work quite ecumenically* with Protestants,* Jews and humanists, all employing similar critical methods.

BIBLIOGRAPHY. *NCE* 12. J. Carmody

Pope, Liston (1909-1974). Congregational* minister,* educator and sociologist. Born in Thomasville, North Carolina, Pope graduated from Duke University (B.A., 1929; B.D., 1932). After

serving as director of religious education (1932-1935) at Wesley Memorial Church, High Point, North Carolina, he was ordained* a Congregational minister (1935) and became pastor of Humphrey Street Congregational Church in New Haven, Connecticut (1935-1938). In 1938 he became lecturer in social ethics at Yale* University Divinty School and completed his Ph.D. in sociology at Yale in 1940. By then he was an assistant professor (1939) and in 1947 became Gilbert Stark Professor of Social Ethics. He was dean of Yale Divinity School from 1949 to 1962.

Pope combined a deep interest in sociology with concern for the role of religion in relation to problems confronting American life. He was a staunch advocate of religious ecumenism* and racial equality. In *The Kingdom Beyond Caste* (1957) he criticized American religious organizations for lagging behind commerce and industry in achieving racial integration. Active in the World Council of Churches,* he frequently traveled and spoke in support of worldwide unity among Protestant* denominations* and with the Catholic Church.* He was also deeply interested in labor relations. His Ph.D. dissertation at Yale, published in 1942 under the title of *Millhands and Preachers: A Study of Gastonia,* is a study of relations between the Church and labor from about 1880 to 1940 in Gastonia, North Carolina. Pope edited *Labor Relations to Church and Community* (1947). From 1944 to 1948 he served as editor of *Social Action,* a monthly magazine of the Congregational Churches of America, treating social and political issues.

BIBLIOGRAPHY. *Current Biography Yearbook* (April 1956), ed. M. Dent; *New York Times* (April 16, 1974):42. R. P. Hesselgrave

Pope, William Burt (1822-1903). Methodist* theologian.* Born in Nova Scotia, the son of an English Methodist missionary* to Horton, Nova Scotia, Pope returned to England for his education. After a stint in his uncle's business in Nova Scotia, he went back to England to attend the Theological Institution, Huxton (1841-1842). In 1867 Pope began teaching theology at Didsbury College, Manchester. It was in that capacity that he published his most influential work, the three-volume *Compendium of Christian Theology* (1875-1876). In 1877 he was elected president of the Methodist Conference in England, and the next year saw the publication of the *Sermons, Addresses and Charges* (1878) he gave while serving in that office. Pope's *Compendium* established him as one of the most significant systematic theologians produced by

Methodism. His *Compendium* endured as a standard theology for Methodists on both sides of the Atlantic long after it left the course of study in 1888.

J. R. Tyson

Porter, Frank Chamberlain (1859-1946). Biblical scholar. Born in Beloit, Wisconsin, Porter was a great-great grandson of Jonathan Edwards.* He attended Beloit College (B.A., 1880; M.A., 1833), Chicago Theological Seminary (1881-1882), Hartford Seminary (1884-1885) and Yale* Divinity School (1885-1886). In 1889 he earned his Ph.D. from Yale Divinity School, with a dissertation on the resurrection in pre-Christian Judaism. He taught at Yale from 1889 until his retirement in 1927. Reinhold Niebuhr* praised Porter as a teacher: "the notes I took in his classes are the only school notes I preserved." H. Richard Niebuhr's* admiration of Jonathan Edwards was fostered by Porter.

Porter valued the historical-critical method and opposed the Princeton Theology.* He was a romanticist who drew inspiration from Aristotle's *Poetics,* Longinus, Wordsworth and Coleridge. For Porter, the Bible had a poetic character with spiritual truths and a sense of wonder which illumines the soul. His critique of George Foote Moore's* *Judaism* was instrumental in re-establishing for modern interpreters the place of apocalyptic thinking in Judaism.

BIBLIOGRAPHY. R. A. Harrisville, *Frank Chamberlain Porter: Pioneer in American Biblical Interpretation* (1976).   J. E. Stanley

Porter, Noah (1811-1892). Congregational* minister,* scholar and president of Yale.* Born in Farmington, Connecticut, Porter graduated from Yale College in 1831 and studied divinity in the new Yale Theological Department under Nathaniel W. Taylor* (whose daughter, Mary, he married in 1836). After 1836 he was pastor of Congregational churches in New Milford, Connecticut, and Springfield, Massachusetts. In 1846 he was made Clark Professor of Moral Philosophy and Metaphysics at Yale and served as president there from 1871 until 1886.

Porter spent most of his career in teaching ethics* and philosophy, always warmly and with a strongly evangelical* bent. He avoided the theological controversies of his age (including those surrounding Nathaniel Taylor), regarding them as barren of result. As president of Yale he recognized that graduates were turning away from the ministry to secular professions, and he sought to accommodate that development by replacing the inculcation

of orthodox doctrine in the college with the building of "Christian character." Porter remained, however, generally conservative in educational philosophy. He strongly resisted the introduction of the elective system and became embroiled in a major dispute in 1879 with W. G. Sumner over the introduction of Sir H. Spencer's *Study of Sociology* as a textbook.

Porter preferred writing to teaching, and he produced several influential textbooks. Although he initially embraced the substance of the Scottish Philosophy* as taught by Taylor, a period of study in Germany in 1853-1854 moved him closer to a rationalist idealism. His major work, *The Human Intellect* (1868), shows him concerned with the power of the mind in determining perceptions of reality. His most important ethical study, *Elements of Moral Science* (1884), presents a strongly rationalist and teleological conception of moral duty.

BIBLIOGRAPHY. *DAB* VII; D. H. Meyer, *The Instructed Conscience: The Shaping of the American National Ethic* (1972); L. Stevenson, *Scholarly Means to Evangelical Ends: The New Haven Scholars, 1830-1890* (1986).

A. C. Guelzo

Portland Deliverance. A statement by the 1892 General Assembly* of the Presbyterian Church (USA)* in Portland, Oregon, requiring ministers to subscribe to a strict understanding of the inspiration and authority* of the Bible.* Conservatives adopted this position to thwart efforts by theological moderates to revise the Westminster Confession* and thus modify the denomination's traditional commitment to Calvinism.* The deliverance, a highwater mark for conservatives, made the Princeton view of Archibald A. Hodge* and Benjamin B. Warfield* the official doctrine of the Church by affirming that "the inspired Word, as it came from God, is without error." All Church officers were mandated to profess the Bible as "the only infallible rule of faith and practice." Any who rejected this doctrine were required to withdraw from the ministry.* Presbyterians reaffirmed biblical inerrancy* several times in the 1890s and made it one of the Five Points* which were declared "essential and necessary" doctrines in 1910. The Portland Deliverance figured prominently in heresy trials* which resulted in the dismissal of Charles A. Briggs* in 1893 and Henry Preserved Smith* in 1894 and the resignation of Arthur C. McGiffert* in 1900.

BIBLIOGRAPHY. L. A. Loetscher, *The Broadening Church* (1954).   W. A. Hoffecker

Positive Thinking. The general belief that optimistic thought can bring beneficial results. Positive thinking is a stream in American life that has been fed by many sources and has produced many tributaries. The immigrant* experience itself—frequently motivated by the hope of a better life—was a major source of optimism. Puritan* theology,* though it emphasized human depravity and the necessity of God's grace for salvation,* also carried a postmillennial* theme. Both Cotton Mather* and Jonathan Edwards,* for example, foresaw divine possibilities for the establishment of the kingdom of God in America.* This optimistic note was emphasized during the revivals* of the First and Second Great Awakenings,* and the Arminian* theology that triumphed in these revivals explicitly encouraged human effort to transform one's will and accept the free offer of salvation. Revivalists such as Charles G. Finney,* Dwight L. Moody* and Billy Sunday* typify this transformation.

Paradoxically, even some who opposed the awakenings contributed to the widening stream of positive thinking. Transcendentalists* such as Ralph Waldo Emerson* articulated a self-consciously optimistic theology. Later, persons like Phineas Quimby* and Mary Baker Eddy* made positive thinking the central affirmation and technique of healing, expressed specifically in Christian Science,* but also informing a host of "new thought" and "mind cure" movements like the Unity School of Christianity.* William James,* in his *Varieties of Religious Experience,* explored the appeal and limitations of such "religion of healthy-mindedness."

In the twentieth century, Norman Vincent Peale's* best seller, *The Power of Positive Thinking* (1952), reclaimed the techniques of self-improvement as an aspect of conventional Protestant piety,* an aspect that is now identified with the television ministry of Robert Schuller's* *Hour of Power.* At the same time, Rabbi Joshua Liebman's *Peace of Mind* (1946) and Bishop Fulton J. Sheen's* *Peace of Soul* (1949) treated similar themes from Jewish and Catholic* perspectives. Humanistic psychologies associated with such persons as Carl Rogers and Abraham Maslow provided secular versions of similar optimistic themes. Though there are significant differences in these various streams of thought, they are all expressions of the continuing appeal of positive thinking in American life.

BIBLIOGRAPHY. D. B. Meyer, *The Positive Thinkers: Popular Religious Psychology from Mary Baker Eddy to Norman Vincent Peale and Ronald Reagan* (1988); R. M. Anker, "Popular Religion and Theories of Self-Help," in *Handbook of American Popular Culture,* vol. 2, ed. M. T. Inge (1980).   R. R. Crocker

Postmillennialism. The belief that the return of Christ will take place after the millennium, which may be a literal period of peace and prosperity or else a symbolic representation of the final triumph of the gospel. This new age will come through Christian teaching and preaching.* The Holy Spirit will use such activity to shape a new world characterized by prosperity, peace and righteousness. Evil will not be totally eliminated, but it will be reduced to a minimum because the moral and spiritual influence of the church will be greatly increased. During the new age Christians will solve many of humankind's most persistent social, economic and educational problems. The millennium will not necessarily be limited to 1,000 years because the number can be used symbolically. The period closes with the Second Coming of Christ, the resurrection of the dead and the last judgment.

Postmillennialism is often dismissed by premillennialists* as a Christian version of the secular idea of progress, but it was actually formulated by Puritan* theologians* in the seventeenth century long before the ideas of the eighteenth-century Enlightenment* popularized the belief in progress. The classic expression of postmillennialism is found in the work of the Anglican* commentator Daniel Whitby (1638-1726). His view was adopted by many later Protestant* ministers* and theologians, including Jonathan Edwards* and the leaders of the Protestant missionary movement* during the nineteenth and early twentieth centuries. Despite the pessimism of recent times, postmillennialism continues to be popular among many in the Reformed* churches.

BIBLIOGRAPHY. L. Boettner, *The Millennium* (1957); R. G. Clouse, ed., *The Meaning of the Millennium: Four Views* (1977); J. J. Davis, *Christ's Victorious Kingdom: Postmillennialism Reconsidered* (1987); I. H. Murray, *The Puritan Hope* (1975).   R. G. Clouse

Posttribulationism. *See* RAPTURE OF THE CHURCH.

Praise the Lord. A verbal exclamation of praise or thanksgiving that God has acted in a special way. It is usually made in response to answered prayer, evangelistic* success or unexpected material and spiritual blessings. Used primarily by Christians of an evangelical* or charismatic* persuasion, the phrase implies a grateful sense of God's work in and through the lives of his people. By nature, it signified an acknowledgement of God's majesty and a sense of fellowship with him. While the exact origin of the phrase is uncertain, the Psalms (e.g., Psalms 148—150) frequently use it as an expression of worship.*   S. A. Wenig

Prayer. Communication with God, usually in verbal form. All Christian traditions find precedent for private and corporate prayer in the Hebrew Scriptures and the New Testament. Christians through the centuries have found private prayer to be an essential aspect of their spiritual life, both as a means of expressing themselves to God and of experiencing his presence. Private and public prayer may be extemporaneous, recited or read from a prayer book. Scripture may also be used as a form of prayer or in contemplative or meditative prayer.

Corporate prayer may take place in a variety of settings: in families, small prayer groups, prayer meetings, worship services and convocations. For many Christians prayer is a daily practice and may take place at the beginning of the day, at mealtime, in the evening, sporadically throughout the day or at set times, such as the canonical hours.*

The most prominent setting for prayer is public worship. Depending on the tradition, this prayer may follow a set liturgical form, be led by the minister with responses from the congregaton, or be extemporaneous. Prayer meetings, either in a church or other settings, are frequently led by lay* people and may be held at regularly scheduled times, at special seasons in the Christian year or in times of crisis.

Particularly in nonliturgical traditions, extemporaneous prayers are preferred for both public and private worship. In these traditions—particularly within the evangelical* tradition—extemporaneous prayers are frequently valued because they are said to arise from the heart—even the Spirit's prompting of the heart. Advocates of extemporaneous prayer often question the use of liturgical prayers, arguing that they easily become rote and meaningless. Proponents of liturgical prayers, on the other hand, argue that extemporaneous prayers are frequently banal and inevitably follow established patterns without the benefit of forethought, inherited wisdom and elegance of expression. Serious practitioners of prayer have learned to benefit from both extemporaneous and liturgical prayers. Prayers are frequently written out of private experience of communion with God and are sometimes published and used by others.

Prayer may take one of several different attitudes

or may combine any number of these into a single occasion of prayer:

Adoration. Offered to God alone, this is the response of creatures who encounter the infinite holiness, majesty and perfection of God. It frequently consists of praising him for who he is.

Confession. Coming before God, who is holy, men and women respond by confessing their own sinfulness and inadequacy to approach him apart from the merit of Jesus Christ.

Intercession. Christians pray on behalf of others, whether for individuals, a group or the world. Intercession may be prayer for those in danger, in sickness or facing a crisis. In the Catholic tradition prayers are offered to the saints and Mary, calling on them to join in intercession.

Petition. This is the prayer of asking, not as a self-interested begging but as a recognition of the believer's creaturely dependence on God for every gift of physical life and spiritual grace. Orthodox Christians believe that God hears and responds to petitions made in accord with his character and will.

Thanksgiving. One of the most prominent types of prayer, Christians give thanks to God for daily food and sustenance and the multitude of blessing they enjoy and receive as coming from the hand of God. While it is difficult to make a rigid distinction, believers frequently view thanksgiving as a response to what God has done and praise or adoration as a response to who God is.

See also PRAYER BREAKFASTS; PRAYER MEETING; SPIRITUALITY.

BIBLIOGRAPHY.   G. Appleton, ed., *Oxford Book of Prayer* (1985); L. A. Bouyer, *A History of Christian Spirituality,* 3 vols. (1982); J. Hastings, *The Doctrine of Prayer* (1915); G. S. Wakefield, *The Westminster Dictionary of Christian Spirituality* (1983).   D. G. Reid

Prayer Breakfasts. Periodic morning prayer* gatherings of laypeople,* frequently including political figures. Methodist minister Abraham Vereide (d.1969) was the originator of the prayer breakfast movement. His first breakfast meeting for Bible study* was held with Seattle businessmen in April 1935. Known as "City Chapel," the gatherings were followed by the first prayer breakfast for political leaders in 1939.

Prayer breakfasts led by Vereide quickly spread to other cities. In 1942 eighty members of Congress attended the capital's first such event. Weekly breakfast groups were then organized in both House and Senate. The first national prayer breakfast, held in 1953, was attended by President

Eisenhower.* Since then, presidents have generally attended, instilling these events with civil-religious* meaning. Similar events are held at local, state and international locations to promote effective Christian leadership. The Vereide-originated ministry has successively been known as the National Committee for Christian Leadership, International Christian Leadership and most recently as Fellowship Foundation.

BIBLIOGRAPHY. N. P. Grubb, *Modern Viking: The Story of Abram Vereide* (1961); J. C. Hefley and E. E. Plowman, *Washington: Christians in the Corridors of Power* (1975); R. V. Pierard, "On Praying with the President," *CCen* 99 (March 10, 1982):262-264.   R. C. Cizik

Prayer Cloths. A method of prayer used primarily by charismatics* and Pentecostals,* especially for physical healing.* The biblical basis for the practice is Acts 19:11-12, in which handkerchiefs taken from the apostle Paul are described as instruments of physical healing. Pentecostal* and charismatic* evangelists,* believing that God desires to work similar miracles today, have adopted the practice. They often encourage people with sick friends to bring cloths to a healing meeting. The evangelist prays, laying hands on the cloth, and then asks the owner to take the cloth to the invalid friend so that God's healing power may be transmitted.

Some prominent healing evangelists, such as Oral Roberts,* have mailed "anointed" cloths to their supporters or invited them to mail cloths to the minister to be prayed over and returned. The use of prayer cloths is easily susceptible to hucksterism, particularly by unscrupulous evangelists whose fantastic claims of healing power bring increased financial contributions from impressed followers.   B. Barron

Prayer in Public Schools. The issue of prayer in public schools is framed by the First Amendment to the U.S. Constitution adopted in 1791: "Congress shall make no law respecting an establishment of religion or prohibiting the free exercise thereof. . . ." This statement of freedom of religion must be interpreted today within the context of a pluralistic* society with a system of public education rooted in religious convictions.

By 1647 evangelical* religion had spawned the Massachusetts Bay Colony township schools—prototype of later public schools in the U.S. Universal education was deemed necessary so that all might read the Bible* and turn to God for salvation.* Religious teaching and prayer* were integral to schooling in that theocratic* environment.

A century later in 1779, Thomas Jefferson's* proposal for public education to the Virginia Assembly argued that public education was necessary for the preservation of liberty through training in republican virtues. While modifying the reasons for public education, Jefferson expanded the vision for state-sponsored education available to all. By 1800 seven of sixteen states had enacted legislation providing for public education. Some of those states (e.g., Massachusetts) required religious practices in their schools while others permitted them.

The nineteenth century saw the rise of the common school. Henry Bernard, Horace Mann and others worked for a system of public education that focused on common values. At the same time Catholic* and Jewish communities objected to Protestant* prayers and the reading of the King James Bible in the schools. This ferment resulted in the deletion of Protestant sectarian religious emphases in public schools. The McGuffy* Eclectic Readers, first published in 1836 and used in thirty-seven states by the end of the century, exemplify this trend. Early editions displayed a theistic* Calvinistic* world view stressing salvation, righteousness and piety. By 1879 the text had been modified to emphasize religious, moral and cultural values without sectarian teaching.

Regional differences have remained a factor since colonial days. By the end of the nineteenth century, prayer in public schools had been banned in six states, including Wisconsin (1890). Yet after 1910 eleven states joined Massachusetts in requiring religious exercises in the public schools. While those practices continued well into the twentieth century, some Far Western states such as California never instituted prayer in public schools at all.

In 1940 the U.S. Supreme Court ruled in *Cantwell* v. *Connecticut* that the states were subject to the First Amendment* through the Fourteenth Amendment. This meant that questions of religious practice in public schools were no longer under state jurisdiction but came under the rule of the U.S. Constitution. Since that time, numerous Supreme Court rulings on religion and public education have been made. Questions of state support for transportation and textbooks for children attending parochial schools,* release time for religious activities on or off public-school grounds, and practices of prayer and Bible reading in the schools have been reviewed by the court.

In 1962 and 1963, three cases reached the U.S. Supreme Court that challenged traditional Bible reading and prayer practiced in some state schools. In *Engel* v. *Vitale* (1962), a school-sponsored prayer composed by the New York State Board of Regents was ruled unconstitutional. A year later recitation of the Lord's Prayer and devotional Bible reading were ruled unconstitutional in the nation's public schools (*Abington* v. *Schempp* and *Murray* v. *Curlett*).

Those decisions engendered national controversy. Three attempts to pass a constitutional amendment that would allow prayer in public schools have failed, the most recent one defeated in 1984 by eleven votes in the U.S. Senate. Attempted legislation aimed at removing the issue of prayer in public schools from the domain of the U.S. Supreme Court has not been adopted.

The Engel and Schempp decisions set the precedent for the relationship of prayer and public education today. The court's interpretation of state neutrality renders school-sponsored prayers and devotional Bible reading illegal. The study of the Bible as literature, the academic teaching of religion and voluntary prayers, however, are acceptable in the public schools.

BIBLIOGRAPHY. D. L. Barr and N. Piediscalzi, eds., *The Bible in American Education* (1982); R. M. McCarthy et al., *Disestablishment a Second Time: Genuine Pluralism for American Schools* (1982); R. C. McMillan, *Religion in the Public Schools: An Introduction* (1984); R. Michaelsen, *Piety in the Public School: Trends and Issues in the Relationship Between Religion and the Public School in the U.S.* (1970).

F. S. Adeney

Prayer Meeting. A meeting convened for the sake of prayer.* Prayer meetings are mentioned occasionally before 1800, but were popularized by Charles G. Finney* and Dwight L. Moody.* In *Lectures* (chapter VII), Finney commented on how to conduct such meetings. An awakening during the years 1857-1858 was even called the "prayer meeting revival."* Moody held noon prayer meetings in conjunction with his campaigns. As a result, by the turn of the century, prayer meetings or midweek services became common in Protestant churches with evangelistic* legacies.

Among seventeenth-century Puritans,* regular gatherings were Sunday* morning and evening, and Thursday morning for a lecture. In the first two awakenings,* preaching* occurred on any night of the week, but on an ad hoc basis. The evangelist preached a night or two, then moved on. Finney and Moody popularized protracted meetings* of two weeks and longer, normally in tents or unheat-

ed tabernacles, and for that reason they were generally held in the summer. The addition of the prayer meeting, frequently held midweek, became a unique feature of the American evangelical* church week. By the middle of the twentieth century, some churches placed more emphasis on teaching or proclamation than on prayer.

BIBLIOGRAPHY. W. G. McLoughlin, *Modern Revivalism: Charles Grandison Finney to Billy Graham* (1959). T. H. Olbricht

Prayer Meeting Revival (1857-1859). The revival originated in the noon prayer meetings* begun by Jeremiah Lanphier on September 23, 1857, in the Dutch Reformed* Church on Fulton Street in New York City. Beginning with six persons praying, the revival of 1857 to 1859 attained proportions that have prompted some students of revivals to term it a major awakening. The movement was given impetus by the financial panic of October 1857, as well as by the ongoing tension over slavery* and from extensive coverage in the secular press. By early 1858 noontime prayer meetings in New York had multiplied to over twenty in number, while in Chicago over two thousand people gathered daily at the Metropolitan Theatre. The movement soon spread to other cities around the nation and gradually made its way to the British Isles and around the world.

In geographical and numerical extent, in fact, the Revival of 1857-1859 has probably never been equaled. Estimates range up to one million or more converts in the U.S., with another million in Great Britain and Ireland, in addition to hundreds of thousands of professed Christians whose lives were deeply affected. Although the immediate dramatic events took place within a relatively brief time span, the results in such areas as evangelism,* missions* and social action continued for several decades. Dwight L. Moody,* William Booth,* A. B. Simpson* and Charles Spurgeon were among the prominent Christian workers who were powerfully affected by the Revival. Among its special characteristics were the prominent role of the laity,* the focus on prayer rather than on preaching* and the close cooperation across denominational lines. *See also* REVIVALISM, PROTESTANT.

BIBLIOGRAPHY. S. I. Prime, *The Power of Prayer* . . . (1859); S. I. Prime, *Fifteen Years of Prayer in the Fulton Street Meeting* (1872); J. E. Orr, *The Fervent Prayer: The Worldwide Impact of the Great Awakening of 1858* (1974); T. L. Smith, *Revivalism and Social Reform in Mid-Nineteenth-Century America* (1957).

N. A. Magnuson

Praying Indian Towns. Towns of settled, Christian Native Americans in colonial Massachusetts. Soon after John Eliot* began his missionary* work among the Massachusetts Native Americans in 1646, he saw the advantage of locating the new converts in separate towns. This protected them from the influences of the heathen Native Americans as well as allowed easy gatherings for worship.* The first such town was at Natick, Massachusetts, in 1651. Such towns soon multiplied. Jonathan Mayhew* was also active in evangelizing among the Native Americans on the island of Martha's Vineyard.

By 1674 there were fourteen such towns in Massachusetts, with a total of twenty-four congregations and about 2,500 converted Native Americans. That same year, however, saw the arrival of King Philip's War,* a bloody conflict between whites and several Native American tribes. The "praying Indians" were distrusted by the white colonists and unconverted Native Americans, and many were abused and killed. Intermarriage with local African-Americans soon reduced the numbers of "praying Indians," and the towns rapidly lost their Native-American identity.

BIBLIOGRAPHY. A. T. Vaughan, *New England Frontier: Puritans and Indians, 1620-1675* (1965).   J. B. North

Preacher. A person, usually of the ordained* clergy,* who regularly preaches sermons. The term is usually used to refer to an ordained minister* of nonliturgical religious groups in which preaching is the primary public function of the clergy. In certain contexts, most notably in the South, a male minister might be addressed as "Preacher" or referred to as "the Preacher." In other contexts, such as urban and suburban white churches, the term is used to refer to one of the several roles of an ordained professional minister who may also serve as teacher, counselor and church administrator. In that context a clergy person may be described as a "good preacher." Theologically speaking, a preacher is one who is called by God to communicate the word of God through speech to a contemporary situation.

See also PREACHING.   D. G. Reid

Preaching in America. The Europeans who invaded North America in the sixteenth and subsequent centuries brought with them their language, their culture and their religious values. They came in search of political and economic freedom and, frequently, in pursuit of spiritual liberty as well. The New England Puritans* in particular were convinced that divine providence was laying a new burden on them: rather than struggling to reform the Church of England, they should cross the sea and establish a new England, with a pure church set in a community governed solely by the laws of God. This "errand into the wilderness" would build a "city set upon a hill," which would serve as a bright beacon not only for the new land but also for the old one.

Leading this venture were their clergy,* who gave voice to the vision and set out to create a "people of the Word." Within settled New England communities, the ministers were generally the best-educated members of the community, respected for their wisdom and learning. In addition, they served as the monitors of morality for the culture. Not only did they control the guidelines of church membership,* but they exercised a weekly role in delivering the sermon—the only regular medium of public communication in their social order. As H. S. Stout has pointed out, "The average weekly churchgoer in New England . . . listened to something like seven thousand sermons in a lifetime, totaling somewhere around fifteen thousand hours of concentrated listening." Given the settled nature of New England's ministers, the high public regard for the pulpit, and the liberty of the minister to apply God's Word to every aspect of life, their power as shapers of cultural values and meanings should not be underestimated.

The Puritan Heritage. Thus, the history of preaching in America begins with the unique office of the settled New England preacher. One of the most prominent of these first-generation pulpiteers was John Cotton,* who had a distinguished career of twenty years in England before coming to Boston. For seventeen years, beginning in 1635, he occupied the pulpit at Boston's First Church, preaching that salvation* rested solely on the eternal, electing grace of God. This election* was manifest in the spiritual and moral condition of the individual, and the community was to be governed only by those who possessed such qualities.

Cotton's was the voice of the Puritan institution, the gathered community of saints settled in covenant* with one another and with God. His sermons tended to be expressed in the clear, direct language of the common people, quietly and carefully analyzing points of doctrine,* occasionally taking note of certain sinful behaviors, always concerned for the salvation of his people's souls. As a preacher his role was to guide the people of New England, to proclaim God's will for them and to encourage them to conduct their lives in ways befitting the chosen people of God.

Other New England pulpiteers shared this approach to preaching and regarded the preparation and delivery of sermons as the principal task of their pastoral charge. Each Sunday they opened the Scriptures and in their "regular sermon" charted the spiritual course of the individual from death in sin to life in Christ. On special weekday events the minister would deliver an "occasional sermon"* in which he would unfold the spiritual meaning and mission of New England. The latter were the sermons that most frequently found their way into print. From New England's birth and through the Revolutionary era, this pattern of regular and occasional sermon remained remarkably consistent.

John Cotton's family lineage included other notable New England preachers. One of his early Boston contemporaries was Richard Mather.* After Cotton's death in 1652, his widow married the recently widowed Mather, whose son Increase* eventually married Cotton's daughter Maria. Of their union was born a son, to whom they gave the ancestral name Cotton Mather.*

In 1685 Cotton Mather became pastor at Boston's Second Church, where his father, Increase, was teacher, a relationship that remained in place until Increase's death in 1723. As a third-generation minister of a distinguished line of preachers, Cotton Mather felt virtually commissioned to advance the sacred cause of New England in his preaching and writing. In his sermons he lamented the decline in moral conduct and spiritual courage in the generations since the founding of New England. In scholarly efforts such as the *Magnalia Christi Americana,** he tirelessly labored to connect the New England experience with the providence of God. As a pastor he visited door to door, leaving with families pamphlets he had written, and preached on Sundays* and midweek to congregations numbering over a thousand. With scholarship, reason and with the passion of a man who believed he could see the old foundations of a faithful community eroding away, Cotton Mather was the quintessential New England preacher.

In 1729, the year after Cotton Mather's death, Jonathan Edwards* became the pastor at Northampton, Massachusetts, succeeding his grandfather Solomon Stoddard.* Edwards was more of a philosopher and theologian than a pastor. He once advised his parishioners that he would be in his study thirteen hours a day and that if they needed him, they knew where to find him; otherwise, they should leave him alone. His carefully crafted sermons on points of biblical doctrine were fashioned in the tradition of New England's best homileticians. Nervous and near-sighted, Edwards read his work to the congregation, occasionally looking up from the manuscript and staring at the bell in the back of the sanctuary.

By temperament and by training, Edwards was an empirical observer of events and behaviors. As a young boy he had been fascinated by spiders, and had taken careful notes on their activities. In his most famous sermon, titled "Sinners in the Hands of an Angry God," Edwards compared the individuals in need of repentance with spiders hanging by a slender, silken thread: only the grace of God suspends them from falling into the fiery pit of hell; only the will of God dangles them above damnation.

In the 1730s Edwards began to notice some startling developments in his congregation. As he read his sermons in his undemonstrative style, parishioners were affected by phenomena such as loud cries, convulsions and fainting spells. Ever the observer, Edwards chronicled these events in four volumes, beginning with *A Faithful Narrative* in 1737 and closing with *A Treatise Concerning the Religious Affections* in 1746. His purpose was to assess whether these physical phenomena could be read as evidence of the work of God within a believer. While he remained skeptical of human ability to draw such direct conclusions, he believed that an individual could receive a new inner perception of God which could be related to changes in outward behavior.

Preaching and the Great Awakening. In other New World colonies, similar spiritual revivals were building toward what would become known as the Great Awakening.* During the 1720s Theodore Jacob Frelinghuysen* had begun preaching an inner experience of conversion to the Dutch settlers in his New Jersey congregations. Signs of spiritual revival seemed to manifest themselves in outpourings of emotion. By mid-decade, Gilbert Tennent* had joined him in working toward spiritual renewal. An intense man, and lacking in pulpit eloquence, Tennent nevertheless spoke directly to the hearts of common people with tremendous effect. Rather than stressing election, this revival preaching stressed the equality of all persons in God's sight. Rooted in the traditions of German Pietism* rather than the Calvinism of the English Puritans, this approach to religious awakening represented a difference of style and theological substance. It also encouraged expressions of religious feeling while discouraging restrictive categories of doctrine and reason.

Meanwhile the colonies were about to experience revival preaching in a style hitherto not seen even in preachers such as Frelinghuysen, Tennent and Edwards. Each of these men were pastors of congregations and based their revival work in their own parish ministries. In 1738 George Whitefield, a twenty-five-year-old itinerant revivalist from England, came to America in the first of seven preaching tours of the colonies (1738-1770).

An Anglican priest with a mixture of theological leanings, Whitefield traveled throughout the colonies, making several different evangelistic forays. Possessing a mighty preaching voice, he could speak to thousands who gathered at once on hillsides or on a town commons. His homiletical* style was vigorous, enthusiastic and intended to provoke emotional responses. Moreover, it was extemporaneous. This style, recommended by Whitefield to New England ministers, became widely influential as preachers discovered the power of direct and spontaneous delivery. Though Whitefield created no enduring institution, either ecclesiastical or educational, his style of preaching left an indelible stamp on the American scene.

Respected by revivalists, on at least one occasion Whitefield was a guest in the Edwards's home, and in 1740 he commissioned Gilbert Tennent to a follow-up tour of his own. Not all New England preachers were impressed however. Charles Chauncy,* for example, who occupied John Cotton's old pulpit in Boston, rejected the "enthusiasts." Maintaining that they defied reason with a pretense of being moved by the Spirit, Chauncy entered into debate with Edwards over the nature of the revivals. In the end Chauncy was pressed to a liberal Arminianism* that placed him outside New England orthodoxy.

Revival Preaching on the American Frontier. Following the success of the American Revolution, preaching in America turned to address new fields for mission, namely the western frontier. Westward expansion was being accomplished faster than the established churches were able to respond, and preachers developed new forms to meet that challenge.

The Methodists invented and virtually institutionalized the most effective approach to the American frontier. Organizing a territory into circuits, they appointed circuit-riding* preachers to travel from point to point, preaching the gospel. Typically these preachers were young, single men with little theological training, who called people to repentance and salvation in simple, emotional terms. They rode on horseback, slept and ate when they could, and generally followed the model of their leader, the circuit-riding Bishop Francis

Asbury.* Best known among these untutored preachers was Peter Cartwright,* a tall man with boundless enthusiasm who insisted that uneducated evangelists like himself were setting the frontier on fire while learned preachers of other denominations were still trying to light their matches.

Another device that preachers found successful on the frontier was the camp meeting.* At these annual events, persons from scattered farms and villages would converge on a certain spot for a week-long marathon of preaching and praying and praising God with song. Hundreds or thousands of persons might gather at a camp meeting at which preachers would occupy pulpits on various spots around the camp and deliver sermons simultaneously. Like a homiletical bazaar, the camp meeting permitted groups to move about, hearing various preachers in an intense immersion into spirituality. Frequent outbursts of religious affections would occur, with listeners shrieking or falling to the ground, all of which meant signs of the Spirit of God at work in the camp meeting atmosphere.

In the 1820s and afterward, Charles G. Finney* raised these events to a new level of sophistication. Finney believed that an effective revival meeting was a combination of the Holy Spirit and human persuasion working together. To that end he developed a set of measures whose purpose was to stimulate spiritual renewal. One such device was the anxious bench,* a front row reserved for those who seemed nervously at the edge of knowing whether God was or was not calling them to repentance and renewal. There, directly in front of the fiery evangelist, they would tend to be overcome with the emotion of the moment. A combination of spiritual management and psychological manipulation, the anxious bench was a widely criticized and enormously successful innovation.

During the century and a half since Finney, his basic approaches have been revised and implemented by preachers including Dwight L. Moody,* Billy Sunday* and Billy Graham.* Remote from the doctrinal precision and cautious judgments exercised by Edwards in New England's Great Awakening, nineteenth and twentieth-century revival preaching has tended to measure its success by its popular appeal to mass audiences.

Preaching in the Black Tradition. In the early years of the new republic, preachers became aware of the continued bondage of one element of the population, the African-American slave. Slavery, with its racism, became an issue which the churches could not long ignore. There was a time when Francis Asbury travelled with an African-

American preacher named Harry Hosier. In settings where there were white folks and African-American folks available to hear the gospel preached, Asbury would assign Hosier and himself to separate racial constituencies. On occasions when Asbury might be invited to spend the night resting in a white slave-owner's home, Hosier would be relegated to the barn or the servant's quarters.

Eventually, more than one schism developed along racial lines. Richard Allen* led a group of African-American Methodists out of St. George's Methodist Episcopal Church in 1787 to form the African Methodist Episcopal Church,* after a number of humiliating encounters within that congregation and with Asbury himself. The African-American church tradition that emerged from this separation, and others like it, cultivated a style of preaching not generally known in white churches. The popular piety of the African-American religious tradition has been intricately related to public worship, an experience often characterized by spirituals, powerful oratory and the famous "answering congregation" in which preacher and congregation carry on a dialog throughout the sermon. More spontaneous and lyrical than reasoned and rhetorical, more evocative of congregational participation than conducive to quiet listening, African-American preaching found a way to tell the biblical story in narrative form. Their preaching mirrored the experiences of Old Testament Israelite slaves seeking freedom and the early Christian martyrs dying and seeking resurrection. It was a spirituality unknown, and perhaps unknowable, by a white majority accustomed to carving out its own city on a hill while oppressively enslaving another race to do the work.

Preaching and Social Conscience. The consequences of slavery could hardly have been more divisive for the church and for preaching in America. Classmates like Theodore Parker* and James Thornwell* at Harvard Divinity School emerged from the same theological curriculum, Parker to be an abolitionist preacher and Thornwell to become a Southern Presbyterian advocate of the rights of slavemasters.

The history of preaching in America was not aloof from the crises confronting the nation. One monumental personality among America's preachers did emerge during this era. Henry Ward Beecher* became pastor of Plymouth Congregational Church in 1847. He brought to the ministry a simple, direct, personal style that applied his formidable pulpit personality to the burning social questions of the day. Beecher, who was the son of the orthodox Puritan Lyman Beecher* and the

brother of Harriet Beecher Stowe,* used no liturgical trappings to adorn or encumber his preaching. The only chancel furniture was a plain lectern or preaching desk, which became his platform to proclaim the Word of God in a unique way. The evils of slavery so incensed him that he raised funds to purchase "Beecher's Bibles" (actually rifles) to use in the fight against proslavery forces in Kansas. He dramatized the situation by raising funds within his congregation to purchase freedom for slaves.

In the forty years of his ministry at the Brooklyn Church, Beecher became a national celebrity, attacking political corruption, applauding women's rights, embracing evolution* and endorsing liberal* biblical scholarship. In the midst of criticism, Beecher remained a towering personality of the pulpit. Declaring himself a free man in 1882, he led his members out of the fold of the Congregational Church.

Preachers as Personalities. Preaching in America had entered a new era. The focus in the late nineteenth century seemed no longer on a set of doctrines or a system of ministerial deployment, but on the social issues of the day as they were being addressed by remarkable pulpit personalities. Henry Ward Beecher was one of the most dominant among these preachers. Another was his contemporary, Phillips Brooks.*

An Anglican priest* and bishop* in Massachusetts, Brooks was by no means a social firebrand. Rather, he provided the classic example of what a thoughtful, scholarly preacher could produce in the progressive and increasingly prosperous culture of late nineteenth-century America. In his Lyman Beecher lectures on preaching at Yale* in 1877, Brooks said that preaching involves the transmission of the eternal truth of the gospel through the contemporary personality of the preacher. In other words, it is the preacher who gives shape and specification to the changeless Christian message in the changing circumstances of the preacher's life and world.

As the twentieth century drew near and dawned, it was the personality of the preacher that became the key element in American homiletics. Neither doctrine nor denomination loomed as large as the impact of an individual. Leaders of the Social Gospel,* like Washington Gladden* who served First Congregational Church in Columbus, Ohio, for nearly three decades, preached across denominational and doctrinal boundaries with a witness that moved Christians to find their mission among the ill and impoverished. Others, like Russell Conwell,* celebrated the promise of American prosperity, endorsing the culture of industrial growth and economic expansion.

Undoubtedly the most indomitable pulpit personality in the U.S. during the first half of the twentieth century was Harry Emerson Fosdick.* Raised in the decades of optimism and progress, Fosdick was an orthodox Baptist* who developed modernist* views in the course of his studies, his ministry and his own emotional crisis. Starting his career at a Baptist church in Montclair, New Jersey, Fosdick became the central figure in a theological debate while preaching at First Presbyterian Church in New York, and spent the crowning portion of his career at the interdenominational Riverside Church, New York City, which was built to house his sermons and his vision of ministry as a seven-day-per-week enterprise to minister to all human needs.

Fosdick developed a new style of preaching, which he called pastoral counseling on a group scale. He began with a need or issue in human life, surrounded it with Scripture, and then crafted his manuscript. He was the first nationally known radio preacher, with messages that reached millions for more than two decades. He exemplified more clearly than anyone else the full meaning of Brooks' judgment that preaching is the proclamation of truth through personality.

In the second half of the twentieth century, that phenomenon took new shape with the so-called electronic church.* A popular image of preaching in America became the televangelist.* Robert Schuller,* who built his celebrated Crystal Cathedral in Garden Grove, California, began by preaching to Southern Californians. But his church soon transcended those limits, becoming a religious television stage from which his sermons could be heard throughout the nation on an electronic network. Other preachers used the same medium at enormous costs to reach enormous numbers of persons. Jimmy Swaggart* of Louisiana developed a television ministry that depended on his personality far more than on his Assembly of God denomination. He continued preaching when his acknowledged moral failures separated him from his denomination. Pat Robertson* created a television network with programming that centered upon his personality without any traditional format for preaching. As host of his 700 Club, he sat in living room furniture, talking and praying with guests, but foregoing pulpit and sermon.

Yet, in the midst of these more notable features of the evolving American pulpit, some groups maintained a commitment to preaching as exposition of Christian Scripture. Usually found within the fundamentalist-evangelical tradition, this form of preaching has focused on expositing Scripture as the written Word of God. Although many within this tradition have effectively combined this concern with an effort to relate their exposition to their contemporary world, others have focused on instilling in their congregations an understanding Scripture and how it supports particular doctrinal formulations. In some instances preaching may, apart from the setting of congregational worship, barely be distinguished from teaching.

Conclusion. The history of preaching in America is the history of an evolving art form which has experienced many transformations since the days of the first European immigrants' arrival. From the days of doctrinal exposition, to camp-meeting revivals, to the electronic personalities of the late twentieth century, the changes have been abundant.

Yet some aspects endure. Preaching in America continues to carry important political implications. The society is such that preachers have continued to discover new ways to acquire political clout for their preaching. Moreover, there remains a moral edge to preaching which assumes a responsibility to speak to and about the ethical issues of the day—from matters of private conduct to issues of global social justice.

Preaching in America will undoubtedly endure even though its familiar forms and institutions may pass away or be radically transformed. New England's theocracy passed away. The mainline denominations that prospered with the nation's growth appear to be waning. The camp meetings have all but disappeared. So, too, will the electronic church give way to other forms and media.

BIBLIOGRAPHY. S. E. Ahlstrom, *A Religious History of the American People* (1972); E. Elliot, *Power and Pulpit in Puritan New England* (1975); C. V. R. George, *Segregated Sabbaths: Richard Allen and the Rise of Independent Black Churches, 1760-1840* (1973); D. T. Holland, *Sermons in American History: Selected Issues in the American Pulpit, 1630-1967* (1971); D. T. Holland, *The Preaching Tradition: a Brief History* (1980); P. Miller, *Jonathan Edwards* (1949); R. M. Miller, *Harry Emerson Fosdick* (1985); H. S. Smith, R. T. Handy, L. A. Loetscher, *American Christianity: An Historical Interpretation and Representative Documents,* 2 vols. (1960-1963); H. S. Stout, *The New England Soul* (1986); P. Tracy, *Jonathan Edwards, Pastor* (1980). W. B. Lawrence

Predestination. In its normal and proper sense, the term refers to the foreordination of moral agents to their eternal ends. That is, the knowledge and choice, made by God before time began, of angels and men as to their final blessedness with God or damnation apart from him.

The doctrine was formulated by Augustine in his controversies with Pelagius (405-418). Augustine held that all persons were predestined either to belief, by the intervention of God's saving grace, or unbelief, by God's permitting them to follow their own ways (reprobation). Pelagius considered election* to refer simply to God's foreknowledge of who would believe. He saw no need for God's intervention to cause belief because he denied that guilt was inherited from Adam's sin.* The later dispute between Calvinism* and Arminianism* (1603-1619) was essentially the same (though Arminius did hold that original righteousness was taken away in the Fall).

Theologically, this doctrine follows from the doctrine of God's eternal knowledge of all events in time and his eternally willing (in the same act, for his will and knowledge are only formally and not really separate) that they be as they are (his decree). The doctrine is also necessary for those who hold that human depravity makes it impossible for people to choose the good, as this would require that God initiate the response of every person who turns to him by giving each the grace to believe. As such, the doctrine is intimately connected with the other cardinal doctrines of soteriology: original sin, election, limited/unlimited atonement,* free will and grace.

Biblically, the doctrine is derived from the Old Testament teaching of God's foreknowledge (Ps 139:4-6), his ordination of events (Is 14:26-27) and his choice of the nation Israel (Deut 10:15; Mal 1:2-3). In the New Testament, God's foreknowledge (1 Pet 1:20) and ordination (Rom 9:11; 1 Cor 2:7; Eph 1:11; 3:11) are understood by some Christians to be specifically applied to individuals (Rom 11:2; Rev 13:8; 17:8). These terms are united in Romans 8:28-30. According to 1 Peter 1:2, predestination is in accordance with foreknowledge.

In American church traditions, there is a broad spectrum of belief about this doctrine. While Catholicism has embraced a range of views on the question, for Protestant churches an understanding or denial of the doctrine has frequently formed an important part of their self-identity. Two views affirm both God's foreknowledge and his choice in predestination:

Dortian, or Extreme Calvinism. The Reformed Tradition (including the Puritan Congregationalists,* Presbyterians,* Reformed churches and Particular Baptists*) has generally held to an Augustinian Calvinism. Jonathan Edwards,* Charles Hodge* and B. B. Warfield* became its most important spokespersons. Here both predestination to eternal life and reprobation to death are affirmed, along with limited atonement and the need for irresistible grace.

Moderate Calvinism. Much of evangelicalism* and some General Baptists* affirm God's choice in election and each person's need for grace to choose God. However, they believe in unlimited atonement, stressing that salvation is hypothetically possible for all, but that God has elected some actually to be saved. Some form of cooperation between people's wills and God's grace is seen. Some also hold that only predestination to life is made, denying any implication that God ordains people to hell.

Two views define predestination as foreknowledge only:

Wesleyan Arminianism. Methodism* has generally held John Wesley's* view that guilt was inherited from Adam, but that this did not affect people's ability to choose God. Hence, predestination was still equated with divine foresight of people's free choice apart from any causal choosing by God.

Arminianism. Quakers,* some General Baptists* and much of the Holiness* and Pentecostal* traditions hold to a classic Arminianism. This position was nurtured by the modified Calvinism of the New Haven Theology* of Nathaniel Taylor* and the revivalism of Charles Finney.* It has penetrated a large and diverse segment of the nation's churches. The Fall is seen to negate persons' original righteousness but not to impair their ability to know and choose God.

Two views deny that God chooses individuals:

*Socianism, or old Unitarianism.** This view maintains that God not only does not choose in predestination but is not able to know the actions of free agents in advance. To do so would be impossible, since freedom is understood to mean absolute random choice.

*Barthianism, or Neo-orthodoxy.** This view has held that Christ was chosen by God and the church was corporately chosen only because it is in Christ. This view avoids the entire issue of free will, determinism and original sin.

BIBLIOGRAPHY. B. G. Armstrong, *Calvinism and the Amyraut Heresy* (1969); L. Berkhof, *A History of Christian Doctrines* (1937); J. Edwards, *Freedom of the Will* (1754); F. H. Foster, *A Genetic History of the New England Theology* (1907); C. Hodge, *Systematic Theology,* vol. 3 (1873); C. Pinnock, ed., *Grace Unlimited* (1975).   N. L. Geisler

Premillennialism. Also called *chiliasm,* this is the belief that there will be a 1,000-year reign of Christ on earth at the end of the present age. This teaching is based on Revelation 20:1-10, elaborated by certain Old Testament texts, such as Isaiah 55—66, which teach that there will be a time of justice, peace and righteousness on earth. Generally, premillennialists believe that the kingdom of Christ will be preceded by certain signs such as the preaching* of the gospel to all nations, a great apostasy, wars, famines, earthquakes, the appearance of the Antichrist and a period of great tribulation. These catastrophes will end with the establishment of Christ's rule over the earth through a sudden and overwhelming display of God's power.

During the millennium the Jews will be converted and will become zealous Christian missionaries, nature will have its curse removed and produce abundant crops, and evil will be restrained through the authoritarian rule of Christ. Despite these idyllic conditions, there is a final rebellion against Christ and his saints. However, God destroys those evil forces, and the eternal states of heaven* and hell are established. Many premillennialists have taught that during the 1,000 years, dead or martyred believers will be resurrected with glorified bodies to intermingle with the other inhabitants of the earth. In the twentieth century, premillennialism has been identified with dispensationalism,* although it is not necessary to follow such a rigid chronology of biblical interpretation to believe in the premillennial view.

BIBLIOGRAPHY. R. G. Clouse, ed., *The Meaning of the Millennium: Four Views* (1977); G. E. Ladd, *The Blessed Hope* (1956); C. C. Ryrie, *Dispensationalism Today* (1965); J. F. Walvoord, *The Millennial Kingdom* (1959).   R. G. Clouse

Presbyterian Church in America. A Conservative Presbyterian* denomination,* organized December 1973 as the National Presbyterian Church. The present name dates from the second general assembly* (1974). The denomination had its origin in the "continuing church" movement, a conservative effort in the Presbyterian Church in the U. S.* (PCUS) (the "Southern Presbyterian" Church) opposed to the denomination's perceived departures from historic doctrines, its membership in the National* and World Councils of Churches* and to social and political pronouncements by church bodies.

The division that gave rise to the new denomination was encouraged mainly by four conservative organizations: *Presbyterian Journal,* Presbyte-

rian Evangelistic Fellowship, Concerned Laymen and Presbyterian Churchmen United. As early as 1969 several hundred ministers* and church sessions* signed a "Declaration of Commitment," opposing union with the United Presbyterian Church in the U.S.A. (UPCUSA),* membership in the Consultation on Christian Union* and substantial change in the doctrinal standards of the PCUS. Several rallies and caucuses were held in the interest of the movement, and the leadership recommended that churches withdraw during 1973 (while the PCUS was engaged in union talks with the UPCUSA and was drafting a possible new confession of faith) by renouncing their membership in the PCUS. Many churches, however, requested and received dismissal.

After plans were laid at a convocation of sessions in Atlanta in May 1973, an advisory convention met in Asheville, North Carolina, in August 1973, and the first general assembly* met in Augusta, Georgia, in December 1973. The first assembly adopted a "Message to All Churches of Jesus Christ throughout the World" which took issue with the PCUS regarding "a diluted theology, a gospel tending towards humanism, an unbiblical view of marriage* and divorce, the ordination of women,* financing of abortion* . . . and numerous other non-Biblical positions . . . all traceable to a different view of Scripture from that we hold and that which was held by the Southern Presbyterian forefathers." The assembly enunciated its stand for the inerrancy* of the Bible,* the Reformed* faith of the Westminster* Standards, the spirituality of the church, the historical Presbyterian view of church government* and "the practice of the principle of purity in the Church visible."

Some independent churches and presbyteries,* as well as congregations from other denominations, have joined the denomination. The denomination was augmented in 1982 by reception of the Reformed Presbyterian Church, Evangelical Synod* (itself the result of a 1965 merger between the Reformed Presbyterian Church, General Synod, and the Evangelical Presbyterian Church). The union also brought Covenant College (Lookout Mountain, Tennessee) and Covenant Seminary (St. Louis, Missouri) into the denomination. Efforts thus far to bring the Orthodox Presbyterian Church* into the denomination have been unsuccessful.

The Presbyterian Church in Amerrica (PCA) is now a national church, the second-largest Presbyterian denomination in the U.S. In 1973 there were about 260 churches, 41,000 members and 196 ministers. In 1986 there were 888 churches,

151,570 members and 1,657 ministers. The PCA is strongly committed to missions,* to the equality in position and authority of ministers and ruling elders* and to the rights of local congregations. The offices of the church are in Decatur, Georgia. *The PCA Messenger,* the denomination's official periodical, is published monthly.

See also PRESBYTERIAN CHURCH IN THE UNITED STATES; REFORMED AND PRESBYTERIAN CHURCHES.

BIBLIOGRAPHY. G. P. Hutchinson, *The History behind the Reformed Presbyterian Church, Evangelical Synod* (1974); F. J. Smith, *The History of the Presbyterian Church in America: The Continuing Church Movement* (1983); M. H. Smith, *How Is the Gold Become Dim: The Decline of the Presbyterian Church, U.S., As Reflected in Its Assembly Actions* (1973); O. Whittaker, *Watchman, Tell It True* (1981).   A. H. Freundt

Presbyterian Church in Canada. Canada's major Presbyterian denomination.* Canadian Presbyterianism* arose first in Nova Scotia in the mid-eighteenth century. It followed the patterns of migration from the U.S. and the United Kingdom, but the predominant numbers and influence came from the Church of Scotland. Indeed, much of Canadian Presbyterian history mirrors that of the Scottish church, the most notable instance being the nineteenth-century schism between Free Church (evangelical* conservative) and Auld Kirk (traditional conservative) movements, which were reconciled in Canada in 1861. In 1875, however, the major Presbyterian bodies in Canada united to form the Presbyterian Church in Canada, a denomination independent of, if still in contact with, the Scottish church.

Fifty years later, the formation of the United Church of Canada* split the Presbyterian church into two groups: the larger one went into union* with the major Methodist* and Congregational* bodies, while about a third remained as "continuing" Presbyterians. No single motive directed all of these latter Presbyterians to remain outside the union. Some strongly preferred traditional Presbyterianism to any admixture with Methodism; others saw the Methodists and Congregationalists as adding harmfully to the growing presence already apparent within Presbyterianism of liberal* theology and the Social Gospel;* a few even saw the United Church as theologically too conservative in its Basis of Union and wanted Canadian Presbyterians to go well beyond it in a liberal direction. The United Church, for its part, saw the Presbyterian Church as having entered the union: those remaining outside were therefore schismatics. In 1939, however, the Canadian Parliament established the right of this latter group to the name "Presbyterian Church in Canada" as it amended the United Church of Canada Act of 1924.

Canadian Presbyterians have a long heritage of distinguished work in missions,* theology and social ministry. Within its ranks, however, there have been different conceptions and practices of each of these works. In the first place, missionaries like the well-known Jonathan Goforth* have gone out in traditional evangelical style; others have served the Social Gospel of the early twentieth century. In the second place, a number of theological traditions have found a home in Canadian Presbyterianism. Liberal theology, emerging in Presbyterian seminaries* around the turn of the twentieth century, remained in those seminaries and increased its influence upon continuing Presbyterianism after the birth of the United Church. Traditional Presbyterian orthodoxy* as well as evangelicalism have characterized other parts of the church. Evangelicalism in particular has been manifest in the recently organized Renewal Fellowship. And Canadian Presbyterianism saw the rise of an indigenous form of neo-orthodox* or dialectical theology,* pre-eminently in the work of W. W. Bryden, former professor and principal of Knox College, Toronto. In the third place, while some twentieth-century evangelicals and others have reacted against what they saw to be an overemphasis on social ministry among some other Presbyterians, the church has always sought to wrestle with the social problems of the day, whether Prohibition,* poor relief, preservation of the Lord's Day Act* or the emancipation of women. To be sure, the Church has comprised a variety of opinions about each of these issues, but it has maintained that involvement in such issues is a Christian duty.

Once the largest Protestant denomination in Canada, like the other mainline Canadian churches the Presbyterian Church has lost members steadily since the early 1960s. In the late 1980s it claimed over 1,000 churches and an inclusive membership of over 200,000. It is a member of the World Alliance of Reformed Churches* (Presbyterian and Congregational) and of the Canadian* and World Councils of Churches.*

BIBLIOGRAPHY. N. K. Clifford, *The Resistance to Church Union in Canada, 1904-1939* (1985); J. S. Moir, *Enduring Witness: A History of the Presbyterian Church in Canada* (1974); N. G. Smith et al., *A Short History of the Presbyterian Church in Canada* (n.d.).   J. G. Stackhouse

Presbyterian Church in the United States. Commonly known as the "Southern Presbyterian Church," a Reformed* denomination, formed from the Presbyterian Church in the Confederate States of America (1861-1866) and Presbyterians who had belonged to border synods* of the Old School* branch of the Presbyterian Church in the U.S.A. A few members also came from congregations that had belonged to the New School* Assembly before that denomination split in 1857 and its Southern side withered.

As other Presbyterian denominations, the Presbyterian Church in the United States (PCUS) based its theology* on Scripture,* as interpreted through the *Westminster Confession of Faith** and its accompanying catechisms* (1648). In the twentieth century some few amendments to the Westminster Standards passed; and a "Declaration of Faith," composed by a committee of the PCUS to reflect contemporary theology, received attention in liturgy* though not formal adoption during the 1970s.

As other Presbyterian denominations, the PCUS adopted a *Book of Church Order* specifying in detail church courts, their powers and procedures for decision making. A denomination-wide general assembly* meeting annually was to oversee work of state-wide synods,* presbyteries* within them, and the "particular churches" that comprised each presbytery. Distinctive for the PCUS was the requirement that three-fourths of its presbyteries concur with any decision of General Assemblies to change the *Book of Church Order.* The difficulty in having three-fourths of the presbyteries agree on anything assured a conservative stance on the part of the denomination.

In many respects the PCUS resembled other Presbyterian denominations throughout the world. Emphasis on the sermon in worship,* on the celebration of infant baptism* and at least quarterly Communion* and on the balance of power between teaching elders* (ministers) and ruling elders (lay leaders) remained typical of connectional, Reformed Christianity.

The PCUS was also characterized by engagements in foreign and domestic missions* throughout the nineteenth and into the twentieth centuries. Mission efforts in China and the Belgian Congo (now Zaire) were especially significant, supplementing initial and important efforts in Brazil, where early missionaries also served ex-Confederate colonists for a time. Among home missions activities, those in the Appalachian highlands were particularly noteworthy.

During much of its existence, the PCUS stood for a doctrine of "the spirituality of the church," contending that corporate involvement in social and political issues was inappropriate (though individual Christians should vote and otherwise participate in moral and ethical matters). In fact, many of the presbyteries and synods, as well as most general assemblies, did take stands on such issues as Sabbath* observance and temperance.* Beginning in the 1930s, the assemblies began to speak and act more widely on such matters as patriotism and legislation concerning children. Issues like civil rights,* women's rights and national foreign policy came to occupy more attention during the 1950s and thereafter.

Growing in numbers from 80,000 members in 1869 to more than 1 million in 1962, the PCUS began to decline, in part from the withdrawal of dissidents who formed the Presbyterian Church in America* in 1973. Involvement of the church in civil rights and other "political matters," the ordination of women* and theological departures from strict Calvinism were reasons most often named for departures. Their departure also enabled the PCUS, which had rejected union with the Presbyterian Church in the U.S.A. and the United Presbyterian Church in North America in the 1950s, to join with the United Presbyterian Church in the U.S.A.* to form the Presbyterian Church (U.S.A.)* in 1983.

See also PRESBYTERIAN CHURCH IN AMERICA; PRESBYTERIAN CHURCH (U.S.A.); REFORMED AND PRESBYTERIAN CHURCHES; REFORMED TRADITION.

BIBLIOGRAPHY. A. C. Piepkorn, *Profiles in Belief,* vol. 2 (1978); E. T. Thompson, *Presbyterians in the South,* 3 vols. (1965); R. E. Thompson, *A History of the Presbyterian Churches in the United States* (1895); L. J. Trinterud, *The Forming of an American Tradition* (1949).   L. B. Weeks

Presbyterian Church (U.S.A.). A mainline* Presbyterian denomination formed from 1983 to 1987 by the union of the United Presbyterian Church in the United States of America (UPCUSA)* and the Presbyterian Church in the United States (PCUS),* also known as the "Southern Presbyterian Church."

The present-day Presbyterian Church (U.S.A.) (PCUSA) can trace its roots back to 1788 and the formation of the Presbyterian General Assembly,* and further yet to the Presbytery,* gathered in 1706. Representing the connectional side of Puritanism* and the Scottish Presbyterian* traditions, the Presbytery constituted itself a synod* in 1716 and grew during colonial times to become a significant force in American religion. Throughout the varied fortunes of the Presbyterian Church, the General Assembly has remained the major judicatory body among Presbyterian bodies from 1788 until the present day.

The Second Great Awakening* proved costly for the Presbyterians, whose leadership opposed the emotional demonstrations of conversion* and the lack of attention to theology.* Many members left to join the Restoration Movement,* which led to the forming of the Disciples of Christ* and other "Campbellite" bodies. Other Presbyterians became Baptists,* Methodists* and even Shakers.* In 1803-1810 members of this body withdrew to form the Cumberland Presbyterian Church,* a separate body whose General Assembly voted in 1906 to rejoin what had by then come to be called the Presbyterian Church in the U.S.A. (PC-USA) (about two-thirds of them did). In the 1830s disputes in the PC-USA about theology, relations with other Christian bodies, and reform* methods regarding slavery,* led to another split—into Old School* and New School* assemblies. Generally more parochial in missionary* programs, Old School Presbyterians also proved less willing to work against slavery and more closely tied to the *Westminster Confession of Faith.**

Though Presbyterians in the South belonged to both New and Old School assemblies, most were Old School. Under the tensions that led to the Civil War,* New School Presbyterians divided in 1857 into Northern and Southern denominations, but the Old School remained one until after the taking of Fort Sumpter and the secession of several states to form the Confederacy in 1861. The Old School in the South became the Presbyterian Church in the Confederate States of America, later taking the name, Presbyterian Church in the U.S. (PCUS) in 1866. After the Civil War, Old and New School assemblies in the North reunited into one denomination, the PC-USA (1870), and their mission work in the South among blacks soon led to the PC-USA again being a truly national religious body. After the reunion with most of the Cumberland Presbyterians, the PC-USA numbered 1.4 million in 1910.

The United Presbyterian Church in the United States of America (UPCUSA), emerged from the union of the PC-USA and the United Presbyterian Church of North America (UPCNA) in 1958. The UPCNA had been formed in 1858 by Scottish Covenanter Presbyterians that had come to terms with their American environment and joined together.

By the late nineteenth century, the major Presbyterian bodies in the North and South had changed, becoming more tightly organized both at congregational and at regional and national levels. Churches hired staff members for leading music, Christian education* and visitation. Sunday-school* classes, women's and men's programs, mission activities, stewardship, evangelism* and many other portions of the life of churches became increasingly formal, specialized and led by bureaucracies.

The PC-USA, more than other Reformed* denominations, was the scene of struggles between fundamentalists* and so-called modernists.* (*See* Fundamentalist-Modernist Controversy.) One major source of the struggle, the conservative Princeton Theology,* had been taught at Princeton and other seminaries through much of the nineteenth century. Charles Hodge,* his son Archibald A. Hodge* and Benjamin B. Warfield,* together enunciated principles including a fully developed doctrine of the inerrancy* of Scripture that later characterized much of American Protestant thought. When J. Gresham Machen,* also a proponent of the Princeton Theology, started an Independent Board of Foreign Missions, the General Assembly censured him, and he moved to found the Presbyterian Church of America in 1936. Forced by court action to discontinue the use of that name, since 1939 it has been known as the Orthodox Presbyerian Church.* A group withdrew from that body in 1937 to form the Bible Presbyterian Church. The PCUS suffered the withdrawal of a number of conservative members and congregations in the 1970s. Objecting to a number of changes in the church's policies and doctrinal emphases, as well as attempts to join with the more liberal UPCUSA, they left to join the newly formed Presbyterian Church in America.*

Their departure enabled the PCUS, which had previously rejected union with the Northern Presbyterians in the 1950s, to join with the UPCUSA to form the Presbyterian Church (U.S.A.) on June 10, 1983. The gradual process of consolidating national offices, boards and agencies, as well as merging overlapping synods and presbyteries, continued into the late 1980s. In 1986 the PCUSA reported 11,554 congregations with an inclusive membership of 3,048,235.

See also CIVIL WAR AND THE CHURCHES; PRESBYTERIAN CHURCH IN THE UNITED STATES; REFORMED AND PRESBYTERIAN CHURCHES; REFORMED TRADITION;UNITED PRESBYTERIAN CHURCH IN THE UNITED STATES OF AMERICA.

BIBLIOGRAPHY. A. C. Piepkorn, *Profiles in Belief,* vol. 2 (1978); R. E. Thompson, *A History of the Presbyterian Churches in the United States* (1895); L. J. Trinterud, *The Forming of an American Tradition* (1970); L. B. Weeks, *To Be a Presbyterian* (1983). L. B. Weeks

Presbytery. The legislative and judicial body of a geographical district in Presbyterian* church government.* A district, or presbytery, is made up of a given number of congregations. While problems confined to an individual church are usually resolved in a session* consisting of ministers* (teaching elders) and lay* elders* (ruling elders) of a local congregation,* disputes or issues concerning the churches within a district are referred to the presbytery, the title given to the adjudicating body. This body consists of an equal number of teaching and ruling elders* from each church, all of whom have the power to cast a vote.

The presbytery examines and ordains ministers, oversees congregations within its jurisdiction, serves as a court of appeal for decisions made by sessions and transmits petitions and overtures to the general assembly.* The churches within the represented district are obliged to heed the decisions of their presbytery. The classis* of Reformed churches* is the equivalent to a presbytery.

See also CHURCH GOVERNMENT: PRESBYTERIAN.

BIBLIOGRAPHY. L. Trinterud, *The Forming of an American Tradition* (1949).   K. P. Minkema

Press, Catholic. A 1986 statistical profile helps illustrate the shape of the Catholic* press in America. There are six U.S. national Catholic newspapers with a circulation of 463,429, and 157 U.S. diocesan newspapers with a circulation of 4,893,094. Two Canadian Catholic national newspapers and fourteen regional and diocesan newspapers have a circulation of 234,305. A combination of 367 U.S. Catholic magazines and twenty more from Canada have a circulation of 21,546,782. Thirty-two U.S. and eleven more Canadian publications for Catholics in languages other than English have a circulation of 697,150. A total of 609 Catholic newspapers, magazines and publications have a circulation of 27,834,760 in North America.

The Irish-born Bishop John England,* of Charleston, South Carolina, is regarded as the father, or founder, of the Catholic press in the U.S. His *U.S. Catholic Miscellany* (1827-1861) served as something of a national Catholic paper. With several title changes, the Boston *Pilot* (1829-) is considered the oldest of the U.S. Catholic newspapers. In Cincinnati, Bishop Edward D. Fenwick* founded the *Catholic Telegraph* in 1831. It, like the *Pittsburgh Catholic* (1844), continues to the present. In New York, the *Freeman's Journal* (1840-1918) began as a diocesan newspaper but was soon sold by Bishop John Hughes* to James A. McMaster, who became one of the best-known

lay editors of the nineteenth century. Orestes A. Brownson's* *Brownson's Quarterly Review* (1844-1875, with one suspension) and Isaac Hecker's* *Catholic World* (1865-) are among the most notable publications of this period. The Civil War* split the press, with papers like the *Catholic Telegraph* in Cincinnati supporting Lincoln* and emancipation, while the New Orleans *Le Propagateur Catholique* was pro-Confederacy. Catholic publications proliferated in the nineteenth century, with some entering vigorously into the intramural and extramural debates of the Catholic community. A notable quarterly in this period was the *American Catholic Quarterly Review* (1876-1924), which was based in Philadelphia.

Pope Leo XIII's* encyclical,* *Testem Benevolentiae,* condemned Americanism* in 1899, and while the alleged heresy* condemned under that name is regarded as a phantom heresy, one real consequence of the condemnation was a general quieting of Catholic debate and the Catholic press. The Catholic Press Association was formed in 1911 with forty-seven charter members.

In the period from 1900 through World War 2,* the U.S. Catholic press evolved into the character that has endured into the present. It is multifaceted and Church-controlled and operated. The independent publications once common in the nineteenth century have become a rarity. Official diocesan newspapers have predominated, helped by the National Catholic News Service, which began in 1920. There is also a profusion of magazines sponsored by religious orders. During this period two large Catholic newspaper chains were born: *Our Sunday Visitor,* which has been the official organ of twenty dioceses, and *The National Catholic Register,* which has served thirty-five dioceses. *Our Sunday Visitor* deserves particular praise for its defense of Catholics against the calumnies of the Ku Klux Klan. Some of the most distinguished of Catholic publications have their origin in this period. The Jesuit* weekly, *America* (1909), the lay-edited and independent *Commonweal* (1924), the *Brooklyn Tablet* (1908) and Dorothy Day's* *Catholic Worker* (1933).

Following World War 2, the education benefits of the G.I. Bill gave a major boost to the Catholic community, and a notable growth in professionalization began in the Catholic press. In 1964 *The National Catholic Reporter,* with a network of "stringers" that made it free of any dependence on the bishops' National Catholic News Service, became a publishing phenomenon when it expanded from an initial 10,000 subscribers to more than 50,000 in one year. The National Catholic

News Service was faulted by some, such as Monsignor Salvatore Adamo in his columns on the Catholic Press in *America* in this period, for National Catholic News's occasional omission of coverage of some embarrassing stories and its excess of diplomacy in the coverage of others. It became certain that *The National Catholic Reporter* and the secular press, whose professionalism and interest in the coverage of religious news had blossomed, would cover these stories. Because of this and also because of the principled professionalism of most persons at NC News, for some years NC News has been respected for its judicious but truly comprehensive coverage.

The *Catholic Digest,* founded on the model of the *Reader's Digest* in the 1930s, is the most widely circulated Catholic publication today. The *St. Anthony's Messenger,* founded by the Franciscans,* and *U.S. Catholic,* founded by the Claretians, are widely circulated and more venturesome publications than *Catholic Digest.* Matured Catholic scholarship in the U.S. is reflected in journals such as *Theological Studies,* published by the Jesuits; the *Catholic Biblical Quarterly,* published by the Catholic Biblical Association;* and the *Catholic Historical Review,* published by the Catholic Historical Association. *Horizons* is the semi-annual publication of the College Theology Society. Fordham University's *Thought* and the independent and lay-edited *Cross Currents* are also notable scholarly journals. One generally finds a progressive viewpoint in *America, Commonweal* and the *National Catholic Reporter,* and a cautious-to-conservative viewpoint in *Our Sunday Visitor,* the *National Catholic Register* and especially *The Wanderer.*

The history of the Catholic press in Canada begins in 1806 when *Le Canadien* appeared in Quebec. Since all French-speaking Canadians were then Catholics, it was regarded as a Catholic publication. The first English diocesan weekly was begun in 1826 by Bishop Alexander MacDonell, who brought it to his Kingston diocese* in 1830 and gave it the title of the *Catholic.* Most Catholic publications, however, date from the late nineteenth century and even more from the early twentieth century.

Canada's first chain of diocesan newspapers, the *Canadian Register,* was founded in 1941, when the archbishops* of Ontario amalgamated five diocesan weeklies. The lay-edited *Western Catholic Reporter* was launched in 1965 in Edmonton, Alberta. The Catholic hierarchy of Canada created a national French news service in 1953 and an English service in 1955. The English-language Catholic press is linked with that of the U.S. through its membership in the Catholic Press Association.

In Canada, a notable recent development is the *Catholic New Times,* a national Catholic independent paper founded in Toronto in 1976. A significant but slender bimonthly appearing since 1962, is *The Ecumenist,* a journal for promoting Christian unity which is a collaborative effort of the Paulist* Press and the faculty of religious studies of McGill University in Montreal.

In summary, the Catholic press is quite vigorous in North America. For journals of opinion and some newspapers, circulation is probably a good measure of readership. For many diocesan newspapers, especially those in so-called guaranteed subscription plans, the extent that some essentially non-paying subscribers are real readers is questionable.

BIBLIOGRAPHY. G. Laviolette, "Catholic Press: Canada," *NCE* 3; James A. Doyle, ed., *Catholic Press Directory* (1986); *Catholic Press Annual;* W. L. Lucey et al., "Catholic Press: U.S." *NCE* 3; J. G. Deedy, Jr., "The Catholic Press," in Martin E. Marty et al., *The Religious Press in America* (1963).

R. Van Allen

Press, Protestant. The first religious magazine in America is generally considered to have been Thomas Prince's* *The Christian History* (1743-1745), which was published in Boston and documented the popular piety* of the Great Awakening* by collecting and transmitting ministerial reports of revival as they occurred in America and Europe. But properly speaking, no religious press existed in colonial America. Newspapers and periodicals, while reflecting religious views, did not consciously distinguish between society and the established Congregational* Church in New England or Anglican* Church in the South. The actual birth of the Protestant religious press in America came during the Second Great Awakening* of the early nineteenth century. For example, in 1800 the *Connecticut Evangelical Magazine* began publication, reporting on and encouraging the revivals in New England. Its success encouraged the founding of the *Virginia Religious Magazine* (1804).

On the advancing western edge of the new nation, Protestant denominations were faced with the breakdown of established religion and the challenge of an ever-expanding frontier. In this new setting the Methodists,* Baptists* and Disciples of Christ* mobilized itinerant* preachers* who moved from community to community, evangelizing* and ministering* as they went. But these efforts were unable to provide ongoing instruction in the faith and instill a sense of belonging to a larger body of kindred spirits. Without ongoing nurture, a Baptist convert might easily fall prey to the proselytizing efforts of a Methodist circuit rider* during the weeks or months when the Baptist preacher was ministering elsewhere, and vice versa. This missionary and pastoral need was met by the rise of the religious press. The Industrial Revolution, a burgeoning population, reduced postal rates and the lowered costs of large print runs all contributed to make the print media a more accessible means of disseminating religion. But it has been argued that, more than any other factor, the evangelical* missionary* impulse to publish for the masses may have been the impetus behind the growth of the mass media in North America.

The Restoration Movement* in particular found journalism to be an effective tool for growth. Alexander Campbell,* the principal leader of the movement, edited first *The Christian Baptist* (1823-1830) and then *The Millenial Harbinger* (1830-1866). Campbell's co-religionist, Walter Scott,* edited the *Evangelist* (1832-1835; 1838-1844) and the *Protestant Unionist* (1844-1850). This heritage of Christian journalism was to prove an important feature of the movement that would become the Churches of Christ and Christian Churches. In a movement of independent churches not bound by denominational structures, journals such as the *Gospel Advocate* (1866-) and *Firm Foundation* (1884-) have been very influential, with their editors functioning as de facto bishops. The same can be said for the Southern Baptist Convention. Though historically it has been more centralized in its structure than most Baptist associations, the absence of a national publication has left the state papers and their editors with remarkable influence.

Denominational organs are a part of nearly every religious body in America, making them the most common form of religious journalism. An efficient means for disseminating denominational news, they also serve to reinforce the common goals of the body and provide commentary on contemporary issues. Some of these denominational papers have supported the ethnic nature of their respective denominations. In 1847 the African Methodist Episcopal Church,* perceiving the need to secure its self-identity, began publishing a weekly magazine which became *The Christian Recorder,* the oldest African-American newspaper in the world. Likewise, German-speaking Lutherans* in St. Louis

read the popular periodical *Der Lutheraner,* edited by Carl F. W. Walther* from 1844 to 1887, while around 1836 German-speaking Mennonites in Pennsylvania read *Der Evangelische Botschafter.* Later, more acculturated Mennonites would read John F. Funk's *Herald of Truth,* which began publication in 1864. The first Methodist church-wide weekly newspaper, the *Christian Advocate,* began publication in New York City in 1826 and remained in existence until 1939. Within its first two years, its paying subscribers reached 20,000.

A further impetus to publish was the rise of the nineteenth-century voluntary religious societies, each addressing itself to a particular goal or cause. These special-interest groups stood outside the established denominational structures and could not depend on denominational organs to reach or expand their constituencies. Orange Scott,* the Methodist abolitionist,* found that his only access to publication was through founding his own periodical, *The Wesleyan Quarterly Review* (1838), later known as the *American Wesleyan Observer* (1839). The American Colonization Society,* intent on helping freed slaves return to Africa, published the *African Repository* (1825-1849). The American Tract Society,* in its day the most innovative and powerful distributor of Christian literature, nurtured its extensive nationwide organization by means of the *American Tract Magazine* (begun in 1824). Other publications, such as *The Massachusetts Missionary Magazine* (1803-1808), *The American Biblical Repository* (1839-1850) and *The American Missionary* (1857-1860), served the interests of Protestant foreign mission* societies.

The Holiness Movement,* an evangelical and transdenominational movement which arose during the later half of the nineteenth century, utilized the printed word in spreading its message and method of spirituality.* Phoebe Palmer,* a leading figure in the early years of the Holiness Movement, disseminated her ideas through her books and her widely circulated magazine *Guide to Holiness* (1864-1874). Charles Cullis* published his views on the higher life* and faith healing* through his periodicals *Times of Refreshing* (1869), *The Word of Life* (1873) and *Service for Jesus* (1885). Daniel Sidney Warner,* the early leader of what would become the Church of God (Anderson, Indiana), edited the *Herald of Gospel Freedom,* which eventually became the *Gospel Trumpet* (1881), and played an important role in spreading the message of an avowedly nonsectarian branch of the Holiness Movement. In 1879 the National Camp Meeting Association for the Promotion of Holiness* began publishing what would become its principal periodical for the next seventy-five years, the *Christian Witness and Advocate of Bible Holiness.* One brand of Holiness teaching, called the "victorious life,"* would later find a suitable platform in an established evangelical weekly, *The Sunday School Times.* Charles G. Trumbull,* inheriting the editorial desk from his father, Henry Clay Trumbull,* utilized the *Times* to promote the movement beginning in 1910.

As with the Holiness Movement, the Pentecostal Movement* came to rely on periodicals to inform, instruct and inspire what was soon to become a far-flung movement. Florence Crawford's* *Apostolic Faith* magazine, taken over from William J. Seymour* by 1908, boasted a circulation of 80,000 after only one year. G. B. Cashwell* began circulating *The Bridegroom's Messenger* in 1907 and the successful *Latter Rain Evangel* was begun in 1908 by William H. Piper at Chicago's Stone Church. Aimee Semple McPherson's* *Bridal Call* began in 1917 and in 1964 became the *Foursquare Magazine.* But these are just a sample of the beginnings of a flood of periodical literature that would flow from churches, denominations and independent evangelists. The offspring of the Pentecostal Movement, the charismatic movement,* has been nourished and informed by a variety of publications, including Daniel Malachuk's now-defunct *Logos Journal* (1971-1981). More successful has been Stephen Strang's *Charisma* (1975-), which in 1987 merged with *Christian Life* to become *Charisma and Christian Life* (circ. 220,000).

The premillenialist* movement of the late nineteenth and early twentieth century depended on their own publications to disseminate their eschatological* perspective across denominational lines. Prophetic magazines such as Robert Cameron's* the *Watchword and Truth* (1898-1921), a merger of A. J. Gordon's* millenarian journal *Watchword* (1878-1897) and James H. Brookes's* dispensational magazine *The Truth* (1874-1897), served a wide audience. Arno Gaebelein,* a missionary to Jews and a leading figure in North American dispensationalism,* founded *Our Hope* (1894-1957), a magazine devoted to Jewish missions* and prophetic study. *The Christian Herald,* a magazine still published today (circ. 200,000), was originally founded in 1878 as *The Christian Herald and Signs of the Times.* Originally a premillennialist magazine, it began to lose that emphasis around the turn of the century as it became increasingly focused on evangelical social work and even labor issues. Its broader appeal led to an increased readership (250,000 by 1910).

Other periodicals arose to serve twentieth-century fundamentalism,* such as William B. Riley's* *Christian Fundamentals in School and Church* (1918), later called the *Christian Fundamentalist,* which became the official organ of the World's Christian Fundamentals Association* and the Baptist weekly, the *Watchman-Examiner,* which from 1913, under the editorship of Curtis Lee Laws,* voiced evangelical orthodox Baptist principles. John R. Rice's* *Sword of the Lord* (circ. 200,000), an influential fundamentalist weekly, has attacked modernism* and neo-evangelicalism.* And beginning in the early 1940s, Carl McIntire's* *Christian Beacon* warned fundamentalists of the dangers of liberalism and called for separation from apostate liberal denominations. These were set beside periodicals of a less pungent nature, including the *Moody Bible Institute Monthly* (now *Moody Monthly,* circ. 230,000), *The King's Business* and Donald Grey Barnhouse's* monthly magazine *Revelation* (1931), which was renamed *Eternity* in 1950 and ceased publication in January 1989.

Within the mainline* Protestant sector, there have been many denominational house organs, but by far the outstanding religious journal of twentieth-century mainline religion has been *The Christian Century* * (circ. 37,000). The magazine began in 1884 as the *Christian Oracle,* published by the Disciples of Christ.* In 1900 it was optimistically renamed *The Christian Century* and began to achieve prominence when Charles Clayton Morrison* became editor (1908-1947). Morrison expanded the focus and audience of the journal, dropping its denominational affiliation in 1916 and calling his effort "An Undenominational Journal of Religion." Headquartered in Chicago, by the 1920s the *Century* had become a barometer of liberal Protestant thought and a forum for the opinions of leading figures in American Protestantism. A significant though less widely distributed competitor has been *Christianity and Crisis* (circ. 20,000). Founded prior to World War 2 under the leadership of Reinhold Niebuhr,* this periodical was meant to be a corrective to the pacifism of the *Century* and has since continued to stress issues of social justice.

The leading periodical of evangelical opinion during the latter half of the twentieth century was originally launched in 1956 as an orthodox alternative to *The Christian Century.* Founded largely by the initiative of Billy Graham* and his father-in-law, L. Nelson Bell,* *Christianity Today* (CT, circ. 185,000) was aimed at ministers and thoughtful laymen, especially those who were holding forth, or could be won back to, the historic faith within the major denominations. The founding editor, Carl Henry,* supplied the magazine with an initial burst of progressive and intellectual leadership. CT has continued to foster a broader evangelical engagement with culture and society, though it has generally taken a conservative political stance. More than any other evangelical periodical, CT has reflected and reported the evangelical resurgence of the second half of the twentieth century. More recently, Jerry Falwell's* magazine *The Fundamentalist Journal* (circ. 70,000) has spoken for the growing new fundamentalism that has been gaining in prominence and political power since the late 1970s.

Far more popular in its appeal, *Guideposts* started in 1946 as a four-page weekly leaflet of inspirational testimonies edited by Norman Vincent Peale* and distributed through his ministry. By the 1950s it had developed into a monthly magazine featuring the religious faith of celebrities and ordinary lay people. By 1975 it claimed to have more paying subscribers (3.1 million) than any other inspirational magazine in the world.

BIBLIOGRAPHY. J. S. Duke, *Religious Publishing and Communications* (1955); M. E. Marty et al., *The Religious Press in America* (1963); D. P. Nord, *The Evangelical Origins of Mass Media in America, 1815-1835* (1984); L. B. Wright, *Culture on the Moving Frontier* (1955). The Editors

Preston, John (1587-1628). English Reformed* theologian* influential among New England Puritans.* From a humble family but exceedingly ambitious, Preston excelled at Kings and then as fellow of Queens College, Cambridge University. He abandoned goals in business and government after his 1611 conversion* during a sermon by John Cotton,* who became a leading New England minister. Later, Preston sent students to finish their theological education under Cotton at his church in Boston, England. Preston's theological studies included Calvin and Aquinas. In 1615 he won the admiration of King James at a university debate. Preston capitalized on friendships among nobility to pull strings for evangelical* preachers* and to advance the Puritan cause at Cambridge, even securing his own appointment as chaplain* to the future king, Prince Charles.

Preston devoted most of his time to preaching and advanced from one prominent post to another. In 1620 he was dean and catechist* of Queens College; in 1622 he succeeded John Donne as preacher at Lincoln's Inn, London, and became master of Emmanuel College, Cambridge, training ground of early New England pastors. Huge crowds gathered to hear him, prompting limiting of access to his sermons and the enlargement of chapel buildings. Thomas Shepherd,* future pastor in Cambridge, Massachusetts, converted under Preston's preaching at Emmanuel, called him "the most searching preacher in the world." He took little time to write during his meteoric career, preaching extemporaneously, but auditors copied and circulated sermon notes. After his death of "a consumption" at the age of forty-one, several disciples, including future New Haven pastor John Davenport,* edited his sermons for publication and fought the pirated editions rushed into print. His works went through numerous editions and were on the shelves of New England pastors.

BIBLIOGRAPHY. W. Haller, *The Rise of Puritanism* (1938); P. Miller, *The New England Mind* (1939); N. Pettit, *The Heart Prepared* (1966). C. E. Hambrick-Stowe

Preston, Thomas Scott (1824-1891). Catholic* priest* and apologist. Born in Hartford, Connecticut, Preston studied for the Episcopal* priesthood at Washington (later Trinity) College and General Theological Seminary in New York. His high church* sympathies deferred his ordination* until 1847. In 1849 he and his brother, William, became Catholics and were received into the Church by fellow convert, Reverend James Roosevelt Bayley.* Preston studied for the priesthood at St. Joseph's Seminary at Fordham and was ordained by Archbishop* John Hughes* in 1850. He served for a time as a curate at Old St. Patrick's and a parish* in Yonkers. In 1853 he was appointed secretary to Hughes and in 1855 diocesan chancellor. Appointed pastor* of St. Ann's Church in New York in 1862, he remained there until his death. Preston helped found the Sisterhood of Divine Compassion with Mother Veronica Starr. Preston achieved distinction as an apologist* and lecturer for Roman Catholicism. Many of his sermons and conferences were published, including *Lectures on Reason and Revelation* (1868), *Protestantism and the Church* (1882) and *God and Reason* (1884).

BIBLIOGRAPHY. M. Teresa, *The Fruits of His Compassion: The Life of Mother Mary Veronica* (1962). S. M. Avella

Presuppositionalism. A term describing a particular approach to philosophy and theology, it argues that all systems of knowledge are founded on unprovable assumptions about God, human nature and reality. Theoretical thought must, therefore, begin with a conscious appraisal of these assumptions. In this view, claims of objectivity as found in empiricism, rationalism or scientism are little more than pretensions resting on unexamined assumptions.

Among Christians, presuppositionalism began in the 1930s through the efforts of two Calvinist* thinkers, Herman Dooyeweerd* in the Netherlands, and Cornelius Van Til* in the U.S. They argued that Christians must radically reject all nonbiblical assumptions. In their voluminous writings they sought to demonstrate that most Christian thinkers had compromised their methodology by using nonbiblical assumptions in their theology, anthropology and epistemology. This practice, they argued, yields a distorted theology.

Perhaps the most crucial methodological factor for presuppositionalists is the question of authority. Their unequivocal answer is that the self-attesting triune God revealed in Scripture is the authority in all things. Believers must think analogically, thinking God's thoughts after him. This means that presuppositionalists consciously and constantly looked to Scripture for norms in all theoretical matters. Presuppositionalists have, therefore, vigorously attacked reason and experience as principles of authority, arguing that they are merely human constructs. Rationalism and empiricism thus fail as viable methodological stances for Christians. As a practical matter, this means that presuppositionalists reject Princeton Theology* and Thomism,* maintaining that they are rooted in rationalistic assumptions.

BIBLIOGRAPHY. H. Dooyeweerd, *A New Critique of Theoretical Thought,* 4 vols. (1953-1958); C. Van Til, *A Christian Theory of Knowledge* (1969).

L. J. Van Til

Pretribulationalism. *See* RAPTURE OF THE CHURCH.

Price, Charles Sydney (c.1880-1947). Healing* revivalist.* A native Englishman, Price earned an Oxford law degree before moving to Canada. Converted in a Free Methodist* mission in Spokane, Washington, Price entered the Methodist* ministry* in the Northwest until he left the Methodist Church to pastor a Congregational* church in Valdez, Alaska. By World War 1* he had become a popular speaker in San Francisco and then assumed a Congregational pastorate in Lodi, California. In 1920 he became a Pentecostal,* receiving the Spirit baptism* under Aimee Semple McPherson's* preaching. In 1922 Price launched a successful independent healing ministry, with meetings in Oregon, Victoria, Vancouver, Calgary, Edmonton, Winnipeg, Toronto, Minneapolis, Duluth, St. Louis and Belleville (Illinois). In later years he traveled overseas, holding meetings in Europe and the Middle East. Price refused to identify with the conflicts that arose among the emerging Pentecostal groups. In 1925 he began publishing *Golden Grain,* an excellent source for studying healing revivalism.*

Like all healing ministries, Price's work encountered financial hardships in the 1930s. Foreshadowing later years, Price maintained his ministry by reaching non-Pentecostals. At his death in 1947, according to advocates of healing revivalism, Price prophesied the emergence of the post-World War 2 healing revival. Demos Shakarian,* a leader of that movement, was a close friend and follower of Price. Price was one of the most successful and influential healing revivalists of the 1920s.

BIBLIOGRAPHY. D. E. Harrell, Jr., *All Things Are Possible* (1975); C. S. Price, *The Story of My Life* (1944).

C. D. Weaver

Price, Joseph Charles (1854-1893). African-American clergyman,* educator and civil rights* advocate. Born in Elizabeth City, North Carolina, to a slave father and free mother, Price studied as a child in freedmen's schools. He was licensed* to preach* in the African Methodist Episcopal Zion Church* in 1875, ordained* an elder* in 1881, studied for a time at Shaw University and was valedictorian at Lincoln University, Pennsylvania, in 1879. Price was a delegate four times to the general conference of his denomination,* and was also a representative to the Ecumenical Conference of Methodism in London (1881). While lecturing in England he obtained $10,000 in pledges for the Zion Wesley Institute in Salisbury, North Carolina, which was incorporated in 1885 as Livingstone College. Under his leadership, Livingstone (named for the famous missionary to Africa, David Livingstone) became one of the important liberal arts colleges for Southern African-Americans. A nationally known preacher and powerful orator, Price also campaigned for prohibition* and civil rights. In 1890, he became chairman of the Citizens' Equal Rights Association of Washington, D.C., and president of the National Afro-American League. Even as he forcefully challenged Southern racism, Price was also respected by white leaders. Succumbing to Bright's disease at forty years of age, Price left a widow and four small children.

BIBLIOGRAPHY. W. J. Walls, *Joseph Charles Price, Educator and Race Leader* (1943); A. Meier, *Negro Thought in America, 1880-1915* (1963).

W. Gravely and D. Nelson

Priest. *See* HOLY ORDERS.

Priesthood of Believers. A Protestant* principle whereby each believer has immediate access to God through the one mediator, Jesus Christ. One of the great principles of the sixteenth-century Protestant Reformation, as expounded by Martin Luther, was the priesthood of all believers. Joined with justification* by faith alone and the authority* of Scripture alone, it cut through the tangles of medieval Catholicism that tended to place barriers between the individual Christian and God. The implications of the principle were that no priest* was necessary, no saints,* no Blessed Virgin Mary,* to intercede for the ordinary believer. The whole medieval system of salvation, so dependent on a strong distinction between laity* and clergy* and the power of the latter to administer or withhold the sacraments,* was thus for Protestants abolished.

The general effects of this Protestant principle were at least threefold. First, it meant that laypeople* prayed directly to God through Jesus Christ, thus increasing lay involvement in private and public worship.* Second, it meant that God communicated directly to the individual Christian through his Word, the Bible, thus encouraging the production of vernacular versions of Scripture and the pursuit of lay Bible study.* Third, it meant a new sense of Christian liberty for the ordinary Christian, who felt no longer bound by the authority of extrabiblical traditions or by ecclesiastical hierarchies.

Transported to the American environment, without bishoprics and generally established churches, the priesthood of all believers provided a basis for greater lay influence than had characterized European Christianity. In many instances churches could form only where ministers had sufficient powers of persuasion to gather a lay following. In Puritan* settings it was not uncommon for regular "private meetings" of laypeople to have as much influence as the church services and to comprise a church within the church. In some groups, such as the Quakers* and later the Plymouth Brethren,* the priesthood of believers came to mean that there was no recognized clergy at all.

On the negative side, the American expression of the priesthood of believers could manifest itself in a lack of reverence and in a lack of respect for the institutional church. It has contributed also to the spawning of numerous parachurch* organizations, many of which have special effectiveness but frequently lack accountability.

BIBLIOGRAPHY. W. S. Hudson, *Religion in America* (1965); L. Ryken, *Worldly Saints: The Puritans As They Really Were* (1906); C. E. Hambrick-Stowe,

The Practice of Piety: Puritan Devotional Disciplines in Seventeenth-Century New England (1982).   W. S. Barker

Priestley, Joseph (1733-1804). Noted English scientist, philosopher and Unitarian* minister.* Born in Fieldhead, England, Priestley's exposure to open debate on questions of dogma* while a divinity* student at Daventry Academy, a Dissenting institution, induced him to abandon the Calvinist* orthodoxy* of his upbringing. Although Priestley was engaged as pastor* by a succession of congregations, his iconoclastic doctrinal views, along with his hot temper and tendency to stammer, led to repeated difficulties. A diligent experimental scientist whose investigations of electrical phenomena earned him induction into the Royal Society in 1766, Priestley is best remembered today for his discovery of oxygen in 1774. Reflecting the same materialist mindset were theological treatises such as Priestley's first published work, *The Scripture Doctrine of Remission* (1761), rejecting traditional views of the atonement;* and especially his *Disquisitions Relating to Matter and Spirit* (1777), which questioned conventional notions of the soul. Priestley's widely read *History of the Corruptions of Christianity* (1782), which treated the doctrine of the Trinity as one such corruption; and his *History of Early Opinions Concerning Jesus Christ* (4 vols., 1789), which denied Christ's infallibility and sinlessness, were highly regarded by deists* such as Thomas Jefferson.*

Priestley's outspoken defense of the French Revolution, reflecting his radical political sympathies, incited a mob to torch his chapel* and sack his home in Birmingham in 1791. This assault precipitated Priestley's eventual decision to immigrate to America, where his writings had already proved influential with James Freeman and other leaders of nascent New England Unitarianism. Hailed as something of a martyr on his arrival in New York in June 1794, Priestley found his subsequent reception more problematic. In Philadelphia his addresses in Elhanan Winchester's* Universalist* meetinghouse* drew respectable crowds, but ensuing efforts to organize a local Unitarian congregation met with only modest results. Priestley spent his final decade in Northumberland, Pennsylvania, preaching* infrequently in local churches and in the end reduced to presiding over worship* services in his own home. Feared in England as an atheist* and derided on the Continent for daring to defend even a dilute tincture of historic Christianity, Priestley was ultimately judged irrelevant by American Christians drawn to the rationalism* of Scottish Common Sense Philosophy* and caught up in the fervor of the Second Great Awakening.*

BIBLIOGRAPHY. *AAP* 8; *DAB* VIII; *DARB;* E. M. Geffen, *Philadelphia Unitarianism, 1796-1861* (1961); F. W. Gibbs, *Joseph Priestley: Adventurer in Science and Champion of Truth* (1965); J. Priestley, *The Memoirs of Dr. Joseph Priestley . . . with a continuation, to the time of his decease, by his son, Joseph Priestley* (1806).   G. W. Harper

Priests of St. Sulpice. *See* SULPICIANS.

Primitive Baptists. Baptist* churches and associations generally characterized by rigid predestinarianism and a desire to recapture the original faith and order of the New Testament apostles. Emerging in the early nineteenth century, these Baptists used Particular Baptist* confessions to develop a rigid Calvinism* and an opposition to organized missions.* The Kehuckee Association (North Carolina), which first articulated their position (1826), said missionary organizations promoted a nonpredestinarian theology,* undermined local church autonomy and encouraged a paid clergy.* Most Primitive Baptists oppose church auxiliaries not found in Scripture,* such as Bible/tract societies,* seminaries* and Sunday schools.* Their churches group only in associations which meet annually and correspond with each other by letter or messenger. Their church order has been characterized by simple, monthly worship* meetings, closed communion, refusal to accept members without Primitive Baptist immersion and untrained/unsalaried, bivocational ministers.

Five main groups survive. The rigidly predestinarian* Absoluters publish *Signs of the Times* and *Zion's Landmark* (6,495 members, 380 churches in 1980). Old Liners, who allow human responsibility in predestination, publish *Advocate and Messenger, Baptist Witness* and *The Primitive Baptist* (48,980 members, 1,426 churches in 1980). Progressive Primitive Baptists, the least rigidly predestinarian, meet weekly, pay ministerial salaries and conduct Sunday schools (11,043 members, 163 churches in 1980). Over one million National Primitive Baptists, with headquarters in Huntsville, Alabama, comprise the African-American convention. A few descendants of Daniel Parker's* "Two-Seed-in-the-Spirit Predestinarian Baptists" (c.1826) still exist in Texas and Louisiana.

BIBLIOGRAPHY. H. L. McBeth, *The Baptist Heritage* (1987); A. C. Piepkorn, "The Primitive Baptists of North America," *CTM* XLII, no. 5 (1971); A. C.

Piepkorn, *Profiles in Belief,* vol. 2 (1978).
                                                      J. T. Spivey

Primitivism. The impulse to restore the primitive or original order of things as revealed in Scripture,* free from the accretions of church history and tradition. This is the general meaning of the term as it has come to be used by scholars of American religion, though some have preferred the terms *restorationism* or *restitutionism.*

The theme of primitivism can be found in America's national history and is reflected in Thomas Paine's* suggestion that "we have it in our power to begin the world over again." For the early colonists of the Atlantic seaboard and the later settlers of the Western frontier, America promised a land of fresh beginnings and new opportunities such as had not been offered since the paradise of Eden's garden. As the British philosopher John Locke (1632-1714) observed, "in the beginning, all the world was America."

Primitivism has been a vital force in American religion, though its meaning and implications have not been the same in every religious tradition. The New England Puritan* ideal was to establish the "original," "primitive" or "ancient" order and doctrine in their Congregational* life and worship.* Puritan millennialism* was arguably primitivist in its hope for the restoration of primordial purity and simplicity. Other European traditions transplanted in American soil would mingle primitivism with church tradition. Methodism,* for example, retained elements of its Anglican* heritage. Yet in its itinerant* ministers,* its modified episcopal church government* and its emphasis on lay* participation in class meetings, it was a movement self-consciously pursuing John Wesley's* ideal of restoring apostolic Christianity. Baptists* also were embued with the primitivist impulse in their own dependence on Scripture for the model of New Testament faith and order.

The most outstanding examples of primitivism are the religious traditions indigenous to America, such as the Churches of Christ* and Pentecostalism.* The Churches of Christ began in the early nineteenth century as a quest for Christian unity—a unity based not on creeds* but on the essential truths of Christianity as expressed in the New Testament. Alexander Campbell,* one of the founding fathers of what came to be known as the Restoration Movement,* expressed its goal in his thirty articles entitled "A Restoration of the Ancient Order of Things."

Pentecostalism, on the other hand, has expressed primitivism in its claims to a twentieth-century restoration of apostolic power and order, and the full gospel of salvation,* healing,* Spirit baptism* and Christ's imminent return. Early Pentecostals believed they had direct access to the true meaning of God's Word—the blueprint for the church today. Their experience of the outpouring of God's Spirit, accompanied by miraculous gifts, gave them ample reason to believe that the apostolic faith had leaped nearly nineteen centuries of church history and reinstated itself in their midst. Primitivism has continued to be a recurring theme in twentieth-century American religion, a prominent example being the Jesus Movement* of the 1960s.

BIBLIOGRAPHY. T. D. Bozeman, *To Live Ancient Lives: The Primitivist Dimension in New England Puritanism* (1988); S. S. Hill, "A Typology of American Restitutionism: From Frontier Revivalism and Mormonism to the Jesus Movement," *JAAR* 44 (March 1976):65-76; R. T. Hughes, ed., *The American Quest for the Primitive Church* (1988). R. T. Hughes and C. L. Allen, *Illusions of Innocence: Protestant Primitivism in America, 1693-1875* (1988). The Editors

Prince, Thomas (1687-1758). Congregational* minister* and historian. Born in Sandwich, Massachusetts, into a prominent family, Prince graduated from Harvard* (1709), where he had a pious reputation. He traveled for two years in the West Indies and Europe and preached* in England before returning to Massachusetts in 1717. From among several offers, he accepted a call to a copastorate with Joseph Sewall at Boston's Third Church (Old South), where he was ordained* in 1718 and remained until his death. The next year he married Deborah Denny, with whom he had four children.

In a position of such influence, Prince quickly emerged as a central figure in eighteenth-century New England's religious and political history. Associated with the Mather* family on most public issues, in 1721 Prince endorsed Dr. Zabdiel Boylston's innovative program of smallpox inoculation for which chief supporter Cotton Mather* was so vilified. During the Great Awakening* of the 1740s he was a New Light* and engaged in friendly controversy with the revival's leading opponent, Charles Chauncy.* He was among those who invited evangelist George Whitefield* to preach in Boston. He started America's first religious magazine, *The Christian History,* to report on local revivals in America and Europe. Prince published a number of occasional sermons,* including funeral orations, election sermons, thanksgiving

sermons and discourses on current events such as earthquakes. An avid bibliophile, he was especially committed to collecting material on the history of New England, including the Mather family papers. Prince's most memorable work was as an historian, for he published *A Chronological History of New England* (1736). His last work was a revision of *The New England Psalm Book* (*See* Bay Psalm Book) in 1758.

BIBLIOGRAPHY. *AAP* 1; *DAB* VII; *NCAB* 7; J. L. Sibley, *Biographical Sketches of the Graduates of Harvard University,* 8 vols. (1873-1951).

C. E. Hambrick-Stowe

Princeton Theology. A Presbyterian* and Reformed* theological tradition developed at Princeton Theological Seminary. American Presbyterianism's most dominant theology* was propagated at Princeton Seminary from its founding in 1812 until its reorganization in 1921. Princeton Theological Seminary was founded by Old School Presbyterians in order to provide ministerial training for Presbyterians. The seminary filled a gap left by the declining theological leadership and commitment to ministerial training on the part of the College of New Jersey* and its president until 1812, Samuel Stanhope Smith.

For over a century Princeton was the domain of prominent professors—Archibald Alexander,* Charles Hodge,* Archibald A. Hodge,* Benjamin B. Warfield* and J. Gresham Machen*—who taught a demanding theological curriculum to over 6,000 students, defended Reformed interpretations of Scripture* and laid intellectual and spiritual foundations for twentieth-century evangelicalism.*

Princeton's theologians advocated a Reformed confessionalism.* They taught that human depravity resulted from an historical Fall and that the imputation of Adam's sin* resulted in a fallen race which could only be saved by Christ's sacrificial atonement.* God worked out his plan of covenantal redemption through election* and predestination.* In his famous remark that "a new idea never originated in this Seminary," Charles Hodge epitomized Princeton's claim to be merely a bearer of an unbroken and unaltered Calvinism.* The Princeton men treated Christian teaching as an unchanging whole by delineating their Calvinism back through the Westminster* standards, Swiss theologian Francois Turretin (1623-1687), Augustine (354-430), early church fathers and ultimately to New Testament writers. While they displayed little sensitivity to historical conditions shaping doctrines* and to the necessity of contextualizing faith for each generation, they were committed to retaining the Reformed biblical world view as foundational for all Christian teaching.

As modern theologians mounted hostile attacks against orthodoxy,* each Princeton generation responded by refining its predecessors' view of Scripture. After Alexander defended the Bible* against deism* and Charles Hodge met the first onslaught of European biblical criticism, A. A. Hodge and Warfield taught that God's verbal and plenary inspiration produced a Scripture inerrant* in the original autographs. In numerous articles and reviews Warfield defended Scripture as divine in origin yet possessing human characteristics. While fully supporting critical inquiry of Scripture because God gifted human reason to unlock the treasures of revelation, Warfield adamantly opposed criticism predicated on naturalistic premises. Modern scholarship distorted Christianity's essence by denying biblical supernaturalism.

Princeton's defense of Scripture relied heavily on the principles of Scottish Common Sense Philosophy* that empirical induction is the primary source of truth and that all reasonable people intuit moral absolutes. Princeton's apologists proposed to refute secularism by establishing God's existence, the Scripture's veracity and authenticity and the necessity of biblical religion. Occasionally Princetonians even intruded induction into systematic* theology by defining theology as a science in which theologians garner facts from the Bible as scientists investigate facts of nature. Critics have pointed out Princeton's failure to recognize the areligious nature of scientism and the conflict between Scottish Philosphy's principles and Calvin's teaching that the noetic effect of sin precludes any natural theology.* In affirming Scottish philosophy as basic to their apologetic,* the Princeton men uncritically followed the lead of nineteenth-century American culture. Usually, however, Princeton theologians evaluated philosophy through the lens of biblical revelation and not vice versa.

In practical matters they taught Christian nurture as the basis for piety,* prayer* and the sacraments* as means of grace, and Christian vocation as the means by which believers contribute to God's kingdom.* Alexander and the elder Hodge kept detailed diaries of their spirituality.* They enumerated internal evidences for the divinity of Scriptures which they associated with illumination of the Holy Spirit. Critical of the emotional excesses of American revivals* and the blatant subjectivism of later liberalism,* Princetonians nevertheless pronounced regeneration* and conversion* as indispensable prerequisites of a subdued but genuine piety. Valid religious experience* flows from a prior profession of faith in biblical doctrine.

The Princeton men disseminated their perspectives outside the classroom through voluminous writing. Alexander wrote on religious experience and a detailed work, *Evidences of the Authenticity, Inspiration, and Canonical Authority of the Holy Scriptures* (1836). Charles Hodge brought European scholarship to America and engaged competing theological perspectives in lively debate by editing the prestigious *Biblical Repertory and Reformed Review.* His three-volume *Systematic Theology* (1872-1873) became a standard text in conservative seminaries, as did A. A. Hodge's popular *Outlines of Theology* (1860). When the liberal-fundamentalist controversy* erupted, Warfield's most valuable contribution to conservatism was subjecting every major theological innovation, both foreign and domestic, to lengthy and trenchant criticism in academic journals. As liberal forces attempted to seize control of America's major denominations,* Machen wrote *Christianity and Liberalism* (1923) to distinguish modernism* and orthodox Christianity as two totally different religions.

Machen was unsuccessful in stemming liberalism at Princeton. When the denomination instituted a more inclusive theological perspective by reorganizing the seminary board, he and several other conservatives resigned and helped found Westminster Theological Seminary in Philadelphia (1929) where their theology was continued, although its evidentialist apologetic was altered (*See* Van Til, Cornelius). The Princeton theology lives on in confessionalist denominations and among many scholars committed to historical evangelicalism. Princeton Theological Seminary continued as the leading seminary of the Presbyterian Church in the U.S.A.,* and since the union of the Presbyterians of the North and South in 1983, it has been affiliated with the new denomination, the Presbyterian Church (U.S.A.).*

BIBLIOGRAPHY. W. A. Hoffecker, *Piety and the Princeton Theologians* (1981); M. A. Noll, "The Founding of Princeton Seminary," *WmTJ* 42 (Fall 1979):72-110; M. A. Noll, ed., *The Princeton Theology 1812-1921* (1983); J. C. VanderStelt, *Philosophy and Scripture: A Study in Old Princeton and Westminster Theology* (1978); D. F. Wells, *Reformed Theology in America* (1985).

W. A. Hoffecker

Princeton University. Educational institution with roots in colonial Presbyterianism.* Princeton was probably the first truly national college in

America and from the late eighteenth century through the nineteenth century perhaps the most influential educational institution in shaping Christian thought in the New World. During the eighteenth century, Scottish* and Scotch-Irish Presbyterians came to America in larger numbers than did any one other immigrant group. Scattered widely throughout the South and West as well as the North, the education-conscious descendants of Scottish Reformer John Knox (1514-1572) and French Reformer John Calvin (1509-1564) originally trained their ministeral candidates in surprisingly effective local "log colleges."* With this apprenticeship system reaching its limits and inspired by the zeal emanating from the First Great Awakening,* the New Light* Presbyterians founded what was originally known as the College of New Jersey, in 1746, to train their future ministers and other public leaders. Relocated in Princeton (and renamed) in 1756, it quickly attracted students from all regions of the country and gained a reputation for training leaders for public life. For example, one-sixth of the members of the Constitutional Convention were Princeton alumni.

No college exceeded Princeton in influencing the development of the nineteenth-century Christian college. Princeton graduates founded and directed many colleges in the South and West, and college leaders everywhere followed the model created by Princeton President John Witherspoon* in introducing the year-long senior instruction in moral and mental philosophy as the most important college course. Drawing on Scottish Common Sense Realism,* Witherspoon's course defended Christian dogma* and morality by means of Enlightenment* rationalism.

Princeton Theological Seminary opened in 1812 as one of the first graduate schools of theology in America. During the nineteenth century it trained more students (over 6,000 by 1912) than did any other seminary, and it articulated one of the most influential theological systems then promoted in America. The Princeton Theology* was a nineteenth-century statement of Reformed* Calvinism as influenced by Common Sense philosophy. It emphasized the trustworthiness of Scripture,* the ability of the human mind to understand Christian truth and the total dependence of man on God for spiritual grace. Its chief spokesmen were Archibald Alexander,* Charles Hodge,* Archibald Alexander Hodge* and Benjamin B. Warfield.*

BIBLIOGRAPHY. J. MacLean, *History of the College of New Jersey,* 2 vols. (1877); M. A. Noll, ed., *The Princeton Theology* (1983); M. A. Noll, *Princeton and the Republic, 1768-1822* (1989); T. J. Werten-

baker, *Princeton, 1746-1896* (1946).

W. C. Ringenberg

Prior/Prioress. The male and female leaders or superiors of a religious house (priory) of men or women who have taken either simple or solemn vows. Most of these communities are Catholic*; some are Anglican.* The term *prior* is first found in the Rule of St. Benedict (c. A.D. 530), founder of the Benedictine* religious order.* The community governed by a prior or prioress is usually an independent priory, although the term may also refer to a subordinate official in an abbey governed by an abbot. The terms are now in use in a number of Catholic religious orders besides Benedictines, such as the Dominicans,* Carmelites and Augustinians.*

BIBLIOGRAPHY. A. Donahue, "Prior" and "Prioress," *NCE* 11.

M. Schneider

Prison Fellowship Ministries. A parachurch* organization dedicated to encouraging and assisting the church in its volunteer ministry to prisoners, ex-prisoners and their families. In 1976 Charles Colson, former special counsel to President Nixon,* started Prison Fellowship Ministries (PFM) in response to the spiritual and emotional needs evident during his Watergate-related prison term.

The ministry is based on the conviction that the only hope for the reformation of criminal offenders is in the redemptive and reconciling power of Christ mediated through the Christian community. At first PFM's program focused on discipleship seminars; small groups of furloughed inmates gathered in Washington, D.C., for leadership training. In 1977 the ministry expanded to include local in-prison seminars, dependent on volunteers to help present an evangelistic* and a Christian-growth message. PFM's outreach mushroomed, by 1986 enlisting the support of some 25,000 volunteers. Other ministry approaches include an extensive pen-pal program, marriage seminars for inmates and spouses, pre-release practical life skills seminars and mentoring programs for recently released prisoners.

Criminal-justice reform is the particular concern of PFM's Justice Fellowship (JF) under the direction of Daniel Van Ness. JF works with public officials and private citizens to make criminal-justice systems more consistent with biblical teaching on justice and righteousness. Believing that crime is first of all committed against a victim, not the state, JF works to institute punishments for nonviolent offenders that will help reduce prison overpopulation and benefit the victim, society and the offender. Programs include restitution and community-service projects which allow prisoners to reduce their sentences by performing community service.

In 1979 Prison Fellowship International was begun as an international association of prison ministries, each member organization being independent, self-supporting and operating under its own national board of directors.

BIBLIOGRAPHY. C. Colson, *Life Sentence* (1979); D. Van Ness, *Crime and Its Victims* (1986).

G. D. Loux

Prison Ministries. Lay* and ordained* ministries* to prisoner, ex-prisoners and their families. The very concept of the modern, Western penitentiary is rooted in American church history. In 1776 the Quakers,* who had been working for criminal-justice reform in England for more than a century, brought their concern to America. Their Philadelphia Society for Relieving Distressed Prisoners looked for humane alternatives to the corporal punishments generally meted out. In 1790 this group overhauled the Philadelphia Walnut Street Jail, placing prisoners in solitary cells where they could meditate and repent (hence the term *penitentiary*). Their reform failed. Madness prevailed over penitence, and yet the penitentiary model, seemingly humane and keeping criminals out of public sight, became the accepted norm.

Although the church spearheaded many nineteenth-century social reforms, ministry to prisoners was relatively quiet and local until after World War 2,* when several large denominations* placed chaplains* in selected institutions. As Ray Hoekstra, known to his radio audience as "Chaplain Ray," brought the needs of prisoners to the attention of the Christian public, he established International Prison Ministries, which has met a need for free distribution of Bibles* and Christian literature in prisons.

The 1970s ushered in a new era for the church, as America's jails and prisons were more generally viewed as a mission field. Jesus' command to visit those in prison was seen in a new light. The spiritual needs of America's prisoners became the overwhelming concern of several prominent men who, through the media, shared their vision with the church. In 1972 former professional football player Bill Glass founded the Bill Glass Prison Ministry, emphasizing crusade evangelism. In 1976 Charles Colson, recently released from prison after his conviction for Watergate-related offenses under the Nixon* administration, founded Prison Fellowship Ministries,* whose array of programs support

local churches in their ministry to prisoners, ex-prisoners and their families. These and many other parachurch* prison ministries have successfully motivated Christians to volunteer time and talent to help meet needs. In ten years, the number of religious volunteers in prison ministries was increased by 200 per cent, with the number of prison ministries more than doubling.

One ministry, Match-Two—matching a mature Christian mentor on the "outside" with an inmate—had a high rate of rehabilitation. Seventy-six per cent of the program's participants were not arrested again in the two years after they were paroled. National statistics from the same period showed that seventy-four per cent of paroled inmates *were* rearrested.

By the late 1980s Christians were involved in a wide variety of prison ministries: evangelism, Bible studies,* church services, discipleship seminars, tutoring, mentoring, counseling, pen-pal programs, literature distribution, correspondence courses, marriage seminars, community service projects and re-entry programs teaching life skills. Increased emphasis was being placed on practical ministry to prisoners' families.

BIBLIOGRAPHY. D. Smarto, *Justice and Mercy* (1987); D. K. Pace, "How Parachurch Groups Serve Prisoners' Needs," *Christian Herald* (May 1980):22-27.

G. D. Loux

Prison Reform, Christians and. Prison reform movements in America have been marked by individuals whose Christian commitment has motivated them to develop, articulate and popularize innovations in the sanctioning of offenders, and has also given content to those reforms.

The first use of imprisonment as punishment was the penitentiary, inaugurated in 1790 in Philadelphia. It was inspired by the Quaker* belief that crime had its roots in the environment of the offender. The remedy, therefore, was to remove convicted offenders from those negative influences by placing them in solitary confinement. Their sole occupations were Bible* reading, conversations with the warden, chaplains* and visiting ministers,* and hand work. This reflection, it was believed, would bring the offenders to repentance; hence, the name *penitentiary.*

However, the Quaker view did not go unchallenged. The first national figure in the prison reform movement was Louis Dwight, founder of the Boston Prison Discipline Society in 1825. His work with the American Bible Society* had taken him into a number of jails, and he was shocked at the miserable conditions he found. He and the

Baptist* and Congregational* ministers who joined his Society held to the Calvinist* doctrine of the innate depravity of human beings. As a result, they argued that reformation came not through solitary reflection, but through revival,* religious training and strictly supervised work performed in silence with other inmates. He succeeded in convincing most states to adopt this approach, known as the "Auburn system," after the New York prison in which it was pioneered in the early 1820s.

Disappointing recidivism rates, serious overcrowding and opposition from the business community led to disenchantment with both the Pennsylvania and Auburn systems. In 1870, Zebulon Brockway, who had been converted during Charles Finney's* revivals, joined with other prison leaders (most of whom were also inspired by their Christian faith) to urge segregating youthful offenders from hardened criminals, and providing them with education and job training. This was known as the "reformatory" movement, and the warden of the first reformatory (built in 1876 in Elmira, New York) was Brockway. However, the old problems of overcrowding and underfunding reduced the effectiveness of the innovation, and reformatories soon became indistinguishable from prisons.

The next major reform movement was the "correctional" or "treatment" model. It held that criminal behavior stemmed from physical or psychological (and not moral or spiritual) problems, and that rehabilitation should follow the model of medical treatment. Although some of its advocates were Christians, the correctional model was influenced less by Christian faith than by medical science. It, too, produced disappointing recidivism rates, chronic overcrowding, underfunding, and public and prisoner resistance to some of its more extreme methods.

In the last two decades, major Christian denominations* and organizations have joined others in questioning the ability of imprisonment to rehabilitate, and have advocated alternative sanctions, such as restitution and community service, as methods of punishing offenders and restoring victims' losses.

See also PRISON MINISTRIES.

BIBLIOGRAPHY. G. A. McHugh, *Christian Faith and Criminal Justice: Toward a Christian Response to Crime and Punishment* (1978); P. B. McKelvey, *American Prisons: A History of Good Intentions* (1977); D. W. Van Ness, *Crime and Its Victims: What We Can Do* (1986).

D. W. Van Ness

Pro Nuncio. *See* PAPAL NUNCIO.

Process Theology. As a theological movement process theology began to receive attention after World War 2, and has had its primary influence in the U.S. The two most influential process philosophers have been Alfred North Whitehead (1861-1947) and Charles Hartshorne (b.1897). Theologians such as Henry Nelson Wieman,* Daniel Day Williams,* Bernard MacDougal Loomer (1912-1985), John Cobb (b.1925), Schubert Ogden (b.1928), Lewis Ford (b.1933) and David R. Griffin (b.1939) have elaborated process motifs for theology.

Christian theologians must deal with at least two distinct cultural settings: the culture of the Bible and the culture of their own age and setting. By its very nature the Christian gospel deals with issues such as God, creation, causality, time, space, history, self-identity and moral values. In order to do theology, theologians require some means of analyzing their contemporary culture and the basic factors in the world view or multiple world views shaping their culture. For this reason theologians have traditionally turned to philosophy. As Augustine employed neo-Platonic thought and Aquinas turned to Aristotelian categories, so process theologians today employ process philosophy in order to structure their presentation of the gospel to our own age.

There are several recurring themes which identify process thought. While each of them may be found in other contemporary philosophies, these motifs combine to form a clearly recognizable constellation which sets process thought apart as a distinct movement. The first motif is radical *empiricism*. Process thought is empirical, considering experience as the ultimate court of appeal, not only for verifying our theories but also for defining their meaning. The empiricism of process thought, however, is radical because the process thinker can find no reason to limit experience to sense perception. And it is radical because the process thinker can find no reason to assume that all genuine experience must be conscious.

Just as animals with primitive nervous systems sustain neither sense perception nor consciousness, and yet clearly experience their worlds, so process thinkers maintain that all life, including human life, rests on primitive, pre-sensual and pre-conscious experience, out of which the capacity for sense perception and consciousness emerges. Process thinkers hold that religious intuitions also are rooted in pre-sensual, pre-conscious modes of experience.

The second central motif of process thought, *relationalism,* maintains that, at these more primitive levels in particular, we directly experience not only things but relations between those things. For example, process thought holds that we directly experience causation and that the very identities of the things related consist, at least in part, in their relationships. If relationships such as causality may be directly experienced at the pre-sensual and pre-conscious level, then it is at least possible that we can directly experience God's working in our lives. The direct experience of divine providence in our lives remains possible even though we have no direct sense perception of an entity called God nor any sense perception of a causal relation between God and us.

Process thought takes its name from the third primary motif, which is *process.* Time, history, change, coming to be, enduring and perishing are among the most important items we can directly experience. Process thought accepts the evolutionary motifs of recent biology and physics, the modern sense of the importance of our past in shaping our present identity, as well as the deep sense of historical movement under God's guidance which permeates the Bible. From the standpoint of process thought, the biblical world view matches, and may even be a significant source of, the evolutionary motifs which have dominated Western intellectual life for the last hundred years.

These three motifs lead to the fourth central motif of process thought: the basic units in our world are "events." Even entities such as rocks or persons may be considered to be ultimately composed of events. It is important to note that the identity of an event (and thus of any "entity" whatsoever) consists, at least in part, in its relationships.

Alfred North Whitehead, the key figure in process thought, provided a speculative interpretation of experience—that is, he created a set of general categories for interpreting our experience where these general ideas are to be logically consistent, forming a balanced and coordinated whole. Whitehead considered his world view a tentative hypothesis to be tested by experience and always open to revision in the light of additional information about the world as discovered by science, religion or other disciplines.

Whitehead's description of God matches each of the major themes of his speculative philosophy. God knows the world through his experience of it. This experience relates God to the world. Whitehead's thesis that an entity's relationships are a part of its identity means that God's knowledge of the world is a part of his identity. Furthermore, as the world changes, God's knowledge changes; and as God's knowledge changes, God himself must change. Thus God can be truly affected by his relations with the world. Yet in other respects God is changeless. As relationships are a *part* of each entity's identity, yet each entity is always more than its relationships, so God includes relationships as *part* of his identity, but he is always far more than his relationships. Process theologians find this concept of a changing God a fitting philosophical description of the biblical God, who enters deeply into the events of history and rejoices over the repentance of one sinner.

Somewhat more difficult to defend on biblical grounds, is Whitehead's view that both God and the world may be described by the "Category of the Ultimate." By this Whitehead seems to mean that there is something—specifically "creativity"—which is more ultimate than God. This means that God is a creature, albeit a unique, universally present and everlastingly indispensable creature. From the standpoint of biblical Christianity, this seems highly problematical. And even distinctly non-evangelical thinkers such as Langdon Gilkey* have objected to this on theological grounds.

The rationalistic metaphysics of Charles Hartshorne represents the second major direction in process thought. Hartshorne's rationalistic stance leads him to affirm the validity of the ontological argument. God, according to Hartshorne, is perfect by definition. But, he argues, the notion of perfection in classical Christian theology is in fact self-contradictory. Thus the classical God "necessarily" fails to exist. Given a proper interpretation of perfection, however, Hartshorne maintains that he can show that God exists "necessarily"—his existence is compatible with any state of affairs in the world and the denial of God's existence always entails a contradiction.

Hartshorne affirms a "di-polar" deity who is both abstract and concrete. God's abstract formal structure consists of those characteristics which never vary and are compatible with any state of affairs in the world. But this abstract, self-identity of God exists only as a necessary element in God; it is not God himself in his full, actual existence.

The concrete pole of God knows the world. As the world grows—as new facts come into existence—God's knowledge, precisely because it is *perfect* knowledge, must also grow. Hartshorne further maintains that the perfect knower must include the object known within himself. Therefore, as the perfect knower of the world, God must include the world within himself. This does not mean that God is to be equated with the world (as in pantheism). But neither is God wholly distinct from and independent of the world (as in classical theism). Rather God, while transcending the world and having his own identity, nonetheless includes the world within himself. Hartshorne calls his view of God pan-en-theism (all-in-God-ism). According to Hartshorne, it is the panentheistic, concrete God who, as Jesus said of his Father, shares the joys and sorrows of each creature, and who loves the world.

The third form of process thought may be associated with Henry Nelson Wieman* and Bernard MacDougal Loomer. Choosing not to engage in either the speculative metaphysics of Whitehead or the rationalistic metaphysics of Hartshorne, these process thinkers adhered closely to felt experience with the goal of describing, articulating and expressing the religious aspects of human life. Wieman, for example, challenged the notion that God is all-powerful on the empiricist grounds that the world as we experience it provides no indication of any such divine omnipotence. Loomer went further, arguing that we have no experiential basis for asserting that God is purely loving.

While most process theologians have concentrated on rethinking the category of God, some theologians have also tried to provide process perspectives on other Christian topics, particularly Christology,* ethics,* love, humanity and the church. Best known among contemporary North American process theologians working in these areas is John B. Cobb, Jr. (1925-). His Christology emphasizes that the term *Christ* connects with the term *Logos*—a universal reality not limited to Jesus and Christianity. While we should not hesitate to consider Jesus as the Christ, Cobb also insists that we should expect to find that other religions also have their Christ figures, such as the cosmic savior, Amida, who is the central reality in the Pure Land traditions of Buddhism. According to Cobb, we should boldly explore these possibilities, open ourselves to encounters with other religions in mutual dialog, and embrace the possibility that this dialog might result in mutual transformation. Cobb argues that this open stance truly fits Christianity because Jesus as the Christ includes within himself the realities of process and transformation.

Process theologians have emphasized the sense of community in their doctrine of the church and in their ethics. Daniel Day Williams* rendered a particularly sensitive analysis of the Christian doctrine of love. In their attempt to provide new ways of looking at the sacraments,* process theologians have emphasized the sense of community and relatedness in the physical bread and wine, and in the water—relatedness both to other Christians as well as relatedness to God and the world.

In the 1980s process theology continued to grow in importance and acceptance among mainline* Protestants* in the U.S. Its continued influence poses a challenge to evangelical* theologians, both as they seek to provide convincing rebuttals to its many sub-biblical claims and as they consider other process themes which may provide a bridge from genuinely biblical perspectives to contemporary ways of experiencing the world.

BIBLIOGRAPHY. D. Brown et al., eds., *Process Philosophy and Christian Thought* (1971); J. B. Cobb, Jr., and D. R. Griffin, *Process Theology: An Introductory Exposition* (1976); S. T. Franklin, *Speaking From the Depths: Alfred North Whitehead's Hermeneutical Metaphysics of Propositions, Experience, Symbolism, Language, and Religion* (1989); B. M. Loomer, "Process Theology: Origins, Strengths, Weaknesses," *Process Studies* 16 (Winter 1987):245-254; G. R. Lucas, Jr., *The Genesis of Modern Process Thought: A Historical Outline with Bibliography* (1983); D. D. Williams, *The Spirit and Forms of Love* (1981).   S. T. Franklin

Professional Ministry. Ministry distinguished from the ministry of all believers, not only by ordination,* but by training and employment by a church* or religious agency. While ordination sets clergy* apart, the secular concept of "profession" links ministry with other occupations. In colonial days it was, with law and medicine, among the learned professions. Proficiency in theology* and ancient languages, plus spiritual vocation,* were the criteria for entry into the profession. The need to train ministers* motivated founding of colleges.* Professionalization involved ministerial meetings for study and support, apprenticeship of young men in the homes of pastors,* regulation of admission to the ministry and attempts to improve terms of call and salaries.

The 1800s saw the rise of modern professions, with the concept of "career" and establishment of specialized graduate schools to award professional degrees. Denominations* assumed institutional authority to credential and foster ministerial careers. At theological seminaries,* beyond Bible* and theology, professional skills were taught. Churches expanded ministries through missionary* and moral reform societies, new colleges* and religious periodicals, creating the need for executives, professors, presidents and editors. A minister or priest's* career might consist of advancement up a ladder of ever-larger parishes or these new positions. Status and success became concerns of the profession. Professionalism implies a lifetime of training for effective ministry and church administration.

Emphasis on professional competence improved but also tended to secularize ministry. Catholics* and Protestants* periodically reminded themselves that while professional training is important, spiritual vocation is essential.

BIBLIOGRAPHY. B. J. Bledstein, *The Culture of Professionalism: The Middle Class and the Development of Higher Education in America* (1976); E. B. Holifield, *The Gentlemen Theologians: American Theology in Southern Culture, 1795-1860* (1978); D. M. Scott, *From Office to Profession: The New England Ministry, 1750-1850* (1978); J. Glasse, *Profession: Minister* (1968).

C. E. Hambrick-Stowe

Progressive Orthodoxy. *See* EVANGELICAL LIBERALISM.

Prohibition Movement (1920-1933). The movement to outlaw the manufacture and sale of alcoholic* beverages by Constitutional amendment, was part of the early twentieth-century Progressive movement for social reform. The roots of the movement go back to the early nineteenth century when increased drinking caused public concern. The pre-Civil War* temperance movement* led to prohibition in at least nine states. After the war restrictive efforts were resumed by the Prohibition Party (1869). Frances Willard,* leader of the Women's Christian Temperance Union (1874), campaigned for restrictive state legislation and scientific instruction in schools on the effects of alcohol. The Anti-Saloon League* (1895) brought effective public pressure on Congress and state legislatures. Led by Methodist* minister* Alpha Kynett,* the League drew its greatest support from Protestant* denominations,* and considered itself "the Church in Action Against the Saloon." Middle-class Protestants attacked the corrupt power of the liquor industry and the urban saloon, gathering place for recent immigrants,* where the atmosphere was deemed a threat to Protestant and democratic* values.

By 1914 over half of the states had adopted some form of prohibition. America's entry into World War 1* aided the cause as Prohibitionists criticized both the use of grain for alcohol production and the German origins of many brewing and distilling interests. The Eighteenth Amendment banned the manufacture, sale or transport of intoxicants, beginning in 1920. Alcoholic consumption de-

clined initially, though enforcement resources were inadequate and a growing illegal liquor traffic mocked the law and aided the growth of organized crime. The Twenty-first Amendment repealed Prohibition in 1933, returning liquor regulation to the states. Similar campaigns occurred in Canada, where every province was dry by 1919, and England, which curtailed liquor sales during the war.

BIBLIOGRAPHY. N. H. Clark, *Deliver Us From Evil: An Interpretation of American Prohibition* (1976); J. H. Timberlake, *Prohibition and the Progressive Movement, 1900-1920* (1963).

D. W. Carlson

Propaganda. *See* SACRED CONGREGATION FOR THE EVANGELIZATION OF PEOPLES OR FOR THE PROPAGATION OF THE FAITH (PROPAGANDA).

Propagation of the Faith. *See* SACRED CONGREGATION FOR THE EVANGELIZATION OF PEOPLES OR FOR THE PROPAGATION OF THE FAITH (PROPAGANDA).

Prophecy, Gift of. A gift of the Holy Spirit; an inspired utterance in vernacular language. The gift of prophecy has been claimed by Christians throughout the centuries, whether officially recognized by the church or practiced in private or sectarian settings. In the post-apostolic church, the gift was widely recognized as a genuine manifestation of the Spirit, being practiced by the orthodox as well as the Montanists and gnostic groups. But with the development of church leadership, the canon and the office of teacher, spontaneous prophecy declined. Nevertheless, the medieval scholastic theologian Thomas Aquinas (1225-1274) recognized the validity of the gift and commented on its usefulness for the church. The Protestant Reformers understood the gift as the right understanding of canonical Scripture,* and within Protestantism as a whole the occasional prophetic claims of the seventeenth and eighteenth centuries were largely outside the mainstream. In America the Shakers* of the late eighteenth and early nineteenth centuries, with their emphasis on the restoration of spiritual gifts in the end time, reportedly exercised the gift of prophecy.

In the modern era, the birth of the Pentecostal Movement in the late nineteenth and early twentieth centuries began to bring the gift of prophecy once again to the church's attention. More recently, with the wider acceptance of Pentecostalism and the growth of the charismatic movement in mainline* churches, the gift has earned wider acceptance and more scholarly attention. Pentecostals and charismatics claim that the gift of prophecy did not cease with the apostolic church and the closing of the biblical canon. They believe that the gift operates under the same conditions as it did in the days of the apostles and should be regulated by principles set forth in the New Testament.

Of the nine gifts of the Holy Spirit listed in 1 Corinthians 12:8-10, prophecy is given special prominence by Paul. In 1 Corinthians 14, prophecy is said to be highly desirable (1 Cor 14:1), since an utterance in the vernacular does not require interpretation as does tongues. Its content may be strengthening to the believers, providing encouragement or comfort (1 Cor 14:3). Episodes of prophetic utterance described in Acts disclose that prediction of future events may have been included (Acts 21:10-14), but Paul did not employ such foreknowledge to obtain personal guidance.

The gift of prophecy should be distinguished from the office of prophet. Paul taught that all in the local assembly may have the privilege of prophesying (1 Cor 14:31), but not all are considered "prophets." Acts 13:1 discloses that at Antioch prophets were one type of leader in the assembly; evidently those who regularly exercised the gift of prophecy. Paul made it clear that prophetic utterances were not infallible. They were to come under the judgment of others present in the assembly, presumably to weigh whether or not the utterance agreed with known apostolic teaching (1 Cor 14:29).

Classical Pentecostals insist that prophetic utterances must come under the judgment of biblical teaching. Just as Paul placed careful limits on prophecy by asserting that the "spirits of prophets are subject to the control of prophets" (1 Cor 14:32), so reason and judgment are believed to be required today for the orderly exercise of such a spiritual manifestation.

BIBLIOGRAPHY. D. Gee, *Concerning Spiritual Gifts* (1980); W. A. Grudem, *The Gift of Prophecy in the New Testament and Today* (1988); H. Horton, *The Gifts of the Spirit* (1971).

W. W. Menzies

Prophetic Conferences. *See* BIBLE AND PROPHETIC CONFERENCE MOVEMENT.

Protestant, Protestantism. The term *Protestant* emerged in the early years of the Reformation of the sixteenth century. In 1529 a group of evangelical princes of Lutheran* and Zwinglian persuasion issued a formal "protest" at the Second Diet of Speyer after an agreement to allow individual German states the right to determine their religious position had been rescinded by the Roman

Catholic* party. In a general sense the term *Protestant* refers to all groups who have separated from the Roman Catholic Church since the Reformation, including those in the Reformed,* Lutheran,* Anglican,* Anabaptist,* Baptist* and Methodist* traditions and a host of smaller groups. Interestingly, the term, which carries the somewhat negative connotation of protest, is rarely used in denominational* labels.

The one belief which serves both as a common denominator and a driving force for all Protestants is the priesthood of all believers.* This doctrinal hallmark of the Reformation implies that the individual Christian has direct access to God and the freedom to think, interpret, pray* and minister independently, and yet many Protestant groups do retain a church hierarchy. Thus, Protestants tend to be independent, and this has proved to be both a strength and a weakness. Such freedom has produced revitalizing new approaches to the formulation of doctrine* and ethics,* and the practice of worship,* missions,* theological education* and hymnody.* On the negative side the Protestant penchant for autonomy has led to numerous denominational splits and a loss of unity.

In North America, Protestantism blossomed in the land of egalitarian democracy* and dominated the religious consciousness of the colonies and the new nation until the mid-nineteenth century. This is illustrated by the fact that until the Civil War* there were no permanent Roman Catholic chaplains* in the U.S. armed forces. American revivalism,* as well as Sunday-school* materials and popular devotional literature, have had a blending influence on Protestantism in the twentieth century, while, on the other hand, the rise of biblical criticism,* Darwinian evolution* and the study of comparative religions has led to the designation *New Protestant* to describe a movement within mainline* churches which stresses tolerance, a more liberal* theology and an emphasis upon the social concerns of the church.

BIBLIOGRAPHY. J. C. Brauer, *Protestantism in America* (1953); J. Dillenberger and C. Welch, *Protestant Christianity, Interpreted through Its Development* (1958); J. H. Nichols, *The Meaning of Protestantism* (1959); M. Marty, *Protestantism* (1972).

N. P. Feldmeth

Protestant Episcopal Church in the U.S.A. Alternately called the Episcopal Church, the Protestant Episcopal Church in the U.S.A. is a member of the world-wide fellowship of Anglican Churches.* It is not joined to other Anglican churches through any established and regulated hierarchical organization. Rather, it is united to the Anglican Communion* by a kinship of faith, government and worship* through mutual association with the mother church in England.

The Episcopal Church began in America as an extension of the Church of England and under its jurisdiction. The first permanently organized Anglican church began in Jamestown, Virginia, under the leadership of Robert Hunt* (1607). Other churches were established in Boston (1689), Philadelphia (1695), New York City (1697) and Newport (1702). By the end of the colonial period, Anglican churches were to be found in all thirteen colonies.

During the American Revolution,* the Church went through a severe crisis. Most clergy in the North, as opposed to their mostly patriotic brethren in the South, remained loyal to the King of England and closed their churches rather than remove prayers for the monarch from the liturgy.* For this loyalty some were put in prison, some banished from the colonies and others escaped to Canada. However, a good many Episcopal lay* people supported the Revolution and two-thirds of the signers of the Declaration of Independence were Episcopalians. In the end those colonies where Anglicanism* had become the legally established religion (Virginia, Maryland, Georgia, North Carolina, South Carolina and certain counties of New York) were forced to revoke this status of the church.

After the Revolution the church gathered its forces to create a denomination* independent and autonomous of the Church of England. The first general convention met in Philadelphia on September 27, 1785, and took preliminary steps toward the establishment of a duly recognized denomination. With no resident American bishop,* the Anglican churches were faced not only with the problem of organizing a national church separate from English monarchial authority but also of securing consecration* for its bishops.

From the start the process took on a distinctly American character. When the general convention met it was attended by laity* as well as clergy* (though without Samuel Seabury* of Connecticut, who, in a controversial move, had recently been consecrated bishop by the Scottish Episcopal Church)—a democratic* arrangement without precedent in England. By the time of the next general convention in Philadelphia on July 28, 1789, two bishops, William White* and Samuel Provost,* had been consecrated in England and the validity of Seabury's consecration was recognized. In the second session of that convention (Sep-

tember 30 to October 16, 1789), a constitution was adopted, canons of the church ratified and a revised version of the *Book of Common Prayer** authorized.

In organization the church is episcopal (*See* Church Government: Episcopal), meaning it is governed by bishops. As in all of the American churches, but distinct from the Church of England, the Episcopal Church is free of state control. Each bishop oversees a diocese* (there are no archbishops* or archdiocese*) consisting of clergy and parishes.* A general convention of bishops and lay people, meeting every three years, presides over the whole church. As in the federal Congress, this body consists of two houses, the House of Bishops (consisting of the bishops of each diocese) and the House of Deputies (consisting of four priests* and four lay persons from every diocese). All actions of the church must be passed by both houses. A national council headed by the elected presiding bishop of the House of Bishops carries out the day-by-day administration of the church. Thus, reflecting American democratic values, lay people have a strong voice in the church, from the vestry* to the national level.

During the nineteenth century the Episcopal Church expanded with the growth and development of the U. S. Missionary* work, carried out by missionary bishops* and priests, extended into the Midwest, the South and the Southwest and between 1829 and 1860 the number of Episcopalians increased from 30,000 to nearly 150,000. Schools were also founded, with General Theological Seminary of New York (1819) representing the high church* movement and the Theological Seminary of Virginia (1824) nourishing the evangelical* movement. Unlike other major American denominations, while the Civil War* separated Episcopalians into Northern and Southern factions, they quietly resumed full relations when the war ended. By 1900 the church had grown to 720,000 communicants.

In the twentieth century the church has been deeply involved in the ecumenical movement.* Its platform for unity, presented by William R. Huntington* in 1870, calls for the union of the church around four basic principles: the Scriptures as the Word of God, the primitive creeds as the rule of faith, the two sacraments* ordained by Christ, and the episcopate. In the twentieth century it was the American Charles Brent,* then Episcopal bishop of the Philippine Islands, who organized and presided over the first meeting of the World Conference on Faith and Order (Lausanne, 1927). The Episcopal Church has remained active in this movement and is a member of the World Council of Churches,* as well as the National Council of Churches* and the Consultation on Church Union.*

Doctrinally the Episcopal Church holds to the ancient creeds, particularly the Apostles' and Nicene Creeds, as appropriate historic symbols of faith. The Thirty-nine Articles* of the Reformation period are loosely held, but are not at all binding on the clergy. A wide variety of interpretation is tolerated in the Episcopal Church, a fact represented by the presence of evangelicals, charismatics,* liberals* and Anglo-Catholics (*See* Tractarianism) in the Church. What binds the church together and defines its unity is its worship,* as articulated in the *Book of Common Prayer* (revised 1979). There is an increasing recognition among other Protestant churches of the West that the *Book of Common Prayer* provides a model of Christian worship that is rooted in biblical-historical tradition and yet pertinent to the modern world. Thus perhaps the single most important contribution the Episcopal Church is making to modern American religion is in the area of liturgy.

From 1955 to 1965 the Episcopal Church enjoyed a twenty per cent gain in membership, followed by a more than sixteen per cent loss in the decade 1965-1975. In the 1980s the membership has stabilized with an inclusive membership of 2,739,422 (with 1,881,250 full communicants) in 7,274 churches reported in 1985.

See also ANGLICAN CHURCH IN CANADA; ANGLICAN CHURCHES IN AMERICA; ANGLICAN COMMUNION; ANGLICANISM.

BIBLIOGRAPHY. R. W. Albright, *A History of the Protestant Episcopal Church* (1964); S. D. McConnell, *History of the American Episcopal Church* (1891); W. W. Manross, *A History of the American Episcopal Church* (1959); J. G. Melton, *The Encyclopedia of American Religions* (1986); C. C. Tiffany, *A History of the Protestant Episcopal Church in the United States of America* (1895).

R. Webber

Protestant Work Ethic. The thesis that there is an affinity between early modern capitalism* and Calvinism.* The concept of the Protestant work ethic originated in a study by the German sociologist Max Weber, *The Protestant Ethic and the Spirit of Capitalism* (1904-1905). Weber's thesis, which has been debated ever since, held that Calvinism (as distinct from Catholicism,* Lutheranism* and Anglicanism*) inculcated in its followers an austere, ascetic outlook on life which systematically suppressed the pursuit of pleasure. At the same time this asceticism, in contrast to medieval Catholicism, was "this-worldly"—believers were encouraged to work hard, discipline themselves and find their salvation in their secular calling. Among other things, Weber argued, this attitude tended to inspire economic productivity, generating income which could not be spent for "frivolous" purposes. Hence it turned into savings or capital.

There have been numerous debates involving applications of the thesis. One claim, for example, is that Catholic culture approved of unproductive expenditures of wealth, such as festivals, lavish art works and rich displays, while Protestant culture did not. Other historians have claimed that Catholic societies historically showed greater compassion for the poor, while the "Protestant ethic" tended to condemn poverty as the result of laziness.

None of the various interpretations of the thesis has ever gained general acceptance. Weber himself erroneously cited John Wesley* and Benjamin Franklin, among others, as Calvinists, and many historians have pointed out the existence of capitalism in Catholic Italy at the time of the Renaissance, albeit not characterized by Weberian austerity.

In recent times the term *Protestant work ethic* has been given attenuated meaning as any tendency to work hard as a way of proving one's personal worth, along with an unease or suspicion concerning rest or enjoyment. Allegedly this represents the secular residuum of older American Puritanism.*

BIBLIOGRAPHY. S. N. Eisenstadt, *The Protestant Ethic and Modernization* (1968); R. W. Green, *Protestantism and Capitalism* (1959); M. Weber, *The Protestant Ethic and the Spirit of Capitalism* (1904-1905, ET 1930). J. F. Hitchcock

Protestant-Catholic Relations, Contemporary. Since the 1960s relations have moved beyond previous mutual hostility to a new spirit of mutual respect. This is based not only on the common recognition of a partially shared Christian life through faith in Christ, the Bible* and baptism,* but also on candor about honest differences. The election of the first Catholic president, John F. Kennedy,* in 1960 signaled a diminishing of hostilities. But it was the U.S. response to the Second Vatican Council* that revolutionized Protestant-Catholic relations.

Vatican II's "Decree on Ecumenism" brought Catholics into the ecumenical movement.* Modern ecumenism* has been at work among Protestants since 1910 and led to the founding of the

World Council of Churches* (WCC) in 1948. Ecumenists believe that God wills them to work for deeper unity among Christians through mutual cooperation and dialog, even if differences make it hard to imagine, humanly speaking, how Christian unity might ever come about. Though some Christians have interpreted their goal as a monolithic super-church, ecumenists prefer to speak of it in terms of diversity and communion. With its political tradition of religious tolerance, and with nearly seventy per cent of its population claiming adherence to one of more than 2,000 Christian denominations, the U.S. provides a unique field for interfaith activity, such as prayer, cooperation in service and dialog. U.S. Protestants formed the National Council of Churches of Christ in the USA* (1950) and the Consultation on Church Union* (1962).

Until 1964 U.S. Catholics had little to do with such activity. Vatican II's seeming about-face on ecumenism—really the outcome of a long twentieth-century development—lent new energy to the movement. U.S. Catholic bishops* responded to the 1964 "Decree on Ecumenism" by establishing the Bishops' Committee for Ecumenical and Interreligious Affairs in the same year. Since then it has cosponsored ongoing bilateral dialogs with U.S. Protestant churches, including the Disciples of Christ,* Episcopal Church,* Lutherans,* Presbyterian* and Reformed* bodies, United Methodists* and Southern Baptists.* Dialogs usually take place among groups of church leaders and theologians who meet periodically to discuss issues that divide and unite them. Recurring topics include baptism,* Eucharist,* ministry,* authority,* creed,* intermarriage, intercommunion, spirituality* and morality. U.S. dialogs have sometimes drawn topics from the results of international efforts such as the 1981 *Final Report* of the Anglican-Roman Catholic International Commission and the WCC's Faith and Order Commission report of 1982, *Baptism, Eucharist and Ministry*

Although the dialogs are cosponsored by the churches involved, their results represent only the participants' consensus and remain to be received by ordinary Christians and church leaders. Nevertheless, the dialogs, along with other ecumenical activities, have helped to create a new spirit among Protestants and Catholics. The Catholic Church is still not an official member of either the WCC or the NCCC, but it does belong to the Faith and Order Commissions of both bodies. With the numerical decline of mainline* denominations (Lutherans, Presbyterians and Episcopalians comprise only fourteen per cent of U.S. Christians) and

the recent resurgence of evangelical* Christianity, the dialog between Catholics and Southern Baptists as the two largest single denominations takes on increased importance.

The Catholic Charismatic* Renewal, begun in the U.S. in 1967, serves as a bridge between Catholics and evangelicals. While the Evangelical-Roman Catholic Dialog on Mission has taken place at the international level, no official U.S. dialog has yet begun. Through the efforts of committed individuals and such bodies as Ann Arbor's Center for Pastoral Renewal, considerable exchange and mutual understanding has taken place between Catholics and evangelicals, who, taken together, make up more than half of the U.S. population. While some pockets of traditional Protestant-Catholic hostility have survived, potential for future conflict seems to lie along transdenominational liberal and conservative religious and political lines, rather than along strictly denominational lines.

See also ECUMENISM; ECUMENICAL MOVEMENT; LUTHERAN-CATHOLIC DIALOG; NATIVISM.

BIBLIOGRAPHY. R. Bellah and F. E. Greenspahn, eds., *Uncivil Religion* (1987); M. D. Lowery, *Ecumenism* (1985); M. A. Noll, "The Eclipse of Old Hostilities between—And the Potential for New Strife among—Catholics and Protestants since Vatican II," *Cushwa Center Working Papers,* 16 (1985); E. L. Unterkoefler and A. Harsanyi, eds., *The Unity We Seek* (1977) N. Ehrenstrom and G. Gassmann, eds., *Confessions in Dialogue,* 3rd ed. (1975). W. L. Portier

Protracted Meeting. *See* FINNEY, CHARLES GRANDISON; REVIVALISM, PROTESTANT.

Provoost, Samuel (1742-1815). Episcopal* bishop* of New York. Born in New York City, the oldest son of John and Eve Rutgers Provoost, he was baptized* in the Dutch Reformed Church. Provoost was one of the seven graduates of King's College* at its first commencement in 1758. In 1761 he went to England and entered St. Peter's College, Cambridge. He was ordained* deacon* on February 23, 1766, at the Chapel Royal of St. James Palace, Westminster, by Bishop Richard Terrick of London, and on March 23, 1766, he was ordained priest* at King's Chapel, Whitehall, by Bishop Edmund Kean of Chester. On June 8, 1766, he married Maria Bousefield at St Mary's Church, Cambridge.

Returning to New York, he was appointed one of the assistant ministers at Trinity Parish, New York, on December 23, 1766. The rector* was the

Rev. Dr. Samuel Auchmuty. Provoost was a supporter of the American colonies and independence, while many at Trinity Parish were Loyalists. Because of his political views he resigned on May 21, 1771, and retired to East Camp, Dutchess County, where he remained for thirteen years, farming and reading. When the colonies had gained their independence and New York was evacuated by the British, he was elected rector of Trinity Parish (Auchmuty having died) on February 5, 1784.

In November 1785 he was chosen Chaplain to the Continental Congress in New York. At the convention of the Diocese* of New York on September 20, 1786, he was elected the first Episcopal bishop of New York. On November 2, 1786, Provoost and William White,* newly elected bishop of Pennsylvania, sailed to England for consecration.* Legislation had been passed by Parliament in 1786 authorizing the consecration of American bishops without their taking an oath of allegiance to England. Provoost, along with White, was consecrated at Lambeth Palace on February 4, 1787, by the Most Rev. John Moore, archbishop of Canterbury.

On his return to New York, he resumed his duties as rector of Trinity Parish and in 1789 became Chaplain* of the U.S. Senate. During these years he was an opponent of Samuel Seabury,* first bishop of the Episcopal Church, especially of Seabury's emphasis on episcopal prerogatives. From September 13, 1792, to September 8, 1795, he was presiding bishop of the Episcopal Church. On September 3, 1801, he resigned as bishop of New York, but the House of Bishops* refused to accept it and approved the election of an assistant bishop. Provoost died on September 6, 1815, and was buried at Trinity Parish.

BIBLIOGRAPHY. *AAP* 5; E. C. Chorley, "Samuel Provoost, First Bishop of New York," *HMPEC* 2 (June 1933):1-25; (September 1933):1-16; *DAB* VIII; *DARB; NCAB* 1; J. N. Norton, *Life of Bishop Provoost of New York* (1859); J. G. Wilson, *The Centennial History of the Protestant Episcopal Church in the Diocese of New York, 1785-1885* (1886).   D. S. Armentrout

Provost. A title of certain ecclesiastical and academic officers. It is derived from the Latin *praepositus,* meaning "head, chief or overseer." The title is used to denote an officer of a cathedral* chapter with duties similar to those of a dean but at times second in authority. The head of some religious orders* or congregations is sometimes called provost general. The title is more commonly used for high-ranking administrative officials of colleges, universities and theological seminaries.* In the colonial period superintendents of Swedish Lutheran* churches on the Delaware River were called provosts.   C. R. Henery

Psychology, Christianity and. The relationship between Christianity and psychology can be illuminated by tracing psychology's roots. The term *psychology* (replacing *psychosophy*) was coined by Marco Marulic prior to 1524 and was for the next 300 years applied as: (1) one of three divisions of *Pneumatologia,* the branch of physics studying spirits and consisting of natural theology, angeology/demonology and psychology; (2) a branch of special metaphysics, the study of special forms of being, which consisted of cosmology, rational theology and psychology. In the eighteenth century, Christian von Wolff (1679-1754) and Immanuel Kant (1724-1804) established the distinction between empirical psychology, the inquiry into our mental states and their operations, which inspired the "new" physiological psychology and rational psychology, the inquiry into the mind itself. In America, psychology was developed and applied primarily by clergy,* leading to a tradition of "clerical psychology."

After 1850 these traditions gradually gave way to an emerging experimental and physiological psychology made possible by advances in the biological and physical sciences. The parent discipline, philosophy, eagerly disowned its rebellious adolescent, experimental psychology. The ties with Christianity were stronger, leading one historian to conclude that "psychology has progressed only as rapidly as it has broken away from theological or religious involvements and become indifferent to them; or made peace with them . . . or overcome them." Because psychology had for several centuries formally been a subdiscipline of areas now designated as "philosophical theology," it is not surprising that theologians* always have considered it a force to be confronted.

Nineteenth-Century Christian Responses. One of the first responses was the delineation of "biblical psychology." Christian anthropology had its roots in the New Testament, and for the first 1900 years had little competition in the Western world. Philosophical histories of psychology generally include the major anthropologies of the Christian tradition. But the presuppositions of Christianity were giving way to other epistemologies, exemplified first in the publication of J. F. Herbart's *Psychologie als Wissenschaft neu gegrundet auf Erfahrung Metaphysic und Mathematik* (1824-1825). Psychological science grounded in experience, metaphysics and mathematics was a far cry from an anthropology grounded in revelation, but the entire philosophical tradition had been moving in this direction.

Medical psychology and *psychological medicine* became familiar English phrases in the 1840s and 1850s, strengthening the connection between the psychic and somatic components of anthropology. These connections became firmly entrenched in the 1870s with Wilhelm Wundt's publication of *Grundzuge der Physiologischen Psychologie* and textbooks by Carl Stumpf, James Sully and Franz Brentano. These European texts and teachers strongly influenced the first generation of American psychologists.

Christian thinkers responded with a clear differentiation of biblical psychology from this new tradition. Thus, the 1860s and 1870s featured the English translation of Delitzsch's *System of Biblical Psychology* (1867) and Johann Beck's *Outlines of Biblical Psychology* (1877), as well as the publication of Charles Ives' *The Bible Doctrine of the Soul* (1873), George Sutherland's *Christian Psychology* (1874) and John Laidlaw's *The Bible Doctrine of Man* (1879), with similar titles occurring for several more decades. An interesting feature of many of these was their assertion of a tripartite human nature, distinguishing between spirit (*pneuma*) and soul (*psyche*). It is possible that this position gained respectability because it preserved a domain not accessible to the experimental psychologists.

A second group of Christians was more explicitly critical of the new psychology. First to offer such critiques, along with strong apologetics* for traditional scholastic psychology, were such Catholic writers as Michael Maher in *Psychology: Empirical and Rational* (1890), Cardinal Mercier in *The Relation of Experimental Psychology to Philosophy* (1902) and Huber Gruender in *Psychology Without a Soul* (1912). Catholic psychologists were eager to preserve their tradition, while using the best of the new psychology. This is illustrated by Edward A. Pace, who began a psychological laboratory at the Catholic University of America as early as 1891.

Twentieth-Century Networks and Institutions. American Christians have been eager from the beginning to utilize the findings of the new psychology. East Coast Episcopalians launched the Emmanuel Movement in Boston in 1905, involving the clergy in psychotherapy. The death of this movement led to the quick rise of clinical/pastoral education and pastoral psychology/psychiatry. Christian mental-health services sprang up in

several other contexts. The Christian Psychopathic Hospital at Cutler Farm (later to become Pine Rest) launched its program of services to the mentally ill shortly after 1910. In 1947 the first patients were admitted to Brook Lane Psychiatric Center under the auspices of the Homes for Mentally Ill Committee of the Mennonite Central Committee.* This work was later assigned to the Mennonite Mental Health Services, leading to the founding of at least a half-dozen psychiatric hospitals. The Bethesda tuberculosis sanitarium, founded by the Christian Reformed Church* and the Reformed Church in America,* was converted into a psychiatric facility in 1948. These were the precursors to the now-common Christian psychiatric units and Christian counseling centers.

Attempts to define a "Christian psychotherapy" came very early. James Murray's *An Introduction to a Christian Psychotherapy* (1938) was quickly imported from England, as were the translation of Alphonse Maeder's *Ways to Psychic Health* (1945) and Wilfried Daim's *Depth Psychology and Salvation* (1954). A significant early effort was the short-lived *Journal of Psychotherapy as a Religious Process,* published from 1954 to 1956 by the Institute for Rankian Psychoanalysis in Dayton, Ohio. Here were featured the ideas of such major thinkers as Paul Tournier, Igor Caruso, Roberto Assagioli, Charles Baudouin, Aleck Dodd, Fritz Kunkel, as well as Daim and Maeder and an assortment of non-Christian religious thinkers. William Rickel, the journal's editor, was a neo-orthodox* Congregationalist* minister whose network of Christian psychotherapists spanned the U.S. and the European continent, but he was at least a decade ahead of his time.

The Journal of Religion and Health, founded in 1961, was more successful, perhaps because the National Academy of Religion and Mental Health, founded in 1955, had the backing of such prominent religious leaders as Sankey L. Blanton, William Menninger, Albert Outler* and Paul Tournier. Apparently many early efforts were made to establish a Christian psychotherapy and to appropriate psychology into spirituality,* evidenced in the founding of such organizations as the Friends Conference on Religion and Psychology (1937), the Christian Association for Psychological Studies (1953), the American Foundation of Religion and Psychiatry (1958), the American Foundation of Religious Therapists (1959), and such meetings as the International Conference on Spiritual Therapy (1956).

The new psychology was eagerly received by Christian educators, establishing a tradition of character education. From 1924 through 1927 the Religious Education Association* and the Institute of Social and Religious Research sponsored the Character Education Inquiry that led to publication of the well-known works of Mark A. May and Hugh Hartshorne. In 1935 the Union College Character Research Project was founded by Ernest Ligon, author of *The Psychology of Christian Personality* (1935). The project led to advances in curriculum development, program development, basic and applied research and cross-disciplinary efforts.

The department of psychology at the Catholic University of America,* founded in 1891, continued to prosper, and many excellent volumes of its Studies in Psychology and Psychiatry were published from 1926 through 1959. Accredited in 1947 by the Education and Training Board of the American Psychological Association for the training of clinical psychologists, it was the first department in a Catholic university to gain such approval. Catholic dialog was enhanced during these early years by such writers as Edward Barrett, Robert Brennan, Thomas V. Moore and Mark Gaffney. In 1947 a group of Catholic psychologists met at the American Psychological Association (APA) meeting to launch what became the American Catholic Psychological Association (ACPA). Chartered in 1948 with 231 members, the ACPA soon incorporated non-Catholic members, eventually becoming Psychologists Interested in Religious Issues, which was formally approved as Division 36 of the APA in 1976.

The Graduate School of Psychology at Fuller Theological Seminary* admitted its first class in the fall of 1964. Offering the Ph.D. in clinical psychology, Fuller's program was accredited by the APA in 1974. The Rosemead Graduate School of Psychology soon followed with its Ph.D. and Psy.D. programs, providing impetus for a variety of Christian training programs around the country. The growing body of Christian psychologists advances its thinking in the pages of several professional journals: *Inward Light: Journal of the Friends Conference on Religion and Psychology* (1937); the *Journal of Religion and Health* (1961); *Insight: Quarterly Review of Religion and Mental Health* (1963); the *Journal of Psychology and Theology* (1973); and the *Journal of Psychology and Christianity* (1982).

One concern of many Christians has been how to bring religion into the college classroom. This led to the publication of Robert B. MacLeod's *Religious Perspectives of College Teaching in Experimental Psychology* (1951) in a series by the Edward W. Hazen Foundation and Joseph D.

Havens' *Psychology* (1964) in the Faith Learning Studies series published by the Faculty Christian Fellowship. More recent efforts along this line include *Psychology and the Christian Faith: An Introductory Reader,* edited by Stanton L. Jones (1984), and *Psychology through the Eyes of Faith* by David G. Myers and Malcolm Jeeves (1987) for the Supplemental Textbook Project of the Christian College Coalition.

Though the alliance with religion has been an uneasy one, apparently it has been easier to re-introduce religion into American psychology than to re-introduce philosophy. In 1987 the membership of Division 24 (Philosophical Psychology) of the APA remained under 600, while the membership of Division 36 (Psychologists Interested in Religious Issues) approached 1,400.

BIBLIOGRAPHY. E. G. Boring, *A History of Experimental Psychology,* 2nd ed. (1950); C. E. Buxton, ed., *Points of View in the Modern History of Psychology* (1985); E. B. Holifield, *A History of Pastoral Care in America: From Salvation to Self-Realization* (1983); S. L. Jones, ed., *Psychology and the Christian Faith: An Introductory Reader* (1986); S. Koch and D. Leary, eds. *A Century of Psychology as Science* (1985); H. Misiak and V. Staudt's *Catholics in Psychology* (1954); R. S. Peters, ed., *Brett's History of Psychology,* 2nd ed. (1974); A. A. Roback, *History of American Psychology* (1964); H. Vande Kemp, "The Tension Between Psychology and Theology: The Etymological Roots," *JPT* 10 (1982):105-112; H. Vande Kemp and H. N. Malony, ed., *Psychology and Theology in Western Thought, 1672-1965: A Historical and Annotated Bibliography* (1984); R. I. Watson, *The Great Psychologists: Aristotle to Freud* (1978).

H. Vande Kemp

Public Education, Religion and. The subject of religion and public education has long been a critical issue in American church-state* relations. As the pattern of the state church gave way to disestablishment and pluralism* in the New World, so the free, secular public school gradually emerged and in time supplanted the sectarian school that dominated during the colonial era and the early decades of the New Republic. With the growth of experimental science, international trade and religious diversity of the population, the religious character of America's schools increasingly became a source of conflict that resulted in an increased demand for secular subjects, without ecclesiastical or sectarian control.

Battles involving the Establishment Clause and the Free Exercise Clause of the First Amendment* have been repeatedly waged over religion and the public schools. Religion in the public schools has been adjudicated on the basis that public schools are necessarily subject to public control and public policy by virtue of the fact that they are tax-supported and, therefore, must be governed by the Establishment Clause of the First Amendment, even if a given program of religion is maintained on a "voluntary" basis. That the Supreme Court's most far-reaching decisions on church and state should have to do with the public schools has been noted as both historically significant and judicially appropriate, since the role played by the public schools is crucial to this nation's being a secular state and a free and pluralistic society. As Justice Felix Frankfurter declared some decades ago, "The public school is at once the symbol of our democracy and the most pervasive means of promoting our common destiny" (*McCollum v. Board of Education*).

The U. S. Supreme Court has rendered nine decisions directly involving religion and public education, all of which have been handed down since 1948; most of them have been rendered by an overwhelming majority. In brief summary, the Court has: struck down "released time," i.e., setting aside a portion of each day for religious instruction by representatives of various faiths, even though attendance in these classes might be on a purely voluntary basis (*McCollum v. Board of Education*, 1948); upheld the practice of "dismissed time," which was essentially the same program reviewed in McCollum except that it was maintained off public school grounds (*Zorach v. Clausen*, 1952); struck down the so-called nondenominational New York State Regents' prayer to be recited in the public schools (*Engel v. Vitale*, 1962); struck down public-school-sponsored devotional* Bible* reading and the recitation of the Lord's Prayer (*Abington v. Schempp*, 1963); struck down an Arkansas law that prohibited the teaching of evolution* in any Arkansas public school or university (*Epperson v. Arkansas*, 1968); struck down a Kentucky law requiring the posting of the Ten Commandments* in public-school classrooms (*Stone v. Graham*, 1980); ruled that the University of Missouri may not deny student religious groups the right to meet on campus if political and social groups do so (*Widmar v. Vincent*, 1981); struck down an 1981 Alabama law requiring a daily moment-of-silence for prayer or meditation (*Wallace v. Jaffree*, 1985); and struck down a Louisiana law mandating the teaching of creation science* whenever evolution is taught (*Edwards v. Aquillard*, 1987). The Court refused to strike down

a program of "Equal Access" in Pennsylvania, but did so not on the basis of the substantive issue but a lack of standing (*Bender v. Williamsport*, 1986).

While efforts continue to be made to permit public-school-sponsored prayer, substitute proposals are being advanced for a moment of silence or meditation. Government neutrality toward religion in the public schools has come to be viewed by many as government hostility toward religion, as has most recently been evidenced by well-organized and repeated efforts toward religious censorship of public-school textbooks which have been charged with promoting the "religion of secular humanism," a charge unanimously ruled invalid by the U. S. Court of Appeals for the Eleventh Circuit on August 26, 1987 (*Smith v. Mobile County Board of Education*). Meanwhile, in the light of the Supreme Court's categorical assertion that "one's education is not complete without a study of . . . religion," earnest efforts are being made by a variety of educators to find ways that are academically and constitutionally appropriate to give greater attention to the teaching *about* religion in the public-school curriculum.

See also SUPREME COURT DECISIONS ON RELIGIOUS ISSUES.

BIBLIOGRAPHY. D. E. Boles, *The Two Swords: Commentaries and Cases in Religion and Education* (1967); R. Michaelsen, *Piety in the Public School: Trends and Issues in the Relationship Between Religion and the Public School in the United States* (1970); R. K. Smith, *Public Prayer and the Constitution: A Case Study in Constitutional Interpretation* (1987); J. E. Wood, Jr., ed., *Religion, the State, and Education* (1984); *Religion and Public Education* (quarterly journal published by the National Council on Religion and Public Education).   J. E. Wood

Public Policy, Christianity and. Despite the legal separation of church and state,* individual Christians and churches have played a significant role in U.S. public policy issues. In early American history European visitors like Alexis de Tocqueville* were surprised that the wall of separation had not deterred the churches in their influence of social life in general and government policies in particular. Though there has always been a lack of unanimity among Christians and churches on particular issues, religious voices have been undaunted in their pursuit of the public good.

The issues alone do not divide Christians. They also disagree over how Christians, churches and religious agencies should interact with government structures. At one end of the spectrum, religious separatists totally remove themselves from involvement with the major social structures. Yet separatists have often played a significant role in public policy, as evidenced by the large number of court cases having to do with the religious practices of extreme separatists such as the Amish* and Jehovah's Witnesses.*

At the other end of the spectrum are the religious groups that forthrightly engage with the social structures and political processes in order to effect change. Often equating particular public policies with Christianity, these social transformers represent a wide spectrum ranging from the Social Gospel Movement* at the turn of the twentieth century to the Moral Majority* and related movements later in the century. Between the transformers and separatists is a widely diverse group of religious bodies seeking to influence public policy, but with less overt political involvement and ideological commitments. Distinctions between these three main approaches center on a theological issue—the normative relationship of Christian faith to society.

A second level of difference regarding public policy has to do with the major goals which religion brings to social life. Robin Lovin in *Religion and American Public Life* notes three major directions. First, there are those who emphasize the goal of order. Religion in this view is seen to provide and maintain patterns of authority* and obedience by which the orderliness of society can be maintained. Second, others have emphasized freedom as the primary goal in linking religion to public life. The major contribution of religion is to ensure freedom of conscience and freedom from totalitarian social structures. Third, still others see justice as the church's major contribution to public policy. Focusing on social rights, the reallocation of resources and the redistribution of power, these groups have attempted to transform social structures to facilitate justice for oppressed and disenfranchised persons.

Throughout American history Christian churches have been engaged in numerous issues of public policy. In the late twentieth century the issues of abortion,* women's rights, ecology, separation of church and state and religion in public education* have been at the forefront. But historically speaking, three major issues have received the greatest attention over the years: war and peace, economic structures and racial justice.

War and Peace. The first significant issue of public policy the American churches faced was the American Revolution* (1775-1783). The churches could not avoid the question, Shall we obey the

powers that be (Rom 13) or go to war to secure freedom and justice? Their answers were by no means unified and can be classified into four different ecclesiastical responses.

The patriots gave whole-hearted support to the revolutionary cause, calling on Christians to join in the struggle for independence. Emphasizing individual liberty and the limitation of power, the patriots found strong support among Congregationalists* and Presbyterians,* both descendants of the Puritans.* A second group, the reformists, supported the patriot cause, but with greater caution and a corollary commitment to extend freedom to the slaves. This approach was popular among Baptists* (especially leaders like Isaac Backus*) as well as among many Presbyterians* and Lutherans.*

The third ecclesiastical response to the Revolution was the loyalist stance which opposed the Revolution and supported Britain. Some estimates claim that one-fifth to one-third of all colonists were loyalists or had loyalist sympathies. This group consisted primarily of Anglicans* and Methodists,* but included church members from other bodies as well. The fourth response was Christian pacifism. Consisting mainly of historic Peace Churches* such as Mennonites,* Church of the Brethren,* Quakers* and Moravians,* these Christians opposed the Revolution on the same grounds that they opposed all warfare.

All four responses to the American Revolution were engaged in public policy debate. The modes of discourse were primarily sermons* and written documents intended to shape individual opinions, which in turn, it was believed, would shape the destiny of the colonies.

The churches' response to the Civil War* (1861-1865) was quite different from their response to the Revolution. Ecclesiastical positions were shaped almost entirely by regional, rather than denominational, commitments, and few debated the justice of the war itself. Both sides equally claimed God for their side, but for different reasons: the North because of the evil of slavery, and the South on principles of freedom and personal choice.

This great national trial tore the nation and churches asunder. Within their respective regions the churches by and large urged the cause of warfare, with each side arguing on biblical grounds for or against slavery. Despite this national and religious factionalism, there were some preachers, church bodies and national leaders (including Abraham Lincoln*) who recognized the war as the judgment of God on both sides. Whatever their positions on the war itself—or on slavery—the churches could not avoid the public issue.

World War 1* (1914-1918) caught the churches and the entire nation by surprise. The optimistic mood of the times and the perception that the U.S. was immune from the old rivalries of Europe, kept war far from the minds of most Americans. Despite President Woodrow Wilson's early attempts at neutrality and non-involvement, the country soon became absorbed in a crusade "to make the world safe for democracy"—a cause most American Christians applauded. The churches' public policy was to engender a spirit of superpatriotism, so contributing to the unbridled antagonism and hatred toward the enemy. In the view of some historians, this paved the way for the later rise of Hitler in a humiliated and beleaguered Germany.

After the U.S. entry into the war in 1917, church leaders helped recruit for the armed forces and staunchly promoted Liberty Bonds used to support the conflict. The mood of the times is reflected in words from Randolph McKim's sermon in the nation's capital:

It is God who has summoned us to this war. It is his war we are fighting. . . . This conflict is indeed a Crusade. The greatest in history—the holiest. It is in the profoundest and truest sense a Holy War.

The mood is also reflected in the down-to-earth language of evangelist* Billy Sunday*:

Our little trouble with Spain was a coon hunt as compared with this scrap we have on hand with that bunch of pretzel-chewing, sauerkraut spawn of blood-thirsty Huns. . . . We can win, we must win . . . so dig down deep and let us fill Uncle Sam's bank vault high with our money and help send a shiver down the crooked spine of the Hohenzollerns who are dancing on the thin, thin crust of hell.

The churches were certainly not alone in exhibiting such attitudes, for they had succumbed to an unbridled nationalism that pervaded the American mind.

The response of the churches to World War 2* (1939-1945) was more restrained. Arguments to enter the war tended to appeal to a theory of just war. As in all American wars, there were significant numbers of conscientious objectors, but their right of conscience was more clearly ensured than in previous wars through the Civilian Public Service Program. By and large, however, most churches wholeheartedly supported American involvement in the war.

In the Vietnam War* churches and individual Christians played a more pivotal role than they had in most previous wars in raising questions of justice and moral discernment. Though many churches, including most evangelical* churches, supported American involvement in Southeast Asia, a few evangelical leaders like Mark Hatfield,* and a significant number of mainline* church leaders, called into question American foreign policy. The role of the church in the anti-war protest movement was perhaps the most significant ecclesiastical challenge to American war policy since the American Revolution.

In recent years Christian involvement in public discourse regarding war has centered on the nuclear threat. Numerous denominations and religious bodies have issued reports and studies on the ethics of using nuclear weapons as well as possessing them for purposes of deterrence. These studies, intended to educate and guide Christians as well as influence public policy, have generally agreed that even a limited nuclear war could not be justified on the grounds of just war theory. However, Christians have been less unanimous regarding the ethics of nuclear deterrence.

Economic Structures. Christian involvement in the American economic system has been centered primarily in two time periods—the Gilded Age (late nineteenth and early twentieth century) and the contemporary era (from the 1960s to the present). The Gilded Age was a period of great economic growth fueled by the Industrial Revolution and unrestrained economic activity. With the flowering of material prosperity came new social problems and ethical issues which drew at least some Christians and churches into the public arena.

The most explicit Christian response to the economic realities of the Gilded Age was the Social Gospel Movement. Under the leadership of people like Walter Rauschenbusch* and Washington Gladden,* the movement attempted to apply the "principles of the kingdom of God" to society, most particularly the economic aspects of society. Four major issues were at the heart of their concern: unrestricted competition flowing from laissez-faire economic theory, conflict between labor and capital, business ethics such as unfair monopolies and problems of urban life arising from the Industrial Revolution (e.g., slum housing, crime, etc.).

The Social Gospel Movement had a significant impact on the American clergy. Its primary means of affecting public policy was through cognitive persuasion rather than boycotts, coercion or even direct political methods such as gaining power in political parties. During the early twentieth century, fundamentalists* strongly reacted to Social Gospel ideals, primarily because they identified the Movement with modernist,* or liberal, theology.

From the 1960s and on into the 1980s, concerns over poverty and world hunger have reached across the theological and ecclesiastical spectrum. Christians have differed over the means of alleviating poverty, with some groups emphasizing relief in terms of food and money and others stressing economic development through education, technology and economic growth. Still others have called for liberation (*See* Liberation Theology), arguing that the old oppressive and inhibiting economic structures must be replaced with new economic structures.

This debate over relief, development and liberation suggests a significant factor dividing Christians seeking an answer to these economic problems—their ideological commitments to particular economic systems. Church groups and individuals focusing on relief or development have by and large been commited to some form of market economics, while those emphasizing liberation have tended to embrace or at least borrow from socialist (*See* Socialism, Christian) economics and Marxist forms of social analysis. Ideological commitments on all sides have often inhibited a clear understanding of the problems and solutions to world hunger and poverty.

Racial Justice. From the time African slaves were first shipped to North America in 1619 until the present, racial justice has been a burning moral and public policy issue. Christians were actively involved in racial policies during two main eras of American history—from 1800 to the Emancipation Proclamation* in 1863 and during the Civil Rights Movement* of the 1950s and 1960s.

The main issue in the nineteenth century was slavery. While numerous churches, especially in the South, defended the institution, many Christians played a significant role in the abolition movement.* Until 1830 there was even an active Christian abolition force in the South, but when secular abolitionists like William Lloyd Garrison* became more radical in their tactics and called for immediate abolition, many Southern reformists retrenched. In the North, however, a strong movement remained, led by evangelical Christians such as Jonathan Blanchard,* the first president of Wheaton College,* and the revivalist* Charles Finney.* Finney, for example, held abolition rallies along with his revivals, and many of his followers became ardent voices within the larger abolition

movement. Their primary mode of social action was to work through voluntary organizations, focussing on legislation and attitudinal changes among the populace.

The racial issues of the 1950s and 1960s can be traced to the late nineteenth century. After the Civil War* the nation's will to make African-American citizenship a meaningful reality was eroded. Segregation, prejudice and racist social policies meant that African-Americans languished far behind whites in attaining the American dream. The plight of the African-American community was intensified through the great migration from the South to Northern cities between World War 1 and 1960. What had been heralded as the promised land turned out to be urban ghettoes that traumatized the new pilgrims and exposed them even further to the realities of a society in which racial equality was still a myth.

Not until the late 1950s (and after the 1954 Supreme Court school desegregation ruling) did the American churches begin addressing the issue. Even then many segments of the church remained entrenched in racism, and some who called for changes were cautious and highly individualistic, addressing personal racial prejudice but not institutional racism. Evangelicals typically followed this latter path. Among those who directly and intentionally addressed the issue in terms of public policy were two main bodies—the white church and the African-American church. The sensitized white churches attempted to address not only their own ecclesiastical institutions, but to call for institutional changes in industry, education, government, housing and hiring practices.

The African-American churches had long preserved many features of the African-American heritage and were the one place in American society where African-Americans controlled their own destiny. Nevertheless, they were often characterized by a somewhat otherworldly aura which in the past had failed to touch deeply their status within American society. In the 1950s, however, the African-American churches began uniting for social change and engendered a heightened sense of dignity and worth within the African-American community. Under the leadership of Martin Luther King, Jr.,* and others, the African-American churches used protests, boycotts, strikes and conventional preaching* to steer public policy toward a more racially just society.

Conclusion. War and peace, economic structures and racial justice historically have been among the major public policy issues the American churches have addressed, but they are by no means the only ones. In each epoch of history, new moral issues, emerge which carry with them implications for social policy. As churches engage with these issues, they are confronted with two major questions. First, what is the relationship of the church to society? The answer to that question determines how churches and individual Christians will attempt to implement their faith within society. Second, what is the major goal of Christian involvement—order, freedom, justice or some combination of the three? The response to that question will shape their public policy agenda, as well as their particular position on the issues.

Churches cannot avoid the public arena, but history reveals pitfalls in their social engagement. A major lesson from the past is that a given public policy can never be equated with the kingdom of God. Christians may well argue that the kingdom propels them in a specific direction, but particular ideological frameworks, policy mechanisms and political party platforms are always finite and fallen. Vested interests (as evidenced in some Christians' defense of slavery), and national or ideological commitments (as evidenced in the churches' acquiescence to unbridled patriotism in World War 1), are among a variety of factors that affect every Christian effort to apply faith to social and political issues. These limitations of the policy-making process have been perennially underestimated by Christians, even in their most laudable public pursuits.

See also POLITICAL THEOLOGY.

BIBLIOGRAPHY. R. H. Abrams, *Preachers Present Arms* (1933); D. Dayton, *Discovering an Evangelical Heritage* (1976); C. H. Hopkins, *The Rise of the Social Gospel in American Protestantism, 1865-1915* (1940); R. Lovin, ed., *Religion and American Public Life* (1986); R. J. Mouw, *Politics and the Biblical Drama* (1976); M. A. Noll, *Christians in the American Revolution* (1977); A. J. Reichley, *Religion in American Public Life* (1985); H. S. Smith, *In His Image But . . . Racism in Southern Religion, 1780-1910* (1972); M. L. Stackhouse, *Public Theology and Political Economy: Christian Stewardship in Modern Society* (1987); R. A. Wells, ed., *The Wars of America: Christian Views* (1981); J. K. Yoder, *The Politics of Jesus* (1972).

D. P. Hollinger

Publishing, Religious. Religious publishing takes place in formats, by many organizations and for many audiences. Among the many different formats are Bibles,* tracts,* music, magazines, newsletters, psalm books, general books, reference works, educational materials and specialized scholarly monographs. Added to these printed materials are now also audio, video and other electronic products. According to recent publishing figures, the annual U.S. book production in religion is approximately 2,500 titles, or five per cent of the total U.S. book production. With an estimated total value of $685 million, it represents approximately six per cent of the total American book industry.

Among the different kinds of religious publishers there are denominations* and other religious bodies with their affiliated organizations, large commercial companies and smaller independent houses, university presses and scholarly societies. Because of the large number of very small publishing organizations, it is difficult to estimate, but a recent survey identified over 750 active participants.

While a few large commercial publishing companies currently dominate the mass markets for best sellers, Bibles and reference books, much of the religious publishing activity is still driven by a strong service orientation in which the Christian mission takes a primary role. This is exemplified by a large, active, creative and highly motivated group of independent publishers.

The many different types of religious publications are most often distributed directly to customers through various methods as well as through a wide network of some four thousand booksellers and distributors. The major Christian publishing and bookselling organizations are the Christian Booksellers Association* (est. 1950, 3,700 members), the Protestant Church-Owned Publishers Association (est. 1951, 34 members), the Evangelical Christian Publishers Association (est. 1974, 75 members).

History. Ever since the Reformation, the close relationship between the printed word and the Christian experience has been firmly established. It is unlikely that the wide spread of Christianity could have taken place without the printing press, while, at the same time, the radical improvements in printing, publishing and distribution would not likely have taken place without the growth of the religious market. The printing press became the agent of change, and the North American experience underscores and reinforces this.

The development of religious publishing in the U.S. and Canada closely follows religious, social and political movements and events. Of these, the major evangelical* movements in the eighteenth, nineteenth and twentieth centuries; mass immigration*; urbanization; the American Revolution*; and the major wars* were probably the most influential. Long under English and continental European influences, North American religious publishing eventually became a major worldwide force by itself.

Religious publishing and bookselling came to America with the Puritans,* who established a printing press in Cambridge, Massachusetts, in 1639. For almost fifty years this press was to be the only one in the New World. Except for New England, literacy levels were not very high, but reading was popular among the literate, and there was a chronic shortage of reading material. Importing books and religious-instructional materials from England was cumbersome and expensive. The result was that the few available products from the Puritan printing press such as *The Whole Book of Psalms* (1640), John Cotton's* *Spiritual Milk* (1656), Michael Wigglesworth's* *The Day of Doom* (1662) and especially the *New England Primer* (1690) dominated American education and general reading tastes. The religious book thus became a strong unifying force in a world with diverse religious, linguistic and social traditions. The Bible was still the most widely distributed book in the colonies. However, printing rights for the King James Version were firmly held in Britain, and during colonial days no English-language edition was produced in America. The Cambridge press was also used for the production of missionary* materials in various Native-American languages. Jesuit* efforts to establish a press in New France (1665, 1683) were unsuccessful.

By 1700 additional printing presses were operating in Boston, New York and Philadelphia, and a small number of publishers and booksellers began to challenge the Puritan monopoly. Reformed* and Lutheran* catechisms* as well as the Anglican* *Book of Common Prayer* (1710) were printed by William Bradford in New York, while Reynier Jansen in Philadelphia produced Baptist* and Quaker* materials.

Books, sermons* and tracts became mass commodities in the American colonies during the Great Awakening.* Charismatic preachers such as Gilbert Tennent,* Jonathan Edwards* and George Whitefield* caused great emotional stirs, and their printed sermons were widely reprinted, distributed and read. The movement resulted in the publication of America's first magazine, *Christian History* (1743-1745). The most popular religious writers in America at the time were British. Books by John Flavel, Isaac Watts and James Hervey were reprinted and distributed in thousands of copies. Religion was also a popular topic in general magazines, which had come on the American

scene in the middle of the eighteenth century.

Publishing was still centered in Boston, New York and Philadelphia, but a significant booktrade network developed throughout the colonies, by which the most popular items were often reprinted in smaller towns taking advantage of the rapid spread of printing technology. The division of tasks among printers, publishers and booksellers was not yet clearly demarcated. Most participants were small artisans and businessmen who were involved in many aspects of the trade. Denominational publishing was rising, but it largely took place through commissions to the existing booktrade. The foreign-language religious press, notably in German, Dutch and French, developed its own small-but-determined markets. In Canada, under British rule after 1763 and effectively cut off from trade with France, one of the first books to be printed was a Roman Catholic* French-language catechism in 1765.

Religious publishing also played a major role during the American Revolution, as the Protestant churchmen for the most part supported the revolt against British tyranny. Fiery sermons were delivered, published and distributed throughout the land. Nonetheless, American reading habits were still dominated by imported books from England, with American entrepreneurs reprinting the most popular ones, mostly without regard to copyright. The first American-produced Bibles appeared on the market after the Revolution, with King James Versions (1791) by Isaiah Thomas of Massachusetts and Isaac Collins of New Jersey (1791), and a Catholic Douay Version (1790) by Matthew Carey of Philadelphia. By 1800 some twenty different editions of the Bible and at least fifteen editions of the New Testament had been printed in America.

The role of the religious printing press during the Second Awakening* was even greater. Cheaper printing presses and paper allowed for proliferation of printing capacity. The existing publishing structure greatly reinforced the spread of the various opinions in a country that now stretched throughout the Mississippi Valley and into the South. During the first few decades of the nineteenth century, a new dimension in religious publishing was established by the newly established volunteer organizations. The missionary need for Bibles, tracts and educational materials stimulated the launching of major interdenominational publishing ventures based on English models, each with its own printing and distribution capacities. The combined publishing efforts of these organizations and their regional subsidiaries had a profound impact on American religious life as well as general education. The American Bible Society* (1816) embarked on several national drives to bring a Bible into each American household. The American Sunday School Union's* (1824) programs included several magazines and a series of weekly lessons which by 1830 had sold more than six million copies. The American Tract Society* (1824) published the highly successful *Christian Almanac* as well as scores of different tracts, some in print runs of 750,000 copies. Publishing took place in many different languages to accommodate new immigrants.

During the same period the major denominations began their own publishing programs, with the Methodists Book Concern (New York, 1804) in the lead. The Presbyterians* followed in 1838 and the Baptists* in 1839. The Congregationalists,* Episcopalians* and Catholics continued to publish through independent, specialized companies. The denominational publishing efforts were especially strong in the publishing of magazines.

Despite the activities of the various Bible societies,* Bible publishing remained a significant commercial enterprise as well. With public interest at high levels, several of the major emerging commercial publishers, such as Harper (1825), Appleton (1831) and Little-Brown (1837), entered the profitable religious market through the publication of books and magazines. The growing American market for religious materials was recognized by Thomas Nelson of London, who established a New York branch in 1854, while German publishers opened up branches in New York, Cincinnati and St. Louis. Book distribution remained in the hands of bookstores and subscription agents, while book peddlers, like the legendary Pastor Weems,* were a major force in the sale of cheap and popular material. The Civil War* and the subsequent failure to reconcile the differences afterward led to long-lasting denominational divisions, resulting in a splintering of their publishing efforts.

Following the rapid rise in population and ever-improving papermaking and printing technology, American book and magazine production tripled in the last quarter of the nineteenth century. New York became the nation's commercial publishing center, while denominational publishing for white and black audiences concentrated in Nashville, Tennessee. Newer American denominations and movements, such as Lutherans, Christian Reformed,* Disciples of Christ,* Seventh-day Adventists* and Jehovah's Witnesses,* established active, long-lasting publishing programs. The first edition of the Book of Mormon appeared in 1867, while

1875 marked the date of Mary Baker Eddy's *Science and Health*. With a rapidly rising immigrant population, Catholic publishers grew and enjoyed substantial sales in books and especially magazines, while the Jewish press began to come into its own with the establishment of the Jewish Publication Society (1888).

During the latter part of the nineteenth century, popular literary taste leaned heavily toward religious, moralistic prose. Examples are Lew Wallace's* *Ben Hur* (1880) and Charles Sheldon's* *In His Steps,* which eventually sold over 30 million copies worldwide. The new Revised Version of the New Testament appeared in 1881. Public interest was so great that the *Chicago Tribune* and the *Chicago Times* published the complete text in their pages immediately after transmittal by telegraph from New York. The American Standard Version (1901) became the leading seller for several decades.

Great public attention was paid to the strife between modernists* and fundamentalists.* As a result of the Social Gospel Movement,* large numbers of books and pamphlets concentrating on poverty, temperance* and other social issues were published. On the other hand three million copies of the twelve-volume *The Fundamentals* (1910-1915) were distributed. Book and magazine sales flourished. Commercial publishers such as Harper, Macmillan and Scribner established religious editorial departments in the 1920s. Religious independents such as Fleming Revell* and William Eerdmans, as well as several denominational publishers, tried to branch out to reach the new wider audiences. Religious broadcasting was introduced during this period.

General sales of religious books declined after the financial crash of 1929, but throughout the next decades the growing strength of the evangelical* movement and the new interest in revised Sunday-school materials spurred new ventures in religious publishing. Gospel Light and Zondervan are examples, but denominational houses such as Southern Baptist, Abingdon, Cokesbury and Benzinger were active as well. Bible sales, stimulated by new popular versions, remained high.

A significant religious revival took place after the Second World War,* touching all major faiths and denominations. On the national best-seller lists were Protestants Billy Graham* and Norman Vincent Peale,* Catholics Fulton Sheen* and Thomas Merton* and the Jewish Rabbi Joshua Liebman. A genuine national religious publishing market emerged. For the first time since the nineteenth century, religious books took their leading place in the mainstream of publishing and bookselling. Denominational and independent religious houses did not stay behind. Aware that a broader publishing base was necessary for successful marketing, many of them entered trade publishing and diversified their lists to appeal to larger audiences.

After the movement peaked in the 1960s, book and magazine sales declined, and a re-configuration of the industry began to take place. Denominational houses curtailed activities when faced with losses, often "spinning off" their general lists to commercial houses. The same applied to independents, where mergers and consolidation became common.

Building on long-term foundations, a substantial new evangelical revival emerged in the 1970s, creating intense public interest. Once again, riding the crest of this movement, religious publishers increased their activities, and scores of new independent companies were founded. Religious publishing expanded into general trade fields especially with titles relating daily life with the Christian experience. Commercial trade houses reentered the religious field with similar books intended for mass audiences. New Bible editions were enormously successful. On the retail side, a large number of new Christian bookstores were opened, often in choice retail locations. Still, a large proportion of the religious materials were sold by mail.

After a decade this revival appeared to have lost its momentum as a national movement. Despite ever-increasing secularism, the total religious publishing market is staying strong, but the pluralistic characteristics of the current religious movements now lead to a widely diversified market. The present-day market is segmented not only by religious preference, but by ethnic origin, geographical location, education, age, income level and other characteristics. Small independent houses function much better in such markets than large corporate entities, and in the late 1980s it appeared that this characterized the situation.

See also PRESS, CATHOLIC; PRESS, PROTESTANT.

BIBLIOGRAPHY. J. S. Duke, *Religious Publishing and Communications* (1981); H. Edelman, "A History of Religious Publishing and Bookselling in the United States and Canada," in J. P. Dessauer et al., *Christian Book Publishing and Distribution in the United States and Canada* (1987); J. A. Hostetler, *God Uses Ink: The Heritage and Mission of the Mennonite Publishing House After Fifty Years* (1958); F. L. Mott, *A History of American Magazines,* 5 vols. (1930-1968); G. L. Parker, *The*

Beginning of the Book Trade in Canada (1985); J. P. Pilkington, *The Methodist Publishing House: A History,* vol. 1, 1789-1870 (1968); P. M. Simms, *The Bible in America* (1936); J. Tebbel, *History of Book Publishing in America,* 4 vols. (1972-1981).

H. Edelman

Pulpit Exchange/Pulpit Supply. The practice of allowing a minister* other than the regular preacher* of a church to deliver the sermon,* either by prior agreement with a minister of another church or because of the absence of the regular preacher. In some communities, a pulpit exchange is an occasional event which allows the members of one church to hear a sermon by a minister of another church, usually from a different denomination.* When a minister is absent from his or her pulpit because of emergency or relocation, a pulpit supply preacher serves until a permanent minister is either appointed by the governing body or elected by the church.

J. M. Glass

Punshon, William Morley (1824-1881). Methodist* minister.* Born in Doncaster, Yorkshire, England, Punshon became a candidate for ministry in the Wesleyan Methodist Conference in 1844 and was ordained* in 1847. After a short period of study at the Methodist Theological Institution at Richmond, he was assigned to what a biographer has described as one of the worst circuits in all Methodism. His effectiveness in this charge, attributed largely to his preaching,* became characteristic of his ministry. After his arrival in Canada in 1868, he was regarded as the leader of the Wesleyan Methodists there. Before returning to England in 1873, he oversaw the building of Toronto's Metropolitan Church, a magnificent and influential architectural accomplishment in its day. A brilliant pulpit orator, Punshon published devotional works such as *Sabbath Chimes* (1868), in addition to sermons and lectures.

BIBLIOGRAPHY. J. Dawson, *William Morley Punshon: The Orator of Methodism* (1906); *DCB* XI; F. W. Macdonald, *The Life of William Morley Punshon, LL.D.* (1887). P. D. Airhart

Purcell, John Baptist (1800-1883). Archbishop* of Cincinnati. Born in Mallow, Cork, Ireland, Purcell immigrated to the U.S. in 1818. He entered Mount St. Mary Seminary in Emmitsburg, Maryland, in 1820 and later spent three years at the Seminary of St. Sulpice in Paris. Ordained* to the priesthood* in Paris, he returned to the U.S. and was made a member of the faculty of Mount St. Mary's

College and Seminary and in 1829 made president of the same. He was consecrated* the second bishop of Cincinnati on October 13, 1833, by Archbishop James Whitfield* of Baltimore. At his installation, the diocese* of Cincinnati comprised the whole state of Ohio. In 1847 the diocese of Cleveland was created, and in 1850 Cincinnati became an archdiocese and Purcell raised to the rank of archbishop.

Purcell was an active and energetic bishop who capably directed the growth and development of a major Midwestern diocese (1833-1860). He welcomed the numerous German Catholics who settled in the city and made provisions for ministry to them. His work among the Catholics involved a building of the archdiocesan infrastructure, with the establishment of parishes,* schools, a cathedral* and a seminary.* He actively crusaded against the anti-Catholic propagandists, forthrightly debating Alexander Campbell,* the founder of the Disciples of Christ.* Later, when nativist* mobs threatened the life of apostolic nuncio* Gaetano Bedini, Purcell confronted the situation directly and defused the violence. His strong support of the Union cause during the Civil War* and his call for the emancipation* of slaves engendered controversy but also distinguished him as a leader of the Northern American bishops. He was in the ranks of the "inopportunists" who deemed the definition of papal infallibility* at Vatican I* to be untimely and withdrew from Rome before the final vote was taken. But when it was formally defined, he accepted it obediently.

The latter years of Purcell's reign were plagued by the consequences of a serious financial scandal in 1878 involving archdiocesan funds managed by his priest-brother Edward Purcell. The seminary was forced to close, and the archdiocese was embroiled in litigation for over twenty years. Purcell retired from active duty in 1880 and died at an Ursuline convent on July 4, 1883.

BIBLIOGRAPHY. *DAB* VII; J. H. Lamott, *History of the Archdiocese of Cincinnati, 1821-1921* (1921); M. E. Hussey, "The 1878 Financial Failure of Archbishop Purcell," *The Cincinnati Historical Society Bulletin* 36 (Spring 1978):6-41.

S. M. Avella

Purgatory. The place, state or condition of departed Christian souls in which they undergo purifying suffering before entering heaven. The Roman Catholic* doctrine of purgatory, while finding some support in apocryphal and biblical texts like 2 Maccabees 12:39-45; Matthew 5:26; Matthew 12:32 and 1 Corinthians 3:11-15, relies chiefly on church tradition for its authority and content. At least as early as the late second century, certain church fathers (notably Clement of Alexandria) were writing about such an intermediate stage, and by Augustine's time the doctrine was widely, if vaguely, understood and taught. The nature and extent of the soul's experience of purgatory has since been disputed widely, but there is general agreement in Roman Catholicism that there are three purposes for it: to make expiation for unforgiven venial sins; to purge the soul of inclination toward sin*; and to undergo the temporal punishment for forgiven venial and mortal sins, the eternal guilt and punishment for which were borne by Christ on the cross.

Besides the existence of purgatory, the Council of Trent declared that the souls in purgatory may be helped by the prayers (*See* Prayers for the Dead) and good works of the faithful on earth. The theological basis is the doctrine of the communion of saints,* by which the action of one member of this community—which stretches beyond the grave to departed Christians—can affect others. Works of piety,* like prayers,* indulgences,* fasting and masses* can be presented to God with the wish that their benefit accrue to those in purgatory. Current Roman Catholic teaching says that God is not bound in some sort of transactional sense to apply the value of these works to these souls, but one can hope that God will respond graciously to such a request.

Eastern Orthodox churches, while agreeing on the existence of purgatory and the efficacy of prayers for the dead, view it in terms of maturation rather than paying a debt. Several recent Catholic theologians have interpreted the doctrine along lines more compatible with the Eastern tradition. Protestant* churches generally have renounced all of these ideas because they are not derived from canonical Scripture, although the Anglican* Church has had to contend with their recurrence in its communion* from time to time.

BIBLIOGRAPHY. J. Le Goff, *The Birth of Purgatory* (1984).

J. G. Stackhouse

Puritanism. Of all the religious movements that helped shape early American culture, none was more important than Puritanism. Yet, for all its recognized importance, the term is notoriously difficult to define. Originally the term appeared in sixteenth-century England as a pejorative one aimed at those reformers who wanted to "purify" the Church of England in more Reformed* Protestant* ways. In time the term encompassed a great plurality of groups and points of view who shared only a common opposition to the established (Anglican*) church of England. At one time or another, Presbyterians,* Quakers,* Ranters, Levellers, Fifth Monarchy Men, Separatists, Independents or Moravians* all fell under the opprobrium of the label *Puritan.*

From the vantage point of American religious history, however, two strands of Puritanism were especially important; the Presbyterians who by the seventeenth century enjoyed great strength and influence in Parliament, and the Independents or Congregationalists* who came to dominate much of the leadership in Oliver Cromwell's New Model Army. Both of these traditions would become particularly influential in colonial New England, where they would stamp the entire region with their identity. In matters of doctrine* these two groups were strongly Reformed in orientation and traced their earliest leaders back to English theologians* who were exiled to Geneva during the reign of Queen Mary. There they studied with John Calvin and absorbed his doctrine of the church* and salvation.* In time, Presbyterians and Independents in England and New England drafted and endorsed the system of doctrine codified in the Westminster Confession of Faith.*

Of all the teachings of the Presbyterian/Independent Puritans, none was more important than that of *Sola Scriptura,*　or "Scripture Alone." In contrast to Roman Catholics* and Anglicans, who emphasized the authority* of tradition alongside the Bible, and in contrast to more radical Puritans, who emphasized an ongoing special revelation through visions or inner lights, the New England Puritans insisted that Scripture alone was a sufficient and all-encompassing guide for all aspects of life and faith relative to this world and the world to come. In the Puritan view, moreover, there were no moral or spiritual issues that could not be resolved infallibly through Scripture.

Given the centrality of Scripture to the Anglo-American Puritan movement, the single-most-important document giving this tradition its identity was not the Westminster Confession of Faith or Calvin's *Institutes,* but the vernacular Bible. In the sixteenth century vernacular translations of the Bible were still in their infancy and were cause for great enthusiasm and controversy. Of the English translations, none was more important to the Puritans than the Geneva Bible, prepared by the Marian exiles during their study with Calvin and first printed in 1560. This Bible would eventually be supplanted by the more familiar Authorized, or King James, Version of 1611, but not before it shaped an entire tradition on both sides of the

Atlantic Ocean. Readers who encountered this document for the first time determined to restructure the church solely in accord with its dictates.

The differences that separated Puritans and Anglicans over *Sola Scriptura* and the place of tradition soon extended to further questions of worship* and preaching.* The Puritan rejection of tradition as an authoritative guide to faith implied a radical redefinition of worship away from the highly ritualized and costumed worship of the Church of England toward simpler forms that eventually rejected liturgy* altogether. Much Anglican worship derived from the Latin Mass,* which, in turn, had evolved from the first centuries of Christian worship. Within Anglican worship the central feature remained for many the Eucharist,* or Lord's Supper. Since the Puritans could find no scriptural warrant for either the "pagan" tradition of the Mass* or the centrality of the Eucharist in weekly worship, they eliminated all liturgy (preferring instead a "directory" for worship). At the same time, they limited the Eucharist to monthly or quarterly celebrations. In place of the Eucharist they reasserted the primacy of the sermon as the center of worship.

By the seventeenth century, Puritan preaching dominated all public assemblies for worship and consecration. In form it assumed a distinctive "Plain Style" that rejected all use of Latin tags or quotations from Church Fathers and limited discourse solely to Scripture commentary. Invariably, Puritan ministers* would begin with a text from which they would extract a "doctrine" or general rule of faith, and then they would "apply" that rule to particular problems and issues the congregation was facing in their corporate life. The Puritan plain style rapidly became the badge of Puritan identity and a form of discourse that was immediately apparent to seventeenth-century listeners.

In church polity,* as in doctrine and preaching, the Puritans evidenced a large debt to the "Reformed" principles they absorbed in Calvin's Geneva. Both Presbyterians and Congregationalists allowed for lay* deacons* and ruling elders* who shared authority with the minister. Among the Presbyterians who dominated the Westminster Assembly and the Puritan faction in Scotland, authority rested primarily at the top in presbyteries* and synods* comprised of representative ministers (teaching elders) and lay ruling elders from every congregation in a given region. In the case of the Congregationalists who dominated New England, the role of the laity was even more pronounced through a system of governance that

[965]

lodged all decision-making power and ruling authority within each particular congregation.

As Puritanism spread from the English universities and parishes* to individual towns and villages throughout England, the household became closely connected to the vernacular Bible. Inevitably, the home emerged alongside the Bible as the primary carrier and locus of Puritan faith. Where the Anglican parish (like the Roman Catholic church) was open seven days a week for Bible readings and prayers,* the Puritan "meetinghouse" was open only on the Sabbath.* For the other six days of the week, the primary place of religious reflection and prayer was the household. Within each home the father was expected to play the role of the minister, leading his family in Bible readings and doctrinal explication. Each child, in turn, was expected to defer to the head of the household as if God himself were speaking. Beyond that, children were expected to learn how to read the Bible for themselves, creating an unprecedented emphasis on schooling and literacy.

By the first decades of the seventeenth century, Puritanism was a mounting wave of dissent that would break in two directions. One wave would break on England itself in the English Civil War or "Puritan Revolution" that led to the execution of King Charles I and the short-lived dictatorship of Oliver Cromwell. The other wave would break on North American shores in the form of Puritan settlements in Bermuda and, more importantly, in New England. Between 1620 and 1640 New England absorbed a "Great Migration" of 20,000 men, women and children—a figure that represented the largest folk migration in the history of New World settlement. The overwhelming majority of these settlers were Puritans, who often came to the New World with their ministers as pre-formed congregations settling the towns in and around Plymouth and Boston.

Among the wave of American-bound Congregationalists, two strains predominated. One, arriving with the Mayflower in 1620, were "Separatists" who settled Plymouth Colony under the governorship of William Bradford.* This group of "Pilgrims"* has been romanticized in American history, but in fact they were the most radical,

unpopular Puritan faction of their age. So adamant was their rejection of Anglican forms and doctrines that they broke fellowship altogether and separated from the Church of England, labeling it "apostate" and beyond all hope of reform.

The other more numerous and powerful strain of Congregationalists was the non-separating Puritans who settled in and around Boston, Hartford and New Haven. This group has often been vilified in American history and national mythology, while in fact they were the more moderate strain of accommodative Congregationalists who refused to give up on the Church of England and worked instead to reform it. These New England Puritans came to the New World less as an escape or attempt to separate from a corrupt Church than to provide a beacon that would reflect back to England and point the Church to the way of reform. These Puritans hoped, in the immortal words of their governor, John Winthrop,* to be as a "City Upon a Hill" that would give light to the whole world, and in particular to their native England.

By the eighteenth century, the term *Puritan* seems to have ceased active connotation with New England Congregationalists. In his classic history of colonial New England—the *Magnalia Christi Americana**—Boston's eminent minister and historian, Cotton Mather,* referred to the recently passed "good old Puritans" of the seventeenth century. Thereafter Congregationalism continued, but it moved in ever-more-democratic* directions that would peak in the mid-eighteenth-century Great Awakening* and in directions the more aristocratic Puritans would have rejected.

In many respects the Puritans continued to cast a long shadow on New England society long after the seventeenth century, through their emphasis on *Sola Scriptura,* lay rule, education, plain speaking and the household of faith. Through their voluminous writings and testimonies, they have continued to influence generations of Americans.

BIBLIOGRAPHY. W. Haller, *The Rise of Puritanism* (1938); E. S. Morgan, *The Puritan Dilemma* (1958); F. Bremer, *The Puritan Experiment* (1976); P. Miller, *The New England Mind: The Seventeenth Century* (1939).   H. S. Stout

Q

Quadragesimo Anno. Papal encyclical* on social reconstruction. Issued in 1931, forty years (the literal rendering of the title) after *Rerum Novarum*,* Pius XI* wrote his encyclical *On the Reconstruction of the Social Order* to "recall . . . and develop" Leo XIII's teachings and comment on his own times. Pius claimed the right to speak to the moral dimensions of the socioeconomic conditions. Rightfully, people could own property to care for their families. On another's property (capital), workers should share in its fruits, provided wages are set according to the workers' family needs, the business's and society's. People should defend their economic rights and aid one another materially and spiritually through associations. They can even, as did American Catholics, separate these goals and join religiously neutral unions. To create a better social order, people should let lesser groups do what they can (*See* Subsidiarity, Principle of*). Then, they should enter worker, capitalist or other associations and cooperate for the common good, as Kennedy's Labor-Management Committee exemplified later. Since socialism and communism deny one's spiritual condition, their power should not be used to resolve conflicts. Rather, acts of justice and charity should accomplish this.

When Pius XI asked that these principles form the workers, Msgrs. John Ryan* and Raymond A. McGowan (1892-1962) of the National Catholic Welfare Council* (now the United States Catholic Conference*) and others taught the workers, set up labor schools and helped them negotiate. Later, at the *Catholic Worker*,* laymen established the Association of Catholic Trade Unionists. In catalyzing these endeavors, *Quadragesimo anno* helped raise such persons as Murray, Brophy and Meany to top labor positions in the U.S.

BIBLIOGRAPHY. Pius XI, "Quadragesimo anno, Encyclical of Pope Pius XI on Reconstruction of the Social Order, May 15, 1931," in *Papal Encyclicals*, vol. 3: 1903-1939, ed. C. Carlen, 5 vols. (1981); R. J. Miller, *Forty Years After: Pius XI and the Social Order* (1947); C. Curran, *American Catholic Social Ethics: 20th Century Approaches* (1984).

W. J. Bracken

Quakers. *See* FRIENDS, RELIGIOUS SOCIETY OF.

Quebec Act (1774). An act of the British Parliament extending religious toleration to the Roman Catholic* majority in the colony, which had been wrested from the French crown in the previous decade. The policy of assimilation under the British Royal Proclamation of 1763 was unsuccessful, and the rising unrest in the American colonies to the south required pacifying the predominately French population. The measures taken were political, cultural and religious. French civil law was re-established, although English criminal law remained in force. The territorial glory of Quebec was restored—to the anger of many in the American colonies, since the lands between the Ohio and Mississippi Rivers were returned to Quebec administration.

Religiously, the Act formally recognized the Catholic hierarchy and granted the Church the right to collect tithes and educate clergy.* It also allowed Roman Catholics to conscientiously enter government office, since references to religion were removed from the oath of allegiance. Although further adjustment of the status quo was required after the influx of thousands of English-speaking Protestants ("United Empire Loyalists") after the American Revolution,* the gains made by the Catholic Church were not lost. Rising tensions between the Roman Catholic French and the largely Protestant English did not lead to the suppression of the former; rather the Constitutional Act of 1791 made room for both by dividing Quebec into Lower Canada (the present Province of Quebec) and Upper Canada (now Ontario).

BIBLIOGRAPHY. H. Neatby, *The Quebec Act* (1972); H. Neatby, *Quebec: The Revolutionary Age, 1760-1791* (1966); H. Plante, *L'Eglise Catholique au Canada* (1970). B. A. McKenzie

Queens College. *See* RUTGERS UNIVERSITY.

Quietism. A term principally applied to one of the extreme forms of Roman Catholic* mysticism* popular in the seventeenth and eighteenth centuries, principally in Spain, France and Italy. It took its inspiration from the teaching of Miguel de Molinos (1640-1697), a Spanish priest,* and his book *Guida Spirituale* (1675). Quietism emphasized the cleansing of the interior life. It was a meditative, passive, nonactive way of life intended to bring one into perfect rest with God. In such a contemplative state, sustained by silent prayer and the infilling of the Spirit of God, the individual abandons personal aspiration and social involvement.

Narrowly restrictive though the teaching was, it spread to other countries. In France its most influential supporter was Madame Guyon (1648-1717), who traveled extensively in her own country seeking converts. Quietism, centering in individual meditative practices, tended to abandon crucial church teaching and ordinances.* When Pope Innocent XI denounced quietism in 1687, Madame Guyon and others were imprisoned.

With their emphasis on the inner light, the Quakers* sometimes showed tendencies toward quietism, but their interest in the improvement of society kept them from extremes.

P. M. Bechtel

Quimby, Phineas (P)arkhurst (1802-1866). Mentalist who transformed magnetic healing into mind cure. A Belfast, Maine, clockmaker, Quimby attended mesmerist Charles Poyen's 1838 public lectures and became fascinated by the possible medical applications of animal magnetism (similar to the hypnotism of today). After careful investigation, Quimby concluded that the success of the magnetic healer lay not in his control of animal magnetism but in the patient's positive mental attitude and his confidence in the healer. Quimby launched a career that soon established his reputation as the foremost mentalist of Portland, Maine. He vicariously experienced his patients' symptoms, visited with them to inspire a positive mental attitude and rubbed their head or manipulated their limbs. Although he practiced healing for less than two decades, he exerted an important influence on the birth of both spiritual healing and mind cure in America. During the two years of 1862 and 1863, three major contributors to the early development of American mind healing— Mary Baker Eddy* (founder of Christian Science*), Warren Felt Evans (widely influential author on mental healing) and Julius A. Dresser (early organizer of New Thought)—studied his unpublished writings and received treatment at his hands.

BIBLIOGRAPHY. A. G. Dresser, *The Philosophy of P. P. Quimby* (0000); C. S. Braden, *Spirits in Rebellion: The Rise and Development of New Thought* (1963). R. B. Schoepflin

Quintard, Charles Todd (1824-1898). Second Protestant Episcopal* bishop* of Tennessee. Born in Stamford, Connecticut, Quintard received the M.D. from University Medical College (New York University) in 1847, practiced medicine several years in Georgia and then joined the faculty of the Memphis Medical College in 1851.

In 1854 Quintard began study for ordination* under James H. Otey,* the first Episcopal bishop of Tennessee. He was ordained priest* in 1856 and served as rector* for two churches in Memphis and Nashville. During the Civil War* he was elected chaplain* of the 1st Tennessee Regiment and also acted as surgeon for that unit.

Quintard succeeded Otey as bishop of Tennessee in 1865. His episcopate was characterized theologically by sympathy with the Oxford* and Ritualist movements, and administratively by efforts to rebuild war-damaged church properties and to educate Episcopal clergy* in the South. Prominent among his accomplishments was the re-establishment in 1868 of the University of the South at Sewanee, Tennessee, where he became vice chancellor. Recognition of Quintard's service to the church was broadened by his fund-raising efforts on behalf of the school in the North and in England. Columbia College conferred on him the D.D. in 1866, and Cambridge University the LL.D. in 1868.

BIBLIOGRAPHY. *DAB* VIII; R. N. Greatwood, *Charles Todd Quintard: His Role and Significance in the Development of the Protestant Episcopal Church in the Diocese of Tennessee and in the South* (unpublished Ph.D. dissertation, Vanderbilt, 1977); A. H. Noll, ed., *Doctor Quintard: Chaplain C.S.A. and Second Bishop of Tennessee* (1905).

T. P. Thigpen

Quitman, Frederick Henry (1760-1832). Lutheran* minister* and theologian.* Born at Iserlohn in Rhineland-Westphalia and educated at Halle, Quitman was ordained* by the Lutheran Consistory of Amsterdam in 1781 for service in Curacao, the West Indies. Revolutionary unrest caused Quitman to leave the Caribbean for New York in 1795. Fluent in Dutch, German and English, Quitman rose rapidly in the American Church. Until his retirement in 1825, he pastored congregations in and near Rhinebeck, New York. In 1807 Quitman was elected the second president of the New York Ministerium.

A Christian Deist,* Quitman attempted to mediate between American rationalism and Lutheran confessionalism.* His major works include *Evangelical Catechism* (1814), *Sermons on the Reformation* (1817) and *Hymn-Book of the Ministerium of New York* (1817). In 1813 Harvard honored him with a D.D. His son, John Anthony Quitman, a Unitarian* layman, was a celebrated soldier, attorney and states-rights advocate. At the time of his death at Rhinebeck, New York, on June 26, 1832, Frederick Quitman was established as the leading theologian of the generation between the Pietism of Henry Melchoir Muhlenberg* and the evangelicalism* of Samuel Simon Schmucker.*

BIBLIOGRAPHY. *AAP* 9; J. F. H. Claiborne, *Life and Correspondence of John A. Quitman* (1860); E. C. Nelson, *The Lutherans in North America* (1975).

C. G. Fry

R

Rader, Paul Daniel (1879-1938). Christian and Missionary Alliance* evangelist,* pastor* and leader. Born in Denver, Colorado, the son of a Methodist* minister and revivalist,* Rader attended the University of Denver, the University of Colorado and the University of Puget Sound. Rader spent some time as athletic director at Hamline University in St. Paul, Minnesota. Entering the ministry, he first pastored a Congregational* church in Boston, Massachusetts, and then in Portland, Oregon (1906-1908), before becoming disillusioned with the ministry. Moving to New York, he became involved with the Christian and Missionary Alliance (CMA). Experiencing a religious awakening in 1911, he began street preaching. From 1912 to 1915 he ministered in Pittsburgh's Christian and Missionary Alliance Tabernacle under E. D. "Daddy" Whiteside.

In 1915 he began his ministry in the Moody Church, Chicago (1915-1921). Rader was elected vice president of the CMA, and upon the death of its founder in 1919 he became president, a position he held until 1924. As president, Rader divided his time between CMA headquarters in New York City and the Moody Church, though he tried to move CMA headquarters to Chicago. In 1922 he began the Chicago Gospel Tabernacle.

Rader urged the CMA to reorganize regionally and promote nondenominational "tabernacalism,"* campaigns in which temporary structures seating 300 to 3,000 persons were erected for special, daily evangelistic efforts which often continued for months. Oswald J. Smith,* pastor of the Parkdale Tabernacle of the CMA, supported the movement. By 1925 both men had left the CMA. Rader went on to organize the Christian World Couriers, a missionary organization, with Smith as the Canadian director. A rugged individualist, Rader was often introduced as a former prospector, prize fighter, bronco buster or football player. He authored two hymns, "Old Time Power" and "Only Believe."

BIBLIOGRAPHY. R. L. Niklaus, J. S. Sawin, S. J. Stoesz, *All for Jesus: God at Work in the Christian and Missionary Alliance over One Hundred Years* (1986); T. Leon, *The Redemption of Paul Rader* (1918).   H. P. Shelly

Radical Catholicism. The radical gospel—the demand of Christ that his followers give themselves unconditionally to their neighbors in need—has long been honored as an ethical ideal. What distinguishes radical gospel movements from individual works of self-sacrificial charity and from institutionalized forms of apostolic service (priesthood,* sisterhood*) is their attempt to make this ideal the foundation of a functioning social order.

Radical Catholicism has existed in the U.S. since 1933, when Dorothy Day* and Peter Maurin* founded the Catholic Worker Movement* and published a penny-a-copy newspaper by the same name. Day had worked a series of jobs with left-wing journals, was an ardent pacifist during World War 1,* and mingled with prominent socialists* and communists* in New York's Greenwich Village before converting* to Catholicism in 1927. The Catholic Worker Houses of Hospitality she established served as newspaper offices, volunteer centers, soup kitchens, boarding houses, schools, places of worship and the center of a far-flung social movement. Maurin, a French peasant, poet and ardent Catholic social theorist, insisted that the value system underlying capitalism* and other secular ideologies could be undermined only by Christians following the perfectionist social ethic* of the radical gospel.

Day and Maurin advocated a social program featuring service to one's immediate neighbors, satisfying and socially useful labor, a rejection of all forms of violence and coercion, and a personal detachment from material goods through the practice of voluntary poverty. The Catholic Worker became a national movement in the 1930s. Houses of Hospitality sprang up in Boston (1934), St. Louis (1935), Chicago (1941) and Cleveland (1941). By the end of World War 2,* there were thirty-two houses in twenty-seven cities in the U.S. Observers first viewed the movement as an effort to fortify the

Catholic urban working class against radical appeals during hard times. But Day and Maurin's long-range solution included a move back to rural communes, or "agronomic universities," as well as support for organized labor, some elements of the New Deal and the social teachings of the bishops.

Although the movement was not well known by the larger Catholic population, its national character afforded the movement the opportunity to establish enduring and influential ties with other American Catholic centers of renewal such as the Liturgical Movement* at St. John's Abbey in Collegeville, Minnesota; the Young Christian Workers; the Grailville Catholic women's community in Loveland, Ohio; and the Catholic Rural Life movement based in Des Moines, Iowa. In this sense the movement was revolutionary in the precedent it set. Lay Catholics in America organized a movement, marched in picket lines, demonstrated at embassies, organized unions and helped integrate all-white facilities in the South. Social historian Mel Piehl has suggested that the radical dissent which characterized the movement was an American Catholic protest against the segregated ordering of human affairs, confining religion and the ideas generated from religion to certain spheres of life.

In the 1960s the radical social activism of Catholic priests Daniel and Philip Berrigan and others in the Catholic Left attracted widespread public notice and underscored this element of social, political and religious extremism in Roman Catholicism. On May 17, 1968, the Berrigan brothers led five men and nine women in a raid on the offices of the Draft Board of Catonsville, Maryland. Television cameras recorded the protest against the Vietnam War* as the small group dumped three hundred draft files into trash baskets and burned them in the office parking lot while intoning prayers* for peace. Other Catholic intellectuals of the Left, including the popular author and Trappist* monk Thomas Merton,* supported such acts of protest by writing numerous books and articles decrying American involvement in the Vietnam War, in the nuclear arms race, in racist policies and laws, and in many other acts of social injustice.

The lay movement* initiated by Dorothy Day had now attracted articulate spokespersons among the clergy and religious. By the late 1970s and early 1980s, even certain members of the American Catholic hierarchy were characterized as radicals by their conservative co-religionists. Perhaps the most prominent of these "peace bishops" was Archbishop Raymond Hunthausen of Seattle, Washington, who publicly denounced the nuclear

arms race and encouraged Washington Catholics to rethink their support of the U.S. defense policy and to reconsider their participation in arms-related industries.

See also PEACE MOVEMENT, CATHOLIC.

BIBLIOGRAPHY. J. T. Baker, *Thomas Merton, Social Critic* (1971); W. V. E. Casey and P. Nobile, eds., *The Berrigans* (1971); M. Piehl, *Breaking Bread: The Catholic Worker and the Origin of Catholic Radicalism in America* (1984).

R. S. Appleby

Rahner, Karl (1904-1984). German Catholic* theologian.* Rahner joined the Jesuits* after high school (1922), studied philosophy and theology* at the University of Freiburg, and taught in Innsbruck (1937-1938; 1949-1964), Munich (1945-1948; 1964-1967) and Munster (1967-1971). Retiring first to Munich (1971-1981) and then Innsbruck (1981-1984), he continued his career as a prolific writer and lecturer, covering the gamut of Catholic doctrinal theology and spirituality.* Rahner was probably the most influential Catholic thinker of his era. His most significant work is found in his twenty-volume *Theological Investigations* (1961-1981) and *Foundations of Christian Faith* (1978).

In an effort to update Catholic theology, Rahner adapted the transcendental method—rooting his thought in the ability of human nature to participate in trans-sensible domains through its intelligence and freedom. He married the dynamic aspects of Thomistic* epistemology to the findings of such modern philosophers as Immanuel Kant (1724-1804), G. W. F. Hegel (1770-1831) and Martin Heidegger (1889-1976), seeking to reformulate the meaning of traditional Catholic theology (of which he had a thorough mastery). Among his special contributions were a Christology* in which the Sonship of Christ was the supreme instance of a vocation shared by all human beings, and a theory of grace that made God present to all people as the lure of their freedom.

Rahner also wrote significant studies of the sacramental nature of the church,* of how the inspiration of Scripture* joins divine and human causalities, and of how death is the consummation of human potential. He has been revered in the U.S. for championing a church free of Roman legalism and for his spiritual writings, which center on the divine mystery.

BIBLIOGRAPHY. L. J. O'Donovan, *A World of Grace: An Introduction to the Themes and Foundations of Karl Rahner's Theology* (1980); H. Vorgrimler, *Karl Rahner: His Life, Thought and*

Works (1966); K. H. Weger, *Karl Rahner: An Introduction to His Theology* (1980).

J. T. Carmody

Railton, George Scott (1849-1913). The first officer officially to begin the work of The Salvation Army in America.* Railton, a Wesleyan* Christian, was attracted to the ministry* of The Christian Mission, the precursor of The Salvation Army, and became secretary of the Mission. A tireless evangelist,* an advocate of the Wesleyan doctrine of holiness,* and a lifelong friend of both William* and Catherine* Booth, he greatly encouraged the change of the organization to The Salvation Army and became its first commissioner.

There had been two tenuous and unofficial beginnings of The Salvation Army in America, and in 1880 Railton and seven women were sent to America. They arrived on March 10, 1880, in New York City "to claim America for God and the Army." They immediately sprang into action, and by the end of May Railton reported that ten corps (churches) had been established, and that two hundred public meetings were being held weekly. By July of 1880 the first Salvation Army publication in America, the *Salvation News*, was printed, and by the end of 1880 the indefatigable Railton had traveled to St. Louis, Missouri, to launch his Western campaign.

He was recalled to London in April 1881. Railton continued as an evangelist, preacher and writer, both inspiring and commanding the work of the Army in many places around the world until his death in 1913.

BIBLIOGRAPHY. E. Douglas and M. Duff, *Commissioner Railton* (n.d.); B. Watson, *Soldier Saint* (1970).

R. J. Green

Ramism. A method of logical analysis based on dichotomies. Stemming from the writings of the French Reformed* philosopher Petrus Ramus (1515-1572), Ramism offered a revision of Aristotelian scholasticism which insisted on the primacy of logic (dialectic) over rhetoric. Ramist logic proceeded by dichotomizing, dividing a subject into two parts, dividing each of these two into two more, and so on. The resulting structure, often visualized in the form of a chart, was thought to represent not just a method of analysis but an accurate description of reality. William Ames,* whose *Marrow of Theology* (1623) and *Cases of Conscience* (1630) weighed heavily on the early Harvard* curriculum, was a thoroughgoing Ramist. So was Samuel Stone (1602-1633), Thomas Hooker's* colleague at Hartford and author of the first systematic theology* written in New England. Stone's convictions are apparent in his simple statement, "all things are dichotomized."

BIBLIOGRAPHY. W. J. Ong, *Ramus, Method, and the Decay of Dialogue* (1958); L. W. Gibbs, trans., *William Ames: Technometry* (1979).

L. B. Tipson

Randall, Benjamin (1749-1808). Founder of New England branch of Free Will Baptists.* Born in New Castle, New Hampshire, Randall went to sea with his ship-captain father until he was about eighteen. He later worked as a sailmaker and tailor, showing little interest in religion as a youth. Upon hearing of the death of George Whitefield* in 1770, whom he had heard preach and whom he had ridiculed, Randall reproached himself, saying, "Whitefield is in heaven, and I am on the road to hell." He professed conversion* and united with the Congregational* Church.

In 1776 Randall joined the Baptists* and soon embarked on an itinerant* evangelistic* ministry. Resisting the strict Calvinistic Baptist emphasis on predestination,* he broke from the Regular Baptists* in 1779, and in 1780 formed a church with seven members at New Durham, New Hampshire. In time this church, and many others like it formed by Randall and his followers, took the name of Free Will Baptists to emphasize their belief that any person is free to believe in Jesus Christ. By 1782 there were twelve such churches, and Randall led them to form a Quarterly Meeting, much like an "association" among Regular Baptists. In 1792 the organizational structure was completed with the addition of a Yearly Meeting. Described as having a loud, clear voice, Randall traveled and preached constantly, although he was never sturdy of health. He is best understood as an example of resistance to strict Calvinism in New England.

BIBLIOGRAPHY. *DAB* VIII; J. Buzzell, *The Life of Elder Benjamin Randall* (1827); F. L. Wiley, *Life and Influence of Rev. Benjamin Randall* (1915); I. D. Stewart, *The History of the Freewill Baptists* (1862); William F. Davidson, *The Free Will Baptists in America, 1727-1984* (1985).

H. L. McBeth

Rankin, Milledge Theron (1894-1953). Southern Baptist* missionary* and missions* leader. Born in South Carolina, the son of a minister, Rankin graduated from Wake Forest College and Southern Baptist Theological Seminary, where he earned the Ph.D.

A long-time missionary to China (1921-1935), he was president of Graves Theological Seminary,

Canton, and then elected secretary for the Orient (1935-1944). Early in World War 2 he was imprisoned by the Japanese for nine months in an internment camp in Hong Kong. From 1945 to 1953 he served as executive secretary of the Foreign Mission Board of the Southern Baptist Convention.

Rankin's tenure coincided with the end of the war, and his goals were to re-enter mission fields vacated due to the war, rebuild Baptist work there and provide relief for the hungry, homeless and sick. Three years later (1948) he proposed a bold program of advance to appoint 1,750 missionaries with an annual budget of $10 million. With his vision and leadership, Southern Baptist missions flourished. In 1945 there were 504 missionaries under appointment, and in 1953, 913 missionaries.

BIBLIOGRAPHY. B. J. Cauthen, *Advance: A History of Southern Baptist Foreign Missions* (1970); J. B. Weatherspoon, *M. Theron Rankin: Apostle of Advance* (1958). W. M. Patterson

Rapp, Johann Georg (1757-1847). Pietist* leader, mystic* and founder of the Harmony Society.* Born in Iptingen, Germany, of peasant origins and trained as a linen weaver, Rapp came under the influence of separatist* Pietism as a young man. By 1785 he refused to attend worship* or communion of the state Reformed* Church. A separatist group formed under his influence attracted thousands of adherents and his strongly millennialist* theology* and unorthodox* views attracted the attention of church officials and later brought persecution.

These conditions led Rapp to immigrate* to western Pennsylvania in 1803-1804, where 5,000 acres had been secured from the U.S. government. The town of Harmony was built and the Harmony Society formed in 1805 after the arrival of several hundred followers from Wurttemberg. The society practiced communitarian living and celibacy (after 1807). "Father" Rapp's undisputed and strict spiritual leadership and the administrative skills of his adopted son, Friedreich (died 1834), enabled the Harmonists to flourish. In 1819 Rapp moved the society further west to a "new Eden" in southern Indiana where the town of New Harmony was built. This village also prospered, but in 1824 he decided to move the Harmonists back to western Pennsylvania where they constructed their third village, Economy.

Rapp's later years were marred by an unfortunate schism (1832) and persistent rumors about his relationship with a young woman in the society. After his death a series of legal suits against the Harmonists resulted in the society's slow demise. Communal ties were dissolved in 1905.

See also NEW HARMONY.

BIBLIOGRAPHY. K. R. J. Arndt, *George Rapp's Harmony Society, 1785-1847,* rev. ed. (1972); *DAB* VIII; J. S. Duss, *George Rapp and His Associates* (1914); *NCAB* 4. D. B. Eller

Rapture of the Church. A phrase premillennialists* use to refer to the "catching up" (from Latin *rapio*) of the church to be with Christ at his Second Coming. All premillennialists trace the doctrine to the same passage (1 Thess 4:15-17) but disagree on when it will occur in relation to the tribulation period, which they identify as the "seventieth week" of Daniel 9:24-27. Historically, premillennialists have divided over whether the rapture will happen before, during or after the tribulation.

Pretribulationism, which is nearly identical with dispensationalism,* argues that the rapture will occur before the tribulation. Though pretribulationists try to find the teaching throughout church history, in about 1830 John Nelson Darby* was the first to divide the Second Coming into two stages: Christ's coming *for* his saints before the tribulation (the rapture) and his coming *with* his saints after it (the Second Coming per se). This view was derived from his total distinction between the church and Israel: The church must be removed from the earth before God can resume his dealings with the Jews and fulfil the prophecies concerning the end times.

Pretribulationists find evidence for their view in Paul's teaching that before Antichrist can be revealed, the "restrainer," which they take as either the church or the Holy Spirit, must be removed (2 Thess 2:6-8); the fact that the church is not mentioned in the eschatological predictions of the Book of Revelation after chapter 3, indicating that the church must have been raptured; and the biblical warning that the rapture is imminent, which means that no prophesied event stands between the present and the coming of Christ for his saints. This view gained ascendancy in American premillennial circles before World War 1,* thanks in large part to The Scofield Reference Bible* (1909), and continues to the present in Hal Lindsey's best-selling *The Late Great Planet Earth* (1970).

Midtribulationism, an alternative view, contends that the church will be raptured halfway through the tribulation. This view, championed by Harold J. Ockenga,* Gleason L. Archer and others, became popular among a relatively small number of premillennialists after World War 2.* Midtribulationalists believe that the frequent mention of forty-two months in key prophetic passages (e.g., Dan 7, 9, and 12; Rev 11 and 12) indicates that only half of Daniel's seventieth week (three and a half years) will experience the terror usually associated with the entire tribulation period (Rev 16—18). In the first half of the seventieth week, the church will remain on earth, witnessing the rise of Antichrist, and experiencing persecution at his hand; but it will be raptured by Christ before God's judgment and wrath are poured out. Advocates claim that their view remedies pretribulationism's shortcomings, which include its insistence that the rapture will be "secret" and its inability to locate the rapture in the Olivet Discourse (Mt 24). Nevertheless, midtribulationism still divides the Second Coming into two phases.

Posttribulationism, which appears to be the oldest premillennialist view, holds that the rapture and the Second Coming of Christ will occur at the same time, at the end of the tribulation. Posttribulationists argue that no scriptural text explicitly divides the Second Coming into two parts. Paul's most explicit passage on the rapture (1 Thess 4) does not mention its time relationship to the tribulation; but its accompanying phenomena (loud command, trumpet of God, gathering of the saints by angels, Christ coming on the clouds) are mentioned in other passages which do place them after the tribulation (Mt 24, Mk 13, Lk 21). Thus advocates of this view expect the church to go through the tribulation, suffering terrible persecution, but not experiencing the wrath of God because of divine protection (Rev 7). In order to come to these conclusions, posttribulationists generally play down the distinction between Israel and the church and the imminence of the rapture. Though eclipsed by pretribulationism before World War 1,* this view has gained many followers since World War 2 through the writings George Ladd,* Robert Gundry and others.

A small number of pretribulationists, led by G. H. Lang, have also argued for a partial rapture theory which contends that only the most faithful Christians will be raptured before the tribulation, with the rest being caught up sometime later, depending on their spiritual condition.

Though such interpretive disagreements may seem inconsequential to outsiders, differences over the timing of the rapture have often produced fierce antagonism among premillennialists, with advocates of one view refusing to associate with those of another.

See also ESCHATOLOGY.

BIBLIOGRAPHY. G. E. Ladd, *The Blessed Hope* (1956); J. F. Walvoord, *The Rapture Question* (1979); J. D. Pentecost, *Things to Come* (1958); G. L. Archer et al, *The Rapture: Pre-, Mid-, or Post-Tribulational?* (1984). T. P. Weber

Ratcliffe, Robert (fl. 1680s). Anglican* minister.* Robert Ratcliffe, M.A. and Fellow of Exeter College, Oxford, was a major contributor to the establishment of Anglicanism in New England. Arriving in Boston, Massachusetts, in 1686, on the same ship that brought the commission to revoke the Massachusetts Bay charter, he became the first minister of the first Anglican church in New England, King's Chapel in Boston, which was organized on June 15, 1686. The month before, he had performed the first marriage* performed by an Anglican clergyman in New England. He was known as "a very excellent preacher, whose matter was good, and the dress in which he put it, extraordinary," and he attracted a large following. It was said that he drew as many as 400 people at a time to daily services in the church.

BIBLIOGRAPHY. W. W. Manross, *A History of the American Episcopal Church* (1959).

G. F. Moran

Rauch, Frederick Augustus (1806-1841). German Reformed educator. Born the son of a Reformed pastor in Kirchbracht, Germany, Rauch was educated in the gymnasia of Hanau and Buedingen before entering the University of Giessen in 1824. In 1827 he was awarded the Ph.D. by the University of Marburg for a dissertation in classics on "The Electra of Sophocles." Later that year he began the study of philosophy at Heidelburg under the right-wing Hegelian Karl Daub who left a permanent stamp upon Rauch. Re-entering Giessen as a student in 1828, Rauch became a university lecturer in 1829 but became embroiled in a lawsuit against another faculty member, which threatened his academic career in Germany and precipitated his immigration* to America in 1831.

Arriving in Pennsylvania, Rauch learned English and taught music in Easton before serving briefly as professor of German at Lafayette College. In 1832 he became principal of the German Reformed Classical School at York, as well as professor of biblical literature at the theological seminary. Both schools were moved to Mercersburg, Pennsylvania, in 1835 and, when the Classical School became Marshall College in 1836, Rauch assumed the presidency.

As a teacher, Rauch was the first to popularize the philosophical idealism of G. W. F. Hegel (1770-1831) in the U.S. His *Psychology* (1840) followed

Daub's philosophical anthropology closely. Although Rauch showed little interest in the Mercersburg* theological themes of ecclesiology, liturgics* and the sacraments,* his philosophical idealism and profound historical consciousness provided a substantial theoretical foundation for the work of John W. Nevin.*

BIBLIOGRAPHY. DAB VIII; *DARB; NCAB* 11; J. H. Nichols, *Romanticism in American Theology* (1961); H. J. B. Ziegler, *Frederick Augustus Rauch: American Hegelian* (1953).

W. B. Evans

Rauschenbusch, Walter (1861-1918). Prophet and theologian* of the Social Gospel.* Born in Rochester, New York, Rauschenbusch was educated in Germany and the U. S. and graduated from the University of Rochester (B.A., 1884) and Rochester Theological Seminary (1886). Following seminary he served for eleven years as pastor of a German Baptist Church (*See* North American Baptist Church) on the edge of "Hell's Kitchen" in New York City. There he encountered the human effects of poverty, unemployment, insecurity, malnutrition, disease and crime. Becoming active in social-reform work, despite increasing deafness, he sought in biblical and theological teachings for resources to counter the individualistic, laissez-faire social philosophies and practices then so rampant. During a leave from his parish* in 1891, he engaged in biblical and sociological studies in Germany and found in the doctrine of the kingdom of God,* particularly as emphasized by Albrecht Ritschl (1822-1889) and his followers, clues for understanding Jesus' teachings and for bringing his evangelical* faith, scholarly interests and social concerns together. A bilingual writer and active participant in Baptist affairs, in 1897 he was called back to Rochester Seminary, becoming in 1902 professor of church history.

In 1907 his book *Christianity and the Social Crisis,* written "to discharge a debt" to the working people among whom he had ministered, became a best seller and made him in great demand as speaker and author until his death from cancer in 1918. He wrote two other major books. *Christianizing the Social Order* (1912) presented a program of progressive, democratic* reformism as moving toward the kingdom of God interpreted as "the progressive transformation of all human affairs by the thought and spirit of Christ." *A Theology for the Social Gospel* (1917) was an effort to provide a vital systematic theology* to undergird the Christian social emphasis. The outbreak of World War 1* had deeply saddened him, contributing to his increased awareness of the reality of sin* in the world and intensifying his stress on the "miraculous" aspects of the kingdom of God as "divine in its origin, progress and consummation."

Rauschenbusch also published many articles and smaller books, notably *For God and the People: Prayers of the Social Awakening* (1910), which shows the depth of his own spirituality,* and *The Social Principles of Jesus* (1916), a study book for college students which received the widest circulation of any of his works. Much of Rauschenbusch's work bears the stamp of its time; H. Shelton Smith* concluded that he was "the foremost molder of American Christian thought in his generation." But later generations also continued to learn from him; Reinhold Niebuhr* called him the "most brilliant and generally satisfying exponent" of social Christianity, and Martin Luther King, Jr.,* observed that "Rauschenbusch gave to American Protestantism a sense of social responsibility that it should never lose." In his own life and writings, the personal and social dimensions of the Christian gospel were never separated.

BIBLIOGRAPHY. *DAB* VIII; *DARB;* D. R. Sharpe, *Walter Rauschenbusch* (1942); K. J. Jaehn, *Rauschenbusch: The Formative Years* (1976); P. M. Minus, *Walter Rauschenbusch: American Reformer* (1988); *NCAB* 19.

R. T. Handy

Ravenscroft, John Stark (1772-1830). Episcopal* bishop.* Born of planter stock in 1772 in Prince George County, Virginia, Ravenscroft was taken by his parents to England and Scotland before his first birthday. Educated in classical schools in Scotland and England, he returned to Virginia in his sixteenth year to reclaim his father's land and to study at the College of William and Mary.* It was the heyday of deism* at William and Mary, and Ravenscroft left the college after a year with neither a degree nor a religious faith. He settled into the life of a worldly Virginia planter.

When he experienced a religious awakening in 1810, Ravenscroft joined the Republican Methodist Church (*see* O'Kelly Schism) and served it as a lay elder.* Concerns about the apostolic succession* and ministerial authority led him into the Episcopal Church five years later. Ordained* deacon* and priest* in 1817, he served as rector* in Mecklenburg County, Virginia, until his election in 1823 as bishop of the tiny and disorganized Episcopal Church of North Carolina.

A Hobartian* high churchman* of striking personality, Ravenscroft emphasized the apostolic character and distinctive teachings of the Episcopal Church. His uncompromising views offended not only Protestants* but also Episcopalians of evangelical* views. Although at his death Episcopalians were still few in number in North Carolina, Ravenscroft had united the diocese and made it more distinctively Anglican.*

BIBLIOGRAPHY. *AAP* 5; *DAB* VIII; L. F. London and S. McC. Lemmon, eds., *The Episcopal Church in North Carolina, 1701-1959* (1987); J. S. Ravenscroft, *The Works of the Rt. Rev. John Stark Ravenscroft*, 2 vols. (1830). D. L. Holmes

Rayburn, James C., Jr. (1909-1970). Founder of Young Life.* After studying engineering and mineralogy at Kansas State University and the University of Colorado, James and Maxine Rayburn were appointed "home missionaries" by the Presbyterian* Board of Missions to New Mexico (1933-1936). Influenced by Lewis Sperry Chafer,* he attended Dallas Theological Seminary* (1936-1939). Seminary "field work" requirements took him to Gainesville, Florida, where he developed "Good News Clubs," later "Miracle Book Clubs," on high-school campuses. Back in Texas, with financial support from Herbert J. Taylor,* he incorporated Young Life Ministries (1941) and started *Young Life* magazine (1944). Taylor provided Star Ranch near Colorado Springs (1946), which became the national headquarters in 1965. Young Life Institute (1951) and additional camps expanded the outreach of the highly pragmatic ministry to youth.* Rayburn retired from Young Life in 1964. Rayburn remained Presbyterian, but Young Life is a parachurch organization.

BIBLIOGRAPHY. E. Cailliet, *Young Life* (1963). D. D. Bundy

RBMU International. Nondenominational foreign missionary* agency. This faith mission* traces its roots to the East London Institute for Home and Foreign Missions (Harley College), founded in 1873 by Irish evangelist H. Grattan Guinness. In 1878 Guinness sent some graduates to the Congo Free State (Zaire) under the newly organized Livingstone Inland Mission, which was subsequently turned over to American Baptists.* In 1888 Guinness initiated a new African venture known as the Congo Balolo Mission. With expansion into other fields, such as Peru and India, the name Regions Beyond Missionary Union was adopted in 1900. In 1948 Ebenezer G. Vine established an American Council and then served as its first General Secretary. By 1971 the U.S. Council became autonomous from its British forebear, and in 1979 the American, Australian and Canadian Councils formed RBMU International, while the British Council retained its older name.

Today the society sponsors frontier evangelism,* church planting, Bible* translation and the training of national church leaders in Chile, Peru, the Philippines, Cameroon, Zaire, Kalimantan Barat and Irian Jaya. The latter field provided the context for RBMU missionary Donald M. Richardson's popular book, *Peace Child* (1974). In recent years new attention has turned to the Delaware Valley as a home mission field surrounding Philadelphia, RBMU International's headquarters in the U.S. Joseph F. Conley serves as executive director of the American Council and oversees 103 full-time missionaries and a total annual income of over $1.2 million. RBMU International is affiliated with the Interdenominational Foreign Mission Association of North America.*

BIBLIOGRAPHY. K. Holmes, *The Cloud Moves* (1967); E. Pritchard, *For Such a Time* (1973). J. A. Patterson

Reagan, Ronald Wilson (1911-). Fortieth U.S. president. Born in Tampico, Illinois, into humble circumstances, Reagan's father was of Irish Catholic* origins, while his mother joined the Christian Church (Disciples of Christ)* just before his birth. Young Ronald was more under her influence, and at age eleven he was baptized* and became quite active in the Disciples congregation in Dixon, Illinois, where he lived as a teen-ager. He also attended a Disciples school, Eureka College (B.A., 1932). After college he went into radio broadcasting and then, in 1937, moved to Hollywood to become a movie actor, where he drifted away from the church as his career developed.

He also was drawn into politics, first as a trade-union activist and then as a conservative speaker. In the 1964 Goldwater campaign, he emerged as a national figure and in 1966 was elected governor of California. He returned somewhat to his religious roots under the influence of evangelical* friends and became quite interested in prayer,* the Bible* and eschatology.* During the late 1970s the New Religious Right,* delighted with the way he mixed conservative politics with an affirmation of evangelical beliefs, adopted him as one of their own and avidly promoted his presidential candidacy in 1980 and 1984.

Although he said the "correct" things in public, his faith was more generalized in nature. He believed that all were the children of God, downplayed sin* and repentance, and stressed optimism, prosperity and assertiveness. He espoused a civil religion* which included faith in America's divine chosenness, his country's spiritual nature and the importance of religion in general to maintain a healthy national existence and to combat Communism. Although he did not attend church, gave little money to charity and even dabbled in astrology in private, he maintained close ties with conservative Protestant* and Catholic* leaders and identified with their causes—school prayer,* aid to nonpublic schools, antiabortion* and combating secular humanism.* In turn, they remained his most loyal supporters throughout his presidency.

BIBLIOGRAPHY. R. V. Pierard, "Ronald Reagan and the Evangelicals," in *Fundamentalism Today,* ed. M. J. Selvidge (1984); R. V. Pierard and R. D. Linder, *Civil Religion and the Presidency* (1988); D. Shepherd, ed., *Ronald Reagan: In God I Trust* (1984); G. Wills, *Reagan's America: Innocents at Home* (1987). R. V. Pierard

Rebaptism. The performing again of the sacrament* or ordinance* of baptism considered to have been valid by one Christian body but invalid by the body administering the rebaptism. Technically, *rebaptism* is a misnomer, since Christians practice a single baptism. Hence, rebaptism relates to debate over what constitutes a valid sacrament or ordinance.

Efficacious baptism usually requires three elements: (1) the Trinitarian formula; (2) water; and (3) faith, either on the part of the adult Christian sponsors of the candidate, or on the part of the recipient. The Council of Arles (A.D. 314) held that the spiritual state of the celebrant does not invalidate the sacrament/ordinance. By the sixth century among Catholics* the baptism of infants was popular, and it became standard practice during the medieval period. Effusion (pouring) and eventually aspersion (sprinkling) replaced the New Testament mode of immersion. Eastern Orthodox* churches continued to baptize persons at various ages by alternate modes. With the sixteenth-century Reformation, radical reformers in Switzerland, Germany and the Netherlands who were committed to biblical restorationism began to question and eventually deny the efficacy of baptisms performed in Catholic and state churches.

Called Anabaptists (from the Greek *anabaptizein*—to baptize again), they taught that baptisms were invalid when the church performing them was "no church," or because the recipients, usually infants, had made no conscious act of faith or appropriation of God's grace and redemption.

After 1560 most emerging "believers" churches* in the Mennonite* and Baptist* traditions practiced the "faith baptism" by immersion of freely confessing and believing persons.

In North America most evangelical* and believers' churches rebaptize if they determine that personal faith was absent at the time a previous sacrament/ordinance was received. Some churches, especially those that teach baptismal regeneration,* hold immersion to be essential for a believer's baptism. A minority of Eastern Orthodox, and some Catholic and Anglican* strict apostolic successionists* reject "alien immersion,"* or "alien baptism." Alien baptism is any baptism which is not performed by that particular denomination.* Alien baptism results in rebaptism of persons who have been baptized as believers by immersion among a minority of Landmark* and Primitive* Baptists in the Southern states, the Pacific Northwest and Western Canada. In recent decades some evangelicals have used rebaptism as a witness to a "recommitment to Christ." This practice is viewed by many as an abuse of the rite.

BIBLIOGRAPHY. G. R. Beasley-Murray, *Baptism Today and Tomorrow* (1966); *BHH* 10.1 (1975); D. Bridge, *The Water that Divides: The Baptismal Debate* (1977); A. Gilmore, ed., *Christian Baptism* (1959). W. F. Ellis

Reconciliation, Sacrament of. *See* PENANCE, SACRAMENT OF.

Reconstructionism, Christian. A fundamentalist*-evangelical* movement, dating from the early 1960s, intent on reconstructing society along lines explicitly set forth in Old Testament law. Leaders include the acknowledged patriarch of the movement, Rousas John Rushdoony; theologian* Greg Bahnsen; and economist Gary North.

Three foundational ideas underlie the Reconstructionist agenda. First, they maintain a presuppositional* apologetic,* believing ultimate truth is not subject to historical or scientific investigation. At the deepest level, reality is approached with a presupposed metaphysic. The real truth—that of God—is found only by presupposing biblical revelation. Second, sometimes referred to as "theonomists," Reconstructionists argue that Old Testament law applies today, in "exhaustive" and "minutial" detail. They anticipate a day when Christians will oversee all aspects of society, using the Bible as their guide. Third, Reconstructionists are postmillennial* in their eschatology, believing the world is now in the millennial age. In the long term, societies are becoming more and more

Christianized. Christ will return at the end of this millennial period to crown the church's triumph.

The Reconstructed society is to be notably different from the contemporary one. Governmentally, Reconstructionists expect to see the death penalty restored across the range of offenses for which it was applied in Old Testament times. This would include, for example, sodomy, Sabbath breaking and incorrigibility in children. Economically, at least some Reconstructionists expect a return to the gold standard, the abolition of property taxes and the restriction of usury (as in Deut 15). Considerable thought has also been devoted to reforming the mass media, the arts and education.

It is difficult to quantify the influence of the Reconstructionist movement, but by the late 1980s it had gained a following among independent Baptist,* separatist Presbyterian* and some charismatic* circles—most notably those within the faith movement.* Spokespersons of the New Religious Right* had, from one degree to another, relied on Reconstructionist literature. In a few instances Reconstructionists ran for political office or were instrumental in the campaigns of other candidates. Finally, Rushdoony and North were frequent guests on religious television programs.

Reconstructionists's appeal among some fundamentalists and evangelicals may be attributed to their reassertion of the social implications of Christianity, their attempt at providing a systematic theory for sociopolitical engagement, and their unswerving intention to submit their thought to biblical revelation. They have been criticized on at least three counts: hermeneutical naiveté, an ecclesiology that encourages triumphalism, and an emphasis on law that subordinates other aspects of biblical revelation and sacrifices the relational aspects of biblical faith to the impersonal qualities of law.

BIBLIOGRAPHY. H. W. House and T. D. Ice, *Dominion Theology: Blessing or Curse?* (1988); R. J. Rushdoony, *The Institutes of Biblical Law* (1973); G. L. Bahnsen, *Theonomy in Christian Ethics* (1977).   R. R. Clapp

Rector. A priest* who is placed in charge of a church* or parish.* The term literally means "one who rules, guides or leads straight" and is commonly used among Episcopalians.* It is less frequently used by Roman Catholics.* Most other traditions refer to the person holding the equivalent office as "pastor." The residence of the rector is called the *rectory,* a term that remains current among both Episcopalians and Catholics. Outside

of the parish context, the head of a Jesuit house may be called a rector, as may the priest in charge of a college or seminary.

The Editors

Redemptorists. A Roman Catholic* community of priests* and lay* brothers dedicated to proclaiming the Word of God by means of missions,* retreats* and novenas,* as well as the administration of parishes.* Officially known as the Congregation of the Most Holy Redeemer (CSSR), it was founded by Alphonsus Liguori in 1732 near Naples, Italy. The name of the congregation refers to the twelve virtues of the Holy Redeemer, one of which is the object of special imitation each month of the year.

Redemptorists first came to North America in the early 1830s, many of them from Germany. Within less than twenty years, they had established an American province and worked from New York to New Orleans among immigrants* from Germany, France and Bohemia. Much of their parish work was originally carried out in the mother tongue of the immigrants—chiefly German—and involved them in education and other efforts to ease the immigrants' transition to the New World while retaining their faith. The Redemptorist Joseph Wissel (1830-1912) was well known for his preaching, having held missions for a period covering more than fifty years. In time American Redemptorists found broader fields of service, with 188 Redemptorists serving as chaplains* in the U.S. military during World War 2* and many Redemptorist missionaries serving in foreign lands beginning in the early-twentieth century. In 1988 there were reported to be 6,344 Redemptorists worldwide.

BIBLIOGRAPHY. J. F. Byrne, *The Redemptorist Centenaries* (1832); T. L. Skinner, *The Redemptorists in the West* (1933); J. Wissel, *The Redemptorist on the American Missions* (1920); *NCE* 12.

D. G. Reid

Redpath, Alan (1907-). Baptist* minister, Bible conference* speaker and writer. English-born, Redpath was influenced by G. Campbell Morgan* and others to leave his position as an accountant in a large English firm and enter the ministry. He pastored the Duke Street Baptist Church in London, building it into a large congregation before coming to America to serve as pastor of Moody Memorial Church in Chicago (1953-1962). Under his leadership Moody Church undertook the "flock" concept of ministry, instituted a Spanish-speaking Sunday-school* class and for the first time received African-Americans into church membership.* In great demand as a conference speaker, he led in the establishment of the first Mid-America Keswick Convention,* held at Moody Church in 1954. In 1962 he resigned the pastorate in Chicago to take a similar position at Charlotte Chapel in Edinburgh, Scotland. He subsequently served as pastoral dean at Capernway Bible School, Lancashire.

BIBLIOGRAPHY. R. G. Flood, *The Story of Moody Church* (1985). R. T. Clutter

Reed, Luther (D)otterer (1873-1972). Lutheran* liturgist.* Born in North Wales, Pennsylvania, Reed graduated from Franklin and Marshall College, Lutheran Theological Seminary, Philadelphia, and received numerous honorary degrees throughout his lifetime. He served as a Lutheran pastor at Allegheny and Jeanette, Pennsylvania, and as director of the library at Lutheran Theological Seminary. There he also served as professor of liturgics and church art (perhaps the first to hold such a post in North America) from 1910 to 1939, when he became president of the seminary (1939-1945).

Reed was the leader of liturgical renewal in the United Lutheran Church in America. He led the commissions that prepared two hymnals and service books. His publications included *The Lutheran Liturgy* (1947-1959) and *Worship* (1959). He was also well known in Protestant circles in the field of church architecture.*

H. F. Horn

Rees, Paul Stromberg (1900-). Minister,* evangelist* and author. Born in Rhode Island, Rees graduated from the University of Southern California (B.A., 1923) and throughout his life was awarded several honorary doctorates. Ordained* in 1921 as a minister of the Evangelical Covenant Church,* he served in the Pilgrim Tabernacle, Pasadena, California (1920-1923) and the Holiness Tabernacle, Detroit, Michigan (1928-1932). He became well known as pastor of First Covenant in Minneapolis, Minnesota (1938-1958) and was elected moderator of the Evangelical Covenant Church for 1948. In the broader evangelical world he held many distinguished positions, serving as vice president of World Evangelical Fellowship* (1950-1955) and president of the National Association of Evangelicals* (1952-1954). He was minister to pastors in the Billy Graham* Crusades from 1954 to 1959 and advisor to the World Council of Churches* assembly in New Delhi (1961). For several years he was vice president of World

Vision* (1958-1975) and editor of *World Vision Magazine* (1964-1972). He also served as associate editor of the *Herald* (1955-1975), trustee of Asbury College (1935-1965) and Asbury Theological Seminary (1967-1980). Rees wrote numerous books on devotional* themes, the practical Christian life and Bible exposition and was a well-known evangelical* statesman and evangelist.

E. E. Cairns

Reform Movements. Movements for the spiritual renewal of the church and of its mission. Three periods of reform stand out in American religious history: the early to mid-nineteenth century, dominated by the question of slavery but marked by a host of other reform efforts as well; the late nineteenth and early twentieth centuries, with the Social Gospel* and related responses to the problems of the emerging urban-industrial America; and the decades after World War 2,* with multifaceted efforts for the renewal of the church.

Expressions of deep concern for reform during the seventeenth and eighteenth centuries included the efforts of the Puritan* Michael Wigglesworth* to call his countrymen back to vital faith and life in *God's Controversy with New England* (1662) and of the Quaker* John Woolman* in opposition to slavery. Revival,* in the sense of supernatural outpourings, has marked most of American history. As Jonathan Edwards* noted for the Northampton, Massachusetts, area in the 1730s, for example, such a "surprising work of God" has continued to work remarkable changes in the churches and in society.

Spiritual Revival and Societal Reform. In the nineteenth century, both the Finney revivals and what some have called the Third Great Awakening—the Prayer Meeting Revival* of 1857-1858—effected similar dramatic changes while serving also as an important undergirding for much of the renewal and reform that occurred during the nineteenth century.

Coinciding with the Second Great Awakening* in the early nineteenth century was a remarkable explosion of energies centered on humane causes. Finney and the Oberlin theology* promoted a Christian perfectionism* that extended beyond individual spirituality* to include the social order. Reflecting a belief that society could be changed and an unwillingness to accept the injustices of the existing social order, Americans organized scores of reform societies in areas such as women's rights,* antislavery,* Sabbath* observance, temperance,* peace,* missions* and prison reform.*

The pioneering British and Foreign Bible Society, founded in 1804, became the pattern for hundreds of societies in England and the U.S. In the U.S. such organizations included the American Board of Commissioners for Foreign Missions* (ABCFM) (1810), the American Tract Society* (1825), the American Education Society (1815), the American Bible Society* (1816), the American Sunday School Union* (1817) and the American Society for the Promotion of Temperance (1826).

By the 1830s Charles G. Finney,* the most prominent of the evangelists of that era, was giving energetic support to the efforts of the various societies, including the antislavery movement that came to overshadow all other reform efforts. By 1838, for example, the American Anti-Slavery Society, begun four years earlier in Finney's meetinghouse, claimed 1,350 auxiliaries and 250,000 members. Theodore Dwight Weld,* Arthur and Lewis Tappan* and Joshua Leavitt, with Finney, were a few of the many prominent evangelicals* lending their earnest support.

Important in the overall effort to elevate the life and morals of the young nation was the establishment, between 1815 and 1860, of about 150 colleges (*See* Higher Education, Protestant). And, in the area of foreign missions, the ABCFM sent out nearly 1,000 missionaries before the Civil War.

Urban Poverty and Urban Missions. The decades following the Civil War produced striking changes in American life, including an accelerating shift from a rural-agricultural to an urban-industrial social and economic order. The poverty and related miseries generated by that transition were intensified by a growing tide of immigrants that by 1920 totalled nearly forty million persons, many of whom settled in the already-troubled cities. Only gradually did the nation awaken to the new poverty and its causes.

Among those who responded early were an increasing number of missionaries who entered the slums of virtually every American city with an evangelistic witness that was soon augmented by practical assistance. Hundreds of individual congregations, along with denominational* agencies and nondenominational institutions, programs and organizations, were among the wide-ranging efforts to meet the needs of the poor of the nation's slums.

Among the largest and best-known of the organizations then operating in American cities, and one that in many ways typified the larger movement, was The Salvation Army.* Originating in the evangelistic outreach of William Booth* in the slums of East London during the mid-1860s, The Salvation Army had by the early 1880s begun a worldwide expansion. In 1880 the first official

Salvationist contingent arrived in the U.S.

Entering the slums to evangelize, the Booths and their coworkers responded to the needs of the poor with increasingly extensive efforts to help. Unstructured personal assistance and simple programs mounted until, in 1890, the publication of William Booth's *In Darkest England and the Way Out* signaled the launching of the Army's ambitious "social scheme." In addition to providing food, shelter, clothing, and medical assistance through shelters, soup kitchens, simple dispensaries and other means, the Army supplied vocational training and employment through schools, factories, farms and "farm colonies." Summer excursions and camps as well as holiday "banquets" ministered, meanwhile, to psyche as well as to body. "Antisuicide" bureaus, searches for missing persons, legal aid, prison ministries* and seasonal distribution of low-cost ice and coal further illustrated the diversified and wide-ranging response of Salvationists and other workers in the slums.

During the same years, through the efforts of Jerry McAuley,* S. H. Hadley,* Emma and Sidney Whittemore,* Charles Nelson Crittenton* and others, hundreds of missions and shelters for outcast men and women were opening in American cities. The Water Street and Bowery* missions in New York City and the Pacific Garden Mission* in Chicago, were among the most prominent of an increasing number of rescue institutions that banded together in what by 1913 had become the International Union of Gospel Missions.* Prominent within the larger movement were the Door of Hope, Florence Crittenton and Salvation Army groups of rescue homes for women. The Woman's Christian Temperance Union,* King's Daughters, Convention of Christian Workers, Christian and Missionary Alliance,* the *Christian Herald* magazine, and many other organizations and individual churches supported similar missions and homes.

Significant for social action were the attitudes of gospel welfare workers toward the poor and outcast. In an era when the vulnerable classes were often oppressed, Salvationists and kindred workers were generally characterized by acceptance of and identification with the poor, issuing in vigorous support across a wide range of social issues. The reform journalist William T. Stead wrote of the popular Salvation Army leader Catherine Booth,* for example, that he knew her as "a Socialist and something more . . . in complete revolt against the established order."

Industrial Reality and Social Gospel. The most well-known facet of the response to the developing urban crisis of the late nineteenth century came to be known as the Social Gospel,* the efforts of American church leaders to apply biblical principles to the emerging problems. Increasingly identified with theological liberalism* and marked by moderately progressive social positions, the Social Gospelers advocated brotherhood and cooperation and opposed the dominant laissez-faire individualism* with its unrestrained competition. They saw in the Old Testament prophets' denunciation of injustice, in the life and teachings of Jesus and in the existence and operation of a God of love, the biblical foundations for a new and just social order. That order was to be realized in the kingdom of God,* a kingdom in which God's will would be accomplished as human lives expressed his love across the range of their personal and institutional activities.

With immediate antecedents in the nineteenth century, the Social Gospel began to take shape during the 1870s and 1880s in response to the first of a series of industrial crises, and in the preaching* of a growing number of Protestant* clergy,* including Washington Gladden,* Josiah Strong* and, after 1890, Walter Rauschenbusch,* who became its most effective and influential proponent.

The zenith of the Social Gospel Movement occurred during the years after 1900, with Lyman Abbott,* Charles Henderson, Shailer Mathews,* Charles Stelzle* and others. In addition, a large number of institutional churches* and other organizations arose. Rauschenbusch, who with other young clergymen had formed the Brotherhood of the Kingdom, came into national prominence with his *Christianity and the Social Crisis* (1907) and other writings. The major denominations not only established commissions, but united to form the Federal Council of Churches* (1908), an agency that gave high priority to addressing the pressing social problems of the new era. Although the Social Gospel continued into the 1930s, it was increasingly undermined by a growing isolationist and reactionary national temper, and by the gradual decline of liberal theology in the mainline* churches.

Social Action and Church Renewal in the Late Twentieth Century. The fading of the Social Gospel Movement did not mean the death of its central emphasis on applying Christian principles to social problems and to human need. In the Civil Rights,* anti-war and feminist* movements of recent decades, and in the social stance of the National* and World* councils of churches, some see continuity with the Social Gospel. Evangelicals

have returned, meanwhile, to the social concern and action that had characterized them until at least World War 1.* In both cases the ongoing social Christianity appears to be less marked by utopianism and narrowly industrial concerns and more by social action than was the Social Gospel itself.

The decades following World War 2* constitute a third major era of reform. A phenomenon which in earlier decades was described by such words as revival, awakening and reform, has been, under the rubric "renewal," one of the dominant concerns of the American church during the latter half of the twentieth century.

Some of the components of that concern for change have been: the radical church renewal movement* of the late 1950s and the 1960s; efforts aimed at personal conversion* and renewal that have included both mass evangelism* and efforts to promote personal evangelism; revivals in the sense of outpourings of the Holy Spirit; the Faith at Work movement, with its stress on relational* Christianity; the charismatic* (or neo-Pentecostal) movement; the youth revival or Jesus movement* of the 1960s; the "young evangelicals" with their strong emphasis on the social dimension of the Christian message; efforts for revitalization that have emanated from individual congregations; and the larger evangelical renaissance, to name only some of the most prominent elements.

Because efforts for renewal are as old as the story of God's people, reformers today, as in earlier centuries, have looked to that story for guidelines by which to revitalize the church. For modern evangelicals the primary models have been the early church, the Reformation and the evangelical awakenings of the post-Reformation era. There are significant antecedents in those models for the major emphases of contemporary renewal movements.

Among those emphases are: the centrality of the Bible,* including the priority of obedience; prayer* and the life of devotion*; the experiential dimension of a living faith rooted in a meaningful personal relationship with God that transforms all other relationships; and the Holy Spirit's role without which there can be no authentic renewal of church or society.

Other emphases of recent decades include quantitative church growth*; the role of the laity*; small groups; both mass and personal evangelism; social concern and action, including structural as well as individual reform; and a renewed stress on the life of the mind as a necessity for reaching and renewing contemporary church and society.

See also ABOLITION MOVEMENT; PRISON REFORM; PROHIBITION MOVEMENT; RENEWAL MOVEMENT, PROTESTANT; SOCIAL GOSPEL; TEMPERANCE MOVEMENT; URBAN MISSIONS; WOMEN'S SUFFRAGE MOVEMENT.

BIBLIOGRAPHY. A. Abell, *The Urban Impact on American Protestantism, 1865-1900* (1943); D. W. Dayton, *Discovering an Evangelical Heritage* (1976); C. H. Hopkins, *The Rise of the Social Gospel in American Protestantism, 1865-19115* (1940); R. F. Lovelace, *Dynamics of Spiritual Life: An Evangelical Theology of Renewal* (1979); N. A. Magnuson, *Salvation in the Slums: Evangelical Social Work, 1865-1920* (1977); D. O. Moberg, *The Great Reversal: Evangelism Versus Social Concern* (1972); B. E. Patterson, ed., *The Stirring Giant: Renewal Forces at Work in the Modern Church* (1971); G. M. Rosell, "Charles Grandison Finney and the Rise of the Benevolence Empire" (unpublished Ph.D. dissertation, University of Minnesota, 1971); T. L. Smith, *Revivalism and Social Reform in Mid-Nineteenth-Century America* (1980). N. A. Magnuson

Reformed and Presbyterian Churches. The diverse assortment of Presbyterian and Reformed denominations in the U.S, and Canada all trace their roots to the Calvinist* branch of the Protestant Reformation in the sixteenth century. The choice between Presbyterian and Reformed for purposes of denominational labeling has been mainly a function of geography; the Reformed Christians of the British Isles chose to identify themselves with reference to their presbyterian* system of church government, while the Calvinists of the European continent preferred to signal their commitment to Reformed theology. Immigrants* from those locales brought their denominational names with them to North America. The differences in nomenclature do not themselves signal any important disagreements about thought or practice: all Presbyterian and Reformed churches profess loyalty to both a presbyterian system of governance and a Reformed theological perspective.

It is the church polity* dimension that actually distinguishes the Reformed and Presbyterian denominations from other Christian groups of Calvinist theological persuasion. For example, in early New England there was a broad consensus on Calvinist teaching regarding human sin* and divine election*; Baptists,* Congregationalists* and even many people of Anglican* sympathies found little to disagree with the Presbyterians on such matters. The major arguments among such groups focused on issues of church governance.

The doctrines* that are usually associated most

directly with Calvinism—predestination* and election*—revolve around the twin themes of divine sovereignty and human depravity. God is viewed as possessing an infinite power that can in no way be limited by the choices of human creatures. Furthermore, the sin of the Fall is understood to have rendered humankind totally incapable of producing a desire to love and to serve God. If the salvation of human beings is to occur, then, it must be initiated from the divine side of things—thus the teaching that God freely chooses out of the whole human race those who will be saved by electing them to eternal life and implanting in them the faith to respond to God's saving mercies.

But these Calvinist teachings are not the exclusive property of a specific family of denominations. What is unique to the Reformed and Presbyterian churches is their traditional insistence that the genius of Calvinism is not limited to the teachings associated with predestination and election narrowly conceived. They have insisted that Calvinist soteriology (doctrine of salvation*) is logically linked to a Reformed ecclesiology (doctrine of the church*): divine election is an election to participation in the life and mission of the redeemed people, the church of Jesus Christ. God's sovereignty shows itself not only in the choosing of individuals to eternal life but also in the formation of a covenant community that is called in this earthly life to manifest the sovereign rule of God over all of life. And the way in which this churchly community organizes its life and mission is not a mere question of habit or convenience, to be decided by an appeal to custom or on pragmatic grounds. Reformed-Presbyterian Christians have been intensely interested in questions of "order" in general and "church order" in particular.

Basic to the presbyterian scheme of church governance is the understanding that ecclesial authority* resides primarily in the local presbytery* or consistory. Here the central "ruling" office is that of elder.* The elders are elected by congregational vote, and they in turn send delegations of local officeholders to broader assemblies, usually called presbyteries and general assemblies* by Presbyterians, and classes (plural of classis*) and synods* by the Reformed. Ruling elders supervise the work of the other two main categories of office holders in the local church: ministers of the Word and sacraments* and the deacons.* While all of these officials are chosen by congregational vote, the patterns of authority are not construed along "congregationalist"* lines: the elders, for example, do not receive their authority from the congregation; rather the congregation is called upon to select those whose gifts are best suited for an office, which is viewed as receiving its authority from God. Nor is the authority of the local session or consistory "handed down" from broader judicatories, although longstanding differences of opinion have been sustained within the Reformed-Presbyterian family over the nature and degree of authority possessed by broader (many strongly resist the use of the word *higher*) assemblies.

The two most prominent "feeder" groups for the Reformed and Presbyterian population in North America have been the Dutch and the Scotch/Scotch-Irish (See Scottish Presbyterians). These are, to be sure, by no means the only ethnic sources. The Presbyterian Church in Canada*—which is the present-day continuation of that portion of Canadian Presbyterianism which did not join the United Church of Canada* in 1925—was originally established by French Huguenots.* The German Reformed have also been an important presence, although they have been for the most part absorbed into other bodies, such as the Reformed Church in America* and the United Church of Christ.* Other churches were established by Reformed groups from Hungary, Czechoslovakia and Italy. Racial segregation also produced in the past several distinct African-American denominational bodies.

The oldest Protestant denomination in North America with a continuous history is the one presently known as the Reformed Church in America. Its first congregation was organized in New Amsterdam (New York City) in 1628. The Dutch Reformed churches in the middle colonies remained under the official control of Classis Amsterdam in the Netherlands until the time of the American Revolution,* but the relationship to the mother church was an uneasy one almost from the beginning. For many decades during the eighteenth century, intense controversy was sustained between the *coetus* and the *conferentie* parties. The former group favored a close alliance of American churches relatively free from direct Dutch control, while the latter advocated very close ties to Classis Amsterdam.

The explicit points of difference between these two parties had to do with the training and licensing of clergy* and matters of doctrinal supervision. But these disputes over polity were symptomatic of deeper disagreements, centering on issues of Americanization. The coetus party was much more open to the influences of American revivalism,* as well as to the broader egalitarian spirit of the New World, which challenged the

stricter European standards of clergy education. Questions of church order, then, were manifestations of an intense wrestling with the patterns of cultural accommodation.

Similar disputes occurred in Anglo-American Presbyterian circles in the eighteenth century. The acceptability of the emphases associated with the Great Awakening* led to a longstanding argument between Old Side* and New Side* Presbyterians, with the former resisting the more emotional and less doctrinally stringent emphases of revivalism and the latter advocating openness to these developments. Some of the same issues characterized the debate, which began in the early nineteenth century, between the Old School* and the New School* Presbyterians. The spirit of the New School was shaped by the frontier experience, where many of the intricacies of traditional thought and practice seemed counterproductive for a vital Christianity. The Old School adherents opposed this rise of "enthusiasm," which they viewed as a serious threat to the maintenance of a distinctive Reformed witness in the New World. These controversies were accentuated by the later debate over slavery and by regionalist impulses which were reinforced by the War between the States. The result was a major split in 1861 between the Northern and Southern Presbyterian churches.

A significant division was also experienced by the Dutch Reformed in the nineteenth century. A group of immigrants from the Netherlands, representing a denomination that had split from the main Reformed body in Holland in 1834, arrived in the Midwest in the 1840s; they chose at midcentury to join the existing Reformed denomination. Before a decade had elapsed, however, a portion of these new congregations withdrew from the Reformed Church to form, along with an earlier splinter group in New Jersey, the denomination now known as the Christian Reformed Church.* Some of the major issues at stake in this separation had to do with questions of Americanization (the use of evangelical* hymns,* liturgical* innovations, revivalist themes); but other items of debate also stemmed from older differences about ecclesiology and soteriology that were imported from the Netherlands.

Controversies that were transported from Europe and the British Isles have contributed to a number of the divisions among the Reformed and Presbyterians in North America. Several small Presbyterian denominations, such as the Reformed Presbyterian Church of North America* and the Associate Reformed Presbyterian Church,* are American outposts of Scotch and Scotch-Irish

Presbyterian Churches

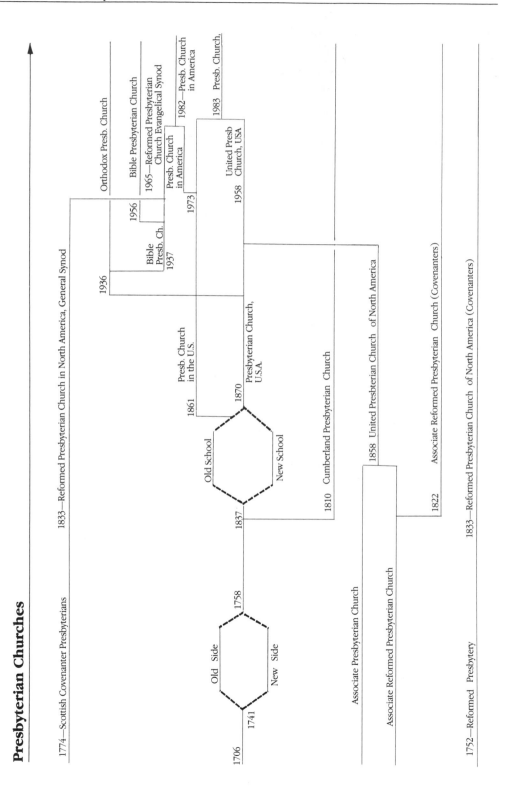

separatist groups (Covenanters and Seceders, respectively). Similar bodies (Netherlands Reformed Churches, Free Reformed Churches, Canadian Reformed Churches) can be found among the Dutch Reformed. But other smaller denominational groups trace their origins to disputes that are more distinctively American. The Cumberland Presbyterian Church,* for example, emerged out of nineteenth-century revivalism in the Southern states; and the Orthodox Presbyterian Church,* along with its offshoot, the Bible Presbyterian Church,* had its origins in a separation from Northern Presbyterianism during the fundamentalist-modernist controversies* of the 1930s.

The second half of the twentieth century has seen some realignment of relationships, especially among Presbyterians. A rather large new denomination was formed when a group of congregations began separating from the Southern church in early 1970, in protest against what were perceived as liberal trends in doctrine and social advocacy. Adopting the name Presbyterian Church in America,* this denomination soon absorbed a number of Northern congregations, as well as the churches belonging to the Reformed Presbyterian Church— Evangelical Synod.

After more than a century of separation, the major Northern and Southern Presbyterian denominations were reunited in June 1983 to form the Presbyterian Church (USA).* This reunited denomination is the largest and most inclusive Reformed-Presbyterian body on the continent, supporting a variety of agencies and an impressive array of theological schools—although it has been experiencing some decline in total membership in recent years.

Most Reformed and Presbyterian groups are also involved in ecumenical* networks. The more mainline* bodies belong to the National* and the World* councils of churches, as well as to the World Alliance of Reformed and Presbyterian Churches.* Many of the more conservative denominations have formed the North American Council of Reformed and Presbyterian Churches, and also belong to the international Reformed Ecumenical Synod. Many discussions that take place within each of these configurations represent a continuing concern over questions that have absorbed the energies of Reformed and Presbyterian Christians from the beginnings of their existence on North American soil.

See also REFORMED TRADITION.

BIBLIOGRAPHY. G. F. DeJong, *The Dutch Reformed Church in the American Colonies* (1978); H. Hageman, *Lily Among the Thorns* (1961); L. A. Loetscher, *The Broadening Church: A Study of Theological Issues in the Presbyterian Church since 1869* (1954); A. C. Piepkorn, *Profiles in Belief: The Religious Bodies of the United States and Canada,* vol. II (1978); A. C. Zenos, *Presbyterianism in America* (1937). R. J. Mouw

Reformed Church in America. The Reformed Church in America has its origin in the formation of a Dutch Reformed congregation on Manhattan Island by Jonas Michaelius* in 1628. The Dutch West India Company, in cooperation with the Reformed Church in the Netherlands, wished to have the spiritual needs of the Dutch settlers served by an ordained* pastor.* Michaelius was followed in time by other pastors as the Dutch settlers moved west into New Jersey, north along the Hudson River to Albany and east into Long Island. Although Dutch settlers virtually ceased coming to America after the Netherlands lost control of New Netherland to the English in 1664, a goodly number of congregations took root in New York and New Jersey.

With the coming of the English, Americanization was inevitable for the Dutch churches as well as for the French and German Reformed congregations which joined the denomination in the later seventeenth and early eighteenth centuries. But the process led to conflict. The churches and pastors were divided between the conferentie, who wished to maintain Dutch ways and remain within the classis of Amsterdam, and the coetus churches, who wished to organize an American body called a "classis"* and educate ministerial recruits in America rather than sending them back to the Netherlands to be educated by the mother church. John H. Livingston,* a promising young minister of the Dutch Church in New York, succeeded in bringing the warring groups together in the Union Convention of 1772.

The American Revolution* and the independence of the thirteen colonies eventually led to the independence of the Dutch Church and their organization into a distinct body in 1792. Livingston took the leadership in this venture as well and also contributed to the establishment in 1784 of a theological seminary* in Brooklyn. In 1810, Livingston moved to New Brunswick, New Jersey, and continued the program of theological education at Queens College,* which had been chartered by coetus* pastors in 1766. In 1856 the seminary at New Brunswick separated from Queens College, which had changed its name to Rutgers College in 1825.

During the eighteenth and nineteenth centuries the Church achieved some strength in New Jersey and New York in spite of ecclesiastical conflicts and a shortage of ministers. Beginning in 1762 in New York, Reformed congregations Americanized to the extent of using English for worship* services. But the failure of the denomination as a whole to join the westward movement in the nineteenth century eventually brought it to a minority status. Although a number of Dutch Reformed people did move to the West and formed congregations in Illinois, Kentucky, Michigan and Wisconsin, the denomination had neither the resources (including a sufficient number of pastors*) nor the will to make decisive moves, and most of these early congregations failed to survive.

But the failure to move west had larger implications. Reformed Christians readily joined the Congregational* and Presbyterian* churches because Reformed congregations were few and far between in the West. Had it not been for the new Dutch migration in the mid nineteenth century, which added many members and new congregations, the old Dutch Reformed Church might have merged with another Reformed denomination by the end of the century and lost its identity. As it was, in 1867 the Dutch Reformed Church dropped the word *Dutch* from its title and began to call itself the Reformed Church in America.

Beginning in 1847 a new surge of Dutch and German Reformed immigrants moved into the Midwest under the leadership of the Reverend Albertus C. Van Raalte and settled in western Michigan. Another group of settlers under the direction of the Reverend Hendrik P. Scholte went to Pella, Iowa. Most of these new settlers had been members of the "Afscheiding," or separatist,* movement, which seceded from the state church of the Netherlands in 1834. Strongly orthodox* and pious, the newcomers immediately formed congregations, and some had already formed congregations in the Netherlands and emigrated *en masse.*

Under Van Raalte's effective leadership, separatists were encouraged to unite with the old Dutch Church in the East. The classis of Holland (Michigan) was accepted into the Dutch Reformed Church in 1850, at a time when the Reformed Church was struggling to move West. This injection of a large number of new Dutch congregations made a profound difference to the future of the denomination. In time, the Western churches were successful in establishing one seminary and three colleges: Western Theological Seminary and Hope College in Holland, Michigan; Central College in Pella, Iowa; and Northwestern College in Orange City, Iowa.

However, the separatist spirit which many Afscheiding settlers brought to America became evident in 1857 when some members showed their dislike of the Union of 1850 by seceding and forming the Christian Reformed Church.* In 1882 a dispute over the issue of allowing Masons to be members of the Reformed Church resulted in a sizeable group leaving the denomination to join the Christian Reformed Church.

This same separatist spirit successfully blocked all merger attempts of the Reformed Church after 1850. The proposed federation with the German Reformed Church in 1892 and the three attempts of the Reformed Church to unite with Presbyterian bodies in the twentieth century failed on the same account. On the other hand, despite resistance of many Midwestern congregations, the Reformed Church in America was a charter member of the Federal Council of Churches* (1908), the World Council of Churches* (1948) and the National Council of Churches (1950).*

A confessional church, since its formal organization in 1792, the denomination has adhered to the Heidelberg Catechism,* the Belgic Confession and the Canons of the Synod of Dort.* Although the denomination holds a conservative, orthodox, Reformed stance, the continual Americanization of the Church shows the effects of other theological trends, such as evangelical liberalism,* fundamentalism* and evangelicalism.* But in spite of the strength of several theological trends contrary to Reformed orthodoxy, only contemporary evangelicalism has made any major impact on the Reformed Church in America. Perhaps surprisingly, the contemporary positive thinking* movement has been most visibly represented by two prominent Reformed ministers, Norman Vincent Peale* and Robert H. Schuller.*

The denomination currently enrolls about 350,000 communicant and baptized members in approximately 950 churches.

See also CHRISTIAN REFORMED CHURCH; IMMIGRATION AND ETHNICITY, PROTESTANT; REFORMED AND PRESBYTERIAN CHURCHES; REFORMED TRADITION IN AMERICA.

BIBLIOGRAPHY. J. D. Bratt, *Dutch Calvinism in Modern America* (1984); A. R. Brouwer, *Reformed Church Roots: Thirty-five Formative Events* (1977); G. F. De Jong, *The Dutch Reformed Church in the American Colonies* (1978); E. M. Eenigenburg, *A Brief History of the Reformed Church in America* (1958); H. Harmelink, III, *Ecumenism and the Reformed Church* (1968).   E. J. Bruins

Reformed Episcopal Church. An evangelical* Episcopal Church organized in 1873 by Bishop

George David Cummins* of Kentucky. In reaction to the influence of the Tractarian Movement* in the Protestant Episcopal Church in the U.S.A.,* evangelical Episcopalians organized a series of protests between 1843 and 1873, beginning with the controversial ordination of A. Carey by Bishop Benjamin T. Onderdonck* and leading up to extended debate on the floor of the 1871 General Convention. Evangelicals clashed with those of Tractarian sympathies over ritual, doctrine and vestments, while calling for a wider Protestant ecumenicity* and greater liberty in the use and meaning of critical passages of the *Book of Common Prayer.* *

These clashes culminated in October 1873 with the public censure of Bishop Cummins by Bishop H. Potter of New York for participating in an ecumenical Communion* service connected with the Evangelical Alliance.* Cummins resigned his office on November 10, 1873, to transfer his episcopate to "another sphere," and organized the Reformed Episcopal Church (REC), with six other clergymen and twenty laymen, on December 2, 1873, for the "purpose of restoring the old paths of their fathers. . . ."

A *Declaration of Principles* (condemning transubstantiation* in the Eucharist,* moral regeneration in baptism* and the exclusive validity of episcopal government*) was issued by Cummins and remains the founding document of the Church. A *Constitution and Canons* and a slightly amended *Book of Common Prayer* were adopted in 1874. By 1876, the REC comprised seven jurisdictions in the U.S. and Canada. It currently has approximately 8,000 members in three synods* and a national missionary* jurisdiction, and is in communion with several other evangelical Anglican* bodies abroad. The orders of the Reformed Episcopal Church have generally been acknowledged as valid by the Episcopal Church.

See also ANGLICAN CHURCHES IN AMERICA; ANGLICANISM.

BIBLIOGRAPHY. B. A. Aycrigg, *Memoirs of the Founding of the Reformed Episcopal Church,* 5th ed. (1880); C. E. Cheney, *What Reformed Episcopalians Believe* (1888); A. C. Guelzo, *The First Thirty Years: A Historical Handbook for the Founding Years of the Reformed Episcopal Church, 1873-1903* (1986).   A. C. Guelzo

Reformed Presbyterian Church, Evangelical Synod.

A conservative denomination existing from 1965 to 1982, the result of a blending of dissenting American Presbyterians (the Bible Presbyterian Church, renamed after 1961 the Evangelical Presbyterian Church) and former Scottish Covenanters (the Reformed Presbyterian Church in North America, General Synod*). The Bible Presbyterian Church (BPC) was a remnant of the 1936 departure of fundamentalists* from the inclusive theological trend within the Presbyterian Church in the U.S.A.* Led by James Oliver Buswell, Jr.,* and Carl McIntire,* the BPC separated, first in 1937 from the Presbyterian Church of America (later the Orthodox Presbyterian Church*). Then in 1955 it split over differences in goals, personalities and autocratic control of agencies.

The Reformed Presbyterian Church in North America, General Synod (RPC, GS) had, by 1965, lost many of its covenanting distinctives, such as exclusive psalmody and nonparticipation in government.

Each denomination maintained a genuine piety,* a testimony against unbelief and a commitment to Reformed* ecumenism.* In order to unite, each had to compromise: the EP gave up its premillennial* amendments to the Westminster* standards and returned to the pre-1903 confessional language. The RPC had already given up the *Reformation Principles Exhibited* in favor of the Westminster standards.

The union of the two denominations in 1965 merged their names, resulting in the Reformed Presbyterian Church, Evangelical Synod (RPC, ES). Feelings of euphoria soon gave way to the challenge of achieving a united Reformed worship* and testimony. The inerrant Bible was central for denominational life, with a subordinate allegiance to the Westminster standards. The RPC, ES stressed national and international missionary efforts. Emphasis was laid on local church autonomy and individual conscience. Higher educational institutions, such as Covenant College and Seminary, were promoted. Widely known men, such as J. Oliver Buswell, Jr., and Francis Schaeffer,* aided the testimony. After seventeen years, the RPC, ES merged with the Presbyterian Church in America* in 1982.

BIBLIOGRAPHY. G. P. Hutchinson, *The History Behind the Reformed Presbyterian Church, Evangelical Synod* (1974); P. R. Gilchrist, *Documents of Synod: Study Papers and Actions of the Reformed Presbyterian Church, Evangelical Synod—1965-1982* (1982).   J. H. Hall

Reformed Presbyterian Church in North America, General Synod.

A Reformed* denomination* with roots in Scottish Presbyterianism* and now absorbed into the Reformed Presbyterian Church, Evangelical Synod.* Although deriving mainly from dissenting Scottish Covenanters coming to America in the 1700s, this denomination officially began in 1833. The Reformed Presbytery, established in 1774, was characterized by exclusive psalm singing, genuine piety* and nonparticipation in any civil government which refused to acknowledge the "crown rights" of Christ.

The nineteenth century began with growth and optimism; but soon after the 1809 formation of the Synod, some leaders began viewing nonparticipation in government (e.g., voting and jury duty) as a hindrance to evangelism.* A division ensued in 1833, in which part of the denomination embraced the government-participation view and were called "new lights." This group adopted the name Reformed Presbyterian Church in North America, General Synod (RPC, GS). The RPC, GS prospered for several decades until a group openly questioned exclusive psalmody. Loss of membership resulted, and the church sought to increase ministerial candidates for seminary by founding Cedarville College in 1894.

The twentieth century was marked by further progress in mission efforts but overall decline in the churches. A growing disinterest among youth, laxity in Sabbath*-keeping and church discipline,* a relinquishing of closed communion and a neglect of tithing contributed to decline. After repeated abortive union efforts, in 1959 the church dropped one of its subordinate standards, *Reformation Principles Exhibited,* and in 1965 united with the Evangelical Presbyterian Church, becoming the Reformed Presbyterian Church, Evangelical Synod.

BIBLIOGRAPHY. R. W. Chesnut, *A Historical Sketch of the Reformed Presbyterian Church, Evangelical Synod* (1945); *Reformation Principles Exhibited* (1807); G. P. Hutchinson, *The History Behind the Reformed Presbyterian Church, Evangelical Synod* (1974).   J. H. Hall

Reformed Tradition in America. The Reformed tradition has played a prominent role within American Christianity and has significantly affected both religious and cultural development in the U.S. Its general principles, such as the Protestant* work ethic* and the sovereignty of God, have helped to shape the American character and ethos; its specific tenets, such as total depravity, limited atonement* and perseverance of the saints, have powerfully influenced American theological understanding. Denominations* and Christian leaders committed to Reformed theology have steadily proclaimed the gospel, labored diligently to develop congregations of dedicated Christians and worked fervently to improve social

conditions in America.

The roots of the Reformed tradition lie in John Calvin's (1509-1564) sixteenth-century Genevan Reformation and secondarily in the work of Theodore Beza (1519-1605), Calvin's successor in Geneva, and Heinrich Bullinger (1504-1575) of Zurich. Calvin's *Institutes of the Christian Religion* (first edition, 1536) expounded the central features of Reformed theology and helped shape its subsequent development. During the sixteenth and seventeenth centuries, Calvinism* spread rapidly among the Swiss, French, Dutch and Germans on the European continent. In the 1550s John Knox (1505-1572) carried Reformed Christianity to Scotland, and in the 1590s Calvinism helped inspire the rise of Puritanism* in England. This broad movement of religious renovation sought to purify the institutional church by reviving New Testament forms of worship* and polity,* teaching Reformed doctrines* and encouraging vital spirituality* among clergy* and laity.* Reformed theological development has been guided by the Heidelberg Catechism (1563), the "Five Points of Calvinism," devised by the Synod of Dort (1619) and especially the Westminster Standards,* which English Puritans framed in the 1640s.

The Reformed Tradition in the New World. Most immigrants to the colonies during the first 150 years following the Puritan settlements at Plymouth and Massachusetts Bay in the 1620s were Reformed Christians from various denominational backgrounds. During these years hundreds of thousands of Dutch, German, Hungarian and Swiss Reformed, as well as French Huguenots,* streamed to the colonies. Different views of church organization divided English Puritans into Congregationalists* and Presbyterians.* These groups, along with Scottish and Scotch-Irish Presbyterians,* came to America in increasing numbers in the years between 1650 and the American Revolution.*

The New England Puritans sought to follow Christ's teachings in their individual lives, founding their congregations on scriptural principles and creating a thoroughly biblical commonwealth for the glory of God. In the Cambridge Platform* of 1640, they adopted the Westminster Standards as their theological basis. The Half-Way Covenant* (1662) was a New England innovation devised to solve a crisis in their religious community. It permitted baptized individuals who had not yet demonstrated clear signs of saving faith (required for church membership*), but had exhibited good behavior, to have their children baptized.* Neither they nor their children, however, were allowed to receive Communion* unless they displayed the marks of conversion.*

The Sunday sermon* was the center of intellectual life in Puritan New England. Preached* in the "plain style," Puritan sermons emphasized theological doctrines, used metaphors from agricultural and artisan life and attempted to apply biblical truth to everyday life. Many Puritan parents taught their children about the Reformed faith by using the Westminster Standards. Contrary to common stereotypes, the Puritans were not glum, cold, stern and repressive. Their marriages were generally caring, compassionate and based on companionship. Many Puritans cultivated a deep and rich experiential piety.* Not without problems, they persecuted dissenters, poorly treated Native Americans, conducted witch trials and incorrectly identified themselves with Old Testament Israel.* Nonetheless, in many ways their individual conduct and social practices were consistent with biblical teachings.

The Reformed Tradition and the Great Awakening. Reformed Christians contributed significantly to the First Great Awakening* of the 1730s and 1740s which helped to stamp evangelical* Christian convictions and mores upon the colonies. Spreading from Georgia to Massachusetts, this revival* flowered especially among three Reformed communities: the Dutch Reformed, Congregationalists and Presbyterians. In New Jersey the ministry of Theodore Frelinghuysen* brought spiritual renewal to many Dutch Reformed. Revival erupted at Northampton, Massachusetts, through the preaching of Congregationalist pastor Jonathan Edwards* and spread from there throughout New England.

Perhaps America's greatest theologian,* Edwards chronicled the activities of the Awakening and defended it as thoroughly biblical. Convinced that human beings did not have the ability to choose Christ as their Savior, he stressed that the Holy Spirit produced conversions and that justification* was by faith alone. His books describing the revival at Northampton, explaining the "distinguishing marks" of a revival and examining religious experience,* set forth a Reformed understanding of these issues. Also important in promoting revival were William Tennent, Sr.,* and his sons, John, William, Jr., and Gilbert,* who along with Jonathan Dickinson* fanned revival fires in Pennsylvania, New Jersey and New York. In the South, the dynamic preaching of Presbyterian pastors like Samuel Davies* of Virginia led to many conversions. The most spectacular aspect of the Awakening was the 1740 preaching tour of the "Grand Itinerant," George Whitefield. Although an ordained* minister* in the Church of England* and friend of the Wesleys,* Whitefield was a committed Calvinist in theology. Thousands of those who came to hear his sermons in New England, New York, Philadelphia, Charleston and Savannah professed faith in Christ.

In the early eighteenth century, Puritan theology had begun to depreciate God's sovereignty and accentuate more strongly human capabilities. Leaders such as Cotton Mather* had sought to revive New England Puritanism through emphasizing broad evangelical piety. The Great Awakening, however, especially the work of Edwards and Whitefield, prompted a resurgence of commitment to and interest in Reformed theology. Edwards's many persuasive and powerful books restated Calvinist conceptions of salvation*—while Whitefield's sermons stressed the role of God's irresistible grace in producing conversion.

At the same time the Awakening caused controversy among Reformed Christians. Conflict between Old Lights* who opposed revival because of its socially disruptive effects, New Lights* who supported revival and renewed evangelical zeal, and Old Calvinists who were caught in the middle, destroyed the Puritan synthesis of theology and spirituality. Dispute over revivalism produced temporary schisms among both Presbyterians and the Dutch Reformed in the mid-eighteenth century.

Reformed Denominations in the Eighteenth Century. Most Reformed denominations grew rapidly during the eighteenth century. Extensive immigration of Scotch-Irish increased the number and vitality of Presbyterians who settled primarily in the Middle Colonies. In the Adopting Act* of 1729 Presbyterians declared the Westminster Standards to be the theological basis of their denomination. By 1788, when Presbyterians established the General Assembly,* their communion consisted of at least 220 congregations organized in sixteen presbyteries,* served by about 180 ministers.

From its founding in America in 1706, the Presbyterian Church embraced two traditions: on the one hand the Scotch-Irish and Scottish desired precise theological formulations and orderly church government,* while the English and Welsh emphasized religious experience and adaptability. Twice the dialectical tension between these two elements produced schisms in the denomination—in the Old Side*/New Side* division of 1741-1758 and the Old School*/New School* division of 1837-1869. Yet most of the time the communion was able to hold together those committed to Pietist revivalism and those devoted to doctrinalist confessionalism.*

Leaders of the German Reformed Church met in 1747 in Philadelphia and adopted the Heidelberg Catechism* as the doctrinal standard of their denomination. By 1791 the church had about 178 congregations scattered between New York City and Virginia. Throughout the eighteenth century most Baptists* were committed to Reformed theology, especially because of the influence of the Philadelphia Baptist Confession of Faith (1742), a modified version of the Westminster Confession adopted by the Philadelphia Baptist Associaton.* During the 1700s Congregationalists, the Reformed Church of America* and two bodies with roots in Scotland—Reformed Presbyterians* and Associate Reformed Presbyterians*—also increased in size and influence.

The Reformed Tradition and the American Revolution. The teachings of the Reformed tradition helped to inspire the American Revolution, and many proponents of Reformed theology supported the Patriot cause. While Revolutionary leaders generally did not appeal directly to the Scriptures or to their religious heritage to justify their revolt against England, Reformed convictions about covenants, history, human nature and the connection between freedom and virtue, helped to reinforce Whig arguments. Moreover, Presbyterian and Congregationalist clergy—especially Ezra Stiles*—led efforts to keep an Anglican bishop out of the colonies. Numerous Reformed clergymen urged the colonists to sever their ties with England, described as the great Babylonian Whore of the book of Revelation, so they could proclaim the light and liberty of the gospel to the world more effectively.

In the years following the Revolutionary War, the complexion and character of American Christianity changed markedly. While Reformed tenets about human nature helped to shape important features of the new nation's Constitution, such as the separation and balance of powers, America became much more pluralistic* denominationally and theologically. During the early national period Baptists and Methodists* grew much more rapidly than did Anglicans, Presbyterians and Congregationalists, who had dominated American religion during the colonial days. Revolt against Calvinism was widespread in the republican environment of the first half of the nineteenth century. Reformed commitments to the doctrines of total depravity, unconditional election,* limited atonement, irresistible grace and perseverance of the saints* has seemed to many Americans to deny human freedom and responsibility and contradict America's democratic* principles. In 1776 about eighty-five per cent of the colonists were affiliated with Reformed denominations; by 1850 seventy per cent of Protestant church members were Baptists or Methodists.

The Reformed Tradition and the Second Awakening. Despite the changing religious environments, Reformed leaders such as President Timothy Dwight* of Yale,* Congregational evangelist Asahel Nettleton* and Lyman Beecher,* the primary architect of the "benevolent empire," helped inspire and direct the Second Great Awakening* of the 1820s and 1830s. But the predominant theology of this Awakening, as it was proclaimed by revivalist Charles G. Finney,* who was first a Presbyterian and later a Congregationalist, was more Arminian* than Calvinist in nature. Stressing the individual's right and ability to choose salvation, Finney promoted his "new measures"*— techniques to be properly applied to sinners rather than awaiting what Calvinists regarded as God's sovereign and surprising work in conversion. Employing the tactics of a trial lawyer, Finney sought to convince sinners of their need of salvation. To foster conversions he introduced an anxious bench (*See* Mourner's Bench) at the front of the sanctuary, community-wide revival campaigns which lasted several weeks and the use of teams to visit people in their homes. From 1801 to 1837 Congregationalists and Presbyterians operating under a Plan of Union* joined their forces in Western expansion. These two Reformed denominations supplied most of the leaders of the numerous societies the Awakening inspired to abolish slavery* and promote temperance,* peace, missions,* education, penal reform and many other good causes.

During the mid-nineteenth century controversy erupted once again, especially among Presbyterians and Congregationalists, over the proper understanding of Reformed theology. Arguing that Calvinism was paralyzing evangelism, Nathaniel W. Taylor,* professor of theology at Yale Divinity School, softened the traditional emphasis on total depravity and stressed humanity's free moral agency. Many Congregationalists and some Presbyterians accepted his New Haven Theology.* Building on Taylor, Finney argued that individuals had the power to choose salvation, avoid all evil acts and achieve "entire sanctification."* Old School* Presbyterian theologian Charles Hodge* and German Reformed church historian Philip Schaff* spoke for the opponents of New Haven Theology. Taylor's claim that people became sinful only by their own sinful acts, Hodge contended, contradicted the biblical teaching that all persons were born with original sin. Schaff, as a representative of the Mercersburg Theology,* criticized Taylorism for focusing too little on the objective work of Christ in redemption and too much on people's own subjective experience. In 1837 the theological dispute over New Haven Theology contributed to the dissolution of the Congregationalist-Presbyterian Plan of Union and to the division of the Presbyterian Church in the U.S.A.* (PC-USA), the largest American Presbyterian body, into two groups—the Old School and New Schools.

From the Civil War* to World War 1* evangelical Protestant institutions flourished in America, despite intensifying secularization* and the increasing religious diversity caused by the arrival of many Catholic* and Jewish immigrants.* During these years evangelical Protestants continued to use interdenominational voluntary organizations* to promote missions and evangelism, distribute Bibles* and tracts,* wage moral crusades and improve social conditions. Reformed Christians still played a major, but no longer the leading, role in such enterprises. By 1930 commitment to Reformed orthodoxy* and the influence of its theological tenets had reached an ebb in America.

The Rise of Four Reformed Schools, 1850-1930. While adherence to the Reformed faith declined between 1850 and 1930, four Reformed schools or emphases took shape during these years that are still influential within American Christianity today. First, and probably most important, was the Princeton Theology* of Archibald Alexander,* Charles Hodge, A. A. Hodge* and B. B. Warfield.* Their teaching at Princeton Theological Seminary, their many books and pamphlets on diverse topics, their periodical articles and their ministry within the PC-USA significantly influenced the views of the Reformed community and, to a lesser degree, evangelical Protestantism in America. Issues such as biblical inspiration, the nature of religious experience and the work of the Holy Spirit were substantially shaped by Princeton Theology.

Dutch Calvinists in the Reformed Church of America* (RCA) and the Christian Reformed Church* (CRC) comprise a second Reformed school. In general, Dutch Calvinists in America have emphasized strict adherence to the Reformed confessions and the lordship of Christ over all of life. In addition, they have sought to establish Christian institutions which can serve as positive biblical models of love and righteousness in society. While the Eastern branch of the RCA has been less distinctly Reformed and more involved

in broad American Protestant crusades, the CRC and the Western branch of the RCA have been more confessionally conscious. During the last one hundred years Dutch Calvinists in America have debated the nature of Christian piety, the proper Christian approach to the world and the teachings of the Neo-Calvinist revival in the Netherlands led by Abraham Kuyper* and Herman Dooyeweerd.*

A third discernable Reformed school is the Southern tradition. The Reformed faith was planted in the South during the colonial period by both Presbyterians and Baptists. In the early nineteenth century two groups—the Cumberland Presbyterians* and the Restoration Movement*—broke away from the Southern Presbyterians. Remaining essentially Old School in character during the nineteenth century, Southern Presbyterians guided by theologians James H. Thornwell* and Robert L. Dabney* subscribed strictly to the Westminster Standards. In 1861 Southern members left the Old School of the PC-USA, forming the Presbyterian Church in the United States. Prior to World War 2* members of this denomination remained strongly committed to orthodox Calvinism, but in the postwar era a drift toward liberalism was detected by many conservatives within the denomination. Finally, in 1973 about 100,000 Southern Presbyterians left their denomination to form the Presbyterian Church in America.*

The fourth and final Reformed emphasis is the Westminster School. Arising in the midst of the fundamentalist-modernist controversy of the 1920s and proposing to continue the Old School Presbyterian tradition of Princeton Theological Seminary, this school became centered at Westminster Theological Seminary in Philadelphia. In 1936 its chief proponent, J. Gresham Machen,* organized the Orthodox Presbyterian Church,* claiming the PC-USA had departed from historic Calvinism.

Reformed themes such as God's sovereignty, human sinfulness, salvation by grace, the significance of Scripture and the centrality of Christ are evident in the neo-orthodoxy* espoused by Reinhold Niebuhr,* H. Richard Niebuhr* and other theologians, pastors and denominational leaders of the post-World War 2 era. Neo-orthodoxy's use of Reformed theology, however, was highly selective.

The Continuing Legacy. There are today eighteen Presbyterian, Reformed and Congregationalist denominations in America with a combined membership of about six million. Substantial numbers of Episcopalians,* Baptists and members of independent churches also espouse Reformed theological convictions. In addition, the influence of the Reformed tradition is strong within the evangelical community because of the role Reformed and Reformed-oriented seminaries (most notably Calvin, Westminster, Biblical, Covenant, Reformed, Gordon-Conwell, Trinity and Fuller*) have played in training evangelical leaders, as well as the influence of Reformed presses, periodicals and publications. While most contemporary American evangelicals reject Calvinist understandings of grace and salvation, many of them agree with the Reformed tradition's emphasis on experiential piety, its defense of biblical authority and inspiration and its commitment to transform culture.

From the founding of Plymouth to the present day, the Reformed tradition has strongly influenced American attitudes toward human nature, humanity's relationship with God, the authority of the Bible and engagement with culture, especially work. By championing the sovereignty and holiness of God, stressing the divine initiative in salvation, denouncing human pride and autonomy and exalting God's absolute standards for nations and individuals, Calvinists have done much to promote biblical Christianity in the U.S.

BIBLIOGRAPHY. F. Hood, *Reformed America; The Middle and Southern States, 1783-1837* (1980); B. Kuklick, *Churchman and Philosophers; From Jonathan Edwards to John Dewey* (1985); L. Loetscher, *The Broadening Church: A Study of Theological Issues in American Presbyterianism since 1869* (1957); G. Marsden, *The Evangelical Mind and the New School Presbyterian Experience* (1970); P. Miller, *Errand into the Wilderness* (1956); L. Ryken, *Worldly Saints: The Puritans As They Really Were* (1986); G. S. Smith. *The Seeds of Secularization: Calvinism, Culture and Pluralism in America, 1870-1915* (1985); E. T. Thompson, *Presbyterians in the South,* 3 vols. (1963); D. F. Wells, ed., *The Reformed Tradition in America* (1985).   G. S. Smith

Reforming Synod (1679). A meeting of Massachusetts clergy* to define and offer solutions to religious declension. By 1679 the elders* of Massachusetts Bay were convinced that contention, pride and a "dying interest in religion" had provoked the Lord to bring his judgments on New England. Citing King Phillip's War* and other difficulties besetting New England society, Increase Mather* called on the elders to assemble a formal synod* to identify the offenses that had angered God and to consider methods of reforming New England. In the published *Result* of the synod, the ministers* condemned lay* people and clergymen* alike for a number of failures and

misdemeanors, including apostasy, contention in the churches, Sabbath*-breaking, swearing and extravagance in apparel. The elders suggested that New England might yet prosper and retain its unique status as God's chosen land, but only if its people reformed their behavior and rededicated themselves to the cause of God and salvation.* To that end the ministers recommended that churches renew their covenants,* increase moral supervision and refamiliarize the laity with the Cambridge Platform* of church government,* a program of reform that most churches apparently followed.

BIBLIOGRAPHY. W. Walker, *The Creeds and Platforms of Congregationalism* (1960); P. Miller, *The New England Mind: From Colony to Province* (1953).   J. F. Cooper

Regeneration. The Bible uses terms like *new birth,** *being born again,** *being a new creature* and *having a renewed mind* to describe the process of spiritual renovation whereby the image of God is restored within fallen people who have become Christians. Thus *regeneration, renovation* and *conversion** are often used as synonyms in the Protestant tradition. Calvin, for example, used *regeneration* to describe the whole inner dimension of salvation,* from conversion through sanctification.* John Wesley* described it as "that great change which God works in the soul by the Holy Spirit" and linked regeneration directly to sanctification. While Christians generally agree on what regeneration ultimately implies, they tend to disagree over how it takes place.

Reflecting the New Testament conjunction of "the washing of rebirth" with "renewal by the Holy Spirit" (Tit 3:5), the Church Fathers and the Catholic* tradition have associated regeneration with the sacrament* of Christian baptism.* Protestants,* on the other hand, typically identify regeneration as the inward renewal beginning with justification* by faith and continuing through the process of sanctification. Thus some Protestants would understand regeneration to be anticipated in the sacramental life of the church and manifested through the work of the church as a nurturing body, while maintaining that it is ultimately connected with conversion under the impact of the Word and Spirit of God.

In America a tension arose between a sacramental, or nurturing, concept of regeneration on the one hand and a voluntaristic* experience of conversion and regeneration on the other. While the early Puritans* emphasized the importance of a personal experience of regeneration and maintained the necessity of the elect showing evidence of regeneration as a condition for joining the body of visible saints as church members,* the Half-Way Covenant* (1662) admitted the children of moral and church-going unregenerate individuals to be baptized. Yet baptism and Christian nurture did not necessarily lead to regeneration, and churches were increasingly filled with unregenerate professing Christians. Alternatives were offered by Boston's Brattle Street Church (1699), which gave full membership to those professing Christian belief and Northampton's Solomon Stoddard,* who redefined the Lord's Supper* as a "converting ordinance" open to all who professed faith, and then preached for revival.*

The Great Awakening* forced those within the Puritan tradition to reconcile experiences of revivalism* with Calvinistic* theology.* One result was the hybrid theology of Samuel Hopkins* which distinguished between regeneration and conversion, thus moderating older Calvinism with an element of human volition. In Hopkins's system the idea of original sin was virtually eliminated, and regeneration referred to an "imperceptible and sovereign work of the Holy Spirit" which creates in one's mind a "hungering and thirsting after righteousness," while the human will remains passive. Conversion, on the other hand, described the exercise of the human will in "turning from sin to God" by embracing the gospel.

Revivalism profoundly shaped Protestant concepts of regeneraton by emphasizing individual personal religious experience over baptism and the nurturing community. Through the revivals *conversion,* or a *personal decision for Christ,* became synonyms for *regeneration.* In the process the sovereign and imperceptible work of the Spirit tended to be supplanted by the voluntaristic work of the human will. The biography of Methodist* evangelist* Peter Cartwright,* for example, chronicles the wave of spiritual excitement, instantaneous conversions and outward manifestations that occurred at camp meetings* under the impact of "vehement" preaching.* Alexander Campbell* distinguished regeneration from conversion. Regeneration was a "change of state" and conversion a "change of life," and both were incorporated into a four-step process of salvation. Charles G. Finney* viewed regeneration as a "baptism of the Holy Spirit"* voluntarily received and marking the beginning of a transition from "entire sinfulness to entire holiness."

Revivalism also engendered reactions like Horace Bushnell's* *Christian Nurture* (1847), which rejected the notion of instantaneous conversion in favor of the process of regeneration, emphasizing the spiritual formation of Christian children. While traditional Protestants like Presbyterian* Charles Hodge* or Methodist John Miley* set regeneration within the larger context of their respective soteriologies, Walter Rauschenbush* countered an individualized conception of regeneration by connecting it with his aim of bringing the transforming power of the kingdom of God* to bear on the evils of an industrialized society: "If we are regenerated, does the scope of so divine a transformation end in our 'going to heaven'? The nexus between our religious experience and humanity seems gone when the Kingdom of God is not present in the idea of regeneration."

Regeneration has played a central role in the message of popular urban evangelists since the Civil War.* Dwight L. Moody* emphasized "the three R's": "ruin by sin, redemption by Christ, regeneration by the Holy Spirit" and looked for instantaneous conversions. He was criticized for using *conversion* and *regeneration* as synonymous terms. R. A. Torrey* refined Moody's approach, insisting that baptism was not the new birth and distinguishing between conversion, regeneration and baptism with the Spirit. For him conversion referred to the outward state of restoration, regeneration to the new life entering the inner person, and baptism with the Spirit a subsequent event bringing the "gifts of the Spirit" and empowerment for Christian service. In recent decades Billy Graham* has often spoken of *being born again* as synonymous with *receiving Christ, being converted* or *making a decision for Christ.* Graham's *How to Be Born Again* (1977) uses *regeneration* and *conversion* as synonyms for describing the presence of Christ or the Holy Spirit in the motivational center of a person, and makes no reference to baptism or the role of the church in that transformation.

See also BORN AGAIN; CONVERSION; NEW BIRTH; SALVATION.

BIBLIOGRAPHY. H. Burkhardt, *The Biblical Doctrine of Regeneration* (1978); E. W. Gritsch, *Born Againism: Perspectives on a Movement* (1982); B. Graham, *How to Be Born Again* (1977); P. Toon, *Born Again* (1987). J. R. Tyson

Regions Beyond Missionary Union. *See* RBMU INTERNATIONAL.

Regular Baptists. Calvinistic* Baptists* opposed to the emotionalism and evangelistic* invitations of the Great Awakening.* In contrast to revivalistic Separate Baptists,* Regular Baptists were more urbane and more orderly in worship,* supported educated and salaried ministers, and discouraged women from ministering publicly. Initially strongest in the Middle Colonies, they were influenced by the Philadelphia Association* (1707), from which itinerant preachers planted churches in Virginia (1740s), North Carolina (1750s), Georgia (1770s) and on the Kentucky-Tennessee frontier (1780s). Also influential were Charleston (1751), Warren (1767), and Kehuckee* (1769) associations.

During the late eighteenth century, a campaign by the Philadelphia and the Warren associations to win General Baptists* over to Calvinism resulted in the "reformation" of most General ministers and churches, but most of the members did not follow. Simultaneously, Free-Will Baptists* became influential. Reacting to the Arminianism* of the Free-Will Baptists, Separates moved closer to the Regulars' Calvinism, which, in turn, Free-Will pressure softened. By 1800 most Regulars and Separates had merged on the basis of the Philadelphia Confession (1742).

Today Regular Baptists comprise a cultural-religious movement that preserves rural folkways through monthly worship, plaintive singing, sing-song preaching, community gatherings and annual association fellowship. They include Old Regular Baptists, mainly of Appalachia (1980: 19,770 members, 366 churches); United Baptists, found from Kentucky through Missouri (1980: 53,665 members, 517 churches); and the General Association of (Duck River) Baptists in Alabama, Tennessee, Georgia and Mississippi (1986: 10,579 members, 81 churches).

BIBLIOGRAPHY. W. L. Lumpkin, *Baptist Foundations in the South* (1961); H. L. McBeth, *The Baptist Heritage* (1987).   J. T. Spivey

Relation. *See* CONVERSION NARRATIVE.

Relational Theology. A recent, largely American theology* stressing the centrality of interpersonal relationships. Unlike traditional orthodoxy,* which emphasizes God's great transactions for mankind, such as the Incarnation, the Cross and the Resurrection, relational theology places emphasis on persons and the quality of their relationships in family, church, community and work.

Pioneers in relational theology were Leslie Weatherhead, Harry Emerson Fosdick* (especially his *On Being a Real Person,* 1943), Samuel Shoemaker* and Norman Vincent Peale.* Numbers of American evangelicals adopted the emphasis in the 1970s. The books of Keith Miller, Bruce Larson, Karl Olsson and Eugenia Price reflect the use of

Scripture* for purposes of personal insight and "healing" of interpersonal relations.

The center of the dissemination of the theology was a movement called Faith at Work, which published a magazine by the same name. Other institutions, however, reflected similar teachings and methods, including Laity Lodge Retreat Center in Texas, and the youth movement called Young Life.*

One of the primary goals of relational theology was to preach, teach, and conduct the life of the local church—or the youth club—so that Christian truth could actually and materially help Christians become better persons who could relate well to other people. The emphases of the movement reflected the impact of psychology,* especially the theory and practice of small groups.

BIBLIOGRAPHY. B. Ramm, "Is It Safe to Shift to 'Interpersonal Theology'?" *Eternity* (December 1972):21-22; B. Peterson and S. Board, "Unmasking: An Interview with Walden Howard," *Eternity* (August 1977):10-15.   B. L. Shelley

Religionless Christianity. In the 1920s Karl Barth* revolted against liberal* theology* and the concept of "religion" which tried to base theology on something "religious" in the human heart. The term *religionless Christianity,* however, is most closely associated with Dietrich Bonhoeffer* and his *Letters and Papers from Prison* (1953; enlarged, 1971). Bonhoeffer rejected "religion" which separated the sacred and secular spheres to promote an "other-worldliness" attitude. Instead he called for a "worldly holiness" that was eminently practical. Bonhoeffer criticized a religion that appealed to a "God of the gaps" to explain what humans cannot. Instead, he argued that we live in a "world come of age" where humanity must take responsibility for its own actions. The challenge of religionless Christianity is to live "as if God himself were not given." The living God who calls for this is the God who suffered and was rejected by the world in Jesus Christ. In the 1960s some theologians used Bonhoeffer's phrase to construct secular theologies that focused strongly on the present world.

BIBLIOGRAPHY. E. Bethge, *Dietrich Bonhoeffer* (1970); T. J. J. Altizer and W. Hamilton, *Radical Theology and the Death of God* (1966); J. A. T. Robinson, *Honest to God* (1963).

D. K. McKim

Religious Education. *See* EDUCATION, CHRISTIAN.

Religious Experience. The concern for religious

experience, for some personal or communal encounter with the Divine, has been an important element of American religion from the beginning. Generations of immigrants brought with them diverse beliefs and practices regarding right relationship with God. Churches,* denominations,* sects,* cults* and other religious groups promoted religious experiences as diverse as dramatic conversions* at camp meetings* and revivals,* the *glossolalia* (speaking in tongues*) of the charismatics,* the silent worship* of the Quakers,* the stately liturgy* of Catholics* and Episcopalians* and the ecstatic chants of the Hare Krishnas. These and other approaches to religious experience reflect the pluralism* of American religion itself. Religious liberty meant that each group was free to promote and search for genuine religious experience uninhibited by interference from the state. Religious experience introduced persons to faith and helped them sustain a continuing communication with the Divine. In America, the quest for experience with God takes many forms.

Evangelical Conversionism. Evangelical conversionism represents one of the most prominent interpretations of religious experience evident in American life. Evangelical Christians insist that every individual must have a personal experience of God's saving grace in order to claim Christian faith and membership* in the church. The need for conversion* is a powerful theme among American Protestants,* from colonial Puritans* to contemporary Pentecostals.* Evangelical preachers from John Cotton and Jonathan Edwards* to Billy Graham* insist that religious experience begins when the sinner is "saved" or "born again,"* thereby turning from sin* and receiving Christ as Savior. Conversion, therefore, is the central religious experience by which the sinner enters into a life of Christian commitment.

While evangelicals agree on the need for conversion, they often differ on the process by which such religious experience occurs. Many colonial evangelicals reflected a more Calvinistic* approach to religious experience based on divine initiative, usually involving a lengthy process of spiritual travail. Salvation originated solely with God who brought grace to those who were predestined* to salvation before the foundation of the world. The salvation process itself involved an awakening to God's commands and a futile attempt to fulfill them "in the flesh." Then came a profound sorrow for sin and the recognition that Christ alone could bring salvation. Finally, the gift of God's irresistible grace was infused in the sinner by the power of the Holy Spirit.

Converts were required to testify publicly through a conversion narrative* to such an experience in order to gain membership in the church. This powerful religious experience was the beginning of a lifelong relationship with God enhanced by prayer,* Bible study,* worship and Christian living. The ability to sustain religious devotion* was evidence of the validity of the conversion experience. Such experiences often characterized religious awakenings and revivals in which large numbers of persons were converted. Debates over revival methods and the role of "religious affections" (emotions) in conversion created frequent controversy and schism among evangelical denominations such as the Presbyterians,* Congregationalists* and Baptists.*

During the nineteenth century, evangelicals continued to proclaim the need for conversion but shortened the process considerably by placing greater stress on individual free will and immediate experience of divine grace. The frontier revival or camp meeting was often the scene of dramatic conversions and various emotional "exercises," including uncontrollable shaking, shouting, running, falling and laughing. Evangelists Charles G. Finney,* Dwight L. Moody,* Billy Sunday* and others contributed to the effort to systematize the conversion experience into specific plans and procedures which might be communicated effectively to mass audiences as well as individuals.

Moody, one of the greatest American evangelists, frequently described religious experience as beginning with "instantaneous regeneration" when the sinner responded freely and immediately to God's grace. Through an act of free will, sinners could instantly receive salvation. Revivals, therefore, became important occasions for proclaiming the gospel and experiencing conversion. Evangelical conversionism continues to be a formative religious experience for many Christian groups in America.

Holiness Perfectionism. For most American evangelicals, however, religious experience does not end with justification* and the initial stage of Christian faith. It continues in sanctification,* the daily growth in Christian faith and holiness. Through this type of religious experience the individual matures as a disciple of Christ in renewed relationship with God. These experiences range from simple prayer and Bible study to ecstatic charismatic events and glossolalia. The holiness movements,* for example, illustrate various ways in which certain groups sought to answer the question, What do you do after conversion? The pursuit of holiness invoked continued confession of sin,* prayer, Bible study and baptism of the Holy Spirit* by which the believer was empowered for holy living. Holiness, or gospel "perfection," generally meant that the individual Christian sought to live in the Spirit, thereby avoiding sin for extended periods of time. Such perfectionism was closely related to the Wesleyan tradition,* as well as the teachings of Charles G. Finney, Phoebe Palmer* and other nineteenth-century Holiness preachers. Palmer was a leading proponent of the Spirit-filled life. Her "meetings for holiness" encouraged continued confession of sin and the experience of a "second blessing"* beyond conversion, by which the individual was sanctified for Christian living.

By the twentieth century, some Christian groups increasingly identified the baptism of the Holy Spirit with an experience of *glossolalia,* or speaking in tongues. The Pentecostal Movement in America began in the early 1900s as individuals seeking holiness came to identify *glossolalia* as primary evidence of the Spirit's baptism and, therefore, a necessary religious experience for all Christian believers. Today, many churches within the Holiness Movement (Free Methodists,* Church of the Nazarene*) remain divided from Pentecostal groups (Assemblies of God;* Church of God,* Cleveland, Tennessee) over the issue of *glossolalia* as a necessary manifestation of the Spirit's baptism. More recently, the charismatic movement* has extended the experience of the baptism of the Spirit, speaking in tongues and other spiritual gifts into the ranks of most contemporary American denominations.

Liturgical Spirituality. Another important expression of religious experience in America is evident in the liturgical* spirituality of certain Christian communions. Lutherans,* Episcopalians, Roman Catholics and others within the liturgical tradition suggest that experience with God is nurtured by the worshiping community of the church. Religious experience for the individual is closely bound to the community of faith. Through baptism, Communion and other sacramental* events, the individual is nurtured into faith and experience with God. Worship is therefore a central element in religious experience. In worship, the church declares and depicts the drama of redemption as it celebrates the Christian year in Advent,* Christmas,* Lent,* Easter,* Pentecost and the continuing life of the people of God. In Word and sacrament Christians continually experience the presence of God within the communion of saints.* Conversion is less a single dramatic event than a life of sacramental nurture into grace.

The Mercersburg Movement* of the mid nineteenth century represents one important reassertion of liturgical spirituality in American Christianity. Mercersburg Theological Seminary in Pennsylvania became a center of liturgical renewal in the German Reformed tradition. John Williamson Nevin,* a professor at the seminary, wrote extensively on the subject, calling American Christians to rediscover religious diversity and liturgical richness in the church's history. Nevin reaffirmed the importance of the sacraments as vehicles of religious experience. Through sacramental renewal he sought to counteract the excessive subjectivism of the evangelical revivalism. Liturgical spirituality recognizes the ancient traditions of the church and the communal nature of religious experience.

Mystical Encounter. Mysticism* represents another form of religious experience which transcends American denominational divisions. Mystics—those who cultivate direct, intense encounter with God—appear in all American religious communions. Mystics often move beyond doctrinal and ecclesiastical distinctions in the quest for intimate experience with the Divine. Such representatives of the mystical life might include the Puritan preacher Jonathan Edwards, the enlightened transcendentalist Ralph Waldo Emerson,* the Quaker teacher Rufus Jones* and the Trappist* monk Thomas Merton.* Mystical experience, or "the practice of the presence of God," often follows a "threefold path" involving awakening to sin, purification of self and union with God. Through prayer and meditation the mystic seeks continued unity with Christ and experience of the divine life. Mystics occupy a minority role in much of American history, but they also reveal valuable lessons regarding contemplation and reflection in religious experience.

New Religions. Recently, diverse forms of religious experience have become more prominent in American life through the so-called New Religions. Some groups stand outside the Judeo-Christian tradition and reflect the influence of other great world religions. Their "newness" is in terms of their growth and impact on American religious life. These include the worship communitarian practices evident in Krishna Consciousness (Hare Krishna), a sect of Hinduism, and the eclectic theology of the Baha'i—whose members claim to combine the best of all world religions. Other groups such as Scientology or EST promote a religious experience which shows the impact of secular theories of group dynamics. The influence of these groups further illustrates the diversity of religious experience in the pluralistic environment of American society.

BIBLIOGRAPHY. N. Pettit, *The Heart Prepared: Grace and Conversion in Puritan Spiritual Life* (1966); W. James, *The Varieties of Religious Experience* (1902); J. Needleman and G. Baker, *Understanding the New Religions* (1978).

B. J. Leonard

Religious Freedom. The alleged reason for many to leave the Old World and come to the New World was to find freedom from established religion. There is evidence that Puritans* left England, Moravians* left Germany and Baptists* left Sweden to attain the goal of religious freedom. However, except for Rhode Island, Maryland and Pennsylvania, established religion was the rule in the colonies, and severe intolerance was shown to Baptists,* Quakers* and Roman Catholics*; all citizens, regardless of their religious convictions, were required to pay church taxes. The Revolutionary War* called for the broadest consensus possible, and with it came a movement toward the disestablishment of religion. Viriginia's state constitution (1776) was the first to mandate religious freedom, and it became a model for the Federal Constitution. The First Amendment* to the Constitution provided the legal means, however, for every citizen to be free of state interference in the practice of personal religious beliefs.

The First Amendment protects the citizenry against any attempt by the government to establish a particular religion. It also guarantees all citizens the "free exercise" of their religious beliefs. Taken together, both aspects promote the voluntary* and pluralistic* nature of religious freedom in America. Any proposal to promote the establishment of any particular religion or Judaeo-Christian* religious synthesis is antithetical to the First Amendment and its protection of pluralism.

See also FIRST AMENDMENT; CHURCH AND STATE, SEPARATION OF; PLURALISM, RELIGIOUS.

BIBLIOGRAPHY. W. S. Hudson, *The Great Tradition of the American Churches* (1953); M. D. Howe, *The Garden and the Wilderness: Religion and Government in American Constitutional History* (1965).

J. E. Johnson

Religious Liberty. *See* RELIGIOUS FREEDOM.

Religious Orders, Catholic Men's. "Religious order" is a term often loosely used in reference to groups of men or women, usually Roman Catho- lic,* committed to a particular religious life. The Catholic Church, however, makes a distinction between religious orders and religious congregations.* The religious life for both orders and congregations is constituted by the traditional vows of poverty, chastity and obedience. The canonical distinction between orders and congregations mainly deals with the ease with which the vows may be dispensed with and the right of members of congregations to retain ownership, but not the use, of private property. Religious orders require the taking of solemn vows, and religious congregations require only simple vows. With minor exceptions, after a year or two of novitiate or spiritual training, the new members of both orders and congregations take temporary vows (for example, for three years) and then later permanent or perpetual vows. Religious, or members of a religious order, are those who have taken the three vows which incorporate them into a religious order. The orders tend to be older and larger than the congregations.

The earliest members of a religious order in the Americas were the Franciscans* who accompanied Columbus.* Jesuits* were among the earliest explorers of the Midwest and Southwest. The Franciscan missionaries in California named most of the places which would later become the state's largest cities. Catholics were distinctly unwelcome in most of the English colonies, but Jesuits ministered to early Catholic settlers in Maryland. Emigration from Catholic countries in the nineteenth century (*See* Immigration and Ethnicity, Roman Catholic) created a need for religious priests* and brothers.* Initially, most of the orders drew their men from Europe, but Europeans were outnumbered by Americans by the end of the century. Growth continued steadily in the early twentieth century, rising to a peak in the years 1945 to 1965. After the Second Vatican Council,* with its emphasis on the role of the laity,* and after the sexual revolution in the U.S., vocations to the religious life fell sharply among men and very sharply among women. Unless the vocation crisis abates, religious orders seem destined to play a decreasing role in American Catholicism.

Currently there are 109 religious orders for clerics* and twenty-eight orders for lay* brothers serving the Catholic Church in the U.S. In the clerical orders most of the members are either priests or seminarians (*See* Seminary Education, Roman Catholic) training for the priesthood, although they generally have a smaller, often much smaller, number of lay brothers who do not plan to take holy orders and are not trained for the priesthood. Orders for brothers do not have priests, or have only a few to tend to their own sacramental needs; orders for brothers do not engage in priestly ministry but usually in education or health care. The religious orders vary considerably in their history, size, structure, training, purpose and ministry so that generalizations are difficult. The older orders especially have developed distinct traditions of spirituality.*

The largest and best-known orders are those founded centuries ago in Europe. Most of these have their international headquarters in Rome and include several provinces as basic administrative units in the U.S. At the head of a province there is usually a provincial superior under whom the superiors of the various houses or communities serve. In some orders the structure is hierarchic, with authority derived from a general superior who usually resides in Rome. Other orders are more democratic, and effective power lies mainly with local units. Aside from small orders which are confined to a single diocese and answer to its bishop, all orders come under papal control through the Sacred Congregation of Religious, one of the administrative divisions of the papal curia.

The largest single order in the U.S. is the Society of Jesus (or Jesuits). In 1986 there were 5,226 American Jesuits in ten provinces. More numerous still are the Franciscans, but they are divided into three separate families or orders, the Order of Friars Minor, the Conventuals and the Capuchins. Less numerous are the other medieval orders of friars such as the Dominicans,* Carmelites,* Augustinians and Servites. Individual houses of the older monastic orders such as the Benedictines,* Cistercians and Carthusians are usually autonomous.

The largest number of orders presently working in the U.S. were founded in the nineteenth century, particularly in France and Italy, and came to the U.S. to help an immigrant Church. Among those with French origins are the Assumptionists, Claretians, the Congregation of Holy Cross,* the Fathers of Mercy, the LaSalette Fathers, the Marianists, Marists* and Resurrectionists. Among those with Italian origins are the Pallotines, Rosminians, Salesians* and Salvatorians. A good number of orders of priests were founded in the U.S., notably the Glenmary Missionaries, Maryknoll Fathers,* Missionaries of the Holy Apostles, Paulists* and the Servants of the Paraclete. Nine different orders of brothers began in the U.S. between 1948 and 1970. The Franciscan Friars of the Atonement began in New York in 1898 as an Anglican* community but joined the Catholic Church in 1909. Some orders

direct their ministry to specific ethnic groups in the U.S. such as Scalabrinians (Italians) or the Congregation of Mother Co-Redemptrix (Vietnamese). Certain orders work with Eastern-Rite Catholics— for example, the Basilian Order of St. Josaphat (for Ukrainians), the Mekhitarist Order (for Armenians), the Basilian Salvatorian Fathers and Maronite Hermits of St. Francis.

The vast majority of American parishes are staffed by the diocesan* clergy, but members of religious orders often take parishes that have special needs, for instance, among African-Americans in the inner cities or Native Americans on reservations. Catholic education (See Parochial Schools, Catholic) is the main ministry of religious priests and brothers. Many orders of brothers, such as Brothers of Christian Instruction, were founded to supply teachers, mainly in secondary schools.

The greatest contribution of the religious orders to the American Catholic Church is a network of Catholic universities; there is nothing comparable elsewhere in the Catholic Church or in Catholic history (See Higher Education, Catholic). Most of these were founded in the nineteenth century but blossomed into real universities only after 1945. Lay professors increasingly outnumbered clerics, and since 1970 most religious orders have turned control over to boards of trustees on which lay persons hold the majority. The Jesuits established nineteen universities, including Georgetown, Fordham, Boston College, St. Louis, Marquette and the three Loyolas. Other notable universities are Dayton (Marianists), DePaul, Niagara and St. John's (Vincentians), LaSalle (Christian Brothers*), Notre Dame* (Congregation of Holy Cross) and Villanova (Augustinians).

After education, foreign missions* are the most important ministry for male religious. In 1988 there were 2,473 American order priests and 532 brothers working in the missions. Of these, 2,104 were in Latin America, 1,356 in the Far East and 944 in Africa. The largest groups were 513 Jesuits working in forty-two countries and 504 Maryknoll Fathers working in twenty-five countries. The three branches of the Franciscans had 390 missionaries.

Other important ministries for male religious are giving retreats,* publishing religious magazines and journals (See Press, Catholic), and working in hospitals and nursing homes, either as chaplains* or health-care specialists. Others serve as military chaplains.* Some religious, such as the Trappists and Carthusians, devote their lives to prayer.

The friars* and Jesuits have been active in Canada since the earliest French settlements. Most of the larger orders found in the U.S. are also

Abbreviations for Roman Catholic Religious Orders and Congregations

A.A. Augustinians of the Assumption: Assumptionists

B.S. Basilian Salvatorian Fathers

C.M.F. *Congregatio Missionariorum Filiorum Immaculati Cordis:* Missionary Sons of the Immaculate Heart of Mary (Claretians)

C.P. *Congregatio Sanctissimi Crucis et Passionis Domini Nostri Jesu Christi:* Congregation of the Passion (Passionists)

C.P.M. *Congregatio Presbyterorum a Misericordia:* Congregation of the Fathers of Mercy

C.R. *Congregatio a Resurrectione Domini Nostri Jesu Christi:* Congregation of the Resurrection (Resurrectionists)

C.S.C. *Congregatio Sanctae Crucis:* Congregation of Holy Cross

C.S.J. *Congregatio Sancti Joseph:* Sisters of St. Joseph

C.S.P. Congregation of the Missionary Society of St. Paul the Apostle (Paulist Fathers)

C.SS.R. *Congregatio Sanctissimi Redemptoris:* Congregation of the Most Holy Redeemer (Redemptorists)

O.S.A. Order of Hermits of St. Augustine: Augustinians

F.M.S. *Fratris Maristarum a Scholis:* Marist Brothers

F.S.C. *Fratres Scholarum Christianorum:* Brothers of the Christian Schools (Christian Brothers)

M.M. Maryknoll Missioners: Catholic Foreign Mission Society of America (Maryknoll Fathers, Maryknoll Brothers, Missionary Sisters of Mary)

M.S. *Missionaires de La Salette:* Missionaries of Our Lady of LaSalette (LaSalette Fathers)

O.Carm. *Ordo Carmelitarum:* Carmelite Nuns of Ancient Observance (Calced Carmelites)

O.Cart. *Ordo Cartusiensis:* Carthusians

O.C.D. *Ordo Carmelitarum Discalceatorum:* Order of Discalced Carmelites

O.C.S.O *Ordo Monialium Cisterciensium Strictioris Observantiae:* Order of Cistercians of the Strict Observance (Trappists); Order of Cistercian Nuns of the Strict Observance (Trappistines)

O.F.M. Order of Friars Minor: Franciscans

O.F.M. Cap. Order of Friars Minor Capuchin: Capuchins

O.F.M. Conv. Order of Friars Minor Conventual: Conventuals

O.S.B.M. *Ordo Sancti Basilii Magni:* Order of St. Basil the Great; Basilian Order of St. Josaphat

O.S.B. Order of St. Benedict: Benedictines

O.S.F. Order of St. Francis: Franciscan Brothers

O.S.M. *Ordo Servorum Mariae:* Order of Servants of Mary (Servites)

O.S.P. Oblate Sisters of Providence

O.S.U. Order of St. Ursula (Ursulines)

P.C. Franciscan Poor Clare Nuns (Poor Clares)

R.S.M. Sisters of Charity

S.A. *Societas Adunationis:* Franciscan Friars of the Atonement

S.A.C. *Societatis Apostolatus Catholici:* Society of the Catholic Apostolate (Pallottines)

S.C.J. *Congregatio Sacerdotum a Corde Jesu:* Congregation of Priests of the Sacred Heart

S.C.S.C. *Sorores a Caritate Sanctae Crucis:* Sisters of Mercy of the Holy Cross

S.D.B. *Societas Sancti Francisci Salesii:* Salesians of St. John Bosco; Society of St. Francis de Sales (Salesians)

S.D.S. Society of the Divine Savior (Salvatorians)

S.J. Society of Jesus (Jesuits)

S.M. Society of Mary (Marists); Society of Mary (Marianists)

S.N.D. Sisters of Notre Dame de Namur

S.O.Cist. *Sacer Ordo Cisterciensis:* Cistercians of the Common Observance

R.S.M. Sisters of Charity

S.S. Society of St. Sulpice (Sulpicians)

S.S.J. *Societas Sancti Joseph Sanctissimi Cordis:* St. Joseph's Society of the Sacred Heart (Josephites)

represented in Canada. Often religious orders in Canada are divided on linguistic lines, with one province or jurisdiction for French speakers, another for English speakers. The Basilian Fathers, with headquarters in Toronto, are more prominent in Canada than in the U.S.

Curiously, there has been very little comparative study of religious orders, either in European or American history. It is a subject seldom given separate treatment in histories of American Catholicism. Better synthetic guides are available for American nuns than for their male counterparts. In contrast, there are many histories of individual religious orders and their work in the U.S.

See also RELIGIOUS ORDERS, PROTESTANT; RELIGIOUS ORDERS, WOMEN'S.

BIBLIOGRAPHY. H. W. Homan, *Knights of Christ* (1957); *Ministries for the Lord: A Resource Guide and Directory of Catholic Church Vocations for Men* (1985); *Religious Community Life in the United States: Proceedings of the Men's Section of the First National Congress of Religious in the United States* (1952). J. P. Donnelly

Religious Orders, Protestant. Protestant* religious communities in America. The revival of the religious life in the churches of the Reformation is one of the significant spiritual movements of the modern age. In the sixteenth century monasticism came under severe criticism from the Protestant Reformers as being nonevangelical, and religious houses were suppressed or eventually declined in Protestant regions. The principle of religious community life, however, had not been rejected outright by the Reformers and new ventures in communal life made their appearance within Protestantism, fostered largely by the pietist* fervor of the seventeenth century. Among the earliest experiments of a monastic nature in North America were the Labadist settlement at Bohemia Manor (1683) on Chesapeake Bay and the Wissahickon hermitage (1696) near Philadelphia. The first influential community was the Ephrata* cloister (1732) in Lancaster County, Pennsylvania, a German Seventh-Day Baptist order of sisters, brethren and householders. Still other semi-monastic experiments in the eighteenth century may be said to include the Moravian Brethren* communities and the Shakers.* In the nineteenth century several more pietist communal societies of an ascetic orientation were established, among them the Rappites and Zoarites.

The nineteenth century also saw the emergence of traditional monastic forms of religious life in the Episcopal Church,* growing out of the Catholic*

and missionary impulses of the period. The first successful communities were sisterhoods, of which the earliest was the Sisterhood of the Holy Communion in New York. It was founded in 1852 as an evangelical association of women living without vows and devoted to works of charity. From this community was later formed in 1865 the first regular order for women, the Community of St. Mary in New York. By 1900 some twenty-three sisterhoods had been formed.

Religious orders for men were later in coming. In 1842 an attempt was made to establish a community for men at Nashotah, Wisconsin, and another a few years later at Valle Crucis, North Carolina. Neither of these foundations long survived, although the Nashotah mission continued as a seminary.* It was not until 1872 that, with the establishment of a branch house of the English Society of St. John the Evangelist at Boston, the first regular order for men was formed. After this, in 1884, the first indigenous community for men, the Order of the Holy Cross, was founded in New York. Today there are no less than forty-six Episcopal or Anglican* religious communities for men and women in North America.

During the late nineteenth century, orders of deaconesses* were also established in many Protestant denominations.* This movement was inspired by the German deaconess community at Kaiserswerth and was introduced to America by Lutherans* in 1849. Between 1870 and 1900 over 140 deaconess houses were organized by Lutherans, Episcopalians, Methodists,* Presbyterians* and others. Deaconess institutions were revived among the Mennonites* in 1908.

Since 1945 there has been a new flowering of community life within American Protestantism, both traditional and experimental in nature. Many of these communities have been influenced by contemporary liturgical* and ecumenical* movements, such as the Lutheran monastic Congregation of the Servants of Christ (1958) in Oxford, Michigan. Other recent communities include the Koinonia Farm (1950) in Americus, Georgia (*See* Jordan, Clarence); Reba Place Fellowship (1957) in Evanston, Illinois; the Ecumenical Institute (1968) in Chicago; and the Sojourners Community* (1975) in Washington, D.C.

BIBLIOGRAPHY. P. F. Anson, *The Call of the Cloister* (1955); D. G. Bloesch, *Wellsprings of Renewal: Promise in Christian Communal Life* (1974); F. Biot, *The Rise of Protestant Monasticism* (1963); F. E. Stoeffler, ed., *Continental Pietism and Early American Christianity* (1976).

C. R. Henery

Religious Orders, Women's. Women's communities with a religious orientation, often with recognized ecclesiastical status and/or vows of poverty, chastity and obedience, have been a feature of Christianity in North America for most of its history, particularly in the Roman Catholic* tradition. There are also Protestant sisterhoods, including Episcopal* sisters, Lutheran,* Mennonite* and Methodist* deaconesses,* and Orthodox* nuns in North America.

From 1693 nuns were present in Canada, but the Ursuline* convent established in French New Orleans in 1727 was the first religious community of women in the present-day U.S. During the colonial period, a number of Maryland Catholic women entered European monasteries. The first women's order founded in the original thirteen colonies was at Port Tobacco, Maryland, where five Discalced Carmelite nuns from the English-speaking monasteries of Antwerp and Hoogstraeten formed a contemplative community there in 1790; it later moved to Baltimore in 1831. Although a few emigrée nuns, individuals and groups came to the U.S. during the French Revolution, their foundations were not lasting. Most American sisterhoods in the period before 1830 were indigenous.

Lacking any institutions for education, health care and social work, the Catholic Church in America looked to new religious foundations to meet this need. In 1799 the Irish-born Teresa Lalor* and her companions formed the nucleus of what eventually became Georgetown Visitation Academy, the first Catholic women's school in the young country. Six more groups, still in existence today, emerged before 1830: the Sisters of Charity* of St. Joseph, under St. Elizabeth Ann Seton* in 1809 in Emmitsburg, Maryland; the Sisters of Loretto at the Foot of the Cross and the Sisters of Charity of Nazareth, both founded in Nelson County, Kentucky, in 1812; the Dominican* Sisters, in St. Catherine, Kentucky, in 1822; the Oblate Sisters of Providence,* the first American community established for African-American women, in Baltimore, Maryland, in 1826; and the Sisters of Charity of Our Lady of Mercy, in Charleston, South Carolina, in 1829. In many frontier situations, sisters provided the only educational or care-giving institutions there were: in 1828, Sisters of Charity from Emmitsburg, Maryland, opened the Saint Louis Mullanphy Hospital, the first hospital west of the Mississippi.

Missionary* foundations began with the pioneering Religious of the Sacred Heart, who arrived from France at St. Charles, Missouri, in 1818, headed by Philippine Duchesne.* In 1833 Sisters of Our Lady of Mt. Carmel from Bourgueil, France, settled in Lacombe, Louisiana, and Sisters of St. Joseph from Lyons in Carondelet, Missouri, in 1836. By the 1840s, European foundations provided a steady influx, sisters following the nineteenth-century immigrants with German, Italian and Eastern European communities succeeding the original French and Irish imports.

Nativist* hostility often focused on sisters who, with their exotic dress and mysterious way of life, seemed to epitomize the foreignness of a European-based church. The most notorious case was the burning of the Ursuline Convent in Charlestown, Massachusetts, in 1834. Not until after the Civil War,* in which they gave outstanding service as nurses and cooks, did sisters become more generally accepted as part of the American scene.

The chief work of sisters in the U.S. has been education—at first in boarding academies accompanied by a free school. Later, they staffed parochial schools,* forming the largest private system of religious education in the world. The second involvement numerically of sisters is health care. Among the only trained nurses in the country, sisters were called into duty in both the Civil War and Spanish American War.* At present the Sisters of Mercy operate one of the larger hospital systems in the U.S. The Catholic sisterhoods dedicated to nursing care for the poor include the Servants of Relief for Incurable Cancer, founded in New York in 1898 by Rose Hawthorne Lathrop, the daughter of Nathaniel Hawthorne.* In 1912 the first American women's missionary congregation, the Maryknoll Sisters of St. Dominic, began in New York.

Contemplative religious life has also flourished in America since its introduction in 1790, now numbering sixty-five monasteries of cloistered Carmelites alone. Other nuns dedicated chiefly to a life of prayer include cloistered Dominicans, Poor Clares, Passionists, Trappestines and others.

The first Catholic college for women, Notre Dame of Maryland, was founded in 1895 under the auspices of the Sisters of Notre Dame de Namur, a mark of the rising trend toward professionalization of teaching and nursing. Women's religious communities experienced intense regularization following World War 1*—internally through the impetus of a newly codified system of Church Law (1918), and professionally through states' efforts to enforce norms for licensing and accreditation. The professional development of sisters, achieved through college and university education, usually on a part-time basis, culminated in the Sister Formation Conference, formally organized in 1957. Change during the 1950s was strongly influenced by the exhortations of Pius XII* for sisters to update and form national associations. The Leadership Conference of Women Religious of the U.S.A. (LCWR) now includes the chief administrators of over three hundred autonomous communities.

With the Catholic Church in general, women religious have experienced great innovation in their way of life and their works since 1960. By the late 1940s, membership in these communities was already inadequate to keep abreast of exploding needs in the school system. Catholic institutions of education and health care, which formed the corporate works of each order, are in crisis. Congregations themselves have suffered drastic numerical loss, declining forty per cent between 1966 and 1982. Total 1987 membership in Catholic sisterhoods in the U.S. is 112,489.

A renewed ecclesiology, coupled with experience in missionary situations and high levels of theological and professional education, has affected sisters' former emphasis on separation from the world. Directed by the Second Vatican Council* to adapt to modern conditions and re-examine the spirit of their founders, Catholic women religious have developed an increasing social consciousness and are in the process of redefining their role in view of a changing church and society.

BIBLIOGRAPHY. M. Ewens, *The Role of the Nun in the Nineteenth Century* (1978); B. Misner, "A Comparative Social Study of the Members and Apostolates of the First Eight Permanent Communities of Women Religious within the Original Boundaries of the United States, 1790-1850" (Unpublished Ph.D. dissertation, Catholic University of America, 1980); M. A. Neal, *Catholic Sisters in Transition from the 1960s to the 1980s* (1984); M. S. Thompson, *The Yoke of Grace: American Nuns and Social Change, 1808-1917* (forthcoming); *Women Religious History Sources: A Guide to Repositories in the United States,* ed., E. Thomas (1983). P. Byrne

Renewal Movements, Catholic. Catholics view renewal as essential to the Church in every age. The Second Vatican Council* taught, ". . . the Church, embracing sinners in her bosom, is at the same time holy and always in need of being purified, and incessantly pursues the path of penance and renewal . . ." (*Lumen Gentium,* no. 8). Renewal, as the word implies, does not mean starting something new (such as a "new" church), but making something old new again or like new. It is a return to faithfulness to what Christ has established. Vatican II's "Decree on Ecumenism"

states, "Every renewal of the Church essentially consists in an increase of fidelity to her own calling . . ." (no. 6). Renewal, then, implies a continuity with the past rather than a break, and a return to what God has established in the Church with increased zeal, fidelity and freshness. Catholics believe that authentic renewal is not a human project, but is an ongoing and necessary work of the Holy Spirit.

Renewal is expressed in an almost infinite variety of ways, because every aspect of the Church's life can be, and needs to be, renewed at one time or another. Renewal in the Church is often sparked and accomplished through particular renewal movements comprised of Christians who believe the Holy Spirit is acting in a particular way to renew the Church. Vatican II's "Decree on Ecumenism," for example, lists forms of renewal that were occurring in the Catholic Church in the early 1960s: "the biblical and liturgical movements, the preaching of the Word of God, catechetics, the apostolate of the laity, new forms of religious life and the spirituality of married life, and the church's social teaching and activity" (no. 6).

Throughout the history of the Catholic Church, there have been movements of renewal. Some of these have been successful in renewing the Church (or some aspect of its life) and were integrated into the Church's life either through changes instituted or occurring "spontaneously" in the Church as a whole (changes in disciplines, practices and observances, attitudes, etc.), or through the official recognition by Church authorities of movements or groups within the Church, such as the formation of religious orders.* Such successful renewal movements include the monastic movement (fourth century onward), the Cluniac and Cistercian renewals of monastic life (tenth and eleventh centuries), the mendicant movement giving rise to the Franciscan* and Dominican* orders (twelfth century), the reforms of the Council of Trent (sixteenth century onwards), Catholic revivalism* in America (nineteenth century) and the recent wave of Catholic renewal ushered in by the Second Vatican Council.

However, not all renewal movements that have emerged within the Catholic Church have been successful. Some have been discerned by Church authority* to be heretical* (e.g., Montanism, Catharism, Jansenism, Quietism), and others have broken from the Catholic Church (e.g., the schisms of the Donatists and the Waldenses). The Protestant Reformation began with the failure of Luther's attempt to renew the Church from within according to his vision.

After the Second Vatican Council, many renewal movements and groups that promise to be successful, have emerged within the Catholic Church including Cursillo,* Focolare, Communion and Liberation, Marriage Encounter,* parish renewal programs and the Catholic charismatic* renewal.

The Catholic charismatic renewal serves as a recent example of the emergence and growth of a Catholic renewal movement. It began in 1967 at Duquesne University in Pittsburgh as a result of contact of some professors with neo-Pentecostal Episcopalians.* On a retreat a number of Duquesne students were "baptized in the Holy Spirit"* and spoke in tongues.* The movement spread quickly and soon Notre Dame University* became a center for annual meetings of "Catholic Pentecostals," culminating in the largest gathering (25,000), in 1974. The movement soon assumed the structured forms of prayer groups and covenant communities.

In 1975, Pope Paul VI* gave his approval to the movement at a gathering of 10,000 charismatic Catholics in Rome, and Pope John Paul II has also encouraged the movement, which stresses a personal relationship with God and experience of the presence of the Holy Spirit in prayer,* service and in the exercise of spiritual gifts (1 Cor 12, Eph 4) in prayer meetings* and in daily life. Like many Catholic renewal movements, the goal of the Catholic charismatic renewal is not to create a distinct or separate group within the Church, but to enable the whole Church to rediscover an aspect of the fullness of Christianity that may have been neglected or forgotten over the course of time.

See also CHARISMATIC MOVEMENT; LAY MOVMENT, MODERN CATHOLIC.

BIBLIOGRAPHY. A. Flannery, ed., *Vatican Council II: The Conciliar and Post-Conciliar Documents* (1975); D. Gelpi, *Pentecostalism: A Theological Viewpoint* (1971); J. P. Dolan, *Catholic Revivalism: The American Catholic Experience, 1830-1900* (1978); K. and D. Ranaghan, *Catholic Pentecostals Today* (1983); A. Schreck, *A Compact History of the Catholic Church* (1987).   A. Schreck

Renewal Movements, Protestant. Movements, usually within larger Protestant* denominations,* seeking to revitalize the church or denomination in some specific way. Such movements are usually concerned with theology* or mission.*

Since the 1920s, when modernity impacted most American denominations, movements for revitalization within Protestant circles have usually been concerned with "evangelical" renewal, a combina-

tion of theology and mission. In the 1930s and 1940s several of these movements among Baptists* and Presbyterians* resulted in new conservative denominations. The Orthodox Presbyterian Church* and the Conservative Baptists* are examples of these. In the 1960s and 1970s, however, movements pressing for renewed commitment to the authority of Scripture* or evangelism* tended to remain within the mainline* denominations.

The Good News movement among United Methodists* began in March 1967, when Charles W. Keysor, a minister in Elgin, Illinois, began publishing a small magazine called *Good News* for evangelicals within the denomination. Regional groups sympathetic with *Good News* soon appeared across the country. By 1970 renewal fellowships were meeting within half of the Methodist annual conferences, and a national convocation meeting during the summer months began to press for changes in the publications, seminaries* and mission agencies of the denomination.

Renewal within the Episcopal Church* has been more diverse, including Anglo-Catholic,* evangelical* and charismatic* efforts. One evangelical center is The Fellowship of Witness, stimulated by the clergyman John Guest and encouraged by the magazine *Kerygma.* From this fellowship in Pennsylvania came Trinity Episcopal School for Ministry, founded in 1976. The church's other eleven seminaries have slowly admitted increasing numbers of Episcopal evangelicals influenced by the Fellowship and Trinity.

Presbyterians can claim four evangelical renewal organizations: (1) The Covenant Fellowship of Presbyterians, largely a lay movement encouraging evangelism, was started in 1969. (2) The Presbyterian Lay Committee seeks greater emphasis on the Bible* within the denomination and a check on the leftward drift of the denominational leadership. (3) Presbyterians for Democracy and Religious Freedom, the youngest of the evangelical renewal groups, seeks to correct the liberal political positions supported by denominational leaders. And (4) Presbyterians United for Biblical Concerns, which began in 1966 to resist the Confession of 1967,* continues to stress the authority of Scripture and spiritual renewal.

Among American Baptists, the American Baptist Fellowship pressed for evangelical renewal in the 1960s, but since the death of Lawrence T. Slaght interest has waned. Within the Disciples of Christ* two organizations press for renewal: the National Evangelistic Association of the Christian Church (Disciples of Christ) and the Conference on Spiritual Renewal. The most vigorous renewal group within the United Church of Christ* is the Biblical Witness Fellowship, which assists local churches in securing evangelical leaders and seminarians in placement for ministry.

BIBLIOGRAPHY. R. H. Nash, ed., *Evangelical Renewal in the Mainline Churches* (1987).

B. L. Shelley

Republican Methodists. *See* O'KELLY SCHISM.

Rerum Novarum. Papal encyclical* outlining Catholic* social principles. Issued by Leo XIII* on May 15, 1891, *Rerum Novarum* was a response to the growing social movement within the Catholic Church. Though not the sole or even most significant impetus for the encyclical, events in the U.S. had attracted the attention of the papacy and invited a response.

The Knights of Labor,* a labor organization with Catholic involvement, had attracted the criticism of numerous bishops who wished to have it condemned. But in 1887 Cardinal Gibbons* had submitted to the Vatican* that such a move would be mistaken, arguing that the Knights were a legitimate organization seeking redress for the rights of workers. Conservative prelates had also sought a public condemnation of Henry George's *Progress and Poverty* (1879), fearing its teachings would undermine the right to private property. Gibbons again, supported by men such as John Ireland,* John J. Keane* and John Lancaster Spalding,* had convinced the Vatican of the futility of such a move.

The encyclical upheld the natural right of private property and rejected socialism, thereby satisfying the conservatives. Yet it affirmed the principle of a just wage and the efforts of workers to seek wage settlements. The role of the state was affirmed in protecting private property, seeking to avoid strikes, regulating working conditions and encouraging a broad distribution of property. The encyclical also emphasized the role of the church in social issues, both in practicing charity and upholding justice. Finally, the document supported the organization of labor unions and other religious bodies devoted to the good of society. *Rerum Novarum* was acclaimed as an important affirmation of the emerging Catholic social movement.

With other issues, such as Americanism,* taking center stage, the encyclical did not launch a crusade for social justice among American Catholics. More frequently it was appealed to by opponents of socialism, who neglected the encyclical's criticism of capitalism. The appearance of *Rerum Novarum* was commemorated forty years later, on May 15, 1931, when Pope Pius XI* issued the social encyclical *Quadragesimo Anno.*

BIBLIOGRAPHY. A. I. Abell, *American Catholicism and Social Action* (1960); A. I. Abell, "The Reception of Leo XIII's Labor Encyclical in America, 1891-1919," *Review of Politics* 7 (1945):464-495; M. Piehl, *Breaking Bread: The Catholic Worker and the Origin of Catholic Radicalism* (1982); L. Watt, *A Handbook to Rerum Novarum* (1941). D. G. Reid

Rescue Mission Movement. The spread of urban missions* designed to present the gospel and offer food and lodging to street people. During the late nineteenth century, the forces of immigration,* industrialization and urbanization brought unprecedented problems to America. Although these changes created economic opportunities and vaulted America to a position of economic and military superiority, some people were left homeless and helpless in the wake of these changes. Poverty became a national problem, especially in cities. And homeless people—usually called "tramps"—multiplied, especially during periods of economic recession and depression. Some of these people suffered from alcoholism and drug addiction; many of them were plagued by malnutrition; and all were drifting from place to place in search of shelter.

A few sensitive evangelicals* looked at this street-people phenomenon and saw it as an opportunity. Rather than criticize the drifters for laziness and drunkenness, or attack society for creating these people's plight, an energetic group of evangelicals took their cue from evangelicals in Great Britain. Reaching out to these hurting people, they provided them with meals, temporary lodging and secondhand clothing. They not only met immediate physical needs, they took the opportunity to preach the gospel of Jesus Christ.

One of the first of its kind was the Helping Hand for Men Mission in New York City's Bowery district. Founded in 1872 by Jerry McAuley,* and renamed the Water Street Mission* soon thereafter, this relief and evangelistic* ministry was popularized by *Jerry McAuley's Newspaper,* a weekly periodical that reported on the spiritual and benevolent work done in this Lower East Side facility. Evangelicals across urban America read the little paper, and numerous communities were inspired to begin similar programs.

Although McAuley is usually credited with beginning the movement, Rachel Bradley in Chicago began a similar storefront mission the same year (1872). Bradley's facility became known as the Olive Branch Mission. Like the Water Street Mission and the famous Bowery Mission, it not only exists to this day, it became a model that was imitated by other communities.

Chicago's Pacific Garden Mission* is not the nation's oldest, but it is considered to be the parent of more rescue missions than any other facility. Founded in 1877, this still-thriving mission has been extremely influential for several reasons. First, it is located in a major city where it has attracted attention. Second, two of its converts, Melvin Trotter* and Billy Sunday,* devoted their post-conversion lives to evangelistic ministries which included the planting and encouraging of rescue missions across America. Indeed, Trotter founded many missions, doing so until his death in 1940. Billy Sunday also devoted much energy to rescue mission promotion until his death in 1935. And after that time Mrs. Sunday continued in his footsteps until her death in 1957.

Contemporary missions in such cities as Los Angeles, California; Denver, Colorado; Grand Rapids, Michigan and Aurora, Illinois; acknowledge the debt of their origins to Mel Trotter or Billy Sunday. It is little wonder then that Pacific Garden Mission, with its still-popular "Unshackled" radio program, is viewed as the most important city mission founded in the United States.

See also URBAN CHURCHES AND MINISTRIES; URBAN MISSIONS.

BIBLIOGRAPHY. N. Magnuson, *Salvation in the Slums: Evangelical Social Work, 1865-1920* (1977); J. R. Adair, *The Old Lighthouse: The Story of the Pacific Garden Mission* (1966); L. W. Dorsett, *The Denver Rescue Mission: A Brief History* (1983); B. R. Skaggs, *Inasmuch: The Wayside Cross Rescue Mission of Aurora, 1928-1978* (1978).

L. W. Dorsett

Restitutionism. *See* PRIMITIVISM.

Restoration Movement. A religious movement, beginning about 1800, to reform the churches by restoring New Testament teaching about the church. The movement that its followers refer to as *the Restoration Movement* developed in America about the turn of the nineteenth century. Though its origins were diverse, it represented a common pattern of religion arising from the appeal of primitivism* on the early American frontier. Numerous people were looking back to the New Testament as the basis for Christianity. Two basic thrusts mark the beginnings of this movement: a commitment to the practice of Christian unity and a commitment to the authority* of the Bible*

(specifically the New Testament) as the only guidebook for the faith and practice of the church.

Origins. The Restoration Movement had several different origins. One source began in the Southern states around 1792 when James O'Kelly* separated from the Methodist Episcopal* Church because of a dispute over the authority of Bishop Francis Asbury* in appointing preachers* to their circuits.* His followers, first called *Republican Methodists* in 1793, by 1794 had chosen the title *Christians* to the exclusion of other labels. They emphasized local church autonomy, equality between all clergy* and even equality between clergy and laity.*

A similar group began in New England about 1801 under the leadership of Abner Jones* and Elias Smith. They came out of a Baptist background, but were disenchanted with the Baptist name, some Baptist doctrine (particularly predestination*) and the organization of Baptist churches into associations. Desiring to follow the Bible only and work for Christian unity with like-minded Christians, by 1811 they had become aware of some of the O'Kelly group and formed a union with them.

In 1803 Barton W. Stone* and several other clergy in Kentucky left the Presbyterians* and formed their own group, the Presbytery of Springfield.* Within a year, however, they decided that presbyteries* were unscriptural, and they disbanded. They took the name *Christian,* committed themselves to local church autonomy and desired to work for the cause of Christian unity among all Christians. When Stone met members of the Smith Jones movement in 1826, they united in fellowship without the encumbrance of a formal merger.

Thomas Campbell* was a Scottish Seceder Presbyterian minister who came to western Pennsylvania from Northern Ireland in 1807. He could not accept the petty denominational jealousies he discovered, and in 1808 he left his denomination to function as an independent minister. By 1809 he had coined the phrase, "Where the Bible speaks, we speak; where it is silent, we are silent." Organizing the Christian Association of Washington, he wrote *The Declaration and Address* to enunciate his commitment to the principles of Christian unity and exclusive biblical authority. That same year his son, Alexander Campbell,* joined him from Northern Ireland, and soon became the major voice in the Campbellite Movement.

Their commitment to biblical authority* as the basis for all church teachings and practices led them to question infant baptism* by 1812. Finding

Restoration Movement

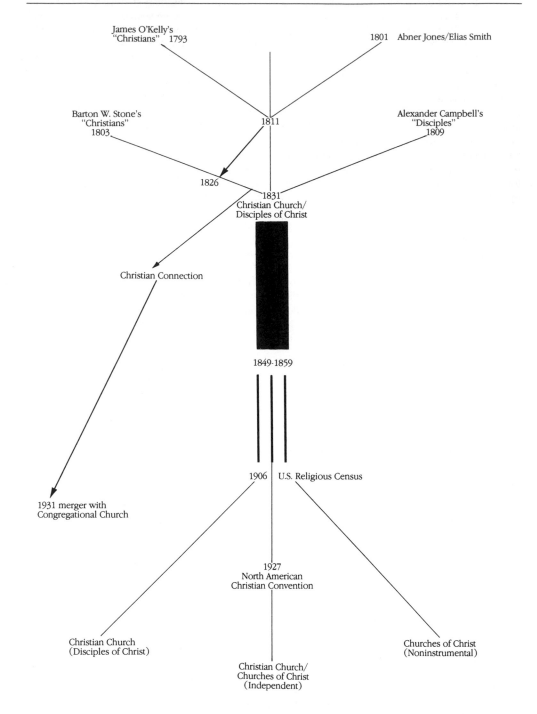

James O'Kelly's "Christians" 1793

1801 Abner Jones/Elias Smith

Barton W. Stone's "Christians" 1803

1811

Alexander Campbell's "Disciples" 1809

1826

1831 Christian Church/ Disciples of Christ

Christian Connection

1849-1859

1906 | U.S. Religious Census

1931 merger with Congregational Church

1927 North American Christian Convention

Christian Church (Disciples of Christ)

Christian Church/ Churches of Christ (Independent)

Churches of Christ (Noninstrumental)

no biblical support for the practice, they decided in favor of believers' baptism by immersion. This made them appear to be Baptists, and from 1815 to about 1830, the Campbells worked among the Baptists, until the Baptists began to exclude them. Baptist leaders were concerned about the Campbells's emphasis on baptism by immersion "for remission of sins." In addition, the Campbells rejected the typical Calvinist* teaching on the necessity of the special regenerating work of the Holy Spirit on the sinner's heart before he could even come to faith in Christ. The Campbells rejected any concept of "baptismal regeneration," but they also insisted that sinners could accept Christ's salvation without any miraculous activity of the Holy Spirit or a special gift of faith by the Spirit. Their churches also developed a uniform practice of weekly observance of the Lord's Supper.*

Development. When the followers of Barton Stone and the Campbells met each other, they discovered they held very similar views on many points of belief and practice. In 1831 they joined forces in central Kentucky. However, about half of Stone's movement of Christians distrusted the Campbells' emphasis on baptism for remission of sins, considered them guilty of baptismal regeneration and refused to follow their leader into the union with the "Campbellites." Instead, they remained united with the Smith-Jones movement in New England and the Christian Connection.*

Since Alexander Campbell preferred the name *Disciples of Christ,* that was often the label by which the movement came to be known, although Stone's use of *Christian Church* was just as common. The movement expanded at a significant rate, achieving 118,000 followers by 1850, and 192,000 by 1860, making it the sixth-largest religious group in the country. They refused to call themselves a denomination, however, feeling such identifications were unbiblical and meant an acceptance of religious division.

Division. Some evidence of the growth of the movement was indicated in 1849 when the American Christian Missionary Society formed. This was to facilitate the spread of the gospel through organized missions, but many members of the movement opposed this methodology. "Where the Bible speaks, we speak," they echoed. Where had the Bible spoken in terms of authorizing missionary societies? Since the societies were unscriptural, they could only be rejected. Perhaps the most controversial issue came in 1859 when a church in Midway, Kentucky, was the first to use instrumental music* to accompany congregational singing in worship.*

This became the *cause celebre,* for it represented the use of an unscriptural means of worship. Conservatives saw both missionary societies and musical instruments as apostasy* from the original commitment to the Bible as the only basis for the life and practice of the church. Others saw them as tools to aid the work of the churches, tools which were not *prohibited* in the New Testament and were therefore expedients in the area of opinions. The real issue was neither missionary societies nor musical instruments, but how to apply biblical teaching, particularly the rule of biblical silence. The more conservative churches, usually located in the area of the Southern Confederacy, refused to follow the innovations. Both sides often used the societies and the instruments as tests of fellowship, and the inevitable occurred in 1906 when the U.S. Census Bureau began to list the noninstrumental Churches of Christ separately from the Christian Churches, or the Disciples of Christ.

A second problem emerged in the late nineteenth century with the impact of theological liberalism.* The new views of higher biblical criticism undercut the authority of the Scriptures, and the young men who went to graduate seminaries* and accepted the new teachings found themselves in opposition to older evangelicals* who still accepted the "fundamentals." Gradually, liberals began to take on offices in the missionary societies and other organized agencies among the Christian Churches. Inquiries were made regarding what was being taught in some of the movement's schools, particularly the College of the Bible in Lexington, Kentucky, in 1917. New professors with new learning had replaced the older generation of teachers, and theological liberalism was being presented in the classroom.

The conservatives tried to resist this, as well as the application of liberalism in missionary practices. The practice of open membership—receiving unimmersed persons as members of Christian Churches—convinced many conservatives that ministers at home and missionaries abroad were now committed to the new liberalism. Resolutions to prohibit liberal practices were adopted in national conventions, but were reinterpreted by the official leadership and rendered harmless. As a result, the conservatives felt betrayed and in 1927 developed their own convention, the North American Christian Convention.* They ceased supporting the organized missionary societies and sent out missionaries directly, often called "independent" missionaries representing "independent" churches. Thus a further division developed between the independent Christian Churches and the Disciples of Christ, with the latter oriented toward liberalism. These divisions have led to an ongoing confusion over the names of the various branches of the movement. In some parts of the country the terms *Christian Churches* and *Churches of Christ* are completely interchangeable; in other areas they have distinct meanings.

Current Status. For a movement founded in the name of Christian unity to now exist in three separate parts has been an acute embarrassment. Statistics are hard to come by since both the Noninstrumental churches and the Independent Christian Churches lack any central organization. But figures indicate that the Noninstrumental churches number somewhat under two million members, while the other two groups, the Independent Christian Church and Disciples of Christ, number just over one million each, for a cumulative total of about four million members.

The Disciples of Christ restructured their organization in 1968 and now have centralized headquarters in Indianapolis. They now have a hierarchy of ministerial structure, a delegate convention, organized funding and promotion and denominational status. They continue their concern for Christian unity with activity in the Consultation on Christian Union and their continuing merger negotiations with the United Church of Christ.* Most Disciples leaders are theologically liberal, with a commitment to social action and reform,* though many Disciples still retain a conservative, evangelical orientation.

The Independent Christian Churches are normally identified with their North American Christian Convention, a publishing house in Cincinnati, and over thirty regional Bible colleges.* The Noninstrumental churches of Christ have no central organization but find leadership in a few large churches, periodicals and college lectureships. Recently, the Noninstrumentalists and the Independent Christians have discovered their theological and historical similarities may be more important than their differences regarding societies and musical instruments and have begun a series of tentative meetings. The result for the present is still a divided movement, reflecting an inability to agree on "where the Bible speaks."

See also CHRISTIAN CHURCHES/CHURCHES OF CHRIST (INDEPENDENT); CHURCHES OF CHRIST (NONINSTRUMENTAL); CHRISTIAN CHURCH (DISCIPLES OF CHRIST); NORTH AMERICAN CHRISTIAN CONVENTION.

BIBLIOGRAPHY. E. E. Dowling, *The Restoration Movement* (1964); L. Garrett, *The Stone-Campbell Movement: An Anecdotal History of Three Churches* (1981); L. G. McAllister and W. E. Tucker,

Journey in Faith: A History of the Christian Church (Disciples of Christ) (1975); J. D. Murch, *Christians Only: A History of the Restoration Movement* (1962); R. Richardson, *Memoirs of Alexander Campbell,* 2 vols. (1868, 1870); E. I. West, *The Search for the Ancient Order: A History of the Restoration Movement,* 3 vols. (1949, 1950, 1979); C. A. Young, ed., *Historical Documents Advocating Christian Union* (1904). J. B. North

Restorationism. *See* PRIMITIVISM.

Retreats, Religious. Times of withdrawal from the normal affairs of life to cultivate a deepened personal relationship with God. Christians find precedence for retreats in Jesus' own practice of withdrawing, either privately or with his disciples, for prayer and spiritual renewal. Spiritual-life retreats vary greatly—they may be private or corporate, silent or dialogical, guided or unguided, long or short.

Many regard the ideal length of a retreat to be a weekend from Friday evening through Sunday noon—forty-four hours. The most frequent type of retreat is the reflective one which is observed in silence, broken only by occasional teaching or worship periods. Private overnight or one-day retreats are increasingly common. Regular quiet days are being observed by more and more Christian leaders.

Whatever the length, individuals are encouraged to make use of many kinds of spiritual disciplines to enhance their communion with God. Prayer* and the devotional reading of Scripture are the two foundational disciplines. They are often accompanied by reflecting in silence, listening to worship music, reading classics of devotion, writing in a journal about the experience, memorizing key Scriptures, participating in a communion service and counseling with a spiritual director. In the case of corporate retreats, these exercises are sometimes interspersed with periods of group interaction and affirmation of one another. Occasionally the prayer experience is accompanied by fasting.*

The retreat movement has a long history in the Roman Catholic Church,* going back to St. Ignatius in the sixteenth century, and in the Church of England,* going back to its first retreats, both held in 1856—one in February at Chislehurst led by the Society of the Holy Cross and one led in July by E. B. Pusey (1800-1882) at Oxford. Since World War 2,* however, retreats have flourished among many Protestant* groups as one of many important renewal* movements growing out of that period. Among Protestants, retreat centers have largely been a parachurch* phenomenon, but increasingly local churches are establishing such centers as extensions of their ministry. Among these are the Dayspring Retreat Center of the Church of the Savior in Washington, D.C., and the Mt. Olivet Retreat Center of Mount Olivet Lutheran Church, Minneapolis, Minnesota. The offering of such retreats to its members supplements the work of the church by providing a time for longer periods of spiritual reflection in places psychologically different from one's normal environment and with many immediate stimuli available for personal spiritual growth.

In the U.S. there may now be as many as one thousand retreat centers or places used for spiritual-life retreats. Many of them are identified in the *Ecumenical Directory of Retreat and Conference Centers* (1984). Two networks of retreat directors meet regularly, the North American Retreat Directors Association and Retreats International. These groups have regular meetings and publications to foster the retreat movement in America.

BIBLIOGRAPHY. N. Goodacre, *Experiment in Retreats* (1969); T. H. Green, *A Vacation with the Lord* (1986); N. Shawchuck et al., *How to Conduct a Spiritual Retreat* (1986); H. C. Swift, *A Living Room Retreat* (1981).   C. H. Lundquist

Reu, (J)ohann (M)ichael (1869-1943). Lutheran* pastor,* theologian,* and churchman. Born in Diebach, Bavaria, Reu was educated in the Latin school Öttingen and the mission seminary Neuendettelsau, Bavaria. He immigrated* to America and was ordained* in 1889, serving as a pastor in Illinois until 1899, when he became professor at Wartburg Seminary Dubuque, Iowa. There he served until his death, teaching dogmatics,* homiletics,* catechetics,* exegesis* and other subjects.

In 1910 Reu was honored with a Th.D. from the University of Erlangen for his extensive research on religious education in the Reformation era which was published in German in four volumes between 1904 and 1935. Reu authored numerous other works in German and English, including *Thirty-five Years of Luther Research* (1917), *Catechetics* (1918), *Homiletics* (1922), *Dr. Martin Luther's Small Catechism* (1929) and *The Augsburg Confession* (1930). From 1904 he edited *Kirchliche Zeitschrift,* contributing articles and reviewing hundreds of books. He was a delegate to three Lutheran World Conventions and member of numerous committees of the Iowa Synod (until 1929) and the American Lutheran Church (after 1930). He died in Rochester, Minnesota, October 14, 1943.

BIBLIOGRAPHY. A. Pilger, "Johann Michael Reu," in *Johann Michael Reu: A Book of Remembrance, Kirchliche Zeitschrift, 1876-1943* (1945).
                                                    J. L. Schaaf

Revell, Fleming Hewitt (1849-1931). Protestant* publisher. Born in Chicago, the son of Fleming H. and Emma (Manning) Revell, Revell left school at the age of ten to help support his mother and three sisters. One of his sisters, Emma, married Dwight L. Moody,* and it was Moody who encouraged Revell, not yet twenty years of age, to begin publishing religious literature. In fact the business, one of the first wholly independent and undenominational religious publishing houses in America, was firmly established by the publication of Moody's sermons and tracts.

The Chicago Fire in 1871 destroyed his establishment, but he started again. Revell opened a branch in New York in 1887, and by 1890 Fleming H. Revell Company was one of the largest publishers of religious literature in America. Moving to New York about 1906, he established his headquarters there. Revell was a Presbyterian layman, a trustee of Northfield Seminary and Wheaton College,* a director of New York Life Insurance Co. and of the New York YMCA* and treasurer of the American Mission to Lepers. He was active in the Niagara Conference* and published many of the books, pamphlets and journals of premillennialist* and fundamentalist* authors.

BIBLIOGRAPHY. *DAB* VIII; "Revell: Seventy-Five Years of Religious Book Publishing," *Publisher's Weekly* (December 9, 1944):2232-2236.
                                                    P. C. Wilt

Revels, Hiram Rhoades (1822-1901). African-American Methodist* minister,* politician and educator. Born of free parentage in North Carolina, Revels went to Quaker* institutions in Indiana and Ohio and to Knox College in Illinois. In 1845 he entered the ministry of the African Methodist Episcopal Church* (AME), serving churches in the Midwest and border states. A local church dispute in St. Louis resulted in his shift to an African-American Presbyterian* congregation in Baltimore in 1858. During the Civil War,* he recruited for African-American regiments, served as a chaplain,* helped set up Freedmen's Bureau schools in Mississippi and rejoined the AME Church. In 1868 he changed his clerical status to the Methodist Episcopal Church (ME), which had returned South for missions among the freedpeople. During Reconstruction, Revels advanced from local political roles in Mississippi to the state Senate until he became the first of his race to serve in the U.S. Senate (January 1870 to March 1871). Elected president of Alcorn University, he spent the remainder of his career in education, as a contributor to the church press and as a pastor* and presiding elder.* A representative to the General Conference of the ME Church in 1876, he fought unsuccessfully against the policy to permit a color line in the denomination.*

BIBLIOGRAPHY. J. A. Borome, ed., "The Autobiography of Hiram Rhodes Revels Together with Some Letters By and About Him," *Midwest Journal* 5 (1952-1953):79-92; W. B. Gravely, ed., "Hiram Revels Protests Racial Separation in the Methodist Episcopal Church (1876)," *MH* 8 (1970):13-20.   W. B. Gravely

Revivalism, Catholic. In the first half of the nineteenth century, revivals of religion became a permanent fixture in the U.S. Revivals spread like wildfire, setting cities and towns ablaze with religious enthusiasm. These revivals changed the way people thought about God by emphasizing the importance of individual conversion* and the personal experience of religion. Calvinism* gave way to evangelicalism,* and as this happened American Protestantism* was permanently altered. But revivals of religion were not an exclusively Protestant phenomenon in nineteenth-century America. Roman Catholics* were also involved in religious revivals, and these Catholic revivals, known at that time as parish missions,* also changed the way people thought about God. Catholics acquired a more evangelical understanding of God and religion, and like their Protestant neighbors, they began to emphasize the importance of conversion and the personal experience of religion.

The Catholic revival was not made in America. Its origin was in sixteenth-century Europe, the era of the Reformation, when the Roman Catholic Church was attempting to renew the piety* of the people. Religious order* preachers* such as the Jesuits* traveled across Europe preaching revivals or missions as they called them. The golden age of parish missions was in the early eighteenth century, and after that a noticeable decline set in. Then in the early nineteenth century, in the decade of the thirties, parish missions became popular once again, as bishops* and clergy* sought to revitalize the piety of the people. When Catholic priests* immigrated to the U.S., they brought with them the idea of the parish mission.

Like Protestant revivals parish missions were a technique used in the evangelization of the people. They were ideally suited for the immigrant Catholic community in the antebellum period because this community was, as far as the clergy was concerned, in dire need of religious conversion. Having emigrated from Ireland and Germany, a large majority of these Catholic newcomers were not actively practising their religion. The parish mission sought to remedy that, and it is fair to say that it did so rather successfully. Because of its increasing popularity, the parish mission became a standard event in Catholic communities. The movement peaked in the late nineteenth century, lost momentum in the twentieth century and disappeared in the post-World War 2 era. In the 1970s and 1980s, a new form of the parish mission, now referred to as a revival, came into vogue with its goal being much the same as in prior centuries, the evangelization of the people.

The Catholic version of the religious revival took place over a period of time—one or two weeks, possibly even a month. The preachers belonged to one of the major religious orders, such as the Jesuits, Redemptorists,* or Vincentians. Considered specialists in their work, they traveled from parish to parish preaching revivals. Walter Elliott* of the Paulists* and Francis X. Weninger,* a German-speaking Jesuit, were two noted nineteenth-century preachers. An early-morning Mass* and sermon* began a typical day in the course of the revival; during the day some catechesis* would take place, generally with the young people. Then in the evening came the main event, a lengthy sermon that was aimed at a heartfelt conversion. Preachers used rituals and music,* as well as the spoken word, to gain conversions. One of the most elaborate rituals was the closing of the mission. Candlelight processions, renewal of vows made at baptism* and taking the temperance* pledge highlighted the evening.

In Catholic revivals the sawdust trail* led to the confessional, where individuals, convicted of sin,* renounced their evil ways and sought pardon of their sins. This ritual of penance,* which took place in the church every evening, was a sacramental ratification of the individual's conversion. It was a distinctive part of the Roman Catholic tradition and indicated that even though Catholic revivals nurtured an evangelical piety rooted in the religious experience* of personal conversion, they remained distinctly Catholic. Thus, Catholic revivalism blended the gospel of evangelicalism with the ritual of the sacraments*; the result was a sacramental evangelicalism. This gave Catholic piety a new tone by placing the heart above the head, feeling over reason. Through the revival the personal experience of religion became an important aspect in the Catholic pursuit of holiness.*

The Catholic revival also sought to strengthen the institutional church by building up the local parish community. It emphasized the importance of orthodox* religious behavior and the importance of attending Mass and receiving the sacraments in the local parish church. Mission preachers often acted as boosters of Catholic schools* and on occasion were called in to heal parish dissensions and schisms. In this manner the parish mission fostered the growth and consolidation of the Roman Catholic Church in the U.S.

BIBLIOGRAPHY. J. P. Dolan, *Catholic Revivalism: The American Experience, 1830-1900* (1978); J. Wissel, *The Redemptorist on the American Missions,* 3 vols. (1978). J. P. Dolan

Revivalism, German-American. Beginning in the late seventeenth and early eighteenth centuries, large numbers of Germans immigrated* to the American Middle Colonies of Pennsylvania, Maryland and western New York, as well as western Virginia. Many sought religious and economic freedom from the ravages resulting from Europe's Thirty Years' War (1618-1648). The majority came from the Rhineland states of Southwestern Germany, as well as Switzerland. Their formal religious identity was either Lutheran* or Reformed,* though a significant number were sectarian Christians representing the Mennonites,* Dunkers* (*See* Church of the Brethren), Schwenkfelders* and others. They were concentrated in the rural area west of Philadelphia, where, with the dearth of opportunities for formal education, they developed the vernacular "Pennsylvania-Dutch" (from *Deutsch* or *German*) dialect that is still in use.

The impact of New England's Great Awakening* rippled through the German communities in the years following the revival,* although the main influence on the spirituality* of these communities derived from the literature of German Pietism,* such as that expressed in Johann Arndt's *True Christianity.* However, in general the spiritual life of these German-Americans was at a low ebb in the decades preceding and during the American Revolution,* and sectarian infighting resulted in serious religious fragmentation, particularly in southeastern Pennsylvania. In 1741 the Moravian leader* Count Nicholas von Zinzendorf* attempted to unify the Pennsylvania-German sects,* forming the Congregation of God in the Spirit. But his ambitious plan to achieve unity among the sects was soon aborted.

In 1726 Philip William Otterbein* arrived in Pennsylvania. A German Reformed missionary,* he became the leader of the revivalist wing of his church and cofounder of the first indigenous German-American revivalist denomination, the Church of the United Brethren in Christ.* Before the era of camp meetings,* lay* evangelists* began to appear in the German communities. The Mennonite* Martin Boehm* was an outstanding example, addressing a "big meeting" (*grosse Versammlung*) held in the Isaac Long barn on Pentecost in 1767. Otterbein, pastor of the nearby German Reformed congregation in Lancaster, was in attendance. Following Boehm's spiritual testimony*—an experience closely paralleling Otterbein's own new birth* in Christ (*Wiedergeburt*) under the Reformed Pietists at Haborn—Otterbein embraced Boehm with the announcement "Wir sind Bruder!" ("We are brethren"). Here was forged a unity of brethren in Christ that transcended, if it did not displace, commitments to their historic church bodies. It was a uniquely American phenomenon, bringing together in voluntary* association adherents of church bodies that had long been enemies in Europe.

The long-term result of this ecumenical* effort was the formation of a separate revivalist denomination.* But this occurred after 1800, partially under Methodist* influence. As a result of the Methodist's reticence to minister in the German language, a separate body was formed that more closely resembled Methodist doctrine and polity, the Evangelical Association (1809). Its founder, the lay revivalist Jacob Albright,* initiated a work directed at the successive waves of nineteenth-century German immigrants. In 1850 the Evangelicals also launched an ambitious program of missionary activity in Germany itself, resulting in a major free church* movement there, *Die Evangelische Gemeinschaft.* In addition, the first German Methodist Conference within the Methodist Episcopal* Church was launched in Ohio in 1832, the most prominent leader being Wilhelm Nast (1807-1889). These German Conferences were absorbed into the English conferences of the Methodist Episcopal Church prior to 1939.

For the most part, Lutherans, German Reformed and Mennonites resisted nineteenth-century revivalism. Fearful of the subjective, individual Piety* of the revivalistic "bush meeting Dutch," who rapidly expanded through their camp meetings, the Lutheran and Reformed "church Dutch" renewed their emphasis on their confessions* and sacraments.* Mennonite and Amish "plain Dutch," on the other hand, renewed their emphasis on legal and ethical norms. The major fruit of German-American revivalism, the Evangelicals and the United Brethren, were largely assimilated into American culture during the early twentieth century prior to their union with each other in 1946 and the United Methodist Church* in 1968.

BIBLIOGRAPHY. B. Behney and P. Eller, *History of the Evangelical United Brethren Church* (1979); J. S. O'Malley, *Pilgrimage of Faith: The Legacy of the Otterbeins* (1973); J. S. O'Malley, *Touched by Godliness; Bishop John Seybert and the Evangelical Heritage* (1985); D. Yoder, *Pennsylvania Spirituals* (1961).   J. S. O'Malley

Revivalism, Protestant. Revivalism is the movement that promotes periodic spiritual intensity in church life, during which the unconverted come to Christ and the converted* are shaken out of their spiritual lethargy. Often leading to social and moral reform* activities, revivalism was one of the chief characteristics of American Protestantism in the eighteenth and nineteenth centuries and still retains a powerful influence in many quarters. Unevenly distributed among the denominations,* revivalism has been strongest in Baptist,* Methodist,* Holiness* and Pentecostal* groups and weakest among Lutherans* and Episcopalians.* Theologically, it has been closer to conservative evangelicalism* and fundamentalism* than to liberalism.*

Debate over the meaning of terms like *revival, awakening* and *renewal* has prompted much dialog, but confining revivalism to frontier* conditions and emotional appeals is an unhistorical understanding of the movement. Revivalism is both urban* and rural, rational and emotional, cutting across all class lines.

Renewal often refers to changes in church life that include revivals but also include other changes like liturgical* and parish* movements as well. *Revival* and *awakening* are virtually synonymous terms, though *awakening* is usually used to refer to extensive revival movements. When do local revival movements become general awakenings? The question is variously answered, some even doubting whether general awakenings have occurred. At the very least, general awakenings are never total in their reach, whether vertically through socioeconomic levels or horizontally in their geographic extension. In historical parlance, however, the conventions of Great Awakening* in the mid-eighteenth century, Second Awakening* early in the nineteenth century and the Prayer Meeting Revival,* or Awakening, of 1857-1858 are standard descriptions.

The general sources of revivalism are the Protestant emphasis on preaching,* the Puritan* emphasis on a noticeable conversion experience and the pietistic* emphasis on warmhearted faith. To these may be added Solomon Stoddard's* belief that the Spirit works in "seasons of harvest." By the early eighteenth century, the notion of periodic awakenings in reponse to preaching and resulting in renewed spiritual life had emerged.

The Beginnings of Revivalism. The Great Awakening of the 1730s and 1740s traces its beginning to 1720, with the arrival of Theodore Frelinghuysen* in New Jersey. A Dutch Reformed* pastor influenced by Puritanism,* his preaching divided the Dutch congregations but also led to revival in several of the churches in his charge. At about that same time, the Tennent family—William, Sr.,* and his four sons, most notably Gilbert*— preached a revival message that influenced Reformed and Presbyterian* churches in Pennsylvania and New Jersey in the 1720s and 1730s. Similar effects were realized during the years 1734-1735 in the Congregational* church in Northampton, Massachusetts, under the ministry of Jonathan Edwards,* successor to his grandfather Solomon Stoddard.

Though the revival in Northampton waned fairly quickly, Edwards was extremely influential because of the books he wrote on revival issues. His work, substantial portions of which were reprinted and commented on by John Wesley* in England, laid out several important principles: the whole heart (intellect, will, emotion) is affected by conversion; revivals are surprising works of God; the true marks of conversion are in a holy life; and changed hearts have social effects (thereby laying the groundwork for social and moral reform movements).

The Great Awakening reached its zenith in the 1740s with the preaching tours of the Grand Itinerant, George Whitefield.* His powerful delivery and strong appeals, often given in outdoor settings, made him a popular and effective preacher and set the model for other itinerants to follow. Whitefield continued to itinerate, and the revival moved South in the 1740s and 1750s, but by 1750 its influence had ebbed.

The effects of the Great Awakening were clear enough. Belief in awakenings became the commonly held legacy of the movement, based largely on Edwards's apologetic work and on the experience in scores of churches. Detractors also came to the fore, producing Old* (anti-revival) and New* (pro-revival) Lights, indicative of the dividing effects that revivalism was always to have among American Protestants. Education* also was affected, with several colleges founded by revival advocates. And in many congregations experiential piety replaced the religious formalism that had threatened Protestantism earlier in the century.

Whether the Great Awakening created the national consciousness needed for the Revolution* is debated, but it clearly created a church consciousness among the majority of Protestants that helped make revivalism the staple of church life it became in the Second Awakening.

Revivalism Reaches Maturity. Instances of revival occurred throughout the revolutionary generation, with strong local expressions at times, but the Second Awakening is usually dated from 1800, with the appearance of the camp meeting.* The Cane Ridge,* Kentucky, meeting in the summer of 1801 was attended by thousands and set the stage for the camp-meeting approach with its emotional appeals, use of the mourner's bench* and the holding of periodic meetings at which the Spirit moved. Begun by Presbyterians and Baptists as well as Methodists, the camp meeting became an almost exclusive Methodist domain after 1810. It also moved East, became more settled and eventually merged into Bible camps* and conference* grounds as it assumed more permanence.

Revival came to New England after 1800 as well, both in the cities and towns and at the schools, such as the series of revivals at Yale* during the presidency of Timothy Dwight, grandson of Jonathan Edwards. New England revivalism was more sedate than its Western counterpart, producing debate on the nature of revivals that was settled, but never fully resolved, by the career of Charles G. Finney.*

Converted as an adult, Finney was ordained* a Presbyterian minister* in 1824 and soon began his evangelistic work. By 1835 his revivalist career had peaked, though he continued holding meetings even after his attachment to Oberlin College* in that year. In his *Lectures on Revival,* Finney argued that the Scriptures* laid out the principles which, when followed, would result in revival. A revival was not a miracle (a surprising work); God used the regular agencies of providence, the Holy Spirit and human beings to bring about revival.

Finney created opposition when he elaborated the role that persons could play as God's agents and when he hinted that revival could come as often as every year. The means that Finney was faulted for—called "new measures"*—included prayer language that was over-familiar with God; the public naming of saints and sinners who needed spiritual change; preaching for immediate decision; and the use of the anxious (mourner's)

bench,* an area at the front of the meeting place where those who were anxious about their souls' condition could struggle through to resolution.

Finney believed that the crucial component in human nature was the will. A person begins life in a morally neutral state, with the will facing decisions posed by the sensibilities and the understanding: "Sin is in the sinning," not in the person as original sin. At conversion, the will is faced with a decision and, aided by the grace of God, the right moral choice can be made. Finney's emphasis on the will laid the groundwork for the new measures: the church and the revivalist arranged the situation in which the decision can be made.

Finney stated that means would not produce a revival without the blessing of God on them, and he used new measures in a relatively restrained manner. Some revivalists were not so careful. But from the time of Finney on, most advocates of revivalism believed that revival could be "worked up"; revivals were not simply "sent down" from God. Modern revivalism was now fixed: protracted meetings* held once or twice yearly; preaching for decision; professional itinerating revivalists; techniques for the preparation and conducting of meetings; and even a special musical form, the gospel song.*

Revivalism moved through the frontier camp meeting into towns and small cities and into large urban centers. The move to the urban center was embodied in the Awakening of 1857-1858, sometimes referred to as the Prayer Meeting Revival, or Laymen's Revival. Beginning in New York City in the fall of 1857, run by local businessmen, the revival soon spread to other East Coast and then to Midwestern cities. Aided by the telegraph and various branches of the YMCA,* both of which dated from the 1830s, the movement peaked in the spring of 1858, when thousands were meeting each noontime for prayer and witness, and the effects spilled over into the churches as well. Perhaps a million members were added to church rolls as a result of the Awakening.

Revivalism in the Modern Era. After the Awakening of 1857-1858. it is difficult to find instances of general awakening. But revivalism continued in the years following, and some of the most noteworthy names in revival history made their appearance.

Dwight L. Moody* was the premier revivalist in the last third of the nineteenth century. Raised in New England, converted in Boston, he early moved to Chicago in the booming West. Successful as a businessman, he was also in Sunday school* and YMCA work, and by 1875, after two years of campaigning in England, he became a full-time evangelist.* To some extent the epitome of a late-nineteenth-century businessman, Moody's simple and low-key approach was heard by millions in many citywide campaigns.

Moody was only the best known of late nineteenth-century evangelists. Hundreds of others crisscrossed the continent, lacing the nation with revival meetings. African-American churches and denominations were as actively revivalistic as white ones. The Holiness Movement* that began in Methodist bodies before the Civil War* was revivalistic in nature. By the end of the century the first glimmerings of the Pentecostal Movement* appeared—it too arose out of and perpetuated the revivalistic tradition. While evangelicals were just beginning the fight against burgeoning liberalism, revivalism remained at the core of most Protestant churches.

In some ways, certainly in the popular press, post-Civil War revivalism reached its apogee in the career of Billy Sunday,* the flamboyant revivalist of the Progressive Era. He continued to hold meetings until the year of his death, but after the hugely successful New York meeting in 1917, his career gradually diminished. Sunday's style was uncharacteristic of a generation of revivalists who flourished after Moody and maintained the revival tradition in a variety of ways.

Revivalism continued between the two world wars, though with less influence in the general culture and with the stereotypical evangelist, as in Sinclair Lewis's *Elmer Gantry,* a staple of the media. At the same time, new forces were at work. Radio's rise in the 1920s led to ministries like those of Charles Fuller*; Pentecostal denominations grew; missionary* activity, especially faith missions,* increased, leading to the further export of American revivalism. Many evangelists continued to itinerate, others settled into semipermanent "tabernacle" ministries that advocated continuous revival, the logical extension of the idea that revival could be a constant and not just a recurring feature in the churches.

With the revival of religion after World War 2 came a resurgence in revivalism. Both Oral Roberts* and Billy Graham* came on the national scene in the late 1940s, Roberts representing Pentecostal healing* revivals and Graham initially representing fundamentalism, the movement that included the majority of conservative Protestants after World War 1.* Fundamentalism went through some changes in the 1950s with the rise of neo-evangelicalism* (more recently simply called evangelicalism) in its ranks, and Graham eventually aligned with the more culturally affirming neo-

evangelicalism, thereby bringing revivalism back to a more central place in American life.

The revival of religion faded after 1960, but revivalism remains a strong feature of important segments of contemporary Protestantism and, despite the televangelist* scandals of the 1980s, seems unlikely to disappear from the American church scene for the foreseeable future.

Characteristics of Revivalism. Revivalism has undergone theological change over the years, moving from a rather strong Calvinism in the Great Awakening to the "Calvinized Arminianism" of the last two centuries. Interestingly enough, opposition to revivalism has come from both the conservative side—for example, Charles Hodge* and some of the nineteenth-century Princetonians*—and the liberal side of the theological spectrum. But even where it has been opposed, the emphasis on conversion and warmhearted faith has been strong. Thus to some extent even its opponents have accepted at least some of revivalism's basic beliefs. Revivalism has often been attached to a particular view of sanctification,* ranging from Wesleyan forms of perfectionism,* as in the teaching of nineteenth-century Holiness leader Phoebe Palmer,* to the extremely influential Keswick* Higher Life movement,* begun in 1875. At times the anxious bench and its later equivalents have been used to call persons forward for sanctification as much as for regeneration.*

Revivalism has kept up with the technology of the day also, the use of satellites and computers being the most recent in a long line of advances in communication being adopted by revivalists. Though at times decrying the surrounding culture, revivalists have seen technology as a neutral force in advancing the gospel.

Social and moral reform are intimately tied to revivalism, reaching a peak of influence in the "benevolent empire" of reform societies in the antebellum era. But there is always a social result from revivalism. Beginning with changes in social life reported by Jonathan Edwards in Northampton during the 1730s, seen through evidences of the softening of frontier life, noted in the late-nineteenth-century societies organized to combat urban social ills, it continued in the resurgence of social and political awareness that began in the 1960s. Education has also been a constant feature as revivalism has made its social impact, from the colleges of pre-revolutionary America and the scores of schools founded in the antebellum era, to the Bible institute* movement begun late in the nineteenth century and the institutions founded more recently.

[1014]

Finally, there has been a close tie between revivalism and missions.* College revivals* provided impetus and personnel for the modern missionary movement that began around 1810. Revivalism also gave support to the lay, student and faith mission* movements of the nineteenth and early twentieth centuries. Supported by both denominational and independent missions, the tie between revivalism and missions remains strong down to the present.

BIBLIOGRAPHY. D. D. Bruce, *And They All Sang Hallelujah: Plain-Folk Camp-Meeting Religion, 1800-1845* (1974); R. Carwardine, *Transatlantic Revivalism: Popular Evangelicalism in Britain and America, 1790-1865* (1979); J. Edwards, *A Faithful Narrative of the Surprising Work of God* (1737); C. C. Goen, ed., *The Great Awakening* (1972); J. F. Findlay, Jr., *Dwight L. Moody: American Evangelist, 1837-1899* (1969); K. J. Hardman, *Charles Grandison Finney, 1792-1875* (1987); D. E. Harrell, Jr., *All Things Are Possible: The Healing and Charismatic Revivals in Modern America* (1975); W. G. McLoughlin, Jr., *Modern Revivalism: Charles Grandison Finney to Billy Graham* (1959); S. S. Sizer, *Gospel Hymns and Social Religion: The Rhetoric of Nineteenth Century Revivalism* (1978); T. L. Smith, *Revivalism and Social Reform: Protestantism on the Eve of the Civil War* (1980).

W. G. Travis

Revolution, American. *See* AMERICAN REVOLUTION, CHRISTIANITY AND THE.

Rice, ("Father") David (1733-1816). Presbyterian* minister,* anti-revivalist and abolitionist* leader. Born in colonial Virginia, Rice became a Presbyterian under Samuel Davies.* In 1763 he married Mary Blair, daughter of Samuel Blair, another prominent Presbyterian, and served congregations in Hanover and Bedford counties before pioneering in Kentucky in 1783. Rice organized Presbyterian congregations at Danville, Fork of Dix River and Cane Run. He also worked with other groups and congregations to form the Transylvania Presbytery (1796), the parent body of Presbyterianism in the Midwest.

Rice initiated higher education in Kentucky, working with members of his extended family and with close friends. The Transylvania Seminary (later Transylvania University) was begun in his house, with a son-in-law as its first professor.

"Father" Rice opposed slavery and revivals* alike. In 1792, he was elected to the convention to fashion a state constitution, solely to oppose the legalizing of slavery. He lost that vote and retired from active politics. When the Great Kentucky Revival began in 1799-1800, he criticized the emotional preaching and the "bodily agitations" that accompanied it.

BIBLIOGRAPHY. *AAP* 3; R. H. Bishop, *An Outline of the History of the Church in the State of Kentucky . . . together with the Memoirs of "Father" David Rice, D.D.* (1824); *DAB* VIII; L. B. Weeks, *Kentucky Presbyterians* (1983).

L. B. Weeks

Rice, John Holt (1777-1831). Presbyterian* minister* and educator. Born in Bedford County, Virginia, Rice read theology* with Archibald Alexander* after teaching school and marrying Anne Smith Morton. Licensed* by Hanover Presbytery and ordained* in 1804, Rice served the Cub Creek Presbyterian Church, farmed and formed a school for boys. He also raised funds for the beginning of a theological school at Hampden-Sydney.

In 1812, Rice was called to Richmond, Virginia, and organized the First Presbyterian Church in that community. With others he founded the Virginia Bible Society in 1813 and the American Bible Society* in 1816 to provide the Scriptures "without note or comment" for as many Americans as possible.

After experimenting with a predecessor, Rice began in 1818 to publish the *Virginia Evangelical and Literary Magazine,* a significant religious monthly that continued for ten years. During this period Rice moved from an active, anti-slavery position to one that became quietly supportive of the South's "peculiar institution." Rice likewise fought unsuccessfully for evangelical* control of the University of Virginia.

Elected moderator of the Presbyterian General Assembly in 1819, Rice turned down an invitation to become the president of the College of New Jersey* three years later. He did accept the call in 1824 to be president of the Theological Seminary at Hampden-Sydney (later Union Theological Seminary in Virginia) and by the time of his death he was able to put the school on a sound intellectual and financial footing.

Rice mixed Calvinism* with humane care for those who differed in Christian conviction. He especially directed his energies toward those who had not heard the gospel, and his lobbying for Presbyterian missions* led in part to the forming of the Board of World Missions by the denomination. Rice wrote several books and pamphlets, among them *Irenicum or the Peacemaker* (1820).

BIBLIOGRAPHY. *AAP* 4; *DAB* VIII; W. Maxwell, *A*

Memoir of the Rev. John H. Rice, D.D. (1835); *NCAB* 2; P. B. Price, *The Life of the Reverend John Holt Rice, D.D.* (1887).   L. B. Weeks

Rice, John R. (1895-1980). Baptist* fundamentalist,* evangelist,* editor and controversialist. Born in Texas and raised a Southern Baptist,* Rice attended Decatur (Texas) Baptist College, Baylor University and Southwestern Baptist Seminary. He left the Southern Baptist Convention in the 1920s and remained an outspoken critic of Baptist denominationalism.*

Rice served as pastor of the Fundamentalist Baptist Church in Dallas (1932-1940). In 1934 he founded *The Sword of the Lord,* an "independent Christian weekly," promoting fundamentalist theology and attacking modernism* and liberalism in church and government. The headquarters of the *Sword of the Lord* was later moved to Murfreesboro, Tennessee, and Rice continued as its editor and a full-time evangelist until his death. *The Sword of the Lord* soon became an influential fundamentalist periodical, particularly among independent Baptists.

Rice was a colorful preacher and prolific author. He was well known for his polemical response to theological modernism, Catholicism,* Communism* and the Civil Rights Movement,* as well as dancing, smoking, movies and alcohol.*

BIBLIOGRAPHY. R. Summer, *A Man Sent from God* (1960).   B. J. Leonard

Rice, Luther (1783-1836). Baptist* denominational* leader, promoter of missions* and education.* Born in Northborough, Massachusetts, Rice studied at Leicester Academy and graduated from Williams College (1810). Ordained* for missionary service by Congregationalists,* he embarked for India in 1812. After intense study of baptism* on shipboard, he rejected infant baptism, became a Baptist and was immersed in Calcutta in November 1812, by William Ward, an English Baptist missionary.

Returning to America in 1813, Rice severed ties with the Congregationalists and began to stir up Baptist interest in missions. His extensive travels and enthusiastic preaching resulted in the formation of the General Convention of the Baptist Denomination in the United States for Foreign Missions, in May 1814. Known as the Triennial Convention,* it was the first national body of Baptists in America.

Rice's missionary vision led him to advocate the founding of Baptist colleges, beginning in 1821 with Columbian College in Washington, D.C. In 1818 he started the *Latter Day Luminary,* a mis-

sions monthly and first national Baptist periodical, and in 1821 he began *The Columbian Star* (1821), a religious weekly. Rice was instrumental in founding the Baptist General Tract Society (1824). His travels were marked with success in raising funds for missions and education.

By the mid-1820s Columbian College faced financial difficulties due to overexpansion, and Rice came under criticism. Powerful personalities, inevitable reaction and ecclesiological differences contributed to the problem. Though vindicated, his influence became circumscribed. Rice left no published works, though his journal and letters remain. However, few men have exerted a greater or more lasting influence on the Baptist denomination. One historian said, "The coming of Luther Rice was the most important event in Baptist history in the nineteenth century." He is buried at Pine Pleasant Church, Washington, South Carolina.

BIBLIOGRAPHY. *AAP* 6; L. Rice, *Dispensations of Providence: Journal and Letters of Luther Rice,* ed., W. H. Brackney (1984); *DAB* VIII; *DARB;* H. L. McBeth, *The Baptist Heritage* (1987); E. W. Thompson, *Luther Rice: Believer in Tomorrow* (1967).   W. M. Patterson

Richard, Gabriel (1767-1832). Catholic* educator and missionary.* Born at Saintes, France, Richard studied at the Seminary of St. Sulpice in Paris. Because of the anticlericalism* of the French Revolution, he was secretly ordained* priest* in the fall of 1791 and sent to Baltimore the following spring. Not needed to teach at the seminary there, he was assigned as a missionary to the Illinois country. In the spring of 1798, he moved to Detroit to work in the outlying missions. After the Detroit fire of 1805, Richard became the sole priest there, building up St. Anne's Parish and helping with the development of the new Michigan Territory. Acquiring a printing press, he made possible Detroit's first newspaper. Imprisoned briefly by the British during the War of 1812, he returned to develop schools for the settlers and the Native Americans and especially the Catholepistemiad, the forerunner of the University of Michigan. In 1824 he won election to Congress as the territorial delegate from Michigan, the only priest before the twentieth century to have a seat in the House of Representatives. On his return to Detroit, he was suggested as bishop* for a proposed see at Detroit, but he died September 13, 1832, six months before the diocese was established.

BIBLIOGRAPHY. *DAB* VIII; F. B. Woodford and A. Hyma, *Gabriel Richard: Frontier Ambassador* (1958).   J. W. Bowen

Richards, George Warren (1869-1955). Reformed* theologian and educator. Born in Farmington, Pennsylvania, Richards graduated from Franklin and Marshall College (B.A., 1887; M.A., 1890; D.D., 1902) and was ordained to the ministry of the Reformed Church in the U.S. in 1890 and, following a pastorate in Allentown, Pennslyvania (1890-1899), studied theology at the universities of Berlin and Erlangen and received the Th.D. from Heidelberg (1925). Richards joined the faculty of the Theological Seminary of the Reformed Church in the U.S. at Lancaster, Pennsylvania, in 1899 and became its president (1920-1937). His major writings included *The Heidelberg Catechism— Historical and Doctrinal Studies* (1913), *Beyond Fundamentalism and Modernism: The Gospel of God* (1934) and *Creative Controversies in Christianity* (1938). He also wrote a history of the Lancaster seminary and edited the *Reformed Church Review* (1904-1911).

Richards was an exponent of Barthian, or neo-orthodox,* theology, which he considered to be an alternative to both liberalism* and fundamentalism.* Aside from his own historical and theological work, Richards helped introduce Karl Barth* to North Americans through his translations of many of Barth's sermons (*Come, Creator Spirit,* 1933; and *God's Search for Man,* 1935). As a churchman Richards was involved with his own denomination at the national level and in the ecumenical movement. He was a member of the continuation committee of the World Conference on Faith and Order and vice president of the Federal Council of Churches (1934-1936).   J. F. Johnson

Rigdon, Sidney (1793-1876). Early Mormon* leader. Born in Piny Fork, Pennsylvania, Rigdon became a Baptist* minister* and served congregations in Warren, Ohio (1819-1820), and Pittsburgh, Pennsylvania (1820-1824). After this he worked as a tanner (1824-1826) and as a minister (1824-1826) associated with the Mahoning Baptist Association in Ohio.

Attracted to the restorationism of Alexander Campbell,* Rigdon found opportunity to work alongside Campbell as early as 1821. He rode with Campbell to the Campbell-Maccalla Debate in 1823 and later transcribed that debate for the publication. By 1828 Rigdon had joined the Campbellites and was serving as a minister in Mentor, Ohio (1828-1830).

In 1830, Rigdon was one of the earliest converts to Mormonism, soon becoming a spokesman for Joseph Smith* and an ardent evangelist for the Mormon Church. Involved in the building of the first temple at Kirtland, Ohio, Rigdon fled with other Mormons to Missouri in 1838 and then to Nauvoo, Illinois. A brilliant speaker, though not always trusted by his fellow Mormons, Rigdon considered himself a serious claimant to the leadership of the church after Smith's death in 1844. When Brigham Young* assumed leadership of the church, Rigdon led a small group of dissidents to Pittsburgh, where they called themselves the Church of Christ. Eventually, the group dwindled away and Rigdon, rejecting overtures of peace from the Utah Mormons, lived out his years in poverty and disappointment.

BIBLIOGRAPHY. *DAB* VIII; F. M. McKiernan, *Voice of One Crying in the Wilderness: Sidney Ridgon, Religious Reformer* (1971); *NCAB* 16.
    T. L. Miethe

Riggs, Stephen Return (1812-1883). Missionary* and linguist among the Dakota Indians. Born at Steubenville, Ohio, and educated at Jefferson College in Pennsylvania and at the Western Seminary in Allegheny, Pennsylvania, Riggs was ordained* to the Presbyterian* ministry* in 1836. In 1837 he was sent by the American Board of Commissioners for Foreign Missions* to the Lac Qui Parle mission near Ft. Snelling, Minnesota.

Riggs worked there and at nearby missions until the outbreak of the Sioux Wars in 1862. After this uprising, he continued his work among the Dakotas imprisoned at Mankato, Minnesota, and later when they were confined to reservations in the Dakota Territory. Over the course of his forty-five years among the Dakotas, Riggs became an authority on their language, reducing it to written form, and producing primers, grammars and a variety of educational and religious literature, including a Dakota New Testament in 1865 and the entire Bible in 1880. In his later years, he lived in Beloit, Wisconsin, and supervised the work of other missionaries, making frequent visits to the Dakota reservation. He died in Beloit in 1883.

BIBLIOGRAPHY. *DAB* VIII; *DARB; NCAB* 3; S. R. Riggs, *Mary and I: Forty Years with the Sioux* (1880); S. R. Riggs, *Tah-koo Wah-kan, or the Gospel Among the Dakotas* (1869).
    M. S. Joy

Right to Life. A movement opposed to the taking of innocent human life at any time from conception to natural death. The term *pro-life* is often used as well. Arising as a reaction to the movement for liberalized abortion,* the first permanent group was founded in New York in 1966. From early on, however, Right to Life groups were concerned with the question of euthanasia as well and came to devote more of their energies to this subject during the 1980s.

The Supreme Court* decision of January 22, 1973, overthrowing all existing abortion laws, led to an enormous growth in the movement.The National Right to Life Committee which had been founded in 1968 under the auspices of the National Conference of Catholic Bishops,* in 1973 became autonomous and non-sectarian. It is the largest and most influential national organization, with well over two thousand local affiliates by the 1980s. A large number of other groups appeared as well, many the product of splits within the movement over strategy and tactics (e.g., American Life Lobby, Pro-Life Action League) and others appealing to specific constituencies (e.g., National Youth ProLife Coalition, Feminists for Life, Lutherans for Life). The movement is diverse, its members representing a wide range of religious and political viewpoints, and is monolithic only in its rejection of killing the innocent.

While the Right to Life movement from its beginning has had members of a variety of religions, it was initially heavily Roman Catholic* in composition. The later 1970s saw a huge influx of evangelical* Protestants* and this helped propel it to new prominence and political impact. The movement developed in Canada as well. The Alliance for Life was founded in 1968 and by the 1980s represented over two hundred local affiliates.

See also ABORTION.

BIBLIOGRAPHY. D. Andrusko, *To Rescue the Future: The Pro-Life Movement in the 1980's* (1983); J. T. Burtchaell, *Rachel Weeping and Other Essays on Abortion* (1982); S. M. Krason, *Abortion: Politics, Morality and the Constitution* (1984).

K. M. Cassidy

Riley, William Bell (1861-1947). Baptist* pastor* and fundamentalist* leader. Born in Green County, Indiana, less than thirty days before the outbreak of the Civil War,* Riley, like Lincoln* before him, came to know the hardships of a Kentucky cabin and dawn-to-dark hoeing. He found time, however, to join other youngsters on the county courthouse steps to listen to summertime trials, and to dream of speaking someday to huge audiences. By sixteen he had become an able public speaker.

In August 1875, during an evangelistic* meeting, Riley made a public profession of faith in Christ. After his immersion, he was received into the Dallesburg, Kentucky, Baptist church. In 1879

young Riley entered normal school at Valparaiso, Indiana. He intended to pursue a law career, but "a divine voice" indicated that he should enter the ministry* instead. As a result Riley moved to the Presbyterian College at Hanover, Indiana, and graduated in 1885. Three years later he earned his theological degree from the Southern Baptist Theological Seminary* in Louisville, Kentucky. He was ordained* in 1883 and a series of pastorates along the Ohio River followed. Later he moved to Lafayette, Indiana; Bloomington, Illinois; and Chicago, before settling in 1897 at the First Baptist Church of Minneapolis. After only a short time in the Twin Cities area, he founded the Northwestern Bible and Missionary Training School. In 1935 he established Northwestern Evangelical Seminary and in 1944 Northwestern College.

Riley's childhood dream of debating was fulfilled when he entered the modernist-fundamentalist controversy.* His most prominent contests were in defense of the Bible* against the evolutionary theory.* He debated, among others, Maynard Shipley of the Science League of America and J. C. McCabe, the English rationalist.

BIBLIOGRAPHY. *DAB* 4; M. A. Riley, *The Dynamic of a Dream* (1938); C. A. Russell, *Voices of American Fundamentalism* (1976); F. M. Szasz, "Three Fundamentalist Leaders" (unpublished Ph.D. dissertaton, University of Rochester, 1969).

B. L. Shelley

Rimmer, Harry (1890-1952). Presbyterian minister* and Christian apologist. A native of San Francisco, Rimmer attended Hahnemann College of the Pacific, Whittier College and the Bible Institute of Los Angeles. He was ordained* as a minister of the Society of Friends* and served as pastor of the First Friends Church in Los Angeles and as a chaplain* during World War 1.*

In 1920 he started the Research Science Bureau, Inc., in Denver, Colorado, through which he brought forward scientific evidence in support of the authenticity of the Bible.* He undertook archaeological expeditions, studied manuscripts in British and Egyptian museums and lectured at hundreds of college and university campuses on the harmony of science* and Scripture. He later became a Presbyterian and served as pastor* of the First Presbyterian Church, Duluth, Minnesota (1934-1939).

Rimmer was the author of twenty-nine books, among which were: *The Harmony of Science and Scripture* (1938); *Modern Science and the Genesis Record* (1938) and *Internal Evidence of Inspiration* (1939). He also served as associate editor of

Christian Faith and Life, as contributing editor of *Kings Business, Religious Digest, Northwest Pilot* and *Moody Monthly.* The recepient of several honorary degrees, he also served on the board of directors of John Brown University and radio station HCJB in Quito, Ecuador, where the Rimmer Memorial Hospital stands in honor of his fund-raising activity on behalf of Indian health care.

BIBLIOGRAPHY. *NCAB* 41.   D. G. Buss

Ripley, George (1802-1880). Transcendental-ist,* editor, literary critic and reformer. Born in Greenfield, Massachusetts, Ripley graduated from Harvard College* in 1823 and Harvard* Divinity School in 1826. He was ordained* a Unitarian pastor in 1826 and installed in the newly organized Purchase Street Church in Boston.

In 1836 the first meeting of the "Transcendental Club" was held in Ripley's home, and when that group first began publishing *The Dial* in 1840, he assisted in writing and editing it. During this period Ripley studied German theology* and philosophy, especially the works of Schleiermach-er, Herder and Kant. One fruit of his study was the *Specimens of Foreign Standard Literature,* a series of translations of European scholarship which he edited with C. F. Hedge beginning in 1838.

After extended controversy with more conserva-tive Unitarian colleagues, Ripley finally withdrew from the ministry* in 1841. That same year he established a farming cooperative in West Roxbury, Massachusetts, nine miles outside of Boston. "Brook Farm,"* as it was called, attempted to apply what Ripley considered the New Testament social order. He hoped that the community would inspire others to imitate its pattern of communal property and mutual toleration, but the farm sank into heavy debt and was finally dissolved in 1847.

Ripley moved next to a long career in journal-ism, exerting significant influence on the American public's opinion of new writers such as Nathaniel Hawthorne* and Charles Darwin. In 1849 Ripley became literary editor of the *New York Tribune,* and in 1850 he and others founded Harper's *New Monthly Magazine.* His most popular work was the *New American Cyclopedia,* sixteen volumes pro-duced between 1858 and 1863 with Charles A. Dana. The first two editions of this reference work sold more than three million copies.

BIBLIOGRAPHY. *DAB* VIII; *DARB;* O. B. Fro-thingham, *George Ripley* (1882); L. Swift, *Brook Farm: Its Members, Scholars, and Visitors* (1900).

T. P. Thigpen

Ritter, Joseph Elmer (1892-1967). Cardinal* of St. Louis. Born at New Albany, Indiana, Ritter was educated at St. Meinrad Abbey in his native state, where he was ordained* to the priesthood* in 1917. Ritter did pastoral work in the diocese of Indianapolis, becoming rector* of the cathedral* in 1924 and auxiliary bishop* in 1933. He became bishop of the diocese the following year and in 1944 its first archbishop.*

In 1946 Ritter was transferred to St. Louis, where he almost immediately established the character of his episcopacy by ordering the racial desegrega-tion of all Catholic schools and parishes,* a decision which was fought bitterly by some Catholics. This occurred seven years before the Supreme Court* case striking down segregation in the public schools, all of which were still segregat-ed in the St. Louis archdiocese in 1947.

During the 1950s Archbishop Ritter quietly encouraged newer movements within the church, such as greater lay* participation in the liturgy,* and especially the cause of racial justice. The 1950s were also a time of unprecedented growth for the Catholic Church. The St. Louis archbishop founded numerous new parishes and directed a major building program of churches, schools and other religious institutions. He also inaugurated a system whereby St. Louis priests served in the Latin American missions.

Ritter was made a cardinal by Pope John XXIII* at the end of 1960 and was one of the leading American delegates to the Second Vatican Coun-cil.* At Vatican II Ritter almost always supported the "progressive" program, including ecumenical* relations with other religious bodies, liturgical reform and social justice. At the same time he began implementing these changes in his own archdiocese. As cardinal he also participated in the election of Pope Paul VI* in 1963.

In the turmoil immediately following the Coun-cil, Cardinal Ritter clashed with some of his priests and lay people over interpretations of the council's decrees. But his death in 1967 preceded post-conciliar crisis in American Catholicism.

BIBLIOGRAPHY. W. B. Faherty, *Dream by the River: Two Centuries of St. Louis Catholicism* (1971); J. Johnson, *Joseph Cardinal Ritter* (1964).   J. F. Hitchcock

Roberts, Benjamin Titus (1823-1893). Found-er of the Free Methodist Church.* As a young preacher* Roberts became involved in a reform movement in the Genessee annual conference of the Methodist Episcopal Church (*See* Methodist Churches). When the movement failed Roberts and a number of others were expelled from the church. In 1860 Roberts and the other expelled ministers were joined by sympathetic laymen* in founding the Free Methodist Church. He served as general superintendent* of the denomination from its founding until his death. His ministry was characterized by a vigorous advocacy of the Wesleyan* doctrine of entire sanctification* and by active promotion of abolition,* the rights of women and bimetallism. He wrote four books, edited the *Earnest Christian* and founded Chili Seminary, which after his death was renamed Roberts Wesleyan College (Rochester, New York).

BIBLIOGRAPHY. B. T. Roberts, *Why Another Sect* (1879); C. H. Zahniser, *Earnest Christian: Life and Works of Benjamin Titus Roberts* (1957).

C. E. White

Roberts, Granville Oral (1918-). Pentecostal* evangelist,* college president and television minister. Born in Pontotoc County, Oklahoma, Roberts is the son of Ellis Roberts, a minister in the Pentecostal Holiness Church. Roberts rebelled against his religious upbringing, but in 1935 he had a conversion* experience and, a few days later, experienced what he believed was a divine healing* from tuberculosis. During the next dozen years, he became a well-known evangelist and pastor* in the Pentecostal Holiness Church.

In 1947 Roberts launched an independent ministry based on divine healing. Riding a wave of Pentecostal ecumenism* after World War 2,* he conducted huge tent revivals* and pioneered sophisticated methods of mass mailing. Roberts was the ablest of a group of revivalists who built large financial empires in the 1950s and 1960s. In 1954 he greatly broadened his influence by televising his healing crusades.

Healing revivalism began to wane in the late 1950s, but Roberts skillfully used new methods to sustain his ministry. In 1960 he announced plans to build a university in Tulsa, and Oral Roberts University opened in 1965. In the late 1960s Roberts made other dramatic changes in his ministry. He stopped holding crusades in 1968. He canceled his television program in 1967, but in 1969 he returned in a series of prime-time specials that featured well-known personalities from the entertainment field. Roberts left the Pentecostal Holiness Church in 1968 and was ordained a minister in the United Methodist Church.* During these years, Roberts de-emphasized his extreme Pentecostal views, and he became a key figure in the emergence of the charismatic movement* in the traditional churches.

Around 1975 Roberts appeared to begin a journey back to his roots. He angered some people, particularly in Tulsa, when he added a number of graduate programs to his university, including a medical school. Even more controversial was his construction of a hospital and medical-research center called the City of Faith. Faced with huge financial obligation, Roberts resorted to high-pressure fund-raising techniques, often launching his campaigns with controversial personal revelations from God. By the late 1980s the Roberts empire was valued at around $500,000,000, but the evangelist and his son and heir apparent, Richard, were often criticized by the media. More and more, Roberts associated himself with the radical leaders of the charismatic movement known as the "Faith Teachers" (*See* Faith Movement).

Aside from the institutions he has founded in Tulsa, Oklahoma, Roberts has contributed to modern religious history in important ways. He was a key figure in communicating the Pentecostal healing message, as well as the emphasis on the gifts of the Holy Spirit, to mainstream Christians. Roberts also pioneered many of the techniques which led to the explosion of religious television; particularly important was his use of sophisticated production methods and entertainment formats. Finally, at the City of Faith, Roberts brought together a variety of people interested in the relationship of religion and healing, including physicians and researchers. Although his public image has suffered in recent years, his permanent contributions to the shaping of the Pentecostal and charismatic movements are beyond dispute.

See also ELECTRONIC CHURCH; FAITH HEALING; PENTECOSTAL MOVEMENT.

BIBLIOGRAPHY. D. E. Harrell, Jr., *Oral Roberts: An American Life* (1985); O. Roberts, *The Call* (1972); E. Roberts, *His Darling Wife, Evelyn* (1976); W. A. Robinson, *Oral: The Warm, Intimate, Unauthorized Portrait of a Man of God* (1976); J. Sholes, *Give Me That Prime-Time Religion* (1979).

D. E. Harrell

Robertson, Archibald Thomas (1863-1934). Southern Baptist* Greek scholar, professor of New Testament and author. Son of an impoverished physician, Robertson received his M.A. from Wake Forest College in 1885. Converted* at thirteen years of age, he felt called to the gospel ministry at seventeen, and preached his first sermon in an African-American church in North Carolina. Though hindered by a speech impediment, he nevertheless applied himself with unflagging diligence to preparation for the ministry.* At Southern Baptist Theological Seminary, where he received his Th.M. degree in 1888, he distinguished himself as a gifted and brilliant student. In 1894 he married Ella Broadus, daughter of his beloved mentor, John A. Broadus.*

Robertson became the most widely respected Southern Baptist scholar of his time. His "big grammar," *A Grammar of the Greek New Testament in the Light of Historical Research* (1914), established him as the foremost New Testament Greek scholar of his day. He authored forty-four other books, including four grammars, fourteen commentaries, six volumes of *Word Pictures of the New Testament* (1930) and eleven historical and ten biographical studies. His *A Harmony of the Gospels* (1922) and *An Introduction to the Textual Criticism* (1925) became the most widely used of his many books.

Robertson combined a demand for academic excellence and a deep Christian devotion.* Upon at least one occasion he worked as a counselor in a revival* meeting in Louisville, Kentucky, conducted by Dwight L. Moody* and was in demand as a speaker at religious assemblies in England and America.

BIBLIOGRAPHY. Everet Gill, *A. T. Robertson* (1943); W. A. Mueller, *A History of Southern Baptist Theological Seminary* (1959).

W. R. Estep

Robertson, James (1839-1902). Presbyterian* missions* leader in Canada. Born in Scotland, Robertson immigrated to Canada in 1855, where he taught school before studying at the University of Toronto, Princeton Seminary* and Union Theological Seminary (New York).* After ordination* by the Presbyterian Church of Canada* in 1869, he ministered at Norwich in rural Ontario until he accepted a call to the city of Winnipeg on the developing prairies of western Canada. In 1881 he became superintendent of Presbyterian missions on the prairies.

When he began as "the Presbyterian bishop," the denomination* had but four congregations. During his tenure the denominational presence increased to over one hundred forty established churches in addition to 226 mission charges which served over a thousand communities. Robertson received a D.D. from the Presbyterian College in Montreal in 1888, and in 1895 he was honored by election as the moderator of the Presbyterian Church.

BIBLIOGRAPHY. C. W. Gordon, *The Life of James Robertson* (1908); I. McFadden, *He Belonged to the West: James Robertson* (1958).

B. A. McKenzie

Robertson, Marion Gordon "Pat" (1930-). Religious television broadcaster and politician. Born in Lexington, Virginia, the son of U.S. Senator A. Willis Robertson, young Pat graduated cum laude from Washington and Lee University in 1950. After a brief tour of Marine duty, he returned to school in 1952, pursuing a law degree from Yale University* Law School. Three years later, after graduation, Robertson failed the New York bar exam.

After a brief venture in the business world, Robertson became a Christian in 1956 and turned toward a full-time commitment to ministry.* In September he entered the Biblical Seminary of New York (renamed in 1965 to New York Theological Seminary). While a student, Robertson became a pioneer of the modern charismatic movement.* His work over the next thirty years helped that movement gain strength among members of traditional evangelical* churches.

After seminary, Robertson purchased a small UHF television station in Norfolk, Virginia. Working on a shoestring budget, he supported his efforts in religious broadcasting by taking a job as a Southern Baptist* associate minister in a nearby church. In 1963 he began a campaign to get 700 listeners to pledge $10.00 per month so that he could meet his monthly budget. The "700 Club" was born. Two years later, shortly after Jim and Tammy Bakker* came to work for Robertson, the Christian Broadcasting Network (CBN) hosted its first successful fund-raising telethon. In the late 1970s Robertson moved his headquarters to Virginia Beach and established a full graduate university. By 1987 the annual budget of CBN exceeded two hundred million dollars, and its television signal reached over 190 different stations in the U.S. and overseas.

Robertson's initial involvement in politics came as a result of the successful "Washington for Jesus" rally he helped organize in 1980. The secular press estimated the crowd to be just over 200,000 strong. Believing that such a showing indicated Christians could influence American political life for the better, Robertson began to mobilize Christian support for various political issues.

On September 17, 1986, he announced that he would become a candidate for the U.S. presidency if he could, within one year, obtain the signatures of three million Americans who would commit to work, pray and provide financial support for his campaign. His goal met, he declared his intention to run just short of one year later. After early successes, his campaign faltered, and he withdrew before the summer Republican Convention.

Though Robertson's 1988 campaign met with only limited success, and though he has returned to religious broadcasting, he will likely remain active in presidential politics for many years to come.

BIBLIOGRAPHY. D. E. Harrell, Jr., *Pat Robertson: A Personal, Religious, and Political Portrait* (1988); P. Robertson, *Shout It from the Housetop* (1972); M. G. Toulouse, "Pat Robertson: Apocalyptic Theology and American Foreign Policy," *JCS* 31 (Winter 1989):73-99.   M. G. Toulouse

Robinson, Edward (1794-1863). Biblical scholar and geographer. Born in Southington, Connecticut, Robinson graduated from Hamilton College, Clinton, New York (B.A., 1816), studied law and then tutored in Greek and mathematics at Hamilton College. In 1821, while in Andover, Massachusetts, he met Moses Stuart,* the Andover Seminary* Hebrew scholar. Stuart persuaded Robinson to pursue the study of Hebrew, and by 1823 Robinson was instructing in Hebrew at Andover. In 1826 he went to Germany for a period of four years, during which he studied at the universities of Göttingen, Halle and Berlin.

Returning to America, Robinson became professor extraordinary of biblical literature and librarian at Andover. There he also founded and edited the *American Biblical Repository* (1831), a journal of biblical studies which was later incorporated into *Bibliotheca Sacra* (1851). Plagued by epilepsy, Robinson left his post at Andover in 1833 and moved to Boston, where he continued his scholarly labors. In 1836 he published his translation and revision of Gesenius's *A Hebrew and English Lexicon of the Old Testament* as well as *A Greek and English Lexicon of the New Testament.*

In 1837 he accepted an invitation to the chair of biblical literature at Union Theological Seminary,* New York, and was simultaneously given leave to undertake a geographical expedition to Palestine, Sinai and southern Syria (March-July 1838). Returning to Berlin, he published the results of his research in the three-volume *Biblical Researches in Palestine, Mount Sinai and Arabia Petraea* (1841). This work established him as the foremost historical geographer of the Holy Land. Two subsequent expeditions to Palestine in 1852 and 1856 led to further published results. His *Greek Harmony of the Gospels* (1845) was regarded as the best Greek harmony of its day, and his incomplete *Physical Geography of the Holy Land* was published posthumously in 1865.

BIBLIOGRAPHY. *DAB* VIII; H. B. Smith and R. D. Hitchcock, *The Life, Writings, and Character of Edward Robinson* (1863).   D. G. Reid

Robinson, John (1575-1625). English separatist* minister.* Born at Sturton-le-Steeple and educated at Corpus Christi College, Cambridge (B.A. 1596, M.A. 1599), Robinson served as fellow of the college and as minister at St. Andrews, Norwich. Through these early years he was an active Puritan.* About 1605 he was suspended from his ministry for nonconformity, and his opinions moved toward the more extreme position of separatism. The Separatist Puritans declared that the Church of England was fatally corrupt and withdrew into their own separated congregations. Robinson joined the separatist congregation at Scrooby, eventually becoming the minister. Disillusioned with England, Robinson's group in 1608 immigrated to the Netherlands in search of freedom.

After a short sojourn in Amsterdam, the Robinson church in 1609 moved to Leiden. This Leiden congregation became the mother church of the American Pilgrims,* when in 1620 a group from Leiden immigrated on the *Mayflower* to Plymouth in New England. Robinson stayed with the larger portion who remained in Holland. Although never an American, Robinson's standing as the pastor of the American Pilgrims gives him a place in American history.

Robinson was one of the most creative theologians* of Separatism, a forerunner of Congregationalism.* He wrote many books, chief among them was *A Justification of Separation* (1610). Although committed to the separatist ideals of church purity,* he urged a generous and broad spirit of religion. As the Pilgrims moved to America, he advised them to "close with the godly party" of non-Separatist Puritans for some common concerns. Prophetically, he told that "the Lord had more truth and light yet to break forth out of his holy word."

BIBLIOGRAPHY. T. George, *John Robinson and the Separatist Tradition* (1982); W. H. Burgess, *The Pastor of the Pilgrims: A Biography of John Robinson* (1920).   K. L. Sprunger

Robinson, Stuart (1814-1881). Southern Presbyterian* minister. Born in County Tyrone, Ireland, of Scotch-Irish parents, Robinson immigrated* to the U.S. with his family when he was two, eventually settling in Virginia. Robinson was educated at Amherst College (B.A., 1836), Union Theological Seminary in Virginia (1836-1837) and Princeton Theological Seminary* (1839-1840). Ordained* into the Presbyterian ministry in 1842, he served as the pastor of the Presbyterian Church at Kanawha-Salines, Virginia (1842-1847); the Presbyterian

Church at Frankfort, Kentucky (1847-1852); Fayette Street Church (Independent) in Baltimore (1852-1853); and Central Presbyterian Church, Baltimore (1853-1856). In 1856 he became professor of church government* and pastoral theology at the Danville Theological Seminary, Danville, Kentucky. In 1858 he left his teaching post to become pastor of Second Presbyterian Church of Louisville, Kentucky, where he remained until his death. During his pastoral career he also edited *The True Presbyterian*.

A gifted preacher, noted for his exegetical, expository sermons, Robinson was an ardent defender of Old School* Presbyterianism. He was also a strong proponent of the distinctive Southern Presbyterian doctrine of the "spirituality of the church" which asserted that the church should only deal with spiritual matters and avoid all political statements. He was suspected of Confederate sympathies and spent part of the Civil War* years in Canada. After the War he was active in relief work for the South. In 1869 he led the majority of the synod of Kentucky out of the Northern church and into the Southern church. Robinson was an outspoken opponent of reunion with the Northern church. In addition to his sermons, he published several polemical theological works.

BIBLIOGRAPHY. *DAB* VIII, E. T. Thompson, *Presbyterians in the South,* vol. 2 (1965).

J. R. Wiers

Robinson, William (?-1746). Presbyterian* evangelist* to Virginia and North Carolina. Born near Carlisle, in England, Robinson immigrated to America out of fear of parental censure after having spent a period in youthful dissipation in London. In New Jersey he found employment as a teacher, but following Christian conversion* he determined to take up the ministry and studied at the Tennents's* "Log College"* on Neshaminy Creek.

Robinson was ordained* to the Presbyterian ministry by the New Brunswick Presbytery on August 4, 1741. The following year he embarked as an evangelist to Presbyterian settlements in the Shenandoah Valley, on the south side of the James River in Virginia and along the Haw River in North Carolina. Persuaded to visit Hanover County, Virginia, Robinson's sermon of July 6, 1743, marked the first appearance of a Presbyterian minister in the eastern part of the colony and prefaced a triumphant four-day visitation. He then ministered along upper Chesapeake Bay, but his health rapidly declined, and he died in 1746 on the eve of taking up work in Delaware.

Robinson is said to have earlier been a victim of smallpox which cost the sight of one eye and left his face badly scarred, hence the oft-used sobriquet "one-eyed Robinson." His importance to Presbyterianism rests almost entirely on the success of his southern missionary* journey in 1743, which paved the way for an extensive Presbyterian revival* in Virginia and the larger work, beginning there in 1747, of his former pupil Samuel Davies.*

BIBLIOGRAPHY. A. Alexander, *Biographical Sketches of the Founder and Principal Alumni of the Log College* (1845); *AAP* 3; W. H. Foote, *Sketches of Virginia* (First Series) (1850).

W. J. Wade

Rodeheaver, Homer Alvan (1880-1955). Songleader for Billy Sunday,* music publisher and hymn* tune composer. Born in Ohio and reared in Tennessee, Rodeheaver first used his music in Tennessee's Regimental Band of the Spanish American War.* Playing his trombone, he served as Billy Sunday's songleader for many years (1910-1930). In that role, as well as through his instructional books, such as *Song Leadership: A Practical Manual for All Who Want to Help Folks Sing* (1941), he established the enduring style of evangelistic* song leading. Rodeheaver frequently told song and hymn stories to his audiences, many of which are preserved in his *Hymnal Handbook for Standard Hymns and Gospel Songs* (1931) and *Song Stories of the Sawdust Trail* (1917). A prophetic voice for gospel music, he defended it against its detractors and composed gospel song tunes, including the solo "Then Jesus Came." He was founder of the Summer School of Sacred Music at Winona Lake and co-owner of the Rodeheaver-Hall-Mack Music Publishing Co.

BIBLIOGRAPHY. H. A. Rodeheaver, *Twenty Years with Billy Sunday* (1936). R. J. Stanislaw

Rodgers, James Burton (1865-1944). First regularly appointed permanent Protestant* missionary* to the Philippines. Born in Albany, New York, Rodgers received degrees from Hamilton College and Auburn Theological Seminary. After his marriage to Anna Van Vechten Bigelow and ordination* in 1889, the Presbyterian Church in the U.S.A. appointed Rodgers a missionary to Brazil. After serving two terms in Brazil, he was transferred to the Philippines in June 1898. Because of fighting around Manila, Rodgers left his family in Hong Kong and arrived in Manila alone on April 21, 1889. Shortly thereafter, on May 7, 1899, he preached* his first sermon* in the Philippines at the home of a Mr. Poblete. The congregation of seven included four members of the Paulino Zamora family, which would play a major role in the beginnings of Philippine Protestant churches. On October 22, 1899, Rodgers baptized* his first Filipino converts.

From his arrival in Manila in 1899 until his retirement in 1935, Rodgers participated actively in evangelistic,* educational and ecumenical* ministries. In addition to serving as head of the Presbyterian mission, Rodgers played instrumental roles in the founding of the Evangelical Union and the comity agreement in 1901; in the founding of Union Theological Seminary, Manila, in 1907; and in the founding of the United Evangelical Church in 1929. He also taught theology* at Union Seminary, Manila, from 1908 to 1932.

His service beyond the Philippines included membership in the 1922 Presbyterian deputation visit to Mexico, the 1926 China Evaluation Conference and the 1936 deputation to Korea. In 1905 Union University in Jackson, Tennessee, conferred an honorary D.D. on Rodgers. After 1935 Rodgers lived in retirement in the Philippines. In 1940 he published *Forty Years in the Philippines.* He died in Baguio City in April 1944, during the Japanese occupation.

BIBLIOGRAPHY. K. J. Clymer, *Protestant Missionaries in the Philippines, 1898-1916* (1986).

G. J. Bekker

Roman Catholicism. Roman Catholicism arrived in what is now the U.S. with sixteenth- and seventeenth-century Spanish and French explorers. Spain's colonies made a long arc from Florida to California, with settlements centered on military presidios and mission churches. Every effort, including force, was used to have Native Americans live in mission villages, where they were evangelized with music, art and Spanish-language religious instruction (*See* Spanish Missions to North America).

A French arc intersected the Spanish. In the North it was anchored by Montreal and Quebec on the St. Lawrence and in the South by New Orleans in the Mississippi Delta. Settlements were few. New France was devoted to the fur trade, and only the necessary settlers were wanted in the hinterland. The missionary* approach differed from that of the Spanish: priests lived with the Native Americans, spoke their languages and adapted to their lifestyles (*See* French Missions to North America).

Catholics in the South and Southwest. The first permanent settlement in the continental U.S. was at St. Augustine, Florida, in 1565, and the first

Catholic parish,* founded by secular priests,* was called Nombre de Dios. Franciscan friars worked among Florida and Georgia tribes, but Spanish missions ended when Florida became British in 1763. Few Catholics remained to greet the American arrival in 1821.

Twentieth-century Catholic growth in this region owes much to the influx of retired people from Northern states and Canada and to immigrants and refugees from Latin America and the Caribbean. One-third of the Roman Catholic priests in Florida are Irish-born. In other Southeastern and South Central states, Catholics have been since colonial days a minority, although well represented in port cities and in Louisiana, which has Creole descendants of French and Spanish settlers, Cajun descendants of French Catholics exiled from Canada in 1755 (*See* Acadian Expulsion) and the largest concentration in the nation of African American Catholics. Immigration from Mexico as well as industrial and business immigration to the Sunbelt have increased the Catholic population.

In the Southwest, Spanish Catholic influence remains strong in New Mexico (where Santa Fe dates from 1609) and Arizona. Pueblos were the earliest Native-American Catholics; Mexican and Native American elements mingle in the Southwestern Church, where, after 1848, French and other missionaries institutionalized the community along nineteenth-century European lines. Colonial Spain neglected California until the latter half of the eighteenth century when Russians moving southward along the coast spurred establishment of presidios and the chain of twenty-one missions, one day's journey apart, which reached over six-hundred miles from San Diego to San Francisco Solano. A tiny Mexican population was overwhelmed after the American takeover in 1847 and the gold rush which began a year later.

In the regions of former Spanish influence, the culture became predominantly Protestant,* and a mixed Catholic population built a Church staffed in many areas by Irish priests. Irish Catholics came to the mines and cities; Italians and Croatians to orchards, farms and vineyards; Portuguese to the fishing fleet. Late in the nineteenth century, Mexicans began their massive and still-continuing northward migration. Across the old Spanish arc, and far to the north of it, the religious style first brought by conquistadores four centuries earlier has, in the late twentieth century, begun to make a lasting mark on Roman Catholic religious culture in the U.S.

Catholics in the North. Establishment of Catholicism in American sections of the old French empire came after the American Revolution* as settlers moved across the Appalachians and into the Ohio and Mississippi Valleys. Anglo-American Catholics from Maryland moved to Kentucky in 1785, and some pushed on to Missouri, but the major Catholic centers were cities like Cincinnati, St. Louis, Chicago and Milwaukee, with large populations of Irish and German nineteenth-century immigrants, soon followed by Poles, Lithuanians, Hungarians, Croatians, Slovaks and Italians, who came to work in the mills and factories of what has become the American "rust belt," as well as in mining areas from Pennsylvania westward.

Formal church structure in the future U.S. began with Maryland, founded in 1634 by a Catholic, Lord Baltimore (*See* Colonial Catholicism). Roman Catholics were never a majority in the colony, but for the first twenty years they controlled Maryland and introduced a policy almost unique in Christendom: religious toleration for all. This ended with the Puritan* revolt in 1654, and the Anglican Church* was eventually established, but similar religious toleration, the only possible policy for a minority government, was obtained when Roman Catholics controlled New York (1683-1689). Scattered Catholics settled elsewhere but had no priests. Quaker* Pennsylvania was an exception, with a polyglot city parish in Philadelphia and missions among "Pennsylvania Dutch" Catholics.

Catholic congregations developed during the Revolution in East Coast cities; the Middle Atlantic States waited until the inflow of nineteenth-century immigrants to develop substantial communities. There were few colonial Catholics in New England, except the Maine Abenakis who made it a condition of their support for the Revolution that the Americans provide them with priests, a problem solved with the help of the new nation's French allies. Nineteenth-century immigrants from Ireland, Italy, Portugal and Quebec built the strongest regional concentration of Roman Catholics in the country in the homeland of the Pilgrims* and Puritans.

Catholics and the New Republic. In 1776 American Catholics numbered about 25,000, one per cent of the population of English America. There were twenty-three priests, all former members of the Jesuit* order which Pope Clement XIV had suppressed three years earlier. The church had been nominally subject to a bishop* in London, but in 1784 Rome took the advice of Benjamin Franklin, U.S. representative in France, and named an American ex-Jesuit, John Carroll,* "superior of the missions." He was elected Bishop

of Baltimore in 1789 and became archbishop* there in 1808. Franklin had met Carroll in 1776 when the priest accompanied an unsuccessful diplomatic mission to Canada.

A more diversified post-Revolution Catholic population and the free republican air of the new nation brought national rivalries to a head, and frequent conflicts arose over the role in church management of bishops, clergy* and lay trustees (*See* Trusteeism). As a result the authority of the bishops was strengthened at the expense of both local clergy and laity.* Seminary education* began with arrival in 1790 of members of the Society of St. Sulpice, a group dedicated to training future priests, while church-related education of the laity began around the same time with the "academy" at Georgetown on the Potomac. Elizabeth Ann Seton,* later canonized as the first American-born saint,* founded the American Sisters of Charity, committed to schools as well as to protective and health-care institutions. Other native sisterhoods sprang up in the "holy land" of Kentucky (*See* Religious Orders, Catholic Women's).

The nation expanded rapidly, and more Catholics were added by the Louisiana Purchase (1803), annexation of Texas (1845), agreement with Britain on the Oregon Territory (1848) and the Mexican cession (1848). Church organization followed the flag, with the American bishops meeting triennially in Baltimore to plan and supervise the process (*See* Baltimore, Councils of). Missionaries from the Jesuit, Benedictine* and Sacred Heart orders worked with Native Americans across the plains and in the Northwest. Meanwhile, an immigrant flood transformed American Catholicism (*See* Immigration and Ethnicity, Catholic).

Catholics and Nineteenth-Century Immigration. Between 1820 and 1920, ten million Catholics arrived from Europe. Irish and Germans came first. The Irish settled in East-Coast and Midwestern cities; few became farmers. The Germans who arrived had a greater preference for the shores of the Great Lakes and the Ohio and Mississippi Valleys, and many became farmers. In terms of numbers, the Roman Catholic Church was the largest in the country by 1850, but it lived in a culture that was Protestant and evangelical* and in which there was a strong measure of anti-foreign and anti-Catholic feeling (*See* Nativism).

Catholic converts like the philosopher Orestes Brownson* and the priest Isaac Hecker* urged the compatibility of Catholicism and Americanism,* but many immigrants, especially in Eastern cities, tended to a defensive isolation which lasted until, in a first phase, they mustered enough political power to assert themselves on the municipal level. Later, their descendants moved up in terms of education and took their places in the American mainstream. One result of nineteenth-century Catholic isolationism was a heavy investment of financial and personnel resources in schools (*See* Parochial Schools), hospitals and other institutions which often paralleled those of the state.

Catholic immigrants who scrambled for the bottom rung of the economic ladder with American blacks showed little interest in pre-Civil War* abolition movements,* but when war came they soldiered on both sides, while Catholic nuns nursed in Union and Confederate hospitals and Catholic bishops undertook diplomatic missions for both governments. Post-War efforts at evangelization of Southern blacks were patchy, and work among Native Americans was impeded by President Grant's "Peace Policy" (1870) which neglected existing religious situations in assigning reservations to various churches. But in the far West and in Midwestern and Eastern cities many Catholics shared in the prosperity of the "Gilded Age," while they were being joined by new waves of immigrants, now increasingly from Eastern Europe and southern Italy.

These formed ethnic neighborhoods, with their own churches and schools. Often they came into conflict with older German or Irish co-religionists. The church's bishops were largely of Irish descent, with a few Germans; many newcomers found the religious style alien. At the turn of the century, Lithuanian and Polish national churches seceded from the Roman Catholic community, as did substantial numbers in the church's Eastern rites* who transferred their allegiance to Eastern Orthodoxy.* Priests, as well as vowed religious sisters and brothers, accompanied all the immigrant groups, and they were instrumental in fashioning a more pluralistic mosaic of American Catholicism.

Catholics and Americanization. The turn of the century saw internal conflict among American Roman Catholics over the pace and extent of the church's Americanization. Newer immigrants, as well as German leaders and many Northeastern Irish, were cautious. Schools frequently served the double purpose of preserving both religious doctrine and the language and culture of immigrant homelands. Americanists praised separation of church and state;* they were less enthusiastic about church-controlled schools, although the Catholic University of America* (1889), sponsored by the nation's bishops, was their project. They championed primitive unions like the Knights of Labor* and favored the New York priest Edward

McGlynn,* to whom Walter Rauschenbusch* paid tribute as a precursor of the Social Gospel.*

Papal letters in 1895 and 1899 dampened their enthusiasms, the first (*See Longinqua Oceani*) cautioning against idealizing the American religious system and indicating a Roman preference for church-state union; the second (*See Testem benevolentiae*) warning about an excessively activistic religious approach. Pope Pius X's* condemnation of the European development he named "modernism,"* coupled with a string of repressive regulations, had a chilling effect on intellectual development.

Catholic sisters had returned to military hospitals during the Spanish-American War,* and World War 1* saw a high percentage of Catholics in uniform. Between the world wars, immigration patterns changed, allowing space for consolidating the church community. Nationally, the bishops were organized under the umbrella of the National Catholic Welfare Conference,* complete with Washington offices and agencies. Major building projects sprouted in a prosperous, confident community, the picture marred only by the anti-Catholicism of the renewed Ku Klux Klan and by religious undertones that contributed to the 1928 defeat of Catholic Alfred E. Smith* in the presidential election.

The 1930s witnessed rising Catholic influence in labor circles, and radical movements like the personalist, communitarian Catholic Worker* Movement* flourished. Interracial committees and programs to foster family life spread, as did the nationwide "Legion of Decency," publishing moral evaluations of motion pictures. While most American Catholics were supporters of Franklin D. Roosevelt, who reciprocated by appointing Catholics to public office in record numbers, the decade also saw the popularity of populist Michigan priest Charles E. Coughlin,* whose increasingly shrill radio broadcasts attracted millions and who forged a novel political alliance in the 1936 presidential election with extreme right-wing Protestants not usually friendly to Roman Catholics. Only a tiny number of Catholics were conscientious objectors in World War 2. Millions of Catholics served in the armed forces, and Archbishop Francis J. Spellman* became a familiar figure by his visits to battlefronts.

Catholics and the Post-War Era. Post-War Catholics shared in the socio-economic upswing, the move to the suburbs and the religious revival of the 1950s. Archbishop Fulton J. Sheen* popularized religious philosophy weekly on television. And with the election (1960) of Roman Catholic John F. Kennedy* as president, Catholic youth shared in idealistic visions, finding outlets in the Peace Corps and like agencies. They also participated in the Civil Rights Movement* and moved from that into opposition of the Vietnam War.* Nuns* and priests became fixtures in protest movements (*See* Peace Movement, Catholic), and many, dissatisfied with the pace of church involvement, moved on to secular careers.

The Second Vatican Council (1962-1965), called by Pope John XXIII,* was a catalyst for extensive change. As American Catholics moved to suburbs, the role of the parish as social center declined. Parochial school costs rose. A downward trend in vocations to religious communities, the broader range of ministries (but not priesthood) open to women, and increased lay participation (*See* Lay Ministries, Catholic) altered institutional appearances, while virtual abandonment of Latin* and greater informality in worship* changed age-old patterns.

A sharper ideological spectrum has emerged. On the far right, small schisms emerged of those discontented with worship reforms and what they see as a leftward political drift in the Church. The "pro-life" anti-abortion* activists count many Catholics among them. While most American Catholics are religiously centrist, there is greater liberalism in ethical areas and in judging what is, or is not, sinful—and more reliance on individual conscience instead of unquestioning obedience to church directives. Both social-activist liberals and right-wing intellectuals actively propagate their ideas in journals and in Washington D.C. "think-tanks." There is growing interest in personal spirituality,* nourished by groups which promote Bible study,* charismatic* prayer and family and parish renewal.* Houses of prayer and spiritual retreat* centers flourish.

A third age of Catholicism in the U.S. is developing, following the colonial and federal periods. As they integrate new Catholic immigrants from Latin America, Haiti and Southeast Asia, American Roman Catholics find themselves better integrated into the national life and less defensive about their religion. But a structure and style for the third age are still being worked out.

BIBLIOGRAPHY. J. P. Dolan, *The American Catholic Experience* (1985); J. T. Ellis, *American Catholicism* (1969); A. M. Greeley, *The American Catholic: A Social Portrait* (1977); J. Hennesey, *American Catholics* (1981); T. T. McAvoy, *A History of the Catholic Church* (1969); M. E. Marty, *An Invitation to American Catholic History* (1986).

J. Hennesey

Romanticism, Catholic (1840-1888). Catholic Romanticism refers to a movement in apologetical* literature and religious piety* that emphasized divine immanence in creation, history, tradition and the Church, as well as the role of intuition and religious feelings in apprehending the divine.

Romanticism had its origins in late eighteenth-century European thought and had little impact upon American sensibilities and patterns of thought until the 1840s. From the 1840s until the death of Isaac Thomas Hecker* (1888), a few Catholic apologists (e.g., John Hughes,* Martin John Spalding,* Orestes Brownson,* Isaac Hecker*) appropriated elements of Romanticism in their accounts of Catholic life and thought.

Although apologists continued to defend the doctrines of the Council of Trent (1545-1563) and Catholic polity during the period, their apologetical literature reflected a shift from the rational, objective and individualistic concerns of the Enlightenment* to the intuitive, subjective and organic concerns of Romanticism. The Romantic apologetic had two major emphases. First, it reasserted the centrality of the Incarnation, making the divine presence in history and tradition the ultimate source of the Church's authority and organic unity. In this view, Catholicism was perceived as the guarantor of high culture and the primary agent for the development of Western civilization.

Second, the Romantic apologetic asserted that intuition and feeling, not reason, was the primary human agency for understanding the Divine. The emphasis on intuition and feeling did not lead to subjectivism, the apologists claimed, because intuition and feeling had an objective as well as a subjective referent. The individual person was always a part of a synthetic whole. To be authentic, the individual's subjective religious intuitions and experiences had to be in harmony with the objective and communal sacramental* expressions of the divine presence.

The revival of American Catholic piety during the 1840s also manifested the Romantic temperament. Romantic piety, emphasizing the cult of the saints* and a variety of para-liturgical religious devotions, was a strong reaction to the bland moralism of Enlightenment piety. Through parish revival-like missions,* Catholic preachers tried to bring about individual religious conversions and to strengthen the converts' sacramental lives, thereby intensifying the converts' ties with the Church. This "sacramental evangelicalism," as Jay P. Dolan called it, was central to the Romantic revival of Catholic piety. It emphasized religious feelings and institutional identification.

The Romantic Movement in American Catholic thought did not survive the onslaught of liberalism, but its emphasis upon the organic and providential nature of history did contribute to the rise of Americanism* in late nineteenth-century American Catholicism. Romantic forms of piety, however, would continue to inform Catholic religious sensibilities until the 1960s.

See also ENLIGHTENMENT CATHOLICISM; PIETY, POPULAR CATHOLIC; ROMANTICISM, PROTESTANT.

BIBLIOGRAPHY. P. W. Carey, ed., *American Catholic Religious Thought* (1987); J. P. Dolan, *Catholic Revivalism: The American Experience, 1830-1900* (1979); A. Taves, *The Household of Faith: Roman Catholic Devotionalism in Mid-Nineteenth-Century America* (1986).

P. W. Carey

Romanticism, Protestant (1836-1860). *Romanticism* is the name commonly applied to Western intellectual history of the first half of the nineteenth century. It stressed the importance of human feelings, intuition and emotion and was expressed in numerous disciplines, including literature, art, music, philosophy and religion. The term is vague, and interpreters frequently call it a mood or outlook rather than a system of thought. In the religious arena it created no American denomination,* but it did provide an ethos for important new ways of understanding Christian faith.

The Romantic Movement. In Europe, romanticism followed the Enlightenment* (1750-1800) and preceded the era of realism (1860-1900). It eventually had a powerful influence on American thought as well, though its full impact was not felt until about 1836, a year which, among other things, witnessed the anonymous publication of Ralph Waldo Emerson's *Nature.* Romantic notions were advocated by a cluster of creative European thinkers, including Goethe (1749-1832), Immanuel Kant (1724-1804), G. W. F. Hegel (1770-1831), Friedrich Schlegel (1772-1829) and Friedrich Schleiermacher (1768-1834) in Germany; and Robert Burns (1759-1796), George Byron (1788-1824), William Blake (1757-1827), Percy Shelley (1792-1822), Samuel Coleridge (1772-1834), Thomas Carlyle (1795-1881) and William Wordsworth (1770-1850) in Britain. Americans such as Ralph Waldo Emerson* and James Marsh*—the latter publishing an edition of Coleridge's *Aids to Reflection* in 1829 and his translation of Johann Gottfried Herder's (1744-1803) *Spirit of Hebrew Poetry* in 1833—helped to transmit European romanticism into the fabric of American culture.

Romanticism was very diverse, but several characteristic themes recur. Feelings and intuition were central to romantic understanding. Jean-Jacques Rousseau (1712-1778), often considered the founder of romanticism, expressed the sentiment in his novel *Emile* (1762), declaring, "If it is by reason that man is made, it is his feelings that guide him." The heart was seen to be the best path to truth. To truly know God, nature and humankind, one must go beyond the reason and logic advocated by the Enlightenment and rely on inner feelings. Closely allied with the significance placed on feeling was the romantic emphasis on individual freedom and expression. Political changes—the revolutionary fervor in France and the forming of the new American republic—produced a mood of optimism and an accompanying desire to organize social reforms, including education, women's rights and abolition of slavery. In short, it instilled a desire to perfect society.

Whereas the Enlightenment looked at the world in terms of natural law and stressed its order, romantics saw nature as a source of personal inspiration. Modern historical research and writing was created in the romantic era. Over the following generations the notion of organic development would become a very powerful tool of understanding. Virtually everything would be seen, not as fixed but as having developed in history, including church,* dogma* and Scripture.* Hegel provided a philosophical understanding of history, and Ferdinand Christian Baur (1792-1860) interpreted Christian beginnings in terms of struggle, development and change.

Romantics reveled in the remote and exotic. The Enlightenment had discredited the Middle Ages as the source of intellectual bondage, but romantics were enthusiastic about the idealized Middle Ages, reflected in the novels of Sir Walter Scott (1771-1832). Romantics also found truth in remote cultures, exemplified by James Freeman Clarke's* introduction of Americans to Oriental beliefs in *Ten Great Religions* (1871-1873). They also embraced the non-rational aspects of human experience—as in the works of Edgar Allan Poe (1809-1849). And despite the romantic criticism of Enlightenment assumptions, romanticism built on Enlightenment views of government, individual freedom and optimism.

Romanticism and American Protestantism. Christian thought was deeply influenced by romanticism. The leading Protestant theologian in the era of romanticism was Friedrich Schleiermacher, whose views were so important that he is often called the founder of modern theology.

Schleiermacher wrote that religion is not primarily a matter of doctrinal orthodoxy* nor is it primarily right behavior. Instead, he urged that the essence of religion comes from the heart: it is a feeling and an intuition of absolute dependence on God. Thus the romantic impulse helped to give a new focus to Christian thought. Jesus Christ experienced absolute consciousness of God, and his mission was to awaken a similar experience in others. In England, Coleridge urged that sensory and scientific knowledge of the world comprised only one aspect of human experience. Knowledge of spiritual matters is of a different order, and the evidence for God is found within, fixed in the religious consciousness.

Transcendentalism* was one major expression of romantic religion. The Transcendalists were a society of intellectuals, organized in Boston in 1836 and led by Ralph Waldo Emerson,* who himself exercised enormous influence through speeches and essays, notably "Nature," "The American Scholar" and "The Divinity School Address." Emerson developed the idea that everything in nature is the product of one spirit, and the recognition of this notion awakens the religious sentiment. Religion can never be received second-hand; it must come directly to the heart. Man must have self-reliance and must accept only what is true. Emerson criticized deadening dogma and advocated recognition of the potential of humans, who were a microcosm of the All. The Unitarian* Theodore Parker's* famous published sermon *A Discourse on the Transient and Permanent in Christianity* (1841) provided a vehicle of interpretation which allowed the hearer to accept the teaching of the Scripture without accepting all of its cultural forms. Parker was an early American advocate of the higher-critical study of Scripture and an outspoken champion of the abolition* of slavery. Much of Transcendentalist thought was eventually absorbed into Unitarianism.

The romantic period in American literature produced some of the nation's most significant writers. Nathaniel Hawthorne* and Herman Melville* probed deeply the nature of man and sin.* Their works have been read by generations of American students, as have the essays of Emerson, and have left an enduring legacy in the consciousness of the nation.

The romantic impulse spawned important Catholic movements within American Protestantism. The Oxford, or Tractarian, Movement* defended the Anglican Church* as a true church and understood the sacraments* to be a means of grace. The notion of the historic apostolic succession* of the

ministry was given new emphasis, as was attention to neo-Gothic architecture and to ceremonial features of worship.* Bishop Henry Hobart,* president of the Episcopal Church's General Theological Seminary in New York City, led the Anglo-Catholic,* or high church,* movement in the U.S., advocating traditional prayer-book liturgy* and the saving power of the sacraments.

John W. Nevin* and Philip Schaff* shaped the new Mercersburg Theology at the German Reformed Mercersburg Seminary during the era 1840-1860. Nevin published the *Anxious Bench* (1843), an attack on the manipulative methods of many revivalists. His major work, *The Mystical Presence* (1846), criticized popular memorial views of the Lord's Supper.* Schaff's *The Principle of Protestantism* (1845) stressed the continuity of Reformation thought with Medieval Catholicism—an alarming idea for many Protestants who were caught up in an era of intense nativism.* Moreover, Schaff's magnificent *Creeds of Christendom* (1877) showed profound appreciation for the great variety of confessional* traditions. In short, his outlook was inclusive, catholic and ecumenical.* The Mercersburg theology was not widely influential, but it did provide an important alternative to evangelical revivalism* for Protestant self-understanding at mid-century.

Another highly significant dimension of romantic religion was the theological work of Horace Bushnell,* pastor at North Church in Hartford, Connecticut, from 1833 to 1859. Bushnell was deeply influenced by Coleridge and Schleiermacher, and he sought to reshape theology so that the gospel would speak to his urban congregation which believed in self-improvement and reform and was affronted by orthodox Calvinism.* Bushnell's reconstruction laid the basis for liberal* Protestant thought in America.

Revivalism, which emphasized radical conversion* of the depraved sinner, was by mid-century an enormously popular way of bringing people into Protestant churches. Bushnell's earliest work, *Christian Nurture* (1847), critiqued revivalism and suggested an alternative. He argued that children should never know a time when they were not Christian and that the family should nurture Christian growth. Conversion should be seen as a long process of development and growth. This view offered an alternative to the Calvinist emphasis on depravity and original sin and became perhaps the single-most-influential theoretical basis for Protestant religious education* in the twentieth century.

A second contribution of Bushnell lay in his

notion of the nature of religious language. In the preface to his *God in Christ* (1849), he argued that religious language cannot be exact and scientific. Words are to God like a water pot to water. They are a vehicle to define God but cannot be equated with God. Language is symbolic. Literal appeals to Scripture or to creeds* cannot locate truth—mere words cannot express the divine. Protestant theologians had assumed the precision of words since the seventeenth century, but Bushnell raised the linguistic issue—a question that has remained problematic for modern theology into the twentieth century.

Recognizing the plurality of theologies and denominations, Bushnell believed that comprehensiveness was a useful approach for theology: one should be open to insights from many traditions since no one theology possessed all truth. Bushnell's influence on American Protestantism was enormous, and he has been called the father of American religious liberalism.

Romanticism produced numerous important new ideas. If the Mercersburg and Tractarian movements were limited in their direct influence, the writings of Transcendentalists and of American romantics have become a part of the American literary canon. Moreover, in the century following Bushnell, liberalism influenced virtually the entire sweep of American Protestant traditions.

BIBLIOGRAPHY. S. E. Ahlstrom, *A Religious History of the American People* (1972); W. Clebsch, *American Religious Thought* (1973); B. M. Cross, *Horace Bushnell* (1958); P. Miller, *The American Transcendentalists* (1957); J. H. Nichols, *Romanticism in American Theology* (1961).

W. L. Pitts

Roots, Logan Herbert (1870-1945). Episcopal* missionary* and bishop* of Hankow, China. Born in Illinois and educated at Harvard* (B.S., 1891) and the Episcopal Theological School (B.D., 1896), Roots went to China as a missionary in 1896. He spent his entire China career (1896-1938) in the cities of Hankow and Wuchang on the Yangtse River. He was consecrated* bishop of Hankow in 1904, and retired as bishop in 1937. In the 1910s and 1920s he was a leader in the ecumenical movement* in China, and held leading posts in several ecumenical bodies. In the 1930s Roots maintained personal contact with several foreign and Chinese leftist journalists and political leaders, such as Edgar Snow, Agnes Smedley and Chou En-lai. Some called him the "Red Bishop," but he was not himself a political activist; he was also on good terms with Chiang Kai-shek's government. Roots

lived in New York City from 1938 until his death.

D. H. Bays

Rosary. The term derives from *rosarium*, meaning a "rose garden." It commonly refers to a set of beads divided into five sets of ten separated by single beads. The rosary is used as a counter of prayers and, as such, bears a general resemblance to the prayer beads of Buddhists and Muslims or the "rope" or "cord" used by Eastern Orthodox* Christians for the recitation of the Jesus Prayer. In the Roman Catholic* Church, the rosary is a devotion* in honor of the Virgin Mary.*

The origins of the rosary are somewhat obscure and complex. Early in the medieval period, illiterates were encouraged to say a Pater (i.e., the Lord's Prayer) for each psalm said by the monks in their communal worship.* Since the entire psalter was said over the course of a week (or, in some cases, a day), beads were developed to keep count of the Paters. Later, there developed the custom of a parallel practice in honor of the Blessed Virgin Mary. The common belief that the rosary was the gift of Saint Dominic after a vision from the Virgin is pure legend, although the Dominicans were influential in spreading the devotion.

The current rosary custom goes back only to the sixteenth century. The complete rosary consists of 150 Hail Marys in sets of ten (called "decades"), with each introduced by the Lord's Prayer and ended with the short prayer "Glory be to the Father, etc." To each decade of the rosary, there is assigned a scriptural meditation (fifteen in all) which are subdivided into the sorrowful, joyful and glorious mysteries. Typically, a person would recite one third of the rosary each day (with fifty Aves) consisting of five decades of the total. The rosary used by most Catholics has fifty beads; those used by religious* (and often worn on the belt or cord) have the total 150 beads.

The combination of meditation and recitation has made the rosary one of the most popular and characteristic devotions in the Roman Catholic Church. Until recently it was very common for families to recite the rosary together in the home every evening.

See also PIETY, POPULAR CATHOLIC.

L. S. Cunningham

Royce, Josiah (1855-1916). Harvard* idealist philosopher. Born in California, Royce was the son of English immigrants* who moved West during the Gold Rush. After earning a B.A. in 1875 at the University of California at Berkeley, Royce studied philosophy in Germany, then enrolled in the newly formed Johns Hopkins University and received a Ph.D. in 1878. He returned to teach at Berkeley until he became a professor at Harvard* in 1882. From then until his death in 1916, Royce was part of a distinguished faculty of Harvard philosophers which included William James,* Hugo Munsterberg (1863-1916) and George Santayana (1863-1952).

Royce was one of the first men in America to earn a doctorate and engage in professional philosophy. Out of his use of logic to explore the meaning of religious ideas and values, Royce evolved a system of absolute idealism, based on the premise that individual experience was part of and validated by a universal consciousness. A student of German idealists such as Immanuel Kant (1724-1804) and G. W. F. Hegel (1770-1831) and a contemporary of American pragmatists such as Charles S. Pierce (1839-1914) and William James,* Royce uniquely combined concerns with the theoretical grounds of belief and practical ethics.

Though Royce rejected the evangelical* Christianity of his parents, religious questions shaped his philosophy. To respond to the determinism of Darwinian* naturalism, Royce stressed voluntarism in cognition and social activity. In *The Religious Aspect of Philosophy* (1885), he argued that human effort was grounded in an absolute consciousness, the existence of which he demonstrated by his seminal proof of the possibility of error. To underscore the limits of science, Royce wrote in *The Spirit of Modern Philosophy* (1892) that the outer "world of description" merely expressed the inner "world of appreciation" through which men were linked to the infinite.

Royce's philosophy is notable for its consistency over time, yet his thought also grew through dialog with critics. Reservations about his monism, expressed by James and others, informed Royce's re-emphasis of the individual after 1890, particularly in *The World and the Individual* (1901-1902). More important, as philosophical pragmatism gained prestige, Royce wrote increasingly on applied ethics. His argument that human salvation* depended on individual loyalty to a universal "beloved" community dominated his last works, especially *The Problem of Christianity* (1913).

BIBLIOGRAPHY. J. Clendenning, *The Life and Thought of Josiah Royce* (1985); J. J. McDermott, ed., *The Basic Writings of Josiah Royce*, 2 vols., (1969); B. Kuklick, *The Rise of American Philosophy: Cambridge, Massachusetts, 1860-1930* (1977). A. C. Rose

Rozhdestvensky, Platon Porphyry (1866-1934). Russian Orthodox* metropolitan*-archbishop* in America. Born in the Kursk region of Russia, where he received his early education, Platon was ordained* a priest* in 1887 and served as a parish* priest in Lukashevsky. After the death of his wife, he became a monk in 1894 and continued his studies at the Kiev Theological Academy. He became rector of the Academy and was ordained a vicar bishop of Kiev in 1902. He was transferred to America to replace Archbishop Tikhon* in 1907. Returning to Russia in 1914, he occupied a number of sees before being appointed Metropolitan of Kherson and Odessa. Following the Bolshevik Revolution, he fled Odessa and returned to America in 1922 and was subsequently reappointed head of the North American archdiocese, which was deeply divided and financially weak due to the developments in Russia.

Platon continued to head the archdiocese after it became a "temporarily self-governing Church," independent from the beleaguered Church of Russia in 1924. Composed of about two hundred and fifty parishes, it became known as the Russian Orthodox Greek Catholic Church, or the "Metropolia." It was not reconciled with the Church of Russia until 1970, when it formally was granted an autocephalous* status and the name *The Orthodox Church in America*. Its autocephaly, however, is not recognized by all Orthodox autocephalous churches.

BIBLIOGRAPHY. J. H. Tarasar and John Erickson, eds., *Orthodox America, 1784-1976* (1975).

T. E. FitzGerald

Ruffner, Henry (1789-1861). Presbyterian* minister* and educator. Born in Page County, Virginia, Ruffner grew up in the western frontier of Virginia. In 1813, after graduating from Washington College in Lexington, Virginia, he studied theology* with the college president and was licensed* to preach* in 1815. He was ordained* in 1818 and shortly thereafter organized the first Presbyterian church in what is now Charleston, West Virginia. During his lifetime he served in a number of pastorates in the area.

Ruffner eventually returned to Washington College to teach, and over a thirty-year period he served twelve years as president (1836-1848) and taught nearly every subject offered by the college. His publications include: *A Discourse on the Duration of Future Punishment* (1823) and *Against Universalism* (1833); a romance entitled *Judith Bensaddi*, published in the *Southern Literary Messenger* in 1839; and the two-volumed *The*

Fathers of the Desert (1850) on the origins and practice of monasticism.

In 1842, at a state education convention, Ruffner submitted his comprehensive plan for a public school system. It drew praise from the U.S. Commissioner of Education as the most valuable piece on Virginia education since Thomas Jefferson's* work. Ruffner's influential antislavery pamphlet was a dispassionate analysis, written by a slaveholder, detailing the system's evils and economic disadvantages while recommending gradual emancipation.

BIBLIOGRAPHY. E. T. Thompson, *Presbyterians in the South, 1607-1861,* vol. I (1963).

S. E. Berk

Russell, Charles Taze (1852-1916). Founder of the Watch Tower Bible and Tract Society. Born in Pittsburgh, Pennsylvania, into a devout Presbyterian* family, Russell seems to have been a zealous Christian until around the age of sixteen when, while engaged in evangelistic* endeavors, he encountered rationalism and experienced a profound loss of faith. He recovered by moving first to Congregationalism* and then to Adventist* meetings before starting his own Bible study* groups. These groups attracted like-minded members who rejected traditional Christian doctrines, such as the Trinity (Christ is a created and exalted being, and Jesus was not God incarnate), the resurrection of Christ and belief in hell,* and which emphasized the Second Advent of Christ. Russell maintained that Christ had spiritually returned to earth in 1874, and Russell himself was regarded by his followers as the end-time messenger. Russell's intricate eschatology required believers to preach judgment to the nations and await God's defeat of Satan at the battle of Armageddon. The end of all things would come in 1914.

Russell was successful in promulgating his views through publications and his constant travels. Eventually he became the pastor of a number of these groups—known by names such as Russellites, Millennial Dawnists or International Bible Students—and in 1884 founded the Watch Tower Bible and Tract Society. The movement grew through his tireless evangelism and prolific publications (with his sermons syndicated in approximately fifteen hundred newspapers) so that by the time of his death he was the head of a worldwide network of loosely associated groups of Bible Students, the majority of whom became Jehovah's Witnesses* under the leadership of J. F. Rutherford.* Russell died on October 31, 1916, in Pampa,

Texas, on the last of his many pastoral trips.

BIBLIOGRAPHY. *DAB* VIII; *DARB; NCAB* 12; J. Penton, *Apocalypse Delayed: The Story of Jehovah's Witnesses* (1985); T. White, *A People for His Name: A History of the Jehovah's Witnesses* (1968).

I. Hexham

Russell, Howard Hyde (1855-1946). Congregational* clergyman* and founder of the Anti-Saloon League.* After an erratic career as a clerk, cowboy, teacher, newspaper editor and lawyer, Russell experienced a religious conversion* in 1883 and was ordained* a Congregational minister* in 1885. He received a B.D. from the Oberlin* Theological Seminary in 1888. The Oberlin environment, staunchly anti-liquor, and his brother's alcoholism led him to a lifelong crusade against the liquor traffic.

In 1888 he directed a successful campaign to persuade the Ohio legislature to permit townships to restrict or forbid the sale of alcoholic* beverages. A pastorate in Kansas City, Missouri, and directorship of a mission in Chicago further revealed to him the destructive power of alcohol. Returning to Ohio, he and Oberlin associates organized, in September 1893, the Ohio Anti-Saloon League, and he effectively served as superintendent from 1893 to 1897. The League utilized Protestant congregations as League units and focused on the single issue of prohibition, refusing to align with any political party.

The "Ohio model" attracted national attention and a national league, later named the Anti-Saloon League of America, was formed in December 1895 in Washington, D.C. Because of his leadership as general superintendent (1895-1903), Russell is considered the founder of the national league. He organized state leagues in thirty-six states, eventually serving as superintendent of the New York league from 1901 to 1909. His implementation of the techniques and tactics pioneered in Ohio made the Anti-Saloon League the dominant organization in the national Prohibition Movement.* The ratification of the Eighteenth Amendment, which prohibited the manufacture, sale or transportation of intoxicating beverages beginning in January 1920, was a triumph not only for the League but also for Russell. In 1919 he helped to organize the World League Against Alcoholism and served as its first American president. In the 1920s and 1930s, he held only a minor administrative post in the Anti-Saloon League but served as a publicist and fund-raiser. Even after repeal of the Eighteenth Amendment in 1933, he believed that a "dry" America would someday be achieved.

BIBLIOGRAPHY. E. H. Cherrington, ed., *Standard Encyclopedia of the Alcohol Problem* 5 (1929); P. H. Odegard, *Pressure Politics: The Story of the Anti-Saloon League* (1928); K. A. Kerr, *Organized for Prohibition: A New History of the Anti-Saloon League* (1985).   G. F. Goodwin

Russian Orthodox Church in America. This label applies to three church organizations in North America. The most widespread one, known officially as The Orthodox Church in America, originated around 1800 in missionary* work by Russian priests* in Alaska. From there activity spread, first southward to California and then eastward across the continent. The result is an organization now numbering about 850,000 members who are led by the Metropolitan of All America and Canada with offices in Washington. In 1970 this church received recognition from other churches of the Orthodox family as an independent (autocephalous*) American church body. It aspires to transcend its Russian past and unite all American Orthodox Christians, whatever their original national roots. Its seminary is St. Vladimir's in Crestwood, New York.

The two other Russian Orthodox churches in North America are The Russian Orthodox Church Outside of Russia and The Patriarchal Russian Orthodox Church in the U.S.A. Their identity includes political overtones which have to do with the 1917 Communist Revolution in Russia. The 150,000-member Russian Orthodox Church Outside of Russia consists of congregations created by emigrés who fled revolutionary Russia and condemned the accommodation to Communist rule made by the church hierarchy that remained behind. One expression of its abiding anti-Communism was its ceremony in New York in 1981 to canonize the last tsar, Nicholas. Its seminary is in Jordanville, New York. The other group, comprising thirty-eight parishes with about 10,000 members, is the American branch of the Russian Orthodox Church headed by the Patriarch of Moscow. It continues its Christian work within the limitations imposed by the Soviet government.

See also ORTHODOX TRADITION; MISSIONS, RUSSIAN ORTHODOX TO ALASKA.

BIBLIOGRAPHY. *Orthodox America, 1794-1976* (1975); D. Grigorieff, "The Orthodox Church in America from the Alaska Mission to Autocephaly," *Saint Vladimir's Theological Quarterly* 14 (1970):196-219; A. C. Piepkorn, *Profiles in Belief,* vol. 1 (1977).   P. D. Steeves

Rutgers University. Institution of higher education with origins in the Dutch Reformed* Church. Formerly called Queens College, the institution was chartered in New Jersey in 1766. Its formation was the result of a theological split within the Dutch Reformed Church. In November 1771, Queens opened at New Brunswick with Jacob R. Hardenbergh as its first president. The college's broadly tolerant charter can be ascribed to the influence of the Great Awakening's* interdenominationalism, as well as the need to placate opposition groups in order to obtain a royal charter.

After closing during the Revolutionary War,* the college re-established itself in 1778. As a result of the lack of students and funds, it was forced to suspend classes from 1795 to 1807, with only the grammar school continuing in operation. After a second suspension of operation beginning in 1817, it reopened in 1825 as a result of the proceeds of a lottery and a gift of $5,000 from Colonel Henry Rutgers of New York, whose name it bore from that year on.

While Queens was largely free from denominational control at its inception, it gradually came under the control of the Reformed Church in the first third of the nineteenth century. This control waned during the last half of the century, especially after Rutgers became New Jersey's Land Grant institution in 1862. In 1917 the Land Grant sections of Rutgers were designated as the state university by the New Jersey legislature, as was the whole institution in 1926. In 1956 the charter was amended to give the state formal control.

The university presently maintains campuses in New Brunswick, Newark and Camden. It consists of numerous undergraduate, graduate and professional schools, offering bachelor's, master's, doctoral and advanced professional degrees.

BIBLIOGRAPHY. R. P. McCormick, *Rutgers: A Bicentennial History* (1966); G. P. Schmidt, *Princeton and Rutgers* (1964).   F. M. Perko

Rutherford, Joseph Franklin "Judge" (1869-1942). Leader of the Watch Tower Bible and Tract Society and true founder of the Jehovah's Witnesses* theocratic* organization. Born in Morgan County, Missouri, Rutherford grew up in a Baptist* farming family and became a lawyer. He became associated with C. T. Russell's* Bible Students in 1894 and joined the group in 1906. After Russell's death in 1916, Rutherford became president of Jehovah's Witnesses (this title dates to 1931). Under his leadership (1917-1942) the loose and undogmatic organization of Bible Students was gradually reorganized and turned into the highly disciplined, dogmatic bureaucracy.

Believing the millennium* to have begun in 1914, Rutherford led the Society in forming a pacifist stance in the face of World War 1.* They reasoned that to fight was to fight on Satan's side. On June 21, 1918, Rutherford was convicted of violating the Espionage Act and sentenced to twenty years in a federal penitentiary. While in prison he started publishing the journal *Golden Age,* which later became *Awake!* In March 1919 he was released on bail and his case was eventually dropped—but he was perceived as a hero within the movement. Rutherford published numerous books, started the Society's radio station and broadcast, and emphasized the necessity for every member to be a witness. Under his leadership the Jehovah's Witnesses grew from one thousand members in the U.S. in 1918 to thirty thousand in the U.S. (fifty thousand worldwide) by 1942.

He died on January 8, 1942, at Beth-Sarim ("House of Princes"), a house he had built in San Diego, California, in order to house Abraham and the prophets.

BIBLIOGRAPHY. *DAB* 3; *DARB;* J. Penton, *Apocalypse Delayed: The Story of Jehovah's Witnesses* (1985); T. White, *A People for His Name: A History of the Jehovah's Witnesses* (1968).

I. Hexham

Ryan, John Augustine (1869-1945). Catholic* priest* and social theorist. Ryan grew up on a farm in Minnesota and studied at St. Thomas Seminary* (1887-1892) and St. Paul Seminary, Minnesota (1892-1898). After his ordination* for the archdiocese* of St. Paul in 1898, he started graduate studies in moral theology* at the Catholic University of America,* receiving his doctorate in 1906. He taught moral theology at St. Paul Seminary from 1902 until 1915 when he joined the faculty of Catholic University. During his years in Washington, he also conducted courses in political science and economics at Trinity College. Ryan became the founding editor of the *Catholic Charities Review* in 1917, and two years later he was elected to the first of several terms as dean of the School of Sacred Theology. In 1920 he was appointed director of the Social Action Department of the newly organized National Catholic Welfare Council,* a position he held until his death.

Ryan decisively influenced Catholic theory and practice concerning social, political and economic issues. He brought a fresh perspective to the question of economic rights and social justice in an industrial society when he argued in his books *A Living Wage: Its Ethical and Economic Aspects* (1906) and *Distributive Justice* (1916) that em-

ployees had a right to a minimum level of compensation for their work and that the state could legitimately involve itself in sustaining the rights of labor and capital. In 1919 Ryan wrote the first draft of the "Bishops' Program of Social Reconstruction,"* a document calling for major reforms and increased government intervention. In the 1930s he criticized Hoover's policies but strongly supported the New Deal programs of Roosevelt, particularly against the attacks of Father Charles Coughlin.* Ryan's involvement with such organizations as the Federal Council of Churches* and the American Civil Liberties Union also did much to break down stereotypes of Catholics as conservative and aloof from contemporary life.

BIBLIOGRAPHY. F. Broderick, *Right Reverend New Dealer: John A. Ryan* (1963); *DAB* 3; *DARB; NCAB* C; J. A. Ryan, *Social Doctrine in Action: A Personal History* (1941). W. P. Leahy

Ryerson, Adolphus Egerton (1803-1882). Canadian Methodist* leader and educator. Born to a Loyalist family of Dutch extraction which fled New Jersey after the American Revolution,* as a half-pay officer his father received an extensive grant of land on the north shore of Lake Erie, where he was prominent and prosperous. Egerton, the most famous of the numerous sons, imbibed the love of the British constitution which was his heritage. Thus, however much he might advocate specific measures that appeared to partake of reform sentiment, at base his principles were conservative.

Converted among the Methodists, he matured quickly when he was accordingly disinherited by his father. He still sought to acquire the best education available and then became a Methodist circuit* minister. In 1826 and 1828 he ably rebutted the charges of Anglican* Archdeacon John Strachan* that Methodists were ignorant American enthusiasts. These public letters were widely read throughout Upper Canada (Ontario), and Ryerson became a hero in many quarters. He argued for a British-style Christian nation, without an established church and with full religious liberty.

Ryerson was appointed first editor of the Methodist newspaper, the *Christian Guardian,* in 1829, and for a decade was the Methodist spokesman on all major public issues. He was the first principal of Methodist Victoria College and the founding superintendent of the Ontario public-school system which he developed and administered brilliantly for several decades. It was described as a Christian public-school system which was universal, tuition-free, comprehensive (both elementary and secondary) and which had strong British roots. In later years Ryerson returned to his earlier involvements. In 1874 his years of active Methodist life were crowned by his election as president of the largely reunited Canadian Methodism, while this was followed by the writing and publication of volumes on the Loyalists.

BIBLIOGRAPHY. *DCB* XI.

I. S. Rennie

S

Sabbatarianism. The rigid and scrupulous observance of the Sabbath as a divinely ordained day of rest. This view contends that people should abstain from all activity on the Sabbath, except for what is necessary for the benefit of society and is based on a strict understanding of Old Testament Law. Its most rigorous form arose out of the Scottish and English Reformation and was transferred to the New World by the Puritans.* In both England and the American colonies, Sabbatarianism was intended to glorify God and enhance the covenant* blessings which he promised to his people.

The origin of Anglo-American Sabbatarianism can be traced to the publication of Nicolas Bound's *True Doctrine of the Sabbath* (1595), which advocated a strict Sunday Sabbatarianism. Many Puritans embraced its ideas and sought to impose them on England and, eventually, on colonial American society. In England the Puritan Sabbath was enforced by successive acts of legislation (1644, 1645, 1655) which prohibited any kind of work or recreation on Sunday. After the Restoration of the Stuart monarchy (1660), restrictions on recreation were relaxed when Parliament passed the Act for the Better Observance of the Lord's Day (1677). Following the evangelical* revival of the eighteenth century, however, Sabbatarianism regained its vigor in the Lord's Day Observance Act (1781), which prohibited any entertainment or debate involving an exchange of money.

In the colonies the first generation of Puritans enacted legislation against the desecration of the Sunday Sabbath and imposed severe penalties for violations. Contemporary Sunday restrictions and so-called blue laws in various states reflect its long-term impact upon American society.

See also LORD'S DAY ACT.

BIBLIOGRAPHY. K. Strand, ed., *The Sabbath in Scripture and History* (1982); W. Solberg, *Redeem the Time: The Puritan Sabbath in Early America* (1977). S. A. Wenig

Sabbath. *See* SABBATARIANISM.

Sacramentals. Predominantly a Catholic* term for sacred signs signifying spiritual effects obtained by the intercession of the Church. Each of the sacraments* is surrounded by subsidiary actions and signs meant to enrich the believer's participation in the sacraments. Examples are ritual actions such as anointings,* readings, laying on of hands* and signs of the cross* performed during the catechumenate and in connection with baptism.* According to the Constitution on the Sacred Liturgy, the function of these sacred signs is to dispose believers to receive the chief effects of the sacraments and to render holy various occasions in daily life. Through their designations as sacramentals, material things and persons become signs and instruments of grace. As sacred signs instituted by the Church rather than directly by Christ, they are always subject to revision and adaptation to the requirements of changing times.

BIBLIOGRAPHY. A. G. Martimort, "Sacred Signs," in *The Church at Prayer. Introduction to the Liturgy,* ed. A. G. Martimort (1968). C. Waddell

Sacramentary. The liturgical* book of the Roman Catholic Church* containing all the Mass* texts required for the celebrant at Mass, exclusive of the readings and chants reserved to other ministers* and singers. Consisting originally of booklets or *libelli* of Mass prayers* grouped nonsystematically, these random collections of Mass-formulas led to a more systematic compilation, as in the early seventh-century "Leonine" sacramentary, composed chiefly of fifth- and sixth-century Roman formularies grouped by months. More important for the future medieval evolution are the Gregorian and Gelasian sacramentaries. The Gregorian tradition provided the basic material for the Missal of Pius V (1570), which was normative for the Roman Rite until the promulgation of the *Missale Romanum* by Pope Paul VI* in 1970. The latter draws freely on sources ancient, medieval and modern. C. Waddell

Sacraments and Ordinances. Catholics* in America have affirmed seven sacraments (baptism,* confirmation,* the Eucharist,* penance,* extreme unction,* ordination* and matrimony), which, in accord with the Council of Trent (1545-1563), they defined as efficacious means of grace. Eastern Orthodox* Christians accepted the same seven sacraments, though some Orthodox theologians* emphasized that other "holy acts" also possessed a sacramental character. Protestants* accepted only the sacraments of baptism and the Lord's Supper,* with Baptists* and heirs of the continental Anabaptist* traditions preferring to designate the rites as *ordinances,* performed because Jesus ordained their use, rather than as means of grace.

The Sacramental Spectrum. American Christians have maintained a spectrum of sacramental doctrines and practices, corresponding always to their views of the church.* In the nineteenth century the differences were especially pronounced. In defining baptism, for example, Catholics insisted that the sacrament contained and conferred the grace of justification,* which was normally available only within the church. High-church* Episcopalians* preferred to say that it conferred regeneration* by admitting infants into the church. Confessional* Lutherans* viewed it as a divine promise of salvation.* But groups in the middle of the spectrum felt uneasy about suggesting that baptism conveyed regeneration: Methodists,* Congregationalists* and Presbyterians*— along with Episcopal and Lutheran evangelicals*— usually spoke of baptism as a seal to a divine promise or as a visible form of the Word.

Most Methodist writers defined it as the seal of a universal but conditional covenant* requiring future faith, though some viewed it merely as a parental pledge. Reformed* churches typically agreed that the rite sealed a conditional covenant—requiring future faith—for all infants and adults who were baptized, but they added that it also sealed an absolute covenant ensuring salvation for God's elect.* But Baptists, who understood the church as a community exclusively of believers, thought of the rite as an ordinance commanded by Christ to signify their obedience and faith, and Quakers* believed that all external sacraments corrupted spiritual purity. In short, groups defining the church as a community formed by the inner experience of new birth* tended to move away from any view of baptism as an efficacious rite.

A similar spectrum marked doctrines of the Eucharist, or Lord's Supper. Catholics believed that

through the miracle of transubstantiation,* the elements of bread and wine became in substance the real body and blood of Christ, who was then offered in the Mass. Confessional Lutherans, while rejecting transubstantiation, also insisted on a corporeal presence of Christ, as did high-church Episcopalians, who called for the retrieval of Catholic sacramental rituals. Lutheran and Episcopal evangelicals reacted against this insistence on the Real Presence; they spoke of Christ as spiritually present to the faithful, and they feared that traditional Catholic ritual forms hindered true sacramental devotion.* In the other denominations* the issue was usually whether to accept a doctrine of the spiritual presence of Christ or to claim only that the Lord's Supper served as a rite of commemoration. Churches that required an inward experience of rebirth as a prerequisite for membership tended to celebrate the Lord's Supper primarily as an ordinance of remembrance for the faithful.

Early Sacramental Debates. The earliest American sacramental debates occurred within those churches. As early as the 1650s sacramental issues divided New England Puritans.* A 1662 synod* in Boston finally decided that baptized but unconverted members could present their children for baptism, though neither they nor their children could receive the Lord's Supper without offering a credible narration* of their conversion.* Opponents derided this Half-Way Covenant.* The debate displayed intense feeling about sacramental practices, so it was not surprising when New England printers soon published an array of sacramental manuals, nurturing a piety* that found eloquent expression in the meditations of the poet Edward Taylor.* But the Lord's Supper also became the subject of renewed controversy when Solomon Stoddard* of Northampton defined it as a "converting ordinance" that could move the hearts of the unconverted.

In the Chesapeake colonies, meanwhile, the institution of slavery generated another kind of sacramental question: Only after securing legal confirmation that baptism could not confer temporal liberty—and sometimes inserting such a disclaimer in the ceremony—did the clergy* gradually gain free access to the slaves. And the Great Awakening* prompted further sacramental debate in both New England and the South, for revivalist* congregations occasionally repudiated the baptism of infants.

Sacraments and Revivalism. Revivalist piety by no means entailed a disdain for sacraments: the revivalistic Methodists broke from the Anglican Church* in 1784 partly because it would not permit unordained American Methodist preachers to administer the Lord's Supper. A series of "sacramental meetings," moreover, helped spark the later frontier* revivals in the South. But revivalism did diminish interest in traditional sacramental doctrines and liturgies.* By 1792, for example, the Methodist *Discipline* drastically abbreviated John Wesley's* rite for the administration of the Lord's Supper. The revivalist ethos and the yearning to recover primitive biblical patterns also encouraged innovative baptismal doctrines. Alexander Campbell* attracted converts to his Christian Movement by preaching that the baptism of believers by immersion was necessary for the remission of sins. Joseph Smith* carried his Mormon* community beyond the boundaries of Christian tradition by revealing, among other new doctrines, the possibility of proxy baptism for the dead. And the Landmarkers* among Southern Baptists* insisted by 1851 that baptism by immersion, administered by preachers* who had themselves been properly immersed, was a necessary mark of a true church.

The flowering of nineteenth-century sacramental thought and piety, however, came from groups uncomfortable with revivalism. After 1838 American Episcopal Tractarians,* influenced by the Oxford Movement in England, occasionally affirmed older Catholic interpretations of the sacraments, and reformers like William Muhlenberg* at the Church of the Holy Communion in New York City redefined congregational worship* by introducing a weekly Eucharist. In the German Reformed Church, John Williamson Nevin,* a teacher at the seminary in Mercersburg,* Pennsylvania, announced in *The Mystical Presence* (1846) that sacramental doctrine extended "in its bearings and consequences, to the farthest limits of theology,"* and that the Reformed tradition affirmed the presence of both the divine and the human natures of Christ in the Lord's Supper. After 1855, when so-called American Lutherans discarded traditional Lutheran doctrines of baptismal regeneration and the physical presence of Christ in the Eucharist, confessional Lutherans, led by Charles Porterfield Krauth,* reasserted the older views and formed in 1867 their own General Council of churches.

Sacraments in the Twentieth Century. Sacramental issues have remained divisive: The claim advanced in 1913 by "oneness" or "Jesus only" Pentecostal* groups that churches could baptize only in the name of Jesus Christ rather than with the Trinitarian formula created an enduring division within Pentecostalism. But the sacraments have also served as means of renewal* and symbols of unity. At St. John's Benedictine Abbey in

Collegeville, Minnesota, Virgil Michel* helped guide a revitalizing of the Catholic liturgy, and his journal *Orate Fratres* (1926), later renamed *Worship,* encouraged the emphasis in the Catholic Liturgical Movement* on lay* participation in the Eucharist—an emphasis symbolized architecturally* by a move away from the building of elaborate altars and confirmed theologically by Vatican II.* Among Protestants as well, the turn toward a renewed sacramental piety found architectural expression as early as the 1930s, when even congregations outside the traditionally liturgical denominations—the Episcopal and Lutheran churches—began to push the pulpit to one side and elevate the Communion table* to a central platform in the front of the sanctuary.

A growing Protestant interest in sacramental liturgy found expression in a new Presbyterian *Book of Common Worship* in 1946 and in a decision by Episcopalians three years later gradually to revise their *Book of Common Prayer.* By 1964 as many as nine Protestant denominations that had often included sacramental disagreements among the reasons for their disunity were able to formulate statements on the "One Baptism" and the "One Table" as a basis for further cooperation. Methodists, Episcopalians, Presbyterians, Disciples of Christ,* Lutherans and the United Church of Christ* subsequently prepared new sacramental liturgies that recovered traditions from both the Reformation and earlier Christian worship. After Vatican II, moreover, the Catholic Church revised its sacramental liturgies in accordance with new understandings of worship and the Church. By the late twentieth century, therefore, an increasing number of American churches encouraged the full and active participation of the laity in frequent sacramental services that embodied ancient Christian traditions.

BIBLIOGRAPHY. J. G. Davies, ed., *The New Westminster Dictionary of Liturgy and Worship* (1986); E. B. Holifield, *The Covenant Sealed: The Development of Puritan Sacramental Theology in Old and New England, 1570-1720* (1974); C. P. Krauth, *The Conservative Reformation and Its Theology* (1899); J. W. Nevin, *The Mystical Presence: A Vindication of the Reformed or Calvinistic Doctrine of the Holy Eucharist* (1966); J. F. White, *Sacraments as God's Self-Giving* (1983).

E. B. Holifield

Sacred. A term referring to the quality of otherness or holiness.* The term *sacred* refers to objects, places, times and events that are holy or religious in nature. Such sacred categories are usually distinguished in opposition to objects that are profane or objects that are ordinary (lacking in holy qualities). In addition, the term *sacred* can refer to a perception of reality—how one views the world—and, thus, to how one lives in the world. As such, a sacred world view orients a person to a world governed by the Divine while a profane world view locates a person in a world without reference to divine or holy categories.

The idea of the sacred was suggested by Rudolf Otto in *Das Heilige* (1917). Otto recognized a mysterious numinous quality that pervades religious experience* and that is characterized by radical otherness. When human beings stand in the presence of this otherness, they are reduced to nothingness. In other words, the term *sacred* refers to those qualities of the holy that confront human beings and remind them of their humanness by creating in them awe and fear.

The most common use of the term comes in connection with time and space. Sacred times and sacred spaces become times set apart for God and spaces that are inhabited by the Holy. Thus, in the Christian tradition, rituals (such as regular Sunday* worship,* events such as baptism* or celebrations of festivals in the church year*) and ritualistic sites (such as churches* and cathedrals*) define the idea of the sacred, because through the ritual, time and space become receptacles of the divine.

In the study of American religions, the term *sacred* is used often in the description of the relationship between American religion and culture and in connection to the perceived transition of America from a sacred to a secular society.

BIBLIOGRAPHY. C. Colpe, "The Sacred and the Profane," in *The Encyclopedia of Religion,* ed. Mircea Eliade (1987); M. Eliade, *The Sacred and the Profane* (1959); R. Otto, *The Idea of the Holy* (1923).   C. E. Ostwalt

Sacred Congregation for the Evangelization of Peoples or for the Propagation of the Faith (Propaganda).

A Roman curial congregation coordinating the missionary* activity of the Catholic Church.* The Congregation was established in 1622 by Gregory XV to take control of the missionary work then languishing under the Spanish and Portuguese patronages. It was made up of thirteen cardinals,* who provided the property and funds, two prelates and one secretary. In 1809 Napoleon seized all its possessions. When re-established in 1817, it regained control of mission work but no longer funded it.

The Propaganda developed under the popes* of the nineteenth and twentieth centuries, receiving reports, dividing territories, appointing apostolic vicars and prefects, assigning territories to various religious orders, etc. At the end of the nineteenth century, its competence covered all matters in its territories. In the twentieth century this competence was limited, although on the eve of Vatican II* it had ordinary administration and executive power over 740 dioceses, vicariates or prefectures. Since 1968, in addition to the cardinals appointed by the pope, the Congregation consists of twelve prelates from the missions, four prelates from other regions to represent the universal church, four superiors of clerical missionary institutes and four heads of pontifical missionary works. It also includes the secretariats for promoting Christian unity, for non-Christians and for non-believers. The U.S. was removed from the jurisdiction of the Congregation in 1908, when the American Catholic missionary movement* began.

See also MISSIONS, ROMAN CATHOLIC FOREIGN.

BIBLIOGRAPHY. R. Song, *The Sacred Congregation for the Propagation of the Faith* (1961); J. Metzler, *Sacrae Congregationis de Propaganda Fide Memoria Rerum, 1622-1972* (1971); R. Hoffman, "Propagation of the Faith, Congregation for the," *NCE* 11.   L. Nemer

Sacred Congregations. Administrative bodies in the Catholic Church* that the pope* uses to implement his judicial, legislative and executive office as head of the Church. Their specific powers are set out in the Code of Canon Law* and postcode documents. These congregations, whose history is centuries old, make up what is known as the Roman or Papal Curia. Their number has varied over the centuries according to the needs of the moment, and congregations were added or eliminated according to circumstances. The most recent reforms of these bodies, whose duties and jurisdictions began to overlap, were those of Pius X* who precisely defined each congregation's duties and jurisdiction, and that of Pope Paul VI* which were initiated at the close of Vatican II.* All decisions of Sacred Congregations require papal approval, unless special authority* is delegated by the pope. The Congregations are usually concerned with matters of faith, morals and canonical discipline, and with several exceptions, are presided over by a cardinal* prefect aided by a secretary and undersecretary.

C. E. Ronan

Sacred Heart of Jesus. A theology, popular devotion and official liturgical feast. The language of the Bible speaks of the heart as the seat, or principal part, of the human being. The theology and devotion of the sacred heart is primarily based on two New Testament texts. In John 7:37-38 Jesus speaks of streams of life-giving water that will flow from within him. In John 19:34 the soldier's spear piercing Jesus' side brings forth blood and water. In Asia Minor these texts were interpreted in the sacramental sense, the water signifying baptism,* the blood the Eucharist.* The church was seen as being born from the wounded side of Christ. In Alexandria, under the influence of Origen, a more spiritual interpretation of John 7 understood the living water as the saving knowledge (*gnosis*).

In the Middle Ages a distinctly new approach was developed. The wounded heart of Jesus was understood not so much as the source of grace as it was the explicit, direct object of personal devotion. St. Margaret Mary Alacoque (1647-1690) played a decisive role in the popularization of this latter devotion, the one most familiar to American Catholics today. The Sacred Heart did not become a liturgical feast until 1765, and only in 1856 was this feast extended to the whole Western Church. As a reprise of Good Friday,* it is celebrated on a Friday, in the second week after Pentecost.* Many religious orders* of men and women and many religious institutions such as parishes* and schools* are named in honor of the Sacred Heart. Popular devotions* were widespread, especially novenas,* litanies* and the practice of receiving Holy Communion* on nine consecutive first Fridays. A representation of the sacred heart has frequently been installed in a place of honor in Catholic households, signifying Christ's sovereignty over the family and as a focus of devotion. As with many such popular devotions, its practice has been decreasing since the 1960s. The entire complex of the Sacred Heart emphasizes the incarnational principle of Christianity—that the love of God for the world is truly present in the historical heart of Jesus.

See also PIETY, POPULAR CATHOLIC.

BIBLIOGRAPHY. J. Stierli, ed., *Heart of the Savior* (1957). R. L. Kress

Saint Vincent de Paul. *See* SOCIETY OF SAINT VINCENT DE PAUL.

Saint-Vallier, Jean Baptiste de la Croix de Chevières de (1653-1727). Second Bishop* of Quebec. Born in Grenoble, France, and educated at the seminary of Saint-Sulpice in Paris, he was appointed almoner to Louis XIV in 1676. Well known for his moral rigor, austerity and generosity to the poor, he was nominated by Bishop Laval* to

succeed him in Quebec. He arrived in Canada in 1685 as vicar-general of the diocese* and in 1688 was consecrated bishop.

Energetic and enterprising, he was also zealous and undiplomatic. Accordingly, he was in constant conflict with the civil authorities, the seminary of Quebec, and the Jesuits* over ecclesiastical jurisdiction and the moral tone of the colony. By unceasing activity he visited all the parishes in his vast American diocese, established several hospitals, constructed new churches and set up a rudimentary welfare service. His pastoral letters condemn libertinism, drunkenness, trafficking in spirits, immodest dress and cabarets. Even though his enemies often accused him of Pelagianism and Jansenism, his published writings, *Catéchisme du diocèse de Québec* (1702) and *Rituel du diocèse de Québec* (1703), attest to his orthodoxy.*

Through his piety,* untiring service to the poor and breadth of legislation, Saint-Vallier favorably contributed to the establishment of the Catholic Church in North America.

BIBLIOGRAPHY. G. Plante, *Le rigorisme au XVIIe siècle: Mgr. de Saint-Vallier et le sacrement de pénitence* (1971); A. Rambaud, "La vie orageuse et douloureuse de Mgr. de Saint-Vallier, deuxième évêque de Québec (1653-1727)," *RUL* 9 (1954): 90-108. D. A. Scalberg

Saints, Cult of the. In the Catholic tradition the term *saints* may refer to (1) the comparatively few well-known or canonized* deceased holy ones; (2) the many deceased holy ones celebrated on the feast of "All Saints"; or (3) the many living, faithful believers in Christ. The *cult of the saints* is a broad term for various kinds of honor directed by the third group toward the first group especially, and less often toward the second. The practice has three main aspects: veneration, or giving honor to the saints; invocation, or praying* for their intercession with God; and imitation, or acting on their inspiration and example. The cult of the saints is based theologically on the doctrine of the communion of saints,* which displays confidence in the bond of unity existing among all those who live in Christ, including even those whose lives on earth are ended.

A longstanding Catholic tradition holds that Mary* and the apostles were venerated from the time of their deaths. Certainly a blossoming of popular veneration of saints occurred in the fourth and fifth centuries in conjunction with Christians' trust that their beloved martyrs (those who had suffered death for their faith in Christ) were enjoying heavenly bliss. Awareness and veneration of martyrs, which flourished among all social classes, mitigated death's sting and reminded believers of their own promised final destiny with God. With that, the way was opened for many other Christians who were outstanding in virtue to be venerated as saints after their deaths. The Second Council of Nicaea (787) helpfully distinguished between the adoration owed to God alone (*latreia*) and the veneration due the saints (*dulia*).

The reformer Martin Luther, reviving a New Testament practice, regularly called living Christian believers *saints*. At the same time, he venerated and imitated some celebrated and canonized saints, including some notable and canonized ones (e.g., Mary, apostles, biblical figures, Francis of Assisi). He turned against the practice of invoking saints of heaven, however, on account of devotional abuses which seemed to him to substitute the saints for Christ.

In the centuries since the Reformation, devotion to the saints has served as a distinctive hallmark of Roman Catholicism. At the same time, the virtual absence of such devotion characterized much of Protestant church life. This area has come in for reappraisal by various churches in recent years. The Roman Church's Second Vatican Council,* in words which show strong concern that the cult of the saints never detract from the unique adoration to be given to the triune God, clearly upheld the value of all three main aspects of the cult of the saints. Some late twentieth-century Protestants may be more inclined than were their parents and grandparents to venerate and imitate at least some renowned saints, but for most Protestants the invocation of saints remains controversial.

BIBLIOGRAPHY. L. Cunningham, *The Meaning of Saints* (1980); R. Kieckhefer and G. D. Bond, eds., *Sainthood: Its Manifestations in World Religions* (1988); P. Molinari, *Saints: Their Place in the Church* (1965); Vatican Council II, *Dogmatic Constitution on the Church,* ch. VII (1969).

G. P. Evans

Salem Witch Trial. The infamous Salem witch trial of 1692 began innocently enough when several young girls gathered to gaze into a crystal ball and see their futures. When caught in the act, they immediately claimed they had been assaulted by witches. Instead of correcting the children, the parents believed their charges and began searching for the witches in their midst. As hysteria mounted, the local pastor, Samuel Parris (himself a newcomer to the colonies from England), failed to quiet his parishioners' fears. Instead, he actually heightened tensions by suggesting that the witches

might be far closer than anyone dared imagine. "In this very church," Parris warned ominously from his pulpit, "God knows how many Devils there are."

With that ringing accusation the witch hunt was on. Before the panic subsided and the neighboring ministers intervened to bring a halt to the judicial proceedings, over 150 suspected witches had been imprisoned and nineteen hanged at "Witches Hill" on the western side of town. Many of the accused were middle-aged women and social misfits. Others were members of powerful families who had opposed Parris's ministry in Salem Village. Hardly any were to be found among the young or middle-aged men.

Despite the fact that the Salem witch trials led to no new laws and did nothing to change prevailing beliefs in witchcraft, they belong in every account of Puritan New England as a lesson in misdirected zeal. As the most dramatic instance of social pathology and moral cowardice, Salem stands as a symbol of all people's vulnerability to mass suggestion and scapegoating. The accused witches were never engaged in Satan worship, but they were people caught on the fringes of their society who, in uncertain and angry times, were isolated for attack and execution. To their credit, most of the Puritan clergy recognized that the real evil was in the accusers, not the accused, and never again would witches be executed in New England.

BIBLIOGRAPHY. P. Boyer and S. Nissenbaum, *Salem Possessed: The Social Origins of Witchcraft* (1974); C. Hansen, *Witchcraft at Salem* (1969); D. Levin, ed., *What Happened in Salem* (1960).

H. S. Stout

Saliba, Philip (1931-). Antiochian Orthodox* archbishop* of New York. The Lebanese-born Saliba came to the U.S. in 1956 to advance his training in history and theology.* Following a single pastorate in Cleveland, where he became deeply involved in various civic and humanitarian projects, he stood as the overwhelming favorite of the clergy* and laity* to succeed Antony Bashir* as Antiochian archbishop of New York when the latter died in 1966.

As metropolitan, he early concentrated on improving the financial stability of his church and the lot of his clergy in particular, on upgrading the level of theological training required of candidates for the priesthood* and on further organizing the women and youth of the archdiocese. In 1978 he purchased land in Ligonier, Pennsylvania, to establish the Antiochian Village. First a modest summer camp for youth, it was augmented in 1983 with a Heritage and Learning Center to promote knowledge of the Middle East and the roots of Christianity there. Among his greatest frustrations has been the inability, despite friendship with presidents and other government officials, to obtain justice for the land of his birth.

One of the most vocal spokesmen for Orthodox unity and outreach in America, he initiated steps to realize these. In 1975 he and Archbishop Michael Shaheen, head of the rival Toledo Archdiocese, succeeded in ending a forty-one-year-old rift to form a united Antiochian Archdiocese. He suggested formation of a Bilateral Commission with the Orthodox Church in America,* the jurisdiction whose outlook most closely matched his own. In 1987 he received into canonical Orthodoxy some 2,000 evangelical* Christians in seventeen communities who for ten years had been studying the post-biblical development of ancient Christianity.

P. D. Garrett

Salvation. In biblical usage *salvation* describes the full range of divine activity in physical and spiritual deliverance, both past, present and future. It includes and integrates other more specific terms such as *justification,* redemption, reconciliation, regeneration,* sanctification* and the final eschatological* deliverance from death and judgment and into the life to come.

Among Roman Catholics* salvation is linked to the sacramental* ministries of the Church and the purifying effects of purgatory.* In churches of the Reformed tradition,* like the New England Puritans,* salvation was connected to covenant theology,* eternal predestination* and election.* Under this formulation *predestination* describes God's decree by which he chooses individuals to be included in the community of the elect, while *election* describes an effectual divine calling of irresistible grace that irrevocably joins Christians to Christ. In churches of the Wesleyan*-Arminian* tradition, salvation is considered to be conditional since it could be lost through faithlessness, and justification is inextricably linked to sanctification or holiness.*

Revivalism* made American Protestant conceptions of salvation increasingly individualistic* and experiential. These adjustments made *being saved* a synonym for *justification* or *being converted* in popular parlance. Although evangelicalism* drew a close connection between personal salvation and opposition to social evils such as slavery* and poverty, the rise of popular millennialism*—evidenced by the emergence of groups as diverse as the Millerites* (who predicted the end of the world in 1843) and the Seventh-day Adventists*—caused the popular conception of salvation to become increasingly futuristic and other-worldly.

As revivalism waned, conservative theologians, such as the Presbyterian Charles Hodge* and the Methodist John Miley,* expressed the soteriological distinctives of their respective traditions. Liberalism* also offered various correctives to revivalism, seeking to sever salvation from individualism, instantaneous conversion and futurism. Horace Bushnell's* *Christian Nurture* (1847) associated salvation with the role of the Christian community as a nuturing body. The birth of Institutional Churches,* like Thomas Beecher's* famous Park Church in Elmira, New York, sought to provide care for the entire life of the person; soon gymnasiums, libraries, dispensaries, sewing rooms and kitchens became a part of American churches' attempts to meet people's physical, social, mental and spiritual needs. Walter Rauschenbush,* the father of the Social Gospel Movement,* pointed beyond individualism to the importance of *Christianizing the Social Order* (1912). His *A Theology for the Social Gospel* (1917) championed a corporate Christianity that was committed to bringing the kingdom of God* to bear on this world. Charles M. Sheldon* captured the mood and imagination of the period by recasting soteriology in practical, ethical terms. His fictional approach, *In His Steps* (1896), sold over six million copies and is still in print.

The extent of salvation has been the subject of periodic controversy. New England liberals attacked the Calvinistic doctrines of original sin and election in the mid-eighteenth century. And Charles Chauncy,* minister of Boston's First Church, argued against the doctrine of eternal damnation, maintaining a universalism* in which all humanity would evenually be redeemed. His arguments, set forth in *The Mystery Hidden from Ages and Generations* as early as the 1750s, were not published until 1784. Universalism's official beginning in America came in 1770 with the arrival of the British Universalist John Murray.* During the Revolutionary* period Universalism found a ready companion in an optimistic democratic* millenialism that prevailed. During the nineteenth century Universalism as promoted by individuals such as Hosea Ballou,* who maintained some evangelical characteristics, though the movement itself grew increasingly closer to Unitarianism.* Liberal theology of the twentieth century has always had its proponents of various types of Universalism, and some recent Roman Catholic theologians have begun to speak of the salvation of "anonymous

Christians" (Karl Rahner*)—the devout adherents of other faiths.

Contemporary trends in American Christianity show some continuity with these same emphases. Mainline* ministers often define salvation in terms of social, psychological, physical and spiritual welfare. Universalism is frequently maintained, particularly in the face of increasing religious pluralism.* Liberation theologies identify salvation with deliverance from social oppression, discrimination and prejudice. The experiences of Native Americans like Vine Deloria (*God Is Red,* 1973), African-Americans like James Cone (*A Black Theology of Liberation,* 1970) and feminists like Rosemary Ruether (*Sexism and God-Talk,* 1983) have produced theologies which set salvation in the context of the problems of contemporary society and which parallel theologies from Latin America and South Africa.

Most evangelicals continue to emphasize the personal aspects of salvation, often echoing themes shaped by revivalism in the evangelical, Arminian tradition. A few evangelicals, reflecting on the themes of liberation theology and the biblical basis for a more wholistic view of salvation, have sought to define salvation in more comprehensive terms. A recent debate among some evangelicals has been the relationship between salvation and the lordship of Christ. Some evangelicals have maintained that salvation is granted to those who have trusted Christ for salvation at any point in their lives, regardless of their subsequent behavior or lack of faith. Those who show no visible signs of redemption, known as "carnal Christians," nevertheless enjoy the benefits of an eternally secure* salvation. Opponents have called this an "easy-believism," selectively adopting elements of both Arminian revivalism and Calvinistic election, but neglecting the gospel demand to submit to the lordship of Christ. In turn, these critics are accused of holding a "lordship salvation" that adds demands of obedience to the simple response of faith.

The theme of salvation is at the heart of the Christian faith, but its various expressions in America—some plausibly biblical and others not—have continued to reflect the impulses, ideals and demands of their American cultural environment.

See also ETERNAL SECURITY; LIBERATION THEOLOGY; REGENERATION; REVIVALISM; UNIVERSALISM.

BIBLIOGRAPHY. B. Graham, *How to Be Born Again* (1977); D. W. Frank, *Less Than Conquerors: How Evangelicals Entered the Twentieth Century* (1986); Z. C. Hodges, *The Gospel under Seige* (1981); B. J. Leonard, "Getting Saved in America: Conversion Event in a Pluralistic Culture," *RE* (1985):111-127; D. Robinson, *The Unitarians and the Universalists* (1985); D. F. Wells, *The Search for Salvation* (1978).   J. R. Tyson

Salvation Army, The. Holiness* denomination.* The mission that became The Salvation Army was established in the slums of London, England, in 1865 by William Booth,* an independent evangelist* trained in Wesleyan* doctrine, and his wife Catherine. The mission was given its present military form in 1878, after which its spread throughout Britain and overseas was very rapid. Although zealous Salvationist immigrants launched unofficial outposts on their own in North America, the Army's official missionaries* "opened fire" on the U.S. in March 1880, and on Canada in July 1882.

Although The Salvation Army may be described as a Protestant* and evangelical* denomination, it is more than that. Beginning in 1890 all Salvationists have been required to accept and sign the Army's "Articles of War," which pledge its members to evangelistic fervor and to a disciplined lifestyle in support of "Salvation* warfare," which since Victorian times has meant a wide range of energetic activities designed to save souls and relieve human suffering. Its members, both clergy ("Officers") and lay* persons ("Soldiers"), are called "Salvationists." They subscribe to eleven specific doctrines, with an emphasis on the Wesleyan doctrine of sanctification.* They do not observe the Lord's Supper* or baptism.* The purpose of The Salvation Army from the start has been to make converts for Christ from among those elements in society not touched by other forms of religion.

Practical charitable activities formed an important part of the Army's ministry from its earliest days. In recent years social relief work has come to occupy a large part of the time and energy of Army personnel and to figure prominently in the organization's public relations campaigns. Officially Salvation Army leaders are not troubled by the role that social welfare plays in the movement: Social work is intended to supplement evangelism, is an expression of God's love for fallen personhood and is a direct response to the command of Christ to care in his name for the poor and weak. One practical consequence of this emphasis has been, however—especially in the U.S.—that The Salvation Army is regarded by most of the general public as a charitable, rather than as a religious, organization.

The organization currently operates in eighty-six

countries, but the branches in English-speaking countries are particularly strong. The American Salvation Army is by far the largest, with 3,600 active officers (twenty-two per cent of the world's total) and 79,000 "Senior Soldiers" (adult members). There are 1,088 "Corps" in the United States (local churches, which in the U.S. almost always form part of a larger community-center complex), whose religious services are analogous to those held in other evangelical denominations. About one-third of the Corps in the United States have brass bands to provide congregational music, and a few still conduct the street-corner services for which the movement was once famous.

The Salvation Army's social welfare services are especially well developed in the U.S. These include personal counseling, family welfare, day care, summer camps, senior citizens' residences, Christmas relief, assistance in times of natural disaster and an extensive residential program for homeless alcoholics carried on in the Army's 118 Adult Rehabilitation Centers and eighteen Harbor Light Centers. These institutions provided for ninety-two per cent of the 148,325 clients cared for in the Army's residential alcoholic programs in 1985.

BIBLIOGRAPHY. E. H. McKinley, *Marching to Glory: The History of The Salvation Army in the United States, 1880-1980* (1980); E. H. McKinley, *Somebody's Brother: A History of The Salvation Army Men's Social Service Department in the U.S., 1891-1985* (1986). E. H. McKinley

Salzburgers. Members of a colony of Lutheran* refugees from Austria who settled in colonial Georgia. In the sixteenth century Lutheranism established a foothold among subjects of the archbishop* of Salzburg and persisted despite attempts to suppress it. When Count von Firmian became archbishop in 1727 he decided to wipe out this heresy,* especially strong among workers in the productive salt mines. He believed that firm measures would cow the remaining Protestants. However, registration showed that thousands were willing to adhere to their faith. In October 1731, Firmian issued an Edict of Expulsion, mandating that all unpropertied Protestants* must leave within eight days; those with property were given thirty days to depart. This contravened the international agreements reached at the Treaties of Westphalia (1648), which gave emigrating dissenters three years to arrange their affairs.

Some twenty thousand Lutherans were driven out amidst much suffering, exciting the compassion of Protestant Europe. Most of the exiles were resettled in Prussia, following the generous and shrewd invitation of Frederick William I. Others were aided by Samuel Urlsperger, Lutheran pastor in Augsburg, who interceded on their behalf with English authorities. With help from the Society for Promoting Christian Knowledge (SPCK),* some three hundred emigrants in four groups were sent between 1734 and 1741 to the newly founded colony of Georgia. The first colony was Ebenezer (named after the memorial "stone of help" referred to in 1 Sam 7:12) on the Savannah River, established under the leadership of two able pastors, Johann Martin Boltzius and Israel Christian Gronau, both trained at the Pietist* center of Halle. After initial difficulties, the colonies of Lutheran exiles prospered until the Revolutionary War* era.

BIBLIOGRAPHY. G. F. Jones, *The Salzburger Saga: Religious Exiles and Other Germans Along the Savannah* (1984). D. F. Durnbaugh

Sampey, John Richard (1863-1946). President of Southern Baptist Theological Seminary and professor of Old Testament and Hebrew. Sampey was converted* at fourteen years of age and two years later entered Howard College, Birmingham, Alabama, as a ministerial student, from which he graduated with his A.B. degree. He entered Southern Baptist Theological Seminary in 1882 to prepare for foreign missionary* service but was persuaded to remain and teach at the seminary upon his graduation in 1885.

Upon John A. Broadus's* death Sampey succeeded him as a member of the International Sunday School Lesson Committee and became chairman of the Committee in 1921. Sampey served continuously on the Committee for forty-six years. He was also one of the founders of the Baptist World Alliance* and throughout his long career continued to take a lively interest in Baptists around the world. Sampey took several preaching* tours to Brazil where he found some fulfillment of his earlier desire to become a foreign missionary.

When Edgar Y. Mullins* died in 1928,* Sampey, then sixty-six, became president of the seminary. In 1942 he resigned from his post after fifty-seven years of continuous service to the seminary. In his years as professor and president of the seminary, he wrote several books, including *The First Thirty Years of Southern Baptist Theological Seminary* (1890), *The Ethical Teachings of Jesus* (1909) and *The Heart of the Old Testament* (1922).

An effective churchman, in 1935 Sampey was elected president of the Southern Baptist Convention and was re-elected for two succeeding terms. Internationally, his reputation took him to the

Conference on Life and Work in Oxford and the Conference on Faith and Order in Edinburgh in 1937, as well as the Congress of the Baptist World Alliance, where he spoke in 1939.

BIBLIOGRAPHY. *ESB* 2; W. A. Mueller, *A History of Southern Baptist Theological Seminary* (1959). W. R. Estep

Sanctification. To make or be made holy. In biblical theology and religion,* objects, occasions, places and persons are sanctified or set apart for sacred use. Sanctification is the act or process by which they are made to correspond with God's holiness. In the context of personal redemption as it is set forth in the New Testament, sanctification is the process by which believers are made holy.

Protestants* have understood sanctification as distinguishable from, and logically subsequent to, justification,* whereas Catholics have used the term *justification* to refer to both the event (*justification* in Protestant terminology) and the process (*sanctification* in Protestant terminology). The Catholic tradition has produced many outstanding examples of men and women who have sought after holiness with methods and understanding that invite comparison with later Protestant proponents of sanctification (*See* Spirituality: Roman Catholic). Eastern Orthodoxy has also spoken of the pursuit of holiness, placing a distinctive emphasis on the attainment of the "divine nature" (dependent on 2 Pet 1:4), or likeness of God (*See* Spirituality: Eastern Orthodox). But no tradition of spirituality in America has placed more emphasis on the term *sanctification,* nor thereby had more influence on American religion, than evangelicalism.

Evangelical Protestants have been divided over three issues: (1) whether or not entire sanctification or perfection* can be attained in this life, (2) whether or not sanctification is a gradual lifelong experience that can be achieved or advanced by momentous experiences of grace, and (3) the means by which believers achieve sanctification.

Traditional Calvinists* have held that, while Christians are called to righteous living, the total depravity of humanity, even justified and regenerate humanity, limits the possibilities for sanctification in this life. Justification frees the believer from the guilt of sin* while sanctification, flowing out of justification, frees from the power of sin. Both are the work of God's grace, but sanctification is God's continuous work in the believer that manifests itself in a holy and moral life. In the Puritan* view, this process was characterized by an intense, lifelong struggle involving spiritual discipline and a reliance on God's grace. This legacy of Reformed* theology* was handed down through the Puritan tradition and reaffirmed in the theology of Presbyterian theologians* such as Charles Hodge* and Benjamin B. Warfield.*

In American religious history no tradition has been more vocal in its doctrine of sanctification than the Wesleyan,* or Methodist,* tradition. "Justification," said John Wesley,* "God does for us; sanctification, God does in us." Thus far he agreed with the Reformed tradition. But Wesley also believed that sanctification culminated in the dramatic experience of a second work of grace, given by God and appropriated by faith, whereby the believer attained Christian perfection. This was not a sinless perfection, nor did it preclude the believer's growth in grace, but was defined as freedom from all conscious, or intentional, sin—a perfection of motives and desires—manifested in "perfect love." Sinless perfection was to be attained only after death.

Concern for holy living became a central theme of the camp meetings* and revivals* that characterized so much of the religious life of the nineteenth-century American frontier.* Instrumental in providing a theological rationale for this revivalism were Charles Finney* and Asa Mahan* of Oberlin College.* Synthesizing elements found in both the Reformed and Wesleyan views of sanctification, they introduced a version of the doctrine of sanctification emphasizing Christian obedience to the moral law of God. Finney, popularizing the revised Calvinism of Yale's* Nathaniel W. Taylor,* reckoned that since sin was a voluntary act, it was at least theoretically avoidable. This made entire sanctification a human possibility. Finney, who was a New School Presbyterian,* thus challenged the conservative Calvinist* view of sanctification and introduced a form of perfectionism into Presbyterianism.*

Sanctification was not the exclusive property of evangelicalism,* however. Nineteenth-century social radical John Humphrey Noyes's* communal experiment at Oneida was founded on an ideology that included a perfectionism he claimed was inspired by Nathaniel Taylor's call for "holiness of heart and life." And the Unitarian* rebellion against Calvinism did not jettison the Puritan ideal of the life of sanctification. In a series of sermons, William Ellery Channing* argued that the central point of Christianity was to purify the soul of all sin, though a Puritan would have warned that any attempt to do so apart from a work of grace is futile.

Nineteenth-century American Catholicism also had

features remarkably similar to Protestant revivalism. Catholic revivalism* in the form of parish missions* combined a reliance on the means of grace and a call to righteousness. In a series of meetings, the counterpart of the Protestant revival,* mission preachers exhorted their audiences to repent of their sins and forsake wickedness. At the end of a week of such sermons, penitents were invited to make confession in preparation for receiving the sacrament.* A righteous life was the expected consequence.

Radical Wesleyans of the nineteenth century, such as Phoebe Palmer,* interpreted Wesley as saying sanctification could be entire and, having obtained sanctification, Christians need no longer sin. Palmer spoke of a dramatic second blessing,* achieved by a three-step process, in which the believer layed "all on the altar" and so achieved entire sanctification. Palmer's many books, her widely circulated *Guide to Holiness* and her extensive speaking tours were instrumental in shaping the emerging Holiness denominations, such as the Wesleyan Methodists, the Free Methodists* and the Church of the Nazarene.* Traditional Methodists, on the other hand, emphasized other aspects of Wesley's doctrine of sanctification and stressed the means of grace for the gradual attainment of holiness.

By the 1870s this Holiness Movement* had made significant inroads into evangelical Christianity. Presbyterian minister William E. Boardman* was influenced by both Oberlin Theology* and the Wesleyan tradition, particularly as it was popularized by Phoebe Palmer. In *The Higher Christian Life* (1859), he commended a method for achieving a "second conversion" characterized by a higher life of Christian joy and rest. Hannah Whitall Smith* and her husband, Robert Pearsall Smith,* both from a Quaker* background, promoted a holiness view of sanctification popularly expressed in her *The Christian's Secret of a Happy Life* (1875). The popularity of these views is evident in the gospel hymns* of the period, which frequently and sentimentally invoke the theme of total surrender to Christ.

By about 1875 Asa Mahan, as well as William Boardman and Pearsall Smith were promoting their Holiness views at conferences held at Keswick, England, the beginning of the famous Keswick Movement.* Their doctrine was soon modified in British hands, their basically Wesleyan view of the eradication of sin being substituted by a more Reformed emphasis on the suppression of the sinful nature by Christ's righteousness. The British Keswick teachers tended to avoid the Wesleyan emphasis on a singular perfectionist experience and preferred to speak of a crisis experience followed by repeated "surrenders" and "fillings" with the Holy Spirit. It was this experience that separated "carnal" from "spiritual" Christians. As with most mainstream Holiness teachings, the goal of sanctification was Christian service. This modified Keswick view of sanctification was popularized in America by Dwight L. Moody,* adopted by many evangelical leaders and widely disseminated through the notes of The Scofield Reference Bible.*

The Pentecostal Movement, arising around the turn of the century, grew out of the Holiness Movement. Early Pentecostals, in speaking of the baptism of the Holy Spirit, described the experience as a third step in the two-step Wesleyan formula of salvation and sanctification. But in 1910 a dispute arose over non-Wesleyan, or "Reformed," Pentecostals such as William H. Durham,* who emphasized the sufficiency of salvation, the progressive work of sanctification (as opposed to a second blessing) and the baptism of the Holy Spirit as crisis enduement of power. This view came to characterize the Assemblies of God.*

Sanctification continues to be an essential theological and devotional theme among contemporary Christians—particularly those in the evangelical tradition. Countless books are written on the subject, and it remains a popular topic at Bible conferences* and youth gatherings. Though not as controversial as eschatology,* views of sanctification have tended to distinguish leaders within the evangelical and fundamentalist movements, with certain institutions representing particular theologies of sanctification.

See also HIGHER CHRISTIAN LIFE; HOLINESS; HOLINESS MOVEMENT; KESWICK MOVEMENT; OBERLIN THEOLOGY; PENTECOSTAL MOVEMENT; PERFECTIONISM; SECOND BLESSING; VICTORIOUS CHRISTIAN LIFE.

BIBLIOGRAPHY. M. Dieter et al., *Five Views on Sanctification* (1987); T. L. Smith, "Righteousness and Hope: Christian Holiness and the Millennial Vision in America, 1800-1900," *AQ* 31 (1979):21-45; J. P. Dolan, *Catholic Revivalism: The American Experience, 1830-1900* (1977); G. M. Marsden, *The Evangelical Mind and the New School Presbyterian Experience* (1970); G. M. Marsden, *Fundamentalism and American Culture* (1980); J. L. Peters, *Christian Perfection and American Methodism* (1956).
M. D. Strege

Sanctuary Movement. A network for illegally transporting refugees from Central America into the U.S. and assisting them in establishing themselves.

John Fife, a Presbyterian* minister* in Tucson, Arizona, and Jim Corbett, a Quaker* and a retired rancher, originated the idea of a national sanctuary movement. Fife's Southside Presbyterian Church and five congregations on the east side of San Francisco Bay were the first to declare themselves publicly as sanctuary churches on March 24, 1982. By October 1986 the movement had grown to include over three hundred sanctuary churches or synagogues, twenty-two sanctuary cities and a sanctuary state, New Mexico. The sanctuary movement has received official sanction from several major Protestant* denominations, among them the United Methodist Church* and the Presbyterian Church (USA),* in addition to endorsements from numerous religious leaders.

Members of the movement have justified their actions on one or more of several grounds. They point to the biblical example of providing a place of refuge to those guilty of manslaughter (Numbers 35:6-34) and to the medieval legal precedents for sanctuary to criminals on church territory. They uphold the example of the antebellum abolitionists' "underground railroad" for escaped slaves, which defied federal law in the name of a higher divine mandate. And they contend that U.S. immigration laws are inequitably enforced and contradict the 1967 United Nations Protocol Relating to the Status of Refugees, of which the U.S. is a signatory party. In January 1985 sixteen sanctuary workers from Arizona were indicted for their assistance to illegal aliens after a lengthy undercover investigation of the movement. Eight were later convicted and given suspended sentences. Despite this federal prosecution of sanctuary leaders, the number of sanctuary groups, whether congregational, interdenominational or interfaith, has continued to grow.

BIBLIOGRAPHY. I. Bau, *This Ground Is Holy: Church Sanctuary and Central American Refugees* (1985); A. Crittenden, *Sanctuary: A Story of American Conscience and Law in Collision* (1988); M. Davidson, *Convictions of the Heart: Jim Corbett and the Sanctuary Movement* (1988); R. Golden and M. McConnell, *Sanctuary: The New Underground Railroad* (1986).

M. J. Coalter

Sandeman, Robert (1718-1771). Founder of Sandemanian churches in New England. Born in Scotland, Sandeman was probably still a student at Edinburgh when he came under the influence of John Glas (1695-1773), whose daughter he married. Glas, who had earlier been deposed from the Church of Scotland (1730) for his view that the state

had no authority over the church, argued for a restoration of primitive* Christianity. Sandeman adopted many of Glas's views and became a more forceful proponent than the gentle and kindly Glas. Perceiving an American interest in his writings, Sandeman emigrated in 1764. "Sandemanian" congregations were soon established in Massachusetts, New Hampshire and Connecticut, and doctrines led him to controversies with both Baptists* and Congregationalists.* Danbury, Connecticut, became Sandeman's home, the location of the largest congregation and the place of his death.

Sandeman argued that saving faith issues from the mind accepting the testimony regarding Jesus Christ, thereby rejecting emotional experiences. Belief is possible, however, only for those who are elected. He championed primitive church order, including congregational independence; plurality of elders*; infant baptism*; and weekly closed agape communion (*See* Love Feast), with foot washing* and the holy kiss. Alexander Campbell* read Sandeman's writings but rejected many of his positions. Sometime after a visit by Campbell, the Danbury church transferred to the Disciples* in the 1840s. By 1900 no Sandemanian churches remained in the U.S.

BIBLIOGRAPHY. R. Sandeman, *Some Thoughts on Christianity* (1764); W. Walker, "The Sandemanians of New England," *Annual Report of the American Historical Association, 1901* (1902).

T. H. Olbricht

Sandemanians. *See* SANDEMAN, ROBERT.

Sanford, Elias Benjamin (1843-1932). Congregational* minister* and ecumenical* leader. Born in Westbrook, Connecticut, of seventeenth-century New England Puritan* stock and the son of a Methodist* minister, Sanford studied at Wesleyan University in Connecticut and entered the Methodist ministry himself. In 1867 he reverted to his ancestors' Congregationalism* because it allowed indefinite pastorates. In the 1870s illness, family needs and the financial insecurity of papers he edited caused him to move back and forth between parish work and religious journalism. His longest pastorate was at Westbrook, Connecticut, from 1882 to 1894.

Beginning in 1895 Sanford was the key organizational figure in a series of bodies leading to creation in 1908 of the Federal Council of the Churches.* As secretary of the Open and Institutional Church League* and editor of *The Open Church,* he organized meetings and advanced a platform of free pews,* open churches throughout the week and social service—a practical basis for ecumenical action with potential for advancing the kingdom of God,* whose significance he saw early. In 1901 he became secretary of the successor National Federation of Churches and Christian Workers. His efforts insured the success in 1905 of a Conference on Interchurch Federation at Carnegie Hall* at which the foundational plan for the Federal Council was written. Sanford was the council's first secretary until 1913, and honorary secretary thereafter. A steady vision of denominational* federation, rather than organic union, and skill at gaining confidence and support from people he deemed critical to success, characterized Sanford's unique contribution to Protestant* ecumenicity.

BIBLIOGRAPHY. *DAB* VIII; *DARB*; C. S. Macfarland, *Christian Unity in the Making* (1948); *NCAB* 24; E. B. Sanford, *Origin and History of the Federal Council of the Churches of Christ in America* (1916).   J. H. Dorn

Sankey, Ira David (1840-1908). Singing evangelist* and associate of Dwight L. Moody.* Born in Lawrence County, Pennsylvania, Sankey spent his adolescence in Newcastle, Pennsylvania, where his father was president of the local bank. After serving in the Union Army during the Civil War,* Sankey returned to Newcastle, where music in the Methodist* church and activities in the newly formed YMCA* were his main interests.

In 1870 Moody heard Sankey sing at a YMCA convention in Indianapolis and recruited him for evangelistic work in Chicago. For the next twenty-five years, Sankey was an indispensable part of Moody's revivalistic* work. During Moody's first tour of Great Britain (1873-1875), Sankey contributed significantly to Moody's success. Usually accompanying himself on a small reed organ, Sankey had a pleasant baritone voice whose dramatic quality affected audiences deeply.

Sankey discovered how to supplement the sermon with his music, which contained simple but moving lyrics and easily learned melodies that often borrowed heavily from popular dance and march rhythms. His "story hymns" (e.g., "The Ninety and Nine" and "Jesus of Nazareth Passeth By") carried an emotional evangelistic message of their own. Though he wrote few hymns himself, he edited collections that became ubiquitous in the revivals of Moody and others. His *Sacred Songs and Solos* (1873) and *Gospel Hymns* (6 numbers, 1875-1891) were best sellers, but Sankey never profited from them. All royalties were given to support Moody's Northfield Schools.

Sankey is generally credited with popularizing the "gospel hymn"* and making that musical style a crucial part of modern revivalism. From his day to the present, Sankey has been a model of the revivalist "chorister."

See also GOSPEL HYMNS AND SONGS; MUSIC, CHRISTIAN.

BIBLIOGRAPHY. *DAB* VIII; *DARB;* E. J. Goodspeed, *Moody and Sankey in Great Britain and America* (1876); E. Nason, *The American Evangelists, Dwight L. Moody and Ira D. Sankey* (1877); *NCAB* 7; I. D. Sankey, *My Life and the Story of the Gospel Hymns* (1907); S. S. Sizer, *Gospel Hymns and Social Religion* (1978).   T. P. Weber

Satolli, Francesco (1839-1910). Catholic* cardinal* and first apostolic delegate* to the U.S. Born in Marsciano, Italy, Satolli was ordained* in 1862. After teaching at the seminary* in Perugia, Italy, he became pastor* in his native town (1870). He was professor of theology* in Rome at the College of Propaganda (1880-1892) and at the Roman Seminary (1882-1886). In 1884 he became rector* of the Greek College in Rome and president of the Pontifical Academy of Noble Ecclesiastics. He was a major force in the general renewal of serious scholarship in the Roman Catholic Church, in the promotion of neo-scholasticism* and the revival of interest in the philosophy and theology of Thomas Aquinas.

Satolli visited the U.S. as a papal representative in 1889 and in 1892 for the World's Columbian Exposition in Chicago. In 1892 he expressed support for the school plan of Bishop John Ireland,* who wanted religious and secular education in the public schools. This plan stirred an enormous reaction from American Catholic bishops, particularly Bishop Bernard J. McQuaid* of Rochester, New York, whom Satolli later attempted to silence on this issue. Satolli became a permanent delegate to the U.S. in 1893, only after the American Catholic hierarchy became deeply divided over questions of educational policy and ethnic representation. Satolli successfully reconciled popular dissident priests Edward McGlynn* and Louis Lambert with their bishops. He returned to Rome in 1896 and became the prefect of the Congregation of Studies. His last visit to the U.S. was in 1904 for the St. Louis Exposition.

BIBLIOGRAPHY. R. Trisco, "The Holy See and the First 'Independent Catholic Church' in the United States," in *Studies in Catholic History,* ed., N. Minnisch, R. Eno, R. Trisco (1985).

T. F. Sable

Savage, Mary (fl. 1790s). Freewill Baptist*

preacher.* Late in the eighteenth century, New England's Baptists—the region's most dynamic dissenting sect—faced a series of challenges. Among the new anti-Calvinist groups, none proved more disturbing than the Freewill Baptist schismatics. Founded by Benjamin Randall* in 1780, during the next two decades the Arminian* sect gained thousands of followers in New Hampshire and Vermont. Mary Savage, originally from Woolwich, Maine, joined the Freewill Baptists and began preaching the gospel in 1791. Though she only served as a minister for about a year, she is credited with being the first Baptist woman preacher. Very little is known about her life, but according to one minister who heard her preach, Savage's special ability was helping the most troubled dissenters reconcile their views with Freewill Baptist beliefs. *Freewill Baptists for Half a Century, 1780-1830* (1862). J. M. Craig

Sawdust Trail. In the late nineteenth century, lumbermen of the Pacific Northwest used trails of sawdust to find their way back to camp from various locations in the woods. Applied to evangelistic* meetings, *sawdust trail* became a metaphor for finding one's way to God. Billy Sunday,* at his 1910 meeting in Bellingham, Washington, was apparently the first to use the term. He appealed to members of the audience to hit the sawdust trail, that is, to come forward and shake Sunday's hand as a sign of their conversion.* Terms like *trail-hitting* and *trail-hitters* were common parlance in the later Sunday campaigns. Others, especially newspapermen, picked up the *sawdust trail* phrase and adopted it as a standard way of describing the aisle-walking of would-be converts. By extension, it came to refer to conversion itself. When evangelistic meetings moved out of tents and tabernacles, especially after the 1950s, the term was much less frequently used.

BIBLIOGRAPHY. W. G. McLoughlin, *Billy Sunday Was His Real Name* (1955). W. G. Travis

Saybrook Platform. Congregational* platform of church discipline.* In response to a perceived decline in lay piety and the failure of councils to settle an increasing number of church disputes, Connecticut's General Court authorized and summoned a synod* in Saybrook in 1708 to revise the system of church discipline. Composed of twelve ministers* and four laymen,* the synod constructed a platform of church order that drew its inspiration from Cotton Mather's* *Proposals* for the churches of Massachusetts Bay. The most important provision called for the establishment of consociations made up of lay and clerical representatives that would offer binding judgments on disputes arising within local churches. Ministerial associations* were also created to oversee the clergy* and to approve ministerial candidates. The *Platform* further called for a sentence of noncommunion to be placed on churches that refused to accept the decisions of consociations.

In eliminating the longstanding practice of congregational independence in favor of a system similar to the presbyterian* form of church order, the *Saybrook Platform* marked an important break from the principles of Congregationalism and the *Cambridge Platform** of Massachusetts Bay. Though sanctioned by the General Court and accepted by most ministers and churches in the counties of Hartford, Fairfield, New Haven and New London, many local churches refused to be bound by the decisions of outside consociations, while others silently ignored the *Saybrook Platform*. During the Great Awakening,* many churches, especially those of the Separates* in eastern Connecticut, openly renounced the *Platform* as a product of ministerial tyranny. Nonetheless, the vast majority of churches remained within the consociational system, which survived in Connecticut until the second half of the nineteenth century.

BIBLIOGRAPHY. W. Walker, *The Creeds and Platforms of Congregationalism* (1960).

J. F. Cooper

Sayle, William (?-1671). Puritan* governor of Bermuda and South Carolina. Sayle arrived in Bermuda in 1630 and beginning in 1641 served as occasional governor of that colony. In 1646 he and other Puritan backers obtained a grant for one of the Bahama Islands and planted a shortlived colony there, naming it *Eleuthera* and attempting to establish it on the then-radical principle of complete liberty of conscience. Failing in this experiment, Sayle returned to Bermuda in 1657, where he resumed gubernatorial duties until charges of conflict-of-interest over Eleuthera led to his ouster. In 1670 he was appointed by the proprietors to be first governor of Carolina. By then aged, infirm and of questionable mental ability, he served for only a year before his death. Although Sayles's real influence was limited, he was significant as a visionary and fiery Calvinist* whose politics, like those of his occasional contacts in New England, were closely tied to his Puritan hopes for an experimental society in the New World.

BIBLIOGRAPHY. B. Levy, "Early Puritanism in the

Southern and Island Colonies," in *Proceedings of the American Antiquarian Society* 70 (1960):69-348.

E. C. Nordbeck

Scandinavian Alliance Mission. *See* EVANGELICAL ALLIANCE MISSION, THE.

Scanlan, Patrick F. ("Pat") (1894-1983). Catholic* journalist. Born in New York City, Scanlan grew up in Philadelphia as one of seven children, three of whom became priests.* After some study as a seminarian, he decided against continuing, and completed his education with a B.A. from St. Joseph's College, Philadelphia. Moving to Brooklyn, he became a teacher at St. Peter's High School, Staten Island, and enrolled in a course in apologetics* given by Joseph J. Timmes, who was the managing editor of the *Brooklyn Tablet.* When Timmes joined the armed forces in 1917, he suggested to Bishop Charles E. McDonnell that Scanlan serve as "temporary" managing editor. In fact, Scanlan spent the next fifty-one years as managing editor of the *Tablet.* He became the youngest president of the Catholic Press Association, in 1924, and as his career continued he was widely regarded as the dean of the Catholic press* in the U.S. He wrote a weekly column, "From the Managing Editor's Desk," which appeared in 2,600 consecutive issues, and he wrote many of the *Tablet's* editorials. He was a fierce opponent of Communism,* and was much admired by prelates such as Cardinals Spellman,* O'Hara* and McIntyre. In the 1930s he led the fight, through the *Tablet,* for free public bus service for crippled children attending Catholic schools in New York City. He died in Floral Park, New York.

BIBLIOGRAPHY. D. Zirkil, "Tablet Managing Editor for 51 Years Buried," *Brooklyn Tablet* (April 2, 1983).

R. Van Allen

Scarborough, (L)ee (R)utland (1870-1945). Southern Baptist* denominational* leader and seminary* president. Born in Colfax, Louisiana, Scarborough grew up in West Texas, the son of a Baptist* minister.* Following his experience as a cowboy on a farm ranch, he took degrees from Baylor (1892) and Yale* (1896) universities and attended the Southern Baptist Theological Seminary (1899-1900). He then served as pastor of churches in Cameron and Abilene, Texas.

In 1908 he was appointed to "the chair of fire," as B. H. Carroll referred to the department of evangelism* in the newly organized Southwestern Baptist Theological Seminary in Fort Worth. Scarborough succeeded Carroll as president of South-

western in 1914 and served in this capacity until 1942. In addition to giving formative leadership to the seminary, Scarborough also served in many other denominational posts. He was director of the 75 Million Campaign, a major fund-raising drive among Southern Baptists, served as president of the Southern Baptist Convention (1939-1940) and was active in the Baptist World Alliance.* Scarborough's great passion was for evangelism. He wrote many books on this theme, including *With Christ After the Lost* (1919), *A Search for Souls* (1925) and *How Jesus Won Men* (1926).

BIBLIOGRAPHY. H. E. Dana, *Lee Rutland Scarborough: A Life of Service* (1942); *DAB* 3.

T. F. George

Schaeffer, Francis August (1912-1984). Evangelical* missionary* and apologist.* Born in Philadelphia, Pennsylvania, Schaeffer was raised in a nominally Lutheran* family but during his high-school years became an agnostic. While studying engineering at Drexel Institute, he came to faith and completed his studies at Hampden-Sidney College, a Southern Presbyterian school (B.A., 1935). That same year he married Edith Seville, who would become an able partner in his ministry and a well-known evangelical author in her own right. Schaeffer attended seminary first at Westminster Theological Seminary, where he studied under the apologist Cornelius Van Til,* and then at Faith Theological Seminary (B.D., 1938). In 1938 Schaeffer became the first ordained* minister* of the Bible Presbyterian Church and subsequently pastored churches in Pennsylvania and Missouri.

In 1948 the Schaeffers moved to Switzerland, serving under the Independent Board for Presbyterian Foreign Missions. In 1955 Schaeffer founded L'Abri, an international study center and caring community in the Swiss Alps, where he offered an analysis of modern man's thought and a critique of secular culture from a Christian perspective. Over the years thousands of students and other seekers stayed with the Schaeffers, and through prayer, study and conversation many of them came to Christian faith. The ministry was greatly extended through Schaeffer's writings, and by the 1970s he was widely regarded among American evangelicals as a preeminent apologist for the faith.

In books such as *The God Who Is There* (1968) and *Escape from Reason* (1968), Schaeffer traced the decline of Western humanistic culture to a lack of intellectual and moral absolutes. He claimed that this decline began when the philosopher Hegel replaced the notion that truth is antithetical and therefore absolute with the idea that truth is synthetical and therefore relative. However, Schaeffer contended that relative truth will not provide adequate meaning for life, so secular man has followed Kierkegaard* in abandoning reason and attempting to find significance in drugs, Eastern thought and existentialism.* Finally, Schaeffer argued that this shift from absolutism to relativism had spread three ways: geographically, from Germany to the Continent, England and the U.S.; socially, from intellectuals to the working class and then the middle class; and finally, by disciplines, from philosophy to art, music, general culture and then theology.

In his later writings, such as *How Should We Then Live? The Rise and Decline of Western Thought and Culture* (1976), Schaeffer detailed the political and moral consequences of abandoning absolute truth. Politically, he held that without a Reformation base to unify form and freedom, freedom gives rise to chaos which in turn leads to authoritarian government. In the area of morals, Schaeffer contended that biblical morality has been replaced by sociological law or the view that whatever the majority holds is right. As a result, the belief that man was created in God's image has been replaced by a low view of man, permitting the practice of abortion,* infanticide and euthanasia. Schaeffer held that only a return to biblical absolutes can reverse these trends, and he admonished evangelicals to stand firm on the doctrine of inerrancy* and take a public stand against social and moral evils.

Schaeffer's twenty-four books have sold over three million copies in more that twenty languages. Two film series based on his books were widely viewed in churches. While appreciative of his general argument, some evangelical scholars have argued that Schaeffer's analysis of the disciplines was frequently superficial. His supporters have defended him on the ground that he was an evangelist* and not an academician. By any measure, Schaeffer was a leading figure in the resurgence of evangelicalism during the 1960s and 1970s.

BIBLIOGRAPHY. L. T. Dennis, ed., *Francis A. Schaeffer: Portraits of the Man and His Work* (1986); R. W. Ruegsegger, ed., *Reflections on Francis Schaeffer* (1986); E. Schaeffer, *L'Abri* (1969); F. S. Schaeffer, *The Complete Works of Francis A. Schaeffer: A Christian World View,* 5 vols. (1982).   R. W. Ruegsegger

Schaff, Philip (1819-1893). German Reformed* church historian and ecumenist.* Born in Chur, Switzerland, Schaff received his education at the Universities of Tübingen (1837-1839), Halle (1839-1840) and Berlin (1840-1842), where he came under the influence of such notable scholars as Ferdinand Christian Baur (1792-1860), Friedrich A. G. Tholuck (1799-1877) and Johann A. Neander (1789-1850). Upon completing his studies in 1842, Schaff became *privatdocent* at the University of Berlin. The next year Schaff accepted an invitation by representatives of the newly organized German Reformed* Seminary at Mercersburg,* Pennsylvania, to become a professor there. He arrived to take up his duties in August of 1844, and so began a career of nearly a half-century of scholarship at the forefront of the study of church history. Schaff taught at Mercersburg until 1865, lecturing occasionally at Drew and Hartford seminaries between 1868 and 1871, and in 1870 he accepted a professorship at Union Theological Seminary* in New York, where he remained until his death.

In addition to his pioneering work in church history, Schaff served as secretary of the New York Sabbath Committee and was influential in the reorganization of the American branch of the Evangelical Alliance* in 1866, serving as its corresponding secretary until 1873, and spending hundreds of hours and traveling thousands of miles to organize the World Conference of the Alliance held in New York City, October 2-12, 1873. From 1870 to 1885, Schaff was involved with the committee for the American Revised Bible translation project and served as president of that committee (1872-1885). He founded the American Society of Church History in 1888 and served as president of that organization until his death in 1893.

In addition to these many commitments, Schaff published an astounding number of books and articles. He edited *Der Deutsch Kirchenfreund* (1848-1854), wrote regularly for the *Mercersburg Review,* serving as its co-editor (1857-1861), and founded the German periodical *Evangelische Zeugnisse aus den Deutschen Kirchen in Amerika,* which was issued from 1863 to 1865. His first major work in America was *The Principle of Protestantism* (1845), an expansion of his inaugural address at Mercersburg Seminary. This work, which brought upon Schaff charges of heresy* and Romanism, traced the development of the Christian church through history and emphasized the value of the church in every age. Schaff's assertion that the Reformation was "the legitimate offspring, the greatest act of the Catholic Church" provoked strong protest among the militantly Protestant* wing of the German Reformed clergy.* The next year, Schaff published *What Is Church History?,* a

[1051]

summary of his theology* of the history of the Christian church.

After a decade in Mercersburg, Schaff took a sabbatical leave and returned to Europe, where he presented a series of addresses about his "adopted fatherland." Published in German as *Amerika* (1854), they appeared in English the following year. There Schaff attempted to explain and defend the American system in which church and state* were separated and complete religious liberty enjoyed. In 1858 Schaff published the first volume of his most ambitious work, his *History of the Christian Church,* which ultimately grew to eight volumes (the two on the Middle Ages were written by his son, David, after Schaff's death). On the centennial of the United States Constitution, he issued an interpretation of the constitutional guarantees of religious liberty* entitled *Church and State in the United States.*

As an editor, he presided over the translation of Johann Peter Lange's (1802-1884) massive *Bibelwork,* a project finally completed in 1880 when the last of twenty-five volumes was published. From 1880 to 1886 Schaff edited the first series of fourteen volumes of *A Select Library of the Nicene and Post-Nicene Fathers of the Christian Church,* co-editing with Henry Wace the first two volumes of the second series. In 1877 the first edition of Schaff's three-volume *Creeds of Christendom* appeared. The *Schaff-Herzog Encyclopedia of Religious Knowledge* was published in three volumes (1882-1884). Finally, he originated and organized the American Society of Church History's thirteen-volume American Church History Series. Inspiring all of his prodigious labors was Schaff's ultimate goal to heal the wounds caused by divisions in the church. His epitaph is apt: "He advocated the reunion of Christendom."

See also MERCERSBURG THEOLOGY.

BIBLIOGRAPHY. *DAB* 16; *DARB*; H. W. Bowden, *Church History in the Age of Science* (1971); *NCAB* 3; J. H. Nichols, ed., *The Mercersburg Theology* (1966); J. H. Nichols, *Romanticism in American Theology: Nevin and Schaff at Mercersburg* (1961); D. S. Schaff, *The Life of Philip Schaff* (1897); G. H. Shriver, *Philip Schaff: Christian Scholar and Ecumenical Prophet* (1987).

S. R. Graham

Scherer, Paul Ehrmann (1892-1969). Lutheran* preacher* and homiletics* professor. Born in Pennsylvania and raised in North Carolina, Scherer was the son and grandson of Lutheran ministers in America. His earliest education was directed by his mother, who nurtured him in classical literature. By age four, he was reciting Shakespeare. A formal education in public schools began at age eight and led to a degree from the College of Charleston in 1910. After teaching English and rhetoric and after serving as an assistant principal in Georgia, he returned to Charleston for a master's degree.

Soon afterward, he experienced a call to ministry* that overcame his agnostic views, and in 1913 he enrolled at Mt. Airy Theological Seminary in Philadelphia. Upon graduation, he became assistant pastor at Holy Trinity Lutheran Church in Buffalo, where he met and in 1919 married Lillie Fry Benbow. The following year he was called to be pastor of the Evangelical Lutheran Church of the Holy Trinity, on Central Park West in New York City.

A tall, heavy-set man with a majestic voice, Scherer became a prominent, national figure during his years in New York. From 1932 to 1945, he was the vacation replacement preacher for Harry Emerson Fosdick* on the network radio broadcast called "Sunday Vespers." In 1945 he left his pastorate to become Brown Professor of Homiletics at Union Theological Seminary, New York.* Upon retirement in 1960, he accepted a series of visiting professorships, while continuing to write and preach. He died in an Ohio nursing home in 1969, and his ashes were interred at Princeton.

BIBLIOGRAPHY. "Memorial: Paul Ehrman Scherer, 1892-1969," *PSB* 62 (1969):82-84.

W. B. Lawrence

Schlatter, Michael (1718-1790). Colonial German Reformed* leader. Born at St. Gall, Switzerland, Schlatter's early spiritual mentor was his pastor, Christof Stähelin, who was widely known for his Pietist publications. Comparatively little is known of Michael Schlatter's early education at the local Gymnasium which was temporarily interrupted by his matriculation at the University of Leyden in 1736. Three years later he was ordained* and then recommended to the Dutch Reformed fathers at the Hague by John Caspar Crucinger. Impressed by his gifts, his character and his fluent knowledge of both Dutch and German, the classis* of Amsterdam dispatched him to America with instructions which amounted to the task of overseeing the German Reformed congregations in the American colonies.

After strenuous efforts involving much travel by horseback, he succeeded in organizing the so-called coetus* in 1747, consisting of four ordained ministers and twenty-eight elders who together represented twelve of the thirteen German Reformed congregations. Commissioned by the coetus, he returned to Europe for the purpose of popularizing the spiritual and financial needs of the German Reformed people in America. Having been eminently successful in this endeavor, he returned with six young ministers and a very substantial sum of money (1752). The money was used to start a system of charity schools for the children of German immigrants, a work to which Schlatter gradually devoted most of his energies. Through various misunderstandings these charity schools were less and less appreciated, and Schlatter's relationship with the coetus, as well as with the classis of Amsterdam, became strained. For a time he held a chaplaincy in the Royal American Infantry during the French and Indian War and later ministered independently. Though his relationship to the coetus was never to be restored, his early ministry and leadership were strategic in the organization and growth of the German Reformed churches in Pennsylvania.

BIBLIOGRAPHY. E. T. Corwin, *A Manual of the Reformed Church in America, 1628-1902* (1902); *DAB* VIII; *DARB;* H. Harbaugh, *The Life of the Rev. Michael Schlatter* (1857); W. J. Hinke, *Ministers of the German Reformed Congregations in Pennsylvania and Other Colonies in the Eighteenth Century* (1951).   F. E. Stoeffler

Schmemann, Alexander (1921-1983).

Orthodox* theologian* and dean of St. Vladimir's Theological Seminary. Born in Estonia to Russian parents, Schmemann was educated at St. Serge Orthodox Theological Institute in Paris where he also began his teaching career. His early specialization was in church history, which he approached with a more critical eye than was traditional in the Orthodox East. First under the influence of St. Serge's Cyprian Kern and later under the influence of the French Catholic movement to return to the sources and liturgical movement* that eventually resulted in Vatican II,* Schmemann came to find his heart's desire and devoted his energies to the study of the liturgy.* Through his book *An Introduction to Liturgical Theology* (1966), he assumed a prominent role in the field.

Immigrating to the U.S. in 1951 to join the faculty of St. Vladimir's Theological Seminary, in 1962 Schmemann succeeded Georges Florovsky* as dean and oversaw the school's growth into a pan-Orthodox institution serving most of the jurisdictions in America. As one of the most popular and charismatic Orthodox speakers and writers of the 1960s and 1970s, he traveled widely,

championing liturgical and eucharistic* renewal in the Orthodox churches of America. His scholarly contribution included *The Historical Road of Eastern Orthodoxy* (1966) and *Eucharist* (1988).

Schmemann was also one of the prime players in the negotiations which in 1970 led to the granting of autocephaly* to the Russian Orthodox Greek-Catholic Church of North America (Metropolia), which he saw as the only means of overcoming the ghettoization of Orthodox Christians in diaspora.

BIBLIOGRAPHY. J. Meyendorff, "A Life Worth Living," *SVTQ* 28 (1984):3-10.

P. D. Garrett

Schmucker, Samuel Simon (1799-1873).

Lutheran* theologian* and educator. Born in a parsonage in Hagerstown, Maryland, Schmucker graduated from the University of Pennsylvania (1819) and Princeton Seminary* (1820). Ordained* in 1821, he served five congregations near New Market, Virginia. In 1826 Schmucker was called to be the first president and professor of Gettysburg Seminary, now the oldest Lutheran theological school in America. Prior to his retirement in 1864, Schmucker prepared five hundred men for the ministry.

An advocate of Christian unity, Schmucker pioneered the Lutheran General Synod (1820), proposed cooperation of the major Protestant* denominations* in his *Fraternal Appeal to the American Churches* (1838) and was a delegate to the Evangelical Alliance* in London (1846). A prolific author of liturgies, hymnals, constitutions and catechisms,* his *Elements of Popular Theology* (1834) was the earliest English-language volume on Lutheran theology in America. Opposed to the rationalism* of the Enlightenment,* Schmucker urged a return to the evangelicalism* of the Reformation. He envisioned a Protestant consensus based on the common-core convictions of the Reformers. His "American Lutheranism" called for the revision of the Augsburg Confession* (1530) to remove such Lutheran "peculiarities" as insistence on baptismal regeneration and the real presence in the Eucharist.* These views were circulated widely in the *Definite Synodical Platform* (1855), were repudiated and earned Schmucker the enmity of the "Old" or "Historic Lutherans" who insisted on a strict confessionalism.*

Irenic, ecumenical and evangelical, by the time of his death on July 26, 1873, Schmucker was regarded by many as having been the savior of Lutheranism in the 1820s but its betrayer in the 1850s. A product of German Pietism* and American Puritanism,* Samuel Simon Schmucker was the pre-eminent Lutheran educator and theologian of the mid nineteenth century.

BIBLIOGRAPHY. A. Anstadt, *Life and Times of Rev. S. S. Schmucker* (1896); *DAB* VIII; *DARB;* L. Schmucker, *The Schmucker Family and the Lutheran Church in America* (1937); A. R. Wentz, *Pioneer in Christian Unity* (1967); *NCAB* 5.

C. G. Fry

Schools, Protestant Day. Since the mid 1960s, fundamentalist* and evangelical* Protestants* and their churches,* few of which are affiliated with mainline* denominations,* have been founding so-called Christian day schools or fundamentalist academies at a remarkable rate. Most students of private education estimate that between 8,000 and 10,000 of these schools have been established during the last two decades, with a cumulative current enrollment of approximately one million students (kindergarten through twelfth grade). These independent institutions, which emphasize the Bible,* moral absolutes, spiritual growth, mastery of basic subject matter and varying degrees of separation from contemporary culture, currently account for more than two-thirds of the Protestant day schools in the U.S., and their enrollment amounts to one-fifth of the total private-school-student population. Not only do these schools constitute one of the more robust segments of the American educational enterprise, they also represent the first widespread secession from the public schools since the establishment of Catholic parochial* schools in the nineteenth century.

Protestant-sponsored weekday schooling is not new to American education. Throughout the colonial and early national periods, Protestant churches (e.g., Lutheran,* Friends,* German Reformed,* Anglican,* Moravian* and Baptist*) established day schools for their children and charity schools for children of the poor. During the nineteenth century several denominations (e.g., the Old-School* Presbyterians) experimented with parochial schooling as an alternative to public education. With few exceptions, their success was limited. By 1900 most denominations had abandoned the religious day-school concept. By 1988 only certain Lutheran bodies, particularly the Lutheran Church—Missouri Synod* (1,238 schools and 178,884 students), Wisconsin Evangelical Synod* (388 and 35,422) and Evangelical Lutheran Church in America* (140 and 24,000); the Seventh-day Adventists* (1,145 and 63,411); Christian Reformed* (419 and 86,250); Episcopalians* (373 and 78,438); Friends* (77 and 15,977); Mennonites* (254 and 116,506); and Amish* (683 and

19,358) still maintained a significant number of weekday schools.

Most Protestants have supported public schooling since its inception during the middle decades of the nineteenth century. They approved of early public education because it reflected the Protestant value system of the culture and was viewed as an integral part of the crusade to fashion a Christian America. While the public school, by means of Bible reading, teacher example and the ubiquitous McGuffey* readers, emphasized nondenominational Protestantism, the Sunday school* stressed the particular doctrines of the various denominations. This educational arrangement of parallel institutions was generally satisfactory to most Protestants and precluded the need for denominational day schools.

Much has changed since this dualistic educational strategy was first adopted. No longer does evangelical Protestantism influence the society and the public schools as it did in the nineteenth century. The early decades of the twentieth century witnessed its decline as the moving force behind the dominant cultural and behavioral patterns. By the 1960s the evangelical strain in America's civil religion* had been largely superseded by the more secularistic Enlightenment* theme. Despite this radical alteration of the character of official American culture and the nearly complete secularization of public schooling, most Protestants and their denominations remain wedded to the parallel institutions educational arrangement. The rapid growth of Christian day schools suggests, however, that an increasing number of evangelical Protestants are questioning their historic commitment to public education.

See also PRAYER IN PUBLIC SCHOOLS.

BIBLIOGRAPHY. J. C. Carper and T. C. Hunt, eds., *Religious Schooling in America* (1984); B. S. Cooper, "The Changing Demography of Private Schools," *Education and Urban Society* 16 (1984):429-442; F. X. Curran, *The Churches and the Schools* (1954, 1985); T. C. Hunt, J. C. Carper and C. A. Kniker, eds., *Religious Schools in America: A Selected Bibliography* (1986); L. P. Jorgenson, *The State Non-Public School, 825-1925* (1987).

J. C. Carper

Schuller, Robert Harold (1926-). Reformed Church in America* minister* and televangelist.* Born in Alton, Iowa, Schuller grew up on a farm near Newkirk and was nurtured in the Dutch Calvinism* of the Reformed Church in America. He graduated from his denomination's Hope College (B.A., 1947) and Western Theological Seminary

(B.D., 1950) in Holland, Michigan. In June 1950, he married Arvella De Haan and was ordained* to the ministry at Ivanhoe Reformed Church in Riverside, a Chicago suburb. There he began his ministry, and by the time he left in early 1955 the church had grown from forty to approximately four hundred members.

Having accepted a call to begin a mission church in Orange County, Southern California, Schuller and his family arrived there in February 1955, ready to begin their new ministry. Faced with a shortage of conventional places for holding worship* services, Schuller settled on the idea of renting the Orange Drive-in Theatre. After advertising by sign, brochures and newspaper—including an endorsement by Norman Vincent Peale*—Schuller held the first service of the Garden Grove Community Church on March 27, 1955. From his pulpit mounted on the roof of the theatre's snack bar and with Arvella at the organ, Schuller preached to a congregation seated in fifty cars.

Over the next several years Schuller labored at his ministry and suffered financial hardship. A guest appearance by Norman Vincent Peale, drawing over 1,700 cars and 6,000 people, boosted the visibility of the church. By 1960 the congregation had grown to 700, and a new building served a walk-in congregation while another worship service was continued at the drive-in. With the congregation continually growing, Schuller began to dream of a building that would serve both walk-in and drive-in worshipers. By 1961 the building had become a reality—though not without considerable opposition from within the church. But Schuller began to view opposition as opportunities for him to discover and refine the dynamics of possibility thinking.

Further growth brought additional buildings, including the Tower of Hope (1968) and the spectacular Crystal Cathedral, which was begun in December 1977 and completed in 1980 at a cost of nearly twenty million dollars. As early as 1970 Schuller had begun broadcasting over television his Sunday worship service known as "Hour of Power." Intended to reach the unchurched and orchestrated to hold their attention, by the mid-1970s the program was being aired in major cities across the nation, and by the 1980s it was being broadcast internationally.

Schuller maintains that he preaches the biblical truth of the gospel in a form that touches the mental, social, physical and spiritual needs of men and women for whom the Bible* and the church are obstacles to faith. Calling his own theology* a systematic theology* of self-esteem, he attempts to recast the gospel in a positive form that appeals to the human quest for a positive self-image. In his parlance the Ten Commandments become the "Ten Creative Commandments for Constructive and Creative Living" and the Beatitudes the "Be-Happy Attitudes." While he frequently encourages people to seek success in their lives, he maintains that it is gained only by means of the servanthood modeled by Christ. For Schuller the theme of possibility thinking is a modern restatement of the biblical principle of living by faith.

Since 1969 he has shared the secrets of his success with thousands of ministers and lay leaders through the Robert H. Schuller Institute for Successful Church Leadership. Among his many books are: *Move Ahead with Possibility Thinking* (1967); *Your Church Has Real Possibilities!* (1974); and *Self-Esteem: The New Reformation* (1982). Assailed by many of his fellow Christians, who accuse him of having watered down the gospel, Schuller continues to maintain that he is an evangelical* with a ministry that is faithful to the gospel of Christ and relevant to modern Americans.

BIBLIOGRAPHY. D. Voskuil, *Mountains into Goldmines: Robert Schuller and the Gospel of Success* (1983); M. Nason and D. Nason, *Robert Schuller: The Inside Story* (1983).

D. G. Reid

Schwenkfelders (The Schwenkfelder Church). Followers of the sixteenth-century spiritualist reformer, Caspar Schwenckfeld von Ossig (1489-1561). Schwenckfeld was a well-educated and devout Silesian nobleman who initially embraced the Lutheran* Reformation. Yet he was also an independent thinker with strong mystical leanings and concerns about the fruits of Christian living. He eventually broke with his friend Luther and other reformers, primarily over Christology* and the nature of the Lord's Supper.* Schwenckfeld was forced into a life of traveling exile (1529), although he continued to write and teach. His major writings are found in the *Corpus Schwenckfeldianorum* (19 vols., 1907-1961).

Like the Anabaptists,* Schwenckfeld rejected infant baptism,* participation in war and swearing of oaths; he advocated a strict separation of church and state.* Unlike other radical reformers, however, Schwenkfeld's mysticism* also led him to reject all forms of the "visible church," including believer's baptism. He taught that the sacraments* are to be inwardly and spiritually observed only, a position not unlike the English Quakers* in the next century.

Schwenckfeld did not wish to organize a

church.* Small, informal conventicles, however, developed in Silesia, Swabia and Prussia. Persecution ended the movement in Europe, although a remnant group sought toleration at the Moravian* Brethren town of Herrnhut (Saxony) and finally colonial Pennsylvania (1734). The Society of Schwenkfelders was formed in 1782 (incorporated 1909). In the late 1980s there were five congregations with approximately 2,800 members, all in southeastern Pennsylvania.

BIBLIOGRAPHY. P. C. Erb, *Schwenckfeld in His Reformation Setting* (1975); H. W. Kriebel, *The Schwenkfelders in Pennsylvania* (1904); R. E. McLaughlin, *Caspar Schwenckfeld, Reluctant Radical* (1986); S. G. Schultz, *Caspar Schwenckfeld von Ossig* (1946). D. B. Eller

Science and Christianity. The first two centuries of European settlement in North America coincided with one of the greatest intellectual upheavals in history. The generation of the Pilgrims* lived in a world designed by the ancient philosophers Aristotle and Ptolemy, a stationary home near the center of a finite cosmos. God lived not very far away and often reminded the colonists of his power and presence—to say nothing of his displeasure—by sending lightning and earthquakes, comets and meteors, famine and disease. Frightened—and sometimes repentant—Americans fasted and prayed and clung to the Bible* as the repository of spiritual and temporal truth.

By the time of the American Revolution,* Copernicus, Newton and their fellow scientific revolutionaries had substantially remodeled the world. Earth's residents now whirled through space in an infinite universe, the magnitude and complexity of which telescopes and microscopes daily revealed. The world ran like a giant machine, regulated by immutable natural laws that determined astronomical and meteorological events. As God receded into the distance, some Americans abandoned the notion of miracles and substituted reason for revelation as the surest guide to truth. But the majority seem painlessly to have accommodated the new science to traditional religious beliefs. Few colonial Americans became skeptics or deists;* if religious orthodoxy* declined in the eighteenth century, it resulted more from urban prosperity and complacency than from the secularizing influence of science.

Contrary to still-popular opinion, the American proponents of modern science encountered relatively little religious resistance, though much indifference. In New England, for example, Puritan* clergy* led in the popularization of the Copernican system (which necessitated reinterpreting geocentric biblical passages) and in the promotion of inoculation against smallpox (which called into question the prevailing belief that this loathsome disease was a divine punishment). In colonies to the south, the new science swept almost imperceptibly across the land, rarely arousing religious comment.

The years between the Revolution and Civil War,* especially those after the turn of the century, witnessed the rapid growth of both evangelical* Christianity and scientific inquiry. At the very time Bible-thumping revivalists* were filling the pews of the nation's churches, astronomers and geologists were laboring to substitute a dynamic, naturalistic history of the world for the static, supernatural view found in the Scriptures. Such activity threatened the harmonious relationship between science and Christianity that had characterized the colonial period, but the relatively few conflicts that erupted generally had less to do with geological empiricism versus biblical literalism than with questions of intellectual jurisdiction. The notorious debate between the biblical exegete Tayler Lewis* and the geologist James Dwight Dana,* for example, turned on the question of whether philologists, trained in biblical languages, or geologists, who studied rocks, were better qualified to interpret the Scriptures.

Several factors contributed to peaceful relations in the antebellum period. Such prominent geologists as Dana, Benjamin Silliman* and the Reverend Edward Hitchcock,* all orthodox Christians, went out of their way to harmonize God's Word with his works and to show how the findings of science demonstrated his wisdom and power. They, along with other leaders of American science, also espoused a Baconian philosophy, which emphasized the factual, nontheoretical nature of science and provided concerned Christians with an epistemological tool with which to monitor scientific developments. Rather than inhibiting the growth of science. prevailing Christian values tended to encourage the study of nature, albeit with some restrictions.

The publication of Charles Darwin's *Origin of Species* (1859) provoked considerable debate in Christian circles, but the idea of organic evolution, though clearly incompatible with a literal reading of Genesis, encountered less religious opposition—and more informed criticism—than is commonly believed. Most American scientists, led by the religiously orthodox Asa Gray,* successfully embraced evolution without sacrificing their faith. By the mid 1870s there were only two well-known naturalists in North America, John William Dawson of Montreal and Arnold Guyot of Princeton, who continued to reject organic evolution; neither was a biblical literalist, and both tried to keep explanations relying on supernatural intervention to a minimum. By this time Christian intellectuals, who had earlier tended to dismiss Darwin's views as bad science, were beginning seriously to debate the implications of the transmutation hypothesis. Many liberals,* and not a few evangelicals, came to accept evolution—if not always Darwin's version of it—as God's method of creation, and even conservative intellectuals who rejected organic evolution for being incompatible with natural and revealed religion, rarely invoked a recent, literal, six-day creation. Undoubtedly, the vast majority of inarticulate Christians remained loyal to the doctrine of special creation, but until the twentieth century they also remained largely silent.

During the twentieth century Christians confronted a host of scientific developments, ranging from deterministic psychologies to naturalistic cosmogonies, but no issue elicited such heated discussion as the subject of evolution, especially of humans. During the 1920s and again in the 1970s and 1980s, Christian fundamentalists* and assorted allies sought to inhibit the spread of evolution by legal means, first by outlawing the teaching of evolution in public schools,* later by requiring equal time for "creation science"* whenever "evolution science" was taught. Although they fell considerably short of their goals both times, they succeeded in arousing widespread sympathy for their cause, reflected in a 1982 public-opinion poll that revealed that forty-four per cent of Americans still believed that "God created man pretty much in his present form at one time within the last 10,000 years." At times the creation-evolution controversy took on the appearance of a simple clash between science and conservative Christianity, but even in this case appearances could be deceiving. Hundreds of degree-carrying scientists supported the creationist cause, while hundreds of thousands of orthodox Christians favored the teaching of evolution. Thus clearly no model of "warfare" or "conflict" adequately describes the historical relationship between science and Christianity in America.

See also CREATION SCIENCE; DARWINIAN EVOLUTION AND THE AMERICAN CHURCHES.

BIBLIOGRAPHY. T. D. Bozeman, Protestants in an Age of Science: The Baconian Ideal and Antebellum American Religious Thought (1977); H. Hovenkamp, Science and Religion in America, 1800-1860 (1978); D. C. Lindberg and R. L. Numbers, eds., God and Nature: Historical Essays on the Encounter between Christianity and Science (1986); R. L. Numbers, "Science and Religion," in Historical Writing on American Science: Perspectives and Prospects, ed. S. G. Kohlstedt and M. W. Rossiter (1986); J. H. Roberts, Darwinism and the Divine in America: Protestant Intellectuals and Organic Evolution, 1859-1900 (1988).

R. L. Numbers

Scofield, (C)yrus (I)ngerson (1843-1921).

Bible conference* speaker and defender of dispensational* premillennialism.* Born near Clinton, Michigan, Scofield was raised in the Episcopal Church.* As a child his father moved the family to Lebanon, Tennessee, where Scofield's preparation for college was interrupted by service in the 7th Regiment of the Tennessee infantry during the Civil War.* After the war Scofield settled in St. Louis, married Leontine Cerre and studied law. In the same decade he settled in Atchison, Kansas, pursuing both law (admitted to the Kansas bar in 1869) and politics (1871, representative to the lower house of the Kansas legislature, 4th district; 1872, representative of the 8th district; 1873, U.S. attorney for the district of Kansas). For undisclosed reasons, though likely related to alcohol abuse, Scofield left a promising career and returned to St. Louis in 1879, leaving behind a wife (a divorce was secured in 1883) and two daughters.

The details of this period in his life are, at best, filled with contradictions; in the midst of it, however, he came to an evangelical* conversion.* Shortly thereafter the zealous Scofield assisted in Dwight L. Moody's* campaign in St. Louis, was discipled* by James Hall Brooks* and joined the Pilgrim Congregational Church. He became acting superintendent of the local YMCA* and was licensed* to work in the Hyde Park Congregational Church (1880-1882), in addition to working with railroad men in East St. Louis.

In 1882 Scofield moved to Dallas, Texas, to take a Congregational* mission church, where he was also ordained.* The church grew steadily from fourteen to over eight hundred members when he left in 1895. In addition to establishing other churches and mission stations in the area, Scofield served as denominational superintendent of missions in the South and Southwest, founded the Central American Mission in 1890, began a correspondence course of Bible knowledge that at one time had over 7,000 enrollees (it was sold to Moody Bible Institute* in 1915) and wrote Rightly Dividing the Word of Truth (1888), which established him as a leading defender of dispensational* premillennialism.*

In 1895 Scofield left Dallas for Northfield, Massachusetts, being influenced by D. L. Moody to pastor the local Congregational church. There he became involved in the Northfield conferences,* having already become a regular participant in the Niagara conferences.* In addition, he became president of the Northfield Bible Training School. In 1901, at the Sea Cliff Bible Conference on Long Island, New York, Scofield indicated interest in preparing a reference Bible defending the popular distinctives of the Bible conference movement. Work on the project consumed several years. Scofield, who had initially returned to the Dallas church in 1903, eventually left the church to devote his full time to the project. When the Scofield Reference Bible* was published by Oxford University Press in 1909, it rapidly became the most widely received defense of dispensational premillennialism.

Basking in the popularity of his reference Bible, Scofield severed his connection with the Dallas church (transferring his ministerial connection to the Presbyterian Church in the U.S.* in 1908) and settled near New York City where he operated a correspondence school, the New York Night School of the Bible. In 1914, with Lewis S. Chafer,* he founded the Philadelphia School of the Bible. During this period he edited for Oxford Press the Tercentenary Edition of the Bible (1911) and revised his reference Bible (1917). Though enormously popular in the Bible conference circuit, Scofield suffered from declining health and progressively curtailed his activities, with Chafer continuing much of his work. He died at his home in Douglaston, Long Island, leaving behind a wife and son. In 1922, during the pastorate of L. S. Chafer, the Dallas church (independent since 1908) changed its name to Scofield Memorial Church.

Scofield's influence on the evangelical*/fundamentalist* movement of the early twentieth century was enormous. He not only contributed to the infrastructure of evangelical societies, but his writings defined that segment known as dispensational premillennialism.

BIBLIOGRAPHY. J. M. Canfield, *The Incredible Scofield and His Book* (1988); C. G. Trumbull, *The Life Story of C. I. Scofield* (1920).

J. Hannah

Scofield Reference Bible. A highly influential study Bible providing a dispensational* premillennialist* interpretation of Scripture.* The Scofield Reference Bible was edited by C. I. Scofield,* a lawyer and Congregationalist* minister.* The work was published in 1909 by Oxford University Press, expanded in 1917 and revised in 1967. Scofield believed that the Bible, when interpreted literally, was clear in its divisions and plans for Jews, Gentiles and the church. For example, he argued that the division of law and grace was so distinct "that Scripture never, in any dispensation, mingles these two principles."

Scofield defined a dispensation as "a period of time during which man is tested in respect of obedience to some specific revelation of the will of God." Seven dispensations were delineated in the biblical text: (1) In the dispensation of innocency (Gen 1:28—3:13), God required a simple test of Adam and Eve, warning them of the consequence of disobedience. (2) The dispensation of conscience (Gen 3:23—7:23) required that people do good and abstain from evil according to what their consciences dictated. (3) The dispensation of human government (Gen 8:20—11:9) asked people to govern the world for God, as his stewards. (4) The dispensation of promise (Gen 12:1—Ex 19:8) was specifically Hebrew in intention and seemed to require the faith of Israel in God's promises. (5) The Law (Ex 19:8—Mt 27:53) also applied to Israel, requiring her obedience to the laws given by God to the nation. During this time Gentiles continued to live under the dispensation of human government. (6) The dispensation of grace (Mt 27:35; John 1:17) began with the death and resurrection of Jesus Christ, extends to all people and requires faith in Christ's work of atonement.* (7) At the end of the present dispensation will come the pretribulation rapture* of the church, the great tribulation and Christ's return to establish the millennial kingdom, which is the seventh dispensation, the fullness of times (Eph 1:10; Dan 9:20-27; Rev 20, 21). God's plans for Jews, Gentiles and the church will be brought to fulfillment.

BIBLIOGRAPHY. G. M. Marsden, *Fundamentalism and American Culture* (1980); C. I. Scofield, *Rightly Dividing the Word of Truth* (1888).

C. W. Whiteman

Scopes Trial. The trial of John T. Scopes in 1925 in Dayton, Tennessee, for teaching the biological evolution of humans, became symbolic of fundamentalist* efforts to outlaw such teaching in public schools.*

As soon as Charles Darwin's *Origin of Species* was published in 1859, Christians divided over whether biological evolution contradicted the biblical account of creation. Even some prominent scientists and theologians, such as George Frederick Wright* of Oberlin* and Benjamin B. Warfield* of Princeton Theological Seminary,* who held that the Bible* was inerrant,* allowed that God might have used limited forms of evolutionary development of species as a means of creation. Other conservative Protestants insisted that biological evolution and Genesis were incompatible. Prior to World War 1,* however, such antievolutionary views were rarely used as tests of loyalty to Scripture, except in the South.

After World War 1 a number of prominent leaders in the emerging fundamentalist movement proclaimed that biological evolution undermined faith in the Bible and weakened Christian civilization, since it often was associated with a materialistic philosophy that allowed no place for God. William Jennings Bryan* took up this cause and helped make it a major national movement. A number of Southern states adopted legislation banning the teaching of biological evolution in public schools. The Tennessee bill, passed early in 1925, was one of the strongest, banning "to teach any theory that denies the Story of Divine Creation of man as taught in the Bible, and to teach instead that man has descended from a lower order of animal."

With the backing of the American Civil Liberties Union, John T. Scopes, a young science teacher in Dayton, Tennessee, confessed to having taught the banned views. At his trial in July the ACLU offered a star-studded defense team led by famed trial lawyer and religious skeptic Clarence Darrow. The fundamentalists countered with William Jennings Bryan. The so-called Monkey Trial that ensued was one of the first great media events in history, as reporters packed tiny Dayton, wiring reports all over the world, often ridiculing fundamentalists as rural yokels.

The highlight of the trial was Darrow's cross-examination of Bryan as an expert on the Bible. Bryan's difficulties at answering some of Darrow's village-atheist questions made him vulnerable to further press ridicule. Scopes, however, was convicted; but his conviction was reversed on a technicality by a higher Tennessee court, thus blocking intended further appeals. Bryan died in Dayton a few days after the trial, and the press declared a rout of fundamentalism, an image that has long stuck in the popular imagination, as did the image that fundamentalism simply reflected resentment of undereducated rural people against sophisticated urban culture. Neither fundamentalism nor antievolutionism, however, were seriously slowed by the Scopes Trial. States continued to pass antievolution legislation. Although most such laws were banned by the 1960s, in that same decade antievolution enjoyed a revival with the emergence of a vigorous "creation science"* movement.

See also CREATION SCIENCE; DARWINIAN EVOLUTION AND THE AMERICAN CHURCHES.

BIBLIOGRAPHY. E. J. Larson, *Trial and Error; The American Controversy over Creation and Evolution* (1985); F. M. Szasz, *The Divided Mind of Protestant America, 1880-1930* (1982); L. W. Levine, *Defender of the Faith: William Jennings Bryan* (1965). G. M. Marsden

Scott, Orange (1800-1847). Methodist* minister,* abolitionist* and founder of the Wesleyan Methodist Church. Born in Brookfield, Vermont, Scott was converted* at a camp meeting* at Bane, Vermont, at the age of twenty-one and, with only thirteen months of formal education, became a class leader and licensed* exhorter in the Methodist Episcopal Church.* Following his reception into the membership of the New England Conference in 1822, he became a successful revival* preacher* and a widely known presiding elder.* However, his open support of the antislavery movement caused his popular support to diminish.

Convinced of the vital relationship between personal and social holiness, Scott saw abolition as an inescapable consequence of the Wesleyan* doctrine of entire sanctification.* Hence, he undertook the circulation of 100 copies of the "Liberator," an antislavery tract penned by William Lloyd Garrison, and he sought the abolition of slavery through legislative action in the Methodist Episcopal Church. As chairman of the New England delegation to the General Conference of 1836, he presented abolitionist legislation that was rejected by the majority of that body. However, Scott continued his efforts of persuasion, and became a lecturer for the American Anti-Slavery Society in 1837. Regarded as a radical, he found his only access to publication was through founding his own periodical, *The Wesleyan Quarterly Review* (1838), later known as the *American Wesleyan Observer* (1839).

In the General Conference of 1840 his delegation failed to restore the early Wesleyan doctrine opposing slavery to the *Discipline* of the Methodist Church. Consequently, he and Lucius Matlock organized an antislavery convention that was held in New York. Moving beyond criticism of the Methodist Episcopal leadership, he and his followers organized the American Wesleyan Anti-Slavery Society. Despite poor health, he withdrew from the

Methodist Episcopal Church in 1842 and became the first president of the Wesleyan Methodist Church (*See* Wesleyan Church) and agent for the movement's paper, the *True Wesleyan* (1843-1846).

BIBLIOGRAPHY. *AAP* 7; *DAB* VIII; *DARB*; D. Dayton, *Discovering an Evangelical Heritage* (1976); *NCAB* 2; T. Smith, *Revivalism and Social Reform in Mid-Nineteenth Century America* (1957). J. S. O'Malley

Scott, Peter Cameron (1867-1896). Founder of Africa Inland Mission.* Born in Scotland, Scott immigrated with his family to Philadelphia. His commitment to missionary* service came during a spiritual crisis in Scotland where he had gone for health reasons. After returning to Philadelphia, Scott in 1890 sailed for West Africa under the Missionary Alliance. Poor health forced him to return to America and the British Isles. While kneeling beside the tomb of David Livingstone in Westminster Abbey, Scott's plans for a chain of mission stations stretching from east to central Africa crystallized.

Back in America he met with members of the recently formed Philadelphia Missionary Council. This group agreed to represent the proposed Africa Inland Mission and to channel workers and funds. Committed to the single goal of evangelism,* Scott and his first missionary party sailed in 1895 for East Africa, where he died the following year.

BIBLIOGRAPHY. C. S. Miller, *The Life of Peter Cameron Scott: The Unlocked Door* (1955). J. Gration

Scott, Walter (1796-1861). Early leader of the Restoration Movement.* Born in Moffatt, Scotland, of a family with ten children, Scott studied at the University of Edinburgh (B.A., 1818) and then immigrated to America in 1818 at the suggestion of an uncle, first serving as a Latin tutor in an academy on Long Island. In 1819 he journeyed to Pittsburgh, where he continued to teach school; and he led a congregation influenced by the ideas of Robert Sandeman* as well as Robert and James Haldane. The group, called by some the "kissing Baptists," practiced baptism* by immersion, foot washing* and the "holy kiss."

In 1821 Scott met Alexander Campbell,* a man in whom he recognized a kindred spirit. In 1823 Scott contributed a series of four articles, entitled "A Divinely Authorized Plan of Preaching the Christian Religion," to the first volume of Campbell's *Christian Baptist.* In 1826 Scott moved to Ohio to open an academy and that same year

began attending the meeting of the Mahoning Baptist Association. Later Scott became an evangelist* for the Association. Known for his dynamic speaking ability, Scott never missed an opportunity to preach* and evangelize and is said to have converted over 1,000 persons a year for over a period of three decades. In addition, his editorial voice was heard in two periodicals: *Evangelist* (1832-1835; 1838-1844) and *Protestant Unionist* (1844-1850).

It was Scott who created the Restoration Movement's "five-finger exercise" setting forth the order of conversion: faith, repentance, baptism, remission of sins and the gift of the Holy Spirit. Out of Scott's efforts came a great revival that was very different from the Cane Ridge Revival* of some twenty years earlier. There was no frenzy of emotion but a combination of rationality and authority,* an appeal to common sense and to the absolute authority of the Scripture.* It strongly asserted every man's rational ability to understand what he ought to do and why, and his moral ability to do it. Within one year the total membership of the churches in the Mahoning Association more than doubled, with a net increase of 512 persons.

In 1834 Scott was appointed a trustee of Miami University, Oxford, Ohio, by action of the state legislature. In 1836 when Bacon College (named after Sir Francis Bacon) at Georgetown, Kentucky, was founded, Scott became president for a brief period. His inaugural address was an elaborate application of Bacon's method to the development of a synopsis for a complete system of education. For his forty years of service and leadership, Scott is recognized as one of the Founding Fathers of the Restoration Movement.

BIBLIOGRAPHY. W. Baxter, *Life of Elder Walter Scott* (1873); *DAB* VIII; *DARB; NCAB* 2; D. E. Stevenson, *Walter Scott: Voice of the Golden Oracle* (1946). T. L. Miethe

Scottish Presbyterians in America. While English Puritan* immigration* to New England in the early seventeenth century gave American Presbyterianism* its earliest churches, the influx of Scottish and Scotch-Irish immigration rapidly changed the shape of the colonial church. An early pioneer was Francis Makemie,* an Ulster-bred Glasgow University graduate who, after arriving as a missionary* in 1683, worked tirelessly to establish Presbyterian congregations among the Scotch-Irish of the Middle Colonies.

Because of the rapid increase of Scotch-Irish immigration after 1700, tensions surfaced as New England Puritan-style Presbyterians were quickly outnumbered by the Scotch-Irish, who generally held stricter conceptions of Presbyterian church government* and subscription to the Westminster Confession.* A compromise was effected between the two groups with the approval of the Adopting Act* of 1729, which mandated a qualified confessional* subscription.

Scotch-Irish ranks were split by the emergence of a revivalist* group led by William Tennant, Sr.,* an Ulster-born Scot, which stressed personal conversion* and sanctification.* This Log College* group joined with New England Presbyterians to form the New Side* when the strict subscriptionist Old Side ejected the revivalist party from the synod* in 1741.

Between 1741 and the reunion of the Old and New Sides in 1758, the New Side grew markedly. Of crucial importance for the future of the church was the New Side's founding in 1746 of the institution which came to be known as the College of New Jersey* at Princeton, to which the Scottish churchman John Witherspoon* was called as president in 1768. The only clergyman to sign the Declaration of Independence, Witherspoon introduced Scottish Common Sense Realism,* which soon became the dominant philosophical system in the emerging nation.

Divisions among Presbyterian groups in Scotland were perpetuated in America. The Covenanter tradition, stemming from protests after 1660 against the power of the established church and the restoration of the monarchy, was carried on by groups of settlers arriving after 1720, and a Reformed Presbytery was established in Pennsylvania in 1774. Similarly, the Seceder tradition of those who left the Scottish Kirk in 1733 in the aftermath of the Marrow Controversy was soon represented in America with the formation of an Associate Presbytery in the Susquehanna Valley of Pennsylvania in 1753. Sharing a similar theological and liturgical conservatism, many adherents of the two groups united in 1782 to form the Associate Reformed Synod which, after another merger, became the United Presbyterian Church in North America in 1858. The Covenanter Seceder tradition continues to be represented today by the Reformed Presbyterian Church in North America* and by the Associate Reformed Presbyterian Church.*

BIBLIOGRAPHY. J. G. Craighead, *Scotch and Irish Seeds in American Soil* (1878); G. J. Slosser, ed., *They Seek a Country* (1955); L. J. Trinterud, *The Forming of an American Tradition* (1949).

W. B. Evans

Scottish Realism. Eighteenth-century Scottish philosophy influential in nineteenth-century American Protestantism.* Common Sense philosophy, or Scottish Realism, was the most influential intellectual tradition shaping American Protestantism between the late 1700s and the Civil War.* Developed principally by Scottish philosopher Thomas Reid (1710-1796) in the mid eighteenth century, it sought to refute both the skepticism of David Hume (1711-1776) and the idealism of George Berkeley (1685-1753) by arguing that ordinary people may gain accurate knowledge of the real world through responsible use of their senses. While man's physical senses could discover truth about the outside world through empirical study and induction, an innate "moral sense" common to all humans allowed for intuitive knowledge of certain foundational principles of morality.

Within America, Scottish Realism first gained prominence at the College of New Jersey* during the presidency of John Witherspoon.* Thereafter its influence over American Protestantism grew rapidly as it came to shape the theology* and apologetics* of antebellum Lutherans,* Episcopalians,* Unitarians* and especially Calvinist* evangelicals.* Such widespread acceptance sprang both from Common Sense philosophy's flexibility and its applicability to the epistemological and ethical problems posed by the radical French Enlightenment.* Theologians, moral philosophers, scientists and educators alike employed its essential tenets to counter the dangerous speculations of the French philosophers and to bolster the Protestant case for everything from the harmony of science* and religion (*See* Science and Christianity) to the validity of traditional moral values in the rapidly expanding republic. Overall, Scottish Realism imparted to nineteenth-century Protestants a supreme confidence in their abilities to apprehend and defend the truth, a confidence shaken, but not wholly destroyed, by the social and intellectual challenges of the twentieth century.

See also PRINCETON THEOLOGY.

BIBLIOGRAPHY. S. E. Ahlstrom, "The Scottish Philosophy and American Theology," *CH* 24 (1955):257-272; S. A. Grave, *The Scottish Philosophy of Common Sense* (1960); M. A. Noll, "Common Sense Traditions and American Evangelical Thought," *AQ* 37 (1985):216-238.

R. W. Pointer

Scripture. American Christianity features a wide variety of views about Scripture and the nature of the Bible.* As a theological topic, the doctrine of Scripture includes issues of revelation, canon, authority,* inspiration and the work of the Holy Spirit, as well as the disciplines of hermeneutics and biblical interpretation.* In American Christianity a number of different understandings of Scripture have emerged—many of them rooted in British and continental European theology.* Some, however, have taken on a distinctively American formulation. Heated and sometimes bitter controversies over the nature of Scripture have shaped distinctions and qualifications that often puzzle outside observers, but they are important issues of truth and self-definition for the groups that make them. The following categories are just one approach to understanding what American Christians believe about the Bible.

Roman Catholicism. Catholics have traditionally looked to their Church as the guarantor of the biblical canon. The Church authenticates Scripture by recognizing the authority of the biblical books, but ultimately Scripture is authoritative because it is inspired by God and is what God has intended to reveal to the Church. With the development of the papacy,* Catholicism also stressed the authority of Church tradition as interpreted by the magisterium,* or teaching office, of the Church. The pope, as the vicar of Christ, is the prime interpreter of Scripture in the Church (*See* Papal Infallibility). Since Vatican II,* contemporary Roman Catholicism has focused on the binding together of Scripture and tradition, with the emphasis on their close communication and common goals. Church tradition helps ensure that Scripture is interpreted correctly. Scripture and tradition coinhere as the means by which God guides the Church.

Conservative Protestantism. A number of theological movements in American Christianity would classify themselves as conservative Protestant in their view of Scripture. Generally, this means a firm adherence to Scripture as the authoritative Word of God. Some contemporary adherents to the major confessional traditions of the sixteenth-century Reformation—whether Lutheran or Reformed—look to their historic confessions on Scripture. For Lutherans these formulations are found in *The Book of Concord,* while the *Westminster Confession of Faith* has been particularly significant for American churches in the Presbyterian and Reformed tradition.

The Lutheran tradition has stressed the supreme authority of Scripture as the source and judge of all doctrine, though its confessions are silent on the doctrine of the inspiration of Scripture and the activity of the Holy Spirit in forming the canon. Many Lutherans have argued that the stress of their confessional heritage is not on Scripture as a book, but on its redemptive content. The Reformed confessions likewise emphasize the supreme authority of Scripture, but are more explicit in their definitions of the extent of the canon and the role of the Spirit in inspiration, illumination and interpretation. Traditional Anabaptists have also maintained the supreme authority of Scripture, yet always in direct association with the inner working of the Spirit in the lives of true believers. This "hermeneutic of discipleship" has been a chief distinction between Anabaptists and the confessional churches of the Reformation.

Today, conservative Protestant views often fall into the categories of fundamentalism,* scholasticism and neo-evangelicalism.*

1. *Fundamentalism.* American fundamentalism, as it arose in the late nineteenth and early twentieth centuries, has emphasized Scripture as proposition. The Bible contains divinely inspired and inerrant* propositional truths that God has revealed. Fundamentalists have emphasized the full inspiration of all parts of the Bible, stressing the verbal inspiration of Scripture in their belief that God has directly inspired each word of the biblical text. In addition, inspiration is "plenary," meaning "full" or "complete" and embracing the entire Protestant canon of sixty-six books. Fundamentalism not only upholds the "infallibility," or reliability, of Scripture in all that it addresses, but the "inerrancy" of Scripture, indicating its freedom from falsehood, fraud or deceit of any kind. Fundamentalism has argued that since God is true (Rom 3:4) and God has "breathed out," or "inspired," Scripture (2 Tim 3:16), therefore the Scriptures must be true in all that they teach. What they teach as the revelation of God is revealed in the statements or propositions of Scripture—so characterized because they are directly inspired by God. Often fundamentalism has emphasized a literal reading and interpretation of biblical texts.

2. *Scholastic Theology.* The prominent theologians* of Princeton Seminary* in the nineteenth and early twentieth centuries stressed Scripture as doctrine. Charles Hodge,* Archibald A. Hodge* and Benjamin B. Warfield* presented seventeenth-century Reformed scholastic theology to America. Their emphasis was on Scripture's complete authority arising from its divine inspiration. This means every word of the writers is, in a sense, "divine" and "human." Since inspired writers cannot err, all the Bible teaches as religious and moral truths, as well as all statements of fact, are without error. Princeton theologians spoke of the "original autographs" of Scripture as being "abso-

lutely infallible when interpreted in the sense intended." For this to be disproved, A. A. Hodge and B. B. Warfield argued that two discrepant passages must be shown to have existed in the original autographs, that the interpretation of the apparent discrepancy is the one intended by the passage and that the true sense of the autographic text is "directly and necessarily inconsistent with some certainly known act of history, or truth of science, or some other statement of Scripture certainly ascertained and interpreted." In this view, the Bible functioned as a source for teaching and a system of doctrine for the church.

3. *Neo-Evangelical Theology.* So-called neo-evangelicals* tend to speak of Scripture as message. This movement arose in the late 1940s as a reaction to American fundamentalism and stressed the need for more Christian involvement in societal problems. Forty years later the term is not used as frequently, but it has described a trans-denominational movement that has, among other things, emphasized Scripture's authority and primary purpose as centering on faith and salvation in Jesus Christ. Scripture is the Word of God known by the work of the Holy Spirit. In this view, the central theological purpose of Scripture is stressed. Scripture is a religious document with a theological purpose. It is infallible in that it is completely trustworthy in the self-revelation of God in Jesus Christ. Scripture will not deceive or lead one away from the theological truths God intends to convey. But this infallibility does not entail inerrancy on matters such as history, science or geography. *Error* as "sin" and "deception" is not seen as being in the same category as *error* as "incorrectness." Scripture is God's divine message revealed in human words. The Bible is intended to guide people to salvation and instruct them on how to live the life of faith.

Liberal Theology. American liberal theologians in the early twentieth century emphasized Scripture as experience. Standing in the tradition of Friedrich Schleiermacher (1768-1834), Albrecht Ritschl (1822-1889) and Adolf von Harnack (1851-1930), these theologians sought to reconstruct traditional orthodoxy* to meet the challenges of the modern world. They viewed the Bible as an ancient document written by fallible, human writers who were "religious geniuses." These inspiring writers produced a literature that conveys religious experience* to its readers as it brings them into contact with the great questions of human existence. Thus the liberal pulpiteer Harry Emerson Fosdick* spoke of the Bible as presenting "abiding experiences and changing categories."

This means the basic human experiences of which the Bible speaks will be the same in any age, though expressed in various concepts and frameworks at different periods of history. Theologians must search out the abiding experiences that underlie biblical categories and express them in ways appropriate to the present times. For liberal theology, God is revealed in the events of history and especially in Jesus Christ. Humans may open themselves to this revelation and find the ring of truth in Scripture as biblical experiences coincide with their own religious experiences.

Neo-Orthodox Theology. The Swiss theologians Karl Barth* and Emil Brunner* are associated with neo-orthodox* theology, a movement which characteristically speaks of Scripture as witness. Barth, reacting strongly to the liberal theology in which he was schooled, developed a dialectical* theology that in its early stages stressed the great contrast and distance between the transcendent, holy God and finite, sinful humanity. In Jesus Christ, this gulf was bridged. Christ is God's self-revelation so that to say *revelation* is to say *the Word made flesh.* Barth spoke of the threefold Word of God as the Word revealed (Jesus Christ), the Word written (Scripture) and the Word proclaimed (preaching*). Scripture "becomes" God's Word when, through its proclamation, it witnesses or points to the Word made flesh, Jesus Christ. The inspired writers of Scripture were witnesses to God's revelation. Barth could speak of "verbal inspiration" in the sense that the witnesses to God's revelation recorded their witness in words. But these were fallible words of humans, having "the capacity for errors," yet nevertheless used by God to accomplish his own purposes. Scripture gains authority insofar as the Holy Spirit takes human witnesses and through their witness creates faith and obedience to Jesus Christ.

Existential Theology. Paul Tillich* and Rudolf Bultmann*—two scholars who were heavily influenced by twentieth-century existentialism*—viewed Scripture as living encounter. Tillich in particular taught that humans are estranged from the ground of being (God) and that salvation can come only by God's revelation. This revelation is Jesus the Christ, who reunites humans with the ground of being. God's revelation consists of that which is our "ultimate concern." The Bible is the source for God's revelation and participates in that revelation itself. Its words point to God's revelatory events, which are conveyed in Scripture through religious symbols. The Bible is the catalyst for revelation, so contemporary people can enter into the power of the original revelatory events and share the same ecstatic experiences as the biblical writers. The Bible presents a collage of religious symbols expressing God's revelation. The supreme symbol and God's final revelation is the biblical picture of Jesus as the Christ. In Jesus the Christ, the power of a new being is present as nowhere else. In the living encounter with this symbol of the Christ through Scripture, humans receive God's revelation and the wholeness and health which is their salvation.

Other Views. A number of other theological movements are to be found in modern American Christian thinking. Many of these do not formally discuss the traditional theological categories regarding Scripture but present their views of the Bible through different means. Some of the most prominent of these theologies are the following:

1. *Process Theology.** Process theologians view Scripture as unfolding action. Process theology is built on the process philosophy of Alfred North Whitehead, who viewed all reality and all experiences as related to each other. Whitehead's student, Charles Hartshorne, spoke of God as having two poles or aspects. One is God's abstract essence, which is God's eternal and unchangeable aspect. The other is God's concrete reality, which is God's temporal, changing aspect. In process thought, religious doctrines should be accepted only if they are self-evident and conform to human experience. The Bible is the source of doctrine in that it describes the actions of God in leading the world to what it can be. Scripture also presents possibilities that go beyond normal, societal experience and open new possibilities of relationships. For process philosophy and the Bible, reality is becoming rather than being, in process rather than static. Scripture has authority in that it concurs with one's own self-evident experiences and becomes the source for seeing the unfolding action of God in the world—God as evolving along with creation into future possibilities. Scripture presents this God who is changing along with the world and who responds in love to humans.

2. *Story Theology.* Story, or narrative, theology sees the Bible as the medium for metaphors. The emphasis in this movement is on the importance of narratives and the power of stories in human experience. Metaphoric thinking, is a basic feature of human life and is the ability to spot continuities between two dissimilar objects. The parables of Jesus are prime examples of this type of metaphoric thinking, where common objects, such as lost coins or buried treasure, are compared to the kingdom of God.* In story theology language is seen to have a shaping and participatory power

which draws people into narratives in personal ways. In stories people are confronted with their own possibilities and see their lives in light of their visions of what life can or should be. The Bible provides a central set of metaphors by which one's vision of life can be shaped. Its narrative genre is prominent so it gains authority by calling forth new visions of life. The goal of Scripture is not to find a set of beliefs but to find a way to belief. The Bible is a poetic classic. It is the medium for metaphors in that it invites people to set their own life story in relation to its story. Scripture gives new visions of reality that are validated as they are lived out.

3. *Liberation Theology.* Liberation theology* views the Bible as providing the foundation for freedom. Since 1965 liberation theology has taken on an increasingly prominent place among American theologians. From its origins in the Latin American context, liberation theology now can describe a number of theological orientations identified by geographic location (African; Asian) or special concern (Black theology; feminist theology). The starting point for liberation theology is the poor and oppressed of the world. It emphasizes not the priority of theories but of *praxis,* the practical point "where the pain is." Theology is defined as critical reflection on *praxis.* As such, liberation theologians argue that the Bible shows God on the side of the poor of the world. The poor have an "epistemological privilege" since they can perceive the realities of the world better than the rich. In Scripture, the Exodus liberation event is a paradigm of God's desire to give freedom to the oppressed. The prophetic message of justice and Jesus' proclamation of the kingdom of God confirm this orientation. In liberation theology, Scripture functions as giving a foundation for freedom by providing the paradigms and goals of human liberation and presenting the ultimate human liberator, Jesus Christ.

4. *Feminist Theology.* In many forms of feminist theology, Scripture serves as the mother of models. Those who identify themselves as feminist theologians often speak of the patriarchal biases found in the Bible. On the basis of this, these theologians ask how the Bible can be used as a source for understanding life and how it can serve as a positive resource, especially for women who have been oppressed. Some feminist theologians have sought to reclaim Scripture by reinterpreting biblical texts in light of contemporary feminist consciousness. Some have looked to theological perspectives such as the prophetic tradition to find a central theological theme of liberation for the oppressed. Others have worked on historical

reconstructions that document movements away from egalitarianism toward patriarchalism. For many of these theologians, Scripture is the mother of models in that it serves as an open-ended paradigm to set experiences in motion and to invite life-changing transformations. The Bible can give a new vision of reality—especially in conveying the life and ministry of Jesus. Scripture can be the place where feminist critical consciousness can find congruence with certain of the biblical witnesses.

The plurality of positions about the nature of Scripture and its appropriate interpretation will continue to provoke discussions and at times deep debate in American Christianity. All views have vigorous proponents who will provide opportunities for significant dialog in the years ahead.

See also BIBLE IN AMERICAN CULTURE; BIBLICAL INTERPRETATION; INERRANCY DEBATE.

BIBLIOGRAPHY. P. Achtemeier, *The Inspiration of Scripture* (1980); A. Dulles, *Models of Revelation* (1983); R. Gnuse, *The Authority of the Bible* (1985); N. Hatch and M. A. Noll, eds., *The Bible in America: Essays in Cultural History* (1982); D. H. Kelsey, *The Uses of Scripture in Recent Theology* (1975); D. K. McKim, ed., *A Guide to Contemporary Hermeneutics* (1986); D. K. McKim, ed., *The Authoritative Word: Essays on the Nature of Scripture* (1983); D. K. McKim, *What Christians Believe about the Bible* (1985); J. B. Rogers and D. K. McKim, *The Authority and Interpretation of the Bible: An Historical Approach* (1979); B. Vawter, *Biblical Inspiration* (1972).

D. K. McKim

Scroggie, William Graham (1877-1958). Scottish minister* and author. Born at Malvern, England, of Scottish parents, Scroggie entered business but then felt directed by God to attend Spurgeon's College prior to going into the ministry.* There he gave himself to a mastery of the English Bible. Scroggie held pastorates at London, Halifax, Sunderland and Edinburgh.

While at Edinburgh, Scroggie's consuming passion to share his understanding of "how to know the Bible" led to his development of Bible correspondence courses and a weekly night school. In 1927 the University of Edinburgh awarded him with the doctor of divinity. From 1933 to 1937 Scroggie traveled to North America and worldwide as an evangelist* and Bible teacher, promoting the themes of the Keswick* deeper life movement. His final pastorate was at Spurgeon's Tabernacle (1938-1944), following which time he lectured on the English Bible at Spurgeon's

College. His numerous writings were published and read by North American evangelicals.*

BIBLIOGRAPHY. R. G. Turnbull, *A Treasure of W. Graham Scroggie* (1974).   R. L. Petersen

Scudder, Ida Sophia (1870-1959). Raised in India, Ida was the daughter of Dr. John Scudder, one of a long line of Scudder medical missionaries to India who served under the Reformed Church in America.* Initially she scorned the idea of a missionary career for herself, yearning for more of life's luxuries than life in India offered. It was when she visited her parents as a young adult that she became burdened for the women of India, who were deprived of medical services due to the lack of female physicians.

Returning to America, Ida earned her medical degree at Cornell Medical College and then rejoined her family in India, where she eventually established a medical complex at Vellore which included a clinic, a hospital and the Christian Medical School (1918) established to train women doctors to meet the vast medical needs of India. In all her efforts, she worked closely with Annie Hancock, an evangelist who made contacts with patients after they left the clinic and hospital. Eventually the school became a university and in 1947 it began to train men as well as women. In her Christian faith and service, Ida Scudder was an outstanding missionary of the twentieth century.

BIBLIOGRAPHY. *NAWMP*; D. C. Wilson, *Dr. Ida: The Story of Dr. Ida Scudder of Vellore* (1959).

R. A. Tucker

Scudder, John, Sr. (1793-1855). Medical missionary* to Ceylon and India. After graduating from the College of New Jersey in 1811 and the New York College of Physicians and Surgeons in 1815, Scudder entered private practice in New York. The reading of a tract* so inspired Scudder that he committed himself to missions.* On June 8, 1819, he and his wife left for Ceylon under the American Board of Commissioners for Foreign Missions.* On Ceylon he founded a hospital and several schools. He was the first American foreign medical missionary. He was ordained by a Congregationalist,* a Methodist* and a Baptist* on May 15, 1821.

In 1935 Scudder moved to Madras, India, where he established one of the first medical missions in India, as well as a printing operation for publication of tracts and Tamil Bible translations. Following a period of service back in the U.S. (1842-1846), he moved to Chintodrepettah, near Madras, where he founded the Arcot mission. In 1852 this operation came under the care of the American board and later of the (Dutch) Reformed Church in America.*

Failing health led to a trip to South Africa where he died of a stroke at Wynberg on January 13, 1855. The Scudders had thirteen children, nine of whom lived to adulthood. Of these, seven became medical missionaries and pastors in India. Within three Scudder generations, forty-three family members gave over 1,100 years of missionary service.
See also SCUDDER, IDA SOPHIA.

BIBLIOGRAPHY. *AAP* 9.

G. J. Bekker

Seabury, Samuel (1729-1796). First bishop* of the American Episcopal Church.* Born in Groton, Connecticut, the son of a Congregational* minister* turned Anglican* priest,* young Seabury early on decided on a ministerial career. Graduating from Yale* College (1748), he studied medicine (chiefly at the University of Edinburgh, 1752-1753) before being ordained* in England in 1753. Upon returning to America he served with the Society for Propagating the Gospel* in New Jersey and New York. In the late 1760s and 1770s he was active in the campaign to secure an American bishop. He also gained notoriety for his writings (under the pseudonym A. W. Farmer) opposing American independence. During the Revolution* he was chaplain to a loyalist regiment.

In 1783 the Episcopal clergy* of Connecticut elected him to travel to England to be consecrated bishop. Seabury spent eighteen months trying, but several factors—including questions about Seabury's Connecticut support and problems over waving the oath of allegiance in the English consecration service—proved an impasse. In October 1784 Seabury turned to the Non-Juring Scottish Episcopal Church which had been legally proscribed since the end of the seventeenth century on account of its persevering loyalty to the House of Stuart. On November 14, 1784, Seabury was consecrated by the Scottish bishops. He also signed a concordat accepting for Connecticut Episcopalians the Scottish communion office and the emphasis upon the independence of clergy from laity.*

For both theological and political reasons, Seabury's consecration was strongly criticized by some Episcopal leaders, and not until 1789 were Seabury and the Connecticut church fully integrated into the organization of the Episcopal Church. For the rest of his ministry Seabury worked at organizing the Episcopal Church in both Connecticut and Rhode Island.

BIBLIOGRAPHY. *AAP* 5; E. E. Beardsley, *Life and Correspondence of the Right Reverend Samuel Seabury* (1881); *DAB* VIII; *DARB*; F. V. Mills, Sr., *Bishops by Ballot* (1978); *NCAB* 3; B. E. Steiner, *Samuel Seabury, 1729-1796: A Study in the High Church Tradition* (1971).

R. B. Mullin

Seamands, Earl Arnett (1891-1984). Methodist* missionary* to India. Born in Lexington, Kentucky, Seamands graduated from the University of Cincinnati in civil engineering and sailed for India as a missionary under the Methodist Episcopal Church in 1919. He served with distinction in the South India Annual Conference as engineer, pastor,* evangelist* and superintendent until his retirement in 1957. He was instrumental in inaugurating the famous "Dharur Jathra" in 1923, which today is the largest Christian camp meeting in the world, with an annual attendance of 100,000.

Seamands also promoted the church-building program in the South India Conference and was responsible for the construction of over one hundred seventy-five churches, many of them depicting unusual designs in Indian architecture. Affectionately known as "Thatha" (beloved grandpa), he was named "Missionary of the Century" by his conference at its centennial celebration in 1975. On a visit to India at the age of ninety-two, he died and is buried in the Christian cemetery in Bangalore.

BIBLIOGRAPHY. J. T. Seamands and R. Seamands, *Engineered for Glory* (1984).

J. T. Seamands

Second Blessing. A term used primarily in Holiness* groups for the sanctification* experience. Looking back to John Wesley* and other preachers in the eighteenth century, proponents teach that believers can and should seek a second spiritual experience after being converted.* As a result of various interpretations of sanctification—ranging from sinless perfection to an enduement of power for service—several denominations have come into existence. In Holiness circles it is common for believers to point to a time they were converted and a time they were sanctified (or received the "second blessing").

When the Methodist* Church began to minimize Wesley's "A Plain Account of Christian Perfection" in the mid nineteenth century, others—such as Charles Finney,* William E. Boardman* and Phoebe Palmer*—campaigned for a return to holiness. Their efforts resulted in the formation of new denominations* and the Holiness Movement.* The nineteenth century also saw a marked departure from the traditional view that the "second blessing" was for cleansing; the Keswick view is that the experience is for enduement of power for service. Among those who accepted the Keswick view were Dwight L. Moody,* R. A. Torrey,* A. B. Simpson* and J. Wilbur Chapman.* Pentecostal* groups incorporated both interpretations into their statements of faith.

See also PERFECTIONISM; SANCTIFICATION.

BIBLIOGRAPHY. T. L. Smith, *Called Unto Holiness* (1962); W. W. Menzies, *Anointed to Serve* (1971); V. Synan, *The Holiness-Pentecostal Movement in the United States* (1971).   W. E. Warner

Second Great Awakening. The term *Second Great Awakening* refers to a diverse series of religious revivals* that took place in the U.S., beginning in the latter years of the eighteenth century. Historians have used the term *second* to draw attention to the apparent similarity of the revivals to the Great Awakening* of the 1730s and 1740s. Although this terminological convention can be somewhat misleading, its use is not altogether gratuitous. In both awakenings, Protestant* activists mounted aggressive evangelistic campaigns intended to offer salvation* to the unchurched, convince skeptics of the truths of Christian faith and extend the effects of Christianity over the nation. Not unlike the leaders of the First Awakening—John Wesley,* George Whitefield,* Jonathan Edwards,* Theodore J. Frelinghuysen, and William and Gilbert Tennent*—the leaders of the Second Awakening urged their auditors to search their hearts, repent of their sins* and accept Christ as their Savior. Their homiletic* devices were crafted to maximize their results. Speaking in plain language, they avoided technical, theological disputes that might confuse their listeners. Adopting emotional appeals, they pressed for immediate conversions.* Just as the First Great Awakening had rekindled an interest in salvation among the populace of the Eastern seaboard, the Second Awakening provided the occasion for thousands of Westerners to join churches and the impetus for several new American denominations.*

There were, however, substantive differences between the movements. The first was largely confined to New England and the Middle Colonies, whereas the Second Awakening knew hardly any boundaries. Congregationalists* in New England, Presbyterians* in the Old Northwest, Methodists* and Baptists* on the Southwestern frontier all participated in the nineteenth-century revivals. Nor were the two events theologically congruent. In the First Awakening, Whitefield and Edwards preached a distinctly Calvinistic* gospel; they

exulted in the surprising salvific action of their sovereign, inscrutable God. Many ministers of the Second Awakening, on the other hand, leaned decisively toward theological Arminianism.*

Their far more pragmatic approach to evangelism* was succinctly expressed by Charles G. Finney,* who argued that a revival of religion was not miraculous in any way, but rather the proper application of humanly contrived means. Believing that the chief end of their ministry* was the salvation of their auditors, the Second Awakeners wrenched the initiative formerly thought to be the sole property of the Calvinists' God, and employed a myriad of "new measures"* to attract, convince and "win" the souls of American citizens. Capitalizing on the optimism characteristic in the early Republic, ministers of the Second Awakening forged the tools necessary to their evangelistic task, and combined them to give shape to the new science of revivalism.

Perhaps the best way to organize the diverse events of the Second Great Awakening is to view the movement in its three interconnected phases or theaters: the revivals on the frontier, in New England and in upstate New York.

Revivalism on the American Frontier. In 1796 Presbyterian minister James McGready* took charge of three frontier congregations in Logan County, Kentucky, near the Tennessee border. In 1800 McGready and two other evangelists,* William Hodges and John Rankin, led the first frontier camp meeting.* Other evangelists quickly adopted the successful camp-meeting method in which great numbers of rough-hewn frontiersfolk would gather for a period of days to hear evangelistic preaching.* In August 1801, Barton Stone* led the famous revival in Cane Ridge,* Kentucky, which lasted nearly a week and may have included as many as twenty-five thousand participants. Apart from its size and duration, the Cane Ridge meeting was also remarkable in that many participants experienced strange physical manifestations. Some fell to the ground, "slain in the Spirit," others suffered violent shakings known as the "jerks." The awesome proportions of Cane Ridge notwithstanding, however, the revivals on the frontier had enormous institutional impact. Methodist and Baptist circuit riders* traversed the South and Southwest, building hundreds of churches and several new denominations; the Cumberland Presbyterians* and the Restoration Movement* had their beginnings in this era.

The New England Phase of the Second Awakening. Soon after he became president of Yale College* in 1795, Timothy Dwight* began a vigorous preaching campaign designed to drive student infidelity from the campus. One of his most able students, Lyman Beecher,* recalled that Dwight led a class disputation on the question "Is the Bible the Word of God?" with the result that many students were converted. Student recollections of Dwight's several triumphs at the college have often been used as evidence of the link between the First and Second Awakenings. The New England phases of the Second Awakening, however, have more to do with Beecher and his colleagues than with Dwight's harvests at Yale.

Early in his career Beecher was convinced of the need for evangelistic efforts, but he was extremely wary of the revivalistic techniques that were gaining prominence in the West. Working with his colleague Asahel Nettleton,* he determined to protect New England from unchecked enthusiasm. To Nettleton's dismay, however, Beecher abandoned his opposition to Finney and the frontier evangelists and embraced the new revivalism at the New Lebanon Conference* of 1827. After Beecher left for the West to serve as president of Lane Theological Seminary, other New Englanders—led by the Yale theologian Nathaniel William Taylor*—continued to promote the new revivalism and the social reform* efforts that followed in its wake. Despite the growing popularity of revivalism in New England, some Congregationalist ministers remained skeptical of the innovations of Beecher and Taylor. In an attempt to offset the influence of the new revivalists, Nettleton and Bennet Tyler* helped form the conservative Theological Institute of Connecticut (later Hartford Seminary) in 1833.

"The Burned-Over District." No sketch of the Second Awakening would be complete without some reference to America's first great revivalist, Charles G. Finney.* Converted in 1821 after he had begun a law career, Finney began a preaching tour of upstate New York in which he forged his unique style of evangelism. Over the course of several years Finney refined a set of "new measures" explicitly designed to win Christian converts. In anticipation of an upcoming revival in a distant town, he used advance teams—often made up of women—to pray for and publicize the event. In his exhortations Finney made extensive use of his legal training. He made direct appeals to the reason of his auditors, much as he would to a jury. Persons who were close to making a confession of faith were invited to the front of the church to sit in the "anxious bench" (*See* Mourner's Bench*), a seat not unlike a witness stand, where Finney and others would personally exhort those of unsure

faith. Nor was Finney's work confined to evangelism alone. As often happened during the Second Awakening, men and women converted in the revivals turned their interest to social reform. Under the leadership of Finney and others, abolition* leagues, temperance* societies, missionary* programs and a host of other voluntary* organizations were formed in an effort to bring the salutary effects of Christian faith to citizens in antebellum America.

See also FRONTIER RELIGION; GREAT AWAKENING; REVIVALISM.

BIBLIOGRAPHY. J. B. Boles, *The Great Revival, 1787-1805: The Origins of the Southern Evangelical Mind* (1972); D. D. Bruce, Jr., *And They All Sang Hallelujah: Plain Folk Camp-Meeting Religion, 1800-1845* (1974); W. R. Cross, *The Burned-Over District: The Social and Intellectual History of Enthusiastic Religion in Western New York, 1800-1850* (1950); S. C. Henry, *Unvanquished Puritan: A Portrait of Lyman Beecher* (1973); P. E. Johnson, *A Shopkeeper's Millennium: Society and Revivals in Rochester, New York, 1815-1837* (1978); S. E. Mead, *Nathaniel W. Taylor, 1786-1858: A Connecticut Liberal* (1942).   J. R. Fitzmier

Sect. Sociologically, a minority religious group previously tied to another, more churchly, religious organization. Sects leave the parent body not so much to form a new faith as to reaffirm and re-establish the old one. They are radical in that they often reject the activities and hierarchy of their parent body, while simultaneously emphasizing their separation and distinction from society at large. At the same time, they are conservative in that they seek to reassert authentic religious principles which they claim have been abandoned or compromised. Sects are characterized by strong allegiance to the group and its teachings, a protest orientation, strict adherence to standards (with sanctions applied to the wayward) and a tendency to be anti-sacerdotal. Over a period of time some sectarian groups undergo a process of transformation (institutionalization) in which they evolve into established denominations.*

See also CULT.

BIBLIOGRAPHY. R. Stark and W. S. Bainbridge, *The Future of Religion* (1985); B. Wilson, *Religion in Sociological Perspective* (1982); R. Walis, ed., *Sectarianism* (1975).

     R. Enroth

Secular Clergy. A term for ordained* Catholic* priests* not belonging to a religious order,* society or congregation. Practically speaking, secular clergy and diocesan* priests are one and the same, that is, priests who are ordained to assist the local ordinary bishop* in the pastoral care of a certain portion (usually geographically defined) of the Catholic Church. They are distinguished from both lay* and monastic or religious members of the Church. The latter may also be ordained, but they need not be. The designation *secular* emphasizes that the proper role and service of the secular clergy is in the world, in contrast to monks, whose proper role is a symbolic flight from the world, whatever apostolic work they may nonetheless undertake. R. L. Kress

Secular Humanism. A non-theistic world view based on the belief that humanity is of ultimate importance. Humanism usually refers to a philosophy that emphasizes the importance of humanity in this life. There long have been Christians and other theistic humanists. Secular humanism is distinguished from these views in its atheism or agnosticism, hence leaving the development of humanity as the ultimate value. Such views, although anticipated by Enlightenment* skeptics (who nonetheless were mostly deists*), became common only after the mid nineteenth century.

A central premise of the new secular world view was a thoroughgoing evolutionary naturalism, that is, a belief that reality can be explained only by understanding developing natural forces. While this view might seem to lead toward a pessimistic view of humanity as merely a high-order animal and a product of blind chance, the corollary has been an aggressive assertion of the all-importance of humanity. Secular humanists typically have emphasized the values of human freedom, especially freedom from restrictive or irrational religious traditions, and for educated inquiry leading to development of human potentials, rationally based values and a just society.

Such world views have appeared in many combinations and varieties. In America, during the first three-quarters of the twentieth century, they came to dominate many areas of American public life, especially academia and the media. During this time the term *secular humanism* was only rarely used. More often the more confusing term *humanism* was used, as in the *Humanist Manifesto* I (1933) and II (1973), published by aggressive defenders of such views. The development of such world views was more amorphous and widespread than reference to such organized humanism suggests. The lines were much more blurred because many Americans, including many theists, in practice subscribed to the basic premises of

secular humanism: that businesses, education, research, technical development and public life were best conducted without substantive reference to a deity or formal religious traditions and that the development of human potentials was virtually of ultimate significance.

Since the mid 1970s there has been much discussion as to whether secular humanism is a religion and should be regarded legally as such. This question hinges on one's definition of religion. If belief in a god is necessary to define a religion, secular humanism does not qualify. If on the other hand, religion (or a god) is defined as one's ultimate value, then secular humanism is a religion. In 1961 the United States Supreme Court referred in a footnote to *secular humanism* as being among some non-theistic religions; but the Court did not later develop this view. In the 1970s the emerging New Christian Right* popularized the term *secular humanism,* which they claimed had displaced Christianity as America's unofficially established* religion, especially in public schools. Secular humanism, they were pointing out, was not a neutral ideology. By the 1980s the courts were wrestling with these issues.

BIBLIOGRAPHY. J. Turner, *Without God, without Creed: The Origins of Unbelief in America* (1986); R. E. Webber, *Secular Humanism: Threat and Challenge* (1985); P. Kurtz, ed. *The Humanist Alternative* (1973). G. M. Marsden

Secularism, Secularization. *Secularism* denotes a religious commitment to this world, or anything within it, as ultimate. *Secularization,* a more ambiguous term, refers to a process, a transformation of the way in which a people's traditional religion (e.g., Christianity or Hinduism) relates to their social and intellectual life. Both words reflect the Latin term *saeculum,* which identified the world as a long period of time, an age. Both invoke the traditional and misleading contrast between the secular and the religious.

In North America, secularism indicates that people have taken the affairs and things of the world as the basis and goal of life and that they are indifferent, or opposed, to the message and ministrations of the church. The vast majority of secularists, without fanfare, carry on their lives in devotion to material gain, or to their families, to "the good life," to their careers, to their political parties or labor unions, or perhaps to America or humanity or peace. Their gods are many and their forms of worship are manifold. Only a few belong to any group consciously practicing secularism, such as the Ethical Society, the Humanist Society or an atheist association. Only a very few would claim the title of secular humanist.

The essential message of secularism in North America is that this world is self-revelatory and self-complete, and that the profferings of Christianity are unnecessary for life. Secularism demands the strict separation of life from the influence of traditional religion. The secularist ethos appears most prominently and operates most effectively in the public-school systems, the mega-corporations, the advertising and the entertainment media of the U.S. and Canada. Some would maintain that the American political doctrine of the separation of church and state* favors secularism by prejudicing the public debate against the involvement of Christian discourse (*See* Public Policy, Christianity and). The insertion of Christian commitments into American politics often appears as mere convention or right-wing fanaticism. Canada has no parallel doctrine, and all forms of Christian expression naturally occur in public life.

Secularization sometimes means the process which is turning a Christian society into a merely secular society. Both the U.S. and Canada, as late as the 1950s, could be regarded in some sense as Christian societies, but during the 1950s and thereafter countless voices noted a monumental shift toward the marginalization of the church and of Christian ethics* in economic, educational and political affairs. The "secularization thesis," as defined by sociologists, interpreted the process as inexorable and irreversible, a theory belied by the resilience of religion. A few theologians* urged Christians to consider the process as a blessing for the church, which could now concentrate on spiritual things. Others, by contrast, affirmed that the real domain of any religion worth its name was in the world, and not in church. This latter view echoed the interpretation of secularization as a process—associated with the Reformation—of desacralizing the rocks and trees and of stripping the priests of their powers and giving the laity* access to the mysteries of the universe. In general, this yielded an affirmation of the world as good, and not its denial.

BIBLIOGRAPHY. P. E. Hammond, ed., *The Sacred in a Secular Age* (1985); H. Cox, *The Secular City* (1965); B. Goudzwaard, *Idols of Our Time* (1981).

C. T. McIntire

Seiss, Joseph Augustus (1823-1904). Lutheran* minister* and author. Born of Alsatian stock near Graceham, Maryland, and confirmed in the Moravian Church* when sixteen, Joseph Augustus Seiss ran away from home when his farmer father forbad

him to study for the ministry. Seiss spent two years at Gettysburg Seminary (1839-1841) and was licensed by the Lutheran Virginia Synod to preach when he was nineteen. After pastorates in West Virginia, Virginia and Maryland, Seiss served St. John's Church in Philadelphia (1858-1874), then the largest English-speaking Lutheran congregation in America. In 1874 Seiss founded the Church of the Holy Communion, Philadelphia, pastoring it thirty years until his death in 1904.

An editor of *The Lutheran* (1867-1879), a pioneer of the General Council of the Evangelical Lutheran Church in North America (1867) and its president (1888), Seiss was a popular preacher,* prolific author (publishing more than one hundred titles) on topics as varied as liturgics* and eschatology,* and was hailed as a confessionalist* (though his millenialism* occasioned controversy). Seiss died on June 20, 1904, while tending to his duties as president of the Board of Directors of the Philadelphia Lutheran Seminary.

BIBLIOGRAPHY. *DAB* VIII; *ELC* 3; E. C. Nelson, ed., *The Lutherans in North America* (1975).

C. G. Fry

Selyns (Selijns), Henricus (1636-1701). Dutch Reformed* minister* in New York. Henricus Selyns served two tours of duty in New York, first as minister to the Dutch churches on Long Island from 1660 to 1664 and then from 1682 until his death in 1701 as senior minister in New York City. Selyns corresponded frequently with Cotton Mather* in New England. During the Salem Witch Trials,* he convinced Mather of the specious nature of spectral evidence, and Selyns composed a lengthy poem in 1697 in honor of Mather's *Magnalia Christi Americana.**

Selyns's tenure in New York City coincided with Leisler's Rebellion, occasioned by the Glorious Revolution in England in 1688. When news reached New York the next year, Jacob Leisler mustered many of the Dutch citizens to overthrow the colonial government of King James, the deposed English monarch. Selyns and the other Dutch ministers in the colony, however, together with the more affluent Dutch citizens, opposed Leisler, and that opposition triggered a bitter quarrel in the Dutch churches.

BIBLIOGRAPHY. *AAP* 9; R. H. Balmer, *"A Perfect Babel of Confusion"* (1989); E. T. Corwin, *Manual of the Reformed Church in America,* 5th ed. (1922); *DAB* VIII. R. H. Balmer

Seminary, Catholic Diocesan. The Council of Trent (1545-1565) framed legislation in 1563

creating the seminary (Latin: *seminarium,* or seed-bed) to provide a program for training diocesan, or secular, priests, that is, the priests* who ordinarily perform the tasks of ministry in parishes* under the authority* of the bishop* of the diocese.* The seminary decree enjoined each bishop to sponsor a college at his official church, the cathedral,* to train poor youth for the priesthood. The decree exhorted bishops to provide students with a general education and instruction in the tasks of ministry. The bishop was to determine the specific content of training. The decree did not require a seminary course as a condition for ordination* or determine its length, and it ignored the issue of training priests belonging to religious orders.*

The practice of the diocesan priesthood and the methods of the seminary were deeply influenced by the French school of spirituality* in the seventeenth century. The figures associated with the school, Pierre de Berulle, Charles de Condren and Jean Jacques Olier, developed methods of spiritual preparation for ministry through a lifestyle of self-denial and daily mental prayer in which the seminarian (and the priest) meditated on aspects of Christ's life. By thus configuring himself to Christ, the ordained priest prepared to impart grace through ministering the sacraments.* The seminarian's cultivation of proper spiritual dispositions came to be regarded as more important than formal studies in dogmatic* and moral theology.*

The first Catholic seminary in the U.S. was established at Baltimore in 1791 by priests of the Society of St. Sulpice (Sulpicians),* a French group of diocesan priests who conduct seminaries. The Sulpicians came to America to escape the French Revolution and with the approval of Baltimore's Bishop John Carroll* founded St. Mary's Seminary. As American dioceses were formed in the first half of the nineteenth century, bishops attempted to train priests under various formats: at their small cathedrals or in episcopal residences; at Catholic schools in which seminarians taught part-time while studying theology; or in freestanding seminary institutions. Many such efforts did not survive because of inadequate funding, students or staff.

Notable seminaries that survived informal beginnings to develop as freestanding seminaries serving several dioceses were those of the archdioceses of Philadelphia (1838), Cincinnati (1851), Milwaukee (1855) and New York (1864). Several religious orders, notably the Order of St. Benedict (Benedictines)* and the Congregation of the Mission (Vincentians), trained diocesan priests in seminary programs affiliated with their colleges for laymen in several states. The idea of training diocesan priests abroad was raised and resulted in American Colleges at Louvain, Belgium (1857), and Rome* (1859).

Up to the 1880s the American Catholic community had depended heavily on immigrant priests, despite local seminary activities. The desire to create a clergy from the American-born sons of Catholic immigrants* and to improve the standards of seminary training were major concerns of the American bishops who convened for the last of their national councils of the nineteenth century, the Third Plenary Council of Baltimore,* in 1884 (*See* Conciliar Tradition, American). The bishops issued decrees prescribing programs of six years each for the minor or preparatory seminary and for the major or theological seminary. The bishops established a graduate school, at first offering theology only to priests, which opened in 1889 at Washington, D.C., as the Catholic University of America.* The improved standards were implemented in new seminaries established at Boston (1884), Rochester (1893), St. Louis (1894), St. Paul (1894) and San Francisco (1898). The New York seminary was refounded (1896), and ethnic seminaries opened for Poles in Detroit (1885) and for Germans in Columbus (1892).

The locus of authority for seminaries shifted in the early twentieth century when the Holy See embarked on a policy of imposing greater control on Catholic life to meet the challenges of modernity. This control was demonstrated in the condemnation of theological modernism* in 1907 and the imposition of an oath against modernism on seminary faculties in 1910, thereby discouraging original research and writing in theological and biblical studies. The new Code of Canon Law* took effect throughout the Catholic world in 1918 to provide unity and administrative coherence to church government. The Code contained canons that for the first time outlined the operation of the seminary, named its officers, listed courses and set the length for seminary studies. Seminary training was made a prerequisite for ordination. In the following years Rome's Sacred Congregation of Seminaries and Universities issued supplementary regulations based on the seminary canons. Trent's ideal of making the bishop responsible for the seminary was transformed to make him the local agent of Roman authority.

From 1900 to 1960 the seminary network grew as diocesan institutions opened at Denver, San Antonio, Chicago, New Orleans, Brooklyn, Seattle, Los Angeles, Detroit, Dubuque, Scranton and Miami. Several older seminaries were relocated in larger facilities. Seminary growth stimulated efforts to improve professional standards. By the 1950s seminary educators began to develop, through the National Catholic Educational Association, academic improvements for seminary liberal-arts programs in preparation for accreditation with regional associations.

Vatican II* was a turning point for the Catholic seminary. The Council's "Decree on Priestly Formation" directed each national hierarchy to devise its own program of seminary education within broad guidelines. After consultation with seminary educators, the American bishops issued in 1971 their *Program of Priestly Formation* to guide diocesan seminaries and the seminaries of religious orders. The program provided academic and administrative reforms that conform the seminary to contemporary professional practices. The program introduced pastoral field education and ecumenical* activities that were new to the Catholic seminary. Since the late 1960s, virtually all Catholic seminaries have obtained accreditation with the Association of Theological Schools, the principal accrediting body for seminaries in the U.S., so that Catholic seminaries offer degrees for the professional and theological portions of their programs, and the accredited seminary's development along professional lines is assured.

See also EDUCATION, PROTESTANT THEOLOGICAL; HIGHER EDUCATION, CATHOLIC.

BIBLIOGRAPHY. J. A. O'Donohoe, *Tridentine Seminary Legislation: Its Sources and Its Formation* (1957); T. Heck, *The Curriculum of the Major Seminary in Relation to Contemporary Conditions* (1935); C. J. Kauffman, *Tradition and Transformation in Catholic Culture: History of the Sulpicians in the United States, 1791 to the Present* (1987); National Conference of Catholic Bishops, *The Program of Priestly Formation* (1971); E. A. Walsh, *The Priesthood in the Writings of the French School: Berulle, De Condren, Olier* (1949). J. M. White, *The Diocesan Seminary in the United States: A History from the 1780s to the Present* (1989).

J. M. White

Seminary, Protestant. *See* EDUCATION, PROTESTANT THEOLOGICAL.

Semple, Robert Baylor (1769-1831). Baptist* minister* and denominational leader. Born at Rose Mount, Virginia, Semple received a classical education at a nearby academy, where at sixteen he was made assistant teacher. For a time he pursued the study of law. Converted* in 1789 after a period of skepticism through the vigorous, biblical witness of a Baptist neighbor, Semple was baptized* and then ordained* in 1790. He became pastor* of the Bruington Baptist Church, which he served until his death. For many years he also conducted a school.

Deeply committed to missions, education and denominational service, Semple was active in several societies devoted to these ends, and in 1814 he participated in the founding of the Triennial Convention,* the first national organization of Baptists. He served as its president from 1820 to 1831. In addition, he was the financial agent and president of the board of trustees of Columbian College and the first president of the Baptist General Association of Virginia. He was noted for his understanding of human nature, his diligence in ministerial duties and the practical character of his preaching.*

In 1810 Semple published *A History of the Rise and Progress of the Baptists in Virginia,* an important historical record which was extended and updated by G. W. Beale in 1894.

BIBLIOGRAPHY. *AAP* 6; J. B. Taylor, *Lives of Virginia Baptist Ministers* (1838).

W. M. Patterson

SEND International. A nondenominational evangelical* foreign missionary* agency. During World War 2* some Christians among American military personnel stationed in the Pacific caught an ambitious vision for the evangelization of Asia. At the end of the war, these Christian GIs organized witnessing campaigns in the Philippines and Japan, thus setting the framework for the Far Eastern Gospel Crusade (FEGC), which was established as a faith mission in 1947. FEGC opened its first headquarters in St. Paul, Minnesota, and in 1948 selected Philip E. Armstrong as executive secretary. The agency quickly expanded its presence in the Far East and emphasized evangelism,* church planting, theological education, medicine and support of national churches. FEGC also offered itself as a service organization for other boards by sponsoring educational institutions, loaning missionary personnel, developing language courses and helping to form support ministries like the Pacific Broadcasting Association.

In 1971 Central Alaskan Missions merged with FEGC, thereby creating new opportunities in both Alaska and northwest Canada. FEGC changed its name in 1981 to SEND International to convey a more appropriate image of the mission's geographic scope. In recent years plans have been made to extend operations well beyond the Pacific circle by formulating evangelistic and church-planting strategies for Spain.

Currently Frank M. Severn serves as executive director and administers a total annual income of over $4.5 million and almost 140 North American overseas personnel. North American headquarters are located in Farmington, Michigan, and Downsview, Ontario. SEND International is affiliated with the Interdenominational Foreign Mission Association.*

BIBLIOGRAPHY. P. E. Armstrong, "Far Eastern Gospel Crusade," *The Encyclopedia of Modern Christian Missions,* ed. B. L. Goddard (1967); R. Honeywell and B. Honeywell, *Discovering Our Roots* (n.d.); M. Morehouse and B. Neufeld, *A Branch Made Strong* (1987).

J. A. Patterson

Seneca Falls Woman's Rights Convention (July 19-20, 1848).

A convention held to discuss the social, civil and religious rights of women. Elizabeth Cady Stanton* and Lucretia Mott,* meeting in 1840 at a London anti-slavery convention, discussed women's inequality and agreed on the need for a woman's rights convention. Eight years later Mott and Stanton, along with Martha Wright, Mary Ann McClintock and Jane Hunt, gathered on July 13, 1848, to plan the convention. All but Stanton were Quakers.* According to the published call, the convention's purpose was "to discuss the social, civil and religious rights of woman." Stanton finalized the "Declaration of Sentiments" with eighteen grievances modeled on the Declaration of Independence. Three hundred persons met at the Wesleyan Chapel in Seneca Falls, New York, to discuss the "Declaration" and the twelve resolutions Stanton had also drafted. The "Declaration" denounced woman's subordinate position in both church and state, chastising men who "usurped the Prerogative of Jehovah himself" by assigning women to a limited sphere of action. The "Declaration" and resolutions addressed inequalities in the legal, political and religious arenas. Demands for equality were based on the premise that the Creator endowed woman and man with the same capabilities and intended that woman should be recognized as man's equal. The convention's conveners clearly believed God was on their side. The most controversial resolution of the convention called for woman's suffrage,* but this and the other resolutions eventually passed. Over 100 individuals signed the documents, thus inaugurating the woman's rights movement in the U.S. and setting its agenda.

BIBLIOGRAPHY. *Proceedings of the Woman's Rights Convention Held at Seneca Falls and Rochester, N.Y., July and August 1848;* E. C. Stanton, S. B. Anthony and M. J. Gage, eds., *History of Woman Suffrage,* vol. 1 (1881). S. C. Stanley

Separate Baptists.

Baptists* originating among the pro-revivalists of the Great Awakening.* During the Great Awakening many Baptist churches split into revivalistic* (Separate) and anti-revivalistic (Regular*) factions. The first identifiable Separate Baptist church resulted from such a schism (1743) in Boston. Many revivalistic New Light* Congregationalists also became Separate Baptists. Highly evangelistic* and moderately Calvinistic,* Separate Baptists allowed women to preach, practiced "nine rites," and disdained a learned or paid ministry and confessionalism.* Their emotional worship services typically ended with invitations for salvation.*

Notable pastors included Isaac Backus,* the leading advocate for religious liberty* in Massachusetts; and Richard Furman,* leader of the influential Charleston Association and first president of the Triennial Convention* (1814). Shubal Stearns* and Daniel Marshall* began the first Southern Separate Baptist church (1755) and association (1758) at Sandy Creek, North Carolina. Differences between Regular and Separate Baptists were pronounced in the South, but barriers to fellowship eroded near the end of the eighteenth century. At that time most Separate Baptists moved toward a stronger Calvinism, adopted the Philadelphia Confession and entered Regular Baptist associations. Churches rejecting that union organized six associations in Tennessee, Kentucky, Indiana and Illinois. These formed the General Association of Separate Baptists (1912), which in 1975 added the Christian Unity Association (of North Carolina and Virginia). Generally conservative in theology,* they practice foot washing.* They maintain a mission board and a minister's conference, but no central headquarters, colleges or seminaries. In 1979 they numbered ninety-eight churches with about 9,000 members.

BIBLIOGRAPHY. H. L. McBeth, *The Baptist Heritage* (1987); J. O. Renault, "The Changing Patterns of Separate Baptist Religious Life, 1803-1977," in *BHH* 14 (October 1979):16-25; R. G. Torbet, *A History of the Baptists,* 3rd ed. (1969).

J. T. Spivey

Separates.

A Congregationalist* separatist movement especially prominent in New England during the period 1735-1750. The Separates were strict Congregationalists who desired to return to the original New England ideals of the seventeenth century. Standing for spontaneous, zealous piety,* they maintained that the established New England Congregational churches—clergy* and members —were formal, cold and dead. Over one hundred congregations were formed in New England as a result of splits from the established churches.

Separate congregations overturned the traditional New England parish system and challenged the practice of supporting the clergy with public taxation. Reviving the call for visible sainthood, they demanded that candidates for church membership* show the marks of true conversion before being admitted. Consequently, they adopted the practice of closed Communion.* The Separates supported itinerant* preaching* and encouraged emotional displays of piety amongst both laity* and clergy. Consciously rejecting the moderate theology they saw creeping into New England theology, they stressed the need for a converted ministry rather than an educated ministry, and were willing to break the established rules of ordination.*

The New England Congregational Separate movement died out after about two decades, harassed by the established government and churches. Many of the congregations became Baptist, while other groups moved West to the frontier or were reunited with regular churches. Some became disillusioned with the excesses and irregularities of Separate clergy and laity. The movement was similar to the New Light* movement among Presbyterians* in the Middle Colonies, but the New England phenomenon had a dynamic all its own.

BIBLIOGRAPHY. E. S. Gaustad, *The Great Awakening in New England* (1957); C. C. Goen, *Revivalism and Separatism in New England, 1740-1800* (1962); W. G. McLoughlin, *New England Dissent, 1630-1833: The Baptists and the Separation of Church and State,* 2 vols. (1971).

D. A. Weir

Separatism. Separatism has been a dominant theme of American fundamentalists* in the twentieth century. During the fundamentalist-modernist controversy* of the early decades, the question of separatism came to the fore, especially as it related to the apparent growth of apostasy in mainline* denominations.* Apostasy was defined as the conscious denial of biblical truths such as the virgin birth, deity of Christ and redemption through Christ's atoning sacrifice. Using biblical passages such as 2 Corinthians 6:14-18, Romans 16:17-18 and 1 Timothy 6:3-5, which indicate that believers should separate from impurity, both

doctrinal and moral, fundamentalists argued for separation from theological liberals* and ungodly or worldly living. This became known as first-order separatism and was exemplified by the Baptist Bible Union* (1923) and General Association of Regular Baptist Churches* (1932).

Second-order separatism became the practice of some fundamentalists with the rise of Billy Graham* and the neo-evangelical* movement in the fifties and sixties. These fundamentalists argued that not only should they separate from apostasy but also from those who were either associated with or cooperated with persons of liberal persuasion. For example, Bob Jones, Jr.,* contended in the booklet *Scriptural Separation* that the Bible commands separation from those who compromise with or aid doctrinal impurity. Graham was considered to be compromising with liberals by associating with them in his evangelistic crusades.

Finally, third-order separatism, which developed in the 1970s, taught that fundamentalists should remain separate from other fundamentalists who fail to practice second-order separatism.

BIBLIOGRAPHY. E. Pickering, *Biblical Separation: The Struggle for a Pure Church* (1979).

C. W. Whiteman

Serra, Junipero (1713-1784). Franciscan* missionary* to Mexico and the Southwest. Born in Petra, Majorca, Spain, Serra joined the Franciscans in 1730, taking the name Junipero in 1731 when making his full profession. He studied at Palma, there obtaining a doctorate in philosophy from Lullian University in 1743. Appointed to the Duns Scotus chair of philosophy at Lullian, he could have pursued a promising academic career, but instead devoted himself to missions and rejoiced to join a 1749 Franciscan expedition to the Apostolic College of San Fernando in Mexico City, arriving January 1, 1750.

From 1750 until 1759 Serra pastored Native-American converts in northeast Queretaro, but longed for a pioneering assignment. A proposed mission to Texas, to which he was assigned, never materialized, so Serra spent the next several years (1760-1767) in Mexico City doing administrative work, living ascetically and fervently preaching a rigorous faith to generally indolent audiences.

In 1767 Franciscans replaced Jesuits* (disbanded by papal edict) in Baja (Lower) California, and Serra was appointed *presidente* for the region. The Spanish government, alarmed by British and Russian incursions along the Pacific coast, sought to extend Spanish control into Alta (Upper)

California. This effort required missionaries as well as soldiers. Serra thus joined the expedition led by Gaspar de Portola, which in 1769 established Mission San Diego, the first of nine missions Serra would plant in Alta California. In a region he described as a veritable paradise, he oversaw construction of mission compounds, helped plant flourishing fields around them and saw some 6,000 Native Americans baptized* before he died while visiting Mission San Carlos de Monterey.

See also MISSIONS TO NORTH AMERICA, SPANISH.

BIBLIOGRAPHY. M. Geiger, *The Life and Times of Fray Junipero Serra,* 2 vols. (1959); F. Palou, *Life and Apostolic Labors of the Venerable Father Junipero Serra,* trans. C. S. Williams (1913); A. Repplier, *Junipero Serra* (1962).

G. A. Reed

Session. Presbyterian* decision-making body at the congregational level. Within presbyterian church government the session is the lowest echelon for reaching decisions and resolving disputes on the local level. The minister* or ministers (teaching elders) and lay* elders* (ruling elders) of a local Presbyterian congregation, technically composing a session, meet by request of an aggrieved communicant or to conduct church business. After hearing the complaint or discussing the business, the session votes and hands down its decision, which is binding on the congregation.

See also CHURCH GOVERNMENT: PRESBYTERIAN; PRESBYTERY.

BIBLIOGRAPHY. L. Trinterud, *The Forming of an American Tradition* (1949). K. P. Minkema

Seton, Elizabeth Ann Bayley (1774-1821). Founder of a religious community and Roman Catholic saint. Born in or near New York City, Elizabeth Seton was the second of three daughters of Richard and Catherine (Charlton) Bayley. A brilliant physician, Richard Bayley pioneered research in surgery, diphtheria and yellow fever, from which he died in 1801. Seton's mother had died when Seton was only three, and her rather unhappy childhood perhaps served to foster the early development of a profound piety.*

She married William Magee Seton, of the New York Seton-Curson mercantile firm, in 1794 and bore five children. In 1797, with Isabella Marshall Graham,* she founded the Society for the Relief of Poor Widows with Small Children. By 1800 William Seton's business was in bankruptcy, and on December 27, 1803, he died of tuberculosis at Pisa, Italy. In the months following the death of her husband, Seton became acquainted with the teachings of the Roman Catholic Church through her friendship with the brothers Antonio and Filippo Filicchi. Returning to New York, she became a Catholic on March 15, 1805.

Shunned by her relatives, Seton tried to operate a boarding school in New York in order to support her children, but her religion made her unpopular. At the urging of William Valentine Du Bourg,* a Sulpician* priest,* she opened a girls' school on Paca Street in Baltimore in September 1808. There she began one of the first American religious communities, the Sisters of Charity* of St. Joseph, professing vows on March 25, 1809.

Mother Seton and her companions moved to Emmitsburg in June of 1809. Candidates arrived from Maryland and New York, and the new Community immediately addressed the needs of the young Catholic Church in America by opening St. Joseph's School (a boarding academy) and a free school, as well as nursing the sick and assisting the needy. In 1814 Mother Seton sent sisters to Philadelphia and in 1817 to New York. She died at Emmitsburg in her forty-sixth year. Her sanctity was recognized by contemporaries and officially proclaimed when she was canonized, the first American-born saint, September 14, 1975.

See also RELIGIOUS ORDERS, WOMEN'S; SISTERS OF CHARITY.

BIBLIOGRAPHY. *DAB* VIII; *DARB;* J. I. Dirvin, *Mrs. Seton: Foundress of the American Sisters of Charity* (1962); A. M. Melville, *Elizabeth Bayley Seton, 1774-1821* (1951); *NAW* 3; E. A. Seton, *Elizabeth Seton: Selected Writings,* ed. E. M. Kelly and A. M. Melville (1986). P. Byrne

Settlement House Movement. An urban social reform movement of the late nineteenth and early twentieth centuries. The first settlement house, Toynbee Hall, was established in 1884 in London when Samuel Augustus Barnett, the Vicar of St. Jude's Parish (Anglican), invited several university students to "settle" and live among the poor of East London. Known variously as *social settlements, community centers* or *neighborhood houses,* the idea was transferred to New York City when two Americans, Charles B. Stover and Stanton Coit, visited London and returned to America in 1886 to establish the Neighborhood Guild, or the University Settlement, on New York's Lower East Side.

In 1889 Jane Addams* visited Toynbee Hall and with her friend, Ellen Gates Starr,* returned to Chicago to establish a social settlement house after the British model. Locating a house on the Near Southwest side of the city owned by Charles J. Hull, they purchased the house and named it *Hull House.* Also in 1889 Jane E. Robbins and Jean Fine established the College Settlement, in New York. In 1891 Robert A. Woods and William J. Tucker established Andover House (later, South End House) in Boston. The settlements were generally established in association with a college* or seminary* in order to give students experience in social-reform projects in an urban setting. In 1891 there were only six settlements in the U.S., but by 1910 the number had grown to over 400, with forty-six in Great Britain.

The movement was overwhelmingly Protestant,* and out of 339 settlement workers polled in 1905, eighty-eight per cent were active church members. Typically the workers were young, single women coming from well-to-do families. Staff workers often included vocational counselors, social workers, labor organizers, economists and teachers. Programs were varied and included youth clubs, kindergartens, home economics classes, labor advocacy, cultural events, sanitation inspection and the pursuit of social legislation. Like many of the progressives of the day, settlement workers lobbied for causes such as an eight-hour work day, a six-day work week, the prohibition of child labor, tenement housing reform, unemployment insurance and woman's suffrage. The result was a number of legislative measures that markedly improved the quality of life among the urban poor.

BIBLIOGRAPHY. J. Addams, *Twenty Years at Hull House* (1910); A. F. Davis, *Spearheads for Reform: The Social Settlements and the Progressive Movement, 1890-1914* (1967); J. A. Peterson, "From Social Settlement to Social Agency: Settlement Work in Columbus, Ohio, 1898-1958," *SSR* 39 (1965):191-208.   C. E. Stockwell

Seventh-day Adventists. Christian denomination* originating in the U.S. which emphasizes Saturday as the Sabbath* and the imminent Second Coming of Christ. Seventh-day Adventism arose out of the nineteenth-century Millerite movement, which had predicted Christ's Second Coming about 1843-1844, the last significant date chosen being October 22, 1844. Through the work of James and Ellen White* and Joseph Bates, a small group coalesced in the Northeast around several doctrines. By the early 1850s these distinctive beliefs included the seventh-day Sabbath, the imminent personal advent of Christ, conditional immortality, the investigation judgment (referring to Christ's blotting out of sins, believed to have begun in 1844 in the heavenly sanctuary) and the spirit of prophecy as manifested in the work of

Ellen White. They also adopted such practices as baptism* by immersion and the ordinances* of footwashing* and the Lord's Supper.*

James White had in 1850 begun publishing the *Advent Review and Sabbath Herald,* eventually establishing a publishing house in Rochester, New York, in 1852 and moving it to Battle Creek, Michigan, three years later. Despite opposition among the Sabbatarian Adventists, James and Ellen White pushed for formal church organization. In 1860 the name *Seventh-day Adventist* was chosen and a year later the Michigan churches formed a Conference. By 1863 there were six such state Conferences which in that year established a General Conference. The new denomination had 3,500 members.

Seventh-day Adventism's leaders early established a pattern of working through publishing, educational and medical institutions. In addition to the Review and Herald Publishing Association, it also created in Battle Creek the Western Health Reform Institute (1867), Battle Creek College (1874) and American Medical Missionary College (1895).

Seventh-day Adventism spread throughout the U.S., but most quickly in the West, establishing schools and sanitariums (later hospitals) in many places. Its work among foreign-language groups in the U.S. led to expansion overseas, with the sending of J. N. Andrews to Europe in 1874 as the first officially sponsored missionary. By 1900 there were missionaries on every continent, creating educational, publishing and medical institutions.

The expansion brought pressures that resulted in reorganization in the early twentieth century. General Conference headquarters in 1903 moved from Battle Creek to Takoma Park, a suburb of Washington, D.C. After 1900 a new administrative structure was established; local churches were grouped together into conferences, conferences into unions and the unions into the general conference, each organization based on representation from its constituent bodies. The general conference, a term that refers to both the general church legislative sessions and the denomination's general administrative body, is headed by a president, vice-presidents (each in charge of a geographical area called a division), and secretaries (each responsible for a department, such as education).

In the twentieth century, the primary growth of Seventh-day Adventism has been outside the U.S., although Americans have continued to maintain primary influence within the church. In 1985, out of a worldwide membership of 4,598,935, the U.S.

accounted for 645,952 members.

BIBLIOGRAPHY. J. M. Butler, "Adventism and the American Experience," in *The Rise of Adventism,* ed. E. S. Gaustad (1974); J. M. Butler, "From Millerism to Seventh-day Adventism: Boundlessness to Consolidation," *CH* 55 (1986):50-64. G. G. Land, ed., *Adventism in America: A History* (1986); R. W. Schwarz, *Light Bearers to the Remnant* (1979). G. Land

Seventh-Day Baptists. Baptists* differing from mainstream seventeenth-century Baptists primarily in their strict Sabbath* observance. Some Seventh-Day Baptists are also associated with radical millenarians* such as Fifth Monarchists. Their first known congregation was Mill Yard Church, London, led by Dr. Peter Chamberlen (1653). The earliest American church emerged when Stephen Mumford and seven Sabbatarians left Newport Baptist Church and called William Hiscox as pastor (1671). Initial centers of growth were Rhode Island (where they first held Yearly Meetings), Philadelphia and New Jersey. After 1735 they briefly flourished in Johann Conrad Beissell's* semi-monastic Ephrata* (Pennsylvania) community. During the nineteenth century they opposed alcoholism,* slavery* and secret societies and lost many members to Seventh Day Adventists.*

The General Conference of Seventh-Day Baptists, organized in 1801 with headquarters in Janesville, Wisconsin, maintains societies for missions, publications and education, a Sabbath School Board, a Woman's Executive Board and a Center for Ministerial Education (replacing Alfred University School of Theology). They broadcast "The Word of Truth," publish *The Sabbath Recorder* and support two colleges in West Virginia and Wisconsin. Their "Statement of Belief" (1937) is theologically conservative.

Generally ecumenical, they became concerned about political activities of the National* and World councils of churches* and withdrew in 1973 and 1976 respectively. In 1980 their worldwide membership numbered 52,155 in thirteen countries; but because American membership was declining (5,156 members, 60 churches), the General Conference launched its Decade of Discipleship program in an effort to double membership by 1990.

BIBLIOGRAPHY. H. L. McBeth, *The Baptist Heritage* (1987); A. N. Rogers, *Seventh-Day Baptists in Europe and America* (1972); G. B. Utter, *Manual of the Seventh-Day Baptists* (1958).

J. T. Spivey

Sewall, Samuel (1652-1730). Colonial politician and magistrate. Born in Bishopstoke, Hampshire, England, Sewall migrated to New England with his family in 1661. After his graduation from Harvard College* in 1671, he held a series of political offices that culminated in his appointment in 1691 to the Governor's Council of the Commonwealth of Massachusetts, a position he held until 1725. Appointed a member of the special court convened to try cases of alleged witchcraft* at Salem Village (present-day Danvers) in 1692, Sewall in 1697 made public confession of errors committed while acting in that capacity. Sewall's legal career reached its culmination in 1718 with his appointment as chief justice of the Superior Court of Massachusetts. Sewall served for many years as secretary and treasurer of the Society for the Propagation of the Gospel in New England.* His published works include *Phaenomena Quaedam Apocalyptica ad Aspectum Novi Orbis Configurata* (1697), in which he proposed New England as the site of the New Jerusalem from which Christ; would one day rule over his millennial kingdom; and *The Selling of Joseph* (1700), the first antislavery tract published in America.

BIBLIOGRAPHY. *DAB* VIII; S. Sewall, *The Diary of Samuel Sewall,* 1674-1729, ed. M. H. Thomas (1973); O. E. Winslow, *Samuel Sewall of Boston* (1964). G. W. Harper

Seybert, John (1791-1860). First constitutional bishop* of the Evangelical Church. Born of nominal Lutheran* parentage in Manheim, Pennsylvania, Seybert was converted* at an Evangelical Church camp meeting* in 1810. Soon the zealous Seybert was elected a class leader and then an itinerant* preacher* in Pennsylvania and Ohio. There he developed a deep love for bringing the gospel to the German pioneers along the Western frontiers of the U.S. and Canada. Despite being burdened by malaria, he began a revival* in 1823 at Orwigsburg, Pennsylvania, that swept through his denomination.* After several terms of service as a presiding elder,* he was elected bishop in 1839. Seybert was the first Evangelical leader to hold that post since the death of the founder, Jacob Albright,* who died in 1808, prior to the constitutional organization of the denomination.

As bishop, Seybert traveled throughout the connection and continued in his disciplined, evangelical* zeal for reaching the unconverted. More than anyone, he was responsible for shifting the center of the church from the East to the Midwest, and for initiating the first Evangelical overseas mission,* which was to Germany. Being a bachelor, Seybert was able to give liberally to those in temporal and spiritual need, and he personally distributed thousands of Bibles* and Evangelical publications in his estimated 175,000 miles of travel by horse and buckboard.

See also REVIVALISM, GERMAN-AMERICAN.

BIBLIOGRAPHY. J. S. O'Malley, *Touched by Godliness; Bishop John Seybert and the Evangelical Heritage* (1985); B. Behney and P. Eller, *History of the Evangelical United Brethren Church* (1979).

J. S. O'Malley

Seymour, Richard (fl. c. 1600). Anglican* priest.* The first practical attempt to establish an English Colony on the coast of Maine was made by the Plymouth Company in 1607. This was occurring at the same time that the successful establishment at Jamestown was accomplished. On June 1, 1607, the *Mary and John* under Captain Raleigh Gilbert and the *City of God* under Captain John Popham, left Plymouth for the new world. With the settlers was the Rev. Richard Seymour, thought by good authorities to be the great-grandson of Edward Seymour, Duke of Somerset, who was Lord Protector of England (1547-1550) during the minority of his nephew Edward VI. In August 1607, the company landed on the Island of Monhegan, later known as St. George's Island, near the peninsula of Sabrino in Maine. Here Seymour led the people in worship, using the *Book of Common Prayer.* He was the first Episcopal priest known to have ministered in New England, and his work was contemporaneous with that of Robert Hunt at Jamestown. The settlement at St. George's Island did not persist.

BIBLIOGRAPHY. L. Coleman, *The Church in America* (1895); W. S. Perry, *The History of the American Episcopal Church, 1587-1883,* vol. I (1885). D. S. Armentrout

Seymour, William Joseph (1870-1922). Pentecostal* leader. The son of former slaves, Seymour was born in Centerville, Louisiana. A self-educated man, he worked as a waiter in Indianapolis and then moved to Cincinnati in 1900, where he came under the influence of Martin Knapp, the Methodist* founder of the International Apostolic Holiness Union. Sanctified* among the Evening Light Saints, who had ties to the group which became the Church of God* (Anderson, Indiana), Seymour traveled to Houston, where he settled temporarily. He worked as an itinerant evangelist in association with other black Holiness advocates until he encountered Charles Parham's* short-term Houston Bible school and embraced Pentecostal teaching.

Late in January 1906, Seymour left Houston to accept an invitation to a black Holiness* mission in Los Angeles. His advocacy of the view that tongues* speech always evidenced Spirit baptism resulted in his rejection at the mission. He conducted cottage meetings, and on April 9, participants (including Seymour, who had never had the experience he preached) began to speak in tongues. Large interracial crowds forced the moving of the services to larger facilities in a rundown building at 312 Azusa Street,* where the meetings continued daily, attracting numerous seekers from afar. Seymour's activities in Los Angeles between 1906 and 1909 are generally regarded as having effectively launched American Pentecostalism. After 1909 his influence rapidly waned. The interracial character of the mission changed drastically in 1911. Seymour married one of his faithful assistants, Jennie Moore, and continued to conduct services at Azusa Street until his death in 1922.

See also AZUSA STREET MISSION.

BIBLIOGRAPHY. D. J. Nelson. "For Such a Time as This: The Story of Bishop William J Seymour and the Azusa Street Revival." (unpublished Ph.D dissertation, University of Birmingham [U.K.], 1981); V. Synan, *The Holiness-Pentecostal Movement in the United States* (1971); J. Tinney, "William J. Seymour: Father of Modern-Day Pentecostalism," in R. Burkett and R. Newman, eds., *Black Apostles* (1978). E. L. Blumhofer

Shakarian, Demos (1913-). Founder of Full Gospel Business Men's Fellowship International.* Born in Los Angeles, Demos Shakarian was an Armenian Pentecostal* who prospered in the California dairy industry during the 1940s. A devout layman, he began sponsoring summer revivals* in 1940 and became a friend and disciple of Charles S. Price, a noted Pentecostal healing evangelist.

During the Pentecostal healing revival after World War 2, Shakarian helped organize Oral Roberts's* 1951 Los Angeles campaign and, in turn, Roberts spoke at a small meeting of Pentecostal businessmen. From this meeting the Full Gospel Business Men's Fellowship International was born, with Shakarian as founder and president. Believing his spiritual gift to be that of "helper" (1 Cor 12:28), Shakarian's organization grew rapidly as it supported the healing revival and then served as the organizational cohesion for the charismatic movement in the 1960s.

The recipient of many awards, in 1974 Shakarian was recognized by the Vatican for his work with

Catholic businessmen. In 1986 the North American Congress on the Holy Spirit and World Evangelism acknowledged his key role in spreading the charismatic movement in the non-Pentecostal churches.

See also FULL GOSPEL BUSINESS MEN'S FELLOWSHIP INTERNATIONAL.

BIBLIOGRAPHY. S. Durasoff, *Bright Wind of the Spirit: Pentecostalism Today* (1972); J. Sherrill and E. Sherrill, *The Happiest People on Earth* (1975).

C. D. Weaver

Shakers. Millenarian* communal society. The Shakers (officially, The United Society of Believers in Christ's Second Appearing, or Millennial Church) originated in England as a loose union of enthusiasts under the leadership of Quakers Jane and James Wardley. The group did not fare well until visionary member Ann Lee* led a band of eight Shakers from Manchester to New York in 1774, soon settling in the wilderness at Niskeyuna (near Albany). At first the group experienced severe persecution and financial difficulty, being held suspect because of their British background, their pacifism and their advocation of celibacy. But over time they organized as a community, gained members through missionary* efforts, grew and prospered.

After Mother Ann's death, leadership passed to James Whittaker and at his death (1787) to Joseph Meacham,* the first American-born leader. He soon appointed Lucy Wright (1760-1821) as co-leader, thus beginning the parallel lines of male and female authority that characterized Shaker government. Equally notable was their understanding of God as Father-Mother, a truth they believed was best imaged in their gender-dual structure. But the Shakers are most remembered for their functional and gracefully simple furniture and handicrafts, and the lively Shaker worship,* which included original hymns* and dances.

The Shakers insisted that Christ had already come again, embodied in an embryonic way in the Shaker community. Some believed that Ann Lee was the female counterpart to Jesus, both of them having communicated the Christ Spirit to humankind. Other key teachings included auricular confession, celibacy as the ideal, lust as the root of all sin* and the goal of individual and communal perfection.* The Shakers believed that they were a genuine expression of primitive Christianity and that truth was being ever revealed through their leadership and the communal spiritual experience. Although they disdained creedal* formulations, they were concerned with theological expression and thus published numerous treatises, tracts,* poems and articles explaining their beliefs and lifestyle.

Shaker lifestyle was simple, efficient and regulated, but not austere. Each community contained both male and female members who, though contact was restricted, nevertheless worshiped together, worked cooperatively and were housed on opposite sides of the same dwellings. A sacramental* view of reality and a spirit of creativity resulted in many practical inventions and labor-saving devices. Children which members had brought in with them, as well as orphans and other children left with the Shakers, were included in the Shaker communities.

Some nineteen communities were formed, from Maine to Florida and west to Indiana and Kentucky. The central ministry was located in New Lebanon, New York. An exact count of membership is extremely difficult to make because of the frequent transfers between communities and fluidity of membership, but at its height it may have reached 5,000 members. A few Shakers remain into the late twentieth century, residing in the communities at Sabbathday Lake, Maine, and Canterbury, New Hampshire. The decline, which began at mid-century and was hastened by the Civil War,* can be attributed in large part to the waning of American revivalism* (many Shaker members were drawn from revival converts), as well as to the increasing desertion of rural life for the cities because of American industrialization, and the difficulty of handicrafts competing economically with factory-made goods.

BIBLIOGRAPHY. E. D. Andrews, *The People Called Shakers: A Search for the Perfect Society* (1953); H. Desroches, *The American Shakers: From Neo-Christianity to Presocialism* (1971); R. E. Whitson, ed., *The Shakers: Two Centuries of Spiritual Reflection* (1983); B. S. Youngs, *Testimony of Christ's Second Appearing, Exemplified by the Principles and Practices of the True Church of Christ* (1856).

L. A. Mercadante

Sharing. A verbal expression of ideas or experiences directly related to some aspect of the Christian life. In contemporary evangelical* usage, the term refers to what God has said or done, to what he is doing or to what believers wish him to do. For example, Christians may share the gospel, share their testimonies, share in Bible study* or share prayer requests. It functions as a catalyst for fellowship* and the advance of the gospel.

In Scripture, the term is used of giving physical sustenance to others (Eph 4:28), participating in

God's holiness (Heb 12:10) and sharing in Christ's sufferings (Phil 3:10). The meaning of sharing as a mode of spiritualized, verbal communication, however, derives from both biblical example and teaching (Jn 4:1-42, Acts 20:17-35, Philem 6).

By nature, the term implies a sense of personal involvement with others. Unlike mere talking or discussion, the content and emotions behind the practice of sharing are uniquely Christian. Christ bestows divine life and grace to his people, enabling them to impart this to each other or to unbelievers. Sharing is a means which fosters this process. In the American context, it usually occurs between individuals or within small groups. Its ultimate purpose is to edify other believers, to build the body of Christ and to glorify God.

See also RELATIONAL THEOLOGY.

BIBLIOGRAPHY.   B. Benson, *Come Share the Being* (1974); R. Girard, *Brethren, Hang Together* (1979).

S. A. Wenig

Shaw, Anna Howard (1847-1919). Methodist* minister* and suffragist.* Born in Newcastle-upon-Tyne, England, Shaw grew up in the Michigan wilderness where she learned self-reliance and the value of education. Her oratorical skills were discovered in high school, where she was inspired to consider the ministry* after meeting Universalist* minister Marianna Thompson. Shaw was licensed* to preach* by the Methodist Church and did so for a living while attending Albion College and Boston University's School of Theology. Her request for ordination* was dismissed in 1880 by church officials, but she was ordained that same year by the Methodist Protestants. While pursuing a medical degree, she served parishes in East Dennis and Brewster, Massachusetts. Her work in the slums of Boston, as well as the influence of friends, drew her into the suffrage movement. She was a successful lecturer for the cause, but allowed the National American Woman's Suffrage Association to languish under her presidency between 1904 and 1915. Her last lecture tours were made on behalf of the League of Nations.

BIBLIOGRAPHY.   *DAB* IX; *NAW* 3; A. H. Shaw, *The Story of a Pioneer* (1915); R. Spencer, "Anna Howard Shaw," *MH* 13 (1975):33-51.

B. J. MacHaffie

Shaw, Knowles (1834-1878). Christian Church (Disciples of Christ)* evangelist.* Born in Ohio and raised in poverty in Rush County, Indiana, Shaw had no opportunity for formal education and spent his time learning to play the violin his dying father had given him when he was twelve. By the early 1860s he had become known throughout the frontier, from Michigan to Texas, as the "Singing Evangelist." Before each service he played the organ for a half hour and sang gospel hymns,* many of his own composition. His "Bringing in the Sheaves" is still heard in many churches today.

Shaw's methods heralded a new style of evangelism* later embellished by Billy Sunday.* Shaw often interrupted his sermons by moving theatrically about the stage and suddenly breaking into song. An 1877 New Orleans *Times* newspaper piece described him as the "live preacher." He and Dwight L. Moody* were contemporaries, though Shaw's popular revivalistic* singing preceded by a decade Moody's evangelistic partnership with singer Ira D. Sankey.* In his diary Shaw kept a record of people converted under his preaching, recording more than 11,400 conversions in a little over nineteen years of ministry.* He died in a train wreck while en route from one protracted revival meeting in Dallas to another in McKinney, Texas.

BIBLIOGRAPHY.   W. Baxter, *Life of Knowles Shaw: The Singing Evangelist* (1879).

M. G. Toulouse

Shedd, William Greenough Thayer (1820-1894). Calvinist* theologian* and church historian. A sixth-generation descendant of Massachusetts Puritans,* Shedd appropriated many of the leading intellectual trends of the nineteenth century without sacrificing his commitment to Reformed orthodoxy.* His speculative interests in Romanticism,* historical consciousness and evolution* made him remarkably sensitive to the powerful new thinking of his century. Yet Shedd did not create any controversy, for his firm Calvinist faith was never altered by his novel speculations.

While a student at the University of Vermont, Shedd was profoundly influenced by his philosophy professor, James Marsh. Thereafter his thinking reflected an intimate familiarity with the leading luminaries of European Romanticism. Upon his graduation from Andover Theological Seminary,* Shedd served a Congregational* church in Brandon, Vermont, and later a church in New York City. But his pastoral labors were brief, less than four years in all. The greater part of his career was devoted to teaching. His diversified appointments included seven years as professor of English literature at Vermont, two years as professor of sacred rhetoric at Auburn Theological Seminary and eight years as professor of church history at Andover. In 1863 he accepted a position at Union Theological Seminary* (New York), beginning an affiliation with that institution which would continue for twenty-eight years. After 1874 he served as professor of systematic theology,* succeeding Henry Boynton Smith.*

One of the eminent theologians of his era, Shedd exhibited literary gifts, historical interests and a speculative spirit in his many works, including a *History of Christian Doctrine* (1863) and *Dogmatic Theology* (1889). As an Old School Presbyterian* he opposed any revision of the Westminster* Standards and remained a great advocate of Baconianism and its inductive reasoning.

BIBLIOGRAPHY. *DAB* IX; G. S. Smith, *The Seeds of Secularization* (1985); C. Strout, "Faith and History: The Mind of William G. T. Shedd," *JHI* 15 (1954):153-162.　　　　　　　　S. R. Pointer

Sheen, Fulton J. (1895-1979).

Roman Catholic archbishop,* preacher* and author. Born in El Paso, Illinois, the son of Irish-American farmer Newton Morris Sheen and Delia (Fulton) Sheen, he was baptized *Peter,* but later adopted his mother's maiden name and used it throughout his career. He was educated at St. Viator's College and Seminary at Bourbonnais, Illinois (B.A., 1917; M.A., 1919) and St. Paul's Seminary at St. Paul, Minnesota. On September 20, 1919, he was ordained* to the priesthood* for the Diocese* of Peoria.

Recognized for his intellectual talents, he was sent to continue his education at the Catholic University of America* (J.C.B., 1920), and received his Ph.D. from the University of Louvain in 1923. After further study at the Sorbonne and the Collegio Angelica in Rome (S.T.D., 1924), he taught dogmatic theology* at St. Edmund's College in Ware, England. *God and Intelligence in Modern Philosophy,* his doctoral dissertation, was published in 1925. The first of more than sixty books, it won the Cardinal Mercier Prize for International Philosophy, and Sheen was made an "Agrege en Philosophie" by Louvain, the first American to be so honored.

Upon returning to the U.S., Sheen served briefly as a curate at St. Patrick's Church in Peoria and then joined the faculty of the Catholic University of America in 1926, where he would teach theology and philosophy until 1950. During these years, Sheen attracted widespread attention and won a national reputation as an eloquent and dynamic orator and preacher. He lectured on contemporary issues as well as religion from coast to coast. Adopting the persona of an intellectual popularizer, he became a pioneer of the electronic church* as the featured speaker on NBC radio network's "Catholic Hour Broadcasts," sponsored by the National Council of Catholic Men* (1930-1952). His radio audience was estimated at 4,000,000 listeners.

Sheen's popularity as a media star coincided with his rise in the ranks of the Church as well. He was appointed papal chamberlain in 1934 and elevated to domestic prelate—Right Reverend Monsignor*—the following year. In 1951 he was consecrated titular bishop of Caesariana and auxiliary bishop* of New York.

Widely known as a skilled instructor of Catholic converts, Sheen made headlines when he welcomed many prominent figures into the Church, including journalist Heywood Broun, politician Clare Booth Luce and the former Communist Louis Budenz. In addition, he instructed an entire generation through his best-selling books and lectures on a variety of religious subjects, *Peace of Soul* (1949) and *Life of Christ* (1958) being his most popular books. As an advocate of the Church's program of social justice, he taught that social reconstruction was a by-product of spiritual regeneration. For decades, Sheen was prominent as an outspoken opponent of Marxism, speaking often of the crisis of the times and the worldwide struggle between the forces of Communism* and Christianity.

The decade of the fifties, the culmination of America's post-war religious revival, marked the height of Bishop Sheen's influence and popularity. In 1950 he was appointed national director of the Society for Propagation of the Faith*; for the next sixteen years he raised millions of dollars for Catholic missions.* He edited *World Mission* and *Mission* magazines and wrote two nationally syndicated newspaper columns, "Bishop Sheen Writes" and "God Loves You." Most important, he achieved a phenomenal success as a television star. His television program, "Life Is Worth Living" (1951-1957) reached approximately 30 million viewers each week on the ABC network. In 1952, testimonials to this unusual success included the Emmy Award and the cover of *Time* magazine; a Catholic prelate had become a household name.

At the Second Vatican Council,* Sheen participated as a member of the Commission on the Missions. In 1966, Pope Paul VI appointed him the bishop of Rochester, New York, where he proved himself a controversial innovator. After a short and stormy tenure, he resigned in 1969. The final decade of his life was devoted to continued teaching, lecturing and writing. He died of heart disease on December 9 at the age of eighty-four.

The key to his legendary success on radio and television was his appeal to Americans of all faiths,

Catholic and non-Catholic alike. His talks were a blend of common sense, patriotism and Christian ethics. Having dedicated his life to "working out a Christian response to the challenge of the times," he succeeded admirably as the greatest evangelist* in the history of the Catholic Church in the U.S.

BIBLIOGRAPHY. J. T. Ellis, *Catholic Bishops: A Memoir* (1984); K. R. Fields, "Anti-Communism and Social Justice: The Double-Edged Sword of Fulton Sheen," *RACHAP* 96 (1986):83-91; F. J. Sheen, *Treasure in Clay: The Autobiography of Fulton J. Sheen* (1980).

K. R. Fields

Sheil, Bernard James (1886-1969). Auxiliary bishop* of Chicago, founder of the Catholic Youth Organization.* Born in Chicago, Sheil was ordained* in 1910, named chancellor of the archdiocese* of Chicago by Cardinal* Mundelein* in 1924, and consecrated auxiliary bishop in 1928. He remained an auxiliary for over forty years, serving under four archbishops and never receiving a diocese of his own.

In 1930, Sheil founded the Catholic Youth Organization, a wide-ranging network of religious, athletic and social-welfare organizations for young people. With Cardinal Mundelein's blessing, he involved himself in many controversial activities, such as the organization of CIO industrial unions, the formation of the Back of the Yards Neighborhood Council and the fostering of interracial harmony. Sheil literally would give a beggar the coat off his back. His freespending welfare activities and the controversial causes he championed made him many enemies in the Catholic hierarchy, so he was never named to head a diocese in his own right. He died in virtual exile in Arizona, a largely forgotten but prophetic social-action bishop.

BIBLIOGRAPHY. E. R. Kantowicz, *Corporation Sole* (1982); R. L. Treat, *Bishop Sheil and the CYO* (1951). E. R. Kantowicz

Sheldon, Charles Monroe (1857-1946). Congregational* minister* and Social Gospel* reformer. Born in Wellsville, New York, Sheldon was one of five children born to the Reverend Stewart Sheldon, a Congregational minister who ministered on the South Dakota prairie. Educated at Phillips Academy (graduated 1879), Brown University* (B.A., 1883) and Andover Theological Seminary* (B.D., 1886), he began his ministry in Waterbury, Vermont (1886-1888), and in 1899 accepted what turned out to be a lifelong call to the newly formed Central Congregational Church

in Topeka, Kansas. During the latter portion of his life, he worked for the *Christian Herald,* first as editor-in-chief (1920-1925) and then as contributing editor (1925-1946).

Sheldon was committed to learning as much as possible about the social conditions of the town and did so by living a week at a time with various social groups—railroad men, college students, professional people, African-Americans, newspaper workers and the unemployed. A tireless pastor and reformer, he believed strongly in the major tenet of the Social Gospel: The kingdom of God* is to be established on earth here and now. Striving throughout his life to improve the living and working conditions of others, he argued and fought for the basic rights of African-Americans, women, Jews and all other minorities. He also worked for religious reform, world peace and prohibition, campaigning for the passage of the Eighteenth Amendment.

Sheldon was a folk theologian who focused on the person and work of Jesus, frequently using the medium of story. Though he was a theological liberal,* he managed to stay out of the fundamentalist-modernist controversy,* which reached its peak in the 1920s. Sheldon was perhaps best known as an author of some fifty books and hundreds of articles in religious and secular periodicals as well as poems, hymns* and plays. His most famous work, *In His Steps* (1897), was first published as a series in the religious periodical *Advance.* The story, which soon became a best seller, is about a town that is transformed by the challenge issued by the Rev. Henry Maxwell. Maxwell charges his congregation to do nothing without first asking "What would Jesus do?" and then acting on that answer. Among his other most successful novels are *The Crucifixion of Philip Strong* (1894) and *Robert Hardy's Seven Days* (1899). *Jesus Is Here!* was published in 1913 as the sequel to *In His Steps.* In 1921 Sheldon published *In His Steps Today,* a nonfiction evaluation of the church's progress since 1896.

BIBLIOGRAPHY. *DAB* 4; *DARB; NCAB* 34; C. M. Sheldon, *Charles M. Sheldon: His Life Story* (1925). J. C. Brown

Shepard, Thomas (1605-1649). Puritan* minister.* Born in Towcester, England, Shepard studied at Emmanuel College, Cambridge (B.A., 1623/1624; M.A., 1627), and in 1627 was ordained* priest* in the Church of England. A Nonconformist, he was silenced by Bishop Laud in 1630 and was unable to preach publicly. Thwarted by a storm in October 1634 as he attempted to sail to Boston,

Shepard reached his destination one year later, but he soon lost his first wife to an illness she contracted during the crossing. He married Joanna Hooker, daughter of Thomas Hooker,* in 1637.

In 1636 Shepard accepted a call to be pastor of the church at Newtown (Cambridge). Shepard was one of the most accomplished preachers among the first-generation New England Puritans; his ministry flourished. He was a participant in the founding of Harvard College* at Cambridge in 1636 and continued to support the education of young men. He was also an opponent of antinomianism* and took a keen interest in efforts to evangelize Native Americans, particularly the missionary* work of his friend John Eliot.* Among his published writings were *Theses Sabbaticae* (1649), *The Sincere Convert* (which went through twenty-one editions between 1641 and 1812) and *Church Membership of Children and Their Right to Baptism* (1663). His diary was edited and published by Nehemiah Adam as *The Autobiography of Thomas Shepard* (1832) and offers valuable insights into the life and labors of a Puritan minister. Later generations regarded Shepard as an outstanding Puritan divine* who embodied the ideals of the New England Way.*

BIBLIOGRAPHY. *AAP* 1; J. A. Albro, *The Life of Thomas Shepard* (1847); *DAB* IX; A. Whyte, *Thomas Shepard, Pilgrim Father and Founder of Harvard* (1909).   D. G. Reid

Shepherding Movement (Discipleship Movement). A movement, primarily within charismatic* Christianity, emphasizing strict discipleship* and submission to church leaders. It received its initial impetus in 1970 from four prominent Florida charismatics—Derek Prince, Don Basham, Bob Mumford and Charles Simpson—who felt a need for greater accountability among Christians. Through their widespread influence they encouraged dozens of churches to affiliate with their Christian Growth Ministries and adopt their pyramid-like structure. Each local church member was submitted to an elder, or "shepherd," in the congregation. Each shepherd typically guided eight to twelve persons and in turn submitted to the congregation's pastor or a head elder. The line of authority rose through trans-local shepherds to the Fort Lauderdale teachers. Church membership entailed adherence to a covenant which implied long-term or even permanent commitment.

Abuses quickly appeared: Members seemed unable to make decisions apart from their shepherd's direction and other charismatic leaders charged that shepherding adherents were infiltrating non-shepherding organizations and churches and diverting members' allegiances. Television evangelist Pat Robertson* led the attacks, and during a series of private conferences in 1975-1976, the shepherding leaders admitted they had made some mistakes.

Interaction with Catholic charismatics led to development of similar structures in charismatic communities like the Word of God Community in Ann Arbor, Michigan, and the People of Praise in South Bend, Indiana. Controversy arose in this branch of the movement as well. In 1986 the Catholic archbishop* of New Jersey called on members of the Newark-based People of Hope to leave that community.

The claims of psychological manipulation caused several anti-cult organizations to join in opposing the movement. Derek Prince disassociated himself from shepherding in 1984, and the four founding teachers dissolved their covenant with each other in 1986. Nevertheless, in the late 1980s shepherding remained popular, having spread to many other groups, such as the Crossroads movement in the independent Churches of Christ.*

BIBLIOGRAPHY. K. McDonnell, *Presence, Power, Praise* (1980); B. Ligon, *Discipleship* (1979).

B. Barron

Sherrill, Lewis Joseph (1882-1957). Presbyterian* professor of Christian education.* Born and educated in Texas, Sherrill later received his basic theological training at the Presbyterian Theological Seminary of Kentucky (Louisville). After a four-year pastorate in Tennessee, in 1925 Sherrill returned to Louisville as professor of religious education. Except for a leave to earn his doctorate at Yale,* Sherrill spent the remainder of his career teaching at Louisville (1925-1950) and Union Theological Seminary,* New York (1950-1957). Sherrill's major books demonstrate his changing theology of Christian experience. Originally viewing Christian nurture* as the natural complement of evangelism,* Sherrill came to believe that the process of Christian growth was more important than any single conversion* experience. His preoccupation with process and his reliance on contemporary theories of depth psychology, caused Sherrill to develop a view of Christian education which moved away from evangelical* revivalism.* Rather than a humanistic liberalism,* though, Sherrill's eclectic work demonstrated an appreciation for his faculty colleague Reinhold Niebuhr* and the theology of crisis.*

BIBLIOGRAPHY. L. B. Weeks, "Lewis Sherrill: Christian Educator," *JPH* 51 (1973):235-248; R. W.

Fairchild, "The Contribution of Lewis Sherrill to Christian Education," *RelEd* 53 (1958):403-410. D. M. Strong

Shields, (T)homas (T)odhunter (1873-1955).

Canadian Baptist* pastor* and fundamentalist* leader. Born in England, his father a Baptist pastor, Shields was raised in southwestern Ontario and began to preach with only his father's instruction and model as education. The younger Shields's attention to clear, forceful language, coupled with an impressive build and voice, opened doors to a series of successful pastorates.

In 1910 he became pastor of the largest Baptist church in Canada at the time, Jarvis Street in Toronto. Shields served there for the rest of his life, developing a reputation as the "Canadian Spurgeon." The church grew in numbers, even though it suffered a schism over his leadership in 1921. The church's newspaper, *The Gospel Witness,* under Shields's editorship reached 30,000 subscribers in 60 countries. Shields presided over the Canadian Protestant League in anti-Catholic propaganda during its brief flowering in World War 2,* and helped lead two fundamentalist organizations, the Baptist Bible Union* and the International Council of Christian Churches.*

Shields is best known, however, for his leadership of fundamentalists in the Baptist Convention of Ontario and Quebec. From 1910 to 1926 these Christians opposed a succession of appointments of theological liberals* at the denomination's McMastor University. Largely unsuccessful in their opposition, a number joined Shields in leaving the denomination in 1927. Many of the disaffected would later form the Fellowship of Evangelical Baptist Churches in Canada, but Shields continued his pattern of refusing to compromise and ended up leader only of a tiny denomination, now known as the Association of Regular Baptist Churches of Canada.
See also BAPTIST CHURCHES IN CANADA.

BIBLIOGRAPHY. C. A. Russell, "Thomas Todhunter Shields, Canadian Fundamentalist," *Ontario History* 70 (1978); 263-280; L. K. Tarr, "Another Perspective on T. T. Shields and Fundamentalism," in *Baptists in Canada: Search for Identity amidst Diversity,* ed. J. K. Zeman (1980); L. K. Tarr, *Shields of Canada* (1967). J. G. Stackhouse

Shinn, Asa (1781-1853).

Methodist* preacher,* theologian* and ecclesiastical reformer. Born in New Jersey, Shinn was reared in the wilds of West Virginia and converted* at a Methodist meeting in 1798. He joined the Methodist Episcopal Church

shortly thereafter. Three years later he became an itinerant* preacher. A self-educated man, Shinn is remembered as a powerful orator and a writer whose work reveals a keen mind. His *Essay on the Plan of Salvation* (1813) was the first systematic theology* written by an American Methodist.

Shinn is most famous for his role in the reform movement that resulted in the formation of the Methodist Protestant Church (1830). As the hierarchical polity* of the Methodist Episcopal Church seemed to run counter to the spirit of American populism and Jacksonian democracy,* reformers emerged within Methodism who sought shared authority among ministeral leaders and lay* participation in the Conferences where Church policy was fixed. Shinn was one of the main contributors to the reform-minded journal *Mutual Rights* (1824). When the movement failed at the 1828 General Conference, he withdrew his membership from the Methodist Episcopal Church and labored for the establishment of the Methodist Protestant Church, serving repeatedly as president of his Annual Conference and twice (in 1830, 1842) as president of the Churchwide Methodist Protestant Church General Conference. Throughout his lifetime Shinn suffered several bouts of insanity (1816, 1820, 1828) attributed to a skull fracture he suffered as a child. The final episode came in 1843 and, never recovering, he died in an asylum at Brattleboro, Vermont.

BIBLIOGRAPHY. *AAP* VII; *DAB* IX; R. F. Shinn, *A Tribute to Our Fathers* (1853). J. R. Tyson

Shoemaker, Samuel (M)oor (1893-1963).

Episcopal* clergyman.* Born in Baltimore, Maryland, Shoemaker attended Princeton* University (B.A., 1916) and then served two years as a YMCA* worker in China (1917-1919). After studying at General Theological Seminary and graduating from Union Theological Seminary* in New York (1921), he was ordained* a priest in the Episcopal Church. He later received honorary degrees from Virginia Theological Seminary (D.D.) and Berkeley Divinity School (S.T.D.).

Shoemaker became rector* of Calvary Episcopal Church in New York (1925-1952). His ministry there was marked by a social conscience leading to establishment of the Calvary House in New York and its mission to down-and-outers and alcoholics. Shoemaker assisted the founders of *Alcoholics Anonymous* in formulating their "Twelve Steps." Shoemaker's ministry extended beyond his parish with his twice-weekly broadcasts over 120 ABC radio stations (1945-1946) and Calvary's publication, *Evangel,* which had a circulation of 7,000. In

1945 he opened the Calvary Clergy School which provided training for ministers and those considering ministry.

From 1952 to 1962 Shoemaker was rector of Calvary Episcopal Church, Pittsburgh. There he founded the Pittsburgh Experiment (1955), an attempt to assist lay* persons to witness to their Christian faith in their daily lives, and was one of the early leaders of the small group movement. Committed to ministry to university students, Shoemaker held student conferences at Yale,* Harvard,* Princeton and several other campuses. He was founder of *Faith at Work* magazine and a prolific author. His advice to seminarians and beginning pastors is given in *Beginning Your Ministry* (1963).

BIBLIOGRAPHY. I. D. Harris, *The Breeze of the Spirit: Sam Shoemaker and the Story of Faith at Work* (1978).   D. Macleod

Shuler, Robert Pierce (1880-1965). Fundamentalist* Methodist* minister* and radio preacher*. Born in Grayson County, Virginia, Shuler was educated at Emory and Henry College. He began his ministry in the Methodist Church at Pocahontas, Virginia (1902) and entered the Holston Conference in 1903. He pastored several churches in Virginia and Tennessee until 1906 when he moved to Texas. There he pastored until 1920, when he moved to Trinity Methodist Church in Los Angeles, California. Witty and contentious, under Shuler's ministry the church grew to 5,000 members in the 1930s. Shuler was perhaps the strongest voice for fundamentalism within Methodism and strongly opposed the union of the Southern Methodist Church with the Northern Methodist Church.

Trinity Methodist was among the earliest to own and operate a radio station, KGEF, which the brash pastor used to fight judicial and political corruption as well as moral depravity. His broadcasts attacked many institutions and individuals, including newspaper publisher William Randolph Hearst, local judges, police chiefs and the Roman Catholic Church.* The church was bombed and Shuler was sued, but he continued to preach publicly against evil and enemies. In 1931 the Federal Radio Commission (FRC) refused to renew Shuler's license, and the case established an important precedent in American broadcasting. A year later the colorful preacher lost a bid for U.S. senator on the Prohibition* Ticket, although he amassed over 300,000 votes. Nicknamed "Fighting Bob," he edited *Bob Shuler's Magazine,* the *Fundamentalist* and *The Methodist Challenge.* Among his publications were *Silenced,* his reaction to the FRC's

decision; two books of sermons entitled *Some Dogs I Have Known* and *What New Doctrine is This?* and a book of biographical sketches, *Bob Shuler Met These on the Trail* (1955).

BIBLIOGRAPHY. E. D. Jervey, "Shuler, Robert P.," in N. B. Harmon, ed., *Encyclopedia of World Methodism,* vol II (1974).   Q. J. Schultze

Shuster, George Nathan (1894-1977). Catholic* author, editor and educator. Born in Lancaster, Wisconsin, Shuster was educated at the University of Notre Dame* (B.A., 1915; M.A., 1920) and Columbia University (Ph.D., 1940). After service that included the bloody battle of Chateau-Thierry in World War 1,* he returned to Notre Dame with a deeply matured faith and a broad interest in the life of the Church.

Among the highlights of Shuster's career were his stints as professor of English at Notre Dame until 1924; his writing for and then editing of *Commonweal* until 1937; and his service as president of Hunter College, New York (1940-1961). He was a father figure and mentor to the young Theodore M. Hesburgh at Notre Dame and served as assistant to Hesburgh while the latter was president of Notre Dame. Shuster was also director of Notre Dame's Center for the Study of Man in Contemporary Society.

A man of intellectual vigor, courtesy and principle, Shuster authored twenty-one books on literature, politics, education and religion. He consistently opposed totalitarianism in whatever sphere of life he encountered it. Among the first to recognize the threat of Hitler, he left *Commonweal* because of his principled criticism of Franco. During the years of McCarthyism, he defended academic freedom. In government service he helped to create UNESCO in 1945 and was land commissioner in post-World War 2* Bavaria from 1950 to 1952. He died on January 25, 1977, in South Bend, Indiana.

BIBLIOGRAPHY. V. P. Lannie, ed., *On the Side of Truth: George N. Shuster* (1974); G. N. Shuster, *The Ground I Walked On* (1961, 1969).

R. Van Allen

Sign of the Cross. A devotional* or liturgical* gesture tracing the cross. Tracing the cross on one's forehead with the thumb or index finger was already customary by the end of the second century as a private devotion. Tertullian (c.160-c.220) writes, "At every step and movement, when putting on our clothes and shoes, at the bath, at the table . . . in all the ordinary customs of everyday life we trace the sign" (*De Corona Militus* 3). In the fourth century it apparently came into wide use in liturgy. Augustine (354-430) observed, "Unless the sign of the cross is made on the foreheads of the faithful, as on the water itself wherewith they are regenerated . . . or on the sacrifice with which they are nourished, none of these things is duly performed" (*Tractatus adversus Judaeos* cxviii, in *Joannis Evangelium* xix 24). The Augustinian belief in the sign's necessity for all sacraments* prevailed in the medieval Church but was later rejected by Protestant* reformers. While the sign was originally restricted to the forehead, the large sign of the cross made on forehead, breast and shoulders seems to have been introduced into the monasteries in the tenth century. Currently in the West the crossing of the chest is from left to right, and from right to left in the Eastern Church. The gesture is most noticeably used by Catholics.*

BIBLIOGRAPHY. E. Beresford-Cooke, *The Sign of the Cross in Western Liturgy* (1907); C. E. Pocknee, *Cross and Crucifix* (1962).

D. A. Scalberg

Silliman, Benjamin (1779-1864). Yale* scientist. Born in Trumbull, Connecticut, and raised in Fairfield, Silliman enrolled at Yale at the age of thirteen (1792-1796). In 1799 he began tutoring at Yale. Converted* in the Yale College revival of 1802, Silliman was recruited by Timothy Dwight* to develop the "doxological" aspects of science and thereby counter the perceived threat of French scientific infidelity. Silliman taught geology, chemistry and mineralogy at Yale for decades (his students included James Dwight Dana* and Edward Hitchcock*), lectured widely across the U.S. and edited the *American Journal of Science and Arts*.

Championing Francis Bacon's inductive philosophy in his scientific endeavors, Silliman was convinced that the facts of science contributed to the truth of Christianity. Therefore, for apologetic* purposes he helped popularize the "long day," or "day-age," theory for harmonizing the first chapter of Genesis with the earth's apparent antiquity. He continued to believe there was evidence for a universal deluge but gradually moved from a catastrophic theory to a cautious acceptance of uniformitarian geology. Silliman is widely regarded as the dean of American science in the antebellum period.

BIBLIOGRAPHY. T. D. Bozeman, *Protestants in an Age of Science* (1977); *DAB* IX; H. Hovenkamp, *Science and Religion in America, 1800-1860* (1978); D. N. Livingstone, *Darwin's Forgotten Defenders* (1987). S. R. Pointer

SIM International. Evangelical* foreign mission* agency. SIM International was formed in 1982 in a merger of the Sudan Interior Mission (founded in 1893) and the Andes Evangelical Mission (originally the Bolivian Indian Mission), founded in 1907.

The Sudan Interior Mission (SIM) came into being in response to the need of unevangelized millions who lived some distance away from the more easily accessible coastal regions of Africa. Walter Gowans, the original visionary among SIM's three youthful founders, described in his pamphlet, "Burden of the Soudan" (1893), the plight of some sixty million living apart from Christian witness in Africa's broad middle belt (the Soudan). Gowans, together with fellow Canadian Rowland Bingham* and American Thomas Kent* arrived in Nigeria on December 4, 1893. Their aim was to reach the Hausa of the interior. Gowans and Kent died of fever within a year, and Bingham returned home, his health broken. Bingham, who served as general director of SIM until his death in 1942, returned with another team in 1900, but this attempt was again abandoned because of ill health. A third attempt in 1901, however, resulted in the establishment of the first station at Patigi.

The work of the Bolivian Indian Mission (BIM) was begun by George and Mary Allan, two New Zealanders who began their South American ministry in Argentina in 1899, but whose increasing burden for the Indian peoples of the Andes led to the founding of BIM in 1907. The missionary force during BIM's first decade was primarily made up of Australians, British and New Zealanders, but it came to be increasingly dominated by North Americans in the years following the formation of its New York Council in 1916. In 1989 SIM added Asia to its mission fields through a merger with International Christian Fellowship)a mission agency working largely in South Asia since its beginnings in 1893.

From difficult physical beginnings on two continents, the SIM International unites today some 6,000 congregations in twenty-one countries, with a total church community approaching four million persons. Mission membership in 1987 numbered 1,468 full-time persons from at least fifteen countries (roughly fifty per cent from the U.S.). The mission carries on a broad spectrum of ministries in concert with evangelism and church planting. These include theological education at numerous levels, development and relief work, broadcasting, numerous kinds of health-care ministries, linguistics and Bible translation, literacy, publishing, student ministries and a variety of other educational ministries, including the teaching of the Bible in public schools.

BIBLIOGRAPHY. R. V. Bingham, *Seven Sevens of Years and a Jubilee* (1943); R. J. Davis, *Fire on the Mountains: The Story of a Miracle—The Church in Ethiopia* (1966); M. A. Hudspith, *Ripening Fruit: A History of the Bolivian Indian Mission* (1958); J. H. Hunter, *A Flame of Fire: The Life and Work of R. V. Bingham* (1961).   G. R. Corwin

Simonton, Ashbel Green (1833-1867). Presbyterian* missionary* to Brazil. Born in West Hanover, Pennsylvania, near Harrisburg, Simonton was named for a distinguished clergyman* and chaplain* to Congress, Ashbel Green. After graduating from the College of New Jersey,* he studied at Princeton Theological Seminary, where under the preaching of Charles Hodge* he responded to the call to missionary service. The Presbyterian Church in the U.S.A. ordained him, and he traveled to Brazil under the Presbyterian Board of Foreign Missions in 1859. Settling in Rio de Janeiro, he founded the first Presbyterian church, presbytery and Protestant seminary in that country. Simonton also founded an evangelical newspaper and, in cooperation with other Presbyterians, engaged in extensive evangelistic* campaigns throughout the country. His wife, Helen Murdoch, shared his mission work for a short time before she died in giving birth to their only child. Simonton himself died of yellow fever at the age of thirty-seven.

BIBLIOGRAPHY. P. S. Landes, *Ashbel Green Simonton* (1956).   J. M. Smylie

Simpson, (A)lbert (B)enjamin (1843-1919). Preacher,* hymnwriter and founder of the Christian and Missionary Alliance.* Born on Prince Edward Island, A. B. Simpson was the fourth child of Scottish Covenanter Presbyterian* parents, James and Jane Simpson. He had a conversion* experience in 1858 and three years later dedicated himself to God in a written "covenant." After graduating from Knox College in Toronto in 1865, he accepted a call to Knox Presbyterian Church, Hamilton, Ontario.

In 1873 Simpson was called to the Chestnut Street Presbyterian Church in Louisville, Kentucky. In 1874 after reading W. E. Boardman's* *The Higher Christian Life,* he experienced a spiritual crisis he considered to be the "Baptism of the Holy Ghost." The following year he enlisted the clergy* of the city, divided by the Civil War,* to unite in a one-month campaign for renewal and reconciliation. Major D. W. Whittle served as evangelist and Philip P. Bliss* as soloist and songleader.

In 1879 he became pastor of the Thirteenth Street Presbyterian Church in New York City. From February 1880 to October 1881 he edited his own *Gospel In All Lands.* In 1881 he experienced physical healing* from a weakened heart, received baptism* by immersion and resigned his church. In 1882 he began publishing a periodical which later, under various titles, became the official publication of the Christian and Missionary Alliance and began training classes for workers in his new Gospel Tabernacle.* In 1883 his congregation incorporated, formed their own missionary society called The Missionary Union for the Evangelization of the World. They also opened a "Home for Faith and Physical Healing" (dedicated, Berachah Home in 1884) and began the New York Missionary Training College (now Nyack College and Alliance Theological Seminary), which held its first commencement in 1884.

In 1884 Simpson sent his first missionaries to Congo (Zaire) and held his first October Convention for evangelism, deeper life and missions. At the Convention's Friday evening services, he stressed consecration and healing. To emphasize four essential truths of the gospel, Simpson coined the phrase, "Christ our Saviour, Sanctifier, Healer and Coming King," which became known as the "the Fourfold Gospel."

In 1887 he organized the "Christian Alliance" and the "Evangelical Missionary Alliance" at the Methodist* Campgrounds in Old Orchard, Maine, and the E.M.A. sent missionaries to China that year (the two Alliances would join in 1897 to form the Christian and Missionary Alliance).

A major crisis for the Alliance occurred in 1906 when the Pentecostal experience of tongues* speech became an issue in many Alliance congregations. Although Simpson sought "all the gifts," he never spoke in tongues and had concluded that tongues is not the evidence of the baptism of the Holy Spirit. The consequent departure of many who disagreed with Simpson saddened him.

Simpson authored over one hundred seventy-five hymns, including "Yesterday, Today, Forever," "Jesus Only" and "What Will You Do with Jesus?" *See also* CHRISTIAN AND MISSIONARY ALLIANCE.

BIBLIOGRAPHY. *DAB* IX; D. F. Hartzfeld, and C. Nienkirchen, eds., *The Birth of a Vision* (1986); L. N. Robert et al., *All for Jesus: God at Work in the Christian and Missionary Alliance over One Hundred Years* (1986); A. E. Thompson, *The Life of A. B. Simpson* (1947); A. W. Tozer, *Wingspread* (1943).   H. P. Shelly

Simpson, Matthew (1811-1884). Bishop* of the Methodist Episcopal Church.* Born at Cadiz, Ohio,

Simpson studied medicine but turned to the ministry, joining the Pittsburg Conference of the Methodist Episcopal Church in 1834. Soon thereafter he was appointed to the faculty of Allegheny College in Williamsport, Pennsylvania, and later became president of Indiana Asbury University (now DePauw University).

Simpson was deeply involved in the bitter conflicts beween Methodists regarding abolition.* An ardent opponent of slavery, he sought to repudiate the Plan of Separation by which the Northern and Southern churches had agreed to divide constituencies and assets in 1844, and his aggressive onslaughts on slavery after 1848, as editor of the *Western Christian Advocate,* spread his fame throughout Northern Methodism. He was elected bishop in 1852 and in 1859 was elected president of Garrett Biblical Institute in Evanston, Illinois.

During the Civil War* Simpson exercised great political influence through his friendship with President Lincoln.* He sought to place Methodists in national offices and attempted to use the power of military rule in conquered Southern territory to appropriate properties of the Methodist Episcopal Church, South, for the Northern Church. However, Lincoln's successor, Andrew Johnson, ordered all seized church property to be returned to the Southern Church. The bishop warmly supported Johnson's impeachment. Simpson preached Lincoln's funeral message both in Washington, D.C., and in Springfield, Missouri.

BIBLIOGRAPHY. R. D. Clark, *The Life of Matthew Simpson* (1956); G. R. Crooks, *The Life of Bishop Matthew Simpson* (1890); *DAB* IX; *DARB*; *NCAB* 7; C. T. Wilson, *Matthew Simpson* (1929).

M. E. Dieter

Sin. Theologians* differ over whether sin should be defined as a human privation of good or as purposeful disobedience of God's holy law, but orthodox* theologians are agreed that sin is the human condition that separates humanity from God, who is holy. The reality of sin is one of the basic foundations of biblical Christianity and the doctrine of sin has played an important role in defining each of the major theological traditions of Christianity.

Catholic theologians have made the distinction between mortal and venial sins. Mortal sins are transgressions of divine law in serious matters, made with an awareness of the law and the gravity of the transgression. Venial sins are transgressions that are made with imperfect knowledge of divine law, transgressions of laws of a less binding nature, or transgressions of laws of a serious nature but made with a conscience ignorant of the gravity of the act.

Both Catholics and Protestants have traditionally maintained some form of a doctrine of original sin—the state of sin that has pervaded humanity since the Fall. Catholic theologians have generally followed Augustine in understanding original sin to be a "privation of good" or the loss of sanctifying grace. For Thomas Aquinas, original sin left the human mind and will intact, but deprived men and women of the grace that would enable them to attain their original destiny. The Protestant Reformers, on the other hand, spoke of sin as a perversity encompassing human nature in its entirety, including the mind and will. But Augustine's views regarding the transmission of original sin have had a profound impact on much of Protestant theology. The history of the doctrine in its Protestant expression is particularly noteworthy.

The discussion of sin among orthodox Protestant theologians* has consisted of two foci: the initial act of disobedience by Adam and Eve (resulting in their spiritual separation from God due to a loss of personal righteousness, the inevitability of physical death and the threat of eternal judgment) and the consequences of their sin for their progeny (the entire human race). The issue of the initial disobedience was seldom disputed throughout most of the nineteenth century because most theologians embraced the historicity of the biblical account, but the consequences of Adam's sin for humanity were vigorously debated. The controversy centered on two issues: (1) the manner in which humans participate in Adam's disobedience and (2) its effect on the human race. Theologians questioned whether guilt (i.e., culpability for punishment) is alien—something that is reckoned apart from individual participation—or exclusively the result of personal agency? Does guilt result in depravity which is transmitted through the human race and bears fruit in acts of sin, or is guilt a consequence of either an inherited sinful nature or propensity?

Augustinian Views. In American theology, the most notable discussions of sin have taken place in the Reformed tradition. Within both the Lutheran* and Reformed* traditions, many theologians have built on the Augustinian tradition and adopted a view of the consequences of Adam's first sin that may be termed *immediate* or *antecedent imputation.* The essence of this view is that all people are born already under God's wrath, that their lack of original righteousness results in inherent sin in which all human capacities are corrupted, and that sinful actions, being a result of those corrupted faculties, are not the ground for condemnation.

During the nineteenth century this view evoked considerable discussion. The focus of controversy was the manner in which Adam's progeny participated in his first sin. Federalists (known also as nonparticipationalists or representationalists), such as Charles Hodge* of Princeton* Seminary, advocated a view that had emerged simultaneously with Covenant Theology* in the seventeenth century. They argued that Adam's sin, and no one else's, was the judicial ground of condemnation. Adam's sin was reckoned to be that of the race, though it actually was not, because Adam's act as the first person was judged to be the action of all persons.

Seminalists (also called participationalists or realists), such as James H. Thornwell,* W. G. T. Shedd* and A. H. Strong,* argued that the descendants of Adam directly participated in Adam's sin. Since all were in Adam, all cooperated with Adam in his transgression and therefore justly merited his condemnation. Other theologians, such as Robert L. Dabney* (and more recently John Murray*), have combined facets of both the federalist and the seminalist perspective, suggesting that neither view exclusively expresses the relationship between Adam and the human race.

Another way of understanding the consequences of Adam's first sin on the race is known as *mediate* or *consequent imputation.* On the assumption that guilt arises out of individual freedom, advocates of this perspective have maintained that guilt is strictly personal and is not reckoned apart from human participation in sin. This view was initially set forth by Josua Placaeus, a seventeenth-century theologian of the Reformed school of Saumur (France), and is also known as *dispositionalism* or *transmissionalism.* In essence, it maintains that humans are subject to God's judgment for their own sinful exercises—whether affections, desires, intentions or volitions—that spring from a nature inherited from Adam. Their corrupt capacities are not a result of God's judgment. By participating in Adam the race is born with a bent or propensity toward sin, but with no accompanying liability. It is the actual sin that activates negative potentiality.

Though this view is erroneously said to have been advocated by Jonathan Edwards* in the eighteenth century, it was adopted by many of his followers in the nineteenth century and was a component of the New England Theology.* Theologians such as Samuel Hopkins,* Nathaniel Emmons,* Timothy Dwight,* Leonard Woods,* Moses Stuart* and Nathaniel Taylor* rejected the ideas of imputed guilt and derived depravity, attempting to escape any implication that God was responsible for sin. Contact with New Divinity Congregationalists* brought these ideas into Presbyterian thought and contributed to the 1837 schism between Old* and New* School Presbyterians. Old School Presbyterians followed the lead of Princeton Seminary and Charles Hodge, while New School* Presbyterians, such as Albert Barnes* and Henry B. Smith,* followed the innovations of the New England divines.*

Arminian Views. Theologians within the Arminian* tradition took their cue neither from Augustine or Placaeus, but from John Wesley* and Isaac Watts (1674-1748). The "prince of Wesleyan* theologians," Richard Watson (1781-1833), provides a paradigm for understanding this perspective. Watson attempted the first synthesis of Methodist* theology in his *Theological Institutes* (1823-1824). This work was widely used in American Wesleyan schools such as Vanderbilt, where Thomas O. Summers, professor of theology, published an edition of his work in 1874.

Watson, who seems to have been more dependent on Watts than either Arminius or Wesley, advocated a view of the consequences of Adam's first sin known as *deprivation* or *liability.* In essence, and unlike Wesley who appears Reformed at this point, Watson perceived the result of Adam's sin not as imputed guilt and inherent corruption, but simply as a lack of original righteousness. The consequences of being born neither with penal affliction nor in a state of mere potentiality is that this divinely constituted but deprived state inevitably leads to voluntary depravity because preventative assistance was removed in Adam. While no one is born with alien guilt, all are born without the vital influence of God. The result is that humans are incapable of pleasing God. Watson defined this as the state of spiritual death.

The inability to please God is not sin itself, but it invariably leads to human pollution, corruption and depravity which, in turn, produces actual transgressions. The obstacle of not being able to please God is removed by a prevenient or preparatory grace described as a universal application of Christ's atonement. This makes it possible for individuals to embrace the gospel. Thereafter the will is the only hindrance to procuring redemption. Advocates of this view assert that it preserves the justice of God and the freedom of humanity.

Modern Views. In the twentieth century the concept of sin has been radically reinterpreted. The current theological consensus seems more in harmony with Augustine's fifth-century opponent

Pelagius than with any other source. Pelagius suggested that the relationship between Adam and his progeny was neither organic nor negative; it was environmental, sociological and psychological. The injury of Adam's sin to the race was merely that it set a bad example or precedent that humans have emulated.

Reinhold Niebuhr,* for example, perceived sin as an inevitable result of the tensions between human freedom and human limitation or finitude. It arises out of the personal struggle between what one ought to do and what one personally desires to do and is frequently exhibited in pride and sensuality. Sin is not related to human nature so much as human personality. Paul Tillich* psychologized sin by suggesting that it consists in estrangement from the true self—it is a perceived sense of alienation. Both of these recent attempts to define the human dilemma focus on subjective experience. The traditional views were built on a deeper, objective scenario.

BIBLIOGRAPHY. G. P. Hutchinson, *The Problem of Original Sin in American Presbyterian Theology* (1972); B. Kuklick, *Churchmen and Philosophers* (1985); J. Murray, *The Imputation of Adam's Sin* (1979); B. B. Warfield, "Imputation" in *Studies in Theology* (1988); R. Watson, *Theological Institutes: or, A View of the Evidences, Doctrines, Morals, and Institutions of Christianity,* ed., T. O. Summers (1874); E. Yarnold, *The Theology of Original Sin* (1971).   J. D. Hannah

Sinclair, Upton Beall (1878-1968). American writer and advocate of reform. Born in Baltimore, Maryland, Sinclair grew up in New York City and graduated from the College of the City of New York (B.A., 1897). His writing career began by publishing children's stories while he was a student. He went on to do graduate studies in literature at Columbia University,* though he did not complete a degree.

Sinclair's novel *The Jungle* (1906) brought national acclaim for its exposé of Chicago machine politics and the unsanitary processing of meat products. The description of food processing was so vivid that it led to the passage of pure food laws and is still read as a classic of the reform-novel genre.

His thoughts on religion were expressed in *The Profits of Religion* (1918), Sinclair's manifesto on the evils of the institutional church, published in paperback at his own expense, in simple language and popular illustrations the book argued that Jesus was actually a proletarian rebel against the rich. But within three hundred years of Jesus' death

his revolutionary ministry had been forgotten and the rich and powerful had turned the church into a haven of privilege and hypocrisy. Thereafter, the story of the church was the story of proletarian rebels trying to return the church to Jesus' original vision. Sinclair looked for the day in which this proletarian revolution would take root in America, a day in which "all those men who stay in the Church and pretend to believe nonsense, because it affords an easy living, will suddenly realize that it is possible to earn a living outside." Indeed, he predicted that "by the year 1950 all Catholic authorities will be denying that the Church ever opposed Socialism—true Socialism."

BIBLIOGRAPHY. *DAB* 8; F. Dell, *Upton Sinclair* (1927).   J. E. Mennell

Sister. A woman who publicly professes simple vows or promises, usually obedience, chastity and poverty, in a religious community of women. Most congregations* of sisters are Catholic*; a few are Anglican.* Unlike cloistered nuns,* sisters are actively engaged in education,* social work or the health professions. The majority of Catholic sisters today no longer wear a distinctive dress or habit; those who do wear a modified garb. Their mode of life as vowed, active service within the Church was officially accepted by Rome in 1841 as a new form of religious life when it recognized the Sisters of Mercy.*

BIBLIOGRAPHY. W. B. Ryan, "Sister, Religious," *NCE* 13.   M. L. Schneider

Sisters of Charity. This title includes numerous Catholic sisterhoods of diverse origin, many of whom follow the tradition of St. Vincent de Paul. With St. Louise de Marillac he founded the Daughters of Charity in Paris in 1633. Exempt from cloister, they engaged in educational and social works of charity. Presently, the Daughters of Charity of St. Vincent de Paul include a worldwide membership of more than thirty-two thousand.

Many women's congregations in the U.S. are called Sisters of Charity. The first, the Sisters of Charity of St. Joseph, was founded by Elizabeth Ann Seton* in 1809 at Emmitsburg, Maryland. By 1830 they were in Philadelphia, New York, Baltimore, Boston and St. Louis, where they pioneered in education, health care and social service. In 1850 the Emmitsburg group joined the French Daughters of Charity. This development prompted the formation of several independent congregations of Sisters of Charity, such as in New York and Cincinnati, where sisters or bishops* objected to international jurisdiction or the introduction of

French customs. Six groups in the U.S. trace their roots to Mother Seton: the Daughters of Charity, Emmitsburg, Maryland (1809); and the Sisters of Charity of New York (1846); Halifax (1849); Cincinnati (1852); Convent Station, New Jersey (1859); and Seton Hill (Greensburg), Pennsylvania (1870).

Other American foundations of Sisters of Charity include the Sisters of Charity of Nazareth, Kentucky, established in 1812 near Bardstown. The Sisters of Charity of Leavenworth, Kansas, date to 1828 when a small group of sisters, originally from Nazareth, emigrated from Nashville, Tennessee, to Kansas. The Sisters of Charity of Our Lady of Mercy were founded in 1829 by Bishop John England* in Charleston, South Carolina, and the Sisters of Charity of the Blessed Virgin Mary, Dubuque, Iowa, began in Philadelphia in 1833 with the Irish-born Mary Frances Clarke and four companions. In addition to educational institutions from primary through college levels, the Sisters of Charity have been noted for their service in the Civil* and Spanish American Wars,* in hospitals and in institutions for special needs. Present membership in the mentioned groups is close to thirteen thousand.

BIBLIOGRAPHY. P. Coste, *The Life and Works of St. Vincent de Paul,* 3 vols. (1952); E. M. Kelly, *Numerous Choirs: A Chronicle of Elizabeth Bayley Seton and Her Spiritual Daughters,* vol. 1, *The Seton Years, 1774-1821* (1981).   P. Byrne

Sisters of Mercy. Roman Catholic* congregations of women religious.* The title *Sisters of Mercy* (RSM) includes all those communities of women religious who trace their lineage from, and claim as their founder, Catherine Elizabeth McAuley, whose Institute of Mercy had its inception in Dublin, Ireland, in 1831. In addition to the three simple vows of poverty, chastity and obedience, the Sisters of Mercy bind themselves by a distinctive fourth vow, the service of the poor, the sick and the ignorant.

In 1843, under the intrepid leadership of Sister M. Frances Xavier Warde,* seven Sisters of Mercy heeded the request of Bishop Michael O'Connor, first bishop of Pittsburgh, to respond to the needs of the poor in the near wilderness of western Pennsylvania. From this beginning, Sisters of Mercy now serves throughout the U.S. and its territories, as well as in Central and South America. Comprising many independent congregations as well as various unions, membership in the Federation of the Sisters of Mercy of the Americas presently totals 8,292.

Historically involved in education, health care and various forms of social work, in 1847 Sisters of Mercy established the first permanent hospital west of the Allegheny Mountains in Pittsburgh and now sponsor more than 130 hospitals and health-care facilities. Active in both elementary and secondary education, Sisters of Mercy also sponsor nineteen colleges, which currently enroll almost 30,000 students. Among countless forms of social service, Sisters of Mercy demonstrate a particular commitment to ministries of housing and shelter, ranging from orphanages to residences for the elderly and shelters for the homeless.

BIBLIOGRAPHY. Sr. M. B. Degnan, *Mercy Unto Thousands* (1957); Sr. M. T. A. Carroll, *Leaves from the Annals of the Sisters of Mercy,* 4 vols. (1881).
                                        I. Keiss

Six-Principle Baptists. An Arminian* Baptist tradition maintaining the ordinance* of the laying on of hands.* During the Interregnum some English Baptists adopted Hebrews 6:1-2 as a six-point confessional standard: repentance, faith, baptism,* laying on of hands, the resurrection of the dead and eternal life. Debate arose among General Baptists* concerning whether or not this required a new church ordinance: the laying of hands on new converts. John Griffith's *God's Oracle and Christ's Doctrine* (1655) became the definitive defense for churches affirming this. The Standard Confession (1660) required that new believers submit to the laying on of hands in order to "receive the promise of the Holy Spirit." But because the general assembly refused to adopt the Six Principles as its only official standard, Six-Principle Baptists separated and established their own assembly (1690). Their theology was Arminian, and they practiced closed communion.

Six-Principle Baptists appeared at an early date as minorities among the first Baptist churches in America—Providence and Newport—most of whose members were Calvinistic.* By 1652 they had become the majority at Providence. By 1665 they had left the Newport congregation and formed a church under William Vaughan. Though some Particular Baptists in America laid hands on converts and Regular Baptists* sanctioned it in their Philadelphia Confession (1742), this practice was more characteristic of General Baptists. It visibly symbolized the difference between two traditions known as Five-Principle (Particular) and Six-Principle (General) Baptists. By the 1670s several Rhode Island Six-Principle churches had formed what perhaps was the first Baptist association in America. In the 1940s three churches identified as Six-Principle Baptists listed 280 members, living mostly in Rhode Island and Pennsylvania.

BIBLIOGRAPHY. W. L. Lumpkin, *Baptist Confessions of Faith* (1978); H. L. McBeth, *The Baptist Heritage* (1987). J. T. Spivey

Skelton, Samuel (1584-1634). First pastor of the Congregational* church of Salem, Massachusetts. Born in Lincolnshire, England, Skelton graduated from Clare College, University of Cambridge (B.A., 1611; M.A., 1615). After being Church of England* rector* at Sempringham, he may have served as private Puritan* chaplain* to the Earl of Lincoln. In England he sought to implement rudimentary Congregational ideals by barring unregenerates from the Lord's Supper,* though insisting he was non-separatist. An organizer of the Massachusetts Bay Company, he and his family helped lead the first settlement in 1629. He and Salem colleague Francis Higginson,* who became the church's teacher, organized the church strictly along Congregational lines. The famous Salem covenant reads: "We Covenant with the Lord and one with an other; and doe bynd our selves in the presence of God, to walke together in all his waies, according as he is pleased to reveale himself unto us in his Blessed word of truth." After selection by lay members, Skelton was re-ordained as pastor by "3 or 4 of ye gravest members of ye church." Skelton thus helped set the pattern of New England Congregationalism.

BIBLIOGRAPHY. C. Mather, *Magnalia Christi Americana* (1702); P. Miller, *Orthodoxy in Massachusetts* (1933). C. E. Hambrick-Stowe

Slattery, Charles Lewis (1867-1930). Episcopal* bishop.* Born in Pittsburgh, Pennsylvania, Slattery graduated from Harvard* in 1891 and from the Episcopal Theological School, Cambridge, in 1894. He began his ministry as rector* of St. Andrew's Church, Ayer, Massachusetts. He was dean of the Cathedral of Our Merciful Savior, Faribault, Minnesota (1896-1907), rector of Christ Church Cathedral, Springfield, Massachusetts (1907-1910), and rector of Grace Church, New York (1910-1922). On October 31, 1922, he was consecrated* bishop coadjutor of Massachusetts and became bishop on June 1, 1927, when Bishop William Lawrence retired. Slattery was a sensitive pastor and an outstanding scholar. He wrote twenty-five books and published numerous articles and occasional papers. He was general chairman of the Church Congress in the U.S. and was chairman of the commission on the revision of the *Book of Common Prayer,* which was published in 1928.

BIBLIOGRAPHY. *DAB* IX; H. C. Robbins, *Charles Lewis Slattery* (1931). D. S. Armentrout

Slattery, John Richard (1851-1926). Catholic missionary* to Southern African-Americans and modernist.* Slattery was born in New York City of Irish immigrant parents. In 1873 he left Columbia College School of Law to enter the seminary* for the English Foreign Mission Society at Mill Hill, London, England. Ordained* in 1877 he served successively as rector of St. Francis Xavier Church in Baltimore and U.S. provincial for Mill Hill (1878-1883), evangelist among the African-Americans in the Richmond area (1884-1887) and rector of St. Joseph's Seminary in Baltimore (1888-1902), which he founded to train priests for the African-American missions in the U.S.

In 1892 he arranged the separation from England of five Mill Hill priests who formed St. Joseph's Society of the Sacred Heart, the Josephites, as they are still known today. From 1892 until 1903 Slattery served as the Josephites's first superior general. He published widely on the "Negro question" and came to be recognized as the leading Catholic spokesperson on it, refusing to separate evangelization from the social and educational amelioration of African-Americans. During his twenty-five years as a missionary, Slattery brought unity and vision to Catholic evangelization efforts. Convinced that success required African-American leadership, he championed the cause of African-American priests and integrated St. Joseph's Seminary. He pioneered the use of African-American catechists on the missions and started a college for them in Alabama modeled on Booker T. Washington's* Tuskegee Institute (*See* Black Catholics).

During the 1890s he was closely tied to the progressive or Americanist party. The Vatican's 1899 censure of Americanism,* added to his disillusionment with church support for the missions, precipitated a religious crisis from which he never recovered. By 1904 he had concluded that Catholicism and modern science were irreconcilable. He renounced church and priesthood in 1906, engaged in a few years of religious polemics and then spent the rest of his life as an attorney. He died in Monaco, leaving the modest fortune he had acquired through his inheritance to the New York Public Library.

BIBLIOGRAPHY. W. L. Portier, "John R. Slattery's Vision for the Evangelization of American Blacks," *USCH* 5 (1986):19-44. W. L. Portier

Slavic Gospel Association. An evangelical* mission agency ministering to Soviets and Soviet immigrants. Initially called the Russian Gospel Association, the Slavic Gospel Association was organized in 1934 by Peter Deyneka, Sr., to evangelize* Russian-Slavic emigrés and minister to the church behind the Iron Curtain. Peter Deyneka immigrated to the U.S. from Russia in 1914 and in 1920 became a Christian during a service at Chicago's Moody Memorial Church. After his conversion,* on the encouragement of Dr. Paul W. Rood, he developed a radio and literature ministry. By the mid-1980s Slavic Gospel Association personnel were involved in over ten thousand broadcasts to the Soviet Union from ten international radio stations.

The Slavic Gospel Association is also involved in translating and distributing various types of Christian literature to the Soviet Union and Eastern Europe. It also ministers to immigrants through a Russian Bible Institute in Argentina and an Institute of Slavic Studies in Wheaton, Illinois.

Peter Deyneka, Sr., sometimes called "Peter Dynamite," retired in 1975 and died in July 1987. He was succeeded by his son Peter Deyneka, Jr., as president of the Association. The Slavic Gospel Association presently has its headquarters in Wheaton, Illinois.

BIBLIOGRAPHY. A. Deyneka and P. Deyneka, Jr., *Christians in the Shadow of the Kremlin* (1974); P. Deyneka, Sr., *Traveling with God through Soviet Russia, Siberia and Other Countries* (1937); N. B. Rohrer and P. Deyneka, Jr., *Peter Dynamite: Twice Born Russian* (1975).   G. W. Carlson

Small, Albion Woodbury (1854-1926). Professor of sociology. Born in Buckfield, Maine, to a Baptist* family, Small was educated at Colby College (A.B., 1876), Newton Theological Institute (1876-1879), the universities of Berlin and Leipzig, and Johns Hopkins (Ph.D., 1889), where he studied under Richard Ely. He was professor of political economy at Colby (1881-1888) and later president of the college (1889-1892). When the University of Chicago was founded in 1892, Small was invited to head the sociology department, one of the first in the country. He wrote several books and edited the *American Journal of Sociology.* Like his teacher, Richard Ely, Small's understanding of social science was informed by his religious beliefs. He was concerned with the philosophical bases and the ethical implications of his field, and believed that sociology would teach people how to relate to fellow human beings and solve the problems of society. He frequently lectured on these topics at conferences on the church and social problems.   L. W. Japinga

Smalley, John (1734-1820). New Divinity* Congregational* minister.* Born at Lebanon (now Columbia), Connecticut, Smalley graduated from Yale University* (B.A., 1756) and spent a year studying theology* under Joseph Bellamy,* a prominent New England theologian.* In 1757 he became pastor of the Congregational church at New Britain, Connecticut, a position he held for sixty-three years. He, along with Bellamy, Samuel Hopkins,* Jonathan Edwards the Younger,* Nathaniel Emmons* and Timothy Dwight,* played a part in the New Divinity* Movement. In his *Two Discourses on the Consistency of the Sinner's Inability to Comply with the Gospel,* he developed the "governmental" view of the atonement, arguing that since atonement* flows from divine benevolence, Christ's death makes it possible for God to pardon all men, but it does not make it necessary for him to do so. Smalley exerted a wide influence through his writings and the training of theological students in his home, one of whom was Nathanael Emmons.* He died in New Britain on June 1, 1820.

BIBLIOGRAPHY. *AAP* 1; W. Walker, *A History of the Congregational Churches in the United States* (1894); J. Haroutunian, *Piety v. Moralism: The Passing of the New England Theology* (1964).

R. L. Troutman

Smith, Alfred Emanuel (1873-1944). Governor of New York and first Roman Catholic* presidential nominee. The grandson of Italian, German and Irish immigrants, Smith was born in New York City's Lower East Side. As the protégé of a Tammany Hall precinct boss, Smith was elected to the state assembly in 1903, where he loyally served the machine while simultaneously aligning himself with independent reform groups. A succession of positions in state and city governments culminated in his election as governor in 1918 and re-election in 1922, 1924 and 1926. There he gained national recognition for his reorganization of the state government; improved benefits for workers, women and children; prison reform; a modest public housing program; and limited government regulation of hydroelectric power. These accomplishments, the national publicity given him as New York's governor and the lack of effective opposition gained him the Democratic party's presidential nomination in 1928, making him the first Roman Catholic chosen by a major political party.

Smith's religious affiliation, his opposition to the

Eighteenth Amendment, as well as his urban and immigrant origins alarmed many Protestants,* supporters of national prohibition, and rural and small-town dwellers. A "devoutly pious" Catholic, almost childlike in his faith, Smith responded to religious attacks by pointing out that while he obeyed his Church in matters of faith and morals, he recognized no such authority in social, economic and political affairs. He believed strongly in the separation of church and state.* His stance as a lay* representative of a "liberalized" American Catholicism likely strengthened those tenets within the American Church. Yet, he was unable either to satisfy the honest concerns of non-Catholic Americans or to confound religious bigots. He decisively lost the presidential election of 1928.

Smith's nomination did, however, symbolize the rise of Catholic, urban Americans of recent immigrant origins to the highest level of American politics, thereby furthering his country's evolution from a homogeneous to a heterogeneous society. However, the apparently strong reaction to Smith's religious affiliation revealed that not all Americans accepted these changes. A Roman Catholic presidential nominee was unthinkable for many years to come.

BIBLIOGRAPHY. D. Burner, *The Politics of Provincialism* (1968); *DAB* 3; O. Handlin, *Al Smith and His America* (1958).

G. F. Goodwin

Smith, Amanda Berry (1837-1915). African-American evangelist* and missionary* to India and Africa. Born a slave in Long Green, Maryland, her father purchased his own freedom and that of his family. Smith then worked in domestic service. Her attendance at Phoebe Palmer's* Tuesday meetings may have introduced her to the doctrine of entire sanctification.* In September 1868, while listening to a sermon by Methodist* minister* John Inskip,* she was sanctified. The following year her husband and youngest child died, and thus freed from family responsibilities, she began preaching in African-American churches in the New York and New Jersey area. By 1870 she was a full-time evangelist and a familiar figure on the Holiness* camp meeting* circuit.

In 1878 Smith went to England as an itinerant preacher and left England in 1879 to become a missionary in India for two years. Late in 1881 she returned to England before leaving for Monrovia, Liberia, in 1882, where she worked as a Methodist* missionary until 1889. She spent a year doing evangelistic work in England, Ireland and Scotland

before returning to the U.S. on September 5, 1890.

Smith preached in churches on the East Coast, retiring in 1892 to Harvey, Illinois, outside of Chicago. In 1895 she began building the Amanda Smith Orphan's Home for Colored Children. The orphanage was completed in 1899, and she devoted the rest of her life to its operation.

BIBLIOGRAPHY. A. Smith, *An Autobiography of Mrs. Amanda Smith, The Colored Evangelist* (1893); M. H. Cadbury, *The Life of Amanda Smith* (1916); *NAW* 3.

L. J. Edwards

Smith, Benjamin Mosby (1811-1893). Presbyterian* seminary* professor, church statesman and advocate of public education. Born in Powhatan County, Virginia, he studied at Hampden-Sydney College (B.A., 1829) and then studied theology at Union Theological Seminary (Virginia). He was ordained* in 1835. After a year of study at the University of Halle in Germany (1836-1837), he held pastorates at Danville (1838-1840), Waynesboro (1840-1845) and Staunton (1845-1853), Virginia. In 1854 he was elected professor of Oriental literature at Union Seminary.

Union Seminary was impoverished by the Civil War,* and Smith made numerous journeys to Northern friends, soliciting support. Within the first twelve months after the War, he raised $50,000 and later was instrumental in obtaining munificent gifts from Cyrus H. McCormick* and Mrs. George Brown of Baltimore. A person of irenic disposition and blessed with personal charm, Smith was a moderate among Southern Presbyterians during Reconstruction, willing to discuss reconciliation with the North, but not on terms which would require Southern apology. His election as moderator of his denomination's 1876 General Assembly was indicative of the personal support he enjoyed. Smith was also a strong advocate of public education in Virginia. Following his European study he had prepared a report (1839) on the Prussian educational system and urged a similar plan in Virginia. From 1871 to 1882 he was superintendent of public education in Prince Edward County.

Through his varied career, Smith was to become one of the more influential Southern Presbyterian* leaders of his time.

BIBLIOGRAPHY. *DAB* IX; F. R. Flournoy, *Benjamin Mosby Smith* (1967). W. J. Wade

Smith, Gerald Birney (1868-1929). Liberal* theologian.* Born in Middlefield, Massachusetts, Smith was educated at Brown University* (B.A.,

1891); Columbia University* (M.A., 1898); Union Theological Seminary,* New York (B.D., 1898). He also studied in Marburg, Berlin and Paris. He taught at Oberlin Academy (1892), Worcester Academy (1893-1895) and at the University of Chicago* Divinity School from 1900 until his death in 1929.

Deeply influenced by Albrecht Ritschl (1822-1889) and Wilhelm Herrmann (1846-1922), Smith's theological liberalism emphasized the centrality of human experience and was critical of authoritarianism of any sort. His search for a suitably scientific procedural method in theology—what he called empirical theology*—was advanced in a series of journal articles in *The American Journal of Theology* and again in his essay "Systematic Theology and Christian Ethics" in *A Guide to the Study of the Christian Religion* (1916), which he also edited. His works include: *Social Idealism and the Changing Theology* (1913); *A Guide to the Study of the Christian Religion* (editor) (1916); and *Current Christian Thinking* (1928). With Shailer Mathews he edited *A Dictionary of Religion and Ethics* (1921). Smith was also editor of the *American Journal of Theology* and its successor, the *Journal of Religion,* from 1909 until his death. Smith was an activist in Social Gospel* efforts, and his later emphasis on aesthetics bridged the socio-historical and the naturalist phases of American modernism.*

BIBLIOGRAPHY. *DAB* IX.   K. S. Sawyer

Smith, Gerald L. K. (1898-1976). Disciples of Christ* minister,* politician and nativist.* Born in Padeeville, Wisconsin, Smith became a major figure in the fundamentalist* far-right movement during the 1940s and 1950s. After serving as a pastor* in several Disciples of Christ churches, he began his political career as a spokesperson for Governor Huey Long's *Share the Wealth* program in Louisiana.

Most of Smith's early political rhetoric was aimed at President Roosevelt's New Deal, which he felt led to dictatorial power and the implementation of a planned economy. He associated himself with Francis Townsend's Old Age Revolving Pension Plan and Henry Ford's attack on Jewish influence in American life and politics, expressed in such works as *The International Jew.*

After World War 2,* Smith increasingly alienated himself from mainstream American politics and expressed a paternalistic segregationism, along with an explicit anti-Semitism. His organization, the Christian Nationalist Crusade, was developed on the principle that Christian character "is the

basis of all real Americanism." His platform included a plea for race purity, fear of a Communist influence on the U.S. Supreme Court and dangers of Jewish influence on American social and economic policy.

Smith expressed his anti-Communist ideas in the magazine *The Cross and the Flag* and argued that the "materialists, the secularists, the Jews, the pagans and the Communists realize that they cannot capture America and rule America permanently as long as we remain a Christian nation." He died in California on April 15, 1976.

BIBLIOGRAPHY. L. P. Ribuffo, *The Old Christian Right: The Protestant Far Right from the Great Depression to the Cold War* (1983); G. L. K. Smith, *The Great Issues* (1959).   G. W. Carlson

Smith, Hannah Whitall (1832-1911). Holiness* writer and speaker. Raised in a strict Philadelphia Quaker* home, as a young woman she encountered religious doubts. She married Robert Pearsall Smith* in 1851 and during the 1858 urban prayer meeting revivals,* she and her husband committed their lives to God. Some years later, at a Methodist* camp meeting, Robert experienced an emotional "baptism of the Holy Spirit."* Hannah desperately sought to have a similar ecstatic religious experience,* but it eluded her. Frustrated by her quest for a deeper and emotional confirmation of her faith, she finally admitted she was "a dry old stick." But in 1867 she found the experience she had long sought.

The Smiths held meetings promoting holiness in the U.S., but from 1873 to 1874 they were popular speakers at holiness meetings in England, the immediate predecessors to the famous Keswick conferences.* Though Hannah was highly respected as a devotional* speaker, her ministry was not without controversy. Because of her universalist beliefs, some conference organizers sought to cancel their lectures, but the Smiths' supporters prevailed, and Hannah was later dubbed "the angel of the churches." Her popularity soared, while her husband's quickly faded. In 1875 he was accused of teaching antinomianism* and taking indecent liberties with a young woman. His meetings were cancelled, and he and Hannah returned to America. She continued her public ministry, while he remained in semi-seclusion for most of the remaining twenty-five years of his life.

Although she was not active in the nineteenth-century feminist* movement, Hannah strongly supported women's involvement in ministry. In 1895 she returned to England to participate in a promotional effort for church women. One of nearly two hundred women who preached for a Sunday in chapels in London and neighboring areas, she wrote: "It was a wonderful thing to get an entrance for women into so many places of worship in London, and the funny thing was that when our supply of women failed and we offered men, nobody would have them! No wonder."

The Christian's Secret of a Happy Life, first published in 1875, was influential in its time and remains a popular devotional guide today. Her "secret" can be summed up in her analogy of a Christian as clay: "In order for a lump of clay to be made into a beautiful vessel, it must be entirely abandoned to the potter, and must lie passive in his hands."

See also HIGHER CHRISTIAN LIFE; SANCTIFICATION.

BIBLIOGRAPHY. *DAB* IX; M. Henry, *The Secret Life of Hannah Whitall Smith* (1984); *NAW* 3.

R. A. Tucker

Smith, Henry Boynton (1815-1877). New School* Presbyterian* theologian* and historian. Born of Unitarian* parents in Portland, Maine, Smith was converted* during a revival* at Bowdoin College and later prepared for the ministry* at Andover* and Bangor seminaries. He also studied in Germany from 1838 to 1840, where he was heavily influenced by German philosophy and theology, especially that of Georg W. F. Hegel and the mediating theology of Friedrich A. G. Tholuck, Ernst W. Hengstenberg and Johann A. W. Neander. Smith was appointed professor of mental and moral philosophy at Amherst College in 1847 and moved to Union Theological Seminary* in New York City in 1850 to teach first church history and then systematic theology* (1853-1874).

Smith exercised his greatest influence through his efforts to reconcile the principles of Edwardsean theology and German-inspired philosophy for an American audience. As a historian, he encouraged the teaching of the history of doctrine and discussed the nature of historical progress, consciously modelling himself on German historical thought but also on Jonathan Edwards's *History of the Work of Redemption.* As a theologian, he disagreed sharply with Horace Bushnell's* dismissal of theology as an enterprise irrelevant to faith. However, he conceded that New England Theology* had wasted its energies on abstractions, and he shifted the center of his theological attention away from freedom of the will and other Edwardsean questions to Christology* as the only way to stave off rationalism.

His essays on the New England Theology, as collected in *Faith and Philosophy* (1877), are among the most prescient examples of theological criticism in nineteenth-century Calvinism. His lecture notes were published posthumously by W. S. Karr as *Introduction to Christian Theology* (1883), *Apologetics* (1885) and *System of Christian Theology* (1886).

BIBLIOGRAPHY. *DAB* IX; S. Stearns, *Henry Boynton Smith* (1892); B. Kuklick, *Churchmen and Philosophers* (1985). A. C. Guelzo

Smith, Henry Preserved (1847-1927). Presbyterian* minister,* Old Testament scholar and educator. Born in Troy, Ohio, the son of New England Congregationalists* who became New School* Presbyterians* when they moved west, Smith attended Amherst College as an undergraduate. After graduation in 1869, he studied theology* at Lane Theological Seminary in Cincinnati and then at the University of Berlin. On his return to the U.S. in 1874, Smith taught church history for one year at Lane Seminary before becoming professor of Hebrew. He returned to Germany to study at the University of Leipzig from 1876 to 1877 in order to prepare himself more adequately for his duties at Lane. His efforts were rewarded with his appointment as professor of Old Testament, a position which he held at Lane from 1877 to 1893.

Smith's scholarship led him to accept critical conclusions about the Old Testament which many conservatives in the Presbyterian Church (U.S.A.) regarded as an attack upon the infallibility of the Bible.* Although he rarely published these ideas, Smith made his views known to the public when he defended Charles Augustus Briggs,* a leading protagonist of higher criticism, before the Presbyterian General Assembly* of 1891. Alarmed by his remarks, the Presbytery* of Cincinnati tried Smith for heresy,* found him guilty of denying the verbal inspiration and inerrancy* of the Bible, and suspended him from the ministry in 1892. His views were subsequently published in *Inspiration and Inerrancy* (1893).

Between 1893 and 1898 he held no official position but used this time to publish several studies on the Old Testament. In 1898 he took a position at Amherst College as a professor of biblical literature. In 1907 he moved to Meadville Theological Seminary to teach the history of religions, and then in 1915 he became the librarian at New York's Union Theological Seminary.* In 1925 he retired and lived in Poughkeepsie until his death. Among his publications in Old Testament studies were *A Critical and Exegetical Commentary on the Books of Samuel* (1899), *Old Testament History* (1903) and *The Religion of Israel* (1914).

BIBLIOGRAPHY. *DAB* IX; *DARB;* M. A. Noll, *Between Faith and Criticism* (1986); *NCAB* 23.

D. G. Hart

Smith, Hezekiah (1737-1805). Baptist* pastor. Born on Long Island and reared at Morristown, New Jersey, Smith came under the influence of the Reverend John Gano,* who baptized* him and encouraged him to pursue higher education in preparation for the ministry.* Consequently, he attended Hopewell Academy and the College of New Jersey,* from which he graduated in 1762. Smith went immediately to the South as an itinerant* evangelist.* He toured for fifteen months and was ordained* while in Charleston. After the tour Smith was influential in the founding of Rhode Island College, which later became Brown University.* He served as visiting preacher in many New England churches, and in 1776 became pastor of a Baptist church in Haverhill, Massachusetts.

During a forty-year pastorate, Smith saw the congregation become a large, influential church. He became a leader of Baptists in the region and a strong proponent of missionary* endeavors, including leadership in establishing eighty-six new churches. He was intensely loyal to the causes of national independence and religious liberty.* Smith took leave from his pulpit during the Revolutionary War* to serve as an Army chaplain* under General George Washington,* with whom a close personal friendship developed and was sustained during ensuing years. At age sixty-eight Smith suffered a paralysis and died on January 22, 1805. Smith's journal, which covered the entire forty-two years of his ministry, is a valuable personal account of the Revolutionary era.

BIBLIOGRAPHY. *AAP* 6; *DAB* IX; R. A. Guild, *Chaplain Smith and the Baptists* (1885).

F. A. Teague

Smith, John "Raccoon" (1784-1868). Kentucky farmer and early Restoration Movement* preacher.* Born in Sullivan County, East Tennessee, Smith was raised in great poverty. His nickname, "Raccoon," referred to his habitual raccoonskin cap. Having lost two children to a cabin fire and his wife, Anna, to a deadly illness, as well as having narrowly escaped death to fever himself, Smith became convinced that the Lord had chastened him for his proud ambitions. Influenced by his encounter with Alexander Campbell* in 1824, Smith resolved to "preach the Ancient Gospel" and became a Baptist* farmer-preacher in Kentucky.

Smith was present at the 1831 Christmas meeting in Georgetown, Kentucky, when the Stone and Campbellite movements merged. At the 1832 meeting in Lexington, Kentucky, Smith represented Campbell's "Disciples," while Barton W. Stone* represented the "Christians." Expressing the sentiments of the two movements, Smith urged, "Let us be no longer Campbellites or Stoneites, New Lights* or Old Lights,* or any other kind of lights, but let us come to the Bible,* and to the Bible alone, as the only book in the world that can give us all the Light we need."

Smith then rode with John Rogers, visiting the movments' churches in an effort to cement the union of the two like-minded groups. For three years Smith served the new churches as an evangelist.*

BIBLIOGRAPHY. J. A. Williams, *Life of Elder John Smith: With Some Account of the Rise and Progress of the Current Reformation* (1904).

T. L. Miethe

Smith, Joseph Henry (1855-1946). Methodist* evangelist* and theologian.* Converted,* sanctified* and licensed* to preach* (1874) in the Central Methodist Episcopal Church, Philadelphia, Smith was inspired by William Taylor's* "faith missions" and went to Georgia (1875-1881) as a missionary. Returning to the East Pennsylvania Conference of the Methodist Episcopal Church, he was ordained* (1885) after following a course of independent study. He joined the National Camp-meeting Association for the Promotion of Holiness* (NCAPH) in 1883 and served as an evangelist by conference appointment from 1902 to 1923. Concerned for education, he served as director of the School of Theology at Hale College, Meridian, Mississippi (1907-1912). With the NCAPH he established short-term continuing education courses for clergy* and evangelists known as Itinerant Institutes (or as "School of the Prophets" and "School of Pentecostal Methods"). Smith cooperated with Ida Vennard in the Chicago Evangelistic Institute, where he taught part-time from 1913 to 1944. He became the sixth president of the NCAPH (1925-1928). His publications included *Training in Pentecostal Evangelism* (1897) and *Pauline Perfection* (1913).

BIBLIOGRAPHY. D. R. Rose, *A Theology of Christian Experience* (1965).

D. D. Bundy

Smith, Joseph, Jr. (1805-1844). Founder of The Church of Jesus Christ of Latter Day Saints.* Born near Sharon, Vermont, Smith's parents came from respectable families steeped in religious dissent and the popular piety* of New England but unattached to any church. His mother used to read her children the autobiography of her father, which contained hymns* and religious reflections, giving them a sense of destiny which was increased by her interest in mysticism* and folk religion. Her brother, Jason Mack, may also have influenced Joseph through his religious semi-communistic community in New Brunswick, where he was the patriarch of over thirty families. Joseph's father, who farmed and taught school, lost his mother's substantial dowry, along with his farm, speculating in a scheme to import ginseng from China. Joseph was, therefore, born into poverty and great insecurity. In 1816 the family moved to Palmyra, New York, which proudly boasted good schools, three public libraries and a vigorous intellectual life. It was also in the famous "burned-over district,"* where revival fires sparked many new religious movements.

There Joseph claimed to encounter God the Father and Jesus Christ in human form, who commissioned him to restore the "true church" and "lost priesthood" to earth. He also said an angel, Moroni, showed him an ancient book, which he translated, using magical stones, and published in 1830 as *The Book of Mormon*. On April 6, 1830, he founded his new church and his followers became known as Mormons.

Intense controversy followed these events. Joseph was denounced as a no-good treasure hunter who had used "seer stones" and who indulged in various magical practices to raise money. Joseph's fortunes quickly improved, and a growing following accepted him as a prophet. Local hostility forced him to move to Kirkland, Ohio, in 1832. Persecution followed, but he succeeded in building a temple where his followers could practice religious rituals bearing similarity to Masonic rites. The failure of his attempt to found a banking institution forced him to flee Kirkland in January 1838, and settle in Missouri, but the governor ordered him out of the state. In November 1838, he arrived in Illinois, where he established a new community known as Nauvoo.

During his Nauvoo years Smith prospered; he ran for president of the U.S., established a private army, built a well-planned city, elaborated his theological beliefs, introduced new religious practices and married over forty-nine women, at least twelve of whom had husbands. He extended the practice of polygamy to close followers, but not all accepted it, and a group of ex-members founded *The Nauvoo Expositor* to expose him. Angered by this move, he ordered the destruction of the press. The resulting unrest led to his arrest.

On June 27, 1844, a mob attacked the Carthage jail where he was held, and he and his brother Hyrum were murdered. His death provided his church with a martyr and created the basis for the transformation of an American folk religion into a world faith.

BIBLIOGRAPHY. R. L. Bushman, *Joseph Smith and the Beginnings of Mormonism* (1984); F. M. Brodie, *No Man Knows My History* (1971); *DAB* IX; *DARB; NCAB* 16; J. Tanner and S. Tanner, *Mormonism: Shadow or Reality* (1974).

I. Hexham

Smith, Oswald (J)effrey (1889-1986). Pastor* and missionary* statesman. A native of rural Ontario, Smith was converted* at age sixteen and studied at Toronto Bible College. His decision to become a missionary* was thwarted as the Presbyterian Church of Canada* repeatedly rejected him as a candidate on academic and health grounds. He turned to preaching* and personal evangelism* in rural areas and trained at McCormick Theological Seminary in Chicago.

Ordained* in 1915, his evangelistic and missionary zeal did not sit well with his Presbyterian congregation, and he resigned. Smith started a church in a Toronto YMCA and in 1921 merged it with a struggling Christian and Missionary Alliance* church. Anxious to promote missions, Smith began traveling overseas in 1924, returning home to raise funds and recruit missionaries. In 1928 he began "The People's Church," a large independent mission-oriented church in downtown Toronto. A powerful preacher, Smith was a leading figure in Canadian fundamentalism,* who wrote thirty-five books and had over a hundred of his poems set to music.

BIBLIOGRAPHY. L. Neely, *Fire in His Bones* (1982).

D. M. Lewis

Smith, Robert Pearsall (1827-1899). Holiness* evangelist* and writer. Born in Philadelphia, Smith was raised in a Quaker* home and in 1851 married Hannah Whitall,* also from a Quaker background, with whom he would serve as popular exponent of the "higher Christian life" movement. Both Robert and Hannah committed their lives to God during the 1858 urban prayer meeting revivals.* Their Quaker background did not incline them to propagate experiential religion, but after they heard about the "experience of entire sanctification" in Methodist* Holiness meetings in Philadelphia and southern New Jersey, both became extremely sensitive to the revivalist* emphasis on "heartfelt" religion.

Although it was Mrs. Smith who first testified to a personal faith and wrote about it in *The Christian's Secret of a Happy Life* (1875), Robert gradually yielded to her personal testimony and in true revivalist* fashion "claimed the blessing" during a camp meeting* at Vineland, New Jersey, in 1867. This was an extremely emotional religious experience* for him, and the enthusiasm which resulted led to his prolific involvement in the revival movement.

Smith's greatest contribution to the revival movement was his involvement in Holiness and revival meetings in England, Germany, France and Switzerland. So overwhelming was the response to his message that he returned saying that all of Europe was "at my feet." The moment of triumph soon turned into tragedy, for Smith suffered a nervous breakdown under the pressure. Rumors of heresy* and misconduct circulated, but the truth about his relationship with a young female counselee and his mystical theology did not warrant the exaggerated rumors. The extent of the exhaustion brought on by the gossip is reflected in the fact that after 1876 neither he nor his wife were involved in the revivals in any way. To the requests to preach they simply responded, "Henceforth home and homelife for us. . . . We are done. . . . Somebody else may do it now." Although they were not there to participate, the first meeting of the Keswick* Convention (1875) in Keswick, England, was to a significant degree the result of their emphasis on the higher Christian life in England. Robert Smith published less than his wife and is primarily known for his *Holiness Through Faith: Light on the Way of Holiness* (1870).

BIBLIOGRAPHY. M. E. Dieter, *The Holiness Revival in the Nineteenth Century* (1980); J. C. Pollock, *The Keswick Story: The Authorized History of the Keswick Convention* (1964); B. B. Warfield, *Perfectionism*, 2 vols. (1931). W. S. Gunter

Smith, Rodney ("Gipsy") (1860-1947). British evangelist. Born in a gypsy tent near Epping Forest, England, and receiving no formal education, Smith was influenced by the change that he saw from his father's conversion* to Christianity and by the stories of John Bunyan (1628-1688). In 1876 Smith was converted to evangelical* Christianity and publicly confessed Christ at a Primitive Methodist chapel. Feeling called to the ministry,* he soon came to the attention of William Booth,* who in 1877 enlisted him in his Christian mission.

Booth gave Smith various assignments. While Smith was serving at Hull, as many as 1,500 people at a time gathered to hear him preach. There he

became known as "Gipsy" Smith. In 1882, while preaching at his next station, Hanlay, Smith was dismissed from the now-more-regimented and renamed Salvation Army. He soon after began the first of his many international gospel trips. After 1892 his ministry was called the Gipsy Gospel Wagon Mission. From 1897 to 1912 Smith served as a special missionary for the National Free Church Council in Britain.

In 1889 he made the first of approximately fifty trips to the U.S. in which he held evangelistic meetings in major churches and assembly halls, wooing people to the gospel through his simple messages and gospel solos. His evangelistic work continued until his death at sea en route to the U.S.

BIBLIOGRAPHY. *DARB;* H. Murray, *Sixty Years an Evangelist* (1937); R. Smith, *Gipsy Smith: His Life and Work* (1901). R. L. Petersen

Smith, Wilbur (M)oorehead (1894-1976). Presbyterian* fundamentalist* educator. Born in Chicago to parents who were personal friends of the early fundamentalist leaders, Smith studied at the Moody Bible Institute* for one year (1913-1914), and then at the College of Wooster (Ohio) for three years after that, but earned no academic degrees. He left Wooster in 1917 to assist the pastor of the West Presbyterian Church in Wilmington, Delaware. For the next twenty years Smith pastored Presbyterian congregations in Maryland, Virginia and Pennsylvania.

From 1937 to 1947, Smith taught at the Moody Bible Institute. In 1947 he helped design Fuller Theological Seminary* and then joined its faculty. He departed in 1963 following a controversy over biblical inerrancy,* but was recruited to serve half-time at the Trinity Evangelical Divinity School. Smith finally retired from teaching in 1971.

Smith was a very popular Bible lecturer and a tireless author. He wrote over two dozen books, several hundred short magazine pieces and pamphlets, and thirty-eight annual volumes (1934-1971) of *Peloubet's* Select Notes on the International Bible Lessons for Christian Living.* Smith served on the Revision Committee of the Scofield Reference Bible* from 1954 to 1963, and was at one time or another a contributing editor or columnist for *The Sunday School Times, Moody Monthly, Revelation, Bibliotheca Sacra, His* and *Christianity Today.* Smith's love of books (25,000 in his personal library) and bibliographic talents were without peer in the fundamentalist-evangelical movement of the mid-twentieth century. As a champion of scholarship among fundamentalists, he was an inspiration to a younger generation of scholars who sought to reform fundamentalism.

BIBLIOGRAPHY. G. M. Marsden, *Reforming Fundamentalism: Fuller Seminary and the New Evangelicalism* (1987); W. M. Smith, *Before I Forget* (1971).
J. A. Carpenter

Smith, William (1727-1803). Anglican* minister* and educator. Born in Aberdeen, Scotland, Smith graduated from King's College, University of Aberdeen, in 1747 and four years later (1751) sailed to New York to serve as tutor to the two sons of Colonel Martin of Long Island, a position he held until 1753. During these years he wrote a pamphlet, *A General Idea of the College of Mirania* (1753), a utopian vision setting forth his views on higher education. Smith's ideas attracted the attention of Benjamin Franklin, who at the time was a trustee of the Academy and Charitable School of Philadelphia. In 1754 Smith joined the faculty of the school. The following year he became provost of a newly created college, Academy and Charitable School of Philadelphia, the forerunner of the University of Pennsylvania,* to which he gave twenty-five years of distinguished service.

Smith was influential in other areas as well. As an ardent Anglican* minister,* he worked to secure the appointment of an American bishop* and played an important part in the establishment of the Protestant Episcopal Church.* He also was actively involved in providing schools for German settlers in Pennsylvania. In 1757 he established a literary magazine, the *American Magazine and Monthly Chronicle for the British Colonies* (1757), which provided an outlet for young authors. Smith was a loyalist and did not favor American independence, but he did speak out against British policies. He died in Philadelphia on May 14, 1803.

BIBLIOGRAPHY. *DAB* IX; T. F. Jones, *A Pair of Lawn Sleeves: A Biography of William Smith (1727-1803)* (1972).
R. L. Troutman

Smyth, Newman (1843-1925). Congregational* minister* and theologian.* Born in Brunswick, Maine, Smyth was educated at both Phillips Academy and Bowdoin College. After serving as a lieutenant in the Civil War,* he entered Andover Seminary,* graduating in 1867. At Andover he became dissatisfied with the New England Theology* of Edwards Amasa Park* and in 1869 continued his theological studies at the German universities at Halle and Berlin where he was greatly influenced by Friedrich Tholuck (1799-1877) and Isaac Dorner (1809-1884). Smyth became an early proponent of the New Theology*

and in books such as *The Religious Feeling* (1877) and *Orthodox Theology Today* (1881) argued that the new approach could better respond to the modern era than the older New England Theology.

In 1881 he was elected as Park's successor but declined due to opposition from Andover's board of visitors (the board's action precipitating the Andover Controversy*). Smyth always considered himself a pastor-theologian, serving for twenty-six years (1882-1908) at Center Church, New Haven. While there he studied in the Yale biological laboratory, and the connection between modern science and religion was a continuing theme in his work. In his later years, most pointedly in *Passing Protestantism and Coming Catholicism* (1908), Smyth advocated the need for church unity* and labored vainly for the union of the Congregational and Episcopal* churches.

See also MUNGER, THEODORE THORNTON.

BIBLIOGRAPHY. *DAB* IX; N. Smyth, *Recollections and Reflections* (1926); J. W. Buckham, *Progressive Religious Thought in America* (1919).
R. B. Mullin

Smyth, Thomas (1808-1873). Southern Presbyterian* minister.* Born in Belfast, Ireland, Smyth spent his youth in Northern Ireland and began his higher education at Belfast College (1827-1829). In 1829 he entered Highbury College, London, where he continued his studies in classics and theology.* Due to financial setbacks, his family immigrated* to the U.S., and he continued his theological education at Princeton Theological Seminary* (1830-1831). Ordained* in 1831, he became pastor* of Second Presbyterian Church, Charleston, South Carolina, where he remained the rest of his life.

Smyth was famous as a scholarly pastor, amassing one of the largest private collections of theological books in the U.S. An Old School* Presbyterian, he wrote a number of theological works, many of them polemical. The majority of these were in the area of ecclesiology. His love of scholarship induced him to leave an endowment for the Smyth Lectureship at Columbia Theological Seminary. An ardent Confederate, he saw the early Northern defeats in the Civil War* as evidence of divine judgment and predicted a speedy victory for the South. His *Complete Works* have been collected in ten volumes (1908-1912).

BIBLIOGRAPHY. *DAB* IX; T. Smyth, *Autobiographical Notes, Letters and Reflections* (1914).
J. R. Wiers

Snake Handling. The religious practice of handling deadly vipers as a demonstration of special anointing by God. The practice is today largely limited to particular Pentecostal* churches in the rural Appalachian region. It developed out of the serious consideration of Mark 16:18, where the resurrected Christ announces that his disciples "will pick up snakes with their hands; and when they drink deadly poison, it will not hurt them at all. . . ." This passage belongs to the longer ending of Mark which, though missing from the best manuscripts and considered by most scholars to be an inauthentic saying of Jesus, appears in most English Bibles.*

Snake handling first made its appearance among Pentecostals in about 1913. George W. Hensley, having experienced Spirit baptism* in 1910, had meditated on Mark 16:18 and proceeded to handle a timber rattler. Hensley brought the practice into the Church of God* in Cleveland, Tennessee, after he became a member in 1912. At first he enjoyed the approval of the church's leader, A. J. Tomlinson,* who in 1917 declared the practice to be acceptable under certain conditions. However, by 1922 Hensley had left the Church of God. By the late 1930s, snake handling was widely practiced and had moved into some Midwestern states. Considered a public hazard, between 1936 and 1953 it was legally prohibited in Alabama, Georgia, Kentucky, North Carolina, Virginia and Tennessee. By this time the handling of serpents was accompanied by the drinking of poison (often diluted strychnine) and the handling of fire.

Practitioners freely handle the snakes, usually during weeknight evening-worship services in an atmosphere of physical movement and loud music. When deaths occur they may be attributed to either a lack of Spirit anointing or to the will of God, who is sometimes thought to have punished the individual through the deadly bite.

BIBLIOGRAPHY. K. W. Carden and R. W. Pelton, *The Persecuted Prophets* (1976); S. M. Kane, "Holy Ghost People: The Snake-Handlers of Southern Appalachia," *Appalachian Journal* 1 (Spring 1974): 255-262.   D. G. Reid

Social Creed of the Churches. A social manifesto principally subscribed to by mainline* American churches. The Federal Council of Churches* (FCC) at its first meeting in 1908 adopted, with additions, a statement approved earlier that year by the Methodist Church,* for whom Harry F. Ward was the chief drafter. Frank Mason North,* also a Methodist, presented the Creed to the FCC. It soon was widely adopted by other Protestant* denominations* and the YMCA* and YWCA.* The original

Creed, confined largely to questions of industrial relations (such as reductions in the workday and workweek), was modified by the FCC in 1912 to include other social concerns. It remained unchanged until 1932 when the implications for governmental programs were spelled out more clearly, anticipating the New Deal. It then continued without formal changes. Many of the principles have appeared in legislation. "Social Creed," the popular name, reflects the ongoing parallel tradition of the statement in the Methodist Church (until 1972). "The Social Ideals of the Churches" was the actual FCC title. It is regarded as a classic statement of the goals of the Social Gospel.

BIBLIOGRAPHY. C. H. Hopkins, *The Rise of the Social Gospel in American Protestantism* (1940); A. D. Ward, *The Social Creed of the Methodist Church* (1961); H. F. Ward, *The Social Creed of the Churches* (1914).   S. C. Mott

Social Ethics. *Social ethics* is typically contrasted with *personal ethics** as a way of marking off two complementary areas of ethical concern. The distinction is a useful one, even though it is sometimes difficult to draw clear boundary lines between the two areas of investigation. Abortion* is certainly a social issue; but it is also an intensely personal matter for many women. Phenomena such as gambling, pornography, racial prejudice and the use of sexist language have a similar status; each can be viewed as an item that is both personal and social in nature. The two areas are found on a spectrum of moral deliberation, and they shade into each other. But a topic can be said to fall properly within the domain of social ethics if it deals with issues of moral value—rightness, goodness, virtue—as they arise in group or institutional contexts. Thus, when a question about sexual behavior or race relations is considered from the perspective of social policy, or when it is viewed in a group or institutional context, it has clearly become an appropriate topic for social ethics.

Social ethics should not be viewed as being coextensive with political ethics. Sometimes when people talk about "social concerns" or "social action," they are thinking primarily about the issues of political life. Social ethics includes a focus on the political, but it also covers a much larger territory. The question of how we ought to deal with poverty, for example, is a social-ethical topic which includes a political dimension: What are the state's obligations toward the poor, and what strategies are most fitting for a government to pursue in combatting poverty? But there are other "ought" questions about poverty that have little or nothing to do with governments: How ought churches to serve the poor? What moral obligations do medical professionals have to the poor of their communities? How does a concern for the disadvantaged and oppressed fit into the mission of a Christian educational institution?

Human social interaction takes place in a variety of group and institutional settings: family, school, church, hospital, factory, the military, athletic teams and so on. Questions about right and wrong, good and bad, virtue and vice, arise in all of these areas. Many interesting questions of social ethics also have to do with the relationships *between* specific spheres of social interaction: In what ways must a journalist respect a professional athlete's or a politician's right-to-privacy? May parents refuse medical treatment for a critically ill teen-ager on the grounds of religious belief? What obligations do employers have to provide child care for employees?

North America has been an especially lively setting for debating the issues of social ethics, since Canada and the U.S. have been characterized by a high degree of pluralism.* Immigrant* groups have brought a vast array of religious and denominational* allegiances with them, along with a rich variety of cultural mores and practices. The spiritual environment of North America has also been conducive to the spawning of home-grown cults* and sects.* The resultant mix of religious movements, ethnic conclaves and new cultural experiments has produced not only doctrinal diversity, but also a plurality of perspectives on family and educational values, sexual expression and physical health, group authority-patterns and political obligation.

The difficulties of carefully evaluating these differences on the level of moral principle are obvious. Thus a spirit of pragmatism has often ruled the day in the public arena. A commitment to political compromise and a fondness for temporary ad hoc solutions have sometimes been closely associated with attitudes that approximate moral relativism and even cynicism. But these tendencies have been held in check—often, at least—by religious visions in which "the democratic spirit" is placed in the context of a larger world view. The role of the churches has been significant in this regard.

On some accounts of the differences between the two "parties" in North American Protestantism,* the so-called mainline* liberals* have specialized in social ethics while the conservative evangelicals* have emphasized matters of personal morality. This portrayal of the two ethical styles gains plausibility from the fact that the mainstream churches (at least their denominational leaders and educators) have paid much explicit attention to social concerns in the twentieth century. The Social Gospel Movement* of the first few decades of the century, followed by Reinhold Niebuhr's* influential Christian realism and the more recent interest in the varieties of liberation theology,* have all helped to give social concerns high visibility in the major denominations.

Evangelical Protestants have regularly criticized this emphasis, arguing that liberalism reduces the gospel to a social program. In the name of Bible-believing* Christianity, conservatives have preached the necessity of individual conversion* and of a life of personal holiness.* But for all of that, they too have promoted a set of social concerns. Rather than ignoring social issues, they have sometimes offered individualist* solutions to problems caused by injustice and oppression: "Changed hearts will change societies." They have also pleaded for legislative solutions regarding a select number of social sins: the use of alcohol,* gambling, pornography and the teaching of biological evolution.* And they have fostered their own kinds of social ministries, often with a strong sense of identification with the needs of the disadvantaged: the rescue mission movement* is an important case in point, as is the ministry of The Salvation Army.*

The events of the 1960s had a special impact on Christian social ethics in North America. Due to Martin Luther King, Jr.'s,* leadership in the Civil Rights Movement,* the questions of racial justice were formulated in inescapably Christian terms. Church leaders were also prominent in protests against the Vietnam War.* The teaching of social ethics in college* and seminaries* had a special poignancy during this period; courses dealing with the application of ethical principles to specific practical issues, such as race relations, war and civil disobedience, were much in demand.

Conservative Protestants were not unaffected by these developments. The 1970s saw the appearance of a more assertive evangelical social conscience. The Chicago Declaration of Evangelical Social Concerns,* issued in 1973, pledged more serious efforts in combatting racism, militarism and economic injustice. A few years later the "born again politics" of the New Christian Right* began to command public attention; led by Jerry Falwell,* founder of the Moral Majority,* previously a-political Christians of conservative convictions began to address a broad agenda of social issues, especially those pertaining to family concerns and sexual legislation.

As evangelicals of various political leanings reflected seriously on social-ethical matters, they began to explore various traditions of the past in search of moral and theological resources. Some focused on traditional Anabaptist* or Reformed* contributions; others have looked to the commitment to social reform in early Wesleyanism,* or to the Puritan* theocratic* perspective; the African-American church tradition, in which personal piety and social concern have seldom been kept separate, has also been a source of inspiration.

The public ethical dialog in North America, a discussion that has always drawn heavily on religious themes and concerns, has for the most part been couched in very Protestant terms—although this has been less so in Canada, where French-speaking Catholics* have always been an important cultural presence. But in the decades following World War 2,* Roman Catholic ethical thought gained a new prominence. One noteworthy development is the increasing public attention given to official Catholic teachings about specific areas of social concern. Some of this attention has been primarily negative—due to publicly stated disagreements by many Catholics with their Church's policies on such matters as birth control,* abortion,* divorce and homosexuality.* But many Catholic social documents, notably Pope John XXIII's* encyclical *Pacem in Terris* and several pastoral letters* published in the 1980s by bishops in the U.S. and Canada, have stimulated widespread and appreciative ecumenical responses.

Catholic liberation theology,* as it has been developed in Latin America, has also had a significant impact on Christian social thought in North America, among Protestants as well as Roman Catholics. Even though the Marxist categories of some (but not all) liberation theologians have not been greeted with the same enthusiasm as they might be accorded in some Latin American environs, the liberationists' insistence on serious attention to the Bible's concern for the poor and the oppressed has made its mark on North American social ethics.

Yet another Catholic contribution has been channeled through the renewed interest in traditional spirituality.* Christians of various denominations have come to see, for example, the spirituality of the monastic tradition as an important resource for the Christian quest for justice and peace. The Franciscan* strain of Catholic piety,*

with its emphasis on simple living and a concern for the poor—an important influence on Dorothy Day* and her Catholic Worker Movement*—has received new attention in Christian social thought. The traditions of Eastern Orthodoxy* and Anglicanism* have also attracted interest, as Christians have explored the connections between social action and such spiritual discipline as prayer,* contemplation and fasting.

The resources of the past, however, have not been deemed fully adequate for dealing with the issues of the present. The feminist movement,* awareness of ecological issues, the AIDS crisis and radical new developments in medical technology are only some of the factors which have made it necessary for Christians to challenge and stretch traditional frameworks for ethical decision making.

The ethical agenda has also been drastically altered by an increasing global awareness that has come to characterize the mood and the substance of Christian social ethics in the late decades of the twentieth century. Calls for an American isolationism may have had their impact in the past, but they have been effectively silenced by the unavoidable fact of a world community that is linked by intricate economic ties, instant communication, complex and speedy transportation systems and the fear of nuclear destruction.

Global awareness has been reinforced by increasing opportunities for crosscultural dialog. The successes of the missionary movements* (an important factor for both the evangelical and Roman Catholic communities, where evangelism* continues to be a matter of strong interest), along with various international Christian networks for facilitating cooperation and dialog, have forced North American Christians to revise their own ethical schemes and agendas in the light of challenges and obligations posed from other cultural perspectives.

Social ethics in North America is a vitally important area of discussion for the Christian community, one that has increasingly become a matter of dialog with the traditions of the past and with contemporary Christians who represent a variety of theological persuasions and cultural contexts. In this setting many central theological concerns of the past continue to be of pressing importance, even though they may appear in new forms in these newer situations. The issue of where the ultimate authority resides in moral decision-making will always loom large for those Christians who seek to know and to do the will of the biblical God in all of life, including the complex spheres of social interaction.

[1103]

See also ABORTION; BIOETHICS; ETHICS, CATHOLIC PERSONAL; ETHICS, PROTESTANT PERSONAL; EUTHANASIA; PACEM IN TERRIS; PACIFISM; PEACE MOVEMENT, CATHOLIC; POLITICAL THEOLOGY; PUBLIC POLICY, CHRISTIANITY AND; QUADRAGESIMO ANNO; RERUM NOVARUM; SOCIAL GOSPEL MOVEMENT.

BIBLIOGRAPHY. J.-Y. Calvez and J. Perrin, *The Church and Social Justice: The Social Teaching of the Popes from Leo XIII to Pius XII, (1878-1967)* (1969); C. E. Curran and R. A. McCormick, ed., *Official Catholic Social Teaching* (1986); R. T. Handy, *The Social Gospel in America, 1870-1920* (1966); E. L. Long, *A Survey of Christian Ethics* (1967); H. R. Niebuhr, *Christ and Culture* (1951).
R. J. Mouw

Social Gospel Movement. The term *Social Gospel* came into prominence only at the beginning of the twentieth century, when it was used primarily to refer to a movement among North American Protestants* to relate biblical and theological insights to the need for social reform. In an age of rapid economic change, the full impact of the Industrial Revolution, with its vast manufacturing productivity, its concentrations of economic power and its stimulus to the burgeoning of urban centers, created serious social and labor problems as wide inequalities in the distribution of wealth increased. In various countries of Europe, especially in Great Britain, Christian social movements emerged which had an influence on the rise of similar movements in North America. There the predominance of individualistic and conservative social philosophies had long had a strong hold on patterns of ethical thought among church people, so that the Christian social movements which arose in the last half of the nineteenth century were highly controversial.

Early leading figures in the emergence of social Christianity in the U.S. included such ministers as Washington Gladden,* the widely known pastor of Columbus, Ohio; Josiah Strong,* former home missionary,* who turned his great abilities to an effort to lead the Evangelical Alliance* toward social concerns and then focused on cooperative Christianity; and Charles M. Sheldon,* who wrote a series of novels that conveyed a social message, especially *In His Steps: What Would Jesus Do?* (1896). Some prominent members of the laity* also contributed to the emerging social Christian movement, notably Henry George, author of the seminal *Progress and Poverty* (1879); Richard T. Ely,* the economist who wrote two works that significantly contributed to the rise of the Social Gospel, *Social Aspects of Christianity* (1889) and

The Social Law of Service (1896); and Jane Addams,* founder of Chicago's famous social settlement* Hull House, who gave the movement her support.

One wing of the social Christian movement remained oriented to conservative evangelical* Protestantism, as in the rescue missions,* The Salvation Army* and the Volunteers of America.* While these movements were not noted for directly challenging individualistic social ethics,* most did identify with the needy, and some sharply criticized the social order and pled for a greater measure of justice. There was also a radical side to the movement among groups which took a reconstructionist rather than reformist position, some embracing political socialism. Well known in their time were William D. P. Bliss,* who in the 1890s was the central figure in a Society of Christian Socialists and editor of *The Dawn*; George D. Herron,* who pursued a meteoric career across the social Christian spectrum before being forced out of the ministry; and Vida D. Scudder, a Wellesley professor who was active in such groups as the Christian Socialist Fellowship and the (Episcopal) Church Socialist League. Small and short-lived in themselves, these groups challenged the churches to face social issues more squarely.

By the turn of the century the term *Social Gospel* became especially attached to the more moderate, reformist elements in the churches, most of which were influenced by liberal* theology and progressive social thought. The veteran Washington Gladden, who also was a popularizer of the historical approach to the Bible* and echoed the cry of the ancient prophets for justice and righteousness, continued to be active in the movement he helped to create, but its outstanding prophet became seminary* professor Walter Rauschenbusch,* whose book *Christianity and the Social Crisis* (1907) thrust both him and the Social Gospel into national prominence. In the pre-war years it became a highly visible, controversial movement that gained considerable influence, especially in Congregational,* Episcopal,* Baptist,* Methodist* and Presbyterian* churches—notably in the Northern branches of the latter three, though it also had advocates in the South, especially among Methodists. The Social Gospel called for cooperation among the churches so that the work of Christianizing society could be more effectively done, and its influence was strong in the formation of the Federal Council of the Churches of Christ in America* in 1908.

Theologically, Social Gospel leaders looked to the historical Jesus, believing he could be known through biblical scholarship and declaring that his principles were reliable guides for personal and social life in any age. At the center of his teaching they identified the doctrine of the kingdom of God,* which they interpreted as a historical possibility that would soon come to earth in some fullness, bringing with it social harmony and ending gross injustices. They were inclined to emphasize the immanence rather than the transcendence of God, to find the divine at work in the regular processes of nature and history and to minimize the distinction between sacred and secular realms. While the Social Gospel leaders emphasized progress, they usually did not refer to it as automatic or inevitable, but viewed it as conditioned by human response to the divine will. But their estimate of human potential was consistently high so that in most cases they believed humans could be guided to make the right choices and so contribute to "the building of the kingdom."

At the practical level, the movement encouraged increased social action by the churches, especially as it benefited underpaid industrial workers. By the early twentieth century it found congenial the major emphases of political progressivism which sought to engage more citizens in the democratic process and so worked for measures such as the direct primary and direct election of senators, the initiative, referendum and recall. Social Gospelers normally chose to work in a non-partisan way and were especially concerned with getting the laboring masses into the political process. They backed the rights of unions at a time when that was very controversial. A clear statement of Social Gospel principles arose out of Methodist auspices as the "Social Creed of the Churches,"* which was formally adopted by the Federal Council in 1912. In this same period many theological seminaries added courses in ethics* and the sociology of religion, in which the Social Gospel was taught to prospective ministers. Leading figures in the young but growing discipline of religious education* adopted progressive views in both their educational and social teachings.

In the early years Social Gospelers were drawn especially to the plight of wage-earners and the problems of capital and labor. As the movement matured some of its advocates added other concerns to the agenda. Gladden and Rauschenbusch gradually became more aware of the plight of African-Americans, then still largely concentrated in the South under the harsh realities of enforced segregation. A Social Gospel perspective was evident in Willis D. Weatherford's pioneering *Negro Life in the South* (1910), and a number of prominent African-American preachers injected the social emphasis into their public work.

Though the Social Gospel emerged as a Protestant movement, there was also a distinctive social Catholicism* which was deeply concerned about the social problems that troubled the lives of many immigrants,* most of whom were Catholics after 1880. Father Edward McGlynn* campaigned for Henry George as mayor of New York City in 1886 and pointed to the social relevance of Catholic doctrine. In 1887 James Cardinal Gibbons was able to keep the first national labor union, the Catholic-run Knights of Labor, from being condemned by Rome. The encyclical *Rerum novarum** (1891) of Pope Leo XIII encouraged socially minded Catholics to support the rights of wage-earners. A conspicuous leader in the development of Catholic social thought and action was an able, articulate priest, John A. Ryan,* who published *A Living Wage* in 1906.

In Canada, the Social Gospel became a significant movement which combined indigenous as well as British and American influences. The Canadian movement actually had a wider impact on the numerically much smaller nation than did its sister movement in the U.S. No major Protestant body escaped its impact, and its political influence was more direct. The most prominent Canadian leader of Social Gospel thought was Salem G. Bland,* while J. S. Woodsworth was its outstanding practitioner. As in the U.S., the movement was committed to cooperative work among the denominations, and played a role in the formation of the United Church of Canada* in 1925, a union of Methodists, Congregationalists and about half the Presbyterians.

After World War 1* the optimism that had characterized the early thrust of the Social Gospel began to fade. Its liberal theological basis was challenged both by conservatives who stressed the premillennialist* interpretation of the kingdom of God* and by neo-orthodox* realists who criticized it as overly idealistic and naive. Yet it remained an important force in many denominations and in interdenominational movements until mid century and beyond, and left a permanent stamp on North American religious life as many of its emphases were adopted by other causes and theologies. Hence, though the peak of the historic Social Gospel Movement was reached in the early decades of the century, as a general term the *Social Gospel* persists as a label for social Christianity in general.

BIBLIOGRAPHY. A. I. Abell, *American Catholi-*

cism and Social Action: A Search for Social Justice, 1865-1950 (1963); R. Allen, *The Social Passion: Religion and Social Reform in Canada, 1914-1928* (1971); P. A. Carter, *The Decline and Revival of the Social Gospel: Social and Political Liberalism in American Protestant Churches, 1920-1940* (1971); R. T. Handy, ed., *The Social Gospel in America, 1870-1920: Gladden, Ely, Rauschenbusch* (1966); C. H. Hopkins, *The Rise of the Social Gospel in American Protestantism, 1865-1915* (1940); N. A. Magnuson, *Salvation in the Slums: Evangelical Social Work, 1865-1900* (1977); H. F. May, *Protestant Churches and Industrial America* (1949); R. C. White, Jr., and C. H. Hopkins, *The Social Gospel: Religion and Reform in Changing America* (1976).   R. T. Handy

Socialism, Christian. During the first half of the nineteenth century, Christian socialism consisted mainly of a succession of failed utopian colonies led by such European eccentrics as the German Weitling and the Frenchmen Cabet and Considérant. In 1874 followers of the sixteenth-century reformer Jakob Hutter established communitarian settlements in the Northwest, and 25,000 Hutterites* remain to this day in the U.S. and Canada, including several flourishing communes in the eastern U.S.

During the latter half of the century, a more contemporary form of Christian socialism appeared in the Christian Labor Union* (1872-1878) and in such diverse personalities as Washington Gladden,* national moderator of the Congregational* Church; Edward Bellamy (1850-1898), author of *Looking Backward*; the Episcopal* minister* William Dwight Porter Bliss,* founder of the Society of Christian Socialists (1889-1896) and editor of its newspaper, *The Dawn*; and Frances Willard,* president of the Women's Christian Temperance Union.*

In the first two decades of the twentieth century, socialism reached the peak of its popularity in the U.S. in the presidential campaigns of Eugene Debs. This popularity was largely due to the excessive self-aggrandizement of the Vanderbilts, Goulds and Rockefellers, in contrast with the poverty of the workers. Almost as popular as Debs was George Herron,* a spellbinder and cofounder of the Socialist Party in 1901, who lost his Congregational pulpit when he divorced his wife to marry a wealthy heiress.

A Methodist* minister, Edward Ellis Carr, edited *The Christian Socialist* (1903-1922) and built its circulation to 20,000, including 2,000 ministers. He founded the Christian Socialist Fellowship* (1906-

1917), which had 1,500 members in twenty-seven chapters. Carr was twice expelled from the Socialist Party for criticizing the sexual mores of SP leaders.

Less controversial figures were Richard Ely,* an Episcopalian* and founder of the American Economic Association; Walter Rauschenbusch,* the German Baptist* leader of the Social Gospel Movement* whose book *Christianity and the Social Crisis* (1907) embodied a non-Marxist, cooperative brand of Christian socialism and became an international best seller; and Vida Scudder, Anglican professor at Wellesley and author of popular books. Christian socialism died during the 1920s, only to be revived by Reinhold Niebuhr* in the Fellowship of Socialist Christians* (1931-1948) and its periodical, *Radical Religion*. However, Niebuhr became disillusioned with Marxism, particularly as it was practiced in the Soviet Union.

From 1974 to 1983 there existed a U.S. branch of Christians for Socialism, the international organization inspired by liberation* theologians of Latin America. Since 1977 a group has operated within the Democratic Socialists of America under the name Religion and Socialism Commission, DSA. It publishes a quarterly, *Religious Socialism*, which has tried to develop a non-Marxist form of socialism with more emphasis on worker cooperatives.

In Canada, where the New Democratic Party provides a more prominent socialist presence, Christian socialism has been an even more significant factor. The party was founded in 1932 by J. S. Woodsworth, a Methodist minister, supported by a Christian socialist movement that existed under various names up to 1945. The opposition of the Catholic Church* to socialism, also prominent in the U.S., has evaporated in recent years as statements of the Socialist International and the Vatican* have become more and more similar.

BIBLIOGRAPHY. J. C. Cort, *Christian Socialism* (1988); G. Baum, *Catholics and Canadian Socialism* (1980).

J. C. Cort

Society for Propagating the Gospel among the Indians and Others in North America. Missionary* society. Founded in Boston in 1787, the Society is the oldest continuing missionary organization in the Americas, though in recent times its emphasis has shifted more to educational than strictly missionary endeavors. Its primary function has been to act as a funding or supporting agency for missionary and educational works among Native Americans, but it has also aided works among other disadvantaged or unchurched peoples in America.

Though in the beginning the membership of the Society was primarily composed of ministers* and active laymen* in the Congregational churches* of New England, it has supported missionaries and works from several Protestant* denominations.* Beginning almost immediately after its founding, the Society helped to provide ministers among the white population in newly-settled regions, such as along the eastern Maine coast and on the western frontier in Illinois. Aid was also given at times for schools among the African-Americans in the South. Since the mid nineteenth century, however, the Society's work has primarily been with Native Americans, and at various times missionaries affiliated with the Society have worked among virtually every tribe in the U.S.

In the early twentieth century, the work of the Society centered on the Indian reservations throughout the country—including the urban Native Americans of the Northeast—providing assistance in matters of health and general welfare, as well as continuing its religious and educational efforts. In recent years, the resources of the Society have been focused on scholarship assistance to Native American students, primarily pre-theological students enrolled at the Cook Christian Training School in Tempe, Arizona.

See also MISSIONS TO NATIVE AMERICAN INDIANS.

BIBLIOGRAPHY. J. F. Hunnewell, The Society for Propagating the Gospel among the Indians and Others in North America, 1787-1887 (1887).

M. S. Joy

Society for the Promotion of Christian Knowledge.

An Anglican* missionary* society supplying libraries for clergy* and parishes* overseas. English evangelizing in the colonies began early, with the founding of the Society for the Propagation of the Gospel in New England* (1649). But the vagaries of English politics and, in America, King Philip's War,* curtailed extensive activity. With the ascendancy of William and Mary to the throne in 1689, Anglicans in both England and America were encouraged to press for more zealous supervision and promotion of the church in the colonies. In 1696 Henry Compton, Bishop of London, appointed Thomas Bray* as commissary to Maryland, an office designed to accomplish these objectives.

Discovering in his recruitment efforts that only the poorer clergy were willing to emigrate, and that few of these had resources adequate to their mission, Bray determined to provide them with the

proper volumes. His efforts resulted in the founding of the Society for the Promotion of Christian Knowledge (SPCK), a voluntary organization that would both publish and distribute significant theological works. In 1700 a brief journey to Maryland convinced Bray that a separate missionary society was essential to promote the interests of the church in America. Two years later he secured a charter for the Society for the Propagation of the Gospel in Foreign Parts* (SPG), for which the SPCK became a sponsor. Thereafter the SPG had primary responsibility for evangelizing the colonies. Nevertheless, the SPCK continued to provide resources for some fifty libraries from New York to the Carolinas and Bermuda; the largest of these, in Annapolis, Maryland, was one of America's earliest lending libraries. As the harbinger of a more aggressive Anglican presence throughout the colonies, both the SPCK and the SPG generated opposition and apprehension in America, especially among Congregationalists* and other Free Church members. The SPCK continues its work in the late twentieth century.

BIBLIOGRAPHY. B. C. Steiner, ed., Rev. Thomas Bray: His Life and Selected Works (1901); H. P. Thompson, Thomas Bray (1954).

E. C. Nordbeck

Society for the Propagation of the Gospel in Foreign Parts.

Anglican* missionary* society. The Society for the Propagaton of the Gospel (SPG) was founded in 1701 by Thomas Bray* to achieve two objectives: (1) supply an educated and well-qualified ministry* for Anglican parishes* in the English colonies; and (2) provide the vanguard of the Anglican outreach to Native Americans. During the eighteenth century the SPG was active in Bermuda and the American and Canadian colonies, admirably supporting the Anglican cause and establishing some three hundred new churches.

In 1702 the Society sent the acerbic George Keith,* a converted Quaker* who did not shun confrontation, to survey the status of the colonial churches. Keith exemplified the new aggressiveness of imperial Anglicanism as did the expansion of the society's work into Puritan* New England. Though the "Great Defection" of Yale* rector* Timothy Cutler* and others to the Church of England in 1722 was not the direct result of SPG influence, Cutler returned to America after his ordination* as an SPG missionary. The society enthusiastically supported the founding of the Georgia colony in which John Wesley* served in the 1730s under SPG auspices.

The missions to Native Americans* were hampered by barriers of language and war, so the society turned its attention to the conversion* of the African slaves, enjoying so much success that wary colonial legislatures passed laws that explicitly renounced baptism* as a means of manumission. With the coming of the American Revolution,* the largely loyalist missionaries fled to Nova Scotia where one of their members, Charles Inglis,* became the first Anglican bishop in the New World. In the nineteenth century, the SPG continued its expansion into other areas of British colonial rule.

BIBLIOGRAPHY. C. F. Pascoe, *Two Hundred Years of the SPG, 1701-1900* (1901); H. P. Thompson, *Into All Lands* (1951).

R. M. Payne

Society for the Propagation of the Gospel in New England. A colonial mission* agency. Efforts to formally organize missionary* efforts among the Native Americans of New England were realized in 1649 with the granting of a charter by the English Parliament to a group of sixteen philanthropic Englishmen led by Edward Winslow. Their organization, officially chartered as The Society for the Promoting and Propagating the Gospel of Jesus Christ in New England, was the first formal overseas Christian mission agency. The corporation was to be headquartered in London, where charitable funds were to be raised and sent to America for the evangelization of New England's Native-American population. All parish ministers in England and Wales were legally required to announce the establishment of the Society and solicit funds for the cause from parishioners. Tracts* written by New England divines* relating conversions* among Native Americans paved the way for the Society to be well received, and fundraising efforts during the first decade were quite successful.

A handful of American Puritan* evangelists relied on the support of the Society, the most notable being John Eliot,* whose expansive views of Christianizing Native Americans prevailed. To Christianize was to civilize, and the accoutrements of civilization were thought necessary to keep the New England natives from reverting to barbarism. Fortified by support from the Society, Eliot established Natick, Massachusetts, as the first of several "praying towns"* for Native-American converts who were also taught the English way of life. Following Eliot's translation work, the Society provided funding for the printing of Scripture in the Native-American language. The Society was rechartered as "The New England Company" following the restoration of the English monarchy in 1660, and its activities continued until the time of the American Revolution.* From 1750 the New England Company helped support Jonathan Edwards* in his mission outpost at Stockbridge, Massachusetts. At the time of the Revolution, the mission channeled its remaining resources into reaching Native Americans in Canada, where it still supports the education of Native Americans.

BIBLIOGRAPHY. S. E. Morison, *Builders of the Bay Colony* (1930); F. J. Bremer, *The Puritan Experiment* (1976). A. M. Carden

Society of Biblical Literature, The. A North American association of biblical scholars. Founded in 1880, during a period in which several other scholarly societies were being founded, in view of American interest in the Scriptures it is not surprising that the first major scholarly religious society focused on the Bible. Instrumental in the founding were Frederic Gardiner, Charles A. Briggs* and Philip Schaff.* There were thirty-two male charter members, mostly seminary* and college professors; all were Protestants* from the Northeast. By the turn of the century, Jews, Catholics* and women had been inducted. The purpose of the society as it was stated in 1884 has remained essentially unchanged: "The object of the Society shall be to stimulate the critical study of the Scriptures by presenting, discussing, and publishing original papers on biblical topics."

Papers at the annual meetings, later published in the *Journal of Biblical Literature,* focused on philology, exegesis, archaeology, text and translation, and literary criticism. Most of the articles were moderate in regard to criticism and non-polemical, with controversies over higher criticism appearing in church-related journals. Since 1910 the papers have reflected trends and positions in international critical scholarship.

The Society has expanded by establishing regional sections; publishing monographs, dissertations, texts and translations, an additional journal entitled *Semeia;* and cooperating in placement and other services under the umbrella of Scholars Press. The members of the Society represent the full diversity of those teaching the Judeo-Christian Scriptures in seminaries, universities, colleges and biblical institutes, as well as those serving churches and synagogues in North America. In the late 1980s there were approximately seven thousand members, with the Society's offices located in Decatur, Georgia.

BIBLIOGRAPHY. E. W. Saunders, *Searching the*

Scriptures, A History of the Society of Biblical Literature, 1880-1980 (1982).

T. H. Olbricht

Society of Jesus. Catholic religious order.* The Society of Jesus, better known as the Jesuits, is the largest Roman Catholic* religious order for men both in the world and in the U.S. Founded by St. Ignatius of Loyola and approved by Pope Paul III in 1540, the Jesuits soon spread to most of the Catholic countries of Europe.

Jesuit spirituality* flows largely from Loyola's *Spiritual Exercises.* The early Jesuits excelled as retreat* directors and teachers. By 1626 the Jesuits operated 544 colleges and seminaries*; by 1749 they operated 894, of which twenty-four were universities. Jesuit training was long and demanding, traditionally involving three years of spiritual training, two years of humanities, three years of philosophy, three years of teaching experience and four years of theology.*

One of Loyola's early companions was the first and greatest Jesuit missionary, St. Francis Xavier. By the end of the sixteenth century, there were Jesuit missionaries* working in India, China, Japan and most of Latin America. Many Jesuits made important contributions to early modern theology, philosophy, literature, science and art. In 1600 there were 8,519 Jesuits; by 1749 there were 22,589. During the Enlightenment, Jesuit influence was opposed by Jansenists; philosophes; and the absolutist kings of France, Spain, Portugal and Naples. The kings pressured Clement XIV to suppress the Order in 1773.

The Romantic period brought in a religious revival and the restoration of the Jesuits in 1814. Thereafter growth was steady, peaking at 36,036 in 1965. Then came a decline to 25,382 by 1986. By that year the two countries with the most Jesuits were the U.S. (5,226) and India (3,118).

Jesuit roots in the U.S. go back to 1566 when three Jesuits tried to land on the Florida coast and were killed by Native Americans. The explorations of Father Jacques Marquette* down the Mississippi River and of Father Eusebio Kino* in the Southwest are well known. The most important Jesuit ministry in the U.S. has long been education (*See* Education, Catholic Higher). By 1814 there were fourteen Jesuits at Georgetown College (now Georgetown University). Currently there are nineteen Jesuit universities and nine colleges in the U.S. Even more numerous are the Jesuit high schools. Jesuit schools are concentrated in large cities, particularly the older cities of the East and Midwest. In the early 1970s control of most Jesuit colleges and universities was turned over to trustees, who number more lay* persons than Jesuits.

Presently the American Jesuits are divided into ten provinces. There are two Jesuit provinces in Canada, one for French speakers (381 members) and one for English speakers (304 members). Education is a relatively less important Jesuit apostolate in Canada.

Worldwide the Jesuits publish 1,400 periodicals. Jesuits such as the late Karl Rahner* and Bernard Lonergan* are esteemed theologians. Some American Jesuits, for example Daniel Berrigan, have become political activists, usually for liberal causes; while in Latin America Jesuits have contributed to the development of Liberation Theology,* which combines Marxist analysis with Christian principles. Jesuits disagree sharply about the wisdom of such developments. Superiors have tended to allow considerable freedom to individual Jesuits in their writing on social and political issues but have discouraged Jesuits from holding political office. When the liberal Jesuit general Pedro Arrupe suffered a stroke in 1981, Pope John Paul II* appointed a conservative Jesuit to run the order until a General Congregation in 1983 elected a new general, the Dutchman Peter-Hans Kolvenbach. His first years in office suggest that he will steer a middle course.

BIBLIOGRAPHY. J. C. H. Aveling, *The Jesuits* (1981); W. Bangert, *A History of the Society of Jesus* (1972); G. Garraghan, *The Jesuits of the Middle United States,* 3 vols. (1938).

J. P. Donnelly

Society of St. John the Evangelist. Anglican* monastic order. Also known as Cowley Fathers, the Society was the first officially recognized Anglican monastic order. Ideologically, the origin of the society can be traced back to the Oxford Movement* in the mid-nineteenth century, which emphasized the "Catholic" side of the Anglican confession. The actual founder and first head of the order was Richard Meux Benson (1824-1915), the village vicar of Cowley. On December 27, 1866, Benson and two confreres took vows of poverty, chastity and obedience. They combined a life of contemplative prayer* with active social ministry.

The order became established in Boston in 1870. In addition, successful missions were sent to India and South Africa. Today the society is organized into three branches: English, American and Canadian. Its membership consists mostly of Anglican (Episcopalian*) priests. In its theological

[1109]

emphasis it focuses on the centrality of the Trinity and the Incarnation, somewhat reminiscent of Eastern Orthodoxy.* It encourages a mystical* spirituality* based on discipline and prayer. The Society spreads this approach to the Christian life by sponsoring retreats,* though it also continues to stress active ministry in modern society.

BIBLIOGRAPHY. M. L. Smith, ed., *Benson of Cowley* (1980).   W. Corduan

Society of St. Vincent de Paul.

An international Roman Catholic-sponsored association of lay* persons seeking to help the poor. Frederic Ozanam (1813-1853), a Catholic layman, founded the group in Paris in 1833. Its patron is Vincent de Paul, the priest of seventeenth-century France who attended valiantly to social problems. From the beginning its charitable acts have been nonpartisan and not restricted to Catholics.

The Society came to North America in 1845 and quickly made its mark. "Vincentians" founded or helped to found the first Catholic institutions for children, struggled for just wages for workers and were among the first Catholics to recognize and cooperate with efforts of other Christians to contribute to the public welfare.

Active members gather for regular (often weekly) meetings in "conferences" of about seven to ten members. Meetings, frequently held in parish* settings, provide for prayer,* mutual support and common consideration of needs. Conferences are linked by diocesan, national and international councils. There are now over 750,000 members—men, women and youth—in 112 countries. In the U.S. and Canada there are more than 34,000 members in over 4,300 conferences. There are also associate members and contributing members, which in some parts of the world include non-Catholic Christians. The genius of the Society lies in its localization and person-to-person care, always according to particular needs, places and circumstances. Nevertheless, local conferences often help Vincentian endeavors worldwide.

In the United States and Canada, some of the larger projects which many conferences also support include furniture and clothing stores, food supply, shelters, children's camps, job placement and elderly services. Vincentians seek above all to bear witness to the love of Christ and strive to see his face in the faces of the poor.

BIBLIOGRAPHY. C. H. Murphy, *The Spirit of the Society of St. Vincent de Paul* (1940); D. T. McColgan, *A Century of Charity*, 2 vols. (1951); *The Rule of the Society of St. Vincent de Paul.*
G. P. Evans

Society of the Woman in the Wilderness.

See KELPIUS, JOHANNES.

Sockman, Ralph Washington (1889-1970).

Methodist* preacher.* Born and raised on a farm in Ohio, after graduating from high school (1906) Sockman spent one year teaching school and working on the family farm. Graduating from Ohio Wesleyan (1911), he entered graduate school at Columbia University* and studied political science (M.A., 1913) in preparation for a career of college teaching. During that time he worked as intercollegiate secretary of the YMCA.*

While studying in New York, Sockman worshiped at the Madison Avenue Methodist Episcopal Church, where pastors persuaded him to enter seminary. The church hired him as a part-time assistant minister when he began his studies at Union Theological Seminary* in 1913, and when he graduated in 1916 he joined the church staff. The following year, while studying for a Ph.D. at Columbia University, Sockman was asked to become the senior minister of the church. There he remained until his retirement in 1961.

During his early years as pastor, the Madison Avenue congregation merged with another Methodist church nearby. A new landmark building called Christ Church, Methodist, was then constructed on Park Avenue in Manhattan. Begun in 1929, its completion was delayed by the impact of the Great Depression* and World War 2,* and it was not finished until 1949. A frequent traveler, Sockman preached and spoke around the country, yet never once in forty-four years did he fail to deliver a scheduled Sunday sermon at Christ Church. In his concern to communicate the relevance for Christian faith to his day, Sockman was greatly influenced by his fellow liberal* pulpiteer Harry Emerson Fosdick.*

Sockman published twenty books, including *The Highway of God* (1942), *How to Believe* (1953), *The Meaning of Suffering* (1961) and *Recoveries in Religion* (1938). He served as president of the Methodist Board of World Peace (1928-1960), wrote a weekly newspaper column and for twenty-five years was the voice of the National Radio Pulpit. He taught at Yale* Divinity School and Union Theological Seminary, and served a term as president of the Federal Council of Churches.* Among his loyal parishioners were J. C. Penney, the department store magnate, and Alfred P. Sloan, the head of General Motors. One of his most loyal radio listeners was J. Edgar Hoover.

After retiring in 1961 he continued to write and preach. His last sermon at Christ Church was delivered on July 26, 1970. He died five weeks later at his Park Avenue apartment.

BIBLIOGRAPHY. F. J. Barton, "Ralph Washington Sockman: Twentieth Century Circuit Rider" in *American Public Address* (1961); *DARB;* E. D. Jones, *The Royalty of the Pulpit* (1951); *NCAB* G.

W. B. Lawrence

Sojourners Community. A community of Christians committed to a life of radical discipleship. The community had its origins with a group of seminarians at Trinity Evangelical Divinity School (Chicago, Illinois) who in the fall of 1971 started publishing a magazine entitled the *Post-American* under the leadership of Jim Wallis. This effort became the basis for a formal establishment one year later of the community known as the People's Christian Coalition. The community stayed briefly in a poor area of north Chicago called Uptown before moving in 1975 to Washington, D.C., its current base of operations. Subsequently, it changed the name of its magazine to *Sojourners* to reflect the belief that the church is an "alien society" of God's people "fully present in the world, but committed to a whole different order of things."

Believing that the church's mission is to challenge the social and political establishment on issues of war, civil religion,* materialism, and economic and racial oppression, the Sojourners Community is highly critical of what it regards as the "cultural conformity" of twentieth-century Christianity. It calls for and seeks to live out a pattern of discipleship characterized by a sharing of material resources, identification with the poor and disenfranchised of society and commitment to the values of social peace and reconciliation. In the late 1980s the Sojourners Community had a core membership of sixty individuals. It serves as the basis for a wide range of community-based programs, including a teaching and worship* ministry; children's programs; a food cooperative and ministries to the poor in the form of emergency food and clothing distribution. In addition, it is socially and politically active in public campaigns which challenge government policies on housing for the poor, nuclear arms and U.S. support of repressive regimes.

BIBLIOGRAPHY. W. Michaelson, "Crucible of Community; Interview: A Dialogue on the Shaping of Sojourners," *Sojourners* 6 (January 1977):14-21; J. Wallis, "Celebrating 15 Years (Sojourners Community)," *Sojourners* 15 (November 1986):5-6; J. Roos, "Sojourners Fellowship, Washington, D.C.," in *Living More Simply,* ed. R. J. Sider (1980).

R. P. Hesselgrave

Sola Scriptura. A Latin phrase (literally "by Scripture alone") describing the Protestant* theological principle that Scripture* is the final norm in all judgments of faith and practice. Church traditions and customs, pronouncements of church officials, civil law or any other purely human source, including human reason, must yield to clear scriptural pronouncements. Initially used by Protestant theologians* as a polemical device in their debates with Roman Catholics,* *sola scriptura* soon became a fundamental tenet of lay* people as well. In America this principle was manifest in the New England Puritan* "Bible* Commonwealth," as well as the primitive* or restorationist* impulse which sought to bypass the centuries of Christian institutional, liturgical and doctrinal development and restore the primitive church in the New World. The principle enunciated by Thomas Campbell* in 1809, "Where the Bible speaks, we speak; Where it is silent, we are silent," well expressed an indigenous American adaptation of a Reformation principle.

The application of *sola scriptura* has often proved problematic. Does it allow the continuance of church practices not plainly forbidden by the Bible (as many of Luther's followers were inclined to argue), or should any practice without explicit biblical sanction be condemned (as some more radical Reformers believed)? Does the Bible speak clearly on every controversial issue, or might it sometimes appear ambiguous, even contradictory and vague as to detail? The history of Protestantism provides countless occasions when people of good will, agreeing on the principle of *sola scriptura,* have been unable to agree on its application in a particular instance.

The historian seeking to understand how an individual or group derives a particular theological position from a scriptural foundation must consider the principles of biblical interpretation* (hermeneutics) at work. Is the Bible understood as a series of propositional statements, all of roughly equal weight and any of which can be used as a "proof text" in support of a position? Is the text read contextually, in its original language, with an understanding of its historical and literary milieu? Does an understanding of certain critical texts inform the interpretation of all other texts (as their understanding of Jesus' statements about the kingdom of God* did for adherents of the Social Gospel*)? Positions based on the principle of *sola scriptura* have varied according to the hermeneutical principles utilized by interpreters and communities of faith.

BIBLIOGRAPHY. R. M. Brown, *The Spirit of Prot-*

estantism (1961); N. O. Hatch and M. A. Noll, eds., *The Bible in America: Essays in Cultural History* (1982).

L. B. Tipson

Sommer, Peter Nicholas (1709-1795). Colonial Lutheran* pastor.* Sommer received his theological education in Germany before immigrating to America and ministering in the Schoharie Valley in New York. Along with his father-in-law, Willam C. Berkenmeyer,* he was a staunch proponent of Lutheran orthodoxy* and opponent of Pietism,* insisting on the acceptance of all the Lutheran confessional writings and not just the Augsburg Confession.*

Because of this he was one of the few German pastors not to cooperate with Henry Melchior Muhlenberg* in establishing the Pennsylvania Ministerium,* and refused to cooperate with the evangelistic work of George Whitefield.* During the American Revolution* he remained loyal to the crown until the English defeat was inevitable. Blind for the last twenty years of his life, he remained active in parish* ministry to the end, with the aid of assistant pastors.

BIBLIOGRAPHY. E. C. Nelson, ed., *The Lutherans in North America* (1975); J. L. Neve and W. D. Allbeck, *History of the Lutheran Church in America* (1934).

J. D. Sutherland

Sorin, Edward Frederick (1838-1893). Founder and first president of University of Notre Dame.* Born in Ahuillé, France, Sorin studied at the diocesan seminary of Le Mans, was ordained in 1838 and in 1840 joined the Congregation of Holy Cross* (C.S.C.). In 1841 he was sent to America to establish the Congregation in the Diocese of Vincennes, Indiana. In 1842 he established the University of Notre Dame near South Bend, where he served as president (1842-1865) and first chairman of its board of trustees (1865-1893). Nativism,* in the form of local Know-Nothing harassment in the late 1840s, greeted him upon his arrival in northern Indiana. Sorin offset this hostility by holding county-wide Fourth of July celebrations at the University. He likewise demonstrated his Americanism* by becoming a U.S. citizen as early as 1858, being elected to public office, serving as a local postmaster and sending eight Holy Cross priests* and eighty Holy Cross sisters to serve, respectively, as chaplains* and nurses in the Union Army during the Civil War.*

By the 1860s Sorin had come to believe that European Catholicism, beset as it was with political revolution, ideological factionalism and timid clerical leadership, had become a sterile, ossified, moribund faith. Much like American Catholics Isaac Hecker* and Orestes A. Brownson* (whom Sorin sought to add to his Notre Dame faculty), he concluded that the future of Catholic Christianity lay not in the Old World but in the New World. His international administration of the Congregation of Holy Cross as that community's superior general (1868-1893) bolstered this belief as he moved the community's international headquarters from France to Notre Dame from where he directed the Congregation's educational and missionary activities in Canada, France and Bengal, as well as the U.S.

Sorin typified much that historians see in the nineteenth-century American character: mobility (making fifty-two trans-Atlantic voyages); ambitious, inner-directed individualism (he was the head of his first university at age twenty-eight); and energetic, resourceful entrepreneurialism (in addition to being a priest,* missionary,* college president, religious superior and papal diplomat, he was also a land speculator in Nebraska, clarinetist, railroad investor, magazine publisher, historian, playwright, farmer and civic leader). Apart from founding Notre Dame, Sorin founded or administered six other Catholic institutions of higher education* in America.

BIBLIOGRAPHY. T. J. Schlereth, *The University of Notre Dame: A Portrait of Its History and Campus* (1976).

T. J. Schlereth

Soul Winning. Revivalistic* and evangelistic* term referring to the activity of making converts to Christianity. One who is particularly successful at evangelism is sometimes called a "soul winner." Based on a biblical understanding that individuals apart from faith in Christ are eternally lost, the task of evangelism came to be viewed as rescuing people, or "souls" from the bondage of the world and bringing, or "winning," them to Christ. This use of *soul,* however, suggests and promotes an unbiblical dualism.

It is not known who first coined the expressions *soul winner* and *soul winning,* but they fit well the evangelical revivalism of the nineteenth century and probably originated within that movement, with its emphasis on means and results in evangelism. Books by R. A. Torrey* and England's C. H. Spurgeon seem to be the first written specifically on "soul winning."

R. L. Petersen

South America Mission. A nondenominational mission agency founded to evangelize unreached tribal peoples. The missionary organization that would become the South American Mission (SAM) originated in 1914 out of the vision of Joseph A.

Davis, a young minister concerned with the native peoples beyond the reach of civilization. Davis established his initial station in Paraguay. When he met a Scottish missionary, John Hay, their two missions united in 1919 as the Inland South America Missionary Union. After a decade Hay and his associates withdrew, and in 1939 the mission's name was changed to the South America Indian Mission.

The group's efforts to reach the tribal groups of the Amazon basin have required sacrificial persistence and deprivation. Work was begun in Brazil in 1919, in Peru in 1921, in Bolivia in 1922 and in Colombia in 1934. Two members of the mission were killed in an attack on a station in Brazil in 1930, resulting in the redoubling of efforts to finish the work the martyrs had begun. By the 1940s the mission consisted of almost one hundred workers operating out of thirty stations and reaching thirty tribes. In order to prepare national leadership, SAM has maintained training schools and has placed scores of indigenous people in places of ministry. In support of its evangelistic efforts, the mission has opened day schools and numerous dispensaries and clinics. In 1970, as the mission increasingly reached partially acculturated tribal peoples, it deleted the term *Indian* from its name.

BIBLIOGRAPHY. J. H. Kane, *Faith, Mighty Faith* (1956); S. Wilson, ed., *Mission Handbook*, 13th edition (1986).   E. A. Wilson

Southern Baptist Convention. Largest Baptist* body in the U.S. The Southern Baptist Convention (SBC) is comprised of fifteen million baptized believers in about thirty-eight thousand churches in all fifty states of the U.S., making it the largest Protestant* denomination* in the U.S. Approximately half of all Baptists in the U.S. belong to churches affiliated with the Southern Baptist Convention.

The convention was organized on May 8, 1845, in Augusta, Georgia. Its separation from the General Missionary Convention of the Baptist Denomination in the U.S. for Foreign Missions [Triennial Convention*] and the American Baptist* Home Mission Society was due to issues arising out of the abolition movement* in the U.S. Other factors, such as the freedom to carry on missionary* activities without regard to the slavery issue and differences over the nature of denominational structure, were also contributing factors.

Theologically, most Southern Baptists are evangelicals* and subscribe to the authority of the Bible* in determining their ecclesiology and social action. They baptize* by immersion believers who publicly profess faith; they hold that neither baptism nor the Lord's Supper* convey sacramental* grace. A heavy evangelistic* and missionary emphasis has helped to shape the denomination into one of the most aggressive missionary bodies in Christendom. In their doctrine of salvation, Southern Baptists can be generally classified as modified Calvinists,* being heirs of the Free Church* tradition which includes both Calvinist and Arminian* strains. Southern Baptists are not bound by a creed* but share a confession of faith based on The New Hampshire Confession,* first adopted by the Convention in 1925 and revised in 1963.

Southern Baptist worship* is nonliturgical. Preaching* is the central act of worship while music constitutes an important element in the worship life of the churches. Great emphasis is placed upon congregational singing. Many churches have a graded choir* program and some feature orchestras in addition to pianos, organs and bell choirs.

A strong congregational ecclesiology, coupled with a sense of destiny and a conservative theology, have helped to determine the Convention's relationship with other Christian communions. Southern Baptists have steadfastly refused to join the National* and World* Councils of Churches. Its agencies, however, cooperate with various programs of the National Council of Churches on projects of mutual interest. Although not a member of the World Council of Churches, the Southern Baptist Convention took the lead in bringing disparate Baptist unions and conventions together into the Baptist World Alliance* in 1905.

The organization of the SBC seems simple but is, in reality, very complex. Southern Baptists jealously guard the autonomy of the local church. The local church is the highest judicature in Southern Baptist life. Yet the principle of cooperation commands the loyalty of most Southern Baptists. Local congregations are related to the SBC in the same way they are related to the state conventions and local associations. Congregations also send messengers to area associations and state conventions, each of which is an autonomous body but closely interrelated. The state conventions sponsor educational and benevolent institutions, such as hospitals, orphanages and retirement villages, as well as mission programs, within their respective states.

The relationship between the congregations, the state convention and the SBC is both voluntary and financial. Churches may send to the annual meeting of the SBC up to ten "messengers." The number is determined by the size of church membership and the amount of money given to denominational causes. The messengers then report back to their churches on the actions of the annual meeting. The Convention has no authority over the churches but is free to recommend and promote convention-wide programs. The churches then may support either completely or partially the programs recommended by the associations, state conventions and the SBC. Without the cooperation and financial support of the local churches, the SBC could not function.

The work of the Convention is delegated to four boards, seven commissions, and six seminaries. Of these agencies the Foreign and Home Mission Boards sponsor 7,556 missionaries (1987). Missionary work in the U.S. is performed in eighty-seven different languages under the direction of the Home Mission Board. In 1987 the Foreign Mission Board supported 3,816 missionaries who served in 108 countries.

Responsibility for colleges and seminaries of the denomination is divided between the SBC, which sponsors the seminaries, and the state conventions which operate the colleges and universities. For the 1986-1987 school year, the fifty-one colleges enrolled 161,108 students and the six seminaries had a total enrollment of 10,910.

See also BAPTIST CHURCHES.

BIBLIOGRAPHY. R. A. Baker, *The Southern Baptist Convention and Its People, 1607-1972 (1974)*; W. Barnes, *The Southern Baptist Convention* (1954); L. McBeth, *The Baptist Heritage* (1987); *Encyclopedia of Southern Baptists,* vols. 1-4 (1958-1982); *Southern Baptist Convention Annual* (1986).

W. R. Estep

Southern Christian Leadership Conference (SCLC). An organization advocating nonviolent social change, particularly in the area of civil rights. Although it was only one of several local desegregation campaigns of the mid-1950s, the Montgomery bus boycott of 1955-1956 was distinctive as the triggering event in the formation of a Southwide nonviolent movement. Sparked by the refusal of Rosa Parks, an African-American seamstress, to yield her bus seat to a white man, as law and custom required, the 381-day boycott led by the Montgomery Improvement Association (MIA) became both a model and an experiential center for the convergence of many local efforts. In January 1957 some sixty people, mostly African-American ministers, met at the Ebenezer Baptist Church in Atlanta to consider the possibility of continuing the "Montgomery way" in an organized

regional association. Subsequent meetings in New Orleans and Montgomery in the same year resulted in the formation of the Southern Christian Leadership Conference. Dr. Martin Luther King, Jr.,* pastor of the Dexter Avenue Baptist Church in Montgomery and president of the MIA, was elected president of SCLC.

The guiding principle of SCLC was nonviolence, derived in part from the tactics of Mohandas K. Gandhi in India, but in a broader sense from the religious faith of its members. The SCLC chose not to be a membership organization but a loose network of "affiliates." At the outset SCLC, with its headquarters on Auburn Avenue in Atlanta, had affiliates in eleven states.

SCLC is best known for its leadership of nonviolent campaigns in Albany (1962), Birmingham (1963), St. Augustine (1964) and Selma (1965). The Birmingham and Selma campaigns were very instrumental in moving the Congress to enact the 1964 Civil Rights Act and the 1965 Voting Rights Act. But SCLC also had significant impact through its programs of educational and economic improvement. After 1965 SCLC's efforts to extend its outreach into Chicago (1966) and other Northern cities had less obvious results.

King's death slowed the momentum both of the nonviolent movement and SCLC. His successor, Ralph David Abernathy (president from 1968 to 1977), continued the basic program of nonviolent direct action. Abernathy was succeeded by Dr. Joseph E. Lowery, a Methodist minister, who began a rebuilding program that had visible results by the end of the seventies. In the early 1980s SCLC campaigned for extension of the Voting Rights Act (1982) and a variety of economic and social reforms. Youth programs were expanded, and SCLC/WOMEN was added. Occasionally, SCLC also spoke out on foreign-affairs issues, as King had done in opposing the Vietnam War.

BIBLIOGRAPHY. A. Fairclough, *To Redeem the Soul of America: The Southern Christian Leadership Conference and Martin Luther King, Jr.* (1987); D. J. Garrow, *Bearing the Cross: Martin Luther King, Jr., and the Southern Christian Leadership Conference* (1986); T. R. Peake, *Keeping the Dream Alive: A History of the Southern Christian Leadership Conference from King to the Nineteen-Eighties* (1987). T. R. Peake

Southern Christianity. Recognized as a distinctive religious region in North America, the South is dominated by Protestantism*—particularly conservative or evangelical* forms of it. Baptists* are by far the largest and most influential tradition within both white and African-American populations.

The Span of Popular Southern Christianity.
What truly distinguishes the South is the span of
popular forms of Christianity. It extends as far as
the Presbyterians* on the classical end but knows
no boundaries on the innovative or radical end.
That is to say, fundamentalists,* Restorationists,*
independents and Holiness* and Pentecostal*
churches and people are plentiful, and, while
regarded by the majority as having gone too far
with their zeal, are viewed as basically on the right
track. In the substantial middle are the major
Baptist denominations and the Methodists.*

Of course others are present: the Episcopal
Church* in towns and cities everywhere; Lutheran-
ism* in certain parts of the Carolinas, Virginia and
Texas; the United Church of Christ* and the
Society of Friends* here and there, especially in
North Carolina; the Restoration Movement in the
form of the Disciples of Christ* in Kentucky,
Virginia and North Carolina especially, and the
Churches of Christ* in great strength, especially in
middle and west Tennessee and certain areas of
Texas and Arkansas.

Roman Catholicism,* despite the early settlement of the Spanish* and the French* in the lower
South, has always been weaker in the region than
anywhere else in the nation. In the late twentieth
century, active immigration from other regions has
expanded centers of Catholic strength to many
places—beyond its traditional strongholds in
Maryland, Kentucky, Louisiana and, more recently,
south Texas and south Florida. Fears and suspicions toward the Catholic Church and Catholics,
long widespread and sometimes quite hostile,
have abated notably. A major reason for this is the
presence of the Catholic community within most
people's orbits of acquaintance. This new set of
conditions marks a sharp break with the Southern
nativism* and triumphal Protestantism that shaped
cultural values for so long. The Southern faithful
are still willing to do battle, but the enemy is
hardly ever the Catholic Church anymore.

From the beginning of Southern society, Protestantism has been the region's religious form. The
Church of England* was the established church in
all the colonies throughout the colonial period. A
small number of Catholics were scattered through
the thinly populated areas of La Florida, from the
Atlantic to the Mississippi River. A larger number,
but still a minority, lived in Maryland. Protestant
diversity emerged as Congregationalists,* Quakers,
Baptists and Presbyterians moved in from England,
New England, Ulster and Scotland. During the
middle third of the eighteenth century, German

Lutherans, Anabaptists* and Moravians* settled in
Virginia and the Carolinas. Methodists appeared in
the South about as early as they did anywhere; and
people of Wesleyan* persuasion and style were
surfacing in and out of Anglican parish churches in
the 1760s.

The "big three" Southern denominations had
staked out the high ground before the Revolutionary War.* Baptists and Methodists proliferated with
such force that they had claimed the field, both on
the Western frontier and in the older seaboard
areas, by the 1830s. Presbyterians were never as
large, but they were a familiar component and
formidable in their influence almost everywhere.
What these numbers and proportions signified was
that, during the period of the Old South, Protestantism of the center and left-of-center acquired
normative status. Presbyterians anchored this
spectrum on its traditionalist end, and the Baptists
energized it through their dynamic and innovative
means.

The enlarging African-American population
became a part of the Protestant company in the
antebellum South. Black Baptists and Methodists
were numerous; church and faith became a central
force in personal and social life for the entire
community. The presence of these culturally
distinctive people in the services and organizational life of the white-run churches affected the
modes of white Protestantism.

After the Civil War,* separate, independent
African-American congregations and denominations appeared with remarkable speed. This
contributed to the South's becoming an even more
intensely religious culture. Religious interaction
between the two racial societies was infrequent—
indeed, taboo—but they shared in building a
cohesive evangelical culture. In terms of their
familiarity and ready acceptability, African-American and white forms alike were thoroughly accredited.

Around 1900 even more conservative (non-
traditional) brands of religion appeared among
whites and African-Americans, sometimes in mixed
congregations, but especially in the vicinity of the
southern Appalachian highlands and among the
poor and powerless. Pentecostal and Holiness
practices characterized those groups and managed
to distinguish them as "off brand" and extreme by
the lights of most religious, as well as social,
circles. Fundamentalism also made its appearance,
both in regionally traditional modes such as the
Churches of Christ, and through movements that
held the line against new intellectual and scientific
currents.

[1115]

The Changing Face of Southern Christianity. In the late 1980s the region continued to reflect the strength and cultural dominance of the popular Southern religion forged around 1830 by the Baptists and Methodists—and to a degree by the Presbyterians also. But the span had widened and extended leftward to include several million Pentecostal, Holiness and fundamentalist people who were no longer confined to the margins of the society or its religious life. On the more traditional end, it stretched to embrace Catholics, Lutherans and Episcopalians, as well as the liberal bodies. The center of gravity remained well to the left of the center of the traditional Christian heritage and the pull was, if anything, somewhat more to the left. The Southern Baptist Convention,* the nation's largest Protestant body, was feeling the effect of that pull in the protracted struggle (threatening its unity) between "moderate conservatives" and "fundamental conservatives."

The South's dominant forms of Protestant Christianity are correctly described as "evangelical." But, as always, the use of that complex term calls for refinement. Southern evangelicalism is, for the greater part, conversionist rather than confessional. That is, its orientation is toward direct personal experience of God in a specifiable event of conversion.* Confessionalism,* that is, subscription to a creed* or to doctrine* as constitutive of faith, is recessive. Where fundamentalism exists, assent to a stated list of doctrines as well as to the inerrancy* of Scripture,* is absolutely required. In the Presbyterian Church in America,* a conservative body created in 1973, a particular version of Calvinist* scholasticism prevails. But classical forms of Calvinist or Lutheran confessionalism, so influential in Northern evangelicalism, are somewhat eccentric in the South.

The revival* is the technique that brought so much of the Southern population into the churches' folds from the 1740s and 1750s and the Great Revival of 1799-1810 (*See* Second Great Awakening), through to the end of the nineteenth century. Conversionist theologies are correlated with revivalist measures. Knowing in one's heart that he or she has been saved in the datable, memorable—and sometimes intensely dramatic— event of conversion, is the hallmark of Christian identification. This is most notably true within the evangelistic white communions. In the African-American church the focus does not fall on a moment that demarcates entry into the saved life, but on the continual exposure to and enjoyment of the Spirit's presence in one's heart. The distinction between "in" and "out" is sharper in the white church than in the African-American church, but the assurance of human access to God is powerful and central in both cases. Moreover, both these groups of Christians believe that one's identity as a Christian is a matter of fact—as a badge and practice among whites and as a practice in the African-American churches.

A "limited options culture" is about as concise a characterization of historic Southernness as any. Homogeneity with respect to ethnicity, politics and forms of commerce has been joined by religion in Southern society and culture from the Old South down to World War 2.* Since then, the racial desegregation of the region has driven a wedge into this homogeneity. In addition, since the 1950s diversity in population and in economic and political life have made a heavy imprint. But for a very long time, religious homogeneity (the narrow center-to-left span of Protestant Christianity) prevailed. Few extraneous options were available and Baptist and Baptist-like forms were the center of gravity. It is this transition from limited to multiple options, their availability and popularity, that is occasioning severe strains within the denominations and the proliferation of hyperconservative bodies in regional life.

The charge that religion has been captive to culture in the American South has plausibility but is only partially true. On the one hand, church and theology have supported slavery and segregation and reinforced regional identity. Moreover, indigenous forms of white Christianity have not been exported easily or widely. And, we have noted, versions of evangelicalism strong elsewhere have not managed a firm hold in the South. On the other hand, the African-American churches have typically been prophetic, challenging the status quo. White Christianity too has shown a reform-mindedness on such issues as the dangers of alcoholic* beverages, gambling, mistreatment of slaves and separation of church and state.* A vocal minority has always been present to condemn economic and social injustices, including slavery and segregation, corruption in government and inferior education. Thus it is accurate to note an effective symbiosis between church and culture in the South, but misleading to suggest an uncritical relationship between them.

Christianity in the American South has stronger claim to a cultural establishment than it does anywhere in historic Christendom—but among the traditionally Protestant societies in particular. In the late twentieth century, it faces major disruptions and dislocations but persists in great numerical strength and major social and cultural impact.

BIBLIOGRAPHY. D. E. Harrell, ed., *Varieties of Southern Evangelicalism* (1981); S. S. Hill, *Southern Churches in Crisis* (1967); S. S. Hill, *Encyclopedia of Southern Religion* (1984); E. B. Holifield, *The Gentlemen Theologians* (1978); D. G. Mathews, *Religion in the Old South* (1979); C. R. Wilson, ed., *Religion in the South* (1985).

S. S. Hill

Southern Presbyterians. *See* PRESBYTERIAN CHURCH IN THE UNITED STATES.

Southern Sociological Congress. The Congress was called by Governor Ben Hooper of Tennessee to meet in Nashville on May 7-10, 1912, for the purpose of addressing the "social, civic and economic problems" of sixteen Southern states. As the Congress outlined its social program, it asked "for the closest cooperation between the church and all social agencies." Furthermore, the Congress issued "a challenge to the Church to prove her right to social mastery by a universal and unselfish social ministry." Invited to speak at this first Congress was Washington Gladden,* a prominent leader in the Social Gospel Movement,* along with other Protestant* and Catholic* clergy.* When the Congress met the following year, further stress was placed on the ways in which the church could advance social service. Speakers at the 1913 Congress included Walter Rauschenbusch,* a prominent Social Gospeller; Charles S. Macfarland, secretary of the Federal Council of Churches*; and other clergy who were prominent in the arena of social service and action. The Congress met until 1920, when it moved its headquarters to Washington, D. C., and changed its name to the Southern Cooperative League of Education and Social Service.

The Southern Sociological Congress was an example of government, social agencies and the church working together for social betterment. It demonstrated the church's willingness to use the techniques of social service, and it gave evidence that secular agencies recognized the important role the church could play in addressing social needs, such as child welfare, justice, public health, African-American needs and education. The Congress had its roots in the Social Gospel Movement and turned to the movement for its initial inspiration and for help in implementing its program.

BIBLIOGRAPHY. L. M. Brooks and A. L. Bertrand, *History of the Southern Sociological Society* (1962); Southern Sociological Congress, *The Call of the New South* (1912); Southern Sociological Congress, *The South Mobilizing for Social Service* (1913).

D. B. Chesebrough

Spalding, John Lancaster (1840-1916). Bishop of Peoria. Born in Lebanon, Kentucky, and descended from a Maryland Catholic family which arrived in the colonies in 1650, Spalding was the nephew of Cardinal* Martin J. Spalding* of Louisville. Young Spalding went to local primary schools, graduated from St. Mary's College, Kentucky, in 1859, then attended Mount St. Mary's Seminary of the West at Cincinnati, and was sent for further study at the American College at Rome* and the American College at Louvain. Ordained* in 1863, he continued to study in Europe until 1865.

Upon returning to the U.S. Spalding became curate of the cathedral* in Louisville, attended the Second Plenary Council at Baltimore* in 1866, organized the first African-American parish* in Louisville in 1869 and became chancellor of the diocese* in 1871. In 1872 the Paulist* Fathers called him to be assistant at St. Michael's Church in New York City. During that time Spalding developed a distinct dislike for cities, called them morally depraved, urged Catholics to avoid work in factories and in mines, and advocated their resettlement in rural life. Spalding also led in the Catholic prohibition movement,* as he believed that drink destroyed work and moral ethics.

In 1877 Pope Pius IX* named him to the See at Peoria, Illinois. Spalding joined liberal Catholic leaders at the Third Council at Baltimore in 1884 in support of the Irish Colonization Society to help Catholics move West. Active in educational circles, in 1898 he opened a boy's school, the Spalding Institute, and he was instrumental in the promotion of and the founding of The Catholic University of America.* He wrote many books and educational essays, including a biography of his uncle Martin J. Spalding (1873) and the political work *The Religious Mission of the Irish People and Catholic Colonization* (1880).

President Theodore Roosevelt appointed him to the Anthracite Coal Commission in 1902, in which capacity this scion of a patrician Kentucky family spoke against the poor treatment of miners. After suffering a stroke in 1905, Spalding curtailed his work, resigned his See in 1908 and retired to live in Peoria.

BIBLIOGRAPHY. *DAB* IX; *DARB;* J. T. Ellis, *John Lancaster Spalding* (1961); *NCAB* 10; D. F. Sweeney, *The Life of John Lancaster Spalding* (1965).

J. L. Wakelyn

Spalding, Martin John (1810-1872). Bishop* of Louisville, archbishop* of Baltimore and Catholic* apologist.* Born into a devout Catholic family in Kentucky, Martin and his brother Benedict became priests.* After graduating from St. Mary's College (1826), Spalding earned a seminary* degree from St. Thomas in Bardstown, Kentucky (1830), and a doctorate in theology from Urban College in Rome (1834). Returning to Kentucky in 1834, he served as pastor at Bardstown (1834-1838, 1841-1848) and Lexington (1840-1841), Kentucky, as rector of St. Joseph's College (1838-1840) and as vicar-general (1844-1848) and then bishop of Louisville (1848-1864). In 1864 he became archbishop of Baltimore.

During his Kentucky years Spalding wrote frequently for Catholic magazines, including the *Catholic Advocate* and *The Metropolitan,* both of which he later edited. Spalding earned national fame as a lecturer and writer of Catholic apologetics* and history. Among his publications were the oft-reprinted lectures *General Evidences of Catholicity* (1847), his essays published in *Miscellanea* (1855) and several histories of Catholics and the church in Kentucky, as well as of the Reformation in Europe. Spalding also supported the Catholic Publication Society in an effort to provide Catholics with their own literature, free of Protestant* influences. As bishop of Louisville, his pastorals on the sacraments,* marriage and education attracted national attention; so too did his personal and written opposition to the anti-Catholic and nativist* attacks of the 1850s. As priest and bishop, Spalding reached out to African-Americans, established orphanages and charities, and introduced several religious orders* to Kentucky.

Throughout his life Spalding argued that education was the foundation of faith and civic responsibility. To that end, he built parochial schools,* promoted the American colleges in Louvain and in Rome,* urged the creation of a national Catholic university, and, while archbishop of Baltimore, supported postemancipation schools for African-Americans and founded St. Mary's Industrial School in Baltimore. During the Civil War* Spalding espoused a neutral position for Catholics, despite his own personal Southern sympathies. His pamphlet *Dissertazione nella Guerra Civile Americana* (1863), influenced European Catholic opinion toward neutrality regarding the American Civil War. After the war, he played a leading role in organizing Catholic relief in the South and encouraging the Josephite Fathers in their missions to African-Americans.

Spalding believed that a strong Catholicism best protected Catholics in America. Strength derived from unity in doctrine* and practice and submission to church authority.* As archbishop of Baltimore, Spalding called the Second Plenary Council

(1866), which codified ecclesiastical discipline and church legislation, much of it drafted by Spalding, and established rules for doctrinal uniformity. Spalding defended the Syllabus of Errors and advocated defining papal infallibility* at the Vatican Council* in 1870, and then endorsed the dogma in his writings. He died in 1872 and was buried at the cathedral* in Baltimore.

BIBLIOGRAPHY. J. L. Spalding, *The Life of the Most Rev. M. J. Spalding, D. D., Archbishop of Baltimore* (1873); T. W. Spalding, *Martin John Spalding: American Churchman* (1973); and A. A. Micek, *The Apologetics of Martin John Spalding* (1915). R. M. Miller

Spangenberg, Augustus Gottlieb (1704-1792). Moravian* bishop* and assistant to Count Nikolaus L. Zinzendorf.* Born at Klettenberg, Germany, the son of a Lutheran* minister,* Spangenberg was educated at the University of Jena (M.A., 1726). He taught at Jena (1726-1732) and Halle (1732-1733) before joining the Moravians in 1733 and becoming Zinzendorf's assistant. In 1735 Spangenberg led the Moravian colonists to Georgia and then moved to Pennsylvania in 1736, where he remained until 1739. For several years (1739-1744) he conducted mission* work in Europe and was instrumental in establishing a Moravian work in England.

Spangenberg was with Zinzendorf at the early meetings of the Pennsylvania synods* and wrote a theme hymn for them. In 1744 he was consecrated* bishop and put in charge of the settlement at Bethlehem, Pennsylvania, from 1744 until 1748. Instrumental in establishing the economic structure for the town, he provided a base for support of the Moravian mission and extension work in the colonies. In 1752 he led Moravians in settling the Wachau district of North Carolina. Following another brief period in Europe, he returned to America in 1754, where he remained until 1762 when he was summoned to return to Herrnhut, Saxony, following the death of Zinzendorf. The remainder of his life was spent in Europe, leading Moravian missionary* activity. Spangenberg wrote an extensive biography of Zinzendorf, published in eight volumes (1772-1775), and his *Idea Fidei Fratrum* (1779) set forth the Moravian vision of Christian piety. Called "Brother Joseph" by his brethren because of his kind and faithful care of them, he is remembered for the motto he left the American Moravian Church: "Together we pray, together we labor, together we suffer, together we rejoice."

BIBLIOGRAPHY. *DAB* IX; *DARB; NCAB* 1. A. H. Frank

Spanish-American War and the American Churches. When Cuban insurgents rebelled against Spanish rule in 1895, most Americans sympathized with the revolutionaries who, in their view, had long been wrongly oppressed. Although Christians expressed humanitarian concerns as reason for intervention, they also spoke of ensuing commercial advantages if Cuban insurgency proved successful. But there was mixed reaction to questions of whether the U.S. should officially recognize a status of belligerency. Christian leaders supported intervention in Cuba through diplomatic means. American churches rather overwhelmingly opposed both U.S. attempts to annex Cuba or filibustering as a means of settling the conflict.

In 1898 after the sinking of the *Maine,* the religious press, unlike the yellow press, counseled patience pending full investigation. After the American Court of Inquiry judged that an external explosion from a submarine mine destroyed the *Maine* but refused to fix blame on either the Spanish or Cuban rebels, American churches supported these findings. More damaging in turning churches against Spain than the *Maine* disaster was a speech delivered by Vermont's respected Senator Redfield Procter, who, after touring war-stricken Cuba, returned to give graphic descriptions of what he had observed.

After the official U.S. declaration of war in April 1898, the churches strongly supported the war effort. Some Christians viewed it as a holy crusade. Victories against the Spanish at Manila, Philippines, and Santiago, Cuba, it was said, were signs that God was on the American side. The U.S. had been chosen as a nation called to chastise the evil Spaniards. At the same time churchmen denounced the yellow press, ardently hoped for a speedy end to the conflict, and prayed that the altruistic motives which prompted U.S. intervention not be compromised or put aside as Americans waged war on Spain.

After the war, the American religious press manifested great interest in the individuals named to the American Peace Commission. This press applauded the selection of Justice Eduard D. White, a Catholic* who, it was said, embraced the same faith as the natives of the newly acquired possessions. The *Christian Register* stated that the appointment gave evidence "of the desire of the United States to give due and impartial consideration to all the interests that were involved in the conflict."

Most churches agreed with the decision that Cuba should be given independence, while Puerto Rico should be annexed. Philippine annexation generated significant debate. Some churchmen argued that much work remained to be done at home and that annexation violated America's democratic ideals. One minister reminded his hearers of American treatment of its own Native Americans, thus implying that there should be no repeat performance.

The preponderant opinion, however, favored Philippine annexation. Churches saw an opportunity to extend the gospel to a "barbarous" people. President William McKinley,* a devout Methodist,* may well have reflected the sentiments of most churchmen when he described how he had repeatedly sought God's guidance and then one night it came to him that "there was nothing left for us to do but to take them all, and to educate the Filipinos, and uplift and civilize and Christianize them, and by God's grace do the very best we could by them, as our fellow men for whom Christ also died." After that revelation, said the president, "I went to bed, and went to sleep and slept soundly."

BIBLIOGRAPHY. W. A. Karraker, "The American Churches and the Spanish-American War" (unpublished Ph.D. dissertation, University of Chicago, 1940); J. W. Pratt, *Expansionists of 1898* (1936); A. G. Cerillo, Jr., "The Spanish-American War," in *The Wars of America: Christian Views,* ed. R. A. Wells (1981).   R. Bolt

Speer, Robert Elliott (1867-1947). Evangelist* and Presbyterian* missions* leader. Born in Pennsylvania, graduated from Princeton University* in 1889, Speer worked for the Student Volunteer Movement* for one year before attending Princeton Theological Seminary* (1889-1891). From 1891 until his retirement in 1937, he served as a lay* secretary of the Presbyterian Board of Foreign Missions in New York. In 1893 he married Emma Doll Bailey, later a leader in the Presbyterian Church and in the world YMCA.*

Speer's interest in missions was shaped by attending Dwight L. Moody's* Northfield Conferences* and by his friend John R. Mott.* His own thinking is well illustrated in his *The Unfinished Task of Foreign Missions* (1926). For Speer the purpose of foreign missions was "to plant and set in the way to autonomy and self-maintenance the Christian Church in nations where it does not exist." He also wrote about the social conditions in Asia and Latin America during the period of 1890 to 1930 and the work of the Presbyterian missions and churches in those areas. An advocate of the unique authority of Christ amid the religions of the world, his book *The Finality of Christ* (1933) was widely influential. A prolific author, he wrote over sixty-seven books and pamphlets and numerous articles.

An ecumenist, Speer was a leader in the Federal Council of Churches*—elected as its president in 1920—as well as in the Foreign Missionary Conference of North America* and the International Missionary Council, a parent body of the World Council of Churches.* His own denomination, the Presbyterian Church in the U.S.A., elected him moderator of the General Assembly in 1927. However, conservatives within his own denomination were not all happy with his policies, and he was sharply criticized by J. Gresham Machen* for sending theologically liberal missionaries overseas.

BIBLIOGRAPHY. *DAB* 4; *DARB*; H. M. Goodpasture, "Robert E. Speer's Legacy," *IBMR* 2 (1978):38-41; *NCAB* 36; W. R. Wheeler, *A Man Sent From God: A Biography of Robert E. Speer* (1956).

H. M. Goodpasture

Spellman, Francis Joseph (1889-1967).

Catholic* archbishop* of New York. The son of a Whitman, Massachusetts, grocer, Spellman graduated from Fordham University in 1911 and went to the North American College in Rome* where he was ordained* in 1916. Not an impressive figure in his personal appearance or in the pulpit, Spellman's power lay in his personal connections and his abilities in diplomacy, administration and finance. His rise to prominence within the American Church is all the more amazing in that his superiors, Cardinal* William O'Connell* of Boston chief among them, often tried to bury him in obscure positions. But Spellman's carefully cultivated personal connections enabled him to return to Rome in 1925, where he was attached to the Vatican Secretariat of State. Of the many contacts he made between 1925 and his return to Boston as auxiliary bishop in 1932, the most significant was his close friendship with Eugenio Pacelli, who, from 1939 until his death in 1958, served as Pope Pius XII.* Within months of his election, Pacelli appointed Spellman archbishop of New York.

Italian participation in World War 2* on the side of the Axis combined with the Vatican's neutrality, lent considerable diplomatic importance to Spellman's role under Pacelli as the Vatican's chief contact with the U.S. government. As New York's archbishop, Spellman was also Military Vicar, or Bishop Ordinary of the Army and Navy, a post he relished. President Roosevelt took advantage of the Military Vicar's freedom of movement to enlist him as an unofficial envoy representing U.S. interests in various parts of the globe. At war's end, he nearly became Vatican Secretary of State, and Pacelli named him a cardinal in 1946.

Spellman's stature in New York politics was equally formidable. He took controversial public stands on birth control,* movie censorship and public aid to private schools, and defended the rightful place of Catholics in American society. His American nationalism was matched by the ardor of his anti-Communism. In addition to his public support for Joseph McCarthy and his general opposition to unions, Spellman's anti-Communism led him to continue his diplomatic activities on behalf of the U.S. in Latin America and Southeast Asia. With Pacelli's death, the election of John F. Kennedy* in 1960, and the general mood swing of the 1960s, Spellman's power began to wane.

Kennedy all but squashed the campaign Spellman had waged since 1939 for formal diplomatic recognition of the Vatican by the U.S. Spellman patronized Ngo Dinh Diem and his rise to the presidency of South Vietnam, and as Military Vicar he gave strong support to the U.S. cause in Vietnam.* At Vatican 2* Spellman was personally responsible for bringing Jesuit* theologian* John Courtney Murray* to Rome. During conciliar debates he lent his support to the "Declaration on Religious Freedom," fathered by Murray and generally acknowledged as the chief contribution of American Catholicism to the council's work.

Spellman combined genuine thoughtfulness toward others with an instinct for the right career move in a way that makes it easy to dismiss him as inordinately ambitious. He was blessed with a near-photographic memory, endearing him to the many whose names and faces he always remembered, and an extraordinary gift for languages. Although he published a novel, some poetry and translations of Italian theology, his chief gift with words lay in his facility for learning and speaking other languages. During a period known for the "Romanization" of the Catholic hierarchy in the U.S., Spellman, for better or worse, succeeded, where his Americanist* predecessors had failed, in bringing Catholics into the American mainstream. He was one of the most politically influential churchmen in U.S. history.

BIBLIOGRAPHY. J. Cooney, *The American Pope: The Life and Times of Francis Cardinal Spellman* (1986); *DARB*; J. T. Ellis, *CHR* 72 (1986):676-681; G. P. Fogarty, *The Vatican and the American Hierarchy from 1870 to 1965* (1985); R. I. Gannon, *The Cardinal Spellman Story* (1962); *NCAB* F.

W. L. Portier

Spirit Baptism. *See* BAPTISM IN THE SPIRIT.

Spiritual Director. A person whose ministry is to guide a fellow believer into deeper Christian experience. Normally spiritual direction takes place on an individual or small-group basis. A spiritual director does not necessarily carry out other ministerial tasks, such as preaching or administering the sacraments,* unless such is part of his or her broader ministry. Two historical roots may be identified for the modern work of the spiritual director. The calling originated out of the system of confession and penance* in which individuals allowed their spiritual welfare to be guided by a priest.* Furthermore, in the contemplative (mystical) traditions of spirituality, the person with greater experience gives direction to the novice. Spiritual directors must be knowledgeable in Christian belief as well as sensitive in dealing with people. Above all, they must have attained a recognizable level of maturity themselves. This office is most widely recognized in the Roman Catholic* and Anglican* traditions.

BIBLIOGRAPHY. F. De Sales, *Introduction to the Devout Life* (1959); T. Merton, *Spiritual Direction and Meditation* (1975). W. Corduan

Spirituality: Catholic. The goal of Catholic spirituality is the profound union of the individual with God in prayer,* something which can never be earned or achieved by human effort, but which is a pure gift from God. The predisposing conditions for and obstacles against such a union, as well as the means and methods conducive to it are all subjects of Catholic spiritual writings throughout the centuries. Since Catholics believe that God is accessible to the individual, Catholic spirituality is always incarnational, sacramental,* integrative and unitive. Until recently, American Catholic spirituality reflected Western European traditions that developed after the Council of Trent (1545-1563) rather than any specific American adaptations.

Colonial Domestic Spirituality, 1565-1776. The three major nations that vied for control of North America each had Catholic colonists. Spain and France transplanted a state-sponsored Church and a national culture permeated with Catholicism. Priests* were sent to minister to colonists and also to evangelize Native Americans. Some of the most creative expressions of spirituality at the time attempted to reconcile European Catholic piety* with compatible elements of Native American religion. Meanwhile, Spanish and French settlers brought their spirituality from the mother country, but mediated it through home and family because of the scarcity of clergy* and parishes.*

This domestic spirituality was particularly evident in the English colonies where Catholicism was a small minority amidst a decidedly anti-Catholic culture. Catholic clergy, parishes and laity were few and far between. Itinerant Jesuits* (numbering between five and twenty-three at any one time) made sporadic visits to pockets of Catholics in the rural areas, ministering out of homes rather than churches. Domestic Catholic piety expressed itself through private devotional* reading, family prayers* and special dietary practices (e.g., meatless Fridays). Religious education of youth took place in the home with parents and relatives. English colonial spirituality was private, personal, unobtrusive, discrete and domestic. Except among the Native Americans, no attempt was made in colonial America to harmonize the American experience with European spirituality.

Devotional Spirituality, 1776-1960. With the birth of the nation came the separation of church and state,* religious freedom,* voluntarism* and pluralism.* From the 1830s waves of Catholic immigrants* crowded into urban parishes which became the focal points of their spiritual lives, although in the South older patterns of domestic piety often remained. Catholics from Ireland, Germany, Poland, Italy and other European countries carried with them their devotional spirituality, which gave them a sense of security amidst a new and often-unwelcoming American environment. This devotionalism emphasized private rote prayer (such as the Rosary*), the sacraments* (such as confession), eucharistic* adoration (such as benediction*), the Blessed Virgin Mary,* specific saints* as personal patrons, festivals and processions. After 1900 it became more standardized, institutionalized and Romanized. Until 1960, with the exception of a few individuals (John Carroll,* Isaac Hecker,* John Keane,* Dorothy Day*), American Catholics made little attempt to integrate Catholic spirituality with American culture.

Post-Vatican II Spirituality, 1960 to the Present. In the 1960s a "spiritual earthquake" in American Catholicism began to produce a new expression of spirituality that was liturgical,* scriptural, historical and mystical.* This was precipitated by several events, including shifts in American culture and changes initiated by Vatican Council II.* Rather than a carbon copy of Western European thought and practice, this new piety was informed by American culture.

Since Vatican II's revision of the liturgy, no longer is the Mass* a priest's prayer in Latin which the laity observed with devotion, but a communal celebration in the vernacular with broad participation by all. The new spirituality focuses on Scripture, something de-emphasized in the older devotionalism. More Scripture is read at the liturgy as well as in private, with Scripture study groups meeting in many parishes. New Catholic congregational hymns* express scriptural themes and, most importantly, Catholic preaching* is now based primarily on Scripture.

The new spirituality is also historical. The history of spirituality is studied with renewed interest and insight while trying to integrate this understanding with American cultural identity. The most latent development is mysticism.* The popularity of American spiritual writers (such as Thomas Merton*), the charismatic movement,* parish prayer groups and spiritual renewal groups (such as Cursillo*) all testify to the quest for mysticism. Disenchantment with modernity has resulted in a hunger for spiritual values, for the mystical, which is expressed both individually and communally. Recent emphasis on lay involvement, social justice and preference for the poor must all be informed and sustained by the life of the Spirit.

The implications of Vatican II for Catholic spirituality continue to unfold. The shift from devotional spirituality to a new expression continues to produce pain, confusion and anxiety for some Catholics. Yet this new spirituality is potentially both more Catholic and more American than any previous expression of American spirituality. *See also* PIETY, CATHOLIC POPULAR.

BIBLIOGRAPHY. J. P. Chinnici, ed., *Devotion to the Holy Spirit in American Catholicism* (1985); R. E. Curran, ed., *American Jesuit Spirituality: The Maryland Tradition, 1634-1900* (1988); J. P. Dolan, *The American Catholic Experience: A History from Colonial Times to the Present* (1985); J. Farina, *An American Experience of God: The Spirituality of Isaac Hecker* (1981); A. Taves, *The Household of Faith: Roman Catholic Devotions in Mid-Nineteenth Century America* (1986).

M. J. McNally

Spirituality: Orthodox. For Orthodox* Christians spirituality is a way of living and thinking centered on the mystery of the risen Christ as encountered through personal prayer,* the reading of Scripture,* the sacraments* and devotional practices of the Orthodox Church. Its basis is the experience of new creation in Christ by the power of the Holy Spirit and its goal is *theosis* (deification or divinization), understood as glorification by participation in the eternal resurrection light commonly shared by the Holy Trinity. Orthodox spirituality is closely related to Orthodox piety,* from which it cannot be empirically separated because both are at once deeply rooted in the same worship,* theology and life of the Orthodox Church as a living community guided by the Holy Spirit.

Orthodox spirituality is marked by a variety of accents, yet a profound coherence of vision. The ascetic accent (fasting, sleeping on the ground, harsh dress and struggle against demons) is typified by Anthony the Great (250-356). Purification of the mind or intellect from distracting and sinful thoughts through pure prayer in order to attain to union with God is emphasized in somewhat Platonist terms by Origen (185-253) and Evagrius (345-399). The biblical accent on the cleansing of the heart as the way to experiential knowledge of God is found in the *Spiritual Homilies* (fifth or sixth century), attributed to Macarius of Egypt (c. fourth century). A focus on spiritual wisdom and prudent conduct is provided by Dorotheos of Gaza (sixth century). A charismatic dimension, including new birth through "baptism by the Spirit" and vision of the uncreated light of God, is offered by Symeon the New Theologian (949-1022). The sacramental connection is represented by Nicholas Cabasilas (1322-c.1387).

The coherent vision of Orthodox spirituality is grounded on commonly shared basic features such as biblical personalism, christocentrism, Trinitarianism, union with God through prayer, a high estimation of discernment and spiritual wisdom and a strong synergistic and eschatological outlook. These features are fundamentally reflective of the Pauline, Johannine and Wisdom Literature of Scripture—the chief sources of Orthodox spirituality.

In the context of American culture, Orthodox spirituality presents a diverse picture. On the one hand, Alexander Schmemann* pronounced the "spiritual problem," that is, the unconscious embrace of secular ideas about personhood, marriage, family, profession, leisure and even religion, as well as the progressive surrender to secular values such as affluence, status, profit and prestige, as the ultimate problem of Orthodoxy in America. On the other hand, the publication of books and translations on Orthodox spirituality in English, including the acclaimed *Philokalia,* as well as the hesychastic practice of the Jesus Prayer among clergy* and laity* alike, are signs of renewed interest in Orthodox spirituality. Indeed, there are positive new emphases derived from efforts toward liturgical renewal, rediscovery of Scripture through study groups and a missionary spirit. The revival of Orthodox spirituality in America is closely linked to the whole concern about Orthodox identity, spiritual renewal in the parishes, the establishment of monastic centers and the challenge of translating the monastic cast of traditional spirituality into terms and practices useful to lay people.

BIBLIOGRAPHY. P. Evdokimov, *Struggle with God* (1966); M. Oleksa, ed., *Alaskan Missionary Spirituality* (1987); G. E. H. Palmer et al., eds., *The Philokalia: The Complete Text,* 5 vols. (1979-). A. Schmemann, "Problems of Orthodoxy in America: The Spiritual Problem," *St. Vladimir's Seminary Quarterly* 9 (1965):171-193; T. Spidlik, *The Spirituality of the Christian East* (1986); K. Ware, *The Orthodox Way* (1979).   T. Stylianopoulos

Spirituality: Protestant. The term *spirituality* is used in a variety of ways. It may refer to the state of being immaterial or consisting of pure spirit, such as God's existence. Centuries ago it could refer to tithes or property belonging to the church. Even today theologians may speak of the spirituality of the church, referring to the deeper nature and reality of the people of God. In current usage *spirituality* commonly embraces the beliefs, attitudes and practices by which individuals and communities commune with God or other perceived spiritual realities. This definition is admittedly vague, but its general reference has been shaped by the need to include the variety of religious lifestyles and devotions encountered in religiously pluralistic societies.

Protestant spirituality generally emphasizes the priority of God's saving grace—the spiritual life begins with God justifying believers and granting them assurance of the forgiveness of sins. Catholic* spirituality, on the other hand, typically lays more emphasis on the role of believers in seeking to purge their souls from sin in order to attain illumination. The experience of complete forgiveness of sins awaits the life to come. But even within Protestantism there is a breadth of spiritual traditions. Two issues tend to dominate Protestant spirituality: the proper role of human effort and divine grace in attaining personal holiness,* and the proper goal of spirituality in this life.

Anglican Spirituality. Anglican* spirituality has been shaped primarily by the Bible* and the *Book of Common Prayer*—in near-equal emphasis. The Prayer Book is much more than a liturgical directory, it is a daily spiritual companion and guide. Unless nurtured by Puritanism,* Colonial Anglican spirituality was not conversion*-oriented and tended to be ordered, shunning the extempore.

Anglicans might be aided in their inner spiritual growth by popular spiritual works such as Jeremy Taylor's *Holy Living* (1650) and *Holy Dying* (1651) or the anonymous work *The Whole Duty of Man* (1657). The latter emphasized a common Anglican spiritual theme—that the Christian life without morality is only superstition. As the *Book of Common Prayer* put it, to live Christianly is to live a "godly, righteous and sober life." Yet, given the bipolar Protestant and Catholic nature of the Anglican tradition, it is particularly difficult to generalize regarding Anglican spirituality, whether past or present.

Evangelical* Anglicans have practiced a spirituality characterized by private, extemporaneous prayer* and meditation on Scripture much like that of the Puritans. On the other end of the spectrum, Anglo-Catholic* spirituality has revived a sacramentalism that, as exemplified in the nineteenth-century Tractarian Movement,* was characterized by a quest for holiness that utilized the church year,* the daily office and the Eucharist,* all pervaded by a sense of mystery and an emphasis on the transforming presence of Christ in men and women. On the other hand, Anglican spirituality has sometimes emphasized reason, order and transcendence over piety,* feelings and immanence. Thus, in the Early Republic, deism* was able to take hold among Anglicans.

Lutheran Spirituality. In the Middle Colonies the Lutherans* introduced a spirituality centered around the doctrine of justification.* The sinner, having been justified by God's redeeming grace, is simultaneously righteous and sinful. While not neglecting the doctrine of progressive sanctification,* the Lutheran theology of the spiritual life has been reluctant to emphasize it for fear of introducing human works into a process that is God's from first to last. Lutheran spirituality is and was worked out in the context of a person's calling: first, as a child of God and second, within a station in life. Thus day-to-day spirituality might best be fulfilled in carrying out one's labors well. In corporate worship* the spirituality of believers is nourished by the sacraments,* understood as a true means of grace. In the church's catechetical* role, believers are reminded of the commandments and instructed in the creed.* In prayer—particularly in the "Our Father," or Lord's Prayer—believers are reminded of their utter dependency on God. Often suspicious of subjective quests for the holy life, Lutheran spirituality has tended to center on the confidence of faith and a liberty of conscience in the pilgrimage of faith. But though Lutherans have generally been resistant to the conversion-oriented revivalism that has come to be the common spiritual currency of American religion, some Lutherans have found it spiritually compatible with their faith.

Reformed *Spirituality*. The spiritual descendants of John Calvin inherited a spirituality that placed more emphasis on the process of sanctification than did that of their Lutheran cousins. Calvin himself had an acute sense of the bond between true piety and theology,* and his entire *Institutes* is a spiritual guide for Christian living as individuals, as the church and in the world.

The foundation for Reformed spirituality is union by faith with the exalted Christ, who is the believer's holiness. Christ and his work are alone the sufficient basis for the sanctification of believers. Believers are united with him and through the Spirit share in his spiritual resources, becoming dead to sin and alive with Christ. In the Calvinist understanding a Christian simultaneously experiences faith, regeneration* and baptism with the Spirit, thus beginning a lifelong process of sanctification that is not consummated until the moment of glorification in the life to come. Sanctification— a major theme in Reformed spirituality—is essentially a Spirit-enabled process of working out the practical consequences of being a new creation in Christ. Yet it takes place within a cosmic context of redemption in which spiritual warfare is a constant personal and corporate reality.

The spiritual means for fighting this battle are founded on what Calvinists would call a realistic evaluation of believers, who are united with Christ. They are at once highly valued in their new identity and destiny in Christ, yet defiled by sin and worthy of death in themselves. From this perspective believers cooperate with the sanctifying grace of God in putting to death (mortifying) their sinful nature and conforming to the image of Christ. The primary means for this work of grace is God's Word (whether preached or read), which convicts believers of sin and instructs them in the way of righteous living. But Calvinists also view the circumstances of life as God's providential means for shaping them into conformity with Christ. Moreover, the church through its fellowship, its instruction, its prayer, its discipline and its sacraments nurtures believers in their spiritual growth toward Christlikeness.

Pietist Spirituality. The Continental Pietists* who came to the New World were Old World spiritual reformers of Lutheran and Reformed orthodoxy,* which they felt had become an arid intellectualism. Arguing that the Lutheran emphasis on justification spoke only to the guilt of sin

and not its power, Pietists emphasized a rebirth by which the image of God is restored in a person and the power of sin, conquered. The reborn participate in the divine nature (2 Pet 1:4), though they are not without sin. The spiritual life is one of conflict and victory over concrete sins, chiefly by means of prayer and the training of the will. The sanctified life bears fruit in particular spiritual graces such as faith, love, patience, humility and good works. The spiritual classics of this tradition are Philip Jakob Spener's (1635-1705) *Pia Desideria* (1675) and Johan Arndt's (1555-1621) *True Christianity*. The hymns of pietists, such as those of the Moravians,* have been a significant contribution to Protestant Christian spirituality as a whole.

Pietists also emphasized the importance of spiritual societies or conventicles in which believers through prayer and Bible study* could build one another up in their spiritual life. Frequently ecumenical, these societies served as a spiritual renewal movement within the church at large. Among some Pietist groups, particularly Conrad Beissel's* followers in Pennsylvania, communal societies were formed that were reminiscent of monasticism. Some, like the Schwenkfelders,* adopted a mystical spirituality.

Quaker Spirituality. The most radical of all the spiritual traditions broadly labeled "Protestant" belonged to the Society of Friends,* or Quakers, many of whom settled in Pennsylvania. Originating with George Fox,* the movement grew out of a disillusionment with all forms of religion and a conviction that true religion consists of the "divine light of Christ" in the inner person. This divine light overwhelms the sinful self and, for some, this inner light has been of greater authority than Scripture itself. Possessed with the Spirit of Christ, Quakers could claim sinless perfection and viewed their mission as being Christ in the world, living humble lives and not partaking in its violence. Yet the spirituality of William Penn,* Pennsylvania's founder, was more moderate in tone and came to emphasize honesty, simplicity, tolerance, sobriety and the spiritual rewards of suffering (an attitude summarized in Penn's words "No cross, no crown"). Later Quakers would play an influential role by means of a spirituality that incorporated pacifism, philanthropy* and social justice—particularly in their participation in the anti-slavery movement. For some Quakers the doctrine of the inner light took them toward silent worship and mysticism,* while evangelical Quakers, such as the Gurneyites,* came to anchor their spirituality in Christ and his atonement.*

Anabaptist Spirituality. Anabaptists made their entrance into the New World beginning in the seventeenth century and later still in the migrations of the nineteenth and twentieth centuries. Better known as Brethren, Mennonites* and Amish,* they brought with them a spirituality that was characterized by separation from the world and a commitment to radical discipleship.* Focusing on an experience of regeneration signified by the outward act of believer's baptism,* Anabaptists have viewed this turning point in each believer's life as not only an inner transformation, but a renunciation of worldly ways and a pledge to a life of discipleship. This emphasis has frequently led them to resist cultural influences and cultivate a simple life and piety that is often community-centered, scripturally based and characterized by a call to obedience despite its costs. As pacifists who strongly oppose the influence of the state on the church, their spirituality has at times been publicly demonstrated in their practice of non-resistance. In the late-nineteenth and twentieth centuries, some Anabaptists were spiritually influenced by the Holiness* and fundamentalist* movements. The twentieth century, however, has also seen a revival of the traditional Anabaptist vision and spirituality. This has in turn influenced the spirituality of others who share a similar vision of justice in human relationships and society as a whole.

Puritan Spirituality. The leading theme of Protestant spirituality in America was set by the Puritans. No other immigrant group so clearly represents the ideals and spiritual impulses that would come to shape the typically American spirituality of the ensuing centuries. The Puritan spirituality was, as historian Perry Miller noted "the Augustinian* strain of piety"—a spirituality deeply rooted in the conviction that humanity, though separated from God by sin, was created to enjoy communion with God and is restless until it attains that end. While consciously Reformed in its emphases, its particular expressions are significant for understanding later forms of American spirituality.

The Puritans did not separate the spiritual from the secular. All of life was under the canopy of the sacred and the life of the spirit was no more demanded of so-called divines* than it was of the blacksmith at his forge or the housewife at her hearth. The Puritan ideal was that spirituality be integrated into ordinary daily life, thus creating a sort of worldly asceticism. Rejecting the Anglo-Catholic canonical hours and Christian year with its feast days, Puritans celebrated every Sunday* as the Lord's Day and sanctified every other day by honest labor as well as morning and evening prayers, both in private and as a family.

As in all of Puritan life and worship, spirituality was marked by simplicity and discipline, and was deeply personal. While methodical and practical, it was also passionate and lacked ostentatious display. For the Puritans the mind was the avenue to both the heart and will. Firmly believing in the authority of Scripture for faith and life, Puritan spirituality centered around the written Word and depended on a literate laity and an educated clergy, the latter serving as spiritual guides for individuals and covenanted community. Personal Bible study and meditation were important disciplines, as were the attentive listening to sermons and instruction, and the discussion of spiritual matters with like-minded Christians. Infant baptism and the Lord's Supper were sacramental ordinances,* the latter requiring individual spiritual preparation. Devotional literature also played an important role in the practice of piety, whether it be reading a printed sermon from a New England divine, spiritual meditations such as Richard Baxter's *The Saints' Everlasting Rest* or a biblical commentary by an English Puritan mentor.

The spiritual life was one of warfare under the cross of Christ—a continual struggle between good and evil (the enemy consisting of the world, the flesh and the devil) requiring watchful and disciplined living. It was a spirituality that knew the cost of faithfulness, reminded itself of those who had paid the price before and counted life in this world as spiritual pilgrimage, full of lessons and conflicts preparing the faithful for a life beyond. But the fulfillment of holiness was reserved for the life to come.

Puritan devotional practices were frequently introspective, based on a realistic assessment of the wiles of sin and the soul's seemingly infinite capacity for self-deception. The pathway to holiness was a spiral, leading through succeeding rounds of strenuous self-examination, confession of sin, mortification of the flesh, and acceptance of God's forgiving grace in Christ. The effect was a piety composed of humility and self-suspicion, accompanied by discipline and self-control. Yet there was always the expectation of a fresh renewing work of the Spirit.

Puritans expected true spirituality to do more than shape the interior life, although this process could be charted with some precision by Puritan spiritual masters. Spirituality was also to express itself in effective action in the reformation of life. Good works were the visible evidence of election,* regeneration and the sanctifying grace of the Holy Spirit.

Wesleyan Spirituality. Though originating within the Church of England, Wesleyanism* was far more influenced by Pietism than it was by the Anglican tradition. While Wesleyan spirituality agreed with the Calvinist emphasis on justification by faith as the starting point for the Christian pilgrimage, it sought an additional release from the power of sin. Wesleyans maintain that sanctification, rather than a process which cannot reach its goal of perfection in this life, can culminate in a this-worldly experience of complete sanctification—a state Wesley himself never claimed to have achieved. This is perfection defined as a perfect love, free of any known sin against God or humanity. Yet it is an experience to be sought through the means of grace, which include prayer (private, family and public), fasting, the Lord's Supper, Scripture reading and meditation, and spiritual association with other believers through Methodist societies and class meetings.

Wesley himself was well read in the spiritual classics, including those of Pietism and the Eastern church. His brother Charles (1707-1788), who produced a rich treasury of hymns* expressing evangelical doctrine* and spirituality, has had a lasting influence in shaping two centuries of evangelical spirituality. In early nineteenth-century America, the chief conduit of Wesleyan spirituality was the rapidly growing Methodist Church. But during the latter half of the century, Wesleyan spirituality would become a potent force through the Holiness Movement and a variety of Higher Life* movements that would have a profound effect on evangelicalism.

Evangelical Spirituality. A highly influential form of New World spirituality grew out of the Puritan tradition and the new impetus it received in the Great Awakening* of the mid-eighteenth century. Puritan spirituality had, in the eyes of many, become a dead and formulaic orthodoxy. The leaders of the Awakening—men such as Jonathan Edwards* and George Whitefield*— revived the conversion-oriented spirituality of the Puritan tradition, but did so with a fresh sense of possibilities for religious experience and a new style that bypassed the conventional and clerically controlled means of established religion. Edwards, the great theoretician of the revival, understood the fruit of the Awakening not as a new catalog of religious excess but true regeneration characterized by a Spirit-given apprehension of God, a purified heart, a humble character and an outflow of good works. Whitefield preached a gospel that emphasized the New Birth,* and through his preaching many came to experience this work of

grace in their hearts. An ecumenical, lay-oriented movement, The Great Awakening was the beginning of America's most significant spiritual tradition, evangelicalism.

Conversion and the revival of dormant religion became the focus of the early-nineteenth-century evangelical movement known as the Second Great Awakening. On the western frontier, camp meetings separated people from the routine of everyday living and exposed them to a concentrated period of evangelistic preaching. Conversions and extraordinary ecstatic behavior frequently characterized these meetings. But more notable for evangelicalism was the increasing influence of Arminianism, which focused attention on the human will and its role in conversion and religious experience. Unlike the Puritans, who waited for God's grace to invade their lives, evangelicalism began to foster a spirituality that sought, through the proper environment and means, to produce religious experience. In the end, popular evangelicalism ran the risk of making extraordinary religious experience the hallmark of spirituality, with spiritual vitality being marked by repeated crisis experiences.

On the other hand, attention was increasingly focused on the doctrine of sanctification. By the early 1840s Charles G. Finney,* who was reputedly within the Reformed Tradition, was championing an essentially Wesleyan spirituality of entire sanctification. Within Methodism* the nascent Holiness Movement was reviving Wesleyan perfectionism. By 1848 Phoebe Palmer had published her formula for holiness, encouraging believers to figuratively place themselves on the altar and receive by faith the second blessing of entire sanctification. Other evangelicals such as William E. Boardman* and Hannah Whitall Smith* urged believers on to new heights of Christian spirituality characterized by victory over the constant cycle of sin and repentance.

Whether they used the slogans of "higher Christian life" or "victorious Christian life," the effect was a pervasive form of evangelical spirituality that was clearly more Wesleyan than Calvinist. While the elements of prayer and Bible study were ongoing spiritual disciplines, this movement enumerated spiritual principles that would give access to the higher life. In order to attain the victorious Christian life, for example, believers were enjoined to surrender every sin (known and unknown) and all of their life plans to God. This surrender was to be accompanied by faith that confidently believed God would honor his word and give the victory. But victory was not a permanent state, and further sin called for immediate repentance and a reclamation of the victory.

Pentecostal and Charismatic Spirituality. The Pentecostal Movement* grew out of the sectarian edge of the Holiness Movement, where leaders began to speak of a second spiritual crisis experience beyond conversion: baptism in the Spirit evidenced by speaking in tongues. Pentecostal spirituality is thus oriented toward the expectation of an individual's emotional experience, which is attributed to the work of the Holy Spirit. This being the case, Pentecostals have valued spontaneity, particularly in corporate worship. In addition, earlier Pentecostalism was particularly otherworldly and separatist in its relationship to culture, a feature that has notably receded as the movement has gained social acceptance.

Particular expressions of Pentecostal spirituality are the laying on of hands* in intercessory prayer, the raising of hands* in worship, dancing in the Spirit, oral exclamations such as "Praise the Lord,"* and the experience of the charismatic gifts of visions, prophecy,* healing* and speaking in tongues. Though its spiritual tradition has generally been passed on orally, it highly regards the authority of the Bible and is primitivist* in its desire to restore the spirituality of the early church, particularly as it was expressed at Pentecost.* These same values pervade charismatic spirituality to one degree or another, though in nearly every case charismatics will tend to be less expressive in their outward display.

African-American Spirituality. African-American spirituality has traditionally been oriented toward the conversion experience, anchored in biblical narrative and expressed in the spirituals that gave swelling cadence to the soul's deepest longings. The slaves brought with them an African cultural heritage that viewed reality as a unified whole, with no separation between the sacred and the secular, spirit and nature. Worship was offered to the gods in an expressive and rhythmic style often translated into dance and usually accompanied by music.

When slaves became Christians, their spirituality was typically expressed through these same means—though for the most part only in secret. Prayers were offered and songs were sung by groups gathered in slave cabins or in secluded thickets. Heavy hearts cried out for God to deliver them from servitude, a theme that was expounded from the biblical narratives by their own preachers and found its way into the texture of their songs. In this way the message of liberation became the leading motif of African-American spirituality and has been maintained throughout the struggle for civil rights in the 1960s and the African-American theology and spirituality of the ensuing decades. Liberation, for African-American spirituality, is seen most clearly in the face of Christ who was born and died under oppression and so reflects God's closeness and concern for African-American people and their history.

Conclusion. In the late 1970s and throughout the 1980s, spirituality was an increasingly popular subject among Protestants. A growing awareness of the variety of spiritual traditions within Christendom encouraged some to choose spiritual paths other than the familiar and well-worn avenues of their inherited spiritual traditions. For many, the variety of spiritualities seemed to offer a smorgasbord of options and avenues, and one more arena in which they could unself-consciously work out the perennial American religious impulse of expressive individualism.*

BIBLIOGRAPHY. D. L. Alexander, *Christian Spirituality: Five Views of Sanctification* (1989); J. Farina, ed., "Sources of American Spirituality," multi-volume series (1978-); C. E. Hambrick-Stowe, *The Practice of Piety: Puritan Devotional Disciplines in Seventeenth-Century New England* (1982); C. Jones et al., ed., *The Study of Spirituality* (1986); R. F. Lovelace, *Dynamics of Spiritual Life* (1979); R. Lundin and M. A. Noll, eds., *Voices from the Heart: Four Centuries of American Piety* (1987); F. S. Senn, ed., *Protestant Spiritual Traditions* (1986); R. P. Spittler, "Spirituality, Pentecostal and Charismatic," in *Dictionary of Pentecostal and Charismatic Movements* (1988); G. S. Wakefield, *The Westminster Dictionary of Christian Spirituality* (1983).

D. G. Reid

Sprague, William (B)uell (1795-1876). Presbyterian* minister,* author, orator and biographer. Born in Andover, Connecticut, Sprague was educated at Yale College* (M.A., 1815) and Princeton Theological Seminary* (B.D., 1819). Ordained* to minister at the Congregational* church in West Springfield, Massachusetts, he served there from 1820 to 1829, first as a colleague of Joseph Lathrop and then as Lathrop's successor as senior minister. Called to Second Presbyterian Church in Albany, New York, in 1829, Sprague remained there until 1869.

Known as an outstanding preacher,* he was also a prolific author. Among his many books was his *Life of Timothy Dwight* of Yale (1844), but his greatest achievement was his nine-volume *Annals of the American Pulpit* (1857-1869), an interdenominational collection of memoranda of American clergymen up to 1855. A full collection of his works is kept in the Speer Library of Princeton

Theological Seminary.

BIBLIOGRAPHY. *DAB* IX. D. Macleod

Spring, Gardiner (1785-1873). Presbyterian* minister. Born in Newburyport, Massachusetts, Spring attended Berwick Academy in Maine and Yale University* (B.A., 1805). He studied law and taught school before being convinced that he should enter the ministry*; he attended Andover Seminary* in 1809. In 1810 Spring was called as pastor to Brick Church (old First Presbyterian Church) in New York City. He remained there for sixty-three years, until his death.

Spring was very active in denominational politics. He objected to the "Excision Act" of 1837, which precipitated the New School*/Old School* schism. Nonetheless, Spring kept his church in the Old School, always seeking to be a voice of moderation within that body. Preaching* was his first concern, and he believed that sermons ought to result in genuine and thorough conversions.* Spring published many of his sermons and addresses. In New York, he was active in numerous religious and charitable associations, particularly missions.* Spring also led Brick Church to a major move from downtown to a magnificent new building at Fifth Avenue and 37th Street.

He is perhaps best known for the so-called Spring Resolutions, which he presented at the General Assembly of 1861. This Assembly, meeting in an atmosphere of national tension, was divided along sectional lines over the question of supporting the federal government in its suppression of secession. While Spring had been opposed to antislavery agitation, which he considered extreme, he nonetheless felt strongly that the lawful government in Washington should be supported now that a crisis was at hand. Spring's resolutions affirmed that churches should "do all in their power to strengthen, uphold, and encourage the federal government." By adopting these resolutions, the Old School Assembly broke its traditional silence on political issues. Consequently, the Southern group withdrew and formed their own Assembly. During the War, the Old School/New School dispute in the North lost much of its urgency. In 1869 Spring pled powerfully for reunion and was pleased to see it accomplished before his death.

BIBLIOGRAPHY. *DAB* IX; *DARB*; *NCAB* 5; G. Spring, *Personal Reminiscences of the Life and Times of Gardiner Spring,* 2 vols. (1866); L. G. VanderVelde, *The Presbyterian Churches and the Federal Union, 1861-1869* (1932).

D. M. Strong

Springfield Will and Testament (1804). Document dating the beginning of the Christian Churches in America. When the Second Great Awakening* swept through the frontier in 1801, the Presbyterian* Synod* of Kentucky took a firm stand against it. Five Presbyterian ministers* seceded from the Synod and in 1803 formed their own presbytery, that of Springfield, Ohio. Within a year, however, they decided their organization was unscriptural and a barrier to the union of all Christians which they desired. They willed their death in "The Last Will and Testament of the Springfield Presbytery." Major themes in the brief document are a concern for Christian union, an adherence to the Scriptures* alone as the rule for faith and practice and an insistence on local church autonomy. Initially no organization resulted from the group, only a loose fellowship of churches and ministers. Barton W. Stone* soon emerged as the major leader of what was called Christian Churches or Churches of Christ.* Other names were New Lights, and Christian Connection.*

See also RESTORATION MOVEMENT.

BIBLIOGRAPHY. B. W. Stone, *The Biography of Eld. Barton Warren Stone, Written by Himself* (1847). J. B. North

Stam, Elizabeth Alden Scott ("Betty") (1906-1934). Missionary* martyr. Born in Albion, Michigan, Stam was taken to China before her first birthday. Her parents, The Rev. and Mrs. Charles Ernest Scott, were missionaries with the Presbyterian Church U.S.A.* Stam attended the North China American School near Peking and high school in Springfield, Massachusetts; she graduated from Wilson College in Chambersburg, Pennsylvania. She then went to Moody Bible Institute,* where she met John C. Stam (1907-1934), who was from New Jersey. Already accepted as a missionary by China Inland Mission,* Betty returned to China in 1931. John followed in 1932. They were married in October 1933, at the home of her parents at Tsinan, Shantung. Their daughter, Helen Priscilla, was born September 11, 1934. On December 7, 1934, Betty and John Stam were executed by Communist bandits who invaded their station at Tsingteh, Anhui. Helen was saved by a Chinese pastor and his wife, who carried her seventy miles on foot, finding nursing mothers and a tin of powdered milk to sustain her along the way. Regarded as martyrs for the cause of Christ, their example inspired others to give of their lives and resources to the evangelical* mission movement.

BIBLIOGRAPHY. M. G. Taylor, *Triumph of John and Betty Stam* (1949). N. A. Hardesty

Standing Conference of Canonical Orthodox Bishops in America. An association of Orthodox* jurisdictions in the U.S. The various Orthodox episcopal jurisdictions (dioceses* and archdioceses*) established in the U.S. since the late eighteenth century were related either directly or indirectly to one of the autocephalous* Orthodox churches of Eastern Europe and the Middle East. Especially after the great waves of immigration of the late nineteenth and early twentieth centuries, each of these jurisdictions generally served the needs of specific groups of Orthodox. Although united in the same faith, there was very little contact and cooperation among these jurisdictions, chiefly because of the linguistic, ethnic and cultural differences of the immigrants.

A shortlived effort to establish an association of six jurisdictions, The Federated Orthodox Greek Catholic Primary Jurisdictions in America, was initiated in 1943. This voluntary federation failed chiefly because it was limited to those jurisdictions which had a direct canonical link with one of the autocephalous Orthodox churches.

The Standing Conference (SCOBA) was established in 1960 by the primates of eleven jurisdictions, with Archbishop Iakovos* of the Greek Orthodox Archdiocese (Ecumenical Patriarchate) serving as the chairman. From the start, SCOBA was essentially a voluntary association of the major jurisdictions, designed to foster cooperation and to coordinate a united Orthodox witness, especially in the ecumenical movement.*

SCOBA is presently composed of nine jurisdictions, which contain the majority of five million Orthodox in the U.S. SCOBA coordinates a number of commissions and committees. It sponsors the formal, bilateral theological consultations between American Orthodox theologians and the Roman Catholics,* the Anglican* and the Lutheran* churches in the U.S. SCOBA is viewed as the preliminary step toward the ultimate establishment of a provincial synod* of bishops recognized by the Ecumenical Patriarchate of Constantinople and the other autocephalous churches.

BIBLIOGRAPHY. S. Surrency, *The Quest for Orthodox Church Unity in America* (1973).

T. E. FitzGerald

Stanton, Elizabeth Cady (1815-1902). Women's rights leader. Born in Johnstown, New York, Stanton's interest in the condition of women developed early in life as she experienced her father's preference for her brothers, the plight of women who sought his legal advice and the assertiveness of her mother. Despite reservations, her parents permitted her to attend Emma Willard's* Female Seminary in Troy, New York (from which she graduated in 1832), and to read widely. Her marriage to abolitionist* Henry Stanton brought her into close contact with antebellum reform movements, including the nascent women's rights movement nurtured by Lucretia Mott.* Although she became devoted to the cause of women, she struggled for years with the competing demands of private and public life.

In the 1840s she campaigned successfully for a Married Women's Property Act in New York state. She helped to organize the first women's rights convention in Seneca Falls,* New York, in 1848 and drafted its "Declaration of Sentiments," in which she called for female suffrage, along with other notable changes in woman's status. This broad feminism* came to characterize Stanton's position for the remainder of her life. In the years following Seneca Falls, Stanton did not assume the role of public reformer but instead wrote letters, editorials, speeches and articles from her home. She became the chief architect of the movement's ideology.

Her fifty-year friendship with Susan B. Anthony,* whom she met in 1851, was the main impetus for Stanton's increasingly public role as orator and leader of the women's rights movement. Stanton organized a number of groups to promote women's suffrage* and equal rights and edited a controversial journal, *Revolution.* After her children were grown, she undertook an ambitious series of lecture tours in the Midwest. She remained angered by the abolitionists' focus on African-American male suffrage and never altered her message that women must seek divorce reform and access to the professions as well as the vote. In the 1880s she helped edit the voluminous *History of Woman Suffrage* and began work on *The Woman's Bible.* Stanton's religious pilgrimage took her from the revivalism* of Charles G. Finney* to Unitarianism* and skepticism. At the end of her life she concluded that there was little in the Old and New Testaments to benefit women and, thus, little which could be called divine truth.

BIBLIOGRAPHY. *DAB* IX; *DARB;* E. Griffith, *In Her Own Right: The Life of Elizabeth Cady Stanton* (1984); *NAW* 3; E. Cady Stanton, *Eighty Years and More* (1898); T. Stanton and H. Blatch, eds., *Elizabeth Cady Stanton as Revealed in Her Letters, Diary and Reminiscences,* 2 vols. (1922).

B. J. MacHaffie

Stanton, Robert Livingston (1810-1885). Presbyterian* minister,* church statesman, educator and writer. Born at Griswold, Connecticut, Stanton attended Lane Seminary, graduating in 1836. He was ordained* by the Mississippi Presbytery and served pastorates at Pine Ridge and Woodville, Mississippi, and Second Church of New Orleans, Louisiana. From 1851 to 1854 he was president of Oakland College (Mississippi) and then pastor* at Chillicothe, Ohio. In 1862 he became professor of pastoral theology and homiletics* at Danville Theological Seminary (Kentucky).

An advisor to Lincoln on Southern affairs, Stanton emerged during the Civil War* as a leader of the strongly nationalistic Midwestern faction of Presbyterian clergymen. In *The Church and the Rebellion* (1864), they argued the responsibility of church leaders in promoting the spirit of secession. Stanton's own election as moderator of the 1866 Old School* General Assembly* (St. Louis) signaled the triumph of radical forces in the church, especially in regard to postwar policies for Southern congregations.

In 1866 Stanton assumed the presidency of Miami University (Ohio), an institution faltering for lack of students and financial support. Unable to increase the enrollment or strengthen its finances, he left in 1871 to become an editor of the New York *Independent,* followed by the Cincinnati *Herald and Presbyter* (1872-1878). Later, he moved to Washington, D.C., was attracted to faith-healing* and wrote *Gospel Parallelisms: Illustrated in the Healing of Body and Soul* (1884). Ill with malaria, Stanton sailed for England in 1885 to attend a faith-healing conference and died on the voyage. He was buried at sea.

BIBLIOGRAPHY. *NCAB* 26; L. G. Vander Velde, *The Presbyterian Churches and the Federal Union, 1861-1869* (1932).   W. J. Wade

Starr, Ellen Gates (1859-1940). Cofounder of Hull House. Born on a farm near Laona, Illinois, Starr grew up in a Unitarian* family, but she was deeply influenced by her aunt Eliza Allen Starr, a lecturer on Christian art and a devout convert to Roman Catholicism.* Starr spent 1877 at Rockford Seminary in Rockford, Illinois, where she became a close friend of Jane Addams.* While on a trip to Europe together, schoolteachers Starr and Addams conceived Hull House, which they founded in 1889. Always interested in art, Starr started reading clubs, art history classes and an art gallery at Hull House. She was skilled in various arts and crafts, which she taught there. She also battled child labor, became a charter member of the Illinois branch of the National Women's Trade Union League and a Christian Socialist.* In 1916 she ran for alderman. Seeking spiritual nurture, Starr attended Chicago's Church of the Unity for a time and then became an Episcopalian* in 1884. She came to consider herself Anglo-Catholic.* In 1920 she converted to Roman Catholicism and eventually became an oblate of the Third Order of St. Benedict at the Convent of the Holy Child in Suffern, New York, where she died February 10, 1940.

BIBLIOGRAPHY. J. Addams, *Twenty Years at Hull House* (1910); *NAW* 3.   N. A. Hardesty

Stations of the Cross. A representation of Christ's progressive suffering from condemnation by Pilate to burial in the tomb, erected for devotional purposes. The origin of this practice lies with pilgrims to the Holy Land who traced the steps of Jesus along the *via dolorosa* in Jerusalem. The stations can be set up in churches and other consecrated areas by marking them with fourteen crosses and optional placards, constituting a "way of the cross." The person moves from station to station and meditates on Christ's suffering, saying prayers or making responses to an officiating priest.

The fourteen standardized stations are: (1) Jesus is condemned by Pilate. He is flagellated and crowned with thorns; (2) Jesus is forced to carry his own cross; (3) Jesus falls for the first time; (4) Jesus encounters Mary, his mother; (5) Simon of Cyrene is made to carry Jesus' cross for him; (6) Veronica wipes Jesus' face; (7) Jesus falls for a second time; (8) Jesus addresses the women of Jerusalem; (9) Jesus falls for a third time; (10) Jesus is stripped and made to drink gall; (11) Jesus is nailed to the cross; (12) Jesus dies on the cross; (13) Jesus is removed from the cross and mourned; (14) Jesus is placed into the tomb.

The stations combine biblical information with pious legend. In traditional Roman Catholic devotion, proper placement and execution of the symbolic pilgrimage is rewarded with indulgences.

BIBLIOGRAPHY. H. Thurston, *The Stations of the Cross* (1906).   W. Corduan

Stearns, Lewis French (1847-1892). Congregational* theologian.* Born in Newburyport, Massachusetts, Stearns graduated from Princeton College* (B.A., 1867) and later studied at the Columbia School of Law (1867-1869). In preparing for the ministry he attended Princeton Theological Seminary* (1869-1870) and Union Theological Seminary, New York* (1871-1872), with a year at the universities of Leipzig and Berlin (1870-1871).

After a few years as a Presbyterian* minister in Norwood, New Jersey (1873-1876), he taught history and literature at Albion College, Michigan (1876-1879). Resigning from the faculty because of eye trouble, he turned his energies toward theological reconstruction while recuperating. That reconstruction involved rejecting the Calvinist* emphasis on divine sovereignty and election* and the adoption of a distinctively liberal* Christology* that highlighted the humanity of Jesus while not denying his divinity. In the experience of the human Jesus, Stearns believed, one had a way to interpret human suffering, a model for recognizing that all were part of one human family and a basis for the liberal Protestant* insistence on the immanence of God and progress in human social development. Stearns resumed teaching in 1880, this time at Bangor Theological Seminary, a Congregationalist institution in Maine, where he remained until his death.

BIBLIOGRAPHY. *DARB;* G. L. Prentiss, "Biographical Sketch" in L. F. Stearns, *Present Day Theology* (1893). C. H. Lippy

Stearns, Shubal (1706-1771). Baptist* separate* in North Carolina. Born in Boston, Stearns moved in his youth to Tolland, Connecticut, where he joined the Congregational Church.* During George Whitefield's* second tour of New England in 1745, Stearns was converted.* In 1751, after a thorough study of the Scriptures,* he became a Baptist and persuaded enough of his fellow church members to withdraw from Congregationalism to form a Baptist church in Tolland. In May the church ordained* Stearns as pastor. He served the church for three years.

Seeking a special place to preach the gospel, Stearns moved first to Virginia and then, when he received word about the spiritual hunger of people in the Piedmont section of North Carolina, he moved there. Late in 1755 Stearns led a company of fifteen, including his sister and brother-in-law Daniel Marshall,* to Sandy Creek in Guilford (now Randolph) County, North Carolina. Within three years the Sandy Creek Church, started by the New Englanders, had planted two sister churches and formed the Sandy Creek Association.

The key to the growth of these Separate Baptists in the South was Stearns's itinerant* ministry. Although he lacked formal preparation for the ministry, he was a man of vision, action and unusual preaching skill. Baptist historian Morgan Edwards* reports that his voice was "musical and strong" and he could use it "to make soft impressions on the heart" or "to throw the animal system into tumults."

Stearns died in 1771, completing his sixteen-year mission to the South. The next year his associates counted forty-two churches and one hundred twenty-five ministers who had arisen from the Sandy Creek Church.

BIBLIOGRAPHY. *DAB* IX; *DARB;* M. Edwards, *Materials Towards a History of the Baptists,* 2 vols. (1770-1792); W. L. Lumpkin, *Baptist Foundations in the South* (1961). B. L. Shelley

Stebbins, George Coles (1846-1945). Composer, hymnwriter and music evangelist.* A farm boy from upstate New York, Stebbins early studied music in Buffalo and Rochester. In 1867 he married Elma Miller, who would later assist in women's meetings. The couple moved to Chicago where Stebbins worked for Lyon & Healy, a music store which is still famous. As music director of First Baptist Church, he became acquainted with George F. Root,* Philip P. Bliss* and Dwight L. Moody.*

Following the Chicago fire, Stebbins moved (1874) to Boston's Clarendon Street Baptist Church where A. J. Gordon* was pastor. In 1876 he moved to Tremont Temple with George C. Lorimer, spending summers in Northfield, Massachusetts, with Moody. The twenty-five-year association with Moody also led to work with George F. Pentecost and Major D. W. Whittle. He led the singing of thousands in Madison Square Garden and Carnegie Hall in connection with Christian Endeavor* and YMCA* meetings.

With James McGranahan and Ira D. Sankey,* Stebbins edited several editions of *Gospel Hymns,* which sold over 10 million copies, with the profit of $357,388 going to the Northfield Schools Trust Fund. Stebbins also compiled *The Northfield Hymnal* (1904). Some of his enduring hymns and tunes are: "Jesus is Tenderly Calling," "I've Found a Friend," "Take Time to Be Holy" and "Have Thine Own Way."

BIBLIOGRAPHY. J. H. Hall, *Biography of Gospel Song and Hymn Writers* (1914).

R. J. Stanislaw

Steinmeyer, Ferdinand "Farmer" (1720-1786). Colonial Catholic* missionary.* Born in Wurttemberg, Germany, Steinmeyer joined the Society of Jesus* in 1743. After ordination* he was selected as a missionary for German immigrants* in the American colonies. Steinmeyer arrived in Lancaster, Pennsylvania, in 1752 where he began his ministry,* frequently known under the pseudonym of Ferdinand Farmer.

In 1758 Fr. Steinmeyer took up residence at St.

Joseph's Church in Philadelphia, which served as a central base for his mission journeys throughout eastern Pennsylvania. Gradually he extended his labors into New Jersey and Delaware, where he gathered German Catholics into congregations. When British troops occupied Philadelphia, General Howe offered Steinmeyer an appointment as chaplain* in the British Army, which he declined. He did, however, minister to Hessian troops under Howe's command. After 1778 Steinmeyer extended his missionary trips into the state of New York, visiting as far up the Hudson as Fishkill and secretly saying Mass* in New York City. His popularity among Philadelphians of all denominations* led to his election as a trustee of the University of Pennsylvania* and to membership in the American Philosophical Society.

BIBLIOGRAPHY. J. T. Ellis, *Catholics in Colonial America* (1965). L. R. Riforgiato

Stelzle, Charles (1869-1941). Presbyterian* minister* and social reformer. Born in New York City, Stelzle spent most of his childhood in the Bowery—a poor, tenement area on the Lower East Side of Manhattan. At the age of eight, he stripped tobacco leaves in a sweatshop. From 1885 to 1893 he worked as a machinist and was a member of the International Association of Machinists. These experiences would give his ministry a commitment to improving the relationship between the church and the working classes. After attending Moody Bible Institute* (1894-1895), he served in several churches, first as a lay worker at Hope Chapel in Minneapolis (1895-1897) and Hope Chapel in New York (1897-1899), where he had attended as a boy, and then as pastor* of Markham Memorial Church in St. Louis (1899-1903). He was ordained* in 1900.

In 1903 he began a special mission to workers under the auspices of the Presbyterian Board of Home Missions. The project became the Department of Church and Labor in 1906. Stelzle served as superintendent of this agency, the first established by any denomination* primarily to implement social Christianity. Stelzle gave lectures, attended labor meetings, served as a fraternal delegate to the national conventions of the American Federation of Labor and wrote articles for the labor press. In 1910 he organized the Labor Temple on the East Side, which ministered to the spiritual, intellectual and social needs of the workers. He also worked for the Men and Religion Forward Movement,* taking surveys and speaking on social service. Stelzle resigned his position in 1913 when budget cuts and reorganization threat-

ened to limit his activities. From then on he did public relations work, was a social service field secretary for the Federal Council of Churches* and worked for the Red Cross in Washington, D.C. He wrote several books in his lifetime, including *The Workingman and Social Problems* (1903). Throughout his ministry he maintained that Christianity should be concerned with everyday affairs, and particularly with the lives of working-class people.

BIBLIOGRAPHY. *DAB* II; *DARB; NCAB* C; C. Stelzle, *A Son of the Bowery* (1926).

L. W. Japinga

Stephan, Martin (1777-1846). Original leader of the Saxon Lutheran* immigrants to Missouri in 1839. Born at Stramberg, Moravia, Stephan was educated at the universities of Halle and Leipzig. Earlier pietistic* influences made him critical of the rationalism dominating those institutions and the state church. After a brief pastorate in Bohemia, he was appointed to St. John's Church in Dresden, where he conducted a bilingual ministry—in Bohemian (his native tongue) as well as in German. His theological* orientation combined Pietism with some elements of conservative, confessional* Lutheranism.

With earnest preaching,* sensitive counseling and personal magnetism, Stephan attracted many followers, including clergy* as well as laity.* They granted him ever-increasing authority, both temporal and spiritual, in the movement that was growing up around him.

By their criticism of rationalistic teaching and practices and by their insistence on holding unauthorized religious gatherings, Stephan and his followers were increasingly in trouble with both civil and ecclesiastical authorities. Sensing that his dismissal was imminent, he convinced many of his followers that they were the last remnant of authentic Christianity in Germany and that their only hope of preserving their salvation was to flee to America.

Shortly after his arrival in Missouri in 1838 with 612 followers, Stephan was expelled from the group on charges of sexual immorality. He moved to Horse Prairie, Illinois, where he served a congregation until his death. After several years of turmoil his followers regrouped under the leadership of C. F. W. Walther* and founded the denomination now known as The Lutheran Church—Missouri Synod.*

BIBLIOGRAPHY. W. O. Forster, *Zion on the Mississippi* (1953); C. S. Mundinger, *Government in the Missouri Synod* (1947). M. L. Rudnick

Stetson, Augusta Emma (Simmons) (1842-1928). Christian Science* leader and schismatic. Born in Waldoboro, Maine, Stetson graduated from Mary Baker Eddy's* Massachusetts Metaphysical College in 1884. In 1886 she went to New York City and founded the city's First Church of Christ, Scientist (1887) and the New York City Christian Science Institute (1891) for training practitioners. Her charismatic leadership stimulated the growth of Christian Science, especially among the wealthier classes, and led church officials to fear that her popularity might supplant the authority of Eddy and the Boston church. Actions taken in 1902 restricted her official, activities, and a heresy trial in 1909 led to her excommunication for deviant teachings and for trying "to control and to injure persons by mental means."

Stetson came to understand her expulsion as a necessary step in the formation of a purified Christian Science she called the "Church Triumphant." Through lectures and the publication of sermons and correspondence, Stetson spread her message of reform and chastised church leaders for tolerating spiritual decline and accommodating to state medical laws. She published her major work, *Sermons Which Spiritually Interpret the Scriptures and Other Writings on Christian Science* (1924), in the midst of a largely unsuccessful radio and print campaign to reactivate the interest of her dwindling followers.

BIBLIOGRAPHY. *DAB* IX; *NAW* 3; A. K. Swihart, *Since Mrs. Eddy* (1931).   R. B. Schoepflin

Stevenson, Joseph Ross (1866-1939). Presbyterian* minister and Princeton Seminary* president. Born at Ligonier, Pennsylvania, Stevenson graduated from Washington and Jefferson College (1886) and McCormick Theological Seminary (1890). After pastoring in Sedalia, Missouri, in 1894, he returned to McCormick as church history professor. He pastored Fifth Avenue Church in New York City from 1902 until 1909 and then went to Baltimore's Brown Memorial Church for five years.

Stevenson is best known for serving as Princeton Seminary president from 1914 to 1936—tumultuous years in the school's history. While theologically conservative, Stevenson had an irenic approach toward the presence of liberalism* within Presbyterianism, believing the Seminary should concentrate on preparing ministers for the entire denomination.* To more militant faculty members, including conservative leader J. Gresham Machen,* this smacked of an unacceptable inclusivism. After years of conflict and a denominational investigation, in 1929 the seminary government was reorganized to ensure broader representation of theological views and to increase the president's powers. This was a major victory for Stevenson. However, Machen and his supporters withdrew to found Westminster Seminary.

BIBLIOGRAPHY. R. T. Clutter, "The Reorientation of Princeton Theological Seminary, 1900-1929" (unpublished Th.D. dissertation, Dallas Theological Seminary, 1982); L. A. Loetscher, *The Broadening Church: A Study of Theological Issues in the Presbyterian Church Since 1869* (1954).

W. V. Trollinger

Steward. The chief overseer of the everyday affairs of a local Methodist* church. Stewards were elected by the charge conference, based on nominations made by the preacher in charge. Required to be men of "solid piety," stewards were to know the theology* and polity* of the Methodist Church and to "transact the temporal business of the Church."

In effect stewards were the executive secretaries of the local church: "to make estimates of expenses and provision for the support of the gospel"; to handle all monies to care for the needy, informing the preacher of illness; "to tell the preachers what they think wrong in them"; to prepare and assist in the Lord's Supper.* Stewards of each circuit and station formed a standing committee to arrange for housing and other necessities of life for their preachers.

Stewards were accountable to the quarterly conference, and each charge was entitled to one steward for every thirty members. Where Methodist societies were small, each society was entitled to one steward and each circuit, to seven.

By the time of the Evangelical United Brethren and Methodist merger, which formed the United Methodist Church* (1968), the steward's responsibilities had been replaced by bodies such as the pastor/parish relations committee, the administrative board, the program council and the worship committee. Parallel in function to these local stewards were the district stewards, who were responsible to the annual conference.

P. A. Mickey

Stewart, Charles James (1775-1837). Canadian Anglican* bishop.* Son of the Earl of Galloway, he was raised, as were so many of the Scottish aristocracy, as an Anglican. He graduated from Oxford and was rector* of an English parish* for eight years. Sensing a definite missionary* call to Canada, in 1807, under the auspices of the Society for the Propagation of the Gospel,* he became rector of St. Armand, which had its center in the village of Frelighsburg, southeast of Montreal, almost on the American border.

Although he never identified himself exclusively with any ecclesiastical party in the Church of England, he had close ties with the evangelicals.* This influence was evident in his preaching,* in the zealous evangelistic outreach which was always part of his ministry and in his ability to value and learn from Christians who were not Anglicans. He continually itinerated throughout the English-speaking Eastern townships of Quebec, as well as "across the line" into Vermont.

From 1818 to 1826 his ministry under the Society was entirely itinerant, covering many of the settled areas of Lower and Upper Canada (Quebec and Ontario). In 1826 Stewart became the second bishop of Quebec, with oversight for all of Quebec and Ontario. Here his outstanding ministerial qualities were particularly to the fore, and in a period when Anglican claims to establishment in Canada were rousing much general opposition, he probably did more than anyone to demonstrate that the Church of England did not depend for its existence on government support. He was responsible for opening many new parishes and raised money to build some forty church structures.

BIBLIOGRAPHY. T. R. Millman, *The Life of the Right Reverend the Honourable Charles James Stewart, D.D. Oxon., Second Anglican Bishop of Quebec* (1953).   I. S. Rennie

Stewart, Lyman (1840-1923) and Milton (1838-1923). Fundamentalist* businessmen and philanthropists.* The Stewart brothers grew up in the region of Pennsylvania in which oil was first discovered. While both brothers were involved in numerous oil-related business enterprises, Lyman was the more active in taking entrepreneurial risks (including some disastrous failures) and in developing new oil production technology and products. Both men were active Presbyterians,* concerned with using their resources for the support of Christian work.

Lyman Stewart came to California before the turn of the century and was a pioneer oil developer in that state. He was one of the founders and long-time president of the Union Oil Company. Both men were concerned about modernism* within American Christendom and developed and supported projects to extend fundamentalist influence. Notable projects included development of a Bible* publishing house in Los Angeles, the support of missionaries* in China and funding for Chinese Bibles, and the establishment in 1908 of

the Bible Institute of Los Angeles (now Biola University). Perhaps the most famous Stewart project was the publication of a twelve-volume series of booklets called *The Fundamentals.** These volumes, published between 1910 and 1915, contained articles written by a variety of conservative theologians* on issues considered of fundamental importance to the historic Christian faith. The Stewarts' plan, largely accomplished, was to send a free set of these booklets to every pastor and Christian worker in the English-speaking world. It is likely that the term *fundamentalism* came into common usage as a result of these volumes.   A. M. Carden

Stiles, Ezra (1727-1795). Congregational* minister* and president of Yale College.* Born in North Haven, Connecticut, Stiles graduated from Yale at the age of nineteen, and began to prepare for a law career. From 1749 to 1755 he was a tutor at Yale, and he struggled with skepticism and his leanings toward deism.* Rational arguments persuaded him that the Bible* accurately revealed the word of God, and eventually he was able to embrace the tenets, if not the rigidity, of his father's Calvinism.* In 1755 Stiles accepted a call as pastor of the Second Congregational Church in Newport, Rhode Island, where he remained until war forced him to evacuate in 1776. Stiles's habit of forming friendships that ignored denominational* differences continued in Newport, where he often attended services at the local synagogue. As his intellectual and social worlds expanded, his preaching* began to move beyond reasoned demonstration to include more evangelical* appeals to the heart.

During his presidency at Yale (1778-1795), Stiles raised academic standards and helped reconcile warring factions, allowing the institution to begin to grow from a sectarian college to a university. Although he was known for his expertise in Semitic languages and his efforts in ecclesiastical history, he published little. But his vast correspondence and dozens of notebooks, diaries and journals reveal a man of wide-ranging interests and insatiable curiosity—from temperature records and silkworms, to New England culture and the Stamp Act Crisis. Stiles was a religious moderate for whom tolerance was a matter of both principle and temperament. Although he tried to avoid political controversy, he strongly supported American independence and the French Revolution.

BIBLIOGRAPHY. *AAP* 1; F. B. Bowditch, ed., *The Literary Diary of Ezra Stiles,* 3 vols. (1901); F. B. Bowditch, *Extracts from the Itineraries and Other*

Miscellanies of Ezra Stiles with a Selection from his Correspondence (1916); *DAB* IX; *DARB*; A. Holmes, *The Life of Ezra Stiles, D.D. LL.D.* (1798); E. S. Morgan, *The Gentle Puritan: A Life of Ezra Stiles, 1727-1795* (1962); *NCAB* 7.

C. Grasso

Stillman, Samuel (1737-1807). Baptist* minister*. Born and raised in Charleston, South Carolina, in an environment that fostered moral and intellectual growth, Stillman was converted under the preaching of Oliver Hart, and he directed his education toward preparation for the ministry. He preached* his first sermon in 1758, was ordained* the next year and immediately began work as an evangelist.* Stillman became pastor on James Island, near Charleston, where he served for about two years. During this period he traveled to Philadelphia, where he met and married the daughter of Dr. John Morgan, a noted physician and professor of medicine. While in the region he was awarded honorary degrees from The College of Philadelphia* and from Harvard.* In 1761 Stillman moved to Bordertown, New Jersey, and then to Boston in 1763, where he assisted the pastor of Second Baptist Church. In 1765 he became pastor of First Baptist Church of Boston, a post he occupied for the rest of his life. His forty-two-year pastorate was regarded as a remarkable success. The church was in decline when he arrived, but Stillman's emphasis on evangelism, combined with a number of successful revivals,* ushered in extended periods of growth and progress. The church was held in high regard and was visited by presidents, generals and governors. Stillman died on March 12, 1807, after suffering a paralyzing stroke.

BIBLIOGRAPHY. *AAP* 6; I. Backus, *A History of New England With Particular Reference to the Denomination of Christians Called Baptists* (1871); *DAB* IX.

F. A. Teague

Stoddard, Solomon (1643-1729). Colonial minister.* Born in Boston and educated at Harvard* (1662), Stoddard was the second pastor* of the Congregational* church in Northampton, Massachusetts. The town was small in 1672 when he arrived, but by the 1720s his strong leadership was felt throughout the Connecticut Valley, and the church grew to be the largest outside of Boston.

Preaching* was Stoddard's great strength, and he presided over several "harvests" during his forty-seven-year pastorate. Stoddard struggled with the normal concerns of frontier pastors—insufficient pay and the necessity of entering into business on the side. He had a fine theological mind and possessed one of the better personal libraries in western New England. The historian Perry Miller analyzed Stoddard as the typical country parson, the ambassador of culture and sound doctrine to a hardworking frontier.

The desire to teach sound doctrine* led Stoddard into several widely known controversies with the Mathers* and other Boston clergy.* While Stoddard remained the annual speaker at the Harvard graduation ceremonies through much of his ministry, the conflicts over the Half-Way Covenant* put him at odds with the Boston clergy, and the Mather family in particular. Stoddard found it necessary to baptize the children of church members, despite the fact that these parents had not yet experienced a personal "awakening" or "new birth."* He believed that communion* could be a "converting ordinance"* and therefore entreated those without church membership* to participate and thereby be exposed to his evangelical preaching style. Although this controversial doctrinal stance did not meet with the approval of the Boston Mathers, Stoddard achieved great success in controlling his society and seeing people come to "new birth" eventually.

In 1727 Stoddard presided over the calling of Jonathan Edwards,* his grandson, to an associate pastorate in Northampton. When Stoddard died two years later, his well-trained congregation was prepared for repeated harvests which would be known as the Great Awakening.*

BIBLIOGRAPHY. *AAP* 1; *DAB* IX; *DARB;* P. Miller, "Solomon Stoddard, 1643-1729," *HTR* 34 (1941): 277-320; *NCAB* 7; H. S. Stout, *The New England Soul* (1986).

J. H. Edwards

Stoever, John Casper, Jr. (1707-1779). Pioneer Lutheran* pastor.* Born in the Lower Palatinate, Stoever immigrated with his father to Pennsylvania in 1728. Although not yet ordained,* a pressing need for ministers* among German Lutherans moved him to offer his services almost immediately. He finally secured ordination in 1733. Stoever served a large number of parishes* as pastor, in most places beginning their first record books, which list hundreds of infant baptisms,* confirmations, marriages* and funerals* under his ministry. After 1735 he extended his ministerial labors beyond the Susquehannah River, preaching also in Maryland and Virginia. Unfortunately, he was not accepted as a full colleague by Henry M. Muhlenberg,* who in 1742 was sent by the Pietists* at Halle to bring order among Lutheranism in Pennsylvania. It was not until 1763 that Stoever's name was placed on the roll of the Lutheran ministerium, although he had been for decades the colony's senior pastor. An energetic, forceful and controversial personality, his critics charged him with being authoritarian, greedy and given to strong drink. Nevertheless, he was above all fondly regarded as a pastor by hundreds of Lutherans.

BIBLIOGRAPHY. C. H. Glatfelter, *Pastors and People: German Lutheran and Reformed Churches in the Pennsylvania Field, 1717-1793,* vols. I-II (1980-1981); R. L. Winters, *John Casper Stoever: Colonial Pastor and Founder of Churches* (1948).

D. F. Durnbaugh

Stone, Barton Warren (1772-1844). Leader of the "Stonite" wing of the early Restoration Movement.* Born near Port Tobacco, Maryland, in 1793, Stone completed the classical course at a private academy run by David Caldwell, a Presbyterian minister. After his conversion* at age nineteen, he dedicated his life to the ministry* and applied in 1793 to the Orange Presbytery for a license* to preach,* which was not granted until 1796. After a short period of preaching in North Carolina, Virginia and Tennessee, Stone began preaching for the Presbyterian congregations at Cane Ridge and Concord, Kentucky. The congregations then issued a call to ministry through the Transylvania Presbytery and an examination for ordination was called for October 4, 1790.

Even at this point Stone had questions about traditional Calvinist* doctrines such as predestination.* But when asked by the presbytery, "Do you receive and adopt the (Westminster) Confession of Faith* as containing the system of doctrine taught in the Bible?" he replied: "I do, as far as I see it consistent with the word of God." So satisfying the presbytery, he was ordained to the Presbyterian ministry.

In 1801 Stone visited a revival* in Logan County and was impressed by the "religious exercises" he observed (falling, jerking, dancing, barking, running, laughing and singing), believing them to be authentic manifestations of God's presence. These "religious exercises" were increasingly seen in his own famous revival at Cane Ridge,* which eventually attracted thousands.

With his revival methods bringing increasing tension between him and the Presbyterian Synod of Kentucky, Stone and several other revivalists organized their own body in January 1804, calling it the Springfield Presbytery. Within a few months they began questioning the validity of presbyteries and in June 1804 desolved theirs by writing and signing "The Last Will and Testament of the Springfield Presbytery."* The group then agreed to be known as "Christians only," and to follow only the Bible. In 1807 they adopted the practice of baptism* by immersion for the remission of sins, though they did not make it a test for fellowship.

From 1826 until his death, Stone extended his influence through his monthly journal, *Christian Messenger.* In 1830 Stone met Alexander Campbell* and, finding a common ground, the next year Stone and most of his followers united with the Campbellites to form a group which became known as the Christian Church (Disciples of Christ).*

See also RESTORATION MOVEMENT.

BIBLIOGRAPHY. *DAB* IX; *DARB;* B. W. Stone, *The Biography of Eld. Barton Warren Stone. Written by Himself* (1847); C. C. Ware, *Barton Warren Stone* (1932).

T. L. Miethe

Stone, John Timothy (1868-1954). Presbyterian* minister.* A graduate of Amherst College and Auburn Theological Seminary, Stone was pastor of such prominent churches as Brown Memorial in Baltimore and Fourth Presbyterian in Chicago. During Stone's tenure from 1909 to 1930, Fourth Presbyterian quadrupled in membership* and erected the Gothic structure it has since occupied on Chicago's Gold Coast. Stone's evangelistic* commitment expressed itself in his books (*Recruiting for Christ,* 1910; *George Whitefield,* 1914; and *Winning Men: Studies in Soul-Winning,* 1946), his support for the YMCA* and Moody Bible Institute,* and in his chairmanship of the Committee on Evangelism of the Men and Religion Forward Movement* (1911). A respected figure in the Presbyterian Church in the U.S.A.,* he was elected moderator of its General Assembly* (1913), chaired a committee that reorganized its General Boards (1921-1923) and headed McCormick* Theological Seminary (1928-1940). He was also president of the Chicago Bible Society and director of the Chicago Sunday Evening Club.

BIBLIOGRAPHY. "In Memoriam," *Presbyterian Life* 7 (July 24, 1954).

J. H. Dorn

Stone, Lucy (1818-1893). Pioneer in the women's rights movement. Born near West Brookfield, Massachusetts, Lucy taught school until she had saved enough money to enter Oberlin College.* Unable to believe that the Bible* endorsed women's subjugation or that the Congregationalists* were right to accept her as a member and then deny her a vote, she had vowed in her childhood to learn Greek and Hebrew in order to understand the Scriptures.* At Oberlin she mastered the biblical languages, became a Unitarian* and graduated with honors in 1847. She lectured for the Anti-Slavery Society and spoke increasingly for women's rights. In 1855 she married Henry Blackwell, issuing a protest against the legal disabilities of women and choosing to keep her own name. When the suffragists* split in 1869, she became head of the American Woman's Suffrage Association and editor of the *Woman's Journal.* She saw the movement reunified as the National American Women's Suffrage Association in 1890 and delivered her last speech in 1893 at the Chicago World's Columbian Exposition.

BIBLIOGRAPHY. A. S. Blackwell, *Lucy Stone, Pioneer of Women's Rights* (1930); *DAB* IX; E. R. Hays, *Morning Star: A Biography of Lucy Stone* (1961); *NAW* 3.   K. K. Kidd

Stonehouse, Ned Bernard (1902-1962). Presbyterian* biblical scholar. Born in Grand Rapids, Michigan, and educated at Calvin College, Princeton Seminary* and the Free University of Amsterdam (Th.D. in New Testament, 1929), Stonehouse was a member of the original faculty of Westminster Theological Seminary, Philadelphia, where he remained until his death. He was also prominent in the formation of the Orthodox Presbyterian Church* and in time became one of its most highly regarded leaders, with a special concern for its ecumenical vision. In his *J. Gresham Machen: A Biographical Memoir* (1954), he told the story of the eminent founder of both Westminster and the Orthodox Presbyterian Church.

Combining a cordial commitment to Reformed* theology* with breadth of learning, Stonehouse was among the more widely respected conservative New Testament scholars of his day. He wrote on a wide range of New Testament topics, but his particular area of expertise was the synoptic Gospels, as demonstrated in his *Origin of the Synoptic Gospels* (1963). Perhaps his most enduring contribution, as expressed in *The Witness of Matthew and Mark to Christ* (1944) and *The Witness of Luke to Christ* (1951), was his anticipation of the rise of redaction criticism. Basing his work on a high view of Scripture, he drew attention to the theologically distinctive editorial activity of each of the synoptic writers.

BIBLIOGRAPHY. M. A. Noll, *Between Faith and Criticism* (1986); M. Silva, "Ned B. Stonehouse and Redaction Criticism," *WmTJ* 40 (Fall 1977):77-88 and (Spring 1978):281-303.

R. B. Gaffin

Stough, Henry Wellington (1870-1939). Evan-gelist* and founder of the America-Israel movement. After study at Oberlin College* (1888-1891), Moody Bible Institute* (1891-1893) and Chicago Theological Seminary (1893-1896), Stough was ordained* to the Congregational* ministry* and pastored in Oak Park, Illinois (1894-1901). In 1901 he became an independent evangelist, working under the title of his "Stough Evangelistic Campaigns" (1901-1939). He was active in the Interdenominational Evangelists Association (secretary/treasurer, 1906-1912) and the healing* movement, founding the Society of the Healing Christ (1926). Stough lectured and campaigned for the Anglo-Saxon Federation of America (1932) and prohibitionist* causes. Moving to Knoxville, Tennessee, he founded and was national director of the restorationist America-Israel movement and associate editor of the periodical, *America-Israel Message.* Among his publications were *Against the Deadline of Amusements* (1912) and *Faith and Prayer in their Conflict against Unbelief* (1913).   D. D. Bundy

Stowe, Harriet Elizabeth Beecher (1811-1896). Author. One of nine children born to the Calvinist* clergyman Lyman Beecher* and his first wife, Roxanna Foote, Harriet moved from Litchfield, Connecticut, to Cincinnati, Ohio, in 1832, when her father became director of Lane Theological Seminary, a center of abolitionist* sentiment. While in Ohio she once visited a slave-run plantation in Kentucky.

In 1836 she married a professor at Lane, Calvin E. Stowe, and in 1850 they moved to Bowdoin College in Maine. There, after having borne seven children, she wrote *Uncle Tom's Cabin,* drawing on her experiences in Ohio to depict the evils of slavery. The book was published in serial form in 1852 in the *National Era,* an anti-slavery newspaper in Washington, D.C. Not an abolitionist herself, Stowe nonetheless intended her book to lead to the eventual eradication of slavery. Her hopes were realized in its immediate, unprecedented popular success, although its factual inaccuracies as a portrayal of slavery were criticized in both the North and South. In 1853 the family moved to Andover, Massachusetts, where her husband taught at Andover Theological Seminary.*

Stowe wrote *Uncle Tom's Cabin* when she was forty years old. She produced thirty more books in the next thirty years, including a volume of verse (1867) containing what was to be a popular hymn, "Still, Still with Thee," and a controversial treatise on Lord Byron (*Lady Byron Vindicated,* 1870). Her father, husband and five of her brothers (including

Henry Ward Beecher,* to whom she was especially close) were ministers. A Calvinistic moral earnestness and romantic pathos pervaded her work. Late in her life, Stowe affiliated with the Episcopal Church* and was active in its mission in Florida and in Hartford, Connecticut, where she had homes.

BIBLIOGRAPHY. J. R. Adams, *Harriet Beecher Stowe* (1963); J. W. Ashton, *Harriet Beecher Stowe: A Reference Guide* (1977); *DAB* IX; *DARB; NAW* 3; *NCAB* 1; F. Wilson, *Crusader in Crinoline: The Life of Harriet Beecher Stowe* (1941).

R. R. Crocker

Strachan, John (1778-1867). Educator and first Anglican* bishop* of Toronto. Born in Scotland, raised a Presbyterian* and educated at St. Andrews and Aberdeen universities, Strachan came to Upper Canada (Ontario) in 1799. He founded an influential grammar school at Cornwall in 1803 which trained many of Upper Canada's leaders of the nineteenth century.

Taking Anglican orders, he rose to become archdeacon of York in 1825 and bishop of the newly created Diocese* of Toronto in 1839. A member of the provincial government for more than twenty years, his central concerns were the preservation of the proceeds from the clergy reserves* for the Anglican Church, the establishment of an autonomous Canadian church and the founding of Christian universities. In fulfillment of the latter interest he was instrumental in the birth of McGill University and Trinity College and was first president of King's College, later known as the University of Toronto. Strachan was also a devoted pastor and distinguished himself in caring for the city during the War of 1812 and the cholera outbreaks of the 1830s.

BIBLIOGRAPHY. J. L. H. Henderson, ed., *John Strachan: Documents and Opinions; A Selection* (1969); J. L. H. Henderson, *John Strachan, 1778-1867* (1969). J. G. Stackhouse

Strachan, Robert Kenneth (1910-1965). Director of the Latin America Mission.* Raised in Latin America, Strachan was the son of a well-known missionary father, Harry S. Strachan, the founder of Latin American Mission (LAM). His schooling included studies at Wheaton College* and Dallas Theological Seminary.* He married Wheaton student Elizabeth Walker in 1940 and received the Th.D. from Princeton Theological Seminary* in 1943. Strachan assumed the directorship of LAM after the death of his father. An intense, energetic and intellectually restless figure, Kenneth Strachan

directed LAM from 1945 to 1965. During these years following World War 2,* the mission moved in the direction of Latin American control, which was finally achieved in 1971. Strachan's major contribution was Evangelism-in-Depth,* a concept of mobilizing resources in order to concentrate evangelical efforts in a highly visible, unifying display of Christian conviction in a given Latin American republic. Evangelism-in-Depth began in Nicaragua in 1960 and was extended to other Latin American countries through the rest of the decade. At the time of his death, Strachan was a visiting professor of missions at Fuller Theological Seminary.*

BIBLIOGRAPHY. E. Elliot, *Who Shall Ascend; The Life of R. Kenneth Strachan of Costa Rica* (1968); W. D. Roberts, *Strachan of Costa Rica* (1971); R. K. Strachan, *The Inescapable Calling* (1968).

E. A. Wilson

Straton, John Roach (1875-1929). Fundamentalist* preacher* and social-rights activist. Born in Evansville, Indiana, Straton attended Mercer University and the Southern Baptist Theological Seminary. He was ordained* a Baptist minister (1900), later holding pastorates in Maryland, Virginia and Illinois (1905-1917) prior to his outspoken ministry at Calvary Baptist Church, New York City (1918-1929). There he championed Christian fundamentals from the pulpit and founded the Fundamentalist League of Greater New York (1922).

Straton's attack on modernism* and his anti-denominational policies led to tension within the Baptist World Alliance* and his own withdrawal from the Northern Baptist Convention* (1926). Straton fought political corruption, sought justice for minorities and encouraged censorship of entertainment. In his preaching and social activism he made wide use of the media, including pioneer work in radio broadcasting. His books outline a vision of the kingdom of God* on earth, differing from that of Rauschenbusch* in its emphasis upon a deeper reality accorded to "regeneration, not reform; soteriology, not sociology." This combination of emphases earned him the titles "Pope of fundamentalism" and "prophet of social rightousness."

BIBLIOGRAPHY. *DAB* IX; C. A. Russell, *Voices of American Fundamentalism: Seven Biographical Studies* (1976). R. L. Petersen

Stringfellow, Frank William (1928-1985). Lawyer, Episcopal* lay* theologian* and social activist. Born in Johnston, Rhode Island, Stringfellow graduated from Bates College (B.A., 1949), attended the London School of Economics (1950) and studied law at Harvard University* (LL.B., 1956). Admitted to the New York bar in 1957, he entered private practice (1957-1960) and then became a partner in a law firm in 1961.

An adamant supporter of equal rights, Stringfellow was uncompromising in his belief that the gospel demands identification with the disenfranchised of society. His works in ethics and theology (i.e., *Free in Obedience,* 1954; *Dissenter in a Great Society,* 1966; *An Ethic for Christians and Other Aliens in a Strange Land,* 1973; *Conscience and Obedience,* 1977; *The Politics of Spirituality,* 1984) are marked by a frequent denunciation of both church and nation for promoting the "collective evils" of racism, sexism, national idolatry and military imperialism.

Stringfellow's efforts as an attorney and social activist were often the subject of controversy. During his years of private law practice in East Harlem, New York (1957-1960), he defended the poor in housing and welfare cases, drug users, homosexuals and sex offenders. He later defended Bishop James Pike* against the charge of heresy* by the Episcopal Church hierarchy. This event and Stringfellow's close friendship with that controversial theologian led to two other books, *The Bishop Pike Affair* (1967) and *The Death and Life of Bishop Pike* (1976).

Throughout the 1960s Stringfellow was a frequent advisor to those who faced criminal charges for resisting the Vietnam War.* Among these was the Roman Catholic* priest-activist Daniel Berrigan, who had gone into hiding following his arrest in 1968 for destroying military draft records. In 1970 Stringfellow was indicted for "harboring a fugitive," but the charges against him were later dropped. This experience is recounted in *Suspect Tenderness: The Ethics of the Berrigan Witness* (1971). Stringfellow was also known for his strong and often vehement espousal of women's ordination.* It is largely due to his efforts that the General Convention of the Episcopal Church voted in 1976 to recognize the ordination of women priests.

BIBLIOGRAPHY. D. Straub, "William Stringfellow," *Contemporary Authors,* New Revision Series, vol. 9, ed. A. Every and L. Metzger (1983); J. Wallis, ed., "William Stringfellow: Keeper of the Word," (Special Issue) *Sojourners* 14 (December 1985): 12-29. R. P. Hesselgrave

Stritch, Samuel Alphonsus (1887-1958). Cardinal* archbishop* of Chicago. Born in Nashville, Tennessee, Stritch completed high school work by age fourteen. He studied for the priesthood* at St. Gregory's Seminary in Cincinnati and was later sent by his bishop* to the Urban College of the Propaganda in Rome, where he completed doctorates in philosophy and theology.* He was ordained* to the priesthood in 1910 at the Lateran Basilica.

Stritch was first sent as a curate to St. Patrick's Parish in Memphis. In 1916 he returned to Nashville where he became the bishop's personal secretary. Later he was appointed chancellor, superintendent of schools and rector* of the cathedral.* In 1921 he was named the second bishop of Toledo, Ohio, and was consecrated* a bishop by Archbishop Henry Moeller of Cincinnati on November 30, 1921. During his years in Toledo (1921-1930) he gave great attention to issues of education, establishing a teacher's training college and a central Catholic high school.

In 1930 he succeeded Archbishop Sebastian Messmer of Milwaukee. During his years in Milwaukee (1930-1939) he coped with the effects of the Great Depression* by inaugurating a highly successful charity drive. There he also urged the establishment of teacher-training institutions for the major sisterhoods in Milwaukee. Stritch was a strong supporter of official Catholic Action* movements, and he federated the Holy Name Societies in Milwaukee, using them for an extensive program which included sports programs for youth, adult education and devotional rallies. When he was transferred to Chicago in 1940, he continued these activities.

Since 1930 he had been an active member of the Administrative Board of the National Catholic Welfare Conference* (NCWC). In 1940 he became chairman of the board and later its treasurer. One of his tasks was the chairmanship of a committee on the Papal Peace Points, which led him to an active interest in the issue of post-war reconstruction. His support of the NCWC was important to its survival and credibility, and he generously allowed Chicago priests to serve in full-time positions for the Conference.

His elevation to cardinal in 1946 coincided with tremendous population and building booms in the archdiocese of Chicago. There he directed a major program of parochial and institutional expansion of the diocese. He also gave serious attention to the problems of the urban church, working to preserve urban Catholic communities and quietly but firmly dealing with Catholic resistance to African-American admittance in Catholic schools, hospitals and neighborhoods.

Though generally permissive toward his priests and laity, he was not kindly disposed to ecumenical or interfaith gatherings and prohibited Catholic participation in the World Council of Churches* meeting held in Evanston* in 1954. In 1958 Pope Pius XII* appointed him pro-prefect of the curial office for the Propagation of the Faith.* Stritch reluctantly left his archdiocese in April 1958. Soon after arriving in Rome, he suffered the amputation of his right arm. He died of a stroke in Rome on May 23, 1958.

BIBLIOGRAPHY. S. M. Avella, "Stritch: The Milwaukee Years," *Salesianum* 81 (Spring/Summer 1986):9-14; *DAB* 6; T. Stritch, "Four Catholic Bishops from Tennessee," in *The Catholic Church in Tennessee* (1987).   S. M. Avella

Strong, Augustus Hopkins (1836-1921). Northern Baptist* theologian.* Born in Rochester, New York, the son of a wealthy newspaperman. The brother of the founder and president of the Eastman Kodak Company and a close friend of John D. Rockefeller, Strong moved easily among the rich and powerful. He bore an authoritative, if not aristocratic, demeanor that propelled him into positions of ecclesiastical and academic leadership. After graduating from Yale College* in 1857 and Rochester Theological Seminary in 1859, Strong briefly served Baptist churches in Haverhill, Massachusetts, and Cleveland, Ohio. In 1872 he moved back to Rochester where he spent the next forty years as president of the seminary and professor of systematic theology.* During those years he also served as president of numerous organizations such as the American Baptist Foreign Mission Society (1892-1895) and the General Convention of Baptists of North America (1905-1910). From about 1885 to 1910, Strong reigned as the most influential Northern Baptist and one of the most influential conservative Protestant theologians in the U.S.

Generations of Protestant* seminarians began their study of theology with Strong's *Systematic Theology.* First published in 1876, this substantial volume passed through eight editions and thirty printings. But his most creative and speculative work appeared in a series of essays published as *Christ in Creation and Ethical Monism* (1899). Here Strong articulated an idealist metaphysical position similar to those propounded by Hermann Lotze (1817-1881) in Germany and Borden Parker Bowne* at Boston University. Throughout his long life Strong endeavored to avoid theological controversy, but by 1916 his apprehension over the havoc that modernism* seemed to be wreaking on the mission* field prompted him to publish *A Tour of the Missions.* The uncharacteristically polemical

tone of this volume, coupled with its revelations of theological drift among Baptist foreign missionaries, did more than a little to precipitate the fundamentalist-modernist controversy* in the 1920s.

Assessments of Strong's work have varied. Some have understood him to be a closet liberal, and still others have concluded he was simply confused. The best explanation seems to be that as he grew older and confronted biblical higher criticism and the arguments for human evolution,* he was forced to change his mind in key respects. There is no evidence that he ever seriously compromised, much less jettisoned, any of the cardinal doctrines of Reformed orthodoxy, but he did come to see that the epistemic foundations of all doctrines, including his own, were conditioned by the historical setting in which they had emerged. So for Strong the challenge was to hold the faith of the fathers intact on one side and the best of modern philosophical, social and scientific thought on the other. To some extent he was a tragic figure, forced to come to terms with seemingly incompatible, yet equally cogent, conceptual worlds.

BIBLIOGRAPHY. *DAB* IX; *DARB;* C. Douglas, ed., *Autobiography of Augustus Hopkins Strong* (1981); C. F. H. Henry, *Personal Idealism and Strong's Theology* (1951); *NCAB* 12; G. Wacker, *Augustus H. Strong and the Dilemma of Historical Consciousness* (1985).   G. Wacker

Strong, Josiah (1847-1916). Social Gospel Movement* leader, expansionist, interdenominationalist. Born in Naperville, Illinois, educated at Western Reserve College (B.A., 1869) and Lane Seminary (1869-1871) and ordained a Congregational* minister in 1871, Strong served in pastoral, college-chaplaincy* and home-mission* roles for fifteen years. He became famous for the controversial book *Our Country: Its Possible Future and Its Present Crisis* (1885), which outlined seven perils confronting America (immigration,* Romanism,* Mormonism,* intemperance, socialism, wealth and cities), and called for reform led by Anglo-Saxons, representatives of civil liberty and "pure, *spiritual* Christianity."

As general secretary of the Evangelical Alliance* (1886-1898), he displayed exceptional organizational abilities, setting up three major national conferences devoted to Social Gospel* themes. His growing concerns for cooperative Christianity led to a parting of ways, and he organized and became president of what became known as the American Institute for Social Service. He advocated a larger American role in international affairs, expressed vigorously in *Expansion Under New World Conditions* (1900). As he worked for a wider unity among Protestant* churches and missionary* agencies, he played an important part in the formation of the Federal Council of the Churches of Christ in America* (1908). In his last book, *Our World: The New World Religion* (1915), he combined expansionism with Christian social reform, fearing a resurgence of barbarism in the increasingly urbanized civilization of his country. A magnetic platform speaker and the author of eleven books, he was a conspicuous figure for three decades in Protestant mission, reform and unitive movements.

BIBLIOGRAPHY. *DAB* IX; *DARB;* P. R. Meyer, "The Fear of Cultural Decline: Josiah Strong's Thought about Reform and Expansion," *CH* 42 (1973):396-405; J. Strong, *My Religion in Everyday Life* (1910); *NCAB* 9.   R. T. Handy

Strong, Nathan (1748-1816). Congregational* clergyman. A native of Connecticut, Strong graduated from Yale College* in 1769 and then did further study in both law and theology.* He taught at Yale for a year before becoming pastor of the First Congregational Church of Hartford, a post he held for over forty years. During the American Revolution* he authored a number of influential political treatises, often sarcastic in character, favorable to the American position. Strong was known as a commanding pulpit orator whose later sermons* were often revivalistic* in nature. His interest in evangelism* was further evidenced by his leadership of the Connecticut Missionary Society,* which he helped establish in 1798. A man of varied interests and talents, Strong also compiled a hymnal,* published in 1799 as the *Hartford Collection of Hymns,* which included several anthems of his own composition. Two volumes of his sermons were published between 1798 and 1800, although his most notable work was *The Doctrine of Eternal Misery Consistent with the Infinite Benevolence of God* (1796).

BIBLIOGRAPHY. *AAP* 2; F. H. Foster, *A Genetic History of the New England Theology* (1907).
                                        A. M. Carden

Stuart, George Hay (1816-1890). Philadelphia merchant and evangelical* philanthropist.* Born near Belfast, Stuart immigrated to the U.S. at age fifteen. Without formal education he became a successful banker and dry goods wholesaler in Philadelphia.

When the Civil War* began, Stuart was serving as chairman of the central committee of the vigorous-

ly evangelistic YMCA.* During an informal convention of YMCA supporters in 1861, the United States Christian Commission* was born, with Stuart as chairman. The aim was to promote "the spiritual good of the soldiers in the army, and incidentally their intellectual improvement and social and physical comfort." The Commission enlisted lay* "delegates" as "ambassadors for Jesus" who followed the troops into the field, preaching,* holding prayer meetings, distributing Bibles,* tracts,* hymnbooks, hospital supplies, food and other material aid. Stuart collected six million dollars and enlisted 5,000 volunteers. One and a half million Bibles were distributed, along with nine million other books and thirty million tracts.

Following the War, Dwight L. Moody's* successes at urban evangelism* turned Stuart into an enthusiastic supporter. When the Chicago Fire of 1871 burned Moody's church and Sunday-school* buildings, Stuart collected money from former Christian Commission supporters to rebuild.

After refusing several offers to join Grant's cabinet, in 1869 Stuart accepted an appointment to the Board of Indian Commissioners where, as purchasing agent, he fought corruption.

BIBLIOGRAPHY. G. H. Stuart, *The Life of George Hay Stuart* (1890); L. Moss, *Annals of the United States Christian Commission* (1868); R. H. Bremner, *The Public Good: Philanthropy and Welfare in the Civil War Era* (1980).
                                        R. E. Selleck

Stuart, John (c.1740-1811). Anglican* clergyman and missionary.* Born and educated in Pennsylvania, Stuart was early on an Anglican missionary to Mohawk Indians in New York. Violent reactions to his Loyalist sympathies forced him to leave for Montreal in 1781, and there he set up a school while serving as an army chaplain.* In 1785, however, he and his family moved to Cataraqui (Kingston, Ontario) to stay. Stuart was the first Anglican missionary (to both whites and Native Americans) in the western settlements. He opened the first school west of the Ottawa River, pastored the congregation of St. George's until his death and from 1792 on served as chaplain of the legislative council. John Strachan* called him the "Father of the Episcopal Church in this Province."

BIBLIOGRAPHY. A. Young, *The Revd. John Stuart of Kingston and His Family* (1921).
                                        J. G. Stackhouse

Stuart, Moses (1780-1852). Biblical scholar and Trinitarian opponent of Unitarianism.* Born in Wilton, Connecticut, Stuart graduated first in his class in math at Yale* (1799) after only two years of study. He then taught at two academies in Connecticut and completed a law degree at Newton. Although he passed the Bar, instead of practicing law he studied religion under President Timothy Dwight* at Yale and was ordained* a Congregational* minister* at First Church in New Haven. Under his ministry the revival spirit of the Second Great Awakening* was strongly manifest during 1807-1808. Nathaniel W. Taylor* succeeded him in the pulpit when Stuart was called as professor of sacred literature to the newly founded Andover Theological Seminary.* There he remained until his retirement in 1848.

An indefatigable scholar, Stuart revolutionized American biblical studies. He taught himself German and Hebrew, translated Gesenius's grammar and then wrote his own, which he distributed to his students in manuscript form so they could copy it by hand. Conservative colleagues viewed with suspicion his introduction of European biblical studies to America because Germans were arriving at unorthodox conclusions in biblical criticism. But Stuart gradually won recognition at home and abroad for his comprehensive and conservative scholarship.

In the early 1800s Stuart contributed mightily on behalf of orthodoxy* in New England's tumultuous Unitarian Controversy.* He championed Trinitarian theology against William Ellery Channing* and Henry Ware* by adducing biblical evidence. He claimed reason's task is not to pass judgment on the Bible* but to accept and understand its content. As New England drifted away from Calvinism,* many recalled Stuart's prescient remark that Unitarianism is but a halfway house on the road to infidelity.

BIBLIOGRAPHY. M. Stuart, *Letters to the Rev. W. E. Channing, Containing Remarks on His Sermon Recently Preached and Published at Baltimore* (1819); J. H. Giltner, *Moses Stuart: The Father of Biblical Science in America* (1988).

W. A. Hoffecker

Stub, Hans Gerhard (1849-1931). Lutheran* pastor, professor and synodical leader. Following a pastorate in Minnesota, Stub served as professor of Luther Seminary (1878-1896), located first in Madison, Wisconsin, and then in Robbinsdale, Minnesota. He was then a pastor and professor at Decorah, Iowa, for two decades. Stub carried elective office in his Norwegian Synod and was a founder of the Norwegian Lutheran Church in America (a 1917 merger of three Norwegian-American church bodies), serving as its first

president for eight years. He also took an active part in the formation of the National Lutheran Council in 1910 and for two years served as its first president. In this connection and during discussions of the principles to govern inter-Lutheran cooperation, Stub authored a doctrinal statement which became the "Chicago Theses." This document was instrumental in showing the divergence in attitude toward cooperation and unity between Midwestern Lutherans and the United Lutheran Church in America.

BIBLIOGRAPHY. E. C. Nelson and E. L. Fevold, *The Lutheran Church among Norwegian-Americans* (1960); E. C. Nelson, ed., *The Lutherans in North America* (1975).

F. K. Wentz

Student Foreign Missions Fellowship. An association of college and university students interested in foreign missions. Dissatisfaction with long-evident trends in the fifty-year-old Student Volunteer Movement* led in 1936 to the beginning of the Student Foreign Missions Fellowship (SFMF), primarily through the energies of students at Wheaton College* in Illinois and Columbia Bible College in South Carolina. Though the purpose was to spark interest in foreign missionary service on college campuses in general, favorable reception was largely limited to evangelical* campuses (including seminaries*). Within four years there were more than seventeen hundred members and twenty-nine chapters. Meanwhile InterVarsity Christian Fellowship* (IVCF) was being started in Canada (1934) and the U.S. (1939), with a focus on evangelism and discipleship, including the challenge of missions, on secular campuses.

Given the complementary purposes of the two movements, merger was smoothly effected in 1945, and ever since SFMF (under a variety of local names) has been the student arm of IVCF on Christian campuses. By the mid-1980s they numbered about 130 campus groups. In addition, regional weekend conferences and summer training camps have been sponsored with varying regularity and attended by students from both Christian and secular schools. The national head of SFMF has also been the missions director for IVCF, charged with seeing that all IVCF staff and students receive a missions challenge. The principal means for doing this have been the great Urbana Student Missionary Conventions,* held triennially since 1946.

BIBLIOGRAPHY. H. W. Norton, *To Stir the Church: A Brief History of the SFMF, 1936-1986*

(1986); A. Poyner, *From the Campus to the World: Stories from the First Fifty Years of SFMF* (1986).

D. G. Tinder

Student Volunteer Movement for Foreign Missions. Student voluntary association promoting world missions.* The Student Volunteer Movement (SVM), spurred by the YMCA* and YWCA,* was conceived in the summer of 1886 at a conference led by Dwight L. Moody* at Mount Hermon, Massachusetts. By the end of the conference one hundred students had signified their intention to become missionaries. An early leader was Robert P. Wilder,* who carried the spirit of Mount Hermon to colleges and seminaries in the U.S. and abroad.

Within the first year of his travels, over one thousand students had signed the pledge, "It is my purpose, if God permit, to become a foreign missionary." By 1888 the SVM was formally organized, with John R. Mott* as chairman and Robert E. Speer* as traveling secretary. In 1891 the SVM held the first of its long series of large conventions, called "Quadrennials." The SVM produced mission books and study programs which influenced many students and teachers. The Movement quickly spread in the 1890s and early 1900s to Great Britain, Europe and Asia.

The Movement's watchword, "the evangelization of the world in this generation," challenged students to dedicate their lives to the task of world evangelization. After the 1920 Quadrennial the SVM began to decline. Organizational and leadership problems, combined with a general loss of its original vision and a shift in student concerns, all contributed to its demise. In 1959 the SVM merged with two other bodies to form the National Student Christian Federation, which became part of the University Christian Movement in 1966. The Movement was then dissolved in 1969.

Within its history the SVM stimulated an estimated 20,000 North American college students to be Christian missionaries. In 1936, feeling the need for a new organization reflecting the SVM's original evangelical* missionary concerns, a group of students founded the Student Foreign Mission Fellowship.* *See also* MOUNT HERMON ONE HUNDRED.

BIBLIOGRAPHY. R. W. Braisted, *In This Generation: The Story of Robert P. Wilder* (1941); B. Harder, "The Student Volunteer Movement for Foreign Missions and Its Contribution to 20th C. Missions," *Missiology* 8 (1980):141-154; C. P. Shedd, *Two Centuries of Student Christian Movements* (1934); R. P. Wilder, *The Student Volunteer Movement* (1935). H. M. Goodpasture

Stuyvesant, Peter (Petrus) (c.1610-1672). Dutch soldier and last governor of New Netherland. Born in Scherpenzeel, near Wolvega, Friesland, Netherlands, Peter Stuyvesant was the son of Dutch Reformed* Church pastor Balthazar Johannes Stuyvesant and Margaretha Hardenstein. Raised in a Frisian parsonage and educated in the highest grades of the Latin school and then at Franeker University (1629-1630), Stuyvesant was slated by heritage and training for the parish* ministry.* But religious controversies between Calvinists* and Remonstrants, which the Calvinists won at the Synod of Dordrecht (1618-1619), together with the constricting society of Friesland in the *ancien regime,* repulsed him from a religious career. The maverick entered Dutch military service and never returned to Friesland, much to his father's sorrow.

His Frisian background molded his personality for life, which was characterized by paternalism, fierce determination, a compulsion for orderly action and an active commitment to traditional institutions—the Dutch Reformed Church, the Orange Monarchy and the Dutch West India Company. In 1635, Stuyvesant joined the Company, rising in the ranks by 1643 to governor of Curacao and adjacent West Indies islands. While defending his territories against a Portuguese attack in 1644, Stuyvesant suffered a wound in his right leg, which was later amputated and replaced by a famed silver-ornamented wooden prosthesis. In 1645, while recuperating in the Netherlands, he married Judith Bayard (1608-1687) in the Walloon (French Reformed) church of Breda, Noord Brabant Province. A year later the States General of the Netherlands commissioned him director-general of New Netherland, Curacao, Bonnaire and Aruba.

Stuyvesant governed New Netherland from May 11, 1647, to September 8, 1664, when an invading English naval force compelled him to surrender the colony to the English Duke of York. Although not appreciated for his aristocratic leadership, he brought honest, efficient administration to the stumbling colony. He reformed city government in New Amsterdam (later New York City) and improved the city infrastructure; stoutly defended the Reformed faith against Lutherans,* Quakers* and other nonconformists; expanded the colony by conquering New Sweden (later Delaware) in 1655; settled the boundary dispute between Connecticut and New Netherland; improved relations with Native Americans and stamped out smuggling.

Failure to gain popular support for the government was his main shortcoming. But the rapid growth and expansion of the New England colony into the Connecticut Valley and Long Island doomed the small Dutch colony anyway. It was merely a matter of time before the Yankees absorbed the Yorkers. Stuyvesant retired on his Manhattan Island farm and was buried there at his death. St. Mark's Episcopal Church now stands on the site. "Silver-Leg" Stuyvesant remains a symbol of Dutch colonization in North America.

BIBLIOGRAPHY. *DAB* IX; S. J. Fockema, "Data on the Dutch Background of Peter Stuyvesant," *Halve Maen* 39 (1964):5-6; O. A. Rink, *Holland on the Hudson* (1986); G. L. Smith, *Religion and Trade in New Netherland* (1973).   R. P. Swierenga

Subscription Controversy. Eighteenth-century dispute within the Presbyterian Church.* The subscription controversy concerned whether candidates for church membership* and, more importantly, whether candidates for Presbyterian ordination* ought to be required to subscribe or assent to doctrinal creeds* or articles of church government.* Proponents of subscription, such as John Thompson of the New Castle Presbytery, generally demanded that candidates assent to the Westminster Confession* and Directory, arguing that these requirements would help prevent the spread of heresy* and erroneous opinions. Opponents, including Jonathan Dickinson,* insisted that the Bible* alone should serve as a guide to significant questions of doctrine* and practice; creeds represented human interpretations of Scripture* and cast doubt on the sufficiency of the Bible. Antisubscriptionists recognized creeds as useful tools for understanding the Scriptures but insisted that only the Bible itself could serve as a binding standard.

Divisions over these issues plagued Presbyterians in Scotland and Ireland in the first years of the eighteenth century and surfaced among American Presbyterians in the 1720s. The controversy exacerbated pre-existing tensions within the American Presbyterian Church between Scotch-Irish newcomers (*See* Scottish Presbyterians) who favored subscription, and Presbyterians hearkening to the traditions of Puritan* New England, who opposed the practice. The controversy also contributed to the bitter disputes that divided American Presbyterians during the Great Awakening.* Most subscriptionists identified with opponents of the revivals,* while antisubscriptionists supported the Awakening and won support from revivalist preachers such as Gilbert Tennent.*

BIBLIOGRAPHY. L. J. Trinterud, *The Forming of an American Tradition* (1949).

J. F. Cooper

Subsidiarity, Principle of. The principle of subsidiarity is expressed by Pope Pius XI* in his encyclical *Quadragessimo Anno** (1931), so named because it was promulgated on the fortieth anniversary of Leo XIII's* great social encyclical, *Rerum Novarum.** This principle means that the state or lesser, intermediate organizations should never intervene to do for a lower group—including the family or even the individual—what that lower group can do for itself.

D. T. DeMarco

Sudermann, Leonhard (1821-1900). A leader of the Mennonite* emigration* from Russia to North America in the 1870s. Sudermann moved from Prussia to Russia in 1841, settling in Berdyansk in 1843, where he was elected minister* and then elder* of the Mennonite Church. In the 1860s Sudermann and his friend Cornelius Jansen* were among those who came quickly to believe that new laws threatened the Mennonites's century-old exemption from military service and other privileges. Sudermann led a delegation to St. Petersburg in 1871 and participated in a second to learn about the impact on Mennonites of the new military law. In 1873 he was part of a twelve-person delegation of Mennonites and Hutterites* from Russia and Prussia who traveled to North America to investigate possibilities for settlement. His *Deputationsreise* describes the trip. On his return, Sudermann advocated emigration and defended the principle of nonresistance for which Mennonites were willing to emigrate.

Sudermann and his family emigrated in 1876. After six months in Summerfield, Illinois, they established a permanent residence in Butler County, Kansas, joining Prussian Mennonite settlers who had founded the Emmaus Mennonite Church. Sudermann served that congregation as elder and was active in conference work until his death.

BIBLIOGRAPHY. L. Sudermann, *Eine Deputationsreise von Russland nach Amerika vor vierundswanzig Jahren* (1897), ET, *From Russia to America* (1947); T. F. Schlabach, *Faith, Peace, Nation: Mennonites and Amish in 19th Century America* (1988); G. Leibbrandt, "The Emigration of the German Mennonites from Russia to the United States and Canada in 1873-1880, I, II," *MQR* 6.4 (October 1932):205-226, 7.1 (January 1933):5-41.   J. D. Weaver

Sulpicians/Priests of Saint Sulpice. A group of diocesan* priests* released by their bishops* to serve in the formation of priests and future priests.

Forming a community under a general superior (they are not a religious order*), they take no special vows and work in each of their houses as a collegial* body. The Sulpicians grew out of the French school of spirituality* which, among other figures, produced Jean-Jacques Olier (1608-1657), the Sulpician founder. After working as a spiritual director* and a preacher of missions,* Olier was called in 1642 to accept the pastorate of St. Sulpice, the largest parish* in the city of Paris. To guarantee an adequate supply of priests to serve the parish, he moved a year-old seminary program into the parish house, and this developed into a system of seminaries throughout France.

When the anticlericalism of the French Revolution threatened to destroy the Sulpician efforts in France, Superior General Jacques-Andre Emery arranged with newly ordained* Bishop John Carroll* to found a Sulpician seminary in the U.S. In 1791 he sent four priests, five seminarians and seed money to establish St. Mary's Seminary in Baltimore. A number of the early faculty and alumni served as pioneer missionaries* and bishops. The Sulpicians conducted a lay* college for a half century; were involved in the founding of Mount St. Mary's College at Emmitsburg, Maryland; and helped establish several religious communities of women: Elizabeth Seton's* Daughters of Charity,* Jean-Baptiste David's Sisters of Charity* of Nazareth (Kentucky) and the first African-American community, the Oblate Sisters of Providence.*

Over the past two centuries the Sulpicians have spread from Baltimore to direct seminaries in Boston, New York, San Francisco, Seattle, Detroit, Louisville, Honolulu and Washington, D.C. In addition to forming thousands of American priests and bishops, they were involved in the formation of the Catholic University of America* and of the National Catholic Welfare Conference* and have been in the forefront of theological and biblical studies. In 1988 the U.S. province numbered one hundred members.

BIBLIOGRAPHY. C. J. Kauffman, *Tradition and Transformation in Catholic Culture: The Priests of Saint Sulpice in the United States from 1791 to the Present* (1988); C. G. Herbermann, *The Sulpicians in the United States* (1916). J. W. Bowen

Sunday. A Christian holy day. The early Jewish Christians continued to observe the Sabbath, the seventh day of the week, but gradually began to observe Sunday as a holy day. As the early Christians distinguished themselves from Judaism, they emphasized Sunday as the Lord's Day, the day of

the resurrection. Sometimes they called it the "eighth day," meaning that it was the first day of the new creation.

English Puritanism* insisted on a strictly observed Christian Sabbath (Sunday), and this idea was brought to New England. In 1656 when New Haven, Connecticut, enacted a set of laws pertaining to Sunday activity, they were printed in England on blue paper. Henceforth these laws were popularly known as "blue laws."* After the American Revolution and the disestablishment of the church, many Protestants* desired to maintain a strict Christian Sabbath in American society. This reserved time for worship and was perceived as a clear sign of a Christian civilization. One threat to this so-called Puritan Sabbath was the mid-nineteenth-century immigration of Lutherans* and Roman Catholics,* who played and drank alcohol* on Sunday, thus creating the expression *continental Sunday.*

Not all Christian groups regard Sunday as a holy day; some have maintained the sanctity of the seventh day—Saturday. In 1671 Stephen Munford founded a Seventh-Day Baptist church* in Newport, Rhode Island, and in 1728 Johann Conrad Beissel* of the Church of the Brethren* founded the Seventh-Day Dunkers or Ephrata Community* in Pennsylvania. In 1844 Mrs. Rachel Oaks Preston, a Seventh-Day Baptist,* convinced some Adventists* in Washington, New Hampshire, of the Sabbatarian position. This resulted in the formation of the Seventh-Day Adventists.*

Most American Christians regard Sunday as a holy day because of the resurrection of Jesus Christ. They hold their major worship service on this day, as well as their church schools. Many of the evangelical* churches will have a Sunday-evening* worship service. Many American Christians still regard it as a day of rest and a special time for the family, but the day is rapidly becoming secularized.

See also BLUE LAWS; SABBATARIANISM.

BIBLIOGRAPHY. P. K. Jewett, *The Lord's Day* (1971); H. B. Porter, *The Day of Light* (1960); W. Rordorf, *Sunday* (1968).

D. S. Armentrout

Sunday, William (Billy) Ashley (1862-1935). Urban evangelist.* Born on a farm near Ames, Iowa, Sunday was known in his lifetime as "the baseball evangelist." Receiving little formal schooling, Sunday began a career as a major league baseball player in 1883. Three years later he surrendered his life to Christ at Chicago's Pacific Garden Rescue Mission.* By 1891 the talented ball player walked away from his sports career to devote his full time to Christian ministry.* In 1896, after working for the YMCA* and two traveling evangelists, Sunday was invited to Garner, Iowa, to conduct a revival.* From that time on he was never without invitations to preach.

Sunday was licensed* by the Presbyterian Church* in 1898, and in 1903 he was ordained.* During the early years of his ministry his campaigns were held in small Midwestern towns. By the eve of World War 1,* however, he was preaching in larger cities all over the U.S., including Chicago, Boston and New York City. By the time of his death on November 6, 1935, the itinerant evangelist had preached thousands of sermons in over two hundred campaigns. Millions of people heard his message and approximately three-hundred thousand men and women were led to faith in Christ in his meetings.

Until the advent of Billy Graham,* no American evangelist ever preached to as many people and counted as many conversions for his efforts as Billy Sunday. His unorthodox preaching style—flamboyant antics, theatrical poses and impassioned gestures—attracted attention of the press and helped make him a household name. But much of his success was due to the organizational talents of his wife, Helen Amelia Thompson, whom he married in 1888. Despite the fact that she raised four children, she found time to select the cities where he preached, arrange the pre-campaign machinery and organize the campaigns themselves.

Thanks to his preaching skill and Mrs. Sunday's managerial talent, Sunday went from obscurity to national prominence, and from poverty to modest wealth. The common people admired his pluck and no doubt took vicarious delight in his popularity and success. To be sure he made enemies. Many churchmen loathed his down-home style, especially his backwoods vocabulary. And ultraconservatives found his promulgation of women's rights and his outreach to African-Americans to be as distasteful as the liquor interests found his battle for prohibition.*

Sunday is credited with helping passage of the Prohibition Amendment. He is also remembered for helping raise millions of dollars for the American military effort in World War 1. What cannot be measured is his impact on the nation's morality, let alone his actual effectiveness as an evangelist. Nevertheless, the evidence is overwhelming that Sunday left countless changed lives in the wake of his campaigns.

BIBLIOGRAPHY. *DAB* IX; W. T. Ellis, *Billy Sun-*

day, The Man and His Message (1936); W. G. McLaughlin, Jr., *Billy Sunday Was His Real Name* (1955); H. Rodeheaver, *Twenty Years with Billy Sunday* (1936). L. W. Dorsett

Sunday and Adult School Union. *See* AMERICAN SUNDAY SCHOOL UNION.

Sunday-School Movement. Originating in England, the Sunday school is traced to the efforts of Robert Raikes (1735-1811), the editor of the *Gloucester Journal,* who hired teachers to aid children in desperate circumstances. Raikes gained popular and ecclesiastical support for the idea of the Sunday school. Transported to the U.S., the institution was aided by movements for social reform. Schools were founded in Virginia in 1785, and in the 1790s Sunday schools spread to Boston, New York, Philadelphia, Rhode Island and New Jersey. They were intended to aid children who had no other opportunities for education, many of whom were employed in factories. The Pawtucket, Rhode Island, school brought education to the workplace, being founded on the property of the first U.S. cotton mill. The early schools were primarily led by laity* and community leaders. The text was the Bible,* and the curriculum included reading, writing and moral values. These Sunday schools paved the way for the development of public schools.

After 1800 the purposes for the Sunday school became both instruction and evangelism.* With a waning church-going population, efforts to extend religion were made by voluntary* associations, like the Sunday school. These groups combined commitment to Christianity with the democratic* spirit of the emerging nation. The first national Sunday-school effort was founded in 1824, the American Sunday-School Union.* Its purpose was to both evangelize and civilize. It organized Sunday-school leaders, published a significant amount of literature and formed thousands of Sunday schools through the Mississippi Valley Enterprise in 1880 and a subsequent campaign in the Southern Atlantic states.

A lack of theological clarity among the voluntary Sunday-school unions, however, led many denominations* in the 1820s and 1830s to initiate their own competing unions. From 1820 through the 1870s, with the rise of public education, the Sunday school existed in two forms: as the mission Sunday school, it evangelized children in rural and inner-city areas, and as the church Sunday school, it taught denominational distinctives to the children of members.

Beginning in 1869 efforts to extend the influence of Sunday schools came from National Sunday School Conventions (renamed International Sunday School Conventions in 1875). With leaders like the Baptist layman, B. F. Jacobs,* and the Methodist* pastor, John H. Vincent,* a system was organized to encourage Sunday-school work and a committee established to provide the International Uniform Lesson curriculum. This nondenominational system provided the energy as the church Sunday school became the norm. It reformed the use of time and space in the church, and extended the Sunday school into foreign missions.* By the late 1800s, eighty per cent of all new members were introduced to the church through Sunday schools.

Conflicts over denominational control of Sunday schools and over their educational and theological rationale stimulated new associations. Denominations founded boards of education, the convention system was formalized in 1905 into the International Sunday School Association* (ISSA), the Religious Education Association* was formed in 1903, and in 1910 the Sunday School Council of Evangelical Denominations (SSCED) was established. For twenty years competing forces fought to define the role of the Sunday school in educating persons in an increasingly pluralistic* society. The debate exaggerated differences, making the Sunday school stand for evangelism and the church school for instruction. In 1922 the ISSA and the SSCED merged into the International Sunday School Council of Religious Education (later becoming in 1950 the Division of Christian Education of the National Council of Churches*). Through this action, the Sunday school was defined as only one strategy in the program of church education.

Since that time, conflicts have reoccurred over the purposes, theology* and educational procedures for the church's education. Many now recognize that during the height of the Sunday-school movement in the last century, the Sunday school succeeded because it was supported by a broader system of Protestant education, including revival,* church publishing,* public school* and family. Today the Sunday school continues in churches as a primary means of education. Evangelical* denominations find it an effective means of evangelism and nurture within an educational program, and mainline* denominations are putting new energies into discovering its particular role within church education.

See also CATECHETICS, CATHOLIC; CHRISTIAN EDUCATION; CONFRATERNITY OF CHRISTIAN DOCTRINE.

BIBLIOGRAPHY. A. M. Boylan, *Sunday School: The Formation of an American Institution* (1988); R. W. Lynn and E. Wright, *The Big Little School* (1980); J. L. Seymour, *From Sunday School to Church School: Continuities in Protestant Church Education in the United States, 1860-1929* (1982).

J. L. Seymour

Sunderland, La Roy (1804-1885). Methodist* abolitionist* minister and one of the founders of the Wesleyan Methodist Church. Born in Exeter, Rhode Island, Sunderland became a minister in the New England Annual Conference of the Methodist Episcopal Church* in 1826, but withdrew from the ministry in 1833. He was one of that Church's most ardent abolitionists. As founder of the American Anti-Slavery Society (1833), Sunderland published "An Appeal on the Subject of Slavery," *Zion's Herald* (Dec. 5, 1834), which decried slavery as utterly opposed to the Bible,* to the *Discipline* of the Methodist Episcopal Church and to the teachings of John Wesley.* His efforts, along with those of Orange Scott,* brought the slavery issue to the Church's attention. In January 1836 Sunderland established the weekly *Zion's Watchman,* a platform for the abolitionist cause.

The General Conference of 1836 passed no resolutions against slavery and condemned "modern abolitionism" by a vote of 123 to 15. At the same conference Nathan Bangs* emerged as Sunderland's able opponent. In the next four years Sunderland was six times acquitted in church councils of "slander and falsehood," but on April 6, 1840, was found guilty. Sunderland subsequently withdrew his membership from the M. E. Church and joined Orange Scott* in February 1843 at the first Conference of the Wesleyan Methodist Church, held at Andover, Massachusetts, to found a church that was "free from episcopacy and slavery." But Sunderland did not join the new denomination. Moving from one reformatory cause to another, he invented a naturalistic faith he called *Panthetism* and drifted into what his former colleagues termed *infidelity.*

BIBLIOGRAPHY. *DAB* IX; L. C. Matlack, *The History of American Slavery and Methodism from 1780-1849* (1849); E. D. Jervey, "La Roy Sunderland: Zion's Watchman," *MH* 6 (April 1968):16-32.

J. R. Tyson

Superintendent. A Methodist* pastoral administrator responsible for a district. Appointed by the resident bishop,* the district superintendent has pastoral responsibilities to (1) travel the district, preaching and directing its spiritual and temporal affairs; (2) have charge of ministers and preachers in the absence of the bishop; (3) preside at the charge conference for each parish; (4) assure compliance by the local congregation with *The Discipline*; (5) counsel with local pastors regarding their pastoral and personal responsibilities; (6) recruit candidates for the ministry.

The superintendents of an episcopal area, together with pastors of special assignment under the direct supervision of the bishop, constitute a conference cabinet that meets regularly as an executive council with the bishop. Program, pastoral appointments and terminations, and pastoral concern for preachers of the conference are the immediate corporate responsibility for the conference cabinet.

Superintendents receive annual reports for each charge and consult with the pastor/parish relations committees of the churches under their care regarding pastoral effectiveness and program development among the charges. Superintendents are appointed for a maximum of a six-year term and may not succeed themselves but may, at a later date, serve again. Bishops are considered *general superintendents*.   P. A. Mickey

Supreme Court Decisions on Religious Issues. Religious liberty,* which is the cornerstone of the American Bill of Rights, was fundamental in the development of American civilization. The principle of complete religious liberty has long been viewed by Americans as being near the center of their national life. There is perhaps no more fundamental or distinctive feature of American political as well as religious life than the relationship between religion, the state and society. Supreme Court decisions on religion are generally based on the religion clauses of the First Amendment:* "Congress shall make no law respecting an establishment of religion or prohibiting the free exercise thereof." The only other reference to religion in the Constitution is to be found in Clause 3 of Article VI: "No religious test shall ever be required as a qualification to any office or public trust under the authority of the United States."

Free-Exercise Clause Cases. While state courts from their beginning have been frequently called upon to resolve questions bearing upon the free exercise of religion and the separation of church and state,* very few U. S. Supreme Court decisions on religion and state were handed down during the first century of the nation's history. The first several religion cases taken by the court either did not involve the First Amendment or were dis-

missed on appeal. Not until *Watson* v. *Jones* (1872) did the Court render an opinion based on the religion clauses of the First Amendment. It did so by ruling that it could not involve itself in deciding which of two factions represented the true faith in a church dispute. The Court declared, "The law knows no heresy,* and is committed to the support of no dogma,* the establishment of no sect.*"

The first major church-state case in America involved the Mormons* in *Reynolds* v. *United States* (1878), in which the Court rejected the contention of the plaintiff that his practice of polygamy was a religious obligation. As Chief Justice Morrison Waite wrote for the Court, "Laws are made for the government of actions, and while they cannot interfere with mere religious belief and opinions, they may with practices." Quoting Thomas Jefferson,* the Court affirmed that the purpose of the First Amendment was to build "a wall of separation between Church and State," but that this did not deprive the State of the right to limit actions based on religious beliefs. Other Mormon cases that followed, *Davis* v. *Beason* (1890) and *Church of Christ of Latter-Day Saints* v. *U.S.* (1892), were also aimed at prohibiting the practice of polygamy by the Mormon Church.

In a landmark church-state case, *Cantwell* v. *Connecticut* (1940), the Court unanimously upheld the right of Jehovah's Witnesses* to propagate their faith in public and to engage in door-to-door solicitation without a permit or "certificate of approval." For the first time, the Court specifically "incorporated" the Free-Exercise Clause into the Fourteenth Amendment, thus making the Clause applicable to the states. That same year the Court upheld the expulsion of children of a Jehovah's Witness from the public schools of Minersville, Pennsylvania, in *Minersville School District* v. *Gobitis* (1940), for refusing to salute the flag and to recite the Pledge of Allegiance. This decision was overturned three years later in *West Virginia Board of Education* v. *Barnette,* in which the Court declared, "If there is any fixed star in our constitutional constellation, it is that no official, high or petty, can prescribe what shall be orthodox* in politics, nationalism, religion, or other matters of opinion or force citizens to confess by word or act their faith therein. If there are any circumstances which permit an exception, they do not now occur to us." Far out of proportion to their numerical membership or institutional strength, Jehovah's Witnesses have been responsible for more cases concerned with religious liberty than any other group in America and far too numerous to be included here.

In *United States* v. *Ballard* (1944), the Court ruled that no agency of the State has the competence or the power to determine "the truth or falsity of the beliefs or doctrines" of anyone even though those beliefs "might seem incredible, if not preposterous to most people." Again, the Court affirmed that while freedom to believe is absolute, freedom to act on that belief is not absolute.

In adjudicating the "free exercise of religion," the Court has attempted to set forth two judicial standards for regulating actions based on religious beliefs: the "compelling interest" rule and the "alternate means" test. The first specific Supreme Court case to "balance" freedom of religion with compelling public or state interest came in *Prince* v. *Commonwealth of Massachusetts* (1944), in which the Court upheld a state child labor law and thereby denied the right of a Jehovah's Witness to have her nine-year-old niece accompany her in selling religious literature on the street. First advanced in *Braunfeld* v. *Brown* (1961), the "alternate means" test was used in *Sherbert* v. *Verner* (1963) to invalidate the denial of unemployment compensation by the state of South Carolina to a Seventh-Day Adventist* because she refused to work on Saturday. The state's unwillingness to find "alternate means" readily available to it, the Court said, imposed a religious burden on the appellant in that it forced her to choose between following her religious convictions and, thus, forfeiting her employment compensation or abandoning her religious principles in order to accept employment. This decision is widely regarded as the "highwater mark" in the Court's interpretation of the Free Exercise Clause. Other decisions by the Court on religion and the right to work include: *Trans World Airlines* v. *Hardison* (1977), *Thomas* v. *Review Board of Indiana Employment Security Division* (1981) and *Ohio Civil Rights Commission* v. *Dayton Christian Schools* (1986).

In more than a half dozen cases, the Court has applied the Free Exercise Clause to conscientious objection to war. While exemption of conscientious objectors from combatant services is a precedent going back to colonial times, it is nowhere guaranteed as a constitutional right as in the case of freedom of religion, freedom of assembly or freedom of speech. The Court has repeatedly affirmed the supremacy of the defense of the State against a foreign enemy as taking precedence over constitutional guarantees of civil liberties and individual rights. In a famous case, *United States* v. *Macintosh* (1931), the Court

repudiated as "astonishing" the claim that it is a "fixed principle of our Constitution . . . that a citizen cannot be forced and need not bear arms in a war if he has conscientious religious scruples against doing so." Both *United States* v. *Schwimmer* (1929) and *Hamilton* v. *Regents of the University of California* (1934) were decided on the basic premise of the power of the state to conscript its citizens for military service. Macintosh was overturned by the Court's ruling in *Girouard* v. *United States* (1946), not on constitutional grounds but on the basis that Congress had not intended to make conscientious objection a bar to citizenship.

Conscientious objection did not become a serious legal question until there was a universal or national conscription for military service at the time of World War 1.* First restricted to members of peace churches,* Congress extended it in 1948 to those with "religious training and belief." In *United* v. *Seeger* (1965), the Court broadly interpreted this provision to include those whose religious beliefs may not be theistic in nature, but who possess "a sincere and meaningful belief which occupies in the life of its possessor a place parallel to that filled by God of those qualifying for exemption." In June 1967, Congress deleted the Supreme Being clause as a basis for conscientious objection. In *Welsh* v. *United States* (1970), the Court extended conscientious objection status to those with beliefs that occupy "a place parallel to that filled by . . . God."

The ratification of the Constitution did not mark an end to state laws of religious tests for public office, since Article VI prohibiting any religious tests applied only to the federal government and federal elections. A landmark case bearing on religious tests for state office came in *Torcaso* v. *Watkins* (1961), in which the Court unanimously held unconstitutional a Maryland law requiring "a declaration of belief in the existence of God" for state office. The significance of Torcaso is that the Court categorically denied religious tests for office at any level of government and any preferential treatment of theistic over nontheistic faiths, or religion over against nonreligion as a qualification for public office. In a case out of Tennessee, the last of the state laws barring clergy from state office was unanimously declared unconstitutional by the Court in *McDaniel* v. *Paty* (1978).

Establishment Clause Cases. During the twentieth century, no church-state issues have provoked as much discussion or prompted as much litigation as the relation of the State to church schools and the role of religion in state schools. Since the latter is treated elsewhere in this volume (*See* Religion and Public Education), it is appropriate here to limit this review to the relation of the State to church schools. In *Pierce* v. *Society of Sisters* (1925), the Court outlawed an Oregon statute that required all parents to send their children to public schools and affirmed that the right to maintain and attend a church or private school is constitutionally guaranteed. The Court based its decision, however, on the Fourteenth Amendment, under the Due-Process Clause, not the Free-Exercise Clause of the First Amendment, which had not yet been declared applicable to the states. Similarly, in *Cochran* v. *Board of Education* (1930), based on the Due-Process Clause of the Fourteenth Amendment, the Court upheld a Louisiana law authorizing the purchase of state-approved textbooks for children in nonpublic schools.

Government aid to church schools has been the subject of more than a dozen decisions by the Court based upon the Establishment Clause of the First Amendment. In *Everson* v. *Board of Education* (1947), the Court upheld a New Jersey law providing for bus transportation of pupils in parochial schools.* This landmark decision marked the first time that the Court attempted to define the Establishment Clause and to "incorporate" it into the Fourteenth Amendment and thereby make it applicable to the states. In another split decision, *Board of Education* v. *Allen* (1968), the Court upheld a New York statute providing state-approved textbooks for nonpublic schools.

In approximately a dozen cases since 1971 involving the Establishment Clause, the Court has applied a three-pronged test in judging the constitutionality of legislation or a government act: The statute must have a "secular legislative purpose"; it must have a "primary effect that neither advances nor inhibits religion"; and its administration must avoid "excessive entanglement" with religion. With few exceptions, all of these cases have had to do with tax aid to religious schools. Not until *Lemon* v. *Kurtzman* (1971) and *Earley* v. *DiCenso* (1971) did the Court have occasion to strike down legislation authorizing public funds for church schools; the ruling of the former was unanimous and the latter was eight to one.

Two years later in three separate opinions (*PEARL* v. *Nyquist; Levitt* v. *PEARL*; and *Sloan* v. *Lemon*), the Court again denied the use of public funds for nonpublic schools. In these three cases the Court specifically struck down five programs of public assistance to parochial schools. The Court substantially restricted still further the use of

public funds for parochial schools in *Meek* v. *Pittenger* (1975). In *Wolman* v. *Walter* (1977), the Court declared the loan of instructional materials and equipment to parochial schools to be unconstitutional. In a split decision, *PEARL* v. *Regan* (1980), the Court upheld a New York state court decision authorizing public funds for grading state-mandated and state-prepared examinations on secular subjects as reimbursement to parochial schools for the cost incurred in meeting the requirements of state record-keeping. In still another split decision, *Mueller* v. *Allen* (1983), the Court upheld the constitutionality of Minnesota's tuition tax-deduction system. Two years later, in twin cases, *School District of the City of Grand Rapids* v. *Ball and Aquilar* v. *Felton,* the Court struck down a state-funded parochial program for teaching remedial and enrichment courses in Grand Rapids church schools and a federally funded program for "educationally deprived" children in New York City's parochial schools.

In the case of church-related colleges and universities, the Court's position has appeared to many to be far less clear, and, indeed, to be far more lenient than with tax aid to elementary and secondary schools. Even here, however, the Court has denied the constitutionality of tax funds to church colleges or universities that are sectarian or pervasively religious and not primarily secular in character. The Court has rendered three decisions directly bearing upon church-related colleges or universities. In *Tilton* v. *Richardson* (1971) the Court gave qualified approval of the use of federal funds for the construction of church college facilities not used, nor or at any time in the future, for religious purposes and where the primary purpose of the college was found to be secular, not religious. Two years later, in *Hunt* v. *McNair,* the Court upheld a South Carolina statute that authorized the issuance of bonds to finance college facilities not used for religious purposes. In the most important of three decisions, *Roemer* v. *Board of Public Works* (1976), the court upheld the constitutionality of a Maryland law authorizing an annual subsidy to private colleges, including church schools, with the proviso that none of the state funds may be used for "sectarian purposes." Eligibility for these funds also rested on the findings of the Court that the colleges in question were not found to be "pervasively sectarian," but that they performed "essentially secular functions" and were neither controlled nor financed by the church.

With regard to tax exemption and religious institutions, the Court in its only decision directly bearing on tax exemption of church property upheld tax exemptions for churches in *Walz* v. *Tax Commission* (1970). In two cases involving the balancing of free exercise claims against congressional power to tax, the Court upheld the government's contention that no statutory exemption based on religion applies to an employer and his employees in the payment of Social Security taxes (*United States* v. *Lee*, 1982). Tax exemption was denied in *Bob Jones University* v. *United States* and *Goldsboro Christian Schools* v. *United States* (1983) on the ground that beyond meeting the requirements of the Internal Revenue code, entitlement requires "meeting certain common law standards of charity—namely, that an institution seeking tax-exempt status must serve a public purpose and not be contrary to established public policy."

In 1961, in a series of Sunday* law cases (*McGown* v. *Maryland, Two Guys from Harrison-Allentown, Inc.* v. *McGinley; Gallagher* v. *Crown Kosher Super Market of Massachusetts*; and *Braunfeld* v. *Brown*), the Court upheld Sunday closing laws in three states to be constitutional since it determined that the Sunday laws were not religious laws but social welfare laws. In *Thornton* v. *Caldor* (1985), the Court invalidated a Connecticut law that exempted employees from work on their Sabbath.

In addition to decisions on religion and public education, which are treated elsewhere in this volume, the Court has addressed a wide range of other church-state issues on the basis of the Establishment Clause. In *N.L.R.B.* v. *Catholic Bishop of Chicago* (1979), the Court denied the claim of jurisdiction by the National Labor Relations Board over parochial schools. The Court denied the constitutionality of an amendment to Minnesota's Charitable Solicitation Act directed against new religions as violative of both the Establishment Clause and the Free Exercise Clause in *Larson* v. *Valente* (1982). The practice of paid legislative chaplains* and offering prayers* at the opening of each session of the Nebraska legislature was upheld in *Marsh* v. *Chambers* (1983), although primarily on the basis of historical precedent rather than on purely constitutional grounds. Overturning the decisions of two lower federal courts, the Court affirmed in *Lynch* v. *Donnelly* (1984) the constitutionality of a nativity scene erected by the city of Pawtucket, Rhode Island, in front of its city hall.

The decisions of the Court during the 1980s seem to reaffirm, to the delight of some and the dismay of others, that the "wall of separation" is,

in the words of former Chief Justice Warren E. Burger, "a blurred, indistinct and variable barrier."

BIBLIOGRAPHY. P. G. Rauper, *Religion and the Constitution* (1964); P. B. Kurland, ed., *Church and State: The Supreme Court and the First Amendment* (1975); L. W. Levy, ed., *Encyclopedia of the American Constitution,* 4 vols. (1986); R. T. Miller and R. B. Flowers, *Toward Benevolent Neutrality: Church, State, and the Supreme Court* (1982); L. Pfeffer, *God, Caesar, and the Constitution: The Court as a Referee of Church-State Confrontation* (1975); A. P. Stokes and L. Pfeffer, *Church and State in the United States* (1975); *Journal of Church and State.*

J. E. Wood

Sverdrup, Georg (1848-1907). Lutheran* churchman and theologian.* Born into a leading family in Norway, Sverdrup became professor of theology (1874) and then president for thirty-one years of Augsburg Seminary in Minneapolis. Among various groups of Norwegian-American Lutherans, Sverdrup was the leader of those who resisted any church organizational control beyond the local congregation. Thus he was instrumental in the formation of the Lutheran Free Church in 1897 and participated in conflicts over the control of Augsburg Seminary and theological education for Norwegian-American clergy. A seminal thinker, his ideas have received wider recognition in recent decades. He taught that the church is the body of Christ which finds its full organizational expression in the local congregation. He had a broad grasp of the way in which the Christian life relates to all of life and maintained that ministerial training should encompass general education beyond secondary levels.

BIBLIOGRAPHY. *DAB* IX; M. A. Helland, ed. and trans., *The Heritage of Faith: Selections from the Writings of Georg Sverdrup* (1969); E. C. Nelson and E. L. Fevold, *The Lutheran Church Among Norwegian-Americans* (1960).

F. K. Wentz

Swaggart, Jimmy Lee (1935-). Pentecostal* evangelist* and gospel singer. Born near Ferriday, Louisiana, in the same year as his cousin Jerry Lee Lewis, the future star of rock n' roll, Swaggart grew up in the Assemblies of God* church where his father, a grocer, would occasionally preach.* Swaggart began preaching at the age of six and experienced conversion* and the baptism of the Spirit* at the age of eight. With his cousin Jerry Lee, he honed his musical skills, but the two cousins parted ways in their teens when Swaggart, who had dropped out of high school, felt the call to be an evangelist. He committed himself to full-time ministry on January 1, 1958, and began itinerating with his wife, Francis, and his two-year-old son. Swaggart's ministry began to prosper when he publicized his relationship to Jerry Lee Lewis.

In 1964 Swaggart, by then ordained* by the Assemblies of God, began to preach extended revivals* in his denomination's churches. In 1969, having already released several gospel-music record albums, he launched *The Camp Meeting Hour,* a radio show that was broadcast over hundreds of stations. As sales of his records grew, he was able to invest in further radio broadcasts. In 1972 he began holding crusades in civic auditoriums, and in 1973 he began a weekly television show. By the late 1980s *The Jimmy Swaggart Telecast* was broadcast nationwide through more than 200 stations and was reaching some 1,880,000 households each week. In addition, some fifteen million of his gospel albums had been sold, and his monthly magazine, *The Evangelist,* had a circulation of 800,000. His headquarters in Baton Rouge, Louisiana, became the location for a 7,000-seat Family Worship Center and the Jimmy Swaggart Bible College.

An ardent exponent of right-wing politics, Swaggart was a supporter of Pat Robertson's* bid for the 1988 Republican presidential nomination. His combination of lively gospel music, theatrical preaching and "old-fashioned gospel Holy Ghost message" made him perhaps the most effective televangelist* in North America. His message is frequently punctuated by attacks on Catholics,* Protestant* liberals* and secular humanists,* and in the spring of 1987 he launched an attack on fellow televangelist Jim Bakker,* accusing him of adultery. Some months later Swaggart himself was accused of voyeuristic engagements with a prostitute, an activity he admitted and confessed on his television show. When his ordination was withdrawn by his denomination in April 1988, Swaggart nevertheless continued his ministry.

BIBLIOGRAPHY. C. Moritz, ed., *Current Biography Yearbook* (1987); J. Swaggart with R. P. Lamb, *To Cross a River* (1977). D. G. Reid

Swain, Clara A. (1834-1910). Medical missionary* to India. Born in Elmira, New York, Swain graduated from the Women's Medical College in Philadelphia, and sailed for India in 1869. She was the first woman missionary doctor in the world, serving under the Woman's Foreign Missionary Society of the Methodist Episcopal Church.* Arriving in Bareilly, North India, she went straight

to work and was soon overcome with more patients than she or her facilities could handle.

A Mogul ruler, the Nawab of Rampur, impressed by her dedication, donated forty acres of land, including a palatial residence. By 1872 the first women's hospital in Asia was opened under Swain's direction. Today the same hospital, now a modern medical facility, bears her name. In 1885, after two terms at Bareilly, Swain became a physician in the palace of the Rajah of Khetri. There, in an area previously unevangelized, she ministered until 1895 and then retired to Castile, New York.

BIBLIOGRAPHY. *DAB* IX; *NAW* 3; C. A. Swain, *A Glimpse of India, Extracts from the Letters of Dr. Clara A. Swain* (1909); D. C. Wilson, *Palace of Healing* (1968). J. T. Seamands

Swedenborg. *See* CHURCH OF THE NEW JERUSALEM.

Swedish Baptist General Conference. *See* BAPTIST GENERAL CONFERENCE.

Sweet, William Warren (1881-1959). Methodist* minister* and American church historian. Born in Baldwin City, Kansas, Sweet grew up in Baldwin and Salina, where his father taught in Methodist colleges. Himself a product of the late frontier, Sweet's later work as a historian would emphasize indigenous factors and the role of religion on the frontier.* He attended Ohio Wesleyan University and then Drew Theological Seminary, graduating in 1906. Ordained* in the Methodist Church, Sweet held pastorates in Willow Grove and Langhorne, Pennsylvania, while attending Crozer Theological Seminary and the University of Pennsylvania (Ph.D., 1912). After teaching at Ohio Wesleyan and then at DePauw University, in 1927 he went to the Divinity School at the University of Chicago,* where his chair in the History of American Christianity was the first such post in the country.

As the first professionally trained historian to specialize in the study of American religion, Sweet led a pioneering effort in gathering vital source documents (*Religion on the American Frontier,* 4 vols.) and trained many of the scholars who influenced the study of American religion into the next generation. Sweet's own writings, most notably *The Story of Religion in America* (1930), called attention to the importance of religion within the broader field of American history. On the frontier, he argued, the churches that adapted best to the needs of a demanding environment came to the forefront; there the Methodists, Baptists* and Presbyterians* emerged as the leading Protestant denominations and served as important civilizing agents in newly settled regions.

Though avoiding the hagiography of earlier denominational historians, Sweet tended to focus narrowly on the major Protestant groups to the neglect of others. Yet over the course of his long career, he had a substantial impact on the developing field of American religion as a recognized historical discipline.

BIBLIOGRAPHY. J. L. Ash, *Protestantism and the American University: An Intellectual Biography of William Warren Sweet* (1982); *DARB;* S. E. Mead, "Prof. Sweet's Religion and Culture in America: A Review Article," *CH* 23 (1953):33-49.

M. S. Joy

Sweet Daddy Grace. *See* GRACE, CHARLES MANUEL.

Swing, David (1830-1894). Presbyterian,* later independent, pastor in Chicago. Born in Cincinnati, Ohio, Swing graduated from Miami University at Oxford, Ohio (1852), studied theology* under Nathan Lewis Rice in Cincinnati and taught classical languages at Miami from 1854 to 1866. In 1866 he went to Chicago to pastor Westminster Presbyterian Church, which in 1869 consolidated with North Church as the Fourth Presbyterian Church.

A popular preacher* who attracted several thousand worshipers every Sunday,* Swing came to national attention in 1874 when Francis L. Patton,* editor of *The Interior* of Chicago, accused him of heresy.* Patton's main charge was that Swing's sermons and his book *Truths for Today* (1874) denied basic evangelical* doctrines* and the teachings of the denominational standard, the Westminster Confession.* Swing's defense rested principally on his often-repeated argument that creeds* as human expressions are necessarily imperfect and therefore must be constantly revised to keep pace with ever-changing cultural conditions. The Presbytery of Chicago acquitted Swing of all charges, but when Patton threatened to appeal to the Northern Illinois Synod, Swing withdrew from the denomination.*

In 1875 Swing became the pastor of the newly organized and independent Central Church of Chicago, a congregation founded on simple declaration of commitment to Christ as the Savior and leader of people. For nearly two decades Swing preached weekly to 3,000 or more worshipers and was widely respected across the nation. His liberal evangelicalism and proclamation of traditional beliefs in poetic language helped give rise to the "new theology" of the latter years of the nineteenth century. And his pulpit eloquence made him one of the most celebrated and contro-

versial preachers of the second half of the nineteenth century.

BIBLIOGRAPHY. *DAB* IX; *DARB;* W. R. Hutchison, *The Modernist Impulse in American Protestantism* (1976); *NCAB* 3; J. F. Newton, *David Swing: Poet-Preacher* (1909).

G. S. Smith

Synod. A meeting of ministers* and lay* representatives from the congregations within several presbyteries* or associations. In the context of the Presbyterian Church,* a synod is an assembly of all ministers and ruling elders who are members of the constituent presbyteries. A synod is one level below the highest judicatory body, the General Assembly.

The Congregational* churches of New England also had periodic synods, where ministers and lay delegates addressed problems concerning the collective churches. However, these synods were viewed with suspicion by many congregations because they posed a threat to the autonomy of the particular churches. Thus, a synod was seen only as an occasional necessity. In contrast to the Presbyterian system of church government, the recommendations of the Congregational synods were not binding on the churches, and changes in polity or doctrine had to be presented to the churches for approval.

In episcopal forms of church government, a synod may refer to a periodic gathering of the clergy of a diocese called by the bishop. In the Roman Catholic Church the pontiff may call a Synod of Bishops, most often an international gathering of bishops in Rome called to discuss the procedures of the church in a collegial manner.*

Titles of American Lutheran denominations have included the term *synod* (as in Wisconsin Synod and Missouri Synod). In many cases this use of the term indicates an organization of like-minded, or ethnically homogeneous, Lutheran congregations, joined together as a conference or federation of churches. In some Lutheran denominations the term *synod* refers to a geographical district within the denomination. The authority of a synod may vary. The Lutheran Church—Missouri Synod (which is not a geographical designation) is the most congregational among major American Lutheran denominations and no action of the synod is considered binding on the congregations if they consider it contrary to the Word of God or inexpedient in their particular case.

See also CHURCH GOVERNMENT.

BIBLIOGRAPHY. A. C. Piekorn, *Profiles in Belief,* vol. 2 (1978); L. Trinterud, *The Forming of an American Tradition* (1949); W. Walker, ed., *The*

Creeds and Platforms of Congregationalism (1960).   K. P. Minkema

Syrian Orthodox Church of Antioch. The book of Acts (11:26) confirms that the disciples were first called Christians in Antioch, capital of ancient Syria. According to ancient tradition, St. Peter the Apostle established the See of Antioch and served as the See's first patriarch from A.D. 33 to 40. Since the fourth century the authority of the See of Antioch has extended over all the territory between the Mediterranean Sea and the Persian Gulf and was eventually extended as far as India and the Far East by the church's missionary endeavors. By 1236 the Syrian Orthodox Church of Antioch numbered some twenty thousand parishes and had established a history of great educational institutions.

The Syrian Orthodox Church of Antioch participated in and fully accepted the teaching of Nicea (325), Constantinople (381) and Ephesus (431) but rejected the terminology of the Council of Chalcedon (451). The Church believes and confesses that Christ is of one nature and is indivisible into two separate natures, he being fully God and fully man in the unique oneness of his person and nature without mixture or confusion.

The Syrian Orthodox Church of Antioch is in full communion with the Armenian, Coptic and Ethiopian Churches, being one of what are referred to as the Oriental Orthodox Churches. The Church is a member of both the World Council of Churches,* as well as the National Council of the Churches of Christ in the United States of America.* Today, the seat of the Syrian Orthodox Patriarchate of Antioch is in Damascus, Syria.

The presence of the Syrian Orthodox Church of Antioch in America dates back to the late nineteenth century, when religious persecution forced immigration from Ottoman Turkey to the U.S. Frequently locating according to their skills and trade, families from Diyarbakir, Turkey, settled in New Jersey where there was a silk industry; those from Harput, Turkey, were drawn to Massachusetts; families from the Turkish province of Tur 'Abdin established themselves in Rhode Island as employees in local weaving mills. Later families from the vicinity of Homs, Syria, settled in the Detroit, Michigan, area.

In 1907 the Very Reverend Hanna Koorie was ordained* to serve as the first Syrian Orthodox priest* in the U.S. and stationed in New Jersey. By 1923 the number of faithful living in Worcester, Massachusetts, officially organized themselves into a parish in the name of the Virgin Mary. In the late 1920s Archbishop Mar Severius Ephrem Barsoum, then Syrian Orthodox metropolitan* of Syria and Lebanon, consecrated* a church built by local faithful in west New York and New Jersey, and established a formal congregation in Detroit. Within this period of time, parish churches were likewise built in both Worcester, Massachusetts, and Central Falls, Rhode Island. In the years following, a few of the Detroit faithful were to move to Jacksonville and Miami, Florida.

On January 29, 1949, His Eminence Archbishop Mar Athanasius Yeshue Samuel, then Syrian Orthodox metropolitan of Jerusalem, arrived in the U.S. and began to minister to the spiritual needs of the faithful in North America. On May 13, 1952, His Holiness Patriarch Ignatius Ephrem I appointed Archbishop Samuel patriarchal vicar to the U.S. and Canada; and on November 15, 1957, Patriarch Ignatius Yacoub III officially established the Archdiocese of the Syrian Orthodox Church in the U.S. and Canada with His Eminence Archbishop Samuel as primate, then in residence in Hackensack, New Jersey. On September 7, 1958, Archbishop Samuel consecrated a cathedral* for the archdiocese in Hackensack in the name of St. Mark. The 1960s saw new congregations organized in Los Angeles, California, and Chicago, Illinois. By the 1980s new parishes had been established in West Roxbury, Massachusetts; Portland, Oregon; and California. The North American archdiocese has also established a number of Malankarese parishes, composed of faithful who have come from India, beginning with Mar Gregorios Syrian Orthodox Church of Staten Island, New York, in 1975. There are presently twenty-six parishes and approximately twenty-five thousand faithful, served by twenty-eight priests. The archdiocesan headquarters is presently located in Lodi, New Jersey.

The Church has translated a number of church service books from Syriac, the Church's official language, into English. The American experience has also encouraged the Church to actively participate in ecumenical activities, such as the Church's role in the current dialog between the National Conference of Catholic Bishops and the Standing Conference of the Oriental Orthodox Churches in America.

BIBLIOGRAPHY. A. S. Atiya, *History of Eastern Christianity* (1967); Mar Ignatius Zakka I Iwas, *The Syrian Orthodox Church of Antioch at a Glance* (1983); P. Kadavil, *The Orthodox Syrian Church* (1973); R. F. Taft, ed., *The Oriental Orthodox Churches in the United States* (1986).

                                    J. Meno

Systematic Theology. The intellectual reflection, within a specific world-view context, on the act and context of Christian faith, including its expression in beliefs, practices and institutions.

The term *theology,* derived from the Greek words *theos* (God) and *logos* (word, teaching or study), was originally used to denote the sayings of the Greek philosophers and poets concerning divine matters. In the Middle Ages, theology (as the doctrine of God) comprised one subtopic of "dogmatics."* The meaning was broadened in the nineteenth century to include all the various aspects of the study of the Bible* and the church, and was divided into three categories: biblical, systematic and practical.

In America the older term, *dogmatics,* has generally been replaced by *systematic theology,* or even *constructive* or *doctrinal theology.* Its task focuses on the intellectual reflection on faith, especially the belief system itself (doctrine), but also the nature of believing and the integration of commitment and life are subjects for systematic inquiry. The result is a coherent presentation of the themes of Christian faith. Traditionally these include God, humanity and creation, Jesus Christ, salvation, the Holy Spirit, the church and the consummation. It is not to be equated with religious studies, for theology is pursued within the context of a faith stance.

Theology is an on-going task. It articulates its subject within a specific context, thereby explicating an unchanging faith commitment in thought-forms that are culturally conditioned. Generally, a systematic theology is developed from a particular perspective, as one or more central motifs is employed to illumine the whole. Its goal, however, often goes beyond description of the Christian belief system, for theology seeks to be applied, that is, to assist in producing Christian life and practice which is faithful to the Christian faith-commitment.

Theological construction utilizes Scripture as its primary and normative source. The enterprise must be pursued with a view toward other sources as well: the history of doctrine, human reason and scientific inquiry, and contemporary experience.

Since colonial times the Reformed tradition* has been influential in America. The leading theologian* of the eighteenth century was the Calvinist Jonathan Edwards.* Although that tradition was maintained in the nineteenth century by Charles Hodge* and the Princeton Theology,* other approaches, such as Arminianism,* also became significant. In the twentieth century a variety of theological orientations, including liberalism,* neo-orthodoxy,* process* and more recently liberation,* feminist, and narrative theologies, have become prominent. The 1960s brought a reaction against the attempt to construct theological systems, in part because such systems appeared to have little connection with life. Interest in the enterprise and its relationship to Christian living has re-emerged in recent years.

BIBLIOGRAPHY. F. G. Healey, ed., *What Theologians Do* (1970); T. W. Jennings, Jr., ed., *The Vocation of the Theologian* (1985).

S. J. Grenz

T

Tache, Alexandre-Antonin (1823-1894). Roman Catholic* missionary bishop* in western Canada. From its base among the French-Canadian half-breeds, or *metis,* in the Red River (Winnipeg) area, Roman Catholicism hoped to make western Canada Francophone and Catholic. The key figure in the attempt to realize this ideal was A. A. Tache. Born in Quebec, Tache possessed a distinguished family connection. He could claim the famous explorer Joliette* and La Verendrye as ancestors, and his uncle was a father of Confederation. Bishop Bourget* of Montreal, with his ultramontane* enthusiasm, was welcoming clergy* from France in considerable numbers and from various orders. The first Oblates arrived in Montreal in 1841 and soon began to fan out in missionary service. In 1845 the first Oblate arrived in Winnipeg, accompanied by the novice Tache. He was soon ordained* and developed missionary stations among the native people in northern Saskatchewan and northern Alberta. At twenty-seven years of age, he was named coadjutor to Bishop Provencher, and before he was thirty he was Provencher's successor.

Tache gradually built up an establishment on the Red River, imported teaching orders, persuaded many of the metis to give up their nomadic life and settle, and sought to send Francophone missionaries across western Canada. A strong supporter of the movement for Canadian confederation, he did much to mitigate the Riel Rebellion at Red River in 1870. At the same time his vision was being eroded by the vast influx of English-speaking settlers. What was even worse was the settlement of the Manitoba School Question in 1890, which deprived the Roman Catholics of a government-supported separate school system which had been granted when Manitoba entered Confederation. In spite of these disappointments, he laid the foundations of a strong western Canadian Roman Catholicism with all its ethnic diversity.

BIBLIOGRAPHY. J. S. Moir, *The Church in the British Era: From the British Conquest to Confed-* *eration* (1972); J. W. Grant, *The Church in the Canadian Era: The First Century of Confederation* (1972).

I. S. Rennie

Talbot, John (1645-1727). Anglican* missionary* in colonial America. Born in Wymondham, Norfolk, England, Talbot was educated at Christ's College, Cambridge (B.A., 1664; M.A., 1671). After serving as fellow of Peterhouse (1664-1668), he became rector* of churches in Icklingham, Suffolk (1673-1689), and in Fretherne, Gloucestershire (1695-1701). In 1702 he left England for America, arriving in Boston as chaplain* of the *Centurion* in the company of George Keith* and Patrick Gordon, the first two missionaries sent by the Society for the Propagation of the Gospel in Foreign Parts* to the colonies.

Appointed a missionary of the Society in September 1702, he and Keith traveled 800 miles from Maine to North Carolina, preaching* to large crowds in New Jersey, New York and Pennsylvania, and establishing the first formal presence of the Anglican Church in several colonies. In 1704 he helped found St. Mary's Church, Burlington, New Jersey, and remained as its rector. He soon became involved in efforts to establish an American bishop* and went to England to plead the cause. Returning to the colonies in 1708, he aroused criticism for his high church* views and Stuart sympathies, and was promptly removed from his Burlington church for three years. Once reinstated, he continued to press for an American bishopric, encountering opposition from all sides. He was an untiring missionary and proselytized in all parts of New Jersey. He died at the age of eighty-two and was buried in St. Mary's Church, Burlington.

BIBLIOGRAPHY. *AAP* 5; *DAB* IX; *NCAB* 3; E. L. Pennington, *Apostle of New Jersey: John Talbot, 1645-1727* (1938); J. Woolverton, *Colonial Anglicanism in North America* (1984).

G. F. Moran

Talbot, Louis Thomson (1889-1976). Evangelical* minister* and president of the Bible Institute of Los Angeles. Born the sixth of eight children to John and Elizabeth Freyling Talbot, Louis grew up near Sydney, Australia. He was a graduate of Newington College in Australia and Moody Bible Institute* in Chicago. Talbot served as pastor of the First Congregational Church of Paris, Texas, before and after he studied at McCormick Seminary.

During his seminary years Talbot started the Madison Street Church in Oak Park, Illinois. Then Talbot took pastorates in Presbyterian* churches at Keokuk, Iowa (1921-1925), and Minneapolis, Minnesota (1925-1929). In 1929 he was called to the Philpott Tabernacle in Hamilton, Ontario (*See* Philpott, Peter W.). From 1932 to 1948 he was pastor of the Church of the Open Door and president of the Bible Institute of Los Angeles (1932-1952). At that time both institutions were on one location at the corner of Hope and Sixth Streets in Los Angeles. Talbot rescued the work from bankruptcy in 1938 through a radio fund drive. After 1953 he served as chancellor of Biola College (now Biola University) and the board named the newly founded Talbot Seminary in his honor.

Among Talbot's publications were: *God's Plan of the Ages* (1936), *The Prophecies of Daniel in the Light of the Past, Present and Future Events* (1940) and *Christ in the Tabernacle* (1942). He received a D.D. from Wheaton College (Illinois) and a D.Laws from John Brown University. During his later years Talbot actively promoted evangelical foreign mission* endeavors through his extensive travels in Asia, Africa and Latin America.

BIBLIOGRAPHY. C. Talbot, *For This I Was Born: The Captivating Story of Louis T. Talbot* (1977).
D. G. Buss

Talmage, (T)homas DeWitt (1832-1902).
Dutch Reformed* and Presbyterian* preacher.* Talmage was born near Bound Brook, New Jersey, and was the son of a farmer. He had three brothers, a brother-in-law and two uncles who were ministers in the Dutch Reformed Church. After attending school in New Brunswick, New Jersey, at the age of nineteen he entered the University of the City of New York to study law. Talmage never completed his law course, turning instead to the study of theology at the New Brunswick Theological Seminary of the Dutch Reformed Church, from which he graduated in 1856.

Ordained* in 1856, Talmage pastored the Dutch Reformed Church at Belleville, New Jersey, until 1859. He then served the Dutch Reformed Church in Syracuse, New York (1859-1862), followed by a pastorate at the Second Dutch Reformed Church of

Philadelphia (1862-1869). Accepting a call from the badly divided Central Presbyterian Church in Brooklyn, New York (1869), he remained there until 1895, developing it into one of the largest churches in the U.S. During his tenure there he attracted considerable attention and became involved in lecturing and journalism, in addition to his preaching. Three times during his Brooklyn pastorate the church building burned down, and each time his middle- and upper-class congregation replaced it with a larger and more impressive edifice, the final two with seating in excess of 5,000. Shortly after the last building burned, he moved to Washington, D.C., where he pastored the First Presbyterian Church (1895-1899).

Probably the most popular preacher during the last quarter of the nineteenth century, Talmage's sermons were published in 3,500 newspapers. They also appeared in the journals *Christian at Work* (1874-1876), *Frank Leslie's Sunday Magazine* (1881-1889) and *Christian Herald* (1890-1902), all of which were edited by Talmage. Considered a master of sensational rhetoric and having an unconventional style of organizing and delivering his sermons, he was both strongly admired and criticized. The substance of the criticism was that he mishandled texts by badly pulling them out of context and that he mistook assertion for proof. His admirers appreciated his florid rhetoric and his ability to communicate to the cultured urban dwellers of the Gilded Age. Not an innovator in theology and an outspoken critic of Darwinism,* he was nonetheless accused in 1879 before the Brooklyn Presbytery "of falsehood and deceit and . . . using improper methods of preaching which tend to bring religion into contempt." Talmage was acquitted of these charges by a close vote, but the fact that he was charged demonstrates the controversial nature of his preaching. His collected sermons fill twenty volumes.

BIBLIOGRAPHY. C. E. Banks, *Authorized and Authentic Life and Works of T. DeWitt Talmage* (1902); *DAB* IX; *DARB; NCAB* 4; J. Rusk, *The Authentic Life of T. DeWitt Talmage* (1902); M. Talmage, ed., *500 Selected Sermons,* 20 vols. (1900).
J. R. Wiers

Tanner, Benjamin Tucker (1835-1923).
African Methodist Episcopal* editor and bishop.* Born a free African-American in Pittsburgh, Pennsylvania, Tanner attended Avery Institute (later Avery College) from 1852 to 1857 and then studied for three years at Western Theological Seminary, where he learned the conservative Presbyterian*

orthodoxy* he espoused for the rest of his career. Licensed* to preach* in 1858 and ordained* to the ministry of the African Methodist Episcopal Church (AME) in 1860, he briefly served the First Colored (later the Fifteenth Street) Presbyterian Church in Washington, D.C., and then held a series of AME appointments in the Washington-Baltimore area, among them the prominent Bethel Church in Baltimore.

At the AME general conference of 1868, he was elected editor of the denomination's widely influential newspaper, the *Christian Recorder.* After sixteen years at this post, in 1884 he was elected founding editor of the *A.M.E. Church Review,* a quarterly he quickly established as a leading cultural journal among African-Americans. In 1888 he was elected bishop, a position he held until his retirement in 1908. A bookish man with a great taste for intellectual debate, Tanner, in scores of articles, editorials and a dozen books and pamphlets, energetically defended the authority of Scripture,* the full humanity and past greatness of the Negro race (*The Negro's Origin, or Is He Cursed of God?* 1869), and the independence of the AME Church (*An Apology for African Methodism,* 1867). He and his wife, Sarah E. Miller, whom he married in 1858, had two sons and five daughters, the most notable among them being the well-known painter Henry Ossawa Tanner.

BIBLIOGRAPHY. *DAB* IX; *DARB; NCAB* 3; R. R. Wright, *The Bishops of the A.M.E. Church* (1963).

D. W. Wills

Tant, (J)efferson (D)avis (1861-1941). Church of Christ* evangelist* and debater. Born in Paulding County, Georgia, the Tant family moved to Texas in 1876. Tant, a Methodist* boy preacher at the age of fourteen, began to ride circuits in North Texas. By 1881 he had come under the influence of Church of Christ preachers and in 1885 was rebaptized* and became a member of that group.

A colorful and controversial figure, Tant was a farmer and preacher for most of his life and participated in over 350 debates, with three pending at the time of his death. He frequently debated Methodists and Baptists* with little preparation, saying he was ready to affirm anything they denied or deny anything they affirmed. He also disputed with those of his own fellowship, opposing every unscriptural innovation. His familiar warning was "Brethren, we are drifting."

As an evangelist Tant received one hundred invitations a year to hold meetings. There was an urgency about his evangelism, and in his lifetime he baptized eight thousand people. Because of his limited formal education, many considered him rough and uncouth, while others regarded him as a colorful character.

BIBLIOGRAPHY. F. Y. Tant, *J. D. Tant—Texas Preacher* (1958).

L. B. Sullivan

Tappan, Arthur (1786-1865), and Lewis (1788-1873). Evangelical* businessmen and social reformers. Born in Northampton, Massachusetts, the Tappan brothers eventually became partners in a silk business in New York City. But they are best known for their careers in evangelical social reform, expressed in a Calvinistic* activism inherited from their mother and harking back to Jonathan Edwards.* Unlike many contemporary reformers for whom eradication of social evil was an end in itself, the Tappans' primary concern was that the Christian faith be accepted and obeyed. Evil cried out for reform because it was logically incompatible with the will of God, which took precedence over every activity to which they were committed. The brothers gave liberally of their administrative talents and wealth gained in business to movements for revival,* missions,* tract* and Bible* distribution, Sunday schools,* education, Sabbath* observance, temperance* and the banning of tobacco. They helped build Charles G. Finney's* Broadway Tabernacle, the Chatham Street Chapel and the Magdalen Asylum.

In response to slavery they turned from colonization to abolition,* and shared in organizing the American Anti-Slavery Society (1833) and the American and Foreign Anti-Slavery Society (1840). Displaying impressive talents as speaker, organizer, administrator, writer, editor and propagandist, Lewis attracted lasting national attention to the slavery issue through his "Great Postal Campaign" (1835) and his role in the Amistad case. On Christian principle he opposed racism and segregation with a consistency rare even for abolitionists. The brothers supported Lane Seminary and helped establish Oberlin* Seminary and Kenyon College.

BIBLIOGRAPHY. C. W. Bowen, *Arthur and Lewis Tappan* (1883); *DAB* IX; *DARB; NCAB* 2; L. Tappan, *The Life of Arthur Tappan* (1870); B. Wyatt-Brown, *Lewis Tappan and the Evangelical War against Slavery* (1969).

R. M. Healey

Tappan, David (1752-1803). Congregationalist* minister* and Harvard* professor. Born in Manchester, Massachusetts, the son of a traditional New England pastor, Tappan studied divinity* after graduation from Harvard in 1771 and became pastor of the church in Newbury, Massachusetts, in

1774. He identified himself with those who became known as "Old Calvinists," persons wary of the revivalism* that had divided New England Congregationalists since the Great Awakening* but who insisted on the centrality of an experience of regeneration.* Tappan was also critical of the more liberal trends in Congregationalism that eventually gave birth to Unitarianism.* He became the third Hollis Professor of Divinity at Harvard in 1792, where he remained a respected proponent of moderate Calvinism* until his death. Controversy erupted over designating Tappan's successor. When the more orthodox* could not agree on a candidate, the naming of liberal Henry Ware* to the post in 1805 led to the Unitarian ascendancy at Harvard.

BIBLIOGRAPHY. *AAP* 2.   C. H. Lippy

Taschereau, Elzear Alexandre (1820-1898). Roman Catholic* archbishop of Quebec and first Canadian Cardinal.* Born into a family that had distinguished itself in law, Taschereau exhibited a legal mind characteristized by thoughtfulness, objectivity and probity. His family also represented the seigneurial tradition, and once again he seemed to embody this heritage with its emphasis upon stability and history. The family roots were in the Beauce district south of Quebec City, and instinctively he seemed to grasp the unique French emphasis for which it was famous. During an outstanding academic career at the old and prestigious Quebec Seminary, which spanned the years from childhood to priesthood, he was exposed to a rigorously classical education. He also obtained a doctorate in canon law* in Rome in 1856. With the exception of his period in Europe, he served the Quebec Seminary as teacher, director, prefect of studies and supervisor. He helped found Laval University in Quebec City, and was rector for a time before his consecration* as archbishop of Quebec in 1870.

Taschereau was almost immediately in conflict with the ultramontanes* led by Bishop Bourget* of Montreal. They wished to restore the religious and social world of the High Middle Ages with its extravagant claims of ecclesiastical power. The Archbishop was as conservative in many ways as his opponents, but his was a different kind of conservatism. It represented long-standing French Gallicanism,* which recognized various spheres of sovereignty. While ultramontanism was activistic, overstated and overreaching, Taschereau was reserved and even taciturn. But he held his ground. He defended Laval University against attack before the papacy and sought to moderate the excessive claims to clerical influence in politics. He retained in Quebec City a different tradition than Montreal, and when he was created cardinal in 1890, it proved his point that there was more than one legitimate heritage in French-Canadian Catholicism.

BIBLIOGRAPHY. J. W. Grant, *The Church in the Canadian Era: The First Century of Confederation* (1972).   I. S. Rennie

Taylor, Clyde W. (1904-1988). Evangelical* statesman. Born in Fort Smith, Arkansas, Taylor attended Nyack Missionary Institute (1924) and graduated from Gordon College (Th.B., 1931) and later Boston University (M.A., 1942). In his lifetime he was granted several honorary degrees. Taylor was a missionary* with the Christian and Missionary Alliance* to Peru (1925-1927) and Colombia, South America (1931-1941). He then pastored Central Baptist Church in Quincy, Massachusetts (1942-1944).

His career with the National Association of Evangelicals (NAE) began in 1944. For more than forty years, Taylor, known widely as "Mr. NAE," served American evangelicals through this premier unifying organization. His many leadership positions at NAE included secretary of NAE's Washington office—later called Office of Public Affairs— (1944-1963), executive secretary of the Evangelical Foreign Missions Association* (1944-1974), general director of the NAE (1963-1974) and general secretary of the World Evangelical Fellowship* (1970-1974).

Taylor's leadership was particularly important in the early days of NAE. In 1943 he began working in Washington, D.C., to assist foreign mission* agencies. He also helped write key immigration legislation and resisted the Federal Council of Churches's attempts to obtain a monopoly on religious broadcasting time. Taylor's extensive travels, which took him to more than ninety-two countries, contributed to the creation of national evangelical fellowships in Asia, Africa and Latin America and raised awareness of the world's needs, physical as well as spiritual.

BIBLIOGRAPHY. B. L. Shelley, *Evangelicalism in America* (1967); J. D. Murch, *Cooperation Without Compromise* (1956).   R. C. Cizik

Taylor, Edward (c.1645-1729). Puritan* minister* and poet. Born in Leicestershire, England, Taylor reportedly was taught by a Nonconformist schoolmaster. After Taylor taught school for some time, his Puritan commitments led him to immigrate to Boston in 1668. There he enrolled in

Harvard College* as a sophomore, where he was a roommate and friend of Samuel Sewall* and graduated in 1671. Taylor was called to the church at Westfield, Massachusetts, in 1671—though King Philip's War* prevented his being ordained until 1679—and remained there until his death, serving the town as both minister and physician. Taylor's life in a frontier town was not notable by all outward appearances, though he was an opponent of the Half-Way Covenant* practiced by his nearby neighbor in Northampton, Solomon Stoddard. It was not until 1937 that his manuscripts were discovered, having been deposited in the Yale College* Library by his grandson Ezra Stiles,* who had maintained his grandfather's will that they never be published.

Taylor was a poet whose skillful verse explores the soul's journey to salvation against the background of Puritan cosmology and covenant theology. His longest work, "God's Determinations Touching His Elect," describes the contest between Christ and Satan for the human soul. A series of "Preparatory Meditations" were poetic meditations written as spiritual exercises prior to the Lord's Supper. The discovery of Taylor's poetry established him as the most accomplished American poet of his era.

BIBLIOGRAPHY. *AAP* 1; *DAB* I; T. H. Johnson, ed., *The Poetical Works of Edward Taylor* (1939); J. L. Sibley, *Biographical Sketches of Graduates of Harvard University,* vol. 2 (1881).

D. G. Reid

Taylor, Graham (1851-1938). Dutch Reformed* and later Congregational* minister,* sociologist. Born in Schenectady, New York, Taylor was a descendant of four generations of ministers in the Dutch Reformed Church. He graduated from Rutgers College (B.A., 1870), attended the Reformed Theological Seminary in New Brunswick, New Jersey (B.D., 1873), and in 1873 became pastor of Hopewell Dutch Reformed Church in New York. In 1880 he moved to the Fourth Congregational Church in Hartford, Connecticut, where he also became professor of practical theology at the Hartford Seminary.

While at Hartford, Taylor became interested in the settlement house* movement. In 1892 Taylor joined the faculty of the Chicago Theological Seminary as professor of Christian sociology and English Bible in what was the first department of Christian sociology in the U.S. In 1894 Taylor, his family and four students moved into a poor westside Chicago community and established "Chicago Commons," a settlement house which

achieved a wide reputation. There he developed a great variety of social and educational programs, at one time hosting forty courses with 400 students enrolled. Taylor also served the community in a large number of civic capacities. Well known for his lectures on the social teachings of Jesus, he was also a firm believer in training seminarians in sociology, as well as in giving them practical experience in urban and industrial settings. Taylor remained associated with the seminary until 1924. He was associate editor of *The Survey,* a Social Gospel journal, and wrote weekly columns on social issues for the *Chicago Daily News* from 1902 to 1938. He also authored several books, including *Religion in Social Action* (1913); *Pioneering on Social Frontiers* (1930); and *Chicago Commons Through Forty Years* (1936). Through his activism, teaching and writing, Taylor achieved a national reputation as a sociologist and advocate of the Social Gospel.*

BIBLIOGRAPHY. *DAB* 2; A. F. Davis, *Spearheads for Reform: The Social Settlements and the Progressive Movement, 1890-1914* (1985).

C. E. Stockwell

Taylor, Herbert John (1893-1978). Businessman and philanthropist.* Born in Pickford, Michigan, and converted* in a Methodist* church, Taylor studied at Northwestern University (B.A., 1917). When World War 1* broke out, Taylor was already in France working with the YMCA.* During the war he served with the U.S. Navy reserve in Brest, France, resuming his YMCA work after the war. In 1919 he married Gloria Forbrich and moved to Paul's Valley, Oklahoma, where he worked one year for the Sinclair Oil Company and then operated a lease-brokerage, insurance and real estate office for three years.

In 1924 he moved to Barrington, Illinois, to work at the Jewel Tea Co. (1924-1931), where he eventually became executive vice president. In 1930 Taylor was called in to rescue Club Aluminum Company from bankruptcy, where he eventually became president (1932-1952) and chairman of the board (1952-1968). He developed the "Four-Way Test" as a business strategy: (1) Is it the truth? (2) Is it fair to all concerned? (3) Will it build goodwill and better friendships? (4) Will it be beneficial for all concerned? In 1942 the Four-Way Test was adopted by Rotary International.

Taylor supported a wide variety of evangelical* and other organizations, including: Young Life* (which he served as chairman of the board), Christian Workers Foundation (which he founded), Creation House Publishers, National Methodist

Foundation for Higher Education, Christian Life, Child Evangelism,* InterVarsity Christian Fellowship* and Rotary International. He also served on the boards of Young Life Institute, Christian Camps Foundation, Fuller Theological Seminary* and the American Institute of Holy Land Studies. Known for his "can do" spirit and belief that God has a plan for each person, Taylor was widely known as a man of both evangelical and civic commitment.

BIBLIOGRAPHY. H. J. Taylor, *God Has a Plan for You* (1968); H. J. Taylor, *The Herbert J. Taylor Story* (1968).   D. D. Bundy

Taylor, John (1752-1835). Pioneer Baptist* preacher,* missionary* and author. Born in Fauquier County, Virginia, Taylor grew up in that region, joined a Baptist church at age twenty, and started preaching shortly thereafter. In 1779 he moved west to Kentucky to engage in mission work. During the 1880s he became a strong proponent of mission endeavors in the whole region then known as the West and was a frequent spokesman in opposition to the work of Alexander Campbell.* Taylor's work was characterized by the starting of new churches on the frontier and then the pastoring of each new church for a number of years. He is credited with being the major force in the establishment of several Baptist churches in Kentucky, including the Clear Creek church (1785), the Bullittsburg church (1795), the Corn Creek church (1802), the Frankfort church (1816) and the Buck Run church (1818).

Taylor published *History of Ten Baptist Churches* (1823), which gives unique insight into the functioning of frontier churches, and *Thoughts on Missions* (1820), which was written to educate and build support for Western mission work. He also wrote several short biographies of frontier churchmen. Taylor died at Frankfort, Kentucky.

BIBLIOGRAPHY. *AAP* 6; W. Catheart, ed., *The Baptist Encyclopedia* (1883); *DAB* VIII; W. L. Lumpkin, *Baptist Foundations in the South* (1961).
                                    F. A. Teague

Taylor, Nathaniel William (1786-1858). Congregational* minister* and theologian.* Born in Connecticut and educated at Yale College,* Taylor served from 1811 to 1822 as the pastor of New Haven's First Church. In 1822 Taylor became the first incumbent of the Dwight Professorship of Didactic Theology at the newly formed Yale Divinity School, where he remained until 1857. From this prestigious position at the heart of Connecticut Congregationalism, Taylor developed a distinct theological outlook known as "Taylor-

ism" or "New Haven Theology."* More than any other New England theologian of the period, Taylor helped shape a synthetic theological system that borrowed from two of New England's most prominent religious traditions: Congregationalism and nineteenth-century revivalism.*

Several theological disputes within New England shaped Taylor's theology.* During his college years at Yale, Taylor served as President Timothy Dwight's personal amanuensis—a position of honor few undergraduates attained. As Dwight's hand-picked protégé, Taylor became familiar with his mentor's attempts to forge a moderate position between hyper-Calvinism, the New Divinity* movement and the revivalistic Arminianism* that was becoming increasingly popular in New England. Continuing Dwight's efforts, Taylor became an apologist for a version of American Calvinism that preserved many of the emphases of traditional Reformed* theology and yet encouraged aggressive evangelistic efforts. Despite his concern for maintaining contact with the broad Reformed tradition, however, Taylor was wary of slavish adherence to dated theological perspectives. Upon observing the bitter theological struggles between New England's Trinitarians and Unitarians, he noted that Leonard Woods's* defense of Trinitarianism had set the cause of Congregational orthodoxy* back by fifty years.

Taylor first made his progressive theology evident in his *Concio Ad Clerum,* a lecture he delivered to the annual gathering of Congregational clergy* in 1828. Therein, Taylor forthrightly rejected the classical Reformed notion that human depravity resulted from humanity's legal connection with Adam. This traditional position, he argued, paralyzed evangelism* and was offensive to the individualistic* democratic* ideology that had captured the American imagination. Moral depravity, Taylor insisted, did not consist in the constitutional nature of the human heart, or in human disposition or tendency to do evil. Rather, sin and depravity resulted from individual moral choices. As Taylor noted, "there is no such thing as sinning without acting." In other words, sin is in the sinning. Although Taylor believed sin was inevitable, he also affirmed that people "had power to the contrary."

Having loosed New England theology* from its traditional ties to the Reformed doctrine of innate or imputed depravity, Taylor encouraged progressive Congregationalist efforts, many of which were already underway, to engage in aggressive revivalism and social reform. Taylor's liberalizing efforts earned him the respect of many forward-looking evangelicals. As New England became increasingly attracted to the "new measures"* revival techniques of Charles G. Finney,* Taylor's views were hailed as a theological foundation on which such efforts could be grounded. But Taylor's theology was also severely criticized. Many conservative American Calvinists believed he had abandoned both the orthodox Puritan* tradition and the Presbyterian* Westminister Confession of Faith.*

Taylor's writings were collected and published after his death in *Practical Sermons* (1858); *Essays, Lectures, Etc. upon Select Topics in Revealed Theology* (1859); and *Lectures on the Moral Government of God* (1859).

See also NEW ENGLAND THEOLOGY; NEW HAVEN THEOLOGY.

BIBLIOGRAPHY. *DAB* IX; *DARB*; S. E. Mead, *Nathaniel W. Taylor, 1786-1858: A Connecticut Liberal* (1942); *NCAB* 7. J. R. Fitzmier

Taylor, William (1821-1902). Methodist* missionary bishop.* Born in Rockbridge County, Virginia, Taylor was converted at a Methodist camp meeting* and received his first ministerial appointment in 1845. He received his first missionary assignment in 1847, to the gold fields of California. There he conducted open-air meetings and organized the first Methodist church in San Francisco. His published account, *Seven Year's Street Preaching in San Francisco* (1856), was the first of the many such volumes which would support his ventures over the next fifty years.

After an itinerant ministry in North America (1856-1861), Taylor literally made the world his parish by evangelizing and establishing missions on six continents. Successive assignments took him to England and Australia (1862-1866) and South Africa (1866)—where his Methodist message of entire sanctification* attracted the attention of Andrew Murray of later Keswick* fame. In 1870 he went to India at the invitation of James M. Thoburn,* where he remained until 1875. There his method of establishing self-supporting mission congregations was most successful. In 1875 he ministered with Dwight L. Moody* in England. From 1877 to 1884 he developed Methodist missions in South America—chiefly Peru, Chile and Brazil. In 1884 Taylor was elected missionary bishop of Africa, where he worked primarily in the Congo and Liberia (1884-1896). Taylor was a member of the National Holiness Association,* a group of Methodist pastors dedicated to Holiness* evangelism.* He received significant support from the hundreds of state and local Holiness associations associated with the Association. Taylor retired in 1896 due to failing

health and died in 1902. Taylor University in Upland, Indiana, is named after him.

BIBLIOGRAPHY. *DAB* IX; E. Davies, *The Bishop of Africa* (1885); J. Paul, *The Soul Digger, Or the Life and Times of William Taylor* (1928); W. Taylor, *Story of My Life* (1896). M. E. Dieter

Taylorism. *See* NEW HAVEN THEOLOGY.

Teen Challenge. A drug rehabilitation agency for adolescents. After reading a 1958 *Life* magazine account of seven young boys on trial for murder, Pentecostal* minister* David R. Wilkerson drove from his church in Philipsburg, Pennsylvania, into the unfamiliar scene of New York City, where he hoped to have opportunity to meet the young defendants and to present them with the gospel. Though unsuccessful, his encounter with the plight of inner-city youth, and particularly members of teen-age gangs, led him to leave the rural pastorate and form an outreach ministry to young people. In 1960 Wilkerson met with a number of interested New York City clergymen and officially organized the ministry of Teen Challenge. By the end of that same year, the first Teen Challenge Center opened its doors.

Approximately one hundred Teen Challenge Centers have been established across the U.S., caring for the needs of teens, particularly those addicted to drugs. Approximately one hundred and fifty ministries have been established in foreign countries. These homes provide an atmosphere of love and caring and an opportunity to hear the gospel and confront biblical values. In addition, young people are given vocational training and academic tutoring so that they are equipped to re-enter society when their rehabilitation period is completed. Teen Challenge also conducts street outreaches, drug prevention programs for younger neighborhood children and family counseling sessions. It was one of the first agencies outside of the federal government to work with drug addicts in a residential program. A 1973 study conducted by the National Institute of Drug Abuse found that eighty-six per cent of those who had completed the Teen Challenge drug program remained free of drugs for more than seven years after completing the program.

BIBLIOGRAPHY. F. M. Reynolds, "Teen Challenge at the Quarter-Century Mark," *Pentecostal Evangel* (June 19, 1983); D. Wilkerson, *The Cross and the Switchblade* (1963). B. E. Brown

Tekakwitha, Katherine (Kateri Tegah-Kouita, also Tegawita) (c. 1656- 1680). Native American and Roman Catholic* convert. Born in the Iroquois country of upper New York, the daughter of a Christian Algonquin mother and a non-Christian Mohawk father, Tekakwitha's parents died in a smallpox epidemic, c. 1670. Jesuit* missionaries who came among the tribes in 1667 deeply influenced her, and in 1676 she was baptized* by Jacques de Lamberville.

Her conversion met with much hostility among her tribe, and in 1677 she fled to live among a village of Christian Native Americans at Sault Ste. Louis, on the St. Lawrence River near Montreal. There she became widely known for her life of deep spirituality* and asceticism. Upon her death, the story of her life spread, and her grave became the site of many pilgrimages among both Christian Native Americans and the French colonists. In 1932 she became the first North American Indian to be proposed for canonization* in the Roman Catholic Church.

BIBLIOGRAPHY. M. C. Buehrle, *Kateri of the Mohawks* (1954); *DARB; NAW* 3; *NCE* 13; E. Walworth, *The Life and Times of Kateri Tekakwitha* (1891). M. S. Joy

Temperance Movement (1820s-1860). The initial phase of the century-long effort to curb consumption of alcoholic* beverages in America. Drinking was common in America from earliest settlement; both distilled and fermented beverages were considered invigorating and nourishing if used temperately. After America's independence, gradual changes in attitude, along with increasing consumption, set the stage for the temperance movement. Benjamin Rush, noted Philadelphia physician, wrote a pamphlet in 1784 warning of the harmful effects of alcohol. But as the population moved west and grain production increased, so also did alcoholic consumption, since grain was more easily marketed as liquor. Barrels of whiskey often served as a medium of exchange.

Intemperance posed a serious threat to a nation extolling individualism,* democracy* and Christianity* as its foundation. "Intemperance is the sin of our land," declared evangelist* Lyman Beecher* in one of his *Six Sermons on Intemperance,* "and if anything shall defeat the hopes of the world, which hang upon our experiment in civil liberty, it is that river of fire . . . rolling through the land and extending around an atmosphere of death." Drunkenness ruined individual lives, imposed suffering on families, threatened democracy and impeded the gospel.

The American Temperance Society (ATS) was founded in Boston in 1826 to promote voluntary total abstinence* from distilled liquor and to act as a clearinghouse for information on the temperance societies forming in every state. Protestant* churches provided major support, and seven of the sixteen founders of the ATS were clergymen. Temperance enthusiasm often followed on the heels of religious revivals*; the movement was one manifestation of the perfectionist* impulse of the era. Temperance literature abounded, like the popular stories of Timothy Shay Arthur, advocating the virtues and rewards of abstinence.

By the late 1830s more radical leaders like Beecher began attacking the state licensing system, which regulated liquor sales. Petitions to repeal license laws inundated state legislatures in 1839, usually to no avail. The legal campaigns caused internal division in the movement and external opposition, leaving temperance a faltering crusade by 1840.

The ATS was aimed at the moderate drinker. In 1840 the Washingtonian movement, founded by six reformed drunkards in Baltimore, addressed the inebriate. Meetings featured testimonials and group activities to substitute for those of the tavern. The movement soon waned for lack of organization, but temperance enthusiasm revived two years later with the formation of the Sons of Temperance, a fraternal organization that spread throughout the U.S., Canada and England. Membership in the U.S. peaked in 1850 at more than 238,000. The Sons took no stand on liquor legislation, but imposed on members a strict code of total abstinence.

In the 1850s the "Maine Law," a prohibition statute enacted through the efforts of Neal Dow, became the model for state prohibition campaigns throughout the country. At least nine other states enacted similar laws, though most were repealed or declared unconstitutional by 1857. Despite these failures, the temperance movement proved to be the most widespread reform effort of the antebellum era. After the Civil War* temperance efforts were resumed by groups like the Women's Christian Temperance Union* and the Anti-Saloon League,* efforts aimed more at national legislation and which prepared the way for the Eighteenth Amendment in 1917.

See also ALCOHOL; ANTI-SALOON LEAGUE; PROHIBITION MOVEMENT; WOMEN'S CHRISTIAN TEMPERANCE UNION.

BIBLIOGRAPHY. J. A. Krout, *The Origins of Prohibition* (1925); W. J. Rorabaugh, *The Alcoholic Republic: An American Tradition* (1979); S. R. Tyrrell, *Sobering Up: From Temperance to Prohibition in Antebellum America, 1800-1860* (1979). D. W. Carlson

Templin, Terah (1742?-1818). Pioneer Presbyterian* minister* of Kentucky. Raised on a farm near Peaks of Otter, Bedford County, Virginia, Templin was attracted to the ministry* by David Rice,* a Presbyterian evangelist* who had settled in the vicinity. Given a basic education by Rice, Templin attended Liberty Hall Academy and was licensed* to preach* by Hanover Presbytery in 1780. He followed Rice in immigrating to Kentucky and in 1785 was ordained* *sine titulo* by a commission of Hanover Presbytery. On October 17, 1786, he was admitted to Transylvania Presbytery at its formative meeting. Settling in Washington County and making his home with General John Caldwell, a benefactor, Templin ministered in central Kentucky for some fifteen years, preaching and establishing churches. About 1800 he moved with General Caldwell to Livingston County in western Kentucky, but upon the general's death Templin returned to Washington County, where he died in 1818.

Neither a powerful intellect nor a charismatic preacher,* Templin's gifts lay in the consistent and sacrificial dedication of his service to the church over a long period of time. He never received a regular salary, was regarded by his colleagues as a "plain practical preacher," orthodox* in theology* and respected for his integrity and unassuming modesty. In the controversies surrounding the Cumberland Presbytery, Templin was staunch in his loyalty to the orthodox party. He never married; a fiancée of his youth having died, it is conjectured that he remained celibate in loyalty to her memory.

BIBLIOGRAPHY. R. Davidson, *History of the Presbyterian Church in the State of Kentucky* (1847).
W. J. Wade

Ten Boom, Corrie (1892-1983). World War 2* Nazi death camp survivor and popular evangelical* author. Born in Holland, ten Boom lived an uneventful life in Holland until the outbreak of World War 2,* when her country was invaded and her family became leaders in the Dutch Underground. Her home became "the Hiding Place" for Jews who were seeking to escape the terror of the Nazis. Many of them found safety through her family's hospitality, but as a result of their involvement in this underground activity, she and her sister were sent to a Nazi concentration camp at Ravensbruck.

There she witnessed indescribable atrocities of countless other prisoners and the agonizing death of her sister. Yet, trusting God, she organized a clandestine Bible study* group that grew steadily during her internment. Many lives were changed and Barracks 28 was referred to as "the crazy place where there is hope." Surviving the terrors of the camp, when she was released she began sharing her testimony through her writing and worldwide speaking tours that took her to more than sixty countries. She became a very popular figure among American evangelicals through her widely circulated book and film, *The Hiding Place,* which details her wartime activities and life in the Nazi death camp. A second book, *Tramp for the Lord,* tells of her ministry which began at Ravensbruck and continued in the years that followed.

BIBLIOGRAPHY. C. ten Boom, *The Hiding Place* (1971); C. ten Boom, *Tramp for the Lord* (1974).
R. A. Tucker

Tennent, Gilbert (1703-1764). Presbyterian* minister* and revivalist* during the Great Awakening.* Born in County Armagh, Ireland, Gilbert was the eldest son of William Tennent.* The Tennent family immigrated to the American colonies in 1718. Gilbert studied at Yale,* receiving his M.A. in 1725. In that same year he was licensed by the Presbytery of Philadelphia. Later that year he briefly served a church in Newcastle, Delaware, and then assumed a pastorate in New Brunswick, New Jersey.

In New Brunswick he met the Dutch Reformed* minister Theodorus Frelinghuysen,* whose emphasis on personal piety* and evangelistic* fervor had a dramatic and lasting impact on young Tennent. In the late 1720s and early 1730s, Tennent was involved with his father's efforts at the Log College* and this involvement, coupled with his revival zeal, made him the leader of a vigorous minority within the Presbyterian Church. Tennent's influence was such that George Whitefield* sought him out when he arrived in the Middle Colonies, bringing the Great Awakening with him. Whitefield first preached for Tennent in New Brunswick on November 13, 1739.

Tennent became the chief spokesman for supporters of the Great Awakening and is frequently remembered for his sermon "The Danger of an Unconverted Ministry," preached at Nottingham, Pennsylvania, on March 8, 1740. This sermon, assailing opponents of the Awakening, contributed to the spirit of animosity which produced the first split in the Presbyterian Church between the Old Side* and the New Side.* In 1743 Tennent moved to Philadelphia to become pastor of a New Side congregation and, while continuing to support the Awakening, thereafter led the attempt to bring reconciliation, admitting publicly that his own censoriousness had contributed to the schism in the Church. His efforts were successful and, in 1758, the two sides were reunited, with the New Side dominant in numbers and influence.

BIBLIOGRAPHY. *AAP* 3; *DAB* IX; *DARB;* L. J. Trinterud, *The Forming of an American Tradition: A Re-examination of Colonial Presbyterianism* (1949). S. T. Logan

Tennent, William (1673-1746). Presbyterian* minister* and educator. Tennent was probably born in Ireland, although inadequate records leave open the possibility that he was born in Scotland. He was trained at the University of Edinburgh, from which he received his M.A. (1693). Formally received by the general synod of Ulster in 1701, he married in 1702 and took orders in the Church of England* in 1704. In 1718 he immigrated to Pennsylvania and on September 16 of that year applied for admission to the Presbyterian Church,* the synod of which was then meeting in Philadelphia. Between 1720 and 1727 he served pastorates in New York, and in 1727 he moved to Neshaminy, Pennsylvania, to assume a pastorate there.

In the late 1720s, with controversy building in the Presbyterian Church over ministerial subscription to the Westminster Confession* (*See* Adopting Act), and out of concern for "experimental orthodoxy," Tennent began tutoring young men (including his four sons) who were preparing to enter the Presbyterian ministry. By 1735 these efforts had become sufficiently formalized that Tennent built a simple log building which became known as the Log College.* Until his death in 1746, he continued to be very influential in the work of the Presbyterian Church, particularly in the debates over the role of graduates of the Log College in the Presbyterian Church and in the Old Side*/New Side* controversy, during which he always sided with the New Side party. His son Gilbert Tennent* was a noted leader of the New Side Presbyterians.

BIBLIOGRAPHY. *AAP* 3; A. Alexander, *The Log College: Biographical Sketches of William Tennent and His Students, Together with an Account of the Revivals under Their Ministries* (1845); *DAB* IX; *DARB;* L. J. Trinterud, *The Forming of an American Tradition: A Re-Examination of Colonial Presbyterianism* (1949). S. T. Logan

Tent Meetings. The religious camp meetings* of the nineteenth century, with their emphasis on open-air activities, required participants to be away from home for several days. These forest revivals* became popular on the American frontier and attracted crowds from near and far. The site layout required an open space where the preaching took place, a designated area for cooking and a place to park the wagons and erect tents for sleeping. If the area was suitable, the crowds kept returning to the same place each year and eventually a large tabernacle was constructed to house the crowds during the preaching* services. The Methodists* developed camp meetings and campgrounds to a fine art, and the annual summer trek to the camp meetings was an anticipated event.

Borrowing from that tradition, some itinerant evangelists* took a tent with them, setting it up wherever they decided to hold meetings. Charles Finney* had an enormous tent erected on the campus of Oberlin College when he arrived there in 1835. The early Oberlin campus revival meetings were conducted in that tent which had a banner waving on top entitled "Holiness Unto The Lord." Tents provided an economical and portable means of accommodating the crowds that attended preaching and revival services. Enthusiastic singing, aisles layered with woodchips forming a "sawdust trail"* to the altar* and fiery preaching characterized the tent-meeting atmosphere.

Though tent-meeting crusades were very popular in the late nineteenth and early twentieth centuries, they were still used extensively after World War 2. Large tent meetings were held by healing revivalists such as Oral Roberts* and others, some of whom were known to boast of having the largest tent. The most prominent evangelist of the latter half of the twentieth century, Billy Graham, held his first widely publicized crusade (Los Angeles, 1949) in a tent. With the development of the electronic medium of television and the growth of the televangelists' followings, most successful itinerant revivalists and evangelists gave up the tent for the coliseum, the auditorium and the broadcast studio. Nevertheless, tents are still used occasionally by some itinerant revivalists, particularly in the South.

BIBLIOGRAPHY. C. A. Johnson, *The Frontier Camp Meeting* (1985); W. W. Sweet, *The Story of Religion in America* (1950). J. E. Johnson

Terry, Milton Spenser (1846-1914). Methodist* minister,* theologian* and biblical commentator. Born in Coeymans, New York, Terry studied at the New York Conference Seminary, Charlotteville, New York (1857-1859), and Yale* Divinity School (1862-1863) and then devoted himself to intensive personal study. After serving pastorates in New York (1863-1884), in 1884 he went to Garrett Biblical Institute, Evanston, Illinois, as professor of Christian doctrine and head of the department of Hebrew and Old Testament exegesis. Terry was an effective teacher and prolific writer whose long career was dedicated to the task of integrating modern trends in biblical interpretation* with Methodist theology.

Terry's *Biblical Hermeneutics* (1883) reflected this theological task. It showed his appreciation for higher and lower criticism, and also emphasized the interpreter's reliance on the Holy Spirit as both creator and communicator of the meaning of biblical texts. He produced numerous Old Testament commentaries and several doctrinal works, including *A Primer of Christian Doctrine* (1906) and *Biblical Dogmatics* (1907). The latter was a significant effort to inform Methodist doctrine* through the application of modern biblical hermeneutics. Writing at the height of the fundamentalist-modernist controversy,* Terry's work soon drew reaction from conservative elements in the Church. L. W. Munhall's *Breakers! Methodism Adrift* (1913) for example, reflected his belief that through the efforts of Terry and others, the Church was entering dangerous waters, anchorless without scriptural authority. Terry died in Los Angeles, California.

BIBLIOGRAPHY. *DAB* IX.   J. R. Tyson

Testem Benevolentiae. An apostolic letter, dated January 22, 1899, addressed by Pope Leo XIII* to James Gibbons,* Cardinal* Archbishop* of Baltimore, and communicated to all the bishops* of the U.S. Although it mentions the term only once, this letter is remembered as the Vatican's condemnation of "Americanism."* It is a brief treatise, framed in neo-scholastic categories, on the relationship between the Church and the modern age.

Americanism, according to the letter, is based on the false principle that Catholicism's adaptation to modern civilization requires not only changes in church discipline* but also in doctrine.* This liberalism derives its supposedly American character from the proposal that, in imitation of recent developments in secular states, a certain false liberty be introduced into the Church. Supporting this proposal was the claim that the first Vatican Council's* definition of papal infallibility* secured for Catholics a greater freedom to follow their natural inclinations. From these proposals followed six suspicious consequences, having chiefly to do with the role of the Holy Spirit in Christian life and the nature of Christian virtue. In his reply, not published until 1944, Gibbons claimed that no Catholic leader in the U.S. had ever held such opinions. Scholars have continued to debate this question.

BIBLIOGRAPHY. J. T. Ellis, ed., *Documents of American Catholic History* (1956); W. L. Portier, "Isaac Hecker and *Testem Benevolentiae:* A Study in Theological Pluralism," in *Hecker Studies,* ed. J. Farina (1983); S. J. Thomas, "The American Periodical Press and the Apostolic Letter *Testem Benevolentiae,*" *CHR* 62 (1976):408-423.

W. L. Portier

Testimony Meeting. A gathering where individuals are invited to share their personal religious experience in the presence of the entire assembly. This practice may have its roots in the biblical tradition (e.g., Pss 40:8-10; 107:2), but it became firmly established in America through the early Puritan* requirement that every prospective member* of the church confess his or her experience of faith in a clear and believable manner. Although testimonies tended to become stereotyped by the late seventeenth century, the practice was revived by the Great Awakening* of the mid-eighteenth century and was supported by the Moravian* and Methodist* tradition of "love feasts" and "watch nights" as well as camp meetings* of the nineteenth century and the "new measures" of evangelist* Charles G. Finney.* In the twentieth century the abundance of trained clergy,* the emphasis on Christian education,* preaching,* liturgy* and more structured worship* have all combined to diminish the role of the testimony meeting in many denominations.

T. R. Albin

Thanksgiving Day. A legal holiday, celebrated in the U.S. on the fourth Thursday of November and in Canada on the second Monday of October. It is a day on which people assemble to express gratitude to God. Churches* and synagogues hold special services; interfaith observances are common. Food is gathered and distributed to the poor, and families come together for a dinner of uniquely North American foods, including turkey, squash and pumpkin.

In the U.S. Thanksgiving commemorates the celebration of the Pilgrims* in 1621 after their first harvest in Plymouth. After 1630 Thanksgiving was celebrated annually and became common in the New England colonies. In the eighteenth and nineteenth centuries U.S. presidents proclaimed national thanksgiving days. In 1789 George Washington* named Thursday, November 26, a day of thanks for the ratification of the Constitution, and another in 1795 for general benefits. James Madison in 1815 asked the nation to give thanks for peace. In 1863 Abraham Lincoln* began the practice of a national proclamation, setting the fourth Thursday in November as Thanksgiving Day. Subsequent presidents carried out the practice, fixing various Thursdays in November. A 1941 resolution by Congress set the fourth Thursday in November as Thanksgiving.

In Canada Thanksgiving has its own history. Regular annual observance began in 1879 on the sixth of November of that year. After World War 1* it was combined with Armistice Day. Since a 1957 Parliamentary proclamation, it has been observed on the second Monday in October.

BIBLIOGRAPHY. J. M. Hatch, ed., *The American Book of Days* (1978).   A. M. Clifford

Theism. In America belief in God has included almost every kind of faith imaginable. But in general the story of how Americans have conceived of God reflects the ways in which a democratic and pragmatic people have developed, and in some cases reacted against, the Puritan* understanding of a sovereign, yet intimate, God. Though foreign influences—first British, then German—have been present, American thinkers have characteristically adapted these ideas under unique domestic pressures.

Orthodox Theism. Theism in the narrow sense, the orthodox* view of God as the personal creator and sustainer of the world, has been the dominant view of God throughout American history. This belief is well summarized in the Westminster* Shorter Catechism: "God is a Spirit, infinite, eternal, and unchangeable in his being, wisdom, power, holiness, justice, goodness and truth."

The form in which theism first arrived in British North America was what the Puritan divines called Covenant* Theology.* Though the influence of Calvin's view of God as sovereign and holy was central to this formulation, it was the covenanting of God with his people in the new American situation that was determinative. As a result, Puritan theology had a Christocentric focus and emphasized the knowledge and experience of God possible through conversion* and the life of faith. Cotton Mather,* echoing William Ames,* summed up his understanding of Christianity in this way: "It is most certain, that the Christian religion is nothing other than the doctrine of living unto God through Christ; and further, that it is more a practical than a theoretical science, of which the goal is the animation of real, solid, living piety,* and the calling forth of men who are dead in sin* unto a pious, sober and righteous life." This righteous life was understood in terms of the covenant between God and his people that was to be reflected in all aspects of life.

At the beginning of the eighteenth century, the scientific synthesis of Isaac Newton and the psychology of John Locke changed the way Europeans thought about theology. These influences encouraged an emphasis on the "reasonableness" of Christianity that found its characteristic formulation in Deism.* But in Jonathan Edwards* these influences came to a more orthodox expression.

Edwards adapted Locke's empiricism religiously; rather than matter acting upon our senses, he reasoned, it is God who acts to give us experience. Rejecting the deistic notion of the unmoved mover, Edwards believed God was everywhere active, creating the world at every moment. The whole material world is really a divine language, a divine light which our minds, dimmed by the effects of sin, could not see unless converted by the Holy Spirit. For Edwards, grace was revealed in feelings, emotions and impulses to action, as well as in intellectual understanding. While holding to a fully Reformed* view of God, he mined a portion of the Augustinian/Platonic tradition that the reformers had rejected, stressing God's creativity in terms of emanations (God created out of himself rather than *ex nihilo*) that seemed at times to have an affinity with pantheism.

In spite of Edwards's early death, his influence continued to dominate American theology, especially among those thinkers known as the "New Divinity."* While continuing Edwards's support of revivalism* and individualism,* these theologians place more stress on the transcendence of God and freedom of humanity. Through a God-ordained natural law, creation was ordered and could be rationally known through science, a view which found its most characteristic expression in Scottish Common Sense philosophy.* This realism affirmed the axioms of logic and the first principles of morality as self-evident.

Common Sense philosophy had decisive impact on Charles Hodge,* whose formulation of Reformed theology has been formative for much evangelical* theology, even into the latter part of the twentieth century. Unlike the more optimistic New Divinity men, Hodge stressed the reality of human sin,* though he broadened the covenant of grace to include infants and most professed Christians. His discussion of the attributes of God recalls Protestant scholasticism, rather than the practical focus of the Puritans.

Liberal Reactions to Puritan Theology. Locke's emphasis on "reasonable" Christianity led in Britain to Deism, a view of God as first cause, including belief in immortality and, above all, an emphasis on virtuous living. During the American

Revolution, these ideas spread rapidly in America through tracts, free-thinking newspapers and lectureships. Benjamin Franklin popularized a noncontroversial form of Deism in his maxims. As he told Ezra Stiles,* he had no objection to believing Jesus was God, as long as it had the practical effect of making a person more virtuous. Thomas Paine,* in *The Age of Reason* (1794), represented the influence of a more controversial French form of Deism that was actively hostile toward organized religion. Paine accepted only those truths about God which passed the test of reason, often identified with the pure (i.e., noninstitutionalized) teachings of Jesus.

Charles Chauncy,* a prominent eighteenth-century Boston minister, pioneered a movement that was to have a more far-reaching influence than Deism, and indeed was partly a reaction against Deism's distant and detached God. Chauncy emphasized God as the epitome of love, with the consequence that he downplayed the depravity of human nature and the threat of eternal judgment. His views would eventually lead to the emergence of Unitarianism.*

The father of American Unitarian theology was William Ellery Channing,* whose spiritual awakening at Harvard* led him to discover "the glory of the Divine disinterestedness . . . [and] the sublimity of devotedness to the will of Infinite Love." His Puritan-flavored liberalism* was based on Scripture* as God's Word interpreted within the limits of reason. The divine Christ, though not God, was central to his theology. The divine will of the personal God was manifested in a person through the Holy Spirit. Most distinctive was his view of the "essential sameness" of God and humanity and hence the perfectibility of persons.

Although Ralph Waldo Emerson* called Channing "our bishop," the Unitarians were appalled with what the next generation did with their ideas. Emerson and his party of hope were especially attracted to the Unitarian idea of the unity of God and humanity. As he wrote in his essay *The Oversoul,* "Ineffable is the union of man and God in every act of the soul. The simplest person who in his integrity worships God, becomes God . . . the Highest dwells with him; the sources of nature are in his own mind, if the sentiment of duty is there." Nature, then, was God as he showed himself to mankind; we for our part discover him as we seek in nature the regeneration of our souls. This was not the God of Puritan theology and yet, as Anne Rose has put it, "deep down . . . the Transcendentalists* were evangelical Protestants, concerned with the individual soul."

Progressive Orthodoxy. Not all of Edwards's heirs among the New Divinity men maintained his orthodoxy. The growing emphasis on God's "disinterested benevolence" culminated in the thought of Nathaniel W. Taylor.* Seeking to adapt New England theology* to the nineteenth-century American mind, the concept of a sovereign, almighty God gave way to God as the moral governor of the universe. Consistent with Common Sense philosophy and democratic values, God did not decree sin, only a world in which people make real ethical decisions. Sin was certain but not necessary, actual but not imputed. This, Taylor believed, was the only way to account for God's moral government in the world. Taylor's emphasis on moral agency was to have lasting influence, especially in revivalists* Lyman Beecher* and Charles Grandison Finney.*

Though he had sat in Taylor's classes at Yale,* Horace Bushnell* came to realize that Common Sense philosophy could not address the problems of mid-nineteenth-century America. The year 1859 marked the change of an era with the publication of Darwin's *Origin of Species.* Fitted to this new scientific view of origins were the developmental and evolutionary categories of German idealism. Soon to replace Scottish Common Sense philosophy as the dominant philosophical framework, this new orientation signaled a distinct move away from orthodox theology. Scottish realism had assumed a view of God consistent with an orderly, law-governed universe. Darwin's world was one of chance adaptation and chaos. Moreover, the organic, anti-individualistic thrust of evolutionary thought made it necessary to explain God's relationship to the world in different ways.

The one who best adapted his thought to these currents was Horace Bushnell, who adapted the Transcendentalist's notion of the interconnectedness of reality for more Christian purposes. For Bushnell, regeneration was made possible by Christ's vicarious and objective atonement.* But it worked its effect within humanity, much like other creative human impulses. Regeneration was thus seen as analogous to God working supernaturally from outside nature but also from within the natural order. Both the natural and supernatural, action and reaction "taken as one, [are] the true system of God."

Twentieth-Century Theism and Atheism. Bushnell's influence on the New Theology* and eventually on twentieth-century liberalism was large. His evolutionary and communitarian* emphases prepared the way for the social theology of Walter Rauschenbusch,* and even in a sense, for the political theology* of Reinhold Niebuhr.* But while these thinkers did much for our understanding of Christian involvement in society, their view of God was often a function of their social and political views. Rauschenbusch argued somewhat vaguely that our view of God has been "democraticised," or made relevant to the people. Neibuhr noted in 1926, "We may be able to put God back in nature by a little serious thought, but we cannot put God back in society without much crossbearing." H. Richard Niebuhr* made a creative attempt to stress the centrality of a personal God in his ethics* of responsibility.

Though the formulations of the progressive orthodoxy and twentieth-century liberalism differed from their Puritan ancestors, there is a clear continuity as well. New England theology had a grand conception of Christian faith as world forming and God's purposes as decisive for all of life. John Dewey (1859-1952) too was raised in this environment. In the evolutionary process, Dewey reasoned, God embodied himself in matter just as the body incarnated the individual soul. In the 1890s he came to believe that God imparted grace not to individuals, but rather to institutions and cultures that embraced Christian virtues. Like many other twentieth-century intellectuals, Dewey later lost faith in a transcendent, personal God. But in *A Common Faith* (1934) he revealed his hope in the possibility of a spiritualized society, promoting a nonreligious faith.

John Dewey symbolizes both the strength and the weakness of the New England tradition of theology in America. He was able to maintain its world-forming faith but only at the cost of its incorporation into a scientific conception of humanity and nature. As result, the religious values and the scientific world view survive the theology of a living and active God who gives both the values and the world view their meaning. The continuing challenge for orthodox theism has been to maintain its biblical dynamic, while being open to the cultural currents in which that faith must be expressed.

BIBLIOGRAPHY. S. E. Ahlstrom, "Theology in America," *The Shaping of American Religion,* ed. J. W. Smith and A. L. Jamison (1961); R. B. Edwards, *A Return to Moral and Religious Philosophy in Early America* (1982); B. Kuklick, *Churchmen and Philosophers: From Jonathan Edwards to John Dewey* (1985). W. A. Dyrness

Theocracy. A term literally meaning "rule by God." The term has been used to describe the government of New England in the seventeenth

century because of the way in which scriptural principles were employed not only in the polity* of the church, but also in the civil realm, particularly in the Massachusetts Bay Colony. If the term is understood as civil rule by the clergy* or by the church as an institution, then it is inaccurate to apply it to seventeenth-century New England.

Most New England Puritans* tended to see themselves as similar to Old Testament Israel, much as John Foxe had taught Elizabethan England to see herself as an elect nation in his *Book of Martyrs.* This did not mean that New England was to be equated with Israel, but that a similar role in God's providence was to be played out responsibly. The sovereignty of God applied not only to God's gracious initiative in the plan of redemption, but also to the government of society in which the civil magistrate was to apply the biblical laws of God. The Westminster Confession* of 1647 declared that the civil government was still to be guided by the judicial laws of Old Testament Israel as far as "the general equity thereof may require."

Boston minister* John Cotton* argued in 1636 that God did not ordain democracy* but set up theocracy "as the best form of government in the commonwealth, as well as in the church." This meant that only members of the church could hold civil office and exercise the vote, a stipulation that eventually led to lowering of requirements for church membership,* as in the Half-Way Covenant* of 1662.

In a literary debate with Cotton from 1643 to 1652, Roger Williams* disputed the propriety of the civil magistrate's enforcing the first four of the Ten Commandments. Williams' contention was that the New Testament did not countenance coercion of the individual's conscience* in the area of religious belief.

The views of Williams were eventually to prevail. The lasting heritage of the New England concept of theocracy was a limitation of the power of the civil government, which was viewed as always subject to the sovereignty of God.

BIBLIOGRAPHY. E. S. Morgan, ed., *Puritan Political Ideas, 1558-1794* (1965); L. Ziff, *Puritanism in America: New Culture in a New World* (1973); A. Heimert and A. Delbanco, eds., *The Puritans in America: A Narrative Anthology* (1985).

W. S. Barker

Theologian. A person who systematically studies theology or some aspect of theology.* Throughout Christian history the title *theologian* or its equivalent has frequently been reserved for the professional scholar or minister who, as teacher, thinker and writer, identifies the central tenets of the Christian faith, ranks subtopics in respect to those centers and systematically fleshes out interrelations and further subdivisions in the light of Scripture,* Christian tradition and contemporary culture. In Colonial America theologians were usually learned pastors who might also instruct prospective ministers in private or in a college setting. With the development of seminaries* in the nineteenth century, theologians as a whole tended to become professional academicians and specialists, leaving their previous role of providing an integrating center for the academic community. Prominent American theologians have been Jonathan Edwards,* Nathaniel Taylor,* Charles Hodge,* Philip Schaff* and Reinhold Niebuhr.*

Early Americans followed the their use of the Latin-derived term *divine* for one who studied *divinity.** By the late nineteenth century, the continental preference for the Greek-derived term *theologian* won out in Great Britain as well as in America. *Theology* now serves as an umbrella term for numerous subdivisions—both traditional and non-traditional—such as biblical,* systematic,* practical, historical, mission, moral and feminist theology. Americans in the revivalist* and restorationist* traditions have tended to suspect, even denounce, theologians, favoring instead various modes of popular theological and biblical formulations.

BIBLIOGRAPHY. M. J. Erickson, *Christian Theology* (1983-1985); G. D. Kaufmann, *Systematic Theology* (1969); B. Kuklick, *Churchmen and Philosophers* (1985).   T. H. Olbricht

Theology. The study of God and of his relationship with created reality. While the term *theology* may refer even to simple and unsophisticated statements and ideas about God and his relationships, it most frequently refers to the academic disciplines of professional theologians* and ministerial students. In the Reformed Tradition,* for example, a student preparing for the ministry might be said to be "studying theology." In recent years theologians have spoken of their vocation as "doing theology."

From time to time American religious leaders and evangelists* within the revivalist* and Pietist* traditions have characterized theology as a pretentious exercise carried out by intellectually elite but spiritually cold academics. Pitting the simple gospel message against theology, they have identified with the popular current of anti-intellectualism. Properly speaking, however, these individuals

have also formulated a theology.

Academic theology is frequently broken down into a variety of sub-disciplines including systematic,* biblical,* historical, practical (or pastoral), philosophical,* moral,* natural,* spiritual and liturgical. In some cases these qualifiers refer to the basis on which theological reflection is carried out—whether it be natural, philosophical, biblical or confessional. Theology may also be described in terms of its alignment with a principal tradition such as Reformed, Wesleyan,* Arminian,* liberal,* Roman Catholic* or Eastern Orthodox* theology. A dominant motif or organizing principle may also describe theology, as in the case of covenant* and dispensational* theology, and, more recently, process, narrative, liberation* and feminist* theologies.

BIBLIOGRAPHY. F. Whaling, "The Development of the Word 'Theology,' " *SJT* 34 (1981):289-312.
                                               The Editors

Theonomy. *See* RECONSTRUCTIONISM, CHRISTIAN.

Thiessen, Henry Clarence (1883-1947). Evangelical* biblical scholar and educator. Born in Hamilton, Nebraska, Thiessen served as a Baptist pastor in Pandora, Ohio (1909-1916), and then became an instructor (1916-1923) and principal (1919-1923) of Fort Wayne Bible School. He then attended Northern Baptist Seminary (Th.B., 1925) and taught there as an assistant professor (1925-1926) and earned successive degrees from Northwestern University (A.B., 1927), Northern Baptist Seminary (B.D., 1928) and Southern Baptist Seminary, where he studied under A. T. Robertson* (Ph.D., 1929). He was then dean of the College of Theology at the Evangelical University in New Jersey (1929-1931); professor at Dallas Theological Seminary* (1931-1935); and then successively associate professor of Bible and philosophy (1935-1936), professor of New Testament literature and exegesis (1936-1946) and first dean of the Graduate School (1946) at Wheaton College.* He accepted a call to become president of Los Angeles Baptist Seminary with the hope of finding relief from the asthmatic attacks that had troubled him in Illinois. Thiessen authored the widely used *Introduction to the New Testament* (1943) and *Introductory Lectures in Systematic Theology* (1949; rev. ed. 1979). A conscientious and exacting scholar with a dispensational* orientation, Thiessen's area of expertise was the New Testament.

                                               E. E. Cairns

Third Awakening. *See* PRAYER MEETING REVIVAL.

Thirty-Nine Articles of Religion. Anglican* statement of faith adopted by the Episcopal Church* in 1801. In 1551 English Archbishop* of Canterbury Thomas Cranmer prepared a set of theological articles in which he attempted to sketch out a Protestant* middle ground between Roman Catholicism* and Anabaptism.* Cranmer's articles formed the basis for the Forty-Two Articles of Edward VI (1553) and the Thirty-Nine Articles of Elizabeth I (1562, 1571).

Colonial Anglican clergy* in America and Canada accepted "all things contained" in "all and every article" as a precondition for ordination.* By the time of the American Revolution,* however, some opposed subscription.* New England Anglicans, wishing to distinguish themselves from Congregationalists* and Wesleyan* Arminianism,* objected most strongly to the seventeenth article, which took a Calvinist* position on predestination.*

In 1784 John Wesley* prepared an abbreviated Twenty-Five Articles for use by the Methodist Episcopal Church in America, omitting any reference to predestination. William White* and other Anglicans who were then organizing the Episcopal Church did not reach a consensus on the subject until 1801, when the general convention adopted the Articles with a few minor political changes. The Convention, however, requires no subscription beyond conformity to the "doctrine, discipline, and worship" required in the church's constitution. It also adopted (1804) Gilbert Burnet's *Exposition of the Thirty-Nine Articles,* a seventeenth-century commentary which argued that a close reading of the articles allowed either a Calvinist or an Arminian interpretation.

BIBLIOGRAPHY. *Book of Common Prayer* (1979); C. Hardwick, *A History of the Articles of Religion* (1852).   R. W. Prichard

Thoburn, James Mills (1836-1922). Methodist* missionary* to India. Born in St. Clairsville, Ohio, Thoburn graduated from Allegheny College in Meadville, Pennsylvania, and sailed as a missionary to north India in 1859, under appointment by the Methodist Episcopal Church.* He was the cofounder of *The Indian Witness* (1871) and helped to establish the Methodist Church in Burma (1879), Malaysia (1885), and the Philippines (1899). In 1888 he was elected the first Methodist missionary bishop* in Asia and was the first of his church to perceive the significance of "people movements." A keen student of the religions of India, he wrote several books and articles. He retired in 1908 after a long and distinguished career.

BIBLIOGRAPHY. *DAB* IX; W. F. Oldham, *Thoburn—Called of God* (1918); J. M. Thoburn: *My Missionary Apprenticeship* (1884).
J. T. Seamands

Thomas, Norman (M)attoon (1884-1968). Presbyterian* minister,* social activist and leader of the Socialist Party in America. Born in Marion, Ohio, the son of a Presbyterian minister, Thomas was educated at Bucknell University (1901-1902), Princeton University* (B.A., 1905) and the Union Theological Seminary* (New York) (B.D., 1911). Thomas served as an assistant minister and social worker in New York City and became well acquainted with the slum conditions of the city's "Little Italy." After ordination* in 1911 he ministered at the East Harlem Presbyterian Church and was director of the American Parish, a federation of Presbyterian churches that addressed Social issues in the city.

Thomas formed the Association of Pacifist Ministers in 1914, and in 1917 he joined the Fellowship of Reconciliation,* serving as its executive secretary and editor of *The World Tomorrow* (1918-1922).* Perceiving conscientious objection as a watershed issue, since the draft seemed to repress the freedom of conscience and civil liberties, he became one of the founders of the American Civil Liberties Union. In 1918 Thomas resigned his pastorate and joined the Socialist Party, assuming leadership from 1926 to 1950. He ran for governor of New York in 1924, mayor of the city of New York in 1925 and 1929, and was six times a presidential candidate for the Socialist Party from 1928 to 1948. Intellectually, Thomas was eclectic, borrowing from the Social Gospel,* progressivism and moderate Socialist thinkers.

BIBLIOGRAPHY. *DARB*; J. C. Duran, "In Defense of Conscience: Norman Thomas as an Exponent of Christian Pacifism during WWI," *JPH* 52 (1974):19-32; H. Fleischman, *Norman Thomas: A Biography* (1969).   C. E. Stockwell

Thomas, Samuel (c.1672-1706). First SPG missionary* to South Carolina. Samuel Thomas was sent by the Society for the Propagation of the Gospel* (SPG) to serve as its first missionary to the Yamassee Indians of South Carolina. Arriving in the colony in 1702, Thomas was prevented from fulfilling this mission because of continuous warfare between the tribes. Governor Nathaniel Johnson convinced him to go instead to the Cooper River area, with Goose-Creek as his principal locale. In a manner both selfless and politically astute, Thomas justified his actions to the SPG by noting the large number of uneducated whites in the parish,* in addition to one thousand African-American and Native American slaves, most of whom could speak English and thus be receptive to the gospel. Thomas was well-liked in the province, saw a significant increase in the number of communicants in his area, convinced the SPG to send several additional ministers to South Carolina and showed a great sensitivity toward the plight of both Native Americans and African-Americans. Thomas's death in 1706 was considered a great loss to the province.

BIBLIOGRAPHY. F. Dalcho, *An Historical Account of the Protestant Episcopal Church in South-Carolina* (1820); *The South Carolina Historical and Genealogical Magazine* (1903-1904).

N. L. Erickson

Thomas, (W)illiam (H)enry Griffith (1861-1924). Evangelical* Anglican* clergyman.* Born in Oswestry, Shropshire, Thomas overcame financial and educational handicaps to study for the Church of England ministry.* He earned degrees from King's College, London (Associate, 1885) and Christ Church, Oxford (B.D., 1895; M.A., 1898; D.D., 1906). Ordained* in 1885, he served curacies in London and Oxford. His fame as vicar of St. Paul's, Portman Square (London) (1896-1905), brought him the principalship of Wycliffe Hall, Oxford, in 1905. From 1910 to 1919 he was professor of Old Testament (also systematic theology* from 1915) at Wycliffe College, Toronto. Both schools trained evangelical Anglican ordinands. His last five years were spent in the U.S. as an itinerant teacher and Bible conference* speaker. He died in Philadelphia.

Thomas united Anglican churchmanship and Augustinian Protestantism* with dispensationalism* and support of the "higher"* or "victorious"* Christian life. He spoke often at Keswick* and prophetic gatherings in England and North America, helping found Dallas Theological Seminary,* where but for death he would have taught. Adept at popular scholarship, he wrote many books, articles and reviews on the Bible,* theology,* apologetics* and Christian living. He fought Roman Catholicism,* high church* Anglicanism, Protestant legalism,* German biblical criticism and B. B. Warfield's* view of Keswick. He had earlier given the Stone Lectures at Princeton Seminary* on the Holy Spirit (material once rejected for the Bampton Lectures at Oxford). He contributed to *The Fundamentals** (1910), wrote regularly for *Bibliotheca Sacra* and produced weekly columns for *The Sunday School Times* and *The Toronto Globe.*

BIBLIOGRAPHY. M. G. Clark, *W. H. Griffith Thomas* (1949); J. I. Packer, "New Lease of Life: A Preface to *Principles of Theology* by W. H. Griffith Thomas," *Churchman* 92 (1978):44-52.

E. W. Kennedy

Thomism. A philosophical system derived from the writings of Thomas Aquinas. The philosophy of St. Thomas Aquinas (1225-1274) is not a closed, deductive system like Cartesianism, nor an ideology like Marxism, but part of the "perennial philosophy" *(philosophia perennis)* contributed to by Socrates, Plato, Aristotle, Plotinus, Dionysius, Augustine, Boethius, Avicenna, Maimonides and others. Though clearly distinguished from theology, it is in symbiosis with and service to it.

Thomism is distinguished by (1) a high reliance on reason (e.g., to prove God's existence and know the natural moral law [vs. fideism*]); (2) a metaphysics emphasizing the primacy of *esse,* the act of existing, and the real distinction between essence and existence (vs. essentialism); (3) an epistemology setting forth an objective realism (vs. Kantian subjective idealism) and empiricism (vs. Platonic intellectualism), in which all knowledge begins in sensation; and (4) a philosophical psychology stressing the substantial unity of body and soul (vs. Platonic and Cartesian dualism).

Though using Aristotle's terminology and doctrines extensively, Aquinas did not hesitate to correct and refute him wherever he contradicted Christianity (e.g., denying divine providence, creation and, apparently, individual immortality), and quoted Augustine as frequently as Aristotle.

Thomas's philosophy, popular in his lifetime, declined after the bishop of Paris condemned some of his (misunderstood) propositions in 1277; was revived by the Council of Trent, which placed his *Summa* next to the Bible on the altar, and again by Pope Leo XIII's* encyclical "Aeterni Patris" in 1878. Thomism was often taught in a very artificial and doctrinaire way by "manuals," until Etienne Gilson and others revived Thomism by going back to Thomas, and Jacques Maritain and others by applying his principles to modern issues. Thomism, very popular in American Catholic schools in the 1950s, drastically declined in the 1960s and 1970s and is today enjoying a modest resurgence.

BIBLIOGRAPHY. G. K. Chesterton, *St. Thomas Aquinas* (1933); E. Giloson, *The Christian Philosophy of St Thomas Aquinas* (1956).

P. J. Kreeft

Thompson, Charles Lemuel (1839-1924). Presbyterian* minister* and home mission* board executive. Born in Lehigh County, Pennsylvania, Thompson moved with his parents to the Wisconsin frontier in the late 1840s. Thompson attended Carroll College (B.A., 1858), and studied theology* at Princeton Theological Seminary* (1858-1860) and Theological Seminary of the Northwest (later McCormick) (B.D., 1861). Ordained* by the Presbyterian Church in the U.S.A.* in 1861, from then until 1888, he served churches in Wisconsin, Ohio, Illinois, Pennsylvania and Missouri. In 1888 he was called to the Madison Avenue Presbyterian Church, New York City. His denomination* elected him moderator in 1888, and in 1898 he left his pastorate to become secretary of the Board of Home Missions, a position he held until 1914.

Thompson's pastorates in various parts of the country prepared him for his work, but the challenges of home missions extended his vision and made him the champion of ministries to Native Americans,* the immigrants* filling American cities, rural churches and the Hispanic* population. He developed various departments of his board to meet these challenges. Though he was evangelical* in conviction, Thompson was more interested in mission than doctrine* and deplored the heresy* trials of ministers such as David Swing* and Charles A. Briggs.* His concern for cooperation and comity among various denominations involved him in the Home Missions Council* (chairman, 1908-1914) and the Federal Council of Churches of Christ.* He interpreted his work in his various writings, including *The Soul of America* (1919) and *The Religious Foundations of America* (1917). Though he displayed his own white Anglo-Saxon orientation in his dream of creating a Christian culture in America, he also had an understanding and appreciation for American pluralism. At the time of his death he was recognized as the "Home Missionary Statesman" of his generation.

BIBLIOGRAPHY. *DARB*; *NCAB* 10; E. O. Thompson, ed., *Charles Lemuel Thompson, An Autobiography* (1924). J. M. Smylie

Thoreau, Henry David (1817-1862). New England Transcendental* essayist and philosopher. Born in Concord, Massachusetts, Thoreau lived there nearly all of his life, traveling, as he put it, a good deal in Concord. Although he made few journeys beyond his native village, his ideas—couched in elegant prose—have inspired and challenged, and sometimes angered, his readers. He insisted that life should consist of more than the acquisition of material objects; that humans could enrich life by finding a sympathy with the natural world; that all human beings possessed dignity and worth; that governments could be, and often were, oppressive; and that, on occasion, the truly moral act might be illegal.

During his career he published two books, *A Week on the Concord and Merrimack Rivers* (1849) and *Walden* (1854), and he wrote numerous essays and a journal which is an acknowledged masterpiece. In the first book he employed the travelog format to piece together his interest in flora and fauna, his enthusiasm for local customs and people, and his views on numerous topics, including fishing, Christianity, Chaucer, nature, art and the social issues of his day. In *Walden* Thoreau explored similar themes, using the framework of an extended stay in a cabin he built himself on Ralph Waldo Emerson's* property on Walden Pond. In this classic, Thoreau gathers together his personal, intellectual and social positions to focus on the central question of how a person ought to live. In this profoundly moral book, Thoreau mines his New England heritage (including its Puritan* roots) for radical answers to the problems clamoring for social reform and the issues confronting individuals striving to live morally in an increasingly materialistic society. Claiming that he went to the woods in order to find out whether life was worth living, and if it were, then to drink deeply, he chided his neighbors for having decided too quickly on priorities that undermined their essential humanity.

Thoreau's most famous essay, "Resistance to Civil Government," is read most frequently under the title of "Civil Disobedience." Published anonymously in his own lifetime, it became a key document in later American social conflicts and has received recognition from around the world. Perhaps America's best and best-known prose essayist, Thoreau received little sympathy for his personal philosophy and his social views during his own lifetime.

BIBLIOGRAPHY. W. Harding, *The Days of Henry Thoreau: A Biography* (1965); S. Paul, *The Shores of America: Thoreau's Inward Exploration* (1958). J. E. Barcus

Thornwell, James Henley (1812-1862). Southern Presbyterian* theologian* and educator. Born in the Marlborough District of South Carolina, Thornwell graduated from South Carolina College (1831) and served as a schoolteacher for two years. During that time he experienced a dramatic conversion and, in turn, a call to the ministry. He studied theology* at Andover* and briefly at Harvard* (1834) and then pastored churches in and around Lancaster, South Carolina (1835-1838). He then accepted a call as professor of philosophy at South Carolina College (1838-1839). Returning to the pastorate for a brief period (First Presbyterian Church, Columbia, 1839-1841), he soon returned to the College as chaplain* and professor of sacred literature and Christian evidences (1841-1851) and from 1852 to 1855 served as president of the College. From 1855 to 1862 Thornwell occupied the chair of theology at Columbia Theological Seminary and served as supply pastor of the Columbia Church during most of this time.

A leader in the formation of the Presbyterian Church in the United States* (1861), he wrote the "Address to All the Churches of Jesus Christ throughout the Earth," justifying its separation from the Northern Church. Thornwell was founding editor of the *Southern Presbyterian Review* (1847) and editor of the *Southern Quarterly Review* (1855-1857). Most of his writings appear in his *Collected Writings* (4 volumes, 1871-1873).

Thornwell had a passion for orthodoxy* and a sense of duty to truth and sought to defend traditional institutions and standards against liberal and ungodly assaults. He defended the South and its institutions, including slavery.* He was a unionist until the election of Abraham Lincoln,* after which he championed the Confederacy. His theology,* which he supported with immense learning, was essentially that of the Westminster* Standards. He defined theology as "the system of doctrine in its logical connection and dependence, which, when spiritually discerned, produces true piety.*" Following Scottish Common Sense* philosophy and Old School* Presbyterian orthodoxy, Thornwell believed that the task of theological scholarship was to show the complete harmony of sound philosophy and theology as one system of truth. He had few views not shared with other Old School theologians, unless it was in making justification* the central principle of all theology and in the large place he gave to Christian ethics* as a section of systematic theology.* He died before he could develop a complete systematic theology.

Thornwell's influence was more lasting in the area of ecclesiology. He developed a *jure divino* view of Presbyterianism, which Charles Hodge called "hyper-High Church* Presbyterianism." Thornwell believed that the polity* of the Church, as well as its doctrine, is limited to scriptural teaching. He viewed the lay elder* as just as much a presbyter in the biblical sense as the minister. Elders should share equally with ministers in the government of the Church and in the ordination*

of ministers. Since the Church cannot surrender the discharge of its own divinely assigned responsibilities, it should not use boards or voluntary societies* to carry out its mission. This should be done through committees subject to Church courts. Nor should the Church become embroiled in political controversies or give its endorsement to movements for social reform.* The Church can only enforce scriptural duties, and slavery was considered a political matter which the Church could neither enjoin nor condemn.

A brilliant Old School preacher,* theologian and churchman, he was the youngest General Assembly* moderator ever (1847) and perhaps the most influential Southern minister before the Civil War.*

BIBLIOGRAPHY. *DAB* IX; *DARB;* J. O. Farmer, Jr., *The Metaphysical Confederacy; James Henley Thornwell and the Synthesis of Southern Values* (1986); P. L. Garber, "A Centennial Appraisal of James Henley Thornwell," *A Miscellany of American Christianity,* ed. S. C. Henry (1963); E. B. Holifield, *The Gentlemen Theologians; American Theology in Southern Culture, 1795-1860* (1978); B. M. Palmer, *The Life and Letters of James Henley Thornwell* (1875); J. H. Thornwell, *The Collected Writings of J. H. Thornwell,* J. B. Adger and J. L. Girardeau, eds., 4 vols. (1871-1873).

A. H. Freundt

Tichenor, (I)saac (T)aylor (1825-1902). Southern Baptist* preacher,* educator, agriculturalist and denominational* leader. Born in Spencer County, Kentucky, young Tichenor was a popular preacher, sometimes called "the boy orator of Kentucky." In 1847 he became a representative of the American Indian Mission Association. A year later he was ordained* and became pastor* of a Baptist church in Columbus, Mississippi. He later served as pastor of First Baptist Church, Montgomery, Alabama (1852-1867).

During the Civil War,* Tichenor was both a chaplain* and a combat soldier, fighting at the Battle of Shiloh. After the war, he served as president of the Alabama Agricultural and Mechanical College, later Auburn University (1871-1882). His agricultural and industrial expertise were widely recognized. In 1882 Tichenor assumed leadership of the Home Mission Board of the Southern Baptist Convention. During his seventeen years in that position, Tichenor strengthened the mission board financially and extended its ministry among blacks and Native Americans, as well as in Appalachia. His work helped to stabilize the Southern Baptist Convention after the Civil War.

BIBLIOGRAPHY. *DAB* IX; J. S. Dill, *Isaac Taylor Tichenor: The Home Mission Statesman* (1908).

B. J. Leonard

Tillet, Wilbur Fisk (1854-1936). Methodist* theologian* and hymnwriter. Tillet graduated from Randolph-Macon College (B.A., 1877) and Princeton Theological Seminary* (B.D., 1880), and became professor of systematic theology* at Vanderbilt University in 1886. He quickly emerged as one of the leading theologians of the Methodist Episcopal Church, South.* From 1886 he served as dean of the Vanderbilt Divinity School and shepherded it through the crisis brought about by charges that the school was disseminating heretical teaching. When the Methodist Episcopal Church took steps to bring the school under increased control, a lawsuit ensued and the church lost ownership of the institution. Vanderbilt continued independently and the Methodist Episcopal Church supported divinity schools at Southern Methodist University (Dallas) and Emory University (Atlanta).

Tillet considered himself "a modern-minded man, possessed of an open attitude toward the results of an honest and sincere spirit of truth-seeking." He authored several books, including *Personal Salvation* (1902), *Paths that Lead to God* (1924) and *Providence, Prayer, and Power* (1926). He also served on the joint hymnal committee for the Methodist Episcopal Church, both North and South, and wrote the hymn "O Son of God Incarnate," which continues in the current *United Methodist Hymnal.* J. R. Tyson

Tillich, Paul Johannes Oskar (1886-1965). Lutheran* theologian.* Born in the Prussian town of Starzeddel, Tillich was the son of a Lutheran pastor. He took a doctorate in philosophy from the University of Breslau in 1911. His licentiate in theology from Halle came in 1912, the same year as his ordination* to the Lutheran ministry.* He served as a chaplain (1914-1918) with the German military forces in World War 1, a period that convinced him even modern people need the category of the demonic if they are to understand their world. Tillich described himself as living "on the boundary" between, for example, the rural, history-drenched life of his youth and the urban, cosmopolitan life of his maturity, between philosophy's drive for human autonomy and theology's recognition of an ultimate beyond human life, and between European and North American cultures.

Between 1919 and 1932, Tillich was privatdozent at the University of Berlin (1919-1924);

professor of theology at the universities of Marburg (1924-1925), Dresden and Leipzig (1925-1929); and professor of philosophy at the University of Frankfurt-am-Main (1929-1933). His opposition to the Nazis resulted in his removal from his professorship in philosophy at the University of Frankfurt. Through the efforts of Reinhold Niebuhr,* however, Union Theological Seminary* in New York City offered Tillich an academic position, where he stayed from 1933 until 1955. From 1955 to 1962 he taught at Harvard University,* and from 1962 until his death in 1965, he was professor of theology at the University of Chicago.*

Tillich's theological works included *The Courage to Be* (1952) and *Dynamics of Faith* (1956), but his most significant work was his three-volume *Systematic Theology* (1951, 1957, 1963), in which he employed his method of correlation by which philosophy and other modes of "autonomous" human reflection uncover certain problems in human existence. Revelation provides answers to these problems. Tillich did not derive religious answers from a philosophical analysis of the world. While nature and human experience contain certain problems which a careful analysis will reveal, nature and human experience do not contain, implicitly or explicitly, the answers to those problems. Religious answers are *answers* which only revelation can provide.

Tillich divided his *Systematic Theology* into five basic sections: "Reason and the Quest for Revelation," "Being and the Question of God," "Existence and the Quest for the Christ," "Life, Its Ambiguities and the Quest for Unambiguous Life" and "History and the Kingdom of God." In each section, a philosophical analysis of the first-mentioned term uncovers fundamental problems that cannot be resolved from within human experience. Throughout, Tillich provides a complete analysis of the major symbols or topics of the Christian faith, always with an eye on how these symbols answer the problems uncovered by his philosophic analysis of the twentieth-century human situation.

The term *ultimate concern* plays a key role in Tillich's theology. An ultimate concern is not one concern among the many other concerns of life but is the dimension of depth that is present when any of our ordinary concerns impinge on our entire pattern of meaning and purpose. Two formal criteria determine whether or not a proposition is theological: if it connects with our ultimate concern and if it bears on the question of our being or nonbeing—that which determines our entire world of significance, value and meaning.

Christian theology presupposes that Christians have found in the gospel of Jesus Christ the full and adequate expression of their ultimate concern. In addition to the two formal criteria, Christian theology needs the "material norm" of "the new being in Jesus as the Christ." The adequacy of theology as a Christian endeavor hangs on its ability to articulate, structure and express salvation in Jesus Christ.

Tillich was the last major theologian to argue that theology had something to say to all of culture. He believed that a deep-level commitment to the creation of culture and to the living of our personal lives puts us into contact with the realm of theology. Theology, without violating the autonomy of culture's disciplines in their status as preliminary, surface concerns, can provide insights into the religious character of all serious cultural creation. Tillich's theology of culture has elicited stiff resistance from those who wish to deny that scientific or artistic or other "secular" activity needs any religious foundation. Precisely these insights into the religious identity of all serious culture, however, may be one of his more lasting accomplishments.

BIBLIOGRAPHY. R. C. Crossman, *Paul Tillich: A Comprehensive Bibliography (1983)*; *DARB*; R. May, *Paulus: Reminiscences of a Friendship* (1973); W. Pauck, *Paul Tillich: His Life and Thought* (1976); W. L. Rowe, *Religious Symbols and God: A Critical Study of Tillich's Theology* (1968); R. P. Scharlemann, *Reflection and Doubt in the Thought of Paul Tillich* (1969); H. Tillich, *From Time to Time* (1973). S. T. Franklin

Tilly, Dorothy Eugenia Rogers (1883-1970). Methodist* civil rights* activist. Born in Hampton, Georgia, Tilly was educated at Reinhardt College (1899) and Wesleyan College (1901). In 1903 she married Milton Eben Tilly, a chemical salesman. Active in the Woman's Missionary Society in the North Georgia Conference, she was put in charge of the children's work committee in 1916.

Tilly's major concern was race relations, organizing interracial projects for children and special classes for African-American youth, lecturing in churches and frequently speaking on race relations. She was one of the first Georgians to join the Association of Southern Women for the Prevention of Lynching. Tilly, along with the group's founder, Methodist Jessie Daniel Ames,* traveled from county to county securing pledges from law officers that they would not tolerate lynchings in their communities and educating the public about the real causes of lynching—racism.

Defying opposition from the Georgia legislature, Tilly was responsible for the establishment of a school for delinquent African-American girls. She was also active in the peace movement and president of the Georgia Chapter of the Committee on the Cause and Cure of War. In 1944 she was a founding member of the Southern Regional Council, which replaced the Commission on Interracial Cooperation which had denied African-Americans positions of leadership. With her connections throughout the South, she was invaluable to the organization. In response to the rise of the Ku Klux Klan, she formed The Fellowship of the Concerned, in 1949, an activist group which addressed lynchings and promoted integration. She was attacked as un-American, and the Klan threatened to bomb her house. Undeterred, she continued traveling—even when confined to a wheelchair— to speak about the human potential to make the world a better place. She was the embodiment of one of her favorite beliefs: There have always been Southerners who put humanity above color.

BIBLIOGRAPHY. *NAWMP*; A. Shankman, "Dorothy Tilly, Civil Rights, and the Methodist," *MH* 18 (January 1980):95-108; B. MacKay, "Dorothy Tilly: Pioneer," *The Church Woman* (March 1964); H. H. Smith, "Mrs. Tilly's Crusade," *Colliers*, CXXVI (December 30, 1950). J. C. Brown

Tittle, Ernest Fremont (1885-1949). Methodist* minister.* Born in Springfield, Ohio, of old stock Methodist parents, Tittle was educated at Wittenberg College (1903-1904), Ohio Wesleyan (B.A., 1906) and Drew Theological Seminary (B.D., 1908). An intense, intelligent and ambitious young man, Tittle was ordained* in 1910 and experienced a rapid succession of appointments to Methodist pastorates in Christiansburg (1908-1910), Dayton (1910-1913), Delaware (1913-1916) and Columbus (1916-1918), Ohio. These were a tribute to his mounting reputation as a theological liberal* and Social Gospel* prophet.

When the U.S. entered World War 1,* Tittle served as a YMCA* secretary in France. His searing experience of the realities of war contributed to his later position of absolute pacifism*—a conviction unshaken even by Pearl Harbor. In late 1918 he returned to the U.S. and to a new pastorate, the First Methodist Church of Evanston, Illinois. Tittle's Evanston ministry of thirty-one years was one of continuing trials, due to his prophetic preaching on economic and racial injustice and the sinfulness of prideful nationalism and international war. He was under constant assault, yet he refused to soften his jeremiads.*

The First Church congregation, heavily wealthy and Republican, upheld the freedom of the pulpit because of their love for their pastor. Under Tittle's leadership First Church was transformed physically into an impressive Gothic sanctuary, the "Cathedral of Methodism." Membership mounted steadily; congregations averaging 1,500 gathered every Sunday for public worship,* and each week some 6,000 individuals utilized the church's facilities. First Church was then a major force in the life of Northwestern University; Garrett Biblical Institute, Evanston; and the Chicago area. Under Tittle's guidance, the worship services were formally structured and conducted with majesty and solemnity, breaking with early Methodism's emphasis on freedom and subjectivism. A skilled and respected preacher, he published twelve volumes of his sermons, perhaps the most enduring being *A Mighty Fortress* (1950). Tittle became the recognized leader of Methodism's liberal and pacifist ministers; his voice carried weight in denominational as well as interdenominational affairs. A concerned, compassionate, conscientious man, he suffered a long series of coronary troubles, culminating in a fatal heart attack at age sixty-three. His ashes were buried in the chapel of First Church.

BIBLIOGRAPHY. *DARB*; R. M. Miller, *How Shall They Hear Without a Preacher? The Life of Ernest Fremont Tittle* (1971). Rob. M. Miller

Tocqueville, Alexis de (1805-1859). French political thinker and observor of nineteenth-century America. As a Catholic* and an aristocrat whose grandfather had been guillotined during the Revolution, Tocqueville feared the excesses to which democracy* might run, but he wanted his native France to have stable democratic institutions such as those he admired in England. In 1832, preparing an official report for the French government on prisons in America, Tocqueville and a companion traveled throughout the U.S. interviewing persons at all levels of society. He concluded that three countervailing forces—the law, voluntary associations and religion—kept American society from degenerating into selfishness and materialism. Impressed by the universal opinion that religion was indispensable to democracy, he observed "While the law permits the Americans to do what they please, religion prevents them from conceiving, and forbids them to commit, what is rash or unjust."

Contrary to the European opinion that America's apparent religious anarchy would lead to atheism, Tocqueville found "on a shelf formed of a roughly hewn plank" in a log cabin deep in the wilderness "a Bible, the first six books of Milton, and two of Shakespeare's plays." This strength of religious feeling in America, he concluded, was due to the separation of church and state.* In France, where the old religion was deeply involved in conservative politics, reformers became anticlerical. In the U.S., however, even Catholic priests* credited the separation of church and state for producing the religious "habits of the heart" which made democracy work. Tocqueville's classic *Democracy in America* remains one of the best studies of American democracy and of the relationship between liberty and religion.

BIBLIOGRAPHY. R. Bellah et al., *Habits of the Heart* (1986); D. S. Goldstein, *Trial of Faith: Religion and Politics in Tocqueville's Thought* (1975); A Jardin, *Tocqueville: A Biography* (1988); G. W. Pierson, *Tocqueville and Beaumont in America* (1938); A. de Tocqueville, *Democracy in America,* 2 vols. (1832, 1834).

D. R. Williams

Toews, David (1870-1947). General Conference Mennonite* Church leader in Canada. Born in Russia, Toews was the son of a Mennonite minister* who had emigrated from Prussia to escape military service for his sons. As a boy of ten, Toews accompanied his parents on the ill-fated trek to Turkestan led by apocalyptist* Claas Epp. Disillusioned with Epp, the Toews family immigrated to America, reaching Newton, Kansas, in October 1884. David Toews attended public schools and the Mennonite school at Halstead, Kansas. He taught in several Kansas towns and four years in Manitoba. After a year's further study in Winnipeg, Manitoba, Toews moved with his family to Saskatchewan as both homesteader and teacher. In 1904 he cofounded the German-English Academy at Rosthern, which became the rallying point for Mennonite progressives. Toews served as principal until 1917, and was president of the school corporation for many years.

The Rosenort congregation ordained Toews a minister in 1900 and an elder in 1913. A church statesman of considerable repute, Toews was moderator of the Conference of Mennonites in Central Canada, member of various conference structures, founder and chairman of the Canadian Mennonite Board of Colonization, which settled more than 20,000 Russian Mennonite immigrants in 1923-1930, and a vigorous advocate of Mennonite nonresistance during both world wars.

BIBLIOGRAPHY. F. H. Epp, *Mennonite Exodus: The Rescue and Resettlement of the Russian Mennonites since the Communist Revolution* (1962);

F. H. Epp, *Mennonites in Canada 1786-1920* (1974).

J. D. Weaver

Toleration, Act of (Maryland, 1649). Legislation providing for religious toleration of Trinitarian Christians. The Act of Toleration passed by the Maryland Assembly in 1649 gave legal protection to the religious freedoms* of the colony's Catholics* and Protestants.* Although liberal by seventeenth-century standards, the bill did not go beyond what had been common practice in Maryland from its founding in 1634. Moreover, it retreated from the wider liberties guaranteed by a toleration act passed in 1639, since unlike this earlier legislation, it limited its benefits to Trinitarian Christians.

Under the 1649 act, deniers of the Trinity were subject to the death penalty while those who profaned the Sabbath* could be fined. Both of these stipulations were probably concessions to the colony's growing Puritan* element and revealed part of the motivation behind the bill. Promoted by the colony's proprietor, Lord Baltimore, at a time when English Catholics faced a tenuous future amid civil war and when Protestants had become a clear-cut majority in Maryland, the bill was a compromise measure designed to continue Catholic religious liberty, to placate Protestant demands and to attract new settlers.

Its concern with preserving religious harmony and avoiding religious controversy was readily evident in its third article, which banned the use of "reproachful names" such as *papist, heretick* and *puritan.* Yet within five years, the 1649 Toleration Act was repealed following a Protestant takeover of the colony's government. The bill was re-enacted in 1657 when the rule of Lord Baltimore was restored, only to be repealed once again after England's Glorious Revolution and the establishment of Anglicanism* in Maryland.

BIBLIOGRAPHY. T. O. Hanley, *Their Rights and Liberties: The Beginnings of Religious and Political Freedom in Maryland* (1959).

R. W. Pointer

Tolton, Augustine (1854-1897). Roman Catholic* priest.* Born to Catholic African-American slave parents in Rails County, Missouri, Tolton was baptized with his three siblings. After his father died, Tolton's mother escaped slavery to settle in Quincy, Illinois, where the young boy worked in a tobacco factory for the next twelve years. Earning attention from his priest, Tolton was admitted to parish schools,* where Franciscans* tutored him in subjects necessary to prepare for the priesthood. In 1877 Michael Richardt, a priest, made him catechist* for African-American children, afterwards recommending to Bishop* Peter J. Baltes that Tolton be admitted to the College of the Propagation of the Faith in Rome.

Tolton matriculated in 1880, was ordained,* and on Easter Sunday 1886, celebrated Mass* at the high altar at St. Peter's in Rome. On returning to Quincy, Tolton took charge of St. Joseph's Catholic Church for Negroes. Soon he was in demand as a speaker, including the First Catholic Colored Congress in Washington in 1889. The same year he moved to Chicago to pastor St. Monica's Church for the Colored. His chapel, built in 1893, remained the center of African-American Catholic life in the city for the next three decades. Tolton did not live to see the success, dying in 1897 at the age of forty-three.

BIBLIOGRAPHY. A. Foley, *God's Men of Color* (1955); W. J. Simmons, *Men of Mark* (1887).

W. B. Gravely and C. White

Tomlinson, Ambrose Jessup (1865-1943). Pentecostal* minister* and founder of the Church of God of Prophecy. Born near Westfield, Indiana, Tomlinson attended Westfield Academy and around 1889, shortly after marrying, was converted* and began working as a Sunday-school* superintendent at a Quaker* congregation. He soon learned of the doctrine of divine healing* from a tract written by Carrie Judd Montgomery,* and of the Holiness* view of sanctification* from several sources.

On June 13, 1903, Tomlinson joined and immediately became pastor of a small band that had been organized in May 1902 by Richard Spurling, Jr., and W. F. Bryant. Soon Tomlinson was pastoring three or four affiliated congregations and co-editing a paper entitled *The Way.* He moderated the first annual meeting of the group in 1906 and by 1909 he was elected the full-time leader of the fledgling denomination* now know as the Church of God.* Tomlinson's personal Spirit-baptism* with tongues* (specifically *xenolalia* [known foreign tongues]) came in January 1908 through the ministry of G. B. Cashwell.* It was simply a matter of time before the church completely moved from the Holiness Movement* into the Holiness segment of the Pentecostal Movement.

For the next fourteen years Tomlinson traveled widely, holding numerous revival* campaigns, organizing local churches and leading the development of the principal ministries of the Church of God, including its official periodical (*The Church of God Evangel*), its missions* enterprise, its doctrinal formulations, its Bible Training School and orphanages. A controversy in 1922-1923 resulted in Tomlinson leaving the Church of God and starting over with approximately 2,000 adherents. This body, later (1952) legally designated the Church of God of Prophecy, was kept outside the Pentecostal mainstream largely due to an ecclesiastical structure granting Tomlinson ultimate authority in all matters. By the time of Tomlinson's death in 1943, membership was nearly 32,000.

BIBLIOGRAPHY. L. Duggar, *A. J. Tomlinson* (1964). H. D. Hunter

Tongues, Speaking in. Speaking in tongues, as practiced by Christians, particularly those within the Pentecostal* and charismatic* movements, has two principal manifestations: *glossolalia* refers to a speech pattern with which humans are not familiar and *xenolalia* refers to the miraculous use of a known language not learned by traditional methods. Another phenomenon, *akolalia,* refers to a miracle of hearing. While practitioners argue that these are genuine manifestations of the gifts of the Holy Spirit, they also discern human imitations and diabolically inspired representations. Tongues speech may occur in Pentecostal or charismatic public worship,* small-group gatherings and private devotion.

In some non-Pentecostal and noncharismatic Christian circles, the phenomenon of tongues speech has been controversial. Critics of the phenomenon have taken various approaches, some arguing theologically, as did Benjamin B. Warfield,* that the gift of tongues was a sign intended to authenticate the apostolic message. No longer necessary with the completion of the biblical canon, they ceased with the apostolic age. Those that hold this view regard the present-day phenomenon as at best a harmless emotional release and at worst a demonic delusion. Others have studied the phenomenon from the standpoint of the social sciences and have viewed it as either arising from an altered mental state or as nonlinguistic learned behavior. Other Christians are open to the authenticity of tongues speech, though they may not practice it themselves. Their attitude may be summarized in the words of A. B. Simpson: "Seek not, forbid not." At the same time, Pentecostal and charismatic scholars have become increasingly more sophisticated in their defense of speaking in tongues, answering their critics' objections.

A study of historical data demonstrates that speaking in tongues was not only the experience of the early church at Pentecost (Acts 2:1-13), but

seems to have been experienced by certain Christians through the centuries. The seventeenth-century Camisards of France are credited with glossolalia and bringing the phenomena to the attention of John Wesley* in England. In America, the United Society of Believers in Christ's Second Appearing, better known as the "Shakers,"* attested to a variety of extraordinary phenomena, including speaking in tongues. Mother Ann Lee* was obviously exaggerating when she claimed to have been empowered by the Spirit to speak in seventy-two languages, but her testimony places the phenomenon within the eighteenth century. Mormons* are also reputed to have spoken in tongues and continue to support the practice.

In the early nineteenth century, a North Carolina Presbyterian congregation manifested tongues-speech during the summer of 1801, while related phenomena may have occurred in the 1801 Cane Ridge revival* in Kentucky. The so-called Gift People discovered tongues-speech in 1874, as did W. Jethro Walthell in 1879. Tongues-speech has been claimed as part of the early ministries of the faith-healing evangelist Maria B. Woodworth Etter,* The Salvation Army,* and the Christian and Missionary Alliance.* In the 1890s tongues speech was known to individuals such as Daniel Awrey, John Thompson and C. M. Hanseon, a group in Virginia and a revival at Camp Creek, North Carolina.

With the dawning of the twentieth century came the most extensive practice of tongues speech. As this experience arose among those Holiness groups that had come to speak of their experience of perfectionist sanctification in terms of Spirit baptism, Pentecost and enduement with power, tongues speech came to be regarded as the initial outward evidence of Spirit baptism. Speaking in tongues has been a distinctive feature of the Pentecostal Movement ever since, and a characteristic tenet of the Movement has been the belief that tongues is the initial evidence of Spirit baptism.

Historians have frequently dated the birth of this movement to New Year's Day 1901, when Agnes Ozman* spoke in tongues at Charles Parham's* Bible school in Topeka, Kansas. Though this was not the first occurrence of tongues speech in America, the incident set off a remarkable chain of events that brought tongues speech and other phenomenon of the Spirit to the public's attention. In more recent times the charismatic movement, beginning with the mainline* Protestant* churches in the early 1960s and then the Roman Catholic Church* since about 1967, has made tongues speech a more common and acceptable religious practice in America. However, charismatics generally do not regard tongues as the initial evidence of Spirit baptism, frequently viewing it as one of several possible gifts given to Spirit-baptized believers.

See also CHARISMATIC MOVEMENT; PENTECOSTAL MOVEMENT.

BIBLIOGRAPHY. S. H. Frodsham, *With Signs Following* (1946); M. T. Kelsey, *Tongue Speaking* (1968); K. McDonnell, *Charismatic Renewal and the Churches* (1976); G. H. Williams and E. Waldvogel, "A History of Speaking in Tongues and Related Gifts," in *The Charismatic Movement*, ed. M. P. Hamilton (1975). H. D. Hunter

Torrey, (C)harles (C)utler (1863-1956). Biblical scholar and Semitist. Born in East Hardwick, Vermont, the son of a Congregational minister, Torrey graduated from Bowdoin College (B.A., 1884; M.A., 1887). He then attended Andover Theological Seminary* (B.D., 1889), where he studied Semitic philology, Arabic and Aramaic under George Foot Moore.* Following graduation from Andover he earned a Ph.D. in Arabic Studies at the University of Strasbourg (1892) and returned to Andover to teach Semitic languages, biblical theology and history (1892-1900). The remainder of his career was spent as professor of Semitic languages and literature at Yale* (1900-1932). Torrey established, and was the first director in Jerusalem (1900-1901), of the American School of Archaeology (later the American School of Oriental Research). He conducted archaeological excavations at Sidon and co-edited the *Journal of the American Oriental Society* (1900-1917). Torrey's interest in the intertestamental period perhaps influenced him to date Old Testament books late (Ezekiel and Chronicles in the third century B.C.) and New Testament books early (the Gospels and Revelation written before 70 A.D.). His ideas were often controversial (e.g., the nonexistence of Ezra), and although few scholars agree with him, his creative brilliance cannot be ignored.

BIBLIOGRAPHY. M. Burrows, "A Sketch of Charles Cutler Torrey's Career," *BASOR* (1953); *DAB* 6; H. A. Wolfson, "Charles Cutler Torrey," *Speculum* 22 (July 1957):648-649.

S. Meier

Torrey, (R)euben (A)rcher (1856-1928). Evangelist* and Congregational* minister.* Born in Hoboken, New Jersey, Torrey received his education at Walnut Hill School, Geneva, New York; Yale* (A.B., 1875) and Yale Divinity School (B.D., 1878). He was ordained* into the Congregational ministry in 1878 and installed as pastor in Garretts-

ville, Ohio, where he remained until 1882. Torrey spent the 1882-1883 academic year in Germany, where he studied at Leipzig and Erlangen. During the next six years he served in Minneapolis, first as pastor of the Open Door Congregational Church (1883-1886) and then as superintendent of the City Missionary Society and pastor of the People's Church (1886-1889).

In 1889 Torrey became superintendent of Moody's Chicago Training Institute (later called Moody Bible Institute*), and remained there until 1908. From 1894 until 1906 he was also pastor of the Chicago Avenue Church. Although he remained in charge of Chicago Training Institute, much of the administrative work of the school fell to others, particularly after 1900 when Torrey began an increasingly demanding evangelistic ministry. Between 1902 and 1905, accompanied by singer Charles M. Alexander* and pianist Robert Harkness, he conducted a worldwide evangelistic tour, during which he preached to more than 15 million persons in England, Scotland, Ireland, Germany, France, Australia, New Zealand, Tasmania, India, China and Japan. His 1905 London campaign, in Royal Albert Hall, lasted five months and led to an estimated seventeen thousand conversions. From 1906 to 1911 he conducted numerous campaigns in the U.S. and Canada, revisiting England, Scotland and Ireland in 1911.

Torrey returned to educational work in 1912 when he accepted the position of dean of the Bible Institute of Los Angeles (Biola). Three years later he became pastor of the Church of the Open Door in Los Angeles while retaining his position at the Institute. During these years he carried out a broad preaching ministry, including conferences for missionaries in China (1919-1921). After leaving Biola and his pastorate in 1924, he spent the remaining years of his life as an itinerant Bible teacher and evangelist, and as a guest lecturer at Moody Bible Institute. He died at his home in Biltmore, North Carolina, in 1928.

Torrey was one of the most prolific writers among the evangelicals* of his generation. He wrote or edited forty books and scores of booklets and articles on a wide range of subjects, devoting special attention to the defense of the authenticity of Scripture and the cardinal doctrines of the Christian faith. He edited *The Institute Tie* (Moody Bible Institute) and *The King's Business* (Bible Institute of Los Angeles) and served on the editorial committee for *The Fundamentals,** editing the last two volumes in that series. He founded the Montrose Bible Conference at Montrose, Pennsylvania (1908), and played a prominent role in the founding of the World's Christian Fundamentals Association.*

See also ALEXANDER, CHARLES M.

BIBLIOGRAPHY. G. T. B. Davis, *Torrey and Alexander* (1905); R. Harkness, *Reuben Archer Torrey, the Man, His Message* (1929); H. T. Hight, *A Critical Analysis of the Published Sermons of Reuben Archer Torrey* (1969); R. Martin, *R. A. Torrey: Apostle of Certainty* (1976); *NCAB* 21; T. P. Weber, *Living in the Shadow of the Second Coming* (1979).

P. C. Wilt

Toth, Alexis Georgievich (1853-1909). Archpriest of the Russian Orthodox* Diocese of Alaska and the Aleutian Islands. Born near Eperjes (Presov) in the region of Slovakia (then part of the Austro-Hungarian Empire), Father Toth was educated at the Roman Catholic Seminary of Esztergom, the United Greek Catholic Seminary of Ungvar (Uzhorod) and the University of Presov, from which he received a degree in theology.* Ordained* to the priesthood of the Greek Catholic Church in 1878, he served in several important positions prior to his being sent in 1889 to the U.S. to serve as a missionary to Greek Catholic immigrants.*

In Europe, Greek Catholics worshiped* according to their own Byzantine Rite, allowed married clergy* and were presided over by their own bishops.* The situation was different in the U.S., where they were placed under the jurisdiction of the local Roman Catholic* bishops in whose dioceses* their parishes* were located. Father Toth, newly assigned as the first resident pastor* of St. Mary's Church in Minneapolis, was thus required to present his credentials to the Americanist* Archbishop John Ireland* of St. Paul-Minneapolis. Archbishop Ireland, however, refused to recognize his catholicity when they met in December 1889. After being refused again, Toth presided over the first consultation of Greek Catholic clergy on October 20, 1890, at Wilkes-Barre, Pennsylvania. With no satisfactory resolution achieved, he seized the initiative by establishing communications with the Russian Orthodox Bishop Vladimir (Sokolovsky) of San Francisco by the end of 1890. On March 25, 1891, Father Toth and the entire St. Mary's parish earned notoriety by being the first Greek Catholics in America to come over to the Orthodox Church.*

In the year that followed, Father Toth continued in his mission to the immigrants, traveling extensively and encouraging them to accept Orthodoxy. By the time of his death in 1909, he was credited with organizing seventeen parishes in Pennsyl-

vania and bringing whole parishes to the Orthodox faith. Of the some 29,000 souls who came to Orthodoxy in the years up until 1909, more than half of them did so as a result of Father Toth's efforts. He was elevated to the rank of archpriest prior to his death.

BIBLIOGRAPHY. K. Russin, "Father Alexis G. Toth and the Wilkes-Barre Litigations," *SVTQ* 16 (1972):128-148; C. Tarasar, ed., *Orthodox America, 1794-1976* (1975). C. M. Elliott

Townsend, William Cameron (1896-1982). Founder of Wycliffe Bible Translators* and the Summer Institute of Linguistics. Born and raised in a Presbyterian* home in California, Townsend enrolled in Occidental College in Los Angeles. While studying there he joined the Student Volunteer Movement (SVM).* The SVM and a message by John R. Mott* were instrumental in his decision to become involved in foreign missions.* When the Bible House of Los Angeles issued an appeal for Bible salesmen to go to Central America, Townsend applied and was sent to Guatemala with a colleague in 1917. Working in rural areas he became burdened for the large number of Indians who could not read Spanish. The question of a Cakchiquel Indian ("If your God is so smart, why doesn't he speak Cakchiquel?") crystalized his thinking.

After marrying Elvira Malmstrom, a first-term missionary to Guatemala, Townsend joined the Central American Mission (CAM) and took up work among the Cakchiquels. Without linguistic training, he embarked on a program of language learning, reducing the language to writing and translating the New Testament. After over ten years of labor, Townsend presented a copy of the New Testament, the first book published in the Cakchiquel language, to the president of Guatemala.

During his tenure in Guatemala, Townsend had begun various ministries, but his overriding concern was for translation work—a priority not shared by CAM leadership. Townsend resigned and, with L. L. Letgers, in 1934 founded Camp Wycliffe in Arkansas. Out of this small beginning emerged the Summer Institute of Linguistics (SIL) and Wycliffe Bible Translators (WBT), destined to become the largest independent Protestant* mission in the world. The war years and their aftermath proved to be decisive in this growth pattern. Townsend's first wife died in 1944, and two years later he married his second wife, Elaine, who proved to be a most able helper. America's international involvement grew dramatically, as did that of WBT. From a total of about 100 personnel in its early days and a focus on South and Central America, the mission increased its involvement to cover the world and grew to a force of almost 5,000 members by the late 1980s.

Throughout his life Townsend remained an innovator. In his approach to linguistics he was ahead of his times. And his constant quest and discovery of new groups without a written language quickly dated his statistics. His missionary strategies, such as his openness to working with mainline* denominations, his promotion of literacy in alliance with foreign governments, and the sending of single women to remote tribes, occasioned controversy among his largely evangelical* constituency. When he died in April 1982, half of the world's over 5,000 languages still had no portion of the Bible, but half did. This remarkable fact was in no small part due to "Uncle Cam" Townsend and his translators.

BIBLIOGRAPHY. J. and M. Hefley, *Uncle Cam: The Story of William Cameron Townsend, Founder of the Wycliffe Bible Translators and the Summer Institute of Linguistics* (1974); E. E. Wallis and M. A. Bennett, *Two Thousand Tongues to Go: The Story of the Wycliffe Bible Translators* (1959).

D. J. Hesselgrave

Toy, Crawford Howell (1836-1919). Baptist* professor of Old Testament and Hebrew. Raised in Virginia, Toy graduated from the University of Virginia in 1856 and taught for three years at the Albemarle Female Institute in Charlottesville, Virginia, before entering Southern Baptist Theological Seminary in Greenville, South Carolina. His plans to become a missionary* to Japan were interrupted by the Civil War,* when he served for a time as a chaplain* in the Confederate army. After the War he pursued two years of graduate study in Berlin (1866-1868). In 1869 Toy became professor of Old Testament interpretation at Southern Baptist Theological Seminary.

It soon became evident, however, that Toy had embraced Darwin's theory of evolution* and favored the Kuenen-Wellhausen theory of pentateuchal criticism. He was asked by the trustees of the seminary to cease teaching these theories, but in spite of growing dissatisfaction on the part of the trustees, he persisted and was finally forced to resign in 1879. Toy left the seminary without bitterness and spent the following year as literary editor of the New York *Independent* before becoming Hancock Professor of Hebrew and other Oriental languages at Harvard* University in 1880. A regular contributor to scholarly journals, he authored several books, including *Quotations in*

the New Testament (1884); *Judaism and Christianity* (1890); *A Critical and Exegetical Commentary on the Book of Proverbs* (1899) and *Introduction to the History of Religions* (1913). At Harvard Toy became a recognized scholar in his field, giving three decades (1880-1919) to his teaching and scholarship both in the University and the Divinity School.

BIBLIOGRAPHY. R. A. Baker, *The Southern Baptist Convention and Its People, 1607-1972* (1974); *DAB* IX; *DARB;* W. A. Mueller, *A History of Southern Baptist Theological Seminary* (1959); *NCAB* 6.

W. R. Estep

Tozer, (A)iden (W)ilson (1897-1963). Christian and Missionary Alliance* minister* and popular evangelical* author and mystic. Tozer's conversion* in 1915 was marked, as he wrote, by "an old-fashioned Biblical invasion of my nature by the Holy Spirit." Active in witnessing thereafter, he was ordained* in 1920. Self-educated, Tozer read widely, with a special love for poetry, the Church Fathers and the mystics* of the church. Tozer pastored churches in West Virginia, Ohio, Indiana and, for more than thirty years (1928-1959), the Southside Alliance Church of Chicago, before becoming preaching* minister of the Avenue Road Alliance Church of Toronto, Canada (1959-1963). Elected vice president of the Alliance in 1946 and re-elected in 1949, he resigned that position in 1950, the year he became editor of the *Alliance Weekly* (later *Alliance Witness* and currently *Alliance Life*). A prolific writer, Tozer wrote approximately thirty books. His first published volume, *Wingspread* (1943), was a biography of A. B. Simpson,* founder of the Alliance. Other volumes included *The Pursuit of God* (1948), *The Root of the Righteous* (1955), *The Knowledge of the Holy* (1961) and *The Christian Book of Mystical Verse* (1963). As editor, author and speaker, Tozer ministered to the evangelical* community in North America and abroad, making him one of the most influential American evangelicals of the mid-twentieth century.

BIBLIOGRAPHY. D. J. Fant, *A. W. Tozer; A Twentieth-Century Prophet* (1964).

N. A. Magnuson

Tract. A short pamphlet written with a religious or evangelistic* message. Tracts usually consist of two to eight pages and are designed for easy distribution, quick reading and immediate comprehension. Primarily used in evangelism, they are also used to encourage a change in doctrinal* belief. Tracts first appeared long before the invention of the printing press and were used extensively during the Reformation. The American Tract Society* (1825) was the earliest national tract distribution society in America. In Roman Catholic* usage, *tract* refers to an anthem consisting of verses of Scripture sung on certain occasions after the gradual in the Mass.*   J. M. Glass

Tractarianism. Common name for the movement also known as the Oxford Movement or Puseyism, which was concerned with asserting the spiritual nature of the Church of England (*See* Anglican Church) and its independence over against Parliament. It is commonly seen as arising from John Keble's Assize sermon (July 1833), "National Apostasy." The name *Tractarianism* is derived from the *Tracts for the Times*, the most famous literary product of the early movement, authored by its most noted leaders: John Henry Newman (1801-1890), John Keble (1792-1866), Richard Hurrell Froude (1803-1836) and E. B. Pusey (1800-1882). In contrast to the worldliness and antidogmatic Erastianism then strong in the Church of England, the Tract writers emphasized the importance of dogma,* the true catholicity of the church (and in particular the importance of apostolic succession*), and the need for an increased spirit of holiness. The movement's openness to Catholic theology* and piety* led by the end of the 1830s to increasing criticism from Anglican evangelicals.* In particular the last of the tracts, *Tract 90*, which attempted to reconcile the Anglican Thirty-nine Articles* with the Council of Trent, provoked great outrage. One may see the termination of the Tractarian Movement in 1845, with the secession of Newman and a number of others to Roman Catholicism. Tractarian ideals, however, would be reflected in the succeeding Anglo-Catholicism.*

American Episcopalians,* far removed from the political and intellectual milieu that gave birth to English Tractarianism, only gradually became interested in the movement. Excerpts from the tracts appeared in America as early as 1835, and a full American edition was published in 1839-1840, but their immediate influence in America has been debated. Clearly in certain parts of the American church where the high church* tradition was strongest, particularly in the diocese* of New York and General Theological Seminary, an interest in Tractarian teachings did emerge, and the bishop* of New York, Benjamin T. Onderdonk,* became a strong defender of the message of the Tracts. In the long run Tractarianism did contribute to the erosion of the older Hobartian (*See* Hobart, John

Henry) high church tradition among some American Episcopalians in favor of the emerging Anglo-Catholicism. Yet another affect of Tractarianism among American Episcopalians was in increasing the high church/low church* polarization of the communion. Episcopal bishops such as William Meade* (Virginia) and Charles P. McIlvaine* (Ohio) were vigorous in their denunciation of the movement. The decade of the 1840s saw great debates over the teachings of the *Tracts*. One indirect result of these debates was a series of ecclesiastical trials of the leading pro-Tractarian bishops on various moral charges, which resulted in the suspension of two high-church bishops, including Benjamin T. Onderdonk, and the secession of another (Levi Silliman Ives*) to Roman Catholicism.*

Tractarianism had largely a negative effect on the rest of American Protestantism.* Leading Protestant theologians such as Horace Bushnell,* Edwards Amasa Park* and Albert Barnes* all publicly attacked the movement. The one major exception to this was among the proponents of the Mercersburg Theology.* Both Philip Schaff* and John W. Nevin* expressed cautious sympathy for some of the Tractarian critique of extreme Protestantism, but faulted the movement for its underestimation of the true value of the Reformation heritage.

See also ANGLICANISM; ANGLO-CATHOLICISM.

BIBLIOGRAPHY. O. Chadwick, ed., *The Mind of the Oxford Movement* (1960); E. C. Chorley, *Men and Movements in the American Episcopal Church* (1950); R. W. Church, *The Oxford Movement: Twelve Years, 1833-1845* (1891); G. B. DeMille, *The Catholic Movement in the American Episcopal Church*, 2nd ed. (1951); R. B. Mullin, *Episcopal Vision/American Reality* (1986).

R. B. Mullin

Transcendentalism. A broad-ranging intellectual reform movement centered in New England. Although the movement away from the philosophy of the Enlightenment* had begun in the U.S. as early as 1820, it was not until 1836 that it took definite shape. That year witnessed the publication of the manifesto of Transcendentalism—Ralph Waldo Emerson's* *Nature*—as well as Orestes Brownson's* social critique *New Views of Christianity, Society and the Church;* the beginning of George Ripley's* controversy with Andrews Norton* over the nature of miracles; and the first meeting in Boston of the Transcendentalist Club. For the next decade Transcendentalism exerted a major effect on American literature, art, religion and social reform.*

The movement was an American manifestation of the Romantic* mood that had transformed European intellectual life during the first third of the nineteenth century. It stressed a return to idealism over against the sensism of the Enlightenment, as epitomized by Locke, looking instead to Plato and Kant for inspiration. The religious dimensions of the movement were pronounced. Its leaders were young Unitarian* clergy* who revolted against the "corpse cold" religion of their fathers and the negative anthropology of Calvinism.* They asserted instead the importance of sentiment, the reality of the individual's abilities to intuit religious truth and the fluid nature of revelation, stressing always the notion of God as Spirit. In addition to European Romantics they read the mystical writings of Swedenborg, Boehme and some of the earliest English translations of the great Hindu and Buddhist holy books. The movement's greatest impact, however, came in literature where it gave rise to the first great indigenous American fiction.

See also ROMANTICISM, CATHOLIC; ROMANTICISM, PROTESTANT.

BIBLIOGRAPHY. W. R. Hutchison, *The Transcendentalist Ministers: Church Reform in the New England Renaissance* (1959); P. Miller, *The Transcendentalists: An Anthology* (1959); A. C. Rose, *Transcendentalism as a Social Movement* (1981).

J. Farina

Transubstantiation. Catholic* doctrine* concerning the Eucharist.* The Roman Catholic Church from early times has taught that Jesus intended his statement "This is my Body. . . . This is my blood" to be understood literally. Among scriptural passages offered to support this are: Matthew 26:26-28; Mark 14:22-24; Luke 22:19-20; John 6:50-67 and 1 Corinthians 11:23-25. In the early centuries of the Church, theologians* like Ignatius of Antioch tended simply to state that the eucharistic bread and wine are the body and blood of Christ, without further elaboration. However, by the fourth century Gregory of Nyssa taught that in the Eucharist the bread and wine are "transformed" into Christ's body and blood. The Benedictine monk Paschasius Radbertus (c.785-c.860) is usually credited with being the first explicit proponent of a doctrine of transubstantiation.

In the mid-eleventh century, Berengarius of Tours taught that the bread and wine are symbolic representations of Christ's body and blood. He was made to retract and to acknowledge that in Communion* the faithful actually consume that body

and blood. Subsequently, the Fourth Lateran Council (1215) proclaimed that the bread and wine are "substantially changed."

The first use of a term equivalent to *transubstantiation* seems to have been around A.D. 1130. Literally, the term means "substance crossing over" or "substance changing" and denotes the belief that the bread and wine are transformed into Christ's body and blood. The new term was the result of the rediscovery in the West of the philosophy of Aristotle. Aristotelian metaphysics held that the underlying reality of a being is its substance, by which it is what it is. Its tangible characteristics (size, color, shape, etc.) are its accidents.

The standard Catholic doctrine was formulated by Thomas Aquinas in the thirteenth century—in the Eucharist the substance of bread and wine are miraculously transformed into the body and blood of Christ, while the accidents remain unchanged. While the use of the term seems to imply acceptance of Aristotelian metaphysics—which is not required of Catholics—it is also commonly used in a looser sense, designed to emphasize merely that a real and complete physical change has taken place in the Eucharistic elements.

The Protestant Reformers all rejected this Catholic doctrine to one degree or another. Martin Luther stayed closest to it, holding that Christ is indeed present "with, in and under" the bread and the wine, but does not replace them (*See* Consubstantiation). The Council of Trent (1545-1563), as part of its general refutation of Protestant doctrine, strongly reaffirmed transubstantiation.

Practical implications of the doctrine include the adoration of the reserved sacrament, the belief that Christ's bodily presence in no way depends on the faith of the recipient (hence, sacrilege is possible), and the belief that every particle of the eucharistic elements is Christ's body.

For various reasons, attempts have been made in recent times to reformulate the doctrine, not least because of a movement away from Aristotelian metaphysics. Although the Catholic Church permits other terms and other formulations of Christ's sacramental presence, any truly Catholic alternative must retain the idea of complete physical transformation.

See also MASS, THE.

BIBLIOGRAPHY. S. Bonano, *The Concept of Substance and the Development of Eucharistic Theology to the 13th Century* (1960); R. A. Tartre, ed., *The Eucharist Today* (1967); C. Vollert, "The Eucharist: Controversy on Transubstantiation," *TS* 22 (1961):391-425.

J. F. Hitchcock

Trappists. Popular name for the Order of Cistercians of the Strict Observance, a Roman Catholic* religious order* known for its austerity and dedication to prayer. The Cistercians began as a reform movement in 1098 which dedicated the French monastery of Molesme to pristine observance of the Benedictine* Rule. During the next six centuries various relaxations were introduced into Cistercian practice. Armand Jean de Rancé (1626-1700), abbot of La Trappe (whence the name "Trappists"), restored silence, seclusion, manual labor and stringent abstinence from meat. Later this strict observance spread to monasteries in Switzerland, Spain, Belgium, England, Italy and the U.S.

French Trappists arrived in the U.S. in 1803, but most returned to France in 1814. Lasting monasteries were set up at Gethsemani, Kentucky, in 1848 and New Melleray, Iowa, in 1849. Rapid expansion came to the order after World War 2,* as it did to many religious orders. Trappist austerity offered a clear alternative to modern materialism. Interest in the Trappists was spurred by Thomas Merton,* a monk at Gethsemani, whose writings explained the monastic and contemplative ideal to modern Americans. So did more than twenty books on a popular level by another Trappist, Father Raymond, especially in his *The Man Who Got Even with God* (1941). Currently there are Trappist monasteries at Spencer, Massachusetts; Gethsemani, Kentucky; Conyers, Georgia; Moncks Corner, South Carolina; Berryville, Virginia; Ava, Missouri; New Melleray, Iowa; Lafayette, Oregon; Huntsville, Utah; Vina, California; and Snowmass, Colorado. Communities average about thirty monks, rather evenly divided between priests* and lay* brothers, who support themselves mainly by manual work on their farms.

BIBLIOGRAPHY. A. J. Krailsheimer, *Rancé and the Trappist Legacy* (1985); L. J. Lekai, *The Rise of the Cistercians of Strict Observance in Seventeenth-Century France* (1968); T. Merton, *The Waters of Siloe* (1949). J. P. Donnelly

Triennial Convention. First national organization of Baptists in the U.S. Founded in Philadelphia on May 18, 1814, its proper name was The General Missionary Convention of the Baptist Denomination in the United States for Foreign Missions, and its first president was Richard Furman* of South Carolina. Organized by thirty-three delegates from eleven states, it became the first national body of Baptists. It met every three years, hence the name "Triennial Convention." The leading spirit in its formation was Luther Rice* who challenged Baptists to organize in order to sponsor Adoniram and Ann Judson,* American missionaries laboring in India and later, Burma.

Although its primary impulse was foreign missions,* in 1817 its work was broadened to include home missions and education. In that year John Mason Peck* and James Welch were appointed as missionaries to Missouri, and in 1818 Columbian College (later, George Washington University) was founded.

In 1826 the Convention returned to its first emphasis of foreign missions. The ministry of home missions was picked up by the formation of The American Baptist Home Mission Society in 1832. In 1845 the Triennial Convention was renamed the American Baptist Missionary Union, and in 1910 it became the American Baptist Foreign Mission Society. In 1845 Baptists in the South were separated from this body, when they organized the Southern Baptist Convention.*

BIBLIOGRAPHY. W. Shurden, "The Development of Baptist Associations in America, 1707-1814," *BHH* 4 (1969):31-39.

W. M. Patterson

Trifa, Valerian (1914-1987). Romanian Orthodox* archbishop.* Arriving from Italy as a displaced person in 1950, Trifa rose quickly from editor of *Solia*, the journal of the Romanian Orthodox episcopate to its bishopric, to succeed Policarp Morusca, then detained in Romania by the Communists. Through *Solia*'s pages and other writings, and through the youth programs he instituted at the Vatra Center, he brought vitality to a failing Church. In 1960 he affiliated it with the Russian Metropolia, and in 1970 became a founding father of the Orthodox Church in America. He served on the ruling boards of both the National* and World councils of churches.*

Trifa's strident anticommunism and organizational success made him a target for political attacks from Bucharest and its faction in this country. They succeeded in convincing the U.S. government to declare as "Nazi" the patriotic student organization he had led in the volatile days between the two world wars, thereby warranting his deportation. After years of legal battle which financially exhausted his followers, he renounced his citizenship and accepted exile to Portugal, steadfastly denying the charges leveled against him.

BIBLIOGRAPHY. G. Bobango, *Religion and Politics: Bishop Valerian Trifa and His Times* (1981).

P. D. Garrett

Trinitarianism. *See* THEISM.

Trotman, Dawson Earle (1906-1956). Founder of The Navigators.* Born in Bisbee, Arizona, Trotman joined the Presbyterian Church* after his conversion* in Los Angeles but withdrew (1931) because of liberalism* within the Church. He studied at the Bible Institute of Los Angeles and Los Angeles Baptist Seminary. To evangelize* seamen in Los Angeles, he began (1933) a Bible study* in his home and developed a discipleship* process emphasizing Bible memorization, prayer,* personal evangelism and conservative Christian lifestyle. The group was called "Navigators" in 1934 and legally incorporated in 1943. Throughout World War 2,* evangelistic efforts focused on military personnel. After the War, the ministry moved to the university and college campuses. Trotman developed the follow-up program of the Billy Graham Evangelistic Association* which has been used since the Shreveport Crusade of 1951. He served on the Board of Wycliffe Bible Translators* (1942-1956). He died of a heart attack while rescuing a swimmer at a summer Navigator conference in the Adirondacks.

BIBLIOGRAPHY. E. Wallis, *Lengthened Cords: How Dawson Trotman, Founder of the Navigators, Also Helped Extend the Worldwide Outreach of the Wycliffe Bible Translators* (1958); B. L. Skinner, *Daws: The Story of Dawson Trotman, Founder of the Navigators* (1974). D. D. Bundy

Trotter, Melvin Ernest (1870-1940). Evangelist* and founder of urban rescue missions.* Born in Orangeville, Illinois, one of seven children, Trotter had little formal schooling before going to work as a bartender and barber. Addicted to alcohol Trotter would frequently leave his wife as he went on drinking binges. After the death of their two-year-old child, one such trip led to Chicago in January 1897. Broke, shoeless and coatless, Trotter wandered into the Pacific Garden Mission* where he heard a sermon by Harry Monroe and was converted.*

Trotter's repentance was not short-lived. Immediately he took up barbering, sent for his wife and began volunteering his spare time at the mission. Eventually he became a traveling evangelist with Harry Monroe. The two men started a city mission in Grand Rapids, Michigan. Eventually named the Mel Trotter Mission, this ministry was headed by Trotter, who also planted urban missions* in states such as Minnesota, Michigan, Ohio and California. Until his death on September 11, 1940, Mel Trotter built missions and worked as an itinerant evangelist.

BIBLIOGRAPHY. M. E. Trotter, *These Forty Years* (1939); F. Zarfas, *Mel Trotter, A Biography* (1950); E. Reese, *Mel Trotter* (n.d.). L. W. Dorsett

Truett, George Washington (1867-1944). Baptist* pastor and denominational* leader. Born near Hayesville, North Carolina, he attended the Hayesville Academy (1875-1885) and then taught in a one-room school. To earn funds to study law, he opened a school in Hiawassee, Georgia, in 1887, which in two years grew to 300 students and three teachers.

Converted* in 1886 during revival* services, Truett joined the Hayesville Baptist Church. In 1889 he moved with his family to Whitewright, Texas, where he became active in the Baptist church and was ordained* in 1890. Soon after, he was chosen financial agent of Baylor University and in twenty-three months raised sufficient funds to rid the school of a $92,000 debt.

In 1893 he entered Baylor as a student and in 1897 received his B.A. While in college he served the East Waco Baptist Church, and upon his graduation he became pastor of the First Baptist Church, Dallas, where he remained until his death. During his forty-seven-year pastorate, membership increased from 715 to 7,804 with a total of 19,531 new members actually received and contributions in excess of $6 million.

Truett's ministry was distinguished by pulpit eloquence, pastoral effectiveness and outstanding leadership in his denomination. He served as president of the Southern Baptist Convention* for three years (1927-1929) and as president of the Baptist World Alliance* (1934-1939). He was active in founding the first Baptist hospital in Texas, invited by President Woodrow Wilson* to preach to American troops in Europe in 1918 and elected in 1919 to lead in raising $75 million for denominational causes. On May 16, 1920, he preached his famous sermon, "Baptists and Religious Liberty," to 15,000 people from the Capitol steps in Washington.

For fifty years Truett's ministry was woven into the life of Texas Baptists. Held in greatest esteem by all Baptists, he was viewed as an example of what a preacher and Southern Christian gentleman ought to be.

BIBLIOGRAPHY. P. W. James, *George W. Truett: A Biography* (1939); *DAB* 3. W. M. Patterson

Trumbull, Charles Gallaudet (1872-1941). Leader of American Keswick movement.* Born in Hartford, Connecticut, Trumbull graduated from Yale* in 1893 and went to work with his father, Henry Clay Trumbull,* editor of the *Sunday School*

Times. After his father's death in 1903, Trumbull assumed the editorship. In 1910 he converted to Keswick sanctification* and turned his editorial energies to promoting the message that Spirit-filled believers could have victory over sin and power for service. Trumbull also organized the Victorious Life* Testimony, which conducted summer conferences at a variety of locations until 1924, when a permanent conference was established at Keswick Grove, New Jersey. Thanks to Trumbull's promotional labors, numerous similar conferences were established throughout North America.

Trumbull also participated in the post-World War 1 fundamentalist* movement, and wrote both a glowing biography of C. I. Scofield* and weekly Sunday-school lessons for numerous newspapers. But Trumbull's most significant contribution was his role in gaining widespread acceptance for Keswick Holiness* teachings among American and Canadian evangelicals.

BIBLIOGRAPHY. D. W. Frank, *Less Than Conquerors: How Evangelicals Entered the Twentieth Century* (1986); E. R. Sandeen, *The Roots of Fundamentalism: British and American Millenarianism, 1800-1930* (1970).

W. V. Trollinger

Trumbull, David (1819-1889). First Protestant* American missionary* to Chile. A Congregational* minister and son of a governor of Connecticut, Trumbull completed studies at Yale* and Princeton Seminary* before responding to an appeal from the foreign residents of Valparaiso for a resident Protestant pastor. He was sent jointly by the Foreign Evangelical Society and the Seaman's Friend Society, arriving in 1845. His winsomeness, as well as the liberal attitude of the Chilean authorities, allowed him to work freely even among the Roman Catholic* population. A church for Chileans in his home resulted in the acquisition of property and completion of a chapel* by 1856. Trumbull's cooperation with all denominations has been credited with the absence of sectarian divisions in Chile that have afflicted missionary work in the neighboring republics. His efforts to influence legislation contributed to the granting of religious toleration in 1865, the opening of cemeteries to Protestants in 1883 and civil marriage in 1884. Trumbull took Chilean citizenship in 1886, and when he died three years later, the Chilean congress suspended its sessions in a display of respect.

BIBLIOGRAPHY. J. B. A. Kessler, Jr., *A Study of the Older Protestant Missions and Churches in Peru*

and Chile (1967); W. R. Wheeler et al., *Modern Missions in Chile and Brazil* (1926).

E. A. Wilson

Trumbull, Henry Clay (1830-1903). Leader in the American Sunday-school movement.* Born at Stonington, Connecticut, Trumbull was educated at the Stonington Academy and Williston Seminary in Massachusetts. After working for the railroads (1851-1858), he began his lifelong work with the Sunday-school movement. Trumbull was ordained* a Congregational* minister (1862) and then served as chaplain* in the Union army. After the Civil War* (1865) he became secretary for the New England department of the Sunday School Union.

At first dissuaded in this by Horace Bushnell,* Trumbull was later given unqualified support. As chair of the Fifth National Sunday School Convention (1872), Trumbull promoted the International Uniform Sunday School Lessons. A prolific author, he became editor of the *Sunday School Times* in 1875 and wrote numerous books on topics dealing with Christian education as well as theology. In 1888 he delivered the Lyman Beecher* Lectures at Yale,* later published as *The Sunday School: Its Origin, Mission, Methods, and Auxiliaries* (1893). There he defended the thesis that the Sunday school is "an agency approved of God for the evangelizing and the religious training of the race . . . pre-eminently adapted to the needs of our American communities." His son, Charles G. Trumbull,* later succeeded him as editor of the *Sunday School Times* and became a noted leader in the Holiness Movement.*

BIBLIOGRAPHY. *DAB* X; P. E. Howard, *The Life Story of Henry Clay Trumbull* (1905).

R. L. Petersen

Trusteeism. A lay* movement seeking to adapt European Catholicism* to American republican values, trusteeism emphasized the centrality of lay participation at the congregational level and exclusive lay control of ecclesiastical temporalities. Catholic bishops* and many pastors* vigorously resisted the movement, insisting that congregational lay leaders had usurped episcopal* and pastoral authority* within the church. Lay and clerical claims and counterclaims gave rise to a series of contracted debates and hostilities within a number of Catholic congregations during the antebellum period.

Lay trusteeism arose from a variety of sources, but it was legally grounded in the trustee system. According to American law, every congregation that wanted legal protection for its property had to elect a board of trustees who would be responsible for ecclesiastical temporalities. The elected trustees were corporately accountable for church debts, pastors' salaries, and for hiring and firing those who worked for the church (e. g., sextons, organists, teachers, building contractors). From Boston to New Orleans, lay Catholics during the antebellum period formed congregations according to this American legislation and thereby received legal sanction for many of their powers within the congregations. These legal sanctions, the general republican atmosphere, the congregational practices of other Christian denominations and the European Catholic practice of patronage gave many of the elected lay trustees support for their demands for lay leadership and even control of their congregations.

Lay trustees throughout the country argued, as did members of other ecclesiastical traditions, that the Church in the U.S. should be distinctively American in its manner of government. Within the Catholic Church this meant that temporal ecclesiastical concerns should be under the control of the laity and spiritual concerns under the authority of the clergy.* This division of powers within the Church corresponded to ancient Catholic as well as American distinctions. As the congregations' elected representatives, many lay trustees asserted that they had the right and duty to select their pastors, establish a description of the pastoral role and fire them when they proved incompetent or unacceptable in the congregation. The trustees' claims reflected the aspirations of many Americans at the time: the voice of the people is the voice of God—in church as in state.

The trustees' republican-based arguments for lay authority within the Church were reinforced by arguments from the Catholic tradition. They claimed that the ancient Catholic practice of lay patronage should be instituted in the U.S. in a way that acknowledged American voluntaryism.* Lay patronage in the European Catholic legal tradition had acknowledged that those who built or financially supported congregations had the right to select and reject pastors. The Catholic people who supported their churches through their free-will offerings, therefore, should be acknowledged as legal patrons in the U.S. The claims for the lay role in the Church were thus consistent, the trustees argued, with the Catholic as well as the American republican traditions.

The anti-trustee party, those who joined the bishops in opposition to the trustees' demands, charged that the trustees' claims, if fully implemented, would destroy Catholic identity. The trustees had identified Catholicism with a republicanism and Protestantism* which asserted that all authority, ecclesiastical as well as political, arose from the people. This was absolutely contrary to the Catholic view, which held that all ecclesiastical authority arose from divine commission. The trustees' administration of congregational temporalities, most bishops asserted, could be tolerated as long as their authority was subordinate in all things to that of the pastors and bishops. They could not claim an independent authority within the congregations. To do so, the bishops argued, would produce a republican captivity of the Church.

The antitrustees believed that the American separation of church and state* provided a providential opportunity for the Catholic Church to be freed from excessive lay and governmental interference in ecclesiastical affairs and to develop episcopal authority without any lay restraints. In Europe, lay interference had frequently impinged upon ecclesiastical freedom. Lay intervention in pastoral appointments represented the worst kind of tyranny, made pastors slaves of congregational whim and at times imprisoned the preaching* of the gospel. Under trustee circumstances not only would pastoral authority be practically eliminated, but the Church's message would be utterly dependent upon the cultural and political condition of the congregation.

From 1829 to 1855, the bishops—through individual efforts, conciliar* legislation, papal support and new American laws—were able to crush the republican lay assertiveness behind trusteeism and to gain for themselves legal control over ecclesiastical properties and temporalities. Lay trustees continued to function in many congregations, but they did so under the pastoral and episcopal arm.

The tensions created by trusteeism had a significant effect upon the development of American Catholicism. The memories of the antebellum battles were almost indelibly etched upon clerical consciousness. Trusteeism unwittingly aided the formation of a strong centralized episcopal authority in American Catholicism, made the subsequent episcopacy suspicious of lay participation in ecclesiastical government and supported American nativists' charges that Catholicism and republicanism were ideologically and practically incompatible. Because elements of republicanism were not appropriated in ecclesiastical government, American Catholicism after the Civil War* was periodically disturbed by lay-clerical tensions, repeated calls for lay rights and attempts to create a more effective constitutional balance of powers within the Church.

See also HOGAN SCHISM.

BIBLIOGRAPHY. P. Carey, *People, Priests and Prelates: Ecclesiastical Democracy and the Tensions of Trusteeism* (1987); V. J. Fecher, *A Study of the Movement for German National Parishes in Philadelphia and Baltimore (1787-1802)* (1985); D. Gerber, "Modernity in the Service of Tradition: Catholic Lay Trustees at Buffalo's St. Louis Church and the Transformation of European Communal Traditions, 1829-1855," *JSH* 15 (1983):655-684; R. McNamara, "Trusteeism in the Atlantic States, 1785-1863," *CHR* 30 (1944):135-54; F. E. Tourscher, *The Hogan Schism and Trustee Troubles in St. Mary's Church, Philadelphia, 1820-1829* (1930).

P. W. Carey

Truth, Sojourner (Isabella Baumfree) (c.1797-1883). Abolitionist* and women's rights lecturer. Born an African-American slave to a Dutch master in Ulster County, New York, Isabella Baumfree, called "Bell," was separated from her family and sold twice before she was twelve years old. Emancipated by her master in 1827, by 1829 she was supporting herself as a domestic helper in New York City, where she became associated with Elijah Pierson, a religious visionary who in 1833 began a commune with Isabella and others. The venture failed within about two years.

Isabella left New York on June 1, 1843, in response to a vision of God telling her to "travel up an' down the land showin' the people their sins an' bein' a sign unto them." Asking God for a new name to complement her mission, she became "Sojourner Truth." Tall and stout, head wrapped in a Madras handkerchief turban, unable to read or write, Sojourner Truth spread the abolitionist message of freedom, using biblical references and stories in her heavy Dutch accent. She became famous throughout the North as an itinerant preacher,* abolitionist and advocate for the poor and women's rights.

At age sixty-seven she toured Indiana, lecturing before hostile audiences for the National Woman's Loyal League, ignoring a new law forbidding African-Americans from entering the state. In the fall of 1864 she met with President Lincoln.* At the end of the Civil War* she became a counselor for the National Freedmen's Relief Association and lived in the Freedmen's Village in Arlington Heights, Virginia. Later she worked in the Freedmen's Hospital in Washington, D.C.

In her old age Sojourner Truth settled in Battle Creek, Michigan, but she remained an active advocate of women's rights, Reconstruction policies to protect and educate the freed slaves, and resettlement of freed slaves in the West. She died at Battle Creek in November 1883.

BIBLIOGRAPHY. *DARB;* A. H. Fauset, *Sojourner Truth: God's Faithful Pilgrim* (1971); O. Gilbert, *Narrative of Sojourner Truth. A Northern Slave* (1850); *NAW* 3; V. Ortiz, *Sojourner Truth: A Self-Made Woman* (1974); H. E. Pauli, *Her Name Was Sojourner Truth* (1962).

L. J. Edwards

Tucker, Henry St. George (1874-1959). Episcopalian* missionary bishop* and ecclesiastical statesman. Born in Warsaw, Virginia, Tucker followed in his father's footsteps as a church leader. He was trained at the University of Virginia (M.A., 1895) and the Virginia Theological Seminary (B.D. and D.D., 1899). In 1899 he went as a missionary* to northern Honshu, Japan, moving in 1902 to Tokyo as president of what has become Rikkyo Daigaku (St. Paul's University). In 1912 he became missionary bishop of Kyoto, where a visitor years later remembered him as "tall [and] young." With time out for military service in Siberia during World War 1,* he remained in Kyoto until 1923 when he returned to Virginia to teach pastoral theology at Virginia Theological Seminary. Elected bishop* of Virginia in 1927 and presiding bishop in 1937, he became in 1942 the most prominent American Protestant* voice, as president of the Federal Council of the Churches of Christ in America.* An outspoken critic of social injustice, he articulated the American conscience in the fateful 1930s and 1940s.

BIBLIOGRAPHY. H. S. Tucker, *Exploring the Silent Shore of Memory* (1951); *DAB* 6.

J. F. Howes

Tucker, William Jewett (1839-1926). Congregationalist* theologian* and educator. Born in Griswold, Connecticut, Tucker was educated at Dartmouth* (B.A., 1861) and Andover Theological Seminary* (B.D., 1866). He worked with the United States Christian Commission* during the Civil War,* and the American Home Missionary Society* before assuming pastorates in Manchester, New Hampshire (1867-1875), and New York City (1875-1879). In 1880 Tucker became professor of sacred rhetoric at Andover Seminary, in which position he developed pastoral courses in sociology (then a novelty in American seminaries). In 1891 he founded a social settlement in Boston's South End (Andover House) which, modeled on London's Toynbee Hall, elicited widespread notice and imitation.

At Andover Tucker also became one of the foremost leaders in a liberal theological movement sweeping Congregationalism, known as the "New Theology."* This movement eventuated in Tucker and four other professors publishing the *Andover Review* (1884), one of the most famous Protestant* journals in nineteenth-century America. The *Review's* publication in 1886 of a number of its most important articles under the title "Progressive Orthodoxy" quickly attracted the unfavorable attention of the conservative wing of Congregationalism. Because of its doctrine of a "second probation" for non-Christians, it was particularly disturbing to leaders of the missionary movement.* Tucker and the other editors were tried and acquitted in 1886 by the Seminary Board of Visitors.

In 1893 Tucker became president of Dartmouth College, where his educational vision and business acumen made that struggling college into a nationally respected institution. Tucker's autobiography, *My Generation* (1919), is generally considered an invaluable resource on late nineteenth-century liberal* Protestantism.

BIBLIOGRAPHY. *DAB* X; *DARB*; *NCAB* 24; D. D. Williams, *The Andover Liberals* (1941).

M. S. Massa

Turkevich, Leonty (1876-1965). Russian Orthodox* Metropolitan* of All America and Canada. Recruited from his mission* among the Nestorians in Persia in 1906 by Bishop Tikhon Bellavin,* for nearly six decades Turkevich was to provide leadership in the Russian Mission and later in the Metropolia. He authored its statutes, led its councils, edited its publications and advanced the somewhat unpopular cause of theological education. As the first dean of the North American Seminary in Minneapolis, he modified the prescribed Russian curriculum to fit the American situation, lectured over twenty hours a week and bore the brunt of administration—all while pastoring one of the largest parishes* in the diocese* and writing extensively in the major church journals of his day. In old age he served as president of St. Vladimir's Seminary in New York and launched a major faculty-development drive.

As America's delegate to the 1917 All-Russian Council in Moscow, he experienced firsthand the power of such gatherings. At the next four All-American Councils, held between 1924 and 1955, his was often the decisive voice. In controversy with the other, smaller factions of the Russian Church throughout the 1940s, 1950s and early 1960s, Turkevich championed the Metropolia's

anticommunism, while at the same time eschewing the Synod Abroad's pan-Russianism, in favor of Tikhon's vision of a missionary-minded territorial Orthodox Church in America. Advanced to the episcopacy in 1933, he served the diocese* of Chicago until his elevation to the metropolitan throne following the death of Theophilus Pashkovsky in 1950.

BIBLIOGRAPHY. *DAB* 7; "A Life of Service," *St. Vladimir's Seminary Quarterly* (Summer 1965); Russian Orthodox Church in America, *The Life and Work of the Most Reverend Metropolitan Leonty* [in Russian] (1969).

P. D. Garrett

Turner, Henry McNeal (1834-1915). Born a free African-American at Newberry Courthouse, South Carolina, Turner joined the Methodist Episcopal Church,* South, in 1848 and was licensed* to preach* in 1853. He then became a popular revivalist* in Georgia and other Southern states. Joining the African Methodist Episcopal Church (AME)* in 1858, he filled pastorates in Baltimore and Washington, D.C., until, in 1863 during the Civil War,* he helped recruit the first United States Colored Troops and was appointed the regiment's chaplain.* He was present at the Battle of Petersburg and numerous other engagements in Virginia and North Carolina.

During Reconstruction, Turner was the chief organizer of the AME Church in Georgia. He was elected to the Georgia State House of Representatives in 1868 and briefly served as U.S. Postmaster in Macon, Georgia, in 1869, returning to the state legislature in 1870. After Reconstruction, he returned to full-time church work, filling various local and national church offices before being elected a bishop* of the AME Church in 1880.

A vigorous human rights advocate, he denounced Supreme Court decisions in 1883 and 1896 denying federal civil rights* protection to African-Americans. During the 1890s, he made four trips to Africa, helping to organize AME churches in Liberia, Sierra Leone and South Africa. Turner strongly supported "back to Africa" movements in the U.S., and is now widely recognized as a precursor of modern-day black theology* for his 1898 statement that "God is a Negro." Increasingly embittered in his later years toward his country of birth, he died in Windsor, Ontario, in 1915.

BIBLIOGRAPHY. *DAB* X; E. S. Redkey, ed., *Respect Black: The Writings and Speeches of Henry McNeal Turner* (1971); R. R. Wright, Jr., *The Bishops of the African Methodist Episcopal Church* (1963).

S. W. Angell

Turner, Nat (1800-1831). Leader of a slave revolt and lay* preacher.* Turner was born in Southampton County, Virginia, in the same year that Gabriel and Samson Prosser led an insurrection nearby. A slave of Benjamin Turner, Nat's father ran away. In 1821 Nat escaped, but voluntarily returned, earning a sale to Thomas Moore, and eight years later to Joseph Travis. Turner was depicted as deeply religious, living an ascetic life filled with messianic notions. He assumed the role of exhorter or lay preacher, heard by whites as well as slaves. One account tells of a white overseer baptizing* him in 1825.

Inspired by certain biblical texts, Turner began to receive visions and signs that he would liberate his people. Astrological events led him to choose August 22, 1831, for the revolt, when about sixty men joined him in killing fifty-seven white Virginians. Within a day most of the group was captured or killed, but Turner remained at large until October 30. Jailed at Jerusalem, Virginia, he was tried, found guilty and executed on November 11. Folk traditions in black America revered Turner's memory, composing songs and narratives about the feats of this apocalyptically obsessed, militant slave. His story also inspired *Dred*, by Harriet Beecher Stowe,* and *Nat Turner's Confessions*, by William Styron, both white novelists.

BIBLIOGRAPHY. J. H. Clarke, ed., *William Stryon's Nat Turner* (1968); *DAB* X; H. I. Tragle, *The Southampton Slave Revolt of 1831* (1971).

W. B. Gravely and C. White

Tuttle, Daniel Sylvester (1837-1923). Episcopal* bishop.* Born in Windham, New York, Tuttle graduated from Columbia College* in 1857 and General Theological Seminary in 1862. In 1863 he was ordained* priest* and served until 1867 in the rural parish* of Morris, New York.

To his surprise, Tuttle was elected missionary bishop* of Montana in 1866, though he had not yet reached the canonical age of thirty. He was consecrated* in 1867, and then left his wife and infant son behind to set out for the Rocky Mountain Jurisdiction, which included Montana, Idaho and Utah. The new territory, which had been established by the 1865 general convention, stretched out across 340,000 square miles without even a single ordained priest.

For the next nineteen years "Bishop Dan" labored in his pioneering ministry, often preaching* in mining towns or stocktenders' stations where clergy had never traveled. Most of his work was concentrated in an arc that stretched from Salt Lake City through Boise to Helena. In 1868 he was elected bishop of Missouri but declined the position because he believed that his labors in the West had just begun. The next year he settled his family in Salt Lake City, where he earned the respect of Mormon* leaders by his philanthropic activities.

Churches in the territory soon developed under Tuttle's care, and in 1872 he established St. Mark's Hospital. He also founded a number of schools. By 1886, when he gave in to urgent requests from the diocese* of Missouri to become bishop there, he had traveled more than forty thousand miles by stagecoach across his episcopal territory. Tuttle spent the rest of his life serving in St. Louis, and in 1903 became presiding bishop of the church, the last to do so by reason of seniority.

BIBLIOGRAPHY. *DAB* X; *DARB*; *NCAB* 6; D. S. Tuttle, *Reminiscences of a Missionary Bishop* (1906). T. P. Thigpen

Tyler, Bennet (1783-1858). Congregational* minister,* educator and theologian.* A native of Connecticut and trained at Yale College* (B.A., 1804), Tyler studied theology* under Asahel Hooker at Goshen, Connecticut, pastored at South Britain, Connecticut (1801-1822), and then served as president of Dartmouth College* (1822-1828). He later served as a pastor in Portland, Maine (1828-1834). Tyler became famous in 1829 when he engaged in a dispute with Yale theologian Nathaniel W. Taylor.* In his *Concio ad Clerum* (1828), Taylor sought to revise the traditional notions of human depravity and original sin.* For Taylor, human nature was not morally disabled because of Adam's first sin. Rather, "sin was in the sinning"; individual immoral acts constituted human depravity, not the primeval fall of Adam.

Tyler viewed such progressive theology as a dangerous defection from traditional Calvinism.* In response to this threat, he mounted a campaign to defend traditional Congregationalism* from the encroachment of liberal "Taylorism." Joining with other conservatives, notably Leonard Woods* of Andover Seminary,* Tyler attempted to revive the theological outlooks of the Puritan* tradition and Jonathan Edwards.* This complex theological paper war between New England's progressives and conservatives—an important chapter in the history of Reformed theology in America—soon was given the name *the Tyler-Taylor controversy.*

In 1833, in an attempt to offset the growing influence of Taylor and Lyman Beecher* (known as the *New Haven theologians*), the conservative party formed a new seminary.* Located in East Windsor, Connecticut, the Theological Institute of

Connecticut (later renamed Hartford Theological Seminary) became a bastion of conservative Congregationalism in the antebellum period. Tyler served as president of the Institute from its opening until his death in 1858.

BIBLIOGRAPHY. *DAB* X; *DARB*; S. E. Mead, *Nathaniel William Taylor, 1786-1858: A Connecticut Liberal* (1942); *NCAB* 9; B. Tyler, *Letters on the Origins and Progress of the New Haven Theology From a New England Minister to One at the South* (1837). J. R. Fitzmier

Tyler-Taylor Controversy. *See* TYLER, BENNET.

Tyng, Stephen Higginson, Jr. (1839-1898). Evangelical* Episcopal* rector* and premillennialist* leader. Born in Philadelphia, the son of the Rev. Stephen H. Tyng,* he graduated from Williams College, Massachusetts, in 1858 and continued his studies in the Protestant Episcopal Seminary of Virginia. The outbreak of the Civil War* interrupted his studies in his senior year. He was ordained* a deacon of the Protestant Episcopal Church* on May 8, 1861, and for two years served as his father's assistant at St. George's Episcopal Church in New York City. On Sept. 11, 1863, he was ordained* priest* and installed as rector of the Church of the Mediator in New York.

Following the Civil War Tyng organized the Church of the Holy Trinity in New York City. There he developed an outstanding church, combining a strong evangelical witness and an effective outreach to the urban poor. Tyng became one of the leading Protestants of the 1860s and 1870s, and his church has been called "one of the great mission churches of America" during its time. Like his father, Stephen Tyng, Jr. was a premillennialist, authoring a book entitled *He Will Come* (1877). He organized the first International Prophetic Conference in 1878, which was held in his church.

Tyng retired from the ministry in 1881 because of ill health. To support his family after leaving the ministry, he entered the business world and spent a number of years in Paris as a representative of the Equitable Life Assurance Society of New York and as European manager of the Mutual Reserve Fund Life Association of New York. He died in Paris in 1898.

BIBLIOGRAPHY. *NCAB* 2. P. C. Wilt

Tyng, Stephen Higginson, Sr. (1800-1885). Episcopal* minister.* Born in Newburyport, Massachusetts, Tyng graduated from Harvard College* at the age of seventeen and after two years in business left to prepare for ministry in the Episcopal Church. He studied theology* under Alexander V. Griswold* and was ordained* deacon* in 1821 and priest* in 1824. Tyng's fifty-seven years in the ministry took him to St. John's Church, Georgetown, D.C. (1821-1823); Queen Anne's Parish, Prince George County, Maryland (1823-1829); St. Paul's Church, Philadelphia (1829-1834); Church of the Epiphany, Philadelphia (1834-1845) and St. George's Church, New York City (1845-1878).

A convinced evangelical* low churchman,* Tyng was a vehement opponent of both the Tractarian Movement* and broad-church* liberalism.* Perhaps because of his outspoken convictions, he never rose in church leadership. Yet he was a commanding orator and pulpiteer. Henry Ward Beecher* described him as "the one man that I am afraid of. When he speaks first I do not care to follow him." Thousands flocked to hear Tyng at St. Paul's in Philadelphia (known as "Tyng's Theatre"). He was also a vigorous promoter of Sunday schools,* attracting more than two thousand children to his own Sunday school in Philadelphia.

A premillenialist* and nearly a perfectionist* in his view of sanctification,* Tyng nevertheless carried out a strong commitment to social work, as evidenced in his promotion of the American Female Guardian Society and Home for the Friendless in New York City. His son, Stephen H. Tyng, Jr.,* an Episcopal minister in New York City, shared in his father's evangelical convictions and commitment to urban social work.

BIBLIOGRAPHY. *DAB* X; C. R. Tyng, *Record of the Life and Work of the Rev. Stephen Higginson Tyng, D.D.* (1890). D. G. Reid

U

UFM International. Nondenominational foreign missionary* agency. Unevangelized Fields Mission (UFM) began as a faith mission in London in 1931, comprising several missionaries who had earlier ministered in Brazil and the Congo with Worldwide Evangelization Crusade. In the same year, Edwin J. Pudney and his wife established an autonomous North American headquarters in Toronto. The Pudneys' leadership shaped the mission for the next thirty years. In 1941 they opened a new headquarters in Philadelphia, which was later moved to suburban Bala Cynwyd in 1954. Over the years UFM has grown through several mergers, incorporating the World Christian Crusade (Dominican Republic) in 1949, the Alpine Mission to France in 1962 and the Mexican Indian Mission in 1971. In addition, the society developed other fields in several European countries as well as Haiti, Guyana, Indonesia, Quebec, South Africa and the Philippines. In 1977 the Australian, British and North American branches of UFM recognized each other as separate, independent organizations with their respective mission fields. The North American agency officially changed its name to UFM International in 1980.

Currently UFM emphasizes evangelism,* church planting, training national leadership, Bible* translation, medicine and radio broadcasting in seventeen foreign countries, as well as in New Mexico and Puerto Rico. Expansion on the European front is anticipated in Portugal. Since 1966 Alfred Larson has held the office of general director, and he manages a full-time missionary corps of over 300 and a total annual income of close to $5 million. The mission is affiliated with the Interdenominational Foreign Mission Association of North America.*

BIBLIOGRAPHY. M. Odman, "Unevangelized Fields Mission," *The Encyclopedia of Modern Christian Missions,* ed. B. L. Goddard; C. E. Piepgrass, "50 Years Retrospect," *Lifeline* 43 (February 1981):1-12.   J. A. Patterson

Ukrainian Catholics in America. Christians whose church is under the jurisdiction of the pope* of Rome but whose church law is that of Eastern Orthodoxy.* They are also called *Ruthenian Catholics, Byzantine Rite Catholics* or *Uniates.* The church's history began with the Union of Brest in 1596, when many Russian Orthodox churches within the expanding Polish kingdom agreed to accept Rome's authority in exchange for the right to retain their Orthodox practices, most notably the use of Slavonic instead of Latin in the liturgy* and the tradition of allowing priests* to be married.

In the late 1800s, people from these churches began to immigrate to the U.S. The first such emigrants* from the Austrian Empire were known as *Ruthenians.* Many later emigrants from the Russian Empire had begun calling themselves *Ukrainian,* and eventually this name was accepted. In North America, Ukrainian Catholics experienced considerable religious conflict. Latin rite* Catholics tried to compel them to give up their Eastern traditions and follow Western ways. Eventually a papal decree in 1929 confirmed their right to maintain their distinct religious practices. After World War 2,* new emigration from Soviet-controlled territories increased their numbers. The Soviet state declared the Ukrainian Catholic Church illegal.

The more than 200,000 Ukrainian Catholics in America are led by a metropolitan* archbishop* with his cathedral* in Philadelphia and by annual synods of their bishops.* Ukrainians have been requesting that the pope approve an international patriarchal administration for all Ukrainian Catholics (over 4 million worldwide), but until now it has been denied. Part of the reason for this denial is that the Church remains illegal in its native territorial base.

BIBLIOGRAPHY. B. P. Procko, *Ukrainian Catholics in America* (1982).   P. D. Steeves

Ultradispensationalism. A movement within dispensationalism* which argues that the church began after the Day of Pentecost. All dispensationalists make a sharp distinction between Israel and the church and are thus concerned to show when the administration of God's redemptive plan shifted from one to the other. Most believe that the shift occurred in the events described in Acts 2, on the Day of Pentecost. But some others, labelled "ultra" by the majority, point to later times (Acts 13 or 28).

Acts 28 dispensationalism was championed by Ethelbert W. Bullinger (1837-1913), who found three phases in the transition from Israel to the church. The first encompassed the period of the Gospels in which Christ offered the kingdom to the Jews, whose acceptance was marked by water baptism. The second comprised the transitional time in Acts and the early epistles when the apostles invited Jews to join the "bride church" by accepting both water and Spirit baptism.* The third began toward the end of Paul's ministry (Acts 28:26-28 and the prison epistles) when Jews and Gentiles were brought into the body of Christ through Spirit baptism alone. Consequently, followers of "Bullingerism" do not practice the Lord's Supper* or water baptism because they do not belong to the dispensation of the completed church of Jew and Gentile.

According to Acts 13 dispensationalism, as taught by Charles F. Baker, Cornelius R. Stam and others, the church began when Paul started his mission to both Jews and Gentiles (Acts 13:2). Unlike Acts 28 dispensationalists, Baker argues for the uniformity of Paul's teachings about the church throughout his epistles and accepts the continuing relevance of the Lord's Supper for the church age. However, this view still sees water baptism as a transitional practice meant for Jews, but not for Gentiles entering the church (1 Cor 1:13-17), for whom Spirit baptism is sufficient.

See also DISPENSATIONALISM.

BIBLIOGRAPHY. E. W. Bullinger, *How to Enjoy the Bible* (1900); C. F. Baker, *A Dispensational Theology* (1971); C. C. Ryrie, *Dispensationalism Today* (1965). T. P. Weber

Ultramontanism. The movement in Roman Catholicism to centralize authority in the papacy.* Meaning literally "over the mountains," it initially referred to those in the French Church who resisted Gallicanism* and looked over the Alps to the pope for direction. Ultramontanism grew greatly in the nineteenth century and found strong defenders in both Canada and the U.S. In Quebec, under the leadership of bishops such as Jean-Jacques Lartigue,* Ignace Bourget* and Louis-Francois Lafleche, a very conservative ultra-

montanism became the most vocal and influential sector of the Church. It sought to reform society along Roman Catholic lines. The *programme catholique* of 1871 gave expression to some of these ultramontane ideas. These provoked fierce conflict both within and without the Church and became a major factor in Quebec politics. Ultramontanism also became an important element in the development of French Canadian nationalism. A central contention of ultramontanism—papal infallibility*—was affirmed by the First Vatican Council* (1869-1870).

See also VATICAN—U.S. CATHOLIC CHURCH RELATIONS.

BIBLIOGRAPHY. J. W. Grant, *The Church in the Canadian Era* (1972). K. M. Cassidy

Unction. The sacrament* of healing in the Roman Catholic* and Eastern Orthodox* churches, based on the New Testament (Mk 6:13 and Jas 5:14-16) and on early Christian tradition, such as Hippolytus' *Apostolic Tradition* and Serapion of Thmuis' *Euchologion.* A consistent tradition shows its use in various forms to the present.

Medieval practice in Western Christianity limited the sacrament to those who were dying, hence, the name *Extreme Unction.* Vatican II* restored it to its earlier healing purpose. In the Orthodox tradition the rite consisted of two prayers,* one of consecration* and one of anointing* as part of a eucharistic* service until the twelfth century. At that time it was extensively developed. It may be that this development took place when, in Byzantium, the church lost control of its hospitals. There has been a renewal of interest in spiritual healing and the sacrament of unction in the latter part of the twentieth century.

BIBLIOGRAPHY. S. S. Harakas, "The Eastern Orthodox Tradition," *Caring and Curing: Health and Medicine in the Western Religious Traditions,* ed. R. L. Numbers and D. W. Amundsen (1986); P. F. Palmer, *Sacraments and Forgiveness: History and Doctrinal Development of Penance, Extreme Unction and Indulgences* (1959).

S. S. Harakas

Unevangelized Fields Mission. *See* UFM INTERNATIONAL.

Unger, Merrill F. (1909-1980). Old Testament scholar, writer and popular conference speaker. Born in Baltimore, Maryland, Unger was educated at Johns Hopkins University (A.B., 1930; Ph.D., 1947), where he did his doctorate in Semitics and biblical archaeology, and at Dallas Theological Seminary* (Th.M., 1943; Th.D., 1945). He began his teaching career at Gordon College of Theology and Missions and Gordon Divinity School (1947-1948), teaching Greek and Old Testament studies respectively. From 1948 to 1967 he served as professor of Semitics and Old Testament at Dallas Theological Seminary. In addition to teaching he pastored several churches (Buffalo, New York, 1934-1940; Dallas, Texas, 1943-1944; Baltimore, Maryland (1944-1947), and published widely. His major books include *Introductory Guide to the Old Testament* (1951), *Biblical Demonology* (1952), *Archaeology and the Old Testament* (1954), *Unger's Bible Dictionary* (1957) and *Demons in the World Today* (1971). He served as assistant editor of *Bibliotheca Sacra* after 1956, becoming a regular contributor to it as well as to numerous other religious periodicals. His teaching and writings reflect the theological orientation of the school he served: dispensational* premillennialism.*

J. D. Hannah

Uniates. *See* Eastern-Rite Catholics.

Unification Church, The. A new religious movement founded in 1954. The founder of The Unification Church, the Reverend Sun Myung Moon, was born of Presbyterian* parents in Korea, January 6, 1920. Although the movement's first American churches were established in the 1960s, it was during the 1970s that Moon first toured the U.S. and his group achieved visibility in the media as increasing numbers of young adults joined. Followers of Moon, popularly known as Moonies, became known for their zealous recruitment tactics and fund-raising efforts. Critics charged that the organization engaged in brainwashing and other authoritarian practices. Parents sometimes attempted to deprogram or coercively remove members from the group. Moonies claimed persecution by the press, the government and anti-cultists.

Moon's doctrine can be traced to a dramatic experience he claims took place on Easter morning in 1936 when Jesus appeared to him on a Korean mountainside and told him he was chosen to complete the earthly mission that Jesus failed to carry out fully. For the next nine years, Moon received a series of revelations which comprise the core of the movement's major book, *Divine Principle* (1966, 1973). According to Unification theology, restoration (salvation) will be accomplished by the Lord of the Second Advent or Messiah, who will help unite all religions. Followers of Moon believe that he is that messenger of

God. In order to pursue their religious goals and to achieve legitimation in the larger society, Unificationists founded a seminary in New York State, sponsor many ecumenical and academic conferences, and promote anti-Communist forums. The church is also involved in various publishing and business enterprises.

Bibliography. J. I. Yamamoto, *The Puppet Master* (1977); F. Sontag, *Sun Myung Moon and the Unification Church* (1977); J. T. Biermans, *The Odyssey of New Religious Movements* (1986).

R. Enroth

Union Theological Seminary (New York). Protestant* mainline* seminary. Founded in 1836 by a group of New School* Presbyterian* leaders, the school quickly became one of the nation's larger seminaries, in great measure because of the prominence of biblical scholar Edward Robinson* and theologian Henry Boynton Smith.* Originally an independent institution that welcomed ministerial candidates of all evangelical* denominations,* Union became affiliated with the (Northern) Presbyterian Church when the Old and New School branches united in 1870 and gathered a strong faculty, including the famous historian Philip Schaff.* It reclaimed its independence in 1892 when that denomination was moving toward suspending from the ministry Charles Briggs,* controversial pioneer of biblical criticism. Twelve years later it became a fully nondenominational seminary. In 1910 the school moved with its strong faculty to new buildings on Morningside Heights, adjacent to Columbia University.*

Among Union's notable professors of the twentieth century have been Francis Brown,* Arthur C. McGiffert,* Harry Emerson Fosdick,* Henry Sloane Coffin,* Henry P. Van Dusen,* Reinhold Niebuhr,* Paul Tillich,* James Muilenburg, Mary Ely Lyman, Wilhelm Pauck,* Cyril C. Richardson, John Knox, John C. Bennett,* Daniel D. Williams,* Roger L. Shinn, Raymond E. Brown, Beverly Harrison and James H. Cone.* It has been open to a variety of theological trends, including liberal evangelical,* liberal,* ecumenical,* neo-orthodox* and liberation* movements. It is renowned for its theological library of more than half a million volumes, preeminent in the Western hemisphere. In its student body are not only those studying for church ministries, but also many in doctoral programs (some jointly with Columbia University) preparing for seminary and university teaching in religion.

Bibliography. H. S. Coffin, *A Half Century of Union Theological Seminary, 1896-1945: An*

Informal History (1954); R. T. Handy, *A History of Union Theological Seminary in New York* (1987).

R. T. Handy

Unitarian Controversy. The series of theological debates (1805-1825) between orthodox* Calvinists* and liberals* that split Massachusetts Congregationalism* and led to the formation of the American Unitarian Association.* Theological dispute had been building within Puritan* Congregationalism throughout the late eighteenth century, but the controversy was sharpened dramatically with the 1805 election of Henry Ware* as Hollis Professor of Divinity at Harvard.* The appointment was widely regarded as a key to the theological direction of Harvard, and the election of Ware suggested that the liberals were in ascendance. In response to Ware's election, the orthodox founded Andover Seminary* in 1808 to preserve the Calvinist viewpoint. The liberals responded over the next decade by the formation of a program for theological education at Harvard and the erection of Divinity Hall there. The controversy was deepened in 1815 when Jedediah Morse* reprinted an English account of the growth of Unitarian ideas in America under the title *American Unitarianism.*

Jeremiah Evarts used a review of the pamphlet as an occasion to attack the gradual and secretive growth of Unitarian views in Boston, and thereby raised the ire of many of the liberals. William Ellery Channing* was thrust into the leadership of the liberal defense with his *Letter to the Rev. Samuel Cooper Thacher* (1815) and his manifesto *Unitarian Christianity* (1819). The Orthodox position was expounded by Moses Stuart* in his *Letters to the Rev. Wm. E. Channing* (1819).

Another series of pamphlet debates was conducted by Ware and the orthodox spokesman Leonard Woods.* The controversy also reached the parish* level in many of the churches in eastern Massachusetts. A dispute over a ministerial appointment in Dedham* led to a court decision in 1820 through which many historic New England churches became Unitarian. By this time the liberals had begun to accept their identity as a separate movement, and in 1825, the American Unitarian Association, a forerunner of the present Unitarian Universalist Association,* was formed.

Underlying the institutional division of Massachusetts Congregationalism in these years was a profound theological difference, centering on two key issues: the nature of biblical interpretation and authority,* and the extent of human capacity for spiritual development. The Unitarians, strongly influenced by German scholarship, moved increasingly toward historically and rationally conditioned biblical interpretation. And in rejecting the Calvinist doctrine of innate sinful* depravity, the Unitarians stressed the cultivation of the spiritual resources inherent in the self, which had to be exhibited through a life of constant probation. These same issues would be debated later in many other American denominations, a suggestion that the Unitarian controversy was the first entry of modernism* into the American theological mainstream.

BIBLIOGRAPHY. C. C. Wright, "The Election of Henry Ware," *Harvard Library Bulletin* 17 (July 1969):245-278; C. Forman, " 'Elected Now by Time,' " in C. Wright, ed., *A Stream of Light* (1975); C. C. Wright, "The Controversial Career of Jedidiah Morse," *Harvard Library Bulletin* 31 (Winter 1983): 64-87; D. M. Robinson, *The Unitarians and the Universalists* (1985).

D. M. Robinson

Unitarian Universalist Association. The Unitarian Universalist Association (UUA) was established in 1961 with the merger of the American Unitarian Association* and the Universalist Church of America. Both were small denominations,* primarily of New England origin, that exemplified two separate courses of the development of religious liberalism* in America.

Unitarianism refers most generally to a belief that God is one Person rather than a trinity. Some free spirits of the Reformation era, such as Michael Servetus (1511-1553) and Lelius Socinus (1525-1604) and Faustus Socinus (1539-1604) held such beliefs, which flourished mainly in Poland, Hungary and Transylvania. English Unitarianism, based on philosophical materialism, came to America with the scientist Joseph Priestley* in the Revolutionary* era. American Unitarianism, however, had its most immediate origins among a group of mid-eighteenth-century Boston-area clergy* who became skeptical both of the revivalism* of the Great Awakening* and also of traditional Puritan* Calvinism.* These men, led by Charles Chauncy,* Ebenezer Gay* and Jonathan Mayhew,* were New England Arminians* who were especially hostile to the doctrine of original sin.* The first open rejection of the doctrine of the Trinity, however, came not from them but from Boston's Anglican* King's Chapel, which in 1785 prepared an edition of the Book of Common Prayer* devoid of Trinitarian references.

Although these Boston liberals did not wish to break formally with Puritan Congregationalism,* their hand was forced by conservatives such as

Jedidiah Morse,* who precipitated the first Unitarian controversy* during the early decades of the nineteenth century. The appointment of the liberal Henry Ware* as Hollis Professor at Harvard* in 1805 was a major victory. William Ellery Channing,* the movement's most eloquent spokesman, outlined the liberal position publicly in his Baltimore sermon of 1819. In 1825 the rift between factions of Congregationalists had become irreconcilable. The American Unitarian Association was founded in Boston as a loose institutional alliance of liberals and included eighty-eight of the hundred oldest congregations in eastern Massachusetts.

Meanwhile, another liberal movement was taking shape, not in cosmopolitan Boston, but primarily in smaller towns along the Atlantic coast. Universalism,* the doctrine that all of humanity would ultimately be saved, was first preached in New England by John Murray.* In Philadelphia, a "Society of Universal Baptists" was founded by Elhanan Winchester* and based on a similar optimistic message. Universalism was soon given systematic theological articulation and leadership through the work of Hosea Ballou* in writings such as his *Treatise on the Atonement* (1805) and his ministry* in Boston. Although the movement resisted tight organization, legal pressures led to the forming of the Universalist Church of America in 1833. The denomination found its greatest strength in small towns and rural areas, expanding from its bases in New England and the Mid-Atlantic States into the South and beyond. Its maximum strength, attained around the turn of the twentieth century, was about 65,000.

Unitarianism attained its greatest influence in early nineteenth-century Boston, where it rapidly became the church of the intelligentsia and the civic and commercial leadership, with Harvard and its Divinity School as its academic center. A challenge to its establishment status and its espousal of the Scottish Common Sense* philosophy soon came from a fellowship of thinkers and writers, influenced by German idealism and Oriental religion, who acquired the nickname of "Transcendentalists."* A second Unitarian controversy was precipitated by Ralph Waldo Emerson's* address to the graduating class at the Harvard Divinity School in 1838. Emerson's attack on the Unitarian insistence that Jesus had worked miracles as an authentication of his mission provoked a sharp attack from Harvard's Andrews Norton.* Although Unitarians had rejected traditional Christian claims that Jesus was divine, few were prepared to abandon the idea that Christianity was

historically unique and based on specific divine revelation. Transcendentalism had few institutional consequences but did raise questions of Unitarian inclusiveness which were echoed in the founding of the Free Religious Association in 1867 by dissidents unwilling to identify themselves as Christians. Unitarians in the Midwest, led by Jenkin Lloyd Jones (1843-1918), shared similar qualms and later gave rise to the humanist movement, which did not affirm the existence of a personal god.

By the twentieth century the appeal of the two denominations had been challenged by several factors. Such traditional liberal ideas as the benevolence of God, the exemplary character of Jesus and the possibilities for human growth through personal moral cultivation had become widely accepted through the spread of Protestant liberalism in many seminaries* and pulpits. Spokesmen for both denominations espoused the Social Gospel,* but were hardly alone in their advocacy. Agnosticism* also became socially acceptable, and descendants of prominent Unitarian families, such as Henry Adams, were openly unchurched. Both Unitarians and Universalists also faced the question of coming to terms with the nontheistic humanist movement within their own ranks, and were further undermined by administrative problems and the financial impact of the Great Depression.*

One response by Unitarians was the Lay Fellowship Plan of 1948, which helped small groups of liberals to organize worship* and discussion societies without having to found a church and support a minister. A more definitive solution came with the merger of the two denominations in 1961 to form the Unitarian-Universalist Association. Since their differences had always been more sociological than theological, the resultant UUA made considerable organizational sense. Its headquarters are in Boston, and it recognizes three seminaries: Harvard (interdenominational), Meadville-Lombard in Chicago, and Starr King in Berkeley. Polity is congregational,* with a national board of trustees composed of delegates from twenty-three districts in the U.S. and Canada, and others elected at large. Membership in the late 1980s stood at about 180,000, with approximately 1,000 churches and fellowships and 1,100 clergy. The UUA is vocal in its commitment to progressive social issues, including environmentalism, feminism and gay rights. It imposes no creedal tests, and recognizes its roots both in the Judaeo-Christian tradition* as well as in humanistic sources. Although New England remains a bastion

United Church of Canada

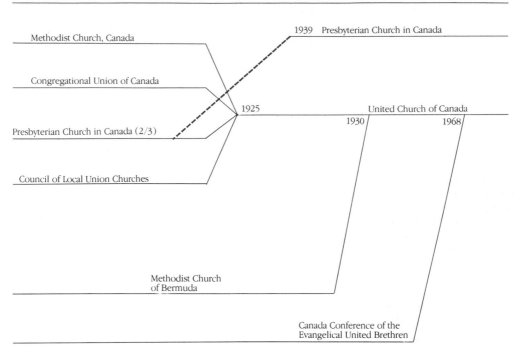

Methodist Church, Canada

Congregational Union of Canada

Presbyterian Church in Canada (2/3)

Council of Local Union Churches

1925

1939   Presbyterian Church in Canada

United Church of Canada

1930   1968

Methodist Church
of Bermuda

Canada Conference of the
Evangelical United Brethren

of numerical strength, Unitarian Universalists can be found throughout the nation, especially in urban areas, academic communities and "high tech" centers.

BIBLIOGRAPHY. S. E. Ahlstrom and J. S. Carey, eds., *An American Reformation: A Documentary History of Unitarian Christianity* (1984); D. Robinson, *The Unitarians and the Universalists* (1985); C. C. Wright, *The Beginnings of Unitarianism in America* (1955); C. C. Wright, ed., *A Stream of Light* (1975). C. E. Wright, ed., *American Unitarianism, 1805-1865* (1989).

P. W. Williams

Unitarianism. *See* UNITARIAN CONTROVERSY; UNITARIAN UNIVERSALIST ASSOCIATION.

United Church of Canada, The. Canada's largest Protestant* denomination.* The United Church of Canada was formed officially on June 10, 1925, out of the union of the following groups: the Methodist* Church, Canada (representing the large majority of Canadian Methodists); the Congregational Union of Canada (representing virtually all Canadian Congregationalists*); the Council of Local Union Churches (numbering about 3,000 congregations at the time, albeit many relatively

small ones); and about two-thirds of the Presbyterian* Church in Canada. Some joined the Church in the interests of sparking a renewal of evangelical* piety* and outreach; others saw it as the beginning of a national church that would manifest the concerns of the modern mainline* ecumenical movement;* still others, especially on the prairies, saw it as a way of avoiding the costly duplication of resources, whether pastors* or church buildings, in small communities.

The union capped several decades of negotiations among these churches. These negotiations saw, especially among the Presbyterians (who had by far the largest number of dissenters and so offered the most lively debate), idealism and principle mixed with less inspiring politicking and maneuvering. The resulting denomination was the first modern church in the world fully to unite such diverse traditions in one religious body. The Church later was augmented by the additions of the Wesleyan Methodist Church of Bermuda (1930) and the Canada Conference of the Evangelical United Brethren (1968).

The Church's polity* combines elements from the constituent churches, but most resembles Presbyterianism.* The Church is governed by a General Council which meets every two years. A moderator, elected for the same period, directs the General Council and represents the Church between Councils. The secretary of the General Council holds the other most important administrative post. The various ministries of the Church are centralized under boards and administrators in Toronto, but the boards are duplicated at the conference, presbytery and, often, individual church levels. Church courts are also established at the conference and presbytery levels. An official board, chaired by the pastor, combines the session and board of stewards in the local church.

The United Church's "Basis of Union" set forth a statement of faith which agreed with the basic evangelical doctrines held in common by its constituent traditions, but the Church also took in a large number of the most influential Canadian liberal* theologians* and church leaders of the time. Since then its leadership, including its theological seminaries,* has been characterized generally by liberal or neo-orthodox* theology* and a strong commitment to social issues and the mainline ecumenical movement. The Renewal Fellowship, comprised of a number of evangelicals within the Church, was formed in the early 1960s to protest the "New Curriculum" developed for the Church's Sunday schools,* a curriculum opposed by many evangelicals within and without the Church. Since then the Renewal Fellowship has sought generally to influence the Church away from what it sees to be unorthodox theology and in directions which are, in its view, more in keeping with the heritage of the particular traditions which went into the Church and of evangelical Christianity in general.

The United Church is a member of the World Methodist Council, the World Alliance of Reformed Churches* (Presbyterian and Congregational), and the Canadian* and World Councils of Churches.* Declining in numbers since the early 1960s, the Church claimed over 4,000 congregations, over 1 million adult members, and over 2 million affiliated Canadians in the late 1980s.

BIBLIOGRAPHY. N. K. Clifford, *The Resistance to Church Union in Canada, 1904-1939* (1985); J. W. Grant, *The Canadian Experience of Church Union* (1967); C. E. Silcox, *Church Union in Canada: Its Causes and Consequences* (1933).

J. G. Stackhouse

United Church of Christ, The. Formed in 1957, the United Church of Christ (UCC) was a merger of the Congregational Christian Churches and the Evangelical and Reformed Church. Through its denominational* traditions the Congregational

wing of the UCC goes back to the original Congregationalism* of Puritan* New England. But though they were one of the major forces in early-American religious history, Congregationalists did not have a distinct denominational identity until the mid-nineteenth century because their congregational form of government* valued the autonomy of individual congregations. Although Congregationalists joined forces in creating the American Board of Commissioners for Foreign Mission* (1812) and the American Missionary Association* (1846), it was not until 1871 that Congregationalists founded the National Council of Congregational Churches (NCCC). In 1892 the NCCC was joined by a body of Congregational Methodist* churches in Georgia and Alabama, and in 1925 the Evangelical Protestant Churches, a group of Ohio Valley congregations, also joined the NCCC.

In 1931 the General Convention of the Christian Church, or Christian Connection,* united with the NCCC to form the General Council of Congregational and Christian Churches. The General Convention of the Christian Church, a body arising from the nineteenth-century Restoration Movement,* had been seeking union with other Protestant churches since 1924.

The other church tradition represented in the UCC union of 1957, the Evangelical and Reformed Church, was itself the product of a union of two church traditions, both of them tracing their histories back to German immigrants* to America. On the one hand the General Synod of the Reformed Church in the United States (a name they adopted in 1863) had originated in the organizing efforts of John Philip Boehm* and Michael Schlatter,* who organized German Reformed* congregations in Pennsylvania in the early 1700s and formed their first coetus* in 1747 under the jurisdiction of the Dutch Reformed Church. The other member of this 1934 union, the Evangelical Synod of North America, was a product of several Midwestern immigrant congregations of the Evangelical Union of Prussia, itself a German Lutheran* and Reformed amalgamation brought about by King Frederick William III (1770-1840). The Evangelical Synod and the Reformed Church began exploring their common ground in the late 1920s, finally becoming one denomination on June 26, 1934.

The General Council of the Congregational Christian Churches and the Evangelical and Reformed Church began exploring the possibilities of union in the early 1940s, a process that concluded in the birth of the UCC at a meeting in Cleveland, Ohio, on June 25-27, 1957. Three

United Church of Christ/Congregationalists

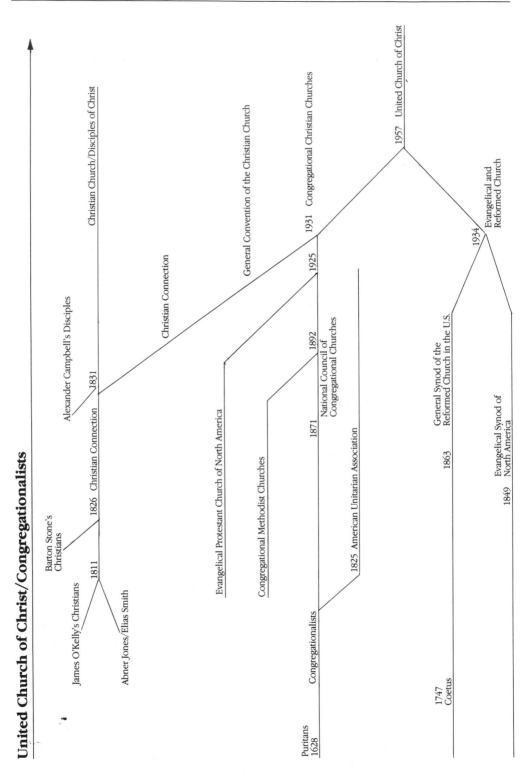

James O'Kelly's Christians

Barton Stone's
Christians

1811

Abner Jones/Elias Smith

1826 Christian Connection

Alexander Campbell's Disciples

1831

Christian Connection

Christian Church/Disciples of Christ

Evangelical Protestant Church of North America

Congregational Methodist Churches

General Convention of the Christian Church

1871

National Council of
Congregational Churches

1892

1925

1931 Congregational Christian Churches

Puritans
1628

Congregationalists

1825 American Unitarian Association

1957 United Church of Christ

1934

Evangelical and
Reformed Church

1747
Coetus

1863

General Synod of the
Reformed Church in the U.S.

1849

Evangelical Synod of
North America

formative documents define the United Church of Christ: the "Basis of Union with Interpretations," adopted in 1957; the "UCC Statement of Faith," adopted in 1959 at the second General Synod and "The Preamble and Constitution of the United Church of Christ," also adopted in 1959. These documents express the center of the UCC, which in its theological spectrum encompasses churches and individuals ranging from liberal* to moderately evangelical.* Its national and conference leadership would be classified as predominantly liberal in theology.* Evangelical renewal* efforts since the 1970s have resulted in a conservative (UCC People for Biblical Witness) and a charismatic* fellowship (Fellowship of Charismatic Christians in the UCC). In the 1980s, concern for theological revitalization has brought about the Biblical Witness Fellowship and the Biblical-Theological-Liturgical Group. The Fifteenth General Synod of the UCC (1985) added the two new priorities of "Spiritual Renewal" and "Justice and Peace." A new Statement of Faith was scheduled for 1989.

The contemporary UCC denomination is noted for its social consciousness, having been influenced by the Social Gospel Movement* of the early twentieth century. It seeks to work for peace, the slowing of the arms race, human rights, defeat of apartheid and reduction of violence. Out of its concept of a functional clergy* and the ministry of all believers, it ordains women,* a practice Congregationalists instituted over one hundred years ago with the ordination of Antoinette Brown in 1853. Local church autonomy, the vocation of all believers and ecumenism* continue to characterize the UCC. In the late 1980s the UCC reported an inclusive membership of 1,676,105 in 6,406 congregations throughout the United States.

See also CONGREGATIONALISM; REFORMED TRADITION.

BIBLIOGRAPHY. D. Horton, *The United Church of Christ: Its Origins, Organization and Role in the World Today* (1962); R. L. Shinn and D. D. Williams, *We Believe: An Interpretation of the United Church of Christ Statement of Faith* (1966); L. H. Gunnemann, *The Shaping of the United Church of Christ* (1977); R. S. Paul, *Freedom with Order. The Doctrine of the Church in the United Church of Christ* (1987). L. E. Wilshire

United Council for Christian Democracy. A nondenominational, social activist organization. The organization of the United Council was an attempt to bring together the more radical Christians from various denominations who were concerned with the inequities in the social and economic order, most of whom were calling for extensive government action and social planning and some of whom were avowedly socialist. Organized in November 1936, at Columbus, Ohio, the United Council for Christian Democracy formed the umbrella for such left-wing groups as the Methodist Federation for Social Service, the Church League for Industrial Democracy and other similar organizations.

Eighty-five ministers and six laymen constituted the founders. The Council included representation from the Methodists,* Presbyterians,* Episcopalians,* Congregationalists* and evangelicals,* with Baptists,* Disciples* and Unitarians* joining later. Reinhold Niebuhr,* a socialist and outspoken critic of the capitalistic system, served as its chairman. Endorsing socialism and rejecting capitalism,* the Council served as a focus for Protestant radicals and stimulated the formation of social activist groups in other denominations. Though outside the mainstream of mainline* Protestantism,* the Council did valuable work in the areas of labor relations and civil liberties.

BIBLIOGRAPHY. R. M. Miller, *American Protestantism and Social Issues, 1919-1939* (1958).
G. DeVries

United Domestic Missionary Society. See NEW YORK MISSIONARY SOCIETY.

United Holy Church of America. A predominantly African-American Holiness* denomination. The United Holy Church of America was founded on May 1, 1886, in Method, a suburb of Raleigh, North Carolina. The chief purpose of the early meetings was to seek the "deeper life of sanctification" and recover the lost zeal of the mainline* evangelical* churches. A trinitarian body, it accepts the faith confessed in the Apostle's Creed and delimited by the Protestant Reformation. Tremendous emphasis is placed on sanctification* as essential for Christian life. Equal emphasis is placed on Spirit baptism* which, like sanctification, is regarded as subsequent to conversion.* The United Holy Church practices charismatic manifestations of the Spirit, including speaking in tongues.* The Church does not, however, insist on speaking in tongues as the "necessary evidence" of Spirit baptism.

This Holiness church emerged during a period when lynching, dire poverty, racial segregation and limited educational opportunities affected the lives of African Americans. The Church responded with an emphasis on holiness that preserved a focus on inner-transformation and high scriptural standards for ethics. Spiritual empowerment was the source for holy living, and a prophetic social consciousness judged the culture and kept the cause of the dispossessed foremost in the practical programs of the Church. Early leaders drawn from Methodist* churches included L. M. Mason, W. H. Fulford, H. L. Fisher,* R. H. White and J. D. Diggs, while G. J. Branch came from the Free-Will Baptist Church.* Early women in the movement included Bettie Thompson, E. E. Craig and Julia A. Delk.

The Church experienced unsurpassed growth in the first half of the century through a program of evangelism* and missions* centered in district convocations. Convocations established in the Southeast, Northeast, Midwest, West Coast and Bermuda became magnets for drawing those of like faith and social station. Following licensing* or ordination,* workers were sent out from these centers. Convocations, under the leadership of bishops, served as adjudicating bodies for handling grievances and agencies for sponsoring missionaries to other countries, as well as for educational work, Bible* training, youth work and social relief. The greatest concentration of membership remains along the East Coast, and the present headquarters are located in Greensboro, North Carolina.

BIBLIOGRAPHY. H. L. Fisher, *The History of the United Holy Church of America, Inc.* (1945); W. C. Turner, Jr., "The United Holy Church of America" (unpublished Ph.D. dissertation, Duke University, Durham, North Carolina, 1984); C. Gregory, *The United Holy Church of America, Inc., 1886-1986.*
W. Turner

United Methodist Church. The United Methodist Church came into existence in 1968 through a union between the Methodist Church* and the Evangelical United Brethren—two denominations* that traced their roots to revivals* in eighteenth-century Britain and America.

The name *Methodist* originated as a satirical allusion to the order and regularity of behavior in the Holy Club to which John Wesley* belonged as a student at Oxford University. Wesley retained it as a name for the societies, classes and bands that he began to organize in 1739 within the Church of England (*See* Anglicanism) to provide worship,* discipline and nurture for the converts attracted by his evangelistic* sermons. Impressed by the tradition of "holy living" within Anglican piety,* by the accent on free grace in Reformation theology* and Moravian* pietism* and by accounts of the Christian life in Greek and Syrian patristic writings, Wesley encouraged a devotion that blended confidence in justification* by grace with a commitment to a holiness* that could, by God's grace, find its fulfillment in the perfecting of love.

Possibly as early as 1763 the Methodist lay exhorter* Robert Strawbridge brought this message to the American Chesapeake colonies; by 1766 the lay preacher* Philip Embury* carried it to New York, and in the following year Methodists there formed the first American society. In 1769 the British conference, under Wesley's leadership, officially sent missionaries* to America. Two years later it sent Francis Asbury,* who helped direct a revival that by 1784 had attracted 14,988 members under the care of eighty-four itinerant* preachers and numerous lay* class leaders.

Restless because their unordained preachers could not administer the Sacraments,* many American Methodists were by 1779 demanding the formation of a separate denomination. In 1784 Wesley agreed to ordain* elders and set apart Asbury and Thomas Coke* as "superintendents"* of the Methodists in America. On December 24, the American preachers convened for the "Christmas Conference"* at the Lovely Lane Chapel in Baltimore to form the Methodist Episcopal Church.

From the beginning, the Methodists nurtured a close relationship with Dutch and German Pietists,* who shared their revivalist fervor. Philip William Otterbein,* a Dutch Reformed* minister* from Pennsylvania, participated in the service that made Asbury a bishop.* In 1800 Otterbein and Martin Boehm,* a German Mennonite,* formed the Church of the Brethren in Christ, but both they and some of their converts maintained close ties to the Methodists. One such convert, Jacob Albright,* became a Methodist lay preacher before organizing in Pennsylvania in 1807 a "Newly-Formed Methodist Church," renamed in 1816 as the *Evangelische Gemeinschaft* (Evangelical Community). The Brethren and Albright's group would eventually merge and then join in the union that formed the United Methodist Church.

After 1784 the Methodist Episcopal Church grew especially through the agency of circuit riders,* who traveled on horseback to organize classes and congregations on the frontier,* and of camp meetings,* which maintained the revivalist* zeal. It benefited also from a disciplined ministry: bishops assigned the itinerant preachers to their circuits. Such episcopal power generated discontent—the followers of James O'Kelly* withdrew in 1796, and the Methodist Protestant Church resulted from a similar separation in 1830—but by 1840 the Methodist Episcopal Church, with 580,098 members, was the largest Protestant denomination in America.

Growth continued even after debate over slavery divided the denomination in 1844 into two regional denominations, but after the Civil War* the Northern Church outstripped its Southern counterpart. By 1880 it could boast 1,743,000 members, compared to 848,000 in the Methodist Episcopal Church, South, which had suffered the loss of 158,964 African-American members after emancipation. Increasingly, new Methodists came from the middle classes in the countryside and the small towns; by 1900 President Theodore Roosevelt could call the Northern Methodists "the most representative church in America." And the new members began to demand an educated ministry and more refined styles of worship. But the Church did not entirely forget its origins among the poor. During the labor crises of the 1880s, the Northern bishops addressed the problems of the workers, and in 1908 the Northern Church adopted a Social Creed* calling for just treatment of the labor force.

By that time, calls for reconciliation could be heard in both North and South, and in 1939 the two regional churches, along with the Methodist Protestant Church, reunited as the Methodist Church. Seven years later, when the Church of the United Brethren in Christ and the Evangelical Church (the successor to the *Evangelische Gemeinschaft*) joined together as the Evangelical United Brethren Church. G. Bromley Oxnam,* a Methodist bishop, suggested a further merger, which was realized in 1968 at a uniting conference in Dallas. Delegates for the eight hundred thousand Evangelical United Brethren members joined with representatives of ten million Methodists to form the United Methodist Church.

See also REVIVALISM, GERMAN-AMERICAN; METHODIST CHURCHES; WESLEYAN TRADITION.

BIBLIOGRAPHY. E. Bucke, ed., *History of American Methodism,* 3 vols. (1964); N. B. Harmon, ed., *Encyclopedia of World Methodism,* 2 vols. (1974); F. A. Norwood, *The Story of American Methodism* (1974).   E. B. Holifield

United Pentecostal Church, International. Oneness* Pentecostal* denomination.* Formed in 1945 by the merger of the Pentecostal Assemblies of Jesus Christ and the Pentecostal Church, Inc., the United Pentecostal Church is the largest white oneness Pentecostal denomination. Its two constituent bodies had separated from the Pentecostal Assemblies of the World in 1924 in a secession in part motivated by racial tension. Earlier, some of its prominent leaders had left the Assemblies of God* in a 1916 dispute over the baptismal formula and the nature of the Godhead. With headquarters in

Hazelwood, Missouri, the denomination sponsors a radio program "Harvestime" and operates a publishing house. The group's doctrinal distinctives include the insistence that water baptism* by immersion must be administered "in the name of Jesus" and the belief that there is only one Person in the Godhead, Jesus Christ. As with the Assemblies of God, they hold to the "finished work of grace," believing that sanctification* begins at conversion* and progresses toward perfection* throughout one's lifetime. The denomination endorses a more rigorous social behavior code than do white Trinitarian Pentecostal denominations of similar size. In 1987 there were 3,410 congregations with an inclusive membership of approximately five hundred thousand. The denomination supports over four hundred missionaries in more than one hundred countries.

BIBLIOGRAPHY. A. Clanton, *United We Stand—A History of Oneness Organizations* (1970); F. Foster, *Think It Not Strange: A History of the Oneness Movement* (1965).   E. L. Blumhofer

United Presbyterian Church in the United States of America. *See* PRESBYTERIAN CHURCH U.S.A.).

United Society of Believers in Christ's Second Appearing. *See* SHAKERS.

United States Catholic Conference, The. The public policy* agency of the Catholic* bishops* of America. As an organization of Catholic lay* people, clergy* and religious,* The United States Catholic Conference (USCC) serves as a consultative body for the American Catholic Church in such areas as education, social action and immigration.* Formed in 1966 out of the post-Vatican II* restructuring of the National Catholic Welfare Conference,* the American bishops officially divided the Conference into the National Council of Catholic Bishops* (NCCB) and the United States Catholic Conference. The two conferences serve distinct but complementary responsibilities. Both are served by a general secretariat, which maintains a staff of about four hundred in the Washington, D.C., headquarters.

Three USCC committees (communication, education, and social development and world peace) recommend policy for developing the Catholic Church within society. Through their various departments the committees oversee, respectively, the Church's apostolate* of print and electronic media in producing television and radio programs, promotional material and staffing a Catholic news

[1203]

service; leadership programs in religious education of children and adults, as well as youth activities and campus ministry; programs to aid developing countries in rural and urban issues, human rights, economic concerns, and military and political affairs. Several other Catholic self-supporting agencies work closely with USCC, especially Catholic Relief Service, Migration and Refugee Services and the American Bishops' Campaign for Human Development.

BIBLIOGRAPHY. NCCB/USCC publications, "NCCB/USCC: Serving the Church and the World" (1987); E. McKeown, "The National Bishops' Conference," *CHR* LXVI (October 1980): 565-83; M. J. Sheehan, "United States Catholic Conference," *NCE* 16.   P. M. Kane

United States Center for World Mission. An evangelical* foreign missions* center in Pasadena, California. Begun in 1976 by Ralph (a professor at Fuller Seminary's* School of World Mission) and Roberta Winter, the United States Center for World Mission (USCWM) was conceived as a strategic center from which the world's 17,000 distinguishable people groups would be reached with the gospel. In order to provide facilities for the Center, the Winters negotiated the purchase of the thirty-five-acre campus of the former Pasadena College for $15 million.

An innovative plan called for one million people to donate $15 each, thus avoiding competition with donations to mission agencies and creating a wide base of support for the vision of the USCWM. The down payment for the property was raised and soon dozens of evangelical mission agencies had bases at the Center, carrying on research and training and mobilizing people for missions. By 1986 there were three hundred full-time workers on campus representing more than seventy mission agencies. By 1988 Winter's fund-raising plan, adjusted to solicit 8,000 pledges of $1,000 "advances" against later small donors, had virtually paid for the property. With renewed dedication, the dozens of specialized mission agencies based at USCWM were sparking efforts to engage the whole church in the task of establishing reproducing congregations in every people group on the planet by the year 2000.

BIBLIOGRAPHY. R. H. Winter, *I Will Do a New Thing* (1987).   D. G. Tinder

United States Christian Commission. Northern Protestant* charitable organization during the Civil War.* The commission was formed under the guidance of the New York YMCA* in 1861 to provide charitable assistance to Union forces. Supported by a broad interdenominational effort and led ably by George H. Stuart,* a Presbyterian* layman* and philanthropist,* the commission sent out nearly 5,000 unpaid volunteer clergymen and laypeople during the war. Their primary purpose was to address the spiritual needs of soldiers through church services, literature and spiritual counsel. But they also provided supplies, assisted with medical care and helped soldiers communicate with families. Over $6 million in money, goods and services were donated and dispersed. The effort was a premier instance of the nineteenth-century Protestant ideal of interdenominational benevolence, occurring in a time of crisis and limited governmental resources.

BIBLIOGRAPHY. E. D. Fite, *Social and Industrial Conditions in the North during the Civil War* (1983); J. Moorhead, *American Apocalypse: Yankee Protestants and the Civil War, 1860-1869* (1978).   D. W. Carlson

Unity School of Christianity. A New Thought religious movement. The Unity School of Christianity traces its origin to Kansas City, Missouri, where, in 1889, its cofounders, Myrtle and Charles Fillmore,* decided to dedicate their lives to the study and teaching of practical Christianity. From modest beginnings, Unity has grown in size and impact so that today it daily affects the lives of over two million persons through its devotional magazine, *The Daily Word.* The Unity movement, through the representation of The Association of Unity Churches (a closely affiliated institution), has 525 field ministries and 275 affiliated study groups. More than four hundred thousand persons receive its monthly denominational magazine, *Unity,* and over two-and-a-half million contact its prayer ministry, Silent Unity, annually. It is by far the largest segment of the New Thought family, while also being unique among New Thought groups in its emphatic claim to be a Christian movement. Unity School is located at Unity Village, an incorporated area (about 1,400 acres) just outside of Kansas City, Missouri.

Unity has discernible theological and historical links with Christian Science* which can be traced through the influence of E. B. Weeks on the Fillmores. In 1886 Weeks, a disciple of Emma Curtis Hopkins* (who had broken ties with Mary Baker Eddy*), was lecturing in Kansas City on mental healing. The Fillmores attended one of the lectures, and as a result Myrtle began a process of healing that by 1888 resulted in a complete healing of her lifelong tuberculosis.

Myrtle's healing precipitated the Fillmores's interest in New Thought, which eventuated in the founding of Unity. Originally established as a healing and publication ministry, Unity soon assumed a sectarian character. Although Unity is nondoctrinal, several foundational teachings are notable: (1) the absolute goodness of God and the unreality of evil; (2) the innate divinity of humanity; (3) the creative nature of consciousness; (4) the freedom of individuals in matters of belief; (5) the acceptance of spiritually interpreted Christian doctrine as normative. Unity's distinctive symbol is a winged globe.

BIBLIOGRAPHY. M. Bach, *The Unity Way* (1982); C. Braden, *Spirits in Rebellion; The Rise and Development of New Thought* (1963); E. Butterworth, *Unity; A Quest for Truth* (1965); J. D. Freeman, *The Story of Unity* (1978).

D. deChant

Universalism. The belief that ultimately all individuals will be saved. Universalism has traditionally sought to defend its viewpoint on the grounds that eternal punishment for sin* is inconsistent, from the standpoint of both Scripture* and reason, with belief in the existence of a loving and merciful God who desires the salvation* of all.

In America, universalism was first espoused by various mystical* and pietistic* groups which arrived from Germany and were influenced by the teachings of George de Benneville (1703-1793). A form of universalism was also held by the New England Congregationalists* Jonathan Mayhew* and Charles Chauncy* (1705-1787), who published his influential *The Salvation of All Men* in 1784. However, the founder of American universalism is considered to be John Murray.* A disciple of John Relly (1720-1778), Murray sought to reconcile Calvinist* presuppositions with belief in the benevolence of God by arguing for the election* of all mankind to salvation. He continued the argument first advanced in Relly's *Union* (1759) that Christ incurred the punishment of all for all eternity through his complete identification with the human race.

In its early years American universalism was faced with controversy over the status of the soul after death. So-called restorationists argued that the soul must go through a period of punishment after death to be purged of all sins committed in this life. This view was advocated by Elhanan Winchester* in his *Dialogues on the Universal Restoration* (1788). Ultra-universalists, on the other hand, affirmed the immediate entrance of the soul into heaven* at death, appealing in support of this view

to the all-sufficiency of Christ's punishment for sins, the infinite love of God and the changed nature of the soul after death. In his pivotal work, *A Treatise on Atonement* (1805), Hosea Ballou* rejected the idea of future punishment. He also argued that the purpose of Christ's work of atonement* was not to reconcile God to man but to reconcile man to God through his eternal love. A strict determinist, Ballou argued that God is the author of sin, but that he uses sin to accomplish his ultimate loving purpose of the salvation of all mankind.

In 1803 the universalist convention adopted the Winchester Profession of Belief. This statement, which was reaffirmed in 1870, asserted a belief in the trustworthiness of the Bible* as God's revelation, the revelation of God through Christ and the final restoration of mankind to holiness* and happiness. However, there were always those within the universalist movement who dissented from this general statement of faith. In the years between the Civil War* and the outbreak of World War 1,* American universalism was buffeted by the intellectual winds of German-English rationalism, biblical criticism,* evolutionism* and the Social Gospel Movement.* Many universalists came to accept the conclusion that the biblical witness is fallible and that God's revelation can take a variety of forms. Many also evidenced a greater appreciation for the social and economic implications of the gospel.

Following the publication of the *Humanist Manifesto* in 1933, universalism struggled with the challenge of humanism.* Although there were those who continued to hold to the necessity of divine intervention through Christ for human salvation, there was a growing trend away from traditional Christian tenets and toward the humanist belief that humanity has the ability to reorder the world. By the 1950s most universalists had come to hold that all religions are to be valued as a means of realizing the potential inherent in all of mankind. This religious inclusivism made possible a greater cooperation with Unitarianism, a relationship which resulted finally in the merging of the Universalist Church of America with the American Unitarian Association and the formation of the Unitarian Universalist Association* in 1961.

BIBLIOGRAPHY. E. Cassara, ed., *Universalism in America: A Documentary History* (1971); C. L. Scott, *The Universalist Church of America: A Short History* (1957); D. Robinson, *The Unitarians and Universalists* (1985); E. A. Robinson, *American Universalism: Its Origins, Organization, and Heritage* (1970). R. P. Hesselgrave

University of Pennsylvania. A secular university with origins in colonial Anglicanism.* Formerly known as the Philadelphia College and Academy, this educational institution traces its origins to a 1740 gathering to erect a charity school in response to the preaching of George Whitefield.* By 1749 this group, which now included Benjamin Franklin, had evolved into the board of trustees of a non-sectarian academy. The institution, however, had an Anglican cast from its inception, since seventy-five per cent of the original trustees belonged to that church.

The year 1751 saw the opening of classes, and in 1755 another charter for the "College, Academy and Charitable School of Philadelphia" was granted, and William Smith became the first provost. Franklin's influence resulted in a curriculum more oriented toward modern subjects than was typical in colonial colleges. The teaching of medical courses began in 1765, making this the nation's first medical school.

A new set of statutes were promulgated in 1779, renaming the institution the "University of the State of Pennsylvania," and constituting a new board. The old faculty and Provost Smith were relieved of their duties. The Pennsylvania Council of Censors in 1788 questioned the validity of these statutes. The reinstatement of the old board resulted in the simultaneous existence of university and college from 1789 to 1791. Need for funds and hope of receiving state aid motivated the institutions to reunite in 1791.

After a time of depression created by lack of students and funding, which continued from 1791 to 1828, the university entered into a renaissance during the tenure of Provosts Charles J. Stille (1868-1880) and William Pepper (1881-1894). In 1872 the university moved to its present location in West Philadelphia. A wide variety of programs offer both undergraduate and graduate education in a number of academic and professional disciplines.

BIBLIOGRAPHY. E. P. Cheyney, *History of the University of Pennsylvania, 1740-1940* (1940).

F. M. Perko

Unruh, Tobias A. (1819-1875). A leader in the emigration of Mennonites* from Russia to North America. Unruh was ordained* in 1853 at Karolswald in Polish Russia and served as district minister and elder.* In 1871 Unruh took part in the delegation to St. Petersburg with Leonard Sudermann* to inquiry about the impact of the new military law on Mennonites and their exemption from military service. He was a conservative member of the

delegation of twelve Mennonites and Hutterites* from Russia and Poland who traveled to North America in 1873 to determine the prospects for Mennonite emigration. Unruh was one of three from the delegation who petitioned U.S. President Ulysses S. Grant at his summer home near New York City. Back in Russia, he aided the emigration effort and served as the leader of a group of emigrants from the Karolswald area. The many hardships they encountered earned them the nickname of "helpless Poles." Unruh and his family emigrated with the last of this group in January 1875. That spring they settled in South Dakota. Unruh died in July of typhoid fever. A number of his people who had settled in McPherson County, Kansas, joined the small Mennonite denomination started by John Holdeman.* Although Unruh lived only a few months in the U.S., he made a significant contribution to the Russian Mennonite immigration to North America.

BIBLIOGRAPHY. A. J. Unruh and V. Unruh, *The Tobias A. Unruh Biography, Diary and Family Record, 1819-1969* (1969); C. Hiebert, *The Holdeman People: The Church of God in Christ, Mennonite, 1859-1969* (1973).

J. D. Weaver

Urban Churches and Ministries. With the British immigration* to America, permanent settlements arose in the New World. They were intended to represent the best of European civilization, leaving the worst of the Old World behind. While the Spanish and French established trading posts and forts like St. Augustine (1560), the Puritans* brought with them an urban vision. In his sermon aboard the Arbella on March 22, 1630, John Winthrop* articulated this vision by proclaiming, "wee must consider that wee shall be as a Citty upon a Hill, the eies of all people are upon us. . . ." Boston was to be the capital of the new holy commonwealth, the foundation for the imminent establishment of the kingdom of God* in America. Winthrop accepted the vision of Calvin's Geneva, a model theocracy* for the world to see.

While the ideal of a "city on a hill" lives on, lingering in the rhetoric of America's political leaders, the reality of the holy city quickly fell prey to secularism—the "private city" of Ben Franklin. Boston quickly lost its Christian vision, as speculation, dissent and factionalism came with the emigration from the Old World. For men such as Winthrop, urban ministry was essentially paternalistic, consisting of the "high and eminent" caring for those who were "mean and in subjection." For example, when Queen Anne's War (1702-1713) reduced one-fifth of Cotton Mather's* Boston congregation to dependency, Mather dispensed food, clothing and wood for heating, but chastised the poor for their "foolish fondness for commodities and fashions" that were above their station in life, as well as their alleged drunkenness and laziness. It was assumed that the godly and the moral would become materially prosperous, while the poor usually deserved their own plight.

The major colonial cities in British North America—Boston, Philadelphia and New York—all experienced growth as commercial and maritime centers. And though the urban population was relatively small—in 1790 the twenty-four urban centers with populations of 2,500 or more made up only 5.1 per cent of the nation's population—even in the seventeenth century cities had begun to feel the social effects of growth. Boston's Brattle Street Church, for example, was established to meet the needs of a growing urban merchant class. But for the most part, religious affiliation was much less a matter of social class and more a matter of regional placement, with the Dutch Reformed* in New York, Congregationalists* in New England, Quakers* and German sectarians in Pennsylvania, Catholics* in Maryland and Anglicans* in the South.

The Second Great Awakening* of the early nineteenth century brought some focus on the cities, with evangelists* such as Lyman Beecher,* Albert Barnes* and Charles G. Finney* conducting urban revivals.* Finney was particularly successful in his revivals in cities like Rochester, New York (1830), later becoming pastor of New York City's Broadway Tabernacle (1832-1835). But the Western frontier,* reflecting America's agrarian ideals, took precedence in home missionary* efforts, and Finney himself would soon respond to Lyman Beecher's "Plea for the West" and accept a chair at Oberlin College* in Ohio. On the other hand, the revivalism of the early nineteenth century united evangelism with social reform in the conviction that the converted person would, out of disinterested benevolence, act for the good of society. This bore fruit in a number of benevolent societies which focused on urban needs.

In New York City a benevolent empire emerged, fueled by revival fires. Various Bible and tract societies* were established, and city missionaries quickly took note of the needs of the urban poor. But many Christians believed that urban poverty was simply the result of intemperance, vice and prodigal living, to be cured by evangelism or moral instruction. Others, such as Ezra Stiles Ely, a city missionary and chaplain* of a New York City

almshouse from 1811 to 1813, argued that poverty was brought on by factors such as low wages forced on widows and spinsters. Similarly, Louis M. Pease of the Five Points House of Industry (1854) offended his peers by seeking to create jobs and skills for the poor and unemployed. But the greatest urban revival of the nineteenth century, the so-called prayer meeting revival* of 1857-1859, was to touch thousands in major cities such as Chicago and New York and eventually give rise to prominent urban revivalists such as Dwight L. Moody.* The results of the revival of 1857-1859 are difficult to measure, and though its impact on missions and social action was to continue for several decades, the revival itself was essentially among the business class.

The greatest growth in urban ministry followed the Civil War*—an era of great social and economic transformation and increased immigration* to America. Cities such as Boston, Philadelphia and New York experienced phenomenal growth between 1860 and 1890, which in turn placed tremendous pressure on urban social and economic order. Western cities also flourished. Chicago, a mere village in 1833, was the fifth largest city in the world by 1890. Reactions to growth were varied. In 1885 the Social Gospel* advocate Josiah Strong* lamented the exodus of the Protestant* church from the urban centers in the face of the rising immigrant population and the threats of Catholicism,* radicalism, urbanization and intemperance. Other Protestants responded in a display of nativistic* hostility toward the newcomers.

New efforts to redeem the city were attempted. Among them, urban evangelists such as Dwight L. Moody and Billy Sunday* argued for conversion, not social reform. On the other hand, advocates of a Social Gospel* established so-called institutional churches* and settlement houses* to educate, train, socialize and Americanize the immigrant poor. During the 1890s key institutional churches such as St. George's Episcopal Church in New York, Baptist Temple in Philadelphia, Plymouth Congregational in Indianapolis, People's Temple in Denver, Ninth Street Baptist Church in Cincinnati and the Markham Memorial Presbyterian Church in St. Louis sought to provide bathing facilities, employment, educational and cultural opportunities, as well as vocational training such as sewing and cooking schools for the immigrant poor. Settlement houses like Andover House in Boston and Chicago Commons in Chicago were also run by ministers and religious leaders.

City rescue missions* also appeared in major cities. In addition to the Five Points House of

Industry, rescue missions like Jerry McAuley's* Water Street Mission* (1876) were established, bringing evangelism, food and vocational training to the poor. The Salvation Army's* gospel of "soup, soap and salvation" likewise illustrated this approach to urban mission. By 1900 there were several hundred rescue missions in America, one of the more successful being Chicago's Pacific Garden Mission,* founded by Col. George Rogers Clarke and his wife, Sarah Dunn Clarke* in 1877. The Clarks combined evangelism with compassion, and employed gospel bands to go into the city and participate in systematic home visitation.

In the twentieth century, a few white churches have chosen to remain in the city, while many have fled to the suburbs. In the wake of the exodus of the white church, blacks,* Asians* and Hispanics* have established their churches in the city. Catholic churches, with their geographically determined parish system, have also remained in the urban centers as transmitters and guardians of religion and immigrant culture.

In the 1960s a resurgence of interest in urban ministry resulted in numerous training programs such as the Institute on the Church in Urban-Industrial Society (ICUIS) and the Urban Training Center in Chicago. In recent decades denominations have been struggling with the issues of cross-cultural ministry which are part of contemporary urban ministry. Numerous specialty training programs in urban ministry have developed, such as the Seminary Consortium for Urban Pastoral Education (SCUPE) in Chicago and other academic urban training programs associated with evangelical seminaries such as Westminster Theological Seminary in Philadelphia, Gordon-Conwell Theological Seminary in the Boston area and the Summer Institute for Urban Mission associated with the Alliance Theological Seminary near New York City.

As early as the 1920s, urban church researcher Harlan Paul Douglas argued that the problem with urban ministry was rooted in the fact that urban churches held on to a rural ideology and pastoral vision and were reluctant to adapt to the pluralism, density and diversity of the city. He pinpointed the historic problem that churches and religious bodies have faced in urban America.

See also RESCUE MISSION MOVEMENT; SOCIAL GOSPEL MOVEMENT.

BIBLIOGRAPHY. C. H. Hopkins, *The Rise of the Social Gospel in American Protestantism, 1865-1915* (1940); N. A. Magnuson, *Salvation in the Slums: Evangelical Social Work, 1865-1920* (1977); H. F. May, *Protestant Churches and Indus-*

trial America (1967); R. M. Miller and T. D. Mardzik, *Immigrants and Religion in Urban America* (1977); C. S. Rosenberg, *Religion and the Rise of the American City: The New York City Mission Movement, 1812-1870* (1971); R. Wade, *The Urban Frontier: The Rise of Western Cities* (1959); G. W. Younger, *From New Creation to Urban Crisis: A History of Action Training Ministries, 1962-1975* (1986).   C. E. Stockwell

Urbana Student Missions Conventions. Triennial missionary conventions sponsored by Inter-Varsity Christian Fellowship* of Canada and the U.S. Beginning in 1946 InterVarsity Christian Fellowship (IVCF) has sponsored missionary conventions intended primarily to challenge college and university students to become a part of the evangelical foreign missions movement. With few exceptions these conventions have been held every three years, always in the period between Christmas and New Year's Day. About 800 were present at the first meeting in Toronto, but this number has grown to 18,000 in the intervening years. Since 1948 the convention has been held on the campus of the University of Illinois at Urbana.

The roster of speakers over the years has featured evangelical* leaders from around the world. In 1957 Harold Ockenga* and Donald Grey Barnhouse* spoke. In later years, international speakers such as Ruben Lores, Philip Teng, Samuel Escobar, Tokunboh Adeyemo and John Stott were featured. In 1973 Elisabeth Elliot became the first woman to address the convention. Evangelist Billy Graham* has spoken at all of the conventions.

The results of the conventions have been an increased number of volunteers joining the evangelical foreign missions movement,* more than through any other student-focused venture since the Student Volunteer Movement.* Many who have attended the conferences have returned to their campuses and churches with an increased interest in missions which they have in turn communicated to others. The conferences have made a significant contribution to the evangelical missions movement by introducing a new generation of evangelical leaders to foreign missions.

BIBLIOGRAPHY. D. M. Howard, *Moving Out: The Story of Student Initiative in World Missions* (1984).   W. A. Detzler

Urshan, Andrew (Bar-) David (1884-1967). Oneness Pentecostal* minister.* Born in Persia, the son of a Presbyterian* minister, Urshan studied at a Presbyterian mission school. He came to America in 1901 and attached himself first to Dwight L.

Moody's* church in Chicago, but after a Pentecostal experience of Spirit baptism* in 1908, he became associated with W. H. Durham's* North Avenue Mission in Chicago. Ordained by Durham in 1910, Urshan returned to Persia as a missionary in 1914 and also traveled throughout Eastern Europe, baptizing and rebaptizing converts with a "Jesus only" formula. He maintained a working relationship with the Assemblies of God* until 1919. Urshan produced several logical points of defense for Oneness Pentecostalism during his long-term ministry as an evangelist and then a pastor. In general, he argued that though many Christian doctrines had been corrupted through the centuries, the way was finally open for a complete return to apostolic faith and practice. Urshan, who had an intense devotion to Jesus and a deep suspicion of complex theological formulas, proved to be an influential thinker among Oneness Pentecostals.

BIBLIOGRAPHY. A. L. Clanton, *United We Stand* (1970); *The First Occasional Symposium on Aspects of the Oneness Pentecostal Movement* (held at Harvard Divinity School, July 5-7, 1984).

H. D. Hunter

Ursulines. A name used to refer to a variety of women's religious* communities, most often engaged in teaching, and identified with St. Angela Merici. Angela, involved in charity hospitals for syphilis in Brescia, Italy, on November 25, 1535, formed the Company of St. Ursula for the protection and Christian education of young girls who, without entering a cloister or leaving their homes, chose a life of consecrated virginity. The original Company included, besides the virgins, mature widows who acted as their guides and educators, male advocates as protectors and a superioress general. The institute received ecclesiastical approval from the Diocese* of Brescia in 1536 and from Pope Paul III in 1544.

In part through pressure from officials scandalized by the novel structure of the Company, the Ursulines gradually evolved into traditional forms of religious life. Some Ursulines lived in community at an early date, and Charles Borromeo, archbishop of Milan from 1566, encouraged a distinctive orientation toward education. Valuable agents of reform, Ursulines were found in France by the 1570s. In 1612 the Paris Ursulines, conforming to legislation of the Council of Trent, adopted a monastic life with strict cloister and solemn vows. This cloistered form extended throughout France, and Ursulines became specialists in women's education.

The first convent of women in the present-day U.S. was Ursuline, established in New Orleans from the monastery of Rennes, France. (They had been founded in Canada by Marie de l'Incarnation Guyart* in 1639.) Expansion from the New Orleans convent, as well as nineteenth-century foundations from Boulogne-sur-Mer, France (1845, 1850), and Straubing, Germany (1858), introduced Ursulines to America. Many of these nuns,* cloistered in Europe, embraced significant modification to their way of life in order to staff the burgeoning parochial school* system, as well as their own academies and colleges. There are presently more than twenty-three hundred Ursulines in the U.S.

BIBLIOGRAPHY. A. Clotilde, *Ursulines of the West* (1936); T. Ledochowska, *Angela Merici and the Company of St. Ursula,* 2 vols. (1969).

P. Byrne

U.S. Catholic Mission Council. *See* MISSIONS, AMERICAN CATHOLIC FOREIGN.

V

Valentine, Milton (1825-1906). Lutheran* theologian* and educator. Born in Uniontown, Maryland, Valentine was educated at the Gettysburg College and Lutheran Theological Seminary (1852). Following several pastorates he became a teacher at the Lutheran Theological Seminary in 1866, president of the College (1868-1884) and president and professor of systematic theology at the Seminary (1884-1903). His publications included *Natural Theology* (1885), *Theological Ethics* (1897), *Christian Faith and Life* (1898) and the widely influential two-volume presentation of his system of theology, *Christian Theology* (1906), edited by his son.

Following the mid-nineteenth-century theological controversy which split the Lutheran General Synod and formed both the General Council and its seminary at Philadelphia (in opposition to Gettysburg Seminary), Valentine became the leading theological figure for the General Synod and its seminary. A moderating influence, Valentine moved away from the earlier evangelical position of Samuel S. Schmucker,* the seminary's founder, by accepting a milder form of the confessionalism* predominant in his day. He advocated complete subscription to the Augsburg Confession, but, in opposition to the General Council and more confessionalist theologians, he denied the necessity of subscription to other confessional statements in the *Book of Concord.* In his thinking and writing, Valentine demonstrated a tolerance both toward theological opponents and the evolutionary* and scientific ideas then emerging in his day.

BIBLIOGRAPHY. A. R. Wentz, *Gettysburg Lutheran Theological Seminary,* 2 vols. (1965); E. C. Nelson, ed., *The Lutherans in North America* (1975).

F. K. Wentz

Van Alstyne, Fanny Jane Crosby. *See* CROSBY (VAN ALSTYNE), FANNY JANE.

Van Cott, Margaret Ann Newton (1830-1914). Methodist* evangelist.* Born in New York City to an affluent family, Maggie Newton was confirmed in the Protestant Episcopal Church* in 1841. In 1848 she married Peter Van Cott and took over as manager of his dry goods business when he became chronically ill in 1850. She began attending prayer meetings* around 1858 and after her husband's death in 1866 joined the Methodist Episcopal Church.

Van Cott became a leader at the Five Points Mission founded by Phoebe Palmer* and began receiving invitations to conduct revivals.* Unusually successful as a soul-winner, she decided to devote herself to evangelism* and was granted a local preacher's license* in 1869—the first American woman licensed to preach from a Methodist pulpit. She traveled the nation for more than thirty years, conducting revivals and organizing prayer groups. An estimated 75,000 persons were converted* under her ministry, and about half of them joined the Methodist Church.

BIBLIOGRAPHY. J. O. Foster, *The Life and Labours of Mrs. Maggie Newton Van Cott* (1872); *NAW* 3; Obituary Notice, *Christian Advocate* (Sept. 3, 1914):26-27. K. K. Kidd

Van Dusen, Henry Pitney (1897-1975). Protestant* theological educator and ecumenical* leader. Born in Philadelphia, Pennsylvania, Van Dusen was educated at Princeton University* (B.A., 1919), Union Theological Seminary,* New York (B.D., 1924) and the University of Edinburgh (Ph.D., 1932). Ordained* a Presbyterian* minister* in 1924, Van Dusen was appointed secretary of the student division of the YMCA.* He returned to Union Seminary in 1926, serving as instructor and then as assistant professor of philosophy of religion* and systematic theology,* as Roosevelt Professor of Systematic Theology, as dean of students and, from 1945 to 1963, as president.

Van Dusen's tenure as president of Union was marked by a significant expansion and diversification of the seminary's faculty, student body and curriculum. Van Dusen led Union to a position of great prominence and prestige among liberal

Protestant seminaries.* He was a leading American Protestant* advocate of the ecumenical movement* and a delegate to the world conference of the Life and Work Movement at Oxford in 1937. Van Dusen actively promoted the formation of the World Council of Churches* (WCC), serving as chair of the WCC study commission and as a member of its executive committee. He attended the first WCC assembly in Amsterdam in 1948.

With Reinhold Niebuhr* and others, Van Dusen was a founder in 1941 of the journal *Christianity and Crisis,* and he served on its editorial board as well as on the boards of the *Presbyterian Tribune,* the *Ecumenical Review* and other journals of American Protestantism. Van Dusen was an important proponent of mainline Protestant missions,* an interest which, along with his concern for Christian unity, was reflected in his many publications.

BIBLIOGRAPHY. *DARB;* R. T. Handy, *A History of Union Theological Seminary in New York* (1987); *NCAB* H; D. K. Thompson, "Henry Pitney Van Dusen: Ecumenical Statesman" (unpublished Ph.D. dissertation, Union Theological Seminary, Richmond, Virginia, 1974).

W. A. Silva

Van Dyke, Henry (1852-1933). Presbyterian* minister,* educator, author and diplomat. Born in Germantown, Pennsylvania, his father, Henry Jackson van Dyke, was a Presbyterian minister. Young Henry was educated at the Brooklyn Polytechnic Institute, Princeton University* (B.A., 1873) and Princeton Theological Seminary* (B.D., 1877). From 1877 to 1879 he traveled abroad, including a period of study in theology* at the University of Berlin under Isaak Dorner (1809-1884). He returned to the U.S. to pastor the United Congregational Church, Newport, Rhode Island (1879-1883). From 1883 to 1899 he was the pastor of the prestigious Brick Presbyterian Church in New York City.

Van Dyke's career began in 1884 with the publication of *The Reality of Religion,* followed by a great variety of works, including poetry, short stories, literary criticism and outdoor life (he was an avid fisherman). His most famous work is *The Story of the Other Wise Man* (1896), which he first presented as Christmas sermons at Brick Church. It was subsequently translated into twenty-eight languages. A gifted preacher, in 1896 he delivered the Yale* Lectures on Preaching, which were published under the title *The Gospel for an Age of Doubt.* His literary renown led to his appointment as Murray Professor of English Literature at Prince-

ton University (1899-1913; 1919-1923). President Woodrow Wilson,* a personal friend of van Dyke's, appointed him ambassador to the Netherlands and Luxembourg (1913-1916). He resigned from that appointment when his strongly pro-Allied sentiments made it difficult for him to remain in a neutral country.

Van Dyke's crowning achievement was his role as chairman of the committee which produced *The Book of Common Worship of the Presbyterian Church* (1906, revised edition 1932). He also served as chairman of the committee which produced the "Brief Statement of the Reformed Faith" (1902), and he was moderator of the General Assembly in 1902.

Van Dyke's theology can best be described as mediating, with a liberal tendency. A leader in the movement for creedal revision, he particularly opposed the traditional Reformed* doctrine of reprobation and was a convinced evolutionist.* A staunch defender of Charles A. Briggs* in the famous heresy trial,* van Dyke found little of value in the issues raised by fundamentalism. Nevertheless, he retained much of the language of evangelical* piety,* though his works may be considered doctrinally imprecise.

BIBLIOGRAPHY. *DAB* X; *DARB; NCAB* 25; H. T. Kerr, ed., *Sons of the Prophets* (1963); T. van Dyke, *Henry Van Dyke, a Biography* (1935); T. van Dyke, *Henry van Dyke* (1935).

J. R. Wiers

Van Til, Cornelius (1895-1987). Reformed apologist. Born at Grootegast, Netherlands, Van Til immigrated with his family to America in 1905. As a member of the Christian Reformed Church,* Van Til attended Calvin College and Calvin Seminary in Grand Rapids, Michigan, followed by studies at Princeton Theological Seminary* and Princeton University.* Ordained* in the Christian Reformed Church (1927), he ministered briefly in Michigan and then taught apologetics* for one year at Princeton Seminary before moving to the newly founded Westminster Theological Seminary in Philadelphia in 1929. Van Til joined the Orthodox Presbyterian Church* soon after its inception in 1936 and remained at Westminster until his retirement in 1975 at the age of eighty.

Van Til built his apologetics around an original application of traditional Reformed* theology.* Borrowing from, as well as correcting, the Princeton traditions of B. B. Warfield* and the Dutch contributions of Abraham Kuyper* and Herman Bavinck, he constructed a presuppositional apologetic based on two fundamental assertions: (1) the Creator-creature distinction that demands human beings presuppose the self-attesting triune God in all their thinking; (2) the reality that unbelievers will resist this obligation in every aspect of life and thought. Insisting that all thought is analogical and self-consciously dependent on the reality of the biblical God and the authority of his revelation, Van Til opposed autonomy, the attempt to think and live by some criterion of truth other than God's Word. All reasoning processes are circular since they must begin with an ultimate, prior religious norm, either for God or against him. Autonomy is self-defeating since its circular reasoning rejects the only basis for its claims, the Word of the living God. Thus Christian apologetics must not yield to any autonomous principle, such as a framework of philosophy or logic abstracted from the Creator God of the Scriptures.

Van Til wrote over twenty books during his teaching career, in addition to over thirty unpublished class syllabi which were widely circulated. Perhaps best known is *The Defense of the Faith* (1955). His views were widely known and debated amongst evangelical* and conservative Reformed theologians and apologists and have been developed by some of his students.

BIBLIOGRAPHY. J. Frame, *Van Til the Theologian* (1976); E. F. Geehan, ed., *Jerusalem and Athens* (1971); W. White, Jr., *Van Til, Defender of the Faith; An Authorized Biography* (1979).

H. M. Conn

Vancouver Assembly. The sixth assembly of the World Council of Churches,* meeting from July 24 to August 10, 1983, in Vancouver, Canada. Meeting on the campus of the University of British Columbia, this was the second assembly in North America (the first was at Evanston,* Illinois, in 1952). The theme of the assembly, "Jesus Christ—The Life of the World," provided occasion to emphasize the life-affirming nature of Christianity and the church's mission to deny the ultimate power of the world's oppression, death and destruction.

This assembly focused on eight issues in contemporary ecumenism: witnessing in a divided world, taking steps toward unity, moving toward participation, healing and sharing life in community, confronting threats to peace and survival, struggling for justice and human dignity, learning in community and communicating credibly. The assembly made statements on several critical issues—peace and justice, human rights, international food disorder—and several critical places—the Middle East, Southern Africa, Central America, Cyprus, the Pacific and Afghanistan. The assembly did not concern itself with substantial reports but

with wide participation and worship.

By far the largest WCC assembly ever held to that date, Vancouver had 4,500 participants, including 847 voting delegates from 301 member churches. Of these, 310 came from North America and Western Europe; 142 from Eastern Europe; and 369 from Africa, Asia, Latin America, the Pacific and the Middle East. Fifteen guests from other religious faiths were active participants. Participants, meeting in a multicolored tent known as "the canvas cathedral," experienced, among others, ancient Orthodox* liturgies,* Caribbean calypso and prayers by Canadian Indians. A Sunday celebration of the so-called Lima Liturgy, presided by the archbishop of Canterbury (Robert C. Runcie), was a liturgical expression of the theological convergence represented in the historic ecumenical document *Baptism, Eucharist, and Ministry* (1982).

BIBLIOGRAPHY. World Council of Churches, *Gathered for Life: Official Report, VI Assembly, World Council of Churches, Vancouver, Canada, 24 July—10 August 1983,* ed. D. Gill (1983).

P. A. Crow

Varick, James (c.1750-1827). Cofounder and first bishop* of the African Methodist Episcopal Zion Church.* Born to a slave mother in the household of the Van Varcks near Newburgh, New York, Varick was a shoemaker in New York City by the close of the American Revolution.* A member of the John Street Methodist* Episcopal (ME) Church, he led the drive for autonomy for African-American members who had formed the Zion Society in 1796. It became one of several African churches in the Methodist Episcopal denomination between 1799 and 1816. From 1806 Varick served as a colored local deacon,* an ordained* but proscribed order of ministry under experimentation by Bishop Francis Asbury.*

An emerging leader of African-Americans in New York City, Varick preached a sermon commemorating the end of the foreign slave trade in 1808, was active in early African-American voluntary societies and became a supporter of ecumenical religious ventures like the American Bible Society.* With the Zion congregation, Varick refused to join the new African Methodist Episcopal* (AME) denomination out of Philadelphia, preferring to form an African conference within the Methodist Episcopal Church. Failing in that effort and other moves to get full ordination for African-American ministers, Varick and his colleagues created an independent organization, another AME Church—the title of *Zion* being officially added in 1848. Varick was the first superintendent (bishop) of the new denomination, which re-elected its chief executives every four years. A church organizer, antislavery advocate, supporter of the first African-American newspaper (*Freedom's Journal*) and activist seeking African-American voting rights, Varick died two weeks after New York abolished slavery in 1827.

BIBLIOGRAPHY. *DAB* X; *DARB;* R. W. Logan, "Varick, James," *Dictionary of American Negro Biography,* ed. R. W. Logan and M. R. Winston (1985); W. J. Walls, *Reality of the Black Church: History of the African Methodist Episcopal Zion Church* (1974).

W. B. Gravely and D. Nelson

Vasey, Thomas (c.1746-1826). Methodist* missionary* to America. A lay* preacher among the Methodist Societies in England until ordained* by John Wesley* for the purpose of establishing a church in America, Vasey joined Thomas Coke,* Richard Whatcoat* and Francis Asbury* in organizing the Methodist Episcopal Church at the 1784 Christmas Conference* in Baltimore. He assisted in the ordination* of Asbury and others as the newly formed church anticipated its ministry throughout the new Republic.

Although described by several as a "great sufferer for the gospel," preaching not only "about Christianity, but Christ," Vasey seemed forever on the periphery—restless and unsatisfied. After just two years, apparently uncertain about the validity of Wesley's ordination, Vasey was re-ordained by Bishop William White* of the recently organized Protestant Episcopal Church in America,* where he served as rector* for a short while before returning to England. Once back on more familiar turf, Vasey served as curate* within the Anglican Church* before again rejoining Wesley and the Methodists in 1789. He remained with the Methodists (serving as "resident clergyman" at Wesley's chapel, London, 1811-1825) until his death on December 27, 1826.

BIBLIOGRAPHY. M. Vasey, *The Life of Thomas Vasey* (1874). R. G. Tuttle

Vassar, Matthew (1792-1868). Baptist* philanthropist* and founder of Vassar College. Born at East Tuddingham, County of Norfolk, England, Vassar immigrated to Dutchess County, New York, in 1796 with his parents James and Anne Vassar. After his father's brewery in Poughkeepsie was destroyed by fire in 1811, Vassar launched an independent brewing business which prospered. On March 7, 1813, he married Catherine Valentine.

In 1845 Vassar and his wife visited Europe. A visit to Guy's Hospital in London "first suggested the idea of devoting a portion of my estate to some charitable purpose." About this time he also took an interest in a girl's school operated by his niece, Lydia Booth. Booth later sold the school to Milo P. Jewett. The business transaction brought Jewett into contact with Vassar and the plan of a college for women began to take shape. In 1861 Vassar provided an endowment of almost unprecedented size ($400,000 hand-delivered in a tin box to the trustees) for the first true liberal arts college for women in America. Vassar College's early board of trustees included Henry Ward Beecher* and Samuel F. B. Morse.*

Committed to an educational experience that was Christian but never sectarian, his purposes in educating women were at least partially expressed in an address to the college trustees on February 23, 1864: ". . . the strongest incentives to goodness and the most valuable religious tendencies, will be found to flow most of all, like an emanation, from the presence of gifted, cultivated Christian women." While addressing the trustees of the college on June 23, 1868, Vassar collapsed and died.

BIBLIOGRAPHY. *DAB* X; M. Vassar, *The Autobiography and Letters of Matthew Vassar,* ed. E. H. Haight (1916). M. D. Floding

Vatican Council I (1869-1870). The First Vatican Council, which met in the north transept of St. Peter's Basilica in Rome from December 8, 1869, until September 1, 1870, is counted by the Roman Catholic* Church as the twentieth ecumenical or general council. Membership was restricted to Roman Catholic cardinals* and bishops,* along with the superiors general of male religious orders.* A total of 793 participated at one time or other in four solemn public sessions and eighty-nine working sessions ("general congregations"). They represented a church with an estimated population of 100 million or some 13.7 per cent of a world Christian population of 731,000,000.

The council considered six draft proposals ("schemata") but accepted only two final documents: a constitution on the interrelationship of faith and reason, known from its initial Latin words as *Dei Filius* (April 24, 1870), and a constitution known as *Pastor Aeternus* (July 18, 1870), declaring the meaning of the "primacy" and "infallibility"* attributed to the pope. In *Dei Filius* the council asserted that God's existence can be known by the natural light of human reason and that, although reason cannot prove the teachings of revelation, it cannot be opposed to them. The constitution reaffirmed the inspiration and divine authorship of Scripture,* as well as the church's authoritative role in determining the meaning of the revealed books.

In *Pastor Aeternus* papal primacy or leadership in the church is assigned the authoritative role of jurisdiction. It is not merely a matter of honor or precedence or of inspection. It means directive power over the whole Church in matters of faith, morals, discipline and government. The descriptive definition of the infallibility that the council attributed to the pope was phrased carefully: The pope must be speaking as a public person, as "supreme pastor and teacher," in his official capacity (*ex cathedra*—literally, "from his official teaching chair"). He must be deliberately exercising his supreme authority; and he must be stating that a given teaching in faith or morals belongs to the revelation given by God.

Arguing from Matthew 16:18 and Luke 22:32, as well as from the tradition of the Church, the council then stated that in such circumstances the pope "possesses through the divine assistance promised him in the person of St. Peter, the infallibility with which the divine Redeemer willed his church to be endowed in defining doctrine concerning faith or morals; and that such definitions of the Roman Pontiff are therefore irreformable because of their nature, but not because of the agreement of the church." The final sentence, added at the last minute, was intended to deny that subsequent acceptance by the Church throughout the world was necessary before an infallible papal statement was considered valid. This had been the argument of the fourth "Gallican* article" adopted by the assembly of the French clergy in 1682.

The council was called by Pope Pius IX* (Giovanni Mastai-Feretti, 1792-1878), whose election as pope in 1846 had been favorably greeted in liberal circles. But he was ousted from Rome by revolutionaries in 1848 and returned in 1850 only under the protection of French troops. The rest of his papacy, which was the longest on record, was spent in conflict with the dominant intellectual and political forces of the age. For a thousand years, the popes had ruled their own kingdom in central Italy. This put them in conflict with the rising Italian nationalism of the nineteenth-century *Risorgimento,* which aimed at a united Italy with Rome as its capital. Pius IX and his immediate predecessors aligned themselves with the more conservative European monarchies and resisted ideas such as popular sovereignty, parliamentary democracy, freedom of the press and of assembly, religious toleration and freedom of conscience.

Pius IX's solemn pronouncement in 1854 that Mary the mother of Jesus had in her conception been preserved free from the original sin that affected all other human beings (Mary's "immaculate conception"*) was an expression of the pope's own piety, but it was also intended to highlight the ancient Christian teaching about the effects of original sin and rebuke the humanitarian optimism of Enlightenment* thinkers and nineteenth-century liberals.

In 1864, Pius IX issued the "syllabus of errors," a digest of papal condemnations. On December 6, 1864, two days before the syllabus appeared, he had informed the cardinals in Rome of his intention to summon a general council. Public announcement was delayed until 1867, and preparations began in earnest that summer. The main focus was to be on contemporary rationalism, which was seen to be challenging religious faith, and on liberal political and intellectual orientations, which weakened the papacy's position in the Church. The council would also have to deal with a division that had grown within Catholicism, between the centralizing forces of "ultramontanism,"* with its Romantic* emphasis on the papacy, and liberal Catholics. Some of the latter emphasized historical and biblical study more than the philosophical approach predominant at Rome, while others were interested in accommodation with the prevailing social, cultural and political currents of the day.

In separate papal letters, Eastern churches not in communion with Rome and "all Protestants* and other non-Catholics" were invited to "return to the truth and to communion with the Catholic Church." Meetings were held throughout Europe at which Protestant bodies framed refusals of the invitation. Many U.S. Protestants ignored the Roman proceedings, but the Presbyterian* General Assembly of 1869 termed the pope's claims "inconsistent with a catholicity more catholic than Rome, the authority of infallible Scripture, and the glorious supremacy of Jesus Christ."

During the council's sessions, American religious writers maintained a substantial interest. Leonard Woolsey Bacon* of the First Congregational* Church of New Haven republished a pamphlet by Archbishop Peter Kenrick* of St. Louis which argued against a definition of papal infallibility. John W. Nevin* of Mercersburg* provided analyses that took the European political situation into account, and Philip Schaff* prepared a history of the council. In secular and religious journals, Protestant scholars analyzed the biblical, historical and theological bases of the doctrines being discussed in Rome and speculated on their impact on the civil loyalties of Roman Catholics. Protestant sympathies lay with the minority of bishops who opposed the infallibility definition. When the council had ended, the Evangelical Alliance* meeting in New York City in 1873 offered a "helping arm and active sympathy" to European "Old Catholics" who had split with Rome over infallibility. Evangelical* leader Roswell Hitchcock lamented Roman Catholic "want of wisdom" in the council's decrees, but he also saw that "a new spiritual power" at Rome was replacing the pope's temporal power, and he was hopeful that the Church would repent so that its last days would be its "best days."

Vatican I was a European council of a European Church. Only fifty-five participants, those from Near-Eastern churches in union with Rome, were of non-European stock. Three-fifths of the council "fathers" were based in Europe; Asia, Africa, Australia and Oceania were represented by missionary bishops* from Europe. Half of these were from France, another quarter from Italy. North and South American bishops, forty-nine of them from the U.S., were all of European origin or birth. Not a single native of East Asia, India or Africa was present. Contrast with the situation a century later is sharp. By the late twentieth century well over half the world's Roman Catholics lived in Third World countries, and their churches are largely led by native bishops.

Although papal infallibility was not on the council's formal agenda, it had been discussed in the committee which prepared the agenda and was the major topic of Roman conversation during the winter of 1869-1870. Petitions which circulated indicated that approximately four-fifths of the council fathers supported the doctrine. Others ("inopportunists") accepted it but felt the time was not right for a pronouncement. A small group opposed the definition because they judged it inadequately grounded in the Church's tradition.

Before formal debate began on infallibility, the council discussed other topics; discipline among bishops and priests* and the possibility of a universal primary catechism.* Nothing came of these discussions, but a formal constitution was adopted on basic tenets of Catholic faith and the relationship of faith and reason. In the debate on infallibility, most U.S. bishops took the "inopportunist" position. The doctrine had not been generally taught in the U.S., and they feared political repercussions from its introduction. A few bishops of French origin were strong pro-infallibilist, while Archbishop Peter Kenrick of St. Louis and Bishops Augustin Verot* of St. Augustine,

Florida; Bernard McQuaid* of Rochester; Richard V. Whelan* of Wheeling, West Virginia; and Michael Domenec of Pittsburgh were strong opponents.

In a test vote on July 13, seven Americans were among eighty-eight negative votes, but only Edward Fitzgerald of Little Rock, Arkansas, remained to cast a "no" vote on July 18, when by a vote of 533-2 papal primacy and infallibility were defined as Roman Catholic dogmas.* The council continued desultory sessions until September 1, but the French garrison had left because of the outbreak on July 19 of the Franco-Prussian War. Italian troops occupied Rome on September 20, ending the independence of the Papal States. The council was suspended on October 20 and never reopened. Although the papal prerogative of infallibility has been used only once, when on November 1, 1950, Pope Pius XII* proclaimed the dogma of Mary's assumption* into heaven, Roswell Hitchcock's judgment proved correct. As papal temporal power disappeared, the pope's "new spiritual power" within Catholicism grew stronger after Vatican I.

See also PAPACY AND U.S. CATHOLICS; PAPAL INFALLIBILITY; VATICAN II AND AMERICAN CATHOLICISM.

BIBLIOGRAPHY. R. Aubert, *Vatican I* (1964); C. Butler, *The Vatican Council, 1869-1870* (1930); A. B. Hasler, *How the Pope Became Infallible* (1981); J. Hennesey, *The First Council of the Vatican, The American Experience* (1963); G. MacGregor, *The Vatican Revolution* (1957); J. H. Smylie, "American Protestants Interpret Vatican Council I," *CH* 38 (1969):459-474.

J. Hennesey

Vatican Council II (1962-1965). The Second Vatican Council had a revolutionary impact on American Catholic practices and self-awareness. It reformed liturgical* patterns, governing styles and ecclesiastical discipline. These changes had an even more significant influence upon the consciousness of many Catholics who had believed that their divinely-established Church was the one bastion of transcendence, stability and divine purpose in a world that was ceaselessly changing, apparently directionless and increasingly secular.

On January 25, 1959, just ninety days after he had been elected pope,* John XXIII* made the surprising announcement that he would call an ecumenical council. The council opened on October 11, 1962, after nearly four years of preparation, and closed on December 8, 1965. Throughout this period the religious and secular press in the U.S. kept Americans well informed about the procedures and results of the conciliar deliberations. For many American Catholics the council's debates and decisions, as reported in the press, were unsettling because they revealed in a public and visible way a great diversity of practice and opinion within the Catholic communion. To some this realization was frightening because it shattered their visions of Catholic unity and uniformity that had been developing in most recent American history. For others, it was a liberating experience, filled with hope for the moral and institutional renewal* of Catholicism.

Vatican II was a pastoral council. It was called to revitalize Christian living among Catholics, to reform changeable ecclesiastical practices and structures, to nurture Christian unity, to engage Catholicism in a compassionate dialog with the modern world, to help promote world peace and social justice and to contribute to whatever advanced the dignity and unity of humanity. Internal and external renewal for the sake of Christian integrity and a more effective Christian mission in the world were the hallmarks of the council's intentions.

The American Contribution. The council enabled the American bishops* to share their pastoral experiences with other bishops. With the help of their own theological experts, the American bishops contributed to the conciliar discussions on a number of issues that had received some pre-conciliar theological reflection.

The Benedictine monks of St. John's Abbey in Collegeville, Minnesota (particularly Godfrey Dickmann, editor of *Worship*), following in the footsteps of Virgil Michel,* had since the 1930s been promoting a renewal of Catholic liturgical life and practice. By the 1960s, moreover, the renewal of biblical studies, occasioned by the papal encyclical* *Divino Afflante Spiritu* (1943), had produced a number of mature American Catholic biblical scholars. Systematic Catholic social thought, initiated by John Ryan,* had also developed in American circles. Prior to the council, furthermore, individual theologians* like Gustave Weigel,* had engaged in and encouraged Catholic theological reflection on the ecumenical movement.* Perhaps the most distinctive and creative American contribution to the conciliar debates was in the area of religious liberty.* John Courtney Murray's* previous twenty-year discussions on religious liberty prepared him to take a leading role in formulating the council's *Declaration on Religious Liberty.*

Although American bishops had, by reflection and experience, some preparation for the conciliar

debates, they were not entirely aware of the theological developments that had been taking place in the European Catholic theological community since World War 2* and were unprepared to discuss some of the issues relative to the new understandings of revelation, tradition and the Church. For these bishops the council was a learning experience because it provided them with an opportunity to discuss and debate new theological perspectives with other bishops and theological experts from around the world and to discover new theological ways of thinking about and understanding their own experiences within the Church and the world.

Conciliar Reforms. The council produced sixteen documents that described the Church's understanding of its role and mission in the modern world. The documents on the liturgy, Church, revelation, ecumenism, religious liberty, and the Church and the modern world were the most significant of the sixteen. They reflected the new biblical, historical and existential* theology* that had been developing in France and Germany, as well as the older rational neo-Thomistic* theology. The very combination of the older and newer theologies provided grounds for both liberal and conservative post-conciliar interpretations of the council's intentions.

Although the documents of Vatican II did not intend to produce new doctrinal* definitions and corresponding anathemas, as had some previous councils, they were not devoid of dogmatic* content. In fact, they not only reaffirmed a number of former dogmatic statements but also represented a new dogmatic sensitivity to the historical and mutable dimensions of human existence and Christian faith.

The council fostered a reform mentality. Pope John XXIII used the Italian term *aggiornamento,** bringing the Church up-to-date, to describe one of the council's chief purposes. For the pope, this meant that the council should enable Catholics to renew their faithfulness to the gospel in the modern world. The conciliar talk of renewal, change and reform, however, represented a dynamic shift of consciousness for many Catholics who were reared in a Church that was accustomed to speaking about the Church's irreformable nature and its unchanging practices.

The conciliar and post-conciliar reform mentality had its origin, in part at least, in the documents' emphasis on the historicity of humanity. Although some documents continued to speak of human nature in the abstract, most of them interpreted human and Christian existence existentially as a vocation and a mission. Revelation and salvation* were also understood historically as a series of events that had a beginning, a development and a fulfillment. This historical view of Christian anthropology helped to produce a new consciousness of the Church's presence in the world.

The council presented the Church as "a kind of sacrament* or sign of intimate union with God, and of the unity of all mankind. She is also an instrument for the achievement of such union and unity." This view represented a fundamental shift from the former emphasis on the Church's juridical and institutional aspects. The council stressed the primacy of the Church's mission within the economy of salvation, with Christ at the head and center. Within this context the Church was distinguished from the kingdom of God, thereby reviving the eschatological dimension of Christian and ecclesial life. The council also acknowledged, for the first time in any official Catholic document, the ecclesial reality of Orthodox* and Protestant* churches.

The council underlined the intimate relationship between the Church and the world, and urged a sympathetic dialog between Catholicism and other Christian churches, other world religions and modernity. The call for dialog ended the post-Tridentine confrontational and polemical posture toward Protestants and modernity. The council also acknowledged the autonomy of earthly affairs, that is, that created things and societies enjoy their own laws and values, which must be respected. This autonomy was a requirement not only of the modern world but also of the Creator's will.

The council affirmed religious liberty as one of the manifestations of the developing consciousness of human dignity and autonomy in the modern world and acknowledged the legitimacy of those modern constitutional practices which protected it for all persons.

Conciliar Reforms and American Realities. Although the council had a significant impact on American Catholics, it was not solely responsible for the post-conciliar revolutionary changes in American Catholicism. Social and cultural transformations in the U.S. and in American Catholicism in particular greatly affected the ways American Catholics interpreted conciliar documents and applied them to the Church's practices and institutions.

Since World War 2 American Catholics were becoming more socially and economically mobile, moving in greater numbers into the suburbs and into the boardrooms of major corporations. In effect, that meant that they were becoming more clearly identified with middle-class cultural and social pluralism. John F. Kennedy's* election to the presidency in 1960 symbolized the social and cultural mobility of Catholics and their acceptance in American life. The state of Catholic isolation from American cultural and political life was coming to an end about the same time that the Second Vatican Council was articulating a new consciousness of the Church's role in the world.

The Civil Rights Movement,* the protests against the Vietnam War,* the student unrest, the campaign for women's liberation and the political crisis of Watergate in the immediate post-Kennedy era affected Catholics as well as other Americans. These cultural changes, coupled with the post-conciliar reforms, contributed to significant transformations in American Catholicism.

The council and the post-conciliar reforms tended to complicate, intensify and justify for many American Catholics the cultural and social dynamics of change, diversity, openness to secularity and freedom during the 1960s and early 1970s. Visible changes in the liturgy, ecclesiastical discipline and piety,* more democratic and lay-involved patterns of governing parish* and diocesan* churches, friendly relations and dialogs with other churches and religions, increased participation of religious and clergy* in political and social-justice movements, new content and methods in catechetics* and theology, and departures of clerics and religious from their active ministries had profound effects upon the American Catholic sense of religious identity. Change itself was becoming a part of Catholic identity, replacing the former sense of permanence and stability.

The reforms that affected the lives and identity of ordinary church-going Catholics the most were those in the liturgy, ecclesiastical discipline and forms of devotional piety. The pre-conciliar sense of Catholic identity was frequently tied to distinctive Catholic practices: Latin* in the liturgy, meatless Fridays, Lenten fastings and abstinence, the cult of the saints* and the regular practice of auricular confession.* When the post-conciliar reforms either eliminated or made optional these specific Catholic ways of being religious, they also removed some of the distinctiveness and separateness of Catholic identity.

The Catholic meaning and symbol system that many American Catholics considered stable and unchanging began to shift. At first alterations in the most visible symbols indicated the shift, but increasingly the new teachings behind the visible transformations began to be promulgated through religious instruction programs. New signs of

Catholic identity and a new catechetics that helped interpret those signs replaced the older ones and began to produce a new sense of Catholic identity for the rising generation.

Social transformations, ecclesiastical reforms and the papal teachings on birth control* combined, sociologists argue, to register a dramatic decline in Catholic participation in the Church's public worship* in the decade following the council. Between 1963 and 1974, weekly Mass* attendance declined by thirty-five per cent and monthly confessions by fifty-five per cent. Significant losses also occurred in commitments to the religious life and priestly ministry. By 1976, 35,000 nuns* and 10,000 priests* had left their religious orders* and the priesthood. The number of seminarians also declined by sixty-four per cent between 1964 and 1975. Significant numbers of Catholics, moreover, have increasingly rejected official Church teachings on birth control, abortion,* remarriage after divorce and papal infallibility.* These changes registered discontent with and alienation from Catholicism.

The experience of change was reinforced by diversity and pluralism within American Catholicism. Catholics had previously experienced internal diversity in ethnic* and social issues, but the postconciliar diversity was qualitatively different. The implementation of the conciliar changes and reforms varied in extent and rapidity throughout the country, giving rise to a great deal of internal visible diversity.

Although the postconciliar reforms were generally accepted, they produced conflicts within the Church that reinforced the dynamics of diversity and change. Reactions to the reforms and interpretations of the council's intentions varied considerably and created new ideological divisions within American Catholicism. Catholic traditionalists, the most reactionary group within American Catholicism, rejected the validity, not just the abuses, of postconciliar liturgical reforms. Other conservatives questioned the extent and uncontrolled pace of the reforms or thought that the elite liberal episcopal* and clerical leadership was imposing reforms that were unwarranted by the council. Liberals thought many of the reforms were minimal and did not really meet the needs of modernity. Many of them sought to extend the implications of Vatican II and also began to revise Catholic theological concepts and methods.

Conflicts within the Church were exacerbated by the publication of the papal encyclical on birth control, *Humanae Vitae,*   in 1968. That issue and a host of other moral issues raised the question of freedom within the Church and the right to dissent to official ecclesiastical proclamations. The issues of freedom and authority within the Church became, thus, a primary focus of much of the postconciliar conflict.

Because of the reforms and new consciousness of the postconciliar era, American Catholics in the 1980s are experiencing more than ever before the full dynamics of American voluntaryism.* The American emphasis on the voluntary nature of religion, which has a tendency to undercut the values of tradition and ecclesiastical authority,* has had a new influence upon American Catholics. Some sociologists argue that many contemporary American Catholics are increasingly selective in their acceptance of a number of controversial official Church teachings, traditional religious practices and styles of Christian spirituality.* Traditionalists as well as liberal Catholics are deciding for themselves what elements of the tradition they will continue to uphold and which elements they will reject. Selective Catholics, too, have discovered new ways of being Catholic as they identify themselves with Pentecostalism,* communalism and a variety of other forms of Christian spirituality.*

Although many American Catholics are selective, they continue to accept and identify with a Catholic ethos that is manifested in the reformed liturgy, Catholic forms of personal prayer* and the fundamental creedal statements. They also remain loyal to parish structures and other ecclesiastical institutions that promote education, social services and missionary* work.

The phenomenon of selective Catholicism troubles some American Catholics because it not only threatens ecclesiastical authority but fosters an individualism* that can destroy commitment to ecclesial unity, Catholic values and to the apostolic tradition itself. The danger of à la carte Catholicism is that the individual becomes the measure of Catholic identity, thereby destroying the meaning of the term *Catholic.*

During the 1980s, in the midst of a conservative swing in politics, conservative American Catholics and Roman authorities increasingly criticized the post-conciliar smorgasbord approach to Catholicism—with its excessive emphasis on change, diversity and freedom—and reasserted the values of ecclesiastical authority, tradition and universal ecclesial unity in doctrine and morals. Roman authorities, too, have disciplined liberal dissidents within American Catholicism to secure unity and a degree of uniformity in theology and ecclesiastical administration. During his two trips to the U.S. in

1979 and 1987, Pope John Paul II* emphasized the universality of the Catholic Church—a warning to those in the American Church who advocated a quasi-independence from the Roman Church—and called upon American Catholics to be faithful to Church teachings in those areas where the greatest disagreements arose in the post-conciliar period.

Vatican II has had, and continues to have, a revolutionary influence upon American Catholicism. The forces of change and continuity, diversity and unity, freedom and authority are locked in conflict and debate in the post-conciliar Church—as they were in the council itself.

See also NEO-CONSERVATIVE CATHOLICISM; VATICAN I; VATICAN-U.S. CATHOLIC CHURCH RELATIONS.

BIBLIOGRAPHY. M. Abbott, ed., *The Documents of Vatican II* (1966); J. T. Ellis, "American Catholicism, 1953-1979: A Notable Change," *Thought* 54 (June 1979):113-131; A. Greeley, *The American Catholic: A Social Portrait* (1977); A. Greeley, *American Catholics since the Council: An Unauthorized Report* (1985); G. Kelly, *The Battle for the American Church* (1979); D. J. O'Brien, *The Renewal of American Catholicism* (1972); E. Schillebeeckx, *The Real Achievement of Vatican II* (1967); W. H. Shannon, *The Lively Debate: Response to Humanae Vitae* (1970); V. A. Yzermans, ed., *American Participation in the Second Vatican Council* (1967). P. W. Carey

Vatican-U.S. Catholic Church Relations. In the Catholic understanding of the Church, the pope,* as the bishop* of Rome, is also the chief pastor* and teacher of the whole Church. His ministry, however, is not meant to replace or impede that of local bishops* who are believed to have their office not by papal delegation, but from Christ through episcopal* ordination.* The pope's pastoral ministry to the whole Church, therefore, does not directly concern the ordinary pastoral care of local churches but the overseeing and building up of the unity of the whole Church in faith and order. Over the centuries, a series of administrative offices or congregations, known collectively as the curia, has been established to assist the bishop of Rome in carrying out his ministry to the universal Church in such areas as evangelization,* doctrine,* liturgical* and sacramental* life, etc. The need to discern the respective pastoral responsibilities of pope, local bishops and the priests* who assist them, as well as the administrative difficulties generated by any large organization, have sometimes created tensions between the Vatican and the Catholic Church in the U.S.

America as Mission Territory. From the Vatican point of view, the new nation was a mission territory and remained under the supervision of the curial office for evangelization until 1908. Religious toleration, combined with disestablishment, presented the Vatican with a novel political situation. Occasionally, from colonial times until the present, the Vatican has intervened in an extraordinary way in matters having to do with Church doctrine or discipline. As the Church expanded from its original one diocese* to its present thirty-four archdioceses* and 150 dioceses, the Vatican was also involved in the erection of new dioceses. But the area of Church life in which it has exercised the greatest influence in the U.S. has been the selection of bishops.

From the popular elections of patristic times to election by cathedral* chapters provided for by the second Lateran Council (1139), selection of bishops had been in the hands of local churches. Lateran II provided for a system of local election or nomination combined with papal confirmation or institution. This legislation was in effect in the eighteenth century, but local election had often fallen into the hands of civil rulers. Although Benjamin Franklin was unofficially involved in the selection of the first Catholic bishop, the U.S. Congress replied to the Vatican's cautious and indirect inquiries that it was without jurisdiction in such matters. At the beginning of the national period, the relative insignificance and isolation of the Catholic Church in the U.S. conspired with the weakness of the papacy to give the Church a certain independence from Vatican influence. In addition, American Catholics successfully communicated to the Vatican their reluctance to offend their fellow citizens by appearing to be unduly subject to foreign influence. Lack of cathedral chapters and virtual government indifference led to a long series of experiments in which the Vatican and the bishops worked out various methods of selecting bishops.

In 1789 the Vatican consented to John Carroll's* election as the first U.S. Catholic bishop by the nation's twenty-six priests. Baltimore became the first and only Catholic diocese. From 1822 until the third and last plenary council of Baltimore* in 1884, a system of nonbinding nomination of bishops by other bishops was in effect. Beginning in 1833, the Vatican, concerned that local priests have a voice, periodically urged the American bishops to regularize their situation by creating cathedral chapters. The bishops preferred consultors. Some system of consultation remained in effect until the revision of the Church's Code of

Canon Law* in 1917. By this time the principle of local election of bishops had all but disappeared and the arrangement of local recommendation and papal appointment, operative in the U.S. since 1822, had become universalized.

Rome and the Emerging American Catholic Identity. As the nineteenth century progressed, the Vatican exerted greater influence on American Church affairs. The papacy had gained in stature on a wave of ultramontane* resistance to state control of the Church in modern Europe. The ensuing trend to Roman centralization of administration grew stronger under Pope Pius IX.* Although it had little to fear from direct government interference, Catholicism in the U.S. would not remain untouched by this trend. A key moment came when the Vatican refused an 1849 request from the American bishops to make the archbishop of Baltimore "primate"* of the Church in the U.S. This would have given him the right to convoke and preside over national councils.

Pius IX's papacy coincided with a period of rapid growth of the American Catholic population due to immigration.* This meant new dioceses and new bishops. Advances in travel and communication facilitated contact between Europe and North America. Bishops were encouraged to send promising students to the newly opened (1859) American College at Rome.* This supplied the Vatican with a ready pool of capable Roman-trained priests from which to choose future American bishops. Until the mid-nineteenth century, with the exception of the Vatican's refusal to grant their request for the right to appoint bishops without clerical elections, the country's mission status left the American bishops relatively free, in a series of councils, to adapt Church discipline to the unique political and cultural conditions of the U.S. When the bishops were unsuccessful in resolving their problems, Rome intervened.

The complex controversies involving lay trustees* for Catholic parish* churches led to a number of such interventions. They included the removal of Philadelphia's bishop in 1826 and the ill-timed visit of Archbishop Gaetano Bedini, cut short by nativist* agitation in 1854. Following this disaster, a series of events, culminating in the First Vatican Council* (1870), brought significant numbers of American bishops to Rome for firsthand contact with the reinvigorated papacy. In addition, the bishops had the task of interpreting to a skeptical American public Pius IX's *Syllabus of Errors* (1864), Vatican I's definition of the infallibility* of the papal teaching office (1870) and consistent Vatican emphasis on a solution to the "Italian question"

that would restore the papal states. After decades of administering the Church according to their own conciliar legislation, the American bishops were now faced by Vatican I and the events leading up to it, with serious theological questions about the limits of their role in Church governance.

At the same time, ultramontanism's devotional revolution with its idealization of the papacy found willing participants in the American Catholic people. During the papacy of Leo XIII, known in the U.S. as the pope of the working man, Vatican administrative centralization was further institutionalized with the establishment in 1893 of an apostolic delegate.* This occurred in spite of the near-unanimous opposition of the American bishops and because of their inability to resolve disputes under the previous conciliar arrangement. Leo's censure of "Americanism"* in 1899 joined with Pius X's* condemnation of modernism* in 1907 to cast a smothering cloud over American Catholicism and its incipient theological gropings. The *New York Review,* a Catholic theological journal, became one of the first casualties of the subsequent hunt for modernists.

There followed a separatist phase which Romanized the hierarchy while Americanizing the Catholic people within the limits of a set of Catholic institutions (schools, hospitals, etc.) parallel to the corresponding public institutions. In 1919 the bishops formed, with Vatican approval, the National Catholic Welfare Council, which eventually evolved into the present National Conference of Catholic Bishops.* In February of 1922 the Vatican disbanded the organization, only to reverse itself a few months later with the stipulation that the organization no longer be called a "council." The bishops decided to call it a "conference" instead. Despite the presence of the conference and the apostolic delegate, Francis J. Spellman,* archbishop of New York from 1939 to 1967, emerged as a dominant figure, and through his close friendship with Pope Pius XII* became the main link between the Vatican and the Church in the U.S.

During this period, the Vatican intervened in the silencing of two Jesuit* priests. The controversies surrounding them involved the question of the Catholic position on religious liberty.* In 1949 a letter from the Vatican's doctrinal congregation to Richard Cushing,* archbishop of Boston, censured Leonard Feeney's* militant position that there was no salvation* outside the Catholic Church. This letter would later be cited approvingly in Vatican II's* *Dogmatic Constitution on the Church* (#16). The year 1949 also saw Paul Blanshard publish *American Freedom and Catholic Power,* a sustained challenge to the compatibility of Catholicism and basic American political freedoms. John Courtney Murray* emerged to defend the Catholic commitment to religious freedom. His thought on Church and state* would eventually help Catholicism to pass from its ghetto phase into the mainstream of American denominationalism.*

Murray presented religious freedom as a positive social good rather than as a situation to be tolerated in the absence of establishment. His Catholic critics in the U.S. accused him of holding the condemned Americanism of 1899. By 1955 his Jesuit superiors in Rome warned Murray that unless he stopped writing on Church and state, he would invite Vatican censure. A decade later, Murray's position would be vindicated in Vatican II's *Declaration on Religious Freedom,* which he helped to draft. The years after the council brought lively attempts to realize its calls for liturgical reform and collegial structures. Ensuing tensions became apparent with widespread dissent by American Catholics over *Humanae Vitae,** Pope Paul VI's* 1968 encyclical* on birth control.*

Recent Relations and Tensions. In addition to increasing participation in Church life at all levels, collegiality* has also brought some tensions to the relationship between pope and bishops as well as some confusion over the role of national bishops' conferences and the regular synod* of bishops at Rome. Re-emphasizing the need for Catholic unity in faith and discipline for the sake of the Church's mission to the world, Pope John Paul II,* who became pope in 1978, has made a number of interventions into the life of the Catholic Church in the U.S., including personal visits in 1979 and 1987. In 1986, at the end of a long investigative process, the Vatican's doctrinal congregation stripped moral theologian Charles Curran of his mission to teach as a Catholic theologian and removed him from his position on the pontifical faculty at the Catholic University of America.* Another moral theologian, John McNeill, was dismissed from the Jesuits when he broke a previously imposed public silence on the topic of homosexuality.* In the same year, expressing dissatisfaction with the state of the Archdiocese of Seattle, the Vatican reassigned some of Archbishop Raymond Hunthausen's episcopal powers to an auxiliary bishop. Through the intervention of a special committee of the NCCB, the Vatican restored Hunthausen to the fullness of his office in 1987 but gave him a coadjutor bishop.

Under Pope John Paul II, the selection of bishops has remained the Vatican's single-most-effective means of influencing the Church in the U.S. The 1983 Code of Canon Law provides for a process of local consultation, involving representatives of the clergy, with the pope's representative playing the key role in the recommending process. Despite historical precedent for popular elections, present Church law provides no role for the people in the selection of their bishops and parochial pastors. With the Vatican's doctrinal commitment to religious freedom, formal diplomatic relations between the U.S. and the Vatican City State, established by President Reagan* in 1984, and the 1985 agreement between the Vatican and the Italian government separating Church and state in Italy, few Americans any longer regard the Vatican's relations with the U.S. Catholic Church as the intrusion of a foreign government inimical to American political institutions.

The Vatican has generally acted slowly and cautiously toward the Catholic Church in the U.S. But the lack of constitutional restraints on the possible abuse of papal power often lends an impression of arbitrariness to Vatican interventions. Nor can it be denied that at times, such as at the turn of the century, these interventions had repressive effects. Nevertheless, by its restraint of extreme factions, its serving as an advocate or court of appeals for disenfranchised groups, including priests and black Catholics,* its check on Church accommodation to some of the excesses of American culture such as nationalism, materialism and sexual permissiveness, the Vatican can in the long view be credited with imparting a broader perspective to, and exercising a moderating influence on, the Catholic Church in the U.S. In general it has served the Petrine function of mediation and preservation of unity.

See also AMERICANISM; CONCILIAR TRADITION, AMERICAN; PAPACY AND UNITED STATES CATHOLICS; TRUSTEEISM.

BIBLIOGRAPHY. C. F. McCarthy, "The Historical Development of Episcopal Nominations in the Catholic Church of the United States (1784-1884)," *RACHAP* 38 (1927):295-354; J. Hennesey, "Papacy and Episcopacy in Eighteenth and Nineteenth-Century America," *RACHAP* 77 (1966):175-189; J. Hennesey, "The Baltimore Council of 1866: An American Syllabus," *RACHAP* 76 (1965):165-172; J. Hennesey, *The First Council of the Vatican, The American Experience, (1963)*; G. P. Fogarty, "Church Councils in the United States and American Legal Institutions," *AHC* 4 (1972):83-105; G. P. Fogarty, *The Vatican and the American Hierarchy from 1870 to 1965* (1985). W. L. Portier

Veniaminov, Innocent (Ivan Veniaminov) (1797-1879). Russian Orthodox* missionary*

bishop.* Siberian born and educated, Veniaminov accepted his bishop's 1822 call to mission in the Aleutian Islands with reluctance, but by the time he left Unalaska ten years later, physically exhausted from his labors, most of the inhabitants of the region were practicing Orthodox Christians. This was the result of his dedication to establishing schools and studying the local language and culture. Veniaminov translated the Gospel of Matthew into Aleut and authored the first tract in that language, *An Indication of the Pathway into the Kingdom of Heaven.* In addition, he amassed an enormous amount of scientific data on the region, which won him membership in the Russian Academy of Sciences. His data received wide use by secular scholars. After another five years ministering with similar methods to the Tlingit Indians around Sitka, he returned to Russia.

Elected bishop for the Russian colonies in 1840, he imposed his enlightened methods on the clergy,* founded a seminary to train native clergy, and traveled widely around the largest diocese in the Russian Church. As it grew apace with the Empire's expansion into Asia, the center of Veniaminov's activities drew him away from America, until in 1868 he succeeded Philaret Drozdov as metropolitan* of Moscow, titular head of the Russian Orthodox Church. There, in old age, he advanced the cause of foreign missions by founding the Russian Orthodox Missionary Society, which functioned until 1917. In 1977 he was canonized by the Russian Orthodox Church as "Apostle to America."

See also MISSIONS TO ALASKA, RUSSIAN ORTHODOX.

BIBLIOGRAPHY. P. Garrett, *St. Innocent, Apostle to America* (1979); M. Oeksa, ed., *Alaskan Native Spirituality* (1987).   P. D. Garrett

Verbeck, Guido Herman Fridolin (1830-1898).

Reformed missionary* to Japan. Born and educated in Holland, Verbeck immigrated to America in 1852. Theological training was received at Auburn Seminary in New York. In 1859 he went to Japan under the mission board of the Reformed Church.* Verbeck was one of the first six Protestant missionaries to arrive in Japan in 1859, the year that four ports were opened to foreigners for trade and residence.

At Nagasaki, in addition to evangelizing,* he taught English and Western technology. Many of his students later held influential positions in the Meiji government. Not long after the Restoration (1868), Verbeck was invited to Tokyo by the new government to help in setting up a new school. There he served as the first president of the school, which developed into what is now Tokyo University. As one of the *oyatoi gaikokujin* (hired foreigners), Verbeck had a prominent role as an adviser to the government. In his position he influenced many promising young men to study in America.

In 1878 he officially severed his government responsibilities and returned to missionary work. For his services to the government, he was officially decorated by the emperor. Verbeck gave the last twenty years of his life to evangelism and Bible translation. He died in Japan and was buried in a plot deeded to his family by officials of the city of Tokyo.

BIBLIOGRAPHY. *DAB* X; W. E. Griffis, *Verbeck of Japan* (1901); H. Sato, "Verbeck, Guido Herman Fridolin," *Kodansha Encyclopedia of Japan,* vol. 8 (1983).   W. N. Browning

Verot, Jean-Pierre Augustin Marcellin (1805-1876).

Bishop* of Savannah and of St. Augustine. Born in Le Puy, France, Jean-Pierre Verot joined the Society of the Priests of St. Sulpice* in Paris after his ordination* in 1828. He came to the U.S. in 1830, first teaching at St. Mary's College and at the Sulpician seminary, both in Baltimore, and from 1852 to 1858 serving as pastor* at Ellicott's Mills, Maryland. In 1858, consecrated a bishop, he was appointed vicar apostolic of Florida. In 1861, while retaining authority in Florida, Verot also was appointed to the See of Savannah.

In time Verot became a social critic, endorsing Southern nationalism, supporting the Confederate war effort and becoming known as the "rebel bishop." In January 1861 he gained national attention for a sermon, later published as *A Tract for the Times: Slavery and Abolitionism* (1861), in which he condemned both abolitionists* and the slave trade. During the Civil War* Verot ministered to both Confederate and Union soldiers. At war's end he claimed, as did several Southern Protestant* ministers, that emancipation* and the South's defeat reflected God's anger for the slaveholders' failure to honor their Christian obligations to the slaves.

During Reconstruction, Verot launched the Church's most ambitious missionary program among the freedmen, which included building special schools for them. He played a major role at the Second Plenary Council of Baltimore* in 1866, mapping ways for the Church to reach out to African-Americans, and at the Vatican Council* of 1870, where he urged the council to recognize that African-Americans had souls. Meanwhile, Verot negotiated an arrangement, known as the "Savannah Plan," whereby Catholic schools were supported by the city.

Conscious of his church's minority status, Verot discouraged any attempts to exaggerate differences between Catholics and Protestants. In 1870 Verot became the first bishop of the newly created diocese* of St. Augustine. He died there as he lived, engaged in a vigorous pastoral ministry.

BIBLIOGRAPHY. M. V. Gannon, *Rebel Bishop: The Life and Era of Augustin Verot* (1964); R. M. Miller, "Roman Catholic Church (in the South)," *ERS;* "Record of the Episcopal Aces of the Rev. Augustin Verot, Bishop of Savannah and Administrator Apostolic of Florida," in *Brief History of St. Augustine, Florida,* ed. B. Roth (1923).

Rob M. Miller

Vesey, Denmark (c.1767-1822). African Methodist* and slave-rebellion leader. Sources vary about Vesey's birthplace, but by 1781 he was a slave in the Dutch West Indies. Slave-trading Captain Joseph Vesey made Denmark his personal servant before retiring to Charleston, South Carolina, in 1783, where his home became a refuge for slaveholders escaping the 1791 uprising in St. Domingue. Denmark's notions of liberation from slavery may have been encouraged by this event.

In 1799 he purchased his freedom, became a successful carpenter and headed an extended family, including wives and children who were still slaves. Active in the small free African-American community in Charleston, Vesey became a lay* leader in the African church movement, first within the Methodist Episcopal Church and after 1817 in the African Methodist Episcopal Church* (AME). Within the metropolitan area, the African church numbered as many as 4500 members. Their independent posture brought conflicts with police, with 469 arrests recorded in 1817 and 140 recorded the next year for Vesey's Hampstead congregation. Citing liberationist and apocalyptic texts like Joshua 6:21 and Zechariah 14:1-3 in his teachings, Vesey planned an elaborate conspiracy for July 14, 1822. Fearful slaves revealed the plot to authorities, who arrested and tried 131 African-Americans, executing thirty-five, deporting forty-three and releasing the remainder. The presiding judge cited Ephesians 6:5-6 and 1 Peter 2:18 as part of Vesey's sentence, contending for a gospel "all whose paths are peace." Hanged on July 2, 1822, with six other class leaders of the African church, Vesey has been honored in the memory of African-Americans as a revolutionary advocate for liberation. The African church disbanded until the AME denomination returned to Charleston in 1865.

BIBLIOGRAPHY. *DAB* X; J. O. Killens, "Introduction," in *The Trial Record of Denmark Vesey* (1970

reprint of 1822 edition); J. Lofton, *Denmark Vesey's Revolt* (1984).

W. B. Gravely and D. Nelson

Vesey, William (1674-1746). Colonial Anglican* rector* in New York City. Raised as a New England Congregationalist* and educated at Harvard* College (B.A., 1693), Vesey's underlying Anglican sympathies prompted his call by the first permanent Anglican church on Manhattan Island. The first rector of Trinity Church in New York City, Vesey served in that post for half a century (1697-1746), overseeing the development of the colony's wealthiest parish and aggressively promoting the interests of the Church of England.

His long tenure at Trinity was characterized by numerous disputes with royal officials and other religious groups, most of which stemmed from Vesey's conservative stance on Anglican prerogatives in the colony. He had particular difficulty with governors like Robert Hunter who refused to use their political clout to aid the Anglican cause. Vesey's own power was enhanced in 1714 when he became the bishop* of London's commissary for New York and New Jersey. He used that power in his last years to oppose the preaching* of George Whitefield* and the revivals* of the Great Awakening.*

BIBLIOGRAPHY. *AAP* 5; *DAB* X; M. Dix et al., *A History of the Parish of Trinity Church in the City of New York,* vol. 1 (1898); C. K. Shipton, *New England Life in the 18th Century* (1963).

R. W. Pointer

Vespers. The evening hour of prayer. Liturgically, vespers is a service of praise and thanksgiving with psalms, another Scripture* reading, a hymn,* the *Magnificat* and a collect. Vespers and Lauds (morning prayer) are the oldest and most important of the seven hours of prayer in the Western liturgy. Following Vatican II* the Roman Catholic* service was revised and translated from Latin into the vernacular. Among other North American churches, the Lutherans* and the Episcopalians* include an evening prayer service in their liturgies. In the Episcopal Church this has traditionally been called Evensong. During the emphasis on liturgical renewal* in the 1970s, both Protestant* churches revised their evening prayer services, modeling them after the traditional Roman Catholic vespers. *See also* EVENING SERVICE. M. D. Floding

Vestry. Originally a room for keeping vestments, the term became attached to the parishioners who administer parish* business in the Episcopal

Church.* The vestry—now known as the sacristy—was a room or a distinct building of the church in which the vestments, and sometimes the vessels and other objects, were kept. Since parishioners met in the vestry to transact the business of the parish, those meeting and the meeting itself came to be called the vestry. During the colonial period the vestries became the center for lay control of the established Anglican Church,* especially in Virginia. An American innovation, vestries controlled the finances, gradually became self-perpetuating and were a source of opposition to an episcopate.* Today the vestry is that body of persons, male and female, in the Episcopal Church that administers the parish.   D. S. Armentrout

Victorious Christian Life. An evangelical* spiritual movement proclaiming the possibility and means for attaining immediate freedom from the whole power of every known sin.* The outreach of the American Wesleyan*/Holiness* tradition to Great Britain in the form of "Union Meetings for the Promotion of Scriptural Holiness" (at Brighton, Oxford and Broadlands) led by Hannah Whitall Smith,* Robert Pearsall Smith* and William E. Boardman* evolved into the spirituality of the Keswick movement.* From 1875 conferences were held annually in the village of Keswick, England. Speakers and writings from Keswick found their way back to North America, especially in connection with evangelists* such as Dwight L. Moody* whose Northfield Conferences* and Moody Bible Institute* became "Keswick" centers, and millenarians* such as Charles G. Trumbull,* editor of the *Sunday School Times.*

Keswick, or victorious life, spirituality emphasizes two steps in attaining spiritual victory in everyday Christian living: (1) Total surrender of self, ambition and every known or unknown sin to God; (2) complete faith in God's promise to grant victory over sin by his Holy Spirit who fills the believer. The promised victory is not a guaranteed continuous state, but depends on the believer's daily surrender and faith. A consequence of the victorious life is service, most specifically soul winning.* For many proponents of the victorious life, the highest calling and expression of spirituality is foreign missionary service.

Victorious Life spirituality became identified with fundamentalism* as expressed in *The Fundamentals.* Trumbull's assistant, Robert C. McQuilkin,* initiated the Victorious Life Conferences, the first of which was held at Oxford, Pennsylvania, July 19-27, 1913, featuring British Keswick leader W. H. Griffith-Thomas.* Later conferences were

held at Princeton, New Jersey (1914-1918); Stonybrook, New York (1919-1923); and thereafter at Keswick Grove, New Jersey. Early Victorious Life Conference lectures were published as *Victory in Christ* (1916), *The Victorious Life* (1918) and *Victorious Christ* (1923).

The perspective has played a profound and often unrecognized role in shaping twentieth-century evangelical spirituality. It has been institutionalized in Columbia Bible College and Theological Seminary; The Christian and Missionary Alliance,* founded by A. B. Simpson*; Prairie Bible Institute in Canada; and many evangelical parachurch* organizations.

BIBLIOGRAPHY. S. Barabas, *So Great Salvation* (1952); D. D. Bundy, *Keswick: A Bibliographic Introduction to the Higher Life Movements* (1975); D. W. Frank, *Less Than Conquerors: How Evangelicals Entered the Twentieth Century* (1986); G. M. Marsden, *Fundamentalism* (1980).

D. D. Bundy

Vietnam War and the American Churches. In 1955 the U.S. began to send financial aid to the government of South Vietnam. American soldiers were then sent to be advisors to South Vietnamese troops. The rationale for this aid was that the government of North Vietnam was Communist and aggressive; if the South should fall, soon Communism would control all Southeast Asia. South Vietnam should be the first line of defense against spreading Communism. The aid accelerated after 1964, when Congress authorized the president to provide military assistance to South Vietnam, although this act was not an official declaration of war. Americans began to engage in combat early in 1965. By March 1973, when the last American troops left Vietnam, 46,397 Americans had been killed and 306,653 wounded. The war had cost $138.9 billion, compared to $18 billion for the Korean war. In addition, huge numbers of Vietnamese were killed, wounded or made refugees, and the countryside was devastated. The war stimulated violent emotions, pro and con, among Americans and was the most unpopular war of the twentieth century. Religious people and institutions participated in the controversy.

The most visible reaction among religious people was opposition. Many who opposed the war for Christian reasons tried to influence the general population and the government through extensive writing. They asserted that the war was immoral for a variety of reasons. It was an intrusion into a civil war between North and South Vietnam. It was a racist war in two senses: It was aggression by a white nation against Oriental people, and the white nation used its own racial underclass to do the bulk of the fighting—the majority of Americans drafted being poor and African.

The war was so expensive that it was debilitating efforts to correct domestic problems such as poverty and the improvement of education. Martin Luther King, Jr.,* the civil rights* leader and president of the Southern Christian Leadership Conference,* forcefully argued that the war was racist and was impeding progress toward desegregation in America by diverting attention from the problem. The Civil Rights Movement did lose momentum as Vietnam increasingly dominated the consciousness of the nation. And, perhaps most basically, the war was illegal because it was undeclared. Denominations and organizations such as the United Church of Christ,* the United Presbyterian Church U.S.A.,* the National Council of Churches* and the Union of American Hebrew Congregations also tried to influence the moral consciousness of the population by passing anti-war resolutions at their conventions.

A number of new organizations were formed to educate the public. Among these were the Clergyman's Emergency Committee for Vietnam, the Catholic Committee on Vietnam, and especially Clergy and Laity Concerned About Vietnam, organized in 1965 by Father Daniel Berrigan, Rabbi Abraham Heschel and Lutheran* pastor Richard J. Neuhaus. In 1968 Clergy and Laity Concerned published *In the Name of America,* which consisted of news accounts of the war and pertinent provisions of international law about the conduct of war. The book vehemently argued that America was in violation of those laws, the principles established at the Nuremberg war crimes trials, and its own Law of Land Warfare contained in the U.S. Army Field Manual.

Opposition took the form of action as well as writing. Religious people conducted marches in the streets and prayer vigils at theological seminaries, churches and synagogues. Others took more direct and controversial action. A group known as the "Catholic Left," the leaders of which were Fathers Daniel and Philip Berrigan, engaged in raiding draft boards and defacing and destroying records. They did the same in FBI offices. Although they destroyed government property, they were nonviolent against persons, since their protest was against the destruction of life. They used their court trials as forums for articulating their Christian anti-war philosophy. This activity was not condoned by the Catholic Church, but it did change the attitudes of many bishops* and lay* people

toward the war. In violation of federal law, many men of draft age burned their draft cards as a protest against the war. This was often done at a public ceremony, sometimes in a church, at which there would be prayers for peace and an address or commentary on the war from the perspective of Judaeo-Christian* ethics. Such meetings were often "media events" and highly controversial.

Many theologians* analyzed the war in the light of the "just war" theory of Christian tradition. A just war must be to avenge injuries, must intend to restore peace with justice, must respect the rights of the enemy, must be conducted by the norm of proportionality (small wrongs should not be avenged by massive destruction) and should be a last resort initiated only after extensive efforts to negotiate a resolution of differences. Opponents believed the Vietnam War met none of those criteria, especially that of proportionality. In addition to being an indictment of the war, this concept had very practical application to conscientious objectors.

Section 6(j) of the Selective Service Law required that one who would be a conscientious objector must object "to participation in war in any form." By 1970, 34,255 individuals had qualified as objectors (as compared with 16,000 in World War 2*). But many had objections to this particular war because it did not fit the "just war" criteria. Because the law would not allow selective conscientious objection, many broke the law by refusing to be inducted. Some went to prison, many more fled to Canada (estimates ranged between 7,000 and 20,000) or Sweden (about 350). Some of those who fled the country were among the approximately 166,500 who deserted the military between 1967 and 1970. Not all did this for religious motivations, but many did: Their sense of Judaeo-Christian morality would not allow them to fight what they understood to be an illegal, immoral and unnecessary war.

By 1970 there were five hundred draft-information centers around the country. Many of these were operated by churches or interdenominational agencies. They were designed to help men think through their attitudes about the war in the light of their faith, to qualify for CO status, or, if they were selective objectors, to leave the U.S. Although many religious leaders, denominations and the World Council of Churches* advocated selective conscientious objection, Congress did not change the law. The Supreme Court* interpreted the criteria for CO status broadly (*U.S. v. Seeger* 380 U.S. 163 [1965]). But it maintained the prohibition of selective objection even against a religious freedom challenge (*Gillette* v. *U.S.* 401 U.S. 437 [1971]).

It should not be thought that all religious people or institutions opposed the war. Many believed America's cause in Southeast Asia was proper as a defense against "godless Communism." America was a defender of liberty and democracy* and thus the war was not inconsistent with Judaeo-Christian moral principles. A highly visible exponent of such a view was Francis Cardinal Spellman,* archbishop* of New York. Although in 1966 the American Catholic Bishops and Pope Paul VI* (in the encyclical *Christi Matri*) declared against the war and begged the participants to make peace, Cardinal Spellman remained a "hawk" until the end, declaring America's cause a "defense of civilization." Many Catholics, and others, believed the war was right. As late as July 1965, sixty-one per cent of a sample felt that it had been right to send troops to Vietnam, while only twenty-four per cent clearly believed it had been a mistake (the remainder were undecided).

But by 1969 the nation had grown weary of the war and perhaps had been sensitized by the religious arguments against it. In a survey, seventy-five per cent of those having no religious preference thought it had been a mistake to send troops, while sixty-four per cent of the Jews, fifty-nine per cent of the Protestants and fifty-three per cent of the Roman Catholics agreed that it had been wrong.

In terms of clergy, it was estimated that only five per cent were active opponents of the war, although they attracted the attention of the media and were influential beyond their numbers. Only about five per cent of the clergy actively supported the war. Observers assumed that the majority of clergy and laity supported the war but did not speak out in favor of it because they believed that religion should not take positions on political issues. Many opponents of the war remained silent, apparently for the same reason, assuming that their refusal to speak for the war was tacit opposition. Surveys showed that most laypeople believed that religion should be for solace, worship* and personal salvation,* rather than for political activism. Consequently, they encouraged their clergy not to speak out on civil rights or the war. Those who did incurred the anger of their constituency.

It was clear that the highly visible religious opponents of the war were primarily denominational bureaucrats, leaders of parachurch* or interdenominational organizations, or academics, rather than local clergy. The further away from being directly accountable to a congregation, the more they were free to express themselves. Many

believed that the war impacted American religion in ways that would be felt for the remainder of the twentieth century, primarily in terms of redefinitions of the role of local clergy in the social arena and the development of theological conservatism as a reaction to the overt radicalism of the 1960s and early 1970s.

BIBLIOGRAPHY. R. M. Brown, A. J. Heschel and M. Novak, *Vietnam: Crisis of Conscience* (1967); M. P. Hamilton, ed., *The Vietnam War: Christian Perspectives* (1967); C. A. Meconis, *With Clumsy Grace: The American Catholic Left, 1961-1975* (1979); R. J. Neuhaus, "The War, the Churches, and Civil Religion," *The Annals of the American Academy of Political and Social Science* 387 (January 1970):128-140; T. E. Quigley, ed., *American Catholics and Vietnam* (1968); J. H. Smylie, "American Religious Bodies, Just War, and Vietnam," *JCS* 11 (Autumn 1969):383-408.   R. B. Flowers

Vincent, John Heyl (1832-1920). Methodist* bishop* and educator. Born in Tuscaloosa, Alabama, Vincent's family moved to central Pennsylvania in 1837. He was ordained* as a Methodist elder* in 1857 and was transferred to the Rock River Conference in Illinois, where he served several churches. In 1861 he held the first Sunday School Teacher's Institute in America. He was an innovator in Sunday-school publications, introducing the use of "lesson leaves." In 1866 he was appointed general agent of the Methodist Episcopal Sunday School Union in recognition of his pioneer work in providing better education for Sunday-school teachers. Vincent's Sunday-school interests led to the founding, with Lewis Miller, of the Chautauqua institutes in 1874. The Chautauqua meetings developed into the most extensive American lay* educational movement of the latter part of the nineteenth century. The movement encompassed people of all denominations* in the classes, lectures, concerts and correspondence courses it sponsored all across the nation. Vincent was elected bishop in 1888 and in 1900 assumed responsibility for the Methodist Episcopal work in Europe, where he took up residence in Zurich, Switzerland.

BIBLIOGRAPHY. L. H. Vincent, *John Heyl Vincent, a Biographical Sketch* (1925).   M. E. Dieter

Virtues, Cardinal. "Virtues" are morally good habits of acting which reside in individual souls. *Cardinal* comes from *carde,* Latin for "hinge." In traditional Catholic philosophy all other virtues hinge, turn or depend on four cardinal virtues because they describe the fundamental structures of health of the soul. First clearly formulated by Plato in *The Republic,* repeated and expanded by Aristotle, they became a classical commonplace and were adopted by all major medieval philosophers. They are also mentioned in Scripture in the deutero-canonical, or apocryphal, *Book of Wisdom of Solomon.*

Their basis is in human nature itself, in the soul, which directs bodily actions in its three parts or functions. First, intelligence, or reason, is perfected by the virtue of prudence, or practical wisdom. Second, will is perfected by the virtue of fortitude, or courage. Third, appetites are perfected by the virtue of moderation, or self-control (*sophrosyne*; there is no good English equivalent to this Greek notion, with its strong aesthetic overtones of harmony and beauty). The fourth and overarching virtue, justice, is the harmony, integration and correct functioning of the three parts. *Rightness* or *righteousness* might be closer to the original meaning, for *justice* connotes to the modern mind almost exclusively social justice, fairness in relations between individuals rather than right relations within a single individual, that is, among parts of the soul.

The cardinal moral virtues are distinguished from the intellectual virtues, or virtues of the speculative intellect (wisdom, science and understanding), and both are distinguished, as natural virtues, from the three supernatural or "theological virtues" which have God as their object: faith, hope and charity.   P. J. Kreeft

Vocation. Derived from the Latin *vocatio,* or "calling," the word is used to describe both God's general election* of his people to salvation* and fellowship in the covenant* community and his particular assignment to serve one's neighbor through daily work. Biblical teaching focuses directly on the former and provides a sound basis for the latter, which was positively articulated by the Protestant reformers.

In the Old Testament, God called Israel as a nation into a covenant relationship with him and claimed them for his service. He also called individuals to specific tasks of obedience, leadership and service. Abraham, David, Jeremiah and Amos illustrate God's elective activity in this regard.

In the New Testament, God calls a new people into being through the redemptive work of Jesus the Messiah. Both Jews and Gentiles are invited to share his fellowship and inherit the blessings and promises of the Messianic kingdom. The New Testament also emphasizes that the Christian life is a holy calling (2 Tim 1:9) in which believers are to become like Jesus in all respects (Eph 4:2). All Christians are called to be saints (Rom 1:7; 1 Cor 1:2) and servants (Jn 13:12-15). Within this general calling to salvation, the Holy Spirit bestows gifts upon individual Christians in order to facilitate the ministry of the church in society (Eph 4:11-13).

Building upon this foundation, Luther, Calvin and other Protestant* divines overthrew the double standard of medieval Christianity which limited vocation to the monastic life. In its place the Reformers stressed that every Christian has a particular calling in a daily occupation. This particular calling is to be carried out in faith and obedience for the good of society and as a ministry to one's neighbors. This concept of vocation, adopted and applied by Puritans,* was to have important consequences for New England's colonial period. Characterized by a this-worldly asceticism (Max Weber) and a strong sense of personal calling and responsibility in their employment, Puritans showed themselves serious and purposeful in their civic and economic affairs. However, this quest for a this-worldly expression of divine calling and holiness carried within it the seeds of secularization. By the late eighteenth century, the concept of vocation had come to refer to one's job without any reference to divine initiation or love of neighbor.

In Roman Catholic terminology, *vocation* usually refers to a person's calling to religious life, particularly that of the priesthood.*

See also PROTESTANT WORK ETHIC.

BIBLIOGRAPHY. J. Cotton, *The Way of Life* (1641); R. Michaelsen, "Changes in the Puritan Concept of Calling or Vocation," *NEQ* 26 (1953):315-336; M. Weber, *The Protestant Ethic and the Spirit of Capitalism* (1958).   S. A. Wenig

Voluntarism. *See* VOLUNTARYISM, VOLUNTARISM.

Voluntary Societies. *See* PARACHURCH GROUPS.

Voluntaryism; Voluntarism. Scholars of American religion have used both *voluntarism* and *voluntaryism* to refer to the principle that individuals are free to choose their religious beliefs and associations without political, ecclesiastical or communal coercion. The *Oxford English Dictionary* defines *voluntarism* as "one or other theory or doctrine which regards will as the fundamental principle or dominant factor in the individual or in the universe." *Voluntaryism* it defines as "the principle or tenet that the Church and educational institutions should be supported by voluntary contributions instead of by the state; any system which rests upon voluntary actions or principles." While a case could be made for the use of either term, *voluntaryism* more accurately describes the phenomenon as it has been observed in American religion.

One of the distinctive traits of American religion, voluntaryism places value on individual choice while assuming the separation of church and state* and a plurality* of voluntary religious denominations* and societies. The concept is closely tied to the development of the denomination in North America, described by Sidney E. Mead as a "voluntary association of like-hearted and like-minded individuals, who are united on the basis of common beliefs for the purpose of accomplishing tangible and defined objectives." Voluntaryism is closely associated with individualism,* another characteristically American trait evident in religion and the culture at large.

While voluntaryism has roots in the Protestant* tradition as a whole, which emphasizes the individual's direct access to God, it received a clear religious impetus from the First* and Second* Great Awakenings. The Awakening of the 1730s and 1740s stressed an experiential religion of the heart rather than an inherited faith or established religion. The Second Awakening of the early-nineteenth century made the human will a focal point of religious conversion* and subsequent affiliation. Prominent revivalists* of the period, such as Charles G. Finney,* emphasized the Arminian* theme of free will and developed effective means for bringing about conversion. These influences profoundly shaped nineteenth-century evangelicalism and may be observed today, for example, in people "making a decision for Christ" or in the slogan "worship at the church of your choice." Religious voluntaryism has shaped and been sustained by related American cultural values such as democracy,* individualism and the entrepreneurial spirit.

Sociologists have noted the growth and development of voluntaryism in the late-twentieth century. For a variety of reasons, the 1960s and 1970s were characterized by a quest for self-fulfillment, accompanied by a declining respect for religious authority and religious institutions. Many Americans found fulfillment in privatized religious experiences—many of them nontraditional—and even traditional religious adherents became increasingly privatized in their beliefs and loyalties. This led some to drop out of institutional religion altogether. Others remained faithful to their traditions but formed significant new voluntary religious alignments. Representing special interests, these associations frequently have cut across denominational lines.

BIBLIOGRAPHY. W. Hudson, *The Great Tradition of the American Churches* (1953); M. E. Marty, *Religion and Republic* (1987); S. E. Mead, *The Lively Experiment* (1963); W. C. Roof and W. McKinney, *American Mainline Religion* (1987); R. Wuthnow, *The Restructuring of American Religion* (1988). The Editors

Volunteers of America. A nondenominational social service organization. The Volunteers of America was founded in March 1896 by the husband and wife team, Ballington* and Maud* Booth. Ballington, the son of Salvation Army* founders William and Catherine Booth, and Maud had been active in the Army but resigned in a disagreement over William Booth's autocratic leadership. The Volunteers of America was similar to The Salvation Army in its mission, but more democratic in its structure. It blended social welfare with evangelism,* and temporal efforts with a strong emphasis on spiritual priorities, while utilizing military organization and garb. Largely due to the great popularity of the Booths, who were to guide the organization for about five decades, the Volunteers grew rapidly to more than 140 posts in twenty states within a year. Earnestly evangelistic, they claimed 15,000 converts during their first three years. Social efforts also expanded rapidly. During 1896 Maud Booth embarked on the prison* work that was to be the organization's most noted emphasis for several decades. Across the next several years the Volunteers gradually developed their wide-ranging social-welfare programs. During the 1980s they have continued to serve a variety of human needs through hundreds of programs in more than 170 communities across the U.S.

BIBLIOGRAPHY. H. E. Wisbey, *History of the Volunteers of America* (1954); J. F. McMahon, *The Volunteers of America* (1972); N. A. Magnuson, *Salvation in the Slums* (1977).

N. A. Magnuson

Voodoo. Rites and beliefs derived from West African religions and syncretized with Catholicism. As an underground African-American church developed in the slave states, a distinctive variety of this "invisible institution" emerged as the voodoo cult associated with South Louisiana. Though most prevalent in the French West Indies, voodoo appeared in New Orleans between 1780 and 1810 with the arrival of slaves and free people of color from the Caribbean, especially refugees from the Haitian revolution.

Adherents, called *voodoos*, worshiped African gods syncretized with Catholic saints.* Voodoo rites were secretive, and most participants were illiterate. Nevertheless, scattered records document communal rituals which typically occurred at night. Enthralling drum music induced dancing and singing around an altar decorated with fetishes and Catholic icons.* The female leader sometimes sacrificed a small animal, releasing its spirit. Aroused by pulsating rhythms, dances and chants, voodoo spirits are believed to possess true believers with frenzied paroxysms and ecstatic trances. Voodoo was also a folk medicine or magic in which conjurers used charms, potions and prayers to work both good and evil. The white community tried to discourage voodoo with legal and religious proscriptions, but vestiges survive.

BIBLIOGRAPHY. A. J. Raboteau, *Slave Religion* (1978); R. Tallant, *Voodoo in New Orleans* (1962). D. B. Touchstone

Vos, Geerhardus (1862-1949). Presbyterian* theologian* and author. Born in Heerenveen, Netherlands, Vos immigrated to the U.S. as a young man. Following theological study at Calvin Theological Seminary and Princeton Theological Seminary,* he studied at the University of Berlin and the University of Strasburg (Ph.D. in Arabic). In 1893 he became the first professor of biblical theology* at Princeton Theological Seminary, where he

remained until retirement in 1932.

Vos was significant for his pioneering work in the discipline of biblical theology, based on a firm commitment to Scripture as God's inerrant Word. Among American orthodox* Protestant* theologians, Vos was among the first to grasp the fundamental significance of the progressive character of God's special, redemptive revelation, and to begin drawing methodological consequences for interpreting Scripture. A controlling emphasis of his work was that the Bible* is not a catalog of truths about God, humans and the world, but that post-Fall verbal revelation accompanies and interprets redemption. Revelation, as an ongoing process, is invariably focused on the history of God's redemptive acts, that redemptive history that reaches its consummation in the coming of Christ. Vos made enduring contributions in both Old Testament and New Testament theology in his *Biblical Theology* (1948), but probably his most important work was on the kingdom teaching of Jesus in *The Teaching of Jesus Concerning the Kingdom of God and the Church* (1903) and on the theology of Paul in *The Pauline Eschatology* (1930). His writings continue to have an influence on conservative Reformed scholarship in America.

BIBLIOGRAPHY. R. B. Gaffin, Jr., ed., *Redemptive History and Biblical Interpretation: The Shorter Writings of Geerhardus Vos* (1980); M. A. Noll, *Between Faith and Criticism* (1986).

R. B. Gaffin

W

Waddel, Moses (1770-1840). Presbyterian* educator in South Carolina and Georgia. Born in Iredell County, North Carolina, of Scotch-Irish parentage, Waddell was first educated at Clio's Nursery, a school conducted by the Reverend James Hall, and then at Hampden-Sydney College (B.A., 1791).

Waddel moved to South Carolina, where he was ordained* and served several Presbyterian churches near Charleston, but soon went to Appling, in northeastern Georgia, and opened a school. In 1804 Waddel established at Willington, in South Carolina near the Savannah River, what was to be one of the most distinguished college-preparatory schools in America. Samuel Stanhope Smith of Princeton considered that its program was equal to any, and it was termed the "American Eton."

In 1819 Waddel became president of Franklin College at Athens, Georgia, a moribund institution of seven students, but he built its enrollment and laid the foundations for what would become the University of Georgia. Retiring in 1829, Waddel suffered a paralytic stroke in 1836 and died at Athens, July 21, 1840. During his lifetime he taught nearly four thousand students, including a dozen members of Congress as well as state governors and numerous lawyers, teachers, ministers and authors. Among the more notable were John C. Calhoun, William H. Crawford, Hugh S. Legare and Augustus Baldwin Longstreet, who described his teacher in the novel *Master William Mitten* (1864).

BIBLIOGRAPHY. *AAP* 4; *DAB* X; J. N. Waddel, *Memorials of an Academic Life* (1891).

W. J. Wade

Walker, Williston (1860-1922). Congregational* churchman and church historian. After graduating from Amherst (1883) and Hartford Theological Seminary (1886), Walker received the Ph.D. at Leipzig (1888), where he was grounded in the seminar method and the study of primary sources in the study of political history. Walker taught at Bryn Mawr College for one year, at Hartford

Theological Seminary from 1889 until 1901 and then served as Titus Street Professor of Ecclesiastical History at Yale University* from 1901 until his death in 1922. Walker was active in denominational, church unity and missionary efforts, but he is best known for his work in Congregational history. He produced many works in this field, including: *The Creeds and Platforms of Congregationalism* (1893), *A History of the Congregational Churches in the United States* (1894) and *Ten New England Leaders* (1901). His *History of the Christian Church* (1918) has gone through many editions and has long served as a standard text in church history.

Walker applied progressive, empirical-historical methods to the study of church history. In contrast to the overtly spiritual interpretations of Philip Schaff* and other contemporaries, Walker emphasized scientific, "secular" explanations of historical causation, with political and naturalistic factors predominating over (but not eliminating) supernatural factors. Walker understood the proper method of the historian to be an approximation of the scientific method, stressing institutions and external, observable events, while charitably interpreting individual motivation as being unavailable to the historian's analysis. Through his studies of American Congregationalism and the broader themes of Western church history, Walker produced careful narratives which avoided sectarian controversies, choosing instead to make moderate claims and tentative conclusions stressing concord and religious toleration.

BIBLIOGRAPHY. *DAB* X.

K. S. Sawyer

Wallace, Foy (E)sco, Jr. (1896-1979). Church of Christ* evangelist,* debater and editor. The son of a well-known Texas preacher, Wallace began preaching at age fifteen and gained a reputation as a boy preacher. He continued to preach for over sixty years, delivering his last sermon a few weeks before his death.

Wallace was best known as a controversialist, a man who refused to compromise with any view he considered wrong. Strongly opposed to premillennialism*—which he considered a threat to the life of the church—he frequently debated its adherents, on one occasion taking on the well-known fundamentalist* Baptist* preacher J. Frank Norris.* Opposition to premillennialism also extended into Wallace's career as an editor. He edited *The Gospel Advocate* (1930-1934) and later edited the *Bible Banner, The Gospel Guardian* and *The Torch*. Wallace also authored fifteen books, most of them on prophecy and the Second Coming of Christ. In his debating, editing and writing, he is credited with stopping the spread of premillennialism among the Churches of Christ.

In the later years of his life he turned his attention to opposing modern translations of the Bible,* identifying them as means by which liberalism* was infiltrating the church. At the height of his career Wallace was considered within his denomination to be the greatest preacher of his time.   L. B. Sullivan

Wallace, Lewis ("Lew") (1827-1905). Religious author. The son of a governor of Indiana, Wallace served in the Mexican War before practicing law and serving in the Indiana State Senate. At the outbreak of the Civil War,* he re-enlisted, was soon promoted to Major-General, and in 1864 at Monocacy he prevented Confederate General Jubal A. Early from completing his advance on Washington. After the war, he practiced law, was ambassador to Turkey and served as the governor of New Mexico.

Ben Hur (1880), his second novel, was conceived while Wallace was on a train arguing with the famous agnostic* Robert Ingersoll about the deity of Christ. Though he wrote six other books, *Ben Hur* was by far his most popular, selling 300,000 copies in ten years. His credible but romantic depiction of the events surrounding the Gospel narratives appealed to the popular imagination and made him perhaps the best-selling religious author in the America of his day, though he was never a member of any church.

BIBLIOGRAPHY. *DAB* X; L. Wallace, *Lew Wallace: An Autobiography* (1906).   D. R. Williams

Walsh, James Anthony (1867-1936). Co-founder and first Superior General of the Catholic Foreign Mission Society of America* (Maryknoll). Born in Cambridge, Massachusetts, of affluent Irish immigrant parents, Walsh spent some time at Boston College and Harvard University* before entering St. John's Seminary, Brighton, Massachusetts, in 1886. He was ordained* a priest* for the Boston archdiocese on May 20, 1892. Parish work engaged him until 1903 when he became director of the diocesan Society of the Propagation of the Faith.*

In 1906, with the aid of three priest friends, he established the Catholic Mission Bureau to publish *Field Afar,* a magazine designed to arouse mission interest and to work for the establishment of a foreign missionary seminary. Beginning in 1910 he and Father Thomas Frederick Price (1860-1919) of Raleigh, North Carolina, actively promoted the establishment of a Catholic Foreign Mission Society of America. It received tentative approval from the U.S. bishops and Rome in 1911, and the seminary was established at Ossining, New York, in 1912.

Walsh organized the seminary and raised funds for it. In 1918 Price led the first group of missionaries to China and died there the following year. Under Walsh's direction the Society grew in numbers, a woman's religious congregation was established, and the Society received definitive approval from Rome. At the general chapter in 1929 he was elected superior general; four years later he was made a bishop.* In 1934 serious sickness set in and his activity gradually stopped. He is buried next to Price in Maryknoll's chapel crypt.

BIBLIOGRAPHY. D. Sargent, *All the Day Long* (1941).   L. Nemer

Walther, Carl Ferdinand Wilhelm (1811-1887). Lutheran Church—Missouri Synod* theologian.* Born in Langenchursdorf, Saxony, Germany, Walther graduated from the University of Leipzig (1833) and there reacted against the predominant rationalism of the Enlightenment.* His theology* developed under the influence of pietistic* friends involved in the revival of Lutheran orthodoxy* and especially as he read Luther extensively during a six-month illness (1831-1832). Disappointed by the indifference and rationalism of his first parish,* in 1838 he joined a band of emigrants led by Pastor Martin Stephan* and settled with them in Perry County, Missouri. After Stephan had betrayed the group's trust, Walther remarshalled its strength by developing a rationale for its existence as a free church* at the Altenburg (Missouri) Disputation in 1841. There he laid out the basis for the congregational* polity, which he would continue to defend, especially against the German confessional* leader J. K. Wilhelm Loehe* and with other immigrant theologians such as Johannes A. A. Grabau.*

Called to his deceased brother's congregation in Saint Louis in 1842, Walther began a popular periodical for Lutherans faithful to the Lutheran

Confessions, *Der Lutheraner*. A group of like-minded pastors and congregations was drawn to him and in 1847 formed the Evangelical Lutheran Synod of Missouri, Ohio, and Other States. Walther served as its president from 1847 to 1850 and from 1864 to 1878. From 1854 to 1887 he served as president of Concordia Seminary, which moved from Perry County to Saint Louis in 1849. In these offices Walther lent his organizational skills to the building of the Synod.* Through his preaching, writing and teaching of seminarians, he created a specific kind of theology and church life for his Synod. He did so with a strong confession of the faith expressed in the Lutheran tradition.* This confession of faith was supported by the creation of an ecclesiastical culture, which provided good pastoral care for its people, met needs for education in its literature and school system, and met other human needs through institutions such as hospitals and orphanages.

Walther's influence spread far beyond his own Synod through his books and his editorial work in *Lehre und Wehre*, a theological periodical founded in 1853. He edited the dogmatic compendium of the orthodox theologian Johann Wilhem Baier and promoted the Saint Louis edition of Luther's Works in order to insure that the Lutheran witness would be available in North America. Walther also promoted popular Lutheran literature through a Bible society* organized in Saint Louis. Striving for agreement among American Lutherans, he fostered a series of free conferences and colloquies among them from 1856 to 1859 and again from 1866 to 1867. He was instrumental in the creation of the Evangelical Lutheran Synodical Conference in 1872, though it split in the late 1870s in a dispute over predestination,* in which Walther defended the point of view of Luther and the Formula of Concord (1577).

Walther's theology was based upon the verbally inspired Scriptures and focused upon God's gracious forgiveness of sins, won through Christ's atoning* death and resurrection, freely given through Word and sacraments.* He instilled in his students the necessity of preaching* God's condemning law sharply and proclaiming his gospel purely, so that believers might be empowered to live out their faith, a program for ministry expressed eloquently in informal lectures to seminarians, published as *The Proper Distinction of Law and Gospel.*

BIBLIOGRAPHY. *DAB* X; C. S. Meyer, ed., *Letters of C. F. W. Walther* (1969); L. W. Spitz, *The Life of Dr. C. F. W. Walther* (1961); A. R. Suelflow, ed., *Selected Writings of C. F. W. Walther*, 6 vols. (1981). R. A. Kolb

Walworth, Clarence Augustus (1820-1900). Catholic* preacher* and pastor.* Born in Plattsburgh, New York, Walworth was admitted to the New York bar in 1841 but gave up the law for the ministry and attended General Theological Seminary. Deeply affected by the Tractarian Movement* in England, he became a Catholic in 1845 and with Isaac Hecker* and James McMaster joined the Redemptorists* and was ordained* for that community in 1848. In 1851 he was sent back to the U.S., where he joined a mission band led by Isaac Hecker and acquired a reputation for compelling and eloquent pulpit oratory. In 1858 he was released from his Redemptorist vows to join Isaac Hecker when the latter formed the new Congregation of St. Paul.* Walworth, however, never joined the group. He withdrew to the diocese of Albany, where he was stationed at St. Peter's Parish in Troy. In 1861 he briefly rejoined his Paulist comrades but the effects of ill health and overwork caused him to withdraw permanently from the Paulists in 1865. He returned to Albany, where he was made pastor of St. Peter's Church. In Albany, Walworth became well known as a spokesman against the abuses of industrialism and a vigorous foe of political corruption. He is perhaps best known for his versed paraphrase of the traditional *Te Deum* in the form of the favorite Catholic hymn "Holy God We Praise Thy Name." He died in Albany on September 19, 1900.

BIBLIOGRAPHY. *DAB* X; C. A. Walworth, *The Oxford Movement in America* (1974).

S. M. Avella

Wanamaker, John (1838-1922). Business entrepreneur, Sunday-school* leader and supporter of evangelical* ministries.* Born in Philadelphia, the son of a brickmaker, Wanamaker had little formal education but grew up in a religious atmosphere. He was converted* at age eighteen at Philadelphia's First Independent Church. There he taught Sunday school* and participated in the 1857 prayer meeting revival.* In 1858 he launched out on his own, founding Bethany Sunday School in a rough neighborhood of the city and becoming the first full-time secretary of the YMCA* in the U.S.

In 1861, Wanamaker resigned his paid secretaryship and began his famous mercantile business. The Wanamaker stores grew into an immense business enterprise, but he never relinquished his Christian work—in fact, his religious undertakings grew as phenomenally as his secular ones. Conservative in temperament, Wanamaker lived by strict Sabbatarian* and temperance* principles. Conservative in politics, he was active in the Republican party. Through the years, Wanamaker was instrumental in supporting the Philadelphia revivals of Dwight L. Moody* and Billy Sunday,* was a national figure in the YMCA and in the Presbyterian Church,* and helped establish the *Sunday School Times* and *The Scholars' Quarterly.*

Wanamaker is perhaps best known for promoting the Sunday-school movement. At Bethany, Wanamaker was a dedicated and concerned Sunday-school superintendent for over sixty years. Through his efforts Bethany became the largest Sunday school in America and provided numerous social and recreational activities for people of all ages and economic levels. A model of an Institutional Church* program, Bethany made full use of educational, reformatory and philanthropic activities as a means of evangelism. As in all his religious endeavors, Wanamaker employed many of the same promotional tactics and entrepreneurial skills that made him one of the nation's most successful retail merchants.

BIBLIOGRAPHY. *DAB* X; H. A. Gibbons, *John Wanamaker,* 2 vols. (1926); L. A. Loetscher, "Presbyterians and Political Reform in Philadelphia from 1870 to 1917," *JPHS* 23 (1945):2-18; 119-136.

D. M. Strong

Ward, Nathaniel (c.1578-1652). Puritan* minister,* legal scholar and author. The son of an English Puritan clergyman,* Ward graduated from Emmanuel College, Cambridge University (B.A., 1599; M.A., 1603), and trained in and practiced law in London for ten years. On a visit to Heidelberg, Calvinist* theologian* David Pareus guided Ward into the ministry. He ministered to British merchants in Prussia and held Church of England* posts in London and Essex until 1633, when he was excommunicated.

Ward joined friends in New England as pastor of the church in Agawam (Ipswich), Massachusetts. Ill health forced his resignation in 1638, but he turned again to law. Ward authored the code of laws adopted in 1641 by the Massachusetts General Court. This Body of Liberties, based on biblical and English common law, helped establish government by law in America. Ward's most famous work, *The Simple Cobler of Agawam* (1647), defended a royalist Puritan view against religious toleration ("poly-piety"), republican government and lavish fashions. Ward posed as a rustic in this witty piece. Back in England he pressed his views before Commons. Ward ended his career serving as an English pastor.

BIBLIOGRAPHY. *AAP* 1; *DAB* X; C. Mather, *Magnalia Christi Americana* (1702); S. E. Morison,

Builders of the Bay Colony (1930).

C. E. Hambrick-Stowe

Warde, Frances (1810-1884). American founder of the Sisters of Mercy.* Born in Abbeyleix, Ireland, Warde became an associate of Catherine McAuley in 1828. In January 1832 she was one of the first seven young women received by McAuley in the new Institute of Mercy, and the first professed by her in 1833. Choosing the name *Mary Frances Xavier, RSM,* she led the first foundation of Sisters of Mercy to the U.S., arriving in Pittsburgh on December 21, 1843. Coming to the U.S. from Carlow, Ireland, at a time of pioneering development of American cities, Frances Warde and successive groups of Sisters of Mercy moved from Maine to California, not the least deterred by the hardships of travel by Conestoga wagon, stage coach and steamer.

Having founded convents in Chicago, Illinois, and in Loretto, Pennsylvania, Warde moved on to serve the poor of Providence, Rhode Island, establishing the first permanent convent in New England, despite the harassment and threats of the nativist* "Know-Nothings." From that city, she established foundations in Hartford and New Haven, Connecticut; Rochester, New York; and Manchester, New Hampshire, where she served as superior until her death in 1884. From Manchester, in addition to responding to requests to provide Sisters of Mercy for Philadelphia and for foundations as widespread as cities in Nebraska, Maine, California, Vermont and New Jersey, Frances Warde sent the first and only Sisters to work among the Penobscot and Passamaquoddy Indians in the state of Maine.

The phenomenal expansion of the Sisters of Mercy in convents, schools, orphanages, hospitals and social-service centers throughout the country was due in no small part to the vitality and organizational genius of this indomitable woman who was responsible for establishing thirty-nine convents in the U.S. within the space of thirty-seven years.

BIBLIOGRAPHY. *DARB*; K. Healy, *Frances Warde: American Founder of the Sisters of Mercy* (1973); *NCE* 14.

I. Keiss

Ware, Henry (1764-1845). Unitarian* theologian.* Born in Sherborn, Massachusetts, Ware grew up on a farm and received an education through the care of his elder brothers, who recognized his intellectual promise. After studying under the Rev. Elijah Brown, Ware attended Harvard College* and graduated (B.A., 1785) valedictorian of his class.

After further study for the ministry, Ware was ordained* pastor* of First Parish Church, Hingham, Massachusetts, where he succeeded Ebenezer Gay.* Like Gay, Ware was a Unitarian and by the time the Hollis Chair of Divinity was vacated by the death of David Tappan, Ware had distinguished himself and was nominated by the Unitarian party to fill the post. Despite strong opposition from Trinitarians, Ware's selection was confirmed on February 14, 1805, and he was inaugurated on May 14, the first Unitarian professor at Harvard. This was the beginning of the Trinitarian Congregationalists' withdrawal from Harvard, and in 1808 they established Andover Theological Seminary.*

The ensuing Unitarian Controversy* was a significant struggle between orthodox Calvinists and the emerging New England Unitarianism. Ware, for his part, engaged in a publishing war with the Trinitarian Leonard Woods* of Andover, which became known as the Wood 'n Ware Controversy.* Under Ware's leadership Harvard took steps toward organizing its own divinity school, which was established in 1816 with Ware as professor of systematic theology* and evidences of Christianity. He resigned his Hollis professorship in 1840 due to a cataract that troubled him, but before he was incapacitated he published his lectures in *An Inquiry into the Foundation, Evidences, and Truths of Religion* (1842). A modest and gentle person, he was nevertheless firm in his convictions. His son, Henry Ware, Jr., was a prominent Unitarian minister and author.

BIBLIOGRAPHY. *AAP* 8; *DAB* X; J. G. Palfrey, *A Discourse on the Life and Character of the Reverend Henry Ware* (1846); C. C. Wright, "The Election of Henry Ware: Two Contemporary Accounts Edited with Commentary," *Harvard Library Bulletin* 17 (July 1969):245-278.

D. G. Reid

Warfield, Benjamin Breckinridge (1851-1921). Princeton* theologian.* Born near Lexington, Kentucky, Warfield graduated from the College of New Jersey* with highest honors in 1871. Entering Princeton Theological Seminary, he studied under Charles Hodge* (B.D., 1876). After traveling and studying in Europe (1876-1877), Warfield ministered at Baltimore's First Presbyterian Church (1877-1878) and then began his teaching career in New Testament at Western Seminary in Allegheny, Pennsylvania (1878-1887). When A. A. Hodge* died in 1887, Warfield succeeded him as professor of didactic and polemic theology at Princeton. Unlike his predecessors, Warfield was not an active churchman, but he maintained

Princeton's reputation for demanding scholarship. Although he did not author a systematic theology,* he left behind a considerable intellectual legacy for Reformed* Christianity. Besides monographs and collections of sermons, his reviews and articles written for learned journals, encyclopedias, dictionaries and the popular press fill more than ten volumes. For more than twenty years (1890-1903) he was editor of *The Princeton Review.*

Warfield's most lasting contribution was his exposure and refutation of liberalism's* naturalistic world view and reinterpretation of traditional Christian teaching. To their acceptance of human autonomy and skepticism of the uniqueness of Christian revelation, Warfield responded by buttressing Princeton's main themes: (1) An authoritative Scripture* and its supernaturalistic world view, and (2) a strict Calvinistic* theology. Warfield honed a rigorous apologetic* method as a prolegomena to theology. Since Christianity's mission was nothing less than to "reason its way to its dominion," Warfield subjected major schools and thinkers, both in Europe and America, to trenchant criticism. He argued that critics' denial of biblical miracles and reinterpretation of the text were without any factual foundation. Their radical conclusions were based on mere hypothetical naturalistic premises which render the Bible's supernaturalism impossible a priori. In denying the biblical world view, which is the only perspective by which Scripture can be correctly interpreted, liberals devalued Christ, overestimated human nature and eliminated biblical teaching on atonement.* In lengthy articles he defended traditional doctrines of the person and work of Christ and the distinctive teachings of Augustine, Calvin and the Westminster* standards.

Warfield also developed a rigorous apologetic for Scripture. In the 1881 article "Inspiration," written in collaboration with A. A. Hodge, Warfield defended a totally trustworthy and inerrant Scripture. In numerous articles and reviews, he described carefully reasoned nuances of the Princeton view by examining biblical data and demonstrating that conservative teaching rested on the Reformed confessions.

In an age preoccupied with religious consciousness, Warfield opposed its multiform subjectivism. He esteemed Augustine's *Confessions* as a model of religious consciousness, and Calvin as the theologian of the Holy Spirit. In place of Friedrich Schleiermacher's* speculative dependence, he proposed Augustine's religion of dependence on an absolutely sovereign God and Calvin's view that Christian piety* is living constantly in the attitude of prayer.* He also denounced Immanuel Kant's* Copernican Revolution for putting categories of human reason in the place of God's revelation and denounced varieties of Protestant* perfectionism* for substituting individual revelatory experiences and "counterfeit miracles" for the completed objective revelation of Scripture. Warfield's most positive reaction to modern thought was his attempt to correlate Calvin's doctrine of God's providence in creation with Darwin's teaching on evolution.*

BIBLIOGRAPHY. *DAB* X; *DARB;* J. E. Meeter, ed., *The Works of Benjamin B. Warfield,* 10 vols. (1927-1932); W. A. Hoffecker, "Benjamin B. Warfield," in *Reformed Theology in America,* ed. D. F. Wells (1985); W. A. Hoffecker, *Piety and the Princeton Theologians* (1981); *NCAB* 20; M. A. Noll, *The Princeton Theology, 1812-1921* (1983).

W. A. Hoffecker

Warner, Anna Bartlett (1827-1915). Hymnwriter and novelist. A native of Westpoint, New York, Warner lived with her lawyer father, Henry W. Warner, and novelist sister, Susan. Together with her sister, she taught Sunday-school* classes at the nearby United States Military Academy. In two collections of verse, Warner expressed her faith and her art: *Hymns of the Church Militant* (1858) and *Wayfaring Hymns, Original and Translated* (1869). The latter is a pocket-sized set of twenty-six refreshing texts. Best known for her song "Jesus Loves Me" (1859, music by William B. Bradbury*), Warner is also remembered for "We Would See Jesus, For the Shadows Lengthen" and "One More Day's Work for Jesus." She also wrote several Victorian novels under the pseudonym, Amy Lothrope, as well as a biography of her sister. The family home, "Good Crag," was willed to the Academy and is now a national shrine. Anna was buried there with military honors.

BIBLIOGRAPHY. *NAW* 3; O. E. Stokes, *Letters and Memories of Susan and Anna Bartlett Warner* (1925).

R. J. Stanislaw

Warner, Daniel Sidney (1842-1925). Founder of the Church of God* (Anderson, Indiana). Born in Bristol (now Marshallville), Ohio, Warner served briefly in the Union army, attended Oberlin College (1865-1866) and taught school. In 1865 he was converted in a revival* led by a minister of the General Eldership of the Churches of God of North America (Winebrennerian). Warner joined that denomination after some consideration and was apparently attracted by its emphasis on Christian unity. Licensed to preach in October 1872, he

pastored in northwestern Ohio for six years, did mission work in Nebraska for two years, and then returned to minister in Ohio.

By 1877 he had come under the influence of Holiness* teaching, and in July 1877 he experienced entire sanctification.* Warner's enthusiastic proclamation of this experience led to his trial and ejection from the Winebrenner Church on January 30, 1878. Setting out to be a Holiness evangelist, he soon affiliated with the Northern Indiana Eldership of the Churches of God, which had previously broken with the General Eldership and was open to Holiness teaching. Warner was invited to edit the group's *Herald of Gospel Freedom,* which eventually became the *Gospel Trumpet* (1881). Originally published in Rome City, Indiana, and then in several other locations, it became an organ for both the local and regional Holiness Movement. Warner, seeking to restore the primitive* church, continued to pursue a nonsectarian Holiness, and in so doing alienated himself from his denomination and the Indiana State Holiness Association.

Accepting this newfound freedom as the fulfillment of his quest, Warner began to organize likeminded individuals into a new movement that propagated its message by means of "the flying scroll" (the magazine) and "flying messengers" (wide-ranging itinerant evangelists*). Throughout the 1880s and early 1890s, the movement was increasingly conceived as an eschatologically momentous reformation of the church. Warner continued to play a key role in the movement, which eventually became the Church of God (Anderson, Indiana).

BIBLIOGRAPHY. J. W. V. Smith, *The Quest for Holiness and Unity* (1980). D. G. Reid

Washington, Booker (T)aliaferro (1856-1915). Educator and founder of the Tuskegee Institute. Born in Franklin County, Virginia, Washington was the son of an African-American slave woman and an unknown white man. In 1865 Washington moved with his mother and stepfather, Washington Ferguson, to Malden, West Virginia, where he worked in the local salt mines and, later, as a house servant. From 1872 to 1875 Washington attended Hampton Normal and Agricultural Institute, a school created by the American Missionary Association.* There he adopted its principles of self-help, Christian morality and technical training. After graduating from Hampton, Washington taught school in Malden for three years and then studied for eight months (1878) at Wayland Seminary in Washington, D.C.

In 1879 Washington returned to Hampton as a teacher and remained there until 1881, when he founded the Tuskegee Institute in Tuskegee, Alabama. In 1895 at the Cotton States and International Exposition in Atlanta, Georgia, Washington delivered his famous "Atlanta Address," in which he encouraged African-American self-reliance in agriculture, mechanics and commerce. This speech and his subsequent autobiography, *Up From Slavery* (1901), gained Washington a national reputation, and he soon found himself the confidant and advisor to presidents McKinley,* Roosevelt and Taft, and prominent American businessmen such as Andrew Carnegie.* Washington used his influence to create an economic climate conducive to African-American organizations such as the National Negro Business League and the "Tuskegee Machine," a network of African-American educators, journalists, politicians and businessmen, all advocates of the Tuskegee philosophy of self-help and racial solidarity.
See also BLACK COLLEGES.

BIBLIOGRAPHY. *DAB* X; *DARB;* L. R. Harlan, *Booker T. Washington: The Making of a Black Leader, 1856-1901,* 3 vols. (1972); *NCAB* 7; E. L. Thornbrough, ed., *Booker T. Washington* (1969).
M. C. Bruce

Washington, George (1732-1799). Statesman, soldier, first U.S. president and key founder of American civil religion.* Born on a farm in Westmoreland County, Virginia, a fourth-generation Virginian, Washington grew up as a member of the local plantation aristocracy. He combined in his career many outstanding achievements in business, warfare and politics, taking the leading part in three great historical events: the American Revolution,* the drafting and ratification of the U.S. Constitution and the establishment of the American republic and its institutions, especially the office of president. It was largely because of his leadership that the thirteen colonies became the U.S., a sovereign and independent nation. In particular, because of his courage and integrity, Washington conferred on the presidency a prestige so great that political leaders afterward considered it the highest distinction in the land to occupy the chair he had honored.

Washington's religious views have been the subject of considerable debate among scholars. As a Virginia aristocrat, he was a member and served as a parish* vestryman of the established Church of England (after the Revolution, the Episcopal Church*). However, he was not devout in the conventional sense and seldom, if ever, took Communion,* often missed services and was not an Anglican* partisan. But he revered the Scriptures,* and frequently expressed a faith in divine providence and a belief that religion is needed to sustain public morality and republican government.

Washington was not an orthodox* Christian,* as some have claimed, nor an orthodox deist,* as others have proposed. His personal theology,* based on his own understanding of the Bible* and his reading of many Enlightenment* thinkers of his time, was most likely broadly Unitarian,* as was that of most deists of his time. Concerning revealed religion and systematic theology,* these deists were either privately skeptical (as Washington may have been), philosophically curious (like Thomas Jefferson*) or belligerently argumentative (like Thomas Paine*). But they all believed in God and generally in life after death. As far as Washington was concerned, God was the Creator of the universe, and human affairs were guided by Providence, the Almighty Being, the Great Author or the Invisible Hand (terms often used by Washington). He highly respected the teachings of Jesus but upheld the right of every religious group—Protestants,* Catholics* and Jews—to freedom of worship* and equality before the law, and condemned all forms of bigotry, intolerance, discrimination and persecution.

The records show that Washington's experiences in the war and later in the presidency deepened his personal religious faith and were the occasion for the development of his civil religion. The Rev. Mason Locke "Parson" Weems* and other early popular biographers attributed to him a degree of pious orthodoxy which he did not possess, and Washington himself encouraged the practice of public religion at the national level. For example, when he was sworn in as the first president at a ceremony in New York City on April 30, 1789, with his right hand resting on a Bible, he not only recited the brief oath prescribed in Article 2 of the Constitution but also added the words "so help me, God" and bent down and kissed the Bible which was held by the secretary of the Senate. Every president since that time has appended this phrase to the oath and sworn it upon a Bible, even though neither is prescribed by the Constitution.

To this, Washington added other acts of public piety and numerous speeches laced with references to the Almighty and the dependency of national morality and public virtue upon religious principles. To this growing body of fact and fiction concerning Washington's faith were added other elements of his personal make-up: his stately bearing and impressive physical stature, his stern code of duty and his strong character. The popular image which emerged made Washington both the first major spokesperson and first practitioner of American civil religion, and after his death a leading figure in the unfolding of the nation's civil theology.

Most striking, after 1799 the first president became one of the most powerful symbols of national unity and a veritable totem of America's public faith. Not only was he regarded as "the father of his country," but also as the American Moses who had led his people, God's New Israel, out of British bondage into the Promised Land of republican America. In sermon after sermon following his death, the clergy* exalted him as the American Moses and the savior of his people. All of this was soon translated into a thousand sacred myths which in turn supported the unifying political superstructure of the nation's public faith.

Washington, therefore, occupied a special place in the development of America's public religion. He gave it a voice, served as the focal point for its formation and encased his presidency in religion by his words and example and through his powerful personality bestowed on the office a sacred aura. Quickly elevated to civil sainthood following his death, he also became the Moses figure who reminded his people that they enjoyed a common heritage and that God had chosen them as his New Israel for a new era. Washington not only provided critical leadership as the key founder of a new nation dedicated to republican ideals and human rights, but also formative leadership as the key founder of the public faith of that new nation.

BIBLIOGRAPHY. V. B. Hampton, *The Religious Background of the White House* (1932); C. P. Nettels, *George Washington and American Independence* (1951); D. S. Freeman, *George Washington,* 7 vols. (1948-1957); J. F. Boller, Jr., *George Washington and Religion* (1963); J. T. Flexner, *George Washington,* 4 vols. (1965-1972); C. L. Albanese, *Sons of the Fathers: The Civil Religion of the American Revolution* (1976); A. J. Menendez, "George Washington and Religious Liberty," *Church and State* 31 (December 1978): 14-16; J. Alden, *George Washington* (1984); R. V. Pierard and R. D. Linder, *Civil Religion and the Presidency* (1988). R. D. Linder

Watchtower Bible and Tract Society. *See* JEHOVAH'S WITNESSES.

Water Street and Bowery Missions. Urban rescue missions. In 1872 an Irish-born immigrant and ex-convict from Sing Sing Prison named Jeremiah McAuley* had a vision to reach lost and drifting people for the Lord. The prompting he felt was to go into Manhattan's Fourth Ward on the Lower East Side and open a facility where drifters could find food, clothing and shelter, and also hear the gospel of Jesus Christ. A Wall Street banker named A. S. Hatch provided the funds for McAuley to bring his dream to fruition. In October 1872 a dance hall property at 316 Water Street was purchased to be a rescue mission. Originally named the "Helping Hand for Men," the facility was enlarged and renamed the McAuley Water Street Mission in 1876.

McAuley's successor at Water Street, S. H. Hadley, assumed leadership in 1886. For the next twenty years he oversaw the lodging, feeding, clothing and evangelizing of thousands of destitute men. Eventually the Water Street Mission became a model for urban missions* all over the U.S. One of the first facilities to pattern itself after McAuley's program was the Bowery Mission, which opened its doors in 1879. As the Bowery district evolved into America's most infamous skid row, the Bowery Mission took on ever-growing responsibilities. In 1895 *Christian Herald* magazine took over this program of evangelism* and service to alcoholics and homeless men. It is still a vital outreach over a century later.

See also RESCUE MISSION MOVEMENT.

BIBLIOGRAPHY. N. A. Magnuson, *Salvation in the Slums: Evangelical Social Work, 1865-1920* (1977). L. W. Dorsett

Way International, Inc., The. Religious group founded on the teachings of Victor Paul Wierwille. Considered a cult* by many observors, The Way International began in the 1940s under Wierwille's radio ministry and assumed its current name in 1974. The movement experienced dramatic growth during the Jesus People era of the late 1960s and continued to expand in the 1970s under Wierwille's leadership. Since his death in 1985, the organization has declined.

Wierwille, formerly a pastor in the Evangelical and Reformed Church (now United Church of Christ*), received a degree from Princeton Theological Seminary* in 1941 and was later awarded a doctorate from an unaccredited correspondence school. In 1953 he developed the first Power for Abundant Living class, which became the cornerstone and chief recruitment device of The Way International. The organization is headquartered in

New Knoxville, Ohio, and operates The Way College in Emporia, Kansas. Many members participate in The Way Corps, a four-year leadership-training program. Known for their aggressive friendship evangelism* and spiritual elitism, The Way does not consider itself a church* or denomination* but prefers to be known as a biblical research and teaching organization. Its belief system derives largely from the writing and teaching of Wierwille who believes that God spoke to him audibly and gave him the only correct interpretation of Scripture* since the first century. Wierwille's views depart from traditional orthodox* Christianity at a number of points. He denied the deity of Jesus Christ and rejected the doctrine of the Trinity. He also denied the distinct personhood of the Holy Spirit and taught that speaking in tongues* is the necessary sign that a person has been "born again."*

BIBLIOGRAPHY. R. Enroth et al., *A Guide to Cults & New Religions* (1983); J. G. Melton, *Encyclopedic Handbook of Cults in America* (1986); J. L. Williams, *Victor Paul Wierwille and The Way International* (1979).   R. Enroth

Wayland, Francis (1796-1865). Baptist* minister* and educator. Born in New York City, the son of a Baptist preacher,* Wayland graduated from Union College in 1813 and studied medicine until 1816. However, a religious experience* altered the course of his preparation, and he entered the ministry.* He enrolled in Andover Theological Seminary* (1816) but soon took a teaching position at Union College (1817), where he remained until 1821.

In 1821 he was called to the First Baptist Church of Boston, Massachusetts, where he served as pastor for five years and acquired a reputation as a man of energy, insight and multiple gifts. Although unimpressive in the pulpit, his two published sermons, "The Moral Dignity of the Missionary Enterprise" (1823) and "The Duties of an American Citizen" (1825), were widely circulated and acclaimed.

In 1827 he began his tenure as the fourth president of Brown University,* Providence, Rhode Island, a position he held until 1855. Wayland brought to the office a forceful personality, a wide range of knowledge and a concern for educational excellence, as well as strong convictions about teaching methods, curricula and textbooks. His determination to initiate change led to a reorganization of the University in 1850 with an expansion of the curriculum to include courses in science, modern languages, economics and a system of elective courses. He also increased endowment, added new buildings and broadened the school's influence.

Respected as an administrator, a teacher and an author, Wayland touched thousands of students with his innovative ideas, intellectual breadth and passion for analysis, combined with a personal interest in them. In addition to his educational achievements, he was involved in a wide array of civic affairs, including public schools, hospital administration, prison reform and community libraries. He also participated actively in Baptist denominational life and was a vigorous advocate of missions.

The diversity of his interests is evident in his publications, which included: *Elements of Moral Science* (1835); *Elements of Political Economy* (1837); *Thoughts on the Present Collegiate System in the United States* (1842); *Domestic Slavery Considered as a Scriptural Institution* (1845); *A Memoir of the Life and Labors of the Reverend Adoniram Judson* (1853); and *Notes on the Principles and Practices of Baptist Churches* (1857). The latter volume argued for the absolute autonomy of local congregations. Wayland's administration at Brown has been referred to as the "golden age of the university."

BIBLIOGRAPHY. *DAB* X; *DARB;* W. Hudson, "Stumbling into Disorder," *Foun* 1 (1958):45-71; J. O. Murray, *Francis Wayland* (1891); *NCAB* 8; F. Wayland, Jr., and H. L. Wayland, *A Memoir of the Life and Labors of Francis Wayland,* 2 vols. (1868).   W. M. Patterson

Wealth, Gospel of. A religious expression of social Darwinism maintaining that wealth is the natural product of moral character and diligence. The gospel of wealth was named after Andrew Carnegie's* essay by the same title published in 1900. A clear expression of social Darwinism and American confidence in progress, it maintained that strong and moral folks grow wealthy, while the poor deserve their fate. Carnegie wrote that in a democracy* the rich have a right to great wealth so long as in return they help build initiative in others. This was a rejection of traditional ideas of charity which, as advocates of the gospel of wealth argued, weakened society. Instead, they maintained, social classes owe nothing to each other and winners need make no room for losers.

The Brooklyn minister* Henry Ward Beecher* joined the gospel of wealth to a Calvinist* theology* of sin,* which further emphasized that people's economic condition was ordained by God and by the person's state of sin. Under this

religious formulation, the law of competition replaced providence. This religious outlook helped shape the development of capitalism* and undergirded the Gilded Age in America. It was opposed by Christian socialists* and the Social Gospel Movement.*
See also POSITIVE THINKING.

BIBLIOGRAPHY. A. Carnegie, *The Gospel of Wealth* (1900); G. Kennedy, ed., *Democracy and the Gospel of Wealth* (1949).

J. C. Brown

Weaver, Rufus Washington (1870-1947). Baptist* minister* and educator. Born in Greensboro, North Carolina, Weaver received the B.A. and M.A. degrees from Wake Forest College and Th.M. and Th.D. degrees from the Southern Baptist Theological Seminary. Ordained* in 1893, he held pastorates in several states prior to his election as president of Mercer University, where he served from 1918 to 1927. Under his leadership the school flourished. Weaver later moved to Washington, D.C., where he was pastor of First Baptist Church (1934-1936) and then executive secretary of the District of Columbia Baptist Convention until 1943.

Weaver's deep concern for religious freedom* is evident in his *Christian Faith at the Nation's Capital* (1936) and *Champions of Religious Liberty* (1946). He also played a major role in organizing the Baptist Joint Committee on Public Affairs, an agency composed of the major Baptist denominations and established to monitor church-state issues in Washington. W. M. Patterson

Wedel, Cornelius H. (1860-1910). Mennonite* educator and historian. In 1874 Wedel immigrated with the entire Alexanderwohl village in southern Russia to central Kansas, where they established a congregation of the same name near Goessel. Wedel's most important higher education took place in the German seminary in Bloomfield, New Jersey, where he studied under German theologian* and historian George Seibert. He then received an M.A. (1893) from Ursinus College. In 1896 and 1898 he made trips to the Netherlands, Germany, Switzerland and Russia in order to research Mennonite history. After teaching for two years in Bloomfield, in 1890 he was ordained* in the Alexanderwohl congregation and accepted an invitation to teach in the Mennonite school at Halstead, Kansas. When Bethel College was established in 1893, Wedel became professor of Bible* and the college's first president, a position he held until his premature death.

Wedel's numerous textbooks presented a com-

prehensive Mennonite world view shaped by German culture. His two books on the Bible and a four-volume series on the history of the Mennonites, *Abriß der Geschichte der Mennoniten,* developed Mennonite history in the context of world history, beginning with creation. He interpreted Mennonites as part of *Gemeindechristentum* (congregational Christendom), a Christendom existing throughout Christian history as a free-church* alternative to state-church Christendom. These six volumes comprise the best and most comprehensive synthesis of Mennonite history of their era. Indeed, Wedel was one of the most significant spokespersons of the Russian Mennonite tradition in North America at the turn of the twentieth century.

BIBLIOGRAPHY. J. C. Juhnke, "Gemeindechristentum and Bible Doctrine: Two Mennonite Visions of the Early Twentieth Century," *MQR* 57.3 (July 1983):206-221; J. C. Juhnke, *Dialogue with a Heritage: Cornelius H. Wedel and the Beginnings of Bethel College* (1987). J. D. Weaver

Wedel, Cynthia Clark (1908-1986). Ecumenical* leader. Born in Dearborn, Michigan, to Arthur Pierson and Elizabeth Haigh Clark, Wedel earned her B.A. (1929) and M.A. (1930) at Northwestern University. Her Ph.D. in psychology was from George Washington University (1957). An Episcopalian,* Wedel's career in church work began as director of Christian education* at St. Luke's, Evanston (1930-1935). From 1931 to 1939 she worked in her church's national headquarters in New York City. In 1939 she married Theodore O. Wedel (d.1970). From 1939 to 1949 she taught at the National Cathedral School for Girls in Washington, D.C.

Wedel served on the national executive board of Episcopal Churchwomen (1946-1952) and the church's national council (1955-1962). She was the first woman to serve as an associate general secretary of the National Council of Churches* (1962-1969), as vice president (1957-1960) and as its president (1969-1972). She also was president of the World Council of Churches* (1975-1983). An ardent volunteer, she served on the national board of the Girl Scouts of America (1960-1966), as chair of volunteers for the American Red Cross (1973-1979), as associate director of the Center for a Voluntary Society (1969-1974), on John F. Kennedy's* Commission on the Status of Women (1961-1963) and the Citizens' Advisory Council on the Status of Women (1963-1968). She was the author of *Citizenship, Our Christian Concern* (1952), *Employed Women of the Church* (1957) and *Faith or Fear and Future Shock* (1974). A leader for racial justice, economic welfare and world peace, she was a staunch advocate of women's full participation in the church and world issues.

BIBLIOGRAPHY. *CCen* (September 24, 1986): 796-797.   N. A. Hardesty

Weems, Mason Locke ("Parson") (1759-1825). Anglican* minister, bookseller and author. Weems was born in Anne Arundel County, Maryland, but little is known of his early life. In 1783-1784 he went abroad to Paris, The Hague and England, where in 1784 he was ordained* by the archbishop of Canterbury for service in the U.S. Weems returned to Maryland in 1784 and served Episcopal* parishes* in Maryland until 1792. He began printing books in 1791, and from 1792 he devoted the rest of his life (thirty-one years) to the selling and writing of books, considering his profession a broadened scope of ministry.

Weems traveled from New York to Georgia, selling his own books and those of the publisher, Matthew Carey, after 1794. His first and most notable work was *The Life and Memorable Actions of George Washington* (1800). By the time of Weems' death, this work had gone through twenty-nine editions, even though it was known to be highly fictional and effusively laudatory. In the fifth edition (1806), the story of young George Washington* cutting down the cherry tree first appeared. Weems also wrote biographies of Francis Marion, Benjamin Franklin and William Penn.* In addition to these biographies, he wrote many moralistic tracts directed against murder, adultery, gambling and drunkenness.

BIBLIOGRAPHY. *DAB* X; P. L. Ford and E. F. Skeel, eds., *Mason Locke Weems, His Works and Ways,* 3 vols. (1929); L. G. Leary, *The Book-Peddling Parson* (1984).   D. B. Chesebrough

Weigel, Gustave (1906-1964). Catholic* ecumenical* theologian.* Born in Buffalo, New York, Weigel received his early education in Buffalo and entered the Society of Jesus* in 1922 and attended Woodstock College, Maryland (B.A., 1928). He was ordained* to the priesthood in 1933, and after receiving his doctorate in theology from the Gregorian University (Rome) in 1937, he taught dogmatic theology* at the Catholic University in Chile. From 1949 until his death he taught ecclesiology at Woodstock College.

Weigel tried to awaken American Catholics to the significance of the movement toward Christian unity, which he saw as "the most striking ecclesi-

ological event since the sixteenth century." He encouraged American Catholics to study Protestant* traditions from their own sources, and published systematic studies of American Protestant theologies, such as *A Survey of Protestant Theology in Our Times* (1954), that he hoped would contribute to a mutual understanding between American Catholics and Protestants. He was pessimistic, though, about the immediate possibilities of Christian unity and believed that his attitude was well grounded in a realistic evaluation of American circumstances. Numerous historical, cultural and theological differences, and an apparent lack of concern for doctrinal unity within the Protestant ecumenical movement,* made Christian union extremely difficult.

Weigel called himself a "middle generation" Catholic ecumenist. He stood between those Catholics who refused to engage in any theological discussions with Protestants and those who would in the future take up the labor of furthering Christian union. His pre-Vatican II* juridical ecclesiology prevented him from acknowledging the ecclesial dimensions of Protestant Christianity, but his openness to the mutual learning that took place in inter-confessional conversations made him one of the earliest American Catholic ecumenists.

BIBLIOGRAPHY. P. W. Collins, "Gustave Weigel: Ecclesiologist and Ecumenist" (unpublished Ph.D. dissertation, Fordham University, 1972); *DARB*; *NCE* 14; G. Weigel, and R. M. Brown, *An American Dialogue: A Protestant Looks at Catholicism and a Catholic Looks at Protestantism* (1961).
                          P. W. Carey

Weld, Theodore Dwight (1803-1895). Revivalist,* abolitionist* and temperance* reformer. Born in Hampton, Connecticut, Weld grew up under the strict Calvinist* teaching of his father, Ludovicus Weld, a Congregational* minister.* Weld was educated at Hamilton College (1825) and Oneida* Institute (1829-1831) and was an accomplished rhetorician. In 1825, while attending Hamilton College, Weld was converted under the ministry of Charles G. Finney* and immediately became a disciple of Finney, urging him to adopt the additional "new measure"* of allowing women to speak in mixed assemblies.

In 1827 Weld left Finney and, under the influence of Charles Stuart, became an abolitionist and temperance lecturer. Having convinced the Tappan* brothers of New York City to support the antislavery struggle, the Tappans in turn sent Weld to the newly opened Lane Seminary in Cincinnati to study theology* (1832-1834). There, in the spring of 1834, Weld staged the famous Lane debates over the issue of slavery, converted a majority of the students to his cause and instituted social programs among the African-American population of Cincinnati. Defying the Lane trustees' injunction against antislavery debate and activism, Ward was expelled from the seminary, and some thirty-two "Lane Rebels" departed for Oberlin College.* Oberlin had recently reorganized with Tappan funding, and under the presidency of Cincinnati pastor Asa Mahan* and the theological professorship of Finney, a radical new college emerged.

Weld, on the other hand, became an agent of the newly founded American Anti-Slavery Society and, adopting the revivalistic techniques of the "protracted meeting" and the "altar call,"* began an itinerant campaign to spread the abolitionist message. He personally trained seventy other itinerants, including his future wife, Angelina Grimké* of South Carolina, a reformer and evangelical* feminist.* After about two years, Weld had suffered permanent damage to his voice and so channeled his efforts into editing and writing material in support of the abolitionist cause. His anonymous tracts, *The Bible Against Slavery* (1837) and *Slavery As It Is* (published in 1839 and selling 100,000 in its first year), influenced other writers, including Charles Dickens and Harriet Beecher Stowe,* author of *Uncle Tom's Cabin.* From 1838 to 1841 Weld lobbied for the antislavery cause in Washington, D.C., feeding information to the radical faction of the Whig party, including John Quincy Adams.

Always modest and avoiding press coverage, Weld preferred to work behind the scenes. After 1840, with disagreement arising over the issue of political action, Theodore and Angelina retired from public life to Belleville, New Jersey, where he farmed (1840-1854), later teaching school in Perth Amboy, New Jersey (1854-1863), and in Lexington, Massachusetts (1864-1867), and only occasionally participating in reform activities. In 1867 he retired to Hyde Park, Massachusetts, where he died at the age of ninety-one. While his role in the abolition movement was for many years overlooked by historians, today many scholars regard Weld as having been the most important of the antislavery crusaders.

BIBLIOGRAPHY. R. H. Abzug, *Passionate Liberator: Theodore Dwight Weld and the Dilemma of Reform* (1980); *DAB* X; *DARB*; *NCAB* 2; B. P. Thomas, *Theodore Weld: Crusader For Freedom* (1950).   C. E. Stockwell

Weninger, Francis1805-1888). Jesuit* missionary*-preacher.* Born in Marburg, Austria, Weninger was ordained* a diocesan priest* in 1828 and earned a doctor of divinity degree two years later. In 1832 he entered the Society of Jesus, eventually becoming a teacher of theology* at the University of Innsbruck and a well-known preacher. Because the Revolution of 1848 led to severe restrictions on Austrian Jesuits, Weninger volunteered for the American missions. Between 1848 and the mid-1880s, he traveled extensively in the U.S. (usually alone), conducting over 800 parish missions* and delivering more than 30,000 sermons.* He became widely known for his work with German-speaking Catholic immigrants,* but his ministry also included other Catholic ethnic groups and African-Americans (he played a key role in the organization of the first African-American congregation in Cincinnati, c.1865). A prolific writer, Weninger published collections of his sermons as well as numerous books and pamphlets concerning catechetics,* liturgy* and papal infallibility.*

BIBLIOGRAPHY. "Father Francis Xavier Weninger," *Woodstock Letters* 18 (1889):43-68; G. J. Garraghan, *Jesuits of the Middle United States,* vol. 2 (1938).   W. P. Leahy

Wesley, John (1703-1791). Founder of Methodism.* Born in Epworth, Lincolnshire, England, in 1703, Wesley was the fifteenth child of high church* Anglican* rector* Samuel Wesley and his wife, Susanna. Wesley was educated at Charterhouse, London, and Christ Church, Oxford (B.A., 1724; M.A., 1727), and was a fellow of Lincoln College (1725-1727) before joining his father as curate in Wroot (being ordained* in 1728). After his father's death Wesley returned to Oxford (1729-1735), where he also directed the Holy Club, a group of serious-minded students who were also called Methodists. The Methodists performed acts of piety* and works of charity until Wesley left for a disastrous missionary* experience in Georgia (1735-1737). On his return, an evangelical* conversion* at a society meeting on Aldersgate Street, London (May 24, 1738), changed his life. He was now convinced that the activities of the Methodists could be empowered by grace (or the work of the Holy Spirit) through faith in Jesus Christ. Less than a year later, a revival* broke out which continued until his death in 1791. In his fifty-two-year itinerant ministry, Wesley preached over 40,000 sermons and averaged 4,000 miles of travel annually.

Wesley's peculiar genius was the formation of societies which gathered and sustained those being awakened and converted. It was these societies that spread to America during the 1760s. Although basically a lay* movement, the Methodist Societies on both sides of the Atlantic had a discipline and style directed by Wesley himself.

In spite of the American Revolution,* which in spirit despised all things British, the Methodists continued to grow, primarily under the leadership of Francis Asbury,* one of several missionaries appointed in England by Wesley to serve in America. In 1784 the American Methodists wrote to Wesley asking for assistance as their numbers increased. Wesley responded immediately by ordaining Thomas Coke* superintendent* (in effect, bishop*) and Thomas Vasey* and Richard Whatcoat* elders to assist Coke in establishing an independent Church in America. These, by Wesley's authority,* could in turn ordain a whole host of itinerants* who up to that point could preach but not serve the sacraments* to thousands of Methodists who were without access to these special means of grace. The famous Christmas Conference* of 1784 saw the Methodist Episcopal Church* in America come to life.

With Coke, Vasey and Whatcoat, Wesley sent documents necessary to organize a church—letters of ordination, an "Open Letter to the People in North America" and an "Abridgement of the English Liturgy." After several ordinations, including Coke's ordination of Asbury as deacon,* elder* and superintendent (soon to be known as bishop), on successive days the conference unanimously approved Wesley's "General Plan," including the standards of doctrine received by British Methodism—Wesley's *Standard Sermons and Notes on the New Testament*—and in addition, the abridged *Articles of Religion,* the abridged "Sunday Service" and "General Rules" for the classes and bands. In one form or another this distinctive Wesleyan flavor remains within most of the Wesleyan traditions to the present.

Although Wesley's theological and spiritual legacy lingers at the heart of Methodism, his direct ecclesiastical authority began to wane soon after the Christmas Conference. As Coke returned for a second visit in 1787, with the strong recommendation from Wesley that Whatcoat be elected bishop, the American Methodists flatly refused. Although they continued to love and revere Wesley, and they held tenaciously to much of his theology, rules for spiritual discipline and polity,* they considered his attempts to make direct judgments on matters relevant only to the new Republic to be inconsistent with the spirit of independence.

Over the years, Wesley's influence could be found in many areas of Methodism. Frequently, one denomination would emphasize only one aspect of the Wesleyan tradition.* Social justice, for example, so crucial for Wesley, has been championed by some, pietistic holiness* by others, evangelism* by still another and discipline* by still others.

BIBLIOGRAPHY. S. Harper, *John Wesley's Message for Today* (1983); P. Mickey, *Essentials of Wesleyan Theology* (1980); A. C. Outler, ed., *John Wesley* (1964); J. Peters, *Christian Perfection and American Methodism* (1985); M. Schmidt, *John Wesley: A Theological Biography,* 2 vols. (1962-1973); T. L. Smith, *Whitefield and Wesley on the New Birth* (1986); R. G. Tuttle, *John Wesley, His Life and Theology* (1978); C. W. Williams, *John Wesley's Theology Today* (1984); W. H. Williams, *Garden of American Methodism* (1984).

R. G. Tuttle

Wesleyan Church. A Holiness* denomination. The Wesleyan Church was formed on June 26, 1968, through the union of the Wesleyan Methodist Church and the Pilgrim Holiness Church. Both bodies had a theological kinship in their acceptance of the Wesleyan Tradition* as it had been transformed through the Holiness Movement of the late-nineteenth century.

The Wesleyan Methodist Church was organized in 1843 by abolitionist* clergy* and lay* people, who had been protesting the tolerance of slavery by the Methodist Episcopal Church.* When Methodist bishops* sought to silence them, twenty-two ministers* and 6,000 members left the denomination and formed the Wesleyan Methodist Connection of America. This took place only one year before the historic split between the Methodist Episcopal Church and the Methodist Episcopal Church, South. The new denomination was also opposed to what it perceived to be abuses of the episcopacy in the mother denomination and drew up an ecclesiastical structure that included lay participation in the annual conference and the election of a president instead of a bishop. The Connection also opposed the use of tobacco and alcohol,* participation in secret societies, and immodest dress. The body did not consider its differences with mainstream Methodism to be reconciled after the Civil War,* and in the latter half of the nineteenth century it was deeply influenced by the Holiness Movement. In 1947 it changed its name to the Wesleyan Methodist Church.

The Pilgrim Holiness Church was a product of the Holiness Movement, originating as the International Holiness Union and Prayer League in 1897 in Cincinnati, Ohio. This movement, formed around holiness,* healing,* evangelism* and pre-millennialism,* had grown into a denomination by 1913 and through several mergers with like-minded bodies became the Pilgrim Holiness Church in 1922.

The denomination has maintained a strong emphasis on foreign missions and now has churches established in thirty-four countries outside of the U.S. and Canada. Membership in the U.S. numbers nearly 110,000 with an additional 5,000 in Canada. The denomination maintains membership in the Christian Holiness Association,* the National Association of Evangelicals* and the World Methodist Council. Its educational institutions include Houghton College in Houghton, New York, and Marion College in Marion, Indiana. The denomination publishes the *Wesleyan Advocate.*

BIBLIOGRAPHY. I. F. McLeister and R. S. Nicholson, *History of the Wesleyan Methodist Church of America* (1959). The Editors

Wesleyan Methodist Church. *See* WESLEYAN CHURCH.

Wesleyan Tradition. Generally speaking, the *Wesleyan tradition in America* identifies the theological impetus for those movements and denominations* in America who trace their roots to a theological tradition finding its initial focus in John Wesley.* Although its primary legacy remains within the various Methodist denominations (e.g., Wesleyan Church*; Free Methodist*; African Methodist Episcopal*; African Methodist Episcopal, Zion*; Christian Methodist Episcopal*; and United Methodist*), the Wesleyan tradition has been redefined and reinterpreted as a catalyst for other movements and denominations as well (e.g., the Holiness Movement* and Pentecostal Movements*).

John Wesley traveled to America from his native England only once, arriving in February 1736 in the newly established colony of Georgia as a missionary* with the Society for the Propagation of the Gospel.* Intending to work among the Native Americans, Wesley found the spiritual needs of the Georgia settlers were so demanding (Wesley claimed that they were more heathen than the Native Americans) as to consume most of his time. The experience was a disaster (to some, almost comical). The young Anglican* priest*—self-righteous and legalistic in the years prior to his heartwarming spiritual conversion* at Aldersgate Street—was not well received by most of the freewheeling colonists. More or less tolerated for two years, he returned to England in early 1738, depressed and disillusioned. Although his American experience was far from successful, Wesley, especially after his 1738 evangelical* conversion, desired to return to America. But that was not to be. Instead, he sent his preachers* (the first few ordained* by himself), who spoke to the people of America as if "he were speaking himself." These preachers were the ones most responsible for establishing the Wesleyan tradition in America.

John Wesley, through men like Francis Asbury,* Thomas Coke* and others, established a tradition among the Methodists that sought to emphasize justification* by faith as the gateway to sanctification* or "scriptural holiness." Briefly stated, the theology of the Wesleyan tradition follows the biblical pattern of creation, Fall, redemption. All are created in the image of God (original righteousness), but because of humanity's fallen nature, that image has been lost (original sin*). The good news is that God is in Jesus Christ reconciling the world, restoring humanity to its original righteousness (Christian perfection).

In other words, Wesley's doctrine of justification (to be contrasted with sanctification that follows from it in Christian experience) is similar to that of the Continental Reformers. (Wesley stated that he and Calvin were but a hair's breadth apart on their theology of justification by faith). Man and woman were created in the image of God's own likeness. Upright and perfect, they dwelt in God and God dwelt in them. God required full and perfect obedience, and they were (in their unfallen state) equal to the task. But having disobeyed God, their righteousness was lost, and they were separated from God. Humanity (as their seed) inherited a corruptible and mortal nature and became dead; dead in spirit, dead in sin, dead to God. In their natural state men and women hasten on to death everlasting. But while they were yet sinners, Christ died for the ungodly, bearing their sins that by his stripes they might be healed. The ungodly, therefore, are justified by faith in the full, perfect and sufficient sacrifice of Christ.

But for Wesley this is only the beginning of the story. His doctrine of sanctification marks a point of departure from the Continental Reformers. Ultimately, for the true Wesleyan, salvation is completed by a return to *original righteousness,* achieved by the work of the Holy Spirit. Though justified by faith alone, believers are sanctified by the Holy Spirit—the Spirit that makes them holy.

Wesley's insistence that *imputed* righteousness must become *imparted* righteousness marks the greatest distinction between the Wesleyan and Reformed* or Lutheran* traditions, both of which maintain that Christian perfection cannot be obtained in this life. God grants the Spirit to those who repent and believe that through faith they might overcome sin, both personal and social. Wesleyans want deliverance from sin, not just from the final judgment. Wesley clearly speaks of a process that culminates in a second, definite work of grace, identified as entire sanctification.

Entire sanctification was defined in terms of "pure or disinterested love." Wesley believed that one could progress in love until—at the moment of entire sanctification—love became devoid of self-interest. Although proponents of "perfectionism"* would later harden these theological lines to the brink of legalism, the basic principles of Wesleyan holiness or sanctification are as follows: Sanctification is received by faith as a work of the Holy Spirit. Beginning at the moment of new birth,* it gradually progresses until the instant of entire sanctification. Its characteristics are: loving God and loving one's neighbor as oneself; living in Christlike meekness and lowliness of heart; abstaining from all appearance of evil and walking in all the commandments of God; being content with any state in life and doing all to the glory of God.

The Wesleyan tradition in America is far more than a theological expression, however. Many who know the movement well have insisted that the Wesleyan tradition's greatest genius was not theological or even evangelistic but related more to Wesley's ability to *organize* struggling Christians into the kind of community that would sustain not only them, but the work of the Holy Spirit. Wesley developed societies, bands and classes specifically for the purpose of discipling those who were earnest about maintaining a lively faith in Jesus Christ. These covenant fellowships became the heart of the Wesleyan revival, both in England and America. Having found that young Christians not properly discipled soon fell away, he developed a style of revival in which preaching was immediately followed by enlisting respondents in a class meeting held that same day. In fact most of those truly converted in the Wesleyan tradition were converted individually within the setting of a class meeting.

All of this was well suited to the American colonial environment and the circumstances of the new Republic that followed. After separating from the Church of England* and establishing an independent Methodist Episcopal Church in 1784, the influence of the Wesleyan tradition grew with amazing speed. Between 1784 and 1840 Methodist membership in the U.S. grew from approximately 18,000 to 580,000, making it the fastest-growing American church in the early nineteenth century. Wesley's preachers on both sides of the Atlantic were enthusiastic, adaptable, totally committed to Christ and his church, and relentless in their determination to spread "Father" Wesley's understanding of scriptural holiness throughout the land. What were "societies" in England simply became "churches" in America. These churches were established wherever two or more were responding to the gospel in any one place. In addition, the early Methodists usually identified with the poor and spoke a language clearly understood by the masses. The legendary circuit rider* extended the influence of the Methodist not only across the frontier* but quite literally throughout the land.

More recently, much of the clarity which marked the earlier movement has been lost. Class meetings, if they exist at all, are no longer required. Furthermore, Wesleyans in America have tended to fragment over a variety of issues. The smaller denominations have traditionally emphasized doctrine. Perfectionism among the Nazarenes,* for example, includes a doctrine of "eradication" (implying that even the temptation to sin is destroyed by the second work of grace) which is not even remotely an issue among the nine million members of the United Methodist Church. Smaller groups (like the Wesleyan Church and Free Methodists) tend to be more evangelical, emphasizing the personal relationship with God by grace through faith in Jesus Christ. It may still be said that Wesleyans in general emphasize worship and singing. Charles Wesley's hymns still enjoy prominence in every Methodist hymn book.

Larger groups tend to be more issue-oriented, focusing on social justice, human rights, racial equality, peace and justice. Unfortunately, many have forgotten that Wesley emphasized both personal and social aspects of the gospel. For many Wesleyans the social aspects of the gospel became associated with liberalism* and many within the Wesleyan tradition overreacted to what they saw as a loss of the personal dimension of the gospel.

There was also a period of division and sectarianism. At the turn of the twentieth century the Wesleyan tradition, then deeply embedded within the Holiness Movement, splintered. Between the 1880s and 1907, the movement experienced a sectarian heyday in which groups formed around issues of ordinances, church order, Holiness theology and Pentecostal experience. The question now remains, how can those who hold to a common tradition recover the balance that began as a movement of the Spirit?

Ecumenism* has had a high priority among the larger United Methodist denomination. As a matter of fact, over the past half-century mergers among the Methodist Episcopal, Methodist Protestant and Evangelical United Brethren culminated in the United Methodist Church in 1968. For the past twenty years, although smaller Wesleyan groups seem to be holding their own, the larger United Methodist Church has been declining at the rate of 100,000 members per year. In spite of attempts to reverse this trend, the decline continues. United Methodists have traditionally been stronger in the South and Midwest, while some of the smaller denominations are stronger in the Far West.

In recent days, many different groups within the Wesleyan tradition in America have underscored Wesley's emphasis on the work of the Holy Spirit. True Wesleyans acknowledge the power of the Holy Spirit available to them by virtue of their faith in Jesus Christ. This power not only saves from sin but empowers them for ministry. Admittedly, there may have been some improvements on Wesley's legacy, but much has been lost as well. Wesley's own question—"how to reunite the two so-long divided, knowledge and vital piety?"—strikes a relevant chord. The principles of scriptural holiness, deeply embedded within the Wesleyan tradition, still have meaning and contain much that is yet relevant and important for today's world.

See also HOLINESS CHURCHES AND ASSOCIATIONS; HOLINESS MOVEMENT; METHODIST CHURCHES; SANCTIFICATION; PERFECTIONISM; WESLEY, JOHN.

BIBLIOGRAPHY. C. Carter, ed., *A Contemporary Wesleyan Theology,* 2 vols. (1983); S. Harper, *John Wesley's Message for Today* (1983); T. Langford, *Practical Divinity, Theology in the Wesleyan Tradition* (1983); F. Norwood, *The Story of American Methodism* (1974); A. Outler, *John Wesley* (1964); J. Peters, *Christian Perfection and American Methodism* (1985); R. Tuttle, *John Wesley, His Life and Theology* (1978).

R. G. Tuttle

West, Nathaniel (1826-1906). Presbyterian* premillennialist* and Bible conference* leader. Born in England, West immigrated* to America as a boy and graduated from the University of Michigan in 1846. He pastored Presbyterian congregations in Cincinnati, Ohio (1855-1862); Brooklyn, New York (1862-1869); Detroit, Michigan (1883-1884); and Louisville, Kentucky (1884-c.1898), and taught at Danville Theological Seminary in Ken-

tucky (1869-1875) and briefly at Moody Bible Institute.* One of the founders of the Niagara Bible Conference,* the first and best known of many Bible and prophecy conferences in the U.S., West was widely admired for his piety,* knowledge of the Scriptures and theological understanding. In the 1890s his charge that the secret rapture* of the church lacked biblical support provoked a major controversy among premillennialists. His numerous writings, especially *The Thousand Years in Both Testaments* (1889), won many to premillenial eschatological* views in the late nineteenth century.

BIBLIOGRAPHY. E. R. Sandeen, *The Roots of Fundamentalism* (1970). G. S. Smith

West, Stephen (1735-1819). New Divinity* Congregational* minister.* A graduate of Yale* College (B.A., 1755) and student of Timothy Woodbridge, West was the pastoral and theological successor to Jonathan Edwards* at Stockbridge, Massachusetts. He spent his entire career (1759-1818) ministering to the whites and Native Americans of this western New England village. There he developed into an effective revivalistic* preacher* as well as a productive theologian.*

His principal writings, *Essay on Moral Agency* (1772), *Scripture Doctrine of the Atonement* (1785) and *Evidence of the Divinity of our Lord Jesus Christ* (1816), all contributed to and reflected the theological distinctions of the New Divinity movement. Specifically, West helped formulate the moral government theory of the atonement* by seeing Christ's sacrifice as originating in God's benevolence and satisfying God's concern for moral justice and order. He likewise sought to uphold "Consistent Calvinism*'" by defending (although also altering) Edwards's position on free will and by attacking the proponents of universal* salvation.

BIBLIOGRAPHY. *AAP* 1; J. A. Conforti, *Samuel Hopkins & The New Divinity Movement* (1981); F. H. Foster, *A Genetic History of the New England Theology* (1963). R. W. Pointer

Westminster Confession of Faith. A Reformed* confessional* document. Most of the colonists until 1776, and most American churches through much of the nineteenth century, were significantly influenced by the Westminster Confession of Faith (WCOF). Presbyterians,* Congregationalists* and Baptists* all subscribed to the WCOF with slight variations. Presbyterians, beginning with the Adopting Act* of 1729, differed only on the WCOF state-over-church posture which was changed after the Revolution. Congregationalists, in their 1648 Cambridge Platform,* excepted only matters of church government* and discipline*; while the Baptists, following the London Confession of 1677, took issue only with church government and infant baptism.*

Historically, Presbyterians firmly subscribed to the WCOF until the 1880s. During that decade Professor Charles Briggs,* through rejecting the inerrancy* of the Bible,* cast doubt on the biblical basis of the WCOF and, during the next decade, sought to revise the document. These broadening efforts of Briggs and others, though opposed by professors A. A. Hodge* and B. B. Warfield,* eventuated in the revisions of the WCOF in 1903, which enabled part of the Cumberland Presbyterian Church* to unite with the Presbyterian Church in the U.S.A.* (PC-USA).

The influence of the WCOF continued to erode, despite the efforts of the conservative majority of the PC-USA General Assemblies of 1910, 1916 and 1923, which declared certain doctrines as salvifically "necessary and essential." An opposing document, the Auburn Affirmation,* signed in 1923 by 1,300 ministers, decried these doctrines as adding to the WCOF. The Confession of 1967* introduced elements regarded by conservatives as neo-orthodox.*

Today, the broadened Presbyterian Church, USA,* gives allegiance to both the WCOF and other documents, while a few smaller conservative Presbyterian bodies continue to maintain a traditional confession of the WCOF.

BIBLIOGRAPHY. C. Hodge, *The Constitutional History of the Presbyterian Church in the United States of America* (1839-1840); J. H. Leith, "The Westminster Confession in American Presbyterianism," in the *Westminster Confession in the Church Today,* ed. A. I. C. Heron (1982); L. A. Loetscher, *The Broadening Church* (1954).

J. H. Hall

Whatcoat, Richard (1736-1806). Methodist* bishop. Born in Gloucestershire, England, Whatcoat became the second elected bishop* of American Methodism. As a business apprentice, Whatcoat began attending Methodist meetings in 1758. Serving first as class leader and then band leader and steward, he eventually became a lay* preacher* itinerating among the Methodists until John Wesley* ordained* him in 1784 for the soon-to-be-established church in America. With Thomas Coke* and Thomas Vasey,* Whatcoat took part in the organizing Christmas Conference* in Baltimore that same year. Assisting in the ordination of

Francis Asbury,* Whatcoat served faithfully, mostly as presiding elder in the circuits of the Middle Atlantic States.

In 1787 the American Methodists refused Wesley's request to elect Whatcoat bishop, but he was then elected bishop in his own right in 1800, narrowly defeating the popular Jesse Lee.* Well known for sermons that were plain, instructive and highly spiritual, Whatcoat soon fell prey to the rigors required of American Methodist bishops, dying July 5, 1806, in Dover, Delaware.

BIBLIOGRAPHY. *AAP* 7; *DAB* X; B. Fry, *The Life of Reverend Richard Whatcoat* (1852); W. Phoebus, *Memoirs on the Reverend Richard Whatcoat* (1828).

R. G. Tuttle

Wheatley, Phillis (c.1753-1784). African-American poet. In 1761 John Wheatley purchased a seven-year old slave girl, christened her *Phillis* and treated her as a member of the family. Encouraged to read the Bible* and classical literature, Wheatley learned to write poetry using the styles of the psalms and neoclassical poetry. In 1770 she published her first work "An Elegiac Poem, on the Death of the Celebrated Divine . . . George Whitefield." That same year she became a member of the Old South Meeting House.

In 1773 the Wheatleys gave Phillis her freedom and took her to London, where she astonished the British aristocracy with her poetry. While there, friends published a volume of her poems demonstrating the role of Christianity in the acculturation of Africans in colonial Africa. Her literary fame, though brief, provided evidence of the African-American intellectual and creative ability and gave her a prominent place in the annals of African-American history and literature. Some time after returning to America, Phillis became estranged from the Wheatley family. In 1778 she married a free African-American named John Peters, but the marriage was not a happy one and she was left to support herself and one child. She worked in a boarding house and died in poverty in 1784.

BIBLIOGRAPHY. *DAB* X; *NAW* 3; J. D. Mason, ed., *The Poems of Phillis Wheatley* (1966); P. Wheatley, *Poems on Various Subjects, Religious and Moral* (1773).

L. J. Edwards

Wheaton College. An independent evangelical* liberal arts college. Originally founded as Illinois Institute in 1848 by Wesleyan Methodists,* an abolitionist* Methodist body, the institution also won the support of Congregationalists.* With Wesleyan financial support declining, the school was rechartered as Wheaton College on January 9,

1860, by Congregationalists, with Jonathan Blanchard* as its president and twenty-nine students enrolled. Land for the campus was donated by Warren Wheaton, one of the founders of Wheaton, Illinois, where the college is located. Blanchard was a strong leader, whose writing and public statements largely shaped the curriculum and laid the Christian foundations of the college. He was a fervent abolitionist,* a temperance* leader, an anti-secret-society crusader and a believer in co-education. Charles Blanchard* followed his father in the presidency in 1882 and served until 1925. Throughout 128 years of its history (1860-1988), Wheaton has had only six presidents.

In the beginning the program of studies was uniformly classical, preparing students for the ministry and the professions. By the turn of the century, the curriculum had become broadly diversified. In 1936 a small graduate program was initiated, which by 1985 enrolled 300 students in masters programs in biblical studies, Christian education* and communications. Following each of the world wars, there was a substantial growth in the undergraduate student body, reaching 2,200 in 1985. Wheaton College now has diversified programs in the humanities, sciences, social sciences, and the arts, and has prepared large numbers of evangelical missionaries,* ministers* and Christian-service workers, in addition to many graduates who have chosen careers in medicine, law, education and business.

Numerous twentieth-century evangelical leaders have been educated at Wheaton, including Billy Graham,* Carl F. H. Henry,* Edward J. Carnell,* Kenneth Taylor, Harold Lindsell and Leighton Ford. Though its early roots were Congregationalist, Wheaton has long been an independent Christian college. Since the 1930s it has been a premier educational institution and intellectual haven, first for a broad, interdenominational fundamentalism* and then for the new evangelicalism* of the latter half of the twentieth century. Within that segment of conservative Protestantism, Wheaton and its environs—in which numerous evangelical parachurch* agencies are headquartered—is regarded as a center of evangelical vision, activity and resources.

See also BILLY GRAHAM CENTER.

BIBLIOGRAPHY. P. M. Bechtel, *Wheaton College: A Heritage Remembered, 1860-1985* (1984).

P. M. Bechtel

Wheaton Declaration. A 1966 consensus statement on evangelical* foreign missions.* In 1966 the Evangelical Foreign Missions Association* and the Interdenominational Foreign Mission Association* sponsored the Congress on the Church's Worldwide Mission, at Wheaton, Illinois. Over nine hundred delegates from seventy-one countries attended, and over two hundred and fifty agencies, mission interest groups and schools were represented. Discussion groups studied position papers, and an editorial team then produced a comprehensive document on the urgency and validity of the missionary task, which the delegates unanimously adopted. The declaration specifically upheld the priority of evangelism,* repudiated both syncretism and universalism,* cautioned against uncritical optimism about changes in the Roman Catholic Church,* and urged greater unity among evangelicals in the missionary enterprise. The Wheaton statement also addressed the issues of proselytism, mission methods, social concern and the hostile forces opposed to missions. The delegates concluded with a pledge to mobilize the church for "the evangelization of the world in this generation."

BIBLIOGRAPHY. H. Lindsell, ed., *The Church's Worldwide Mission* (1966). J. A. Patterson

Wheelock, Eleazar (1711-1779). Colonial missionary* to Native Americans and founder of Dartmouth College.* Born in Windham, Connecticut, Wheelock graduated from Yale College* in 1733. Receiving a license* to preach* in 1734, he became pastor of the Second Congregational Church in Lebanon, Connecticut, a year later. In the 1740s Wheelock emerged with Jonathan Edwards* as the strongest Connecticut supporter of the Great Awakening.* He was one of the most active itinerant preachers in New England, but he also found time to tutor students for college as a way of supplementing his salary.

In 1743 Wheelock began to tutor Samuel Occom,* a Mohegan Indian from New London, Connecticut, and to develop an interest in Native American missions.* He was aided by a neighbor who gave him several buildings and two acres of land to establish a school. In 1754 Wheelock opened Moor's Charity School in Lebanon to instruct both white and Native American missionaries. By the early 1760s, with the English victory in the French and Indian War, Wheelock became interested in the conversion* of the large concentrations of Native Americans in New York and southern Canada. Several Mohawks were sent to him for instruction, and in 1767 Wheelock managed to raise 12,000 pounds in England and Scotland for his school.

With this financial support, Wheelock was able to leave his Lebanon church and move his school to Hanover, New Hampshire. He founded Dartmouth College, naming it after the Earl of Dartmouth—one of his benefactors. Wheelock served as president of the college and of Moor's Charity School. But in Hanover, as in Lebanon, Wheelock did not experience much success in training Native American missionaries. Well before his death in 1779, Wheelock had become primarily interested in training white missionaries.

BIBLIOGRAPHY. *AAP* 1; J. Axtell, "Dr. Wheelock's Little Red School House," in Axtell, *The European and the Indian* (1981); *DAB* X; *DARB;* J. D. McCallum, *Eleazar Wheelock* (1939); D. McClure and E. Parish, *Memoirs of the Rev. Eleazar Wheelock* (1811). J. A. Conforti

Wheelwright, John (1594-1679). Puritan* minister* and major figure in the Antinomian controversy* of 1636-1638. Probably born in Saleby, Lincolnshire, England, Wheelwright graduated from Sidney College, Cambridge (B.A., 1614/1615; M.A., 1618), and was ordained* a priest* in 1619. Succeeding his father-in-law, he was vicar of Bilsby from 1623 to 1633, where he developed his nonconformist views. Silenced in England for his nonconformity, Wheelwright arrived in Boston in 1636 and immediately was caught up in the religious controversy surrounding his sister-in-law (of his second marriage) Anne Hutchinson.* Essentially an orthodox* Puritan, Wheelwright, like Hutchinson, differed from his new ministerial colleagues in placing greater emphasis on God's gift of grace to the unregenerate. An impassioned if ill-advised Fast-day sermon against those "operating under a Covenant of works" alerted others to this dangerous theological aberration; shortly thereafter, Wheelwright was brought to trial and banished. Subsequently, with twenty families of supporters, he trekked northward and founded the town of Exeter, New Hampshire, there establishing a Puritan church and an orderly civil government. Later he founded the town of Wells, Maine, and gathered its first church. Although Wheelwright eventually expressed regret for his hand in the "sharp controversy" of the day, he admitted to no theological error. Six years after his banishment, he sought and was given full reconciliation with the Massachusetts Bay authorities.

BIBLIOGRAPHY. *AAP* 1; E. Battis, *Saints and Sectaries* (1962); *DAB* X; J. Heard, Jr., *John Wheelwright* (1930). E. C. Nordbeck

Whidden, Howard Primrose (1871-1952). Baptist* minister,* politician and educator. Born in Nova Scotia, Whidden was educated at Acadia University, McMaster University, Newton Theological Seminary and the University of Chicago. Whidden taught at both McMaster and Brandon Colleges before entering the Baptist ministry, serving first in Canada and then in Dayton, Ohio. In 1912 he was appointed president of Brandon College, a small Baptist college in Brandon, Manitoba, a position he held until 1923. Strongly supportive of conscription and nonpartisan government during World War 1,* he was elected to the Canadian House of Commons as a Union candidate in 1917. He represented Brandon until 1921.

In 1923 he was appointed chancellor of McMaster University, a Baptist institution then located in Toronto. The move to Hamilton, Ontario, was accomplished in 1930 under Whidden's direction. Whidden and his university became deeply embroiled in the fundamentalist-modernist controversy* which wracked the Ontario-Quebec Baptist Convention in the mid-1920s. After his retirement from McMaster in 1941, Whidden edited the *Canadian Baptist* for three years.

BIBLIOGRAPHY. C. M. Johnston, *McMaster University,* 2 vols. (1976); C. G. Stone and F. J. Garnett, *Brandon College: A History, 1899-1967* (1969). B. M. Moody

Whitaker, Alexander (1585-c.1616). Colonial Anglican* minister.* The son of William Whitaker, Regius Professor of Divinity and master of St. John's College, Cambridge, Alexander Whitaker was educated at Cambridge (B.A., 1605; M.A., 1608) and was ordained* in the Church of England in 1609. He ministered briefly, probably in Yorkshire, before going to Virginia with Sir Thomas Dale in 1611. There he served Dale as chaplain* and as minister to the settlements at Henricopolis and Bermuda Hundreds until Whitaker drowned in March 1616 or 1617.

Like his father, his cousin William Gouge, and his close friend William Crashaw of St. John's, who had helped arrange his removal to Virginia, Whitaker was a moderate Puritan. His influence is generally credited with helping to steer the infant colony's religion toward low church* Anglicanism. His *Good Newes from Virginia* (1613), published by the Virginia Company, extolled Virginia's geography as well as encouraged the company's enterprise on religious grounds, using the text from Ecclesiastes, "Cast thy bread upon the waters: for after many days thou shalt find it." More so than his English peers, Whitaker was impressed by the Native Americans he encountered, whom he called "a very understanding generation, quicke of apprehension, suddaine in their dispatches, subtile in their dealings, exquisite in their inventions, and industrious in their labour." At Dale's request, he taught the English language and the rudiments of Christianity to Pocahontas while she was held captive at Henricopolis, and he baptized* her before her marriage to John Rolfe.

BIBLIOGRAPHY. C. Bridenbaugh, *Jamestown, 1544-1699* (1980); H. C. Porter, "Alexander Whitaker: Cambridge Apostle to Virginia," *WMQ* 14 (July 1957):317-343.   T. T. Taylor

White, Andrew (1579-1656). Catholic* missionary* in Maryland. Born in London, England, White was educated at English colleges on the continent. Ordained* at Douai, France, about 1605, he returned home to labor in the English missions. In 1606 the British government implicated White in the Gunpowder Plot, a supposed attempt to impose Catholic rule on England. With other priests he was banished from the realm. The following year (1607) he entered the Society of Jesus.* Until 1629 White taught theology at English colleges in Lisbon, Portugal, and at Liege and Louvain in Belgium. Relieved of teaching duties because of his rigid conservatism and uncompromising Thomism,* White was sent again to work in the English missions.

When Cecilius Calvert* organized the first colonization voyage to Maryland in 1633, White seized the chance to work in the American missions. With two other Jesuits he sailed on the *Ark,* reaching Maryland in March 1634. As Jesuit superior of the mission from 1634 to 1638, he established the system of self-supporting plantations worked by Jesuit priests as Gentleman Adventurers as mandated by proprietorial law. In 1639 he began ministering to the Native American tribes indigenous to Maryland, a ministry greatly aided by his writing a grammar and dictionary of the Algonquin dialect they spoke and his translation of the catechism* into that language.

In 1644 he was captured and sent to England by invading Virginia Puritans* who tried and acquitted him of violating the penal laws by proving his presence was involuntary. White was again banished to Belgium. Unable to return to Maryland, he returned to England where he ministered to Catholics in the south of the country until his death on December 27, 1656.

BIBLIOGRAPHY. *DAB* X; *DARB.*

L. R. Riforgiato

White, Ellen Gould Harmon (1827-1915). Cofounder of the Seventh-Day Adventist Church.*

Born in Gorham, Maine, Ellen Harmon was reared in Portland. Her formal education essentially ended at age nine when she received a head injury. Her parents were Methodists,* and she was baptized* into their church in 1843. Meanwhile, her family had accepted William Miller's* teaching that the second advent of Christ would take place about the year 1843 and had been forced to leave the Methodist Church as a consequence. When Christ failed to return in 1844, Ellen, then seventeen years of age, experienced the first of over two-thousand visions she would have over the course of her lifetime.

After a second vision, Ellen began traveling among the Millerite (adventist) companies, reporting what she had seen. She soon met James White, an adventist preacher, with whom she worked and eventually married in 1846. That same year, influenced by a pamphlet written by another adventist, Joseph Bates, the Whites began observing Saturday as the Sabbath. The following year, Ellen experienced a vision confirming this new practice. Through their continued travels and several general meetings, called "Sabbath Conferences," the Whites and other adventists developed a set of common beliefs.

Through Ellen's influence, James began publishing the *Review and Herald* (1850), as well as pamphlets reporting her visions. In 1855 the Whites moved from Rochester, New York, to Battle Creek, Michigan. Soon after, Ellen published the first of her extensive *Testimonies for the Church* (1855-1909) and *Spiritual Gifts* (vol. 1, 1858), which she eventually expanded into her major work, *The Great Controversy between Christ and Satan during the Christian Dispensation* (1888).

Ellen's personal experience of illness led to an interest in health. After a vision in 1863 she began promoting health reform within the newly organized Seventh-day Adventist Church. Like other health reformers of the period, she advocated vegetarianism and drugless remedies such as "water treatments," and through her urging the denomination established the Western Health Reform Institute (later Battle Creek Sanitarium) in 1866. Ellen also pushed for educational reform, emphasizing manual as well as intellectual skills, which in part led to the creation of Battle Creek College (later Andrews University) in 1875.

Ellen traveled extensively, calling on the Church to develop a broader vision of its ministry. In 1872 the Whites made their first visit to California. After the death of James in 1881, Ellen traveled to Europe (1885-1887) and Australia (1891-1900). Returning to the U.S. in 1900, she settled in California. Throughout these years she continued writing as well as speaking, producing such books as *The Desire of Ages* (1898), *Education* (1903) and *The Ministry of Healing* (1905). She also took an active part in the 1888 debate among Seventh-day Adventists over righteousness by faith, the reorganization of the Seventh-day Adventist Church in 1901 and the promotion of evangelistic* and educational work among Southern African-Americans. She died on July 16, 1915, at the age of eighty-seven, having suffered a hip fracture several months earlier.

BIBLIOGRAPHY. *DAB* X; *DARB;* D. M. Canright, *Life of Mrs. E. G. White* (1919); *NAW* 3; F. D. Nichol, *Ellen G. White and Her Critics* (1951); R. L. Numbers, *Prophetess of Health: A Study of Ellen G. White* (1976); A. L. White, *Messenger to the Remnant* (1969).   G. Land

White, John Campbell (1870-1962). Presbyterian* minister,* educator and leader of Laymen's Missionary Movement.* Born in Wooster, Ohio, White attended the College of Wooster (B.A., 1890; M.A., 1893). Upon graduating from college White served successively as the college's secretary of the YMCA* (1890-1891), traveling secretary for the Student Volunteer Movement* in the U.S. and Canada (1891-1892) and general secretary for the YMCA in Calcutta (1893-1903). In 1906 White cooperated with Samuel B. Capen in founding the Laymen's Missionary Movement, serving as the general secretary of the movement from 1907 to 1915. The goals of this movement were stated by White as "investigation, agitation, and organization." Lay* interest in missions was investigated, laypeople agitated within their churches for a cohesive missions policy and organized structures to promote missions within their churches.

In 1915 White turned his attention to education, serving first as president of the College of Wooster (1915-1919) and then as vice president (1920-1927) and acting president (1938-1939) of Biblical Seminary in New York. From 1919 to 1920 he was director of the Life and Work Department of the Inter-church World Movement.* He was granted an LL.D. by Ursinus College in 1915.

Much of White's later life was devoted to church ministries. He was general secretary of the Church League of New York (1927-1930), and he served for twelve years as pastor of West 49th Street United Presbyterian Church (1930-1942). Thereafter he returned to his native Ohio as pastor of the First United Presbyterian Church of Mansfield (1942-1947). In 1947 he became executive chairman of Christ for the World Movement.

W. A. Detzler

White, [Mollie] Alma Bridwell (1862-1946). Founder of the Pillar of Fire Church. Born in Lewis County, Kentucky, Mollie Alma Bridwell experienced conversion* as a teen-ager in a revival conducted by William Godbey. Educated at Vanceberg Seminary and Millersburg Female College in Kentucky (1881-1882), she taught school in several states before moving to Denver in 1887, where she married Kent White, a Methodist ministerial student. In 1893 she claimed to have experienced sanctification* by faith. With the empowerment accompanying sanctification, or the second work of grace, White overcame her "man-fearing spirit" and began preaching at her husband's Methodist Episcopal charges. By 1895 both Kent and Alma had withdrawn from the Methodist Church and were conducting revivals* and preaching* at camp meetings,* eventually establishing urban missions* in Colorado, Wyoming and Montana. In 1901 she founded the Pentecostal Union in Denver. The group became known as the Pillar of Fire, the name of her periodical. White's husband embraced Pentecostalism* and eventually left her in 1909 when she refused to accept the doctrine of glossolalia, or speaking in tongues.* She conducted evangelistic services throughout the U.S. and in London and established approximately fifty branches to further her church's goals of evangelism* and education. White wrote over thirty-five books, edited several magazines and purchased two radio stations to spread the gospel.

Combining conservative theology* with political activism, White supported the Ku Klux Klan's anti-Catholicism of the 1920s. She also edited *Woman's Chains,* a periodical advocating passage of the Equal Rights Amendment and women's equality in home, church and state from a biblical basis. In 1910 at the Church's headquarters (1907) in Zarephath, New Jersey, her church consecrated her bishop,* the first woman to occupy that office in any denomination* in the U.S. By the time of her death in 1946, the group numbered over 4,000 adherents.

BIBLIOGRAPHY. *DAB* II; *DARB; NAW* 3; *NCAB* 35; A. White, *The Story of My Life and Pillar of Fire,* 5 vols. (1919-1946).   S. C. Stanley

White, William (1748-1836). Episcopal* bishop.* Born into an affluent Philadelphia family (his sister married Robert Morris, financier of the American Revolution*), White graduated from the College of Philadelphia* in 1765. In 1782 he received the first honorary degree awarded by that institution.

The principal religious influence in his life came

from his mother. Ordained* to the diaconate in London in 1770 and to the priesthood in London in 1772, White became one of the assistant ministers of the United Parishes of Christ Church and St. Peter's Church in Philadelphia, to which St. James Church was added in 1809.

As a supporter of the American cause in the American Revolution,* White succeeded the Tory Jacob Duché as rector* of the United Parishes in 1779. From 1777 until 1789, he served as chaplain* to the Continental Congress, continuing in the same capacity with the Federal Congress until the capital moved from Philadelphia. In 1787 he was consecrated* bishop of Pennsylvania in London's Lambeth Palace. He continued to serve as rector of the United Parishes throughout his episcopate.

In the years following the Revolution, White played the dominant role in guiding and inspiring the scattered Anglican parishes of the thirteen colonies to unite into a national church. Although the Treaty of Paris and the consecration of Samuel Seabury* made its suggestion for temporary presbyterian ordinations unnecessary, White's *The Case of the Episcopal Churches Considered* (1782) largely shaped the form of the Protestant Episcopal Church in the United States of America.* The pamphlet's proposal for representative government at all levels of the denomination and for a division of powers among the clergy* and laity*—subsequently placed in the denomination's constitutions which White drafted—made the Episcopal Church congenial to the new republic.

Unanimously elected president of the first General Convention in 1785, White wrote the appeal to the archbishops* and bishops of the Church of England for episcopal succession. With William Smith,* who was responsible for most of the changes, he adapted the *Book of Common Prayer** for American use. Serving from 1795 on as presiding bishop, he wrote all of the pastoral letters of the House of Bishops* from 1808 until his death and participated in the consecrations of twenty-six bishops.

Theologically a low churchman* of the eighteenth-century type, White's abhorrence of enthusiasm caused him to distance himself from the Episcopal evangelicals* who emerged in the nineteenth century. His call in 1826 for the election of an assistant bishop with the right of succession prompted one of the bitterest struggles between church parties in the history of the Episcopal Church.

White's influence on his contemporaries was substantial. Many of the early leaders of the U.S. attended Christ Church; his relations with George Washington* were especially close. Among the many clergy he helped to train were William Augustus Muhlenberg,* Jackson Kemper, William H. De Lancey and John Henry Hobart*; to the passionate Hobart, his relationship was that of Melanchthon to Luther.

As pre-eminent in the civic affairs of Philadelphia as he was in its religious life, White served as the president, and often as one of the founders, of virtually every public or benevolent institution in the city. The number of societies and institutions that published obituary resolutions and marched in his funeral procession was unprecedented in Philadelphia's history.

Goodness was White's outstanding characteristic. Tactful, conciliatory, scholarly, farsighted and uncommonly conscientious, he was dignified in presence but natural and simple in manner. Although a lackluster preacher, he could fascinate in conversation. Blessed with superb health, he preached every Sunday into his eighties.

In addition to a large number of sermons, addresses, essays, tracts* and pastoral letters, White published several books, including *Comparative Views of the Controversy between the Calvinists and the Arminians* (2 vols., 1817). His autobiographical *Memoirs of the Protestant Episcopal Church in the United States of America* (1828, 1836, 1880) is critical for early Episcopal history, precisely because the history of his life is largely the history of the Episcopal Church during the same period. Not only historically but also spiritually, he is "the Father of the Episcopal Church."

BIBLIOGRAPHY. *AAP* 5; *DARB*; *DAB* X; W. H. Stowe, ed., *Life and Letters of Bishop William White* (1937); B. Wilson, *Memoir of the Life of the Right Reverend William White D.D.* (1839).

D. L. Holmes

Whitefield, George (1715-1770). British itinerant* revivalist* of the Great Awakening.* Born in Gloucester, England, in 1734 Whitefield won admission to Oxford's famed Pembroke College, where he earned his way by serving meals to wealthier fellow students. Among those students were the brothers John* and Charles Wesley, whose renowned piety* would transform Whitefield's life. While parting company with these eventual founders of Methodism* on the issue of free will and predestination* (he remained a Calvinist*), Whitefield imbibed much of the Wesleys's teaching on piety and the necessity of spiritual regeneration,* or New Birth.* Through their influence Whitefield turned his life toward service to God and in 1737 was ordained* a preaching deacon* in the Church of England.*

Immediately on his ordination Whitefield began preaching* to English audiences with enormous success. Not content to preach within Anglican churches, he took his message of spiritual regeneration* to the open fields of England, preaching to all who gathered, regardless of their ecclesiastical affiliation. In what was to become a trademark of his career, Whitefield minimized his connection to the Church of England and proclaimed a message of free grace to all who would hear. In an age when preaching was defined largely in local, settled congregations, Whitefield created an entirely new clerical identity as an itinerant revivalist or "planter" who spent his career traveling from place to place proclaiming the doctrine of the New Birth. He seldom spent more than a day in one town or a month in any one region. The result was a total of over 7,500 sermons preached to audiences of unprecedented size that would total in the millions. Never before had English-speaking audiences heard such a charismatic speaker.

From the start of his itinerant preaching career, Whitefield attracted notice both for his powerful delivery and for his curious habit of preaching without any notes. Extemporaneous preaching, like itinerancy, became identified with Whitefield's ministry and was soon widely imitated by evangelical* speakers from all denominations. Whitefield believed that extemporaneous preaching conformed more closely to the biblical models of preaching handed down by the untutored and unlettered apostles. Beyond this, he argued, extemporaneous preaching compelled the preacher to rely on divine inspiration rather than the text before him. In practice, this mode of preaching proved far more powerful in forging a unique bond between speaker and audience than sermons that were read in classic Anglican fashion.

To sustain a sense of vital engagement, Whitefield generally selected biblical texts for their dramatic setting. Of particular use were Scripture narratives structured around a dialog that Whitefield would expand through the powers of his imagination. Christ's parables, the Sermon on the Mount, or Old Testament stories such as Jonah in the belly of the whale or Abraham sacrificing his son Isaac yielded the dramatic context that Whitefield could turn to serious reflections on the New Birth and the moment of "sudden and instantaneous change" from love of self to love of Christ.

From the fields of England the youthful Whitefield determined to take his novel brand of preaching to the cultural periphery of the British Empire in Scotland and North America. In both of these new worlds, he realized even greater successes than in England. In the American South, where Anglicanism was strongest, Whitefield met with mild success, despite the opposition of the Anglican Commissary, Alexander Garden.* While in Georgia, Whitefield began an orphanage, Bethesda, that would engage his interest and commitment for the remainder of his life. In Philadelphia, Whitefield preached to audiences as large as 20,000. All who heard Whitefield preach marveled at his oratory. Even the skeptical Benjamin Franklin was awestruck. Although never a convert to evangelical faith, Franklin began a lifelong friendship with Whitefield and published many of his sermons.

Whitefield's greatest North American success came in 1740 when he toured urban areas in New England. The way there had been paved by four generations of Puritan preachers, including the renowned revivalist Solomon Stoddard* and his grandson-successor Jonathan Edwards.* By the time Whitefield arrived in Newport in September, word of extraordinary crowds and conversions in Philadelphia preceded him, preparing the region for his exciting and novel brand of mass evangelism.* In a whirlwind forty-five-day tour of central places in Massachusetts and Connecticut, Whitefield delivered over 175 sermons to thousands of hearers that included virtually every New England inhabitant. He generated such excitement that audiences appeared out of control as they "elbowed, shoved, and trampled over themselves to hear of 'divine things' from the famed Whitefield."

In all, Whitefield made seven trips to the American colonies (1738, 1739-1741, 1744-1748, 1751-1752, 1754-1755, 1763-1765, 1769-1770) five of which were speaking tours. Gradually the controversy that marked his first visit diminished but not the public enthusiasm and veneration for the "Grand Itinerant." At the time of his death in Newburyport, Massachusetts, in 1770, he was arguably the best-known and best-loved individual in the American colonies. He was, by all accounts, the greatest English-speaking preacher in the eighteenth century and perhaps the greatest revivalist Anglo-America has ever seen. Although never equaled, his legacy would live on in the lives of countless itinerants whose simple proclamation of the New Birth paved the way for the large evangelical denominations* that would dominate the religious scene in nineteenth-century America.

BIBLIOGRAPHY. *AAP* 5; *DAB* X; A. Dallimore, *George Whitefield: The Life and Times of the Great Evangelist of the Eighteenth-Century Revival,* 2 vols.

(1970, 1979); S. C. Henry, *George Whitefield: Wayfaring Witness* (1954); *NCAB* 5.

H. S. Stout

Whitehead, Alfred North. *See* PROCESS THEOLOGY.

Whitfield, James (1770-1834). Fourth archbishop* of Baltimore. Born in Liverpool, England, Whitfield initially pursued a business career. In 1803 in Lyons, France, he formed a lifelong friendship with Ambrose Marechal,* then rector* of St. Irenaeus Seminary. Whitfield entered the seminary* and was ordained* a priest* in 1809. After some years in England, first as a Jesuit* novice and then as a parish priest, he joined Marechal in 1817 at Baltimore. Following Marechal's consecration* as archbishop, Whitfield was named rector of the cathedral* and in 1828 coadjutor archbishop. Marachal died shortly thereafter, and Whitfield was consecrated archbishop in May 1828. During his brief tenure, he presided over the first provincial council of Baltimore* in 1829 and a second provincial council in 1833. These meetings of the American hierarchy legislated for the growing church in the U.S. and promoted a sense of ecclesial unity. He died in Baltimore on October 19, 1834.

BIBLIOGRAPHY. B. D. Cestello, *James Whitfield, Fourth Archbishop of Baltimore: The Early Years, 1770-1828* (1957).

T. E. Buckley

Whitman, Marcus (1802-1847) and Narcissa (1808-1847). Pioneer missionaries* in the Oregon Territory. Marcus Whitman and Narcissa Prentiss married in 1836, both Presbyterians* and both equally dedicated to missionary work. Marcus, born in Rushville, New York, had studied medicine (1821-1824) and spent several years in medical practice, first in Canada (1825-1829) and then in Wheeler, New York (1830-1834). Narcissa, born in Prattsburg, New York, had taught school in her home town and had been rejected as a missionary candidate in 1834 because she was single.

Commissioned as pioneer missionaries to the Oregon Territory under the American Board of Commissioners for Foreign Missions,* they began their missionary venture in the spring of 1835, traveling westward with the American Fur Company. Accompanying them were Henry and Eliza Spalding. Plans called for a team enterprise, but discord between the two men led to a separation as soon as they arrived at their destination—the Whitmans settling in the lush green valley in Waiilatpu among the Cayuse Indians, and the Spaldings at Lapwai, among the Nez Perce Indians.

The Whitmans encountered sorrow and tragedy, while the Spaldings won many converts through their ministry. Two years after their arrival, the Whitman's only child, Alice, drowned in a nearby stream. They faced discouragement in their mission work as well. The Cayuse Indians bitterly resented the incursion of the whites, and the Whitman mission compound was a symbol of this incursion. Although Dr. Whitman offered his healing ministry to the Native Americans, misfortune struck when even mild vaccinations brought unexpected death to Native Americans, thus confirming their suspicions that he practiced witchcraft. Moreover, his assistance to white immigrants was seen as giving aid to the enemy.

In 1847, less than twelve years after their work in Oregon was initiated, their mission compound was attacked by a small group of Cayuse Indians, and fourteen residents were killed, including Marcus and Narcissa. The five Native Americans involved in the murders were hanged, and all the mission work in the region was suspended on government orders for more than two decades.

BIBLIOGRAPHY. O. S. Allen, *Narcissa Whitman* (1959); *DAB* X; *DARB*; C. M. Drury, *Marcus and Narcissa Whitman and the Opening of Old Oregon,* 2 vols. (1973); N. Jones, *The Great Command: The Story of Marcus and Narcissa Whitman and the Oregon Country Pioneers* (1959); *NAW* 3; *NCAB* 11.

R. A. Tucker

Whitsitt, William Heth (1841-1911). President of Southern Baptist Theological Seminary and professor of church history. Born near Nashville, Tennessee, Whitsitt graduated from Union University in Jackson, Tennessee. In 1861 his life was interrupted by the Civil War,* during which he served as a chaplain* in the Confederate army. After the war he continued his education at the University of Virginia (1866) and the Southern Baptist Theological Seminary (1866-1868), followed by two years of study in the universities of Leipzig and Berlin.

In 1872 Whitsitt gave up his pastorate in Albany, Georgia, to become the professor of ecclesiastical history at Southern Baptist Theological Seminary in Greenville, South Carolina. In 1895 he succeeded John A. Broadus* as president of the seminary. By then the seminary had relocated (1877) in Louisville, Kentucky. Only four years after assuming the presidency, Whitsitt was forced to resign.

The Whitsitt controversy was sparked by the discovery that Whitsitt was the author of an unsigned encyclopedia article which stated that Baptists "invented" immersion in 1641. Whitsitt

[1253]

explained that he had used the word *invent* in the old English sense of "discover" or "uncover"—meaning that in 1641 the Baptists had restored the primitive practice of baptism by immersion.

Nevertheless, Landmarkers,* who believed that Baptists had existed in unbroken succession since the days of John the Baptist, found Whitsitt's arguments unacceptable. Whitsitt, on the other hand, committed to an objective approach to church history, demanded that Baptist claims be supported by documentation. The seminary trustees concluded that harmony could not be restored apart from replacing Whitsitt. In 1899 he resigned both the presidency and his professorship.

Shortly thereafter he became professor of philosophy in Richmond College, Richmond, Virginia, where he taught until his death in 1911. Whitsitt wrote on a number of historically related subjects, including *Position of the Baptists in the History of American Culture* (1872); *The History of the Rise of Infant Baptism* (1878); *A Question in Baptist History* (1896) and *The Origin of the Disciples of Christ* (1888).

BIBLIOGRAPHY. *DAB* X; *ESB* 2; T. Meigs, "The Whitsitt Controversy," *QR* 31 (1971):41-61; W. A. Mueller, *A History of Southern Baptist Theological Seminary* (1959).

W. R. Estep

Whittemore, Emma Mott (1850-1931). Rescue mission* leader and founder of Doors of Hope. Whittemore and her husband, a businessman, were converted at New York's Water Street Mission.* They later worked at this mission as well as others in New York. In 1890 Emma Whittemore established the first Door of Hope "home for fallen and unfortunate women" in New York. An officer in the Christian and Missionary Alliance,* she worked closely with A. B. Simpson,* who provided the location for the first Door of Hope. By the time of her death, ninety-seven homes were in operation. While Whittemore maintained jurisdiction only over the initial home, she formed the Door of Hope Union to band the workers together. She was vice president of the National Federation of Gospel Missions when it became the International Union of Gospel Missions* in 1913 and served as its president from 1914 to 1918. She was also an honorary staff captain in The Salvation Army.* Whittemore engaged in evangelistic work and promoted Door of Hope homes until her death in 1931.

BIBLIOGRAPHY. F. A. Robinson, ed., *Mother Whittemore's Modern Miracles with which is*

Embodied Delia, the Blue-Bird of Mulberry Bend (1947).

S. C. Stanley

Wieman, Henry Nelson (1884-1975). Philosopher of religion.* Born in Rich Hill, Missouri, Wieman was educated at Park College (B.A., 1906) and studied theology* at San Francisco Seminary (B.D., 1910). After graduate studies in Europe at Jena and Heidelberg (1910-1911), he served as a Presbyterian* minister* in Davis, California (1911-1915). In 1917 he earned his Ph.D. from Harvard University* and returned to California to teach philosophy at Occidental College (1917-1927). In 1927 he became professor of philosophy and religion at the University of Chicago Divinity School, where for two decades (1927-1947) he was a prominent figure in the so-called Chicago School.* His writings include *Religious Experience and Scientific Method* (1926), *The Wrestle of Religion with Truth* (1927), *Man's Ultimate Commitment* (1958) and the posthumously published *Creative Freedom: Vocation of Liberal Religion* (C. Peden and L. E. Axel, eds., 1982).

Wieman combined a value-centered religion with an empirical method and a naturalistic world view. The central concern of Wieman's intellectual quest was to discover the force that operates in humanity to transform it in ways in which it cannot transform itself, delivering it from evil and leading it to its full potential. Wieman recognized a condition in this process, which he called *faith,* an act by which men and women give themselves to the transforming and creative power, which he called *God.* For Wieman, God is a dynamic process, revealing itself in events and human experience. His thought reflected the new quest among Protestant* liberals* for a theology consistent with modern methods of thinking, especially as found in the empirical sciences. He was responsible for introducing the empirical metaphysics of Alfred North Whitehead* to the Chicago Divinity School, thus fostering the birth of process theology* as a public and self-conscious theological movement.

BIBLIOGRAPHY. R. W. Bretall, ed., *The Empirical Theology of Henry Nelson Wieman* (1963); *DARB.*

The Editors

Wigglesworth, Michael (1631-1705). Puritan* minister* and poet. Born in Yorkshire, England, Wigglesworth immigrated with his family in 1638 to New Haven, Connecticut. He studied with schoolmaster Ezekiel Cheever, attended Harvard College,* where he underwent conversion,* and graduated in 1651. As a tutor he both taught and ministered to students. Though chronically ill, he accepted a call as pastor* in Maldon, Massachusetts, and married the first of his three wives in 1656. His diary from these years records spiritual struggles with doubt and an acute, overweening sense of his own sinfulness. At Maldon, in addition to what pastoral duties ill health allowed, he studied and practiced medicine.

His most remarkable work was poetic. Wigglesworth put Puritan theology* into verse that was memorized for generations. *The Day of Doom* (1662), describing the final judgment, sold all 1,800 copies and went through numerous editions to become the colonial best seller. Other poetic works include *God's Controversy With New England* and "Meat Out of the Eater; or, Meditations concerning the necessity, end, and usefulness of afflictions unto God's children, all tending to prepare them for and comfort them under the Cross."

BIBLIOGRAPHY. *AAP* 1; *DAB* X; H. T. Meserole, "Michael Wigglesworth," in *Seventeenth-Century American Poetry* (1968); J. L. Sibley, *Biographical Sketches of Graduates of Harvard University,* vols. 1-4 (1873-1885); M. Wigglesworth, *The Diary of Michael Wigglesworth, 1653-1657,* ed. E. S. Morgan (1946).   C. E. Hambrick-Stowe

Wightman, Valentine (1681-1747). Pioneer Baptist* minister* in Connecticut and New York City. Born in North Kingston, Rhode Island, Wightman was a "Six-Principle"* Baptist who rejected many Calvinistic* emphases of the Regular* Baptists. In 1705 he established a church at Groton, Connecticut, the earliest Baptist church in the state except for the fleeting appearance of a Seventh-day* Baptist group in the 1670s. In 1712 he began preaching* in New York City, helping to form the earliest Baptist church there in 1714. This church did not survive, being supplanted in 1726 by a congregation of Regular Baptists. Wightman also formed a number of churches in Connecticut. An advocate of the then-controversial practice of singing in worship, he also conducted a number of public debates on baptism. He married Susanna Holmes in 1703 and left descendants who followed him in the Baptist ministry.

BIBLIOGRAPHY. *AAP* 6; I. Backus, *A History of New England, with Particular Reference to the Denomination of Christians Called Baptists* (1777).   H. L. McBeth

Wilbur, John (1774-1896). Quietist Quaker* minister.* Born in Hopkinton, Rhode Island, Wilbur was recorded as a minister of the Hopkinton Society of Friends in 1812. In a period of the

social transformation of much of American Quakerism into mainstream evangelical* Protestantism,* Wilbur was a conservative and a spokesman for the quietist Friends' tradition of radical dependence on direct leadings of the Spirit. Wilbur's concern for "purity"—a quietist watchword referring to both internal motivation and external behavior—led him to oppose all that smacked of "creaturely activity." Wilbur and other quietists held that preparation and organization in the religious life were a human supplanting of divine initiative and direction.

These quietist convictions brought Wilbur into conflict with the British Quaker Joseph John Gurney,* whose promotion of Bible societies,* Bible schools* and other organized missionary* and philanthropic* endeavors Wilbur regarded as a dangerous innovation. In addition, Gurney's education and ease of interaction with the interdenominational leadership of the evangelical* movement struck Wilbur as "worldly." Theologically, however, Wilbur himself held much in common with evangelicals, including an emphasis on the atonement.* But the dispute between quietists and evangelicals resulted in a parting at the New England Yearly Meeting of 1845, with 500 "Wilburites" being outnumbered by the 6,500 "Gurneyites."* Similar conflicts and divisions followed in New York and Ohio, though Philadelphia Quakers, still in anguish from the painful "Hicksite*-Orthodox" split of 1827-1828, were able to avoid a further disastrous schism.

BIBLIOGRAPHY. *DAB* X; J. Wilbur, *Journal of the Life of John Wilbur* (1859).   M. L. Birkel

Wilder, Robert Parmelee (1863-1938). Missions* leader and Student Volunteer Movement* organizer and promoter. Born to missionary parents in India, Wilder came to the U.S. in 1875 when his father's health forced a family move to Princeton, New Jersey. In 1881 Wilder enrolled at Princeton University* (B.A., 1886), where he helped launch the Princeton Foreign Missionary Society in 1883. After graduation in 1886, he attended Dwight L. Moody's* summer camp for collegians and was instrumental in forming the "Mount Hermon Hundred,"* soon to become the Student Volunteer Movement for Foreign Missions (SVM). Wilder served the SVM as a traveling recruiter, interspersing campus visits with studies at Union Theological Seminary (New York)* (B.D., 1891).

In 1891 Wilder completed his theological training and sailed for England en route to a Presbyterian* missionary appointment in India. He toured several British campuses and assisted in the formation of the Student Volunteer Missionary Union of Great Britain and Ireland. He and his new Norwegian bride, Helene Olsson, arrived in India in 1892 for Wilder's work among students, but ill health ended his tenure in India in 1902, and he eventually accepted a student ministry in Europe. In 1916 Wilder returned to the U.S. to serve as secretary of the Religious Work Department of the International Committee of the YMCA (1916-1919) and as general secretary of the SVM (1919-1927). His last missionary stint took him to Egypt for six years of service as executive secretary of the Near East Christian Council. He retired to Norway in 1933 and died there in 1938.

BIBLIOGRAPHY. R. E. Braisted, *In This Generation: the Story of Robert P. Wilder* (1941); *DARB*. J. A. Patterson

Wiley, Henry Orton (1877-1961). Church of the Nazarene* minister* and theologian.* Born in Marquette, Nebraska, Wiley attended Oregon State Normal School in Ashland, Oregon, and graduated from University of the Pacific, San Jose, California. Wiley earned a B.D. (1910) and S.T.M. (1916) from Pacific Theological Seminary, as well as the S.T.D. from Pacific School of Religion (1929). After pastoring a Nazarene church in Berkeley, California (1905-1909), he served as president of two Nazarene colleges, Pasadena College in Pasadena, California (1910-1916), and Northwest Nazarene College, Nampa, Idaho (1916-1926). Active in the leadership of his denomination, he served as secretary of the General Board of Education and edited the Nazarene publication, *The Herald of Holiness* (1928 1836).

Wiley's most significant publication was his three-volume *Christian Theology* (1941), which has remained the standard systematic theology* for the Church of the Nazarene and others of the Wesleyan*-Arminian* Holiness* tradition. Drawing upon the Scriptures and the Christian tradition, Wiley was particularly influenced by John Wesley* and his latter-day exponents, such as John Miley* and William Burt Pope.* His soteriology reflects the Wesleyan perspective in beginning with prevenient grace that enables—without compelling—fallen people to respond to God, forming the basis of the "synergism or the co-operation of divine grace and human will." Following the Wesleyan-Holiness tradition, Wiley's soteriology moves through reconciliation and regeneration to culminate in "Christian Perfection* or Entire Sanctification."* In a second important work, *Epistle to the Hebrews* (1959), Wiley's exposition

emphasizes the epistle's robust Christology and a soteriology "which not only includes the pardon of actual transgressions, but the cleansing from 'inbred sin' or 'the carnal mind'—a cleansing from all sin." In a 1984 survey of evangelical Wesleyan theologians, Wiley was the author most frequently mentioned as having had the most impact on their academic work. J. R. Tyson

Willard, Frances Elizabeth Caroline (1839-1898). Methodist* educator, temperance* leader, reformer and feminist.* Born in Churchville, New York, Willard graduated from North Western Female College in Evanston, Illinois (1859), and devoted sixteen years to the field of education, culminating in her appointment as president of the Evanston College for Ladies (1871-1873) and then as dean of women (1873-1874) when the college united with Northwestern University. Willard began her involvement with the Woman's Christian Temperance Union* (WCTU) by preaching at daily gospel temperance meetings in the Chicago Loop during the winter of 1874. She was president of the Chicago and Illinois WCTU groups (1874-1877) and also served as first corresponding secretary of the National WCTU (1879-1898).

During 1877 she curtailed her temperance work and led meetings for women in Boston under Dwight L. Moody.* Willard stated on numerous occasions her desire to be ordained,* but the Methodist Episcopal Church, of which she was a member, refused to ordain women then. Willard addressed this issue in *Woman in the Pulpit* (1889). In 1879 Willard assumed the presidency of the National WCTU, a position she held until her death. Under the banner of "home protection," Willard voiced her devotion to the domestic sphere. At the same time, she led WCTU members outside their sphere, pursuing political avenues such as the ballot to protect the home.

Willard was a prominent figure in national reform politics. She was influential in the merger of two parties resulting in the Prohibition Home Protection Party in 1882, although the Prohibition Party resumed its original name two years later. Her genius lay in her ability to combine conservative ideals with a commitment to radical social reform. In her later years she espoused a Christian socialism,* and in this regard she might be recognized as a forerunner of the Social Gospel Movement.*

BIBLIOGRAPHY. *DAB* X; *DARB*; R. Bordin, *Frances Willard* (1986); *NCAB* 1; *NAW* 3; R. Strachey, *Frances Willard: Her Life and Work* (1912); L. J. Trowbridge, *Frances Willard of Evanston* (1938);

F. E. Willard, *Glimpses of Fifty Years* (1899).

S. C. Stanley

Willard, Joseph (1738-1804). Congregational* minister* and president of Harvard College.* Born in Biddeford, Maine, Willard came from a long line of New England ministers reaching back to Samuel Willard,* author of *A Compleat Body of Divinity* (1726). Joseph attended Harvard College (B.A., 1765), and after serving as a tutor at the college for several years, he became pastor of the Beverly, Massachusetts, Congregational Church in 1772. He was an active advocate of the Revolution* and a founding member of the American Academy of Arts and Sciences (1780). For many years he served as the Academy's corresponding secretary and vice president and as one of its leading members. He became famous for his work in astronomy, mathematics and the classics and was considered by John Adams the equal of David Rittenhouse as a scientist.

Willard was inaugurated as the president of Harvard in December 1781, and then devoted himself to the task of repairing the damage to the college wrought by the War. Willard stiffened admission requirements, expanded the curricula and established the medical school. He kept up a steady correspondence with Richard Price, Joseph Priestly* and other European intellectuals, and as a result of his many scientific achievements won membership in several learned societies, including the Royal Society of Göttingen and the Medical Society of London.

BIBLIOGRAPHY. *AAP* 2; *DABX.*

G. F. Moran

Willard, Samuel (1640-1707). New England theologian* and president of Harvard College.* Born in Concord, Massachusetts, Willard was educated at Harvard College (B.A., M.A., 1659). He served as pastor of the frontier congregation of Groton, Massachusetts (1663-1676), and as teacher to the Old South Church, Boston (1676-1707). In 1700 he became vice president of Harvard and in 1701 acting president of the college, a position he held until his death in 1707.

Next to Cotton Mather,* Willard was the most prolific writer of his generation. His major works include *Covenant Keeping, The Way to Blessedness* (1682), his first work; *Mercy Magnified* (1684), which examines the process of conversion* in its entirety; and *Sacramental Meditations* (1711), which celebrates the sacramental* signs of redemption. He was also a tireless preacher* and teacher. From 1688 to his death he delivered

monthly lectures on the Westminster* Assembly's *Shorter Catechism,* lectures that were published posthumously as *Complete Body of Divinity* (1726). This was the first major folio-size book published in America. It was also New England's first and only systematic theology* until the publication of Samuel Hopkins's* *System of Doctrine* (1793). Willard was a transitional figure in American Puritanism*; in his works he combined traditional Puritan interest in predestination* and scriptural authority* with a new concern for human happiness and moral integrity, thus anticipating the thought of Jonathan Edwards* by a generation.

BIBLIOGRAPHY. *AAP* 1; *DAB* X; *DARB*; E. B. Lowrie, *The Shape of the Puritan Mind: The Thought of Samuel Willard* (1974); *NCAB* 6; S. Van Dyken, *Samuel Willard, 1640-1707: Preacher of Orthodoxy in an Era of Change* (1972).

G. F. Moran

Willett, Herbert Lockwood (1864-1944). Disciples of Christ* minister and biblical scholar. Born in Ionia, Michigan, Willet was educated at Bethany College (B.A., 1886; M.A., 1887), Yale University* (1890-1891), the University of Chicago (Ph.D., 1896) and the University of Berlin (1898-1899). He taught at the University of Michigan, but spent most of his career at the University of Chicago (1896-1929). Willett held various pastorates through the years (1886-1944) and was dean of the Disciples Divinity House at the University of Chicago (1896-1921).

Trained in semitics under William Rainey Harper* at Yale and Chicago, Willett's respected scholarship and excellent organizing and speaking skills in the classroom and on the Chautauqua and Lyceum circuits promoted a constructive encounter with biblical criticism. In the face of strong conservative opposition, Willett's modernism* offered a critique of biblical literalism while maintaining a view of biblical inspiration compatible with higher criticism and evolutionary theory. Within his denomination,* the Disciples of Christ, Willett worked tirelessly for increased graduate education and ecumenical cooperation. His books included: *The Prophets of Israel* (1899); *The Bible through the Centuries* (1929) and *The Jew through the Centuries* (1932).

BIBLIOGRAPHY. *DAB* 3. K. S. Sawyer

William and Mary, College of. A College originally founded as a colonial Anglican* institution. Founded at Williamsburg, Virginia, in 1693, the college owes its existence to the Rev. James Blair,* who successfully obtained the royal charter

[1257]

in London and named the school after the joint sovereigns of England. Blair became the college's first president (1693-1743). Initial support came from diverse sources, including the legacy of the scientist Robert Boyle, the contributions of several jailed pirates and a tax levied on Virginia tobacco. Originally established "for the breeding of good Ministers," the college's Anglican* character was reinforced with the 1727 statutes specifying that the president must be ordained.* Twelve of William and Mary's twenty-four presidents have been Anglican divines,* and the chancellorship was held by the archbishop* of Canterbury or bishop of London until 1762.

In 1776 the honorary society Phi Beta Kappa was founded at the college. Closed in 1780 as a result of the Revolutionary War,* William and Mary reopened in 1782 with a large portion of its endowment and lands lost as a result of American independence.

In 1814 the statute requiring the president to be a clergyman was repealed. The nineteenth century saw a continual struggle for existence. Operations were suspended for a year in 1848 because of a lack of students, again from 1861 to 1865 as a result of the Civil War,* and from 1881 to 1888 because of financial difficulties. In 1888 William and Mary was given an annual appropriation from the Virginia legislature which paved the way for it to become a true state institution in 1906.

A 1960 legislative act expanding William and Mary to a multi-campus institution was repealed in 1962. Presently, the college offers degrees in a wide variety of disciplines through the doctoral level. It is the second-oldest college in the U.S.

BIBLIOGRAPHY. W. Kale, *Hark Upon the Gale* (1985); J. E. Morpurgo, *Their Majesties' Royall Colledge* (1976).   F. M. Perko

Williams, Channing Moore (1829-1910). Protestant Episcopal* missionary bishop* to Japan. A sickly child, strengthened by his mother's care and faith, Williams started his career as a merchant but later trained for the Anglican* ministry* at the College of William and Mary* and the Theological Seminary at Alexandria, Virginia. Ordained* a priest* in 1857, he first went to China as a missionary* and then moved to Nagasaki, Japan, in 1859. There he conducted services in the first Japanese Protestant* church building and translated portions of the *Book of Common Prayer.** Consecrated* bishop of Japan and China in 1866, by 1874 he had moved permanently to Japan and given up responsibility for China. He established what later became Rikkyō Daigaku (St. Paul's University)

(1874) and Seikōkai Shingakuin (Central Theological College) (1878), as well as helped found the Seikōkai (1887), the name of the Japanese church formed by the Episcopalian and Anglican missionaries. Quiet and shy, Williams never married. In the words of a later bishop, "his great contribution was the influence exerted by his own faith and character" which led members of the Seikōkai to consider him their "patron saint."

BIBLIOGRAPHY. *DAB* X; H. Kaneko, *A Story of Channing Moore Williams, the Bishop of Yedo* (1965); M. Minor, *Pioneer Missionary in Japan: Channing Moore Williams* (1959).

     J. F. Howes

Williams, Daniel Day (1910-1973). Process* theologian.* Born in Denver, Colorado, Williams was educated at the University of Denver, the University of Chicago,* Chicago Theological Seminary and Columbia University (Ph.D., 1940). Ordained* to ministry* in the Congregational Church* (1936), Williams pastored in Colorado before being called to teach theology,* first at Chicago Theological Seminary and the Federated Theological Faculty at the University of Chicago* (1939-1954) and then at Union Theological Seminary,* New York (1954-1973).

Influenced by the philosophical insights of figures such as Henri Bergson (1859-1941), Alfred North Whitehead and Charles Hartshorne, Williams sought to restate Christian theology in terms of process philosophy. One of his most significant formulations of this came in his book *The Spirit and the Forms of Love* (1968). His other publications included *God's Grace and Man's Hope* (1949) and *What Present-Day Theologians Are Thinking* (1967). Process theologian John Cobb has called him the "senior statesman of process theology."

BIBLIOGRAPHY. D. D. Williams, *Essays in Process Theology,* ed. P. LeFevre (1985).

     R. L. Petersen

Williams, Roger (1603-1683). Christian* minister,* statesman, founder of Rhode Island and first champion of religious liberty* in America. Born in London, probably in 1603, the son of a shopkeeper, Williams studied first at the Charterhouse and later at Pembroke College, Cambridge (B.A., 1627). An Anglican* minister, he became chaplain* to Sir William Masham in Otes, Essex County, where on December 15, 1629, he wedded Mary Barnard, the daughter of a Puritan* clergyman.*

Sometime during his Cambridge experience, Williams apparently became a Puritan, and in 1630 he sailed with his wife from Bristol to Massachusetts, landing at Nantasket on February 5, 1631. On board ship, Williams, after an intensive study of the New Testament, concluded that in order to be truly biblical, the Puritans in New England should explicitly separate from the Church of England. There followed a succession of clashes with the Massachusetts authorities as Williams criticized the Puritan establishment for a variety of practices, especially for expropriating Native American land without negotiations and for having the civil magistrates attempt to enforce the first four of the Ten Commandments. On October 9, 1635, the colonial General Court (legislature) banished him to England, but before he could be deported, he fled with his family and a few companions to the uninhabited regions to the south, outside the limits of Massachusetts, and in the summer of 1636 founded there a settlement which he named Providence.

As leader of the new colony, Williams purchased land from the Narragansett Indians and distributed it for use, befriended the Native Americans and learned their language, and during the Pequot War (1637) served all New England as a negotiator to restore peace to the region. In Providence he adopted the principle that "God requireth not an uniformity of Religion" and saw to it that all individuals and religious bodies enjoyed what he called "soul liberty," that is, religious freedom. In 1642, faced with internal tensions and the expansionist designs of Massachusetts and Connecticut, Williams sailed for England to procure a charter for the cluster of settlements in the Narragansett region. His London trip resulted in the acquisition from Parliament on March 14, 1644, of a charter uniting the several towns into the colony of Rhode Island, fixing its boundaries and guaranteeing its independence, and for the first time in American history granting complete religious liberty to all of its inhabitants. While in London, he also published three books, the most important of which was *The Bloudy Tenent of Persecution* in which he expounded the premises that underlay his lifelong commitment to religious liberty.

Williams was again dispatched to London in November 1651, when internal enemies seemed about to split and perhaps destroy the colony. On this occasion (1651-1654), he not only saved the charter but also became a friend of John Milton and Oliver Cromwell, and published three more volumes, one of which was a reply to John Cotton's response to his earlier work, this one entitled *The Bloudy Tenent Yet More Bloudy.*

Upon his return, Williams served as president

(governor) of the colony (1654-1657), and during his tenure welcomed the first Jews and Quakers* to Rhode Island, even though he disagreed with their views. In 1672 he engaged three Quakers in a tumultuous public debate for four days, publishing the report in Boston in 1676 under the title *George Fox Digg'd out of his Burrowes.* Williams was reduced to poverty when his trade was disrupted by the bloody King Philip's War* (1675-1676), during which Williams, though well over 70, served as a captain in the colonial militia and later as a peace negotiator. He died in Providence sometime between January 16 and March 15, 1683.

In 1639, shortly after settling Providence, Williams became a Baptist,* and during that year joined with a dozen others in forming the first Baptist church on American soil. However, a few months later Williams withdrew from the Baptists and pronounced himself a Seeker, one who had not yet discovered "the true church" as constituted by Jesus Christ in the first century. He agreed with Baptist insistence on religious liberty and separation of church and state,* but he could not accept the Baptist claim that their congregations constituted "the true church" which could only be entered through their "true baptism."

For the remainder of his life Williams would be a religious loner searching for a church which he could recognize as created in the image of the first apostles. In the end, he clung tenaciously to his basic Calvinist theology and to his belief in religious liberty and separation of church and state, and died an independent evangelical* Christian without a denomination.

Williams' original influence was greatest among his near co-religionists, the Baptists. It was through the Baptists that Williams's thought and reputation was transmitted to the young nation for whom Williams became a folk hero in the nineteenth century. In many ways, Williams's Rhode Island, with its stress on freedom, individualism* and being a place "where no man should be molested for his conscience"—and not Puritan New England with its emphasis on order, community and the mission of a "city on a hill"—was the prototype of the future American republic.

BIBLIOGRAPHY. T. D. Bozeman, "Religious Liberty and the Problem of Order in Early Rhode Island," *NEQ* 45 (March 1971):44-64; S. H. Brocknuier, *Irrepressible Democrat: Roger Williams* (1940); M. Calamandrei, "Neglected Aspects of Roger Williams' Thought," *CH* 21 (1952):239-259; J. Garrett, *Roger Williams: Witness Beyond Christendom* (1970); W. C. Gilpin, *The Millenarian Piety of Roger Williams* (1979). P. Miller, *Roger*

Williams: His Contribution to the American Tradition (1953); E. S. Morgan, *Roger Williams: The Church and the State* (1967); H. J. Schultz, "Roger Williams, Delinquent Saint: The Religious Odyssey of the Providence Prophet," *Baptist Quarterly* 19 (April 1962):253-269; R. Williams, *The Complete Writings of Roger Williams* 7 vols. (1963); O. E. Winslow, *Master Roger Williams* (1957).

R. D. Linder

Williams, Samuel Wells (1812-1884). Missionary* to China, diplomat and Sinologist. Born in Utica, New York, Williams was sent to China by the American Board of Commissioners for Foreign Missions* in 1833 as a printer for the Canton mission press. There he developed an extraordinary knowledge of the Chinese language as he worked closely with Elijah Coleman Bridgman* on *The Chinese Repository* and produced several monographs on the Chinese language and Chinese affairs. From 1845 to 1848 he was in the U.S., where he married Sarah Walworth and gave the lectures which developed into the first edition of his *The Middle Kingdom* (2 vols., 1848). This remained for decades the standard English-language work on China. Williams, who had also learned Japanese, accompanied the Perry expedition to Japan in 1853-1854 and in 1856 became secretary-interpreter in the U.S. legation to China. His connection with the legation continued until 1876. Williams retired to New Haven, Connecticut, in 1877, becoming professor of Chinese at Yale and revising and enlarging *The Middle Kingdom* (2 vols., 1883). His commitment to missions as well as his learning and productivity were a valuable contribution to Protestant missionary efforts in East Asia.

BIBLIOGRAPHY. *DAB* X; F. W. Williams, *The Life and Letters of Samuel Wells Williams* (1889).

D. H. Bays

Williamson, Atkin (fl. 1681-1696). Anglican* missionary* in colonial South Carolina. Atkin Williamson was the first rector* of St. Philip's Church, the first Anglican Church in Charleston, South Carolina, from 1681 to 1696, when he was replaced by Samuel Marshall. He was, apparently, never able to produce satisfactory letters of ordination,* but claimed to have been ordained deacon* by the bishop* of Dublin and priest* by the bishop of Lincoln. His character, it seems, was somewhat suspect, and the parishioners of St. Philips never accepted him as their regular and permanent minister.* He remained in the province for many years, however, and received a small pension from the Assembly in his old age. The first regular

minister in the colony was Samuel Marshall, who arrived in 1696 and became rector of St. Philip's in 1698.

BIBLIOGRAPHY. S. C. Bolton, *Southern Anglicanism: The Church of England in Colonial South Carolina* (1982).

G. F. Moran

Wilson, J. Christy, Sr. (1881-1973). Presbyterian* missionary* to Iran. Born in Columbus, Nebraska, Wilson graduated from Kansas University and was elected to Phi Beta Kappa in 1914. In 1919 he graduated with an M.A. at Princeton University* and a B.D. from Princeton Theological Seminary.* He received a Th.M. from Princeton Seminary in 1926 and two honorary Doctor of Divinity degrees in 1934.

Wilson went as an evangelistic* missionary to Tabriz in Azerbaijan in northwestern Iran under the Presbyterian Board of Foreign Missions in 1919. He served there for twenty years and was chairman of the Near East Relief Committee* for Iran, as well as chairman of the Near East Christian Council. His missionary work also took him to Russia and countries of the Middle East.

Wilson authored several books in Persian, including, at the request of the imperial ministry of education, a textbook on the art, archeology and architecture of Iran. His English publications on Islam included *Introducing Islam* (1958), *The Christian Message to Islam* (1950), *Apostle to Islam: The Biography of Samuel M. Zwemer* (1952) and over twenty encyclopedia articles on Near Eastern subjects. He also wrote a regular missionary column for "The Presbyterian Magazine."

Present in Iran at the beginning of World War 2, in 1939 he returned to the U.S. and became associate professor of ecumenics at Princeton Theological Seminary (1940-1962). There he also directed the field work of ministerial students and wrote *Ministers in Training* (1957).

Following his retirement, he became pastor of visitation at the First Presbyterian Church in Princeton, New Jersey (1962-1963), and later held the same position at the First Presbyterian Church in Monrovia, California (1965-1970). During that time he taught missions courses at Fuller Theological Seminary.*

J. C. Wilson

Wilson, Robert Dick (1856-1930). Presbyterian* Old Testament scholar and educator. Born in western Pennsylvania, Wilson received his undergraduate education at the College of New Jersey* (now Princeton University) and graduated in 1876. From Princeton, he went on to study and teach at Western Theological Seminary in Pittsburgh before attending the University of Berlin (1881-1883), where Wilson did research in Semitic languages. Following his studies in Berlin, Wilson returned to teach at Western, where he produced grammars in Syriac and Hebrew. In 1900 Wilson accepted an appointment at Princeton Seminary* in Semitic philology and Old Testament criticism.

At Princeton, Wilson devoted his scholarship to defending the historical character of the Old Testament in general (*Is the Higher Criticism Scholarly?* 1922) and of the book of Daniel specifically (*Studies in the Book of Daniel*, 1917). In 1929, at the age of seventy-four, Wilson joined his younger colleague J. Gresham Machen* in the establishment of Westminster Theological Seminary in Philadelphia as a response to the controversial reorganization of Princeton Seminary. He died after only one year with the new seminary, taking with him a significant measure of the Old Princeton legacy of biblical scholarship.

BIBLIOGRAPHY. G. L. Haines, "The Princeton Theological Seminary, 1925-1960" (unpublished Ph.D. dissertation, New York University, 1966); J. W. Hart, "Princeton Theological Seminary: The Reorganization of 1929," *JPH* 58 (1980):124-140; M. A. Noll, *Between Faith and Criticism* (1986).

D. G. Hart

Wilson, Thomas Woodrow (1856-1924). Historian, educator, reformer, Presbyterian* churchman and twenty-eighth U.S. president. Descended from Presbyterian clergy* on both sides of his family, Woodrow Wilson was born in Staunton, Virginia, the son of Presbyterian minister* Dr. Joseph Ruggles Wilson. He grew to manhood in the South, where his father served as a pastor and seminary professor. After graduating from Princeton University* (B.A., 1879; M.A., 1882), he launched an unsuccessful law practice in Atlanta, Georgia. On June 24, 1885, he married Ellen Louise Axson of Rome, Georgia, and they eventually became the parents of three daughters. In 1883 Wilson decided on an academic profession and began graduate study in history at the Johns Hopkins University, where he earned a Ph.D. in 1886. In the meantime, he began his teaching career: Bryn Mawr (1885-1888), Wesleyan (1888-1890) and Princeton (1890-1902). At Princeton, he became a popular lecturer and published his major work, *A History of the American People* (1902). In 1902 he became the first layperson* ever chosen as president of the university, a position he held until 1910.

Wilson's statewide reputation as a dynamic educator, his oratorical ability and his abiding interest in politics conjoined to make him the Democratic Party's gubernatorial candidate in 1910. After winning an impressive victory, Wilson launched a successful program of progressive reforms which brought him national attention and made him a leading contender for the Democratic presidential nomination in 1912. Wilson was nominated and won election by enunciating his proposed "New Freedom"—a program to liberate American economic energies by drastically reducing tariffs, strengthening anti-trust laws and reorganizing the banking and credit system.

Wilson's world was shattered in the summer of 1914 by two tragedies: the outbreak in July of a general war in Europe (World War 1,* 1914-1918) and the death of his wife on August 6. He won reelection in 1916, largely because of his successful progressive reforms and the fact that he had kept America out of the European conflict. However, with great reluctance Wilson finally asked for a declaration of war against Germany and its allies in 1917 because of pressures created by unrestricted German submarine warfare and U.S. commercial ties to Britain and France.

Wilson made his greatest contribution to the war effort by formulating war aims that for the first time gave some meaning to the conflict, especially in the enunciation of his Fourteen Points on January 8, 1918, in which he unveiled his liberal plan for a just and lasting peace. It was largely on the basis of Wilson's pronouncements that the Germans finally agreed to an armistice on November 11, 1918. The Versailles Peace Conference, which followed in 1919, betrayed Wilson's program; and in order to save his plan for a League of Nations with responsibility for executing the treaty and preventing future wars, the American president had to compromise his other peace aims. This disappointment was followed by the rejection of the Versailles Treaty with its provision for Wilson's League by a Republican-controlled Congress, despite the president's strenuous efforts to secure acceptance.

His attempt to bring the American public to his side by means of an extensive speaking tour of the Western states came to naught when he collapsed following an address in Pueblo, Colorado, on September 25, 1919, and suffered a debilitating stroke on the following October 2 after his return to the nation's capital. The final blow came with the 1920 election, when the nation chose Republican Warren G. Harding as president, a man who had pledged that he would make a separate peace with Germany and never enter the League. The events of 1919-1920 permanently broke Wilson's health. He retired to his Washington home, where he lived the remainder of his days in seclusion, finally dying on February 3, 1924.

Some scholars consider Wilson to have been "the most God-centered man" ever to be president, while New Jersey Democratic Party boss James Smith once derisively called him "a Presbyterian priest." Whatever the case, there is no doubt that Wilson's political philosophy rested firmly on his understanding of Christianity and that throughout his life he drew his greatest strength from the resources of his Calvinist* faith, with its emphasis on order, reason and righteousness. He was reared in an evangelical Presbyterian home, early introduced to the doctrines of sin,* salvation,* predestination* and free grace, and accepted Christ as his Savior when he was seventeen. A Presbyterian elder,* he had a superb command of Reformed* theology, read the Bible* and prayed daily, and attended church regularly. It was no accident that he never thought about public matters, as well as private ones, without first trying to decide what the teachings of Jesus dictated in such circumstances.

The mainspring of Wilson's public life was his crusading idealism, which grew out of his evangelical faith. He represented the last gasp of both the evangelical urge to reform the nation along Christian lines and the progressive movement in American politics. His drive to establish his New Freedom at home and his impulse to create a peaceful world order based on the League of Nations abroad were both based on his Christian idealism—as was the stubborn certainty that he was right and that his mission came from God. It was also the source of his continuous moralizing about the meaning of American politics. Wilson thus brought to the presidency a moralized political philosophy and a moralized civil religion which stressed obligation, duty and service. He was at heart a "political missionary" who believed that humans could improve the world in which they lived and that America, because of its unique history and place in the divine plan, could serve as the vehicle for world reform.

It is puzzling that Wilson's evangelical Calvinist faith did not inform him more fully of the main roadblock to the realization of his idealistic goals, namely, human nature. In any case, he was a dedicated reformer with a sensitive Christian conscience. If such crusading reformers are often blinded by their own self-righteousness and never wholly succeed, neither do they wholly fail, and they are never forgotten.

BIBLIOGRAPHY. J. M. Blum, *Woodrow Wilson and the Politics of American Morality* (1956); J. M.

Cooper, *The Warrior and the Priest: Woodrow Wilson and Theodore Roosevelt* (1983); E. Fuller and D. E. Green, *God in the White House* (1968); C. T. Grayson, *Woodrow Wilson, An Intimate Memoir* (1960); A. S. Link, *The Higher Realism of Woodrow Wilson and Other Essays* (1971); A. S. Link, *Wilson*, 5 vols. (1947-1965); J. M. Mulder, *Woodrow Wilson: The Years of Preparation* (1978); R. V. Pierard and R. D. Linder, *Civil Religion and the Presidency* (1988).

R. D. Linder

Wimmer, Boniface (1809-1887). Benedictine* archabbot. Born in Thalmassing, Bavaria, Wimmer was educated at Ratisbon, studied law at Munich and prepared for the priesthood at Rome. Ordained* a priest* at Rome (1831), Wimmer worked in the diocese* of Regensburg, Germany, before entering the Benedictine monastery of Metten, Bavaria, in 1833. In 1846 he arrived in New York with several German Benedictine candidates, intending to found a monastery. When the bishop* of Pittsburgh donated to the community some land near Latrobe, Pennsylvania, the community moved there. Eventually St. Vincent Archabbey, College and Seminary were formed at that location, and Wimmer was made archabbot.

Wimmer founded Benedictine parishes* and monasteries across the U.S. with help from Ludwig I of Bavaria, the Ludwig Mission Union and friends in Bavaria. He attended Vatican Council I* in Rome. The Benedictine communities he founded in the U.S., especially St. John's Abbey and University in Collegeville, Minnesota, became powerful forces in the renewal of the liturgy* in the American Roman Catholic Church after 1950. Wimmer was also instrumental in uniting all the Benedictine communities into a single international confederation.

BIBLIOGRAPHY. C. J. Barry, *Worship and Work: St. John's Abbey and University, 1856-1956* (1956); J. Rippinger, "The Origins and Development of Benedictine Monasticism in the United States," in *The Continuing Quest for God*, ed. W. Skudlarek (1982).

T. F. Sable

Winchell, Alexander (1824-1891). Methodist* layman* and natural historian. Born in Dutchess County, New York, Winchell planned to become a physician but, following his graduation from Wesleyan University in 1847, he became a lecturer and author in natural history. He taught in several universities before becoming professor of geology and zoology at Vanderbilt University in 1875.

In most of his 250 articles and books, Winchell

intended to reconcile the apparent conflict between science and religion (*See* Science and Christianity), and he opposed his conservative critics by advocating the compatibility of natural selection and theism.* For him, truth was one, whether it came from Scripture* or the natural sciences. His dismissal from Vanderbilt in 1878 followed the publication of his views in the *Northern Christian Advocate,* where he came under heavy attack from a theological colleague and church editor, Thomas O. Summers. Following his dismissal he became professor at the University of Michigan, where he served until his death. In his later years he was the principal organizer of the Geological Society of America.

BIBLIOGRAPHY. *DAB* X.   J. S. O'Malley

Winchester, (A)lexander (B)rown (1858-1943). Canadian evangelical* Presbyterian* minister. Born in the Aberdeenshire fishing port of Peterhead, just as it was about to be touched by one of the greatest of its many religious revivals,* Winchester soon left Scotland with his parents for Woodstock, Ontario. There he responded to the appeal of Dr. James Robertson,* the great Presbyterian superintendent of missions, for workers in Western Canada. He attended Manitoba College in Winnipeg, but by the time of graduation he felt called as a missionary* to China. Since in 1887 the Canadian Presbyterians would have no work there for another year, he went with the American Presbyterian Board. Returning home on account of his health, after a brief ministry at St. Andrew's, Kitchener, he was asked by his denomination* to organize missions to the Chinese in Victoria and Vancouver, where he remained until he went to Knox Church, Toronto, in 1901.

Knox Church, the oldest Presbyterian congregation in Toronto, was situated in the heart of the city, but its congregation was moving to the suburbs. Winchester did not change the emphasis of his much-respected predecessor, Henry Martyn Parsons,* for he shared the same convictions. His ministry was characterized by biblical exposition within the framework of orthodox* doctrine, a strong missionary program, premillennial* prophetic teaching and a loyalty to presbyterianism which would cause the congregation to be a bulwark of opposition to the church union* scheme which would produce the United Church of Canada* in 1925. He drew around him a remarkable group of people, including John McNicol,* of the Toronto Bible College, as assistant; Sir Mortimer Clark, Lieutenant-Governor of Ontario, as clerk of session; and a host of able folk who were

engaged in evangelistic,* missionary and philanthropic* ministries. In 1907 the congregation relocated to Spadina Avenue, and there it soon doubled in size.

In 1921, while given the title Minister Extra Muros, he devoted himself to full-time itinerant Bible* teaching. During this period he gave time to the World Christian Fundamentals Association* and in 1923 was one of the founders of Dallas Theological Seminary,* where he frequently taught. More than any individual, he may be responsible for the evangelical continuity of Knox Church.

I. S. Rennie

Winchester, Elhanan (1751-1797). Universalist* minister* and evangelist.* Born in Brookline, Massachusetts, Winchester had little formal schooling, but his inquisitive and restless mind led him to acquire his own learning. A profound conversion* experience in 1769 precipitated Winchester's public profession of faith and admission into a Separate* Congregational* church in his hometown of Brookline, Massachusetts. Later that year he received baptism* by immersion and joined a Baptist* church in Canterbury, Connecticut. A gifted orator, Winchester became one of the best-known itinerant* evangelists of his day. Having begun as an open-communion Baptist of Arminian* inclination, he subsequently embraced closed communion* and the hyper-Calvinism* of the British Baptist theologian* John Gill (1697-1771). Finally, in 1780, moved by his reading of *The Everlasting Covenant* by the German mystic Paul Siegvolck, he adopted a view similar to Origen's (c.185-c.254) notion of "universal restoration" and a universalist theory of the atonement.* Nevertheless, Winchester's preaching never lost its evangelical* sense of urgency and from 1787 to 1794 he extended his ministry across the Atlantic to England. The author of numerous books, including several volumes of hymns,* as well as *Dialogues on Universal Restoration* (1788) and *Ten Letters to Thomas Paine, in Reply to his Age of Reason* (1794), Winchester was perhaps the most celebrated exponent of universalism during the nineteenth century.

BIBLIOGRAPHY. *DAB* X; *DARB;* E. M. Stone, *Biography of Rev. Elhanan Winchester* (1836); S. A. Marini, *Radical Sects of Revolutionary New England* (1982).   G. W. Harper

Winebrenner, John (1797-1860). Church of God* leader and social reformer. Born and raised in Maryland, Winebrenner attended Dickinson

College in Carlisle, Pennsylvania (c. 1816), and studied theology under Dr. Samuel Helffenstein, a prominent German Reformed* pastor and teacher in Philadelphia (1817-1820). Appointed to the Harrisburg Reformed Charge in 1820, his adoption of revivalistic* measures, regarded as "extreme" by some in the parish, led to his eventual separation from the German Reformed Church. With a number of like-minded ministers in south-central Pennsylvania, he organized the Church of God (known today as Churches of God, General Conference) in 1830 and remained a leader in the Church until his death in 1860.

During his lifetime Winebrenner was known as an effective speaker, especially in German. He founded in 1835, and edited for a number of years, the Church of God periodical, *The Gospel Publisher* (later, *The Church Advocate*), one of the oldest church papers in continuous existence in the U.S. In the pulpit and through the columns of *The Gospel Publisher,* he advocated the abolition* of slavery, the peace movement and the cause of temperance.* Biblically oriented and evangelical* in his theology, he was also broadly ecumenical in his relationship with other denominations.

Winebrenner's memory is perpetuated today by the Winebrenner Theological Seminary, a theological school in Findlay, Ohio (est. 1942).

BIBLIOGRAPHY. *DAB* X; C. H. Forney, *A History of the Churches of God in North America* (1914); G. R. Kern, *John Winebrenner: Nineteenth Century Reformer* (1974). R. Kern

Winrod, Gerald Burton (1898-1957). Fundamentalist* preacher,* publisher and anti-Semitist. Born in Wichita, Kansas, Winrod used the city as his base of operations throughout his life. Even though he lacked formal theological training, never pastored a local church, and was not affiliated with any denomination,* he became a leader in the fundamentalist movement. In 1925 Winrod organized the Defenders of the Christian Faith to oppose evolution* and modernism.* In 1926 he began publishing *The Defender Magazine* as the voice of the organization and enlisted many prominent fundamentalists to write for it. In turn he was invited to address the World Christian Fundamentals Association,* as well as speak in fundamentalist churches.

A premillennialist,* Winrod wrote many articles on prophetic themes and was especially interested in the place of the Jews in God's plan. His own views led him to see a Jewish conspiracy behind world events. In 1933 he wrote that the Jewish-controlled movie industry, with its emphasis on

sex, crime and violence, was corrupting the moral life of the nation. Calling this conspiracy the "Hidden Hand," he blamed it for World War 1,* the Bolshevik Revolution and the Great Depression.* It was because of his anti-Semitism that Winrod was accused of being a Nazi. Indeed, he had praised Hitler's crackdown on nightclubs and theaters in Germany, as well as his opposition to Communism. However, Winrod criticized Nazism and denied under oath that he was one.

Winrod's involvement in politics began because of his support for Prohibition.* He opposed the presidential candidacies of both Alfred E. Smith* and Franklin Roosevelt, and after Roosevelt's election continued to oppose his policies. Eventually he came to see the New Deal as part of the Jewish conspiracy. In 1938 he became a candidate for U.S. Senator from Kansas, but he was defeated in the primary.

In 1944 his reputation as an anti-Semite and possible Nazi resulted in his becoming one of thirty defendants who were indicted for sedition before a federal grand jury. After eight months of testimony, a mistrial was declared when the judge died. Winrod continued to maintain his theory of a Jewish conspiracy for the rest of his life, blaming it for the major evils in the world.

BIBLIOGRAPHY. *DARB;* L. P. Ribuffo, *The Old Christian Right* (1983). L. B. Sullivan

Winslow, Edward (1595-1655). Puritan* separatist* and Plymouth Colony leader. Born at Droitwich, Worcestershire, England, and one of the signers of the Mayflower Compact,* Edward Winslow served the Colony of Plymouth in a variety of significant ways. He was the Colony's principal envoy to Massasoit; next to William Bradford its most important chronicler (as reflected in his *Good News from New England . . . ,* published in 1624); a lay* leader of the church, preaching* and performing marriages* in the absence of a minister*; one of the Colony's governors (in 1633, 1636 and 1644) and assistants (nearly every year from 1624 to 1646, when he left Plymouth and returned to England for good); and its most active explorer and trader, establishing posts in Maine, on Cape Ann, on Buzzard's Bay, and on the Connecticut River. In 1629 he became the agent for Plymouth and in 1633 the agent for Massachusetts Bay.

In such capacities he returned often to England, defending the two colonies against the charges of Christopher Gardiner, Ferdinando Gorges and others. He also published several important pamphlets in defense of the New England way,* including *Hypocrisie Unmasked by the True Rela-*

tion of the *Proceedings of the Governour and Company of the Massachusetts against Samuel Gorton.* . . . (1646) and *New England's Salamander Discovered by an Irreligious and Scornfull Pamphlet* (1647), a retort to a tract written by John Child. In 1649 he published *The Glorious Progress of the Gospel among the Indians in New England,* which contributed that year to the founding of the Society for the Propagation of the Gospel in New England.* In 1653 he published his last pamphlet, *A Platform of Church Discipline in New England,* and two years later he died of fever while on a military mission from Oliver Cromwell which seized the island of Jamaica from Spain.

BIBLIOGRAPHY. *DAB* X; L. Stephen, ed., *Dictionary of National Biography,* vol. XXI.

G. F. Moran

Winthrop, John (1588-1649). First governor of Massachusetts Bay. Born to a wealthy family in Suffolk County, England, Winthrop entered Trinity College, Cambridge, in 1602. He left college without a degree and married in 1605. At the age of eighteen Winthrop became a justice of the peace and soon established a legal practice in London. In 1626 he was appointed an attorney in the Court of Wards and Liveries. A deeply religious man, Winthrop grew dissatisfied with life in England and with the persecution of the Puritans,* with whom he had identified since his days at Trinity. In 1629 he decided to venture to the New World and, after being elected governor of the Massachusetts Bay Company, he departed aboard the ship *Arbella* in 1630. During passage Winthrop delivered his lay sermon "A Modell of Christian Charity." In the course of describing the goals of the Puritan mission and the means by which to attain them, he offered the famous description of New England as "a citty upon a hill" for the world to witness and to emulate.

Winthrop served as governor of Massachusetts Bay for the periods 1630-1634, 1637-1640, 1642-1644 and 1646-1649. In 1637 he led the opposition to Anne Hutchinson* during the Antinomian controversy,* and his re-election that year marked a turning point in the resolution of that dispute. Winthrop wrote a valuable account of the entire affair, *A Short Story of the Rise, Reign, and Ruine of the Antinomians* (1644). Though cautious in his views of political democracy* and devoted to order, discipline and authority, he was also a man of warmth, charity and unquestioned integrity. Winthrop, as much as anyone, shaped the settlement into a Bible commonwealth,* and he commanded respect and admiration from ministers*

and ordinary churchgoers alike. Throughout his New World career, Winthrop kept a careful record of events affecting the colony. First appearing in 1825-1826, Winthrop's journal, published as *The History of New England from 1630 to 1649,* remains one of the most authoritative accounts of early Massachusetts.

BIBLIOGRAPHY. *DAB* X; *DARB;* E. S. Morgan, *The Puritan Dilemma: The Story of John Winthrop* (1958); *NCAB* 6; R. G. Raymer, *John Winthrop* (1963); R. C. Winthrop, *Life and Letters of John Winthrop,* 2 vols. (1864-1867).

J. F. Cooper

Wisconsin Evangelical Lutheran Synod. Conservative Lutheran* denomination.* Clergy* commissioned in Europe by the Langenberg Mission Society to minister to scattered German Lutheran and Reformed* immigrants* in America founded the Wisconsin Evangelical Lutheran Synod (WELS) in 1850. Chief among these founders was John Muehlhaeuser (1804-1868), the Synod's first president. Efforts to prepare additional church workers were begun in 1865 at Watertown, Wisconsin, with the opening of Northwestern College. In 1878 the denomination established a theological seminary,* which in 1917 was moved from Milwaukee to suburban Wauwatosa and subsequently relocated in Mequon, Wisconsin. Further progress toward denominational status occurred in 1892 when the Synod joined forces with the synods of Minnesota and Michigan for the purpose of cooperation in education and mission work. The members of this federation were amalgamated into the Joint Synod of Wisconsin and Other States in 1917.

Historically, the Wisconsin Synod has moved from a weak confessionalism* to a more staunchly conservative Lutheran stance. Set in the 1860s by John Bading (1824-1913) and Adolf Hoenecke (1835-1908), both of whom insisted on stricter allegiance to the Lutheran confessions and a less tolerant attitude regarding altar* and pulpit fellowship, this trend was reinforced by closer ties with the Lutheran Church—Missouri Synod* in the Evangelical Lutheran Synodical Conference (1872). It was solidified by controversy during the late 1920s when the Synod resisted its own less dogmatic "Wauwatosa Theology" and expelled John Philipp Koehler (1859-1951) from teaching. Charges of "unionism" directed at the Missouri Synod following World War 2* led in 1963 to withdrawal from the Synodical Conference.

In the late 1980s The Wisconsin Synod numbered 419,806 baptized members in 1,194 North

American congregations, with headquarters in Milwaukee, Wisconsin.

BIBLIOGRAPHY. J. P. Koehler, *The History of the Wisconsin Synod,* ed. L. Jordahl (1925).
J. T. Diefenthaler

Wise, John (1652-1725). Congregational* minister.* Raised in Puritan* Massachusetts and a 1673 graduate of Harvard College,* Wise pastored a Congregational church in Ipswich, Massachusetts, from 1683 until his death in 1725. In 1688 Wise was fined, imprisoned and suspended from his ministerial office for leading a local tax revolt against the Dominion of New England, which he justified on the grounds that a representative assembly had not levied the tax in question. His townsmen bought his release, and Wise soon played a role in reorganizing the colony's government. He opposed the way the 1692 witchcraft episodes at Salem were handled, and in 1710 and 1717 Wise authored two influential treatises attacking the Saybrook Platform,* which would place Congregational churches increasingly under the control of ministerial associations.* These writings, which dealt with fundamental issues of government in church and state, advocated democratic* practices on the grounds of both Scripture* and natural law, and by appealing to the Cambridge Platform of 1648. Wise's treatises, among the first to combine covenant theology* with Enlightenment* ideas, were reprinted in the 1770s and used as effective arguments in the colonial struggle with England.

BIBLIOGRAPHY. *AAP* 1; G. A. Cook, *John Wise: Early American Democrat* (1952); *DAB* X; *DARB.*
A. M. Carden

Wishard, Luther Deloraine (1854-1925). Promoter of student Christian work and foreign missions.* Born in Danville, Indiana, Wishard was raised in an evangelical home. He graduated from Princeton University* (B.A., 1877) and attended Princeton Theological Seminary* (1877-1879). Wishard intended to enter the ministry but instead became the catalyst behind a vast expansion of the YMCA's* collegiate program and the world's first full-time Christian worker among students. He was largely responsible for the launching of an intercollegiate YMCA movement at the parent organization's convention in 1877 and became its first secretary (1877-1888). His aims were to evangelize students and involve them in Christian service.

Long hoping that campuses might become enlistment grounds for foreign missions, he persuaded Dwight L. Moody* to hold a summer students' conference at Northfield, Massachusetts, in 1886, at which one hundred students pledged to go abroad. The impulse became contagious, producing over two thousand volunteers by 1887. Thus was born the Student Volunteer Movement,* with its motive of "the evangelization of the world in this generation." Wishard left American student work in 1888 and became foreign secretary until 1898 of the North American YMCA. A world tour from 1888 to 1892 fostered contacts among nascent student Christian groups and prepared the way for John R. Mott* and other missionary leaders. In 1893 he helped organize the Foreign Missions Conference of North America.* His global vision culminated in 1895 in the World's Student Christian Federation,* the direct descendant of the Student Volunteer Movement. Before retiring, he also founded and directed from 1898 to 1902 the Forward Missionary Movement of the Presbyterian and Congregational Churches.

BIBLIOGRAPHY. *DARB*; C. H. Hopkins, *History of the Y. M. C. A. in North America* (1951); C. K. Ober, *Luther D. Wishard: Projector of World Movements* (1927); R. Rouse, *The World's Student Christian Federation: A History of the First Thirty Years* (1948).
J. H. Dorn

Witch Trial. *See* SALEM WITCH TRIAL.

Witherspoon, John (1723-1794). Presbyterian* minister* and educator. Born in Yester, Scotland, Witherspoon received his university education at the University of Edinburgh (M.A., 1739), where he also studied theology (1739-1743). A parish minister in Beith (1745-1757) and Paisley (1757-1768), Scotland, Witherspoon became known as an opponent of the trend in the Scottish Church known as "Moderatism," which tended to de-emphasize the distinctive theological dogmas* of the Church. In his defense of traditional, Reformed* orthodoxy,* Witherspoon made extensive use of Scottish Common Sense Realism,* a brand of philosophy which had been developed by Thomas Reid at the University of Glasgow. Reid had realized that the fundamental truths of Christianity are consistent with "common sense" and that those truths are clearly based on "self-evident axioms."

In 1768 Witherspoon accepted the invitation of New Side* Presbyterians to serve as president of the College of New Jersey.* With him he brought Scottish Common Sense Realism and from that perspective sought to train his students, specifically opposing the lingering elements of New Light* Edwardseanism in the curriculum. Through Witherspoon's influence the Scottish philosophy entered the mainstream of American thought. After the Revolution* Witherspoon helped reorganize the Presbyterian Church and was instrumental in the establishment of its General Assembly (1789), of which he was the first moderator. Witherspoon's influence was not limited to the ecclesiastical sphere, however. He was a delegate to the Continental Congress (1776-1782), the only clergyman* to sign the Declaration of Independence, and a member of the New Jersey state legislature (1783, 1789).

BIBLIOGRAPHY. *AAP* 3; L. B. Butterfield, *John Witherspoon Comes to America* (1953); V. L. Collins, *President Witherspoon*, 2 vols. (1925); *DAB* X; *DARB; NCAB* 5; R. Fechner, "The Godly and Virtuous Commonwealth of John Witherspoon," in *Ideas in America's Cultures,* ed. H. Cravens (1982); M. L. Stohlman, *John Witherspoon: Parson, Politician, Patriot* (1976); J. Scott, ed., *An Annotated Edition of Lectures on Moral Philosophy of John Witherspoon* (1982).

S. T. Logan

Woman's Bible, The A treatise essentially summarizing the religious ideology of Elizabeth Cady Stanton.* The book is divided into two parts—the Pentateuch (1895) and Joshua to Revelation (1898). Selections from the King James Version of the Bible* are followed by commentaries on the text, focusing on those sections of the Bible that mention women or that Stanton thought should have included them. Her main intent was to correct the prevalent anti-female interpretation of the Holy Scriptures.

The Woman's Bible quickly became a best seller, with seven printings within the first six months and translations into several languages. The appearance of the first part of the book, however, caused a considerable amount of turmoil because of its irreverent approach to the biblical passages relating to women. In 1896 the National American Woman Suffrage Association voted to renounce any connection with the publication of the first volume and censured Stanton because it feared that the adverse publicity associated with the book would detract from the principal goal of the women's rights movement of that era. Contributors to the book included Lillie Devereux Blake, Frances Ellen Burr, Lucinda B. Chandler, Clara Berwick Colby, Ellen Battle Dietrick, Matilda Joslyn Gage, Ursula N. Gestefeld, the Reverend Phebe A. Hanford, Clara B. Neyman and Louisa Southworth. But the inspiration (and over sixty per cent of the commentaries) belonged to Elizabeth Cady Stanton.

BIBLIOGRAPHY. E. Griffith, *In Her Own Right: The Life of Elizabeth Cady Stanton* (1984); *The Woman's Bible, Parts I and II* (1895, 1898).

K. E. Guenther

Woman's Christian Temperance Union. Protestant* temperance* organization begun in 1874. The Woman's Christian Temperance Union (WCTU) was a direct outgrowth of the women's crusade that swept across New York and central Ohio during the winter of 1873-1874. Claiming the power of the Holy Spirit, Protestant women visited saloons and demanded their closure.

Viewing alcoholism as a social problem, the WCTU initially devoted itself to the elimination of alcohol.* Frances Willard,* president from 1879 until her death in 1898, introduced a "do everything" policy which incorporated many reforms and resulted in thirty-nine departments by 1896. To Willard, all reform work related to alcohol and home protection. The WCTU, reflecting the interests of Willard, also promoted equal rights for women. Perhaps most noteworthy was her influence in gaining WCTU support for women's suffrage.* She contended that only the vote would give women power to eliminate alcohol and protect the home. The WCTU was both the largest temperance organization and the largest women's organization in the U.S. before 1900. As WCTU members, conservative Christian women expressed their feminist* concerns and became involved in politics as they lobbied for social change. Women evangelists,* rejected by their denominations,* also worked under the auspices of the WCTU.

After Willard's death in 1898, the WCTU reverted to an emphasis on temperance. During prohibition it stressed law enforcement. Since the repeal of prohibition, the WCTU has shifted its focus primarily to alcohol education. In 1900 the national headquarters of the WCTU moved to Evanston, Illinois. Its periodical is the *Union Signal.*

BIBLIOGRAPHY. R. Bordin, *Woman and Temperance: The Quest for Power and Liberty, 1873-1900* (1980); A. D. Hays, *Heritage of Dedication; One Hundred Years of National Woman's Christian Temperance Union, 1874-1974* (1973).

S. C. Stanley

Women's Suffrage Movement. The rise of American feminism had its roots in the Christian reform movements* of the 1830s and 1840s that were in turn generated by the Second Great Awakening.* Following the Civil War,* as the women's movement increasingly focused on the

[1267]

suffrage issue, the traditional link with Christian thought remained strong. Because of the prevailing national attitude that women should represent the spiritual conscience of the family, many suffrage activists argued that granting women the ballot would elevate American politics to a higher moral plane. As Lucia Ames Mead, a president of the Massachusetts Woman Suffrage Association, promised in 1901, the vote for women would usher in a well-ordered, more responsible government simply by adding to the electorate "all the mothers [and] three quarters of the Church members" in the country. Ultimately, this religious argument represented an important part of the women's suffrage position that eventually won the ideological victory and paved the way for the Nineteenth Amendment (passed by Congress in 1919, ratified by the states in 1920).

Many antisuffragists also drew on theological arguments. Basing their position on Genesis and St. Paul, they claimed that a woman's role was to remain subservient and obedient to men. Though the Catholic Church* took no official position on the issue, it was primarily Catholic churchmen who assumed outspoken antisuffragist positions. Protestant* clergymen, on the other hand, were far more likely to support women's suffrage than any other male group. Thus suffragist leaders often took great pains to foster ministerial support.

The controversy over the *Woman's Bible** represents a case in point. When Part I of Elizabeth Cady Stanton's* book appeared in 1895, its repudiation of certain biblical passages alienated many otherwise-sympathetic ministers. But the leading suffragist organization in the U.S., the National American Woman Suffrage Association (NAWSA), in turn repudiated the *Woman's Bible* in order to maintain its crucial Christian support.

The two female activists who assumed leadership over NAWSA between 1900 and the passage of the Nineteenth Amendment, Carrie Chapman Catt and Anna Howard Shaw,* both believed the Bible* was an infallible guide for all Christians. Shaw, an ordained* minister in the Methodist Protestant Church, stressed the consistency between modern Christian ethics* and women's rights. As the brilliant orator observed, "the end of all right institutions," particularly the Church, "is the development of the human soul." By preventing women from voting, American society was inhibiting spiritual development for many individuals. This proved a powerful argument in the struggle for women's suffrage.

BIBLIOGRAPHY. E. Flexner, *Century of Struggle* (1959); A. S. Kraditor, *The Ideas of the Woman's*

Suffrage Movement, 1890-1920 (1965); W. L. O'Neill, *Everyone Was Brave: A History of Feminism in America* (1969).   J. M. Craig

Wood 'n Ware Controversy. A controversy over human nature and the question of freedom between Unitarian* theologian* Henry Ware* and Trinitarian theologian Leonard Woods.* In 1805 Henry Ware* was elected to the vacated chair of divinity* at Harvard* by the liberal-minded president of the university, John T. Kirkland.* The faculty that was built around Ware's leadership was dedicated to advancing the interests of theological liberalism* within the New England Congregational* tradition then embroiled in the Unitarian controversy.* In 1808 Leonard Woods,* a Harvard graduate himself, joined the faculty of the newly established institution intended to counter the rising liberalism at Harvard, Andover Theological Seminary.*

In his *Letters to Unitarians* (1820), Woods challenged the optimistic view of human nature that had been affirmed by the emerging Unitarian leader William Ellery Channing* in his famous Baltimore ordination* sermon of 1819. The Calvinist* orthodoxy that Woods was championing mediated between the so-called consistent Calvinism of Samuel Hopkins,* reflecting the pro-revival position of Jonathan Edwards,* and the "old Calvinists." Essentially, Woods sought to defend the Calvinist view that humanity is sinful* by nature against the accusations that Calvinism maintained either that God created evil or that Adam by a spontaneous and uncaused ability overcame a previously righteous nature. Ware responded to Woods' challenge in a literary debate that lasted for four years and produced five major volumes—two by Woods and three by Ware. Ware defended the essential goodness of humanity and charged that the Andover theology was "immoral." Woods, on the other hand, produced biblical and philosophical arguments in defense of a moderate Calvinist affirmation of human depravity. Though the controversy left no clear winner, it was perhaps the most significant discussion of the doctrine of humanity in American theological history.

See also SIN; UNITARIAN CONTROVERSY.

BIBLIOGRAPHY. B. Kuklick, ed., *The Unitarian Controversy, 1819-1823,* 2 vols. (1987); H. S. Smith, *Changing Conceptions of Original Sin* (1955).   J. S. O'Malley

Woodbridge, Charles Jahleel (1902-). Bible* teacher and church historian. Born in Chinkaing, China, the son of missionary parents, Woodbridge attended Princeton University* (B.A., 1923; M.A.), Princeton Theological Seminary* (Th.B., 1927), the Universities of Berlin and Marburg (1927-1928), the Sorbonne (1932) and Duke University (Ph.D., 1945). Ordained* as a Presbyterian* minister* (1927), he served as a pastor in Flushing, New York (1928-1932). On March 4, 1930, he married Ruth Dunning. The couple went to the French Cameroons, West Africa, as missionaries (1932-1934). Between 1934 and 1937, Woodbridge worked as secretary for the Independent Board for Presbyterian Foreign Missions associated with his seminary mentor, J. Gresham Machen.* When Machen was tried by the New Brunswick Presbytery, Woodbridge acted as one of his trial lawyers. Machen was suspended from the Presbyterian Church, as was Woodbridge eventually.

After pastorates in Salisbury, North Carolina (1937-1945), and Savannah, Georgia (1945-1950), Woodridge taught church history at the newly founded Fuller Theological Seminary* and began a summertime Bible-teaching ministry, particularly with Word of Life, Schroon Lake, New York. In 1958 he left Fuller because of what he perceived to be apostasy among the faculty and concentrated on his popular Bible-teaching ministry. He strongly criticized the emergence of the "New Evangelicalism"* and staunchly defended the principle of separation* from those involved in cooperative evangelism. Fundamentalists* often looked to his book, *The New Evangelicalism* (1969), and his tapes for a justification of their movement's emphasis upon doctrinal purity, separation and biblical inerrancy.*

BIBLIOGRAPHY. G. M. Marsden, *Reforming Fundamentalism* (1987). J. D. Woodbridge

Woodrow, James (1828-1907). Presbyterian* theologian* and scientist. Born in Carlisle, England, the son of a Presbyterian minister* who immigrated to Canada and then Ohio, Woodrow graduated from Jefferson College, Pennsylvania (B.A., 1849), and then taught school in Alabama. He later pursued graduate studies in science at Harvard (1853) and became professor of natural science at Oglethorpe University in Georgia (1853-1861). During this time he pursued further graduate studies at Heidelberg, earning the Ph.D. in 1856. He was ordained* a minister in the Presbyterian Church in 1860.

In 1861 Wilson was made professor of "Natural Science in Connexion with Revelation" at the Presbyterian seminary in Columbia, South Carolina, in order "to evince the harmony of science with the records of our faith, and to refute the objec-

tions of infidel scientists." When the Civil War* came, Woodrow served as a chemist for the Confederate army. During many of his years at the seminary, he served simultaneously as professor of science (1869-1872, 1880-1897) at South Carolina College, and later as president (1891-1897) of that institution. Woodrow was editor of the *Southern Presbyterian Review* (1861-1885), the publisher of the weekly *Southern Presbyterian* (1865-1893) and the denomination's treasurer of foreign missions (1861-1872).

Woodrow held that God's Word and the world both reveal divine truth and that there is no contradiction between them when they are each rightly interpreted. He accepted the inerrancy* of the Bible* but believed that it gave no technical explanation of the origin of Adam's body. After some years of opposition to the evolutionary* hypothesis, Woodrow came to hold that theistic evolution—what he called "mediate creation"—was probably true. An address published in 1884 publicized his views and brought about a storm of protest within the Southern Presbyterian denomination. The seminary board dismissed him when the 1886 General Assembly pronounced that "Adam's body was directly fashioned by Almighty God, without any natural animal parentage." Although he differed with the traditional interpretations of the Bible and the Westminster Confession of Faith,* he was never convicted of heresy* and remained a minister in good standing. Woodrow was the uncle of President Woodrow Wilson.*

BIBLIOGRAPHY. *DAB* X; C. Eaton, "Professor James Woodrow and the Freedom of Teaching in the South," *JSH* 28 (1962):3-17; T. W. Street, "The Evolutionary Controversy in the Southern Presbyterian Church," *JPHS* 37 (1959):232-250; M. W. Woodrow, ed., *Dr. James Woodrow as Seen by His Friends* (1909). A. H. Freundt

Woods, Charles Stacey (1909-1983). Student ministry* leader. Born in Australia and brought up in a Christian home of Plymouth Brethren* background, Woods committed himself to Christ at an early age. Coming to America in 1930, he earned degrees at Wheaton College* and Dallas Theological Seminary.* In 1934, at the age of twenty-five, he took over the leadership of the five-year-old Inter-Varsity Christian Fellowship* of Canada (resigning in 1952). In the fall of 1940 he became the first general secretary of the nascent American movement (resigning in 1960). With a vision for things beyond the success of both of these ministries, Woods went on to become the first general secretary of the International Fellowship of Evangelical Students in 1947. This work led him to move to Switzerland in 1962, where he remained even after his retirement in 1973. Woods also helped to organize the first InterVarsity student missionary convention, held in Toronto during the Christmas vacation of 1946-1947 and later triennially in Urbana,* Illinois, and helped to compile the influential songbook *Hymns* (1950).

BIBLIOGRAPHY. C. S. Woods, *Some Ways of God* (1975); *The Growth of a Work of God* (1978).

J. G. Stackhouse

Woods, Leonard (1774-1854). Congregationalist* minister* and theologian.* Born in Princeton, Massachusetts, Woods graduated from Harvard College* in 1796 and prepared for the Congregational ministry under the tutelage of Charles Backus, a prominent New Divinity* theologian, and Nathaniel Emmons,* the most uncompromising of the Edwardsean* theologians.

Ordained* in the Congregational church of Newbury, Massachusetts, in 1798, Woods went on to distinguish himself by his contributions to the defense of orthodox* Calvinism.* In 1808, when the New Divinity and Old Calvinist factions in Congregationalism agreed to organize a common seminary at Andover, Massachusetts, Woods was selected as the professor of theology, a position he held for thirty-eight years. Although his teaching was neither innovative nor brilliant, his position at Andover Theological Seminary* thrust him into conflict, first with the Unitarians and then with Nathaniel W. Taylor* of Yale.*

In 1820, he replied to William E. Channing's* sermon "Unitarian* Christianity" (1819) with twelve *Letters to Unitarians* which patiently justified Calvinist doctrine on the Trinity, depravity and predestination.* His reply to Channing provoked an attack from Henry Ware,* the Unitarian professor of divinity* at Harvard, initiating the famous "Wood 'n' Ware Controversy"* which lasted until 1824. In 1830 he skillfully chided Taylor, in *Letters to Rev. Nathaniel W. Taylor,* for disingenuously compromising Calvinism in his Convention address, "Concio ad Clerum" (1828). His finest work, *An Essay on Native Depravity* (1835), was specifically pointed against Taylor and the New Haven Theology.*

Woods played important roles in a number of voluntary* religious societies, especially the American Board of Commissioners for Foreign Missions.* His *Works* were collected in five volumes (1850-1851), and his *History of the Andover Seminary* was published posthumously in 1885.

BIBLIOGRAPHY. *AAP* 2; *DAB* X; *DARB;* F. H. Foster, *A Genetic History of the New England Theology* (1907); W. Walker, *Ten New England Leaders* (1901). A. C. Guelzo

Woodward, Samuel Bayard (1787-1850). Asylum superintendent and cofounder of the Association of Medical Superintendents of American Institutions for the Insane (now the American Psychiatric Association). Born at Torrington, Connecticut, Woodward studied medicine with his father. As a general physician, Woodward became involved in the effort to establish an asylum for the humane treatment of the mentally ill in Connecticut. He was instrumental in the founding of the Hartford Retreat (now the Institute of Living) in 1824, and he was appointed superintendent of the Worcester State Hospital in Massachusetts in 1832. Through his annual reports Woodward became a nationally respected authority on the nature and treatment of mental disorders.

Like other physicians of the time, Woodward believed that mental disorders were best treated with medicinal remedies and appropriate psychological interventions. A devout Congregationalist,* he considered proper religious views to be important for mental well-being. He wrote that "the Bible* itself would rarely make a man insane," but he condemned the "new-fangled doctrines" of contemporary religious enthusiasts, such as the Millerites* and the Mormons,* which he believed led to mental instability. Woodward retired from his job at the Worcester asylum in 1846 in poor health and died four years later.

BIBLIOGRAPHY. *DAB* X; H. A. Kelly and W. L. Burrage, eds., *Dictionary of American Medical Biography: Lives of Eminent Physicians of the United States and Canada* (1928, 1978); G. N. Grob, *The State and the Mentally Ill: A History of Worcester State Hospital in Massachusetts, 1830-1920* (1966). S. B. Thielman

Woodworth-Etter, Maria Beulah (1844-1924). Holiness*-Pentecostal* evangelist.* Born near Lisbon, Ohio, Maria was converted and baptized at the age of thirteen and soon felt called to the ministry. Her marriage to P. H. Woodworth and the raising of children postponed that ministry until around 1880 when she first began holding revivals. Preaching and evangelizing first under the auspices of the United Brethren and after 1884 with the Churches of God* (Winebrenner), her ministry after 1912—when she held a major campaign at F.F. Bosworth's* church in Dallas—was primarily with Pentecostal* groups. An ecumenist* at heart, she also believed her meetings should be interracial, even in the South.

People who attended her protracted meetings often "fell in the Spirit," an experience similar to what was seen in the early frontier revivals.* She called it "receiving the power," while her critics called it a trance. In 1885 at a campaign held in Hartford City, Indiana, she began praying for the sick and had apparent success in healing a wide variety of illness. Prophecies and visions also became a regular feature of her meetings. Newspapers often gave generous coverage to her meetings, but their stories were often critical of faith healing* and the trances. By 1889 she owned a tent that would seat 8,000. But as her campaigns took her to South Florida, South Carolina, Indiana, Iowa and Missouri, she frequently found it too small to hold the crowds of followers, critics and curious. One reporter estimated a crowd in Indiana to be twenty thousand strong.

Although she always emphasized evangelism in her meetings and writings, she is best remembered for her charismatic ministries, which included teachings on post-conversion spiritual experience and faith healing. Besides her itinerant ministry, she was also responsible for planting several churches (including what is today the Lakeview Christian Center in Indianapolis) and writing about a dozen books, including *Signs and Wonders God Wrought in the Ministry for Forty Years* (1916) and *Marvels and Miracles; Signs and Wonders* (1922).

Woodworth-Etter became one of the best-known Pentecostal evangelists at the turn of the century and certainly the best-known woman preacher. Her public ministry opened doors for other women, such as Aimee Semple McPherson* and Kathryn Kuhlman.*

BIBLIOGRAPHY. W. E. Warner, *The Woman Evangelist* (1986). W. E. Warner

Woolman, John (1720-1772). Quaker* minister.* Born in Rancocas, New Jersey, Woolman supported himself for a time as a shopkeeper, but perceiving spiritual danger in his success, he apprenticed himself to a tailor and supplemented his income by surveying, drawing wills, keeping orchards and teaching school. A paragon of Quaker quietism, he sought to "divest himself of all self-interest" and obey only the "pure leadings" of God. His *Journal* recounts a pivotal experience in which he was convinced "that true religion consisted in an inward life, wherein the heart doth love and reverence God the Creator and learn to exercise justice and goodness." In 1748 he was

recorded as a minister of the Society of Friends.*

Woolman's life was characterized by an inward and outward motion: searching his heart in silent worship* in order to lay aside his own will and discover God's, and laboring on behalf of the poor and oppressed. From this arose his concerns to live a simple life exemplifying "the right use of things" and to end war, slavery and injustice toward the poor and toward Native Americans—all eloquently expressed in essays such as *Considerations on the Keeping of Negroes,* 2 parts (1754-1762); *A Plea for the Poor* (1793); and *Considerations on the True Harmony of Mankind* (1770).

Woolman's wholehearted devotion to ending slavery was in part a response to the crisis of the French and Indian War of 1755, which he saw as divine judgment on the corruption brought on by wealth and power. The latter had forced Pennsylvania Friends to choose between faithfulness to their traditional peace testimony and their control of the colonial legislature. Part of a movement to reform the Friends, Woolman favored resignation from the assembly. Woolman, like the biblical prophets, used symbolic actions to dramatize the unrighteous condition of society: traveling great distances on foot to visit slave owners to discuss slave keeping with them, paying slaves for services rendered when a guest in a slave owner's household, wearing undyed clothing, refusing to pay war taxes and riding in steerage while journeying to England. Throughout, he was concerned for the oppressor as well as the oppressed and gently urged a conversion of heart in his listeners. His remarkable journey to the Delawares of Wyalusing was made to promote peace and to "feel and understand their life and the spirit they live in, if haply I might receive some instruction from them."

BIBLIOGRAPHY. E. H. Cady, *John Woolman* (1966); *DAB* X; *DARB*; P. Moulton *The Journal and Major Essays of John Woolman* (1971); *NCAB* 1; J. Whitney, *John Woolman: American Quaker* (1942). M. L. Birkel

Worcester, Elwood (1862-1940). Episcopal* clergyman.* Born in Massillton, Ohio, Worcester grew up in Rochester, New York, the son of a wealthy businessman. Worcester experienced a dramatic call to the ministry at age sixteen and subsequently attended Columbia College, General Theological Seminary, and eventually the University of Leipzig where he was influenced by two great pioneers of modern experimental psychology, Wilhelm Wundt and Gustav Theodor Fechner.

In 1904 Worcester was called to Emmanuel

Church in Boston, where he subsequently combined forces with several prominent physicians to evaluate and treat emotionally troubled individuals, using a combination of medical assessment and a liberal Protestant* interpretation of contemporary psychological thought. Worcester viewed this effort, which came to be known as the Emmanuel Movement, as a re-creation in the modern era of the healings of Jesus in the New Testament. The Emmanuel Movement eventually was attacked by men who were involved early in the movement, such as physicians James J. Putnam and Richard C. Cabot, but the effort continued for many years. In 1929 Worcester left Emmanuel Church to devote more time to his psychotherapeutic endeavors. He continued to see troubled people in therapy until the time of his death in 1940.

BIBLIOGRAPHY. *DAB* 2; A. Stokes, *Ministry After Freud* (1985); E. Worcester, S. McComb and I. H. Coriat, *Religion and Medicine: The Moral Control of Nervous Disorders* (1908).   S. B. Thielman

Worcester, Noah (1758-1837). Liberal Congregationalist* pastor* and pacifist.* Born in Hollis, New Hampshire, Worcester received little schooling as a child and was a fifer in the Revolutionary War.* After marrying and settling in Thornton, New Hampshire, Worcester served the town in many capacities and gradually took an interest in the ministry.* Ordained* to the Congregationalist ministry* in 1787, Worcester was pastor in Thornton, New Hampshire, for twenty-two years (1787-1810) and the first missionary* employed by the New Hampshire Missionary Society when it formed. In 1810 Worcester moved to Salisbury, New Hampshire, to assist his ailing brother who was pastor there. That year he also published *Bible News of the Father, Son and Holy Spirit,* which brought criticism from clergy colleagues for its Unitarian* sympathies. In 1813 he moved to Brighton, Massachusetts, to become first editor of the liberal monthly, the *Christian Disciple* (later the *Christian Examiner*), which was supported by William Ellery Channing* and other leading Unitarians. He soon became a convinced pacifist. After he published *A Solemn Review of the Custom of War* in 1814, he helped found the Massachusetts Peace Society and served as its secretary from 1815 until 1828. Harvard* and Dartmouth* granted him honorary degrees.

BIBLIOGRAPHY. *DAB* X; H. Ware, Jr., *Memoirs of the Rev. Noah Worcester, D.D.* (1844).

C. H. Lippy

Worcester, Samuel Austin (1798-1859). Mis-

sionary* among the Cherokee Indians. Born in Worcester, Massachusetts, he was educated at the University of Vermont and Andover Theological Seminary.* After his ordination* in August 1825, he was sent by the American Board of Commissioners for Foreign Missions* to work at Brainerd Mission. In 1827 he moved to the Cherokee capital at New Echota, Georgia, where he worked with Elias Boudinot* in publishing a variety of religious literature in the Cherokee language.

When Georgia, seeking expanded control over Native American affairs within its borders, ordered all whites residing among the Native Americans to swear allegiance to the state, Worcester and Elizur Butler* refused to comply. They were arrested, convicted and in September 1831, were sentenced to four years in prison. Their case was appealed to the U.S. Supreme Court (*Worcester* vs. *Georgia,* 1832), where the state law was held invalid. They were released from prison in January 1833. In April 1835, Worcester went west with some of the Cherokee who were being forced out of Georgia, settling first at the Dwight Mission in Arkansas, and then at the Park Hill Mission in the Indian Territory, where he resided until his death.

BIBLIOGRAPHY. *AAP* 2; A. Bass, *Cherokee Messenger* (1936); *DAB* X; W. G. McLoughlin, "Civil Disobedience and Evangelism Among the Missionaries to the Cherokees, 1829-1839," *JPH* 51 (1973):116-139.   M. S. Joy

Word Movement. *See* FAITH MOVEMENT.

Work Ethic. *See* PROTESTANT WORK ETHIC.

World Alliance for Promoting International Friendship (1914-1948). An organization that developed from a peace conference held in Germany in 1914. The meeting, supported by funds supplied by the Church Peace Union, was quickly adjourned because of the outbreak of World War 1,* but it did succeed in establishing a peace society which met in London and established an international committee to administer its activities.

In addition to encouraging peacemaking, the alliance was one of the precursors of the World Council of Churches.* At its meeting in Holland in 1919, it called for a worldwide council of representatives of the churches to deal with the social and religious problems caused by the war. Ironically, the ecumenical movement* which resulted from such appeals led to the founding of rival groups which represented the churches in a more direct way, causing the dissolution of the alliance in 1948.

BIBLIOGRAPHY. D. P. Gaines, *The World Council of Churches, A Study of Its Background and History* (1966). R. G. Clouse

World Alliance of Reformed Churches. International organization of Presbyterian,* Reformed* and Congregationalist* denominations.* The World Alliance of Reformed Churches was formed in 1970 at Nairobi, Kenya, from a union of two organizations: the World Alliance of Reformed Churches throughout the World Holding the Presbyterian System, and the International Congregational Council. The roots of the denominations comprising the Alliance are in the Protestant Reformation, especially the theology* of John Calvin and Ulrich Zwingli. Member denominations affirm the supreme authority* of the Bible* in matters of faith and morals and hold to classic Reformed creeds.* The parent World Alliance was established in 1875 to further cooperation among Presbyterian and Reformed communions and to promote their common interests and joint endeavors, making its successor the oldest international Protestant confessional body. Today about 160 denominations with congregations in more than eighty countries and approximately 70 million members belong to the Alliance.

A general council, which first met in 1877, and ordinarily meets every five years, makes and administers the policies and programs of the Alliance. Between assemblies an executive committee, which meets annually, directs the work of the Alliance. The headquarters of the Alliance is in Geneva, Switzerland. The Alliance has promoted better understanding among Reformed denominations, held many theological discussions and conducted relief work. Since the mid 1960s Alliance leaders have held conversations with both Roman Catholic* and Lutheran* representatives. In recent years area organizations, including a Caribbean and North American branch, have been formed within the Alliance to provide fellowship, encourage cooperation and foster study. The Alliance publishes a journal, *The Reformed World,* to promote its activities and views.

BIBLIOGRAPHY. M. Pradervand, *A Century of Service: A History of the World Alliance of Reformed Churches, 1875-1975* (1975).

G. S. Smith

World Congress on Evangelism. International evangelical* congress held in Berlin in 1966. Convened to focus attention on the resurgence of evangelical Christianity on the occasion of the tenth anniversary of *Christianity Today,** the Congress was chaired by Carl F. H. Henry* and Billy Graham.* At the beginning a crusade in Berlin, Germany, the Congress brought together 12,000 delegates from one hundred nations, the vast majority of them from outside North America. Anglicans* and Pentecostals* (including evangelist Oral Roberts*) at the ecclesiastical extremes, joined with a broad spectrum of denominational representatives and Roman Catholic,* Jewish and ecumenical* observers as the Congress was addressed by prominent religious figures like Ethiopian Emperor Haile Selassie and John R. W. Stott.

An obvious effort to build on the historic Edinburgh Conference of 1910 that reflected on a century of Protestant missions, the Berlin Congress dramatized the advances made by theologically conservative Protestants in offering leadership in world evangelization. The Congress made an impressive show of unity, convening delegates from Third World churches (many of them from the recently independent African states), Christians from the Communist-bloc countries and theological conservatives from the European and American mainline* denominations. Its evangelical stance was clearly stated in its theme "One Race, One Gospel, One Task." For two weeks the delegates were exposed to reports of evangelistic progress, position papers on strategic theological concerns and plenary sessions that addressed strategies of evangelism. The premillennial* theology of the sponsors was evident in the sense of urgency to complete the task of world evangelization. Billy Graham referred to the "population explosion" that would double the world population during his expected lifetime, and a population "clock" registered the net population increase of more than a million human beings during the duration of the Congress. Though the Congress met with some criticism from within evangelicalism, most evangelical leaders regarded it as one of the most significant evangelical gatherings in the two decades since World War 2.

BIBLIOGRAPHY. B. Graham, "Why the Berlin Congress?" *CT* 11 (1966):131-135; "The Berlin Congress and Missions," *UEA* 25 (1967):11-14; C. F. H. Henry, *Confessions of a Theologian* (1986). E. A. Wilson

World Council of Churches. An ecumenical* organization of Protestant,* Anglican* and Orthodox* bodies on every continent. The vision of a world Christian body that would link the churches together in unity, mission and service was proposed by numerous persons in the nineteenth and twentieth centuries. The formal steps toward a

World Council of Churches, however, took place between 1933 and 1938, with significant meetings in York, England; Princeton, New Jersey; London and Oxford, England; Edinburgh, Scotland; and Utrecht and Amsterdam, Holland. Key Protestant and Anglican leaders in the conception and formation of the World Council of Churches (WCC) were Samuel McCrea Cavert, William Adams Brown* and John R. Mott* in the U.S.A.; William Temple and J. H. Oldham of Great Britain; Marc Boegner of France; and W. A. Visser 't Hooft of Holland. The Orthodox Church was strongly represented by Archbishop Germanos Strenopoulos (Exarch in the West of the Ecumenical Patriarchate) and Stefan Zankov (Bulgaria).

The WCC was to have been formed in 1939, with its first assembly taking place in 1941, but World War 2* delayed these plans. But the WCC "in process of formation," served by a small staff in Geneva, Switzerland, began to care for refugees and the needy and to maintain spiritual communication among the churches. What seemed a delay brought a deeper yearning for unity and common mission.

The nature of the WCC can best be understood in the language of its doctrinal basis, officially approved at the First Assembly at Amsterdam (1948): "The World Council of Churches is a fellowship of churches which accept our Lord Jesus Christ as God and Saviour." At the New Delhi Assembly in 1961, largely at the urging of the Orthodox, it was expanded to its present Trinitarian form: "The World Council of Churches is a fellowship of churches which confess the Lord Jesus Christ as God and Saviour according to the scriptures and therefore seek to fulfill their common calling to the glory of the one God, Father, Son and Holy Spirit."

In its genesis the WCC was the confluence of two expressions of the modern ecumenical movement*—the Universal Christian Council for Life and Work, and the Faith and Order movement. In 1961 the International Missionary Council* brought its missionary* emphasis to the WCC. But eventually new functions and purposes were identified: (1) to call the churches to visible unity in faith and worship*; (2) to facilitate the common witness of the churches; (3) to support the churches in their worldwide missionary and evangelistic task; (4) to express the common concern of the churches for human need, the breaking down of barriers between people and the promotion of justice and peace; (5) to foster the renewal of the churches in unity, worship, mission and service.

These purposes have been the focus of various program subunits. The Faith and Order Commission reflects on the theological issues which continue to divide churches and strives to bring about visible unity. Some of the fruition of this work is brought to realization in the historic convergence text *Baptism, Eucharist, and Ministry* agreed on by the Commission at Lima, Peru, in 1982.

The Commission on World Mission and Evangelism helps the churches proclaim, by word and deed, the whole gospel of Jesus Christ to the whole world—including the struggle for justice and peace. The Commission on Church and Society focuses on the relevance of Christian faith in today's world, especially as it relates to contemporary developments in science and technology.

The Commission on Interchurch Aid, Refugee and World Service helps the churches reach out to others in distress through relief and development. The Commission on the Churches' Participation in Development (CCPD) works for economic justice by expressing solidarity with the struggles of the poor and oppressed for justice and self-reliance.

The Commission of the Churches on International Affairs (CCIA) helps the churches witness in international crises by building understanding with people in other countries and cultures. The Program to Combat Racism sends information about and advocates the incompatibility of racism with the gospel, and draws attention to those governments and transnational corporations which give economic support to racism.

The Ecumenical Institute at Bossey equips persons from many countries, confessions and cultures for ecumenical leadership. Other WCC subunits deal with theological education, the role of women in church and society, and the renewal of congregational life.

Important to the WCC's witness are its assemblies and their themes which testify to the Christological character of ecumenism.* These assemblies and their themes have been: Amsterdam (1948), "Man's Disorder and God's Design"; Evanston* (1954), "Jesus Christ the Hope of the World"; New Delhi (1961), "Jesus Christ the Light of the World"; Uppsala (1968), "Behold, I Make All Things New"; Nairobi (1975), "Jesus Christ Frees and Unites"; and Vancouver* (1983), "Jesus Christ the Life of the World."

The WCC is composed of over three hundred Protestant, Anglican and Orthodox churches from one hundred countries on all six continents. While not a full member, the Roman Catholic Church* does officially participate in the Commission on

Faith and Order and works collaboratively in justice and peace programs. Once an organization dominated by Christians from Europe and North America, the WCC now involves Christians from Africa, Asia, Latin America, the Pacific and the Middle East.

See also INTERNATIONAL COUNCIL OF CHRISTIAN CHURCHES; WORLD EVANGELICAL FELLOWSHIP.

BIBLIOGRAPHY. H. E. Fey, ed., *The Ecumenical Advance: A History of the Ecumenical Movement,* vol. 2: 1948-1968 (1970); R. Rouse and S. Neill, eds., *A History of the Ecumenical Movement,* vol. 1: 1517-1948 (1967); A. J. van der Bent, *Major Studies and Themes in the Ecumenical Movement* (1981); L. Vischer, ed., *A Documentary History of the Faith and Order Movement, 1927-1963* (1963). P. A. Crow

World Evangelical Fellowship. An international alliance of evangelical* bodies serving as a resource and catalyst to help local churches fulfill their scriptural mandate. The historical roots of the World Evangelical Fellowship (WEF) ultimately go back to 1846 and the founding of the World Evangelical Alliance in Britain. The Alliance encouraged unity among evangelical churches, promoted a worldwide week of prayer,* developed missionary* outreach programs and defended persecuted Protestant* minorities. After World War 2* the Alliance sought a closer cooperation among evangelicals around the world. In 1951, led by Harold J. Ockenga* and J. Elwin Wright, an International Convention of Evangelicals was held in the Netherlands with ninety-one delegates from twenty-one countries in attendance. A doctrinal statement was adopted and the World Evangelical Fellowship was officially constituted.

The ruling body of WEF is the general assembly, which meets every six years. The general assembly elects the members of the executive council, the officers who conduct the Fellowship's affairs between assemblies. They, in turn, initiate commissions, appoint the general director and commission executive secretaries. WEF provides both the structure and forum for evangelicals worldwide to join together, defend the faith and cooperate in advancing the gospel. Its activities are directed through commissions on theology,* missions, women's concerns and church renewal.* Its membership now includes fifty-seven autonomous national and regional evangelical bodies, all formed on the initiative of local churches. Currently, David Howard is international director of WEF, based in Singapore since 1987.

BIBLIOGRAPHY. D. M. Howard, *The Dream That Would Not Die* (1986). R. C. Cizik

World Gospel Mission. Holiness* missionary* society. Founded in 1910 by the National Association for the Promotion of Holiness (*See* Christian Holiness Association), the Missionary Bureau of the National Association for the Promotion of Holiness was later changed to National Holiness Missionary Society and since the early 1950s has been known as the World Gospel Mission (WGM). The mission is Wesleyan*-Arminian* in its doctrinal orientation and was created to establish, maintain and conduct interdenominational missions and missionary work in home and foreign fields and to spread scriptural holiness, largely through a properly qualified national ministry.

The WGM's first field of service was Shantung Province in northern China. Today the WGM has a home staff of 62, with 193 missionaries working in Barbados, Burundi, India, Mexico, Argentina, Bolivia, Haiti, Japan, Tanzania, Bangladesh, Brazil, Honduras and Kenya. The major focus of their ministry is evangelism* and Bible* training. WGM operates six Bible-training schools, serving about 200 students; elementary and high schools enrolling about 14,000; two hospitals (in Kenya and Burundi), industrial and agricultural assistance programs; and literature work, such as the Grace Memorial Press in Burundi. The WGM publishes *Call to Prayer for Mission* and is affiliated with the Evangelical Foreign Mission Association.* The home office is located in Marion, Indiana.

BIBLIOGRAPHY. W. W. Cary, *Story of the National Holiness Missionary Society* (1940); L. Trachsel, *Kindled Fires in Africa* (1960); L. Trachsel, *Kindled Fires in Asia* (1961); L. Trachsel, *Kindled Fires in Latin America* (1960). E. Rommen

World Home Bible League. International and interdenominational Bible*-distribution agency. The American Home Bible League was founded in 1938 by William and Betty Chapman for the purpose of placing a Bible in every Bibleless home, that people might be won to Christ. In 1950, as the scope of its evangelistic efforts advanced beyond the borders of the U.S. and into Mexico, Japan and India, the agency changed its name to the World Home Bible League. The League has experienced remarkable growth, distributing Bibles and Bible-study* materials through the ministries of local churches, and placing Scripture in ninety-five countries in over two hundred languages. Working closely with Wycliffe Bible Translators,* the League prints each newly completed Scripture translation and sends copies to the area of need. In the first fifty years of its ministry, the World Home Bible League distributed a total of well over 250 million Bibles, New Testaments and Scripture portions. During 1987 the agency's budget had grown to approximately $9.7 million. Committed to limiting "grievous waste" in Scripture distribution, the League emphasizes strategic placement over mass distribution. Through its programs the League seeks to distribute Scripture through local churches. Its headquarters are located in South Holland, Illinois.

BIBLIOGRAPHY. W. A. Chapman, *The Story without an End* (1970).   B. E. Brown

World Literature Crusade. Evangelical* interdenominational agency dedicated to placing gospel literature in every home in the world. Founded in Canada in 1946, the World Literature Crusade (WLC) opened a U.S. office in 1952. Literature, including tracts* written by national Christians in their own languages, is made available to individual Christians, denominations* and missionaries* who organize and implement their systematic distribution. This is generally done within the framework of the Every Home Crusade (EHC). An EHC national director and a committee of experienced evangelical leaders supervises the printing and distribution of EHC materials in each country. In the case of countries with high illiteracy rates, literature is supplemented with gospel recordings and pictorial tracts. In addition to its focus on homes, WLC also targets high schools, universities, hospitals, prisons, maritime personnel and the blind, for whom braille messages are provided. WLC also produces and administers correspondence courses. Today WLC is active in forty-three countries and has distributed limited amounts of literature in over 200 countries.

The work is supported by many Christians who are engaged in a twenty-four-hour-a-day prayer chain. Information is disseminated by means of a weekly news program broadcast in Canada and the U.S., monthly publications and a semi-annual book, *One Evening World Missionary Tour,* which is designed to keep friends and supporters up to date on major overseas developments. The WLC home office is located in Chatsworth, California.

BIBLIOGRAPHY. A. J. Lee, *Dawn of a New Era* (1962); J. McAlister, *Africa at 6 A.M.* (1963); J. McAlister, *Alaska—Assignment Accomplished* (1960); J. McAlister, *Evangelising Europe—Heart of the World* (1961).   E. Rommen

World Vision. An international and nondenomi-

national Christian humanitarian aid organization. World Vision was founded in 1950 by American evangelist* Bob Pierce,* who pioneered in the use of film to raise relief funds among American churches during the Korean War. After the war, World Vision began raising support for war orphans through a program of child sponsorship. World Vision also hosted pastors' conferences in Korea and other countries around the world.

In the 1950s World Vision expanded its work to various countries of Asia. In the 1960s it began working in Latin America and in the 1970s in Africa. World Vision's work in sponsorship and pastors' conferences grew to include emergency relief and community development, but with a continuing focus on children. A research department (MARC) headed by Edward R. Dayton emphasized world evangelization. During the 1970s World Vision experienced rapid growth from the use of television for fund-raising in the U.S. and Canada. In 1978, under the leadership of W. Stanley Mooneyham and Ted W. Engstrom, World Vision reorganized as an international partnership composed of field and fund-raising offices, with one central coordinating office.

By the late 1980s World Vision was assisting more than half a million children and families in 4,500 projects, with 4,000 staff employed in sixty national offices. In 1987 Robert Seiple assumed leadership of the U.S. office and Don Scott of the Canadian office. Tom Houston was appointed international president in 1984. World Vision's oldest and largest fund-raising office and international headquarters are located in Monrovia, California. The Canadian office is one of fifteen offices on six continents raising funds for World Vision's ministry.

BIBLIOGRAPHY. R. Gehman, *Let My Heart Be Broken* (1960); W. F. Graham and J. Lockerbie, *Bob Pierce, This One Thing I Do* (1983); N. B. Rohrer, *Open Arms* (1987).   N. D. Showalter

World War 1 (1914-1918). The name commonly given to history's most tragic and fateful conflagration, originally called the Great War, and a major watershed in the development of modern civilization. In the generation before 1914, Europeans and Americans, including many theologians, believed themselves heading for a new era of peace and progress in which the benefits of modern science and invention would be more widely diffused and even competitive struggle somehow worked out for the benefit of humanity. Most important, the Western intelligentsia were convinced that humans had matured to the point that they could settle international disputes without resorting to violence. This world view came into serious question when in 1914 the nations of Europe, through arrogance and miscalculation, blundered into a disaster the magnitude of which had hitherto been unknown in human history.

The conflict began in Europe on July 28, 1914, with a declaration of war by the Austro-Hungarian Empire (Austria) against Serbia. This followed the assassination on June 28 in Sarajevo, Bosnia, of the heir apparent to the Austro-Hungarian throne, the Archduke Franz Ferdinand, and his wife, by a Bosnian terrorist acting at the behest of the intelligence section of the Serbian General Staff. The war was fought principally on the European continent but eventually involved the remainder of the world. While previous wars between the British and the French in the period 1689 to 1815 had been extended to North America, Africa and Asia, they remained struggles between European governments and limited in nature. The term *world war* is properly applied to the conflict of 1914-1918 because the various parts of the British Empire on all continents as well as many countries in Asia and North and South America participated in it. For the first time, all the great powers of the world were engaged in the hostilities: Austria, France, Germany, Great Britain, Italy and Russia in Europe; Japan and China in Asia, and the U.S. in North America. It is estimated that by the end of the war about ninety-three per cent of the population of the world was involved.

The incident which touched off the war was, of course, only the spark which ignited the European powder keg. Historians have argued for years over the main cause of the struggle and the concomitant question of national responsibility for the coming of the war. In the period immediately following the war, it was assumed that Germany and, to a lesser extent, its allies were solely responsible for the conflict—and this view was written into the Treaty of Versailles in 1919. Since that time, the finger of war guilt also has been pointed, with varying degrees of plausibility, at Serbia, Austria-Hungary, Russia and France. In 1951 a group of French and German historians even concluded that although no one wanted the war, all accepted it once it came.

The causes of the war are more clear, even though their historical weight has been disputed. First, many historians emphasize what they have called "the international anarchy" created by the two great alliances of the time: the Triple Alliance (Germany, Austria and Italy) and the Triple Entente (France, Russia and Britain). Although Italy

later joined the Entente powers and was replaced in the Triple Alliance by the Ottoman Empire (in an arrangement which became known as the Central Powers), the fact remained that Europe for more than a generation before the war was divided into two hostile armed camps, with a series of complex treaties tying the signatories to each other and to certain weaker states like Serbia in case of European-wide conflict. Thus, when Austria declared war on Serbia in 1914, it activated this alliance system and brought Russia into the conflict on the side of Serbia, then Germany on the side of Austria, then France on the side of Russia, with Britain finally entering the contest against Germany when that nation invaded Britain's ally, Belgium.

Other historians have stressed the fundamental state antipathies which existed, for various historical reasons, on the eve of the war—such as those between France and Germany, Austria and Russia, and Britain and Germany. Still others have pointed to economic causes for the coming of the war, such as the clash of the great European imperialist powers for markets and raw materials in the Middle East and in Africa. Some scholars have emphasized the rampant militarism which had engulfed Europe in the nineteenth century as a cause of the conflict—all of the major powers, with the exception of Britain, had instituted compulsory military training and introduced certain practices calculated to glorify war and the military machine. In addition, some historians have stressed the underlying psychological causes of the conflict, such as the massive boredom resulting from the dehumanization of the workers in the new industrial age, which made many Europeans eager to accept the adventure which they supposed war would bring.

However, it was nationalism—the belief that an individual's highest loyalty belonged to the nationality and to the nation-state created by that nationality—which brought all of these matters to a head in 1914. World War 1 began in the Balkans when the assassination of the archduke brought the nationality question there to a crisis. In the final analysis, war broke out because of the conflict between existing governments and their unhappy minorities, that is, because of the denial of the right of self-determination to large numbers of subject peoples, especially within the Austro-Hungarian Empire. Nationalism also psychologically prepared the population of Europe for war and made it, when it came, not a mere contest of governments but a struggle of peoples. Moreover, rationalistic fervor dictated that the war would be fought by the entire manhood of the belligerent countries and eventually became an all-out effort not only on the part of the military forces but of the civilian homefront as well. All of this helped to make World War I and its aftermath especially brutal.

When the war began in Europe, most Americans assumed that it was just another in a long series of the Old World's conflicts and, therefore, none of their business. However, as the war dragged on and the casualties mounted, so did American interest in the hostilities. Already conditioned to a pro-British viewpoint by common linguistic and cultural ties and by German blundering in diplomatic affairs, and subject to a constant barrage of anti-German propaganda (most of it false) from the British and French press, the majority of Americans gradually moved closer to the Allies in sympathy. Moreover, American munitions-makers and related businesses, as a result of geography and an effective British naval blockade, had access to British and French markets while being denied those of the Central Powers. This meant that as the British and French debts to American businesses escalated, so did the stake of those businesses in an Allied victory. Then, despite President Woodrow Wilson's* efforts to maintain American neutrality, the U.S. was drawn into the conflict when the Germans in January 1917, despite previous promises to the contrary, announced a resumption of unrestricted submarine warfare. In February and March, several American ships were sunk, after which Wilson, urged on by a sizeable segment of American public opinion, asked for a declaration of war against Germany. On April 6, 1917, Congress concurred and the president proclaimed that the U.S. had gone to war "to make the world safe for democracy."

Wilson's earlier stand of neutrality and his subsequent decision to lead the nation into World War 1 can best be understood in light of the political world view which he had forged on the basis of his evangelical* Christian faith. An active Presbyterian* churchman, his political liberalism and international humanitarianism rested, in a large measure, on his understanding of the Scriptures.* His original position of neutrality was based on his desire to serve as a mediator between the belligerents in order to bring the war to a speedy conclusion. Later he justified American entry into the war as a means to preserve democracy and establish peace. By 1917 he became convinced that the war could be shortened with the U.S. as a participant against Germany and its allies, who now seemed more evil than their opponents. Even

so, he was determined to offer the defeated Germans a just and humane peace, a position which he outlined in his celebrated Fourteen Points on January 8, 1918. When the German government approached Wilson concerning an armistice in the autumn of 1918, he was receptive and opposed those who wanted to prolong the war until Allied troops marched into Berlin.

However, the British and French had no intention of abiding by Wilson's idealistic Fourteen Points when the victorious powers—with representatives of none of the defeated countries present—convened the peace conference at Versailles in 1919. Forced to compromise on all of his other points, Wilson preserved the fourteenth, his proposal for a League of Nations, only to have that part of the treaty become the main reason for the U.S. Senate to reject ratification. Wilson's dream of American participation in a congress of nations organized to resist international aggression and to maintain a just peace was repudiated by his fellow Americans when they elected Warren G. Harding as president on an anti-League platform in 1920.

Wilson was supported in his decision to go to war with the Central Powers by the vast majority of America's religious leaders, but not all shared the President's high ideals and humane goals. Although no quantified study has been made of the denominations and their attitudes toward the war effort, it is clear that only a few churches and their leaders actively opposed the conflict. Like the American public, the majority of church leaders could be classified as militants or moderates in their attitude toward the prosecution of the war, with about an equal number taking each position. Moreover, there appears to have been no theological dividing line between these two groups, with conservatives and liberals present in large numbers in each group. However, as Ray Abrams and John F. Piper, Jr., have pointed out in their studies of this subject, the militants were more vocal and more unqualified in their support of the war effort. Thus, evangelist Billy Sunday,* representing the most strident anti-German voice among Protestant ministers, told his listeners, "If you turn hell upside down, you will find 'Made in Germany' stamped on the bottom." Later in a January 1918 prayer in the House of Representatives, he informed God that Germany was "one of the most infamous, vile, greedy, avaricious, bloodthirsty, sensual, and vicious nations that has ever disgraced the pages of history." Not to be outdone, prominent liberal Presbyterian minister Henry Van Dyke* (author of the hymn "Joyful, Joyful, We Adore Thee") advocated hanging "everybody who lifts his voice against America's entering the war." And in April 1917, Cardinal James Gibbons,* primate of the American Catholic Church,* declared that a citizen's loyalty to his nation was "exhibited by an absolute and unreserved obedience to his country's call."

More moderate but nevertheless supportive of America's war effort were the leaders of the Federal Council of Churches* and the National Catholic War Council.* In fact, the majority of denominational leaders shared neither the pacifist nor the militant opinion. Among pulpit ministers, Harry Emerson Fosdick* was perhaps representative of the moderates. Although he later would become a pacifist, Fosdick adopted an essentially Wilsonian attitude toward the war, regarding it as just in its aims but reminding his fellow Christians that in the final analysis Christianity and war were incongruous.

Only a small number of American Christians opposed the war. The historic peace churches* (Mennonites,* Quakers* and Brethren*) maintained their Christian pacifism and a handful of conscientious objectors representing most of the nation's other denominations refused to take part in the conflict. However, before Congress approved legislation permitting alternative service for conscientious objectors in 1918, Christian pacifist draftees were often badly treated in the training camps, and a few even killed. Mennonite pacifists of German background, in particular, were ridiculed, beaten and often court-martialed in the period before alternatives were available. Likewise, Mennonite civilians often suffered indignities, and one Kansas Mennonite was even painted yellow and taken to district court in late 1918 for alleged violation of the Espionage Act when he refused to buy war bonds.

The majority of American church leaders and their followers intimately identified with America's participation in World War 1. Whether this represents a unique and healthful intertwining in American life of religion and democracy in the manner of Tocqueville* or an abject surrender of American Christianity to the god of nationalism will continue to be debated by scholars. What is clear is that during World War 1 nationalism incited Christians to slaughter other Christians and American believers, for the most part, uncritically to join in the carnage.

Based on the most reliable statistics, the total cost of the war was nearly $338 billion. In terms of direct costs—that is, expenditures by the belligerents in carrying out the actual fighting—the average daily expense during the first three years

of the war was $123 million, rising in 1918 to $224 million. The number of casualties in World War 1 far exceeded those of any other war before in history. Civilian deaths from military action, massacre, starvation and exposure between 1914 and 1918 are estimated at 12,618,000. Of the more than 65 million people mobilized by all countries during the war, 57.6 per cent, or more than 37.5 million, became casualties: 8,538,315 dead, 21,219,452 wounded, and 7,750,919 prisoners and missing. U.S. casualties were small in comparison with the total: 126,000 dead, 234,000 wounded, and 4,500 prisoners and missing, or total casualties of 8.2 per cent of the 4,344,000 individuals mobilized.

Above and beyond these stark figures, the war deeply affected nearly all of those who served and badly scarred most of those who saw combat. Moreover, the harshness of the peace terms, coupled with continued violence in eastern Europe, the Balkans, the Middle East and Asia, mutual distrust among the victors, and a sharp recession following the immediate post-war boom, produced a widespread sense of disillusionment in both Europe and America. Some felt that the peacemakers had not been sufficiently idealistic while others thought they had been impractical. The vanquished smarted under the severity of the peace treaty and longed for revenge. Many of the survivors on both sides concluded that the outcome of the war proved that all governments were incapable of acting in the interest of the common person or that an individual's fate was something altogether beyond personal control. Many questioned established authority and almost none thought that the "world had been made safe for democracy." From these various refractory moods emerged an increasingly strong pacifist sentiment, violent nihilist movements like that of the Nazis in Germany, an escapism that gave great popularity to esoteric poets, novelists and painters, and a brooding fatalism that was reflected in the writings of intellectuals like Oswald Spengler and T. S. Eliot.

American Christians, too, were swept along in many of these currents. The war had taught Americans not only to hate the enemy but each other as well. The violence and brutality of the war years and the raw emotions aroused by wartime rhetoric blunted the moral consciences of many Christians and readied them for the internecine religious warfare that was to follow in the modernist-fundamentalist controversy* of the 1920s. The massive mobilization of the American people for war, with its accompanying geographical and social dislocation, the massive relocation of millions of young Americans from hometowns to training camps where they were taught the techniques of modern warfare, the exposure of many of these same young Americans to new and exotic cultures, the diversion of the energies of church leaders from evangelism* and pastoral care to the war effort, and the widespread disillusionment following the war all changed the face of America and of the American churches forever.

BIBLIOGRAPHY. R. H. Abrams, *Preachers Present Arms* (1933); T. A. Bailey, *Woodrow Wilson and the Lost Peace* (1944); R. Bolt, *U.S. Involvement in World War I* (1974); J. S. Hartzler, *Mennonites in the World War* (1922); J. C. Juhnke, "The Victories of Nonresistance: Mennonite Oral Tradition and World War I," *Fides et Historia,* 7 (Fall 1974): 19-25; A. S. Link, *The Higher Realism of Woodrow Wilson* (1971); R. L. Moellering, *Modern War and the American Churches* (1956); J. F. Piper, Jr., *The American Churches in World War I* (1985); R. A. Wells, ed., *The Wars of America: Christian Views* (1961); M. Williams, *American Catholics and the War* (1921).

R. D. Linder

World War 2. Beginning with the German assault on Poland on September 1, 1939, and ending with the Japanese surrender six years later, World War 2 was the greatest conflict in history. Measured in terms of lives lost, damage caused, money expended and countries participating, this struggle was without parallel.

Although the U.S. did not formally enter the War until December 1941, the issue of neutrality or intervention was hotly debated from the outset of hostilities, while the Roosevelt Administration sought through political and economic pressures to counter Japanese expansion in East Asia and gradually aligned itself with the Allies in Europe. By adopting the "Arsenal of Democracy" principle and sending lend-lease aid to Great Britain and the Soviet Union, America was in effect a belligerent; but only with the Japanese raid on Pearl Harbor and the declarations of war by Germany and Italy did it become official. Then the U.S. took the lead in forming a global alliance (the United Nations) against the Axis and devoted its vast industrial potential and seemingly inexhaustible human and physical resources to achieving total victory and a better world.

With a few exceptions, American Christians supported their country's involvement in the War. They saw the cause as a just one because the Axis powers had committed numerous acts of aggression during the previous decade.

Isolationism and Pacifism. The American failure in the 1920s and 1930s to exercise responsible world leadership was a significant factor in the coming of a second global conflict. Although liberal clerics were involved in various peace movements and internationalist causes during the interwar years, they did not really speak for the mass of the American people and could not direct their parishioners away from the path of storm-cellar neutrality which simply abetted the aggressive actions of the rising dictatorships. Among the prominent figures in the peace movement were clerics or persons with theological training, such as Norman Thomas, A. J. Muste, Sherwood Eddy,* Kirby Page, Georgia Harkness,* John Haynes Holmes, Frederick Libby, Harry Emerson Fosdick,* Walter W. Van Kirk and Dorothy Day.* Fundamentalist* leaders distanced themselves from peace activism because of their political conservatism and hatred of modernism.*

The peace movement collapsed after Pearl Harbor. Reactions to Japanese aggression and the Nazi campaign against the Jews depleted its ranks, but a few church organizations and small groups like the Fellowship of Reconciliation* continued and some engaged in humanitarian relief projects. The pacifist press was allowed to criticize government policy and counsel men to refuse service; and, in fact, a larger percentage of young men registered as conscientious objectors (C.O.s) than in World War 1.* Of the 10,022,367 males ordered to report for induction into the armed forces, around 43,000 were classified as C.O.s—25,000 were noncombatants, 11,887 accepted alternative service and 6,086 were imprisoned for refusing induction. (One out of every six federal prisoners was a C.O.)

According to the Selective Service Act, C.O. status would be granted to one who "by reason of religious training and belief, is conscientiously opposed to participation in war in any form." The person would be assigned noncombatant duties or, if he objected to military service of any kind, to "work of national importance under civilian direction." However, most young men who belonged to the historic peace churches did not choose C.O. status. The Mennonites* had the best record—three-fifths were C.O.s, but only one-quarter of young Quakers (Friends)* and less than one-eighth of Church of the Brethren* youth were C.O.s. Men who refused to register for the draft (this included Jehovah's Witnesses*) or who objected to war on political or philosophical grounds were incarcerated.

Threats to Civil Liberties. One of the first victims

of the war effort was civil liberties. By the end of the 1930s partisans of both the political left and right were labeling each other's positions as un-American, subversive and totalitarian, and charges of communism and fascism were flung with abandon. By use of lurid documentary films, books and radio broadcasts and by listing names of alleged subversives, activists spread fear and suspicion. As a result, in 1938 the House of Representatives revived and made permanent its Committee on Un-American Activities, and it conducted numerous hearings to expose radicals.

Liberal churchmen branded fundamentalists as "authoritarians" and "fascists," and a few like Gerald Winrod* even looked favorably on Nazi Germany for a time because of its militant anticommunism and facade of personal morality. Many liberals urged that restrictions be placed on the "native fascists" and supported the Roosevelt Administration's efforts to suppress critics on the right. Under pressure from Washington, Catholic radio preacher Father Charles Coughlin* was silenced by his superior in May 1942.

A serious breach of civil liberties was the mass trial of far-right figures who were charged for conspiring to cause insubordination in the armed forces through the distribution of propaganda. Among the thirty defendants were evangelical* Protestant* figures Winrod, Elizabeth Dilling (Episcopalian* layperson,* author of an exposé of Communists in the churches and public agencies) and Eugene N. Sanctuary (Presbyterian* layperson and publisher of the notorious anti-Jewish tract, *The Talmud Unmasked*). The main religious-right notables not in the dock were Father Coughlin and the rabble-rousing, former Christian Church (Disciples of Christ*) preacher Gerald L. K. Smith,* who had moved increasingly toward anti-Semitism. After seven months the presiding judge died, and a mistrial was ruled. A federal judge finally dismissed the charges in 1946.

The Jehovah's Witnesses were frequent victims of harassment due to their unorthodox views and aggressive proselytizing, but the Supreme Court* ruled in their favor in religious-freedom cases in 1940 and 1942. More important was the Witnesses' refusal to take part in the public schools' flag-salute ceremonies, an issue which stirred patriotic passions. Although they were rebuffed by the court in 1940, three years later in the landmark *West Virginia State Board of Education* v. *Barnette* case, it held on free speech grounds that the children could not be required to salute the flag.

Race and Ethnic Prejudice. World War 2 saw some important gains for minority groups, but there were setbacks as well. The intense hatred for German-Americans that so marked World War 1 did not recur, but the five million Italian-Americans were viewed with suspicion.

Jews, on the other hand, suffered from the effects of popular anti-Semitism. Several ugly anti-Semitic incidents erupted among Irish Catholics in Boston, and Father Coughlin's hate sheet, *Social Justice,* was widely read in urban-Catholic circles. Although Roosevelt had done much to foster tolerance in American life, official policies before 1941 failed to help suffering Jews in Europe. Although by 1942 the terrifying dimensions of the Holocaust* were known in official circles and detailed reports appeared in the religious press, including evangelical magazines, still nothing was done. Finally, in late 1943 when Roosevelt was persuaded to create a War Refugee Board to assist in the rescue and relocation of European Jews, it was too late; six million Jews had perished.

Another target of hostility were Hispanics* in Los Angeles, and the pitifully underpaid Mexican-American farm laborers in the Western states. More significant was the situation of the African-American population who suffered as usual from white oppression during the war years, but African-American leaders, like Baptist preacher and congressman Adam Clayton Powell; Bayard Rustin, a Quaker; James Farmer, graduate of Howard University School of Religion; and A. Philip Randolph, a devout Methodist who headed the Brotherhood of Sleeping Car Porters, sought to make a difference.

Randolph organized the March on Washington Committee in 1941 that induced Roosevelt to set up a Fair Employment Practices Committee. Still, African-Americans were disadvantaged in employment and unrest broke out in various cities, the most serious being the Detroit riots in June 1943. Fundamentalist hatemongers Gerald Smith and J. Frank Norris,* along with local radio preachers and the Ku Klux Klan spread discontent among the poor white Southerners who had moved North and were a thoroughly dislocated element. In the most ferocious race riot in a quarter century, twenty-five African-Americans and nine whites were killed and 800 injured. African-American and white church leaders endeavored to make peace, but federal troops had to be called in to halt the bloodshed.

Segregation was such a way of life in the armed forces that no African-American officer was allowed to outrank or command a white person in any unit. The draft and rapid influx of African-American soldiers made it increasingly difficult to maintain all the old racial barriers. African-Americans still suffered humiliation; clashes frequently took place between white and African-American soldiers; and the army even segregated the blood plasma donated by African-Americans and whites, an action endorsed by the American Red Cross. In the Battle of the Bulge, African-Americans actually did serve in combat, but in platoons assigned to white companies. The navy did better and began integrating ships after May 1944. Some white church figures spoke out against the evils of "Jim Crow" segregation, above all A. J. Muste of the Fellowship of Reconciliation.

The most egregious violation of civil liberties, however, was the internment of 120,000 people of Japanese birth or ancestry, two-thirds of whom were American citizens (the Nisei). Although their "relocation" was ostensibly implemented on the grounds of military necessity, in fact it was due to the pressure of whites and their powerful congressional delegation. Most Japanese were not in occupations vital to national defense, nor did they constitute an espionage threat. Proof of the racist underpinnings of the policy was that the Japanese population of Hawaii was not treated similarly.

During February 1942 President Roosevelt and Secretary Stimson ordered the evacuation of the West Coast Japanese, and on March 27 the army began transporting them to temporary "assembly centers." At the same time, Roosevelt created the War Relocation Authority, and by September the WRA had ten camps in operation in seven Western states, each accommodating 10,000 to 12,000 people in wooden barracks.

Although some liberal clerics criticized the internment (above all, *The Christian Century,** which accused the government of moving in the same direction as Germany was), it was generally accepted in religious circles and local members of the United Council of Church Women worked in the relocation centers to alleviate hardships. Attempts by church groups and liberals to moderate the policy and allow people to leave the camps were stoutly resisted by hardline segregationists in Congress.

Religious Life in the Armed Services. Although servicemen and women were uprooted from their homes and churches, a great deal of religious activity went on in their new environments. The military chaplaincy* underwent a dramatic increase from less than 200 in the interwar years to around 11,000 on active duty. They were apportioned among the faiths in a ratio of 3.7% Jewish, 30.5% Roman Catholic and 65.8% Protestant (a catch-all category which included Eastern Orthodox, Mormons and others), but the quotas were not adhered to strictly. Chapels were built on posts

and provided on ships, and the chaplaincy was clearly ecumenical. As clergy in uniform who provided for the religious needs of service personnel and their dependents, they had to be committed to the war effort.

Many of them served in combat and were killed or wounded. Four army chaplains (two Protestants, a Catholic, and a Jew) who went down with the torpedoed transport ship *Dorchester* on February 3, 1943, after giving their life jackets to men who had none, were among the war's most celebrated heroes. Chaplains also distributed Bibles,* including a New Testament or a collection of readings from the Hebrew Scriptures that contained a foreword from President Roosevelt commending its reading.

The Federal Council of Churches' General Committee on Army and Navy Chaplains and the National Association of Evangelicals* assisted denominations in accrediting ministers for placement. The Federal Council sponsored spiritual retreats for chaplains, preaching missions and seminars in counseling. The International Council of Religious Education created the Service Men's Christian League, which provided popular religious literature and discussion-group materials for use by personnel under the leadership of chaplains and published *The Link,* a monthly magazine emphasizing the bond with local churches. The National Conference of Christians and Jews* sent interfaith teams to over 300 camps to promote mutual understanding among religious groups.

Popular Religion. The war years were marked not only by the typical decline in personal morality but also by thriving popular religiosity. Churches supported the war effort with salvage drives, letters and packages to their "boys" in the service, patriotic sermons and prominently displayed banners with service stars. Youth for Christ,* founded in Chicago in 1944, appealed openly and directly to the patriotic spirit of the country and was the leading edge of the post-war evangelical advance. Religious novels were so popular that for three years in a row they led the fiction best-seller list—A. J. Cronin, *The Keys of the Kingdom* (1941); Franz Werfel, *The Song of Bernadette* (1942); and Lloyd C. Douglas, *The Robe* (1943). Religion and sentimentality were catered to in the screen versions of these, as well as in *Going My Way,* with Bing Crosby and Barry Fitzgerald, which swept the 1944 Academy Awards and was the most successful movie since *Gone with the Wind.*

The War and Missions. When the Nazi government curtailed financial support to German works abroad and the spreading war in Europe left the continental missions cut off from their home bases, the International Missionary Council* and Lutheran World Federation* assisted these "orphaned missions" to continue their work. To head off the impending conflict between their two countries, seventeen American Protestant ecumenical and missionary leaders met with nine of their Japanese Christian counterparts in April 1941, but the effort was futile. As the war progressed, evangelical leaders looked to the future, where they saw a great "open door" for missions, and they used an abundance of military metaphors to challenge potential missionaries to seize the opportunity.

The most vital dimension in the post-war surge of American Protestant missionary activity was the experiences of the "GIs" themselves. They had witnessed conditions overseas and some even came into contact with existing mission enterprises. Many servicemen engaged in grassroots religious activity, such as those in the Philippines who organized an evangelistic outreach to their buddies through a Youth for Christ*-style "GI Gospel Hour" (*See* SEND International) and ministered to the local people with Bible classes, English-language instruction and relief activities. They returned home enthused about missionary work, entered Bible colleges and seminaries in droves, and returned to their former places of service ready to win the world for Christ.

The War and Ecumenism.* In spite of their earlier ties with peace movements, mainline* theologians* generally embraced the effort to crush Nazism. Most notable was Reinhold Niebuhr,* who argued that in a sinful world justice could only be advanced by engaging in armed conflict to protect each life and interest against all others. The person who refused to resist tyranny became a party to the enslavement of nations and the suppression of freedom of thought and life. In early 1941 he helped found *Christianity and Crisis* as the organ of those who wanted to prevent a German victory because, as he wrote, Nazi tyranny intended to annihilate the Jewish people, subject the world to the domination of a master race, extirpate the Christian religion, and destroy the values and fabric of Western civilization. However, the Commission on a Just and Durable Peace, founded in 1941 (*See* Dulles, John Foster), focused its attention on the post-war international structure and generated public support for a United Nations Organization. Three of its people, well-known Protestant ecumenists, served as consultants to the American delegation at the San Francisco Conference in 1945 which created the UN.

Ecumenical figures not only took part in the chaplaincy and alternate service programs but also fostered new church development in the boom towns, participated in USO (United Service Organization for National Defense) programs for service people, provided spiritual help for German war prisoners, assisted in resettling Japanese-Americas and engaged in overseas relief programs. The Church Committee on Overseas Relief and reconstruction coordinated Protestant efforts in the war-torn areas, while the American Council of Voluntary Agencies for Foreign Service was formed on October 7, 1943, as a pioneering interfaith, ecumenical venture to bring the various Protestant, Catholic and Jewish agencies involved in international relief and rehabilitation under one roof. It worked in partnership with the government and thereby fixed the "three faiths" policy in American religious philanthropy abroad. In 1945 about one-third of all private relief funds were being channeled through religious sources, a figure that rose to seventy-five per cent in 1947.

The White House itself expanded the scope of ecumenical relations by establishing unofficial ties with the Holy See. In late 1939 Roosevelt named Myron C. Taylor as his personal envoy to the Vatican* to secure Catholic participation in dealing with refugee problems. His continuing missions to Rome during the War (ostensibly for intelligence purposes) were heavily criticized in Protestant circles as a violation of church-state separation.* In 1943 Roosevelt encouraged the National Catholic Welfare Conference* to create the Catholic War Relief Services (now Catholic Relief Services). It drew heavily on the financial resources of the semiofficial National War Fund for its work and also provided the government with intelligence information through its contacts in Rome and Germany.

Roosevelt and Civil Religion.* A liberal ecumenical Episcopalian, Roosevelt had done much during his presidency to advance interfaith relations. He backed candidates and chose advisers without regard to their religious beliefs, and he addressed Protestant, Catholic and Jewish organizations alike. He saw idealism, patriotism and faith as inseparable, and under his aegis the principle of the "three great faiths" was firmly established in the American civil religion. A public faith characterized by "brotherhood" and civility was the crucial underpinning of American democracy.*

In 1939 Roosevelt declared that the storms abroad challenged the three institutions indispensable to Americans—religion, democracy and international good faith—and wherever democracy was overthrown, free worship disappeared. The defense of religion and democracy was the same fight. In 1941 he identified the "four essential human freedoms"—freedom of speech and worship, and from want and fear—which was the antithesis of the new order which the dictators wished to create. In a later speech he accused Germany of planning to destroy all religions and to create a new "International Nazi Church" to replace the Bible and values of the "God of Love and Mercy" on which America was founded.

During the war he frequently appealed to his people's faith in God and sense of national purpose. While the enemy was guided by brutal cynicism and contempt for the human race, Americans were fighting to cleanse the world of ancient ills and were inspired by the faith that "God created man in his own image." They strove to defend the doctrine that all are equal in the sight of God against an enemy which attempted to create a world in its own image of tyranny, cruelty and serfdom. It was a conflict between good and evil, and only "total victory" could reward the champions of tolerance, decency, freedom and faith.

He also emphasized prayer as a weapon in the struggle. He read a "United Nations" prayer on Flag Day 1942, proclaimed days of prayer on several occasions and recited a prayer to the nation on the evening of the D-Day invasion on June 6, 1944. Utilizing the public faith to bond his people together in a holy and righteous cause, his prayer looked forward to victory and a "world unity" that would allow all people to live in freedom and reap the rewards of their honest toil.

Unresolved Issues. The problems of reconversion and post-war relief occupied much of the churches' concern, but numerous questions with spiritual or moral implications remained unresolved. These included the legitimacy of the saturation bombing of German and Japanese cities and using nuclear weapons in Hiroshima and Nagasaki, the trial of enemy leaders as "war criminals," the treatment of refugees, the quest for a secure homeland for Jewish survivors of the Holocaust, the role of the American churches in a worldwide ecumenical movement* and the strained relationship with the Soviet Union, whose leader, Josef Stalin, was himself a brutal dictator and whose official ideology seemed to threaten all that Christianity and liberal democracy were based on.

See also CHAPLAINS, MILITARY; HOLOCAUST AND THE AMERICAN CHURCHES; WORLD WAR 1.

BIBLIOGRAPHY. J. M. Blum, *V Was for Victory:* *Politics and American Culture during World War II* (1976); A. R. Buchanan, *Black Americans in World War II* (1977); S. M. Cavert, *The American Churches in the Ecumenical Movement, 1900-1968* (1968); H. L. Feingold, *The Politics of Rescue: The Roosevelt Administration and the Holocaust, 1938-1945* (1970); J. B. Nichols, *The Uneasy Alliance: Religion, Refugee Work and U.S. Foreign Policy* (1988); G. Perrett, *Days of Sadness, Years of Triumph: The American People, 1939-1945* (1973); R. V. Pierard, "World War II," in R. A. Wells, ed., *The Wars of America: Christian Views* (1981); R. V. Pierard, "Pax Americana and the Evangelical Missionary Advance," in J. A. Carpenter and W. R. Shenk, eds., *Earthen Vessels: American Evangelicals and Foreign Missions* (1989); R. V. Pierard and R. D. Linder, *Civil Religion and the Presidency* (1988); R. Polenberg, *War and Society: The United States, 1941-1945* (1972); L. P. Ribuffo, *The Old Christian Right: The Protestant Right from the Great Depression to the Cold War* (1983); L. S. Wittner, *Rebels Against War: The American Peace Movement, 1941-1960* (1969). R. V. Pierard

Worldwide Church of God. An adventist* sect.* The founder of the Worldwide Church of God, Herbert W. Armstrong, was ordained* in 1931 by the Oregon Conference of the Church of God (Seventh-Day). In 1934 Armstrong, while still associated with the Church of God, began a radio ministry called the Radio Church of God and began publishing a magazine entitled *The Plain Truth.* A devoted student of the Bible,* Armstrong had by this time come to believe in British Israelism. This doctrine, which identifies the ten lost tribes of Israel with Anglo-Saxons, became part of his church's larger complex of beliefs that includes an emphasis on Old Testament law and the observance of Jewish festivals.

By 1937 Armstrong had withdrawn from the Church of God (Seventh-Day), which had distanced itself from British Israelism and the observance of Jewish feasts. His own following grew, and in 1947 he moved his headquarters to Pasadena, California, where he founded Ambassador College. There the movement continued to prosper, with the radio broadcast (renamed "The World Tomorrow" during the 1960s and hosted by Armstrong's son, Garner Ted Armstrong), followed by a television ministry, reaching an ever-widening audience. By 1974 distribution of *The Plain Truth* had reached 2 million.

The group suffered losses during the 1970s. Schisms among members, alleged scandalous conduct by the leadership, and a lawsuit brought against the church shook the organization. Theological dispute also played a significant role. Armstrong, who viewed himself as God's chosen apostolic messenger of the last days, taught that his church would recapitulate two nineteen-year cycles which he had identified in the early church. These two pre-ordained cycles would restore the knowledge of the gospel. When an eschatological event of cosmic magnitude failed to occur in 1972, at the end of the second nineteen-year cycle of the church's ministry, many members were disappointed. Despite this upheaval, by the mid-1980s the church had stabilized and was once again growing. By 1985 distribution of *The Plain Truth* had surpassed 7,500,000, and in 1984 a correspondence course offered by Ambassador College had enrolled over 300,000.

BIBLIOGRAPHY. H. W. Armstrong, *This Is the Worldwide Church of God* (1971); J. Hopkins, *The Armstrong Empire* (1974); J. G. Melton, *Encyclopedia of American Religions,* 2nd ed. (1986).

The Editors

Worldwide Marriage Encounter Movement. A Catholic*-based movement to enrich marriage and family life. Marriage Encounter began in Spain in the 1950s. A priest,* Fr. Gabriel Calvo, developed a series of conferences geared toward questions that encouraged husbands and wives to improve their communication on a deeper level. In 1962 Fr. Calvo organized twenty-eight Spanish couples for the first "Encuentro Conjugal." The movement grew within the structure of the Christian Family Movement,* spreading through South and Central America.

The Marriage Encounter Movement in the English-speaking world began at the end of the Christian Family Movement conference at the University of Notre Dame in August 1967. A Mexican couple and an American missionary* priest from Mexico presented the encounter program to seven American couples and a few priests and nuns.* By early 1970 an encounter was scheduled in the New York area for every weekend. The movement caught on rapidly across the U.S. By 1985 it included 1.25 million people, with a growth rate of about two hundred thousand a year.

The weekend retreats, led by three married couples and a priest—all of whom are specially trained, stress shared feelings, the sacrament* of marriage and the opportunity to change the world through strengthening marriage and family life. Marriage Encounter neither solves marital problems nor prevents divorce; it seeks to improve existing marriages by challenging spouses to grow through deeper communication and shared feelings.

Follow-up programs include family weekends and premarital instructions. While Encounter weekends are open to all faiths, in 1971 Jewish and Episcopal* movements were begun with support from the Catholic movement. Eventually Methodists,* Lutherans,* Presbyterians,* Reformed* and Mormon churches began their own expressions of Marriage Encounter.

BIBLIOGRAPHY. C. Gallagher, *The Marriage Encounter: As I Have Loved You* (1975).

R. M. Leliaert

World's Christian Fundamentals Association. Interdenominational association of fundamentalist churches. Growing out of a series of prophecy conferences held during World War 1,* the World's Christian Fundamentals Association (WCFA) originated from a group that gathered at a meeting in Philadelphia in 1919. Among the leaders of the nascent movement were William B. Riley,* Reuben A. Torey,* I. M. Haldeman,* Peter W. Philpott,* Lewis S. Chafer,* William L. Pettingill* and John R. Straton.* The participants issued a publication entitled *God Has Spoken; 25 Addresses,* which emphasized the essentials of early fundamentalism* and advocated a program to combat modernism* and evolution.* They encouraged the establishment of Bible conferences* and Bible schools* to meet that goal.

William B. Riley's magazine, *Christian Fundamentals in School and Church,* later called the *Christian Fundamentalist,* became the official organ of the WCFA. Riley and Paul W. Rood guided the organization during most of its existence.

Faced with the threat of liberal theology and the teaching of evolution, the WCFA continually encouraged its supporters to purge their denominations* of heretics and produce theologically sound graduates from their schools. A highlight of their annual meetings came in 1923 in Fort Worth, Texas. Hosted by J. Frank Norris,* they held a full-scale trial of Texas colleges, charging them with teaching rationalism, evolution and higher criticism.

After the famous Scopes Trial* of 1925, the association placed less and less emphasis on combating evolution and modernism and became more of an evangelical* league. The association lasted until the 1940s but gradually weakened and died. During its history it became the first and longest-lasting interdenominational association of fundamentalists.

BIBLIOGRAPHY. S. G. Cole, *The History of Fundamentalism* (1931); N. F. Furniss, *The Fundamentalist Controversy, 1918-1931* (1954); G. W. Dollar, *A History of Fundamentalism in America* (1973).

C. E. Hall

World's Parliament of Religions (1893).

International Congress on Religion held at Chicago Columbian Exposition. The World's Parliament of Religions was the longest, most ambitious, most visited and most admired of the many international meetings that took place during the summer of 1893 as adjunct activities of the World's Fair held in Chicago. A General Committee organized the seventeen-day event. John Henry Barrows, a liberal* pastor* at Chicago's First Presbyterian* Church, chaired the committee, which also contained fifteen other members representing the Episcopal,* Roman Catholic,* Baptist,* Lutheran,* Methodist,* Unitarian* and Universalist* churches, as well as the Society of Friends,* other Christian churches and Judaism.

The international meeting divided its program activities into four distinct groupings. A general program was devoted to the consideration of theism,* Judaism, Islam, Hinduism, Buddhism, Taoism, Confucianism, Shintoism, Zoroastrianism, Catholicism, Greek Orthodoxy* and Protestantism.* A second level of programs focused on "presentations of distinctive faith and achievements, by selected representatives of different churches." The third program consisted of separate meetings for each of the denominations*; these were designed to be informative of the purposes and services of these various faiths. A fourth level involved meetings of religious-related organization or subjects, such as missions,* the YMCA,* the Evangelical Alliance,* Sabbatarianism* and evolution.*

Participating American religious leaders in the World Parliament represented most denominations and sects.* Among those who spoke at the gathering were James Cardinal Gibbons,* Isaac Myer Wise and Lyman Abbott.* Also in attendance was the leader of Christian Science,* Mary Baker Eddy*; the advocate of Theosophy, Annie Besant*; and the spokesperson of the Shakers,* Daniel Offord. Other speakers included Edward Everett Hale,* Washington Gladden,* Richard T. Ely,* Josiah Strong,* Thomas Wentworth Higginson, Sephardic Rabbi H. Pereira Mendes, Bishop John J. Kean,* Frances Willard,* Philip Schaff,* Antoinette Blackwell and W. T. Stead.

BIBLIOGRAPHY. J. H. Barrows, ed., *The World's Parliament of Religions* (1893).

T. J. Schlereth

World's Student Christian Federation.

Ecumenical* association of autonomous Christian student groups. The World's Student Christian Federation (WSCF) grew out of an 1895 meeting which culminated in the union the Student Christian Movements (SCM) of North America, Britain, Germany, Scandinavia and the "mission lands." The WSCF's purpose was to help organize local SCMs, provide ecumenical* training with a view toward preparing future leaders and demonstrating the ecumenicity required by the gospel. Consequently, WSCF efforts were concentrated on calling college and secondary-school students to faith, service and unity.

To achieve its goals the WSCF published two periodicals, *Student World* and *Federation Notes,* as well as numerous books on theology* and mission* strategy. During the course of its development the WSCF has shifted its attention from the pre-World War 1* concern for social involvement to the post-World War 1 question of evangelism* on university campuses. Since 1950 the issues of a post-Christian environment and the onset of technological and political revolutions have occupied the movement.

WSCF conferences have contributed significantly to the ecumenical movement. The 1907 meeting in Tokyo, for example, prepared WSCF leadership for their key role in the 1910 Missions Conference at Edinburgh. On the basis of their experience and contacts, they were able to involve high church Anglicans.* At the 1911 Conference in Constantinople, the way for cooperation with the Orthodox* churches was opened. Thus the WSCF's most enduring contribution seems to have been the training of ecumenical leaders such as Nathan Soderblom (1866-1931) of Sweden, Joseph H. Oldham (1874-1969) and William Temple (1881-1944) of Britain, John R. Mott* of the U.S. and Willem A. Visser't Hooft (1900-) of the Netherlands.

BIBLIOGRAPHY. J. R. Mott, *Addresses and Papers of John R. Mott, vol. II, The World's Student Christian Federation* (1947); R. Rouse, *The World's Student Christian Federation* (1948).

E. Rommen

Worship: Orthodox.

The Eucharist,* generally known as the Divine Liturgy, is the principal service of common worship in the Orthodox Church.* It may be celebrated normally only once a day. It is always celebrated on Sunday* and on major feast days. While the daily celebration is not the norm in parishes,* it may be celebrated on any day with the exception of Good Friday* and most of the weekdays of Lent.*

Consistent with the pattern found in the early church, the Orthodox Eucharist has two major parts. The first is centered on the reading of Scripture* and its explication. The second includes the offering of the bread and wine, the intonation of the Great Eucharistic Prayer (the Anaphora*) and the reception of Holy Communion.* While various themes are found in the prayers* and hymns,* the spirit of joyful thanksgiving for the presence of God and for his mighty acts pervades the rite. The Liturgy of St. John Chrysostom is the form used on most Sundays and feast days. The Liturgy of St. Basil is used chiefly during Lent. Also in use at various times are the liturgies of St. James, of St. Mark and of St. Gregory the Theologian. The Liturgy of the Presanctified Gifts, traditionally ascribed to St. Gregory the Great of Rome, is a lenten vesper* service which includes the distribution of Holy Communion. Many of the hymns and prayers of these rites date back to the early centuries and reflect the liturgical practices of particular centers of the early church.

While not dogmatically defined, it has become common to speak of seven sacraments,* which are often referred to as "mysteries" in the Orthodox Church. All the sacraments are closely related to the Eucharist and were once celebrated in direct conjunction with it. These are Baptism*/Chrismation, Marriage,* Ordination,* Confession (Reconciliation) and Anointing* of the Sick (Unction*). In addition to these rites, there are numerous services and blessings related to the events, needs and tasks of life. All of these emphasize the presence and action of God in the midst of his people.

A cycle of seven daily services of common prayer is found today in some monasteries. In many large parishes, the more ancient practice of daily matins and vespers is preserved. These services are especially common in parishes prior to the Eucharist on Sundays and feast days.

Intimately related to the Eucharist and the other sacraments and services of common worship are highly developed cycles of daily commemorations of particular saints,* celebrations of the great feasts and observances of fasts. Pascha (Easter*), the commemoration of the resurrection, is the most important feast of the liturgical year* and the essential theme of every Sunday celebration. Next in importance are the feasts of Christmas* and the Theophany. The observance of the feasts enables the faithful to enter into the reality of the mighty acts of God in history.

Orthodox worship is expressed not only in words. In addition to the prayers, hymns, Scripture* readings and creed,* the Church makes use of gestures, symbols, processions and the material of creation to involve the entire person—intellect, will, emotions and senses—in the act of worship. All services of common worship are normally sung and done so in the language of the people. While these are minor variations reflecting particular local traditions, the services follow a prescribed order which help to preserve their corporate dimension as well as to maintain a sense of continuity and universality.

The services of common worship are most properly celebrated in sacred space which has been set aside for this purpose. The interior of an Orthodox church building is usually richly adorned with icons* of Christ, the Mother of God and the saints. The icons are a vivid reminder of the presence of the Lord and those close to him.

The worship of the Church is also a means of proclaiming the faith and forming the people in the faith. The Orthodox have sought to maintain a close relationship between worship and authentic teaching. The faith of the Church is expressed in the words and acts of worship. And the services of worship serve not only to glorify God but also to communicate and to strengthen the faith of the people. The word *Orthodox* means both true faith and true worship. The Orthodox believe that their worship forms and informs the faithful as they praise God.

BIBLIOGRAPHY. T. Ware, *The Orthodox Church* (1969); A. Schmemann, *For the Life of the World* (1963); A. Calivas, *Come Before God* (1987); K. FitzGerald, *Religious Formation and Liturgical Life* (1985). T. E. FitzGerald

Worship: Protestant. Protestant* worship in America is rooted in Reformation worship, which in turn traces its lineage back through the worship of the Western church to that of the ancient and apostolic church. Consequently, there is an obvious historical link between Protestant and Catholic* worship. In general the history of Protestant worship can be viewed as a variety of attempts, some of them in successive order, to restore biblical forms of worship. For many Protestants this has been negatively defined as purging their worship of ritual and traditions that are unbiblical. These attempts, beginning with the Protestant worship of the Lutheran,* Reformed,* Anglican* and Anabaptist* varieties and continuing with the Puritans,* the rise of Free Church* and finally charismatic* worship in the twentieth century, constitute the subject of this article. For the sake of organization, denominational traditions are grouped under the headings of Reformation churches and the Free Church movement.

Reformation Churches. The sixteenth-century reformers Martin Luther and John Calvin sought to purge what they considered to be unbiblical practices from the worship they inherited from the medieval Catholic Church. Principally, they rejected (1) the Mass* as a repetition of the sacrifice of Christ and (2) the doctrine of transubstantiation.* They were agreed in restoring (1) the preaching* of the Word and (2) worship in the vernacular.

While Protestants have always agreed with the reformers on these matters, numerous differences which exist in Protestant worship today can also be traced to the Reformation. A fundamental disagreement remains over how much continuity Protestant worship should have with its Catholic past. Lutherans and Anglicans have retained much from their Catholic heritage, while Anabaptists have rejected the past in favor of restoring what they believe to be a simple biblical pattern of worship. The Reformed community, standing in the tradition of John Calvin, has attempted to forge a mediating position. In matters of ceremony Lutherans and Anglicans have been willing to practice what the Bible does not forbid, while the Reformed and Anabaptist traditions have shaped their worship according to what they perceive is the explicit teaching of Scripture.*

Lutheran Worship. Contemporary Lutheran worship is still influenced by the liturgies* produced by Martin Luther in the sixteenth century. These original liturgies, however, went through decisive changes in the eighteenth century. Because of the rise of Pietism,* with its anti-liturgical emphasis, and rationalism with its negative attitude toward mystery and symbol, Lutheran liturgies adopted customs and motifs of Free Church worship. But with the confessional restorationism of Wilhelm Loehe,* which called for a more churchly and sacramental* revival, Lutheran worship on the American frontier began to reflect historic Lutheran worship.

The ecumenical liturgical movement* of the late nineteenth and twentieth centuries resulted in various "high church"* movements in Lutheranism but made its most significant impact in returning Lutheran worship to its roots. In addition, the impact of Catholic liturgical renewal* on Lutheranism has resulted in a Lutheran recovery of the practices of early Catholic Christianity. The changes described above can be seen in the various Lutheran service books. Early Lutheran settlers brought with them liturgies that had been revised through the influences of both Pietism and

rationalism. _The Church Book_ (1868), however, was the first American Lutheran liturgical book to express a return to the sixteenth-century principles of worship. This was the fruit of the earlier labors of the eighteenth-century patriarch of American Lutheranism, Henry Melchior Muhlenberg.* This direction was also evident in _The Common Service_ of 1888 and in _The Common Service Book_ of 1917. This move toward the restoration of more ancient practices of worship has culminated in _The Lutheran Book of Worship_ (1978), a book which reflects the ecumenical* consensus based on the early church sources.

Lutheran worship now reflects the common ecumenical concern for the balance between Word and sacrament, together with the recovery of fuller opening rites, three Scripture* readings, the creed,* the people's prayer,* the kiss of peace and eucharistic* texts based on the canons of the early church.

Episcopal Worship. The parent prayer book for all Anglican churches throughout the world is the litany* of 1544 written by Thomas Cranmer (1489-1556). His aim, similar to that of other Protestant reformers, was to produce a liturgy eliminating the Mass as a sacrifice and the doctrine of transubstantiation.

This prayer book went through a series of changes until the Prayer Book of 1662, the contents of which remained substantially unchanged for 300 more years, and was translated into 210 languages. However, disestablished Episcopalians in Scotland produced a variation on the Prayer Book containing services based on more primitive liturgies. This Scottish Prayer Book was taken as a model by the infant Protestant Episcopal Church of America* and was revised in 1892 and again in 1928. The _Book of Common Prayer_* of 1928 remained the standard form of worship in the Protestant Episcopal Church until it was replaced by the revised _Book of Common Prayer_ in 1979. The 1928 _Book of Common Prayer_ was penitential in tone and did not provide for a weekly Eucharist.* The norm for the Sunday-morning service was set forth in "morning prayer," a beautiful service of hymns,* confessions, prayers, Scripture, versicles and sermons.* The revised Book of 1979 reflects the ecumenical liturgical renewal of the twentieth century.

The Lambeth Conference* of 1920 first called for changes in the liturgy that would meet the demands of the changing world. Since that time changes in Anglican worship have appeared throughout the Anglican Communion. Common to these liturgies and the _Book of Common Prayer_ of

1979 is a pattern of worship that is more distinctly ecumenical and less in keeping with the Anglican heritage and ethos. What has given shape to the new *Book of Common Prayer* is the recovery of early Christian worship with its emphasis on the Word and sacrament. Thus contemporary Episcopal worship follows the early church and the current ecumenical trend in its opening rites, in the service of the Word and its fuller eucharistic prayer.

Reformed Worship. Reformed worship is rooted in the changes made by John Calvin in *The Form of Prayer* (1542). For Calvin, correct worship consisted of a preaching service and the celebration of the Lord's Supper.* The set pattern of worship included an opening Scripture sentence followed by confession of sins, a metrical psalm, a prayer for illumination, the lesson, the sermon, intercessions, the Lord's Prayer, the preparation of bread and wine, the Apostles' Creed, the words of institution, an exhortation, the prayer of consecration, fraction and distribution. During Communion, psalms were sung or read. Communion was followed by a prayer and an Aaronic blessing.

The Reformed community rejected the frequent celebration of Communion, practicing it only four times a year. Consequently Reformed worship became primarily a service of preaching, couched in psalms, hymns and prayers. Reformed worship, such as Presbyterian* worship, became didactic, emphasizing teaching sermons and long prayers. In the nineteenth century, however, the rise of romanticism* and the influence of Tractarianism* in America gave rise to a series of service books reflecting a service of worship less oriented toward teaching and more inclusive of historical elements of worship.

The Presbyterian liturgical aid, *The Worshipbook* (1970), sets forth a service of Word and sacrament as the normative approach to worship. In addition, the Presbyterian Church has published a series of supplemental liturgical resource books in the 1980s, all of which are reflective of the ecumenical consensus of not only Word and sacrament, but of the opening rites, the pattern of three (or two) Scripture readings followed by sermon, creed, intercessory prayer, kiss of peace and an expanded text of the eucharistic prayer which reflects a return to the ancient model.

Anabaptist Worship. Due to the persecution of Anabaptists and their subsequent flight from place to place, little is known of their worship in the sixteenth century. It is generally recognized that they attempted to follow the model of Acts 2:42, stressing the Word, the breaking of bread, prayers and fellowship. In the modern world the Anabaptist traditions expressed in Mennonite Church* and the Church of the Brethren* follows a general Free Church pattern. One major distinction of the Anabaptist Church is the recovery of the ancient *agape* or love feast. It is still in use today and is practiced quarterly. Some groups also practice foot washing and partake of the bread and cup in the context of a fellowship meal. Old Order groups, such as the Amish,* worship in homes.

The Free Church Tradition. The churches belonging to the Free Church tradition were originally part of a movement that broke from the established churches of Europe. In a narrow sense this has come to mean the Anabaptists, Pietists, the Brethren and the Scandinavian Free Churches. Here we use it in its broadest sense to include Puritans, Separatists, Baptists, Quakers, some Methodists and Disciples of Christ. These groups either brought their worship patterns to America or developed on American soil. Most of these established their forms of worship during the seventeenth and eighteenth centuries but underwent a drastic change during the nineteenth century. The emergent nineteenth-century pattern is still used in many nonliturgical churches in America today, particularly among those in the evangelical tradition.

The pattern of worship among the Separatist groups of the early American colonies was as follows: The service began with a fairly long period of prayer. First, there were prayers of thanksgiving, followed by intercessory prayers (the people gave prayer requests either spoken or written). Next, the congregation stood to sing psalms which were lined out (a leader sang a phrase followed by the congregation repeating the phrase). Next, the clergy, standing behind the table, read the Scripture and made commentary on the Scripture as it was read. This was followed by a sermon from the pulpit. These sermons often related to current social issues. After the sermon the preacher sat at the table and answered questions from the congregation. Laypeople were also free to exhort their fellow believers in this part of worship, called witnessing. Finally, the congregation sang more psalms, and the service was closed with the benediction. At least once a month they celebrated the Lord's Table.

This pattern was the normal pattern of Free Church worship during the seventeenth and eighteenth centuries in America. However, during the nineteenth century this pattern underwent significant changes due to the Second Great Awakening* and the adoption of "new measures"* to evangelize the unchurched. The evangelistic model of worship that emerged placed the preacher on a stage and turned the congregation into an audience. Consequently, the lay participation and the place given to social concerns in the earlier model gave way to a more passive approach to worship and a concern for evangelism. Communion came to be practiced less frequently, often being replaced with the altar calls* that increasingly marked the climax of worship.

In the twentieth century, Free Church worship has maintained the structure of evangelistic worship: songs, prayer, Scripture, sermon. In many circles, however, the invitation has been dropped and the evangelistic sermon has been replaced by expository* preaching. The Free Church tradition is increasingly showing an interest in developing its own worship patterns. But most churches and denominations within the tradition lack the necessary leadership. This is largely due to the failure of Free Church seminaries to make worship a significant part of their curriculum and the fact that there are relatively few persons in the Free Church tradition trained in the history, theology and practice of worship.

Baptist. Baptist worship is rooted in the influence of John Smyth, the founder of the General Baptists.* Baptists originally rejected worship books of any kind, including hymn books. They were, according to Smyth, "the Invention of the Man of Sin" because they were incompatible with the spiritual worship of the New Testament, a worship which proceeded from the heart. However, during the seventeenth century Baptists did introduce the singing of metrical psalms, paraphrases and hymns. Eventually, these necessitated the publication of a hymn book. In 1858 a collection of praise music entitled *Psalms and Hymns* was published. In 1900 *The Baptist Church Hymnal* was published (revised in 1933), containing hymns, metrical psalms, traditional canticles, along with prose psalms for chanting and anthems. *The Baptist Hymn Book* of 1962, which contains all these materials, is widely used by the Baptists.

It should be kept in mind that Baptists have no set form of the liturgy, their only widely accepted liturgical book being the hymn book. Liturgical books as such are used only by ministers as guides to prayer and to worship orders for the service of the Word and for the Lord's Supper—usually conducted once a month. Services are adapted to local customs and usages by the consent of each congregation. Furthermore, these books are prepared by individuals rather than denominations. Two such books are James W. Cox's *Minister's Worship Manual* (1969) and John Skoglund's *A Manual of Worship* (1968).

Restoration Movement. The churches arising during the early nineteenth century under the leadership of Barton Stone* and Thomas* and Alexander* Campbell were characterized by their quest to restore the faith and order of the primitive* church. This they did by the principle of adopting practices that were either commanded or set forth by example in the New Testament church. The result was a simple free-church that centered around preaching and a weekly celebration of the Lord's Supper. Other elements of worship included hymns, readings from Scripture, extemporaneous prayers, spiritual songs and a collection. There was no prescribed order, though by the late nineteenth and early twentieth century, a pattern had emerged of opening praise, Scripture lesson, pastoral prayer, Lord's Supper, offering and sermon. The most notable worship characteristic among the churches that emerged from this tradition is that of the noninstrumental Churches of Christ that forbid the use of musical instruments to accompany hymns and other songs of worship.

The tradition has always utilized hymn books, the first being published in 1834, under the leadership of Alexander Campbell. The most recent hymn book, *Hymnbook for Christian Worship* (1970), contains hymns from a wide range of Protestant hymnology, with a strong emphasis on nineteenth-century religious music.

The mainline* denomination that emerged from the tradition, the Disciples of Christ, having no official book of prayers, left the development of the order of worship up to the local pastor and congregation. However, in 1953 the denomination produced an authorized book for voluntary use only, known as *Christian Worship: A Service Book.* This volume represents the work of G. Edwin Osborn (1897-1965), who for more than a third of a century was the denomination's recognized authority on worship. His approach was a psychological one which argued that each service of worship should be organized around a theme. More recently, under the leadership of Keith Watkins, the Disciples have produced a prayer book known as *Thankful Praise.* This prayer book advocates an approach to worship more in keeping with the common understanding of worship drawn from early Christian sources.

Congregationalists and the United Church of Christ. Congregationalists, beginning with the Puritans of New England, have been a part of the Free Church tradition of worship, though heavily influenced by the Reformed tradition. The Puritan style of worship was simple, free from the liturgical ceremony and ritual of the Church of England and focused on the essentials. Its centerpiece was the sermon—plain in style and no less than two hours in length. It might be preceded by confession of sin, prayer for pardon, the singing of a psalm, prayer for illumination and a reading from Scripture. The sermon might then be followed by a prayer, the Apostle's Creed, the psalm-singing and the blessing.

Though the Puritans did not discourage the writing of prayers and their use in worship and were not adverse to worship directories, they rejected the Anglican *Book of Common Prayer*. In America the first official Congregational book of prayer did not come until the twentieth century, when *A Book of Worship for Free Churches* was published in 1948, prepared by the general council of the Congregational Christian Churches.

In 1950 the United Church of Christ was formed, through the union of the Congregational Christian Churches and the Evangelical and Reformed Church. A new commission on worship, led by Louis Gunnemann, produced its first prayer book, known as *The Lord's Day Service,* in 1964, and in 1966 the same commission published *Services of Word and Sacrament.* More recently, the denomination has produced a prayer book known as *Book of Worship: United Church of Christ* (1986). This book reflects the common understanding of worship drawn from early church sources.

Methodist. Although Methodist worship is rooted in the worship proposed by John Wesley,* who was an Anglican, American Methodist worship reflects the nineteenth-century evangelistic model. Methodist preachers crossed the frontier, establishing churches and holding camp meetings* characterized by fervent hymn singing and hellfire preaching. This style of worship spread to other Free Church worshiping communities.

In the twentieth century, Methodist worship has been influenced by the ecumenical liturgical renewal movement. Between 1920 and 1980 an emphasis was placed on choral music, and orders of worship began to appear. In 1944 the first *Book of Worship* appeared, and in 1964 a second was published. In the late 1960s Methodists were engaged in worship experimentation, but during the 1970s and 1980s Methodist worship has been influenced by the spill-over effect of post-Vatican II* reforms. A new *Book of Worship* (1989) reflects the common ecumenical approach to worship found in the more liturgical churches, and it is characterized by contemporary and inclusive language.*

Plymouth Brethren. Both the exclusive and open Brethren practice a similar form of worship, centering around the table of the Lord. A lay leader may begin the service with a hymn, Scripture or exhortation. From there other male lay leaders of the church will spontaneously speak, read Scripture, ask for the singing of a hymn and finally introduce the table of bread and wine with similar prayers, hymns, Scripture and exhortation. All of this takes place without a fixed order. The roots of this service lie in the establishment of the Plymouth Brethren in England about 1831. No substantial change has taken place in this worship from the beginning of the movement.

Quakers. Quaker worship, which is sometimes called "waiting upon the Spirit," does not use an order of worship nor does it practice the sacraments or have an ordained ministry. In worship the community gathers in silence and awaits a word from the Lord. The simple intention of worship is to gather in the presence of Christ and wait for Christ to speak to the gathering through one or more persons who speak Christ's words to the congregation.

Sacraments are shunned in favor of an experience which is completely dependent on the "inner reality." Water baptism is replaced with the baptism of the inner spirit, and communion is achieved in the everyday acts of eating and drinking.

While this form of worship is the original pattern propounded by Robert Barclay, the founder of the Quaker movement, less than half of the Quakers around the world worship this way. Many Quaker churches, having been influence by the Free Church movement, have adopted a Free Church style of worship.

Pentecostal Worship. Pentecostal worship traces its roots back to the 1906 Azusa Street revival* in Los Angeles under the leadership of William J. Seymour,* a black preacher. Unusual characteristics of this revival were the free use of bodily expression such as dance, the laying on of hands for the sick and speaking in tongues. The focus was not on the sermon or music but on the spontaneous leading of the Spirit.

Pentecostal worship represented a pre-literary religious culture that depended on an oral tradition of worship. Pentecostals have thus concentrated on story, parable, witness, prophecy, song and intimate face-to-face encounters rather than liturgical books, set prayers or even hymnbooks.

Nevertheless, Pentecostalism has gone through some very distinct institutionalization as the movement has aged. Some churches, having lost the spontaneity and charismatic quality of worship that characterized its early stage, have institutionalized its form of worship into a controlled spontaneity. Song leaders play an important role in discerning the mood of the audience and building the service to a climax. Body movment and gestures such as raised hands are frequently observed.

Charismatic Worship. The charismatic movement began in the 1960s as a neo-Pentecostal movement among mainline churches and the Roman Catholic Church. Experiencing rapid growth, the movement has spawned a number of large independent charismatic churches. It has made little headway in the more conservative Free Church tradition, especially among those that are self-identified as evangelical.

Charismatic worship is distinguished by singing of scriptural praise choruses, the gesture of lifted hands, the practice of speaking in tongues* and other manifestations of the charismatic gifts of the Spirit. In mainline churches influenced by the movement, these features may be mingled with traditional liturgy. Perhaps the greatest influence of the movement has been its scriptural choruses of praise that are now sung in nearly all denominational and nondenominational churches.

African-American Worship. Rooted in an African heritage, this tradition of worship found early expression in the slaves' secret meetings in the woods and hollows where they gathered at the risk of being severely punished. There they joined to sing, dance, pray and hear "real preaching"—frequently echoing the biblical theme of freedom—as distinguished from the sermons offered by the authorized white ministers who taught them to obey their masters. Attendance at white worship, while frequently encouraged, was not formative and meaningful for the African-American slaves who sought freedom—both spiritual and physical—through worship and prayer. An example of their rhythmic, passionate and expressive worship was the "ring dance"—a shuffle done in a circle to the words and tune of a spiritual. Energetic and lasting sometimes into the middle of the night, these dances were attended by shouts of praise and prayer.

African-American worship was incompatible with the rigid liturgies of Anglicans and Presbyterians but flourished under the looser structures of Baptists and Methodists. There is nothing unique or special about the order of African-American worship. It is distinguished by its unusual freedom of mind, speech and body as well as a powerful expression of dialogic interaction. Vivid in its imaginative style, full of emotive passion and deeply personal, the style has not been greatly influential in other traditions—save for a wide appreciation and use of African-American spirituals. Its lack of influence on white worship is testimony to the continuing divergence between the two cultures and their experience of life.

See also LITURGICAL BOOKS; LITURGICAL MOVEMENT; LITURGIES IN AMERICA; WORSHIP: ROMAN CATHOLIC; WORSHIP: EASTERN ORTHODOX.

BIBLIOGRAPHY. D. Adams, *From Meetinghouse to Campmeeting* (1981); J. Cone, "Black Worship," in *The Study of Spirituality,* ed. C. Jones et al. (1986); G. J. Cuming, *A History of Anglican Liturgy,* rev. ed. (1982); J. G. Davies, ed., *The New Westminster Dictionary of Liturgy and Worship* (1986); F. Hall, ed., *Quaker Worship in North America* (1978); J. Melton, *Presbyterian Worship in America* (1967); W. J. Hollenweger, *The Pentecostals* (1972); L. D. Reed, *The Lutheran Liturgy,* rev. ed. (1959); J. F. White, *Introduction to Christian Worship* (1980).

R. Webber

Worship: Roman Catholic. Public worship in the Catholic tradition is liturgical* in nature and regulated according to norms established by the Roman See. It is centered around the sacraments*—primarily the Eucharist*—the community and the proclaimed Word. When the first Catholic Mass* was celebrated in the New World (1494), it was a worship that had not yet seen the reforms of the Council of Trent (1545-1563). The earliest Spanish missionaries brought with them a worship shaped by the Middle Ages, rich in symbolism and action but subject to the fanciful and even magical notions of folk religion. The liturgical reforms of Trent did much to reform and standardize Catholic worship, particularly the doctrine of the sacraments. For the most part, the worship that was introduced into North America during the later European migrations and missions* of the sixteenth through the nineteenth centuries was post-Tridentine. But even this unity of form and language (Latin) came through an inevitable variety of ethnic expressions—from the Hispanic Catholics of the Southwest to the Polish Catholics of Chicago. Indeed, even a diversity in rites would come to be embraced by the inclusion of Eastern-Rite Catholics* with their own liturgies authorized by Rome.

Movements to reform the Roman liturgy and renew the attitude of the faithful toward worship and its relationship to the Christian life also took place on American soil (*See* Liturgical Movement). As early as 1822 Bishop John England* of Charleston, South Carolina, published an English translation of the Roman Missal, though by 1851 the Roman Congregation of Rites would rule that the ordinary of the Mass should not be translated into the vernacular. The best-known liturgical-reform movement in America was led by the Benedictine* monk Virgil Michel,* who in the 1920s and 1930s emphasized the concept of the Church as the mystical body of Christ,* which through the sacraments expresses the sacrificial worship of Christ and the Church on earth. The laity* was thus encouraged to join in the liturgy through dialog, response, singing and vernacular translation of the ritual. These reforms did not go undisputed, but in 1947 Pope Pius XII* encouraged active participation in the movement, and by the 1950s progressive Catholics had adopted many reforms in their worship.

With the Second Vatican Council* (1962-1965), Catholic worship has undergone extensive revision. Though this revision is complete in its main lines, it is still in process. The *Constitution on the Liturgy* (1963) gave the general principles for the reform and promotion of the liturgy and made specific recommendations for the Eucharist, the other sacraments and sacramentals, the divine office,* the liturgical year,* sacred music, liturgical art* and sacred furnishings.

The Catholic Church sees in the liturgy the most effective way possible for achieving human sanctification* and God's glorification, to which end all the Church's other activities are directed. From this perspective, the Christian is called to participate in the liturgy and pre-eminently in the eucharistic assembly on the Lord's Day, when the memorial of the Lord's resurrection is kept. The Catholic Church views all Christian life as oriented to and from the Lord's Supper because it is at the Eucharist that the body of Christ gathers to encounter its Lord and to be nourished by his word and sacrament for the life of the world. Thus, the pastoral focus of the liturgical reform was the full, conscious and active participation of the faithful in liturgical celebrations.

The task of implementing the council's reform was entrusted to the Consilium (1964-1970), a group composed mainly of bishops* who voted on the proposed reforms and liturgical scholars who prepared them. After the dissolution of the Consilium, the Congregation for Divine Worship* continued the work of implementation. The reform was total and radical in order to restore a coherence to the Church's rituals both individually and in their inter-relatedness. Through historical scholarship and contemporary theological reflection, the Consilium eliminated historical inconsistencies, outmoded world views and questionable theological formulations and emphases that had invaded the rites. Where applicable, a more biblical and patristic understanding was restored. Because this reform took up much of the liturgical agenda that the Council of Trent had regarded as untimely, it has had a great impact on mainline* Protestant* liturgical renewal.

Because the Catholic Church regards every liturgical action as an action of Christ the priest and his body which is the Church, Catholic worship sanctifies the day, the week and the year as well as the important life events of the faithful. It sanctifies the day by praying the Liturgy of the Hours* throughout the day, with particular emphasis on the morning and evening hours as times of public liturgical prayer. It sanctifies the week by the celebration of the memorial of Christ's resurrection on the Lord's Day. Daily celebration of the Eucharist prolongs this Sunday* celebration. It sanctifies the year through the liturgical year which unfolds the whole mystery of Christ in the seasons of Lent*/Easter,* Advent*/Christmas* and ordinary time—those weeks that do not celebrate a specific aspect of the mystery of Christ. The feasts of the Blessed Virgin Mary* and of the saints,* considered to be pre-eminent witnesses to the gospel, are also celebrated throughout the year.

As sacraments of faith, the sacraments are understood to presuppose faith as well as to nourish, strengthen and express it in the lives of the faithful. Thus, the life events of Catholics are celebrated in faith through the rites of initiation, penance or reconciliation,* anointing* of the sick, marriage,* holy orders and burial. All the sacramental celebrations include a liturgy of the word, and each has a fairly extensive lectionary of scriptural readings appropriate to it. In each case, the rite has been made simpler so as to reveal more clearly the grace signified by the sacrament and the meaning of Christian discipleship* associated with it.

Catholic liturgical theology* has emphasized the importance of the assembly as the body of Christ that performs the liturgical action. It is the assembly that initiates, reconciles, anoints and offers the Eucharist rather than the minister* or ministers alone. Christ is also understood to be active in the word that is proclaimed in the Scriptures and the homily. As Christ was the sacrament of God, so the Church is the sacrament of Christ, who continues through the Church his healing and reconciling ministry.

The role of the Holy Spirit as the one who unites the Church and leads it through the Son to the Father has received an increased role in liturgical prayer, most notably in the eucharistic prayer where the Spirit is invoked upon the gifts of bread and wine and upon those who partake of them so that they might become the one body of Christ.

Finally, in the liturgical celebration the principal paradigm placed before Catholics is the paschal mystery of Jesus Christ. The death and resurrection of Jesus Christ are understood through the Jewish feast of Passover, which celebrates God's power to deliver a people from slavery to freedom. Catholic Christians participate in the Passover of the death and resurrection of Christ through the Church's liturgical rites. The ritual of Christian initiation of adults shows the paschal mystery active in those persons who during their conversion* receive pastoral formation. This formation prepares them for baptismal anointing and participation in the eucharistic assembly at the Easter Vigil during the so-called Easter Triduum, the unitive celebration of the passion, death and resurrection of Jesus Christ.

This celebration of the paschal mystery in the lives of persons is understood to be renewed continually at the Christian Eucharist. At the very heart of the Sunday Eucharist, the memorial of Christ's death and resurrection is kept. Catholics participate in this through the eucharistic prayer over the gifts of bread and wine, which recall the supper of the Lord the night before he died, give present nourishment as the Body and Blood of Christ and are already an anticipation of the meal to be taken in the kingdom of heaven.

See also LITURGICAL ART; LITURGICAL BOOKS; LITURGIES IN AMERICA.

BIBLIOGRAPHY. International Commission on English in the Liturgy, *Documents on the Liturgy, 1963-1979, Conciliar, Papal and Curial Texts* (1982); A. G. Martimort, ed., *The Church at Prayer,* 4 vols. (1986-1987); H. Wegman, *Christian Worship in East and West: A Story Guide to Liturgical History* (1985). J. B. Ryan

Wrangel, Karl Magnus von (c. 1730-1786). Lutheran* missionary* in Delaware and Pennsylvania. Born in Sweden about 1730, after graduating from the University of Upsala, Wrangel studied for the Lutheran ministry* at the University of Göttingen in Germany. Ordained* in 1757, Wrangel was appointed court preacher to the Swedish throne. In 1759 he was sent to America as provost of Swedish Lutheran congregations in Delaware and Pennsylvania, including Gloria Dei (Old Swedes) Church in Philadelphia. Wrangel became a close friend and confidant of Henry Melchior Muhlenberg* and took an active role in Muhlen-

berg's German Lutheran Pennsylvania Ministerium.* More politically active than Muhlenberg, Wrangel became an outspoken champion of Pennsylvania German rights, rallying their support to the proprietary party in its struggle against the Quaker*-dominated legislature. In 1764 Governor John Penn dispatched Wrangel, Benjamin Franklin and several others to negotiate with the Paxton Boys, outraged Scotch-Irish and German frontiersmen who were protesting Native American raids. He was instrumental in terminating their march on Philadelphia. Recalled to Sweden in 1768 because of his political activity and association with pietists, he was made pastor of Sala, where he died in 1786.

BIBLIOGRAPHY. L. R. Riforgiato, *Missionary of Moderation: Henry Melchior Muhlenberg and the Lutheran Church in English America* (1980); C. H. Glatfelter, *Pastors and People: German Lutheran and Reformed Churches in the Pennsylvania Field, 1717-1793* (1979). L. R. Riforgiato

Wrieden, Jane Elizabeth (1906-1970). Salvation Army* social worker. Converted* at the age of seventeen, Wrieden joined The Salvation Army and eventually attained the rank of Colonel. Initially involved in evangelistic work, she became convinced that troubled people needed skilled help and earned a master's degree in social work. Wrieden served as an administrator for family services in Buffalo and Brooklyn, New York, and for Salvation Army hospitals in Jersey City, New Jersey, and in Cleveland, Ohio. In 1950 she became its national consultant on women's and children's services. She was a frequent speaker at conferences and institutes on the topic of maternity care and was active in national and international health and welfare and professional organizations. Wrieden helped the Salvationists adapt to the changing pattern of social work by incorporating new methods and scientific discoveries regarding human behavior. S. C. Stanley

Wright, (G)eorge Ernest (1909-1974). Presbyterian* Old Testament scholar and archaeologist. Born in Zanesville, Ohio, Wright graduated from Wooster College (B.A., 1931), studied theology at McCormick Theological Seminary in Chicago (B.D., 1934), and was ordained a Presbyterian minister (1934). After pursuing graduate studies under William F. Albright* at Johns Hopkins University (Ph.D., 1937), he returned to McCormick to teach Old Testament for the next two decades (1939-1958). From 1958 until his death he was Parkman Professor of Divinity at Harvard Divinity School. In addition to directing excavations at Shechem (1956-1964) and Gezer (1964-1965), Wright was founding editor of *The Biblical Archaeologist* and served as president of the American Schools of Oriental Research (1966-1974) and curator of the Harvard Semitic Museum.

Wright figured prominently in the biblical theology movement* and was active in the early post-World War 2* ecumenical movement.* His own theology was enhanced by a concern for archaeological and historical reconstruction of biblical history. The objective reality of the events described in the Bible* was seen by Wright as essential, but the burden of theology was to interpret these events. For Wright the Bible was not primarily the Word of God but the record of the Acts of God accompanied by the human response.

BIBLIOGRAPHY. F. M. Cross, Jr. et al., *Magnalia Dei—The Mighty Acts of God* (1976); R. Lansing Hicks, "G. Ernest Wright and Old Testament Theology," *ATR* 58 (1976):158-178.

S. Meier

Wright, George Frederick (1838-1921). Congregationalist* theologian* and scientist. Born at Whitehall, New York, and educated at Oberlin College* and Seminary, Wright served as a Congregationalist* minister* in New England for almost two decades before accepting a professorship at Oberlin in 1881. Two years later Edwards Amasa Park* entrusted the editorship of *Bibliotheca Sacra* to Wright, who fulfilled that charge by maintaining the highly regarded theological journal until his death in 1921.

Wright's scientific interests prompted him to undertake numerous geological surveys throughout the U.S. and abroad, establishing him as a leading authority in glacial geology. Convinced that an inductive method of discovering truth was vital for both science and the defense of Christianity, Wright ultimately was appointed as professor of the harmony of science and revelation at Oberlin (1892-1907).

Together with Asa Gray,* Wright formed an imposing partnership in their quest to advance the cause of Darwinism* in the U.S. in the late nineteenth century. Their scientific and theological labors were intended to secure a favorable hearing for Darwinism in the American intellectual and religious community but with an emphasis on its theistic (and not its atheistic or agnostic) interpretation.

His prolific writings (sixteen books and almost six hundred articles) reflected a strong apologetic* concern but with interesting variety. They ranged from a defense of Darwinism based on its congrui-

ty with Calvinism (*Studies in Science and Religion,* 1882) to his advocacy of the scientific probability of Noah's flood (*Scientific Confirmations of Old Testament History,* 1906). Finally, his irenic but firm orthodox* faith and lengthy life allowed him to contribute three essays to *The Fundamentals* (1910-1915), which reflected the same unique apologetic diversity.

BIBLIOGRAPHY. *DAB* X; *DARB;* D. N. Livingstone, *Darwin's Forgotten Defenders* (1987); J. R. Moore, *The Post-Darwinian Controversies* (1979); *NCAB* 7; G. F. Wright, *Story of My Life and Work* (1916). S. R. Pointer

Wright, Isaac. *See* COKER, DANIEL.

Wycliffe Bible Translators, Inc. A nondenominational agency devoted to the scientific study of linguistics and the translation of the Bible* for those who lack it in their own languages. Building on the missionary experiences of L. L. Legters and W. Cameron Townsend,* Wycliffe Bible Translators (WBT) (named in honor of the fourteenth-century English reformer associated with the first complete English versions of the Bible) began in 1934 as a summer training program in linguistics, particularly focused on the needs of Bible translators. Education in linguistics has remained a major focus of the organization, though the primary focus of WBT itself is Bible translation. Under its own auspices, field work began with Mexican tribes in 1935, spreading to the Navajo in 1944, to Peru in 1946 and then to several other new locations. In 1953 WBT began work in the Philippines and subsequently elsewhere in Asia and the adjacent islands of the Pacific. Entering Ghana in 1962, it eventually began work in other African locations.

In 1942 a unique dual corporate structure was established, encompassing Wycliffe Bible Translators and the Summer Institute of Linguistics (SIL). The latter is a scientific and educational organization teaching Westerners linguistics and, at the invitation of governments, conducting secular linguistic and literacy work among tribal groups. SIL field workers are also members of WBT.

By the mid-1960s, WBT/SIL had about fourteen hundred members (almost ninety per cent from North America) working in 330 languages in sixteen countries. The remoteness and technical nature of much WBT work has spawned a large network of support personnel, including the separately incorporated Jungle Aviation and Radio Service. By the mid-1980s there were more than five thousand members worldwide drawn from some thirty sending countries. Of these, about three thousand were North Americans serving abroad, while another one thousand served in North America. Wycliffe workers are involved in more than eight hundred languages representing about fifty countries. Nearly three hundred tribes now have the New Testament in their own language as a result of WBT.

BIBLIOGRAPHY. E. F. Wallis and M. A. Bennett, *Two Thousand Tongues to Go* (1959); G. M. Cowan, *The Word That Kindles* (1979).

D. G. Tinder

Y

Yale Band. *See* ILLINOIS BAND.

Yale University and Divinity School. Educational institution with origins in colonial Congregationalism.* Yale came into existence in 1701 in part as a conservative Congregationalist reaction to the growing departure of Harvard* from its traditional Calvinist* orientation. During its first fifteen years the Collegiate School was housed in various Connecticut parsonages until a permanent campus was established at New Haven.

In the early nineteenth century when Harvard clearly embraced Unitarianism,* Yale chose to promote revivalism* and an expansionist Christianity. It was clear that the New Haven, Connecticut, school, together with Princeton* in New Jersey, would emerge as the most influential American colleges (*See* Higher Education, Protestant) during America's greatest boom period of college founding (1800-1860). In this growth era the number of colleges increased from approximately twenty to one hundred eighty, and the college population grew four times as fast as the general population. The primary factor in influencing this growth was the Second Great Awakening,* which in its college phase began at Yale under President Timothy Dwight.* Appropriately, Yale led the Eastern colleges in sending forth spiritually awakened graduates to found and preside over Christian colleges in the South and West, thus earning the reputation as "mother of colleges."

Yale's Divinity School, beginning as a department of theology in 1822, was to become the most potent theological force in nineteenth-century America. Nathaniel W. Taylor,* the first professor of theology in the Yale Divinity School, was prominent in shaping the New Haven Theology,* which provided a theological rationale for the emergent evangelical revivalism* of Jacksonian America. Though Yale would eventually lose its evangelical distinctives, it has continued in the twentieth century to have a distinguished faculty and serve as one of the most prominent centers for theological scholarship in North America.

Nineteenth-century Yale demonstrated its influence in many other ways. In enrollment, as late as the Civil War* era, the number of Yale students made the Connecticut school one of the largest colleges in America. Throughout the nineteenth century, through the famous "Yale Report of 1818" and in other ways, Yale led the movement in American higher education to maintain the traditional prescribed classical curriculum. In governance, to this day the Yale model of institutional control and responsibility by an external board of trustees has been widely adopted by nearly all colleges. In athletics, Yale in the turn-of-the-century period became the chief promoter of intercollegiate football.

See also NEW ENGLAND THEOLOGY; NEW HAVEN THEOLOGY.

BIBLIOGRAPHY. R. H. Bainton, *Yale and the Ministry* (1957); B. M. Kelley, *Yale: A History* (1974); J. T. Wayland, *The Theological Department in Yale College, 1822-1858* (1987).

W. C. Ringenberg

Yeatman, James Erwin (1818-1901). Businessman and philanthropist. The son of a wealthy St. Louis manufacturer, Yeatman early developed a reputation for administrative skill. With the beginning of the Civil War,* two Unitarian* ministers, William Greenleaf Elliot and Henry W. Bellows, independently became concerned with preserving the health of Union troops. The Crimean War had provided fresh evidence that more soldiers were likely to succumb to pestilence than would fall in battle.

Bellows' creation, the United States Sanitary Commission, was organized first under New England leadership. The Western Sanitary Commission* soon followed with Yeatman at its head. The two organizations competed with each other and with the United States Christian Commission* for funds and volunteers.

The Western Sanitary Commission supplied vast quantities of medical and sanitation equipment and material aid to Union troops in Missouri,

Arkansas, Kentucky and Tennessee. Yeatman also toured the Mississippi Valley investigating the plight of the freedmen.

BIBLIOGRAPHY. *DAB* X; *DARB;* W. R. Hodges, *The Western Sanitary Commission* (1906).

R. E. Selleck

Yeo, John (c.1639-1686). Early Anglican* minister* in Delaware and Maryland. A graduate of Exeter College, Oxford, Yeo came to Maryland at a point when the Anglican Church was both small and disorganized. His 1676 letter to Archbishop of Canterbury Gilbert Sheldon, describing the condition of the Church, aroused the interest of Henry Compton, bishop of London, and contributed to a more concerted evangelistic effort on the part of Anglicans.

From 1677 to 1682 Yeo served as the first Anglican clergyman in Delaware, with the English fort at New Castle the focus of his efforts. Interest in the Anglican Church remained strong even after Yeo's departure, and Immanuel Church, New Castle, was the earliest Anglican parish* established in the colony. In 1682 Yeo moved to Calvert County, Maryland, to establish a parish for which a John Eaton had left a bequest of five hundred acres. Yeo apparently remained there until his death in 1686.

BIBLIOGRAPHY. J. F. Woolverton, *Colonial Anglicanism in North America* (1984).

R. W. Prichard

Young, Brigham (1801-1877). Second president of the Church of Jesus Christ of Latter-Day Saints.* Born in Whitingham, Vermont, as a child Young moved with his family to central New York, where he learned such trades as carpentry, masonry and glazing. Though baptized* in the Methodist Church,* he was dissatisfied with the sectarian Protestantism* of the "Burned-Over District"* and embraced Mormonism* in 1832.

In 1835 Joseph Smith,* prophet and leader of the Latter-Day Saints, organized the Quorum of the Twelve Apostles and oversaw Young's ordination* to the apostolate. Young directed the evacuation of Missouri in 1839 and the mission to England in 1840-1841. He rose to the position of senior apostle and became one of a handful of advisors to Smith. After Smith was murdered in 1844, Young's apostolic office, allegiance to the Church and personal charisma resulted in his choice as Smith's successor.

Young led the Mormon exodus from Illinois to the Great Salt Lake Basin (1846-1848) and organized the Mormon effort to build the Kingdom of God* on earth. Contemporaries described Young as a robust, amiable man, sure of himself and his mission. As the head administrator and religious leader of the Saints, he instructed his people in everything from doctrine, architecture and agriculture to fashion and family relations. He used the immense power he possessed as governor of the Utah Territory and Church president to establish some 350 communities and numerous economic ventures. Young was, as one observer noted, the "one chief in Great Salt Lake City."

The comprehensive nature of Young's authority reflected the nineteenth-century Mormon world view. To them, there was no distinction between sacred and secular knowledge, time or space. As the religious head of the Church, Young possessed the authority to supervise every aspect of life. Under his leadership the Mormons worked to establish God's rule on earth and developed a distinctive subculture in America.

BIBLIOGRAPHY. L. J. Arrington, *Brigham Young: American Moses* (1986); N. G. Bringhurst, *Brigham Young and the Expanding American Frontier* (1986); *DAB* X; *DARB; NCAB* 16; J. Shipps, *Mormonism: The Story of a New Religious Tradition* (1985).

B. J. Longfield

Young, Edward Joseph (1907-1968). Presbyterian* Old Testament scholar. Born in San Francisco, Young was educated at Stanford University (B.A., 1929) and Westminster Theological Seminary. Young studied under Albrecht Alt at Leipzig and eventually earned his Ph.D. (1943) at Dropsie College in Philadelphia. Young joined the Old Testament department of Westminster Theological Seminary in 1936, where he taught until his death. A minister in the Orthodox Presbyterian Church,* he was extensively involved in its life and became one of its most admired leaders.

Young combined a deep commitment to Reformed* theology* with a phenomenal linguistic talent. He was widely regarded as the leading evangelical* Old Testament scholar of his day, giving direction especially to the reasoned defense of the authority* and integrity of Scripture* (*Thy Word Is Truth,* 1957) against destructive criticism. His extensive writings, whether scholarly or popular, blended careful exegesis and theological insight with pastoral sensitivity. His *Introduction to the Old Testament* (1949; rev. ed. 1960) was widely used by evangelicals, but his area of expertise was Isaiah, on which he published a three-volume commentary, *The Book of Isaiah* (1965, 1969, 1972). Young was widely in demand, particularly within the North American evangelical* community, as a lecturer, preacher* and conference speaker.

R. B. Gaffin

Young Life. An evangelical* youth movement working primarily with high schoolers. The ministry centers on weekly club meetings consisting of music, skits and a talk based on the Bible.* These weekly clubs are supported by Bible studies* (called Campaigners), camping* experiences and personal conversations with Young Life leaders.

The movement is the result of the ministry* of a young Dallas Theological Seminary* student, Jim Rayburn. In the fall of 1938 Rayburn started driving to Gainsville, Texas, on weekends in order to minister to high schoolers. He started with a Bible club after school on school property, but the next year he initiated a week-night club, meeting in homes. The club grew rapidly. Rayburn had stumbled upon the principles of Young Life: Establish personal relationships with teen-agers; hold meetings in homes, away from school; aim for leaders in the schools; and make meetings enjoyable.

To extend the ministry, Rayburn enlisted other seminarians to organize similar clubs in other towns. Through a seminary friend, Ted Benson, Rayburn gained the financial support of Chicago businessman Herbert J. Taylor* and extended the ministry into other states. With Taylor's backing he also secured a series of camps for summer conferences for young people. Thousands of teen-agers attended every summer. By 1977 the Young Life staff numbered 600 workers and counted over 70,000 teenagers attending Young Life Clubs. The organization's headquarters are in Colorado Springs, Colorado.

BIBLIOGRAPHY. E. Cailliet, *Young Life* (1963); C. Merideth, *It's a Sin to Bore a Kid* (1977); B. L. Shelley, "The Rise of Evangelical Youth Movements," *FH* 18 (1986):47-63.

B. L. Shelley

Young Men's Christian Association. Nondenominational community service organization. Founded in London in 1844 by George Williams, the Young Men's Christian Association (YMCA) provided young men with a wholesome alternative to the evils of urban life. Meeting rooms with suitable reading materials, Bible* classes and assistance in locating good lodging and Christian companions for fellowship and service were among its distinctives. Growing rapidly, it was transplanted to Montreal and Boston in 1851. It quickly became a leading non-sectarian organization in the movement to preach the gospel to the unchurched masses in the burgeoning cities. Along with evangelism,* its members cared for the sick, fed the poor, organized Sunday schools,* worked for temperance,* distributed Bibles and engaged in a host of other good causes.

These activities were expanded to embrace a broad program of spiritual, mental, social and physical development for boys and girls, men and women. In a creative response to society's challenges it added military missions, the Student Volunteer Movement* and industrial missions such as the railroad Y's. Educational programs were developed for youth and adults. The YMCA also developed a variety of human services, including dormitories, physical education and recreation (inventing basketball and volleyball) and camping programs.

Clearly rooted in mainstream evangelical Protestantism, it appealed to the average person's impatience with church rivalries and fine theological distinctions. It forged ahead of most churches in aggressive evangelism. Leaders in the nineteenth century included Dwight L. Moody,* Robert Ross McBurney and Robert Weidensall. Men of prayer, Bible study* and personal evangelism, they had vision, organizational skills and the ability to enlist businessmen to serve, give and train. Moody proved to be the greatest YMCA advocate and fund raiser of the period, repeatedly stating that he owed far more to the YMCA than to any other agency. McBurney was the gifted New York City YMCA administrator and Weidensall the tireless missionary* who developed associations in the West, on the railroads and on college campuses. The mantles of these men fell on the able shoulders of John R. Mott,* Luther Wishard* and many others.

By the 1980s the YMCA had become the largest health and social service agency in the U.S. Its nearly 2,200 organizations reached 12.1 million Americans. Serving 26 million people in ninety-two nations of the world, its spirit, mind and body triangle emblem, with the reference to John 17:21, has been replaced with a small triangle as part of the larger letter *Y.* The movement has revised its objectives over the years, accompanied by strains over policies such as the original evangelical test for membership, the balance of spiritual versus physical needs, the use of volunteer versus professional leadership and local autonomy versus national direction. Those who attend today's "Y" are not necessarily young, men or Christian. The movement has become a flexible community service organization responsive to local needs. Its focus is on goodwill, personal growth and general

Christian values, especially moral, physical, emotional and intellectual growth.

BIBLIOGRAPHY. C. H. Hopkins, *History of the YMCA in North America* (1951); E. Dedmon, *Great Enterprises: 100 Years of the YMCA of Metropolitan Chicago* (1957). C. V. Anderson

Young Women's Christian Association. A movement originally devoted to meeting the social, physical, intellectual and spiritual needs of young Protestant* women. The first Young Women's Christian Association (YWCA) was organized in America in 1866. The original organization stated its goal as helping young women and girls who were "dependent on their own exertions for support" to achieve "those ideals of personal and social living" that arose out of Christian commitment. A nondenominational institution, the YWCA was nevertheless originally understood to be Protestant and evangelical* in character. In time the YWCA took on an increasingly ecumenical* character, and today membership transcends religious faith, being open to all who wish to identify with the movement. Prior to the changes introduced by Vatican II,* the Roman Catholic Church* warned its faithful against membership in the YWCA, stating that it was dangerous to faith and fostered religious indifferentism.

Despite obvious similarities between the two movements, the YWCA has always been completely independent of the YMCA.* Each local YWCA is also independent, though delegates from each YWCA meet every three years for a convention in order to discuss a program and elect a board of 120 women. The board and its staff assist local YWCAs in carrying out the triennial program. In the late 1980s there were approximately four hundred and fifty YWCAs in the U.S. and over fifty in Canada.

BIBLIOGRAPHY. M. S. Sims, *The Y.W.C.A.: An Unfolding Purpose* (1950). The Editors

Youth for Christ, International. An international evangelical* youth organization for evangelism* and Bible study.* The origins of Youth for Christ are nearly impossible to trace. It had no founder; it emerged as an outburst of evangelistic youth rallies. Probably the first youth rally director in America was Lloyd Bryant, who organized weekly rallies for youth in New York City during the early 1930s, but he was soon followed by Jack Wyrtzen, Percy Crawford,* Oscar Gillan, Roger Malsbary and others. By 1943 Saturday-night rallies proliferated in American cities. Torrey Johnson, pastor of the Midwest Bible Church, organized the first rallies in Chicago in 1944.

Some coordination of the ministries came in 1945 when leaders met at Winona Lake, Indiana, and established Youth for Christ, International. Torrey Johnson was elected president. That year Billy Graham* served as a traveling evangelist for the organization. When he brought together his evangelistic team two years later, most of the members had experience in Youth for Christ rallies. During World War 2* and the years immediately following, Youth for Christ made servicemen a special center of concern. Scores of teams went abroad where servicemen were stationed.

In 1948 Bob Cook succeeded Johnson as president of the organization. Under Cook's leadership Youth for Christ turned in the 1950s to high-school Bible clubs (Campus Life) as a more effective way to reach high schoolers. The organization also adopted Youth Guidance Programs, a summer camping ministry to help delinquent young people. By 1986 YFC counted 1,065 Campus Life Clubs in the U.S. and ministries in fifty-six foreign countries.

BIBLIOGRAPHY. J. Hefley, *God Goes to High School* (1970); M. G. Larson, *Twentieth Century Crusade* (1953); M. G. Larson, *Young Man on Fire, The Story of Torrey Johnson and Youth for Christ* (1945); B. L. Shelley, "The Rise of Evangelical Youth Movements," *FH* 18 (1986):47-63.

B. L. Shelley

Youth Ministry/Minister. Today's emphasis on youth ministry in the American church grew out of changing family and cultural patterns in the late 1800s. As public education increasingly grouped children and youth according to ages, a distinct youth culture emerged. Traditional intergenerational approaches were modified. Beginning in urban areas, the YMCA*/YWCA* (1844, 1858) and the Christian Endeavor Society* (1881) emerged in response to this need. Soon, churches also began to plan specific programs and activities for youth. Episcopal* (1883), Presbyterian* (1889), Methodist* (1889), Baptist* (1891) and Lutheran* (1893) youth organizations were typical of this trend. In the early 1900s, local church youth societies met each Sunday evening for Bible* learning, prayer,* socializing and service.

Following World War 2,* the fledgling Young Life* (1941) and Youth for Christ* (c.1944) organizations reached out successfully to youth who were then outside the church through rallies, clubs and camps.* Evangelical* groups such as Pioneer Girls (now Pioneer Clubs*), Christian Service Brigade* and youth clubs worked to teach Scripture and to encourage Christian living. At the same time, most major denominations* established democratically organized and student-led youth fellowships. Camps were purchased and developed. During this period denominational youth ministries were typically structured so that volunteer adults took advisory roles as sponsors, helping youth plan activities furthering faith, witness, fellowship, citizenship and outreach.

During the dramatic societal changes of the late 1960s, the appeal of more structured models of youth work declined. A growing "generation gap" contributed to young peoples' widespread alienation from institutionalized youth organizations. Drugs and rebellion replaced religious activities for many youth who had been raised in the church. Experimental ministries were attempted, including coffeehouses, Christian communes, beach evangelism and Christian folk and rock music. By the early 1970s, the media spoke of the "Jesus Movement,"* a groundswell of open spirituality with a strong emphasis on "experiencing Christ personally." Youth gathered spontaneously to pursue Bible study and sharing,* person-to-person evangelism and a style of praise-singing which combined folk, pop and rock music with scriptural or devotional lyrics. Over time, the anti-institutional tendency of the movement softened. Many of its emphases were channeled into the church, contributing to the development of a more spontaneous and direct approach to youth ministry there.

By the late 1970s, a new style of youth ministry had become an established institution in many American churches. Medium and large-sized congregations commonly had full-time youth ministers or directors to coordinate biblically oriented and openly Christ-centered ministries with youth. Drawn from approaches pioneered by Young Life and Youth for Christ, a forthright focus on Christian discipleship* and evangelism with youth often provided a spark which led to renewal of entire churches. "Incarnational ministry," an influential strategy, encouraged church leaders to enter young peoples' everyday lives and culture in affirming yet uncompromising love, after the pattern of Christ's incarnation. Theme camps which combined fun, humor and Christian formation supplemented this approach, becoming crucial building blocks for ongoing ministries at home. Churches worked to channel maturing youth outward into service projects and peer evangelism. Efforts were made to reintegrate youth ministry into the larger intergenerational context of the congregation.

In the late 1970s and 1980s many youth nurtured in this style of ministry had become Christian leaders who were having a significant impact in the shaping of American religion. Attesting to this impact were a dramatic increase in seminary* and graduate religious studies enrollment, a decade of surging interdenominational college* and university ministries,* and record numbers of American young people pursuing crosscultural missions.

BIBLIOGRAPHY. C. B. Eavey, *History of Christian Education* (1964); R. G. Irving and R. B. Zuck, *Youth and the Church* (1968); E. Caillet, *Young Life* (1963); M. G. Larson, *Youth for Christ* (1947); L. Richards, *Youth Ministry: Its Renewal in the Local Church* (1972); D. Williams, *Call to the Streets* (1972); J. D. Stone, *The Complete Youth Ministries Handbook* (1979). P. W. Butin

Youth With a Mission. A nondenominational and international evangelistic* organization. Established in 1960 by Loren Cunningham, an Assemblies of God* minister, Youth With a Mission (YWAM) is dedicated to presenting Jesus Christ in a loving way to all members of this generation. With 350 permanent centers throughout the world, YWAM operates in over one hundred countries with some six thousand full-time workers, most of whom are engaged in the traditional evangelistic activities of distributing Bibles,* leading open-air meetings, conducting dramatic presentations and sponsoring Christian music groups. Each summer YWAM sends out approximately fifty thousand short-term volunteers from around the world to carry out evangelistic work.

Caring for the physical needs of people is part of YWAM's mercy ministry that is designed to aid people suffering from poverty and to help those recovering from natural disasters. An integral part of this ministry are two ships owned by YWAM that are used to transport mercy cargo throughout the world. To effectively carry out the mercy ministry and evangelism, training is a vital part of the YWAM program. Full-time staff members are required to complete a six-month course at one of over one hundred Discipleship Training Schools. Future YWAM plans include establishing a worldwide, multi-campus school for training Christians to serve in the professions, with the goal of integrating Christianity into all aspects of life, including education, government, media, science, the entertainment fields and the family.

BIBLIOGRAPHY. L. Cunningham, *Is That Really You, God?* (1984); R. M. Wilson, *God's Guerrillas: Youth With a Mission* (1971).

K. L. Staggers

Z

Zahm, John Augustine (1851-1921). Catholic* scientist and educator. Born in New Lexington, Ohio, Zahm was educated at the University of Notre Dame* (B.A., 1871) and after further study (M.A., 1873) became professor of physics and chemistry (1875-1892). Zahm joined the Congregation of Holy Cross* (C.S.C) in 1871 and was ordained* in 1875. Apart from teaching, he also served as the librarian and curator of the University's Scientific Museum, and when he was only twenty-five he assumed the institution's vice-presidency. Zahm's numerous campus projects included an annual public lecture series on modern science; the construction of the university's first science classroom and laboratory building; and the offering of undergraduate and graduate studies in engineering, which made Notre Dame the first American Catholic college to do so.

In 1898 Zahm was elected provincial of his religious congregation* in the U.S., a position he held until 1906. His primary goal in this post was to establish and encourage a group of young priests-scholars to do advanced study at the Catholic University* in Washington, D.C. Zahm's proteges were among the first C.S.C. priests* to take advanced degrees beyond their seminary training.

Zahm published extensively on the geography, history and culture of Colorado, Alaska, the American Southwest and the Hawaiian Islands. He also authored books on subjects as varied as acoustics (*Sound and Music,* 1892), the history of science (*Women in Science,* 1913) and religion (*The Bible, Science, and Faith,* 1894). His most important work was on the relationship between science and faith (*See* Science and Christianity). His best-known work was *Evolution and Dogma* (1896), an attempt to summarize the Catholic view of evolution* and science. The book was a landmark in the intellectual history of both the University of Notre Dame and Zahm's religious community. It was a product of American Catholicism's Chautauqua Movement in the Midwest and a manifesto of the Americanism* of the 1890s. Zahm was the most important nineteenth-century intellectual in the Congregation of Holy Cross and American Catholicism's most erudite and respected writer on the relationship of Darwinian evolution and Christian belief in Victorian America.

BIBLIOGRAPHY. *DAB* X; *DARB; NCAB* 9; *NCE* 14; R. E. Weber, *Notre Dame's John Zahm: American Catholic Apologist and Educator* (1961).

T. J. Schlereth

Zeisberger, David (1721-1808). Moravian* missionary* to Native Americans. Born in Zauchtenthal, Moravia, Zeisberger immigrated to Saxony with his parents at age five. Educated in Holland, he ran away to Georgia to join his parents, who had settled in the Moravian colony there. At Bethlehem, Pennsylvania, he responded to a suggestion by Augustus G. Spangenberg* that he become a missionary to the surrounding Native Americans. After studying the Iroquois language he accompanied Christian Frederick Post in 1745 on a mission to the Mohawk Valley.

Zeisberger spent sixty-four years living, working and preaching among the Delaware Indians in Pennsylvania, New York and Ohio. In Ohio he founded the town of Schönbrunn (Beautiful Spring) in 1772. Throughout the Revolutionary* period he attempted to maintain a pacifistic stance among the Native Americans. Schönbrunn was abandoned in 1777, and the Native Americans at the nearby Gnadenhütten (Tents of Grace) were senselessly massacred by American troops in 1782, while Zeisberger was being held by the British who suspected him of having Revolutionary sympathies. Zeisberger later followed the refugee Native Americans as they were forced to migrate to Canada and Michigan, finally returning to Goshen, Ohio.

Zeisberger's literary efforts in behalf of the Native Americans included a collections of hymns for the Christian Native Americans, a book of sermons to children, translations of some of the Moravian liturgical services, a seven-volume lexicon of the German and Onondaga languages, an Onondaga grammar, a German-Delaware dictionary, a Delaware-English spelling book, a Delaware grammar and a grammatical treatise on Delaware conjugations. Zeisberger's prodigious labors are celebrated by the painting *The Power of the Gospel* by Christian Schussele. He was buried among his Native-American converts at Goshen, Ohio.

BIBLIOGRAPHY. *DAB* X; *DARB; NCAB* 2; W. H. Rice, *David Zeisberger and His Brown Brethren* (1897); E. de Sweinitz, *Life and Times of David Zeisberger* (1871). A. H. Frank

Zinzendorf, Nikolaus Ludwig von (1700-1760). Pietist* and Moravian* leader. Born in Dresden, Germany, Zinzendorf was educated at Halle and the University of Wittenberg. While his family wished him to take up a diplomatic career, the young Count wanted to pursue religious interests. Nevertheless, for several years he served the king of Saxony as a royal counselor (1721-1728). Acquiring an estate in Saxony, he eventually provided a haven for Moravian exiles from Bohemia and Moravia. In 1727 he relinquished his court duties and devoted his time to renewing the *Unitas Fratrum,* otherwise known as the Church of the Brethren, or Moravian Church. The community became known as Hernnhut (The Lord's Protection) and was viewed by Zinzendorf as an ecumenical renewal movement within the church at large. He was ordained* by the group in 1735 and was consecrated a bishop* of the Moravian Church (1737-1741).

From 1732 Zinzendorf devoted both his time and fortune to Moravian mission ventures, visiting the West Indies in 1738-1739. In 1741-1743 he visited America. Arriving in Philadelphia late in 1741 he presided at the Christmas Eve observance at which the community of Bethlehem was named. While in America he served as pastor of a Lutheran congregation in Philadelphia and made three missionary journeys among the Native Americans. He convened and chaired several meetings of German Protestants in Pennsylvania in 1742-1743 in an attempt to bring about ecumenical agreement on work and unity. The gatherings, known as the Pennsylvania synods,* met the resistance of religious leaders such as Henry M. Muhlenberg* and John P. Boehm* and were not successful, but his ecumenical vision spurred other groups to better serve their constituencies in the colony.

A prolific hymnwriter, Zinzendorf left texts for some 2,000 hymns. His personal religious experience* led him to focus on the pietistic theology of the individual's experience of the Savior and shaped his mission theory which guided the early work of the Moravians. The remainder of his life was spent in Moravian ministry in England and Germany. Zinzendorf maintained correspondence with a number of religious leaders in Europe and met with John Wesley on several occasions.

BIBLIOGRAPHY. *DAB* X; *DARB;* A. J. Lewis, *Zinzendorf, The Ecumenical Pioneer* (1962); *NCAB* 2; J. R. Weinlick, *Count Zinzendorf* (1956).

A. H. Frank

Zionism and American Christianity. Derived from the ancient name (Zion) of the mountain site of the fortress city of Jerusalem or the Temple Mount, Zionism as a concept is rooted in the traditions of ancient Israel. It relates to the persistent belief that God's covenant with his people, the Jews, is linked to Palestine and Jerusalem in particular and that the land is rightfully theirs. Biblical references such as Genesis 12:7; 15:18; 35:12; Numbers 34:2-12; Deuteronomy 30:5; Joshua 15:1-12 and Isaiah 11:16 have been frequently used to establish this inextricable connection. Since biblical times, this land tradition has been an integral component of Jewish hopes and dreams, an unshakable expectation during nineteen centuries of exile of returning to Zion.

In the late nineteenth and twentieth centuries Zionism became enfleshed in a movement that has attracted a broad spectrum of American Christians, although they are a minority numerically speaking. Among many conservative evangelical* Christians, Zionism has been accorded a prominent role as a fulfillment of prophecy and as one of the preconditions for the return of Christ. This Second Coming of the Messiah, in line with premillennial* views, will establish the long-awaited kingdom of God,* a kingdom which will last for a thousand years and be followed by the last judgment.

Among early Christian Zionists, William Blackstone* was a formidable figure. Acknowledged as "the father of American Christian Zionism," he worked tirelessly for several decades on behalf of a Jewish homeland in Israel. High visibility was given to his efforts through his endeavor to persuade President Benjamin Harrison to contact world leaders in the interests of an international conference on Zionist aspirations (1891). Over one million copies of his book *Jesus Is Coming* were sold.

Another outstanding leader was Arno C. Gaebelein,* whose journal *Our Hope* (founded 1894) kept readers in touch not only with theological and biblical commentaries on Zionism, but reported on the international prophecy conferences* and political movements related to the restoration of the nation.

Dwight L. Moody* in his own ministry and in the establishment of Moody Bible Institute* in Chicago, gave consistent encouragement and support to the Zionist cause. Other conservative evangelicals who have zealously affirmed the movement toward Jewish rights to a homeland include R. A. Torrey,* James M. Gray,* Jerry Falwell,* Pat Robertson* and Billy Graham.*

Christian Zionism has also been prominent among mainline* Protestants,* as well as Catholics, throughout the twentieth century. Rather than being connected with the fulfillment of biblical prophecy, however, the foundation of their perspective has primarily been a moral commitment to a people grievously persecuted and maltreated through the centuries. The Holocaust,* with its denial to Jews of human dignity and the right to survive, is viewed as the climax of this injustice.

The American Palestine Committee was commenced in 1932, merging with the Christian Council on Palestine, and becoming the American Christian Palestine Committee. By 1942 there were over twelve hundred members, and by 1946 approximately fifteen thousand, including clergy* and lay* members. Throughout the U.S. over one hundred local chapters were organized. Their primary goal was to arouse the American Christian conscience toward a Zionist resolution of a homeland for dispossessed Jews.

Reinhold Niebuhr* was an ardent spokesperson for the American Christian Palestine Committee, advocating a haven for Jewish refugees in Palestine, and subsequently supporting the establishment of the State of Israel in 1948. Other Christian contemporaries of Niebuhr who espoused similar Zionist views were W. F. Albright,* Francis J. McConnell,* Ralph W. Sockman,* Daniel A. Poling and Paul Tillich.* Currently, among the exponents of this heritage are: Franklin H. Littell, Roy and Alice Eckardt, John Pawlikowski, Eugene Fisher, Edward Flannery and Isaac C. Rottenberg. Several have channeled their support through the National Christian Leadership Conference for Israel and the National Conference of Christians and Jews.*

Christian Zionists reject the view that the biblical promises made to ancient Israel were abrogated by the coming of Christ and were superseded by the establishment of the church.

BIBLIOGRAPHY. L. J. Epstein, *Zion's Calls: Christian Contributions to the Origins and Development of Israel* (1984); A. R. Eckardt, *Your People, My People: The Meeting of Jews and Christians* (1974); H. Fishman, *American Protestantism and a Jewish State* (1973); Y. Malachy, *American Fundamentalism and Israel: The Reactions of Fundamentalist Churches to Zionism* (1978); D. A. Rausch, *Zionism within Early American Fundamentalism, 1878-1918: A Convergence of Two Traditions* (1980); A. J. Rudin, *Israel for Christians: Understanding Modern Israel* (1982).   F. B. Nelson

Zouberbuhler, Bartholomew (d.1766). Anglican* minister* in colonial Georgia. Born in Switzerland and raised in South Carolina, Zouberbuhler was ordained* an Anglican priest.* On November 1, 1745, he received an appointment from the trustees of the colony of Georgia as rector* at Christ Church Parish in Savannah. He would serve in that position until his death in 1766. Zouberbuhler was fluent in English, French and German and was particularly suited to the position in Savannah, where he could preach to the nearby German communities of Acton and Vernonburgh as well as to French Protestants located in the area. Always concerned for the general welfare and religious instruction of those in his parish,* Zouberbuhler left much of his estate, which amounted to 3,337 acres of land and 52 slaves, to care for the poor and to support an orphan house, a college and the work of Joseph Ottolenghe, who came to Georgia in 1751 to instruct the slaves. A prodigious worker and successful conciliator, Zouberbuhler is frequently cited as the best and most widely respected Anglican minister in colonial Georgia.

BIBLIOGRAPHY. *Abstracts of Colonial Wills of the State of Georgia, 1733-1777* (1981); A. D. Candler and L. L. Knight, eds., *The Colonial Records of the State of Georgia,* 26 vols., (1904-1916).
                               N. L. Erickson

Zwemer, Samuel Marinus (1867-1952). Reformed* missionary* to the Arab world. Born a minister's* son near Vriesland, Michigan, the thirteenth of fifteen children, Zwemer graduated from Hope College (1887) and the Theological Seminary of the Reformed Church at New Brunswick, New Jersey (1890). Zwemer resolved to become a missionary, due to the influence of Robert P. Wilder* of the Student Volunteer Movement.*

Ordained* by the classis of Iowa in 1890, Zwemer went to Arabia, "the hardest country, the hardest climate, the hardest language, the hardest everything on earth," under the auspices of the Syrian Mission of the Presbyterian Church in the U.S.A. Based in Bahrain, Zwemer evangelized the Gulf from Basra to Muscat, convened the first general conference on Muslim missions in Cairo in 1906, and in 1912 was assigned to literature work in Egypt, attached to the Nile Mission Press.

After seventeen years in Cairo, Zwemer was called to be professor of missions and the history of religion at Princeton Theological Seminary.* Energetic, stately (six feet, 160 pounds), Zwemer was known as "a steam engine in breeches." A prodigious author and editor, Zwemer founded *The Moslem World* (1911) and wrote such classics as *Arabia, the Cradle of Islam* (4 editions, 1900-1912); *The Cross above the Crescent* (1941) and *Islam, a Challenge to Faith* (1907).

An indefatigable traveler, in 1927-1928 Zwemer covered 15,262 miles and once gave 151 addresses in 113 days. Appropriately he died while at work. Following a lecture to InterVarsity Christian Fellowship* in New York, Zwemer had a heart attack and passed away on April 2, 1952, just short of his eighty-fifth birthday. Revered as "the Apostle to Arabia," Zwemer, wrote Sherwood Eddy,* was "unique in our generation . . . a voice in the wilderness calling for the evangelization of Islam."

BIBLIOGRAPHY. C. G. Fry and J. P. Fry, "Samuel Marinus Zwemer, Pioneer Missionary to the Muslims," *Missionary Monthly* 83 (1978):3-5; J. C. Wilson, *Apostle to Islam: A Biography of Samuel M. Zwemer* (1938).

C. G. Fry